# MODERN DRAMA

## PLAYS / CRITICISM / THEORY

# W.B. WORTHEN

is currently professor of English and Theatre
at Northwestern University,
and has taught at the University of Texas at Austin,
Columbia University, and the Bread Loaf
School of English (Middlebury College).
He is the author of *Modern Drama and the Rhetoric of
Theater* (University of California Press, 1992), *The Idea
of the Actor: Drama and the Ethics of Performance*
(Princeton University Press, 1984), and *The HBJ
Anthology of Drama* (Harcourt Brace, 1993), as well as
many articles on modern drama, Shakespeare, and
theories of performance.
He holds degrees in English from the University of
Massachusetts at Amherst (B.A.) and Princeton
University (Ph.D.). Professor Worthen has held research
fellowships from the Guggenheim Foundation and the
National Endowment for the Humanities, and is past
editor of *Theatre Journal.*

# MODERN DRAMA

## PLAYS / CRITICISM / THEORY

**W. B. Worthen**

Northwestern University

**Harcourt Brace College Publishers**

Fort Worth    Philadelphia    San Diego    New York    Orlando    Austin    San Antonio
Toronto    Montreal    London    Sydney    Tokyo

| | |
|---|---|
| Publisher | Ted Buchholz |
| Senior Acquisitions Editor | Stephen T. Jordan |
| Developmental Editor | Karl Yambert |
| Project Editor | Angela Williams |
| Production Manager | Jane Tyndall Ponceti |
| Senior Art Director | David A. Day |
| Photo Editor | Lili Weiner |
| Typographer | Typo-Graphics Inc. |

*Address for Editorial Correspondence*
Harcourt Brace College Publishers, 301 Commerce Street, Suite 3700, Fort Worth, TX 76102

*Address for Orders*
Harcourt Brace & Company, 6277 Sea Harbor Drive, Orlando, FL 32887
1-800-782-4479, or 1-800-433-0001 (in Florida)

Literary credits begin on page 1200.

ISBN: 0-15-501191-X

Library of Congress Catalogue Number: 93-80878

Printed in the United States of America

4  5  6  7  8  9  0  1  2  3     069     9  8  7  6  5  4  3  2  1

# PREFACE

To study modern drama is to undertake a challenging activity. It involves reading the texts of plays, the world-wide dramatic literature of the twentieth century; thinking about the ways that the various strategies of modern theatrical performance help those plays to speak on the stage; and thinking about the complex ways in which theater interacts with the diverse cultures of the modern world. Of course, no anthology can do more than sample the extraordinary richness of modern performance, but *Modern Drama: Plays/Criticism/Theory* engages modern drama in a particularly rich way—treating the drama's participation in the history of world literature, its place in the history of the theater, and some of the ways that drama and theater conduct a theoretical or critical inspection of modern culture at large.

*Modern Drama: Plays/Criticism/Theory* offers a collection of the classic plays of modern European and American drama, a provocative sampling of new work, and a rich gathering of important critical and theoretical essays. The book is divided into five principal parts. The Introduction, "Modernism and the Modern Stage," puts modern drama in the context of literary, artistic, and theatrical innovation in the late-nineteenth and early-twentieth centuries, and suggests some of the ways that modernist esthetics relate to new social and cultural issues facing Western society. The first unit, "The Emergence of Modern Drama: 1850–1950," traces the work of the "first generation" of modern European and American playwrights. Unit 2, "Revolution and Reaction: 1950–1975," covers the revolt against the traditions of realism characteristic of the mid-century decades, and broadens the range of plays to include authors outside the dominant traditions of the West. Unit 3, "Modern / Postmodern: 1975–," considers the effects of "postmodern" production in the theater. The final unit, "Criticism and Theory of the Modern Stage," is a book-within-the-book, a mini-anthology of influential critical and theoretical essays on modern theater, performance, and culture.

At one time, "modern drama" was taken by many teachers and students to label a cast of white male playwrights beginning with Ibsen and ending with Beckett. To think about twentieth-century drama today is to consider how the stage has been shaped from a number of different perspectives, by men and women, by theaters in the Third World as well as the dominant theaters of the West, and by writers working from a variety of positions of racial, ethnic, cultural, and sexual identity. The thirty-nine plays in *Modern Drama: Plays/Criticism/Theory* include plays by Ibsen, Wilde, Chekhov, Strindberg, Shaw, O'Neill, Glaspell, Pirandello, Williams, Brecht, Beckett, Genet, Pinter, Baraka, Handke, and Shepard—playwrights who all challenge the dominant cultural and artistic habits of their time. But more than most anthologies, *Modern Drama: Plays/ Criticism/Theory* enables students and teachers to explore the issues of representation in the modern theater, the ways that culture shapes issues of identity, of gender, of sexuality, of race. Although some of these issues are raised in Unit 1—in the actress and suffragist activist Elizabeth Robins's *Votes for Women!*, in Susan Glaspell's *Trifles*, and in the African-American poet and playwright Angelina Weld Grimké's *Rachel*—they become more prominent in Units 2 and 3, in Caryl Churchill's *Cloud Nine* and *Mad Forest*, Wole Soyinka's *The Lion and the Jewel*, Amiri Baraka's *Dutchman*, Adrienne Kennedy's *Funnyhouse of a Negro*, Luis Valdez's *Los Vendidos*, Marguerite Duras's *India Song*, Griselda Gambaro's *Information for Foreigners*, Ntozake Shange's *spell #7*, Brian Friel's *Translations*, David Henry Hwang's *M. Butterfly*, the Split Britches– Bloolips collaboration *Belle Reprieve*, and Tony Kushner's *Angels in America*. The collection also highlights the extraordinary range of formal innovation characteristic of the modern stage: in the updating of *Antigone* in Fugard, Kani, and Ntshona's *The Island*; in Edward Bond's reworking of Brechtian epic theater in *Bingo*; in Heiner Müller's brilliant pastiche, *Hamletmachine*; in Maria Irene Fornes's filmlike montage in the corrosive political drama, *The Conduct of Life;* and in Anna Deavere Smith's one-woman engagement with racial and ethnic violence, *Fires in the Mirror*. Given its range of inclusion, *Modern Drama: Plays/Criticism/Theory* can be used for a variety of courses in the drama of the twentieth century: courses emphasizing formal and literary issues, courses on performance traditions, courses organized topically or thematically.

Each unit begins with an extensive introduction, placing the drama in the context of the development of twentieth-century culture and the practices of the modern theater. Each play is accompanied by a brief biography of the playwright, a short introduction to the play, and a secondary prose text by the playwright—selections from letters, a prefatory essay about the play, or an interview, for example. The anthology also includes four "Casebooks." Ibsen, Beckett, and Churchill are each represented by two plays, by a more generous sampling of nondramatic prose texts, and by critical essays about their work by prominent critics. Brecht is represented by one play, *Galileo*, by two of his most important theoretical essays, by his reflections on Charles Laughton's work on the role of Galileo, and by Walter Benjamin's seminal essay, "What Is Epic Theater?"

Finally, modern drama is part of a widespread theoretical investigation into the meaning and place of performance in contemporary culture. For this reason, *Modern Drama: Plays/Criticism/Theory* includes an extensive selection of critical and theoretical essays about modern drama, theater, and performance. Some of these essays are themselves classics of the stage, written by some of the modern theater's most influential practitioners: Antonin Artaud, Constantin Stanislavski, and Émile Zola. Others represent some of the important intellectual traditions framing modern theatrical experimentation: essays by Sigmund Freud (psychoanalysis), Jindřich Honzl (semiotics), Fredric Jameson (Marxist theory), Friedrich Nietzsche (philosophy), and Raymond Williams (cultural studies) fall into this category. And several essays consider "performance" to extend beyond the stage, and suggest ways in which drama and theater engage more significantly with the performance of modern culture: Homi Bhabha's essay on mimicry in colonial discourse; Judith Butler and Sue-Ellen Case on performance, gender, and sexuality; Peggy Phelan's remarks on performance art; and the anthropologist Victor Turner's mapping of the relationship between dramatic conventions and social action. These essays— in addition to the essays and interviews by the playwrights themselves throughout the book—can help to provide the critical discourse to frame and explore some of the most suggestive questions raised by the modern theater.

Although many courses in modern drama are taught at an advanced level, *Modern Drama: Plays/Criticism/Theory* is designed both to introduce students to the field of modern drama, and to provide advanced students with the resources for more specialized research. Photographs help to convey a sense of a play's life on the stage, and can help both beginning and advanced students to visualize how the text comes to life in performance. The book also includes a glossary of useful dramatic, theatrical, and literary terms; an extensive bibliography of general works on modern drama and of more specialized studies on individual plays and playwrights; and a list of selected video, film, and sound recordings. John Bell's Instructor's Manual provides a summary and commentary for each play. *Modern Drama: Plays/Criticism/Theory* provides flexible instruments for the exploration of the modern stage and its involvement in the world in which we live.

W. B. W., 1993

## Acknowledgments

Once again, I have the pleasure to thank Stephen T. Jordan of Harcourt Brace for suggesting this project, for imagining this book at its best and for helping to bring it into being. I am also grateful for the excellent advice and help of Karl Yambert and others at Harcourt Brace who have given their care and skill to this book: Eleanor Garner for her grace and persistence in handling permissions; Angela Williams, project editor; David Day, senior art director; and Jane Ponceti, production manager.

Susan Carlson (Iowa State University), Jill Dolan (University of Wisconsin-Madison), and Josephine Lee (Smith College), reviewed the manuscript, and their careful commentary led me to many important corrections, revisions, reflections, and—I hope—improvements. A number of other people also graciously contributed comments and suggestions useful in the planning of a drama anthology: John Glavin (Georgetown University), John Harper (University of Iowa), Keith Hull (University of Wyoming-Laramie), William Hutchings (University of Alabama-Birmingham), Katherine Kelly (Texas A & M University), Dan Kline (Jefferson Community College), Paul Lim (University of Kansas), Keith Newlin (University of North Carolina-Wilmington), Lois More Overbeck (Emory University), Vivian Patraka (Bowling Green University), Steven Putzell (Pennsylvania State University-Wilkes Barre), James Stottlar (University of Illinois-Urbana), and Toby Zinman (University of the Arts).

I am especially grateful to Anna Deavere Smith and her assistant Florence Yoo, to Peggy Shaw and Lois Weaver, and to Kate Davy, for their generosity with information and with unpublished material. I'd also like to thank Sue-Ellen Case, Jill Dolan, Sharon Mazer, Vivian Patraka, Peggy Phelan, and Sandra Richards for talking about this book with me while it was in process, and for giving me some much-needed leads. I am delighted that John Bell agreed to write the Instructor's Manual, and am—as always—impressed by the geniality and intelligence of his work. Finally, I'm grateful to Janelle Reinelt for the conversation and encouragement that helped to keep this project in motion.

# CONTENTS

## UNIT 2: REVOLUTION AND REACTION:1950–1975 . . . 421

## UNIT 4: CRITICISM AND THEORY OF THE MODERN STAGE . . . 1083

# MODERN DRAMA

## PLAYS / CRITICISM / THEORY

# INTRODUCTION

## Modernism and the Modern Stage

IT MAY STRIKE SOME READERS AS ODD that a book on "modern" theater and drama begins with plays written a century ago. Yet to speak of **MODERNISM**[1] is to speak at once of an attitude towards artistic production—"make it new," in the poet Ezra Pound's famous phrase—and of a period in the cultural history of the West. As the literary and cultural critic Raymond Williams noted in an essay entitled "When Was Modernism?" the English word "modern" has undergone a series of subtle changes in meaning and connotation.[2] In the sixteenth and seventeenth centuries, "modern" generally meant "what is happening now, contemporary" and it was often used to distinguish contemporary literature from classical writers, the "ancients"; perhaps the epitome of this usage is in Jonathan Swift's *Battle of the Books* (1697), subtitled "Quarrel of the Ancients and Moderns." Even in Swift's usage, though, the characteristic irony underlying the term "modern," and informing later attitudes, can be felt. On the one hand, "modern" expresses the sense of the new, the progressive, a rejection of the past for something better; yet it also contains an ironic or nostalgic sense that the past is being lost, in favor of an uncertain future. This irony underlies many uses of the term "modern" throughout the eighteenth and nineteenth centuries. Williams notes that while Jane Austen uses the term suspiciously in her 1818 novel *Persuasion* ("a state of alteration, perhaps of improvement"), John Ruskin's *Modern Painters* (1843–1860) defends the paintings of J. M. W. Turner precisely because they are "modern"—new, original, speaking in the accents of contemporary life. This enthusiasm for the "modern"—linked to the rhetoric of social, industrial, scientific "progress"—was captured in the late nineteenth century by the rhetoric of literary and theatrical **NATURALISM,** which called for a new "scientific" approach to writing that would approximate the "modern" methods of the natural sciences in the working of art. As Émile Zola wrote in 1878, epitomizing the linkage between the "modern" and confidence in the power of scientific rationalism: "Naturalism alone corresponds to our social needs; it alone has deep roots in the spirit of our times; and it alone can provide a living, durable formula for our art, because this formula will express the nature of our contemporary intelligence" (Zola's remarks, from "Naturalism in the Theatre," are excerpted in Unit 4).

Although the term "modern" still carries the sense of *now, contemporary,* to speak of "modernism"—or of modern art, modern architecture, modern literature—is now generally to speak in historical terms, of a movement in the arts, architecture, music, that—although its consequences have been far reaching—dates roughly from 1880–1950. In many ways, the world we live in today was born in this period, the period of "modernism" in the arts and of modernization in culture and society. The map of the planet was redrawn by two world wars; by the rise of the United States and the Union of Soviet Socialist Republics as world superpowers; by revolutions in Russia and China; by worldwide liberation from European colonial rule in Mexico, the Philippines, Latin America, Africa, India, and Southeast Asia. These political and social changes, and the esthetics of modernism as well, were fueled by a vigorous technological and industrial revolution. This revolution is expressed not only by inventions—the telephone, radio, film, television, automobile, highway, airplane, rocket, and so on—but more importantly by the changing social relations and new forms of living and working that industrial and technological **MODERNIZATION** brought about: the assembly line and mass production, suburbs and housing developments, trade unions and public corporations, public

---

[1]Terms are defined in the Glossary; many terms raised in the Introduction are also discussed at greater length in the introductory essay to each Unit.

[2]See Raymond Williams, "When Was Modernism?" *The Politics of Modernism,* ed. Tony Pinkney (London and New York: Verso, 1989) 31–36.

education and compulsory retirement, multinational corporations extending their markets and influence around the globe. The landscape of life in the West, and often in the parts of the world dominated by the West, was changed forever, too, by the growth of the modern cityscape, by modern slums, skyscrapers, subways, and even city streets; by massive public projects like the Panama and Suez canals, the Empire State Building, the Eiffel Tower, and their ghastly cousins, the gas chambers of Auschwitz and the nuclear bombing of Hiroshima and Nagasaki.

Many of these revolutions were begun in the nineteenth century, and many of the conceptual revolutions that changed our sense of history, society, and humanity express the continuity between the late nineteenth century and its modern inheritors. For although Thomas Hardy, in his 1902 poem "The Darkling Thrush," spoke of "the Century's corpse," the terms of modern experience were first defined in the nineteenth century and in the early years of the twentieth: geological and biological evolution by Charles Darwin and Sir Charles Lyell; the theory of capital, labor, and communism by Karl Marx, Friedrich Engels, and V. I. Lenin; Albert Einstein's general theory of relativity and the revolution in our understanding of the physical cosmos; Sigmund Freud's discovery of the unconscious. To speak of "modernism" in the arts is similarly to refer to a period of artistic innovation in the arts of Europe ranging from the last decades of the nineteenth century into the first third of the twentieth. These movements in the visual, verbal, and plastic arts are hardly synchronized, of course, but 1921–1922 marks a kind of center in the history of modernism: Marcel Proust's *Remembrances of Things Past*, James Joyce's *Ulysses*, T. S. Eliot's *The Waste Land*, Virginia Woolf's *Mrs. Dalloway*, Luigi Pirandello's *Six Characters in Search of an Author*, and Stravinsky's *Le Sacre du Printemps* all appeared in that brief span.

*Modernism* can be characterized in a variety of ways. It might, for example, best be described as an artistic and cultural response to the impact of *modernization*—the process of industrialization and the social reorganization it entailed that gripped the West in the late nineteenth and early twentieth centuries (on modernism and modernization, see the Introduction to Unit 3). As a result, modernism in the arts was a largely metropolitan, urban phenomenon. Much as the major cities of Europe became international centers governing finance, trade, and extensive economic and political empires, so too they became centers of cultural production, the nexus through which the new artistic experiments of the twentieth century would be driven. The characteristic tone of modernist art, energetic yet enervated, irritable and anxious, rich with the history of Europe yet seeing the poverty of modern life as its consequence, is part of this metropolitan context, as the major modernists coped with a relatively new kind of urban life. To many writers, this sense of crisis was crystallized in the First World War (1914–1917), which epitomized the nightmare of technology rampantly destroying Europe's humanity in the name of "culture." In "Hugh Selwyn Mauberley" (1920), Ezra Pound reflected on the loss of a generation of European youth, all for "two gross of broken statues, /For a few thousand battered books." In *The Waste Land* (1922), T. S. Eliot similarly described a hollowness at the heart of Europe; although he brought the museum of European culture into the poem, the poem finally takes place in the wasted "Unreal City" of modern life. And in Bernard Shaw's *Heartbreak House* (1919), England is bombed while its most attractive, educated, and powerful citizens seem incapable of doing anything to save themselves—indeed, they would prefer to die in the bombing than live on into the barren future that awaits them.

As William Butler Yeats remarked in his famous poem "The Second Coming" (1921), "the centre cannot hold"—and the illusory center provided by the metropolis only marked out the fact that it seemed the center of nothing, a location where the forces of production and technology far outstripped the ability of individual consciousness or action to engage them. The emerging technology of modern life seemed at once an attractive model for art and a repellent and alienating force. While several prewar movements—Vorticism in England, Futurism in Italy, or paintings like Marcel Duchamp's "Nude Descending a Staircase" (1913)—show an affinity for the machine, attempting to rival its speed and flash in a souped-up art, others see modern technology as part of the alien material and social landscape of modern life.

Nonetheless, the modernist arts of the first decades of the twentieth century—whether in the modes of **FUTURISM, CONSTRUCTIVISM, EXPRESSIONISM, CUBISM,** or even in the modes of **REALISM** and **NATURALISM** (terms discussed in Unit 1)—share a certain sensibility. Although composed in various media and various styles, modernist representation tends to represent the world as an interlocking yet mysterious system, a system that is at once disorienting and oppressive, a world in which the search for the self, for personal or cultural vitality or meaning, is thwarted. Technological innovation, political developments, and two major wars encouraged an increasing internationalism across the arts of the West, evident in the "international" style of architecture popularized by Le Corbusier, the Bauhaus, and their followers; in Cubist painting and sculpture; and in modernist writing and music. But this internationalism hardly fostered a single, monolithic sense of "modernism" in the arts. Instead, it gave rise to a series of fragmentary **AVANT-GARDE** movements each with its own ideals, esthetics, and audience, and usually with its own resistant posture toward society as well. The esthetic of avant-gardism—that the arts must adopt a vigorously "modern," resistant posture, rejecting both the arts of the past and the social order of the present—has come to dominate much of the "serious," "high culture" of the twentieth century. As a result, twentieth-century art often has a vaguely oppositional cast. This oppositional sensibility is sometimes reflected in the thematics of modern art, which frequently criticizes modern society, even when its style seems relatively conventional. Literature, drama, and theater in the "realist" mode of, say, Henrik Ibsen, Anton Chekhov, or Eugene O'Neill, adopt the perspective of a "realistic" style in order to criticize the pieties and behavior of the middle classes who represent social power and the oppressive stability of modern society, the normative perspective encoded in "realism" itself. A second line of innovation, and a more important one in the history of modern art, is formal innovation. The development of free verse in poetry, of antinovels like Proust's *Remembrances* or Joyce's *Ulysses* and *Finnegans Wake* (1939); of atonal music, the twelve-tone row, and serial music; of nonrepresentational styles in the visual arts, like Cubism; of the direct representation of the "unconscious" in expressionist and surrealist modes of theater: All of these formal strategies rebel against the hegemony of a "realism" that supports—and is supported by—the bourgeois ideology of the status quo. Finally, many avant-garde movements undertake a specifically ontological and political rejection of the modern world—the nonsense art of the Dadaists is one example, perhaps leading to the nihilism of Beckett's theater of the absurd; the Marxist esthetics of Bertolt Brecht is another.

To place "modernism" in the history of twentieth-century art, then, is to see it both as an attitude toward cultural innovation, and as a phase in the history of twentieth-century culture. In historical terms, modernism is a largely European movement—though embraced in metropolitan centers oriented toward Europe, such as New York, Mexico City, Buenos Aires, Toronto—brought to a crisis by World War I and by the Russian Revolution of 1917. The war came to symbolize the oppressive nature of modern industrial life; the revolution symbolized a harnessing of industry to liberate and change the social order. It flourished in the major capitals of the West in the 1920s, but was challenged by the political and economic strife of the 1930s. The collapse of

Germany, the rise of Hitler to power, a worldwide economic depression, and Stalin's harsh state control in the Soviet Union often made the highly contrived esthetic surface of modernist art seem disengaged from the struggles of daily life. In the **SOCIAL REALISM** advocated by the Communist Party, in Bertolt Brecht's experiments with **EPIC THEATER,** in the oppositional literature that flourished in Europe and the West throughout the 1930s, the formal experimentation of modernism was often replaced by a more pressing sense of social engagement. By the 1950s, however, "modernism" had become part of "official" culture, losing much of its avant-garde, oppositional flavor. The poetry of the modernists was taught in colleges; the paintings of the modern artists were shown in prestigious museums; and the plays of modern playwrights were often in "revival"— modernism had become the classic art of the early twentieth century.

## After Modernism

Not surprisingly, then, "modernism" itself became something to resist, to repudiate. The impact of Antonin Artaud's **THEATER OF CRUELTY,** of the **THEATER OF THE ABSURD** (discussed in Unit 2), of the "new novel" in France, of Jackson Pollock's drip-painting, and— eventually—of the whole dizzying play of **POSTMODERNISM** (discussed in Unit 3) are, in this sense, both implicated in and resistant to the categories of modernism. For the art of the post–World War II period marks out the limitations of modernism in a variety of ways. First, "modernism" was a European affair, enabled by a eurocentric and even imperialist sense of cultural hegemony. But since 1950, this kind of bias has become increasingly untenable. The aftermath of World War II saw the remapping of the planet and increasing resistance to the domination of the Western powers: the independence of India, Pakistan, and many Asian and African nations from colonial rule; liberation movements in the 1980s and 1990s in the Eastern Bloc countries; the founding of Israel and the displacement and resistance of the Palestinians; and wars in Korea, Indochina, the Middle East, Africa, the Persian Gulf, and the Balkans. Those decades also witnessed bitter civil strife in Northern Ireland, Argentina, Chile, the United States, Europe, and elsewhere; the Cuban missile crisis, the building and dismantling of the Berlin Wall; the civil rights movement in the United States and the installation (and, slowly, the waning) of apartheid in South Africa. With the rise of global communications, a global economy, and global political and military interests, such social and political revolutions immediately become the world's business. They reshape the world we live in even as we watch the changes unfold on our flickering television screens. Television, fortunately, has not yet transformed the world's diverse cultures into a single "global village," but local cultures all feel the impact of events around the world. Think of the global effects of environmental disasters like Chernobyl and the deforestation of the rain forests of the Amazon; of medical advances like vaccination and of epidemics like AIDS; of the international effects of social movements like nuclear disarmament, human rights, Amnesty International, feminism, and the peace movement, or, more horrifyingly, of anti-Semitism, racism, and homophobia.

Modernist art—the art, after all, of the turn-of-the-century political and economic empires of the West—tended to appropriate or steal the cultures of the world: think of the "African" motif of Picasso's famous painting "Les Demoiselles D'Avignon" (1906–1907); of Eliot's inclusion of Eastern mysticism in *The Waste Land* ("Shantih shantih shantih"); of the ritualized elements of Stravinsky's *Le Sacre du Printemps;* of the entire sense in which "primitivism" became synonymous in modernist art with the lost vitality of Western culture. But the notion that a "universal" experience could be centered in a central, metropolitan consciousness seems hardly a possibility in the more dispersed, media-responsive, and politically decentered world of the late twentieth century. Since 1950, modernism has been resisted and reshaped in a number of ways: in an art that is often more avowedly political, interested in showing the ways that individual consciousness and artistic representation are bound up in the larger political and economic processes of the world at large—of which the impact of Brecht's Berliner Ensemble is perhaps the best example. But contemporary art has been more determinedly obsessed about the problem of "meaning" itself, about the ways that artistic representation intersects with—or stands apart from—the world at large. This anxious exploration of the materials and processes of artistic representation can be seen to inform a variety of stylistically disparate experiments in the last half of the twentieth century: the nihilism of Beckett; the deformed realism of playwrights like Pinter and Shepard; the antinarratives of novelists like Alain Robbe-Grillet and Don De Lillo, or in the theater, of playwrights like Adrienne Kennedy and Heiner Müller; the movement from Jackson Pollock's fascination with the surface of painting to, say, the distorted portraits of Francis Bacon, or Eric Fischl's uncanny normality. And while modernist art often appropriated "popular culture," more recent art has tended to invade popular culture, to become in some sense part of popular culture—Andy Warhol's "portraits" of Campbell's soup cans are perhaps the best example of this tendency. Art after the 1950s and 1960s most often works to transgress the boundaries that conventionally separate "art" from "life," the boundaries separating fact from fiction, representation from reality.

From the outset, drama and theater have had an unstable relation to the trajectory of modernist innovation in the arts. There are, of course, several fully modernist theatrical innovations—Meyerhold's **CONSTRUCTIVIST THEATER** after the Russian Revolution, for example (see Unit 1)—and several fully modernist reshapings of dramatic style as well—theater of the absurd, epic theater, and so on. But in many respects the kind of formal experimentation that seemed to define modern art seemed more difficult to achieve in the theater and in the drama. This may have something to do with a relatively limited sense of the medium of the stage. The use of human actors—rather than, say, paint, marble, or mere words—seemed to many innovators in the early twentieth century to restrict the theater to verisimilitude; this could be said in a qualified way even of Ibsen, Chekhov, Shaw, or Pirandello. Even the principal reactions against realism in the early decades of the century—**EXPRESSIONISM** and **SURREALISM** (see Unit 1)—were nonetheless focused in the internal, psychological processes of dramatic characters and tended to use relatively "realistic" means to act them out: August Strindberg's *A Dream Play*, while following the elusive logic of a dream, is nonetheless a "narrative" play with a series of characters, who relate to one another in largely realistic ways. Although much of modern literature and visual arts gave up a direct representation of reality, of "characters" and a recognizable world, in order to direct attention to the ways that art constructed itself and mediated a vision of the world, modern theater often remained wedded to these notions: even a play like Pirandello's *Six Characters in Search of an Author*, which does interrogate the medium of theater, does so in the "realistic" mode. Brecht's epic theater of the 1930s undertakes a new way of looking at character and society, but continues the realistic focus on it as well. In fact, many of the most explicitly modernist innovations in twentieth-century theater take place in the sphere of performance, rather than in the sphere of dramatic, "literary" composition: the alogical performances of the Dada cabarets; the abstract, visually oriented productions of the Italian Futurists; or in the innovations of movement and signification we usually associate with modern dance. It might be said that modernist fragmentation and disjunction appears in *drama* most fully in the work of Samuel Beckett and of absurd theater generally, where fragmentation of the body and of the world it inhabits, takes place with an increasingly skeptical regard for narrative, for plot, for the conventional materials of dramatic as well as theatrical composition.

Drama and Theater in the Twentieth Century

This collection traces the trajectory of modern theater and drama, first in relation to modernism, and then through the various reactions to modernism that characterize the contemporary theater. The first unit, "The Emergence of Modern Drama: 1850–1950," outlines the first generation of twentieth-century drama, in particular the impact of realism in the theater. It concludes, however, with Bertolt Brecht's strategic assault on the ways that realism not only shows the world but becomes complicit in reproducing it, and in reproducing its particular strategies of maintaining an oppressive status quo. The second unit, "Revolution and Reaction: 1950–1970," sketches the rise of a series of oppositional modes of theater, not only the arbitrary and aleatory world of theater of the absurd, but the more strategic assaults on the Western representation of reality by writers standing apart from modernism's claim to represent the "universal" truth: women, people of color, writers from the postcolonial "periphery" of modernism's metropolitan consciousness. Although these issues are continued into the third unit, "Modern/Postmodern: 1970–   ," this unit also attempts to examine the ways in which a characteristically "postmodern" interfusion of representational media and representational agendas inflects the work of playwrights and producers.

# UNIT 1

## The Emergence of Modern Drama: 1850-1950

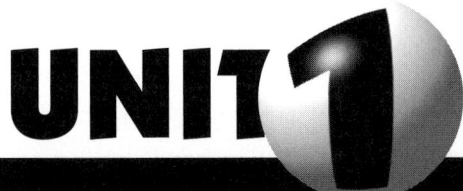

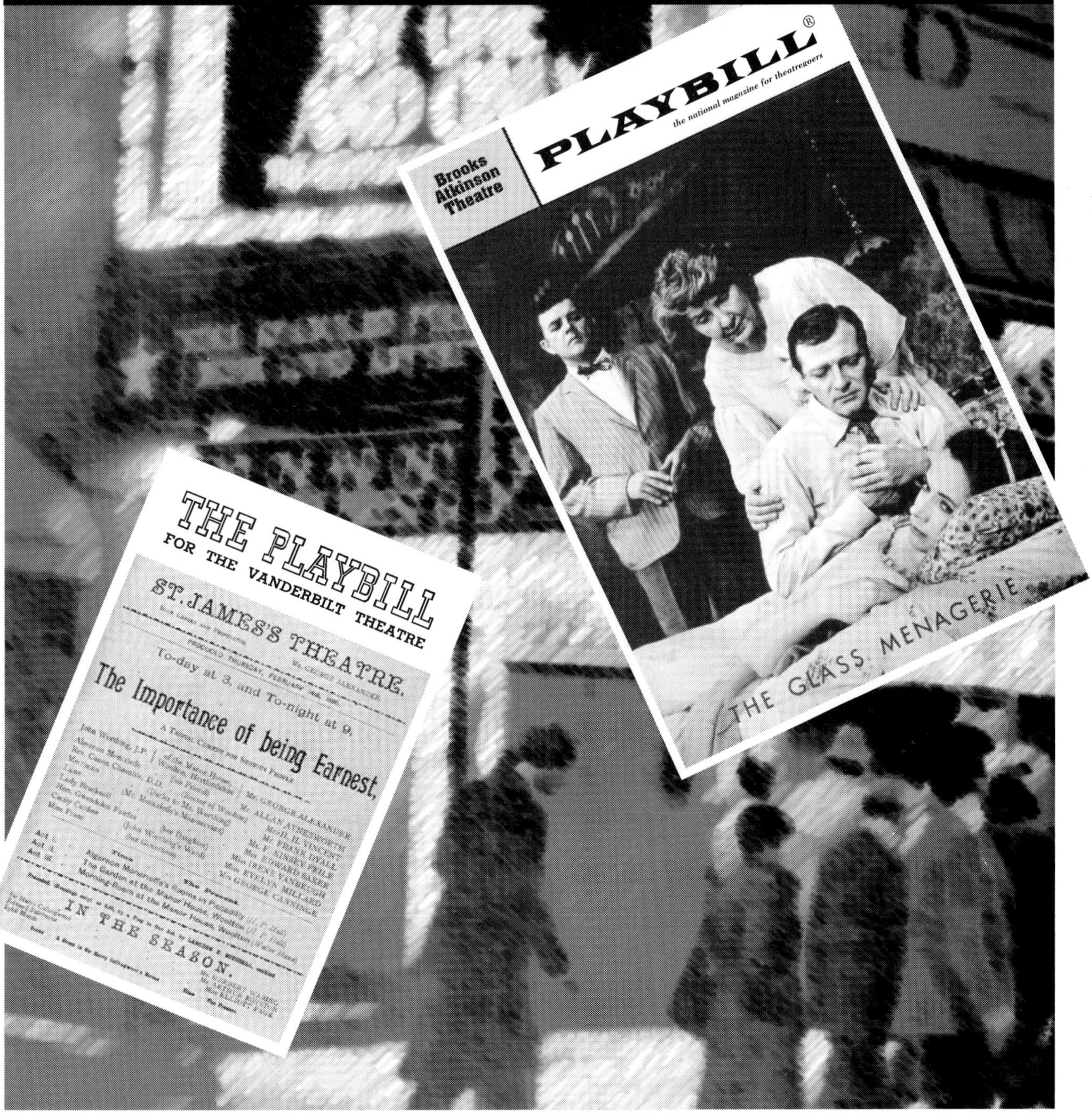


PLAYBILL® is a registered trademark of Playbill Incorporated, N.Y.C. Used by permission.

THEATRICAL INNOVATION ALWAYS TAKES PLACE on three fronts: as technology, as esthetics, and as ideology. The history of the modern theater is in one sense a history of new strategies and techniques for stage production: electric lighting, revolving stages, increasingly spectacular and illusionistic stage machinery, and new techniques of stage design, acting, and direction. But what makes these changes meaningful is how they are used to represent and explain the world around us.

Reviewing the history of nineteenth-century drama, Brander Matthews—the first professor of dramatic literature in the United States—remarked in 1910 that the theater owed more of its innovations to Edison than to Ibsen, that modern drama was "the inevitable consequence of the incandescent bulb." The technological revolutions that brought engines and electricity to the public transformed theater throughout Europe and America: the replacement of the candle lighting and gas lighting of the nineteenth-century theater with more flexible electric lighting; the installation of the **PROSCENIUM** frame, emphasizing the pictorial coherence of the stage; the gradual development of seating the audience in darkened, fan-shaped theaters, emphasizing a perspective view of the stage; elevators to raise and lower sets; revolving stages on which several settings could be placed at one time. This technology could be put to a variety of uses, and the nineteenth-century theaters of Europe and America had an extraordinarily spectacular dimension, fostering a taste for **EXTRAVAGANZAS, MELODRAMAS, NAUTICAL SHOWS, PANTOMIMES,** and **TABLEAUX.** But the use of the modern theater machine came increasingly to be dominated by the notion of **SCENIC UNITY,** the idea that the stage set, the costumes, the behavior of the actors, and the dramatic action all should correspond to a single historical era and social milieu. Shakespeare's actors had mixed contemporary Elizabethan dress with "antique" costumes in the production of plays with classical settings; throughout the eighteenth century actors wore contemporary clothing regardless of the historical era of the play. By the late nineteenth century, however, following the example of Charles Kean and Henry Irving in England, the company of George II, the Duke of Saxe-Meiningen in Germany, and others, productions increasingly strove to establish a unified style on the stage, in which the dialogue, acting style, costumes, setting, and dramatic action all conformed to a single point of view.

The use of a unified theatrical style to assert a thorough **VERISIMILITUDE,** a photographic "slice of life" onstage, became the cornerstone of modern **REALISM** in drama and theater, and of the movement called **NATURALISM** in which it began. In a series of essays calling for a "naturalism in the theater," published in the 1870s, the French novelist and playwright Émile Zola argued that the technology of the late nineteenth-century theater could be used to represent a more clinical or scientific attitude toward the world; he urged the stage to adopt a more lifelike and "naturalistic" style by adopting the "objective" methods and perspective of the natural sciences. By filling the stage with objects— real doors, real walls, pictures, furniture, fireplaces—the theater could place men and women in their "environment" rather than in the idealized "setting" of the classical theater, and the characters could then be seen as influenced by that material environment. In contrast to the ideal heroes of earlier drama, the characters of modern plays would become part of that stage milieu, influenced by the forces of history, society, economy, and psychology. Naturalism, that is, uses the technology of the stage to claim a "scientific" attitude toward social problems, usually emphasizing the determining role that the social environment plays in the characters' actions. Naturalism organized the theater's new technology and the idea of scenic unity it made possible, and provided it with a characteristic kind of meaning: the achievement of verisimilitude.

Naturalism and realism are notoriously difficult to distinguish; here we can describe them as two phases in the history of modern theater and drama. In this sense, naturalism provides the thematic inspiration and many of the dramatic techniques we now associate with modern realistic drama. Realism in the theater is also committed to verisimilitude, but usually develops a more problematic sense of the relationship of character, environment, and theatrical production. While naturalistic plays tend to be preoccupied with the duplication of material reality onstage, realistic plays sometimes distort the verisimilitude of the stage picture in order to dramatize an inner, psychological truth. Ibsen's Master Builder Solness, for example, seems to live in a symbolic landscape where inner fantasy and external "reality" are nearly indistinguishable. Tom, in Tennessee Williams's *The Glass Menagerie,* moves in and out of the realistic setting onstage, between the world of memory, the world of the audience, and the objective social reality of the drama. Realism extends and refines the techniques first explored by Zola's generation of playwrights, directors, and actors: a simple and direct speaking style that usually masks a **SUBTEXT** of subtle, unspoken motives; middle- or lower-class characters; action that revolves around the discovery of some past crime or indiscretion; a three-dimensional stage set, usually a domestic interior. Rather than using the play as a vehicle for a single "star" actor, realistic performance emphasizes the ensemble playing of the cast, so that each character becomes important in the overall action. Onstage, realism often treats the boundary of the proscenium as an invisible **FOURTH WALL** dividing the environment onstage from the audience; the fourth wall prevents the actors from playing to the audience and so from destroying the unity of illusion onstage. Yet even this "fourth wall" convention can be broken to dramatic effect. In Act Two of her suffrage play *Votes for Women!,* Elizabeth Robins breaks the frame of the proscenium by having her heroine Vida Levering deliver an impassioned plea for the vote to an audience onstage that blurs into the offstage audience in the theater seats. In so doing, Robins both confirms and subverts the politics of distance characteristic of pictorial realism in the theater.

Realism has become the dominant mode of Western dramatic performance in the twentieth century, so pervasive that it may be difficult for us to recapture its special excitement and danger when first introduced in the 1880s. For in the first blush of the modern era, the ability to picture an untheatrical, apparently "real" world on the stage was in itself a kind of spectacle, akin to the magic of the new, competing arts of photography and film. Moreover, the first generation of realistic playwrights often adopted a critical posture toward the pieties of the middle-class audience whose attitudes were embodied in the "realistic" vision of the world. Plays like Ibsen's *Ghosts* and *A Doll House,* Strindberg's *Miss Julie,* and even Robins's *Votes for Women!* raised the scandalous topics of sexual betrayal, marital discord, class conflict, sexual freedom, and gender politics in ways that challenged the conventional morality of the bourgeois audience.

The realistic theater developed many of the practices we are familiar with today: new sets and costumes for each production, rather than the same furniture recycled from show to show, in order to create the play's specific environment; the fourth wall; the darkened auditorium. And although realistic drama became pervasive, it first flourished in the small avant-garde theaters of the **INDEPENDENT THEATER MOVEMENT** at the turn of the century. Throughout Europe and the United States, playwrights and directors worked to carve a place for themselves outside the commercial mainstream, which often resisted and sometimes censored the controversial plays of the new realism. André Antoine founded the Théâtre Libre ("Free Theater") in Paris as a subscription theater in 1887; because the shows were open only to subscribers and not to the general public, he was able to avoid censorship and to produce plays like Ibsen's *Ghosts* and Strindberg's *The Father.* Antoine's work was paralleled by the German Freie Bühne ("Free Stage") in 1889. In England, the actress Janet Achurch mounted a production of Ibsen's *A Doll House* in 1889; J. T. Grein's Independent Theater opened in 1891 with a production of

*Ghosts* and went on to produce plays by Ibsen, Shaw, and other contemporary playwrights. In Russia, Constantin Stanislavski and Vladimir Nemirovich-Danchenko founded the Moscow Art Theater in 1898, launching one of the most influential of modern theaters with their production of Chekhov's *The Seagull.* Independent theaters were often part of nationalist movements as well, especially in Norway, Sweden, Italy, and Ireland. In Ireland, W. B. Yeats, Lady Augusta Gregory, John Synge, and a solid cast of amateur actors established a nationalist theater company in 1902, and opened The Abbey Theater in 1904. Here, the artistic resistance of the independent theater was allied to political resistance and national self-definition. The Court Theater, under the management of J. E. Vedrenne and Harley Granville Barker (1904–1907), produced a selection of classics and of new plays for the London intelligentsia and launched the most successful phase of Bernard Shaw's career as a playwright. The influence of these theaters was felt in the United States throughout the first decades of the twentieth century. The **LITTLE THEATER MOVEMENT,** inaugurated by Eugene O'Neill, Susan Glaspell, and their Provincetown Playhouse in 1915, helped establish a repertoire of modern drama in the United States.

The American theater was in some ways peripheral to the energetic traditions of European theater. Although turn-of-the-century Broadway developed a home-grown version of theatrical realism—epitomized by writer/producer David Belasco's *The Governor's Lady* (1912), which reproduced the interior of a familiar theater-district restaurant onstage—European experimentation made its impact on America in more indirect ways, usually only after those experiments had crystallized into a body of theatrical practices and conventions. Many major companies toured the United States: the Abbey Theater came with John Millington Synge's *The Playboy of the Western World* in 1911–1912; the German producer Max Reinhardt brought his spectacular productions to the United States in 1912, 1914, 1924, and 1927–1928; the British director Harley Granville Barker, who sponsored Shaw's plays and had gained fame as an innovative director of Shakespeare, directed in New York in 1915; the Ballets Russes toured in 1916; the Moscow Art Theater—whose disciples Richard Boleslavsky and Maria Ouspenskaya founded the American Laboratory Theater in 1923—performed in 1923–1924.

Some innovation came from the new college and university programs in drama; George Pierce Baker's famous playwriting course at Harvard in the first decades of the century (taken by Eugene O'Neill, among many others) and George T. Montgomery's program for African-American writers and performers at Howard University in the 1920s were only the beginning of a concerted effort to bring theater and drama into the university curriculum and to develop a greater awareness of progressive theater. But it largely fell to the **LITTLE THEATER MOVEMENT** to assimilate this new work and redirect it toward particularly American concerns. Innovation in the American theater came largely from these small companies, committed to mounting new and uncommercial work: the Chicago Little Theater, the Toy Theater of Boston, the Neighborhood Playhouse and the Washington Square Playhouse of New York, and Detroit's Arts and Crafts Theater were all in operation by 1917; the **LITTLE NEGRO THEATER MOVEMENT** was producing plays in Harlem and Washington, D. C., as well.

The Provincetown Playhouse provides a model of the American "little theaters" and their fortunes in the early twentieth century. Founded in 1915 in Provincetown, Massachusetts—an artists' retreat at the tip of Cape Cod—the company was initially a group of young amateurs intent on theater, including the playwright Susan Glaspell, her husband George Cram Cook, and later Eugene O'Neill. In the first year, the players produced plays in their summer homes; in 1916 they converted an old wharf building into a

**European Influence and American Innovation**

small theater, and produced, among other plays, O'Neill's *Bound East for Cardiff*. In the autumn, the players returned to New York and opened a small theater in Greenwich Village. Like their European counterparts, the company could hardly afford complex and expensive sets and made a virtue of necessity, turning their efforts instead toward a simple and realistic kind of performance. Eugene O'Neill's early plays were produced by the Provincetown company, and after he became a successful Broadway playwright, he continued to open many of his plays there. Like all of the "little theaters," the Provincetown had difficulty managing the transition from a small amateur company to the larger demands of a self-sustaining professional company. It went through a series of transformations before closing in 1929, having introduced O'Neill to the stage and having staged works by John Reed, Edna St. Vincent Millay, Susan Glaspell, Djuna Barnes, Edmund Wilson, Paul Green, Wallace Stevens, Theodore Dreiser, August Strindberg, and many others.

In the early decades of the twentieth century, the American theater also confronted—and evaded—the divisive issue of national culture: How could a theater largely in the hands of the white, Anglo, male, middle class adequately represent the diversity of the nation's experience, particularly the experience of the oppressed? As the poet and playwright Langston Hughes suggested in "Notes on Commercial Theater," published in 1940, the stage had in many ways appropriated African-American culture, systematically absorbing it into its own dominant values:

> Yep, you done taken my blues and gone.
> You also took my spirituals and gone.
> You put me in *Macbeth* and *Carmen Jones*
> And all kinds of *Swing Mikados*
> And in everything but what's about me—
> But someday somebody'll
> Stand up and talk about me,
> And write about me—
> Black and beautiful—

Far from representing authentic African-American experience, such theater more often confirmed the discriminatory fantasies already prominent on the stage and in society. Such stereotypes as the boozy Irishman, the dull Swede, the sunny and/or murderous Italian, and the greedy Jew—appearing even in "realistic" plays like Elmer Rice's *Street Scene* (1929)—work to reinforce the "normative" perspective of dominant culture, reflecting the attitudes, behavior, and social practices that oppress such groups in the world outside the theater. It is not surprising, then, that throughout the history of the United States, ethnic theaters have played a prominent part in maintaining the cultural identity of America's minority populations: the Yiddish theater of New York, Polish theaters in Chicago, Scandinavian theaters throughout the Midwest, a thriving circuit of Spanish-language theaters shared by Mexico and southwestern states from Texas to California, Cuban-influenced theater in Florida, and Puerto Rican theater in New York. Some of these theaters produced versions of classic European plays in their own accents, but most developed their own dramatic forms as ways of maintaining themselves in the face of a brutally exclusive "American" culture.

The experience of slavery places African Americans in a different position vis-à-vis the culture of the United States, and the black theater has had a profound impact on the course of the modern stage. Although an African Theater Company was founded in New York in 1821—sponsoring, among others, the brilliant Shakespearean actor Ira Aldridge (1807–1867) who left the United States for a distinguished career in Europe—in the main, African Americans had little direct access to the theater before the twentieth century. Black characters had long figured as stage villains and comic "coons" in American drama. Played by white actors in blackface makeup, these abusive types literally enacted white attitudes toward racial difference: "Jim Crow" was first popularized by the white song-and-dance man T. D. Rice in the 1830s; more "sympathetic" characters, like Tom in the hugely popular stage adaptations of Harriet Beecher Stowe's *Uncle Tom's Cabin* (1832), were devised by white authors and played by white actors; the minstrel troupes that became popular after the Civil War for depicting romanticized vignettes of plantation life were also first performed by white actors. Later, black performers—in minstrel troupes or in the newly popular "Negro musicals"—often had little choice other than to enact these stereotypes themselves, for such roles were the only openings available on the stage (even black theaters were usually financed and operated by white entrepreneurs). Despite inroads like the Lafayette Theater (founded in Harlem in 1915), representing black experience to America at large was almost exclusively the prerogative of white actors, producers, playwrights, and performers. In this regard, the theater—like the institutions of literature, the press, the legal system, and state and federal government—denied African Americans their own voice.

Spurred in part by successful plays by white dramatists that self-consciously attempted to "humanize" black characters for white audiences—O'Neill's *The Emperor Jones* (1920) and *All God's Chillun Got Wings* (1924), Marc Connelly's *The Green Pastures* (1930), Paul Green's *In Abraham's Bosom* (1926), and Dubose and Dorothy Heyward's *Porgy* (1920; transformed into the Gershwin musical *Porgy and Bess* in 1935)—African-American actors and writers became galvanized to "stand up and talk" about themselves, at first through the work of the **LITTLE NEGRO THEATER MOVEMENT.** The Lafayette Theater, for example, opened Willis Richardson's *The Chipwoman's Fortune* in 1923; it later became the first play by an African-American playwright to reach Broadway. In the 1920s and 1930s, plays—often written by women—increasingly addressed the politics of racism in the United States, while also depicting the effect of racism in daily life. Several organizations worked to sponsor drama and theater more effectively. W. E. B. DuBois, a founder of the National Association for the Advancement of Colored People (NAACP), used his *Crisis* magazine—in collaboration with the National Urban League's *Opportunity*—to give a series of prizes to promising black playwrights; winners included Eulalie Spence's *Foreign Mail* (1926), Zora Neale Hurston's *Colorstruck* and *Spears* (1925), and Georgia Douglas Johnson's *Blue Blood* (1926). The NAACP also sponsored the production of plays, including Angelina Weld Grimké's influential drama of a young woman's reaction to the lynching of her father and brother, *Rachel* (1916). *Rachel* was one of the first of a series of plays about lynching. How this important genre of black theater—and a crucial element of black experience in the United States—was both overlooked and distorted by the white theater is the subject of Alice Childress's brilliant play, *Trouble in Mind*, which opened off-Broadway in 1955. Finally, black colleges, universities, and even high schools also became centers for a new dramatic repertory. In 1921, Montgomery T. Gregory formed a department of Dramatic Arts at Howard University in Washington, D. C., and with Alain Locke developed an influential program in acting, playwriting, and theatrical production, offering the first institutionalized training for black writers and performers in the United States.

In a 1926 playbill for Harlem's Krigwa Players, W. E. B. DuBois described the goals of a "Negro theater":

The plays of a real Negro theater must be:
*One: About us.* That is, they must have plots which reveal Negro life as it is. *Two: By us.*

That is, they must be written by Negro authors who understand from birth and continual association just what it means to be a Negro today. *Three: For us.* That is, the theater must cater primarily to Negro audiences and be supported and sustained by their entertainment and approval. *Fourth: Near us.* The theater must be in a Negro neighborhood near the mass of ordinary Negro people.

Throughout the 1930s and 1940s, African-American playwrights and actors came into increasing national prominence, both by developing DuBois's agenda and by working to bring an authentic black drama to a wider audience. Langston Hughes wrote a number of plays in the 1930s, including the well-known *Mulatto* (1935); the Federal Theater Project produced W. E. B. DuBois's *Haiti* at the Lafayette Theater; and plays by playwrights trained at Howard were produced in New York and elsewhere. The founding of companies like the American Negro Theater in 1939, the Negro Playwrights Company in 1940, and the Negro Ensemble Company in 1957 began to meet DuBois's charge, developing the actors, the production experience, and the financing that would sustain the explosive growth of black-American drama after World War II. When Lorraine Hansberry's *A Raisin in the Sun* opened in 1959, it was the first play written by an African-American woman to reach Broadway, the first directed by an African-American director (Lloyd Richards), and the first financed predominantly by African Americans. The success of *Raisin* foretold the success of black theater in the coming decades, as playwrights (see Units 2 and 3)—Amiri Baraka, Adrienne Kennedy, Charles Gordone, Ed Bullins, Charles Fuller, Ntozake Shange, August Wilson, George C. Wolfe, Anna Deavere Smith, and many others—came to shape the modern theater.

## Forms of Modern Drama

The rise of the independent and "little" theaters also points to the theater's fragmentation and its marginalization in modern society. The theater no longer commands the cultural centrality that it had in classical Athens or in London and Paris in the sixteenth and seventeenth centuries; instead, it has become the site for a diverse, sometimes confusing array of artistic experiments. Naturalism and realism were the first dramatic modes to consider themselves not as expressions of the dominant political and ideological order, but as criticizing the values and institutions of middle-class society. The major plays of the realistic canon often tend to criticize modern life, particularly its dehumanizing, exploitative routine. The major heroes of the realistic mode—Master Builder Solness, Chekhov's Prozorov sisters, Hector Hushabye, Laura Wingfield—are all characters whose desire for freedom, vitality, and life is threatened by the deadening, deceptive world in which they live. Because realistic drama usually sees that world as an all-embracing "environment," though, its social themes do not often lead to an effective call for social change. Modern society may be a prison, but the liberation urged by realistic drama is imagined on the individual level; the characters' search for freedom, value, and meaning leaves the world unchanged. Despite its critical stance toward modern society, realistic drama tacitly accepts the world and its values as an unchanging, and unchangeable, environment in which the characters live out their lives.

For this reason, realistic drama has often seemed an inadequate vehicle for a sustained critique of the forces of modern life, and almost from the moment of its inception in the 1880s and 1890s realism inspired antagonistic forms of drama and theater. The history of modern drama is a series of reactions against bourgeois society and its values, and against the realistic drama that seemed to represent it and its vision of the world. Although it was finally concerned with many of the same issues, the **EXPRESSIONIST THEATER** popular from the turn of the century through the 1930s marked an exciting stylistic departure from the realistic mode. Expressionist plays like Strindberg's *A Dream Play,* or American plays like Elmer Rice's *The Adding Machine*, Sophie Treadwell's *Machinal*, or Eugene O'Neill's *The Emperor Jones*, transformed the terms of realistic theater and drama. Rather than showing characters whose inner vitality is crushed by the bourgeois environment, expressionist plays try to show the mind and heart of the character visually, to express it directly in the objects and actions of the stage. The stage set becomes distorted, nearly dreamlike, and it is often peopled by characters who are exaggerated, mechanized, or fantastic, as a way of conveying the emotional coloring of the central character's experience. In Strindberg's *A Dream Play*, for instance, the audience follows the Daughter of Indra through a series of scenes—the growing castle, the law office, Foul Strand and Fair Haven—that seem to blend into each other with the erratic logic of dreams. More often, characters in expressionist drama are unnamed, like the Young Woman of *Machinal* or Mr. Zero of *The Adding Machine*, emphasizing that they have become cogs in the modern social and industrial machine. The action of expressionist drama is episodic and much like morality drama; Ernst Toller even named the scenes of his play *Transfiguration* "stations" to stress the play's likeness to a Christian passion play.

Thematically, expressionist theater resembles realism in its attention to character psychology and in its portrayal—however distorted or exaggerated—of the dehumanizing process of modern life. But the style of expressionism also subverts realism in important ways, challenging both the logical, causal ordering of realistic dramatic action and the visual verisimilitude of the realistic theater. **SYMBOLIST THEATER** also developed antirealistic attitudes toward drama and staging, and extended the expressionist theater's repudiation of the drama of modern life. Written in prose or in verse, symbolic drama created a dim and mysterious other world, sometimes drawn from mythology or simply from the poet's imagination. The Belgian playwright Maurice Maeterlinck created a vogue for this kind of drama at the turn of the century, a drama that finds analogies in the work of Stéphane Mallarmé, August Strindberg, T. S. Eliot, W. B. Yeats, and Samuel Beckett. Yeats's mythological plays—such as *On Baile's Strand*—are typical of this special and influential mode. Relatively static in action, the plays rely on a densely figurative language to enlarge and energize the "poetic" meaning of events onstage.

Finally, an explicitly Marxist theory of the ideologically coercive dimension of realism—the sense that realism claims that its special perspective of the world is *natural,* that is, unavoidable and *real*—stands at the center of modern **EPIC THEATER.** Though usually associated with Bertolt Brecht, many of the techniques of epic theater were developed by Erwin Piscator in Berlin during the 1920s and early 1930s, and in Vsevolod Meyerhold's brilliant experiments with **CONSTRUCTIVIST THEATER** after the Russian Revolution of 1917. Brecht assimilated these techniques to a political purpose that he called epic theater. Rather than claiming to represent reality directly onstage by concealing the workings of the theater, epic theater alerts the audience to the ideological dimension of theater practice by constantly keeping the stage's "means of production" in view. Brecht developed the **ALIENATION EFFECT** as a way of alerting the audience to the constructed nature of stage events. While the realistic theater claims that the theater and drama, actor and character, stage and dramatic locale are the same, epic theater shows how they are different. In so doing, Brecht argued, the epic theater enables the audience to ask how—with what purpose, to what effect—stage practice is making this dramatic effect come about, and so leads the audience to take a more critical view of the process of the theater. Epic acting, then, comments on itself as "acting"; the stage is not unified as a single dramatic locale, but always remains visibly a stage. Brecht also argued that epic drama should be structured differently than realistic plays are. Instead of the apparently organic, "causal" action of realistic drama, Brecht's plays are written in a series of episodes; this technique, Brecht argued, allows the actors and the audience to reconsider the character's possibilities for action and change afresh in each scene. By calling the audience's attention to how the play comes into being onstage, epic theater encourages the audience to develop a dialectical sense of how social reality—in the theater and in the world at large—comes into being, how it is made through the interaction of individual and social forces. Epic theater has had an enormous influence on drama and theater around the world, particularly after World War II.

Stage practice has developed its own rich history, too—again often in reaction to realistic verisimilitude. Throughout the twentieth century, for instance, designers and architects have experimented with different ways of orienting the audience to the stage, in **THEATER-IN-THE-ROUND** and in **ENVIRONMENTAL THEATER,** for instance. To see the dramatic action surrounded by spectators, or to have the play take place among the audience, alters the audience's relationship to both the drama and its performance and changes how the audience can read the production. The **CONSTRUCTIVIST THEATER** experiments of Vsevolod Meyerhold following the Russian Revolution placed a nonrepresentational "construction" onstage, a structure that the actors used as a "machine for acting" rather than as a realistic set. Similarly, experimental performance altered notions of what dramatic and theatrical representation could be like. Following World War I, writers like Tristan Tzara called for an art that was formless and irrational, a process rather than a product; such "Dada"—a nonsense term—poems, plays, and monologues were often performed in **CABARET PERFORMANCE** in Zurich, Berlin, and Paris. **DADA** and **SURREALIST THEATER** developed a kind of hallucinatory intimacy between stage and audience, laying the foundations for Artaud's **THEATER OF CRUELTY** (see Unit 2). In all of these experiments, the theater worked to disperse the visual unity characteristic of the realistic stage, in ways that led to new configurations of the relationship between the audience and the performers, and to new interpretive perspectives on drama and on the possibilities of theater.

*Realism, expressionism, symbolist theater,* and *epic theater*—these useful labels necessarily limit and categorize the rich variety of the stage in ways that are artificial and untrue to the dynamics of change in the modern theater, for new innovations tend to draw their techniques from several of these modes. Modern plays, for instance, often blend representational techniques as a way of challenging the audience's understanding of the drama and its implication in the world. Despite their "realistic" anchoring in a material, lifelike setting, for example, Chekhov's plays sometimes disturb the stability of that illusion with odd, almost "symbolic" effects—the "photograph" scene in *The Three Sisters,* for instance, that stills the cast onstage in an eerie tableau. Shaw's *Heartbreak House* is held together more by its mournful tone and "ship of state" metaphor than by the logic of its plot. In Pirandello's *Six Characters in Search of an Author*—a play indebted in many ways to the "symbolist" theater—the Characters want the Actors to produce a play much in the manner of Ibsen's drama, a realistic drama of hidden crime and its discovery. These labels are useful in helping us describe some of the outlines of a given play, but we should remember that many modern playwrights wrote in a variety of modes and that each play is itself a kind of experiment.

## Acting and Performance

The modern theater's radical redefinitions of the style and purpose of drama required similar redefinitions of acting and performance. At the turn of the century, a theatrical company would have been organized according to each actor's typical **LINE OF BUSINESS.** Something like the company in Pirandello's *Six Characters,* companies had a leading comic actor, a villain or "heavy," a leading man, a leading lady, a comic old man, a comic woman, and a variety of other parts. Actors each played a variety of different characters, but each actor would have elaborated some relatively conventional "business" for acting the kind of character he or she usually played. The unity of illusion demanded by the realistic theater, however, required each character to be more finely individualized. Much as the stage designer provided a new set for each production and the costume designer provided clothing appropriate to the character and his or her setting, so the actors were forced to particularize their performances in new ways.

A second stimulus for this innovation was the drama itself. Playwrights like Ibsen and Chekhov typically created characters against the grain of theatrical stereotypes. Hilde Wangel, for example, seems like a typical **SOUBRETTE** at the opening of *The Master Builder,* the pert and clever young woman of light comedy. But as the play develops, Ibsen challenges this convention, as Hilde's desperate, densely metaphorical struggle to possess Solness seems to move nearly out of the register of realism altogether. Realistic plays frequently ask actors to work against the apparent "type" of the role, to discover the psychological **SUBTEXT** of will and desire beneath the spoken words that motivates the character's actions. Much like the Actors confronted by the baffling Characters of Pirandello's *Six Characters,* actors and actresses at the turn of the century frequently had difficulty reading the new realistic plays, precisely because they could not imagine how to represent the more indirect action and individualized characters of modern plays through the kinds of stage behavior they had been trained to use.

A new kind of drama requires a new kind of acting, and companies throughout Europe developed ways of acting more behavioristically onstage. The most systematic approach to acting was undertaken by the actor and director Constantin Stanislavski at the Moscow Art Theater in the first decades of the twentieth century. Although Stanislavski thought that his techniques could be applied to any play, he discovered the need for such acting largely in his work on Chekhov's drama. Chekhov's plays were frustrating to actors of the old school because the characters did not conform to traditional types, and the action seemed so indirect and inconsequential, and lacked familiar dramatic rhythms and climaxes. Stanislavski developed techniques for approaching each character as an individual, techniques that were later systematized as a "method" of actor training. Stanislavski trained the actor to associate his or her personal history with the invented actions of the dramatic character, so that the actor could tap that emotional spontaneity, a "life in art," as part of the performance. By using the **MAGIC IF**—imagining themselves *as* the character, rather than applying a stock line of business—and using their own **EMOTION MEMORY** to vivify the character's inner life, Stanislavski's actors were taught to bring authentic emotional experience into their performances. Of course, Stanislavski also emphasized the many other abilities that an actor must develop—physical training, vocal control, grace, concentration—but his principal contribution to the modern stage is the emphasis on the actor's emotional reality in performance. The realistic theater uses real objects to create a persuasive material environment, and its characters come alive through the actor's real feeling.

Stanislavski's work has been extremely influential, particularly in the United States, where it was adapted as the school of **METHOD ACTING** in the 1930s, and it remains—in very different and modified forms—at the center of much actor training today. Eventually including Harold Clurman, Cheryl Crawford, Lee Strasberg, Elia Kazan, Sanford Meisner, and many others, the Group Theater of the 1930s at first worked on plays examining the social ferment and hardship of the Great Depression. Much as Chekhov became the centerpiece of Stanislavski's Moscow Art Theater, so the plays of Clifford Odets became the Group's standards: *Awake and Sing!, Waiting for Lefty,* and *Golden Boy.* But the Group's most extensive contribution to the American theater was its systematic importation of Stanislavskian acting techniques. In the Group, and later in the Actors Studio, actors were trained in Stanislavski's approach to emotion memory and **GIVEN**

CIRCUMSTANCES, laying the groundwork for what became a distinctly "American" style of acting: emotionally spontaneous, grounded in subtext, psychologically realistic and nuanced. The Group, the Studio, and the training they devised produced a generation of actors ready to meet the challenges of the burgeoning American drama of the 1940s and 1950s: Marlon Brando, Ben Gazzara, Karl Malden, Geraldine Page, Kim Stanley, Maureen Stapleton, and many others.

The impact of this acting can be seen in the great stage productions of the postwar period. The 1940s and early 1950s saw the development of a distinctively American approach to stage realism, balancing nuanced characterization with a concern for the social environment. Arthur Miller's *Death of a Salesman* and *The Crucible,* Tennessee Williams's *A Streetcar Named Desire* and *The Glass Menagerie,* and Eugene O'Neill's *The Iceman Cometh* and *Long Day's Journey into Night* demanded the subtle realism that became the hallmark of American acting, and of American drama in the world repertoire. These plays—and their descendants, like the plays of Marsha Norman, David Mamet, or Sam Shepard—succeeded by criticizing American ideals and institutions while at the same time exploring the psyche of the American character.

Antirealistic drama also called for the development of new styles of performance. Meyerhold developed BIOMECHANICS as a way to make the actor's performance more physical, less directly concerned with the behavioral and psychological verisimilitude typical of Stanislavskian realistic acting. His work has analogies in the use of dance and ritualized performance in symbolist theater and in the nonrepresentational physicality of Antonin Artaud's theater of cruelty (see Unit 2). Symbolist theater also repudiated the lifelike quality of realistic acting. It required a highly artificial and statuesque stillness from performers, allowing the actors to strike powerful but ethereal poses in order to deliver the densely poetic language of the play without interference. Yeats—whose antipathy to realism was profound—thought of training his actors in barrels, to keep them from moving and gesturing as they would do in everyday life, because the art of the symbolist theater should be emphatically artificial, thoroughly apart from the conduct of life beyond the stage.

Brecht, again, voiced the most thorough critique of realistic acting. To Brecht, the problem of realistic acting was that it showed the "character" as a finished product, a commodity, rather than revealing *how* the character had come into being, both through the social forces described in the drama and through the decisions taken by the actor as part of the performance. Brecht argued that the actor should acknowledge that he or she both empathizes with the character and demonstrates the character to the audience, that acting is both feeling and showing at the same time. This dialectical approach invites the audience to see how the actor is making the "character" and allows the public to interpret both the process and the product of theater art, the dramatic "character" and the actor's labor.

## Women in Modern Drama and Theater

Most readers of modern drama immediately note the prominence of women characters in the plays—Nora in *A Doll House,* Hilde in *The Master Builder,* the three sisters of Chekhov's play, Ellie, Hesione, and Ariadne in *Heartbreak House,* Laura Wingfield in *The Glass Menagerie,* Elizabeth Robins's Vida Levering. Playwrights frequently associated the political and social limitations of middle-class life with male characters and used female characters to pose subversive questions about that social order. But in the drama, as in society, this subversive freedom sometimes emerges as illusory or problematic. Chekhov's three sisters, for all their vivacity, are finally trapped in their illusions of romance; Ibsen's Nora slams the door on her husband, but the world outside her home hardly seems inviting—is there really anywhere for her to go? Many of these women—

Ellie Dunn, Hilde Wangel—are also assigned an erotic power opposed to the "reason" of their male antagonists; while this power, too, can be disruptive, it sometimes also reinforces the political structure of gender opposition and the social categories that support and extend it: woman/man : emotion/reason : nature/culture : bondage/freedom. Feminine erotic power in the drama carries with it other ascribed values, defining women as more emotional, as more subject to the influence of the body, as closer to "nature"; men retain a pragmatic, "rational" authority that places them at the center of society and that defines the arena of culture and civilization as an implicitly male domain. The apparent freedom of these stage women, that is, often signals their deeper captivity to the gendered economy of modern society, a captivity shared by the live women of the theater—actresses, playwrights, managers—in the period as well. As the actress, playwright, and suffragist Elizabeth Robins recognizes in her essay "The Feministe Movement in England," the "fierce tests" of public life familiar to the actress were often taken to be "unnatural" to women, as part of a systematic social, cultural, and ideological effort to position women in a position of privacy, inferiority, powerlessness (at the same time, it was regarded as part of the "natural" process of the law brutally to force-feed imprisoned suffragists who used hunger strikes as their only weapon of resistance). Although this is a period in which actresses—Robins, Sarah Bernhardt, Eleonora Duse, Ellen Terry, Helene Weigel, for example—could earn an international reputation, they worked in a theater in which men greatly outnumbered women in the audience, and in which nearly all of the managers and producers were men. Much of the work of contemporary theater scholars has been to recover the plays of important women playwrights—Susan Glaspell, Angelina Weld Grimké, Zora Neale Hurston, Georgia Douglas Johnson, Elizabeth Robins, Sophie Treadwell, and many others—whose work was not assimilated to the largely white, male "canon" of the "masters of modern drama." In a male-dominated industry like the modern theater, it is not surprising that women onstage—both dramatic characters and performers—reflect fundamentally masculine attitudes about the place of women in society.

To think of European and American theater and drama in the first decades of the twentieth century is to think of an increasingly large and problematic array of dramatic styles, modes of theatrical production, and conceptions of the audience and its world. Many of these innovations were local at first, responding to the social and theatrical conditions of a specific time and place: Brecht's Marxist theater arose in the cabaret culture of Berlin in the late 1920s; Pirandello's **METATHEATER** was part of the lively Italian avant-garde following World War I; Shaw's drama was informed by the progressive politics of the British **FABIAN SOCIETY** and by dramatic conventions drawn from the popular plays of the late Victorian stage. But in many cases, the first generation of "modern" theater and drama strikes a posture of resistant inquiry toward the pieties of contemporary social life. It works both to represent that world and to change it, to affect our ideas about character and personality, about the political realities of our world, and even about the metaphysical certainties we have come to believe.

# Henrik Ibsen

At the turn of the century, Henrik Ibsen (1828–1906) was synonymous with modernity in the European theater; much of the territory of modern drama was first explored in Ibsen's work. Born into a mercantile family in provincial Norway, Ibsen had planned to study medicine; however, after failing to matriculate at the university, he turned to a career as a writer. From 1850 through 1864, Ibsen worked for the nationalist Norwegian Theater in Bergen, and then for the Mollergate Theater in Christiania (now Oslo). As literary manager, stage manager, and assistant to the director, Ibsen learned the craft of practical theater firsthand. He also wrote a series of romantic history plays, some in prose and some in verse. Although his fame now rests on the realistic plays he wrote later in his career, in his own lifetime these history plays—such as *The Vikings at Helgeland* (1858)—were quite popular, especially in Norway.

In 1864, Ibsen left Norway and settled in Rome, where he wrote two pivotal plays, *Brand* (1866) and *Peer Gynt* (1867). The story of an idealistic minister, *Brand* established Ibsen as an important European writer and announced one of his central themes: the cost of moral idealism in the modern world. *Peer Gynt* is often taken as a companion piece to *Brand,* for Peer's picaresque journey throughout Europe is undertaken simply for the purpose of his own self-satisfaction: While Brand's motto is "Be wholly what you are," Peer Gynt's is "To thine own self be . . . enough." In 1877, after extensive work on the Hegelian history drama *Emperor and Galilean,* Ibsen wrote *Pillars of Society,* a prose drama of modern life, inaugurating the stunning series of plays that made him famous and established the contours of modern realistic drama. In *A Doll House* (1879), *Ghosts* (1881), and *An Enemy of the People* (1882), Ibsen explored the conflict between the social and moral restrictions of bourgeois society and the psychological, often unconscious demands of individual freedom. Ibsen adapted the suspenseful, rigorously plotted form of the **WELL-MADE PLAY** (or *pièce bien faite*), popularized throughout Europe by French playwrights Eugène Scribe and Victorien Sardou, and used it in plays of modern life critical of bourgeois morality and society. The well-made play is notoriously difficult to define, even though its features are familiar: a rigorously "causal" plot, a secret gradually revealed to the audience, a "necessary scene" (the *scène-à-faire*) in which the secret is revealed to the characters, a character (the *raisonneur*) who explains and moralizes the action to the others, and a predominance of coincidental events. In his earlier plays, Ibsen takes these formal conventions and makes them function as forces in the dramatic world. The world of the play comes to seem mechanistic, determined by a secret that will out, full of busybodies explaining and interpreting the action. The mechanics of the well-made play, that is, are identified with the deadening force of social convention, which painfully threatens to extinguish the vitality of the central characters. This conflict between deadening social convention and a mysterious inner vitality pervades Ibsen's mature plays as well, which increasingly moved away from the "well-made" form: *The Wild Duck* (1885), *Rosmersholm* (1887), *The Lady from the Sea* (1888), and *Hedda Gabler* (1890). Ibsen's last plays seem more poetic or symbolic, though they take place in the familiar milieu of the realistic stage: *The Master Builder* (1892), *Little Eyolf* (1894), *John Gabriel Borkman* (1896), and the unfinished *When We Dead Awaken* (1900). Ibsen suffered a paralyzing series of strokes in 1900 that left him unable to write; he died in 1906.

Ibsen's effect on his contemporaries and his influence on the course of modern drama were immediate and profound. His plays were rapidly translated into the major European languages, and stage productions—which often inaugurated the new "independent" theaters—frequently became the subject of sensation and controversy. Indeed, "Ibsenism" came to be a catchword for a variety of social causes, though Ibsen himself generally avoided politics. Although Ibsen's plays brought new issues to the stage, it was his practice as a playwright that proved truly revolutionary. Many playwrights had adopted the realistic theater's use of a material stage environment, its emphasis on the burden of the past, and its sense of a mechanized and constricting society. Ibsen not only used this material with powerful subtlety and resonance, he gave the stage its first distinctively modern characters: complex, contradictory individuals driven by a desire for something—the "joy of life," a sense of themselves—that they can barely recognize or name.

## The Wild Duck (1884)

When it first appeared, *The Wild Duck* was taken by many to be an act of self-parody on Ibsen's part; in the benighted moralist Gregers Werle, Ibsen seemed to be criticizing the idealists of his earlier plays: Doctor Stockmann of *An Enemy of the People,* the brooding Osvald of *Ghosts,* perhaps even the clear-eyed and willful Nora of the closing moments of *A Doll House.* Indeed, in *The Wild Duck,* Ibsen seems to undertake a searching reexamination both of the themes of his earlier plays, and—metaphorically—of the materials of realistic theater as well.

In many ways, *The Wild Duck* is exemplary of the "well-made play" genre, gradually releasing a series of "secrets" that seem to determine the lives of the characters, as though "information" could become a kind of fate. In Act One, Gregers becomes suspicious of his father's relations with his former housekeeper Gina. As the play proceeds, a series of well-timed revelations and casual observations—Hedvig's poor eyesight and Werle's failing vision; the proximity of the Ekdals' marriage and Hedvig's birth; Mrs. Sørby's birthday gift—seem to confirm Gregers's suspicion that Werle married his pregnant housekeeper off to the son of the business partner he had ruined. But Ibsen adds a further twist here, for it is Gregers who both produces most of these revelations and seems to provide them with a narrative structure: Gregers acts as a playwright-within-the-play as well as its *raisonneur.* Gregers's blind idealism leads him to believe that by opening all secrets, a "true marriage" can be founded between Hjalmar and Gina. What he fails to recognize is that this idealistic drama completely misjudges the cast of characters, especially the self-indulgent Hjalmar.

Gregers, that is, attempts to produce a kind of "well-made play" in the lives of the Ekdal family; the fact that he fails may suggest the severely limited ways in which the conventional forms of realistic drama can actually represent real life. Ibsen's critique of "well-made" drama is paired with a similar critique of the conventions of the realistic *mise-en-scène.* For *The Wild Duck* is a play that requires its audience to read spatially as well as verbally, to interpret the thematic function of the physical environment on the stage. The play takes place in two locations: Act One in the sumptuous parlor of the Werle family home and Acts Two through Five in the shabby photographic studio of the Ekdal family. But though these two locations mark different social environments, they also reflect one another in unusual ways. Both homes have the same general layout: a downstage room in which secrets are revealed and an upstage room of some mystery. In the Werle house, we see the upstage parlor only intermittently, but the last image we see of that room is of Werle's complacent, bourgeois dinner guests groping for Mrs. Sørby in a game of blindman's buff. In the Ekdal home, the upstage room is the dark garret, where Old Ekdal has rebuilt the Hoidal forest of his youth and spends the day hunting in his dreams. In both cases, the play sets a "realistic" room in the foreground, a room troublingly flanked by an upstage room of desire, blindness, and fantasy.

Ibsen uses this spatial arrangement to undermine the explanatory power of realism in several ways. For in the downstage room where "the facts" become plain, "truth" often seems indistinguishable from lies and deception. It is in the downstage room that Gregers retreats into his crazy idealism, refusing to see the kind of relationship that Werle is pursuing with Mrs. Sørby. In the Ekdal household, the downstage room is a photographic studio—the perfect emblem of realistic verisimilitude—but we never see any photographs taken—they are only retouched. It is also where Relling elaborates his theory of the "life-lie." He persuades the lazy, selfish, and talentless Hjalmar that he is a romantic poet and inventor; the drunken Molvik that he is possessed by demonic spirits rather than by the spirit of drink; and perhaps even persuades himself—equally spuriously— that his "life-lies" amount to a kind of therapy, that he really is a "Doctor" after all.

Indeed, the naturalistic downstage room is where delusion most fully grips the characters. The tragedy of *The Wild Duck* occurs only when Hedvig takes Gregers literally, sacrificing for her father's love the thing she loves most: herself. The characters onstage—Hjalmar, Relling, Gregers—all respond to her death, but all seem finally to misunderstand it, to avoid its power, to dwell on themselves alone. Sacrificing Hedvig in place of the wild duck, Ibsen seems to draw a final, damning comparison between them. The "real" world emerges in *The Wild Duck* as a world of nearly impenetrable solipsism, a world where the "truth" of appearances is nearly always an illusion, a lie we tell ourselves in order to produce the world we want to see. The world we inhabit is, the play seems finally to suggest, a deeply unnatural one, a world that cripples our relationship to nature, to innocence, much as it cripples the wild duck, and kills Hedvig among the tawdry pines of Old Ekdal's potted forest.

# —The Wild Duck—
### Henrik Ibsen
TRANSLATED BY ROLF FJELDE

## —THE CHARACTERS—

HAAKON WERLE, *wholesale merchant and millowner*
GREGERS WERLE, *his son*
OLD EKDAL
HJALMAR EKDAL, *his son, a photographer*
GINA EKDAL, *Hjalmar's wife*
HEDVIG, *their daughter, aged fourteen*
MRS. SØRBY, *housekeeper for the elder Werle*
RELLING, *a doctor*
MOLVIK, *a former divinity student*

GRAABERG, *a bookkeeper*
PETTERSEN, *manservant to the elder Werle*
JENSEN, *a hired waiter*
A FAT MAN
A BALD-HEADED MAN
A NEARSIGHTED MAN
SIX OTHER MEN, *dinner guests at Werle's*
OTHER HIRED SERVANTS

*The first act takes place in* WERLE's *house; the following four acts in* HJALMAR EKDAL's *studio.*

## —ACT ONE—

At WERLE's *house. A richly and comfortably furnished study, with bookcases and upholstered furniture, a writing table, with papers and reports, in the middle of the floor, and green-shaded lamps softly illuminating the room. In the rear wall, open folding doors with curtains drawn back disclose a large, fashionable room, brightly lit by lamps and candelabra. In the right foreground of the study, a small private door leads to the offices. In the left foreground, a fireplace filled with glowing coals, and further back a double door to the dining room.*

WERLE's *manservant,* PETTERSEN, *in livery, and* JENSEN, *a hired waiter, in black, are straightening up the study. In the larger room two or three other hired waiters are moving about, putting things in order and lighting more candles. In from the dining room come laughter and the hum of many voices in conversation; a knife clinks upon a glass; silence; a toast is made; cries of "Bravo," and the hum of conversation resumes.*

PETTERSEN: *(lighting a lamp by the fireplace and putting on the shade)* Ah, you hear that, Jensen. Now the old boy's up on his feet, proposing a long toast to Mrs. Sørby.
JENSEN: *(moving an armchair forward)* Is it really true what people say, that there's something between them?
PETTERSEN: Lord knows.
JENSEN: I've heard he was a real goat in his day.
PETTERSEN: Could be.
JENSEN: But they say it's his son he's throwing this party for.
10 PETTERSEN: Yes. His son came home yesterday.
JENSEN: I never knew before that old Werle had any son.
PETTERSEN: Oh yes, he's got a son. But he spends all his time up at the works in Hoidal. He hasn't been in town all the years I've served in this house.
A HIRED WAITER: *(in the door to the other room)* Say, Pettersen, there's an old guy here who—
PETTERSEN: *(muttering)* What the hell—somebody coming now!

*(Old* EKDAL *appears from the right through the inner room. He is dressed in a shabby overcoat with a high collar, woolen gloves, and in his hand, a cane and a fur cap; under his arm is a bundle wrapped in brown paper. He has a dirty, reddish-brown wig and a little gray moustache.)*

PETTERSEN: *(going toward him)* Good Lord, what do *you* want in here?                                                            20
EKDAL: *(at the door)* Just have to get into the office, Pettersen.
PETTERSEN: The office closed an hour ago, and—
EKDAL: Heard that one at the door, boy. But Graaberg's still in there. Be nice, Pettersen, and let me slip in that way. *(Pointing toward the private entrance.)* I've gone that way before.
PETTERSEN: All right, go ahead, then. *(Opens the door.)* But don't forget now—take the other way out; we have guests.
EKDAL: Got you—hmm! Thanks, Pettersen, good old pal! Thanks. *(To himself.)* Bonehead! *(He goes into the office;* PETTERSEN *shuts the door after him.)*                          30
JENSEN: Is *he* on the office staff too!
PETTERSEN: No, he's just someone who does copying on the outside when it's needed. Still, in his time he was well up in the world, old Ekdal.
JENSEN: Yes, he looks like he's been a little of everything.
PETTERSEN: Oh yes. He was a lieutenant once, if you can imagine.
JENSEN: Good Lord—him a lieutenant!
PETTERSEN: So help me, he was. But then he went into the lumber business or something. They say he must have 40 pulled some kind of dirty deal on the old man once, for the two of them were running the Hoidal works together then. Oh, I know good old Ekdal, all right. We've drunk many a schnapps and bottle of beer together over at Eriksen's.
JENSEN: He can't have much money for standing drinks.
PETTERSEN: My Lord, Jensen, you can bet it's me that stands the drinks. I always say a person ought to act refined toward quality that's come down in life.
JENSEN: Did he go bankrupt, then?

50 PETTERSEN: No, worse than that. He was sent to jail.

JENSEN: To jail!

PETTERSEN: Or maybe it was the penitentiary. (*Laughter from the dining room.*) Hist! They're leaving the table.

(*The dining room door is opened by a pair of servants inside.* MRS. SØRBY, *in conversation with two gentlemen, comes out. A moment later the rest of the guests follow, among them* WERLE. *Last of all come* HJALMER EKDAL *and* GREGERS WERLE.)

MRS. SØRBY: (*to the servant, in passing*) Pettersen, will you have coffee served in the music room.

PETTERSEN: Yes, Mrs. Sørby.

(*She and the two gentlemen go into the inner room and exit to the right.* PETTERSEN *and* JENSEN *leave in the same way.*)

A FAT GUEST: (*to a balding man*) Phew! That dinner—that was a steep bit of work!

THE BALD-HEADED GUEST: Oh, with a little good will a man can
60     do wonders in three hours.

THE FAT GUEST: Yes, but afterward, my dear fellow, afterward.

A THIRD GUEST: I hear we can sample coffee and liqueur in the music room.

THE FAT GUEST: Fine! Then perhaps Mrs. Sørby will play us a piece.

THE BALD-HEADED GUEST: (*in an undertone*) Just so Mrs. Sørby doesn't play us to pieces.

THE FAT GUEST: Oh, now really, Berta wouldn't punish her old friends, would she? (*They laugh and enter the inner room.*)

70 WERLE: (*in a low, depressed tone*) I don't think anyone noticed it, Gregers.

GREGERS: What?

WERLE: Didn't you notice it either?

GREGERS: What should I have noticed?

WERLE: We were thirteen at the table.

GREGERS: Really? Were we thirteen?

WERLE: (*with a glance at* HJALMAR EKDAL) Yes—our usual number is twelve. (*To the others.*) Be so kind, gentlemen.

(*He and those remaining, excepting* HJALMAR *and* GREGERS, *go out to the rear and right.*)

HJALMAR: (*who has heard the conversation*) You shouldn't have
80     sent me the invitation, Gregers.

GREGERS: What! The party's supposed to be for *me*. And then I'm not supposed to have my best and only friend—

HJALMAR: But I don't think your father likes it. Ordinarily I never come to this house.

GREGERS: So I hear. But I had to see you and talk with you, for I'm sure to be leaving soon again. Yes, we two old classmates, we've certainly drifted a long way apart. You know, we haven't seen each other now in sixteen—seventeen years.

90 HJALMAR: Has it been so long?

GREGERS: Yes, all of that. Well, how have you been? You look well. You're almost becoming stout.

HJALMAR: Hm, stout is hardly the word, though I probably look more of a man than I did then.

GREGERS: Yes, you do. The outer man hasn't suffered.

HJALMAR: (*in a gloomier tone*) Ah, but the inner man! Believe me, he has a different look. You know, of course, what misery we've been through, I and my family, since the last time the two of us met.

GREGERS: (*dropping his voice*) How's it going for your father 100 now?

HJALMAR: Oh, Gregers, let's not talk about that. My poor, unhappy father naturally lives at home with me. He's got no one else in the whole world to turn to. But this all is so terribly hard for me to talk about, you know. Tell me, instead, how you've found life up at the mill.

GREGERS: Marvelously solitary, that's what—with a good chance to mull over a great many things. Come on, let's be comfortable.

(*He sits in an armchair by the fire and urges* HJALMAR *down into another by its side.*)

HJALMAR: (*emotionally*) In any case, I'm grateful that you asked 110 me here, Gregers, because it proves you no longer have anything against me.

GREGERS: (*astonished*) How could you think that I had anything against you?

HJALMAR: In those first years you did.

GREGERS: Which first years?

HJALMAR: Right after that awful misfortune. And it was only natural you should. It was just by a hair that your own father escaped being dragged into this—oh, this ugly business.

GREGERS: And that's why I had it in for you? Whoever gave you 120 that idea?

HJALMAR: I know you did, Gregers; it was your father himself who told me.

GREGERS: (*startled*) Father! I see. Hm—is that why I never heard from you—not a single word?

HJALMAR: Yes.

GREGERS: Not even when you went out and became a photographer.

HJALMAR: Your father said it wasn't worth writing you—about anything.                                                                      130

GREGERS: (*looking fixedly ahead*) No, no, maybe he was right there—But tell me, Hjalmar—do you find yourself reasonably content with things as they are?

HJALMAR: (*with a small sigh*) Oh, I suppose I do. What else can I say? At first, you can imagine, it was all rather strange for me. They were such completely different expectations that I came into. But then everything was so different. That immense, shattering misfortune for Father—the shame and the scandal, Gregers—

GREGERS: (*shaken*) Yes, yes. Of course.                                    140

HJALMAR: I couldn't dream of going on with my studies; there wasn't a penny to spare. On the contrary, debts instead—mainly to your father, I think—

GREGERS: Hm—

HJALMAR: Anyway, I thought it was best to make a clean break—and cut all the old connections. It was your father especially who advised me to; and since he'd already been so helpful to me—

GREGERS: He had?

HJALMAR: Yes, you knew that, didn't you? Where could *I* get 150 the money to learn photography and fit out a studio and establish myself? I can tell you, that all adds up.

GREGERS: And all that Father paid for?

HJALMAR: Yes, Gregers, didn't you know? I understood him to say that he'd written you about it.

GREGERS: Not a word saying *he* was the one. Maybe he forgot. We've never exchanged anything but business letters. So that was Father, too—!

HJALMAR: That's right. He never wanted people to know, but he was the one. And he was also the one who put me in a position to get married. Or perhaps—didn't you know that either?

GREGERS: No, not at all. (*Takes him by the arm.*) But Hjalmar, I can't tell you how all this delights me—and disturbs me. Perhaps I've been unfair to my father—in certain ways. Yes, for all this does show good-heartedness, doesn't it? It's almost a kind of conscience—

HJALMAR: Conscience?

GREGERS: Yes, or whatever you want to call it. No, I can't tell you how glad I am to hear this about my father. So you're married, then, Hjalmar. That's further than I'll ever go. Well, I hope you're happy as a married man?

HJALMAR: Oh, absolutely. She's as capable and fine a wife as any man could wish for. And she's not entirely without culture, either.

GREGERS: (*a bit surprised*) No, I'm sure she's not.

HJALMAR: No. Life is a teacher, you see. Associating with me every day—and then there are one or two gifted people who visit us regularly. I can tell you, you wouldn't recognize Gina now.

GREGERS: Gina?

HJALMAR: Yes, Gregers, had you forgotten her name is Gina.

GREGERS: Whose name is Gina? I haven't the faintest idea—

HJALMAR: But don't you remember, she was here in this very house a while—in service?

GREGERS: (*looking at him*) You mean Gina Hansen—?

HJALMAR: Yes, of course. Gina Hansen.

GREGERS: Who was housekeeper for us that last year of Mother's illness?

HJALMAR: Exactly. But my dear Gregers, I know for sure that your father wrote you about my marriage.

GREGERS: (*who has gotten up*) Yes, of course he did. But not that—(*Walks about the floor.*) Yes, wait a minute—it may well be, now that I think of it. My father's letters are always so brief. (*Sits on chair arm.*) Listen, tell me, Hjalmar—this is interesting—how did you come to know Gina?—your wife, I mean.

HJALMAR: Oh, it was all very simple. Gina didn't stay long here in the house; there was so much confusion—your mother's sickness and all. Gina couldn't stand it, so she just up and left. That was the year before your mother died—or maybe it was the same year.

GREGERS: It was the same year. And I was up at the works at the time. But what then?

HJALMAR: Well, then Gina lived at home with her mother, a Mrs. Hansen, a very capable, hardworking woman who ran a little restaurant. She also had a room for rent, a very pleasant, comfortable room.

GREGERS: And you were lucky enough to find it?

HJALMAR: Yes. Actually it was your father who suggested it to me. And it was there, you see—there that I really got to know Gina.

GREGERS: And then your engagement followed?

HJALMAR: Yes. Young people fall in love so easily—hm—

GREGERS: (*getting up and pacing about a little*) Tell me—when you became engaged—was it *then* that my father got you to—I mean, was it then that you started in learning photography?

HJALMAR: That's right. I wanted to get on and set up a home as soon as possible, and both your father and I decided that this photography idea was the most feasible one. And Gina thought so too. Yes, and you see, there was another inducement, a lucky break, in that Gina had already taken up retouching.

GREGERS: That worked out wonderfully all around.

HJALMAR: (*pleased, getting up*) Yes, isn't that so? Don't you think it's worked out wonderfully all around?

GREGERS: Yes, I must say. My father has almost been a kind of providence to you.

HJALMAR: (*with feeling*) He didn't abandon his old friend's son in a time of need. You see, he does have a heart.

MRS. SØRBY: (*entering with* WERLE *on her arm*) No more nonsense, my dear Mr. Werle. You mustn't stay in there any longer, staring at all those lights; it's doing you no good.

WERLE: (*freeing his arm from hers and passing his hand over his eyes*) Yes, I guess you're right about that.

(PETTERSEN *and* JENSEN *enter with trays.*)

MRS. SØRBY: (*to the guests in the other room*) Gentlemen, please—if anyone wants a glass of punch, he must take the trouble to come in here.

THE FAT GUEST: (*comes over to* MRS. SØRBY) But really, is it true you've abolished our precious smoking privilege?

MRS. SØRBY: Yes. Here in Mr. Werle's sanctum, it's forbidden.

THE BALD-HEADED GUEST: When did you pass these drastic amendments to the cigar laws, Mrs. Sørby?

MRS. SØRBY: After the last dinner—when there were certain persons here who let themselves exceed all limits.

THE BALD-HEADED GUEST: And my dear Berta, one isn't permitted to exceed the limits, even a little bit?

MRS. SØRBY: Not in any instance, Mr. Balle.

(*Most of the guests have gathered in the study; the waiters are proffering glasses of punch.*)

WERLE: (*to* HJALMAR, *over by a table*) What is it you're poring over, Ekdal?

HJALMAR: It's only an album, Mr. Werle.

THE BALD-HEADED GUEST: (*who is wandering about*) Ah, photographs! Yes, of course, that's just the thing for you.

THE FAT GUEST: (*seated in an armchair*) Haven't you brought along some of your own?

HJALMAR: No, I haven't.

THE FAT GUEST: You really should have. It's so good for the digestion to sit and look at pictures.

THE BALD-HEADED GUEST: And then it always adds a morsel to the entertainment, you know.

A NEARSIGHTED GUEST: And all contributions are gratefully received.

MRS. SØRBY: These gentlemen mean that if one's invited for dinner, one must also work for the food, Mr. Ekdal.

THE FAT GUEST: Where the larder's superior, *that* is pure joy.

THE BALD-HEADED GUEST: My Lord, it's all in the struggle for existence—

MRS. SØRBY: How right you are! (*They continue laughing and joking.*)

GREGERS: (*quietly*) You should talk with them, Hjalmar.

HJALMAR: (*with a shrug*) What could I talk about?

THE FAT GUEST: Don't you think, Mr. Werle, that Tokay compares favorably as a healthful drink for the stomach?

WERLE: (*by the fireplace*) The Tokay you had today I can vouch for in any case; it's one of the very, very finest years. But you recognized that well enough.

THE FAT GUEST: Yes, it had a remarkably delicate flavor.

HJALMAR: (*tentatively*) Is there some difference between the 280 years?

THE FAT GUEST: (*laughing*) Oh, that's rich!

WERLE: (*smiling*) It certainly doesn't pay to offer you a noble wine.

THE BALD-HEADED GUEST: Tokay wines are like photographs, Mr. Ekdal—sunshine is of the essence. Isn't that true?

HJALMAR: Oh yes, light is very important.

MRS. SØRBY: Exactly the same as with court officials—who push for their place in the sun too, I hear.

THE BALD-HEADED GUEST: Ouch! That was a tired quip.

290 THE NEARSIGHTED GUEST: The lady's performing—

THE FAT GUEST: And at our expense. (*Frowning.*) Mrs. Sørby, Mrs. Sørby!

MRS. SØRBY: Yes, but it certainly is true now that the years can vary enormously. The old vintages are the finest.

THE NEARSIGHTED GUEST: Do you count me among the old ones?

MRS. SØRBY: Oh, far from it.

THE BALD-HEADED GUEST: Ha, you see! But what about *me*, Mrs. Sørby—?

300 THE FAT GUEST: Yes, and me! What years would you put us among?

MRS. SØRBY: I would put you all among the sweet years, gentlemen. (*She sips a glass of punch; the guests laugh and banter with her.*)

WERLE: Mrs. Sørby always finds a way out—when she wants to. Pass your glasses, gentlemen. Pettersen, take care of them. Gregers, I think we'll have a glass together. (GREGERS *does not stir.*) Won't you join us, Ekdal? I had no chance to remember you at the table.

(GRAABERG, *the bookkeeper, peers out from the door to the offices.*)

310 GRAABERG: Beg pardon, Mr. Werle, but I can't get out.

WERLE: What, are you locked in again?

GRAABERG: Yes, and Flakstad's left with the keys—

WERLE: Well, then, go through here.

GRAABERG: But there's someone else—

WERLE: All right, all right, both of you. Don't be shy.

(GRAABERG *and old* EKDAL *come out from the office.*)

WERLE: (*involuntarily*) Oh no!

(*The laughter and small talk die among the guests.* HJALMAR *starts at the sight of his father, sets down his glass, and turns away toward the fireplace.*)

EKDAL: (*without looking up, but bowing slightly to each side and mumbling*) Door locked. Door locked. Beg your pardon. (*He and* GRAABERG *exit in back to the right.*)

320 WERLE: (*between his teeth*) That damned Graaberg!

GREGERS: (*with open mouth, staring at* HJALMAR) But it couldn't have been—!

THE FAT GUEST: What's going on? Who was that?

GREGERS: Oh, no one. Only the bookkeeper and somebody else.

THE NEARSIGHTED GUEST: (*to* HJALMAR) Did *you* know him?

HJALMAR: I don't know—I didn't notice—

THE FAT GUEST: (*getting up*) What in thunder's wrong? (*He goes over to some others, who are talking.*)

MRS. SØRBY: (*whispering to the waiter*) Slip something to him 330 outside, something really fine.

PETTERSEN: (*nodding*) I'll see to it. (*He goes out.*)

GREGERS: (*in a shocked undertone*) Then it really was him!

HJALMAR: Yes.

GREGERS: And yet you stood here and denied you knew him!

HJALMAR: (*whispering fiercely*) But how could I—!

GREGERS: Be recognized by your father?

HJALMAR: (*painfully*) Oh, if you were in my place, then—

(*The hushed conversations among the guests now mount into a forced joviality.*)

THE BALD-HEADED GUEST: (*approaching* HJALMAR *and* GREGERS *amiably*) Ah ha! You over here, polishing up old 340 memories from your student years? Well? Won't you smoke, Mr. Ekdal? Have a light? Oh, that's right, we're not supposed to—

HJALMAR: Thanks, I couldn't—

THE FAT GUEST: Haven't you got a neat little poem to recite for us, Mr. Ekdal? In times past you did that so nicely.

HJALMAR: I'm afraid I can't remember any.

THE FAT GUEST: Oh, that's a shame. Well, Balle, what can we find to do? (*The two men cross the floor into the other room and go out.*) 350

HJALMAR: (*somberly*) Gregers—I'm going! When a man's felt a terrible blow from fate—you understand. Say good night to your father for me.

GREGERS: Yes, of course. Are you going straight home?

HJALMAR: Yes, why?

GREGERS: Well, I may pay you a visit later.

HJALMAR: No, you mustn't. Not to my home. My house is a sad one, Gregers—especially after a brilliant occasion like this. We can always meet somewhere in town.

MRS. SØRBY: (*who has approached; in a low voice*) Are you 360 going, Ekdal?

HJALMAR: Yes.

MRS. SØRBY: Greet Gina.

HJALMAR: Thank you.

MRS. SØRBY: And tell her I'll stop by to see her one day soon.

HJALMAR: Yes. Thanks. (*To* GREGERS.) Stay here. I'd rather disappear without any fuss. (*He strolls around the floor, then into the other room and out to the right.*)

MRS. SØRBY: (*quietly to the waiter, who has returned*) Well, did the old man get something to take home? 370

PETTERSEN: Sure. I slipped him a bottle of cognac.

MRS. SØRBY: Oh, you could have found something better.

PETTERSEN: Not at all, Mrs. Sørby. He knows nothing better than cognac.

THE FAT GUEST: (*in the doorway, holding a score of music*) How about the two of us playing something, Mrs. Sørby?

MRS. SØRBY: All right. Let's.

*(The guests shout approval.* MRS. SØRBY *and the others exit right, through the inner room.* GREGERS *remains standing by the fireplace.* WERLE *looks for something on the writing table, seeming to wish that* GREGERS *would leave; when he fails to stir,* WERLE *crosses toward the door.)*

GREGERS: Father, won't you wait a moment?

WERLE: *(pausing)* What is it?

380 GREGERS: I must have a word with you.

WERLE: Can't it wait till we're alone?

GREGERS: No, it can't, because it just might occur that we never are alone.

WERLE: *(coming closer)* What does *that* mean?

*(Distant piano music is heard from the music room during the following conversation.)*

GREGERS: How could anyone here let that family decay so pitifully?

WERLE: You're referring to the Ekdals, no doubt.

GREGERS: Yes, I mean the Ekdals. Lieutenant Ekdal was once so close to you.

390 WERLE: Yes, worse luck, he was all too close; and for that I've paid a price these many years. He's the one I can thank for putting something of a blot on my good name and reputation.

GREGERS: *(quietly)* Was *he* really the only guilty one?

WERLE: Who else do you mean!

GREGERS: You and he were both in on buying that big stand of timber—

WERLE: But it was Ekdal, wasn't it, who made the survey of the sections—that incompetent survey? He was the one who

400 carried out all the illegal logging on state property. In fact, he was in charge of the whole operation up there. I had no idea of what Lieutenant Ekdal was getting into.

GREGERS: Lieutenant Ekdal himself had no idea of what he was getting into.

WERLE: Very likely. But the fact remains that he was convicted and I was acquitted.

GREGERS: Yes, I'm aware that no proof was found.

WERLE: Acquittal is acquittal. Why do you rake up this ugly old story that's given me gray hair before my time? Is this what

410 you've been brooding about all those years up there? I can assure you, Gregers—here in town the whole business has been forgotten long ago—as far as I'm concerned.

GREGERS: But that miserable Ekdal family!

WERLE: Seriously, what would you have me do for these people? When Ekdal was let out, he was a broken man, beyond any help. There are people in this world who plunge to the bottom when they've hardly been winged, and they never come up again. Take my word for it, Gregers; I've done everything I could, short of absolutely compromising myself

420 and arousing all kinds of suspicion and gossip—

GREGERS: Suspicion—? So that's it.

WERLE: I've gotten Ekdal copying jobs from the office, and I pay him much, much more than his work is worth—

GREGERS: *(without looking at him)* Hm. No doubt.

WERLE: You're laughing? Maybe you think what I'm saying isn't true? There's certainly nothing to show in my books; I don't record such payments.

GREGERS: *(with a cold smile)* No. I'm sure that certain pay-

ments are best left unrecorded.

WERLE: *(surprised)* What do you mean by *that?*   430

GREGERS: *(plucking up his courage)* Did you record what it cost you to have Hjalmar Ekdal study photography?

WERLE: I? Why should I?

GREGERS: I know now it was you who paid for that. And now I know, too, that it was you who set him up so comfortably in business.

WERLE: Well, and I suppose this still means that I've done nothing for the Ekdals! I can assure you, those people have already cost me enough expense.

GREGERS: Have you recorded any of the expenses?   440

WERLE: Why do you ask that?

GREGERS: Oh, there are reasons. Listen, tell me—the time when you developed such warmth for your old friend's son—wasn't that just when he was planning to marry?

WERLE: How the devil—how, after so many years, do you expect me—?

GREGERS: You wrote me a letter then—a business letter, naturally; and in a postscript it said, brief as could be, that Hjalmar Ekdal had gotten married to a Miss Hansen.

WERLE: Yes, that's right; that was her name.   450

GREGERS: But you never said that this Miss Hansen was Gina Hansen—our former housekeeper.

WERLE: *(with a derisive, yet uneasy laugh)* No, it just never occurred to me that you'd be so very interested in our former housekeeper.

GREGERS: I wasn't. But—*(Dropping his voice.)* there were others in the house who were quite interested in her.

WERLE: What do you mean by that? *(Storming at him.)* You're not referring to me!

GREGERS: *(quietly but firmly)* Yes, I'm referring to you.   460

WERLE: And you dare—! You have the insolence—! How could he, that ungrateful dog, that—photographer; how could he have the gall to make such insinuations?

GREGERS: Hjalmar hasn't breathed a word of it. I don't think he has the shadow of a doubt about all this.

WERLE: Then where did you get it from? Who could have said such a thing?

GREGERS: My poor, unhappy mother said it—the last time I saw her.

WERLE: Your mother! Yes, I might have guessed. She and   470 you—you always stuck together. It was she who, right from the start, turned your mind against me.

GREGERS: No. It was everything she had to suffer and endure until she broke down and died so miserably.

WERLE: Oh, she had nothing to suffer and endure—no more, at least, than so many others. But you can't get anywhere with sick, high-strung people. I've certainly learned that. Now you're going around suspecting that sort of thing, digging up all manner of old rumors and slanders against your own father. Now listen, Gregers, I really think that at your   480 age you could occupy yourself more usefully.

GREGERS: Yes, all in due time.

WERLE: Then your mind might be clearer than it seems to be now. What can it lead to, you up there at the works, slaving away year in and year out like a common clerk, never taking a penny over your month's salary. It's pure stupidity.

GREGERS: Yes, if only I were so sure of that.

WERLE: I understand you well enough. You want to be

independent, without obligation to me. But here's the very
490 opportunity for you to become independent, your own man in every way.

GREGERS: So? And by what means—?

WERLE: When I wrote you that it was essential you come to town now, immediately—hmm—

GREGERS: Yes. What is it you really want of me? I've been waiting all day to find out.

WERLE: I'm suggesting that you come into the firm as a partner.

GREGERS: I! In your firm? As a partner?

500 WERLE: Yes. It wouldn't mean we'd need to be together much. You could take over the offices here in town, and then I'd move up to the mill.

GREGERS: You *would?*

WERLE: Yes. You see, I can't take on work now the way I once could. I have to spare my eyes, Gregers; they're beginning to fail.

GREGERS: They've always been weak.

WERLE: Not like this. Besides—circumstances may make it desirable for me to live up there—at least for a while.

510 GREGERS: I never dreamed of anything like this.

WERLE: Listen, Gregers, there are so very many things that keep us apart, and yet, you know—we're father and son still. I think we should be able to reach some kind of understanding.

GREGERS: Just on the surface, is that what you mean?

WERLE: Well, at least that would be something. Think it over, Gregers. Don't you think it ought to be possible? Eh?

GREGERS: (*looking at him coldly*) There's something behind all this.

520 WERLE: How so?

GREGERS: It might be that somehow you're using me.

WERLE: In a relationship as close as ours, one can always be of use to the other.

GREGERS: Yes, so they say.

WERLE: I'd like to have you home with me now for a while. I'm a lonely man, Gregers; I've always felt lonely—all my life through, but particularly now when the years are beginning to press me. I need to have someone around—

GREGERS: You have Mrs. Sørby.

530 WERLE: Yes, I do—and she's become, you might say, almost indispensable. She's witty, even-tempered; she livens up the house—and that's what I need so badly.

GREGERS: Well, then, you've got everything the way you want it.

WERLE: Yes, but I'm afraid it can't go on. The world is quick to make inferences about a woman in her position. Yes, I was going to say, a man doesn't gain by it either.

GREGERS: Oh, when a man gives dinner parties like yours, he can certainly take a few risks.

540 WERLE: Yes, Gregers, but what about her? I'm afraid she won't put up with it much longer. And even if she did—even if, out of her feeling for me, she ignored the gossip and the backbiting and so on—do you still think, Gregers, you with your sharp sense of justice—

GREGERS: (*cutting him off*) Tell me short and sweet just one thing. Are you planning to marry her?

WERLE: And if I *were* planning such a thing—what then?

GREGERS: Yes, that's what I'm asking. What then?

WERLE: Would you be so irreconcilably set against it?

GREGERS: No, not at all. Not in any way.     550

WERLE: Well, I really didn't know whether, perhaps out of regard for your dead mother's memory—

GREGERS: I am not high-strung.

WERLE: Well, you may or may not be, but in any case you've taken a great load off my mind. I'm really very happy that I can count on your support in this.

GREGERS: (*staring intently at him*) Now I see how you want to use me.

WERLE: Use you! That's no way to talk!

GREGERS: Oh, let's not be squeamish in our choice of words. At 560 least, not when it's man to man. (*He laughs brusquely.*) So that's it! That's why I—damn it all!—had to make my personal appearance in town. On account of Mrs. Sørby, family life is in order in this house. Tableau of father with son! That's something new, all right!

WERLE: How dare you speak in that tone!

GREGERS: When has there ever been family life here? Never, as long as I can remember. But *now*, of course, there's need for a little of that. For who could deny what a fine impression it would make to hear that the son—on the wings of 570 piety—came flying home to the aging father's wedding feast. What's left then of all the stories about what the poor dead woman suffered and endured? Not a scrap. Her own son ground them to dust.

WERLE: Gregers—I don't think there's a man in this world you hate as much as me.

GREGERS: I've seen you at too close quarters.

WERLE: You've seen me with your mother's eyes. (*Dropping his voice.*) But you should remember that those eyes were—clouded at times.     580

GREGERS: (*faltering*) I know what you mean. But who bears the guilt for Mother's fatal weakness? You, and all those—! The last of them was that female that Hjalmar Ekdal was fixed up with when you had no more—ugh!

WERLE: (*shrugs*) Word for word, as if I were hearing your mother.

GREGERS: (*paying no attention to him*) . . . and there he sits right now, he with his great, guileless, childlike mind plunged in deception—living under the same roof with that creature, not knowing that what he calls his home is built on 590 a lie. (*Coming a step closer.*) When I look back on all you've done, it's as if I looked out over a battlefield with broken human beings on every side.

WERLE: I almost think the gulf is too great between us.

GREGERS: (*bows stiffly*) So I've observed; therefore I'll take my hat and go.

WERLE: You're going? Out of this house?

GREGERS: Yes. Because now at last I can see a purpose to live for.

WERLE: What purpose is that?     600

GREGERS: You'd only laugh if you heard it.

WERLE: A lonely man doesn't laugh so easily, Gregers.

GREGERS: (*pointing toward the inner room*) Look—your gentleman friends are playing blindman's buff with Mrs. Sørby. Good night and goodbye.

(*He goes out at the right rear. Laughter and joking from the company, which moves into view in the inner room.*)

WERLE: (*muttering contemptuously after* GREGERS) Huh! Poor fool—and he says he's not high-strung!

# —ACT TWO—

HJALMAR EKDAL's *studio. The room, which is fairly spacious, appears to be a loft. To the right is a sloping roof with great panes of glass, half hidden by a blue curtain. In the far right corner is the entrance; nearer on the same side, a door to the living room. Similarly, at the left there are two doors, and between these an iron stove. At the back is a wide double door, designed to slide back to the sides. The studio is simply but comfortably furnished and decorated. Between the right-hand doors, slightly away from the wall, stands a sofa beside a table and some chairs; on the table is a lighted lamp with a shade; by the stove an old armchair. Photographic apparatus and equipment of various sorts are set up here and there in the room. At the left of the double doors stands a bookcase containing a few books, small boxes and flasks of chemicals, various tools, implements, and other objects. Photographs and such small articles as brushes, paper, and the like lie on the table.*

GINA EKDAL *sits on a chair by the table, sewing.* HEDVIG *sits on the sofa, hands shading her eyes, thumbs in her ears, reading*
610 *a book.*

GINA: (*having glanced over several times at* HEDVIG, *as if with anxiety*) Hedvig! (HEDVIG *does not hear.*)

GINA: (*louder*) Hedvig!

HEDVIG: (*removing her hands and looking up*) Yes, Mother?

GINA: Hedvig dear, you mustn't sit and read anymore.

HEDVIG: Oh, but Mother, can't I please read a little longer? Just a little!

GINA: No, no—you must set the book down. Your father doesn't like it; *he* never reads in the evening.

620 HEDVIG: (*closing the book*) No, Daddy's no great one for reading.

GINA: (*lays her sewing aside and takes a pencil and a small notebook from the table*) Do you remember how much we spent for butter today?

HEDVIG: It was one sixty-five.

GINA: That's right. (*Making a note.*) It's awful how much butter gets used in this house. And then so much for smoked sausage, and for cheese—let me see—(*Making more notes.*) and so much for ham—hmm. (*Adds.*) Yes, that adds right up
630 to—

HEDVIG: And then there's the beer.

GINA: Yes, of course. (*Makes another note.*) It mounts up—but it can't be helped.

HEDVIG: Oh, but you and I had no hot food for dinner, 'cause Daddy was out.

GINA: No, and that's to the good. What's more, I also took in eight crowns fifty for photographs.

HEDVIG: No! Was it that much?

GINA: Exactly eight crowns fifty.

(*Silence.* GINA *again picks up her sewing.* HEDVIG *takes paper and pencil and starts to draw, shading her eyes with her left hand.*)

640 HEDVIG: Isn't it something to think that Daddy's at a big din-

ner party at old Mr. Werle's?

GINA: You can't really say that he's at old Mr. Werle's. It was his son who sent him the invitation. (*After a pause.*) We have nothing to do with old Mr. Werle.

HEDVIG: I can hardly wait for Daddy to come home. He promised he'd ask Mrs. Sørby about bringing me a treat.

GINA: Yes, you can bet there are lots of treats to be had in *that* house.

HEDVIG: (*again drawing*) Besides, I'm a little hungry, too.

(*Old* EKDAL, *with a bundle of papers under his arm and another bundle in his coat pocket, comes in through the hall door.*)

GINA: My, but you're late today, Grandfather.                   650

EKDAL: They'd locked the office. Had to wait for Graaberg. And then I had to go through—uhh.

GINA: Did they give you something new to copy, Grandfather?

EKDAL: This whole pile. Just look.

GINA: That's fine.

HEDVIG: And you've got a bundle in your pocket, too.

EKDAL: Oh? Nonsense; that's nothing. (*Puts his cane away in the corner.*) Here's work for a good spell, Gina, this here. (*Pulls one of the double doors slightly open.*) Shh! (*Peers into the room a moment, then carefully closes the door again.*)   660 He, he! They're sound asleep, the lot of them. And she's bedded down in the basket all on her own. He, he!

HEDVIG: Are you sure she won't be cold in the basket, Grandpa?

EKDAL: What a thought! Cold? In all that straw? (*Goes toward the farther door on the left.*) I'll find some matches in here, eh?

GINA: The matches are on the bureau.

(EKDAL *goes into his room.*)

HEDVIG: It's wonderful that Grandpa got all that copying to do.

GINA: Yes, poor old Father; he'll earn himself a little pocket   670 money.

HEDVIG: And he also won't be able to sit the whole morning down in that horrid Mrs. Eriksen's café.

GINA: That too, yes. (*A short silence.*)

HEDVIG: Do you think they're still at the dinner table?

GINA: Lord only knows; it may well be.

HEDVIG: Just think, all the lovely food Daddy's eaten! I'm sure he'll be happy and content when he comes. Don't you think so, Mother?

GINA: Of course. Imagine if we could tell him now that we'd   680 rented out the room.

HEDVIG: But that's not necessary tonight.

GINA: Oh, it could well come in handy, you know. It's no good to us as it is.

HEDVIG: No, I mean it's not necessary because tonight Daddy's feeling good. It's better we have news about the room some other time.

GINA: (*looking over at her*) Are you glad when you have something nice to tell your father when he comes home at night?

HEDVIG: Yes, for things here are pleasanter then.                690

GINA: (*reflecting*) Well, there's something to that.

(*Old* EKDAL *comes in again and starts out through the nearer door to the left.*)

GINA: *(half turning in her chair)* Does Grandfather want something from the kitchen?

EKDAL: I do, yes. Don't stir. *(He goes out.)*

GINA: He never fusses with the fire out there. *(After a moment.)* Hedvig, go see what he's doing.

*(EKDAL reenters with a small jug of steaming water.)*

HEDVIG: Are you after hot water, Grandpa?

EKDAL: Yes, I am. Need it for something. Have to write, and the ink is caked thick as porridge—hmm.

700 GINA: But you ought to have supper first, Grandfather. It's all set and waiting in there.

EKDAL: Never mind about the supper, Gina. Terribly busy, I tell you. I don't want anybody coming into my room—nobody. Hmm. *(He goes into his room. GINA and HEDVIG exchange glances.)*

GINA: *(lowering her voice)* Where do you figure he's gotten money?

HEDVIG: He must have got it from Graaberg.

GINA: Not a chance. Graaberg always sends the pay to me.

710 HEDVIG: Maybe he got a bottle somewhere on credit.

GINA: Poor Grandpa, no one'll give him credit.

*(HJALMAR EKDAL, wearing an overcoat and a gray felt hat, enters from the right.)*

GINA: *(dropping her sewing and getting up)* Ah, Hjalmar, here you are!

HEDVIG: *(jumping up at the same time)* At last you're home, Daddy!

HJALMAR: *(putting his hat down)* Yes, most of them were leaving.

HEDVIG: So early?

HJALMAR: Yes, it was only a dinner party. *(Starts to remove his*
720    *overcoat.)*

GINA: Let me help you.

HEDVIG: Me too.

*(They take off his coat; GINA hangs it up on the rear wall.)*

HEDVIG: Were there many there, Daddy?

HJALMAR: Oh no, not many. We were some twelve, fourteen people at the table.

GINA: And you got to talk with every one of them?

HJALMAR: Oh yes, a little, though Gregers rather monopolized
730    me.

GINA: Is Gregers ugly as ever?

HJALMAR: Well, he doesn't look any better. Isn't the old man home?

HEDVIG: Yes, Grandpa's inside, writing.

HJALMAR: Did he say anything?

GINA: No, what should he say?

HJALMAR: Didn't he mention anything of—I thought I heard that he'd been with Graaberg. I'll go in and have a word with him.

740 GINA: No, no, don't bother.

HJALMAR: Why not? Did he say he wouldn't see me?

GINA: He doesn't want anyone in there this evening.

HEDVIG: *(making signals)* Uh—uh!

GINA: *(not noticing)* He's already been out here and gotten hot water.

HJALMAR: Aha! Is he—?

GINA: Yes, exactly.

HJALMAR: Good Lord, my poor old white-haired father! Well, let him be, enjoying life's pleasures as he may.

*(Old EKDAL in a bathrobe, smoking a pipe, enters from his room.)*

EKDAL: Home, eh? Thought it was your voice I heard.    750

HJALMAR: I just arrived.

EKDAL: You didn't see me at all, did you?

HJALMAR: No, but they said you'd been through—so I thought I'd follow after.

EKDAL: Hm, good of you, Hjalmar. Who were they, all those people?

HJALMAR: Oh, different sorts. There was Flor—he's at the court—and Balle and Kaspersen and, uh—I forget his name, but people at court, all of them—

EKDAL: *(nodding)* Listen to that, Gina! He travels only in the    760 best circles.

GINA: Yes, it's real elegant in that house now.

HEDVIG: Did the court people sing, Daddy? Or give readings?

HJALMAR: No, they just babbled away. Of course they wanted *me* to recite for them, but I couldn't see that.

EKDAL: You couldn't see that, eh?

GINA: That you could easily have done.

HJALMAR: Never. One mustn't be a doormat for every passing foot. *(Walking about the room.)* At least, that's not my way.

EKDAL: No, no, that's not for Hjalmar.    770

HJALMAR: I don't know why I should always provide the entertainment, when I'm out in society so rarely. Let the others make an effort. There those fellows go from one banquet to the next, eating and drinking day in and day out. So let them do their tricks in return for all the good food they get.

GINA: But you didn't say that there?

HJALMAR: *(humming)* Um—um—um—they were told a thing or two.

EKDAL: Right to the nobility!

HJALMAR: I don't see why not. *(Casually.)* Later we had a little    780 quibble about Tokay.

EKDAL: Tokay, you mean? That's a fine wine, that.

HJALMAR: *(coming to a halt)* On occasion. But I must tell you that not all years are equally good. Everything depends strictly on how much sun the grapes have had.

GINA: Really? Oh, Hjalmar, you know everything.

EKDAL: And they could argue about that?

HJALMAR: They tried to. But then they were informed that it's exactly the same with court officials. Among them as well, all years are not equally fine—it was said.    790

GINA: The things you think of!

EKDAL: He—he! So you served that up to them, eh?

HJALMAR: Smack between the eyes they got it.

EKDAL: Hear, Gina! He laid that one smack between the eyes of the nobility.

GINA: Just think, smack between the eyes.

HJALMAR: That's right. But I don't want a lot of talk about this. One doesn't speak of such things. Everything really went off in the most friendly spirit, naturally. They're all pleasant, genial people. How could I hurt their feelings? Never!    800

EKDAL: But smack between the eyes—

HEDVIG: *(ingratiatingly)* How nice to see you in evening clothes, Daddy. You look so well in them.

HJALMAR: Yes, don't you think so? And this one here really fits very well. It's almost as if it were made for me. A bit snug under the arms, maybe—help me, Hedvig. (*Takes off the coat.*) I'd rather wear my jacket. What did you do with my jacket, Gina?

GINA: Here it is. (*Brings the jacket and helps him into it.*)

810 HJALMAR: There! Now don't forget to give Molvik his coat back first thing in the morning.

GINA: (*putting it away*) I'll take care of it.

HJALMAR: (*stretching*) Ah, but this feels much more comfortable. This kind of free and easy dress suits my whole personality better. Don't you think so, Hedvig?

HEDVIG: Yes, Daddy.

HJALMAR: And when I pull my necktie out into a pair of flowing ends—so! Look! What then?

HEDVIG: Yes, it goes so well with your moustache and your
820 long, curly hair.

HJALMAR: Curly? I wouldn't say it's that. I'd call it wavy.

HEDVIG: Yes, but it *is* so curly.

HJALMAR: No—wavy.

HEDVIG: (*after a moment, tugs at his sleeve*) Daddy!

HJALMAR: What is it?

HEDVIG: Oh, you know what.

HJALMAR: No, I don't. Honestly.

HEDVIG: (*laughing fretfully*) Come on, Daddy, don't tease me any longer.

830 HJALMAR: But what is it, then?

HEDVIG: (*shaking him*) Silly! Out with it, Daddy. You know— all the treats you promised me.

HJALMAR: Oh—no! How did I ever forget that?

HEDVIG: No, you can't fool me. Shame on you! Where have you hidden it?

HJALMAR: So help me if I didn't forget. But wait a minute! I've got something else for you, Hedvig. (*Goes over and rummages in his coat pockets.*)

HEDVIG: (*jumping and clapping her hands*) Oh, Mother,
840 Mother!

GINA: You see, if you're only patient enough, then—

HJALMAR: (*returning with a piece of paper*) See, here we have it.

HEDVIG: That? But that's just a piece of paper.

HJALMAR: It's the bill of fare, the complete bill of fare. Here it says "menu"; that means "bill of fare."

HEDVIG: Don't you have anything else?

HJALMAR: I forgot to bring anything else, I tell you. But take my word for it: it's bad business, this doting on sugar candy.
850 Now, if you'll sit down at the table and read the menu aloud, I'll describe for you just how each dish tasted. How's that, Hedvig?

HEDVIG: (*swallowing her tears*) Thanks. (*She sits, but does not read.* GINA *makes gestures at her, which* HJALMAR *notices.*)

HJALMAR: (*pacing about the floor*) What incredible things a family breadwinner is asked to remember; and if he forgets even the tiniest detail—immediately he's met with sour faces. Well, he has to get used to that, too. (*Pauses at the stove beside* EKDAL.) Have you looked inside this evening,
860 Father?

EKDAL: Oh, that you can be sure of. She's gone into the basket.

HJALMAR: No! Into the basket? Then she's begun to get used to it.

EKDAL: Yes. You see, it was just as I predicted. But now there are some little things to do—

HJALMAR: Some improvements, eh?

EKDAL: But they've got to be done, you know.

HJALMAR: All right, let's talk a bit about the improvements, Father. Come, we'll sit here on the sofa.

EKDAL: Very good. Umm—think I'll fill my pipe first. Needs 870 cleaning, too. Hmm. (*He goes into his room.*)

GINA: (*smiling at* HJALMAR) Clean his pipe!

HJALMAR: Ah, now, Gina, let him be. Poor old derelict. Yes, the improvements—it's best we get those off our hands tomorrow.

GINA: Tomorrow you won't have time, Hjalmar—

HEDVIG: (*interrupting*) Oh yes, he will, Mother!

GINA: Remember those prints that need retouching. They've been called for so many times already.

HJALMAR: Oh yes, those prints again. They'll be finished in no 880 time. Did any new orders come in?

GINA: No such luck. For tomorrow, I have nothing except those two portrait sittings you know about.

HJALMAR: Nothing else? Ah, well, if people won't even try, then naturally—

GINA: But what else can I do? I've put ads in the papers time and again.

HJALMAR: Yes, ads, ads—you see what a help they are. And of course nobody's been to look at the spare room either?

GINA: No, not yet. 890

HJALMAR: That was to be expected. If one doesn't keep wide awake—Gina, you've simply got to pull yourself together.

HEDVIG: (*going to him*) Let me bring you your flute, Daddy.

HJALMAR: No, no flute. I want no pleasures in this world. (*Pacing about.*) Ah, yes, work—I'll be deep in work tomorrow; there'll be no lack of *that*. I'll sweat and slave as long as my strength holds out—

GINA: But Hjalmar dear, I didn't mean it that way.

HEDVIG: Can't I get you a bottle of beer, then?

HJALMAR: Absolutely not. There's nothing I need. (*Stopping.*) 900 Beer? Did you say beer?

HEDVIG: (*vivaciously*) Yes, Daddy, lovely cool beer.

HJALMAR: Well—if you really insist, I suppose you could bring in a bottle.

GINA: Yes, do that. Then we'll have it cozy.

(HEDVIG *runs toward the kitchen door.* HJALMAR *by the stove stops her, gazes at her, clasps her about the head and hugs her to him.*)

HJALMAR: Hedvig! Hedvig!

HEDVIG: (*with tears of joy*) Oh, my dearest Daddy!

HJALMAR: No, don't call me that. There I sat, helping myself at a rich man's table, gorging myself with all good things—! I could at least have remembered— 910

GINA: (*sitting at the table*) Oh, nonsense, Hjalmar.

HJALMAR: Yes, I could! But you mustn't be too hard on me. You both know I love you anyway.

HEDVIG: (*throwing her arms around him*) And we love you too, so much!

HJALMAR: And if I should seem unreasonable at times, then— good Lord—remember that I am a man assailed by a host of cares. Ah, yes! (*Drying his eyes.*) No beer at a time like this. Bring me my flute. (HEDVIG *runs to the bookcase and fetches*

920    *it.*) Thank you. There—so. With flute in hand, and you two close by me—ah!

(HEDVIG *sits at the table by* GINA, HJALMAR *walks back and forth, then forcefully begins to play a Bohemian folk dance, but in a slow elegiac tempo with sentimental intonation. After a moment he breaks off the melody and extends his left hand to* GINA.)

HJALMAR: (*with feeling*) So what if we skimp and scrape along under this roof, Gina—it's still our home. And I'll say this: it's good to be here. (*He starts playing again; immediately there comes a knock on the hall door.*)

GINA: (*getting up*) Shh, Hjalmar. I think someone's there.

HJALMAR: (*returning the flute to the bookcase*) What, again! (GINA *goes over and opens the door.*)

GREGERS WERLE: (*out in the hallway*) Excuse me—

930   GINA: (*drawing back slightly*) Oh!

GREGERS: But doesn't Mr. Ekdal, the photographer, live here?

GINA: Yes, that's right.

HJALMAR: (*going toward the door*) Gregers! Is it really you? Well, come right in.

GREGERS: (*entering*) I said I was going to drop in on you.

HJALMAR: But tonight? Have you left the party?

GREGERS: Left both party and family home. Good evening, Mrs. Ekdal. I don't know whether you recognize me.

GINA: Oh yes. Young Mr. Werle is not so hard to recognize.

940   GREGERS: No. I look like my mother, and you remember her, no doubt.

HJALMAR: Did you say you'd left your home?

GREGERS: Yes, I've moved into a hotel.

HJALMAR: I see. Well, now that you've come, take off your things and sit down.

GREGERS: Thank you. (*Removes his overcoat. He is dressed now in a simple grey suit of somewhat rustic cut.*)

HJALMAR: Here, on the sofa. Make yourself at home.

(GREGERS *sits on the sofa,* HJALMAR *on a chair at the table.*)

GREGERS: (*looking around*) So this is where you work, then, 950   Hjalmar. And you live here as well.

HJALMAR: This is the studio, as you can see—

GINA: There's more room in here, so we like it better.

HJALMAR: We had a better place before; but this apartment has one great advantage: it has such wonderful adjoining rooms—

GINA: And so we have a room on the other side of the hall that we can rent out.

GREGERS: (*to* HJALMAR) Ah, then you have lodgers, too.

HJALMAR: No, not yet. It's not that easy, you know. One has to 960   keep wide awake. (*To* HEDVIG.) But how about that beer?

(HEDVIG *nods and goes into the kitchen.*)

GREGERS: So that's your daughter, then?

HJALMAR: Yes, that's Hedvig.

GREGERS: An only child?

HJALMAR: She's the only one, yes. She's the greatest joy of our lives, and—(*Lowering his voice.*) also our deepest sorrow, Gregers.

GREGERS: What do you mean?

HJALMAR: Yes. You see, there's the gravest imminent danger of her losing her sight.

GREGERS: Going blind!    970

HJALMAR: Yes. So far only the first signs are present, and things may go well for a while. All the same, the doctor has warned us. It will come inevitably.

GREGERS: What a dreadful misfortune! How did this happen?

HJALMAR: (*sighing*) Heredity, most likely.

GREGERS: (*startled*) Heredity?

GINA: Hjalmar's mother also had bad eyes.

HJALMAR: Yes, so my father says. I don't remember her.

GREGERS: Poor child. And how is she taking it?

HJALMAR: Oh, you can well imagine, we haven't the heart to tell 980   her. She suspects nothing. She's carefree, gay, and singing like a tiny bird, she's fluttering into life's eternal night. (*Overcome.*) Oh, it's a brutal blow for me, Gregers.

(HEDVIG *brings in beer and glasses on a tray, which she sets down on the table.*)

HJALMAR: (*stroking her head*) Thanks. Thanks, Hedvig.

(HEDVIG *puts her arms around his neck and whispers in his ear.*)

HJALMAR: No. No bread and butter now. (*Looking over.*) Or maybe Gregers will have a piece?

GREGERS: (*making a gesture of refusal*). No. No, thanks.

HJALMAR: (*his tone still mournful*) Well, you can bring in a little anyway. If you have a crust, that would be fine. And please, put enough butter on, too.    990

(HEDVIG *nods contentedly and returns to the kitchen.*)

GREGERS: (*after following her with his eyes*). In every other respect she looks so strong and healthy.

GINA: Yes, thank God, she's got nothing else wrong with her.

GREGERS: She'll certainly look like you when she grows up, Mrs. Ekdal. How old is she now?

GINA: Hedvig is almost fourteen exactly; her birthday's the day after tomorrow.

GREGERS: Rather tall for her age.

GINA: Yes, she's shot right up this past year.

GREGERS: Nothing like the growth of a child to show us how 1000   old we're getting. How long is it you've been married now?

GINA: We've been married now for—yes, near fifteen years.

GREGERS: No, truly! Has it been that long?

GINA: (*looking at him, becoming wary*) Yes, no doubt about it.

HJALMAR: That's right. Fifteen years, short a few months. (*Changing the subject.*) They must have been long years for you, Gregers, up there at the works.

GREGERS: They were long while I was living them—but now I scarcely know what became of the time.

(Old EKDAL *enters from his room, without his pipe, but with his old military cap on his head; his walk is a bit unsteady.*)

EKDAL: There, now, Hjalmar. Now we can settle down and talk 1010   about that—umm. What was it again?

HJALMAR: (*going toward him*) Father, someone is here. Gregers Werle. I don't know if you remember him.

EKDAL: (*regarding* GREGERS, *who has gotten up*) Werle? That's the son, isn't it? What does he want with me?

HJALMAR: Nothing; it's me he's come to see.

EKDAL: Well, then nothing's up, eh?

HJALMAR: No, of course not.

EKDAL: *(swinging his arms)* It's not that I'm scared of anything, you know, but—

GREGERS: *(going over to him)* I just want to greet you from your old hunting grounds, Lieutenant Ekdal.

EKDAL: Hunting grounds?

GREGERS: Yes, up there around the Hoidal works.

EKDAL: Oh, up there. Yes, I was well known there once.

GREGERS: In those days you were a tremendous hunter.

EKDAL: So I was. Still am, maybe. You're looking at my uniform. I ask nobody permission to wear it in here. As long as I don't walk in the streets with it—(HEDVIG *brings a plate of buttered bread, which she places on the table.*)

HJALMAR: Sit down, Father, and have a glass of beer. Help yourself, Gregers.

*(EKDAL stumbles, muttering, over to the sofa.* GREGERS *sits on the chair nearest him,* HJALMAR *on the other side of* GREGERS. GINA *sits near the table and sews;* HEDVIG *stands beside her father.*)

GREGERS: Do you remember, Lieutenant Ekdal, when Hjalmar and I would come up to visit you summers and at Christmas?

EKDAL: Did you? No, no, no, I don't recall. But I'll tell you something: I've been a first-rate hunter. Bear—I've shot them, too. Shot nine in all.

GREGERS: *(looking sympathetically at him)* And now you hunt no more.

EKDAL: Oh, I wouldn't say *that*, boy. Get some hunting in now and then. Yes, but not that kind there. The woods, you see—the woods, the woods—*(Drinks.)* How do the woods look up there?

GREGERS: Not so fine as in your time. They've been cut into heavily.

EKDAL: Cut into? *(More quietly, as if in fear.)* It's a dangerous business, that. It catches up with you. The woods take revenge.

HJALMAR: *(filling his glass)* Here, a little more, Father.

GREGERS: How can a man like you—such an outdoorsman—live in the middle of a stuffy city, cooped up in these four walls?

EKDAL: *(half laughs and glances at* HJALMAR*)* Oh, it's not so bad here. Not bad at all.

GREGERS: But all those other things, the very roots of your soul—that cool, sweeping breeze, that free life of the moors and forests, among the animals and birds—?

EKDAL: *(smiling)* Hjalmar, should we show him?

HJALMAR: *(quickly and a bit embarrassed)* No, no, Father, not tonight.

GREGERS: What's that he wants to show me?

HJALMAR: Oh, it's only a sort of—you can see it some other time.

GREGERS: *(speaking again to* EKDAL*)* Yes, my point was this, Lieutenant Ekdal, that now you might as well return with me to the works, for I'm sure to be leaving very soon. Without a doubt, you could get some copying to do up there; and here you've nothing in the world to stir your blood and make you happy.

EKDAL: *(staring at him, astonished)* I have nothing, nothing at all—!

GREGERS: Of course you have Hjalmar, but then again, he has

his own. And a man like you, who's always felt himself so drawn to whatever is free and wild—

EKDAL: *(striking the table)* Hjalmar, now he's *got* to see it!

HJALMAR: But Father, is it worth it now? It's dark, you know—

EKDAL: Nonsense! There's moonlight. *(Getting up.)* I say he's got to see it. Let me by. Come and help me, Hjalmar!

HEDVIG: Oh yes, do that, Father!

HJALMAR: *(getting up)* Well—all right.

GREGERS: *(to* GINA*)* What's this all about?

GINA: Oh, you really mustn't expect anything special.

*(EKDAL *and* HJALMAR *have gone to the back wall to push aside the two halves of the double door;* HEDVIG *helps her grandfather, while* GREGERS *remains standing by the sofa and* GINA *sits, imperturbably sewing. The doorway opens on an extensive, irregular loft room with many nooks and corners, and two separate chimney shafts ascending through it. Clear moonlight streams through skylights into certain parts of the large room; others lie in deep shadow.*)

EKDAL: *(to* GREGERS*)* All the way over here, please.

GREGERS: *(going over to them)* What *is* it, then?

EKDAL: See for yourself—hmm.

HJALMAR: *(somewhat self-conscious)* All this belongs to Father, you understand.

GREGERS: *(peering in at the doorway)* So you keep poultry, Lieutenant Ekdal!

EKDAL: I'll say we keep poultry! They're roosting now; but you just ought to see our poultry by daylight!

HEDVIG: And then there's a—

EKDAL: Shh, shh—don't say anything yet.

GREGERS: And you've got pigeons too, I see.

EKDAL: Oh yes, it might just be we've got some pigeons. They have their nesting boxes up there under the eaves; pigeons like to perch high, you know.

HJALMAR: They're not ordinary pigeons, all of them.

EKDAL: Ordinary! No, I should say not! We have tumblers, and we have a couple of pouters also. But look here! Can you see that hutch over there by the wall?

GREGERS: Yes. What do you use that for?

EKDAL: The rabbits sleep there at night, boy.

GREGERS: Well, so you have rabbits too?

EKDAL: Yes, what the devil do you think we have but rabbits! He asks if we have rabbits, Hjalmar! Hmm! But now listen, this is really something! This is it! Out of the way, Hedvig. Stand right here—that's it—and look straight down there. Do you see a basket there with straw in it?

GREGERS: Yes, and there's a bird nesting in the basket.

EKDAL: Hmm! "A bird"—

GREGERS: Isn't it a duck?

EKDAL: *(hurt)* Yes, of course it's a duck.

HJALMAR: But what *kind* of duck?

HEDVIG: It's not just any old duck—

EKDAL: Shh!

GREGERS: And it's no exotic breed, either.

EKDAL: No, Mr.—Werle, it's not any exotic breed—because it's a wild duck.

GREGERS: No, is it really? A wild duck?

EKDAL: Oh yes, that's what it is. That "bird" as you said—that's a wild duck. That's our wild duck, boy.

HEDVIG: *My* wild duck—I own it.

GREGERS: And it can survive up here indoors? And do well?

EKDAL: You've got to understand, she's got a trough of water to splash around in.

HJALMAR: Fresh water every other day.

GINA: *(turning to* HJALMAR*)* Hjalmar dear, it's freezing cold in
1130 here now.

EKDAL: Hmm, let's close up, then. Doesn't pay to disturb their rest either. Lend a hand, Hedvig dear. *(*HJALMAR *and* HEDVIG *push the double doors together.)* Another time you can get a proper look at her. *(Sits in the armchair by the stove.)* Oh, they're most curious, the wild ducks, you know.

GREGERS: But how did you capture it, Lieutenant Ekdal?

EKDAL: Didn't capture it myself. There's a certain man here in town we can thank for it.

GREGERS: *(starts slightly)* That man—it wouldn't be my
1140 father?

EKDAL: Exactly right—your father. Hmm.

HJALMAR: It was odd you were able to guess that, Gregers.

GREGERS: Well, you said before that you owed Father for so many different things, so I thought here too—

GINA: But we didn't get the duck from Mr. Werle himself—

EKDAL: We might just as well thank Haakon Werle for her anyhow, Gina. *(To* GREGERS.*)* He was out in his boat—follow me?—and he shot for her, but he sees so bad now, your father, that—hm—he only winged her.

1150 GREGERS: I see. She took some shot in her body.

HJALMAR: Yes, some one, two—three pieces.

HEDVIG: She got it under the wing, and so she couldn't fly.

GREGERS: Ah, so she dived right for the bottom, eh?

EKDAL: *(sleepily, with a thick voice)* You can bet on that. They always do, the wild ducks—streak for the bottom, deep as they can get, boy—bite right into the weeds and sea moss— and all that devil's beard that grows down there. And then they never come up again.

GREGERS: But Lieutenant Ekdal, *your* wild duck came up
1160 again.

EKDAL: He had such a remarkably clever dog, your father. And that dog—he dove down and brought her up.

GREGERS: *(turning to* HJALMAR*)* And then you got her here.

HJALMAR: Not directly. First she went home to your father's, but there she didn't do well, so Pettersen got his orders to put an end to her—

EKDAL: *(half asleep)* Hm—yes, Pettersen—that bonehead—

HJALMAR: *(speaking more softly)* That's the way we got her, you see. Father knows Pettersen a bit and when he heard all this
1170 about the wild duck, he arranged to have her handed over to us.

GREGERS: And now she's absolutely thriving in that attic room.

HJALMAR: Yes, it's incredible. She's gotten fat. I think she's been in there so long, too, that she's forgotten her old wild life, and that's what it all comes down to.

GREGERS: You're certainly right there, Hjalmar. Just don't let her ever catch sight of the sea and the sky—But I mustn't stay any longer, for I think your father's asleep.

HJALMAR: Oh, don't bother about that.

1180 GREGERS: But incidentally—you said you had a room for rent, a free room?

HJALMAR: Yes. Why? Do you know someone, perhaps—?

GREGERS: Could I take that room?

HJALMAR: You?

GINA: No, not *you*, Mr. Werle—

GREGERS: Could I take the room? If so, I'll move in first thing in the morning.

HJALMAR: By all means, with the greatest pleasure—

GINA: No, but Mr. Werle, it's not at all the room for *you*.

HJALMAR: But Gina, how can you say that? 1190

GINA: Oh, the room isn't large enough, or light enough, and—

GREGERS: That really doesn't matter, Mrs. Ekdal.

HJALMAR: I think it's a very pleasant room, and it's not badly furnished, either.

GINA: But remember those two who live right below.

GREGERS: What two are those?

GINA: Oh, one of them's been a private tutor—

HJALMAR: That's Molvik, from the university.

GINA: And then there's a doctor named Relling.

GREGERS: Relling? I know him somewhat. He practiced a 1200 while up in Hoidal.

GINA: They're a pretty wild pair, those fellows. They go out on the town evenings and then come home in the dead of night, and they're not always so—

GREGERS: One gets used to that soon enough. I'm hoping things will go for me the same as with the wild duck—

GINA: Well, I think you ought to sleep on it first, anyway.

GREGERS: You're not very anxious to have me in the house, Mrs. Ekdal.

GINA: Goodness, what makes you think that? 1210

HJALMAR: Yes, Gina, this is really peculiar of you. *(To* GREGERS.*)* But tell me, do you expect to stay here in town till the first?

GREGERS: *(putting on his overcoat)* Yes, now I expect to stay on.

HJALMAR: But not at home with your father? What do you plan to do with yourself?

GREGERS: Yes, if I only knew that—then I'd be doing all right. But when one is cursed with being called Gregers— "Gregers"—and then "Werle" coming after—have you ever 1220 heard anything so disgusting?

HJALMAR: Oh, I don't agree at all.

GREGERS: Ugh! Phew! I feel I'd like to spit on any man with a name like that. But when one has to *live* with that curse of being called Gregers, as I do—

HJALMAR: *(laughing)* If you weren't Gregers Werle, who would you want to be?

GREGERS: If I could choose, above all else I'd like to be a clever dog.

GINA: A dog! 1230

HEDVIG: *(involuntarily)* Oh no!

GREGERS: Yes. A really fantastic, clever dog, the kind that goes to the bottom after wild ducks when they dive under and bite fast into the weeds down in the mire.

HJALMAR: You know, Gregers—I can't follow a word you're saying.

GREGERS: Never mind. There's really nothing very remarkable in it. But tomorrow morning, early, I'll be moving in. *(To* GINA.*)* I won't be any trouble to you; I do everything for myself. *(To* HJALMAR.*)* The rest we can talk over tomorrow. 1240 Good night, Mrs. Ekdal. *(Nods to* HEDVIG.*)* Good night.

GINA: Good night, Mr. Werle.

HEDVIG: Good night.

HJALMAR: *(who has lit a lamp)* Just a minute. I'd better light your way; it's quite dark on the stairs.

(GREGERS *and* HJALMAR *go out through the hall.*)

GINA: (*gazing into space, her sewing in her lap*) Wasn't that a queer business, his wanting to be a dog?

HEDVIG: I'll tell you something, Mother—it seemed to me he meant something else by that.

1250 GINA: What else could he mean?

HEDVIG: I don't know—but it was just as if he meant something else from what he said, all the time.

GINA: Do you think so? It was strange, all right.

HJALMAR: (*coming back*) The light was still lit. (*Putting out the lamp and setting it down.*) Ah, at last one can get a bite to eat. (*Beginning on the bread and butter.*) Well, now you see, Gina—if you simply keep wide awake, then—

GINA: What do you mean, wide awake?

HJALMAR: Well, it was lucky, then, that we got the room rented
1260 out for a while at last. And think—to a person like Gregers—a good old friend.

GINA: Yes. I don't know what to say. I don't.

HEDVIG: Oh, Mother, you'll see. It'll be fun.

HJALMAR: You really are peculiar. Before you were so eager to rent, and now you don't like it.

GINA: Yes, Hjalmar, if it could only have been somebody else. What do you think the old man will say?

HJALMAR: Old Werle? This doesn't concern him.

GINA: But you can bet that something has come up be-
1270 tween them, since the son is moving out. You know how those two get along together.

HJALMAR: Yes, that may well be, but—

GINA: And now maybe the old man thinks it's you that's behind—

HJALMAR: He can think that as much as he likes! Old Werle has done a tremendous amount for me. God knows, I'm aware of that. But even so, I can't make myself eternally dependent on him.

GINA: But Hjalmar dear, that can have its effect on Grand-
1280 father. He may now lose that miserable little income he gets from Graaberg.

HJALMAR: I could almost say, so much the better! Isn't it rather humiliating for a man like me to see his gray-haired father go around like an outcast? But now time is gathering to a ripeness, I think. (*Takes another piece of bread and butter.*) Just as sure as I've got a mission in life, I'm going to carry it out!

HEDVIG: Oh yes, Daddy! Do!

GINA: Shh! Don't wake him up.

1290 HJALMAR: (*more quietly*) I *will* carry it out, I tell you. There will come a day when—And that's why it's good we got the room rented out, for now I'm more independently fixed. Any man *must* be that, who's got a mission in life. (*Over by the armchair; emotionally.*) Poor old white-haired Father—lean on your Hjalmar. He has broad shoulders—powerful shoulders, in any case. One fine day you'll wake up and—(*To* GINA.) You do believe that, don't you?

GINA: (*getting up*) Yes, of course I do. But first let's see about getting him to bed.

1300 HJALMAR: Yes, let's do that.

(*Gently they lift up the old man.*)

—ACT THREE—

HJALMAR EKDAL's *studio. It is morning. Daylight streams through the large window in the sloping roof; the curtain is drawn back.*

HJALMAR *is sitting at the table, busy retouching a photograph; many other pictures lie in front of him. After a moment* GINA, *wearing a hat and coat, enters by the hall door; she has a covered basket on her arm.*

HJALMAR: Back so soon, Gina?

GINA: Oh yes. Got to keep moving. (*She sets the basket on a chair and takes her coat off.*)

HJALMAR: Did you look in on Gregers?

GINA: Um-hm, I certainly did. Looks real nice in there. The moment he came, he got his room in beautiful shape.

HJALMAR: Oh?

GINA: Yes. He wanted to do everything himself, he said. So he starts building a fire in the stove, and the next thing he's closed down the damper so the whole room is full of smoke. 1310 Phew! What a stink, enough to—

HJALMAR: Oh no!

GINA: But that's not the best part! So then he wants to put it out, so he empties his whole water pitcher into the stove and now the floor's swimming in the worst muck.

HJALMAR: That's a nuisance.

GINA: I got the janitor's wife to come and scrub up after him, the pig; but it'll be unfit to live in till afternoon.

HJALMAR: What's he doing with himself in the meantime?

GINA: Thought he'd take a little walk, he said. 1320

HJALMAR: I was in to see him for a moment too—after you left.

GINA: I heard that. You asked him for lunch.

HJALMAR: Just the tiniest little midday snack, you understand. It's the very first day—we could hardly avoid it. You always have something in the house.

GINA: I'll see what I can find.

HJALMAR: But now don't make it too skimpy. Because Relling and Molvik are dropping in too, I think. I just met Relling on the stairs, you see, so of course I had to—

GINA: Oh? Must we have those two also? 1330

HJALMAR: Good Lord, a couple of sandwiches more or less; what's the difference?

EKDAL: (*opening his door and looking in*) Say, listen, Hjalmar—(*Noticing* GINA.) Oh, well.

GINA: Is there something Grandfather wants?

EKDAL: Oh no. Let it be. Hmm. (*Goes in again.*)

GINA: (*picking up the basket*) Keep a sharp eye on him so he doesn't go out.

HJALMAR: Oh yes, I'll do that. Listen, Gina, a little herring salad would be awfully good—because Relling and Molvik were 1340 out on a binge last night.

GINA: Just so they don't come before I'm ready—

HJALMAR: Not a chance. Take your time.

GINA: That's fine, then—and meanwhile you can get a little work done.

HJALMAR: Can't you see how I'm working! I'm working for all I'm worth!

GINA: Because then you'll have *those* off your hands, you know. (*She carries the basket out to the kitchen.* HJALMAR *sits for a while, tinting the photograph in a glum and listless manner.*) 1350

EKDAL: (*peeks in, peers about the studio, and whispers*) Are you busy, boy?

HJALMAR: Of course. I'm sitting here struggling with these pictures—

EKDAL: Oh well, don't bother. If you're so busy, then—Hm! (*He reenters his room, leaving the door ajar.*)

HJALMAR: (*continues a moment in silence, then puts down the brush and goes over to the door*) Father, are *you* busy?

EKDAL: (*grumbling from within*) When you're busy—I'm busy too. Huh!

1360

HJALMAR: Yes, of course. (*Returns to his work.*)

EKDAL: (*a moment later, coming in again*) Hm. Well, now, Hjalmar, I'm really not *that* busy.

HJALMAR: I thought you had copying to do.

EKDAL: Oh, the devil! Can't he, Graaberg, wait a day or two? I'm sure it's no matter of life or death.

HJALMAR: No, and you're no slave, either.

EKDAL: And then there was that other business inside—

HJALMAR: Yes, that's just it. Maybe you want to go in? Shall I open it up for you?

1370

EKDAL: Wouldn't be a bad idea, really?

HJALMAR: (*getting up*) And then we'd have *that* off our hands.

EKDAL: Yes, exactly. And it has to be ready first thing tomorrow. But it *is* tomorrow, isn't it?

HJALMAR: It certainly is tomorrow.

(*HJALMAR and EKDAL each push back one of the double doors. Within, morning sunlight shines through the skylights. A few doves fly back and forth; others perch, cooing, on the rafters. Chickens cackle now and then from back in the loft.*)

HJALMAR: There, now you can get in, Father.

EKDAL: (*going in*) Aren't you coming along?

HJALMAR: Well, you know what—I almost think—(*Sees GINA in the kitchen doorway.*) I? No, I haven't the time; I've got to work. But that means our new mechanism—

1380

(*He pulls a cord; inside a curtain descends, its lower portion composed of a strip of old sailcloth, the upper part being a piece of worn-out fishnetting. By this means, the floor of the loft is rendered invisible.*)

HJALMAR: (*returning to the table*) That's that. Now at last I can work in peace for a while.

GINA: Is he in there, romping around again?

HJALMAR: Isn't that better than having him run down to Mrs. Eriksen's? (*Sitting.*) Is there anything you want? You look so—

GINA: I only wanted to ask, do you think we can set the lunch table in here?

HJALMAR: Well, we haven't any portraits scheduled that early, have we?

1390

GINA: No. I don't expect anybody except that couple who want to be taken together.

HJALMAR: Why the devil can't they be taken together some other day?

GINA: Now, Hjalmar dear, I've got them booked for during your midday nap.

HJALMAR: Well, that's fine, then. So we'll eat in here.

GINA: All right. But there's no hurry about setting the table; you can certainly use it a while longer.

1400

HJALMAR: Oh, it's obvious I'm using the table as much as I can!

GINA: Because then you'll be free later on, you know. (*She goes back into the kitchen. A short pause.*)

EKDAL: (*at the door to the loft, behind the net*) Hjalmar!

HJALMAR: —Well?

EKDAL: 'Fraid we'll have to move the water trough after all.

HJALMAR: Yes, that's what I've been saying all along.

EKDAL: Hm—hm—hm. (*Disappears from the doorway.*)

(*HJALMAR works a bit, glances toward the loft, and half rises. HEDVIG enters from the kitchen.*)

HJALMAR: (*hurriedly sitting again*) What do you want?

HEDVIG: I was just coming in to you, Father.

HJALMAR: (*after a moment*) You seem to be kind of snooping around. Are you checking up, maybe?

1410

HEDVIG: No, not at all.

HJALMAR: What's Mother doing out there now?

HEDVIG: Oh, she's half through the herring salad. (*Going over to the table.*) Don't you have some little thing I could help you with, Daddy?

HJALMAR: Oh no. It's better just to leave me alone with all this—so long as my strength holds out. Nothing to worry about, Hedvig—if only your father can keep his health—

HEDVIG: Oh, Daddy, no. That's horrid; you musn't talk like that. (*She wanders about a little, stops by the loft doorway, and looks in.*)

1420

HJALMAR: What's he trying to do now?

HEDVIG: It must be a new pathway up to the water trough.

HJALMAR: He can't possibly rig that up on his own! And I'm condemned to sit here—!

HEDVIG: (*going to him*) Let *me* take the brush, Daddy. I know I can.

HJALMAR: Oh, nonsense, you'll only ruin your eyes.

HEDVIG: No such thing. Give me the brush.

1430

HJALMAR: (*getting up*) Well, it'll only be for a minute or two.

HEDVIG: Pooh! How could that hurt me? (*Takes the brush.*) There now. (*Sitting.*) And here's one to go by.

HJALMAR: But don't ruin your eyes! Hear me? I won't take the blame; you can take the blame yourself—you hear me?

HEDVIG: (*at work retouching*) Yes, yes, sure I will.

HJALMAR: You're wonderfully clever, Hedvig. Just for a couple of minutes now.

(*He slips around the edge of the curtain into the loft. HEDVIG sits at her work. HJALMAR and EKDAL are heard arguing inside.*)

HJALMAR: (*appearing behind the net*) Hedvig, just hand me the pliers from the shelf. And the chisel, please. (*Turning over his shoulder.*) Yes, now you'll see, Father. Will you give me a chance to show you the way I mean! (*HEDVIG fetches the desired tools from the bookcase and passes them in to him.*) Ah, thanks. See, dear, it was a good thing I came. (*He vanishes from the doorway; sounds of carpentry and bantering are heard. HEDVIG remains, looking in at them. A moment later, a knock at the hall door; she fails to notice it.*)

1440

GREGERS: (*bareheaded, and without his overcoat, enters, hesitating slightly at the door*) Hm—

HEDVIG: (*turning and going toward him*) Good morning. Please come in.

1450

GREGERS: Thanks. (*Looking at the loft.*) You seem to have workmen in the house.

HEDVIG: No, that's only Father and Grandfather. I'll go tell them.

GREGERS: No, no, don't bother. I'd rather wait a bit. (*He sits on the sofa.*)

HEDVIG: It's so messy here—(*Starts to remove the photographs.*)

1460 GREGERS: Oh, they can stay. Are those some pictures that have to be finished?

HEDVIG: Yes, it's a little job I'm helping Daddy with.

GREGERS: Please don't let me disturb you.

HEDVIG: All right. (*She gathers her materials around her and sets to work again;* GREGERS *meanwhile regards her in silence.*)

GREGERS: Did the wild duck sleep well last night?

HEDVIG: Yes, I'm sure she did, thanks.

GREGERS: (*turning toward the loft*) It looks so very different by
1470 daylight than it did by moonlight.

HEDVIG: Yes, it can change so completely. In the morning it looks different from in the afternoon; and when it rains it's different from when it's clear.

GREGERS: Have you noticed that?

HEDVIG: Sure. You can't help it.

GREGERS: And do you like it in there with the wild duck, too?

HEDVIG: Yes, whenever I can be there—

GREGERS: But of course you don't have much free time; you do go to school, don't you?

1480 HEDVIG: No, not anymore. Daddy's afraid I'll hurt my eyes.

GREGERS: Oh. Then he reads to you himself.

HEDVIG: Daddy's promised to read to me, but he hasn't found time for that yet.

GREGERS: But isn't there anyone else to help you a little?

HEDVIG: Sure, there's Mr. Molvik, but he isn't always exactly, really—well—

GREGERS: He gets drunk, eh?

HEDVIG: He *certainly* does.

GREGERS: Well, then you do have time to yourself. And
1490 inside—I'll bet in there it's just like a world of its own—am I right?

HEDVIG: Oh, completely! And then there are so many wonderful things.

GREGERS: Really?

HEDVIG: Yes, big cupboards with books in them; and lots of the books have pictures.

GREGERS: Ah!

HEDVIG: And then there's an old cabinet with drawers and compartments, and a huge clock with figures that are sup-
1500 posed to come out. But the clock doesn't go anymore.

GREGERS: Even time doesn't exist in there—with the wild duck.

HEDVIG: Yes. And then there's an old watercolor set and things like that. And then all the books.

GREGERS: And of course you read the books?

HEDVIG: Oh yes, whenever I can. But they're mostly in English, and I don't understand that. But then I look at the pictures. There's one just enormous book called *Harryson's History of London;* it must be a hundred years old, and it's
1510 got ever so many pictures in it. At the front there's a picture of Death with an hourglass and a girl. I think that's horrible. But then there are all the other pictures of churches and castles and streets and great ships sailing on the ocean.

GREGERS: But tell me, where did all these rare things come from!

HEDVIG: Oh, an old sea captain lived here once, and he brought them home. They called him "the flying Dutchman"—and that's the strangest thing, because he wasn't a Dutchman at all.

GREGERS: No? 1520

HEDVIG: No. But then he didn't come back finally, and he left all these things behind.

GREGERS: Listen, tell me—when you sit in there and look at pictures, don't you ever want to go out and see the real world all for yourself?

HEDVIG: No, never! I'm going to stay at home always and help Daddy and Mother.

GREGERS: You mean finishing photographs?

HEDVIG: No, not just that. Most of all, I'd like to learn how to engrave pictures like those in the English books. 1530

GREGERS: Hm. What does your father say to that?

HEDVIG: I don't think he likes it. Daddy's so funny about such things. Just think, he talks about me learning basketmaking and wickerwork! But I don't see anything in *that.*

GREGERS: Oh no, I don't either.

HEDVIG: But Daddy's right when he says that if I'd learned how to make baskets, I could have made the new basket for the wild duck.

GREGERS: You could have, yes—and that really was up to you.

HEDVIG: Yes, because it's *my* wild duck. 1540

GREGERS: Yes, of course it is.

HEDVIG: Uh-huh, I own it. But Daddy and Grandpa can borrow it as much as they want.

GREGERS: Oh? What do they do with it?

HEDVIG: Oh, they look after it and build things for it and so on.

GREGERS: I can well imagine. The wild duck rules supreme in there, doesn't she?

HEDVIG: Yes, she does, and that's because she's a real wild bird. And then it's so sad for her; the poor thing has no one to turn to. 1550

GREGERS: No family, like the rabbits—

HEDVIG: No. Even the chickens have all the others that they were baby chicks with, but she's so completely apart from any of her own. So you see, everything is so really mysterious about the wild duck. There's no one who knows her, and no one who knows where she's come from, either.

GREGERS: And actually, she's been in the depths of the sea.

HEDVIG: (*glances at him, suppresses a smile, and asks*) Why did you say "depths of the sea"?

GREGERS: What else should I say? 1560

HEDVIG: You could have said "bottom of the sea"—or "the ocean's bottom"?

GREGERS: But couldn't I just as well say "depths of the sea"?

HEDVIG: Sure. But to me it sounds so strange when someone else says "depths of the sea."

GREGERS: But why? Tell me why?

HEDVIG: No, I won't. It's something so stupid.

GREGERS: It couldn't be. Now tell me why you smiled.

HEDVIG: That was because always, when all of a sudden—in a flash—I happen to think of that in there, it always seems to 1570 me that the whole room and everything in it is called "the depths of the sea"! But that's all so stupid.

GREGERS: Don't you dare say that.

HEDVIG: Oh yes, because it's only an attic.

GREGERS: Are you so sure of that?

HEDVIG: (*astonished*) That it's an attic!

GREGERS: Yes. Do you know that for certain?

(HEDVIG, *speechless, stares at him open-mouthed.* GINA *enters from the kitchen with a tablecloth.*)

GREGERS: (*getting up*) I'm afraid I've come too early for you.

GINA: Oh, you can find yourself a spot; it's almost ready now.
1580    Clear the table, Hedvig.

(HEDVIG *puts away the materials; during the following dialogue, she and* GINA *set the table.* GREGERS *settles in the armchair and pages through an album.*)

GREGERS: I hear you can retouch photographs, Mrs. Ekdal.

GINA: (*with a side-glance*) Um-hm, so I can.

GREGERS: That's really very lucky.

GINA: Why "lucky"?

GREGERS: With Hjalmar a photographer, I mean.

HEDVIG: Mother can take pictures, too.

GINA: Oh yes, I even got lessons in that.

GREGERS: So we might say it's you who runs the business.

GINA: Yes, when my husband hasn't the time himself—

1590 GREGERS: He finds himself so taken up with his old father, I suppose.

GINA: Yes, and then a man like Hjalmar shouldn't have to go snapping pictures of every Tom, Dick and Harry.

GREGERS: I agree; but once he's chosen this line of work, then—

GINA: Mr. Werle, you must realize that my husband is not just any old photographer.

GREGERS: Well, naturally; but even so—

(*A shot is fired in the loft.*)

GREGERS: (*jumping up*) What's that!

1600 HEDVIG: They go hunting.

GREGERS: What! (*Going to the loft doorway.*) Have you gone hunting, Hjalmar?

HJALMAR: (*behind the net*) Are you here? I didn't realize; I was so occupied—(*To* HEDVIG.) And you, you didn't tell us. (*Comes into the studio.*)

GREGERS: Do you go shooting in the loft?

HJALMAR: (*producing a double-barreled pistol*) Oh, only with this here.

GINA: Yes, some day you and Grandfather'll have an accident
1610    with that there gun.

HJALMAR: (*annoyed*) I believe I've remarked that this type of firearm is called a pistol.

GINA: I don't see that that makes it any better.

GREGERS: So you've turned out a "hunter" as well, Hjalmar?

HJALMAR: Just a little rabbit hunt, now and then. It's mainly for Father's sake, you understand.

GINA: Men are so funny, really; they've always got to have their little diversities.

HJALMAR: (*angrily*) That's right, yes—they always have to have
1620    their little diversions.

GINA: Yes, that's just what I was saying.

HJALMAR: Oh, well! (*To* GREGERS.) So that's it, and then we're very lucky in the way the loft is placed—nobody can hear us when we're shooting. (*Puts the pistol on the highest book-*

*shelf.*) Don't touch the pistol, Hedvig! One barrel's still loaded, don't forget.

GREGERS: (*peering through the netting*) You've got a hunting rifle too, I see.

HJALMAR: Yes, that's Father's old rifle. It won't shoot anymore; something's gone wrong with the lock. But it's a lot of fun to 1630 have anyway, because we can take it all apart and clean it and grease it and put it together again—Of course, it's mostly Father who fools around with that sort of thing.

HEDVIG: (*crossing to* GREGERS) Now you can really see the wild duck.

GREGERS: I was just now looking at her. She seems to drag one wing a little.

HJALMAR: Well, no wonder; she took a bad wound.

GREGERS: And then she limps a little. Isn't that so?

HJALMAR: Maybe just a tiny bit.                                        1640

HEDVIG: Yes, that was the foot the dog bit her in.

HJALMAR: But she hasn't a thing wrong with her otherwise; and that's simply remarkable when you think that she's had a charge of shot in her and been held by the teeth of a dog—

GREGERS: (*with a glance at* HEDVIG) And been in the depths of the sea—so long.

HEDVIG: (*smiling*) Yes.

GINA: (*arranging the table*) Oh, that sacred duck—there's fuss enough made over her.

HJALMAR: Hm. Are you nearly ready?                                    1650

GINA: Yes, right away. Hedvig, now you can come and help me.

(GINA *and* HEDVIG *exit into the kitchen.*)

HJALMAR: (*in an undertone*) I don't think it's so good that you stand there, watching my father. He doesn't like it. (GREGERS *comes away from the loft doorway.*) And it's better, too, that I close up before the others come. (*Shooing away the menagerie with his hands.*) Hssh! Hssh! Go 'way now! (*With this he raises the curtain and draws the double doors together.*) I invented these contraptions myself. It's really great fun to have such things around to take care of and fix when they get out of whack. And besides, it's ab- 1660 solutely necessary, you know; Gina doesn't go for rabbits and chickens out here in the studio.

GREGERS: Of course not. And I suppose it *is* your wife who manages here?

HJALMAR: My general rule is to delegate the routine matters to her, and that leaves me free to retire to the living room to think over more important things.

GREGERS: And what sort of things are these, Hjalmar?

HJALMAR: I've been wondering why you haven't asked me that before. Or maybe you haven't heard about my invention.   1670

GREGERS: Invention? No.

HJALMAR: Oh? Then you haven't? Well, no, up there in that waste and wilderness—

GREGERS: Then you've really invented something!

HJALMAR: Not completely invented it yet, but I'm getting very close. You must realize that when I decided to dedicate my life to photography, it wasn't my idea to spend time taking pictures of a lot of nobodies.

GREGERS: Yes, that's what your wife was just now saying.

HJALMAR: I swore that if I devoted my powers to the craft, I 1680 would then exalt it to such heights that it would become both an art and a science. That's when I decided on this amazing invention.

GREGERS: And what does this invention consist of? What's its purpose?

HJALMAR: Yes, Gregers, you mustn't ask for details like that yet. It takes time, you know. And you mustn't think it's vanity that's driving me, either. I'm certainly not working for my- self. Oh no, it's my life's work that stands before me day and 1690 night.

GREGERS: What life's work is that?

HJALMAR: Remember the silver-haired old man?

GREGERS: Your poor father. Yes, but actually what can you do for him?

HJALMAR: I can raise his self-respect from the dead—by restor- ing the Ekdal name to dignity and honor.

GREGERS: So that's your life's work.

HJALMAR: Yes. I am going to rescue that shipwrecked man. That's just what he suffered—shipwreck—when the storm 1700 broke over him. When all those harrowing investigations took place, he wasn't himself anymore. That pistol, there— the one we use to shoot rabbits with—it's played a part in the tragedy of the Ekdals.

GREGERS: Pistol! Oh?

HJALMAR: When he was sentenced and facing prison, he had that pistol in his hand—

GREGERS: You mean he—!

HJALMAR: Yes. But he didn't dare. He was a coward. That shows how broken and degraded he'd become by then. Can 1710 you picture it? He, a soldier, a man who'd shot nine bears and was directly descended from two lieutenant colonels— I mean, one after the other, of course. Can you picture it, Gregers?

GREGERS: Yes, I can picture it very well.

HJALMAR: Well, I can't. And then that pistol intruded on our family history once again. When he was under lock and key, dressed like a common prisoner—oh, those were agonizing times for me, you can imagine. I kept the shades of both my windows drawn. When I looked out, I saw the sun shining 1720 the same as ever. I couldn't understand it. I saw the people going along the street, laughing and talking of trivial things. I couldn't understand it. I felt all creation should be stand- ing still, like during an eclipse.

GREGERS: I felt that way when my mother died.

HJALMAR: During one of those times Hjalmar Ekdal put a pis- tol to his own breast.

GREGERS: You were thinking of—

HJALMAR: Yes.

GREGERS: But you didn't shoot?

1730 HJALMAR: No. In that critical moment I won a victory over my- self. I stayed alive. But you can bet it takes courage to choose life in those circumstances.

GREGERS: Well, that depends on your point of view.

HJALMAR: Oh, absolutely. But it was all for the best, because now I've nearly finished my invention; and then Dr. Relling thinks, just as I do, that they'll let Father wear his uniform again. That's the only reward I'm after.

GREGERS: So it's really the uniform that he—?

HJALMAR: Yes, that's what he really hungers and craves for. 1740 You've no idea how that makes my heart ache. Every time we throw a little family party—like my birthday, or Gina's, or whatever—then the old man comes in, wearing that uni-

form from his happier days. But if there's even a knock at the door, he goes scuttering back in his room fast as the old legs will carry him. You see, he doesn't dare show himself to strangers. What a heartrending spectacle for a son!

GREGERS: Approximately when do you think the invention will be finished?

HJALMAR: Oh, good Lord, don't hold me to a timetable. An in- 1750 vention, that's something you can hardly dictate to. It de- pends a great deal on inspiration, on a sudden insight—and it's nearly impossible to say in advance when that will occur.

GREGERS: But it is making progress?

HJALMAR: Of course it's making progress. Every single day I think about my invention. I'm brimming with it. Every af- ternoon, right after lunch, I lock myself in the living room where I can meditate in peace. But it's no use driving me; it simply won't work. Relling says so too.

GREGERS: And you don't think all those contraptions in the loft distract you and scatter your talents? 1760

HJALMAR: No, no, no, on the contrary. You mustn't say that. I can't always go around here, brooding over the same nerve- racking problems. I need some diversion to fill in the time. You see, inspiration, the moment of insight—when that comes, nothing can stop it.

GREGERS: My dear Hjalmar, I suspect you've got a bit of the wild duck in you.

HJALMAR: Of the wild duck? What do you mean?

GREGERS: You've plunged to the bottom and clamped hold of the seaweed. 1770

HJALMAR: I suppose you mean that near-fatal shot that brought down Father—and me as well?

GREGERS: Not quite that. I wouldn't say you're wounded; but you're wandering in a poisonous swamp, Hjalmar. You've got an insidious disease in your system, and so you've gone to the bottom to die in the dark.

HJALMAR: Me? Die in the dark! You know what, Gregers— you'll really have to stop that talk.

GREGERS: But never mind. I'm going to raise you up again. You know, I've found my purpose in life, too. I found it 1780 yesterday.

HJALMAR: Yes, that may well be; but you can just leave me out of it. I can assure you that—apart from my quite under- standable melancholy—I'm as well off as any man could wish to be.

GREGERS: And your thinking so is part of the sickness.

HJALMAR: Gregers, you're my old friend—please—don't talk any more about sickness and poison. I'm not used to that kind of conversation. In my house nobody talks to me about ugly things. 1790

GREGERS: That's not hard to believe.

HJALMAR: Yes, because it isn't good for me. And there's no swamp air here, as you put it. In a poor photographer's house, life is cramped; I know that. My lot is a poor one— but, you know, I'm an inventor. And I'm the family bread- winner, too. *That's* what sustains me through all the pettiness. Ah, here they come with the lunch.

(GINA and HEDVIG *bring in bottles of beer, a decanter of brandy, glasses, and the like. At the same time,* RELLING *and* MOLVIK *enter from the hall. Neither wears a hat or overcoat;* MOLVIK *is dressed in black.*)

GINA: *(setting things down on the table).* Well, the two of them—right on time.

1800 RELLING: Molvik was positive he could smell that herring salad, and there was just no holding him back. 'Morning for the second time, Ekdal.

HJALMAR: Gregers, I'd like you to meet Mr. Molvik. And Dr.—ah, but don't you know Relling?

GREGERS: Yes, slightly.

RELLING: Well, Mr. Werle junior. Yes, we've had a few run-ins together up at the Hoidal works. You've just moved in, haven't you?

GREGERS: I moved in this morning.

1810 RELLING: And Molvik and I live downstairs; so you're not very far from a doctor and a priest, if you ever have need of such.

GREGERS: Thanks; that could happen. After all, we had thirteen at the table last night.

HJALMAR: Oh, don't start in on ugly subjects again!

RELLING: You don't have to worry, Hjalmar; Lord knows this doesn't involve you.

HJALMAR: I hope not, for my family's sake. But let's sit down and eat and drink and be merry.

GREGERS: Shouldn't we wait for your father?

1820 HJALMAR: No, he'll have his lunch sent in to him later. Come now!

*(The men sit at the table, eating and drinking.* GINA *and* HEDVIG *go in and out, serving the food.)*

RELLING: Last night Molvik was tight as a tick, Mrs. Ekdal.

GINA: Oh? Last night again?

RELLING: Didn't you hear him when I finally brought him home?

GINA: No, can't say I did.

RELLING: That's lucky—because Molvik was revolting last night.

GINA: Is that so, Molvik?

1830 MOLVIK: Let's draw a veil over last night's activities. They have no bearing on my better self.

RELLING: *(to* GREGERS*)* All of a sudden he's possessed by an impulse; and then I have to take him out on a bat. You see, Mr. Molvik is demonic.

GREGERS: Demonic?

RELLING: Molvik is demonic, yes.

GREGERS: Hm.

RELLING: And demonic natures aren't made to go through life on the straight and narrow; they've got to take detours every 1840 so often. Well—and you're still sticking it out there at that dark, hideous mill.

GREGERS: I've stuck it out till now.

RELLING: And did you ever collect on that "summons" you were going around with?

GREGERS: Summons? *(Understanding him.)* Oh, that.

HJALMAR: Were you serving summonses, Gregers?

GREGERS: Nonsense.

RELLING: Oh, but he was, definitely. He was going around to all the farms and cabins with copies of something he called 1850 "Summons to the Ideal."

GREGERS: I was young then.

RELLING: You're right, there. You were very young. And that summons to the ideal—it wasn't ever honored during my time up there.

GREGERS: Nor later, either.

RELLING: Well, I guess you've learned enough to cut down your expectations a bit.

GREGERS: Never—when I meet a man who's a real man.

HJALMAR: Yes, that seems quite reasonable to me. A little butter, Gina. 1860

RELLING: And then a piece of pork for Molvik.

MOLVIK: Ugh, no pork!

*(There is a knock at the loft door.)*

HJALMAR: Open it, Hedvig; Father wants to get out.

*(*HEDVIG *goes to open the door a little; old* EKDAL *enters with a fresh rabbit skin. He closes the door after him.)*

EKDAL: Good morning, gentlemen. Good hunting today. Shot a big one.

HJALMAR: And you went ahead and skinned it without waiting for me!

EKDAL: Salted it, too. It's nice tender meat, this rabbit meat. And it's so sweet. Tastes like sugar. Enjoy your food, gentlemen! *(He goes into his room.)* 1870

MOLVIK: *(getting up)* Pardon—I, I can't—got to go downstairs right—

RELLING: Drink soda water, man!

MOLVIK: *(rushing out the hall door)* Ugh—ugh!

RELLING: *(to* HJALMAR*)* Let's empty a glass to the old hunter.

HJALMAR: *(clinking glasses with him)* Yes, to the gallant sportsman on the brink of the grave.

RELLING: To the old, gray-haired—*(Drinks.)* Tell me something, is it gray hair he's got, or is it white?

HJALMAR: It's really a little of both. But as a matter of fact, he's 1880 scarcely got a hair on his head.

RELLING: Well, fake hair will take you through life, good as any. You know, Ekdal, you're really a very lucky man. You have your high mission in life to fight for—

HJALMAR: And I am fighting for it, too.

RELLING: And then you've got this clever wife of yours, padding around in her slippers and waggling her hips and keeping you neat and cozy.

HJALMAR: Yes, Gina—*(Nodding at her.)* you're a good companion for life's journey, you are. 1890

GINA: Oh, don't sit there deprecating me.

RELLING: And what about your Hedvig, Ekdal?

HJALMAR: *(stirred)* My child, yes! My child above all. Hedvig, come here to me. *(Caresses her head.)* What day is tomorrow, dear?

HEDVIG: *(shaking him)* Oh, don't talk about it, Daddy!

HJALMAR: It's like a knife turning in my heart when I think how bare it's all going to be, just the tiniest celebration out in the loft—

HEDVIG: Oh, but that will be just wonderful! 1900

RELLING: And wait till that marvelous invention comes to the world, Hedvig!

HJALMAR: Ah, yes—then you'll see! Hedvig, I've resolved to make your future secure. As long as you live, you'll live in style. I'll assure you of something, one way or another. That will be the poor inventor's sole reward.

HEDVIG: *(whispering, with her arms around his neck)* Oh, you dear, dear Daddy!

RELLING: *(to* GREGERS*)* Well, now, isn't it good for a change to

1910 be sitting around a well-spread table in a happy family circle?

HJALMAR: Yes, I really prize these hours around the table.

GREGERS: I, for my part, don't thrive in marsh gas.

RELLING: Marsh gas?

HJALMAR: Oh, don't start that rubbish again!

GINA: Lord knows there isn't any marsh gas here, Mr. Werle; every blessed day I air the place out.

GREGERS: (leaving the table) You can't air out the stench I mean.

1920 HJALMAR: Stench!

GINA: What about that, Hjalmar!

RELLING: Beg pardon—but it wouldn't be you who brought that stench in with you from the mines up there?

GREGERS: It's just like you to call what I'm bringing into this house a stench.

RELLING: (crossing over to him) Listen, Mr. Werle junior, I've got a strong suspicion that you're still going around with the uncut version of that "Summons to the Ideal" in your back pocket.

1930 GREGERS: I've got it written in my heart.

RELLING: I don't care where the devil you've got it; I wouldn't advise you to play process-server here as long as I'm around.

GREGERS: And what if I do anyway?

RELLING: Then you'll go head first down the stairs, that's what.

HJALMAR: (getting up) Come, now, Relling!

GREGERS: Yes, just throw me out—

GINA: (coming between them) You can't do that, Relling. But I'll tell you this, Mr. Werle—that you, who made all that mess with your stove, have no right to come to me talking

1940 about smells.

(A knock at the hall door.)

HEDVIG: Mother, somebody's knocking.

GINA: I'll go—(She crosses and opens the door, gives a start, shudders and shrinks back.) Uff! Oh no!

(Old WERLE, in a fur coat, steps into the room.)

WERLE: Excuse me, but I think my son is living in this house.

GINA: (catching her breath) Yes.

HJALMAR: (coming closer) If Mr. Werle will be so good as to—

WERLE: Thanks, I'd just like to talk with my son.

GREGERS: Yes, why not? Here I am.

WERLE: I'd like to talk with you in your room.

1950 GREGERS: In my room—fine—(Starts in.)

GINA: No. Good Lord, that's in no condition for—

WERLE: Well, out in the hall, then. This is just between us.

HJALMAR: You can talk here, Mr. Werle. Come into the living room, Relling.

(HJALMAR and RELLING go out to the right; GINA takes HEDVIG with her into the kitchen.)

GREGERS: (after a brief interval) Well, now it's just the two of us.

WERLE: You dropped a few remarks last night—And since you've now taken a room with the Ekdals, I must assume that you're planning something or other against me.

1960 GREGERS: I'm planning to open Hjalmar Ekdal's eyes. He's going to see his situation just as it is—that's all.

WERLE: Is that the mission in life you talked about yesterday?

GREGERS: Yes. You haven't left me any other.

WERLE: Am I the one that spoiled your mind, Gregers?

GREGERS: You've spoiled my entire life. I'm not thinking of all that with Mother. But you're the one I can thank for my going around, whipped and driven by this guilt-ridden conscience.

WERLE: Ah, it's your conscience that's gone bad.

GREGERS: I should have taken a stand against you when the trap was laid for Lieutenant Ekdal. I should have warned him, for I had a pretty good idea what was coming off. 1970

WERLE: Yes, you really should have spoken up then.

GREGERS: I didn't dare; I was so cowed and frightened. I was unspeakably afraid of you—both then and for a long time after.

WERLE: That fright seems to be over now.

GREGERS: It is, luckily. The harm done to old Ekdal, both by me and—others, can never be undone; but Hjalmar I can free from all the lies and evasions that are smothering him here.

WERLE: You believe you'd be doing him good by that? 1980

GREGERS: That's what I believe.

WERLE: Maybe you think Ekdal's the kind of man who'll thank you for that friendly service?

GREGERS: Yes! He is that kind of man.

WERLE: Hmm—we'll see.

GREGERS: And besides—if I'm ever to go on living, I'll have to find a cure for my sick conscience.

WERLE: It'll never be sound. Your conscience has been sickly from childhood. It's an inheritance from your mother, Gregers—the only inheritance she left you. 1990

GREGERS: (with a wry half-smile) You've never been able to accept the fact, have you, that you calculated wrong when you thought she'd bring you a fortune?

WERLE: Let's not get lost in irrelevancies. Then you're still intent on this goal of putting Ekdal on what you suppose is the right track?

GREGERS: Yes, I'm intent on that.

WERLE: Well, then I could have saved myself the walk up here. For there's no point in asking if you'll move back home with me? 2000

GREGERS: No.

WERLE: And you won't come into the business either?

GREGERS: No.

WERLE: Very well. But since I'm now planning a second marriage, the estate, of course, will be divided between us.

GREGERS: (quickly) No, I don't want that.

WERLE: You don't want it?

GREGERS: No, I wouldn't dare, for the sake of my conscience.

WERLE: (after a pause) You going back to the works again?

GREGERS: No. I consider that I've retired from your service. 2010

WERLE: But what are you going to do, then?

GREGERS: Simply carry out my life's mission; nothing else.

WERLE: Yes, but afterwards? What will you live on?

GREGERS: I have some of my salary put aside.

WERLE: Yes, that won't last long!

GREGERS: I think it will last my time.

WERLE: What do you mean by that?

GREGERS: I'm not answering any more.

WERLE: Good-bye then, Gregers.

GREGERS: Good-bye. 2020

(Old WERLE *goes out.*)

HJALMAR: (*peering out*) Has he gone?

GREGERS: Yes.

(HJALMAR *and* RELLING *come in.* GINA *and* HEDVIG *also return from the kitchen.*)

RELLING: There's one lunch gone to the dogs.

GREGERS: Put your things on, Hjalmar; you've got to take a long walk with me.

HJALMAR: Yes, gladly. What did your father want? Was it anything to do with me?

GREGERS: Just come. We have some things to talk over. I'll go and get my coat. (*He leaves by the hall door.*)

2030 GINA: You mustn't go out with him, Hjalmar.

RELLING: No, don't go. Stay where you are.

HJALMAR: (*getting his hat and overcoat*) But why? When a childhood friend feels a need to open his mind to me in private—

RELLING: But damn it all! Can't you see the man's mad, crazy, out of his skull!

GINA: Yes, that's the truth, if you'd listen. His mother, off and on, had those same conniption fits.

HJALMAR: That's just why he needs a friend's watchful eye on
2040 him. (*To* GINA.) Be sure dinner's ready in plenty of time. See you later. (*Goes out the hall door.*)

RELLING: It's really a shame that fellow didn't go straight to hell down one of the Hoidal mines.

GINA: Mercy—why do you say that?

RELLING: (*muttering*) Oh, I've got my reasons.

GINA: Do you think Gregers Werle is really crazy?

RELLING: No, worse luck. He's no crazier than most people. But he's got a disease in his system all the same.

GINA: What is it that's wrong with him?

2050 RELLING: All right, I'll tell you, Mrs. Ekdal. He's suffering from an acute case of moralistic fever.

GINA: Moralistic fever?

HEDVIG: Is that a kind of disease?

RELLING: Oh yes, it's a national disease, but it only breaks out now and then. (*Nodding to* GINA.) Thanks for lunch. (*He goes out through the hall door.*)

GINA: (*walking restlessly around the room*) Ugh, that Gregers Werle—he was always a cold fish.

HEDVIG: (*standing by the table, looking searchingly at her*)
2060 This is all so strange to me.

—ACT FOUR—

HJALMAR EKDAL'S *studio. A photograph has just been taken; a portrait camera covered with a cloth, a stand, a couple of chairs, a console table, among other things, stand well out in the room. Late afternoon light; it is near sunset; somewhat later it begins to grow dark.*

GINA *is standing in the hall doorway with a plate-holder and a wet photographic plate in her hand, talking with someone outside.*

GINA: Yes, that's definite. When I promise something, I keep my word. On Monday the first dozen will be ready. Goodbye. Good-bye. (*Footsteps are heard descending the stairs.*

GINA *closes the door, puts the plate into the holder, and slips both back into the covered camera.*)

HEDVIG: (*coming in from the kitchen*) Are they gone?

GINA: (*tidying up*) Yes, thank goodness, at last I'm rid of them.

HEDVIG: But why do you suppose Daddy isn't home yet?

GINA: Are you sure he's not below with Relling?

HEDVIG: No, he's not there. I ran down the back stairs just now 2070 and asked.

GINA: And his dinner's standing and getting cold, too.

HEDVIG: Just imagine—Daddy's always sure to be on time for dinner.

GINA: Oh, he'll be right along, you'll see.

HEDVIG: Oh, I wish he would come! Everything's so funny around here.

GINA: (*calling out*) There he is!

(HJALMAR *comes in by the hall door.*)

HEDVIG: (*running toward him*) Daddy! Oh, we've waited ages for you! 2080

GINA: (*eyeing him*) You've been out pretty long, Hjalmar.

HJALMAR: (*without looking at her*) I've been a while, yes. (*He takes off his overcoat.* GINA *and* HEDVIG *start to help him; he waves them away.*)

GINA: Did you eat with Werle, maybe?

HJALMAR: (*hanging his coat up*) No.

GINA: (*going toward the kitchen*) I'll bring your dinner in, then.

HJALMAR: No, the dinner can wait. I don't want to eat now.

HEDVIG: (*coming closer*) Don't you feel well, Daddy?

HJALMAR: Well? Oh yes, well enough. We had an exhausting 2090 walk, Gregers and I.

GINA: You shouldn't do that, Hjalmar; you're not used to it.

HJALMAR: Hm. There are a lot of things a man's got to get used to in this world. (*Walking about the room a bit.*) Did anyone come while I was out?

GINA: No one but that engaged couple.

HJALMAR: No new orders?

GINA: No, not today.

HEDVIG: You'll see, there'll be some tomorrow, Daddy.

HJALMAR: I certainly hope so, because tomorrow I'm going to 2100 throw myself into my work—completely.

HEDVIG: Tomorrow! But don't you remember what day tomorrow is?

HJALMAR: Oh yes, that's right. Well, the day after tomorrow, then. From now on, I'm doing everything myself; I just want to be left alone with all the work.

GINA: But Hjalmar, what's the point of that? It'll only make your life miserable. Let me handle the photographing, and then you'll be free to work on the invention.

HEDVIG: And free for the wild duck, Daddy—and for all the 2110 chickens and rabbits—

HJALMAR: Don't talk to me about that rubbish! Starting tomorrow I shall never again set foot in that loft.

HEDVIG: Yes, but Daddy, you promised me tomorrow there'd be a celebration.

HJALMAR: Hm, that's true. Well, the day after, then. That infernal wild duck—I'd almost like to wring its neck!

HEDVIG: (*crying out*) The wild duck!

GINA: What an idea!

HEDVIG: (*shaking him*) Yes, but Daddy—it's my wild duck! 2120

HJALMAR: That's why I won't do it. I haven't the heart—for

your sake, Hedvig. I haven't the heart. But deep inside me I feel I ought to. I shouldn't tolerate under my roof a creature that's been in that man's hands.

GINA: My goodness, just because Grandfather got her from that worthless Pettersen—

HJALMAR: *(pacing the floor)* There are certain standards—what should I call them—ideal standards, let's say—certain claims on us that a man can't put aside without damaging his soul.

HEDVIG: *(following him)* But think—the wild duck—the poor wild duck!

HJALMAR: *(stopping)* You heard me say I'd spare it—for your sake. It won't be hurt, not a hair on its—well, anyway, I'll spare it. There are more important matters to settle. But Hedvig, now you better get out for your afternoon walk; it's already pretty dark for you.

HEDVIG: No, I don't want to go out now.

HJALMAR: Yes, go on. You seem to be blinking your eyes so. All these fumes in here aren't good for you; the air here under this roof is bad.

HEDVIG: All right, then, I'll run down the back stairs and take a little walk. My coat and hat? Oh, they're in my room. Daddy—promise you won't hurt the wild duck while I'm out.

HJALMAR: There won't be a feather ruffled on its head. *(Drawing her to him.)* You and I, Hedvig—we two! Now run along, dear.

*(HEDVIG nods to her parents and goes out through the kitchen.)*

HJALMAR: *(walking around without looking up)* Gina.

GINA: Yes?

HJALMAR: From tomorrow on—or let's say the day after tomorrow—I'd prefer to keep the household accounts myself.

GINA: You want to keep the household accounts, too?

HJALMAR: Yes, or budget the income, in any case.

GINA: Lord love us, there's nothing to that.

HJALMAR: One wouldn't think so. It seems to me you can make our money stretch remarkably far. *(Stopping and looking at her.)* How *is* that?

GINA: Hedvig and I, we don't need much.

HJALMAR: Is it true that Father gets such good pay for the copying he does for Werle?

GINA: I don't know how good it is. I don't know rates for such things.

HJALMAR: Well, what does he get, just roughly? Tell me!

GINA: It's never the same. I suppose it's roughly what he costs us, with a little pocket money thrown in.

HJALMAR: What he costs us! That's something you've never told me before!

GINA: No, I never could. You were always so happy thinking he got everything from you.

HJALMAR: And instead it comes from Mr. Werle.

GINA: Oh, but he's got plenty to spare, that one.

HJALMAR: Let's have the lamp lit!

GINA: *(lighting it)* And then we can't know if it really is the old man; it could well be Graaberg—

GINA: No, I don't know. I just thought—

HJALMAR: Hm!

GINA: You know it wasn't me that got Grandfather the copying. It was Berta, that time she came here.

HJALMAR: Your voice sounds so shaky.

GINA: *(putting the shade on the lamp)* It does?

HJALMAR: And then your hands are trembling. Or aren't they?

GINA: *(firmly)* Say it straight out, Hjalmar. What is it he's gone and said about me?

HJALMAR: Is it true—can it possibly be that—that there was some kind of involvement between you and Mr. Werle while you were in service there?

GINA: That's not true. Not then, there wasn't. Werle was after me, all right. And his wife thought there was something to it, and she made a big fuss and bother, and she roasted me coming and going, she did—so I quit.

HJALMAR: But then what!

GINA: Yes, so then I went home. And Mother—well, she wasn't all you took her to be, Hjalmar; she ran on telling me one thing and another, because Werle was a widower by then.

HJALMAR: Yes. And then!

GINA: Well, you might as well know it all. He didn't give up till he had his way.

HJALMAR: *(with a clap of his hands)* And this is the mother of my child! How could you keep that hidden from me!

GINA: Yes, I did the wrong thing; I really should have told you long ago.

HJALMAR: Right at the start, you mean—so I could have known what sort you are.

GINA: But would you have married me anyway?

HJALMAR: How can you think that?

GINA: No. But that's why I didn't dare say anything then. Because I'd come to be so terribly in love with you, as you know. And then how could I make myself utterly miserable—

HJALMAR: *(walking about)* And this is my Hedvig's mother! And then to know that everything I see around me— *(Kicking at a table.)* my whole home—I owe to a favored predecessor. Ah, that charmer Werle!

GINA: Do you regret the fourteen, fifteen years we've lived together?

HJALMAR: *(stopping in front of her)* Tell me—don't you every day, every hour, regret this spider web of deception you've spun around me? Answer me that! Don't you really go around in a torment of remorse?

GINA: Hjalmar dear, I've got so much to think about just with the housework and the day's routine—

HJALMAR: Then you never turn a critical eye on your past!

GINA: No. Good Lord, I'd almost forgotten that old affair.

HJALMAR: Oh, this dull, unfeeling content! To me there's something outrageous about it. Just think—not one regret!

GINA: But Hjalmar, tell me now—what would have happened to you if you hadn't found a wife like me?

HJALMAR: Like you—!

GINA: Yes, because I've always been a bit more hardheaded and resourceful than you. Well, of course I'm a couple of years older.

HJALMAR: What would have happened to me?

GINA: You were pretty bad off at the time you met me; you can't deny that.

HJALMAR: "Pretty bad off" you call it. Oh, you have no idea what a man goes through when he's deep in misery and despair—especially a man of my fiery temperament.

GINA: No, that may be. And I shouldn't say nothing about it,

2240 either, because you turned out such a good-hearted husband as soon as you got a house and home—and now we've made it so snug and cozy here, and pretty soon both Hedvig and I could begin spending a little on food and clothes.

HJALMAR: In the swamp of deception, yes.

GINA: Ugh, that disgusting creature, tracking his way through our house!

HJALMAR: I also thought this home was a good place to be. That was a pipe dream. Now where can I find the buoyancy I need to carry my invention into reality? Maybe it'll die with
2250 me; and then it'll be your past, Gina, that killed it.

GINA: (close to tears) No, you mustn't ever say such things, Hjalmar. All my days I've only wanted to do what's best for you!

HJALMAR: I wonder—what happens now to the breadwinner's dream? When I lay in there on the sofa pondering my invention, I had a hunch it would drain my last bit of strength. I sensed that the day I took the patent in my hand—that would be the day of—departure. And it was my dream that then *you* would go on as the departed inventor's prosperous
2260 widow.

GINA: (drying her eyes) No, don't say that, Hjalmar. Lord knows I never want to see the day I'm a widow.

HJALMAR: Oh, what does it matter? Everything's over and done with now. Everything!

(GREGERS *cautiously opens the hall door and looks in.*)

GREGERS: May I come in?

HJALMAR: Yes, do.

GREGERS: (advancing with a beaming countenance, hands out-stretched as if to take theirs) Now, you dear people—! (Looks from one to the other, then whispers to HJALMAR.)
2270 But isn't it done, then?

HJALMAR: (resoundingly) It's done.

GREGERS: It is?

HJALMAR: I've just known the bitterest hour of my life.

GREGERS: But also the most exalted, I think.

HJALMAR: Well, anyway, it's off our hands for the moment.

GINA: God forgive you, Mr. Werle.

GREGERS: (with great surprise) But I don't understand this.

HJALMAR: What don't you understand?

GREGERS: With this great rapport—the kind that forges a
2280 whole new way of life—a life, a companionship in truth with no more deception—

HJALMAR: Yes, I know, I know all that.

GREGERS: I was really positive that when I came through that door I'd be met by a transfigured light in both your faces. And what do I see instead but this gloomy, heavy, dismal—

GINA: How true. (She removes the lampshade.)

GREGERS: You don't want to understand me, Mrs. Ekdal. No, no, you'll need time— But you yourself, Hjalmar? You must have gained a sense of high purpose out of this great
2290 unburdening.

HJALMAR: Yes, naturally. That is—more or less.

GREGERS: Because there's nothing in the world that compares with showing mercy to a sinner and lifting her up in the arms of love.

HJALMAR: Do you think a man can recover so easily from the bitter cup I've just emptied!

GREGERS: Not an ordinary man, no. But a man like you—!

HJALMAR: Good Lord, yes, I know that. But you mustn't be driving me, Gregers. You see, these things take time.

GREGERS: You've *lots* of the wild duck in you, Hjalmar. 2300

(RELLING *has entered through the hall door.*)

RELLING: Aha! The wild duck's flying again, eh?

HJALMAR: Yes, the wounded trophy of old Werle's hunt.

RELLING: Old Werle? Is it him you're talking about?

HJALMAR: Him and—all of us.

RELLING: (under his breath to GREGERS) The devil take you!

HJALMAR: What'd you say?

RELLING: I merely expressed my heartfelt desire that this quack would cut out for home. If he stays here, he's just the man to ruin you both.

GREGERS: They won't be ruined, Mr. Relling. Regarding Hjal- 2310 mar, I'll say nothing. We know him. But she, too, surely, in the depths of her being, has something authentic, something sincere.

GINA: (near tears) Well, if I *was* that, why didn't you leave me alone?

RELLING: (to GREGERS) Would it be nosy to ask what you're really trying to do in this house?

GREGERS: I want to establish a true marriage.

RELLING: Then you don't think Ekdal's marriage is good enough as it is? 2320

GREGERS: It's about as good a marriage as most, unfortunately. But it isn't yet a *true* marriage.

HJALMAR: You don't believe in ideals in life, Relling.

RELLING: Nonsense, sonny boy! Excuse me, Mr. Werle, but how many—in round numbers—how many "true marriages" have you seen in your time?

GREGERS: I believe I've hardly seen a single one.

RELLING: And I likewise.

GREGERS: But I've seen innumerable marriages of the opposite kind. And I've had a chance to see at close range what such 2330 a marriage can destroy in two people.

HJALMAR: A man's whole moral foundation can crumble under his feet; that's the dreadful thing.

RELLING: Well, I've never really exactly been married, so I'm no judge of these things. But I do know this, that the child is part of the marriage too. And you've got to leave the child in peace.

HJALMAR: Ah, Hedvig! My poor Hedvig!

RELLING: Yes, you'll please see that Hedvig's left out of it. You're both grown people; you're free, God knows, to slop 2340 up your private lives all you want. But I tell you, you've got to be careful with Hedvig, or else you might do her some serious harm.

HJALMAR: Harm!

RELLING: Yes, or she could do harm to herself—and possibly others as well.

GINA: But how can you know that, Relling?

HJALMAR: There's no immediate threat to her eyes, is there?

RELLING: This has nothing to do with her eyes. Hedvig arrived at a difficult age. She's open to all kinds of erratic 2350 ideas.

GINA: You know—she is at that! She's begun to fool around something awful with the fire in the kitchen stove. She calls it playing house afire. I'm often scared she *will* set the house on fire.

RELLING: See what I mean? I knew it.

GREGERS: *(to RELLING)* But how do you explain something like that?

RELLING: *(brusquely)* Her voice is changing, junior.

2360 HJALMAR: As long as the child has *me!* As long as I'm above the sod.

*(A knock is heard at the door.)*

GINA: Shh, Hjalmar, someone's in the hall. *(Calling out.)* Come on in!

*(MRS. SØRBY, wearing street clothes, enters.)*

MRS. SØRBY: Good evening!

GINA: *(going toward her)* Is it you, Berta!

MRS. SØRBY: Oh yes, it's me. But perhaps I came at an awkward time?

HJALMAR: Oh, not at all; a messenger from *that* house—

MRS. SØRBY: *(to GINA)* As a matter of fact, I'd hoped that I

2370 wouldn't find your menfolk in at this hour, so I ran over just to have a word with you and say good-bye.

GINA: Oh? Are you going away?

MRS. SØRBY: Yes, tomorrow, early—up to Hoidal. Mr. Werle left this afternoon. *(Casually to GREGERS.)* He sends his regards.

GINA: Just think!

HJALMAR: So Mr. Werle has left? And you're following him?

MRS. SØRBY: Yes, what do you say to that, Ekdal?

HJALMAR: I say watch out.

2380 GREGERS: Let me explain. My father is marrying Mrs. Sørby.

HJALMAR: He's marrying her!

GINA: Oh, Berta, it's come at last!

RELLING: *(his voice quavering slightly)* This really can't be true.

MRS. SØRBY: Yes, my dear Relling, it's completely true.

RELLING: You want to marry again?

MRS. SØRBY: Yes, so it seems. Werle has gotten a special license, and we're going to have a very quiet wedding up at the works.

2390 GREGERS: So I ought to wish you happiness, like a good stepson.

MRS. SØRBY: Thank you, if you really mean it. I'm hoping it will bring us happiness, both Werle and me.

RELLING: That's a reasonable hope. Mr. Werle never gets drunk—as far as *I* know; and he's certainly not given to beating up his wives the way the late horse doctor did.

MRS. SØRBY: Oh, now let Sørby rest in peace. He did have some worthy traits, you know.

RELLING: Old Werle's traits are worth rather more, I'll bet.

2400 MRS. SØRBY: At least he hasn't wasted the best that's in him. Any man who does *that* has to take the consequences.

RELLING: Tonight I'm going out with Molvik.

MRS. SØRBY: You shouldn't, Relling. Don't do it—for my sake.

RELLING: What else is left? *(To HJALMAR.)* If you'd care to, you could come too.

GINA: No, thanks. Hjalmar never goes dissipating.

HJALMAR: *(in an angry undertone)* Can't you keep quiet!

RELLING: Good-bye, Mrs.—Werle. *(He goes out the hall door.)*

GREGERS: *(to MRS. SØRBY)* It would seem that you and Dr.

2410 Relling know each other quite intimately.

MRS. SØRBY: Yes, we've known each other for many years. At one time something might have developed between us.

GREGERS: It was certainly lucky for you that it didn't.

MRS. SØRBY: Yes, that's true enough. But I've always been wary of following my impulses. After all, a woman can't just throw herself away.

GREGERS: Aren't you even a little bit afraid that I'll drop my father a hint about this old friendship?

MRS. SØRBY: You can be sure I've told him myself.

2420 GREGERS: Oh?

MRS. SØRBY: Your father knows every last scrap of gossip that holds any grain of truth about me. I told him all of those things; it was the first thing I did when he made his intentions clear.

GREGERS: Then I think you're more frank than most people.

MRS. SØRBY: I've always been frank. In the long run, it's the best thing for us women to be.

HJALMAR: What do you say to that, Gina?

GINA: Oh, women are all so different. Some live one way and

2430 some live another.

MRS. SØRBY: Well, Gina, I do think it's wisest to handle things as I have. And Werle, for his part, hasn't held back anything either. Really, it's this that's brought us so close together. Now he can sit and talk to me as freely as a child. He's never had that chance before. He, a healthy, vigorous man, had to spend his whole youth and all his best years hearing nothing but sermons on his sins. And generally those sermons were aimed at the most imaginary failings—at least from what *I* could see.

2440 GINA: Yes, that's just as true as you say.

GREGERS: If you women are going to explore this subject, I'd better leave.

MRS. SØRBY: You can just as well stay, for that matter; I won't say another word. But I did want you to understand that I haven't done anything sly or in any way underhanded. I suppose it looks like I've had quite a nice piece of luck, and that's true enough, up to a point. But, anyway, what I mean is that I'll not be taking any more than I give. One thing I'll never do is desert him. And I can be useful to him and care for him now better than anyone else after he's helpless.

2450

HJALMAR: After he's helpless?

GREGERS: *(to MRS. SØRBY)* All right, don't talk about that here.

MRS. SØRBY: No need to hide it any longer, much as he'd like to. He's going blind.

HJALMAR: *(astounded)* He's going blind? But that's peculiar. Is he going blind too?

GINA: Lots of people do.

MRS. SØRBY: And you can imagine what that means for a businessman. Well, I'll try to make my eyes do for his as well as I can. But I mustn't stay any longer; I've so much to take 2460 care of now. Oh yes, I was supposed to tell you this, Ekdal— that if there's anything Werle can do for you, please just get in touch with Graaberg.

GREGERS: That offer Hjalmar Ekdal will certainly decline.

MRS. SØRBY: Come, now, I don't think that in the past he's—

GINA: No, Berta, Hjalmar doesn't need to take anything from Mr. Werle now.

HJALMAR: *(slowly and ponderously)* Would you greet your future husband from me and say that I intend very shortly to call on his bookkeeper, Graaberg— 2470

GREGERS: What! Is that what you want?

HJALMAR: To call on his bookkeeper Graaberg, as I said, to request an itemized account of what I owe his employer. I shall repay this debt of honor—(*Laughs.*) That's a good name for it, "debt of honor"! But never mind. I shall repay every penny of it, with five percent interest.

GINA: But Hjalmar dear, God knows we don't have the money for that.

2480 HJALMAR: Will you tell your husband-to-be that I'm working away relentlessly at my invention. Would you tell him that what keeps my spirits up through this grueling ordeal is the desire to be quit of a painful burden of debt. That's why I'm making my invention. The entire proceeds will be devoted to shedding my monetary ties with your imminent partner.

MRS. SØRBY: Something has really happened in this house.

HJALMAR: Yes, it certainly has.

MRS. SØRBY: Well, good-bye, then. I still have a little more to talk about with you, Gina, but that can keep till another time. Good-bye.

(HJALMAR *and* GREGERS *silently nod;* GINA *accompanies* MRS. SØRBY *to the door.*)

2490 HJALMAR: Not across the threshold, Gina!

(MRS. SØRBY *leaves;* GINA *closes the door behind her.*)

HJALMAR: There, now, Gregers—now I've got that pressing debt off my hands.

GREGERS: You will soon, anyway.

HJALMAR: I believe my attitude could be called correct.

GREGERS: You're the man I always thought you were.

HJALMAR: In certain circumstances it's impossible not to feel the summons of the ideal. As the family provider, you know, I've got to write and groan beneath it. Believe you me, it's really no joke for a man without means to try and pay off a 2500 long-standing debt over which the dust of oblivion, so to speak, had fallen. But it's got to be, all the same; my human self demands its rights.

GREGERS: (*laying one hand on his shoulder*) Ah, Hjalmar—wasn't it a good thing I came?

HJALMAR: Yes.

GREGERS: Getting a clear picture of the whole situation—wasn't that a good thing?

HJALMAR: (*a bit impatiently*) Of course it was good. But there's one thing that irks my sense of justice.

2510 GREGERS: What's that?

HJALMAR: It's the fact that—oh, I don't know if I dare speak so freely about your father.

GREGERS: Don't hold back on my account.

HJALMAR: Well, uh—you see, I find something so irritating in the idea that I'm not the one, he's the one who's going to have the true marriage.

GREGERS: How can you say such a thing!

HJALMAR: But it's true. Your father and Mrs. Sørby are entering a marriage based on complete trust, one that's whole-2520 hearted and open on both sides. They haven't bottled up any secrets from each other; there isn't any reticence between them; they've declared—if you'll permit me—a mutual forgiveness of sins.

GREGERS: All right. So what?

HJALMAR: Yes, but that's the whole thing, then. You said yourself that the reason for all these difficulties was the founding of a true marriage.

GREGERS: But that marriage is a very different sort, Hjalmar. You certainly wouldn't compare either you or her with those two—well, you know what I mean.

HJALMAR: Still, I can't get over the idea that there's something in all this that violates my sense of justice. It really seems as if there's no just order to the universe.

GINA: Good Lord, Hjalmar, you mustn't say such things.

GREGERS: Hm, let's not start on that question.

HJALMAR: But then, on the other hand, I can definitely make out what seems to be the meticulous hand of fate. He's going blind.

GINA: Oh, that's not for sure.

HJALMAR: That is indisputable. Anyway, we oughtn't to doubt 2540 it, because it's precisely this fact that reveals the just retribution. Years back he abused the blind faith of a fellow human being—

GREGERS: I'm afraid he's done that to many others.

HJALMAR: And now a pitiless, mysterious something comes and claims the old man's eyes in return.

GINA: What a horrible thing to say! It really frightens me.

HJALMAR: It's useful sometimes to go down deep into the night side of existence.

(HEDVIG, *in her hat and coat, comes in, happy and breathless, through the hall door.*)

GINA: Back so soon?

HEDVIG: Yes, I got tired of walking, and it was just as well, 'cause then I met someone down at the door.

HJALMAR: That must have been Mrs. Sørby.

HEDVIG: Yes.

HJALMAR: (*pacing back and forth*) I hope that's the last time you'll see her.

(*Silence,* HEDVIG *glances timidly from one to the other, as if trying to read their feelings.*)

HEDVIG: (*coaxingly, as she approaches*) Daddy.

HJALMAR: Well—what is it, Hedvig?

HEDVIG: Mrs. Sørby brought along something for me.

HJALMAR: (*stopping*) For you?

HEDVIG: Yes. It's something meant for tomorrow.

GINA: Berta's always brought some little gift for your birthday.

HJALMAR: What is it?

HEDVIG: No, you can't know that yet, because Mother has to bring it to me in bed first thing in the morning.

HJALMAR: Oh, all this conspiracy that I'm left out of!

HEDVIG: (*hurriedly*) Oh, you can see it all right. It's a big letter. (*She takes the letter out of her coat pocket.*)

HJALMAR: A letter, too?

HEDVIG: Well, it's only the letter. I guess the rest will come later. But just think—a letter! I've never gotten a real letter before. And on the outside there, it says "Miss." (*She reads.*) "Miss Hedvig Ekdal." Just think—that's me.

HJALMAR: Let me see the letter.

HEDVIG: (*handing it over*) See, there.

HJALMAR: That's old Werle's writing.

GINA: Are you positive, Hjalmar?

HJALMAR: See for yourself.

GINA: Oh, how would I know?

HJALMAR: Hedvig, mind if I open the letter—and read it?

HEDVIG: Sure. If you want to, go right ahead.

GINA: No, not tonight, Hjalmar. It's meant for tomorrow.

HEDVIG: *(softly)* Oh, won't you let him read it! It's got to be something good, and then Daddy'll be happy and things will be pleasant again.

HJALMAR: May I open it, then?

2590 HEDVIG: Yes, please do, Daddy. It'll be fun to find out what it is.

HJALMAR: Good. *(He opens the envelope, takes out a sheet of paper, and reads it through with growing bewilderment.)* Now what's this all about?

GINA: But what does it say?

HEDVIG: Oh yes, Daddy—tell us!

HJALMAR: Be quiet. *(He reads it through once more, turns pale, then speaks with evident restraint.)* This is a deed of gift, Hedvig.

2600 HEDVIG: Honestly? What am I getting?

HJALMAR: Read for yourself.

*(HEDVIG goes over to the lamp and reads for a moment.)*

HJALMAR: *(clenching his fists, in almost a whisper)* The eyes! The eyes—and now that letter!

HEDVIG: *(interrupting her reading)* Yes, but I think the gift is for Grandfather.

HJALMAR: *(taking the letter from her)* Gina—do you understand this?

GINA: I know nothing at all about it. Just tell me.

HJALMAR: Mr. Werle writes Hedvig to say that her old grand-
2610 father needn't trouble himself any longer with copying work, but that henceforth he can draw one hundred crowns a month from the office—

GREGERS: Aha!

HEDVIG: One hundred crowns, Mother! I read that.

GINA: That'll be nice for Grandfather.

HJALMAR: One hundred crowns, as long as he needs it. That means till death, of course.

GINA: Well, then he's provided for, poor dear.

HJALMAR: But there's more. You didn't read far enough, Hed-
2620 vig. Afterwards this gift passes over to you.

HEDVIG: To me! All of it?

HJALMAR: You're assured the same income for the rest of your life, he writes. Hear that, Gina?

GINA: Yes, of course I heard.

HEDVIG: Imagine me getting all that money! *(Shaking HJAL-MAR.)* Daddy, Daddy, aren't you glad?

HJALMAR: *(disengaging himself)* Glad! *(Walking about the room.)* Ah, what vistas—what perspectives it offers me. Hedvig is the one, she's the one he remembers so
2630 bountifully.

GINA: Of course, because it's Hedvig's birthday.

HEDVIG: And anyway, you'll have it, Daddy. You know that I'll give all the money to you and Mother.

HJALMAR: To Mother, yes! There we have it.

GREGERS: Hjalmar, this is a trap that's been set for you.

HJALMAR: You think it could be another trap?

GREGERS: When he was here this morning, he said, "Hjalmar Ekdal is not the man you think he is."

HJALMAR: Not the man—!

2640 GREGERS: "You'll find that out," he said.

HJALMAR: Find out if I could be bought off for a price, eh—!

HEDVIG: But Mother, what's this all about?

GINA: Go and take your things off.

*(HEDVIG, close to tears, goes out the kitchen door.)*

GREGERS: Yes, Hjalmar—now we'll see who's right, he or I.

HJALMAR: *(slowly tearing the paper in half and putting both pieces on the table)* That is my answer.

GREGERS: What I expected.

HJALMAR: *(going over to GINA, who is standing by the stove, and speaking quietly)* And now no more pretenses. If that thing between you and him was all over when you—came to be so 2650 terribly in love with me, as you put it—then why did he give us the means to get married?

GINA: Maybe he thought he could come and go here.

HJALMAR: Is that all? Wasn't he afraid of a certain possibility?

GINA: I don't know what you mean.

HJALMAR: I want to know if—your child has the right to live under my roof.

GINA: *(draws herself up, her eyes flashing)* And you can ask that?

HJALMAR: Just answer me this: does Hedvig belong to me—or? 2660 Well!

GINA: *(regarding him with chill defiance)* I don't know.

HJALMAR: *(with a slight quaver)* You don't know!

GINA: How would *I* know that? A woman of my sort—

HJALMAR: *(softly, turning from her)* Then I have nothing more to do in this house.

GREGERS: You must think about this, Hjalmar.

HJALMAR: *(putting on his overcoat)* There's nothing to think about for a man like me.

GREGERS: Oh, there's so very much to think about. You three 2670 have got to stay together if you're ever going to win through to a self-sacrificial, forgiving spirit.

HJALMAR: I don't want that. Never, never! My hat! *(Takes his hat.)* My home is down in ruins around me. *(Breaks into tears.)* Gregers, I have no child!

HEDVIG: *(who has opened the kitchen door)* What are you saying! *(Running toward him.)* Daddy, Daddy!

GINA: Now look!

HJALMAR: Don't come near me, Hedvig! Keep away. I can't bear seeing you. Oh, the eyes! Goodbye. *(Starts for the door.)* 2680

HEDVIG: *(clinging fast to him and shrieking)* Oh no! Oh no! Don't leave me.

GINA: *(crying out)* Look out for the child, Hjalmar! Look out for the child!

HJALMAR: I won't. I can't. I've got to get out—away from all this! *(He tears himself loose from HEDVIG and goes out through the hall door.)*

HEDVIG: *(with desperate eyes)* He's left us, Mother! He's left us! He'll never come back again!

GINA: Now don't cry, Hedvig, Daddy's coming back. 2690

HEDVIG: *(throws herself, sobbing, on the sofa)* No, no, he'll never come home to us again.

GREGERS: Will you believe I've wanted everything for the best, Mrs. Ekdal?

GINA: Yes, I think I believe that—but God have mercy on you all the same.

HEDVIG: *(lying on the sofa)* I think I'll die from all this. What did I do to him? Mother, you've got to make him come home!

2700 GINA: Yes, yes, yes, just be calm, and I'll step out and look for him. (*Putting on her coat.*) Maybe he's gone down to Relling's. But now don't you lie there, wailing away. Will you promise?

HEDVIG: (*sobbing convulsively*) Yes, I'll be all right—if only Daddy comes back.

GREGERS: (*to* GINA, *about to leave*) Wouldn't it be better, though, to let him fight through his painful battle first?

GINA: Oh, he can do that later. First of all, we've got to comfort the child. (*She goes out the hall door.*)

2710 HEDVIG: (*sitting up and drying her tears*) Now you have to tell me what it's all about. Why does Daddy not want to see me anymore?

GREGERS: That's something you mustn't ask until you're big and grown-up.

HEDVIG: (*catching her breath*) But I can't go on being so horribly unhappy till I'm big and grown-up. I bet I know what it is. Perhaps I'm really not Daddy's child.

GREGERS: (*disturbed*) How could that ever be?

HEDVIG: Mother could have found me. And now maybe Dad-
2720 dy's found out. I've read about these things.

GREGERS: Well, but if that was the—

HEDVIG: Yes, I think he could love me even so. Or maybe more. The wild duck was sent us as a present too, and I'm terribly fond of it, all the same.

GREGERS: (*divertingly*) Of course, the wild duck, that's true. Let's talk a bit about the wild duck, Hedvig.

HEDVIG: The poor wild duck. He can't bear to see her again, either. Imagine, he wanted to wring her neck!

GREGERS: Oh, he certainly wouldn't do that.

2730 HEDVIG: No, but that's what he said. And I think it was awful for Daddy to say, because each night I make a prayer for the wild duck and ask that she be delivered from death and everything evil.

GREGERS: (*looking at her*) Do you always say your prayers at night?

HEDVIG: Uh-huh.

GREGERS: Who taught you that?

HEDVIG: I taught myself, and that was once when Daddy was so sick and had leeches on his neck, and then he said he was
2740 in the jaws of death.

GREGERS: Oh yes?

HEDVIG: So I said a prayer for him when I went to bed. And I've kept it up ever since.

GREGERS: And now you pray for the wild duck, too?

HEDVIG: I thought it was best to put the wild duck in, because she was ailing so at the start.

GREGERS: Do you say morning prayers, too?

HEDVIG: No, not at all.

GREGERS: Why not morning prayers as well?

2750 HEDVIG: In the morning it's light, and so there's nothing more to be afraid of.

GREGERS: And the wild duck you love so much—your father wants to wring her neck.

HEDVIG: No. He said it would be the best thing for him if he did, but for my sake he would spare her; and that was good of Daddy.

GREGERS: (*coming closer*) But what if you now, of your own free will, sacrificed the wild duck for *his* sake.

HEDVIG: (*springing up*) The wild duck!

GREGERS: What if you, in a sacrificing spirit, gave up the dear- 2760 est thing you own and know in the whole world?

HEDVIG: Do you think that would help?

GREGERS: Try it, Hedvig.

HEDVIG: (*softly, with shining eyes*) Yes, I'll try it.

GREGERS: And the strength of mind, do you think you have it?

HEDVIG: I'll ask Grandpa to shoot the wild duck for me.

GREGERS: Yes, do that. But not a word to your mother about all this!

HEDVIG: Why not?

GREGERS: She doesn't understand us. 2770

HEDVIG: The wild duck? I'll try it tomorrow, early.

(GINA *comes in through the hall door.*)

HEDVIG: (*going toward her*) Did you find him, Mother?

GINA: No. But I heard he'd looked in downstairs and gotten Relling along.

GREGERS: Are you sure of that?

GINA: Yes, I asked the janitor's wife. And Molvik was with them, she said.

GREGERS: And this, right when his mind needs nothing so much as to wrestle in solitude—!

GINA: (*taking off her coat*) Oh, men are strange ones, they are. 2780 God knows where Relling has led him! I ran over to Mrs. Eriksen's café, but they weren't there.

HEDVIG: (*struggling with her tears*) Oh, what if he never comes back again!

GREGERS: He *will* come back. I'll get a message to him tomorrow, and then you'll see just how quick he comes. Believe that, Hedvig, and sleep well. Good night. (*He goes out the hall door.*)

HEDVIG: (*throwing herself, sobbing, into* GINA'*s arms*) Mother, Mother! 2790

GINA: (*pats her on the back and sighs*) Ah, me, Relling was right. That's the way it goes when these crazy people come around, summoning up their ideals.

## —ACT FIVE—

HJALMAR EKDAL'*s studio. A cold, gray morning light filters in; wet snow lies on the huge panes of the skylight.* GINA, *wearing a pinafore, comes in from the kitchen, carrying a feather duster and a cleaning cloth, and makes for the living room door. At the same moment* HEDVIG *rushes in from the hallway.*

GINA: (*stopping*) Well?

HEDVIG: You know, Mother, I'm pretty sure he's down at Relling's—

GINA: There, you see!

HEDVIG: 'Cause the janitor's wife said she heard Relling had two others with him when he came in last night.

GINA: That's about what I thought. 2800

HEDVIG: But it's still no good if he won't come up to us.

GINA: At least I can go down there and talk with him.

(EKDAL, *in dressing gown and slippers, smoking a pipe, appears in the doorway to his room.*)

EKDAL: Say, Hjalmar—Isn't Hjalmar home?

GINA: No, he's gone out, I guess.

EKDAL: So early? In a raging blizzard like this? Oh, well, never mind; I'll take my morning walk alone, that's all.

(*He pulls the loft door ajar,* HEDVIG *helping him. He goes in; she closes up after him.*)

HEDVIG: (*lowering her voice*) Just think, Mother, when Grandpa finds out that Daddy's leaving us.

GINA: Go on, Grandpa won't hear anything of the kind. It was
2810  a real stroke of providence he wasn't here yesterday in all that racket.

HEDVIG: Yes, but—

(GREGERS *comes in the hall entrance.*)

GREGERS: Well? Had any reports on him?

GINA: He should be down at Relling's, they tell me.

GREGERS: With Relling! Did he really go out with those fellows?

GINA: Apparently.

GREGERS: Yes, but he who needed so much to be alone to pull himself together—!

2820  GINA: Yes, just as you say.

(RELLING *enters from the hall.*)

HEDVIG: (*going toward him*) Is Daddy with you?

GINA: (*simultaneously*) Is he there?

RELLING: Yes, of course he is.

HEDVIG: And you never told us!

RELLING: Oh, I'm a beast. But first of all, I had that other beast to manage—you know, the demonic one, him—and then, next, I fell so sound asleep that—

GINA: What's Hjalmar been saying today?

RELLING: He's said absolutely nothing.

2830  HEDVIG: Hasn't he talked at all?

RELLING: Not a blessed word.

GREGERS: No, no, I can well understand that.

GINA: But what's he doing, then?

RELLING: He's laid out on the sofa, snoring.

GINA: Oh? Yes, Hjalmar's great at snoring.

HEDVIG: He's asleep? Can he sleep?

RELLING: Well, so it seems.

GREGERS: It's conceivable—when all that strife of spirit has torn him.

2840  GINA: And then he's never been used to roaming around the streets at night.

HEDVIG: Maybe it's a good thing that he's getting some sleep, Mother.

GINA: I think so too. But then it's just as well we don't rouse him too soon. Thanks a lot, Relling. Now I've got to clean and straighten up here a bit, and then— Come and help me, Hedvig.

(GINA *and* HEDVIG *disappear into the living room.*)

GREGERS: (*turning to* RELLING) Have you an explanation for the spiritual upheaval taking place within Hjalmar Ekdal?

2850  RELLING: For the life of me, I can't remember any spiritual upheaval in him.

GREGERS: Wait! At a time of crisis like this, when his life has been recast? How can you believe that a rare personality like Hjalmar—?

RELLING: Pah! Personality—him! If he's ever had a tendency toward anything so abnormal as what you call personality, it

was ripped up, root and vine, by the time he was grown, and that's a fact.

GREGERS: That's rather surprising—with all the loving care he    2860
had as a child.

RELLING: From those two warped, hysterical maiden aunts, you mean?

GREGERS: I want to tell you they were women who always summoned themselves to the highest ideals—yes, now of course you'll start mocking me again.

RELLING: No, I'm hardly in a mood for that. Besides, I'm well informed here; he's regurgitated any amount of rhetoric about his "twin soul-mothers." I really don't believe he has much to thank them for. Ekdal's misfortune is that in his cir-    2870
cle he's always been taken for a shining light—

GREGERS: And isn't he, perhaps, exactly that? In his heart's core, I mean?

RELLING: I've never noticed anything of the kind. His father thinks so—but that's nothing; the old lieutenant's been a fool all his life.

GREGERS: He has, all his life, been a man with a childlike awareness; and that's something you just don't understand.

RELLING: Oh, sure! But back when our dear, sweet Hjalmar became a student of sorts, right away he got taken up by his classmates as the great beacon of the future. Oh, he was    2880
good-looking, the lout—pink and white—just the way little moon-eyed girls like boys. And then he had that excitable manner and that heart-winning tremor in his voice, and he was so cute and clever at declaiming other people's poems and ideas—

GREGERS: (*indignantly*) Is it Hjalmar Ekdal you're speaking of that way?

RELLING: Yes, with your permission. That's an inside look at him, this idol you're groveling in front of.

GREGERS: I really didn't think I was utterly blind.    2890

RELLING: Well, you're not far from it. Because you're a sick man, you are. You know that.

GREGERS: There you're right.

RELLING: Oh yes. Your case has complications. First there's this virulent moralistic fever; and then something worse— you keep going off in deliriums of hero worship; you always have to have something to admire that's outside of yourself.

GREGERS: Yes, I certainly have to look for it outside myself.

RELLING: But you're so woefully wrong about these great miraculous beings you think you see and hear around you.    2900
You've simply come back to a cotter's cabin with your summons to the ideal; there's no one but fugitives here.

GREGERS: If you've got no higher estimate of Hjalmar Ekdal than this, how can you ever enjoy seeing him day after day?

RELLING: Good Lord, I *am* supposed to be some kind of doctor, I'm ashamed to say. Well, then I ought to look after the poor sick people I live with.

GREGERS: Oh, come! Is Hjalmar Ekdal sick, too?

RELLING: Most of the world is sick, I'm afraid.

GREGERS: And what's your prescription for Hjalmar?    2910

RELLING: My standard one. I try to keep up the life-lie in him.

GREGERS: The life-lie? I don't think I heard—

RELLING: Oh yes, I said the life-lie. The life-lie, don't you see— that's the animating principle of life.

GREGERS: May I ask what kind of lie has infected Hjalmar?

RELLING: No, thanks, I don't betray secrets like that to quacks.

You'd just be able to damage him all the more for me. My method is tested, though. I've also used it on Molvik. I made him "demonic." That was my remedy for him.

2920 GREGERS: Then he isn't demonic?

RELLING: What the devil does it mean to be demonic? That's just some hogwash I thought up to keep life going in him. If I hadn't done that, the poor innocent mutt would have given in years ago to self-contempt and despair. And then take the old lieutenant! But he really discovered his own cure himself.

GREGERS: Lieutenant Ekdal? How so?

RELLING: Well, what do you think of this bear hunter going into a dark loft to stalk rabbits? There isn't a happier sports-

2930 man in the world than the old man when he's prowling around in that junkyard. Those four or five dried-out Christmas trees he's got—to him they're like all the green forests of Hoidal; the hens and the rooster—they're the game birds up in the fir tops; and the rabbits hopping across the floor— they're the bears that call up his youth again, out in the mountain air.

GREGERS: Poor, unhappy old Ekdal, yes. He certainly had to pare down his early ideals.

RELLING: While I remember it, Mr. Werle junior—don't use

2940 that exotic word *ideals*. Not when we've got a fine native word—*lies*.

GREGERS: You're implying the two have something in common?

RELLING: Yes, about like typhus and typhoid fever.

GREGERS: Dr. Relling, I won't rest till I've gotten Hjalmar out of your clutches.

RELLING: So much the worse for him. Deprive the average man of his vital lie, and you've robbed him of happiness as well. (*To* HEDVIG, *entering from the living room.*) Well, little

2950 wild-duck mother, now I'll go down and see if Papa's still lying and pondering his marvelous invention. (*He goes out the hall door.*)

GREGERS: (*approaching* HEDVIG) I can see by your face that it isn't done.

HEDVIG: What? Oh, about the wild duck. No.

GREGERS: Your courage failed you when the time came to act, I suppose.

HEDVIG: No, it's not exactly that. But when I woke up this morning early and thought of what we talked about, then it

2960 seemed so strange to me.

GREGERS: Strange?

HEDVIG: Yes, I don't know— Last night, right at the time, there was something so beautiful about it, but after I'd slept and then thought it over, it didn't seem like so much.

GREGERS: Ah, no, you couldn't grow up here without some taint in you.

HEDVIG: I don't care about that; if only Daddy would come up, then—

GREGERS: Oh, if only your eyes were really open to what makes

2970 life worth living—if only you had the true, joyful, coura- geous spirit of self-sacrifice, *then* you'd see him coming up to you. But I still have faith in you. (*He goes out the hall door.*)

(HEDVIG *wanders across the room, then starts into the kitchen. At that moment a knock comes on the loft door,* HEDVIG *goes*

*over and opens it a space;* EKDAL *slips out, and she slides it shut again.*)

EKDAL: Hm, a morning walk alone is no fun at all.

HEDVIG: Don't you want to go hunting, Grandpa?

EKDAL: The weather's no good for hunting. Awfully dark in there; you can hardly see ahead of you.

HEDVIG: Don't you ever want to shoot at anything but rabbits? 2980

EKDAL: Aren't rabbits good enough, eh?

HEDVIG: Yes, but the wild duck, say?

EKDAL: Ha, ha! You're afraid I'll shoot the wild duck for you? Never in this world, dear. Never!

HEDVIG: No, you couldn't do that. It must be hard to shoot wild ducks.

EKDAL: Couldn't? I certainly could!

HEDVIG: How would you go about it, Grandpa?—I don't mean with *my* wild duck, but with others.

EKDAL: I'd be sure to shoot them in the breast, understand; 2990 that's the safest. And then they've got to be shot *against* the feathers, you see—not *with* the feathers.

HEDVIG: They die then, Grandpa?

EKDAL: Oh yes, they do indeed—if you shoot them right. Well, got to go in and clean up. Hm—you understand—hm. (*He goes into his room.*)

(HEDVIG *waits a moment, glances at the living room door, goes to the bookcase, stands on tiptoe, takes down the double-barreled pistol from the shelf and looks at it.* GINA, *with duster and cloth, comes in from the living room.* HEDVIG *hastily sets down the pistol, unnoticed.*)

GINA: Don't mess with your father's things, Hedvig.

HEDVIG: (*leaving the bookcase*) I was just straightening up a little.

GINA: Go out in the kitchen instead and make sure the coffee's 3000 still hot; I'll take a tray along to him when I go down.

(HEDVIG *goes out;* GINA *begins to dust and clean up the studio. After a moment the hall door is cautiously opened, and* HJAL-MAR *peers in. He wears his overcoat, but no hat. He is un-washed, with tousled, unruly hair; his eyes are dull and inert.*)

GINA: (*standing rooted with duster in hand, looking at him*) Don't tell me, Hjalmar—are you back after all?

HJALMAR: (*steps in and answers in a thick voice*) I'm back—but only for one moment.

GINA: Oh yes, I'm sure of that. But my goodness—what a sight you are!

HJALMAR: Sight?

GINA: And then your good winter coat! Well, it's done for.

HEDVIG: (*at the kitchen door*) Mother, should I—(*Seeing* HJAL- 3010 MAR, *giving a squeal of delight, and running toward him.*) Oh, Daddy, Daddy!

HJALMAR: (*turning from her and waving her off*) Get away! Get away! (*To* GINA.) Make her get away from me, will you!

GINA: (*in an undertone*) Go in the living room, Hedvig.

(HEDVIG *silently goes out.*)

HJALMAR: (*with a busy air, pulling out the table drawer*) I must have my books along. Where are my books?

GINA: What books?

HJALMAR: My scientific works, of course—the technical jour-
3020 nals I use for my invention.

GINA: *(looking over the bookshelves)* Are these them, the ones
without covers?

HJALMAR: Yes, exactly.

GINA: *(putting a stack of booklets on the table)* Could I get
Hedvig to cut the pages for you?

HJALMAR: Nobody has to cut pages for me. *(A short silence.)*

GINA: Then it's definite that you're moving out, Hjalmar?

HJALMAR: *(rummaging among the books)* Yes, that would seem
to me self-evident.

3030 GINA: I see.

HJALMAR: How could I go on here and have my heart shattered
every hour of the day!

GINA: God forgive you for thinking so badly of me.

HJALMAR: Show me proof—

GINA: I think *you're* the one to show proof.

HJALMAR: After your kind of past? There are certain standards—I'd like to call them ideal standards—

GINA: But Grandfather? What'll happen to him, poor dear?

HJALMAR: I know my duty; that helpless old soul leaves with
3040 me. I'm going downtown and make arrangements—hm—
*(Hesitantly.)* Did anybody find my hat on the stairs?

GINA: No. Have you lost your hat?

HJALMAR: I had it on, naturally, when I came in last night; I'm
positive of that. But today I couldn't find it.

GINA: My Lord, where did you go with those two stumble-
bums?

HJALMAR: Oh, don't bother me with petty questions. Do you
think I'm in a mood to remember details?

GINA: I just hope you didn't catch cold, Hjalmar. *(She goes out
3050 into the kitchen.)*

HJALMAR: *(muttering to himself in exasperation, as he empties
the table drawer)* You're a sneak, Relling! A barbarian, that's
what! Oh, snake in the grass! If I could just get someone to
strangle you! *(He puts some old letters to one side, discovers
the torn deed of the day before, picks it up and examines the
pieces. He hurriedly puts them down as* GINA *enters.)*

GINA: *(setting a breakfast tray on the table)* Here's a drop of
something hot, if you care for it. And there's some bread and
butter and a little salt meat.

3060 HJALMAR: *(glancing at the tray)* Salt meat? Never under this
roof! Of course I haven't enjoyed going without food for
nearly twenty-four hours; but that doesn't matter—My
notes! My unfinished memoirs! Where can I find my journal and my important papers? *(Opens the living room door,
then draws back.)* There she is again!

GINA: Well, goodness, the child has to be somewhere.

HJALMAR: Come out. *(He stands aside, and* HEDVIG, *terrified,
comes into the studio.)*

HJALMAR: *(with his hand on the doorknob, says to* GINA*)* These
3070 last moments I'm spending in my former home, I'd like to
be free from intruders—*(Goes into the living room.)*

HEDVIG: *(rushing to her mother, her voice hushed and trembling)* Does he mean me?

GINA: Stay in the kitchen, Hedvig. Or, no—go into your own
room instead. *(Speaking to* HJALMAR *as she goes in to him.)*
Just a minute, Hjalmar. Don't muss up the bureau like that;
I know where everything is. (HEDVIG *stands for a moment as
if frozen by fright and bewilderment, biting her lips to keep*

*the tears back; then she clenches her fists convulsively.)*

HEDVIG: *(softly)* The wild duck. *(She steals over and takes the* 3080
*pistol from the shelf, sets the loft door ajar, slips in and
draws the door shut after her.* HJALMAR *and* GINA *start arguing in the living room.)*

HJALMAR: *(reenters with some notebooks and old loose papers,
which he lays on the table)* Oh, what good is that traveling
bag! I've got a thousand things to take with me.

GINA: *(following with the traveling bag)* So leave everything
else for the time being, and just take a shirt and a pair of
shorts with you.

HJALMAR: Phew! These agonizing preparations! *(Takes off his* 3090
*overcoat and throws it on the sofa.)*

GINA: And there's your coffee getting cold, too.

HJALMAR: Hm. *(Unthinkingly takes a sip and then another.)*

GINA: The hardest thing for you will be to find another room
like that, big enough for all the rabbits.

HJALMAR: What! Do I have to take all the rabbits with me, too?

GINA: Yes, Grandfather couldn't live without the rabbits, I'm
sure.

HJALMAR: He's simply got to get used to it. The joys of life *I*
have to renounce are higher than rabbits. 3100

GINA: *(dusting the bookcase)* Should I put your flute in the
traveling bag?

HJALMAR: No. No flute for me. But give me the pistol!

GINA: You want your pistol along?

HJALMAR: Yes. My loaded pistol.

GINA: *(looking for it)* It's gone. He must have taken it inside.

HJALMAR: Is he in the loft?

GINA: Of course he's in the loft.

HJALMAR: Hm—lonely old man. *(He takes a piece of bread and
butter, eats it, and finishes the cup of coffee.)* 3110

GINA: Now if we only hadn't rented the room, you could have
moved in there.

HJALMAR: I should stay on under the same roof as—! Never!
Never!

GINA: But couldn't you put up in the living room just for a day
or two? You've got everything you need in there.

HJALMAR: Never within these walls!

GINA: Well, how about down with Relling and Molvik?

HJALMAR: Don't mention those barbarians' names! I can almost
lose my appetite just thinking about them. Oh no, I've got to 3120
go out in sleet and snow—tramp from house to house and
seek shelter for Father and me.

GINA: But you haven't any hat, Hjalmar! You've lost your hat.

HJALMAR: Oh, those two vermin, wallowing in sin! The hat will
have to be bought. *(Taking another piece of bread and butter.)* Someone's got to make arrangements. I certainly don't
intend to risk my life. *(Looking for something on the tray.)*

GINA: What are you looking for?

HJALMAR: Butter.

GINA: Butter's coming right up. *(Goes into the kitchen.)* 3130

HJALMAR: *(calling after her)* Oh, never mind; I can just as easily eat dry bread.

GINA: *(bringing in a butter dish)* Look. It's fresh today. *(She
passes him another cup of coffee. He sits on the sofa, spreads
more butter on the bread, eats and drinks a moment in
silence.)*

HJALMAR: Could I—without being annoyed by anybody—anybody at all—put up in the living room just for a day or two?

GINA: Yes, of course you could, if you want to.

3140 HJALMAR: Because I can't see any possibility of getting all Father's things out in one trip.

GINA: And then there's this, too, that you've first got to tell him you're not living with us any longer.

HJALMAR: (pushing the coffee cup away) That too, yes. All these intricate affairs to unravel. I've got to clear my thinking; I need a breathing spell; I can't shoulder all these burdens in one day.

GINA: No, and not when the weather's like it is out.

HJALMAR: (picking up WERLE's letter) I see this letter's still

3150 kicking around.

GINA: Yes, I haven't touched it.

HJALMAR: This trash is nothing to me—

GINA: Well, I'm not going to use it for anything.

HJALMAR: All the same, there's no point in throwing it around helter-skelter. In all the confusion of my moving, it could easily—

GINA: I'll take good care of it, Hjalmar.

HJALMAR: First and foremost, the deed of gift is Father's; it's really his affair whether or not he wants to use it.

3160 GINA: (sighing) Yes, poor old Father—

HJALMAR: Just for safety's sake—where would I find some paste?

GINA: (going to the bookcase) Here's the pastepot.

HJALMAR: And then a brush.

GINA: Here's a brush, too. (Bringing both.)

HJALMAR: (taking a pair of scissors) A strip of paper down the back, that's all. (Cutting and pasting.) Far be it from me to take liberties with another's property—least of all, a penniless old man's. No, nor with—the other person's. There,

3170 now. Let it lie a while. And when it's dry, then take it away. I don't want to set eyes on that document again. Ever!

(GREGERS enters from the hall.)

GREGERS: (somewhat surprised) What? Are you lounging in here, Hjalmar?

HJALMAR: (springing up) I was overcome by fatigue.

GREGERS: Still, you've had breakfast, I see.

HJALMAR: The body makes its claims now and then too.

GREGERS: What have you decided to do?

HJALMAR: For a man like me there's only one way open. I'm in the process of assembling my most important things. But

3180 that takes time, don't you know.

GINA: (a bit impatient) Should I get the room ready for you, or should I pack your bag?

HJALMAR: (after a vexed glance at GREGERS) Pack—and get the room ready!

GINA: (taking the traveling bag) All right, then I'll put in the shirt and the rest. (She goes into the living room, shutting the door behind her.)

GREGERS: (after a short silence) I never dreamed that things would end like this. Is it really necessary for you to leave

3190 house and home?

HJALMAR: (pacing restlessly about) What would you have me do? I wasn't made to be unhappy, Gregers. I've got to have it snug and secure and peaceful around me.

GREGERS: But why can't you, then? Give it a try. Now I'd say you have solid ground to build on—so make a fresh start. And don't forget you have your invention to live for, too.

HJALMAR: Oh, don't talk about the invention. That seems such a long way off.

GREGERS: Oh?

HJALMAR: Good Lord, yes. What would you really have me in- 3200 vent? Other people have invented so much already. It gets more difficult every day—

GREGERS: And you've put so much work in it.

HJALMAR: It was that dissolute Relling who got me started.

GREGERS: Relling?

HJALMAR: Yes, he was the one who first made me aware that I had a real talent for inventing something in photography.

GREGERS: Aha—that was Relling!

HJALMAR: Oh, I was so blissfully happy as a result. Not so much from the invention itself, but because Hedvig believed in 3210 it—believed in it with all the power and force of a child's mind. Yes, in other words, fool that I am, I've gone around imagining that she believed in it.

GREGERS: You can't really think that Hedvig could lie to you!

HJALMAR: Now I can think anything. It's Hedvig that ruins it all. She's managed to blot the sun right out of my life.

GREGERS: Hedvig! You mean Hedvig? How could she ever do that?

HJALMAR: (without answering) How inexpressibly I loved that child! How inexpressibly happy I was whenever I came 3220 home to my poor rooms and she came flying to meet me with those sweet, fluttering eyes. I was so unspeakably fond of her—and so I dreamed and deluded myself into thinking that she, too, was fond of me beyond words.

GREGERS: Can you call that just a delusion?

HJALMAR: How can I tell? I can't get anything out of Gina; and besides, she has no feeling at all for the ideal phase of these complications. But with you, Gregers, I feel impelled to open my mind. There's this horrible doubt—maybe Hedvig never really, truly has loved me. 3230

GREGERS: She may perhaps give you proof that she has. (Listening.) What's that? I thought I heard the wild duck cry.

HJALMAR: The duck's quacking. Father's in the loft.

GREGERS: Is he? (His face radiates joy.) I tell you, you may yet have proof that your poor, misjudged Hedvig loves you!

HJALMAR: Oh, what proof could she give me? I don't dare hope to be reassured from that quarter.

GREGERS: Hedvig's completely free of deceit.

HJALMAR: Oh, Gregers, that's just what I can't be sure of. Who knows what Gina and this Mrs. Sørby have whispered and 3240 gossiped about in all the times they've sat here? And Hedvig uses her ears, you know. Maybe the deed of gift wasn't such a surprise, after all. In fact, I seemed to get that impression.

GREGERS: What is this spirit that's gotten into you?

HJALMAR: I've had my eyes opened. Just wait—you'll see; the deed of gift is only the beginning. Mrs. Sørby has always cared a lot for Hedvig, and now she has the power to do what she wants for the child. They can take her away from me any time they like. 3250

GREGERS: You're the last person in the world Hedvig would leave.

HJALMAR: Don't be too sure of that. If they stand beckoning her with all they have—? Oh, I who've loved her so inexpressibly! I who'd find my highest joy in taking her tenderly by the hand and leading her as one leads a child terrified of the dark through a huge, empty room! I can feel it now with such gnawing certainty; the poor photographer up in this attic has never meant much to her. She's merely been clever

3260  to keep on a good footing with him till the right time came.

GREGERS: You really don't believe that, Hjalmar.

HJALMAR: The worst thing is precisely that I don't know what to believe—that I'll never know. But can you honestly doubt that it's just what I'm saying? (*With a bitter laugh.*) Ah, you're just too idealistic, my dear Gregers! Suppose the others come with their hands full of riches and call out to the child: Leave him. Life waits for you here with us—

GREGERS: (*quickly*) Yes, then what?

HJALMAR: If I asked her then: Hedvig, are you willing to give

3270  up life for me? (*Laughs derisively.*) Yes, thanks—you'd hear all right what answer I'd get!

(*A pistol shot is heard in the loft.*)

GREGERS: (*with a shout of joy*) Hjalmar!

HJALMAR: Hear that. He's got to go hunting as well.

GINA: (*coming in*) Oh, Hjalmar, it sounds like Grandfather's shooting up the loft by himself.

HJALMAR: I'll take a look—

GREGERS: (*animated and exalted*) Wait now! Do you know what that was?

HJALMAR: Of course I know.

3280  GREGERS: No, you don't know. But *I* do. That was the proof!

HJALMAR: What proof?

GREGERS: That was a child's sacrifice. She's had your father shoot the wild duck.

HJALMAR: Shoot the wild duck!

GINA: No, really—!

HJALMAR: What for?

GREGERS: She wanted to sacrifice to you the best thing she had in the world, because she thought then you'd have to love her again.

3290  HJALMAR: (*stirred, gently*) Ah, that child!

GINA: Yes, the things she thinks of!

GREGERS: She only wants your love again, Hjalmar; she felt she couldn't live without it.

GINA: (*struggling with tears*) There you are, Hjalmar.

HJALMAR: Gina, where's she gone?

GINA: (*sniffling*) Poor thing. I guess she's out in the kitchen.

HJALMAR: (*going over and flinging the kitchen door open*) Hedvig, come! Come here to me! (*Looking about.*) No, she's not there.

3300  GINA: Then she's in her own little room.

HJALMAR: (*out of sight*) No, she's not there either. (*Coming back in.*) She may have gone out.

GINA: Yes, you didn't want her around anywhere in the house.

HJALMAR: Oh, if only she comes home soon—so I can just let her know—! Things will work out now, Gregers—for now I really believe we can start life over again.

GREGERS: (*quietly*) I knew it; through the child everything rights itself.

(*EKDAL appears at the door to his room; he is in full uniform and is absorbed in buckling his sword.*)

HJALMAR: (*astonished*) Father! Are you there?

3310  GINA: Were you out gunning in your room?

EKDAL: (*approaching angrily*) So you've been hunting alone,

eh, Hjalmar?

HJALMAR: (*baffled and anxious*) Then it wasn't you who fired a shot in the loft?

EKDAL: Me, shoot? Hm!

GREGERS: (*shouting to* HJALMAR) She's shot the wild duck herself!

HJALMAR: What is all this! (*Rushes to the loft doors, throws them open, looks in and cries:*) Hedvig!

GINA: (*running to the door*) Lord, what now!  3320

HJALMAR: (*going in*) She's lying on the floor!

GINA: (*simultaneously*) Hedvig! (*Going into the loft.*) No, no, no!

EKDAL: Ha, ha! So she's a hunter, too.

(*HJALMAR, GINA, and GREGERS carry HEDVIG into the studio; her right hand hangs down and her fingers curve tightly about the pistol.*)

HJALMAR: (*distraught*) The pistol's gone off. She's wounded herself. Call for help! Help!

GINA: (*running into the hall and calling downstairs*) Relling! Relling! Dr. Relling, come up as quick as you can!

EKDAL: (*hushed*) The woods take revenge.

HJALMAR: (*on his knees by her*) She's just coming to now. She's  3330  coming to now—oh yes, yes.

GINA: (*who has returned*) Where is she wounded? I can't see anything—

(*RELLING hurries in, and right after him,* MOLVIK, *who is without vest or tie, his dress coat open.*)

RELLING: What's up here?

GINA: They say Hedvig shot herself.

HJALMAR: Come here and help.

RELLING: Shot herself! (*He shoves the table to one side and begins to examine her.*)

HJALMAR: (*kneeling still, looking anxiously up at him*) It can't be serious? Huh, Relling? She's hardly bleeding. It can't be  3340  serious?

RELLING: How did this happen?

HJALMAR: Oh, how do I know—

GINA: She wanted to shoot the wild duck.

RELLING: The wild duck?

HJALMAR: The pistol must have gone off.

RELLING: Hm. I see.

EKDAL: The woods take revenge. But I'm not scared, even so. (*He goes into the loft, shutting the door after him.*)

HJALMAR: But Relling—why don't you say something?  3350

RELLING: You can see for yourself that Hedvig is dead.

GINA: (*breaking into tears*) Oh, my child, my child!

GREGERS: (*hoarsely*) In the depths of the sea—

HJALMAR: (*jumping up*) No, no, she *must* live! Oh, in God's name, Relling—just for a moment—just enough so I can tell her how inexpressibly I loved her all the time!

RELLING: It's reached the heart. Internal hemorrhage. She died on the spot.

HJALMAR: And I drove her from me like an animal! And she crept terrified into the loft and died out of love for me.  3360  (*Sobbing.*) Never to make it right again! Never to let her know—! (*Clenching his fists and crying to heaven.*) Oh, you up there—if you *do* exist. Why have you done this to me!

GINA: Hush, hush, you mustn't carry on like that. We just

didn't deserve to keep her, I guess.

MOLVIK: The child isn't dead; she sleepeth.

RELLING: Rubbish!

HJALMAR: (*becoming calm, going over to the sofa to stand, arms folded, looking at* HEDVIG) There she lies, so stiff and still.

3370 RELLING: (*trying to remove the pistol*) She holds it so tight, so tight.

GINA: No, no, Relling, don't break her grip. Let the gun be.

HJALMAR: She should have it with her.

GINA: Yes, let her. But the child shouldn't lie displayed out here. She ought to go into her own little room, she should. Give me a hand, Hjalmar.

(HJALMAR *and* GINA *lift* HEDVIG *between them.*)

HJALMAR: (*as they carry her off*) Oh, Gina, Gina, how can you bear it!

GINA: We must try to help each other. For now she belongs to 3380 us both, you know.

MOLVIK: (*outstretching his arms and mumbling*) Praise be to God. Dust to dust, dust to dust—

RELLING: (*in a whisper*) Shut up, you fool; you're drunk.

(HJALMAR *and* GINA *carry the body out through the kitchen door.* RELLING *closes it after them.* MOLVIK *steals out the hall door.*)

RELLING: (*going over to* GREGERS) Nobody's ever going to sell me the idea that this was an accident.

GREGERS: (*who has stood in a convulsive fit of horror*) Who can say how this awful thing happened?

RELLING: There are powder burns on her blouse. She must have aimed the pistol point-blank at her breast and fired.

GREGERS: Hedvig did not die in vain. Did you notice how grief 3390 freed the greatness in him?

RELLING: The grief of death brings out greatness in almost everyone. But how long do you think this glory will last with *him?*

GREGERS: I should think it would last and grow all his life.

RELLING: In less than a year little Hedvig will be nothing more to him than a pretty theme for recitations.

GREGERS: You dare say that about Hjalmar Ekdal!

RELLING: We'll be lectured on this when the first grass shows on her grave. Then you can hear him spewing out phrases 3400 about "the child torn too soon from her father's heart," and you'll have your chance to watch him souse himself in conceit and self-pity. Wait and see.

GREGERS: If you're right, and I'm wrong, then life isn't worth living.

RELLING: Oh, life would be good in spite of all, if we only could have some peace from these damned shysters who come badgering us poor people with their "summons to the ideal."

GREGERS: (*staring straight ahead*) In that case, I'm glad my destiny is what it is. 3410

RELLING: Beg pardon—but what *is* your destiny?

GREGERS: (*about to leave*) To be the thirteenth man at the table.

RELLING: Oh, the hell you say.

## The Master Builder (1892)

As a portrait of an aging creator reinvigorated by his brush with an attractive younger woman, *The Master Builder* is easily read as a portrait of Ibsen's later career, where the eminent playwright had several similar encounters. But *The Master Builder* goes far beyond autobiography to inaugurate a powerful reading of the work of desire in the structure of the self. As in *The Wild Duck*, the "past" returns to haunt the present of *The Master Builder*. But in this play, Ibsen lends that past a more urgently allegorical, even symbolic force. Solness, for example, no sooner mentions his fear of being displaced by a younger generation, his fear of youth "knocking at the door," than there *is* a knock at the door and the mysterious Hilde Wangel appears. Hilde seems in many ways a figure of Solness's fear and desire. She tells the story of his building of a church in Lysanger, climbing to the top of the spire to crown it with a wreath, and, later in the evening, throwing his arms around her, bending her over backward, and kissing her. What is odd is that Solness at first seems not to re-member this incident, as though Ibsen were trying to blur the line between the historical past of the play and the fantasy life of Solness's—or Hilde's—imagination. Throughout the play, Ibsen emphasizes the power of desire and the ways it distorts and reshapes everyday reality. Solness be-lieves himself to be haunted by "helpers and servers" that mysteriously enact his will while at the same time plunging him into the painful torment of guilt; Solness's brooding wife Aline seems to be grieving the death of her children, but in fact mourns the loss of her dolls, dolls more alive to her than the people who inhabit her bleak world; Hilde dreams of being carried off by lusty Vikings; and Hilde and Solness imagine, and want to inhabit, their "castles in the air."

In *The Master Builder,* that is, the "self" seems a vertiginous abyss, where desire and fantasy blend inextricably with history, with "reality." For there is, of course, an external reality in the play, and Ibsen carefully establishes the narrative of Solness's trip to Lysanger, the lucky fire in Aline's family home that enabled him to begin his career, as a way to place these powerfully disorienting characters in a recognizable world. But Ibsen's staging—as in *The Wild Duck*—works subversively here as well. For although many realistic plays argue that the present is the inevitable consequence of the past, in *The Master Builder* the past merges inseparably with the illusions of memory, with fantasy. Did Solness climb the tower in Lysanger, shaking his fist at God while watching Hilde dance dizzyingly below? Or did Hilde manufacture this story, appealing to the fearfully aging builder with a tale of his youthful courage, daring, and seduction? The play finally makes this "source" in the past unreliable, while at the same time reenacting it at the end of the play, as Sol-ness "again" climbs to the top of the tower, cheered on by the maddening Hilde. As the play moves forward in stage time, Solness seems to move deeper into some shared, primal fantasy of erotic self-possession, the place where he possesses himself, Hilde, "castles in the air." And when he falls from the tower, only Hilde continues to stare aloft, as though her "master builder" had finally learned to climb where he builds.

# — The Master Builder —

## Henrik Ibsen

TRANSLATED BY ROLF FJELDE

### —THE CHARACTERS—

HALVARD SOLNESS, *Master Builder*
ALINE SOLNESS, *his wife*
DR. HERDAL, *the family doctor*
KNUT BROVIK, *former architect, now assistant to* SOLNESS
RAGNAR BROVIK, *his son, a draftsman*
KAJA FOSLI, *his niece, a bookkeeper*
MISS HILDA WANGEL
SOME LADIES
A CROWD IN THE STREET

*The action takes place in and around* SOLNESS's *house.*

### —ACT ONE—

*A plainly furnished workroom in* SOLNESS's *house. Folding doors in the wall to the left lead to the entryway. To the right is a door to the inner rooms. In the rear wall a door stands open on the drafting room. Downstage left, a desk with books, papers, and writing materials. Upstage, beyond the folding doors, a stove. In the right-hand corner, a sofa with a table and a couple of chairs. On the table, a carafe of water and a glass. A smaller table with a rocker and an armchair in the right foreground. Lights for working lit over the drafting room table, on the table in the corner, and on the desk.*

*In the drafting room* KNUT BROVIK *and his son* RAGNAR *are sitting, busy with blueprints and calculations. At the desk in the workroom* KAJA FOSLI *stands, writing in a ledger.* KNUT BROVIK *is a gaunt old man with white hair and beard. He wears a rather threadbare but well-preserved black coat, glasses, and a white muffler somewhat yellowed by age.* RAGNAR BROVIK *is in his thirties, well-dressed, blond, with a slight stoop.* KAJA FOSLI *is a delicate young girl of twenty some years, trimly dressed, but rather sickly in appearance. She is wearing a green eyeshade. All three work on for a time in silence.*

KNUT BROVIK: *(suddenly stands up from the drafting table, as if in fright, his breathing heavy and labored as he comes forward into the doorway)* No, I can't go on much longer!
KAJA: *(moves over to him)* Are you feeling quite bad tonight, Uncle?
BROVIK: Oh, I think it gets worse every day.
RAGNAR: *(having risen and approached them)* Father, you'd better go home. Try to get some sleep—
BROVIK: *(impatiently)* Take to my bed, hm? You want to have
10    me suffocate for good!
KAJA: Go out for a little walk, then.

RAGNAR: Yes, go on. I'll walk with you.
BROVIK: *(vehemently)* I won't go till he's back! Tonight I'm putting it straight up to—*(With suppressed resentment.)* to him—to the chief.
KAJA: *(upset)* Oh no, Uncle—please, let it wait!
RAGNAR: Yes, Father, wait a while!
BROVIK: *(struggling for breath)* Uhh—uhh! I haven't much time to wait.
KAJA: *(listening)* Shh! I hear him down on the stairs. *(All three*    20    *return to work. Short silence.)*

*(*HALVARD SOLNESS *comes in from the entry hall. He is a middle-aged man, strong and forceful, with close-cropped, curly hair, a dark moustache and thick, dark eyebrows. His jacket, gray-green with wide lapels, is buttoned, with the collar turned up. On his head is a soft gray felt hat, and under his arm a couple of portfolios.)*

SOLNESS: *(by the door, pointing at the drafting room and whispering)* Are they gone?
KAJA: *(softly, shaking her head)* No. *(She removes the eyeshade.* SOLNESS *crosses the room, tosses his hat on a chair, sets the folios on the sofa table and then comes back toward the desk.* KAJA *steadily continues writing, but seems nervous and ill at ease.)*
SOLNESS: *(aloud)* What's that you're putting down there, Miss Fosli?    30
KAJA: *(with a start)* Oh, it's just something that—
SOLNESS: Here, let me see. *(Bends over her, pretending to examine the ledger, and whispers.)* Kaja?
KAJA: *(softly, as she writes)* Yes.
SOLNESS: Why do you always take off that shade when I'm around?
KAJA: *(as before)* You know it makes me look so ugly.
SOLNESS: *(smiling)* And you don't want that, do you, Kaja?
KAJA: *(half glancing up at him)* Not for all the world. Not for *you* to see.    40
SOLNESS: *(lightly stroking her hair)* Poor, poor little Kaja—
KAJA: *(ducking her head)* Shh—they can hear you!

*(*SOLNESS *strolls across the room to the right, turns, and pauses at the drafting room door.)*

SOLNESS: Has anyone been in to see me?
RAGNAR: *(getting up)* Yes, the young couple that want to build out at Lovstrand.
SOLNESS: *(growling)* Oh, them. Well, they can wait. I'm not quite clear on the plans yet.
RAGNAR: *(coming forward and rather hesitantly)* They did want so badly to have those drawings soon.
SOLNESS: *(as before)* Good God—they all want that!    50
BROVIK: *(looking up)* They said they had such a longing to

move into their own place.

SOLNESS: All right, all right—we know that! So they'll make do with anything—any kind of a—a roost. Just a peg to hang their hats. But not a home. No—no, thanks! They can go find somebody else. Tell them that when they come again.

BROVIK: *(pushing his glasses up on his forehead and staring at him in amazement)* Find somebody else? You'd turn that commission down?

60 SOLNESS: *(impatiently)* Yes, damn it all, yes! If that's how it's going to be—It's better than slapping a shack together. *(Exploding.)* What do I know about these people!

BROVIK: They're good solid people. Ragnar knows them. He's like one of the family. Very solid people.

SOLNESS: Ahh, solid—solid! That's not what I mean. Lord—don't *you* understand me either? *(Sharply.)* I'll have nothing to do with strangers. They can find anyone they please, for all I care!

BROVIK: *(rising)* Seriously, you mean that?

70 SOLNESS: *(sullenly)* Yes—for once. *(He paces across the room.)*

*(BROVIK exchanges a look with RAGNAR, who makes a warning gesture. He then comes into the workroom.)*

BROVIK: May I have a word or two with you?

SOLNESS: Gladly.

BROVIK: *(to KAJA)* Kaja, go inside a while.

KAJA: *(uneasily)* Oh, but Uncle—

BROVIK: Do as I say, child. And close the door after you.

*(KAJA goes reluctantly into the drafting room and, with a fearful and imploring look at SOLNESS, shuts the door.)*

BROVIK: *(dropping his voice)* I don't want the poor children knowing how sick I am.

SOLNESS: Yes, you're looking quite done in these days.

80 BROVIK: It's almost over with me. My strength—it's less every day.

SOLNESS: Sit down, rest a bit.

BROVIK: Thanks—may I?

SOLNESS: *(adjusting the armchair)* Here, please. Well?

BROVIK: *(having seated himself with difficulty)* Yes, well, it's Ragnar; he's on my mind. What's going to happen with him?

SOLNESS: Your son, he can stay on here with me, naturally, as long as he wants.

BROVIK: But that's just the thing: it's not what he wants. He 90 thinks he can't—now, any longer.

SOLNESS: Well, I'd say he's got a very nice salary. But if he's out for a little more, I wouldn't be averse to—

BROVIK: No, no, it isn't that! *(Impatiently.)* But he needs a chance to work on his own.

SOLNESS: *(not looking at him)* Do you think Ragnar has really enough talent for that?

BROVIK: Don't you see, *that's* the worst of it. That I'm beginning to have my doubts about the boy. For you've never said so much as—as one word of encouragement about him. 100 But then I think it can't be any other way—he *must* have the talent.

SOLNESS: Well, but he hasn't learned anything yet—nothing basic. Nothing but drafting.

BROVIK: *(looking at him with veiled hatred, his voice hoarse)* You hadn't learned anything either, back when you worked for me. But you got along all right. *(Breathing heavily.)*

Pushed your way up. Cut the ground out from under me—and so many others.

SOLNESS: Well—I had luck on my side.

BROVIK: True enough. Everything was on your side. But you 110 can't have the heart, then, to let me die—without seeing what Ragnar can do. And then, I'd like so much to see them married—before I'm gone.

SOLNESS: *(sharply)* Is she the one who wants that?

BROVIK: Not so much Kaja. But Ragnar talks of it every day. *(Beseeching him.)* You must—you *must* help him get some independent work now! I've got to see something the boy has done. You hear me!

SOLNESS: *(angrily)* What the hell—you think I can pull down commissions out of the moon for him! 120

BROVIK: He could have a fine commission right now. A big piece of work.

SOLNESS: *(surprised and disconcerted)* He could?

BROVIK: If you'd give permission.

SOLNESS: What work is that?

BROVIK: *(hesitating a bit)* He could build that house at Lovstrand.

SOLNESS: That! But I'm building that!

BROVIK: Oh, but you have no more interest in it.

SOLNESS: *(flaring up)* No interest! Me! Who says so? 130

BROVIK: You said it yourself just now.

SOLNESS: Oh, don't listen to what I—say. Would they give Ragnar that job?

BROVIK: Yes. He knows the family. And then, just for fun, he's worked out the plans and the estimate, the whole thing—

SOLNESS: And they like the plans? Those people—?

BROVIK: Yes. So if you'd just go over them and give your approval, then—

SOLNESS: Then they'd invite Ragnar to build their home.

BROVIK: They really liked what he wants to do. They thought it 140 was completely new and different—that's what they said.

SOLNESS: Aha! New! Modern! None of the old-fashioned stuff I build!

BROVIK: They thought it was something—different.

SOLNESS: *(with suppressed bitterness)* And they came here to Ragnar—while I was out!

BROVIK: They came to see you—and also to ask if you'd be willing to give up—

SOLNESS: *(erupting)* Give up! I!

BROVIK: That is, if you found Ragnar's plans— 150

SOLNESS: I—give up for your son!

BROVIK: Give up the commission, they meant.

SOLNESS: Oh, it's one and the same. *(With a wry laugh.)* So that's it! Halvard Solness—he ought to start giving up now! Make room for youth. For even the youngest. Just make room! Room!

BROVIK: Good Lord, there's room enough here for more than one man—

SOLNESS: There's not that much room here anymore. But, never mind—I'm not giving up! I never give ground. Not 160 voluntarily. Never in this world, never!

BROVIK: *(rising with effort)* And I—must I give up life without hope? Without joy? Without faith and trust in Ragnar? Without seeing a single one of his works? Is that it?

SOLNESS: *(half turning away, in a whisper)* Don't ask any more now.

BROVIK: Yes, answer me. Shall I go into death so poor?

SOLNESS: (*after an inner struggle, he speaks at last in a low but firm voice*) You have to face death the best you can.

170 BROVIK: Then that's it. (*He walks away.*)

SOLNESS: (*following him, half in desperation*) Don't you see— what else can I do! I'm made the way I am! I can't change myself over!

BROVIK: No, no, I guess you can't. (*Stumbles and halts by the sofa table.*) May I have a glass of water?

SOLNESS: Please. (*Pours and hands him the glass.*)

BROVIK: Thanks. (*Drinks and sets the glass down.*)

SOLNESS: (*going over and opening the door to the drafting room*) Ragnar—come take your father home.

(RAGNAR *quickly gets up. He and* KAJA *come into the workroom.*)

180 RAGNAR: Father, what is it?

BROVIK: Give me your arm. Then we'll go.

RAGNAR: All right. You get your things too, Kaja.

SOLNESS: Miss Fosli will have to stay on a moment—I've a letter to be written.

BROVIK: (*looking at* SOLNESS) Good night. Sleep well—if you can.

SOLNESS: Good night.

(BROVIK *and* RAGNAR *leave by way of the entry hall.* KAJA *goes over to the desk.* SOLNESS *stands, head bent, to the right by the armchair.*)

KAJA: (*hesitating*) Is there a letter—?

SOLNESS: (*brusquely*) Of course not. (*With a fierce look at her.*)
190    Kaja!

KAJA: (*frightened, softly*) Yes?

SOLNESS: (*decisively, beckoning her*) Over here! Quick!

KAJA: (*reluctantly*) Yes.

SOLNESS: (*as before*) Closer!

KAJA: (*obeying*) What do you want of me?

SOLNESS: (*looking at her a moment*) Are you at the root of all this?

KAJA: No, no, don't believe that!

SOLNESS: But marriage—that's what you want now.

200 KAJA: (*quietly*) Ragnar and I have been engaged four or five years, and so—

SOLNESS: So you think it just can't go on forever—isn't that it?

KAJA: Ragnar and Uncle tell me I must—so I think I'll have to give in.

SOLNESS: (*more gently*) Kaja, don't you really care a little for Ragnar too?

KAJA: I cared very much for Ragnar once—before I came here to you.

SOLNESS: But no more? Not at all?

210 KAJA: (*passionately, extending her clasped hands out toward him*) Oh, you know I care now for one, only one! Nobody else in this whole world. I'll never care for anyone else!

SOLNESS: Yes, you say that. And then you desert me all the same. Leave me to struggle with everything alone.

KAJA: But couldn't I stay on with you even if Ragnar—?

SOLNESS: No, no, that's out of the question. If Ragnar goes out on his own, he'll be needing you himself.

KAJA: (*wringing her hands*) Oh, I don't see how I *can* ever part from you! It's just so completely impossible.

SOLNESS: Then try to rid Ragnar of these stupid ideas. Marry 220 him as much as you like—(*Changing his tone.*) Well, I mean—don't let him throw over a good job here with me. Because—then I can keep *you* too, Kaja dear.

KAJA: Oh yes, how lovely that would be, if only we could manage it!

SOLNESS: (*caressing her head with both hands and whispering*) Because I can't be without you. You understand? I've got to have you close to me every day.

KAJA: (*shivering with excitement*) Oh, God! God!

SOLNESS: (*kissing her hair*) Kaja—Kaja!    230

KAJA: (*sinks down before him*) Oh, how good you are to me! How incredibly good you are!

SOLNESS: (*intensely*) Get up! Get up now, I—I hear someone coming!

(*He helps her up. She falters over to the desk.* MRS. SOLNESS *enters by the door on the right. She looks thin and careworn, but traces of former beauty still show. Blonde ringlets. Dressed stylishly, entirely in black. Speaks rather slowly in a plaintive voice.*)

MRS. SOLNESS: (*in the doorway*) Halvard!

SOLNESS: (*turning*) Oh, is it you, dear—?

MRS. SOLNESS: (*with a glance at* KAJA) I'm afraid I'm intruding.

SOLNESS: Not a bit. Miss Fosli has one short letter to write.

MRS. SOLNESS: Yes—I see that.

SOLNESS: What did you want me for, Aline?    240

MRS. SOLNESS: I just wanted to say that Dr. Herdal's in the living room. Maybe you could join us, Halvard?

SOLNESS: (*looks suspiciously at her*) Hm—is the doctor so anxious to talk with me?

MRS. SOLNESS: No, not exactly anxious. He stopped by to see me, but he'd like to say hello to you too.

SOLNESS: (*laughing to himself*) Yes, I can imagine. Well, then you'd better ask him to wait a while.

MRS. SOLNESS: And you'll look in on him later?

SOLNESS: Possibly. Later—later, dear. In a while.    250

MRS. SOLNESS: (*glancing again at* KAJA) Don't forget now, Halvard. (*She leaves, closing the door after her.*)

KAJA: (*softly*) Oh, my Lord—she must think the worst of me!

SOLNESS: Oh, certainly not. No more than usual, anyway. Still, it's best if you go now, Kaja.

KAJA: Yes, I've *got* to go now.

SOLNESS: (*sternly*) And then you'll settle up that business for me—you hear!

KAJA: Oh, if only it were just up to *me*, then—

SOLNESS: Listen, I want it settled! Tomorrow the latest!    260

KAJA: (*apprehensively*) If it doesn't work out, then I'd rather break off with him.

SOLNESS: (*explosively*) Break off with him! Are you crazy, completely! You'd break it off?

KAJA: (*in desperation*) Yes. I have to—have to stay here with you! I can't ever leave you! Ever! That's impossible!

SOLNESS: (*in an outburst*) But damn it—Ragnar! Ragnar's the one that I—

KAJA: (*looking at him with terrified eyes*) Is it more for Ragnar's sake that—that you—?    270

SOLNESS: (*checking himself*) Of course not! Oh, you don't see what I mean either. (*Gently and softly.*) Obviously, it's you that I need here. You above all, Kaja. But that's precisely why you have to make Ragnar hang onto his job. There, there—run along home now.

KAJA: All right—good night, then.

SOLNESS: Good night. (*As she starts out.*) Oh, wait—are Ragnar's drawings in there?

KAJA: Yes, I don't think he took them along.

280 SOLNESS: See if you can locate them for me. I could give them a look maybe, after all.

KAJA: (*in delight*) Oh yes, please do!

SOLNESS: For your sake, Kaja, my sweet. Now let's have them in a hurry, you hear?

(KAJA *runs into the drafting room, rummages anxiously in the table drawer, pulls out a portfolio and brings it.*)

KAJA: All the drawings are here.

SOLNESS: Fine. Lay them over there on the table.

KAJA: (*does so*) Good night. (*Imploringly.*) And please—think well of me.

SOLNESS: Oh, you know I do, always. Good night, my dear lit-
290 tle Kaja. (*Glancing to the right.*) Go on now—go!

(MRS. SOLNESS *and* DR. HERDAL *enter through the door on the right. He is a plump, elderly man with a round, complacent face, smooth shaven; he has light, thinning hair, and gold spectacles.*)

MRS. SOLNESS: (*standing in the doorway*) Halvard, I can't keep the doctor any longer.

SOLNESS: Well, come in, then.

MRS. SOLNESS: (*to* KAJA, *who is dimming the desk lamp*) All finished with the letter, Miss Fosli?

KAJA: (*confused*) The letter—?

SOLNESS: Yes, it was very short.

MRS. SOLNESS: I'm sure it was terribly short.

SOLNESS: You may as well leave, Miss Fosli. And be here on
300 time in the morning.

KAJA: I certainly will. Good night, Mrs. Solness. (*She goes out by the hall door.*)

MRS. SOLNESS: You've certainly been in luck, Halvard, to have gotten hold of that girl.

SOLNESS: Oh yes. She's useful in all kinds of ways.

MRS. SOLNESS: She looks it.

HERDAL: A clever bookkeeper, too?

SOLNESS: Well—she's had a lot of experience these past two years. And then she's willing and eager to take on anything.

310 MRS. SOLNESS: Yes, that must be such a great comfort—

SOLNESS: It is—especially when one's so used to doing without.

MRS. SOLNESS: (*in a tone of mild reproach*) Can *you* really say *that*, Halvard?

SOLNESS: Ah, my dear Aline, no, no. I beg your pardon.

MRS. SOLNESS: Don't trouble yourself. Well, Doctor, so you'll stop in again later and have some tea with us?

HERDAL: As soon as I've made that house call, I'll be back.

MRS. SOLNESS: Thank you. (*She goes out the door right.*)

320 SOLNESS: Are you pressed for time, Doctor?

HERDAL: No, not a bit.

SOLNESS: May I have a few words with you?

HERDAL: Yes, by all means.

SOLNESS: Then let's sit down. (*He motions the doctor toward the rocker, and after seating himself in the armchair, looks at him sharply.*) Tell me—did you notice anything about Aline?

HERDAL: Just now, you mean, when she was here?

SOLNESS: Yes. With respect to me. Did you notice anything?

HERDAL: (*smiling*) Well, really—one could hardly help notic- 330
ing that your wife—hm—

SOLNESS: Go on.

HERDAL: That your wife doesn't think very much of this Miss Fosli.

SOLNESS: Nothing else? I could tell that myself.

HERDAL: And, after all, it's not so very surprising.

SOLNESS: What?

HERDAL: That she isn't exactly pleased that you enjoy another woman's company every day.

SOLNESS: That's true, you're right—and so is Aline. But it can't 340
be changed.

HERDAL: Couldn't you hire a man instead?

SOLNESS: Just anyone off the street? No, thanks—that isn't the way I work.

HERDAL: But what if your wife—? When she *is* so delicate, what if she can't endure this thing?

SOLNESS: Even so—I'm tempted to say it can't make a bit of difference. I've got to keep Kaja Fosli. Nobody else will do.

HERDAL: Nobody else?

SOLNESS: (*curtly*) No, nobody else.                        350

HERDAL: (*draws his chair in closer*) If I may, Mr. Solness, I'd like to ask you something, just between us.

SOLNESS: Yes, go ahead.

HERDAL: Women, you know—in certain areas they do have a painfully keen intuition—

SOLNESS: That they do. So—?

HERDAL: Well. All right, then. If your wife simply can't bear this Kaja Fosli—

SOLNESS: Yes, what then?

HERDAL: Hasn't she perhaps some tiny grounds for this in- 360
stinctive dislike?

SOLNESS: (*looks at him and rises*) Aha!

HERDAL: Now don't get excited. But really—hasn't she?

SOLNESS: (*his voice clipped and decisive*) No.

HERDAL: Not the slightest grounds?

SOLNESS: Nothing, except her own suspicious mind.

HERDAL: I realize you've known a good many women in your life.

SOLNESS: I have, yes.

HERDAL: And thought very well of some of them, too.          370

SOLNESS: Oh yes, that also.

HERDAL: But in this case—there's nothing of that kind involved?

SOLNESS: No. Nothing whatever—on my side.

HERDAL: But on hers?

SOLNESS: I don't think you've any right to ask about that, Doctor.

HERDAL: We were discussing your wife's intuition.

SOLNESS: We were, yes. And for that matter—(*Dropping his voice.*) Aline's intuition, as you call it—you know, to a cer- 380
tain extent it's proved itself.

HERDAL: There—see!

SOLNESS: Dr. Herdal—let me tell you a strange story. That is, if you don't mind listening.

HERDAL: I like listening to strange stories.

SOLNESS: Ah, that's good. I guess you remember how I took on Knut Brovik and his son here—that time when the old man nearly went under.

HERDAL: I vaguely remember, yes.

390 SOLNESS: Because, you know, they're really a clever pair, those two. They've got ability, each in his own way. But then the son went out and got engaged. And then, of course, he was all for getting married—and launching his own career as a builder. Because the young people today, that's all they ever think about.

HERDAL: (*laughing*) Yes, they have this bad habit of pairing off.

SOLNESS: Well, but *I* can't be bothered by that. You see, I need Ragnar—and the old man as well. He has a real knack for calculating stresses, cubic content—all that damned detail 400 work.

HERDAL: Of course, that's important too.

SOLNESS: Yes, it is. But Ragnar, he felt he wanted and he had to be out on his own. There just wasn't any reasoning with him.

HERDAL: Even so, he stayed on with you.

SOLNESS: Yes, but now listen to what happened. One day she came in, this Kaja Fosli, on some errand for them. First time she'd ever been here. And when I saw those two, how completely wrapped up in each other they were, then the 410 thought struck me: suppose I could get her here in the office, then maybe Ragnar would stay put too.

HERDAL: That was reasonable enough.

SOLNESS: But I didn't breathe a word of any of this then—just stood looking at her—every ounce of me wishing that I had her here. I made a little friendly conversation about one thing or another. And then she went away.

HERDAL: So?

SOLNESS: But the next day, in the late evening, after old Brovik and Ragnar had gone, she came by to see me again, acting 420 as if we'd already struck a bargain.

HERDAL: Bargain? What about?

SOLNESS: About precisely what I'd been standing there wishing before—even though I hadn't uttered a word of it.

HERDAL: That *is* strange.

SOLNESS: Yes, isn't it? So she wanted to know what her job would be—and whether she'd be starting the very next morning. Things like that.

HERDAL: Don't you think she did that to be with her fiancé?

SOLNESS: I thought so too, at first. But no, that wasn't it. From 430 the moment she came here to work, she started drifting away from him.

HERDAL: And over to you?

SOLNESS: Yes, completely. If I look at her when her back is turned, I can tell she feels it. She trembles and quivers if I even come near her. What do you make of it?

HERDAL: Hm—it's easy enough to explain.

SOLNESS: Well, but the rest of it, then? The fact that she thought I'd told her what I had only wished and willed—all in silence, inwardly. To myself. What do you say about that? 440 Can you explain such a thing, Dr. Herdal?

HERDAL: No, I wouldn't attempt to.

SOLNESS: I thought as much. That's why I've never cared to discuss it till now. But you see, as time goes on, I'm finding it such a damned nuisance. Here, day after day, I have to keep on pretending that I'm—And then, poor girl, it's not fair to her. (*Furiously.*) But I can't help it! If she runs off—then Ragnar will follow, out on his own.

HERDAL: And you haven't told your wife this whole story.

SOLNESS: No.

HERDAL: Why in the world haven't you?     450

SOLNESS: (*looking intently at him, his voice constrained*) Because I feel that there's almost a kind of beneficial self-torment in letting Aline do me an injustice.

HERDAL: (*shaking his head*) I don't understand one blessed word of this.

SOLNESS: Yes, don't you see—it's rather like making a small payment on a boundless, incalculable debt—

HERDAL: To your wife?

SOLNESS: Yes. And it always eases the mind a bit. Then you can breathe more freely for a while, you know.     460

HERDAL: God help me if I understand a word—

SOLNESS: (*breaking in, and again getting up*). Yes, all right—so we won't speak of it anymore, then. (*He meanders across the room, comes back, and stops by the table. Looks at the doctor with a quiet smile.*) Now you really think you've done a neat job of drawing me out, hm, Doctor?

HERDAL: (*somewhat upset*) Drawing you out? Mr. Solness, I'm still very much in the dark.

SOLNESS: Oh, come now—confess. Because really, you know, it's been so obvious to me!     470

HERDAL: *What's* so obvious to you?

SOLNESS: (*slowly, in an undertone*) That behind this genial manner, you're keeping your eye on me.

HERDAL: Am I! Why on earth should I do that?

SOLNESS: Because you think I'm—(*Explosively.*) Oh, damn it! You think the same as Aline about me.

HERDAL: But what does she think of you, then?

SOLNESS: She's begun to think that I'm—somewhat ill.

HERDAL: Ill! YOU! She's never breathed a word of it to me. What is it that's wrong with you, then?     480

SOLNESS: (*leans over the back of the chair and whispers*) Aline's got the idea that I'm mad. *That's* what she thinks.

HERDAL: (*rising*) But my dear Mr. Solness—!

SOLNESS: Yes, on my soul she does! And she has you thinking the same. Oh, I tell you, Doctor—I can see it in you so clear, so clear. Because I'm not so easily fooled, I'm not, I can tell you that.

HERDAL: (*stares at him, amazed*) I've never, Mr. Solness—never had the least inkling of anything like this.

SOLNESS: (*with a skeptical smile*) Really? Not at all?     490

HERDAL: No, never! And your wife certainly hasn't either—I'd almost swear to that.

SOLNESS: Well, you'd better not. Because, you know, maybe, in a way—maybe she's not so far off.

HERDAL: Look, I'm telling you now, really—!

SOLNESS: (*breaking in, with a sweep of his hand*) All right there, Doctor—then let's not go on with this. Each to his own, that's the best. (*His tone changes to quiet amusement.*) But now listen, Doctor—hm—

HERDAL: Yes?     500

SOLNESS: If you don't think, then, that I'm, somehow—ill—or crazy or mad and that sort of thing—

HERDAL: Then what, hm?

SOLNESS: Then I guess you must imagine that I'm a very happy man.

HERDAL: Is *that* no more than imagination?

SOLNESS: *(with a laugh)* Oh no, not a chance! God forbid! Just think—to be Solness, the master builder! Halvard Solness! Oh, thanks a lot!

510 HERDAL: Yes, I must say, to *me* it seems that you've had luck with you to an incredible degree.

SOLNESS: *(masking a wan smile)* So I have. Can't complain of that.

HERDAL: First, that hideous old robbers' den burned down for you. And that was really a stroke of luck.

SOLNESS: *(seriously)* It was Aline's family home that burned—don't forget.

HERDAL: Yes, for *her* it must have been a heavy loss.

SOLNESS: She hasn't recovered right to this day. Not in all these 520 twelve—thirteen years.

HERDAL: What followed after, that must have been the worst blow for her.

SOLNESS: The two together.

HERDAL: But you yourself—*you* rose from those ashes. You began as a poor boy from the country—and now you stand the top man in your field. Ah, yes, Mr. Solness, you've surely had luck on your side.

SOLNESS: *(glancing nervously at him)* Yes, but that's exactly why I've got this horrible fear.

530 HERDAL: Fear? For having luck on your side?

SOLNESS: It racks me, this fear—it racks me, morning and night. Because someday things have to change, you'll see.

HERDAL: Oh, rot! Where's this change coming from?

SOLNESS: *(with firm conviction)* From the young.

HERDAL: Hah! The young! I'd hardly say that you're obsolete. No, you've probably never been better established than you are now.

SOLNESS: The change is coming. I can sense it. And I feel that it's coming closer. Someone or other will set up the cry: Step 540 back for *me!* And all the others will storm in after, shaking their fists and shouting: Make room—make room—make room! Yes, Doctor, you better look out. Someday youth will come here, knocking at the door—

HERDAL: *(laughing)* Well, good Lord, what if they do?

SOLNESS: What if they do? Well, then it's the end of Solness, the master builder.

*(A knock at the door to the left.)*

SOLNESS: *(with a start)* What's that? Did you hear it?

HERDAL: Somebody's knocking.

SOLNESS: *(loudly)* Come in!

*(HILDA WANGEL enters from the hall. She is of medium height, supple and well-formed. Slight sunburn. Dressed in hiking clothes, with shortened skirt, sailor blouse open at the throat, and a little sailor hat. She has a knapsack on her back, a plaid in a strap, and a long alpenstock.)*

550 HILDA: *(goes directly to SOLNESS, her eyes shining with happiness)* Good evening!

SOLNESS: *(looking hesitantly at her)* Good evening—

HILDA: *(laughing)* I almost think you don't recognize me!

SOLNESS: No—really—I must say, just at the moment—

HERDAL: *(coming over)* But I recognize you, young lady—

HILDA: *(delighted)* Oh no! It's you, that—?

HERDAL: That's right, it's me. *(To SOLNESS.)* We met up at one of the mountain lodges last summer. *(To HILDA.)* What happened to all those other ladies?

560 HILDA: Oh, they went off down the west slope.

HERDAL: They didn't quite like all our fun in the evenings.

HILDA: No, they certainly didn't.

HERDAL: *(shaking his finger at her)* Of course, we can't quite say you didn't flirt with us a bit.

HILDA: I'd a lot rather do that than sit knitting knee socks with all the old hens.

HERDAL: *(laughing)* I couldn't agree with you more!

SOLNESS: Did you just get in town this evening?

HILDA: Yes, just now.

570 HERDAL: All by yourself, Miss Wangel?

HILDA: Of course!

SOLNESS: Wangel? Is your name Wangel?

HILDA: *(looks at him with amused surprise)* Well, I should hope so.

SOLNESS: Then aren't you the daughter of the public health officer up at Lysanger?

HILDA: *(still amused)* Sure. Whose daughter did you think I was?

SOLNESS: Ah, so that's where we met, up there. The summer I went up and built a tower on the old church.

580 HILDA: *(more serious)* Yes, it was then.

SOLNESS: Well, that's a long time back.

HILDA: *(her eyes fixed on him)* It's exactly ten years to the day.

SOLNESS: I'd swear you weren't any more than a child then.

HILDA: *(carelessly)* Around twelve—thirteen, maybe.

HERDAL: Is this the first time you've been here in town, Miss Wangel?

HILDA: Yes, that's right.

SOLNESS: And you probably don't know anyone, hm?

590 HILDA: No one but you. Yes, and of course your wife.

SOLNESS: Then you know *her* too?

HILDA: Just slightly. We were together a few days at that health resort.

SOLNESS: Ah, up *there.*

HILDA: She told me please to visit her if I ever came down into town. *(Smiles.)* Even though she really didn't have to.

SOLNESS: Funny she never spoke of it—

*(HILDA puts her stick down by the stove, slips off the knapsack, and sets it and the plaid on the sofa. DR. HERDAL tries to assist. SOLNESS stands, gazing at her.)*

HILDA: *(going up to him)* So now, if I may, I'd like to stay here overnight.

SOLNESS: I'm sure that can be arranged.

600 HILDA: 'Cause I haven't any other clothes, except what I've got on. Oh, and a set of underthings in my knapsack. But they better be washed. They're real grimy.

SOLNESS: Oh, well, that's easy to manage. Just let me speak to my wife—

HERDAL: Then I'll go on to my house call.

SOLNESS: Yes, do that. And stop back again later.

HERDAL: *(playfully, with a glance at HILDA)* Oh, you can bet I will! *(Laughing.)* You read the future all right, Mr. Solness!

610 SOLNESS: How so?

HERDAL: Youth *did* come along, knocking at your door.

SOLNESS: *(buoyantly)* Yes, but that was something else completely.

HERDAL: Oh yes, yes. Definitely!

*(He goes out the hall door.* SOLNESS *opens the door on the right and calls into the room beyond.)*

SOLNESS: Aline! Would you come in here, please. There's a Miss Wangel to see you.

MRS. SOLNESS: *(appearing at the door)* Who did you say? *(Sees* HILDA.*)* Oh, is it you, then? *(Goes over and takes her hand.)* So you've come to town after all.

620 SOLNESS: Miss Wangel's just arrived. And she's wondering if she might stay here overnight.

MRS. SOLNESS: Here with us? Why, of course.

SOLNESS: To get her clothes fixed up a bit, you know.

MRS. SOLNESS: I'll do what I can for you. It's no more than my duty. Is your trunk on the way?

HILDA: I haven't any trunk.

MRS. SOLNESS: Well, it'll all work out, I guess. Now if you'll just make yourself at home here with my husband a while, I'll see about getting a room comfortable for you.

630 SOLNESS: Can't we give up one of the nurseries? They're all ready and waiting.

MRS. SOLNESS: Oh yes. We've more than enough room there. *(To* HILDA.*)* Just sit down and rest a bit. *(She goes out, right.)*

*(*HILDA, *her hands behind her back, wanders around the room, looking at one thing and another.* SOLNESS *stands in front of the table, his hands also behind his back, following her with his eyes.)*

HILDA: *(stops and looks at him)* You have several nurseries?

SOLNESS: There are three nurseries in the house.

HILDA: That's plenty. You must have an awful lot of children.

SOLNESS: No. We have no children. But now you can be the child here for a while.

HILDA: Yes, for tonight. There won't be a peep out of me. I'm
640    going to try to sleep like a stone.

SOLNESS: Yes, you're pretty tired, I'll bet.

HILDA: Oh no! But, after all—You know it is so ravishing just to lie and dream.

SOLNESS: Do you often dream at night?

HILDA: Oh yes! Nearly always.

SOLNESS: What do you dream about most?

HILDA: I won't tell you, not tonight. Some other time—maybe. *(She starts wandering about the room again, stops at the desk, and fingers the books and papers a little.)*

650 SOLNESS: *(approaching her).* Something you're looking for?

HILDA: No, it's only to see all this here. *(Turning.)* But I shouldn't, maybe?

SOLNESS: Yes, go ahead.

HILDA: Is it you that writes in this big ledger?

SOLNESS: No, that's the bookkeeper.

HILDA: A woman?

SOLNESS: *(smiles)* Of course.

HILDA: Someone you have working here?

SOLNESS: Yes.

660 HILDA: Is she married?

SOLNESS: No, she's single.

HILDA: I see.

SOLNESS: But I understand she's getting married now quite soon.

HILDA: That's very nice—for her.

SOLNESS: But not so nice for me. Because then I'll have no one to help me.

HILDA: Can't you find somebody else who's just as good?

SOLNESS: Maybe you'd like to stay here and—and write in the ledger?    670

HILDA: *(giving him a dark look).* Yes, wouldn't that suit you! No, thanks—we're not having any of that. *(She strolls across the room again and settles into the rocker.* SOLNESS *follows her over to the table.* HILDA *goes on in the same tone.)* Because there are plenty of other things to be done around here. *(Looks up at him, smiling.)* Don't you think so too?

SOLNESS: Why, of course. First of all, I expect you'll want to tour the shops and do yourself up in style.

HILDA: *(amused)* No, somehow I think I'll pass that up.

SOLNESS: Oh?    680

HILDA: Yes—since, you see, I'm completely broke.

SOLNESS: *(laughing).* No trunk, or money either!

HILDA: Nothing of both. But shoot! What's the difference, anyway?

SOLNESS: Ah, I really like you for that!

HILDA: Only for that?

SOLNESS: Among other things. *(Sits in the armchair.)* Is your father still living?

HILDA: Yes, still living.

SOLNESS: And are you thinking of studying here now?    690

HILDA: No, that's not what I'd thought.

SOLNESS: But you *are* staying here for some time, I suppose?

HILDA: Depends how things go. *(A pause, while she sits rocking and looking at him half seriously, half with a suppressed smile. She then takes off her hat and places it on the table before her.)* Mr. Solness?

SOLNESS: Yes?

HILDA: Are you very forgetful?

SOLNESS: Forgetful? No, not as far as *I* know.

HILDA: But do you absolutely not want to talk to me about what    700 happened up there?

SOLNESS: *(with a momentary start)* Up at Lysanger? *(Carelessly.)* Well, there's not much to talk about, I'd say.

HILDA: *(gazing reproachfully at him)* How can you sit there and say that!

SOLNESS: All right, *you* tell me about it then.

HILDA: When the tower was finished, we had a big function in town.

SOLNESS: Yes, that's one day I won't soon forget.

HILDA: *(smiling)* Won't you? So good of you!    710

SOLNESS: Good?

HILDA: They had music in the churchyard. And there were hundreds and hundreds of people. We schoolgirls were all dressed in white, and we had flags, all of us.

SOLNESS: Oh yes, the flags—I remember them, all right.

HILDA: Then you climbed straight up the scaffolding, straight to the very top—and you had a great wreath with you—and you hung it up high on the weather vane.

SOLNESS: *(interrupting brusquely)* I did that back in those days. It's an old custom.    720

HILDA: It was so wonderfully thrilling to stand below, looking up at you. What if he slipped and fell—he, the master builder himself!

SOLNESS: *(as if thrusting the subject aside)* Yes, all right, that could have happened too. Because one of those little devils in white—how she carried on screaming up at me—

HILDA: (*eyes sparkling in delight*) "Hurray for Mr. Solness, the master builder!" Yes!

SOLNESS: Waving her flag and flourishing it till my—my head
730  nearly spun at the sight of it.

HILDA: (*growing more quiet and serious*) That little devil—that was *me*.

SOLNESS: (*peering fixedly at her*) I'm sure of that now.

HILDA: (*vivacious again*) It was so terribly thrilling and lovely. I'd never dreamt that anywhere in the world there was a builder who could build a tower so high. And then, that you could stand there right at the top, large as life! And that you weren't the least bit dizzy! That's what made me so—almost dizzy to realize.

740  SOLNESS: What makes you so sure I wasn't—?

HILDA: (*deprecatingly*) Oh, honestly—come on! I felt it within me. How else could you stand up there singing?

SOLNESS: (*stares astonished at her*) Singing? I sang?

HILDA: Yes, really you did.

SOLNESS: (*shaking his head*) I've never sung a note in my life.

HILDA: Yes, you were singing then. It sounded like harps in the air.

SOLNESS: (*thoughtfully*) It's something very peculiar—this.

HILDA: (*silent a moment, then looking at him and speaking
750  softly*) But then—afterwards—came the *real* thing.

SOLNESS: The real thing?

HILDA: (*her vivacity kindling again*) Oh, now I don't have to remind you of that!

SOLNESS: Better give me a little reminder there, too.

HILDA: Don't you remember a big banquet for you at the club?

SOLNESS: Of course. That must have been the same afternoon—because I left the next morning.

HILDA: And after the club, you were asked home to our place for the evening.

760  SOLNESS: You're right, Miss Wangel. Amazing how you can keep all these details clear in your mind.

HILDA: Details! Oh, you! I suppose it was just another detail that I was alone in the room when you came in?

SOLNESS: Were you?

HILDA: (*not answering him*) You didn't call me any little devil then.

SOLNESS: No, I guess not.

HILDA: You said I was lovely in my white dress-and that I looked like a little princess.

770  SOLNESS: I'm sure you did, Miss Wangel. And then, feeling the way I did that day, so light and free—

HILDA: And then you said that when I grew up, I could be *your* princess.

SOLNESS: (*with a short laugh*) Really—I said that too?

HILDA: Yes, you did. And when I asked how long I should wait, then you said you'd come back in ten years, like a troll, and carry me off—to Spain or someplace. And there you promised to buy me a kingdom.

SOLNESS: (*as before*) Well, after a good meal one's not in a
780  mood to count pennies. But did I really *say* all that?

HILDA: (*laughing softly*) Yes, and you also said what the kingdom would be called.

SOLNESS: Oh? What?

HILDA: It was going to be the Kingdom of Orangia, you said.

SOLNESS: Ah, that's a delectable name.

HILDA: No, I didn't like it at all. It was as if you were out to make fun of me.

SOLNESS: But I hadn't the slightest intention to.

HILDA: No, it wouldn't seem so—not after what you did next—

SOLNESS: What on earth did I do next?  790

HILDA: Well, this is really the limit if you've even forgotten *that!* A thing like that I think anybody ought to remember.

SOLNESS: All right, just give me a tiny hint, then, maybe—hm?

HILDA: (*looking intently at him*) You caught me up and kissed me, Mr. Solness.

SOLNESS: (*open-mouthed, getting up*) I did!

HILDA: Oh yes, that you did. You held me in both your arms and bent me back and kissed me—many times.

SOLNESS: But, my dear Miss Wangel—!

HILDA: (*rising*) You can't deny it, can you?  800

SOLNESS: Yes, I most emphatically do deny it!

HILDA: (*looking scornfully at him*) I see. (*She turns and walks slowly over close by the stove and remains standing motionless, face averted from him, hands behind her back. A short pause.*)

SOLNESS: (*going cautiously over behind her*) Miss Wangel—? (*HILDA stays silent, not moving.*) Don't stand there like a statue. These things you've been saying—you must have dreamed them. (*Putting his hand on her arm.*) Now listen— (*HILDA moves her arm impatiently. SOLNESS appears struck  810 by a sudden thought.*) Or else—wait a minute! There's something strange in back of all this, you'll see! (*In a hushed but emphatic voice.*) This all must have been in my thoughts. I must have willed it. Wished it. Desired it. And so— Doesn't that make sense? (HILDA *remains still.* SOLNESS *speaks impatiently.*) Oh, all right, for God's sake—so I *did* the thing too!

HILDA: (*turning her head a bit, but without looking at him*) Then you confess?

SOLNESS: Yes. Whatever you please.  820

HILDA: That you threw your arms around me?

SOLNESS: All right!

HILDA: And bent me back.

SOLNESS: Way over back.

HILDA: And kissed me.

SOLNESS: Yes, I did it.

HILDA: Many times?

SOLNESS: As many as you ever could want.

HILDA: (*whirling about to face him, the sparkle once again in her delighted eyes*) There, you see—I did get it out of you in  830 the end!

SOLNESS: (*with a thin smile*) Yes—imagine my forgetting something like that.

HILDA: (*sulking a little once more, moving away from him*) Oh, you've kissed a good many in your time, I think.

SOLNESS: No, you mustn't think that of me.

(HILDA *sits in the armchair.* SOLNESS *stands leaning on the rocking chair, watching her closely.*)

SOLNESS: Miss Wangel?

HILDA: Yes.

SOLNESS: How was it, now? What went on next—with us?

HILDA: Nothing else went on. You know that well enough. Be-  840 cause then all the others came in, and—ffft!

SOLNESS: That's right. The others came. And I could forget

that too.

HILDA: Oh, you haven't forgotten a thing. You're just a little ashamed. Nobody forgets this kind of thing.

SOLNESS: No, it wouldn't seem likely.

HILDA: (*looking at him, vivacious again*) Or maybe you've even forgotten what day it was?

SOLNESS: What day—?

850 HILDA: Yes, what day you hung the wreath on the tower? Well? Quick, say it!

SOLNESS: Hm—I guess I've forgotten the actual date. I only know it was ten years ago. Sometime in the fall.

HILDA: (*nodding her head slowly several times*) It was ten years ago. The nineteenth of September.

SOLNESS: Ah, yes, it must have been about then. So you've re-membered that too! (*Hesitates.*) But wait a minute—! Yes—today it's also the nineteenth of September.

HILDA: Yes, it is. And the ten years are up. And you didn't
860 come—as you promised me.

SOLNESS: Promised you? Threatened, don't you mean?

HILDA: It never struck me as some kind of threat.

SOLNESS: Well, teased that I would, then.

HILDA: Is that all you wanted? To tease me?

SOLNESS: Well, or to joke a bit with you, then! Lord knows I don't remember. But it must have been something like that—for you were only a child at the time.

HILDA: Oh, maybe I wasn't so much of a child either. Not quite the little kitten you thought.

870 SOLNESS: (*looks searchingly at her*) Did you really in all seri-ousness get the idea I'd be coming back?

HILDA: (*hiding a rather roguish smile*) Of course! That's what I expected.

SOLNESS: That I'd come to your home and carry you off with me?

HILDA: Just like a troll, yes.

SOLNESS: And make you a princess?

HILDA: It's what you promised.

SOLNESS: And give you a kingdom, too?

880 HILDA: (*gazing at the ceiling*) Why not? After all, it didn't have to be the everyday, garden-variety kingdom.

SOLNESS: But something else that was just as good.

HILDA: Oh, at least just as good. (*Glancing at him.*) If you could build the highest church tower in the world, it seemed to me you certainly should be able to come up with some kind of kingdom, too.

SOLNESS: (*shaking his head*) I just can't figure you out, Miss Wangel.

HILDA: You can't? I think it's so simple.

890 SOLNESS: No, I can't make out whether you mean all you say—or whether you're just having some fun—

HILDA: (*smiles*) Fooling around—and teasing, maybe. I too?

SOLNESS: Exactly. Making fools—of both of us. (*Looking at her.*) How long have you known I was married?

HILDA: Right from the start. Why do you ask about *that*?

SOLNESS: (*casually*) Oh, nothing—just wondered. (*Lowering his voice, with a straight look at her.*) Why have you come?

HILDA: I want my kingdom. Time's up.

SOLNESS: (*laughing in spite of himself*) You are the limit!

900 HILDA: (*gaily*) Give us the kingdom, come on! (*Drumming with her fingers.*) One kingdom, on the line!

SOLNESS: (*pushing the rocking chair closer and sitting*) Seri-ously now—why have you come? What do you really want

to do here?

HILDA: Oh, to begin with, I want to go around and look at everything you've built.

SOLNESS: That'll keep you going a while.

HILDA: Yes, you've built such an awful lot.

SOLNESS: I have, yes. Mainly these later years.

HILDA: Many more church towers? Enormously high ones?  910

SOLNESS: No, I don't build any church towers now. Nor churches either.

HILDA: What *do* you build then?

SOLNESS: Homes for human beings.

HILDA: (*reflectively*) Couldn't you put a small—a small church tower up over the homes as well?

SOLNESS: (*with a start*) What do you mean by that?

HILDA: I mean—something pointing—free, sort of, into the sky. With a weather vane way up in the reeling heights.

SOLNESS: (*musing*) How odd that you should say that. It's ex-  920
actly what, most of all, I've wanted.

HILDA: (*impatiently*) But why don't you do it, then!

SOLNESS: (*shaking his head*) Because people won't have it.

HILDA: Imagine—not to want that!

SOLNESS: (*more lightly*) But I'm building a new home now—right opposite this.

HILDA: For yourself?

SOLNESS: Yes. It's almost ready. And it has a tower.

HILDA: A high one?

SOLNESS: Yes.  930

HILDA: Very high?

SOLNESS: People are bound to say, too high. At least for a home.

HILDA: I'll be out looking at that tower first thing in the morn-ing.

SOLNESS: (*sitting with his hand propping his cheek, gazing at her*) Miss Wangel, tell me—what's your name? Your first name, I mean?

HILDA: You know—it's Hilda.

SOLNESS: (*as before*) Hilda? So?  940

HILDA: You don't remember *that?* You called me Hilda your-self—the day when you acted up.

SOLNESS: I did that, too?

HILDA: But then you said "little Hilda," and I didn't care for that.

SOLNESS: So, Miss Hilda, you didn't care for that.

HILDA: Not at such a time, no. But—Princess Hilda—that's going to sound quite nice, I think.

SOLNESS: No doubt. Princess Hilda of—of that kingdom, what was it called?  950

HILDA: Ish! I'm through with that stupid kingdom! I want a dif-ferent one, completely.

SOLNESS: (*who has leaned back in his chair, goes on studying her*) Isn't it strange—? The more I think about it, the more it seems to me that all these years I've been going around tormented by—hm—

HILDA: By what?

SOLNESS: By a search for something—some old experience I thought I'd forgotten. But I've never had an inkling of what it could be.  960

HILDA: You should have tied a knot in your handkerchief, Mr. Solness.

SOLNESS: Then I'd only wind up puzzling over what the knot might mean.

HILDA: Yes, there's even that kind of troll in the world too.

SOLNESS: (*slowly gets up*) It's really so good that you've come to me now.

HILDA: (*with a probing look*) Is it?

SOLNESS: I've been so alone here—and felt so utterly helpless watching it all. (*Dropping his voice.*) I should tell you—I've begun to grow afraid—so awfully afraid of the young.

HILDA: (*sniffing scornfully*) Pooh! Are the young anything to fear!

SOLNESS: Decidedly. That's why I've locked and bolted myself in. (*Mysteriously.*) Wait and see, the young will come here, thundering at the door! Breaking in on me!

HILDA: Then I think you should go out and open your door to the young.

SOLNESS: Open the door?

HILDA: Yes. Let them come in to you—as friends.

SOLNESS: No, no, no! The young—don't you see, they're retribution—the spearhead of change—as if they came marching under some new flag.

HILDA: (*rises, looks at him, her lips trembling as she speaks*) Can you find a use for *me*, Mr. Solness?

SOLNESS: Oh, of course I can! Because I feel that you've come, too, almost—under some new flag. And then it's youth against youth—!

(DR. HERDAL *comes in by the hall door.*)

HERDAL: So? You and Miss Wangel still here?

SOLNESS: Yes. We've had a great many things to talk about.

HILDA: Both old and new.

HERDAL: Oh, have you?

HILDA: Really, it's been such fun. Because Mr. Solness—he's got just a fantastic memory. He remembers the tiniest little details in a flash.

(MRS. SOLNESS *enters by the door to the right.*)

MRS. SOLNESS: All right, Miss Wangel, your room's all ready for you now.

HILDA: Oh, how kind of you.

SOLNESS: (*to his wife*) Nursery?

MRS. SOLNESS: Yes, the middle one. But first we ought to have a bite to eat, don't you think?

SOLNESS: (*nodding to* HILDA) So Hilda sleeps in the nursery, then.

MRS. SOLNESS: (*looking at him*) Hilda?

SOLNESS: Yes, Miss Wangel's name is Hilda. I knew her when she was small.

MRS. SOLNESS: No, did you really, Halvard? Well—shall we? Supper's waiting.

(*She takes* DR. HERDAL'*s arm and they go out, right.* HILDA *meanwhile gathers up her hiking gear.*)

HILDA: (*softly and quickly to* SOLNESS) Is that true, what you said? *Can* you find a use for me?

SOLNESS: (*taking her things away from her*) You're the one person I've needed the most.

HILDA: (*clasping her hands and looking at him with wondering eyes full of joy*) Oh, you beautiful, big world—!

SOLNESS: (*tensely*) What—?

HILDA: Then I have my kingdom!

SOLNESS: (*involuntarily*) Hilda—!

HILDA: (*her lips suddenly trembling again*) Almost—that's

what I meant.

(*She goes out to the right, with* SOLNESS *following.*)

## —ACT TWO—

*An attractively furnished small living room in* SOLNESS'*s house. A glass door in the back wall opens on the veranda and garden. Diagonally cutting the right-hand corner is a broad bow window with flower stands before it. The left-hand corner is similarly cut by a wall containing a door papered to match. In each of the side walls, an ordinary door. In the right foreground, a console table and a large mirror. Flowers and plants richly displayed. In the left foreground, a sofa, along with table and chairs. Further back, a bookcase. Out in the room in front of the bow window, a little table and a couple of chairs. It is early in the morning.*

SOLNESS *is sitting at the little table with* RAGNAR BROVIK'*s portfolio open before him. He is leafing through the drawings and now and then looks sharply at one.* MRS. SOLNESS *moves silently about with a small watering can, freshening the flowers. She wears black, as before. Her hat, coat, and parasol lie on a chair by the mirror. Unnoticed by her,* SOLNESS *follows her several times with his eyes. Neither of them speaks.*

KAJA FOSLI *comes quietly in by the door on the left.*

SOLNESS: (*turns his head and speaks with careless indifference*) Oh, is that you?

KAJA: I just wanted to tell you I'm here.

SOLNESS: Yes, that's fine. Isn't Ragnar there too?

KAJA: No, not yet. He had to wait a bit for the doctor. But he'll be along soon to find out—

SOLNESS: How's the old man getting on?

KAJA: Poorly. He's so very sorry, but he can't leave his bed today.

SOLNESS: Of course not. He mustn't stir. But you go on to your work.

KAJA: Yes. (*Pauses at the door.*) Will you want to speak to Ragnar when he gets in?

SOLNESS: No—I've nothing special to say.

(KAJA *goes out again to the left.* SOLNESS *continues to sit and leaf through the drawings.*)

MRS. SOLNESS: (*over by the plants*). I wonder if he won't die now, he too.

SOLNESS: (*looking at her*) He—and who else?

MRS. SOLNESS: (*not answering*) Yes, old Brovik—he's going to die now too, Halvard. You wait and see.

SOLNESS: Aline dear, couldn't you do with a little walk?

MRS. SOLNESS: Yes, I really suppose I could. (*She goes on tending the flowers.*)

SOLNESS: (*bent over the drawings*) Is she still sleeping?

MRS. SOLNESS: (*looking at him*) Is it Miss Wangel you're sitting there thinking about?

SOLNESS: (*casually*) I just happened to remember her.

MRS. SOLNESS: Miss Wangel's been up for hours.

SOLNESS: Oh, she has?

MRS. SOLNESS: When I looked in, she was busy arranging her things. (*She goes to the mirror and begins slowly putting her hat on.*)

SOLNESS: *(after a short silence)* So we did find use for one of the nurseries after all, Aline.

MRS. SOLNESS: Yes, we did.

SOLNESS: And I think that's better really, than all of them standing empty.

MRS. SOLNESS: You're right—that emptiness, it's horrible.

SOLNESS: *(closes the portfolio, rises, and approaches her)* You're only going to see *this*, Aline—that from now on things'll go better for us. Much pleasanter. Life will be eas-
1060   ier—especially for you.

MRS. SOLNESS: *(looking at him)* From now on?

SOLNESS: Yes, believe me, Aline—

MRS. SOLNESS: You mean—because *she's* come?

SOLNESS: *(restraining himself)*. I mean, of course, once we're in the new house.

MRS. SOLNESS: *(taking her coat)* Yes, do you think so, Halvard? That things will go better there?

SOLNESS: I'm sure of it. And you, don't you have the same feeling?

1070   MRS. SOLNESS: I feel absolutely nothing about the new house.

SOLNESS: *(dejected)* Well, that's certainly hard for me to hear. It's mostly for your sake that I built it. *(He makes a motion toward helping her on with her coat.)*

MRS. SOLNESS: *(evading him)* As it is, you do all too much for my sake.

SOLNESS: *(rather heatedly)* No, no, Aline, don't talk like that! I can't stand hearing you say such things.

MRS. SOLNESS: All right, then I won't say them, Halvard.

SOLNESS: But I swear I'm right. You'll see, it'll go so well for
1080   you over there.

MRS. SOLNESS: Oh, Lord—so well for me—!

SOLNESS: *(eagerly)* Oh yes, it will! Just trust that it will. Because over there—you'll see, there'll be so very much to remind you of your own old home—

MRS. SOLNESS: Of what was Mother and Father's—that burned to the ground.

SOLNESS: *(gently)* Yes, my poor Aline. That was a terrible blow for you.

MRS. SOLNESS: *(breaking out in lamentation)* You can build as
1090   much as you ever want, Halvard—but for *me* you can never build up a real home again.

SOLNESS: *(pacing across the room)* Then, for God's sake, let's not discuss it anymore.

MRS. SOLNESS: We don't ordinarily discuss it at all. Because you only push it aside—

SOLNESS: *(stops short and looks at her)* Do I? And why should I do that? Push it aside?

MRS. SOLNESS: Oh, don't you think I know you, Halvard? You want so much to spare me—to find excuses for me, all that
1100   you can.

SOLNESS: *(eyes wide in amazement)* For *you!* Is it you—yourself you're talking of, Aline?

MRS. SOLNESS: Yes, it has to be me, of course.

SOLNESS: *(involuntarily, to himself)* That, too!

MRS. SOLNESS: After all, with the old house—it couldn't have happened otherwise. Once disaster's on the wind, then—

SOLNESS: Yes, you're right. There's no running away from trouble—they say.

MRS. SOLNESS: But it's the horror after the fire—*that's* the
1110   thing! That, that, that!

SOLNESS: *(vehemently)* Don't think about it, Aline!

MRS. SOLNESS: Oh, but it's what I have to think about, exactly that. And finally talk about for once, too. Because I don't see how I can bear it any longer. And then, never the least chance to forgive myself—!

SOLNESS: *(exclaiming)* Yourself!

MRS. SOLNESS: Yes, you know I had my duties on both sides—both to you and to the babies. I should have made myself strong. Not let fear take hold of me so. Or grief either, because my old home had burned. *(Wringing her hands.)* Oh, 1120
if I'd only been strong enough, Halvard!

SOLNESS: *(softly, moved, coming closer)* Aline—you must promise me never to think these thoughts again. Promise me now.

MRS. SOLNESS: Good heavens—promise! Promise! Anyone can promise—

SOLNESS: *(clenching his fists and crossing the room)* Oh, how hopeless it is! Never a touch of sun! Not the least glimmer of light in this home!

MRS. SOLNESS: This is no home, Halvard.                               1130

SOLNESS: No, that's true enough. *(Heavily.)* And God knows if you're not right that it'll be no better for us in the new place.

MRS. SOLNESS: It can never be different. Just as empty—just as barren—there as here.

SOLNESS: *(fiercely)* But why in the world did we build it, then? Tell me that.

MRS. SOLNESS: No, that answer you'll have to find in yourself.

SOLNESS: *(glancing at her suspiciously)* What do you mean by *that*, Aline?

MRS. SOLNESS: What do I mean?                                          1140

SOLNESS: Yes, damn it—! You said it so strangely—as if you were holding something back.

MRS. SOLNESS: No, I can assure you—

SOLNESS: *(coming closer)* Ah, thanks a lot! I know what I know. I've got eyes and ears, Aline, don't forget.

MRS. SOLNESS: But what's this about? What is it?

SOLNESS: *(planting himself in front of her)* Aren't you out to discover some sly, hidden meaning in the most innocent thing I say?

MRS. SOLNESS: *I*, you say? *I* do that?                             1150

SOLNESS: *(laughing)* Of course that's only natural, Aline—when you've got a sick man around to deal with—

MRS. SOLNESS: *(anxiously)*. Sick? Are you ill, Halvard?

SOLNESS: *(in an outburst)*. Half mad, then. A crazy man. Anything you want to call me.

MRS. SOLNESS: *(groping for a chair and sitting)* Halvard—for God's sake—!

SOLNESS: But you're wrong, both of you. Both you and the doctor. It's no such thing with me. *(He paces back and forth,*
MRS. SOLNESS *following him anxiously with her eyes, until he* 1160
*goes over and speaks quietly to her.)* In fact, there's nothing the matter with me at all.

MRS. SOLNESS: No, of course not. But what is it, then, that's upsetting you?

SOLNESS: It's this, that I often feel that I'm going to sink under this awful burden of debt—

MRS. SOLNESS: Debt? But you're not in debt to anyone, Halvard.

SOLNESS: *(softly, with emotion)* Infinitely in debt to you—to you, Aline—to you.                                                  1170

MRS. SOLNESS: (*rising slowly*) What's back of all this? Might as well tell me it right now.

SOLNESS: But nothing's back of it. I've never done anything against you—not that I've ever known. And yet—there's this sense of some enormous guilt hanging over me, crushing me down.

MRS. SOLNESS: A guilt toward *me?*

SOLNESS: Toward you most of all.

MRS. SOLNESS: Then you are—ill, after all, Halvard.

1180 SOLNESS: (*wearily*) I suppose so—something like that. (*Looks toward the door to the right, as it opens.*) Ah! But it's brightening up.

(HILDA WANGEL *comes in. She has made some changes in her clothes and let down her skirt.*)

HILDA: Good morning, Mr. Solness!

SOLNESS: (*nodding*) Sleep well?

HILDA: Beautifully! Like a child in a cradle. Oh—I lay and stretched myself like—like a princess.

SOLNESS: (*smiling a little*) Quite comfortable, then.

HILDA: I'll say.

SOLNESS: And I suppose you dreamed?

1190 HILDA: Oh yes. But that was awful.

SOLNESS: So?

HILDA: Yes, 'cause I dreamed I was falling over a terribly high, steep cliff. *You* ever dream such things?

SOLNESS: Oh yes—now and then—

HILDA: It's wonderfully thrilling—just to fall and fall.

SOLNESS: It makes my blood run cold.

HILDA: You pull your legs up under you while you fall?

SOLNESS: Of course, as high as possible.

HILDA: Me too.

1200 MRS. SOLNESS: (*taking her parasol*) I've got to go down into town now, Halvard. (*To* HILDA.) And I'll try to pick up a few of the things you need.

HILDA: (*about to throw her arms around her*) Oh, Mrs. Solness, you're a dear! You're really too kind—terribly kind—

MRS. SOLNESS: (*deprecatingly, freeing herself*) Oh, not at all. It's simply my duty, so I'm quite happy to do it.

HILDA: (*piqued and pouting*) Actually, I don't see any reason why I can't go out myself—with my clothes all neat again. Why can't I?

1210 MRS. SOLNESS: To tell the truth, I rather think people would be staring at you a bit.

HILDA: (*sniffing*) Pooh! Is that all? But that's fun.

SOLNESS: (*with suppressed bad temper*) Yes, but you see people might get the idea that *you* were mad too.

HILDA: Mad? Are there so many mad people in town here?

SOLNESS: (*points at his forehead*) Here's one, at least.

HILDA: You—Mr. Solness!

MRS. SOLNESS: Oh, Halvard, really!

SOLNESS: You mean you haven't noticed *that?*

1220 HILDA: No, I certainly have not. (*Reflects a moment and laughs a little.*) Well, maybe in just one thing.

SOLNESS: Ah, hear that, Aline?

MRS. SOLNESS: What sort of thing, Miss Wangel?

HILDA: I'm not saying.

SOLNESS: Oh yes, come on!

HILDA: No thanks—I'm not *that* crazy.

MRS. SOLNESS: When Miss Wangel and you are alone, I'm sure she'll tell you, Halvard.

SOLNESS: Oh—you think so?

MRS. SOLNESS: Why, of course. After all, you've known her so 1230 well in the past. Ever since she was a child—you tell me. (*She goes out by the door on the left.*)

HILDA: (*after a brief pause*) Does your wife not like me at all?

SOLNESS: Does it seem so to you?

HILDA: Couldn't you see it yourself?

SOLNESS: (*evasively*) These last years Aline's become very shy around people.

HILDA: Has she really?

SOLNESS: But if only you got to know her well—Because underneath, she's so kind—so good—such a fine person— 1240

HILDA: (*impatiently*) But if she *is* all that—why does she run on so about duty!

SOLNESS: Duty?

HILDA: Yes. She said she'd go out and buy me some things because that was her *duty.* Oh, I can't stand that mean, ugly word!

SOLNESS: Why not?

HILDA: No, it sounds so cold and sharp and cutting. Duty, duty, duty! Don't you feel it too? As if it's made to cut.

SOLNESS: Hm—never thought of it, really. 1250

HILDA: But it's true! And if she's so kind—the way you say— why would she put it like that?

SOLNESS: But, my Lord, what would you want her to say?

HILDA: She could have said she'd do it because she liked me a lot. Something like that she could have said. Something really warm and straight from the heart—you know?

SOLNESS: (*looking at her*) Is *that* what you'd want?

HILDA: Yes, just that. (*She strolls around the room, stopping at the bookcase and examining the books.*)

HILDA: You have an awful lot of books. 1260

SOLNESS: Oh, I've picked up a fair number.

HILDA: Do you read them all, too?

SOLNESS: I used to try, in the old days. Do *you* do much reading?

HILDA: No, never! At least, not now. I can't connect with them anymore.

SOLNESS: It's exactly the same for me.

(HILDA *wanders about a little, stops by the small table, opens the portfolio and turns over some sketches.*)

HILDA: Did you do all these designs?

SOLNESS: No, they're done by a young man I've had helping me. 1270

HILDA: Someone you've been teaching.

SOLNESS: Oh yes, I guess he's learned something from me, all right.

HILDA: (*sitting*) Then he must be quite clever, hm? (*Studies one of the sketches a moment.*) Isn't he?

SOLNESS: Oh, could be worse. For *my* work, though—

HILDA: Oh yes! He must be dreadfully clever.

SOLNESS: You think you can see it in the drawings?

HILDA: Ffft! These scribbles! But if he's been studying with *you,* then— 1280

SOLNESS: Oh, for that matter, there've been plenty of others who've studied with me, and none of them have ever come to much.

HILDA: (*looks at him, shaking her head*) For the life of me, I don't understand how you can be so stupid.

SOLNESS: Stupid? You really think I'm so stupid?

HILDA: Yes, really I do. When you can take time to go on teaching these fellows—

SOLNESS: (*with a start*) Well, why not?

1290 HILDA: (*rising, half serious, half laughing*) Oh, come on, Mr. Solness! What's the point of it? Nobody but you should have a right to build. You should be all alone in that. Have the field to yourself. Now you know.

SOLNESS: (*involuntarily*) Hilda—!

HILDA: Well?

SOLNESS: What on earth gave you that idea?

HILDA: Am I so very wrong, then?

SOLNESS: No, that's not it. But let me tell you something.

HILDA: What?

1300 SOLNESS: Here, in my solitude and silence—endlessly—I've been brooding on that same idea.

HILDA: Well, it seems only natural to me.

SOLNESS: (*looks rather sharply at her*) And I'm sure you've already noticed it.

HILDA: No, not a bit.

SOLNESS: But before—when you said you thought I was—unbalanced, there was one thing—

HILDA: Oh, I was thinking of something quite different.

SOLNESS: What do you mean, different?

1310 HILDA: Never you mind, Mr. Solness.

SOLNESS: (*crossing the room*) All right—have it your way. (*Stops at the bow window.*) Come over here, and I'll show you something.

HILDA: (*approaching*) What's that?

SOLNESS: You see—out there in the garden—?

HILDA: Yes?

SOLNESS: (*pointing*) Right above that big quarry?

HILDA: The new house, you mean?

SOLNESS: The one under construction, yes. Nearly finished.

1320 HILDA: I think it's got a very high tower.

SOLNESS: The scaffolding's still up.

HILDA: That's your new house?

SOLNESS: Yes.

HILDA: The one you're about to move into?

SOLNESS: Yes.

HILDA: (*looking at him*) Are there nurseries in that house too?

SOLNESS: Three, same as here.

HILDA: And no children.

SOLNESS: Not now—nor ever.

1330 HILDA: (*half smiling*) So, isn't that just what I said—?

SOLNESS: Namely—?

HILDA: Namely, that you are a little—sort of mad, after all.

SOLNESS: Was that what you were thinking of?

HILDA: Yes, of all those empty nurseries I slept in.

SOLNESS: (*dropping his voice*) We did have children—Aline and I.

HILDA: (*looking intently at him*) You did—?

SOLNESS: Two little boys. Both the same age.

HILDA: Twins.

1340 SOLNESS: Yes, twins. That's some eleven, twelve years ago now.

HILDA: (*cautiously*) And both of them are—? The twins— they're not with you anymore?

SOLNESS: (*with quiet feeling*) We had them only about three weeks. Not even that. (*In an outburst.*) Oh, Hilda, how amazingly lucky for me that you've come! Now at last I've got someone I can talk to.

HILDA: You can't talk with—*her?*

SOLNESS: Not about this. Not the way I want to and need to. (*Heavily.*) And there's so much else I can never talk out.

1350 HILDA: (*her voice subdued*) Was that all you meant when you said you needed me?

SOLNESS: Mostly that, I guess. Yesterday, anyhow. Today I'm not so sure—(*Breaking off.*) Come here, Hilda, and let's get settled. Sit there on the sofa—then you can look out in the garden. (HILDA *sits in the corner of the sofa.* SOLNESS *draws over a chair.*) Would you care to hear about it?

HILDA: Yes, I like listening to you.

SOLNESS: (*sitting*) Then I'll give you the whole story.

1360 HILDA: Now I'm looking at both the garden and you, Mr. Solness. So tell me. Please!

SOLNESS: (*pointing out the bow window*) Over on that ridge there—where you see the new house—

HILDA: Yes.

SOLNESS: That's where Aline and I lived in those early years. There was an old house up there then, one that had belonged to her mother—and then passed on to us. And this whole enormous garden came with it.

HILDA: Did that house have a tower too?

1370 SOLNESS: No, not at all. From the outside it was an ugly, dark, overgrown packing case. And yet, for all that, it was snug and cozy enough inside.

HILDA: Did you tear the old crate down, then?

SOLNESS: No, it burned.

HILDA: To the ground?

SOLNESS: Yes.

HILDA: Was it a terrible loss for you?

SOLNESS: Depends how you look at it. As a builder, the fire put me in business—

HILDA: Well, but—?

1380 SOLNESS: We'd just had the two little boys at the time—

HILDA: The poor little twins, yes.

SOLNESS: They'd come so plump and healthy into life. And every day you could see them growing.

HILDA: Babies grow fast at the start.

SOLNESS: There was nothing finer in the world to see than Aline, lying there, holding those two— But then it came, the night of the fire—

HILDA: (*excitedly*) What happened? Go on! Was anyone burned?

1390 SOLNESS: No, not that. They were all rescued out of the house—

HILDA: Well, but then what—?

SOLNESS: The fright shook Aline to the core. The alarms—getting out of the house—and all the confusion—the whole thing at night, in the freezing cold to boot. They had to be carried out just as they lay—both she and the babies.

HILDA: And they didn't survive?

SOLNESS: Oh, *they* pulled through it all right. But Aline came down with fever—and it affected her milk. Nurse them herself, she had to do that. It was her duty, she said. And both 1400 of our little boys, they—(*Knotting his hands.*) they—oh!

HILDA: They couldn't take that as well.

SOLNESS: No, they couldn't take that as well. It's how we lost them.

HILDA: It must have been terribly hard for you.

SOLNESS: Hard enough for me—but ten times harder for Aline. (*Clenching his fists in suppressed fury.*) Oh, why do such things have to happen in life! (*Brusquely and firmly.*) From the day I lost them, I never wanted to build another 1410 church.

HILDA: And the church tower in our town—you disliked doing that?

SOLNESS: Very much. I remember when it was finished how relieved I felt.

HILDA: *I* remember too.

SOLNESS: And now I'll never build those things anymore—never! No church towers, or churches.

HILDA: (*nodding slowly*) Only houses for people to live in.

SOLNESS: Homes for human beings, Hilda.

1420 HILDA: But homes with high towers and spires on them.

SOLNESS: If possible. (*In a lighter tone.*) Anyhow—as I said before—the fire put me in business. As a builder, I mean.

HILDA: Why don't you call yourself an architect like the others?

SOLNESS: Never went through the training. Almost all I know I've had to find out for myself.

HILDA: But still you've made a success.

SOLNESS: Out of the fire, yes. I subdivided nearly the whole garden into small lots, where I could build exactly the way I wanted. And after that, things really began to move for me.

1430 HILDA: (*looking at him searchingly*) How happy you must be—with the life you've made.

SOLNESS: (*darkly*) Happy? You say it too? Same as all the others.

HILDA: Yes, you have to be, I really think so. If you just could stop thinking about the little twins—

SOLNESS: (*slowly*) The little twins—they're not so easy to forget, Hilda.

HILDA: (*with some uncertainty*) They really still bother you? After so many years?

1440 SOLNESS: (*regarding her steadily, without answering*) A happy man, you said—

HILDA: Yes, but aren't you—I mean, otherwise?

SOLNESS: (*continues to look at her*) When I told you all that about the fire—

HILDA: Yes?

SOLNESS: Did nothing strike you then—nothing special?

HILDA: (*puzzling a moment*) No. Was there something special?

SOLNESS: (*quietly stressing his words*) By means of that fire, and that alone, I won my chance to build homes for human 1450 beings. Snug, cozy, sunlit homes, where a father and mother and a whole drove of children could live safe and happy, feeling what a sweet thing it is to be alive in this world. And mostly, knowing they belonged to each other—in the big things and the small.

HILDA: (*animated*) Yes, but isn't it really a joy for you then, to create these beautiful homes?

SOLNESS: The price, Hilda. The awful price I've had to pay for that chance.

HILDA: But can you never get over that?

1460 SOLNESS: No. For this chance to build homes for others, I've had to give up—absolutely give up any home of my own—a real home, I mean, with children.

HILDA: (*delicately*) But did you have to? Absolutely, that is?

SOLNESS: (*slowly nodding*) That was the price for my famous

luck. Luck—hm. This good luck, Hilda—it couldn't be bought for less.

HILDA: (*as before*) But still, mightn't it all work out?

SOLNESS: Never in this world. Never. That also comes out of the fire. And Aline's sickness after.

HILDA: (*looks at him with an enigmatic expression*) And so you 1470 go and build all these nurseries.

SOLNESS: (*seriously*) Have you ever noticed, Hilda, how the impossible—how it seems to whisper and call to you?

HILDA: (*reflecting*) The impossible? (*Vivaciously.*) Oh yes! *You* know it too?

SOLNESS: Yes.

HILDA: Then I guess there's—something of a troll in you as well?

SOLNESS: Why a troll?

HILDA: Well, what would *you* call it, then? 1480

SOLNESS: (*getting up*) Hm, yes, could be. (*Furiously.*) But why shouldn't the troll be in me—the way things go for me all the time, in everything! In everything!

HILDA: What do you mean?

SOLNESS: (*hushed and inwardly stirred*) Pay attention to what I tell you, Hilda. All I've been given to do, to build and shape into beauty, security, a good life—into even a kind of splendor—(*Knotting his fists.*) Oh, how awful just to think of it—!

HILDA: What's so awful?

SOLNESS: That I've got to make up for it all. Pay up. Not with 1490 money, but with human happiness. And not just my own happiness. With others', too. You understand, Hilda! That's the price my name as an artist has cost me—and others. And every single day I've got to look on here and see that price being paid for me again and again—over and over, and over, endlessly!

HILDA: (*rises, looking intently at him*) Now you're thinking of—of her.

SOLNESS: Yes, mostly of Aline. Because Aline—she had her lifework too—just as I had mine. (*His voice trembles.*) But 1500 *her* lifework had to be cut down, crushed, broken to bits, so that mine could win through to—to some kind of great victory. Aline, you know—she had a talent for building too.

HILDA: She! For building?

SOLNESS: (*shaking his head*) Not houses and towers and spires—the kind of thing I do—

HILDA: What, then?

SOLNESS: (*gently, with feeling*) For building up the souls of children, Hilda. Building those souls up to stand on their own, poised, in beautiful, noble forms—till they'd grown 1510 into the upright human spirit. *That's* what Aline had a talent for. And now, there it lies, all of it—unused and useless forever. And for what earthly reason. Just like charred ruins after a fire.

HILDA: Yes, but even if this were so—?

SOLNESS: It *is* so! It *is!* I know.

HILDA: Well, but in any case it's not *your* fault.

SOLNESS: (*fixing his eyes on her and nodding slowly*) Ah, you see—that's the enormous, ugly riddle—the doubt that gnaws at me day and night. 1520

HILDA: That?

SOLNESS: Put it this way. Suppose it *was* my fault, in some sense.

HILDA: You! For the fire?

SOLNESS: For everything, the whole business. And yet, per-haps—completely innocent all the same.

HILDA: (*looks at him anxiously*) Mr. Solness—when you can talk like that, then it sounds like you are—ill, after all.

1530 SOLNESS: Hm—I don't think I'll ever be quite sound in that department.

(RAGNAR BROVIK *cautiously opens the small corner door at the left.* HILDA *crosses the room.*)

RAGNAR: (*on seeing* HILDA) Oh—excuse me, Mr. Solness. (*He starts to leave.*)

SOLNESS: No, no, don't go. Let's be done with it.

RAGNAR: Yes, if we only could!

SOLNESS: Your father's no better, I hear.

RAGNAR: He's going downhill fast now. And that's why I'm beg-ging you, please—give me a good word or two, just some-thing on one of the drawings for Father to read before he—

1540 SOLNESS: (*explosively*) Stop talking to me about those drawings of yours!

RAGNAR: Have you looked them over?

SOLNESS: Yes—I have.

RAGNAR: And they're worthless? And no doubt I'm worthless too?

SOLNESS: (*evasively*) You stay on here with me, Ragnar. You'll get everything the way you want it. You can marry Kaja then and have it easy—happy even. Just don't think about doing your own building.

RAGNAR: Oh, sure, I should go home and tell that to my father.
1550 Because I promised to. *Shall* I tell him that—before he dies?

SOLNESS: (*with a groan*) Oh, tell him—tell him—don't ask me what to say! Anything. Better still to say nothing. (*In an out-burst.*) I can't do any more than I'm doing, Ragnar.

RAGNAR: May I take along my drawings, then?

SOLNESS: Yes, take them—help yourself! They're on the table.

RAGNAR: (*going to the table*) Thanks.

HILDA: (*putting her hand on the portfolio*) No, no, leave them.

SOLNESS: Why?

1560 HILDA: Because *I* want to see them too.

SOLNESS: But you've already—(*To* RAGNAR.) All right, then, just leave them.

RAGNAR: Gladly.

SOLNESS: And go right home to your father.

RAGNAR: Yes, I really ought to.

SOLNESS: (*with an air of desperation*) Ragnar—don't ask me for what I can't give! You hear, Ragnar? You mustn't!

RAGNAR: No, no. Excuse me—(*He bows and goes out through the corner door.* HILDA *goes over and sits on a chair by the*
1570 *mirror.*)

HILDA: (*looking angrily at* SOLNESS) That was really mean of you.

SOLNESS: You think so too?

HILDA: Yes, it was terribly mean. And hard and wicked and cruel.

SOLNESS: You don't know my side of it.

HILDA: All the same. No, you shouldn't be like that.

SOLNESS: You were only just now saying that no one but me should be allowed to build.

1580 HILDA: *I* can say that—but *you* mustn't.

SOLNESS: But I can, most of all—when I've paid such a price

for my recognition.

HILDA: That's right—with what you think of as the comfortable life—that sort of thing.

SOLNESS: And my inner peace in the bargain.

HILDA: (*rising*) Inner peace! (*Intensely.*) Yes, yes, you're right! Poor Mr. Solness—you imagine that—

SOLNESS: (*with a quiet laugh*) Sit down again, Hilda—if you want to hear something funny.

HILDA: (*expectantly, sitting down*) Well?   1590

SOLNESS: It sounds like such a ridiculous little thing. You see, the whole business revolves about no more than a crack in a chimney.

HILDA: Nothing else?

SOLNESS: No; at least, not at the start. (*He moves a chair closer to* HILDA *and sits.*)

HILDA: (*impatiently, tapping her knee*) So—the crack in the chimney!

SOLNESS: I'd noticed that tiny opening in the flue long, long be-fore the fire. Every time I was up in the attic, I checked to   1600 see that it was still there.

HILDA: And was it?

SOLNESS: Yes. Because no one else knew.

HILDA: And you said nothing?

SOLNESS: No. Nothing.

HILDA: Never thought of fixing the flue, either?

SOLNESS: I thought, yes—but never got to it. Every time I wanted to start repairing it, it was exactly as if a hand were there, holding me back. Not today, I'd think. Tomorrow. So nothing came of it.   1610

HILDA: But why did you keep on postponing?

SOLNESS: Because I went on thinking. (*Slowly, in an under-tone.*) Through that little black opening in the chimney I could force my way to success—as a builder.

HILDA: (*looking straight ahead of her*) That must have been thrilling.

SOLNESS: Irresistible, almost. Completely irresistible. Because the whole thing, then, seemed so easy and obvious to me. I wanted it to happen on some winter's day, a little before noon. I'd be out with Aline for a drive in the sleigh. The peo-   1620 ple at home would have fires blazing in the stoves—

HILDA: Yes, because the day should be bitterly cold—

SOLNESS: Yes, quite raw. And they'd want it snug and warm for Aline when she got in.

HILDA: Because I'm sure her temperature's normally low.

SOLNESS: It is, you know. So then, driving home it was, that we were supposed to see the smoke.

HILDA: Only the smoke?

SOLNESS: The smoke first. But when we'd pull in at the garden gate, there the old packing case would stand, a roaring in-   1630 ferno. At least, that's how I wanted it.

HILDA: Oh, but if it only could have gone that way!

SOLNESS: Yes, you can say that well enough, Hilda.

HILDA: But wait a minute, Mr. Solness—how can you be so sure the fire started from that little crack in the chimney?

SOLNESS: I can't, not at all. In fact, I'm absolutely certain it had nothing whatever to do with the fire.

HILDA: What!

SOLNESS: It's been proved without a shadow of a doubt that the fire broke out in a clothes closet, in quite another part of the   1640 house.

HILDA: Then what's the point in all this sitting and mooning around about a cracked chimney!

SOLNESS: You mind if I go on talking a bit, Hilda?

HILDA: No, if only you'll talk sense—

SOLNESS: I'll try. (*He moves his chair in closer.*)

HILDA: So—go on then, Mr. Solness.

SOLNESS: (*confidingly*) Don't you believe with me, Hilda, that there are certain special, chosen people who have a gift and
1650 power and capacity to *wish* something, *desire* something, *will* something—so insistently and so—so inevitably—that at last it *has* to be theirs? Don't you believe that?

HILDA: (*with an inscrutable look in her eyes*) If that's true, then we'll see someday—if *I'm* one of the chosen.

SOLNESS: It's not one's self alone that makes great things. Oh no—the helpers and servers—they've got to be with you if you're going to succeed. But they never come by themselves. One has to call on them, incessantly—within oneself, I mean.

1660 HILDA: What are these helpers and servers?

SOLNESS: Oh, we can talk about that some other time. Let's stay with the fire now.

HILDA: Don't you think the fire still would have come—even if you hadn't wished it?

SOLNESS: If old Knut Brovik had owned the house, it never would have burned down so conveniently for him—I'm positive of that. Because he doesn't know how to call on the helpers, or the servers either. (*Gets up restlessly.*) So you see, Hilda—it *is* my fault that the twins had to die. And isn't
1670 it my fault, too, that Aline's never become the woman she could have and should have been? And wanted to be, more than anything?

HILDA: Yes, but if it's really these helpers and servers, then—?

SOLNESS: Who called for the helpers and servers? I did! And they came and did what I willed. (*In rising agitation.*) That's what all the nice people call "having the luck." But I can tell you what this luck feels like. It feels as if a big piece of skin had been stripped, right here, from my chest. And the helpers and servers go on flaying the skin off other people to
1680 patch *my* wound. But the wound never heals—never! Oh, if you knew how sometimes it leeches and burns.

HILDA: (*looking at him attentively*) You *are* ill, Mr. Solness. Very ill, I almost think.

SOLNESS: Insane. You can say it. It's what you mean.

HILDA: No, I don't think you've lost your reason.

SOLNESS: *What*, then? Out with it!

HILDA: I'm wondering if maybe you didn't enter life with a frail conscience.

SOLNESS: A frail conscience? What in hell's name does that
1690 mean?

HILDA: I mean your conscience is very fragile. Overrefined, sort of. It isn't made to struggle with things—to pick up what's heavy and bear it.

SOLNESS: (*growling*) Hm! And what kind of conscience do you recommend?

HILDA: I could wish that your conscience was—well, quite robust.

SOLNESS: Oh? Robust? And I suppose *you* have a robust conscience?

1700 HILDA: Yes, I think so. I've never noticed it wasn't.

SOLNESS: I'd say you've never had a real test to face up to, either.

HILDA: (*with tremulous lips*) Oh, it wasn't so easy to leave Father, when I'm so terribly fond of him.

SOLNESS: Come on! Just for a month or two—

HILDA: I'm never going home again.

SOLNESS: Never? Why did you leave home, then?

HILDA: (*half serious, half teasing*) You still keep forgetting that the ten years are up?

SOLNESS: Nonsense. Was something wrong there at home? 1710 Hm?

HILDA: (*fully serious*) It was inside me, something goading and driving me here. Coaxing and luring me, too.

SOLNESS: (*eagerly*) That's it! That's it, Hilda! There's a troll in you—same as in me. It's that troll in us, don't you see— that's what calls on the powers out there. And then we *have* to give in—whether we want to or not.

HILDA: I almost believe you're right, Mr. Solness.

SOLNESS: (*walking about the room*) Oh, Hilda, there are so many devils one can't see loose in the world!                  1720

HILDA: Devils, too?

SOLNESS: (*stops*) Good devils and bad devils. Blond devils and black-haired ones. And if only you always knew if the light or the dark ones had you! (*Pacing about; with a laugh.*) Wouldn't it be simple then!

HILDA: (*her eyes following him*) Or if you had a really strong conscience, brimming with health—so you could dare what you most wanted.

SOLNESS: (*stopping by the console table*) Still, I think most people, in this respect, are just as weak as I am.                  1730

HILDA: Probably.

SOLNESS: (*leaning against the table*) In the sagas—Ever done any reading in the old sagas?

HILDA: Oh yes! In the days when I used to read books—

SOLNESS: In the sagas it tells about Vikings that sailed to foreign countries and plundered and burned and killed the men—

HILDA: And captured the women—

SOLNESS: And carried them off-

HILDA: Took them home in their ships—                  1740

SOLNESS: And treated them like—like the worst of trolls.

HILDA: (*looking straight ahead with half-veiled eyes*) I think that must have been thrilling.

SOLNESS: (*with a short, deep laugh*) Capturing women, hm?

HILDA: *Being* captured.

SOLNESS: (*studying her a moment*) I see.

HILDA: (*as if breaking the train of thought*) But what are you getting at with all these Vikings, Mr. Solness?

SOLNESS: Just that there's your robust conscience—in *those* boys! When they got back home, they went on eating and 1750 drinking and living lighthearted as children. And the women as well! They soon had no urge, most of them, ever to give up their men. Does that make sense to you, Hilda?

HILDA: Those women make perfect sense to me.

SOLNESS: Aha! Perhaps you could go and do likewise?

HILDA: Why not?

SOLNESS: Live, of your own free will, with a barbarian like that?

HILDA: If it was a barbarian that I really loved—

SOLNESS: But *could* you ever love one?

HILDA: My Lord, you don't just plan whom you're going to 1760 love.

SOLNESS: (*gazing thoughtfully at her*) No—I suppose it's the troll within that decides.

HILDA: (*half laughing*) Yes, and all those enchanting little devils—your friends. The blond and the black-haired both.

SOLNESS: (*with quiet warmth*) Then I'll ask that the devils choose tenderly for you, Hilda.

HILDA: For me they've already chosen. Now and forever.

SOLNESS: (*looks at her probingly*) Hilda—you're like some wild bird of the woods.

HILDA: Hardly. I don't go hiding away under bushes.

SOLNESS: No. No, there's more in you of the bird of prey.

HILDA: More that—perhaps. (*With great vehemence.*) And why not a bird of prey? Why shouldn't I go hunting as well? Take the spoil I'm after? If I can once set my claws in it and have my own way.

SOLNESS: Hilda—you know what you are?

HILDA: Yes, I'm some strange kind of bird.

SOLNESS: No. You're like a dawning day. When I look at you—then it's as if I looked into the sunrise.

HILDA: Tell me, Mr. Solness—are you quite sure that you've never called for me? Within yourself, I mean?

SOLNESS: (*slowly and softly*) I almost think I must have.

HILDA: What did you want with me?

SOLNESS: You, Hilda, are youth.

HILDA: (*smiles*) Youth that you're so afraid of?

SOLNESS: (*nodding slowly*) And that, deep within me, I'm so much hungering for.

(*HILDA rises, goes over to the small table, and takes up RAGNAR BROVIK's portfolio.*)

HILDA: (*holding the portfolio out toward him*) Then, about these drawings—

SOLNESS: (*sharply, waving them aside*) Put those things away! I've seen enough of them.

HILDA: Yes, but you've got to write your comment on them.

SOLNESS: Write a comment! Never!

HILDA: But now, with that poor old man near death! Can't you do him and his son a kindness before they're parted? And maybe later he could build from these drawings.

SOLNESS: Yes, that's exactly what he would do. The young pup's made sure of that.

HILDA: But, my Lord, if that's all—then can't you tell a little white lie?

SOLNESS: A lie? (*Furious.*) Hilda—get away with those damned drawings!

HILDA: (*pulls back the portfolio a bit*) Now, now, now—don't bite me. You talk about trolls. I think you're acting like a troll yourself. (*Glancing about.*) Where's your pen and ink?

SOLNESS: Haven't got any.

HILDA: (*going toward the door*) But out there where that girl works—

SOLNESS: Hilda, stay here—! You said I could lie a little. Well, I guess, for the old man's sake, I could manage it. I did beat him down in his time—and broke him—

HILDA: Him too?

SOLNESS: I had to have room for myself. But this Ragnar—he mustn't be given the least chance to rise.

HILDA: Poor boy, his chances are slim enough—if he simply hasn't got it in him—

SOLNESS: (*comes closer, looks at her and whispers*) If Ragnar Brovik gets his chance, he'll hammer me to the ground. Break me—same as I broke his father.

HILDA: Break you? Can he do that?

SOLNESS: You bet he can! He's all the youth that's waiting to come thundering at my door—to do away with master builder Solness.

HILDA: (*with a quietly reproachful look*) And so you'll still try to lock him out. For shame, Mr. Solness!

SOLNESS: It's cost me heart's blood enough to fight my battle. And then—the helpers and servers, I'm afraid they won't obey me anymore.

HILDA: Then you'll have to get along on your own, that's all.

SOLNESS: Hopeless, Hilda. The change, it's coming. Maybe a little sooner, maybe later. But the retribution—it's inescapable.

HILDA: (*pressing her hands to her ears in fright*) Don't say those things! You want to kill me? You want to take what's even more than my life?

SOLNESS: And what's that?

HILDA: I want to see you great. See you with a wreath in your hand—high, high up on a church tower! (*Calm again.*) So—out with your pencil. You do have a pencil on you?

SOLNESS: (*brings one out with his pocket sketchbook*). Here's one.

HILDA: (*puts the portfolio down on the table*) Good. Now let's get settled here, Mr. Solness, the two of us.

(*SOLNESS sits at the table. HILDA, behind him, leans over the back of his chair.*)

HILDA: And now let's write on these drawings—something really warm and nice—for this stupid Roar—or whoever he is.

SOLNESS: (*writes a few lines, then turns his head and looks up at her*) Tell me one thing, Hilda.

HILDA: Yes?

SOLNESS: If you've really been waiting for me all these ten years—

HILDA: Then what?

SOLNESS: Why didn't you write to me? I could have answered you then.

HILDA: (*hurriedly*) No, no, no! That's just what I didn't want.

SOLNESS: Why not?

HILDA: I was afraid then the whole thing'd be ruined—But we should be writing on the drawings, Mr. Solness.

SOLNESS: Yes, of course.

HILDA: (*bends forward, watching as he writes*) Something heartfelt and kind. Oh, how I hate—how I hate this Roald—

SOLNESS: (*writing*). Have you never really loved anyone, Hilda?

HILDA: (*harshly*) What did you say?

SOLNESS: Have you never loved anyone?

HILDA: Anyone else. Is that what you mean?

SOLNESS: (*glancing up at her*) Anyone else, yes. You never have—in ten whole years? Never?

HILDA: Oh yes, now and then. When I was really furious at you for not coming.

SOLNESS: So you did care for others too?

HILDA: A little bit—for a week or so. Oh, honestly, Mr. Solness, you ought to know that kind of thing.

SOLNESS: Hilda—what are you here for?

HILDA: Don't waste time talking. That poor old man could easily be dying on us.

SOLNESS: Answer me, Hilda. What do you want from me?

HILDA: I want my kingdom.

SOLNESS: Hm—

*(He gives a quick glance toward the door on the left and resumes writing on the drawings. At the same moment MRS. SOLNESS enters; she has several packages with her.)*

1880 MRS. SOLNESS: I brought along a little something here for you, Miss Wangel. They'll send the big parcels out later.

HILDA: Oh, how wonderfully kind of you!

MRS. SOLNESS: No more than my duty, that's all.

SOLNESS: *(reading over his comments)* Aline.

MRS. SOLNESS: Yes?

SOLNESS: Did you notice if she—if the bookkeeper's out there?

MRS. SOLNESS: Oh, *she's* there, don't worry.

SOLNESS: *(sliding the drawings back in the portfolio)* Hm—

MRS. SOLNESS: She's right at her desk, as she always is—when-
1890 ever *I* go through the room.

SOLNESS: *(getting up)* Then I'll give her this, and tell her that—

HILDA: *(taking the portfolio from him)* Oh no, let me have the pleasure. *(Goes toward the door, then turns.)* What's her name?

SOLNESS: Miss Fosli.

HILDA: Ah, that's much too cold! I mean her first name.

SOLNESS: Kaja—I think.

HILDA: *(opens the door and calls)* Kaja, come in here! Hurry up! The master builder wants to speak to you.

1900 *(KAJA FOSLI appears at the door.)*

KAJA: *(looking fearfully at him)* Here I am—?

HILDA: *(handing her the portfolio)* See here, Kaja— you can have this now. The master builder's written his opinion.

KAJA: Oh, at last!

SOLNESS: Get it to old Brovik soon as you can.

KAJA: I'll go right over with it.

SOLNESS: Yes, go on. Now Ragnar can do some building.

KAJA: Oh, can he stop by and thank you for all—?

SOLNESS: *(sharply)* I want no thanks! Tell him that, with my respects.

1910 KAJA: Yes, I'll—

SOLNESS: And tell him as well that hereafter I won't be needing his services. Nor yours, either.

KAJA: *(her voice low and quavering)* Nor mine, either?

SOLNESS: You'll have other things to think about now. A lot to do. And that's only right. So run along home with the drawings, Miss Fosli. Quick! Hear me?

KAJA: *(as before)* Yes, Mr. Solness. *(She goes out.)*

MRS. SOLNESS: My, what scheming eyes she has.

SOLNESS: She? That poor little fool.

1920 MRS. SOLNESS: Oh—I see just what I see, Halvard. Are you really letting them go?

SOLNESS: Yes.

MRS. SOLNESS: Her too?

SOLNESS: Isn't that the way you wanted it?

MRS. SOLNESS: But to get rid of *her*—? Oh, well, Halvard, I'm sure you have one in reserve.

HILDA: *(playfully)* As for me, I just can't function behind a desk.

SOLNESS: There, there, now—it'll all work out, Aline. Don't

think of anything now except moving into the new home— 1930 as soon as you can. We'll be hanging the wreath up this evening—*(Turning to HILDA.)* way up high at the top of the tower. What do you say to that, Miss Hilda?

HILDA: *(gazing at him with sparkling eyes)* It'll be so marvelous seeing you high up there again!

SOLNESS: Me!

MRS. SOLNESS: For heaven's sake, Miss Wangel, what are you thinking of! My husband—who gets so dizzy!

HILDA: He dizzy? Impossible!

MRS. SOLNESS: Oh yes, it's true, though. 1940

HILDA: But I've seen him myself, right at the top of a high church tower!

MRS. SOLNESS: Yes, I've heard people talk about that. But it's so completely impossible—

SOLNESS: *(forcefully)* Impossible—yes, impossible! But all the same I stood there!

MRS. SOLNESS: Oh, Halvard, how can you say that? You can't even bear going out on the second-story balcony here. You've always been like that.

SOLNESS: Maybe this evening you'll see something new. 1950

MRS. SOLNESS: *(terrified)* No, no, no, I hope to God I never see that! I'm getting in touch with the doctor right away. He'll know how to stop you from this.

SOLNESS: But Aline—!

MRS. SOLNESS: Yes, because you know you're sick, Halvard. This only proves it! God—oh, God! *(She goes hurriedly out to the right.)*

HILDA: *(looking intently at him)* Is it true, or isn't it?

SOLNESS: That I get dizzy?

HILDA: That my master builder dares not—and *can* not climb 1960 as high as he builds?

SOLNESS: Is that the way you see it?

HILDA: Yes.

SOLNESS: I think soon I won't have a corner in me safe from you.

HILDA: *(looking toward the bow window)* So then, up. Right up there.

SOLNESS: *(coming closer)* In the topmost room of the tower— that's where you could live, Hilda—live like a princess.

HILDA: *(ambiguously; half playing, half serious)* Sure, it's what 1970 you promised.

SOLNESS: Did I really?

HILDA: Oh, come on, Mr. Solness! You said I'd be a princess— and you'd give me a kingdom. So you went and—well?

SOLNESS: *(warily)* Are you quite positive this isn't some kind of dream—some fantasy that's taken hold of you?

HILDA: *(caustically)* Meaning you didn't do it, hm?

SOLNESS: I hardly know myself. *(Dropping his voice.)* But one thing I know for certain—that I—

HILDA: That you—? Go on! 1980

SOLNESS: That I *ought* to have done it.

HILDA: *(exclaiming spiritedly)* You could never be dizzy!

SOLNESS: So we'll hang the wreath this evening—Princess Hilda.

HILDA: *(with a wry face)* Over your new home, yes.

SOLNESS: Over the new house—that'll never be home for me. *(He goes out by the garden door.)*

HILDA: *(looks straight ahead with a veiled look, whispering to herself. The only words heard are:)* Terribly thrilling—

## —ACT THREE—

*A large, broad veranda, part of* SOLNESS's *house. A portion of the house, with a door leading onto the veranda, is visible left. A railing along the veranda to the right. Far back at the end of the veranda, steps lead down to the garden below. Huge old trees in the garden spread their branches over the veranda and toward the house. Through the trees at the far right, a glimpse of the lower structure of the new house, scaffolding rising around the base of the tower. In the background, the garden is bordered by an old wooden fence. Beyond the fence, a street with small, low, dilapidated houses. The evening sky is streaked with sunlit clouds.*

*On the veranda a garden bench stands along the wall of the house, and in front of the bench a long table. On the other side of the table are an armchair and some stools. All the furniture is wickerwork.*

MRS. SOLNESS, *wrapped in a large white crepe shawl, sits resting in the armchair and gazing off to the right. After a moment* HILDA WANGEL *comes up the steps from the garden. She is dressed the same as before and is wearing her hat. On her blouse she has a little bouquet of small common flowers.*

1990 MRS. SOLNESS: *(turning her head slightly)* Have you had a walk in the garden, Miss Wangel?

HILDA: Yes, I've been having a look around.

MRS. SOLNESS: And found some flowers too, I see.

HILDA: Oh yes! They're just growing thick in through the bushes.

MRS. SOLNESS: Oh, are they really? Still? I hardly ever get down there, you know.

HILDA: *(approaching)* Honestly? You don't run down to the garden every day?

2000 MRS. SOLNESS: *(with a faint smile)* I don't "run" any place, not anymore.

HILDA: Well, but don't you go down even once in a while and visit all those lovely things?

MRS. SOLNESS: It's grown so strange to me, all of it. I'm almost frightened of seeing it again.

HILDA: Your own garden!

MRS. SOLNESS: I don't feel it's mine anymore.

HILDA: What's *that* mean—?

MRS. SOLNESS: No, no, it isn't. Not what it used to be, in
2010    Mother and Father's time. They've taken so much of the garden away, it's painful, Miss Wangel. Can you imagine—they've cut it up and built houses for strangers. People I don't know. And they can sit at their windows and look in on me.

HILDA: *(her face lighting up)* Mrs. Solness?

MRS. SOLNESS: Yes?

HILDA: May I stay here a while with you?

MRS. SOLNESS: Yes, of course, if you want to.

HILDA: *(moving a stool over to the armchair and sitting)* Ah—
2020    you can sit and really sun yourself here, like a cat.

MRS. SOLNESS: *(laying her hand gently on* HILDA's *neck)* It's kind of you to want to sit with me. I thought you'd be going in to my husband.

HILDA: What would I want with him?

MRS. SOLNESS: To help him, I thought.

HILDA: No, thanks. Besides, he's not in. He's over there with

the workmen. But he looked so ferocious I didn't dare speak to him.

MRS. SOLNESS: Oh, underneath he's so mild and softhearted.

HILDA: *Him!*

MRS. SOLNESS: You hardly know him yet, Miss Wangel.    2030

HILDA: *(looking at her warmly)* Are you happy to be moving into the new place?

MRS. SOLNESS: I *should* be happy. It's what Halvard wants—

HILDA: Oh, but not just for that reason.

MRS. SOLNESS: Oh yes, Miss Wangel. For that's no more than my duty, giving in to him. But it isn't always so easy forcing your thoughts to obey.

HILDA: I'm sure it can't be.

MRS. SOLNESS: Believe me, it's not. When one's no better a person than I am, then—    2040

HILDA: You mean, when one's gone through all the sorrow you have—

MRS. SOLNESS: How did you hear of that?

HILDA: Your husband told me.

MRS. SOLNESS: With me he hardly ever mentions those things. Yes, I've been through more than my share in life, Miss Wangel.

HILDA: *(regarding her sympathetically and slowly nodding)* Poor Mrs. Solness. First you had the fire—

MRS. SOLNESS: *(with a sigh)* Yes. Everything of mine burned.    2050

HILDA: And then what was worse followed.

MRS. SOLNESS: *(looks questioningly at her)* Worse?

HILDA: The worst of all.

MRS. SOLNESS: What do you mean?

HILDA: *(softly)* You lost your two little boys.

MRS. SOLNESS: Oh, *them,* yes. Yes, you see, that's something quite different, that. That was an act of Providence, you know. And there one can only bow one's head and submit. And be grateful.

HILDA: And are you?    2060

MRS. SOLNESS: Not always, I'm afraid. I know very well it's my duty. But all the same, I *can't.*

HILDA: Of course not. That's only natural.

MRS. SOLNESS: And time and again I have to remind myself that it was a just punishment for me—

HILDA: Why?

MRS. SOLNESS: Because I wasn't staunch enough under misfortune.

HILDA: But I don't see that—

MRS. SOLNESS: Oh no, no, Miss Wangel. Don't talk anymore to    2070 me about the two little boys. We can only be happy for them. Because they're well off—so well off now. No, it's the small losses in life that strike at your heart. Losing all of those things that other people value at next to nothing.

HILDA: *(laying her arms on* MRS. SOLNESS's *knee and looking up at her fondly)* Dear Mrs. Solness—what sort of things? Tell me.

MRS. SOLNESS: As I say—just little things. There were all the old portraits on the walls that burned. And all the old silk dresses. They'd been in the family for ever so long, genera-    2080 tions—they burned. And all Mother's and Grandmother's lace—that burned too. And just think—their jewels! *(Heavily.)* And then, all the dolls.

HILDA: The dolls?

MRS. SOLNESS: *(choking with tears)* I had nine beautiful dolls.

HILDA: And they burned also?

MRS. SOLNESS: All of them. Oh, that was hard—so hard for me.

HILDA: Were they dolls that you'd had put away, ever since you were little?

MRS. SOLNESS: Not put away. I and the dolls had gone on living 2090 together.

HILDA: After you'd grown up?

MRS. SOLNESS: Yes, long after that.

HILDA: After you were married, too?

MRS. SOLNESS: Oh yes. As long as he didn't see them, then— But then, poor things, they were all burned up. No one ever thought about saving *them.* Oh, it's so sad to remember. Now you mustn't laugh at me, Miss Wangel.

HILDA: I'm not laughing a bit.

MRS. SOLNESS: Because, you see, in a way there was life in them 2100 too. I used to carry them under my heart. Just like little unborn children.

(DR. HERDAL, *with his hat in his hands, comes out through the door and spots* MRS. SOLNESS *and* HILDA.)

DR. HERDAL: So you're out here, Mrs. Solness, catching yourself a cold, hm?

MRS. SOLNESS: It seems so nice and warm here today.

DR. HERDAL: All right. But is something the matter? I got a note from you.

MRS. SOLNESS: (*getting up*) Yes, there's something I have to talk to you about.

DR. HERDAL: Fine. Perhaps we'd better go in, then. (*To* HILDA.) 2110 Still dressed for climbing mountains, hm?

HILDA: (*gaily, rising*) That's right—full gear! But I won't be climbing and breaking my neck today. We two are going to stay quietly down below and watch, Doctor.

DR. HERDAL: Watch what?

MRS. SOLNESS: (*to* HILDA, *in a low, frightened voice*) Shh, shh— for God's sake! He's coming. Just try and get him out of this wild idea. And then, do let's be friends, Miss Wangel. Can't we be?

HILDA: (*throwing her arms impetuously around* MRS. SOLNESS) 2120 Oh—if we only could!

MRS. SOLNESS: (*gently disengaging herself*) Oh-oh-oh! There he is, Doctor. We've got to talk.

DR. HERDAL: Is this about *him?*

MRS. SOLNESS: Of course it is. Just come inside.

(*She and* DR. HERDAL *enter the house. A moment after,* SOLNESS *comes up the steps from the garden. A serious look comes over* HILDA's *face.*)

SOLNESS: (*glancing toward the door of the house, carefully being closed from within*) Have you noticed something, Hilda—that the moment I come, she goes?

HILDA: I've noticed that the moment you come, you *make* her go.

2130 SOLNESS: Maybe so. But I can't help that. (*Scrutinizing her.*) Are you cold, Hilda? You rather look it to me.

HILDA: I've just come up out of a tomb.

SOLNESS: Now what's that mean?

HILDA: That I've been chilled right to the bone, Mr. Solness.

SOLNESS: (*slowly*) I think I understand—

HILDA: What do you want here now?

SOLNESS: I caught sight of you from over there.

HILDA: But then you must have seen her too, hm?

SOLNESS: I knew she'd leave immediately if I came.

HILDA: Is it very hard on you, that she keeps on avoiding you like this? 2140

SOLNESS: In a way it's almost a relief.

HILDA: That you don't have her right under your eyes?

SOLNESS: Yes.

HILDA: And you're not always seeing how she broods over this business of the children?

SOLNESS: Yes. Mostly that.

(HILDA *saunters across the veranda with her hands behind her back, takes a stance at the railing, and looks out over the garden.*)

SOLNESS: (*after a short pause*) Did you talk with her quite a while? (*Hilda remains motionless, without answering.*) I'm asking, did you talk quite a while? (HILDA *says nothing.*) What did she talk about, Hilda? (HILDA *stays silent.*) Poor 2150 Aline! It was the twins, I suppose. (HILDA *shudders nervously, then quickly nods several times.*) She'll never get over it. Never in this world. (*Coming closer.*) Now you're standing there like a statue again. The same as last night.

HILDA: (*turns and looks at him with great, serious eyes*) I'm going away.

SOLNESS: (*sharply*) Away!

HILDA: Yes.

SOLNESS: But I won't let you!

HILDA: What can I do here now? 2160

SOLNESS: Just *be* here, Hilda!

HILDA: (*looking him up and down*) Sure, thanks a lot. You know it wouldn't stop there.

SOLNESS: (*wildly*) So much the better.

HILDA: (*with intensity*) I just *can't* hurt somebody I *know!* Or take away something that's really hers—

SOLNESS: Who wants you to?

HILDA: A stranger, yes. Because that's different, completely! Someone I never laid eyes on. But somebody I've gotten close to—! No, not that! Never! 2170

SOLNESS: But what have I ever suggested?

HILDA: Oh, master builder, you know so well what would happen. And that's why I'm going away.

SOLNESS: And what'll become of me when you're gone? What'll I have to live for then? Afterwards?

HILDA: (*with the inscrutable look in her eyes*) There's no real problem for you. You have your duties to her. Live for those duties.

SOLNESS: Too late. These powers—these—these—

HILDA: Devils— 2180

SOLNESS: Yes, devils! And the troll inside me too—they've sucked all the lifeblood out of her. (*With a desperate laugh.*) They did it to make me happy! Successful! And now she's dead—thanks to me. And I'm alive, chained to the dead. (*In anguish.*) I—I, who can't go on living without joy in life!

(HILDA *goes around the table and sits on the bench with her elbows on the table and her head propped in her hands.*)

HILDA: (*after watching him a while*) What are you building next?

SOLNESS: (*shaking his head*) Don't think I'll build much more now.

HILDA: No more warm, happy homes for mothers and 2190 fathers—and droves of children?

SOLNESS: Who knows if there'll be any use for such homes in

the future.

HILDA: Poor master builder! And you who've gone all these ten years and put your life into—nothing but that.

SOLNESS: Yes, you might as well say it, Hilda.

HILDA: *(in an outburst)* Oh, it's just so senseless, really, so senseless—the whole thing!

SOLNESS: What whole thing?

2200 HILDA: Not daring to take hold of one's own happiness. Of one's own life! Just because someone you know is there, standing in the way.

SOLNESS: Someone you have no right to leave.

HILDA: Who knows if you really don't have a right. And still, all the same— Oh, to sleep the whole business away! *(She lays her arms down flat on the table, rests her head on her hands, and shuts her eyes.)*

SOLNESS: *(turning the armchair and sitting by the table)* Was yours a warm, happy home—up there with your father, 2210 Hilda?

HILDA: *(motionless, answering as if half asleep)* I only had a cage.

SOLNESS: And you won't go back in?

HILDA: *(as before)* Wild birds never like cages.

SOLNESS: They'd rather go hunting in the open sky—

HILDA: *(still as before)* Birds of prey like hunting best—

SOLNESS: *(letting his eyes rest on her)* Oh, to have had the Viking spirit—

HILDA: *(in her usual voice, opening her eyes, but not moving)*
2220 And the other? Say what that was!

SOLNESS: A robust conscience.

*(HILDA sits up on the bench, vivacious once more. Her eyes again have their happy, sparkling look.)*

HILDA: *(nods to him)* I know what you're going to build next!

SOLNESS: Then you know more than I do, Hilda.

HILDA: Yes, master builders—they're really so dumb.

SOLNESS: All right, what's it going to be?

HILDA: *(nods again)* The castle.

SOLNESS: What castle?

HILDA: *My* castle, of course.

SOLNESS: Now you want a castle?

2230 HILDA: Let me ask you—don't you owe me a kingdom?

SOLNESS: If I listen to you, I do.

HILDA: So. You owe me this kingdom, then. And who ever heard of a kingdom without a castle!

SOLNESS: *(more and more animated)* Yes, they usually do go together.

HILDA: Good. So build it for me! Right now!

SOLNESS: *(laughing)* Is everything always "right now"?

HILDA: That's right! Because the ten years, they're up—and I'm not going to wait any longer. So, come on, Mr. Solness—
2240 fork over the castle!

SOLNESS: It's not easy owing you anything, Hilda.

HILDA: You should've thought of that before. It's too late now. Come on—*(Drumming on the table.)* one castle on the table! It's *my* castle! I want it *now!*

SOLNESS: *(more serious, leaning nearer her, with his arms on the table)* What sort of castle did you imagine for yourself, Hilda?

HILDA: *(her expression veiling itself more and more, as if she were peering deep within herself; then, slowly)* My castle
2250 must stand up—very high up—and free on every side. So I

can see far—far out.

SOLNESS: And I suppose it'll have a high tower?

HILDA: A terribly high tower. And at the highest pinnacle of the tower there'll be a balcony. And out on that balcony I'll stand—

SOLNESS: *(instinctively clutching his forehead)* How you can want to stand at those dizzy heights—!

HILDA: Why not! I'll stand right up there and look down on the others—the ones who build churches. And homes for mothers and fathers and droves of children. And you must come 2260 up and look down on them too.

SOLNESS: *(his voice low)* Will the master builder be allowed to come up to the princess?

HILDA: If he wants to.

SOLNESS: *(lower still)* Then I think he'll come.

HILDA: *(nods)* The master builder—he'll come.

SOLNESS: But never build anymore—poor master builder.

HILDA: *(full of life)* Oh, but he will! We two, we'll work together. And that way we'll build the loveliest—the most beautiful thing anywhere in the world. 2270

SOLNESS: *(caught up)* Hilda—tell me, what's that!

HILDA: *(looks smilingly at him, shakes her head a little, purses her lips, and speaks as if to a child)* Master builders, they are very—very stupid people.

SOLNESS: Of course they're stupid. But tell me what it is! What's the world's most beautiful thing that we're going to build together?

HILDA: *(silent a moment, then says, with an enigmatic look in her eyes)* Castles in the air.

SOLNESS: Castles in the air? 2280

HILDA: *(nodding)* Yes, castles in the air! You know what a castle in the air is?

SOLNESS: It's the loveliest thing in the world, you say.

HILDA: *(rising impatiently, with a scornful gesture of her hand)* Why, yes, of course! Castles in the air—they're so easy to hide away in. And easy to build too. *(Looking contemptuously at him.)* Especially for builders who have a—dizzy conscience.

SOLNESS: *(getting up)* From this day on we'll build together, Hilda. 2290

HILDA: *(with a skeptical smile)* A real castle in the air?

SOLNESS: Yes. One with solid foundations.

*(RAGNAR BROVIK comes out of the house. He carries a large green wreath with flowers and silk ribbons.)*

HILDA: *(in an outcry of joy)* The wreath! Oh, that'll be magnificent!

SOLNESS: *(surprised)* Are you bringing the wreath, Ragnar?

RAGNAR: I promised the foreman I would.

SOLNESS: *(relieved)* Oh. Then I suppose your father's better?

RAGNAR: No.

SOLNESS: Didn't he get a lift from what I wrote?

RAGNAR: It came too late. 2300

SOLNESS: Too late!

RAGNAR: When she got back with it, he was in a coma. He'd had a stroke.

SOLNESS: But go home to him, then! Look after your father!

RAGNAR: He doesn't need me anymore.

SOLNESS: But you need to be with him.

RAGNAR: *She's* sitting by his bed.

SOLNESS: *(somewhat uncertain)* Kaja?

RAGNAR: *(giving him a dark look)* Yes—Kaja, yes.

2310 SOLNESS: Go home, Ragnar, to both of them. Let *me* have the wreath.

RAGNAR: *(suppresses a mocking smile)* You don't mean you're going to—

SOLNESS: I'll take it down myself, thanks. *(Takes the wreath from him.)* And go along home. We won't be needing you today.

RAGNAR: I'm aware that you won't be needing me permanently. But today I'm staying.

SOLNESS: Well, then stay, if—you're so anxious to.

2320 HILDA: *(at the railing)* Mr. Solness—I'll stand here and watch you.

SOLNESS: Watch me!

HILDA: It'll be terribly thrilling.

SOLNESS: *(in an undertone)* We'll talk about that later, Hilda. *(He goes, with the wreath, down the steps and off through the garden.)*

HILDA: *(looking after him, then turning to* RAGNAR*)* It seems to me you might at least have thanked him.

RAGNAR: Thanked him? Should I have thanked *him?*

2330 HILDA: Yes, you absolutely should have!

RAGNAR: If anything, it's probably you I should thank.

HILDA: Why do you say that?

RAGNAR: *(without answering)* But just look out for yourself, miss. Because, actually, you hardly know him yet.

HILDA: *(fiercely)* Oh, I know him the best!

RAGNAR: *(with a bitter laugh)* Thank him, when he's held me down year after year! He, who made my own father doubt me. Made me doubt myself— And all that, just so he could—

2340 HILDA: *(as if surmising something)* He could—? Say it out!

RAGNAR: So he could keep her with him.

HILDA: *(with a start toward him)* The girl at the desk!

RAGNAR: Yes.

HILDA: *(threateningly, with fists clenched)* It isn't true! You're lying about him!

RAGNAR: I didn't want to believe it either, before today—when she said it herself.

HILDA: *(as if beside herself)* What did she say! I've got to know! Now! Right now!

2350 RAGNAR: She said he'd taken possession of her mind—completely. That all her thoughts are caught up in him, only him. She says she'll never let him go—that she wants to stay here where *he* is—

HILDA: *(her eyes flashing)* She won't be allowed to!

RAGNAR: *(searchingly)* Who won't allow her?

HILDA: *(quickly)* He won't either.

RAGNAR: Oh no—I understand everything now. From here on she could only be, shall we say—an inconvenience.

HILDA: You understand nothing—when you can talk like that!

2360 No, *I'll* tell you why he kept her.

RAGNAR: Why?

HILDA: So he could keep *you.*

RAGNAR: Did he tell you that?

HILDA: No, but it's true! It *must* be true! *(Wildly.)* I will—I *will* have it that way!

RAGNAR: But just the moment you come by—is when he drops her.

HILDA: *You*—you're the one he dropped. What do you think he cares about strange girls like her?

RAGNAR: *(reflectively)* You suppose he's really been afraid of 2370 me all along?

HILDA: Him afraid? I wouldn't be so conceited if I were you.

RAGNAR: Oh, I think he's suspected for a long time that I had it in me all right. Besides—*afraid*—that's exactly what he is, you know.

HILDA: Him! Oh, don't give me that!

RAGNAR: In certain ways he's afraid—this great master builder. When it comes to stealing other people's happiness in life—like my father's and mine—there he's not afraid. But if it's a matter of climbing up a measly piece of scaffolding—watch 2380 him take God's own sweet time getting around to it!

HILDA: Oh, if you'd only seen him as I did once—way, high up in the spinning sky!

RAGNAR: You've seen that?

HILDA: Of course I have. How proud and free he looked, standing there, tying the wreath to the weather vane!

RAGNAR: I heard that he'd once gone up—just that once in his lifetime. Among us younger men, talking about it—it's almost a legend now. But no power on earth could get him to do it again. 2390

HILDA: He'll do it again today.

RAGNAR: *(scornfully)* Sure—tell me another!

HILDA: We're going to see it!

RAGNAR: Neither you nor I will ever see that.

HILDA: *(in a frenzy)* I *will* see it! I *will* and I *must* see it!

RAGNAR: But he's not going to do it. He simply doesn't dare. He's got this disability now, and that's it.

*(*MRS. SOLNESS *comes out on the veranda.)*

MRS. SOLNESS: *(looking about)* Isn't he here? Where has he gone?

RAGNAR: Mr. Solness is down with the men. 2400

HILDA: He took the wreath over.

MRS. SOLNESS: *(terrified)* He took the wreath! Oh, God, no! Brovik—go down to him! Try to get him back up here!

RAGNAR: Should I say you'd like to speak with him?

MRS. SOLNESS: Oh yes, dear, do that. No, no—don't say *I'd* like anything! You can say that somebody's here—and he should come at once.

RAGNAR: Good. I'll take care of it, Mrs. Solness. *(He goes down the steps and out through the garden.)*

MRS. SOLNESS: Oh, Miss Wangel, you can't imagine how anx- 2410 ious I am about him.

HILDA: But is there anything here, really, to be so frightened about?

MRS. SOLNESS: Of course. It's obvious. Suppose he goes through with this seriously—and tries to climb that scaffolding?

HILDA: *(thrilled)* You think he might?

MRS. SOLNESS: One just never knows what he'll come up with. He could easily do anything.

HILDA: Ah, so you do think that he's—somewhat—? 2420

MRS. SOLNESS: I don't know what to think about him anymore. The doctor's been telling me so much now, and when I put it all together with one thing and another that I've heard him say—

*(*DR. HERDAL *opens the door and looks out.)*

DR. HERDAL: Isn't he coming right up?

MRS. SOLNESS: Yes, I guess so. In any case, I've sent after him.

DR. HERDAL: *(approaching)* But I think you'd better go in, Mrs. Solness—

MRS. SOLNESS: No, no. I'll stay out here and wait for Halvard.

2430 DR. HERDAL: Yes, but some ladies are here asking for you—

MRS. SOLNESS: Good grief, that too? And right at this moment!

DR. HERDAL: They say they absolutely must see the ceremony.

MRS. SOLNESS: Oh, well, I suppose I ought to go in to them after all. It *is* my duty.

DR. HERDAL: Can't you just invite them to move on?

MRS. SOLNESS: No, that wouldn't do. Now that they're here, it's my duty to make them welcome. *(To* HILDA.*)* But you stay here a while—until he comes.

DR. HERDAL: And try to hold him here talking as long as
2440     possible—

MRS. SOLNESS: Yes, do try, Miss Wangel, dear. Hold him, as hard as you can.

HILDA: Aren't you the one who ought to be doing that?

MRS. SOLNESS: Lord, yes—it's my duty, I know. But when you have duties in so many directions, then—

DR. HERDAL: *(looking toward the garden)* There he comes!

MRS. SOLNESS: Oh, my—and I have to go in!

DR. HERDAL: *(to* HILDA*)* Don't say anything about my being here.

2450 HILDA: Don't worry. I'm sure I can find something else to talk to him about.

MRS. SOLNESS: And hold him, no matter what. I'm sure *you* can do it best.

*(*MRS. SOLNESS *and* DR. HERDAL *go into the house.* HILDA *remains standing on the veranda.* SOLNESS *comes up the steps from the garden.)*

SOLNESS: I hear someone wants me.

HILDA: Yes, I'm the someone, Mr. Solness.

SOLNESS: Oh, it's you, Hilda. I was afraid it'd be Aline and the doctor.

HILDA: You're pretty easily frightened, I guess!

SOLNESS: You think so?

2460 HILDA: Yes, people say you're afraid to go clambering around—like up on scaffolds.

SOLNESS: Well, that's a special case.

HILDA: But you *are* afraid—it's true, then?

SOLNESS: Yes, I am.

HILDA: Afraid of falling and killing yourself?

SOLNESS: No, not that.

HILDA: What, then?

SOLNESS: Afraid of retribution, Hilda.

HILDA: Of retribution? *(Shaking her head.)* I don't follow that.

2470 SOLNESS: Sit down and I'll tell you something.

HILDA: Yes, do! Right now! *(She sits on a stool by the railing and looks expectantly at him.)*

SOLNESS: *(tosses his hat on the table)* You know that I first started out with building churches.

HILDA: *(nods)* I know that, of course.

SOLNESS: Because, you see, as a boy I came from a pious home out in the country. That's why the building of churches seemed to me the noblest thing I could do with my life.

HILDA: Go on.

2480 SOLNESS: And I think I can say that I built those poor country churches in so honest and warm and fervent a spirit that—that—

HILDA: That—what?

SOLNESS: Well, that I feel He should have been pleased with me.

HILDA: He? Who's "He"?

SOLNESS: He who was to have the churches, of course. He whose honor and glory they served.

HILDA: I see! But are you sure that—that He wasn't—well, pleased with you?     2490

SOLNESS: *(scoffingly)* He pleased with me! What are you saying, Hilda? He who turned the troll in me loose to stuff its pockets. He who put on call, right around the clock for me, all these—these—

HILDA: Devils—

SOLNESS: Yes—both kinds. Oh no, I pretty well got the idea that He wasn't pleased with me. *(Mysteriously.)* Actually, that's why He had the old house burn.

HILDA: That was why—?

SOLNESS: Yes, don't you see? He wanted me to have the chance     2500 to become a complete master in my own realm—and enhance His glory with still greater churches. At first I didn't understand what He was after—but then, all at once, it dawned on me.

HILDA: When was that?

SOLNESS: When I was building the church tower in Lysanger.

HILDA: I thought so.

SOLNESS: For you see, Hilda, up in those strange surroundings I used to go around musing and pondering inside myself. And I saw then, clearly, why He'd taken my children from     2510 me. It was to keep me from becoming attached to anything else. I was only to be a master builder, nothing else. And all my life through, I was to go on building for Him. *(Laughs.)* But that never got very far.

HILDA: What did you do then?

SOLNESS: First, I searched my heart—tested myself—

HILDA: And then?

SOLNESS: Then I did the impossible. I no less than He.

HILDA: The impossible?

SOLNESS: I'd never in my life been able to climb straight up to     2520 a great height. But that day I could.

HILDA: *(jumping up)* Yes, yes, you could!

SOLNESS: And when I stood right up at the very top, hanging the wreath, I said to Him: Hear me, Thou Almighty! From this day on, I'll be a free creator—free in my own realm, as you are in yours.

HILDA: *(with great, luminous eyes)* That was the singing I heard in the air!

SOLNESS: Yes—but His mill went right on grinding.

HILDA: What do you mean by *that?*     2530

SOLNESS: *(looking despondently at her)* This building homes for human beings—it's not worth a bent pin, Hilda!

HILDA: You really feel that now?

SOLNESS: Yes, because now I see it. Human beings don't know how to use these homes of theirs. Not for being happy in. And I couldn't have found use for a home like that either— if I'd had one. *(With a quiet, bitter laugh.)* So that's the sum total, as far, as far back as I can see. Nothing really built. And nothing sacrificed for the chance to build, either. Nothing, nothing—it all comes to nothing.     2540

HILDA: Then will you never build anything again?

SOLNESS: *(animated)* Why, I'm just now beginning!

HILDA: With what? What'll you build? Tell me now!

SOLNESS: The one thing human beings can be happy in—that's what I'm building now.

HILDA: *(looking intently at him)* Master builder—you mean our castles in the air.

SOLNESS: Castles in the air, yes.

HILDA: I'm afraid you'd be dizzy before we got halfway up.

2550 SOLNESS: Not if I went hand in hand with you, Hilda.

HILDA: *(with a touch of suppressed resentment)* Only with me? Won't we have company?

SOLNESS: Who else?

HILDA: Oh, her—that Kaja at the desk. Poor thing—don't you want her along too?

SOLNESS: Ah, so she was the subject of Aline's little talk.

HILDA: Is it true, or isn't it?

SOLNESS: *(hotly)* I wouldn't answer a question like that! You'll have to trust me, absolutely!

2560 HILDA: For ten years I've trusted you utterly—utterly—

SOLNESS: You'll have to keep on trusting me.

HILDA: Then let me see you high and free, up there!

SOLNESS: *(wearily)* Oh, Hilda—I'm not up to that every day.

HILDA: *(passionately)* I want you to! I want that! *(Imploring.)* Just once more, master builder! Do the impossible again!

SOLNESS: *(looking deep into her eyes)* If I did try it, Hilda, I'd stand up there and talk to Him the same as before.

HILDA: *(with mounting excitement)* What would you say to Him?

2570 SOLNESS: I'd say: Hear me, Almighty God—you must judge me after your own wisdom. But from now on, I'll build only what's most beautiful in all this world—

HILDA: *(enraptured)* Yes—yes—yes!

SOLNESS: Build it together with a princess that I love—

HILDA: Oh, tell Him that! Tell Him!

SOLNESS: Yes. And then I'll say to Him: I'm going down now and throw my arms about her and kiss her—

HILDA: —many times! Say that!

SOLNESS: —many, many times, I'll say.

2580 HILDA: And then—?

SOLNESS: Then I'll swing my hat in the air—and come down to earth, here—and do as I said.

HILDA: *(with outstretched arms)* Now I see you again as if there was singing in the air!

SOLNESS: *(looks at her with bowed head)* How did you ever become what you are, Hilda?

HILDA: How have you made me into what I am?

SOLNESS: *(decisively)* The princess shall have her castle.

HILDA: *(jubilant, clapping her hands)* Oh, Mr. Solness—! My 2590 lovely, lovely castle. Our castle in the air!

SOLNESS: On a solid foundation.

*(Out in the street, faintly visible through the trees, a* CROWD OF PEOPLE *has gathered. Distant music of a brass band is heard from behind the new house.* MRS. SOLNESS, *with a fur stole around her neck,* DR. HERDAL, *with her white shawl on his arm, and several* LADIES *come out onto the veranda.* RAGNAR BROVIK *comes up at the same time from the garden.)*

MRS. SOLNESS: *(to* RAGNAR*)* There'll be music too?

RAGNAR: Yes. They're from the Building Trades Association. *(To* SOLNESS.*)* I'm supposed to tell you from the foreman that he's ready to go up now with the wreath.

SOLNESS: *(taking his hat)* Good. I'll go down myself.

MRS. SOLNESS: *(anxiously)* What are you going to do there, Halvard?

SOLNESS: *(brusquely)* I've got to be down below with the men.

MRS. SOLNESS: Yes, down below. Please, stay down below. 2600

SOLNESS: Don't I always—as a normal rule? *(He goes down the steps and off across the garden.)*

MRS. SOLNESS: *(calling after him from the railing)* But you must tell the man to be careful climbing! Promise me, Halvard.

DR. HERDAL: *(to* MRS. SOLNESS*)* You see, I was right. He's forgotten all about that craziness.

MRS. SOLNESS: Oh, what a relief! We've had men fall there twice now, and both times they were killed on the spot. *(Turning to* HILDA.*)* Thank you so much, Miss Wangel, for taking hold of him like that. I'm sure I never could have 2610 managed it.

DR. HERDAL: *(roguishly)* You know, Miss Wangel—you have a gift for taking hold of a man that you shouldn't hide!

*(*MRS. SOLNESS *and* DR. HERDAL *move across to the* LADIES, *who stand nearer the steps, looking out over the garden.* HILDA *remains standing at the railing in the foreground.* RAGNAR *goes over to her.)*

RAGNAR: *(with stifled laughter, dropping his voice)* Miss Wangel—do you see all the young people, down there in the street?

HILDA: Yes.

RAGNAR: They're my fellow students, come for a look at the master.

HILDA: Why do they want to look at *him?* 2620

RAGNAR: They want to see him afraid to climb up on his own house.

HILDA: So, that's what the boys want!

RAGNAR: *(with seething scorn)* He's kept us down so long—now we're going to see him have the pleasure of keeping himself down.

HILDA: You're not going to see it. Not today.

RAGNAR: *(smiling)* Really? And where will we see him?

HILDA: High—high up by the weather vane, that's where.

RAGNAR: *(laughs)* Him! Oh, you bet! 2630

HILDA: His will—is to climb straight to the top. And that's where you'll see him, too.

RAGNAR: His *will*, yes, sure—that I believe. But he simply can't do it. His head would be swimming before he was even halfway up. He'd have to crawl down again on his hands and knees.

DR. HERDAL: *(pointing)* Look! There goes the foreman up the ladder.

MRS. SOLNESS: And he's got the wreath to carry, too. Oh, if he'll only take care. 2640

RAGNAR: *(crying out in astonishment)* But it's—!

HILDA: *(in an outburst of joy)* It's the master builder himself!

MRS. SOLNESS: *(with a shriek of terror)* Yes, it's Halvard! Oh, my God! Halvard! Halvard!

DR. HERDAL: Shh. Don't shout at him!

MRS. SOLNESS: *(half distracted)* I'll go to him. Get him down again!

DR. HERDAL: *(restraining her)* All of you—don't move!

HILDA: *(motionless, following* SOLNESS *with her eyes)* He's climbing and climbing. Always higher. Always higher! Look! 2650

Just look!

RAGNAR: *(breathlessly)* Now he's got to turn back. It's all he can do.

HILDA: He's climbing and climbing. He's almost there.

MRS. SOLNESS: Oh, I'll die of fright. I can't bear to look.

DR. HERDAL: Then don't watch him.

HILDA: There he is, on the highest planks! Straight to the top!

DR. HERDAL: Nobody move—you hear me!

HILDA: *(exulting with quiet intensity)* At last! At last! Now I can
2660     see him great and free again.

RAGNAR: *(nearly speechless)* But this is—

HILDA: All these ten years I've seen him like this. How strong
he stands! Terribly thrilling, after all. Look at him! Now he's
hanging the wreath on the vane!

RAGNAR: I feel like I'm seeing something here that's—that's
impossible.

HILDA: Yes, it's the impossible, now, that he's doing! *(With the
inscrutable look in her eyes.)* Do you see anyone up there
with him?

2670     RAGNAR: There's nobody else.

HILDA: Yes, there's someone he's struggling with.

RAGNAR: You're mistaken.

HILDA: You don't hear singing in the air, either?

RAGNAR: It must be the wind in the treetops.

HILDA: I hear the singing—a tremendous music! *(Crying out
in wild exultation.)* Look, look! He's waved his hat! He's
waving to us down here! Oh, wave—wave back up to him
again—because now, now, it's fulfilled! *(Snatches the white
shawl from the doctor, waves it, and calls out.)* Hurray for
2680     master builder Solness!

DR. HERDAL: Stop! Stop! In God's name—!

*(The* LADIES *on the veranda wave their handkerchiefs, and
shouts of "Hurray" fill the street below. Suddenly they are cut
short, and the* CROWD *breaks into a cry of horror. A human
body, along with some planks and splintered wood, is indistinctly seen plunging down between the trees.)*

MRS. SOLNESS AND THE LADIES: *(as one)* He's falling! He's
falling!

*(MRS. SOLNESS sways and sinks back in a faint; the* LADIES *catch
her up amid cries and confusion. The* CROWD *in the street
breaks the fence down and storms into the garden.* DR. HERDAL
*also rushes down below. A short pause.)*

HILDA: *(stares fixedly upward and speaks as if petrified)* My
master builder.

RAGNAR: *(leans, trembling, against the railing)* He must have
been smashed to bits. Killed on the spot.

ONE OF THE LADIES: *(as* MRS. SOLNESS *is carried into the house)*
Run down to the doctor—

RAGNAR: I can't move—     2690

ANOTHER LADY: Call down to someone, then!

RAGNAR: *(trying to call)* How is it? Is he alive?

A VOICE: *(down in the garden)* Mr. Solness is dead.

OTHER VOICES: *(nearer)* His whole head's been crushed—He
fell right into the quarry.

HILDA: *(turns to* RAGNAR *and says quietly)* I can't see him up
there anymore.

RAGNAR: How horrible this is. And so, after all—he really
couldn't do it.

HILDA: *(as if out of a hushed, dazed triumph)* But he went 2700
straight, straight to the top. And I heard harps in the air.
*(Swings the shawl up overhead and cries with wild intensity.)* My—my master builder!

# CASEBOOK ON IBSEN

Henrik Ibsen

Letters on
*The Wild Duck*
(1884)

TRANSLATED BY
MARY MORISON

*In these letters—to the eminent Danish literary critic Georg Brandes, to the Norwegian poet Theodor Caspari, and to Ibsen's publisher, Frederick Hegel—Ibsen alludes to the process of composing the play. What is striking is the offhand, casual attitude Ibsen has to the complexity of his own composition. Despite his reputation for creating subtle and nuanced characters, Ibsen clearly regards refining the plot of the play as the most difficult phase of composition, where his labor as a playwright is the most intensive.*

*To George Brandes*

Rome, 25th June 1884.

Dear Brandes,—My best thanks for your letter, which I ought to have answered long ago, especially as I know that you keep strict accounts in the matter of correspondence—although you assure me that you have changed somewhat in this respect. . . .

I have finished the first sketch of my new work, a play in five acts, and am now engrossed in elaborating it—moulding the language more carefully, and individualizing the characters and speeches more thoroughly. In a day or two I go to Gossensass in the Tyrol, expecting to put the finishing touches to it there in the course of the summer. My wife and son go to Norway.

Please excuse this hurried letter. Remember us most kindly to your wife and your little girls.—Your attached friend,

Henrik Ibsen.

*To Theodor Caspari*

Rome, 27th June 1884.

Dear Mr. Caspari,—I do not remember whether I told you, when we were together here, that one of my faults was dilatoriness in the matter of answering letters. At any rate you have now been made aware of it by experience. I have had your kind letter and beautiful, warm-hearted verses lying on my table since the middle of April, and have looked at them every day, with the good intention of writing to you "tomorrow." And not until now has my resolution become performance! Forgive the delay, and accept my warmest thanks for the poem, which moves me every time I read it—and I read it often, for there is something in it which speaks to me of home.

You are greatly mistaken in imagining it to be my desire that you should break your lyre in pieces. It most certainly is not. There is not a single poem of yours which I could wish unwritten; and I hope that you will produce much in the future in the domain of metre and rhyme; for it seems to me that it is for this your natural gifts qualify you. I have not forgotten certain disrespectful utterances of my own on the subject of the metrical art; but they were merely the expression of my own temporary attitude to that art. I gave up universal standards long ago, because I ceased believing in the justice of applying them. I believe that there is nothing else and nothing better for us all to do than in spirit and in truth to realise ourselves. This, in my opinion, constitutes real liberalism; and you can therefore understand why the so-called Liberals are in so many ways thoroughly antipathetic to me.

All this winter I have been revolving some new follies in my brain; I went on doing it until they assumed dramatic form; and now I have just completed a play in five acts—that is to say, the rough draft of it; now comes the elaboration, the more energetic individualisation of the persons and their mode of expression. In order to find the quiet and solitude necessary for this work, I am going in a day or two to Gossensass in the Tyrol. My wife and son go to Norway. I wish I could have accompanied them; but that is not possible. At my age a man must make use of his time for his work; the work will never be finished; he "will not have time to write the last verse"; but still, one wishes to get as much done as possible.

I wish you and Mrs. Caspari a pleasant summer! You may be sure that we shall not forget either of you. Thanking you again, I remain—Yours very sincerely,

Henrik Ibsen.

*To Frederik Hegel*

Gossensass, *2nd September* 1884.

Dear Mr. Hegel,—Along with this letter I send you the manuscript of my new play, *The Wild Duck.* For the last four months I have worked at it every day; and it is not without a certain feeling of regret that I part from it. Long, daily association with the persons in this play has endeared them to me, in spite of their manifold failings; and I am not without hope that they may find good and kind friends among the great reading public, and more particularly among the actor tribe—to whom they offer rôles which will well repay the trouble spent on them. The study and representation of these characters will not be an easy task; therefore it is desirable that the book should be offered to the theatres as early as possible in the season; I shall send the letters, which you will be good enough to despatch along with the different copies.

In some ways this new play occupies a position by itself among my dramatic works; in its method it differs in several respects from my former ones. But I shall say no more on this subject at present. I hope that my critics will discover the points alluded to; they will, at any rate, find several things to squabble about and several things to interpret. I also think that *The Wild Duck* may very probably entice some of our young dramatists into new paths; and this I consider a result to be desired.

I shall now take a thorough rest, until new plans begin to announce themselves importunately. Where we shall spend the winter I do not yet know. If cholera breaks out in Rome or the neighborhood, we shall not be able to go there for some time. For the present I am staying on here, where, in spite of the altitude, we are still having real summer weather.

As you probably know, the Björnsons are at Schwaz, two or three hours by rail north of Gossensass. I have accepted an invitation to go and see them; it is now more than twenty years since we met. Perhaps Jonas Lie will come to them at the same time, from Berchtesgaden; but this is quite uncertain.

Please accept my best thanks for all the kindness and attention shown by you and your family to my wife and son during their stay in Copenhagen. They have been at the North Cape, and are now spending the summer at the Lake of Selbo, near Trondhjem. It is uncertain yet when they come south.

With kindest regards to yourself and your family, I remain—Yours sincerely and gratefully,

Henrik Ibsen.

## Bernard Shaw
(1856–1950)

FROM *The Quintessence
of Ibsenism*
(1913)

RESPONDING *to the extraordinary controversy surrounding Ibsen's plays, Bernard Shaw delivered a lecture to the Fabian Society in 1890 on the subject of socialism in contemporary literature. Over the course of the next two years these insights were expanded into the book-length study* The Quintessence of Ibsenism. *Shaw tended to read Ibsen's plays as socialist allegories, plays that were specifically intended to undermine the complacent pieties of bourgeois life; he saw* A Doll House *as a play on the subject of women's rights, for example. But though Shaw saw in Ibsen's work the reflection of his own interests as a playwright, his observations on Ibsen's drama were both influential and richly provocative. First published in 1892, Shaw revised* The Quintessence of Ibsenism *again after the death of Ibsen.*

*The Wild Duck, 1884*

After *An Enemy of the People,* Ibsen, as I have said, left the vulgar ideals for dead, and set about the exposure of those of the choicer spirits, beginning with the incorrigible idealists who had idealized his very self, and were becoming known as Ibsenites. His first move in this direction was such a tragicomic slaughtering of sham Ibsenism that his astonished victims plaintively declared that *The Wild Duck,* as the new play was called, was a satire on his former works; whilst the pious, whom he had disappointed so severely by his interpretation of Brand, began to hope that he was coming back repentant to the fold. The household to which we are introduced in *The Wild Duck* is not, like Mrs Alving's, a handsome one made miserable by superstitious illusions, but a shabby one made happy by romantic illusions. The only member of it who sees it as it really is is the wife, a good-natured Philistine who desires nothing better. The husband, a vain, petted, spoilt dawdler, believes that he is a delicate and high-souled man, devoting his life to redeeming his old father's name from the disgrace brought on it by imprisonment for breach of the forest laws. This redemption he proposes to effect by making himself famous as a great inventor some day when he has the necessary inspiration. Their daughter, a girl in her teens, believes intensely in her father and in the promised invention. The disgraced grandfather cheers himself by drink whenever he can get it; but his chief resource is a wonderful garret full of rabbits and pigeons. The old man has procured a number of second-hand Christmas trees; and with these he has turned the garret into a sort of toy forest, in which he can play at bear hunting, which was one of the sports of his youth and prosperity. The weapons employed in the hunting expeditions are a gun which will not go off, and a pistol which occasionally brings down a rabbit or a pigeon. A crowning touch is given to the illusion by a wild duck, which, however, must not be shot, as it is the special property of the girl, who reads and dreams whilst her mother cooks, washes, sweeps, and carries on the photographic work which is supposed to be the business of her husband. Mrs Ekdal does not appreciate Hjalmar's highly strung sensitiveness of character, which is constantly suffering agonizing jars from her vulgarity; but then she does not appreciate that other fact that he is a lazy and idle imposter. Downstairs there is a disgraceful clergyman named Molvik, a hopeless drunkard; but even he respects himself and is tolerated because of a special illusion invented for him by another lodger, Dr Relling, upon whom the lesson of the household above has not been thrown away. Molvik, says the doctor, must break out into drinking fits because he is daimonic, an imposing explanation which completely relieves the reverend gentleman from the imputation of vulgar tippling.

Into this domestic circle there comes a new lodger, an idealist of the most advanced type. He greedily swallows the daimonic theory of the clergyman's drunkenness, and enthusiastically accepts the photographer as the high-souled hero he supposes himself to be; but he is troubled because the relations of the man and his wife do not constitute an ideal marriage. He happens to know that the woman, before her marriage, was the cast-off mistress of his own father; and because she has not told her husband this, he conceives her life as founded on a lie, like that of Bernick in *Pillars of Society*. He accordingly sets himself to work out the woman's salvation for her, and establish ideally frank relations between the pair, by simply blurting out the truth, and then asking them, with fatuous self-satisfaction, whether they do not feel much the better for it. This wanton piece of mischief has more serious results than a mere domestic scene. The husband is too weak to act on his bluster about outraged honor and the impossibility of his ever living with his wife again; and the woman is merely annoyed with the idealist for telling on her; but the girl takes the matter to heart and shoots herself. The doubt cast on her parentage, with her father's theatrical repudiation of her, destroy her ideal place in the home, and make her a source of discord there; so she sacrifices herself, thereby carrying out the teaching of the idealist mischief-maker, who has talked a good deal to her about the duty and beauty of self-sacrifice, without foreseeing that he might be taken in mortal earnest. The busybody thus finds that people cannot be freed from their failings from without. They must free themselves. When Nora is strong enough to live out of the doll's house, she will go out of it of her own accord if the door stands open; but if before that period you take her by the scruff of the neck and thrust her out, she will only take refuge in the next establishment of the kind that offers to receive her. Woman has thus two enemies to deal with; the old-fashioned one who wants to keep the door locked, and the new-fashioned one who wants to thrust her into the street before she is ready to go. In the cognate case of a hypocrite and liar like Bernick, exposing him is a mere police measure; he is none the less a liar and hypocrite when you have exposed him. If you want to make a sincere and truthful man of him, all you can wisely do is to remove what you can of the external obstacles to his exposing himself, and then wait for the operation of his internal impulse to confess. If he has no such impulse, then you must put up with him as he is. It is useless to make claims on him which he is not yet prepared to meet. Whether, like Brand, we make such claims because to refrain would be to compromise with evil, or, like Gregers Werle, because we think their moral beauty must recommend them at sight to every one, we shall alike incur Relling's impatient assurance that 'life would be quite tolerable if we could only get rid of the confounded duns that keep on pestering us in our poverty with the claims of the ideal.'

Ibsen now lays down the completed task of warning the world against its idols and anti-idols, and passes into the shadow of death, or rather into the splendor of his sunset glory; for his magic is extraordinarily potent in these four plays, and his purpose more powerful. And yet the shadow of

*Down Among the Dead Men*

death is here; for all four, except *Little Eyolf,* are tragedies of the dead, deserted and mocked by the young who are still full of life. The Master Builder is a dead man before the curtain rises: the breaking of his body to pieces in the last act by its fall from the tower is rather the impatient destruction of a ghost of whose delirious whisperings Nature is tired than of one who still counts among the living. Borkman and the two women, his wife and her sister, are not merely dead: they are buried; and the creatures we hear and see are only their spirits in torment. 'Never dream of life again,' says Mrs. Borkman to her husband, 'lie quiet where you are.' And the last play of all is frankly called *When We Dead Awaken.* Here the quintessence of Ibsenism reaches its final distillation; morality and reformation give place to mortality and resurrection; and the next event is the death of Ibsen himself: he, too, creeping ghost-like through the blackening mental darkness until he reaches his actual grave, and can no longer make Europe cry with pity by sitting at a copybook, like a child, trying to learn again how to write, only to find that divine power gone for ever from his dead hand. He, the crustiest, grimmest hero since Beethoven, could not die like him, shaking his fist at the thunder and alive to the last: he must follow the path he had traced for Solness and Borkman, and survive himself. But as these two were dreamers to the last, and never so luminous in their dreams as when they could no longer put the least of them into action; so we may believe that when Ibsen could no longer remember the alphabet, or use a dictionary, his soul may have been fuller than ever before of the unspeakable. Do not snivel, reader, over the contrast he himself drew between the man who was once the greatest writer in the world, and the child of seventy-six trying to begin again at pothooks and hangers. Depend on it, whilst there was anything left of him at all there was enough of his iron humor to grin as widely as the skeleton with the hour-glass who was touching him on the shoulder.

*The Master Builder,*
*1892*

Halvard Solness is a dead man who has been a brilliantly successful builder, and, like the greatest builders, his own architect. He is sometimes in the sublime delirium that precedes bodily death, and sometimes in the horror that varies the splendors of delirium. He is mortally afraid of young rivals; of the younger generation knocking at the door. He has built churches with high towers (much as Ibsen built great historical dramas in verse). He has come to the end of that and built 'homes for human beings' (much as Ibsen took to writing prose plays of modern life). He has come to the end of that too, as men do at the end of their lives; and now he must take to dead men's architecture, the building of castles in the air. Castles in the air are the residences not only of those who have finished their lives, but of those who have not yet begun them. Another peculiarity of castles in the air is that they are so beautiful and so wonderful that human beings are not good enough to live in them: therefore when you look round you for somebody to live with you in your castle in the air, you find nobody glorious enough for that sanctuary. So you resort to the most dangerous of all the varieties of idolization: the idolization of the person you are most in love with; and you take him or her to live with you in your castle. And as imaginative young people, because they are young, have no illusions about youth, whilst old people, because they are old, have no illusions about age, elderly gentlemen very often idolize adolescent girls, and adolescent girls idolize elderly gentlemen. When the idolization is not reciprocal, the idolizer runs terrible risks if the idol is selfish and unscrupulous. Cases of girls enslaved by elderly gentlemen whose scrupulous respect for their maiden purity is nothing but an excuse for getting a quantity of secretarial or domestic service out of them that is limited only by their physical endurance, without giving them anything in return, are not at all so rare as they would be if the theft of a woman's youth and devotion were as severely condemned by public opinion as the comparatively amiable and negligible theft of a few silver spoons and forks. On the other hand doting old gentlemen are duped and ruined by designing young women who care no more for them than a Cornish fisherman cares for a conger eel. But sometimes, when the two natures are poetic, we have scenes of Bettina and Goethe, which are perhaps wholesome as well as pleasant for both parties when they are good enough and sensible enough to face the inexorable on the side of age and to recognize the impossible on the side of youth. On these conditions, old gentlemen are indulged in fancies for poetic little girls; and the poetic little girls have their emotions and imaginations satisfied harmlessly until they find a suitable mate.

But the master builder, though he gets into just such a situation, does not get out of it so cheaply, because he is not outwardly an old, or even a very elderly gentleman. 'He is a man no longer young, but healthy and vigorous, with closely cut curly hair, dark moustache, and dark thick eyebrows.' Also he is daimonic, not sham daimonic like Molvik in *The Wild Duck*, but really daimonic, with luck, a star, and mystic 'helpers and servers,' who find the way through the maze of life for him. In short, a very fascinating man, whom nobody, himself least of all, could suspect of having shot his bolt and being already dead. Therefore a man for whom a girl's castle in the air is a very dangerous place, as she may easily thrust upon him adventures that would tax the prime of an unexhausted man, and are mere delirious madness for a spent one.

Grasp this situation and you will be able to follow a performance of *The Master Builder* without being puzzled; though to the unprepared theatregoer it is a bewildering business. You see Solness in his office, ruthlessly exploiting the devotion of the girl secretary Kaia, who idolizes him, and giving her nothing in return but a mesmerizing word occasionally. You see him with equal ruthlessness apparently, but really with the secret terror of 'the priest who slew the slayer and shall himself be slain,' trying to suppress a young rival who is as yet only a draughtsman in his employment. To keep the door shut against the younger generation already knocking at it: that is all he can do now, except build castles in the air; for, as I have said, the effective part of the man is dead. Then there is his wife, who, knowing that he is failing in body and mind, can do nothing but look on in helpless terror. She cannot make a happy home for Solness, because her own happiness has been sacrificed to his genius. Or rather, her own genius, which is for 'building up the souls of little children,' has been sacrificed to his. For they began their family life in an old house that was part of her property: the sort of house that may be hallowed by old family associations and memories of childhood, but that it pays the speculative builder to pull down and replace by rows of villas. Now the ambitious Solness knows this but dares not propose such a thing to his wife, who cherishes all the hallowing associations, and even keeps her dolls: nine lovely dolls, feeling them 'under her heart, like little unborn children.' Everything in the house is precious to her: the old silk dresses, the lace, the portraits. Solness knows that to touch these would be tearing her heart up by the roots. So he says nothing; does nothing; only notes a crack in the old chimney which should be repaired if the house is to be safe against fire, and does not repair it. Instead, he pictures to himself a fire, with his wife out in the sledge with his two children, and nothing but charred ruins facing her when she returns; but what matter, since the children have escaped and are still with her? He even calls upon his helpers and servers to consider whether this vision might not become a reality. And it does. The house is burnt; the villas rise on its site and cover the park; and Halvard Solness becomes rich and successful.

But the helpers and servers have not stuck to the program for all that. The fire did not come from the crack in the chimney when all the domestic fires were blazing. It came at night when the fires were low, and began in a cupboard quite away from the chimney. It came when Mrs. Solness and the children were in bed. It shattered the mother's health; it killed the children she was nursing; it devoured the portraits and the silk dresses and the old lace; it burnt the nine lovely dolls; and it broke the heart under which the dolls had lain like little unborn children. That was the price of the master builder's success. He is married to a dead woman; and he is trying to atone by building her a new villa: a new tomb to replace the old home; for he is gnawed with remorse.

But the fire was not only a good building speculation: it also led to his obtaining commissions to build churches. And one triumphant day, when he was celebrating the completion of the giant tower he had added to the old church at Lysanger, it suddenly flashed on him that his house had been burnt, his wife's life laid waste, and his own happiness destroyed, so that he might become a builder of churches. Now it happens that one of his difficulties as a builder is that he has a bad head for heights, and cannot venture even on a second floor balcony. Yet in the fury of that thought he mounts to the pinnacle of his tower, and there, face to face with God, who has, he feels, wasted the wife's gift of building up the souls of little children to make the husband a builder of steeples, he declares that he will never set hand to church-building again, and will henceforth build nothing but homes for happier men than he. Which vow he keeps, only to find that the home, too, is a devouring idol, and that men and women have no longer any use for it.

In spite of his excitement, he very nearly breaks his neck after all; for among the crowd below there is a little devil of a girl who waves a white scarf and makes his head swim. This tiny animal is no other than the younger stepdaughter of Ellida, *The Lady from the Sea*, Hilda Wangel, of whose taste for 'thrilling' sensations we had a glimpse in that play. On the same evening Solness is entertained at a club banquet, in consequence of which he is not in the most responsible condition when he returns to sup at the house of Dr. Wangel, who is putting him up for the night. He meets the imp there; thinks her like a little princess in her white dress; kisses her; and promises her to come back in ten years and carry her off to the kingdom of Orangia. Perhaps it is only just to mention that he stoutly denies these indiscretions afterwards; though he admits that when he wishes something to happen between himself and somebody else, the somebody else always imagines it actually has happened.

The play begins ten years after the climbing of the tower. The younger generation knocks at the door with a vengeance. Hilda, now a vigorous young woman, and a great builder of castles in the air, bursts in on him and demands her kingdom; and very soon she sends him up a tower again (the tower of the new house) and waves her scarf to him as madly as ever. This time he really does break his neck; and so the story ends.

## Raymond Williams
(1921–1988)

FROM *Modern Tragedy*
(1966)

*THE Marxist cultural critic Raymond Williams wrote extensively on drama. In* Modern Tragedy, *Williams invites us to see tragedy not as a universal form or experience, but as something local, an experience that must be discovered and defined anew as the historical circumstances of its surrounding society change. Williams was also the author of several groundbreaking books, including* Culture and Society *(1958),* Drama from Ibsen to Brecht *(1968), and* The Country and the City *(1973).*

Liberal tragedy, at its full development, drew from all the sources that have been named, but in a new form and pressure created a new and specific structure of feeling. It is important, at this stage, not to try to fragment it, when it appears in Ibsen. The humanist exploration of the unknown reaches of life; the bourgeois preoccupation with humanitarianism and with money; the romantic intensities of alienation, remorse and perverted desire; the social recognition of dead institutions and limiting beliefs: all these are present in Ibsen, but in active combination, not as separate influences. To try to resolve his work into one of these lines has been a common practice in criticism: Ibsen the social critic; Ibsen the romantic or existentialist: each has been plausibly presented. But the real interest lies, where the work lies, in the struggle of these forces and in their composition into a particular drama.

Ibsen creates again and again in his plays, with an extraordinary richness of detail, false relationships, a false society, a false condition of man. The marks along this scale are often difficult to discern. The immediate lie is almost always present, but there is great variation in its ultimate reference: sometimes to an alterable condition; sometimes to an absolute condition; often, ambiguously, between these. Yet the generalising reference, in whatever kind, is persistent; the lie is never merely local, for it is seen as a symptom of a general condition. Characteristically, for liberal tragedy, the fight against the lie is individual; a man fights for his own life. Brand's vocation is 'All or Nothing,' and compromise is personally impossible:

> *One thing is yours you may not spend,*
> *Your very inmost self of all,*
> *You may not bind it, may not bend,*
> *Nor stem the river of your call.*

Or again:

> *Self completely to fulfil,*
> *That's a valid right of man,*
> *And no more than that I will.*

At the same time, the 'right' is also the 'call':

> *A great one gave me charge. I must.*

The call to wholeness is seen as self-fulfilment, and yet also as necessary. The right and the duty coincide in self-fulfilment, as in the classic liberal statements.

Yet the whole point about self-fulfilment is that it challenges, to the death, the existing compromise order. For here the lie is actual: men are afraid of wholeness and of self-fulfilment. As the Provost argues:

> *The surest way to destroy a man*
> *Is to turn him into an individual.*

Men have settled for a fragmentary life, as the easiest way, but this settlement is the sickness of their own personal lives and of their society. Routine is destructive, but so also are the wild breaks from routine, the simple refusals. What is needed is a new and total assent, for

> *Our time, our generation, that is sick*
> *And must be cured.*

Thus the individual, fulfilling himself absolutely, becomes, or offers himself as, the liberator. This position is reached again and again in Ibsen, but the resolution varies. In *Pillars of Society, A Doll's House, Enemy of the People,* the refusal of compromise is unambiguously carried through, if not to liberation, at least to positive individual defiance. In *Peer Gynt,* what looks like the quest for self-fulfilment is shown in the end to be simple evasion: the self alone, detached from the reality of world and relationships, withers and is wasted, to be redeemed only by return. More commonly, in varying degrees of emphasis, the individual's struggle is seen as both necessary and tragic. The evasion of fulfilment, by compromise, breeds false relationships and a sick society, but the attempt at fulfilment ends again and again in tragedy: the individual is destroyed in his attempt to climb out of his partial world.

This is the crux of liberal tragedy, and it is in many ways difficult to understand. The simple position is that of the heroic liberator opposed and destroyed by a false society: the liberal martyr. It is clear that Ibsen knew this feeling; it finds memorable expression in Stockmann. But it is not in this pattern that Ibsen takes his heroes to their deaths. Stockmann, faced only by this, is stronger and survives:

> The strongest man in the world is he who stands most alone.

Nor is it merely by accident and complication that the hero dies. The tragedy, in fact, is built into the form of the aspiration, in the significant concept of *debt.*

In the action and imagery of the plays, the nature of debt is persistently explored. Just as aspiration cannot be reduced simply to social reform, to a religious calling, or to self-expression, but remains obstinately general—the liberation of human spirit and energy—so debt cannot be reduced to inherited obligations, to a society burdened by compromises, or to original sin. These are often the forms in which aspiration and debt appear, but the actual works are more often explorations of the conflicting forces than definitions of them. Thus while in *Brand* there is a simple fatalism—

> *Blood of children must be spilt*
> *To atone for parents' guilt*

—it is also clear that new debts are contracted in the act of refusal of compromise; it is Brand himself, and not merely Brand the son or the human being, who is eventually guilty. The position would be simpler if this guilt were then condemned, if the voice through the final avalanche—'He is the God of love'—were a verdict. But this is not the case. Brand had to do what he did, and yet had to come to this point. This is not ethical tragedy, where a different choice would have brought safety. The choice and the fate admit no real alternatives.

What happens, again and again in Ibsen, is that the hero defines an opposing world, full of lies and compromises and dead positions, only to find, as he struggles against it, that as a man he belongs to this world, and has its destructive inheritance in himself. Ibsen turned this way and that, looking for a way out of this tragic deadlock, but normally he returned to it, and confessed its terrible power:

> Ghosts! . . . I almost believe we are all ghosts, Pastor Manders. It is not only what we have inherited from our fathers and mothers that walks in us. It is every kind of dead idea, lifeless old beliefs and so on. They are not alive, but they cling to us for all that, and we can never rid ourselves of them. Whenever I read a newspaper I seem to see ghosts stealing between the lines. There must be ghosts the whole country over, as thick as the sands of the sea. And then we are all of us so wretchedly afraid of the light.

This position, so often stated, is not a gloss for surrender to the darkness. The cry for light, the desire to climb out of such a world, is persistent and emphatic:

> Give me air and the blaze of day . . .
> Through darkness to light . . .
> A summer night on the uplands . . .
> The joy of life . . . always, always the joy of life—light and sunshine
>     and glorious air . . .
> Mother, give me the sun.

But as the last phrase, the dying cry of Osvald, reminds us, the light is only a breaking aspiration, at the limits of human endurance. The death of Julian the Apostate, not the death of Christ, is the significant ending:

> Beautiful earth, beautiful life . . . O, Helios, Helios, why hast thou betrayed me?

There is no turning away from life to death, no tragic resignation. Ibsen's heroes, characteristically, die fighting and struggling and climbing: the aspiration to light is confirmed, not contradicted, by their deaths. In this sense, they are still heroes, but also they are tragic heroes. The ghosts

> cling to us . . . we can never rid ourselves of them.

Or as the liberal Rosmer puts it:

> We can never escape them, we of this house.

Ibsen seems to depend, as some of his language certainly depends, on a traditional idea of original sin. But the effect of his whole work is in fact a transformation of this. He never gives up the idea of the false society, even when he has realised that its complications eat into the lives of those opposing it. Nor, truly, does he ever mean 'sin' by 'debt.' The debts that count, in bringing his heroes down, are incurred in the struggle for life and light, however wayward this is often shown to be. When we have said 'sin,' of Adam's desire, we have discounted human life, in any aspiring sense. But this desire, in Ibsen, is deep and valid. This is most clearly shown in *Emperor and Galilean,* where the false world of power and the false doctrine of resignation are alike rejected, in the struggle for the 'third empire,' in which 'the spirit of men shall re-enter on its heritage.' It is the false condition of spirit against flesh that Julian fights, because

> all that is human has become unlawful since the day when the seer of Galilee became ruler of the world. Through him, life has become death.

The desire fails, or is broken, but is never denied. Ibsen's world, from his historical dramas to his domestic plays, is recognisable always by this fact: the struggle of individual desire, in a false and compromising situation, to break free and know itself. This is why we must not render him back to a dramatic tradition which would show the desire as false or unlawful. In the best sense, this is still a liberal world.

It is also, however, the world of liberal tragedy. Implacably, in most of his plays, the affirmed desire is brought to a breaking-point

—a tight place where you stick fast. There is no going forward or backward—

and the hero, if not the desire itself, is broken. Why should this be so? Why, repeatedly, should so powerful a struggle of human desire fail to break through? It is not any force outside man that breaks him. As Rosmer says, going to his death:

There is no judge over us, and therefore we must do justice upon ourselves.

But the justice, still, is death. The conviction of guilt, and of necessary retribution, is as strong as ever it was when imposed by an external design.

And this is the heart of liberal tragedy, for we have moved from the heroic position of the individual liberator, the aspiring self against society, to a tragic position, of the self against the self. Guilt, that is to say, has become internal and personal, just as aspiration was internal and personal. The internal and personal fact is the only general fact, in the end. Liberalism, in its heroic phase, begins to pass into its twentieth-century breakdown: the self-enclosed, guilty and isolated world; the time of man his own victim.

We are still in this world, and it is doubtful if we can clearly name all its pressures. A characteristic ideology has presented it as truth and even as science, until argument against it has come to seem hopeless. A structure of feeling as deep as this enacts a world, as well as interpreting it, so that we learn it from experience as well as from ideology. All we can say, reflecting on Ibsen's tragedy, is that the deadlock reached there, the heroic deadlock in which men die still struggling to climb, was indeed necessary. For there is no way out, there is only an inevitable tragic consciousness, while desire is seen as essentially individual. We have to push past Ibsen's undoubted social consciousness to discover, at its roots, this same individual consciousness. Certainly there is to be reform, the 'sick earth' is to be 'made whole,' but this is to happen, always, by an individual act: the liberal conscience, *against* society. Change is never to be *with* people; if others come, they can at most be led. But also change, significantly often, is against people; it is against their wills that the liberator is thrown, and disillusion is then rapid. He speaks for human desire, as a general fact, but he knows this only as individual fulfilment. The self then makes its most terrible discovery: that there is not only a world outside it, resisting it, but other selves, capable of similar suffering, and desire. It is possible then for fulfilment to be re-defined: a getting away from the world and from others; the loneliness of the high mountains. But desire had included the joy of life: the life of earth, and of men and women, which the hero is still governed by, even while he drives himself to reject it. The conflict is then indeed internal: a desire for relationship when all that is known of relationship is restricting; desire narrowing to an image in the mind, until it is realised that the search for warmth and light has ended in cold and darkness. Every move towards relationship ends in guilt. It is significant that nowhere in Ibsen is there a loving, active, lasting relationship; the image of it, at the end of *Peer Gynt*, is as much a relapse from effort, a return to the mother, as a discovery of a loving equal. More often, the tie to the parent is not even relapse. There is a kind of terror in natural inheritance itself. As later in Freudian psychology, the parent-child relationship is guilty as such, and the revelation of the face or feeling of father and mother, behind the adult self, is in itself horrifying. That inescapable connection haunts, quite literally, the liberal idea of the self. In this sense, to be born is to be guilty, and inheritance is inevitably 'debt.' For the identity of the 'free' self is limited and impugned by the necessary physical inheritance. That connection to others is involuntary, and is in the blood. To the liberal self this is not connection but tainting.

Then, driven by individual desire, which cannot admit any final connection, Ibsen's adult persons simply involve and damage each other, beyond the possibility of fulfilment. Freedom is defined as getting away from this net, or exposing it, in the name of truth. But there is nowhere to get away to, except by renunciation of the individual life and desire which are still active and compelling. Desire, consistently, betrays desire. The most active search to fulfil the self leads away from the persons in whom fulfilment is desired. It was this that Ibsen recognised, in his last plays; most notably in the Dramatic Epilogue:

> We see the irretrievable only when . . .
> When? . . .
> When we dead awaken.
> What do we really see then?
> We see that we have never lived.

The search for self-fulfilment has ended in the denial of life:

> It was self-murder, a deadly sin against myself. And that sin I can never expiate.

It is the final tragic recognition: that the self, which is all that is known as desire, leads away from fulfilment, and to its own breakdown.

From this recognition, there is no way out, within the liberal consciousness. There is either the movement to common desire, common aspiration, which politically is socialism, or there is the acceptance, reluctant at first but strengthening and darkening, of failure and breakdown as common and inevitable. In one way or the other, a total condition is asserted, and the differentiated self becomes dramatically rare. It is true that Shaw, in *Saint Joan* and elsewhere, could retain the simpler pattern, of the heroic and liberating individual destroyed by a false society. Numerically, many other plays have repeated this, but, at least in European drama, this pattern has commonly failed to include any of the deepest human energies and problems. The heroic individual, as in Shaw, survives only as a romantic portrait, emptied of personality so that the positive role can be played without complications. The act of liberation, correspondingly, is in the narrow sense historical or political; it is not an absolute human demand, but a limited cause here and there. The problem of the frustrated individual is masked by his theatrical transformation into a movement, leaving all the deeper problems, of history and personality, untouched.

# Oscar Wilde

Oscar Fingal O'Flahertie Willis Wilde (1854–1900) is best known as the aesthete's asthete of 1880s and 1890s London, famous for his epigrammatic wit, for his novel *The Picture of Dorian Gray* (1890) and the moody symbolist drama *Salomé* (1892), for the highly polished dramas he produced in the 1890s—*Lady Windermere's Fan* (1892), *A Woman of No Importance* (1893), *An Ideal Husband* (1895)—capped by his transcendent "trivial comedy for serious people," *The Importance of Being Earnest* (1895). But Wilde is also remembered for the tragedy of his life as well, the terrible trial in which he was convicted of homosexual practices and sentenced to two years' hard labor, and for the poverty, isolation, and rejection that ensued.

Wilde was born in Dublin, the second son of Sir William Wilde—an author, oculist, and surgeon—and Jane Francesca Elgee, a poet and translator. He was educated at the Portora Royal School, read classics at Trinity College, Dublin, and then matriculated at Magdalen College, Oxford, where he continued to study classics. Leaving Oxford in 1876, Wilde began a career as a poet—his poem "Ravenna" won the Newdigate prize in 1878—and occasional critic on artistic subjects. By 1881, his wit, his pose, his green carnation (already part of the vestimentary code of Victorian gay culture) were so well known that he could be satirized as Bunthorne in Gilbert and Sullivan's operetta *Patience*. In the early 1880s he perfected his lecture performance on tour throughout the United States and Canada, but once he was married to Constance Lloyd in 1884—his two sons Cyril and Vyvyan were born in 1885 and 1886—Wilde had need of an income as a regular reviewer and essayist. Through the late 1880s, Wilde gained additional fame as the paradoxical spokesman of aestheticism, writing a brilliant series of articles for the *Pall Mall Gazette*, the *Dramatic Review, Nineteenth Century,* and other magazines, notably "The Decay of Lying" (1889), "The Artist as Critic" (1890), and "The Truth of Masks" (1885).

The posed, paradoxical, masked quality of Wilde's public *persona* had another dimension, for Wilde's homosexuality forced him to lead an elaborate double life. The passage of the Criminal Law Amendment Act in 1885 made homosexual activity illegal, and Wilde risked—and eventually suffered—both social rejection and legal punishment. As his career and public visibility began to crest in the early 1890s with the publication of *The Picture of Dorian Gray* and the success of his first plays, Wilde became involved with a young man, Lord Alfred Douglas. In 1895, Douglas's father, the Marquess of Queensberry left a card at Wilde's club, addressed to Oscar Wilde, "posing as a somdomite" [*sic*]. Against the advice of his friends, Wilde prosecuted the Marquess for criminal libel, but when Queensberry was acquitted, Wilde was arrested for "acts of gross indecency with other male persons" and subjected to two jury trials, in which a series of young men were put on the stand, testifying to their sexual relations with Wilde. In the first trial, the jury was unable to reach a verdict; in the second, Wilde was found guilty and given the maximum sentence of two years' hard labor. Although he was eventually moved from hard labor in Pentonville to Wandsworth prison, and then finally to Reading Gaol, prison broke Wilde's health. Constance changed the last names of Cyril and Vyvyan to avoid association with Wilde, and when he was released in 1897 he was bankrupt and alone. Although Wilde's sexual orientation had long been known or suspected by many of his friends, most were unwilling to associate with Wilde after such public scandal, and when Wilde returned to society he was cruelly and systematically shunned. He settled first in France, then joined Alfred Douglas briefly in Italy; in 1898 he published *The Ballad of Reading Gaol* and settled in Paris, where he died two years later.

## The Importance of Being Earnest
## (1895)

Despite its energetic "triviality," *The Importance of Being Earnest* is deeply, symbolically involved in the contours of Wilde's life. The opening of *Earnest* in February of 1895 at George Alexander's fashionable St. James's Theatre was something of a society event; fearing the publicity of Wilde's trial, Alexander closed the hugely successful play only weeks later. But *The Importance of Being Earnest* seems to resonate with Wilde's life in other ways as well. For in an important sense, *The Importance of Being Earnest* is a play about masking. Much as Wilde's sexual identity had constantly to be negotiated behind the fictive "conventions" of polite society—his sexuality could be tolerated only as long as it was kept discreetly offstage, disacknowledged, unspoken—so in *Earnest* the process of social life in general seems to depend on a tissue of acceptable lies, which occasionally verge on truth: Algernon Moncrieff invents "an invaluable permanent invalid called Bunbury" so that he will have an excuse to escape London; Jack Worthing invents a wastrel younger brother named Ernest as an excuse to escape the country; Cecily invents scenes for her diary and Gwendolen keeps hers handy to "have something sensational to read on the train"; Jack and Algy, both vying to be baptized "Ernest," turn out to be brothers; and Jack, a foundling, turns out to named Ernest after all.

As Algy remarks in Act One, "The truth is rarely pure and never simple. Modern life would be very tedious if it were either, and modern literature a complete impossibility!" In *Earnest*, Wilde carefully constructs a comedy in which the deceptive surfaces of experience, the manifest fictions and deceptions of "modern life" turn out to provide the only vehicle for truth the play has to offer. For beneath the constricted, yet infinitely manipulable conventions of polite society surges the powerful force of desire. It is manifest in the elaborate verbal sparring between Jack, Algy, Gwendolen, and Cecily; in the manic, adolescent energy that drives Jack and Algy to the brink of baptism; even in the appetitive fury of the muffin scene. One final way in which these social conventions are marked is through their connection to the conventions of comedy itself—conventions that are forced to the forefront of the audience's attention throughout the play. *Earnest* comes to a climax in a paroxysm of artificiality. Making a mockery of the recognition scene between long-lost siblings of romantic comedy, Wilde's Jack Worthing turns out to *be* his fictitious brother Ernest after all. In *The Importance of Being Earnest*, all convention—both social and comic—is shown to be a kind of mask, a fiction that sometimes enables the expression of truth.

# — The Importance of Being Earnest —
## Oscar Wilde

### —CHARACTERS—

| | |
|---|---|
| JOHN WORTHING, J.P. | LADY BRACKNELL |
| ALGERNON MONCRIEFF | HON. GWENDOLEN FAIRFAX |
| REV. CANON CHASUBLE, D.D. | CECILY CARDEW |
| MERRIMAN, *Butler* | MISS PRISM, *Governess* |
| LANE, *Manservant* | |

THE SCENES OF THE PLAY.

ACT I:  Algernon Moncrieff's Flat in Half-Moon Street, W.

ACT II:  The Garden at the Manor House, Woolton.

ACT III:  Drawing-Room of the Manor House, Woolton.

*Time.—The Present.*      *Place.—London.*

### —ACT ONE—

SCENE.—*Morning-room in* ALGERNON's *flat in Half-Moon Street. The room is luxuriously and artistically furnished. The sound of a piano is heard in the adjoining room. (*LANE *is arranging afternoon tea on the table, and after the music has ceased,* ALGERNON *enters.)*

ALGERNON: Did you hear what I was playing, Lane?

LANE: I didn't think it polite to listen, sir.

ALGERNON: I'm sorry for that, for your sake. I don't play accurately—anyone can play accurately—but I play with wonderful expression. As far as the piano is concerned, sentiment is my forte. I keep science for Life.

LANE: Yes, sir.

ALGERNON: And, speaking of the science of Life, have you got the cucumber sandwiches cut for Lady Bracknell?

10  LANE: Yes, sir. *(Hands them on a salver.)*

ALGERNON: *(inspects them, takes two, and sits down on the sofa)* Oh! . . . by the way, Lane, I see from your book that on Thursday night, when Lord Shoreman and Mr. Worthing were dining with me, eight bottles of champagne are entered as having been consumed.

LANE: Yes, sir; eight bottles and a pint.

ALGERNON: Why is it that at a bachelor's establishment the servants invariably drink the champagne? I ask merely for information.

20  LANE: I attribute it to the superior quality of the wine, sir. I have often observed that in married households the champagne is rarely of a first-rate brand.

ALGERNON: Good Heavens! Is marriage so demoralizing as that?

LANE: I believe it *is* a very pleasant state, sir. I have had very little experience of it myself up to the present. I have only been married once. That was in consequence of a misunderstanding between myself and a young woman.

ALGERNON: *(languidly)* I don't know that I am much interested

30  in your family life, Lane.

LANE: No, sir; it is not a very interesting subject. I never think of it myself.

ALGERNON: Very natural, I am sure. That will do, Lane, thank you.

LANE: Thank you, sir. *(*LANE *goes out.)*

ALGERNON: Lane's views on marriage seem somewhat lax. Really, if the lower orders don't set us a good example, what on earth is the use of them? They seem, as a class, to have absolutely no sense of moral responsibility.

*(Enter* LANE.*)*

LANE: Mr. Ernest Worthing.     40

*(Enter* JACK. LANE *goes out.)*

ALGERNON: How are you, my dear Ernest? What brings you up to town?

JACK: Oh, pleasure, pleasure! What else should bring one anywhere? Eating as usual, I see, Algy!

ALGERNON: *(stiffly)* I believe it is customary in good society to take some slight refreshment at five o'clock. Where have you been since last Thursday?

JACK: *(sitting down on the sofa)* In the country.

ALGERNON: What on earth do you do there?

JACK: *(pulling off his gloves)* When one is in town one amuses  50 oneself. When one is in the country one amuses other people. It is excessively boring.

ALGERNON: And who are the people you amuse?

JACK: *(airily)* Oh, neighbours, neighbours.

ALGERNON: Got nice neighbours in your part of Shropshire?

JACK: Perfectly horrid! Never speak to one of them.

ALGERNON: How immensely you must amuse them! *(Goes over and takes sandwich.)* By the way, Shropshire is your county, is it not?

JACK: Eh? Shropshire? Yes, of course. Hallo! Why all these  60 cups? Why cucumber sandwiches? Why such reckless extravagance in one so young? Who is coming to tea?

ALGERNON: Oh! merely Aunt Augusta and Gwendolen.

JACK: How perfectly delightful!

ALGERNON: Yes, that is all very well; but I am afraid Aunt Augusta won't quite approve of your being here.

JACK: May I ask why?

ALGERNON: My dear fellow, the way you flirt with Gwendolen is perfectly disgraceful. It is almost as bad as the way Gwendolen flirts with you.     70

JACK: I am in love with Gwendolen. I have come up to town expressly to propose to her.

ALGERNON: I thought you had come up for pleasure? . . . I call that business.

JACK: How utterly unromantic you are!

ALGERNON: I really don't see anything romantic in proposing. It is very romantic to be in love. But there is nothing romantic about a definite proposal. Why, one may be accepted. One usually is, I believe. Then the excitement is all over. The very essence of romance is uncertainty. If ever I get married, I'll certainly try to forget the fact.

JACK: I have no doubt about that, dear Algy. The Divorce Court was specially invented for people whose memories are so curiously constituted.

ALGERNON: Oh! there is no use speculating on that subject. Divorces are made in Heaven—(JACK *puts out his hand to take a sandwich.* ALGERNON *at once interferes.*) Please don't touch the cucumber sandwiches. They are ordered specially for Aunt Augusta. (*Takes one and eats it.*)

JACK: Well, you have been eating them all the time.

ALGERNON: That is quite a different matter. She is my aunt. (*Takes plate from below.*) Have some bread and butter. The bread and butter is for Gwendolen. Gwendolen is devoted to bread and butter.

JACK: (*advancing to table and helping himself*) And very good bread and butter it is, too.

ALGERNON: Well, my dear fellow, you need not eat as if you were going to eat it all. You behave as if you were married to her already. You are not married to her already, and I don't think you ever will be.

JACK: Why on earth do you say that?

ALGERNON: Well, in the first place girls never marry the men they flirt with. Girls don't think it right.

JACK: Oh, that is nonsense!

ALGERNON: It isn't. It is a great truth. It accounts for the extraordinary number of bachelors that one sees all over the place. In the second place, I don't give my consent.

JACK: Your consent!

ALGERNON: My dear fellow, Gwendolen is my first cousin. And before I allow you to marry her, you will have to clear up the whole question of Cecily. (*Rings bell.*)

JACK: Cecily! What on earth do you mean? What do you mean, Algy, by Cecily? I don't know anyone of the name of Cecily.

(*Enter* LANE.)

ALGERNON: Bring me that cigarette case Mr. Worthing left in the smoking-room the last time he dined here.

LANE: Yes, sir. (LANE *goes out.*)

JACK: Do you mean to say you have had my cigarette case all this time? I wish to goodness you had let me know. I have been writing frantic letters to Scotland Yard about it. I was very nearly offering a large reward.

ALGERNON: Well, I wish you would offer one. I happen to be more than usually hard up.

JACK: There is no good offering a large reward now that the thing is found.

(*Enter* LANE *with the cigarette case on a salver.* ALGERNON *takes it at once.* LANE *goes out.*)

ALGERNON: I think that is rather mean of you, Ernest, I must say. (*Opens case and examines it.*) However, it makes no matter, for, now that I look at the inscription, I find that the thing isn't yours after all.

JACK: Of course it's mine. (*Moving to him.*) You have seen me with it a hundred times, and you have no right whatsoever to read what is written inside. It is a very ungentlemanly thing to read a private cigarette case.

ALGERNON: Oh! it is absurd to have a hard-and-fast rule about what one should read and what one shouldn't. More than half of modern culture depends on what one shouldn't read.

JACK: I am quite aware of the fact, and I don't propose to discuss modern culture. It isn't the sort of thing one should talk of in private. I simply want my cigarette case back.

ALGERNON: Yes; but this isn't your cigarette case. This cigarette case is a present from someone of the name of Cecily, and you said you didn't know anyone of that name.

JACK: Well, if you want to know, Cecily happens to be my aunt.

ALGERNON: Your aunt!

JACK: Yes. Charming old lady she is, too. Lives at Tunbridge Wells. Just give it back to me, Algy.

ALGERNON: (*retreating to back of sofa*) But why does she call herself little Cecily if she is your aunt and lives at Tunbridge Wells? (*Reading.*) "From little Cecily with her fondest love."

JACK: (*moving to sofa and kneeling upon it*) My dear fellow, what on earth is there in that? Some aunts are tall, some aunts are not tall. That is a matter that surely an aunt may be allowed to decide for herself. You seem to think that every aunt should be exactly like your aunt! That is absurd! For Heaven's sake give me back my cigarette case. (*Follows* ALGERNON *round the room.*)

ALGERNON: Yes. But why does your aunt call you her uncle? "From little Cecily, with her fondest love to her dear Uncle Jack." There is no objection, I admit, to an aunt being a small aunt, but why an aunt, no matter what her size may be, should call her own nephew her uncle, I can't quite make out. Besides, your name isn't Jack at all; it is Ernest.

JACK: It isn't Ernest; it's Jack.

ALGERNON: You have always told me it was Ernest. I have introduced you to everyone as Ernest. You answer to the name of Ernest. You look as if your name was Ernest. You are the most earnest looking person I ever saw in my life. It is perfectly absurd your saying that your name isn't Ernest. It's on your cards. Here is one of them. (*Taking it from case.*) "Mr. Ernest Worthing, B 4, The Albany." I'll keep this as a proof your name is Ernest if ever you attempt to deny it to me, or to Gwendolen, or to anyone else. (*Puts the card in his pocket.*)

JACK: Well, my name is Ernest in town and Jack in the country, and the cigarette case was given to me in the country.

ALGERNON: Yes, but that does not account for the fact that your small Aunt Cecily, who lives at Tunbridge Wells, calls you her dear uncle. Come, old boy, you had much better have the thing out at once.

JACK: My dear Algy, you talk exactly as if you were a dentist. It is very vulgar to talk like a dentist when one isn't a dentist. It produces a false impression.

ALGERNON: Well, that is exactly what dentists always do. Now, go on! Tell me the whole thing. I may mention that I have always suspected you of being a confirmed and secret Bunburyist; and I am quite sure of it now.

JACK: Bunburyist? What on earth do you mean by a Bunburyist?

ALGERNON: I'll reveal to you the meaning of that incomparable expression as soon as you are kind enough to inform me why you are Ernest in town and Jack in the country.

190

JACK: Well, produce my cigarette case first.

ALGERNON: Here it is. (*Hands cigarette case.*) Now produce your explanation, and pray make it improbable. (*Sits on sofa.*)

JACK: My dear fellow, there is nothing improbable about my explanation at all. In fact it's perfectly ordinary. Old Mr. Thomas Cardew, who adopted me when I was a little boy, made me in his will guardian to his grand-daughter, Miss Cecily Cardew. Cecily, who addresses me as her uncle from motives of respect that you could not possibly appreciate, lives at my place in the country under the charge of her admirable governess, Miss Prism.

200

ALGERNON: Where is that place in the country, by the way?

JACK: That is nothing to you, dear boy. You are not going to be invited. . . . I may tell you candidly that the place is not in Shropshire.

ALGERNON: I suspected that, my dear fellow! I have Bunburyed all over Shropshire on two separate occasions. Now, go on. Why are you Ernest in town and Jack in the country?

210 JACK: My dear Algy, I don't know whether you will be able to understand my real motives. You are hardly serious enough. When one is placed in the position of guardian, one has to adopt a very high moral tone on all subjects. It's one's duty to do so. And as a high moral tone can hardly be said to conduce very much to either one's health or one's happiness, in order to get up to town I have always pretended to have a younger brother of the name of Ernest, who lives in the Albany, and gets into the most dreadful scrapes. That, my dear Algy, is the whole truth pure and simple.

220 ALGERNON: The truth is rarely pure and never simple. Modern life would be very tedious if it were either, and modern literature a complete impossibility!

JACK: That wouldn't be at all a bad thing.

ALGERNON: Literary criticism is not your forte, my dear fellow. Don't try it. You should leave that to people who haven't been at a University. They do it so well in the daily papers. What you really are is a Bunburyist. I was quite right in saying you were a Bunburyist. You are one of the most advanced Bunburyists I know.

230 JACK: What on earth do you mean?

ALGERNON: You have invented a very useful younger brother called Ernest, in order that you may be able to come up to town as often as you like. I have invented an invaluable permanent invalid called Bunbury, in order that I may be able to go down into the country whenever I choose. Bunbury is perfectly invaluable. If it wasn't for Bunbury's extraordinary bad health, for instance, I wouldn't be able to dine with you at Willis's to-night, for I have been really engaged to Aunt Augusta for more than a week.

240 JACK: I haven't asked you to dine with me anywhere tonight.

ALGERNON: I know. You are absolutely careless about sending out invitations. It is very foolish of you. Nothing annoys people so much as not receiving invitations.

JACK: You had much better dine with your Aunt Augusta.

ALGERNON: I haven't the smallest intention of doing anything of the kind. To begin with, I dined there on Monday, and once a week is quite enough to dine with one's own relatives. In the second place, whenever I do dine there I am always treated as a member of the family, and sent down with either no woman at all, or two. In the third place, I know

250

perfectly well whom she will place me next to, tonight. She will place me next Mary Farquhar, who always flirts with her own husband across the dinner-table. That is not very pleasant. Indeed, it is not even decent . . . and that sort of thing is enormously on the increase. The amount of women in London who flirt with their own husbands is perfectly scandalous. It looks so bad. It is simply washing one's clean linen in public. Besides, now that I know you to be a confirmed Bunburyist I naturally want to talk to you about Bunburying. I want to tell you the rules.

260

JACK: I'm not a Bunburyist at all. If Gwendolen accepts me, I am going to kill my brother, indeed I think I'll kill him in any case. Cecily is a little too much interested in him. It is rather a bore. So I am going to get rid of Ernest. And I strongly advise you to do the same with Mr. . . . with your invalid friend who has the absurd name.

ALGERNON: Nothing will induce me to part with Bunbury, and if you ever get married, which seems to me extremely problematic, you will be very glad to know Bunbury. A man who marries without knowing Bunbury has a very tedious time of it.

270

JACK: That is nonsense. If I marry a charming girl like Gwendolen, and she is the only girl I ever saw in my life that I would marry, I certainly won't want to know Bunbury.

ALGERNON: Then your wife will. You don't seem to realize, that in married life three is company and two is none.

JACK: (*sententiously*) That, my dear young friend, is the theory that the corrupt French Drama has been propounding for the last fifty years.

ALGERNON: Yes; and that the happy English home has proved in half the time.

280

JACK: For heaven's sake, don't try to be cynical. It's perfectly easy to be cynical.

ALGERNON: My dear fellow, it isn't easy to be anything now-a-days. There's such a lot of beastly competition about. (*The sound of an electric bell is heard.*) Ah! that must be Aunt Augusta. Only relatives, or creditors, ever ring in that Wagnerian manner. Now, if I get her out of the way for ten minutes, so that you can have an opportunity for proposing to Gwendolen, may I dine with you to-night at Willis's?

290

JACK: I suppose so if you want to.

ALGERNON: Yes, but you must be serious about it. I hate people who are not serious about meals. It is so shallow of them.

(*Enter* LANE.)

LANE: Lady Bracknell and Miss Fairfax. (ALGERNON *goes forward to meet them. Enter* LADY BRACKNELL *and* GWENDOLEN.)

LADY BRACKNELL: Good afternoon, dear Algernon, I hope you are behaving very well.

ALGERNON: I'm feeling very well, Aunt Augusta.

LADY BRACKNELL: That's not quite the same thing. In fact the two things rarely go together. (*Sees* JACK *and bows to him with icy coldness.*)

300

ALGERNON: (*to* GWENDOLEN) Dear me, you are smart!

GWENDOLEN: I am always smart! Aren't I, Mr. Worthing?

JACK: You're quite perfect, Miss Fairfax.

GWENDOLEN: Oh! I hope I am not that. It would leave no room for developments, and I intend to develop in *many directions*. (GWENDOLEN *and* JACK *sit down together in the corner.*)

310 LADY BRACKNELL: I'm sorry if we are a little late, Algernon, but I was obliged to call on dear Lady Harbury. I hadn't been there since her poor husband's death. I never saw a woman so altered; she looks quite twenty years younger. And now I'll have a cup of tea, and one of those nice cucumber sandwiches you promised me.

ALGERNON: Certainly, Aunt Augusta. (*Goes over to tea-table.*)

LADY BRACKNELL: Won't you come and sit here, Gwendolen?

GWENDOLEN: Thanks, mamma, I'm quite comfortable where I am.

320 ALGERNON: (*picking up empty plate in horror*). Good heavens! Lane! Why are there no cucumber sandwiches? I ordered them specially.

LANE: (*gravely*) There were no cucumbers in the market this morning, sir. I went down twice.

ALGERNON: No cucumbers!

LANE: No, sir. Not even for ready money.

ALGERNON: That will do, Lane, thank you.

LANE: Thank you sir. (*Goes out.*)

ALGERNON: I am greatly distressed, Aunt Augusta, about there
330 being no cucumbers, not even for ready money.

LADY BRACKNELL: It really makes no matter, Algernon. I had some crumpets with Lady Harbury, who seems to me to be living entirely for pleasure now.

ALGERNON: I hear her hair has turned quite gold from grief.

LADY BRACKNELL: It certainly has changed its colour. From what cause I, of course, cannot say. (ALGERNON *crosses and hands tea.*) Thank you. I've quite a treat for you to-night, Algernon. I am going to send you down with Mary Farquhar. She is such a nice woman, and so attentive to her husband.
340 It's delightful to watch them.

ALGERNON: I am afraid, Aunt Augusta, I shall have to give up the pleasure of dining with you to-night after all.

LADY BRACKNELL: (*frowning*) I hope not, Algernon. It would put my table completely out. Your uncle would have to dine upstairs. Fortunately he is accustomed to that.

ALGERNON: It is a great bore, and, I need hardly say, a terrible disappointment to me, but the fact is I have just had a telegram to say that my poor friend Bunbury is very ill again. (*Exchanges glances with* JACK.) They seem to think I should
350 be with him.

LADY BRACKNELL: It is very strange. This Mr. Bunbury seems to suffer from curiously bad health.

ALGERNON: Yes; poor Bunbury is a dreadful invalid.

LADY BRACKNELL: Well, I must say, Algernon, that I think it is high time that Mr. Bunbury made up his mind whether he was going to live or to die. This shilly-shallying with the question is absurd. Nor do I in any way approve of the modern sympathy with invalids. I consider it morbid. Illness of any kind is hardly a thing to be encouraged in others. Health
360 is the primary duty of life. I am always telling that to your poor uncle, but he never seems to take much notice . . . as far as any improvement in his ailments goes. I should be much obliged if you would ask Mr. Bunbury, from me, to be kind enough not to have a relapse on Saturday, for I rely on you to arrange my music for me. It is my last reception and one wants something that will encourage conversation, particularly at the end of the season when everyone has practically said whatever they had to say, which, in most cases, was probably not much.

ALGERNON: I'll speak to Bunbury, Aunt Augusta, if he is still 370 conscious, and I think I can promise you he'll be all right by Saturday. You see, if one plays good music, people don't listen, and if one plays bad music people don't talk. But I'll run over the programme I've drawn out, if you will kindly come into the next room for a moment.

LADY BRACKNELL: Thank you, Algernon. It is very thoughtful of you. (*Rising, and following* ALGERNON.) I'm sure the programme will be delightful, after a few expurgations. French songs I cannot possibly allow. People always seem to think that they are improper, and either look shocked, which is 380 vulgar, or laugh, which is worse. But German sounds a thoroughly respectable language, and indeed, I believe is so. Gwendolen, you will accompany me.

GWENDOLEN: Certainly, mamma. (LADY BRACKNELL *and* ALGERNON *go into the music-room,* GWENDOLEN *remains behind.*)

JACK: Charming day it has been, Miss Fairfax.

GWENDOLEN: Pray don't talk to me about the weather, Mr. Worthing. Whenever people talk to me about the weather, I always feel quite certain that they mean something else. 390 And that makes me so nervous.

JACK: I do mean something else.

GWENDOLEN: I thought so. In fact, I am never wrong.

JACK: And I would like to be allowed to take advantage of Lady Bracknell's temporary absence . . .

GWENDOLEN: I would certainly advise you to do so. Mamma has a way of coming back suddenly into a room that I have often had to speak to her about.

JACK: (*nervously*) Miss Fairfax, ever since I met you I have admired you more than any girl . . . I have ever met since . . . I 400 met you.

GWENDOLEN: Yes, I am quite aware of the fact. And I often wish that in public, at any rate, you had been more demonstrative. For me you have always had an irresistible fascination. Even before I met you I was far from indifferent to you. (JACK *looks at her in amazement.*) We live, as I hope you know, Mr. Worthing, in an age of ideals. The fact is constantly mentioned in the more expensive monthly magazines, and has reached the provincial pulpits I am told: and my ideal has always been to love some one of the name of 410 Ernest. There is something in that name that inspires absolute confidence. The moment Algernon first mentioned to me that he had a friend called Ernest, I knew I was destined to love you.

JACK: You really love me, Gwendolen?

GWENDOLEN: Passionately!

JACK: Darling! You don't know how happy you've made me.

GWENDOLEN: My own Ernest!

JACK: But you don't really mean to say that you couldn't love me if my name wasn't Ernest? 420

GWENDOLEN: But your name is Ernest.

JACK: Yes, I know it is. But supposing it was something else? Do you mean to say you couldn't love me then?

GWENDOLEN: (*glibly*) Ah! that is clearly a metaphysical speculation, and like most metaphysical speculations has very little reference at all to the actual facts of real life, as we know them.

JACK: Personally, darling, to speak quite candidly, I don't much care about the name of Ernest . . . I don't think that name
430    suits me at all.

GWENDOLEN: It suits you perfectly. It is a divine name. It has a music of its own. It produces vibrations.

JACK: Well, really, Gwendolen, I must say that I think there are lots of other much nicer names. I think, Jack, for instance, a charming name.

GWENDOLEN: Jack? . . . No, there is very little music in the name Jack, if any at all, indeed. It does not thrill. It produces absolutely no vibration. . . . I have known several Jacks, and they all, without exception, were more than usually plain.
440    Besides, Jack is a notorious domesticity for John! And I pity any woman who is married to a man called John. She would probably never be allowed to know the entrancing pleasure of a single moment's solitude. The only really safe name is Ernest.

JACK: Gwendolen, I must get christened at once—I mean we must get married at once. There is no time to be lost.

GWENDOLEN: Married, Mr. Worthing?

JACK: (astounded) Well . . . surely. You know that I love you, and you led me to believe, Miss Fairfax, that you were not
450    absolutely indifferent to me.

GWENDOLEN: I adore you. But you haven't proposed to me yet. Nothing has been said at all about marriage. The subject has not even been touched on.

JACK: Well . . . may I propose to you now?

GWENDOLEN: I think it would be an admirable opportunity. And to spare you any possible disappointment, Mr. Worthing, I think it only fair to tell you quite frankly beforehand that I am fully determined to accept you.

JACK: Gwendolen!

460 GWENDOLEN: Yes, Mr. Worthing, what have you got to say to me?

JACK: You know what I have got to say to you.

GWENDOLEN: Yes, but you don't say it.

JACK: Gwendolen, will you marry me? (Goes on his knees.)

GWENDOLEN: Of course I will, darling. How long you have been about it! I am afraid you have had very little experience in how to propose.

JACK: My own one, I have never loved anyone in the world but you.

470 GWENDOLEN: Yes, but men often propose for practice. I know my brother Gerald does. All my girl-friends tell me so. What wonderfully blue eyes you have, Ernest! They are quite, quite blue. I hope you will always look at me just like that, especially when there are other people present.

(Enter LADY BRACKNELL.)

LADY BRACKNELL: Mr. Worthing! Rise, sir, from this semi-recumbent posture. It is most indecorous.

GWENDOLEN: Mamma! (He tries to rise; she restrains him.) I must beg you to retire. This is no place for you. Besides, Mr. Worthing has not quite finished yet.

480 LADY BRACKNELL: Finished what, may I ask?

GWENDOLEN: I am engaged to Mr. Worthing, mamma. (They rise together.)

LADY BRACKNELL: Pardon me, you are not engaged to anyone. When you do become engaged to some one, I, or your father, should his health permit him, will inform you of the fact. An engagement should come on a young girl as a surprise, pleasant or unpleasant, as the case may be. It is hardly a matter that she could be allowed to arrange for herself. . . . And now I have a few questions to put to you, Mr. Worthing. While I am making these inquiries, you,
490 Gwendolen, will wait for me below in the carriage.

GWENDOLEN: (reproachfully) Mamma!

LADY BRACKNELL: In the carriage, Gwendolen! (GWENDOLEN goes to the door. She and JACK blow kisses to each other behind LADY BRACKNELL's back. LADY BRACKNELL looks vaguely about as if she could not understand what the noise was. Finally turns round.) Gwendolen, the carriage!

GWENDOLEN: Yes, mamma. (Goes out, looking back at JACK.)

LADY BRACKNELL: (sitting down) You can take a seat, Mr. Worthing. (Looks in her pocket for note-book and pencil.)
500 JACK: Thank you, Lady Bracknell, I prefer standing.

LADY BRACKNELL: (pencil and note-book in hand) I feel bound to tell you that you are not down on my list of eligible young men, although I have the same list as the dear Duchess of Bolton has. We work together, in fact. However, I am quite ready to enter your name, should your answers be what a really affectionate mother requires. Do you smoke?

JACK: Well, yes, I must admit I smoke.

LADY BRACKNELL: I am glad to hear it. A man should always have an occupation of some kind. There are far too many
510 idle men in London as it is. How old are you?

JACK: Twenty-nine.

LADY BRACKNELL: A very good age to be married at. I have always been of opinion that a man who desires to get married should know either everything or nothing. Which do you know?

JACK: (after some hesitation) I know nothing, Lady Bracknell.

LADY BRACKNELL: I am pleased to hear it. I do not approve of anything that tampers with natural ignorance. Ignorance is like a delicate exotic fruit; touch it and the bloom is gone.
520 The whole theory of modern education is radically unsound. Fortunately in England, at any rate, education produces no effect whatsoever. If it did, it would prove a serious danger to the upper classes, and probably lead to acts of violence in Grosvenor Square. What is your income?

JACK: Between seven and eight thousand a year.

LADY BRACKNELL: (makes a note in her book) In land, or in investments?

JACK: In investments, chiefly.

LADY BRACKNELL: That is satisfactory. What between the du-
530 ties expected of one during one's life-time, and the duties exacted from one after one's death, land has ceased to be either a profit or a pleasure. It gives one position, and prevents one from keeping it up. That's all that can be said about land.

JACK: I have a country house with some land, of course, attached to it, about fifteen hundred acres, I believe; but I don't depend on that for my real income. In fact, as far as I can make out, the poachers are the only people who make anything out of it.
540

LADY BRACKNELL: A country house! How many bedrooms? Well, that point can be cleared up afterwards. You have a town house, I hope? A girl with a simple, unspoiled nature, like Gwendolen, could hardly be expected to reside in the country.

JACK: Well, I own a house in Belgrave Square, but it is let by the year to Lady Bloxham. Of course, I can get it back whenever I like, at six months' notice.

LADY BRACKNELL: Lady Bloxham? I don't know her.

550 JACK: Oh, she goes about very little. She is a lady considerably advanced in years.

LADY BRACKNELL: Ah, now-a-days that is no guarantee of respectability of character. What number in Belgrave Square?

JACK: 149.

LADY BRACKNELL: (*shaking her head*) The unfashionable side. I thought there was something. However, that could easily be altered.

JACK: Do you mean the fashion, or the side?

LADY BRACKNELL: (*sternly*) Both, if necessary, I presume.
560     What are your politics?

JACK: Well, I am afraid I really have none. I am a Liberal Unionist.

LADY BRACKNELL: Oh, they count as Tories. They dine with us. Or come in the evening, at any rate. Now to minor matters. Are your parents living?

JACK: I have lost both my parents.

LADY BRACKNELL: Both? . . . That seems like carelessness. Who was your father? He was evidently a man of some wealth. Was he born in what the Radical papers call the purple of
570     commerce, or did he rise from the ranks of the aristocracy?

JACK: I am afraid I really don't know. The fact is, Lady Bracknell, I said I had lost my parents. It would be nearer the truth to say that my parents seem to have lost me . . . I don't actually know who I am by birth. I was . . . well, I was found.

LADY BRACKNELL: Found!

JACK: The late Mr. Thomas Cardew, an old gentleman of a very charitable and kindly disposition, found me, and gave me the name of Worthing, because he happened to have a first-class ticket for Worthing in his pocket at the time. Worthing
580     is a place in Sussex. It is a seaside resort.

LADY BRACKNELL: Where did the charitable gentleman who had a first-class ticket for this seaside resort find you?

JACK: (*gravely*) In a hand-bag.

LADY BRACKNELL: A hand-bag?

JACK: (*very seriously*) Yes, Lady Bracknell. I was in a hand-bag—a somewhat large, black leather hand-bag, with handles to it—an ordinary hand-bag in fact.

LADY BRACKNELL: In what locality did Mr. James, or Thomas, Cardew come across this ordinary hand-bag?

590 JACK: In the cloak-room at Victoria Station. It was given to him in mistake for his own.

LADY BRACKNELL: The cloak-room at Victoria Station?

JACK: Yes. The Brighton line.

LADY BRACKNELL: The line is immaterial. Mr. Worthing, I confess I feel somewhat bewildered by what you have just told me. To be born, or at any rate bred, in a hand-bag, whether it had handles or not, seems to me to display a contempt for the ordinary decencies of family life that remind one of the worst excesses of the French Revolution. And I presume
600     you know what that unfortunate movement led to? As for the particular locality in which the hand-bag was found, a cloak-room at a railway station might serve to conceal a social indiscretion—has probably, indeed, been used for the purpose before now—but it could hardly be regarded as an

assured basis for a recognized position in good society.

JACK: May I ask you then what you would advise me to do? I need hardly say I would do anything in the world to ensure Gwendolen's happiness.

LADY BRACKNELL: I would strongly advise you, Mr. Worthing, to try and acquire some relations as soon as possible, and to 610 make a definite effort to produce at any rate one parent, of either sex, before the season is quite over.

JACK: Well, I don't see how I could possibly manage to do that. I can produce the hand-bag at any moment. It is in my dressing-room at home. I really think that should satisfy you, Lady Bracknell.

LADY BRACKNELL: Me, sir! What has it to do with me? You can hardly imagine that I and Lord Bracknell would dream of allowing our only daughter—a girl brought up with the utmost care—to marry into a cloak-room, and form an alliance 620 with a parcel? Good morning, Mr. Worthing! (LADY BRACKNELL *sweeps out in majestic indignation.*)

JACK: Good morning! (ALGERNON, *from the other room, strikes up the Wedding March.* JACK *looks perfectly furious, and goes to the door.*) For goodness' sake don't play that ghastly tune, Algy! How idiotic you are! (*The music stops, and* ALGERNON *enters cheerily.*)

ALGERNON: Didn't it go off all right, old boy? You don't mean to say Gwendolen refused you? I know it is a way she has. She is always refusing people. I think it is most ill-natured of 630 her.

JACK: Oh, Gwendolen is as right as a trivet. As far as she is concerned, we are engaged. Her mother is perfectly unbearable. Never met such a Gorgon . . . I don't really know what a Gorgon is like, but I am quite sure that Lady Bracknell is one. In any case, she is a monster, without being a myth, which is rather unfair. . . . I beg your pardon, Algy, I suppose I shouldn't talk about your own aunt in that way before you.

ALGERNON: My dear boy, I love hearing my relations abused. It is the only thing that makes me put up with them at all. Re- 640 lations are simply a tedious pack of people, who haven't got the remotest knowledge of how to live, nor the smallest instinct about when to die.

JACK: Oh, that is nonsense!

ALGERNON: It isn't!

JACK: Well, I won't argue about the matter. You always want to argue about things.

ALGERNON: That is exactly what things were originally made for.

JACK: Upon my word, if I thought that, I'd shoot myself . . . (*A* 650 *pause.*) You don't think there is any chance of Gwendolen becoming like her mother in about a hundred and fifty years, do you, Algy?

ALGERNON: All women become like their mothers. That is their tragedy. No man does. That's his.

JACK: Is that clever?

ALGERNON: It is perfectly phrased! and quite as true as any observation in civilized life should be.

JACK: I am sick to death of cleverness. Everybody is clever now-a-days. You can't go anywhere without meeting clever 660 people. The thing has become an absolute public nuisance. I wish to goodness we had a few fools left.

ALGERNON: We have.

JACK: I should extremely like to meet them. What do they talk about?

ALGERNON: The fools? Oh! about the clever people, of course.

JACK: What fools!

ALGERNON: By the way, did you tell Gwendolen the truth about your being Ernest in town, and Jack in the country?

670 JACK: *(in a very patronizing manner)* My dear fellow, the truth isn't quite the sort of thing one tells to a nice, sweet, refined girl. What extraordinary ideas you have about the way to behave to a woman!

ALGERNON: The only way to behave to a woman is to make love to her, if she is pretty, and to someone else if she is plain.

JACK: Oh, that is nonsense.

ALGERNON: What about your brother? What about the profligate Ernest?

JACK: Oh, before the end of the week I shall have got rid of
680 him. I'll say he died in Paris of apoplexy. Lots of people die of apoplexy, quite suddenly, don't they?

ALGERNON: Yes, but it's hereditary, my dear fellow. It's a sort of thing that runs in families. You had much better say a severe chill.

JACK: You are sure a severe chill isn't hereditary, or anything of that kind?

ALGERNON: Of course it isn't!

JACK: Very well, then. My poor brother Ernest is carried off suddenly in Paris, by a severe chill. That gets rid of him.

690 ALGERNON: But I thought you said that . . . Miss Cardew was a little too much interested in your poor brother Ernest? Won't she feel his loss a good deal?

JACK: Oh, that is all right. Cecily is not a silly, romantic girl, I am glad to say. She has got a capital appetite, goes for long walks, and pays no attention at all to her lessons.

ALGERNON: I would rather like to see Cecily.

JACK: I will take very good care you never do. She is excessively pretty, and she is only just eighteen.

ALGERNON: Have you told Gwendolen yet that you have an ex-
700 cessively pretty ward who is only just eighteen?

JACK: Oh! one doesn't blurt these things out to people. Cecily and Gwendolen are perfectly certain to be extremely great friends. I'll bet you anything you like that half an hour after they have met, they will be calling each other sister.

ALGERNON: Women only do that when they have called each other a lot of other things first. Now, my dear boy, if we want to get a good table at Willis's, we really must go and dress. Do you know it is nearly seven?

JACK: *(irritably)* Oh! it always is nearly seven.

710 ALGERNON: Well, I'm hungry.

JACK: I never knew you when you weren't. . .

ALGERNON: What shall we do after dinner? Go to a theatre?

JACK: Oh, no! I loathe listening.

ALGERNON: Well, let us go to the Club?

JACK: Oh, no! I hate talking.

ALGERNON: Well, we might trot round to the Empire at ten?

JACK: Oh, no! can't bear looking at things. It is so silly.

ALGERNON: Well, what shall we do?

JACK: Nothing!

720 ALGERNON: It is awfully hard work doing nothing. However, I don't mind hard work where there is no definite object of any kind.

*(Enter LANE.)*

LANE: Miss Fairfax.

*(Enter GWENDOLEN. LANE goes out.)*

ALGERNON: Gwendolen, upon my word!

GWENDOLEN: Algy, kindly turn your back. I have something very particular to say to Mr. Worthing.

ALGERNON: Really, Gwendolen, I don't think I can allow this at all.

GWENDOLEN: Algy, you always adopt a strictly immoral attitude towards life. You are not quite old enough to do that. 730 *(ALGERNON retires to the fireplace.)*

JACK: My own darling!

GWENDOLEN: Ernest, we may never be married. From the expression on mamma's face I fear we never shall. Few parents now-a-days pay any regard to what their children say to them. The old-fashioned respect for the young is fast dying out. Whatever influence I ever had over mamma, I lost at the age of three. But although she may prevent us from becoming man and wife, and I may marry someone else, and marry often, nothing that she can possibly do can alter my 740 eternal devotion to you.

JACK: Dear Gwendolen.

GWENDOLEN: The story of your romantic origin, as related to me by mamma, with unpleasing comments, has naturally stirred the deeper fibers of my nature. Your Christian name has an irresistible fascination. The simplicity of your character makes you exquisitely incomprehensible to me. Your town address at the Albany I have. What is your address in the country?

JACK: The Manor House, Woolton, Hertfordshire. (ALGERNON, 750 *who has been carefully listening, smiles to himself, and writes the address on his shirt-cuff. Then picks up the Railway Guide.)*

GWENDOLEN: There is a good postal service, I suppose? It may be necessary to do something desperate. That, of course, will require serious consideration. I will communicate with you daily.

JACK: My own one!

GWENDOLEN: How long do you remain in town?

JACK: Till Monday. 760

GWENDOLEN: Good! Algy, you may turn round now.

ALGERNON: Thanks, I've turned round already.

GWENDOLEN: You may also ring the bell.

JACK: You will let me see you to your carriage, my own darling?

GWENDOLEN: Certainly.

JACK: *(to LANE, who now enters)* I will see Miss Fairfax out.

LANE: Yes, sir. (JACK *and* GWENDOLEN *go off.* LANE *presents several letters on a salver to* ALGERNON. *It is to be surmised that they are bills, as* ALGERNON, *after looking at the envelopes, tears them up.)* 770

ALGERNON: A glass of sherry, Lane.

LANE: Yes, sir.

ALGERNON: To-morrow, Lane, I'm going Bunburying.

LANE: Yes, sir.

ALGERNON: I shall probably not be back till Monday. You can put up my dress clothes, my smoking jacket, and all the Bunbury suits . . .

LANE: Yes, sir. *(Handing sherry.)*

ALGERNON: I hope to-morrow will be a fine day, Lane.

LANE: It never is, sir. 780

ALGERNON: Lane, you're a perfect pessimist.

LANE: I do my best to give satisfaction, sir.

*(Enter JACK. LANE goes off.)*

JACK: There's a sensible, intellectual girl! the only girl I ever cared for in my life. (ALGERNON *is laughing immoderately.*) What on earth are you so amused at?

ALGERNON: Oh, I'm a little anxious about poor Bunbury, that's all.

JACK: If you don't take care, your friend Bunbury will get you into a serious scrape some day.

790 ALGERNON: I love scrapes. They are the only things that are never serious.

JACK: Oh, that's nonsense, Algy. You never talk anything but nonsense.

ALGERNON: Nobody ever does. (JACK *looks indignantly at him, and leaves the room.* ALGERNON *lights a cigarette, reads his shirt-cuff and smiles.*)

### —ACT TWO—

SCENE.—*Garden at the Manor House. A flight of gray stone steps leads up to the house. The garden, an old-fashioned one, full of roses. Time of year, July. Basket chairs, and a table covered with books, are set under a large yew tree.*

(MISS PRISM *discovered seated at the table.* CECILY *is at the back watering flowers.*)

MISS PRISM: *(calling)* Cecily, Cecily! Surely such a utilitarian occupation as the watering of flowers is rather Moulton's duty than yours? Especially at a moment when intellectual 
800 pleasures await you. Your German grammar is on the table. Pray open it at page fifteen. We will repeat yesterday's lesson.

CECILY: *(coming over very slowly)* But I don't like German. It isn't at all a becoming language. I know perfectly well that I look quite plain after my German lesson.

MISS PRISM: Child, you know how anxious your guardian is that you should improve yourself in every way. He laid particular stress on your German, as he was leaving for town yesterday. Indeed, he always lays stress on your German when 
810 he is leaving for town.

CECILY: Dear Uncle Jack is so very serious! Sometimes he is so serious that I think he cannot be quite well.

MISS PRISM: *(drawing herself up)* Your guardian enjoys the best of health, and his gravity of demeanour is especially to be commended in one so comparatively young as he is. I know no one who has a higher sense of duty and responsibility.

CECILY: I suppose that is why he often looks a little bored when we three are together.

MISS PRISM: Cecily! I am surprised at you. Mr. Worthing has 
820 many troubles in his life. Idle merriment and triviality would be out of place in his conversation. You must remember his constant anxiety about that unfortunate young man, his brother.

CECILY: I wish Uncle Jack would allow that unfortunate young man, his brother, to come down here sometimes. We might have a good influence over him, Miss Prism. I am sure you certainly would. You know German, and geology, and things of that kind influence a man very much (CECILY *begins to write in her diary.*)

830 MISS PRISM: *(shaking her head)* I do not think that even I could produce any effect on a character that, according to his own brother's admission, is irretrievably weak and vacillating. In-

deed, I am not sure that I would desire to reclaim him. I am not in favour of this modern mania for turning bad people into good people at a moment's notice. As a man sows so let him reap. You must put away your diary, Cecily. I really don't see why you should keep a diary at all.

CECILY: I keep a diary in order to enter the wonderful secrets of my life. If I didn't write them down I should probably forget all about them. 
840

MISS PRISM: Memory, my dear Cecily, is the diary that we all carry about with us.

CECILY: Yes, but it usually chronicles the things that have never happened, and couldn't possibly have happened. I believe that Memory is responsible for nearly all the three volume novels that Mudie sends us.

MISS PRISM: Do not speak slightingly of the three-volume novel, Cecily. I wrote one myself in earlier days.

CECILY: Did you really, Miss Prism? How wonderfully clever you are! I hope it did not end happily? I don't like novels 850 that end happily? They depress me so much.

MISS PRISM: The good ended happily, and the bad unhappily. That is what Fiction means.

CECILY: I suppose so. But it seems very unfair. And was your novel ever published?

MISS PRISM: Alas! no. The manuscript unfortunately was abandoned. I use the word in the sense of lost or mislaid. To your work, child, these speculations are profitless.

CECILY: *(smiling)* But I see dear Dr. Chasuble coming up through the garden. 
860

MISS PRISM: *(rising and advancing)* Dr. Chasuble! This is indeed a pleasure.

(*Enter* CANON CHASUBLE.)

CHASUBLE: And how are we this morning? Miss Prism, you are, I trust, well?

CECILY: Miss Prism has just been complaining of a slight headache. I think it would do her so much good to have a short stroll with you in the park, Dr. Chasuble.

MISS PRISM: Cecily, I have not mentioned anything about a headache.

CECILY: No, dear Miss Prism, I know that, but I felt instinc- 870 tively that you had a headache. Indeed I was thinking about that, and not about my German lesson, when the Rector came in.

CHASUBLE: I hope, Cecily, you are not inattentive.

CECILY: Oh, I am afraid I am.

CHASUBLE: That is strange. Were I fortunate enough to be Miss Prism's pupil, I would hang upon her lips. (MISS PRISM *glares.*) I spoke metaphorically.—My metaphor was drawn from bees. Ahem! Mr. Worthing, I suppose, has not returned from town yet? 
880

MISS PRISM: We do not expect him till Monday afternoon.

CHASUBLE: Ah yes, he usually likes to spend his Sunday in London. He is not one of those whose sole aim is enjoyment, as, by all accounts, that unfortunate young man, his brother, seems to be. But I must not disturb Egeria and her pupil any longer.

MISS PRISM: Egeria? My name is Lætitia, Doctor.

CHASUBLE: *(bowing)* A classical allusion merely, drawn from the Pagan authors. I shall see you both no doubt at Even-song. 
890

MISS PRISM: I think, dear Doctor, I will have a stroll with you. I find I have a headache after all, and a walk might do it good.

CHASUBLE: With pleasure, Miss Prism, with pleasure. We might go as far as the schools and back.

MISS PRISM: That would be delightful. Cecily, you will read your Political Economy in my absence. The chapter on the Fall of the Rupee you may omit. It is somewhat too sensational. Even these metallic problems have their melodramatic side.

(*Goes down the garden with* DR. CHASUBLE.)

900   CECILY: (*picks up books and throws them back on table*) Horrid Political Economy! Horrid Geography! Horrid, horrid German!

(*Enter* MERRIMAN *with a card on a salver.*)

MERRIMAN: Mr. Ernest Worthing has just driven over from the station. He has brought his luggage with him.

CECILY: (*takes the card and reads it*) "Mr. Ernest Worthing, B 4 The Albany, W." Uncle Jack's brother! Did you tell him Mr. Worthing was in town?

MERRIMAN: Yes, Miss. He seemed very much disappointed. I mentioned that you and Miss Prism were in the garden. He

910   said he was anxious to speak to you privately for a moment.

CECILY: Ask Mr. Ernest Worthing to come here. I suppose you had better talk to the housekeeper about a room for him.

MERRIMAN: Yes, Miss. (MERRIMAN *goes off.*)

CECILY: I have never met any really wicked person before. I feel rather frightened. I am so afraid he will look just like everyone else.

(*Enter* ALGERNON, *very gay and debonair.*)

He does!

ALGERNON: (*raising his hat*) You are my little cousin Cecily, I'm sure.

920   CECILY: You are under some strange mistake. I am not little. In fact, I am more than usually tall for my age. (ALGERNON *is rather taken aback.*) But I am your cousin Cecily. You, I see from your card, are Uncle Jack's brother, my cousin Ernest, my wicked cousin Ernest.

ALGERNON: Oh! I am not really wicked at all, cousin Cecily. You musn't think that I am wicked.

CECILY: If you are not, then you have certainly been deceiving us all in a very inexcusable manner. I hope you have not been leading a double life, pretending to be wicked and

930   being really good all the time. That would be hypocrisy.

ALGERNON: (*looks at her in amazement*) Oh! of course I have been rather reckless.

CECILY: I am glad to hear it.

ALGERNON: In fact, now you mention the subject, I have been very bad in my own small way.

CECILY: I don't think you should be so proud of that, though I am sure it must have been very pleasant.

ALGERNON: It is much pleasanter being here with you.

CECILY: I can't understand how you are here at all. Uncle Jack

940   won't be back till Monday afternoon.

ALGERNON: That is a great disappointment. I am obliged to go up by the first train on Monday morning. I have a business appointment that I am anxious . . . to miss.

CECILY: Couldn't you miss it anywhere but in London?

ALGERNON: No; the appointment is in London.

CECILY: Well, I know, of course, how important it is not to keep a business engagement, if one wants to retain any sense of the beauty of life, but still I think you had better wait till Uncle Jack arrives. I know he wants to speak to you about your emigrating.                                                   950

ALGERNON: About my what?

CECILY: Your emigrating. He has gone up to buy your outfit.

ALGERNON: I certainly wouldn't let Jack buy my outfit. He has no taste in neckties at all.

CECILY: I don't think you will require neckties. Uncle Jack is sending you to Australia.

ALGERNON: Australia! I'd sooner die.

CECILY: Well, he said at dinner on Wednesday night, that you would have to choose between this world, the next world, and Australia.                                                     960

ALGERNON: Oh, well! The accounts I have received of Australia and the next world, are not particularly encouraging. This world is good enough for me, cousin Cecily.

CECILY: Yes, but are you good enough for it?

ALGERNON: I'm afraid I'm not that. That is why I want you to reform me. You might make that your mission, if you don't mind, cousin Cecily.

CECILY: I'm afraid I've not time, this afternoon.

ALGERNON: Well, would you mind my reforming myself this afternoon?                                                          970

CECILY: That is rather Quixotic of you. But I think you should try.

ALGERNON: I will. I feel better already.

CECILY: You are looking a little worse.

ALGERNON: That is because I am hungry.

CECILY: How thoughtless of me. I should have remembered that when one is going to lead an entirely new life, one requires regular and wholesome meals. Won't you come in?

ALGERNON: Thank you. Might I have a button-hole first? I never have any appetite unless I have a button-hole first.   980

CECILY: A Maréchal Niel? (*Picks up scissors.*)

ALGERNON: No, I'd sooner have a pink rose.

CECILY: Why? (*Cuts a flower.*)

ALGERNON: Because you are like a pink rose, cousin Cecily.

CECILY: I don't think it can be right for you to talk to me like that. Miss Prism never says such things to me.

ALGERNON: Then Miss Prism is a short-sighted old lady. (CECILY *puts the rose in his button-hole.*) You are the prettiest girl I ever saw.

CECILY: Miss Prism says that all good looks are a snare.      990

ALGERNON: They are a snare that every sensible man would like to be caught in.

CECILY: Oh! I don't think I would care to catch a sensible man. I shouldn't know what to talk to him about.

(*They pass into the house.* MISS PRISM *and* DR. CHASUBLE *return.*)

MISS PRISM: You are too much alone, dear Dr. Chasuble. You should get married. A misanthrope I can understand—a womanthrope, never!

CHASUBLE: (*with a scholar's shudder*) Believe me, I do not 1000 deserve so neologistic a phrase. The precept as well as the practice of the Primitive Church was distinctly against matrimony.

MISS PRISM: (*sententiously*) That is obviously the reason why the Primitive Church has not lasted up to the present day. And you do not seem to realize, dear Doctor, that by persistently remaining single, a man converts himself into a permanent public temptation. Men should be careful; this very celibacy leads weaker vessels astray.

1010  CHASUBLE: But is a man not equally attractive when married?

MISS PRISM: No married man is ever attractive except to his wife.

CHASUBLE: And often, I've been told, not even to her.

MISS PRISM: That depends on the intellectual sympathies of the woman. Maturity can always be depended on. Ripeness can be trusted. Young women are green. (DR. CHASUBLE *starts.*) I spoke horticulturally. My metaphor was drawn from fruits. But where is Cecily?

CHASUBLE: Perhaps she followed us to the schools.

*(Enter* JACK *slowly from the back of the garden. He is dressed in the deepest mourning, with crepe hatband and black gloves.)*

1020  MISS PRISM: Mr. Worthing!

CHASUBLE: Mr. Worthing?

MISS PRISM: This is indeed a surprise. We did not look for you till Monday afternoon.

JACK: (*shakes* MISS PRISM's *hand in a tragic manner*) I have returned sooner than I expected. Dr. Chasuble, I hope you are well?

CHASUBLE: Dear Mr. Worthing, I trust this garb of woe does not betoken some terrible calamity?

JACK: My brother.

1030  MISS PRISM: More shameful debts and extravagance?

CHASUBLE: Still leading his life of pleasure?

JACK: (*shaking his head*) Dead!

CHASUBLE: Your brother Ernest dead?

JACK: Quite dead.

MISS PRISM: What a lesson for him! I trust he will profit by it.

CHASUBLE: Mr. Worthing, I offer you my sincere condolence. You have at least the consolation of knowing that you were always the most generous and forgiving of brothers.

JACK: Poor Ernest! He had many faults, but it is a sad, sad blow.

1040  CHASUBLE: Very sad indeed. Were you with him at the end?

JACK: No. He died abroad; in Paris, in fact. I had a telegram last night from the manager of the Grand Hotel.

CHASUBLE: Was the cause of death mentioned?

JACK: A severe chill, it seems.

MISS PRISM: As a man sows, so shall he reap.

CHASUBLE: (*raising his hand*) Charity, dear Miss Prism, charity! None of us are perfect. I myself am peculiarly susceptible to draughts. Will the interment take place here?

JACK: No. He seems to have expressed a desire to be buried in
1050  Paris.

CHASUBLE: In Paris! (*Shakes his head.*) I fear that hardly points to any very serious state of mind at the last. You would no doubt wish me to make some slight allusion to this tragic domestic affliction next Sunday. (JACK *presses his hand convulsively.*) My sermon on the meaning of the manna in the wilderness can be adapted to almost any occasion, joyful, or, as in the present case, distressing. (*All sigh.*) I have preached it at harvest celebrations, christenings, confirmations, on days of humiliation and festal days. The last time I
1060  delivered it was in the Cathedral, as a charity sermon on behalf of the Society for the Prevention of Discontentment among the Upper Orders. The Bishop, who was present, was much struck by some of the analogies I drew.

JACK: Ah, that reminds me, you mentioned christenings I think, Dr. Chasuble? I suppose you know how to christen all right? (DR. CHASUBLE *looks astounded.*) I mean, of course, you are continually christening, aren't you?

MISS PRISM: It is, I regret to say, one of the Rector's most constant duties in this parish. I have often spoken to the poorer classes on the subject. But they don't seem to know what 1070 thrift is.

CHASUBLE: But is there any particular infant in whom you are interested, Mr. Worthing? Your brother was, I believe, unmarried, was he not?

JACK: Oh, yes.

MISS PRISM: (*bitterly*) People who live entirely for pleasure usually are.

JACK: But it is not for any child, dear Doctor. I am very fond of children. No! the fact is, I would like to be christened myself, this afternoon, if you have nothing better to do. 1080

CHASUBLE: But surely, Mr. Worthing, you have been christened already?

JACK: I don't remember anything about it.

CHASUBLE: But have you any grave doubts on the subject?

JACK: I certainly intend to have. Of course, I don't know if the thing would bother you in any way, or if you think I am a little too old now.

CHASUBLE: Not at all. The sprinkling, and, indeed, the immersion of adults is a perfectly canonical practice.

JACK: Immersion! 1090

CHASUBLE: You need have no apprehensions. Sprinkling is all that is necessary, or indeed I think advisable. Our weather is so changeable. At what hour would you wish the ceremony performed?

JACK: Oh, I might trot around about five if that would suit you.

CHASUBLE: Perfectly, perfectly! In fact I have two similar ceremonies to perform at that time. A case of twins that occurred recently in one of the outlying cottages on your own estate. Poor Jenkins the carter, a most hard-working man.

JACK: Oh! I don't see much fun in being christened along with 1100 other babies. It would be childish. Would half-past five do?

CHASUBLE: Admirably! Admirably! (*Takes out watch.*) And now, dear Mr. Worthing, I will not intrude any longer into a house of sorrow. I would merely beg you not to be too much bowed down by grief. What seem to us bitter trials at the moment are often blessings in disguise.

MISS PRISM: This seems to me a blessing of an extremely obvious kind.

*(Enter* CECILY *from the house.)*

CECILY: Uncle Jack! Oh, I am pleased to see you back. But what horrid clothes you have on! Do go and change them. 1110

MISS PRISM: Cecily!

CHASUBLE: My child! my child! (CECILY *goes towards* JACK; *he kisses her brow in a melancholy manner.*)

CECILY: What is the matter, Uncle Jack? Do look happy! You look as if you had a toothache and I have such a surprise for you. Who do you think is in the dining-room? Your brother!

JACK: Who?

CECILY: Your brother Ernest. He arrived about half an hour ago.

JACK: What nonsense! I haven't got a brother. 1120

CECILY: Oh, don't say that. However badly he may have

behaved to you in the past he is still your brother. You couldn't be so heartless as to disown him. I'll tell him to come out. And you will shake hands with him, won't you, Uncle Jack? (*Runs back into the house.*)

CHASUBLE: These are very joyful tidings.

MISS PRISM: After we had all been resigned to his loss, his sudden return seems to me peculiarly distressing.

JACK: My brother is in the dining-room? I don't know what it 1130  all means. I think it is perfectly absurd.

(*Enter* ALGERNON *and* CECILY *hand in hand. They come slowly up to* JACK.)

JACK: Good heavens! (*Motions* ALGERNON *away.*)

ALGERNON: Brother John, I have come down from town to tell you that I am very sorry for all the trouble I have given you, and that I intend to lead a better life in the future. (JACK *glares at him and does not take his hand.*)

CECILY: Uncle Jack, you are not going to refuse your own brother's hand?

JACK: Nothing will induce me to take his hand. I think his coming down here disgraceful. He knows perfectly well why.

1140  CECILY: Uncle Jack, do be nice. There is some good in everyone. Ernest has just been telling me about his poor invalid friend, Mr. Bunbury, whom he goes to visit so often. And surely there must be much good in one who is kind to an invalid, and leaves the pleasures of London to sit by a bed of pain.

JACK: Oh, he has been talking about Bunbury, has he?

CECILY: Yes, he has told me all about poor Mr. Bunbury, and his terrible state of health.

JACK: Bunbury! Well, I won't have him talk to you about Bun-1150  bury or about anything else. It is enough to drive one perfectly frantic.

ALGERNON: Of course I admit that the faults were all on my side. But I must say that I think that Brother John's coldness to me is peculiarly painful. I expected a more enthusiastic welcome, especially considering it is the first time I have come here.

CECILY: Uncle Jack, if you don't shake hands with Ernest I will never forgive you.

JACK: Never forgive me?

1160  CECILY: Never, never, never!

JACK: Well, this is the last time I shall ever do it. (*Shakes hands with* ALGERNON *and glares.*)

CHASUBLE: It's pleasant, is it not, to see so perfect a reconciliation? I think we might leave the two brothers together.

MISS PRISM: Cecily, you will come with us.

CECILY: Certainly, Miss Prism. My little task of reconciliation is over.

CHASUBLE: You have done a beautiful action to-day, dear child.

MISS PRISM: We must not be premature in our judgments.

1170  CECILY: I feel very happy. (*They all go off.*)

JACK: You young scoundrel, Algy, you must get out of this place as soon as possible. I don't allow any Bunburying here.

(*Enter* MERRIMAN.)

MERRIMAN: I have put Mr. Ernest's things in the room next to yours, sir. I suppose that is all right?

JACK: What?

MERRIMAN: Mr. Ernest's luggage, sir. I have unpacked it and put it in the room next to your own.

JACK: His luggage?

MERRIMAN: Yes, sir. Three portmanteaus, a dressing-case, two hat-boxes, and a large luncheon-basket.          1180

ALGERNON: I am afraid I can't stay more than a week this time.

JACK: Merriman, order the dog-cart at once. Mr. Ernest has been suddenly called back to town.

MERRIMAN: Yes, sir. (*Goes back into the house.*)

ALGERNON: What a fearful liar you are, Jack. I have not been called back to town at all.

JACK: Yes, you have.

ALGERNON: I haven't heard anyone call me.

JACK: Your duty as a gentleman calls you back.

ALGERNON: My duty as a gentleman has never interfered with 1190  my pleasures in the smallest degree.

JACK: I can quite understand that.

ALGERNON: Well, Cecily is a darling.

JACK: You are not to talk of Miss Cardew like that. I don't like it.

ALGERNON: Well, I don't like your clothes. You look perfectly ridiculous in them. Why on earth don't you go up and change? It is perfectly childish to be in deep mourning for a man who is actually staying for a whole week with you in your house as a guest. I call it grotesque.          1200

JACK: You are certainly not staying with me for a whole week as a guest or anything else. You have got to leave . . . by the four-five train.

ALGERNON: I certainly won't leave you so long as you are in mourning. It would be most unfriendly. If I were in mourning you would stay with me, I suppose. I should think it very unkind if you didn't.

JACK: Well, will you go if I change my clothes?

ALGERNON: Yes, if you are not too long. I never saw anybody take so long to dress, and with such little result.          1210

JACK: Well, at any rate, that is better than being always overdressed as you are.

ALGERNON: If I am occasionally a little over-dressed, I make up for it by being always immensely over-educated.

JACK: Your vanity is ridiculous, your conduct an outrage, and your presence in my garden utterly absurd. However, you have got to catch the four-five, and I hope you will have a pleasant journey back to town. This Bunburying, as you call it, has not been a great success for you. (*Goes into the house.*)          1220

ALGERNON: I think it has been a great success. I'm in love with Cecily, and that is everything. (*Enter* CECILY *at the back of the garden. She picks up the can and begins to water the flowers.*) But I must see her before I go, and make arrangements for another Bunbury. Ah, there she is.

CECILY: Oh, I merely came back to water the roses. I thought you were with Uncle Jack.

ALGERNON: He's gone to order the dog-cart for me.

CECILY: Oh, is he going to take you for a nice drive?

ALGERNON: He's going to send me away.          1230

CECILY: Then have we got to part?

ALGERNON: I am afraid so. It's a very painful parting.

CECILY: It is always painful to part from people whom one has known for a very brief space of time. The absence of old friends one can endure with equanimity. But even a momentary separation from anyone to whom one has just been introduced is almost unbearable.

ALGERNON: Thank you.

*(Enter* MERRIMAN.*)*

MERRIMAN: The dog-cart is at the door, sir. (ALGERNON *looks* 1240    *appealingly at* CECILY.*)*

CECILY: It can wait, Merriman . . . for . . . five minutes.

MERRIMAN: Yes, miss. *(Exit* MERRIMAN.*)*

ALGERNON: I hope, Cecily, I shall not offend you if I state quite frankly and openly that you seem to me to be in every way the visible personification of absolute perfection.

CECILY: I think your frankness does you great credit, Ernest. If you will allow me I will copy your remarks into my diary. *(Goes over to table and begins writing in diary.)*

ALGERNON: Do you really keep a diary? I'd give any thing to 1250    look at it. May I?

CECILY: Oh, no. *(Puts her hand over it.)* You see, it is simply a very young girl's record of her own thoughts and impressions, and consequently meant for publication. When it appears in volume form I hope you will order a copy. But pray, Ernest, don't stop. I delight in taking down from dictation. I have reached "absolute perfection." You can go on. I am quite ready for more.

ALGERNON: *(somewhat taken aback)* Ahem! Ahem!

CECILY: Oh, don't cough, Ernest. When one is dictating one 1260    should speak fluently and not cough. Besides, I don't know how to spell a cough. *(Writes as* ALGERNON *speaks.)*

ALGERNON: *(speaking very rapidly)* Cecily, ever since I first looked upon your wonderful and incomparable beauty, I have dared to love you wildly, passionately, devotedly, hopelessly.

CECILY: I don't think that you should tell me that you love me wildly, passionately, devotedly, hopelessly. Hopelessly doesn't seem to make much sense, does it?

ALGERNON: Cecily!

*(Enter* MERRIMAN.*)*

1270    MERRIMAN: The dog-cart is waiting, sir.

ALGERNON: Tell it to come round next week, at the same hour.

MERRIMAN: *(looks at* CECILY, *who makes no sign).* Yes, sir.

*(*MERRIMAN *retires.)*

CECILY: Uncle Jack would be very much annoyed if he knew you were staying on till next week, at the same hour.

ALGERNON: Oh, I don't care about Jack. I don't care for anybody in the whole world but you. I love you, Cecily. You will marry me, won't you?

CECILY: You silly you! Of course. Why, we have been engaged for the last three months.

1280    ALGERNON: For the last three months?

CECILY: Yes, it will be exactly three months on Thursday.

ALGERNON: But how did we become engaged?

CECILY: Well, ever since dear Uncle Jack first confessed to us that he had a younger brother who was very wicked and bad, you of course have formed the chief topic of conversation between myself and Miss Prism. And of course a man who is much talked about is always very attractive. One feels there must be something in him after all. I daresay it was foolish of me, but I fell in love with you, Ernest.

1290    ALGERNON: Darling! And when was the engagement actually settled?

CECILY: On the 14th of February last. Worn out by your entire ignorance of my existence, I determined to end the matter one way or the other, and after a long struggle with myself I accepted you under this dear old tree here. The next day I bought this little ring in your name, and this is the little bangle with the true lover's knot I promised you always to wear.

ALGERNON: Did I give you this? It's very pretty, isn't it?

CECILY: Yes, you've wonderfully good taste, Ernest. It's the excuse I've always given for your leading such a bad life. And 1300    this is the box in which I keep all your dear letters. *(Kneels at table, opens box, and produces letters tied up with blue ribbon.)*

ALGERNON: My letters! But my own sweet Cecily, I have never written you any letters.

CECILY: You need hardly remind me of that, Ernest. I remember only too well that I was forced to write your letters for you. I wrote always three times a week, and sometimes oftener.

ALGERNON: Oh, do let me read them, Cecily? 1310

CECILY: Oh, I couldn't possibly. They would make you far too conceited. *(Replaces box.)* The three you wrote me after I had broken off the engagement are so beautiful, and so badly spelled, that even now I can hardly read them without crying a little.

ALGERNON: But was our engagement ever broken off?

CECILY: Of course it was. On the 22nd of last March. You can see the entry if you like. *(Shows diary.)* "Today I broke off my engagement with Ernest. I feel it is better to do so. The weather still continues charming." 1320

ALGERNON: But why on earth did you break it off? What had I done? I had done nothing at all. Cecily, I am very much hurt indeed to hear you broke it off. Particularly when the weather was so charming.

CECILY: It would hardly have been a really serious engagement if it hadn't been broken off at least once. But I forgave you before the week was out.

ALGERNON: *(crossing to her, and kneeling)* What a perfect angel you are, Cecily.

CECILY: You dear romantic boy. *(He kisses her, she puts her fin-* 1330    *gers through his hair.)* I hope your hair curls naturally, does it?

ALGERNON: Yes, darling, with a little help from others.

CECILY: I am so glad.

ALGERNON: You'll never break off our engagement again, Cecily?

CECILY: I don't think I could break it off now that I have actually met you. Besides, of course, that is the question of your name.

ALGERNON: Yes, of course. *(Nervously.)* 1340

CECILY: You must not laugh at me, darling, but it had always been a girlish dream of mine to love some one whose name was Ernest. (ALGERNON *rises,* CECILY *also.)* There is something in that name that seems to inspire absolute confidence. I pity any poor married woman whose husband is not called Ernest.

ALGERNON: But, my dear child, do you mean to say you could not love me if I had some other name?

CECILY: But what name?

ALGERNON: Oh, any name you like—Algernon, for instance. . . . 1350

CECILY: But I don't like the name of Algernon.

ALGERNON: Well, my own dear, sweet, loving little darling, I really can't see why you should object to the name of Algernon. It is not at all a bad name. In fact, it is rather an aristocratic name. Half of the chaps who get into the Bankruptcy Court are called Algernon. But seriously, Cecily . . . (*Moving to her*) . . . if my name was Algy, couldn't you love me?

CECILY: (*rising*) I might respect you, Ernest, I might admire your character, but I fear that I should not be able to give
1360  you my undivided attention.

ALGERNON: Ahem! Cecily! (*Picking up hat.*) Your Rector here is, I suppose, thoroughly experienced in the practice of all the rites and ceremonials of the church?

CECILY: Oh, yes. Dr. Chasuble is a most learned man. He has never written a single book, so you can imagine how much he knows.

ALGERNON: I must see him at once on a most important christening—I mean on most important business.

CECILY: Oh!

1370  ALGERNON: I sha'n't be away more than half an hour.

CECILY: Considering that we have been engaged since February the 14th, and that I only met you to-day for the first time, I think it is rather hard that you should leave me for so long a period as half an hour. Couldn't you make it twenty minutes?

ALGERNON: I'll be back in no time. (*Kisses her and rushes down the garden.*)

CECILY: What an impetuous boy he is. I like his hair so much. I must enter his proposal in my diary.

(*Enter* MERRIMAN.)

1380  MERRIMAN: A Miss Fairfax has just called to see Mr. Worthing. On very important business, Miss Fairfax states.

CECILY: Isn't Mr. Worthing in his library?

MERRIMAN: Mr. Worthing went over in the direction of the Rectory some time ago.

CECILY: Pray ask the lady to come out here; Mr. Worthing is sure to be back soon. And you can bring tea.

MERRIMAN: Yes, miss. (*Goes out.*)

CECILY: Miss Fairfax! I suppose one of the many good elderly women who are associated with Uncle Jack in some of his
1390  philanthropic work in London. I don't quite like women who are interested in philanthropic work. I think it is so forward of them.

(*Enter* MERRIMAN.)

MERRIMAN: Miss Fairfax.

(*Enter* GWENDOLEN. *Exit* MERRIMAN.)

CECILY: (*advancing to meet her*) Pray let me introduce myself to you. My name is Cecily Cardew.

GWENDOLEN: Cecily Cardew? (*Moving to her and shaking hands.*) What a very sweet name! Something tells me that we are going to be great friends. I like you already more than I can say. My first impressions of people are never
1400  wrong.

CECILY: How nice of you to like me so much after we have known each other such a comparatively short time. Pray sit down.

GWENDOLEN: (*still standing up*) I may call you Cecily, may I not?

CECILY: With pleasure!

GWENDOLEN: And you will always call me Gwendolen, won't you?

CECILY: If you wish.

GWENDOLEN: Then that is all quite settled, is it not?    1410

CECILY: I hope so. (*A pause. They both sit down together.*)

GWENDOLEN: Perhaps this might be a favorable opportunity for my mentioning who I am. My father is Lord Bracknell. You have never heard of papa, I suppose?

CECILY: I don't think so.

GWENDOLEN: Outside the family circle, papa, I am glad to say, is entirely unknown. I think that is quite as it should be. The home seems to me to be the proper sphere for the man. And certainly once a man begins to neglect his domestic duties he becomes painfully effeminate, does he not? And I don't  1420 like that. It makes men so very attractive. Cecily, mamma, whose views on education are remarkably strict, has brought me up to be extremely short-sighted; it is part of her system; so do you mind my looking at you through my glasses?

CECILY: Oh, not at all, Gwendolen. I am very fond of being looked at.

GWENDOLEN: (*after examining* CECILY *carefully through a lorgnette*) You are here on a short visit, I suppose.

CECILY: Oh, no, I live here.

GWENDOLEN: (*severely*) Really? Your mother, no doubt, or  1430 some female relative of advanced years, resides here also?

CECILY: Oh, no. I have no mother, nor, in fact, any relations.

GWENDOLEN: Indeed?

CECILY: My dear guardian, with the assistance of Miss Prism, has the arduous task of looking after me.

GWENDOLEN: Your guardian?

CECILY: Yes, I am Mr. Worthing's ward.

GWENDOLEN: Oh! It is strange he never mentioned to me that he had a ward. How secretive of him! He grows more interesting hourly. I am not sure, however, that the news inspires  1440 me with feelings of unmixed delight. (*Rising and going to her.*) I am very fond of you, Cecily; I have liked you ever since I met you. But I am bound to state that now that I know that you are Mr. Worthing's ward, I cannot help expressing a wish you were—well, just a little older than you seem to be—and not quite so very alluring in appearance. In fact, if I may speak candidly—

CECILY: Pray do! I think that whenever one has anything unpleasant to say, one should always be quite candid.

GWENDOLEN: Well, to speak with perfect candour, Cecily, I  1450 wish that you were fully forty-two, and more than usually plain for your age. Ernest has a strong upright nature. He is the very soul of truth and honour. Disloyalty would be as impossible to him as deception. But even men of the noblest possible moral character are extremely susceptible to the influence of the physical charms of others. Modern, no less than Ancient History, supplies us with many most painful examples of what I refer to. If it were not so, indeed, History would be quite unreadable.

CECILY: I beg your pardon, Gwendolen, did you say Ernest?    1460

GWENDOLEN: Yes.

CECILY: Oh, but it is not Mr. Ernest Worthing who is my guardian. It is his brother—his elder brother.

GWENDOLEN: (*sitting down again*). Ernest never mentioned to me that he had a brother.

CECILY: I am sorry to say they have not been on good terms for a long time.

GWENDOLEN: Ah! that accounts for it. And now that I think of

it I have never heard any man mention his brother. The sub-
1470 ject seems distasteful to most men. Cecily, you have lifted a
load from my mind. I was growing almost anxious. It would
have been terrible if any cloud had come across a friendship
like ours, would it not? Of course you are quite, quite sure
that it is not Mr. Ernest Worthing who is your guardian?

CECILY: Quite sure. (*A pause.*) In fact, I am going to be his.

GWENDOLEN: (*enquiringly*) I beg your pardon?

CECILY: (*rather shy and confidingly*) Dearest Gwendolen,
there is no reason why I should make a secret of it to you.
Our little county newspaper is sure to chronicle the fact next
1480 week. Mr. Ernest Worthing and I are engaged to be
married.

GWENDOLEN: (*quite politely, rising*) My darling Cecily, I think
there must be some slight error. Mr. Ernest Worthing is engaged to me. The announcement will appear in the *Morning Post* on Saturday at the latest.

CECILY: (*very politely, rising*) I am afraid you must be under
some misconception. Ernest proposed to me exactly ten
minutes ago. (*Shows diary.*)

GWENDOLEN: (*examines diary through her lorgnette carefully*)
1490 It is certainly very curious, for he asked me to be his wife
yesterday afternoon at 5.30. If you would care to verify the
incident, pray do so. (*Produces diary of her own.*) I never
travel without my diary. One should always have something
sensational to read in the train. I am so sorry, dear Cecily, if
it is any disappointment to you, but I am afraid *I* have the
prior claim.

CECILY: It would distress me more than I can tell you, dear
Gwendolen, if it caused you any mental or physical anguish,
but I feel bound to point out that since Ernest proposed to
1500 you he clearly has changed his mind.

GWENDOLEN: (*meditatively*) If the poor fellow has been entrapped into any foolish promise I shall consider it my duty
to rescue him at once, and with a firm hand.

CECILY: (*thoughtfully and sadly*) Whatever unfortunate entanglement my dear boy may have got into, I will never reproach him with it after we are married.

GWENDOLEN: Do you allude to me, Miss Cardew, as an entanglement? You are presumptuous. On an occasion of this
kind it becomes more than a moral duty to speak one's
1510 mind. It becomes a pleasure.

CECILY: Do you suggest, Miss Fairfax, that I entrapped Ernest
into an engagement? How dare you? This is no time for
wearing the shallow mask of manners. When I see a spade I
call it a spade.

GWENDOLEN: (*satirically*) I am glad to say that I have never
seen a spade. It is obvious that our social spheres have been
widely different.

(*Enter* MERRIMAN, *followed by the footman. He carries a
salver, tablecloth, and plate-stand.* CECILY *is about to retort.
The presence of the servants exercises a restraining influence,
under which both girls chafe.*)

MERRIMAN: Shall I lay tea here as usual, miss?

CECILY: (*sternly, in a calm voice*) Yes, as usual. (MERRIMAN *be-*
1520 *gins to clear and lay cloth. A long pause.* CECILY *and* GWEN-
DOLEN *glare at each other.*)

GWENDOLEN: Are there many interesting walks in the vicinity,
Miss Cardew?

CECILY: Oh, yes, a great many. From the top of one of the hills
quite close one can see five counties.

GWENDOLEN: Five counties! I don't think I should like that. I
hate crowds.

CECILY: (*sweetly*) I suppose that is why you live in town?
(GWENDOLEN *bites her lip, and beats her foot nervously with
her parasol.*)
1530
GWENDOLEN: (*looking round*) Quite a well-kept garden this is,
Miss Cardew.

CECILY: So glad you like it, Miss Fairfax.

GWENDOLEN: I had no idea there were any flowers in the
country.

CECILY: Oh, flowers are as common here, Miss Fairfax, as people are in London.

GWENDOLEN: Personally I cannot understand how anybody
manages to exist in the country, if anybody who is anybody
does. The country always bores me to death.
1540
CECILY: Ah! This is what the newspapers call agricultural depression, is it not? I believe the aristocracy are suffering very
much from it just at present. It is almost an epidemic
amongst them, I have been told. May I offer you some tea,
Miss Fairfax?

GWENDOLEN: (*with elaborate politeness*) Thank you. (*Aside.*)
Detestable girl! But I require tea!

CECILY: (*sweetly*) Sugar?

GWENDOLEN: (*superciliously*) No, thank you. Sugar is not fashionable any more. (CECILY *looks angrily at her, takes up the* 1550
*tongs and puts four lumps of sugar into the cup.*)

CECILY: (*severely*) Cake or bread and butter?

GWENDOLEN: (*in a bored manner*) Bread and butter, please.
Cake is rarely seen at the best houses nowadays.

CECILY: (*cuts a very large slice of cake, and puts it on the tray*)
Hand that to Miss Fairfax. (MERRIMAN *does so, and goes out
with footman.* GWENDOLEN *drinks the tea and makes a grimace. Puts down cup at once, reaches out her hand to the
bread and butter, looks at it, and finds it is cake. Rises in indignation.*)
1560
GWENDOLEN: You have filled my tea with lumps of sugar, and
though I asked most distinctly for bread and butter, you
have given me cake. I am known for the gentleness of my
disposition, and the extraordinary sweetness of my nature,
but I warn you, Miss Cardew, you may go too far.

CECILY: (*rising*) To save my poor, innocent, trusting boy from
the machinations of any other girl there are no lengths to
which I would not go.

GWENDOLEN: From the moment I saw you I distrusted you. I
felt that you were false and deceitful. I am never deceived 1570
in such matters. My first impressions of people are invariably right.

CECILY: It seems to me, Miss Fairfax, that I am trespassing on
your valuable time. No doubt you have many other calls of a
similar character to make in the neighbourhood.

(*Enter* JACK.)

GWENDOLEN: (*catching sight of him*) Ernest! My own Ernest!

JACK: Gwendolen! Darling! (*Offers to kiss her.*)

GWENDOLEN: (*drawing back*) A moment! May I ask if you are
engaged to be married to this young lady? (*Points to
CECILY.*) 1580

JACK: (*laughing*) To dear little Cecily! Of course not! What could have put such an idea into your pretty little head?

GWENDOLEN: Thank you. You may. (*Offers her cheek.*)

CECILY: (*very sweetly*) I knew there must be some misunderstanding, Miss Fairfax. The gentleman whose arm is at present around your waist is my dear guardian, Mr. John Worthing.

GWENDOLEN: I beg your pardon?

CECILY: This is Uncle Jack.

1590 GWENDOLEN: (*receding*) Jack! Oh!

(*Enter* ALGERNON.)

CECILY: Here is Ernest.

ALGERNON: (*goes straight over to* CECILY *without noticing anyone else*) My own love! (*Offers to kiss her.*)

CECILY: (*drawing back*) A moment, Ernest! May I ask you—are you engaged to be married to this young lady?

ALGERNON: (*looking round*) To what young lady? Good heavens! Gwendolen!

CECILY: Yes, to good heavens, Gwendolen, I mean to Gwendolen.

1600 ALGERNON: (*laughing*) Of course not! What could have put such an idea into your pretty little head?

CECILY: Thank you. (*Presenting her cheek to be kissed.*) You may. (ALGERNON *kisses her.*)

GWENDOLEN: I felt there was some slight error, Miss Cardew. The gentleman who is now embracing you is my cousin, Mr. Algernon Moncrieff.

CECILY: (*breaking away from* ALGERNON) Algernon Moncrieff! Oh! (*The two girls move towards each other and put their arms round each other's waists as if for protection.*)

1610 CECILY: Are you called Algernon?

ALGERNON: I cannot deny it.

CECILY: Oh!

GWENDOLEN: Is your name really John?

JACK: (*standing rather proudly*) I could deny it if I liked. I could deny anything if I liked. But my name certainly is John. It has been John for years.

CECILY: (*to* GWENDOLEN) A gross deception has been practised on both of us.

GWENDOLEN: My poor wounded Cecily!

1620 CECILY: My sweet, wronged Gwendolen!

GWENDOLEN: (*slowing and seriously*) You will call me sister, will you not? (*They embrace.* JACK *and* ALGERNON *groan and walk up and down.*)

CECILY: (*rather brightly*) There is just one question I would like to be allowed to ask my guardian.

GWENDOLEN: An admirable idea! Mr. Worthing, there is just one question I would like to be permitted to put to you. Where is your brother Ernest? We are both engaged to be married to your brother Ernest, so it is a matter of some

1630 importance to us to know where your brother Ernest is at present.

JACK: (*slowly and hesitatingly*) Gwendolen—Cecily—it is very painful for me to be forced to speak the truth. It is the first time in my life that I have ever been reduced to such a painful position, and I am really quite inexperienced in doing anything of the kind. However I will tell you quite frankly that I have no brother Ernest. I have no brother at all. I never had a brother in my life, and I certainly have not the smallest intention of ever having one in the future.

CECILY: (*surprised*) No brother at all?   1640

JACK: (*cheerily*) None!

GWENDOLEN: (*severely*) Had you never a brother of any kind?

JACK: (*pleasantly*) Never. Not even of any kind.

GWENDOLEN: I am afraid it is quite clear, Cecily, that neither of us is engaged to be married to anyone.

CECILY: It is not a very pleasant position for a young girl suddenly to find herself in. Is it?

GWENDOLEN: Let us go into the house. They will hardly venture to come after us there.

CECILY: No, men are so cowardly, aren't they? (*They retire into*  1650 *the house with scornful looks.*)

JACK: This ghastly state of things is what you call Bunburying, I suppose?

ALGERNON: Yes, and a perfectly wonderful Bunbury it is. The most wonderful Bunbury I have ever had in my life.

JACK: Well, you've no right whatsoever to Bunbury here.

ALGERNON: That is absurd. One has a right to Bunbury anywhere one chooses. Every serious Bunburyist knows that.

JACK: Serious Bunburyist! Good heavens!

ALGERNON: Well, one must be serious about something, if one  1660 wants to have any amusement in life. I happen to be serious about Bunburying. What on earth you are serious about I haven't got the remotest idea. About everything, I should fancy. You have such an absolutely trivial nature.

JACK: Well, the only small satisfaction I have in the whole of this wretched business is that your friend Bunbury is quite exploded. You won't be able to run down to the country quite so often as you used to do, dear Algy. And a very good thing, too.

ALGERNON: Your brother is a little off colour, isn't he, dear  1670 Jack? You won't be able to disappear to London quite so frequently as your wicked custom was. And not a bad thing, either.

JACK: As for your conduct towards Miss Cardew, I must say that your taking in a sweet, simple, innocent girl like that is quite inexcusable. To say nothing of the fact that she is my ward.

ALGERNON: I can see no possible defence at all for your deceiving a brilliant, clever, thoroughly experienced young lady like Miss Fairfax. To say nothing of the fact that she is  1680 my cousin.

JACK: I wanted to be engaged to Gwendolen, that is all. I love her.

ALGERNON: Well, I simply wanted to be engaged to Cecily. I adore her.

JACK: There is certainly no chance of your marrying Miss Cardew.

ALGERNON: I don't think there is much likelihood, Jack, of you and Miss Fairfax being united.

JACK: Well, that is no business of yours.   1690

ALGERNON: If it was my business, I wouldn't talk about it. (*Begins to eat muffins.*) It is very vulgar to talk about one's business. Only people like stock-brokers do that, and then merely at dinner parties.

JACK: How you can sit there, calmly eating muffins, when we are in this horrible trouble, I can't make out. You seem to me to be perfectly heartless.

ALGERNON: Well, I can't eat muffins in an agitated manner. The butter would probably get on my cuffs. One should

1700 always eat muffins quite calmly. It is the only way to eat them.

JACK: I say it's perfectly heartless your eating muffins at all, under the circumstances.

ALGERNON: When I am in trouble, eating is the only thing that consoles me. Indeed, when I am in really great trouble, as anyone who knows me intimately will tell you, I refuse everything except food and drink. At the present moment I am eating muffins because I am unhappy. Besides, I am particularly fond of muffins. *(Rising.)*

1710 JACK: *(rising)* Well, that is no reason why you should eat them all in that greedy way. *(Takes muffin from* ALGERNON.*)*

ALGERNON: *(offering tea-cake)* I wish you would have tea-cake instead. I don't like tea-cake.

JACK: Good heavens! I suppose a man may eat his own muffins in his own garden.

ALGERNON: But you have just said it was perfectly heartless to eat muffins.

JACK: I said it was perfectly heartless of you, under the circumstances. That is a very different thing.

1720 ALGERNON: That may be. But the muffins are the same. *(He seizes the muffin dish from* JACK.*)*

JACK: Algy, I wish to goodness you would go.

ALGERNON: You can't possibly ask me to go without having some dinner. It's absurd. I never go without my dinner. No one ever does, except vegetarians and people like that. Besides I have just made arrangements with Dr. Chasuble to be christened at a quarter to six under the name of Ernest.

JACK: My dear fellow, the sooner you give up that nonsense the better. I made arrangements this morning with Dr. Cha-
1730 suble to be christened myself at 5.30, and I naturally will take the name of Ernest. Gwendolen would wish it. We can't both be christened Ernest. It's absurd. Besides, I have a perfect right to be christened if I like. There is no evidence at all that I ever have been christened by anybody. I should think it extremely probable I never was, and so does Dr. Chasuble. It is entirely different in your case. You have been christened already.

ALGERNON: Yes, but I have not been christened for years.

JACK: Yes, but you have been christened. That is the important
1740 thing.

ALGERNON: Quite so. So I know my constitution can stand it. If you are not quite sure about your ever having been christened, I must say I think it rather dangerous your venturing on it now. It might make you very unwell. You can hardly have forgotten that someone very closely connected with you was very nearly carried off this week in Paris by a severe chill.

JACK: Yes, but you said yourself that a severe chill was not hereditary.

1750 ALGERNON: It usedn't to be, I know—but I daresay it is now. Science is always making wonderful improvements in things.

JACK: *(picking up the muffin-dish)* Oh, that is nonsense; you are always talking nonsense.

ALGERNON: Jack, you are at the muffins again! I wish you wouldn't. There are only two left. *(Takes them.)* I told you I was particularly fond of muffins.

JACK: But I hate tea-cake.

ALGERNON: Why on earth then do you allow tea-cake to be served up for your guests? What ideas you have of hos-     1760 pitality!

JACK: Algernon! I have already told you to go. I don't want you here. Why don't you go?

ALGERNON: I haven't quite finished my tea yet, and there is still one muffin left. *(*JACK *groans, and sinks into a chair.* ALGERNON *still continues eating.)*

## C U R T A I N

## —ACT THREE—

SCENE.—*Morning-room at the Manor House.* GWENDOLEN *and* CECILY *are at the window, looking out into the garden.*

GWENDOLEN: The fact that they did not follow us at once into the house, as anyone else would have done, seems to me to show that they have some sense of shame left.

CECILY: They have been eating muffins. That looks like repen-     1770 tance.

GWENDOLEN: *(after a pause)* They don't seem to notice us at all. Couldn't you cough?

GWENDOLEN: They're looking at us. What effrontery!

CECILY: They're approaching. That's very forward of them.

GWENDOLEN: Let us preserve a dignified silence.

CECILY: Certainly. It's the only thing to do now.

*(Enter* JACK, *followed by* ALGERNON. *They whistle some dreadful popular air from a British opera.)*

GWENDOLEN: This dignified silence seems to produce an unpleasant effect.

CECILY: A most distasteful one.     1780

GWENDOLEN: But we will not be the first to speak.

CECILY: Certainly not.

GWENDOLEN: Mr. Worthing, I have something very particular to ask you. Much depends on your reply.

CECILY: Gwendolen, your common sense is invaluable. Mr. Moncrieff, kindly answer me the following question. Why did you pretend to be my guardian's brother?

ALGERNON: In order that I might have an opportunity of meeting you.

CECILY: *(to* GWENDOLEN*)* That certainly seems a satisfactory     1790 explanation, does it not?

GWENDOLEN: Yes, dear, if you can believe him.

CECILY: I don't. But that does not affect the wonderful beauty of his answer.

GWENDOLEN: True. In matters of grave importance, style, not sincerity, is the vital thing. Mr. Worthing, what explanation can you offer to me for pretending to have a brother? Was it in order that you might have an opportunity of coming up to town to see me as often as possible?

JACK: Can you doubt it, Miss Fairfax?     1800

GWENDOLEN: I have the gravest doubts upon the subject. But I intend to crush them. This is not the moment for German scepticism. *(Moving to* CECILY.*)* Their explanations appear to be quite satisfactory, especially Mr. Worthing's. That seems to me to have the stamp of truth upon it.

CECILY: I am more than content with what Mr. Moncrieff said.

His voice alone inspires one with absolute credulity.

GWENDOLEN: Then you think we should forgive them?

CECILY: Yes. I mean no.

1810 GWENDOLEN: True! I had forgotten. There are principles at stake that one cannot surrender. Which of us should tell them? The task is not a pleasant one.

CECILY: Could we not both speak at the same time?

GWENDOLEN: An excellent idea! I nearly always speak at the same time as other people. Will you take the time from me?

CECILY: Certainly. (GWENDOLEN *beats time with uplifted finger.*)

GWENDOLEN *and* CECILY: (*speaking together*) Your Christian names are still an insuperable barrier. That is all!

1820 JACK *and* ALGERNON: (*speaking together*) Our Christian names! Is that all? But we are going to be christened this afternoon.

GWENDOLEN: (*to* JACK) For my sake you are prepared to do this terrible thing?

JACK: I am.

CECILY: (*to* ALGERNON) To please me you are ready to face this fearful ordeal?

ALGERNON: I am!

GWENDOLEN: How absurd to talk of the equality of the sexes! Where questions of self-sacrifice are concerned, men are in-

1830 finitely beyond us.

JACK: We are. (*Clasps hands with* ALGERNON.)

CECILY: They have moments of physical courage of which we women know absolutely nothing.

GWENDOLEN: (*to* JACK) Darling!

ALGERNON: (*to* CECILY) Darling! (*They fall into each other's arms.*)

(*Enter* MERRIMAN. *When he enters he coughs loudly, seeing the situation.*)

MERRIMAN: Ahem! Ahem! Lady Bracknell!

JACK: Good heavens!

(*Enter* LADY BRACKNELL: *The couples separate in alarm. Exit* MERRIMAN.)

LADY BRACKNELL: Gwendolen! What does this mean?

1840 GWENDOLEN: Merely that I am engaged to be married to Mr. Worthing, Mamma.

LADY BRACKNELL: Come here. Sit down. Sit down immediately. Hesitation of any kind is a sign of mental decay in the young, of physical weakness in the old. (*Turns to* JACK.) Apprised, sir, of my daughter's sudden flight by her trusty maid, whose confidence I purchased by means of a small coin, I followed her at once by a luggage train. Her unhappy father is, I am glad to say, under the impression that she is attending a more than usually lengthy lecture by the Uni-

1850 versity Extension Scheme on the Influence of a Permanent Income on Thought. I do not propose to undeceive him. Indeed I have never undeceived him on any question. I would consider it wrong. But of course, you will clearly understand that all communication between yourself and my daughter must cease immediately from this moment. On this point, as indeed on all points, I am firm.

JACK: I am engaged to be married to Gwendolen, Lady Bracknell!

LADY BRACKNELL: You are nothing of the kind, sir. And now, as

1860 regards Algernon! . . . Algernon!

ALGERNON: Yes, Aunt Augusta.

LADY BRACKNELL: May I ask if it is in this house that your invalid friend Mr. Bunbury resides?

ALGERNON: (*stammering*) Oh, no! Bunbury doesn't live here. Bunbury is somewhere else at present. In fact, Bunbury is dead.

LADY BRACKNELL: Dead! When did Mr. Bunbury die? His death must have been extremely sudden.

ALGERNON: (*airily*) Oh, I killed Bunbury this afternoon. I mean poor Bunbury died this afternoon.    1870

LADY BRACKNELL: What did he die of?

ALGERNON: Bunbury? Oh, he was quite exploded.

LADY BRACKNELL: Exploded! Was he the victim of a revolutionary outrage? I was not aware that Mr. Bunbury was interested in social legislation. If so, he is well punished for his morbidity.

ALGERNON: My dear Aunt Augusta, I mean he was found out! The doctors found out that Bunbury could not live, that is what I mean—so Bunbury died.

LADY BRACKNELL: He seems to have had great confidence in 1880 the opinion of his physicians. I am glad, however, that he made up his mind at the last to some definite course of action, and acted under proper medical advice. And now that we have finally got rid of this Mr. Bunbury, may I ask, Mr. Worthing, who is that young person whose hand my nephew Algernon is now holding in what seems to me a peculiarly unnecessary manner?

JACK: That lady is Miss Cecily Cardew, my ward. (LADY BRACKNELL *bows coldly to* CECILY.)

ALGERNON: I am engaged to be married to Cecily, Aunt Au- 1890 gusta.

LADY BRACKNELL: I beg your pardon?

CECILY: Mr. Moncrieff and I are engaged to be married, Lady Bracknell.

LADY BRACKNELL: (*with a shiver, crossing to the sofa and sitting down*) I do not know whether there is anything peculiarly exciting in the air of this particular part of Hertfordshire, but the number of engagements that go on seems to me considerably above the proper average that statistics have laid down for our guidance. I think some pre- 1900 liminary enquiry on my part would not be out of place. Mr. Worthing, is Miss Cardew at all connected with any of the larger railway stations in London? I merely desire information. Until yesterday I had no idea that there were any families or persons whose origin was a Terminus. (JACK *looks perfectly furious, but restrains himself.*)

JACK: (*in a clear, cold voice*) Miss Cardew is the granddaughter of the late Mr. Thomas Cardew of 149, Belgrave Square, S.W.; Gervase Park, Dorking, Surrey; and the Sporran, Fifeshire, N.B.    1910

LADY BRACKNELL: That sounds not unsatisfactory. Three addresses always inspire confidence, even in tradesmen. But what proof have I of their authenticity?

JACK: I have carefully preserved the Court Guide of the period. They are open to your inspection, Lady Bracknell.

LADY BRACKNELL: (*grimly*) I have known strange errors in that publication.

JACK: Miss Cardew's family solicitors are Messrs. Markby, Markby, and Markby.

LADY BRACKNELL: Markby, Markby, and Markby? A firm of the 1920

very highest position in their profession. Indeed I am told that one of the Mr. Markbys is occasionally to be seen at dinner parties. So far I am satisfied.

JACK: (*very irritably*) How extremely kind of you, Lady Bracknell! I have also in my possession, you will be pleased to hear, certificates of Miss Cardew's birth, baptism, whooping cough, registration, vaccination, confirmation, and the measles; both the German and the English variety.

LADY BRACKNELL: Ah! A life crowded with incident, I see; 1930 though perhaps somewhat too exciting for a young girl. I am not myself in favour of premature experiences. (*Rises, looks at her watch.*) Gwendolen! the time approaches for our departure. We have not a moment to lose. As a matter of form, Mr. Worthing, I had better ask you if Miss Cardew has any little fortune?

JACK: Oh, about a hundred and thirty thousand pounds in the Funds. That is all. Good-bye, Lady Bracknell. So pleased to have seen you.

LADY BRACKNELL: (*sitting down again*) A moment, Mr. Wor- 1940 thing. A hundred and thirty thousand pounds! And in the Funds! Miss Cardew seems to me a most attractive young lady, now that I look at her. Few girls of the present day have any really solid qualities, any of the qualities that last, and improve with time. We live, I regret to say, in an age of surfaces. (*To* CECILY.) Come over here, dear. (CECILY *goes across.*) Pretty child! your dress is sadly simple, and your hair seems almost as Nature might have left it. But we can soon alter all that. A thoroughly experienced French maid produces a really marvellous result in a very brief space of 1950 time. I remember recommending one to young Lady Lancing, and after three months her own husband did not know her.

JACK: (*aside*) And after six months nobody knew her.

LADY BRACKNELL: (*glares at* JACK *for a few moments. Then bends, with a practised smile, to* CECILY) Kindly turn round, sweet child. (CECILY *turns completely round.*) No, the side view is what I want. (CECILY *presents her profile.*) Yes, quite as I expected. There are distinct social possibilities in your profile. The two weak points in our age are its want of prin- 1960 ciple and its want of profile. The chin a little higher, dear. Style largely depends on the way the chin is worn. They are worn very high, just at present. Algernon!

ALGERNON: Yes, Aunt Augusta!

LADY BRACKNELL: There are distinct social possibilities in Miss Cardew's profile.

ALGERNON: Cecily is the sweetest, dearest, prettiest girl in the whole world. And I don't care twopence about social possibilities.

LADY BRACKNELL: Never speak disrespectfully of society, Al- 1970 gernon. Only people who can't get into it do that. (*To* CE-CILY.) Dear child, of course you know that Algernon has nothing but his debts to depend upon. But I do not approve of mercenary marriages. When I married Lord Bracknell I had no fortune of any kind. But I never dreamed for a moment of allowing that to stand in my way. Well, I suppose I must give my consent.

ALGERNON: Thank you, Aunt Augusta.

LADY BRACKNELL: Cecily, you may kiss me!

CECILY: (*kisses her*) Thank you, Lady Bracknell.

1980 LADY BRACKNELL: You may also address me as Aunt Augusta

for the future.

CECILY: Thank you, Aunt Augusta.

LADY BRACKNELL: The marriage, I think, had better take place quite soon.

ALGERNON: Thank you, Aunt Augusta.

CECILY: Thank you, Aunt Augusta.

LADY BRACKNELL: To speak frankly, I am not in favour of long engagements. They give people the opportunity of finding out each other's character before marriage, which I think is never advisable. 1990

JACK: I beg your pardon for interrupting you, Lady Bracknell, but this engagement is quite out of the question. I am Miss Cardew's guardian, and she cannot marry without my consent until she comes of age. That consent I absolutely decline to give.

LADY BRACKNELL: Upon what grounds, may I ask? Algernon is an extremely, I may almost say an ostentatiously, eligible young man. He has nothing, but he looks everything. What more can one desire?

JACK: It pains me very much to have to speak frankly to you, 2000 Lady Bracknell, about your nephew, but the fact is that I do not approve at all of his moral character. I suspect him of being untruthful. (ALGERNON *and* CECILY *look at him in indignant amazement.*)

LADY BRACKNELL: Untruthful! My nephew Algernon? Impossible! He is an Oxonian.

JACK: I fear there can be no possible doubt about the matter. This afternoon, during my temporary absence in London on an important question of romance, he obtained admission to my house by means of the false pretence of being my 2010 brother. Under an assumed name he drank, I've just been informed by my butler, an entire pint bottle of my Perrier-Jouet, Brut, '89; a wine I was specially reserving for myself. Continuing his disgraceful deception, he succeeded in the course of the afternoon in alienating the affections of my only ward. He subsequently stayed to tea, and devoured every single muffin. And what makes his conduct all the more heartless is, that he was perfectly well aware from the first that I have no brother, that I never had a brother, and that I don't intend to have a brother, not even of any kind. I 2020 distinctly told him so myself yesterday afternoon.

LADY BRACKNELL: Ahem! Mr. Worthing, after careful consideration I have decided entirely to overlook my nephew's conduct to you.

JACK: That is very generous of you, Lady Bracknell. My own decision, however, is unalterable. I decline to give my consent.

LADY BRACKNELL: (*to* CECILY) Come here, sweet child. (CECILY *goes over.*) How old are you, dear?

CECILY: Well, I am really only eighteen, but I always admit to 2030 twenty when I go to evening parties.

LADY BRACKNELL: You are perfectly right in making some slight alteration. Indeed, no woman should ever be quite accurate about her age. It looks so calculating. . . . (*In meditative manner.*) Eighteen, but admitting to twenty at evening parties. Well, it will not be very long before you are of age and free from the restraints of tutelage. So I don't think your guardian's consent is, after all, a matter of any importance.

JACK: Pray excuse me, Lady Bracknell, for interrupting you again, but it is only fair to tell you that according to the terms 2040 of her grandfather's will Miss Cardew does not come legally of age till she is thirty-five.

LADY BRACKNELL: That does not seem to me to be a grave objection. Thirty-five is a very attractive age. London society is full of women of the very highest birth who have, of their own free choice, remained thirty-five for years. Lady Dumbleton is an instance in point. To my own knowledge she has been thirty-five ever since she arrived at the age of forty, which was many years ago now. I see no reason why our dear Cecily should not be even still more attractive at the age you mention than she is at present. There will be a large accumulation of property.

CECILY: Algy, could you wait for me till I was thirty-five?

ALGERNON: Of course I could, Cecily. You know I could.

CECILY: Yes, I felt it instinctively, but I couldn't wait all that time. I hate waiting even five minutes for anybody. It always makes me rather cross. I am not punctual myself, I know, but I do like punctuality in others, and waiting, even to be married, is quite out of the question.

ALGERNON: Then what is to be done, Cecily?

CECILY: I don't know, Mr. Moncrieff.

LADY BRACKNELL: My dear Mr. Worthing, as Miss Cardew states positively that she cannot wait till she is thirty-five—a remark which I am bound to say seems to me to show a somewhat impatient nature—I would beg of you to reconsider your decision.

JACK: But my dear Lady Bracknell, the matter is entirely in your own hands. The moment you consent to my marriage with Gwendolen, I will most gladly allow your nephew to form an alliance with my ward.

LADY BRACKNELL: (rising and drawing herself up) You must be quite aware that what you propose is out of the question.

JACK: Then a passionate celibacy is all that any of us can look forward to.

LADY BRACKNELL: That is not the destiny I propose for Gwendolen. Algernon, of course, can choose for himself. (Pulls out her watch.) Come, dear, (GWENDOLEN rises) we have already missed five, if not six, trains. To miss any more might expose us to comment on the platform.

(Enter DR. CHASUBLE.)

CHASUBLE: Everything is quite ready for the christenings.

LADY BRACKNELL: The christenings, sir! Is not that somewhat premature?

CHASUBLE: (looking rather puzzled, and pointing to JACK and ALGERNON) Both these gentlemen have expressed a desire for immediate baptism.

LADY BRACKNELL: At their age? The idea is grotesque and irreligious! Algernon, I forbid you to be baptised. I will not hear of such excesses. Lord Bracknell would be highly displeased if he learned that that was the way in which you wasted your time and money.

CHASUBLE: Am I to understand then that there are to be no christenings at all this afternoon?

JACK: I don't think that, as things are now, it would be of much practical value to either of us, Dr. Chasuble.

CHASUBLE: I am grieved to hear such sentiments from you, Mr. Worthing. They savour of the heretical views of the Anabaptists, views that I have completely refuted in four of my unpublished sermons. However, as your present mood seems to be one peculiarly secular, I will return to the church at once. Indeed, I have just been informed by the pew-opener that for the last hour and a half Miss Prism has been waiting for me in the vestry.

LADY BRACKNELL: (starting) Miss Prism! Did I hear you mention a Miss Prism?

CHASUBLE: Yes, Lady Bracknell. I am on my way to join her.

LADY BRACKNELL: Pray allow me to detain you for a moment. This matter may prove to be one of vital importance to Lord Bracknell and myself. Is this Miss Prism a female of repellent aspect, remotely connected with education?

CHASUBLE: (somewhat indignantly) She is the most cultivated of ladies, and the very picture of respectability.

LADY BRACKNELL: It is obviously the same person. May I ask what position she holds in your household?

CHASUBLE: (severely) I am a celibate, madam.

JACK: (interposing) Miss Prism, Lady Bracknell, has been for the last three years Miss Cardew's esteemed governess and valued companion.

LADY BRACKNELL: In spite of what I hear of her, I must see her at once. Let her be sent for.

CHASUBLE: (looking off) She approaches; she is nigh.

(Enter MISS PRISM hurriedly.)

MISS PRISM: I was told you expected me in the vestry, dear Canon. I have been waiting for you there for an hour and three-quarters. (Catches sight of LADY BRACKNELL, who has fixed her with a stony glare. MISS PRISM grows pale and quails. She looks anxiously round as if desirous to escape.)

LADY BRACKNELL: (in a severe, judicial voice) Prism! (MISS PRISM bows her head in shame.) Come here, Prism! (MISS PRISM approaches in a humble manner.) Prism! Where is that baby? (General consternation. The Canon starts back in horror. ALGERNON and JACK pretend to be anxious to shield CECILY and GWENDOLEN from hearing the details of a terrible public scandal.) Twenty-eight years ago, Prism, you left Lord Bracknell's house, Number 104, Upper Grosvenor Street, in charge of a perambulator that contained a baby, of the male sex. You never returned. A few weeks later, through the elaborate investigations of the Metropolitan police, the perambulator was discovered at midnight, standing by itself in a remote corner of Bayswater. It contained the manuscript of a three-volume novel of more than usually revolting sentimentality. (MISS PRISM starts in involuntary indignation.) But the baby was not there! (Everyone looks at MISS PRISM.) Prism, where is that baby? (A pause.)

MISS PRISM: Lady Bracknell, I admit with shame that I do not know. I only wish I did. The plain facts of the case are these. On the morning of the day you mention, a day that is forever branded on my memory, I prepared as usual to take the baby out in its perambulator. I had also with me a somewhat old but capacious hand-bag in which I had intended to place the manuscript of a work of fiction that I had written during my few unoccupied hours. In a moment of mental abstraction, for which I never can forgive myself, I deposited the manuscript in the bassinette, and placed the baby in the hand-bag.

JACK: (who has been listening attentively) But where did you deposit the hand-bag?

MISS PRISM: Do not ask me, Mr. Worthing.

JACK: Miss Prism, this is a matter of no small importance to me. I insist on knowing where you deposited the hand-bag that contained that infant.

2160 MISS PRISM: I left it in the cloak-room of one of the larger railway stations in London.

JACK: What railway station?

MISS PRISM: *(quite crushed)* Victoria. The Brighton line. *(Sinks into a chair.)*

JACK: I must retire to my room for a moment. Gwendolen, wait here for me.

GWENDOLEN: If you are not too long, I will wait here for you all my life.

*(Exit JACK in great excitement.)*

CHASUBLE: What do you think this means, Lady Bracknell?

2170 LADY BRACKNELL: I dare not even suspect, Dr. Chasuble. I need hardly tell you that in families of high position strange coincidences are not supposed to occur. They are hardly considered the thing. *(Noises heard overhead as if someone was throwing trunks about. Everybody looks up.)*

CECILY: Uncle Jack seems strangely agitated.

CHASUBLE: Your guardian has a very emotional nature.

LADY BRACKNELL: This noise is extremely unpleasant. It sounds as if he was having an argument. I dislike arguments of any kind. They are always vulgar, and often convincing.

2180 CHASUBLE: *(looking up)* It has stopped now. *(The noise is redoubled.)*

LADY BRACKNELL: I wish he would arrive at some conclusion.

GWENDOLEN: The suspense is terrible. I hope it will last.

*(Enter JACK with a hand-bag of black leather in his hand.)*

JACK: *(rushing over to MISS PRISM)* Is this the hand-bag, Miss Prism? Examine it carefully before you speak. The happiness of more than one life depends on your answer.

MISS PRISM: *(calmly)* It seems to be mine. Yes, here is the injury it received through the upsetting of a Gower Street omnibus in younger and happier days. Here is the stain on the 2190 lining caused by the explosion of a temperance beverage, an incident that occurred at Leamington. And here, on the lock, are my initials. I had forgotten that in an extravagant mood I had had them placed there. The bag is undoubtedly mine. I am delighted to have it so unexpectedly restored to me. It has been a great inconvenience being without it all these years.

JACK: *(in a pathetic voice)* Miss Prism, more is restored to you than this hand-bag. I was the baby you placed in it.

MISS PRISM: *(amazed)* You?

2200 JACK: *(embracing her)* Yes . . . mother!

MISS PRISM: *(recoiling in indignant astonishment)* Mr. Worthing! I am unmarried!

JACK: Unmarried! I do not deny that is a serious blow. But after all, who has the right to cast a stone against one who has suffered? Cannot repentance wipe out an act of folly? Why should there be one law for men and another for women? Mother, I forgive you. *(Tries to embrace her again.)*

MISS PRISM: *(still more indignant)* Mr. Worthing, there is some error. *(Pointing to LADY BRACKNELL.)* There is the lady who 2210 can tell you who you really are.

JACK: *(after a pause)* Lady Bracknell, I hate to seem inquisitive, but would you kindly inform me who I am?

LADY BRACKNELL: I am afraid that the news I have to give you will not altogether please you. You are the son of my poor sister, Mrs. Moncrieff, and consequently Algernon's elder brother.

JACK: Algy's elder brother! Then I have a brother after all. I knew I had a brother! I always said I had a brother! Cecily,—how could you have ever doubted that I had a brother? *(Seizes hold of ALGERNON.)* Dr. Chasuble, my un- 2220 fortunate brother. Miss Prism, my unfortunate brother. Gwendolen, my unfortunate brother. Algy, you young scoundrel, you will have to treat me with more respect in the future. You have never behaved to me like a brother in all your life.

ALGERNON: Well, not till to-day, old boy, I admit. I did my best, however, though I was out of practice. *(Shakes hands.)*

GWENDOLEN: *(to JACK)* My own! But what own are you? What is your Christian name, now that you have become someone else? 2230

JACK: Good heavens! . . . I had quite forgotten that point. Your decision on the subject of my name is irrevocable, I suppose?

GWENDOLEN: I never change, except in my affections.

CECILY: What a noble nature you have, Gwendolen!

JACK: Then the question had better be cleared up at once. Aunt Augusta, a moment. At the time when Miss Prism left me in the hand-bag, had I been christened already?

LADY BRACKNELL: Every luxury that money could buy, including christening, had been lavished on you by your fond and 2240 doting parents.

JACK: Then I was christened! That is settled. Now, what name was I given? Let me know the worst.

LADY BRACKNELL: Being the eldest son you were naturally christened after your father.

JACK: *(irritably)* Yes, but what was my father's Christian name?

LADY BRACKNELL: *(meditatively)* I cannot at the present moment recall what the General's Christian name was. But I have no doubt he had one. He was eccentric, I admit. But only in later years. And that was the result of the Indian cli- 2250 mate, and marriage, and indigestion, and other things of that kind.

JACK: Algy! Can't you recollect what our father's Christian name was?

ALGERNON: My dear boy, we were never even on speaking terms. He died before I was a year old.

JACK: His name would appear in the Army Lists of the period, I suppose, Aunt Augusta?

LADY BRACKNELL: The General was essentially a man of peace, except in his domestic life. But I have no doubt his name 2260 would appear in any military directory.

JACK: The Army Lists of the last forty years are here. These delightful records should have been my constant study. *(Rushes to bookcase and tears the books out.)* M. Generals . . . Mallam, Maxbohm, Magley, what ghastly names they have—Markby, Migsby, Mobbs, Moncrieff! Lieutenant 1840, Captain, Lieutenant-Colonel, Colonel, General 1869, Christian names, Ernest John. *(Puts book very quietly down and speaks quite calmly.)* I always told you, Gwendolen, my name was Ernest, didn't I? Well, it is Ernest after all, I mean 2270 it naturally is Ernest.

LADY BRACKNELL: Yes, I remember the General was called

Ernest. I knew I had some particular reason for disliking the name.

GWENDOLEN: Ernest! My own Ernest! I felt from the first that you could have no other name!

JACK: Gwendolen, it is a terrible thing for a man to find out suddenly that all his life he has been speaking nothing but the truth. Can you forgive me?

2280 GWENDOLEN: I can. For I feel sure that you are sure to change.

JACK: My own one!

CHASUBLE (*to* MISS PRISM) Lætitia! (*Embraces her.*)

MISS PRISM: (*enthusiastically*) Frederick! At last!

ALGERNON: Cecily! (*Embraces her.*) At last!

JACK: Gwendolen! (*Embraces her.*) At last!

LADY BRACKNELL: My nephew, you seem to be displaying signs of triviality.

JACK: On the contrary, Aunt Augusta, I've now realized for the first time in my life the vital Importance of Being Earnest.

## T A B L E A U
## C U R T A I N

*WILDE first published "The Critic as Artist" as an article in* Nineteenth Century, *under the title "The True Function and Value of Criticism"; the essay uses the dialogue form to explore the relationship between criticism and artistic activity. In the essay, Wilde's interest in the truth of appearances, in the power of artifice to represent an inarticulate reality, lays the groundwork for the more explicitly formalist literary and dramatic experiments of the early twentieth century*

## Oscar Wilde
FROM "The Critic as Artist"
(1890)

*With Some Remarks upon the Importance of Doing Nothing*

A DIALOGUE

PART I.
PERSONS: *Gilbert and Ernest.*

SCENE: *the library of a house in Piccadilly, overlooking the Green Park.*

. . . ERNEST: Yes; I see now what you mean. . . . Surely, the higher you place the creative artist, the lower must the critic rank.

GILBERT: Why so?

ERNEST: Because the best that he can give us will be but an echo of rich music, a dim shadow of clear-outlined form. It may, indeed, be that life is chaos, as you tell me that it is; that its martyrdoms are mean and its heroisms ignoble; and that it is the function of Literature to create, from the rough material of actual existence, a new world that will be more marvellous, more enduring, and more true than the world that common eyes look upon, and through which common natures seek to realise their perfection. But surely, if this new world has been made by the spirit and touch of a great artist, it will be a thing so complete and perfect that there will be nothing left for the critic to do. I quite understand now, and indeed admit most readily, that it is far more difficult to talk about a thing than to do it. But it seems to me that this sound and sensible maxim, which is really extremely soothing to one's feelings, and should be adopted as its motto by every Academy of Literature all over the world, applies only to the relations that exist between Art and Life, and not to any relations that there may be between Art and Criticism.

GILBERT: But, surely, Criticism is itself an art. And just as artistic creation implies the working of the critical faculty, and, indeed, without it cannot be said to exist at all, so Criticism is really creative in the highest sense of the word. Criticism is, in fact, both creative and independent.

ERNEST: Independent?

GILBERT: Yes; independent. Criticism is no more to be judged by any low standard of imitation or resemblance than is the work of poet or sculptor. The critic occupies the same relation to the work of art that he criticises as the artist does to the visible world of form and colour, or the unseen world of passion and of thought. He does not even require for the perfection of his art the finest materials. Anything will serve his purpose. And just as out of the sordid and sentimental amours of the silly wife of a small country doctor in the squalid village of Yonville-l'Abbaye, near Rouen, Gustave Flaubert was able to create a classic, and make a masterpiece of style, so, from subjects of little or of no importance, such as the pictures in this year's Royal Academy, or in any year's Royal Academy for that matter, Mr. Lewis Morris's poems, M. Ohnet's novels, or the plays of Mr. Henry Arthur Jones,[1] the true critic can, if it be his pleasure so to direct or waste his faculty of

---

[1] Sir Lewis Morris (1833–1907) was a mediocre but popular English writer of religious and mythological poetry. Georges Ohnet (1848–1918) was a popular late-nineteenth-century French novelist. Henry Arthur Jones (1851–1929) was a popular English dramatist whose greatest successes were the melodramatic *The Silver King* (1882), *The Case of Rebellious Susan* (1894), and *Michael and His Last Angel* (1896), which was praised by the critics, including Shaw, but was a box-office failure. His chief success in comedy came with *The Liars* in 1897.

contemplation, produce work that will be flawless in beauty and instinct with intellectual subtlety. Why not? Dulness is always an irresistible temptation for brilliancy, and stupidity is the permanent *Bestia Trionfans* that calls wisdom from its cave. To an artist so creative as the critic, what does subject-matter signify? No more and no less than it does to the novelist and the painter. Like them, he can find his motives everywhere. Treatment is the test. There is nothing that has not in it suggestion or challenge.

ERNEST: But is Criticism really a creative art?

GILBERT: Why should it not be? It works with materials, and puts them into a form that is at once new and delightful. What more can one say of poetry? Indeed, I would call criticism a creation within a creation. For just as the great artists, from Homer and Aeschylus, down to Shakespeare and Keats, did not go directly to life for their subject-matter, but sought for it in myth, and legend, and ancient tale, so the critic deals with materials that others have, as it were, purified for him, and to which imaginative form and colour have been already added. Nay, more, I would say that the highest Criticism, being the purest form of personal impression, is in its way more creative than creation, as it has least reference to any standard external to itself, and is, in fact, its own reason for existing, and, as the Greeks would put it, in itself, and to itself, an end. Certainly, it is never trammelled by any shackles of verisimilitude. No ignoble considerations of probability, that cowardly concession to the tedious repetitions of domestic or public life, affect it ever. One may appeal from fiction unto fact. But from the soul there is no appeal.

ERNEST: From the soul?

GILBERT: Yes, from the soul. That is what the highest criticism really is, the record of one's own soul. It is more fascinating than history, as it is concerned simply with oneself. It is more delightful than philosophy, as its subject is concrete and not abstract, real and not vague. It is the only civilised form of autobiography, as it deals not with the events, but with the thoughts of one's life; not with life's physical accidents of deed or circumstance, but with the spiritual moods and imaginative passions of the mind. I am always amused by the silly vanity of those writers and artists of our day who seem to imagine that the primary function of the critic is to chatter about their second-rate work. The best that one can say of most modern creative art is that it is just a little less vulgar than reality, and so the critic, with his fine sense of distinction and sure instinct of delicate refinement, will prefer to look into the silver mirror or through the woven veil, and will turn his eyes away from the chaos and clamour of actual existence, though the mirror be tarnished and the veil be torn. His sole aim is to chronicle his own impressions. It is for him that pictures are painted, books written, and marble hewn into form.

ERNEST: I seem to have heard another theory of Criticism.

GILBERT: Yes: it has been said by one whose gracious memory we all revere, and the music of whose pipe once lured Proserpina from her Sicilian fields, and made those white feet stir, and not in vain, the Cumnor cowslips, that the proper aim of Criticism is to see the object as in itself it really is. But this is a very serious error, and takes no cognisance of Criticism's most perfect form, which is in its essence purely subjective, and seeks to reveal its own secret and not the secret of another. For the highest Criticism deals with art not as expressive but as impressive purely.

ERNEST: But is that really so?

GILBERT: Of course it is. Who cares whether Mr. Ruskin's views on Turner are sound or not? What does it matter? That mighty and majestic prose of his, so fervid and so fiery-coloured in its noble eloquence, so rich in its elaborate symphonic music, so sure and certain, at its best, in subtle choice of word and epithet, is at least as great a work of art as any of those wonderful sunsets that bleach or rot on their corrupted canvases in England's [Tate] Gallery; greater indeed, one is apt to think at times, not merely because its equal beauty is more enduring, but on account of the fuller variety of its appeal, soul speaking to soul in those long-cadenced lines, not through form and colour alone, though through these, indeed, completely and without loss, but with intellectual and emotional utterance, with lofty passion and with loftier thought, with imaginative insight, and with poetic aim; greater, I always think, even as Literature is the greater art. Who, again, cares whether Mr. Pater has put into the portrait of Monna Lisa something that Lionardo never dreamed of? The painter may have been merely the slave of an archaic smile, as some have fancied, but whenever I pass into the cool galleries of the Palace of the Louvre, and stand before that strange figure "set in its marble chair in that cirque of fantastic rocks, as in some faint light under sea," I murmur to myself, "She is older than the rocks among which she sits; like the vampire, she has been dead many times, and learned the secrets of the grave; and has been a diver in deep seas, and keeps their fallen day about her; and trafficked for strange webs with Eastern merchants; and, as Leda, was the mother of Helen of Troy, and, as St. Anne, the mother of Mary; and all this has been to her but as the sound of lyres and flutes, and lives only in the delicacy with which it has moulded the changing lineaments, and tinged the eyelids and the hands." And I say to my friend, "The presence that thus so strangely rose beside the waters is expressive of what in the ways of a thousand years man had come to desire"; and he answers me, "Hers is the head upon which all 'the ends of the world are come,' and the eyelids are a little weary."

And so the picture becomes more wonderful to us than it really is, and reveals to us a secret of which, in truth, it knows nothing, and the music of the mystical prose is as sweet in our ears as was that flute-player's music that lent to the lips of La Gioconda those subtle and poisonous curves. Do you ask me what Lionardo would have said had any one told him of this picture that "all the thoughts and experience of the world had etched and moulded there in that which they had of power to refine and make expressive the outward form, the animalism of Greece, the lust of Rome, the reverie of the Middle Age with its spiritual ambition and imaginative loves, the return of the Pagan world, the sins of the Borgias?" He would probably have answered that he had contemplated none of these things, but had concerned himself simply with certain arrangements of lines and masses, and with new and curious colour-harmonies of blue and green. And it is for this very reason that the criticism which I have quoted is criticism of the highest kind. It treats the work of art simply as a starting-point for a new creation. It does not confine itself—let us at least suppose so for the moment—to discovering the real intention of the artist and accepting that as final. And in this it is right, for the meaning of any beautiful created thing is, at least, as much in the soul of him who looks at it, as it was in his soul who wrought it. Nay, it is rather the beholder who lends to the beautiful thing its myriad meanings, and makes it marvellous for us, and sets it in some new relation to the age, so that it becomes a vital portion of our lives, and a symbol of what we pray for, or perhaps of what, having prayed for, we fear that we may receive. The longer I study, Ernest, the more clearly I see that the beauty of the visible arts is, as the beauty of music, impressive primarily, and that it may be marred, and indeed often is so, by any excess of intellectual intention on the part of the artist. For when the work is finished it has, as it were, an independent life of its own, and may deliver a message far other than that which was put into its lips to say. Sometimes, when I listen to the overture to *Tannhäuser*, I seem indeed to see that comely knight treading delicately on the flower-strewn grass, and to hear the voice of Venus calling to him from the caverned hill. But at other times it speaks to me of a thousand different things, of myself, it may be, and my own life, or of the lives of others whom one has loved and grown weary of loving, or of the passions that man has known, or of the passions that man has not known, and so has sought for. To-night it may fill one with that ΕΡΩΣ ΤΩΝ ΑΔΥΝΑΤΩΝ, that *Amour de l'Impossible*, which falls like a madness on many who think they live securely and out of reach of harm, so that they sicken suddenly with the poison of unlimited desire, and, in the infinite pursuit of what they may not obtain, grow faint and swoon or stumble. Tomorrow, like the music of which Aristotle and Plato tell us, the noble Dorian music of the Greek, it may perform the office of a physician, and give us an anodyne against pain, and heal the spirit that is wounded, and "bring the soul into harmony with all right things." And what is true about music is true about all the arts. Beauty has as many meanings as man has moods. Beauty is the symbol of symbols. Beauty reveals everything, because it expresses nothing. When it shows us itself, it shows us the whole fiery-coloured world.

ERNEST: But is such work as you have talked about really criticism?

GILBERT: It is the highest Criticism, for it criticises not merely the individual work of art, but Beauty itself, and fills with wonder a form which the artist may have left void, or not understood, or understood incompletely.

ERNEST: The highest Criticism, then, is more creative than creation, and the primary aim of the critic is to see the object as in itself it really is not; that is your theory, I believe?

GILBERT: Yes, that is my theory. To the critic the work of art is simply a suggestion for a new work of his own, that need not necessarily bear any obvious resemblance to the thing it criticises.

The one characteristic of a beautiful form is that one can put into it whatever one wishes, and see in it whatever one chooses to see; and the Beauty, that gives to creation its universal and aesthetic element, makes the critic a creator in his turn, and whispers of a thousand different things which were not present in the mind of him who carved the statue or painted the panel or graved the gem.

It is sometimes said by those who understand neither the nature of the highest Criticism nor the charm of the highest Art, that the pictures that the critic loves most to write about are those that belong to the anecdotage of painting, and that deal with scenes taken out of literature or history. But this is not so. Indeed, pictures of this kind are far too intelligible. As a class, they rank with illustrations, and even considered from this point of view are failures, as they do not stir the imagination, but set definite bounds to it. For the domain of the painter is, as I suggested before, widely different from that of the poet. To the latter belongs life in its full and absolute entirety; not merely the beauty that men look at, but the beauty that men listen to also; not merely the momentary grace of form or the transient gladness of colour, but the whole sphere of feeling, the perfect cycle of thought. The painter is so far limited that it is only through the mask of the body that he can show us the mystery of the soul; only through conventional images that he can handle ideas; only through its physical equivalents that he can deal with psychology. And how inadequately does he do it then, asking us to accept the torn turban of the Moor for the noble rage of Othello, or a dotard in a storm for the wild madness of Lear! Yet it seems as if nothing could stop him. Most of our elderly English painters spend their wicked and wasted lives in poaching upon the domain of the poets, marring their motives by clumsy treatment, and striving to render, by visible form or colour, the marvel of what is invisible, the splendour of what is not seen. Their pictures are, as a natural consequence, insufferably tedious. They have degraded the invisible arts into the obvious arts, and the one thing not worth looking at is the obvious. I do not say that poet and painter may not treat of the same subject. They have always done so, and will always do so. But while the poet can be pictorial or not, as he chooses, the painter must be pictorial always. For a painter is limited, not to what he sees in nature, but to what upon canvas may be seen.

And so, my dear Ernest, pictures of this kind will not really fascinate the critic. He will turn from them to such works as make him brood and dream and fancy, to works that possess the subtle quality of suggestion, and seem to tell one that even from them there is an escape into a wider world. It is sometimes said that the tragedy of an artist's life is that he cannot realise his ideal. But the true tragedy that dogs the steps of most artists is that they realise their ideal too absolutely. For, when the ideal is realised, it is robbed of its wonder and its mystery, and becomes simply a new starting-point for an ideal that is other than itself. This is the reason why music is the perfect type of art. Music can never reveal its ultimate secret. This, also, is the explanation of the value of limitations in art. The sculptor gladly surrenders imitative colour, and the painter the actual dimensions of form, because by such renunciations they are able to avoid too definite a presentation of the Real, which would be mere imitation, and too definite a realisation of the Ideal, which would be too purely intellectual. It is through its very incompleteness that Art becomes complete in beauty, and so addresses itself, not to the faculty of recognition nor to the faculty of reason, but to the aesthetic sense alone, which, while accepting both reason and recognition as stages of apprehension, subordinates them both to a pure synthetic impression of the work of art as a whole, and, taking whatever alien emotional elements the work may possess, uses their very complexity as a means by which a richer unity may be added to the ultimate impression itself. You see, then, how it is that the aesthetic critic rejects those obvious modes of art that have but one message to deliver, and having delivered it become dumb and sterile, and seeks rather for such modes as suggest reverie and mood, and by their imaginative beauty make all interpretations true, and no interpretation final. Some resemblance, no doubt, the creative work of the critic will have to the work that has stirred him to creation, but it will be such resemblance as exists, not between Nature and the mirror that the painter of landscape or figure may be supposed to hold up to her, but between Nature and the work of the decorative artist. Just as on the flowerless carpets of Persia, tulip and rose blossom indeed and are lovely to look on, though they are not reproduced in visible shape or line; just as the pearl and purple of the sea-shell is echoed in the church of St. Mark at Venice; just as the vaulted ceiling of the wondrous chapel at Ravenna is made gorgeous by the gold and green and sapphire of the peacock's tail, though the birds of Juno fly not across it; so the critic reproduces the work that he criticises in a mode that is never imitative, and part of whose charm may really consist in the rejection of resemblance, and shows us in this way not merely the meaning but also the mystery of Beauty, and, by transforming each art into literature, solves once for all the problem of Art's unity.

But I see it is time for supper. After we have discussed some Chambertin and a few ortolans, we will pass on to the question of the critic considered in the light of the interpreter.

ERNEST: Ah! you admit, then, that the critic may occasionally be allowed to see the object as in itself it really is.

GILBERT: I am not quite sure. Perhaps I may admit it after supper. There is a subtle influence in supper.

# Anton Chekhov

The work of Anton Chekhov (1860–1904) is noted for its objectivity, its sympathetic yet almost clinical examination of turn-of-the-century Russian life. Born in the provincial town of Taganrog, Chekhov trained for a career in medicine and began practicing as a physician in the mid–1880s. At that time he also began to write his first short stories. Throughout his career as a physician, Chekhov continued to write, and he developed a reputation as a modern master of the short story in addition to writing an extraordinary series of plays. In his fiction, as in his later plays, Chekhov adopted a mildly ironic attitude toward his subjects, one that resisted sensation and melodrama in favor of a more neutral stance; as he wrote in a letter, "It is necessary that on stage everything should be as complex and as simple as in life. People are having dinner, and while they're having it, their future happiness may be decided or their lives may be about to be shattered." Chekhov's life was shattered in just this way, simply, suddenly, and casually. In 1884 he coughed up blood, the sure sign that he had contracted tuberculosis. The disease could not be cured and required repeated periods of convalescence; an early death was a certainty.

Chekhov began writing plays in the 1880s as well, mainly short comic sketches he called "vaudevilles," among them *The Bear* (1888), *The Proposal* (1889), and *The Wedding* (1890). In 1896 the Alexandrinsky Theater in St. Petersburg performed his full-length drama *The Seagull*. The play's indirect plotting and its avoidance of the conventional climaxes of melodrama confused actors and audiences alike, and it failed. Chekhov was persuaded by Constantin Stanislavski and Vladimir Nemirovich-Danchenko to mount the play in their newly founded Moscow Art Theater (MAT) in 1898. Stanislavski's commitment to a restrained style of performance, emphasizing psychological complexity and balanced playing by the entire ensemble is generally credited with making the MAT production a success; a seagull became the company's signature. Chekhov produced three more major plays with the MAT. He revised *The Wood Demon* (1889) as *Uncle Vanya* in 1899, and then produced *The Three Sisters* (1901) and *The Cherry Orchard* (1904). He married the actress Olga Knipper—who played leading roles in his plays, including Masha in *The Three Sisters* and Madame Ranevskaya in *The Cherry Orchard*—in 1901, and spent the final years of his life convalescing in Yalta.

## The Three Sisters
## (1901)

The action of Chekhov's plays is usually indirect, not progressive and consequential in the manner of Ibsen's work. Instead, a Chekhov play generally opens with the arrival of some well-to-do characters in the provincial scene of the play and closes with their departure: Yelena and Serbryakov in *Uncle Vanya*, Madame Ranevskaya and her entourage in *The Cherry Orchard*, and the regiment and its romantic Lieutenant Vershinin in *The Three Sisters*.

*The Three Sisters* is very much an ensemble play, and though it focuses our attention on the fortunes of the three Prozorov sisters, it implicates the sisters richly in the lives of the characters who surround them. The play is haunted by Irina's lyrical desire to return "to Moscow," and it is a measure of Chekhov's irony that this romantic wish itself lies at the heart of the sisters' unhappiness. For romantic fantasies seduce many characters in the play, fantasies that replace the reality of their lives. Irina, for instance, is seduced by dreams of a life of work together with Tuzenbach, but is unable to "love" him, to see their life together as enough; it might be said that she nearly drives him to the suicidal duel with the monstrous Solyony. Andrei's youthful vision of a university position in Moscow has been replaced by the petulant desire for a seat on the District Board, and an increasingly unhappy marriage to the village girl Natasha—who seems to be pursuing her own romance with Mr. Protopopov just offstage.

It is Masha's story, though, that brings the destructive potential of such romantic illusions into sharp focus. Married to the warm, kindly, foolish schoolmaster Kulygin, Masha is swept away by the lovelorn Lieutenant Vershinin. In the course of the play, they become more intimate, and finally become lovers, escaping late in Act Three while Kulygin comically searches for them. Chekhov's stagecraft at this moment in the play points up the play's complex and ironic tone.

Everyone leaves the stage: Olga and Irina's room is empty. The fire alarm continues to ring, and Kulygin sticks his head in the door, "Where is Masha? Isn't she here? What an extraordinary business!" It is an extraordinary, alarming business, for the price that Masha pays for her tryst is her life itself. Vershinin will move on to the next town with his regiment, and the story of his unhappy marriage and sad children will no doubt charm another interesting and sophisticated woman trapped in the boring hinterlands. But Masha is left *here*, able to see only the empty and loveless horizon of her future and taste the bitterness of Kulygin's loving forgiveness.

That is, *The Three Sisters* is a romantic drama that casts a cold eye on the unreality of romance. Vershinin plays an important role in this dimension of the play, too. Vershinin is no cad, not the heartless, rapacious recruiting officer of countless melodramas. But his tendency to "philosophize" makes him particularly dangerous to the dreamy Prozorov sisters. Even in his final scene, waiting to say goodbye to Masha, he remarks, "What more can I say to you in parting? What can I philosophize about? . . . *[Laughs]* Life is hard. It presents itself to many of us as desolate and hopeless, and yet, one must admit that it keeps getting clearer and easier, and the day is not far off when it will be wholly bright." Such "philosophizing" seems troubling in two ways. First, it is as though Vershinin is merely filling the time with words, as though the meaning of his "philosophy" were irrelevant. But there is a second, harder lesson here, in the complete rupture between Vershinin's vision of a "clearer and easier" future and the future that faces the ravaged Masha. Rather than enabling him to live more richly, more authentically, Vershinin's philosophy, like Masha's poetry and novels, like the romantic illusions that grip all three sisters, blinds him to the consequences of his actions, to the suffering he creates, and finally to the world in which he lives.

# —The Three Sisters—
## *A Drama in Four Acts*
### Anton Chekhov

TRANSLATED BY ANN DUNNIGAN

## —CHARACTERS IN THE PLAY—

PROZOROV, ANDREI SERGEYEVICH
NATALYA IVANOVNA, *his fiancée, later his wife*
OLGA  
MASHA } *his sisters*  
IRINA  
KULYGIN, FYODOR ILYICH, *a high-school teacher, husband of Masha*
VERSHININ, ALEKSANDR IGNATYEVICH, *Lieutenant Colonel, Battery Commander*
BARON TUZENBACH, NIKOLAI LVOVICH, *Lieutenant*
SOLYONY, VASSILY VASSILYEVICH, *Staff Captain*
CHEBUTYKIN, IVAN ROMANOVICH, *Army doctor*
FEDOTIK, ALEKSEI PETROVICH, *Second Lieutenant*
RODAY, VLADIMIR KARLOVICH, *Second Lieutnant*
FERAPONT, *porter of the District Board, an old man*
ANFISA, *the nurse, an old woman of eighty*

*The action takes place in a provincial town.*

## —ACT ONE—

*(In the PROZOROVS' house. A drawing room with columns, beyond which a large reception room is visible. Midday: it is bright and sunny outside. In the reception room a table is being set for lunch.* OLGA, *in the dark blue uniform of a girls' high-school teacher, is correcting exercise books, standing or walking about as she does so;* MASHA, *in a black dress, her hat on her lap, sits reading a book;* IRINA, *in a white dress, stands lost in thought.)*

OLGA: Father died just a year ago today, on the fifth of May—your name day, Irina. It was snowing then, and very cold. I felt as though I should never live through it, and you lay in a dead faint. But now, a year has gone by, and we think of it calmly; you're already wearing white, and your face is radiant. *(The clock strikes.)* The clock was striking then, too. *(Pause)* I remember there was music when Father was carried out, and they fired a salute at the cemetery. He was a general, in command of a brigade, yet there were very few people walking behind his coffin. But then, it was raining. Heavy rain and snow.

10

IRINA: Why recall it?

*(*BARON TUZENBACH, CHEBUTYKIN, *and* SOLYONY *appear behind the columns near the table in the reception room.)*

OLGA: It's so warm today we can keep the windows wide open, but the birches are not yet in leaf. . . . Father was given a brigade and left Moscow eleven years ago, and I remember perfectly that by this time, at the beginning of May in Moscow, everything was in bloom, it was warm, all bathed in sunshine. Eleven years have passed, but I remember it all as though we had left there yesterday. Oh, God! This morning I woke up, I saw this flood of sunlight, saw the spring, and joy stirred in my soul, I had a passionate longing to go home again.

20

CHEBUTYKIN: Like hell he did!

TUZENBACH: Of course, that's nonsense.

*(*MASHA, *absorbed in her book, softly whistles a tune.)*

OLGA: Don't whistle, Masha. How can you! *(Pause)* Being in school every day, then giving lessons till evening, my head aches continually, and I'm beginning to think like an old woman. In fact, these four years that I've been teaching in the high school, day by day I feel my youth and strength draining out of me. Only one dream keeps growing stronger and stronger . . .

30

IRINA: To go to Moscow. To sell the house, make an end of everything here, and go to Moscow. . . .

OLGA: Yes! To go to Moscow as soon as possible.

*(*CHEBUTYKIN *and* TUZENBACH *laugh.)*

IRINA: Brother will probably become a professor; in any case, he won't go on living here. So there's nothing to stop us but poor Masha.

OLGA: Masha will come and spend the whole summer in Moscow every year.

*(*MASHA *softly whistles a tune.)*

IRINA: God grant it all works out! *(Looking out the window)* The weather is lovely today. I don't know why I feel so lighthearted! This morning I remembered that it was my name day, and suddenly I felt joyful, and thought of our childhood, when Mama was still alive. And I was stirred by such wonderful thoughts . . . such thoughts!

40

OLGA: You are radiant today, more beautiful than ever. And Masha looks beautiful, too. Andrei would be handsome if he hadn't grown so stout, it doesn't suit him. But I've grown old and terribly thin, probably because I get so cross with the girls at school. Today I am free, I'm at home, and my head doesn't ache, I feel younger than yesterday. I'm only twenty-eight. . . . It's all good, all from God, but it seems to me that if I had married and stayed at home all day, it would have been better. *(Pause)* I should have loved my husband.

50

TUZENBACH: *(to* SOLYONY) You talk such nonsense I'm tired of listening to you. *(Coming into the drawing room)* I forgot to tell you, our new battery commander, Vershinin, is going to call on you today. (*Sits down at the piano.*)

OLGA: Really? I shall be delighted.

60 IRINA: Is he old?

TUZENBACH: No, not particularly. Forty or forty-five at most. Seems to be a nice fellow. Not stupid, that's certain. Only he talks a lot.

IRINA: An interesting man?

TUZENBACH: Yes, rather, but there's a wife, a mother-in-law, and two girls. What's more, he's married for the second time. He calls on everyone and tells them he has a wife and two little girls. He'll tell you, too. The wife seems a bit crazy, wears her hair in a long braid like a girl, talks only of lofty
70 matters, philosophizes, and frequently attempts suicide— evidently to make it hot for her husband. I'd have left such a woman long ago, but he puts up with it and merely complains.

SOLYONY: (*coming into the drawing room with* CHEBUTYKIN) With one hand I can lift only fifty pounds, but with two I can lift a hundred and eighty or even two hundred pounds. From this I conclude that two men are not just twice as strong as one, but three times as strong, or even more. . . .

CHEBUTYKIN: (*reading a newspaper as he comes in*) For falling
80 hair . . . two ounces of naphthaline to half a bottle of spirits . . . dissolve and apply daily. . . . (*Writes in a notebook.*) Must make a note of that. (*To* SOLYONY) So, as I was telling you, you stick a little cork into a bottle and pass a glass tube through it. . . . Then you take a pinch of plain ordinary alum . . .

IRINA: Ivan Romanych, dear Ivan Romanych!

CHEBUTYKIN: What is it, my child, my joy?

IRINA: Tell me, why am I so happy today? It's just as though I were sailing before the wind, with the broad blue sky above,
90 and great white birds floating overhead. Why is that? Why?

CHEBUTYKIN: (*kisses both her hands tenderly*) My little white bird. . . .

IRINA: When I woke up this morning, I got up and washed, and suddenly I felt as though everything in this world was clear to me, and that I knew how one ought to live. Dear Ivan Romanych, I know everything. Man must work, he must toil by the sweat of his brow, no matter who he is, and in this alone lies the meaning and purpose of his life, his happiness, his ecstasy. How good to be a workman who gets up at dawn
100 and breaks stones in the street, or a shepherd, or a schoolmaster teaching children, or an engineer on a railroad. . . . Oh, Lord, to say nothing of man, it's better to be an ox, better to be a mere horse, if only one works, than to be a young woman who wakes up at twelve o'clock, has coffee in bed, and then spends two hours dressing. . . . Oh, how dreadful that is! In the same way that one has a craving for water in hot weather, I have a craving for work. And if I don't get up early and work, you can give me up as a friend, Ivan Romanych.

110 CHEBUTYKIN: I will, I'll give you up. . . .

OLGA: Father trained us to get up at seven. Now Irina wakes up at seven and lies in bed at least till nine thinking. And she looks so serious! (*Laughs.*)

IRINA: You're used to thinking of me as a little girl, so it seems strange to you when I look serious. I am twenty years old!

TUZENBACH: The longing for work, oh, my God, how well I understand it! I have never in my life worked. I was born in Petersburg, cold, idle Petersburg, into a family that knew nothing of work or worry of any kind. I remember, when I used to come home from cadet school a footman would pull 120 off my boots, I'd make it difficult for him, and my mother would gaze at me with adoration, surprised that others didn't do the same. I was shielded from work. Though I doubt if they succeeded in shielding me completely, I doubt it! The time has come, something tremendous is hanging over our heads, a powerful, invigorating storm is gathering; it is coming, it's already near, and will blow away the indolence, the indifference, the prejudice against work, the rotten boredom of our society. I am going to work, and in another twenty-five or thirty years everyone will work. 130 Everyone!

CHEBUTYKIN: I'm not going to work.

TUZENBACH: You don't count.

SOLYONY: Twenty-five years from now you'll no longer be here, thank God. In two or three years you'll die of apoplexy, or I'll lose my temper and put a bullet through your head, my angel. (*Takes a bottle of scent out of his pocket and sprinkles his chest and hands.*)

CHEBUTYKIN: As a matter of fact, I never have done anything. I haven't lifted a finger since the day I left the university, 140 haven't even read a book, only newspapers. . . . (*Takes another newspaper out of his pocket.*) Here . . . I know from the newspapers, for instance, that there was a person called Dobrolyubov, but what he wrote—I don't know. . . . (*Sound of knocking on the floor downstairs.*) There . . . I'm being called from downstairs, someone has come to see me. I'll be right back . . . wait. . . . (*Goes out hurriedly, combing his beard.*)

IRINA: He's up to something.

TUZENBACH: Yes. He looked so elated when he went out that 150 it's obvious he's about to bring you a present.

IRINA: I wish he wouldn't!

OLGA: Yes, it's awful. He's always doing something foolish.

MASHA: "A green oak by a curved seashore, upon that oak a golden chain . . . upon that oak a golden chain"° . . . (*Gets up, humming softly.*)

OLGA: You're not very cheerful today, Masha.

(MASHA, *humming, puts on her hat.*)

OLGA: Where are you going?

MASHA: Home.

IRINA: Strange . . . 160

TUZENBACH: Leaving a name-day party!

MASHA: Never mind . . . I'll come back in the evening. Goodbye, my lovely one. . . . (*Kisses* IRINA.) Once again, I wish you health and happiness. In the old days, when Father was alive, thirty or forty officers used to come to our name-day parties and there was a real racket, but today there's only a man and a half, and it's silent as a desert. . . . I'm going. . . . I'm in the doldrums today, not very cheerful, so don't listen to me. (*Laughing through her tears*) Later we'll have a talk,

---

°The quotation is from the Prologue of *Ruslan and Ludmilla* by Aleksandr Sergeyevich Pushkin (1799–1837).

170    but good-bye for now, darling, I'll go off somewhere. . . .

IRINA: *(annoyed)* Oh, you're so . . .

OLGA: *(tearfully)* I understand you, Masha.

SOLYONY: If a man philosophizes, you'll get philosophy, or at least sophistry, but if a woman, or a couple of women, start philosophizing—it's like pulling taffy!

MASHA: What do you mean by that, you impossibly dreadful man?

SOLYONY: Nothing. He no sooner cried "Alack" than the bear was on his back.

*(A Pause)*

180    MASHA: *(to* OLGA, *angrily)* Don't bawl!

*(Enter* ANFISA *and* FERAPONT *with a cake.)*

ANFISA: This way, my dear. Come in, your boots are clean. *(To* IRINA*)* From the District Board, from Protopopov—Mikhail Ivanych . . . a cake.

IRINA: Thank you. Thank him for me. *(Takes cake.)*

FERAPONT: How's that?

IRINA: *(louder)* Thank him for me!

OLGA: Nurse dear, give him some pie. Go along, Ferapont, they'll give you some pie.

FERAPONT: How's that?

190    ANFISA: Come along, Ferapont Spiridonych, my dear. Come along . . . *(Goes out with* FERAPONT.*)*

MASHA: I don't like Protopopov, that Mikhail Potapych, or Ivanych. He shouldn't be invited here.

IRINA: I didn't invite him.

MASHA: Good.

*(Enter* CHEBUTYKIN, *followed by a soldier carrying a silver samovar; there is a murmur of astonishment and displeasure.)*

OLGA: *(covers her face with her hands)* A samovar! *(Goes out to the table in the reception room.)*

IRINA: Dear Ivan Romanych, what have you done!

TUZENBACH: I told you.

200    MASHA: Ivan Romanych, you are simply shameless!

CHEBUTYKIN: My dear ones, my darlings, you are all I have, you are dearer to me than anything in the world. I'll soon be sixty, I'm an old man, a lonely, good-for-nothing old man. . . . There's nothing good about me but this love for you, and if it weren't for you, I'd have been dead long ago. . . . *(To* IRINA*)* My dear child, I have known you since the day you were born . . . I carried you in my arms. . . . I loved your dear mother. . . .

IRINA: But why such expensive presents!

210    CHEBUTYKIN: *(through his tears, angrily)* Expensive presents! Why, you're completely—*(to the orderly)* Take the samovar in there. . . . *(Mimicking)* Expensive presents . . . *(The orderly carries the samovar into the reception room.)*

ANFISA: *(passing through the drawing room)* My dears, there's a colonel, a stranger! He's already taken off his overcoat, children, he is coming in here. Irinushka, now you be nice and polite. . . . *(Going out)* And it's high time we had lunch. . . . Mercy on us!

TUZENBACH: Vershinin, I suppose.

*(Enter* VERSHININ.*)*

220    TUZENBACH: Lieutenant Colonel Vershinin!

VERSHININ: *(to* MASHA *and* IRINA*)* I have the honor to introduce myself: Vershinin. I am very, very happy to be in your house at last. How you have grown! Ay! Ay!

IRINA: Please sit down. We are delighted to see you.

VERSHININ: *(gaily)* How glad I am, how glad I am! But there were three sisters. I remember—three little girls. The faces I no longer remember, but that your father, Colonel Prozorov, had three little girls, I remember perfectly, I saw them with my own eyes. How time passes! Oh, oh, how time passes!    230

TUZENBACH: Aleksandr Ignatyevich is from Moscow.

IRINA: From Moscow? You are from Moscow?

VERSHININ: Yes, from Moscow. Your father was a battery commander there, and I was an officer in the same brigade. *(To* MASHA*)* Your face, now, I do seem to remember.

MASHA: I don't remember you.

IRINA: Olya! Olya! *(Calling into the reception room)* Olya, come here!

*(*OLGA *comes from the reception room into the drawing room.)*

IRINA: Lieutenant Colonel Vershinin, it turns out, is from Moscow.    240

VERSHININ: You must be Olga Sergeyevna, the eldest . . . and you are Maria . . . and you are Irina—the youngest. . . .

OLGA: You're from Moscow?

VERSHININ: Yes. I studied in Moscow and went into the service in Moscow. I served there a long time, and at last I have been given a battery here—and have moved here, as you see. I don't exactly remember you, I only remember that there were three sisters. Your father I remember very well; I can close my eyes and see him as plain as life. I used to visit you in Moscow.    250

OLGA: I thought I remembered everyone, and all at once I—

VERSHININ: My name is Aleksandr Ignatyevich.

IRINA: Aleksandr Ignatyevich, you are from Moscow. . . . What a surprise!

OLGA: You see, we are going to move there.

IRINA: We hope to be there by autumn. It's our native town, we were born there . . . on Old Basmannaya Street. . . . *(They both laugh delightedly.)*

MASHA: Suddenly we see someone from our own town. *(Animatedly)* Now I remember! Olya, you remember, at    260 home they used to talk of "the lovelorn major." You were a lieutenant then, and in love, and for some reason they used to call you major to tease you. . . .

VERSHININ: *(laughing)* Yes, yes . . . "the lovelorn major," that's right. . . .

MASHA: You had only a moustache then. . . . Oh, how much older you look! How much older!

VERSHININ: Yes, when I was called "the lovelorn major," I was still young, I was in love. It's different now.

OLGA: But you haven't a single gray hair. You've grown older,    270 but you're still not old.

VERSHININ: Nevertheless, I am in my forty-third year. Is it long since you left Moscow?

IRINA: Eleven years. But why are you crying, Masha, you funny girl? *(Through tears)* I'm starting to cry, too. . . .

MASHA: I'm all right. And what street did you live on?

VERSHININ: On Old Basmannaya.

OLGA: We did, too.

VERSHININ: At one time I lived on Nemyetskaya Street. I used to walk from there to the Krasny Barracks. There's a gloomy-looking bridge on the way, and under the bridge the water roars. It makes a lonely man feel sick at heart. *(Pause)* But here, what a broad, magnificent river! A wonderful river!

OLGA: Yes, except that it's cold. It's cold here, and there are mosquitoes.

VERSHININ: Really! But it's such a fine, healthy, Russian climate. The woods, the river . . . and then there are birch trees here. Sweet, modest birches, of all trees I love them best. It's good to live here. Only it's strange that the railway station is twenty versts away. . . . And no one knows why that is.

SOLYONY: I know why it is. *(Everyone looks at him.)* Because if the station had been near, then it wouldn't have been far, and since it is far, it can't be near.

*(An awkward silence)*

TUZENBACH: You're a wag, Vassily Vassilyich.

OLGA: Now I remember you. I remember.

VERSHININ: I knew your mother.

CHEBUTYKIN: She was a lovely woman `. . . God rest her soul.

IRINA: Mama is buried in Moscow.

OLGA: In the Novo-Dyevichy. . . .

MASHA: Imagine, I'm already beginning to forget her face. And we won't be remembered either. We'll be forgotten.

VERSHININ: Yes, we'll be forgotten. Such is our fate, we can do nothing about it. What to us seems serious, significant, highly important—a time will come when it will be forgotten, or seem unimportant. *(Pause)* And it's interesting that now we absolutely cannot know just what will be considered great, important, and what pitiful, absurd. Didn't the discoveries of Copernicus, or, let us say, Columbus, at first seem worthless and absurd, while the shallow nonsense written by some crank appeared to be the truth? And it may be that our present life, to which we are so reconciled, will in time seem strange, inconvenient, stupid, not pure enough, perhaps even sinful. . . .

TUZENBACH: Who can tell? Perhaps our age will be called great and be remembered with respect. Today there are no torture chambers, no executions, no invasions, and yet, how much suffering!

SOLYONY: *(in a high-pitched voice)* Peep, peep, peep. . . . Don't give the Baron his porridge, just let him philosophize a little.

TUZENBACH: Vassily Vassilyich, I beg you to leave me alone. *(Moves to another chair.)* After all, it's boring.

SOLYONY: *(in a high-pitched voice)* Peep, peep, peep. . . .

TUZENBACH: *(to VERSHININ)* The suffering that can be observed today—and there is so much of it—does speak for a certain moral development which our society has attained.

VERSHININ: Yes, yes, of course.

CHEBUTYKIN: You said just now, Baron, that our age will be called great; but people are small, all the same. . . . *(Gets up.)* Look how small I am. It would only be to console me if you called my life a great, understandable thing.

*(Someone is playing a violin offstage.)*

MASHA: That's Andrei, our brother.

IRINA: He's the scholar in the family. He's probably going to be a professor. Papa was a military man, but his son has chosen an academic career.

MASHA: In accordance with Papa's wish.

OLGA: We haven't stopped teasing him all day. He seems to be slightly in love.

IRINA: With a local girl. She'll very likely call on us today.

MASHA: Oh, how she dresses! It's not just that her clothes are ugly and out of style, they're simply awful. A queer, gaudy, yellowish skirt with some sort of vulgar fringe and a red blouse. And such scrubbed, scrubbed cheeks! Andrei's not in love—I can't believe that, after all, he does have taste—he's simply teasing us, fooling. Yesterday I heard that she was marrying Protopopov, the chairman of the District Board. And a very good thing, too. . . . *(At a side door)* Andrei, come here. Just for a minute, dear.

*(Enter ANDREI)*

OLGA: This is my brother, Andrei Sergeyich.

VERSHININ: Vershinin.

ANDREI: Prozorov. *(Wipes his perspiring face.)* You are our new battery commander?

OLGA: Just imagine, Aleksandr Ignatych is from Moscow!

ANDREI: Yes? Well, I congratulate you; now my little sisters will give you no peace.

VERSHININ: I'm afraid your sisters must be getting tired of me already.

IRINA: Look at the little picture frame Andrei gave me today. *(Shows the frame.)* He made it himself.

VERSHININ: *(looking at the frame, not knowing what to say)* Yes . . . it's quite . . .

IRINA: And you see the frame above the piano, he made that, too.

*(ANDREI, with a gesture of impatience, moves away.)*

OLGA: He's not only a scholar, but he plays the violin and makes all sorts of things out of wood—in fact, he's good at everything. Andrei, don't go! He has a way of always going off. Come here!

*(MASHA and IRINA take hold of his hands and, laughing, lead him back.)*

MASHA: Come on, come on!

ANDREI: Leave me alone, please.

MASHA: You're so funny! Aleksandr Ignatyevich used to be called "the lovelorn major," and he didn't mind in the least . . .

VERSHININ: Not in the least.

MASHA: And I'm going to call you the lovelorn violinist!

IRINA: Or the lovelorn professor!

OLGA: He's in love! Andryusha is in love!

IRINA: *(clapping her hands)* Bravo, bravo! Bis! Andryusha is in love!

CHEBUTYKIN: *(comes up behind ANDREI and puts both arms around his waist)* For love alone has nature put us in this world! *(Laughs loudly, still holding his newspaper.)*

ANDREI: Come, that's enough. *(Wipes his face.)* I haven't slept all night, and now I'm not quite myself, as they say. I read till four o'clock and then went to bed, but it was no use. I kept thinking of one thing and another, and at the crack of dawn the sun simply poured into my bedroom. During the summer, while I'm here, I'd like to translate a book from the English.

390 VERSHININ: You read English, then?

ANDREI: Yes. Father—God rest his soul—oppressed us with education. It's ridiculous and stupid, but all the same I must confess that after his death I began to fill out, and now, in one year, I've grown fat, as if a weight had been lifted from my body. Thanks to Father, my sisters and I know French, German, and English, and Irina knows Italian besides. But at what a cost!

MASHA: In this town, to know three languages is a needless luxury—not even a luxury, but a sort of superfluous ap-
400 pendage, like a sixth finger. We know a great deal that is useless.

VERSHININ: Now, there you are! (*Laughs.*) You know a great deal that is useless! It seems to me that there is not and cannot be a town so dull and depressing that a clever, educated person would be useless. Let us suppose that among the hundred thousand inhabitants of this town, which, of course, is backward and uncouth, there are only three people such as you. It goes without saying that you cannot vanquish the ignorant masses around you; in the course of your
410 life, little by little, you will have to give way and be lost in that crowd of a hundred thousand; life will stifle you, but all the same you will not disappear, you will not be without influence. After you there may appear perhaps six like you, then twelve, and so on, until finally, your kind will become the majority. In two or three hundred years life on this earth will be unimaginably beautiful, wonderful. Man needs such a life, and so long as it is not here, he must foresee it, expect it, dream about it, prepare for it; and for this he will have to see and know more than his grandfather and father knew.
420 (*Laughs.*) And you complain of knowing a great deal that is useless.

MASHA: (*takes off her hat*) I am staying for lunch.

IRINA: (*with a sigh*) Really, all that ought to have been written down. . . .

(ANDREI *is not to be seen; he has gone out unobserved.*)

TUZENBACH: After many years, you say, life on earth will be beautiful, wonderful. That is true. But in order to take part in it now, even from afar, we must prepare for it, we must work. . . .

VERSHININ: (*gets up*) Yes. . . . What a lot of flowers you have!
430 (*Looking around*) And a splendid apartment. I envy you! All my life I've been hanging about little apartments with two chairs and a sofa, and a stove that always smokes. That's exactly what's been lacking in my life, flowers such as these. . . . (*Rubbing his hands*) Well, nothing can be done about it now.

TUZENBACH: Yes, we must work. You're probably thinking: the German is getting sentimental. But, word of honor, I'm a Russian, I don't even speak German. My father was a member of the Orthodox Church. . . . (*Pause*)
440 VERSHININ: (*walking about the stage*) I often think: what if one were to begin life over again, but consciously? If one life, which has already been lived, were only a rough draft, so to say, and the other the final copy! Then each of us, I think, would try above everything not to repeat himself, at least he would create a different setting for his life, he would arrange

an apartment like this for himself, with flowers and plenty of light. . . . I have a wife and two little girls, but then, my wife is not in good health, and so forth and so on, and . . . well, if I were to begin life over again, I wouldn't marry. . . . No, no!

(*Enter* KULYGIN *in the uniform of a schoolteacher.*)

KULYGIN: (*going up to* IRINA) Allow me to congratulate you on 450 your saint's day, dear sister, and to wish you sincerely, from my heart, good health and everything that can be wished for a girl of your age. And then to offer you this little book as a gift. (*Giving her a book*) The history of our high school, covering fifty years, written by myself. A mere trifle, written because I had nothing better to do, but read it, anyway. Good morning, ladies and gentlemen! (*To* VERSHININ) Kulygin, teacher in the local high school, Aulic Councilor. (*To* IRINA) In this little book you will find a list of all those who have graduated from our high school in the last fifty years. *Feci* 460 *quod potui, faciant meliora potentes.* (*Kisses* MASHA.)

IRINA: But you gave me this same book at Easter.

KULYGIN: Impossible! In that case, give it back, or better still, give it to the Colonel. Take it, Colonel. Read it some day when you're bored.

VERSHININ: Thank you. (*About to leave*) I am extremely happy to have made your acquaintance. . . .

OLGA: You aren't going? No, no!

IRINA: You must stay for lunch. Please.

OLGA: Please do! 470

VERSHININ: (*bowing*) I seem to have happened onto a name-day party. Forgive me, I didn't know and have not offered my congratulations. . . . (*Goes with* OLGA *to the reception room.*)

KULYGIN: Today is Sunday, gentlemen, a day of rest, so let us rest, let us enjoy ourselves, each according to his age and position. The carpets ought to be taken up for the summer and put away till winter . . . Persian powder or naphthaline. . . . The Romans were healthy because they knew how to work and knew how to rest, they had *mens sana in corpore sano.* 480 Their life proceeded in accordance with certain forms. Our director says: the chief thing in every life—is its form. That which loses its form comes to an end—and it is the same with our prosaic lives. (*Puts his arm around* MASHA'S *waist, laughing.*) Masha loves me. My wife loves me. . . . And the window curtains, too, along with the carpets. . . . I'm feeling cheerful today, I'm in excellent spirits. Masha, we're to be at the director's house at four o'clock this afternoon. They're organizing a walk for the teachers and their families.

MASHA: I'm not going. 490

KULYGIN: (*hurt*) Masha dear, why not?

MASHA: We'll discuss it later. . . . (*Angrily*) All right, I'll go, only leave me alone, please. . . . (*Walks away.*)

KULYGIN: And afterward we shall spend the evening at the director's. Despite his poor health, this man tries above everything to be sociable. A superior, noble person. A splendid man. Yesterday after the conference he said to me: "I am tired, Fyodor Ilyich! Tired!" (*Looks at the clock on the wall, then at his watch.*) Your clock is seven minutes fast. Yes, he says, I am tired! 500

(*Offstage a violin is heard.*)

OLGA: Please come to lunch, my friends. There's a meat pie!

KULYGIN: Ah, Olga, my dear Olga! Yesterday I worked from early morning to eleven o'clock at night, and was tired out, but today I feel happy. (*Going to the table in the reception room*) My dear . . .

CHEBUTYKIN: (*puts the newspaper into his pocket and combs his beard*) A pie? Splendid!

MASHA: (*to* CHEBUTYKIN, *sternly*) Take care: you're not to drink anything today. Do you hear? It's bad for you to drink.

510  CHEBUTYKIN: Listen to her! I'm past all that. It's two years since I've been on a spree. Anyway, my girl, what does it matter!

MASHA: All the same, don't you dare drink. Don't you dare. (*Angrily, but so that her husband does not hear*) Another of those long, dull evenings at the director's, damn it!

TUZENBACH: If I were in your place I wouldn't go. . . . Very simple.

CHEBUTYKIN: Don't go, my pet.

MASHA: Yes, don't go. . . . This cursed, unbearable life. . . .

520  (*Goes to the reception room.*)

CHEBUTYKIN: (*following her*) Now, now. . . .

SOLYONY: (*goes to the reception room*) Peep, peep, peep. . . .

TUZENBACH: That's enough, Vassily Vassilyich. Drop it!

SOLYONY: Peep, peep, peep. . . .

KULYGIN: (*gaily*) Your health, Colonel! I'm a pedagogue, and one of the family here, Masha's husband. She is kind, very kind. . . .

VERSHININ: I'll have a little of this dark vodka. . . . (*Drinks.*) Your health! (*To* OLGA) It's so good to be here!

(*Only* IRINA *and* TUZENBACH *remain in the drawing room.*)

530  IRINA: Masha is in a bad humor today. She married at eighteen, when he seemed to her the cleverest of men. But now it's different. He's the kindest, but not the cleverest.

OLGA: (*impatiently*) Andrei, will you please come?

ANDREI: (*offstage*) Coming. (*Enters and goes to the table.*)

TUZENBACH: What are you thinking about?

IRINA: Oh, nothing. I don't like that Solyony of yours, I'm afraid of him. He talks nothing but nonsense . . .

TUZENBACH: He's a strange man. I am both sorry for him and annoyed by him, but more sorry. I think he's shy. . . . When

540  I'm alone with him, he can be very intelligent and friendly, but in company he's a crude fellow, a bully. Don't go yet, let them get settled at the table. And let me be near you a little while. What are you thinking about? (*Pause*) You are twenty, I am not yet thirty. How many years lie before us, a long, long succession of days, full of my love for you. . . .

IRINA: Nikolai Lvovich, don't talk to me of love.

TUZENBACH: (*not listening*) I have a passionate thirst for life, for struggle, for work, and that thirst is mingled in my soul with my love for you, Irina, and, just because you are beau-

550  tiful it seems to me that life, too, is beautiful. What are you thinking about?

IRINA: You say life is beautiful. Yes, but what if it only seems so! Life for us three sisters has not been beautiful, it has stifled us, like weeds. . . . Now I have tears in my eyes. I mustn't . . . (*quickly dries her eyes and smiles.*) We must work, work. That's why we're so melancholy and take such a gloomy view of life, because we know nothing of work. We come of people who despised work. . . .

(*Enter* NATALYA IVANOVNA; *she is wearing a pink dress with a green sash.*)

NATASHA: They're already sitting down to lunch . . . I'm late. (*Steals a glance at herself in the mirror and adjusts her* 560 *dress.*)

NATASHA: My hair seems to be all right. . . . (*Seeing* IRINA) Dear Irina Sergeyevna, I congratulate you! (*Gives her a vigorous and prolonged kiss.*) You have such a lot of guests, I really feel awful. . . . How do you do, Baron!

OLGA: (*coming into the drawing room*) Well, here's Natalya Ivanovna. How do you do, my dear! (*Kisses her.*)

NATASHA: Congratulations on the name day. You have so much company, I feel terribly embarrassed. . . .

OLGA: Nonsense, they're all old friends. (*In a shocked under-* 570 *tone*) You're wearing a green sash! My dear, that's not right!

NATASHA: (*plaintively*) Really? But it's not really green, it's more of a neutral color. (*Follows* OLGA *into the reception room.*)

(*Everyone sits down to lunch in the reception room; there is not a soul in the drawing room.*)

KULYGIN: Irina, I wish you a nice fiancé! It's time you married.

CHEBUTYKIN: Natalya Ivanovna, I wish you a nice fiancé, too.

KULYGIN: Natalya Ivanovna already has a fiancé.

MASHA: (*strikes her plate with a fork*) I'll have a little glass of wine. Why not, it's a rosy life, and we only live once!

KULYGIN: Your conduct merits a C minus.                      580

VERSHININ: This is a delicious liquor. What is it made of?

SOLYONY: Cockroaches.

IRINA: (*in a wailing tone*) Ugh! Ugh! How disgusting!

OLGA: For supper we're having roast turkey and apple pie. Thank goodness, I'll be home all day today, and in the evening—home. You must all come back this evening. . . .

VERSHININ: May I come too?

IRINA: Please do.

NATASHA: They are very informal.

CHEBUTYKIN: For love alone has nature put us in this world. 590 (*Laughs.*)

ANDREI: (*angrily*) Stop it, please! Don't you ever get tired of it?

(FEDOTIK *and* RODAY *enter with a big basket of flowers.*)

FEDOTIK: Look, they're already at lunch.

RODAY: (*loudly, speaking with guttural R's*) Really? Yes, they're lunching already.

FEDOTIK: Wait a minute! (*Takes a snapshot.*) One! Wait, just one more! (*Takes another snapshot.*) Two! All over now! (*They pick up the basket and go to the reception room, where they are greeted noisily.*)

RODAY: Congratulations! I wish you everything, everything! 600 The weather today is delightful, absolutely marvelous! I've been out walking all morning with the high-school boys. I teach gymnastics at the high school. . . .

FEDOTIK: You may move now, Irina Sergeyevna, it's all right. (*Taking a snapshot*) You look charming today. (*Takes a top out of his pocket.*) By the way, here's a top. . . . It has an amazing sound. . . .

IRINA: How fascinating!

MASHA: "A green oak by a curved seashore, upon that oak a golden chain . . . upon that oak a golden chain." . . . 610

(*Plaintively*) Why do I keep saying that? This phrase has been haunting me ever since morning. . . .

KULYGIN: Thirteen at the table!

RODAY: (*loudly*) Ladies and gentlemen, can it be that you attach any significance to superstitions? (*Laughter*)

KULYGIN: If there are thirteen at the table it means that someone here is in love. It's not you by any chance, Ivan Romanovich?

CHEBUTYKIN: I'm an old sinner, but why Natalya Ivanovna
620    should be embarrassed I simply cannot understand.

(*Loud laughter;* NATASHA *runs into the drawing room, and* ANDREI *follows her.*)

ANDREI: Come, don't pay any attention! Wait. . . . Stop . . . I beg of you . . .

NATASHA: I feel so ashamed. . . . I don't know what's the matter with me, but they keep making fun of me. I know it was bad manners to leave the table like that, but I can't help it. . . . I can't help it. . . . (*Covers her face with her hands.*)

ANDREI: My darling, I beg of you, I implore you, don't be upset. They are only joking, I assure you, it is not meant unkindly. My darling, my beautiful one, they are all kind, good-
630    hearted people, and they are fond of us both. Come over here to the window, they can't see us here. . . . (*Glances around*)

NATASHA: I'm so unused to being in company!

ANDREI: Oh, youth, wonderful, beautiful youth! My darling, my lovely one, don't be so upset! Believe me, believe me. . . . I feel so happy, my soul is full of love, and ecstasy. . . . Oh, they can't see us! They can't see us! Why, why did I fall in love with you—when did I fall in love—Oh, I don't understand anything. My darling, my lovely, my pure
640    one, be my wife! I love you, love you, as I have never loved anyone before. . . . (*A kiss*)

(*Two officers enter and, seeing the pair kissing, stop in amazement.*)

—ACT TWO—

(*The same set as Act One. Eight o'clock in the evening. Offstage the faint sound of an accordion being played in the street. There are no lights.* NATALYA IVANOVNA *enters in a dressing gown carrying a candle; she comes in and stops at the door leading to* ANDREI'S *room.*)

NATASHA: Andryusha, what are you doing? Reading? Never mind, I was only . . . (*Goes to another door, opens it, and after looking in, closes it.*) If there's a fire anywhere . . .

ANDREI: (*enters with a book in his hand*) What are you doing, Natasha?

NATASHA: Looking to see if there's a fire. . . . It's Carnival Week, and the servants have lost their heads, you have to keep watching to see that nothing happens. Last night at
650    midnight I walked through the dining room, and there was a candle burning. Who lighted it? I couldn't find out. What time is it?

ANDREI: A quarter past eight.

NATASHA: And Olga and Irina are not in yet. They haven't come back. Still hard at work, poor things . . . Olga at the teachers'

meeting, Irina at the telegraph office. . . . (*Sighs.*) This morning I said to your sister: "Take care of yourself, Irina, my dear," I said. But she won't listen. A quarter past eight, you say? I'm afraid our Bobik is not at all well. Why is he so cold? Yesterday he was feverish, and today he is cold all    660
over. . . . I'm so afraid!

ANDREI: It's nothing, Natasha. The boy is all right.

NATASHA: Still it's better to keep him on the diet. I'm afraid. And tonight, they say, the maskers will be here around ten o'clock. It would be better if they didn't come, Andryusha.

ANDREI: I really don't know. They've been invited, you see.

NATASHA: This morning the little fellow wakes up and looks at me, and suddenly he smiles; that means he knows me. "Bobik," I say, "good morning! Good morning, darling!" And he laughs. Children understand, they understand very    670
well. So, then, Andryusha, I'll tell them not to let the maskers in.

ANDREI: (*irresolutely*) But that's up to my sisters. This is their household.

NATASHA: Yes, theirs, too. I'll tell them. They are kind. . . . (*Going*) I've ordered clabber for supper. The doctor says you ought to have nothing but clabber, or you'll never get thin. (*Stops.*) Bobik is cold. I'm afraid his room is too chilly for him. We ought to put him in a different room, at least till the warm weather comes. Irina's room, for instance, is just    680
right for a baby; it's dry, and gets sun all day. I must tell her; she could share Olga's room for a while. . . . She's not at home during the day anyhow, she only sleeps here. . . . (*Pause*) Andryushanchik, why don't you say something?

ANDREI: Oh, I was thinking. . . . Besides, I have nothing to say. . . .

NATASHA: Now there was something I wanted to tell you . . . Oh, yes. Ferapont has come from the District Board and is asking for you.

ANDREI: (*yawning*) Send him in.    690

(NATASHA *goes out;* ANDREI, *bending over the candle which she has forgotten, reads his book. Enter* FERAPONT: *he wears a tattered old overcoat with the collar turned up, and his ears are wrapped up.*)

ANDREI: Good evening, my friend. What have you to say?

FERAPONT: The Chairman has sent you a book and a paper of some kind. Here. . . . (*Hands him a book and a packet.*)

ANDREI: Thank you. Good. Why have you come so late? It's past eight.

FERAPONT: How's that?

ANDREI: (*louder*) I say you came late. It's after eight o'clock.

FERAPONT: Indeed it is. When I came here it was still light, but they wouldn't let me see you. The master is busy, they said. Well, then, if you're busy, you're busy. I'm not going any    700
place. (*Thinking that* ANDREI *has asked him something*) How's that?

ANDREI: Nothing. (*Examining the book*) Tomorrow is Friday. There will be no session, but I'll come anyway . . . and do some work. It's dull at home. . . . (*Pause*) My dear old man, how curiously things change, how life deceives us! Today, out of boredom, having nothing to do, I picked up this book—old university lectures—and I felt like laughing. . . . My God, I'm the Secretary of a District Board, the Board of which Protopopov is Chairman; Secretary, and the very    710 most I can hope for—is to become a member of that Board! I, a member of a District Board, I, who dream every night that I am a professor at the University of Moscow, an illustrious scholar of whom all Russia is proud!

FERAPONT: I wouldn't know . . . I don't hear well. . . .

ANDREI: If you could hear well, I probably wouldn't be talking to you. I must talk to someone, but my wife doesn't understand me, and for some reason I'm afraid of my sisters, I'm afraid they'll laugh at me, make me feel ashamed. . . . I don't 720 drink, I don't like taverns, but right now, how I should enjoy sitting in Tyestov's restaurant in Moscow, or in the Bolshoi Moscovsky, my dear man.

FERAPONT: And in Moscow, so a contractor was saying at the Board the other day, some merchants were eating pancakes; one of them, who ate forty, it seems died. It was either forty or fifty. I don't remember.

ANDREI: You sit in a huge room in a Moscow restaurant, you don't know anyone and no one knows you, and yet you don't feel like a stranger. Here you know everyone, everyone 730 knows you, but you're a stranger, a stranger. . . . A stranger and lonely.

FERAPONT: How's that? *(Pause)* And that same contractor was saying—maybe he was lying—that a rope is stretched all the way across Moscow.

ANDREI: What for?

FERAPONT: I wouldn't know. That's what the contractor said.

ANDREI: Nonsense. *(Reads the book.)* Were you ever in Moscow?

FERAPONT: *(after a pause)* Never was. It was not God's will. 740 *(Pause)* Shall I go now?

ANDREI: You may go. Good-bye. (FERAPONT *goes out.)* Goodbye. *(Reading)* Come back and get these papers tomorrow morning. Go along. . . . *(Pause)* He's gone. *(A bell rings.)* Yes, work. . . . *(Stretches and unhurriedly goes to his own room.)*

*(Behind the scenes a nurse sings, rocking the baby to sleep.* MASHA *and* VERSHININ *enter. While they are talking a maid lights the lamp and candles in the reception room.)*

MASHA: I don't know. *(Pause)* I don't know. Of course, a great deal depends on what one is accustomed to. After Father died, for instance, it took us a long time to get used to having no orderlies in the house. But even apart from habit, I 750 have to say it in all fairness. It may not be so in other places, but in our town the most decent, the most honorable and well-bred people, are all in the army.

VERSHININ: I'm thirsty. I'd like some tea.

MASHA: *(glancing at the clock)* They'll bring it soon. I was married when I was eighteen, and I was afraid of my husband because he was a teacher, and I was hardly out of school. In those days he seemed to me terribly learned, clever, and important. But now, unfortunately, it is different.

VERSHININ: Yes. . . . That's how it is.

760 MASHA: I don't speak of my husband, I've grown used to him, but among civilians generally, there are so many coarse, impolite, ill-bred people. Coarseness upsets and offends me, I suffer when I see that a man is not fine enough, gentle enough, courteous. When I happen to be among teachers, my husband's colleagues, I am simply miserable.

VERSHININ: Yes. . . . But it seems to me that it's all the same whether they're civilians or military men, they're equally uninteresting, in this town at any rate. It's all the same! If you listen to one of the local intelligentsia, either civilian or military, he's sick and tired of everything; either he's 770 sick and tired of his wife, or his home, his estate, or his horses. . . . A Russian is peculiarly given to an exalted way of thinking, but tell me, why is it that in life he falls so short? Why?

MASHA: Why?

VERSHININ: Why is he sick and tired of his children, sick and tired of his wife? And why are his wife and children sick and tired of him?

MASHA: You're not in a very good mood today.

VERSHININ: Perhaps not. I've had no dinner today, nothing to 780 eat since morning. One of my daughters is not very well, and when my little girls are ill, I am seized with anxiety, my conscience torments me for having given them such a mother. Oh, if you could have seen her today! What a worthless creature! We began quarreling at seven o'clock this morning, and at nine I slammed the door and left. *(Pause)* I never talk about this, strangely enough, I complain only to you. *(Kisses her hand.)* Don't be angry with me. Except for you I have no one—no one. . . . *(Pause)*

MASHA: Such a noise in the stove! Just before Father died, 790 there was a wailing in the chimney. There, just like that.

VERSHININ: Are you superstitious?

MASHA: Yes.

VERSHININ: That's strange. *(Kisses her hand.)* You are a splendid, wonderful woman! Splendid, wonderful! It's dark here, but I can see the sparkle of your eyes.

MASHA: *(moves to another chair)* It's lighter here.

VERSHININ: I love you, love you, love you. . . . I love your eyes, your gestures, I dream about them. . . . Splendid, wonderful woman! 800

MASHA: When you talk to me like that, for some reason, I laugh, though I am frightened. Don't do it any more, I beg you. . . . *(In a low voice)* But, say it anyway, I don't mind. . . . *(Covers her face with her hands.)* I don't mind. Someone is coming, talk about something else. . . .

*(*IRINA *and* TUZENBACH *come in through the reception room.)*

TUZENBACH: I've got a triple-barreled name—Baron Tuzenbach-Krone-Altshauer—but I'm Russian, Greek Orthodox, like you. There's very little German left in me, perhaps only this patience and stubbornness that I bore you with. Every evening I see you home. 810

IRINA: How tired I am!

TUZENBACH: And I'll come to the telegraph office and see you home every day, for ten, for twenty years, till you drive me away. . . . *(Delightedly, seeing* MASHA *and* VERSHININ) It's you? Good evening.

IRINA: Here I am, home at last. *(To* MASHA) A lady just came to telegraph her brother in Saratov that her son had died today, and she couldn't remember the address. So she sent it without an address, simply to Saratov. She was crying. And I was rude to her, for no reason whatever. "I haven't got the 820 time," I said. So stupid of me. Are the maskers coming tonight?

MASHA: Yes.

IRINA: *(sits down in an armchair)* I must rest. I'm tired.

TUZENBACH: (*with a smile*) When you come from the office you seem so young, so woebegone. . . . (*Pause*)

IRINA: I'm tired. No, I don't like telegraph work, I don't like it.

MASHA: You've grown thinner. . . . (*Whistles.*) And younger; your face is beginning to look like a little boy's.

830 TUZENBACH: It's the way she wears her hair.

IRINA: I must look for another place, this is not right for me. What I so wanted, what I dreamed of, is the very thing that's lacking. It's work without poetry, without meaning. . . . (*There is a knock on the floor.*) The doctor is knocking. (*To* TUZENBACH) Answer him, dear. I can't . . . I'm too tired. . . .

(TUZENBACH *knocks on the floor.*)

IRINA: He'll come up now. Something must be done about this. Yesterday the doctor and our Andrei were at the club, and they lost again. I hear Andrei lost two hundred rubles.

840 MASHA: (*indifferently*) Well, what's to be done about it now?

IRINA: Two weeks ago he lost, in December he lost. If he would just lose everything quickly, perhaps we'd get away from this town. Oh, my God, I dream of Moscow every night, I'm absolutely like a madwoman. (*Laughs.*) We'll move there in June, that leaves . . . February, March, April, May . . . almost half a year!

MASHA: The only thing is Natasha must not find out about his losses.

IRINA: I don't think she cares.

(CHEBUTYKIN, *who has just got out of bed—he has been resting after dinner—comes into the reception room combing his beard, then sits down at the table and takes a newspaper out of his pocket.*)

850 MASHA: There he is. . . . Has he paid his rent?

IRINA: (*laughs*) No. Not a kopeck for eight months. He's evidently forgotten.

MASHA: (*laughs*) How important he looks sitting there! (*Everyone laughs; a pause.*)

IRINA: Why are you so quiet, Aleksandr Ignatych?

VERSHININ: I don't know. I'd like some tea. Half my life for a glass of tea! I've eaten nothing since morning. . . .

CHEBUTYKIN: Irina Sergeyevna!

IRINA: What do you want?

860 CHEBUTYKIN: Come here, please. *Venez ici.* (IRINA *goes and sits down at the table.*) I can't get along without you.

(IRINA *lays out the cards for a game of patience.*)

VERSHININ: Well, if they won't give us tea, let us at least philosophize a little.

TUZENBACH: Yes, let's. What about?

VERSHININ: What about? Let us dream . . . for instance, of the life that will come after us in two or three hundred years.

TUZENBACH: Well? When we're gone, men will fly in balloons, change the style of their coats, discover a sixth sense, perhaps, and develop it, but life will remain just the same—dif-
870 ficult, full of mysteries, and happy. A thousand years from now man will still be sighing: "Ah, how hard life is!"—Yet he will fear death, exactly as he does now, and be unwilling to die.

VERSHININ: (*after a moment's thought*) How shall I put it? It seems to me that everything on earth must change little by little, and is already changing before our eyes. In two or

three hundred years, let's say a thousand years—the time doesn't matter—a new, happy life will dawn. We'll have no part in that life, of course, but we are living for it now, working, yes, suffering, and creating it—in that alone lies the 880 purpose of our existence, and, if you like, our happiness.

(MASHA *laughs softly.*)

TUZENBACH: Why are you laughing?

MASHA: I don't know. I've been laughing all day today, ever since morning.

VERSHININ: I was graduated from the same school you were, but I didn't go to the academy; I read a great deal, but I don't know how to select books, and perhaps I don't read the right things, nevertheless, the longer I live, the more I want to know. My hair is turning gray, I'm almost an old man now, but I know so little, oh, so little! Yet it seems to me that 890 what is most important and real, I do know, firmly know. How I should like to prove to you that there is no happiness, that there should not and will not be, for us. . . . We must only work and work, and happiness—that is the lot of our remote descendants. (*Pause*) Not for me, but at least for my descendants and those who come after them. . . .

(FEDOTIK *and* RODAY *appear in the reception room; they sit down and softly sing, strumming the guitar.*)

TUZENBACH: According to you, we are not even to dream of happiness! But what if I am happy!

VERSHININ: You're not.

TUZENBACH: (*throwing up his hands and laughing*) Obviously 900 we don't understand each other. Well, how am I to convince you?

(MASHA *laughs softly.*)

TUZENBACH: (*holding up a finger to her*) Laugh! (*To* VERSHININ) Not only in two or three hundred years, but in a million years, life will be just the same as it always was; it doesn't change, it remains constant, following its own laws, which do not concern us, or which, in any case, you will never get to know. Birds of passage, cranes, for example, fly on and on, and no matter what thoughts, great or small, stray through their heads, they will still go on flying, not knowing 910 where or why. They fly and will go on flying no matter what philosophers spring up among them; and let them philosophize as much as they like, so long as they go on flying. . . .

MASHA: But there is a meaning?

TUZENBACH: A meaning . . . Look, it's snowing. What meaning has that? (*Pause*)

MASHA: It seems to me a man must have some faith, or must seek a faith, otherwise his life is empty, empty. . . . To live and not know why the cranes fly, why children are born, why there are stars in the sky . . . Either one knows what one lives 920 for, or it's all futile, worthless. (*Pause*)

VERSHININ: In any case, it is a pity youth is over. . . .

MASHA: Gogol says: It's a bore to live in this world, friends!

TUZENBACH: And I say: It's difficult arguing with you, friends! Well, let it go. . . .

CHEBUTYKIN: (*reading the newspaper*) Balzac was married in Berdichev.

(IRINA *hums softly.*)

CHEBUTYKIN: Must make a note of that. (*Writes.*) Balzac was married in Berdichev. (*Reads newspaper.*)

930 IRINA: (*musing as she lays out cards for a game of patience*) Balzac was married in Berdichev.

TUZENBACH: The die is cast. You know, Maria Sergeyevna, I have sent in my resignation.

MASHA: So I hear. And I see nothing good in that. I don't like civilians.

TUZENBACH: Never mind. . . . (*Gets up.*) I'm not good-looking, what sort of a military man do I make, anyhow? Well, it doesn't matter . . . I'm going to work. If for only one day in my life, to work so that I come home in the evening ex-
940 hausted, fall into bed, and immediately go to sleep. (*Going into the reception room*) Workmen must sleep soundly.

FEDOTIK: (*to* IRINA) I just bought some crayons for you at Pyzhnikov's on Moscow Street. And this little penknife . . .

IRINA: You've got into the habit of treating me as though I were a little girl, but I'm grown up now. . . . (*Gaily takes the crayons and penknife.*) How charming!

FEDOTIK: And I bought a knife for myself . . . look here . . . one blade, another blade, then a third, this to clean your ears, scissors, this to clean your nails . . .

950 RODAY: (*loudly*) Doctor, how old are you?

CHEBUTYKIN: Me? Thirty-two.

(*Laughter*)

FEDOTIK: Now I'll show you another kind of patience. . . . (*Lays out the cards.*)

(*The samovar is brought in;* ANFISA *attends to it; a little later* NATASHA *comes in and also fusses about the table;* SOLYONY *enters and, after greeting the others, sits down at the table.*)

VERSHININ: Really, what a wind!

MASHA: Yes, I'm tired of winter. I've almost forgotten what summer is like.

IRINA: The game is coming out, I see. We shall go to Moscow.

FEDOTIK: No, it's not. You see, the eight falls on the two of spades. (*Laughs.*) That means you won't go to Moscow.

960 CHEBUTYKIN: (*reading from the newspaper*) Tsitsikar. Smallpox is raging here.

ANFISA: (*going up to* MASHA) Masha, have some tea, little one. (*To* VERSHININ) If you please, Your Honor . . . excuse me, sir, I have forgotten your name . . .

MASHA: Bring it here, nurse. I'm not going in there.

IRINA: Nurse!

ANFISA: Com-ing!

NATASHA: (*to* SOLYONY) Little babies understand perfectly. "Good morning, Bobik," I said, "good morning, darling!" He
970 looked at me in a very special way. You think that's just a mother talking, but no, no, I assure you! He is an extraordinary child.

SOLYONY: If that child were mine, I would have fried him in a skillet and eaten him. (*Takes his glass, goes into the drawing room and sits in a corner.*)

NATASHA: (*covering her face with her hands*) Rude, ill-bred man!

MASHA: Happy is he who does not notice whether it's summer or winter. It seems to me that if I were in Moscow now, I'd
980 be indifferent to the weather. . . .

VERSHININ: The other day I was reading the diary of a certain French minister, written in prison. The minister had been convicted of fraud. With what rapture and delight he speaks of the birds he sees from his prison window—birds he had never even noticed when he was a minister. Now that he has been released, of course, he'll no more notice them than he did before. In the same way, you won't notice Moscow when you live there. Happiness is something we never have, but only long for.

TUZENBACH: (*takes a box from the table*) But where's the 990 candy?

IRINA: Solyony ate it.

TUZENBACH: All of it?

ANFISA: (*serving tea*) A letter for you, sir.

VERSHININ: For me? (*Takes the letter.*) From my daughter. (*Reads it.*) Yes, of course. . . . Excuse me, Maria Sergeyevna, I'll just slip out. I won't have any tea. (*Gets up, very much disturbed.*) These eternal scenes . . .

MASHA: What is it? Not a secret, is it?

VERSHININ: (*softly*) My wife has taken poison again. I must go. 1000 I'll slip out without being noticed. Horribly unpleasant all this. (*Kisses* MASHA's *hand.*) My dear, fine, lovely woman . . . I'll slip out here quietly. . . .

ANFISA: Now where is he going? I've just brought him his tea. . . . Such a—

MASHA: (*flaring up*) Leave me alone! You keep pestering, you give one no peace. . . . (*Goes to the table with her cup.*) I'm sick of you, old woman!

ANFISA: Why are you so annoyed? Darling!

(ANDREI's *voice; "Anfisa!"*)

ANFISA: (*mimicking*) Anfisa! He sits in there . . .  1010

MASHA: (*at the table in the reception room, angrily*) Do let me sit down! (*Disarranges the cards on the table.*) You take up the whole table with your cards. Drink your tea!

IRINA: Mashka, you are cross!

MASHA: If I'm cross then don't talk to me. Leave me alone!

CHEBUTYKIN: (*laughing*) Leave her alone, leave her . . .

MASHA: You're sixty years old, but you're like a little boy, always prattling some damned nonsense.

NATASHA: (*sighing*) Masha, dear, why employ such expressions in your conversation? I tell you frankly, with your attractive 1020 appearance you would be simply enchanting in well-bred society if it were not for those words of yours. *Je vous prie, pardonnez moi, Marie, mais vous avez des manières un peu grossières.*

TUZENBACH: (*with suppressed laughter*) Give me . . . give me . . . I think there's some cognac over there. . . .

NATASHA: *Il paraît que mon Bobik déjà ne dort pas,* he's awake. He doesn't seem to be very well today. I must go to him, excuse me. . . . (*Goes out.*)

IRINA: And where has Aleksandr Ignatych gone?  1030

MASHA: Home. Something odd with his wife again.

TUZENBACH: (*goes to* SOLYONY *with the decanter of cognac in his hand*) You're always sitting by yourself, thinking about something—and there's no telling what it is. Come, let's make it up. Let's have some cognac. (*They drink.*) I shall have to play the piano all night tonight—probably play all kinds of trash. . . . So be it!

SOLYONY: Why make it up? I never quarreled with you.

TUZENBACH: You always give me the feeling that something has happened between us. You have a strange character, I 1040 must say.

SOLYONY: (*declaiming*) "I am strange, who is not strange! Be not angry, Aleko!"

TUZENBACH: What's Aleko got to do with it? . . . (*Pause*)

SOLYONY: When I'm alone with someone, it's all right, I'm like anybody else, but in company I'm despondent, timid, and . . . talk all sorts of nonsense. Nevertheless, I am more honest and more noble than many, many others. And I can prove that.

1050 TUZENBACH: I often get angry with you, you're forever trying to pick a quarrel with me when we're in company, but all the same, I like you for some reason. So be it, I'm going to get drunk tonight. Let's drink!

SOLYONY: Let's drink. (*They drink.*) I have never had anything against you, Baron. But I have the temperament of Lermontov. (*Softly*) I even look a little like Lermontov . . . so they say. (*Takes a bottle of scent out of his pocket and pours it on his hands.*)

TUZENBACH: I'm sending in my resignation. *Basta!* I've been

1060 considering it for five years, and at last I've made up my mind. I'm going to work.

SOLYONY: (*declaiming*) "Be not angry, Aleko . . . Forget, forget, thy dreams." . . .

(*While they are talking,* ANDREI *quietly enters with a book and sits down near a candle.*)

TUZENBACH: I'm going to work.

CHEBUTYKIN: (*going into the reception room with* IRINA) And the food, too, was real Caucasian stuff: onion soup, and for the meat course, *chekhartma.*

SOLYONY: *Cheremsha* is not meat at all, but a plant something like our onion.

1070 CHEBUTYKIN: No, my angel. *Chekhartma* is not an onion, it's roast lamb.

SOLYONY: And I tell you *cheremsha* is an onion.

CHEBUTYKIN: And I tell you *chekhartma* is lamb.

SOLYONY: And I tell you *cheremsha* is an onion.

CHEBUTYKIN: Why should I argue with you? You've never been to the Caucasus, and you've never eaten *chekhartma.*

SOLYONY: I've never eaten it because I can't stand it. *Cheremsha* smells just like garlic.

ANDREI: (*imploring*) Enough, gentlemen! Please!

1080 TUZENBACH: When are the maskers coming?

IRINA: They promised to be here by nine; that means any minute now.

TUZENBACH: (*embraces* ANDREI *and sings*) "Oh, my porch, my porch, oh, my new porch." . . .

ANDREI: (*dances and sings*) "New porch, maplewood porch" . . .

CHEBUTYKIN: (*dances*) "Latticework porch!"

(*Laughter*)

TUZENBACH: (*kisses* ANDREI) What the hell, let's drink. Andryusha, let's drink to our friendship. And I'll go to Moscow with you, Andryusha, to the university.

1090 SOLYONY: Which university? There are two in Moscow.

ANDREI: In Moscow there is one university.

SOLYONY: Two, I tell you.

ANDREI: Make it three. So much the better.

SOLYONY: In Moscow there are two universities. (*There is a murmur and hissing.*) In Moscow there are two universities: the old one and the new one. And if you don't care to listen, if my conversation is irritating to you, I can stop talking. I can even go into another room. (*Goes out through one of the doors.*)

TUZENBACH: Bravo, bravo! (*Laughs.*) Let's get started, friends, 1100 I'm going to play! Funny fellow, that Solyony. . . . (*Sits down at the piano and plays a waltz.*)

MASHA: (*waltzing by herself*) The Baron is drunk, the Baron is drunk, the Baron is drunk . . .

(*Enter* NATASHA)

NATASHA: (*to* CHEBUTYKIN) Ivan Romanych! (*Says something to him then quietly goes out.*)

(CHEBUTYKIN *touches* TUZENBACH *on the shoulder and whispers something to him.*)

IRINA: What is it?

CHEBUTYKIN: It's time we were going. Good night.

TUZENBACH: Good night. Time to go.

IRINA: But, look here . . . What about the maskers?   1110

ANDREI: (*embarrassed*) They're not coming. Don't you see, my dear, Natasha says that Bobik is not very well, and so . . . In any case, I don't know anything about it, and I certainly don't care.

IRINA: (*shrugging her shoulders*) Bobik is not well!

MASHA: It's not the first time! If they turn us out, I suppose we must go. (*To* IRINA) It's not Bobik that's sick, but she herself . . . here! (*Taps her forehead.*) Common creature!

(ANDREI *goes out through door on the right to his room;* CHEBUTYKIN *follows him. The others say good-bye in the reception room.*)

FEDOTIK: What a pity! I counted on spending the evening, but if the little fellow is sick, then, of course . . . I'll bring him 1120 some toys tomorrow. . . .

RODAY: (*loudly*) I purposely took a nap after dinner today, I thought I'd be dancing all night. Why, it's only nine o'clock!

MASHA: Let's go out into the street, we can talk there and decide what to do.

(*Voices are heard saying: "Good-bye! Good night!" and* TUZENBACH'S *gay laughter. Everyone goes out.* ANFISA *and a maid clear the table and put out the lights. The nurse sings offstage.* ANDREI, *wearing an overcoat and hat, and* CHEBUTYKIN *enter quickly.*)

CHEBUTYKIN: I never had the time to get married, because life just flashed by like lightning, and because I was madly in love with your mother, who was married. . . .

ANDREI: One shouldn't marry. One shouldn't, because it's boring.   1130

CHEBUTYKIN: That may be so, but what about loneliness? You may philosophize as much as you like, but loneliness is a terrible thing, my boy. . . . Though, as a matter of fact . . . of course, it really doesn't matter.

ANDREI: Let's go quickly.

CHEBUTYKIN: What's the hurry? We have time.

ANDREI: I'm afraid my wife might stop me.

CHEBUTYKIN: Oh!

ANDREI: I'm not going to play tonight, I shall just look on. I don't feel well. . . . What shall I do, Ivan Romanych, for 1140 shortness of breath?

CHEBUTYKIN: Why ask me! I don't remember, my boy. Don't know.

ANDREI: Let's go through the kitchen.

*(They go out. There is a ring, then another ring; voices are heard, and laughter.* IRINA *enters.)*

IRINA: What is it?

ANFISA: *(in a whisper)* The maskers!

*(A ring)*

IRINA: Tell them, nurse dear, that there's no one at home. They must excuse us.

*(*ANFISA *goes out.* IRINA *paces the room, deep in thought: she is perturbed.* SOLYONY *enters.)*

SOLYONY: *(puzzled)* Nobody here. . . . Where is everyone?

1150 IRINA: They've gone home.

SOLYONY: Strange. Are you alone here?

IRINA: Alone. *(Pause)* Good-bye.

SOLYONY: I behaved without sufficient restraint just now, tactlessly. But you are not like the rest of them, you are superior and pure, you see the truth. . . . You alone can understand me. I love you, deeply, infinitely love you. . . .

IRINA: Good-bye! Go away!

SOLYONY: I cannot live without you. *(Following her)* Oh, my bliss! *(Through tears)* Oh, happiness! Magnificent, wonder-
1160 ful, amazing eyes, such as I have never seen in another woman. . . .

IRINA: *(coldly)* Stop it, Vassily Vassilyich!

SOLYONY: For the first time I speak to you of love, and it is as though I were not on this earth, but on another planet. *(Rubs his forehead.)* Well, it's all one. Love cannot be forced, to be sure. . . . But there must be no happy rivals. . . . There must not be . . . I swear to you by all that's holy, I will kill any rival. . . . Oh, wonderful one!

*(*NATASHA *passes with a candle.)*

NATASHA: *(peeps in at one door, then another, and passes by the
1170 door leading into her husband's room)* Andrei is there. Let him read. Excuse me, Vassily Vassilyich, I didn't know you were here, I'm in my dressing gown. . . .

SOLYONY: It's all one. Good-bye! *(Goes out.)*

NATASHA: You are tired, my poor, dear girl! *(Kisses* IRINA.*)* You ought to go to bed a little earlier.

IRINA: Is Bobik asleep?

NATASHA: He's asleep. But he's restless. By the way, dear, I keep meaning to speak to you, but either you are out or I have no time . . . I think the nursery Bobik is in now is cold
1180 and damp. And your room is so nice for a baby. My own dearest, do move in with Olya for a while!

IRINA: *(not understanding)* Where?

*(A troika with bells is heard driving up to the house.)*

NATASHA: You and Olya will be in one room for the time being, and Bobik will be in your room. He's such a darling! Today I said to him: "Bobik, my own! My own baby!" And he looked up at me with his dear little eyes. *(A ring)* That must be Olga. How late she is!

*(The maid comes up to* NATASHA *and whispers in her ear.)*

NATASHA: Protopopov? What a queer man! Protopopov has come to invite me to go for a drive with him in his troika.
1190 *(Laughs.)* How strange these men are! . . . *(A ring)* Someone has come. Maybe I'll go for a little ride, just for a quarter of

an hour. . . . *(To the maid)* Tell him I'll be right there. *(A ring)* The bell . . . It must be Olga. *(Goes out.)*

*(The maid runs out:* IRINA *sits lost in thought;* KULYGIN *and* OLGA *enter, followed by* VERSHININ.*)*

KULYGIN: How do you like that! They said you were going to have a party.

VERSHININ: Strange, when I left a little while ago, half an hour or so, they were expecting the maskers. . . .

IRINA: They have all gone.

KULYGIN: Has Masha gone, too? Where did she go? And why is Protopopov downstairs waiting in a troika? Who is he wait- 1200 ing for?

IRINA: Don't ask questions. . . . I'm tired.

KULYGIN: Well, Miss Caprice . . .

OLGA: The meeting just ended. I'm exhausted. Our head-mistress is ill, and I am to take her place. My head, my head aches, my head . . . *(Sits down.)* Andrei lost two hundred rubles at cards last night. . . . The whole town is talking about it. . . .

KULYGIN: Yes, the meeting tired me, too. *(Sits down.)*

VERSHININ: My wife just took it into her head to frighten me, 1210 she almost poisoned herself. It's all right now, and I'm glad, it's a relief. . . . So, we are to go? Very well, then, I wish you good night. Fyodor Ilyich, let's go somewhere together. I cannot stay at home, I absolutely cannot. . . . Come along!

KULYGIN: I'm tired. I'm not coming. *(Gets up.)* I'm tired. Has my wife gone home?

IRINA: I expect so.

KULYGIN: *(kisses* IRINA'S *hand)* Good-bye. Tomorrow and the day after we can rest the whole day. Good night! *(Going)* I do want some tea. I counted on spending the evening in 1220 pleasant company, and—*O, fallacem hominum spem!* Accusative case exclamatory. . . .

VERSHININ: Well, then, I'll go by myself. *(Goes out with* KULY-GIN, *whistling.)*

OLGA: My head aches, my head . . . Andrei has lost . . . the whole town is talking . . . I'll go and lie down. *(Going)* Tomorrow I shall be free. . . . Oh, Lord, how pleasant that is! Free tomorrow, free the day after. . . . My head aches, my head . . . *(Goes out.)*

IRINA: *(alone)* They have all gone. No one is here.          1230

*(In the street an accordion is heard; the nurse sings a song.)*

NATASHA: *(crosses the reception room in a fur coat and cap, followed by the maid)* I'll be back in half an hour. I'm just going for a little drive. *(Goes out.)*

IRINA: *(left alone, with longing)* Moscow! Moscow! To Moscow!

### —ACT THREE—

*(*OLGA'S *and* IRINA'S *room. To the left and right are beds with screens around them. It is past two o'clock in the morning. Off-stage a fire alarm is ringing for a fire that has been going on for some time. It can be seen that no one in the house has gone to bed.* MASHA *is lying on a sofa dressed, as usual, in black. Enter* OLGA *and* ANFISA.*)*

ANFISA: They're sitting below now, under the stairs. . . . I said to them: "Come upstairs," I said, "you can't sit there like

that." They're crying. "Papa," they say, "we don't know where Papa is. God forbid he's burned!" What an idea! And
1240   there are people in the yard . . . they're without clothes, too.

OLGA: *(taking clothes out of the wardrobe)* Take this gray dress . . . and this one . . . the blouse, too . . . And take this skirt, nurse. . . . My God, what a thing to have happened! Kirsanovsky Street has burned to the ground, apparently. . . . Take this . . . and this. . . . *(Tossing clothes into her arms)* The poor Vershinins had a fright. . . . Their house nearly burned down. They'll have to spend the night here . . . we can't let them go home. . . . Everything was burned at poor Fedotik's, there's nothing left. . . .

1250   ANFISA: You'd better call Ferapont, Olyushka, I won't be able to carry—

OLGA: *(rings)* Nobody comes when I ring. . . . *(At the door)* Come here, whoever is there! *(Through the open door a window can be seen, reflecting the glow of the fire; a fire engine is heard passing the house.)* What a horror this is! And how tiring!

*(Enter FERAPONT.)*

OLGA: Here, take these things downstairs. . . . The Kolotilin young ladies are down there, under the staircase . . . give it to them. And this, too. . . .

1260   FERAPONT: Yes, miss. In 1812 Moscow burned down, too. Oh, good Lord! The French were surprised.

OLGA: Go along now.

FERAPONT: Yes, miss.

OLGA: Nurse, dear, give them everything. We don't need anything, give it all away, nurse. . . . I'm tired, I can hardly stand up. . . . We mustn't let the Vershinins go home. . . . The little girls can sleep in the drawing room, and Aleksandr Ignatych downstairs at the Baron's. . . . Fedotik, too, at the Baron's, or let him stay with us in the reception room. . . .
1270   The doctor, as if on purpose, got drunk, terribly drunk, and we can't put anyone in with him. Vershinin's wife in the drawing room, too. . . .

ANFISA: *(exhausted)* Olyushka, dear, don't send me away! Don't send me away!

OLGA: You're talking nonsense, nurse. Nobody's sending you away.

ANFISA: *(laying her head on OLGA's breast)* My own, my treasure, I work, I work hard. . . . When I get feeble everybody will say: go away! And where will I go? I'm eighty, going on
1280   eighty-two. . . .

OLGA: Sit down, nurse dear. . . . You're tired, you poor thing. . . . *(Seats her in a chair.)* Rest, my dear. How pale you are!

*(Enter NATASHA.)*

NATASHA: They're saying we should form a committee at once to aid the victims of the fire. Why not? It's a fine idea. Indeed, we should always be ready to help the poor, that's the duty of the rich. Bobik and Sofochka are fast asleep, sleeping as if nothing had happened. We've got such a lot of people everywhere, no matter where you turn, the house is full.
1290   There's influenza in town now, I'm afraid the children might catch it.

OLGA: *(not listening to her)* You don't see the fire from this room, it's peaceful here. . . .

NATASHA: Yes . . . I suppose I'm all disheveled. *(In front of the mirror)* They say that I've gained weight . . . but it's not true! Not at all! Masha's sleeping, exhausted, poor thing. . . . *(To ANFISA, coldly)* Don't you dare sit down in my presence! Stand up! Get out of here! *(ANFISA goes out; a pause.)* Why you keep that old woman, I cannot understand!

OLGA: *(taken aback)* Excuse me, but I cannot understand . . .   1300

NATASHA: She's of no use here. She's a peasant, she should live in the country . . . What pampering! I like order in a house! There shouldn't be any useless servants in a house! *(Pats OLGA's cheek.)* Poor dear, you're tired! Our headmistress is tired! When my Sofochka grows up and goes to high school, I'll be afraid of you.

OLGA: I shan't be the headmistress.

NATASHA: You'll be elected, Olechka. That's settled.

OLGA: I shall refuse. I cannot . . . I haven't the strength for it. . . . *(Drinks water.)* You were so rude to nurse just   1310 now. . . . You must excuse me, but I am in no condition to endure . . . I just can't stand it.

NATASHA: *(agitated)* Forgive me, Olya, forgive me . . . I didn't mean to upset you.

*(MASHA gets up, takes her pillow, and goes out angrily.)*

OLGA: You must understand, my dear . . . perhaps we were brought up in a peculiar way, but I cannot bear that. Such an attitude oppresses me, I feel ill, simply sick at heart!

NATASHA: Forgive me, forgive me. . . . *(Kisses her.)*

OLGA: Any rudeness, even the slightest, even a tactless word, upsets me. . . .   1320

NATASHA: I often talk too much, that's true, but you must agree, my dear, that she could just as well live in the country.

OLGA: She has been with us for thirty years.

NATASHA: But now she can't work any more! Either I don't understand, or you don't want to understand me. She is incapable of working, she just sleeps or sits.

OLGA: Then let her sit.

NATASHA: *(astonished)* What do you mean, let her sit? She's a servant, isn't she? *(Through tears)* I don't understand you,   1330 Olya. I have a nurse, I have a wet nurse, we have a maid and a cook . . . what do we keep that old woman for? What for?

*(The fire alarm is heard offstage.)*

OLGA: I have aged ten years tonight.

NATASHA: We must come to an understanding, Olya. You are at school—I am at home; you're doing the teaching—I'm doing the housekeeping. And if I say anything about the servants, then I know what I'm talking about; I-know-what-I-am-talk-ing-about. And by tomorrow that old thief, that old hag, *(stamping her foot)* that old witch, will be gone! Don't you dare cross me! Don't you dare! *(Recovering herself)*   1340 Really, if you don't move downstairs, we shall always be quarreling. It's awful.

*(Enter KULYGIN.)*

KULYGIN: Where is Masha? It's time to go home. They say the fire is subsiding. *(Stretches.)* Only one section burned down, in spite of the fact that there was a wind; at first it looked as if the whole town was on fire. *(Sits down.)* I'm worn out. Olechka, my dear . . . I often think, if it hadn't been for

Masha, I'd have married you, Olechka. You are very good. . . . I'm exhausted. (*Listens.*)

OLGA: What is it?

KULYGIN: Just tonight the doctor had to go on a drinking spree, he's terribly drunk. Just tonight! (*Gets up.*) I think he's coming in here now. . . . Do you hear? Yes, he's coming. . . . (*Laughs.*) Such a fellow, really. . . . I'll hide. (*Goes to the cupboard and stands in the corner.*) What a rascal!

OLGA: He hasn't been drinking for two years, and now all of a sudden he's gone and got drunk. (*Goes with* NATASHA *to the back of the room.*)

(CHEBUTYKIN *comes in; walking as though sober, without staggering, he crosses the room, stops, looks around, then goes to the washstand and begins to wash his hands.*)

CHEBUTYKIN: (*sullenly*) The hell with 'em . . . all of 'em. . . . They think I'm a doctor, that I know how to cure any kind of sickness. I know absolutely nothing, forgot everything I knew, I remember nothing, absolutely nothing. (OLGA *and* NATASHA *go out, unnoticed by him.*) The hell with 'em. Last Wednesday I treated a woman in Zasyp—she died, and it's my fault she died. Yes . . . I used to know a thing or two twenty-five years ago, and now I remember nothing. Nothing. Maybe I'm not even a man, and am just pretending I have arms, and legs, and a head; maybe I don't even exist, and only imagine I'm walking about, eating, sleeping. (*Weeps.*) Oh, if only I didn't exist! (*Stops weeping, sullenly.*) Damn it all. . . . The other day there was a conversation at the club; they were talking about Shakespeare, Voltaire. . . . Never read them, never read them at all, but I tried to look as if I had. And others did the same. Vulgar! Cheap! And that woman I killed Wednesday came to my mind . . . it all came back to me, and in my soul I felt crooked, vile, loathsome . . . and I went out and got drunk. . . .

(*Enter* IRINA, VERSHININ, *and* TUZENBACH; TUZENBACH *is wearing a fashionable new civilian suit.*)

IRINA: Let's sit here. No one will come in here.

VERSHININ: If it weren't for the soldiers, the whole town would have burnt down. Brave boys! (*Rubs his hands with pleasure.*) Salt of the earth! Ah, what a fine lot!

KULYGIN: (*going up to them*) What's the time, gentlemen?

TUZENBACH: Going on four. It's getting light.

IRINA: Everyone's sitting in the reception room, nobody goes. And that Solyony of yours is sitting there, too. . . . (*To* CHEBUTYKIN) You ought to go to bed, Doctor.

CHEBUTYKIN: I'm all right . . . thanks . . . (*Combs his beard.*)

KULYGIN: (*laughs*) You're tipsy, Ivan Romanych! (*Claps him on the shoulder.*) Good boy! *In vino veritas*, as the ancients used to say.

TUZENBACH: Everyone is asking me to arrange a concert for the benefit of the victims of the fire.

IRINA: But who is there to—

TUZENBACH: It could be arranged, if we wanted to. Maria Sergeyevna plays the piano beautifully, in my opinion.

KULYGIN: She does play beautifully.

IRINA: She's forgotten how by now. She hasn't played for three years . . . or perhaps four.

TUZENBACH: Here in this town, absolutely nobody understands music, not a soul; but I do understand it, and I assure you, on my honor, that Maria Sergeyevna plays magnificently, almost with genius.

KULYGIN: You're right, Baron. I love Masha very much. She's lovely.

TUZENBACH: To be able to play so superbly, and at the same time to realize that nobody, nobody understands you. . . .

KULYGIN: (*sighs*) Yes. . . . But would it be proper for her to take part in a concert? (*Pause*) Of course, I know nothing about it, my friends. Perhaps it would even be a good thing. I must admit, our director is a fine man, in fact, a very fine man, most intelligent, but he holds certain views. . . . To be sure, it is none of his affair, nevertheless, if you like, I might have a word with him about it.

(CHEBUTYKIN *picks up a china clock and examines it.*)

VERSHININ: I got covered with dirt at the fire; I look disgraceful. (*Pause*) Yesterday I happened to hear that our brigade might be transferred somewhere far from here. Some say to Poland, others—to Chita.

TUZENBACH: I heard that, too. Well? The town will be quite deserted.

IRINA: And we shall go away!

CHEBUTYKIN: (*drops the clock, which smashes*) Smashed to smithereens!

(*Pause; everyone is upset and embarrassed.*)

KULYGIN: (*picking up the pieces*) To break such an expensive thing—oh, Ivan Romanych, Ivan Romanych! You get minus zero for conduct.

IRINA: That's was Mama's clock.

CHEBUTYKIN: Maybe . . . Mama's, so it was Mama's. Maybe I didn't break it, and it only appears to have been broken. Maybe it only appears that we exist, but, in fact, we are not here. I don't know anything. Nobody knows anything. (*At the door*) Where are your eyes? Natasha is having a little romance with Protopopov, and you don't see it. There you sit, not seeing what's before you, and Natasha is having a little romance with Protopopov. . . . (*Sings.*) "May I offer you this fig?" . . . (*Goes out.*)

VERSHININ: Yes. . . . (*Laughs.*) How strange all this is, really. (*Pause*) When the fire broke out, I ran home as fast as I could; when I got there I saw that our house was safe and sound and in no danger, but my two little girls were standing in the doorway in their underwear, their mother not there, people bustling about, dogs and horses rushing by, and the children's faces full of alarm, terror, entreaty, and I don't know what; it wrung my heart to see those faces. My God, I thought, what will these little girls have to go through in the course of a long life! I picked them up and ran, still thinking the same thing: what more will they have to live through in this world! (*Fire alarm; a pause*) When I got here I found their mother here, shouting, furious.

(MASHA *enters with a pillow and sits down on the sofa.*)

VERSHININ: When my little girls were standing in the doorway in their underwear, the street red with the blaze, and the noise terrible, I thought that something of the sort must have happened many years ago, when the enemy made a sudden raid, plundering, burning. . . . And yet, what a difference between things as they are and as they were. When

a little more time has passed, say, two or three hundred years, then people will look at our present-day life with horror and contempt, and all this will seem awkward, difficult, very uncertain and strange. Oh, what a life that is going to be, what a life! *(Laughs.)* Forgive me, here I am philoso-
1460  phizing again. Please let me go on, my friends. I have a terrific longing to philosophize, now that I am in the mood for it. *(Pause)* It seems everyone is asleep. And so I say: what a life that will be! Try to imagine it. . . . At the present time there are only three of your sort in this town, but in generations to come there will be more and more, a time will come when everything will change to your way, people will live like you, but then later, you, too, will be outmoded, people will appear who will be better than you. . . . *(Laughs.)* I am in a very special mood today. *(Laughs.)* I want desperately
1470  to live. . . . *(Sings.)* "To love at every age we yield, and fruitful are its pangs."° *(Laughs.)*

MASHA: Tram-tam-tam . . .

VERSHININ: Tam-tam . . .

MASHA: Tra-ra-ra . . .

VERSHININ: Tra-ta-ta . . .

*(Laughter. Enter* FEDOTIK.*)*

FEDOTIK: *(dances)* Burnt down, burnt down! All burnt to the ground! *(Laughs)*

IRINA: What sort of a joke is that! Has everything burnt?

FEDOTIK: *(laughs)* Absolutely everything. There's nothing left.
1480  My guitar's burnt, my photography equipment's burnt, and all my letters. . . . Even the little notebook I meant to give you—burnt.

*(Enter* SOLYONY.*)*

IRINA: No, please go, Vassily Vassilyich. You can't stay here.

SOLYONY: Why is it that the Baron can stay and I can't?

VERSHININ: We must go, really. How's the fire?

SOLYONY: Dying down, they say. Yes, it seems decidely odd that the Baron can stay and I can't. *(Takes out a bottle of scent and sprinkles himself.)*

VERSHININ: Tram-tam-tam.
1490  MASHA: Tram-tam.

VERSHININ: *(laughs, to* SOLYONY*)* Let us go into the reception room.

SOLYONY: Ve-ry well, we'll make a note of that. This moral could be made more clear, but might provoke the geese, I fear. . . . *(Fixing his gaze on* TUZENBACH*)* Peep, peep peep. . . . *(Goes out with* VERSHININ *and* FEDOTIK.*)*

IRINA: How that Solyony has smoked up the room. . . . *(Puzzled)* The Baron is asleep! Baron! Baron!

TUZENBACH: *(waking up)* I really am tired. . . . The brickyard
1500  . . . I'm not talking in my sleep, as a matter of fact, I intend to begin work at the brickyard soon. It's already been discussed. *(To* IRINA, *tenderly)* You are so pale, beautiful, enchanting. . . . To me it seems your paleness brightens the dark air like light. . . . You are sad, you're dissatisfied with life. . . . Oh, come with me, let us go away and work together!

MASHA: Nikolai Lvovich, I wish you'd go.

TUZENBACH: *(laughing)* Are you here? I didn't see you. *(Kisses* IRINA's *hand.)* Good-bye, I'm going. . . . As I look at you now, I recall how once, a long time ago on your name day,    1510 you talked of the joy of work, and you were so gay, so confident. . . . What a happy life I dreamed of then! Where is it? *(Kisses* IRINA's *hand.)* There are tears in your eyes. Go to bed, it's growing light . . . the morning has begun. . . . If only I could give my life for you!

MASHA: Nikolai Lvovich, do go! Really, now. . . .

TUZENBACH: I am going. . . . *(Goes out.)*

MASHA: *(lying down)* Are you asleep, Fyodor?

KULYGIN: Eh?

MASHA: You had better go home.    1520

KULYGIN: My dear Masha, my precious Masha. . . .

IRINA: She's exhausted. You ought to let her rest, Fedya.

KULYGIN: I'll go directly. . . . My dear, lovely wife . . . I love you, my one and only. . . .

MASHA: *(irascibly) Amo, amas, amat, amamus, amatis, amant.*

KULYGIN: *(laughs)* Yes, really, she's remarkable. You have been my wife for seven years, but it seems as if we'd been married only yesterday. Word of honor. Yes, really, you are a remarkable woman. I am content, content, content!

MASHA: Bored, bored, bored. . . . *(Sits up.)* I cannot get it out    1530 of my mind. . . . Simply revolting. It's there, like a nail in my head, I can't remain silent. I mean about Andrei. . . . He's mortgaged this house to the bank and his wife got hold of all the money; and after all, the house doesn't belong to him alone, but to the four of us! This is something he ought to realize, if he's a decent man.

KULYGIN: Why bother, Masha? What is it to you? Andryusha owes money to everyone, I'm sorry for him.

MASHA: It's revolting anyhow. *(Lies down.)*

KULYGIN: We're not poor. I work, I teach at the high school and    1540 give private lessons . . . I'm just a plain, honest man. . . . *Omnia mea mecum porto,* as they say.

MASHA: I don't want anything, but the injustice of it revolts me. *(Pause)* Go along, Fyodor.

KULYGIN: *(kisses her)* You're tired; rest for half an hour, and I'll sit out there and wait for you. Sleep. . . . *(Going)* I am content, content, content. *(Goes out.)*

IRINA: Yes, how shallow our Andrei has become, how dull and old he's grown living with that woman! There was a time when he was preparing for a professorship, and yesterday he    1550 boasted of having at last become a member of the District Board. He, a member of the Board, and Protopopov the Chairman. . . . The whole town is laughing and talking about it, and he's the only one who neither sees nor knows anything. . . . And here everyone else has been running to the fire, while he sits in his room taking not the slightest notice. He just plays his violin. *(Nervously)* Oh, it's awful, awful, awful! *(Weeps.)* I can't, I can't bear it any longer! I can't, I can't . . .

*(*OLGA *enters and begins tidying up her dressing table.)*

IRINA: *(sobs loudly)* Turn me out, turn me out, I can't bear any    1560 more!

OLGA: *(alarmed)* What is it, what is it? Darling!

---

°This is from Tchaikovsky's opera *Eugene Onegin.*

IRINA: *(sobbing)* Where? Where has it all gone? Where is it? Oh, my God, my God! I have forgotten everything, I've forgotten . . . it's all muddled in my head. . . . I can't remember how to say window or floor in Italian. I'm forgetting everything, every day I forget, and life is slipping by, never to return, never, we shall never go to Moscow . . . I see that we shall never go. . . .

1570 OLGA: Darling, darling. . . .

IRINA: *(trying to control herself)* Oh, I am miserable . . . I can't work, I won't work. Enough, enough! I've been a telegraph clerk, and now I have a job in the office of the Town Council, and I loathe and despise every single thing they give me to do. . . . I'm nearly twenty-four already, I've been working a long time, and my brain is drying up, I've grown thin and old and ugly, and there is nothing, nothing, no satisfaction of any kind, and time is passing, and I feel that I'm moving away from the real, beautiful life, moving farther and farther 1580 into some sort of abyss. I am in despair, and why I am alive, why I haven't killed myself before now, I don't know. . . .

OLGA: Don't cry, my little one, don't cry. . . . It hurts me.

IRINA: I'm not crying, I'm not crying. . . . That's enough. . . . There, I'm not crying any more. Enough . . . enough!

OLGA: Darling, I'm speaking to you as a sister, as a friend, if you want my advice, marry the Baron!

*(IRINA weeps quietly.)*

After all, you respect him, you value him highly. . . . It's true, he's not good-looking, but he's so honest, so pure. . . . You see, one doesn't marry for love, but to do one's duty. At 1590 least, that's what I think, and I would marry without love. I'd marry anyone who asked me, so long as he was a decent man, I'd even marry an old man. . . .

IRINA: I kept thinking that we'd move to Moscow, and there I'd meet my true love, I dreamed of him, I loved him. . . . But it all turned out to be foolishness, just foolishness. . . .

OLGA: *(embracing her)* My dear, lovely sister, I understand it all; when Baron Nikolai Lvovich left the army and came to see us in civilian clothes, he seemed to me so homely that I actually began to cry. . . . He said: "Why are you crying?" 1600 How could I tell him! But if it were God's will that he should marry you, I'd be happy. That, you see, would be a different matter, quite different.

*(NATASHA, carrying a candle, enters from the door on the right and crosses the stage without speaking.)*

MASHA: *(sitting up)* She goes about looking as if it were she who had started the fire.

OLGA: Masha, you are silly. The silliest one in the family—is you. Forgive me for saying so. *(Pause)*

MASHA: My dear sisters, I want to confess. My soul is in torment. I shall confess to you, and then never again to anyone. . . . I'll tell you right now. *(Softly)* It is my secret, but 1610 you must know everything . . . I cannot remain silent. . . . *(Pause)* I love, love . . . I love that man. . . . You saw him just now. . . . Well, there it is. In short, I love Vershinin.

OLGA: *(goes behind her screen)* Stop that. I can't hear you, anyway.

MASHA: What am I to do! *(Clutching her head)* At first I thought him strange, then I felt sorry for him . . . then I began to love him . . . to love everything about him, his voice, his words, his misfortunes, his two little girls. . . .

OLGA: *(behind the screen)* I'm not listening. Whatever silly 1620 things you may say, it doesn't matter, I shan't hear them.

MASHA: Oh, Olya, you're the one that's silly. I love him—such is my fate. Such is my destiny. . . . And he loves me. . . . All this is frightening. Isn't it? Is it wrong? *(Takes IRINA by the hand, drawing her to her.)* Oh, my darling . . . how are we going to live our life, what will become of us? . . . When you read it in a novel it just seems stale, and all so clear, but when you fall in love yourself, you begin to see that nobody knows anything, that each of us has to resolve everything for himself. . . . My darlings, my sisters . . . I have confessed to 1630 you, now I'll be silent. . . . I shall now be like Gogol's madman. . . . Silence. . . . silence. . . .

*(Enter ANDREI, followed by FERAPONT.)*

ANDREI: *(angrily)* What do you want? I don't understand.

FERAPONT: *(in the doorway, impatiently)* I've told you ten times already, Andrei Sergeyevich.

ANDREI: In the first place, I am not Andrei Sergeyevich to you but Your Honor.

FERAPONT: The firemen, Your Honor, are asking permission to drive through the garden to the river. Otherwise they have to go round and round—a downright nuisance. 1640

ANDREI: All right. Tell them all right. *(FERAPONT goes out.)* I'm fed up with them. Where's Olga? *(OLGA comes out from behind the screen.)* I've come to ask you to give me the key to the cupboard, I've lost mine. You've got one, the little key. *(OLGA gives him the key without speaking; IRINA goes behind her screen; a pause.)* What an enormous fire! It's beginning to die down now. Hang it all, that Ferapont made me lose my temper and I said something stupid to him. . . . Your Honor. . . . *(Pause)* Why don't you speak, Olya? *(Pause)* It's time you dropped this nonsense and gave up sulking for no 1650 reason. . . . You're here, Masha, Irina's here, well, that's fine—let's have it out, once and for all. What are you holding against me? What is it?

OLGA: Let it rest, Andryusha. Tomorrow we'll have a talk. *(Agitated)* What an agonizing night!

ANDREI: *(very much confused)* Don't be upset. I'm asking you quite calmly: what are you holding against me? Tell me frankly.

*(VERSHININ's voice: Tram-tam-tam!)*

MASHA: *(in a loud voice, getting up)* Tra-ta-ta! *(To OLGA)* Goodbye, Olya, God bless you. *(Goes behind screen and kisses 1660 IRINA.)* Sleep well. . . . Good-bye, Andrei. Leave them now, they're tired out. . . . You can have it out tomorrow. . . . *(Goes out.)*

OLGA: Yes, really, Andryusha, let's put it off until tomorrow. . . . *(Goes behind her screen.)* It's time to go to sleep.

ANDREI: I'll just say it and then go. Right now. . . . In the first place, you have something against Natasha, my wife, and I've been aware of this from the very day of my wedding. Natasha is a fine, honest person, straightforward and 1670 noble—that is my opinion! I love and respect my wife, you understand, I respect her, and I insist that others respect her, too. I repeat, she is an honest, noble person, and all your grievances, if you will forgive me, are mere caprice. *(Pause)* In the second place, you seem to be angry because I am not a professor, engaged in academic work. But I serve on the District Board, and I consider this service just as high and sacred as serving science. I am a member of the District Board and I am proud of it, if you want to know. . . . *(Pause)*

1680   In the third place . . . I have something else to say . . . I mortgaged the house without asking your permission. . . . In this I am guilty, yes, and I ask you to forgive me. I was forced to do it because of my debts . . . thirty-five thousand rubles. . . . I am no longer gambling, I gave it up some time ago, but the chief thing I can say to justify myself is that you girls . . . you receive a pension, while I had no . . . emoluments, so to say. . . . *(Pause)*

KULYGIN: *(at the door)* Masha not here? *(Alarmed)* Where could she be? That's strange . . . *(Goes out.)*

1690   ANDREI: They won't listen. Natasha is a superior, honest person. *(Paces the stage in silence, then stops.)* When I married, I thought we should be happy . . . all of us, happy . . . but, my God! *(Weeps.)* My dear sisters, my darling sisters, don't believe me, don't believe me. . . . *(Goes out.)*

KULYGIN: *(at the door, anxiously)* Where is Masha? Isn't she here? What an extraordinary business! *(Goes out.)*

*(Fire alarm; the stage is empty.)*

IRINA: *(behind the screen)* Olya! Who is that knocking on the floor?

OLGA: It's the doctor, Ivan Romanych. He's drunk.

1700   IRINA: What a troubled night! *(Pause)* Olya! *(Looks out from behind the screen.)* Have you heard? The brigade is going to be taken from us, transferred to some place far away.

OLGA: That's only a rumor.

IRINA: We shall be left alone then. . . . Olya!

OLGA: Well?

IRINA: Darling, dearest, I do respect and value the Baron, he is a fine man—I'll marry him, I am willing, only let us go to Moscow! I implore you, let us go! There's nothing in the world better than Moscow! Let us go! Olya! Let us go!

## —ACT FOUR—

*(The old garden of the* PROZOROV *house. At the end of a long avenue of fir trees, the river is seen; on the other side of the river, a wood. To the right is the veranda of the house; there, on the table, bottles and glasses have been set out; apparently they have just been drinking champagne. It is twelve o'clock noon. From time to time people from the street cross the garden on their way to the river; four or five soldiers pass by walking rapidly.*

CHEBUTYKIN, *in an amiable mood, which he maintains throughout the act, sits in an easy chair in the garden, waiting to be called; he wears a military cap and carries a stick.* IRINA, TUZENBACH, *and* KULYGIN, *with a decoration around his neck and no moustache, stand on the veranda saying good-bye to* FEDOTIK *and* RODAY, *who are descending the steps; both officers are in field uniform.)*

1710   TUZENBACH: *(kisses* FEDOTIK*)* You're a good fellow, we got on well together. *(Kisses* RODAY.*)* Once again . . . good-bye, my

dear boy!

IRINA: Till we meet again!

FEDOTIK: It's not till we meet again, but good-bye, we shall never see each other again!

KULYGIN: Who knows! *(Wipes his eyes, smiles.)* Here I am, crying, too.

IRINA: Some day we shall run across one another.

FEDOTIK: In ten or fifteen years, perhaps? By then we shall hardly recognize one another, we'll greet each other 1720 coldly. . . . *(Takes a snapshot.)* Stand still. . . . Once more, for the last time.

RODAY: *(embraces* TUZENBACH*)* We shall not see each other again . . . *(Kisses* IRINA's *hand.)* Thank you for everything, for everything!

FEDOTIK: *(vexed)* Do wait a bit!

TUZENBACH: Please God we'll meet again. But write to us. Be sure to write.

RODAY: *(glancing at the garden)* Good-bye, trees! *(Shouts.)* Yoo-hoo! *(Pause)* Good-bye, echo!                    1730

KULYGIN: I'm afraid you'll get married there in Poland. . . . Your Polish wife will embrace you and say: "Kokhany!" *(Laughs.)*

FEDOTIK: *(looking at his watch)* We have less than an hour. Solyony is the only one out of our battery going on the barge, we're with the rank and file. Three battery divisions are going today, three more tomorrow—then peace and quiet will descend upon the town.

TUZENBACH: And the most dreadful boredom.

RODAY: Where is Maria Sergeyevna?                         1740

KULYGIN: Masha is in the garden.

FEDOTIK: We'll go and say good-bye to her.

RODAY: Good-bye, I must go, or I shall begin to cry. *(Quickly embraces* TUZENBACH *and* KULYGIN, *and kisses* IRINA's *hand.)* It's been splendid living here. . . .

FEDOTIK: *(to* KULYGIN*)* This is a souvenir for you . . . a notebook with a little pencil. . . . We'll go this way to the river. . . . *(As they go off, both look back.)*

RODAY: *(shouts)* Yoo-hoo!

KULYGIN: *(shouts)* Good-bye!                              1750

*(At the rear of the stage* FEDOTIK *and* RODAY *meet* MASHA *and bid her good-bye; she walks off with them.)*

IRINA: They are gone. . . . *(Sits on the bottom step of the veranda.)*

CHEBUTYKIN: They forgot to say good-bye to me.

IRINA: Well, what about you?

CHEBUTYKIN: I forgot, too, somehow. However, I'll see them soon, I'm leaving tomorrow. Yes . . . only one more day. In a year I'll be retired, I'll come back here and spend the rest of my life near you. . . . Only one little year left before I get my pension. . . . *(Puts one newspaper into his pocket and takes out another.)* I'll come here to you and change my life radi- 1760 cally . . . I'll be such a quiet, well- . . . well-behaved, agreeable man . . .

IRINA: Yes, you really ought to change your life, my dear. You really should, somehow.

CHEBUTYKIN: Yes. I feel that. *(Softly sings.)* "Ta-ra-ra boom-de-ay . . . sit on the curb I may" . . .

KULYGIN: Incorrigible Ivan Romanych! Incorrigible!

CHEBUTYKIN: You ought to have taken me in hand. Then I'd

have been reformed.

1770 IRINA: Fyodor has shaved off his moustache. I can't bear to look at him!

KULYGIN: Why?

CHEBUTYKIN: I could tell you what your physiognomy looks like now, but I won't.

KULYGIN: Well! It's the accepted thing, *modus vivendi.* Our director shaved off his moustache, and as soon as I became an inspector, I shaved mine off, too. Nobody likes it, but I don't care. I am content. With a moustache or without a moustache, I am equally content. . . . *(Sits down.)*

*(At the rear of the stage* ANDREI *is wheeling a baby carriage with a sleeping child in it.)*

1780 IRINA: Dear, dear Ivan Romanych, I'm dreadfully worried. You were on the boulevard yesterday, tell me what happened there.

CHEBUTYKIN: What happened? Nothing. Nothing worth talking about. *(Reads newspaper.)* It doesn't matter!

KULYGIN: What they are saying is that Solyony and the Baron met yesterday on the boulevard near the theater—

TUZENBACH: Stop it! Now why, really . . . *(With a wave of his hand, goes into the house.)*

KULYGIN: Near the theater . . . Solyony began badgering him, 1790 and the Baron wouldn't stand for it and said something that offended him. . . .

CHEBUTYKIN: I don't know. It's all nonsense.

KULYGIN: In a certain seminary a teacher wrote "nonsense" on a composition, and the pupil, thinking it was written in Latin, read "consensus". . . . *(Laughs.)* Terribly funny. They say that Solyony is in love with Irina and has conceived a hatred for the Baron. . . . That's understandable. Irina is a very pretty girl. She even resembles Masha, the same pensiveness. Only you, Irina, have a gentler disposition. Though 1800 Masha, too, has a very fine disposition. I love my Masha.

*(At the rear of the garden, offstage:* "Aa-oo! Yoo-hoo!"*)*

IRINA: *(shudders)* Somehow everything frightens me today. *(Pause)* I have all my things ready, after dinner I shall send them off. The Baron and I are getting married tomorrow, leaving tomorrow for the brickyard, and the day after tomorrow I'll be at the school, a new life begins. God will help me somehow! When I passed my teacher's examination, I wept for joy, for pure bliss. . . . *(Pause)* The cart will soon be here for my things. . . .

KULYGIN: That's all very well, only it doesn't seem to be quite 1810 serious. Nothing but ideas and not enough seriousness. However, I wish you well with all my heart.

CHEBUTYKIN: *(moved)* My delightful, lovely . . . my darling. . . . You've gone so far, I can't catch up to you. I've been left behind, like a bird of passage that has grown old and cannot fly. Fly away, my dears, fly away, and God be with you! *(Pause)* It was a mistake, Fyodor Ilyich, to shave off your moustache.

KULYGIN: That'll do! *(Sighs.)* Well, today the military are leaving, and everything will go on again as of old. No matter what they say, Masha is a good, honest woman, I love her 1820 very much and am thankful for my fate. . . . Different people have different destinies. . . . Here in the excise office there is a certain clerk, Kozyryov. He went to school with me, and was expelled from the fifth class in high school be-

cause he simply could not understand *ut consecutivum.* Now he lives in great poverty, he's ill, and whenever we meet I say to him: "Greetings, *ut consecutivum!*" "Yes," he says, "exactly, *consecutivum,*" and then he coughs. . . . And here I've been lucky all my life, I'm happy. I've even been awarded the Order of Stanislav, Second Degree, and now I 1830 am teaching others that *ut consecutivum.* Of course, I'm a clever man, cleverer than a great many other people, but happiness does not consist in that. . . .

*(In the house "The Maiden's Prayer" is being played on the piano.)*

IRINA: Tomorrow evening I shall not be hearing that "Maiden's Prayer," and I shan't be meeting Protopopov. . . . *(Pause)* Protopopov is sitting there in the drawing room, he came again today. . . .

KULYGIN: The headmistress is not here yet?

IRINA: No. They have sent for her. If only you knew how hard it has been for me to live here alone, without Olya. . . . She lives at the high school, as headmistress, she's busy all day 1840 long, but I am alone, I'm bored, I have nothing to do, and the very room I live in is hateful to me. . . . So I have made up my mind: if I am not destined to be in Moscow, then so be it. It is fate. There is nothing to be done. . . . It is all God's will, that is the truth. Nikolai Lvovich proposed to me. . . . Well? I thought it over and made up my mind. He is a good man, it is really amazing how good he is. . . . And suddenly it was as if my soul had grown wings, I rejoiced and grew light-hearted, and again I had a longing for work, for work. . . . Only something happened yesterday, some sort of 1850 mystery is hanging over me. . . .

CHEBUTYKIN: Consensus. Nonsense.

NATASHA: *(at the window)* The headmistress!

KULYGIN: The headmistress has arrived. Let us go! *(Goes into the house with* IRINA.*)*

CHEBUTYKIN: *(reads the newspaper, softly singing to himself)* "Ta-ra-ra boom-de-ay . . . sit on the curb I may" . . .

*(*MASHA *approaches; in the background* ANDREI *is pushing the baby carriage.)*

MASHA: There he sits, just sits . . .

CHEBUTYKIN: What?

MASHA: *(sits down)* Nothing. . . . *(Pause)* Did you love my 1860 mother?

CHEBUTYKIN: Very much.

MASHA: And did she love you?

CHEBUTYKIN: *(after a pause)* That I no longer remember.

MASHA: Is my man here? That's how our cook Marfa used to speak of her policeman: my man. Is my man here?

CHEBUTYKIN: Not yet.

MASHA: When you have to take your happiness in snatches, in bits, and then lose it, as I am losing it, you gradually coarsen, grow bitter. . . . *(With her hand on her breast)* I'm seething 1870 here inside. . . . *(Gazing at* ANDREI, *who is pushing the baby carriage)* Look at Andrei, our little brother. . . . All our hopes vanished. Thousands of people raised the bell, a great deal of money and effort were expended, and suddenly it fell and was shattered. All at once, without rhyme or reason. That's how it was with Andrei. . . .

ANDREI: And when will they finally quiet down in the house?

Such noise.

CHEBUTYKIN: Soon. (*Looks at his watch.*) My watch is an old-
1880 fashioned one, it strikes. . . . (*Winds his watch, it strikes.*)
The first, second, and fifth batteries leave at one o'clock
sharp. (*Pause*) And tomorrow I go.

ANDREI: For good?

CHEBUTYKIN: I don't know. Perhaps I'll come back in a
year. . . . Though, who knows. . . . It doesn't matter. . . .

(*Somewhere in the distance a harp and violin are heard.*)

ANDREI: The town will be empty. As if covered with a hood.
(*Pause*) Something happened yesterday near the theater;
everyone is talking about it, but I don't know what it was.

CHEBUTYKIN: Nothing. Foolishness. Solyony began picking on
1890 the Baron and he lost his temper and insulted him, and it finally got to the point where Solyony had to challenge him to
a duel. (*Looks at his watch.*) It's probably time now. . . . At
half-past twelve in the Crown forest, the one we see from
here, on the other side of the river . . . Piff-paff! (*Laughs.*)
Solyony imagines that he is Lermontov, he even writes
verses. A joke's a joke, but this is the third duel for him.

MASHA: For whom?

CHEBUTYKIN: Solyony.

MASHA: And for the Baron?

1900 CHEBUTYKIN: What about the Baron? (*Pause*)

MASHA: My thoughts are in a tangle. . . . All the same, I tell you,
it shouldn't be allowed. He might wound the Baron, or even
kill him.

CHEBUTYKIN: The Baron is a good fellow, but one Baron more
or less—what does it matter? Let them! It doesn't matter!
(*Beyond the garden a shout: "Aa-oo! Yoo-hoo!"*) You can
wait. That's Skvortsov, the second, shouting. He's in a boat.

ANDREI: In my opinion, to take part in a duel or to be present
at one, even in the capacity of a doctor, is simply immoral.

1910 CHEBUTYKIN: It only seems so. . . . We are not here, there is
nothing in the world, we do not exist, but merely seem to
exist. . . . And it really doesn't matter!

MASHA: Talk, talk, all day long nothing but talk. . . . (*Going*) To
live in such a climate, where you keep thinking it's going to
snow at any minute, and then on top of it these conversations. . . . (*Stopping*) I'm not going into the house, I cannot
go in there. . . . When Vershinin comes, let me know. . . .
(*Goes down the avenue.*) The birds of passage are in flight
already. . . . (*Looks up.*) Swans or geese. . . . My dear, happy
1920 birds. . . . (*Goes out.*)

ANDREI: Our house will be empty. The officers are leaving, you
are going, sister is getting married, and I shall be left alone
in the house.

CHEBUTYKIN: And your wife?

(FERAPONT *enters with some documents.*)

ANDREI: A wife is a wife. She's honest, good . . . well, kind, but
for all that, there's something in her that reduces her to the
level of a small, blind, sort of thick-skinned animal. In any
case, she's not a human being. I am speaking to you as to a
friend, the only person to whom I can open my heart. I love
1930 Natasha, it's true, but sometimes she seems to me extremely
vulgar, and then I feel lost, and I don't understand why, for
what reason, I love her so, or at least, did love her. . . .

CHEBUTYKIN: (*gets up*) I'm going away tomorrow, my boy, per-

haps we shall never see each other again, so here's my advice to you. Put on your hat, you know, take up a walking
stick, and be off . . . walk out, leave, without looking back.
And the farther you go the better.

(SOLYONY *crosses the back of the stage with two officers; seeing*
CHEBUTYKIN, *he turns toward him; the officers walk on.*)

SOLYONY: Doctor, it's time! Half-past twelve. (*Greets* ANDREI.)

CHEBUTYKIN: In a moment. I'm fed up with the lot of you. (*To*
ANDREI) If someone asks for me, Andryusha, say I'll be back 1940
presently. . . . (*Sighs.*) Oh-ho-ho!

SOLYONY: He no sooner cried "Alack" than the bear was on his
back. (*Walks off with him.*) Why are you quacking, old man?

CHEBUTYKIN: Come on!

SOLYONY: How do you feel?

CHEBUTYKIN: (*angrily*) Like a pig in clover.

SOLYONY: The old man upsets himself needlessly. I shall indulge myself a bit, I'll simply shoot him like a snipe. (*Takes
out scent and sprinkles his hands.*) I've used up a whole bottle today, but they still smell. My hands smell like a corpse. 1950
(*Pause*) Yes-s. . . . Remember the poem? "And he, rebellious, seeks the storm, As if in storms lay peace."

CHEBUTYKIN: Yes. He no sooner cried "Alack" than the bear
was on his back. (*Goes out with* SOLYONY.)

(*Cries of "Yoo-hoo" and "Aa-oo" are heard.* ANDREI *and* FER-
APONT *come in.*)

FERAPONT: Papers to sign . . .

ANDREI: (*nervously*) Leave me alone! Leave me alone! I beg of
you! (*Walks away with the baby carriage.*)

FERAPONT: What are papers for, if not to be signed? (*Goes to
the back of the stage.*)

(*Enter* IRINA *and* TUZENBACH, *wearing a straw hat;* KULYGIN
*crosses the stage calling: "Aa-oo, Masha! Aa-oo!"*)

TUZENBACH: That seems to be the only man in town who's glad 1960
the officers are leaving.

IRINA: It's understandable. (*Pause*) Our town is going to be
empty now.

TUZENBACH: Dear, I'll be back shortly.

IRINA: Where are you going?

TUZENBACH: I must go into town . . . to see my comrades off.

IRINA: That's not true. . . . Nikolai, why are you so distracted
today? (*Pause*) What happened yesterday near the theater?

TUZENBACH: (*with a gesture of impatience*) I'll come back in
an hour and be with you again. (*Kisses her hands.*) My 1970
beloved. . . . (*Looks into her face.*) It's five years now that I
have loved you, and I still can't get used to it, and you seem
always more beautiful to me. What lovely, wonderful hair!
What eyes! Tomorrow I shall carry you off, we'll work, and
be rich, and my dreams will come true. You shall be happy.
There is only one thing, only one: you do not love me!

IRINA: That is not within my power! I'll be your wife, faithful
and obedient, but it's not love, I can't help it! (*Weeps.*) I
have never in my life been in love. Oh, how I have dreamed
of love, dreamed of it for a long time now, day and night, but 1980
my soul is like a fine piano that is locked, and the key lost.
(*Pause*) You look troubled.

TUZENBACH: I haven't slept all night. There is nothing in my
life so terrible as to frighten me, only that lost key racks my

soul and will not let me sleep. . . . Tell me something. . . . *(Pause)* Tell me something. . . .

IRINA: What? What shall I say? What?

TUZENBACH: Something.

IRINA: Don't! Don't! *(Pause)*

1990 TUZENBACH: What trifles, what silly little things in life will suddenly, for no reason at all, take on meaning. You laugh at them just as you've always done, consider them trivial, and yet you go on, and you feel that you haven't the power to stop. Oh, let's not talk about that! I feel elated, I see these fir trees, these maples and birches, as if for the first time, and they all gaze at me with curiosity and expectation. What beautiful trees, and, in fact, how beautiful life ought to be with them! *(A shout of: "Aa-oo! Yoo-hoo!")* I must go, it's time. . . . There's a tree that's dead, but it goes on swaying in

2000 the wind with the others. So it seems to me that if I die, I'll still have a part in life, one way or another. Good-bye, my darling. . . . *(Kisses her hands.)* The papers you gave me are on my table, under the calendar.

IRINA: I am coming with you.

TUZENBACH: *(alarmed)* No, no! *(Quickly goes, then stops in the avenue.)* Irina!

IRINA: What?

TUZENBACH: *(not knowing what to say)* I didn't have any coffee this morning. Ask them to make me some. *(Quickly goes*

2010 *out.)*

*(IRINA stands lost in thought, then goes to the back of the stage and sits down on the swing. ANDREI comes in with the baby carriage; FERAPONT appears.)*

FERAPONT: Andrei Sergeyevich, the papers aren't mine, you know, they're official papers. I didn't make them up.

ANDREI: Oh, where is it, where has it all gone, my past, when I was young, gay, clever, when I dreamed and thought with grace, when my present and my future were lighted up with hope? Why is it that when we have barely begun to live, we grow dull, gray, uninteresting, lazy, indifferent, useless, unhappy. . . . Our town has been in existence now for two hundred years, there are a hundred thousand people in it, and

2020 not one who isn't exactly like all the others, not one saint, either in the past or in the present, not one scholar, not one artist, no one in the least remarkable who could inspire envy or a passionate desire to imitate him. . . . They just eat, drink, sleep, and then die . . . others are born and they, too, eat, drink, sleep, and to keep from being stupefied by boredom, they relieve the monotony of life with their odious gossip, with vodka, cards, chicanery, and the wives deceive their husbands, while the husbands lie and pretend not to see or hear anything, and an overwhelmingly vulgar influence

2030 weighs on the children, the divine spark is extinguished in them, and they become the same pitiful, identical corpses as their fathers and mothers. . . . *(Angrily, to FERAPONT)* What do you want?

FERAPONT: How's that? Papers to sign.

ANDREI: I'm fed up with you.

FERAPONT: *(handing him the papers)* The porter from the municipal treasury was saying just now . . . it seems, he says, in Petersburg this winter they had two hundred degrees of frost.

2040 ANDREI: The present is loathsome, but then, when I think of

the future, how good it is! I begin to feel so lighthearted, so free: and in the distance a light begins to dawn, I see freedom, I see how I and my children will be liberated from idleness, from kvas, from goose with cabbage, from after-dinner naps, from base parasitism . . .

FERAPONT: Two thousand people were frozen, it seems. They say everyone was terrified. It was either in Petersburg or Moscow, I don't remember.

ANDREI: *(seized with a feeling of tenderness)* My dear sisters, my wonderful sisters! *(Through tears)* Masha, my sister . . . 2050

NATASHA: *(in the window)* Who's talking so loud out there? Is that you, Andryusha? You'll wake up Sofochka. *Il ne faut pas faire du bruit, la Sofie est dormée déjà. Vous êtes un ours.* *(Getting angry)* If you want to talk, then give the baby carriage to someone else to wheel. Ferapont, take the carriage from your master!

FERAPONT: Yes, ma'am. *(Takes the carriage.)*

ANDREI: *(shamefacedly)* I'm talking quietly.

NATASHA: *(behind the window, caressing her little boy)* Bobik! Little mischief! Naughty Bobik! 2060

ANDREI: *(examining papers)* Very well, I'll look through them and sign what's necessary, and you can take them back to the Board. . . . *(Goes into the house reading papers; FERAPONT pushes the baby carriage to the rear of the garden.)*

NATASHA: *(behind window)* Bobik, what's Mama's name? Darling, darling! And who is this? This is Auntie Olya. Say hello to Auntie Olya!

*(Two street musicians, a man and a girl, play on the violin and harp; VERSHININ, OLGA, and ANFISA come out of the house and listen in silence for a moment; IRINA approaches.)*

IRINA: Our garden's like a public thoroughfare; people keep walking and driving through it. Nurse, give those musicians something. 2070

ANFISA: *(gives money to the musicians)* Go along and God bless you, good people. *(The musicians bow and leave.)* Poor things! You don't go around playing like that if you're well-fed. *(To IRINA)* Good day, Arisha! *(Kisses her.)* Ee-e, little one, what a life I am having! What a life! Living at the high school in a government apartment with Olyusha—that's what God has granted me in my old age. Never in my life have I lived like this, sinner that I am. . . . A big government apartment, a whole room to myself, my own bed. All at government expense. I wake up in the night and—oh, Lord, 2080 Mother of God, there's not a happier person in the world!

VERSHININ: *(looking at his watch)* We shall be leaving directly, Olga Sergeyevna. Time to be off. *(Pause)* I wish you everything, everything. . . . Where is Maria Sergeyevna?

IRINA: She's somewhere in the garden . . . I'll go and look for her.

VERSHININ: Please be so kind. I must hurry.

ANFISA: I'll go look for her, too. *(Calls.)* Mashenka, aa-oo! *(Goes with IRINA to the rear of the garden.)* Aa-oo, aa-oo!

VERSHININ: All things come to an end. Here we are parting. 2090 *(Looks at his watch.)* The town gave us a sort of lunch, we had champagne, the Mayor made a speech, I ate and listened, but in my heart I was here with you. . . . *(Looks around the garden.)* I've grown attached to you.

OLGA: Shall we meet again some day?

VERSHININ: Probably not. *(Pause)* My wife and the two little girls will remain here for another month or two; please, if anything happens, or if they need anything . . .

OLGA: Yes, yes, of course. You needn't worry. *(Pause)* By to- 2100 morrow there won't be a single officer or soldier in town; it will all be a memory, and for us, of course, a new life will begin. . . . *(Pause)* Nothing ever happens the way we want it to. I didn't want to be a headmistress, and yet I became one. It means we are not to be in Moscow . . .

VERSHININ: Well . . . thank you for everything. . . . Forgive me if anything was not quite . . . I have talked so much, far too much—forgive me for that, too, and don't think badly of me. . . .

OLGA: *(drying her eyes)* Oh, why doesn't Masha come. . . .

2110 VERSHININ: What more can I say to you in parting? What can I philosophize about? . . . *(Laughs.)* Life is hard. It presents itself to many of us as desolate and hopeless, and yet, one must admit that it keeps getting clearer and easier, and the day is not far off when it will be wholly bright. *(Looks at his watch.)* Time for me to go, it's time! Formerly mankind was occupied with wars, filling its entire existence with campaigns, invasions, conquests, but now all that has become obsolete, leaving a great void, with nothing to fill it; humanity is passionately seeking something, and, of course, will 2120 find it. Ah, if only it would come soon! *(Pause)* If, don't you know, we could add culture to the love of work, and love of work to culture. *(Looks at his watch.)* I really must go. . . .

OLGA: Here she comes.

*(Enter* MASHA, OLGA *walks off and stands a little to one side so as not to interfere with their leave-taking.)*

MASHA: *(looking into his face)* Good-bye . . . *(A prolonged kiss)*

OLGA: Come, come . . .

*(*MASHA *sobs violently.)*

VERSHININ: Write to me. . . . Don't forget! Let me go . . . it's time. . . . Olga Sergeyevna, take her, I must go now . . . I'm late. . . . *(Deeply moved, he kisses* OLGA's *hand, then embraces* MASHA *again and quickly goes out.)*

2130 OLGA: Come Masha! Stop, darling. . . .

*(Enter* KULYGIN.)*

KULYGIN: *(embarrassed)* Never mind, let her cry, let her . . . My good Masha, my kind Masha . . . you are my wife and I am happy, no matter what. . . . I don't complain, I make not a single reproach . . . Olga here is my witness. . . . We'll begin again to live as we used to, and I won't say a single word to you, nor make any allusion . . .

MASHA: *(restraining her sobs)* "A green oak by a curved seashore, upon that oak a golden chain . . . upon that oak a golden chain." . . . I'm going out of my mind. . . . "A green 2140 oak . . . by a curved seashore" . . .

OLGA: Calm yourself, Masha . . . calm yourself. . . . Give her some water.

MASHA: I'm not crying any more. . . .

KULYGIN: She's not crying any more . . . she is good. . . .

*(The faint sound of a gunshot is heard in the distance.)*

MASHA: "A green oak by a curved seashore, upon that oak a golden chain." . . . A green cat . . . a green oak . . . I'm mixing it up. . . . *(Drinks the water.)* My life is a failure . . . I want

nothing now. . . . I'll be calm in a moment. . . . It doesn't matter. . . . What does that mean, "by a curved seashore"? Why do those words keep running through my head? My 2150 thoughts are all tangled.

*(Enter* IRINA.)*

OLGA: Calm yourself, Masha. Come, that's a good girl. Let's go in.

MASHA: *(angrily)* I'm not going in there. *(Sobs, but instantly stops herself.)* I'm not going into that house any more, I won't go. . . .

IRINA: Let us sit down together, even if we don't talk. You know, I am going away tomorrow. . . . *(Pause)*

KULYGIN: Yesterday I took this beard and moustache away from a boy in the third grade. . . . *(Puts on the beard and 2160 moustache.)* I look like the German teacher. . . . *(Laughs.)* Don't I? Those boys are funny. . . .

MASHA: You really do look like you're German.

OLGA: *(laughs)* Yes.

*(*MASHA *weeps.)*

IRINA: Don't, Masha.

KULYGIN: Very much like him . . .

*(Enter* NATASHA.)*

NATASHA: *(to the maid)* What? Mr. Protopopov will sit with Sofochka, and Andrei Sergeyich can wheel Bobik. So much bother with children. . . . *(To* IRINA) You're going away tomorrow, Irina—such a pity! Stay at least another week. 2170 *(Catching sight of* KULYGIN, *utters a shriek; he laughs and takes off the moustache and beard.)* Oh, you—really, you frightened me! *(To* IRINA) I've grown so used to you—do you think parting from you will be easy for me? I'll have Andrei and his violin moved into your room—he can saw away in there!—and we'll put Sofochka in his room. Marvelous, wonderful child! What an adorable little girl! Today she looked at me with such eyes and said—"Mama"!

KULYGIN: A fine child, that's true.

NATASHA: So tomorrow I shall be all alone here. *(Sighs.)* First 2180 of all I shall have this avenue of fir trees cut down, then that maple. . . . It's so unsightly in the evening. . . . *(To* IRINA) That sash doesn't suit you at all, dear . . . it's not in good taste. You need something a little brighter. And then I'll have flowers planted everywhere—flowers, flowers—and it will be fragrant. . . . *(Severely)* What's a fork doing here on the bench? *(Going into the house, to the maid)* What's a fork doing here on the bench, I'd like to know? *(Shouting)* Hold your tongue!

KULYGIN: She's off again!     2190

*(A band plays a military march offstage; everyone listens.)*

OLGA: They are leaving.

*(Enter* CHEBUTYKIN.)*

MASHA: Our friends are going. Well . . . a happy journey to them! *(To her husband)* We must go home. . . . Where are my hat and cape?

KULYGIN: I took them into the house. . . . I'll get them right away.

OLGA: Yes, now we can all go home. It's time.

CHEBUTYKIN: Olga Sergeyevna!

OLGA: What is it? (*Pause*) What is it?

2200 CHEBUTYKIN: Nothing . . . I don't know how to tell you. . . . (*Whispers in her ear.*)

OLGA: (*shocked*) It's not possible!

CHEBUTYKIN: Yes . . . what a business! . . . I'm worn out, completely exhausted, I don't want to talk any more. . . . (*Irritably*) Besides, it doesn't matter!

MASHA: What has happened?

OLGA: (*puts her arms around* IRINA) This is a terrible day. . . . I don't know how to tell you, my darling . . .

IRINA: What is it? Tell me quickly, what is it? For God's sake! 2210 (*Weeps.*)

CHEBUTYKIN: The Baron has just been killed in a duel.

IRINA: (*quietly weeping*) I knew it, I knew it. . . .

CHEBUTYKIN: (*sits down on a bench at the rear of the stage*) I'm worn out. . . . (*Takes a newspaper out of his pocket.*) Let them cry . . . (*Softly sings.*) "Ta-ra-ra boom-de-ay, sit on the curb I may." . . . As if it mattered!

(*The three sisters stand close to one another.*)

NATASHA: Oh, listen to that music! They are leaving us, one has gone for good, forever; we are left alone to begin our life over again. We must live. . . . We must live. . . .

IRINA: (*lays her head on* OLGA's *breast*) A time will come when 2220 everyone will know what all this is for, why there is all this suffering, and there will be no mysteries; but meanwhile, we must live . . . we must work, only work! Tomorrow I shall go alone, and I shall teach in the school, and give my whole life to those who need it. Now it is autumn, soon winter will come and cover everything with snow, and I shall go on working, working. . . .

OLGA: (*embracing both her sisters*) The music plays so gaily, so valiantly, one wants to live! Oh, my God! Time will pass, and we shall be gone forever, we'll be forgotten, our faces will be 2230 forgotten, our voices, and how many there were of us, but our sufferings will turn into joy for those who live after us, happiness and peace will come to this earth, and then they will remember kindly and bless those who are living now. Oh, my dear sisters, our life is not over yet. We shall live! The music is so gay, so joyous, it seems as if just a little more and we shall know why we live, why we suffer. . . . If only we knew, if only we knew! (*The music grows softer and softer;* KULYGIN, *cheerful, smiling, brings the hat and cape;* ANDREI *pushes the baby carriage with Bobik in it.*) 2240

CHEBUTYKIN: (*softly sings*) "Ta-ra-ra boom-de-ay, sit on the curb I may." . . . It doesn't matter! It doesn't matter!

OLGA: If we only knew, if we only knew!

---

*WRITTEN to various correspondents—the Moscow Art Theater manager Vladimir Nemirovich-Danchenko, the MAT actor A. L. Vishnevsky, his sister Marya, the novelist and playwright Maxim Gorky, the actress Vera Kommissarzhevskaya, and his cousin Georgi Chekhov—Chekhov's letters testify both to the labor of writing and to Chekhov's uncertainty about how his indirect drama would be received.*

## Anton Chekhov

### Letters on *The Three Sisters*

*To Vl. I. Nemirovich-Danchenko*
Yalta.   Nov. 24, 1899.

I am not writing a play at present. I have a plot, "The Three Sisters," but I shall not start on it before I have finished the stories I have on my mind.

*To A. L. Vishnevsky*
Yalta.   August 5, 1900.

I am writing the play; a goodly portion is finished, but as I am not in Moscow I cannot judge it. Perhaps it won't be a play after all, but a Crimean hodge-podge. It is called "The Three Sisters," as you already know. I am writing the part of the high-school director for you; he is the husband of one of the sisters. You will appear in the customary uniform, wearing an order round your neck. The play is not for this season, but I'll have it in shape for the next.

*To His Sister*
Yalta.   Sept. 9, 1900.

"The Three Sisters" is very difficult to write, more difficult than my other plays. Oh well, it doesn't matter; perhaps something will come of it, next season if not this. It's very hard to write in Yalta, by the way: I am interrupted, and I feel as though I had no object in writing; what I wrote yesterday I don't like to-day. . . .

*To Maxim Gorky*
Yalta.   Oct. 16, 1900.

 . . . On the 21st of this month I am going to Moscow, and from there abroad. Can you imagine—I have written a play; but as it will be produced not now, but next season, I have not made a fair copy of it yet. It can lie as it is. It was very difficult to write "The Three Sisters." Three heroines, you see, each a separate type and all the daughters of a general. The action is laid in a provinial town,—it might be Perm,—in the background military, artillery.

*To V. F. Kommissarzhevskaya*
Moscow.    Nov. 13, 1900.

"The Three Sisters" is completed, but its future, at least its immediate future, is obscure to me. The play turned out dull, verbose, and awkward. I say awkward because it has only four female roles, and its mood is duller than dull. Your artists would not take to it if I sent it to them at the Alexandra Theatre. Nevertheless, I shall send it to you. Read it and let me know if it would be a good idea to take it on tour for the summer.

*To G. M. Chekhov*
Yalta.    March 8, 1901.

"The Three Sisters" met with great success. Ah, if only there were three good, young actresses, and actors who know how to wear military uniforms. The play is not intended for the provinces.

# August Strindberg

The Swedish playwright August Strindberg (1849–1912) was a modern Renaissance man—he wrote some fifty plays, several autobiographical novels, and a variety of scientific and occult works as well. A series of tempestuous marriages marked Strindberg's life and are reflected in his corrosively misogynistic attitudes and in his hostility toward Ibsen, who seemed to Strindberg to advocate a new order of feminine domination. Calling *A Doll House* "sick like its father," Strindberg wrote *The Father* (1887) in reply to Ibsen, a play in which a calculating woman drives her husband into madness. Although Strindberg considered the play to be an experiment in the new "naturalism," it is really a kind of psychological thriller; the characters are so consumed by their sexual combat with one another that the worldly environment hardly seems important. Strindberg sent the play to Zola, who found it absorbing and curious, but lacking in the material social reality he demanded of the new drama. Strindberg then wrote *Miss Julie* (1888), and considered the play's use of naturalism in his famous preface to the play. The battle of the sexes is one of Strindberg's preoccupations, examined in a series of plays including *Creditors* (1888) and *The Dance of Death, Parts 1 and 2* (1901).

The battle of the sexes was also the battle that occupied Strindberg's life outside the theater. His three marriages all involved periods of psychological breakdown and creative fertility. Strindberg's breakdown of the mid-1890s after marrying his second wife is documented in *The Inferno* (1897) and is symptomatic of his volatile and unstable frame of mind. Much of Strindberg's manic energy was focused on women—he believed that his wife was attempting to drive him mad by sending rays through the walls. Strindberg also developed a passion for the occult and for alchemy, and in addition to his plays, poems, and novels, he wrote a number of scientific and pseudoscientific treatises. Unlike Ibsen, Strindberg experimented in a variety of dramatic genres throughout his career. Calling himself the "Zola of the occult," Strindberg wrote an influential series of expressionist and symbolic plays; the best known today are *To Damascus* (in three parts, 1898–1901) and *A Dream Play* (1901). He also wrote several important plays on Swedish history, including *Erik XIV* (1899), *Gustav Adolph* (1900), and *Gustav III* (1902). In 1907 he founded a small theater—the Intimate Theater—which brought the independent theater movement to Sweden and produced his intense and often symbolic series of "chamber plays," including *The Ghost Sonata* (1907) and *The Pelican* (1907). When Strindberg died in 1912, he had become not only the most significant literary and theatrical figure in Swedish history, but a major influence on the course of modern drama.

## A Dream Play
## (1901)

Written in 1901 and first staged in Stockholm in 1907, *A Dream Play* often seems to readers a nearly unstageable play, to require the cutting and montage technique of film, a medium still in its infancy when Strindberg wrote the play. Yet *A Dream Play* has been staged many times in Sweden (where it is one of Strindberg's most-often produced plays), in Europe, and in the United States, sometimes produced lavishly, sometimes simply. For although the play's many settings—the "clouds resembling shattered slate cliffs with ruins of castles and fortresses" framing Indra's Daughter in the Prologue, the chrysanthemum-topped castle rising from the manure of the first and last scenes, the Stage Door, the claustral Lawyer's office, Fingal's Cave, Foul Strand and Fair Haven—have an important symbolic function, the vitality of the play on the stage is really not dependent on the densely particularized environment of realism. Instead, as Strindberg suggests in his "Note" to the play, *A Dream Play* is held together by its "musical treatment," in which themes are sounded, amplified, modulated, and counterpointed in the play's rich harmony.

For this reason, too, the play's structure seems more cyclic than linear, as Indra's Daughter progresses from eternity through various scenes of human suffering, loss, and disappointment. *A Dream Play*, that is, maintains a consistent dichotomy between the sorrows of human life and the Daughter's elevated sympathy. As a form of expressionist theater, *A Dream Play* also has a vaguely "morality-play" dimension, as the Daughter proceeds through representative scenes of human life and sorrow to the visionary center of the play in Fingal's Cave, and then returns back to her point of origin in the world, the castle. And Strindberg is also true to his sense that "the characters split, double, multiply, dissolve, condense, float apart, coalesce" in the play. In a sense, the men who accompany the Daughter on her journey—the Officer, the Lawyer, the Poet—all blend into one another, emanations, perhaps, of the mind of the dreamer. To respond closely to the play is to try to feel into its peculiar, repetitive, metaphorical logic, to avoid the kind of materialist narrative logic of realistic theater in order to seek the thematic parallels and symmetries more typically found in poetry. For *A Dream Play* is imagined in the densely analogical register of poetry, a poetry that is for Strindberg at once visual, verbal, narrative, and symbolic, an imagistic poetry perhaps best captured in the play's final vision: *Music. The rear of the stage is lit up by the burning castle and reveals a wall of human faces, questioning, sorrowful, despairing. As the castle burns, the flower bud at the top bursts and blossoms into a huge chrysanthemum.*

# —A Dream Play—
## August Strindberg
TRANSLATED BY EVERT SPRINCHORN

## —PROLOGUE°—

*The backdrop represents banks of clouds resembling shattered slate cliffs with ruins of castles and fortresses.*

*The constellations Leo, Virgo, and Libra can be seen; in their midst the planet Jupiter is shining brightly.°°*

*Indra's Daughter is standing on the highest cloud.*

THE VOICE OF INDRA:
  (*from above*) Where are you, my daughter? Where?
INDRA'S DAUGHTER:
  Here, Father! Here!
THE VOICE OF INDRA:
  You've gone astray, my child. Be careful;
  you're drifting down.
  How did you get there?
INDRA'S DAUGHTER:
10  I followed a flash of lightning from the empyrean,
  riding on a cloud. But the cloud
  sank beneath me, and now I'm drifting down.
  Tell me, Indra, my father, what place is this
  that I have come to? Why is it so stifling,
  so hard to breathe?
THE VOICE OF INDRA:
  You've left the second world and gone into the third.
  You've left Sukra,°°° the morning star, far behind,
  and now you've entered the atmosphere of earth.
20  Regard, my child, the seventh house of the zodiac,
  Libra, the Scales, in which the daystar stands
  as the year tips toward autumn
  and day balances night.
INDRA'S DAUGHTER:
  The earth, you said? This dark and heavy world
  that is lit by the light of the moon?
THE VOICE OF INDRA:
  Earth is the heaviest, the most leaden
  of all the orbs that roam the void.
30 INDRA'S DAUGHTER:
  Tell me, doesn't the sun shine there?
THE VOICE OF INDRA:
  Of course the sun shines there; only not all the time.
INDRA'S DAUGHTER:
  There's a rift in the cloud. I can see all that's below.
THE VOICE OF INDRA:
  And what do you see, my child?
INDRA'S DAUGHTER:
  I see . . . how beautiful it is . . . Green woods,

blue waters, white peaks, golden fields.    40
THE VOICE OF INDRA:
  Yes, beautiful like all Brahma's creations.
  But it was still more beautiful once
  at the dawning of time. Something happened,
  a warping of its orbit—or was it something else?
  A revolt, and in its wake
  crimes that had to be quelled.
INDRA'S DAUGHTER:
  Now I can hear sounds from there . . .
  What sort of beings are they who dwell below?    50
THE VOICE OF INDRA:
  Go down and see for yourself.
  Far be it from me to malign
  the Creator's creatures, but that sound you hear
  is the language they speak.
INDRA'S DAUGHTER:
  It sounds like—. Well, to my ears
  it doesn't ring with joy.
THE VOICE OF INDRA:
  I can well imagine. All their tongues can speak    60
  is the language of complaint. Indeed
  those earthly beings are a bickering, badgering,
  ungrateful race.
INDRA'S DAUGHTER:
  Don't say that. I can hear cries of joy,
  and shots and roars; see flares bursting.
  Bells are ringing, fires blazing,
  and voices, thousands upon thousands,
  singing the praises of heaven.
  (*Pause.*)    70
  You judge them too harshly, Father.
THE VOICE OF INDRA:
  Go down and see. Listen to them.
  Then come back up here and tell me
  if there is any reason, any grounds
  for all their wailing and complaining.
INDRA'S DAUGHTER:
  Very well. I will go down there.
  But you come with me, Father.
THE VOICE OF INDRA:    80
  No, I cannot breathe in those depths.
INDRA'S DAUGHTER:
  The cloud is sinking. The air's so heavy,
  I'm suffocating. It isn't air, it's smoke and water.
  So heavy, heavy, it's dragging me down, down.

---

°This prologue is a later addition to the play. It was written in 1906, in anticipation of the first production of the work, which took place in Stockholm on 17 April 1907.

°°Leo, the Lion, is associated with Hercules and stands for man; Virgo, the Virgin, represents woman; Libra is the balance; and Jupiter is God.

°°°Venus, in Sanskrit.

Now I can see it clearly, wobbling and careening. . . .
No, the third world is not the best of worlds.

THE VOICE OF INDRA:

The best? Of course not. Neither is it the worst.
90      Dust they call it, and it rolls round like the others.
That's why those creatures of dust are always dizzy,
lurching between folly and madness.
Don't be afraid, my child. It's only a test.

INDRA'S DAUGHTER:

(*on her knees, as the cloud descends*) I'm sinking.


[I]

*The backdrop represents a forest of giant hollyhocks in full bloom—white, pink, purple, violet, sulphur-yellow—and over the top of them can be seen the top of a castle crowned with a dome that resembles a flower bud. Beneath the footings of the castle are scattered stacks of straw covering the manure and litter from the stables. The wings and tormentors, which remain unchanged throughout the play, are stylized wall paintings suggesting rooms, buildings, and landscapes simultaneously.*

*The Glazier, an elderly man, and Indra's Daughter enter.*

DAUGHTER: The castle is still growing up out of the earth—you see how much it's grown since last year.

GLAZIER: (*to himself*) I've never seen that castle before in my life—never heard of a castle growing. Oh, well—. (*To the*
100      *Daughter, with complete conviction.*) Yes, indeed, it's grown two yards. That's because they've manured it good. And if you'll notice, another wing is beginning to sprout over there on the sunny side.

DAUGHTER: It's going to bloom soon, isn't it? It's past midsummer.

GLAZIER: Don't you see that flower bud up there?

DAUGHTER: Oh, yes, yes, I do! (*Claps her hands in joy.*) I wonder, why do flowers grow up from dirt?

GLAZIER: (*gently, piously*) They don't like to be in the dirt, so
110      they hurry up into the light as fast as they can—to bloom and die.

DAUGHTER: Who lives in that castle? Do you know?

GLAZIER: I used to know. Can't seem to remember now.

DAUGHTER: I think there's a man imprisoned there. . . . And I'm sure he's waiting for me to come and rescue him.

GLAZIER: Careful. You both might get more than you bargain for.

DAUGHTER: One doesn't haggle over what has to be done! Come on, let's go in!
120  GLAZIER: All right, all right, let's go.


[II]

*They approach the backdrop, which slowly opens up toward the sides.*

*The stage is now a simple, bare room with a table and a few chairs. An Officer in a very unusual modern uniform is sitting in a chair. He is rocking back and forth and striking the table with his saber.*

*The Daughter goes over to the Officer and carefully and gently takes the saber from his hands.*

DAUGHTER: (*as if to a child*) Mustn't do, mustn't do!

OFFICER: Oh, please be nice to me, Agnes; let me keep my saber.

DAUGHTER: No, no! You're chopping the table to pieces! (*To the Glazier.*) You can go down to the harness room and put in the windowpane. I'll meet you later.

(*The Glazier leaves.*)

DAUGHTER: You are a prisoner in your own rooms. I have come to rescue you!

OFFICER: I think I've been expecting this, but I couldn't be sure you'd want to help.      130

DAUGHTER: It's a strong castle—it's got seven walls—but—well, we'll think of something. . . . Well, do you want to or don't you?

OFFICER: To be perfectly frank, I really don't know. Either way I'll be in trouble. You have to pay for every joy in life with twice its price in sorrow. I hate to sit imprisoned here, but if I bought myself some joy and freedom, I'd pay for it three times over in pain and suffering. —Agnes, I'd just as soon put up with it, as long as I can look at you.

DAUGHTER: What do you see in me?      140

OFFICER: Beauty personified, the harmony of the universe. There are curves and lines in your form and features that can't be found anywhere else except in the orbits of the planets, in the strings that vibrate with music, in the trembling pulsations of the light. . . . You've come from heaven.

DAUGHTER: So have you.

OFFICER: Then why do I have to take care of horses? Be a stableboy and carry out manure?

DAUGHTER: So that you'll want to get away from it.

OFFICER: I do want to, I do! I want to rise above it. But it's so  150
difficult, so hard.

DAUGHTER: But, don't you see, it's your duty to find your way to the light.

OFFICER: Duty? Doesn't life owe me something?

DAUGHTER: You think life's been unfair to you? Is that what you think?

OFFICER: Yes! Unfair, unjust. . . .

(*One can now hear voices from behind a partition, which is promptly drawn aside. The Officer and the Daughter look in that direction and then freeze in position, their gestures and expressions frozen, too.*)

(*The Mother, looking very ill, is sitting at a table. In front of her is a lighted tallow candle, which she trims and crops now and again with candle snuffers. On the table are piles of new-made shirts and linen, which she is marking with ink and a quill pen. To the left stands a brown wardrobe or clothespress.*)

(*The Father hands her a silk shawl.*)

FATHER: (*gently*) You mean you don't want it?

MOTHER: A silk shawl—for me? Oh, dearest, what use can I have for a silk shawl? I'm not long for this world.      160

FATHER: Do you believe what the doctor says?

MOTHER: Not only what he says. Most of all I believe the voice I hear inside me.

FATHER: (*gloomily*) Then it's really serious? . . . And here you are thinking only of the children—first, last, and always.

MOTHER: They were my whole life, my reason for living . . . my joy . . . and my sorrow.

FATHER: Forgive me, Christine. . . . For everything.

MOTHER: For what? You must forgive me, my darling. We've
170 been hard on each other. And why? We don't know. We couldn't help ourselves. . . . Anyway, here are new shirts and linen for the children. You must see to it that they change twice a week. Wednesdays and Sundays. And be sure Louisa gives them their baths, and washes them—all over, you understand . . . Are you going out?

FATHER: I have to be up at the school—eleven o'clock.

MOTHER: Would you ask Alfred to come in before you leave?

FATHER: (*pointing at the Officer*) But, dearest, he's standing right here.

180 MOTHER: Can you imagine, I'm beginning to lose my sight, too. . . . Yes, yes, it's getting dark. (*She trims the candlewick.*) Alfred, come here.

.  .  .  .  .  .  .  .  .  .  .  .  .  .  .

(*The Father goes out straight through the wall, nodding good-bye.*)

.  .  .  .  .  .  .  .  .  .  .  .  .  .  .

(*The Officer goes over to his Mother.*)

MOTHER: Who is that girl?

OFFICER: (*whispering*) Why, that's Agnes.

MOTHER: Oh, really, is that Agnes? Do you know what they're saying? That she's the daughter of the god Indra, and that she asked to come down here on earth to find out what life is really like. —Shh! Not a word!

OFFICER: Yes, indeed, she is a child of the gods.

190 MOTHER: (*aloud*) My dearest Alfred, soon I'll have to leave you and the rest of my children. There's something I want to tell you, something I want you to remember all through life.

OFFICER: (*dark and gloomy*) Yes, Mother.

MOTHER: Just one word of advice: don't ever quarrel with God.

OFFICER: I don't understand you, Mother.

MOTHER: You mustn't go around thinking that life has treated you unfairly.

OFFICER: Not even when it has, when I know I've been unjustly accused?

200 MOTHER: I know, I know. You're thinking of the time you were punished because they said you stole a coin and later it turned up.

OFFICER: That's right. It was unjust. It got me started through life on the wrong foot. Things were never the same.

MOTHER: I see. Now you just go over to that wardrobe and—

OFFICER: (*blushing in shame*) You mean you know? You know? That's where—

MOTHER: *The Swiss Family Robinson*. . . . And your—

OFFICER: Please! Don't say any more!

210 MOTHER: —your brother got punished for having torn it up. But it was *you* who tore it up and hid it.

OFFICER: It's strange. That wardrobe is still standing there after twenty years. We've moved so many times since then, and Mother died ten years ago.

MOTHER: Now, what's that got to do with it? There you go—always asking questions. That's how you destroy the best things in life for yourself. . . . Oh, here's Lina!

.  .  .  .  .  .  .  .  .  .  .  .  .  .  .

LINA: (*entering*) Oh, missis, it's awfully kind of you, and I want to thank you, but I can't go to the christening.

MOTHER: But why not, my child?                                         220

LINA: I haven't a thing to wear.

MOTHER: Why, I'll lend you my shawl! —This one.

LINA: Oh, dearest me, I can't take *that!* It wouldn't be right.

MOTHER: I don't understand you. Don't you see, I'll never be going to parties again.

.  .  .  .  .  .  .  .  .  .  .  .  .  .  .

OFFICER: What will Papa say? He gave it to you. It was a gift.

MOTHER: Oh, what small minds!

.  .  .  .  .  .  .  .  .  .  .  .  .  .  .

FATHER: (*sticking his head in*) Don't tell me you're going to lend my present to a scrubwoman?

MOTHER: Don't say that. . . . I was once a maid, too—remem-  230 ber? . . . Why do you have to hurt the feelings of an innocent girl?

FATHER: Why hurt *my* feelings? I'm your husband.

MOTHER: Oh, I give up! If you're nice to somebody, you're mean to someone else. Help one, hurt another. What a life!

(*She trims and crops the candle until it dies. The stage grows dark, and the partition is drawn back in and conceals the scene.*)

.  .  .  .  .  .  .  .  .  .  .  .  .  .  .

DAUGHTER: Yes, what a life. Poor souls, I feel sorry for them.

OFFICER: Do you really?

DAUGHTER: Yes, life is hard. But love—love conquers everything. You'll see! Come.

(*They move toward the rear of the stage.*)

[III]

*The backdrop is drawn up, and a new backdrop is seen, representing a dirty, brick or stone, peeling party wall. In the middle of the wall is a gate opening onto an alleyway that leads out to a bright green area, in the center of which stands a colossal plant—a blue monkshood (Aconitum). The gate functions as a stage door entrance and to the left of it sits the Stage-Door Keeper—a woman wearing a shawl over her head and shoulders. She is working on a huge bedspread with a pattern of stars. To the right is a billboard, and the Billposter is washing it. Leaning against the wall next to him is a dip net with a green handle. Farther to the right is a door with an air hole in the shape of a cloverleaf. Left of the gate stands a small linden tree with a pitch-black trunk and a few pale green leaves. Next to it is a small, round, cellar window.*

DAUGHTER: (*approaching the Stage-Door Keeper*) Haven't you  240 finished that star quilt yet?

STAGE-DOOR KEEPER: Of course not, deary! Twenty-six years is no time at all for a job as big as this.

DAUGHTER: Your fiancé never came back?

STAGE-DOOR KEEPER: No. Wasn't his fault, my dear girl. He *had* to leave, *had* to . . . the poor man. Thirty years it's been.

DAUGHTER: *(to the Billposter)* She was with the ballet, wasn't she? Here in the opera house?

250  BILLPOSTER: She was prima ballerina. But when *he* up and left *her,* he took all her dances with him, you might say. . . . She never got any parts after that . . .

DAUGHTER: All they do is complain. At least with their eyes—and their tone of voice . . .

BILLPOSTER: Oh, I don't. Not like I used to—not since I got my dip net and my green fish pot.

DAUGHTER: That makes you happy?

BILLPOSTER: Yes. So happy, I—I—. It was what I dreamed of when I was a boy, and now it's come true. Of course, I'm fifty years old, but—

260  DAUGHTER: Fifty years for a dip net and a fish pot . . .

BILLPOSTER: Not any fish pot! A *green* one. Green! . . .

. . . . . . . . . . . . . . . . . . . . .

DAUGHTER: *(to the Stage-Door Keeper)* Let me have the shawl. I'll sit here for a while and watch the passing parade. You stand behind me and let me know what's going on. *(She puts on the shawl and sits down at the gate.)*

STAGE-DOOR KEEPER: This is the last day of the opera before it's closed for the season. This is when they find out if they got renewed for next year.

270  DAUGHTER: And those who don't get a place—what about them?

STAGE-DOOR KEEPER: God, I can't bear to see them! I have to cover my face with the shawl, I really do.

DAUGHTER: Those poor people. How awful.

STAGE-DOOR KEEPER: Look, there's one of the girls coming now! . . . She's not one of the lucky ones. Look at her cry.

. . . . . . . . . . . . . . . . . . . . .

*(A Singer enters from the right and hurries through the gate. She is holding her handkerchief to her eyes. She stands for a moment in the passageway outside the gate, and leans her head against the wall. Then rushes out.)*

DAUGHTER: Poor souls, I feel so sorry for them.

. . . . . . . . . . . . . . . . . . . . .

STAGE-DOOR KEEPER: Ah, but look at him! Want to see a really happy man? There he is!

. . . . . . . . . . . . . . . . . . . . .

*(The Officer comes down the alleyway and through the gate. He is wearing a high hat and tails and carrying a bouquet of roses. He is beaming with happiness.)*

STAGE-DOOR KEEPER: He's going to marry Miss Victoria!

280  OFFICER: *(coming downstage, looks upward, and sings out)* Victoria!

STAGE-DOOR KEEPER: Miss Victoria will be down in just a moment.

OFFICER: Good, good! The carriage is waiting, the table is spread, the champagne's on ice—oh, let me kiss you, ladies! *(He embraces the Daughter and the Stage-Door Keeper. Sings out.)* Victoria!

A WOMAN'S VOICE: *(from above, singing out liltingly)* Here I am!

OFFICER: *(beginning to wander up and down)* All right, I'll be 290 waiting!

. . . . . . . . . . . . . . . . . . . . .

DAUGHTER: Don't you recognize me?

OFFICER: No, for me there's only one woman in the whole world—Victoria! —For seven years I've walked up and down here, waiting for her. In the morning when the sun reached the chimney tops, and in the evening as night began to fall. . . . Look here in the asphalt; you can see the path worn by true love. Hurrah, hurrah! She's mine, she's all mine! *(Calls out.)* Victoria!

*(No answer.)*

Hm, I guess she must be getting dressed. . . . *(To the Bill-* 300 *poster.)* I see you've got a dip net. Everybody at the opera is crazy about dip nets—or should I say, about fish. You know why? No voices, that's why. No competition. —How much does a thing like that cost?

BILLPOSTER: Pretty expensive.

OFFICER: *(singing out)* Victoria! . . . *(Shakes the linden tree.)* It's blooming again! Look! For the eighth time. . . . *(Singing out.)* Victoria! . . . Now she's combing her bangs. . . . *(To the Daughter.)* Oh, come on now, my good woman, let me go up and fetch my bride!     310

STAGE-DOOR KEEPER: Sorry, no one's allowed backstage.

OFFICER: Seven years I've been walking and waiting! Seven years! Seven times three hundred and sixty-five makes two thousand five hundred and fifty-five. *(Stops and pokes with his cane at the door with the cloverleaf air hole.)* And I've looked at this door two thousand five hundred and fifty-five times without ever finding out where it leads to. And that cloverleaf hole to let in light—who's in there who needs to have light? Is there anyone in there? Someone live there?

STAGE-DOOR KEEPER: I don't know. I've never seen anyone 320 open that door.

OFFICER: It looks like a door to a pantry I saw when I was four years old and nanny took me out one Sunday afternoon to visit her friends. Out—other families, other maids—but I never got farther than the kitchen—had to sit there and wait between the water barrel and the salt tub—I've seen so many kitchens in my time—and the pantry was always out next to the porch—with round holes bored through it and a cloverleaf. . . . But an opera house can't have a pantry—there's no kitchen! *(Singing out.)* Victoria! . . . Say, she 330 couldn't possibly leave the theater by some other door, could she?

STAGE-DOOR KEEPER: Oh, no, dearie, there's no other way out.

OFFICER: Good, then I can't miss her!

*(The Actors and Dancers come pouring out. The Officer looks them all over.)*

. . . . . . . . . . . . . . . . . . . . .

OFFICER: She's got to come along pretty soon. . . . Madame—that blue flower out there—that monkshood. I remember it from the time I was a child. Can't be the same one, can it? . . . It was at the parsonage, I remember, the minister's house—the garden. I was seven years old. . . . Fold back the top petals—the pistil and stamen look like two doves. We 340

used to do that as children. . . . But this time a bee came—
went into the flower. "Got you!" I said. And I pinched the
flower together. And the bee stung me . . . And I cried . . .
Then the minister's wife came and put mud on my
finger. . . . Later we had strawberries and cream for dessert
at supper. . . . I do believe it's getting dark already. —Where
are you off to?

BILLPOSTER: Home. Time for my supper.

OFFICER: *(rubbing his eyes)* Supper?! At this time of day? —
350  Say, wait a minute! Do you mind if I make a phone call to
"the growing castle"? Take just a minute.

DAUGHTER: Why, what do you have to do?

OFFICER: I have to tell the glazier to put in the storm windows.
Winter's almost here, and I'm freezing to death. *(He goes
into the Stage-Door Keeper's office.)*

· · · · · · · · · · · · · · · ·

DAUGHTER: Who is this Victoria he keeps calling for?

STAGE-DOOR KEEPER: His sweetheart. The dearest person in
the world to him.

DAUGHTER: I understand. What she may be to us or to anyone
360  else doesn't concern him at all. Whatever he sees in her,
that's what she really is.

*(It grows dark very suddenly.)*

STAGE-DOOR KEEPER: *(lights a lamp)* It's getting dark so early
today.

DAUGHTER: For the gods in heaven a year is only a minute.

STAGE-DOOR KEEPER: And for us here on earth a minute can
seem like a year . . .

· · · · · · · · · · · · · · · ·

*(The Officer returns. He looks rather dusty and dirty. The
roses have withered.)*

OFFICER: Hasn't she come down yet?

STAGE-DOOR KEEPER: No.

OFFICER: She will, she will. I know *she'll* come! *(Walks up and
370  down.)* But it's true, the sensible thing for me to do, I suppose, is to cancel the dinner reservation anyway—since it's
already nighttime. . . . Yes—yes, that's what I'll do. *(Goes in
to telephone.)*

· · · · · · · · · · · · · · · ·

STAGE-DOOR KEEPER: *(to the Daughter)* I guess I'd better take
my shawl back now.

DAUGHTER: No, no this is your time off. I'll do your work for
you. . . . I want to learn all about people and this life on
earth—I want to find out if it is as hard as they say it is.

STAGE-DOOR KEEPER: You know you can't sleep at this post,
380  don't you? Can't ever sleep—neither day nor night.

DAUGHTER: Not sleep at night?

STAGE-DOOR KEEPER: Well, you can try—with a string from the
doorbell tied to your arm. You see, they've got watchmen on
duty backstage, and they spell each other every three hours.

DAUGHTER: Forced to stay awake—sounds like torture!

STAGE-DOOR KEEPER: You think so? I know a lot of people who
would be glad to have my job. You don't know how they
envy me!

DAUGHTER: Envy you! Envy someone who's being tortured?

390  STAGE-DOOR KEEPER: Well, they do. . . . Darling, I haven't told

you the worst part. The worst part isn't slaving all day and
staying awake all night, or sitting in the draft, getting cold
and damp—it's to have to listen, like I have to, to all their
sad stories. All the actors, all the dancers, they all come to
me and pour their hearts out. Why do they come to me? I
guess it's these wrinkles. What I've suffered is scrawled
all over my face, and that's what makes them confide in
me. . . . In this shawl, dearie, there's thirty years of suffering,
my own and others', all tucked away.

DAUGHTER: It's so heavy—and it stings like nettles . . .         400

STAGE-DOOR KEEPER: Wear it if you want to, dearie. If it gets
too heavy, give a call, and I'll come and relieve you.

DAUGHTER: You run along. If you can bear it, I certainly should
be able to.

STAGE-DOOR KEEPER: You be kind to my friends now. Don't let
their complaining get you down. *(She disappears down the
passageway.)*

*(Complete blackout while the scene changes. The linden tree is
stripped bare of all its leaves. The monkshood is virtually dead
and withered. And when it grows light again, the green patch
seen through the perspective of the alleyway has turned
autumn-brown.)*

*(The Officer enters when the lights come up. Now his hair and
beard are gray. His clothes are shabby and threadbare. His de-
tachable shirt collar is badly soiled and limp as a rag. The roses
have fallen from his bouquet so that nothing is left but a bunch
of twigs. He wanders up and down.)*

OFFICER: No doubt about it. Everything points to the fact that
summer is over and autumn is on its way. I can tell from the
linden tree—and the monkshood. *(Wanders up and down.)*  410
So what! Autumn is spring for me! That's when the theater
opens again. And then she's got to come! —My dear lady,
would you mind if I sat down on that chair a few minutes?

DAUGHTER: No, of course not. I can stand for a while.

OFFICER: *(sitting down)* If I could grab forty winks, I'd feel better. . . . *(He falls asleep for a moment, then wakes up with a
start and begins to pace up and down. Stops in front of the
cloverleaf door and pokes at it.)* That door . . . can't get it out
of my mind. . . . What's behind it? There's got to be something behind it.                                                           420

*(From above one can hear the soft strains of ballet music.)*

Ah ha! The rehearsals have begun!

*(The stage is lit up in flashes as if by the revolving lamp in a
lighthouse.)*

What's going on? *(In time with the flashes.)* Light and
dark—light and dark!

DAUGHTER: Day and night—day and night! . . . A merciful
providence wants to shorten the time you have to wait. The
days are flying by, chasing the nights.

*(The flashes die away, and the light becomes constant. The
Billposter enters with his dip net and his paste bucket, paste
brush, and the rest of his equipment.)*

OFFICER: The billposter, with his net. —Make a good catch?

BILLPOSTER: Sure did! It was a hot summer and it dragged on
a bit. . . . The net was all right, I guess, but it wasn't exactly

430     what I'd imagined.

OFFICER: *(stressing the words)* "Not exactly what I'd imagined." Perfectly put! Nothing is as I imagined it to be. You see, the thought is greater than the deed, finer than the thing itself . . . *(Paces up and down and slaps the rose bouquet against the wall so that the last few petals fall off.)*

BILLPOSTER: You mean to say she hasn't come down yet?

OFFICER: No, not yet. She's on her way, on her way. . . . Say, you don't happen to know what's behind that door, do you?

BILLPOSTER: No, can't say as I do. Never saw that door open.

440   OFFICER: Well, I think it's about time. I'm going to phone for a locksmith to come and open it. *(Goes in to telephone.)*

*(The Billposter pastes up a poster and moves out to the right.)*

DAUGHTER: What was the matter with the dip net?

BILLPOSTER: Matter? Nothing. There wasn't anything really the matter—it just wasn't exactly like I imagined it would be. So the pleasure wasn't all *that* great.

DAUGHTER: How had you imagined it would be?

BILLPOSTER: How had I—? Well, it's hard to say . . .

DAUGHTER: Let me say it. You had imagined it *different* from what it was. It was supposed to be green, but not *that* green!

450   BILLPOSTER: That's right. It just wasn't the same. You know what it's like, don't you? You really do—and that's why everybody comes to you with their troubles. . . . Maybe you'd listen to me too . . . sometime?

DAUGHTER: Of course I will. . . . Come in here and pour out your heart . . . *(She goes into the Stage-Door Keeper's cage.)*

*(The Billposter stands outside and talks to her through the window.)*

. . . . . . . . . . . . . . . . . . . . . .

*(Complete blackout again. When the lights come up, the linden tree is leafy, the monkshood is in full bloom, and the sun is shining on the green place at the end of the alleyway.)*

*(The Officer comes in. He is old and completely gray-haired. Clothes ragged and torn, shoes full of holes. Carries the bare twigs of what was once the bouquet of roses. Walks up and down—slowly, like an old man. He studies the poster.)*

. . . . . . . . . . . . . . . . . . . . . .

*(A Ballet Girl enters from the right.)*

OFFICER: Has Victoria left?

BALLET GIRL: No, she's still here.

OFFICER: Good, I'll wait. You think she'll be leaving soon?

BALLET GIRL: *(earnestly)* I'm sure she will.

460   OFFICER: Don't run off now or you won't get to see what's behind this door. I've sent for a locksmith.

BALLET GIRL: How exciting! I'd love to see that door opened. That door gets me—and that growing castle. —Do you know the growing castle?

OFFICER: Do I? Who do you think was imprisoned there?

BALLET GIRL: No! Was that you?! —Tell me, why did they have so many horses there?

OFFICER: Because they had all those stalls—why do you think?

BALLET GIRL: *(hurt; almost crying)* Oh, I'm so dumb! Why
470   didn't I think of that?

. . . . . . . . . . . . . . . . . . . . . .

*(A Singer from the Chorus enters from the right.)*

OFFICER: Has Miss Victoria left?

SINGER: *(earnestly)* Of course she hasn't left. She never leaves.

OFFICER: That's because she loves me!—Don't go away before the locksmith gets here. He's going to open this door.

SINGER: Really? The door's going to be opened? Hey, that's great! —Excuse me, I want to ask the doorkeeper something.

. . . . . . . . . . . . . . . . . . . . . .

*(The Prompter enters from the right.)*

OFFICER: Has Miss Victoria left?

PROMPTER: Not as far as I know.

OFFICER: You see! What did I tell you, didn't I say she was wait-   480
ing for me? —Don't go, don't go, the door's going to be opened.

PROMPTER: What door?

OFFICER: What door? Is there more than one door?

PROMPTER: Oh, that one! The door with the cloverleaf! Don't worry, of course I'll stay for that. —Just have to say a few words to the doorkeeper.

. . . . . . . . . . . . . . . . . . . . . .

*(The Ballet Girl, the Chorus Singer, and the Prompter group themselves beside the Billposter outside the window to the Stage-Door Keeper's cage, and they all take turns talking to the Daughter.)*

*(The Glazier enters through the gate.)*

OFFICER: Are you the locksmith?

GLAZIER: No, he couldn't come; he had company. I'm a glazier and I can handle it just as well.                                   490

OFFICER: Of course . . . of course. . . . But do you have your diamond with you?

GLAZIER: Naturally! A glazier without his diamond! What do you take me for?

OFFICER: Never mind, never mind. —All right, let us proceed! *(Claps his hands.)*

*(Everyone gathers in a circle around the door. Singers from the Chorus in "Die Meistersinger" and Ballet Dancers and Extras from "Aida," both groups in costume, pour onstage from the right.)*

. . . . . . . . . . . . . . . . . . . . . .

OFFICER: Locksmith—or glazier, or whatever you are: do your duty!

*(The Glazier comes forward with his diamond.)*

OFFICER: Moments like this recur very seldom in one's life, my good friends, and therefore I urge you strongly to—to—   500
consider carefully what—

. . . . . . . . . . . . . . . . . . . . . .

*(Policemen come forward.)*

POLICEMAN: In the name of the law I forbid the opening of this door!

OFFICER: Oh, my God, what a lot of fuss and feathers whenever you want to do something new and great! . . . All right, we'll take it to court! We'll get a lawyer. We'll see what the law has to say! They can't stop us! To the lawyer!

## [IV]

*In full view of the audience, the set is changed to the Lawyer's office in the following way. The gate remains standing but now functions as the gate in the office railing, which runs straight across the stage. The Stage-Door Keeper's office or cage remains as the Lawyer's small inner office with his desk, but the opening of the office now faces downstage. The linden tree, stripped of its leaves, serves as a hat tree. The billboard is now a bulletin board covered with government decrees and court decisions. The cloverleaf door now belongs to a filing cabinet.*

*The Lawyer, dressed in white tie and tails, is sitting at a high desk, completely covered with papers and documents, just to the left inside the gate. His appearance suggests he has experienced indescribable suffering in his life. His face is white as chalk and scarred with deep wrinkles, and the hollows of his face are filled with purple shadows.*

*He looks hideous, his face reflecting all the crimes and sins his profession has brought him in contact with.*

*He has two Clerks, one of whom has only one eye, the other only one arm.*

*The crowd that had gathered for the opening of the door remain in their places, but now they seem to be clients waiting to see the Lawyer, and they appear to have been standing there always.*

*The Daughter, wearing the shawl, and the Officer are far downstage.*

LAWYER: *(goes down to the Daughter)* Excuse me, Sister Agnes, but may I have that shawl? I'll hang it in my office
510    until I get a fire going in the stove. Then I'll burn it, and send all the sorrows it contains up in smoke.

DAUGHTER: Not just yet, Brother Axel. First I want to fill it to bursting. Above all, I want to gather up all your pains, all the confessions you've had to take to your heart, of crimes and vices, false arrests, libels, slanders . . .

LAWYER: My dear friend, your shawl wouldn't be nearly large enough. Look at these walls—black with the soot of sin. Look at these legal briefs: one miscarriage of justice after another. Look at *me!* No one comes to me with a smile on
520    his face. They glare at me, bare their teeth, shake their fists. They spew their venom at me, their malice, their envy, their suspicions. Look at my hands—black, and I can never wash them clean. Cracked and bleeding. My clothes have to be cleaned almost every day, they smell so of crime. Sometimes I fumigate the office with sulphur, but it doesn't help. I sleep on a couch in the next room, and all I dream about is crime. Right now I've got a murder case on my hands. That's all right; I can get through that. What's much worse—the worst of all—is divorce. A divorce case is like a cry from the
530    center of the earth, a shriek heard in heaven. Because it goes against nature itself, against the source of all good, against love. And what's the cause of it all? When both parties have filled reams of paper with mutual accusations and finally some dear soul grabs one of them, looks him—or

her—straight in the eye, and gently asks, "Come now, what have you really got against your husband—or wife?"—that person will stand there tongue-tied, unable to offer one good explanation. One time—yes, one time all the trouble started over a vegetable salad. Another time, a single wrong word. Most times, nothing at all. But the anguish, the pain! 540 It all falls on me. Look at my face! Look at me. No woman could love me; I look like the worst sort of criminal. Do you think anyone wants me as a friend? No; I'm the man who makes them pay up—either for their debts or their sins. I tell you it's a wretched business. Living, I mean.

DAUGHTER: Poor souls. I feel so sorry for them.

LAWYER: Well you might! What do they live on? They get married on an income of ten thousand a year when they know they need twenty thousand. They borrow, of course, everybody borrows. They scrimp and scrape—live on credit— 550 until the day they die. Who finally pays? Can you tell me that?

DAUGHTER: What of the birds of the air and the lilies of the field? Someone has his eye on them.

LAWYER: Yes. Perhaps He should take His eye off them, come down to earth and take a look at human beings. Then He might have pity for them.

DAUGHTER: Poor souls. I do feel sorry for them.

LAWYER: Who wouldn't? *(To the Officer.)* What can I do for you? 560

. . . . . . . . . . . .

OFFICER: I just wanted to find out if Miss Victoria has left.

LAWYER: No, she hasn't, I assure you. You can put your mind at ease about that. —Why are you poking at my filing cabinet?

OFFICER: This cloverleaf—it's just like—

LAWYER: Oh, no, no. Oh no.

*(Church bells begin to ring.)*

. . . . . . . . . . . .

OFFICER: Is there a funeral today?

LAWYER: No, commencement exercises at the university! I'm just about to receive my degree: Doctor of Laws. —Say, maybe you might like to come along, get a degree and wear 570 a mortarboard.

OFFICER: Yes, why not? Might help to break up the day a bit.

LAWYER: Excellent! Time to get ready to march in the procession. —Hurry and change your clothes!

## [V]

*The Officer exits. Blackout onstage while the following changes are made. The office railing remains standing, but it now serves as the railing to the choir in a cathedral. The bulletin board becomes a hymn board with numbers of the psalms to be sung. The linden tree/hat tree becomes a candelabrum. The Lawyer's high desk in its niche becomes the dais and lectern for the Dean conferring the degrees. The cloverleaf door now leads to the sacristy of the cathedral.*

*The Singers from "Die Meistersinger" become Heralds with staffs, and the Extras in "Aida" carry the laurel crowns that are to be given to the degree candidates. The rest of the company are spectators.*

*The backdrop is pulled up, and the new drop represents immensely high organ pipes; at bottom, the console and the organist's mirror.*

*Music is heard. The faculties of philosophy, theology, medicine, and law are grouped at the sides of the stage. The rest of the stage is empty for a moment.*

*The Heralds enter from the right. Following them come the Extras from "Aida," carrying the laurel crowns on their outstretched arms.*

*Three Doctoral Candidates enter one after the other from the left, are invested, crowned with laurel wreaths, and go out to the right.*

*The Lawyer comes forward to receive his laurel crown. The Extras turn their backs on him, refusing to give him one. They leave. The Lawyer, shattered, leans against a pillar. Everyone leaves. The Lawyer is left alone.*

. . . . . . . . . . . . . . . . . . .

*(The Daughter enters. She is wearing a white veil over her head and shoulders.)*

DAUGHTER: Do you see? I've washed the shawl. —Why are you standing here? Didn't you get the laurel crown?

LAWYER: No, I wasn't worthy of it.

DAUGHTER: Why on earth not? Because you spoke up for the poor, put in a good word for the criminal, lightened the bur-
580 den of the guilty, sought to pardon the condemned? . . . What wretched people! They're not angels, are they? Still, I feel sorry for them.

LAWYER: Don't say anything bad about human beings. I'm going to take their case.

DAUGHTER: *(leaning against the organ)* Why do they spit in the face of anyone who tries to help them?

LAWYER: Because they don't know any better.

DAUGHTER: Can't we teach them? Will you help? You and I together!

590 LAWYER: They don't want to be taught. . . . Oh, if only our grievances could be heard by the gods in heaven—!

DAUGHTER: They shall be heard, they shall reach the highest throne! *(Standing before the organ.)* Do you know what I see in that mirror? —The world—right way round. Because in reality it's backwards.

LAWYER: How did it get turned around?

DAUGHTER: When the copy was made—

LAWYER: How right you are! A copy . . . I'd always suspected it was a bad copy. And when I began to recollect the original
600 image, everything was a disappointment to me. People said I did nothing but complain and that I had bits of the devil's mirror in my eyes°—and so on . . .

DAUGHTER: It's a mad world. Just look at the four faculties of the university. The conservative government pays the salaries of all four of them. Theology, the study of God, which is always being attacked and ridiculed by philosophy, which sets itself up to be the essence of wisdom. And medicine, which is always challenging philosophy and dismissing

religion from the learned disciplines and calling it superstition. And yet they all sit together on the University Council 610 which is supposed to teach the youth of the land respect—for the university. It's a madhouse. Heaven help him who first comes to his senses.

LAWYER: The first ones to do so are the theologians. As undergraduates they study philosophy, which teaches them that theology is nonsense. Then they go on to study theology, where they learn that philosophy is nonsense. Fools, aren't they?

DAUGHTER: And the law! Serving everyone—everyone who can afford to have servants! 620

LAWYER: And the poor judges!—when they try to execute justice, they end up executing people. Justice—so often unjust.

DAUGHTER: What a mess you children of God have made of your earthly lives. Children, little children! . . . Come here. I shall give you a crown—one that becomes you better. *(She places a crown of thorns on his head.)* And I shall play for you! *(She seats herself at the organ and plays a Kyrie. But instead of organ notes human voices well up.)*

VOICES OF CHILDREN: Lord Almighty! Lord Almighty! *(The last note is held.)* 630

VOICES OF WOMEN: Have mercy on us! *(The last note is held.)*

VOICES OF MEN: Show us thy mercy and deliver us! *(The last note is held.)*

VOICES OF MEN: *(basses)* Spare us, oh Lord! Be not angry with your children.

. . . . . . . . . . . . . . . . . . .

EVERYONE: Have mercy on us! Listen to our voices! Pity us mortals! . . . Oh, Almighty One, why art thou so far away? . . . From the depths we call to you: mercy, oh Almighty One! Lay not too heavy a burden on thy children! Hear our voices! Hear! 640

[VI]

*The stage grows dark. The Daughter rises and approaches the Lawyer. By means of lighting, the organ is transformed into Fingal's Cave. The waves of the sea wash in under the basalt pillars, producing a choir of wind and waves.*

LAWYER: Where are we, Agnes?

DAUGHTER: Don't you hear—?

LAWYER: I hear . . . drops . . . falling.

DAUGHTER: Those are tears. . . . People are crying. What else do you hear?

LAWYER: Sighing . . . wailing . . . moaning . . .

DAUGHTER: The complaints of mortals. They reach this far and no farther. Why are they always complaining? Are there no joys in life at all?

LAWYER: Yes, yes! The sweetest thing in life. And the most bit- 650 ter! Love. A wife and a home. The best of life and the worst.

DAUGHTER: I want to know it. I want to know everything, try everything.

LAWYER: With me?

DAUGHTER: With you. You know where the dangerous corners

---

° See H. C. Andersen's fairy tale *The Snow Queen.*

are, the stumbling blocks. We can avoid them.

LAWYER: I'm a poor man. Haven't a penny.

DAUGHTER: What does that matter, as long as we have each other? A little joy and beauty doesn't cost anything.

660 LAWYER: What if we don't like the same things? You like what I dislike?

DAUGHTER: We'll have to learn to get along with each other.

LAWYER: Suppose we get bored with each other?

DAUGHTER: A baby will come. We'll be too busy to be bored.

LAWYER: You really want to marry me? Me—a poor and ugly man, cast out, despised by all?

DAUGHTER: Yes. Let us unite our destinies.

LAWYER: If you wish. So be it.


[VII]

*A very plain and simple room adjacent to the Lawyer's office. To the right, a large four-poster double bed with tester and hangings. A window near it. To the left, a kitchen stove with pots and pans on it. Christine is busy sealing up the inner window of the double window, using strips of paper as weather stripping. In the rear the door to the office stands open; through it can be seen a group of poor clients waiting to see the Lawyer.*

CHRISTINE: I'm pasting and sealing. I'm pasting and sealing!

670 DAUGHTER: (*pale and haggard, is sitting at the stove*) You're shutting out all the air. I'm suffocating.

CHRISTINE: Just one little crack left.

DAUGHTER: I've got to have air! Air! I can't breathe.

CHRISTINE: I'm pasting and sealing. I'm pasting and sealing!

LAWYER: That's right, Christine. You're doing fine. Heat's expensive.

DAUGHTER: Oh, I feel as if you were sealing up my mouth.

LAWYER: (*standing in the doorway to his office with papers in his hand*) Is the baby asleep?

680 DAUGHTER: Yes—finally!

LAWYER: (*gently*) I'm sorry. It's just that his bawling frightens away my clients.

DAUGHTER: (*without harshness*) I don't know what we can do about it, do you?

LAWYER: Nothing.

DAUGHTER: We'll have to get a larger apartment.

LAWYER: With what?

DAUGHTER: Do you mind if I open the window? This stale air is suffocating me.

690 LAWYER: You'll let all the heat out. You want to sit here and freeze to death?

DAUGHTER: I don't know. It's awful. . . . Maybe at least we could scrub the floor out there?

LAWYER: You're not up to scrubbing any floors now. I'm not either. And Christine's got to go on pasting. She's got to seal up the whole house—every crack—in the ceiling, in the floor, in the walls.

DAUGHTER: I expected to be poor, but I didn't expect to be dirty.

700 LAWYER: The poor are always relatively dirty.

DAUGHTER: It's worse than I ever dreamed it could be.

LAWYER: We don't have it the worst. There's still food in the pot.

DAUGHTER: Do you call that food?

LAWYER: What's wrong with cabbage? It's cheap—nourishing—tastes good—

DAUGHTER: —If you happen to like cabbage! It makes me sick.

LAWYER: Well, why didn't you say so?

DAUGHTER: Because I want you to be happy. I don't mind giving up something I like for you. 710

LAWYER: All right, then I have to give up something I like: cabbage. The sacrifices have to be mutual.

DAUGHTER: Then what will we eat? Fish? You hate fish.

LAWYER: It is also expensive.

DAUGHTER: I never imagined it would be like this.

LAWYER: (*making a joke of it*) You don't have to imagine any longer—you can see for yourself. . . . What about the baby? It was supposed to be a blessing. It's going to be the death of us.

DAUGHTER: Darling . . . dearest. . . . I'll die in this air, in this 720 room, with nothing to look at but a backyard—with the baby crying for hours on end and never a moment's sleep—with all those people out there, always complaining, quarreling, accusing one another. I can't stand it any longer. I'll die in here.

LAWYER: My poor beautiful flower—without sun, without air . . .

DAUGHTER: And you say some people have got it even worse!

LAWYER: In this part of town I'm envied.

DAUGHTER: I think I could stand anything, if only I could have 730 some beauty in my home.

LAWYER: I know, I know. A flower—a heliotrope—that's what you want! But it costs as much as six quarts of milk or half a bushel of potatoes.

DAUGHTER: I wouldn't mind starving if I could have flowers to look at.

LAWYER: Well, now that you mention it, there is one kind of beauty that doesn't cost anything. And a man with a sense of beauty misses it more than anything else when he can't find it in his home. 740

DAUGHTER: What's that?

LAWYER: No, you'll get mad.

DAUGHTER: No, I won't! We've agreed not to get mad.

LAWYER: So we have. We can say whatever's on our minds—as long as we don't snap at each other. So far we haven't.

DAUGHTER: And never will.

LAWYER: Never, as far as I'm concerned.

DAUGHTER: All right, now tell me what you were going to say.

LAWYER: All right. When I come into somebody's house, the first thing I look at is the curtains, to see if they're hanging 750 straight. (*He goes over to the window and straightens the curtain.*) If they hang like strings or old rags, I leave—right away. The next thing I look at is the chairs. If they're grouped properly, I stay. (*He adjusts the position of a chair against the wall.*) And then I look at the candles in the candlesticks. If they're crooked, it's a sign the whole house needs straightening. (*He straightens a candle on the chest of drawers.*) There, you see! Now that, my friend, is the kind of beauty that doesn't cost a cent!

DAUGHTER: (*lowering her head to her bosom*) You're being 760 snappish!

LAWYER: I am not being snappish!

DAUGHTER: Yes, you are!

LAWYER: Oh, for Christ's sake—!!

DAUGHTER: You see?! Listen to you!

LAWYER: I'm sorry, Agnes . . . but I've suffered just as much from your untidiness as you have from the dirt. And I haven't dared to tidy up things myself, because then you'd think I was reproaching you and you'd get mad. —Oh, 770 what's the use! We'll stop right now. Not a word more. All right?

DAUGHTER: It's awfully hard to be married. It's the hardest thing of all. I guess you have to be an angel.

LAWYER: I guess so.

DAUGHTER: I think I'll begin to hate you after this.

LAWYER: Heaven help us! . . . I tell you what: let's forestall the hate before it comes! I promise I'll never make any more remarks about your housekeeping . . . although it is sheer torture to me.

780 DAUGHTER: And I'll eat cabbage—although it makes me sick.

LAWYER: Fine! We'll live together and make each other sick. Your pleasure—my pain; and vice versa.

DAUGHTER: We poor souls. I feel sorry for us.

LAWYER: You've come to realize that, have you?

DAUGHTER: Yes. But in the name of God, let's avoid the dangerous corners, since we know exactly where they are.

LAWYER: Let's! After all, we're humane, reasonable, enlightened people. We should be able to make allowances, forget and forgive—

790 DAUGHTER: —Laugh at the small things—

LAWYER: That's right. If anyone can, we can! . . . You know, I read in *The Times* this morning that—by the way, where is the paper?

DAUGHTER: (abashed) Which paper?

LAWYER: (snappishly) Do I get more than one?

DAUGHTER: Smile! And don't bark at me. —I used the paper to start the fire.

LAWYER: (sharply) Oh, for Christ's sake!

DAUGHTER: Come on now, smile. —I hate that paper. It makes 800 fun of everything that I love and respect.

LAWYER: And that I hate and detest! —Ohhh! (Throws up his arms, unable to contain himself.) All right, I'll smile. Grin and bear it. I'll be humane, reasonable, and keep my opinions to myself, and say yes to everything, and be sneaky and hypocritical! . . . So you burned up my paper. . . . How about that! . . . (He adjusts the bed hangings.) Look at me! Here I am tidying up again and making you mad. . . . Agnes, the whole thing's impossible.

DAUGHTER: It certainly is.

810 LAWYER: But we still have to go on with it. Not because of the promises we swore to each other, but because of the child.

DAUGHTER: That's true. For the sake of the child. (Sighing deeply.) We have to go on with it . . .

LAWYER: And I've got to go to work. My clients are waiting for me. Listen to them. Growling with impatience to get at one another's throats, tear each other to pieces, force each other to pay penalties and go to jail. . . . Cursed creatures . . .

DAUGHTER: Poor, wretched people. . . . And this pasting, pasting . . . (She bows her head in silent despair.)

820 CHRISTINE: I'm pasting and sealing! I'm pasting and sealing!

*(The Lawyer stands at the door, nervously twisting the doorknob.)*

DAUGHTER: Oh, how that doorknob squeals. It's as if you were squeezing my heart . . .

LAWYER: I squeeze, I squeeze . . .

DAUGHTER: Don't! Don't!

LAWYER: I squee-ee-ze . . .

DAUGHTER: No, no!

LAWYER: I—

. . . . . . . . . . . . . . . . . . . . . . .

OFFICER: (from inside the office, grabbing the doorknob from the other side) May I come in?

LAWYER: (letting go of the doorknob) Help yourself! You're a 830 big shot! You've got your doctor's degree!

OFFICER: That's right. The world is at my feet. I can go where I want, do what I want. I've climbed Parnassus, won the laurel crown. Honor, fame, immortality, it's all mine!

LAWYER: And what are you going to live on?

OFFICER: Live on?

LAWYER: Yes. Clothing, housing, food?

OFFICER: Oh, you can always make out, as long as there is someone who loves you and wants you to be happy.

LAWYER: Oh, sure! Sure! . . . Paste away, Christine! Paste until 840 they suffocate! (He is moving out backward, nodding his head.)

CHRISTINE: I'm pasting and sealing. I'm pasting and sealing! Until they suffocate!

. . . . . . . . . . . . . . . . . . . . . . .

OFFICER: Well, are you coming along?

DAUGHTER: Right away! Where are we going?

OFFICER: To Fair Haven! It's summer there, the sun is shining. There's youth and happiness, children and flowers, singing and dancing, picnics and parties!

DAUGHTER: That's where I want to go!                                      850

OFFICER: Well, come on!

. . . . . . . . . . . . . . . . . . . . . . .

LAWYER: (reenters) Now I shall go back to my first hell. This here was the second hell—and the greatest. The most beautiful was the greatest hell of all. . . . Look, she's been dropping hairpins on the floor again . . . (He is picking them off the floor.)

OFFICER: Good Lord! He's found out about the hairpins too.

LAWYER: Too? Of course! There are two prongs, but one hairpin. Two making one. If I straighten it out, it's one single piece. If I bend it, it's two, without ceasing to be one. This 860 means the two are one. But if I break one off—like this— then the two are two. (He breaks the hairpin and throws away the pieces.)

OFFICER: Marvelous! He's understood the whole thing! —But before you can break it, the prongs must diverge. If they converge, they stay together.

LAWYER: And if they're parallel, they never meet. It neither breaks nor holds.

OFFICER: The hairpin is absolutely the most nearly perfect of all created things. A straight line that is the same as two par- 870 allel lines!

LAWYER: A lock that holds when it's open.

OFFICER: Holds a free band of hair that remains free when

it closes.

LAWYER: Like this door! When I close it, I open the way—for you, Agnes! (*He withdraws and closes the door.*)

. . . . . . . . . . . . . . . . .

DAUGHTER: And now what?

[VIII]

*Scene change. The four-poster with its tester and hangings is transformed into a tent. The stove remains where it was. The backdrop is drawn up. In the foreground to the right are charred hills covered with the red brush and black and white tree stumps remaining after a forest fire; also red pigsties and privies. At the foot of this is an open-air gymnasium for invalids and convalescents where the patients exercise on mechanical contraptions and machines that resemble instruments of torture. To the left in the foreground are some of the open sheds of the quarantine station, housing the boilers, piping systems, and furnaces used in the disinfecting processes. Beyond the foreground is a strait of water. The backdrop represents a beautiful wooded shore lined with docks decorated with flags. White boats, some with sails hoisted, others not, are moored alongside. Between the trees one can catch glimpses of small Italian-style villas, with pavilions, belvederes, and marble statues.*

*Dressed up like a Moor, the Medical Inspector of the quarantine station is walking along the shore. The Officer goes over and shakes his hand.*

OFFICER: Well, I'll be darned, if it isn't old Gabby himself! So this is where you disappeared to!

880  MEDICAL INSPECTOR: That's right. Here I am!

OFFICER: Is this Fair Haven or isn't it?

MEDICAL INSPECTOR: No, Fair Haven is on the opposite shore. You're in Foul Strand.

OFFICER: Oops! We've come the wrong way.

MEDICAL INSPECTOR: We?—Ah, yes! Aren't you going to introduce me?

OFFICER: Can't. Just wouldn't do. (*Sotto voce.*) She's the daughter of Indra himself!

MEDICAL INSPECTOR: Indra? Don't you mean Varuna himself?

890  —Well, what do you say? Aren't you surprised my face is black?

OFFICER: Dear boy, I'm fifty years old. At that age nothing surprises you. I guessed right away that you were going to a masquerade tonight.

MEDICAL INSPECTOR: Right on the head! Why don't you come along? How about it?

OFFICER: Great idea! This place isn't—. Can't say it attracts me. . . . What sort of people live here, anyway?

MEDICAL INSPECTOR: The sick ones here, the healthy ones over

900  on the other side.

OFFICER: You mean these are all poor people here?

MEDICAL INSPECTOR: Don't be ridiculous! The rich ones here. Look at the fellow on the rack. He's eaten too much *pâté de foie gras*, and drunk so much Burgundy he's got knotted feet.

OFFICER: Knotted?

MEDICAL INSPECTOR: That's right; feet like knotted wood. . . . And that fellow over there lying on the guillotine—he's drunk so much cognac, we've got to straighten out his spine by putting him through the mangle.  910

OFFICER: Don't like the sound of that!

MEDICAL INSPECTOR: Fact is, on this side everyone's got some sort of problem he wants to hide. Look at the one who's coming now. A real dilly!

(*An elderly Dandy enters in a wheelchair, pushed by an Attendant. Accompanying him is a scrawny, ugly, sixty-year-old Coquette, dressed in the height of fashion. She in turn is accompanied by the "Friend," a man in his early forties.*)

OFFICER: Why, there's the Major himself! Went to school with us, didn't he?

MEDICAL INSPECTOR: Yes, that's him: Don Juan! Look at him— he's still in love with that skinny spook at his side. He can't see that she's grown old—that she's ugly, faithless, cruel!

OFFICER: That's real love for you. I never thought that old play-  920 boy could ever be so deeply in love, so seriously in love.

MEDICAL INSPECTOR: You do see the bright side of things, I must say.

OFFICER: Well, you see, I've been in love myself. Victoria. . . . Yes, yes, I'm still walking up and down in that corridor waiting for her.

MEDICAL INSPECTOR: Don't tell me you're the stage-door Johnny waiting in the corridor!

OFFICER: That's me.

MEDICAL INSPECTOR: Well, well. Have you got the door open  930 yet?

OFFICER: No, the case is still pending in the courts. The lawyers are fighting it out. . . . Trouble is that the billposter is out fishing with his net, as you might have known, so he's not available to give evidence . . . And in the meantime, the glazier has put the windowpanes in the castle, which has grown half a story. . . . It's really been a very good year this year. . . . Very warm and humid.

MEDICAL INSPECTOR: You don't know what heat is. I've got heat like nobody else!  940

OFFICER: How hot does it get in those ovens anyway?

MEDICAL INSPECTOR: When we're disinfecting cholera carriers, we get it up to one hundred forty degrees.

OFFICER: Not another cholera epidemic?

MEDICAL INSPECTOR: Yes, didn't you know?

OFFICER: Of course I knew. My trouble is I keep forgetting what I know.

MEDICAL INSPECTOR: I wish I could forget—at least forget myself. That's why I dress up, go to masquerades, Halloween parties, play charades.  950

OFFICER: What have you been up to anyway?

MEDICAL INSPECTOR: If I tell you, you'll say I'm bragging. If I don't, you'll call me a hypocrite.

OFFICER: I get it. That's why you painted your face black!

MEDICAL INSPECTOR: That's right. A little blacker than I really am!

OFFICER: Who's that coming this way?

MEDICAL INSPECTOR: That, my friend, is a real live poet. On his way to his mud bath.

(*The Poet comes in. He is walking with his eyes fixed on the heavens, and he is carrying a bucket of mud.)*

960 OFFICER: Mud? Damnation! He should be bathing himself in light and air!

MEDICAL INSPECTOR: Oh, no. He's got his head in the clouds so much of the time, he gets homesick for the mud. Wallowing in the mud makes his skin tough—same as with pigs. After that he doesn't feel the gadflies stinging.

OFFICER: What a strange world! All contradictions!

.  .  .  .  .  .  .  .  .  .  .  .  .  .  .  .  .  .  .  .

POET: *(ecstatically)* Out of clay the god Ptah created man on a potter's wheel, a turning lathe—*(Skeptically.)* or what the hell was it? *(Ecstatically.)* Out of clay the sculptor creates 970 his more or less imperishable masterpieces—*(Skeptically.)* or are they only junk? *(Ecstatically.)* Out of clay are created for the world's kitchens and pantries those indispensable vessels known under the generic name of pots, plates, and— *(Skeptically.)* actually, I really don't care what they're called. *(Ecstatically.)* I say to you: lo, here is clay! In its liquid state, it's called mud.—And that's where I come in. *(Calls out.)* Lina!

.  .  .  .  .  .  .  .  .  .  .  .  .  .  .  .  .  .  .  .

*(Lina enters with a bucket.)*

POET: Lina, come here and let Agnes have a look at you. She knew you ten years ago, when you were young, happy, 980 and—let's say—pretty. . . . Look at her now! Five kids—and a husband who beats her! Scrimping, slaving, starving! All her beauty faded, all her joy withered, while she was being a good mother and wife—which should have given her an inner satisfaction, a sense of fulfillment that should have found expression in a radiant smile on her face and the glow of contentment in her eyes—

MEDICAL INSPECTOR: *(puts his hand over the Poet's mouth)* Shut up, you fool! Shut up!

POET: That's what they all say! And if you shut up, they say, 990 "Speak out, man, speak out!" Crazy people. No rhyme or reason

.  .  .  .  .  .  .  .  .  .  .  .  .  .  .  .  .  .  .  .

DAUGHTER: *(moves over to Lina)* What's the matter? I want to know.

LINA: No, I don't dare. They'll punish me. Make things worse for me.

DAUGHTER: Who would be that cruel?

LINA: I don't dare tell you. They'll beat me!

POET: That's the truth! But I can talk—even if this big Moor here knocks my teeth out.—Let me tell you, Agnes, daugh-1000 ter of the gods, about injustice. Do you hear music and dancing up there on the hill? You know who that's for? That's for Lina's sister. She's just come home from the big city. When she was in the big city, she wasn't exactly a good girl, if you know what I mean. But now they've slaughtered the fatted calf for her. And Lina, who stayed at home, has to carry the buckets to feed the pigs!

DAUGHTER: Don't you see? They're happy because the girl was going astray and she found her way back, not because she's come home. What's wrong with that?

POET: Then why not give a party every night for the blameless 1010 working girl who never went dancing down the primrose path? Why not? Where's Lina's party? When she quits work, she has to go to a prayer meeting and be preached at for not being perfect. Is that fair?

DAUGHTER: I don't know. It's hard to say because—because there are always unforeseen circumstances.

POET: That's what the famous caliph realized, too: Harun al-Rashid, Harun the Just sat quietly on his throne, and from up there he could never see how the others had to live way down here. But finally some complaints floated up to his 1020 sublime ear. Then one fine day he climbed down from his throne, disguised himself, and took his place with the crowds in the street to learn all about justice in this world.

DAUGHTER: You surely don't take me for Harun the Just, do you?

OFFICER: Let's change the subject.—Look at the new arrivals.

*(Gliding into the strait from the left comes a white boat shaped like a dragon, with a pale blue, silken sail hoist on a golden arm and a rose-colored pennant flying from a golden masthead. Sitting at the helm with their arms around each other are He and She.)*

OFFICER: Now just look at that, will you? Look at that! There's real happiness, boundless bliss, the ecstasy of young love!

*(The stage grows bright.)*

.  .  .  .  .  .  .  .  .  .  .  .  .  .  .  .  .  .  .  .

HE: (stands up in the boat and sings)

> *Hail to thee, my beautiful bay,*     1030
> *Where in my green seasons*
> *I dreamed my golden dreams.*
> *I've come back to you,*
> *Not alone as I was then.*
> *Blue water, blue skies,*
> *Sparkling bays, shady bowers,*
> *Greet the girl of my dreams—*
> *My love, my bride,*
> *My sunshine, my life!*

*(The flags on the docks at Fair Haven dip in salute. White handkerchiefs can be seen waving from the villas and from the shore. An arpeggio of harps and violins ripples across the water.)*

POET: See how the world is lit up by love. Listen to the music 1040 ringing across the water!—Eros!

OFFICER: Why, that's Victoria!

MEDICAL INSPECTOR: Now you've had it!

OFFICER: That's *his* Victoria. I've got my own all to myself. And my Victoria—nobody can see her! She's mine! . . . All right, time to hoist the quarantine flag, and I'll haul in our catch.

*(The Medical Inspector waves a yellow flag. The Officer tugs on a line that makes the boat head in toward Foul Strand.)*

OFFICER: Put in! Put in! Come ashore! Come ashore!

*(He and She suddenly notice the hideous landscape and utter cries of fear and loathing.)*

MEDICAL INSPECTOR: Yes, I know, it's pretty tough on you,

but everyone who comes from infected places has got to
go through this station. You've got to be inspected and
fumigated.

POET: How can you talk that way, how can you act this way?!
They're two people deeply in love. Leave them alone. Let
the lovers be. Meddling with true love is a capital crime . . .
Why does everything beautiful have to be dragged down,
dragged through the mud?

*(Ashamed and downcast, He and She come ashore.)*

HE: What do you want with us? What have we done?

MEDICAL INSPECTOR: Who says you've done anything? You
needn't have done anything to have to suffer the little vexa-
tions of life.

SHE: Happiness never lasts.

HE: How long do we have to stay here?

MEDICAL INSPECTOR: Forty days and nights.

SHE: I'd rather end it all!

HE: Yes. Live here among charred hills and pigsties? Not a
chance!

POET: Wait! Love conquers everything—including sulphur
fumes and carbolic acid!

. . . . . . . . . . . . . . . .

MEDICAL INSPECTOR: *(lights the stove. Blue sulphur fumes rise
up)* I'm getting the sulphur going. Now, if you don't mind,
please step in.

SHE: But this blue dress will lose its color!

MEDICAL INSPECTOR: And turn white! And those red roses will
turn white!

HE: And your cheeks, too. Forty days! Forty nights!

SHE: *(to the Officer)* I hope you're satisfied! This is just what
you wanted!

OFFICER: No, not at all!—It's true that your happiness was the
source of my unhappiness, but—well, it doesn't matter anymore. I've got my degree from the university, and I've got a
very good position right across there. . . . Ho, ho, yes, yes,
I'm doing all right! . . . And this fall I'll be teaching in a
school. . . . Teaching class to the little boys, the same lessons
I read all the time I was a child . . . all my youth . . . And now
I'll have to read the same old assignments, the same old
lessons over and over again while I pass through middle
age. . . . And then through old age . . . the same old assignments. How much is two times two? How many times does
two go into four? . . . Until they retire me. . . . Nothing to do
but wait for the next meal and the morning paper and the
evening paper. . . . Until by and by I'm hauled out to the cre-
matory and burned to ashes. . . . Don't you have any retired
people out here? That's the worst thing, you know—after
two times two is four—to start in grade school again after
you've been through the university—to ask the same questions over and over again until you die . . .

*(A Middle-aged Man walks by with his hands clasped behind
his back.)*

There goes a retired man, living on his pension, and waiting
for his life to trickle out. Probably an army captain who
never got to be major. Or a CPA who never quite made it to
office manager. Many are called but few are chosen. . . .
Walking and waiting for his breakfast—

MIDDLE-AGED MAN: No! For my paper. My morning paper!

OFFICER: And he's only fifty-four. He can go on for another
twenty years like that, waiting for his meals and his papers.
. . . It's enough to make you sick.

MIDDLE-AGED MAN: What is there in life that doesn't make you
sick? Tell me that, will you? Tell me that.

OFFICER: I wish someone could. . . . Now I've got to go and
study with little boys—two times two is four—how many
times does two go into four? *(He grabs his head in desperation.)*—Oh, Victoria, Victoria! I loved her and wanted her to
be the happiest girl in the world. Now she is happy, as happy
as she can be. And that makes my heart ache—ache—ache!

. . . . . . . . . . . . . . . .

SHE: Do you really think I can be happy when I see how you
suffer? How can you think that? Maybe your heart won't
ache so much when you see me sitting here like a prisoner
for forty days and nights? Maybe you won't suffer so much?

OFFICER: Maybe yes, maybe no. It can't make me happy to see
you suffer. Ohhh . . .

HE: How do you think I feel? How can I build a happy life out
of your agony?

OFFICER: We are poor lost souls—all of us!

EVERYONE: *(stretching their arms toward heaven and giving
out a cry or shriek like a dissonant chord)* Ohhhh—!

DAUGHTER: Almighty One, listen to them! Life is cruel! Poor
lost souls! Take pity on them!

EVERYONE: *(as before)* Ohhh—!

[IX]

*Blackout for a moment while all those onstage either leave or
change places. When the lights come up again the shoreline of
Foul Strand is in the back and lying in shadow. The strait lies
between it and Fair Haven, which is now in the foreground.
Both Fair Haven and the strait are brightly lit. To the right,
one corner of a ballroom, its windows wide open, can be seen.
Couples are dancing within. Standing on an empty box outside
the ballroom are three Young Girls, holding one another
around the waist and looking in at the dance. On the terrace
steps to the casino is a bench on which Ugly Edith is sitting,
bareheaded, melancholy-looking, with her hair like a wild
mop. In front of her is a grand piano with its lid raised. To the
left, a yellow frame house. Outside it two Children, in summer
clothes, are playing catch.*

*Back of the foreground is a pier with white boats tied up and
with flags flying from flagpoles. Lying at anchor out in the
strait is a white ship of war, square-rigged, gunports open.*

*But the landscape as a whole suggests winter, with snow on the
ground and on the bare trees.*

*The Daughter and the Officer enter.*

DAUGHTER: How wonderful! This is vacation land! Everybody's resting and happy! No work for anybody—parties
every day—everybody's dressed in their finest clothes—
music and dancing even before lunch! *(To the three Young
Girls.)* Why aren't you girls in there dancing?

YOUNG GIRLS: Us?

OFFICER: Don't you see they're chambermaids?

DAUGHTER: Oh, of course! . . . But why is Edith sitting out here? Why isn't she dancing?

(*Edith hides her face in her hands.*)

OFFICER: Don't embarrass her! She's been sitting there for three hours and nobody's asked her to dance. (*He goes into the yellow house at the left.*)

1140 DAUGHTER: What a cruel game!

. . . . . . . . . . . . . . . . . . . . . .

MOTHER: (*in a low-cut dress, comes out and goes over to Edith*) What are you doing out here? Why don't you go in and dance like I told you?

EDITH: Please, Mother! . . . I can't be forward like the other girls, I can't. I know I'm ugly, I know that no one wants to dance with me. Why do you have to remind me of it all the time? (*She begins to play on the piano Johann Sebastian Bach's "Toccata con Fuga," in D Minor, BWV 913.*)

(*From within the ballroom the waltz can be heard softly at first, then growing louder, as if it were competing with Bach's Toccata. But Edith outplays it, and reduces the waltz to silence. The guests at the ball can be seen in the doorway listening to her play. Everyone on the stage stands entranced by her playing.*)

(*Then a Navy Lieutenant grabs Alice, one of the guests at the ball, around the waist, and rushes off with her down to the pier.*)

NAVY LIEUTENANT: Come on, let's get out of here!

(*Edith breaks off playing, rises and follows them with her eyes, her face registering her heartache. She remains standing as if turned to stone.*)

. . . . . . . . . . . . . . . . . . . . . .

(*Now a wall of the yellow frame house is lifted away and we see the interior of a small schoolhouse and three benches with small boys sitting on them. Among them is the Officer, looking troubled and ill at ease. Standing in front of them is the Teacher, wearing glasses, a piece of chalk in one hand and a ruler in the other. He handles the ruler as if threatening punishment.*)

1150 TEACHER: (*to the Officer*) Now, boy, tell me: how much is two times two?

(*The Officer remains sitting. Searches desperately for the answer.*)

TEACHER: Stand up when I ask you a question!

OFFICER: (*in torment, gets to his feet*) Two . . . times two . . . is—let me see now, it's . . . it's two—two!

TEACHER: I see. I see. You haven't learned your lesson.

OFFICER: (*ashamed*) Yes, I have, it's just that . . . well, I know how to do it, but I—I just can't tell you.

TEACHER: Don't try to wiggle out of it!—So you know what it is, but you just can't say it. Well, now, maybe I can help you. (*He grabs the Officer by the hair and shakes him.*) Maybe 1160 that will shake it out of you!

OFFICER: My God, this is disgraceful! Disgraceful!

TEACHER: It's disgraceful to see a big boy like you turning into a lazy—

OFFICER: (*hurt and stung*) A *big* boy?! Yes, I am big, much bigger than these boys. I've finished school—(*As if waking up.*) I've got my doctor's degree. What am I doing sitting here? Don't I have my doctorate?

TEACHER: Certainly you do. But you've got to sit here and mature. You've got to mature. —Don't you think that's right? 1170

OFFICER: (*his hand on his forehead*) Yes, of course. That's right; you've got to mature. . . . Yes. . . . Two times two—. Two times two—is two! Yes! I shall prove it by means of analogy, the highest form of proof. Follow carefully. One times one is one; therefore two times two is two. What applies to one applies to the other.

TEACHER: Your proof is completely in accord with the laws of logic. But the answer is wrong!

OFFICER: Whatever is in accord with the laws of logic can't be wrong. Let's test it. One goes into one once; therefore two 1180 goes into two twice!

TEACHER: Absolutely right according to analogy. But now tell me how much is one times three?

OFFICER: Three!

TEACHER: It therefore follows that two times three is also three!

OFFICER: (*pondering*) No, that can't be right. . . . It can't be. . . . Or maybe . . . (*Sits down, looking lost and hopeless.*) I guess I'm not mature yet.

TEACHER: You're not nearly mature enough! Not nearly!       1190

OFFICER: How long will I have to sit here?

TEACHER: How long here? Do you think time and space exist? Suppose time exists. Then you should be able to tell me what time is. All right, what is time?

OFFICER: Time. . . . (*Thinking.*) I can't exactly tell you, but I know what it is. Ergo, I can know how much two times two is without being able to tell you! Can Teacher tell us what time it is?

TEACHER: Of course I can!

ALL THE BOYS: Tell us! Tell us!       1200

TEACHER: Time . . . ? Let me think. (*Stands motionless with his finger alongside his nose.*) While we're talking, time is flying. Therefore time is something that flies while I'm talking!

ONE OF THE BOYS: (*stands up*) Teacher, now you're talking, and while Teacher is talking, I'm going to fly from here. Therefore I am time! (*He flees from the classroom.*)

TEACHER: Absolutely correct according to the laws of logic!

OFFICER: Then the laws of logic are crazy. Johnny who flew away can't be time!

TEACHER: That, too, is absolutely correct according to the laws 1210 of logic, even though it's crazy.

OFFICER: Then logic is crazy!

TEACHER: It does seem so, doesn't it? But if logic is crazy, then the whole world's crazy. And I'll be damned if I'll sit here and teach these boys how to act crazy! What do you say? If someone will treat me to a drink, we'll go for a swim!

OFFICER: That's a *posterus prius* or the world upside down! You're supposed to take a swim first and a drink after.

Stupid old fool!

1220 TEACHER: Don't get arrogant with me, Doctor!

OFFICER: Colonel, if you don't mind! I'm an army officer. And I don't understand why I have to sit here and be scolded and insulted and treated like a schoolboy.

TEACHER: (*raising his finger*) We have to mature!

. . . . . . . . . . . . . . . . . .

MEDICAL INSPECTOR: (*enters*) We're all under quarantine as of now!

OFFICER: Ah, there you are! Where have you been? Do you realize this fellow here has been making me sit on this bench with the other boys—and I've got a Ph.D.

1230 MEDICAL INSPECTOR: Really? Why don't you just get up and leave?

OFFICER: Leave! That's a good one! . . . Easier said than done!

TEACHER: You know it, boy! Just you try to leave!

OFFICER: (*to the Medical Inspector*) Save me! Hide me from his eyes!

MEDICAL INSPECTOR: Well, come on, never mind! Come and help us dance and make merry. Dance before the plague breaks out! We've got to dance!

OFFICER: Will the warship sail then?

1240 MEDICAL INSPECTOR: That's the first thing! The ship will sail away. What a lot of sobbing and crying there'll be.

OFFICER: Always crying. When the ship comes in and when it puts to sea. . . . Well, let's go!

(*They leave the schoolhouse. The Teacher continues teaching silently.*)

. . . . . . . . . . . . . . . . . .

(*The three Young Girls, who were watching the dance through the window, move sadly down to the pier. Edith, who has been standing as if turned to stone at the piano, follows them slowly.*)

DAUGHTER: (*to the Officer*) You mean there isn't a single happy person in this paradise?

OFFICER: Yes, there is. Two of them. A newlywed couple. Listen to them.

(*The Newlywed Couple enters.*)

HUSBAND: (*to his Wife*) I'm so happy I want to die.

WIFE: Die because you're happy?

1250 HUSBAND: Yes. "There lives within the very flame of love a kind of wick or snuff that will abate it."° And knowing what's to come turns my love to ashes when it burns most brightly.

WIFE: Then let's die together. Now, before it's too late.

HUSBAND: Die? Why not? I'm afraid of happiness. A mirage, made to lure us on.

(*They go down toward the sea.*)

. . . . . . . . . . . . . . . . . .

DAUGHTER: (*to the Officer*) What a cruel world! And the poor

souls who live in it!

OFFICER: You think so? Look at this man who's coming now. Of all the mortals in this place he's the most envied.

(*A Blind Mind is led in.*)

He owns every one of these hundred villas. The bays and 1260 harbors, the beaches and woods are all his, including the fish in the water, the birds in the air, and the beasts in the woods. All these thousands of people are nothing more than his tenants. The sun rises on his waters and sets on his lands—

DAUGHTER: So? Does he have something to complain about, too?

OFFICER: Yes, and with good reason: he can't see.

MEDICAL INSPECTOR: He's totally blind.

DAUGHTER: The most envied of them all!

OFFICER: He's come to see the warship sail. His son is on 1270 board.

. . . . . . . . . . . . . . . . . .

BLIND MAN: I can't see it, but I can hear it. I can hear the claws of the anchor tearing at the mud at the bottom of the sea. Sounds like the hook when it's pulled out of the fish and the heart is ripped out through the throat. . . . My son, my one and only child, is leaving me to travel far from home, to sail the seven seas; and all I can do is follow him in my thoughts. . . . I can hear the anchor chain clanking and scraping. . . . And there's something flapping and snapping like wet sheets on the line whipped by the wind . . . handkerchiefs 1280 wet with tears, hm? . . . And I can hear sighing and sobbing and sniffling, like people crying . . . maybe little waves lapping against the hull, maybe the girls on the shore . . . the girls that get left behind . . . with nothing to console them. . . . I once asked a little boy why the sea was salt, and the boy, whose father was away on a long journey, said right away, "The sea is salt because the sailors cry so much." "But why do the sailors cry so much?" I asked. "Because," he said, "they always have to go away from home—and that's why they're always drying their handkerchiefs up on the mast- 1290 head!" And then I asked him, "But why do people cry when they're sad?" And he said, "That's because they have to wash the glasses of their eyes so they can see better."

(*The warship has gotten under sail and glides away. The Girls on the shore are alternately waving goodbye with their handkerchiefs and drying their tears with them. Suddenly, a signal flag with red, white, and blue stripes°° signifying "Yes" is hoisted on a halyard to the yardarm of the foremast. Alice jubilantly waves her answer back with her handkerchief.*)

DAUGHTER: (*to the Officer*) What does the flag mean?

OFFICER: It means "Yes." It's the lieutenant's way of writing "yes" with the red blood of his heart on the blue cloth of heaven.

DAUGHTER: What does "No" look like?

OFFICER: A blue and white checkerboard—tainted blood and anemia.°°° —Look at Alice! Have you ever seen anyone 1300 look so happy?

---

°Strindberg does not quote this passage from *Hamlet* (IV. vii) but seems to echo it.

°°In the original, a red ball on a white field, which most people today would take for the Japanese flag.

°°°A blue flag in the original. The translator has followed the modern International Code of Signals.

DAUGHTER: Look at Edith! Have you ever seen anyone look so sad?

BLIND MAN: Coming and going—meeting each other and leaving each other—that's life. I met his mother one day—and then she left me. But at least I had my son with me. Now he's gone!

DAUGHTER: But he'll surely come again!

BLIND MAN: Who are you? I've heard your voice before . . . in 1310 my dreams . . . in my youth . . . when summer vacation began . . . when I was a newlywed . . . when my child was born. . . . Every time life smiled on me, I heard that voice, like a softly stirring south wind, like harps from heaven, like the songs I imagine the angels sang the first Christmas . . .

·  ·  ·  ·  ·  ·  ·  ·  ·  ·  ·  ·  ·  ·  ·  ·

*(The Lawyer enters, goes over to the Blind Man, and whispers in his ear.)*

BLIND MAN: Is that so!

LAWYER: The honest truth! *(He approaches the Daughter.)* You've seen just about everything there is to see, but you haven't experienced the worst thing we've got to live through.

1320 DAUGHTER: The worst! What can that be?

LAWYER: Repeating everything . . . going through it again! Going back to the beginning! . . . Having to learn your lesson all over again! —Come on!

DAUGHTER: Where?

LAWYER: Back to your duties!

DAUGHTER: Duties? What are my duties?

LAWYER: Everything you shy away from. Everything you hate to do and have to do! It means doing without, giving up, denying yourself. It means everything unpleasant, disgust-
1330 ing, and painful.

DAUGHTER: You mean there aren't any pleasant duties?

LAWYER: Yes. After you've done them, they're pleasant.

DAUGHTER: You mean when they don't exist. If duty is everything that's unpleasant, then what's pleasure?

LAWYER: What's pleasant is sin.

DAUGHTER: Sin?

LAWYER: That's right. And sin is something to be punished for. If I have a good time, the next day I have a bad conscience and suffer the torments of hell.

1340 DAUGHTER: Strange!

LAWYER: But true. I wake up in the morning with a headache, and then I have to go through the whole thing again, repeat everything, but in a perverted way. So that all the beauty, fun, and wit of the night before appears, in the light of the morning after, to be ugly, disgusting, and stupid. The good times turn sour; the laughter rings hollow. It's the same with success. Success just sets you up to be knocked down. All the successes I had were the death of me. Because people instinctively hate to see someone get lucky. They think it's
1350 unfair that fate should favor any one person, so they try to make things even by switching the dice or changing the rules. Take talent, for instance. A real handicap. If you've got a real gift, you can easily starve to death. —Why are we talking? You've got to go back to your duties! Or else I'll take you to court—county, state, federal, and Supreme Court, if necessary.

DAUGHTER: Go back! To the kitchen stove, with the cabbage stinking up the place, the diapers in the sink—

LAWYER: That's right, my dear! We've got a big wash today—all the handkerchiefs! 1360

DAUGHTER: Oh, no, I can't go through it again!

LAWYER: That's what life is—going through it again and again. —Look at the teacher in there. He got his doctor's degree yesterday, was crowned with the laurel, honored with a ten-gun salute, climbed Parnassus, and got a medal from the king. And today he begins school all over again, asking how much two times two is, and he'll keep on asking until the day he dies. . . . That's how it is. Now come back with me, back to your chores.

DAUGHTER: I'd rather die! 1370

LAWYER: You mean kill yourself? You can't. The game isn't played that way. Suicide is a disgrace—in the first place—so much so that one's corpse is defiled. And in the second place—you'll send yourself to perdition; it's a mortal sin.

DAUGHTER: It isn't easy to be a human being, is it?

·  ·  ·  ·  ·  ·  ·  ·  ·  ·  ·  ·  ·  ·  ·  ·

EVERYONE: Bravo! Hear, hear!

·  ·  ·  ·  ·  ·  ·  ·  ·  ·  ·  ·  ·  ·  ·  ·

DAUGHTER: I won't go back with you. I won't sink back and be treated like dirt. I want to rise. I want to rise to the place I first came from. . . . But before I go, I want the door to be opened so that I shall know the secret. I want the door to be 1380 opened!

LAWYER: Then you'll have to double back on your tracks, go back the same way you came, and suffer through all the horrors of a trial and lawsuit, the hearings and rehearings, the repetitions and transcriptions, the recapitulations and summations!

DAUGHTER: If that's the way it has to be, very well. But first I want to be alone. I want to go out into the wilderness where I can find myself. We'll see each other soon. *(To the Poet.)* Come along with me. 1390

*(Distant cries, wails, and moans are heard from the rear.)*

DAUGHTER: What is that?

LAWYER: The lost souls of Foul Strand.

DAUGHTER: Why are they complaining more than ever now?

LAWYER: Because the sun is shining *here*, because there's music *here*, and dancing *here*, and youth and life *here*. That's why they feel their misery so much more deeply.

DAUGHTER: We must set them free!

LAWYER: Go ahead. Try! Someone once came to set them free. They hanged him on a cross.

DAUGHTER: Who did? 1400

LAWYER: *They* did. All the right-minded, well-meaning people.

DAUGHTER: Who are *they*?

LAWYER: You mean you don't know the right-minded, well-meaning people? You soon will!

DAUGHTER: Were they the ones who turned against you at the university?

LAWYER: Yes.

DAUGHTER: I know them!

[X]

*The Riviera.° In the foreground to the left stands a white wall, over the top of which the fruit-laden branches of an orange tree can be seen. In the rear are villas and a casino. On the terrace of the casino are tables with parasols. To the right is a huge pile of coal, and near it two wheelbarrows. In the rear to the right one can catch a glimpse of the blue ocean.*

*Two Coal Haulers, naked to the waist, their faces, hands, and bodies blackened with coal soot, are sitting, hunched in tired despair, on the wheelbarrows.*

*The Daughter and the Lawyer enter at the rear.*

DAUGHTER: Oh! This is paradise!

1410 FIRST COAL HAULER: This is hell.

SECOND COAL HAULER: Hundred twenty in the shade.

FIRST COAL HAULER: Let's go for a swim.

SECOND COAL HAULER: Can't. Police will stop you. No swimming allowed.

FIRST COAL HAULER: What about picking an orange?

SECOND COAL HAULER: Can't. Police will come.

FIRST COAL HAULER: But I can't work in this heat. I've had it! I'm getting out of here.

SECOND COAL HAULER: Can't. Police will stop you. *(Pause.)* Be-
1420    sides, you'd starve to death.

FIRST COAL HAULER: Starve to death? We do most of the work and we get the least to eat. And the rich who don't do nothing get the most. . . . Wouldn't it be fair to say—without being too blunt about it—something's wrong somewhere? Daughter of the gods, what do you say?

. . . . . . . . . . . . . . . . . . . . . .

DAUGHTER: I have no answer. . . . But tell me, what have you done? Why are you so black? Why do you have to work so hard?

FIRST COAL HAULER: What have we done? We picked the
1430    wrong parents—poor and disreputable. . . . And maybe we got arrested and sentenced a couple of times.

DAUGHTER: Sentenced?

FIRST COAL HAULER: Sure. Some get away with it and some don't. Those who get away with it are sitting up there in the casino eating eight-course dinners—with wine.

DAUGHTER: *(to the Lawyer)* Can that be true?

LAWYER: Generally speaking, yes.

DAUGHTER: You mean that everybody at one time or another broke some law and could have been sent to prison?

1440 LAWYER: Yes.

DAUGHTER: Even you?

LAWYER: Even I.

. . . . . . . . . . . . . . . . . . . . . .

DAUGHTER: Is it true that the poor folks can't go swimming here?

LAWYER: That's right—not even with their clothes on. Only those who try to drown themselves get away without paying. But don't worry, they have to settle up in court.

DAUGHTER: Why can't they go outside the town, out in the country for a swim?

LAWYER: There isn't any open country; it's all fenced in.        1450

DAUGHTER: I mean way out, where there aren't any fences, where the land is free.

LAWYER: There isn't any free land. It's all owned and occupied.

DAUGHTER: The ocean, the wide-open sea—

LAWYER: Everything! You can't even take a boat out or come ashore without signing a piece of paper and paying money. Neat, isn't it?

DAUGHTER: This is no paradise.

LAWYER: I can promise you that!

DAUGHTER: Why don't the people do something to change    1460 things?

LAWYER: They do. But all who want to make the world better end up in prison or in the madhouse.

DAUGHTER: Who puts them in prison?

LAWYER: All the right-thinking, fair-minded—

DAUGHTER: But not the madhouse?

LAWYER: Their own despair puts them there when they realize how hopeless it all is.

DAUGHTER: Hasn't it occurred to anyone that there might be a good reason why things are the way they are?        1470

LAWYER: Yes, as a matter of fact. Everyone who is well-off believes that.

DAUGHTER: Believes that things are best as they are?

. . . . . . . . . . . . . . . . . . . . . .

FIRST COAL HAULER: You see in us the foundation of society. If we didn't carry the coal, the kitchen stoves would go out, the rooms you live in would grow cold, the factories would close down. The lights in your streets, your stores, your homes would die. Darkness and cold would fall upon you. Yet we sweat like the damned in hell to carry the black coal. . . . What wilt thou do for us?        1480

LAWYER: *(to the Daughter)* Do something for them. . . . *(Pause.)* I realize that complete equality is impossible, but why, why must there be such great inequality?

. . . . . . . . . . . . . . . . . . . . . .

*(A Man and his Wife cross the stage.)*

WIFE: Are you going to join us for a game of cards?

MAN: No, I've got to take my constitutional. Got to work up an appetite.

. . . . . . . . . . . . . . . . . . . . . .

FIRST COAL HAULER: Work up an appetite!

SECOND COAL HAULER: Work up—!

. . . . . . . . . . . . . . . . . . . . . .

*(Some Children come running in. When they see the coal-blackened workers, they cry and scream in terror.)*

FIRST COAL HAULER: One look at us and they scream! They scream . . . !        1490

SECOND COAL HAULER: God damn it! It's a sick society. I say it's

---

° In Strindberg's manuscript the Riviera scene has been added as an afterthought.

time to operate on it—with the guillotine!
FIRST COAL HAULER: Damn right! (*He spits in disgust.*)

. . . . . . . . . . . . . . . . . . .

LAWYER: (*to the Daughter*) Something's wrong. Anyone can
    see that. People aren't so bad. It's just that—
DAUGHTER: Just what?
LAWYER: The system. The organization.
DAUGHTER: (*hides her face and leaves*) It's no paradise!
BOTH COAL HAULERS: No. It's hell.


[XI]

*Fingal's Cave. Long green waves roll gently into the cavern. In
the foreground a red whistling buoy rocks on the waves, but
the bell does not sound except when indicated.*

*The music of the winds. The music of the waves.*

*The Daughter and the Poet onstage.*

1500 POET: Where have you brought me?
    DAUGHTER: Far from the murmuring and moaning of human
        beings—to the outermost edge of the world and the sea—
        to this grotto we call Indra's Ear. For it is said that here the
        god of the skies and sovereign of the heavens listens to the
        pleas and petitions of mortals.
    POET: Listens? How?
    DAUGHTER: Don't you see that this grotto is built like a
        seashell? You see it is. Don't you know that your ear is
        shaped like a seashell? You know it is, but you never thought
1510    about it before. (*She picks up a shell from the shore.*) When
        you were a child, did you never hold a shell to your ear and
        listen? Listen to the singing of your blood, to the swirling of
        the thoughts in your brain, to the thousands of tiny little ex-
        plosions as the wornout threads in the fabric of your body
        snap and break? . . . If you can hear all that in such a little
        shell, imagine what you can hear in this great big one!
    POET: (*listening*) I don't hear anything, except the sighing of
        the wind . . .
    DAUGHTER: Let me help you. I'll be the interpreter. Listen.
1520    . . . The lament of the winds. (*Recitative to the accompani-
        ment of soft music.*)

> Born in the clouds,
> chased by Indra's lightning,
> we fled to clayey earth.
> The mulch in the fields
> sullied our feet.
> The dust of the road,
> the smoke of the city
> we had to endure—
1530 > foul smell of crowds,
> stale beer, sour wine.
> Out to the open sea we swept
> to breathe clean air,
> to flutter our wings,
> to bathe our feet.
> Indra, ruler of heaven,
> listen to us.
> Hear out sighs.
> The earth is not clean,
1540 > life is not kind.

> Man is not evil,
> nor is he good.
> People live as best they can,
> one day at a time.
> Living in ashes and dust,
> they breed and die:
> ashes to ashes, dust to dust.
> Feet for plodding
> were they given,
> not wings for flying.            1550
> So the dust covers them
> Is the fault theirs
> or yours?

. . . . . . . . . . . . . . . . .

POET: Once long ago I heard the same—
DAUGHTER: Shhh! The winds are still singing. (*Recitative to the
    accompaniment of soft music.*)

> We are the winds.
> It is we who carry
> man's complaints.
> On autumn nights you heard us          1560
> whistling in chimneys,
> howling in the stove,
> as the autumn rain
> cried on the roof.
> On winter nights you heard us
> whisper in the snow-laden trees.
> Out on the storm-swept sea
> you heard our whining
> in the ropes and sails.
> You heard us,                          1570
> creatures of air,
> who learned our songs
> in passing through
> the lungs of men.
> The hospital, the battlefield
> taught us what to sing.
> Most we learned in the nursery
> where the newborn cry,
> mewl, and scream
> with the pain of coming alive.         1580
> We are the winds,
> howling, whining,
> whistling, wailing.

. . . . . . . . . . . . . . . . . .

POET: I believe that once before—
DAUGHTER: Shh! Now the waves are singing. (*Recitative to the
    accompaniment of soft music.*)

> We are the waves.
> We cradle the winds
> and lull the winds
> to sleep.                              1590
> Green cradles, wet and salt,
> shaped like flames,
> flames of water,
> slaking, burning,
> cleansing, bathing,
> spuming, spawning.
> We are the waves.

*We cradle the winds*
*and lull the winds*
*to sleep.*

1600

. . . . . . . . . . . . . . . . . . .

DAUGHTER: False and faithless waves! Everything on earth that doesn't get burned up gets drowned—in the waves. —Do you see what I mean? Look. *(She points to a scrap heap.)* Look at what the sea has pillaged and plundered and destroyed. . . . All that's left of the sunken ships are these figureheads—and their names. The good ships *Justice, Friendship, The Golden Peace, Hope*—here's all that's left of *Hope*—deceptive *Hope* . . . leeboards, oarlocks, bailing buckets . . . ! And there's the life buoy. It saved itself and let the souls in distress go down.

1610

POET: *(poking around in the scrap heap)* Here's the nameplate of the *Justice*. It must be the same one that sailed from Fair Haven with the Blind Man's son. It must have gone down. And on board was Alice's fiancé, too, the lieutenant Edith loves so hopelessly.

DAUGHTER: Blind Man? Fair Haven? I must have dreamed all that. And Alice's lieutenant, ugly Edith, Foul Strand and the quarantine, sulphur and phenol. Graduation exercises in the cathedral, the lawyer's office, the corridor and Victoria, the growing castle and the officer—it's all a dream I've dreamed.

1620

POET: It's all in a poem I once wrote.

DAUGHTER: Then you know what poetry is.

POET: I know what dreams are. What is poetry?

DAUGHTER: Not reality. Something more than reality. Not dreams, but wide-awake dreams.

POET: And people, innocent earthlings, believe that we poets merely play and pretend and make it all up.

DAUGHTER: And a good thing, too, my friend. Else no one would believe there was any point to living and working, and the world would go to rack and ruin. Everyone would lie on his back and look at the sky. No one would lift a hand to use a plow or rake, pick or shovel.

1630

POET: You admit that, do you? You the daughter of Indra, whose home is the heavens?

DAUGHTER: You're right to reproach me. I've been down here on earth too long and taken too many of your mud baths. My thoughts refuse to take wing. My wings are laden with clay, my feet are heavy with dirt and earth. . . . And, as for myself—*(She lifts her arms up high.)* I'm sinking, sinking. . . . Help me, Father, God of heaven, help me! *(Silence.)* I can no longer hear him. The ether cannot carry the sound of his voice from his lips to the sounding shell of my ear. The silver cord is broken. . . . I am earthbound . . . earthbound.

1640

POET: Do you intend to rise from earth soon?

DAUGHTER: As soon as I have burned away the ashes and dust that cling to me, for not all the water in the world can wash me clean. Why do you ask?

POET: Because I—I have a prayer and a plea—

1650 DAUGHTER: What sort of plea?

POET: A petition on behalf of humanity, addressed to the ruler of the world, and drawn up by a dreamer.

DAUGHTER: And to be conveyed and presented by—?

POET: By Indra's daughter.

DAUGHTER: Can you say the words of your poem?

POET: I can.

DAUGHTER: Then say them.

POET: Better if you did.

DAUGHTER: Where are they?

POET: In my thoughts. And here. *(He hands her a scroll.)* 1660

DAUGHTER: Very well, I shall say them. *(She takes the scroll but recites without looking at it.)*

. . . . . . . . . . . . . . . . . . .

DAUGHTER : "Why are we born in pain,
we human beings? Why
do we hurt our mothers
when we should be giving them
the greatest of joys?
Why do we come crying hither,
why do we greet the light,
wailing in pain and wrath? 1670
Why do we not laugh and smile?
The gift of life should be full of joy.
Why are we, the progeny of angels,
the image of God, born like beasts?
Our souls would have a vesture
other than this of blood and filth.
Must the paragon of created beings
cut his eyeteeth and descend into the flesh?"

You presume too much! The work should praise its creator.°
No one has yet solved the riddle of life and being. 1680

"Now the passage through life begins,
over thorns, thistles, sharp stones.
If you find a smooth, well-worn path,
there will soon be detours through the rough.
If flowers will make your journey lighter,
they will cost you more than you can pay.
To make your way you'll have to fight
the crowd and step on someone's toes.
No matter: soon the others will step
on yours to keep the race a close one. 1690
Every joy that comes to you will leave
some poor soul depressed and sadder.
But sorrow breeds no happiness;
all goes one way: from joy to pain,
and the world's cup fills up with sorrow.
So shall it be even when you're dead:
your grave will be the digger's bread."

Is this how you hope to approach the throne of the Almighty?

POET: How can a man of earth like me 1700
find words bright enough, pure enough,
light enough to fly from earth?
Child of the gods, will you
render our lament in the tongue
the immortals best comprehend?

DAUGHTER: I will.

---

°The Daughter alludes to a saying, "The work praises the master," not uncommon in Swedish, from Ecclesiasticus, an apocryphal book of the Bible. The standard version in English is ineffective: "For the hand of the artificer the work shall be commended."

POET: *(indicating the whistling buoy)* What is that floating there? A buoy?

DAUGHTER: Yes.

1710 POET: It looks like a human lung with the larynx attached.

DAUGHTER: It's the watchman of the sea. When danger lurks, it sings.

POET: I think the sea is rising now. The waves are turning white.

DAUGHTER: I believe you are right!

POET: There's trouble ahead. Do you see what I see? A ship—out beyond the reef.

DAUGHTER: What ship can that be?

POET: It looks to me like the ghost ship.

1720 DAUGHTER: The ghost ship?

POET: *The Flying Dutchman.*

DAUGHTER: Is that the *Dutchman?* . . . Why was he punished so harshly? And why does he never put in to land?

POET: Because he had seven unfaithful wives.

DAUGHTER: Why should he be punished for that?

POET: All the right-thinking people condemned him.

DAUGHTER: Strange world! . . . How can he be freed from his curse?

POET: Freed? Best beware setting anyone free—

1730 DAUGHTER: Why?

POET: Because that—. No, it isn't the *Dutchman,* after all. It's an ordinary ship in distress! —Why doesn't the buoy sound off and warn them? Before it's too late! —Look, the sea is rising, the waves are mounting higher. In a minute we'll be trapped in this cave! —The ship's bells are ringing! Abandon ship! —Won't be long before we can add another figurehead to the pile! —Cry out, buoy! Come on! Do your duty, sentinel of the sea!

*(The whistling buoy sings out with a four-tone chord of a fifth and sixth, the sound resembling foghorns.)*

POET: The crew is waving for us to help—but we ourselves are 1740    drowning!

DAUGHTER: I thought you wanted to be set free!

POET: Yes, of course I do. But not now! And not in water!

. . . . . . . . . . . . . . . . . . .

THE CREW: *(singing in four-part harmony)* Christ Kyrie!

POET: Now they're calling. And the sea is calling. But no one hears.

THE CREW: *(as before)* Christ Kyrie!

DAUGHTER: Who is that out there coming toward us?

POET: Walking on water? There's only one who walks on water—certainly not Peter "the rock"; he sank like a stone.

*(A white glow appears out on the water.)*

1750 THE CREW: *Christ Kyrie!*

DAUGHTER: Is that he?

POET: Yes, that is He, the Crucified One . . .

DAUGHTER: Why—tell me now, why was he crucified?

POET: Because He wanted to set all men free . . .

DAUGHTER: And who—I have forgotten—who wanted to crucify Him?

POET: All the right-thinking ones.

DAUGHTER: It is a strange world!

POET: The sea is rising. Darkness is falling. The storm rages.

*(The Crew screams.)*

POET: The sailors scream in terror when they see their Saviour. 1760    . . . And now . . . they're jumping overboard—afraid of their Redeemer!

*(The Crew screams again.)*

POET: Now they're screaming because they're about to die. They scream when they're born and they scream when they die!

*(The rising waves threaten to drown them in the cave.)*

DAUGHTER: If I could only be certain that it is a ship—

POET: I see what you mean—I don't think it is. It's a two-story house, with trees around it—and—a telephone communication tower—a tower reaching up to the skies. It's a modern Tower of Babel, sending its wires upward—to let those 1770    up there know—

DAUGHTER: You know better than that. Thoughts do not need metal threads to move from place to place. Devout prayers can force their way through all the world. I say it's definitely not a Tower of Babel. If you want to storm the walls of heaven, besiege it with your prayers.

POET: No, it's not a house . . . not a telephone tower. . . . You see what it is?

DAUGHTER: No, what do you see?

POET: I see a plain covered with snow—a drill field. . . . The 1780    winter sun is shining behind a church on a hill, and the church tower casts a long shadow on the snow . . . a platoon of soldiers is marching across the field—marching across the tower—up the spire—now they're on the cross—I have a feeling that the first one who steps on the weathercock at the top must die—they're getting closer—the corporal's leading the way. —Ha! a cloud is sweeping over the plain, blotting out the sun, naturally—it's all disappeared—the wet cloud put out the sun's fire. The light of the sun created the dark tower, but the cloud's dark shadow smothered the 1790    tower's dark shadow . . .

[XII]

*While the Poet has been speaking, the set has changed back to the theater corridor.*

DAUGHTER: *(to the Stage-Door Keeper)* Has the president of the university arrived yet?

STAGE-DOOR KEEPER: No, he hasn't.

DAUGHTER: The deans of the colleges and faculties?

STAGE-DOOR KEEPER: No.

DAUGHTER: Well then, you'd better call them. Right away! Because the door is going to be opened.

STAGE-DOOR KEEPER: Is it really so urgent?

1800 DAUGHTER: Yes, very urgent. A lot of people have come to suspect that the key to the mystery of the universe is kept there. So if you don't mind, call the president and the deans at once.

*(The Stage-Door Keeper pulls out a whistle and blows on it.)*

DAUGHTER: And don't forget the glazier and his diamond. Without him there can be no opening of the door.

. . . . . . . . . . . . . . . . . . . . . . .

*(The Actors and Dancers come in from the left, as at the beginning of the play.)*

. . . . . . . . . . . . . . . . . . . . . . .

OFFICER: *(enters from the rear, wearing top hat and tails, carrying a bouquet of roses, radiantly happy)* Victoria!

STAGE-DOOR KEEPER: Miss Victoria will be down in just a moment.

1810 OFFICER: Good, good! The carriage is waiting, the table is spread, the champagne's on ice. Oh, let me kiss you, madame! *(He embraces the Stage-Door Keeper.)* Victoria!

. . . . . . . . . . . . . . . . . . . . . . .

A WOMAN'S VOICE: *(from above, singing out liltingly)* Here I am!

OFFICER: *(beginning to pace back and forth)* Very good. I'll be waiting!

. . . . . . . . . . . . . . . . . . . . . . .

POET: I have a strange feeling I've been through this before.

DAUGHTER: Me too.

POET: Maybe I dreamed it . . . ?

1820 DAUGHTER: Or wrote it in a poem, maybe?

POET: Or wrote it in a poem.

DAUGHTER: Then you know what poetry is.

POET: Then I know what dreams are.

DAUGHTER: And I have the strange feeling that we once stood somewhere else and said these same words.

POET: Then it shouldn't take you long to figure out what reality is.

DAUGHTER: Or dreams!

POET: Or poetry!

. . . . . . . . . . . . . . . . . . . . . . .

*(Enter the President of the University, the Dean of the Theological Seminary, the Dean of the Faculty of Philosophy, the Dean of the School of Medicine, and the Dean of the School of Law.)*

1830 PRESIDENT: You all know what brings us here: the opening of the door. Let me call first upon the Dean of the Theological Seminary. What is your view of the matter?

DEAN OF THEOLOGY: I don't have any views; I believe! — *Credo*—

DEAN OF PHILOSOPHY: I postulate—

DEAN OF MEDICINE: I know—

DEAN OF LAW: I object—until I've seen the evidence and heard the witnesses.

PRESIDENT: Here we go! Quarreling already! . . . Let me begin 1840 again. What does the Dean of Theology *believe*?

DEAN OF THEOLOGY: I believe that this door should not be opened. It obviously conceals dangerous truths.

DEAN OF PHILOSOPHY: The truth is never dangerous!

DEAN OF MEDICINE: What is truth?

DEAN OF LAW: Whatever two witnesses testify to.

DEAN OF THEOLOGY: With two false witnesses anything can be proved—by a shyster!

DEAN OF PHILOSOPHY: Truth is wisdom; and wisdom and knowledge constitute philosophy itself. Philosophy is the science of sciences, the knowledge of knowledge; and all 1850 other branches of learning are its servants.

DEAN OF MEDICINE: The only science is natural science. Philosophy is not science; it's only empty speculation.

DEAN OF THEOLOGY: Bravo!

DEAN OF PHILOSOPHY: *(to Dean of Theology)* Bravo, you say! What do you think you are? You're the archenemy of all knowledge. You're the very antithesis of science. You're ignorance and obscurantism itself—!

DEAN OF MEDICINE: Bravo!

DEAN OF THEOLOGY: *(to Dean of Medicine)* Bravo, you say! You 1860 of all people! Who can't see farther than the end of your nose in a magnifying glass—you, who don't believe in anything but what your deceptive senses tell you—what your eyes tell you, for example, even though you may be farsighted or near-sighted; cross-eyed, wall-eyed, or one-eyed; color blind, red-blind, green-blind.

DEAN OF MEDICINE: You blithering idiot!

DEAN OF THEOLOGY: Jackass!

*(They start fighting.)*

PRESIDENT: Stop that! Let's not have you birds pecking each other's eyes out.                                              1870

DEAN OF PHILOSOPHY: Well, if I had to choose between those two—theology and medicine—I would choose—neither!

DEAN OF LAW: And if I sat on the bench and you three were brought before me, I'd sentence—all three of you! You can't agree on a single point, and you never could. . . . Let's get back to business. Mr. President, what is your own view on the opening of this door?

PRESIDENT: My view? I don't have any views. I have simply been appointed by the state to see to it that during our executive meetings you don't tear one another to pieces— 1880 while you're educating our youth. Views? Ah, no, indeed, I'm very careful not to have any views. There was a time when I had a few, but they were quickly refuted. Views are always quickly refuted—by those with the opposite views, you understand. . . . And now, perhaps we might proceed to the opening of the door, even at the risk of revealing some dangerous truths?

DEAN OF LAW: What is truth? What is *the* truth?

DEAN OF THEOLOGY: I am the truth, the way, and the life—

DEAN OF PHILOSOPHY: I am knowledge of knowledge—    1890

DEAN OF MEDICINE: I am exact knowledge—

DEAN OF LAW: I object!

*(They all start to fight.)*

. . . . . . . . . . . . . . . . . . . . . . .

DAUGHTER: Aren't you ashamed? You, the teacher of our youth!

DEAN OF LAW: Mr. President! As the representative of the government and as the head of the faculty, you must bring charges against this woman for her remarks. She said we ought to be ashamed. Now that's an insult. And when she referred to us as the teacher of the young, her ironic tone of voice implied that we were incapable. Now that's slander!

1900 DAUGHTER: Heaven help the students!

DEAN OF LAW: Do you hear? She's excusing the students! — That's the same as accusing us. Mr. President, I insist that you prosecute her!

DAUGHTER: Yes, that's right. I accuse you, you as a group, of sowing doubt and breeding skepticism in the minds of our youth.

DEAN OF LAW: Listen to her! There she stands telling the students to have no respect for our authority, and yet she has

1910 the gall to accuse us of breeding skepticism! If that isn't a criminal act, what is? I put it to you, all you good, right-thinking people.

· · · · · · · · · · · · · · · ·

ALL THE RIGHT-THINKING PEOPLE: Yes, yes, absolutely criminal!

DEAN OF LAW: There! All the right-thinking people have condemned you! —Now go in peace and be content with thy gain. Otherwise—!

DAUGHTER: My gain? —Otherwise! Otherwise what??

DEAN OF LAW: Otherwise thou shall be stoned.

1920 POET: Or crucified.

DAUGHTER: Very well, I'll go. —Come with me and I'll give you the answer to the riddle.

POET: What riddle?

DAUGHTER: What did he mean by "my gain"?°

POET: Probably nothing. Just a lot of hot air, as we say. Talking through his hat.

DAUGHTER: But nothing could have hurt me more.

POET: I suppose that's why he said it. That's how people are.

· · · · · · · · · · · · · · · ·

ALL THE RIGHT-THINKING PEOPLE: Hooray! The door is open!

· · · · · · · · · · · · · · · ·

1930 PRESIDENT: What lay hidden behind the door?

GLAZIER: I can't see anything.

PRESIDENT: You can't see anything? Well, I can't say I'm surprised—. Learned deans, what lay hidden behind the door?

DEAN OF THEOLOGY: Nothing. That is the key to the riddle of the world. In the beginning God created heaven and earth out of nothing.

DEAN OF PHILOSOPHY: Nothing comes of nothing.

DEAN OF MEDICINE: Bosh! Nothing. Period.

DEAN OF LAW: I object to the whole thing. It's a clear case of

1940 fraud. I appeal to all the right-thinking people!

DAUGHTER: (to the Poet) What are the right-thinking people?

POET: I wish I knew. They usually turn out to be a party of one. Today it's me and my side—tomorrow it's you and your side. . . . You get appointed—or rather, you're self-appointed.

· · · · · · · · · · · · · · · ·

ALL THE RIGHT-THINKING PEOPLE: We've been swindled!

Tricked!

PRESIDENT: And who has swindled you?

ALL THE RIGHT-THINKING PEOPLE: She did! The Daughter!

PRESIDENT: (to the Daughter) Would you be so good as to tell us what you had in mind with this door-opening? 1950

DAUGHTER: No, good people, I won't. "If I tell you, ye will not believe."

DEAN OF MEDICINE: But there's nothing—nothing at all.

DAUGHTER: You say right. But you understand not.

DEAN OF MEDICINE: She's talking nonsense!

EVERYONE: Nonsense! Boo!

DAUGHTER: (to the Poet) Poor lost souls. I feel sorry for them.

POET: You serious?

DAUGHTER: Always serious.

POET: Do you also feel sorry for the right-thinking people? 1960

DAUGHTER: Perhaps most of all for them.

POET: And what about the four learned faculties?

DAUGHTER: Them too, no less than the others. Four heads on one body, four minds! Who created the monster?

EVERYONE: She's not answering us!

PRESIDENT: Down with her!

DAUGHTER: But I have answered you!

PRESIDENT: Don't you talk back to me!

EVERYONE: Listen to her! She's talking back!

DAUGHTER: Answer or not answer, I can't win. . . . Come with 1970 me, you poet and seer, and I shall tell you—somewhere far from here—the answer to the riddle. Somewhere, out in the desert, where no one can hear us, no one see us. Because—

· · · · · · · · · · · · · · · ·

LAWYER: (coming forward and grabbing the Daughter by the arm) Have you forgotten your responsibilities?

DAUGHTER: God knows I haven't. But I have more important responsibilities.

LAWYER: What about your child?

DAUGHTER: My child—oh yes! What about her?

LAWYER: Your child is crying for you. 1980

DAUGHTER: My child! How that child ties me down! I feel chained to the earth. . . . And I have this pain in my breast, this feeling of anguish. What is it?

LAWYER: Don't you know?

DAUGHTER: No.

LAWYER: The pangs of conscience.

DAUGHTER: Is that what it is? The pangs of conscience?

LAWYER: That's right. They show up after every duty you neglect, after every pleasure you enjoy, however innocent—if there are any innocent pleasures (which I doubt), and after 1990 every harm you do your friends and neighbors.

DAUGHTER: And there's no cure for these pangs, I suppose?

LAWYER: Oh, yes; but only one. You must discharge your duty without a moment's hesitation.

DAUGHTER: You know, you look just like a demon when you say that word "duty." —But what am I supposed to do if I have two duties to discharge?

LAWYER: Simple! First you discharge one, and then the other.

DAUGHTER: The most important one first. —So I leave my child in your care, while I go to discharge my first duty. 2000

_____

° The exchange between the Dean of Law and the Daughter evidently reflects the words of Paul, I Timothy 6:1–6, with the Dean turning Paul's admonition against the Daughter.

LAWYER: But the child needs you; you'll break its heart. Can you bear to know that someone is suffering on account of you?

DAUGHTER: You're turning me against myself. You've broken my heart in two and it's pulling me both ways.

LAWYER: Life is full of little conflicts like that.

DAUGHTER: Oh, how my heart is torn. I don't know which way to turn.

. . . . . . . . . . . . . . . . . . . .

POET: If you knew how much sorrow and misery I caused by
2010 discharging the obligations I owed to my calling in life—notice: my calling, the most important duty of all—you would shun me.

DAUGHTER: Why? What did you do?

POET: My father placed all his hopes in me. I was his only son and he dreamed about how I would carry on the business he had built up. I ran away from business school and my father never got over it. My mother wanted me to study religion, but I didn't have the heart for it. So she disowned me. I had a friend who gave me a helping hand when I was down and
2020 out. But my friend had different political views, fought against the causes I spoke for and fought for. I had to cut down my best friend and benefactor in order to be true to myself. Since then I've never known any peace. They call me disloyal, a stinker. And a fat lot of good it does me to hear my conscience tell me, "You did right," because the next moment it's telling me how wrong I was. And that's life for you.

. . . . . . . . . . . . . . . . . . . .

DAUGHTER: Come with me out into the desert.

LAWYER: Your child! Your child!

2030 DAUGHTER: (*indicating all those present*) Here are my children! Taken one by one, they're good and gentle. But put them together and they fight with one another and turn into demons. . . . Goodbye . . .


[XIII]

*Outside the castle. Same set as in the first scene of the first act. Only now the ground below the footings is covered with flowers (blue monkshood or aconite). At the very top of the castle, surmounting its tower and lantern, is a chrysanthemum bud ready to burst into bloom. The windows have candles burning in them.*

*The Daughter and the Poet are onstage.*

DAUGHTER: The time has nearly come when with the help of the fire I shall rise and return to the empyrean. This is what you call death, what you approach with fear in your hearts.

POET: Fear of the unknown.

DAUGHTER: Which you really know.

POET: Who knows?

2040 DAUGHTER: Everyone! Why do you not believe your prophets?

POET: Prophets have never been believed. I wonder why?—"If God has spoken, why will men not believe?" His power to persuade must surely be irresistible!

DAUGHTER: Have you always been a skeptic?

POET: No. Many a time I've had absolute faith and certitude, but it always faded away after a while, like a dream upon awakening.

DAUGHTER: It isn't easy to be a human being. I know that.

POET: You have come to realize that, have you, and admit it?

DAUGHTER: Yes.    2050

POET: Tell me something. Was it not Indra who once sent his son here to earth to hear the complaints of mankind?

DAUGHTER: Yes, it was. And how did the people receive him?

POET: What did he do to accomplish his mission?—to answer with a question.

DAUGHTER: To answer with another question: was not the condition of mankind improved as a result of his visit to earth? Tell me truly.

POET: Improved? Yes, a little. Very little! —Now, instead of asking questions, will you solve the riddle?    2060

DAUGHTER: I could. But what good would it do? You wouldn't believe the answer.

POET: You, I will believe. I know who you are.

DAUGHTER: Very well, I shall tell you. . . . At the dawn of time before the sun shone, Brahma, the divine primal potency, went forth and let himself be seduced by Maya, the creative mother of the world, so that he might propagate himself. The divine element thus joined with earthly matter. This was the fall of heaven. Consequently, the world and its inhabitants and life itself are nothing more than phantoms, 2070 mirages, images in a dream—

POET: My dream!

DAUGHTER: A dream come true. Now, to free themselves from earthly matter the progeny of Brahma seek deprivation and suffering. There you have suffering as the redeemer. But this yearning for suffering comes into conflict with the craving for pleasure. Which is love. Now do you understand what love is, offering the most sublime joys along with the most profound suffering, sweetest when it is most bitter? Do you understand what woman is? Woman, through whom 2080 sin and death entered into life?

POET: I do understand. And the upshot?

DAUGHTER: I don't have to tell you. Constant strife between the anguish of joy and the pleasure of suffering, the torments of remorse and the delights of sensuality.

POET: Strife—is that all we can hope for?

DAUGHTER: The conflict between opposites produces energy, just as fire and water generate steam power.

POET: And peace? And rest?

DAUGHTER: I've said enough. You mustn't ask any more, and I 2090 mustn't answer. . . . The altar is decked for the sacrifice. . . . The flowers keep watch, the lights are lit. . . . The funeral wreaths hang in the windows and doors.°

POET: You say that as calmly and coolly as if you didn't know what it means to suffer.

DAUGHTER: Not know? I have suffered all that mortal man suffers but felt it a hundred times more, because my senses are keener.

---

° In place of the funeral wreaths, the original has "white sheets in the windows, pine cuttings on the walk"—once customary features at Swedish funerals.

POET: Tell me what you suffered.

2100 DAUGHTER: You're a poet, but could even you tell me your troubles in words that said it all? Was there ever a time when your words and your thoughts were in perfect harmony? A time when your words soared to the level of your thoughts?

POET: No, you're right. Before my own thoughts I stood deaf and dumb. And when the crowd listened in admiration to my song, it sounded like bawling to me. I guess that's why I always blushed when I heard my praises sung.

DAUGHTER: And yet you expect me to—? Look me in the eye!

2110 POET: I can't. Your gaze is too intense.

DAUGHTER: And so would my words be if I spoke in my own tongue.

POET: At least tell me—before you go—what was the hardest thing to endure—down here?

DAUGHTER: Being, just being. Feeling my sight clouded by these eyes, my hearing muffled by these ears, and my thoughts, my bright, airy thoughts trapped in the labyrinth of coiled fat. You know what a brain looks like—what crooked ways, what secret passages!

2120 POET: I know. I suppose that's why all the right-thinking people think crooked.

DAUGHTER: Always ready with sarcasm. That's how you all are.

POET: What do you expect?

DAUGHTER: Now I'm going to shake the dust off my feet first— the earth, the clay. (*She takes off her shoes and lays them on the fire.*)

·  ·  ·  ·  ·  ·  ·  ·  ·  ·  ·  ·  ·  ·  ·  ·

STAGE-DOOR KEEPER: (*enters and lays her shawl on the fire*) Maybe you wouldn't mind if I added my shawl to the fire, would you, deary? (*Exits.*)

2130 OFFICER: (*enters*) And I my roses? Nothing left but thorns. (*Exits.*)

BILLPOSTER: (*enters*) The posters can go. But my dip net, never! (*Exits.*)

GLAZIER: (*enters*) The diamond glass cutter that opened the door! Goodbye! (*Exits.*)

LAWYER: (*enters*) The minutes of the great lawsuit concerning the pope's beard or the diminishing water supply in the sources of the Ganges River. (*Exits.*)

MEDICAL INSPECTOR: (*enters*) Only a small contribution: the

2140 black mask that made me black against my will. (*Exits.*)

VICTORIA: (*enters*) My beauty—my sorrow! (*Exits.*)

EDITH: (*enters*) My ugliness—my sorrow! (*Exits.*)

BLIND MAN: (*enters, sticks his hand into the fire*) I give my hand in place of my eye! (*Exits.*)

(*The old Don Juan enters in his wheelchair, accompanied by the Coquette and the "Friend."*)

DON JUAN: Hurry up! Hurry up! Life is short! (*Exits with the others.*)

·  ·  ·  ·  ·  ·  ·  ·  ·  ·  ·  ·  ·  ·  ·  ·

POET: I once read that when life nears its end, everything in it comes rushing past in single file. Is this the end?

DAUGHTER: It is for me. Goodbye.

2150 POET: Not even a few parting words?

DAUGHTER: There's nothing I can say. Do you still believe that your words can express our thoughts?

·  ·  ·  ·  ·  ·  ·  ·  ·  ·  ·  ·  ·  ·  ·  ·

DEAN OF THEOLOGY: (*enters, raging mad*) I've been repudiated by my God, I'm persecuted by the people, disowned by the administration, ridiculed by my colleagues! How can I have faith, how can I believe, when no one else does? How can I fight for a God who does not fight for his own? Junk! That's what it is—junk! (*He throws a book on the fire and leaves.*)

·  ·  ·  ·  ·  ·  ·  ·  ·  ·  ·  ·  ·  ·  ·  ·

POET: (*snatching the book from the fire*) You know what it is? A martyrology. It lists a martyr for each day of the year.    2160

DAUGHTER: Martyr?

POET: Yes—someone who was tortured and put to death for his beliefs. And why? —Do you think that everyone who is tortured suffers, and that everyone who is put to death feels pain? Doesn't suffering melt our chains and doesn't death set us free?

·  ·  ·  ·  ·  ·  ·  ·  ·  ·  ·  ·  ·  ·  ·  ·

CHRISTINE: (*enters with her strips of paper and weatherstripping*) I'm going to paste and seal and paste and seal until there's nothing more to paste and seal!

POET: And if heaven itself split wide open, you'd try to paste 2170 and seal that too! Go away!

CHRISTINE: Aren't there any inner windows in the castle for me to seal up?

POET: No, there certainly aren't! Not there!

CHRISTINE: (*leaving*) Well, then I'm leaving.

·  ·  ·  ·  ·  ·  ·  ·  ·  ·  ·  ·  ·  ·  ·  ·

DAUGHTER: It's time! Give me your hand, my friend,
Farewell, you human being, you dreamer,
you poet, who knows best how to live,
soaring on wings above the earth,
swooping down when you feel like it,                          2180
to graze the dust, not to drown in it.
Now when I must leave, how hard it is
to say goodbye, to bid farewell.
One longs for all that one has loved,
regrets all that one has offended.
Now, now I know what it means to live;
I feel the pain of being human.
You miss what you never wanted;
regret even misdeeds never done.
You want to leave, you want to stay;                           2190
your heart's drawn and quartered, torn apart
by conflicting wishes, indecision, doubt.
Goodbye, my friend! Tell your fellow men
that where I'm going I shall think of them
and that in your name I shall convey
their plaints and protests to the throne on high.
Farewell!

(*She enters the castle. Music. The rear of the stage is lit up by the burning castle and reveals a wall of human faces, questioning, sorrowful, despairing.*)

(*As the castle burns, the flower bud at the top bursts and blossoms into a huge chrysanthemum.*)

August
Strindberg

*"A Dream Play:* A Note
from the Author"
(1901)

TRANSLATED BY
EVERT SPRINCHORN

*A Note from the
Author*

*In this preface to his play, Strindberg describes the relationship between characters, dramatic form, and the "dreamer" that he hoped to achieve in the play.*

Following the example of my previous dream play *To Damascus,* I have in this present dream play sought to imitate the incoherent but ostensibly logical form of our dreams. Anything can happen; everything is possible and probable. Time and space do not exist. Working with some insignificant real events as a background, the imagination spins out its threads of thoughts and weaves them into new patterns—a mixture of memories, experiences, spontaneous ideas, impossibilities, and improvisations.

The characters split, double, multiply, dissolve, condense, float apart, coalesce. But one mind stands over and above them all, the mind of the dreamer; and for him there are no secrets, no inconsistencies, no scruples, no laws. He does not condemn, does not acquit; he only narrates the story. And since the dream is more often painful than cheerful, a tone of melancholy and of sympathy with all living creatures runs through the pitching and swaying narrative. Sleep, which should free the dreamer, often plagues and tortures him instead. But when the pain is most excruciating, the moment of waking comes and reconciles the dreamer to reality, which, however agonizing it may be, is a joy and a pleasure at that moment compared with the painful dream.

The idea that life is a dream° seemed to us in the past to be no more than a poetic dream of Calderon's. But when Shakespeare in *The Tempest* has Prospero say that "we are such stuff as dreams are made on," and when elsewhere this wise Briton, speaking through Macbeth, talks about life as "a tale told by an idiot," we should probably give the matter some more thought.

Whoever during these brief hours follows the sleepwalking author on his wanderings may find a certain similarity between the apparent jumble of a dream and the disordered and mottled cloth of life, woven by the great World Weaver, who winds the warp of human destinies and then fills the woof using our conflicting aims and changeable passions. Anyone who notes the similarity is surely entitled to think that there may be some substance to it.

As far as the loose, disconnected shape of the play is concerned, that too is only apparent. On closer examination, the composition is seen to be quite firm and solid—a symphony, polyphonic, now and then like a fugue with a constantly recurring main theme, which is repeated in all registers and varied by the more than thirty voices. There are no solos with accompaniments, that is, no big parts, no characters—or rather, no caricatures; no intrigue; no strong curtains demanding applause. The voice parts are subjected to strict musical treatment; and in the sacrificial scene of the finale, all that has happened passes in review, with the themes once again repeated, just as a man's life with all its incidents is said to do at the moment of death. Yet another similarity!

Now it is time to see the play itself—and to hear it. With a little goodwill on your part, the battle is half-won. That is all we ask of you.

Curtain going up!

---

°This paragraph and the ones following were written in 1907 in connection with the first staging of the play. They were inserted in the director's copy of the play but not printed at that time. —Trans.

# Elizabeth Robins

Elizabeth Robins (1862–1952) was a radical reformer on two fronts. A significant actress, one of the first female actor-managers in England, a significant force in the Ibsen movement in the 1890s, and friend of Henry James, Bernard Shaw, and Harley Granville Barker, Robins played a critical role in politicizing theater and theatrical performance. Moreover, Robins was also an important figure in the woman suffrage movement in England. Robins wrote the stage play *Votes for Women!* (1907) and then expanded it into the novel *The Convert* (1907); she helped to organize the Actresses' Franchise League in 1908, recruiting the most important actresses (and some actors) of the era—Ellen Terry, Mrs. Patrick Campbell, among others—to the cause; she gathered a series of lectures on women, politics, and the vote in *Way Stations* (1913); and she wrote an important investigation of the social and philosophical construction of gender relations in society, *Ancilla's Share: An Indictment of Sex Antagonism* (1924).

Robins was born in Kentucky and studied at Putnam Female Seminary before going to Vassar College to study medicine; she soon left Vassar for the stage and toured the United States as an actress. In Boston, she married an actor, George Richmond Parkes, but refused to give up acting. He committed suicide shortly thereafter, pitching himself into the Charles River in a suit of stage armor. In the 1880s she traveled to Norway with the widow of the violinist Ole Bull. When she arrived in London late in the decade, she played a variety of theatrical roles to support herself while organizing a company to produce Ibsen's plays. A woman with a mission, Robins quickly gained the—by no means unequivocal—support of William Archer, Henry James, Bernard Shaw, and others; she brought *Hedda Gabler* and *The Master Builder* to England, creating Hedda and Hilde Wangel on the London stage.

In *Ibsen and the Actress* (1924), Robins recounted her struggle both to bring Ibsen to the English theater and to gain financial and institutional power in a theatrical system entirely governed by men. Her suffrage play *Votes for Women!* marks in many ways Robins's entrance onto a new phase of her life, as an important figure in the British suffrage movement. Robins was early converted to the militant programs of Emmeline Pankhurst and her daughter Christabel and of the Women's Social and Political Union (formed in Manchester in 1903). The Pankhursts orchestrated demonstrations, besieged members of Parliament, and developed hunger strikes among imprisoned suffragettes as a mode of agitating for the vote. Robins's skills as a propagandist and speaker were invaluable, and her career on the stage became important in other respects. She donated the profits from *Votes for Women!* and *The Convert* to buy a farm, which was initially used as a rest home for suffragettes who had been force-fed during imprisonment, and was later used to house women studying medicine. Throughout the rest of her career—as polemicist, essayist, novelist—Robins remained committed to the cause of women's equality.

## Votes for Women! (1907)

Although the Actresses' Franchise League would eventually produce plays on women and suffrage, when Robins wrote *Votes for Women!*, the League had yet to be founded. She produced the play at the Court Theatre in 1907, where—given the prominence of the Court's repertoire under the Barker-Vedrenne management—its politics were certain to make a keen impact on the theatergoing public.

To audiences in 1907, the outlines of Robins's plot—suffrage aside—would have marked the play as part of a familiar theatrical type: the "problem play." Part of a genre that includes plays from Arthur Wing Pinero's *The Second Mrs. Tanqueray* (1892) (and Bernard Shaw's send-up of 1893, *Mrs. Warren's Profession*) to John Galsworthy's *The Skin Game* (1920), this drama uses the heroine's sexuality to motivate the narrative. Some "secret" sexual encounter or relationship is revealed in the play and usually becomes the cause of the heroine's demise: Paula Tanqueray shoots herself when her stepdaughter falls in love with one of Paula's former lovers; Galsworthy's Chloe throws herself into a gravel pit when her own "past" is revealed to her family.

In *Votes for Women!*, however, Robins appropriates this design as a means of empowering her heroine, not destroying her. For Vida Levering has a "past" of her own, the deeply coded story of how she had been involved with a man who would not marry her, became pregnant, and escaped to the country for an abortion. But when her "past"—in the person of the new Member of Parliament, Geoffrey Stonor—returns to her life, Vida is galvanized into action. Her "experience" becomes the force behind her political awakening, rather than the cause of a sentimental suicide. Despite a horror of "publicity," she takes the stage at a suffrage rally in Trafalgar Square and speaks so movingly of women's sexual exploitation in male-dominated society that Stonor's fiancée Jean guesses that Stonor was the man involved. In Act Three, Jean and Vida combine to persuade Stonor to press for women's suffrage in Parliament.

Robins modeled Vida Levering on the charismatic Christabel Pankhurst, and reviewers of the 1907 production were unanimous in finding the central rally scene in Trafalgar Square a theatrical masterpiece. This is, of course, the scene in which Vida Levering finally takes the stage, moving from the protected sphere of domestic life into the public sphere of politics. Speaking to the audience onstage, Vida also speaks directly to the audience in the theater; Vida Levering is, perhaps, the best image of Robins's lifelong effort to fuse her two voices, the voice of the actress and the voice of the activist.

# —Votes for Women!—
### Elizabeth Robins

## —CHARACTERS—

LORD JOHN WYNNSTAY
LADY JOHN WYNNSTAY, *his wife*
MRS HERIOT, *sister of Lady John*
MISS JEAN DUNBARTON, *niece to Lady John and Mrs Heriot*
THE HON. GEOFFREY STONOR, *Unionist M.P. affianced to Jean Dunbarton*
MR ST JOHN GREATOREX, *Liberal M.P.*
THE HON. RICHARD FARNBOROUGH
MR FREDDY TUNBRIDGE
MRS FREDDY TUNBRIDGE
MR ALLEN TRENT
MISS ERNESTINE BLUNT, *a Suffragette*
MR PILCHER, *a working man*
A WORKING WOMAN
MISS VIDA LEVERING
PERSONS IN THE CROWD
SERVANTS IN THE TWO HOUSES

*The Entire Action of the Play takes place between Sunday noon and six o'clock in the evening of the same day.*

## —ACT ONE—

*Hall of Wynnstay House.*

*Twelve o'clock, Sunday morning, end of June. With the rising of the curtain, enter the* BUTLER. *As he is going, with majestic port, to answer the door, enter briskly from the garden, by the lower French window,* LADY JOHN WYNNSTAY, *flushed, and flapping a garden hat to fan herself. She is a pink-cheeked woman of fifty-four, who has plainly been a beauty, keeps her complexion, but is "gone to fat."*

LADY JOHN: Has Miss Levering come down yet?
BUTLER: *(pausing)* I haven't seen her, m'lady.
LADY JOHN: *(almost sharply as* BUTLER *turns)* I won't have her disturbed if she's resting. *(To herself as she goes to the writing table.)* She certainly needs it.
BUTLER: Yes, m'lady.
LADY JOHN: *(sitting at the writing table, her back to the front door)* But I want her to know the moment she comes down that the new plans arrived by the morning post.
10 BUTLER: *(pausing nearly at the door)* Plans, m'la—
LADY JOHN: She'll understand. There they are. *(Glancing at the clock.)* It's very important she should have them in time to look over before she goes—

*(*BUTLER *opens the door.)*

*(Over her shoulder.)* Is that Miss Levering?
BUTLER: No, m'lady. Mr Farnborough.

*(Exit* BUTLER.*)*

*(Enter the* HON. R. FARNBOROUGH. *He is twenty-six; reddish hair, high-coloured, sanguine, self-important.)*

FARNBOROUGH: I'm afraid I'm scandalously early. It didn't take me nearly as long to motor over as Lord John said.
LADY JOHN: *(shaking hands)* I'm afraid my husband is no authority on motoring—and he's not home yet from church.
FARNBOROUGH: It's the greatest luck finding *you*. I thought 20 Miss Levering was the only person under this roof who was ever allowed to observe Sunday as a real Day of Rest.
LADY JOHN: If you've come to see Miss Levering—
FARNBOROUGH: Is she here? I give you my word I didn't know it.
LADY JOHN: *(unconvinced)* Oh?
FARNBOROUGH: Does she come every weekend?
LADY JOHN: Whenever we can get her to. But we've only known her a couple of months.
FARNBOROUGH: And I have only known her three weeks! Lady 30 John, I've come to ask you to help me.
LADY JOHN: *(quickly)* With Miss Levering? I can't do it!
FARNBOROUGH: No, no—all that's no good. She only laughs.
LADY JOHN: *(relieved)* Ah!—she looks upon you as a boy.
FARNBOROUGH: *(firing up)* Such rot! What do you think she said to me in London the other day?
LADY JOHN: That she was four years older than you?
FARNBOROUGH: Oh, I knew that. No. She said she knew she was all the charming things I'd been saying, but there was only one way to prove it—and that was to marry some one 40 young enough to be her son. She'd noticed that was what the *most* attractive women did—and she named names.
LADY JOHN: *(laughing)* You were too old!
FARNBOROUGH: *(nods)* Her future husband, she said, was probably just entering Eton.
LADY JOHN: Just like her!
FARNBOROUGH: *(waving the subject away)* No. I wanted to see you about the Secretaryship.
LADY JOHN: You didn't get it, then?
FARNBOROUGH: No. It's the grief of my life.              50
LADY JOHN: Oh, if you don't get one you'll get another.
FARNBOROUGH: But there *is* only one.
LADY JOHN: Only one vacancy?
FARNBOROUGH: Only one man I'd give my ears to work for.
LADY JOHN: *(smiling)* I remember.
FARNBOROUGH: *(quickly)* Do I always talk about Stonor? Well, it's a habit people have got into.
LADY JOHN: I forget, do you know Mr Stonor personally, or *(smiling)* are you just dazzled from afar?
FARNBOROUGH: Oh, I know him. The trouble is he doesn't 60 know me. If he did he'd realise he can't be sure of winning his election without my valuable services.
LADY JOHN: Geoffrey Stonor's re-election is always a foregone conclusion.

FARNBOROUGH: That the great man shares that opinion is precisely his weak point. (*Smiling.*) His only one.

LADY JOHN: You think because the Liberals swept the country the last time—

FARNBOROUGH: How can we be sure any Conservative seat is
70 safe after—(As LADY JOHN *smiles and turns to her papers:*) Forgive me, I know you're not interested in politics *qua* politics. But this concerns Geoffrey Stonor.

LADY JOHN: And you count on my being interested in him like all the rest of my sex.

FARNBOROUGH: (*leans forward*) Lady John, I've heard the news.

LADY JOHN: What news?

FARNBOROUGH: That your little niece—the Scotch heiress—is going to become Mrs Geoffrey Stonor.

80 LADY JOHN: Who told you that?

FARNBOROUGH: Please don't mind my knowing.

LADY JOHN: (*visibly perturbed*) She had set her heart upon having a few days with just her family in the secret, before the flood of congratulations breaks loose.

FARNBOROUGH: Oh, that's all right. I always hear things before other people.

LADY JOHN: Well, I must ask you to be good enough to be very circumspect. I wouldn't have my niece think that I—

FARNBOROUGH: Oh, of course not.

90 LADY JOHN: She will be here in an hour.

FARNBOROUGH: (*jumping up delighted*) What? Today? The future Mrs Stonor!

LADY JOHN: (*harassed*) Yes. Unfortunately we had one or two people already asked for the weekend—

FARNBOROUGH: And I go and invite myself to luncheon! Lady John, you can buy me off. I'll promise to remove myself in five minutes if you'll—

LADY JOHN: No, the penalty is you shall stay and keep the others amused between church and luncheon, and so leave me
100 free. (*Takes up the plan.*) Only remember—

FARNBOROUGH: Wild horses won't get a hint out of me! I only mentioned it to you because—since we've come back to live in this part of the world you've been so awfully kind—I thought, I hoped maybe you—you'd put in a word for me.

LADY JOHN: With—?

FARNBOROUGH: With your nephew that is to be. Though I'm *not* the slavish satellite people make out, you can't doubt—

LADY JOHN: Oh, I don't doubt. But you know Mr Stonor inspires a similar enthusiasm in a good many young—

110 FARNBOROUGH: They haven't studied the situation as I have. They don't know what's at stake. They don't go to that hole Dutfield as I did just to hear his Friday speech.

LADY JOHN: Ah! But you were rewarded. Jean—my niece—wrote me it was "glorious."

FARNBOROUGH: (*judicially*) Well, you know, *I* was disappointed. He's too content just to criticise, just to make his delicate pungent fun of the men who are grappling—very inadequately, of course—still *grappling* with the big questions. There's a carrying power (*gets up and faces an imag-*
120 *inary audience*)—some of Stonor's friends ought to point it out—there's a driving power in the poorest constructive policy that makes the most brilliant criticism look barren.

LADY JOHN: (*with good-humoured malice*) Who told you that?

FARNBOROUGH: You think there's nothing in it because *I* say it.

But now that he's coming into the family, Lord John or somebody really ought to point out—Stonor's overdoing his rôle of magnificent security.

LADY JOHN: I don't see even Lord John offering to instruct Mr Stonor.

FARNBOROUGH: Believe me, that's just Stonor's danger! No-  130 body saying a word, everybody hoping he's on the point of adopting some definite line, something strong and original that's going to fire the public imagination and bring the Tories back into power.

LADY JOHN: So he will.

FARNBOROUGH: (*hotly*) Not if he disappoints meetings—goes calmly up to town—and leaves the field to the Liberals.

LADY JOHN: When did he do anything like that?

FARNBOROUGH: Yesterday! (*With a harassed air.*) And now that he's got this other preoccupation—                                    140

LADY JOHN: You mean—

FARNBOROUGH: Yes, your niece—that spoilt child of Fortune. Of course! (*Stopping suddenly.*) She kept him from the meeting last night. Well! (*Sits down.*) If that's the effect she's going to have it's pretty serious!

LADY JOHN: (*smiling*) You are!

FARNBOROUGH: I can assure you the election agent's more so. He's simply tearing his hair.

LADY JOHN: (*more gravely and coming nearer*) How do you know?                                                                    150

FARNBOROUGH: He told me so himself—yesterday. I scraped acquaintance with the agent just to see if—if—

LADY JOHN: It's not only here that you manœuvre for that Secretaryship!

FARNBOROUGH: (*confidentially*) You can never tell when your chance might come! That election chap's promised to keep me posted.

(*The door flies open and* JEAN DUNBARTON *rushes in.*)

JEAN: Aunt Ellen—here I—

LADY JOHN: (*astonished*) My dear child!

(*They embrace. Enter* LORD JOHN *from the garden—a benevolent, silver-haired despot of sixty-two.*)

LORD JOHN: I thought that was you running up the avenue.    160

(JEAN *greets her uncle warmly, but all the time she and her aunt talk together.* "How did you get here so early?" "I knew you'd be surprised—wasn't it clever of me to manage it? I don't deserve all the credit." "But there isn't any train between—" "Yes, wait till I tell you." "You walked in the broiling sun—" "No, no." "You must be dead. Why didn't you telegraph? I ordered the carriage to meet the 1.10. Didn't you say the 1.10? Yes, I'm sure you did—here's your letter.*")

LORD JOHN: (*has shaken hands with* FARNBOROUGH *and speaks through the torrent*) Now they'll tell each other for ten minutes that she's an hour earlier than we expected.

(LORD JOHN *leads* FARNBOROUGH *towards the garden.*)

FARNBOROUGH: The Freddy Tunbridges said *they* were coming to you this week.

LORD JOHN: Yes, they're dawdling through the park with the Church Brigade.

FARNBOROUGH: Oh! (*With a glance back at* JEAN.) I'll go and meet them.

(*Exit* FARNBOROUGH.)

170    LORD JOHN: (*as he turns back*) That discreet young man will get
on.

LADY JOHN: (*to* JEAN) But *how* did you get here?

JEAN: (*breathless*) "He" motored me down.

LADY JOHN: Geoffrey Stonor? (JEAN *nods.*) Why, where is he,
then?

JEAN: He dropped me at the end of the avenue and went on to
see a supporter about something.

LORD JOHN: You let him go off like that without—

LADY JOHN: (*taking* JEAN's *two hands*) Just tell me, my child, is
180    it all right?

JEAN: My engagement? (*Radiantly.*) Yes, absolutely.

LADY JOHN: Geoffrey Stonor isn't going to be—a little too old
for you?

JEAN: (*laughing*) Bless me, am I such a chicken?

LADY JOHN: Twenty-four used not to be so young—but it's become so.

JEAN: Yes, we don't grow up so quick. (*Gaily.*) But on the other
hand we *stay* up longer.

LORD JOHN: You've got what's vulgarly called "looks," my dear,
190    and that will help to *keep* you up!

JEAN: (*smiling*) I know what Uncle John's thinking. But I'm not
the only girl who's been left "what's vulgarly called" money.

LORD JOHN: You're the only one of our immediate circle who's
been left so beautifully much.

JEAN: Ah, but remember Geoffrey could—everybody *knows*
he could have married any one in England.

LADY JOHN: (*faintly ironic*) I'm afraid everybody does know
it—not excepting Mr Stonor.

LORD JOHN: Well, how spoilt is the great man?

200    JEAN: Not the least little bit in the world. You'll see! He so
wants to know my best-loved relations better. (*Another embrace.*) An orphan has so few belongings, she has to make
the most of them.

LORD JOHN: (*smiling*) Let us hope he'll approve of us on more
intimate acquaintance.

JEAN: (*firmly*) He will. He's an angel. Why, he gets on with my
grandfather!

LADY JOHN: *Does* he? (*Teasing.*) You mean to say Mr Geoffrey
Stonor isn't just a tiny bit—"superior" about Dissenters.

210    JEAN: (*stoutly*) Not half as much as Uncle John and all the rest
of you! My grandfather's been ill again, you know, and
rather difficult—bless him! (*Radiantly.*) But Geoffrey—
(*Clasps her hands.*)

LADY JOHN: He must have powers of persuasion!—to get that
old Covenanter to let you come in an abhorred motor car—
on Sunday, too!

JEAN: (*half whispering*) Grandfather didn't know!

LADY JOHN: Didn't know?

JEAN: I honestly meant to come by train. Geoffrey met me on
220    my way to the station. We had the most glorious run. Oh,
Aunt Ellen, we're so happy! (*Embracing her.*) I've so looked
forward to having you to myself the whole day just to talk to
you about—

LORD JOHN: (*turning away with affected displeasure*) Oh, very
well—

JEAN: (*catches him affectionately by the arm*) You'd find it

dreffly dull to hear me talk about Geoffrey the whole
blessed day!

LADY JOHN: Well, till luncheon, my dear, you mustn't mind if
I—(*To* LORD JOHN, *as she goes to the writing table.*) Miss    230
Levering wasn't only tired last night, she was ill.

LORD JOHN: I thought she looked very white.

JEAN: Who is Miss—You don't mean to say there are other
people?

LADY JOHN: One or two. Your uncle's responsible for asking
that old cynic. St. John Greatorex, and I—

JEAN: (*gravely*) Mr. Greatorex—he's a Radical, isn't he?

LORD JOHN: (*laughing*) Jean! Beginning to "think in parties"!

LADY JOHN: It's very natural now that she should—

JEAN: I only meant it was odd he should be here. Naturally at    240
my grandfather's—

LORD JOHN: It's all right, my child. Of course we expect now
that you'll begin to think like Geoffrey Stonor, and to feel
like Geoffrey Stonor, and to talk like Geoffrey Stonor. And
quite proper too.

JEAN: (*smiling*) Well, if I do think with my husband and feel
with him—as, of course, I shall—it will surprise me if I ever
find myself talking a tenth as well—(*Following her uncle to
the French window.*) You should have heard him at Dutfield—(*Stopping short, delighted.*) Oh! The Freddy Tun-    250
bridges. What? Not Aunt Lydia! Oh-h! (*Looking back
reproachfully at* LADY JOHN, *who makes a discreet motion "I
couldn't help it."*)

(*Enter the* TUNBRIDGES. MR FREDDY, *of no profession and of independent means. Well-groomed, pleasant-looking; of few
words. A "nice man" who likes "nice women," and has married
one of them.* MRS FREDDY *is thirty. An attractive figure, delicate
face, intelligent grey eyes, over-sensitive mouth, and naturally
curling dust-coloured hair.*)

MRS FREDDY: What a delightful surprise!

JEAN: (*shaking hands warmly*) I'm so glad. How d'ye do, Mr
Freddy?

(*Enter* LADY JOHN's *sister,* MRS HERIOT—*smart, pompous,
fifty—followed by* FARNBOROUGH.)

MRS HERIOT: My dear Jean! My darling child!

JEAN: How do you do, aunt?

MRS HERIOT: (*sotto voce*) I wasn't surprised. I always prophe-
sied—                                                          260

JEAN: Sh! *Please!*

FARNBOROUGH: We haven't met since you were in short skirts.
I'm Dick Farnborough.

JEAN: Oh, I remember.

(*They shake hands.*)

MRS FREDDY: (*looking round*) Not down yet—the Elusive
One?

JEAN: Who is the Elusive One?

MRS FREDDY: Lady John's new friend.

LORD JOHN: (*to* JEAN) Oh, I forgot you hadn't seen Miss Levering; such a nice creature! (*To* MRS FREDDY.)—don't you    270
think?

MRS FREDDY: Of course I do. You're lucky to get her to come
so often. She won't go to other people.

LADY JOHN: She knows she can rest here.

FREDDY: *(who has joined* LADY JOHN *near the writing table)* What does she do to tire her?

LADY JOHN: She's been helping my sister and me with a scheme of ours.

MRS HERIOT: She certainly knows how to inveigle money out of the men.

LADY JOHN: It would sound less equivocal, Lydia, if you added that the money is to build baths in our Shelter for Homeless Women.

MRS FREDDY: Homeless women?

LADY JOHN: Yes, in the most insanitary part of Soho.

FREDDY: Oh—a—really.

FARNBOROUGH: It doesn't sound quite in Miss Levering's line!

LADY JOHN: My dear boy, you know as little about what's in a woman's line as most men.

FREDDY: *(laughing)* Oh, I say!

LORD JOHN: *(indulgently to* MR FREDDY *and* FARNBOROUGH*)* Philanthropy in a woman like Miss Levering is a form of restlessness. But she's a *nice* creature; all she needs is to get some "nice" fella to marry her.

MRS FREDDY: *(laughing as she hangs on her husband's arm)* Yes, a woman needs a balance wheel—if only to keep her from flying back to town on a hot day like this.

LORD JOHN: Who's proposing anything so—

MRS FREDDY: The Elusive One.

LORD JOHN: Not Miss—

MRS FREDDY: Yes, before luncheon!

*(Exit* FARNBOROUGH *to the garden.)*

LADY JOHN: She must be in London by this afternoon, she says.

LORD JOHN: What for in the name of—

LADY JOHN: Well, *that* I didn't ask her. But *(consults her watch)* I think I'll just go up and see if she's changed her plans.

*(Exit* LADY JOHN*.)*

LORD JOHN: Oh, she must be *made* to. Such a nice creature! All she needs—

*(Voices outside. Enter fussily, talking and gesticulating,* ST JOHN GREATOREX, *followed by* MISS LEVERING *and* FARNBOROUGH. GREATOREX *is sixty, wealthy, a county magnate, and Liberal MP. He is square, thick-set, square-bearded. His shining bald pate has two strands of coal-black hair trained across his crown from left ear to right and securely pasted there. He has small, twinkling eyes and a reputation for telling good stories after dinner when ladies have left the room. He is carrying a little book for* MISS LEVERING. *She (parasol over shoulder), an attractive, essentially feminine, and rather "smart" woman of thirty-two, with a somewhat foreign grace; the kind of whom men and women alike say, "What's her story? Why doesn't she marry?")*

GREATOREX: I protest! Good Lord! what are the women of this country coming to? I *protest* against Miss Levering being carried off to discuss anything so revolting. Bless my soul! what can a woman like you *know* about it?

MISS LEVERING: *(smiling)* Little enough. Good morning.

GREATOREX: *(relieved)* I should think so indeed!

LORD JOHN: *(aside)* You aren't serious about going—

GREATOREX: *(waggishly breaking in)* We were so happy out there in the summer-house, weren't we?

MISS LEVERING: Ideally.

GREATOREX: And to be haled out to talk about Public *Sanitation* forsooth! *(Hurries after* MISS LEVERING *as she advances to speak to the* FREDDYS *& co.)* Why, God bless my soul, do you realise that's *drains?*

MISS LEVERING: I'm dreadfully afraid it is! *(Holds out her hand for the small book* GREATOREX *is carrying.)*

GREATOREX *returns* MISS LEVERING'S *book open; he has been keeping the place with his finger. She opens it and shuts her handkerchief in.)*

GREATOREX: And we in the act of discussing Italian literature! Perhaps you'll tell me that isn't a more savoury topic for a lady.

MISS LEVERING: But for the tramp population less conducive to savouriness, don't you think, than—baths?

GREATOREX: No, I can't understand this morbid interest in vagrants. *You're* much too—leave it to the others.

JEAN: What others?

GREATOREX: *(with smiling impertinence)* Oh, the sort of woman who smells of indiarubber. The typical English spinster. *(To* MISS LEVERING.*) You* know—Italy's full of her. She never goes anywhere without a mackintosh and a collapsible bath—rubber. When you look at her, it's borne in upon you that she doesn't only smell of rubber. *She's* rubber too.

LORD JOHN: *(laughing)* This is my niece, Miss Jean Dunbarton, Miss Levering.

JEAN: How do you do? *(They shake hands.)*

GREATOREX: *(to* JEAN*)* I'm sure *you* agree with me.

JEAN: About Miss Levering being too—

GREATOREX: For that sort of thing—*much* too—

MISS LEVERING: What a pity you've exhausted the more eloquent adjectives.

GREATOREX: But I haven't!

MISS LEVERING: Well, you can't say to me as you did to Mrs Freddy: "You're too young and too happily married—and too—"*(Glances round smiling at* MRS FREDDY, *who, oblivious, is laughing and talking to her husband and* MRS HERIOT.*)*

JEAN: For what was Mrs Freddy too happily married and all the rest?

MISS LEVERING: *(lightly)* Mr Greatorex was repudiating the horrid rumour that Mrs Freddy had been speaking in public; about Women's Trade Unions—wasn't that what you said, Mrs Heriot?

LORD JOHN: *(chuckling)* Yes, it isn't made up as carefully as your aunt's parties usually are. Here we've got Greatorex *(takes his arm)* who hates political women, and we've got in that mild and inoffensive looking little lady—*(Motion over his shoulder towards* MRS FREDDY.*)*

GREATOREX: *(shrinking down stage in comic terror)* You don't mean she's *really*—

JEAN: *(simultaneously and gaily rising)* Oh, and you've got me!

LORD JOHN: *(with genial affection)* My dear child, he doesn't hate the charming wives and sweethearts who help to win seats.

*(*JEAN *makes her uncle a discreet little signal of warning.)*

MISS LEVERING: Mr Greatorex objects only to the unsexed creatures who—a—

LORD JOHN: *(hastily to cover up his slip)* Yes, yes, who want to act independently of men.

MISS LEVERING: Vote, and do silly things of that sort.

LORD JOHN: *(with enthusiasm)* Exactly.

MRS HERIOT: It will be a long time before we hear any more of *that* nonsense.

JEAN: You mean that rowdy scene in the House of Commons?

MRS HERIOT: Yes. No decent woman will be able to say "Suffrage" without blushing for another generation, thank
380     Heaven!

MISS LEVERING: *(smiling)* Oh? I understood that so little I almost imagined people were more stirred up about it than they'd ever been before.

GREATOREX: *(with a quizzical affectation of gallantry)* Not people like you.

MISS LEVERING: *(teasingly)* How do you know?

GREATOREX: *(with a start)* God bless my soul!

LORD JOHN: She's saying that only to get a rise out of you.

GREATOREX: Ah, yes, your frocks aren't serious enough.

390 MISS LEVERING: I'm told it's an exploded notion that the Suffrage women are all dowdy and dull.

GREATOREX: Don't you believe it!

MISS LEVERING: Well, of course we know you've been an authority on the subject for—let's see, how many years is it you've kept the House in roars whenever Woman's Rights are mentioned?

GREATOREX: *(flattered but not entirely comfortable)* Oh, as long as I've known anything about politics there have been a few discontented old maids and hungry widows—

400 MISS LEVERING: "A few!" That's really rather forbearing of you, Mr Greatorex. I'm afraid the number of the discontented and the hungry was 96,000—among the mill operatives alone. *(Hastily.)* At least the papers said so, didn't they?

GREATOREX: Oh, don't ask me; that kind of woman doesn't interest me, I'm afraid. Only I am able to point out to the people who lose their heads and seem inclined to treat the phenomenon seriously that there's absolutely nothing new in it. There have been women for the last forty years who haven't had anything more pressing to do than petition Par-
410     liament.

MISS LEVERING: *(reflectively)* And that's as far as they've got.

LORD JOHN: *(turning on his heel)* It's as far as they'll ever get.

*(Meets the group coming down.)*

MISS LEVERING: *(chaffing GREATOREX)* Let me see, wasn't a deputation sent to you not long ago? *(Sits)*

GREATOREX: H'm! *(Irritably.)* Yes, yes.

MISS LEVERING: *(as though she has just recalled the circumstances)* Oh, yes, I remember. I thought at the time, in my modest way, it was nothing short of heroic of them to go asking audience of their arch opponent.

420 GREATOREX: *(stoutly)* It didn't come off.

MISS LEVERING: *(innocently)* Oh! I thought they insisted on bearding the lion in his den.

GREATOREX: Of course I wasn't going to be bothered with a lot of—

MISS LEVERING: You don't mean you refused to go out and face them!

GREATOREX: *(with a comic look of terror)* I wouldn't have done it for worlds. But a friend of mine went and had a look at 'em.

MISS LEVERING: *(smiling)* Well, did he get back alive?   430

GREATOREX: Yes, but he advised me not to go. "You're quite right," he said. "Don't you think of bothering," he said. "I've looked over the lot," he said, "and there isn't a weekender among 'em."

JEAN: *(gaily precipitates herself into the conversation)* You remember Mrs Freddy's friend who came to tea here in the winter? *(To GREATOREX.)* He was a member of Parliament too—quite a little young one—he said women would never be respected till they had the vote!

*(GREATOREX snorts, the other men smile and all the women except MRS HERIOT.)*

MRS HERIOT: *(sniffing)* I remember telling him that he was too   440 young to know what he was talking about.

LORD JOHN: Yes, I'm afraid you all sat on the poor gentleman.

LADY JOHN: *(entering)* Oh, *there* you are! *(Greets MISS LEVERING.)*

JEAN: It was such fun. He was flat as a pancake when we'd done with him. Aunt Ellen told him with her most distinguished air she didn't want to be "respected."

MRS FREDDY: *(with a laugh of remonstrance)* My *dear* Lady John!

FARNBOROUGH: Quite right! Awful idea to think you're re-   450 *spected!*

MISS LEVERING: *(smiling)* Simply revolting.

LADY JOHN: *(at writing-table)* Now, you frivolous people, go away. We've only got a few minutes to talk over the terms of the late Mr Soper's munificence before the carriage comes for Miss Levering—

MRS FREDDY: *(to FARNBOROUGH)* Did you know she'd got that old horror to give Lady John £8,000 for her charity before he died?

MRS FREDDY: Who got him to?   460

LADY JOHN: Miss Levering. He wouldn't do it for me, but she brought him round.

FREDDY: Yes. Bah-ee Jove! I expect so.

MRS FREDDY: *(turning enthusiastically to her husband)* Isn't she wonderful?

LORD JOHN: *(aside)* Nice creature. All she needs is—

*(MR and MRS FREDDY and FARNBOROUGH stroll off to the garden. LADY JOHN is on the far side of the writing-table. MRS HERIOT is at the top. JEAN and LORD JOHN on the left.)*

GREATOREX: *(on divan centre, aside to MISS LEVERING)* Too "wonderful" to waste your time on the wrong people.

MISS LEVERING: I shall waste less of my time after this.

GREATOREX: I'm relieved to hear it. I can't see you wheedling   470 money for shelters and rot of that sort out of retired grocers.

MISS LEVERING: You see, you call it rot. We couldn't have got £8,000 out of *you.*

GREATOREX: *(very low)* I'm not sure.

*(MISS LEVERING looks at him.)*

GREATOREX: If I gave you that much—for your little projects— what would you give me?

MISS LEVERING: *(speaking quietly)* Soper didn't ask that.

GREATOREX: *(horrified)* Soper! I should think not!

LORD JOHN: *(turning to MISS LEVERING)* Soper? You two still talking Soper? How flattered the old beggar'd be!   480

LORD JOHN: *(lower)* Did you hear what Mrs Heriot said about him? "So kind; so munificent—so *vulgar,* poor soul, we couldn't know him in London—*but we shall meet him in heaven.*"

(GREATOREX *and* LORD JOHN *go off laughing.*)

LADY JOHN: *(to* MISS LEVERING*)* Sit over there, my dear. *(Indicating chair in front of the writing table.)* You needn't stay, Jean. This won't interest you.

MISS LEVERING: *(in the tone of one agreeing)* It's only an effort to meet the greatest evil in the world.

490  JEAN: *(pausing as she's following the others)* What do you call the greatest evil in the world?

(*Looks pass between* MRS HERIOT *and* LADY JOHN.)

MISS LEVERING: *(without emphasis)* The helplessness of women.

(JEAN *stands still.*)

LADY JOHN: *(rising and putting her arm about the girl's shoulder)* Jean, darling, I know you can think of nothing but *(aside)* him—so just go and—

JEAN: *(brightly)* Indeed, indeed, I can think of everything better than I ever did before. He has lit up everything for me—made everything vivider, more—more significant.

500  MISS LEVERING: *(turning round)* Who has?

JEAN: Oh, yes, I don't care about other things less but a thousand times more.

LADY JOHN: You *are* in love.

MISS LEVERING: Oh, that's it! *(Smiling at* JEAN.*)* I congratulate you.

LADY JOHN: *(returning to the outspread plan)* Well—*this,* you see, obviates the difficulty you raised.

MISS LEVERING: Yes, quite.

MRS HERIOT: But it's going to cost a great deal more.

510  MISS LEVERING: It's worth it.

MRS HERIOT: We'll have nothing left for the organ at St Pilgrim's.

LADY JOHN: My dear Lydia, we're putting the organ aside.

MRS HERIOT: *(with asperity)* We can't afford to "put aside" the elevating effect of music.

LADY JOHN: What we must make for, first, is the cheap and humanely conducted lodging-house.

MRS HERIOT: There are several of those already, but poor St Pilgrim's—

520  MISS LEVERING: There are none for the poorest women.

LADY JOHN: No, even the excellent Soper was for multiplying Rowton Houses. You can never get men to realise—you can't always get women—

MISS LEVERING: It's the work least able to wait.

MRS HERIOT: I don't agree with you, and I happen to have spent a great deal of my life in works of charity.

MISS LEVERING: Ah, then you'll be interested in the girl I saw dying in a Tramp Ward a little while ago. *Glad* her cough was worse—only she mustn't die before her father. Two

530  reasons. Nobody but her to keep the old man out of the workhouse—and "father is so proud." If she died first, he would starve; worst of all he might hear what had happened up in London to his girl.

MRS HERIOT: She didn't say, I suppose, how she happened to fall so low.

MISS LEVERING: Yes, she had been in service. She lost the train

back one Sunday night and was too terrified of her employer to dare ring him up after hours. The wrong person found her crying on the platform.

MRS HERIOT: She should have gone to one of the Friendly So-  540  cieties.

MISS LEVERING: At eleven at night?

MRS HERIOT: And there are the Rescue Leagues. I myself have been connected with one for twenty years—

MISS LEVERING: *(reflectively)* "Twenty years!" Always arriving "after the train's gone"—after the girl and the Wrong Person have got to the journey's end.

(MRS HERIOT'S *eyes flash.*)

JEAN: Where is she now?

LADY JOHN: Never mind.

MISS LEVERING: Two nights ago she was waiting at a street cor-  550  ner in the rain.

MRS HERIOT: Near a public-house, I suppose.

MISS LEVERING: Yes, a sort of "public-house." She was plainly dying—she was told she shouldn't be out in the rain. "I mustn't go in yet," she said. "*This* is what he gave me," and she began to cry. In her hand were two pennies silvered over to look like half-crowns.

MRS HERIOT: I don't believe that story. It's just the sort of thing some sensation-monger trumps up—now, who tells you such—  560

MISS LEVERING: Several credible people. I didn't believe them till—

JEAN: Till—?

MISS LEVERING: Till last week I saw for myself.

LADY JOHN: *Saw?* Where?

MISS LEVERING: In a low lodging-house not a hundred yards from the church you want a new organ for.

MRS HERIOT: How did *you* happen to be there?

MISS LEVERING: I was on a pilgrimage.

JEAN: A pilgrimage?  570

MISS LEVERING: Into the Underworld.

LADY JOHN: *You* went?

JEAN: How *could* you?

MISS LEVERING: I put on an old gown and a tawdry hat— *(Turns to* LADY JOHN.*)* You'll never know how many things are hidden from a woman in good clothes. The bold, free look of a man at a woman he believes to be destitute—you must *feel* that look on you before you can understand—a good half of history.

MRS HERIOT: *(rises)* Jean!—  580

JEAN: But where did you go—dressed like that?

MISS LEVERING: Down among the homeless women—on a wet night looking for shelter.

LADY JOHN: *(hastily)* No wonder you've been ill.

JEAN: *(under her breath)* And it's like that?

MISS LEVERING: No.

JEAN: No?

MISS LEVERING: It's so much worse I dare not tell about it— even if you weren't here I couldn't.

MRS HERIOT: *(to* JEAN*)* You needn't suppose, darling, that those  590  wretched creatures feel it as we would.

MISS LEVERING: The girls who need shelter and work aren't all serving-maids.

MRS HERIOT: *(with an involuntary flash)* We know that all the women who—*make mistakes* aren't.

MISS LEVERING: *(steadily)* That is why *every* woman ought to take an interest in this—every girl too.

JEAN                                    Yes—oh, yes!
            *(simultaneously)*
LADY JOHN                                No. This is a matter for
600                                      us older—

MRS HERIOT: *(with an air of sly challenge)* Or for a person who has some special knowledge. *(Significantly.)* We can't pretend to have access to such sources of information as Miss Levering.

MISS LEVERING: *(meeting* MRS HERIOT's *eye steadily)* Yes, for I can give you access. As you seem to think, I have some first-hand knowledge about homeless girls.

LADY JOHN: *(cheerfully turning it aside)* Well, my dear, it will all come in convenient. *(Tapping the plan.)*

610 MISS LEVERING: It once happened to me to take offence at an ugly thing that was going on under my father's roof. Oh, *years* ago! I was an impulsive girl. I turned my back on my father's house—

LADY JOHN: *(for* JEAN's *benefit)* That was ill-advised.

MRS HERIOT: Of course, if a girl does *that*—

MISS LEVERING: That was what all my relations said *(with a glance at* JEAN*)*, and I couldn't explain.

JEAN: Not to your mother?

MISS LEVERING: She was dead. I went to London to a small 620 hotel and tried to find employment. I wandered about all day and every day from agency to agency. I was supposed to be educated. I'd been brought up partly in Paris; I could play several instruments, and sing little songs in four different tongues. *(Slight pause.)*

JEAN: Did nobody want you to teach French or sing the little songs?

MISS LEVERING: The heads of schools thought me too young. There were people ready to listen to my singing, but the terms—they were too hard. Soon my money was gone. I 630 began to pawn my trinkets. *They* went.

JEAN: And still no work?

MISS LEVERING: No; but by that time I had some real education—an unpaid hotel bill, and not a shilling in the world. *(Slight pause.)* Some girls think it hardship to have to earn their living. The horror is not to be allowed to—

JEAN: *(bending forward)* What happened?

LADY JOHN: *(rises)* My dear *(to* MISS LEVERING*)* have your things been sent down? Are you quite ready?

MISS LEVERING: Yes, all but my hat.

640 JEAN: Well?

MISS LEVERING: Well, by chance I met a friend of my family.

JEAN: That was lucky.

MISS LEVERING: I thought so. He was nearly ten years older than I. He said he wanted to help me. *(Pause.)*

JEAN: And didn't he?

*(*LADY JOHN *lays her hand on* MISS LEVERING's *shoulder.)*

MISS LEVERING: Perhaps after all he did. *(With sudden change of tone.)* Why do I waste time over myself? I belonged to the little class of armed women. My body wasn't born weak, and my spirit wasn't broken by the *habit* of slavery. But, as Mrs 650 Heriot was kind enough to hint, I do know something about the possible fate of homeless girls. I found there were pleasant parks, museums, free libraries in our great rich London—and not one single place where destitute women can be sure of work that isn't killing or food that isn't worse than prison fare. That's why women ought not to sleep o' nights till this Shelter stands spreading out wide arms.

JEAN: No, no—

MRS HERIOT: *(gathering up her gloves, fan, prayer-book, etc.)* Even when it's built—you'll see! Many of those creatures will prefer the life they lead. They *like* it.                   660

MISS LEVERING: A woman told me—one of the sort that knows—told me many of them "like it" so much that they are indifferent to the risk of being sent to prison. "*It gives them a rest,*" she said.

LADY JOHN: A rest!

*(*MISS LEVERING *glances at the clock as she rises to go upstairs.)*

*(*LADY JOHN *and* MRS HERIOT *bend their heads over the plan, covertly talking.)*

JEAN: *(intercepting* MISS LEVERING*)* I want to begin to understand something of—I'm horribly ignorant.

MISS LEVERING: *(Looks at her searchingly)* I'm a rather busy person—

JEAN: *(interrupting)* I have quite a special reason for wanting 670 *not* to be ignorant. *(Impulsively.)* I'll go to town tomorrow, if you'll come and lunch with me.

MISS LEVERING: Thank you—I *(catches* MRS HERIOT's *eye)*—I must go and put my hat on.

*(Exit upstairs.)*

MRS HERIOT: *(aside)* How little she minds all these horrors!

LADY JOHN: They turn me cold. Ugh! *(Rising, harassed.)* I wonder if she's signed the visitors' book!

MRS HERIOT: For all her Shelter schemes, she's a hard woman.

JEAN: Miss Levering is?

MRS HERIOT: Oh, of course *you* won't think so. She has angled 680 very adroitly for your sympathy.

JEAN: She doesn't look hard.

LADY JOHN: *(glancing at* JEAN *and taking alarm)* I'm not sure but what she does. Her mouth—always like this . . . as if she were holding back something by main force!

MRS HERIOT: *(half under her breath)* Well, so she is.

*(Exit* LADY JOHN *into the lobby to look at the visitors' book.)*

JEAN: Why haven't I seen her before?

MRS HERIOT: Oh, she's lived abroad. *(Debating with herself.)* You don't know about her, I suppose?

JEAN: I don't know how Aunt Ellen came to know her.          690

MRS HERIOT: That was my doing. But I didn't bargain for her being introduced to you.

JEAN: She seems to go everywhere. And why shouldn't she?

MRS HERIOT: *(quickly)* You mustn't ask her to Eaton Square.

JEAN: I have.

MRS HERIOT: Then you'll have to get out of it.

JEAN: *(with a stubborn look)* I must have a reason. And a very good reason.

MRS HERIOT: Well, it's not a thing I should have preferred to tell you, but I know how difficult you are to guide . . . so I 700 suppose you'll have to know. *(Lowering her voice.)* It was ten or twelve years ago. I found her horribly ill in a lonely Welsh farmhouse. We had taken the Manor for that August. The farmer's wife was frightened, and begged me to go and see what I thought. I soon saw how it was—I thought she was dying.

JEAN: *Dying!* What was the—

MRS HERIOT: I got no more out of her than the farmer's wife did. She had had no letters. There had been no one to see her except a man down from London, a shady-looking doc-tor—nameless, of course. And then this result. The farmer and his wife, highly respectable people, were incensed. They were for turning the girl out.

JEAN: *Oh!* but—

MRS HERIOT: Yes. Pitiless some of these people are! I insisted they should treat the girl humanely, and we became friends . . . that is, "sort of." In spite of all I did for her—

JEAN: What did you do?

MRS HERIOT: I—I've told you, and I lent her money. No small sum either.

JEAN: Has she never paid it back?

MRS HERIOT: Oh, yes, after a time. But I *always* kept her se-cret—as much as I knew of it.

JEAN: But you've been telling me!

MRS HERIOT: That was my duty—and I *never* had her full con-fidence.

JEAN: Wasn't it natural she—

MRS HERIOT: Well, all things considered, she might have wanted to tell me who was responsible.

JEAN: Oh! Aunt Lydia!

MRS HERIOT: All she ever said was that she was ashamed— (*los-ing her temper and her fine feeling for the innocence of her auditor*)—ashamed that she "hadn't had the courage to re-sist"—not the original temptation but the pressure brought to bear on her "not to go through with it," as she said.

JEAN: (*wrinkling her brows*) You are being so delicate—I'm not sure I understand.

MRS HERIOT: (*irritably*) The only thing you need understand is that she's not a desirable companion for a young girl.

(*Pause.*)

JEAN: When did you see her after—after—

MRS HERIOT: (*with a slight grimace*) I met her last winter at the Bishop's. (*Hurriedly.*) She's a connection of his wife's. They'd got her to help with some of their work. Then she took hold of ours. Your aunt and uncle are quite foolish about her, and I'm debarred from taking any steps, at least till the Shelter is out of hand.

JEAN: I do rather wonder she can bring herself to talk about—the unfortunate women of the world.

MRS HERIOT: The effrontery of it!

JEAN: Or . . . the courage! (*Puts her hand up to her throat as if the sentence had caught there.*)

MRS HERIOT: Even presumes to set *me* right! Of course I don't *mind* in the least, poor soul . . . but I feel I owe it to your dead mother to tell you about her, especially as you're old enough now to know something about life—

JEAN: (*slowly*) —and since a girl needn't be very old to suffer for her ignorance. (*Moves a little away.*) I *felt* she was rather wonderful.

MRS HERIOT: *Wonderful!*

JEAN: (*pausing*) . . . To have lived through *that* when she was . . . how old?

MRS HERIOT: (*rising*) Oh, nineteen or thereabouts.

JEAN: Five years younger than I. To be abandoned and to come out of it like this!

MRS HERIOT: (*laying her hand on the girl's shoulder*) It was too bad to have to tell you such a sordid story today of all days.

JEAN: It is a very terrible story, but this wasn't a bad time. I feel very sorry today for women who aren't happy.

(*Motor horn heard faintly.*)

(*Jumping up.*) That's Geoffrey!

MRS HERIOT: Mr Stonor! What makes you think . . . ?

JEAN: Yes, yes. I'm sure, I'm sure—

(*Checks herself as she is flying off. Turns and sees* LORD JOHN *entering from the garden.*)

(*Motor horn louder.*)

LORD JOHN: Who do you think is motoring up the drive?

JEAN: (*catching hold of him*) Oh, dear! How am I ever going to be able to behave like a girl who isn't engaged to the only man in the world worth marrying?

MRS HERIOT: You were expecting Mr Stonor all the time!

JEAN: He promised he'd come to luncheon if it was humanly possible; but I was afraid to tell you for fear he'd be pre-vented.

LORD JOHN: (*laughing as he crosses to the lobby*) You felt we couldn't have borne the disappointment.

JEAN: I felt I couldn't.

(*The lobby door opens.* LADY JOHN *appears radiant, followed by a tall figure in a dustcoat, etc., no goggles. He has straight, firm features, a little blunt; fair skin, high coloured; fine, straight hair, very fair; grey eyes, set somewhat prominently and heavy when not interested; lips full, but firmly moulded.* GEOFFREY STONOR *is heavier than a man of forty should be, but otherwise in the pink of physical condition. The* FOOTMAN *stands waiting to help him off with his motor coat.*)

LADY JOHN: Here's an agreeable surprise!

(JEAN *has gone forward only a step, and stands smiling at the approaching figure.*)

LORD JOHN: How do you do? (*As he comes between them and briskly shakes hands with* STONOR.)

(FARNBOROUGH *appears at the French window.*)

FARNBOROUGH: Yes, by Jove! (*Turning to the others clustered round the window.*) What gigantic luck!

(*Those outside crane and glance, and then elaborately turn their backs and pretend to be talking among themselves, but betray as far as manners permit the enormous sensation the ar-rival has created.*)

STONOR: How do you do?

(*Shakes hands with* MRS HERIOT, *who has rushed up to him with both hers outstretched. He crosses to* JEAN, *who meets him half way; they shake hands, smiling into each other's eyes.*)

JEAN: Such a long time since we met!

LORD JOHN: (*to* STONOR) You're growing very enterprising. I could hardly believe my ears when I heard you'd motored all the way from town to see a supporter on Sunday.

STONOR: I don't know how we covered the ground in the old days. (*To* LADY JOHN.) It's no use to stand for your borough any more. The American, you know, he "runs" for Congress. By and by we shall all be flying after the thing we want. (*Smiles at* JEAN.)

JEAN: Sh! (*Smiles and then glances over her shoulder and speaks low.*) All sorts of irrelevant people here.

800 FARNBOROUGH: (*unable to resist the temptation, comes forward*) How do you do, Mr Stonor?

STONOR: Oh—how d'you do.

FARNBOROUGH: Some of them were arguing in the smoking-room last night whether it didn't hurt a man's chances going about in a motor.

LORD JOHN: Yes, we've been hearing a lot of stories about the unpopularity of motor cars—among the class that hasn't got 'em, of course. What do you say?

LADY JOHN: I'm sure you gain more votes by being able to reach 810    so many more of your constituency than we used—

STONOR: Well, I don't know—I've sometimes wondered whether the charm of our presence wasn't counterbalanced by the way we tear about smothering our fellow-beings in dust and running down their pigs and chickens, not to speak of their children.

LORD JOHN: (*anxiously*) What on the whole are the prospects?

(FARNBOROUGH *cranes forward.*)

STONOR: (*gravely*) We shall have to work harder than we realised.

FARNBOROUGH: Ah! (*Retires towards group.*)

820 JEAN: (*in a half-aside as she slips her arm in her uncle's and smiles at* GEOFFREY) He says he believes I'll be able to make a real difference to his chances. Isn't it angelic of him?

STONOR: (*in a jocular tone*) Angelic? Macchiavelian. I pin all my hopes on your being able to counteract the pernicious influence of my opponent's glib wife.

JEAN: You want me to have a *real* share in it all, don't you, Geoffrey?

STONOR: (*smiling into her eyes*) Of course I do.

(FARNBOROUGH *drops down again on pretence of talking to* MRS HERIOT.)

LORD JOHN: I don't gather you're altogether sanguine. Any 830    complication?

(JEAN *and* LADY JOHN *stand close together, the girl radiant, following* STONOR *with her eyes and whispering to the sympathetic elder woman.*)

STONOR: Well, (*taking Sunday paper out of pocket*) there's this agitation about the Woman Question. Oddly enough, it seems likely to affect the issue.

LORD JOHN: Why should it? Can't you do what the other four hundred have done?

STONOR: (*laughs*) Easily. But, you see, the mere fact that four hundred and twenty members have been worried into promising support—and then once in the House have let the matter severely alone—

840 LORD JOHN: (*to* STONOR) Let it alone! Bless my soul, I should think so indeed.

STONOR: Of course. Only it's a device that's somewhat worn.

(*Enter* MISS LEVERING, *with hat on; gloves and veil in her hand.*)

LORD JOHN: Still if they think they're getting a future Cabinet Minister on their side—

STONOR: . . . it will be sufficiently embarassing for the Cabinet Minister.

(STONOR *turns to speak to* JEAN. *He stops dead seeing* MISS LEVERING.)

JEAN: (*smiling*) You know one another?

MISS LEVERING: (*looking at* STONOR *with intentness but quite calmly*) Everybody in this part of the world knows Mr Stonor, but he doesn't know me.    850

LORD JOHN: Miss Levering.

(*They bow.*)

(*Enter* GREATOREX, *sidling in with an air of giving* MRS FREDDY *a wide berth.*)

JEAN: (*to* MISS LEVERING *with artless enthusiasm*) Oh, have you been hearing him speak?

MISS LEVERING: Yes, I was visiting some relations near Dutfield. They took me to hear you.

STONOR: Oh—the night the Suffragettes made their customary row.

MISS LEVERING: The night they asked you—

STONOR: (*flying at the first chance of distraction, shakes hands with* MRS FREDDY) Well, Mrs Freddy, what do you think of 860 your friends now?

MRS FREDDY: My friends?

STONOR: (*offering her the Sunday paper*) Yes, the disorderly women.

MRS FREDDY: (*with dignity*) They are not my friends, but I don't think you must call them—

STONOR: Why not? (*Laughs.*) I can forgive them for worrying the late Government. But they *are* disorderly.

MISS LEVERING: (*quietly*) Isn't the phrase consecrated to a different class?    870

GREATOREX: (*who has got hold of the Sunday paper*) He's perfectly right. How do you do? Disorderly women! That's what they are!

FARNBOROUGH: (*reading over his shoulder*) Ought to be locked up! Every one of 'em.

GREATOREX: (*assenting angrily*) Public nuisances! Going about with dog whips and spitting in policemen's faces.

FREDDY: (*with a harassed air*) I wonder if they did spit?

GREATOREX: (*exulting*) Of *course* they did.

MRS FREDDY: (*turns on him*) You're no authority on what they 880 do. *You* run away.

GREATOREX: (*trying to turn the laugh*) Run away? Yes. (*Backing a few paces.*) And if ever I muster up courage to come back, it will be to vote for better manners in public life, not worse than we have already.

MRS FREDDY: (*meekly*) So should I. Don't think that *I* defend the Suffragette methods.

JEAN: (*with cheerful curiosity*) Still, you *are* an advocate of the Suffrage, aren't you?

MRS FREDDY: Here? (*Shrugs.*) I don't beat the air.    890

GREATOREX: *(mocking)* Only policemen.

MRS FREDDY: *(plaintively)* If you cared to know the attitude of the real workers in the reform, you might have noticed in any paper last week we lost no time in dissociating ourselves from the little group of hysterical—*(Catches her husband's eye, and instantly checks her flow of words.)*

MRS HERIOT: They have lowered the whole sex in the eyes of the entire world.

JEAN: *(joining* GEOFFREY STONOR*)* I can't quite see what they want—those Suffragettes.

GREATOREX: Notoriety.

FARNBOROUGH: What they want? A good thrashin'—that's what I'd give 'em.

MRS HERIOT: *(murmurs)* Spirited fellow!

LORD JOHN: Well, there's one sure thing—they've dished their goose. (GREATOREX *chuckles, still reading the account.)* I believe these silly scenes are a pure joy to you.

GREATOREX: Final death-blow to the whole silly business!

JEAN: *(mystified, looking from one to the other)* The Suffragettes don't seem to *know* they're dead.

GREATOREX: They still keep up a sort of death-rattle. But they've done for themselves.

JEAN: *(clasping her hands with fervour)* Oh, I hope they'll last till the election's over.

FARNBOROUGH: *(stares)* Why?

JEAN: Oh, we want them to get the working man to—*(stumbling and a little confused)*—to vote for . . . the Conservative candidate. Isn't that so?

*(Looking round for help. General laughter.)*

LORD JOHN: Fancy, Jean—!

GREATOREX: The working man's a good deal of an ass, but even he won't listen to—

JEAN: *(again appealing to the silent* STONOR*)* But he *does* listen like anything! I asked why there were so few at the Long Mitcham meeting, and I was told, 'Oh, they've all gone to hear Miss—'

STONOR: Just for a lark, that was.

LORD JOHN: It has no real effect on the vote.

GREATOREX: Not the smallest.

JEAN: *(wide-eyed to* STONOR*)* Why, I thought you said—

STONOR: *(hastily, rubbing his hand over the lower part of his face and speaking quickly)* I've a notion a little soap and water wouldn't do me any harm.

LORD JOHN: I'll take you up. You know Freddy Tunbridge.

*(*STONOR *pauses to shake hands. Exeunt all three.)*

JEAN: *(perplexed, as* STONOR *turns away, says to* GREATOREX*)* Well, if women are of no importance in politics, it isn't for the reason you gave. There is now and then a weekender among them.

GREATOREX: *(shuffles about uneasily)* Hm—Hm. *(Finds himself near* MRS FREDDY.*)* Lord! The perils that beset the feet of man! *(With an air of comic caution, moves away, left.)*

JEAN: *(to* FARNBOROUGH, *aside, laughing)* Why does he behave like that?

FARNBOROUGH: His moral sense is shocked.

JEAN: Why, I saw him and Mrs Freddy together at the French Play the other night—as thick as thieves.

MISS LEVERING: Ah, that was before he knew her revolting views.

JEAN: What revolting views?

GREATOREX: Sh! Sunday.

*(As* GREATOREX *sidles cautiously further away.)*

JEAN: *(laughing in spite of herself)* I can't believe women are so helpless when I see men so afraid of them.

GREATOREX: The great mistake was in teaching them to read and write.

JEAN: *(over* MISS LEVERING'S *shoulder, whispers) Say* something.

MISS LEVERING: *(to* GREATOREX, *smiling)* Oh no, that wasn't the worst mistake.

GREATOREX: Yes, it was.

MISS LEVERING: No. Believe me. The mistake was in letting women learn to talk.

GREATOREX: Ah! *(Wheels about with sudden rapture.)* I see now what's to be the next great reform.

MISS LEVERING: *(holding up the little volume)* When women are all dumb, no more discussions of the 'Paradiso.'

GREATOREX: *(with a gesture of mock rapture)* The thing itself! *(Aside.)* That's a great deal better than talking about it, as I'm sure *you* know.

MISS LEVERING: Why do you think I know?

GREATOREX: Only the plain women are in any doubt.

*(*JEAN *joins* MISS LEVERING.*)*

GREATOREX: Wait for me, Farnborough. I cannot go about unprotected.

*(Exeunt* FARNBOROUGH *and* GREATOREX.*)*

MRS FREDDY: It's true what that old cynic says. The scene in the House has put back the reform a generation.

JEAN: I wish I'd been there.

MRS FREDDY: I *was*.

JEAN: Oh, was it like the papers said?

MRS FREDDY: Worse. I've never been so moved in public. No tragedy, no great opera ever gripped an audience as the situation in the House did that night. There we all sat breathless—with everything more favourable to us than it had been within the memory of women. Another five minutes and the Resolution would have passed. Then . . . all in a moment—

LORD JOHN: *(to* MRS HERIOT*)* Listen—they're talking about the female hooligans.

MRS HERIOT: No, thank you! *(Sits apart with the "Church Times.")*

MRS FREDDY: *(excitedly)* All in a moment a horrible dingy little flag was poked through the grille of the Woman's Gallery— cries—insults—scuffling—the police—the ignominious turning out of the women—*us* as well as the—Oh, I can't *think* of it without—*(Jumps up and walks to and fro. Pauses.)* Then the next morning! The people gloating. Our friends antagonised—people who were wavering—nearly won over—all thrown back—heart breaking! Even my husband! Freddy's been an angel about letting me take my share when I felt I must—but of course I've always known he doesn't really like it. It makes him shy. I'm sure it gives him a horrid twist inside when he sees my name among the speakers on the placards. But he's always been an angel about it before this. After the disgraceful scene he said, "It just shows how unfit women are for any sort of coherent thinking or concerted action."

JEAN: To think that it should be women who've given the Cause the worst blow it ever had!

MRS FREDDY: The work of forty years destroyed in five minutes!

1010 JEAN: They must have felt pretty sick when they woke up the next morning—the Suffragettes.

MRS FREDDY: I don't waste any sympathy on *them*. I'm thinking of the penalty *all* women have to pay because a handful of hysterical—

JEAN: Still I think I'm sorry for them. It must be dreadful to find you've done such a lot of harm to the thing you care most about in the world.

MISS LEVERING: Do you picture the Suffragettes sitting in sackcloth?

MRS FREDDY: Well, they can't help realising *now* what they've 1020 done.

MISS LEVERING: (*quietly*) Isn't it just possible they realise they've waked up interest in the Woman Question so that it's advertised in every paper and discussed in every house from Land's End to John O'Groats? Don't you think *they* know there's been more said and written about it in these ten days since the scene, than in the ten years before it?

MRS FREDDY: You aren't saying you think it was a good way to get what they wanted?

MISS LEVERING: (*shrugs*) I'm only pointing out that it seems not 1030 such a bad way to get it known they *do* want something—and (*smiling*) "want it bad."

JEAN: (*getting up*) Didn't Mr Greatorex say women had been politely petitioning Parliament for forty years?

MISS LEVERING: And men have only laughed.

JEAN: But they'd come round. (*She looks from one to the other.*) Mrs Tunbridge says, before that horrid scene, everything was favourable at last.

MISS LEVERING: At last? Hadn't it been just as "favourable" before?

1040 MRS FREDDY: No. We'd never had so many members pledged to our side.

MISS LEVERING: I thought I'd heard somebody say the Bill had got as far as that, time and time again.

JEAN: Oh no. Surely not—

MRS FREDDY: (*reluctantly*) Y—yes. This was only a Resolution. The Bill passed a second reading thirty-seven years ago.

JEAN: (*with wide eyes*) And what difference did it make?

MISS LEVERING: The men laughed rather louder.

MRS FREDDY: Oh, it's got as far as a second reading several 1050 times—but we never had so many friends in the House before—

MISS LEVERING: (*with a faint smile*) "Friends!"

JEAN: Why do you say it like that?

MISS LEVERING: Perhaps because I was thinking of a funny story—he said it was funny—a Liberal Whip told me the other day. A Radical Member went out of the House after his speech in favour of the Woman's Bill, and as he came back half an hour later, he heard some Members talking in the Lobby about the astonishing number who were going to 1060 vote for the measure. And the Friend of Woman dropped

his jaw and clutched the man next to him: "My God!" he said, "you don't mean to say they're going to give it to them!"

JEAN: Oh!

MRS FREDDY: You don't think all men in Parliament are like that!

MISS LEVERING: I don't think all men are burglars, but I lock my doors.

JEAN: (*below her breath*) You think that night of the scene—you think the men didn't *mean* to play fair?

MISS LEVERING: (*her coolness in contrast to the excitement of* 1070 *the others*) Didn't the women sit quiet till ten minutes to closing time?

JEAN: Ten minutes to settle a question like that!

MISS LEVERING: (*quietly to* MRS FREDDY) Couldn't you see the men were at their old game?

LADY JOHN: (*coming forward*) You think they were just putting off the issue till it was too late?

MISS LEVERING: (*in a detached tone*) I wasn't there, but I haven't heard anybody deny that the women waited till ten minutes to eleven. Then they discovered the policeman 1080 who'd been sent up at the psychological moment to the back of the gallery. Then, I'm told, when the women saw they were betrayed once more, they utilised the few minutes left, to impress on the country at large the fact of their demands—did it in the only way left them. (*Sits leaning forward reflectively smiling, chin in hand.*) It does rather look to the outsider as if the well-behaved women had worked for forty years and made less impression on the world then those fiery young women made in five minutes.

MRS FREDDY: Oh, come, be fair!     1090

MISS LEVERING: Well, you must admit that, next day, every newspaper reader in Europe and America knew there were women in England in such dead earnest about the Suffrage that the men had stopped laughing at last, and turned them out of the House. Men even advertised how little they appreciated the fun by sending the women to gaol in pretty sober earnest. And all the world was talking about it.

(MRS HERIOT *lays down the "Church Times" and joins the others.*)

LADY JOHN: I have noticed, whenever the men aren't there, the women sit and discuss that scene.

JEAN: (*cheerfully*) I shan't have to wait till the men are gone. 1100 (*Leans over* LADY JOHN's *shoulder and says half aside*) He's in sympathy.

LADY JOHN: How do you know?

JEAN: He told the interrupting women so.

(MRS FREDDY *looks mystified. The others smile.*)

LADY JOHN: Oh!

(MR FREDDY *and* LORD JOHN *appear by the door they went out of. They stop to talk.*)

MRS FREDDY: Here's Freddy! (*Lower, hastily to* MISS LEVERING) You're judging from the outside. Those of us who have been working for years—we all realise it was a perfectly lunatic proceeding. Why, *think!* The only chance of our getting what we want is by *winning over* the men. 1110 (*Her watchful eye, leaving her husband for a moment, catches* MISS LEVERING's *little involuntary gesture.*) What's the matter?

MISS LEVERING: "Winning over the men" has been the woman's way for centuries. Do you think the result should make us proud of our policy? Yes? Then go and walk in Piccadilly at midnight. (*The older women glance at* JEAN.) No, I forgot—

MRS HERIOT: (*with majesty*) Yes, it's not the first time you've forgotten.

1120 MISS LEVERING: I forgot the magistrate's ruling. He said no decent woman had any business to be in London's main thoroughfare at night unless she has *a man with her*. I heard that in Nine Elms, too. "You're obliged to take up with a chap!" was what the woman said.

MRS HERIOT: (*rising*) JEAN! Come!

(*She takes* JEAN *by her arm and draws her to the window, where she signals* GREATOREX *and* FARNBOROUGH. MRS FREDDY *joins her husband and* LORD JOHN.)

LADY JOHN: (*kindly, aside to* MISS LEVERING) My dear, I think Lydia Heriot's right. We oughtn't to do anything or *say* anything to encourage this ferment of feminism, and I'll tell you why: it's likely to bring a very terrible thing in its train.

1130 MISS LEVERING: What terrible thing?

LADY JOHN: Sex antagonism.

MISS LEVERING: (*rising*) It's here.

LADY JOHN: (*very gravely*) Don't say that.

(JEAN *has quietly disengaged herself from* MRS HERIOT, *and the group at the window returns and stands behind* LADY JOHN, *looking up into* MISS LEVERING'S *face.*)

MISS LEVERING: (*to* LADY JOHN) You're so conscious it's here, you're afraid to have it mentioned.

LADY JOHN: (*turning and seeing* JEAN. *Rising hastily*) If it's here, it is the fault of those women agitators.

MISS LEVERING: (*gently*) No woman *begins* that way. (*Leans forward with clasped hands looking into vacancy.*) Every

1140 woman's in a state of natural subjection (*smiles at* JEAN)— no, I'd rather say allegiance to her idea of romance and her hope of motherhood. They're embodied for her in man. They're the strongest things in life—till man kills them. (*Rousing herself and looking into* LADY JOHN'S *face.*) Let's be fair. Each woman knows why that allegiance died.

(LADY JOHN *turns hastily, sees* LORD JOHN *coming down with* MR FREDDY *and meets them at the foot of the stairs.* MISS LEVERING *has turned to the table looking for her gloves, etc., among the papers; unconsciously drops the handkerchief she had in her little book.*)

JEAN: (*in a low voice to* MISS LEVERING) All this talk against the wicked Suffragettes—it makes me want to go and hear what they've got to say for themselves.

MISS LEVERING: (*smiling with a noncommittal air as she finds*

1150 *the veil she's been searching for*) Well, they're holding a meeting in Trafalgar Square at three o'clock.

JEAN: This afternoon? But that's no use to people out of town—Unless I could invent some excuse . . .

LORD JOHN: (*benevolently*) Still talking over the Shelter plans?

MISS LEVERING: No. We left the Shelter some time ago.

LORD JOHN: (*to* JEAN) Then what's all the chatterment about?

(JEAN, *a little confused, looks at* MISS LEVERING.)

MISS LEVERING: The latest thing in veils. (*Ties hers round her hat.*)

GREATOREX: The invincible frivolity of woman!

LORD JOHN: (*genially*) Don't scold them. It's a very proper 1160 tonic.

MISS LEVERING: (*whimsically*) Oh, I was afraid you'd despise us for it.

BOTH MEN: (*with condescension*) Not at all—not at all.

JEAN: (*to* MISS LEVERING *as* FOOTMAN *appears*) Oh, they're coming for you. Don't forget your book. (FOOTMAN *holds out a salver with a telegram on it for* JEAN.) Why, it's for me!

MISS LEVERING: But it's time I was—

(*She crosses to the table.*)

JEAN: (*opening the telegram*) May I? (*Reads, and glances over the paper at* MISS LEVERING.) I've got your book. (*Crosses to* 1170 MISS LEVERING, *and, looking at the back of the volume*) Dante! Whereabouts are you? (*Opening at the marker.*) Oh, the "Inferno."

MISS LEVERING: No; I'm in a worse place.

JEAN: I didn't know there was a worse.

MISS LEVERING: Yes; it's worse with the Vigliacchi.

JEAN: I forget. Were they Guelf or Ghibelline?

MISS LEVERING: (*smiling*) They weren't either, and that was why Dante couldn't stand them. (*More gravely.*) He said there was not place in Heaven nor in Purgatory—not even 1180 a corner in Hell—for the souls who had stood aloof from strife. (*Looking steadily into the girl's eyes.*) He called them "wretches who never lived," Dante did, because they'd never felt the pangs of partizanship. And so they wander homeless on the skirts of limbo among the abortions and off-scourings of Creation.

JEAN: (*a long breath after a long look. When* MISS LEVERING *has turned away to make her leisurely adieux* JEAN'S *eyes fall on the open telegram*) Aunt Ellen, I've got to go to London.

(STONOR, *re-entering, hears this, but pretends to talk to* MR FREDDY, *etc.*)

LADY JOHN: My dear child! 1190

MRS HERIOT: Nonsense! Is your grandfather worse?

JEAN: (*folding the telegram*) No-o. I don't think so. But it's necessary I should go, all the same.

MRS HERIOT: Go away when Mr Stonor—

JEAN: He said he'd have to leave directly after luncheon.

LADY JOHN: I'll just see Miss Levering off, and then I'll come back and talk about it.

LORD JOHN: (*to* MISS LEVERING) Why are you saying goodbye as if you were never coming back?

MISS LEVERING: (*smiling*) One never knows. Maybe I shan't 1200 come back. (*To* STONOR.) Goodbye.

(STONOR *bows ceremoniously. The others go up laughing.* STONOR *comes down.*)

JEAN: (*impulsively*) There mayn't be another train! Miss Levering—

STONOR: (*standing in front of her*) What if there isn't? I'll take you back in the motor.

JEAN: (*rapturously*) Will you? (*Inadvertently drops the telegram.*) I must be there by three!

STONOR: (*picks up the telegram and a handkerchief lying near,*

1210 *glances at the message)* Why, it's only an invitation to dine— Wednesday!

JEAN: Sh! *(Takes the telegram and puts it in her pocket.)*

STONOR: Oh, I see! *(Lower, smiling.)* It's rather dear of you to arrange our going off like that. You *are* a clever little girl!

JEAN: It's not that I was arranging. I want to hear those women in Trafalgar Square—the Suffragettes.

STONOR: *(incredulous, but smiling)* How perfectly absurd! *(Looking after* LADY JOHN.*)* Besides, I expect she wouldn't like my carrying you off like that.

JEAN: Then she'll have to make an excuse and come too.

1220 STONOR: Ah, it wouldn't be quite the same—

JEAN: *(rapidly thinking it out)* We could get back here in time for dinner.

*(GEOFFREY STONOR glances down at the handkerchief still in his hand, and turns it half mechanically from corner to corner.)*

JEAN: *(absent-mindedly)* Mine?

STONOR: *(hastily, without reflection)* No. *(He hands it to* MISS LEVERING *as she passes)*: Yours.

*(MISS LEVERING, on her way to the lobby with* LORD JOHN *seems not to notice.)*

JEAN: *(takes the handkerchief to give it to her, glancing down at the embroidered corner; stops)* But that's not an L! It's Vi—!

*(GEOFFREY STONOR suddenly turns his back and takes up the newspaper.)*

LADY JOHN: *(from the lobby)* Come, Vida, since you will go.

1230 MISS LEVERING: Yes; I'm coming.

*(Exit* MISS LEVERING.*)*

JEAN: *I* didn't know her name was Vida; how did you?

*(STONOR stares silently over the top of his paper.)*

## —ACT TWO—

*Scene: the north side of the Nelson Column in Trafalgar Square. The Curtain rises on an uproar. The crowd, which momentarily increases, is composed chiefly of weedy youths and wastrel old men. There are a few decent artisans; three of four "beery" out-o'-works; three or four young women of the domestic servant or Strand restaurant cashier class; one aged woman in rusty black peering with faded, wondering eyes, consulting the faces of men and laughing nervously and apologetically from time to time; one or two quiet-looking, business-like women, thirty to forty; two middle-class men, who stare and whisper and smile. A quiet old man with a lot of unsold Sunday papers under one arm stands in an attitude of rapt attention, with the free hand round his deaf ear. A brisk-looking woman of forty-five or so, wearing pince-nez, goes round with a pile of propagandist literature on her arm. Many of the men smoking cigarettes—the old ones pipes. On the outskirts of this crowd, of several hundred, a couple of smart men in tall shining hats hover a few moments, single eyeglass up, and then saunter off. Against the middle of the Column, where it rises above the stone platform, is a great red banner, one supporting pole upheld by a grimy sandwichman, the other by a small, dirty boy of eight. If practicable only the lower portion of the banner need be seen, bearing the final words of the legend—*"VOTES FOR WOMEN!"* in immense white letters. It will be well to get, to the full, the effect of the height above the crowd of the straggling group of speakers on the pedestal platform. These are, as the Curtain rises, a working-class woman who is waving her arms and talking very earnestly, her voice for the moment blurred in the uproar. She is dressed in brown serge and looks pinched and sallow. At her side is the* CHAIRMAN *urging that she be given a fair hearing.* ALLEN TRENT *is a tall, slim, brown-haired man of twenty-eight, with a slight stoop, an agreeable aspect, well-bred voice, and the gleaming brown eye of the visionary. Behind these two, looking on or talking among themselves, are several other carelessly dressed women; one, better turned out than the rest, is quite young, very slight and gracefully built, with round, very pink cheeks, full, scarlet lips, naturally waving brown hair, and an air of childish gravity. She looks at the unruly mob with imperturbable calm. The* CHAIRMAN'S *voice is drowned.*

WORKING WOMAN: *(with lean, brown finger out and voice raised shriller now above the tumult)* I've got boys o' me own and we laugh at all sorts o' things, but I should be ashymed and so would they if ever they was to be'yve as you're doin' to-d'y.

*(In laughter the noise dies.)*

People 'ave been sayin' this is a middle-class woman's movement. It's a libel. I'm a workin' woman myself, the wife of a working man. *(Voice:* "Pore devil!"*)* I'm a Poor Law Guardian and a— 1240

NOISY YOUNG MAN: Think of that, now—gracious me!

*(Laughter and interruption.)*

OLD NEWSVENDOR: *(to the noisy young man near him)* Oh, shut up, cawn't yer?

NOISY YOUNG MAN: Not fur *you!*

VOICE: Go 'ome and darn yer old man's stockens!

VOICE: Just clean yer *own* doorstep!

WORKING WOMAN: It's a pore sort of 'ousekeeper that leaves 'er doorstep till Sunday afternoon. Maybe that's when you would do *your* doorstep. I do mine in the mornin' before you men are awake. 1250

OLD NEWSVENDOR: It's true, wot she says!—every word.

WORKING WOMAN: You say we women 'ave got no business servin' on boards and thinkin' about politics. Wot's *politics?*

*(A derisive roar.)*

It's just 'ousekeepin' on a big scyle. 'Oo among you [workin'] men 'as the most comfortable 'omes? Those of you that gives yer wives yer wyges.

*(Loud laughter and jeers.)*

VOICES: } That's it!
} Wantin' our money.
} Lord 'Igh 'Ousekeeper of England.

WORKING WOMAN: If it wus only to use fur *our* comfort, d'ye 1260 think many o' you workin' men would be found turnin' over their wyges to their wives? No! Wot's the reason thousands do—and the best and the soberest? Because the workin' man knows that wot's a pound to '*im* is twenty shillin's to 'is wife. And she'll myke every penny in every one o' them shillin's *tell*. She gets more fur '*im* out of 'is wyges than wot 'e can! Some o' you know wot the 'omes is like where the men don't let the women manage. Well, the Poor Laws and the 'ole Government is just in the same muddle because the men 'ave tried to do the national 'ousekeepin' without the women.

1270

(*Roars.*)

But, like I told you before, it's a libel to say it's only the well-off women wot's wantin' the vote. Wot about the 96,000 textile workers? Wot about the Yorkshire tailoresses? I can tell you wot plenty o' the poor women think about it. I'm one of them, and I can tell you we see there's reforms needed. *We ought to 'ave the vote* (*jeers*), and we know 'ow to appreciate the other women 'oo go to prison fur tryin' to get it fur us!

(*With a little final bob of emphasis and a glance over shoulder at the old woman and the young one behind her, she seems about to retire, but pauses as the murmur in the crowd grows into distinct phrases.* "They get their 'air cut free." "Naow they don't, that's only us!" "Silly Suffragettes!" "Stop at 'ome!" "['Inderin'] policemen—mykin' rows in the streets!")

VOICE: (*louder than the others*) They sees yer ain't fit t'ave—

1280 OTHER VOICES: "Ha, ha!" "Shut up." "Keep quiet, cawn't yer."
(*General uproar.*)
CHAIRMAN: You evidently don't know what had to be done by *men* before the extension of the Suffrage in '67. If it hadn't been for demonstrations of violence. (*His voice is drowned.*)
WORKING WOMAN: (*coming forward again, her shrill note rising clear*) You s'y woman's plyce is 'ome! Don't you know there's a third of the women o' this country can't afford the luxury of stayin' in their 'omes? They *got* to go out and 'elp make money to p'y the rent and keep the 'ome from bein'
1290 sold up. Then there's all the women that 'aven't got even miseerable 'omes. They 'aven't got any 'omes *at all*.
NOISY YOUNG MAN: You said *you* got one. W'y don't you stop in it?
WORKING WOMAN: Yes, that's like a man. If one o' you is all right, he thinks the rest don't matter. We women—
NOISY YOUNG MAN: The lydies! God bless 'em!

(*Voices drown her and the* CHAIRMAN.)

OLD NEWSVENDOR: (*to* NOISY YOUNG MAN) Oh, take that extra 'alf pint 'ome and *sleep it off!*
WORKING WOMAN: P'r'aps *your* 'omes are all right. P'r'aps you
1300 aren't livin', old and young, married and single, in one room. I come from a plyce where many fam'lies 'ave to live like that if they're to go on livin' *at all*. If you don't believe me, come and let me show you! (*She spreads out her lean arms.*) Come with me to Canning Town!—come with me to Bromley—come to Poplar and to Bow! No. You won't even *think* about the overworked women and the underfed children and the 'ovels they live in. And you want that we shouldn't think neither—
A VAGRANT: We'll do the thinkin'. You go 'ome and nuss the
1310 byby.

WORKING WOMAN: I do nurse my byby! I've nursed seven. What 'ave you done for yours? P'r'aps your children never goes 'ungry, and maybe you're satisfied—though I must say I wouldn't a' thought it from the *look* o' you.
VOICE: Oh, I s'y!
WORKING WOMAN: But we women are not satisfied. We don't only want better things for our own children. We want better things for all. *Every* child is our child. We know in our 'earts we oughtn't to rest till we've mothered 'em every one.
VOICE: "Women"—"children"—wot about the *men*? Are *they* 1320 all 'appy?

(*Derisive laughter and* "No! no!" "Not precisely." "'Appy? Lord!")

WORKING WOMAN: No, there's lots o' you men I'm sorry for (*Shrill Voice:* "Thanks awfully."), an' we'll 'elp you if you let us.
VOICE: 'Elp us? You tyke the bread out of our mouths. You women are blackleggin' the men!
WORKING WOMAN: W'y does any woman tyke less wyges than a man for the same work? Only because we can't get anything better. That's part the reason w'y we're yere to-d'y. Do you reely think we tyke them low wyges because we got a 1330 *lykin'* for low wyges? No. We're just like you. We want as much as ever we can get. ("*Ear!* '*Ear!*" *and laughter.*) We got a gryte deal to do with our wyges, we women has. We got the children to think about. And w'en we got our rights, a woman's flesh and blood won't be so much cheaper than a man's that employers can get rich on keepin' you out o' work, and sweatin' us. If you men only could see it, we got the *syme* cause, and if you 'elped us you'd be 'elpin yerselves.
VOICES: "Rot!" "Drivel." 1340
OLD NEWSVENDOR: True as gospel!

(*She retires against the banner with the others. There is some applause.*)

A MAN: (*patronisingly*) Well, now, that wusn't so bad—fur a woman.
ANOTHER: Nnaw. *Not fur a woman.*
CHAIRMAN: (*speaking through this last*) Miss Ernestine Blunt will now address you.

(*Applause, chiefly ironic, laughter, a general moving closer and knitting up of attention.* ERNESTINE BLUNT *is about twenty-four, but looks younger. She is very downright, not to say pugnacious—the something amusing and attractive about her is there, as it were, against her will, and the more fetching for that. She has no conventional gestures, and none of any sort at first. As she warms to her work she uses her slim hands to enforce her emphasis, but as though unconsciously. Her manner of speech is less monotonous than that of the average woman-speaker, but she, too, has a fashion of leaning all her weight on the end of the sentence. She brings out the final word or two with an effort of underscoring, and makes a forward motion of the slim body as if the better to drive the last nail in. She evidently means to be immensely practical—the kind who is pleased to think she hasn't a grain of sentimentality in her composition, and whose feeling, when it does all but master her, communicates itself magnetically to others.*)

MISS ERNESTINE BLUNT: Perhaps I'd better begin by explaining a little about our "tactics."

(*Cries of "Tactics! We know!" "Mykin' trouble!" "Public scandal!"*)

1350 To make you understand what we've done, I must remind you of what others have done. Perhaps you don't know that women first petitioned Parliament for the Franchise as long ago as 1866.

VOICE: How do *you* know?

(*She pauses a moment, taken off her guard by the suddenness of the attack.*)

VOICE: You wasn't there!

VOICE: That was the trouble. Haw! haw!

MISS ERNESTINE BLUNT: And the petition was presented—

VOICE: Give 'er a 'earin' now she 'as got out of 'er crydle.

MISS ERNESTINE BLUNT: —presented to the House of Commons by that great Liberal, John Stuart Mill. (*Voice:* "Mill?
1360 Who is he when he's at home?") Bills or Resolutions have been before the House on and off for the last thirty-six years. That, roughly, is our history. We found ourselves, towards the close of the year 1905, with no assurance that if we went on in the same way any girl born into the world in this generation would live to exercise the rights of citizenship, though she lived to be a hundred. So we said all this has been in vain. We must try some other way. How did the working man get the Suffrage, we asked ourselves? Well, we turned up the records, and we *saw*—
1370 VOICES: "Not by scratching people's faces!" . . . "Disraeli give it 'em!" "Dizzy? Get out!" "Cahnty Cahncil scholarships!" "Oh, Lord, this education." "Chartists riots, she's thinkin' of!" (*Noise in the crowd.*)

MISS ERNESTINE BLUNT: But we don't *want* to follow such a violent example. We would much rather *not*—but if that's the only way we can make the country see we're in earnest, we are prepared to show them.

VOICE: An' they'll show you!—Give you another month 'ard.

MISS ERNESTINE BLUNT: Don't think that going to prison has
1380 any fears for us. We'd go *for life* if by doing that we could get freedom for the rest of the women.

VOICES: "Hear, hear!" "Rot!" "W'ye don't the men 'elp ye to get your rights?"

MISS ERNESTINE BLUNT: Here's some one asking why the men don't help. It's partly they don't understand yet—they *will* before we've done! (*Laughter.*) Partly they don't understand yet what's at stake—

RESPECTABLE OLD MAN: (*chuckling*) Lord, they're a 'educatin' of us!

1390 VOICE: Wot next?

MISS ERNESTINE BLUNT: —and partly that the bravest man is afraid of ridicule. Oh, yes; we've heard a great deal all our lives about the timidity and the sensitiveness of women. And it's true. We *are* sensitive. But I tell you, ridicule crumples a man up. It steels a woman. We've come to know the value of ridicule. We've educated ourselves so that we welcome ridicule. We owe our sincerest thanks to the comic writers. The cartoonist is our unconscious friend. Who cartoons people who are of no importance? What advertisement is so
1400 sure of being remembered?

POETIC YOUNG MAN: I admit that.

MISS ERNESTINE BLUNT: If we didn't know it by any other sign, the comic papers would tell us *we've arrived!* But our greatest debt of gratitude we owe, to the man who called us female hooligans.

(*The crowd bursts into laughter.*)

We aren't hooligans, but we hope the fact will be overlooked. If everybody said we were nice, well-behaved women, who'd come to hear us? *Not the men.*

(*Roars.*)

Men tell us it isn't womanly for us to care about politics. How do they know what's womanly? It's for women to de- 1410 cide that. Let the men attend to being manly. It will take them all their time.

VOICE: Are we down-'earted? Oh no!

MISS ERNESTINE BLUNT: And they say it would be dreadful if we got the vote, because then we'd be pitted against men in the economic struggle. But that's come about already. Do you know that out of every hundred women in this country eighty-two are wage-earning women? It used to be thought unfeminine for women to be students and to aspire to the arts—that bring fame and fortune. But nobody has ever said 1420 it was unfeminine for women to do the heavy drudgery that's badly paid. That kind of work had to be done by *some*body—and the men didn't hanker after it. Oh, no.

(*Laughter and interruption.*)

A MAN ON THE OUTER FRINGE: She can talk—the little one can.

ANOTHER: Oh, they can all "talk."

A BEERY, DIRTY FELLOW OF FIFTY: I wouldn't like to be 'er 'usban'. Think o' comin' 'ome to *that!*

HIS PAL: I'd soon learn 'er!

MISS ERNESTINE BLUNT: (*speaking through the noise*) Oh, no! *Let* the women scrub and cook and wash. That's all right! 1430 But if they want to try their hand at the better paid work of the liberal professions—oh, very unfeminine indeed! Then there's another thing. Now I want you to listen to this, because it's *very* important. Men say if we persist in competing with them for the bigger prizes, they're dreadfully afraid we'd lose the beautiful protecting chivalry that—Yes, I don't wonder you laugh. We laugh. (*Bending forward with lit eyes.*) But the women I found at the Ferry Tin Works working for five shillings a week—I didn't see them laughing. The beautiful chivalry of the employers of women doesn't 1440 prevent them from paying women tenpence a day for sorting coal and loading and unloading carts—doesn't prevent them from forcing women to earn bread in ways worse still. So we won't talk about chivalry. It's being over-sarcastic. We'll just let this poor ghost of chivalry go—in exchange for a little plain justice.

VOICE: If the House of Commons won't give you justice, why don't you go to the House of Lords?

MISS ERNESTINE BLUNT: What?

VOICE: Better 'urry up. Case of early closin'. 1450

(*Laughter. A man at the back asks the speaker something.*)

MISS ERNESTINE BLUNT: (*unable to hear*) You'll be allowed to ask any question you like at the end of the meeting.

NEWCOMER: (*boy of eighteen*) Oh, is it question time? I s'y, Miss, 'oo killed cock robin?

(*She is about to resume, but above the general noise the voice of a man at the back reaches her indistinct but insistent. She leans forward trying to catch what he says. While the indistinguishable murmur has been going on* GEOFFREY STONOR *has appeared on the edge of the crowd, followed by* JEAN *and* LADY JOHN *in motor veils.*)

JEAN: (*pressing forward eagerly and raising her veil*) Is she one of them? That little thing!

STONOR: (*doubtfully*) I—I suppose so.

JEAN: Oh, ask some one, Geoffrey. I'm so disappointed. I did so hope we'd hear one of the—the worst.

1460  MISS ERNESTINE BLUNT: (*to the interrupter—on the other side*) What? What do you say? (*She screws up her eyes with the effort to hear, and puts a hand up to her ear. A few indistinguishable words between her and the man.*)

LADY JOHN: (*who has been studying the figures on the platform through her lorgnon, turns to a working man beside her*) Can you tell me, my man, which are the ones that—a—that make the disturbances?

WORKING MAN: Don't you be took in, Miss.

MISS ERNESTINE BLUNT: Oh, yes—I see. There's a man over
1470  here asking—

A YOUNG MAN: *I've got a question, too. Are—you—married?*

ANOTHER: (*sniggering*) Quick! There's yer chawnce. 'E's a bachelor.

(*Laughter.*)

MISS ERNESTINE BLUNT: (*goes straight on as if she had not heard*) —man asking: if the women get full citizenship, and a war is declared, will the women fight?

POETIC YOUNG MAN: No, really—no, really, now!

(*The Crowd: "Haw! Haw!" "Yes!" "Yes, how about that?"*)

MISS ERNESTINE BLUNT: (*smiling*) Well, you know, some people say the whole trouble about us is that we *do* fight. But it
1480  is only hard necessity makes us do that. We don't *want* to fight—as men seem to—just for fighting's sake. Women are for peace.

VOICE: Hear, hear.

MISS ERNESTINE BLUNT: And when we have a share in public affairs there'll be less likelihood of war. But that's not to say women can't fight. The Boer women did. The Russian women face conflicts worse than any battlefield can show. (*Her voice shakes a little, and the eyes fill, but she controls her emotion gallantly, and dashes on.*) But we women know
1490  all that is evil, and we're for peace. Our part—we're proud to remember it—our part has been to go about after you men in war time, and—*pick up the pieces!*

(*A great shout.*)

Yes—seems funny, doesn't it? You men blow them to bits, and then we come along and put them together again. If you know anything about military nursing, you know a good deal of our work has been done in the face of danger—*but it's always been done.*

OLD NEWSVENDOR: That's so. That's so.

MISS ERNESTINE BLUNT: You complain that more and more

we're taking away from you men the work that's always been
1500  yours. You can't any longer keep women out of the industries. The only question is upon what terms shall she continue to be in? As long as she's in on bad terms, she's not only hurting herself—she's hurting you. But if you're feeling discouraged about our competing with you, we're willing to leave you your trade in war. *Let* the men take life! We *give* life! (*Her voice is once more moved and proud.*) No one will pretend ours isn't one of the dangerous trades either. I won't say any more to you now, because we've got others to speak to you, and a new woman helper that I want you to
1510  hear.

(*She retires to the sound of clapping. There's a hurried consultation between her and the* CHAIRMAN. *Voices in the Crowd: "The little 'un's all right" "Ernestine's a corker," etc.*)

JEAN: (*looking at* STONOR *to see how he's taken it*) Well?

STONOR: (*smiling down at her*) Well—

JEAN: Nothing reprehensible in what *she* said, was there?

STONOR: (*shrugs*) Oh, reprehensible!

JEAN: It makes me rather miserable all the same.

STONOR: (*draws her hand protectingly through his arm*) You mustn't take it as much to heart as all that.

JEAN: I can't help it—I can't indeed, Geoffrey. I shall *never* be
1520  able to make a speech like that!

STONOR: (*taken aback*) I hope not, indeed.

JEAN: Why, I thought you said you wanted me—?

STONOR: (*smiling*) To make nice little speeches with composure—so I did! So I—(*Seems to lose his thread as he looks at her.*)

JEAN: (*with a little frown*) You said—

STONOR: That you have very pink cheeks? Well, I stick to that.

JEAN: (*smiling*) Sh! Don't tell everybody.

STONOR: And you're the only female creature I ever saw who
1530  didn't look a fright in motor things.

JEAN: (*melted and smiling*) I'm glad you don't think me a fright.

CHAIRMAN: I will now ask (*name indistinguishable*) to address the meeting.

JEAN: (*as she sees* LADY JOHN: *moving to one side*) Oh, don't go yet, Aunt Ellen.

LADY JOHN: Go? Certainly not. I want to hear another. (*Craning her neck.*) I can't believe, you know, she was really one of the worst.

(*A big, sallow Cockney has come forward. His scanty hair grows in wisps on a great bony skull.*)

VOICE: That's Pilcher.

ANOTHER: 'Oo's Pilcher?
1540
ANOTHER: If you can't afford a bottle of Tatcho, w'y don't you get yer 'air cut.

MR. PILCHER: (*not in the least discomposed*) I've been addressin' a big meetin' at 'Ammersmith this morning, and w'en I told 'em I was comin' 'ere this awfternoon to speak fur the women—well—then the usual thing began!

(*An appreciative roar from the crowd.*)

In these times if you want peace and quiet at a public meetin'—

(*The crowd fills in the hiatus with laughter.*)

1550 There was a man at 'Ammersmith, too, talkin' about women's sphere bein' 'ome. *'Ome* do you call it? You've got a kennel w'ere you can munch your tommy. You've got a corner w'ere you can curl up fur a few hours till you go out to work again. No, my man, there's too many of you ain't able to *give* the women 'omes—fit to live in, too many of you in that fix fur you to go on jawin' at those o' the women 'oo want to myke the 'omes a little decenter.

VOICE: If the vote ain't done us any good, 'ow'll it do the women any good?

1560 MR. PILCHER: Looke 'ere! Any men here belongin' to the Labour Party?

*(Shouts and applause.)*

Well, I don't need to tell these men the vote 'as done us *some* good. They know it. And it'll do us a lot more good w'en you know 'ow to use the power you got in your 'and.

VOICE: Power! It's those fellers at the bottom o' the street that's got the power.

MR. PILCHER: It's you, and men like you, that gave it to 'em. You carried the Liberals into Parliament Street on your own shoulders.

*(Complacent applause.)*

1570 You believed all their fine words. You never asked yourselves, "Wot's a Liberal, anyw'y?"

A VOICE: He's a jolly good fellow.

*(Cheers and booing.)*

MR. PILCHER: No, 'e ain't, or if 'e is jolly, it's only because 'e thinks you're such silly codfish you'll go swellin' his majority again. *(Laughter, in which* STONOR *joins.)* It's enough to make any Liberal jolly to see sheep like you lookin' on, proud and 'appy, while you see Liberal leaders desertin' Liberal principles.

*(Voices in agreement and protest.)*

You show me a Liberal, and I'll show you a Mr Fycing-both-W'ys. Yuss.

*(STONOR moves closer with an amused look.)*

1580 'E sheds the light of 'is warm and 'andsome smile on the working man, and round on the other side 'e's tippin' a wink to the great landowners. That's to let 'em know 'e's standin' between them and the Socialists. Huh! Socialists. Yuss, *Socialists!*

*(General laughter, in which* STONOR *joins.)*

The Liberal, 'e's the judicial sort o'chap that sits in the middle—

VOICE: On the fence!

MR PILCHER: Tories one side—Socialists the other. Well it ain't always so comfortable in the middle. You're like to get 1590 squeezed. Now, I s'y to the women, the Conservatives don't promise you much but what they promise they *do!*

STONOR: *(to* JEAN*)* This fellow isn't half bad.

MR. PILCHER: The Liberals—they'll promise you the earth, and give yer . . . the whole o' nothing.

*(Roars of approval.)*

JEAN: *Isn't* it fun? Now, aren't you glad I brought you?

STONOR: *(laughing)* This chap's rather amusing!

MR PILCHER: We men 'ave seen it 'appen over and over. But the women can tyke a 'int quicker 'n what we can. They won't stand the nonsense men do. Only they 'aven't got a fair chawnce even to agitate fur their rights. As I wus comin' 1600 up 'ere I 'eard a man sayin', "Look at this big crowd." W'y, we're all *men!* If the women want the vote w'y ain't they 'ere to s'y so? Well, I'll tell you w'y. It's because they've 'ad to get the dinner fur you and me, and now they're washin' up the dishes.

A VOICE: D'you think *we* ought to st'y 'ome and wash the dishes?

MR PILCHER: *(laughs good-naturedly)* If they'd leave it to us once or twice per'aps we'd understand a little more about the Woman Question. I know w'y *my* wife isn't here. It's be- 1610 cause she *knows* I ain't much use round the 'ouse, and she's 'opin' I can talk to some purpose. Maybe she's mistaken. Any'ow, here I am to vote for her and all the other women.

VOICES: "Hear! hear!", "Oh-h!"

MR PILCHER: And to tell you men what improvements you can expect to see when women 'as the share in public affairs they *ought* to 'ave!

VOICE: What do you know about it? You can't even talk grammar.

MR PILCHER: *(is dashed a fraction of a moment, for the first and* 1620 *only time)* I'm not 'ere to talk grammar but to talk Reform. I ain't defendin' my grammar—but I'll say in pawssing that if my mother 'ad 'ad 'er rights, maybe my grammar would have been better.

*(STONOR and JEAN exchange smiles. He takes her arm again and bends his head to whisper something in her ear. She listens with lowered eyes and happy face. The discreet love-making goes on during the next few sentences. Interruption. One voice insistent but not clear. The speaker waits only a second and then resumes. "Yes, if the women," but he cannot instantly make himself heard. The boyish* CHAIRMAN *looks harassed and anxious.* MISS ERNESTINE BLUNT *alert, watchful.)*

MR PILCHER: Wait a bit—'arf a minute, my man!

VOICE: 'Oo yer talkin' to? I ain't your man.

MR PILCHER: Lucky for me! There seems to be a *gentleman* 'ere who doesn't think women ought to 'ave the vote.

VOICE: One? Oh-h!

*(Laughter.)*

MR PILCHER: Per'aps 'e doesn't know much about women?    1630

*(Indistinguishable repartee.)*

Oh, the gentleman says 'e's married. Well, then, fur the syke of 'is wife we mustn't be too sorry 'e's 'ere. No doubt she's s'ying: "'Eaven by prysed those women are mykin' a Demonstrytion in Trafalgar Square, and I'll 'ave a little peace and quiet at 'ome for one Sunday in my life."

*(The crowd laughs and there are jeers for the interruptor—and at the speaker.)*

*(Pointing.)* Why, you're like the man at 'Ammersmith this morning. 'E was awskin' me: "'Ow would you like men to

st'y at 'ome and do the family washin'?"

(*Laughter.*)

1640   I told 'im I wouldn't advise it. I 'ave too much respect fur— me clo'es.

VAGRANT: It's their place—the women ought to do the washin'.

MR PILCHER: I'm not sure you ain't right. For a good many o' you fellas, from the look o' you—you cawn't even wash yer-selves.

(*Laughter.*)

VOICE: (*threatening*) 'Oo are you talkin' to?

(CHAIRMAN *more anxious than before—movement in the crowd.*)

THREATENING VOICE: Which of us d'you mean?

MR PILCHER: (*coolly looking down*) Well, it takes about ten of your sort to myke a man, so you may take it I mean the lot of you.

(*Angry indistinguishable retorts and the crowd sways.* MISS ERNESTINE BLUNT, *who has been watching the fray with seri-ous face, turns suddenly, catching sight of someone just arrived at the end of the platform.* MISS BLUNT *goes right with alacrity, saying audibly to* PILCHER *as she passes, "Here she is," and proceeds to offer her hand helping some one to get up the im-provised steps. Laughter and interruption in the crowd.*)

LADY JOHN: Now, there's another woman going to speak.

1650   JEAN: Oh, is she? Who? Which? I do hope she'll be one of the wild ones.

MR PILCHER: (*speaking through this last. Glancing at the new arrival whose hat appears above the platform.*) That's all right, then. (*Turns to the left.*) When I've attended to this microbe that's vitiating the air on my right—

(*Laughter and interruptions from the crowd.*)

(STONOR *stares, one dazed instant, at the face of the new ar-rival; his own changes.*)

(JEAN *withdraws her arm from his and quite suddenly presses a shade nearer the platform.* STONOR *moves forward and takes her by the arm.*)

STONOR: We're going now.

JEAN: Not yet—oh, please not yet. (*Breathless, looking back.*) Why I—I do believe—

1660   STONOR: (*to* LADY JOHN, *with decision*) I'm going to take Jean out of this mob. Will you come?

LADY JOHN: What? Oh yes, if you think—(*Another look through her glasses.*) But isn't that—surely it's—!!!

(VIDA LEVERING *comes forward. She wears a long, plain, dark green dustcloak. Stands talking to* ERNESTINE BLUNT *and glancing a little apprehensively at the crowd.*)

JEAN: Geoffrey!

STONOR: (*trying to draw* JEAN *away*) Lady John's tired—

JEAN: But you don't see who it is, Geoffrey—! (*Looks into his face, and is arrested by the look she finds there.*)

(LADY JOHN *has pushed in front of them amazed, transfixed, with glass up.* GEOFFREY STONOR *restrains a gesture of annoy-ance, and withdraws behind two big policemen.* JEAN *from*

time to time turns to look at him with a face of perplexity.*)

MR PILCHER: (*resuming through a fire of indistinct interrup-tion*) I'll come down and attend to that microbe while a lady will say a few words to you (*raises his voice*)—if she can 1670 myke 'erself 'eard.

(PILCHER *retires in the midst of booing and cheers.*)

CHAIRMAN: (*harassed and trying to creat a diversion*) Some one suggests—and it's such a good idea I'd like you to listen to it—

(*Noise dies down.*)

that a clause shall be inserted in the next Suffrage Bill that shall expressly reserve to each Cabinet Minister, and to any respectable man, the power to prevent the Franchise being given to the female members of his family on his public de-claration of their lack of sufficient intelligence to entitle them to vote.   1680

VOICES: Oh! oh.

CHAIRMAN: Now, I ask you to listen, as quietly as you can, to a lady who is not accustomed to speaking—a—in Traflagar Square—or a . . . as a matter of fact, at all.

VOICES: "A dumb lady!" "Hooray!" "Three cheers for the dumb lady!"

CHAIRMAN: A lady who, as I've said, will tell you, if you'll be-have yourselves, her impressions of the administration of police court justice in this country.

(JEAN *looks wondering at* STONOR'S *sphinx-like face as* VIDA LEVERING *comes to the edge of the platform.*)

MISS LEVERING: Mr Chairman, men and women—   1690

VOICES: (*off*) Speak up.

(MISS LEVERING: *flushes, comes quite to the edge of the plat-form and raises her voice a little.*)

MISS LEVERING: I just wanted to tell you that I was—I was—present in the police court when the women were charged for creating a disturbance.

VOICE: Y' oughtn't t' get mixed up in wot didn't concern you.

MISS LEVERING: I—I—(*Stumbles and stops.*)

(*Talking and laughing increases. "Wot's 'er name?" "Mrs or Miss?" "Ain't seen this one before."*)

CHAIRMAN: (*anxiously*) Now, see here, men; don't interrupt—

A GIRL: (*shrilly*) I don't like this one's 'at. Ye can see she ain't one of 'em.

MISS LEVERING: (*trying to recommence*) I—   1700

VOICE: They're a disgrace—them women be'ind yer.

A MAN WITH A FATHERLY AIR: It's the w'y they goes on as mykes the Government keep ye from gettin' yer rights.

CHAIRMAN: (*losing his temper*) It's the way *you* go on that—

(*Noise increases.* CHAIRMAN *drowned, waves his arms and moves his lips.* MISS LEVERING *discouraged, turns and looks at* ERNESTINE BLUNT *and pantomimes "It's no good. I can't go on."* ERNESTINE BLUNT *comes forward, says a word to the* CHAIRMAN, *who ceases gyrating, and nods.*)

MISS ERNESTINE BLUNT: (*facing the crowd*) Look here. If the Government withhold the vote because they don't like the way some of us ask for it—*let them give it to the Quiet Ones.*

Does the Government want to punish *all* women because they don't like the manners of a handful? Perhaps that's you men's notion of justice. It isn't women's.

1710 VOICES: Haw! haw!

MISS LEVERING: Yes. Thi—this is the first time I've ever 'gone on,' as you call it, but they never gave me a vote.

MISS ERNESTINE BLUNT: (*with energy*) No! And there are one—two—three—four women on this platform. Now, we all want the vote, as you know. Well, we'd agree to be disfranchised all our lives, if they'd give the vote to all the other women.

VOICE: Look here, you made one speech, give the lady a
1720 chawnce.

MISS ERNESTINE BLUNT: (*retires smiling*) That's *just* what I wanted *you* to do!

MISS LEVERING: Perhaps you—you don't know—you don't know—

VOICE: (*sarcastic*) 'Ow 're we goin' to know if you can't tell us?

MISS LEVERING: (*flushing and smiling*) Thank you for that. We couldn't have a better motto. How *are* you to know if we can't somehow manage to tell you? (*With a visible effort she goes on.*) Well, I certainly didn't know before that the
1730 sergeants and policemen are instructed to deceive the people as to the time such cases are heard. You ask, and you're sent to Marlborough Police Court instead of to Marylebone.

VOICE: They ought ter sent yer to 'Olloway—do y' good.

OLD NEWSVENDOR: You go on, Miss, don't mind 'im.

VOICE: Wot d'you expect from a pig but a grunt?

MISS LEVERING: You're told the case will be at two o'clock, and it's really called for eleven. Well, I took a great deal of trouble, and I didn't believe what I was told—

(*Warming a little to her task.*)

Yes, that's almost the first thing we have to learn—to get
1740 over our touching faith that, because a man tells us something, it's true. I got to the right court, and I was so anxious not to be late, I was too early. The case before the women's was just coming on. I heard a noise. At the door I saw the helmets of two policemen, and I said to myself: "What sort of crime shall I have to sit and hear about? Is this a burglar coming along between the two big policemen, or will it be a murderer? What sort of felon is to stand in the dock before the women whose crime is they ask for the vote?" But, try as I would, I couldn't see the prisoner. My heart misgave me.
1750 Is it a woman, I wondered? Then the policemen got nearer, and I saw—(*she waits an instant*)—a little, thin, half-starved boy. What do you think he was charged with? Stealing. What had he been stealing—that small criminal? *Milk.* It seemed to me as I sat there looking on, that the men who had the affairs of the world in their hands from the beginning, and who've made so poor a business of it—

VOICES: Oh! oh! Pore benighted man! Are we down-'earted? *Oh,* no!

MISS LEVERING: —so poor a business of it as to have the poor
1760 and the unemployed in the condition they're in today—when your only remedy for a starving child is to hale him off to the police court—because he had managed to get a little milk—well, I *did* wonder that the men refuse to be helped with a problem they've so notoriously failed at. I began to say to myself: "Isn't it time the women lent a hand?"

A VOICE: Would you have women magistrates?

(*She is stumped by the suddenness of the demand.*)

VOICES: Haw! Haw! Magistrates!

ANOTHER: Women! Let 'em prove first they deserve—

A SHABBY ART STUDENT: (*his hair longish, soft hat, and flowing
1770 tie*) They study music by thousands; where's their Beethoven? Where's their Plato? Where's the woman Shakespeare?

ANOTHER: Yes—what 'a' they ever *done?*

(*The speaker clenches her hands, and is recovering her presence of mind, so that by the time the CHAIRMAN can make himself heard with, "Now men, give this lady a fair hearing—don't interrupt"—she, with the slightest of gestures, waves him aside with a low "It's all right.")*

MISS LEVERING: (*steadying and raising her voice*) These questions are quite proper! They are often asked elsewhere; and I would like to ask in return: Since when was human society held to exist for its handful of geniuses? How many Platos are there here in this crowd?

A VOICE: (*very loud and shrill*) Divil a wan!

(*Laughter.*)

MISS LEVERING: Not one. Yet that doesn't keep you men off the
1780 register. How many Shakespeares are there in all England today? Not one. Yet the State doesn't tumble to pieces. Railroads and ships are built—homes are kept going, and babies are born. The world goes on! (*Bending over the crowd.*) It goes on *by virtue of its common people.*

VOICES: (*subdued*) Hear! hear!

MISS LEVERING: I am not concerned that you should think we women can paint great pictures, or compose immortal music, or write good books. I am content that we should be
1790 classed with the common people—who keep the world going. But (*Straightening up and taking a fresh start.*) I'd like the world to go a great deal better. We were talking about justice. I have been inquiring into the kind of lodging the poorest class of homeless women can get in this town of London. I find that only the men of that class are provided for. Some measure to establish Rowton Houses for women has been before the London County Council. They looked into the question "very carefully," so their apologists say. And what did they decide? They decided that *they could do
1800 nothing.*

LADY JOHN: (*having forced her way to STONOR's side*) Is that true?

STONOR: (*speaking through MISS LEVERING's next words*) I don't know.

MISS LEVERING: Why could that great, all-powerful body do nothing? Because, if these cheap and decent houses were opened, they said, the homeless women in the streets would make use of them! You'll think I'm not in earnest. But that was actually the decision and the reason given for it. Women
1810 that the bitter struggle for existence has forced into a life of horror—

STONOR: (*sternly to LADY JOHN*): You think this is the kind of thing—(*A motion of the head towards JEAN.*)

MISS LEVERING:—the outcast women might take advantage of the shelter these decent, cheap places offered. But the *men,*

I said! Are all who avail themselves of Lord Rowton's hostels, are *they* all angels? Or does wrong-doing in a man not matter? Yet women are recommended to depend on the chivalry of men.

(*The two policemen, who at first had been strolling about, have stood during this scene in front of* GEOFFREY STONOR. *They turn now and walk away, leaving* STONOR *exposed. He, embarrassed, moves uneasily, and* VIDA LEVERING's *eye falls upon his big figure. He still has the collar of his motor coat turned up to his ears. A change passes over her face, and her nerve fails her an instant.*)

1820 MISS LEVERING: Justice and chivalry!! (*She steadies her voice and hurries on.*) —they both remind me of what those of you who read the police court news—(I have begun only lately to do that)—but you've seen the accounts of the girl who's been tried in Manchester lately for the murder of her child. Not pleasant reading. Even if we'd noticed it, we wouldn't speak of it in my world. A few months ago I should have turned away my eyes and forgotten even the headline as quickly as I could. But since that morning in the police court, I read these things. This, as you'll remember, was 1830 about a little working girl—an orphan of eighteen—who crawled with the dead body of her new born child to her master's back door, and left the baby there. She dragged herself a little way off and fainted. A few days later she found herself in court, being tried for the murder of her child. Her master—a married man—had of course reported the "find" at his back door to the police, and he had been summoned to give evidence. The girl cried out to him in the open court, "You are the father!" He couldn't deny it. The Coroner at the jury's request censured the man, and regret-1840 ted that the law didn't make him responsible. But he went scot-free. And that girl is now serving her sentence in Strangeways Gaol.

(*Murmuring and scraps of indistinguishable comment in the crowd, through which only* JEAN's *voice is clear.*)

JEAN: (*who has wormed her way to* STONOR's *side*) Why do you dislike her so?

STONOR: I? Why should you think—

JEAN: (*With a vaguely frightened air*) I never saw you look as you did—as you do.

CHAIRMAN: Order, please—give the lady a fair—

MISS LEVERING: (*signing to him "It's all right"*) Men make 1850 boast that an English citizen is tried by his peers. What woman is tried by hers?

(*A sombre passion strengthens her voice and hurries her on.*)

A woman is arrested by a man, brought before a man judge, tried by a jury of men, condemned by men, taken to prison by a man, and by a man she's hanged! Where in all this were *her* "peers"? Why did men so long ago insist on trial by "a jury of their peers"? So that justice shouldn't miscarry—wasn't it? A man's peers would best understand his circumstances, his temptation, the degree of his guilt. Yet there's no such unlikeness between different classes of men as ex-1860 ists between man and woman. What man has the knowledge that makes him a fit judge of woman's deeds at that time of anguish—that hour—(*lowers her voice and bends over the*

crowd)—that hour that some woman struggled through to put each man here into the world. I noticed when a previous speaker quoted the Labour Party you applauded. Some of you here—I gather—call yourselves Labour men. Every woman who has borne a child is a Labour woman. No man among you can judge what she goes through in her hour of darkness—

JEAN: (*with frightened eyes on her lover's set, white face, whis-* 1870 *pers*) Geoffrey—

MISS LEVERING: (*catching her fluttering breath, goes on very low*) —in that great agony when, even under the best conditions that money and devotion can buy, many a woman falls into temporary mania, and not a few go down to death. In the case of this poor little abandoned working girl, what man can be the fit judge of her deeds in that awful moment of half-crazed temptation? Women know of these things as those know burning who have walked through fire.

(STONOR *makes a motion towards* JEAN *and she turns away fronting the audience. Her hands go up to her throat as though she suffered a choking sensation. It is in her face that she "knows."* MISS LEVERING *leans over the platform and speaks with a low and thrilling earnestness.*)

I would say in conclusion to the women here, it's not enough 1880 to be sorry for these unfortunate sisters. We must get the conditions of life made fairer. We women must organise. We must learn to work together. We have all (rich and poor, happy and unhappy) worked so long and so exclusively for *men*, we hardly know how to work for one another. But we must learn. Those who can, may give money—

VOICES: (*grumbling*) Oh, yes—Money! Money!

MISS LEVERING: Those who haven't pennies to give—even those people aren't so poor they can't give some part of their labour—some share of their sympathy and support. (*Turns* 1890 *to hear something the* CHAIRMAN *is whispering to her.*)

JEAN: (*low to* LADY JOHN) Oh, I'm glad I've got power!

LADY JOHN: (*bewildered*) Power!—*you?*

JEAN: Yes, all that money—

(LADY JOHN *tries to make her way to* STONOR.)

MISS LEVERING: (*suddenly turning from the* CHAIRMAN *to the crowd*) Oh, yes, I hope you'll all join the Union. Come up after the meeting and give your names.

LOUD VOICE: You won't get many men.

MISS LEVERING: (*with fire*) Then it's to the women I appeal!

(*She is about to retire when, with a sudden gleam in her lit eyes, she turns for the last time to the crowd, silencing the general murmur and holding the people by the sudden concentration of passion in her face.*)

I don't mean to say it wouldn't be better if men and women 1900 did this work together—shoulder to shoulder. But the mass of men won't have it so. I only hope they'll realise in time the good they've renounced and the spirit they've aroused. For I know as well as any man could tell me, it would be a bad day for England if all women felt about all men *as I do.*

(*She retires in a tumult. The others on the platform close about her. The* CHAIRMAN *tries in vain to get a hearing from the excited crowd.*)

JEAN *tries to make her way through the knot of people surging round her.*)

STONOR: *(calls)* Here—Follow me!

JEAN: No—no—I—

STONOR: You're going the wrong way.

JEAN: *This* is the way I must go.

1910 STONOR: You can get out quicker on this side.

JEAN: I don't *want* to get out.

STONOR: What! Where are you going?

JEAN: To ask that woman to let me have the honour of working with her.

*(She disappears in the crowd. Curtain.)*

—ACT THREE—

*Scene: The drawing room at old* MR DUNBARTON'S *house in Eaton Square. Six o'clock the same evening. As the Curtain rises the door opens and* JEAN *appears on the threshold. She looks back into her own sitting room, then crosses the drawing room, treading softly on the parquet spaces between the rugs. She goes to the window and is in the act of parting the lace curtains when the folding doors are opened by the* BUTLER.

JEAN: *(to the Servant)* Sh!

*(She goes softly back to the door she has left open and closes it carefully. When she turns, the* BUTLER *has stepped aside to admit* GEOFFREY STONOR, *and departed, shutting the folding doors.* STONOR *comes rapidly forward.)*

*(Before he gets a word out.)* Speak low, please.

STONOR: *(angrily)* I waited about a whole hour for you to come back.

*(*JEAN *turns away as though vaguely looking for the nearest chair.)*

If you don't mind leaving *me* like that you might have con-
1920 sidered Lady John.

JEAN: *(pausing)* Is she here with you?

STONOR: No. My place was nearer than this, and she was very tired. I left her to get some tea. We couldn't tell whether you'd be here, or *what* had become of you.

JEAN: Mr Trent got us a hansom.

STONOR: Trent?

JEAN: The Chairman of the meeting.

STONOR: "Got us—"?

JEAN: Miss Levering and me.

1930 STONOR: *(incensed)* MISS L—

BUTLER: *(opens the door and announces)* Mr Farnborough.

*(Enter* MR RICHARD FARNBOROUGH—*more flurried than ever.)*

FARNBOROUGH: *(seeing* STONOR*)* At last! You'll forgive this incursion, Miss Dunbarton, when you hear—*(Turns abruptly back to* STONOR.*)* They've been telegraphing you all over London. In despair they set me on your track.

STONOR: Who did? What's up.

FARNBOROUGH: *(lays down his hat and fumbles agitatedly in his breast pocket)* There was the devil to pay at Dutfield last night. The Liberal chap tore down from London and took

over your meeting!    1940

STONOR: Oh?—Nothing about it in the Sunday paper *I* saw.

FARNBOROUGH: Wait till you see the Press tomorrow morning! There was a great rally and the beggar made a rousing speech.

STONOR: What about?

FARNBOROUGH: Abolition of the Upper House—

STONOR: They were at that when I was at Eton!

FARNBOROUGH: Yes. But this new man has got a way of putting things!—the people went mad. *(Pompously.)* The Liberal platform as defined at Dutfield is going to make a big dif- 1950 ference.

STONOR: *(drily)* You think so.

FARNBOROUGH: Well, your agent says as much. *(Opens telegram.)*

STONOR: My—*(Taking telegram.)* "Try find Stonor"—Hm! Hm!

FARNBOROUGH: *(pointing)*—"tremendous effect of last night's Liberal manifesto ought to be counteracted in tomorrow's papers." *(Very earnestly.)* You see, Mr. Stonor, it's a battle cry we want.    1960

STONOR: *(turns on his heel)* Claptrap!

FARNBOROUGH: *(a little dashed)* Well, they've been saying we have nothing to offer but personal popularity. No practical reform. No—

STONOR: No truckling to the masses. I suppose. *(Walks impatiently away.)*

FARNBOROUGH: *(snubbed)* Well, in these democratic days— *(Turns to* JEAN *for countenance.)* I hope you'll forgive my bursting in like this. *(Struck by her face.)* But I can see you realise the gravity—*(Lowering his voice with an air of* 1970 *speaking for her ear alone.)* It isn't as if he were going to be a mere private member. Everybody knows he'll be in the Cabinet.

STONOR: *(drily)* It may be a Liberal Cabinet.

FARNBOROUGH: Nobody thought so up to last night. Why, even your brother—but I am afraid I'm seeming officious. *(Takes up his hat.)*

STONOR: *(coldly)* What about my brother?

FARNBOROUGH: I met Lord Windlesham as I rushed out of the Carlton.    1980

STONOR: Did he say anything?

FARNBOROUGH: I told him the Dutfield news.

STONOR: *(impatiently)* Well?

FARNBOROUGH: He said it only confirmed his fears.

STONOR: *(half under his breath)* Said that, did he?

FARNBOROUGH: Yes. Defeat is inevitable, he thinks, unless— *(Pause.)*

*(*GEOFFREY STONOR *who has been pacing the floor, stops but doesn't raise his eyes.)*

unless you can "manufacture some political dynamite within the next few hours." Those were his words.

STONOR: *(resumes his walking to and fro, raises his head and* 1990 *catches sight of* JEAN'S *white, drawn face. Stops short)* You are very tired.

JEAN: No. No.

STONOR: *(to* FARNBOROUGH*)* I'm obliged to you for taking so much trouble. *(Shakes hands by way of dismissing* FARNBOROUGH.*)* I'll see what can be done.

FARNBOROUGH: (*offering the reply-paid form*) If you'd like to wire I'll take it.

STONOR: (*faintly amused*) You don't understand, my young friend. Moves of this kind are not rushed at by responsible politicians. I must have time for consideration.

FARNBOROUGH: (*disappointed*) Oh, well, I only hope someone else won't jump into the breach before you—(*Watch in hand.*) I tell you. (*To* JEAN.) I'll find out what time the newspapers go to press on Sunday. Goodbye (*To* STONOR.) I'll be at the Club just *in case* I can be of any use.

STONOR: (*firmly*) No, don't do that. If I should have anything new to say—

FARNBOROUGH: (*feverishly*) B-b-but with our party, as your brother said—"heading straight for a vast electoral disaster—"

STONOR: If I decide on a counterblast I shall simply telegraph to headquarters. Goodbye.

FARNBOROUGH: Oh—a—g-goodbye. (*A gesture of "The country's going to the dogs."*)

(JEAN *rings the bell. Exit* FARNBOROUGH.)

STONOR: (*studying the carpet*) "Political dynamite," eh? (*Pause.*) After all . . . women are much more conservative than men—aren't they?

(JEAN *looks straight in front of her, making no attempt to reply.*)

Especially the women the property qualification would bring in. (*He glances at* JEAN *as though for the first time conscious of her silence.*) You see now (*He throws himself into the chair by the table.*) one reason why I've encouraged you to take an interest in public affairs. Because people like us don't go screaming about it, is no sign we don't (some of us) see what's on the way. However little they want to, women of our class will have to come into line. All the best things in the world—everything that civilisation has won will be in danger if—when this change comes—the only women who have practical political training are the women of the lower classes. Women of the lower classes, and (*His brows knit heavily.*)—women inoculated by the Socialist virus.

JEAN: Geoffrey.

STONOR: (*draws the telegraph form towards him*) Let us see, how we shall put it—when the time comes—shall we? (*He detaches a pencil from his watch chain and bends over the paper, writing.*)

(JEAN *opens her lips to speak, moves a shade nearer the table and then falls back upon her silent, half-incredulous misery.*)

STONOR: (*holds the paper off, smiling*) Enough dynamite in that! Rather too much, isn't there, little girl?

JEAN: Geoffrey, I know her story.

STONOR: Whose story?

JEAN: Miss Levering's

STONOR: *Whose?*

JEAN: Vida Levering's

(STONOR *stares speechless. Slight pause.*)

(*The words escaping from her in a miserable cry.*) Why did you desert her?

STONOR: (*staggered*) I! I?

JEAN: Oh, why did you do it?

STONOR: (*bewildered*) What in the name of—What has she been saying to you?

JEAN: Someone else told me part. Then the way you looked when you saw her at Aunt Ellen's—Miss Levering's saying you didn't know her—then your letting out that you knew even the curious name on the handkerchief—Oh, I pieced it together—

STONOR: (*with recovered self-possession*) Your ingenuity is undeniable!

JEAN: —and then, when she said that at the meeting about "the dark hour" and I looked at your face—it flashed over me—Oh, *why* did you desert her?

STONOR: I *didn't* desert her.

JEAN: Ah-h! (*Puts her hands before her eyes.*)

(STONOR *makes a passionate motion towards her, is checked by her muffled voice saying.*)

I'm glad—I'm glad!

(*He stares bewildered.* JEAN *drops her hands in her lap and steadies her voice.*)

She went away from you, then?

STONOR: You don't expect me to enter into—

JEAN: She went away from you?

STONOR: (*with a look of almost uncontrollable anger*) Yes!

JEAN: Was that because you wouldn't marry her?

STONOR: I couldn't marry her—and she knew it.

JEAN: Did you want to?

STONOR: (*an instant's angry scrutiny and then turning away his eyes*) I thought I did—*then*. It's a long time ago.

JEAN: And why "couldn't" you?

STONOR: (*a movement of strong irritation cut short*) Why are you catechising me? It's a matter that concerns another woman.

JEAN: If you're saying that it doesn't concern me, you're saying—(*her lip trembles*)—that *you* don't concern me.

STONOR: (*commanding his temper with difficulty*) In those days I—I was absolutely dependent on my father.

JEAN: Why, you must have been thirty, Geoffrey.

STONOR: (*slight pause*) What? Oh—thereabouts.

JEAN: And everybody says you're so clever.

STONOR: Well, everybody's mistaken.

JEAN: (*drawing nearer*) It must have been terribly hard—

(STONOR *turns towards her.*)

for you both—

(*He arrests his movement and stands stonily.*)

that a man like you shouldn't have had the freedom that even the lowest seem to have.

STONOR: Freedom?

JEAN: To marry the woman they choose.

STONOR: She didn't break off our relations because I couldn't marry her.

JEAN: Why was it, then?

STONOR: You're too young to discuss such a story. (*Half turns away.*)

JEAN: I'm not so young as she was when—

STONOR: (*wheeling upon her*) Very well, then, if you will have it! The truth is, it didn't seem to weigh upon her, as it seems to on you, that I wasn't able to marry her.

2100 JEAN: Why are you so sure of that?

STONOR: Because she didn't so much as hint such a thing when she wrote that she meant to break off the—the—

JEAN: What made her write like that?

STONOR: (*with suppressed rage*) Why *will* you go on talking of what's so long over and ended?

JEAN: What reason did she give?

STONOR: If your curiosity has so got the upper hand—*ask her*.

JEAN: (*her eyes upon him*) You're afraid to tell me.

STONOR: (*putting pressure on himself to answer quietly*) I still
2110 hoped—at *that* time—to win my father over. She blamed me because (*goes to the window and looks blindly out and speaks in a low tone.*) if the child had lived it wouldn't have been possible to get my father to—to overlook it.

JEAN: (*faintly*) You wanted it *overlooked?* I don't underst—

STONOR: (*turning passionately back to her*) Of course you don't. (*He seizes her hand and tries to draw her to him.*) If you did, you wouldn't be the beautiful, tender, innocent child you are—

JEAN: (*has withdrawn her hand and shrunk from him with an
2120 impulse—slight as is its expression—so tragically eloquent, that fear for the first time catches hold of him*) I am glad you didn't mean to desert her, Geoffrey. It wasn't your fault after all—only some misunderstanding that can be cleared up.

STONOR: *Cleared up?*

JEAN: Yes. Cleared up.

STONOR: (*aghast*) You aren't thinking that this miserable old affair I'd as good as forgotten—

JEAN: (*in a horror struck whisper, with a glance at the door
2130 which he doesn't see*) Forgotten!

STONOR: No, no. I don't mean exactly forgotten. But you're torturing me so I don't know what I'm saying. (*He goes closer.*) You aren't—Jean! you—you aren't going to let it come between you and me!

JEAN: (*presses her handkerchief to her lips, and then, taking it away, answers steadily*) I can't make or unmake what's past. But I'm glad, at least, that you didn't *mean* to desert her in her trouble. You'll remind her of that first of all, won't you? (*Moves to the door.*)

2140 STONOR: Where are you going? (*Raising his voice.*) Why should I remind anybody of what I want only to forget?

JEAN: (*finger on lip*) Sh!

STONOR: (*with eyes on the door*) You don't mean that *she's*—

JEAN: Yes. I left her to get a little rest.

(*He recoils in an access of uncontrollable rage. She follows him. Speechless, he goes to get his hat.*)

Geoffrey, don't go before you hear me. I don't know if what I think matters to you now—but I hope it does. (*With tears.*) You can still make me think of you without shrinking—if you will.

STONOR: (*fixes her a moment with his eyes. Then sternly*) What
2150 is it you are asking of me?

JEAN: To make amends, Geoffrey.

STONOR: (*with an outburst*) You poor little innocent!

JEAN: I'm poor enough. But (*locking her hands together.*) I'm not so innocent but what I know you must right that old wrong now, if you're ever to right it.

STONOR: You aren't insane enough to think I would turn round in these few hours and go back to something that ten years ago was ended for ever! Why, it's stark, staring madness!

JEAN: No. (*Catching on his arm*) What you did ten years ago—
*that* was mad. This is paying a debt.                                      2160

STONOR: Look here, Jean, you're dreadfully wrought up and excited—tired too—

JEAN: No, not tired—though I've travelled so far today. I know you smile at sudden conversions. You think they're hysterical—worse—vulgar. But people must get their revelation how they can. And, Geoffrey, if I can't make you see this one of mine—I shall know your love could never mean strength to me. Only weakness. And I shall be afraid. So afraid I'll never dare to give you the *chance* of making me loathe myself. I shall never see you again.                                        2170

STONOR: How right *I* was to be afraid of that vein of fanaticism in you. (*Moves towards the door.*)

JEAN: Certainly you couldn't make a greater mistake than to go away now and think it any good ever to come back. (*He turns.*) Even if I came to feel different, I couldn't *do* anything different. I should know all this couldn't be forgotten. I should know that it would poison my life in the end. Yours too.

STONOR: (*with suppressed fury*) She has made good use of her time? (*With a sudden thought.*) What has changed her? Has     2180
*she* been seeing visions too?

JEAN: What do you mean?

STONOR: Why is she intriguing to get hold of a man that, ten years ago, she flatly refused to see, or hold any communication with?

JEAN: "Intriguing to get hold of." She hasn't mentioned you!

STONOR: *What!* Then how in the name of Heaven do you know—that she wants—what you ask?

JEAN: (*firmly*) There can't be any doubt about that.

STONOR: (*with immense relief*) You absurd, ridiculous child!     2190
Then all this is just your own unaided invention. Well—I could thank God! (*Falls into the nearest chair and passes his handkerchief over his face.*)

JEAN: (*perplexed, uneasy*) For what are you thanking God?

STONOR: (*trying to think out his plan of action*) Suppose, (I'm not going to risk it)—but suppose—(*He looks up and at the sight of* JEAN's *face a new tenderness comes into his own. He rises suddenly.*) Whether I deserve to suffer or not—it's quite certain *you* don't. Don't cry, dear one. It never was the real thing. I had to wait till I knew you before I understood.     2200

JEAN: (*lifts her eyes brimming*) Oh, is that true? (*Checks her movement towards him.*) Loving you has made things clear to me I didn't dream of before. If I could think that because of me you were able to do this—

STONOR: (*seizes her by the shoulders and says hoarsely*) Look here! Do you seriously ask me to give up the girl I love—to go and offer to marry a woman that even to think of—

JEAN: You cared for her once. You'll care about her again. She is beautiful and brilliant—everything. I've heard she could win any man she set herself to—                                           2210

STONOR: (*pushing* JEAN *from him*) She's bewitched you!

JEAN: Geoffrey, Geoffrey, you aren't going away like that. This isn't *the end!*

STONOR: (*darkly—hesitating*) I suppose even if she refused me, you'd—

JEAN: She won't refuse you.

STONOR: She did once.

JEAN: She didn't refuse to *marry* you—

(JEAN *is going to the door.*)

STONOR: (*catches her by the arm*) Wait!—a—(*Hunting for*
2220   *some means of gaining time.*) Lady John is waiting all this
while for the car to go back with a message.

JEAN: *That's* not a matter of life and death—

STONOR: All the same—I'll go down and give the order.

JEAN: (*stopping quite still on a sudden*) Very well. (*Sits.*) You'll
come back if you're the man I pray you are. (*Breaks into a
flood of silent tears, her elbows on the table, her face in her
hands.*)

STONOR: (*returns, bends over her, about to take her in his
arms*) Dearest of all the world—

(*Door opens softly and* VIDA LEVERING *appears. She is arrested
at the sight of* STONOR, *and is in the act of drawing back when,
upon the slight noise,* STONOR *looks round. His face darkens, he
stands staring at her and then with a look of speechless anger
goes silently out.* JEAN, *hearing him shut the door, drops her
head on the table with a sob.* VIDA LEVERING *crosses slowly to
her and stands a moment silent at the girl's side.*)

2230   MISS LEVERING: What is the matter?

JEAN: (*lifting her head and drying her eyes*) I—I've been seeing Geoffrey.

MISS LEVERING: (*with an attempt at lightness*) Is this the effect
seeing Geoffrey has?

JEAN: You see, I know now (*as* MISS LEVERING *looks quite un-
comprehending*)—how he (*drops her eyes*)—how he
spoiled some one else's life.

MISS LEVERING: (*quickly*) Who tells you that?

JEAN: Several people have told me.

2240   MISS LEVERING: Well, you should be very careful how you believe what you hear.

JEAN: (*passionately*) You *know* it's true.

MISS LEVERING: I know that it's possible to be mistaken.

JEAN: I see! You're trying to shield him—

MISS LEVERING: Why should I—what is it to me?

JEAN: (*with tears*) Oh-h, how you must love him!

MISS LEVERING: Listen to me—

JEAN: (*rising*) What's the use of your going on denying it? (MISS
LEVERING, *about to break in, is silenced.*) Geoffrey doesn't.

(JEAN, *struggling to command her feelings, goes to window.*
VIDA LEVERING *relinquishes an impulse to follow, and sits left
centre.* JEAN *comes slowly back with her eyes bent on the floor,
does not lift them till she is quite near* VIDA. *Then the girl's self-
absorbed face changes.*)

2250   Oh, don't look like that! I shall bring him back to you!
(*Drops on her knees beside the other's chair.*)

MISS LEVERING: You would be impertinent (*softening*) if you
weren't a romantic child. You can't bring him back.

JEAN: Yes, he—

MISS LEVERING: But there's something you *can* do—

JEAN: What?

MISS LEVERING: Bring him to the point where he recognises
that he's in our debt.

JEAN: In *our* debt?

MISS LEVERING: In debt to women. He can't repay the one he   2260
robbed—

JEAN: (*wincing and rising from her knees*) Yes, yes.

MISS LEVERING: (*sternly*) No, he can't repay the dead. But
there are the living. There are the thousands with hope still
in their hearts and youth in their blood. Let him help *them.*
Let him be a Friend to Women.

JEAN: (*rising on a wave of enthusiasm*) Yes, yes—I understand.
That too!

(*The door opens. As* STONOR *enters with* LADY JOHN, *he makes
a slight gesture towards the two as much as to say, "You see."*)

JEAN: (*catching sight of him*) Thank you!

LADY JOHN: (*in a clear, commonplace tone to* JEAN) Well, you   2270
rather gave us the slip. Vida, I believe Mr. Stonor wants to
see you for a few minutes (*glances at watch*)—but I'd like a
word with you first, as I must get back. (*To* STONOR.) Do you
think the car—your man said something about re-charging.

STONOR: (*hastily*) Oh, did he? I'll see about it.

(*As* STONOR *is going out he encounters the* BUTLER. *Exit*
STONOR.)

BUTLER: Mr Trent has called, Miss, to take Miss Levering to
the meeting.

JEAN: Bring Mr Trent into my sitting room. I'll tell him—you
can't go tonight.

(*Exeunt* BUTLER *centre,* JEAN *left.*)

LADY JOHN: (*hurriedly*) I know, my dear, *you're* not aware of   2280
what that impulsive girl wants to insist on.

MISS LEVERING: Yes, I am aware of it.

LADY JOHN: But it isn't with your sanction, surely, that she goes
on making this extraordinary demand.

MISS LEVERING: (*slowly*) I didn't sanction it at first, but I've
been thinking it over.

LADY JOHN: Then all I can say is I am greatly disappointed in
you. You threw this man over years ago for reasons—whatever they were—that seemed to you good and sufficient.
And now you come between him and a younger woman—   2290
just to play Nemesis, so far as I can make out!

MISS LEVERING: Is that what he says?

LADY JOHN: He says nothing that isn't fair and considerate.

MISS LEVERING: I can see he's changed.

LADY JOHN: And you're unchanged—is that it?

MISS LEVERING: I've changed even more than he.

LADY JOHN: But (*pity and annoyance blended in her tone*)—
you care about him still, Vida?

MISS LEVERING: No.

LADY JOHN: I see. It's just that you wish to marry somebody—   2300

MISS LEVERING: Oh, Lady John, there are no men listening.

LADY JOHN: (*surprised*) No, I didn't suppose there were.

MISS LEVERING: Then why keep up that old pretence?

LADY JOHN: What pre—

MISS LEVERING: That to marry *at all costs* is every woman's
dearest ambition till the grave closes over her. You and I
*know* it isn't true.

LADY JOHN: Well, but—Oh! it was just the unexpected sight of
him bringing it back—*That* was what fired you this afternoon! (*With an honest attempt at sympathetic understand-*   2310
*ing.*) Of course. The memory of a thing like that can never

die—can never even be dimmed—*for the woman.*

MISS LEVERING: I mean her to think so.

LADY JOHN: (*bewildered*) Jean!

(MISS LEVERING *nods.*)

LADY JOHN: And it *isn't so?*

MISS LEVERING: You don't seriously believe a woman with anything else to think about, comes to the end of ten years still *absorbed* in a memory of that sort?

LADY JOHN: (*astonished*) You've got over it, then!

2320 MISS LEVERING: If the newspapers didn't remind me I shouldn't remember once a twelvemonth that there was ever such a person as Geoffrey Stonor in the world.

LADY JOHN: (*with unconscious rapture*) Oh, I'm *so* glad!

MISS LEVERING: (*smiles grimly*) Yes. I'm glad too.

LADY JOHN: And if Geoffrey Stonor offered you—what's called 'reparation'—you'd refuse it?

MISS LEVERING: (*smiles a little contemptuously*) Geoffrey Stonor! For me he's simply one of the far back links in a chain of evidence. It's certain I think a hundred times of
2330 other women's present unhappiness, to once that I remember that old unhappiness of mine that's past. I think of the nail and chain makers of Cradley Heath. The sweated girls of the slums. I think of the army of ill-used women whose very existence I mustn't mention—

LADY JOHN: (*interrupting hurriedly*) Then why in Heaven's name do you let poor Jean imagine—

MISS LEVERING: (*bending forward*) Look—I'll trust you, Lady John. I don't suffer from that old wrong as Jean thinks I do, but I shall coin her sympathy into gold for a greater cause
2340 than mine.

LADY JOHN: I don't understand you.

MISS LEVERING: Jean isn't old enough to be able to care as much about a principle as about a person. But if my half-forgotten pain can turn her generosity into the common treasury—

LADY JOHN: What do you propose she shall do, poor child?

MISS LEVERING: Use her hold over Geoffrey Stonor to make him help us!

LADY JOHN: Help you?

2350 MISS LEVERING: The man who served one woman—God knows how many more—very ill, shall serve hundreds of thousands well. Geoffrey Stonor shall make it harder for his son, harder still for his grandson, to treat any woman as he treated me.

LADY JOHN: How will he do that?

MISS LEVERING: By putting an end to the helplessness of women.

LADY JOHN: (*ironically*) You must think he has a great deal of power—

2360 MISS LEVERING: Power? Yes, men have too much over penniless and frightened women.

LADY JOHN: (*impatiently*) What nonsense! You talk as though the women hadn't their share of human nature. *We* aren't made of ice any more than the men.

MISS LEVERING: No, but all the same we have more self-control.

LADY JOHN: Than men?

MISS LEVERING: You know we have.

LADY JOHN: (*shrewdly*) I know we mustn't admit it.

MISS LEVERING: For fear they'd call us fishes!    2370

LADY JOHN: (*evasively*) They talk of our lack of self-control—but it's the last thing they *want* women to have.

MISS LEVERING: Oh, we know what they want us to have. So we make shift to have it. If we don't, we go without hope—sometimes we go without bread.

LADY JOHN: (*shocked*) Vida—do you mean to say that you—

MISS LEVERING: I mean to say that men's vanity won't let them see it, but the thing's largely a question of economics.

LADY JOHN: (*shocked*) You *never* loved him, then!

MISS LEVERING: Oh yes. I loved him—*once*. It was my help-  2380 lessness turned the best thing life can bring, into a curse for both of us.

LADY JOHN: I don't understand you—

MISS LEVERING: Oh, being "understood!"—that's too much to expect. When people come to know I've joined the Union—

LADY JOHN: But you won't—

MISS LEVERING: —who is there who will resist the temptation to say, "Poor Vida Levering! What a pity she hasn't got a husband and a baby to keep her quiet"? The few who know about me, they'll be equally sure that it's not the larger view  2390 of life I've gained—my own poor little story is responsible for my new departure. (*Leans forward and looks into* LADY JOHN's *face.*) My best friend, she will be surest of all, that it's a private sense of loss, or, lower yet, a grudge—! But I tell you the only difference between me and thousands of women with husbands and babies is that I'm free to say what I think. *They aren't.*

LADY JOHN: (*rising and looking at her watch*) I must get back—my poor ill-used guests.

MISS LEVERING: (*rising*) I won't ring. I think you'll find Mr  2400 Stonor downstairs waiting for you.

LADY JOHN: (*embarrassed*) Oh—a—he will have left word about the car in any case.

(MISS LEVERING *has opened the door.* ALLEN TRENT *is in the act of saying goodbye to* JEAN *in the hall.*)

MISS LEVERING: Well, Mr Trent, I didn't expect to see you this evening.

TRENT: (*comes and stands in the doorway*) Why not? Have I ever failed?

MISS LEVERING: Lady John, this is one of our allies. He is good enough to squire me through the rabble from time to time.

LADY JOHN: Well, I think it's very handsome of you, after what  2410 she said today about men. (*Shakes hands.*)

TRENT: I've no great opinion of most men myself. I might add—or of most women.

LADY JOHN: Oh! Well, at any rate I shall go away relieved to think that Miss Levering's plain speaking hasn't alienated *all* masculine regard.

TRENT: Why should it?

LADY JOHN: That's right, Mr Trent! Don't believe all she says in the heat of propaganda.

TRENT: I do believe all she says. But I'm not cast down.    2420

LADY JOHN: (*smiling*) Not when she says—

TRENT: (*interrupting*) Was there never a misogynist of my sex who ended by deciding to make an exception?

LADY JOHN: (*smiling significantly*) Oh, if *that's* what you build on!

TRENT: Well, why shouldn't a man-hater on your side prove

equally open to reason?

MISS LEVERING: That part of the question doesn't concern me. I've come to a place where I realise that the first battles of
2430 this new campaign must be fought by women alone. The only effective help men could give—amendment of the law—they refuse. The rest is nothing.

LADY JOHN: Don't be ungrateful, Vida. Here's Mr Trent ready to face criticism in publicly championing you.

MISS LEVERING: It's an illusion that I as an individual need Mr Trent. I am quite safe in the crowd. Please don't wait for me, and don't come for me again.

TRENT: (*flushes*) Of course if you'd rather—

MISS LEVERING: And that reminds me. I was asked to thank you
2440 and to tell you, too, that they—the women of the Union—they won't need your chairmanship any more—though that, I beg you to believe, has nothing to with any feeling of mine.

TRENT: (*hurt*) Of course. I know there must be other men ready—better known men—

MISS LEVERING: It isn't that. It's simply that they find a man can't keep a rowdy meeting in order as well as a woman.

(*He stares.*)

LADY JOHN: You aren't serious?

MISS LEVERING: (*to* TRENT) Haven't you noticed that all their worst disturbances come when men are in charge?

2450 TRENT: Well—a—(*laughs a little ruefully as he moves to the door.*) I hadn't connected the two ideas. Goodbye.

MISS LEVERING: Goodbye.

(JEAN *takes him downstairs, right centre.*)

LADY JOHN: (*as* TRENT *disappears*) That nice boy's in love with you.

(MISS LEVERING *simply looks at her.*)

Goodbye. (*They shake hands.*) I wish you hadn't been so unkind to that nice boy!

MISS LEVERING: Do you?

LADY JOHN: Yes, for then I would be more certain of your telling Geoffrey Stonor that intelligent women don't nurse
2460 their wrongs and lie in wait to punish them.

MISS LEVERING: You are *not* certain?

LADY JOHN: (*goes close up to* VIDA) Are you?

(VIDA *stands with her eyes on the ground, silent, motionless.* LADY JOHN, *with a nervous glance at her watch and a gesture of extreme perturbation, goes hurriedly out.* VIDA *shuts the door. She comes slowly back, sits down and covers her face with her hands. She rises and begins to walk up and down, obviously trying to master her agitation. Enter* GEOFFREY STONOR.)

MISS LEVERING: Well, have they primed you? Have you got your lesson (*with a little broken laugh*) by heart at last?

STONOR: (*looking at her from immeasurable distance*) I am not sure I understand you. (*Pause.*) However unpropitious your mood may be—I shall discharge my errand. (*Pause. Her silence irritates him.*) I have promised to offer you what I believe is called "amends."

2470 MISS LEVERING: (*quickly*) You've come to realise, then—after all these years—that you owed me something?

STONOR: (*on the brink of protest, checks himself*) I am not here

to deny it.

MISS LEVERING: (*fiercely*) Pay, then—*pay.*

STONOR: (*a moment's dread as he looks at her, his lips set. Then stonily*) I have promised that, if you exact it, I will.

MISS LEVERING: Ah! If I insist you'll "make it all good"! (*Quite low.*) Then don't you know you must pay me in kind?

STONOR: What do you mean.

MISS LEVERING: Give me back what you took from me: my old 2480 faith. Give me that.

STONOR: Oh, if you mean to make phrases—(*A gesture of scant patience.*)

MISS LEVERING: (*going closer*) Or give me back mere kindness—or even tolerance. Oh, I don't mean *your* tolerance! Give me back the power to think fairly of my brothers—not as mockers—thieves.

STONOR: I have not mocked you. And I have asked you—

MISS LEVERING: Something you knew I should refuse! Or (*her eyes blaze*) did you dare to be afraid I wouldn't? 2490

STONOR: I suppose, if we set our teeth, we could—

MISS LEVERING: I couldn't—not even if I set my teeth. And you wouldn't dream of asking me, if you thought there was the smallest chance.

STONOR: I can do no more than make you an offer of such reparation as is in my power. If you don't accept it—(*He turns with an air of "That's done."*)

MISS LEVERING: Accept it? No! . . . Go away and live in debt! Pay and pay and pay—and find yourself still in debt!—for a thing you'll never be able to give me back. (*Lower.*) And 2500 when you come to die, say to yourself, "I paid all creditors but one."

STONOR: I'm rather tired, you know, of this talk of debt. If I hear that you persist in it I shall have to—

MISS LEVERING: What? (*She faces him.*)

STONOR: No. I'll keep to my resolution. (*Turning to the door.*)

MISS LEVERING: (*intercepting him*) What resolution?

STONOR: I came here, under considerable pressure, to speak of the future—not to re-open the past.

MISS LEVERING: The Future and the Past are one. 2510

STONOR: You talk as if that old madness was mine alone. It is the woman's way.

MISS LEVERING: I know. And it's not fair. Men suffer as well as we by the woman's starting wrong. We are taught to think the man a sort of demigod. If he tells her: "go down into Hell"—down into Hell she goes.

STONOR: Make no mistake. Not the woman alone. *They go down together.*

MISS LEVERING: Yes, they go down together, but the man comes up alone. As a rule. It is more convenient so—for 2520 him. And for the Other Woman.

(*The eyes of both go to* JEAN's *door.*)

STONOR: (*angrily*) My conscience is clear. I know—and so do you—that most men in my position wouldn't have troubled themselves. I gave myself endless trouble.

MISS LEVERING: (*with wondering eyes*) So you've gone about all these years feeling that you'd discharged every obligation.

STONOR: Not only that. I stood by you with a fidelity that was nothing short of Quixotic. If, woman like, you *must* recall the Past—I insist on your recalling it correctly.

MISS LEVERING: (*very low*) You think I don't recall it correctly? 2530

STONOR: Not when you make—other people believe that I deserted you. (*With gathering wrath.*) It's a curious enough charge when you stop to consider—(*Checks himself, and with a gesture of impatience sweeps the whole thing out of his way.*)

MISS LEVERING: Well, when we *do*—just for five minutes out of ten years—when we do stop to consider—

STONOR: We remember it was *you* who did the deserting! Since you had to rake the story up, you might have had the 2540 fairness to tell the facts.

MISS LEVERING: You think "the facts" would have excused you! (*She sits.*)

STONOR: No doubt you've forgotten them, since Lady John tells me you wouldn't remember my existence once a year if the newspapers didn't—

MISS LEVERING: Ah, you minded that!

STONOR: (*with manly spirit*) I minded your giving false impressions. (*She is about to speak, he advances on her.*) Do you deny that you returned my letters unopened?

2550 MISS LEVERING: (*quietly*) No.

STONOR: Do you deny that you refused to see me—and that, when I persisted, you vanished?

MISS LEVERING: I don't deny any of those things.

STONOR: Why, I had no trace of you for years!

MISS LEVERING: I suppose not.

STONOR: Very well, then. What *could* I do?

MISS LEVERING: Nothing. It was too late to do anything.

STONOR: It wasn't too late! You knew—since you "read the papers"—that my father died that same year. There was no 2560 longer any barrier between us.

MISS LEVERING: Oh yes, there was a barrier.

STONOR: Of your own making, then.

MISS LEVERING: I had my guilty share in it—but the barrier (*her voice trembles*)—the barrier was your invention.

STONOR: It was no "invention." If you had ever known my father—

MISS LEVERING: Oh, the echoes! The echoes! How often you used to say, if I "knew your father!" But you said, too (*lower*)—you called the greatest barrier by another name.

2570 STONOR: What name?

MISS LEVERING: (*very low*) The child that was to come.

STONOR: (*hastily*) That was before my father died. While I still hoped to get his consent.

MISS LEVERING: (*nods*) How the thought of that all-powerful personage used to terrorise me! What chance had a little unborn child against "the last of the great feudal lords," as you called him.

STONOR: You *know* the child would have stood between you and me!

2580 MISS LEVERING: I know the child *did* stand—

STONOR: (*with vague uneasiness*) It *did* stand—

MISS LEVERING: Happy mothers teach their children. Mine had to teach me.

STONOR: You talk as if—

MISS LEVERING: —teach me that a woman may do a thing for love's sake that shall kill love.

(*A silence.*)

STONOR: (*fearing and putting from him fuller comprehension, rises with an air of finality*) You certainly made it plain you had no love left for me.

MISS LEVERING: I had need of it all for the child.    2590

STONOR: (*stares—comes closer, speaks hurriedly and very low*) Do you mean then that, after all—it lived?

MISS LEVERING: No; I mean that it was sacrificed. But it showed me no barrier is so impassable as the one a little child can raise.

STONOR: (*a light dawning*) Was that why you . . . was *that* why?

MISS LEVERING: (*nods, speechless a moment*) Day and night there it was!—between my thought of you and me. (*He sits again, staring at her.*) When I was most unhappy I would wake, thinking I heard it cry. It was my own crying I heard, 2600 but I seemed to have it in my arms. I suppose I was mad. I used to lie there in that lonely farmhouse pretending to hush it. It was so I hushed myself.

STONOR: I never knew—

MISS LEVERING: I didn't blame you. You couldn't risk being with me.

STONOR: You agreed that for both our sakes—

MISS LEVERING: Yes, you had to be very circumspect. You were so well known. Your autocratic father—your brilliant political future—    2610

STONOR: Be fair. *Our* future—as I saw it then.

MISS LEVERING: Yes, it all hung on concealment. It must have looked quite simple to you. You didn't know that the ghost of a child that had never seen the light, the frail thing you meant to sweep aside and forget—*have* swept aside and forgotten—you didn't know it was strong enough to push you out of my life. (*Lower with an added intensity.*) It can do more. (*Leans over him and whispers.*) It can push that girl out. (STONOR's *face changes.*) It can do more still.

STONOR: Are you threatening me?    2620

MISS LEVERING: No. I am preparing you.

STONOR: For what?

MISS LEVERING: For the work that must be done. Either with *your help*—or *that girl's.*

(STONOR *lifts his eyes a moment.*)

One of two things. Either her life, and all she has, given to this new service—or a Ransom, if I give her up to you.

STONOR: I see. A price. Well—?

MISS LEVERING: (*looks searchingly in his face, hesitates and shakes her head*) Even if I could trust you to pay—no, it would be a poor bargain to give her up for anything you 2630 could do.

STONOR: (*rising*) In spite of your assumption—she may not be your tool.

MISS LEVERING: You are horribly afraid she is! But you are wrong. Don't think it's merely I that have got hold of Jean Dumbarton.

STONOR: (*angrily*) Who else?

MISS LEVERING: The New Spirit that's abroad.

(STONOR *turns away with an exclamation and begins to pace, sentinel-like, up and down before* JEAN's *door.*)

How else should that inexperienced girl have felt the new loyalty and responded as she did?    2640

STONOR: (*under his breath*) "New" indeed—however little loyal.

MISS LEVERING: Loyal above all. But no newer than electricity was when it first lit up the world. It had been there since the world began—waiting to do away with the dark. *So has the thing you're fighting.*

STONOR: *(his voice held down to its lowest register)* The thing I'm fighting is nothing more than one person's hold on a highly sensitive imagination. I consented to this interview with the hope—*(A gesture of impotence.)* It only remains for me to show her your true motive is revenge.

MISS LEVERING: Once say that to her and you are lost!

*(STONOR motionless; his look is the look of a man who sees happiness slipping away.)*

I know what it is that men fear. It even seems as if it must be through fear that your enlightenment will come. That is why I see a value in Jean Dumbarton far beyond her fortune.

*(STONOR lifts his eyes dully and fixes them on VIDA's face.)*

More than any girl I know—if I keep her from you—that gentle, inflexible creature could rouse in men the old half-superstitious fear—

STONOR: "Fear?" I believe you are mad.

MISS LEVERING: "Mad." "Unsexed." These are the words of today. In the Middle Ages men cried out "Witch!" and burnt her—the woman who served no man's bed or board.

STONOR: You want to make that poor child believe—

MISS LEVERING: She sees for herself we've come to a place where we find there's a value men see in them. You teach us not to look to you for some of the things we need most. If women must be freed by women, we have need of such as—*(Her eyes go to JEAN's door.)*—who knows? She may be the new Joan of Arc.

STONOR: *(aghast)* That *she* should be the sacrifice!

MISS LEVERING: You have taught us to look very calmly on the sacrifice of women. Men tell us in every tongue it's "a necessary evil."

*(STONOR stands rooted, staring at the ground.)*

One girl's happiness—against a thing nobler than happiness for thousands—who can hesitate?—*Not Jean.*

STONOR: Good God! Can't you see that this crazed campaign you'd start her on—even if it's successful, it can only be so through the help of men? What excuse shall you make your own soul for not going straight to the goal?

MISS LEVERING: You think we wouldn't be glad to go straight to the goal?

STONOR: I do. I see you'd much rather punish me and see her revel in a morbid self-sacrifice.

MISS LEVERING: You say I want to punish you only because, like most men, you won't take the trouble to understand what we do want—or how determined we are to have it. You can't kill this new spirit among women. *(Going nearer.)* And you couldn't make a greater mistake than to think it finds a home only in the exceptional, or the unhappy. It's so strange, Geoffrey, to see a man like you as much deluded as the Hyde Park loafers who say to Ernestine Blunt, "Who's hurt *your* feelings?" Why not realise *(Going quite close to him.)* this is a thing that goes deeper than personal experience? And yet *(Lowering her voice and glancing at the door.)* if you take only the narrowest personal view, a good deal depends on what you and I agree upon in the next five minutes.

STONOR: *(bringing her farther away from the door)* You recommend my realising the larger issues. But in your ambition to attach that girl to the chariot wheels of "Progress," you quite ignore the fact that people fitter for such work—the men you look to enlist in the end—are ready waiting to give the thing a chance.

MISS LEVERING: Men are ready! What men?

STONOR: *(avoiding her eyes, picking his words)* Women have themselves to blame that the question has grown so delicate that responsible people shrink—for the moment—from being implicated in it.

MISS LEVERING: We have seen the "shrinking."

STONOR: Without quoting any one else, I might point out that the New Antagonism seems to have blinded you to the small fact that I, for one, am not an opponent.

MISS LEVERING: The phrase *has* a familiar ring. We have heard it from four hundred and twenty others.

STONOR: I spoke, if I may say so, of some one who would count. Some one who can carry his party along with him—or risk a seat in the Cabinet.

MISS LEVERING: *(quickly)* Did you mean you are ready to do that?

STONOR: An hour ago I was.

MISS LEVERING: Ah! . . . an hour ago.

STONOR: Exactly. You don't understand men. They can be led. They can't be driven. Ten minutes before you came into the room I was ready to say I would throw in my political lot with this Reform.

MISS LEVERING: And now . . . ?

STONOR: Now you block my way by an attempt at coercion. By forcing my hand you give my adherence an air of bargain-driving for a personal end. Exactly the mistake of the ignorant agitators of your "Union," as you call it. You have a great deal to learn. This movement will go forward, not because of the agitation, but in spite of it. There are men in Parliament who would have been actively serving the Reform today . . . as actively as so vast a constitutional change—

MISS LEVERING: *(smiles faintly)* And they haven't done it because—

STONOR: Because it would have put a premium on breaches of decent behaviour. *(He takes a crumpled piece of paper out of his pocket.)* Look here!

MISS LEVERING: *(flushes with excitement as she reads the telegram)* This is very good. I see only one objection.

STONOR: Objection!

MISS LEVERING: You haven't sent it.

STONOR: *That* is your fault.

MISS LEVERING: When did you write this?

STONOR: Just before you came in—when—*(He glances at the door.)*

MISS LEVERING: Ah! It must have pleased Jean—that message. *(Offers him back the paper.)*

*(STONOR astonished at her yielding it up so lightly, and remembering JEAN had not so much as read it. He throws himself heavily into a chair and drops his head in his hands.)*

I could drive a hard-and-fast bargain with you, but I think I won't. If *both* love and ambition urge you on, perhaps—*(She gazes at the slack, hopeless figure with its sudden look of age—goes over silently and stands by his side.)* After all, life hasn't been quite fair to you—

(*He raises his heavy eyes.*)

You fall out of one ardent woman's dreams into another's.

STONOR: You may as well tell me—do you mean to—?

MISS LEVERING: To keep you and her apart? No.

STONOR: (*for the first time tears come into his eyes. After a moment he holds out his hand*) What can I do for you?

(MISS LEVERING *shakes her head—speechless.*)

2760 For the real you. Not the Reformer, or the would-be politician—for the woman I so unwillingly hurt. (*As she turns away, struggling with her feelings, he lays a detaining hand on her arm.*) You may not believe it, but now that I understand, there is almost nothing I wouldn't do to right that old wrong.

MISS LEVERING: There's nothing to be done. You can never give me back my child.

STONOR: (*at the anguish in* VIDA's *face his own has changed*) Will that ghost give you no rest?

2770 MISS LEVERING: Yes, oh, yes. I see life is nobler than I knew. There is work to do.

STONOR: (*stopping her as she goes towards the folding doors*) Why should you think that it's only you, these ten years have taught something to? Why not give even a man credit for a willingness to learn something of life, and for being sorry—profoundly sorry—for the pain his instruction has cost others? You seem to think I've taken it all quite lightly. That's not fair. All my life, ever since you disappeared, the thought of you has hurt. I would give anything I possess to know

2780 you—were happy again.

MISS LEVERING: Oh, happiness!

STONOR: (*significantly*) Why shouldn't you find it still.

MISS LEVERING: (*stares an instant*) I see! She couldn't help telling about Allen Trent—Lady John couldn't.

STONOR: You're one of the people the years have not taken from, but given more to. You are more than ever . . . You haven't lost your beauty.

MISS LEVERING: The gods saw it was so little effectual, it wasn't worth taking away. (*She stands looking out into the void.*) One woman's mishap?—what is that? A thing as trivial to 2790 the great world as it's sordid in most eyes. But the time has come when a woman may look about her, and say, "What general significance has my secret pain? Does it 'join on' to anything?" And I find it does. I'm no longer merely a woman who has stumbled on the way. I'm one (*She controls with difficulty the shake in her voice.*) who has got up bruised and bleeding, wiped the dust from her hands and the tears from her face, and said to herself not merely, "Here's one luckless woman! but—here is a stone of stumbling to many. Let's see if it can't be moved out of other women's way." And she calls 2800 people to come and help. No mortal man, let alone a woman, *by herself,* can move that rock of offence. But (*with a sudden sombre flame of enthusiasm*) if many help, Geoffrey, the thing can be done.

STONOR: (*looks at her with wondering pity*) Lord! how you care!

MISS LEVERING: (*touched by his moved faced*) Don't be so sad. Shall I tell you a secret? Jean's ardent dreams needn't frighten you, if she has a child. *That*—from the beginning, it was not the strong arm—it was the weakest—the little, lit- 2810 tle arms that subdued the fiercest of us.

(STONOR *puts out a pitying hand uncertainly towards her. She does not take it, but speaks with great gentleness.*)

You will have other children, Geoffrey—for me there was to be only one. Well, well—(*She brushes her tears away.*)—since men alone have tried and failed to make a decent world for the little children to live in—it's as well some of us are childless. (*Quietly taking up her hat and cloak.*) Yes, *we* are the ones who have no excuse for standing aloof from the fight.

STONOR: Vida!

MISS LEVERING: What? 2820

STONOR: You've forgotten something. (*As she looks back he is signing the message.*) This.

(*She goes out silently with the "political dynamite" in her hand.*)

**CURTAIN**

Elizabeth
Robins

"The Feministe
Movement in England"
(1913)

ONE *of many essays Robins wrote on the treatment and behavior of women in male-dominated society, "The Feministe Movement in England" speaks particularly to Robins's own position as an actress in a society that defined women's sphere as essentially domestic and private, outside the reach of public or political life.*

I am one of those who, until comparatively recently, was an ignorant opponent of Woman Suffrage. I felt that what we women needed was more education, more discipline, rather than more liberty, not realising that the higher discipline can come only through liberty.

I was not alone in my error. It turns out that not only have men a great deal still to learn about women, but that women have a great deal to learn about themselves. I have been prosecuting my education in this direction almost daily since a certain memorable afternoon in Trafalgar Square when I first heard women talking politics in public. I went out of shamefaced curiosity, my head full of masculine criticism as to woman's limitations, her well-known inability to stick to the point, her poverty in logic and in humour, and the impossibility, in any case, of her coping with the mob.

I had found in my own heart hitherto no firm assurance that these charges were not anchored in fact. But on that Sunday afternoon, in front of Nelson's Monument, a new chapter was begun for me in the lesson of faith in the capacities of women. Talking about it afterward with a well-known London editor, I found him sorrowfully admitting the day was coming when the vote could no longer be withheld from women. "But when they get it," he asked, "won't we find they've lost more than they've gained?" He spoke of the deteriorating effect of public life on men. If it bore so hardly on the stronger masculine fibre, what effect must it have on the delicate, impressionable nature of woman? How shall she preserve what is best in character after tasting the intoxication of political victory or the humiliation of political defeat?

"I am ready to believe you," he said, "when you tell me these Suffragists can rule and sway the London crowds. But isn't it very bad for women, all this publicity and concentration of attention on themselves?"

I answered that I was perhaps not so bad a person to whom to put that question, since I had spent a good part of my adult existence under conditions where I could see the effect on character of just these fierce tests, save that in the theatre they operate innocent of political significance.

In common with many others of my old craft, I had seen how the actor's necessary preoccupation with things of the imagination may divorce him from the larger realities of life. His necessary concern about himself tends to impoverish his intellectual life, narrowing down existence till for him all the world's a stage in very truth, and all men merely "parts." But the great difference, in the common effect on character, between doing work on the stage and doing it in the political arena, seems accounted for by the difference between the ambition that is obliged to concern itself with one's own advantage, and the ambition that is obliged to concern itself with the advantage of other people.

If I am to judge by the women I see working to win the suffrage in England, there is something civilising, ennobling, in giving up your life to the furtherance of a great impersonal object. When women, such as these I speak of, stand up in public to talk reform, their high earnestness, their forgetfulness of themselves, lends them a dignity that made my answer to the question of the London editor as easy as it was honourable to the disfranchised sex.

We have come to a point in England where there is little need, and indeed little opportunity, to combat argument. The opponents of Woman's Suffrage own, with engaging frankness, that their prejudices against the innovation are irremovable. If these obstructionists are not too old in years or in spirit, they will presently be advancing to the stool of repentance. If, however, their prejudices are indeed irremovable, they themselves are not. Those who, in the natural order, are to take their place will see the matter otherwise, for the future is on the side of woman's freedom. So keenly is this felt that in the hundreds of meetings, public and private, held throughout England for the ventilation of the subject, the prime difficulty encountered of late in getting up a debate is to find anybody who can be induced to oppose the notion. Has it been discovered that all the telling arguments, witty or wise, are on the side of the reform?

The old-fashioned opponent, with his jargon about "short hair and the shrieking sisterhood," sees all his poor little dingy rags of ridicule blown to the winds of heaven, and he seems able to find nothing new.

One of the signs of the reserve force behind the movement is that everything ministers to it. The police magistrate sends groups of unknown women to Holloway Gaol. They come out public characters, hot with tales of abuses in the prison system and the crying need for matrons and women inspectors. The authorities try to avoid repeating their error by making all such inconvenient prisoners thereafter first-class misdemeanants, and thus ensure their seeing less and having less material with which to stir the public conscience. But the public is quick to detect the fear behind the seeming leniency of the authorities.

Then again, at a later stage of the agitation, the police magistrate, in trying a fresh batch of prisoners, endeavours to rouse public indignation against the leaders of the movement by sternly rebuking them for allowing a mill girl of seventeen to come up from the provinces to assist in a London demonstration, in the course of which the girl was arrested,—that being nothing less than what she had come for. She was a Lancashire delegate, representative of hundreds more who could not come themselves. The magistrate was full of a noble rage at "the cruelty of turning a girl of such tender age loose in London," as he expressed it. He seemed to count on setting men's hearts aflame at the bare idea of a young girl in the streets without her mother. That she should be in the London streets to testify to her interest in the laws governing women's honest work, that was indeed shameful!

"Why, this child," said the Magistrate, "should be at school!" And the outburst of wise and manly tenderness was reported in every paper in the land.

The working women opened incredulous eyes. They are so used to hearing their own ignorance urged against their claim to vote, that they were stark amazed to find how strangely benighted are these great London gentlemen about the conditions governing the lives of the women they make laws for. School at seventeen? Why, this girl, like many more, had been earning her living in a mill since she was twelve, rising in the dawn, tramping cold and half-fed, to her work, and returning wearily through slums whose haggard realism left this prematurely old "hand" of seventeen little to learn from London, even if she had no friends here, which of course is not the case. No woman, however lonely, who joins the English Suffrage Movement but has friends. . . .

# Susan Glaspell

Susan Glaspell (1882–1948) was born in Iowa, studied at Drake University and the University of Chicago, and then briefly pursued a career as a journalist. With her husband George Cram Cook, she founded the Provincetown Playhouse and wrote many of the plays it produced: *Suppressed Desires* (1914, written with Cook), a spoof of the vogue for psychoanalysis among New York's intellectual elite; *Trifles* (1916); *Close the Book* (1917); *A Woman's Honor* (1918); and *Tickless Time* (1918, again written with Cook). After the reorganization of the Provincetown in 1921, Glaspell wrote a series of full-length, often experimental, plays: *Inheritors* (1920), *The Verge* (1921), and *Alison's House* (1930). *Alison's House*, based loosely on Emily Dickinson and her family, won Glaspell the Pulitzer Prize in 1930. Glaspell then retired from playwriting and largely from the theater as well, returning briefly to serve as the director of the Mid-West Play Bureau for the Federal Theater Project.

## Trifles (1916)

*Trifles* is an important play in the development of American realism. It poses a distinct contrast to Eugene O'Neill's early plays, with which it shared the Provincetown stage. O'Neill's realistic plays attempt to filter an abstract, metaphysical longing into the drab world of his down-and-out drifters and sailors. Glaspell's drama more directly examines the values and behavior of the society she brings to the stage. In *Trifles*—and in the short story "A Jury of Her Peers," which she adapted from the play the following year—Glaspell considers the relationship between truth, power, and gender. The play is a murder mystery. A local man, John Wright, has been found dead, and his wife, Minnie, is suspected of killing him. Called to investigate, the County Attorney George Henderson, the Sheriff Henry Peters, and a neighbor, Lewis Hale, readily assume a masculine prerogative to discover the truth of George Wright's murder, telling their wives to remain in the kitchen out of the way. But the truth of the crime is in fact concealed *in* the kitchen, and only the women are able to discover it. For Glaspell shows the audience that the "trifles" of the women's world are the signs of a reality wholly unreadable to the men, precisely because it is a world they regard as feminine, and therefore unimportant and uninteresting. *Trifles,* that is, works to subvert our notions of reality and truth by suggesting how such ideas are constructed within a specific social order—the masculine order of modern society.

# — Trifles —

## A Play in One Act

### Susan Glaspell

## —CHARACTERS—

GEORGE HENDERSON, *County Attorney*
HENRY PETERS, *Sheriff*
LEWIS HALE, *A Neighboring Farmer*
MRS. PETERS
MRS. HALE

THE SETTING: *The kitchen in the now abandoned farmhouse of* JOHN WRIGHT

SCENE: *The kitchen in the now abandoned farmhouse of John Wright, a gloomy kitchen, and left without having been put in order—unwashed pans under the sink, a loaf of bread outside the breadbox, a dish towel on the table—other signs of incompleted work. At the rear the outer door opens and the* SHERIFF *comes in followed by the* COUNTY ATTORNEY *and* HALE. *The* SHERIFF *and* HALE *are men in middle life, the* COUNTY ATTORNEY *is a young man; all are much bundled up and go at once to the stove. They are followed by the two women—the* SHERIFF's *wife first; she is a slight wiry woman, a thin nervous face.* MRS. HALE *is larger and would ordinarily be called more comfortable looking, but she is disturbed now and looks fearfully about as she enters. The women have come in slowly, and stand close together near the door.*

COUNTY ATTORNEY: (*Rubbing his hands*) This feels good. Come up to the fire, ladies.

MRS. PETERS: (*After taking a step forward*) I'm not—cold.

SHERIFF: (*Unbuttoning his overcoat and stepping away from the stove as if to mark the beginning of official business*) Now, Mr. Hale, before we move things about, you explain to Mr. Henderson just what you saw when you came here yesterday morning.

COUNTY ATTORNEY: By the way, has anything been moved? Are things just as you left them yesterday?

SHERIFF: (*Looking about*) It's just the same. When it dropped below zero last night I thought I'd better send Frank out this morning to make a fire for us—no use getting pneumonia with a big case on, but I told him not to touch anything except the stove—and you know Frank.

COUNTY ATTORNEY: Somebody should have been left here yesterday.

SHERIFF: Oh—yesterday. When I had to send Frank to Morris Center for that man who went crazy—I want you to know I had my hands full yesterday, I knew you could get back from Omaha by today and as long as I went over everything here myself—

COUNTY ATTORNEY: Well, Mr. Hale, tell just what happened when you came here yesterday morning.

HALE: Harry and I had started to town with a load of potatoes. We came along the road from my place and as I got here I said, "I'm going to see if I can't get John Wright to go in with me on a party telephone." I spoke to Wright about it once before and he put me off, saying folks talked too much anyway, and all he asked was peace and quiet—I guess you know about how much he talked himself; but I thought maybe if I went to the house and talked about it before his wife, though I said to Harry that I didn't know as what his wife wanted made much difference to John—

COUNTY ATTORNEY: Let's talk about that later, Mr. Hale. I do want to talk about that, but tell me now just what happened when you got to the house.

HALE: I didn't hear or see anything; I knocked at the door, and still it was all quiet inside. I knew they must be up, it was past eight o'clock. So I knocked again, and I thought I heard somebody say, "Come in." I wasn't sure, I'm not sure yet, but I opened the door—this door (*indicating the door by which the two women are still standing*) and there in that rocker—(*pointing to it*) sat Mrs. Wright.

(*They all look at the rocker.*)

COUNTY ATTORNEY: What—was she doing?

HALE: She was rockin' back and forth. She had her apron in her hand and was kind of—pleating it.

COUNTY ATTORNEY: And how did she—look?

HALE: Well, she looked queer.

COUNTY ATTORNEY: How do you mean—queer?

HALE: Well, as if she didn't know what she was going to do next. And kind of done up.

COUNTY ATTORNEY: How did she seem to feel about your coming?

HALE: Why, I don't think she minded—one way or other. She didn't pay much attention. I said, "How do, Mrs. Wright, it's cold ain't it?" And she said, "Is it?"—and went on kind of pleating at her apron. Well, I was surprised; she didn't ask me to come up to the stove, or to set down, but just sat there, not even looking at me, so I said, "I want to see John." And then she—laughed. I guess you would call it a laugh. I thought of Harry and the team outside, so I said a little sharp: "Can't I see John?" "No," she says, kind o' dull like. "Ain't he home?" says I. "Yes," says she, "he's home." "Then why can't I see him?" I asked her, out of patience. "'Cause he's dead," says she. "*Dead?*" says I. She just nodded her head, not getting a bit excited, but rockin' back and forth. "Why—where is he?" says I, not knowing what to say. She just pointed upstairs—like that (*Himself pointing to the room above.*) I got up, with the idea of going up there. I walked from there to here—then I says, "Why, what did he die of?" "He died of a rope round his neck," says she, and just went on pleatin' at her apron. Well, I went out and called Harry. I thought I might—need help. We went upstairs and there he was lyin'—

COUNTY ATTORNEY: I think I'd rather have you go into that upstairs, where you can point it all out. Just go on now with the rest of the story.

HALE: Well, my first thought was to get that rope off. It looked . . . (*Stops, his face twitches*) . . . but Harry, he went up to him, and he said, "No, he's dead all right, and we'd better not touch anything." So we went back down stairs. She was still sitting that same way, "Has anybody been notified?" I asked. "No," says she, unconcerned. "Who did this, Mrs. Wright?" said Harry. He said it businesslike—and she stopped pleatin' of her apron. "I don't know," she says. "You don't *know*?" says Harry. "No," says she. "Weren't you sleepin' in the bed with him?" says Harry. "Yes," says she, "but I was on the inside." "Somebody slipped a rope round his neck and strangled him and you didn't wake up?" says Harry. "I didn't wake up," she said after him. We must 'a looked as if we didn't see how that could be, for after a minute she said, "I sleep sound." Harry was going to ask her more questions but I said maybe we ought to let her tell her story first to the coroner, or the sheriff, so Harry went fast as he could to Rivers' place, where there's a telephone.

COUNTY ATTORNEY: And what did Mrs. Wright do when she knew that you had gone for the coroner?

HALE: She moved from that chair to this one over here (*Pointing to a small chair in the corner*) and just sat there with her hands held together and looking down. I got a feeling that I ought to make some conversation, so I said I had come in to see if John wanted to put in a telephone, and at that she started to laugh, and then she stopped and looked at me—scared. (*The* COUNTY ATTORNEY, *who has had his notebook out, makes a note.*) I dunno, maybe it wasn't scared. I wouldn't like to say it was. Soon Harry got back, and then Dr. Lloyd came, and you, Mr. Peters, and so I guess that's all I know that you don't.

COUNTY ATTORNEY: (*Looking around*) I guess we'll go upstairs first—and then out to the barn and around there. (*To the* SHERIFF) You're convinced that there was nothing important here—nothing that would point to any motive.

SHERIFF: Nothing here but kitchen things.

(*The* COUNTY ATTORNEY *after again looking around the kitchen, opens the door of a cupboard closet. He gets up on a chair and looks on a shelf. Pulls his hand away, sticky.*)

COUNTY ATTORNEY: Here's a nice mess.

(*The women draw nearer.*)

MRS. PETERS: (*to the other woman*) Oh, her fruit; it did freeze. (*To the* COUNTY ATTORNEY) She worried about that when it turned so cold. She said the fire'd go out and her jars would break.

SHERIFF: Well, can you beat the women! Held for murder and worryin' about her preserves.

COUNTY ATTORNEY: I guess before we're through she may have something more serious than preserves to worry about.

HALE: Well, women are used to worrying over trifles.

(*The two women move a little closer together.*)

COUNTY ATTORNEY: (*With the gallantry of a young politician*) And yet, for all their worries, what would we do without the ladies? (*The women do not unbend. He goes to the sink, takes a dipperful of water from the pail and pouring it into a basin, washes his hands. Starts to wipe them on the roller towel, turns it for a cleaner place*) Dirty towels! (*Kicks his foot against the pans under the sink*) Not much of a housekeeper, would you say, ladies?

MRS. HALE: (*Stiffly*) There's a great deal of work to be done on a farm.

COUNTY ATTORNEY: To be sure. And yet (*With a little bow to her*) I know there are some Dickson county farmhouses which do not have such roller towels.

(*He gives it a pull to expose its full length again.*)

MRS. HALE: Those towels get dirty awful quick. Men's hands aren't always as clean as they might be.

COUNTY ATTORNEY: Ah, loyal to your sex, I see. But you and Mrs. Wright were neighbors. I suppose you were friends, too.

MRS. HALE: (*Shaking her head*) I've not seen much of her of late years. I've not been in this house—it's more than a year.

COUNTY ATTORNEY: And why was that? You didn't like her?

MRS. HALE: I liked her all well enough. Farmers' wives have their hands full, Mr. Henderson. And then—

COUNTY ATTORNEY: Yes—?

MRS. HALE: (*Looking about*) It never seemed a very cheerful place.

COUNTY ATTORNEY: No—it's not cheerful. I shouldn't say she had the homemaking instinct.

MRS. HALE: Well, I don't know as Wright had, either.

COUNTY ATTORNEY: You mean that they didn't get on very well?

MRS. HALE: No, I don't mean anything. But I don't think a place'd be any cheerfuller for John Wright's being in it.

COUNTY ATTORNEY: I'd like to talk more of that a little later. I want to get the lay of things upstairs now.

(*He goes to the left, where three steps lead to a stair door.*)

SHERIFF: I suppose anything Mrs. Peters does'll be all right. She was to take in some clothes for her, you know, and a few little things. We left in such a hurry yesterday.

COUNTY ATTORNEY: Yes, but I would like to see what you take, Mrs. Peters, and keep an eye out for anything that might be of use to us.

MRS. PETERS: Yes, Mr. Henderson.

(*The women listen to the men's steps on the stairs, then look about the kitchen.*)

MRS. HALE: I'd hate to have men coming into my kitchen, snooping around and criticising.

(*She arranges the pans under sink which the* COUNTY ATTORNEY *had shoved out of place.*)

MRS. PETERS: Of course it's no more than their duty.

MRS. HALE: Duty's all right, but I guess that deputy sheriff that came out to make the fire might have got a little of this on.

*(Gives the roller towel a pull)* Wish I'd thought of that sooner. Seems mean to talk about her for not having things slicked up when she had to come away in such a hurry.

MRS. PETERS: *(Who has gone to a small table in the left rear corner of the room, and lifted one end of a towel that covers a pan)* She had bread set.

*(Stands still)*

MRS. HALE: *(Eyes fixed on a loaf of bread beside the breadbox, which is on a low shelf at the other side of the room. Moves slowly toward it)* She was going to put this in there. *(Picks up loaf, then abruptly drops it. In a manner of returning to familiar things)* It's a shame about her fruit. I wonder if it's all gone. *(Gets up on the chair and looks)* I think there's some here that's all right, Mrs. Peters. Yes—here; *(Holding it toward the window)* this is cherries, too. *(Looking again)* I declare I believe that's the only one. *(Gets down, bottle in her hand. Goes to the sink and wipes it off on the outside)* She'll feel awful bad after all her hard work in the hot weather. I remember the afternoon I put up my cherries last summer.

*(She puts the bottle on the big kitchen table, center of the room. With a sigh, is about to sit down in the rocking-chair. Before she is seated realizes what chair it is; with a slow look at it, steps back. The chair which she has touched rocks back and forth.)*

MRS. PETERS: Well, I must get those things from the front room closet. *(She goes to the door at the right, but after looking into the other room, steps back.)* You coming with me, Mrs. Hale? You could help me carry them.

*(They go in the other room; reappear, MRS. PETERS carrying a dress and skirt, MRS. HALE following with a pair of shoes.)*

MRS. PETERS: My, it's cold in there.

*(She puts the clothes on the big table, and hurries to the stove.)*

MRS. HALE: *(Examining the skirt)* Wright was close. I think maybe that's why she kept so much to herself. She didn't even belong to the Ladies Aid. I suppose she felt she couldn't do her part, and then you don't enjoy things when you feel shabby. She used to wear pretty clothes and be lively, when she was Minnie Foster, one of the town girls singing in the choir. But that—oh, that was thirty years ago. This all you was to take in?

MRS. PETERS: She said she wanted an apron. Funny thing to want, for there isn't much to get you dirty in jail, goodness knows. But I suppose just to make her feel more natural. She said they was in the top drawer in this cupboard. Yes, here. And then her little shawl that always hung behind the door. *(Opens stair door and looks)* Yes, here it is.

*(Quickly shuts door leading upstairs)*

MRS. HALE: *(Abruptly moving toward her)* Mrs. Peters?

MRS. PETERS: Yes, Mrs. Hale?

MRS. HALE: Do you think she did it?

MRS. PETERS: *(In a frightened voice)* Oh, I don't know.

MRS. HALE: Well, I don't think she did. Asking for an apron and her little shawl. Worrying about her fruit.

MRS. PETERS: *(Starts to speak, glances up, where footsteps are heard in the room above. In a low voice)* Mr. Peters says it looks bad for her. Mr. Henderson is awful sarcastic in a speech and he'll make fun of her sayin' she didn't wake up.

MRS. HALE: Well, I guess John Wright didn't wake when they was slipping that rope under his neck.

MRS. PETERS: No, it's strange. It must have been done awful crafty and still. They say it was such a—funny way to kill a man, rigging it all up like that.

MRS. HALE: That's just what Mr. Hale said. There was a gun in the house. He says that's what he can't understand.

MRS. PETERS: Mr. Henderson said coming out that what was needed for the case was a motive, something to show anger, or—sudden feeling.

MRS. HALE: *(Who is standing by the table)* Well, I don't see any signs of anger around here. *(She puts her hand on the dish towel which lies on the table, stands looking down at table, one half of which is clean, the other half messy.)* It's wiped to here. *(Makes a move as if to finish work, then turns and looks at loaf of bread outside the breadbox. Drops towel. In that voice of coming back to familiar things)* Wonder how they are finding things upstairs. I hope she had it a little more red-up up there. You know, it seems kind of *sneaking.* Locking her up in town and then coming out here and trying to get her own house to turn against her!

MRS. PETERS: But Mrs. Hale, the law is the law.

MRS. HALE: I s'pose 'tis. *(Unbuttoning her coat)* Better loosen up your things, Mrs. Peters. You won't feel them when you go out.

*(MRS. PETERS takes off her fur tippet, goes to hang it on hook at back of room, stands looking at the under part of the small corner table.)*

MRS. PETERS: She was piecing a quilt.

*(She brings the large sewing basket and they look at the bright pieces.)*

MRS. HALE: It's log cabin pattern. Pretty, isn't it? I wonder if she was goin' to quilt it or just knot it?

*(Footsteps have been heard coming down the stairs. The SHERIFF enters followed by HALE and the COUNTY ATTORNEY.)*

SHERIFF: They wonder if she was going to quilt it or just knot it!

*(The men laugh; the women look abashed.)*

COUNTY ATTORNEY: *(Rubbing his hands over the stove)* Frank's fire didn't do much up there, did it? Well, let's go out to the barn and get that cleared up.

*(The men go outside.)*

MRS. HALE: *(Resentfully)* I don't know as there's anything so strange, our takin' up our time with little things while we're waiting for them to get the evidence. *(She sits down at the big table smoothing out a block with decision.)* I don't see as it's anything to laugh about.

MRS. PETERS: *(Apologetically)* Of course they've got awful important things on their minds.

*(Pulls up a chair and joins MRS. HALE at the table)*

MRS. HALE: *(Examining another block)* Mrs. Peters, look at this

260   one. Here, this is the one she was working on, and look at that sewing! All the rest of it has been so nice and even. And look at this! It's all over the place! Why, it looks as if she didn't know what she was about!

*(After she has said this they look at each other, then start to glance back at the door. After an instant* MRS. HALE *has pulled at a knot and ripped the sewing.)*

MRS. PETERS: Oh, what are you doing, Mrs. Hale?

MRS. HALE: *(Mildly)* Just pulling out a stitch or two that's not sewed very good. *(Threading a needle)* Bad sewing always made me fidgety.

MRS. PETERS: *(Nervously)* I don't think we ought to touch things.

270   MRS. HALE: I'll just finish up this end. *(Suddenly stopping and leaning forward)* Mrs. Peters?

MRS. PETERS: Yes, Mrs. Hale?

MRS. HALE: What do you suppose she was so nervous about?

MRS. PETERS: Oh—I don't know. I don't know as she was nervous. I sometimes sew awful queer when I'm just tired. (MRS. HALE *starts to say something, looks at* MRS. PETERS, *then goes on sewing.)* Well, I must get these things wrapped up. They may be through sooner than we think. *(Putting apron and other things together)* I wonder where I can find

280   a piece of paper, and string.

MRS. HALE: In that cupboard, maybe.

MRS. PETERS: *(Looking in cupboard)* Why, there's a birdcage. *(Holds it up)* Did she have a bird, Mrs. Hale?

MRS. HALE: Why, I don't know whether she did or not—I've not been here for so long. There was a man around last year selling canaries cheap, but I don't know as she took one; maybe she did. She used to sing real pretty herself.

MRS. PETERS: *(Glancing around)* Seems funny to think of a bird here. But she must have had one, or why would she have a

290   cage? I wonder what happened to it.

MRS. HALE: I s'pose maybe the cat got it.

MRS. PETERS: No, she didn't have a cat. She's got that feeling some people have about cats—being afraid of them. My cat got in her room and she was real upset and asked me to take it out.

MRS. HALE: My sister Bessie was like that. Queer, ain't it?

MRS. PETERS: *(Examining the cage)* Why, look at this door. It's broke. One hinge is pulled apart.

MRS. HALE: *(Looking too)* Looks as if someone must have been

300   rough with it.

MRS. PETERS: Why, yes.

*(She brings the cage forward and puts it on the table.)*

MRS. HALE: I wish if they're going to find any evidence they'd be about it. I don't like this place.

MRS. PETERS: But I'm awful glad you came with me, Mrs. Hale. It would be lonesome for me sitting here alone.

MRS. HALE: It would, wouldn't it? *(Dropping her sewing)* But I tell you what I do wish, Mrs. Peters. I wish I had come over sometimes when *she* was here. I—*(Looking around the room)*—wish I had.

310   MRS. PETERS: But of course you were awful busy, Mrs. Hale—your house and your children.

MRS. HALE: I could've come. I stayed away because it weren't cheerful—and that's why I ought to have come. I—I've never liked this place. Maybe because it's down in a hollow and you don't see the road. I dunno what it is, but it's a lonesome place and always was. I wish I had come over to see Minnie Foster sometimes. I can see now—

*(Shakes her head)*

MRS. PETERS: Well you mustn't reproach yourself, Mrs. Hale. Somehow we just don't see how it is with other folks until—something comes up.   320

MRS. HALE: Not having children makes less work—but it makes a quiet house, and Wright out to work all day, and no company when he did come in. Did you know John Wright, Mrs. Peters?

MRS. PETERS: Not to know him; I've seen him in town. They say he was a good man.

MRS. HALE: Yes—good; he didn't drink, and kept his word as well as most, I guess, and paid his debts. But he was a hard man, Mrs. Peters. Just to pass the time of day with him—*(Shivers)* Like a raw wind that gets to the bone. *(Pauses, her*   330 *eye falling on the cage)* I should think she would 'a wanted a bird. But what do you suppose went with it?

MRS. PETERS: I don't know, unless it got sick and died.

*(She reaches over and swings the broken door, swings it again. Both women watch it.)*

MRS. HALE: You weren't raised round here, were you? (MRS. PETERS *shakes her head.)* You didn't know—her?

MRS. PETERS: Not till they brought her yesterday.

MRS. HALE: She—come to think of it, she was kind of like a bird herself—real sweet and pretty, but kind of timid and—fluttery. How—she—did—change. *(Silence; then as if struck by a happy thought and relieved to get back to every day*   340 *things)* Tell you what, Mrs. Peters, why don't you take the quilt in with you? It might take up her mind.

MRS. PETERS: Why, I think that's a real nice idea, Mrs. Hale. There couldn't possibly be any objection to it, could there? Now, just what would I take? I wonder if her patches are in here—and her things.

*(They look in the sewing basket.)*

MRS. HALE: Here's some red. I expect this has got sewing things in it. *(Brings out a fancy box)* What a pretty box. Looks like something somebody would give you. Maybe her scissors are in here. *(Opens box. Suddenly puts her hand to her nose)*   350 Why—(MRS. PETERS *bends nearer, then turns her face away.)* There's something wrapped up in this piece of silk.

MRS. PETERS: Why, this isn't her scissors.

MRS. HALE: *(Lifting the silk)* Oh, Mrs. Peters—its—

(MRS. PETERS *bends closer.)*

MRS. PETERS: It's the bird.

MRS. HALE: *(Jumping up)* But, Mrs. Peters—look at it! Its neck! Look at its neck! It's all—other side *to.*

MRS. PETERS: Somebody—wrung—its—neck.

*(Their eyes meet. A look of growing comprehension, of horror. Steps are heard outside.* MRS. HALE *slips box under quilt pieces, and sinks into her chair. Enter* SHERIFF *and* COUNTY ATTORNEY. MRS. PETERS *rises.)*

COUNTY ATTORNEY: *(As one turning from serious things to little*

360   *pleasantries)* Well, ladies, have you decided whether she was going to quilt it or knot it?

MRS. PETERS: We think she was going to—knot it.

COUNTY ATTORNEY: Well, that's interesting, I'm sure. *(Seeing the birdcage)* Has the bird flown?

MRS. HALE: *(Putting more quilt pieces over the box)* We think the—cat got it.

COUNTY ATTORNEY: *(Preoccupied)* Is there a cat?

*(MRS. HALE glances in a quick covert way at MRS. PETERS.)*

MRS. PETERS: Well, not *now*. They're superstitious, you know. They leave.

370   COUNTY ATTORNEY: *(to SHERIFF PETERS continuing an interrupted conversation)* No sign at all of anyone having come from the outside. Their own rope. Now let's go up again and go over it piece by piece. *(They start upstairs.)* It would have to have been someone who knew just the—

*(MRS. PETERS sits down. The two women sit there not looking at one another, but as if peering into something and at the same time holding back. When they talk now it is in the manner of feeling their way over strange ground, as if afraid of what they are saying, but as if they cannot help saying it.)*

MRS. HALE: She liked the bird. She was going to bury it in that pretty box.

MRS. PETERS: *(In a whisper)* When I was a girl—my kitten—there was a boy took a hatchet, and before my eyes—and before I could get there—*(Covers her face an instant)* If 380   they hadn't held me back I would have—*(Catches herself, looks upstairs where steps are heard, falters weakly)*—hurt him.

MRS. HALE: *(With a slow look around her)* I wonder how it would seem never to have had any children around. *(Pause)* No, Wright wouldn't like the bird—a thing that sang. She used to sing. He killed that, too.

MRS. PETERS: *(Moving uneasily)* We don't know who killed the bird.

MRS. HALE: I knew John Wright.

390   MRS. PETERS: It was an awful thing was done in this house that night, Mrs. Hale. Killing a man while he slept, slipping a rope around his neck that choked the life out of him.

MRS. HALE: His neck. Choked the life out of him.

*(Her hand goes out and rests on the birdcage.)*

MRS. PETERS: *(With rising voice)* We don't know who killed him. We don't know.

MRS. HALE: *(Her own feeling not interrupted)* If there'd been years and years of nothing, then a bird to sing to you, it would be awful—still, after the bird was still.

MRS. PETERS: *(Something within her speaking)* I know what 400   stillness is. When we homesteaded in Dakota, and my first baby died—after he was two years old, and me with no other then—

MRS. HALE: *(Moving)* How soon do you suppose they'll be through, looking for the evidence?

MRS. PETERS: I know what stillness is. *(Pulling herself back)* The law has got to punish crime, Mrs. Hale.

MRS. HALE: *(Not as if answering that)* I wish you'd seen Minnie Foster when she wore a white dress with blue ribbons and stood up there in the choir and sang. *(A look around the*

*room)* Oh, I *wish* I'd come over here once in a while! That 410   was a crime! That was a crime! Who's going to punish that?

MRS. PETERS: *(Looking upstairs)* We mustn't—take on.

MRS. HALE: I might have known she needed help! I know how things can be—for women. I tell you, it's queer, Mrs. Peters. We live close together and we live far apart. We all go through the same things—it's all just a different kind of the same thing. *(Brushes her eyes; noticing the bottle of fruit, reaches out for it)* If I was you I wouldn't tell her her fruit was gone. Tell her it *ain't*. Tell her it's all right. Take this in to prove it to her. She—she may never know whether it was 420   broke or not.

MRS. PETERS: *(Takes the bottle, looks about for something to wrap it in, takes petticoat from the clothes brought from the other room, very nervously begins winding this around the bottle. In a false voice)* My, it's a good thing the men couldn't hear us. Wouldn't they just laugh! Getting all stirred up over a little thing like a—dead canary. As if that could have anything to do with—with—wouldn't they laugh!

*(The men are heard coming down stairs.)*

MRS. HALE: *(Under her breath)* Maybe they would—maybe 430   they wouldn't.

COUNTY ATTORNEY: No, Peters, it's all perfectly clear except a reason for doing it. But you know juries when it comes to women. If there was some definite thing. Something to show—something to make a story about—a thing that would connect up with this strange way of doing it—

*(The women's eyes meet for an instant. Enter HALE from outer door.)*

HALE: Well, I've got the team around. Pretty cold out there.

COUNTY ATTORNEY: I'm going to stay here a while by myself. *(To the SHERIFF)* You can send Frank out for me, can't you? I want to go over everything. I'm not satisfied that we can't 440   do better.

SHERIFF: Do you want to see what Mrs. Peters is going to take in?

*(The COUNTY ATTORNEY goes to the table, picks up the apron, laughs.)*

COUNTY ATTORNEY: Oh, I guess they're not very dangerous things the ladies have picked out. *(Moves a few things about, disturbing the quilt pieces which cover the box. Steps back)* No, Mrs. Peters doesn't need supervising. For that matter, a sheriff's wife is married to the law. Ever think of it that way, Mrs. Peters?

MRS. PETERS: Not—just that way. 450

SHERIFF: *(Chuckling)* Married to the law. *(Moves toward the other room)* I just want you to come in here a minute, George. We ought to take a look at these windows.

COUNTY ATTORNEY: *(Scoffingly)* Oh, windows!

SHERIFF: We'll be right out, Mr. Hale.

*(HALE goes outside. The SHERIFF follows the COUNTY ATTORNEY into the other room. Then MRS. HALE rises, hands tight together, looking intensely at MRS. PETERS, whose eyes make a slow turn, finally meeting MRS. HALE's. A moment MRS. HALE holds her, then her own eyes point the way to where the box is*

*concealed. Suddenly* MRS. PETERS *throws back quilt pieces and tries to put the box in the bag she is wearing. It is too big. She opens box, starts to take bird out, cannot touch it, goes to pieces, stands there helpless. Sound of a knob turning in the other room.* MRS. HALE *snatches the box and puts it in the pocket of her big coat. Enter* COUNTY ATTORNEY *and* SHERIFF.)

COUNTY ATTORNEY: *(Facetiously)* Well, Henry, at least we found out that she was not going to quilt it. She was going to—what is it you call it, ladies?

MRS. HALE: *(her hand against her pocket)* We call it—knot it, Mr. Henderson.                                         460

## Susan Glaspell:

"A Jury of Her Peers"
(1917)

*AFTER the success of* Trifles, *Glaspell wrote a short, narrative version of the play, which has been justly celebrated for the ways it deploys a woman's narrative "point of view." Moreover, the short story also dramatizes the different resources that the theater and narrative fiction have available in order to tell the "same" story.*

When Martha Hale opened the storm-door and got the north wind, she ran back for her big woollen scarf. As she hurriedly wound that round her head her eye made a scandalized sweep of her kitchen. It was no ordinary thing that called her away—it was probably farther from ordinary than anything that had ever happened in Dickson County. But her kitchen was in no shape for leaving: bread ready for mixing, half the flour sifted and half unsifted.

She hated to see things half done; but she had been at that when they stopped to get Mr. Hale, and the sheriff came in to say his wife wished Mrs. Hale would come too—adding, with a grin, that he guessed she was getting scarey and wanted another woman along. So she had dropped everything right where it was.

"Martha!" now came her husband's impatient voice. "Don't keep folks waiting out here in the cold."

She joined the three men and the one woman waiting for her in the sheriff's car.

After she had the robes tucked in she took another look at the woman beside her. She had met Mrs. Peters the year before, at the county fair, and the thing she remembered about her was that she didn't seem like a sheriff's wife. She was small and thin and didn't have a strong voice. Mrs. Gorman, sheriff's wife before Gorman went out and Peters came in, had a voice that seemed to be backing up the law with every word. But if Mrs. Peters didn't look like a sheriff's wife, Peters made it up in looking like a sheriff—a heavy man with a big voice, who was particularly genial with the law-abiding, as if to make it plain that he knew the difference between criminals and non-criminals. And right there it came into Mrs. Hale's mind that this man who was so lively with all of them was going to the Wrights' now as a sheriff.

"The country's not very pleasant this time of year," Mrs. Peters at last ventured.

Mrs. Hale scarcely finished her reply, for they had gone up a little hill and could see the Wright place, and seeing it did not make her feel like talking. It looked very lonely this cold March morning. It had always been a lonesome-looking place. It was down in a hollow, and the poplar trees around it were lonely-looking trees. The men were looking at it and talking about what had happened. The county attorney was bending to one side, scrutinizing the place as they drew up to it.

"I'm glad you came with me," Mrs. Peters said nervously, as the two women were about to follow the men in through the kitchen door.

Even after she had her foot on the doorstep, Martha Hale had a moment of feeling she could not cross this threshold. And the reason it seemed she couldn't cross it now was because she hadn't crossed it before. Time and time again it had been in her mind, "I ought to go over and see Minnie Foster"—she still thought of her as Minnie Foster, though for twenty years she had been Mrs. Wright. And then there was always something to do and Minnie Foster would go from her mind. But *now* she could come.

The men went over to the stove. The women stood close together by the door. Young Henderson, the county attorney, turned around and said, "Come up to the fire, ladies."

Mrs. Peters took a step forward, then stopped. "I'm not—cold," she said.

And so the two women stood by the door, at first not even so much as looking around the kitchen.

The men talked about what a good thing it was the sheriff had sent his deputy out that morning to make a fire for them, and then Sheriff Peters stepped back from the stove, unbuttoned his outer coat, and leaned his hands on the kitchen table in a way that seemed to mark the beginning of official business. "Now, Mr. Hale," he said in a sort of semi-official voice, "before we move things about, you tell Mr. Henderson just what it was you saw when you came here yesterday morning."

The county attorney was looking around the kitchen.

"By the way," he asked, "has anything been moved?" He turned to the sheriff. "Are things just as you left them yesterday?"

Peters looked from cupboard to sink; to a small worn rocker a little to one side of the kitchen table.

"It's just the same."

"Well, Mr. Hale," said the county attorney, "tell just what happened when you came here yesterday morning."

Mrs. Hale, still leaning against the door, had that sinking feeling of the mother whose child is about to speak a piece. Lewis often wandered along and got things mixed up in a story. She hoped he would tell this straight and plain, and not say unnecessary things that would make it harder for Minnie Foster. He didn't begin at once, and she noticed that he looked queer, as if thinking of what he had seen here yesterday.

"Yes, Mr. Hale?" the county attorney reminded.

"Harry and I had started to town with a load of wood," Mrs. Hale's husband began.

Harry was Mrs. Hale's oldest boy. He wasn't with them now, for the wood never got to town yesterday and he was taking it this morning, so he hadn't been home when the sheriff stopped to say he wanted Mr. Hale to come over to the Wright place and tell the county attorney his story there, where he could point it all out. With all Mrs. Hale's other emotions came the fear Harry wasn't dressed warm enough—they hadn't any of them realized how that north wind did bite.

"We come along this road," Hale was going on, "and as we got in sight of the house I says to Harry, 'I'm goin' to see if I can't get John Wright to take a telephone.' You see," he explained to Henderson, "unless I can get somebody to go in with me they won't come out this branch road except for a price I can't pay. I'd spoke to Wright about it before; but he put me off, saying folks talked too much anyway, and all he asked was peace and quiet—guess you know about how much he talked himself. But I thought maybe if I went to the house and talked about it before his wife, and said all the women-folks liked the telephones, and that in this lonesome stretch of road it would be a good thing—well, I said to Harry that that was what I was going to say—though I said at the same time that I didn't know as what his wife wanted made much difference to John—"

Now, there he was!—saying things he didn't need to say. Mrs. Hale tried to catch her husband's eye, but fortunately the county attorney interrupted with:

"Let's talk about that a little later, Mr. Hale. I do want to talk about that, but I'm anxious now to know just what happened when you got here."

When he began this time, it was deliberately, as if he knew it were important.

"I didn't see or hear anything. I knocked at the door. And still it was all quiet inside. I knew they must be up—it was past eight o'clock. So I knocked again, louder, and I thought I heard somebody say, 'Come in.' I wasn't sure—I'm not sure yet. But I opened the door—this door," jerking a hand toward the door by which the two women stood, "and there, in that rocker"—pointing to it—"sat Mrs. Wright."

Everyone in the kitchen looked at the rocker. It came into Mrs. Hale's mind that this chair didn't look in the least like Minnie Foster—the Minnie Foster of twenty years before. It was a dingy red, with wooden rungs up the back, and the middle rung gone; the chair sagged to one side.

"How did she—look?" the county attorney was inquiring.

"Well," said Hale, "she looked—queer."

"How do you mean—queer?"

He took out note-book and pencil. Mrs. Hale did not like the sight of that pencil. She kept her eye on her husband, as if to keep him from saying unnecessary things that would go into the book and make trouble.

Hale spoke guardedly: "Well, as if she didn't know what she was going to do next. And kind of—done up."

"How did the seem to feel about your coming?"

"Why, I don't think she minded—one way or other. She didn't pay much attention. I said, 'Ho' do, Mrs. Wright. It's cold, ain't it?' And she said, 'Is it?'—and went on pleatin' of her apron.

"Well, I was surprised. She didn't ask me to come up to the stove, but just set there, not even lookin' at me. And so I said, 'I want to see John.'

"And then she—laughed. I guess you would call it a laugh.

"I thought of Harry and the team outside, so I said, a little sharp, 'Can I see John?' 'No,' says she—kind of dull like. 'Ain't he home?' says I. Then she looked at me.'Yes,' says she, 'he's home.' 'Then why can't I see him?' I asked her, out of patience with her now. ''Cause he's dead,' says she, just as quiet and dull—and fell to pleatin' her apron. 'Dead?' says I, like you do when you can't take in what you've heard.

"She just nodded her head, not getting a bit excited, but rockin' back and forth.

"'Why—where is he?" says I, not knowing *what* to say.

"She just pointed upstairs—like this"—pointing to the room above.

"I got up, with the idea of going up there myself. By this time I—didn't know what to do. I walked from there to here, then I says "Why, what did he die of?"

"'He died of a rope round his neck,' says she; and just went on pleatin' at her apron."

Hale stopped speaking, staring at the rocker. Nobody spoke; it was as if all were seeing the woman who had sat there the morning before.

"And what did you do then?" the attorney asked.

"I went out and called Harry. I thought I might—need help. I got Harry in, and we went upstairs." His voice fell almost to a whisper. "There he was—lying over the—"

"I think I'd rather have you go into that upstairs," the county attorney interrupted, "where you can point it all out. Just go on now with the rest of the story."

"Well, my first thought was to get that rope off. It looked—"

He stopped; he did not say how it looked.

"But Harry, he went up to him and he said, 'No, he's dead all right, and we'd better not touch anythin'.' So we went downstairs.

"She was still sitting that same way. 'Has anybody been notified?' I asked. 'No,' says she, unconcerned.

"'Who did this, Mrs. Wright?' said Harry. He said it business-like, and she stopped pleatin' at her apron. 'I don't know,' she says. 'You don't *know*?' says Harry. 'Weren't you sleepin' in the bed with him?' 'Yes,' says she, 'but I was on the inside.' 'Somebody slipped a rope round his neck and strangled him, and you didn't wake up?' says Harry. 'I didn't wake up,' she said after him.

"We may have looked as if we didn't see how that could be, for after a minute she said, 'I sleep sound.'

"Harry was going to ask her more questions, but I said maybe that weren't our business; maybe we ought to let her tell her story first to the coroner or the sheriff. So Harry went fast as he could over to High Road—the Rivers' place, where there's a telephone."

"And what did she do when she knew you had gone for the coroner?"

"She moved from that chair to this one over here, and just sat there with her hands held together and looking down. I got a feeling that I ought to make some conversation, so I said I had come in to see if John wanted to put in a telephone; and at that she started to laugh, and then she stopped and looked at me—scared."

At sound of a moving pencil the man who was telling the story looked up.

"I dunno—maybe it wasn't scared; I wouldn't like to say it was. Soon Harry got back, and then Dr. Lloyd came, and you, Mr. Peters, and so I guess that's all I know that you don't."

He said this with relief, moved as if relaxing. The county attorney walked to the stair door.

"I guess we'll go upstairs first—then out to the barn and around there."

He paused and looked around the kitchen.

"You're convinced there was nothing important here?" he asked the sheriff. "Nothing that would—point to any motive?"

The sheriff too looked all around. "Nothing here but kitchen things," he said, with a little laugh for the insignificance of kitchen things.

The county attorney was looking at the cupboard. He opened the upper part and looked in. After a moment he drew his hand away sticky.

"Here's a nice mess," he said resentfully.

The two women had drawn nearer, and now the sheriff's wife spoke.

"Oh—her fruit," she said, looking to Mrs. Hale for understanding. "She worried about that when it turned so cold last night. She said the fire would go out and her jars might burst."

Mrs. Peters' husband broke into a laugh.

"Well, can you beat the women! Held for murder, and worrying about her preserves!"

The young attorney set his lips.

"I guess before we're through with her she may have something more serious than preserves to worry about."

"Oh, well," said Mrs. Hale's husband, with good-natured superiority, "women are used to worrying over trifles."

The two women moved a little closer together. Neither of them spoke. The county attorney seemed to remember his manners—and think of his future.

"And yet," said he, with the gallantry of a young politician, "for all their worries, what would we do without the ladies?"

The women did not speak. He went to the sink to wash his hands, turned to wipe them on the roller towel, pulled it for a cleaner place.

"Dirty towels! Not much of a housekeeper, would you say, ladies?" He kicked his foot against some dirty pans under the sink.

"There's a great deal of work to be done on a farm," said Mrs. Hale stiffly.

"To be sure. And yet"—with a little bow to her—"I know there are some Dickson County farm-houses that do not have such roller towels."

"Those towels get dirty awful quick. Men's hands aren't always as clean as they might be."

"Ah, loyal to your sex, I see," he laughed. He gave her a keen look. "But you and Mrs. Wright were neighbours. I suppose you were friends too."

Martha Hale shook her head.

"I've seen little enough of her of late years. I've not been in this house—it's more than a year."

"And why was that? You didn't like her?"

"I liked her well enough," she replied with spirit. "Farmers' wives have their hands full, Mr. Henderson. And then—" She looked around the kitchen.

"Yes?" he encouraged.

"It never seemed a very cheerful place," said she, more to herself than to him.

"No," he agreed; "I don't think anyone would call it cheerful. I shouldn't say she had the home-making instinct."

"Well, I don't know as Wright had either," she muttered.

"You mean they didn't get on very well?"

"No; I don't mean anything," she answered, with decision. "But I don't think a place would be any the cheerfuler for John Wright's bein' in it."

"I'd like to talk to you about that a little later, Mrs. Hale." He moved towards the stair door, followed by the two men.

"I suppose anything Mrs. Peters does'll be all right?" the sheriff inquired. "She was to take in some clothes for her, you know—and a few little things. We left in such a hurry yesterday."

The county attorney looked at the two women they were leaving alone among the kitchen things.

"Yes—Mrs. Peters," he said, his glance resting on the woman who was not Mrs. Peters, the big farmer woman who stood behind the sheriff's wife. "Of course Mrs. Peters is one of us," he added in a manner of entrusting responsibility. "And keep your eye out, Mrs. Peters, for anything that might be of use. No telling; you women might come upon a clue to the motive—and that's the thing we need."

Mr. Hale rubbed his face in the fashion of a slow man getting ready for a pleasantry. "But would the women know a clue if they did come upon it?" he said. Having delivered himself of this, he followed the others through the stair door.

The women stood motionless, listening to the footsteps, first upon the stairs, then in the room above them.

Then, as if releasing herself from something too strange, Mrs. Hale began to arrange the dirty pans under the sink, which the county attorney's disdainful push of the foot had upset.

"I'd hate to have men coming into my kitchen, snoopin' round and criticizing."

"Of course it's no more than their duty," said the sheriff's wife, in her timid manner.

"Duty's all right, but I guess that deputy sheriff that come out to make the fire might have got a little of this on." She gave the roller towel a pull. "Wish I'd thought of that sooner! Seems mean to talk about her for not having things slicked up, when she had to come away in such a hurry."

She looked around the kitchen. Certainly it was not "slicked up." Her eye was held by a bucket of sugar on a low shelf. The cover was off the wooden bucket, and beside it was a paper bag—half full.

Mrs. Hale moved towards it.

"She was putting this in there," she said to herself—slowly.

She thought of the flour in her kitchen at home—half sifted, half not sifted. She had been interrupted, and had left things half done. What had interrupted Minnie Foster? Why had that work been left half done? She made a move as if to finish it—unfinished things always bothered her, and then she saw that Mrs. Peters was watching her, and she didn't want Mrs. Peters to get that feeling she had of work begun and then—for some reason—not finished.

"It's a shame about her fruit," she said, going to the cupboard. "I wonder if it's all gone.

"Here's one that's all right," she said at last. She held it towards the light. "This is cherries, too," She looked again. "I declare I believe that's the only one.

"She'll feel awful bad, after all her hard work in the hot weather. I remember the afternoon I put up my cherries last summer."

She put the bottle on the table, and was about to sit down in the rocker. But something kept her from sitting in that chair. She stood looking at it, seeing the woman who had sat there "pleatin' at her apron."

The thin voice of the sheriff's wife broke in upon her: "I must be getting those things from the front room closet." She opened the door into the other room, started in, stepped back. "You coming with me, Mrs. Hale?" she asked nervously. "You—you could help me get them."

They were soon back. "My!" said Mrs. Peters, dropping the things on the table and hurrying to the stove.

Mrs. Hale stood examining the clothes the woman who was being detained in town had said she wanted.

"Wright was close!" she exclaimed, holding up a shabby black skirt that bore the marks of much making over. "I think maybe that's why she kept so much to herself. I s'pose she felt she couldn't do her part; and then, you don't enjoy things when you feel shabby. She used to wear pretty clothes and be lively—when she was Minnie Foster, one of the town girls, singing in the choir. But that—oh, that was twenty years ago."

With a carefulness in which there was something tender, she folded the shabby clothes and piled them at one corner of the table. She looked up at Mrs. Peters, and there was something in the other woman's look that irritated her.

"She don't care," she said to herself. "Much difference it makes to her whether Minnie Foster had pretty clothes when she was a girl."

Then she looked again, and she wasn't so sure; in fact, she hadn't at any time been sure about Mrs. Peters. She had that shrinking manner, and yet her eyes looked as if they could see a long way into things.

"This all you was to take in?" asked Mrs. Hale.

"No," said the sheriff's wife; "she said she wanted an apron. Funny thing to want," she ventured in her nervous way, "for there's not much to get you dirty in jail, goodness knows. But I suppose just to make her feel more natural. She said they were in the bottom drawer of this cupboard. Yes—here they are. And then her little shawl that always hung on the stair door."

She took the small grey shawl from behind the door leading upstairs.

Suddenly Mrs. Hale took a quick step towards the other woman.

"Mrs. Peters!"

"Yes, Mrs. Hale?"

"Do you think she—did it?"

Mrs. Peters looked frightened. "Oh, I don't know," she said, in a voice that seemed to shrink from the subject.

"Well, I don't think she did," affirmed Mrs. Hale. "Asking for an apron, and her little shawl. Worryin' about her fruit."

"Mr. Peters says—" Footsteps were heard in the room above; she stopped, looked up, then went on in a lowered voice: "Mr. Peters says—it looks bad for her. Mr. Henderson is awful sarcastic in a speech, and he's going to make fun of her saying she didn't wake up."

For a moment Mrs. Hale had no answer. Then, "Well, I guess John Wright didn't wake up—when they was slippin' that rope under his neck," she muttered.

"No, it's *strange*," breathed Mrs. Peters. "They think it was such a—funny way to kill a man."

"That's just what Mr. Hale said," said Mrs. Hale, in a resolutely natural voice. "There was a gun in the house. He says that's what he can't understand."

"Mr. Henderson said, coming out, that what was needed for the case was a motive. Something to show anger—or sudden feeling."

"Well, I don't see any signs of anger around here," said Mrs. Hale. "I don't—"

She stopped. Her eye was caught by a dishtowel in the middle of the kitchen table. Slowly she moved towards the table. One half of it was wiped clean, the other half untidy. Her eyes made a slow, almost unwilling turn to the bucket of sugar and the half-empty bag beside it. Things begun—and not finished.

She stepped back. "Wonder how they're finding things upstairs? I hope she had it in better shape up there. Seems kind of *sneaking*, locking her up in town and coming out here to get her own house to turn against her!"

"But, Mrs. Hale," said the sheriff's wife, "the law is the law."

"I s'pose it is," answered Mrs. Hale shortly.

She turned to the stove, saying something about that fire not being much to brag of.

"The law is the law—and a bad stove is a bad stove. How'd you like to cook on this?" with the poker pointing to the broken lining. She opened the oven door. The thought of Minnie Foster trying to bake in that oven—and the thought of her never going over to see Minnie Foster—

She was startled by hearing Mrs. Peters say, "A person gets discouraged—and loses heart."

The sheriff's wife had looked from the stove to the sink—the pail of water which had been carried in from outside. The two women stood there silent, above them the footsteps of the men who were looking for evidence against the woman who had worked in that kitchen. That look of seeing into things, of seeing through a thing to something else, was in the eyes of the sheriff's wife now. When Mrs. Hale next spoke to her, it was gently.

"Better loosen up your things, Mrs. Peters. We'll not feel them when we go out."

Mrs. Peters went to the back of the room to hang up the fur tippet she was wearing. "Why, she was piecing a quilt," she exclaimed, and held up a large sewing basket piled high with quilt pieces.

Mrs. Hale spread some of the blocks on the table.

"It's log-cabin pattern," she said, putting several of them together. "Pretty, isn't it?"

They were so engaged with the quilt that they did not hear the footsteps on the stairs. As the stair door opened Mrs. Hale was saying, "Do you suppose she was going to quilt it, or just knot it?"

The sheriff threw up his hands.

"They wonder whether she was going to quilt it, or just knot it!"

There was a laugh for the ways of women, a warming of hands over the stove, and then the county attorney said briskly, "Well, let's go right out to the barn and get that cleared up."

"I don't see as there's anything so strange," Mrs. Hale said resentfully, after the outside door had closed on the three men—"our taking up our time with little things while we're waiting for them to get the evidence. I don't see as it's anything to laugh about."

"Of course they've got awful important things on their minds," said the sheriff's wife apologetically.

They returned to an inspection of the blocks for the quilt. Mrs. Hale was looking at the fine, even sewing, preoccupied with thoughts of the woman who had done that sewing, when she heard the sheriff's wife say, in a startled tone, "Why, look at this one."

"The sewing," said Mrs. Peters, in a troubled way. "All the rest of them have been so nice and even—but—this one. Why, it looks as if she didn't know what she was about!"

Their eyes met—something flashed to life, passed between them; then, as if with an effort, they seemed to pull away from each other. A moment Mrs. Hale sat there, her fingers upon those stitches so unlike the rest of the sewing. Then she had pulled a knot and drawn the threads.

"Oh, what are you doing, Mrs. Hale?" asked the sheriff's wife.

"Just pulling out a stitch or two that's not sewed very good," said Mrs. Hale mildly.

"I don't think we ought to touch things," Mrs. Peters said.

"I'll just finish up this end," answered Mrs. Hale.

She threaded a needle and started to replace bad sewing with good. Then in that thin, timid voice, she heard: "Mrs. Hale!"

"Yes, Mrs. Peters?"

"What do you suppose she was so—nervous about?"

"Oh, I don't know," said Mrs. Hale, as if dismissing a thing not important enough to spend much time on. "I don't know as she was—nervous. I sew awful queer sometimes when I'm just tired."

"Well, I must get these clothes wrapped. They may be through sooner than we think. I wonder where I could find a piece of paper—and string."

"In that cupboard, maybe," suggested Mrs. Hale.

One piece of the crazy sewing remained unripped. Mrs. Peters' back turned, Martha Hale scrutinized that piece, compared it with the dainty, accurate stitches of the other blocks. The difference was startling. Holding this block it was hard to remain quiet, as if the distracted thoughts of the woman who had perhaps turned to it to try and quiet herself were communicating themselves to her.

"Here's a bird-cage," Mrs. Peters said. "Did she have a bird, Mrs. Hale?"

"Why, I don't know whether she did or not." She turned to look at the cage Mrs. Peters was holding up. "I've not been here in so long." She sighed. "There was a man round last year selling canaries cheap—but I don't know as she took one. Maybe she did. She used to sing real pretty herself."

"Seems kind of funny to think of a bird here. But she must have had one—or why would she have a cage? I wonder what happened to it."

"I suppose maybe the cat got it," suggested Mrs. Hale, resuming her sewing.

"No; she didn't have a cat. She's got that feeling some people have about cats—being afraid of them. When they brought her to our house yesterday, my cat got in the room, and she was real upset and asked me to take it out."

"My sister Bessie was like that," laughed Mrs. Hale.

The sheriff's wife did not reply. The silence made Mrs. Hale turn. Mrs. Peters was examining the bird-cage.

"Look at this door," she said slowly. "It's broke. One hinge has been pulled apart."

Mrs. Hale came nearer.

"Looks as if someone must have been—rough with it."

Again their eyes met—startled, questioning, apprehensive. For a moment neither spoke nor stirred. Then Mrs. Hale, turning away, said brusquely, "If they're going to find any evidence, I wish they'd be about it. I don't like this place."

"But I'm awful glad you came with me, Mrs. Hale." Mrs. Peters put the bird-cage on the table and sat down. "It would be lonesome for me—sitting here alone."

"Yes, it would, wouldn't it?" agreed Mrs. Hale. She had picked up the sewing, but now it dropped to her lap, and she murmured: "But I tell you what I *do* wish, Mrs. Peters. I wish I had come over sometimes when she was here. I wish—I had."

"But of course you were awful busy, Mrs. Hale. Your house—and your children."

"I could've come. I stayed away because it weren't cheerful—and that's why I ought to have come. I"—she looked around—"I've never liked this place. Maybe because it's down in a hollow and you don't see the road. I don't know what it is, but it's a lonesome place, and always was. I wish I had come over to see Minnie Foster sometimes. I can see now—"

"Well, you mustn't reproach yourself. Somehow we just don't see how it is with other folks till—something comes up."

"Not having children makes less work," mused Mrs. Hale, "but it makes a quiet house. And Wright out to work all day—and no company when he did come in. Did you know John Wright, Mrs. Peters?"

"Not to know him. I've seen him in town. They say he was a good man."

"Yes—good," conceded John Wright's neighbour grimly. "He didn't drink, and kept his word as well as most, I guess, and paid his debts. But he was a hard man, Mrs. Peters. Just to pass the time of day with him—" She shivered. "Like a raw wind that gets to the bone." Her eye fell upon the cage on the table before her, and she added, "I should think she would've wanted a bird!"

Suddenly she leaned forward, looking intently at the cage. "But what do you s'pose went wrong with it?"

"I don't know," returned Mrs. Peters; "unless it got sick and died."

But after she said this she reached over and swung the broken door. Both women watched it.

"You didn't know—her?" Mrs. Hale asked.

"Not till they brought her yesterday," said the sheriff's wife.

"She—come to think of it, she was kind of like a bird herself. Real sweet and pretty, but kind of timid and—fluttery. How—she—did—change."

Finally, as if struck with a happy thought and relieved to get back to every-day things: "Tell you what, Mrs. Peters, why don't you take the quilt in with you? It might take up her mind."

"Why, I think that's a real nice idea, Mrs. Hale. There couldn't possibly be any objection to that, could there? Now, just what will I take? I wonder if her patches are in here?" They turned to the sewing basket.

"Here's some red," said Mrs. Hale, bringing out a roll of cloth. Underneath this was a box. "Here, maybe her scissors are in here—and her things." She held it up. "What a pretty box! I'll warrant that was something she had a long time ago—when she was a girl."

She held it in her hand a moment; then, with a little sigh, opened it.

Instantly her hand went to her nose. "Why!"

Mrs. Peters drew nearer—then turned away.

"There's something wrapped up in this piece of silk," faltered Mrs. Hale.

"This isn't her scissors," said Mrs. Peters, in a shrinking voice.

Mrs. Hale raised the piece of silk. "Oh, Mrs. Peters!" she cried. "It's—"

Mrs. Peters bent closer.

"It's the bird," she whispered.

"But, Mrs. Peters!" cried Mrs. Hale. "*Look* at it! Its *neck*—look at its neck! It's all—other side *to*."

The sheriff's wife again bent closer.

"Somebody wrung its neck," said she, in a voice that was slow and deep.

The eyes of the two women met—this time clung together in a look of dawning comprehension, of growing horror. Mrs. Peters looked from the dead bird to the broken door of the cage. Again their eyes met. And just then there was a sound at the outside door.

Mrs. Hale slipped the box under the quilt pieces in the basket. The county attorney and sheriff came in.

"Well, ladies," said the attorney, as one turning from serious things to little pleasantries, "have you decided whether she was going to quilt it or knot it?"

"We think," said the sheriff's wife hastily, "that she was going to knot it."

"Well, that's very interesting, I'm sure." He caught sight of the cage. "Has the bird flown?"

"We think the cat got it," said Mrs. Hale in a prosaic voice.

He was walking up and down, as if thinking something out.

"Is there a cat?" he asked absently.

Mrs. Hale shot a look up at the sheriff's wife.

"Well, not *now*," said Mrs. Peters. "They're superstitious, you know; they leave."

The county attorney did not heed her. "No sign at all of anyone having come in from the outside," he said to Peters, continuing an interrupted conversation. "Their own rope. Now let's go upstairs again and go over it, piece by piece. It would have to have been someone who knew just the—"

The stair door closed behind them and their voices were lost.

The two women sat motionless, not looking at each other, but as if peering into something and at the same time holding back. When they spoke now it was as if they were afraid of what they were saying, but could not help saying it.

"She liked the bird," said Martha Hale. "She was going to bury it in that pretty box."

"When I was a girl," said Mrs. Peters, under her breath, "my kitten—there was a boy took a hatchet, and before my eyes—before I could get there—" She covered her face an instant. "If they hadn't held me back I would have"—she caught herself, and finished weakly—"hurt him."

Then they sat without speaking or moving.

"I wonder how it would seem," Mrs. Hale began, as if feeling her way over strange ground— "never to have had any children around." Her eyes made a sweep of the kitchen. "No, Wright wouldn't like the bird—a thing that sang. She used to sing. He killed that too."

Mrs. Peters moved. "Of course we don't know who killed the bird."

"I knew John Wright," was the answer.

"It was an awful thing was done in this house that night, Mrs. Hale," said the sheriff's wife. "Killing a man while he slept—slipping a thing round his neck that choked the life out of him."

Mrs. Hale's hand went to the bird-cage. "His neck. Choked the life out of him."

"We don't *know* who killed him," whispered Mrs. Peters wildly. "We don't *know.*"

Mrs. Hale had not moved. "If there had been years and years of nothing, then a bird to sing to you, it would be awful—still, after the bird was still."

"I know what stillness is," whispered Mrs. Peters. "When we homesteaded in Dakota, and my first baby died—after he was two years old—and me with no other then—"

Mrs. Hale stirred. "How soon do you suppose they'll be through looking for the evidence?"

"I know what stillness is," repeated Mrs. Peters. Then she too pulled back. "The law has got to punish crime, Mrs. Hale."

"I wish you'd seen Minnie Foster when she wore a white dress with blue ribbons, and stood up there in the choir and sang."

The picture of that girl, the thought that she had lived neighbour to her for twenty years, and had let her die for lack of life, was suddenly more than the woman could bear.

"Oh, I *wish* I'd come over here once in a while!" she cried. "That was a crime! That was a crime! Who's going to punish *that?*"

"We mustn't—take on," said Mrs. Peters, with a frightened look towards the stairs.

"I might 'a' *known* she needed help! I tell you, it's *queer,* Mrs. Peters. We live close together, and we live far apart. We all go through the same things—it's all just a different kind of the same thing! If it weren't—why do you and I *know*—what we know this minute?"

Seeing the jar of fruit on the table, she reached for it. "If I was you I wouldn't *tell* her her fruit was gone! Tell her it *ain't.* Tell her it's all right—all of it. Here—take this in to prove it to her! She—she may never know whether it was broke or not."

Mrs. Peters took the bottle of fruit as if glad to take it—as if touching a familiar thing, having something to do, could keep her from something else. She looked about for something to wrap the fruit in, took a petticoat from the pile of clothes she had brought from the front room, nervously started winding that round the bottle.

"My!" she began, in a high voice, "it's a good thing the men couldn't hear us! Getting all stirred up over a little thing like a—dead canary. As if that could have anything to do with—with— My, wouldn't they *laugh?*"

There were footsteps on the stairs.

"Maybe they would," muttered Mrs. Hale—"maybe they wouldn't."

"No, Peters," said the county attorney, "it's all perfectly clear, except the reason for doing it. But you know juries when it comes to women. If there was some definite thing—something to *show.* Something to make a story about. A thing that would connect up with this clumsy way of doing it."

Mrs. Hale looked at Mrs. Peters. Mrs. Peters was looking at her. Quickly they looked away from one another. The outer door opened and Mr. Hale came in.

"I've nailed back that board we ripped off," he said.

"Much obliged, Mr. Hale," said the sheriff. "We'll be getting along now."

"I'm going to stay here awhile by myself," the county attorney suddenly announced. "You can send Frank out for me, can't you?" he asked the sheriff. "I want to go over everything. I'm not satisfied we can't do better."

Again, for one brief moment, the women's eyes met.

The sheriff came up to the table.

"Did you want to see what Mrs. Peters was going to take in?"

The county attorney picked up the apron. He laughed.

"Oh, I guess they're not very dangerous things the ladies have picked out."

Mrs. Hale's hand was on the sewing basket in which the box was concealed. She felt that she ought to take her hand off the basket. She did not seem able to. She picked up one of the quilt blocks she had piled on to cover the box. She had a fear that if he took up the basket she would snatch it from him.

But he did not take it. With another laugh he turned away, saying, "No, Mrs. Peters doesn't need supervising. For that matter, a sheriff's wife is married to the law. Ever think of it that way, Mrs. Peters?"

Mrs. Peters had turned her face away. "Not—just that way," she said.

"Married to the law!" chuckled Mrs. Peters' husband. He moved towards the door into the front room, and said to the county attorney, "I just want you to come here a minute, George. We ought to take a look at these windows."

"Oh—windows!" scoffed the county attorney.

"We'll be leaving in a second, Mr. Hale," Mr. Peters told the farmer, as he followed the county attorney into the other room.

"Can't be leavin' too soon to suit me," muttered Hale, and went out.

Again, for one final moment, the two women were alone in that kitchen.

Martha Hale sprang up, her hands tight together, looking at that other woman, with whom it rested. At first she could not see her eyes, for the sheriff's wife had not turned back since she turned away at that suggestion of being married to the law. Slowly, unwillingly, Mrs. Peters turned her head until her eyes met the eyes of the other woman. There was a moment when they held each other in a steady, burning look in which there was no evasion nor flinching. Then Martha Hale's eyes pointed the way to the basket in which was hidden the thing that would convict the third woman—that woman who was not there, and yet who had been there with them through that hour.

For a moment Mrs. Peters did not move. And then she did it. Threw back the quilt pieces, got the box, tried to put it in her hand-bag. It was too big. Desperately she opened it, started to take the bird out. But there she broke—she could not touch the bird. She stood there helpless, foolish.

There was a sound at the door. Martha Hale snatched the box from the sheriff's wife and got it in the pocket of her big coat just as the sheriff and the county attorney came back into the kitchen.

"Well, Henry," said the county attorney, facetiously, "at least we found out that she was not going to quilt it. She was going to—what is it you call it, ladies?"

Mrs. Hale's hand was against the pocket of her coat.

"We call it—knot it," was her answer.

**T H E   E N D**

# Angelina Weld Grimké

Angelina Weld Grimké (1880–1958) was an important African-American poet, essayist, and writer of short fiction in the early decades of the twentieth century. Her only play, *Rachel* (1916), is one of the earliest American plays to address the subject of lynching and the more general oppression of African Americans. Grimké was born and largely raised in the Boston area. Her father, Archibald Grimké, was the illegitimate, black son of a white South Carolina slaveholder, Henry Grimké, and his slave Nancy Weston. Her mother, who was white, left the Grimké family soon after Angelina was born, and Grimké was raised mainly by her father.

Educated at the Fairmount Grammar School in Hyde Park, Massachusetts, Carleton Academy in Minnesota, and at the Cushing Academy and the Girls' Latin School in Massachusetts, Grimké took her degree in physical education from the Boston Normal School of Gymnastics in 1902. She pursued a teaching career, first at the Armstrong Manual Training School in Washington, D.C., and then at the M Street High School, later renamed Dunbar High School, before retiring and moving to New York City in 1926.

Grimké's writing dates mainly from the 1910s and 1920s. Although *Rachel* is the only work she published in book form, her poetry, essays, and stories were printed frequently in magazines, journals, and anthologies during her lifetime. Grimké was a lesbian, and appears to have recognized her sexual orientation early in life; many of her love poems are openly addressed to women. Her fiction and nonfiction prose is more concerned with the themes of racism in the United States, and stories like "The Closing Door" and "Blackness"—later revised as "Goldie"—directly condemn the lynchings of African Americans common in the United States in the first third of the twentieth century.

Like many African-American women writers—Zora Neale Hurston is perhaps the best example—Grimké was well known in her lifetime, but her works were not readily assimilated to the canon of American literature. *The Selected Works of Angelina Weld Grimké* was published in 1991, as a part of the Schomburg Library of Nineteenth-Century Black Women Writers series. This excellent collection, edited by Carolivia Herron, is the first collection to bring Grimké's important body of writing together for modern readers.

## Rachel (1916)

*Rachel* is an important play in the canon of American drama, in part because it links a critique of overt racism—the lynching that killed Rachel's father and half-brother, the taunts of "nigger" that follow her brother Tom and her adopted son Jimmy—with an account of the more subtle racism that oppresses the Loving family in other ways.

From the outset, Grimké establishes the Loving family as honest, hard-working, and upwardly mobile. Much as in Ibsen's plays, *Rachel* layers the class and the aspirations of the Lovings into their domestic environment. When the curtain rises, the audience sees a spare, unprepossessing room decorated with the ornaments of middle-class respectability: prints of famous artwork (Millais, Burne-Jones, Raphael), a full and well-used bookcase, a piano. And, although Mrs. Loving supports her children on her meager wages as a seamstress, they seem bursting with vitality and potential. Yet in the course of Act One, Mrs. Loving reveals the cause of her distracted behavior. Ten years earlier, on this date, her husband and their step-brother had been seized and lynched outside their home in the South. Grimké makes it plain that such lynchings are both commonplace and supported by the majority of whites. The men who lynched Loving and seven-year-old George were not aberrant criminals; they were "all church members in good standing—the best people" of the community.

The violence of the South is, in *Rachel,* only a more explicit version of the institutionalized racism that pervades American culture as a whole, North and South. Even in Act One, Tom reports being called a "nigger" by his white rival for quarterback, and that a white girl—once apparently his girlfriend—has begun to ignore him, now that she has become friends with two girls recently moved from the South. Finally, John Strong, a polite, college-educated family friend, has been able to find work only as a waiter—"he had the tremendous handicap of being colored," as Mrs. Loving reminds her children.

"We sing a song at school, I believe," Rachel remarks, "about 'The land of the free and the home of the brave.' What an amusing nation it is." But the "amusing nation" is clearly a nation of real freedom only for its white citizens. Its black citizens can be lynched with impunity in this "white Christian nation," and men like Tom and John Strong face equally certain discrimination; despite talent, effort, and education, they are able to find only relatively menial employment. As Tom says, "In the South, they make it as impossible as they can for us to get an education. . . . In the North, they make a pretence of liberality: they give us the ballot and a good education, and then—snuff us out." And as the play shows, the schools themselves are where the lessons of racism are both taught and learned.

Writing the play, Grimké had toyed with calling it *The Pervert, The Daughter,* and *Blessed Are the Barren* before deciding on *Rachel.* These draft titles point to the most difficult dimension of Grimké's play for modern readers: that Rachel's act of resistance in the play is to refuse to bear children, to refuse to bring more black children into a world in which they will be systematically oppressed. As a strategy of resistance, Rachel's act implies a kind of autogenocide oddly complicit with the racism she wants to oppose. Yet as Grimké suggests in her article on the play, Rachel's refusal is meant to signify the extent to which white, racist culture is itself unnatural. By making Rachel refuse the life she seems so naturally to desire—the life of wife and mother—Grimké hopes to make "the white women of this country . . . see, feel, understand just what effect their prejudice and the prejudice of their fathers, brothers, husbands, sons were having on the sons of colored mothers everywhere."

Grimké, that is, attempts to forge a "natural" union among women—black and white—to oppose the unnatural, racist culture of the United States. Throughout *Rachel,* Grimké urgently resists the dramatic stereotypes applied by white authors to African-American characters onstage. While Grimké deftly shows notions of "race" to be socially constructed, though, her assumptions about gender remain more deeply rooted in her sense of an "essential" nature distinguishing men from women. Grimké uses Rachel in something like the way Elizabeth Robins uses Vida Levering in her play *Votes for Women!* She brings Rachel's "natural" feminine experience into conflict with the dominant (white, male) social order, in order to expose the unnatural ways in which that order deforms and destroys women. It will remain for later playwrights—Caryl Churchill in *Cloud Nine,* Ntozake Shange in *spell #7,* for example—to suggest that notions of both "race" and "gender" are ideologically conditioned ways of representing a particular social order and a particular structure of social power.

# —Rachel—
## A Play in Three Acts
### Angelina W. Grimké

## —CHARACTERS—

MRS. MARY LOVING, *a widow*
RACHEL LOVING, *her daughter*
THOMAS LOVING, *her son*
JIMMY MASON, *a small boy*
JOHN STRONG, *a friend of the family*
MRS. LANE, *a caller*
ETHEL LANE, *her daughter*

MARY
NANCY
EDITH
JENNY    } *little friends of Rachel*
LOUISE
MARTHA

*Time: The first decade of the Twentieth Century.*

*Act I. October 16th.*
*Act II. October 16th, four years later.*
*Act III. One week later.*

*Place: A northern city. The living room in the small apartment of Mrs. Loving.*

*All of the characters are colored.*

## —ACT ONE—

The scene is a room scrupulously neat and clean and plainly furnished. The walls are painted green, the woodwork, white. In the rear at the left an open doorway leads into a hall. Its bare, green wall and white baseboard are all that can be seen of it. It leads into the other rooms of the flat. In the centre of the rear wall of the room is a window. It is shut. The white sash curtains are pushed to right and left as far as they will go. The green shade is rolled up to the top. Through the window can be seen the red bricks of a house wall, and the tops of a couple of trees moving now and then in the wind. Within the window, and just below the sill, is a shelf upon which are a few potted plants. Between the window and the door is a bookcase full of books and above it, hanging on the wall, a simply framed, inexpensive copy of Millet's "The Reapers." There is a run extending from the right center to just below the right upper entrance. It is the vestibule of the flat. Its open doorway faces the left wall. In the right wall near the front is another window. Here the sash curtains are drawn together and the green shade is partly lowered. The window is up from the bottom. Through it street noises can be heard. In front of this window is an open, threaded sewing-machine. Some frail, white fabric is lying upon it. There is a chair in front of the machine and at the machine's left a small table covered with a green cloth. In the rear of the left wall and directly opposite to the entrance to the flat is the doorway leading into the kitchenette, dishes on shelves can be seen behind glass doors.

In the center of the left wall is a fireplace with a grate in it for coals; over this is a wooden mantel painted white. In the

center is a small clock. A pair of vases, green and white in coloring, one at each end, complete the ornaments. Over the mantel is a narrow mirror; and over this, hanging on the wall, Burne-Jones' "Golden Stairs," simply framed. Against the front end of the left wall is an upright piano with a stool in front of it. On top is music neatly piled. Hanging over the piano is Raphael's "Sistine Madonna." In the center of the floor is a green rug, and in the center of this, a rectangular dining-room table, the long side facing front. It is covered with a green table-cloth. Three dining-room chairs are at the table, one at either end and one at the rear facing front. Above the table is a chandelier with four gas jets enclosed by glass globes. At the right front center is a rather shabby arm-chair upholstered in green.

*Left and right from the spectator's point of view.*

Before the sewing-machine, Mrs. Loving is seated. She looks worried. She is sewing swiftly and deftly by hand upon a waist in her lap. It is a white, beautiful thing and she sews upon it delicately. It is about half-past four in the afternoon; and the light is failing. Mrs. Loving pauses in her sewing, rises and lets the window-shade near her go up to the top. She pushes the sash-curtains to either side, the corner of a red brick house wall being thus brought into view. She shivers slightly, then pushes the window down at the bottom and lowers it a trifle from the top. The street noises become less distinct. She takes off her thimble, rubs her hands gently, puts the thimble on again, and looks at the clock on the mantel. She then reseats herself, with her chair as close to the window as possible and begins to sew. Presently a key is heard, and the door opens and shuts noisily.

*Rachel comes in from the vestibule. In her left arm she carries four or five books strapped together; under her right, a roll of music. Her hat is twisted over her left ear and her hair is falling in tendrils about her face. She brings into the room with her the spirit of abounding life, health, joy, youth. Mrs. Loving pauses, needle in hand, as soon as she hears the turning key and the banging door. There is a smile on her face. For a second, mother and daughter smile at each other. Then Rachel throws her books upon the dining-room table, places the music there also, but with care, and rushing to her mother, gives her a bear hug and a kiss.*

RACHEL: Ma dear! dear, old Ma dear!

MRS. LOVING: Look out for the needle, Rachel! The waist! Oh, Rachel!

RACHEL: *(On her knees and shaking her finger directly under her mother's nose.)* You old, old fraud! You know you adore being hugged. I've a good mind . . .

MRS. LOVING: Now, Rachel, please! Besides, I know your tricks. You think you can make me forget you are late. What time is it?

10 RACHEL: *(Looking at the clock and expressing surprise)* Jiminy Xmas! *(Whistles)* Why, it's five o'clock!

MRS. LOVING: *(Severely)* Well!

RACHEL: *(Plaintively)* Now, Ma dear, you're going to be horrid and cross.

MRS. LOVING: *(Laughing)* Really, Rachel, that expression is not particularly affecting, when your hat is over your ear, and you look, with your hair over your eyes, exactly like some one's pet poodle. I wonder if you are ever going to grow up and be ladylike.

20 RACHEL: Oh! Ma dear, I hope not, not for the longest time, two long, long years at least. I just want to be silly and irresponsible, and have you to love and torment, and, of course, Tom, too.

MRS. LOVING: *(Smiling down at Rachel)* You'll not make me forget, young lady. Why are you late, Rachel?

RACHEL: Well, Ma dear, I'm your pet poodle, and my hat is over my ear, and I'm late, for the loveliest reason.

MRS. LOVING: Don't be silly, Rachel.

RACHEL: That may sound silly, but it isn't. And please don't
30 "Rachel" me so much. It was honestly one whole hour ago when I opened the front door down stairs. I know it was, because I heard the postman telling some one it was four o'clock. Well, I climbed the first flight, and was just starting up the second, when a little shrill voice said, "'Lo!" I raised my eyes, and there, half-way up the stairs, sitting in the middle of a step, was just the dearest, cutest, darlingest little brown baby boy you ever saw. "'Lo! yourself," I said. "What are you doing, and who are you anyway?" "I'm Jimmy; and I'm widing to New York on the choo-choo tars." As he
40 looked entirely too young to be going such a distance by himself, I asked him if I might go too. For a minute or two he considered the question and me very seriously, and then he said, "'Es," and made room for me on the step beside him. We've been everywhere: New York, Chicago, Boston, London, Paris and Oshkosh. I wish you could have heard him say that last place. I suggested going there just to hear him. Now, Ma dear, is it any wonder I am late? See all the places we have been in just one "teeny, weeny" hour? We

would have been traveling yet, but his horrid, little mother came out and called him in. They're in the flat below, the 50 new people. But before he went, Ma dear, he said the "cunningest" thing. He said, "Will you tum out an' p'ay wif me aden in two minutes?" I nearly hugged him to death, and it's a wonder my hat is on my head at all. Hats are such unimportant nuisances anyway!

MRS. LOVING: Unimportant nuisances! What ridiculous language you do use, Rachel! Well, I'm no prophet, but I see very distinctly what is going to happen. This little brown baby will be living here night and day. You're not happy unless some child is trailing along in your rear. 60

RACHEL: *(Mischievously)* Now, Ma dear, whose a hypocrite? What? I suppose you don't like children! I can tell you one thing, though, it won't be my fault if he isn't here night and day. Oh, I wish he were all mine, every bit of him! Ma dear, do you suppose that "she woman" he calls mother would let him come up here until it is time for him to go to bed? I'm going down there this minute. *(Rises impetuously.)*

MRS. LOVING: Rachel, for Heaven's sake! No! I am entirely too busy and tired today without being bothered with a child romping around in here. 70

RACHEL: *(Reluctantly and a trifle petulantly)* Very well, then. *(For several moments she watches her mother, who has begun to sew again. The displeasure vanishes from her face).* Ma dear!

MRS. LOVING: Well.

RACHEL: Is there anything wrong today?

MRS. LOVING: I'm just tired, chickabiddy, that's all.

RACHEL: *(Moves over to the table. Mechanically takes off her hat and coat and carries them out into the entryway of the flat. She returns and goes to the looking glass over the fire-* 80 *place and tucks in the tendrils of her hair in rather a preoccupied manner. The electric doorbell rings. She returns to the speaking tube in the vestibule. Her voice is heard answering.)* Yes!—Yes!—No, I'm not Mrs. Loving. She's here, yes!—What? Oh! come right up! *(Appearing in the doorway).* Ma dear, it's some man, who is coming for Mrs. Strong's waist.

MRS. LOVING: *(Pausing and looking at Rachel)* It is probably her son. She said she would send for it this afternoon. *(Rachel disappears. A door is heard opening and closing. There is* 90 *the sound of a man's voice. Rachel ushers in Mr. John Strong.)*

STRONG: *(Bowing pleasantly to Mrs. Loving)* Mrs. Loving? *(Mrs. Loving bows, puts down her sewing, rises and goes toward Strong.)* My name is Strong. My mother asked me to come by and get her waist this afternoon. She hoped it would be finished.

MRS. LOVING: Yes, Mr. Strong, it is all ready. If you'll sit down a minute, I'll wrap it up for you. *(She goes into hallway leading to other rooms in flat.)* 100

RACHEL: *(Manifestly ill at ease at being left alone with a stranger; attempting, however, to be the polite hostess)* Do sit down, Mr. Strong. *(They both sit.)*

RACHEL: *(Nervously after a pause)* It's a very pleasant day, isn't it, Mr. Strong?

STRONG: Yes, very. *(He leans back composedly, his hat on his knee, the faintest expression of amusement in his eyes.)*

RACHEL: *(After a pause)* It's quite a climb up to our flat, don't you think?

110 STRONG: Why, no! It didn't strike me so. I'm not old enough yet to mind stairs.

RACHEL: (*Nervously*) Oh! I didn't mean that you are old! Anyone can see you are quite young, that is, of course, not too young, but,—(*Strong laughs quietly*). There! I don't blame you for laughing. I'm always clumsy just like that.

MRS. LOVING: (*Calling from the other room*) Rachel, bring me a needle and the sixty cotton, please.

RACHEL: All right, Ma dear! (*Rummages for the cotton in the machine drawer, and upsets several spools upon the floor.*

120 *To Strong:*) You see! I can't even get a spool of cotton without spilling things all over the floor. (*Strong smiles, Rachel picks up the spools and finally gets the cotton and needle*). Excuse me! (*Goes out door leading to other rooms. Strong left to himself, looks around casually. The "Golden Stairs" interests him and the "Sistine Madonna."*)

RACHEL: (*Reenters, evidently continuing her function of hostess*) We were talking about the climb to our flat, weren't we? You see, when you're poor, you have to live in a top flat. There is always a compensation, though; we have bully—I

130 mean nice air, better light, a lovely view, and nobody "thud-thudding" up and down over our heads night and day. The people below have our "thud-thudding," and it must be something *awful*, especially when Tom and I play "Ivanhoe" and have a tournament up here. We're entirely too old, but we still play. Ma dear rather dreads the climb up three flights, so Tom and I do all the errands. We don't mind climbing the stairs, particularly when we go up two or three at a time,—that is—Tom still does. I can't, Ma dear stopped me. (*Sighs.*) I've got to grow up it seems.

140 STRONG: (*Evidently amused*) It is rather hard being a girl, isn't it?

RACHEL: Oh, no! It's not hard at all. That's the trouble; they won't let me be a girl. I'd love to be.

MRS. LOVING: (*Reentering with parcel. She smiles*) My chatterbox, I see, is entertaining you, Mr. Strong. I'm sorry to have kept you waiting, but I forgot, I found, to sew the ruching in the neck. I hope everything is satisfactory. If it isn't, I'll be glad to make any changes.

STRONG: (*Who has risen upon her entrance*) Thank you, Mrs.

150 Loving, I'm sure everything is all right. (*He takes the package and bows to her and Rachel. He moves towards the vestibule, Mrs. Loving following him. She passes through the doorway first. Before leaving, Strong turns for a second and looks back quietly at Rachel. He goes out too. Rachel returns to the mirror, looks at her face for a second, and then begins to touch and pat her hair lightly and delicately here and there. Mrs. Loving returns*).

RACHEL: (*Still at the glass*) He *was* rather nice, wasn't he, Ma dear?—for a man? (*Laughs*). I guess my reason's a vain

160 one,—he let me do all the talking. (*Pauses.*) Strong? Strong? Ma dear, is his mother the little woman with the sad, black eyes?

MRS. LOVING: (*Resuming her sewing; sitting before the machine*) Yes. I was rather curious, I confess, to see this son of hers. The whole time I'm fitting her she talks of nothing else. She worships him. (*Pauses.*) It's rather a sad case, I believe. She is a widow. Her husband was a doctor and left her a little money. She came up from the South to educate this

boy. Both of them worked hard and the boy got through col-

170 lege. Three months he hunted for work that a college man might expect to get. You see he had the tremendous handicap of being colored. As the two of them had to live, one day, without her knowing it, he hired himself out as a waiter. He has been one now for two years. He is evidently goodness itself to his mother.

RACHEL: (*Slowly and thoughtfully*) Just because he is *colored*! (*Pauses*). We sing a song at school, I believe, about "The land of the free and the home of the brave." What an amusing nation it is.

180 MRS. LOVING: (*Watching Rachel anxiously*) Come, Rachel, you haven't time for "amusing nations." Remember, you haven't practised any this afternoon. And put your books away; don't leave them on the table. You didn't practise any this morning either, did you?

RACHEL: No, Ma dear,—didn't wake up in time. (*Goes to the table and in an abstracted manner puts books on the bookcase; returns to the table; picks up the roll of sheet music she has brought home with her; brightens; impulsively.*) Ma dear, just listen to this lullaby. It's the sweetest thing. I was

190 so "daffy" over it, one of the girls at school lent it to me. (*She rushes to the piano with the music and plays the accompaniment through softly and then sings, still softly and with great expression, Jessie Gaynor's "Slumber Boat"*)—

> Baby's boat the silver moon;
> Sailing in the sky,
> Sailing o'er the sea of sleep,
> While the clouds float by.

> Sail, baby, sail,
> Out upon that sea,
200 Only don't forget to sail
> Back again to me.

> Baby's fishing for a dream,
> Fishing near and far,
> His line a silver moonbeam is,
> His bait a silver star.

> Sail, baby, sail, etc.

Listen, Ma dear, right here. Isn't it lovely? (*Plays and sings very softly and slowly*)

> "Only don't forget to sail
> Back again to me." 210

(*Pauses; in hushed tones*) Ma dear, it's so beautiful—it—it hurts.

MRS. LOVING: (*Quietly*) Yes, dear, it is pretty.

RACHEL: (*For several minutes watches her mother's profile from the piano stool. Her expression is rather wistful*) Ma dear!

MRS. LOVING: Yes, Rachel.

RACHEL: What's the matter?

MRS. LOVING: (*Without turning*) Matter! What do you mean?

RACHEL: I don't know. I just *feel* something is not quite right 220 with you.

MRS. LOVING: I'm only tired—that's all.

RACHEL: Perhaps. But—(*Watches her mother a moment or two longer; shakes her head; turns back to the piano. She is thoughtful; looks at her hands in her lap*). Ma dear, wouldn't it be nice if we could keep all the babies in the world—always little babies? Then they'd be always little, and cunning, and lovable; and they could never grow up, then, and—and—be bad. I'm so sorry for mothers, whose little babies—grow up—and—and—are bad.

MRS. LOVING: (*Startled; controlling herself, looks at Rachel anxiously, perplexedly. Rachel's eyes are still on her hands. Attempting a light tone*) Come, Rachel, what experience have you had with mothers whose babies have grown up to be bad? You—you talk like an old, old woman.

RACHEL: (*Without raising her eyes, quietly*) I *know* I'm not old; but, just the same I know that is true. (*Softly*) And I'm so sorry for the mothers.

MRS. LOVING: (*With a forced laugh*) Well, Miss Methuselah, how do you happen to know all this? Mothers whose babies grow up to be bad don't, as a rule, parade their faults before the world.

RACHEL: That's just it—that's *how* you know. They don't talk at all.

MRS. LOVING: (*Involuntarily*) Oh! (*Ceases to sew; looks at Rachel sharply; she is plainly worried. There is a long silence. Presently Rachel raises her eyes to Raphael's "Madonna" over the piano. Her expression becomes rapt; then, very softly, her eyes still on the picture, she plays and sings Nevin's "Mighty Lak A Rose"*)—

> Sweetest li'l feller,
> Ev'rybody knows;
> Dunno what to call him,
> But he mighty lak' a rose!
> Lookin' at his Mammy
> Wid eyes so shiny blue,
> Mek' you think that heav'n
> Is comin' clost ter you!
>
> W'en [he's] dar a sleepin'
> In his li'l place
> Think I see de angels
> Lookin' thro' de lace:
> W'en de dark is fallin',
> W'en de shadders creep,
> Den dey comes on tip-toe,
> Ter kiss him in his sleep.
>
> Sweetest li'l feller, etc.

(*With head still raised, after she has finished, she closes her eyes. Half to herself and slowly*) I think the loveliest thing of all the lovely things in this world is just (*almost in a whisper*) being a mother!

MRS. LOVING: (*Turns and laughs*) Well, of all the startling children, Rachel! I am getting to feel, when you're around as though I'm shut up with dynamite. What next? (*Rachel rises, goes slowly to her mother, and kneels down beside her. She does not touch her mother*). Why so serious, chickabiddy?

RACHEL: (*Slowly and quietly*) It is not kind to laugh at sacred things. When you laughed, it was as though you laughed—at God!

MRS. LOVING: (*Startled*) Rachel!

RACHEL: (*Still quietly*) It's true. It was the best in me that said that—it was God! (*Pauses*). And, Ma dear, if I believed that I should grow up and not be a mother, I'd pray to die now. I've thought about it a lot, Ma dear, and once I dreamed, and a voice said to me—oh! it was so real—"Rachel, you are to be a mother to little children." Wasn't that beautiful? Ever since I have known how Mary felt at the "Annunciation." (*Almost in a whisper*) God spoke to me through some one, and I believe. And it has explained so much to me. I know now why I just can't resist any child. I have to love it—it calls me—it—draws me. I want to take care of it, wash it, dress it, live for it. I want the feel of its little warm body against me, its breath on my neck, its hands against my face. (*Pauses thoughtfully for a few moments.*) Ma dear, here's something I don't understand: I love the little black and brown babies best of all. There is something about them that—that—clutches at my heart. Why—why—should they be—oh!—pathetic? I don't understand. It's dim. More than the other babies, I feel that I must protect them. They're in danger, but from what? I don't know. I've tried so hard to understand, but I can't. (*Her face radiant and beautiful*). Ma dear, I think their white teeth and the clear whites of their big black eyes and their dimples everywhere—are—are (*Breaks off*). And, Ma dear, because I love them best, I pray God every night to give me, when I grow up, little black and brown babies—to protect and guard. (*Wistfully*). Now, Ma dear, don't you see why you must never laugh at me again? Dear, dear, Ma dear? (*Buries her head in her mother's lap and sobs.*)

MRS. LOVING: (*For a few seconds, sits as though dazed, and then instinctively begins to caress the head in her lap. To herself*) And I suppose my experience is every mother's. Sooner or later—of a sudden she finds her own child a stranger to her. (*To Rachel, very tenderly*) Poor little girl! Poor little chickabiddy!

RACHEL: (*Raising her head*) Why do you say, "Poor little girl," like that? I don't understand. Why, Ma dear, I never saw tears in your eyes before. Is it—is it—because you know the things I do not understand? Oh! it *is* that.

MRS. LOVING: (*Simply*) Yes, Rachel, and I cannot save you.

RACHEL: Ma dear, you frighten me. Save me from *what*?

MRS. LOVING: Just life, my little chickabiddy!

RACHEL: Is life so terrible? I had found it mostly beautiful. How can life be terrible, when the world is full of little children?

MRS. LOVING: (*Very sadly*) Oh, Rachel! Rachel!

RACHEL: Ma dear, what have I said?

MRS. LOVING: (*Forcing a smile*) Why, the truth, of course, Rachel. Life is not terrible when there are little children— and you—and Tom—and a roof over our heads—and work—and food—and clothes—and sleep at night. (*Pauses*). Rachel, I am not myself today. I'm tired. Forget what I've said. Come, chickabiddy, wipe your eyes and smile. That's only an imitation smile, but it's better than none. Jump up now, and light the lamp for me, will you? Tom's late, isn't he? I shall want you to go, too, for the rolls and pie for supper.

RACHEL: (*Rises rather wearily and goes into the kitchenette. While she is out of the room Mrs. Loving does not move. She sits staring in front of her. The room for some time has been growing dark. Mrs. Loving can just be seen when Rachel reenters with the lamp. She places it on the small table near her mother, adjusts it, so the light falls on her mother's work, and then lowers the window shades at the windows. She still droops. Mrs. Loving, while Rachel is in the room, is industrious. Rachel puts on her hat and coat listlessly. She does not look in the glass.)* Where is the money, Ma dear? I'm ready.

350 MRS. LOVING: Before you go, Rachel, just give a look at the meat and see if it is cooking all right, will you, dearie?

RACHEL: *(Goes out into the kitchenette and presently returns)* It's all right, Ma dear.

MRS. LOVING: *(While Rachel is out of the room, she takes her pocket-book out of the machine-drawer, opens it, takes out money and gives it to Rachel upon her return)* A dozen brown rolls, Rachel. Be sure they're brown! And, I guess,— an apple pie. As you and Tom never seem to get enough apple pie, get the largest she has. And here is a quarter. Get

360 some candy—any kind *you* like, Chickabiddy. Let's have a party tonight, I feel extravagant. Why, Rachel! why are you crying?

RACHEL: Nothing, dear Ma dear. I'll be all right when I get in the air. Goodbye! *(Rushes out of the flat. Mrs. Loving sits idle. Presently the outer door of the flat opens and shuts with a bang, and Tom appears. Mrs. Loving begins to work as soon as she hears the banging door.)*

TOM: 'Lo, Ma! Where's Sis,—out? The door's off the latch. *(Kisses his mother and hangs hat in entryway).*

370 MRS. LOVING: *(Greeting him with the same beautiful smile with which she greeted Rachel)* Rachel just went after the rolls and pie. She'll be back in a few minutes. You're late, Tommy.

TOM: No, Ma—you forget—it's pay day. *(With decided shyness and awkwardness he hands her his wages.)* Here, Ma!

MRS. LOVING: *(Proudly counting it)* But, Tommy, this is every bit of it. You'll need some.

TOM: Not yet! *(Constrainedly)* I only wish—. Say, Ma, I hate to see you work so hard. *(Fiercely)* Some day—some

380 day—. *(Breaks off.)*

MRS. LOVING: Son, I'm as proud as though you had given me a million dollars.

TOM: *(Emphatically)* I may some day,—you see. *(Abruptly changing the subject)* Gee! Ma, I'm hungry. What's for dinner? Smell's good.

MRS. LOVING: Lamb and dumplings and rice.

TOM: Gee! I'm glad I'm living—and a pie too?

MRS. LOVING: Apple pie, Tommy.

TOM: Say, Ma, don't wake me up. And shall "muzzer's" own lit-

390 tle boy set the table?

MRS. LOVING: Thank you, Son.

TOM: *(Folds the green cloth, hangs it over the back of the arm-chair, gets white table-cloth from kitchenette and sets the table. The whole time he is whistling blithely a popular air. He lights one of the gas jets over the table)* Ma!

MRS. LOVING: Yes, Son.

TOM: I made "squad" today—I'm quarterback. Five other fellows tried to make it. We'll all have to buy new hats, now.

MRS. LOVING: *(With surprise)* Buy new hats! Why?

400 TOM: *(Makes a ridiculous gesture to show that his head and hers are both swelling)* Honest, Ma, I had to carry my hat in my hand tonight,—couldn't even get it to perch aloft.

MRS. LOVING: *(Smiling)* Well, I for one, Son, am not going to say anything to make you more conceited.

TOM: You don't *have* to say anything. Why, Ma, ever since I told you, you can almost look down your own back your head is so high. What? *(Mrs. Loving laughs. The outer door of the flat opens and shuts. Rachel's voice is heard.)*

RACHEL: *(Without)* My! that was a "drefful" climb, wasn't it? Ma, I've got something here for you. *(Appears in the door-* 410 *way carrying packages and leading a little boy by the hand. The little fellow is shy but smiling.)* Hello, Tommy! Here, take these things for me. This is Jimmy. Isn't he a dear? Come, Jimmy. *(Tom carries the packages into the kitchenette. Rachel leads Jimmy to Mrs. Loving.)* Ma dear, this is my brown baby. I'm going to take him right down stairs again. His mother is as sweet as can be, and let me bring him up just to see you. Jimmy, this is Ma dear. *(Mrs. Loving turns expectantly to see the child. Standing before her, he raises his face to hers with an engaging smile. Suddenly,* 420 *without word or warning, her body stiffens; her hands grip her sewing convulsively; her eyes stare. She makes no sound.)*

RACHEL: *(Frightened)* Ma dear! What is the matter? Tom! Quick! *(Tom reenters and goes to them).*

MRS. LOVING: *(Controlling herself with an effort and breathing hard)* Nothing, dears, nothing. I must be—I am—nervous tonight. *(With a forced smile)* How do-you-do, Jimmy? Now, Rachel—perhaps—don't you think—you had better take him back to his mother? Good-night, Jimmy! *(Eyes the* 430 *child in a fascinated way the whole time he is in the room. Rachel, very much perturbed, takes the child out.)* Tom, open that window, please! There! That's better! *(Still breathing deeply).* What a fool I am!

TOM: *(Patting his mother awkwardly on the back)* You're all pegged out, that's the trouble—working entirely too hard. Can't you stop for the night and go to bed right after supper?

MRS. LOVING: I'll see, Tommy dear. Now, I must look after the supper.                                                                          440

TOM: Huh! Well, I guess not. How old do you think Rachel and I are anyway? I see; you think we'll break some of this beau-ti-ful Hav-i-land china, we bought at the "Five and Ten Cent Store." *(To Rachel who has just reentered wearing a puzzled and worried expression. She is without hat and coat.)* Say, Rachel, do you think you're old enough?

RACHEL: Old enough for what, Tommy?

TOM: To dish up the supper for Ma.

RACHEL: *(With attempted sprightliness)* Ma dear thinks nothing can go on in this little flat unless she does it. Let's show 450 her a thing or two. *(They bring in the dinner. Mrs. Loving with trembling hands tries to sew. Tom and Rachel watch her covertly. Presently she gets up.)*

MRS. LOVING: I'll be back in a minute, children. *(Goes out the door that leads to the other rooms of the flat. Tom and Rachel look at each other.)*

RACHEL: *(In a low voice keeping her eyes on the door)* Why do you suppose she acted so strangely about Jimmy?

TOM: Don't know—nervous, I guess,—worn out. I wish— *(Breaks off).*                                                                        460

RACHEL: *(Slowly)* It may be that; but she hasn't been herself this afternoon. I wonder—. Look out! Here she comes!

TOM: *(In a whisper)* Liven her up. *(Rachel nods. Mrs. Loving*

*reenters. Both rush to her and lead her to her place at the right end of the table. She smiles and tries to appear cheerful. They sit down, Tom opposite Mrs. Loving and Rachel at the side facing front. Mrs. Loving asks grace. Her voice trembles. She helps the children bountifully, herself sparingly. Every once in a while she stops eating and stares*
470 *blankly into her plate; then, remembering where she is suddenly, looks around with a start and goes on eating. Tom and Rachel appear not to notice her.)*

TOM: Ma's "some" cook, isn't she?

RACHEL: Is she! Delmonico's isn't in it.

TOM: *(Presently)* Say, Rachel, do you remember that Reynolds boy in the fourth year?

RACHEL: Yes. You mean the one who is flat-nosed, freckled, and who squints and sneers?

TOM: *(Looking at Rachel admiringly)* The same.

480 RACHEL: *(Vehemently)* I hate him!

MRS. LOVING: Rachel, you do use such violent language. Why hate him?

RACHEL: I do—that's all.

TOM: Ma, if you saw him just once, you'd understand. No one likes him. But, then, what can you expect? His father's in "quod" doing time for something, I don't know just what. One of the fellows says he has a real decent mother, though. She never mentions him in any way, shape or form, he says. Hard on her, isn't it? Bet I'd keep my head shut too;—you'd
490 never get a yap out of me. *(Rachel looks up quickly at her mother; Mrs. Loving stiffens perceptibly, but keeps her eyes on her plate. Rachel catches Tom's eye; silently draws his attention to their mother; and shakes her head warningly at him).*

TOM: *(Continuing hastily and clumsily)* Well, anyway, he called me "Nigger" today. If his face isn't black, his eye is.

RACHEL: Good! Oh! Why did you let the other one go?

TOM: *(Grinning)* I knew he said things behind my back; but today he was hopping mad, because I made quarterback.
500 He didn't!

RACHEL: Oh, Tommy! How lovely! Ma dear, did you hear that? *(Chants)* Our Tommy's on the team! Our Tommy's on the team!

TOM: *(Trying not to appear pleased)* Ma dear, what did I say about er—er "capital" enlargements?

MRS. LOVING: *(Smiling)* You're right, Son.

TOM: I hope you got that "capital," Rachel. How's that for Latin knowledge? Eh?

RACHEL: I don't think much of your knowledge, Tommy dear;
510 but *(continuing to chant)* Our Tommy's on the team! Our Tommy's on the team! Our— *(Breaks off)*. I've a good mind to kiss you.

TOM: *(Threateningly)* Don't you dare.

RACHEL: *(Rising and going toward him)* I will! I will! I will!

TOM: *(Rising, too, and dodging her)* No, you don't, young lady. *(A tremendous tussle and scuffle ensues.)*

MRS. LOVING: *(Laughing)* For Heaven's sake! children, do stop playing and eat your supper. *(They nod brightly at each other behind her back and return smiling to the table).*

520 RACHEL: *(Sticking out her tongue at Tom)* I will!

TOM: *(Mimicking her)* You won't!

MRS. LOVING: Children! *(They eat for a time in silence).*

RACHEL: Ma dear, have you noticed Mary Shaw doesn't come

here much these days?

MRS. LOVING: Why, that's so, she doesn't. Have you two quarreled?

RACHEL: No, Ma dear. *(Uncomfortably.)* I—think I know the reason—but I don't like to say, unless I'm certain.

TOM: Well, I know. I've seen her lately with those two girls who have just come from the South. Twice she bowed stiffly, and   530 the last time made believe she didn't see me.

RACHEL: Then you think—? Oh! I was afraid it was that.

TOM: *(Bitterly)* Yes—we're "niggers"—that's why.

MRS. LOVING: *(Slowly and sadly)* Rachel, that's one of the things I can't save you from. I worried considerably about Mary, at first—you do take your friendships so seriously. I knew exactly how it would end. *(Pauses)*. And then I saw that if Mary Shaw didn't teach you the lesson—some one else would. They don't want you, dearies, when you and they grow up. You may have everything in your favor—but   540 they don't *dare* to like you.

RACHEL: I know all that is generally true—but I had hoped that Mary— *(Breaks off)*.

TOM: Well, I guess we can still go on living even if people don't speak to us. I'll never bow to *her* again—that's certain.

MRS. LOVING: But, Son, that wouldn't be polite, if she bowed to you first.

TOM: Can't help it. I guess I can be blind, too.

MRS. LOVING: *(Wearily)* Well—perhaps you are right—I don't know. It's the way I feel about it too—but—but I wish my   550 son always to be a *gentleman*.

TOM: If being a *gentleman* means not being a *man*—I don't wish to be one.

RACHEL: Oh! well, perhaps we're wrong about Mary—I hope we are. *(Sighs.)* Anyway, let's forget it. Tommy guess what I've got. *(Rises, goes out into entryway swiftly, and returns holding up a small bag.)* Ma dear treated. Guess!

TOM: Ma, you're a thoroughbred. Well, let's see—it's—a dozen dill pickles?

RACHEL: Oh! stop fooling.   560

TOM: I'm not. Tripe?

RACHEL: Silly!

TOM: Hog's jowl?

RACHEL: Ugh! Give it up—quarter-back.

TOM: Pig's feet?

RACHEL: *(In pretended disgust)* Oh! Ma dear—send him from the table. It's CANDY!

TOM: Candy? Funny, I never thought of that! And I was just about to say some nice, delicious chitlings. Candy! Well! Well! *(Rachel disdainfully carries the candy to her mother,*   570 *returns to her own seat with the bag and helps herself. She ignores Tom.)*

TOM: *(In an aggrieved voice)* You see, Ma, how she treats me. *(In affected tones)* I have a good mind, young lady to punish you, er—er corporeally speaking. Tut! Tut! I have a mind to master thee—I mean—you. Methinks that if I should advance upon you, apply, perchance, two or three digits to your glossy locks and extract—aha!—say, a strand—you would no more defy me. *(He starts to rise.)*

MRS. LOVING: *(Quickly and sharply)* Rachel! give Tom the   580 candy and stop playing. *(Rachel obeys. They eat in silence. The old depression returns. When the candy is all gone, Rachel pushes her chair back, and is just about to rise, when her mother, who is very evidently nerving herself for something, stops her.)* Just a moment, Rachel. *(Pauses, continuing slowly and very seriously.)* Tom and Rachel! I have been trying to make up my mind for some time whether a certain thing is my duty or not. Today—I have decided it is. You are old enough, now,—and I see you ought to be told. Do you

590 know what day this is? *(Both Tom and Rachel have been watching their mother intently.)* It's the sixteenth of October. Does that mean anything to either of you?

TOM *and* RACHEL: *(Wonderingly)* No.

MRS. LOVING: *(Looking at both of them thoughtfully, half to herself)* No—I don't know why it should. *(Slowly)* Ten years ago—today—your father and your half-brother died.

TOM: I do remember, now, that you told us it was in October.

RACHEL: *(With a sigh)* That explains—today.

MRS. LOVING: Yes, Rachel. *(Pauses.)* Do you know—how

600 they—died?

TOM *and* RACHEL: Why, no.

MRS. LOVING: Did it ever strike you as strange—that they—died—the same day?

TOM: Well, yes.

RACHEL: We often wondered, Tom and I; but—but somehow we never quite dared to ask you. You—you—always refused to talk about them, you know, Ma dear.

MRS. LOVING: Did you think—that—perhaps—the reason—I—I—wouldn't   talk   about   them—was—because,

610 because—I was ashamed—of them? *(Tom and Rachel look uncomfortable.)*

RACHEL: Well, Ma dear—we—we—did—wonder.

MRS. LOVING: *(Questioningly)* And you thought?

RACHEL: *(Haltingly)* W-e-l-l—

MRS. LOVING: *(Sharply)* Yes?

TOM: Oh! come, now, Rachel, you know we haven't bothered about it at all. Why should we? We've been happy.

MRS. LOVING: But when you have thought—you've been ashamed? *(Intensely)* Have you?

620 TOM: Now, Ma, aren't you making a lot out of nothing?

MRS. LOVING: *(Slowly)* No. *(Half to herself)* You evade—both—of you. You *have* been ashamed. And I never dreamed until today you *could* take it this way. How blind—how almost criminally blind, I have been.

RACHEL: *(Tremulously)* Oh! Ma dear, don't! *(Tom and Rachel watch their mother anxiously and uncomfortably. Mrs. Loving is very evidently nerving herself for something.)*

MRS. LOVING: *(Very slowly, with restrained emotion)* Tom—and Rachel!

630 TOM: Ma!

RACHEL: Ma dear! *(A tense, breathless pause.)*

MRS. LOVING: *(Bracing herself)* They—they—were lynched!!

TOM and RACHEL: *(In a whisper)* Lynched!

MRS. LOVING: *(Slowly, laboring under strong but restrained emotion)* Yes—by Christian people—in a Christian land. We found out afterwards they were all church members in good standing—the best people. *(A silence.)* Your father was a man among men. He was a fanatic. He was a Saint!

TOM: *(Breathing with difficulty)* Ma—can you—will you—tell

640 us—about it?

MRS. LOVING: I believe it to be my duty. *(A silence.)* When I married your father I was a widow. My little George was seven years old. From the very beginning he worshiped your

father. He followed him around—just like a little dog. All children were like that with him. I myself have never seen anybody like him. "Big" seems to fit him better than any other word. He was big-bodied—big-souled. His loves were big and his hates. You can imagine, then, how the wrongs of the Negro—ate into his soul. *(Pauses.)* He was utterly fearless. *(A silence.)* He edited and owned, for several years, a 650 small negro paper. In it he said a great many daring things. I used to plead with him to be more careful. I was always afraid for him. For a long time, nothing happened—he was too important to the community. And then—one night—ten years ago—a mob made up of the respectable people in the town lynched an innocent black man—and what was worse—they knew him to be innocent. A white man was guilty. I never saw your father so wrought up over anything: he couldn't eat; he couldn't sleep; he brooded night and day over it. And then—realizing fully the great risk he was run- 660 ning, although I begged him not to—and all his friends also—he deliberately and calmly went to work and published a most terrific denunciation of that mob. The old prophets in the Bible were not more terrible than he. A day or two later, he received an anonymous letter, very evidently from an educated man, calling upon him to retract his words in the next issue. If he refused his life was threatened. The next week's issue contained an arraignment as frightful, if not more so, than the previous one. Each word was white-hot, searing. That night, some dozen masked men came to 670 our house.

RACHEL: *(Moaning)* Oh, Ma dear! Ma dear!

MRS. LOVING: *(Too absorbed to hear)* We were not asleep—your father and I. They broke down the front door and made their way to our bedroom. Your father kissed me—and took up his revolver. It was always loaded. They broke down the door. *(A silence. She continues slowly and quietly)* I tried to shut my eyes—I could not. Four masked men fell—they did not move any more—after a little. *(Pauses.)* Your father was finally overpowered and dragged out. In the hall—my little 680 seventeen-year-old George tried to rescue him. Your father begged him not to interfere. He paid no attention. It ended in their dragging them both out. *(Pauses.)* My little George—was—a man! *(Controls herself with an effort.)* He never made an outcry. His last words to me were: "Ma, I am glad to go with Father." I could only nod to him. *(Pauses.)* While they were dragging them down the steps, I crept into the room where you were. You were both asleep. Rachel, I remember, was smiling. I knelt down by you—and covered my ears with my hands—and waited. I could not pray—I 690 couldn't for a long time—afterwards. *(A silence.)* It was very still when I finally uncovered my ears. The only sounds were the faint rustle of leaves and the "tap-tapping of the twig of a tree" against the window. I hear it still—sometimes in my dreams. *It was the tree—where they were. (A silence.)* While I had knelt there waiting—I had made up my mind what to do. I dressed myself and then I woke you both up and dressed you. *(Pauses.)* We set forth. It was a black, still night. Alternately dragging you along and carrying you—I walked five miles to the house of some friends. They took us 700 in, and we remained there until I had seen my dead laid comfortably at rest. They lent me money to come North—I couldn't bring you up—in the South. *(A silence.)* Always re-

member this: There never lived anywhere—or at any time—any two whiter or more beautiful souls. God gave me one for a husband and one for a son and I am proud. (*Brokenly*) You—must—be—proud—too. (*A long silence. Mrs. Loving bows her head in her hands. Tom controls himself with an effort. Rachel creeps softly to her mother, kneels be-*
710  *side her and lifts the hem of her dress to her lips. She does not dare touch her. She adores her with her eyes.*)

MRS. LOVING: (*Presently raising her head and glancing at the clock*) Tom, it's time, now, for you to go to work. Rachel and I will finish up here.

TOM: (*Still laboring under great emotion goes out into the entryway and comes back and stands in the doorway with his cap. He twirls it around and around nervously*) I want you to know, Ma, before I go—how—how proud I am. Why, I didn't believe two people could be like that—and live. And
720  then to find out that one—was your own father—and one—your own brother.—It's wonderful! I'm—not much yet, Ma, but—I've—I've just got to be something now. (*Breaks off.*) (*His face becomes distorted with passion and hatred.*) When I think—when I think—of those devils with white skins—living somewhere today—living and happy—I—see—red! I—I—goodbye! (*Rushes out, the door bangs.*)

MRS. LOVING: (*Half to herself*) I was afraid—of just that. I wonder—if I did the wise thing—after all.

RACHEL: (*With a gesture infinitely tender, puts her arms
730  around her mother*) Yes, Ma dear, you did. And, hereafter, Tom and I share and share alike with you. To think, Ma dear, of ten years of this—all alone. It's wicked! (*A short silence.*)

MRS. LOVING: And, Rachel, about that dear, little boy, Jimmy.

RACHEL: Now, Ma dear, tell me tomorrow. You've stood enough for one day.

MRS. LOVING: No, it's better over and done with—all at once. If I had seen that dear child suddenly any other day than this—I might have borne it better. When he lifted his little
740  face to me—and smiled—for a moment—I thought it was the end—of all things. Rachel, he is the image of my boy—my George!

RACHEL: Ma dear!

MRS. LOVING: And, Rachel—it will hurt—to see him again.

RACHEL: I understand, Ma dear. (*A silence. Suddenly*) Ma dear, I am beginning to see—to understand—so much. (*Slowly and thoughtfully*) Ten years ago, all things being equal, Jimmy might have been—George? Isn't that so?

MRS. LOVING: Why—yes, if I understand you.

750  RACHEL: I guess that doesn't sound very clear. It's only getting clear to me, little by little. Do you mind my thinking out loud to you?

MRS. LOVING: No, chickabiddy.

RACHEL: If Jimmy went South now—and grew up—he might be—a George?

MRS. LOVING: Yes.

RACHEL: Then, the South is full of tens, hundreds, thousands of little boys, who, one day may be—and some of them with certainty—Georges?

760  MRS. LOVING: Yes, Rachel.

RACHEL: And the little babies, the dear, little, helpless babies, being born today—now—and those who will be, tomorrow, and all the tomorrows to come—have *that* sooner or later to

look forward to? They will laugh and play and sing and be happy and grow up, perhaps, and be ambitious—just for *that*!

MRS. LOVING: Yes, Rachel.

RACHEL: Then, everywhere, everywhere, throughout the South, there are hundreds of dark mothers who live in fear,  770
terrible, suffocating fear, whose rest by night is broken, and whose joy by day in their babies on their hearts is three parts—pain. Oh, I know this is true—for this is the way I should feel, if I were little Jimmy's mother. How horrible! Why—it would be more merciful—to strangle the little things at birth. And so this nation—this white Christian nation—has deliberately set its curse upon the most beautiful—the most holy thing in life—motherhood! Why—it—makes—you doubt—God!

MRS. LOVING: Oh, hush! little girl. Hush!

RACHEL: (*Suddenly with a great cry*) Why, Ma dear, *you know.*  780
*You* were a *mother, George's mother.* So, this is what it means. Oh, Ma dear! Ma dear! (*Faints in her mother's arms.*)

## —ACT TWO—

TIME: *October sixteenth, four years later; seven o'clock in the morning.*

SCENE: *The same room. There have been very evident improvements made. The room is not so bare; it is cosier. On the shelf, before each window, are potted red geraniums. At the windows are green denim drapery curtains covering fresh white dotted Swiss inner curtains. At each doorway are green denim portieres. On the wall between the kitchenette and the entrance to the outer rooms of the flat, a new picture is hanging, Millet's "The Man With the Hoe." Hanging against the side of the run that faces front is Watts's "Hope." There is another easy-chair at the left front. The table in the center is covered with a white table-cloth. A small asparagus fern is in the middle of this. When the curtain rises there is the clatter of dishes in the kitchenette. Presently Rachel enters with dishes and silver in her hands. She is clad in a bungalow apron. She is noticeably all of four years older. She frowns as she sets the table. There is a set expression about the mouth. A child's voice is heard from the rooms within.*

JIMMY: (*Still unseen*) Ma Rachel!

RACHEL: (*Pauses and smiles*) What is it, Jimmy boy?

JIMMY: (*Appearing in rear doorway, half-dressed, breathless, and tremendously excited over something. Rushes toward Rachel*) Three guesses! Three guesses! Ma Rachel!

RACHEL: (*Her whole face softening*) Well, let's see—maybe there is a circus in town.  790

JIMMY: No siree! (*In a sing-song*) You're not right! You're not right!

RACHEL: Well, maybe Ma Loving's going to take you somewhere.

JIMMY: No! (*Vigorously shaking his head*) It's—

RACHEL: (*Interrupting quickly*) You said I could have three guesses, honey. I've only had two.

JIMMY: I thought you had three. How many are three?

RACHEL: (*Counting on her fingers*) One! Two! Three! I've only

800 had one! two!—See? Perhaps Uncle Tom is going to give you some candy.

JIMMY: (*Dancing up and down*) No! No! No! (*Catches his breath*) I leaned over the bath-tub, way over, and got hold of the chain with the button on the end, and dropped it into the little round place in the bottom. And then I runned lots and lots of water in the tub and climbed over and fell in splash! just like a big stone; (*Loudly*) and took a bath all by myself alone.

RACHEL: (*Laughing and hugging him*) All by yourself, honey?

810 You ran the water, too, boy, not "runned" it. What I want to know is, where was Ma Loving all this time?

JIMMY: I stole in "creepy-creep" and looked at Ma Loving and she was awful fast asleep. (*Proudly*) Ma Rachel, I'm a "nawful," big boy now, aren't I? I are almost a man, aren't I?

RACHEL: Oh! Boy, I'm getting tired of correcting you—"I am almost a man, am I not?" Jimmy, boy, what will Ma Rachel do, if you grow up? Why, I won't have a little boy any more! Honey, you mustn't grow up, do you hear? You mustn't.

JIMMY: Oh, yes, I must; and you'll have me just the same, Ma

820 Rachel. I'm going to be a policeman and make lots of money for you and Ma Loving and Uncle Tom, and I'm going to buy you some trains and fire-engines, and little, cunning ponies, and some rabbits, and some great 'normous banks full of money—lots of it. And then, we are going to live in a great, big castle and eat lots of ice cream, all the time, and drink lots and lots of nice pink lemonade.

RACHEL: What a generous Jimmy boy! (*Hugs him.*) Before I give you "morning kiss," I must see how clean my boy is. (*Inspects teeth, ears and neck.*) Jimmy, you're sweet and clean

830 enough to eat. (*Kisses him; he tries to strangle her with hugs.*) Now the hands. Oh! Jimmy, look at those nails! Oh! Jimmy! (*Jimmy wriggles and tries to get his hands away.*) Honey, get my file off of my bureau and go to Ma Loving; she must be awake by this time. Why, honey, what's the matter with your feet?

JIMMY: I don't know. I thought they looked kind of queer, myself. What's the matter with them?

RACHEL: (*Laughing*) You have your shoes on the wrong feet.

JIMMY: (*Bursts out laughing*) Isn't that most 'normously funny?

840 I'm a case, aren't I—(*pauses thoughtfully*) I mean—am I not, Ma Rachel?

RACHEL: Yes, honey, a great big case of molasses. Come, you must hurry now, and get dressed. You don't want to be late for school, you know.

JIMMY: Ma Rachel! (*Shyly*) I—I have been making something for you all the morning—ever since I waked up. It's awful nice. It's—stoop down, Ma Rachel, please—a great, big (*puts both arms about her neck and gives her a noisy kiss. Rachel kisses him in return, then pushes his head back. For*

850 *a long moment they look at each other; and, then, laughing joyously, he makes believe he is a horse, and goes prancing out of the room. Rachel, with a softer, gentler expression, continues setting the table. Presently, Mrs. Loving, bent and worn-looking, appears in the doorway in the rear. She limps a trifle.*)

MRS. LOVING: Good morning, dearie. How's my little girl, this morning? (*Looks around the room.*) Why, where's Tom? I was certain I heard him running the water in the tub, sometime ago. (*Limps into the room.*)

RACHEL: (*Laughing*) Tom isn't up yet. Have you seen Jimmy? 860

MRS. LOVING: Jimmy? No. I didn't know he was awake, even.

RACHEL: (*Going to her mother and kissing her*) Well! What do you think of that! I sent the young gentleman to you, a few minutes ago, for help with his nails. He is very much grown up this morning, so I suppose that explains why he didn't come to you. Yesterday, all day, you know, he was a puppy. No one knows what he will be by tomorrow. All of this, Ma dear, is preliminary to telling you that Jimmy boy has stolen a march on you, this morning.

MRS. LOVING: Stolen a march! How? 870

RACHEL: It appears that he took his bath all by himself and, as a result, he is so conceited, peacocks aren't in it with him.

MRS. LOVING: I heard the water running and thought, of course, it was Tom. Why, the little rascal! I must go and see how he has left things. I was just about to wake him up.

RACHEL: Rheumatism's not much better this morning, Ma dear. (*Confronting her mother*) Tell me the truth, now, did you or did you not try that liniment I bought you yesterday?

MRS. LOVING: (*Guiltily*) Well, Rachel, you see—it was this way, I was—I was so tired, last night,—I—I really forgot it. 880

RACHEL: I thought as much. Shame on you!

MRS. LOVING: As soon as I walk around a bit it will be all right. It always is. It's bad, when I first get up—that's all. I'll be spry enough in a few minutes. (*Limps to the door; pauses*) Rachel, I don't know why the thought should strike me, but how very strangely things turn out. If any one had told me four years ago that Jimmy would be living with us, I should have laughed at him. Then it hurt to see him; now it would hurt not to. (*Softly*) Rachel, sometimes—I wonder—if, perhaps, God—hasn't relented a little—and given me back my 890 boy,—my George.

RACHEL: The whole thing was strange, wasn't it?

MRS. LOVING: Yes, God's ways are strange and often very beautiful; perhaps all would be beautiful—if we only understood.

RACHEL: God's ways are certainly very mysterious. Why, of all the people in this apartment-house, should Jimmy's father and mother be the only two to take the smallpox, and the only two to die! It's queer!

MRS. LOVING: It doesn't seem like two years ago, does it? 900

RACHEL: Two years, Ma dear! Why it's three the third of January.

MRS. LOVING: Are you sure, Rachel?

RACHEL: (*Gently*) I don't believe I could ever forget that, Ma dear.

MRS. LOVING: No, I suppose not. That is one of the differences between youth and old age—youth attaches tremendous importance to dates,—old age does not.

RACHEL: (*Quickly*) Ma dear, don't talk like that. You're not old.

MRS. LOVING: Oh! yes, I am, dearie. It's sixty long years since I 910 was born; and I am much older than that, much older.

RACHEL: Please, Ma dear, please!

MRS. LOVING: (*Smiling*) Very well, dearie, I won't say it any more. (*A pause*). By the way,—how—does Tom strike you, these days?

RACHEL: (*Avoiding her mother's eye*) The same old, bantering, cheerful Tom. Why?

MRS. LOVING: I know he's all that, dearie, but it isn't possible for him to be really cheerful. (*Pauses; goes on wistfully*)

920 When you are little, we mothers can kiss away all the trouble, but when you grow up—and go out—into the world—and get hurt—we are helpless. There is nothing we can do.

RACHEL: Don't worry about Tom, Ma dear, he's game. He doesn't show the white feather.

MRS. LOVING: Did you see him, when he came in, last night?

RACHEL: Yes.

MRS. LOVING: Had he had—any luck?

RACHEL: No. (*Firmly*) Ma dear, we may as well face it—it's hopeless, I'm afraid.

930 MRS. LOVING: I'm afraid—you are right. (*Shakes her head sadly*) Well, I'll go and see how Jimmy has left things and wake up Tom, if he isn't awake yet. It's the waking up in the mornings that's hard. (*Goes limping out rear door. Rachel frowns as she continues going back and forth between the kitchenette and the table. Presently Tom appears in the door at the rear. He watches Rachel several moments before he speaks or enters. Rachel looks grim enough.*)

TOM: (*Entering and smiling*) Good-morning, "Merry Sunshine"! Have you, perhaps, been taking a—er—prolonged
940 draught of that very delightful beverage—vinegar? (*Rachel, with a knife in her hand, looks up unsmiling. In pretended fright*) I take it all back, I'm sure. May I request, humbly, that before I press my chaste, morning salute upon your forbidding lips, that you—that you—that you—er—in some way rid yourself of that—er—knife? (*Bows as Rachel puts it down.*) I thank you. (*He comes to her and tips her head back; gently*) What's the matter with my little Sis?

RACHEL: (*Her face softening*) Tommy dear, don't mind me. I'm getting wicked, I guess. At present I feel just like—like cur-
950 dled milk. Once upon a time, I used to have quite a nice disposition, didn't I, Tommy?

TOM: (*Smiling*) Did you, indeed! I'm not going to flatter you. Well, brace yourself, old lady. Ready, One! Two! Three! Go! (*Kisses her, then puts his hands on either side of her face, and raising it, looks down into it.*) You're a pretty, decent little sister, Sis, that's what T. Loving thinks about it; and he knows a thing or two. (*Abruptly looking around*) Has the paper come yet?

RACHEL: I haven't looked, it must have, though, by this time.
960 (*Tom, hands in his pockets, goes into the vestibule. He whistles. The outer door opens and closes, and presently he saunters back, newspaper in hand. He lounges carelessly in the arm-chair and looks at Rachel.*)

TOM: May T. Loving be of any service to you?

RACHEL: Service! How?

TOM: May he run, say, any errands, set the table, cook the breakfast? Anything?

RACHEL: (*Watching the lazy figure*) You look like working.

TOM: (*Grinning*) It's at least—polite—to offer.

970 RACHEL: You can't do anything; I don't trust you to do it right. You may just sit there, and read your paper—and try to behave yourself.

TOM: (*In affectedly meek tones*) Thank you, ma'am. (*Opens the paper, but does not read. Jimmy presently enters riding around the table on a cane. Rachel peeps in from the kitchenette and smiles. Tom puts down his paper.*) 'Lo! Big Fellow, what's this?

JIMMY: (*Disgustedly*) How can I hear? I'm miles and miles away yet. (*Prances around and around the room; presently*

stops near Tom, attempting a gruff voice) Good-morning! 980

TOM: (*Lowering his paper again*) Bless my stars! Who's this? Well, if it isn't Mr. Mason! How-do-you-do, Mr. Mason? That's a beautiful horse you have there. He limps a trifle in his left, hind, front foot, though.

JIMMY: He doesn't!

TOM: He does!

JIMMY: (*Fiercely*) He doesn't!

TOM: (*As fiercely*) I say he does!

MRS. LOVING: (*Appearing in the doorway in the rear*) For Heaven's sake! What is this? Good-morning, Tommy. 990

TOM: (*Rising and going toward his mother, Jimmy following astride of the cane in his rear*) Good-morning, Ma. (*Kisses her; lays his head on her shoulder and makes believe he is crying; in a high falsetto*) Ma! Jimmy says his horse doesn't limp in his hind, front right leg, and I say he does.

JIMMY: (*Throws his cane aside, rolls on the floor and kicks up his heels. He roars with laughter*) I think Uncle Tom is funnier than any clown in the "Kickus."

TOM: (*Raising his head and looking down at Jimmy; Rachel stands in the kitchenette doorway*) In the *what*, Jimmy? 1000

JIMMY: In the "kickus," of course.

TOM: "Kickus"! "Kickus"! Oh, Lordy! (*Tom and Rachel shriek with laughter; Mrs. Loving looks amused; Jimmy, very much affronted, gets upon his feet again. Tom leans over and swings Jimmy high in the air.*) Boy, you'll be the death of me yet. Circus, son! Circus!

JIMMY: (*From on high, soberly and with injured dignity*) Well, I thinks "Kickus" and circus are very much alike. Please put me down.

RACHEL: (*From the doorway*) We laugh, honey, because we 1010 love you so much.

JIMMY: (*Somewhat mollified, to Tom*) Is that so, Uncle Tom?

TOM: Surest thing in the world! (*Severely*) Come, get down, young man. Don't you know you'll wear my arms out? Besides, there is something in my lower vest pocket, that's just dying to come to you. Get down, I say.

JIMMY: (*Laughing*) How can I get down? (*Wriggles around.*)

TOM: How should I know? Just get down, of course. (*Very suddenly puts Jimmy down on his feet. Jimmy tries to climb up over him.*) 1020

JIMMY: Please sit down, Uncle Tom.

TOM: (*In feigned surprise*) Sit down! What for?

JIMMY: (*Pummeling him with his little fists, loudly*) Why, you said there was something for me in your pocket.

TOM: (*Sitting down*) So I did. How forgetful I am!

JIMMY: (*Finding a bright, shiny penny, shrieks*) Oh! Oh! Oh! (*Climbs up and kisses Tom noisily.*)

TOM: Why, Jimmy! You embarrass me. My! My!

JIMMY: What is 'barrass?

TOM: You make me blush. 1030

JIMMY: What's that?

MRS. LOVING: Come, come, children! Rachel has the breakfast on the table. (*Tom sits in Jimmy's place and Jimmy tries to drag him out.*)

TOM: What's the matter, now?

JIMMY: You're in *my* place.

TOM: Well, can't you sit in mine?

JIMMY: (*Wistfully*) I wants to sit by my Ma Rachel.

TOM: Well, so do I.

1040 RACHEL: Tom, stop teasing Jimmy. Honey, don't you let him bother you; ask him please prettily.

JIMMY: Please prettily, Uncle Tom.

TOM: Oh! well then. (*Gets up and takes his own place, They sit as they did in Act I, only Jimmy sits between Tom, at the end, and Rachel.*)

JIMMY: (*Loudly*) Oh, goody! goody! goody! We've got sau-sa-ges.

MRS. LOVING: Sh!

JIMMY: (*Silenced for a few moments; Rachel ties a big napkin*
1050  *around his neck, and prepares his breakfast. He breaks forth again suddenly and excitedly*) Uncle Tom!

TOM: Sir?

JIMMY: I took a bath this morning, all by myself alone, in the bath-tub, and I ranned, no (*Doubtfully*) I runned, I think— the water all in it, and got in it all by myself; and Ma Loving thought it was you; but it was *me*.

TOM: (*In feignedly severe tones*) See here, young man, this won't do. Don't you know I'm the only one who is allowed to do that here? It's a perfect waste of water—that's what
1060  it is.

JIMMY: (*Undaunted*) Oh! no, you're not the only one, 'cause Ma Loving and Ma Rachel and me—alls takes baths every single morning. So, there!

TOM: You 'barrass me. (*Jimmy opens his mouth to ask a question; Tom quickly*) Young gentleman, your mouth is open. Close it, sir; close it.

MRS. LOVING: Tom, you're as big a child exactly as Jimmy.

TOM: (*Bowing to right and left*) You compliment me. I thank you, I am sure.

(*They finish in silence.*)

1070 JIMMY: (*Sighing with contentment*) I'm through, Ma Rachel.

MRS. LOVING: Jimmy, you're a big boy, now, aren't you? (*Jimmy nods his head vigorously and looks proud.*) I wonder if you're big enough to wash your own hands, this morning?

JIMMY: (*Shrilly*) Yes, ma'am.

MRS. LOVING: Well, if they're beautifully clean, I'll give you another penny.

JIMMY: (*Excitedly to Rachel*) Please untie my napkin, Ma Rachel! (*Rachel does so.*) "Excoose" me, please.

MRS. LOVING and RACHEL: Certainly. (*Jimmy climbs down and*
1080  *rushes out at the rear doorway.*)

MRS. LOVING: (*Solemnly and slowly; breaking the silence*) Rachel, do you know what day this is?

RACHEL: (*Looking at her plate; slowly*) Yes, Ma dear.

MRS. LOVING: Tom.

TOM: (*Grimly and slowly*) Yes, Ma.

(*A silence.*)

MRS. LOVING: (*Impressively*) We must never—as long—as we live—forget this day.

RACHEL: No, Ma dear.

TOM: No, Ma.

(*Another silence.*)

1090 TOM: (*Slowly; as though thinking aloud*) I hear people talk about God's justice—and I wonder. There, are you, Ma. There isn't a sacrifice—that you haven't made. You're still working your fingers to the bone—sewing—just so all of us

may keep on living. Rachel is a graduate in Domestic Science; she was high in her class; most of the girls below her in rank have positions in the schools. I'm an electrical engineer—and I've tried steadily for several months—to practice my profession. It seems our educations aren't of much use to us: we aren't allowed to make good—because our skins are dark. (*Pauses.*) And, in the South today, there are 1100 white men—(*Controls himself.*) They have everything; they're well-dressed, well-fed, well-housed; they're prosperous in business; they're important politically; they're pillars in the church. I know all this is true—I've inquired. Their children (our ages, some of them) are growing up around them; and they are having a square deal handed out to them—college, position, wealth, and best of all, freedom, without galling restrictions, to work out their own salvations. With ability, they may become—anything; and all this will be true of their children's children after them. (*A pause.*) 1110 Look at us—and look at them. We are destined to failure— they, to success. Their children shall grow up in hope; ours, in despair. Our hands are clean;—theirs are red with blood—red with the blood of a noble man—and a boy. They're nothing but low, cowardly, bestial murderers. The scum of the earth shall succeed. —God's justice, I suppose.

MRS. LOVING: (*Rising and going to Tom; brokenly*) Tom, promise me—one thing.

TOM: (*Rises gently*) What is it, Ma?

MRS. LOVING: That—you'll try—not to lose faith—in God. I've 1120 been where you are now—and it's black. Tom, we don't understand God's ways. My son, I know, now—He is beautiful. Tom, won't you try to believe, again?

TOM: (*Slowly, but not convincingly*) I'll try, Ma.

MRS. LOVING: (*Sighs*) Each one, I suppose, has to work out his own salvation. (*After a pause*) Rachel, if you'll get Jimmy ready, I'll take him to school. I've got to go down town shopping for a customer, this morning. (*Rachel rises and goes out the rear doorway; Mrs. Loving, limping very slightly now, follows. She turns and looks back yearningly at Tom, who* 1130 *has seated himself again, and is staring unseeingly at his plate. She goes out. Tom sits without moving until he hears Mrs. Loving's voice within and Rachel's faintly; then he gets the paper, sits in the arm-chair and pretends to read.*)

MRS. LOVING: (*From within*) A yard, you say, Rachel? You're sure that will be enough. Oh! you've measured it. Anything else?—What?—Oh! all right. I'll be back by one o'clock, anyway. Good-bye. (*Enters with Jimmy. Both are dressed for the street. Tom looks up brightly at Jimmy.*)

TOM: Hello! Big Fellow, where are you taking *my* mother, I'd 1140 like to know? This is a pretty kettle of fish.

JIMMY: (*Laughing*) Aren't you funny, Uncle Tom! Why, I'm not taking her anywhere. She's taking me. (*Importantly*) I'm going to school.

TOM: Big Fellow, come here. (*Jimmy comes with a rush*). Now, where's that penny I gave you? No, I don't want to see it. All right. Did Ma Loving give you another? (*Vigorous noddings of the head from Jimmy.*) I wish you to promise me solemnly—Now, listen! Here, don't wriggle so! not to buy— Listen! too many pints of ice-cream with my penny. Under- 1150 stand?

JIMMY: (*Very seriously*) Yes, Uncle Tom, cross my "tummy"! I promise.

TOM: Well, then, you may go. I guess that will be all for the present. (*Jimmy loiters around looking up wistfully into his face.*) Well?

JIMMY: Haven't you—aren't you—isn't you—forgetting something?

TOM: (*Grabbing at his pockets*) Bless my stars! what now?

1160 JIMMY: If you could kind of lean over this way. (*Tom leans forward*). No, not that way. (*Tom leans toward the side away from Jimmy*). No, this way, this way! (*Laughs and pummels him with his little fists.*) This way!

TOM: (*Leaning toward Jimmy*) Well, why didn't you say so, at first?

JIMMY: (*Puts his arms around Tom's neck and kisses him*) Good-bye, dear old Uncle Tom. (*Tom catches him and hugs him hard.*) I likes to be hugged like that—I can taste—sau-sa-ges.

1170 TOM: You 'barrass me, son. Here, Ma, take your boy. Now remember all I told you, Jimmy.

JIMMY: I 'members.

MRS. LOVING: God bless you, Tom. Good luck.

JIMMY: (*To Tom*) God bless you, Uncle Tom. Good luck!

TOM: (*Much affected, but with restraint, rising*) Thank you—Good-bye. (*Mrs. Loving and Jimmy go out through the vestibule. Tom lights a cigarette and tries to read the paper. He soon sinks into a brown study. Presently Rachel enters humming. Tom relights his cigarette; and Rachel proceeds to clear the table. In the midst of this, the bell rings three dis-*
1180 *tinct times.*)

RACHEL *and* TOM: John!

TOM: I wonder what's up—It's rather early for him.—I'll go. (*Rises leisurely and goes out into the vestibule. The outer door opens and shuts. Men's voices are heard. Tom and John Strong enter. During the ensuing conversation Rachel finishes clearing the table, takes the fern off, puts on the green table-cloth, places a doily carefully in the centre, and replaces the fern. She apparently pays no attention to the con-*
1190 *versation between her brother and Strong. After she has finished, she goes to the kitchenette. The rattle of dishes can be heard now and then.*)

RACHEL: (*Brightly*) Well, stranger, how does it happen you're out so early in the morning?

STRONG: I hadn't seen any of you for a week, and I thought I'd come by, on my way to work, and find out how things are going. There is no need of asking how you are, Rachel. And the mother and the boy?

RACHEL: Ma dear's rheumatism still holds on. —Jimmy's fine.

1200 STRONG: I'm sorry to hear that your mother is not well. There isn't a remedy going that my mother doesn't know about. I'll get her advice and let you know. (*Turning to Tom*) Well, Tom, how goes it? (*Strong and Tom sit.*)

TOM: (*Smiling grimly*) There's plenty of "go," but no "git there."

STRONG: I was hoping for better news.

TOM: If I remember rightly, not so many years ago, you tried—and failed. Then, a colored man had hardly a ghost of a show;—now he hasn't even the ghost of a ghost.

(RACHEL *has finished and goes into the kitchenette.*)

1210 STRONG: That's true enough. (*A pause.*) What are you going to do?

TOM: (*Slowly*) I'll do this little "going act" of mine the rest of the week; (*pauses*) and then, I'll do anything I can get to do. If necessary, I suppose, I can be a "White-wing."

STRONG: Tom, I came— (*Breaks off; continuing slowly*) Six years ago, I found I was up against a stone wall—your experience, you see, to the letter. I couldn't let my mother starve, so I became a waiter. (*Pauses.*) I studied waiting; I made a science of it, an art. In a comparatively short time, I'm a head-waiter and I'm up against another stonewall. I've 1220 reached my limit. I'm thirty-two now, and I'll die a head-waiter. (*A pause.*) College friends, so-called, and acquaintances used to come into the restaurant. One or two at first—attempted to commiserate with me. They didn't do it again. I waited upon them—I did my best. Many of them tipped me. (*Pauses and smiles grimly.*) I can remember my first tip, still. They come in yet; many of them are already powers, not only in this city, but in the country. Some of them make a personal request that I wait upon them. I am an artist, now, in my proper sphere. They tip me well, ex- 1230 tremely well—the larger the tip, the more pleased they are with me. Because of me, in their own eyes, they're philanthropists. Amusing, isn't it? I can stand their attitude now. My philosophy—learned hard, is to make the best of everything you can, and go on. At best, life isn't so very long. You're wondering why I'm telling you all this. I wish you to see things exactly as they are. There are many disadvantages and some advantages in being a waiter. My mother can live comfortably; I am able, even, to see that she gets some of the luxuries. Tom, it's this way—I can always get you a job 1240 as a waiter; I'll teach you the art. If you care to begin the end of the week—all right. And remember this, as long as I keep my job—this offer holds good.

TOM: I—I— (*Breaks off*) Thank you. (*A pause; then smiling wryly*) I guess it's safe enough to say, you'll see me at the end of the week. John you're— (*Breaking off again. A silence interrupted presently by the sound of much vigorous rapping on the outer door of the flat. Rachel appears and crosses over to the vestibule.*) Hear the racket! My kiddies gently begging for admittance. It's about twenty minutes of 1250 nine, isn't it? (*Tom nods.*) I thought so. (*Goes into the entryway; presently reappears with a group of six little girls ranging in age from five to about nine. All are fighting to be close to her; and all are talking at once. There is one exception: the smallest tot is self-possessed and self-sufficient. She carries a red geranium in her hand and gives it her full attention.*)

LITTLE MARY: It's my turn to get "Morning kiss" first, this morning, Miss Rachel. You kissed Louise first yesterday. You said you'd kiss us "alphabetically." (*Ending in a shriek.*) 1260 You promised! (*Rachel kisses Mary, who subsides.*)

LITTLE NANCY: (*Imperiously*) Now, me. (*Rachel kisses her, and then amid shrieks, recriminations, pulling of hair, jostling, etc., she kisses the rest. The small tot is still oblivious to everything that is going on.*)

RACHEL: (*Laughing*) You children will pull me limb from limb; and then I'll be all dead; and you'll be sorry—see, if you aren't. (*They fall back immediately. Tom and John watch in amused silence. Rachel loses all self-consciousness, and seems to bloom in the children's midst.*) Edith! come here 1270 this minute, and let me tie your hair ribbon again. Nancy,

I'm ashamed of you, I saw you trying to pull it off. (*Nancy looks abashed but mischievous.*) Louise, you look as sweet as sweet, this morning; and Jenny, where did you get the pretty, pretty dress?

LITTLE JENNY: (*Snuffling, but proud*) My mother made it. (*Pauses with more snuffles.*) My mother says I have a very bad cold. (*There is a brief silence interrupted by the small tot with the geranium.*)

1280  LITTLE MARTHA: (*In a sweet, little voice*) I—have—a—pitty—'ittle flower.

RACHEL: Honey, it's beautiful. Don't you want "Morning kiss" too?

LITTLE MARTHA: Yes, I do.

RACHEL: Come, honey. (*Rachel kisses her.*) Are you going to give the pretty flower to Jenny's teacher? (*Vigorous shakings of the head in denial.*) Is it for—mother? (*More shakings of the head.*) Is it for—let's see—Daddy? (*More shakings of the head.*) I give up. To whom are you going to

1290  give the pretty flower, honey?

LITTLE MARTHA: (*Shyly*) "Oo."

RACHEL: You, darling!

LITTLE MARTHA: Muzzer and I picked it—for "oo." Here 't is. (*Puts her finger in her mouth, and gives it shyly.*)

RACHEL: Well, I'm going to pay you with three big kisses. One! Two! Three!

LITTLE MARTHA: I can count, One! Two! Free! Tan't I? I am going to school soon; and I wants to put the flower in your hair.

1300  RACHEL: (*Kneels*) All right, baby. (*Little Martha fumbles and Rachel helps her.*)

LITTLE MARTHA: (*Dreamily*) Miss Rachel, the 'ittle flower loves you. It told me so. It said it wanted to lie in your hair. It is going to tell you a pitty 'ittle secret. You listen awful hard—and you'll hear. I wish I were a fairy and had a little wand, I'd turn everything into flowers. Wouldn't that be nice, Miss Rachel?

RACHEL: Lovely, honey!

LITTLE JENNY: (*Snuffling loudly*) If I were a fairy and had a

1310  wand, I'd turn you, Miss Rachel, into a queen—and then I'd always be near you and see that you were happy.

RACHEL: Honey, how beautiful!

LITTLE LOUISE: I'd make my mother happy—if I were a fairy. She cries all the time. My father can't get anything to do.

LITTLE NANCY: If I were a fairy, I'd turn a boy in my school into a spider. I hate him.

RACHEL: Honey, why?

LITTLE NANCY: I'll tell you sometime—I hate him.

LITTLE EDITH: Where's Jimmy, Miss Rachel?

1320  RACHEL: He went long ago; and chickies, you'll have to clear out, all of you, now, or you'll be late. Shoo! Shoo! (*She drives them out prettily before her. They laugh merrily. They all go into the vestibule.*)

TOM: (*Slowly*) Does it ever strike you—how pathetic and tragic a thing—a little colored child is?

STRONG: Yes.

TOM: Today, we colored men and women, everywhere—are up against it. Every year, we are having a harder time of it. In the South, they make it as impossible as they can for us to

1330  get an education. We're hemmed in on all sides. Our one safeguard—the ballot—in most states, is taken away al-

ready, or is being taken away. Economically, in a few lines, we have a slight show—but at what a cost! In the North, they make a pretence of liberality: they give us the ballot and a good education, and then—snuff us out. Each year, the problem just to live, gets more difficult to solve. How about these children—if we're fools enough to have any? (*RACHEL reenters. Her face is drawn and pale. She returns to the kitchenette.*)

STRONG: (*Slowly, with emphasis*) That part—is damnable! (*A  1340 silence.*)

TOM: (*Suddenly looking at the clock*) It's later than I thought. I'll have to be pulling out of here now, if you don't mind. (*Raising his voice*) Rachel! (*Rachel still drawn and pale, appears in the doorway of the kitchenette. She is without her apron.*) I've got to go now, Sis. I leave John in your hands.

STRONG: I've got to go, myself, in a few minutes.

TOM: Nonsense, man! Sit still. I'll begin to think, in a minute, you're afraid of the ladies.

STRONG: I am.  1350

TOM: What! And not ashamed to acknowledge it?

STRONG: No.

TOM: You're lots wiser than I dreamed. So long! (*Gets hat out in the entry-way and returns; smiles wryly.*) "Morituri Salutamus." (*They nod at him—Rachel wistfully. He goes out. There is the sound of an opening and closing door. Rachel sits down. A rather uncomfortable silence, on the part of Rachel, ensues. Strong is imperturbable.*)

RACHEL: (*Nervously*) John!

STRONG: Well?  1360

RACHEL: I—I listened.

STRONG: Listened! To what?

RACHEL: To you and Tom.

STRONG: Well,—what of it?

RACHEL: I didn't think it was quite fair not to tell you. It—it seemed, well, like eavesdropping.

STRONG: Don't worry about it. Nonsense!

RACHEL: I'm glad—I want to thank you for what you did for Tom. He needs you, and will need you. You'll help him?

STRONG: (*Thoughtfully*) Rachel, each one—has his own little  1370 battles. I'll do what I can. After all, an outsider doesn't help much.

RACHEL: But friendship—just friendship—helps.

STRONG: Yes. (*A silence.*) Rachel, do you hear anything encouraging from the schools? Any hope for you yet?

RACHEL: No, nor ever will be. I know that now. There's no more chance for me than there is for Tom,—or than there was for you—or for any of us with dark skins. It's lucky for me that I love to keep house, and cook, and sew. I'll never get anything else. Ma dear's sewing, the little work Tom has  1380 been able to get, and the little sewing I sometimes get to do—keep us from the poorhouse. We live. According to your philosophy, I suppose, make the best of it—it might be worse.

STRONG: (*Quietly*) You don't want to get morbid over these things, you know.

RACHEL: (*Scornfully*) That's it. If you see things as they are, you're either pessimistic or morbid.

STRONG: In the long run, do you believe, that attitude of mind—will be—beneficial to you? I'm ten years older than  1390 you. I tried your way. I know. Mine is the only sane one.

*(Goes over to her slowly; deliberately puts his hands on her hair, and tips her head back. He looks down into her face quietly without saying anything.)*

RACHEL: *(Nervous and startled)* Why, John, don't! *(He pays no attention, but continues to look down into her face.)*

STRONG: *(Half to himself)* Perhaps—if you had—a little more fun in your life, your point of view would be—more normal. I'll arrange it so I can take you to some theatre, one night, this week.

RACHEL: *(Irritably)* You talk as though I were a—a jellyfish. You'll take me, how do you know *I'll* go?

STRONG: You will.

RACHEL: *(Sarcastically)* Indeed! *(*STRONG *makes no reply.)* I wonder if you know how—how—maddening you are. Why, you talk as though my will counts for nothing. It's as if you're trying to master me. I think a domineering man is detestable.

STRONG: *(Softly)* If he's, perhaps, *the* man?

RACHEL: *(Hurriedly, as though she had not heard)* Besides, some of these theatres put you off by yourself as though you had leprosy. I'm not going.

STRONG: *(Smiling at her)* You know I wouldn't ask you to go, under those circumstances. *(A silence.)* Well, I must be going now. *(He takes her hand, and looks at it reverently. Rachel, at first resists; but he refuses to let go. When she finds it useless, she ceases to resist. He turns his head and smiles down into her face.)* Rachel, I am coming back to see you, this evening.

RACHEL: I'm sure *we'll* all be very glad to see you.

STRONG: *(Looking at her calmly)* I said—*you.* *(Very deliberately, he turns her hand palm upwards, leans over and kisses it; then he puts it back into her lap. He touches her cheek lightly.)* Good-bye—little Rachel. *(Turns in the vestibule door and looks back, smiling.)* Until tonight. *(He goes out. Rachel sits for some time without moving. She is lost in a beautiful day-dream. Presently she sighs happily, and after looking furtively around the room, lifts the palm John has kissed to her lips. She laughs shyly and jumping up, begins to hum. She opens the window at the rear of the room and then commences to thread the sewing-machine. She hums happily the whole time. A light rapping is heard at the outer door. Rachel listens. It stops, and begins again. There is something insistent, and yet hopeless in the sound. Rachel looking puzzled, goes out into the vestibule . . . The door closes. Rachel, a black woman, poorly dressed, and a little ugly, black child come in. There is the stoniness of despair in the woman's face. The child is thin, nervous, suspicious, frightened.)*

MRS. LANE: *(In a sharp, but toneless voice)* May I sit down? I'm tired.

RACHEL: *(Puzzled, but gracious; draws up a chair for her)* Why, certainly.

MRS. LANE: No, you don't know me—never even heard of me—nor I of you. I was looking at the vacant flat on this floor—and saw your name—on your door,—"Loving!" It's a strange name to come across—in this world. —I thought, perhaps, you might give me some information. *(The child hides behind her mother and looks around at Rachel in a frightened way.)*

RACHEL: *(Smiling at the woman and child in a kindly manner)* I'll be glad to tell you anything, I am able Mrs.—

MRS. LANE: Lane. What I want to know is, how do they treat the colored children in the school I noticed around the corner? *(The child clutches at her mother's dress.)*

RACHEL: *(Perplexed)* Very well—I'm sure.

MRS. LANE: *(Bluntly)* What reason have you for being sure?

RACHEL: Why, the little boy I've adopted goes there; and he's very happy. All the children in this apartment-house go there too; and I know they're happy.

MRS. LANE: Do you know how many colored children there are in the school?

RACHEL: Why, I should guess around thirty.

MRS. LANE: I see. *(Pauses.)* What color is this little adopted boy of yours?

RACHEL: *(Gently)* Why—he's brown.

MRS. LANE: Any black children there?

RACHEL: *(Nervously)* Why—yes.

MRS. LANE: Do you mind if I send Ethel over by the piano to sit? N—no, certainly not. *(Places a chair by the piano and goes to the little girl holding out her hand. She smiles beautifully. The child gets farther behind her mother.)*

MRS. LANE: She won't go to you—she's afraid of everybody now but her father and me. Come Ethel. *(Mrs. Lane takes the little girl by the hand and leads her to the chair. In a gentler voice)* Sit down, Ethel. *(Ethel obeys. When her mother starts back again toward Rachel, she holds out her hands pitifully. She makes no sound.)* I'm not going to leave you, Ethel. I'll be right over here. You can see me. *(The look of agony on the child's face, as her mother leaves her, makes Rachel shudder.)* Do you mind if we sit over here by the sewing-machine? Thank you. *(They move their chairs.)*

RACHEL: *(Looking at the little, pitiful figure watching its mother almost unblinkingly)* Does Ethel like apples, Mrs. Lane?

MRS. LANE: Yes.

RACHEL: Do you mind if I give her one?

MRS. LANE: No. Thank you, very much.

RACHEL: *(Goes into the kitchenette and returns with a fringed napkin, a plate, and a big, red apple, cut into quarters. She goes to the little girl, who cowers away from her; very gently)* Here, dear, little girl, is a beautiful apple for you. *(The gentle tones have no appeal for the trembling child before her.)*

MRS. LANE: *(Coming forward)* I'm sorry, but I'm afraid she won't take it from you. Ethel, the kind lady has given you an apple. Thank her nicely. Here! I'll spread the napkin for you, and put the plate in your lap. Thank the lady like a good little girl.

ETHEL: *(Very low)* Thank you. *(They return to their seats. Ethel with difficulty holds the plate in her lap. During the rest of the interview between Rachel and her mother, she divides her attention between the apple on the plate and her mother's face. She makes no attempt to eat the apple, but holds the plate in her lap with a care that is painful to watch. Often, too, she looks over her shoulder fearfully. The conversation between Rachel and her mother is carried on in low tones.)*

MRS. LANE: I've got to move—it's *Ethel.*

RACHEL: What is the matter with that child? It's—it's

heartbreaking to see her.

MRS. LANE: I understand how you feel,—I don't feel anything, myself, any more. (A pause.) My husband and I are poor, and we're ugly and we're black. Ethel looks like her father more than she does like me. We live in 55th Street—near the railroad. It's a poor neighborhood, but the rent's cheap. My husband is a porter in a store; and, to help out, I'm a caretaker. (Pauses.) I don't know why I'm telling you all this.

1520 We had a nice little home—and the three of us were happy. Now we've got to move.

RACHEL: Move! Why?

MRS. LANE: It's Ethel. I put her in school this September. She stayed two weeks. (Pointing to Ethel) That's the result.

RACHEL: (In horror) You mean—that just two weeks—in school—did that?

MRS. LANE: Yes. Ethel never had a sick day in her life—before. (A brief pause.) I took her to the doctor at the end of the two weeks. He says she's a nervous wreck.

1530 RACHEL: But what could they have done to her?

MRS. LANE: (Laughs grimly and mirthlessly) I'll tell you what they did the first day. Ethel is naturally sensitive and backward. She's not assertive. The teacher saw that, and, after I had left, told her to sit in a seat in the rear of the class. She was alone there—in a corner. The children, immediately feeling there was something wrong with Ethel because of the teacher's attitude, turned and stared at her. When the teacher's back was turned they whispered about her, pointed their fingers at her and tittered. The teacher divided

1540 the class into two parts, divisions, I believe, they are called. She forgot all about Ethel, of course, until the last minute, and then, looking back, said sharply: "That little girl there may join this division," meaning the group of pupils standing around her. Ethel naturally moved slowly. The teacher called her sulky and told her to lose a part of her recess. When Ethel came up—the children drew away from her in every direction. She was left standing alone. The teacher then proceeded to give a lesson about kindness to animals. Funny, isn't it, *kindness to animals?* The children

1550 forgot Ethel in the excitement of talking about their pets. Presently, the teacher turned to Ethel and said disagreeably: "Have you a pet?" Ethel said, "Yes," very low. "Come, speak up, you sulky child, what is it?" Ethel said: "A blind puppy." They all laughed, the teacher and all. Strange, isn't it, but Ethel loves that puppy. She spoke up: "It's mean to laugh at a little blind puppy. I'm glad he's blind." This remark brought forth more laughter. "Why are you glad?" the teacher asked curiously. Ethel refused to say. (Pauses.) When I asked her why, do you know what she told me? "If

1560 he saw me, he might not love me any more." (A pause.) Did I tell you that Ethel is only seven years old?

RACHEL: (Drawing her breath sharply) Oh! I didn't believe any one could be as cruel as that—to a little child.

MRS. LANE: It isn't very pleasant, is it? When the teacher found out that Ethel wouldn't answer, she said severely: "Take your seat!" At recess, all the children went out. Ethel could hear them playing and laughing and shrieking. Even the teacher went too. She was made to sit there all alone—in that big room—because God made her ugly—and black.

1570 (Pauses.) When the recess was half over the teacher came back. "You may go now," she said coldly. Ethel didn't stir.

"Did you hear me?" "Yes'm." "Why don't you obey?" "I don't want to go out, please." "You don't, don't you, you stubborn child! Go immediately!" Ethel went. She stood by the school steps. No one spoke to her. The children near her moved away in every direction. They stopped playing, many of them, and watched her. They stared as only children can stare. Some began whispering about her. Presently one child came up and ran her hand roughly over Ethel's face. She looked at her hand and Ethel's face and ran screaming

1580 back to the others, "It won't come off! See!" Other children followed the first child's example. Then one boy spoke up loudly: "I know what she is, she's a nigger!" Many took up the cry. God or the devil interfered—the bell rang. The children filed in. One boy boldly called her "Nigger!" before the teacher. She said, "That isn't nice,"—but she smiled at the boy. Things went on about the same for the rest of the day. At the end of school, Ethel put on her hat and coat—the teacher made her hang them at a distance from the other pupils' wraps; and started for home. Quite a crowd escorted

1590 her. They called her "Nigger!" all the way. I *made* Ethel go the next day. I complained to the authorities. They treated me lightly. I was determined not to let them force my child out of school. At the end of two weeks—I had to take her out.

RACHEL: (Brokenly) Why,—I never—in all my life—heard anything—so—pitiful.

MRS. LANE: Did you ever go to school here?

RACHEL: Yes. I was made to feel my color—but I never had an experience like that.

1600 MRS. LANE: How many years ago were you in the graded schools?

RACHEL: Oh!—around ten.

MRS. LANE: (Laughs grimly) Ten years! Every year things are getting worse. Last year wasn't as bad as this. (Pauses.) So they treat the children all right in this school?

RACHEL: Yes! Yes! I know that.

MRS. LANE: I can't afford to take this flat here, but I'll take it. I'm going to have Ethel educated. Although, when you think of it,—it's all rather useless—this education! What are our

1610 children going to do with it, when they get it? We strive and save and sacrifice to educate them—and the whole time—down underneath, we know—they'll have no chance.

RACHEL: (Sadly) Yes, that's true, all right.—God seems to have forgotten us.

MRS. LANE: God! It's all a lie about God. I know.—This fall I sent Ethel to a white Sunday-school near us. She received the same treatment there she did in the day school. Her being there, nearly broke up the school. At the end, the superintendent called her to him and asked her if she didn't

1620 know of some nice colored Sunday-school. He told her she must feel out of place, and uncomfortable there. That's your Church of God!

RACHEL: Oh! how unspeakably brutal. (Controls herself with an effort; after a pause) Have you any other children?

MRS. LANE: (Dryly) Hardly! If I had another—I'd kill it. It's kinder. (Rising presently) Well, I must go, now. Thank you, for your information—and for listening. (Suddenly) You aren't married, are you?

RACHEL: No.

1630 MRS. LANE: Don't marry—that's my advice. Come, Ethel.

*(Ethel gets up and puts down the things in her lap, carefully upon her chair. She goes in a hurried, timid way to her mother and clutches her hand.)* Say good-bye to the lady.

ETHEL: *(Faintly)* Good-bye.

RACHEL: *(Kneeling by the little girl—a beautiful smile on her face)* Dear little girl, won't you let me kiss you good-bye? I love little girls. *(The child hides behind her mother; continuing brokenly)* Oh!—no child—ever did—that to me—
1640 before!

MRS. LANE: *(In a gentler voice)* Perhaps, when we move in here, the first of the month, things may be better. Thank you, again. Good-morning! You don't belie your name. *(All three go into the vestibule. The outside door opens and closes. Rachel as though dazed and stricken returns. She sits in a chair, leans forward, and clasping her hands loosely between her knees, stares at the chair with the apple on it where Ethel Lane has sat. She does not move for some time. Then she gets up and goes to the window in the rear center*
1650 *and sits there. She breathes in the air deeply and then goes to the sewing-machine and begins to sew on something she is making. Presently her feet slow down on the pedals; she stops; and begins brooding again. After a short pause, she gets up and begins to pace up and down slowly, mechanically, her head bent forward. The sharp ringing of the electric bell breaks in upon this. Rachel starts and goes slowly into the vestibule. She is heard speaking dully through the tube.)*

RACHEL: Yes!—All right! Bring it up! *(Presently she returns*
1660 *with a long flower box. She opens it listlessly at the table. Within are six, beautiful crimson rosebuds with long stems. Rachel looks at the name on the card. She sinks down slowly on her knees and leans her head against the table. She sighs wearily)* Oh! John! John!—What are we to do?—I'm— I'm—afraid! Everywhere—it is the same thing. My mother! My little brother! Little, black, crushed Ethel! *(In a whisper)* Oh! God! You who I have been taught to believe are so good, so beautiful how could—You permit—these— things? *(Pauses, raises her head and sees the rosebuds. Her*
1670 *face softens and grows beautiful, very sweetly.)* Dear little rosebuds—you—make me think—of sleeping, curled up, happy babies. Dear beautiful, little rosebuds! *(Pauses; goes on thoughtfully to the rosebuds)* When—I look—at you—I believe—God is beautiful. He who can make a little exquisite thing like this, and this can't be cruel. Oh! He can't mean me—to give up—love—and the hope of little children. *(There is the sound of a small hand knocking at the outer door. Rachel smiles.)* My Jimmy! It must be twelve o'clock. *(Rises.)* I didn't dream it was so late. *(Starts for the*
1680 *vestibule.)* Oh! the world can't be so bad. I don't believe it. I won't. I *must* forget that little girl. My little Jimmy is happy—and today John—sent me beautiful rosebuds. Oh, there are lovely things, yet. *(Goes into the vestibule. A child's eager cry is heard; and Rachel carrying Jimmy in her arms comes in. He has both arms about her neck and is hugging her. With him in her arms, she sits down in the armchair at the right front.)*

RACHEL: Well, honey, how was school today?

JIMMY: *(Sobering a trifle)* All right, Ma Rachel. *(Suddenly sees*
1690 *the roses)* Oh! look at the pretty flowers. Why, Ma Rachel, you forgot to put them in water. They'll die.

RACHEL: Well, so they will. Hop down this minute, and I'll put them in right away. *(Gathers up box and flowers and goes into the kitchenette. Jimmy climbs back into the chair. He looks thoughtful and serious. Rachel comes back with the buds in a tall, glass vase. She puts the fern on top of the piano, and places the vase in the centre of the table.)* There, honey, that's better, isn't it? Aren't they lovely?

JIMMY: Yes, that's lots better. Now they won't die, will they? 1700 Rosebuds are just like little "chilyun," aren't they, Ma Rachel? If you are good to them, they'll grow up into lovely roses, won't they? And if you hurt them, they'll die. Ma Rachel do you think all peoples are kind to little rosebuds?

RACHEL: *(Watching Jimmy shortly)* Why, of course. Who could hurt little children? Who would have the heart to do such a thing?

JIMMY: If you hurt them, it would be lots kinder, wouldn't it, to kill them all at once, and not a little bit and a little bit?

RACHEL: *(Sharply)* Why, honey boy, why are you talking like this? 1710

JIMMY: Ma Rachel, what is a "Nigger"?

*(Rachel recoils as though she had been struck.)*

RACHEL: Honey boy, why—why do you ask that?

JIMMY: Some big boys called me that when I came out of school just now. They said: "Look at the little nigger!" And they laughed. One of them runned, no ranned, after me and threw stones; and they all kept calling "Nigger! Nigger! Nigger!" One stone struck me hard in the back, and it hurt awful bad; but I didn't cry, Ma Rachel. I wouldn't let them make me cry. The stone hurts me there, Ma Rachel; but what they called me hurts and hurts here. What is a "Nigger," Ma 1720 Rachel?

RACHEL: *(Controlling herself with a tremendous effort. At last she sweeps down upon him and hugs and kisses him)* Why, honey boy, those boys didn't mean anything. Silly, little, honey boy! They're rough, that's all. How *could* they mean anything?

JIMMY: You're only saying that, Ma Rachel, so I won't be hurt. I know. It wouldn't ache here like it does—if they didn't mean something.

RACHEL: *(Abruptly)* Where's Mary, honey? 1730

JIMMY: She's in her flat. She came in just after I did.

RACHEL: Well, honey, I'm going to give you two big cookies and two to take to Mary; and you may stay in there and play with her, till I get your lunch ready. Won't that be jolly?

JIMMY: *(Brightening a little)* Why, you never give me but one at a time. You'll give me two?—One? Two? *(Rachel gets the cookies and brings them to him. Jimmy climbs down from the chair.)* Shoo! now, little honey boy. See how many laughs you can make for me, before I come after you. Hear? Have a good time, now. *(Jimmy starts for the door quickly;* 1740 *but he begins to slow down. His face gets long and serious again. Rachel watches him.)*

RACHEL: *(Jumping at him)* Shoo! Shoo! Get out of here quickly, little chicken. *(She follows him out. The outer door opens and shuts. Presently she returns. She looks old and worn and grey; calmly. Pauses.)* First, it's little, black Ethel—and then's it's Jimmy. Tomorrow, it will be some other little child. The blight—sooner or later—strikes all. My little Jimmy, only seven years old poisoned! *(Through*

1750 *the open window comes the laughter of little children at play. Rachel, shuddering, covers her ears.)* And once I said, centuries ago, it must have been: "How can life be so terrible, when there are little children in the world?" Terrible! Terrible! *(In a whisper, slowly)* That's the reason it *is* so terrible. *(The laughter reaches her again; this time she listens.)* And, suddenly, some day, from out of the black, the blight shall descend, and shall still forever—the laughter on those little lips, and in those little hearts. *(Pauses thoughtfully.)* And the loveliest thing—almost, that ever happened to me, 1760 that beautiful voice, in my dream, those beautiful words: "Rachel, you are to be the mother to little children." *(Pauses, then slowly and with dawning surprise.)* Why, God, you were making a mock of me; you were laughing at me. I didn't believe God could laugh at our sufferings, but He can. We are accursed, accursed! We have nothing, absolutely nothing. *(Strong's rosebuds attract her attention. She goes over to them, puts her hand out as if to touch them, and then shakes her head, very sweetly)* No, little rosebuds, I may not touch you. Dear, little, baby rosebuds,—I am ac-1770 cursed. *(Gradually her whole form stiffens, she breathes deeply; at last slowly.)* You God!—You terrible, laughing God! Listen! I swear—and may my soul be damned to all eternity, if I do break this oath—I swear—that no child of mine shall ever lie upon my breast, for I will not have it rise up, in the terrible days that are to be—and call me cursed. *(A pause, very wistfully; questioningly.)* Never to know the loveliest thing in all the world—the feel of a little head, the touch of little hands, the beautiful utter dependence—of a little child? *(With sudden frenzy)* You can laugh, Oh God! 1780 Well, so can I. *(Bursts into terrible, racking laughter)* But I can be kinder than You. *(Fiercely she snatches the rosebuds from the vase, grasps them roughly, tears each head from the stem, and grinds it under her feet. The vase goes over with a crash; the water drips unheeded over the table-cloth and floor.)* If I kill, You Mighty God, I kill at once—I do not torture. *(Falls face downward on the floor. The laughter of the children shrills loudly through the window.)*

### —ACT THREE—

TIME: *Seven o'clock in the evening, one week later.*

PLACE: *The same room. There is a coal fire in the grate. The curtains are drawn. A lighted oil lamp with a dark green porcelain shade is in the center of the table. Mrs. Loving and Tom are sitting by the table, Mrs. Loving sewing, Tom reading. There is the sound of much laughter and the shrill screaming of a child from the bedrooms. Presently Jimmy clad in a flannelet sleeping suit, covering all of him but his head and hands, chases a pillow, which has come flying through the doorway at the rear. He struggles with it, finally gets it in his arms, and rushes as fast as he can through the doorway again. Rachel jumps at him with a cry. He drops the pillow and shrieks. There is a tussle for possession of it, and they disappear. The noise grows louder and merrier. Tom puts down his paper and grins. He looks at his mother.*

TOM: Well, who's the giddy one in this family now?

MRS. LOVING: *(Shaking her head in a troubled manner)* I don't

like it. It worries me. Rachel—*(Breaks off).* 1790

TOM: Have you found out, yet—

MRS. LOVING: *(Turning and looking toward the rear doorway, quickly interrupting him)* Sh! *(Rachel, laughing, her hair tumbling over her shoulders, comes rushing into the room. Jimmy is in close pursuit. He tries to catch her, but she dodges him. They are both breathless.)*

MRS. LOVING: *(Deprecatingly)* Really, Rachel, Jimmy will be so excited he won't be able to sleep. It's after his bedtime, now. Don't you think you had better stop?

RACHEL: All right, Ma dear. Come on, Jimmy; let's play "Old 1800 Folks" and sit by the fire. *(She begins to push the big armchair over to the fire. Tom jumps up, moves her aside, and pushes it himself. Jimmy renders assistance.)*

TOM: Thanks, Big Fellow, you are "sure some" strong. I'll remember you when these people around here come for me to move pianos and such things around. Shake! *(They shake hands.)*

JIMMY: *(Proudly)* I am awful strong, am I not?

TOM: You "sure" are a Hercules. *(Hurriedly, as Jimmy's mouth and eyes open wide.)* And see here! don't ask me tonight 1810 who that was. I'll tell you the first thing tomorrow morning. Hear? *(Returns to his chair and paper.)*

RACHEL: *(Sitting down)* Come on, honey boy, and sit in my lap.

JIMMY: *(Doubtfully)* I thought we were going to play "Old Folks."

RACHEL: We are.

JIMMY: Do old folks sit in each other's laps?

RACHEL: Old folks do anything. Come on.

JIMMY: *(Hesitatingly climbs into her lap, but presently snuggles down and sighs audibly from sheer content; Rachel starts to* 1820 *bind up her hair)* Ma Rachel, don't please! I like your hair like that. You're—you're pretty. I like to feel of it; and it smells like—like—oh!—like a barn.

RACHEL: My! how complimentary! I like that. Like a barn, indeed!

JIMMY: What's "complimentary"?

RACHEL: Oh! saying nice things about me. *(Pinching his cheek and laughing)* That my hair is like a barn, for instance.

JIMMY: *(Stoutly)* Well, that is "complimentary." It smells like hay—like the hay in the barn you took me to, one day, last 1830 summer. 'Member?

RACHEL: Yes honey.

JIMMY: *(After a brief pause)* Ma Rachel!

RACHEL: Well?

JIMMY: Tell me a story, please. It's "story-time," now, isn't it?

RACHEL: Well, let's see. *(They both look into the fire for a space; beginning softly)* Once upon a time, there were two, dear, little boys, and they were all alone in the world. They lived with a cruel, old man and woman, who made them work hard, very hard—all day, and beat them when they did 1840 not move fast enough, and always, every night, before they went to bed. They slept in an attic on a rickety, narrow bed, that went screech! screech! whenever they moved. And, in summer, they nearly died with the heat up there, and in winter, with the cold. One wintry night, when they were both weeping very bitterly after a particularly hard beating, they suddenly heard a pleasant voice saying: "Why are you crying, little boys?" They looked up, and there, in the moonlight, by their bed, was the dearest, little old lady. She was

1850 dressed all in gray, from the peak of her little pointed hat to her little, buckled shoes. She held a black cane much taller than her little self. Her hair fell about her ears in tiny, grey corkscrew curls, and they bobbed about as she moved. Her eyes were black and bright—as bright as—well, as that lovely, white light there. No, there! And her cheeks were as red as the apple I gave you yesterday. Do you remember?

JIMMY: *(Dreamily)* Yes.

RACHEL: "Why are you crying, little boys?" she asked again, in a lovely, low, little voice. "Because we are tired and sore and
1860 hungry and cold; and we are all alone in the world; and we don't know how to laugh any more. We should so like to laugh again." "Why, that's easy," she said, "it's just like this." And she laughed a little, joyous, musical laugh. "Try!" she commanded. They tried, but their laughing boxes were very rusty, and they made horrid sounds. "Well," she said, "I advise you to pack up, and go away, as soon as you can, to the Land of Laughter. You'll soon learn there, I can tell you." "Is there such a land?" they asked doubtfully. "To be sure there is," she answered the least bit sharply. "We never heard of
1870 it," they said. "Well, I'm sure there must be plenty of things you never heard about," she said just the "leastest" bit more sharply. "In a moment you'll be telling me flowers don't talk together, and the birds." "We never heard of such a thing," they said in surprise, their eyes like saucers. "There!" she said, bobbing her little curls. "What did I tell you? You have much to learn." "How do you get to the Land of Laughter?" they asked. "You go out of the eastern gate of the town, just as the sun is rising; and you take the highway there, and follow it; and if you go with it long enough, it will bring you to
1880 the very gates of the Land of Laughter. It's a long, long way from here; and it will take you many days." The words had scarcely left her mouth, when, lo! the little lady disappeared, and where she had stood was the white square of moonlight—nothing else. And without more ado these two little boys put their arms around each other and fell fast asleep. And in the grey, just before daybreak, they awoke and dressed; and, putting on their ragged caps and mittens, for it was a wintry day, they stole out of the house and made for the eastern gate. And just as they reached it, and passed
1890 through, the whole east leapt into fire. All day they walked, and many days thereafter, and kindly people, by the way, took them in and gave them food and drink and sometimes a bed at night. Often they slept by the roadside, but they didn't mind that for the climate was delightful—not too hot, and not too cold. They soon threw away their ragged little mittens. They walked for many days, and there was no Land of Laughter. Once they met an old man, richly dressed, with shining jewels on his fingers, and he stopped them and asked: "Where are you going so fast, little boys?" "We are
1900 going to the Land of Laughter," they said together gravely. "That," said the old man, "is a very foolish thing to do. Come with me, and I will take you to the Land of Riches. I will cover you with garments of beauty, and give you jewels and a castle to live in and servants and horses and many things besides." And they said to him: "No, we wish to learn how to laugh again; we have forgotten how, and we are going to the Land of Laughter." "You will regret not going with me. See, if you don't," he said; and he left them in quite a huff. And they walked again, many days, and again they met an old

man. He was tall and imposing-looking and very dignified. 1910 And he said: "Where are you going so fast, little boys?" "We are going to the Land of Laughter," they said together very seriously. "What!" he said, "that is an extremely foolish thing to do. Come with me, and I will give you power. I will make you great men: generals, kings, emperors. Whatever you desire to accomplish will be permitted you." And they smiled politely: "Thank you very much, but we have forgotten how to laugh, and we are going there to learn how." He looked upon them haughtily, without speaking, and disappeared. And they walked and walked more days; and they met an- 1920 other old man. And he was clad in rags, and his face was thin, and his eyes were unhappy. And he whispered to them: "Where are you going so fast, little boys?" "We are going to the Land of Laughter," they answered, without a smile. "Laughter! Laughter! that is useless. Come with me and I will show you the beauty of life through sacrifice, suffering for others. That is the only life. I come from the Land of Sacrifice." And they thanked him kindly, but said: "We have suffered long enough. We have forgotten how to laugh. We would learn again." And they went on; and he looked after 1930 them very wistfully. They walked more days, and at last they came to the Land of Laughter. And how do you suppose they knew this? Because they could hear, over the wall, the sound of joyous laughter,—the laughter of men, women, and children. And one sat guarding the gate, and they went to her. "We have come a long, long distance; and we would enter the Land of Laughter." "Let me see you smile, first," she said gently. "I sit at the gate; and no one who does not know how to smile may enter the Land of Laughter." And they tried to smile, but could not. "Go away and practice," 1940 she said kindly, "and come back tomorrow." And they went away, and practiced all night how to smile; and in the morning they returned, and the gentle lady at the gate said: "Dear little boys, have you learned how to smile?" And they said: "We have tried. How is this?" "Better," she said, "much better. Practice some more, and come back tomorrow." And they went away obediently and practiced. And they came the third day. And she said: "Now try again." And tears of delight came into her lovely eyes. "Those were very beautiful smiles," she said. "Now, you may enter." And she un- 1950 locked the gate, and kissed them both, and they entered the Land—the beautiful Land of Laughter. Never had they seen such blue skies, such green trees and grass; never had they heard such birds songs. And people, men, women and children, laughing softly, came to meet them, and took them in, and made them as home; and soon, very soon, they learned to sleep. And they grew up here, and married, and had laughing, happy children. And sometimes they thought of the Land of Riches, and said: "Ah! well!" and sometimes of the Land of Power, and sighed a little; and sometimes of 1960 the Land of Sacrifice—and their eyes were wistful. But they soon forgot, and laughed again. And they grew old, laughing. And then when they died—a laugh was on their lips. Thus are things in the beautiful Land of Laughter. *(There is a long pause.)*

JIMMY: I like that story, Ma Rachel. It's nice to laugh, isn't is? Is there such a land?

RACHEL: *(Softly)* What do you think, honey?

JIMMY: I thinks it would be awful nice if there was. Don't you?

1970 RACHEL: *(Wistfully)* If there only were! If there only were!

JIMMY: Ma Rachel.

RACHEL: Well?

JIMMY: It makes you think—kind of—doesn't it—of sunshine medicine?

RACHEL: Yes, honey,—but it isn't medicine there. It's always there—just like—well—like our air here. It's *always* sunshine there.

JIMMY: Always sunshine? Never any dark?

RACHEL: No, honey.

1980 JIMMY: You'd—never—be—afraid there, then, would you? Never afraid of nothing?

RACHEL: No, honey.

JIMMY: *(With a big sigh)* Oh!—Oh! I *wish* it was here—not there. *(Puts his hand up to Rachel's face; suddenly sits up and looks at her.)* Why, Ma Rachel dear, you're crying. Your face is all wet. Why! Don't cry! Don't cry!

RACHEL: *(Gently)* Do you remember that I told you the lady at the gate had tears of joy in her eyes, when the two, dear, little boys smiled that beautiful smile?

1990 JIMMY: Yes.

RACHEL: Well, these are tears of joy, honey, that's all—tears of joy.

JIMMY: It must be awful queer to have tears of joy, 'cause you're happy. I never did. *(With a sigh.)* But, if you say they are, dear Ma Rachel, they must be. You knows everything, don't you?

RACHEL: *(Sadly)* Some things, honey, some things. *(A silence.)*

JIMMY: *(Sighing happily)* This is the beautiful-est night I ever knew. If you would do just one more thing, it would be lots

2000 more beautiful. Will you, Ma Rachel?

RACHEL: Well, what, honey?

JIMMY: Will you sing—at the piano, I mean, it's lots prettier that way—the little song you used to rock me to sleep by? You know, the one about the "Slumber Boat"?

RACHEL: Oh! honey, not tonight. You're too tired. It's bedtime now.

JIMMY: *(Patting her face with his little hand; wheedlingly)* Please! Ma Rachel, please! pretty please!

RACHEL: Well, honey boy, this once, then. Tonight, you shall

2010 have the little song—I used to sing you to sleep by *(half to herself)* perhaps, for the last time.

JIMMY: Why, Ma Rachel, why the last time?

RACHEL: *(Shaking her head sadly, goes to the piano; in a whisper)* The last time. *(She twists up her hair into a knot at the back of her head and looks at the keys for a few moments; then she plays the accompaniment of the "Slumber Boat" through softly, and, after a moment, sings. Her voice is full of pent-up longing, and heartbreak, and hopelessness. She ends in a little sob, but attempts to cover it by singing, lightly*

2020 *and daintily, the chorus of "The Owl and the Moon" . . . Then softly and with infinite tenderness, almost against her will, she plays and sings again the refrain of the "Slumber Boat"):*

> *"Sail, baby, sail*
> *Out from that sea,*
> *Only don't forget to sail*
> *Back again to me."*

*(Presently she rises and goes to Jimmy, who is lolling back happily in the big chair. During the singing, Tom and Mrs. Loving*

apparently do not listen; when she sobs, however, Tom's hand on his paper tightens; Mrs. Loving's needle poises for a moment in mid-air. Neither looks at Rachel. Jimmy evidently has not noticed the sob.)*

RACHEL: *(Kneeling by Jimmy)* Well, honey, how did you like it?

JIMMY: *(Proceeding to pull down her hair from the twist)* It was lovely, Ma Rachel. *(Yawns audibly.)* Now, Ma Rachel, I'm 2030 just beautifully sleepy. *(Dreamily)* I think that p'r'aps I'll go to the Land of Laughter tonight in my dreams. I'll go in the "Slumber Boat" and come back in the morning and tell you all about it. Shall I?

RACHEL: Yes, honey. *(Whispers)*

> *"Only don't forget to sail*
> *Back again to me."*

TOM: *(Suddenly)* Rachel! *(Rachel starts slightly.)* I nearly forgot. John is coming here tonight to see how you are. He told me to tell you so. 2040

RACHEL: *(Stiffens perceptibly, then in different tones)* Very well. Thank you. *(Suddenly with a little cry she puts her arms around Jimmy)* Jimmy! honey! don't go tonight. Don't go without Ma Rachel. Wait for me, honey. I do so wish to go, too, to the Land of Laughter. Think of it, Jimmy; nothing but birds always singing, and flowers always blooming, and skies always blue—and people, all of them, always laughing, laughing. You'll wait for Ma Rachel, won't you, honey?

JIMMY: Is there really and truly, Ma Rachel, a Land of 2050 Laughter?

RACHEL: Oh! Jimmy, let's hope so; let's pray so.

JIMMY: *(Frowns)* I've been thinking— *(Pauses.)* You have to smile at the gate, don't you, to get in?

RACHEL: Yes, honey.

JIMMY: Well, I guess I couldn't smile if my Ma Rachel wasn't somewhere close to me. So I couldn't get in after all, could I? Tonight, I'll go somewhere else, and tell you all about it. And then, some day, we'll go together, won't we?

RACHEL: *(Sadly)* Yes, honey, some day—some day. *(A short si-* 2060 *lence).* Well, this isn't going to "sleepy-sleep," is it? Go, now, and say good-night to Ma Loving and Uncle Tom.

JIMMY: *(Gets down obediently, and goes first to Mrs. Loving. She leans over, and he puts his little arms around her neck. They kiss; very sweetly)* Sweet dreams! God keep you all the night!

MRS. LOVING: The sweetest of sweet dreams to you, dear little boy! Good-night *(Rachel watches, unwatched, the scene. Her eyes are full of yearning.)*

JIMMY: *(Going to Tom, who makes believe he does not see him)* 2070 Uncle Tom!

TOM: *(Jumps as though tremendously startled; Jimmy laughs)* My! how you frightened me. You'll put my gizzard out of commission, if you do that often. Well, sir, what can I do for you?

JIMMY: I came to say good-night.

TOM: *(Gathering Jimmy up in his arms and kissing him; gently and with emotion)* Good-night, dear little Big Fellow! Good-night!

JIMMY: Sweet dreams! God keep you all the night! *(Goes se-* 2080 *dately to Rachel, and holds out his little hand.)* I'm ready, Ma Rachel. *(Yawns)* I'm so nice and sleepy.

RACHEL: *(With Jimmy's hand in hers, she hesitates a moment, and then approaches Tom slowly. For a short time she stands looking down at him; suddenly leaning over him)* Why, Tom, what a pretty tie! Is it new?

TOM: Well, no, not exactly. I've had it about a month. It is rather a beauty, isn't it?

RACHEL: Why, I never remember seeing it.

2090 TOM: *(Laughing)* I guess not. I saw to that.

RACHEL: Stingy!

TOM: Well, I am—where my ties are concerned. I've had experience.

RACHEL: *(Tentatively)* Tom!

TOM: Well?

RACHEL: *(Nervously and wistfully)* Are you—will you—I mean, won't you be home this evening?

TOM: You've got a long memory, Sis. I've that engagement, you know. Why?

2100 RACHEL: *(Slowly)* I forgot; so you have.

TOM: Why?

RACHEL: *(Hastily)* Oh! nothing—nothing. Come on, Jimmy boy, you can hardly keep those little peepers open, can you? Come on, honey. *(Rachel and Jimmy go out the rear doorway. There is a silence.)*

MRS. LOVING: *(Slowly, as though thinking aloud)* I try to make out what could have happened; but it's no use—I can't. Those four days, she lay in bed hardly moving, scarcely speaking. Only her eyes seemed alive. I never saw such a

2110 wide, tragic look in my life. It was as though her soul had been mortally wounded. But how? how? What could have happened?

TOM: *(Quietly)* I don't know. She generally tells me everything; but she avoids me now. If we are alone in a room—she gets out. I don't know what it means.

MRS. LOVING: She will hardly let Jimmy out of her sight. While he's at school, she's nervous and excited. She seems always to be listening, but for what? When he returns, she nearly devours him. And she always asks him in a frightened sort of

2120 way, her face as pale and tense as can be: "Well, honey boy, how was school today?" And he always answers, "Fine, Ma Rachel, fine! I learned—"; and then he goes on to tell her everything that has happened. And when he has finished, she says in an uneasy sort of way: "Is—is that all?" And when he says "Yes," she relaxes and becomes limp. After a little while she becomes feverishly happy. She plays with Jimmy and the children more than ever she did—and she played a good deal, as you know. They're here, or she's with them. Yesterday, I said in remonstrance, when she came in, her

2130 face pale and haggard and black hollows under her eyes: "Rachel, remember you're just out of a sickbed. You're not well enough to go on like this." "I know," was all she would say, "but I've go to. I can't help myself. This part of their little lives must be happy—it just must be." *(Pauses.)* The last couple of nights, Jimmy has awakened and cried most pitifully. She wouldn't let me go to him; said I had enough trouble, and she could quiet him. She never will let me know why he cries; but she stays with him, and soothes him until, at last, he falls asleep again. Every time she has come out

2140 like a rag; and her face is like a dead woman's. Strange isn't it, this is the first time we have ever been able to talk it over? Tom, what could have happened?

TOM: I don't know, Ma, but I feel, as you do; something terrible and sudden has hurt her soul; and, poor little thing, she's

trying bravely to readjust herself to life again. *(Pauses, looks at his watch and then rises, and goes to her. He pats her back awkwardly).* Well, Ma, I'm going now. Don't worry too much. Youth, you know, gets over things finally. It takes them hard, that's all—. At least, that's what the older heads tell us. *(Gets his hat and stands in the vestibule doorway.)* 2150 Ma, you know, I begin with John tomorrow. *(With emotion)* I don't believe we'll ever forget John. Good-night! *(Exit. Mrs. Loving continues to sew. Rachel, her hair arranged, reenters through the rear doorway. She is humming.)*

RACHEL: He's sleeping like a top. Aren't little children, Ma dear, the sweetest things, when they're all helpless and asleep? One little hand is under his cheek; and he's smiling. *(Stops suddenly, biting her lips. A pause)* Where's Tom?

MRS. LOVING: He went out a few minutes ago.

RACHEL: *(Sitting in Tom's chair and picking up his paper. She* 2160 *is exceedingly nervous. She looks the paper over rapidly; presently trying to make her tone casual)* Ma,—you—you— aren't going anywhere tonight, are you?

MRS. LOVING: I've got to go out for a short time about half-past eight. Mrs. Jordan, you know. I'll not be gone very long, though. Why?

RACHEL: Oh! nothing particular. I just thought it would be cosy if we could sit here together the rest of the evening. Can't you—can't you go tomorrow?

MRS. LOVING: Why, I don't see how I can. I've made the en- 2170 gagement. It's about a new reception gown; and she's exceedingly exacting, as you know. I can't afford to lose her.

RACHEL: No, I suppose not. All right, Ma dear. *(Presently, paper in hand, she laughs, but not quite naturally.)* Look! Ma dear! How is that for fashion, anyway? Isn't it the "limit"? *(Rises and shows her mother a picture in the paper. As she is in the act, the bell rings. With a startled cry.)* Oh! *(Drops the paper, and grips her mother's hand.)*

MRS. LOVING: *(Anxiously)* Rachel, your nerves are right on edge; and your hand feels like fire. I'll have to see a doctor 2180 about you; and that's all there is to it.

RACHEL: *(Laughing nervously, and moving toward the vestibule)* Nonsense, Ma dear! Just because I let out a whoop now and then, and have nice warm hands? *(Goes out, is heard talking through the tube)* Yes! *(Her voice emitting tremendous relief.)* Oh! bring it right up! *(Appearing in the doorway)* Ma dear, did you buy anything at Goddard's today?

MRS. LOVING: Yes; and I've been wondering why they were so late in delivering it. I bought it early this morning. *(Rachel* 2190 *goes out again. A door opens and shuts. She reappears with a bundle.)*

MRS. LOVING: Put it on my bed, Rachel, please. *(Exit Rachel rear doorway; presently returns empty-handed; sits down again at the table with the paper between herself and mother; sinks in a deep revery. Suddenly there is the sound of many loud knocks made by numerous small fists. Rachel drops the paper, and comes to a sitting posture, tense again. Her mother looks at her, but says nothing. Almost immediately Rachel relaxes.)* 2200

RACHEL: My kiddies! They're late, this evening. *(Goes out into the vestibule. A door opens and shuts. There is the shrill, excited sound of childish voices. Rachel comes in surrounded by the children, all trying to say something to her at once. Rachel puts her finger on her lip and points toward the doorway in the rear. They all quiet down. She sits on the floor in the front of the stage, and the children all cluster around her. Their conversation takes place in a half-whisper. As they enter they nod brightly at Mrs. Loving, who smiles in return.)* Why so late, kiddies? It's long past "sleepy-time."

LITTLE NANCY: We've been playing "Hide and Seek," and having the mostest fun. We promised, all of us, that if we could play until half-past seven tonight we wouldn't make any fuss about going to bed at seven o'clock the rest of the week. It's awful hard to go. I *hate* to go to bed!

LITTLE MARY, LOUISE *and* EDITH: So do I! So do I! So do I!

LITTLE MARTHA: I don't. I love bed. My bed, after my muzzer tucks me all in, is like a nice warm bag. I just stick my nose out. When I lifts my head up I can see the light from the dining-room come in the door. I can hear my muzzer and fazzer talking nice and low; and then, before I know it, I'm fast asleep, and I dream pretty things, and in about a minute it's morning again. I love my little bed, and I love to dream.

LITTLE MARY: *(Aggressively)* Well, I guess I love to dream too. I wish I could dream, though, without going to bed.

LITTLE NANCY: When I grow up, I'm never going to bed at night! *(Darkly)* You see.

LITTLE LOUISE: "Grown-ups" just love to poke their heads out of windows and cry, "Child'run, it's time for bed now; and you'd better hurry, too, I can tell you." They "sure" are queer, for sometimes when I wake up, it must be about twelve o'clock, I can hear by big sister giggling and talking to some silly man. If it's good for me to go to bed early—I should think—

RACHEL: *(Interrupting suddenly)* Why, where is my little Jenny? Excuse me, Louise dear.

LITTLE MARTHA: Her cold is awful bad. She coughs like this *(giving a distressing imitation)* and snuffles all the time. She can't talk out loud, and she can't go to sleep. Muzzer says she's fev'rish—I thinks that's what she says. Jenny says she knows she could go to sleep, if you would come and sit with her a little while.

RACHEL: I certainly will. I'll go when you do, honey.

LITTLE MARTHA: *(Softly stroking Rachel's arm)* You're the very nicest "grown-up," *(loyally)* except my muzzer, of course, I ever knew. You knows all about little chil'run and you can be one, although you're all grown up. I think you would make a lovely muzzer. *(To the rest of the children)* Don't you?

ALL: *(In excited whispers)* Yes, I do.

RACHEL: *(Winces, then says gently)* Come, kiddies, you must go now, or your mothers will blame me for keeping you. *(Rises, as do the rest. Little Martha puts her hand into Rachel's.)* Ma dear, I'm going down to sit a little while with Jenny. I'll be back before you go, though. Come, kiddies, say good-night to my mother.

ALL: *(Gravely)* Good-night! Sweet dreams! God keep you all the night.

MRS. LOVING: Good-night dears! Sweet dreams, all!

*(Exeunt Rachel and the children. Mrs. Loving continues to sew. The bell presently rings three distinct times. In a few moments, Mrs. Loving gets up and goes out into the vestibule. A door opens and closes. Mrs. Loving and John Strong come in. He is a trifle pale but his imperturbable self. Mrs. Loving,*

*somewhat nervous, takes her seat and resumes her sewing. She motions Strong to a chair. He returns to the vestibule, leaves his hat, returns, and sits down.)*

STRONG: Well, how is everything?

MRS. LOVING: Oh! about the same, I guess. Tom's out. John, we'll never forget you—and your kindness.

STRONG: That was nothing. And Rachel?

MRS. LOVING: She'll be back presently. She went to sit with a sick child for a little while.

STRONG: And how is she?

MRS. LOVING: She's not herself yet, but I think she is better.

STRONG: *(After a short pause)* Well, what *did* happen—exactly?

MRS. LOVING: That's just what I don't know.

STRONG: When you came home—you couldn't get in—was that it?

MRS. LOVING: Yes. *(Pauses.)* It was just a week ago today. I was down town all the morning. It was about one o'clock when I got back. I had forgotten my key. I rapped on the door and then called. There was no answer. A window was open, and I could feel the air under the door, and I could hear it as the draught sucked it through. There was no other sound. Presently I made such a noise the people began to come out into the hall. Jimmy was in one of the flats playing with a little girl named Mary. He told me he had left Rachel here a short time before. She had given him four cookies, two for him and two for Mary, and had told him he could play with her until she came to tell him his lunch was ready. I saw he was getting frightened, so I got the little girl and her mother to keep him in their flat. Then, as no man was at home, I sent out for help. Three men broke the door down. *(Pauses.)* We found Rachel unconscious, lying on her face. For a few minutes I thought she was dead. *(Pauses.)* A vase had fallen over on the table and the water had dripped through the cloth and onto the floor. There had been flowers in it. When I left, there were no flowers here. What she could have done to them, I can't say. The long stems were lying everywhere, and the flowers had been ground into the floor. I could tell that they must have been roses from the stems. After we had put her to bed and called the doctor, and she had finally regained consciousness, I very naturally asked her what had happened. All she would say was, "Ma dear, I'm too—tired—please." For four days she lay in bed scarcely moving, speaking only when spoken to. That first day, when Jimmy came in to see her, she shrank away from him. We had to take him out, and comfort him as best we could. We kept him away, almost by force, until she got up. And, then, she was utterly miserable when he was out of her sight. What happened, I don't know. She avoids Tom, and she won't tell me. *(Pauses.)* Tom and I both believe her soul has been hurt. The trouble isn't with her body. You'll find her highly nervous. Sometimes she is very much depressed; again she is feverishly gay—almost reckless. What do you think about it, John?

STRONG: *(Who has listened quietly)* Had anybody been here, do you know?

MRS. LOVING: No, I don't. I don't like to ask Rachel; and I can't ask the neighbors.

STRONG: No, of course not. *(Pauses.)* You say there were

some flowers?

MRS. LOVING: Yes.

STRONG: And the flowers were ground into the carpet?

MRS. LOVING: Yes.

2320 STRONG: Did you happen to notice the box? They must have come in a box, don't you think?

MRS. LOVING: Yes, there was a box in the kitchenette. It was from "Marcy's." I saw no card.

STRONG: (*Slowly*) It is rather strange. (*A long silence, during which the outer door opens and shuts. Rachel is heard singing. She stops abruptly. In a second or two she appears in the door. There is an air of suppressed excitement about her.*)

RACHEL: Hello! John. (*Strong rises, nods at her, and brings for-*
2330 *ward for her the big arm-chair near the fire.*) I thought that was your hat in the hall. It's brand new, I know—but it looks—"Johnlike." How are you? Ma! Jenny went to sleep like a little lamb. I don't like her breathing, though. (*Looks from one to the other; flippantly*) Who's dead? (*Nods her thanks to Strong for the chair and sits down.*)

MRS. LOVING: Dead, Rachel?

RACHEL: Yes. The atmosphere here is so funereal,—it's positively "crapey."

STRONG: I don't know why it should be—I was just asking how
2340 you are.

RACHEL: Heavens! Does the mere inquiry into my health precipitate such an atmosphere? Your two faces were as long, as long—(*Breaks off*). Kind sir, let me assure you, I am in the very best of health. And how are you, John?

STRONG: Oh! I'm always well. (*Sits down.*)

MRS. LOVING: Rachel, I'll have to get ready to go now. John, don't hurry. I'll be back shortly, probably in three-quarters of an hour—maybe less.

RACHEL: And maybe more, if I remember Mrs. Jordan. How-
2350 ever, Ma dear, I'll do the best I can—while you are away. I'll try to be a credit to your training. (*Mrs. Loving smiles and goes out the rear doorway.*) Now, let's see—in the books of etiquette, I believe, the properly reared young lady, always asks the young gentleman caller—you're young enough, aren't you, to be classed still as a "young gentleman caller?" (*No answer.*) Well, anyway, she always asks the young gentleman caller sweetly something about the weather. (*Primly*) This has been an exceedingly beautiful day, hasn't it, Mr. Strong? (*No answer from Strong, who, with his head*
2360 *resting against the back of the chair, and his knees crossed is watching her in an amused, quizzical manner.*) Well, really, every properly brought up young gentleman, I'm sure, ought to know, that it's exceedingly rude not to answer a civil question.

STRONG: (*Lazily*) Tell me what to answer, Rachel.

RACHEL: Say, "Yes, very"; and look interested and pleased when you say it.

STRONG: (*With a half-smile*) Yes, very.

RACHEL: Well, I certainly wouldn't characterize that as a par-
2370 ticularly animated remark. Besides, when you look at me through half-closed lids like that—and kind of smile—what are you thinking? (*No answer*) John Strong, are you deaf or—just plain stupid?

STRONG: Plain stupid, I guess.

RACHEL: (*In wheedling tones*) What were you thinking, John?

STRONG: (*Slowly*) I was thinking—(*Breaks off*).

RACHEL: (*Irritably*) Well?

STRONG: I've changed my mind.

RACHEL: You're not going to tell me?

STRONG: No.    2380

(*Mrs. Loving dressed for the street comes in.*)

MRS. LOVING: Goodbye, children. Rachel, don't quarrel so much with John. Let me see—if I have my key. (*Feels in her bag.*) Yes, I have it. I'll be back shortly. Good-bye. (*Strong and Rachel rise. He bows.*)

RACHEL: Good-bye, Ma dear. Hurry back as soon as you can, won't you? (*Exit Mrs. Loving through the vestibule. Strong leans back again in his chair, and watches Rachel through half-closed eyes. Rachel sits in her chair nervously.*)

STRONG: Do you mind, if I smoke?

RACHEL: You know I don't.    2390

STRONG: I am trying to behave like—Reginald—"the properly reared young gentleman caller." (*Lights a cigar; goes over to the fire, and throws his match away. Rachel goes into the kitchenette, and brings him a saucer for his ashes. She places it on the table near him.*) Thank you. (*They both sit again, Strong very evidently enjoying his cigar and Rachel.*) Now this is what I call cosy.

RACHEL: Cosy! Why?

STRONG: A nice warm room—shut in—curtains drawn—a cheerful fire crackling at my back—a lamp, not an electric 2400 or gas one, but one of your plain, old-fashioned kerosene ones—

RACHEL: (*Interrupting*) Ma dear would like to catch you, I am sure, talking about *her* lamp like that. "Old-fashioned! plain!"—You have nerve.

STRONG: (*Continuing as though he had not been interrupted*) A comfortable chair—a good cigar—and not very far away, a little lady, who is looking charming, so near, that if I reached over, I could touch her. You there—and I here.— It's living.    2410

RACHEL: Well! of all things! A compliment—and from *you!* How did it slip out, pray? (*No answer.*) I suppose that you realize that a conversation between two persons is absolutely impossible, if one has to do her share all alone. Soon my ingenuity for introducing interesting subjects will be exhausted; and then will follow what, I believe, the story books call, "an uncomfortable silence."

STRONG: (*Slowly*) Silence—between friends—isn't such a bad thing.

RACHEL: Thanks awfully. (*Leans back; cups her cheek in her* 2420 *hand, and makes no pretense at further conversation. The old look of introspection returns to her eyes. She does not move.*)

STRONG: (*Quietly*) Rachel! (*Rachel starts perceptibly*) You must remember I'm here. I don't like looking into your soul—when you forget you're not alone.

RACHEL: I hadn't forgotten.

STRONG: Wouldn't it be easier for you, little girl, if you could tell—some one?

RACHEL: No. (*A silence*)    2430

STRONG: Rachel,—you're fond of flowers,—aren't you?

RACHEL: Yes.

STRONG: Rosebuds—red rosebuds—particularly?

RACHEL: (*Nervously*) Yes.

STRONG: Did you—dislike—the giver?

RACHEL: (*More nervously; bracing herself*) No, of course not.

STRONG: Rachel,—why—why—did you—kill the roses—then?

RACHEL: (*Twisting her hands*) Oh, John! I'm so sorry, Ma dear
2440   told you that. She didn't know, you sent them.

STRONG: So I gathered. (*Pauses and then leans forward; quietly*) Rachel, little girl, why—did you kill them?

RACHEL: (*Breathing quickly*) Don't you believe—it—a—a—kindness—sometimes—to kill?

STRONG: (*After a pause*) You—considered—it—a—kindness—to kill them?

RACHEL: Yes. (*Another pause.*)

STRONG: Do you mean—just—the roses?

RACHEL: (*Breathing more quickly*) John!—Oh! must I say?

2450   STRONG: Yes, little Rachel.

RACHEL: (*In a whisper*) No. (*There is a long pause. Rachel leans back limply, and closes her eyes. Presently Strong rises, and moves his chair very close to hers. She does not stir. He puts his cigar on the saucer.*)

STRONG: (*Leaning forward; very gently*) Little girl, little girl, can't you tell me why?

RACHEL: (*Wearily*) I can't—It hurts—too much—to talk about it yet,—please.

STRONG: (*Takes her hand; looks at it a few minutes and then at
2460   her quietly*) You—don't—care, then? (*She winces*) Rachel!—Look at me, little girl! (*As if against her will, she looks at him. Her eyes are fearful, hunted. She tries to look away, to draw away her hand; but he holds her gaze and her hand steadily.*) Do you?

RACHEL: (*Almost sobbing*) John! John! don't ask me. You are drawing my very soul out of my body with your eyes. You must not talk this way. You mustn't look—John, don't! (*Tries to shield her eyes.*)

STRONG: (*Quietly takes both of her hands, and kisses the backs
2470   and the palms slowly. A look of horror creeps into her face. He deliberately raises his eyes and looks at her mouth. She recoils as though she expected him to strike her. He resumes slowly*) If—you—do—care, and I know now—that you do—nothing else, *nothing* should count.

RACHEL: (*Wrenching herself from his grasp and rising. She covers her ears; she breathes rapidly*) No! No! No!—You *must* stop. (*Laughs nervously; continues feverishly*) I'm not behaving very well as a hostess, am I? Let's see. What shall I do? I'll play you something, John. How will that do? Or I'll
2480   sing to you. You used to like to hear me sing; you said my voice, I remember, was sympathetic, didn't you? (*Moves quickly to the piano.*) I'll sing you a pretty little song. I think it's beautiful. You've never heard it, I know. I've never sung it to you before. It's Nevin's "At Twilight." (*Pauses, looks down, before she begins, then turns toward him and says quietly and sweetly*) Sometimes—in the coming years—I want—you to remember—I sang you this little song.—Will you?—I think it will make it easier for me—when I—when I—(*Breaks off and begins the first chords. Strong goes
2490   slowly to the piano. He leans there watching intently. Rachel sings*):

"The roses of yester-year
Were all of the white and red;

It fills my heart with silent fear
To find all their beauty fled.

The roses of white are sere,
All faded the roses red,
And one who loves me is not here
And one that I love is dead."

(*A long pause. Then Strong goes to her and lifts her from the piano-stool. He puts one arm around her very tenderly and pushes her head back so he can look into her eyes. She shuts them, but is passive.*)

STRONG: (*Gently*) Little girl, little girl, don't you know that sug-    2500
gestions—suggestions—like those you are sending yourself constantly—are wicked things? You, who are so gentle, so loving, so warm—(*Breaks off and crushes her to him. He kisses her many times. She does not resist, but in the midst of his caresses she breaks suddenly into convulsive laughter. He tries to hush the terrible sound with his mouth; then brokenly*) Little girl—don't laugh—like that.

RACHEL: (*Interrupted throughout by her laughter*) I have to.— God is laughing.—We're his puppets.—He pulls the wires,—and we're so funny to Him.—I'm laughing too—    2510
because I can hear—my little children—weeping. They come to me generally while I'm asleep,—but I can hear them now.—They've begged me—do you understand?— begged me—not to bring them here;—and I've promised them—not to.—I've promised. I can't stand the sound of their crying.—I have to laugh—Oh! John! laugh!—laugh too!—I can't drown their weeping.

(*Strong picks her up bodily and carries her to the armchair.*)

STRONG: (*Harshly*) Now, stop that!

RACHEL: (*In sheer surprise*) W-h-a-t?

STRONG: (*Still harshly*) Stop that!—You've lost your self-    2520
control.—Find yourself again!

(*He leaves her and goes over to the fireplace, and stands looking down into it for some little time. Rachel, little by little, becomes calmer. Strong returns and sits beside her again. She doesn't move. He smoothes her hair back gently, and kisses her forehead—and then, slowly, her mouth. She does not resist; simply sits there, with shut eyes, inert, limp.*)

STRONG: Rachel!—(*Pauses.*) There is a little flat on 43rd Street. It faces south and overlooks a little park. Do you remember it?—it's on the top floor?—Once I remember your saying—you liked it. That was over a year ago. That same day—I rented it. I've never lived there. No one knows about it—not even my mother. It's completely furnished now— and waiting—do you know for whom? Every single thing in it, I've bought myself—even to the pins on the little bird's-eye maple dresser. It has been the happiest year I have ever    2530
known. I furnished it—one room at a time. It's the prettiest, the most homelike little flat I've ever seen. (*Very low*) Everything there—breathes love. Do you know for whom it is waiting? On the sitting-room floor is a beautiful, Turkish rug—red, and blue and gold. It's soft—and rich—and do you know for whose little feet it is waiting? There are delicate curtains at the windows and a bookcase full of friendly, eager, little books.—Do you know for whom they are waiting? There are comfortable leather chairs, just the right size,

and a beautiful piano—that I leave open—sometimes, and lovely pictures of Madonnas. Do you know for whom they are waiting? There is an open fireplace with logs of wood, all carefully piled on gleaming andirons—and waiting. There is a bellows and a pair of shining tongs—waiting. And in the kitchenette painted blue and white, and smelling sweet with paint is everything: bright pots and pans and kettles, and blue and white enamel-ware, and all kinds of knives and forks and spoons—and on the door—a roller-towel. Little girl, do you know for whom they are all waiting? And somewhere—there's a big, strong man—with broad shoulders. And he's willing and anxious to do anything—everything, and he's waiting very patiently. Little girl, is it to be—yes or no?

RACHEL: (*During Strong's speech life has come flooding back to her. Her eyes are shining; her face, eager. For a moment she is beautifully happy*) Oh! you're too good to me and mine, John. I—didn't dream any one—could be—so good. (*Leans forward and puts his big hand against her cheek and kisses it shyly.*)

STRONG: (*Quietly*) Is it—yes—or no, little girl?

RACHEL: (*Feverishly, gripping his hands*) Oh, yes! yes! yes! and take me quickly, John. Take me before I can think any more. You mustn't let me think, John. And you'll be good to me, won't you? Every second of every minute, of every hour, of every day, you'll have me in your thoughts, won't you? And you'll be with me every minute that you can? And, John, John!—you'll keep away the weeping of my little children. You won't let me hear it, will you? You'll make me forget everything—won't you? Life is so short, John. (*Shivers and then fearfully and slowly*) And eternity so—long. (*Feverishly again*) And, John, after I am dead—promise me, promise me you'll love me more. (*Shivers again.*) I'll need love then. Oh! I'll need it. (*Suddenly there comes to their ears the sound of a child's weeping. It is monotonous, hopeless, terribly afraid. Rachel recoils.*) Oh! John!—Listen!—It's my boy, again.—I—John—I'll be back in a little while. (*Goes swiftly to the door in the rear, pauses and looks back. The weeping continues. Her eyes are tragic. Slowly she kisses her hand to him and disappears. John stands where she has left him looking down. The weeping stops. Presently Rachel appears in the doorway. She is haggard, and grey. She does not enter the room. She speaks as one dead might speak—tonelessly, slowly.*)

RACHEL: Do you wish to know why Jimmy is crying?

STRONG: Yes.

RACHEL: I am twenty-two—and I'm old; you're thirty-two—and you're old; Tom's twenty-three—and he is old. Ma dear's sixty—and she said once she is much older than that. She is. We are all blighted; we are all accursed—all of us,—everywhere, we whose skins are dark—our lives blasted by the white man's prejudice. (*Pauses*) And my little Jimmy—seven years old, that's all—is blighted too. In a year or two, at best, he will be made old by suffering. (*Pauses.*) One week ago, today, some white boys, older and larger than my little Jimmy, as he was leaving the school—called him "Nigger"! They chased him through the streets calling him, "Nigger! Nigger! Nigger!" One boy threw stones at him. There is still a bruise on his little back where one struck him. That will get well; but they bruised his soul—and that—will never—get well. He asked me what "Nigger"

meant. I made light of the whole thing, laughed it off. He went to his little playmates, and very naturally asked them. The oldest of them is nine!—and they knew, poor little things—and they told him. (*Pauses.*) For the last couple of nights he has been dreaming—about these boys. And he always awakes—in the dark—afraid—afraid—of the now—and the future—I have seen that look of deadly fear—in the eyes—of other little children. I know what it is myself.—I was twelve—when some big boys chased me and called me names.—I never left the house afterwards—without being afraid. I was afraid, in the streets—in the school—in the church, everywhere, always, afraid of being hurt. And I—was not—afraid in vain. (*The weeping begins again.*) He's only a baby—and he's blighted. (*To Jimmy*) Honey, I'm right here. I'm coming in just a minute. Don't cry. (*To Strong*) If it nearly kills me to hear my Jimmy's crying, do you think I could stand it, when my own child, flesh of my flesh, blood of my blood—learned the same reason for weeping? Do you? (*Pauses.*) Ever since I fell here—a week ago—I am afraid—to go—to sleep, for every time I do—my children come—and beg me—weeping—not to—bring them here—to suffer. Tonight, they came—when I was awake. (*Pauses.*) I have promised them again, now—by Jimmy's bed. (*In a whisper*) I have damned—my soul to all eternity—if I do. (*To Jimmy*) Honey, don't! I'm coming. (*To Strong*) And John,—dear John—you see—it can never be—all the beautiful, beautiful things—you have—told me about. (*Wistfully*) No—they—can never be—now. (*Strong comes toward her*) No,—John dear,—you—must not—touch me—any more. (*Pauses.*) Dear, this—is—"Good-bye."

STRONG: (*Quietly*) It's not fair—to you, Rachel, to take you—at your word—tonight. You're sick; you've brooded so long, so continuously,—you've lost—your perspective. Don't answer, yet. Think it over for another week and I'll come back.

RACHEL: (*Wearily*) No,—I can't think—any more.

STRONG: You realize—fully—you're sending me—for always?

RACHEL: Yes.

STRONG: And you care?

RACHEL: Yes.

STRONG: It's settled, then for all time—"Good-bye!"

RACHEL: (*After a pause*) Yes.

STRONG: (*Stands looking at her steadily a long time, and then moves to the door and turns, facing her; with infinite tenderness*) Good-bye, dear, little Rachel—God bless you.

RACHEL: Good-bye, John! (*Strong goes out. A door opens and shuts. There is finality in the sound. The weeping continues. Suddenly; with a great cry*) John! John! (*Runs out into the vestibule. She presently returns. She is calm again. Slowly*) No! No! John. Not for us. (*A pause; with infinite yearning*) Oh! John,—if it only—if it only—(*Breaks off, controls herself. Slowly again; thoughtfully*) No—No sunshine—no laughter—always, always—darkness. That is it. Even our little flat—(*In a whisper*) John's and mine—the little flat—that calls, calls us—through darkness. It shall wait—and wait—in—vain—in darkness. Oh, John! (*Pauses.*) And my little children! my little children! (*The weeping ceases; pauses.*) I shall never—see—you—now. Your little, brown, beautiful bodies—I shall never see.—Your dimples—everywhere—your laughter—your tears—the beautiful, lovely feel of you here. (*Puts her hands against her heart.*)

Never—never—to be. *(A pause, fiercely)* But you are some-where—and wherever you are you are mine! You are mine! All of you! Every bit of you! Even God can't take you away. *(A pause; very sweetly; pathetically)* Little children!—My little children!—No more need you come to me—weeping—weeping. You may be happy now—you are safe. Little weeping, voices, hush! hush! *(The weeping begins again. To Jimmy, her whole soul in her voice)* Jimmy! My lit-tle Jimmy! Honey! I'm coming.—Ma Rachel loves you so. *(Sobs and goes blindly, unsteadily to the rear doorway; she leans her head there one second against the door; and then stumbles through and disappears. The light in the lamp flickers and goes out. . . . It is black. The terrible, heart-breaking weeping continues.)* 2670

**T H E   E N D**

*First printed in* Competitor *in January 1920, Angelina Weld Grimké's description of* Rachel *outlines several of her goals in writing the play, particularly her sense of Rachel's complex refusal of motherhood in the play's finale.*

Since it has been understood that "Rachel" preaches race suicide, I would emphasize that that was not my intention. To the contrary, the appeal is not primarily to the colored people, but to the whites.

Because of environment and certain inherent qualities each of us reacts correspondingly and logically to the various forces about us. For example, if these forces be of love we react with love, and if of hate with hate. Very naturally all of us will not react as strongly or in the same manner— that is impossible.

Now the colored people in this country form what may be called the "submerged tenth." From morning until night, week in week out, year in year out, until death ends all, they never know what it means to draw one clean, deep breath free from the contamination of the poison of that enveloping force which we call race prejudice. Of necessity they react to it. Some are embittered, made resentful, belligerent, even dangerous; some are made hopeless, indifferent, submissive, lacking in initiative; some again go to any extreme in a search for temporary pleasures to drown their memory, thought, etc.

Now the purpose was to show how a refined, sensitive, highly-strung girl, a dreamer and an idealist, the strongest instinct in whose nature is a love for children and a desire some day to be a mother herself—how this girl would react to this force.

The majority of women, everywhere, although they are beginning to awaken, form one of the most conservative elements of society. They are, therefore, opposed to changes. For this reason and for sex reasons the white women of this country are about the worst enemies with which the colored race has to contend. My belief was, then, that if a vulnerable point in their armor could be found, if their hearts could be active or passive enemies, they might become, at least, less inimical and possibly friendly.

Did they have a vulnerable point and, if so, what was it? I believed it to be motherhood. Certainly all the noblest, finest, most sacred things in their lives converge about this. If anything can make all women sisters underneath their skins it is motherhood. If, then, the white women of this country could see, feel, understand just what effect their prejudice and the prejudice of their fathers, brothers, husbands, sons were having on the souls of the colored mothers everywhere, and upon the mothers that are to be, a great power to affect public opinion would be set free and the battle would be half won.

This was the main purpose. There is a subsidiary one as well. Whenever you say "colored person" to a white man he immediately, either through an ignorance that is deliberate or stupid, conjures up in his mind the picture of what he calls "the darkey." In other words, he believes, or says he does, that all colored people are a grinning, white-toothed, shiftless, carefree set, given to chicken-stealing, watermelon-eating, always, under all circumstances, properly obsequious to a white skin and always amusing. Now, it is possible that this type is to be found among the colored people; but if the white man is honest and observant he will have to acknowledge that the same type can be duplicated in his own race. Human nature, after all, is the same. And if the white man only cared to find out he would know that, type for type, he could find the same in both races. Certainly colored people are living in homes that are clean, well-kept with many evidences of taste and refinement about them. They are many of them well educated, cultivated and cultured; they are well-mannered and, in many instances, more moral than the whites; they love beauty; they have ideals and ambitions, and they do not talk—this educated type—in the Negro dialect. All the joys and sorrows and emotions the white people feel they feel; their feelings are as sensitive; they can be hurt as easily; they are as proud. I drew my characters, then, from the best type of colored people.

Now as to the play itself. In the first act Rachel, loving, young, joyous and vital, caring more to be a mother than anything else in the world, comes suddenly and terribly face to face with what motherhood means to the colored woman in the South. Four years elapse between the first and second acts. Rachel has learned much. She is saddened, disillusioned and embittered. She knows

Angelina Weld
Grimké

*"Rachel*—The Play of
the Month: The Reason
and Synopsis by the
Author"
(1920)

*The Reason and
Synopsis by the Author*

now that organized society in the North has decreed that if a colored man or woman is to be an economic factor, then he or she must, with comparatively few exceptions, remain in the menial class. This has been taught her by her own experience, by the experience of her brother, Tom, and by the experience of John Strong, the man she loves. She has learned that she may not go to a theater for an evening's entertainment without having it spoiled for her since, because of her color she must sit as an outcast, a pariah in a segregated section. And yet in spite of all this youth in her dies hard and hope and the desire for motherhood. She loves children, if anything, more than ever. It is in this act that she feels certain, for the first time, that John Strong loves her. She is made very happy by this knowledge, but in the midst of her joy there comes a knocking at the door. And very terribly and swiftly again it is brought home to her what motherhood means, this time to the colored woman in the North. The lesson comes to her through a little black girl and her own little adopted son, Jimmy. Not content with maiming and marring the lives of colored men and women she learns this baneful thing, race prejudice, strikes at the souls of little colored children. In her anguish and despair at the knowledge she turns against God, believing that He has been mocking at her by implanting in her breast this desire for motherhood, and she swears by the most solemn oath of which she can think never to bring a child here to have its life blighted and ruined.

A week elapses between Acts II and III. During the time Rachel has been very ill, not in body, but in mind and soul. She is up and about again, but is in a highly overwrought, nervous state. John Strong, whom she has not seen since she has been sick, comes to see her. She knows what his coming means and tries unsuccessfully to ward off his proposal. He pleads so well that, although she feels she is doing a wicked thing she finally yields. Just at the moment of her surrender, however, the sound of little Jimmy's heartbreaking weeping comes to her ears. She changes immediately and leaves him to go to Jimmy. Every night since Jimmy has undergone that searing experience in the previous act he has dreamed of it and awakens weeping. With that sound in her ears and soul she finds that she cannot break her oath. She returns and tells John Strong she cannot marry him. He is inclined, at first, not to take her seriously; but she shows him that this time her answer is final. Although her heart is breaking she sends him away. The play ends in blackness and with the inconsolable sounds of little Jimmy weeping.

---

Reprinted from the *Competitor* 1 (Jan. 1920): 51–52.

# Bernard Shaw

George Bernard Shaw (1856–1950)—Shaw disliked the name "George" and never used it—was a man of wide-ranging passions and huge abilities. By his fortieth birthday he had written five novels, three volumes of classic music criticism, and three volumes of incendiary theater reviews; he had become visible in the influential socialist political organization, the Fabian Society; he had written the first books in English on Wagner's operas and on Ibsen's plays; and he had just started his career as a dramatist, a career that would eventually include over fifty plays.

Shaw was born in Dublin, and like Jonathan Swift, Richard Brinsley Sheridan, and Oscar Wilde, Shaw retained the satiric perspective of the Irish outsider in England. His mother was a music teacher and his sister was a promising singer when they left for London while Shaw was in his teens; he followed them to London in 1876. A shy and self-effacing young man, Shaw took a variety of jobs that brought him into contact with the public, and he used the opportunity of lecturing for the **FABIAN SOCIETY** to develop the brilliantly articulate persona we recognize today as "G. B. S." Throughout the 1880s, Shaw worked with the Fabians, adopting their plan of gradual social reform in place of a more rigorously Marxist call for social revolution. The Fabians strove to change society through a strategy of permeation, working to get their members elected into prominent offices, where their educational and social reforms might be put into effect. Shaw was deeply influenced by the Fabians' gradualist scheme for social improvement, a scheme that underlies the utopian project of his greatest plays. For Fabian gradualism synchronized with Shaw's other passion, creative evolution. Appalled by what he regarded as the mindless mechanism of Darwinian natural selection, Shaw resisted the notion that human evolution followed a random and inevitable process. He urged instead that humanity take command of its future by willing itself to evolve in certain humane directions, and he advocated eugenics, capital punishment, and other ideas in the interest of the development of the species. Shaw attempted an uneasy synthesis of the Fabian socialist project of gradual social evolution with the individualist metaphysics of creative evolution: the improvement of society through the improvement of each of its members.

Shaw's friend William Archer once described seeing Shaw in the British Museum reading room simultaneously reading Karl Marx's *Capital* and the score of Richard Wagner's *Ring of the Niebelung* cycle, and the blending of political substance with a rich and deeply harmonized verbal music became a constant feature of Shaw's drama. Writing as a theater critic in the 1890s, Shaw became the champion of Ibsen in England. Vowing to lay siege to the conventions of the nineteenth-century theater, he touted Ibsen's plays and lambasted the corny tearjerkers, simplistic melodramas, and overstuffed Shakespearean productions that were the theater's common fare. Not incidentally, he worked to create a taste for his own plays, an operatic drama of the intellectual passions.

Shaw's career as a playwright falls into three main phases. Shaw's earliest plays—*Widowers' Houses* (1892) and *Mrs Warren's Profession* (1893)—attacked specific social problems, like slum landlords and international prostitution. But Shaw more often linked social ills to the smug pieties of conventional morality. His plays generally work to disillusion his main characters—and his audience—from the ready acceptance of bourgeois **IDEOLOGY** as a natural "reality." This process of disillusionment informs Shaw's lighter comedies of the 1890s, plays like *Arms and the Man* (1894), *Candida* (1894), and *Caesar and Cleopatra* (1898). After the turn of the century, however, Shaw entered on his maturity as a playwright, undertaking a series of major comedies that place this process of disillusionment directly in conflict with society's most important institutions: marriage and sexuality in *Man and Superman* (1903); British imperialism in Ireland in *John Bull's Other Island* (1904); salvation, damnation, and raw power in *Major Barbara* (1905); medicine in *The Doctor's Dilemma* (1906); language and class in *Pygmalion* (1912). Several of these plays were first produced at the Court Theater, under the management of Shaw's close friend Harley Granville Barker, who originated the part of Cusins in *Major Barbara* and other Shavian roles. Under Barker and his partner J. E. Vedrenne, the Court Theater in 1904–1907 became the most influential theater in London before World War I. Through its efforts, and Shaw's own energy as playwright, director, and advisor, the Court made Shaw's reputation as a major dramatist. With the coming of World War I, and the violent waste of civilization it brought with it, Shaw's confidence in the eventual perfection of humanity was deeply shaken, and the plays of his final half-century are much bleaker, more uncertain in tone: his magnificent "fantasia in the Russian manner on English themes," *Heartbreak House* (1919), modeled on Chekhov's *The Cherry Orchard; Saint Joan* (1923), perhaps his best-loved play; his five-play "metabiological pentateuch" on the origin and future of the species, *Back to Methuselah* (1921); and many others. In contrast to the confidence of Shaw's earlier plays, the later dramas generally seem to ask the question that Shaw gave to his Saint Joan, "O God that madest this beautiful earth, when will it be ready to receive Thy saints? How long, O Lord, how long?"

## Heartbreak House (1919)

Shaw was born before the publication of Darwin's *Origin of Species* in 1859, and died after the dropping of the first atomic bomb on Hiroshima, and he worked indefatigably throughout his life for the betterment of society. But the zeal with which Shaw pursued his utopian vision of a better world flagged as the horror of World War I destroyed Europe, rent the fabric of English society at home, and made "gradual" social change seem even more intangible. The war was personally brutal for Shaw. Publication of his 1914 pacifist pamphlet *Common Sense About the War* left him reviled and isolated; his friend, the actor Robert Lorraine was severely wounded in fighting; Alan Campbell—the son of the actress Mrs. Patrick Campbell, one of Shaw's life-long romances—was killed, as was William Archer's son, Tom, whom Shaw had known since childhood. Usually a rapid writer, Shaw made slow progress on *Heartbreak House,* beginning the play in 1913 on the eve of the war, but finishing it only five years later.

Subtitled "A Fantasia in the Russian Manner on English Themes," *Heartbreak House* is indebted to the indirect and elegiac music of Chekhov's plays, though given a full, Shavian orchestration. Much as the characters in *Three Sisters* seem trapped in the web of romantic illusion, so in Shaw's play the denizens of Heartbreak House seem caught in a world of dreams. The opening of the play establishes this motif clearly and effectively, as Ellie Dunn arrives at Heartbreak House, waits to be received, opens her copy of *Othello,* and falls asleep—only to be met by the dotty Nurse Guinness and the confusing Captain Shotover. Throughout *Heartbreak House,* sleep is a prominent activity: Hesione has failed to meet Ellie because she fell asleep upstairs; Boss Mangan is hypnotized onstage; Mazzini Dunn spends much of the play in his pyjamas; and just as the bombs are about to fall in Act Three, everyone onstage seems to be fitfully dozing. The characters are irresistibly drawn to sleep, but even when they are awake their lives are absorbed in dreams, fictions, lies. Hector Hushabye, for instance, seduces Ellie with his fictive exploits as "Marcus Darnley"; Shotover's mystical "seventh degree of concentration" turns out to be rum-induced; the social reformer Mazzini Dunn (named for the Italian revolutionary), is finally captive to the machinations of Boss Mangan; even the thief Billy Dunn turns out to be no thief—he works hard to get caught, so that he can blackmail his victims into buying their way out of scandal; even Hesione's beautiful hair is false. As Hector suggests near the end of the play, the characters have a nearly ghostly unreality: "We do not live in this house: we haunt it."

But as Shaw's stage-design—a house designed to look like a ship, the ship of state foundering rudderless on the rocks—suggests, *Heartbreak House* is not merely about a group of English eccentrics gathering for the weekend. *Heartbreak House* is Shaw's anatomy of "cultured, leisured Europe before the war." Shaw's critique of this class is profoundly pessimistic. For in Shaw's view, the inhabitants of Heartbreak House ought to be England's saviors, the educated, professional, moneyed elite that could provide the moral, intellectual, and spiritual leadership to move the state into a better future. What cripples them in part is their lack of effective agency, the fact that the intellectual elite has been separated from the powerful, executive elite of England. Shaw symbolizes this disjunction between culture and power through the simple device of pairing opposite characters, opposing Mangan the industrialist to Mazzini the reformer, Hastings Utterword to Hector Hushabye, the drinking to the thinking Dunns. "Heartbreak" could provide a solution, a powerful disillusionment that might lead the characters back into effective, worldly action, and throughout the play, the characters are exposed, unmasked, given the chance to make this transformation. But when these lies are revealed, nothing happens. When Hector is exposed as "Marcus Darnley," he dons his extravagant Arabian costume; when Boss Mangan's fictive power is exploded, he runs out to the heath only to explode again.

Near the center of the play, Shotover and Ellie have a crucial dialogue on the subject of "heartbreak":

> CAPTAIN SHOTOVER: Heartbreak? Are you one of those who are so sufficient to themselves that
>    they are only happy when they are stripped of everything, even of hope?
> ELLIE: (*gripping the hand*) It seems so; for I feel now as if there was nothing I could not do,
>    because I want nothing.
> CAPTAIN SHOTOVER: That's the only real strength. That's genius. That's better than rum.

To "want nothing," to be free of the illusions of romantic desire is, in the economy of *Heartbreak House*, to be poised at the point where action is possible, where it may be possible to break out of this haunted, miserable house. Yet, finally, when action becomes possible, it is only the act of self-destruction. When the Zeppelins are heard above, the "splendid drumming in the sky" seems like an apocalyptic music to the haunted souls of Heartbreak House. Their best response is to beg for annihilation. As with much else in the play, even this desire is thwarted, ironically disappointed. The bombs fall elsewhere, killing the play's unimportant villains, but leaving its heroes in a state of disillusioned, disappointed half-life. England's saviors are left poised on the edge of destruction. At the play's end, we hear the mournful tune of "Keep the Home Fires Burning," the ballad of the war about to begin. The shattering consequences of England's inability to awaken lie just over the horizon.

# — Heartbreak House —
## Bernard Shaw

## —ACT ONE—

*The hilly country in the middle of the north edge of Sussex, looking very pleasant on a fine evening at the end of September, is seen through the windows of a room which has been built so as to resemble the after part of an old-fashioned high-pooped ship with a stern gallery; for the windows are ship built with heavy timbering, and run right across the room as continuously as the stability of the wall allows. A row of lockers under the windows provides an unupholstered window-seat interrupted by twin glass doors, respectively half-way between the stern post and the sides. Another door strains the illusion a little by being apparently in the ship's port side, and yet leading, not to the open sea, but to the entrance hall of the house. Between this door and the stern gallery are bookshelves. There are electric light switches beside the door leading to the hall and the glass doors in the stern gallery. Against the starboard wall is a carpenter's bench. The vice has a board in its jaws; and the floor is littered with shavings, overflowing from a waste-paper basket. A couple of planes and a centrebit are on the bench. In the same wall, between the bench and the windows, is a narrow doorway with a half door, above which a glimpse of the room beyond shows that it is a shelved pantry with bottles and kitchen crockery.*

*On the starboard side, but close to the middle, is a plain oak drawing-table with drawing-board, T-square, straight-edges, set squares, mathematical instruments, saucers of water color, a tumbler of discolored water, Indian ink, pencils, and brushes on it. The drawing-board is set so that the draughtsman's chair has the window on its left hand. On the floor at the end of the table, on his right, is a ship's fire bucket. On the port side of the room, near the bookshelves, is a sofa with its back to the windows. It is a sturdy mahogany article, oddly upholstered in sailcloth, including the bolster, with a couple of blankets hanging over the back. Between the sofa and the drawing-table is a big wicker chair, with broad arms and a low sloping back, with its back to the light. A small but stout table of teak, with a round top and gate legs, stands against the port wall between the door and the bookcase. It is the only article in the room that suggests (not at all convincingly) a woman's hand in the furnishing. The uncarpeted floor of narrow boards is caulked and holystoned like a deck.*

*The garden to which the glass doors lead dips to the south before the landscape rises again to the hills. Emerging from the hollow is the cupola of an observatory. Between the observatory and the house is a flagstaff on a little esplanade, with a hammock on the east side and a long garden seat on the west.*

*A young lady, gloved and hatted, with a dust coat on, is sitting in the window-seat with her body twisted to enable her to look out of the view. One hand props her chin; the other hangs down with a volume of the Temple Shakespeare in it, and her finger stuck in the page she has been reading.*

*A clock strikes six.*

*The young lady turns and looks at her watch. She rises with an air of one who waits and is almost at the end of her patience. She is a pretty girl, slender, fair, and intelligent looking, nicely but not expensively dressed, evidently not a smart idler.*

*With a sigh of weary resignation she comes to the draughtsman's chair; sits down; and begins to read Shakespeare. Presently the book sinks to her lap; her eyes close; and she dozes into a slumber.*

*An elderly womanservant comes in from the hall with three unopened bottles of rum on a tray. She passes through and disappears in the pantry without noticing the young lady. She places the bottles on the shelf and fills her tray with empty bottles. As she returns with these, the young lady lets her book drop, awakening herself, and startling the womanservant so that she all but lets the tray fall.*

THE WOMANSERVANT: God bless us! (*The young lady picks up the book and places it on the table.*) Sorry to wake you, miss, I'm sure; but you are a stranger to me. What might you be waiting here for now?

THE YOUNG LADY: Waiting for somebody to show some signs of knowing that I have been invited here.

THE WOMANSERVANT: Oh, you're invited, are you? And has nobody come? Dear! dear!

THE YOUNG LADY: A wild-looking old gentleman came and looked in at the window; and I heard him calling out, 10 "Nurse, there is a young and attractive female waiting in the poop. Go and see what she wants." Are you the nurse?

THE WOMANSERVANT: Yes, miss: I'm Nurse Guinness. That was old Captain Shotover, Mrs Hushabye's father. I heard him roaring; but I thought it was for something else. I suppose it was Mrs Hushabye that invited you, ducky?

THE YOUNG LADY: I understood her to do so. But really I think I'd better go.

NURSE GUINNESS: Oh, don't think of such a thing, miss. If Mrs Hushabye has forgotten all about it, it will be a pleasant sur- 20 prise for her to see you, won't it?

THE YOUNG LADY: It has been a very unpleasant surprise to me to find that nobody expects me.

NURSE GUINNESS: You'll get used to it, miss: this house is full of surprises for them that don't know our ways.

CAPTAIN SHOTOVER: (*looking in from the hall suddenly: an ancient but still hardy man with an immense white beard, in a reefer jacket with a whistle hanging from his neck*) Nurse, there is a hold-all and a hand-bag on the front steps for everybody to fall over. Also a tennis racquet. Who the devil 30 left them there?

THE YOUNG LADY: They are mine, I'm afraid.

THE CAPTAIN: (*advancing to the drawing-table*) Nurse, who is this misguided and unfortunate young lady?

NURSE GUINNESS: She says Miss Hessy invited her, sir.

THE CAPTAIN: And had she no friend, no parents, to warn her against my daughter's invitations? This is a pretty sort of house, by heavens! A young and attractive lady is invited here. Her luggage is left on the steps for hours; and she her-
40    self is deposited in the poop and abandoned, tired and starving. This is our hospitality. These are our manners. No room ready. No hot water. No welcoming hostess. Our visitor is to sleep in the toolshed, and to wash in the duckpond.

NURSE GUINNESS: Now it's all right, Captain: I'll get the lady some tea; and her room shall be ready before she has finished it. (*To the young lady.*) Take off your hat, ducky; and make yourself at home (*she goes to the door leading to the hall*).

THE CAPTAIN: (*as she passes him*) Ducky! Do you suppose,
50    woman, that because this young lady has been insulted and neglected, you have the right to address her as you address my wretched children, whom you have brought up in ignorance of the commonest decencies of social intercourse?

NURSE GUINNESS: Never mind him, doty. (*Quite unconcerned, she goes out into the hall on her way to the kitchen.*)

THE CAPTAIN: Madam, will you favor me with your name? (*He sits down in the big wicker chair.*)

THE YOUNG LADY: My name is Ellie Dunn.

THE CAPTAIN: Dunn! I had a boatswain whose name was Dunn.
60    He was originally a pirate in China. He set up as a ship's chandler with stores which I have every reason to believe he stole from me. No doubt he became rich. Are you his daughter?

ELLIE: (*indignant*) No, certainly not. I am proud to be able to say that though my father has not been a successful man, nobody has ever had one word to say against him. I think my father is the best man I have ever known.

THE CAPTAIN: He must be greatly changed. Has he attained the seventh degree of concentration?

70 ELLIE: I don't understand.

THE CAPTAIN: But how could he, with a daughter? I, madam, have two daughters. One of them is Hesione Hushabye, who invited you here. I keep this house: she upsets it. I desire to attain the seventh degree of concentration: she invites visitors and leaves me to entertain them. (*Nurse Guinness returns with the tea-tray, which she places on the teak table.*) I have a second daughter who is, thank God, in a remote part of the Empire with her numskull of a husband. As a child she thought the figure-head of my ship, the
80    Dauntless, the most beautiful thing on earth. He resembled it. He had the same expression: wooden yet enterprising. She married him, and will never set foot in this house again.

NURSE GUINNESS: (*carrying the table, with the tea-things on it, to Ellie's side*) Indeed you never were more mistaken. She is in England this very moment. You have been told three times this week that she is coming home for a year for her health. And very glad you should be to see your own daughter again after all these years.

THE CAPTAIN: I am not glad. The natural term of the affection
90    of the human animal for its offspring is six years. My daughter Ariadne was born when I was forty-six. I am now eighty-eight. If she comes, I am not at home. If she wants anything,

let her take it. If she asks for me, let her be informed that I am extremely old, and have totally forgotten her.

NURSE GUINNESS: That's no talk to offer to a young lady. Here, ducky, have some tea; and don't listen to him (*she pours out a cup of tea*)

THE CAPTAIN: (*rising wrathfully*) Now before high heaven they have given this innocent child Indian tea: the stuff they tan their own leather insides with. (*He seizes the cup and the* 100 *tea-pot and empties both into the leathern bucket.*)

ELLIE: (*almost in tears*) Oh, please! I am so tired. I should have been glad of anything.

NURSE GUINNESS: Oh, what a thing to do! The poor lamb is ready to drop.

THE CAPTAIN: You shall have some of my tea. Do not touch that fly-blown cake: nobody eats it here except the dogs. (*He disappears into the pantry.*)

NURSE GUINNESS: There's a man for you! They say he sold himself to the devil in Zanzibar before he was a captain; and the 110 older he grows the more I believe them.

A WOMAN'S VOICE: (*in the hall*) Is anyone at home? Hesione! Nurse! Papa! Do come, somebody; and take in my luggage.

(*Thumping heard, as of an umbrella, on the wainscot.*)

NURSE GUINNESS: My gracious! It's Miss Addy, Lady Utterword, Mrs Hushabye's sister: the one I told the captain about. (*Calling.*) Coming, Miss, coming.

(*She carries the table back to its place by the door and is hurrying out when she is intercepted by Lady Utterword, who bursts in much flustered. Lady Utterword, a blonde, is very handsome, very well dressed, and so precipitate in speech and action that the first impression [erroneous] is one of comic silliness.*)

LADY UTTERWORD: Oh, is that you, Nurse? How are you? You don't look a day older. Is nobody at home? Where is Hesione? Doesn't she expect me? Where are the servants? Whose luggage is that on the steps? Where's papa? Is every- 120 body asleep? (*Seeing Ellie.*) Oh! I beg your pardon. I suppose you are one of my nieces. (*Approaching her with outstretched arms.*) Come and kiss your aunt, darling.

ELLIE: I'm only a visitor. It is my luggage on the steps.

NURSE GUINNESS: I'll go get you some fresh tea, ducky. (*She takes up the tray.*)

ELLIE: But the old gentleman said he would make some himself.

NURSE GUINNESS: Bless you! he's forgotten what he went for already. His mind wanders from one thing to another. 130

LADY UTTERWORD: Papa, I suppose?

NURSE GUINNESS: Yes, Miss.

LADY UTTERWORD: (*vehemently*) Don't be silly, Nurse. Don't call me Miss.

NURSE GUINNESS: (*placidly*) No, lovey (*she goes out with the tea-tray*).

LADY UTTERWORD: (*sitting down with a flounce on the sofa*) I know what you must feel. Oh, this house, this house! I come back to it after twenty-three years; and it is just the same: the luggage lying on the steps, the servants spoilt and im- 140 possible, nobody at home to receive anybody, no regular meals, nobody ever hungry because they are always gnawing bread and butter or munching apples, and, what is worse,

the same disorder in ideas, in talk, in feeling. When I was a child I was used to it: I had never known anything better, though I was unhappy, and longed all the time—oh, how I longed!—to be respectable, to be a lady, to live as others did, not to have to think of everything for myself. I married
150 at nineteen to escape from it. My husband is Sir Hastings Utterword, who has been governor of all the crown colonies in succession. I have always been the mistress of Government House. I have been so happy: I had forgotten that people could live like this. I wanted to see my father, my sister, my nephews and nieces (one ought to, you know), and I was looking forward to it. And now the state of the house! the way I'm received! the casual impudence of that woman Guinness, our old nurse! really Hesione might at least have been here: *some* preparation might have been made for me. You must excuse my going on in this way; but I am really
160 very much hurt and annoyed and disillusioned: and if I had realized it was to be like this, I wouldn't have come. I have a great mind to go away without another word (*she is on the point of weeping*).

ELLIE: (*also very miserable*) Nobody has been here to receive me either. I thought I ought to go away too. But how can I, Lady Utterword? My luggage is on the steps; and the station fly has gone.

(*The captain emerges from the pantry with a tray of Chinese lacquer and a very fine tea-set on it. He rests it provisionally on the end of the table; snatches away the drawing-board, which he stands on the floor against table legs; and puts the tray in the space thus cleared. Ellie pours out a cup greedily.*)

THE CAPTAIN: Your tea, young lady. What! another lady! I must fetch another cup (*he makes for the pantry*).
170 LADY UTTERWORD: (*rising from the sofa, suffused with emotion*) Papa! Don't you know me? I'm your daughter.
THE CAPTAIN: Nonsense! my daughter's upstairs asleep. (*He vanishes through the half door.*)

(*Lady Utterword retires to the window to conceal her tears.*)

ELLIE: (*going to her with a cup*) Don't be so distressed. Have this cup of tea. He is very old and very strange: he has been just like that to me. I know how dreadful it must be: my own father is all the world to me. Oh, I'm sure he didn't mean it.

(*The captain returns with another cup.*)

THE CAPTAIN: Now we are complete. (*He places it on the tray.*)
LADY UTTERWORD: (*hysterically*) Papa, you can't have forgot-
180 ten me. I am Ariadne. I'm little Paddy Patkins. Won't you kiss me? (*She goes to him and throws her arms round his neck.*)
THE CAPTAIN: (*woodenly enduring her embrace*) How can you be Ariadne? You are a middle-aged woman: well preserved, madam, but no longer young.
LADY UTTERWORD: But think of all the years and years I have been away, Papa. I have had to grow old, like other people.
THE CAPTAIN: (*disengaging himself*) You should grow out of kissing strange men: they may be striving to attain the sev-
190 enth degree of concentration.
LADY UTTERWORD: But I'm your daughter. You haven't seen me for years.
THE CAPTAIN: So much the worse! When our relatives are at

home, we have to think of all their good points or it would be impossible to endure them. But when they are away, we console ourselves for their absence by dwelling on their vices. That is how I have come to think my absent daughter Ariadne a perfect fiend; so do not try to ingratiate yourself here by impersonating her (*he walks firmly away to the other side of the room.*)
200
LADY UTTERWORD: Ingratiating myself indeed! (*With dignity.*) Very well, papa. (*She sits down at the drawing-table and pours out tea for herself.*)
THE CAPTAIN: I am neglecting my social duties. You remember Dunn? Billy Dunn?
LADY UTTERWORD: Do you mean that villainous sailor who robbed you?
THE CAPTAIN: (*introducing Ellie*) His daughter. (*He sits down on the sofa.*)
ELLIE: (*protesting*) No—
210

(*Nurse Guinness returns with fresh tea.*)

THE CAPTAIN: Take that hogwash away. Do you hear?
NURSE: You've actually remembered about the tea! (*To Ellie.*) Oh, miss, he didn't forget you after all! You *have* made an impression.
THE CAPTAIN: (*gloomily*) Youth! beauty! novelty! They are badly wanted in this house. I am excessively old. Hesione is only moderately young. Her children are not youthful.
LADY UTTERWORD: How can children be expected to be youthful in this house? Almost before we could speak we were filled with notions that might have been all very well for 220 pagan philosophers of fifty, but were certainly quite unfit for respectable people of any age.
NURSE: You were always for respectability, Miss Addy.
LADY UTTERWORD: Nurse, will you please remember that I am Lady Utterword, and not Miss Addy, nor lovey, nor darling, nor doty? Do you hear?
NURSE: Yes, ducky: all right. I'll tell them all they must call you My lady. (*She takes her tray out with undisturbed placidity.*)
LADY UTTERWORD: What comfort? what sense is there in hav- 230 ing servants with no manners?
ELLIE: (*rising and coming to the table to put down her empty cup*) Lady Utterword, do you think Mrs Hushabye really expects me?
LADY UTTERWORD: Oh, don't ask me. You can see for yourself that I've just arrived; her only sister, after twenty-three years' absence! and it seems that *I* am not expected.
THE CAPTAIN: What does it matter whether the young lady is expected or not? She is welcome. There are beds: there is food. I'll find a room for her myself (*he makes for the door*). 240
ELLIE: (*following him to stop him*) Oh, please—(*He goes out.*) Lady Utterword, I don't know what to do. Your father persists in believing that my father is some sailor who robbed him.
LADY UTTERWORD: You had better pretend not to notice it. My father is a very clever man; but he always forgot things; and now that he is old, of course he is worse. And I must warn you that it is sometimes very hard to feel quite sure that he really forgets.

(*Mrs. Hushabye bursts into the room tempestuously and*

*embraces Ellie. She is a couple of years older than Lady Utterword, and even better looking. She has magnificent black hair, eyes like the fishpools of Heshbon, and a nobly modelled neck, short at the back and low between her shoulders in front. Unlike her sister she is uncorseted and dressed anyhow in a rich robe of black pile that shows off her white skin and statuesque contour.)*

250 MRS HUSHABYE: Ellie, my darling, my pettikins *(kissing her),* how long have you been here? I've been at home all the time: I was putting flowers and things in your room; and when I just sat down for a moment to try how comfortable the armchair was I went off to sleep. Papa woke me and told me you were here. Fancy your finding no one, and being neglected and abandoned. *(Kissing her again.)* My poor love! *(She deposits Ellie on the sofa. Meanwhile Ariadne has left the table and come over to claim her share of attention.)* Oh! you've brought someone with you. Introduce me.

260 LADY UTTERWORD: Hesione, is it possible that *you* don't know me?

MRS HUSHABYE: *(conventionally)* Of course I remember your face quite well. Where have we met?

LADY UTTERWORD: Didn't Papa tell you I was here? Oh! this is really too much. *(She throws herself sulkily into the big chair.)*

MRS HUSHABYE: Papa!

LADY UTTERWORD: Yes, Papa. Our papa, you unfeeling wretch! *(Rising angrily.)* I'll go straight to a hotel.

270 MRS HUSHABYE: *(seizing her by the shoulders)* My goodness gracious goodness, you don't mean to say that you're Addy!

LADY UTTERWORD: I certainly am Addy; and I don't think I can be so changed that you would not have recognized me if you had any real affection for me. And Papa didn't think me even worth mentioning!

MRS HUSHABYE: What a lark! Sit down *(she pushes her back into the chair instead of kissing her, and posts herself behind it).* You *do* look a swell. You're much handsomer than you used to be. You've made the acquaintance of Ellie, of course. She

280 is going to marry a perfect hog of a millionaire for the sake of her father, who is as poor as a church mouse; and you must help me to stop her.

ELLIE: Oh, please, Hesione!

MRS HUSHABYE: My pettikins, the man's coming here today with your father to begin persecuting you; and everybody will see the state of the case in ten minutes; so what's the use of making a secret of it?

ELLIE: He is not a hog, Hesione. You don't know how wonderfully good he was to my father, and how deeply grateful I am

290 to him.

MRS HUSHABYE: *(to Lady Utterword)* Her father is a very remarkable man, Addy. His name is Mazzini Dunn. Mazzini was a celebrity of some kind who knew Ellie's grandparents. They were both poets, like the Brownings; and when her father came into the world Mazzini said, "Another soldier born for freedom!" So they christened him Mazzini; and he has been fighting for freedom in his quiet way ever since. That's why he is so poor.

ELLIE: I am proud of his poverty.

300 MRS HUSHABYE: Of course you are, pettikins. Why not leave him in it, and marry someone you love?

LADY UTTERWORD: *(rising suddenly and explosively)* Hesione, are you going to kiss me or are you not?

MRS HUSHABYE: What do you want to be kissed for?

LADY UTTERWORD: I *don't* want to be kissed; but I do want you to behave properly and decently. We are sisters. We have been separated for twenty-three years. You *ought* to kiss me.

MRS HUSHABYE: To-morrow morning, dear, before you make up. I hate the smell of powder. 310

LADY UTTERWORD: Oh! you unfeeling—*(she is interrupted by the return of the captain).*

THE CAPTAIN: *(to Ellie)* Your room is ready. *(Ellie rises.)* The sheets were damp; but I have changed them *(he makes for the garden door on the port side).*

LADY UTTERWORD: Oh! What about *my* sheets?

THE CAPTAIN: *(halting at the door)* Take my advice: air them: or take them off and sleep in blankets. You shall sleep in Ariadne's old room.

LADY UTTERWORD: Indeed I shall do nothing of the sort. That 320 little hole! I am entitled to the best spare room.

THE CAPTAIN: *(continuing unmoved)* She married a numskull. She told me she would marry anyone to get away from home.

LADY UTTERWORD: You are pretending not to know me on purpose. I will leave the house.

*(Mazzini Dunn enters from the hall. He is a little elderly man with bulging credulous eyes and earnest manners. He is dressed in a blue serge jacket suit with an unbuttoned mackintosh over it, and carries a soft black hat of clerical cut.)*

ELLIE: At last! Captain Shotover, here is my father.

THE CAPTAIN: This! Nonsense! not a bit like him *(he goes away through the garden, shutting the door sharply behind him).*

LADY UTTERWORD: I will not be ignored and pretended to be 330 somebody else. I will have it out with Papa now, this instant. *(To Mazzini.)* Excuse me. *(She follows the captain out, making a hasty bow to Mazzini, who returns it.)*

MRS HUSHABYE: *(hospitably shaking hands)* How good of you to come, Mr Dunn! You don't mind Papa, do you? He is as mad as a hatter, you know, but quite harmless and extremely clever. You will have some delightful talks with him.

MAZZINI: I hope so. *(To Ellie.)* So here you are, Ellie, dear. *(He draws her arm affectionately through his.)* I must thank you, Mrs Hushabye, for your kindness to my daughter. I'm afraid 340 she would have had no holiday if you had not invited her.

MRS HUSHABYE: Not at all. Very nice of her to come and attract young people to the house for us.

MAZZINI: *(smiling)* I'm afraid Ellie is not interested in young men, Mrs Hushabye. Her taste is on the graver, solider side.

MRS HUSHABYE: *(with a sudden rather hard brightness in her manner)* Won't you take off your overcoat, Mr Dunn? You will find a cupboard for coats and hats and things in the corner of the hall.

MAZZINI: *(hastily releasing Ellie)* Yes—thank you—I had bet- 350 ter—*(he goes out).*

MRS HUSHABYE: *(emphatically)* The old brute!

ELLIE: Who?

MRS HUSHABYE: Who! Him. He. It *(pointing after Mazzini).* "Graver, solider tastes," indeed!

ELLIE: *(aghast)* You don't mean that you were speaking like that of my father!

MRS HUSHABYE: I was. You know I was.

360 ELLIE: *(with dignity)* I will leave your house at once. *(She turns to the door.)*

MRS HUSHABYE: If you attempt it, I'll tell your father why.

ELLIE: *(turning again)* Oh! How can you treat a visitor like this, Mrs Hushabye?

MRS HUSHABYE: I thought you were going to call me Hesione.

ELLIE: Certainly not now?

MRS HUSHABYE: Very well: I'll tell your father.

ELLIE: *(distressed)* Oh!

MRS HUSHABYE: If you turn a hair—if you take his part against
370 me and against your own heart for a moment, I'll give that
born soldier of freedom a piece of my mind that will stand
him on his selfish old head for a week.

ELLIE: Hesione! My father selfish! How little you know—

*(She is interrupted by Mazzini, who returns, excited and perspiring.)*

MAZZINI: Ellie, Mangan has come: I thought you'd like to
know. Excuse me, Mrs. Hushabye, the strange old gentleman—

MRS HUSHABYE: Papa. Quite so.

MAZZINI: Oh, I beg your pardon, of course: I was a little confused by his manner. He is making Mangan help him with
380 something in the garden; and he wants me too—

*(A powerful whistle is heard.)*

THE CAPTAIN'S VOICE: Bosun ahoy! *(the whistle is repeated).*

MAZZINI: *(flustered)* Oh dear! I believe he is whistling for me.
*(He hurries out.)*

MRS HUSHABYE: Now *my* father is a wonderful man if you like.

ELLIE: Hesione, listen to me. You don't understand. My father
and Mr Mangan were boys together. Mr Ma—

MRS HUSHABYE: I don't care what they were: we must sit down
if you are going to begin as far back as that. *(She snatches at
Ellie's waist, and makes her sit down on the sofa beside her.)*
390 Now, pettikins, tell me all about Mr Mangan. They call him
Boss Mangan, don't they? He is a Napoleon of industry and
disgustingly rich, isn't he? Why isn't your father rich?

ELLIE: My poor father should never have been in business. His
parents were poets; and they gave him the noblest ideas; but
they could not afford to give him a profession.

MRS HUSHABYE: Fancy your grandparents, with their eyes in
fine frenzy rolling! And so your poor father had to go into
business. Hasn't he succeeded in it?

ELLIE: He always used to say he could succeed if he only had
400 some capital. He fought his way along, to keep a roof over
our heads and bring us up well; but it was always a struggle:
always the same difficulty of not having capital enough. I
don't know how to describe it to you.

MRS HUSHABYE: Poor Ellie! I know. Pulling the devil by the tail.

ELLIE: *(hurt)* Oh, no. Not like that. It was at least dignified.

MRS HUSHABYE: That made it all the harder, didn't it? *I*
shouldn't have pulled the devil by the tail with dignity. I
should have pulled hard—*(between her teeth)* hard. Well?
Go on.

410 ELLIE: At last it seemed that all our troubles were at an end. Mr
Mangan did an extraordinarily noble thing out of pure
friendship for my father and respect for his character. He

asked him how much capital he wanted, and gave it to him.
I don't mean that he lent it to him, or that he invested it in
his business. He just simply made him a present of it.
Wasn't that splendid of him?

MRS HUSHABYE: On condition that you married him?

ELLIE: Oh, no, no, no! This was when I was a child. He had
never even seen me: he never came to our house. It was absolutely disinterested. Pure generosity.                        420

MRS HUSHABYE: Oh! I beg the gentleman's pardon. Well, what
became of the money?

ELLIE: We all got new clothes and moved into another house.
And I went to another school for two years.

MRS HUSHABYE: Only two years?

ELLIE: That was all: for at the end of two years my father was
utterly ruined.

MRS HUSHABYE: How?

ELLIE: I don't know. I never could understand. But it was
dreadful. When we were poor my father had never been in   430
debt. But when we launched out into business on a large
scale, he had to incur liabilities. When the business went
into liquidation he owed more money than Mr Mangan had
given him.

MRS HUSHABYE: Bit off more than he could chew, I suppose.

ELLIE: I think you are a little unfeeling about it.

MRS HUSHABYE: My pettikins, you mustn't mind my way of talking. I was quite as sensitive and particular as you once; but I
have picked up so much slang from the children that I am
really hardly presentable. I suppose your father had no head   440
for business, and made a mess of it.

ELLIE: Oh, that just shows how entirely you are mistaken about
him. The business turned out a great success. It now pays
forty-four per cent after deducting the excess profits tax.

MRS HUSHABYE: Then why aren't you rolling in money?

ELLIE: I don't know. It seems very unfair to me. You see, my
father was made bankrupt. It nearly broke his heart, because he had persuaded several of his friends to put money
into the business. He was sure it would succeed; and events
proved that he was quite right. But they all lost their money.   450
It was dreadful. I don't know what we should have done but
for Mr Mangan.

MRS HUSHABYE: What! Did the Boss come to the rescue again,
after all his money being thrown away?

ELLIE: He did indeed, and never uttered a reproach to my father. He bought what was left of the business—the buildings and the machinery and things—from the official
trustee for enough money to enable my father to pay six and
eightpence in the pound and get his discharge. Everyone
pitied papa so much, and saw so plainly that he was an hon-  460
orable man, that they let him off at six-and-eight-pence instead of ten shillings. Then Mr Mangan started a company
to take up the business, and made my father a manager in it
to save us from starvation; for I wasn't earning anything
then.

MRS HUSHABYE: Quite a romance. And when did the Boss develop the tender passion?

ELLIE: Oh, that was years after, quite lately. He took the chair
one night at a sort of people's concert. I was singing there.
As an amateur, you know: half a guinea for expenses and   470
three songs with three encores. He was so pleased with my
singing that he asked might he walk home with me. I never

saw anyone so taken aback as he was when I took him home and introduced him to my father, his own manager. It was then that my father told me how nobly he had behaved. Of course it was considered a great chance for me, as he is so rich. And—and—we drifted into a sort of understanding— I suppose I should call it an engagement—(*she is distressed and cannot go on*).

480 MRS HUSHABYE: (*rising and marching about*) You may have drifted into it; but you will bounce out of it, my pettikins, if I am to have anything to do with it.

ELLIE: (*hopelessly*) No: it's no use. I am bound in honor and gratitude. I will go through with it.

MRS HUSHABYE: (*behind the sofa, scolding down at her*) You know, of course, that it's not honorable or grateful to marry a man you don't love. Do you love this Mangan man?

ELLIE: Yes. At least—

MRS HUSHABYE: I don't want to know about "at least": I want to know the worst. Girls of your age fall in love with all sorts of impossible people, especially old people.

ELLIE: I like Mr Mangan very much; and I shall always be—

MRS HUSHABYE: (*impatiently completing the sentence and prancing away intolerantly to starboard*) —grateful to him for his kindness to dear father. I know. Anybody else?

ELLIE: What do you mean?

MRS HUSHABYE: Anybody else? Are you in love with anybody else?

ELLIE: Of course not.

500 MRS HUSHABYE: Humph! (*The book on the drawing-table catches her eye. She picks it up, and evidently finds the title very unexpected. She looks at Ellie, and asks, quaintly*) Quite sure you're not in love with an actor?

ELLIE: No, no. Why? What put such a thing into your head?

MRS HUSHABYE: This is yours, isn't it? Why else should you be reading Othello?

ELLIE: My father taught me to love Shakespeare.

MRS HUSHABYE: (*flinging the book down on the table*) Really! your father does seem to be about the limit.

510 ELLIE: (*naïvely*) Do you never read Shakespeare, Hesione? That seems to me so extraordinary. I like Othello.

MRS HUSHABYE: Do you, indeed? He was jealous, wasn't he?

ELLIE: Oh, not that. I think all the part about jealousy is horrible. But don't you think it must have been a wonderful experience for Desdemona, brought up so quietly at home, to meet a man who had been out in the world doing all sorts of brave things and having terrible adventures, and yet finding something in her that made him love to sit and talk with her and tell her about them?

520 MRS HUSHABYE: That's your idea of romance, is it?

ELLIE: Not romance, exactly. It might really happen.

(*Ellie's eyes show that she is not arguing, but in a daydream. Mrs Hushabye, watching her inquisitively, goes deliberately back to the sofa and resumes her seat beside her.*)

MRS HUSHABYE: Ellie darling, have you noticed that some of those stories that Othello told Desdemona couldn't have happened?

ELLIE: Oh, no. Shakespeare thought they could have happened.

MRS HUSHABYE: Hm! Desdemona thought they could have happened. But they didn't.

ELLIE: Why do you look so enigmatic about it? You are such a sphinx: I never know what you mean. 530

MRS HUSHABYE: Desdemona would have found him out if she had lived, you know. I wonder was that why he strangled her!

ELLIE: Othello was not telling lies.

MRS HUSHABYE: How do you know?

ELLIE: Shakespeare would have said if he was. Hesione, there are men who have done wonderful things: men like Othello, only, of course, white, and very handsome, and—

MRS HUSHABYE: Ah! Now we're coming to it. Tell me all about him. I knew there must be somebody, or you'd never have 540 been so miserable about Mangan: you'd have thought it quite a lark to marry him.

ELLIE: (*blushing vividly*) Hesione, you are dreadful. But I don't want to make a secret of it, though of course I don't tell everybody. Besides, I don't know him.

MRS HUSHABYE: Don't know him! What does that mean?

ELLIE: Well, of course I know him to speak to.

MRS HUSHABYE: But you want to know him ever so much more intimately, eh?

ELLIE: No, no: I know him quite—almost intimately. 550

MRS HUSHABYE: You don't know him; and you know him almost intimately. How lucid!

ELLIE: I mean that he does not call on us. I—I got into conversation with him by chance at a concert.

MRS HUSHABYE: You seem to have rather a gay time at your concerts, Ellie.

ELLIE: Not at all: I talk to everyone in the greenroom waiting for our turns. I thought he was one of the artists: he looked so splendid. But he was only one of the committee. I happened to tell him that I was copying a picture at the National 560 Gallery. I make a little money that way. I can't paint much; but as it's always the same picture I can do it pretty quickly and get two or three pounds for it. It happened that he came to the National Gallery one day.

MRS HUSHABYE: One students' day. Paid sixpence to stumble about through a crowd of easels, when he might have come in next day for nothing and found the floor clear! Quite by accident?

ELLIE: (*triumphantly*) No. On purpose. He liked talking to me. He knows lots of the most splendid people. Fashionable 570 women who are all in love with him. But he ran away from them to see me at the National Gallery and persuade me to come with him for a drive round Richmond Park in a taxi.

MRS HUSHABYE: My pettikins, you have been going it. It's wonderful what you good girls can do without anyone saying a word.

ELLIE: I am not in society, Hesione. If I didn't make acquaintances in that way I shouldn't have any at all.

MRS HUSHABYE: Well, no harm if you know how to take care of yourself. May I ask his name? 580

ELLIE: (*slowly and musically*) Marcus Darnley.

MRS HUSHABYE: (*echoing the music*) Marcus Darnley! What a splendid name!

ELLIE: Oh, I'm so glad you think so. I think so too; but I was afraid it was only a silly fancy of my own.

MRS HUSHABYE: Hm! Is he one of the Aberdeen Darnleys?

ELLIE: Nobody knows. Just fancy! He was found in an antique chest—

MRS HUSHABYE: A what?

590  ELLIE: An antique chest, one summer morning in a rose garden, after a night of the most terrible thunderstorm.

MRS HUSHABYE: What on earth was he doing in the chest? Did
he get into it because he was afraid of the lightning?

ELLIE: Oh, no, no: he was a baby. The name Marcus Darnley
was embroidered on his baby clothes. And five hundred
pounds in gold.

MRS HUSHABYE: (*looking hard at her*) Ellie!

ELLIE: The Garden of the Viscount—

MRS HUSHABYE: —de Rougemont?

600  ELLIE: (*innocently*) No: de Larochejaquelin. A French family.
A vicomte. His life has been one long romance. A tiger—

MRS HUSHABYE: Slain by his own hand?

ELLIE: Oh, no: nothing vulgar like that. He saved the life of the
tiger from a hunting party: one of King Edward's hunting
parties in India. The King was furious: that was why he
never had his military services properly recognized. But he
doesn't care. He is a Socialist and despises rank, and has
been in three revolutions fighting on the barricades.

MRS HUSHABYE: How can you sit there telling me such lies?
610  You, Ellie, of all people! And I thought you were a perfectly
simple, straightforward, good girl.

ELLIE: (*rising, dignified but very angry*) Do you mean to say
you don't believe me?

MRS HUSHABYE: Of course I don't believe you. You're inventing
every word of it. Do you take me for a fool?

(*Ellie stares at her. Her candor is so obvious that Mrs
Hushabye is puzzled.*)

ELLIE: Goodbye, Hesione. I'm very sorry. I see now that it
sounds very improbable as I tell it. But I can't stay if you
think that way about me.

MRS HUSHABYE: (*catching her dress*) You shan't go. I couldn't
620  be so mistaken: I know too well what liars are like. Somebody has really told you all this.

ELLIE: (*flushing*) Hesione, don't say that you don't believe him.
I couldn't bear that.

MRS HUSHABYE: (*soothing her*) Of course I believe him, dearest. But you should have broken it to me by degrees. (*Drawing her back to her seat.*) Now tell me all about him. Are you
in love with him?

ELLIE: Oh, no. I'm not so foolish. I don't fall in love with people. I'm not so silly as you think.

630  MRS HUSHABYE: I see. Only something to think about—to give
some interest and pleasure to life.

ELLIE: Just so. That's all, really.

MRS HUSHABYE: It makes the hours go fast, doesn't it? No tedious waiting to go to sleep at nights and wondering
whether you will have a bad night. How delightful it makes
waking up in the morning! How much better than the happiest dream! All life transfigured! No more wishing one had
an interesting book to read, because life is so much happier
than any book! No desire but to be alone and not to have to
640  talk to anyone: to be alone and just think about it.

ELLIE: (*embracing her*) Hesione, you are a witch. How do you
know? Oh, you are the most sympathetic woman in the
world!

MRS HUSHABYE: (*caressing her*) Pettikins, my pettikins, how I
envy you! and how I pity you!

ELLIE: Pity me! Oh, why?

(*A very handsome man of fifty, with mousquetaire moustaches,
wearing a rather dandified curly brimmed hat, and carrying
an elaborate walking-stick, comes into the room from the hall,
and stops short at sight of the women on the sofa.*)

ELLIE: (*seeing him and rising in glad surprise*) Oh! Hesione:
this is Mr Marcus Darnley.

MRS HUSHABYE: (*rising*) What a lark! He is my husband.

ELLIE: But now—(*she stops suddenly: then turns pale and*  650
*sways*)

MRS HUSHABYE: (*catching her and sitting down with her on the
sofa*). Steady, my pettikins.

THE MAN: (*with a mixture of confusion and effrontery, deposit-
ing his hat and stick on the teak table*) My real name, Miss
Dunn, is Hector Hushabye. I leave you to judge whether
that is a name any sensitive man would care to confess so. I
never use it when I can possibly help it. I have been away for
nearly a month; and I had no idea you knew my wife, or that
you were coming here. I am none the less delighted to find  660
you in our little house.

ELLIE: (*in great distress*) I don't know what to do. Please, may
I speak to papa? Do leave me. I can't bear it.

MRS HUSHABYE: Be off, Hector.

HECTOR: I—

MRS HUSHABYE: Quick, quick. Get out.

HECTOR: If you think it better—(*he goes out, taking his hat
with him but leaving the stick on the table*).

MRS HUSHABYE: (*laying Ellie down at the end of the sofa*) Now,
pettikins, he is gone. There's nobody but me. You can let  670
yourself go. Don't try to control yourself. Have a good cry.

ELLIE: (*raising her head*) Damn!

MRS HUSHABYE: Splendid! Oh, what a relief! I thought you
were going to be broken-hearted. Never mind me. Damn
him again.

ELLIE: I am not damning him. I am damning myself for being
such a fool. (*Rising.*) How could I let myself be taken in so?
(*She begins prowling to and fro, her bloom gone, looking curiously older and harder.*)

MRS HUSHABYE: (*cheerfully*) Why not, pettikins? Very few  680
young women can resist Hector. I couldn't when I was your
age. He is really rather splendid, you know.

ELLIE: (*turning on her*) Splendid! Yes, splendid *looking*, of
course. But how can you love a liar?

MRS HUSHABYE: I don't know. But you can, fortunately. Otherwise there wouldn't be much love in the world.

ELLIE: But to lie like that! To be a boaster! a coward!

MRS HUSHABYE: (*rising in alarm*) Pettikins, none of that, if you
please. If you hint the slightest doubt of Hector's courage,
he will go straight off and do the most horribly dangerous  690
things to convince himself that he isn't a coward. He has a
dreadful trick of getting out of one third-floor window and
coming in at another, just to test his nerve. He has a whole
drawerful of Albert Medals for saving people's lives.

ELLIE: He never told me that.

MRS HUSHABYE: He never boasts of anything he really did: he
can't bear it; and it makes him shy if anyone else does. All
his stories are made-up stories.

ELLIE: (*coming to her*) Do you mean that he is really brave, and
really has adventures, and yet tells lies about things that he  700

never did and that never happened?

MRS HUSHABYE: Yes, pettikins, I do. People don't have their virtues and vices in sets: they have them anyhow: all mixed.

ELLIE: (staring at her thoughtfully) There's something odd about this house, Hesione, and even about you. I don't know why I'm talking to you so calmly. I have a horrible fear that my heart is broken, but that heartbreak is not like what I thought it must be.

MRS HUSHABYE: (fondling her) It's only life educating you, pet-
710   tikins. How do you feel about Boss Mangan now?

ELLIE: (disengaging herself with an expression of distaste) Oh, how can you remind me of him, Hesione?

MRS HUSHABYE: Sorry, dear. I think I hear Hector coming back. You don't mind now, do you, dear?

ELLIE: Not in the least. I am quite cured.

(Mazzini Dunn and Hector come in from the hall.)

HECTOR: (as he opens the door and allows Mazzini to pass in) One second more, and she would have been a dead woman!

MAZZINI: Dear! dear! what an escape! Ellie, my love, Mr Hushabye has just been telling me the most extraordinary—

720 ELLIE: Yes, I've heard it (she crosses to the other side of the room).

HECTOR: (following her) Not this one: I'll tell it to you after din-ner. I think you'll like it. The truth is I made it up for you, and was looking forward to the pleasure of telling it to you. But in a moment of impatience at being turned out of the room, I threw it away on your father.

ELLIE: (turning at bay with her back to the carpenter's bench, scornfully self-possessed) It was not thrown away. He be-lieves it. I should not have believed it.

730 MAZZINI: (benevolently) Ellie is very naughty, Mr Hushabye. Of course she does not really think that. (He goes to the bookshelves, and inspects the titles of the volumes.)

(Boss Mangan comes in from the hall, followed by the captain. Mangan, carefully frock-coated as for church or for a directors' meeting, is about fifty-five, with a careworn, mistrustful ex-pression, standing a little on an entirely imaginary dignity, with a dull complexion, straight, lustreless hair, and features so entirely commonplace that it is impossible to describe them.)

CAPTAIN SHOTOVER: (to Mrs Hushabye, introducing the new-comer) Says his name is Mangan. Not able-bodied.

MRS HUSHABYE: (graciously) How do you do, Mr Mangan?

MANGAN: (shaking hands) Very pleased.

CAPTAIN SHOTOVER: Dunn's lost his muscle, but recovered his nerve. Men seldom do after three attacks of delirium tremens (he goes into the pantry).

740 MRS HUSHABYE: I congratulate you, Mr Dunn.

MAZZINI: (dazed) I am a lifelong teetotaler.

MRS HUSHABYE: You will find it far less trouble to let papa have his own way than try to explain.

MAZZINI: But three attacks of delirium tremens, really!

MRS HUSHABYE: (to Mangan) Do you know my husband, Mr Mangan (she indicates Hector)?

MANGAN: (going to Hector, who meets him with outstretched hand). Very pleased. (Turning to Ellie.) I hope, Miss Ellie, you have not found the journey down too fatiguing. (They
750   shake hands.)

MRS HUSHABYE: Hector, show Mr Dunn his room.

HECTOR: Certainly. Come along, Mr Dunn. (He takes Mazzini out.)

ELLIE: You haven't shown me my room yet, Hesione.

MRS HUSHABYE: How stupid of me! Come along. Make yourself quite at home, Mr Mangan. Papa will entertain you. (She calls to the captain in the pantry.) Papa, come and explain the house to Mr Mangan.

(She goes out with Ellie. The captain comes from the pantry.)

CAPTAIN SHOTOVER: You're going to marry Dunn's daughter. Don't. You're too old.    760

MANGAN: (staggered) Well! That's fairly blunt, Captain.

CAPTAIN SHOTOVER: It's true.

MANGAN: She doesn't think so.

CAPTAIN SHOTOVER: She does.

MANGAN: Older men than I have—

CAPTAIN SHOTOVER: (finishing the sentence for him)—made fools of themselves. That, also, is true.

MANGAN: (asserting himself) I don't see that this is any business of yours.

CAPTAIN SHOTOVER: It is everybody's business. The stars in 770 their courses are shaken when such things happen.

MANGAN: I'm going to marry her all the same.

CAPTAIN SHOTOVER: How do you know?

MANGAN: (playing the strong man) I intend to. I mean to. See? I never made up my mind to do a thing yet that I didn't bring it off. That's the sort of man I am; and there will be a better understanding between us when you make up your mind to that, Captain.

CAPTAIN SHOTOVER: You frequent picture palaces.

MANGAN: Perhaps I do. Who told you?    780

CAPTAIN SHOTOVER: Talk like a man, not like a movy. You mean that you make a hundred thousand a year.

MANGAN: I don't boast. But when I meet a man that makes a hundred thousand a year, I take off my hat to that man, and stretch out my hand to him and call him brother.

CAPTAIN SHOTOVER: Then you also make a hundred thousand a year, hey?

MANGAN: No. I can't say that. Fifty thousand, perhaps.

CAPTAIN SHOTOVER: His half brother only (he turns away from Mangan with his usual abruptness, and collects the empty 790 tea-cups on the Chinese tray).

MANGAN: (irritated) See here, Captain Shotover. I don't quite understand my position here. I came here on your daugh-ter's invitation. Am I in her house or in yours?

CAPTAIN SHOTOVER: You are beneath the dome of heaven, in the house of God. What is true within these walls is true out-side them. Go out on the seas; climb the mountains; wander through the valleys. She is still too young.

MANGAN: (weakening) But I'm very little over fifty.

CAPTAIN SHOTOVER: You are still less under sixty. Boss Mangan, 800 you will not marry the pirate's child (he carries the tray away into the pantry).

MANGAN: (following him to the half door) What pirate's child? What are you talking about?

CAPTAIN SHOTOVER: (in the pantry) Ellie Dunn. You will not marry her.

MANGAN: Who will stop me?

CAPTAIN SHOTOVER: (emerging) My daughter (he makes for the door leading to the hall).

810 MANGAN: (*following him*) Mrs Hushabye! Do you mean to say she brought me down here to break it off?

CAPTAIN SHOTOVER: (*stopping and turning on him*) I know nothing more than I have seen in her eye. She will break it off. Take my advice: marry a West Indian negress: they make excellent wives. I was married to one myself for two years.

MANGAN: Well, I am damned!

CAPTAIN SHOTOVER: I thought so. I was, too, for many years. The negress redeemed me.

820 MANGAN: (*feebly*) This is queer. I ought to walk out of this house.

CAPTAIN SHOTOVER: Why?

MANGAN: Well, many men would be offended by your style of talking.

CAPTAIN SHOTOVER: Nonsense! It's the other sort of talking that makes quarrels. Nobody ever quarrels with me.

(*A gentleman, whose first-rate tailoring and frictionless manners proclaim the wellbred West Ender, comes in from the hall. He has an engaging air of being young and unmarried, but on close inspection is found to be at least over forty.*)

THE GENTLEMAN: Excuse my intruding in this fashion, but there is no knocker on the door and the bell does not seem to ring.

830 CAPTAIN SHOTOVER: Why should there be a knocker? Why should the bell ring? The door is open.

THE GENTLEMAN: Precisely. So I ventured to come in.

CAPTAIN SHOTOVER: Quite right. I will see about a room for you (*he makes for the door*).

THE GENTLEMAN: (*stopping him*) But I'm afraid you don't know who I am.

CAPTAIN SHOTOVER: Do you suppose that at my age I make distinctions between one fellowcreature and another? (*He goes out. Mangan and the newcomer stare at one another.*)

840 MANGAN: Strange character, Captain Shotover, sir.

THE GENTLEMAN: Very.

CAPTAIN SHOTOVER: (*shouting outside*) Hesione, another person has arrived and wants a room. Man about town, well dressed, fifty.

THE GENTLEMAN: Fancy Hesione's feelings! May I ask are you a member of the family?

MANGAN: No.

THE GENTLEMAN: I am. At least a connection.

(*Mrs Hushabye comes back.*)

MRS HUSHABYE: How do you do? How good of you to come!

850 THE GENTLEMAN: I am very glad indeed to make your acquaintance, Hesione. (*Instead of taking her hand he kisses her. At the same moment the captain appears in the doorway.*) You will excuse my kissing your daughter, Captain, when I tell you that—

CAPTAIN SHOTOVER: Stuff! Everyone kisses my daughter. Kiss her as much as you like (*he makes for the pantry*).

THE GENTLEMAN: Thank you. One moment, Captain. (*The captain halts and turns. The gentleman goes to him affably.*) Do you happen to remember—but probably you don't, as it occurred many years ago—that your younger daughter married a numskull?

860 CAPTAIN SHOTOVER: Yes. She said she'd marry anybody to get away from this house. I should not have recognized you:

your head is no longer like a walnut. Your aspect is softened. You have been boiled in bread and milk for years and years, like other married men. Poor devil! (*He disappears into the pantry.*)

MRS HUSHABYE: (*going past Mangan to the gentleman and scrutinizing him*) I don't believe you are Hastings Utterword.

THE GENTLEMAN: I am not.    870

MRS HUSHABYE: Then what business had you to kiss me?

THE GENTLEMAN: I thought I would like to. The fact is, I am Randall Utterword, the unworthy younger brother of Hastings. I was abroad diplomatizing when he was married.

LADY UTTERWORD: (*dashing in*) Hesione, where is the key of the wardrobe in my room? My diamonds are in my dressing-bag: I must lock it up—(*recognizing the stranger with a shock*) Randall, how dare you? (*She marches at him past Mrs Hushabye, who retreats and joins Mangan near the sofa.*)    880

RANDALL: How dare I what? I am not doing anything.

LADY UTTERWORD: Who told you I was here?

RANDALL: Hastings. You had just left when I called on you at Claridge's; so I followed you down here. You are looking extremely well.

LADY UTTERWORD: Don't presume to tell me so.

MRS HUSHABYE: What is wrong with Mr Randall, Addy?

LADY UTTERWORD: (*recollecting herself*) Oh, nothing. But he has no right to come bothering you and papa without being invited (*she goes to the window-seat and sits down, turning    890 away from them ill-humoredly and looking into the garden, where Hector and Ellie are now seen strolling together*).

MRS HUSHABYE: I think you have not met Mr Mangan, Addy.

LADY UTTERWORD: (*turning her head and nodding coldly to Mangan*) I beg your pardon. Randall, you have flustered me so: I make a perfect fool of myself.

MRS HUSHABYE: Lady Utterword. My sister. My younger sister.

MANGAN: (*bowing*) Pleased to meet you, Lady Utterword.

LADY UTTERWORD: (*with marked interest*) Who is that gentleman walking in the garden with Miss Dunn?    900

MRS HUSHABYE: I don't know. She quarrelled mortally with my husband only ten minutes ago; and I didn't know anyone else had come. It must be a visitor. (*She goes to the window to look.*) Oh, it is Hector. They've made it up.

LADY UTTERWORD: Your husband! That handsome man?

MRS HUSHABYE: Well, why shouldn't my husband be a handsome man?

RANDALL: (*joining them at the window*) One's husband never is, Ariadne (*he sits by Lady Utterword, on her right*).

MRS HUSHABYE: One's sister's husband always is, Mr Randall.    910

LADY UTTERWORD: Don't be vulgar, Randall. And you, Hesione, are just as bad.

(*Ellie and Hector come in from the garden by the starboard door. Randall rises. Ellie retires into the corner near the pantry. Hector comes forward; and Lady Utterword rises looking her very best.*)

MRS HUSHABYE: Hector, this is Addy.

HECTOR: (*apparently surprised*) Not this lady.

LADY UTTERWORD: (*smiling*) Why not?

HECTOR: (*looking at her with a piercing glance of deep but respectful admiration, his moustache bristling*) I thought— (*pulling himself together*). I beg your pardon, Lady Utterword. I am extremely glad to welcome you at last

920 under our roof (*he offers his hand with grave courtesy*).

MRS HUSHABYE: She wants to be kissed, Hector.

LADY UTTERWORD: Hesione! (*But she still smiles.*)

MRS HUSHABYE: Call her Addy; and kiss her like a good brother-in-law; and have done with it. (*She leaves them to themselves.*)

HECTOR: Behave yourself, Hesione. Lady Utterword is entitled not only to hospitality but to civilization.

LADY UTTERWORD: (*gratefully*) Thank you, Hector. (*They shake hands cordially.*)

(*Mazzini Dunn is seen crossing the garden from starboard to port.*)

930 CAPTAIN SHOTOVER: (*coming from the pantry and addressing Ellie*) Your father has washed himself.

ELLIE: (*quite self-possessed*) He often does, Captain Shotover.

CAPTAIN SHOTOVER: A strange conversion! I saw him through the pantry window.

(*Mazzini Dunn enters through the port window door, newly washed and brushed, and stops, smiling benevolently, between Mangan and Mrs Hushabye.*)

MRS HUSHABYE: (*introducing*) Mr Mazzini Dunn, Lady Ut— oh, I forgot: you've met. (*Indicating Ellie*) Miss Dunn.

MAZZINI: (*walking across the room to take Ellie's hand, and beaming at his own naughty irony*) I have met Miss Dunn also. She is my daughter. (*He draws her arm through his ca-*

940 *ressingly.*)

MRS HUSHABYE: Of course: how stupid! Mr Utterword, my sister's—er—

RANDALL: (*shaking hands agreeably*) Her brother-in-law, Mr Dunn. How do you do?

MRS HUSHABYE: This is my husband.

HECTOR: We have met, dear. Don't introduce us any more. (*He moves away to the big chair, and adds*) Won't you sit down, Lady Utterword? (*She does so very graciously.*)

MRS HUSHABYE: Sorry. I hate it: it's like making people show

950 their tickets.

MAZZINI: (*sententiously*) How little it tells us, after all! The great question is, not who we are, but what we are.

CAPTAIN SHOTOVER: Ha! What are you?

MAZZINI: (*taken aback*) What am I?

CAPTAIN SHOTOVER: A thief, a pirate, and a murderer.

MAZZINI: I assure you you are mistaken.

CAPTAIN SHOTOVER: An adventurous life; but what does it end in? Respectability. A ladylike daughter. The language and appearance of a city missionary. Let it be a warning to all of

960 you (*he goes out through the garden*).

DUNN: I hope nobody here believes that I am a thief, a pirate, or a murderer. Mrs Hushabye, will you excuse me a moment? I must really go and explain. (*He follows the captain.*)

MRS HUSHABYE: (*as he goes*) It's no use. You'd really better— (*but Dunn has vanished*). We had better all go out and look for some tea. We never have regular tea; but you can always get some when you want: the servants keep it stewing all day. The kitchen veranda is the best place to ask. May I show you? (*She goes to the starboard door.*)

970 RANDALL: (*going with her*) Thank you, I don't think I'll take any tea this afternoon. But if you will show me the garden—

MRS HUSHABYE: There's nothing to see in the garden except papa's observatory, and a gravel pit with a cave where he

keeps dynamite and things of that sort. However, it's pleasanter out of doors; so come along.

RANDALL: Dynamite! Isn't that rather risky?

MRS HUSHABYE: Well, we don't sit in the gravel pit when there's a thunderstorm.

LADY UTTERWORD: That's something new. What is the dyna-  980 mite for?

HECTOR: To blow up the human race if it goes too far. He is trying to discover a psychic ray that will explode all the explosive at the will of a Mahatma.

ELLIE: The captain's tea is delicious, Mr Utterword.

MRS HUSHABYE: (*stopping in the doorway*) Do you mean to say that you've had some of my father's tea? that you got round him before you were ten minutes in the house?

ELLIE: I did.

MRS HUSHABYE: You little devil! (*She goes out with Randall.*)

MANGAN: Won't you come, Miss Ellie?  990

ELLIE: I'm too tired. I'll take a book up to my room and rest a little. (*She goes to the bookshelf.*)

MANGAN: Right. You can't do better. But I'm disappointed. (*He follows Randall and Mrs Hushabye.*)

(*Ellie, Hector, and Lady Utterword are left. Hector is close to Lady Utterword. They look at Ellie, waiting for her to go.*)

ELLIE: (*looking at the title of a book*) Do you like stories of adventure, Lady Utterword?

LADY UTTERWORD: (*patronizingly*) Of course, dear.

ELLIE: Then I'll leave you to Mr Hushabye. (*She goes out through the hall.*)

HECTOR: That girl is mad about tales of adventure. The lies I  1000 have to tell her!

LADY UTTERWORD: (*not interested in Ellie*) When you saw me what did you mean by saying that you thought, and then stopping short? What did you think?

HECTOR: (*folding his arms and looking down at her magnetically*) May I tell you?

LADY UTTERWORD: Of course.

HECTOR: It will not sound very civil. I was on the point of saying, "I thought you were a plain woman."

LADY UTTERWORD: Oh, for shame, Hector! What right had you  1010 to notice whether I am plain or not?

HECTOR: Listen to me, Ariadne. Until today I have seen only photographs of you; and no photograph can give the strange fascination of the daughters of that supernatural old man. There is some damnable quality in them that destroys men's moral sense, and carries them beyond honor and dishonor. You know that, don't you?

LADY UTTERWORD: Perhaps I do, Hector. But let me warn you once for all that I am a rigidly conventional woman. You may think because I'm a Shotover that I'm a Bohemian, because  1020 we are all so horribly Bohemian. But I'm not. I hate and loathe Bohemianism. No child brought up in a strict Puritan household ever suffered from Puritanism as I suffered from our Bohemianism.

HECTOR: Our children are like that. They spend their holidays in the houses of their respectable schoolfellows.

LADY UTTERWORD: I shall invite them for Christmas.

HECTOR: Their absence leaves us both without our natural chaperones.

LADY UTTERWORD: Children are certainly very inconvenient  1030 sometimes. But intelligent people can always manage, unless they are Bohemians.

HECTOR: You are no Bohemian; but you are no Puritan either: your attraction is alive and powerful. What sort of woman do you count yourself?

LADY UTTERWORD: I am a woman of the world, Hector; and I can assure you that if you will only take the trouble always to do the perfectly correct thing, and to say the perfectly correct thing, you can do just what you like. An ill-conducted, careless woman gets simply no chance. An ill-conducted, careless man is never allowed within arm's length of any woman worth knowing.

HECTOR: I see. You are neither a Bohemian woman nor a Puritan woman. You are a dangerous woman.

LADY UTTERWORD: On the contrary, I am a safe woman.

HECTOR: You are a most accursedly attractive woman. Mind, I am not making love to you. I do not like being attracted. But you had better know how I feel if you are going to stay here.

LADY UTTERWORD: You are an exceedingly clever lady-killer, Hector. And terribly handsome. I am quite a good player, myself, at that game. Is it quite understood that we are only playing?

HECTOR: Quite. I am deliberately playing the fool, out of sheer worthlessness.

LADY UTTERWORD: (rising brightly) Well, you are my brother-in-law. Hesione asked you to kiss me. (He seizes her in his arms and kisses her strenuously.) Oh! that was a little more than play, brother-in-law. (She pushes him suddenly away.) You shall not do that again.

HECTOR: In effect, you got your claws deeper into me than I intended.

MRS HUSHABYE: (coming in from the garden) Don't let me disturb you; I only want a cap to put on daddiest. The sun is setting; and he'll catch cold (she makes for the door leading to the hall).

LADY UTTERWORD: Your husband is quite charming, darling. He has actually condescended to kiss me at last. I shall go into the garden: it's cooler now (she goes out by the port door).

MRS HUSHABYE: Take care, dear child. I don't believe any man can kiss Addy without falling in love with her. (She goes into the hall.)

HECTOR: (striking himself on the chest). Fool! Goat!

(Mrs Hushabye comes back with the captain's cap.)

HECTOR: Your sister is an extremely enterprising old girl. Where's Miss Dunn!

MRS HUSHABYE: Mangan says she has gone up to her room for a nap. Addy won't let you talk to Ellie: she has marked you for her own.

HECTOR: She has the diabolical family fascination. I began making love to her automatically. What am I to do? I can't fall in love; and I can't hurt a woman's feelings by telling her so when she falls in love with me. And as women are always falling in love with my moustache I get landed in all sorts of tedious and terrifying flirtations in which I'm not a bit in earnest.

MRS HUSHABYE: Oh, neither is Addy. She has never been in love in her life, though she has always been trying to fall head over ears. She is worse than you, because you had one real go at least, with me.

HECTOR: That was a confounded madness. I can't believe that such an amazing experience is common. It has left its mark on me. I believe that is why I have never been able to repeat it.

MRS HUSHABYE: (laughing and caressing his arm) We were frightfully in love with one another, Hector. It was such an enchanting dream that I have never been able to grudge it to you or anyone else since. I have invited all sorts of pretty women to the house on the chance of giving you another turn. But it has never come off.

HECTOR: I don't know that I want it to come off. It was damned dangerous. You fascinated me; but I loved you; so it was heaven. This sister of yours fascinates me; but I hate her; so it is hell. I shall kill her if she persists.

MRS HUSHABYE: Nothing will kill Addy; she is as strong as a horse. (Releasing him.) Now I am going off to fascinate somebody.

HECTOR: The Foreign Office toff? Randall?

MRS HUSHABYE: Goodness gracious, no! Why should I fascinate him?

HECTOR: I presume you don't mean the bloated capitalist, Mangan?

MRS HUSHABYE: Hm! I think he had better be fascinated by me than by Ellie. (She is going into the garden when the captain comes in from it with some sticks in his hand.) What have you got there, daddiest?

CAPTAIN SHOTOVER: Dynamite.

MRS HUSHABYE: You've been to the gravel pit. Don't drop it about the house, there's a dear. (She goes into the garden, where the evening light is now very red.)

HECTOR: Listen, O sage. How long dare you concentrate on a feeling without risking having it fixed in your consciousness all the rest of your life?

CAPTAIN SHOTOVER: Ninety minutes. An hour and a half. (He goes into the pantry.)

(Hector, left alone, contracts his brows, and falls into a daydream. He does not move for some time. Then he folds his arms. Then, throwing his hands behind him, and gripping one with the other, he strides tragically once to and fro. Suddenly he snatches his walkingstick from the teak table, and draws it; for it is a swordstick. He fights a desperate duel with an imaginary antagonist, and after many vicissitudes runs him through the body up to the hilt. He sheathes his sword and throws it on the sofa, falling into another reverie as he does so. He looks straight into the eyes of an imaginary woman; seizes her by the arms; and says in a deep and thrilling tone, "Do you love me!" The captain comes out of the pantry at this moment; and Hector, caught with his arms stretched out and his fists clenched, has to account for his attitude by going through a series of gymnastic exercises.)

CAPTAIN SHOTOVER: That sort of strength is no good. You will never be as strong as a gorilla.

HECTOR: What is the dynamite for?

CAPTAIN SHOTOVER: To kill fellows like Mangan.

HECTOR: No use. They will always be able to buy more dynamite than you.

CAPTAIN SHOTOVER: I will make a dynamite that he cannot explode.

HECTOR: And that you can, eh?

CAPTAIN SHOTOVER: Yes: when I have attained the seventh degree of concentration.

HECTOR: What's the use of that? You never do attain it.

CAPTAIN SHOTOVER: What then is to be done? Are we to be kept forever in the mud by these hogs to whom the universe is nothing but a machine for greasing their bristles and filling 1140 their snouts?

HECTOR: Are Mangan's bristles worse than Randall's love-locks?

CAPTAIN SHOTOVER: We must win powers of life and death over them both. I refuse to die until I have invented the means.

HECTOR: Who are we that we should judge them?

CAPTAIN SHOTOVER: What are they that they should judge us? Yet they do, unhesitatingly. There is enmity between our seed and their seed. They know it and act on it, strangling our souls. They believe in themselves. When we believe in 1150 ourselves, we shall kill them.

HECTOR: It is the same seed. You forget that your pirate has a very nice daughter. Mangan's son may be a Plato: Randall's a Shelley. What was my father?

CAPTAIN SHOTOVER: The damnedst scoundrel I ever met. (*He replaces the drawing-board; sits down at the table; and begins to mix a wash of color.*)

HECTOR: Precisely. Well, dare you kill his innocent grand-children?

CAPTAIN SHOTOVER: They are mine also.

1160 HECTOR: Just so. We are members one of another. (*He throws himself carelessly on the sofa.*) I tell you I have often thought of this killing of human vermin. Many men have thought of it. Decent men are like Daniel in the lion's den; their survival is a miracle; and they do not always survive. We live among the Mangans and Randalls and Billie Dunns as they, poor devils, live among the disease germs and the doctors and the lawyers and the parsons and the restaurant chefs and the tradesmen and the servants and all the rest of the parasites and blackmailers. What are our terrors to theirs? 1170 Give me the power to kill them; and I'll spare them in sheer—

CAPTAIN SHOTOVER: (*cutting in sharply*) Fellow feeling?

HECTOR: No. I should kill myself if I believed that. I must believe that my spark, small as it is, is divine, and that the red light over their door is hell fire. I should spare them in simple magnanimous pity.

CAPTAIN SHOTOVER: You can't spare them until you have the power to kill them. At present they have the power to kill you. There are millions of blacks over the water for them to 1180 train and let loose on us. They're going to do it. They're doing it already.

HECTOR: They are too stupid to use their power.

CAPTAIN SHOTOVER: (*throwing down his brush and coming to the end of the sofa*) Do not deceive yourself: they do use it. We kill the better half of ourselves every day to propitiate them. The knowledge that these people are there to render all our aspirations barren prevents us having the aspirations. And when we are tempted to seek their destruction they bring forth demons to delude us, disguised as pretty daugh-1190 ters, and singers and poets and the like, for whose sake we spare them.

HECTOR: (*sitting up and leaning towards him*) May not Hesione be such a demon, brought forth by you lest I should slay you?

CAPTAIN SHOTOVER: That is possible. She has used you up, and left you nothing but dreams, as some women do.

HECTOR: Vampire women, demon women.

CAPTAIN SHOTOVER: Men think the world well lost for them, and lose it accordingly. Who are the men that do things? The husbands of the shrew and of the drunkard, the men 1200 with the thorn in the flesh. (*Walking distractedly away towards the pantry.*) I must think these things out. (*Turning suddenly.*) But I go on with the dynamite none the less. I will discover a ray mightier than any X-ray: a mind ray that will explode the ammunition in the belt of my adversary before he can point his gun at me. And I must hurry. I am old: I have no time to waste in talk (*he is about to go into the pantry, and Hector is making for the hall, when Hesione comes back*).

MRS HUSHABYE: Daddiest, you and Hector must come and help 1210 me to entertain all these people. What on earth were you shouting about?

HECTOR: (*stopping in the act of turning the door handle*) He is madder than usual.

MRS HUSHABYE: We all are.

HECTOR: I must change (*he resumes his door opening*).

MRS HUSHABYE: Stop, stop. Come back, both of you. Come back. (*They return, reluctantly.*) Money is running short.

HECTOR: Money! Where are my April dividends?

MRS HUSHABYE: Where is the snow that fell last year? 1220

CAPTAIN SHOTOVER: Where is all the money you had for that patent lifeboat I invented?

MRS HUSHABYE: Five hundred pounds; and I have made it last since Easter!

CAPTAIN SHOTOVER: Since Easter! Barely four months! Monstrous extravagance! I could live for seven years on £500.

MRS HUSHABYE: Not keeping open house as we do here, daddiest.

CAPTAIN SHOTOVER: Only £500 for that lifeboat! I got twelve thousand for the invention before that. 1230

MRS HUSHABYE: Yes, dear; but that was for the ship with the magnetic keel that sucked up submarines. Living at the rate we do, you cannot afford life-saving inventions. Can't you think of something that will murder half Europe at one bang?

CAPTAIN SHOTOVER: No. I am ageing fast. My mind does not dwell on slaughter as it did when I was a boy. Why doesn't your husband invent something? He does nothing but tell lies to women.

HECTOR: Well, that is a form of invention, is it not? However, 1240 you are right: I ought to support my wife.

MRS HUSHABYE: Indeed you shall do nothing of the sort: I should never see you from breakfast to dinner. I want my husband.

HECTOR: (*bitterly*) I might as well be your lapdog.

MRS HUSHABYE: Do you want to be my breadwinner, like the other poor husbands?

HECTOR: No, by thunder! What a damned creature a husband is anyhow!

MRS HUSHABYE: (*to the captain*) What about that harpoon 1250 cannon?

CAPTAIN SHOTOVER: No use. It kills whales, not men.

MRS HUSHABYE: Why not? You fire the harpoon out of a

cannon. It sticks in the enemy's general; you wind him in; and there you are.

HECTOR: You are your father's daughter, Hesione.

CAPTAIN SHOTOVER: There is something in it. Not to wind in generals: they are not dangerous. But one could fire a grapnel and wind in a machine gun or even a tank. I will think it out.

1260

MRS HUSHABYE: (squeezing the captain's arm affectionately) Saved! You are a darling, daddiest. Now we must go back to these dreadful people and entertain them.

CAPTAIN SHOTOVER: They have had no dinner. Don't forget that.

HECTOR: Neither have I. And it is dark: it must be all hours.

MRS HUSHABYE: Oh, Guinness will produce some sort of dinner for them. The servants always take jolly good care that there is food in the house.

1270 CAPTAIN SHOTOVER: (raising a strange wail in the darkness) What a house! What a daughter!

MRS HUSHABYE: (raving) What a father!

HECTOR: (following suit) What a husband!

CAPTAIN SHOTOVER: Is there no thunder in heaven?

HECTOR: Is there no beauty, no bravery, on earth?

MRS HUSHABYE: What do men want? They have their food, their firesides, their clothes mended, and our love at the end of the day. Why are they not satisfied? Why do they envy us the pain with which we bring them into the world, and make

1280 strange dangers and torments for themselves to be even with us?

CAPTAIN SHOTOVER: (weirdly chanting)
I built a house for my daughters, and opened the doors thereof,
That men might come for their choosing, and their betters spring from their love;
But one of them married a numskull;

HECTOR: (taking up the rhythm)
The other a liar wed;

1290 MRS HUSHABYE: (completing the stanza)
And now must she lie beside him, even as she made her bed.

LADY UTTERWORD: (calling from the garden) Hesione! Hesione! Where are you?

HECTOR: The cat is on the tiles.

MRS HUSHABYE: Coming, darling, coming (she goes quickly into the garden).

(The captain goes back to his place at the table.)

HECTOR: (going out into the hall) Shall I turn up the lights for you?

1300 CAPTAIN SHOTOVER: No. Give me deeper darkness. Money is not made in the light.

### —ACT TWO—

The same room, with the lights turned up and the curtains drawn. Ellie comes in, followed by Mangan. Both are dressed for dinner. She strolls to the drawing-table. He comes between the table and the wicker chair.

MANGAN: What a dinner! I don't call it a dinner: I call it a meal.

ELLIE: I am accustomed to meals, Mr Mangan, and very lucky to get them. Besides, the captain cooked some maccaroni for me.

MANGAN: (shuddering liverishly) Too rich: I can't eat such things. I suppose it's because I have to work so much with my brain. That's the worst of being a man of business: you are always thinking, thinking, thinking. By the way, now that we are alone, may I take the opportunity to come to a little 1310 understanding with you?

ELLIE: (settling into the draughtsman's seat) Certainly. I should like to.

MANGAN: (taken aback) Should you? That surprises me; for I thought I noticed this afternoon that you avoided me all you could. Not for the first time either.

ELLIE: I was very tired and upset. I wasn't used to the ways of this extraordinary house. Please forgive me.

MANGAN: Oh, that's all right: I don't mind. But Captain Shotover has been talking to me about you. You and me, you 1320 know.

ELLIE: (interested) The captain! What did he say?

MANGAN: Well, he noticed the difference between our ages.

ELLIE: He notices everything.

MANGAN: You don't mind, then?

ELLIE: Of course I know quite well that our engagement—

MANGAN: Oh! you call it an engagement.

ELLIE: Well, isn't it?

MANGAN: Oh, yes, yes: no doubt it is if you hold to it. This is the first time you've used the word; and I didn't quite know 1330 where we stood: that's all. (He sits down in the wicker chair; and resigns himself to allow her to lead the conversation.) You were saying—?

ELLIE: Was I? I forget. Tell me. Do you like this part of the country? I heard you ask Mr Hushabye at dinner whether there are any nice houses to let down here.

MANGAN: I like the place. The air suits me. I shouldn't be surprised if I settled down here.

ELLIE: Nothing would please me better. The air suits me too. And I want to be near Hesione.                                    1340

MANGAN: (with growing uneasiness) The air may suit us; but the question is, should we suit one another? Have you thought about that?

ELLIE: Mr Mangan, we must be sensible, mustn't we? It's no use pretending that we are Romeo and Juliet. But we can get on very well together if we choose to make the best of it. Your kindness of heart will make it easy for me.

MANGAN: (leaning forward, with the beginning of something like deliberate unpleasantness in his voice) Kindness of heart, eh? I ruined your father, didn't I?                              1350

ELLIE: Oh, not intentionally.

MANGAN: Yes I did. Ruined him on purpose.

ELLIE: On purpose!

MANGAN: Not out of ill-nature, you know. And you'll admit that I kept a job for him when I had finished with him. But business is business; and I ruined him as a matter of business.

ELLIE: I don't understand how that can be. Are you trying to make me feel that I need not be grateful to you, so that I may choose freely?

MANGAN: (rising aggressively) No. I mean what I say.          1360

ELLIE: But how could it possibly do you any good to ruin my father? The money he lost was yours.

MANGAN: *(with a sour laugh)* Was mine! It is mine, Miss Ellie, and all the money the other fellows lost too. *(He shoves his hands into his pockets and shows his teeth.)* I just smoked them out like a hive of bees. What do you say to that? A bit of shock, eh?

ELLIE: It would have been, this morning. Now! you can't think how little it matters. But it's quite interesting. Only, you
1370 must explain it to me. I don't understand it. *(Propping her elbows on the drawing-board and her chin on her hands, she composes herself to listen with a combination of conscious curiosity with unconscious contempt which provokes him to more and more unpleasantness, and an attempt at patronage of her ignorance.)*

MANGAN: Of course you don't understand: what do *you* know about business? You just listen and learn. Your father's business was a new business; and I don't start new businesses: I let other fellows start them. They put all their money and
1380 their friends' money into starting them. They wear out their souls and bodies trying to make a success of them. They're what you call enthusiasts. But the first dead lift of the thing is too much for them; and they haven't enough financial experience. In a year or so they have either to let the whole show go bust, or sell out to a new lot of fellows for a few deferred ordinary shares: that is, if they're lucky enough to get anything at all. As likely as not the very same thing happens to the new lot. They put in more money and a couple of years' more work; and then perhaps they have to sell out to
1390 a third lot. If it's really a big thing the third lot will have to sell out too, and leave their work and their money behind them. And that's where the real business man comes in: where *I* come in. But I'm cleverer than some: I don't mind dropping a little money to start the process. I took your father's measure. I saw that he had a sound idea, and that he would work himself silly for it if he got the chance. I saw that he was a child in business, and was dead certain to outrun his expenses and be in too great a hurry to wait for his market. I knew that the surest way to ruin a man who doesn't
1400 know how to handle money is to give him some. I explained my idea to some friends in the city, and they found the money; for I take no risks in ideas, even when they're my own. Your father and the friends that ventured their money with him were no more to me than a heap of squeezed lemons. You've been wasting your gratitude: my kind heart is all rot. I'm sick of it. When I see your father beaming at me with his moist, grateful eyes, regularly wallowing in gratitude, I sometimes feel I must tell him the truth or burst. What stops me is that I know he wouldn't believe me. He'd
1410 think it was my modesty, as you did just now. He'd think anything rather than the truth, which is that he's a blamed fool, and I am a man that knows how to take care of himself. *(He throws himself back into the big chair with large self-approval.)* Now what do you think of me, Miss Ellie?

ELLIE: *(dropping her hands)* How strange! that my mother, who knew nothing at all about business, should have been quite right about you! She always said—not before papa, of course, but to us children—that you were just that sort of man.

1420 MANGAN: *(sitting up, much hurt)* Oh! did she? And yet she'd have let you marry me.

ELLIE: Well, you see, Mr Mangan, my mother married a very

good man—for whatever you may think of my father as a man of business, he is the soul of goodness—and she is not at all keen on my doing the same.

MANGAN: Anyhow, you don't want to marry me now, do you?

ELLIE: *(very calmly)* Oh, I think so. Why not?

MANGAN: *(rising aghast)* Why not!

ELLIE: I don't see why we shouldn't get on very well together.

MANGAN: Well, but look here, you know—*(he stops, quite at* 1430 *a loss).*

ELLIE: *(patiently)* Well?

MANGAN: Well, I thought you were rather particular about people's characters.

ELLIE: If we women were particular about men's characters, we should never get married at all, Mr Mangan.

MANGAN: A child like you talking of "we women"! What next! You're not in earnest?

ELLIE: Yes, I am. Aren't you?

MANGAN: You mean to hold me to it? 1440

ELLIE: Do you wish to back out of it?

MANGAN: Oh, no. Not exactly back out of it.

ELLIE: Well?

*(He has nothing to say. With a long whispered whistle, he drops into the wicker chair and stares before him like a beggared gambler. But a cunning look soon comes into his face. He leans over towards her on his right elbow, and speaks in a low steady voice.)*

MANGAN: Suppose I told you I was in love with another woman!

ELLIE: *(echoing him)* Suppose I told you I was in love with another man!

MANGAN: *(bouncing angrily out of his chair)* I'm not joking.

ELLIE: Who told you I was?

MANGAN: I tell you I'm serious. You're too young to be serious; but you'll have to believe me. I want to be near your friend 1450 Mrs Hushabye. I'm in love with her. Now the murder's out.

ELLIE: I want to be near your friend Mr Hushabye. I'm in love with him. *(She rises and adds with a frank air)* Now we are in one another's confidence, we shall be real friends. Thank you for telling me.

MANGAN: *(almost beside himself)* Do you think I'll be made a convenience of like this?

ELLIE: Come, Mr Mangan! you made a business convenience of my father. Well, a woman's business is marriage. Why shouldn't I make a domestic convenience of you? 1460

MANGAN: Because I don't choose, see? Because I'm not a silly gull like your father. That's why.

ELLIE: *(with serene contempt)* You are not good enough to clean my father's boots, Mr Mangan; and I am paying you a great compliment in condescending to make a convenience of you, as you call it. Of course you are free to throw over our engagement if you like; but, if you do, you'll never enter Hesione's house again: I will take care of that.

MANGAN: *(gasping)* You little devil, you've done me. *(On the point of collapsing into the big chair again he recovers him-* 1470 *self.)* Wait a bit, though: you're not so cute as you think. You can't beat Boss Mangan as easy as that. Suppose I go straight to Mrs Hushabye and tell her that you're in love with her husband.

ELLIE: She knows it.

MANGAN: You told her!!!

ELLIE: She told me.

MANGAN: (*clutching at his bursting temples*) Oh, this is a crazy house. Or else I'm going clean off my chump. Is she making a swop with you—she to have your husband and you to have hers?

ELLIE: Well, you don't want us both, do you?

MANGAN: (*throwing himself into the chair distractedly*) My brain won't stand it. My head's going to split. Help! Help me to hold it. Quick: hold it: squeeze it. Save me. (*Ellie comes behind his chair; clasps his head hard for a moment; then begins to draw her hands from his forehead back to his ears.*) Thank you. (*Drowsily.*) That's very refreshing. (*Waking a little.*) Don't you hypnotize me, though. I've seen men made fools of by hypnotism.

ELLIE: (*steadily*) Be quiet. I've seen men made fools of without hypnotism.

MANGAN: (*humbly*) You don't dislike touching me, I hope. You never touched me before, I noticed.

ELLIE: Not since you fell in love naturally with a grown-up nice woman, who will never expect you to make love to her. And I will never expect him to make love to me.

MANGAN: He may, though.

ELLIE: (*making her passes rhythmically*) Hush. Go to sleep. Do you hear? You are to go to sleep, go to sleep, go to sleep; be quiet, deeply deeply quiet; sleep, sleep, sleep, sleep, sleep.

(*He falls asleep. Ellie steals away; turns the light out; and goes into the garden.*)

(*Nurse Guinness opens the door and is seen in the light which comes in from the hall.*)

GUINNESS: (*speaking to someone outside*) Mr Mangan's not here, duckie: there's no one here. It's all dark.

MRS HUSHABYE: (*without*) Try the garden. Mr Dunn and I will be in my boudoir. Show him the way.

GUINNESS: Yes, ducky. (*She makes for the garden door in the dark; stumbles over the sleeping Mangan and screams.*) Ahoo! O Lord, sir! I beg your pardon, I'm sure: I didn't see you in the dark. Who is it? (*She goes back to the door and turns on the light.*) Oh, Mr Mangan, sir, I hope I haven't hurt you plumping into your lap like that. (*Coming to him.*) I was looking for you, sir. Mrs Hushabye says will you please—(*noticing that he remains quite insensible*) Oh, my good Lord, I hope I haven't killed him. Sir! Mr Mangan! Sir! (*She shakes him; and he is rolling inertly off the chair on the floor when she holds him up and props him against the cushion.*) Miss Hessy! Miss Hessy! Quick, doty darling. Miss Hessy! (*Mrs Hushabye comes in from the hall, followed by Mazzini Dunn.*) Oh, Miss Hessy, I've been and killed him.

(*Mazzini runs round the back of the chair to Mangan's right hand, and sees that the nurse's words are apparently only too true.*)

MAZZINI: What tempted you to commit such a crime, woman?

MRS HUSHABYE: (*trying not to laugh*) Do you mean you did it on purpose?

GUINNESS: Now is it likely I'd kill any man on purpose? I fell over him in the dark; and I'm a pretty tidy weight. He never spoke nor moved until I shook him; and then he would have dropped dead on the floor. Isn't it tiresome?

MRS HUSHABYE: (*going past the nurse to Mangan's side, and inspecting him less credulously than Mazzini*) Nonsense! he is not dead: he is only asleep. I can see him breathing.

GUINNESS: But why won't he wake?

MAZZINI: (*speaking very politely into Mangan's ear*) Mangan! My dear Mangan! (*he blows into Mangan's ear.*)

MRS HUSHABYE: That's no good (*she shakes him vigorously.*) Mr Mangan, wake up. Do you hear? (*He begins to roll over.*) Oh! Nurse, nurse: he's falling: help me.

(*Nurse Guinness rushes to the rescue. With Mazzini's assistance, Mangan is propped safely up again.*)

GUINNESS: (*behind the chair; bending over to test the case with her nose*) Would he be drunk, do you think, pet?

MRS HUSHABYE: Had he any of papa's rum?

MAZZINI: It can't be that: he is most abstemious. I am afraid he drank too much formerly, and has to drink too little now. You know, Mrs Hushabye, I really think he has been hypnotized.

GUINNESS: Hip no what, sir?

MAZZINI: One evening at home, after we had seen a hypnotizing performance, the children began playing at it; and Ellie stroked my head. I assure you I went off dead asleep; and they had to send for a professional to wake me up after I had slept eighteen hours. They had to carry me upstairs; and as the poor children were not very strong, they let me slip; and I rolled right down the whole flight and never woke up. (*Mrs Hushabye splutters.*) Oh, you may laugh, Mrs Hushabye; but I might have been killed.

MRS HUSHABYE: I couldn't have helped laughing even if you had been, Mr Dunn. So Ellie has hypnotized him. What fun!

MAZZINI: Oh no, no, no. It was such a terrible lesson to her: nothing would induce her to try such a thing again.

MRS HUSHABYE: Then who did it? *I* didn't.

MAZZINI: I thought perhaps the captain might have done it unintentionally. He is so fearfully magnetic: I feel vibrations whenever he comes close to me.

GUINNESS: The captain will get him out of it anyhow, sir: I'll back him for that. I'll go fetch him (*she makes for the pantry*).

MRS HUSHABYE: Wait a bit. (*To Mazzini.*) You say he is all right for eighteen hours?

MAZZINI: Well, *I* was asleep for eighteen hours.

MRS HUSHABYE: Were you any the worse for it?

MAZZINI: I don't quite remember. They had poured brandy down my throat, you see; and—

MRS HUSHABYE: Quite. Anyhow, you survived. Nurse, darling: go and ask Miss Dunn to come to us here. Say I want to speak to her particularly. You will find her with Mr Hushabye probably.

GUINNESS: I think not, ducky: Miss Addy is with him. But I'll find her and send her to you. (*She goes out into the garden.*)

MRS HUSHABYE: (*calling Mazzini's attention to the figure on the chair*) Now, Mr Dunn, look. Just look. Lood hard. Do you still intend to sacrifice your daughter to that thing?

MAZZINI: (*troubled*) You have completely upset me, Mrs Hushabye, by all you have said to me. That anyone could imagine that I—I, a consecrated soldier of freedom, if I may say so—could sacrifice Ellie to anybody or anyone, or that I should ever have dreamed of forcing her inclinations in any way, is a most painful blow to my—well, I suppose you would say to my good opinion of myself.

MRS HUSHABYE: (*rather stolidly*) Sorry.

MAZZINI: (*looking forlornly at the body*) What is your objection to poor Mangan, Mrs Hushabye? He looks all right to me. But then I am so accustomed to him.

MRS HUSHABYE: Have you no heart? Have you no sense? Look at the brute! Think of poor weak innocent Ellie in the clutches of this slavedriver, who spends his life making thousands of rough violent workmen bend to his will and sweat for him: a man accustomed to have great masses of iron beaten into shape for him by steam-hammers! to fight with women and girls over a halfpenny an hour ruthlessly! a captain of industry, I think you call him, don't you? Are you going to fling your delicate, sweet, helpless child into such a beast's claws just because he will keep her in an expensive house and make her wear diamonds to show how rich he is?

MAZZINI: (*staring at her in wide-eyed amazement*) Bless you, dear Mrs Hushabye, what romantic ideas of business you have! Poor dear Mangan isn't a bit like that.

MRS HUSHABYE: (*scornfully*) Poor dear Mangan indeed!

MAZZINI: But he doesn't know anything about machinery. He never goes near the men: he couldn't manage them: he is afraid of them. I never can get him to take the least interest in the works: he hardly knows more about them than you do. People are cruelly unjust to Mangan: they think he is all rugged strength just because his manners are bad.

MRS HUSHABYE: Do you mean to tell me he isn't strong enough to crush poor little Ellie?

MAZZINI: Of course it's very hard to say how any marriage will turn out; but speaking for myself, I should say that he won't have a dog's chance against Ellie. You know, Ellie has remarkable strength of character. I think it is because I taught her to like Shakespeare when she was very young.

MRS HUSHABYE: (*contemptuously*) Shakespeare! The next thing you will tell me is that you could have made a great deal more money than Mangan. (*She retires to the sofa, and sits down at the port end of it in the worst of humors.*)

MAZZINI: (*following her and taking the other end*) No: I'm no good at making money. I don't care enough for it, somehow. I'm not ambitious! that must be it. Mangan is wonderful about money: he thinks of nothing else. He is so dreadfully afraid of being poor. I am always thinking of other things: even at the works I think of the things we are doing and not of what they cost. And the worst of it is, poor Mangan doesn't know what to do with his money when he gets it. He is such a baby that he doesn't know even what to eat and drink: he has ruined his liver eating and drinking the wrong things; and now he can hardly eat at all. Ellie will diet him splendidly. You will be surprised when you come to know him better: he is really the most helpless of mortals. You get quite a protective feeling towards him.

MRS HUSHABYE: Then who manages his business, pray?

MAZZINI: I do. And of course other people like me.

MRS HUSHABYE: Footling people, you mean.

MAZZINI: I suppose you'd think us so.

MRS HUSHABYE: And pray why don't you do without him if you're all so much cleverer?

MAZZINI: Oh, we couldn't: we should ruin the business in a year. I've tried; and I know. We should spend too much on everything. We should improve the quality of the goods and make them too dear. We should be sentimental about the hard cases among the workpeople. But Mangan keeps us in order. He is down on us about every extra halfpenny. We could never do without him. You see, he will sit up all night thinking of how to save sixpence. Won't Ellie make him jump, though, when she takes his house in hand!

MRS HUSHABYE: Then the creature is a fraud even as a captain of industry!

MAZZINI: I am afraid all the captains of industry are what *you* call frauds, Mrs Hushabye. Of course there are some manufacturers who really do understand their own works; but they don't make as high a rate of profit as Mangan does. I assure you Mangan is quite a good fellow in his way. He means well.

MRS HUSHABYE: He doesn't look well. He is not in his first youth, is he?

MAZZINI: After all, no husband is in his first youth for very long, Mrs Hushabye. And men can't afford to marry in their first youth nowadays.

MRS HUSHABYE: Now if *I* said that, it would sound witty. Why can't *you* say it wittily? What on earth is the matter with you? Why don't you inspire everybody with confidence? with respect?

MAZZINI: (*humbly*) I think that what is the matter with me is that I am poor. You don't know what that means at home. Mind: I don't say they have ever complained. They've all been wonderful: they've been proud of my poverty. They've even joked about it quite often. But my wife has had a very poor time of it. She has been quite resigned—

MRS HUSHABYE: (*shuddering involuntarily*)!!

MAZZINI: There! You see, Mrs Hushabye. I don't want Ellie to live on resignation.

MRS HUSHABYE: Do you want her to have to resign herself to living with a man she doesn't love?

MAZZINI: (*wistfully*) Are you sure that would be worse than living with a man she did love, if he was a footling person?

MRS HUSHABYE: (*relaxing her contemptuous attitude, quite interested in Mazzini now*) You know, I really think you must love Ellie very much; for you become quite clever when you talk about her.

MAZZINI: I didn't know I was so very stupid on other subjects.

MRS HUSHABYE: You are, sometimes.

MAZZINI: (*turning his head away; for his eyes are wet*) I have learnt a good deal about myself from you, Mrs Hushabye; and I'm afraid I shall not be the happier for your plain speaking. But if you thought I needed it to make me think of Ellie's happiness you were very much mistaken.

MRS HUSHABYE: (*leaning towards him kindly*) Have I been a beast?

MAZZINI: (*pulling himself together*) It doesn't matter about me, Mrs Hushabye. I think you like Ellie; and that is enough for me.

MRS HUSHABYE: I'm beginning to like you a little. I perfectly loathed you at first. I thought you the most odious, self-satisfied, boresome elderly prig I ever met.

MAZZINI: (*resigned, and now quite cheerful*) I daresay I am all that. I never have been a favorite with gorgeous woman like you. They always frighten me.

MRS HUSHABYE: *(pleased)* Am I a gorgeous woman, Mazzini? I shall fall in love with you presently.

MAZZINI: *(with placid gallantry)* No, you won't, Hesione. But you would be quite safe. Would you believe it that quite a lot of women have flirted with me because I am quite safe?

1710 But they get tired of me for the same reason.

MRS HUSHABYE: *(mischievously)* Take care. You may not be so safe as you think.

MAZZINI: Oh yes, quite safe. You see, I have been in love really: the sort of love that only happens once. *(Softly.)* That's why Ellie is such a lovely girl.

MRS HUSHABYE: Well, really, you *are* coming out. Are you quite sure you won't let me tempt you into a second grand passion?

MAZZINI: Quite. It wouldn't be natural. The fact is, you don't

1720 strike on my box, Mrs Hushabye; and I certainly don't strike on yours.

MRS HUSHABYE: I see. Your marriage was a safety match.

MAZZINI: What a very witty application of the expression I used! I should never have thought of it.

*(Ellie comes in from the garden, looking anything but happy.)*

MRS HUSHABYE: *(rising)* Oh! here is Ellie at last. *(She goes behind the sofa.)*

ELLIE: *(on the threshold of the starboard door)* Guinness said you wanted me: you and papa.

MRS HUSHABYE: You have kept us waiting so long that it almost

1730 came to—well, never mind. Your father is a very wonderful man *(she ruffles his hair affectionately)*: the only one I ever met who could resist me when I made myself really agreeable. *(She comes to the big chair, on Mangan's left.)* Come here. I have something to show you. *(Ellie strolls listlessly to the other side of the chair.)* Look.

ELLIE: *(contemplating Mangan without interest)* I know. He is only asleep. We had a talk after dinner; and he fell asleep in the middle of it.

MRS HUSHABYE: You did it, Ellie. You put him asleep.

1740 MAZZINI: *(rising quickly and coming to the back of the chair)* Oh, I hope not. Did you, Ellie?

ELLIE: *(wearily)* He asked me to.

MAZZINI: But it's dangerous. You know what happened to me.

ELLIE: *(utterly indifferent)* Oh, I daresay I can wake him. If not, somebody else can.

MRS HUSHABYE: It doesn't matter, anyhow, because I have at least persuaded your father that you don't want to marry him.

ELLIE: *(suddenly coming out of her listlessness, much vexed)*

1750 But why did you do that, Hesione? I do want to marry him. I fully intend to marry him.

MAZZINI: Are you quite sure, Ellie? Mrs Hushabye has made me feel that I may have been thoughtless and selfish about it.

ELLIE: *(very clearly and steadily)* Papa. When Mrs. Hushabye takes it on herself to explain to you what I think or don't think, shut your ears tight; and shut your eyes too. Hesione knows nothing about me: she hasn't the least notion of the sort of person I am, and never will. I promise you I won't do

1760 anything I don't want to do and mean to do for my own sake.

MAZZINI: You are quite, quite sure?

ELLIE: Quite, quite sure. Now you must go away and leave me

to talk to Mrs Hushabye.

MAZZINI: But I should like to hear. Shall I be in the way?

ELLIE: *(inexorable)* I had rather talk to her alone.

MAZZINI: *(affectionately)* Oh, well, I know what a nuisance parents are, dear. I will be good and go. *(He goes to the garden door.)* By the way, do you remember the address of that professional who woke me up? Don't you think I had better

telegraph to him? 1770

MRS HUSHABYE: *(moving towards the sofa)* It's too late to telegraph tonight.

MAZZINI: I suppose so. I do hope he'll wake up in the course of the night. *(He goes out into the garden.)*

ELLIE: *(turning vigorously on Hesione the moment her father is out of the room)* Hesione, what the devil do you mean by making mischief with my father about Mangan?

MRS HUSHABYE: *(promptly losing her temper)* Don't you dare speak to me like that, you little minx. Remember that you

are in my house. 1780

ELLIE: Stuff! Why don't you mind your own business? What is it to you whether I choose to marry Mangan or not?

MRS HUSHABYE: Do you suppose you can bully me, you miserable little matrimonial adventurer?

ELLIE: Every woman who hasn't any money is a matrimonial adventurer. It's easy for you to talk: you have never known what it is to want money; and you can pick up men as if they were daisies. I am poor and respectable—

MRS HUSHABYE: *(interrupting)* Ho! respectable! How did you pick up Mangan? How did you pick up my husband? You 1790 have the audacity to tell me that I am a—a—a—

ELLIE: A siren. So you are. You were born to lead men by the nose: if you weren't, Marcus would have waited for me, perhaps.

MRS HUSHABYE: *(suddenly melting and half laughing)* Oh, my poor Ellie, my pettikins, my unhappy darling! I am so sorry about Hector. But what can I do? It's not my fault: I'd give him to you if I could.

ELLIE: I don't blame you for that.

MRS HUSHABYE: What a brute I was to quarrel with you and call 1800 you names! Do kiss me and say you're not angry with me.

ELLIE: *(fiercely)* Oh, don't slop and gush and be sentimental. Don't you see that unless I can be hard—as hard as nails— I shall go mad? I don't care a damn about your calling me names: do you think a woman in my situation can feel a few hard words?

MRS HUSHABYE: Poor little woman! Poor little situation!

ELLIE: I suppose you think you're being sympathetic. You are just foolish and stupid and selfish. You see me getting a smasher right in the face that kills a whole part of my life: 1810 the best part that can never come again; and you think you can help me over it by a little coaxing and kissing. When I want all the strength I can get to lean on: something iron, something stony, I don't care how cruel it is, you go all mushy and want to slobber over me. I'm not angry; I'm not unfriendly; but for God's sake do pull yourself together; and don't think that because you're on velvet and always have been, women who are in hell can take it as easily as you.

MRS HUSHABYE: *(shrugging her shoulders)* Very well. *(She sits down on the sofa in her old place.)* But I warn you that when 1820 I am neither coaxing and kissing nor laughing, I am just wondering how much longer I can stand living in this cruel, damnable world. You object to the siren: well, I drop the siren. You want to rest your wounded bosom against a grindstone. Well (*folding her arms,*) here is the grindstone.

ELLIE: (*sitting down beside her, appeased*) That's better: you really have the trick of falling in with everyone's mood; but you don't understand, because you are not the sort of woman for whom there is only one man and only one
1830   chance.

MRS HUSHABYE: I certainly don't understand how your marrying that object (*indicating Mangan*) will console you for not being able to marry Hector.

ELLIE: Perhaps you don't understand why I was quite a nice girl this morning, and am now neither a girl nor particularly nice.

MRS HUSHABYE: Oh, yes, I do. It's because you have made up your mind to do something despicable and wicked.

ELLIE: I don't think so, Hesione. I must make the best of my
1840   ruined house.

MRS HUSHABYE: Pooh! You'll get over it. Your house isn't ruined.

ELLIE: Of course I shall get over it. You don't suppose I'm going to sit down and die of a broken heart, I hope, or be an old maid living on a pittance from the Sick and Indigent Roomkeepers' Association. But my heart is broken, all the same. What I mean by that is that I know that what has happened to me with Marcus will not happen to me ever again. In the world for me there is Marcus and a lot of other men
1850   of whom one is just the same as another. Well, if I can't have love, that's no reason why I should have poverty. If Mangan has nothing else, he has money.

MRS HUSHABYE: And are there no *young* men with money.

ELLIE: Not within my reach. Besides, a young man would have the right to expect love from me, and would perhaps leave me when he found I could not give it to him. Rich young men can get rid of their wives, you know, pretty cheaply. But this object, as you call him, can expect nothing more from me than I am prepared to give him.

1860 MRS HUSHABYE: He will be your owner, remember. If he buys you, he will make the bargain pay him and not you. Ask your father.

ELLIE: (*rising and strolling to the chair to contemplate their subject*) You need not trouble on that score, Hesione. I have more to give Boss Mangan than he has to give me: it is I who am buying him, and at a pretty good price too, I think. Women are better at that sort of bargain than men. I have taken the Boss's measure; and ten Boss Mangans shall not prevent me doing far more as I please as his wife than I have
1870   ever been able to do as a poor girl. (*Stooping to the recumbent figure.*) Shall they, Boss? I think not. (*She passes on to the drawing-table, and leans against the end of it, facing the windows.*) I shall not have to spend most of my time wondering how long my gloves will last, anyhow.

MRS HUSHABYE: (*rising superbly*) Ellie, you are a wicked, sordid little beast. And to think that I actually condescended to fascinate that creature there to save you from him! Well, let me tell you this: if you make this disgusting match, you will never see Hector again if I can help it.

1880 ELLIE: (*unmoved*) I nailed Mangan by telling him that if he did not marry me he should never see you again (*she lifts herself on her wrists and seats herself on the end of the table*).

MRS HUSHABYE: (*recoiling*) Oh!

ELLIE: So you see I am not unprepared for your playing that trump against me. Well, you just try it: that's all. I should have made a man of Marcus, not a household pet.

MRS HUSHABYE: (*flaming*) You dare!

ELLIE: (*looking almost dangerous*) Set him thinking about me if *you* dare.

MRS HUSHABYE: Well, of all the impudent little fiends I ever 1890 met! Hector says there is a certain point at which the only answer you can give to a man who breaks all the rules is to knock him down. What would you say if I were to box your ears?

ELLIE: (*calmly*) I should pull your hair.

MRS HUSHABYE: (*mischievously*) That wouldn't hurt me. Perhaps it comes off at night.

ELLIE: (*so taken aback that she drops off the table and runs to her*) Oh, you don't mean to say, Hesione, that your beautiful black hair is false?                                             1900

MRS HUSHABYE: (*patting it*) Don't tell Hector. He believes in it.

ELLIE: (*groaning*) Oh! Even the hair that ensnared him false! Everything false!

MRS HUSHABYE: Pull it and try. Other women can snare men in their hair; but I can swing a baby on mine. Aha! you can't do that, Goldylocks.

ELLIE: (*heartbroken*) No. You have stolen my babies.

MRS HUSHABYE: Pettikins, don't make me cry. You know what you said about my making a household pet of him is a little true. Perhaps he ought to have waited for you. Would any 1910 other woman on earth forgive you?

ELLIE: Oh, what right had you to take him all for yourself! (*Pulling herself together.*) There! You couldn't help it: neither of us could help it. He couldn't help it. No, don't say anything more: I can't bear it. Let us wake the object. (*She begins stroking Mangan's head, reversing the movement with which she put him to sleep.*) Wake up, do you hear? You are to wake up at once. Wake up, wake up, wake—

MANGAN: (*bouncing out of the chair in a fury and turning on them*) Wake up! So you think I've been asleep, do you? (*He* 1920 *kicks the chair violently back out of his way, and gets between them.*) You throw me into a trance so that I can't move hand or foot—I might have been buried alive! it's a mercy I wasn't—and then you think I was only asleep. If you'd let me drop the two times you rolled me about, my nose would have been flattened for life against the floor. But I've found you all out, anyhow. I know the sort of people I'm among now. I've heard every word you've said, you and your precious father, and (*to Mrs Hushabye*) you too. So I'm an object, am I? I'm a thing, am I? I'm a fool that hasn't sense 1930 enough to feed myself properly, am I? I'm afraid of the men that would starve if it weren't for the wages I give them, am I? I'm nothing but a disgusting old skinflint to be made a convenience of by designing women and fool managers of my works, am I? I'm—

MRS HUSHABYE: (*with the most elegant aplomb*) Sh-sh-sh-sh-sh! Mr Mangan, you are bound in honor to obliterate from your mind all you heard while you were pretending to be asleep. It was not meant for you to hear.

MANGAN: Pretending to be asleep! Do you think if I was only 1940 pretending that I'd have sprawled there helpless, and listened to such unfairness, such lies, such injustice and plotting and backbiting and slandering of me, if I could have up and told you what I thought of you! I wonder I didn't burst.

MRS HUSHABYE: (*sweetly*) You dreamt it all, Mr Mangan. We were only saying how beautifully peaceful you looked in your sleep. That was all, wasn't it, Ellie? Believe me, Mr Mangan, all those unpleasant things came into your mind in the last half second before you woke. Ellie rubbed your hair the wrong way; and the disagreeable sensation suggested a disagreeable dream.

MANGAN: (*doggedly*) I believe in dreams.

MRS HUSHABYE: So do I. But they go by contraries, don't they?

MANGAN: (*depths of emotion suddenly welling up in him*) I shan't forget, to my dying day, that when you gave me the glad eye that time in the garden, you were making a fool of me. That was a dirty low mean thing to do. You had no right to let me come near you if I disgusted you. It isn't my fault if I'm old and haven't a moustache like a bronze candlestick as your husband has. There are things no decent woman would do to a man—like a man hitting a woman in the breast.

(*Hesione, utterly shamed, sits down on the sofa and covers her face with her hands. Mangan sits down also on his chair and begins to cry like a child. Ellie stares at them. Mrs Hushabye, at the distressing sound he makes, takes down her hands and looks at him. She rises and runs to him.*)

MRS HUSHABYE: Don't cry: I can't bear it. Have I broken your heart? I didn't know you had one. How could I?

MANGAN: I'm a man, ain't I?

MRS HUSHABYE: (*half coaxing, half rallying, altogether tenderly*) Oh no: not what I call a man. Only a Boss: just that and nothing else. What business has a Boss with a heart?

MANGAN: Then you're not a bit sorry for what you did, nor ashamed?

MRS HUSHABYE: I was ashamed for the first time in my life when you said that about hitting a woman in the breast, and I found out what I'd done. My very bones blushed red. You've had your revenge, Boss. Aren't you satisfied?

MANGAN: Serve you right! Do you hear? Serve you right! You're just cruel. Cruel.

MRS HUSHABYE: Yes: cruelty would be delicious if one could only find some sort of cruelty that didn't really hurt. By the way (*sitting down beside him on the arm of the chair*), what's your name? It's not really Boss, is it?

MANGAN: (*shortly*) If you want to know, my name's Alfred.

MRS HUSHABYE: (*springs up*) Alfred!! Ellie, he was christened after Tennyson!!!

MANGAN: (*rising*) I was christened after my uncle, and never had a penny from him, damn him! What of it?

MRS HUSHABYE: It comes to me suddenly that you are a real person: that you had a mother, like anyone else. (*Putting her hands on his shoulders and surveying him.*) Little Alf!

MANGAN: Well, you have a nerve.

MRS HUSHABYE: And you have a heart, Alfy, a whimpering little heart, but a real one. (*Releasing him suddenly.*) Now run and make it up with Ellie. She has had time to think what to say to you, which is more than I had (*she goes out quickly into the garden by the port door*).

MANGAN: That woman has a pair of hands that go right through you.

ELLIE: Still in love with her, in spite of all we said about you?

MANGAN: Are all women like you two? Do they never think of anything about a man except what they can get out of him? You weren't even thinking that about me. You were only thinking whether your gloves would last.

ELLIE: I shall not have to think about that when we are married.

MANGAN: And you think I am going to marry you after what I heard there!

ELLIE: You heard nothing from me that I did not tell you before.

MANGAN: Perhaps you think I can't do without you.

ELLIE: I think you would feel lonely without us all, now, after coming to know us so well.

MANGAN: (*with something like a yell of despair*) Am I never to have the last word?

CAPTAIN SHOTOVER: (*appearing at the starboard garden door*) There is a soul in torment here. What is the matter?

MANGAN: This girl doesn't want to spend her life wondering how long her gloves will last.

CAPTAIN SHOTOVER: (*passing through*) Don't wear any. I never do (*he goes into the pantry*).

LADY UTTERWORD: (*appearing at the port garden door, in a handsome dinner dress*) Is anything the matter?

ELLIE: This gentleman wants to know is he never to have the last word.

LADY UTTERWORD: (*coming forward to the sofa*) I should let him have it, my dear. The important thing is not to have the last word, but to have your own way.

MANGAN: She wants both.

LADY UTTERWORD: She won't get them, Mr Mangan. Providence always has the last word.

MANGAN: (*desperately*) Now you are going to come religion over me. In this house a man's mind might as well be a football. I'm going. (*He makes for the hall, but is stopped by a hail from the Captain, who has just emerged from his pantry.*)

CAPTAIN SHOTOVER: Whither away, Boss Mangan?

MANGAN: To hell out of this house: let that be enough for you and all here.

CAPTAIN SHOTOVER: You were welcome to come: you are free to go. The wide earth, the high seas, the spacious skies are waiting for you outside.

LADY UTTERWORD: But your things, Mr Mangan. Your bag, your comb and brushes, your pyjamas—

HECTOR: (*who has just appeared in the port doorway in a handsome Arab costume*) Why should the escaping slave take his chains with him?

MANGAN: That's right, Hushabye. Keep the pyjamas, my lady, and much good may they do you.

HECTOR: (*advancing to Lady Utterword's left hand*) Let us all go out into the night and leave everything behind us.

MANGAN: You stay where you are, the lot of you. I want no company, especially female company.

ELLIE: Let him go. He is unhappy here. He is angry with us.

CAPTAIN SHOTOVER: Go, Boss Mangan; and when you have found the land where there is happiness and where there are no women, send me its latitude and longitude; and I will join you there.

LADY UTTERWORD: You will certainly not be comfortable without your luggage, Mr Mangan.

ELLIE: *(impatient)* Go, go: why don't you go? It is a heavenly
2060 night: you can sleep on the heath. Take my waterproof to lie
on: it is hanging up in the hall.

HECTOR: Breakfast at nine, unless you prefer to breakfast with
the captain at six.

ELLIE: Good night, Alfred.

HECTOR: Alfred! *(He runs back to the door and calls into the
garden.)* Randall, Mangan's Christian name is Alfred.

RANDALL: *(appearing in the starboard doorway in evening
dress)* Then Hesione wins her bet.

*(Mrs Hushabye appears in the port doorway. She throws her
left arm round Hector's neck: draws him with her to the back
of the sofa: and throws her right arm round Lady Utterword's
neck.)*

MRS HUSHABYE: They wouldn't believe me, Alf.

*(They contemplate him.)*

2070 MANGAN: Is there any more of you coming in to look at me, as
if I was the latest thing in a menagerie?

MRS HUSHABYE: You are the latest thing in this menagerie.

*(Before Mangan can retort, a fall of furniture is heard from up-
stairs: then a pistol shot, and a yell of pain. The staring group
breaks up in consternation.)*

MAZZINI'S VOICE: *(from above)* Help! A burglar! Help!

HECTOR: *(his eyes blazing)* A burglar!!!

MRS HUSHABYE: No, Hector: you'll be shot *(but it is too late; he
has dashed out past Mangan, who hastily moves towards the
bookshelves out of his way).*

CAPTAIN SHOTOVER: *(blowing his whistle)* All hands aloft! *(He
strides out after Hector.)*

2080 LADY UTTERWORD: My diamonds! *(She follows the captain.)*

RANDALL: *(rushing after her)* No, Ariadne. Let me.

ELLIE: Oh, is papa shot? *(She runs out.)*

MRS HUSHABYE: Are you frightened, Alf?

MANGAN: No. It ain't my house, thank God.

MRS HUSHABYE: If they catch a burglar, shall we have to go into
court as witnesses, and be asked all sorts of questions about
our private lives?

MANGAN: You won't be believed if you tell the truth.

*(Mazzini, terribly upset, with a duelling pistol in his hand,
comes from the hall, and makes his way to the drawing-table.)*

MAZZINI: Oh, my dear Mrs Hushabye, I might have killed him.
2090 *(He throws the pistol on the table and staggers round to the
chair.)* I hope you won't believe I really intended to.

*(Hector comes in, marching an old and villainous looking man
before him by the collar. He plants him in the middle of the
room and releases him.)*
*(Ellie follows, and immediately runs across to the back of her
father's chair and pats his shoulders.)*

RANDALL: *(entering with a poker)* Keep your eye on this door,
Mangan. I'll look after the other *(he goes to the starboard
door and stands on guard there).*

*(Lady Utterword comes in after Randall, and goes between
Mrs Hushabye and Mangan.)*
*(Nurse Guinness brings up the rear, and waits near the door,
on Mangan's left.)*

MRS HUSHABYE: What has happened?

MAZZINI: Your housekeeper told me there was somebody upstairs, and gave me a pistol that Mr Hushabye had been
practicing with. I thought it would frighten him; but it went
off at a touch.

THE BURGLAR: Yes, and took the skin off my ear. Precious near 2100
took the top off my head. Why don't you have a proper revolver instead of a thing like that, that goes off if you as
much as blow on it?

HECTOR: One of my duelling pistols. Sorry.

MAZZINI: He put his hands up and said it was a fair cop.

THE BURGLAR: So it was. Send for the police.

HECTOR: No, by thunder! It was not a fair cop. We were four
to one.

MRS HUSHABYE: What will they do to him?

THE BURGLAR: Ten years. Beginning with solitary. Ten years off 2110
my life. I shan't serve it all: I'm too old. It will see me out.

LADY UTTERWORD: You should have thought of that before you
stole my diamonds.

THE BURGLAR: Well, you've got them back, lady, haven't you?
Can you give me back the years of my life you are going to
take from me?

MRS HUSHABYE: Oh, we can't bury a man alive for ten years for
a few diamonds.

THE BURGLAR: Ten little shining diamonds! Ten long black
years! 2120

LADY UTTERWORD: Think of what it is for us to be dragged
through the horrors of a criminal court, and have all our
family affairs in the papers! If you were a native, and Hastings could order you a good beating and send you away, I
shouldn't mind; but here in England there is no real protection for any respectable person.

THE BURGLAR: I'm too old to be give a hiding, lady. Send for the
police and have done with it. It's only just and right you
should.

RANDALL: *(who has relaxed his vigilance on seeing the burglar* 2130
*so pacifically disposed, and comes forward swinging the
poker between his fingers like a well-folded umbrella)* It is
neither just nor right that we should be put to a lot of inconvenience to gratify your moral enthusiasm, my friend.
You had better get out, while you have the chance.

THE BURGLAR: *(inexorably)* No. I must work my sin off my conscience. This has come as a sort of call to me. Let me spend
the rest of my life repenting in a cell. I shall have my reward
above.

MANGAN: *(exasperated)* The very burglars can't behave natu- 2140
rally in this house.

HECTOR: My good sir, you must work out your salvation at
somebody else's expense. Nobody here is going to charge
you.

THE BURGLAR: Oh, you won't charge me, won't you?

HECTOR: No. I'm sorry to be inhospitable; but will you kindly
leave the house?

THE BURGLAR: Right. I'll go to the police station and give
myself up. *(He turns resolutely to the door: but Hector
stops him.)* 2150

HECTOR: } { Oh no. You mustn't do that.
RANDALL: } { No, no. Clear out, man, can't you; and
} { don't be a fool.
MRS HUSHABYE: } { Don't be so silly. Can't you repent at
} { home?

LADY UTTERWORD: You will have to do as you are told.

THE BURGLAR: It's compounding a felony, you know.

MRS HUSHABYE: This is utterly ridiculous. Are we to be forced to prosecute this man when we don't want to?

2160 THE BURGLAR: Am I to be robbed of my salvation to save you the trouble of spending a day at the sessions? Is that justice? Is it right? Is it fair to me?

MAZZINI: (*rising and leaning across the table persuasively as if it were a pulpit desk or a shop counter*) Come, come! let me show you how you can turn your very crimes to account. Why not set up as a locksmith? You must know more about locks than most honest men?

THE BURGLAR: That's true, sir. But I couldn't set up as a lock-smith under twenty pounds.

2170 RANDALL: Well, you can easily steal twenty pounds. You will find it in the nearest bank.

THE BURGLAR: (*horrified*) Oh, what a thing for a gentleman to put into the head of a poor criminal scrambling out of the bottomless pit as it were! Oh, shame on you, sir! Oh, God forgive you! (*He throws himself into the big chair and covers his face as if in prayer.*)

LADY UTTERWORD: Really, Randall!

HECTOR: It seems to me that we shall have to take up a collection for this inopportunely contrite sinner.

2180 LADY UTTERWORD: But twenty pounds is ridiculous.

THE BURGLAR: (*looking up quickly*) I shall have to buy a lot of tools, lady.

LADY UTTERWORD: Nonsense: you have your burgling kit.

THE BURGLAR: What's a jimmy and a centrebit and an acetylene welding plant and a bunch of skeleton keys? I shall want a forge, and a smithy, and a shop, and fittings. I can't hardly do it for twenty.

HECTOR: My worthy friend, we haven't got twenty pounds.

THE BURGLAR: (*now master of the situation*) You can raise it 2190 among you, can't you?

MRS HUSHABYE: Give him a sovereign, Hector, and get rid of him.

HECTOR: (*giving him a pound*) There! Off with you.

THE BURGLAR: (*rising and taking the money very ungratefully*) I won't promise nothing. You have more on you than a quid: all the lot of you, I mean.

LADY UTTERWORD: (*vigorously*) Oh, let us prosecute him and have done with it. I have a conscience too, I hope; and I do not feel at all sure that we have any right to let him go, es-2200 pecially if he is going to be greedy and impertinent.

THE BURGLAR: (*quickly*) All right, lady, all right. I've no wish to be anything but agreeable. Good evening, ladies and gen-tlemen; and thank you kindly.

(*He is hurrying out when he is confronted in the doorway by Captain Shotover.*)

CAPTAIN SHOTOVER: (*fixing the burglar with a piercing regard*) What's this? Are there two of you?

THE BURGLAR: (*falling on his knees before the captain in abject terror*) Oh, my good Lord, what have I done? Don't tell me it's your house I've broken into, Captain Shotover.

(*The captain seizes him by the collar: drags him to his feet: and leads him to the middle of the group, Hector falling back beside his wife to make way for them.*)

CAPTAIN SHOTOVER: (*turning him towards Ellie*) Is that your daughter? (*He releases him.*)    2210

THE BURGLAR: Well, how do I know, Captain? You know the sort of life you and me has led. Any young lady of that age might be my daughter anywhere in the wide world, as you might say.

CAPTAIN SHOTOVER: (*to Mazzini*) You are not Billy Dunn. This is Billy Dunn. Why have you imposed on me?

THE BURGLAR: (*indignantly to Mazzini*) Have you been giving yourself out to be me? You, that nigh blew my head off! Shooting yourself, in a manner of speaking!

MAZZINI: My dear Captain Shotover, ever since I came into this 2220 house I have done hardly anything else but assure you that I am not Mr William Dunn, but Mazzini Dunn, a very dif-ferent person.

THE BURGLAR: He don't belong to my branch, Captain. There's two sets in the family: the thinking Dunns and the drinking Dunns, each going their own ways. I'm a drinking Dunn: he's a thinking Dunn. But that didn't give him any right to shoot me.

CAPTAIN SHOTOVER: So you've turned burglar, have you?

THE BURGLAR: No, Captain: I wouldn't disgrace our old sea 2230 calling by such a thing. I am no burglar.

LADY UTTERWORD: What were you doing with my diamonds?

GUINNESS: What did you break into the house for if you're no burglar?

RANDALL: Mistook the house for your own and came in by the wrong window, eh?

THE BURGLAR: Well, it's no use my telling you a lie: I can take in most captains, but not Captain Shotover, because he sold himself to the devil in Zanzibar, and can divine water, spot gold, explode a cartridge in your pocket with a glance of his 2240 eye, and see the truth hidden in the heart of man. But I'm no burglar.

CAPTAIN SHOTOVER: Are you an honest man?

THE BURGLAR: I don't set up to be better than my fellow-crea-tures, and never did, as you well know, Captain. But what I do is innocent and pious. I enquire about for houses where the right sort of people live. I work it on them same as I worked it here. I break into the house; put a few spoons or diamonds in my pocket; make a noise; get caught; and take up a collection. And you wouldn't believe how hard it is to 2250 get caught when you're actually trying to. I have knocked over all the chairs in a room without a soul paying any at-tention to me. In the end I have had to walk out and leave the job.

RANDALL: When that happens, do you put back the spoons and diamonds?

THE BURGLAR: Well, I don't fly in the face of Providence, if that's what you want to know.

CAPTAIN SHOTOVER: Guinness, you remember this man?

GUINNESS: I should think I do, seeing I was married to him, the 2260 blackguard!

HESIONE:            } *exclaiming*   { Married to him!
LADY UTTERWORD:    } *together*     { Guinness!!

THE BURGLAR: It wasn't legal. I've been married to no end of women. No use coming that over me.

CAPTAIN SHOTOVER: Take him to the forecastle (*he flings him to the door with a strength beyond his years*).

GUINNESS: I suppose you mean the kitchen. They won't have

him there. Do you expect servants to keep company with thieves and all sorts?

CAPTAIN SHOTOVER: Land-thieves and water-thieves are the same flesh and blood. I'll have no boatswain on my quarter-deck. Off with you both.

THE BURGLAR: Yes, Captain. (*He goes out humbly.*)

MAZZINI: Will it be safe to have him in the house like that?

GUINNESS: Why didn't you shoot him, sir? If I'd known who he was, I'd have shot him myself. (*She goes out.*)

MRS HUSHABYE: Do sit down, everybody. (*She sits down on the sofa.*)

(*They all move except Ellie. Mazzini resumes his seat. Randall sits down in the window-seat near the starboard door, again making a pendulum of his poker, and studying it as Galileo might have done. Hector sits on his left, in the middle. Mangan, forgotten, sits in the port corner. Lady Utterword takes the big chair. Captain Shotover goes into the pantry in deep abstraction. They all look after him: and Lady Utterword coughs consciously.*)

MRS HUSHABYE: So Billy Dunn was poor nurse's little romance. I knew there had been somebody.

RANDALL: They will fight their battles over again and enjoy themselves immensely.

LADY UTTERWORD: (*irritably*) You are not married; and you know nothing about it, Randall. Hold your tongue.

RANDALL: Tyrant!

MRS HUSHABYE: Well, we have had a very exciting evening. Everything will be an anticlimax after it. We'd better all go to bed.

RANDALL: Another burglar may turn up.

MAZZINI: Oh, impossible! I hope not.

RANDALL: Why not? There is more than one burglar in England.

MRS HUSHABYE: What do you say, Alf?

MANGAN: (*huffily*) Oh, I don't matter. I'm forgotten. The burglar has put my nose out of joint. Shove me into a corner and have done with me.

MRS HUSHABYE: (*jumping up mischievously, and going to him*) Would you like a walk on the heath, Alfred? With me?

ELLIE: Go, Mr Mangan. It will do you good. Hesione will soothe you.

MRS HUSHABYE: (*slipping her arm under his and pulling him upright*) Come, Alfred. There is a moon: it's like the night in Tristan and Isolde. (*She caresses his arm and draws him to the port garden door.*)

MANGAN: (*writhing but yielding*) How you can have the face—the heart—(*he breaks down and is heard sobbing as she takes him out*).

LADY UTTERWORD: What an extraordinary way to behave! What is the matter with the man?

ELLIE: (*in a strangely calm voice, staring into an imaginary distance*) His heart is breaking: that is all. (*The captain appears at the pantry door, listening.*) It is a curious sensation: the sort of pain that goes mercifully beyond our powers of feeling. When your heart is broken, your boats are burned: nothing matters any more. It is the end of happiness and the beginning of peace.

LADY UTTERWORD: (*suddenly rising in a rage, to the astonishment of the rest*) How dare you?

HECTOR: Good heavens! What's the matter?

RANDALL: (*in a warning whisper*) Tch—tch—tch! Steady.

ELLIE: (*surprised and haughty*) I was not addressing you particularly, Lady Utterword. And I am not accustomed to being asked how dare I.

LADY UTTERWORD: Of course not. Anyone can see how badly you have been brought up.

MAZZINI: Oh, I hope not, Lady Utterword. Really!

LADY UTTERWORD: I know very well what you meant. The impudence!

ELLIE: What on earth do you mean?

CAPTAIN SHOTOVER: (*advancing to the table*) She means that her heart will not break. She has been longing all her life for someone to break it. At last she has become afraid she has none to break.

LADY UTTERWORD: (*flinging herself on her knees and throwing her arms round him*) Papa, don't say you think I've no heart.

CAPTAIN SHOTOVER: (*raising her with grim tenderness*) If you had no heart how could you want to have it broken, child?

HECTOR: (*rising with a bound*) Lady Utterword, you are not to be trusted. You have made a scene (*he runs out into the garden through the starboard door*).

LADY UTTERWORD: Oh! Hector, Hector! (*she runs out after him*).

RANDALL: Only nerves, I assure you. (*He rises and follows her, waving the poker in his agitation.*) Ariadne! Ariadne! For God's sake, be careful. You will—(*he is gone*).

MAZZINI: (*rising*) How distressing! Can I do anything, I wonder?

CAPTAIN SHOTOVER: (*promptly taking his chair and setting to work at the drawing-board*) No. Go to bed. Good-night.

MAZZINI: (*bewildered*) Oh! Perhaps you are right.

ELLIE: Good-night, dearest. (*She kisses him.*)

MAZZINI: Good-night, love. (*He makes for the door, but turns aside to the bookshelves.*) I'll just take a book (*he takes one*). Good-night. (*He goes out, leaving Ellie alone with the captain.*)

(*The captain is intent on his drawing. Ellie, standing sentry over his chair, contemplates him for a moment.*)

ELLIE: Does nothing ever disturb you, Captain Shotover?

CAPTAIN SHOTOVER: I've stood on the bridge for eighteen hours in a typhoon. Life here is stormier; but I can stand it.

ELLIE: Do you think I ought to marry Mr Mangan?

CAPTAIN SHOTOVER: (*never looking up*) One rock is as good as another to be wrecked on.

ELLIE: I am not in love with him.

CAPTAIN SHOTOVER: Who said you were?

ELLIE: You are not surprised?

CAPTAIN SHOTOVER: Surprised! At my age!

ELLIE: It seems to me quite fair. He wants me for one thing: I want him for another.

CAPTAIN SHOTOVER: Money?

ELLIE: Yes.

CAPTAIN SHOTOVER: Well, one turns the cheek: the other kisses it. One provides the cash: the other spends it.

ELLIE: Who will have the best of the bargain, I wonder?

CAPTAIN SHOTOVER: You. These fellows live in an office all day. You will have to put up with him from dinner to breakfast; but you will both be asleep most of that time. All day you will be quit of him; and you will be shopping with his money. If that is too much for you, marry a seafaring man: you will be bothered with him only three weeks in the year, perhaps.

2380 ELLIE: That would be best of all, I suppose.

CAPTAIN SHOTOVER: It's a dangerous thing to be married right up to the hilt, like my daughter's husband. The man is at home all day, like a damned soul in hell.

ELLIE: I never thought of that before.

CAPTAIN SHOTOVER: If you're marrying for business, you can't be too businesslike.

ELLIE: Why do women always want other women's husbands?

CAPTAIN SHOTOVER: Why do horse-thieves prefer a horse that is broken-in to one that is wild?

2390 ELLIE: *(with a short laugh)* I suppose so. What a vile world it is!

CAPTAIN SHOTOVER: It doesn't concern me. I'm nearly out of it.

ELLIE: And I'm only just beginning.

CAPTAIN SHOTOVER: Yes; so look ahead.

ELLIE: Well, I think I am being very prudent.

CAPTAIN SHOTOVER: I didn't say prudent. I said look ahead.

ELLIE: What's the difference?

CAPTAIN SHOTOVER: It's prudent to gain the whole world and lose your own soul. But don't forget that your soul sticks to 2400 you if you stick to it; but the world has a way of slipping through your fingers.

ELLIE: *(wearily, leaving him and beginning to wander restlessly about the room)* I'm sorry, Captain Shotover; but it's no use talking like that to me. Old-fashioned people are no use to me. Old-fashioned people think you can have a soul without money. They think the less money you have, the more soul you have. Young people nowadays know better. A soul is a very expensive thing to keep; much more so than a motor car.

2410 CAPTAIN SHOTOVER: Is it? How much does your soul eat?

ELLIE: Oh, a lot. It eats music and pictures and books and mountains and lakes and beautiful things to wear and nice people to be with. In this country you can't have them without lots of money: that is why our souls are so horribly starved.

CAPTAIN SHOTOVER: Mangan's soul lives on pig's food.

ELLIE: Yes: money is thrown away on him. I suppose his soul was starved when he was young. But it will not be thrown away on me. It is just because I want to save my soul that I 2420 am marrying for money. All the women who are not fools do.

CAPTAIN SHOTOVER: There are other ways of getting money. Why don't you steal it?

ELLIE: Because I don't want to go to prison.

CAPTAIN SHOTOVER: Is that the only reason? Are you quite sure honesty has nothing to do with it?

ELLIE: Oh, you are very very old-fashioned, Captain. Does any modern girl believe that the legal and illegal ways of getting money are the honest and dishonest ways? Mangan robbed 2430 my father and my father's friends. I should rob all the money back from Mangan if the police would let me. As they won't, I must get it back by marrying him.

CAPTAIN SHOTOVER: I can't argue: I'm too old: my mind is made up and finished. All I can tell you is that, old-fashioned or new-fashioned, if you sell yourself, you deal your soul a blow that all the books and pictures and concerts and scenery in

the world won't heal *(he gets up suddenly and makes for the pantry)*.

ELLIE: *(running after him and seizing him by the sleeve)* Then why did you sell yourself to the devil in Zanzibar?     2440

CAPTAIN SHOTOVER: *(stopping, startled)* What?

ELLIE: You shall not run away before you answer. I have found out that trick of yours. If you sold yourself, why shouldn't I?

CAPTAIN SHOTOVER: I had to deal with men so degraded that they wouldn't obey me unless I swore at them and kicked them and beat them with my fists. Foolish people took young thieves off the streets; flung them into a training ship where they were taught to fear the cane instead of fearing God; and thought they'd made men and sailors of them by private subscription. I tricked these thieves into believing 2450 I'd sold myself to the devil. It saved my soul from the kicking and swearing that was damning me by inches.

ELLIE: *(releasing him)* I shall pretend to sell myself to Boss Mangan to save my soul from the poverty that is damning *me* by inches.

CAPTAIN SHOTOVER: Riches will damn you ten times deeper. Riches won't save even your body.

ELLIE: Old-fashioned again. We know now that the soul is the body, and the body the soul. They tell us they are different because they want to persuade us that we can keep our souls 2460 if we let them make slaves of our bodies. I am afraid you are no use to me, Captain.

CAPTAIN SHOTOVER: What did you expect? A Savior, eh? Are you old-fashioned enough to believe in that?

ELLIE: No. But I thought you were very wise, and might help me. Now I have found you out. You pretend to be busy, and think of fine things to say, and run in and out to surprise people by saying them, and get away before they can answer you.

CAPTAIN SHOTOVER: It confuses me to be answered. It discour- 2470 ages me. I cannot bear men and women. I *have* to run away. I must run away now *(he tries to)*.

ELLIE: *(again seizing his arm)* You shall not run away from me. I can hypnotize you. You are the only person in the house I can say what I like to. I know you are fond of me. Sit down. *(She draws him to the sofa.)*

CAPTAIN SHOTOVER: *(yielding)* Take care: I am in my dotage. Old men are dangerous: it doesn't matter to them what is going to happen to the world.

*(They sit side by side on the sofa. She leans affectionately against him with her head on his shoulder and her eyes half closed.)*

ELLIE: *(dreamily)* I should have thought nothing else mattered 2480 to old men. They can't be very interested in what is going to happen to themselves.

CAPTAIN SHOTOVER: A man's interest in the world is only the overflow from his interest in himself. When you are a child your vessel is not yet full; so you care for nothing but your own affairs. When you grow up, your vessel overflows; and you are a politician, a philosopher, or an explorer and adventurer. In old age the vessel dries up: there is no overflow: you are a child again. I can give you the memories of my ancient wisdom: mere scraps and leavings; but I no longer 2490 really care for anything but my own little wants and hobbies. I sit here working out my old ideas as a means of destroying my fellow-creatures. I see my daughters and their men living foolish lives of romance and sentiment and snobbery. I see you, the younger generation, turning from their romance and sentiment and snobbery to money and comfort and hard common sense. I was ten times happier on the bridge in the typhoon, or frozen into Arctic ice for months in darkness, than you or they have ever been. You are look-2500 ing for a rich husband. At your age I looked for hardship, danger, horror, and death, that I might feel the life in me more intensely. I did not let the fear of death govern my life; and my reward was, I had my life. You are going to let the fear of poverty govern your life; and your reward will be that you will eat, but you will not live.

ELLIE: (*sitting up impatiently*) But what can I do? I am not a sea captain: I can't stand on bridges in typhoons, or go slaughtering seals and whales in Greenland's icy mountains. They won't let women be captains. Do you want me to be a 2510 stewardess?

CAPTAIN SHOTOVER: There are worse lives. The stewardesses could come ashore if they liked; but they sail and sail and sail.

ELLIE: What could they do ashore but marry for money? I don't want to be a stewardess: I am too bad a sailor. Think of something else for me.

CAPTAIN SHOTOVER: I can't think so long and continuously. I am too old. I must go in and out. (*He tries to rise.*)

ELLIE: (*pulling him back*) You shall not. You are happy here, 2520 aren't you?

CAPTAIN SHOTOVER: I tell you it's dangerous to keep me. I can't keep awake and alert.

ELLIE: What do you run away for? To sleep?

CAPTAIN SHOTOVER: No. To get a glass of rum.

ELLIE: (*frightfully disillusioned*) Is that it? How disgusting! Do you like being drunk?

CAPTAIN SHOTOVER: No; I dread being drunk more than anything in the world. To be drunk means to have dreams; to go soft; to be easily pleased and deceived; to fall into the 2530 clutches of women. Drink does that for you when you are young. But when you are old: very very old, like me, the dreams come by themselves. You don't know how terrible that is: you are young: you sleep at night only, and sleep soundly. But later on you will sleep in the afternoon. Later still you will sleep even in the morning; and you will awake tired, tired of life. You will never be free from dozing and dreams; the dreams will steal upon your work every ten minutes unless you can awaken yourself with rum. I drink now to keep sober; but the dreams are conquering; rum is not 2540 what it was: I have had ten glasses since you came; and it might be so much water. Go get me another: Guinness knows where it is. You had better see for yourself the horror of an old man drinking.

ELLIE: You shall not drink. Dream. I like you to dream. You must never be in the real world when we talk together.

CAPTAIN SHOTOVER: I am too weary to resist, or too weak. I am in my second childhood. I do not see you as you really are. I can't remember what I really am. I feel nothing but the accursed happiness I have dreaded all my life long: the happi-2550 ness that comes as life goes, the happiness of yielding and dreaming instead of resisting and doing, the sweetness of the fruit that is going rotten.

ELLIE: You dread it almost as much as I used to dread losing my dreams and having to fight and do things. But that is all over for me: my dreams are dashed to pieces. I should like to marry a very old, very rich man. I should like to marry you. I had much rather marry you than marry Mangan. Are you very rich?

CAPTAIN SHOTOVER: No. Living from hand to mouth. And I have a wife somewhere in Jamaica: a black one. My first 2560 wife. Unless she's dead.

ELLIE: What a pity! I feel so happy with you. (*She takes his hand, almost unconsciously, and pats it.*) I thought I should never feel happy again.

CAPTAIN SHOTOVER: Why?

ELLIE: Don't you know?

CAPTAIN SHOTOVER: No.

ELLIE: Heartbreak. I fell in love with Hector, and didn't know he was married.

CAPTAIN SHOTOVER: Heartbreak? Are you one of those who are 2570 so sufficient to themselves that they are only happy when they are stripped of everything, even of hope?

ELLIE: (*gripping the hand*) It seems so; for I feel now as if there was nothing I could not do, because I want nothing.

CAPTAIN SHOTOVER: That's the only real strength. That's genius. That's better than rum.

ELLIE: (*throwing away his hand*) Rum! Why did you spoil it?

(*Hector and Randall come in from the garden through the starboard door.*)

HECTOR: I beg your pardon. We did not know there was anyone here.

ELLIE: (*rising*) That means that you want to tell Mr Randall the 2580 story about the tiger. Come, Captain: I want to talk to my father; and you had better come with me.

CAPTAIN SHOTOVER: (*rising*) Nonsense! the man is in bed.

ELLIE: Aha! I've caught you. My real father has gone to bed; but the father you gave me is in the kitchen. You knew quite well all along. Come. (*She draws him out into the garden with her through the port door.*)

HECTOR: That's an extraordinary girl. She has the Ancient Mariner on a string like a Pekinese dog.

RANDALL: Now that they have gone, shall we have a friendly 2590 chat?

HECTOR: You are in what is supposed to be my house. I am at your disposal.

(*Hector sits down in the draughtsman's chair, turning it to face Randall, who remains standing, leaning at his ease against the carpenter's bench.*)

RANDALL: I take it that we may be quite frank. I mean about Lady Utterword.

HECTOR: You may. I have nothing to be frank about. I never met her until this afternoon.

RANDALL: (*straightening up*) What! But you are her sister's husband.

HECTOR: Well, if you come to that, you are her husband's 2600 brother.

RANDALL: But you seem to be on intimate terms with her.

HECTOR: So do you.

RANDALL: Yes: but I *am* on intimate terms with her. I have known her for years.

HECTOR: It took her years to get to the same point with you that she got to with me in five minutes, it seems.

RANDALL: (*vexed*) Really, Ariadne is the limit (*he moves away huffishly towards the windows*).

2610 HECTOR: (*coolly*) She is, as I remarked to Hesione, a very enterprising woman.

RANDALL: (*returning, much troubled*) You see, Hushabye, you are what women consider a good-looking man.

HECTOR: I cultivated that appearance in the days of my vanity; and Hesione insists on my keeping it up. She makes me wear these ridiculous things (*indicating his Arab costume*) because she thinks me absurd in evening dress.

RANDALL: Still, you do keep it up, old chap. Now, I assure you I have not an atom of jealousy in my disposition—

2620 HECTOR: The question would seem to be rather whether your brother has any touch of that sort.

RANDALL: What! Hastings! Oh, don't trouble about Hastings. He has the gift of being able to work sixteen hours a day at the dullest detail, and actually likes it. That gets him to the top wherever he goes. As long as Ariadne takes care that he is fed regularly, he is only too thankful to anyone who will keep her in good humor for him.

HECTOR: And as she has all the Shotover fascination, there is plenty of competition for the job, eh?

2630 RANDALL: (*angrily*) She encourages them. Her conduct is perfectly scandalous. I assure you, my dear fellow, I haven't an atom of jealousy in my composition; but she makes herself the talk of every place she goes to by her thoughtlessness. It's nothing more: she doesn't really care for the men she keeps hanging about her; but how is the world to know that? It's not fair to Hastings. It's not fair to me.

HECTOR: Her theory is that her conduct is so correct—

RANDALL: Correct! She does nothing but make scenes from morning till night. *You* be careful, old chap. She will get you
2640 into trouble: that is, she would if she really cared for you.

HECTOR: Doesn't she?

RANDALL: Not a scrap. She may want your scalp to add to her collection; but her true affection has been engaged years ago. You had really better be careful.

HECTOR: Do you suffer much from this jealousy?

RANDALL: Jealousy! I jealous! My dear fellow, haven't I told you that there is not an atom of—

HECTOR: Yes. And Lady Utterword told me she never made scenes. Well, don't waste your jealousy on my moustache.
2650 Never waste jealousy on a real man: it is the imaginary hero that supplants us all in the long run. Besides, jealousy does not belong to your easy man-of-the-world pose, which you carry so well in other respects.

RANDALL: Really, Hushabye, I think a man may be allowed to be a gentleman without being accused of posing.

HECTOR: It is a pose like any other. In this house we know all the poses: our game is to find out the man under the pose. The man under your pose is apparently Ellie's favorite, Othello.

2660 RANDALL: Some of your games in this house are damned annoying, let me tell you.

HECTOR: Yes: I have been their victim for many years. I used to writhe under them at first; but I became accustomed to them. At last I learned to play them.

RANDALL: If it's all the same to you I had rather you didn't play

them on me. You evidently don't quite understand my character, or my notions of good form.

HECTOR: Is it your notion of good form to give away Lady Utterword?

RANDALL: (*a childishly plaintive note breaking into his huff*) I 2670 have not said a word against Lady Utterword. This is just the conspiracy over again.

HECTOR: What conspiracy?

RANDALL: You know very well, sir. A conspiracy to make me out to be pettish and jealous and childish and everything I am not. Everyone knows I am just the opposite.

HECTOR: (*rising*) Something in the air of the house has upset you. It often does have that effect. (*He goes to the garden door and calls Lady Utterword with commanding emphasis.*) Ariadne!                                                                                  2680

LADY UTTERWORD: (*at some distance*) Yes.

RANDALL: What are you calling her for? I want to speak—

LADY UTTERWORD: (*arriving breathless*) Yes. You really are a terribly commanding person. What's the matter?

HECTOR: I do not know how to manage your friend Randall. No doubt you do.

LADY UTTERWORD: Randall: have you been making yourself ridiculous, as usual? I can see it in your face. Really, you are the most pettish creature.

RANDALL: You know quite well, Ariadne, that I have not an 2690 ounce of pettishness in my disposition. I have made myself perfectly pleasant here. I have remained absolutely cool and imperturbable in the face of a burglar. Imperturbability is almost too strong a point of mine. But (*putting his foot down with a stamp, and walking angrily up and down the room*) I *insist* on being treated with a certain consideration. I will not allow Hushabye to take liberties with me. I will not stand your encouraging people as you do.

HECTOR: The man has a rooted delusion that he is your husband.                                                                                            2700

LADY UTTERWORD: I know. He is jealous. As if he had any right to be! He compromises me everywhere. He makes scenes all over the place. Randall: I will not allow it. I simply will not allow it. You had no right to discuss me with Hector. I will not be discussed by men.

HECTOR: Be reasonable, Ariadne. Your fatal gift of beauty forces men to discuss you.

LADY UTTERWORD: Oh indeed! what about *your* fatal gift of beauty?

HECTOR: How can I help it?                                                                   2710

LADY UTTERWORD: You could cut off your moustache: I can't cut off my nose. I get my whole life messed up with people falling in love with me. And then Randall says I run after men.

RANDALL: I—

LADY UTTERWORD: Yes you do: you said it just now. Why can't you think of something else than women? Napoleon was quite right when he said that women are the occupation of the idle man. Well, if ever there was an idle man on earth, his name is Randall Utterword.                                                    2720

RANDALL: Ariad—

LADY UTTERWORD: (*overwhelming him with a torrent of words*) Oh yes you are: it's no use denying it. What have you ever done? What good are you? You are as much trouble in the house as a child of three. You couldn't live without your valet.

RANDALL: This is—

LADY UTTERWORD: Laziness! You are laziness incarnate. You are selfishness itself. You are the most uninteresting man on 2730 earth. You can't even gossip about anything but yourself and your grievances and your ailments and the people who have offended you. (*Turning to Hector.*) Do you know what they call him, Hector?

HECTOR ⎱ (*speaking* ⎰ Please don't tell me.
RANDALL ⎰ *together*) ⎱ I'll not stand it—

LADY UTTERWORD: Randall the Rotter: that is his name in good society.

RANDALL: (*shouting*) I'll not bear it, I tell you. Will you listen to me, you infernal—(*he chokes*).

2740 LADY UTTERWORD: Well: go on. What were you going to call me? An infernal what? Which unpleasant animal is it to be this time?

RANDALL: (*foaming*) There is no animal in the world so hateful as a woman can be. You are a maddening devil. Hushabye, you will not believe me when I tell you that I have loved this demon all my life; but God knows I have paid for it (*he sits down in the draughtsman's chair, weeping*).

LADY UTTERWORD: (*standing over him with triumphant contempt*) Cry-baby!

2750 HECTOR: (*gravely, coming to him*) My friend, the Shotover sisters have two strange powers over men. They can make them love; and they can make them cry. Thank your stars that you are not married to one of them.

LADY UTTERWORD: (*haughtily*) And pray, Hector—

HECTOR: (*suddenly catching her round the shoulders: swinging her right round him and away from Randall: and gripping her throat with the other hand*) Ariadne, if you attempt to start on me, I'll choke you: do you hear? The cat-and-mouse game with the other sex is a good game; but I can play your 2760 head off at it. (*He throws her, not at all gently, into the big chair, and proceeds, less fiercely but firmly.*) It is true that Napoleon said that woman is the occupation of the idle man. But he added that she is the relaxation of the warrior. Well, I am the warrior. So take care.

LADY UTTERWORD: (*not in the least put out, and rather pleased by his violence*) My dear Hector, I have only done what you asked me to do.

HECTOR: How do you make that out, pray?

LADY UTTERWORD: You called me in to manage Randall, didn't 2770 you? You said you couldn't manage him yourself.

HECTOR: Well, what if I did? I did not ask you to drive the man mad.

LADY UTTERWORD: He isn't mad. That's the way to manage him. If you were a mother, you'd understand.

HECTOR: Mother! What are you up to now?

LADY UTTERWORD: It's quite simple. When the children got nerves and were naughty, I smacked them just enough to give them a good cry and a healthy nervous shock. They went to sleep and were quite good afterwards. Well, I can't 2780 smack Randall: he is too big; so when he gets nerves and is naughty, I just rag him till he cries. He will be all right now. Look: he is half asleep already (*which is quite true*).

RANDALL: (*waking up indignantly*) I'm not. You are most cruel, Ariadne. (*Sentimentally.*) But I suppose I must forgive you, as usual (*he checks himself in the act of yawning*).

LADY UTTERWORD: (*to Hector*) Is the explanation satisfactory, dread warrior?

HECTOR: Some day I shall kill you, if you go too far. I thought you were a fool.

LADY UTTERWORD: (*laughing*) Everybody does, at first. But I 2790 am not such a fool as I look. (*She rises complacently.*) Now, Randall, go to bed. You will be a good boy in the morning.

RANDALL: (*only very faintly rebellious*) I'll go to bed when I like. It isn't ten yet.

LADY UTTERWORD: It is long past ten. See that he goes to bed at once, Hector. (*She goes into the garden.*)

HECTOR: Is there any slavery on earth viler than this slavery of men to women?

RANDALL: (*rising resolutely*) I'll not speak to her tomorrow. I'll not speak to her for another week. I'll give her *such* a lesson. 2800 I'll go straight to bed without bidding her good-night. (*He makes for the door leading to the hall.*)

HECTOR: You are under a spell, man. Old Shotover sold himself to the devil in Zanzibar. The devil gave him a black witch for a wife; and these two demon daughters are their mystical progeny. I am tied to Hesione's apron-string; but I'm her husband; and if I did go stark staring mad about her, at least we became man and wife. But why should *you* let yourself be dragged about and beaten by Ariadne as a toy donkey is dragged about and beaten by a child? What do you 2810 get by it? Are you her lover?

RANDALL: You must not misunderstand me. In a higher sense—in a Platonic sense—

HECTOR: Psha! Platonic sense! She makes you her servant; and when pay-day comes round, she bilks you: that is what you mean.

RANDALL: (*feebly*) Well, if I don't mind, I don't see what business it is of yours. Besides, I tell you I am going to punish her. You shall see: *I* know how to deal with women. I'm really very sleepy. Say good-night to Mrs Hushabye for me, 2820 will you, like a good chap. Good-night. (*He hurries out.*)

HECTOR: Poor wretch! Oh women! women! women! (*He lifts his fists in invocation to heaven.*) Fall. Fall and crush. (*He goes out into the garden.*)

## —ACT THREE—

*In the garden, Hector, as he comes out through the glass door of the poop, finds Lady Utterword lying voluptuously in the hammock on the east side of the flagstaff, in the circle of light cast by the electric arc, which is like a moon in its opal globe. Beneath the head of the hammock, a campstool. On the other side of the flagstaff, on the long garden seat, Captain Shotover is asleep, with Ellie beside him, leaning affectionately against him on his right hand. On his left is a deck chair. Behind them in the gloom, Hesione is strolling about with Mangan. It is a fine still night, moonless.*

LADY UTTERWORD: What a lovely night! It seems made for us.

HECTOR: The night takes no interest in us. What are we to the night? (*He sits down moodily in the deck chair.*)

ELLIE: (*dreamily, nestling against the captain*) Its beauty soaks into my nerves. In the night there is peace for the old and hope for the young. 2830

HECTOR: Is that remark your own?

ELLIE: No. Only the last thing the captain said before he went to sleep.

CAPTAIN SHOTOVER: I'm not asleep.

HECTOR: Randall is. Also Mr Mazzini Dunn. Mangan, too, probably.

MANGAN: No.

HECTOR: Oh, you are there. I thought Hesione would have sent you to bed by this time.

2840 MRS HUSHABYE: *(coming to the back of the garden seat, into the light, with Mangan)* I think I shall. He keeps telling me he has a presentiment that he is going to die. I never met a man so greedy for sympathy.

MANGAN: *(plaintively)* But I have a presentiment. I really have. And you wouldn't listen.

MRS HUSHABYE: I was listening for something else. There was a sort of splendid drumming in the sky. Did none of you hear it? It came from a distance and then died away.

MANGAN: I tell you it was a train.

2850 MRS HUSHABYE: And *I* tell *you*, Alf, there is no train at this hour. The last is nine forty-five.

MANGAN: But a goods train.

MRS HUSHABYE: Not on our little line. They tack a truck on to the passenger train. What can it have been, Hector?

HECTOR: Heaven's threatening growl of disgust at us useless futile creatures. *(Fiercely.)* I tell you, one of two things must happen. Either out of that darkness some new creation will come to supplant us as we have supplanted the animals, or the heavens will fall in thunder and destroy us.

2860 LADY UTTERWORD: *(in a cool instructive manner, wallowing comfortably in her hammock)* We have not supplanted the animals, Hector. Why do you ask heaven to destroy this house, which could be made quite comfortable if Hesione had any notion of how to live? Don't you know what is wrong with it?

HECTOR: We are wrong with it. There is no sense in us. We are useless, dangerous, and ought to be abolished.

LADY UTTERWORD: Nonsense! Hastings told me the very first day he came here, nearly twenty-four years ago, what is 2870 wrong with the house.

CAPTAIN SHOTOVER: What! The numskull said there was something wrong with my house!

LADY UTTERWORD: I said Hastings said it; and he is not in the least a numskull.

CAPTAIN SHOTOVER: What's wrong with my house?

LADY UTTERWORD: Just what is wrong with a ship, papa. Wasn't it clever of Hastings to see that?

CAPTAIN SHOTOVER: The man's a fool. There's nothing wrong with a ship.

2880 LADY UTTERWORD: Yes, there is.

MRS HUSHABYE: But what is it? Don't be aggravating, Addy.

LADY UTTERWORD: Guess.

HECTOR: Demons. Daughters of the witch of Zanzibar. Demons.

LADY UTTERWORD: Not a bit. I assure you, all this house needs to make it a sensible, healthy, pleasant house, with good appetites and sound sleep in it, is horses.

MRS HUSHABYE: Horses! What rubbish!

LADY UTTERWORD: Yes: horses. Why have we never been able 2890 to let this house? Because there are no proper stables. Go anywhere in England where there are natural, wholesome, contented, and really nice English people; and what do you always find? That the stables are the real centre of the household; and that if any visitor wants to play the piano the whole room has to be upset before it can be opened, there are so many things piled on it. I never lived until I learned to ride; and I shall never ride really well because I didn't begin as a child. There are only two classes in good society in England: the equestrian classes and the neurotic classes. It isn't mere convention: everybody can see that the people 2900 who hunt are the right people and the people who don't are the wrong ones.

CAPTAIN SHOTOVER: There is some truth in this. My ship made a man of me; and a ship is the horse of the sea.

LADY UTTERWORD: Exactly how Hastings explained your being a gentleman.

CAPTAIN SHOTOVER: Not bad for a numskull. Bring the man here with you next time: I must talk to him.

LADY UTTERWORD: Why is Randall such an obvious rotter? He is well bred; he has been at a public school and a university; 2910 he has been in the Foreign Office; he knows the best people and has lived all his life among them. Why is he so unsatisfactory, so contemptible? Why can't he get a valet to stay with him longer than a few months? Just because he is too lazy and pleasure-loving to hunt and shoot. He strums the piano, and sketches, and runs after married women, and reads literary books and poems. He actually plays the flute; but I never let him bring it into my house. If he would only—*(she is interrupted by the melancholy strains of a flute coming from an open window above. She raises herself 2920 indignantly in the hammock).* Randall, you have not gone to bed. Have you been listening? *(The flute replies pertly.)*

How vulgar! Go to bed instantly, Randall: how dare you? *(The window is slammed down. She subsides.)* How can anyone care for such a creature!

MRS HUSHABYE: Addy: do you think Ellie ought to marry poor Alfred merely for his money?

MANGAN: *(much alarmed)* What's that? Mrs Hushabye, are my affairs to be discussed like this before everybody?

LADY UTTERWORD: I don't think Randall is listening now.   2930

MANGAN: Everybody is listening. It isn't right.

MRS HUSHABYE: But in the dark, what does it matter? Ellie doesn't mind. Do you, Ellie?

ELLIE: Not in the least. What is your opinion, Lady Utterword? You have so much good sense.

MANGAN: But it isn't right. It—*(Mrs Hushabye puts her hand on his mouth.)* Oh, very well.

LADY UTTERWORD: How much money have you, Mr Mangan?

MANGAN: Really—No: I can't stand this.

LADY UTTERWORD: Nonsense, Mr Mangan! It all turns on your 2940 income, doesn't it?

MANGAN: Well, if you come to that, how much money has she?

ELLIE: None.

LADY UTTERWORD: You are answered, Mr Mangan. And now, as you have made Miss Dunn throw her cards on the table, you cannot refuse to show your own.

MRS HUSHABYE: Come, Alf! out with it! How much?

MANGAN: *(baited out of all prudence)* Well, if you want to know, I have no money and never had any.

2950 MRS HUSHABYE: Alfred, you mustn't tell naughty stories.

MANGAN: I'm not telling you stories. I'm telling you the raw truth.

LADY UTTERWORD: Then what do you live on, Mr Mangan?

MANGAN: Travelling expenses. And a trifle of commission.

CAPTAIN SHOTOVER: What more have any of us but travelling expenses for our life's journey?

MRS HUSHABYE: But you have factories and capital and things?

MANGAN: People think I have. People think I'm an industrial Napoleon. That's why Miss Ellie wants to marry me. But I 2960 tell you I have nothing.

ELLIE: Do you mean that the factories are like Marcus's tigers? That they don't exist?

MANGAN: They exist all right enough. But they're not mine. They belong to syndicates and shareholders and all sorts of lazy good-for-nothing capitalists. I get money from such people to start the factories. I find people like Miss Dunn's father to work them, and keep a tight hand so as to make them pay. Of course I make them keep me going pretty well; but it's a dog's life; and I don't own anything.

2970 MRS HUSHABYE: Alfred, Alfred, you are making a poor mouth of it to get out of marrying Ellie.

MANGAN: I'm telling the truth about my money for the first time in my life; and it's the first time my word has ever been doubted.

LADY UTTERWORD: How sad! Why don't you go in for politics, Mr Mangan?

MANGAN: Go in for politics! Where have you been living? I *am* in politics.

LADY UTTERWORD: I'm sure I beg your pardon. I never heard 2980 of you.

MANGAN: Let me tell you, Lady Utterword, that the Prime Minister of this country asked me to join the Government without even going through the nonsense of an election, as the dictator of a great public department.

LADY UTTERWORD: As a Conservative or a Liberal?

MANGAN: No such nonsense. As a practical business man. *(They all burst out laughing.)* What are you all laughing at?

MRS HUSHABYE: Oh, Alfred, Alfred!

ELLIE: You! who have to get my father to do everything for you!

2990 MRS HUSHABYE: You! who are afraid of your own workmen!

HECTOR: You! with whom three women have been playing cat and mouse all the evening!

LADY UTTERWORD: You must have given an immense sum to the party funds, Mr Mangan.

MANGAN: Not a penny out of my own pocket. The syndicate found the money: they knew how useful I should be to them in the Government.

LADY UTTERWORD: This is most interesting and unexpected, Mr Mangan. And what have your administrative achieve-3000 ments been, so far?

MANGAN: Achievements? Well, I don't know what you call achievements; but I've jolly well put a stop to the games of the other fellows in the other departments. Every man of them thought he was going to save the country all by himself, and do me out of the credit and out of my chance of a title. I took good care that if they wouldn't let me do it they shouldn't do it themselves either. I may not know anything about my own machinery; but I know how to stick a ramrod

into the other fellow's. And now they all look the biggest fools going. 3010

HECTOR: And in heaven's name, what do you look like?

MANGAN: I look like the fellow that was too clever for all the others, don't I? If that isn't a triumph of practical business, what is?

HECTOR: Is this England, or is it a madhouse?

LADY UTTERWORD: Do you expect to save the country, Mr Mangan?

MANGAN: Well, who else will? Will your Mr Randall save it?

LADY UTTERWORD: Randall the rotter! Certainly not.

MANGAN: Will your brother-in-law save it with his moustache 3020 and his fine talk?

HECTOR: Yes, if they will let me.

MANGAN: *(sneering)* Ah! *Will* they let you?

HECTOR: No. They prefer you.

MANGAN: Very well then, as you're in a world where I'm appreciated and you're not, you'd best be civil to me, hadn't you? Who else is there but me?

LADY UTTERWORD: There is Hastings. Get rid of your ridiculous sham democracy; and give Hastings the necessary powers, and a good supply of bamboo to bring the British native to 3030 his senses: he will save the country with the greatest ease.

CAPTAIN SHOTOVER: It had better be lost. Any fool can govern with a stick in his hand. *I* could govern that way. It is not God's way. The man is a numskull.

LADY UTTERWORD: The man is worth all of you rolled into one. What do you say, Miss Dunn?

ELLIE: I think my father would do very well if people did not put upon him and cheat him and despise him because he is so good.

MANGAN: *(contemptuously)* I think I see Mazzini Dunn getting 3040 into parliament or pushing his way into the Government. We've not come to that yet, thank God! What do you say, Mrs Hushabye?

MRS HUSHABYE: Oh, *I* say it matters very little which of you governs the country so long as we govern you.

HECTOR: We? Who is we, pray?

MRS HUSHABYE: The devil's granddaughters, dear. The lovely women.

HECTOR: *(raising his hands as before)* Fall, I say, and deliver us from the lures of Satan! 3050

ELLIE: There seems to be nothing real in the world except my father and Shakespeare. Marcus's tigers are false; Mr Mangan's millions are false; there is nothing really strong and true about Hesione but her beautiful black hair; and Lady Utterword's is too pretty to be real. The one thing that was left to me was the Captain's seventh degree of concentration; and that turns out to be—

CAPTAIN SHOTOVER: Rum.

LADY UTTERWORD: *(placidly)* A good deal of my hair is quite genuine. The Duchess of Dithering offered me fifty guineas 3060 for this *(touching her forehead)* under the impression that it was a transformation; but it is all natural except the color.

MANGAN: *(wildly)* Look here: I'm going to take off all my clothes *(he begins tearing off his coat).*

LADY UTTERWORD: ⎱
CAPTAIN SHOTOVER: ⎰ *(in consternation)* ⎱ Mr Mangan!
HECTOR: ⎱ ⎰ What's that?
ELLIE: ⎰ ⎱ Ha! ha! Do. Do.
⎰ Please don't.

MRS HUSHABYE: *(catching his arm and stopping him)* Alfred,

3070 for shame! Are you mad?

MANGAN: Shame! What shame is there in this house? Let's all strip stark naked. We may as well do the thing thoroughly when we're about it. We've stripped ourselves morally naked: well, let us strip ourselves physically naked as well, and see how we like it. I tell you I can't bear this. I was brought up to be respectable. I don't mind the women dyeing their hair and the men drinking: it's human nature. But it's not human nature to tell everybody about it. Every time one of you opens your mouth I go like this (*he cowers as if* 3080 *to avoid a missile*), afraid of what will come next. How are we to have any self-respect if we don't keep it up that we're better than we really are?

LADY UTTERWORD: I quite sympathize with you, Mr Mangan. I have been through it all; and I know by experience that men and women are delicate plants and must be cultivated under glass. Our family habit of throwing stones in all directions and letting the air in is not only unbearably rude, but positively dangerous. Still, there is no use catching physical colds as well as moral ones; so please keep your clothes on.

3090 MANGAN: I'll do as I like: not what you tell me. Am I a child or a grown man? I won't stand this mothering tyranny. I'll go back to the city, where I'm respected and made much of.

MRS HUSHABYE: Goodbye, Alf. Think of us sometimes in the city. Think of Ellie's youth!

ELLIE: Think of Hesione's eyes and hair!

CAPTAIN SHOTOVER: Think of this garden in which you are not a dog barking to keep the truth out!

HECTOR: Think of Lady Utterword's beauty! her good sense! her style!

3100 LADY UTTERWORD: Flatterer. Think, Mr. Mangan, whether you can really do any better for yourself elsewhere: that is the essential point, isn't it?

MANGAN: (*surrendering*) All right: all right. I'm done. Have it your own way. Only let me alone. I don't know whether I'm on my head or my heels when you all start on me like this. I'll stay. I'll marry her. I'll do anything for a quiet life. Are you satisfied now?

ELLIE: No. I never really intended to make you marry me, Mr Mangan. Never in the depths of my soul. I only wanted to 3110 feel my strength: to know that you could not escape if I chose to take you.

MANGAN: (*indignantly*) What! Do you mean to say you are going to throw me over after my acting so handsome?

LADY UTTERWORD: I should not be too hasty, Miss Dunn. You can throw Mr Mangan over at any time up to the last moment. Very few men in his position go bankrupt. You can live very comfortably on his reputation for immense wealth.

ELLIE: I cannot commit bigamy, Lady Utterword.

| MRS HUSHABYE: | | Bigamy! Whatever on earth are you talking about, Ellie? |
| LADY UTTERWORD: | | Bigamy! What do you mean, Miss Dunn? |
| MANGAN: | (*exclaiming all together*) | Bigamy! Do you mean to say you're married already? |
| HECTOR: | | Bigamy! This is some enigma. |

ELLIE: Only half an hour ago I became Captain Shotover's

white wife. 3130

MRS HUSHABYE: Ellie! What nonsense! Where?

ELLIE: In heaven, where all true marriages are made.

LADY UTTERWORD: Really, Miss Dunn! Really, papa!

MANGAN: He told me *I* was too old! And him a mummy!

HECTOR: (*quoting Shelley*).
"Their altar the grassy earth outspread,
And their priest the muttering wind."

ELLIE: Yes: I, Ellie Dunn, give my broken heart and my strong sound soul to its natural captain, my spiritual husband and second father. 3140

(*She draws the captain's arm through hers, and pats his hand. The captain remains fast asleep.*)

MRS HUSHABYE: Oh, that's very clever of you, pettikins. Very clever. Alfred, you could never have lived up to Ellie. You must be content with a little share of me.

MANGAN: (*sniffing and wiping his eyes*) It isn't kind—(*his emotion chokes him*).

LADY UTTERWORD: You are well out of it, Mr Mangan. Miss Dunn is the most conceited young woman I have met since I came back to England.

MRS HUSHABYE: Oh, Ellie isn't conceited. Are you, pettikins?

ELLIE: I know my strength now, Hesione. 3150

MANGAN: Brazen, I call you. Brazen.

MRS HUSHABYE: Tut, tut, Alfred: don't be rude. Don't you feel how lovely this marriage night is, made in heaven? Aren't you happy, you and Hector? Open your eyes: Addy and Ellie look beautiful enough to please the most fastidious man: we live and love and have not a care in the world. We women have managed all that for you. Why in the name of common sense do you go on as if you were two miserable wretches?

CAPTAIN SHOTOVER: I tell you happiness is no good. You can be happy when you are only half alive. I am happier now I am 3160 half dead than ever I was in my prime. But there is no blessing on my happiness.

ELLIE: (*her face lighting up*) Life with a blessing! that is what I want. Now I know the real reason why I couldn't marry Mr Mangan: there would be no blessing on our marriage. There is a blessing on my broken heart. There is a blessing on your beauty, Hesione. There is a blessing on your father's spirit. Even on the lies of Marcus there is a blessing; but on Mr Mangan's money there is none.

MANGAN: I don't understand a word of that. 3170

ELLIE: Neither do I. But I know it means something.

MANGAN: Don't say there was any difficulty about the blessing. I was ready to get a bishop to marry us.

MRS HUSHABYE: Isn't he a fool, pettikins?

HECTOR: (*fiercely*) Do not scorn the man. We are all fools.

(*Mazzini, in pyjamas and a richly colored silk dressing-gown, comes from the house, on Lady Utterword's side.*)

MRS HUSHABYE: Oh! here comes the only man who ever resisted me. What's the matter, Mr Dunn? Is the house on fire?

MAZZINI: Oh, no: nothing's the matter: but really it's impossible to go to sleep with such an interesting conversation 3180 going on under one's window, and on such a beautiful night too. I just had to come down and join you all. What has it all been about?

MRS HUSHABYE: Oh, wonderful things, soldier of freedom.

HECTOR: For example, Mangan, as a practical business man, has tried to undress himself and has failed ignominiously; whilst you, as an idealist, have succeeded brilliantly.

MAZZINI: I hope you don't mind my being like this, Mrs Hushabye. (*He sits down on the campstool.*)

3190 MRS HUSHABYE: On the contrary, I could wish you always like that.

LADY UTTERWORD: Your daughter's match is off, Mr Dunn. It seems that Mr Mangan, whom we all supposed to be a man of property, owns absolutely nothing.

MAZZINI: Well, of course I knew that, Lady Utterword. But if people believe in him and are always giving him money, whereas they don't believe in me and never give me any, how can I ask poor Ellie to depend on what I can do for her?

MANGAN: Don't you run away with this idea that I have 3200 nothing. I—

HECTOR: Oh, don't explain. We understand. You have a couple of thousand pounds in exchequer bills, 50,000 shares worth tenpence a dozen, and half a dozen tabloids of cyanide of potassium to poison yourself with when you are found out. That's the reality of your millions.

MAZZINI: Oh no, no, no. He is quite honest: the businesses are genuine and perfectly legal.

HECTOR: (*disgusted*) Yah! Not even a great swindler!

MANGAN: So you think. But I've been too many for some hon-3210 est men, for all that.

LADY UTTERWORD: There is no pleasing you, Mr Mangan. You are determined to be neither rich nor poor, honest nor dishonest.

MANGAN: There you go again. Ever since I came into this silly house I have been made to look like a fool, though I'm as good a man in this house as in the city.

ELLIE: (*musically*) Yes: this silly house, this strangely happy house, this agonizing house, this house without foundations. I shall call it Heartbreak House.

3220 MRS HUSHABYE: Stop, Ellie; or I shall howl like an animal.

MANGAN: (*breaks into a low snivelling*)!!!

MRS HUSHABYE: There! you have set Alfred off.

ELLIE: I like him best when he is howling.

CAPTAIN SHOTOVER: Silence! (*Mangan subsides into silence.*) I say, let the heart break in silence.

HECTOR: Do you accept that name for your house?

CAPTAIN SHOTOVER: It is not my house: it is only my kennel.

HECTOR: We have been too long here. We do not live in this house: we haunt it.

3230 LADY UTTERWORD: (*heart torn*) It is dreadful to think how you have been here all these years while I have gone round the world. I escaped young; but it has drawn me back. It wants to break my heart too. But it shan't. I have left you and it behind. It was silly of me to come back. I felt sentimental about papa and Hesione and the old place. I felt them calling to me.

MAZZINI: But what a very natural and kindly and charming human feeling, Lady Utterword!

LADY UTTERWORD: So I thought, Mr Dunn. But I know now 3240 that it was only the last of my influenza. I found that I was not remembered and not wanted.

CAPTAIN SHOTOVER: You left because you did not want us. Was

there no heartbreak in that for your father? You tore yourself up by the roots; and the ground healed up and brought forth fresh plants and forgot you. What right had you to come back and probe old wounds?

MRS HUSHABYE: You were a complete stranger to me at first, Addy; but now I feel as if you had never been away.

LADY UTTERWORD: Thank you, Hesione; but the influenza is quite cured. The place may be Heartbreak House to you, 3250 Miss Dunn, and to this gentleman from the city who seems to have so little self-control; but to me it is only a very ill-regulated and rather untidy villa without any stables.

HECTOR: Inhabited by—?

ELLIE: A crazy old sea captain and a young singer who adores him.

MRS HUSHABYE: A sluttish female, trying to stave off a double chin and an elderly spread, vainly wooing a born soldier of freedom.

MAZZINI: Oh, really, Mrs Hushabye— 3260

MANGAN: A member of His Majesty's Government that everybody sets down as a nincompoop: don't forget him, Lady Utterword.

LADY UTTERWORD: And a very fascinating gentleman whose chief occupation is to be married to my sister.

HECTOR: All heartbroken imbeciles.

MAZZINI: Oh no. Surely, if I may say so, rather a favorable specimen of what is best in our English culture. You are very charming people, most advanced, unprejudiced, frank, humane, unconventional, democratic, free-thinking, and 3270 everything that is delightful to thoughtful people.

MRS HUSHABYE: You do us proud, Mazzini.

MAZZINI: I am not flattering, really. Where else could I feel perfectly at ease in my pyjamas? I sometimes dream that I am in very distinguished society, and suddenly I have nothing on but my pyjamas! Sometimes I haven't even pyjamas. And I always feel overwhelmed with confusion. But here, I don't mind in the least: it seems quite natural.

LADY UTTERWORD: An infallible sign that you are now not in really distinguished society, Mr Dunn. If you were in my 3280 house, you would feel embarrassed.

MAZZINI: I shall take particular care to keep out of your house, Lady Utterword.

LADY UTTERWORD: You will be quite wrong, Mr Dunn. I should make you very comfortable; and you would not have the trouble and anxiety of wondering whether you should wear your purple and gold or your green and crimson dressing-gown at dinner. You complicate life instead of simplifying it by doing these ridiculous things.

ELLIE: Your house is not Heartbreak House: is it, Lady 3290 Utterword?

HECTOR: Yet she breaks hearts, easy as her house is. That poor devil upstairs with his flute howls when she twists his heart, just as Mangan howls when my wife twists his.

LADY UTTERWORD: That is because Randall has nothing to do but have his heart broken. It is a change from having his head shampooed. Catch anyone breaking Hastings' heart!

CAPTAIN SHOTOVER: The numskull wins, after all.

LADY UTTERWORD: I shall go back to my numskull with the greatest satisfaction when I am tired of you all, clever as 3300 you are.

MANGAN: (*huffily*) I never set up to be clever.

LADY UTTERWORD: I forgot you, Mr Mangan.

MANGAN: Well, I don't see that quite, either.

LADY UTTERWORD: You may not be clever, Mr Mangan; but you are successful.

MANGAN: But I don't want to be regarded merely as a successful man. I have an imagination like anyone else. I have a presentiment—

3310 MRS HUSHABYE: Oh, you are impossible, Alfred. Here I am devoting myself to you; and you think of nothing but your ridiculous presentiment. You bore me. Come and talk poetry to me under the stars. (*She drags him away into the darkness.*)

MANGAN: (*tearfully, as he disappears*) Yes: it's all very well to make fun of me; but if you only knew—

HECTOR: (*impatiently*) How is all this going to end?

MAZZINI: It won't end, Mr Hushabye. Life doesn't end; it goes on.

3320 ELLIE: Oh, it can't go on forever. I'm always expecting something. I don't know what it is; but life must come to a point sometime.

LADY UTTERWORD: The point for a young woman of your age is a baby.

HECTOR: Yes, but, damn it, I have the same feeling; and *I* can't have a baby.

LADY UTTERWORD: By deputy, Hector.

HECTOR: But I *have* children. All that is over and done with for me: and yet I too feel that this can't last. We sit here talking,

3330 and leave everything to Mangan and to chance and to the devil. Think of the powers of destruction that Mangan and his mutual admiration gang wield! It's madness: it's like giving a torpedo to a badly brought up child to play at earthquakes with.

MAZZINI: I know. I used often to think about that when I was young.

HECTOR: Think! What's the good of thinking about it? Why didn't you do something?

MAZZINI: But I did. I joined societies and made speeches and

3340 wrote pamphlets. That was all I could do. But, you know, though the people in the societies thought they knew more than Mangan, most of them wouldn't have joined if they had known as much. You see they had never had any money to handle or any men to manage. Every year I expected a revolution, or some frightful smash-up: it seemed impossible that we could blunder and muddle on any longer. But nothing happened, except, of course, the usual poverty and crime and drink that we are used to. Nothing ever does happen. It's amazing how well we get along, all things con-

3350 sidered.

LADY UTTERWORD: Perhaps somebody cleverer than you and Mr Mangan was at work all the time.

MAZZINI: Perhaps so. Though I was brought up not to believe in anything, I often feel that there is a great deal to be said for the theory of an over-ruling Providence, after all.

LADY UTTERWORD: Providence! I meant Hastings.

MAZZINI: Oh, I beg your pardon, Lady Utterword.

CAPTAIN SHOTOVER: Every drunken skipper trusts to Providence. But one of the ways of Providence with drunken

3360 skippers is to run them on the rocks.

MAZZINI: Very true, no doubt, at sea. But in politics, I assure you, they only run into jellyfish. Nothing happens.

CAPTAIN SHOTOVER: At sea nothing happens to the sea. Nothing happens to the sky. The sun comes up from the east and goes down to the west. The moon grows from a sickle to an arc lamp, and comes later and later until she is lost in the light as other things are lost in the darkness. After the typhoon, the flying-fish glitter in the sunshine like birds. It's amazing how they get along, all things considered. Nothing happens, except something not worth mentioning.    3370

ELLIE: What is that, O Captain, O my captain?

CAPTAIN SHOTOVER: (*savagely*) Nothing but the smash of the drunken skipper's ship on the rocks, the splintering of her rotten timbers, the tearing of her rusty plates, the drowning of the crew like rats in a trap.

ELLIE: Moral: don't take rum.

CAPTAIN SHOTOVER: (*vehemently*) That is a lie, child. Let a man drink ten barrels of rum a day, he is not a drunken skipper until he is a drifting skipper. Whilst he can lay his course and stand on his bridge and steer it, he is no drunkard. It is the    3380 man who lies drinking in his bunk and trusts to Providence that I call the drunken skipper, though he drank nothing but the waters of the River Jordan.

ELLIE: Splendid! And you haven't had a drop for an hour. You see you don't need it: your own spirit is not dead.

CAPTAIN SHOTOVER: Echoes: nothing but echoes. The last shot was fired years ago.

HECTOR: And this ship that we are all in? This soul's prison we call England?

CAPTAIN SHOTOVER: The captain is in his bunk, drinking bottled 3390 ditch-water; and the crew is gambling in the forecastle. She will strike and sink and split. Do you think the laws of God will be suspended in favor of England because you were born in it?

HECTOR: Well, I don't mean to be drowned like a rat in a trap. I still have the will to live. What am I to do?

CAPTAIN SHOTOVER: Do? Nothing simpler. Learn your business as an Englishman.

HECTOR: And what may my business as an Englishman be, pray?    3400

CAPTAIN SHOTOVER: Navigation. Learn it and live; or leave it and be damned.

ELLIE: Quiet, quiet: you'll tire yourself.

MAZZINI: I thought all that once, Captain; but I assure you nothing will happen.

(*A dull distant explosion is heard.*)

HECTOR: (*starting up*) What was that?

CAPTAIN SHOTOVER: Something happening (*he blows his whistle*). Breakers ahead!

(*The light goes out.*)

HECTOR: (*furiously*) Who put that light out? Who dared put that light out?    3410

NURSE GUINNESS: (*running in from the house to the middle of the esplanade*) I did, sir. The police have telephoned to say we'll be summoned if we don't put that light out: it can be seen for miles.

HECTOR: It shall be seen for a hundred miles (*he dashes into the house*).

NURSE GUINNESS: The rectory is nothing but a heap of bricks, they say. Unless we can give the rector a bed he has nowhere to lay his head this night.

3420 CAPTAIN SHOTOVER: The Church is on the rocks, breaking up.
I told him it would unless it headed for God's open sea.

NURSE GUINNESS: And you are all to go down to the cellars.

CAPTAIN SHOTOVER: Go there yourself, you and all the crew.
Batten down the hatches.

NURSE GUINNESS: And hide beside the coward I married! I'll go
on the roof first. (*The lamp lights up again.*) There! Mr
Hushabye's turned it on again.

THE BURGLAR: (*hurrying in and appealing to Nurse Guinness*)
Here: where's the way to that gravel pit? The boot-boy says
3430 there's a cave in the gravel pit. Them cellars is no use.
Where's the gravel pit, Captain?

NURSE GUINNESS: Go straight on past the flagstaff until you fall
into it and break your dirty neck. (*She pushes him contemptuously towards the flagstaff, and herself goes to the foot of
the hammock and waits there, as it were by Ariadne's
cradle.*)

(*Another and louder explosion is heard. The burglar stops and
stands trembling.*)

ELLIE: (*rising*) That was nearer.

CAPTAIN SHOTOVER: The next one will get us. (*He rises.*) Stand
by, all hands, for judgment.

3440 THE BURGLAR: Oh my Lordy God! (*He rushes away frantically
past the flagstaff into the gloom.*)

MRS HUSHABYE: (*emerging panting from the darkness*) Who
was that running away? (*She comes to Ellie.*) Did you hear
the explosions? And the sound in the sky: it's splendid: it's
like an orchestra: it's like Beethoven.

ELLIE: By thunder, Hesione: it is Beethoven.

(*She and Hesione throw themselves into one another's arms in
wild excitement. The light increases.*)

MAZZINI: (*anxiously*) The light is getting brighter.

NURSE GUINNESS: (*looking up at the house*) It's Mr Hushabye
turning on all the lights in the house and tearing down the
3450 curtains.

RANDALL: (*rushing in his pyjamas, distractedly waving a flute*)
Ariadne, my soul, my precious, go down to the cellars: I beg
and implore you, go down to the cellars!

LADY UTTERWORD: (*quite composed in her hammock*) The governor's wife in the cellars with the servants! Really, Randall!

RANDALL: But what shall I do if you are killed?

LADY UTTERWORD: You will probably be killed, too, Randall.
Now play your flute to show that you are not afraid; and be
good. Play us "Keep the home fires burning."

3460 NURSE GUINNESS: (*grimly*) They'll keep the home fires burning
for us: them up there.

RANDALL: (*having tried to play*) My lips are trembling. I can't
get a sound.

MAZZINI: I hope poor Mangan is safe.

MRS HUSHABYE: He is hiding in the cave in the gravel pit.

CAPTAIN SHOTOVER: My dynamite drew him there. It is the
hand of God.

HECTOR: (*returning from the house and striding across to his
former place*) There is not half light enough. We should be
3470 blazing to the skies.

ELLIE: (*tense with excitement*) Set fire to the house, Marcus.

MRS HUSHABYE: My house! No.

HECTOR: I thought of that; but it would not be ready in time.

CAPTAIN SHOTOVER: The judgment has come. Courage will not
save you; but it will show that your souls are still live.

MRS HUSHABYE: Sh-sh! Listen: do you hear it now? It's magnificent.

(*They all turn away from the house and look up, listening.*)

HECTOR: (*gravely*) Miss Dunn, you can do no good here. We of
this house are only moths flying into the candle. You had
better go down to the cellar.                                   3480

ELLIE: (*scornfully*) I don't think.

MAZZINI: Ellie, dear, there is no disgrace in going to the cellar.
An officer would order his soldiers to take cover. Mr
Hushabye is behaving like an amateur. Mangan and the bur-
glar are acting very sensibly; and it is they who will survive.

ELLIE: Let them. I shall behave like an amateur. But why
should you run any risk?

MAZZINI: Think of the risk those poor fellows up there are running!

NURSE GUINNESS: Think of *them*, indeed, the murdering black-   3490
guards! What next?

(*A terrific explosion shakes the earth. They reel back into their
seats, or clutch the nearest support. They hear the falling of the
shattered glass from the windows.*)

MAZZINI: Is anyone hurt?

HECTOR: Where did it fall?

NURSE GUINNESS: (*in hideous triumph*) Right in the gravel pit:
I seen it. Serve un right! I seen it (*she runs away towards the
gravel pit, laughing harshly*).

HECTOR: One husband gone.

CAPTAIN SHOTOVER: Thirty pounds of good dynamite wasted.

MAZZINI: Oh, poor Mangan!

HECTOR: Are you immortal that you need pity him? Our         3500
turn next.

(*They wait in silence and intense expectation. Hesione and
Ellie hold each other's hand tight.*) A distant explosion is
heard.

MRS HUSHABYE: (*relaxing her grip*) Oh! they have passed us.

LADY UTTERWORD: The danger is over, Randall. Go to bed.

CAPTAIN SHOTOVER: Turn in, all hands. The ship is safe. (*He sits
down and goes asleep.*)

ELLIE: (*disappointedly*) Safe!

HECTOR: (*disgustedly*) Yes, safe. And how damnably dull the
world has become again suddenly! (*He sits down.*)

MAZZINI: (*sitting down*) I was quite wrong, after all. It is we
who have survived; and Mangan and the burglar—          3510

HECTOR: —the two burglars—

LADY UTTERWORD: the two practical men of business—

MAZZINI: —both gone. And the poor clergyman will have to get
a new house.

MRS HUSHABYE: But what a glorious experience! I hope they'll
come again tomorrow night.

ELLIE: (*radiant at the prospect*) Oh, I hope so.

(*Randall at last succeeds in keeping the home fires burning on
his flute.*)

## Bernard Shaw

FROM the Preface
to *Heartbreak House*
(1919)

*Where Heartbreak
House stands*

*SHAW frequently used a disquisitory preface to elaborate the political and social themes of his plays. Here, he explains the political functions of* Heartbreak House *and* Horseback Hall.

Heartbreak House is not merely the name of the play which follows this preface. It is cultured, leisured Europe before the war. When the play was begun not a shot had been fired; and only the professional diplomatists and the very few amateurs whose hobby is foreign policy even knew that the guns were loaded. A Russian playwright, Tchekov, had produced four fascinating dramatic studies of Heartbreak House, of which three, *The Cherry Orchard, Uncle Vanya,* and *The Seagull,* had been performed in England. Tolstoy, in his *Fruits of Enlightenment,* had shown us through it in his most ferociously contemptuous manner. Tolstoy did not waste any sympathy on it: it was to him the house in which Europe was stifling its soul; and he knew that our utter enervation and futilization in that overheated drawing-room atmosphere was delivering the world over to the control of ignorant and soulless cunning and energy, with the frightful consequences which have now overtaken it. Tolstoy was no pessimist: he was not disposed to leave the house standing if he could bring it down about the ears of its pretty and amiable voluptuaries; and he wielded the pickaxe with a will. He treated the case of the inmates as one of opium poisoning, to be dealt with by seizing the patients roughly and exercising them violently until they were broad awake. Tchekov, more of a fatalist, had no faith in these charming people extricating themselves. They would, he thought, be sold up and sent adrift by the bailiffs; and he therefore had no scruple in exploiting and even flattering their charm.

*The inhabitants*

Tchekov's plays, being less lucrative than swings and roundabouts, got no further in England, where theatres are only ordinary commercial affairs, than a couple of performances by the Stage Society. We stared and said, "How Russian!" They did not strike me in that way. Just as Ibsen's intensely Norwegian plays exactly fitted every middle and professional class suburb in Europe, these intensely Russian plays fitted all the country houses in Europe in which the pleasures of music, art, literature, and the theatre had supplanted hunting, shooting, fishing, flirting, eating, and drinking. The same nice people, the same utter futility. The nice people could read; some of them could write; and they were the sole repositories of culture who had social opportunities of contact with our politicians, administrators, and newspaper proprietors, or any chance of sharing or influencing their activities. But they shrank from that contact. They hated politics. They did not wish to realize Utopia for the common people: they wished to realize their favorite fictions and poems in their own lives; and, when they could, they lived without scruple on incomes which they did nothing to earn. The women in their girlhood made themselves look like variety theatre stars, and settled down later into the types of beauty imagined by the previous generation of painters. They took the only part of our society in which there was leisure for high culture, and made it an economic, political, and, as far as practicable, a moral vacuum; and as Nature, abhorring the vacuum, immediately filled it up with sex and with all sorts of refined pleasures, it was a very delightful place at its best for moments of relaxation. In other moments it was disastrous. For prime ministers and their like, it was a veritable Capua.

*Horseback Hall*

But where were our front benchers to nest if not here? The alternative to Heartbreak House was Horseback Hall, consisting of a prison for horses with an annex for the ladies and gentlemen who rode them, hunted them, talked about them, bought them and sold them, and gave nine-tenths of their lives to them, dividing the other tenth between charity, churchgoing (as a substitute for religion), and conservative electioneering (as a substitute for politics). It is true that the two establishments got mixed at the edges. Exiles from the library, the music room, and the picture gallery would be found languishing among the stables, miserably discontented; and hardy horsewomen who slept at the first chord of Schumann were born, horribly misplaced, into the garden of Klingsor; but sometimes one came upon horsebreakers and heartbreakers who could make the best of both worlds. As a rule, however, the two were apart and knew little of one another; so the prime minister folk had to choose between barbarism and Capua. And of the two atmospheres it is hard to say which was the more fatal to statesmanship.

*Revolution on the shelf*

Heartbreak House was quite familiar with revolutionary ideas on paper. It aimed at being advanced and freethinking, and hardly ever went to church or kept the Sabbath except by a little extra fun at weekends. When you spent a Friday to Tuesday in it you found on the shelf in your bedroom not only the books of poets and novelists, but of revolutionary biologists and even economists. Without at least a few plays by myself and Mr Granville Barker, and a few stories by Mr H. G. Wells, Mr Arnold Bennett, and Mr John Galsworthy, the house would have been out of the movement. You would find Blake among the poets, and beside him Bergson, Butler, Scott Haldane, the poems of Meredith and Thomas Hardy, and, generally speaking, all the literary implements for forming the mind of the perfect modern Socialist and Creative Evolutionist. It was a curious experience to spend Sunday in dipping into these books, and on Monday morning to read in the daily paper that the country had just been brought to the verge of anarchy because a new Home Secretary or chief of police without an idea in his head that his great-grandmother might not have had to apologize for, had refused to "recognize" some powerful Trade Union, just as a gondola might refuse to recognize a 20,000-ton liner.

In short, power and culture were in separate compartments. The barbarians were not only literally in the saddle, but on the front bench in the House of Commons, with nobody to correct their incredible ignorance of modern thought and political science but upstarts from the counting-house, who had spent their lives furnishing their pockets instead of their minds. Both, however, were practised in dealing with money and with men, as far as acquiring the one and exploiting the other went; and although this is as undesirable an expertness as that of the medieval robber baron, it qualifies men to keep an estate or a business going in its old routine without necessarily understanding it, just as Bond Street tradesmen and domestic servants keep fashionable society going without any instruction in sociology.

*The Cherry Orchard*

The Heartbreak people neither could nor would do anything of the sort. With their heads as full of the Anticipations of Mr H. G. Wells as the heads of our actual rulers were empty even of the anticipations of Erasmus or Sir Thomas More, they refused the drudgery of politics, and would have made a very poor job of it if they had changed their minds. Not that they would have been allowed to meddle anyhow, as only through the accident of being a hereditary peer can anyone in these days of Votes for Everybody get into parliament if handicapped by a serious modern cultural equipment; but if they had, their habit of living in a vacuum would have left them helpless and ineffective in public affairs. Even in private life they were often helpless wasters of their inheritance, like the people in Tchekov's *Cherry Orchard*. Even those who lived within their incomes were really kept going by their solicitors and agents, being unable to manage an estate or run a business without continual prompting from those who have to learn how to do such things or starve.

From what is called Democracy no corrective to this state of things could be hoped. It is said that every people has the Government it deserves. It is more to the point that every Government has the electorate it deserves; for the orators of the front bench can edify or debauch an ignorant electorate at will. Thus our democracy moves in a vicious circle of reciprocal worthiness and unworthiness.

*Nature's long credits*

Nature's way of dealing with unhealthy conditions is unfortunately not one that compels us to conduct a solvent hygiene on a cash basis. She demoralizes us with long credits and reckless overdrafts, and then pulls us up cruelly with catastrophic bankruptcies. Take, for example, common domestic sanitation. A whole city generation may neglect it utterly and scandalously, if not with absolute impunity, yet without any evil consequences that anyone thinks of tracing to it. In a hospital two generations of medical students may tolerate dirt and carelessness, and then go out into general practice to spread the doctrine that fresh air is a fad, and sanitation an imposture set up to make profits for plumbers. Then suddenly Nature takes her revenge. She strikes at the city with a pestilence and at the hospital with an epidemic of hospital gangrene, slaughtering right and left until the innocent young have paid for the guilty old, and the account is balanced. And then she goes to sleep again and gives another period of credit, with the same result.

This is what has just happened in our political hygiene. Political science has been as recklessly neglected by Governments and electorates during my lifetime as sanitary science was in the days of Charles the Second. In international relations diplomacy has been a boyishly lawless affair of family intrigues, commercial and territorial brigandage, torpors of pseudo-goodnature produced by laziness and spasms of ferocious activity produced by terror. But in these islands we muddled through. Nature gave us a longer credit than she gave to France or Germany or Russia. To British centenarians who died in their beds in 1914, any dread of having to hide underground in London from the shells of an enemy seemed more remote and fantastic than a dread of the appearance of a colony of cobras and rattlesnakes in Kensington Gardens. In the prophetic works of Charles Dickens we were warned against many evils which have since come to pass; but of the evil of being slaughtered by a foreign foe on our own doorsteps there was no shadow. Nature gave us a very long credit; and we abused it to the utmost. But when she struck at last she struck with a vengeance. For four years she smote our first-born and heaped on us plagues of which Egypt never dreamed. They were all as preventible as the great Plague of London, and came solely because they had not been prevented. They were not undone by winning the war. The earth is still bursting with the dead bodies of the victors.

*The wicked half century*

It is difficult to say whether indifference and neglect are worse than false doctrine; but Heartbreak House and Horseback Hall unfortunately suffered from both. For half a century before the war civilization had been going to the devil very precipitately under the influence of a pseudo-science as disastrous as the blackest Calvinism. Calvinism taught that as we are predestinately saved or damned, nothing that we can do can alter our destiny. Still, as Calvinism gave the individual no clue as to whether he had drawn a lucky number or an unlucky one, it left him a fairly strong interest in encouraging his hopes of salvation and allaying his fear of damnation by behaving as one of the elect might be expected to behave rather than as one of the reprobate. But in the middle of the nineteenth century naturalists and physicists assured the world, in the name of Science, that salvation and damnation are all nonsense, and that predestination is the central truth of religion, inasmuch as human beings are produced by their environment, their sins and good deeds being only a series of chemical and mechanical reactions over which they have no control. Such figments as mind, choice, purpose, conscience, will, and so forth, are, they taught, mere illusions, produced because they are useful in the continual struggle of the human machine to maintain its environment in a favorable condition, a process incidentally involving the ruthless destruction or subjection of its competitors for the supply (assumed to be limited) of subsistence available. We taught Prussia this religion; and Prussia bettered our instruction so effectively that we presently found ourselves confronted with the necessity of destroying Prussia to prevent Prussia destroying us. And that has just ended in each destroying the other to an extent doubtfully reparable in our time.

It may be asked how so imbecile and dangerous a creed ever came to be accepted by intelligent beings. I will answer that question more fully in my next volume of plays, which will be entirely devoted to the subject. For the present I will only say that there were better reasons than the obvious one that such sham science as this opened a scientific career to very stupid men, and all the other careers to shameless rascals, provided they were industrious enough. It is true that this motive operated very powerfully; but when the new departure in scientific doctrine which is associated with the name of the great naturalist Charles Darwin began, it was not only a reaction against a barbarous pseudo-evangelical teleology intolerably obstructive to all scientific progress, but was accompanied, as it happened, by discoveries of extraordinary interest in physics, chemistry, and that lifeless method of evolution which its investigators called Natural Selection. Howbeit, there was only one result possible in the ethical sphere, and that was the banishment of conscience from human affairs, or, as Samuel Butler vehemently put it, "of mind from the universe."

*Hypochondria*

Now Heartbreak House, with Butler and Bergson and Scott Haldane alongside Blake and the other major poets on its shelves (to say nothing of Wagner and the tone poets), was not so completely blinded by the doltish materialism of the laboratories as the uncultured world outside. But being an idle house it was a hypochondriacal house, always running after cures. It would stop eating meat, not on valid Shelleyan grounds, but in order to get rid of a bogey called Uric Acid; and it would actually let you pull all its teeth out to exorcise another demon named Pyorrhea. It was superstitious, and addicted to table-rapping, materialization seances, clairvoyance, palmistry, crystalgazing and the like to such an extent that it may be doubted whether ever before in the history of the world did soothsayers, astrologers, and unregistered therapeutic specialists of all sorts flourish as they did during this half century of the drift to the abyss. The registered doctors and surgeons were hard put to it to compete with the unregistered. They were not clever enough to appeal to the imagination and sociability of the Heartbreakers by the arts of the actor, the orator, the poet, the winning conversationalist. They had to fall back coarsely on the terror of infection and death. They prescribed inoculations and operations. Whatever part of a human being could be cut out without necessarily killing him they cut out; and he often died (unnecessarily of course) in consequence. From such trifles as uvulas and tonsils they went on to ovaries and appendices until at last no one's inside was safe. They explained that the human intestine was too long, and that nothing could make a child of Adam healthy except short circuiting the pylorus by cutting a length out of the lower intestine and fastening it directly to the stomach. As their mechanist theory taught them that medicine was the business of the chemist's laboratory, and surgery of the carpenter's shop, and also that Science (by which they meant their practices) was so important that no consideration for the interests of any individual creature, whether frog or philosopher, much less the vulgar commonplaces of sentimental ethics, could weigh for a moment against the remotest off-chance of an addition to the body of scientific knowledge, they operated and vivisected and inoculated and lied on a stupendous scale, clamoring for and actually acquiring such legal powers over the bodies of their fellow-citizens as neither king, pope, nor parliament dare ever have claimed. The Inquisition itself was a Liberal institution compared to the General Medical Council.

Heartbreak House was far too lazy and shallow to extricate itself from this palace of evil enchantment. It rhapsodized about love; but it believed in cruelty. It was afraid of the cruel people; and it saw that cruelty was at least effective. Cruelty did things that made money, whereas Love did nothing but prove the soundness of Larochefoucauld's saying that very few people would fall in love if they had never read about it. Heartbreak House, in short, did not know how to live, at which point all that was left to it was the boast that at least it knew how to die: a melancholy accomplishment which the outbreak of war presently gave it practically unlimited opportunities of displaying. Thus were the firstborn of Heartbreak House smitten; and the young, the innocent, the hopeful expiated the folly and worthlessness of their elders.

*Those who do not know how to live must make a merit of dying*

Only those who have lived through a first-rate war, not in the field, but at home, and kept their heads, can possibly understand the bitterness of Shakespeare and Swift, who both went through this experience. The horror of Peer Gynt in the madhouse, when the lunatics, exalted by illusions of splendid talent and visions of a dawning millennium, crowned him as their emperor, was tame in comparison. I do not know whether anyone really kept his head completely except those who had to keep it because they had to conduct the war at first hand. I should not have kept my own (as far as I did keep it) if I had not at once understood that as a scribe and speaker I too was under the most serious public obligation to keep my grip on realities; but this did not save me from a considerable degree of hyperaesthesia. There were of course some happy people to whom the war meant nothing: all political and general matters lying outside their little circle of interest. But the ordinary war-conscious civilian went mad, the main symptom being a conviction that the whole order of nature had been reversed. All foods, he felt, must now be adulterated. All schools must be closed. No advertisements must be sent to the newspapers, of which new editions must appear and be bought up every ten minutes. Travelling must be stopped, or, that being impossible, greatly hindered. All pretences about fine art and culture and the like must be flung off as an intolerable affectation; and the picture galleries and museums and schools at once occupied by war workers. The British Museum itself was saved only by a hair's breadth. The sincerity of all this, and of much more which would not be believed if I chronicled it, may be established by one conclusive instance of the general craziness. Men were seized with the illusion that they could win the war by giving away money. And they not only subscribed millions to Funds of all sorts with no discoverable object, and to ridiculous voluntary organizations for doing what was plainly the business of the civil and military authorities, but actually handed out money to any thief in the street who had the presence of mind to pretend that he (or she) was "collecting" it for the annihilation of the enemy. Swindlers were emboldened to take offices; label themselves Anti-Enemy Leagues; and simply pocket the money that was heaped on them. Attractively dressed young women found that they had nothing to do but parade the streets, collectingbox in hand, and live gloriously on the profits. Many months elapsed before, as a first sign of returning sanity, the police swept an Anti-Enemy secretary into prison *pour*

*War delirium*

*encourager les autres,* and the passionate penny collecting of the Flag Days was brought under some sort of regulation.

*Madness in court*

The demoralization did not spare the Law Courts. Soldiers were acquitted, even on fully proved indictments for wilful murder, until at last the judges and magistrates had to announce that what was called the Unwritten Law, which meant simply that a soldier could do what he liked with impunity in civil life, was not the law of the land, and that a Victoria Cross did not carry with it a perpetual plenary indulgence. Unfortunately the insanity of the juries and magistrates did not always manifest itself in indulgence. No person unlucky enough to be charged with any sort of conduct, however reasonable and salutary, that did not smack of war delirium, had the slightest chance of acquittal. There were in the country, too, a certain number of people who had conscientious objections to war as criminal or unchristian. The Act of Parliament introducing Compulsory Military Service thoughtlessly exempted these persons, merely requiring them to prove the genuineness of their convictions. Those who did so were very ill-advised from the point of view of their own personal interest; for they were persecuted with savage logicality in spite of the law; whilst those who made no pretence of having any objection to war at all, and had not only had military training in Officers' Training Corps, but had proclaimed on public occasions that they were perfectly ready to engage in civil war on behalf of their political opinions, were allowed the benefit of the Act on the ground that they did not approve of this particular war. For the Christians there was no mercy. In cases where the evidence as to their being killed by ill treatment was so unequivocal that the verdict would certainly have been one of wilful murder had the prejudice of the coroner's jury been on the other side, their tormentors were gratuitously declared to be blameless. There was only one virtue, pugnacity; only one vice, pacifism. That is an essential condition of war; but the Government had not the courage to legislate accordingly; and its law was set aside for Lynch law.

The climax of legal lawlessness was reached in France. The greatest Socialist statesman in Europe, Jaurés, was shot and killed by a gentleman who resented his efforts to avert the war. M. Clemenceau was shot by another gentleman of less popular opinions, and happily came off no worse than having to spend a precautionary couple of days in bed. The slayer of Jaurés was recklessly acquitted: the would-be slayer of M. Clemenceau was carefully found guilty. There is no reason to doubt that the same thing would have happened in England if the war had begun with a successful attempt to assassinate Keir Hardie, and ended with an unsuccessful one to assassinate Mr Lloyd George.

*The long arm of war*

The pestilence which is the usual accompaniment of war was called influenza. Whether it was really a war pestilence or not was made doubtful by the fact that it did its worst in places remote from the battlefields, notably on the west coast of North America and in India. But the moral pestilence, which was unquestionably a war pestilence, reproduced this phenomenon. One would have supposed that the war fever would have raged most furiously in the countries actually under fire, and that the others would be more reasonable. Belgium and Flanders, where over large districts literally not one stone was left upon another as the opposed armies drove each other back and forward over it after terrific preliminary bombardments, might have been pardoned for relieving their feelings more emphatically ·han by shrugging their shoulders and saying, "C'est la guerre." England, inviolate for so many centuries that the swoop of war on her homesteads had long ceased to be more credible than a return of the Flood, could hardly be expected to keep her temper sweet when she knew at last what it was to hide in cellars and underground railway stations, or lie quaking in bed, whilst bombs crashed, houses crumbled, and aircraft guns distributed shrapnel on friend and foe alike until certain shop windows in London, formerly full of fashionable hats, were filled with steel helmets. Slain and mutilated women and children, and burnt and wrecked dwellings, excuse a good deal of violent language, and produce a wrath on which many suns go down before it is appeased. Yet it was in the United States of America, where nobody slept the worse for the war, that the war fever went beyond all sense and reason. In European Courts there was vindictive illegality: in American Courts there was raving lunacy. It is not for me to chronicle the extravagances of an Ally: let some candid American do that. I can only say that to us sitting in our gardens in England, with the guns in France making themselves felt by a throb in the air as unmistakeable as an audible sound, or with tightening hearts studying the phases of the moon in London in their bearing on the chances whether our houses would be standing or ourselves alive next morning, the newspaper accounts of the sentences American Courts were passing on young girls and old men alike for the expression of opinions which were being uttered amid thundering applause before huge audiences in England, and the more private records of the methods by which the American War Loans were raised, were so amazing that they put the guns and the possibilities of a raid clean out of our heads for the moment.

Not content with these rancorous abuses of the existing law, the war maniacs made a frantic rush to abolish all constitutional guarantees of liberty and well-being. The ordinary law was superseded by Acts under which newspapers were seized and their printing machinery destroyed by simple police raids *à la Russe,* and persons arrested and shot without any pretence of trial by jury or publicity of procedure or evidence. Though it was urgently necessary that production should be increased by the most scientific organization and economy of labor, and though no fact was better established than that excessive duration and intensity of toil reduces production heavily instead of increasing it, the factory laws were suspended, and men and women recklessly over-worked until the loss of their efficiency became too glaring to be ignored. Remonstrances and warnings were met either with an accusation of pro-Germanism or the formula, "Remember that we are at war now." I have said that men assumed that war had reversed the order of nature, and that all was lost unless we did the exact opposite of everything we had found necessary and beneficial in peace. But the truth was worse than that. The war did not change men's minds in any such impossible way. What really happened was that the impact of physical death and destruction, the one reality that every fool can understand, tore off the masks of education, art, science and religion from our ignorance and barbarism, and left us glorying grotesquely in the licence suddenly accorded to our vilest passions and most abject terrors. Ever since Thucydides wrote his history, it has been on record that when the angel of death sounds his trumpet the pretences of civilization are blown from men's heads into the mud like hats in a gust of wind. But when this scripture was fulfilled among us, the shock was not the less appalling because a few students of Greek history were not surprised by it. Indeed these students threw themselves into the orgy as shamelessly as the illiterate. The Christian priest joining in the war dance without even throwing off his cassock first, and the respectable school governor expelling the German professor with insult and bodily violence, and declaring that no English child should ever again be taught the language of Luther and Goethe, were kept in countenance by the most impudent repudiations of every decency of civilization and every lesson of political experience on the part of the very persons who, as university professors, historians, philosophers, and men of science, were the accredited custodians of culture. It was crudely natural, and perhaps necessary for recruiting purposes, that German militarism and German dynastic ambition should be painted by journalists and recruiters in black and red as European dangers (as in fact they are), leaving it to be inferred that our own militarism and our own political constitution are millennially democratic (which they certainly are not); but when it came to frantic denunciations of German chemistry, German biology, German poetry, German music, German literature, German philosophy, and even German engineering, as malignant abominations standing towards British and French chemistry and so forth in the relation of heaven to hell, it was clear that the utterers of such barbarous ravings had never really understood or cared for the arts and sciences they professed and were profaning, and were only the appallingly degenerate descendants of the men of the seventeenth and eighteenth centuries who, recognizing no national frontiers in the great realm of the human mind, kept the European comity of that realm loftily and even ostentatiously above the rancors of the battle-field. Tearing the Garter from the Kaiser's leg, striking the German dukes from the roll of our peerage, changing the King's illustrious and historically appropriate surname (for the war was the old war of Guelph against Ghibelline, with the Kaiser as Arch-Ghibelline) to that of a traditionless locality. One felt that the figure of St. George and the Dragon on our coinage should be replaced by that of the soldier driving his spear through Archimedes. But by that time there was no coinage: only paper money in which ten shillings called itself a pound as confidently as the people who were disgracing their country called themselves patriots.

The mental distress of living amid the obscene din of all these carmagnoles and corobberies was not the only burden that lay on sane people during the war. There was also the emotional strain,

*The rabid watchdogs of liberty*

*The sufferings of the sane*

complicated by the offended economic sense, produced by the casualty lists. The stupid, the selfish, the narrow-minded, the callous and unimaginative were spared a great deal. "Blood and destruction shall be so in use that mothers shall but smile when they behold their infantes quartered by the hands of war," was a Shakespearean prophecy that very nearly came true; for when nearly every house had a slaughtered son to mourn, we should all have gone quite out of our senses if we had taken our own and our friend's bereavements at their peace value. It became necessary to give them a false value; to proclaim the young life worthily and gloriously sacrificed to redeem the liberty of mankind, instead of to expiate the heedlessness and folly of their fathers, and expiate it in vain. We had even to assume that the parents and not the children had made the sacrifice, until at last the comic papers were driven to satirize fat old men, sitting comfortably in club chairs, and boasting of the sons they had "given" to their country.

No one grudged these anodynes to acute personal grief; but they only embittered those who knew that the young men were having their teeth set on edge because their parents had eaten sour political grapes. Then think of the young men themselves! Many of them had no illusions about the policy that led to the war: they went clear-sighted to a horribly repugnant duty. Men essentially gentle and essentially wise, with really valuable work in hand, laid it down voluntarily and spent months forming fours in the barrack yard, and stabbing sacks of straw in the public eye, so that they might go out to kill and maim men as gentle as themselves. These men, who were perhaps, as a class, our most efficient soldiers (Frederick Keeling, for example), were not duped for a moment by the hypocritical melodrama that consoled and stimulated the others. They left their creative work to drudge at destruction, exactly as they would have left it to take their turn at the pumps in a sinking ship. They did not, like some of the conscientious objectors, hold back because the ship had been neglected by its officers and scuttled by its wreckers. The ship had to be saved, even if Newton had to leave his fluxions and Michael Angelo his marbles to save it; so they threw away the tools of their beneficent and ennobling trades, and took up the blood-stained bayonet and the murderous bomb, forcing themselves to pervert their divine instinct for perfect artistic execution to the effective handling of these diabolical things, and their economic faculty for organization to the contriving of ruin and slaughter. For it gave an ironic edge to their tragedy that the very talents they were forced to prostitute made the prostitution not only effective, but even interesting; so that some of them were rapidly promoted, and found themselves actually becoming artists in war, with a growing relish for it, like Napoleon and all the other scourges of mankind, in spite of themselves. For many of them there was not even this consolation. They "stuck it," and hated it, to the end.

# Eugene O'Neill

Born the son of a turn-of-the-century stage "star," the actor James O'Neill, Eugene O'Neill (1888–1953) became America's most famous dramatist. Much of O'Neill's younger life is described in his late play, *Long Day's Journey Into Night:* how he spent his first several years touring with his family following his father's career on the stage; his stints in boarding school and at Princeton; some time spent working on ships sailing to South America and Africa, and bumming around in Buenos Aires and New York; a serious bout with tuberculosis. In the play, O'Neill leaves the future of his young poet-hero uncertain, but in fact illness provided O'Neill with the time to begin writing seriously. When he recovered, O'Neill attended George Pierce Baker's playwriting classes at Harvard. He worked briefly in Greenwich Village and then joined the Provincetown Playhouse company on Cape Cod in 1916, where his first plays were produced.

O'Neill had a long and tumultuous career in the theater. An admirer of Strindberg's drama, and widely read in Nietzsche, Freud, and Jung, O'Neill experimented in a variety of different theatrical styles, always searching for new ways to reveal the complex working of a character's psychology. He wrote a series of short realistic plays that were produced at the Provincetown and other "little theaters," the best of which concern life at sea: *Bound East for Cardiff* (1916), *Fog* (1917), *In the Zone* (1917), *The Long Voyage Home* (1917), and *The Moon of the Caribbees* (1918). His first Broadway production, *Beyond the Horizon* (1920) won him the first of four Pulitzer Prizes; he later won for *Anna Christie* (1921), *Strange Interlude* (1928), and *Long Day's Journey Into Night* (awarded posthumously in 1956). Throughout the 1920s, the period of his greatest success in the theater, O'Neill both wrote realistic plays like *Desire Under the Elms* (1924) and experimented in a variety of other modes. He tried expressionistic techniques in *The Hairy Ape* (1922) and *The Emperor Jones* (1920); masks in *The Great God Brown* (1926); and revealing "asides" in *Strange Interlude,* in which characters speak their unspoken "thoughts" directly to the audience. He also took a chance with comedy in *Ah, Wilderness!* (1932), something of a study for *Long Day's Journey.*

O'Neill's decade of success was followed by a series of impressive failures. Some of these plays are nonetheless fascinating. Although it played well in 1928, the asides and length (more than eight hours) of *Strange Interlude* have militated against many revivals; the parallels between Aeschylus' *Oresteia* and O'Neill's *Mourning Becomes Electra* (1931) still attract comment and discussion. But much of O'Neill's work from the late 1920s and 1930s is inflated and bombastic, and plays like *Lazarus Laughed* (1928), *Marco Millions* (1929), *Dynamo* (1929), and *Days Without End* (1934) seemed to mark his flagging powers as a writer. When O'Neill won the Nobel Prize in 1936, his career was widely regarded as finished. His plays had become empty and grandiose, and he suffered from Parkinson's disease, which made it increasingly difficult for him to write. Throughout the 1930s and 1940s, though, O'Neill planned a massive cycle of plays concerning the fortunes of an American family, called *A Tale of Possessors Self-Dispossessed;* of these he completed only *A Touch of the Poet* (written 1935–1942) and a draft of *More Stately Mansions* (1935–1940). But in the 1940s, O'Neill also wrote his greatest plays, realistic dramas based for the most part on his family's history and on his own life. These hard-won plays may have been out of keeping with the upbeat national mood in the aftermath of World War II. When *The Iceman Cometh* opened in 1946, it ran for only 136 performances, and *A Moon for the Misbegotten* (1947) closed in Ohio before reaching New York. Yet when *Iceman* was revived in 1956, directed by José Quintero, it was a huge success and prompted a widespread reevaluation of O'Neill's drama.

Raised on his father's melodramatic portrayal of *The Count of Monte Cristo,* it is not surprising that O'Neill was at times also infected with the spirit of melodrama. O'Neill's plays often recall melodrama's emphasis on the passions of the characters, its striking moments of stage action, its penchant for the romantic and the sentimental. O'Neill's experimentation and sure sense of the stage enabled him to achieve an unparalleled body of work and to define the course of drama in the United States in the first half of the twentieth century.

## The Emperor Jones (1920)

*The Emperor Jones* was one of O'Neill's earliest successes, and one of the first plays with a black hero to be produced with a mixed-race cast in the United States. O'Neill cast Charles Gilpin—a successful actor in the Harlem theater—in the role of the Emperor Jones, and when the play moved from the bohemian milieu of Greenwich Village to the "legitimate" precincts of Broadway, he insisted that Gilpin remain in the part. During the play's revival in 1926, O'Neill cast Paul Robeson as Jones, a role Robeson played in the film version as well.

*The Emperor Jones* epitomizes the difficulties of staging black Americans in the white theater. O'Neill's use of expressionistic techniques—the drums, the formless fears, the dreamlike scenes of his past—as a way of collapsing Jones's individual and racial history makes for powerful and effective theater. Yet, despite O'Neill's fascination with his main character, the play raises the question of the use of racial stereotypes. Jones's speech, for instance, is firmly in the dialect tradition of stage-blacks dating back to the minstrel shows and beyond. Charles Gilpin angered O'Neill by cutting the word "nigger" from his performances and substituting other less pejorative epithets. Gilpin seems to have recognized the extent to which *The Emperor Jones* potentially confirmed the racist attitudes of the audience, attitudes perhaps implicit in the structure of the play itself. For by tracing Jones's flight back through his personal history to a racial memory of Africa, the play may imply that Jones is somehow closer to "nature," more "primitive" in some essential way than the white characters or the largely white audience of the play. From a contemporary perspective, Jones may seem to emerge as an exoticized "other," whose powerful humanity nonetheless remains outside the privileged values of white culture.

*The Emperor Jones,* that is, may raise different kinds of issues for contemporary audiences than it did in the 1920s. To the play's first Broadway audiences, *The Emperor Jones* brought what seemed an authentic black experience to the stage. Not only did O'Neill succeed in bringing important African-American actors into the Broadway theater, he forced his audience to confront black experience in new ways, to confront the institutions of slavery and discrimination through the experience of a powerful, psychologically complex African-American man.

# —The Emperor Jones—
## Eugene O'Neill

### —CHARACTERS—

BRUTUS JONES, *Emperor*
HENRY SMITHERS, *a Cockney Trader*
AN OLD NATIVE WOMAN
LEM, A NATIVE CHIEF
SOLDIERS, ADHERENTS OF SUN

THE LITTLE FORMLESS FEARS
JEFF
THE NEGRO CONVICTS
THE PRISON GUARD
THE PLANTERS
THE AUCTIONEER
THE SLAVES
THE CONGO WITCH-DOCTOR
THE CROCODILE GOD

*The action of the play takes place on an island in the West Indies, as yet un-self-determined by white marines. The form of native government is, for the time being, an Empire.*

SCENE I

*The audience chamber in the palace of the Emperor—a spacious, high-ceilinged room with bare, white-washed walls. The floor is of white tiles. In the rear, to the left of center, a wide archway giving out on a portico with white pillars. The palace is evidently situated on high ground, for beyond the portico nothing can be seen but a vista of distant hills, their summits crowned with thick groves of palm trees. In the right wall, center, a smaller arched doorway leading to the living quarters of the palace. The room is bare of furniture with the exception of one huge chair, made of uncut wood, which stands at center, its back to rear. This is very apparently the Emperor's throne. It is painted a dazzling, eye-smiting scarlet. There is a brilliant orange cushion on the seat and another smaller one is placed on the floor to serve as a footstool. Strips of matting, dyed scarlet, lead from the foot of the throne to the two entrances.*

*It is late afternoon, but the sunlight still blazes yellowly beyond the portico, and there is an oppressive burden of exhausting heat in the air. As the curtain rises a native negro woman sneaks in cautiously from the entrance on the right. She is very old, dressed in cheap calico, barefooted, a red bandana handkerchief covering all but a few stray wisps of white hair. A bundle bound in colored cloth is carried over her shoulder on the end of a stick. She hesitates beside the doorway, peering back as if in extreme dread of being discovered. Then she begins to glide noiselessly, a step at a time, toward the doorway in the rear. At this moment Smithers appears beneath the portico.*

*Smithers is a tall, stoop-shouldered man about forty. His bald head, perched on a long neck with an enormous Adam's apple, looks like an egg. The tropics have tanned his naturally pasty face with its small, sharp features to a sickly yellow, and native rum has painted his pointed nose to a startling red. His little washy-blue eyes are red-rimmed, and dart about like a ferret's. His expression is one of unscrupulous meanness, cowardly and dangerous. His attitude toward Jones is that of one who will give vent to a nourished grudge against all superiority—as far as he dares. He is dressed in a worn riding suit of dirty white drill, puttees, spurs, and wears a white cork helmet. A cartridge belt with an automatic revolver is around his waist. He carries a riding whip in his hand. He sees the woman and stops to watch her suspiciously. Then, making up his mind, he steps quickly on tiptoe into the room. The woman, looking back over her shoulder continually, does not see him until it is too late. When she does, Smithers springs forward and grabs her firmly by the shoulder. She struggles to get away, fiercely but silently.*

SMITHERS: (*tightening his grasp—roughly*) Easy! None o' that, me birdie. You can't wriggle out now. I got me 'ooks on yer.

WOMAN: (*seeing the uselessness of struggling, gives away to frantic terror and sinks to the ground, embracing his knees supplicatingly*) No tell him! No tell him, Mister!

SMITHERS: (*with great curiosity*) Tell 'im (*then scornfully*) Oh, you mean 'is bloomin' Majesty. What's the gaime, any 'ow? What are you sneakin' away for? Been stealin' a bit, I s'pose. (*He taps her bundle with his riding whip significantly.*)

WOMAN: (*shaking her head vehemently*) No, me no steal.    10

SMITHERS: Bloody liar! But tell me what's up. There's somethin' funny goin' on. I smelled it in the air first thing I got up this mornin'. You blacks are up to some devilment. This palace of 'is is like a bleedin' tomb. Where's all the 'ands? (*The woman keeps sullenly silent. Smithers raises his whip threateningly.*) Ow, yer won't, won't yer? I'll show yer what's what.

WOMAN: (*coweringly*) I tell, Mister. You no hit. They go—all go. (*She makes a sweeping gesture toward the hills in the distance.*)    20

SMITHERS: Run away—to the 'ills?

WOMAN: Yes, Mister. Him Emperor—Great Father—(*She touches her forehead to the floor with a quick, mechanical jerk.*) Him sleep after eat. Then they go—all go. Me old woman. Me left only. Now me go, too.

SMITHERS: (*his astonishment giving way to an immense mean satisfaction*) Ow! So that's the ticket! Well, I know bloody well wot's in the air—when they runs orf to the 'ills. The tom-tom 'll be thumping out there bloomin' soon. (*With extreme vindictiveness*) And I'm bloody glad of it, for one!    30 Serve 'im right! Puttin' on airs, the stinkin' nigger! 'Is Majesty! Gawd blimey! I only 'opes I'm there when they takes 'im out to shoot 'im. (*Suddenly*) 'E's still 'ere all right, ain't 'e?

WOMAN: Yes. Him sleep.

SMITHERS: 'E's bound to find out soon as 'e wakes up. 'E's cunnin' enough to know when 'is time's come. (*He goes to the doorway on right and whistles shrilly with his fingers in his mouth. The old woman springs to her feet and runs out* 40 *of the doorway, rear. Smithers goes after her, reaching for his revolver.*) Stop or I'll shoot! (*Then stopping indifferently.*) Pop orf, then, if yer like, yer black cow! (*He stands in the doorway, looking after her.*)

(*Jones enters from the right. He is a tall, powerfully-built, full-blooded negro of middle age. His features are typically negroid, yet there is something decidedly distinctive about his face—an underlying strength of will, a hardy, self-reliant confidence in himself that inspires respect. His eyes are alive with a keen, cunning intelligence. In manner he is shrewd, suspicious, evasive. He wears a light-blue uniform coat, sprayed with brass buttons, heavy gold chevrons on his shoulders, gold braid on the collar, cuffs, etc. His pants are bright red, with a light-blue stripe down the side. Patent leather laced boots with brass spurs, and a belt with a long-barreled, pearl-handled revolver in a holster, complete his make-up. Yet there is something not altogether ridiculous about his grandeur. He has a way of carrying it off.*)

JONES: (*not seeing anyone—greatly irritated and blinking sleepily—shouts*) Who dare whistle dat way in my palace? Who dare wake up de Emperor? I'll git de hide frayled off some o' you niggers sho'!

SMITHERS: (*showing himself—in a manner half-afraid and half-defiant*) It was me whistled to yer. (*As Jones frowns an-* 50 *grily.*) I got news for yer.

JONES: (*putting on his suavest manner, which fails to cover up his contempt for the white man*) Oh, it's you, Mister Smithers. (*He sits down on his throne with easy dignity.*) What news you got to tell me?

SMITHERS: (*coming close to enjoy his discomfiture*) Don't you notice nothin' funny to-day?

JONES: (*coldly*) Funny? No, I ain't perceived nothin' of de kind!

SMITHERS: Then you ain't so foxy as I thought you was. Where's all your court? (*Sarcastically*) the Generals and the Cabinet 60 Ministers and all?

JONES: (*imperturbably*) Where dey mostly runs to minute I closes my eyes—drinkin' rum and talkin' big down in de town. (*Sarcastically*) How come you don't know dat? Ain't you sousin' with 'em most every day?

SMITHERS: (*stung, but pretending indifference—with a wink*) That's part of the day's work. I got ter—ain't I—in my business?

JONES: (*contemptuously*) Yo' business!

SMITHERS: (*imprudently enraged*) Gawd blimey, you was glad 70 enough for me ter take you in on it when you landed here first. You didn' 'ave no 'igh and mighty airs in them days!

JONES: (*his hand going to his revolver like a flash—menacingly*) Talk polite, white man! Talk polite, you heah me! I'm boss heah now, is you forgettin'? (*The Cockney seems about to challenge this last statement with the facts, but something in the other's eyes holds and cows him.*)

SMITHERS: (*in a cowardly whine*) No 'arm meant, old top.

JONES: (*condescendingly*) I accepts yo' apology. (*Lets his hand fall from his revolver.*) No use'n you rakin' up ole times. 80 What I was den is one thing. What I is now's another. You

didn't let me in on yo' crooked work out o' no kind feelin' dat time. I done de dirty work fo' you—and most o' de brain work, too, fo' dat matter—and I was wu'th money to you, dat's de reason.

SMITHERS: Well, blimey, I give yer a start, didn't I—when no one else would. I wasn't afraid to hire yer like the rest was—'count of the story about your breakin' jail back in the States.

JONES: No, you didn't have no s'cuse to look down on me fo' dat. You been in jail yo'self more'n once.

SMITHERS: (*furiously*) It's a lie! (*Then trying to pass it off by an* 90 *attempt at scorn*) Garn! Who told yer that fairy tale?

JONES: Dey's some things I ain't got to be tole. I kin see 'em in folks eyes. (*Then after a pause—meditatively*) Yes, you sho' give me a start. And it didn't take long from dat time to git dese fool woods' niggers right where I wanted dem. (*With pride*) From stowaway to Emperor in two years! Dat's goin' some!

SMITHERS: (*with curiosity*) And I bet you got er pile o' money 'id safe someplace.

JONES: (*with satisfaction*) I sho' has! And it's in a foreign bank 100 where no pusson don't ever get it out but me, no matter what come. You don't s'pose I was holdin' down dis Emperor job for de glory in it, did you? Sho'! De fuss and glory part of it, dat's only to turn de heads o' de low-flung bush niggers dat's here. Dey wants de big circus show for deir money. I gives it to 'em an' I gits de money. (*With a grin.*) De long green, dat's me every time! (*Then rebukingly*) But you ain't got no kick agin me, Smithers. I'se paid you back all you done for me many times. Ain't I pertected you and winked at all de crooked tradin' you been doin' right out in 110 de broad day? Sho' I has—and me makin' laws to stop it at de same time! (*He chuckles.*)

SMITHERS: (*grinning*) But, meanin' no 'arm, you been grabbin' right and left yourself, ain't you? Look at the taxes you've put on 'em! Blimey! You've squeezed 'em dry.

JONES: (*chuckling*) No dey ain't *all* dry yet. I'se still heah, ain't I?

SMITHERS: (*smiling at his secret thought*) They're dry right now, you'll find out. (*Changing the subject abruptly*) And as for me breaking laws, you've broke 'em all yerself just as fast 120 as yer made 'em.

JONES: Ain't I de Emperor? De laws don't go for him. (*Judiciously*) You heah what I tells you, Smithers. Dere's little stealin' like you does, and dere's big stealin' like I does. For de little stealin' dey gits you in jail soon or late. For de big stealin' dey makes you Emperor and puts you in de Hall o' Fame when you croaks. (*Reminiscently*) If dey's one thing I learns in ten years on de Pullman ca's listenin' to de white quality talk, it's dat same fact. And when I gits a chance to use it I winds up Emperor in two years. 130

SMITHERS: (*unable to repress the genuine admiration of the small fry for the large*) Yes, you turned the bleedin' trick, all right. Blimey, I never seen a bloke 'as 'ad the bloomin' luck you 'as.

JONES: (*severely*) Luck? What you mean—luck?

SMITHERS: I suppose you'll say as that swank about the silver bullet ain't luck—and that was what first got the fool blacks on yer side the time of the revolution, wasn't it?

JONES: (*with a laugh*) Oh, dat silver bullet! Sho' was luck! But I makes dat luck, you heah? I loads de dice! Yessuh! When 140 dat murderin' nigger ole Lem hired to kill me takes aim ten feet away and his gun misses fire and I shoots him dead, what you heah me say?

SMITHERS: You said yer'd got a charm so's no lead bullet 'd kill yer. You was so strong only a silver bullet could kill yer, you told 'em. Blimey, wasn't that swank for yer—and plain, fat-'eaded luck?

JONES: *(proudly)* I got brains and I uses 'em quick. Dat ain't luck.

150 SMITHERS: Yer knew they wasn't 'ardly liable to get no silver bullets. And it was luck 'e didn't 'it you that time.

JONES: *(laughing)* And dere all dem fool bush niggers was kneelin' down and bumpin' deir heads on de ground like I was a miracle out o' de Bible. Oh, Lawd, from dat time on I has dem all eatin' out of my hand. I cracks de whip and dey jumps through.

SMITHERS: *(with a sniff)* Yankee bluff done it.

JONES: Ain't a man's talkin' big what makes him big—long as he makes folks believe it. Sho' I talks large when I ain't got 160 nothin' to back it up, but I ain't talkin' wild just de same. I knows I kin fool 'em—I *knows* it—and dat's backin' enough fo' my game. And ain't I got to learn deir lingo and teach some of dem English befo' I kin talk to 'em? Ain't dat wuk? You ain't never learned ary word er it, Smithers, in de ten years you been heah, dough yo' knows it's money in yo' pocket tradin' wid 'em if you does. But yo' too shiftless to take de trouble.

SMITHERS: *(flushing)* Never mind about me. What's this I've 'eard about yer really 'avin' a silver bullet moulded for 170 yourself?

JONES: It's playin' out my bluff. I has de silver bullet moulded and I tells 'em when de time comes I kills myself wid it. I tells 'em dat's 'cause I'm de on'y man in de world big enuff to git me. No use'n deir tryin'. And dey falls down and bumps deir heads. *(He laughs.)* I does dat so's I kin take a walk in peace widout no jealous nigger gunnin' at me from behind de trees.

SMITHERS: *(astonished)* Then you 'ad it made—'onest?

JONES: Sho' did. Heah she be. *(He takes out his revolver,* 180 *breaks it, and takes the silver bullet out of one chamber.)* Five lead an' dis silver baby at de last. Don't she shine pretty? *(He holds it in his hand, looking at it admiringly, as if strangely fascinated.)*

SMITHERS: Let me see. *(Reaches out his hand for it.)*

JONES: *(harshly)* Keep yo' hands whar dey b'long, white man. *(He replaces it in the chamber and puts the revolver back on his hip.)*

SMITHERS: *(snarling)* Gawd blimey! Think I'm a bleedin' thief, you would.

190 JONES: No. 'Tain't dat. I knows you'se scared to steal from me. On'y I ain't 'lowin' nary body to touch dis baby. She's my rabbit's foot.

SMITHERS: *(sneering)* A bloomin' charm, wot? *(Venomously)* Well, you'll need all the bloody charms you 'as before long, s' 'elp me!

JONES: *(judicially)* Oh, I'se good for six months yit 'fore dey gits sick o' my game. Den, when I sees trouble comin', I makes my get-a-way.

SMITHERS: Ho! You got it all planned, ain't yer?

200 JONES: I ain't no fool. I knows dis Emperor's time is sho't. Dat why I make hay when de sun shine. Was you thinkin' I'se aimin' to hold down dis job for life? No, suh! What good is gittin' money if you stays back in dis raggedy country? I wants action when I spends. And when I sees dese niggers gittin' up deir nerve to tu'n me out, and I'se got all de money in sight, I resigns on de spot and beats it quick.

SMITHERS: Where to?

JONES: None o' yo' business.

SMITHERS: Not back to the bloody States, I'll lay my oath.

JONES: *(suspiciously)* Why don't I? *(Then with an easy laugh)* 210 You mean 'count of dat story 'bout me breakin' from jail back dere? Dat's all talk.

SMITHERS: *(skeptically)* Ho, yes!

JONES: *(sharply)* You ain't 'sinuatin' I'se a liar, is you?

SMITHERS: *(hastily)* No, Gawd strike me! I was only thinkin' o' the bloody lies you told the blacks 'ere about killin' white men in the States.

JONES: *(angered)* How come dey're lies?

SMITHERS: You'd 'ave been in jail if you 'ad, wouldn't yer then? *(With venom)* And from what I've 'eard, it ain't 'ealthy for a 220 black to kill a white man in the States. They burn 'em in oil, don't they?

JONES: *(with cool deadliness)* You mean lynchin' 'd scare me? Well, I tells you, Smithers, maybe I does kill one white man back dere. Maybe I does. And maybe I kills another right heah 'fore long if he don't look out.

SMITHERS: *(trying to force a laugh)* I was on'y spoofin' yer. Can't yer take a joke? And you was just sayin' you'd never been in jail.

JONES: *(in the same tone—slightly boastful)* Maybe I goes to 230 jail dere for gettin' in an argument wid razors ovah a crap game. Maybe I gits twenty years when dat colored man die. Maybe I gits in 'nother argument wid de prison guard who was overseer ovah us when we're walkin' de roads. Maybe he hits me wid a whip an' I splits his head wid a shovel an' runs away an' files de chain off my leg an' gits away safe. Maybe I does all dat an' maybe I don't. It's a story I tells you so's you knows I'se de kind of man dat if you evah repeats one word of it, I ends yo' stealin' on dis yearth mighty damn quick! 240

SMITHERS: *(terrified)* Think I'd peach on yer? Not me! Ain't I always been yer friend?

JONES: *(suddenly relaxing)* Sho' you has—and you better be.

SMITHERS: *(recovering his composure—and with it his malice)* And just to show yer I'm yer friend, I'll tell yer that bit o' news I was goin' to.

JONES: Go ahead! Shoot de piece. Must be bad news from de happy way you look.

SMITHERS: *(warningly)* Maybe it's gettin' time for you to re-sign—with that bloomin' silver bullet, wot? *(He finishes* 250 *with a mocking grin.)*

JONES: *(puzzled)* What's dat you say? Talk plain.

SMITHERS: Ain't noticed any of the guards or servants about the place to-day, I 'aven't.

JONES: *(carelessly)* Dey're all out in de garden sleepin' under de trees. When I sleeps, dey sneaks a sleep, too, and I pre-tends I never suspicions it. All I got to do is to ring de bell an' dey come flyin', makin' a bluff dey was wukin' all de time.

SMITHERS: *(in the same mocking tone)* Ring the bell now an' 260 you'll bloody well see what I means.

JONES: (*startled to alertness, but preserving the same careless tone*) Sho' I rings. (*He reaches below the throne and pulls out a big common dinner bell which is painted the same vivid scarlet as the throne. He rings this vigorously—then stops to listen. Then he goes to both doors, rings again, and looks out.*)

SMITHERS: (*watching him with malicious satisfaction—after a pause—mockingly*) The bloody ship is sinkin' an' the
270  bleedin' rats 'as slung their 'ooks.

JONES: (*in a sudden fit of anger flings the bell clatteringly into a corner*) Low-flung, woods niggers! (*Then catching Smithers' eye on him, he controls himself and suddenly bursts into a low, chuckling laugh.*) Reckon I overplays my hand dis once! A man can't take de pot on a bob-tailed flush all de time. Was I sayin' I'd sit in six months mo'? Well, I'se changed my mind, den. I cashes in and resigns de job of Emperor right dis minute.

SMITHERS: (*with real admiration*) Blimey, but you're a cool
280  bird, and no mistake.

JONES: No use'n fussin'. When I knows de game's up I kisses it good-bye widout no long waits. Dey've all run off to de hills, ain't dey?

SMITHERS: Yes—every bleedin' manjack of 'em.

JONES: Den de revolution is at de post. And de Emperor better git his feet smokin' up de trail. (*He starts for the door in rear.*)

SMITHERS: Goin' out to look for your 'orse? Yer won't find any. They steals the 'orses first thing. Mine was gone when I
290  went for 'im this mornin'. That's wot first give me a suspicion of wot was up.

JONES: (*alarmed for a second, scratches his head, then philosophically*) Well, den I hoofs it. Feet, do yo' duty! (*He pulls out a gold watch and looks at it.*) Three-thuty. Sundown's at six-thuty or dereabouts. (*Puts his watch back—with cool confidence.*) I got plenty o' time to make it easy.

SMITHERS: Don't be so bloomin' sure of it. They'll be after you 'ot and 'eavy. Ole Lem is at the bottom o' this business an' 'e 'ates you like 'ell. 'E'd rather do for you than eat 'is dinner,
300  'e would!

JONES: (*scornfully*) Dat fool no-count nigger! Does you think I'se scared o' him? I stands him on his thick head more'n once befo' dis, and I does it again if he come in my way—(*fiercely*). And dis time I leave him a dead nigger fo' sho'!

SMITHERS: You'll 'ave to cut through the big forest—an' these blacks 'ere can sniff and follow a trail in the dark like 'ounds. You'd 'ave to 'ustle to get through that forest in twelve hours even if you knew all the bloomin' trails like a native.

JONES: (*with indignant scorn*) Look-a-heah, white man! Does
310  you think I'm a natural bo'n fool? Give me credit fo' havin' some sense, fo' Lawd's sake! Don't you s'pose I'se looked ahead and made sho' of all de chances? I'se gone out in dat big forest, pretendin' to hunt so many times dat I knows it high an' low like a book. I could go through on dem trails wid my eyes shut. (*With great contempt*) Think dese ig'nerent bush niggers dat ain't got brains enuff to know deir own names even can catch Brutus Jones? Huh! I s'pects not! Not on yo' life! Why, man, de white men went after me wid bloodhounds where I come from an' I jes' laughs at 'em. It's
320  a shame to fool dese black trash around heah, dey're so easy.

You watch me, man. I'll make dem look sick, I will. I'll be 'cross de plain to de edge of de forest by time dark comes. Once in de woods in de night, dey got a swell chance o' findin' dis baby! Dawn tomorrow I'll be out at de oder side and on de coast whar dat French gunboat is stayin'. She picks me up, take me to de Martinique when she go dar, and dere I is safe wid a mighty big bankroll in my jeans. It's easy as rollin' off a log.

SMITHERS: (*maliciously*) But s'posin' somethin' 'appens wrong
330  an' they do nab yer?

JONES: (*decisively*) Dey don't. Dat's de answer.

SMITHERS: But just for argument's sake—what'd you do?

JONES: (*frowning*) I'se got five lead bullets in dis gun good enuff fo' common bush niggers—an' after dat I got de silver bullet left to cheat 'em out o' gittin' me.

SMITHERS: (*jeeringly*) Ho, I was fergettin' that silver bullet. You'll bump yourself orf in style, won't yer? Blimey!

JONES: (*gloomily*) Yo' kin bet yo' whole roll on one thing, white man. Dis baby plays out his string to de end and when he
340  quits, he quits wid a bang de way he ought. Silver bullet ain't none too good for him when he go, dat's a fac'! (*Then shaking off his nervousness—with a confident laugh*) Sho'! What is I talkin' about? Ain't come to dat yit an' I never will—not wid trash niggers like dese yere. (*Boastfully*) Silver bullet bring me luck, anyway. I kin outguess, outrun, outfight, an' outplay de whole lot o' dem all ovah de board any time o' de day er night! Yo' watch me!

(*From the distant hills comes the faint, steady thump of a tom-tom, low and vibrating. It starts at a rate exactly corresponding to normal pulse-beat—72 to the minute—and continues at a gradually accelerating rate from this point uninterruptedly to the very end of the play.*)
(*Jones starts at the sound; a strange look of apprehension creeps into his face for a moment as he listens. Then he asks, with an attempt to regain his most casual manner:*)

What's dat drum beatin' fo'?

SMITHERS: (*with a mean grin*) For you. That means the bleedin' ceremony 'as started. I've 'eard it before and I
350  knows.

JONES: Cer'mony? What cer'mony?

SMITHERS: The blacks is 'oldin' a bloody meetin', 'avin' a war dance, gettin' their courage worked up b'fore they starts after you.

JONES: Let dem! Dey'll sho' need it!

SMITHERS: And they're there 'oldin' their 'eathen religious service—makin' no end of devil spells and charms to 'elp 'em against your silver bullet. (*He guffaws loudly.*) Blimey, but they're balmy as 'ell.
360

JONES: (*a tiny bit awed and shaken in spite of himself*) Huh! Takes more'n dat to scare dis chicken!

SMITHERS: (*scenting the other's feeling—maliciously*) Ternight when it's pitch black in the forest, they'll 'ave their pet devils and ghosts 'oundin' after you. You'll find yer bloody 'air 'll be standin' on end before to-morrow mornin'. (*Seriously*) It's a bleedin' queer place, that stinkin' forest, even in daylight. Yer don't know what might 'appen in there, it's that rotten still. Always sends the cold shivers down my back minute I gets in it.
370

JONES: (*with a contemptuous sniff*) I ain't no chicken-liver like you is. Trees an' me, we's friends, an' dar's a full moon comin' bring me light. And let dem po' niggers make all de fool spells dey'se a min' to. Does yo' s'pect I'se silly enuff to b'lieve in ghosts an' ha'nts an' all dat ole woman's talk? G' long, white man! You ain't talkin' to me. (*With a chuckle*) Doesn't you knows dey's got to do wid a man who was member in good standin' o' de Baptist Church. Sho' I was dat when I was porter on de Pullman, an' befo' I gits into my lit-

380　tle trouble. Let dem try deir heathen tricks. De Baptist Church done pertect me an' land dem all in hell. (*Then with more confident satisfaction*) An' I'se got little silver bullet o' my own, don't forgit.

SMITHERS: Ho! You 'aven't give much 'eed to your Baptist Church since you been down 'ere. I've 'eard myself and 'ad turned yer coat an' was taken' up with their blarsted witchdoctors, or whatever the 'ell yer calls the swine.

JONES: (*vehemently*) I pretends to! Sho' I pretends! Dat's part o' my game from de fust. If I finds out dem niggers believes

390　dat black is white, den I yells it out louder 'n deir loudest. It don't git me nothin' to do missionary work for de Baptist Church. I'se after de coin, an' I lays my Jesus on de shelf for de time bein'. (*Stops abruptly to look at his watch—alertly.*) But I ain't got de time to waste no mo'e fool talk wid you. I'se gwine away from heah dis secon'. (*He reaches in under the throne and pulls out an expensive Panama hat with a bright multi-colored band and sets it jauntily on his head.*) So long, white man! (*With a grin*) See you 'n jail some time, maybe!

400　SMITHERS: Not me, you won't. Well, I wouldn't be in yer bloody boots for no bloomin' money, but 'ere's wishin' yer luck just the same.

JONES: (*contemptuously*) You're de frightenedest man evah I see! I tells you I'se safe 's'f I was in New York City. It take dem niggers from now to dark to git up de nerve to start somethin'. By dat time I'se got a head start dey never kotch up wid.

SMITHERS: (*maliciously*) Give my regards to any ghosts yer meets up with.

410　JONES: (*grinning*) If dat ghost got money, I'll tell him never ha'nt you less'n he wants to lose it.

SMITHERS: (*flattered*) Garn! (*Then curiously*) Ain't yer takin' no luggage with yer?

JONES: I travels light when I wants to move fast. And I got tinned grub buried on de edge o' de forest. (*Boastfully*) Now say dat I don't look ahead an' use my brains! (*With a wide, liberal gesture*) I will all dat's left in de palace to you an' you better grab all you kin sneak away wid befo' dey gits here.

SMITHERS: (*gratefully*) Righto—and thanks ter yer. (*As Jones*

420　*walks toward the door in rear—cautioningly*) Say! Look 'ere, you ain't goin' out that way, are yer?

JONES: Does you think I'd slink out de back door like a common nigger? I'se Emperor yit, ain't I? And de Emperor Jones leaves de way he comes, and dat black trash don't dare stop him—not yit, leastways. (*He stops for a moment in the doorway, listening to the far-off but insistent beat of the tom-tom.*) Listen to dat roll-call, will you? Must be mighty big drum carry dat far. (*Then with a laugh*) Well, if dey ain't no whole brass band to see me off, I sho' got de drum part

430　of it. So long, white man. (*He puts his hands in his pockets and with studied carelessness, whistling a tune, he saunters*

out of the doorway and off to the left.)

SMITHERS: (*looks after him with a puzzled admiration*) 'E's got 'is bloomin' nerve with 'im, s'elp me! (*Then angrily*) Ho— the bleedin' nigger—puttin' on 'is bloody airs! I 'opes they nabs 'im an' gives 'im what's what! (*Then putting business before the pleasure of his thought, looking around him with cupidity.*) A bloke ought to find a 'ole lot in this palace that 'd go for a bit of cash. Let's take a look, 'Arry, me lad. (*He starts for the doorway on right as*)　440

*The Curtain Falls*

SCENE II: NIGHTFALL

(*The end of the plain where the Great Forest begins. The foreground is sandy, level ground, dotted by a few stones and clumps of stunted bushes cowering close against the earth to escape the buffeting of the trade wind. In the rear the forest is a wall of darkness dividing the world. Only when the eye becomes accustomed to the gloom can the outlines of separate trunks of the nearest trees be made out, enormous pillars of deeper blackness. A somber monotone of wind lost in the leaves moans in the air. Yet this sound serves but to intensify the impression of the forest's relentless immobility, to form a background throwing into relief its brooding, implacable silence.*)

(*Jones enters from the left, walking rapidly. He stops as he nears the edge of the forest, looks around him quickly, peering into the dark as if searching for some familiar landmark. Then, apparently satisfied that he is where he ought to be, he throws himself on the ground, dog-tired.*)

Well, heah I is. In de nick o' time, too! Little mo' an' it'd be blacker'n de ace of spades heahabouts. (*He pulls a bandana handkerchief from his hip pocket and mops off his perspiring face.*) Sho! Gimme air! I'se tuckered out sho' 'nuf. Dat soft Emperor job ain't no trainin' fo' a long hike ovah dat plain in de brilin' sun (*Then with a chuckle*) Cheah up, nigger, der worst is yet to come. (*He lifts his head and stares at the forest. His chuckle peters out abruptly. In a tone of awe:*) My goodness, look at dem woods, will you? Dat no-count Smithers said dey'd be black an' he sho' called de turn. 450 (*Turning away from them quickly, and looking down at his feet, he snatches at a chance to change the subject—solicitously:*) Feet, yo' is holdin' up yo' end fine an' I sutinly hopes you ain't blisterin' none. It's time you git a rest. (*He takes off his shoes, his eyes studiously avoiding the forest. He feels of the soles of his feet gingerly.*) You is still in de pink—only a little mite feverish. Cool you' self. Remember yo' done got a long journey yit befo' yo'. (*He sits in a weary attitude, listening to the rhythmic beating of the tom-tom. He grumbles in a loud tone to cover up a growing uneasiness.*) Bush nig-　460 gers! Wonder dey wouldn't git sick o' beatin' dat drum. Sound louder, seem like. I wonder if dey's startin' after me? (*He scrambles to his feet, looking back across the plain.*) Couldn't see dem now, nohow, if dey was hundred feet away. (*Then shaking himself like a wet dog to get rid of these depressing thoughts.*) Sho', dey's miles an' miles behind. What yo' gittin' fidgetty about? (*But he sits down and begins to lace up his shoes in great haste, all the time muttering*

*reassuringly.*) You know what? Yo' belly is empty, dat's
470    what's de matter wid you. Come time to eat! Wid nothin'
but wind on yo' stumach, o' course yo' feels jiggedy. Well,
we eats right heah an' now soon's I gits dese pesky shoes
laced up. (*He finishes lacing up his shoes.*) Dere! Now le's
see! (*Gets on his hands and knees and searches the ground
around him with his eyes.*) White stone, white stone, where
is yo'? (*He sees the first white stone and crawls to it—with
satisfaction.*) Heah yo' is! I knowed dis was de right place.
Box of grub, come to me. (*He turns over the stone and feels
in under it—in a tone of dismay*) Ain't heah! Gorry, is I in
480    de right place or isn't I? Dere's 'nother stone. Guess dat's it.
(*He scrambles to the next stone and turns it over.*) Ain't
heah, neither! Grub, whar is yo'? Ain't heah. Gorry, has I got
to go hungry into dem woods—all de night? (*While he is
talking he scrambles from one stone to another, turning
them over in frantic haste. Finally he jumps to his feet excitedly.*) Is I lost de place? Must have! But how dat happen
when I was followin' de trail across de plain in broad daylight? (*Almost plaintively*) I'se hungry, I is! I gotta git my
feed. Whar's my strength gonna come from if I doesn't?
490    Gorry, I gotta find dat grub high an' low somehow! Why it
come dark so quick like dat? Can't see nothin'. (*He scratches
a match on his trousers and peers about him. The rate of the
beat of the far-off tom-tom increases perceptibly as he does
so. He mutters in a bewildered voice.*) How come all dese
white stones come heah when I only remembers one? (*Suddenly, with a frightened gasp, he flings the match on the
ground and stamps on it.*) Nigger, is yo' gone crazy mad? Is
you lightin' matches to show dem whar you is? Fo' Lawd's
sake, use yo' haid. Gorry, I'se got to be careful! (*He stares at
500    the plain behind him apprehensively, his hand on his revolver.*) But how come all dese white stones? And whar's dat
tin box o' grub I hid all wrapped up in oilcloth?

(*While his back is turned, the Little Formless Fears creep out
from the deeper blackness of the forest. They are black, shapeless; only their glittering little eyes can be seen. If they have any
describable form at all it is that of a grubworm about the size
of a creeping child. They move noiselessly, but with deliberate,
painful effort, striving to raise themselves on end, failing and
sinking prone again. Jones turns about to face the forest. He
stares up at the tops of the trees, seeking vainly to discover his
whereabouts by their conformation.*)

Can't tell nothin' from dem trees! Gorry, nothin' 'round
heah look like I evah seed it befo'. I'se done lost de place
sho' 'nuff! (*With mournful foreboding*) It's mighty queer!
It's mighty queer! (*With sudden forced defiance—in an
angry tone*) Woods, is yo' tryin' to put somethin' ovah on me?

(*From the formless creatures on the ground in front of him
comes a tiny gale of low mocking laughter like a rustling of
leaves. They squirm upward toward him in twisted attitudes.
Jones looks down, leaps backward with a yell of terror, yank-
ing out his revolver as he does so—in a quavering voice.*)

What's dat? Who's dar? What's you? Git away from me befo'
I shoots yo' up! Yo' don't?—

(*He fires. There is a flash, a loud report, then silence, broken
only by the far-off quickened throb of the tom-tom. The formless creatures have scurried back into the forest. Jones remains*

*fixed in his position, listening intently. The sound of the shot,
the reassuring feel of the revolver in his hand have somewhat
restored his shaken nerve. He addresses himself with renewed
confidence:*)

Dey're gone. Dat shot fix 'em. Dey was only little animals—    510
little wild pigs, I reckon. Dey've maybe rooted out yo' grub
an' eat it. Sho', yo' fool nigger, what yo' think dey is—ha'nts?
(*Excitedly*) Gorry, you give de game away when yo' fire dat
shot. Dem niggers heah dat fo' su'tin! Time yo' beat it in de
woods widout no long waits. (*He starts for the forest—hesitates before the plunge—then urging himself in with manful
resolution.*) Git in, nigger! What yo' skeered at? Ain't nothin'
dere but de trees! Git in! (*He plunges boldly into the forest.*)

SCENE III

(*Nine o'clock. In the forest. The moon has just risen. Its beams
drifting through the canopy of leaves make a barely percepti-
ble, suffused eerie glow. A dense low wall of underbrush and
creepers is in the nearer foreground fencing in a small triangular clearing. Beyond this is the massed blackness of the forest like an encompassing barrier. A path is dimly discerned
leading down to the clearing from left, rear, and winding away
from it again toward the right. As the scene opens nothing can
be distinctly made out. Except for the beating of the tom-tom,
which is a trifle louder and quicker than in the previous scene,
there is silence, broken every few seconds by a queer, clicking
sound. Then gradually the figure of the negro Jeff can be discerned crouching on his haunches at the rear of the triangle.
He is middle-aged, thin, brown in color, is dressed in a Pullman porter's uniform, cap, etc. He is throwing a pair of dice on
the ground before him, picking them up, shaking them, casting
them out with the regular, rigid, mechanical movements of an
automaton. The heavy, plodding footsteps of some one approaching along the trail from the left are heard, and Jones'
voice, pitched in a slightly higher key and strained in a cheering effort to overcome its own tremors.*)

De moon's rizen. Does yo' heah dat, nigger? Yo' gits more
light from dis out. No mo' buttin' yo' fool head agin' de    520
trunks an' scratchin' de hide off yo' legs in de bushes. Now
yo' sees whar yo's gwine. So cheer up! From now on yo' has
a snap. (*He steps just to the rear of the triangular clearing
and mops off his face on his sleeve. He has lost his Panama
hat. His face is scratched, his brilliant uniform shows several
large rents.*) What time's it gittin' to be, I wonder? I dassent
light no match to find out. Phoo'. It's wa'm, an' dat's a fac'!
(*Wearily*) How long I been makin' tracks in dese woods?
Must be hours an' hours. Seems like fo'evah! Yit can't be,
when de moon's jes' riz. Dis am a long night fo' yo', yo'    530
Majesty! (*With a mournful chuckle*) Majesty! Der ain't
much majesty 'bout dis baby now. (*With attempted cheerfulness*) Never min'. It's all part o' de game. Dis night come
to an end like everythin' else. An' when yo' gits dar safe an'
has dat bankroll in yo' hands, yo' laughs at all dis. (*He starts
to whistle, but checks himself abruptly.*) What yo' whistlin'
for, yo' po' dope? Want all de worl' to heah yo'? (*He stops
talking to listen.*) Heah dat ole drum! Sho' gits nearer from
de sound. Dey're packin' it along wid 'em. Time fo' me to
move. (*He takes a step forward, then stops—worriedly.*)    540

What's dat odder queer clicketty sound I heah? Der it is! Sound close! Sound like—fo' God sake, sound like some nigger was shakin' crap! *(Frightenedly)* I better beat it quick when I gits dem notions. *(He walks quickly into the clear space—then stands transfixed as he sees Jeff—in a terrified gasp.)* Who dar? Who dat? Is dat yo', Jeff? *(Starting toward the other, forgetful for a moment of his surroundings and really believing it is a living man that he sees—in a tone of happy relief.)* Jeff! I'se sho' mighty glad to see yo'! Dey tol'

550 me yo' done died from dat razor cut I gives you. *(Stopping suddenly, bewilderedly)* But how come you to be heah, nigger? *(He stares fascinatedly at the other, who continues his mechanical play with the dice. Jones' eyes begin to roll wildly. He stutters)* Ain't you gwine—look up—can't you speak to me? Is you—is you—a ha'nt? *(He jerks out his revolver in a frenzy of terrified rage.)* Nigger, I kills yo' dead once. Has I got to kill yo' agin? You take it, den. *(He fires. When the smoke clears away Jeff has disappeared. Jones stands trembling—then with a certain reassurance)* He's

560 gone, anyway. Ha'nt or no ha'nt, dat shot fix him. *(The beat of the far-off tom-tom is perceptibly louder and more rapid. Jones becomes conscious of it—with a start, looking back over his shoulder.)* Dey's gittin' near! Dey're comin' fast! An' heah I is shootin' shots to let 'em know jes' whar I is. Oh, Gorry, I'se got to run. *(Forgetting the path, he plunges wildly into the underbrush in the rear and disappears in the shadow.)*

Scene IV

*(Eleven o'clock. In the forest. A wide dirt road runs diagonally from right, front, to left, rear. Rising sheer on both sides the forest walls it in. The moon is now up. Under its light the road glimmers ghastly and unreal. It is as if the forest had stood aside momentarily to let the road pass through and accomplish its veiled purpose. This done, the forest will fold in upon itself again and the road will be no more. Jones stumbles in from the forest on the right. His uniform is ragged and torn. He looks about him with numbed surprise when he sees the road, his eyes blinking in the bright moonlight. He flops down exhaustedly and pants heavily for a while. Then, with sudden anger:)*

I'm meltin' wid heat! Runnin' an' runnin' an' runnin'! Damn dis heah coat! Like a straitjacket! *(He tears off his coat and*

570 *flings it away from him, revealing himself stripped to the waist.)* Dere! Dat's better! Now I kin breathe! *(Looking down at his feet, the spurs catch his eye.)* An' to hell wid dese high-fangled spurs. Dey're what's been a-trippin' me up an' breakin' my neck. *(He unstraps and flings them away disgustedly.)* Dere! I gits rid o' dem frippety Emperor trappin's an' I travels lighter. Lawd! I'se tired! *(After a pause, listening to the insistent beat of the tom-tom in the distance.)* I must 'a put some distance between myself an' dem—runnin' like dat—an' yet—dat damn drum sound jes' de

580 same—nearer, even. Well, I guess I a'most holds my lead, anyhow. Dey won't never kotch up. *(With a sigh)* If on'y my fool legs stands up. Oh, I'se sorry I evah went in for dis. Dat Emperor job is sho' hard to shake. *(He looks around him suspiciously.)* How'd dis road evah git heah? Good, level road, too. I never remembers seein' it befo'. *(Shaking his head apprehensively.)* Dese woods is sho' full o' de queerest

things at night. *(With sudden terror)* Lawd God, don't let me see no more o' dem ha'nts. Dey gits my goat! *(Then trying to talk himself into confidence.)* Ha'nts! Yo' fool nigger, dey ain't no such things! Don't de Baptist parson tell you dat 590 many time? Is yo' civilized, or is yo' like dese ign'rent black niggers heah? Sho'! Dat was all in yo' own head. Wasn't nothin' there! Wasn't no Jeff! Know what? Yo' jus' get seein' dem thing 'cause yo' belly's empty an' you's sick wid hunger inside. Hunger 'fects yo' head an' yo' eyes. Any fool know dat. *(Then pleading fervently)* But bless God, I don't come across no more o' dem, whatever dey is! *(Then cautiously)* Rest! Don't talk! Rest! You needs it. Den yo' gits on yo' way again. *(Looking at the moon)* Night's half gone a'most. Yo' hits de coast in de mawning! Den you'se all safe. 600

*(From the right forward a small gang of negroes enter. They are dressed in striped convicts suits, their heads are shaven, one leg drags limpingly, shackled to a heavy ball and chain. Some carry picks, the others shovels. They are followed by a white man dressed in the uniform of a prison guard. A Winchester rifle is slung across his shoulders and he carries a heavy whip. At a signal from the guard they stop on the road opposite to where Jones is sitting. Jones, who has been staring up at the sky, unmindful of their noiseless approach, suddenly looks down and sees them. His eyes pop out, he tries to get to his feet and fly, but sinks back, too numbed by fright to move. His voice catches in a choking prayer.)*

Lawd Jesus!

*(The prison guard cracks his whip—noiselessly—and at that signal all the convicts start to work on the road. They swing their picks, they shovel, but not a sound comes from their labor. Their movements, like those of Jeff in the preceding scene, are those of automatons—rigid, slow, and mechanical. The prison guard points sternly at Jones with his whip, motions him to take his place among the other shovelers. Jones gets to his feet in a hypnotized stupor. He mumbles subserviently:)*

Yes, suh! Yes, suh! I'se comin'!

*(As he shuffles, dragging one foot, over to his place, he curses under his breath with rage and hatred.)*

God damn yo' soul, I gits even wid yo' yit, sometime.

*(As if there was a shovel in his hands, he goes through weary, mechanical gestures of digging up dirt and throwing it to the roadside. Suddenly the guard approaches him angrily, threateningly. He raises his whip and lashes Jones viciously across the shoulders with it. Jones winces with pain and cowers abjectly. The guard turns his back on him and walks away contemptuously. Instantly Jones straightens up. With arms upraised, as if his shovel were a club in his hands, he springs murderously at the unsuspecting guard. In the act of crashing down his shovel on the white man's skull, Jones suddenly becomes aware that his hands are empty. He cries despairingly:)*

Whar's my shovel? Gimme my shovel 'till I splits his damn head! *(Appealing to his fellow convicts)* Gimme a shovel, one o' yo' fo' God's sake!

*(They stand fixed in motionless attitudes, their eyes on the ground. The guard seems to wait expectantly, his back turned*

*to the attacker. Jones bellows with baffled terrified rage, tugging frantically at his revolver.)*

I kills you, you white debil, if it's de last thing I evah does! Ghost or debil, I kill you agin!

*(He frees the revolver and fires pointblank at the guard's back. Instantly the walls of the forest close in from both sides, the road and the figures of the convict gang are blotted out in an enshrouding darkness. The only sounds are a crashing in the underbrush as Jones leaps away in mad flight and the throbbing of the tom-tom, still far distant, but increased in volume of sound and rapidity of beat.)*

SCENE V

*(One o'clock. A large circular clearing, enclosed by the serried ranks of lofty, gigantic trunks of tall trees whose tops are lost to view. In the center is a big dead stump, worn by time into a curious resemblance to an auction block. The moon floods the clearing with a clear light. Jones forces his way in through the forest on the left. He looks wildly about the clearing with hunted, fearful glances. His pants are in tatters, his shoes cut and misshapen, flapping about his feet. He slinks cautiously to the stump in the center and sits down in a tense position, ready for instant flight. Then he holds his head in his hands and rocks back and forth, moaning to himself miserably.)*

Oh, Lawd, Lawd! Oh Lawd, Lawd! *(Suddenly he throws*
610 *himself on his knees and raises his clasped hands to the sky—in a voice of agonized pleading.)* Lawd, Jesus, heah my prayer! I'se a poor sinner, a poor sinner! I knows I done wrong, I knows it! When I cotches Jeff cheatin' wid loaded dice my anger overcomes me an' I kills him dead! Lawd, I done wrong! When dat guard hits me wid de whip, my anger overcomes me, and I kills him dead. Lawd, I done wrong! An' down heah whar dese fool bush niggers raises me up to the seat o' de mighty, I steals all I could grab. Lawd, I done wrong! I knows it! I'se sorry! Forgive me, Lawd! Forgive dis
620 po' sinner! *(Then beseeching terrifiedly)* An' keep dem away, Lawd! Keep dem away from me! An' stop dat drum soundin' in my ears! Dat begin to sound ha'nted, too. *(He gets to his feet, evidently slightly reassured by his prayer— with attempted confidence)* De Lawd'll preserve me from dem ha'nts after dis. *(Sits down on the stump again.)* I ain't skeered o' real men. Let dem come. But dem odders— *(He shudders—then looks down at his feet, working his toes inside the shoes—with a groan)* Oh, my po' feet! Dem shoes ain't no use no more 'ceptin' to hurt. I'se better off widout
630 dem. *(He unlaces them and pulls them off—holds the wrecks of the shoes in his hand and regards them mournfully.)* You was real A-one patin' leather, too. Look at yo' now. Emperor, you'se gittin' mighty low!

*(He sighs dejectedly and remains with bowed shoulders, staring down at the shoes in his hands as if reluctant to throw them away. While his attention is thus occupied, a crowd of figures silently enter the clearing from all sides. All are dressed in Southern costumes of the period of the fifties of the last century. There are middle-aged men who are evidently well-to-do planters. There is one spruce, authoritative individual—the Auctioneer. There are a crowd of curious spectators, chiefly young belles and dandies who have come to the slave market*

*for diversion. All exchange courtly greetings in dumb show and chat silently together. There is something stiff, rigid, unreal, marionettish about their movements. They group themselves about the stump. Finally a batch of slaves are led in from the left by an attendant—three men of different ages, two women, one with a baby in her arms, nursing. They are placed to the left of the stump, beside Jones.)*

*(The white planters look them over appraisingly as if they were cattle, and exchange judgments on each. The dandies point with their fingers and make witty remarks. The belles titter bewitchingly. All this in silence save for the ominous throb of the tom-tom. The Auctioneer holds up his hand, taking his place at the stump. The groups strain forward attentively. He touches Jones on the shoulder peremptorily, motioning for him to stand on the stump—the auction block. Jones looks up, sees the figures on all sides, looks wildly for some opening to escape, sees none, screams and leaps madly to the top of the stump to get as far away from them as possible. He stands there, cowering, paralyzed with horror. The Auctioneer begins his silent spiel. He points to Jones, appeals to the planters to see for themselves. Here is a good field hand, sound in wind and limb, as they can see. Very strong still, in spite of his being middle-aged. Look at that back. Look at those shoulders. Look at the muscles in his arms and his sturdy legs. Capable of any amount of hard labor. Moreover, of a good disposition, intelligent and tractable. Will any gentleman start the bidding? The planters raise their fingers, make their bids. They are apparently all eager to possess Jones. The bidding is lively, the crowd interested. While this has been going on, Jones has been seized by the courage of desperation. He dares to look down and around him. Over his face abject terror gives way to mystification, to gradual realization—stutteringly:)*

What yo' all doin', white folks? What's all dis? What yo' all lookin' at me fo'? What yo' doin' wid me, anyhow? *(Suddenly convulsed with raging hatred and fear)* Is dis a auction? Is yo' sellin' me like dey uster befo' de war? *(Jerking out his revolver just as the Auctioneer knocks him down to one of the planters—glaring from him to the purchaser)* An' you sells me? An' you buys me? I shows you I'se a free nig- 640 ger, damn yo' souls! *(He fires at the Auctioneer and at the planter with such rapidity that the two shots are almost simultaneous. As if this were a signal, the walls of the forest fold in. Only blackness remains and silence broken by Jones as he rushes off, crying with fear—and by the quickened, ever louder beat of the tom-tom.)*

SCENE VI

*(Three o'clock. A cleared space in the forest. The limbs of the trees meet over it, forming a low ceiling about five feet from the ground. The interlocked ropes of creepers reaching upward to entwine the tree trunks give an arched appearance to the sides. The space this encloses is like the dark, noisome hold of some ancient vessel. The moonlight is almost completely shut out and only a vague, wan light filters through. There is the noise of some one approaching from the left, stumbling and crawling through the undergrowth. Jones' voice is heard between chattering moans.)*

Oh, Lawd, what I gwine do now? Ain't got no bullet left on'y de silver one. If mo' o' dem ha'nts come after me, how I

gwine skeer dem away? Oh, Lawd, on'y de silver one left—
650 an' I gotta save dat fo' luck. If I shoots dat one I'm a goner
sho'! Lawd, it's black heah! Whar's de moon? Oh, Lawd,
don't dis night evah come to an end? *(By the sounds he is
feeling his way cautiously forward.)* Dere! Dis feels like a
clear space. I gotta lie down an' rest. I don't care if dem niggers does catch me. I gotta rest.

*(He is well forward now where his figure can be dimly made
out. His pants have been so torn away that what is left of them
is no better than a breech cloth. He flings himself full length,
face downward on the ground, panting with exhaustion. Gradually it seems to grow lighter in the enclosed space, and two
rows of seated figures can be seen behind Jones. They are sitting in crumpled, despairing attitudes, hunched facing one another, with their backs touching the forest walls as if they were
shackled to them. All are negroes, naked save for loin cloths. At
first they are silent and motionless. Then they begin to sway
slowly forward toward each other and back again in unison, as
if they were laxly letting themselves follow the long roll of a
ship at sea. At the same time, a low, melancholy murmur rises
among them, increasing gradually by rhythmic degrees, which
seem to be directed and controlled by the throb of the tom-tom
in the distance, to a long, tremendous wail of despair that
reaches a certain pitch, unbearably acute, then falls by slow
gradations of tone into silence and is taken up again. Jones
starts, looks up, sees the figures, and throws himself down
again to shut out the sight. A shudder of terror shakes his
whole body as the wail rises up about him again. But the next
time, his voice, as if under some uncanny compulsion, starts
with the others. As their chorus lifts he rises to a sitting posture
similar to the others, swaying back and forth. His voice reaches
the highest pitch of sorrow, of desolation. The light fades out,
the other voices cease, and only darkness is left. Jones can be
heard scrambling to his feet and running off, his voice sinking
down the scale and receding as he moves farther and farther
away in the forest. The tom-tom beats louder, quicker, with a
more insistent, triumphant pulsation.)*

SCENE VII

*(Five o'clock. The foot of a gigantic tree by the edge of a great
river. A rough structure of boulders like an altar is by the tree.
The raised river bank is in the nearer background. Beyond this
the surface of the river spreads out brilliant and unruffled in
the moonlight, blotted out and merged into a veil of bluish mist
in the distance. Jones' voice is heard from the left, rising and
falling in the long, despairing wail of the chained slaves, to the
rhythmic beat of the tom-tom. As his voice sinks into silence he
enters the open space. The expression of his face is fixed and
stony, his eyes have an obsessed glare, he moves with a strange
deliberation like a sleep-walker or one in a trance. He looks
around at the tree, the rough stone altar, the moonlit surface of
the river beyond, and passes his hand over his head with a
vague gesture of puzzled bewilderment. Then, as if in obedience to some obscure impulse, he sinks into a kneeling,
devotional posture before the altar. Then he seems to come to
himself partly, to have an uncertain realization of what he is
doing, for he straightens up and stares about him horrifiedly—
in an incoherent mumble.)*

What—what is I doin'? What is—dis place? Seems like—

seems like I know dat tree—an' dem stones—an' de river. I
remember—seems like I been heah befo'. *(Tremblingly)*
Oh, Gorry, I'se skeered in dis place! I'se skeered! Oh, Lawd,
pertect dis sinner!                                              660

*(Crawling away from the altar, he cowers close to the ground,
his face hidden, his shoulders heaving with sobs of hysterical
fright. From behind the trunk of the tree, as if he had sprung
out of it, the figure of the Congo witch-doctor appears. He is
wizened and old, naked except for the fur of some small animal
tied about his waist, its bushy tail hanging down in front. His
body is stained all over a bright red. Antelope horns are on
each side of his head, branching upward. In one hand he carries a bone rattle, in the other a charm stick with a bunch of
white cockatoo feathers tied to the end. A great number of glass
beads and bone ornaments are about his neck, ears, wrists, and
ankles. He struts noiselessly with a queer prancing step to a position in the clear ground between Jones and the altar. Then
with a preliminary, summoning stamp of his foot on the earth,
he begins to dance and to chant. As if in response to his summons the beating of the tom-tom grows to a fierce, exultant
boom whose throbs seem to fill the air with vibrating rhythm.
Jones looks up, starts to spring to his feet, reaches a half-kneel-
ing, half-squatting position, and remains rigidly fixed there,
paralyzed with awed fascination by this new apparition. The
witch-doctor sways, stamping with his foot, his bone rattle
clicking the time. His voice rises and falls in a weird, monotonous croon, without articulate word division. Gradually his
dance becomes clearly one of a narrative in pantomime, his
croon is an incantation, a charm to allay the fierceness of some
implacable deity demanding sacrifice. He flees, he is pursued
by devils, he hides, he flees again. Ever wilder and wilder becomes his flight, nearer and nearer draws the pursuing evil,
more and more the spirit of terror gains possession of him. His
croon, rising to intensity, is punctuated by shrill cries. Jones
has become completely hypnotized. His voice joins in the incantation, in the cries; he beats time with his hands and sways
his body to and fro from the waist. The whole spirit and meaning of the dance has entered into him, has become his spirit. Finally the theme of the pantomime halts, on a howl of despair,
and is taken up again in a note of savage hope. There is a salvation. The forces of evil demand sacrifice. They must be appeased. The witch-doctor points with his wand to the sacred
tree, the river beyond, to the altar, and finally to Jones with a
ferocious command. Jones seems to sense the meaning of this.
It is he who must offer himself for sacrifice. He beats his forehead abjectly to the ground, moaning hysterically.)*

Mercy, Oh Lawd! Mercy! Mercy on dis po' sinner!

*(The witch-doctor springs to the river bank. He stretches out
his arms and calls to some god within its depths. Then he starts
backward slowly, his arms remaining out. A huge head of a
crocodile appears over the bank and its eyes, glittering greenly,
fasten upon Jones. He stares into them fascinatedly. The witch-
doctor prances up to him, touches him with his wand, motions
with hideous command toward the waiting monster. Jones
squirms on his belly nearer and nearer, moaning continually:)*

Mercy, Lawd! Mercy!

*(The crocodile heaves more of his enormous hulk onto the land.
Jones squirms toward him. The witch-doctor's voice shrills out*

*in furious exultation, the tom-tom beats madly. Jones cries out in fierce, exhausted spasms of anguished pleading:)*

Lawd, save me! Lawd Jesus, heah my prayer!

*(Immediately, in answer to his prayer, comes the thought of the one bullet left him. He snatches at his hip, shouting defiantly:)*

De silver bullet! Yo' don't git me yit!

*(He fires at the green eyes in front of him. The head of the crocodile sinks back behind the river bank, the witch-doctor springs behind the sacred tree and disappears. Jones lies with his face to the ground, his arms outstretched, whimpering with fear as the throb of the tom-tom fills the silence about him with a somber pulsation, a baffled but revengeful power.)*

Scene VIII

*(Dawn. Same as Scene Two, the dividing line of forest and plain. The nearest tree trunks are dimly revealed, but the forest behind them is still a mass of glooming shadow. The tom-tom seems on the very spot, so loud and continuously vibrating are its beats. Lem enters from the left, followed by a small squad of his soldiers, and by the Cockney trader, Smithers. Lem is a heavy-set, ape-faced old savage of the extreme African type, dressed only in a loin cloth. A revolver and cartridge belt are about his waist. His soldiers are in different degrees of rag-concealed nakedness. All wear broad palm leaf hats. Each one carries a rifle. Smithers is the same as in Scene One. One of the soldiers, evidently a tracker, is peering about keenly on the ground. He grunts and points to the spot where Jones entered the forest. Lem and Smithers come to look.)*

SMITHERS: *(after a glance, turns away in disgust.)* That's where 'e went in right enough. Much good it'll do yer. 'E's miles orf by this an' safe to the coast, damn 'is 'ide! I tole yer ye'd lose 'im, didn't I?—wastin' the 'ole bloomin' night beatin' yer bloody drum and castin' yer silly spells! Gawd blimey, wot
670 a pack!

LEM: *(gutterally)* We kotch him. You see. *(He makes a motion to his soldiers, who squat down on their haunches in a semi-circle.)*

SMITHERS: *(exasperatedly)* Well, ain't yer goin' in an' 'unt 'im in the woods? What the 'ell's the good of waitin'?

LEM: *(imperturbably—squatting down himself)* We kotch him.

SMITHERS: *(turning away from him contemptuously)* Aw! Garn! 'E's a better man than the lot o' you put together. I
680 'ates the sight o' 'im, but I'll say that for 'im.

*(A sound of snapping twigs comes from the forest. The soldiers jump to their feet, cocking their rifles alertly. Lem remains sitting with an imperturbable expression, but listening intently. The sound from the woods is repeated. Lem makes a quick*

signal with his hand. His followers creep quickly but noiselessly into the forest, scattering so that each enters at a different spot.)*

SMITHERS: *(in the silence that follows—in a contemptuous whisper)* You ain't thinkin' that would be 'im, I 'ope?

LEM: *(calmly)* We kotch him.

SMITHERS: Blarsted fat 'eads! *(Then after a second's thought—wonderingly)* Still an' all, it might happen. If 'e lost 'is bloody way in these stinkin' woods 'e'd likely turn in a circle without 'is knowin' it. They all does.

LEM: *(peremptorily)* S-s-s-h-h!

*(The report of several rifles sounds from the forest, followed a second later by savage, exultant yells. The beating of the tom-tom abruptly ceases. Lem looks up at the white man with a grin of satisfaction.)*

We kotch him. Him dead.

SMITHERS: *(with a snarl)* 'Ow d'yer know it's 'im an' 'ow d'yer 690 know 'e's dead?

LEM: My men's dey got 'um silver bullets. Dey kill him shore.

SMITHERS: *(astonished)* They got silver bullets?

LEM: Lead bullet no kill him. He got um strong charm. I took um money, make um silver bullet, make um strong charm, too.

SMITHERS: *(light breaking upon him)* So that's wot you was up to all night, wot? You was scared to put after 'im till you'd molded silver bullets, eh?

LEM: *(simply stating a fact)* Yes. Him got strong charm. Lead 700 no good.

SMITHERS: *(slapping his thigh and guffawing)* Haw-haw! If yer don't beat al 'ell! *(Then recovering himself—scornfully)* I'll bet you it ain't 'im they shot at all, yer bleedin' looney!

LEM: *(calmly)* Dey come bring him now.

*(The soldiers come out of the forest, carrying Jones' limp body. There is a little reddish-purple hole under his left breast. He is dead. They carry him to Lem, who examines his body with great satisfaction. Smithers leans over his shoulder—in a tone of frightened awe:)*

Well, they did for yer right enough, Jonesy, me lad! Dead as a 'erring! *(Mockingly)* Where's yer 'igh an' mighty airs now, yer bloomin' Majesty? *(Then with a grin)* Silver bullets! Gawd blimey, but yer died in the 'eight o' style, any'ow!

*(Lem makes a motion to the soldiers to carry the body out left. Smithers speaks to him sneeringly)*

SMITHERS: And I s'pose you think it's yer bleedin' charms 710 and yer silly beatin' the drum that made 'im run in a circle when 'e'd lost 'imself, don't yer? *(But Lem makes no reply, does not seem to hear the question, walks out left after his men. Smithers looks after him with contemptuous scorn.)* Stupid as 'ogs, the lot of 'em! Blarsted niggers!

**C U R T A I N   F A L L S**

*ALTHOUGH* The Emperor Jones *is not one of the plays in which O'Neill used masks, the idea of masking is fundamental to O'Neill's approach to character. O'Neill's characters often have a kind of public persona, fashioned to meet and dominate the public world of others; but when the mask is removed, what remains beneath is not an alternate, authentic "self," but a kind of absence, the still-fresh scars of some long-distant wound. In these three essays, which initially appeared in* The American Spectator *between November 1932 and January 1933, O'Neill takes the "mask" as an emblem for the character's complex negotiation—and evasion—of demands arising both in the outer world and in the depths of the psyche.*

Not masks for all plays, naturally. Obviously not for plays conceived in purely realistic terms. But masks for certain types of plays, especially for the new modern play, as yet only dimly foreshadowed in a few groping specimens, but which must inevitably be written in the future. For I hold more and more surely to the conviction that the use of masks will be discovered eventually to be the freest solution of the modern dramatist's problem as to how—with the greatest possible dramatic clarity and economy of means—he can express those profound hidden conflicts of the mind which the probings of psychology continue to disclose to us. He must find some method to present this inner drama in his work, or confess himself incapable of portraying one of the most characteristic preoccupations and uniquely significant, spiritual impulses of his time. With his old—and more than a bit senile!—standby of realistic technique, he can do no more than, at best, obscurely hint at it through a realistically disguised surface symbolism, superficial and misleading. But that, while sufficiently beguiling to the sentimentally mystical, is hardly enough. A comprehensive expression is demanded here, a chance for eloquent presentation, a new form of drama projected from a fresh insight into the inner forces motivating the actions and reactions of men and women (a new and truer characterization, in other words), a drama of souls, and the adventures of "Free wills," with the masks that govern them and constitute their fates.

For what, at bottom, is the new psychological insight into human cause and effect but a study in masks, an exercise in unmasking? Whether we think the attempted unmasking has been successful, or has only created for itself new masks, is of no importance here. What is valid, what is unquestionable, is that this insight has uncovered the mask, has impressed the idea of mask as a symbol of inner reality upon all intelligent people of today; and I know they would welcome the use of masks in the theatre as a necessary, dramatically revealing new convention, and not regard them as any "stunty" resurrection of archaic props.

This was strikingly demonstrated for me in practical experience by *The Great God Brown*, which ran in New York for eight months, nearly all of that time in Broadway theatres—a play in which the use of masks was an integral part of the theme. There was some misunderstanding, of course. But so is there always misunderstanding in the thing beyond what is contained in a human-interest newspaper story. In the main, however, *The Great God Brown* was accepted and appreciated by both critics and public—a fairly extensive public, as its run gives evidence.

I emphasize this play's success because the fact that a mask drama, the main values of which are psychological, mystical, and abstract, could be played in New York for eight months, has always seemed to me a more significant proof of the deeply responsive possibilities in our public than anything that has happened in our modern theatre before or since.

2

Looked at from even the most practical standpoint of the practicing playwright, the mask *is* dramatic in itself, *has always* been dramatic in itself, *is* a proven weapon of attack. At its best, it is more subtly, imaginatively, suggestively dramatic than any actor's face can ever be. Let anyone who doubts this study the Japanese Noh masks, or Chinese theatre masks, or African primitive masks—or right here in America the faces of the big marionettes Robert Edmond Jones made for the production of Stravinsky's *Oedipus*, or Benda's famous masks, or even photographs of them.

3

*Dogma for the new masked drama.* One's outer life passes in a solitude haunted by the masks of others; one's inner life passes in a solitude hounded by the masks of oneself.

4

With masked mob a new type of play may be written in which the Mob as King, Hero, Villain, or Fool will be the main character—The Great Democratic Play!

5

Why not give all future Classical revivals entirely in masks? *Hamlet*, for example. Masks would liberate this play from its present confining status as exclusively a "star vehicle." We would be able to see the great drama we are now only privileged to read, to identify ourselves with the figure of Hamlet as a symbolic projection of a fate that is in each of us, instead of merely watching a star giving us his version of a great acting role. We would even be able to hear the sublime poetry as the innate expression of the spirit of the drama itself, instead of listening to it as realistic recitation—or ranting—by familiar actors.

6

Consider Goethe's *Faust*, which, psychologically speaking, should be the closest to us of all the Classics. In producing this play, I would have Mephistopheles wearing the Mephistophelean mask of the face of Faust. For is not the whole of Goethe's truth *for our time* just that Mephistopheles and Faust are one and the same—*are* Faust?

*Second thoughts*     What would I change in past productions of my plays if I could live through them again? Many things. In some plays, considerable revision of the writing of some of the scenes would strike me as imperative. Other plays—*The First Man, Gold, Welded, The Fountain*—I would dismiss as being too painfully bungled in their present form to be worth producing at all.

But one thing I most certainly would not change: the use of masks in *The Hairy Ape*, in my arrangement of Coleridge's "Ancient Mariner," in *All God's Chillun Got Wings* (the symbol of the African primitive mask in the last part of the play, which, in the production in Russian by the Moscow Kamerny Theatre I saw in Paris, is dramatically intensified and emphasized), in *The Great God Brown* and, finally, in *Lazarus Laughed,* in which all the characters except Lazarus remain masked throughout the play. I regard this use of masks as having been uniformly successful.

The change I would make would be to call for more masks in some of these productions and to use them in other productions where they were not used before. In *The Emperor Jones*, for example. All the figures in Jones's flight through the forest should be masked. Masks would dramatically stress their phantasmal quality, as contrasted with the unmasked Jones, intensify the supernatural menace of the tom tom, give the play a more complete and vivid expression. In *The Hairy Ape* a much more extensive use of masks would be of the greatest value in emphasizing the theme of the play. From the opening of the fourth scene, where Yank begins to think he enters into a masked world; even the familiar faces of his mates in the forecastle have become strange and alien. They should be masked, and the faces of everyone he encounters thereafter, including the symbolic gorilla's.

In *All God's Chillun Got Wings*, all save the seven leading characters should be masked; for all the secondary figures are part and parcel of the Expressionistic background of the play, a world at first indifferent, then cruelly hostile, against which the tragedy of Jim Harris is outlined. In *The Great God Brown* I would now make the masks symbolize more definitely the abstract theme of the play instead of, as in the old production, stressing the more superficial meaning that people wear masks before other people and are mistaken by them for their masks.

In *Marco Millions* all the people of the East should be masked—Kublai, the Princess Kukachin, all of them! For anyone who has been in the East, or who has read Eastern philosophy, the reason for this is obvious. It is an exact dramatic expression of West confronted by East. Moreover, it is the only possible way to project this contrast truthfully in the theatre, for Western actors cannot convey Eastern character realistically, and their only chance to suggest it convincingly is with the help of masks.

As for *Strange Interlude*, that is an attempt at the new masked psychological drama which I have discussed before, without masks—a successful attempt, perhaps, in so far as it concerns only surfaces and their immediate subsurfaces, but not where, occasionally, it tries to probe deeper.

With *Mourning Becomes Electra,* masks were called for in one draft of the three plays. But the Classical connotation was too insistent. Masks in that connection demand great language to speak—which let me out of it with a sickening bump! So it evolved ultimately into the "masklike faces," which expressed my intention tempered by the circumstances. However, I should like to see *Mourning Becomes Electra* done entirely with masks, now that I can view it solely as a psychological play, quite removed from the confusing preoccupations the Classical derivation of its plot once caused me. Masks would emphasize the drama of the life and death impulses that drive the characters on to their fates and put more in its proper secondary place, as a frame, the story of the New England family.

I advocate masks for stage crowds, mobs—wherever a sense of impersonal, collective mob psychology is wanted. This was one reason for such an extensive use of them in *Lazarus Laughed.* In masking the crowds in that play, I was visualizing an effect that, intensified by dramatic lighting, would give an audience visually the sense of the Crowd, not as a random collection of individuals, but as a collective whole, an entity. When the Crowd speaks, I wanted an audience to hear the voice of Crowd mind, Crowd emotion, as one voice of a body composed of, but quite distinct from, its parts.

*A dramatist's notebook*

And, for more practical reasons, I wanted to preserve the different crowds of another time and country from the blighting illusion-shattering recognitions by an audience of the supers on the stage. Have you ever seen a production of *Julius Caesar*? Did the Roman mob ever suggest to you anything more Roman than a gum-chewing Coney Island Mardi Gras or, in the case of a special all-star revival, a gathering of familiar-faced modern actors masquerading uncomfortably in togas? But with masks—and the proper intensive lighting—you would have been freed from these recognitions; you would have been able to imagine a Roman mob; you would not even have recognized the Third Avenue and Brooklyn accents among the supers, so effectively does a mask change the quality of a voice.

It was interesting to watch, in the final rehearsals of *The Great God Brown,* how after using their masks for a time the actors and actresses reacted to the demand made by the masks that their bodies become alive and expressive and participate in the drama. Usually it is only the actors' faces that participate. Their bodies remain bored spectators that have been dragged off to the theatre when they would have much preferred a quiet evening in the upholstered chair at home.

Meaning no carping disrespect to our actors. I have been exceedingly lucky in having had some exceptionally fine acting in the principal roles in my plays, for which I am exceedingly grateful. Also some damned poor acting. But let that pass. Most of the poor acting occurred in the poor plays, and there I hold only myself responsible. In the main, wherever a part challenged the actors' or actresses' greatest possibilities, they have reacted to the challenge with a splendid creative energy and skill. Especially, and this is the point I want to make now, where the play took them away from the strictly realistic parts they were accustomed to playing. They always welcomed any opportunity that gave them new scope for their talents. So when I argue here for a non-realistic imaginative theatre I am hoping, not only for added scope for playwright and director and scenic designer, but also for a chance for the actor to develop his art beyond the narrow range to which our present theatre condemns it. Most important of all, from the standpoint of future American culture, I am hoping for added imaginative scope for the audience, a chance for a public I know is growing yearly more numerous and more hungry in its spiritual need to participate in imaginative interpretations of life rather than merely identify itself with faithful surface resemblances of living.

I harp on the word "imaginative"—and with intention! But what do I mean by an "imaginative" theatre—(where I hope for it, for example, in the subtitle of *Lazarus Laughed:* A Play for an Imaginative Theatre)? I mean the one true theatre, the age-old theatre, the theatre of the Greeks and Elizabethans, a theatre that could dare to boast—without committing a farcical sacrilege—that it is a legitimate descendant of the first theatre that sprang, by virtue of man's imaginative interpretation of life, out of his worship of Dionysus. I mean a theatre returned to its highest and sole significant function as a Temple where the religion of a poetical interpretation and symbolical celebration of life is communicated to human beings, starved in spirit by their soul-stifling daily struggle to exist as masks among the masks of living!

But I anticipate the actors' objection to masks: that they would extinguish their personalities and deprive them of their greatest asset in conveying emotion by facial expression. I claim, however, that masks would give them the opportunity for a totally new kind of acting, that they would learn many undeveloped possibilities of their art if they appeared, even if only for a season or two, in masked roles. After all, masks did not extinguish the Greek actor, nor have they kept the acting of the East from being an art.

*From* The American Spectator, *November 1932 ("Memoranda on Masks"); December 1932 ("Second Thoughts"); January 1933 ("A Dramatist's Notebook").*

# Luigi Pirandello

Luigi Pirandello (1867–1936) created a diverse and influential body of plays, but his work is now most often associated with the preoccupations of his *Six Characters in Search of an Author*. Like *Six Characters*, Pirandello's plays use **METATHEATER**—roleplaying, plays-within-plays, and a flexible sense of the limits of stage illusion—to examine a highly theatricalized vision of identity. Can any of us be certain of our identity when others hold radically different perspectives on our actions, on who we are?

Pirandello was born in Sicily; he studied language and literature and received his doctorate in 1891 from the University of Rome. He then married the daughter of his father's business partner, but the collapse of the business forced him into a career as a writer. He wrote hundreds of stories, as well as critical and scholarly articles, in the 1890s and in the first decades of the twentieth century. Pirandello's dramatic interest in the uncertainty of identity can be traced partly to his troubled marriage. His wife suffered a long mental illness and constantly accused him of adultery, despite his careful and constant attention to her health. In a sense, Pirandello was caught between his own sense of himself and the role he was given in this domestic tragedy.

Pirandello's use of the theater as a metaphor for representing this conflict pervades his mature plays: *Six Characters in Search of an Author* (1921; extensively revised 1925), *Enrico IV* (1922), *Each in His Own Way* (1924), and *Tonight We Improvise* (1930). In these plays, the struggle to discover and maintain identity is subjected to the pressure of performance in the world, performance that renders the "self" a kind of fiction. Yet while all behavior seems to verge on mere "acting," undermining our confidence in the authority or reality of a "self," Pirandello's plays do not seem nostalgic for the fixed and determined characters of realistic drama. For in Pirandello's drama, the "self" can also become a kind of prison, a role that traps the individual in a single and confining performance. This is the tragedy that the nameless hero of *Enrico IV* discovers at the close of that play, much as the hero of *When One Is Somebody* (1933)—a famous author like Pirandello himself—is gradually transformed from a man into a statue by the force of his admirers' adulation.

Pirandello became the director of his own company, the Art Theater of Rome, in 1924, and his major plays entered the world repertoire almost immediately. Pirandello's company toured throughout Europe and the Americas, influencing a generation of playwrights with the power of his theatrical conception of modern life. In addition to his short stories and criticism, Pirandello wrote over forty plays. He was awarded the Nobel Prize in 1934 in recognition of his achievement in the modern theater.

## Six Characters in Search of an Author (1922, 1925)

*Six Characters* seems at first to elaborate a simple and striking idea: what would happen if a cast of dramatic "characters" confronted the actors who gave them life on the stage. Pirandello had toyed with the idea for some time, and had sketched it out as a short story. Onstage, though, the story develops a new and challenging dimension, for the confrontation between the Characters and Actors explores the nature of theatrical representation itself. As the play proceeds, it becomes clear that the Actors and Characters represent opposed versions of reality and of the theater, and their contest calls our understanding of the difference between them into question. The Characters need completion. Their melodramatic incest drama has defined each of them in an imprisoning role, as though the climactic moment of their unfinished play—when the Father nearly (or does he?) procures the Stepdaughter in Madame Pace's brothel—were definitive of the identity of each character. That is, Pirandello questions our fundamental notions of how dramatic characters represent the lives of real people, how they represent the rich complexity of a "life" through a short series of a few typical deeds. As the Father asks at one point, who among us would want his or her life summed-up in one moment, one act?

The Actors, on the other hand, seem even less real than the Characters. Although the Characters are "fixed" by the design of their common story, that very consistency gives them a coherence and weight that the flighty Actors seem to lack. The Actors are entirely absorbed in the conventions of their lines of business and the petty jealousies of working together; the Leading

Actor must always be "acting" the "Leading Actor," whether he is onstage or not, and so on through the rest of the cast. Oddly enough, then, *Six Characters* does not seem to allow us to choose between the Actors or Characters, to decide which kind of representation—narrative or stage performance—provides a more accurate depiction of "reality": The drama of *Six Characters* arises from the unresolved collision between these two perspectives. In the theater, the process of *Six Characters* insistently disorients its audience from the stable categories of "reality" and "illusion," which is perhaps why audiences rioted when the play was first produced. The Characters are, of course, played by actors, while the Actors are clearly "characters" to the audience. Are we, in the audience any more "real"? Are we outside the play looking in, or has Pirandello managed to place *us* onstage, showing the audience also to be playing a role in the endless roleplaying of the theater? For this reason, when reading the play we should resist locating its "meanings" in the Father's philosophical monologues, those moments of *pirandellismo* that seem to sum up the play's confrontation between illusion and reality. The play's meaning arises through the entire process of its action, the baffling, inconclusive, and frustrating confrontation between Characters, Actors, and audience, a confrontation that finally prevents the Characters' drama from ever taking the stage.

# — Six Characters —
# in Search of an Author
## Luigi Pirandello
TRANSLATED BY JOHN LINSTRUM

## —THE CHARACTERS—

THE FATHER
THE MOTHER
THE STEPDAUGHTER
THE SON
THE BOY (non-speaking)
THE LITTLE GIRL (non-speaking)
MADAME PACE

## —THE ACTORS—

THE PRODUCER
THE LEADING ACTRESS
THE LEADING ACTOR
THE SECOND ACTRESS
THE YOUNG ACTRESS
THE YOUNG ACTOR
OTHER ACTORS AND ACTRESSES (a variable number)
THE STAGE MANAGER
THE PROMPTER
THE PROPERTY MAN
THE STAGE-HAND
THE PRODUCER'S SECRETARY
THE DOORKEEPER
OTHER THEATRE STAFF

*The action of the play takes place on the stage of a theatre. There are no act or scene divisions, but there are two interruptions: when the Producer and the Characters go to the office to write the scenario, giving the Actors a break in rehearsal, and when a stage-hand lowers the front curtain by mistake.*

*References to "prompt-box," "curtains" and "letting down trees" will need to be altered if they are not appropriate to the theatre where the performance is taking place.*

## —ACT ONE—

*When the audience enters, the curtain is already up and the stage is just as it would be during the day. There is no set; it is empty, in almost total darkness. This is so that from the beginning the audience will have the feeling of being present, not at a performance of a properly rehearsed play, but at a performance of a play that happens spontaneously. Two small sets of steps, one on the right and one on the left, lead up to the stage from the auditorium. On the stage, the top is off the*

PROMPTER's *box and is lying next to it. Downstage, there is a small table and a chair with arms for the* PRODUCER: *it is turned with its back to the audience.*

*Also downstage there are two small tables, one a little bigger than the other, and several chairs, ready for the rehearsal if needed. There are more chairs scattered on both left and right for the* ACTORS: *to one side at the back and nearly hidden is a piano.*

*When the houselights go down the* STAGE HAND *comes on through the back door. He is in blue overalls and carries a tool bag. He brings some pieces of wood on, comes to the front, kneels down and starts to nail them together.*

*The* STAGE MANAGER *rushes on from the wings.*

STAGE MANAGER: Hey! What are you doing?
STAGE HAND: What do you think I'm doing? I'm banging nails in.
STAGE MANAGER: Now? (*He looks at his watch.*) It's half-past ten already. The Producer will be here in a moment to rehearse.
STAGE HAND: I've got to do my work some time, you know.
STAGE MANAGER: Right—but not now.
STAGE HAND: When?
STAGE MANAGER: When the rehearsal's finished. Come on, get 10 all this out of the way and let me set for the second act of *"The Rules of the Game."*

(*The* STAGE HAND *picks up his tools and wood and goes off, grumbling and muttering. The* ACTORS *of the company come in through the door, men and women, first one then another, then two together and so on: there will be nine or ten, enough for the parts for the rehearsal of a play by Pirandello, "The Rules of the Game," today's rehearsal. They come in, say their "Good-mornings" to the* STAGE MANAGER *and each other. Some go off to the dressing-rooms; others, among them the* PROMPTER *with the text rolled up under his arm, scatter about the stage waiting for the* PRODUCER *to start the rehearsal. Meanwhile, sitting or standing in groups, they chat together; some smoke, one complains about his part, another one loudly reads something from "The Stage." It would be as well if the* ACTORS *and* ACTRESSES *were dressed in colourful clothes, and this first scene should be improvised naturally and vivaciously. After a while somebody might sit down at the piano and play a song; the younger* ACTORS *and* ACTRESSES *start dancing.*)

STAGE MANAGER: (*clapping his hands to call their attention*) Come on everybody! Quiet please. The Producer's here.

(*The piano and the dancing both stop. The* ACTORS *turn to look out into the theatre and through the door at the back comes the*

PRODUCER; *he walks down the gangway between the seats and, calling "Good-morning" to the* ACTORS, *climbs up one of the sets of stairs onto the stage. The* SECRETARY *gives him the post, a few magazines, a script. The* ACTORS *move to one side of the stage.*)

PRODUCER: Any letters?

SECRETARY: No. That's all the post there is. (*Giving him the script.*)

PRODUCER: Put it in the office. (*Then looking round and turning to the* STAGE MANAGER.) I can't see a thing here. Let's
20 have some lights please.

STAGE MANAGER: Right. (*Calling.*) Workers please!

(*In a few seconds the side of the stage where the* ACTORS *are standing is brilliantly lit with white light. The* PROMPTER *has gone into his box and spread out his script.*)

PRODUCER: Good. (*Clapping hands.*) Well then, let's get started. Anybody missing?

STAGE MANAGER: (*heavily ironic*) Our leading lady.

PRODUCER: Not again! (*Looking at his watch.*) We're ten minutes late already. Send her a note to come and see me. It might teach her to be on time for rehearsals. (*Almost before he has finished, the* LEADING ACTRESS's *voice is heard from the auditorium.*)
30 LEADING ACTRESS: Morning everybody. Sorry I'm late. (*She is very expensively dressed and is carrying a lap-dog. She comes down the aisle and goes up on to the stage.*)

PRODUCER: You're determined to keep us waiting, aren't you?

LEADING ACTRESS: I'm sorry. I just couldn't find a taxi anywhere. But you haven't started yet and I'm not on at the opening anyhow. (*Calling the* STAGE MANAGER, *she gives him the dog.*) Put him in my dressing-room for me will you?

PRODUCER: And she's even brought her lap-dog with her! As if we haven't enough lap-dogs here already. (*Clapping his*
40 *hands and turning to the* PROMPTER.) Right then, the second act of "*The Rules of the Game.*" (*Sits in his arm-chair.*) Quiet please! Who's on?

(*The* ACTORS *clear from the front of the stage and sit to one side, except for three who are ready to start the scene—and the* LEADING ACTRESS. *She has ignored the* PRODUCER *and is sitting at one of the little tables.*)

PRODUCER: Are you in this scene, then?

LEADING ACTRESS: No—I've just told you.

PRODUCER: (*annoyed*) Then get off, for God's sake. (*The* LEADING ACTRESS *goes and sits with the others. To the* PROMPTER.) Come on then, let's get going.

PROMPTER: (*reading his script*) "The house of Leone Gala. A peculiar room, both dining-room and study."
50 PRODUCER: (*to the* STAGE MANAGER). We'll use the red set.

STAGE MANAGER: (*making a note*) The red set—right.

PROMPTER: (*still reading*) "The table is laid and there is a desk with books and papers. Bookcases full of books and china cabinets full of valuable china. An exit at the back leads to Leone's bedroom. An exit to the left leads to the kitchen. The main entrance is on the right."

PRODUCER: Right. Listen carefully everybody: there, the main entrance, there, the kitchen. (*To the* LEADING ACTOR *who plays Socrates.*) Your entrances and exits will be from there.

(*To the* STAGE MANAGER.) We'll have the French windows 60 there and put the curtains on them.

STAGE MANAGER: (*making a note*) Right.

PROMPTER: (*reading*) "Scene One. Leone Gala, Guido Venanzi, and Filippo, who is called Socrates." (*To* PRODUCER.) Have I to read the directions as well?

PRODUCER: Yes, you have! I've told you a hundred times.

PROMPTER: (*reading*) "When the curtain rises, Leone Gala, in a cook's hat and apron, is beating an egg in a dish with a little wooden spoon. Filippo is beating another and he is dressed as a cook too. Guido Venanzi is sitting listening." 70

LEADING ACTOR: Look, do I really have to wear a cook's hat?

PRODUCER: (*annoyed by the question*) I expect so! That's what it says in the script. (*Pointing to the script.*)

LEADING ACTOR: If you ask me it's ridiculous.

PRODUCER: (*leaping to his feet furiously*). Ridiculous? It's ridiculous, is it? What do you expect me to do if nobody writes good plays any more and we're reduced to putting on plays by Pirandello? And if you can understand them you must be very clever. He writes them on purpose so nobody enjoys them, neither actors nor critics nor audience. (*The* 80 ACTORS *laugh. Then crosses to* LEADING ACTOR *and shouts at him.*) A cook's hat and you beat eggs. But don't run away with the idea that that's all you are doing—beating eggs. You must be joking! You have to be symbolic of the shells of the eggs you are beating. (*The* ACTORS *laugh again and start making ironical comments to each other.*) Be quiet! Listen carefully while I explain. (*Turns back to* LEADING ACTOR.) Yes, the shells, because they are symbolic of the empty form of reason, without its content, blind instinct! You are reason and your wife is instinct: you are playing a game where you 90 have been given parts and in which you are not just yourself but the puppet of yourself. Do you see?

LEADING ACTOR: (*spreading his hands*) Me? No.

PRODUCER: (*going back to his chair*) Neither do I! Come on, let's get going; you wait till you see the end! You haven't seen anything yet! (*Confidentially.*) By the way, I should turn almost to face the audience if I were you, about three-quarters face. Well, what with the obscure dialogue and the audience not being able to hear you properly in any case, the whole lot'll go to hell. (*Clapping hands again.*) Come on. 100 Let's get going!

PROMPTER: Excuse me, can I put the top back on the prompt-box? There's a bit of a draught.

PRODUCER: Yes, yes, of course. Get on with it.

(*The* STAGE DOORKEEPER, *in a braided cap, has come into the auditorium, and he comes all the way down the aisle to the stage to tell the* PRODUCER *the* SIX CHARACTERS *have come, who, having come in after him, look about them a little puzzled and dismayed. Every effort must be made to create the effect that the* SIX CHARACTERS *are very different from the* ACTORS *of the company. The placings of the two groups, indicated in the directions, once the* CHARACTERS *are on the stage, will help this; so will using different coloured lights. But the most effective idea is to use masks for the* CHARACTERS, *masks specially made of a material that will not go limp with perspiration and light enough not to worry the actors who wear them: they should be made so that the eyes, the nose and the mouth are all free. This is the way to bring out the deep significance of the play. The* CHARACTERS *should not appear as ghosts, but as created realities, timeless creations of the imagination, and so more real and consistent than the changeable realities of the* ACTORS. *The masks are designed to give the impression of figures constructed by art, each one fixed forever in its own fundamental emotion; that is, Remorse for the* FATHER, *Revenge for the* STEPDAUGHTER, *Scorn for the* SON, *Sorrow for the* MOTHER. *Her mask should have wax tears in the corners of the eyes and down the cheeks like the sculptured or painted weeping Madonna in a church. Her dress should be of a plain material, in stiff folds, looking almost as if it were carved and not of an ordinary material you can buy in a shop and have made up by a dressmaker.)*

*(The* FATHER *is about fifty: his reddish hair is thinning at the temples, but he is not bald: he has a full moustache that almost covers his young-looking mouth, which often opens in an uncertain and empty smile. He is pale, with a high forehead: he has blue oval eyes, clear and sharp: he is dressed in light trousers and a dark jacket: his voice is sometimes rich, at other times harsh and loud.)*

*(The* MOTHER *appears crushed by an intolerable weight of shame and humiliation. She is wearing a thick black veil and is dressed simply in black; when she raises her veil she shows a face like wax, but not suffering, with her eyes turned down humbly.)*

*(The* STEPDAUGHTER, *who is eighteen years old, is defiant, even insolent. She is very beautiful, dressed in mourning as well, but with striking elegance. She is scornful of the timid, suffering, dejected air of her* YOUNG BROTHER, *a grubby little boy of fourteen, also dressed in black; she is full of a warm tenderness, on the other hand, for the* LITTLE SISTER, *a girl of about four, dressed in white with a black silk sash round her waist.)*

*(The* SON *is twenty-two, tall, almost frozen in an air of scorn for the* FATHER *and indifference to the* MOTHER: *he is wearing a mauve overcoat and a long green scarf round his neck.)*

DOORMAN: Excuse me, sir.

PRODUCER: *(angrily)* What the hell is it now?

DOORMAN: There are some people here—they say they want to see you, sir.

*(The* PRODUCER *and the* ACTORS *are astonished and turn to look out into the auditorium.)*

PRODUCER: But I'm rehearsing! You know perfectly well that
110    no-one's allowed in during rehearsals. *(Turning to face out front.)* Who are you? What do you want?

FATHER: *(coming forward, followed by the others, to the foot of one of the sets of steps)* We're looking for an author.

PRODUCER: *(angry and astonished)* An author? Which author?

FATHER: Any author will do, sir.

PRODUCER: But there isn't an author here because we're not rehearsing a new play.

STEPDAUGHTER: *(excitedly as she rushes up the steps)* That's better still, better still! We can be your new play.

120 ACTORS: *(lively comments and laughter from the* ACTORS) Oh, listen to that, etc.

FATHER: *(going up on the stage after the* STEPDAUGHTER) Maybe, but if there isn't an author here . . . *(To the* PRODUCER.) Unless you'd like to be . . .

*(Hand in hand, the* MOTHER *and the* LITTLE GIRL, *followed by the* LITTLE BOY, *go up on the stage and wait. The* SON *stays sullenly behind.)*

PRODUCER: Is this some kind of joke?

FATHER: Now, how can you think that? On the contrary, we are bringing you a story of anguish.

STEPDAUGHTER: We might make your fortune for you!

PRODUCER: Do me a favour, will you? Go away. We haven't time to waste on idiots.    130

FATHER: *(hurt but answering gently)* You know very well, as a man of the theatre, that life is full of all sorts of odd things which have no need at all to pretend to be real because they are actually true.

PRODUCER: What the devil are you talking about?

FATHER: What I'm saying is that you really must be mad to do things the opposite way round: to create situations that obviously aren't true and try to make them seem to be really happening. But then I suppose that sort of madness is the only reason for your profession.    140

*(The* ACTORS *are indignant.)*

PRODUCER: *(getting up and glaring at him)* Oh, yes? So ours is a profession of madmen, is it?

FATHER: Well, if you try to make something look true when it obviously isn't, especially if you're not forced to do it, but do it for a game . . . Isn't it your job to give life on the stage to imaginary people?

PRODUCER: *(quickly answering him and speaking for the* ACTORS *who are growing more indignant)* I should like you to know, sir, that the actor's profession is one of great distinction. Even if nowadays the new writers only give us dull 150 plays to act and puppets to present instead of men, I'd have you know that it is our boast that we have given life, here on this stage, to immortal works.

*(The* ACTORS, *satisfied, agree with and applaud the* PRODUCER.)

FATHER: *(cutting in and following hard on his argument)* There! You see? Good! You've given life! You've created living beings with more genuine life than people have who breathe and wear clothes! Less real, perhaps, but nearer the truth. We are both saying the same thing.

*(The* ACTORS *look at each other, astonished.)*

PRODUCER: But just a moment! You said before . . .

FATHER: I'm sorry, but I said that before, about acting for fun, 160 because you shouted at us and said you'd no time to waste on idiots, but you must know better than anyone that Nature uses human imagination to lift her work of creation to even higher levels.

PRODUCER: All right then: but where does all this get us?

FATHER: Nowhere. I want to try to show that one can be thrust into life in many ways, in many forms: as a tree or a stone, as water or a butterfly—or as a woman. It might even be as a character in a play.

PRODUCER: *(ironic, pretending to be annoyed)* And you, and 170 these other people here, were thrust into life, as you put it, as characters in a play?

FATHER: Exactly! And alive, as you can see.

*(The* PRODUCER *and the* ACTORS *burst into laughter as if*

*at a joke.*)

FATHER: I'm sorry you laugh like that, because we carry in us, as I said before, a story of terrible anguish as you can guess from this woman dressed in black.

(*Saying this, he offers his hand to the* MOTHER *and helps her up the last steps and, holding her still by the hand, leads her with a sense of tragic solemnity across the stage which is suddenly lit by a fantastic light.*)

(*The* LITTLE GIRL *and the* BOY *follow the* MOTHER: *then the* SON *comes up and stands to one side in the background: then the* STEPDAUGHTER *follows and leans against the proscenium arch: the* ACTORS *are astonished at first, but then, full of admiration for the "entrance," they burst into applause—just as if it were a performance specially for them.*)

PRODUCER: (*at first astonished and then indignant*) My God! Be quiet all of you. (*Turns to the* CHARACTERS.) And you lot get out! Clear off! (*To the* STAGE MANAGER.) Jesus! Get them
180    out of here.
STAGE MANAGER: (*comes forward but stops short as if held back by something strange*) Go on out! Get out!
FATHER: (*to* PRODUCER) Oh no, please, you see, we . . .
PRODUCER: (*shouting*) We came here to work, you know.
LEADING ACTOR: We really can't be messed about like this.
FATHER: (*resolutely, coming forward*) I'm astonished! Why don't you believe me? Perhaps you are not used to seeing the characters created by an author spring into life up here on the stage face to face with each other. Perhaps it's
190    because we're not in a script? (*He points to the* PROMPTER's *box.*)
STEPDAUGHTER: (*coming down to the* PRODUCER, *smiling and persuasive*) Believe me, sir, we really are six of the most fascinating characters. But we've been neglected.
FATHER: Yes, that's right, we've been neglected. In the sense that the author who created us, living in his mind, wouldn't or couldn't make us live in a written play for the world of art. And that really is a crime sir, because whoever has the luck to be born a character can laugh even at death. Because a
200    character will never die! A man will die, a writer, the instrument of creation: but what he has created will never die! And to be able to live for ever you don't need to have extraordinary gifts or be able to do miracles. Who was Sancho Panza? Who was Prospero? But they will live for ever because—living seeds—they had the luck to find a fruitful soil, an imagination which knew how to grow them and feed them, so that they will live for ever.
PRODUCER: This is all very well! But what do you want here?
FATHER: We want to live, sir.
210    PRODUCER: (*ironically*) For ever!
FATHER: No, no: only for a few moments—in you.
AN ACTOR: Listen to that!
LEADING ACTRESS: They want to live in us!
YOUNG ACTOR: (*pointing to the* STEPDAUGHTER) I don't mind . . . so long as I get her.
FATHER: Listen, listen: the play is all ready to be put together

and if you and your actors would like to, we can work it out now between us.
PRODUCER: (*annoyed*) But what exactly do you want to do? We don't make up plays like that here! We present comedies 220 and tragedies here.
FATHER: That's right, we know that of course. That's why we've come.
PRODUCER: And where's the script?
FATHER: It's in us, sir. (*The* ACTORS *laugh.*) The play is in us: we are the play and we are impatient to show it to you: the passion inside us is driving us on.
STEPDAUGHTER: (*scornfully, with the tantalising charm of deliberate impudence*) My passion, if only you knew! My passion for him! (*She points at the* FATHER *and suggests that she* 230 *is going to embrace him: but stops and bursts into a screeching laugh.*)
FATHER: (*with sudden anger*) You keep out of this for the moment! And stop laughing like that!
STEPDAUGHTER: Really? Then with your permission, ladies and gentlemen; even though it's only two months since I became an orphan, just watch how I can sing and dance.

(*The* ACTORS, *especially the younger, seem strangely attracted to her while she sings and dances and they edge closer and reach out their hands to catch hold of her.° She eludes them, and when the* ACTORS *applaud her and the* PRODUCER *speaks sharply to her she stays still quite removed from them all.*)

ACTOR 1: Very good! etc.
PRODUCER: (*angrily*) Be quiet! Do you think this is a nightclub? (*Turns to* FATHER *and asks with some concern.*) Is she 240 a bit mad?
FATHER: Mad? Oh no—it's worse than that.
STEPDAUGHTER: (*suddenly running to the* PRODUCER) Yes. It's worse, much worse! Listen please! Let's put this play on at once, because you'll see that at a particular point I—when this darling little girl here—(*Taking the* LITTLE GIRL *by the hand from next to the* MOTHER *and crossing with her to the* PRODUCER.) Isn't she pretty? (*Takes her in her arms.*) Darling! Darling! (*Puts her down again and adds, moved very deeply but almost without wanting to.*) Well, this lovely lit- 250 tle girl here, when God suddenly takes her from this poor Mother: and this little idiot here (*Turning to the* LITTLE BOY *and seizing him roughly by the sleeve.*) does the most stupid thing, like the half-wit he is,—then you will see me run away! Yes, you'll see me rush away! But not yet, not yet! Because, after all the intimate things there have been between him and me (*In the direction of the* FATHER, *with a horrible vulgar wink.*) I can't stay with them any longer, to watch the insult to this mother through that supercilious cretin over there. (*Pointing to the* SON.) Look at him! Look at him! Con- 260 descending, stand-offish, because he's the legitimate son, him! Full of contempt for me, for the boy and for the little girl: because we are bastards. Do you understand? Bastards. (*Running to the* MOTHER *and embracing her.*) And this poor mother—she—who is the mother of all of us—he doesn't want to recognise her as his own mother—and he looks

---

°Suggested songs: Eartha Kitt's *Old Fashioned Millionaire;* Theme Song from *The Moon is Blue, I'm Gonna Wash That Man Right Out Of My Hair* from *South Pacific.*

down on her, he does, as if she were only the mother of the three of us who are bastards—the traitor. *(She says all this quickly, with great excitement, and after having raised her voice on the word "bastards" she speaks quietly, half-spitting the word "traitor."*

270

MOTHER: *(with deep anguish to the* PRODUCER*)* Sir, in the name of these two little ones, I beg you . . . *(Feels herself grow faint and sways.)* Oh, my God.

FATHER: *(rushing to support her with almost all the* ACTORS *bewildered and concerned)* Get a chair someone . . . quick, get a chair for this poor widow.

*(One of the* ACTORS *offers a chair: the others press urgently around. The* MOTHER, *seated now, tries to stop the* FATHER *lifting her veil.)*

ACTORS: Is it real? Has she really fainted? etc.

FATHER: Look at her, everybody, look at her.

280

MOTHER: No, for God's sake, stop it.

FATHER: Let them look!

MOTHER: *(lifting her hands and covering her face, desperately)* Oh, please, I beg you, stop him from doing what he is trying to do; it's hateful.

PRODUCER: *(overwhelmed, astounded)* It's no use, I don't understand this any more. *(To the* FATHER.*)* Is this woman your wife?

FATHER: *(at once)* That's right, she is my wife.

PRODUCER: How is she a widow, then, if you're still alive?

*(The* ACTORS *are bewildered too and find relief in a loud laugh.)*

290

FATHER: *(wounded, with rising resentment)* Don't laugh! Please don't laugh like that! That's just the point, that's her own drama. You see, she had another man. Another man who ought to be here.

MOTHER: No, no! *(Crying out.)*

STEPDAUGHTER: Luckily for him he died. Two months ago, as I told you: we are in mourning for him, as you can see.

FATHER: Yes, he's dead: but that's not the reason he isn't here. He isn't here because—well just look at her, please, and you'll understand at once—hers is not a passionate drama of

300

the love of two men, because she was incapable of love, she could feel nothing—except, perhaps a little gratitude (but not to me, to him). She's not a woman; she's a mother. And her drama—and, believe me, it's a powerful one—her drama is focused completely on these four children of the two men she had.

MOTHER: I had them? How dare you say that I had them, as if I wanted them myself? It was him, sir! He forced the other man on me. He made me go away with him!

STEPDAUGHTER: *(leaping up, indignantly)* It isn't true!

310

MOTHER: *(bewildered)* How isn't it true?

STEPDAUGHTER: It isn't true, it just isn't true.

MOTHER: What do you know about it?

STEPDAUGHTER: It isn't true. *(To the* PRODUCER.*)* Don't believe it! Do you know why she said that? She said it because of him, over there. *(Pointing to the* SON.*)* She tortures herself, she exhausts herself with worry and all because of the indifference of that son of hers. She wants to make him believe that she abandoned him when he was two years old because the Father made her do it.

320

MOTHER: *(passionately)* He did! He made me! God's my

witness. *(To the* PRODUCER.*)* Ask him if it isn't true. *(Pointing to the* FATHER.*)* Make him tell our son it's true. *(Turning to the* STEPDAUGHTER.*)* You don't know anything about it.

STEPDAUGHTER: I know that when my father was alive you were always happy and contented. You can't deny it.

MOTHER: No, I can't deny it.

STEPDAUGHTER: He was always full of love and care for you. *(Turning to the* LITTLE BOY *with anger.)* Isn't it true? Admit it. Why don't you say something, you little idiot?

330

MOTHER: Leave the poor boy alone! Why do you want to make me appear ungrateful? You're my daughter. I don't in the least want to offend your father's memory. I've already told him that it wasn't my fault or even to please myself that I left his house and my son.

FATHER: It's quite true. It was my fault.

LEADING ACTOR: *(to other actors)* Look at this. What a show!

LEADING ACTRESS: And we're the audience.

YOUNG ACTOR: For a change.

PRODUCER: *(beginning to be very interested)* Let's listen to them! Quiet! Listen!

340

*(He goes down the steps into the auditorium and stands there as if to get an idea of what the scene will look like from the audience's viewpoint.)*

SON: *(without moving, coldly, quietly, ironically)* Yes, listen to his little scrap of philosophy. He's going to tell you all about the Daemon of Experiment.

FATHER: You're a cynical idiot, and I've told you so a hundred times. *(To the* PRODUCER *who is now in the stalls.)* He sneers at me because of this expression I've found to defend myself.

SON: Words, words.

FATHER: Yes words, words! When we're faced by something we don't understand, by a sense of evil that seems as if it's going to swallow us, don't we all find comfort in a word that tells us nothing but that calms us?

350

STEPDAUGHTER: And dulls your sense of remorse, too. That more than anything.

FATHER: Remorse? No, that's not true. It'd take more than words to dull the sense of remorse in me.

STEPDAUGHTER: It's taken a little money too, just a little money. The money that he was going to offer as payment, gentlemen.

*(The* ACTORS *are horrified.)*

SON: *(contemptuously to his stepsister)* That's a filthy trick.

360

STEPDAUGHTER: A filthy trick? There it was in a pale blue envelope on the little mahogany table in the room behind the shop at Madame Pace's. You know Madame Pace, don't you? One of those Madames who sell "Robes et Manteaux" so that they can attract poor girls like me from decent families into their workroom.

SON: And she's bought the right to tyrannise over the whole lot of us with that money—with what he was going to pay her: and luckily—now listen carefully—he had no reason to pay it to her.

370

STEPDAUGHTER: But it was close!

MOTHER: *(rising up angrily)* Shame on you, daughter! Shame!

STEPDAUGHTER: Shame? Not shame, revenge! I'm desperate, desperate to live that scene! The room . . . over here the

showcase of coats, there the divan, there the mirror, and the screen, and over there in front of the window, that little mahogany table with the pale blue envelope and the money in it. I can see it all quite clearly. I could pick it up! But you should turn your faces away, gentlemen: because I'm nearly
380 naked! I'm not blushing any longer—I leave that to him. (*Pointing at the* FATHER.) But I tell you he was very pale, very pale then. (*To the* PRODUCER.) Believe me.

PRODUCER: I don't understand any more.

FATHER: I'm not surprised when you're attacked like that! Why don't you put your foot down and let me have my say before you believe all these horrible slanders she's so viciously telling about me.

STEPDAUGHTER: We don't want to hear any of your long winded fairy-stories.

390 FATHER: I'm not going to tell any fairy-stories! I want to explain things to him.

STEPDAUGHTER: I'm sure you do. Oh, yes! In your own special way.

(*The* PRODUCER *comes back up on stage to take control.*)

FATHER: But isn't that the cause of all the trouble? Words! We all have a world of things inside ourselves and each one of us has his own private world. How can we understand each other if the words I use have the sense and the value that I expect them to have, but whoever is listening to me inevitably thinks that those same words have a different sense
400 and value, because of the private world he has inside himself too. We think we understand each other: but we never do. Look! All my pity, all my compassion for this woman (*Pointing to the* MOTHER.) she sees as ferocious cruelty.

MOTHER: But he turned me out of the house!

FATHER: There, do you hear? I turned her out! She really believed that I had turned her out.

MOTHER: You know how to talk. I don't . . . But believe me, sir, (*Turning to the* PRODUCER.) after he married me . . . I can't think why! I was a poor, simple woman.

410 FATHER: But that was the reason! I married you for your simplicity, that's what I loved in you, believing—(*He stops because she is making gestures of contradiction. Then, seeing the impossibility of making her understand, he throws his arms wide in a gesture of desperation and turns back to the* PRODUCER.) No, do you see? She says no! It's terrifying, sir, believe me, terrifying, her deafness, her mental deafness. (*He taps his forehead.*) Affection for her children, oh yes. But deaf, mentally deaf, deaf, sir, to the point of desperation.

420 STEPDAUGHTER: Yes, but make him tell you what good all his cleverness has brought us.

FATHER: If only we could see in advance all the harm that can come from the good we think we are doing.

(*The* LEADING ACTRESS, *who has been growing angry watching the* LEADING ACTOR *flirting with the* STEPDAUGHTER, *comes forward and snaps at the* PRODUCER.)

LEADING ACTRESS: Excuse me, are we going to go on with our rehearsal?

PRODUCER: Yes, of course. But I want to listen to this first.

YOUNG ACTOR: It's such a new idea.

YOUNG ACTRESS: It's fascinating.

LEADING ACTRESS: For those who are interested. (*She looks meaningfully at the* LEADING ACTOR.)    430

PRODUCER: (*to the* FATHER) Look here, you must explain yourself more clearly. (*He sits down.*)

FATHER: Listen then. You see, there was a rather poor fellow working for me as my assistant and secretary, very loyal: he understood her in everything. (*Pointing to the* MOTHER.) But without a hint of deceit, you must believe that: he was good and simple, like her: neither of them was capable even of thinking anything wrong, let alone doing it.

STEPDAUGHTER: So instead he thought of it for them and did it too!    440

FATHER: It's not true! What I did was for their good—oh yes and mine too, I admit it! The time had come when I couldn't say a word to either of them without there immediately flashing between them a sympathetic look: each one caught the other's eye for advice, about how to take what I had said, how not to make me angry. Well, that was enough, as I'm sure you'll understand, to put me in a bad temper all the time, in a state of intolerable exasperation.

PRODUCER: Then why didn't you sack this secretary of yours?

FATHER: Right! In the end I did sack him! But then I had to    450 watch this poor woman wandering about in the house on her own, forlorn, like a stray animal you take in out of pity.

MOTHER: It's quite true.

FATHER: (*suddenly, turning to her, as if to stop her*) And what about the boy? Is that true as well?

MOTHER: But first he tore my son from me, sir.

FATHER: But not out of cruelty! It was so that he could grow up healthy and strong, in touch with the earth.

STEPDAUGHTER: (*pointing to the* SON *jeeringly*) And look at the result!    460

FATHER: (*quickly*) And is it my fault, too, that he's grown up like this? I took him to a nurse in the country, a peasant, because his mother didn't seem strong enough to me, although she is from a humble family herself. In fact that was what made me marry her. Perhaps it was superstitious of me; but what was I to do? I've always had this dreadful longing for a kind of sound moral healthiness.

(*The* STEPDAUGHTER *breaks out again into noisy laughter.*)

Make her stop that! It's unbearable.

PRODUCER: Stop it will you? Let me listen, for God's sake.

(*When the* PRODUCER *has spoken to her, she resumes her previous position . . . absorbed and distant, a half-smile on her lips. The* PRODUCER *comes down into the auditorium again to see how it looks from there.*)

FATHER: I couldn't bear the sight of this woman near me.    470 (*Pointing to the* MOTHER.) Not so much because of the annoyance she caused me, you see, or even the feeling of being stifled, being suffocated that I got from her, as for the sorrow, the painful sorrow that I felt for her.

MOTHER: And he sent me away.

FATHER: With everything you needed, to the other man, to set her free from me.

MOTHER: And to set yourself free!

FATHER: Oh, yes, I admit it. And what terrible things came out of it. But I did it for the best, and more for her than for me:    480 I swear it! (*Folds his arms: then turns suddenly to the*

MOTHER.) I never lost sight of you did I? Until that fellow, without my knowing it, suddenly took you off to another town one day. He was idiotically suspicious of my interest in them, a genuine interest, I assure you, without any ulterior motive at all. I watched the new little family growing up round her with unbelievable tenderness, she'll confirm that. (*He points to the* STEPDAUGHTER.)

STEPDAUGHTER: Oh yes, I can indeed. I was a pretty little girl,
490 　you know, with plaits down to my shoulders and my little frilly knickers showing under my dress—so pretty—he used to watch me coming out of school. He came to see how I was maturing.

FATHER: That's shameful! It's monstrous.

STEPDAUGHTER: No it isn't! Why do you say it is?

FATHER: It's monstrous! Monstrous. (*He turns excitedly to the* PRODUCER *and goes on in explanation.*) After she'd gone away (*Pointing to the* MOTHER.), my house seemed empty. She'd been like a weight on my spirit but she'd filled the
500 　house with her presence. Alone in the empty rooms I wandered about like a lost soul. This boy here, (*Indicating the* SON.) growing up away from home—whenever he came back to the home—I don't know—but he didn't seem to be mine any more. We needed the mother between us, to link us together, and so he grew up by himself, apart, with no connection to me either through intellect or love. And then—it must seem odd, but it's true—first I was curious about and then strongly attracted to the little family that had come about because of what I'd done. And the thought of
510 　them began to fill all the emptiness that I felt around me. I needed, I really needed to believe that she was happy, wrapped up in the simple cares of her life, lucky because she was better off away from the complicated torments of a soul like mine. And to prove it, I used to watch that child coming out of school.

STEPDAUGHTER: Listen to him! He used to follow me along the street; he used to smile at me and when we came near the house he'd wave his hand—like this! I watched him, wide-eyed, puzzled, I didn't know who he was. I told my mother
520 　about him and she knew at once who it must be. (MOTHER *nods agreement.*) At first, she didn't let me go to school again, at any rate for a few days. But when I did go back, I saw him standing near the door again—looking ridiculous—with a brown paper bag in his hand. He came close and petted me: then he opened the bag and took out a beautiful straw hat with a hoop of rosebuds round it—for me!

PRODUCER: All this is off the point, you know.

SON: (*contemptuously*) Yes . . . literature, literature.

FATHER: What do you mean, literature? This is real life: real
530 　passions.

PRODUCER: That may be! But you can't put it on the stage just like that.

FATHER: That's right you can't. Because all this is only leading up to the main action. I'm not suggesting that this part should be put on the stage. In any case, you can see for yourself, (*Pointing at the* STEPDAUGHTER.) she isn't a pretty little girl any longer with plaits down to her shoulders.

STEPDAUGHTER:—and with frilly knickers showing under her frock.

540 FATHER: The drama begins now: and it's new and complex.

STEPDAUGHTER: (*coming forward, fierce and brooding*) As soon as my father died . . .

FATHER: (*quickly, not giving her time to speak*) They were so miserable. They came back here, but I didn't know about it because of the Mother's stubbornness. (*Pointing to the* MOTHER.) She can't really write you know; but she could have got her daughter to write, or the boy, or tell me that they needed help.

MOTHER: But tell me, sir, how could I have known how he felt?

FATHER: And hasn't that always been your fault? You've never 550 known anything about how I felt.

MOTHER: After all the years away from him and after all that had happened.

FATHER: And was it my fault if that fellow took you so far away? (*Turning back to the* PRODUCER.) Suddenly, overnight, I tell you, he'd found a job away from here without my knowing anything about it. I couldn't possibly trace them; and then, naturally I suppose, my interest in them grew less over the years. The drama broke out, unexpected and violent, when they came back: when I was driven in misery by the needs 560 of my flesh, still alive with desire . . . and it is misery, you know, unspeakable misery for the man who lives alone and who detests sordid, casual affairs; not old enough to do without women, but not young enough to be able to go and look for one without shame! Misery? Is that what I called it. It's horrible, it's revolting, because there isn't a woman who will give her love to him any more. And when he realises this, he should do without . . . It's easy to say though. Each of us, face to face with other men, is clothed with some sort of dignity, but we know only too well all the unspeakable things 570 that go on in the heart. We surrender, we give in to temptation: but afterwards we rise up out of it very quickly, in a desperate hurry to rebuild our dignity, whole and firm as if it were a gravestone that would cover every sign and memory of our shame, and hide it from even our own eyes. Everyone's like that, only some of us haven't the courage to talk about it.

STEPDAUGHTER: But they've all got the courage to do it!

FATHER: Yes! But only in secret! That's why it takes more courage to talk about it! Because if a man does talk about 580 it—what happens then?—everybody says he's a cynic. And it's simply not true; he's just like everybody else; only better perhaps, because he's not afraid to use his intelligence to point out the blushing shame of human bestiality, that man, the beast, shuts his eyes to, trying to pretend it doesn't exist. And what about woman—what is she like? She looks at you invitingly, teasingly. You take her in your arms. But as soon as she feels your arms round her she closes her eyes. It's the sign of her mission, the sign by which she says to a man, "Blind yourself—I'm blind!" 590

STEPDAUGHTER: And when she doesn't close her eyes any more? What then? When she doesn't feel the need to hide from herself any more, to shut her eyes and hide her own shame. When she can see instead, dispassionately and dry-eyed this blushing shame of a man who has blinded himself, who is without love. What then? Oh, then what disgust, what utter disgust she feels for all these intellectual complications, for all this philosophy that points to the bestiality of man and then tries to defend him, to excuse him . . . I can't listen to him, sir. Because when a man says he needs to "sim- 600 plify" life like this—reducing it to bestiality—and throws away every human scrap of innocent desire, genuine feeling, idealism, duty, modesty, shame, then there's nothing more contemptible and nauseating than his remorse—crocodile tears!

PRODUCER: Let's get to the point, let's get to the point. This is all chat.

FATHER: Right then! But a fact is like a sack—it won't stand up if it's empty. To make it stand up, first you have to put in it 610 all the reasons and feelings that caused it in the first place. I couldn't possibly have known that when that fellow died they'd come back here, that they were desperately poor and that the Mother had gone out to work as a dressmaker, nor that she'd gone to work for Madame Pace, of all people.

STEPDAUGHTER: She's a very high-class dressmaker—you must understand that. She apparently has only high-class customers, but she has arranged things carefully so that these high-class customers in fact serve her—they give her a respectable front . . . without spoiling things for the other 620 ladies at the shop, who are not quite so high-class at all.

MOTHER: Believe me, sir, the idea never entered my head that the old hag gave me work because she had an eye on my daughter . . .

STEPDAUGHTER: Poor Mummy! Do you know what that woman would do when I took back the work that my mother had been doing? She would point out how the dress had been ruined by giving it to my mother to sew: she bargained, she grumbled. So, you see, I paid for it, while this poor woman here thought she was sacrificing herself for me and these 630 two children, sewing dresses all night for Madame Pace.

(The ACTORS make gestures and noises of disgust.)

PRODUCER: (quickly) And there one day, you met . . .

STEPDAUGHTER: (pointing at the FATHER) Yes, him. Oh, he was an old customer of hers! What a scene that's going to be, superb!

FATHER: With her, the mother, arriving—

STEPDAUGHTER: (quickly, viciously)—Almost in time!

FATHER: (crying out)—No, just in time, just in time! Because, luckily, I found out who she was in time. And I took them all back to my house, sir. Can you imagine the situation now, 640 for the two of us living in the same house? She, just as you see her here: and I, not able to look her in the face.

STEPDAUGHTER: It's so absurd! Do you think it's possible for me, sir, after what happened at Madame Pace's, to pretend that I'm a modest little miss, well brought up and virtuous just so that I can fit in with his damned pretensions to a "sound moral healthiness"?

FATHER: This is the real drama for me; the belief that we all, you see, think of ourselves as one single person: but it's not true: each of us is several different people, and all these peo- 650 ple live inside us. With one person we seem like this and with another we seem very different. But we always have the illusion of being the same person for everybody and of always being the same person in everything we do. But it's not true! It's not true! We find this out for ourselves very clearly when by some terrible chance we're suddenly stopped in the middle of doing something and we're left dangling there, suspended. We realise then, that every part of us was not involved in what we'd been doing and that it would be a dreadful injustice of other people to judge us only by this 660 one action as we dangle there, hanging in chains, fixed for

all eternity, as if the whole of one's personality were summed up in that single, interrupted action. Now do you understand this girl's treachery? She accidentally found me somewhere I shouldn't have been, doing something I shouldn't have been doing! She discovered a part of me that shouldn't have existed for her: and now she wants to fix on me a reality that I should never have had to assume for her: it came from a single brief and shameful moment in my life. This is what hurts me most of all. And you'll see that the play will make a tremendous impact from this idea of mine. But 670 then, there's the position of the others. His . . . (Pointing to the SON.)

SON: (shrugging his shoulders scornfully) Leave me out of it. I don't come into this.

FATHER: Why don't you come into this?

SON: I don't come into it and I don't want to come into it, because you know perfectly well that I wasn't intended to be mixed up with you lot.

STEPDAUGHTER: We're vulgar, common people, you see! He's a fine gentleman. But you've probably noticed that every 680 now and then I look at him contemptuously, and when I do, he lowers his eyes—he knows the harm he's done me.

SON: (not looking at her) I have?

STEPDAUGHTER: Yes, you. It's your fault, dearie, that I went on the streets! Your fault! (Movement of horror from the ACTORS.) Did you or didn't you, with your attitude, deny us— I won't say the intimacy of your home—but that simple hospitality that makes guests feel comfortable? We were intruders who had come to invade the country of your "legitimacy"! (Turning to the PRODUCER.) I'd like you to have seen 690 some of the little scenes that went on between him and me, sir. He says that I tyrannised over everyone. But don't you see? It was because of the way he treated us. He called it "vile" that I should insist on the right we had to move into his house with my mother—and she's his mother too. And I went into the house as its mistress.

SON: (slowly coming forward) They're really enjoying themselves, aren't they, sir? It's easy when they all gang up against me. But try to imagine what happened: one fine day, there is a son sitting quietly at home and he sees arrive as 700 bold as brass, a young woman like this, who cheekily asks for his father, and heaven knows what business she has with him. Then he sees her come back with the same brazen look in her eye accompanied by that little girl there: and he sees her treat his father—without knowing why—in a most ambiguous and insolent way—asking him for money in a tone that leads one to suppose he really ought to give it, because he is obliged to do so.

FATHER: But I was obliged to do so: I owed it to your mother.

SON: And how was I to know that? When had I ever seen her 710 before? When had I ever heard her mentioned? Then one day I see her come in with her (Pointing at the STEPDAUGHTER.), that boy and that little girl: they say to me, "Oh, didn't you know? This is your mother, too." Little by little I began to understand, mostly from her attitude (Points to STEPDAUGHTER.) why they'd come to live in the house so suddenly. I can't and I won't say what I feel, and what I think. I wouldn't even like to confess it to myself. So I can't take any active part in this. Believe me, sir, I am a character who has not been fully developed dramatically, and I feel 720 uncomfortable, most uncomfortable, in their company. So please leave me out of it.

FATHER: What! But it's precisely because you feel like this . . .

SON: *(violently exasperated)* How do you know what I feel? When have you ever bothered yourself about me?

FATHER: All right! I admit it! But isn't that a situation in itself? This withdrawing of yourself, it's cruel to me and to your mother: when she came back to the house, seeing you almost for the first time, not recognising you, but know-730  ing that you're her own son . . . *(Turning to point out the* MOTHER *to the* PRODUCER.*)* There, look at her: she's weeping.

STEPDAUGHTER: *(angrily, stamping her foot)* Like the fool she is!

FATHER: *(quickly pointing at the* STEPDAUGHTER *to the* PRODUCER*)* She can't stand that young man, you know. *(Turning and referring to the* SON.*)* He says that he doesn't come into it, but he's really the pivot of the action! Look here at this little boy, who clings to his mother all the time, fright-740  ened, humiliated. And it's because of him over there! Perhaps this little boy's problem is the worst of all: he feels an outsider, more than the others do; he feels so mortified, so humiliated just being in the house,—because it's charity, you see. *(Quietly.)* He's like his father: timid; he doesn't say anything . . .

PRODUCER: It's not a good idea at all, using him: you don't know what a nuisance children are on the stage.

FATHER: He won't need to be on the stage for long. Nor will the little girl—she's the first to go.

750 PRODUCER: That's good! Yes. I tell you all this interests me—it interests me very much. I'm sure we've the material here for a good play.

STEPDAUGHTER: *(trying to push herself in)* With a character like me you have!

FATHER: *(driving her off, wanting to hear what the* PRODUCER *has decided)* You stay out of it!

PRODUCER: *(going on, ignoring the interruption)* It's new, yes.

FATHER: Oh, it's absolutely new!

PRODUCER: You've got a nerve, though, haven't you, coming760  here and throwing it at me like this?

FATHER: I'm sure you understand. Born as we are for the stage . . .

PRODUCER: Are you amateur actors?

FATHER: No! I say we are born for the stage because . . .

PRODUCER: Come on now! You're an old hand at this, at acting!

FATHER: No I'm not. I only act, as everyone does, the part in life that he's chosen for himself, or that others have chosen for him. And you can see that sometimes my own passion gets a bit out of hand, a bit theatrical, as it does with770  all of us.

PRODUCER: Maybe, maybe . . . But you do see, don't you, that without an author . . . I could give you someone's address . . .

FATHER: Oh no! Look here! You do it.

PRODUCER: Me? What are you talking about?

FATHER: Yes, you. Why not?

PRODUCER: Because I've never written anything!

FATHER: Well, why not start now, if you don't mind my suggesting it? There's nothing to it. Everybody's doing it. And780  your job is even easier, because we're here, all of us, alive before you.

PRODUCER: That's not enough.

FATHER: Why isn't it enough? When you've seen us live our drama . . .

PRODUCER: Perhaps so. But we'll still need someone to write it.

FATHER: Only to write it down, perhaps, while it happens in front of him—live—scene by scene. It'll be enough to sketch it out simply first and then run through it.

PRODUCER: *(coming back up, tempted by the idea)* Do you know I'm almost tempted . . . just for fun . . . it might work. 790

FATHER: Of course it will. You'll see what wonderful scenes will come right out of it! I could tell you what they will be!

PRODUCER: You tempt me . . . you tempt me! We'll give it a chance. Come with me to the office. *(Turning to the* ACTORS.*)* Take a break: but don't go far away. Be back in a quarter of an hour or twenty minutes. *(To the* FATHER.*)* Let's see, let's try it out. Something extraordinary might come out of this.

FATHER: Of course it will! Don't you think it'd be better if the others came too? *(Indicating the other* CHARACTERS.*)*       800

PRODUCER: Yes, come on, come on. *(Going, then turning to speak to the* ACTORS.*)* Don't forget: don't be late: back in a quarter of an hour.

*(The* PRODUCER *and the* SIX CHARACTERS *cross the stage and go. The* ACTORS *look at each other in astonishment.)*

LEADING ACTOR: Is he serious? What's he going to do?

YOUNG ACTOR: I think he's gone round the bend.

ANOTHER ACTOR: Does he expect to make up a play in five minutes?

YOUNG ACTOR: Yes, like the old actors in the commedia del'arte!

LEADING ACTRESS: Well if he thinks I'm going to appear in that 810 sort of nonsense . . .

YOUNG ACTOR: Nor me!

FOURTH ACTOR: I should like to know who they are.

THIRD ACTOR: Who do you think? They're probably escaped lunatics—or crooks.

YOUNG ACTOR: And is he taking them seriously?

YOUNG ACTRESS: It's vanity. The vanity of seeing himself as an author.

LEADING ACTOR: I've never heard of such a thing! If the theatre, ladies and gentlemen, is reduced to this . . .      820

FIFTH ACTOR: I'm enjoying it!

THIRD ACTOR: Really? We shall have to wait and see what happens next I suppose.

*(Talking, they leave the stage. Some go out through the back door, some to the dressing-rooms.)*
*(The Curtain stays up.)*
*(The interval lasts twenty minutes.)*

### —ACT TWO—

*The theatre warning-bell sounds to call the audience back. From the dressing-rooms, the door at the back and even from the auditorium, the* ACTORS, *the* STAGE MANAGER, *the* STAGE HANDS, *the* PROMPTER, *the* PROPERTY MAN *and the* PRODUCER, *accompanied by the* SIX CHARACTERS *all come back on to the stage.*

*The house lights go out and the stage lights come on again.*

PRODUCER: Come on, everybody! Are we all here? Quiet now!

Listen! Let's get started! Stage manager?

STAGE MANAGER: Yes, I'm here.

PRODUCER: Give me that little parlour setting, will you? A couple of plain flats and a door flat will do. Hurry up with it!

(*The* STAGE MANAGER *runs off to order someone to do this immediately and at the same time the* PRODUCER *is making arrangements with the* PROPERTY MAN, *the* PROMPTER, *and the* ACTORS: *the two flats and the door flat are painted in pink and gold stripes.*)

830 PRODUCER: (*to* PROPERTY MAN) Go see if we have a sofa in stock.

PROPERTY MAN: Yes, there's that green one.

STEPDAUGHTER: No, no, not a green one! It was yellow, yellow velvet with flowers on it: it was enormous! And so comfortable!

PROPERTY MAN: We haven't got one like that.

PRODUCER: It doesn't matter! Give me whatever there is.

STEPDAUGHTER: What do you mean, it doesn't matter? It was Mme. Pace's famous sofa.

PRODUCER: It's only for a rehearsal! Please, don't interfere. (*To* 840 *the* STAGE MANAGER.) Oh, and see if there's a shop window, will you—preferably a long, low one.

STEPDAUGHTER: And a little table, a little mahogany table for the blue envelope.

STAGE MANAGER: (*to the* PRODUCER) There's that little gold one.

PRODUCER: That'll do—bring it.

FATHER: A mirror!

STEPDAUGHTER: And a screen! A screen, please, or I won't be able to manage, will I?

850 STAGE MANAGER: All right. We've lots of big screens, don't you worry.

PRODUCER: (*to* STEPDAUGHTER) Then don't you want some coat-hangers and some clothes racks?

STEPDAUGHTER: Yes, lots of them, lots of them.

PRODUCER: (*to the* STAGE MANAGER). See how many there are and have them brought up.

STAGE MANAGER: Right; I'll see to it.

(*The* STAGE MANAGER *goes off to do it: and while the* PRODUCER *is talking to the* PROMPTER, *the* CHARACTERS *and the* ACTORS, *the* STAGE MANAGER *is telling the* SCENE SHIFTERS *where to set up the furniture they have brought.*)

PRODUCER: (*to the* PROMPTER) Now you, go sit down, will you? Look, this is an outline of the play, act by act. (*He hands him* 860 *several sheets of paper.*) But you'll need to be on your toes.

PROMPTER: Shorthand?

PRODUCER: (*pleasantly surprised*) Oh, good! You know shorthand?

PROMPTER: I don't know much about prompting, but I do know about shorthand.

PRODUCER: Thank God for that anyway! (*He turns to a* STAGE HAND.) Go fetch me some paper from my office—lots of it—as much as you can find!

(*The* STAGE HAND *goes running off and then comes back shortly with a bundle of paper that he gives to the* PROMPTER.)

PRODUCER: (*crossing to the* PROMPTER) Follow the scenes, one 870 after another, as they are played and try to get the lines

down . . . at least the most important ones. (*Then turning to the* ACTORS.) Get out of the way everybody! Here, go over to the prompt side (*Pointing to stage left.*) and pay attention!

LEADING ACTRESS: But, excuse me, we . . .

PRODUCER: (*anticipating her*) You won't be expected to improvise, don't worry!

LEADING ACTOR: Then what are we expected to do?

PRODUCER: Nothing! Just go over there, listen and watch. You'll all be given your parts later written out. Right now we're going to rehearse, as well as we can. And they will be 880 doing the rehearsal. (*He points to the* CHARACTERS.)

FATHER: (*rather bewildered, as if he had fallen from the clouds into the middle of the confusion on the stage*) We are? Excuse me, but what do you mean, a rehearsal?

PRODUCER: I mean a rehearsal—a rehearsal for the benefit of the actors. (*Pointing to the* ACTORS.)

FATHER: But if we are the characters . . .

PRODUCER: That's right, you're "the characters": but characters don't act here, my dear chap. It's actors who act here. The characters are there in the script—(*Pointing to the* 890 PROMPTER.) that's when there is a script.

FATHER: That's the point! Since there isn't one and you have the luck to have the characters alive in front of you . . .

PRODUCER: Great! You want to do everything yourselves, do you? To act your own play, to produce your own play!

FATHER: Well yes, just as we are.

PRODUCER: That would be an experience for us, I can tell you!

LEADING ACTOR: And what about us? What would we be doing then?

PRODUCER: Don't tell me you think you know how to act! Don't 900 make me laugh! (*The* ACTORS *in fact laugh.*) There you are, you see, you've made them laugh. (*Then remembering.*) But let's get back to the point! We need to cast the play. Well, that's easy: it almost casts itself. (*To the* SECOND ACTRESS.) You, the mother. (*To the* FATHER.) You'll need to give her a name.

FATHER: Amalia.

PRODUCER: But that's the real name of your wife isn't it? We can't use her real name.

FATHER: But why not? That is her name . . . But perhaps if this 910 lady is to play the part . . . (*Indicating the* ACTRESS *vaguely with a wave of his hand.*) I think of her as Amalia . . . (*Pointing to the* MOTHER.) But do as you like . . . (*A little confused.*) I don't know what to say . . . I'm already starting to . . . how can I explain it . . . to sound false, my own words sound like someone else's.

PRODUCER: Now don't worry yourself about it, don't worry about it at all. We'll work out the right tone of voice. As for the name, if you want it to be Amalia, then Amalia it shall be: or we can find another. For the moment we'll refer to the 920 characters like this: (*To the* YOUNG ACTOR, *the juvenile lead.*) you are The Son. (*To the* LEADING ACTRESS.) You, of course, are The Stepdaughter.

STEPDAUGHTER: (*excitedly*) What did you say? That woman is me? (*Bursts into laughter.*)

PRODUCER: (*angrily*) What are you laughing at?

LEADING ACTRESS: (*indignantly*) Nobody has ever dared to laugh at me before! Either you treat me with respect or I'm walking out! (*Starting to go.*)

STEPDAUGHTER: I'm sorry. I wasn't really laughing at you.     930

PRODUCER: (*to the* STEPDAUGHTER) You should feel proud to be played by . . .

LEADING ACTRESS: (*quickly, scornfully*) . . . that woman!

STEPDAUGHTER: But I wasn't thinking about her, honestly. I was thinking about me: I can't see myself in you at all . . . you're not a bit like me!

FATHER: Yes, that's right: you see, our meaning . . .

PRODUCER: What are you talking about, "our meaning"? Do you think you have exclusive rights to what you represent? 940 Do you think it can only exist inside you? Not a bit of it!

FATHER: What? Don't we even have our own meaning?

PRODUCER: Not a bit of it! Whatever you mean is only material here, to which the actors give form and body, voice and gesture, and who, through their art, have given expression to much better material than what you have to offer: yours is really very trivial and if it stands up on the stage, the credit, believe me, will all be due to my actors.

FATHER: I don't dare to contradict you. But you for your part, must believe me—it doesn't seem trivial to us. We are suf-950 fering terribly now, with these bodies, these faces . . .

PRODUCER: (*interrupting impatiently*) Yes, well, the make-up will change that, make-up will change that, at least as far as the faces are concerned.

FATHER: Yes, but the voices, the gestures . . .

PRODUCER: That's enough! You can't come on the stage here as yourselves. It is our actors who will represent you here: and let that be the end of it!

FATHER: I understand that. But now I think I see why our author who saw us alive as we are here now, didn't want to put 960 us on the stage. I don't want to offend your actors. God forbid that I should! But I think that if I saw myself represented . . . by I don't know whom . . .

LEADING ACTOR: (*rising majestically and coming forward, followed by a laughing group of* YOUNG ACTRESSES) By me, if you don't object.

FATHER: (*respectfully, smoothly*) I shall be honoured, sir. (*He bows.*) But I think, that no matter how hard this gentleman works with all his will and all his art to identify himself with me . . . (*He stops, confused.*)

970 LEADING ACTOR: Yes, go on.

FATHER: Well, I was saying the performance he will give, even if he is made up to look like me . . . I mean with the difference in our appearance . . . (*All the* ACTORS *laugh.*) it will be difficult for it to be a performance of me as I really am. It will be more like—well, not just because of his figure—it will be more an interpretation of what I am, what he believes me to be, and not how I know myself to be. And it seems to me that this should be taken into account by those who are going to comment on us.

980 PRODUCER: So you are already worrying about what the critics will say, are you? And I'm still waiting to get this thing started! The critics can say what they like: and we'll worry about putting on the play. If we can! (*Stepping out of the group and looking around.*) Come on, come on! Is the scene set for us yet? (*To the* ACTORS *and* CHARACTERS.) Out of the way! Let's have a look at it. (*Climbing down off the stage.*) Don't let's waste any more time. (*To the* STEPDAUGHTER.) Does it look all right to you?

STEPDAUGHTER: What? That? I don't recognise it at all.

990 PRODUCER: Good God! Did you expect us to reconstruct the room at the back of Mme. Pace's shop here on the stage? (*To the* FATHER.) Did you say the room had flowered wallpaper?

FATHER: White, yes.

PRODUCER: Well it's not white: it's striped. That sort of thing doesn't matter at all! As for the furniture, it looks to me as if we have nearly everything we need. Move that little table a bit further downstage. (*A* STAGE HAND *does it. To the* PROPERTY MAN.) Go and fetch an envelope, pale blue if you can find one, and give it to that gentleman there. (*Pointing to the* 1000 FATHER.)

STAGE HAND: An envelope for letters?

PRODUCER: }
FATHER: } Yes, an envelope for letters!

STAGE HAND: Right. (*He goes off.*)

PRODUCER: Now then, come on! The first scene is the young lady's. (*The* LEADING ACTRESS *comes to the centre.*) No, no, not yet. I said the young lady's. (*He points to the* STEPDAUGHTER.) You stay there and watch.

STEPDAUGHTER: (*adding quickly*) . . . how I bring it to life. 1010

LEADING ACTRESS: (*resenting this*) I shall know how to bring it to life, don't you worry, when I am allowed to.

PRODUCER: (*his head in his hands*) Ladies, please, no more arguments! Now then. The first scene is between the young lady and Mme Pace. Oh! (*Worried, turning round and looking out into the auditorium.*) Where is Mme. Pace?

FATHER: She isn't here with us.

PRODUCER: So what do we do now?

FATHER: But she is real. She's real too!

PRODUCER: All right. So where is she? 1020

FATHER: May I deal with this? (*Turns to the* ACTRESSES.) Would each of you ladies be kind enough to lend me a hat, a coat, a scarf or something?

ACTRESSES: (*some are surprised or amused*) What? My scarf? A coat? What's he want my hat for? What are you wanting to do with them? (*All the* ACTRESSES *are laughing.*)

FATHER: Oh, nothing much, just hang them up here on the racks for a minute or two. Perhaps someone would be kind enough to lend me a coat?

ACTORS: Just a coat? Come on, more! The man must be mad. 1030

AN ACTRESS: What for? Only my coat?

FATHER: Yes, to hang up here, just for a moment. I'm very grateful to you. Do you mind?

ACTRESSES: (*taking off various hats, coats, scarves, laughing and going to hang them on the racks*) Why not? Here you are. I really think it's crazy. Is it to dress the set?

FATHER: Yes, exactly. It's to dress the set.

PRODUCER: Would you mind telling me what you are doing?

FATHER: Yes, of course: perhaps, if we dress the set better, she will be drawn by the articles of her trade and, who knows, 1040 she may even come to join us . . . (*He invites them to watch the door at the back of the set.*) Look! Look!

(*The door at the back opens and* MME. PACE *takes a few steps downstage: she is a gross old harridan wearing a ludicrous carroty-coloured wig with a single red rose stuck in at one side, Spanish fashion: garishly made-up: in a vulgar but stylish red silk dress, holding an ostrich-feather fan in one hand and a cigarette between two fingers in the other. At the sight of this Apparition, the* ACTORS *and the* PRODUCER *immediately jump off the stage with cries of fear, leaping down into the auditorium and up the aisles. The* STEPDAUGHTER, *however, runs across to* MME. PACE, *and greets her respectfully, as if she were the mistress.)*

STEPDAUGHTER: *(running across to her)* Here she is! Here she is!

FATHER: *(smiling broadly)* It's her! What did I tell you? Here she is!

PRODUCER: *(recovering from his shock, indignantly)* What sort of trick is this?

1050  LEADING ACTOR: *(almost at the same time as the others)* What the hell is happening?

JUVENILE LEAD: Where on earth did they get that extra from?

YOUNG ACTRESS: They were keeping her hidden!

LEADING ACTRESS: It's a game, a conjuring trick!

FATHER: Wait a minute! Why do you want to spoil a miracle by being factual. Can't you see this is a miracle of reality, that is born, brought to life, lured here, reproduced, just for the sake of this scene, with more right to be alive here than you have? Perhaps it has more truth than you have yourselves. Which actress can improve on Mme. Pace there? Well?
1060  That is the real Mme. Pace. You must admit that the actress who plays her will be less true than she is herself—and there she is in person! Look! My daughter recognised her straight away and went to meet her. Now watch—just watch this scene.

*(Hesitantly, the* PRODUCER *and the* ACTORS *move back to their original places on the stage.)*
*(But the scene between the* STEPDAUGHTER *and* MME. PACE *has already begun while the* ACTORS *were protesting and the* FATHER *explaining: it is being played under their breaths, very quietly, very naturally, in a way that is obviously impossible on stage. So when the* ACTORS' *attention is recalled by the* FATHER *they turn and see that* MME. PACE, *has just put her hand under the* STEPDAUGHTER's *chin to make her lift her head up: they also hear her speak in a way that is unintelligible to them. They watch and listen hard for a few moments, then they start to make fun of them.)*

PRODUCER: Well?

LEADING ACTOR: What's she saying?

LEADING ACTRESS: Can't hear a thing!

JUVENILE LEAD: Louder! Speak up!

STEPDAUGHTER: *(leaving* MME. PACE *who has an astonishing*
1070  *smile on her face, and coming down to the* ACTORS*)* Louder? What do you mean, "Louder"? What we're talking about you can't talk about loudly. I could shout about it a moment ago to embarrass him *(Pointing to the* FATHER.) to shame him and to get my own back on him! But it's a different matter for Mme. Pace. It would mean prison for her.

PRODUCER: What the hell are you on about? Here in the theatre you have to make yourself heard! Don't you see that? We can't hear you even from here, and we're on the stage with you! Imagine what it would be like with an audience out front! You need to make the scene go! And after all, you
1080  would speak normally to each other when you're alone, and you will be, because we shan't be here anyway. I mean we're only here because it's a rehearsal. So just imagine that there you are in the room at the back of the shop, and there's no one to hear you.

*(The* STEPDAUGHTER, *with a knowing smile, wags her finger and her head rather elegantly, as if to say no.)*

PRODUCER: Why not?

STEPDAUGHTER: *(mysteriously, whispering loudly)* Because there is someone who will hear if she speaks normally.

*(Pointing to* MME. PACE.*)*

PRODUCER: *(anxiously)* You're not going to make someone else appear are you?                                                    1090

*(The* ACTORS *get ready to dive off the stage again.)*

FATHER: No, no. She means me. I ought to be over there, waiting behind the door: and Mme. Pace knows I'm there, so excuse me will you: I'll go there now so that I shall be ready for my entrance.

*(He goes towards the back of the stage.)*

PRODUCER: *(stopping him)* No, no wait a minute! You must remember the stage conventions! Before you can go on to that part . . .

STEPDAUGHTER: *(interrupts him)* Oh yes, let's get on with that part. Now! Now! I'm dying to do that scene. If he wants to go through it now, I'm ready!                                          1100

PRODUCER: *(shouting)* But before that we must have, clearly stated, the scene between you and her. *(Pointing to* MME. PACE.*)* Do you see?

STEPDAUGHTER: Oh God! She's only told me what you already know, that my mother's needlework is badly done again, the dress is spoilt and that I shall have to be patient if I want her to go on helping us out of our mess.

MME. PACE: *(coming forward, with a great air of importance)* Ah, yes, sir, for that I do not wish to make a profit, to make advantage.                                                        1110

PRODUCER: *(half frightened)* What? Does she really speak like that?

*(All the* ACTORS *burst out laughing.)*

STEPDAUGHTER: *(laughing too)* Yes, she speaks like that, half in Spanish, in the silliest way imaginable!

MME. PACE: Ah it is not good manners that you laugh at me when I make myself to speak, as I can, English, senor.

PRODUCER: No, no, you're right! Speak like that, please speak like that, madam. It'll be marvellous. Couldn't be better! It'll add a little touch of comedy to a rather crude situation. Speak like that! It'll be great!                                        1120

STEPDAUGHTER: Great! Why not? When you hear a proposition made in that sort of accent, it'll almost seem like a joke, won't it? Perhaps you'll want to laugh when you hear that there's an "old senor" who wants to "amuse himself with me"—isn't that right, Madame?

MME. PACE: Not so old . . . but not quite young, no? But if he is not to your taste . . . he is, how you say, discreet!

*(The* MOTHER *leaps up, to the astonishment and dismay of the* ACTORS *who had not been paying any attention to her, so that when she shouts out they are startled and then smilingly restrain her: however she has already snatched off* MME. PACE's *wig and flung it on the floor.)*

MOTHER: You witch! Witch! Murderess! Oh, my daughter!

STEPDAUGHTER: *(running across and taking hold of the*

1130    MOTHER) No! No! Mother! Please!

FATHER: *(running across to her as well)* Calm yourself, calm yourself! Come and sit down.

MOTHER: Get her away from here!

STEPDAUGHTER: *(to the PRODUCER who has also crossed to her)* My mother can't bear to be in the same place with her.

FATHER: *(also speaking quietly to the PRODUCER)* They can't possibly be in the same place! That's why she wasn't with us when we first came, do you see! If they meet, everything's given away from the very beginning.

1140    PRODUCER: It's not important, that's not important! This is only a first run-through at the moment! It's all useful stuff, even if it is confused. I'll sort it all out later. *(Turning to the MOTHER and taking her to sit down on her chair.)* Come on my dear, take it easy, take it easy: come and sit down again.

STEPDAUGHTER: Go on, Mme. Pace.

MME. PACE: *(offended)* Oh no, thank-you! I no longer do nothing here with your mother present.

STEPDAUGHTER: Get on with it, bring in this "old senor" who wants to "amuse himself with me"! *(Turning majestically to*
1150    *the others.)* You see, this next scene has got to be played out—we must do it now. *(To MME. PACE.)* Oh, you can go!

MME. PACE: Ah, I go, I go—I go! Most probably I go!

*(She leaves banging her wig back into place, glaring furiously at the ACTORS who applaud her exit, laughing loudly.)*

STEPDAUGHTER: *(to the FATHER)* Now you come on! No, you don't need to go off again! Come back! Pretend you've just come in! Look, I'm standing here with my eyes on the ground, modestly—well, come on, speak up! Use that special sort of voice, like somebody who has just come in. "Good afternoon, my dear."

PRODUCER: *(off the stage by now)* Look here, who's the direc-
1160    tor here, you or me? *(To the FATHER who looks uncertain and bewildered.)* Go on, do as she says: go upstage—no, no don't bother to make an entrance. Then come down stage again.

*(The FATHER does as he is told, half mesmerised. He is very pale but already involved in the reality of his recreated life, smiles as he draws near the back of the stage, almost if he genuinely is not aware of the drama that is about to sweep over him. The ACTORS are immediately intent on the scene that is beginning now.)*

THE SCENE

FATHER: *(coming forward with a new note in his voice)* Good afternoon, my dear.

STEPDAUGHTER: *(her head down trying to hide her fright)* Good afternoon.

FATHER: *(studying her a little under the brim of her hat which partly hides her face from him and seeing that she is very*
1170    *young, he exclaims to himself a little complacently and a little guardedly because of the danger of being compromised in a risky adventure)* Ah . . . but . . . tell me, this won't be the first time, will it? The first time you've been here?

STEPDAUGHTER: No, sir.

FATHER: You've been here before? *(And after the STEPDAUGH-TER has nodded an answer.)* More than once? *(He waits for her reply: tries again to look at her under the brim of her hat:*

*smiles: then says.)* Well then . . . it shouldn't be too . . . May I take off your hat?

STEPDAUGHTER: *(quickly, to stop him, unable to conceal her* 1180 *shudder of fear and disgust)* No, don't! I'll do it!

*(She takes it off unsteadily.)*

*(The MOTHER watches the scene intently with the SON and the two smaller children who cling close to her all the time: they make a group on one side of the stage opposite the ACTORS. She follows the words and actions of the FATHER and the STEP-DAUGHTER in this scene with a variety of expressions on her face—sadness, dismay, anxiety, horror: sometimes she turns her face away and sobs.)*

MOTHER: Oh God! Oh God!

FATHER: *(he stops as if turned to stone by the sobbing; then he goes on in the same tone of voice)* Here, give it to me. I'll hang it up for you. *(He takes the hat in his hand.)* But such a pretty, dear little head like yours should have a much smarter hat than this! Would you like to help me choose one, then, from these hats of Madame's hanging up here? Would you?

YOUNG ACTRESS: *(interrupting)* Be careful! Those are our hats! 1190

PRODUCER: *(quickly and angrily)* For God's sake, shut up! Don't try to be funny! We're rehearsing! *(Turns back to the STEPDAUGHTER.)* Please go on, will you, from where you were interrupted.

STEPDAUGHTER: *(going on)* No, thank you, sir.

FATHER: Oh, don't say no to me please! Say you'll have one—to please me. Isn't this a pretty one—look! And then it will please Madame too, you know. She's put them out here on purpose, of course.

STEPDAUGHTER: No, look, I could never wear it.                 1200

FATHER: Are you thinking of what they would say at home when you went in wearing a new hat? Goodness me! Don't you know what to do? Shall I tell you what to say at home?

STEPDAUGHTER: *(furiously, nearly exploding)* That's not why! I couldn't wear it because . . . as you can see: you should have noticed it before. *(Indicating her black dress.)*

FATHER: You're in mourning! Oh, forgive me. You're right, I see that now. Please forgive me. Believe me, I'm really very sorry.

STEPDAUGHTER: *(gathering all her strength and making herself* 1210 *overcome her contempt and revulsion)* That's enough. Don't go on, that's enough. I ought to be thanking you and not letting you blame yourself and get upset. Don't think any more about what I told you, please. And I should do the same. *(Forcing herself to smile and adding.)* I should try to forget that I'm dressed like this.

PRODUCER: *(interrupting, turning to the PROMPTER in the box and jumping up on the stage again)* Hold it, hold it! Don't put that last line down, leave it out. *(Turning to the FATHER and the STEPDAUGHTER.)* It's going well! It's going well! 1220 *(Then to the FATHER alone.)* Then we'll put in there the bit that we talked about. *(To the ACTORS.)* That scene with the hats is good, isn't it?

STEPDAUGHTER: But the best bit is coming now! Why can't we get on with it?

PRODUCER: Just be patient, wait a minute. *(Turning and moving across to the ACTORS.)* Of course, it'll all have to be made a lot more light-hearted.

LEADING ACTOR: We shall have to play it a lot quicker, I think.

1230 LEADING ACTRESS: Of course: there's nothing particularly difficult in it. (*To the* LEADING ACTOR.) Shall we run through
it now?

LEADING ACTOR: Yes right . . . Shall we take it from my entrance? (*He goes to his position behind the door upstage.*)

PRODUCER: (*to the* LEADING ACTRESS) Now then, listen, imagine the scene between you and Mme. Pace is finished. I'll
write it up myself properly later on. You ought to be over
here I think—(*She goes the opposite way.*) Where are you
going now?

1240 LEADING ACTRESS: Just a minute, I want to get my hat—(*She
crosses to take her hat from the stand.*)

PRODUCER: Right, good, ready now? You are standing here
with your head down.

STEPDAUGHTER: (*very amused*) But she's not dressed in black!

LEADING ACTRESS: Oh, but I shall be, and I'll look a lot better
than you do, darling.

PRODUCER: (*to the* STEPDAUGHTER) Shut up, will you! Go over
there and watch! You might learn something! (*Clapping his
hands.*) Right! Come on! Quiet please! Take it from his en-
1250 trance.

(*He climbs off stage so that he can see better. The door opens
at the back of the set and the* LEADING ACTOR *enters with the
lively, knowing air of an ageing rouet. The playing of the following scene by the* ACTORS *must seem from the very beginning
to be something quite different from the earlier scene, but without having the faintest air of parody in it.*)
(*Naturally the* STEPDAUGHTER *and the* FATHER, *unable to see
themselves in the* LEADING ACTOR *and* LEADING ACTRESS, *hearing their words said by them, express their reactions in different ways, by gestures, or smiles or obvious protests so that we
are aware of their suffering, their astonishment, their disbelief.
The* PROMPTER'S *voice is heard clearly between every line in the
scene, telling the* ACTORS *what to say next.*)

LEADING ACTOR: Good afternoon, my dear.

FATHER: (*immediately, unable to restrain himself*) Oh, no!

(*The* STEPDAUGHTER, *watching the* LEADING ACTOR *enter this
way, bursts into laughter.*)

PRODUCER: (*furious*) Shut up, for God's sake! And don't you
dare laugh like that! We're never going to get anywhere at
this rate.

STEPDAUGHTER: (*coming to the front*) I'm sorry, I can't help it!
The lady stands exactly where you told her to stand and she
never moved. But if it were me and I heard someone say
good afternoon to me in that way and with a voice like that
1260 I should burst out laughing—so I did.

FATHER: (*coming down a little too*) Yes, she's right, the whole
manner, the voice . . .

PRODUCER: To hell with the manner and the voice! Get out of
the way, will you, and let me watch the rehearsal!

LEADING ACTOR: (*coming down stage*) If I have to play an old
man who has come to a knocking shop—

PRODUCER: Take no notice, ignore them. Go on please! It's
going well, it's going well! (*He waits for the* ACTOR *to begin
again*). Right, again!

1270 LEADING ACTOR: Good afternoon, my dear.

LEADING ACTRESS: Good afternoon.

LEADING ACTOR: (*copying the gestures of the* FATHER, *looking

under the brim of the hat, but expressing distinctly the two
emotions, first, complacent satisfaction and then anxiety*)
Ah! But tell me . . . this won't be the first time I hope.

FATHER: (*instinctively correcting him*) Not "I hope"—"will it,"
"will it."

PRODUCER: Say "will it"—and it's a question.

LEADING ACTOR: (*glaring at the* PROMPTER) I distinctly heard
him say "I hope." 1280

PRODUCER: So what? It's all the same, "I hope" or "isn't it." It
doesn't make any difference. Carry on, carry on. But perhaps it should still be a little bit lighter; I'll show you—watch
me! (*He climbs up on the stage again, and going back to the
entrance, he does it himself.*) Good afternoon, my dear.

LEADING ACTRESS: Good afternoon.

PRODUCER: Ah, tell me . . . (*He turns to the* LEADING ACTOR *to
make sure that he has seen the way he has demonstrated of
looking under the brim of the hat.*) You see—surprise . . .
anxiety and self-satisfaction. (*Then, starting again, he turns* 1290
*to the* LEADING ACTRESS.) This won't be the first time, will it?
The first time you've been here? (*Again turns to the* LEAD-
ING ACTOR, *questioningly.*) Right? (*To the* LEADING AC-
TRESS.) And then she says, "No, sir." (*Again to* LEADING
ACTOR.) See what I mean? More subtlety. (*And he climbs off
the stage.*)

LEADING ACTRESS: No, sir.

LEADING ACTOR: You've been here before? More than once?

PRODUCER: No, no, no! Wait for it, wait for it. Let her answer
first. "You've been here before?" 1300

(*The* LEADING ACTRESS *lifts her head a little, her eyes closed in
pain and disgust, and when the* PRODUCER *says "Now" she
nods her head twice.*)

STEPDAUGHTER: (*involuntarily*) Oh, my God! (*And she immediately claps her hand over her mouth to stifle her laughter.*)

PRODUCER: What now?

STEPDAUGHTER: (*quickly*) Nothing, nothing!

PRODUCER: (*to* LEADING ACTOR) Come on, then, now it's you.

LEADING ACTOR: More than once? Well then, it shouldn't be
too . . . May I take off your hat?

(*The* LEADING ACTOR *says this last line in such a way and adds
to it such a gesture that the* STEPDAUGHTER, *even with her hand
over her mouth trying to stop herself laughing, can't prevent a
noisy burst of laughter.*)

LEADING ACTRESS: (*indignantly turning*) I'm not staying any
longer to be laughed at by that woman!

LEADING ACTOR: Nor am I! That's the end—no more! 1310

PRODUCER: (*to* STEPDAUGHTER, *shouting*) Once and for all, will
you shut up! Shut up!

STEPDAUGHTER: Yes, I'm sorry . . . I'm sorry.

PRODUCER: You're an ill-mannered little bitch! That's what you
are! And you've gone too far this time!

FATHER: (*trying to interrupt*) Yes, you're right, she went too
far, but please forgive her . . .

PRODUCER: (*jumping on the stage*) Why should I forgive her?
Her behaviour is intolerable!

FATHER: Yes, it is, but the scene made such a peculiar impact 1320
on us . . .

PRODUCER: Peculiar? What do you mean peculiar? Why
peculiar?

FATHER: I'm full of admiration for your actors, for this gentle-man *(To the* LEADING ACTOR.*)* and this lady. *(To the* LEADING ACTRESS.*)* But, you see, well . . . they're not us!

PRODUCER: Right! They're not! They're actors!

FATHER: That's just the point—they're actors. And they are acting our parts very well, both of them. But that's what's 1330 different. However much they want to be the same as us, they're not.

PRODUCER: But why aren't they? What is it now?

FATHER: It's something to do with . . . being themselves, I sup-pose, not being us.

PRODUCER: Well we can't do anything about that! I've told you already. You can't play the parts yourselves.

FATHER: Yes, I know, I know . . .

PRODUCER: Right then. That's enough of that. *(Turning back to the* ACTORS.*)* We'll rehearse this later on our own, as we usu-1340 ally do. It's always a bad idea to have rehearsals with authors there! They're never satisfied. *(Turns back to the* FATHER *and the* STEPDAUGHTER.*)* Come on, let's get on with it; and let's see if it's possible to do it without laughing.

STEPDAUGHTER: I won't laugh any more, I won't really. My best bit's coming up now, you wait and see!

PRODUCER: Right: when you say "Don't think any more about what I told you, please. And I should do the same." *(Turning to the* FATHER.*)* then you come in immediately with the line "I understand, ah yes, I understand" and then 1350 you ask . . .

STEPDAUGHTER: *(interrupting)* Ask what? What does he ask?

PRODUCER: Why you're in mourning.

STEPDAUGHTER: No! No! That's not right! Look: when I said that I should try not to think about the way I was dressed, do you know what he said? "Well then, let's take it off, we'll take it off at once, shall we, your little black dress."

PRODUCER: That's great! That'll be wonderful! That'll bring the house down!

STEPDAUGHTER: But it's the truth!

1360 PRODUCER: The truth! Do me a favour will you? This is the the-atre you know! Truth's all very well up to a point but . . .

STEPDAUGHTER: What do you want to do then?

PRODUCER: You'll see! You'll see! Leave it all to me.

STEPDAUGHTER: No. No I won't. I know what you want to do! Out of my feeling of revulsion, out of all the vile and sordid reasons why I am what I am, you want to make a sugary lit-tle sentimental romance. You want him to ask me why I'm in mourning and you want me to reply with the tears run-ning down my face that it is only two months since my father 1370 died. No. No. I won't have it! He must say to me what he re-ally did say. "Well then, let's take it off, we'll take it off at once, shall we, your little black dress." And I, with my heart still grieving for my father's death only two months before, I went behind there, do you see? Behind that screen and with my fingers trembling with shame and loathing I took off the dress, unfastened my bra . . .

PRODUCER: *(his head in his hands)* For God's sake! What are you saying!

STEPDAUGHTER: *(shouting excitedly)* The truth! I'm telling you 1380 the truth!

PRODUCER: All right then. Now listen to me. I'm not denying it's the truth. Right. And believe me I understand your hor-ror, but you must see that we can't really put a scene like that on the stage.

STEPDAUGHTER: You can't? Then thanks very much. I'm not stopping here.

PRODUCER: No, listen . . .

STEPDAUGHTER: No, I'm going. I'm not stopping. The pair of you have worked it all out together, haven't you, what to put in the scene. Well, thank you very much! I understand 1390 everything now! He wants to get to the scene where he can talk about his spiritual torments but I want to show you my drama! Mine!

PRODUCER: *(shaking with anger)* Now we're getting to the real truth of it, aren't we? Your drama—yours! But it's not only yours, you know. It's drama for the other people as well! For him *(Pointing to the* FATHER.*)* and for your mother! You can't have one character coming on like you're doing, tram-pling over the others, taking over the play. Everything needs to be balanced and in harmony so that we can show what has 1400 to be shown! I know perfectly well that we've all got a life in-side us and that we all want to parade it in front of other peo-ple. But that's the difficulty, how to present only the bits that are necessary in relation to the other characters: and in the small amount we show, to hint at all the rest of the inner life of the character! I agree, it would be so much simpler, if each character, in a soliloquy or in a lecture could pour out to the audience what's bubbling away inside him. But that's not the way we work. *(In an indulgent, placating tone.)* You must restrain yourself, you see. And believe me, it's in your 1410 own interests: because you could so easily make a bad im-pression, with all this uncontrollable anger, this disgust and exasperation. That seems a bit odd, if you don't mind my saying so, when you've admitted that you'd been with other men at Mme. Pace's and more than once.

STEPDAUGHTER: I suppose that's true. But you know, all the other men were all him as far as I was concerned.

PRODUCER: *(not understanding)* Uum—? What? What are you talking about?

STEPDAUGHTER: If someone falls into evil ways, isn't the re-1420 sponsibility for all the evil which follows to be laid at the door of the person who caused the first mistake? And in my case, it's him, from before I was even born. Look at him: see if it isn't true.

PRODUCER: Right then! What about the weight of remorse he's carrying? Isn't that important? Then, give him the chance to show it to us.

STEPDAUGHTER: But how? How on earth can he show all his long-suffering remorse, all his moral torments as he calls them, if you don't let him show his horror when he finds me 1430 in his arms one fine day, after he had asked me to take my dress off, a black dress for my father who had just died: and he finds that I'm the child he used to go and watch as she came out of school, me, a woman now, and a woman he could buy. *(She says these last words in a voice trembling with emotion.)*

*(The* MOTHER, *hearing her say this, is overcome and at first gives way to stifled sobs: but then she bursts out into uncon-trollable crying. Everyone is deeply moved. There is a long pause.)*

STEPDAUGHTER: *(as soon as the* MOTHER *has quietened herself she goes on, firmly and thoughtfully)* At the moment we are here on our own and the public doesn't know about us. But 1440 tomorrow you will present us and our story in whatever way you choose, I suppose. But wouldn't you like to see the real drama? Wouldn't you like to see it explode into life, as it really did?

PRODUCER: Of course, nothing I'd like better, then I can use as much of it as possible.

STEPDAUGHTER: Then persuade my mother to leave.

MOTHER: (*rising and her quiet weeping changing to a loud cry*) No! No! Don't let her! Don't let her do it!

PRODUCER: But they're only doing it for me to watch—only for 1450 me, do you see?

MOTHER: I can't bear it, I can't bear it!

PRODUCER: But if it's already happened, I can't see what's the objection.

MOTHER: No! It's happening now, as well: it's happening all the time. I'm not acting my suffering! Can't you understand that? I'm alive and here now but I can never forget that terrible moment of agony, that repeats itself endlessly and vividly in my mind. And these two little children here, you've never heard them speak have you? That's because 1460 they don't speak any more, not now. They just cling to me all the time: they help to keep my grief alive, but they don't really exist for themselves any more, not for themselves. And she (*Indicating the* STEPDAUGHTER.) . . . she has gone away, left me completely, she's lost to me, lost . . . you see her here for one reason only: to keep perpetually before me, always real, the anguish and the torment I've suffered on her account.

FATHER: The eternal moment, as I told you, sir. She is here (*Indicating the* STEPDAUGHTER.) to keep me too in that mo- 1470 ment, trapped for all eternity, chained and suspended in that one fleeting shameful moment of my life. She can't give up her role and you cannot rescue me from it.

PRODUCER: But I'm not saying that we won't present that bit. Not at all! It will be the climax of the first act, when she (*He points to the* MOTHER.) surprises you.

FATHER: That's right, because that is the moment when I am sentenced: all our suffering should reach a climax in her cry. (*Again indicating the* MOTHER.)

STEPDAUGHTER: I can still hear it ringing in my ears! It was that 1480 cry that sent me mad! You can have me played just as you like: it doesn't matter! Dressed, too, if you want, so long as I can have at least an arm—only an arm—bare, because, you see, as I was standing like this (*She moves across to the* FATHER *and leans her head on his chest.*) with my head like this and my arms round his neck, I saw a vein, here in my arm, throbbing: and then it was almost as if that throbbing vein filled me with a shivering fear, and I shut my eyes tightly like this, like this and buried my head in his chest. (*Turning to the* MOTHER.) Scream, Mummy, scream. (*She buries her* 1490 *head in the* FATHER's *chest, and with her shoulders raised as if to try not to hear the scream, she speaks with a voice tense with suffering.*) Scream, as you screamed then!

MOTHER: (*coming forward to pull them apart*) No! She's my daughter! My daughter! (*Tearing her from him.*) You brute, you animal, she's my daughter! Can't you see she's my daughter?

PRODUCER: (*retreating as far as the footlights while the* ACTORS *are full of dismay*) Marvellous! Yes, that's great! And then curtain, curtain!

FATHER: (*running downstage to him, excitedly*) That's it, that's 1500 it! Because it really was like that!

PRODUCER: (*full of admiration and enthusiasm*) Yes, yes, that's got to be the curtain line! Curtain! Curtain!

(*At the repeated calls of the* PRODUCER, *the* STAGE MANAGER *lowers the curtain, leaving on the apron in front, the* PRODUCER *and the* FATHER.)

PRODUCER: (*looking up to heaven with his arms raised*). The idiots! I didn't mean now! The bloody idiots—dropping it in on us like that! (*To the* FATHER, *and lifting up a corner of the curtain.*) That's marvellous! Really marvellous! A terrific effect! We'll end the act like that! It's the best tag line I've heard for ages. What a First Act ending! I couldn't have done better if I'd written it myself! 1510

(*They go through the curtain together.*)

## —ACT THREE—

*When the curtain goes up we see that the* STAGE MANAGER *and* STAGE HANDS *have struck the first scene and have set another, a small garden fountain.*

*From one side of the stage the* ACTORS *come on and from the other the* CHARACTERS. *The* PRODUCER *is standing in the middle of the stage with his hand over his mouth, thinking.*

PRODUCER: (*after a short pause, shrugging his shoulders*) Well, then: let's get on to the second act! Leave it all to me, and everything will work out properly.

STEPDAUGHTER: This is where we go to live at his house (*Pointing to the* FATHER.) in spite of the objections of him over there. (*Pointing to the* SON.)

PRODUCER: (*getting impatient*) All right, all right! But leave it all to me, will you?

STEPDAUGHTER: Provided that you make it clear that he objected! 1520

MOTHER: (*from the corner, shaking her head*) That doesn't matter! The worse it was for us, the more he suffered from remorse.

PRODUCER: (*impatiently*) I know, I know! I'll take it all into account. Don't worry!

MOTHER: (*pleading*) To set my mind at rest, sir, please do make sure it's clear that I tried all I could—

STEPDAUGHTER: (*interrupting her scornfully and going on*)— to pacify me, to persuade me that this despicable creature wasn't worth making trouble about! (*To the* PRODUCER.) Go 1530 on, set her mind at rest, because it's true, she tried very hard. I'm having a whale of a time now! You can see, can't you, that the meeker she was and the more she tried to worm her way into his heart, the more lofty and distant he became! How's that for a dramatic situation!

PRODUCER: Do you think that we can actually begin the Second Act?

STEPDAUGHTER: I won't say another word! But you'll see that it won't be possible to play everything in the garden, like you want to do. 1540

PRODUCER: Why not?

STEPDAUGHTER: (*pointing to the* SON) Because to start with, he stays shut up in his room in the house all the time! And then all the scenes for this poor little devil of a boy happen in the house. I've told you once.

PRODUCER: Yes, I know that! But on the other hand we can't put up a notice to tell the audience where the scene is taking place, or change the set three or four times in each Act.

LEADING ACTOR: That's what they used to do in the good
1550  old days.

PRODUCER: Yes, when the audience was about as bright as that little girl over there!

LEADING ACTRESS: And it makes it easier to create an illusion.

FATHER: (*leaping up*) An illusion? For pity's sake don't talk about illusions! Don't use that word, it's especially hurtful to us!

PRODUCER: (*astonished*) And why, for God's sake?

FATHER: It's so hurtful, so cruel! You ought to have realised that!

1560 PRODUCER: What else should we call it? That's what we do here—create an illusion for the audience . . .

LEADING ACTOR: With our performance . . .

PRODUCER: A perfect illusion of reality!

FATHER: Yes, I know that, I understand. But on the other hand, perhaps you don't understand us yet. I'm sorry! But you see, for you and for your actors what goes on here on the stage is, quite rightly, well, it's only a game.

LEADING ACTRESS: (*interrupting indignantly*) A game! How dare you! We're not children! What happens here is serious!

1570 FATHER: I'm not saying that it isn't serious. And I mean, really, not just a game but an art, that tries, as you've just said, to create the perfect illusion of reality.

PRODUCER: That's right!

FATHER: Now try to imagine that we, as you see us here, (*He indicates himself and the other* CHARACTERS.) that we have no other reality outside this illusion.

PRODUCER: (*astonished and looking at the* ACTORS *with the same sense of bewilderment as they feel themselves*) What the hell are you talking about now?

1580 FATHER: (*after a short pause as he looks at them, with a faint smile*) Isn't it obvious? What other reality is there for us? What for you is an illusion you create, for us is our only reality. (*Brief pause. He moves towards the* PRODUCER *and goes on.*) But it's not only true for us, it's true for others as well, you know. Just think about it. (*He looks intently into the* PRODUCER's *eyes.*) Do you really know who you are? (*He stands pointing at the* PRODUCER.)

PRODUCER: (*a little disturbed but with a half smile*) What? Who I am? I am me!

1590 FATHER: What if I told you that that wasn't true: what if I told you that you were me?

PRODUCER: I would tell you that you were mad!

(*The* ACTORS *laugh.*)

FATHER: That's right, laugh! Because everything here is a game! (*To the* PRODUCER.) And yet you object when I say that it is only for a game that the gentleman there (*Pointing to the* LEADING ACTOR.) who is "himself" has to be "me," who, on the contrary, am "myself." You see, I've caught you in a trap.

(*The* ACTORS *start to laugh.*)

PRODUCER: Not again! We've heard all about this a little
1600  while ago.

FATHER: No, no. I didn't really want to talk about this. I'd like

you to forget about your game, (*Looking at the* LEADING ACTRESS *as if to anticipate what she will say.*) I'm sorry—your artistry! Your art!—that you usually pursue here with your actors; and I am going to ask you again in all seriousness, who are you?

PRODUCER: (*turning with a mixture of amazement and annoyance, to the* ACTORS) Of all the bloody nerve! A fellow who claims he is only a character comes and asks me who I am!

FATHER: (*with dignity but without annoyance*) A character, my 1610 dear sir, can always ask a man who he is, because a character really has a life of his own, a life full of his own specific qualities, and because of these he is always "someone." While a man—I'm not speaking about you personally, of course, but man in general—well, he can be an absolute "nobody."

PRODUCER: All right, all right! Well, since you've asked me, I'm the Director, the Producer—I'm in charge! Do you understand?

FATHER: (*half smiling, but gently and politely*) I'm only asking 1620 to try to find out if you really see yourself now in the same way that you saw yourself, for instance, once upon a time in the past, with all the illusions you had then, with everything inside and outside yourself as it seemed then—and not only seemed, but really was! Well then, look back on those illusions, those ideas that you don't have any more, on all those things that no longer seem the same to you. Don't you feel that not only this stage is falling away from under your feet but so is the earth itself, and that all these realities of today are going to seem tomorrow as if they had been an illusion? 1630

PRODUCER: So? What does that prove?

FATHER: Oh, nothing much. I only want to make you see that if we (*Pointing to himself and the other* CHARACTERS.) have no other reality outside our own illusion, perhaps you ought to distrust your own sense of reality: because whatever is a reality today, whatever you touch and believe in and that seems real for you today, is going to be—like the reality of yesterday—an illusion tomorrow.

PRODUCER: (*deciding to make fun of him*) Very good! So now you're saying that you as well as this play you're going to 1640 show me here, are more real than I am?

FATHER: (*very seriously*) There's no doubt about that at all.

PRODUCER: Is that so?

FATHER: I thought you'd realised that from the beginning.

PRODUCER: More real than I am?

FATHER: If your reality can change between today and tomorrow—

PRODUCER: But everybody knows that it can change, don't they? It's always changing! Just like everybody else's!

FATHER: (*crying out*) But ours doesn't change! Do you see? 1650 That's the difference! Ours doesn't change, it can't change, it can never be different, never, because it is already determined, like this, for ever, that's what's so terrible! We are an eternal reality. That should make you shudder to come near us.

PRODUCER: (*jumping up, suddenly struck by an idea, and standing directly in front of the* FATHER) Then I should like to know when anyone saw a character step out of his part and make a speech like you've done, proposing things, explaining things. Tell me when, will you? I've never seen it 1660 before.

FATHER: You've never seen it because an author usually hides all the difficulties of creating. When the characters are alive, really alive and standing in front of their author, he has only to follow their words, the actions that they suggest to him: and he must want them to be what they want to be: and it's his bad luck if he doesn't do what they want! When a character is born he immediately assumes such an independence even of his own author that everyone can imagine him in scores of situations that his author hadn't even thought of putting him in, and he sometimes acquires a meaning that his author never dreamed of giving him.

PRODUCER: Of course I know all that.

FATHER: Well, then. Why are you surprised by us? Imagine what a disaster it is for a character to be born in the imagination of an author who then refuses to give him life in a written script. Tell me if a character, left like this, suspended, created but without a final life, isn't right to do what we are doing now, here in front of you. We spent such a long time, such a very long time, believe me, urging our author, persuading him, first me, then her, *(Pointing to the* STEPDAUGHTER.*)* then this poor Mother . . .

STEPDAUGHTER: *(coming down the stage as if in a dream)* It's true, I would go, would go and tempt him, time after time, in his gloomy study just as it was growing dark, when he was sitting quietly in an armchair not even bothering to switch a light on but leaving the shadows to fill the room: the shadows were swarming with us, we had come to tempt him. *(As if she could see herself there in the study and is annoyed by the presence of the* ACTORS.*)* Go away will you! Leave us alone! Mother there, with that son of hers—me with the little girl—that poor little kid always on his own—and then me with him *(Pointing to the* FATHER.*)* and then at last, just me, on my own, all on my own, in the shadows. *(She turns quickly as if she wants to cling on to the vision she has of herself, in the shadows.)* Ah, what scenes, what scenes we suggested to him! What a life I could have had! I tempted him more than the others!

FATHER: Oh yes, you did! And it was probably all your fault that he did nothing about it! You were so insistent, you made too many demands.

STEPDAUGHTER: But he wanted me to be like that! *(She comes closer to the* PRODUCER *to speak to him in confidence.)* I think it's more likely that he felt discouraged about the theatre and even despised it because the public only wants to see . . .

PRODUCER: Let's get on, for God's sake, let's get on. Come to the point will you?

STEPDAUGHTER: I'm sorry, but if you ask me, we've got too much happening already, just with our entry into his house. *(Pointing to the* FATHER.*)* You said that we couldn't put up a notice or change the set every five minutes.

PRODUCER: Right! Of course we can't! We must combine things, group them together in one continuous flowing action: not the way you've been wanting, first of all seeing your little brother come home from school and wander about the house like a lost soul, hiding behind the doors and brooding on some plan or other that would—what did you say it would do?

STEPDAUGHTER: Wither him . . . shrivel him up completely.

PRODUCER: That's good! That's a good expression. And then you "can see it there in his eyes, getting stronger all the time"—isn't that what you said?

STEPDAUGHTER: Yes, that's right. Look at him! *(Pointing to him as he stands next to his* MOTHER.*)*

PRODUCER: Yes, great! And then, at the same time, you want to show the little girl playing in the garden, all innocence. One in the house and the other in the garden—we can't do it, don't you see that?

STEPDAUGHTER: Yes, playing in the sun, so happy! It's the only pleasure I have left, her happiness, her delight in playing in the garden: away from the misery, the squalor of that sordid flat where all four of us slept and where she slept with me—with me! Just think of it! My vile, contaminated body close to hers, with her little arms wrapped tightly round my neck, so lovingly, so innocently. In the garden, whenever she saw me, she would run and take my hand. She never wanted to show me the big flowers, she would run about looking for the "little weeny" ones, so that she could show them to me; she was so happy, so thrilled! *(As she says this, tortured by the memory, she breaks out into a long desperate cry, dropping her head on her arms that rest on a little table. Everybody is very affected by her. The* PRODUCER *comes to her almost paternally and speaks to her in a soothing voice.)*

PRODUCER: We'll have the garden scene, we'll have it, don't worry: and you'll see, you'll be very pleased with what we do! We'll play all the scenes in the garden! *(He calls out to a* STAGE HAND *by name.)* Hey. . . . , let down a few bits of tree, will you? A couple of cypresses will do, in front of the fountain. *(Someone drops in the two cypresses and a* STAGE HAND *secures them with a couple of braces and weights.)*

PRODUCER: *(to the* STEPDAUGHTER*)* That'll do for now, won't it? It'll just give us an idea. *(Calling out to a* STAGE HAND *by name again.)* Hey . . . , give me something for the sky will you?

STAGE HAND: What's that?

PRODUCER: Something for the sky! A small cloth to come in behind the fountain. *(A white cloth is dropped from the flies.)* Not white! I asked for a sky! Never mind: leave it! I'll do something with it. *(Calling out.)* Hey lights! Kill everything will you? Give me a bit of moonlight—the blues in the batten and a blue spot on the cloth . . . *(They do.)* That's it! That'll do! *(Now on the scene there is the light he asked for, a mysterious blue light that makes the* ACTORS *speak and move as if in the garden in the evening under a moon. To the* STEPDAUGHTER.*)* Look here now: the little boy can come out here in the garden and hide among the trees instead of hiding behind the doors in the house. But it's going to be difficult to find a little girl to play the scene with you where she shows you the flowers. *(Turning to the* LITTLE BOY.*)* Come on, come on, son, come across here. Let's see what it'll look like. *(But the* BOY *doesn't move.)* Come on will you, come on. *(Then he pulls him forward and tries to make him hold his head up, but every time it falls down again on his chest.)* There's something very odd about this lad . . . What's wrong with him? My God, he'll have to say something sometime! *(He comes over to him again, puts his hand on his shoulder and pushes him between the trees.)* Come a bit nearer: let's have a look. Can you hide a bit more? That's it. Now pop your head out and look round. *(He moves away to look at the effect and as the* BOY *does what he has been told to do, the* ACTORS *watch impressed and a little disturbed.)* Ahh, that's good, very good . . . (*He turns to the* STEPDAUGHTER.) How about having the little girl, surprised to see him there, run across. Wouldn't that make him say something?

STEPDAUGHTER: (*getting up*) It's no use hoping he'll speak, not as long as that creature's there. (*Pointing to the* SON.) You'll have to get him out of the way first.

SON: (*moving determinedly to one of the sets of steps leading off the stage*) With pleasure! I'll go now! Nothing will please me better!

PRODUCER: (*stopping him immediately*) Hey, no! Where are you going? Hang on!

(*The* MOTHER *gets up, anxious at the idea that he is really going and instinctively raising her arms as if to hold him back, but without moving from where she is.*)

SON: (*at the footlights, to the* PRODUCER *who is restraining him there*) There's no reason why I should be here! Let me go will you? Let me go!

PRODUCER: What do you mean there's no reason for you to be here?

STEPDAUGHTER: (*calmly, ironically*) Don't bother to stop him. He won't go!

FATHER: You have to play that terrible scene in the garden with your mother.

SON: (*quickly, angry and determined*) I'm not going to play anything! I've said that all along! (*To the* PRODUCER.) Let me go will you?

STEPDAUGHTER: (*crossing to the* PRODUCER) It's all right. Let him go. (*She moves the* PRODUCER'*s hand from the* SON. *Then she turns to the* SON *and says.*) Well, go on then! Off you go!

(*The* SON *stays near the steps but as if pulled by some strange force he is quite unable to go down them: then to the astonishment and even the dismay of the* ACTORS, *he moves along the front of the stage towards the other set of steps down into the auditorium: but having got there, he again stays near and doesn't actually go down them. The* STEPDAUGHTER *who has watched him scornfully but very intently, bursts into laughter.*)

STEPDAUGHTER: He can't, you see? He can't! He's got to stay here! He must. He's chained to us for ever! No, I'm the one who goes, when what must happen does happen, and I run away, because I hate him, because I can't bear the sight of him any longer. Do you think it's possible for him to run away? He has to stay here with that wonderful father of his and his mother there. She doesn't think she has any other son but him. (*She turns to the* MOTHER.) Come on, come on, Mummy, come on! (*Turning back to the* PRODUCER *to point her out to him.*) Look, she's going to try to stop him . . . (*To the* MOTHER, *half compelling her, as if by some magic power.*) Come on, come on. (*Then to the* PRODUCER *again.*) Imagine how she must feel at showing her affection for him in front of your actors! But her longing to be near him is so strong that—look! She's going to go through that scene with him again! (*The* MOTHER *has now actually come close to the* SON *as the* STEPDAUGHTER *says the last line: she gestures to show that she agrees to go on.*)

SON: (*quickly*) But I'm not! I'm not! If I can't get away then I suppose I shall have to stay here; but I repeat that I will not have any part in it.

FATHER: (*to the* PRODUCER, *excitedly*) You must make him!

SON: Nobody's going to make me do anything!

FATHER: I'll make you!

STEPDAUGHTER: Wait! Just a minute! Before that, the little girl has to go to the fountain. (*She turns to take the* LITTLE GIRL, *drops on her knees in front of her and takes her face between her hands.*) My poor little darling, those beautiful eyes, they look so bewildered. You're wondering where you are, aren't you? Well, we're on a stage, my darling! What's a stage? Well, it's a place where you pretend to be serious. They put on plays here. And now we're going to put on a play. Seriously! Oh, yes! Even you . . . (*She hugs her tightly and rocks her gently for a moment.*) Oh, my little one, my little darling, what a terrible play it is for you! What horrible things have been planned for you! The garden, the fountain . . . Oh, yes, it's only a pretend fountain, that's right. That's part of the game, my pretty darling: everything is pretends here. Perhaps you'll like a pretends fountain better than a real one: you can play here then. But it's only a game for the others; not for you, I'm afraid, it's real for you, my darling, and your game is in a real fountain, a big beautiful green fountain with bamboos casting shadows, looking at your own reflection, with lots of baby ducks paddling about, shattering the reflections. You want to stroke one! (*With a scream that electrifies and terrifies everybody.*) No, Rosetta, no! Your mummy isn't watching you, she's over there with that selfish bastard! Oh, God, I fell as if all the devils in hell were tearing me apart inside . . . And you . . . (*Leaving the* LITTLE GIRL *and turning to the* LITTLE BOY *in the usual way.*) What are you doing here, hanging about like a beggar? It'll be your fault too, if that little girl drowns; you're always like this, as if I wasn't paying the price for getting all of you into this house. (*Shaking his arm to make him take his hand out of his pocket.*) What have you got there? What are you hiding? Take it out, take your hand out! (*She drags his hand out of his pocket and to everyone's horror he is holding a revolver. She looks at him for a moment, almost with satisfaction: then she says, grimly.*) Where on earth did you get that? (*The* BOY, *looking frightened, with his eyes wide and empty, doesn't answer.*) You idiot, if I'd been you, instead of killing myself, I'd have killed one of those two: either or both, the father and the son. (*She pushes him towards the cypress trees where he then stands watching: then she takes the* LITTLE GIRL *and helps her to climb in to the fountain, making her lie so that she is hidden: after that she kneels down and puts her head and arms on the rim of the fountain.*)

PRODUCER: That's good! It's good! (*Turning to the* STEPDAUGHTER.) And at the same time . . .

SON: (*scornfully*) What do you mean, at the same time? There was nothing at the same time! There wasn't any scene between her and me. (*Pointing to the* MOTHER.) She'll tell you the same thing herself, she'll tell you what happened.

(*The* SECOND ACTRESS *and the* JUVENILE LEAD *have left the group of* ACTORS *and have come to stand nearer the* MOTHER *and the* SON *as if to study them so as to play their parts.*)

MOTHER: Yes, it's true. I'd gone to his room . . .

SON: Room, do you hear? Not the garden!

PRODUCER: It's not important! We've got to reorganise the events anyway. I've told you that already.

SON: (*glaring at the* JUVENILE LEAD *and the* SECOND ACTRESS) What do you want?

1890 JUVENILE LEAD: Nothing. I'm just watching.

SON: (*turning to the* SECOND ACTRESS) You as well! Getting ready to play her part are you? (*Pointing to the* MOTHER.)

PRODUCER: That's it. And I think you should be grateful—they're paying you a lot of attention.

SON: Oh, yes, thank you! But haven't you realised yet that you'll never be able to do this play? There's nothing of us inside you and you actors are only looking at us from the outside. Do you think we could go on living with a mirror held up in front of us that didn't only freeze our reflection for ever, but

1900 froze us in a reflection that laughed back at us with an expression that we didn't even recognise as our own?

FATHER: That's right! That's right!

PRODUCER: (*to* JUVENILE LEAD *and* SECOND ACTRESS) Okay. Go back to the others.

SON: It's quite useless. I'm not prepared to do anything.

PRODUCER: Oh, shut up, will you, and let me listen to your mother. (*To the* MOTHER.) Well, you'd gone to his room, you said.

MOTHER: Yes, to his room. I couldn't bear it any longer. I

1910 wanted to empty my heart to him, tell him about all the agony that was crushing me. But as soon as he saw me come in . . .

SON: Nothing happened. I got away! I wasn't going to get involved. I never have been involved. Do you understand?

MOTHER: It's true! That's right!

PRODUCER: But we must make up the scene between you, then. It's vital!

MOTHER: I'm ready to do it! If only I had the chance to talk to him for a moment, to pour out all my troubles to him.

1920 FATHER: (*going to the* SON *and speaking violently*) You'll do it! For your Mother! For your Mother!

SON: (*more than ever determined*) I'm doing nothing!

FATHER: (*taking hold of his coat collar and shaking him*) For God's sake, do as I tell you! Do as I tell you! Do you hear what she's saying? Haven't you any feelings for her?

SON: (*taking hold of his* FATHER) No I haven't! I haven't! Let that be the end of it!

(*There is a general uproar. The* MOTHER *frightened out of her wits, tries to get between them and separate them.*)

MOTHER: Please stop it! Please!

FATHER: (*hanging on*) Do as I tell you! Do as I tell you!

1930 SON: (*wrestling with him and finally throwing him to the ground near the steps. Everyone is horrified*) What's come over you? Why are you so frantic? Do you want to parade our disgrace in front of everybody? Well, I'm having nothing to do with it! Nothing! And I'm doing what our author wanted as well—he never wanted to put us on the stage.

PRODUCER: Then why the hell did you come here?

SON: (*pointing to the* FATHER) He wanted to, I didn't.

PRODUCER: And aren't you here now?

SON: He was the one who wanted to come and he dragged all

1940 of us here with him and agreed with you in there about what to put in the play: and that meant not only what had really happened, as if that wasn't bad enough, but what hadn't

happened as well.

PRODUCER: All right, then, you tell me what happened. You tell me! Did you rush out of your room without saying anything?

SON: (*after a moment's hesitation*) Without saying anything. I didn't want to make a scene.

PRODUCER: (*needling him*) What then? What did you do then?

SON: (*he is now the centre of everyone's agonised attention and he crosses the stage*) Nothing . . . I went across the gar- 1950 den . . . (*He breaks off gloomy and absorbed.*)

PRODUCER: (*urging him to say more, impressed by his reluctance to speak*) Well? What then? You crossed the garden?

SON: (*exasperated, putting his face into the crook of his arm*) Why do you want me to talk about it? It's horrible! (*The* MOTHER *is trembling with stifled sobs and looking towards the fountain.*)

PRODUCER: (*quietly, seeing where she is looking and turning to the* SON *with growing apprehension*) The little girl?

SON: (*looking straight in front, out to the audience*) There, in 1960 the fountain . . .

FATHER: (*on the floor still, pointing with pity at the* MOTHER) She was trailing after him!

PRODUCER: (*to the* SON, *anxiously*) What did you do then?

SON: (*still looking out front and speaking slowly*) I dashed across. I was going to jump in and pull her out . . . But something else caught my eye: I saw something behind the tree that made my blood run cold: the little boy, he was standing there with a mad look in his eyes: he was standing looking into the fountain at his little sister, floating there, drowned. 1970

(*The* STEPDAUGHTER *is still bent at the fountain hiding the* LITTLE GIRL, *and she sobs pathetically, her sobs sounding like an echo.*)

(*There is a pause.*)

SON: (*continued*) I made a move towards him: but then . . .

(*From behind the trees where the* LITTLE BOY *is standing there is the sound of a shot.*)

MOTHER: (*with a terrible cry she runs along with the* SON *and all the* ACTORS *in the midst of a great general confusion*) My son! My son! (*And then from out of the confusion and crying her voice comes out.*) Help! Help me!

PRODUCER: (*amidst the shouting he tries to clear a space whilst the* LITTLE BOY *is carried by his feet and shoulders behind the white skycloth.*) Is he wounded? Really wounded?

(*Everybody except the* PRODUCER *and the* FATHER *who is still on the floor by the steps, has gone behind the skycloth and stays there talking anxiously. Then independently the* ACTORS *start to come back into view.*)

LEADING ACTRESS: (*coming from the right, very upset*) He's dead! The poor boy! He's dead! What a terrible thing!    1980

LEADING ACTOR: (*coming back from the left and smiling*) What do you mean, dead? It's all make-believe. It's a sham! He's not dead. Don't you believe it!

OTHER ACTORS FROM THE RIGHT: Make-believe? It's real! Real! He's dead!

OTHER ACTORS FROM THE LEFT: No, he isn't He's pretending! It's all make-believe.

FATHER: (*running off and shouting at them as he goes*) What do you mean, make-believe? It's real! It's real, ladies and

1990 gentlemen! It's reality! (*And with desperation on his face he too goes behind the skycloth.*)

PRODUCER: (*not caring any more*) Make-believe?! Reality?! Oh, go to hell the lot of you! Lights! Lights! Lights!

(*At once all the stage and auditorium is flooded with light. The* PRODUCER *heaves a sigh of relief as if he has been relieved of a terrible weight and they all look at each other in distress and with uncertainty.*)

PRODUCER: God! I've never known anything like this! And we've lost a whole day's work! (*He looks at the clock.*) Get off with you, all of you! We can't do anything now! It's too late to start a rehearsal. (*When the* ACTORS *have gone, he calls out.*) Hey, lights! Kill everything! (*As soon as he has said this, all the lights go out completely and leave him in the* 2000 *pitch dark.*) For God's sake!! You might have left the workers! I can't see where I'm going!

(*Suddenly, behind the skycloth, as if because of a bad connection, a green light comes up to throw on the cloth a huge sharp shadow of the* CHARACTERS, *but without the* LITTLE BOY *and the* LITTLE GIRL. *The* PRODUCER, *seeing this, jumps off the stage, terrified. At the same time the flood of light on them is switched off and the stage is again bathed in the same blue light as before. Slowly the* SON *comes on from the right, followed by the* MOTHER *with her arms raised towards him. Then from the left, the* FATHER *enters.*)

(*They come together in the middle of the stage and stand there as if transfixed. Finally from the left the* STEPDAUGHTER *comes on and moves towards the steps at the front: on the top step she pauses for a moment to look back at the other three and then bursts out in a raucous laugh, dashes down the steps and turns to look at the three figures still on the stage. Then she runs out of the auditorium and we can still hear her manic laughter out into the foyer and beyond.*)

(*After a pause the curtain falls slowly.*)

If a work of art is to produce a state of mind, it seems evident that the more intense and harmonious the various contributing elements are, the more complete the final effect will be. Also in esthetics the sum total is the result of the individual terms. The analysis of each particular expression, one by one, will give the measure of the general expression. *Now since the perfect reproduction of a state of mind, which is just what esthetic beauty consists of, is an emotional fact which can only result from the sum total of a number of feelings represented, then the psychological analysis of a work of art is the necessary foundation of any esthetic evaluation.*[4]

Speaking about the present essay, in connection with Baldensperger's study, "Les Définitions de l'humour," Croce is pleased to say that Baldensperger mentions also the studies made by Cazamian, a Bergsonian, who argues that humor eludes scientific inquiry because its typical and constant elements are few in number and are, above all, negative, whereas its variable elements are countless.[5] As a result, the task for criticism is to study the content and tone of each example of humor, that is, the personality of each humorist. According to Mr. Baldensperger, *there is no such thing as humor, there are only humorists.* And Croce hastens to conclude that "the question is thus exhausted."

Exhausted? But we ask and shall ask again and again how it is that, if humor does not exist and cannot be defined, there are writers who can be identified and defined as humorists. On what basis can they be recognized and identified as such? There is no *humor*, there are only humorists; the *comic* does not exist, there are only comic writers. Fine! And if someone mistakes a certain humorist for a comic writer, how can I show him that he is mistaken and that the author in question is indeed a humorist and not a comic writer?

Croce postulates a procedural obstacle regarding the possibility of defining a concept. I, in turn, put a specific case to him and raise the question of how could he prove to Arcoleo, for instance, that Don Abbondio is not a comic character, as he asserts, but a humoristic character, if he did not have a clear idea in his mind of what humor is and of how it should be understood. But then Croce says that, after all, he is not really attacking the definitions, and that he can reject all of them, on the philosophical level, by way of accepting them on the empirical level. This acceptance includes also my definition of humor, which moreover is not, nor was it meant to be, a definition, but is rather an explanation of the inner process which takes place, and must inevitably take place, in all the writers called humorists.

Croce's esthetics is so abstract and negative that to apply it to literary criticism is absolutely impossible unless it is repeatedly to reject it, as he himself does when he accepts those so-called empirical concepts which, having been chased out the door, come back on him through the window.

Oh, how beautifully satisfying philosophy can be!

// Let us see, then, without further digression, what is the process that results in the particular representation which is customarily called humor; let us see if this representation has its own distinctive traits, and what is their origin, and if there exists a special way of looking at the world which constitutes precisely the substance and explanation of humor.

Ordinarily, as I have written elsewhere[6] and must necessarily repeat now, the work of art is created by the free movement of inner life which organizes the ideas and images into a harmonious form, in which all the elements correspond with one another and with the generating idea that coordinates them. Reflection does not remain inactive, of course, during the conception and during the execution of the work of art: it is present at the birth and throughout the development of the work, follows its progressive phases and derives pleasure from it, and brings all the various elements together, coordinating and comparing them. Consciousness does not illuminate the whole realm of the spirit; particularly in a creative artist consciousness is not an inner light distinct from

---

[4]G. A. Cesarco, "La critica estetica," *Critica militante* (Messina: Trimarchi, 1907), p. 11. [tr.]

[5]Croce, *La Critica*, VII (1909), 219–23. For the Baldensperger reference, see his "Les définitions de l'humour," *Etudes d'historie littéraire* (Paris: Hachette, 1907), pp. 176–222. The article by L. Cazamian, "Pourquoi nous ne pouvons définir l'humour" is in *Revue germanique*, II (1906), 601–634.

[6]See "Un critico fantastico," which I cited earlier, in my volume *Arte e scienza*.

thought, which might allow the will to draw from its images and ideas as if from a rich source. Consciousness, in short, is not a creative power, but an inner mirror in which thought contemplates itself. One could say rather that consciousness is thought which sees itself watching over what it does spontaneously. As a rule, in the moment of artistic conception, reflection is hidden and remains, as it were, invisible: in the artist, reflection is almost a form of feeling. While the work is slowly taking shape, reflection criticizes it, not coldly and without feeling, as an impartial judge would do in analyzing it, but suddenly, thanks to the impression that it receives from the work.

This is what happens as a rule. Let us see now whether—as a result of the natural temperament of those writers called humorists and as a result of their peculiar way of intuiting and considering man and life—this same process occurs in the conception of the work of humor; that is, let us see whether reflection plays in it the role just described or whether it acquires a special function.

Now, we shall see that during the conception of all works of humor, reflection is not hidden, it does not remain invisible: it is not, that is, almost a form of feeling or almost a mirror in which feeling contemplates itself; rather, it places itself squarely before the feeling, in a judging attitude, and, detaching itself from it, analyzes it and disassembles its imagery; from this analysis and decomposition, however, there arises or emerges a new feeling which could be called and in fact I call the *feeling of the opposite.*

I see an old lady whose hair is dyed and completely smeared with some kind of horrible ointment; she is all made-up in a clumsy and awkward fashion and is all dolled-up like a young girl. I begin to laugh. I *perceive* that she is *the opposite* of what a respectable old lady should be. Now I could stop here at this initial and superficial comic reaction: the comic consists precisely of this *perception of the opposite.* But if, at this point, reflection interferes in me to suggest that perhaps this old lady finds no pleasure in dressing up like an exotic parrot, and that perhaps she is distressed by it and does it only because she pitifully deceives herself into believing that, by making herself up like that and by concealing her wrinkles and gray hair, she may be able to hold the love of her much younger husband—if reflection comes to suggest all this, then I can no longer laugh at her as I did at first, exactly because the inner working of reflection has made me go beyond, or rather enter deeper into, the initial stage of awareness: from the beginning *perception of the opposite,* reflection has made me shift to a *feeling of the opposite.* And herein lies the precise difference between the comic and humor.

Another illustration: "Oh sir, my dear sir! Perhaps all this seems *ludicrous* to you as it does to others; perhaps I am only burdening you with the stupid and trivial details of my domestic life, but it is not a laughing matter to me, because I feel it all . . . "[7] This is what Marmeladoff cries out to Raskolnikoff in the tavern amid the laughter of the drunken customers. This outcry is precisely the painful and exasperated protest of a humoristic character against someone who, right there before him, dwells on an initial superficial perception of his situation and only succeeds in seeing its comic side.

---

[7]Dostoevski, *Crime and Punishment,* 1, Chap. 1. [tr.]

# Tennessee Williams

Like Amanda Wingfield in *The Glass Menagerie*, Tennessee Williams (1911–1983) regarded himself as a product of the Old South, and its genteel, rural, and—finally—obsolete traditions. Born Thomas Lanier Williams to a traveling shoe-salesman and his wife, Williams was raised in Mississippi before moving as a child to the tenements of St. Louis. As a child, Williams contracted diphtheria which briefly paralyzed his legs and left him frail and homebound for some time. During his convalescence, Williams read and wrote avidly, and published his first story at the age of sixteen. After high school, he briefly attended the University of Missouri, but withdrew when his poor health prevented him from passing the ROTC course. He then worked for three years in a shoe factory, then tried Washington University in St. Louis, but again dropped out. He finally took his degree in playwriting from the University of Iowa in 1938, when he changed his name to "Tennessee." In the 1930s, Williams's embattled relation to the world was deepened by the "loss" of his beloved sister Rose. Rose became chronically depressed, and Williams's mother, unable to cope with her erratic and wild behavior, consented to have a lobotomy performed. Rose was left docile but inert, and became the prototype of several of Williams's most memorable dramatic characters, women whose often-fantasized sense of inner beauty seems too delicate to be disclosed to the world. At this time Williams also recognized his own homosexuality, a recognition that deepened his sense of isolation from American society.

Coming of age in the Depression was formative for Williams's drama, particularly the range of themes associated with his mature work: a sexual tension surging beneath the surface of the characters' lives, the collapse of a sustaining family and social order, his attraction to misfits destroyed by a world that will not accept them. Williams wrote several plays in the late 1930s, and *Battle of Angels* (1940; later revised as *Orpheus Descending* in 1957) was produced by the Theater Guild in Boston, where it failed. But Williams scored a major success with his next play, *The Glass Menagerie* (1944), and continued his success with a series of important dramas: *Summer and Smoke* (1947), *A Streetcar Named Desire* (1947), *The Rose Tattoo* (1951), *Camino Real* (1953), *Cat on a Hot Tin Roof* (1955), *Sweet Bird of Youth* (1959), *Night of the Iguana* (1961). In his later years, Williams's drama because increasingly gothic and sensational, and his personal life suffered as well; Williams became an alcoholic and was institutionalized on several occasions. He continued to write plays to the end of his life, developing his characteristic strengths: a feel for the nuances of character and a flair for dramatizing the victims of an unfeeling world.

## The Glass Menagerie (1945)

First performed in 1944, *The Glass Menagerie* looks back to the 1930s. Its characters are reminiscent of Williams and his family, and their grinding poverty recalls the Depression-era plays of Elmer Rice and Clifford Odets. In many ways, *The Glass Menagerie* is a play in the realistic tradition. Laura's menagerie recalls how Ibsen, Chekhov, and Strindberg used stage objects (the wild duck in Ibsen's play, Chekhov's cherry orchard, Miss Julie's bird) to evoke and symbolize the characters' motives and sensibilities. But Williams also uses the device of the "memory play" to disrupt the linearity of realistic drama. Tom constructs the scene and the characters for the audience, and slide projections of phrases and images often illustrate the action as it takes place. These devices lend *The Glass Menagerie* the flavor of symbolist theater. Moreover, Tom's anticipation of the Spanish Civil War and of World War II sets the play in a larger social and political context that looms forebodingly over the fragile and self-absorbed characters. Amanda and Laura seem doomed never to escape the drab apartment, and even Tom, wandering the world, finally cannot escape it either. Deeply personal, *The Glass Menagerie* also provides a kind of study for Williams's later plays, for it includes a typical panoply of Williams's characters: the blunt, sexually aggressive, emotionally stunted Jim; Amanda, captive to her faded-Southern-belle persona; Laura, more crippled emotionally than physically; and Tom, who falls in love with long distance yet never succeeds in escaping his past or in finding his future.

# — The Glass Menagerie —
## Tennessee Williams

## —PRODUCTION NOTES—

Being a "memory play," *The Glass Menagerie* can be presented with unusual freedom of convention. Because of its considerably delicate or tenuous material, atmospheric touches and subtleties of direction play a particularly important part. Expressionism and all other unconventional techniques in drama have only one valid aim, and that is a closer approach to truth. When a play employs unconventional techniques, it is not, or certainly shouldn't be, trying to escape its responsibility of dealing with reality, or interpreting experience, but is actually or should be attempting to find a closer approach, a more penetrating and vivid expression of things as they are. The straight realistic play with its genuine Frigidaire and authentic ice-cubes, its characters who speak exactly as its audience speaks, corresponds to the academic landscape and has the same virtue of a photographic likeness. Everyone should know nowadays the unimportance of the photographic in art: that truth, life, or reality is an organic thing which the poetic imagination can represent or suggest, in essence, only through transformation, through changing into other forms than those which were merely present in appearance.

These remarks are not meant as a preface only to this particular play. They have to do with a conception of a new, plastic theatre which must take the place of the exhausted theatre of realistic conventions if the theatre is to resume vitality as a part of our culture.

THE SCREEN DEVICE: There is *only one important difference between the original and the acting version of the play* and that is the *omission* in the latter of the device that I tentatively included in my *original* script. This device was the use of a screen on which were projected magic-lantern slides bearing images or titles. I do not regret the omission of this device from the original Broadway production. The extraordinary power of Miss Taylor's performance made it suitable to have the utmost simplicity in the physical production. But I think it may be interesting to some readers to see how this device was conceived. So I am putting it into the published manuscript. These images and legends, projected from behind, were cast on a section of wall between the front-room and dining-room areas, which should be indistinguishable from the rest when not in use.

The purpose of this will probably be apparent. It is to give accent to certain values in each scene. Each scene contains a particular point (or several) which is structurally the most important. In an episodic play, such as this, the basic structure or narrative line may be obscured from the audience; the effect may seem fragmentary rather than architectural. This may not be the fault of the play so much as a lack of attention in the audience. The legend or image upon the screen will strengthen the effect of what is merely allusion in the writing and allow the primary point to be made more simply and lightly than if the entire responsibility were on the spoken lines. Aside from this structural value, I think the screen will have a definite emotional appeal, less definable but just as important. An imaginative producer or director may invent many other uses for this device than those indicated in the present script. In fact the possibilities of the device seem much larger to me than the instance of this play can possibly utilize.

THE MUSIC: Another extra-literary accent in this play is provided by the use of music. A single recurring tune, "The Glass Menagerie," is used to give emotional emphasis to suitable passages. This tune is like circus music, not when you are on the grounds or in the immediate vicinity of the parade, but when you are at some distance and very likely thinking of something else. It seems under those circumstances to continue almost interminably and it weaves in and out of your preoccupied consciousness; then it is the lightest, most delicate music in the world and perhaps the saddest. It expresses the surface vivacity of life with the underlying strain of immutable and inexpressible sorrow. When you look at a piece of delicately spun glass you think of two things: how beautiful it is and how easily it can be broken. Both of those ideas should be woven into the recurring tune, which dips in and out of the play as if it were carried on a wind that changes. It serves as a thread of connection and allusion between the narrator with his separate point in time and space and the subject of his story. Between each episode it returns as reference to the emotion, nostalgia, which is the first condition of the play. It is primarily Laura's music and therefore comes out most clearly when the play focuses upon her and the lovely fragility of glass which is her image.

THE LIGHTING: The lighting in the play is not realistic. In keeping with the atmosphere of memory, the stage is dim. Shafts of light are focused on selected areas or actors, sometimes in contradistinction to what is the apparent center. For instance, in the quarrel scene between Tom and Amanda, in which Laura has no active part, the clearest pool of light is on her figure. This is also true of the supper scene, when her silent figure on the sofa should remain the visual center. The light upon Laura should be distinct from the others, having a peculiar pristine clarity such as light used in early religious portraits of female saints or madonnas. A certain correspondence to light in religious paintings, such as El Greco's, where the figures are radiant in atmosphere that is relatively dusky, could be effectively used throughout the play. (It will also permit a more effective use of the screen.) A free, imaginative use of light can be of enormous value in giving a mobile, plastic quality to plays of a more or less static nature.

*Tennessee Williams*

### —THE CHARACTERS—

AMANDA WINGFIELD (*the mother*)
A little woman of great but confused vitality clinging frantically to another time and place. Her characterization must be carefully created, not copied from type. She is not paranoiac, but her life is paranoia. There is much to admire in Amanda, and as much to love and pity as there is to laugh at. Certainly she has endurance and a kind of heroism, and though her foolishness makes her unwittingly cruel at times, there is tenderness in her slight person.

LAURA WINGFIELD (*her daughter*)
Amanda, having failed to establish contact with reality, continues to live vitally in her illusions, but Laura's situation is even graver. A childhood illness has left her crippled, one leg slightly shorter than the other, and held in a brace. This defect need not be more than suggested on the stage. Stemming from this, Laura's separation increases till she is like a piece of her own glass collection, too exquisitely fragile to move from the shelf.

TOM WINGFIELD (*her son*)
And the narrator of the play. A poet with a job in a warehouse. His nature is not remorseless, but to escape from a trap he has to act without pity.

JIM O'CONNOR (*the gentleman caller*)
A nice, ordinary, young man.

SCENE: *An Alley in St. Louis*

*Part I. Preparation for a Gentleman Caller.*
*Part II. The Gentleman calls.*

*Time: Now and the Past.*

### SCENE I

*The Wingfield apartment is in the rear of the building, one of those vast hive-like conglomerations of cellular living-units that flower as warty growths in overcrowded urban centers of lower middle-class population and are symptomatic of the impulse of this largest and fundamentally enslaved section of American society to avoid fluidity and differentiation and to exist and function as one interfused mass of automatism.*

*The apartment faces an alley and is entered by a fire escape, a structure whose name is a touch of accidental poetic truth, for all of these huge buildings are always burning with the slow and implacable fires of human desperation. The fire escape is part of what we see—that is, the landing of it and steps descending from it.*

*The scene is memory and is therefore nonrealistic. Memory takes a lot of poetic license. It omits some details; others are exaggerated, according to the emotional value of the articles it touches, for memory is seated predominantly in the heart. The interior is therefore rather dim and poetic.*

*At the rise of the curtain, the audience is faced with the dark, grim rear wall of the Wingfield tenement. This building is flanked on both sides by dark, narrow alleys which run into murky canyons of tangled clotheslines, garbage cans, and the sinister latticework of neighboring fire escapes. It is up and down these side alleys that exterior entrances and exits are made during the play. At the end of Tom's opening commentary, the dark tenement wall slowly becomes transparent and reveals the interior of the ground-floor Wingfield apartment.*

*Nearest the audience is the living room, which also serves as a sleeping room for Laura, the sofa unfolding to make her bed. Just beyond, separated from the living room by a wide arch or second proscenium with transparent faded portieres (or second curtain), is the dining room. In an old-fashioned whatnot in the living room are seen scores of transparent glass animals. A blown-up photograph of the father hangs on the wall of the living room, to the left of the archway. It is the face of a very handsome young man in a doughboy's First World War cap. He is gallantly smiling, ineluctably smiling, as if to say "I will be smiling forever."*

*Also hanging on the wall, near the photograph, are a typewriter keyboard chart and a Gregg shorthand diagram. An upright typewriter on a small table stands beneath the charts.*

*The audience hears and sees the opening scene in the dining room through both the transparent fourth wall of the building and the transparent gauze portieres of the dining-room arch. It is during this revealing scene that the fourth wall slowly ascends, out of sight. This transparent exterior wall is not brought down again until the very end of the play, during Tom's final speech.*

*The narrator is an undisguised convention of the play. He takes whatever license with dramatic convention is convenient to his purposes.*

*(Tom enters, dressed as a merchant sailor, and strolls across to the fire escape. There he stops and lights a cigarette. He addresses the audience.)*

TOM: Yes, I have tricks in my pocket, I have things up my sleeve. But I am the opposite of a stage magician. He gives you illusion that has the appearance of truth. I give you truth in the pleasant disguise of illusion. To begin with, I turn back time. I reverse it to that quaint period, the thirties, when the huge middle class of America was matriculating in a school for the blind. Their eyes had failed them, or they had failed their eyes, and so they were having their fingers pressed forcibly down on the fiery Braille alphabet of a dissolving economy.
In Spain there was revolution. Here there was only shouting and confusion. In Spain there was Guernica. Here there were disturbances of labor, sometimes pretty violent, in otherwise peaceful cities such as Chicago, Cleveland, Saint

10

Louis . . . This is the social background of the play.

(*Music begins to play.*)

The play is memory. Being a memory play, it is dimly lighted, it is sentimental, it is not realistic. In memory everything seems to happen to music. That explains the fiddle in the wings.

I am the narrator of the play, and also a character in it. The other characters are my mother, Amanda, my sister, Laura, and a gentleman caller who appears in the final scenes. He is the most realistic character in the play, being an emissary from a world of reality that we were somehow set apart from. But since I have a poet's weakness for symbols, I am using this character also as a symbol; he is the long-delayed but always expected something that we live for.

There is a fifth character in the play who doesn't appear except in this larger-than-life-size photograph over the mantel. This is our father who left us a long time ago. He was a telephone man who fell in love with long distances; he gave up his job with the telephone company and skipped the light fantastic out of town . . .

The last we heard of him was a picture postcard from Mazatlan, on the Pacific coast of Mexico, containing a message of two words: "Hello—Goodbye!" and no address.

I think the rest of the play will explain itself. . . .

(*Amanda's voice becomes audible through the portieres.*)

(*Legend on screen: "Ou sont les neiges."*)

(*Tom divides the portieres and enters the dining room. Amanda and Laura are seated at a drop-leaf table. Eating is indicated by gestures without food or utensils. Amanda faces the audience. Tom and Laura are seated in profile. The interior has lit up softly and through the scrim we see Amanda and Laura seated at the table.*)

AMANDA: (*calling*) Tom?

TOM: Yes, Mother.

AMANDA: We can't say grace until you come to the table!

TOM: Coming, Mother. (*He bows slightly and withdraws, reappearing a few moments later in his place at the table.*)

AMANDA: (*to her son*) Honey, don't *push* with your *fingers*. If you have to push with something, the thing to push with is a crust of bread. And chew—chew! Animals have secretions in their stomachs which enable them to digest food without mastication, but human beings are supposed to chew their food before they swallow it down. Eat food leisurely, son, and really enjoy it. A well-cooked meal has lots of delicate flavors that have to be held in the mouth for appreciation. So chew your food and give your salivary glands a chance to function!

(*Tom deliberately lays his imaginary fork down and pushes his chair back from the table.*)

TOM: I haven't enjoyed one bite of this dinner because of your constant directions on how to eat it. It's you that make me rush through meals with your hawklike attention to every bite I take. Sickening—spoils my appetite—all this discussion of—animals' secretion—salivary glands—mastication!

AMANDA: (*lightly*) Temperament like a Metropolitan star!

(*Tom rises and walks toward the living room.*)

You're not excused from the table.

TOM: I'm getting a cigarette.

AMANDA: You smoke too much.

(*Laura rises.*)

LAURA: I'll bring in the blanc mange.

(*Tom remains standing with his cigarette by the portieres.*)

AMANDA: (*rising*) No, sister, no, sister—you be the lady this time and I'll be the darky.

LAURA: I'm already up.

AMANDA: Resume your seat, little sister—I want you to stay fresh and pretty—for gentlemen callers!

LAURA: (*sitting down*) I'm not expecting any gentlemen callers.

AMANDA: (*crossing out to the kitchenette, airily*) Sometimes they come when they are least expected! Why, I remember one Sunday afternoon in Blue Mountain—

(*She enters the kitchenette.*)

TOM: I know what's coming!

LAURA: Yes. But let her tell it.

TOM: Again?

LAURA: She loves to tell it.

(*Amanda returns with a bowl of dessert.*)

AMANDA: One Sunday afternoon in Blue Mountain—your mother received—*seventeen!*—gentlemen callers! Why, sometimes there weren't chairs enough to accommodate them all. We had to send the nigger over to bring in folding chairs from the parish house.

TOM: (*remaining at the portieres*) How did you entertain those gentlemen callers?

AMANDA: I understood the art of conversation!

TOM: I bet you could talk.

AMANDA: Girls in those days *knew* how to talk, I can tell you.

TOM: Yes?

(*Image on screen: Amanda as a girl on a porch, greeting callers.*)

AMANDA: They knew how to entertain their gentlemen callers. It wasn't enough for a girl to be possessed of a pretty face and a graceful figure—although I wasn't slighted in either respect. She also needed to have a nimble wit and a tongue to meet all occasions.

TOM: What did you talk about?

AMANDA: Things of importance going on in the world! Never anything coarse or common or vulgar.

(*She addresses Tom as though he were seated in the vacant chair at the table though he remains by the portieres. He plays this scene as though reading from a script.*)

My callers were gentlemen—all! Among my callers were some of the most prominent young planters of the Mississippi Delta—planters and sons of planters!

(*Tom motions for music and a spot of light on Amanda. Her eyes lift, her face glows, her voice becomes rich and elegiac.*)

(*Screen legend: "Ou sont les neiges d'antan?"*)

There was young Champ Laughlin who later became vice-president of the Delta Planters Bank. Hadley Stevenson

100 who was drowned in Moon Lake and left his widow one hundred and fifty thousand in Government bonds. There were the Cutrere brothers, Wesley and Bates. Bates was one of my bright particular beaux! He got in a quarrel with that wild Wainwright boy. They shot it out on the floor of Moon Lake Casino. Bates was shot through the stomach. Died in the ambulance on his way to Memphis. His widow was also well provided-for, came into eight or ten thousand acres, that's all. She married him on the rebound—never loved her—carried my picture on him the night he died!

110 And there was that boy that every girl in the Delta had set her cap for! That beautiful, brilliant young Fitzhugh boy from Greene County!

TOM: What did he leave his widow?

AMANDA: He never married! Gracious, you talk as though all of my old admirers had turned up their toes to the daisies!

TOM: Isn't this the first you've mentioned that still survives?

AMANDA: That Fitzhugh boy went North and made a fortune— came to be known as the Wolf of Wall Street! He had the Midas touch, whatever he touched turned to gold! And I

120 could have been Mrs. Duncan J. Fitzhugh, mind you! But— I picked your *father*!

LAURA: (*rising*) Mother, let me clear the table.

AMANDA: No, dear, you go in front and study your typewriter chart. Or practice your shorthand a little. Stay fresh and pretty!—It's almost time for our gentlemen callers to start arriving. (*She flounces girlishly toward the kitchenette*) How many do you suppose we're going to entertain this afternoon?

(*Tom throws down the paper and jumps up with a groan.*)

LAURA: (*alone in the dining room*) I don't believe we're going

130 to receive any, Mother.

AMANDA: (*reappearing, airily*) What? No one—not one? You must be joking!

(*Laura nervously echoes her laugh. She slips in a fugitive manner through the half-open portieres and draws them gently behind her. A shaft of very clear light is thrown on her face against the faded tapestry of the curtains. Faintly the music of "The Glass Menagerie" is heard as she continues, lightly:*)

Not one gentleman caller? It can't be true! There must be a flood, there must have been a tornado!

LAURA: It isn't a flood, it's not a tornado, Mother. I'm just not popular like you were in Blue Mountains. . . .

(*Tom utters another groan. Laura glances at him with a faint, apologetic smile. Her voice catches a little:*)

Mother's afraid I'm going to be an old maid.

(*The scene dims out with the "Glass Menagerie" music.*)


SCENE II

On the dark stage the screen is lighted with the image of blue roses. Gradually Laura's figure becomes apparent and the screen goes out. The music subsides.

Laura is seated in the delicate ivory chair at the small claw-foot table. She wears a dress of soft violet material for a kimono—

her hair is tied back from her forehead with a ribbon. She is washing and polishing her collection of glass. Amanda appears on the fire escape steps. At the sound of her ascent, Laura catches her breath, thrusts the bowl of ornaments away, and seats herself stiffly before the diagram of the typewriter keyboard as though it held her spellbound. Something has happened to Amanda. It is written in her face as she climbs to the landing: a look that is grim and hopeless and a little absurd. She has on one of those cheap or imitation velvety-looking cloth coats with imitation fur collar. Her hat is five or six years old, one of those dreadful cloche hats that were worn in the late Twenties, and she is clutching an enormous black patent-leather pocketbook with nickel clasps and initials. This is her full-dress outfit, the one she usually wears to the D.A.R. Before entering she looks through the door. She purses her lips, opens her eyes very wide, rolls them upward and shakes her head. Then she slowly lets herself in the door. Seeing her mother's expression Laura touches her lips with a nervous gesture.

LAURA: Hello, Mother, I was—(*She makes a nervous gesture toward the chart on the wall. Amanda leans against the shut door and stares at Laura with a martyred look.*) 140

AMANDA: Deception? Deception? (*She slowly removes her hat and gloves, continuing the sweet suffering stare. She lets the hat and gloves fall on the floor—a bit of acting.*)

LAURA: (*shakily*) How was the D.A.R. meeting?

(*Amanda slowly opens her purse and removes a dainty white handkerchief which she shakes out delicately and delicately touches to her lips and nostrils.*)

Didn't you go to the D.A.R. meeting, Mother?

AMANDA: (*faintly, almost inaudibly*)—No.—No. (*then more forcibly:*) I did not have the strength—to go to the D.A.R. In fact, I did not have the courage! I wanted to find a hole in the ground and hide myself in it forever! (*She crosses slowly to the wall and removes the diagram of the typewriter* 150 *keyboard. She holds it in front of her for a second, staring at it sweetly and sorrowfully—then bites her lips and tears it in two pieces.*)

LAURA: (*faintly*) Why did you do that, Mother?

(*Amanda repeats the same procedure with the chart of the Gregg Alphabet.*)

Why are you—

AMANDA: Why? Why? How old are you, Laura?

LAURA: Mother, you know my age.

AMANDA: I thought that you were an adult; it seems that I was mistaken. (*She crosses slowly to the sofa and sinks down and stares at Laura.*) 160

LAURA: Please don't stare at me, Mother.

(*Amanda closes her eyes and lowers her head. There is a ten-second pause.*)

AMANDA: What are we going to do, what is going to become of us, what is the future?

(*There is another pause.*)

LAURA: Has something happened, Mother?

(*Amanda draws a long breath, takes out the handkerchief again, goes through the dabbing process.*)

Mother, has—something happened?

AMANDA: I'll be all right in a minute, I'm just bewildered—*(She hesitates.)*—by life. . . .

LAURA: Mother, I wish that you would tell me what's happened!

170 AMANDA: As you know, I was supposed to be inducted into my office at the D.A.R. this afternoon.

*(Screen image: A swarm of typewriters.)*

But I stopped off at Rubicam's Business College to speak to your teachers about your having a cold and ask them what progress they thought you were making down there.

LAURA: Oh. . . .

AMANDA: I went to the typing instructor and introduced myself as your mother. She didn't know who you were. "Wingfield," she said, "We don't have any such student enrolled at the school!"

180 I assured her she did, that you had been going to classes since early in January.

"I wonder," she said, "If you could be talking about that terribly shy little girl who dropped out of school after only a few days' attendance?"

"No," I said, "Laura, my daughter, has been going to school every day for the past six weeks!"

"Excuse me," she said. She took the attendance book out and there was your name, unmistakably printed, and all the dates you were absent until they decided that you had 190 dropped out of school.

I still said, "No, there must have been some mistake! There must have been some mix-up in the records!"

And she said, "No—I remember her perfectly now. Her hands shook so that she couldn't hit the right keys! The first time we gave a speed test, she broke down completely—was sick at the stomach and almost had to be carried into the wash room! After that morning she never showed up any more. We phone the house but never got any answer"—While I was working at Famous–Barr, I suppose, demon-200 strating those—

*(She indicates a brassiere with her hands.)*

Oh! I felt so weak I could barely keep on my feet! I had to sit down while they got me a glass of water! Fifty dollars' tuition, all of our plans—my hopes and ambitions for you—just gone up the spout, just gone up the spout like that.

*(Laura draws a long breath and gets awkwardly to her feet. She crosses to the Victrola and winds it up.)*

What are you doing?

LAURA: Oh! *(She releases the handle and returns to her seat.)*

AMANDA: Laura, where have you been going when you've gone out pretending that you were going to business college?

LAURA: I've just been going out walking.

210 AMANDA: That's not true.

LAURA: It is. I just went walking.

AMANDA: Walking? Walking? In winter? Deliberately courting pneumonia in that light coat? Where did you walk to, Laura?

LAURA: All sorts of places—mostly in the park.

AMANDA: Even after you'd started catching that cold?

LAURA: It was the lesser of two evils, Mother.

*(Screen image: Winter scene in a park.)*

I couldn't go back there. I—threw up—on the floor!

AMANDA: From half past seven till after five every day you mean to tell me you walked around in the park, because you 220 wanted to make me think that you were still going to Rubicam's Business College?

LAURA: It wasn't as bad as it sounds. I went inside places to get warmed up.

AMANDA: Inside where?

LAURA: I went in the art museum and the bird houses at the Zoo. I visited the penguins every day! Sometimes I did without lunch and went to the movies. Lately I've been spending most of my afternoons in the Jewel Box, that big glass house where they raise the tropical flowers.                           230

AMANDA: You did all this to deceive me, just for deception? *(Laura looks down.)* Why?

LAURA: Mother, when you're disappointed, you get that awful suffering look on your face, like the picture of Jesus' mother in the museum!

AMANDA: Hush!

LAURA: I couldn't face it.

*(There is a pause. A whisper of strings is heard. Legend on screen: "The Crust of Humility.")*

AMANDA: *(hopelessly fingering the huge pocketbook)* So what are we going to do the rest of our lives? Stay home and watch the parades go by? Amuse ourselves with the glass 240 menagerie, darling? Eternally play those worn-out phonograph records your father left as a painful reminder of him? We won't have a business career—we've given that up because it gave us nervous indigestion! *(She laughs wearily.)* What is there left but dependency all our lives? I know so well what becomes of unmarried women who aren't prepared to occupy a position. I've seen such pitiful cases in the South—barely tolerated spinsters living upon the grudging patronage of sister's husband or brother's wife!—stuck away in some little mousetrap of a room—encouraged by one in- 250 law to visit another—little birdlike women without any nest—eating the crust of humility all their life!

Is that the future that we've mapped out for ourselves? I swear it's the only alternative I can think of! *(She pauses.)* It isn't a very pleasant alternative, is it? *(She pauses again.)* Of course—some girls *do marry.*

*(Laura twists her hands nervously.)*

Haven't you ever liked some boy?

LAURA: Yes, I liked one once. *(She rises.)* I came across his picture a while ago.

AMANDA: *(with some interest)* He gave you his picture?          260

LAURA: No, it's in the yearbook.

AMANDA: *(disappointed)* Oh—a high school boy.

*(Screen image: Jim as the high school hero bearing a silver cup.)*

LAURA: Yes. His name was Jim. *(She lifts the heavy annual from the claw-foot table.)* Here he is in *The Pirates of Penzance.*

AMANDA: *(absently)* The what?

LAURA: The operetta the senior class put on. He had a wonderful voice and we sat across the aisle from each other

Mondays, Wednesdays and Fridays in the Aud. Here he is with the silver cup for debating! See his grin?

270 AMANDA: *(absently)* He must have had a jolly disposition.

LAURA: He used to call me—Blue Roses.

*(Screen image: Blue Roses.)*

AMANDA: Why did he call you such a name as that?

LAURA: When I had that attack of pleurosis—he asked me what was the matter when I came back. I said pleurosis—he thought I said Blue Roses! So that's what he always called me after that. Whenever he saw me, he'd holler, "Hello, Blue Roses!" I didn't care for the girl that he went out with. Emily Meisenbach. Emily was the best-dressed girl at Soldan. She never struck me, though, as being sincere . . . It

280 says in the Personal Section—they're engaged. That's—six years ago! They must be married by now.

AMANDA: Girls that aren't cut out for business careers usually wind up married to some nice man. *(She gets up with a spark of revival.)* Sister, that's what you'll do!

*(Laura utters a startled, doubtful laugh. She reaches quickly for a piece of glass.)*

LAURA: But, Mother—

AMANDA: Yes? *(She goes over to the photograph.)*

LAURA: *(in a tone of frightened apology)* I'm—crippled!

AMANDA: Nonsense! Laura, I've told you never, never to use the word. Why, you're not crippled, you just have a little de-

290 fect—hardly noticeable, even! When people have some slight disadvantage like that, they cultivate other things to make up for it—develop charm—and vivacity—and— charm! That's all you have to do! *(She turns again to the photograph.)* One thing your father had *plenty* of—was charm!

*(The scene fades out with music.)*

SCENE III

*Legend on screen:* "After the fiasco—"

*Tom speaks from the fire escape landing.*

TOM: After the fiasco at Rubicam's Business College, the idea of getting a gentleman caller for Laura began to play a more and more important part in Mother's calculations. It be-

300 came an obsession. Like some archetype of the universal unconscious, the image of the gentleman caller haunted our small apartment. . . .

*(Screen image: A young man at the door of a house with flowers.)*

An evening at home rarely passed without some allusion to this image, this specter, this hope. . . . Even when he wasn't mentioned, his presence hung in Mother's preoccupied look and in my sister's frightened, apologetic manner— hung like a sentence passed upon the Wingfields!

Mother was a woman of action as well as words. She began to take logical steps in the planned direction. Late that winter and in the early spring—realizing that extra money would be needed to properly feather the nest and plume the

310 bird—she conducted a vigorous campaign on the telephone, roping in subscribers to one of those magazines for matrons called *The Homemaker's Companion*, the type of journal that features the serialized sublimations of ladies of letters who think in terms of delicate cuplike breasts, slim, tapering waists, rich, creamy thighs, eyes like wood smoke in autumn, fingers that soothe and caress like strains of music, bodies as powerful as Etruscan sculpture.

*(Screen image: The cover of a glamor magazine.)*

*(Amanda enters with the telephone on a long extension cord. She is spotlighted in the dim stage.)*

AMANDA: Ida Scott? This is Amanda Wingfield! We *missed* you at the D.A.R. last Monday! I said to myself: She's probably 320 suffering with that sinus condition! How is that sinus condition?

Horrors! Heaven have mercy!—You're a Christian martyr, yes, that's what your are, a Christian martyr!

Well, I just now happened to notice that your subscription to the *Companion's* about to expire! Yes, it expires with the next issue, honey!—just when that wonderful new serial by Bessie Mae Hopper is getting off to such an exciting start. Oh, honey, it's something that you can't miss! You remember how *Gone with the Wind* took everybody by storm? You 330 simply couldn't go out if you hadn't read it. All everybody *talked* was Scarlett O'Hara. Well, this is a book that critics already compare to *Gone with the Wind*. It's the *Gone with the Wind* of the post-World-War generation!—What?— Burning?—Oh, honey, don't let them burn, go take a look in the oven and I'll hold the wire! Heavens—I think she's hung up!

*(The scene dims out.)*

*(Legend on screen:* "You think I'm in love with Continental Shoemakers?")

*(Before the lights come up again, the violent voices of Tom and Amanda are heard. They are quarreling behind the portieres. In front of them stands Laura with clenched hands and panicky expression. A clear pool of light is on her figure throughout this scene.)*

TOM: What in Christ's name am I—

AMANDA: *(shrilly)* Don't you use that—

TOM: —supposed to do!                              340

AMANDA: —expression! Not in my—

TOM: Ohhh!

AMANDA: —presence! Have you gone out of your senses?

TOM: I have, that's true, *driven* out!

AMANDA: What is the matter with you, you—big—big— IDIOT!

TOM: Look!—I've got *no* thing, no single thing—

AMANDA: Lower your voice!

TOM: —in my life here that I can call my OWN! Everything is—                                      350

AMANDA: Stop that shouting!

TOM: Yesterday you confiscated my books! You had the nerve to—

AMANDA: I took that horrible novel back to the library—yes! That hideous book by that insane Mr. Lawrence.

*(Tom laughs wildly.)*

I cannot control the output of diseased minds or people who cater to them—

*(Tom laughs still more wildly.)*

BUT I WON'T ALLOW SUCH FILTH BROUGHT INTO MY HOUSE! No, no, no, no, no!

360 TOM: House, house! Who pays rent on it, who makes a slave of himself to—

AMANDA: *(fairly screeching)* Don't you DARE TO—

TOM: No, no, I mustn't say things! I've got to just—

AMANDA: Let me tell you—

TOM: I don't want to hear any more!

*(He tears the portieres open. The dining-room area is lit with a turgid smoky red glow. Now we see Amanda; her hair is in metal curlers and she is wearing a very old bathrobe, much too large for her slight figure, a relic of the faithless Mr. Wingfield. The upright typewriter now stands on the drop-leaf table, along with a wild disarray of manuscripts. The quarrel was probably precipitated by Amanda's interruption of Tom's creative labor. A chair lies overthrown on the floor. Their gesticulating shadows are cast on the ceiling by the fiery glow.)*

AMANDA: You *will* hear more, you—

TOM: No, I won't hear more, I'm going out!

AMANDA: You come right back in—

TOM: Out, out, out! Because I'm—

370 AMANDA: Come back here, Tom Wingfield! I'm not through talking to you!

TOM: Oh, go—

LAURA: *(desperately)*—Tom!

AMANDA: You're going to listen, and no more insolence from you! I'm at the end of my patience!

*(He comes back toward her.)*

TOM: What do you think I'm at? Aren't I supposed to have any patience to reach the end of, Mother? I know, I know. It seems unimportant to you, what I'm *doing*—what I *want* to do—having a little *difference* between them! You don't 
380 think that—

AMANDA: I think you've been doing things that you're ashamed of. That's why you act like this. I don't believe that you go every night to the movies. Nobody goes to the movies night after night. Nobody in their right minds goes to the movies as often as you pretend to. People don't go to the movies at nearly midnight, and movies don't let out at two A.M. Come in stumbling. Muttering to yourself like a maniac! You get three hours' sleep and then go to work. Oh, I can picture the way you're doing down there. Moping, doping, because 
390 you're in no condition.

TOM: *(wildly)* No, I'm in no condition!

AMANDA: What right have you got to jeopardize your job? Jeopardize the security of us all? How do you think we'd manage if you were—

TOM: Listen! You think I'm crazy about the *warehouse?* *(He bends fiercely toward her slight figure.)* You think I'm in love with the Continental Shoemakers? You think I want to spend fifty-five *years* down there in that—*celotex interior!* with—*fluorescent*—*tubes!* Look! I'd rather somebody 
400 picked up a crowbar and battered out my brains—than go back mornings! I *go!* Every time you come in yelling that Goddamn *"Rise and Shine!" "Rise and Shine!"* I say to myself, "How *lucky dead* people are!" But I get up. I *go!* For sixty-five dollars a month I give up all that I dream of doing and being *ever!* And you say self—*self's* all I ever think of.

Why, listen, if self is what I thought of, Mother, I'd be where he is—GONE! *(He points to his father's picture.)* As far as the system of transportation reaches! *(He starts past her. She grabs his arm.)* Don't grab at me, Mother!

AMANDA: Where are you going?    410

TOM: I'm going to the *movies!*

AMANDA: I don't believe that lie!

*(Tom crouches toward her, overtowering her tiny figure. She backs away, gasping.)*

TOM: I'm going to opium dens! Yes, opium dens, dens of vice and criminals' hangouts, Mother. I've joined the Hogan Gang, I'm a hired assassin, I carry a tommy gun in a violin case! I run a string of cat houses in the Valley! They call me Killer, Killer Wingfield, I'm leading a double-life, a simple, honest warehouse worker by day, by night a dynamic *czar* of the *underworld, Mother.* I go to gambling casinos, I spin away fortunes on the roulette table! I wear a patch over one 420 eye and a false mustache, sometimes I put on green whiskers. On those occasions they call me—*El Diablo!* Oh, I could tell you many things to make you sleepless! My enemies plan to dynamite this place. They're going to blow us all sky-high some night! I'll be glad, very happy, and so will you! You'll go up, up on a broomstick, over Blue Mountain with seventeen gentlemen callers! You ugly—babbling old—*witch.* . . .

*(He goes through a series of violent, clumsy movements, seizing his overcoat, lunging to the door, pulling it fiercely open. The women watch him, aghast. His arm catches in the sleeve of the coat as he struggles to pull it on. For a moment he is pinioned by the bulky garment. With an outraged groan he tears the coat off again, splitting the shoulder of it, and hurls it across the room. It strikes against the shelf of Laura's glass collection, and there is a tinkle of shattering glass. Laura cries out as if wounded.)*

*(Music.)*

*(Screen legend: "The Glass Menagerie.")*

LAURA: *(shrilly)* My glass!—menagerie. . . . *(She covers her face and turns away.)*    430

*(But Amanda is still stunned and stupefied by the "ugly witch" so that she barely notices this occurrence. Now she recovers her speech.)*

AMANDA: *(in an awful voice)* I won't speak to you—until you apologize!

*(She crosses through the portieres and draws them together behind her. Tom is left with Laura. Laura clings weakly to the mantel with her face averted. Tom stares at her stupidly for a moment. Then he crosses to the shelf. He drops awkwardly on his knees to collect the fallen glass, glancing at Laura as if he would speak but couldn't.)*

*("The Glass Menagerie" music steals in as the scene dims out.)*

SCENE IV

*The interior of the apartment is dark. There is a faint light in the alley. A deep-voiced bell in a church is tolling the hour of five.*

*Tom appears at the top of the alley. After each solemn boom of the bell in the tower, he shakes a little noisemaker or rattle as if to express the tiny spasm of man in contrast to the sustained power and dignity of the Almighty. This and the unsteadiness of his advance make it evident that he has been drinking. As he climbs the few steps to the fire escape landing light steals up inside. Laura appears in the front room in a nightdress. She notices that Tom's bed is empty. Tom fishes in his pockets for his door key, removing a motley assortment of articles in the search, including a shower of movie ticket stubs and an empty bottle. At last he finds the key, but just as he is about to insert it, it slips from his fingers. He strikes a match and crouches below the door.*

TOM: *(bitterly)* One crack—and it falls through!

*(Laura opens the door.)*

LAURA: Tom! Tom, what are you doing?
TOM: Looking for a door key.
LAURA: Where have you been all this time?
TOM: I have been to the movies.
LAURA: All this time at the movies?
TOM: There was a very long program. There was a Garbo pic-
440   ture and a Mickey Mouse and a travelogue and a newsreel and a preview of coming attractions. And there was an organ solo and a collection for the Milk Fund—simultaneously—which ended up in a terrible fight between a fat lady and an usher!
LAURA: *(innocently)* Did you have to stay through everything?
TOM: Of course! And, oh, I forgot! There was a big stage show! The headliner on this stage show was Malvolio the Magi-cian. He performed wonderful tricks, many of them, such as pouring water back and forth between pitchers. First it
450   turned to wine and then it turned to beer and then it turned to whisky. I know it was whisky it finally turned into because he needed somebody to come up out of the audience to help him, and I came up—both shows! It was Kentucky Straight Bourbon. A very generous fellow, he gave souvenirs. *(He pulls from his back pocket a shimmering rainbow-colored scarf.)* He gave me this. This is his magic scarf. You can have it, Laura. You wave it over a canary cage and you get a bowl of goldfish. You wave it over the goldfish bowl and they fly away canaries. . . . But the wonderfullest trick of all was the
460   coffin trick. We nailed him into a coffin and he got out of the coffin without removing one nail. *(He has come inside.)* There is a trick that would come in handy for me—get me out of this two-by-four situation! *(He flops onto the bed and starts removing his shoes.)*
LAURA: Tom—shhh!
TOM: What're you shushing me for?
LAURA: You'll wake up Mother.
TOM: Goody, goody! Pay 'er back for all those "Rise an' Shines." *(He lies down, groaning.)* You know it don't take much in-
470   telligence to get yourself into a nailed-up coffin, Laura. But who in hell ever got himself out of one without removing one nail?

*(As if in answer, the father's grinning photograph lights up. The scene dims out.)*

*(Immediately following, the church bell is heard striking six. At the sixth stroke the alarm clock goes off in Amanda's room, and*

*after a few moments we hear her calling: "Rise and Shine! Rise and Shine! Laura, go tell your brother to rise and shine!")*

TOM: *(sitting up slowly)* I'll rise—but I won't shine.

*(The light increases.)*

AMANDA: Laura, tell your brother his coffee is ready.

*(Laura slips into the front room.)*

LAURA: Tom!—It's nearly seven. Don't make Mother nervous.

*(He stares at her stupidly.)*

*(beseechingly:)* Tom, speak to Mother this morning. Make up with her, apologize, speak to her!
TOM: She won't to me. It's her that started not speaking.
LAURA: If you just say you're sorry she'll start speaking.
TOM: Her not speaking—is that such a tragedy?          480
LAURA: Please—please!
AMANDA: *(calling from the kitchenette)* Laura, are you going to do what I asked you to do, or do I have to get dressed and go out myself?
LAURA: Going, going—soon as I get on my coat!

*(She pulls on a shapeless felt hat with a nervous, jerky movement, pleadingly glancing at Tom. She rushes awkwardly for her coat. The coat is one of Amanda's, inaccurately made-over, the sleeves too short for Laura.)*

Butter and what else?
AMANDA: *(entering from the kitchenette)* Just butter. Tell them to charge it.
LAURA: Mother, they make such faces when I do that.
AMANDA: Sticks and stones can break our bones, but the ex-   490 pression on Mr. Garfinkel's face won't harm us! Tell your brother his coffee is getting cold.
LAURA: *(at the door)* Do what I asked you, will you, will you, Tom?

*(He looks sullenly away.)*

AMANDA: Laura, go now or just don't go at all!
LAURA: *(rushing out)* Going—going!

*(A second later she cries out. Tom springs up and crosses to the door. Tom opens the door.)*

TOM: Laura?
LAURA: I'm all right. I slipped, but I'm all right.
AMANDA: *(peering anxiously after her)* If anyone breaks a leg on those fire-escape steps, the landlord ought to be sued for   500 every cent he possesses! *(She shuts the door. Now she remembers she isn't speaking to Tom and returns to the other room.)*

*(As Tom comes listlessly for his coffee, she turns her back to him and stands rigidly facing the window on the gloomy gray vault of the areaway. Its light on her face with its aged but childish features is cruelly sharp, satirical as a Daumier print.)*

*(The music of "Ave Maria" is heard softly.)*

*(Tom glances sheepishly but sullenly at her averted figure and slumps at the table. The coffee is scalding hot; he sips it and gasps and spits it back in the cup. At his gasp, Amanda catches her breath and half turns. Then she catches herself and turns*

*back to the window. Tom blows on his coffee, glancing sidewise at his mother. She clears her throat. Tom clears his. He starts to rise, sinks back down again, scratches his head, clears his throat again. Amanda coughs. Tom raises his cup in both hands to blow on it, his eyes staring over the rim of it at his mother for several moments. Then he slowly sets the cup down and awkwardly and hesitantly rises from the chair.)*

TOM: *(hoarsely)* Mother. I—I apologize, Mother.

*(Amanda draws a quick, shuddering breath. Her face works grotesquely. She breaks into childlike tears.)*

I'm sorry for what I said, for everything that I said, I didn't mean it.

AMANDA: *(sobbingly)* My devotion has made me a witch and so I make myself hateful to my children!

TOM: *No, you don't.*

510 AMANDA: I worry so much, don't sleep, it makes me nervous!

TOM: *(gently)* I understand that.

AMANDA: I've had to put up a solitary battle all these years. But you're my right-hand bower! Don't fall down, don't fail!

TOM: *(gently)* I try, Mother.

AMANDA: *(with great enthusiasm)* Try and you will *succeed!* *(The notion makes her breathless.)* Why, you—you're just *full* of natural endowments! Both of my children—they're *unusual* children! Don't you think I know it? I'm so—*proud!* Happy and—feel I've—so much to be thankful for

520 but—promise me one thing, son!

TOM: What, Mother?

AMANDA: Promise, son, you'll—never be a drunkard!

TOM: *(turns to her grinning)* I will never be a drunkard, Mother.

AMANDA: That's what frightened me so, that you'd be drinking! Eat a bowl of Purina!

TOM: Just coffee, Mother.

AMANDA: Shredded wheat biscuit?

TOM: No. No, Mother, just coffee.

530 AMANDA: You can't put in a day's work on an empty stomach. You've got ten minutes—don't gulp! Drinking too-hot liquids makes cancer of the stomach. . . . Put cream in.

TOM: No, thank you.

AMANDA: To cool it.

TOM: No! No, thank you, I want it black.

AMANDA: I know, but it's not good for you. We have to do all that we can to build ourselves up. In these trying times we live in, all that we have to cling to is—each other. . . . That's why it's so important to—Tom, I—I sent out your sister so

540 I could discuss something with you. If you hadn't spoken I would have spoken to you. *(She sits down.)*

TOM: *(gently)* What is it, Mother, that you want to discuss?

AMANDA: *Laura!*

*(Tom puts his cup down slowly.)*

*(Legend on screen: "Laura." Music: "The Glass Menagerie.")*

TOM: —Oh.—Laura . . .

AMANDA: *(touching his sleeve)* You know how Laura is. So quiet but—still water runs deep! She notices things and I think she—broods about them.

*(Tom looks up.)*

A few days ago I came in and she was crying.

TOM: What about?

AMANDA: You.                                                          550

TOM: Me?

AMANDA: She has an idea that you're not happy here.

TOM: What gave her that idea?

AMANDA: What gives her any idea? However, you do act strangely. I—I'm not criticizing, understand *that!* I know your ambitions do not lie in the warehouse, that like everybody in the whole wide world—you've had to—make sacrifices, but—Tom—Tom—life's not easy, it calls for—Spartan endurance! There's so many things in my heart that I cannot describe to you! I've never told you but      560 I—*loved* your father. . . .

TOM: *(gently)* I know that, Mother.

AMANDA: And you—when I see you taking after his ways! Staying out late—and—well, you *had* been drinking the night you were in that—terrifying condition! Laura says that you hate the apartment and that you go out nights to get away from it! Is that true, Tom?

TOM: No. You say there's so much in your heart that you can't describe to me. That's true of me, too. There's so much in my heart that I can't describe to *you!* So let's respect each      570 other's—

AMANDA: But, why—*why,* Tom—are you always so *restless?* Where do you *go* to, nights?

TOM: I—go to the movies.

AMANDA: Why do you go to the movies so much, Tom?

TOM: I go to the movies because—I like adventure. Adventure is something I don't have much of at work, so I go to the movies.

AMANDA: But, Tom, you go to the movies *entirely* too *much!*

TOM: I like a lot of adventure.                                       580

*(Amanda looks baffled, then hurt. As the familiar inquisition resumes, Tom becomes hard and impatient again. Amanda slips back into her querulous attitude toward him.)*

*(Image on screen: A sailing vessel with Jolly Roger.)*

AMANDA: Most young men find adventure in their careers.

TOM: Then most young men are not employed in a warehouse.

AMANDA: The world is full of young men employed in warehouses and offices and factories.

TOM: Do all of them find adventure in their careers?

AMANDA: They do or they do without it! Not everybody has a craze for adventure.

TOM: Man is by instinct a lover, a hunter, a fighter, and none of those instincts are given much play at the warehouse!

AMANDA: Man is by instinct! Don't quote instinct to me! In-      590 stinct is something that people have got away from! It belongs to animals! Christian adults don't want it!

TOM: What do Christian adults want, then, Mother?

AMANDA: Superior things! Things of the mind and the spirit! Only animals have to satisfy instincts! Surely your aims are somewhat higher than theirs! Than monkeys—pigs—

TOM: I reckon they're not.

AMANDA: You're joking. However, that isn't what I wanted to discuss.

TOM: *(rising)* I haven't much time.

AMANDA: *(pushing his shoulders)* Sit down.

TOM: You want me to punch in red at the warehouse, Mother?

AMANDA: You have five minutes. I want to talk about Laura.

(*Screen legend: "Plans and Provisions."*)

TOM: All right! What about Laura?

AMANDA: We have to be making some plans and provisions for her. She's older than you, two years, and nothing has happened. She just drifts along doing nothing. It frightens me terribly how she just drifts along.

TOM: I guess she's the type that people call home girls.

610 AMANDA: There's no such type, and if there is, it's a pity! That is unless the home is hers, with a husband!

TOM: What?

AMANDA: Oh, I can see the handwriting on the wall as plain as I see the nose in front of my face! It's terrifying! More and more you remind me of your father! He was out all hours without explanation!—Then *left!* *Goodbye!* And me with the bag to hold. I saw that letter you got from the Merchant Marine. I know what you're dreaming of. I'm not standing here blindfolded. (*She pauses.*) Very well, then. Then *do* it!

620 But not till there's somebody to take your place.

TOM: What do you mean?

AMANDA: I mean that as soon as Laura has got somebody to take care of her, married, a home of her own, independent—why, then you'll be free to go wherever you please, on land, on sea, whichever way the wind blows you! But until that time you've got to look out for your sister. I don't say me because I'm old and don't matter! I say for your sister because she's young and dependent.

I put her in business college—a dismal failure! Frightened
630 her so it made her sick at the stomach. I took her over to the Young People's League at the church. Another fiasco. She spoke to nobody, nobody spoke to her. Now all she does is fool with those pieces of glass and play those worn-out records. What kind of a life is that for a girl to lead?

TOM: What can I do about it?

AMANDA: Overcome selfishness! Self, self, self is all that you ever think of!

(*Tom springs up and crosses to get his coat. It is ugly and bulky. He pulls on a cap with earmuffs.*)

Where is your muffler? Put your wool muffler on!

(*He snatches it angrily from the closet, tosses it around his neck and pulls both ends tight.*)

Tom! I haven't said what I had in mind to ask you.

640 TOM: I'm too late to—

AMANDA: (*catching his arm—very importunately; then shyly*) Down at the warehouse, aren't there some—nice young men?

TOM: No!

AMANDA: There *must* be—*some* . . .

TOM: Mother—(*He gestures.*)

AMANDA: Find out one that's clean-living—doesn't drink and ask him out for sister!

TOM: What?

650 AMANDA: For *sister!* To *meet!* Get *acquainted!*

TOM: (*stamping to the door*) Oh, my go-osh!

AMANDA: Will you?

(*He opens the door. She says, imploringly:*)

Will you?

(*He starts down the fire escape.*)

Will you? *Will* you, dear?

TOM: (*calling back*) Yes!

(*Amanda closes the door hesitantly and with a troubled but faintly hopeful expression.*)

(*Screen image: The cover of a glamor magazine.*)

(*The spotlight picks up Amanda at the phone.*)

AMANDA: Ella Cartwright? This is Amanda Wingfield! How are you, honey?

How is that kidney condition?

(*There is a five-second pause.*)

Horrors!

(*There is another pause.*)

You're a Christian martyr, yes, honey, that's what you are, a 660 Christian martyr! Well, I just now happened to notice in my little red book that your subscription to the *Companion* has just run out! I knew that you wouldn't want to miss out on the wonderful serial starting in this new issue. It's by Bessie Mae Hopper, the first thing she's written since *Honeymoon for Three.* Wasn't that a strange and interesting story? Well, this one is even lovelier, I believe. It has a sophisticated, society background. It's all about the horsey set on Long Island!

(*The light fades out.*)

## SCENE V

*Legend on the screen: "Annunciation."*

*Music is heard as the light slowly comes on.*

*It is early dusk of a spring evening. Supper has just been finished in the Wingfield apartment. Amanda and Laura, in light-colored dresses, are removing dishes from the table in the dining room, which is shadowy, their movements formalized almost as a dance or ritual, their moving forms as pale and silent as moths. Tom, in white shirt and trousers, rises from the table and crosses toward the fire escape.*

AMANDA: (*as he passes her*) Son, will you do me a favor? 670

TOM: What?

AMANDA: Comb your hair! You look so pretty when your hair is combed!

(*Tom slouches on the sofa with the evening paper. Its enormous headline reads: "Franco Triumphs."*)

There is only one respect in which I would like you to emulate your father.

TOM: What respect is that?

AMANDA: The care he always took of his appearance. He never allowed himself to look untidy.

(*He throws down the paper and crosses to the fire escape.*)

Where are you going?

TOM: I'm going out to smoke. 680

AMANDA: You smoke too much. A pack a day at fifteen cents a pack. How much would that amount to in a month? Thirty times fifteen is how much, Tom? Figure it out and you will be astounded at what you could save. Enough to give you a night-school course in accounting at Washington U.! Just think what a wonderful thing that would be for you, son!

*(Tom is unmoved by the thought.)*

TOM: I'd rather smoke. *(He steps out on the landing, letting the screen door slam.)*

690 AMANDA: *(sharply)* I know! That's the tragedy of it. . . . *(Alone, she turns to look at her husband's picture.)*

*(Dance music: "The World Is Waiting for the Sunrise!")*

TOM: *(to the audience)* Across the alley from us was the Paradise Dance Hall. On evenings in spring the windows and doors were open and the music came outdoors. Sometimes the lights were turned out except for a large glass sphere that hung from the ceiling. It would turn slowly about and filter the dusk with delicate rainbow colors. Then the orchestra played a waltz or a tango, something that had a slow and sensuous rhythm. Couples would come outside, to the relative privacy of the alley. You could see them kissing be-
700 hind ash pits and telephone poles. This was the compensation for lives that passed like mine, without any change or adventure. Adventure and change were imminent in this year. They were waiting around the corner for all these kids. Suspended in the mist over Berchtesgaden, caught in the folds of Chamberlain's umbrella. In Spain there was Guernica! But here there was only hot swing music and liquor, dance halls, bars, and movies, and sex that hung in the gloom like a chandelier and flooded the world with brief, deceptive rainbows. . . . All the world was waiting for bom-
710 bardments!

*(Amanda turns from the picture and comes outside.)*

AMANDA: *(sighing)* A fire escape landing's a poor excuse for a porch. *(She spreads a newspaper on a step and sits down, gracefully and demurely as if she were settling into a swing on a Mississippi veranda.)* What are you looking at?

TOM: The moon.

AMANDA: Is there a moon this evening?

TOM: It's rising over Garfinkel's Delicatessen.

AMANDA: So it is! A little silver slipper of a moon. Have you made a wish on it yet?

720 TOM: Um-hum.

AMANDA: What did you wish for?

TOM: That's a secret.

AMANDA: A secret, huh? Well, I won't tell mine either. I will be just as mysterious as you.

TOM: I bet I can guess what yours is.

AMANDA: Is my head so transparent?

TOM: You're not a sphinx.

AMANDA: No, I don't have secrets. I'll tell you what I wished for on the moon. Success and happiness for my precious chil-
730 dren! I wish for that whenever there's a moon, and when there isn't a moon, I wish for it, too.

TOM: I thought perhaps you wished for a gentleman caller.

AMANDA: Why do you say that?

TOM: Don't you remember asking me to fetch one?

AMANDA: I remember suggesting that it would be nice for your

sister if you brought home some nice young man from the warehouse. I think that I've made that suggestion more than once.

TOM: Yes, you have made it repeatedly.

740 AMANDA: Well?

TOM: We are going to have one.

AMANDA: *What?*

TOM: A gentleman caller!

*(The annunciation is celebrated with music.)*

*(Amanda rises.)*

*(Image on screen: A caller with a bouquet.)*

AMANDA: You mean you have asked some nice young man to come over?

TOM: Yep. I've asked him to dinner.

AMANDA: You really did?

TOM: I did!

AMANDA: You did, and did he—*accept?*

750 TOM: He did!

AMANDA: Well, well—well, well! That's—lovely!

TOM: I thought that you would be pleased.

AMANDA: It's definite then?

TOM: Very definite.

AMANDA: Soon?

TOM: Very soon.

AMANDA: For heaven's sake, stop putting on and tell me some things, will you?

TOM: What things do you want me to tell you?

760 AMANDA: *Naturally* I would like to know when he's *coming!*

TOM: He's coming tomorrow.

AMANDA: *Tomorrow?*

TOM: Yep. Tomorrow.

AMANDA: But, Tom!

TOM: Yes, Mother?

AMANDA: Tomorrow gives me no time!

TOM: Time for what?

AMANDA: Preparations! Why didn't you phone me at once, as soon as you asked him, the minute that he accepted? Then,
770 don't you see, I could have been getting ready!

TOM: You don't have to make any fuss.

AMANDA: Oh, Tom, Tom, Tom, of course I have to make a fuss! I want things nice, not sloppy! Not thrown together. I'll certainly have to do some fast thinking, won't I?

TOM: I don't see why you have to think at all.

AMANDA: You just don't know. We can't have a gentleman caller in a pigsty! All my wedding silver has to be polished, the monogrammed table linen ought to be laundered! The windows have to be washed and fresh curtains put up. And
780 how about clothes? We have to *wear* something, don't we?

TOM: Mother, this boy is no one to make a fuss over!

AMANDA: Do you realize he's the first young man we've introduced to your sister? It's terrible, dreadful, disgraceful that poor little sister has never received a single gentleman caller! Tom, come inside! *(She opens the screen door.)*

TOM: What for?

AMANDA: I want to ask you some things.

TOM: If you're going to make such a fuss, I'll call it off, I'll tell him not to come!

790 AMANDA: You certainly won't do anything of the kind. Nothing offends people worse than broken engagements. It simply

means I'll have to work like a Turk! We won't be brilliant, but we will pass inspection. Come on inside.

*(Tom follows her inside, groaning.)*

Sit down.

TOM: Any particular place you would like me to sit?

AMANDA: Thank heavens I've got that new sofa! I'm also making payments on a floor lamp I'll have sent out! And put the chintz covers on, they'll brighten things up! Of course I'd hoped to have these walls re-papered. . . . What is the young

800     man's name?

TOM: His name is O'Connor.

AMANDA: That, of course, means fish—tomorrow is Friday! I'll have that salmon loaf—with Durkee's dressing! What does he do? He works at the warehouse?

TOM: Of course! How else would I—

AMANDA: Tom, he—doesn't drink?

TOM: Why do you ask me that?

AMANDA: Your father *did!*

TOM: Don't get started on that!

810     AMANDA: He *does* drink, then?

TOM: Not that I know of!

AMANDA: Make sure, be certain! The last thing I want for my daughter's a boy who drinks!

TOM: Aren't you being a little bit premature? Mr. O'Connor has not yet appeared on the scene!

AMANDA: But will tomorrow. To meet your sister, and what do I know about his character? Nothing! Old maids are better off than wives of drunkards!

TOM: Oh, my God!

820     AMANDA: Be still!

TOM: *(leaning forward to whisper)* Lots of fellows meet girls whom they don't marry!

AMANDA: Oh, talk sensibly, Tom—and don't be sarcastic! *(She has gotten a hairbrush.)*

TOM: What are you doing?

AMANDA: I'm brushing that cowlick down! *(She attacks his hair with the brush.)* What is this young man's position at the warehouse?

TOM: *(submitting grimly to the brush and the interrogation)*

830     This young man's position is that of a shipping clerk, Mother.

AMANDA: Sounds to me like a fairly responsible job, the sort of a job *you* would be in if you just had more *get-up.* What is his salary? Have you any idea?

TOM: I would judge it to be approximately eighty-five dollars a month.

AMANDA: Well—not princely, but—

TOM: Twenty more than I make.

AMANDA: Yes, how well I know! But for a family man, eighty-

840     five dollars a month is not much more than you can just get by on. . . .

TOM: Yes, but Mr. O'Connor is not a family man.

AMANDA: He might be, mightn't he? Some time in the future?

TOM: I see. Plans and provisions.

AMANDA: You are the only young man that I know of who ignores the fact that the future becomes the present, the present the past, and the past turns into everlasting regret if you don't plan for it!

TOM: I will think that over and see what I can make of it.

AMANDA: Don't be supercilious with your mother! Tell me 850 some more about this—what do you call him?

TOM: James D. O'Connor. The D. is for Delaney.

AMANDA: Irish on *both* sides! *Gracious!* And doesn't drink?

TOM: Shall I call him up and ask him right this minute?

AMANDA: The only way to find out about those things is to make discreet inquiries at the proper moment. When I was a girl in Blue Mountain and it was suspected that a young man drank, the girl whose attentions he had been receiving, if any girl *was*, would sometimes speak to the minister of his church, or rather her father would if her father was living, 860 and sort of feel him out on the young man's character. That is the way such things are discreetly handled to keep a young woman from making a tragic mistake!

TOM: Then how did you happen to make a tragic mistake?

AMANDA: That innocent look of your father's had everyone fooled! He *smiled*—the world was *enchanted!* No girl can do worse than put herself at the mercy of a handsome appearance! I hope that Mr. O'Connor is not too good looking.

TOM: No, he's not too good-looking. He's covered with freck- 870 les and hasn't too much of a nose.

AMANDA: He's not right-down homely, though?

TOM: Not right-down homely. Just medium homely, I'd say.

AMANDA: Character's what to look for in a man.

TOM: That's what I've always said, Mother.

AMANDA: You've never said anything of the kind and I suspect you would never give it a thought.

TOM: Don't be so suspicious of me.

AMANDA: At least I hope he's the type that's up and coming.

TOM: I think he really goes in for self-improvement.          880

AMANDA: What reason have you to think so?

TOM: He goes to night school.

AMANDA: *(beaming)* Splendid! What does he do, I mean study?

TOM: Radio engineering and public speaking!

AMANDA: Then he has visions of being advanced in the world! Any young man who studies public speaking is aiming to have an executive job some day! And radio engineering? A thing for the future! Both of these facts are very illuminating. Those are the sort of things that a mother should know concerning any young man who comes to call on her daugh- 890 ter. Seriously or—not.

TOM: One little warning. He doesn't know about Laura. I didn't let on that we had dark ulterior motives. I just said, why don't you come and have dinner with us? He said okay and that was the whole conversation.

AMANDA: I bet it was! You're eloquent as an oyster. However, he'll know about Laura when he gets here. When he sees how lovely and sweet and pretty she is, he'll thank his lucky stars he was asked to dinner.

TOM: Mother, you mustn't expect too much of Laura.          900

AMANDA: What do you mean?

TOM: Laura seems all those things to you and me because she's ours and we love her. We don't even notice she's crippled any more.

AMANDA: Don't say crippled! You know that I never allow that word to be used!

TOM: But face facts, Mother. She is and—that's not all—

AMANDA: What do you mean "not all"?

TOM: Laura is very different from other girls.

910 AMANDA: I think the difference is all to her advantage.

TOM: Not quite all—in the eyes of others—strangers—she's terribly shy and lives in a world of her own and those things make her seem a little peculiar to people outside the house.

AMANDA: Don't say peculiar.

TOM: Face the facts. She is.

*(The dance hall music changes to a tango that has a minor and somewhat ominous tone.)*

AMANDA: In what way is she peculiar—may I ask?

TOM: *(gently)* She lives in a world of her own—a world of little glass ornaments, Mother. . . .

*(He gets up. Amanda remains holding the brush, looking at him, troubled.)*

She plays old phonograph records and—that's about all—

920 *(He glances at himself in the mirror and crosses to the door.)*

AMANDA: *(sharply)* Where are you going?

TOM: I'm going to the movies. *(He goes out the screen door.)*

AMANDA: Not to the movies, every night to the movies! *(She follows quickly to the screen door.)* I don't believe you always go to the movies!

*(He is gone. Amanda looks worriedly after him for a moment. Then vitality and optimism return and she turns from the door, crossing to the portieres.)*

Laura! Laura!

*(Laura answers from the kitchenette.)*

LAURA: Yes, Mother.

AMANDA: Let those dishes go and come in front!

*(Laura appears with a dish towel. Amanda speaks to her gaily.)*

Laura, come here and make a wish on the moon!

*(Screen image: The Moon.)*

930 LAURA: *(entering)* Moon—moon?

AMANDA: A little silver slipper of a moon. Look over your left shoulder, Laura, and make a wish!

*(Laura looks faintly puzzled as if called out of sleep. Amanda seizes her shoulders and turns her at an angle by the door.)*

Now! Now, darling, *wish!*

LAURA: What shall I wish for, Mother?

AMANDA: *(her voice trembling and her eyes suddenly filling with tears)* Happiness! Good fortune!

*(The sound of the violin rises and the stage dims out.)*

SCENE VI

*The light comes up on the fire escape landing. Tom is leaning against the grill, smoking.*

*(Screen image: The high school hero.)*

TOM: And so the following evening I brought Jim home to dinner. I had known Jim slightly in high school. In high school Jim was a hero. He had tremendous Irish good nature and

940 vitality with the scrubbed and polished look of white chinaware. He seemed to move in a continual spotlight. He was a star in basketball, captain of the debating club, president of the senior class and the glee club and he sang the male lead in the annual light operas. He was always running or bounding, never just walking. He seemed always at the point of defeating the law of gravity. He was shooting with such velocity through his adolescence that you would logically expect him to arrive at nothing short of the White House by the time he was thirty. But Jim apparently ran into more interference after his graduation from Soldan. His 950 speed had definitely slowed. Six years after he left high school he was holding a job that wasn't much better than mine.

*(Screen image: The Clerk.)*

He was the only one at the warehouse with whom I was on friendly terms. I was valuable to him as someone who could remember his former glory, who had seen him win basketball games and the silver cup in debating. He knew of my secret practice of retiring to a cabinet of the washroom to work on poems when business was slack in the warehouse. He called me Shakespeare. And while the other boys in the 960 warehouse regarded me with suspicious hostility, Jim took a humorous attitude toward me. Gradually his attitude affected the others, their hostility wore off and they also began to smile at me as people smile at an oddly fashioned dog who trots across their path at some distance.

I knew that Jim and Laura had known each other at Soldan, and I had heard Laura speak admiringly of his voice. I didn't know if Jim remembered her or not. In high school Laura had been as unobtrusive as Jim had been astonishing. If he did remember Laura, it was not as my sister, for when 970 I asked him to dinner, he grinned and said, "You know, Shakespeare, I never thought of you as having folks!"

He was about to discover that I did. . . .

*(Legend on screen: "The accent of a coming foot.")*

*(The light dims out on Tom and comes up in the Wingfield living room—a delicate lemony light. It is about five on a Friday evening of late spring which comes "scattering poems in the sky.")*

*(Amanda has worked like a Turk in preparation for the gentleman caller. The results are astonishing. The new floor lamp with its rose silk shade is in place, a colored paper lantern conceals the broken light fixture in the ceiling, new billowing white curtains are at the windows, chintz covers are on the chairs and sofa, a pair of new sofa pillows make their initial appearance. Open boxes and tissue paper are scattered on the floor.)*

*(Laura stands in the middle of the room with lifted arms while Amanda crouches before her, adjusting the hem of a new dress, devout and ritualistic. The dress is colored and designed by memory. The arrangement of Laura's hair is changed; it is softer and more becoming. A fragile, unearthly prettiness has come out in Laura: she is like a piece of translucent glass touched by light, given a momentary radiance, not actual, not lasting.)*

AMANDA: *(impatiently)* Why are you trembling?

LAURA: Mother, you've made me so nervous!

AMANDA: How have I made you nervous?

LAURA: By all this fuss! You make it seem so important!

AMANDA: I don't understand you, Laura. You couldn't be satis-
980    fied with just sitting home, and yet whenever I try to arrange
something for you, you seem to resist it. (*She gets up.*) Now
take a look at yourself. No, wait! Wait just a moment—I
have an idea!

LAURA: What is it now?

(*Amanda produces two powder puffs which she wraps in
handkerchiefs and stuffs in Laura's bosom.*)

LAURA: Mother, what are you doing?

AMANDA: They call them "Gay Deceivers"!

LAURA: I won't wear them!

AMANDA: You will!

LAURA: Why should I?

AMANDA: Because, to be painfully honest, your chest is flat.

900    LAURA: You make it seem like we were setting a trap.

AMANDA: All pretty girls are a trap, a pretty trap, and men expect them to be.

(*Legend on screen: "A pretty trap."*)

Now look at yourself, young lady. This is the prettiest you
will ever be! (*She stands back to admire Laura.*) I've got to
fix myself now! You're going to be surprised by your mother's appearance!

(*Amanda crosses through the portieres, humming gaily. Laura
moves slowly to the long mirror and stares solemnly at herself.
A wind blows the white curtains inward in a slow, graceful motion and with a faint, sorrowful sighing.*)

AMANDA: (*from somewhere behind the portieres*) It isn't dark
enough yet.

(*Laura turns slowly before the mirror with a troubled look.*)

(*Legend on screen: "This is my sister: Celebrate her with
strings!" Music plays.*)

AMANDA: (*laughing, still not visible*) I'm going to show you
1000    something. I'm going to make a spectacular appearance!

LAURA: What is it, Mother?

AMANDA: Possess your soul in patience—you will see! Something I've resurrected from that old trunk! Styles haven't
changed so terribly much after all. . . . (*She parts the
portieres.*) Now just look at your mother! (*She wears a girlish frock of yellowed voile with a blue silk sash. She carries
a bunch of jonquils—the legend of her youth is nearly revived. Now she speaks feverishly:*) This is the dress in which
I led the cotillion. Won the cakewalk twice at Sunset Hill,
1010    wore one Spring to the Governor's Ball in Jackson! See how
I sashayed around the ballroom, Laura? (*She raises her skirt
and does a mincing step around the room.*) I wore it on Sundays for my gentlemen callers! I had it on the day I met your
father. . . . I had malaria fever all that Spring. The change of
climate from East Tennessee to the Delta—weakened resistance. I had a little temperature all the time—not enough
to be serious—just enough to make me restless and giddy!
Invitations poured in—parties all over the Delta! "Stay in
bed," said Mother, "you have a fever!"—but I just wouldn't.
1020    I took quinine but kept on going, going! Evenings, dances!

Afternoons, long, long rides! Picnics—lovely! So lovely, that
country in May—all lacy with dogwood, literally flooded
with jonquils! That was the spring I had the craze for jonquils. Jonquils became an absolute obsession. Mother said,
"Honey, there's no more room for jonquils." And still I kept
on bringing in more jonquils. Whenever, wherever I saw
them, I'd say, "Stop! Stop! I see jonquils!" I made the young
men help me gather the jonquils! It was a joke, Amanda and
her jonquils. Finally there were no more vases to hold them,
every available space was filled with jonquils. No vases to    1030
hold them? All right, I'll hold them myself! And then I—
(*She stops in front of the picture. Music plays.*) met your father! Malaria fever and jonquils and then—this—boy. . . .
(*She switches on the rose-colored lamp.*) I hope they get
here before it starts to rain. (*She crosses the room and places
the jonquils in a bowl on the table.*) I gave your brother a little extra change so he and Mr. O'Connor could take the service car home.

LAURA: (*with an altered look*) What did you say his name was?

AMANDA: O'Connor.    1040

LAURA: What is his first name?

AMANDA: I don't remember. Oh, yes, I do. It was—Jim!

(*Laura sways slightly and catches hold of a chair.*)

(*Legend on screen: "Not Jim!"*)

LAURA: (*faintly*) Not—Jim!

AMANDA: Yes, that was it, it was Jim! I've never known a Jim
that wasn't nice!

(*The music becomes ominous.*)

LAURA: Are you sure his name is Jim O'Connor?

AMANDA: Yes. Why?

LAURA: Is he the one that Tom used to know in high school?

AMANDA: He didn't say so. I think he just got to know him at
the warehouse.    1050

LAURA: There was a Jim O'Connor we both knew in high
school—(*then, with effort*) If that is the one that Tom is
bringing to dinner—you'll have to excuse me, I won't come
to the table.

AMANDA: What sort of nonsense is this?

LAURA: You asked me once if I'd ever liked a boy. Don't you remember I showed you this boy's picture?

AMANDA: You mean the boy you showed me in the yearbook?

LAURA: Yes, that boy.

AMANDA: Laura, Laura, were you in love with that boy?    1060

LAURA: I don't know, Mother. All I know is I couldn't sit at the
table if it was him!

AMANDA: It won't be him! It isn't the least bit likely. But
whether it is or not, you will come to the table. You will not
be excused.

LAURA: I'll have to be, Mother.

AMANDA: I don't intend to humor your silliness, Laura. I've had
too much from you and your brother, both! So just sit down
and compose yourself till they come. Tom has forgotten his
key so you'll have to let them in, when they arrive.    1070

LAURA: (*panicky*) Oh, Mother—*you* answer the door!

AMANDA: (*lightly*) I'll be in the kitchen—busy!

LAURA: Oh, Mother, please answer the door, don't make me
do it!

AMANDA: (*crossing into the kitchenette*) I've got to fix the dressing for the salmon. Fuss, fuss—silliness!—over a gentleman caller!

(*The door swings shut. Laura is left alone.*)

(*Legend on screen: "Terror!"*)

(*She utters a low moan and turns off the lamp—sits stiffly on the edge of the sofa, knotting her fingers together.*)

(*Legend on screen: "The Opening of a Door!"*)

(*Tom and Jim appear on the fire escape steps and climb to the landing. Hearing their approach, Laura rises with a panicky gesture. She retreats to the portieres. The doorbell rings. Laura catches her breath and touches her throat. Low drums sound.*)

AMANDA: (*calling*) Laura, sweetheart! The door!

(*Laura stares at it without moving.*)

JIM: I think we just beat the rain.

1080 TOM: Uh-huh. (*He rings again, nervously. Jim whistles and fishes for a cigarette.*)

AMANDA: (*very, very gaily*) Laura, that is your brother and Mr. O'Connor! Will you let them in, darling?

(*Laura crosses toward the kitchenette door.*)

LAURA: (*breathlessly*) Mother—you go to the door!

(*Amanda steps out of the kitchenette and stares furiously at Laura. She points imperiously at the door.*)

LAURA: Please, please!

AMANDA: (*in a fierce whisper*) What is the matter with you, you silly thing?

LAURA: (*desperately*) Please, you answer it, *please!*

AMANDA: I told you I wasn't going to humor you, Laura. Why

1090 have you chosen this moment to lose your mind?

LAURA: Please, please, please, you go!

AMANDA: You'll have to go to the door because I can't!

LAURA: (*despairingly*) I can't either!

AMANDA: *Why?*

LAURA: I'm *sick!*

AMANDA: I'm sick, too—of your nonsense! Why can't you and your brother be normal people? Fantastic whims and behavior!

(*Tom gives a long ring.*)

Preposterous goings on! Can you give me one reason—(*She

1100 calls out lyrically.*) Coming! Just one second!—why you should be afraid to open a door? Now you answer it, Laura!

LAURA: Oh, oh, oh . . . (*She returns through the portieres, darts to the Victrola, winds it frantically and turns it on.*)

AMANDA: Laura Wingfield, you march right to that door!

LAURA: *Yes—yes, Mother!*

(*A faraway, scratchy rendition of "Dardanella" softens the air and gives her strength to move through it. She slips to the door and draws it cautiously open. Tom enters with the caller, Jim O'Connor.*)

TOM: Laura, this is Jim. Jim, this is my sister, Laura.

JIM: (*stepping inside*) I didn't know that Shakespeare had a sister!

LAURA: (*retreating, stiff and trembling, from the door*) How—how do you do?    1110

JIM: (*heartily, extending his hand*) Okay!

(*Laura touches it hesitantly with hers.*)

JIM: Your hand's *cold,* Laura!

LAURA: Yes, well—I've been playing the Victrola. . . .

JIM: Must have been playing classical music on it! You ought to play a little hot swing music to warm you up!

LAURA: Excuse me—I haven't finished playing the Victrola. . . . (*She turns awkwardly and hurries into the front room. She pauses a second by the Victrola. Then she catches her breath and darts through the portieres like a frightened deer.*)

JIM: (*grinning*) What was the matter?

TOM: Oh—with Laura? Laura is—terribly shy.

JIM: Shy, huh? It's unusual to meet such a shy girl nowadays. I don't believe you ever mentioned you had a sister.    1120

TOM: Well, now you know. I have one. Here is the *Post Dispatch*. You want a piece of it?

JIM: Uh-huh.

TOM: What piece? The comics?

JIM: (*He glances at it.*) Ole Dizzy Dean is on his bad behavior.

TOM: (*uninterested*) Yeah? (*He lights a cigarette and goes over to the fire-escape door.*)

JIM: Where are *you* going?

TOM: I'm going out on the terrace.

JIM: (*going after him*) You know, Shakespeare—I'm going to    1130 sell you a bill of goods!

TOM: What goods?

JIM: A course I'm taking.

TOM: Huh?

JIM: In public speaking! You and me, we're not the warehouse type.

TOM: Thanks—that's good news. But what has public speaking got to do with it?

JIM: It fits you for—executive positions!

TOM: Awww.    1140

JIM: I tell you it's done a helluva lot for me.

(*Image on screen: Executive at his desk.*)

TOM: In what respect?

JIM: In every! Ask yourself what is the difference between you an' me and men in the office down front? Brains?—No!—Ability?—No! Then what? Just one little thing—

TOM: What is that one little thing?

JIM: Primarily it amounts to—social poise! Being able to square up to people and hold your own on any social level!

AMANDA: (*from the kitchenette*) Tom?

TOM: Yes, Mother?    1150

AMANDA: Is that you and Mr. O'Connor?

TOM: Yes, Mother.

AMANDA: Well, you just make yourselves comfortable in there.

TOM: Yes, Mother.

AMANDA: Ask Mr. O'Connor if he would like to wash his hands.

JIM: Aw, no—no—thank you—I took care of that at the warehouse. Tom—

TOM: Yes?

JIM: Mr. Mendoza was speaking to me about you.

TOM: Favorably?    1160

JIM: What do you think?

TOM: Well—

JIM: You're going to be out of a job if you don't wake up.

TOM: I am waking up—

JIM: You show no signs.

TOM: The signs are interior.

*(Image on screen: The sailing vessel with the Jolly Roger again.)*

TOM: I'm planning to change. *(He leans over the fire-escape rail, speaking with quiet exhilaration. The incandescent marquees and signs of the first-run movie houses light his*
1170  *face from across the alley. He looks like a voyager.)* I'm right at the point of committing myself to a future that doesn't include the warehouse and Mr. Mendoza or even a night-school course in public speaking.

JIM: What are you gassing about?

TOM: I'm tired of the movies.

JIM: Movies!

TOM: Yes, movies! Look at them—*(a wave toward the marvels of Grand Avenue)* All of those glamorous people—having adventures—hogging it all, gobbling the whole thing up!
1180  You know what happens? People go to the *movies* instead of *moving!* Hollywood characters are supposed to have all the adventures for everybody in America, while everybody in America sits in a dark room and watches them have them! Yes, until there's a war. That's when adventure becomes available to the masses! *Everyone's* dish, not only Gable's! Then the people in the dark room come out of the dark room to have some adventures themselves—goody, goody! It's our turn now, to go to the South Sea Island—to make a safari—to be exotic, far-off! But I'm not patient. I don't
1190  want to wait till then. I'm tired of the *movies* and I am *about* to *move!*

JIM: *(incredulously)* Move?

TOM: Yes.

JIM: When?

TOM: Soon!

JIM: Where? Where?

*(The music seems to answer the question, while Tom thinks it over. He searches in his pockets.)*

TOM: I'm starting to boil inside. I know I seem dreamy, but inside—well, I'm boiling! Whenever I pick up a shoe, I shudder a little thinking how short life is and what I am doing!
1200  Whatever that means, I know it doesn't mean shoes—except as something to wear on a traveler's feet! *(He finds what he has been searching for in his pockets and holds out a paper to Jim.)* Look—

JIM: What?

TOM: I'm a member.

JIM: *(reading)* The Union of Merchant Seamen.

TOM: I paid my dues this month, instead of the light bill.

JIM: You will regret it when they turn the lights off.

TOM: I won't be here.

1210  JIM: How about your mother?

TOM: I'm like my father. The bastard son of a bastard! Did you notice how he's grinning in his picture in there? And he's been absent going on sixteen years!

JIM: You're just talking, you drip. How does your mother feel about it?

TOM: Shhh! Here comes Mother! Mother is not acquainted

with my plans!

AMANDA: *(coming through the portieres)* Where are you all?

TOM: On the terrace, Mother.

*(They start inside. She advances to them. Tom is distinctly shocked at her appearance. Even Jim blinks a little. He is making his first contact with girlish Southern vivacity and in spite of the night-school course in public speaking is somewhat thrown off the beam by the unexpected outlay of social charm. Certain responses are attempted by Jim but are swept aside by Amanda's gay laughter and chatter. Tom is embarrassed but after the first shock Jim reacts very warmly. He grins and chuckles, is altogether won over.)*

*(Image on screen: Amanda as a girl.)*

AMANDA: *(coyly smiling, shaking her girlish ringlets)* Well, 1220 well, well, so this is Mr. O'Connor. Introductions entirely unnecessary. I've heard so much about you from my boy. I finally said to him, Tom—good gracious!—why don't you bring this paragon to supper? I'd like to meet this nice young man at the warehouse!—instead of just hearing him sing your praises so much! I don't know why my son is so stand-offish—that's not Southern behavior!
Let's sit down and—I think we could stand a little more air in here! Tom, leave the door open. I felt a nice fresh breeze a moment ago. Where has it gone to? Mmm, so warm al- 1230 ready! And not quite summer, even. We're going to burn up when summer really gets started. However, we're having— we're having a very light supper. I think light things are better fo' this time of year. The same as light clothes are. Light clothes an' light food are what warm weather calls fo'. You know our blood gets so thick during th' winter—it takes a while fo' us to *adjust* ou'selves!—when the season changes . . . It's come so quick this year. I wasn't prepared. All of a sudden—heavens! Already summer! I ran to the trunk an' pulled out this light dress—terribly old! 1240 Historical almost! But feels so good—so good an' co-ol, y' know. . . .

TOM: Mother—

AMANDA: Yes, honey?

TOM: How about—supper?

AMANDA: Honey, you go ask Sister if supper is ready! You know that Sister is in full charge of supper! Tell her you hungry boys are waiting for it. *(to Jim)* Have you met Laura?

JIM: She—

AMANDA: Let you in? Oh, good, you've met already! It's rare for 1250 a girl as sweet an' pretty as Laura to be domestic! But Laura is, thank heavens, not only pretty but also very domestic. I'm not at all. I never was a bit. I never could make a thing but angel-food cake. Well, in the South we had so many servants. Gone, gone, gone. All vestige of gracious living! Gone completely! I wasn't prepared for what the future brought me. All of my gentlemen callers were sons of planters and so of course I assumed that I would be married to one and raise my family on a large piece of land with plenty of servants. But man proposes—and woman accepts the proposal! To 1260 vary that old, old saying a little bit—I married no planter! I married a man who worked for the telephone company! That gallantly smiling gentleman over there! *(She points to the picture.)* A telephone man who—fell in love with long-distance! Now he travels and I don't even know where! But what am I going on for about my—tribulations? Tell me yours—I hope you don't have any! Tom?

TOM: *(returning)* Yes, Mother?

AMANDA: Is supper nearly ready?

1270 TOM: It looks to me like supper is on the table.

AMANDA: Let me look—(*She rises prettily and looks through the portieres.*) Oh, lovely! But where is Sister?

TOM: Laura is not feeling well and she says that she thinks she'd better not come to the table.

AMANDA: What? Nonsense! Laura? Oh, Laura!

LAURA: *(from the kitchenette, faintly)* Yes, Mother.

AMANDA: You really must come to the table. We won't be seated until you come to the table! Come in, Mr. O'Connor. You sit over there, and I'll. . . . Laura? Laura Wingfield!

1280 You're keeping us waiting, honey! We can't say grace until you come to the table!

*(The kitchenette door is pushed weakly open and Laura comes in. She is obviously quite faint, her lips trembling, her eyes wide and staring. She moves unsteadily toward the table.)*

*(Screen legend: "Terror!")*

*(Outside a summer storm is coming on abruptly. The white curtains billow inward at the windows and there is a sorrowful murmur from the deep blue dusk.)*

*(Laura suddenly stumbles; she catches at a chair with a faint moan.)*

TOM: Laura!

AMANDA: Laura!

*(There is a clap of thunder.)*

*(Screen legend: "Ah!")*

*(despairingly)* Why, Laura, you *are* ill, darling! Tom, help your sister into the living room, dear! Sit in the living room, Laura—rest on the sofa. Well! *(to Jim as Tom helps his sister to the sofa in the living room)* Standing over the hot stove made her ill! I told her that it was just too warm this evening, but—

*(Tom comes back to the table.)*

1290 Is Laura all right now?

TOM: Yes.

AMANDA: What *is* that? Rain? A nice cool rain has come up! *(She gives Jim a frightened look.)* I think we may—have grace—now . . .
*(Tom looks at her stupidly.)* Tom, honey—you say grace!

TOM: Oh . . . "For these and all thy mercies—"

*(They bow their heads, Amanda stealing a nervous glance at Jim. In the living room Laura, stretched on the sofa, clenches her hand to her lips, to hold back a shuddering sob.)*

God's Holy Name be praised—

*(The scene dims out.)*

## SCENE VII

*It is half an hour later. Dinner is just being finished in the dining room, Laura is still huddled upon the sofa, her feet drawn under her, her head resting on a pale blue pillow, her eyes wide*

and mysteriously watchful. The new floor lamp with its shade of rose-colored silk gives a soft, becoming light to her face, bringing out the fragile, unearthly prettiness which usually escapes attention. From outside there is a steady murmur of rain, but it is slackening and soon stops; the air outside becomes pale and luminous as the moon breaks through the clouds. A moment after the curtain rises, the lights in both rooms flicker and go out.

JIM: Hey, there, Mr. Light Bulb!

*(Amanda laughs nervously.)*

*(Legend on screen: "Suspension of a public service.")*

AMANDA: Where was Moses when the lights went out? Ha-ha. Do you know the answer to that one, Mr. O'Connor?   1300

JIM: No, Ma'am, what's the answer?

AMANDA: In the dark!

*(Jim laughs appreciatively.)*

Everybody sit still. I'll light the candles. Isn't it lucky we have them on the table? Where's a match? Which of you gentlemen can provide a match?

JIM: Here.

AMANDA: Thank you, Sir.

JIM: Not at all, Ma'am!

AMANDA: *(as she lights the candles)* I guess the fuse has burnt out. Mr. O'Connor, can you tell a burnt-out fuse? I know I   1310 can't and Tom is a total loss when it comes to mechanics.

*(They rise from the table and go into the kitchenette, from where their voices are heard.)*

Oh, be careful you don't bump into something. We don't want our gentleman caller to break his neck. Now wouldn't that be a fine howdy-do?

JIM: Ha-ha! Where is the fuse-box?

AMANDA: Right here next to the stove. Can you see anything?

JIM: Just a minute.

AMANDA: Isn't electricity a mysterious thing? Wasn't it Benjamin Franklin who tied a key to a kite? We live in such a mysterious universe, don't we? Some people say that sci-   1320 ence clears up all the mysteries for us. In my opinion it only creates more! Have you found it yet?

JIM: No, Ma'am. All these fuses look okay to me.

AMANDA: Tom!

TOM: Yes, Mother?

AMANDA: That light bill I gave you several days ago. The one I told you we got the notices about?

*(Legend on screen: "Ha!")*

TOM: Oh—yeah.

AMANDA: You didn't neglect to pay it by any chance?

TOM: Why, I—   1330

AMANDA: Didn't! I might have known it!

JIM: Shakespeare probably wrote a poem on that light bill, Mrs. Wingfield.

AMANDA: I might have known better than to trust him with it! There's such a high price for negligence in this world!

JIM: Maybe the poem will win a ten-dollar prize.

AMANDA: We'll just have to spend the remainder of the evening in the nineteenth century, before Mr. Edison made the Mazda lamp!

1340 JIM: Candlelight is my favorite kind of light.

AMANDA: That shows you're romantic! But that's no excuse for Tom. Well, we got through dinner. Very considerate of them to let us get through dinner before they plunged us into everlasting darkness, wasn't it, Mr. O'Connor?

JIM: Ha-ha!

AMANDA: Tom, as a penalty for your carelessness you can help me with the dishes.

JIM: Let me give you a hand.

AMANDA: Indeed you will not!

1350 JIM: I ought to be good for something.

AMANDA: Good for something? (Her tone is rhapsodic.) You? Why, Mr. O'Connor, nobody, *nobody's* given me this much entertainment in years—as you have!

JIM: Aw, now, Mrs. Wingfield!

AMANDA: I'm not exaggerating, not one bit! But Sister is all by her lonesome. You go keep her company in the parlor! I'll give you this lovely old candelabrum that used to be on the altar at the Church of the Heavenly Rest. It was melted a lit-tle out of shape when the church burnt down. Lightning

1360 struck it one spring. Gypsy Jones was holding a revival at the time and he intimated that the church was destroyed be-cause the Episcopalians gave card parties.

JIM: Ha-ha.

AMANDA: And how about you coaxing Sister to drink a little wine? I think it would be good for her! Can you carry both at once?

JIM: Sure. I'm Superman!

AMANDA: Now, Thomas, get into this apron!

(Jim comes into the dining room, carrying the candelabrum, its candles lighted, in one hand and a glass of wine in the other. The door of the kitchenette swings closed on Amanda's gay laughter; the flickering light approaches the portieres. Laura sits up nervously as Jim enters. She can hardly speak from the almost intolerable strain of being alone with a stranger.)

(Screen legend: "I don't suppose you remember me at all!")

(At first, before Jim's warmth overcomes her paralyzing shy-ness, Laura's voice is thin and breathless, as though she had just run up a steep flight of stairs. Jim's attitude is gently hu-morous. While the incident is apparently unimportant, it is to Laura the climax of her secret life.)

JIM: Hello there, Laura.

1370 LAURA: (faintly) Hello.

(She clears her throat.)

JIM: How are you feeling now? Better?

LAURA: Yes. Yes, thank you.

JIM: This is for you. A little dandelion wine. (He extends the glass toward her with extravagant gallantry.)

LAURA: Thank you.

JIM: Drink it—but don't get drunk!

(He laughs heartily. Laura takes the glass uncertainly; she laughs shyly.)

Where shall I set the candles?

LAURA: Oh—oh, anywhere . . .

JIM: How about here on the floor? Any objections?

1380 LAURA: No.

JIM: I'll spread a newspaper under to catch the drippings. I like to sit on the floor. Mind if I do?

LAURA: Oh, no.

JIM: Give me a pillow?

LAURA: What?

JIM: A pillow!

LAURA: Oh . . . (She hands him one quickly.)

JIM: How about you? Don't you like to sit on the floor?

LAURA: Oh—yes.

JIM: Why don't you, then?                                              1390

LAURA: I—will.

JIM: Take a pillow!

(Laura does. She sits on the floor on the other side of the can-delabrum. Jim crosses his legs and smiles engagingly at her.)

I can't hardly see you sitting way over there.

LAURA: I can—see you.

JIM: I know, but that's not fair, I'm in the limelight.

(Laura moves her pillow closer.)

Good! Now I can see you! Comfortable?

LAURA: Yes.

JIM: So am I. Comfortable as a cow! Will you have some gum? 1400

LAURA: No, thank you.

JIM: I think that I will indulge, with your permission. (He mus-ingly unwraps a stick of gum and holds it up.) Think of the fortune made by the guy that invented the first piece of chewing gum. Amazing, huh? The Wrigley Building is one of the sights of Chicago—I saw it when I went up to the Century of Progress. Did you take in the Century of Progress?

LAURA: No, I didn't.

JIM: Well, it was quite a wonderful exposition. What impressed 1410 me most was the Hall of Science. Gives you an idea of what the future will be in America, even more wonderful than the present time is! (There is a pause. Jim smiles at her.) Your brother tells me you're shy. Is that right, Laura?

LAURA: I—don't know.

JIM: I judge you to be an old-fashioned type of girl. Well, I think that's a pretty good type to be. Hope you don't think I'm being too personal—do you?

LAURA: (hastily, out of embarrassment) I believe I *will* take a piece of gum, if you—don't mind. (clearing her throat) Mr. 1420 O'Connor, have you—kept up with your singing?

JIM: Singing? Me?

LAURA: Yes. I remember what a beautiful voice you had.

JIM: When did you hear me sing?

(Laura does not answer, and in the long pause which follows a man's voice is heard singing offstage.)

VOICE:
*O blow, ye winds, heigh-ho,*
*A-roving I will go!*
*I'm off to my love*
*With a boxing glove—*
*Ten thousand miles away!*                                           1430

JIM: You say you've heard me sing?

LAURA: Oh, yes! Yes, very often . . . I—don't suppose—you remember me—at all?

JIM: (smiling doubtfully) You know I have an idea I've seen you before. I had that idea soon as you opened the door. It seemed almost like I was about to remember your name. But the name that I started to call you—wasn't a name! And so I stopped myself before I said it.

LAURA: Wasn't it—Blue Roses?

1440 JIM: *(springing up, grinning)* Blue Roses! My gosh, yes—Blue Roses! That's what I had on my tongue when you opened the door! Isn't it funny what tricks your memory plays? I didn't connect you with high school somehow or other. But that's where it was; it was high school. I didn't even know you were Shakespeare's sister! Gosh, I'm sorry.

LAURA: I didn't expect you to. You—barely knew me!

JIM: But we did have a speaking acquaintance, huh?

LAURA: Yes, we—spoke to each other.

JIM: When did you recognize me?

1450 LAURA: Oh, right away!

JIM: Soon as I came in the door?

LAURA: When I heard your name I thought it was probably you. I knew that Tom used to know you a little in high school. So when you came in the door—well, then I was—sure.

JIM: Why didn't you *say* something, then?

LAURA: *(breathlessly)* I didn't know what to say, I was—too surprised!

JIM: For goodness' sakes! You know, this sure is funny!

LAURA: Yes! Yes, isn't it, though . . .

1460 JIM: Didn't we have a class in something together?

LAURA: Yes, we did.

JIM: What class was that?

LAURA: It was—singing—chorus!

JIM: Aw!

LAURA: I sat across the aisle from you in the Aud.

JIM: Aw.

LAURA: Mondays, Wednesdays, and Fridays.

JIM: Now I remember—you always came in late.

LAURA: Yes, it was so hard for me, getting upstairs. I had that

1470 brace on my leg—it clumped so loud!

JIM: I never heard any clumping.

LAURA: *(wincing at the recollection)* To me it sounded like—thunder!

JIM: Well, well, well, I never even noticed.

LAURA: And everybody was seated before I came in. I had to walk in front of all those people. My seat was in the back row. I had to go clumping all the way up the aisle with everyone watching!

JIM: You shouldn't have been self-conscious.

1480 LAURA: I know, but I was. It was always such a relief when the singing started.

JIM: Aw, yes, I've placed you now! I used to call you Blue Roses. How was it that I got started calling you that?

LAURA: I was out of school a little while with pleurosis. When I came back you asked me what was the matter. I said I had pleurosis—you thought I said *Blue Roses.* That's what you always called me after that!

JIM: I hope you didn't mind.

LAURA: Oh, no—I liked it. You see, I wasn't acquainted with

1490 many—people. . . .

JIM: As I remember you sort of stuck by yourself.

LAURA: I—I—never have had much luck at—making friends.

JIM: I don't see why you wouldn't.

LAURA: Well, I—started out badly.

JIM: You mean being—

LAURA: Yes, it sort of—stood between me—

JIM: You shouldn't have let it!

LAURA: I know, but it did, and—

JIM: You were shy with people!

LAURA: I tried not to be but never could—   1500

JIM: Overcome it?

LAURA: No, I—I never could!

JIM: I guess being shy is something you have to work out of kind of gradually.

LAURA: *(sorrowfully)* Yes—I guess it—

JIM: Takes time!

LAURA: Yes—

JIM: People are not so dreadful when you know them. That's what you have to remember! And everybody has problems, not just you, but practically everybody has got some prob- 1510 lems. You think of yourself as having the only problems, as being the only one who is disappointed. But just look around you and you will see lots of people as disappointed as you are. For instance, I hoped when I was going to high school that I would be further along at this time, six years later, than I am now. You remember that wonderful write-up I had in *The Torch?*

LAURA: Yes! *(She rises and crosses to the table.)*

JIM: It said I was bound to succeed in anything I went into!

*(Laura returns with the high school yearbook.)*

Holy Jeez! *The Torch!*   1520

*(He accepts it reverently. They smile across the book with mutual wonder. Laura crouches beside him and they begin to turn the pages. Laura's shyness is dissolving in his warmth.)*

LAURA: Here you are in *The Pirates of Penzance!*

JIM: *(wistfully)* I sang the baritone lead in that operetta.

LAURA: *(raptly)* So—beautifully!

JIM: *(protesting)* Aw—

LAURA: Yes, yes—beautifully—beautifully!

JIM: You heard me?

LAURA: All three times!

JIM: No!

LAURA: Yes!

JIM: All three performances?   1530

LAURA: *(looking down)* Yes.

JIM: Why?

LAURA: I—wanted to ask you to—autograph my program. *(She takes the program from the back of the yearbook and shows it to him.)*

JIM: Why didn't you ask me to?

LAURA: You were always surrounded by your own friends so much that I never had a chance to.

JIM: You should have just—

LAURA: Well, I—thought you might think I was—   1540

JIM: Thought I might think you was—what?

LAURA: Oh—

JIM: *(with reflective relish)* I was beleaguered by females in those days.

LAURA: You were terribly popular!

JIM: Yeah—

LAURA: You had such a—friendly way—

JIM: I was spoiled in high school.

LAURA: Everybody—liked you!

1550 JIM: Including you?

LAURA: I—yes, I—did, too—(*She gently closes the book in her lap.*)

JIM: Well, well, well! Give me that program, Laura.

(*She hands it to him. He signs it with a flourish.*)

There you are—better late than never!

LAURA: Oh, I—what a—surprise!

JIM: My signature isn't worth very much right now. But some day—maybe—it will increase in value! Being disappointed is one thing and being discouraged is something else. I am disappointed but I am not discouraged. I'm twenty-three

1560 years old. How old are you?

LAURA: I'll be twenty-four in June.

JIM: That's not old age!

LAURA: No, but—

JIM: You finished high school?

LAURA: (*with difficulty*) I didn't go back.

JIM: You mean you dropped out?

LAURA: I made bad grades in my final examinations. (*She rises and replaces the book and the program on the table. Her voice is strained.*) How is—Emily Meisenbach getting

1570 along?

JIM: Oh, that kraut-head!

LAURA: Why do you call her that?

JIM: That's what she was.

LAURA: You're not still—going with her?

JIM: I never see her.

LAURA: It said in the "Personal" section that you were—engaged!

JIM: I know, but I wasn't impressed by that—propaganda!

LAURA: It wasn't—the truth?

1580 JIM: Only in Emily's optimistic opinion!

LAURA: Oh—

(*Legend: "What have you done since high school?"*)

(*Jim lights a cigarette and leans indolently back on his elbows smiling at Laura with a warmth and charm which lights her inwardly with altar candles. She remains by the table, picks up a piece from the glass menagerie collection, and turns it in her hands to cover her tumult.*)

JIM: (*after several reflective puffs on his cigarette*) What have you done since high school?

(*She seems not to hear him.*)

Huh?

(*Laura looks up.*)

I said what have you done since high school, Laura?

LAURA: Nothing much.

JIM: You must have been doing something these six long years.

LAURA: Yes.

JIM: Well, then, such as what?

1590 LAURA: I took a business course at business college—

JIM: How did that work out?

LAURA: Well, not very—well—I had to drop out, it gave me—indigestion—

(*Jim laughs gently.*)

JIM: What are you doing now?

LAURA: I don't do anything—much. Oh, please don't think I sit around doing nothing! My glass collection takes up a good deal of time. Glass is something you have to take good care of.

JIM: What did you say—about glass?

LAURA: Collection I said—I have one—(*She clears her throat* 1600 *and turns away again, acutely shy.*)

JIM: (*abruptly*) You know what I judge to be the trouble with you? Inferiority complex! Know what that is? That's what they call it when someone low-rates himself! I understand it because I had it, too. Although my case was not so aggravated as yours seems to be. I had it until I took up public speaking, developed my voice, and learned that I had an aptitude for science. Before that time I never thought of myself as being outstanding in any way whatsoever! Now I've never made a regular study of it, but I have a friend who says 1610 I can analyze people better than doctors that make a profession of it. I don't claim that to be necessarily true, but I can sure guess a person's psychology, Laura! (*He takes out his gum.*) Excuse me, Laura. I always take it out when the flavor is gone. I'll use this scrap of paper to wrap it in. I know how it is to get it stuck on a shoe. (*He wraps the gum in paper and puts it in his pocket.*) Yep—that's what I judge to be your principal trouble. A lack of confidence in yourself as a person. You don't have the proper amount of faith in yourself. I'm basing that fact on a number of your remarks and 1620 also on certain observations I've made. For instance that clumping you thought was so awful in high school. You say that you even dreaded to walk into class. You see what you did? You dropped out of school, you gave up an education because of a clump, which as far as I know was practically non-existent! A little physical defect is what you have. Hardly noticeable even! Magnified thousands of times by imagination! You know what my strong advice to you is? Think of yourself as *superior* in some way!

LAURA: In what way would I think?                                          1630

JIM: Why, man alive, Laura! Just look about you a little. What do you see? A world full of common people! All of 'em born and all of 'em going to die! Which of them has one-tenth of your good points! Or mine! Or anyone else's, as far as that goes—gosh! Everybody excels in some one thing. Some in many! (*He unconsciously glances at himself in the mirror.*) All you've got to do is discover in *what!* Take me, for instance. (*He adjusts his tie at the mirror.*) My interest happens to lie in electro-dynamics. I'm taking a course in radio engineering at night school, Laura, on top of a fairly re- 1640 sponsible job at the warehouse. I'm taking that course and studying public speaking.

LAURA: Ohhhh.

JIM: Because I believe in the future of television! (*turning his back to her.*) I wish to be ready to go up right along with it. Therefore I'm planning to get in on the ground floor. In fact I've already made the right connections and all that remains is for the industry itself to get under way! Full steam—(*His eyes are starry.*) Knowledge—Zzzzzp! Money—Zzzzzp!— Power! That's the cycle democracy is built on!                    1650

(*His attitude is convincingly dynamic. Laura stares at him, even her shyness eclipsed in her absolute wonder. He suddenly grins.)*

I guess you think I think a lot of myself!

LAURA: No—o-o-o, I—

JIM: Now how about you? Isn't there something you take more interest in than anything else?

LAURA: Well, I do—as I said—have my—glass collection—

*(A peal of girlish laughter rings from the kitchenette.)*

JIM: I'm not right sure I know what you're talking about. What kind of glass is it?

LAURA: Little articles of it, they're ornaments mostly! Most of them are little animals made out of glass, the tiniest little an-
1660    imals in the world. Mother calls them a glass menagerie! Here's an example of one, if you'd like to see it! This one is one of the oldest. It's nearly thirteen.

*(Music: "The Glass Menagerie.")*

*(He stretches out his hand.)*

Oh, be careful—if you breathe, it breaks!

JIM: I'd better not take it. I'm pretty clumsy with things.

LAURA: Go on, I trust you with him! *(She places the piece in his palm.)* There now—you're holding him gently! Hold him over the light, he loves the light! You see how the light shines through him?

JIM: It sure does shine!

1670 LAURA: I shouldn't be partial, but he is my favorite one.

JIM: What kind of a thing is this one supposed to be?

LAURA: Haven't you noticed the single horn on his forehead?

JIM: A unicorn, huh?

LAURA: Mmmm-hmmm!

JIM: Unicorns—aren't they extinct in the modern world?

LAURA: I know!

JIM: Poor little fellow, he must feel sort of lonesome.

LAURA: *(smiling)* Well, if he does, he doesn't complain about it. He stays on a shelf with some horses that don't have horns
1680    and all of them seem to get along nicely together.

JIM: How do you know?

LAURA: *(lightly)* I haven't heard any arguments among them!

JIM: *(grinning)* No arguments, huh? Well, that's a pretty good sign! Where shall I set him?

LAURA: Put him on the table. They all like a change of scenery once in a while!

JIM: Well, well, well, well—*(He places the glass piece on the table, then raises his arms and stretches.)* Look how big my shadow is when I stretch!

1690 LAURA: Oh, oh, yes—it stretches across the ceiling!

JIM: *(crossing to the door)* I think it's stopped raining. *(He opens the fire-escape door and the background music changes to a dance tune.)* Where does the music come from?

LAURA: From the Paradise Dance Hall across the alley.

JIM: How about cutting the rug a little, Miss Wingfield?

LAURA: Oh, I—

JIM: Or is your program filled up? Let me have a look at it. *(He grasps an imaginary card.)* Why, every dance is taken! I'll
1700    just have to scratch some out.

*(Waltz music: "La Golondrina.")*

Ahhh, a waltz! *(He executes some sweeping turns by himself,*

*then holds his arms toward Laura.)*

LAURA: *(breathlessly)* I—can't dance!

JIM: There you go, that inferiority stuff!

LAURA: I've never danced in my life!

JIM: Come on, try!

LAURA: Oh, but I'd step on you!

JIM: I'm not made out of glass.

LAURA: How—how—how do we start?

JIM: Just leave it to me. You hold your arms out a little.    1710

LAURA: Like this?

JIM: *(taking her in his arms)* A little bit higher. Right. Now don't tighten up, that's the main thing about it—relax.

LAURA: *(laughing breathlessly)* It's hard not to.

JIM: Okay.

LAURA: I'm afraid you can't budge me.

JIM: What do you bet I can't? *(He swings her into motion.)*

LAURA: Goodness, yes, you can!

JIM: Let yourself go, now, Laura, just let yourself go.

LAURA: I'm—    1720

JIM: Come on!

LAURA: —trying!

JIM: Not so stiff—easy does it!

LAURA: I know but I'm—

JIM: Loosen th' backbone! There now, that's a lot better.

LAURA: Am I?

JIM: Lots, lots better! *(He moves her about the room in a clumsy waltz.)*

LAURA: Oh, my!

JIM: Ha-ha!    1730

LAURA: Oh, my goodness!

JIM: Ha-ha-ha!

*(They suddenly bump into the table, and the glass piece on it falls to the floor. Jim stops the dance.)*

What did we hit on?

LAURA: Table.

JIM: Did something fall off it? I think—

LAURA: Yes.

JIM: I hope that it wasn't the little glass horse with the horn!

LAURA: Yes. *(She stoops to pick it up.)*

JIM: Aw, aw, aw. Is it broken?

LAURA: Now it is just like all the other horses.    1740

JIM: It's lost its—

LAURA: Horn! It doesn't matter. Maybe it's a blessing in disguise.

JIM: You'll never forgive me. I bet that that was your favorite piece of glass.

LAURA: I don't have favorites much. It's no tragedy, Freckles. Glass breaks so easily. No matter how careful you are. The traffic jars the shelves and things fall off them.

JIM: Still I'm awfully sorry that I was the cause.

LAURA: *(smiling)* I'll just imagine he had an operation. The    1750 horn was removed to make him feel less—freakish!

*(They both laugh.)*

Now he will feel more at home with the other horses, the ones that don't have horns. . . .

JIM: Ha-ha, that's very funny! *(Suddenly he is serious.)* I'm glad to see that you have a sense of humor. You know—you're—well—very different! Surprisingly different from anyone else I know! (*His voice becomes soft and hesitant with a genuine feeling.*) Do you mind me telling you that?

(*Laura is abashed beyond speech.*)

I mean it in a nice way—

(*Laura nods shyly, looking away.*)

1760   You make me feel sort of—I don't know how to put it! I'm usually pretty good at expressing things, but—this is something that I don't know how to say!

(*Laura touches her throat and clears it—turns the broken unicorn in her hands. His voice becomes softer.*)

Has anyone ever told you that you were pretty?

(*There is a pause, and the music rises slightly. Laura looks up slowly, with wonder, and shakes her head.*)

Well, you are! In a very different way from anyone else. And all the nicer because of the difference, too.

(*His voice becomes low and husky. Laura turns away, nearly faint with the novelty of her emotions.*)

I wish that you were my sister. I'd teach you to have some confidence in yourself. The different people are not like other people, but being different is nothing to be ashamed of. Because other people are not such wonderful people.
1770   They're one hundred times one thousand. You're one times one! They walk all over the earth. You just stay here. They're common as—weeds, but—you—well, you're—*Blue Roses!*

(*Image on screen: Blue Roses.*)

(*The music changes.*)

LAURA: But blue is wrong for—roses. . . .
JIM: It's right for you! You're—pretty!
LAURA: In what respect am I pretty?
JIM: In all respects—believe me! Your eyes—your hair—are pretty! Your hands are pretty! (*He catches hold of her hand.*) You think I'm making this up because I'm invited to dinner and have to be nice. Oh, I could do that! I could put on an
1780   act for you, Laura, and say lots of things without being very sincere. But this time I am. I'm talking to you sincerely. I happened to notice you had this inferiority complex that keeps you from feeling comfortable with people. Somebody needs to build your confidence up and make you proud instead of shy and turning away and—blushing. Somebody—ought to—kiss you, Laura!

(*His hand slips slowly up her arm to her shoulder as the music swells tumultuously. He suddenly turns her about and kisses her on the lips. When he releases her, Laura sinks on the sofa with a bright, dazed look. Jim backs away and fishes in his pocket for a cigarette.*)

(*Legend on screen: "A souvenir."*)

Stumblejohn!

(*He lights the cigarette, avoiding her look. There is a peal of girlish laughter from Amanda in the kitchenette. Laura slowly raises and opens her hand. It still contains the little broken glass animal. She looks at it with a tender, bewildered expression.*)

Stumblejohn! I shouldn't have done that—that was way off the beam. You don't smoke, do you?

(*She looks up, smiling, not hearing the question. He sits beside her rather gingerly. She looks at him speechlessly—waiting. He coughs decorously and moves a little farther aside as he considers the situation and senses her feelings, dimly, with perturbation. He speaks gently.*)

Would you—care for a—mint?   1790

(*She doesn't seem to hear him but her look grows brighter even.*)

Peppermint? Life Saver? My pocket's a regular drugstore—wherever I go. . . . (*He pops a mint in his mouth. Then he gulps and decides to make a clean breast of it. He speaks slowly and gingerly.*) Laura, you know, if I had a sister like you, I'd do the same thing as Tom. I'd bring out fellows and—introduce her to them. The right type of boys—of a type to—appreciate her. Only—well—he made a mistake about me. Maybe I've got no call to be saying this. That may not have been the idea in having me over. But what if it was? There's nothing wrong about that. The only trouble is that  1800 in my case—I'm not in a situation to—do the right thing. I can't take down your number and say I'll phone. I can't call up next week and—ask for a date. I thought I had better explain the situation in case you—misunderstood it and—I hurt your feelings. . . .

(*There is a pause. Slowly, very slowly, Laura's look changes, her eyes returning slowly from his to the glass figure in her palm. Amanda utters another gay laugh in the kitchenette.*)

LAURA: (*faintly*) You—won't—call again?
JIM: No, Laura, I can't. (*He rises from the sofa.*) As I was just explaining, I've—got strings on me. Laura, I've—been going steady! I go out all the time with a girl named Betty. She's a home-girl like you, and Catholic, and Irish, and in a  1810 great many ways we—get along fine. I met her last summer on a moonlight boat trip up the river to Alton, on the *Majestic*. Well—right away from the start it was—love!

(*Legend: Love!*)

(*Laura sways slightly forward and grips the arm of the sofa. He fails to notice, now enrapt in his own comfortable being.*)

Being in love has made a new man of me!

(*Leaning stiffly forward, clutching the arm of the sofa, Laura struggles visibly with her storm. But Jim is oblivious; she is a long way off.*)

The power of love is really pretty tremendous! Love is something that—changes the whole world, Laura!

(*The storm abates a little and Laura leans back. He notices her again.*)

It happened that Betty's aunt took sick, she got a wire and had to go to Centralia. So Tom—when he asked me to dinner—I naturally just accepted the invitation, not knowing that you—that he—that I—(*He stops awkwardly.*) Huh—  1820 I'm a stumblejohn!

(*He flops back on the sofa. The holy candles on the altar of Laura's face have been snuffed out. There is a look of almost *infinite desolation. Jim glances at her uneasily.)*

I wish that you would—say something.

*(She bites her lip which was trembling and then bravely smiles. She opens her hand again on the broken glass figure. Then she gently takes his hand and raises it level with her own. She carefully places the unicorn in the palm of his hand, then pushes his fingers closed upon it.)*

What are you—doing that for? You want me to have him? Laura?
*(She nods.)*
What for?

LAURA: A—souvenir. . . .

*(She rises unsteadily and crouches beside the Victrola to wind it up.)*

*(Legend on screen: "Things have a way of turning out so badly!" Or image: "Gentleman caller waving goodbye—gaily.")*

*(At this moment Amanda rushes brightly back into the living room. She bears a pitcher of fruit punch in an old-fashioned cut-glass pitcher, and a plate of macaroons. The plate has a gold border and poppies painted on it.)*

AMANDA: Well, well, well! Isn't the air delightful after the shower? I've made you children a little liquid refreshment.
1830 *(She turns gaily to Jim.)* Jim, do you know that song about lemonade?

> *"Lemonade, lemonade*
> *Made in the shade and stirred with a spade—*
> *Good enough for any old maid!"*

JIM: *(uneasily)* Ha-ha! No—I never heard it.
AMANDA: Why, Laura! You look so serious!
JIM: We were having a serious conversation.
AMANDA: Good! Now you're better acquainted!
JIM: *(uncertainly)* Ha-ha! Yes.
1840 AMANDA: You modern young people are much more serious-minded than my generation. I was so gay as a girl!
JIM: You haven't changed, Mrs. Wingfield.
AMANDA: Tonight I'm rejuvenated! The gaiety of the occasion, Mr. O'Connor! *(She tosses her head with a peal of laughter, spilling some lemonade.)* Oooo! I'm baptizing myself!
JIM: Here—let me—
AMANDA: *(setting the pitcher down)* There now. I discovered we had some maraschino cherries. I dumped them in, juice and all!
1850 JIM: You shouldn't have gone to that trouble, Mrs. Wingfield.
AMANDA: Trouble, trouble? Why, it was loads of fun! Didn't you hear me cutting up in the kitchen? I bet your ears were burning! I told Tom how outdone with him I was for keeping you to himself so long a time! He should have brought you over much, much sooner! Well, now that you've found your way, I want you to be a very frequent caller! Not just occasional but all the time. Oh, we're going to have a lot of gay times together! I see them coming! Mmm, just breathe that air! So fresh, and the moon's so pretty! I'll skip back
1860 out—I know where my place is when young folks are having a—serious conversation!
JIM: Oh, don't go out, Mrs. Wingfield. The fact of the matter is I've got to be going.

AMANDA: Going, now? You're joking! Why, it's only the shank of the evening, Mr. O'Connor!
JIM: Well, you know how it is.
AMANDA: You mean you're a young workingman and have to keep workingmen's hours. We'll let you off early tonight. But only on the condition that next time you stay later. What's the best night for you? Isn't Saturday night the best 1870 night for you workingmen?
JIM: I have a couple of time-clocks to punch, Mrs. Wingfield. One at morning, another one at night!
AMANDA: My, but you *are* ambitious! You work at night, too?
JIM: No, Ma'am, not work but—Betty!

*(He crosses deliberately to pick up his hat. The band at the Paradise Dance Hall goes into a tender waltz.)*

AMANDA: Betty? Betty? Who's—Betty!

*(There is an ominous cracking sound in the sky.)*

JIM: Oh, just a girl. The girl I go steady with!

*(He smiles charmingly. The sky falls.)*

*(Legend: "The Sky Falls.")*

AMANDA: *(a long-drawn exhalation)* Ohhhh . . . Is it a serious romance, Mr. O'Connor?
JIM: We're going to be married the second Sunday in June.     1880
AMANDA: Ohhhh—how nice! Tom didn't mention that you were engaged to be married.
JIM: The cat's not out of the bag at the warehouse yet. You know how they are. They call you Romeo and stuff like that. *(He stops at the oval mirror to put on his hat. He carefully shapes the brim and the crown to give a discreetly dashing effect.)* It's been a wonderful evening, Mrs. Wingfield. I guess this is what they mean by Southern hospitality.
AMANDA: It really wasn't anything at all.
JIM: I hope it don't seem like I'm rushing off. But I promised 1890 Betty I'd pick her up at the Wabash depot, an' by the time I get my jalopy down there her train'll be in. Some women are pretty upset if you keep 'em waiting.
AMANDA: Yes, I know—the tyranny of women! *(She extends her hand.)* Goodbye, Mr. O'Connor. I wish you luck—and happiness—and success! All three of them, and so does Laura! Don't you, Laura?
LAURA: Yes!
JIM: *(taking Laura's hand)* Goodbye, Laura. I'm certainly going to treasure that souvenir. And don't you forget the 1900 good advice I gave you. *(He raises his voice to a cheery shout.)* So long, Shakespeare! Thanks again, ladies. Good night!

*(He grins and ducks jauntily out. Still bravely grimacing, Amanda closes the door on the gentleman caller. Then she turns back to the room with a puzzled expression. She and Laura don't dare to face each other. Laura crouches beside the Victrola to wind it.)*

AMANDA: *(faintly)* Things have a way of turning out so badly. I don't believe that I would play the Victrola. Well, well—well! Our gentleman caller was engaged to be married! *(She raises her voice.)* Tom!
TOM: *(from the kitchenette)* Yes, Mother?
AMANDA: Come in here a minute. I want to tell you something awfully funny.     1910

TOM: *(entering with a macaroon and a glass of the lemonade)* Has the gentleman caller gotten away already?

AMANDA: The gentleman caller has made an early departure. What a wonderful joke you played on us!

TOM: How do you mean?

AMANDA: You didn't mention that he was engaged to be married.

TOM: Jim? Engaged?

AMANDA: That's what he just informed us.

1920 TOM: I'll be jiggered! I didn't know about that.

AMANDA: That seems very peculiar.

TOM: What's peculiar about it?

AMANDA: Didn't you call him your best friend down at the warehouse?

TOM: He is, but how did I know?

AMANDA: It seems extremely peculiar that you wouldn't know your best friend was going to be married!

TOM: The warehouse is where I work, not where I know things about people!

1930 AMANDA: You don't know things anywhere! You live in a dream; you manufacture illusions!

*(He crosses to the door.)*

Where are you going?

TOM: I'm going to the movies.

AMANDA: That's right, now that you've had us make such fools of ourselves. The effort, the preparations, all the expense! The new floor lamp, the rug, the clothes for Laura! All for what? To entertain some other girl's fiancé! Go to the movies, go! Don't think about us, a mother deserted, an unmarried sister who's crippled and has no job! Don't let any-

1940 thing interfere with your selfish pleasure! Just go, go, go—to the movies!

TOM: All right, I will! The more you shout about my selfishness to me the quicker I'll go, and I won't go to the movies!

AMANDA: Go, then! Go to the moon—you selfish dreamer!

*(Tom smashes his glass on the floor. He plunges out on the fire escape, slamming the door. Laura screams in fright. The dance-hall music becomes louder. Tom stands on the fire escape, gripping the rail. The moon breaks through the storm clouds, illuminating his face.)*

*(Legend on screen: "And so goodbye . . . ")*

*(Tom's closing speech is timed with what is happening inside the house. We see, as though through soundproof glass, that Amanda appears to be making a comforting speech to Laura, who is huddled upon the sofa. Now that we cannot hear the mother's speech, her silliness is gone and she has dignity and tragic beauty. Laura's hair hides her face until, at the end of the speech, she lifts her head to smile at her mother. Amanda's gestures are slow and graceful, almost dancelike, as she comforts her daughter. At the end of her speech she glances a moment at the father's picture—then withdraws through the portieres. At the close of Tom's speech, Laura blows out the candles, ending the play.)*

TOM: I didn't go to the moon, I went much further—for time is the longest distance between two places. Not long after that I was fired for writing a poem on the lid of a shoe-box. I left Saint Louis. I descended the steps of this fire escape for a last time and followed, from then on, in my father's footsteps, attempting to find in motion what was lost in 1950 space. I traveled around a great deal. The cities swept about me like dead leaves, leaves that were brightly colored but torn away from the branches. I would have stopped, but I was pursued by something. It always came upon me unawares, taking me altogether by surprise. Perhaps it was a familiar bit of music. Perhaps it was only a piece of transparent glass. Perhaps I am walking along a street at night, in some strange city, before I have found companions. I pass the lighted window of a shop where perfume is sold. The window is filled with pieces of colored glass, tiny transpar- 1960 ent bottles in delicate colors, like bits of a shattered rainbow. Then all at once my sister touches my shoulder. I turn around and look into her eyes. Oh, Laura, Laura, I tried to leave you behind me, but I am more faithful than I intended to be! I reach for a cigarette, I cross the street, I run into the movies or a bar, I buy a drink, I speak to the nearest stranger—anything that can blow your candles out!

*(Laura bends over the candles.)*

For nowadays the world is lit by lightning! Blow out your candles, Laura—and so goodbye. . . .

*(She blows the candles out.)*

WALTER *Wager conducted this interview with Tennessee Williams.*

*How do you literally write a play; where do you begin? Does an idea nurture within you for a long time? Do the characters come first and then the story?*

WILLIAMS: It is almost impossible to pinpoint the start of the play, at least for me. I think that all plays come out of some inner tension in the playwright himself. He is concerned about something, and that concern begins to work itself out in the form of a creative activity. Sometimes I will get up in the morning and feel a little more energetic than usual and I will just start writing.

*With a pen or with a typewriter—how do you work?*

WILLIAMS: Typewriter—I typewrite very rapidly.

*You were saying that sometimes you get up in the morning and start to write dialogue.*

WILLIAMS: Yes, something on a page or two pages of dialogue will spark in the way of characters or situation and I just go along from there. I am a very wasteful writer. I go through several drafts, as many as four or five before I finish a work. I am sure that any playwright would give you practically the same description.

*Albee said to me that he writes a play when it becomes more painful not to write it than to write it.*

WILLIAMS: That's a very good way of putting it, you know.

*Then the subject literally forces itself out?*

WILLIAMS: Yes, some people accuse you of being too personal, you know, in your writing. The truth of the matter is—I don't think you can escape being personal in your writing.

*Impossible.*

WILLIAMS: That doesn't mean that you are one of the characters in the play. What it means simply is that the dynamics of the characters in the play, the tensions correspond to something that you are personally going through—the concerns of the play and the tensions of the play and your own concerns and tensions at the time you wrote it. I have always found that to be true.

*I have noticed that in many of your plays there is poetry or one of your characters is a poet, and I have heard from someone you know, the former drama critic of the St. Louis* Post-Dispatch, *that you began or have done a great deal of poetry writing, and yet you don't write much poetry now. Why have you given up poetry? I have read your poetry and it's excellent.*

WILLIAMS: I found that I had written enough poetry—I mean in the form of poems; I think plays can be just as lyrical as a poem can be; you can use just as much personal lyricism in a play as you can in a poem; and also I have noticed as writers get older—that is, poets—they tend to write less poetry. I think actual poetry is a medium more for the young than for the middle-aged.

*I think the question of age is an interesting one because in the introduction to one of your plays, I think* The Rose Tattoo, *you mention "the continual rush of time that deprives life of dignity and meaning." Does this question of aging trouble you now that you have turned fifty? Is it something that you are going to be writing about?*

WILLIAMS: I think I have always written quite a bit about it. We were having a poker game up here last night and at one point the game got too mixed up and somebody knocked a glass off the table accidently; there was no violence involved; and suddenly all at once I began to talk about age. I said, "I can't believe it, I am fifty-four years old now, and I think the reason it is so incredible to me that I have suddenly reached this age is that each year is not another year to me—it's a play." And sometimes three years are a play and my life seems to be chalked off not in years but in plays and pieces of work, and so I am taken by surprise by how much time has passed and my being as old as I am.

*I am stunned, myself, when I read your biography this afternoon—to see the numbers—your age; but I have no sense of the writing of this being the work of a man of forty or fifty or any age. I have read them as plays; none of that has come through, although some of your recent plays have been concerned with older people, such as the* Slapstick Tragedy, *which is about to open now.*

WILLIAMS: There is no particular age in that.

*There are elderly women in it.*

WILLIAMS: It seems to exist outside of any specific time and, no, they are not elderly women. We are not going to age the women in the plays; they are going to appear the same ages as the actresses actually are playing. Well, the play is so "way out" that it will not have to be pinpointed in time.

*The question of pinpointing them in plays is also an interesting one. Most of your plays, I believe, are set in the South, where you grew up, yet, do you consider yourself a Southern writer, because the questions you raise seem to be universally applicable to me?*

WILLIAMS: I think I am becoming less associated with the South than I was originally. I was a Southern writer because my parents were Southern and I was born in the South. Now, my father was from Tennessee and my mother from Ohio, so it was a sort of split between. Would you say Ohio is the North?

*Well, I guess you would say that it is on the verge of the South.*

WILLIAMS: She was from southern Ohio but she went to East Tennessee when she was a very young girl, so she grew up to be a Southerner.

*Why did you take the name of "Tennessee"?*

WILLIAMS: Because my father's family were Tennesseeans. They were very active in the making of the State of Tennessee.

*And everyone calls you "Tennessee" now?*

WILLIAMS: No, I prefer people to call me "Tom," my real name. Of course, you know in professional meetings people call me "Tennessee."

*Your good friends call you "Tom."*

WILLIAMS: People with whom I am close to, I always ask them to call me "Tom"; it's easier and I like the name "Tom."

*You are the grandchild of an Episcopal minister?*

WILLIAMS: Oh yes, he was almost my closest relation.

*Are you still actively involved in any discernible religion?*

WILLIAMS: Well, I keep a Russian icon by my bed. It was given to me by a dear friend in London for my birthday. It is a very beautiful Russian icon and I don't suppose I would keep it there if I didn't have some religious feeling; it is obvious that I do have religious feeling. It may seem ingenuous to have religious feeling to a lot of people but to me it seems necessary.

*Could you define this religious feeling?*

WILLIAMS: Well, it isn't associated with any particular church. It's just a general feeling of one's dependence upon some superior being of mystic nature.

*Does God or religion come up much in your plays? I haven't seen it specifically.*

WILLIAMS: Oh, yes, I notice the word "God" occurring several times in the recent disaster.

*In one of your interviews you said that in only a few moments of life is there really human contact. Does that mean you feel it is basically a rather lonely existence?*

WILLIAMS: Now, that is probably some quotation that is not an exact quotation, because I certainly don't feel that. I feel that in many, many moments in life there is almost continual contact; under what circumstances I said that I can't imagine, because it isn't what I feel—at least not what I feel *now*.

*When you were a child, I heard an anecdote told that you once were out in the back yard digging.*

WILLIAMS: Oh yes, that was one of my mother's favorite stories.

*What were you digging for—devils?*

WILLIAMS: Yes, she said—I am sure she was telling the truth—it was quite a funny story. She found me digging in the back yard. She said, What are you digging for? I said I was digging for the devil.

*In a sense, do you still think you're digging for the devil in these plays?*

WILLIAMS: In a sense, yes; but I am also digging for the opposite of the devil.

*For the angels?*

WILLIAMS: For God.

*In one of your comments you state the plays represent a struggle between good and evil—of man's struggle between good and evil. How would you define good and evil in our contemporary society?*

WILLIAMS: I don't think it needs definition. It is so obvious. We all know—when I look at the papers that arrive every morning, it is just incredible what is going on; you know that so much is fantastically abominable going on. This whole Vietnam bit is so incomprehensibly evil to me.

*You mean the killing that is going on there?*

WILLIAMS: Yes, the naphtha—what is that?

*Napalm.*

WILLIAMS: The way they burn people alive and the way they spray chemicals over the rice fields so they will starve; I don't need to list the instruments . . .

*You are talking about the cruelty of modern weapons rather than the political connotation.*

WILLIAMS: Yes, they are incredibly cruel and, believe me, nothing that will be won out of this war will be worth the life of a single man who died in it, in my opinion.

*Do you have equally strong feelings about the civil-rights movement in the South?*

WILLIAMS: Yes, equally strong.

*Because you haven't touched that much in your writing, or do I do you an injustice?*

WILLIAMS: I always try to write obliquely. I think the closest I came to writing directly was in *Orpheus Descending* about my feelings about what goes on in certain parts of the country.

*I have found it interesting that a number of the Southern writers, such as yourself and the late Mr. Faulkner, didn't really comment too directly on this question. They were primarily concerned with human struggles of a more general nature.*

WILLIAMS: I don't see the difference between them. I think they were so closely interrelated that I don't see how you can divide the two things.

*Do you think that you would ever write directly on this question?*

WILLIAMS: I am not a direct writer; I am always an oblique writer, if I can be; I want to be allusive; I don't want to be one of these people who hit the nail on the head all the time.

*Have you always been this sort of writer—I mean as a child? By the way, did you write as a child?*

WILLIAMS: I started to write around twelve.

*And did you start writing in this allusive manner then, or probably less so?*

WILLIAMS: Less so, of course, because children are more simple.

*I hate to keep bringing up your past remarks as if to belabor you with them, but in one of the interviews you gave you spoke of the depravity and bestiality in life and went on along those lines— is this a current concern of yours?*

WILLIAMS: I think it is of anyone who pauses to think and who has some perception.

*Now, on the question of perception, I recently read a critical study of your plays that made reference to the obvious influence of Freud on your work. Is that a fair statement? Have you read a lot of Freud?*

WILLIAMS: I looked into maybe a book or two of Freud but I never read any of it.

*You observed it in life?*

WILLIAMS: To the extent that I have any connection with Freud—I think Freud did illuminate many dark areas in the human unconscious, and I think I write mainly from my unconscious mind.

*And do you write day or night? Is there any special time you write?*

WILLIAMS: I find it almost impossible to write any time but the morning, when I have more energy to write.

*Is it early morning, or after breakfast?*

WILLIAMS: Immediately after breakfast.

*And do you require any special conditions?*

WILLIAMS: Oh, yes, I require many special conditions. I have quite a ritual.

*Tell us about it.*

WILLIAMS: Do you want to know about the whole ritual? I think that should be a secret of my own. I think that should be my secret . . . whatever makes it possible for me to work, I should do, because I must work. Up to 1955 I found it much easier to work, and after 1955 I was conscious of a certain fatigue, and now, well, when I get up in the morning . . . let me give you a few little clues— I have anemia, which is rather a problem. I don't know how severe it is, or if anemia is the right word for it, but it is the word that is used; and I have to get up in the morning and give myself an injection, which peps me up sufficiently to get to the goddam desk. And combined with the shot, there's also the two strong cups of coffee; and then I always have one of these martinis on my writing table; I don't take more than one. But I found after 1955, specifically after *Cat on a Hot Tin*

*Roof*—that I needed these things to give me the physical energy to work; and the intelligent thing might have been to stop working, to rest. But I am a compulsive writer. I have tried to stop working and I am bored to death. . . . I don't know what I am here for . . . what is the purpose of my being here.

*I am pleased that you are so compulsive . . . and we all benefit from it every year or two.*

WILLIAMS: Well, occasionally I hope that somebody gets something out of it.

*Do you have any sense of being isolated now or lonely? I have heard somebody say that, that because one or two of your plays haven't been received as some of the earlier plays, that this has troubled you.*

WILLIAMS: I have never been without terrific anxiety about all of my work. You know, it's constitutional with me to be anxious as all hell about all of my work. I'll never get over that and I never hope to; I just have to live with it.

*I guess that's the nature of being a writer—you put your head on the block every time you put a piece of paper into the machine.*

WILLIAMS: Yes, of course you do, and it takes a physical toll of your nervous energies. You've got to do all kinds of things to try to make yourself stand up under it. Now, I am not a self-destructive person; I try to keep myself going. Every afternoon I go to the YMCA and I will swim sixteen or twenty lengths of the pool; that is when I am in New York. When I am in Key West I will swim, I would say, about half a mile in the sea.

*Do you do most of your writing in Key West or here?*

WILLIAMS: I enjoy writing in Key West more than I do here; but I have to be here right now.

*Now, about the other playwrights—first of all, which playwrights do you think have interested you or influenced your work in the past?*

WILLIAMS: Strindberg and Chekhov—if you are talking about master playwrights of the past.

*And which of the current playwrights interest you, American or foreign?*

WILLIAMS: American or foreign—nobody now, because I have my own way which has crystallized for me and nobody influences me anymore.

*Which playwrights interest you rather than influence you?*

WILLIAMS: Interest me? They all interest me if they're good. I think in America Edward Albee is by a good margin the most interesting of the new American playwrights.

*Do you read much in the way of novels?*

WILLIAMS: I don't have much taste for fiction recently—that is, in the last ten years or so, I prefer to read journals and books, collected letters of writers and of the people's biographies. Right now I am reading *The Diary of Anais Nin,* who is one of our very fine writers.

*You don't travel as much as you used to; does this mean you are settling down more in America, you are more at ease in America?*

WILLIAMS: It means, I think, mainly that I don't have the energy to bat around the world like I used to. I went around the world once and lived a good deal of my time during the last fifteen years or more in Rome, Italy, and I saw most of the interesting cities in Europe, cities interesting to me, but now I don't know whether I can resume that sort of traveling or not; I am rather dubious that I can.

*There are two more questions that I would like to ask you. One, you have stated in an earlier interview that you found the state of contemporary society terrifying.*

WILLIAMS: That I am sure I have said because I really do find it so.

*What sort of things do you particularly find terrifying to you?*

WILLIAMS: All the things you see on the front page of the morning paper.

*Violence, cruelty, dishonor?*

WILLIAMS: All those things—the senseless wars going on; you know, so many things—the struggle for civil rights. . . . I'm not a person dedicated primarily to bettering social conditions, because I am not able to, except through my writing, and I doubt whether people will pay enough attention to writing for writing to have any effect.

*You said one more thing. You said, "I don't think America must settle for its present state; you must go forward and be unafraid." In what areas must we go forward, do you think; in what areas must we move?*

WILLIAMS: I think we are moving in some good areas now. We were just talking about the civil rights.

*That's important?*

WILLIAMS: That's very important and we are making progress—not as fast as we might hope for—and there is some very ugly opposition to it; but it seems to me we are making some remarkable progress in that direction. I feel that finally American people have a sense of justice. It may take them a while to formulate it because there are so many false leaders—you know, politicians like Senator Dirksen and Mr. Nixon; and there was the late Senator McCarthy; there are so many people like that who are impeding the spirit of American people—their understanding, I mean.

*On the question of the spirit of American people, do you have any particular feeling about the young people today?*

WILLIAMS: I love what the young people of today are doing. They don't seem to be scared of anything, except their own shadows, maybe, and that's wonderful. It's wonderful how they can go out and face police bullies in the South, Ku Klux Klan, the whole bit, and they do have that courage, and it's marvelous. I think this is one of the great generations of young people that we now have.

*Finally, you said: "I'd rather stay an outsider than adjust to injustice." Do you still think of yourself as an outsider?*

WILLIAMS: Outside of what?

*Outside of the main social stream, in America.*

WILLIAMS: I am very much a part of it, I hope; I hope to be always.

*So you don't feel outside anymore?*

WILLIAMS: No, I never did really; if I said that I was kidding somebody, not myself.

*I thank you very much, Mr. Williams. You were very kind and generous with your time. You make a wicked martini, too.*

WILLIAMS: I hope it made some sense.

# Bertolt Brecht

Bertolt Brecht (1898–1956) changed the course of the modern European theater—and theater around the world—more than any playwright since Ibsen. But Brecht's sphere of influence extends beyond his career as a playwright. As a dramatist, he wrote an unsurpassed body of plays. As a theoretician, Brecht's conception of "alienation" in the epic theater opened the way for sweeping innovation in our understanding of the possibilities of the stage. As a director, Brecht's work with his company, the Berliner Ensemble, made it the most influential and important theater in postwar Europe. The challenge of understanding Brecht is to understand the dialectical interplay between theory and practice that informs his assault on stage realism and on the bourgeois theater itself.

Eugen Berthold Brecht (he later changed his name to Bertolt) was born in Augsburg, Bavaria, in 1898 to a prosperous family. In 1917, he enrolled at Munich University in the natural sciences, and worked as a drama critic on the side; he also began work on several plays, including *Baal* (1917). In 1918 he was conscripted into military service for the remainder of World War I, and worked in a military hospital. He returned briefly to the university after the war, but soon turned his attention full-time to the theater. He moved to Berlin—Germany's theatrical capital at the time—and had the good fortune to work with two influential directors, Max Reinhardt and Erwin Piscator. Piscator advocated the use of new technologies in the theater as a way of developing a kind of performance more responsive to the mechanized and accelerated routines of modern life; Brecht acknowledged that many of his own staging techniques were derived from his work with Piscator in the 1920s. Throughout the 1920s and early 1930s, Brecht wrote a series of plays that brought him notoriety, largely for their satire of the bourgeois establishment: *Drums in the Night* (1919), *In the Jungle of Cities* (1921), *Man Is Man* (1926), and the musical plays he wrote in collaboration with the composer Kurt Weill, *The Threepenny Opera* (1928) and *The Rise and Fall of the City of Mahagonny* (1930).

Brecht also began his serious reading of Marx in the 1920s, and it was his application of a Marxist dialectic to the process of theater that gave rise to his most powerful and original ideas for the stage. From Marx, Brecht adopted a revolutionary posture, not only toward the class struggle, but toward the stage of bourgeois "realism." To Brecht, the realistic theater was not an unbiased window on social reality. Instead, Brecht argued that realistic theater presented a particular political vision, a view of society as inevitably determined by history and evolution, and therefore not susceptible to change. In order to displace "realism," and to demonstrate these hidden politics, Brecht redefined Marx's conception of "alienation" as a theatrical practice.

In *Capital,* Marx argues that the division of labor in modern industrial production has altered the relationship between mankind and the world. Because they now sell their labor rather than producing goods directly, the workers have an estranged relationship to the commodities they make. These commodities, Marx contends, then seem "alien" in that they appear to have arisen magically as a part of the "natural" world. Yet, even as commodities become part of "nature," the workers become dehumanized, incorporated into the machinery of production. They are "alienated" from their labor and from the world in which they live. The prevailing view of the world—in which commodities confront workers as something natural and entirely separate from their makers—is, to Marx, a *false* view, perpetuated within the bourgeois social order to the political advantage of the ruling classes. Brecht's theater works to provide its audience with ways of regarding bourgeois reality—including realistic theater and drama—as "unnatural," as a political vision, as an ideological view of the world produced in the interest of profit. Brecht's theater, that is, works to "alienate" or "estrange" the audience from the commonplace "realities" of daily life—which we have unreflectively come to regard as "natural" and "inevitable"—in order to train us to question the world made by modern capitalism and the society it sustains. As he wrote in "The Modern Theater is the Epic Theater," his theater is based on a "radical separation of the elements" of production, rather than on the scenic unity typical of realism. The seamless illusion of the realistic stage is that theater's most seductive commodity, for it constantly and subliminally urges the audience to accept its "picture" of reality as a natural, apolitical image of the world as it is. Brecht's theater, in contrast, always shows both the dramatic illusion (the character, the setting, the action) and the process of its making (the work of the actor, the machinery of the theater, the activities of the stage). Brecht works to show the "means of production" in his theater, as a way of suggesting that stage realism, like social reality outside the theater, is *made*, not given.

Brecht called this theater by a variety of names, including **EPIC THEATER,** the term now generally used for Brecht's body of theory and technique. Brecht's plays tend to be episodic, a disconnected, open-ended **MONTAGE** of scenes—the audience must arrive at its own understanding of how the events are linked together, rather than being given an apparently inevitable narrative. Brecht generally left the stage bare in his productions, as a way of preventing the audience from seeing a complete illusion of some fictional dramatic locale. He exposed the lights above the stage, so the audience could see how lights influence the mood of the scene and so influence the audience's judgment. Brecht fragmented the "realistic" unity of the setting in other ways, too. Films could be projected on screens above the stage, forcing the audience to hold the drama in counterpoint to more recent events, and placards onstage described the action to take place before the scene began. Finally, Brecht also urged his actors not to empathize entirely with the characters they played, but to strike a balance between a Stanislavskian identification with the character (being "in character," acting the character entirely from his or her point of view) and a more demonstrative attitude, one that enables the actor to represent the character from a variety of perspectives. Through these means, Brecht worked to involve the audience in the process of the play's production. Rather than being seduced by a commodified illusion of reality, the audience of epic theater is invited to consider, and enjoy, how the theater makes its fictions—as a way of teaching the audience to adopt a more critical, "alienated" way of seeing life outside the theater.

Brecht used many of these devices in *The Threepenny Opera* and in the series of plays he wrote in exile. Forced to flee Germany by Nazi purges of left-wing writers in 1933, Brecht spent the greater part of his creative life on the run, living briefly in Sweden, in Finland, and finally in Santa Monica, California, from 1941 to 1947. He worked extensively on *Life of Galileo* in California, collaborating on this English version with the British actor Charles Laughton. He was also questioned by the House Un-American Activities Committee in 1947, as part of its infamous investigation of Communism in the entertainment industry. Brecht was not charged, and left the United States the following day to return to Europe and Germany. During his lengthy exile, with no theater and little support, Brecht wrote his major plays: *Life of Galileo* (1938), *The Good Person of Sezchwan* (1939), *Mother Courage and Her Children* (1939), and *The Caucasian Chalk Circle* (1944); he also wrote his most important theoretical essays, including *A Short Organum for the Theater* (1948).

Brecht returned to East Berlin in 1947 and established his company, the Berliner Ensemble. Brecht's antirealist plays had long been the source of conflict with the **SOCIAL REALISM** advocated by the Communist Party, and even after the war Brecht had to work with a wary eye on the East German authorities. Nonetheless, the Berliner Ensemble—under Brecht's guidance, and with the talents of his wife, Helene Weigel—became the leading European production company of the 1950s, sowing the seeds of innovation in every country they visited. Brecht died in August 1956, just before the Berliner Ensemble's stunning visit to London, but the influence of his conception of theater has become worldwide, visible in plays from Jean Genet's *The Blacks* to Luis Valdez's *Los Vendidos* to Edward Bond's *Bingo* to Caryl Churchill's *Cloud 9*.

## Galileo (1945)

*Life of Galileo* is in many ways typical of Brecht's practice as a playwright and as a theoretician.° As a play in the mode of epic theater, *Life of Galileo* rigorously alienates its audiences from the traditions of romantic drama and performance. As Brecht wrote in "Building up a Part: Laughton's Galileo," the play directly assaults the conventions of historical drama; it "cannot be performed, without drastically changing the present-day style of production, as a historical 'war-horse,' for instance, with a star part." The emphasis of the play is not centrally on "Galileo," as a tragic center of

---

°Brecht originally entitled the play *Life of Galileo* when he wrote the first version in 1938. The translation he made with Charles Laughton—printed here—was called simply *Galileo*. Brecht returned to his original title when he revised the play for the last time in 1955. In the text below, *Life of Galileo* is used to refer to Brecht's play, and *Galileo* refers to the version he produced with Charles Laughton.

the play's action; instead, the play emphasizes Galileo's *life,* and the ways in which the conduct of that life are implicated in the life of Galileo's community. Neither tragedy nor historical romance, *Life of Galileo* encourages its audience to adopt an attitude of "wonder and criticism" toward its protagonist, that dialectical fusion of engagement and distance that is the hallmark of Brecht's thinking about theater.

How does Brecht accomplish this refunctioning of the materials of individualist history? The stylistic devices of epic theater—the titles, the introductory songs, the episodic arrangement of the plot—are much in evidence, of course. But Brecht's assault on how we "read" the character of Galileo, how we interpret his actions is much more subtle and suggestive. For throughout the play, Brecht places Galileo onstage in ways intended to disorient an audience expecting a conventionally heroic figure. In the first scene, for instance, Brecht uses the display of Galileo's body, and his earnest desire to teach Andrea to suggest the appetitive force of scientific inquiry for Galileo. The appetite for food, the appetite for physical pleasure, the appetite for learning are not *different* appetites for Galileo, but are fundamentally the same appetite. If we had expected, Brecht might say, an "intellectual" hero, whose commitment to the things of the mind is strong enough to make him endure the suffering of the flesh, the torture to be threatened by the Inquisition, we have an unrealistic understanding of human nature, and an unrealistic understanding of political nature as well. For much as Brecht dialecticizes the categories "mind" and "body"—taking a conventional opposition and showing the two terms to be interinvolved, mutually interdependent—so he insistently dialecticizes the relationship between individual and social action, and between "scientific" learning and the state.

Brecht addresses this latter issue in the first scene as well. Galileo's ability to practice science depends not on the abstract "value" of his discoveries, but on their monetary "value" to the state. As the Curator of the university remarks, "Only what brings in scudi is worth scudi." Throughout the play, Brecht undermines Galileo's desire to mark out a separate sphere of "pure" research, a kind of intellectual ivory tower. The state—represented here both by the university and by the Church—has an interest in the kind of knowledge that science produces, and has the ability to regulate what kinds of discovery will be tolerated, will be allowed to count as knowledge. Brecht makes this point in Scene 11, one of the most brilliant scenes of the play. In this scene, Cardinal Barberini—a scientist himself—is arrayed in his papal garments; he opens the scene defending both Galileo, and recognizing the need to protect a "pure" science: "I won't permit the multiplication tables to be broken!" But once he is dressed in the robes of authority, he consents to allowing the Inquisitor to display the instruments of torture to Galileo.

Much as *Life of Galileo* argues that all "knowledge" is produced within social institutions which lend it legitimacy, and so lend it the status of "knowledge" or "truth," so the play also works to undermine the notion that scientific inquiry—or *any* inquiry—is a completely individual activity. Galileo opens the play claiming to "foresee in our lifetime people will talk astronomy in the market place," and Brecht emphasizes the extent to which Galileo becomes a figure of revolutionary potential in Scene 9, in which a carnivalesque pageant is concluded with a giant, stuffed figure of "Galileo, the Bible-killer!" and Galileo's discovery that the earth revolves around the sun seems to authorize resistance to political as well as religious authority: "So each of you wake up and do just as he pleases."

To speak of the play in this way, though, is to suggest that Brecht provides us with a "lesson," predigested "truth" about Galileo, science, knowledge, and the state. But the function of epic theater is to engage audiences in a particular, "alienated" process of thinking, not to give them "the answer." For this reason, the play's final three scenes are unusually open-ended. In Scene 12, Galileo recants his discoveries as error and heresy; but when he appears onstage he seems neither the heroic martyr nor the quisling sell-out that he might in a more conventional play. For the scene, after all, has been less about the offstage Galileo than about the responses of the cast onstage, particularly Andrea and Federzoni, his scientific protégés: what have they expected from Galileo, why have they needed *him* to act as a hero, rather than acting simply as a man? If Scene 12 stages the conventional "recantation scene" in a disturbing, unexpected register, Scene 13 stages the "reconciliation scene" in similar ways. Here, Andrea confronts Galileo after years of imprisonment, and discovers that Galileo has continued his scientific work under the watchful eyes of the Church.

Galileo manages to give Andrea the manuscript of the *Discorsi* to smuggle out of Italy. Andrea regards this act as Galileo's subversion of state authority: "You came back: 'I've surrendered but I am alive.' We cried: 'Your hands are stained!' You say: 'Better stained than empty.'" Andrea, that is, makes the standard justification of scientific discovery, that any discovery is worth the addition to abstract "knowledge" that it provides, regardless of the social costs of its production or the consequences of its dissemination. It is a mark of Brecht's irony here that Galileo—not Andrea—recognizes the shallowness of this remark and its damning truth: "'Better stained than empty.' Sounds realistic. Sounds like me. A new science, a new ethics." Brecht's final moment of alienation, though, occurs in the final scene of the play: a scene in which "knowledge"—the manuscript of the *Discorsi*—and not Galileo, is the central character. What does it mean that Galileo's work, science produced under these conditions, in a world rife with superstition, poverty, oppression, will now be disseminated throughout Europe? As Brecht revised the play during and after World War II, these questions took on a new urgency, for Brecht saw the collaboration between the scientific community and the U.S. government in the production of the atomic bomb as an extension of the relationship between science and the state at the center of *Life of Galileo*.

    *Life of Galileo* exemplifies Brecht's attitude toward theater in one other respect. Given Brecht's insistence that "the proof of the pudding is in the eating," it's not surprising that Brecht happily revised his plays for different productions. *Life of Galileo* was first written in German in 1938 and produced in Zurich in 1943. Then, in exile in California, Brecht collaborated with the actor Charles Laughton on an English version in 1944 and 1945; this version, entitled simply *Galileo*, is the version printed here. In this version, Brecht cut several scenes from the earlier German version, rewrote and expanded several scenes, and added several new elements. He made Ludovico an aristocrat, and added Federzoni and Matti. After he returned to Germany, Brecht produced a third version of *Life of Galileo*, translating several elements of the English-language version into German, restoring elements from the first version, and adding some new material. Revising his play for new audiences, new moments in history, Brecht testifies to his sense that the *politics* of "political theater" do not arise solely from the text, but from the work it can accomplish in production on the stage.

# — Galileo —
## Bertolt Brecht
### TRANSLATED BY CHARLES LAUGHTON

■ ■ ■ It is my opinion that the earth is very noble and admirable by reason of so many and so different alterations and generations which are incessantly made therein.

—GALILEO GALILEI

## —CHARACTERS—

GALILEO GALILEI

ANDREA SARTI (*two actors: boy and man*)

MRS. SARTI

LUDOVICO MARSILI

PRIULI, THE CURATOR

SAGREDO, *Galileo's friend*

VIRGINIA GALILEI

TWO SENATORS

MATTI, *an iron founder*

PHILOSOPHER (*later, Rector of the University*)

ELDERLY LADY

YOUNG LADY

FEDERZONI, *assistant to Galileo*

MATHEMATICIAN

LORD CHAMBERLAIN

FAT PRELATE

TWO SCHOLARS

TWO MONKS

INFURIATED MONK

OLD CARDINAL

ATTENDANT MONK

CHRISTOPHER CLAVIUS

LITTLE MONK

TWO SECRETARIES

CARDINAL BELLARMIN

CARDINAL BARBERINI

CARDINAL INQUISITOR

YOUNG GIRL

HER FRIEND

GIUSEPPE

STREET SINGER

HIS WIFE

REVELLER

A LOUD VOICE

INFORMER

TOWN CRIER

OFFICIAL

PEASANT

CUSTOMS OFFICER

BOY

SENATORS, OFFICIALS, PROFESSORS,

LADIES, GUESTS, CHILDREN

*There are two wordless roles: The* DOGE *in Scene Two and* PRINCE COSMO DI MEDICI *in Scene Four. The ballad of Scene Nine is filled out by a pantomime: among the individuals in the pantomimic crowd are three extras (including the* "KING OF HUNGARY"*),* COBBLER'S BOY, THREE CHILDREN, PEASANT WOMAN, MONK, RICH COUPLE, DWARF, BEGGAR, *and* GIRL.

SCENE I

*In the year sixteen hundred and nine*
*Science' light began to shine.*
*At Padua City, in a modest house*
*Galileo Galilei set out to prove*
*The sun is still, the earth is on the move.*

*Galileo's scantily furnished study. Morning. Galileo is washing himself. A bare-footed boy, Andrea, son of his housekeeper, Mrs. Sarti, enters with a big astronomical model.*

GALILEO: Where did you get that thing?

ANDREA: The coachman brought it.

GALILEO: Who sent it?

ANDREA: It said "From the Court of Naples" on the box.

GALILEO: I don't want their stupid presents. Illuminated manuscripts, a statue of Hercules the size of an elephant—they never send money.

ANDREA: But isn't this an astronomical instrument, Mr. Galilei?

GALILEO: That is an antique too. An expensive toy.

10 ANDREA: What's it for?

GALILEO: It's a map of the sky according to the wise men of ancient Greece. Bosh! We'll try and sell it to the university. They still teach it there.

ANDREA: How does it work, Mr. Galilei?

GALILEO: It's complicated.

ANDREA: I think I could understand it.

GALILEO: (*interested*) Maybe. Let's begin at the beginning.

Description!

ANDREA: There are metal rings, a lot of them.

GALILEO: How many?     20

ANDREA: Eight.

GALILEO: Correct. And?

ANDREA: There are words painted on the bands.

GALILEO: What words?

ANDREA: The names of stars.

GALILEO: Such as?

ANDREA: Here is a band with the sun on it and on the inside band is the moon.

GALILEO: Those metal bands represent crystal globes, eight of them.     30

ANDREA: Crystal?

GALILEO: Like huge soap bubbles one inside the other and the stars are supposed to be tacked on to them. Spin the band with the sun on it. (*Andrea does*) You see the fixed ball in the middle?

ANDREA: Yes.

GALILEO: That's the earth. For two thousand years man has chosen to believe that the sun and all the host of stars revolve about him. Well. The Pope, the Cardinals, the princes, the scholars, captains, merchants, housewives, have pictured     40 themselves squatting in the middle of an affair like that.

ANDREA: Locked up inside?

GALILEO: (*triumphant*) Ah!

ANDREA: It's like a cage.

GALILEO: So you sensed that. (*Against the model*) I like to think the ships began it.

ANDREA: Why?

GALILEO: They used to hug the coasts and then all of a sudden they left the coasts and spread over the oceans. A new age was coming. I was on to it years ago. I was a young man, in Siena. There was a group of masons arguing. They had to raise a block of granite. It was hot. To help matters, one of them wanted to try a new arrangement of ropes. After five minutes' discussion, out went a method which had been employed for a thousand years. The millenium of faith is ended, said I, this is the millenium of doubt. And we are pulling out of that contraption. The sayings of the wise men won't wash anymore. Everybody, at last, is getting nosey. I predict that in our time astronomy will become the gossip of the market place and the sons of fishwives will pack the schools.

ANDREA: You're off again, Mr. Galilei. Give me the towel. (*He wipes some soap from Galileo's back*)

GALILEO: By that time, with any luck, they will be learning that the earth rolls round the sun, and that their mothers, the captains, the scholars, the princes and the Pope are rolling with it.

ANDREA: That turning-round-business is no good. I can see with my own eyes that the sun comes up in one place in the morning and goes down in a different place in the evening. It doesn't stand still, I can see it move.

GALILEO: You see nothing, all you do is gawk. Gawking is not seeing. (*He puts the iron washstand in the middle of the room*) Now: that's the sun. Sit down. (*Andrea sits on a chair. Galileo stands behind him*) Where is the sun, on your right or on your left?

ANDREA: Left.

GALILEO: And how will it get to the right?

ANDREA: By your putting it there, of course.

GALILEO: Of course? (*He picks Andrea up, chair and all, and carries him round to the other side of the washstand*) Now where is the sun?

ANDREA: On the right.

GALILEO: And did it move?

ANDREA: I did.

GALILEO: Wrong. Stupid! The chair moved.

ANDREA: But I was on it.

GALILEO: Of course. The chair is the earth, and you're sitting on it.

(*Mrs. Sarti, who has come in with a glass of milk and a roll, has been watching*)

MRS. SARTI: What are you doing with my son, Mr. Galilei?

ANDREA: Now, mother, you don't understand.

MRS. SARTI: You understand, don't you? Last night he tried to tell me that the earth goes round the sun. You'll soon have him saying that two times two is five.

GALILEO: (*eating his breakfast*) Apparently we are on the threshold of a new era, Mrs. Sarti.

MRS. SARTI: Well, I hope we can pay the milkman in this new era. A young gentleman is here to take private lessons and he is well-dressed and don't you frighten him away like you did the others. Wasting your time with Andrea! (*To Andrea*) How many times have I told you not to wheedle free lessons out of Mr. Galilei? (*Mrs. Sarti goes*)

GALILEO: So you thought enough of the turning-round-business to tell your mother about it.

ANDREA: Just to surprise her.

GALILEO: Andrea, I wouldn't talk about our ideas outside.

ANDREA: Why not?

GALILEO: Certain of the authorities won't like it.

ANDREA: Why not, if it's the truth?

GALILEO: (*laughs*) Because we are like the worms who are little and have dim eyes and can hardly see the stars at all, and the new astronomy is a framework of guesses or very little more—yet.

(*Mrs. Sarti shows in Ludovico Marsili, a presentable young man*)

GALILEO: This house is like a marketplace. (*Pointing to the model*) Move that out of the way! Put it down there!

(*Ludovico does*)

LUDOVICO: Good morning, sir. My name is Ludovico Marsili.

GALILEO: (*reading a letter of recommendation he has brought*) You came by way of Holland and your family lives in the Campagna? Private lessons, thirty scudi a month.

LUDOVICO: That's all right, of course, sir.

GALILEO: What is your subject?

LUDOVICO: Horses.

GALILEO: Aha.

LUDOVICO: I don't understand science, sir.

GALILEO: Aha.

LUDOVICO: They showed me an instrument like that in Amsterdam. You'll pardon me, sir, but it didn't make sense to me at all.

GALILEO: It's out of date now.

(*Andrea goes*)

LUDOVICO: You'll have to be patient with me, sir. Nothing in science makes sense to me.

GALILEO: Aha.

LUDOVICO: I saw a brand new instrument in Amsterdam. A tube affair. "See things five times as large as life!" It had two lenses, one at each end, one lens bulged and the other was like that. (*Gesture*) Any normal person would think that different lenses cancel each other out. They didn't! I just stood and looked a fool.

GALILEO: I don't quite follow you. What does one see enlarged?

LUDOVICO: Church steeples, pigeons, boats. Anything at a distance.

GALILEO: Did you yourself—see things enlarged?

LUDOVICO: Yes, sir.

GALILEO: And the tube had two lenses? Was it like this? (*He has been making a sketch*)

(*Ludovico nods*)

GALILEO: A recent invention?

LUDOVICO: It must be. They only started peddling it on the streets a few days before I left Holland.

GALILEO: (*starts to scribble calculations on the sketch; almost friendly*) Why do you bother your head with science? Why don't you just breed horses?

(*Enter Mrs. Sarti. Galileo doesn't see her. She listens to the following*)

LUDOVICO: My mother is set on the idea that science is necessary nowadays for conversation.

GALILEO: Aha. You'll find Latin or philosophy easier. (*Mrs. Sarti catches his eye*) I'll see you on Tuesday afternoon.

LUDOVICO: I shall look forward to it, sir.

GALILEO: Good morning. (*He goes to the window and shouts into the street*) Andrea! Hey, Redhead, Redhead!

160 MRS. SARTI: The curator of the museum is here to see you.

GALILEO: Don't look at me like that. I took him, didn't I?

MRS. SARTI: I caught your eye in time.

GALILEO: Show the curator in.

(*She goes. He scribbles something on a new sheet of paper. The Curator comes in*)

CURATOR: Good morning, Mr. Galilei.

GALILEO: Lend me a scudo. (*He takes it and goes to the window, wrapping the coin in the paper on which he has been scribbling*) Redhead, run to the spectacle-maker and bring me two lenses; here are the measurements. (*He throws the paper out of the window. During the following scene Galileo* 170 *studies his sketch of the lenses*)

CURATOR: Mr. Galilei, I have come to return your petition for an honorarium. Unfortunately I am unable to recommend your request.

GALILEO: My good sir, how can I make ends meet on five hundred scudi?

CURATOR: What about your private students?

GALILEO: If I spend all my time with students, when am I to study? My particular science is on the threshold of important discoveries. (*He throws a manuscript on the table*) Here 180 are my findings on the laws of falling bodies. That should be worth 200 scudi.

CURATOR: I am sure that any paper of yours is of infinite worth, Mr. Galilei. . . .

GALILEO: I was limiting it to 200 scudi.

CURATOR: (*cool*) Mr. Galilei, if you want money and leisure, go to Florence. I have no doubt Prince Cosmo de Medici will be glad to subsidize you, but eventually you will be forbidden to think—in the name of the Inquisition. (*Galileo says nothing*) Now let us not make a mountain out of a molehill. 190 You are happy here in the Republic of Venice but you need money. Well, that's human, Mr. Galilei, may I suggest a simple solution? You remember that chart you made for the army to extract cube roots without any knowledge of mathematics? Now that was practical!

GALILEO: Bosh!

CURATOR: Don't say bosh about something that astounded the Chamber of Commerce. Our city elders are businessmen. Why don't you invent something useful that will bring them a little profit?

200 GALILEO: (*playing with the sketch of the lenses; suddenly*) I see. Mr. Priuli, I may have something for you.

CURATOR: You don't say so.

GALILEO: It's not quite there yet, but . . .

CURATOR: You've never let me down yet, Galilei.

GALILEO: You are always an inspiration to me, Priuli.

CURATOR: You are a great man: a discontented man, but I've always said you are a great man.

GALILEO: (*tartly*) My discontent, Priuli, is for the most part with myself. I am forty-six years of age and have achieved 210 nothing which satisfies me.

CURATOR: I won't disturb you any further.

GALILEO: Thank you. Good morning.

CURATOR: Good morning. And thank you.

(*He goes. Galileo sighs. Andrea returns, bringing lenses*)

ANDREA: One scudo was not enough. I had to leave my cap with him before he'd let me take them away.

GALILEO: We'll get it back some day. Give them to me. (*He takes the lenses over to the window, holding them in the relation they would have in a telescope*)

ANDREA: What are those for?

GALILEO: Something for the senate. With any luck, they will 220 rake in 200 scudi. Take a look!

ANDREA: My, things look close! I can read the copper letters on the bell in the Campanile. And the washerwomen by the river, I can see their washboards!

GALILEO: Get out of the way. (*Looking through the lenses himself*) Aha!

## SCENE II

> *No one's virtue is complete:*
> *Great Galileo liked to eat.*
> *You will not resent, we hope,*
> *The truth about his telescope.*

*The great arsenal of Venice, overlooking the harbor full of ships. Senators and Officials on one side, Galileo, his daughter Virginia and his friend Sagredo, on the other side. They are dressed in formal, festive clothes. Virginia is fourteen and charming. She carries a velvet cushion on which lies a brand new telescope. Behind Galileo are some Artisans from the arsenal. There are onlookers, Ludovico amongst them.*

CURATOR: (*announcing*) Senators, Artisans of the Great Arsenal of Venice; Mr. Galileo Galilei, professor of mathematics at your University of Padua.

(*Galileo steps forward and starts to speak*)

GALILEO: Members of the High Senate! Gentlemen: I have 230 great pleasure, as director of this institute, in presenting for your approval and acceptance an entirely new instrument originating from this our great arsenal of the Republic of Venice. As professor of mathematics at your University of Padua, your obedient servant has always counted it his privilege to offer you such discoveries and inventions as might prove lucrative to the manufacturers and merchants of our Venetian Republic. Thus, in all humility, I tender you this, my optical tube, or telescope, constructed, I assure you, on the most scientific and Christian principles, the product of 240 seventeen years patient research at your University of Padua.

(*Galileo steps back. The senators applaud*)

SAGREDO: (*aside to Galileo*) Now you will be able to pay your bills.

GALILEO: Yes. It will make money for them. But you realize that it is more than a money-making gadget?—I turned it on the moon last night . . .

CURATOR: (*in his best chamber-of-commerce manner*) Gentlemen: Our Republic is to be congratulated not only because

250 this new acquisition will be one more feather in the cap of Venetian culture . . . (*Polite applause*) . . . not only because our own Mr. Galilei has generously handed this fresh product of his teeming brain entirely over to you, allowing you to manufacture as many of these highly saleable articles as you please. . . . (*Considerable applause*) But Gentlemen of the Senate, has it occurred to you that—with the help of this remarkable new instrument—the battlefleet of the enemy will be visible to us a full two hours before we are visible to him? (*Tremendous applause*)

260 GALILEO: (*aside to Sagredo*) We have been held up three generations for lack of a thing like this. I want to go home.

SAGREDO: What about the moon?

GALILEO: Well, for one thing, it doesn't give off its own light.

CURATOR: (*continuing his oration*) And now, Your Excellency, and Members of the Senate, Mr. Galilei entreats you to accept the instrument from the hands of his charming daughter Virginia.

(*Polite applause. He beckons to Virginia who steps forward and presents the telescope to the Doge*)

CURATOR: (*during this*) Mr. Galilei gives his invention entirely into your hands, Gentlemen, enjoining you to construct as
270 many of these instruments as you may please.

(*More applause. The Senators gather round the telescope, examining it, and looking through it*)

GALILEO: (*aside to Sagredo*) Do you know what the Milky Way is made of?

SAGREDO: No.

GALILEO: I do.

CURATOR: (*interrupting*) Congratulations, Mr. Galilei. Your extra five hundred scudi a year are safe.

GALILEO: Pardon? What? Of course, the five hundred scudi! Yes!

(*A prosperous man is standing beside the Curator*)

CURATOR: Mr. Galilei, Mr. Matti of Florence.

280 MATTI: You're opening new fields, Mr. Galilei. We could do with you at Florence.

CURATOR: Now, Mr. Matti, leave something to us poor Venetians.

MATTI: It is a pity that a great republic has to seek an excuse to pay its great men their right and proper dues.

CURATOR: Even a great man has to have an incentive. (*He joins the Senators at the telescope*)

MATTI: I am an iron founder.

GALILEO: Iron founder!

290 MATTI: With factories at Pisa and Florence. I wanted to talk to you about a machine you designed for a friend of mine in Padua.

GALILEO: I'll put you on to someone to copy it for you, I am not going to have the time.—How are things in Florence?

(*They wander away*)

FIRST SENATOR: (*peering*) Extraordinary! They're having their lunch on that frigate. Lobsters! I'm hungry!

(*Laughter*)

SECOND SENATOR: Oh, good heavens, look at her! I must tell my wife to stop bathing on the roof. When can I buy one of these things?

(*Laughter. Virginia has spotted Ludovico among the onlookers and drags him to Galileo*)

VIRGINIA: (*to Ludovico*) Did I do it nicely?    300

LUDOVICO: I thought so.

VIRGINIA: Here's Ludovico to congratulate you, father.

LUDOVICO: (*embarrassed*) Congratulations, sir.

GALILEO: I improved it.

LUDOVICO: Yes, sir. I am beginning to understand science.

(*Galileo is surrounded*)

VIRGINIA: Isn't father a great man?

LUDOVICO: Yes.

VIRGINIA: Isn't that new thing father made pretty?

LUDOVICO: Yes, a pretty red. Where I saw it first it was covered in green.    310

VIRGINIA: What was?

LUDOVICO: Never mind. (*A short pause*) Have you ever been to Holland?

(*They go. All Venice is congratulating Galileo, who wants to go home*)

SCENE III

*January ten, sixteen ten:*
*Galileo Galilei abolishes heaven.*

*Galileo's study at Padua. It is night. Galileo and Sagredo at a telescope.*

SAGREDO: (*softly*) The edge of the crescent is jagged. All along the dark part, near the shiny crescent, bright particles of light keep coming up, one after the other and growing larger and merging with the bright crescent.

GALILEO: How do you explain those spots of light?

SAGREDO: It can't be true . . .

GALILEO: It *is* true: they are high mountains.    320

SAGREDO: On a star?

GALILEO: Yes. The shining particles are mountain peaks catching the first rays of the rising sun while the slopes of the mountains are still dark, and what you see is the sunlight moving down from the peaks into the valleys.

SAGREDO: But this gives the lie to all the astronomy that's been taught for the last two thousand years.

GALILEO: Yes. What you are seeing now has been seen by no other man beside myself.

SAGREDO: But the moon can't be an earth with mountains and 330 valleys like our own any more than the earth can be a star.

GALILEO: The moon *is* an earth with mountains and valleys,—and the earth *is* a star. As the moon appears to us, so we appear to the moon. From the moon, the earth looks something like a crescent, sometimes like a half-globe, sometimes a full-globe, and sometimes it is not visible at all.

SAGREDO: Galileo, this is frightening.

(*An urgent knocking on the door*)

GALILEO: I've discovered something else, something even more astonishing.

(*More knocking. Galileo opens the door and the Curator comes in*)

340  CURATOR: There it is—your "miraculous optical tube." Do you know that this invention he so picturesquely termed "the fruit of seventeen years research" will be on sale tomorrow for two scudi apiece at every street corner in Venice? A shipload of them has just arrived from Holland.

SAGREDO: Oh, dear!

*(Galileo turns his back and adjusts the telescope)*

CURATOR: When I think of the poor gentlemen of the senate who believed they were getting an invention they could monopolize for their own profit. . . . Why, when they took their first look through the glass, it was only by the merest chance
350  that they didn't see a peddler, seven times enlarged, selling tubes exactly like it at the corner of the street.

SAGREDO: Mr. Priuli, with the help of this instrument, Mr. Galilei has made discoveries that will revolutionize our concept of the universe.

CURATOR: Mr. Galilei provided the city with a first rate water pump and the irrigation works he designed function splendidly. How was I to expect this?

GALILEO: *(still at the telescope)* Not so fast, Priuli. I may be on the track of a very large gadget. Certain of the stars appear
360  to have regular movements. If there were a clock in the sky, it could be seen from anywhere. That might be useful for your shipowners.

CURATOR: I won't listen to you. I listened to you before, and as a reward for my friendship you have made me the laughingstock of the town. You can laugh—you got your money. But let me tell you this: you've destroyed my faith in a lot of things, Mr. Galilei. I'm disgusted with the world. That's all I have to say. *(He storms out)*

GALILEO: *(embarrassed)* Businessmen bore me, they suffer so.
370  Did you see the frightened look in his eyes when he caught sight of a world not created solely for the purpose of doing business?

SAGREDO: Did you know that telescopes had been made in Holland?

GALILEO: I'd heard about it. But the one I made for the Senators was twice as good as any Dutchman's. Besides, I needed the money. How can I work, with the tax collector on the doorstep? And my poor daughter will never acquire a husband unless she has a dowry, she's not too bright. And I like
380  to buy books—all kinds of books. Why not? And what about my appetite? I don't think well unless I eat well. Can I help it if I get my best ideas over a good meal and a bottle of wine? They don't pay me as much as they pay the butcher's boy. If only I could have five years to do nothing but research! Come on. I am going to show you something else.

SAGREDO: I don't know that I want to look again.

GALILEO: This is one of the brighter nebulae of the Milky Way. What do you see?

SAGREDO: But it's made up of stars—countless stars.
390  GALILEO: Countless worlds.

SAGREDO: *(hesitating)* What about the theory that the earth revolves round the sun? Have you run across anything about that?

GALILEO: No. But I noticed something on Tuesday that might prove a step towards even that. Where's Jupiter? There are four lesser stars near Jupiter. I happened on them on Monday but didn't take any particular note of their position. On Tuesday I looked again. I could have sworn they had moved.

They have changed again. Tell me what you see.

SAGREDO: I only see three.                                                          400

GALILEO: Where's the fourth? Let's get the charts and settle down to work.

*(They work and the lights dim. The lights go up again. It is near dawn)*

GALILEO: The only place the fourth can be is round at the back of the larger star where we cannot see it. This means there are small stars revolving around a big star. Where are the crystal shells now that the stars are supposed to be fixed to?

SAGREDO: Jupiter can't be attached to anything: there are other stars revolving round it.

GALILEO: There is no support in the heavens. *(Sagredo laughs awkwardly)* Don't stand there looking at me as if it weren't  410 true.

SAGREDO: I suppose it is true. I'm afraid.

GALILEO: Why?

SAGREDO: What do you think is going to happen to you for saying that there is another sun around which other earths revolve? And that there are only stars and no difference between earth and heaven? Where is God then?

GALILEO: What do you mean?

SAGREDO: God? Where is God?

GALILEO: *(angrily)* Not there! Any more than he'd be here—if  420 creatures from the moon came down to look for him!

SAGREDO: Then where is He?

GALILEO: I'm not a theologian: I'm a mathematician.

SAGREDO: You are a human being! *(Almost shouting)* Where is God in your system of the universe?

GALILEO: Within ourselves. Or—nowhere.

SAGREDO: Ten years ago a man was burned at the stake for saying that.

GALILEO: Giordano Bruno was an idiot: he spoke too soon. He would never have been condemned if he could have backed  430 up what he said with proof.

SAGREDO: *(incredulously)* Do you really believe proof will make any difference?

GALILEO: I believe in the human race. The only people that can't be reasoned with are the dead. Human beings are intelligent.

SAGREDO: Intelligent—or merely shrewd?

GALILEO: I know they call a donkey a horse when they want to sell it, and a horse a donkey when they want to buy it. But is that the whole story? Aren't they susceptible to truth as  440 well? *(He fishes a small pebble out of his pocket)* If anybody were to drop a stone . . . *(Drops the pebble)* . . . and tell them that it didn't fall, do you think they would keep quiet? The evidence of your own eyes is a very seductive thing. Sooner or later everybody must succumb to it.

SAGREDO: Galileo, I am helpless when you talk.

*(A church bell has been ringing for some time, calling people to mass. Enter Virginia, muffled up for mass, carrying a candle, protected from the wind by a globe)*

VIRGINIA: Oh, father, you promised to go to bed tonight, and it's five o'clock again.

GALILEO: Why are you up at this hour?

VIRGINIA: I'm going to mass with Mrs. Sarti. Ludovico is going  450 too. How was the night, father?

GALILEO: Bright.

VIRGINIA: What did you find through the tube?

GALILEO: Only some little specks by the side of a star. I must draw attention to them somehow. I think I'll name them after the Prince of Florence. Why not call them the Medicean planets? By the way, we may move to Florence. I've written to His Highness, asking if he can use me as Court Mathematician.

460  VIRGINIA: Oh, father, we'll be at the court!

SAGREDO: (*amazed*) Galileo!

GALILEO: My dear Sagredo, I must have leisure. My only worry is that His Highness after all may not take me. I'm not accustomed to writing formal letters to great personages. Here, do you think this is the right sort of thing?

SAGREDO: (*reads and quotes*) "Whose sole desire is to reside in Your Highness' presence—the rising sun of our great age." Cosmo di Medici is a boy of nine.

GALILEO: The only way a man like me can land a good job is by

470  crawling on his stomach. Your father, my dear, is going to take his share of the pleasures of life in exchange for all his hard work, and about time too. I have no patience, Sagredo, with a man who doesn't use his brains to fill his belly. Run along to mass now.

(*Virginia goes*)

SAGREDO: Galileo, do not go to Florence.

GALILEO: Why not?

SAGREDO: The monks are in power there.

GALILEO: Going to mass is a small price to pay for a full belly. And there are many famous scholars at the court of Flo-

480  rence.

SAGREDO: Court monkeys.

GALILEO: I shall enjoy taking them by the scruff of the neck and making them look through the telescope.

SAGREDO: Galileo, you are traveling the road to disaster. You are suspicious and skeptical in science, but in politics you are as naive as your daughter! How can people in power leave a man at large who tells the truth, even if it be the truth about the distant stars? Can you see the Pope scribbling a note in his diary: "10th of January, 1610, Heaven

490  abolished?" A moment ago, when you were at the telescope, I saw you tied to the stake, and when you said you believed in proof, I smelt burning flesh!

GALILEO: I am going to Florence.

(*Before the next scene a curtain with the following legend on it is lowered*)

■  ■  ■  By setting the name of Medici in the sky, I am bestowing immortality upon the stars. I commend myself to you as your most faithful and devoted servant, whose sole desire is to reside in Your Highness' presence, the rising sun of our great age.

—GALILEO GALILEI

SCENE IV

*Galileo's house at Florence. Well-appointed. Galileo is demonstrating his telescope to Prince Cosmo di Medici, a boy of nine, accompanied by his Lord Chamberlain, Ladies and*

*Gentlemen of the Court and an assortment of university Professors. With Galileo are Andrea and Federzoni, the new assistant (an old man). Mrs. Sarti stands by. Before the scene opens the voice of the Philosopher can be heard.*

VOICE OF THE PHILOSOPHER: Quaedam miracula universi. Orbes mystice canorae, arcus crystallini, circulatio corporum coelestium. Cyclorum epicyclorumque intoxicatio, integritas tabulae chordarum et architectura elata globorum coelestium.

GALILEO: Shall we speak in everyday language? My colleague Mr. Federzoni does not understand Latin.   500

PHILOSOPHER: Is it necessary that he should?

GALILEO: Yes.

PHILOSOPHER: Forgive me. I thought he was your mechanic.

ANDREA: Mr. Federzoni is a mechanic and a scholar.

PHILOSOPHER: Thank you, young man. If Mr. Federzoni insists . . .

GALILEO: I insist.

PHILOSOPHER: It will not be as clear, but it's your house. Your Highness . . . (*The Prince is ineffectually trying to establish contact with Andrea*) I was about to recall to Mr. Galilei  510 some of the wonders of the universe as they are set down for us in the Divine Classics. (*The Ladies "ah"*) Remind him of the "mystically musical spheres, the crystal arches, the circulation of the heavenly bodies—"

ELDERLY LADY: Perfect poise!

PHILOSOPHER: "—the intoxication of the cycles and epicycles, the integrity of the tables of chords and the enraptured architecture of the celestial globes."

ELDERLY LADY: What diction!

PHILOSOPHER: May I pose the question: Why should we go out  520 of our way to look for things that can only strike a discord in this ineffable harmony?

(*The Ladies applaud*)

FEDERZONI: Take a look through here—you'll be interested.

ANDREA: Sit down here, please.

(*The Professors laugh*)

MATHEMATICIAN: Mr. Galilei, nobody doubts that your brain child—or is it your adopted brain child?—is brilliantly contrived.

GALILEO: Your Highness, one can see the four stars as large as life, you know.

(*The Prince looks to the Elderly Lady for guidance*)

MATHEMATICIAN: Ah. But has it occurred to you that an eye-  530 glass through which one sees such phenomena might not be a too reliable eyeglass?

GALILEO: How is that?

MATHEMATICIAN: If one could be sure you would keep your temper, Mr. Galilei, I could suggest that what one sees in the eyeglass and what is in the heavens are two entirely different things.

GALILEO: (*quietly*) You are suggesting fraud?

MATHEMATICIAN: No! How could I, in the presence of His Highness?   540

ELDERLY LADY: The gentlemen are just wondering if Your Highness' stars are really, really there!

(*Pause.*)

YOUNG LADY: (*trying to be helpful*) Can one see the claws on the Great Bear?

GALILEO: And everything on Taurus the Bull.

FEDERZONI: Are you going to look through it or not?

MATHEMATICIAN: With the greatest of pleasure.

(*Pause. Nobody goes near the telescope. All of a sudden the boy Andrea turns and marches pale and erect past them through the whole length of the room. The Guests follow with their eyes*)

MRS. SARTI: (*as he passes her*) What is the matter with you?

ANDREA: (*shocked*) They are wicked.

550 PHILOSOPHER: Your Highness, it is a delicate matter and I had no intention of bringing it up, but Mr. Galilei was about to demonstrate the impossible. His new stars would have broken the outer crystal sphere—which we know of on the authority of Aristotle. I am sorry.

MATHEMATICIAN: The last word.

FEDERZONI: He had no telescope.

MATHEMATICIAN: Quite.

GALILEO: (*keeping his temper*) "Truth is the daughter of Time, not of Authority." Gentlemen, the sum of our knowledge is
560 pitiful. It has been my singular good fortune to find a new instrument which brings a small patch of the universe a little bit closer. It is at your disposal.

PHILOSOPHER: Where is all this leading?

GALILEO: Are we, as scholars, concerned with where the truth might lead us?

PHILOSOPHER: Mr. Galilei, the truth might lead us anywhere!

GALILEO: I can only beg you to look through my eyeglass.

MATHEMATICIAN: (*wild*) If I understand Mr. Galilei correctly, he is asking us to discard the teachings of two thousand
570 years.

GALILEO: For two thousand years we have been looking at the sky and didn't see the four moons of Jupiter, and there they were all the time. Why defend shaken teachings? You should be doing the shaking. (*The Prince is sleepy*) Your Highness! My work in the Great Arsenal of Venice brought me in daily contact with sailors, carpenters, and so on. These men are unread. They depend on the evidence of their senses. But they taught me many new ways of doing things. The question is whether these gentlemen here want to be
580 found out as fools by men who might not have had the advantages of a classical education but who are not afraid to use their eyes. I tell you that our dockyards are stirring with that same high curiosity which was the true glory of Ancient Greece.

(*Pause.*)

PHILOSOPHER: I have no doubt Mr. Galilei's theories will arouse the enthusiasm of the dockyards.

CHAMBERLAIN: Your Highness, I find to my amazement that this highly informative discussion has exceeded the time we had allowed for it. May I remind Your Highness that the
590 State Ball begins in three-quarters of an hour?

(*The Court bows low*)

ELDERLY LADY: We would really have liked to look through your eyeglass, Mr. Galilei, wouldn't we, Your Highness?

(*The Prince bows politely and is led to the door. Galileo follows the Prince, Chamberlain and Ladies towards the exit. The Professors remain at the telescope*)

GALILEO: (*almost servile*) All anybody has to do is look through the telescope, Your Highness.

(*Mrs. Sarti takes a plate with candies to the Prince as he is walking out*)

MRS. SARTI: A piece of homemade candy, Your Highness?

ELDERLY LADY: Not now. Thank you. It is too soon before His Highness' supper.

PHILOSOPHER: Wouldn't I like to take that thing to pieces.

MATHEMATICIAN: Ingenious contraption. It must be quite difficult to keep clean. (*He rubs the lens with his handkerchief* 600 *and looks at the handkerchief*)

FEDERZONI: We did not paint the Medicean stars on the lens.

ELDERLY LADY: (*to the Prince, who has whispered something to her*) No, no, no, there is nothing the matter with your stars!

CHAMBERLAIN: (*across the stage to Galileo*) His Highness will of course seek the opinion of the greatest living authority: Christopher Clavius, Chief Astronomer to the Papal College in Rome.

SCENE V

> *Things take indeed a wondrous turn*
> *When learned men do stoop to learn.*
> *Clavius, we are pleased to say,*
> *Upheld Galileo Galilei.*

*A burst of laughter is heard and the curtains reveal a ball in the Collegium Romanum. High Churchmen, monks and Scholars standing about talking and laughing. Galileo by himself in a corner.*

FAT PRELATE: (*shaking with laughter*) Hopeless! Hopeless! Hopeless! Will you tell me something people won't believe? 610

A SCHOLAR: Yes, that you don't love your stomach!

FAT PRELATE: They'd believe that. They only do not believe what's good for them. They doubt the devil, but fill them up with some fiddle-de-dee about the earth rolling like a marble in the gutter and they swallow it hook, line, and sinker. Sancta simplicitas!

(*He laughs until the tears run down his cheeks. The others laugh with him. A group has formed whose members boisterously begin to pretend they are standing on a rolling globe*)

A MONK: It's rolling fast, I'm dizzy. May I hold on to you, Professor? (*He sways dizzily and clings to one of the scholars for support*)

THE SCHOLAR: Old Mother Earth's been at the bottle again. 620 Whoa!

MONK: Hey! Hey! We're slipping off! Help!

SECOND SCHOLAR: Look! There's Venus! Hold me, lads. Whee!

SECOND MONK: Don't, don't hurl us off on to the moon. There are nasty sharp mountain peaks on the moon, brethren!

VARIOUSLY: Hold tight! Hold tight! Don't look down! Hold tight! It'll make you giddy!

FAT PRELATE: And we cannot have giddy people in Holy Rome.

*(They rock with laughter. An infuriated Monk comes out from a large door at the rear holding a Bible in his hand and pointing out a page with his finger)*

INFURIATED MONK: What does the Bible say—"Sun, stand thou
630 still on Gideon and thou, moon, in the valley of Ajalon." Can the sun come to a standstill if it doesn't ever move? Does the Bible lie?

FAT PRELATE: How did Christopher Clavius, the greatest astronomer we have, get mixed up in an investigation of this kind?

INFURIATED MONK: He's in there with his eye glued to that diabolical instrument.

FAT PRELATE: *(to Galileo, who has been playing with his pebble and has dropped it)* Mr. Galilei, something dropped
640 down.

GALILEO: Monsignor, are you sure it didn't drop up?

INFURIATED MONK: As astronomers we are aware that there are phenomena which are beyond us, but man can't expect to understand everything!

*(Enter a very old Cardinal leaning on a Monk for support. Others move aside)*

OLD CARDINAL: Aren't they out yet? Can't they reach a decision on that paltry matter? Christopher Clavius ought to know his astronomy after all these years. I am informed that Mr. Galilei transfers mankind from the center of the universe to somewhere on the outskirts. Mr. Galilei is therefore an
650 enemy of mankind and must be dealt with as such. Is it conceivable that God would trust this most precious fruit of His labor to a minor frolicking star? Would He have sent His Son to such a place? How can there be people with such twisted minds that they believe what they're told by the slave of a multiplication table?

FAT PRELATE: *(quietly to Cardinal)* The gentleman is over there.

OLD CARDINAL: So you are the man. You know my eyes are not what they were, but I can see you bear a striking resem-
660 blance to the man we burned. What was his name?

MONK: Your Eminence must avoid excitement, the doctor said. . . .

OLD CARDINAL: *(disregarding him)* So you have degraded the earth despite the fact that you live by her and receive everything from her. I won't have it! I won't have it! I won't be a nobody on an inconsequential star briefly twirling hither and thither. I tread the earth, and the earth is firm beneath my feet, and there is no motion to the earth, and the earth is the center of all things, and I am the center of the earth,
670 and the eye of the creator is upon me. About me revolve, affixed to their crystal shells, the lesser lights of the stars and the great light of the sun, created to give light upon me that God might see me—Man, God's greatest effort, the center of creation. "In the image of God created He him." Immortal . . . *(His strength fails him and he catches for the Monk for support)*

MONK: You mustn't overtax your strength, Your Eminence.

*(At this moment the door at the rear opens and Christopher Clavius enters followed by his Astronomers. He strides hastily across the hall, looking neither to right nor left. As he goes by we hear him say—)*

CLAVIUS: He is right.

*(Deadly silence. All turn to Galileo)*

OLD CARDINAL: What is it? Have they reached a decision? *(No one speaks)*
680
MONK: It is time that Your Eminence went home.

*(The hall is emptying fast. One little Monk who had entered with Clavius speaks to Galileo)*

LITTLE MONK: Mr. Galileo, I heard Father Clavius say: "Now it's for the theologians to set the heavens right again." You have won.

*(Before the next scene a curtain with the following legend on it is lowered)*

■ ■ ■ . . . . . . As these new astronomical charts enable us to determine longitudes at sea and so make it possible to reach the new continents by the shortest routes, we would beseech Your Excellency to aid us in reaching Mr. Galilei, mathematician to the Court of Florence, who is now in Rome . . . . . .

—FROM A LETTER WRITTEN BY A MEMBER OF THE
GENOA CHAMBER OF COMMERCE AND NAVIGATION
TO THE PAPAL LEGATION.

## SCENE VI

> When Galileo was in Rome
> A Cardinal asked him to his home
> He wined and dined him as his guest
> And only made one small request.

*Cardinal Bellarmin's house in Rome. Music is heard and the chatter of many guests. Two Secretaries are at the rear of the stage at a desk. Galileo, his daughter Virginia, now 21, and Ludovico Marsili, who has become her fiancé, are just arriving. A few Guests, standing near the entrance with masks in their hands, nudge each other and are suddenly silent. Galileo looks at them. They applaud him politely and bow.)*

VIRGINIA: O father! I'm so happy. I won't dance with anyone but you, Ludovico.

GALILEO: *(to a Secretary)* I was to wait here for His Eminence.

FIRST SECRETARY: His Eminence will be with you in a few minutes.

VIRGINIA: Do I look proper?
690
LUDOVICO: You are showing some lace.

*(Galileo puts his arms around their shoulders)*

GALILEO: *(quoting mischievously)*
> Fret not, daughter, if perchance
> You attract a wanton glance.
> The eyes that catch a trembling lace
> Will guess the heartbeat's quickened pace.
> Lovely woman still may be
> Careless with felicity.

VIRGINIA: *(to Galileo)* Feel my heart.

700 GALILEO: *(to Ludovico)* It's thumping.

VIRGINIA: I hope I always say the right thing.

LUDOVICO: She's afraid she's going to let us down.

VIRGINIA: Oh, I want to look beautiful.

GALILEO: You'd better. If you don't they'll start saying all over again that the earth doesn't turn.

LUDOVICO: *(laughing)* It *doesn't* turn, sir.

*(Galileo laughs)*

GALILEO: Go and enjoy yourselves. *(He speaks to one of the Secretaries)* A large fête?

FIRST SECRETARY: Two hundred and fifty guests, Mr. Galilei.
710 We have represented here this evening most of the great families of Italy, the Orsinis, the Villanis, the Nuccolis, the Soldanieris, the Canes, the Lecchis, the Estensis, the Colombinis, the . . .

*(Virginia comes running back)*

VIRGINIA: Oh father, I didn't tell you: you're famous.

GALILEO: Why?

VIRGINIA: The hairdresser in the Via Vittorio kept four other ladies waiting and took me first. *(Exit)*

GALILEO: *(at the stairway, leaning over the well)* Rome!

*(Enter Cardinal Bellarmin, wearing the mask of a lamb, and Cardinal Barberini, wearing the mask of a dove)*

SECRETARIES: Their Eminences, Cardinals Bellarmin and Bar-
720 berini.

*(The Cardinals lower their masks)*

GALILEO: *(to Bellarmin)* Your Eminence.

BELLARMIN: Mr. Galilei, Cardinal Barberini.

GALILEO: Your Eminence.

BARBERINI: So you are the father of that lovely child!

BELLARMIN: Who is inordinately proud of being her father's daughter.

*(They laugh)*

BARBERINI: *(points his finger at Galileo)* "The sun riseth and setteth and returneth to its place," saith the Bible. What saith Galilei?
730 GALILEO: Appearances are notoriously deceptive, Your Eminence. Once when I was so high, I was standing on a ship that was pulling away from the shore and I shouted, "The shore is moving!" I know now that it was the ship which was moving.

BARBERINI: *(laughs)* You can't catch that man. I tell you, Bellarmin, his moons around Jupiter are hard nuts to crack. Unfortunately for me I happened to glance at a few papers on astronomy once. It is harder to get rid of than the itch.

BELLARMIN: Let's move with the times. If it makes navigation
740 easier for sailors to use new charts based on a new hypothesis let them have them. We only have to scotch doctrines that contradict Holy Writ.

*(He leans over the balustrade of the well and acknowledges various Guests)*

BARBERINI: But Bellarmin, you haven't caught on to this fellow. The scriptures don't satisfy him. Copernicus does.

GALILEO: Copernicus? "He that withholdeth corn the people shall curse him." Book of Proverbs.

BARBERINI: "A prudent man concealeth knowledge." Also Book of Proverbs.

GALILEO: "Where no oxen are, the stable is clean, but much in-
750 crease is by the strength of the ox."

BARBERINI: "He that ruleth his spirit is better than he that taketh a city."

GALILEO: "But a broken spirit drieth up the bones." *(Pause)* "Doth not wisdom cry?"

BARBERINI: "Can one walk on hot coals and his feet not be scorched?"—Welcome to Rome, Friend Galileo. You recall the legend of our city's origin? Two small boys found sustenance and refuge with a she-wolf and from that day we have paid the price for the she-wolf's milk. But the place is not
760 bad. We have everything for your pleasure—from a scholarly dispute with Bellarmin to ladies of high degree. Look at that woman flaunting herself. No? He wants a weighty discussion! All right! *(To Galileo)* You people speak in terms of circles and ellipses and regular velocities—simple movements that the human mind can grasp—very convenient—but suppose Almighty God had taken it into his head to make the stars move like that . . . *(He describes an irregular motion with his fingers through the air)* . . . then where would you be?

GALILEO: My good man—the Almighty would have endowed
770 us with brains like that . . . *(Repeats the movement)* . . . so that we could grasp the movements . . . *(Repeats the movement)* . . . like that. I believe in the brain.

BARBERINI: I consider the brain inadequate. He doesn't answer. He is too polite to tell me he considers *my* brain inadequate. What is one to do with him? Butter wouldn't melt in his mouth. All he wants to do is to prove that God made a few boners in astronomy. God didn't study his astronomy hard enough before he composed Holy Writ. *(To the Secretaries)* Don't take anything down. This is a scientific discus-
780 sion among friends.

BELLARMIN: *(to Galileo)* Does it not appear more probable—even to you—that the Creator knows more about his work than the created?

GALILEO: In his blindness man is liable to misread not only the sky but also the Bible.

BELLARMIN: The interpretation of the Bible is a matter for the ministers of God. *(Galileo remains silent)* At last you are quiet. *(He gestures to the Secretaries. They start writing)* Tonight the Holy Office has decided that the theory ac-
790 cording to which the earth goes around the sun is foolish, absurd, and a heresy. I am charged, Mr. Galilei, with cautioning you to abandon these teachings. *(To the First Secretary)* Would you repeat that?

FIRST SECRETARY: *(reading)* "His Eminence, Cardinal Bellarmin, to the aforesaid Galilei: The Holy Office has resolved that the theory according to which the earth goes around the sun is foolish, absurd, and a heresy. I am charged, Mr. Galilei, with cautioning you to abandon these teachings."
800 GALILEO: *(rocking on his base)* But the facts!

BARBERINI: *(consoling)* Your findings have been ratified by the Papal Observatory, Galilei. That should be most flattering to you . . .

BELLARMIN: *(cutting in)* The Holy Office formulated the decree without going into details.

GALILEO: *(to Barberini)* Do you realize, the future of all scientific research is . . .

BELLARMIN: *(cutting in)* Completely assured, Mr. Galilei. It is
810     not given to man to know the truth: it is granted to him to
seek after the truth. Science is the legitimate and beloved
daughter of the Church. She must have confidence in the
Church.

GALILEO: *(infuriated)* I would not try confidence by whistling
her too often.

BARBERINI: *(quickly)* Be careful what you're doing—you'll be
throwing out the baby with the bath water, friend Galilei.
*(Serious)* We need you more than you need us.

BELLARMIN: Well, it is time we introduced our distinguished
820     friend to our guests. The whole country talks of him!

BARBERINI: Let us replace our masks, Bellarmin. Poor Galilei
hasn't got one.

*(He laughs. They take Galileo out)*

FIRST SECRETARY: Did you get his last sentence?

SECOND SECRETARY: Yes. Do you have what he said about believing in the brain?

*(Another cardinal—the Inquisitor—enters)*

INQUISITOR: Did the conference take place?

*(The First Secretary hands him the papers and the Inquisitor
dismisses the Secretaries. They go. The Inquisitor sits down
and starts to read the transcription. Two or three Young
Ladies skitter across the stage; they see the Inquisitor and
curtsy as they go)*

YOUNG GIRL: Who was that?

HER FRIEND: The Cardinal Inquisitor.

*(They giggle and go. Enter Virginia. She curtsies as she goes.
The Inquisitor stops her)*

INQUISITOR: Good evening, my child. Beautiful night. May I
830     congratulate you on your betrothal? Your young man comes
from a fine family. Are you staying with us here in Rome?

VIRGINIA: Not now, Your Eminence. I must go home to prepare for the wedding.

INQUISITOR: Ah. You are accompanying your father to Florence. That should please him. Science must be cold
comfort in a home. Your youth and warmth will keep him
down to earth. It is easy to get lost up there. *(He gestures to
the sky)*

VIRGINIA: He doesn't talk to me about the stars, Your Emi-
840     nence.

INQUISITOR: No. *(He laughs)* They don't eat fish in the fisherman's house. I can tell you something about astronomy. My
child, it seems that God has blessed our modern astronomers with imaginations. It is quite alarming! Do you
know that the earth—which we old fogies supposed to be so
large—has shrunk to something no bigger than a walnut,
and the new universe has grown so vast that prelates—and
even cardinals—look like ants. Why, God Almighty might
lose sight of a Pope! I wonder if I know your Father Con-
850     fessor.

VIRGINIA: Father Christopherus, from Saint Ursula's at
Florence, Your Eminence.

INQUISITOR: My dear child, you father will need you. Not so
much now perhaps, but one of these days. You are pure, and
there is strength in purity. Greatness is sometimes, indeed

often, too heavy a burden for those to whom God has
granted it. What man is so great that he has no place in a
prayer? But I am keeping you, my dear. Your fiancé will be
jealous of me, and I am afraid your father will never forgive
me for holding forth on astronomy. Go to your dancing and 860
remember me to Father Christopherus.

*(Virginia kisses his ring and runs off. The Inquisitor resumes
his reading)*

SCENE VII

> *Galileo, feeling grim,*
> *A young monk came to visit him.*
> *The monk was born of common folk.*
> *It was of science that they spoke.*

*Garden of the Florentine Ambassador in Rome. Distant hum of
a great city. Galileo and the Little Monk of Scene Five are
talking.*

GALILEO: Let's hear it. That robe you're wearing gives you the
right to say whatever you want to say. Let's hear it.

LITTLE MONK: I have studied physics, Mr. Galilei.

GALILEO: That might help us if it enabled you to admit that two
and two are four.

LITTLE MONK: Mr. Galilei, I have spent four sleepless nights
trying to reconcile the decree that I have read with the
moons of Jupiter that I have seen. This morning I decided
to come to see you after I had said Mass.     870

GALILEO: To tell me that Jupiter has no moons?

LITTLE MONK: No, I found out that I think the decree a wise
decree. It has shocked me into realizing that free research
has its dangers. I have had to decide to give up astronomy.
However, I felt the impulse to confide in you some of the
motives which have impelled even a passionate physicist to
abandon his work.

GALILEO: Your motives are familiar to me.

LITTLE MONK: You mean, of course, the special powers invested in certain commissions of the Holy Office? But there 880
is something else. I would like to talk to you about my family. I do not come from the great city. My parents are peasants in the Campagna, who know about the cultivation of
the olive tree, and not much about anything else. Too often
these days when I am trying to concentrate on tracking
down the moons of Jupiter, I see my parents. I see them sitting by the fire with my sister, eating their curded cheese. I
see the beams of the ceiling above them, which the smoke
of centuries has blackened, and I can see the veins stand out
on their toil-worn hands, and the little spoons in their hands. 890
They scrape a living, and underlying their poverty there is a
sort of order. There are routines. The routine of scrubbing
the floors, the routine of the seasons in the olive orchard,
the routine of paying taxes. The troubles that come to them
are recurrent troubles. My father did not get his poor bent
back all at once, but little by little, year by year, in the olive
orchard; just as year after year, with unfailing regularity,
childbirth has made my mother more and more sexless.
They draw the strength they need to sweat with their loaded
baskets up the stony paths, to bear children, even to eat, 900
from the sight of the trees greening each year anew, from
the reproachful face of the soil, which is never satisfied, and

from the little church and Bible texts they hear there on Sunday. They have been told that God relies upon them and that the pageant of the world has been written around them that they may be tested in the important or unimportant parts handed out to them. How could they take it, were I to tell them that they are on a lump of stone ceaselessly spinning in empty space, circling around a second-rate star? 910 What, then, would be the use of their patience, their acceptance of misery? What comfort, then, the Holy Scriptures, which have mercifully explained their crucifixion? The Holy Scriptures would then be proved full of mistakes. No, I see them begin to look frightened. I see them slowly put their spoons down on the table. They would feel cheated. "There is no eye watching over us, after all," they would say. "We have to start out on our own, at our time of life. Nobody has planned a part for us beyond this wretched one on a worthless star. There is no meaning in our misery. Hunger is just 920 not having eaten. It is no test of strength. Effort is just stooping and carrying. It is not a virtue." Can you understand that I read into the decree of the Holy Office a noble motherly pity and a great goodness of the soul?

GALILEO: (*embarrassed*) Hm, well at least you have found out that it is not a question of the satellites of Jupiter, but of the peasants of the Campagna! And don't try to break me down by the halo of beauty that radiates from old age. How does a pearl develop in an oyster? A jagged grain of sand makes its way into the oyster's shell and makes its life unbearable. 930 The oyster exudes slime to cover the grain of sand and the slime eventually hardens into a pearl. The oyster nearly dies in the process. To hell with the pearl, give me the healthy oyster! And virtues are not exclusive to misery. If your parents were prosperous and happy, they might develop the virtues of happiness and prosperity. Today the virtues of exhaustion are caused by the exhausted land. For that my new water pumps could work more wonders than their ridiculous super-human efforts. Be fruitful and multiply: for war will cut down the population, and our fields are barren! (*A* 940 *pause*) Shall I lie to your people?

LITTLE MONK: We must be silent from the highest of motives: the inward peace of less fortunate souls.

GALILEO: My dear man, as a bonus for not meddling with your parents' peace, the authorities are tendering me, on a silver platter, persecution-free, my share of the fat sweated from your parents, who, as you know, were made in God's image. Should I condone this decree, my motives might not be disinterested: easy life, no persecution and so on.

LITTLE MONK: Mr. Galilei, I am a priest.

950 GALILEO: You are also a physicist. How can new machinery be evolved to domesticate the river water if we physicists are forbidden to study, discuss, and pool our findings about the greatest machinery of all, the machinery of the heavenly bodies? Can I reconcile my findings on the paths of falling bodies with the current belief in the tracks of witches on broom sticks? (*A pause*) I am sorry—I shouldn't have said that.

LITTLE MONK: You don't think that the truth, if it is the truth, would make its way without us?

960 GALILEO: No! No! No! As much of the truth gets through as we push through. You talk about the Campagna peasants as if they were the moss on their huts. Naturally, if they don't get

a move on and learn to think for themselves, the most efficient of irrigation systems cannot help them. I can see their divine patience, but where is their divine fury?

LITTLE MONK: (*helpless*) They are old!

(*Galileo stands for a moment, beaten; he cannot meet the little monk's eyes. He takes a manuscript from the table and throws it violently on the ground*)

LITTLE MONK: What is that?

GALILEO: Here is writ what draws the ocean when it ebbs and flows. Let it lie there. Thou shalt not read. (*Little Monk has picked up the manuscript*) Already! An apple of the tree of 970 knowledge, he can't wait, he wolfs it down. He will rot in hell for all eternity. Look at him, where are his manners?— Sometimes I think I would let them imprison me in a place a thousand feet beneath the earth where no light could reach me, if in exchange I could find out what stuff that is: "Light." The bad thing is that, when I find something, I have to boast about it like a lover or a drunkard or a traitor. That is a hopeless vice and leads to the abyss. I wonder how long I shall be content to discuss it with my dog!

LITTLE MONK: (*immersed in the manuscript*) I don't under- 980 stand this sentence.

GALILEO: I'll explain it to you, I'll explain it to you.

(*They are sitting on the floor*)

## SCENE VIII

> *Eight long years with tongue in cheek*
> *Of what he knew he did not speak.*
> *Then temptation grew too great*
> *And Galileo challenged fate.*

*Galileo's house in Florence again. Galileo is supervising his Assistants Andrea, Federzoni, and the Little Monk who are about to prepare an experiment. Mrs. Sarti and Virginia are at a long table sewing bridal linen. There is a new telescope, larger than the old one. At the moment it is covered with a cloth.*

ANDREA: (*looking up a schedule*) Thursday. Afternoon. Floating bodies again. Ice, bowl of water, scales, and it says here an iron needle. Aristotle.

VIRGINIA: Ludovico likes to entertain. We must take care to be neat. His mother notices every stitch. She doesn't approve of father's books.

MRS. SARTI: That's all a thing of the past. He hasn't published a book for years. 990

VIRGINIA: That's true. Oh Sarti, it's fun sewing a trousseau.

MRS. SARTI: Virginia, I want to talk to you. You are very young, and you have no mother, and your father is putting those pieces of ice in water, and marriage is too serious a business to go into blind. Now you should go to see a real astronomer from the university and have him cast your horoscope so you know where you stand. (*Virginia giggles*) What's the matter?

VIRGINIA: I've been already.

MRS. SARTI: Tell Sarti. 1000

VIRGINIA: I have to be careful for three months now because the sun is in Capricorn, but after that I get a favorable ascendant, and I can undertake a journey if I am careful of

Uranus, as I'm a Scorpion.

MRS. SARTI: What about Ludovico?

VIRGINIA: He's a Leo, the astronomer said. Leos are sensual.

*(Giggles)*

*(There is a knock at the door, it opens. Enter the Rector of the University, the philosopher of Scene Four, bringing a book)*

RECTOR: *(to Virginia)* This is about the burning issue of the moment. He may want to glance over it. My faculty would appreciate his comments. No, don't disturb him now, my dear. Every minute one takes of your father's time is stolen from Italy. *(He goes)*

VIRGINIA: Federzoni! The rector of the university brought this.

*(Federzoni takes it)*

GALILEO: What's it about?

FEDERZONI: *(spelling)* De maculis in sole.

ANDREA: Oh, it's on the sun spots!

*(Andrea comes one side, and the Little Monk the other, to look at the book)*

ANDREA: A new one!

*(Federzoni resentfully puts the book into their hands and continues with the preparation of the experiment)*

ANDREA: Listen to this dedication. *(Quotes)* "To the greatest living authority on physics, Galileo Galilei."—I read Fabricius' paper the other day. Fabricius says the spots are clusters of planets between us and the sun.

LITTLE MONK: Doubtful.

GALILEO: *(noncommittal)* Yes?

ANDREA: Paris and Prague hold that they are vapors from the sun. Federzoni doubts that.

FEDERZONI: Me? You leave me out. I said "hm," that was all. And don't discuss new things before me. I can't read the material, it's in Latin. *(He drops the scales and stands trembling with fury)* Tell me, can I doubt anything?

*(Galileo walks over and picks up the scales silently. Pause)*

LITTLE MONK: There is happiness in doubting, I wonder why.

ANDREA: Aren't we going to take this up?

GALILEO: At the moment we are investigating floating bodies.

ANDREA: Mother has baskets full of letters from all over Europe asking his opinion.

FEDERZONI: The question is whether you can afford to remain silent.

GALILEO: I cannot afford to be smoked on a wood fire like a ham.

ANDREA: *(surprised)* Ah. You think the sun spots may have something to do with that again? *(Galileo does not answer)*

ANDREA: Well, we stick to fiddling about with bits of ice in water. They can't hurt you.

GALILEO: Correct.—Our thesis!

ANDREA: All things that are lighter than water float, and all things that are heavier sink.

GALILEO: Aristotle says—

LITTLE MONK: *(reading out of a book, translating)* "A broad and flat disk of ice, although heavier than water, still floats, because it is unable to divide the water."

GALILEO: Well, now I push the ice below the surface. I take away the pressure of my hands. What happens?

*(Pause.)*

LITTLE MONK: It rises to the surface.

GALILEO: Correct. It seems to be able to divide the water as it's coming up, doesn't it?

LITTLE MONK: Could it be lighter than water after all?

GALILEO: Aha!

ANDREA: Then all things that are lighter than water float, and all things that are heavier sink. Q. e. d.

GALILEO: Not at all. Hand me that iron needle. Heavier than water? *(They all nod)* A piece of paper. *(He places the needle on a piece of paper and floats it on the surface of the water. Pause)* Do not be hasty with your conclusion. *(Pause)* What happens?

FEDERZONI: The paper has sunk, the needle is floating.

VIRGINIA: What's the matter?

MRS. SARTI: Every time I hear them laugh it sends shivers down my spine.

*(There is a knocking at the outer door)*

MRS. SARTI: Who's that at the door?

*(Enter Ludovico. Virginia runs to him. They embrace. Ludovico is followed by a servant with baggage)*

MRS. SARTI: Well!

VIRGINIA: Oh! Why didn't you write that you were coming?

LUDOVICO: I decided on the spur of the moment. I was over inspecting our vineyards at Bucciole. I couldn't keep away.

GALILEO: Who's that?

LITTLE MONK: Miss Virginia's intended. What's the matter with your eyes?

GALILEO: *(blinking)* Oh yes, it's Ludovico, so it is. Well! Sarti, get a jug of that Sicilian wine, the old kind. We celebrate.

*(Everybody sits down. Mrs. Sarti has left, followed by Ludovico's Servant.)*

GALILEO: Well, Ludovico, old man. How are the horses?

LUDOVICO: The horses are fine.

GALILEO: Fine.

LUDOVICO: But those vineyards need a firm hand. *(To Virginia)* You look pale. Country life will suit you. Mother's planning on September.

VIRGINIA: I suppose I oughtn't, but stay here, I've got something to show you.

LUDOVICO: What?

VIRGINIA: Never mind. I won't be ten minutes. *(She runs out)*

LUDOVICO: How's life these days, sir?

GALILEO: Dull.—How was the journey?

LUDOVICO: Dull.—Before I forget, mother sends her congratulations on your admirable tact over the latest rumblings of science.

GALILEO: Thank her from me.

LUDOVICO: Christopher Clavius had all Rome on its ears. He said he was afraid that the turning around business might crop up again on account of these spots on the sun.

ANDREA: Clavius is on the same track! *(To Ludovico)* My mother's baskets are full of letters from all over Europe asking Mr. Galilei's opinion.

GALILEO: I am engaged in investigating the habits of floating

1100    bodies. Any harm in that?

*(Mrs. Sarti re-enters, followed by the Servant. They bring wine and glasses on a tray)*

GALILEO: *(hands out the wine)* What news from the Holy City, apart from the prospect of my sins?

LUDOVICO: The Holy Father is on his death bed. Hadn't you heard?

LITTLE MONK: My goodness! What about the succession?

LUDOVICO: All the talk is of Barberini.

GALILEO: Barberini?

ANDREA: Mr. Galilei knows Barberini.

LITTLE MONK: Cardinal Barberini is a mathematician.

1110 FEDERZONI: A scientist in the chair of Peter!

*(Pause.)*

GALILEO: *(cheering up enormously)* This means change. We might live to see the day, Federzoni, when we don't have to whisper that two and two are four. *(To Ludovico)* I like this wine. Don't you, Ludovico?

LUDOVICO: I like it.

GALILEO: I know the hill where it is grown. The slope is steep and stony, the grape almost blue. I am fond of this wine.

LUDOVICO: Yes, sir.

GALILEO: There are shadows in this wine. It is almost sweet but
1120    just stops short.—Andrea, clear that stuff away, ice, bowl and needle.—I cherish the consolations of the flesh. I have no patience with cowards who call them weaknesses. I say there is a certain achievement in enjoying things.

*(The Pupils get up and go to the experiment table)*

LITTLE MONK: What are we to do?

FEDERZONI: He is starting on the sun.

*(They begin with clearing up)*

ANDREA: *(singing in a low voice)*
The Bible proves the earth stands still,
The Pope, he swears with tears:
The earth stands still. To prove it so
1130    He takes it by the ears.

LUDOVICO: What's the excitement?

MRS. SARTI: You're not going to start those hellish goings-on again, Mr. Galilei?

ANDREA: And gentlefolk, they say so too.
Each learned doctor proves,
(If you grease his palm): The earth stands still.
And yet—and yet it moves.

GALILEO: Barberini is in the ascendant, so your mother is uneasy, and you're sent to investigate me. Correct me if I am
1140    wrong, Ludovico. Clavius is right: these spots on the sun interest me.

ANDREA: We might find out that the sun also revolves. How would you like that, Ludovico?

GALILEO: Do you like my wine, Ludovico?

LUDOVICO: I told you I did, sir.

GALILEO: You really like it?

LUDOVICO: I like it.

GALILEO: Tell me, Ludovico, would you consider going so far as to accept a man's wine or his daughter without insisting
1150    that he drop his profession? I have no wish to intrude, but have the moons of Jupiter affected Virginia's bottom?

MRS. SARTI: That isn't funny, it's just vulgar. I am going for Virginia.

LUDOVICO: *(keeps her back)* Marriages in families such as mine are not arranged on a basis of sexual attraction alone.

GALILEO: Did they keep you back from marrying my daughter for eight years because I was on probation?

LUDOVICO: My future wife must take her place in the family pew.

GALILEO: You mean, if the daughter of a bad man sat in your 1160 family pew, your peasants might stop paying the rent?

LUDOVICO: In a sort of way.

GALILEO: When I was your age, the only person I allowed to rap me on the knuckles was my girl.

LUDOVICO: My mother was assured that you had undertaken not to get mixed up in this turning around business again, sir.

GALILEO: We had a conservative Pope then.

MRS. SARTI: Had! His Holiness is not dead yet!

GALILEO: *(with relish)* Pretty nearly.                               1170

MRS. SARTI: That man will weigh a chip of ice fifty times, but when it comes to something that's convenient, he believes it blindly. "Is His Holiness dead?"—"Pretty nearly!"

LUDOVICO: You will find, sir, if His Holiness passes away, the new Pope, whoever he turns out to be, will respect the convictions held by the solid families of the country.

GALILEO: *(to Andrea)* That remains to be seen.—Andrea, get out the screen. We'll throw the image of the sun on our screen to save our eyes.

LITTLE MONK: I thought you'd been working at it. Do you know 1180 when I guessed it? When you didn't recognize Mr. Marsili.

MRS. SARTI: If my son has to go to hell for sticking to you, that's my affair, but you have no right to trample on your daughter's happiness.

LUDOVICO: *(to his Servant)* Giuseppe, take my baggage back to the coach, will you?

MRS. SARTI: This will kill her. *(She runs out, still clutching the jug)*

LUDOVICO: *(politely)* Mr. Galilei, if we Marsilis were to countenance teachings frowned on by the church, it would un- 1190 settle our peasants. Bear in mind: these poor people in their brute state get everything upside down. They are nothing but animals. They will never comprehend the finer points of astronomy. Why, two months ago a rumor went around, an apple had been found on a pear tree, and they left their work in the fields to discuss it.

GALILEO: *(interested)* Did they?

LUDOVICO: I have seen the day when my poor mother has had to have a dog whipped before their eyes to remind them to keep their place. Oh, you may have seen the waving corn 1200 from the window of your comfortable coach. You have, no doubt, nibbled our olives, and absentmindedly eaten our cheese, but you can have no idea how much responsibility that sort of thing entails.

GALILEO: Young man, I do not eat my cheese absentmindedly. *(To Andrea)* Are we ready?

ANDREA: Yes, sir.

GALILEO: *(leaves Ludovico and adjusts the mirror)* You would not confine your whippings to dogs to remind your peasants to keep their places, would you, Marsili?                          1210

LUDOVICO: *(after a pause)* Mr. Galilei, you have a wonderful brain, it's a pity.

LITTLE MONK: *(astonished)* He threatened you.

GALILEO: Yes. And he threatened you too. We might unsettle his peasants. Your sister, Fulganzio, who works the lever of the olive press, might laugh out loud if she heard the sun is not a gilded coat of arms but a lever too. The earth turns because the sun turns it.

1220 ANDREA: That could interest his steward too and even his money lender—and the seaport towns. . . .

FEDERZONI: None of them speak Latin.

GALILEO: I might write in plain language. The work we do is exacting. Who would go through the strain for less than the population at large!

LUDOVICO: I see you have made your decision. It was inevitable. You will always be a slave of your passions. Excuse me to Virginia, I think it's as well I don't see her now.

GALILEO: The dowry is at your disposal at any time.

LUDOVICO: Good afternoon. *(He goes followed by the Servant)*

1230 ANDREA: Exit Ludovico. To hell with all Marsilis, Villanis, Orsinis, Canes, Nuccolis, Soldanieris. . . .

FEDERZONI: . . . who ordered the earth stand still because their castles might be shaken loose if it revolves . . .

LITTLE MONK: . . . and who only kiss the Pope's feet as long as he uses them to trample on the people. God made the physical world, God made the human brain. God will allow physics.

ANDREA: They will try to stop us.

GALILEO: Thus we enter the observation of these spots on the

1240 sun in which we are interested, at our own risk, not counting on protection from a problematical new Pope . . .

ANDREA: . . . but with great likelihood of dispelling Fabricius' vapors, and the shadows of Paris and Prague, and of establishing the rotation of the sun . . .

GALILEO: . . . and with *some* likelihood of establishing the rotation of the sun. My intention is not to prove that I was right but to find out *whether* I was right. "Abandon hope all ye who enter—an observation." Before assuming these phenomena are spots, which would suit us, let us first set about

1250 proving that they are not—fried fish. We crawl by inches. What we find today we will wipe from the blackboard tomorrow and reject it—unless it shows up again the day after tomorrow. And if we find anything which would suit us, that thing we will eye with particular distrust. In fact, we will approach this observing of the sun with the implacable determination to prove that the earth stands still and only if hopelessly defeated in this pious undertaking can we allow ourselves to wonder if we may not have been right all the time: the earth revolves. Take the cloth off the telescope

1260 and turn it on the sun.

*(Quietly they start work. When the corruscating image of the sun is focused on the screen, Virginia enters hurriedly, her wedding dress on, her hair disheveled, Mrs. Sarti with her, carrying her wedding veil. The two women realize what has happened. Virginia faints. Andrea, Little Monk and Galileo rush to her. Federzoni continues working)*

## SCENE IX

> On April Fool's Day, thirty two,
> Of science there was much ado.
> People had learned from Galilei:
> They used his teaching in their way.

*Around the corner from the market place a Street Singer and his Wife, who is costumed to represent the earth in a skeleton globe made of thin bands of brass, are holding the attention of a sprinkling of representative citizens, some in masquerade who were on their way to see the carnival procession. From the market place the noise of an impatient crowd.*

BALLAD SINGER: *(accompanied by his Wife on the guitar)*
> When the Almighty made the universe
> He made the earth and then he made the sun.
> Then round the earth he bade the sun to turn—
> That's in the Bible, Genesis, Chapter One.
> And from that time all beings here below
> Were in obedient circles meant to go:
> > Around the pope the cardinals
> > Around the cardinals the bishops
> > Around the bishops the secretaries
> > Around the secretaries the aldermen     1270
> > Around the aldermen the craftsmen
> > Around the craftsmen the servants
> > Around the servants the dogs, the chickens, and the beggars.

*(A conspicuous reveller—henceforth called the Spinner—has slowly caught on and is exhibiting his idea of spinning around. He does not lose dignity, he faints with mock grace)*

BALLAD SINGER:
> Up stood the learned Galileo
> Glanced briefly at the sun
> And said: "Almighty God was wrong
> In Genesis, Chapter One!"
> > Now that was rash, my friends, it is no matter small     1280
> > For heresy will spread today like foul diseases.
> > Change Holy Writ, forsooth? What will be left at all?
> > Why: each of us would say and do just what he pleases!

*(Three wretched Extras, employed by the chamber of commerce, enter. Two of them, in ragged costumes, moodily bear a litter with a mock throne. The third sits on the throne. He wears sacking, a false beard, a prop crown, he carries a prop orb and sceptre, and around his chest the inscription "The King of Hungary." The litter has a card with "No. 4" written on it. The litter bearers dump him down and listen to the Ballad Singer)*

BALLAD SINGER:
> Good people, what will come to pass
> If Galileo's teachings spread?
> No altar boy will serve the mass
> No servant girl will make the bed.
> > Now that is grave, my friends, it is no matter small:
> > For independent spirit spreads like foul diseases!     1290
> > (Yet life is sweet and man is weak and after all—
> > How nice it is, for a little change, to do just as one pleases!)

*(The Ballad Singer takes over the guitar. His Wife dances around him, illustrating the motion of the earth. A Cobbler's Boy with a pair of resplendent lacquered boots hung over his shoulder has been jumping up and down in mock excitement. There are three more children, dressed as grownups among the spectators, two together and a single one with mother. The Cobbler's Boy takes the three Children in hand, forms a chain*

*and leads it, moving to the music, in and out among the spectators, "whipping" the chain so that the last child bumps into people. On the way past a Peasant Woman, he steals an egg from her basket. She gestures to him to return it. As he passes her again he quietly breaks the egg over her head. The King of Hungary ceremoniously hands his orb to one of his bearers, marches down with mock dignity, and chastises the Cobbler's Boy. The parents remove the three Children. The unseemliness subsides)*

BALLAD SINGER:
> The carpenters take wood and build
> Their houses—not the church's pews.
> And members of the cobblers' guild
> Now boldly walk the streets—in shoes.
> The tenant kicks the noble lord
> 1300    Quite off the land he owned—like that!
> The milk his wife once gave the priest
> Now makes (at last!) her children fat.
> Ts, ts, ts, ts, my friends, this is no matter small
> For independent spirit spreads like foul diseases
> People must keep their place, some down and some on
> top!
> (Though it is nice, for a little change, to do just as one
> pleases!)

*(The Cobbler's Boy has put on the lacquered boots he was carrying. He struts off. The Ballad Singer takes over the guitar again. His Wife dances around him in increased tempo. A Monk has been standing near a rich Couple, who are in subdued costly clothes, without masks: shocked at the song, he now leaves. A Dwarf in the costume of an astronomer turns his telescope on the departing Monk, thus drawing attention to the rich Couple. In imitation of the Cobbler's Boy, the Spinner forms a chain of grownups. They move to the music, in and out, and between the rich Couple. The Spinner changes the Gentleman's bonnet for the ragged hat of a Beggar. The Gentleman decides to take this in good part, and a Girl is emboldened to take his dagger. The Gentleman is miffed, throws the Beggar's hat back. The Beggar discards the Gentleman's bonnet and drops it on the ground. The King of Hungary has walked from his throne, taken an egg from the Peasant Woman, and paid for it. He now ceremoniously breaks it over the Gentleman's head as he is bending down to pick up his bonnet. The Gentleman conducts the Lady away from the scene. The King of Hungary, about to resume his throne, finds one of the Children sitting on it. The Gentleman returns to retrieve his dagger. Merriment. The Ballad Singer wanders off. This is part of his routine. His Wife sings to the Spinner)*

WIFE:
> 1310    Now speaking for myself I feel
> That I could also do with a change.
> You know, for me . . . (Turning to a reveller) . . . you have
> appeal
> Maybe tonight we could arrange . . .

*(The Dwarf-Astronomer has been amusing the people by focusing his telescope on her legs. The Ballad Singer has returned)*

BALLAD SINGER:
> No, no, no, no, no, stop, Galileo, stop!

> For independent spirit spreads like foul diseases
> People must keep their place, some down and some on
> top!
> (Though it is nice, for a little change, to do just as one    1320
> pleases!)

*(The Spectators stand embarrassed. A Girl laughs loudly)*

BALLAD SINGER AND HIS WIFE:
> Good people who have trouble here below
> In serving cruel lords and gentle Jesus
> Who bids you turn the other cheek just so . . . (With
> mimicry)
> While they prepare to strike the second blow:
> Obedience will never cure your woe
> So each of you wake up and do just as he pleases!

*(The Ballad Singer and his Wife hurriedly start to try to sell pamphlets to the spectators)*

BALLAD SINGER: Read all about the earth going round the sun,    1330
two centesimi only. As proved by the great Galileo. Two
centesimi only. Written by a local scholar. Understandable
to one and all. Buy one for your friends, your children and
your aunty Rosa, two centesimi only. Abbreviated but complete.
Fully illustrated with pictures of the planets, including
Venus, two centesimi only.

*(During the speech of the Ballad Singer we hear the carnival procession approaching followed by laughter. A Reveller rushes in)*

REVELLER: The procession!

*(The litter bearers speedily joggle out the King of Hungary. The Spectators turn and look at the first float of the procession, which now makes its appearance. It bears a gigantic figure of Galileo, holding in one hand an open Bible with the pages crossed out. The other hand points to the Bible, and the head mechanically turns from side to side as if to say "No! No!")*

A LOUD VOICE: Galileo, the Bible killer!

*(The laughter from the market place becomes uproarious. The Monk comes flying from the market place followed by delighted Children)*

## SCENE X

> *The depths are hot, the heights are chill*
> *The streets are loud, the court is still.*

*Ante-Chamber and staircase in the Medicean palace in Florence. Galileo, with a book under his arm, waits with his Daughter to be admitted to the presence of the Prince.*

VIRGINIA: They are a long time.

GALILEO: Yes.    1340

VIRGINIA: Who is that funny looking man? *(She indicates the Informer who has entered casually and seated himself in the background, taking no apparent notice of Galileo)*

GALILEO: I don't know.

VIRGINIA: It's not the first time I have seen him around. He gives me the creeps.

GALILEO: Nonsense. We're in Florence, not among robbers in the mountains of Corsica.

VIRGINIA: Here comes the Rector.

(*The Rector comes down the stairs*)

1350 GALILEO: Gaffone is a bore. He attaches himself to you.

(*The Rector passes, scarcely nodding*)

GALILEO: My eyes are bad today. Did he acknowledge us?

VIRGINIA: Barely. (*Pause*) What's in your book? Will they say it's heretical?

GALILEO: You hang around church too much. And getting up at dawn and scurrying to mass is ruining your skin. You pray for me, don't you?

(*A Man comes down the stairs*)

VIRGINIA: Here's Mr. Matti. You designed a machine for his Iron Foundries.

MATTI: How were the squabs, Mr. Galilei? (*Low*) My brother
1360 and I had a good laugh the other day. He picked up a racy pamphlet against the Bible somewhere. It quoted you.

GALILEO: The squabs, Matti, were wonderful, thank you again. Pamphlets I know nothing about. The Bible and Homer are my favorite reading.

MATTI: No necessity to be cautious with me, Mr. Galilei. I am on your side. I am not a man who knows about the motions of the stars, but you have championed the freedom to teach new things. Take that mechanical cultivator they have in Germany which you described to me. I can tell you, it will
1370 never be used in this country. The same circles that are hampering you now will forbid the physicians at Bologna to cut up corpses for research. Do you know, they have such things as money markets in Amsterdam and in London? Schools for business, too. Regular papers with news. Here we are not even free to make money. I have a stake in your career. They are against iron foundries because they say the gathering of so many workers in one place fosters immorality! If they ever try anything, Mr. Galilei, remember you have friends in all walks of life including an iron founder.
1380 Good luck to you.

(*He goes*)

GALILEO: Good man, but need he be so affectionate in public? His voice carries. They will always claim me as their spiritual leader particularly in places where it doesn't help me at all. I have written a book about the mechanics of the firmament, that is all. What they do or don't do with it is not my concern.

VIRGINIA: (*loud*) If people only knew how you disagreed with those goings-on all over the country last All Fools day.

GALILEO: Yes. Offer honey to a bear, and lose your arm if the
1390 beast is hungry.

VIRGINIA: (*low*) Did the prince ask you to come here today?

GALILEO: I sent word I was coming. He will want the book, he has paid for it. My health hasn't been any too good lately. I may accept Sagredo's invitation to stay with him in Padua for a few weeks.

VIRGINIA: You couldn't manage without your books.

GALILEO: Sagredo has an excellent library.

VIRGINIA: We haven't had this month's salary yet—

GALILEO: Yes. (*The Cardinal Inquisitor passes down the stair-*
1400 *case. He bows deeply in answer to Galileo's bow*) What is he doing in Florence? If they try to do anything to me, the new

Pope will meet them with an iron NO. And the Prince is my pupil, he would never have me extradited.

VIRGINIA: Psst. The Lord Chamberlain.

(*The Lord Chamberlain comes down the stairs*)

LORD CHAMBERLAIN: His Highness had hoped to find time for you, Mr. Galilei. Unfortunately, he has to leave immediately to judge the parade at the Riding Academy. On what business did you wish to see His Highness?

GALILEO: I wanted to present my book to His Highness.

LORD CHAMBERLAIN: How are your eyes today? 1410

GALILEO: So, so. With His Highness' permission, I am dedicating the book . . .

LORD CHAMBERLAIN: Your eyes are a matter of great concern to His Highness. Could it be that you have been looking too long and too often through your marvelous tube? (*He leaves without accepting the book*)

VIRGINIA: (*greatly agitated*) Father, I am afraid.

GALILEO: He didn't take the book, did he? (*Low and resolute*) Keep a straight face. We are not going home, but to the house of the lens-grinder. There is a coach and horses in his 1420 backyard. Keep your eyes to the front, don't look back at that man.

(*They start. The Lord Chamberlain comes back*)

LORD CHAMBERLAIN: Oh, Mr. Galilei, His Highness has just charged me to inform you that the Florentine Court is no longer in a position to oppose the request of the Holy Inquisition to interrogate you in Rome.

## SCENE XI

### *The Pope*

*A chamber in the Vatican. The Pope, Urban VIII—formerly Cardinal Barberini—is giving audience to the Cardinal Inquisitor. The trampling and shuffling of many feet is heard throughout the scene from the adjoining corridors. During the scene the Pope is being robed for the conclave he is about to attend: at the beginning of the scene he is plainly Barberini, but as the scene proceeds he is more and more obscured by grandiose vestments.*

POPE: No! No! No!

INQUISITOR: (*referring to the owners of the shuffling feet*) Doctors of all chairs from the universities, representatives of the special orders of the Church, representatives of the clergy as 1430 a whole who have come believing with child-like faith in the word of God as set forth in the Scriptures, who have come to hear Your Holiness confirm their faith: and Your Holiness is really going to tell them that the Bible can no longer be regarded as the alphabet of truth?

POPE: I will not set myself up against the multiplication table. No!

INQUISITOR: Ah, that is what these people say, that it is the multiplication table. Their cry is, "The figures compel us," but where do these figures come from? Plainly they come from 1440 doubt. These men doubt everything. Can society stand on doubt and not on faith? "Thou art my master, but I doubt whether it is for the best." "This is my neighbor's house and my neighbor's wife, but why shouldn't they belong to me?"

After the plague, after the new war, after the unparalleled disaster of the Reformation, your dwindling flock look to their shepherd, and now the mathematicians turn their tubes on the sky and announce to the world that you have not the best advice about the heavens either—up to now your only uncontested sphere of influence. This Galilei started meddling in machines at an early age. Now that men in ships are venturing on the great oceans—I am not against that of course—they are putting their faith in a brass bowl they call a compass and not in Almighty God.

POPE: This man is the greatest physicist of our time. He is the light of Italy, and not just any muddle-head.

INQUISITOR: Would we have had to arrest him otherwise? This bad man knows what he is doing, not writing his books in Latin, but in the jargon of the market place.

POPE: (occupied with the shuffling feet) That was not in the best of taste. (A pause) These shuffling feet are making me nervous.

INQUISITOR: May they be more telling than my words, Your Holiness. Shall all these go from you with doubt in their hearts?

POPE: This man has friends. What about Versailles? What about the Viennese court? They will call Holy Church a cesspool for defunct ideas. Keep your hands off him.

INQUISITOR: In practice it will never get far. He is a man of the flesh. He would soften at once.

POPE: He has more enjoyment in him than any man I ever saw. He loves eating and drinking and thinking. To excess. He indulges in thinking-bouts! He cannot say no to an old wine or a new thought. (Furious) I do not want a condemnation of physical facts. I do not want to hear battle cries: Church, church, church! Reason, reason, reason! (Pause) These shuffling feet are intolerable. Has the whole world come to my door?

INQUISITOR: Not the whole world, Your Holiness. A select gathering of the faithful.

(Pause)

POPE: (exhausted) It is clearly understood: he is not to be tortured. (Pause) At the very most, he may be shown the instruments.

INQUISITOR: That will be adequate, Your Holiness. Mr. Galilei understands machinery.

(The eyes of Barberini look helplessly at the Cardinal Inquisitor from under the completely assembled panoply of Pope Urban VIII)

SCENE XII

> June twenty second, sixteen thirty three,
> A momentous date for you and me.
> Of all the days that was the one
> An age of reason could have begun.

*Again the garden of the Florentine Ambassador at Rome, where Galileo's assistants wait the news of the trial. The Little Monk and Federzoni are attempting to concentrate on a game of chess. Virginia kneels in a corner, praying and counting her beads.*

LITTLE MONK: The Pope didn't even grant him an audience.

FEDERZONI: No more scientific discussions.

ANDREA: The "Discorsi" will never be finished. The sum of his findings. They will kill him.

FEDERZONI: (stealing a glance at him) Do you really think so?

ANDREA: He will never recant.

(Silence)

LITTLE MONK: You know when you lie awake at night how your mind fastens on to something irrelevant. Last night I kept thinking: if only they would let him take his little stone in with him, the appeal-to-reason-pebble that he always carried in his pocket.

FEDERZONI: In the room *they'll* take him to, he won't have a pocket.

ANDREA: But he will not recant.

LITTLE MONK: How can they beat the truth out of a man who gave his sight in order to see?

FEDERZONI: Maybe they can't.

(Silence)

ANDREA: (speaking about Virginia) She is praying that he will recant.

FEDERZONI: Leave her alone. She doesn't know whether she's on her head or on her heels since they got hold of her. They brought her Father Confessor from Florence.

(The Informer of Scene Ten enters)

INFORMER: Mr. Galilei will be here soon. He may need a bed.

FEDERZONI: Have they let him out?

INFORMER: Mr. Galilei is expected to recant at five o'clock. The big bell of Saint Marcus will be rung and the complete text of his recantation publicly announced.

ANDREA: I don't believe it.

INFORMER: Mr. Galilei will be brought to the garden gate at the back of the house, to avoid the crowds collecting in the streets. (He goes)

(Silence)

ANDREA: The moon is an earth because the light of the moon is not her own. Jupiter is a fixed star, and four moons turn around Jupiter, therefore we are not shut in by crystal shells. The sun is the pivot of our world, therefore the earth is not the center. The earth moves, spinning about the sun. And he showed us. You can't make a man unsee what he has seen.

(Silence)

FEDERZONI: Five o'clock is one minute.

(Virginia prays louder)

ANDREA: Listen all of you, they are murdering the truth.

(He stops up his ears with his fingers. The two other pupils do the same. Federzoni goes over to the Little Monk, and all of them stand absolutely still in cramped positions. Nothing happens. No bell sounds. After a silence, filled with the murmur of Virginia's prayers, Federzoni runs to the wall to look at the clock. He turns around, his expression changed. He shakes his head. They drop their hands)

FEDERZONI: No. No bell. It is three minutes after.

LITTLE MONK: He hasn't.

ANDREA: He held true. It is all right, it is all right.

LITTLE MONK: He did not recant.

1530 FEDERZONI: No.

*(They embrace each other, they are delirious with joy)*

ANDREA: So force cannot accomplish everything. What has been seen can't be unseen. Man is constant in the face of death.

FEDERZONI: June 22, 1633: dawn of the age of reason. I wouldn't have wanted to go on living if he had recanted.

LITTLE MONK: I didn't say anything, but I was in agony. Oh, ye of little faith!

ANDREA: I was sure.

FEDERZONI: It would have turned our morning to night.

1540 ANDREA: It would have been as if the mountain had turned to water.

LITTLE MONK: *(kneeling down, crying)* Oh God, I thank Thee.

ANDREA: Beaten humanity can lift its head. A man has stood up and said "no."

*(At this moment the bell of Saint Marcus begins to toll. They stand like statues. Virginia stands up)*

VIRGINIA: The bell of Saint Marcus. He is not damned.

*(From the street one hears the Town Crier reading Galileo's recantation)*

TOWN CRIER: I, Galileo Galilei, Teacher of Mathematics and Physics, do hereby publicly renounce my teaching that the earth moves. I foreswear this teaching with a sincere heart and unfeigned faith and detest and curse this and all other

1550 errors and heresies repugnant to the Holy Scriptures.

*(The lights dim; when they come up again the bell of Saint Marcus is petering out. Virginia has gone but the Scholars are still there waiting)*

ANDREA: *(loud)* The mountain did turn to water.

*(Galileo has entered quietly and unnoticed. He is changed, almost unrecognizable. He has heard Andrea. He waits some seconds by the door for somebody to greet him. Nobody does. They retreat from him. He goes slowly and, because of his bad sight, uncertainly, to the front of the stage where he finds a chair, and sits down)*

ANDREA: I can't look at him. Tell him to go away.

FEDERZONI: Steady.

ANDREA: *(hysterically)* He saved his big gut.

FEDERZONI: Get him a glass of water.

*(The Little Monk fetches a glass of water for Andrea. Nobody acknowledges the presence of Galileo, who sits silently on his chair listening to the voice of the Town Crier, now in another street)*

ANDREA: I can walk. Just help me a bit.

*(They help him to the door)*

ANDREA: *(in the door)* "Unhappy is the land that breeds no hero."

GALILEO: No, Andrea: "Unhappy is the land that needs a hero."

*(Before the next scene a curtain with the following legend on it is lowered)*

■ ■ ■ You can plainly see that if a horse were to fall from a height of three or four feet, it could break its bones, whereas a dog would not suffer injury. The same applies to a cat from a height of as much as eight or ten feet, to a grasshopper from the top of a tower, and to an ant falling down from the moon. Nature could not allow a horse to become as big as twenty horses nor a giant as big as ten men, unless she were to change the proportions of all its members, particularly the bones. Thus the common assumption that great and small structures are equally tough is obviously wrong.

—FROM THE "DISCORSI"

SCENE XIII

*1633–1642.*
*Galileo Galilei remains a prisoner*
*of the Inquisition until his death.*

*A country house near Florence. A large room simply furnished. There is a huge table, a leather chair, a globe of the world on a stand, and a narrow bed. A portion of the adjoining anteroom is visible, and the front door which opens into it. An Official of the Inquisition sits on guard in the anteroom. In the large room, Galileo is quietly experimenting with a bent wooden rail and a small ball of wood. He is still vigorous but almost blind. After a while there is a knocking at the outside door. The Official opens it to a peasant who brings a plucked goose. Virginia comes from the kitchen. She is past forty.*

PEASANT: *(handing the goose to Virginia)* I was told to deliver 1560 this here.

VIRGINIA: I didn't order a goose.

PEASANT: I was told to say it's from someone who was passing through.

*(Virginia takes the goose, surprised. The Official takes it from her and examines it suspiciously. Then, reassured, he hands it back to her. The Peasant goes. Virginia brings the goose in to Galileo)*

VIRGINIA: Somebody who was passing through sent you something.

GALILEO: What is it?

VIRGINIA: Can't you see it?

GALILEO: No. *(He walks over)* A goose. Any name?

VIRGINIA: No.                                                    1570

GALILEO: *(weighing the goose)* Solid.

VIRGINIA: *(cautiously)* Will you eat the liver, if I have it cooked with a little apple?

GALILEO: I had my dinner. Are you under orders to finish me off with food?

VIRGINIA: It's not rich. And what is wrong with your eyes again? You should be able to see it.

GALILEO: You were standing in the light.

VIRGINIA: I was not.—You haven't been writing again?

1580 GALILEO: (*sneering*) What do you think?

(*Virginia takes the goose out into the anteroom and speaks to the Official*)

VIRGINIA: You had better ask Monsignor Carpula to send the doctor. Father couldn't see this goose across the room.—Don't look at me like that. He has not been writing. He dictates everything to me, as you know.

OFFICIAL: Yes?

VIRGINIA: He abides by the rules. My father's repentance is sincere. I keep an eye on him. (*She hands him the goose*) Tell the cook to fry the liver with an apple and an onion. (*She goes back into the large room*) And you have no business to 1590 be doing that with those eyes of yours, father.

GALILEO: You may read me some Horace.

VIRGINIA: We should go on with your weekly letter to the Archbishop. Monsignor Carpula to whom we owe so much was all smiles the other day because the Archbishop had expressed his pleasure at your collaboration.

GALILEO: Where were we?

VIRGINIA: (*sits down to take his dictation*) Paragraph four.

GALILEO: Read what you have.

VIRGINIA: "The position of the Church in the matter of the un-1600 rest at Genoa. I agree with Cardinal Spoletti in the matter of the unrest among the Venetian ropemakers . . . "

GALILEO: Yes. (*Dictates*) I agree with Cardinal Spoletti in the matter of the unrest among the Venetian ropemakers: it is better to distribute good nourishing food in the name of charity than to pay them more for their bellropes. It being surely better to strengthen their faith than to encourage their acquisitiveness. St. Paul says: Charity never faileth.—How is that?

VIRGINIA: It's beautiful, father.

1610 GALILEO: It couldn't be taken as irony?

VIRGINIA: No. The Archbishop will like it. It's so practical.

GALILEO: I trust your judgment. Read it over slowly.

VIRGINIA: "The position of the Church in the matter of the unrest . . . "

(*There is a knocking at the outside door. Virginia goes into the anteroom. The Official opens the door. It is Andrea*)

ANDREA: Good evening. I am sorry to call so late, I'm on my way to Holland. I was asked to look him up. Can I go in?

VIRGINIA: I don't know whether he will see you. You never came.

ANDREA: Ask him.

(*Galileo recognizes the voice. He sits motionless. Virginia comes in to Galileo*)

1620 GALILEO: Is that Andrea?

VIRGINIA: Yes. (*Pause*) I will send him away.

GALILEO: Show him in.

(*Virginia shows Andrea in. Virginia sits, Andrea remains standing*)

ANDREA: (*cool*) Have you been keeping well, Mr. Galilei?

GALILEO: Sit down. What are you doing these days? What are you working on? I heard it was something about hydraulics in Milan.

ANDREA: As he knew I was passing through, Fabricius of Amsterdam asked me to visit you and inquire about your health.

(*Pause.*)

GALILEO: I am very well.

ANDREA: (*formally*) I am glad I can report you are in 1630 good health.

GALILEO: Fabricius will be glad to hear it. And you might inform him that, on account of the depth of my repentance, I live in comparative comfort.

ANDREA: Yes, we understand that the church is more than pleased with you. Your complete acceptance has had its effect. Not one paper expounding a new thesis has made its appearance in Italy since your submission.

(*Pause*)

GALILEO: Unfortunately there are countries not under the wing of the church. Would you not say the erroneous con-1640 demned theories are still taught—there?

ANDREA: (*relentless*) Things are almost at a standstill.

GALILEO: Are they? (*Pause*) Nothing from Descartes in Paris?

ANDREA: Yes. On receiving the news of your recantation, he shelved his treatise on the nature of light.

GALILEO: I sometimes worry about my assistants whom I led into error. Have they benefited by my example?

ANDREA: In order to work I have to go to Holland.

GALILEO: Yes.

ANDREA: Federzoni is grinding lenses again, back in some 1650 shop.

GALILEO: He can't read the books.

ANDREA: Fulganzio, our little monk, has abandoned research and is resting in peace in the church.

GALILEO: So. (*Pause*) My superiors are looking forward to my spiritual recovery. I am progressing as well as can be expected.

VIRGINIA: You are doing well, father.

GALILEO: Virginia, leave the room.

(*Virginia rises uncertainly and goes out*)

VIRGINIA: (*to the Official*) He was his pupil, so now he is his 1660 enemy.—Help me in the kitchen.

(*She leaves the anteroom with the Official*)

ANDREA: May I go now, sir?

GALILEO: I do not know why you came, Sarti. To unsettle me? I have to be prudent.

ANDREA: I'll be on my way.

GALILEO: As it is, I have relapses. I completed the "Discorsi."

ANDREA: You completed what?

GALILEO: My "Discorsi."

ANDREA: How?

GALILEO: I am allowed pen and paper. My superiors are intel-1670 ligent men. They know the habits of a lifetime cannot be broken abruptly. But they protect me from any unpleasant consequences: they lock my pages away as I dictate them. And I should know better than to risk my comfort. I wrote the "Discorsi" out again during the night. The manuscript is in the globe. My vanity has up to now prevented me from destroying it. If you consider taking it, you will shoulder the entire risk. You will say it was pirated from the original in the hands of the Holy Office.

(*Andrea, as in a trance, has gone to the globe. He lifts the upper half and gets the book. He turns the pages as if wanting to devour them. In the background the opening sentences of the "Discorsi" appear:* MY PURPOSE IS TO SET FORTH A VERY NEW SCIENCE DEALING WITH A VERY ANCIENT SUBJECT— MOTION. . . . AND I HAVE DISCOVERED BY EXPERIMENT SOME PROPERTIES OF IT WHICH ARE WORTH KNOWING. . . . )

1680 GALILEO: I had to employ my time somehow.

(*The text disappears*)

ANDREA: Two new sciences! This will be the foundation stone of a new physics.

GALILEO: Yes. Put it under your coat.

ANDREA: And we thought you had deserted. (*In a low voice*) Mr. Galilei, how can I begin to express my shame. Mine has been the loudest voice against you.

GALILEO: That would seem to have been proper. I taught you science and I decried the truth.

ANDREA: Did you? I think not. Everything is changed!

1690 GALILEO: What is changed?

ANDREA: You shielded the truth from the oppressor. Now I see! In your dealings with the Inquisition you used the same superb common sense you brought to physics.

GALILEO: Oh!

ANDREA: We lost our heads. With the crowd at the street corners we said: "He will die, he will never surrender!" You came back: "I surrendered but I am alive." We cried: "Your hands are stained!" You say: "Better stained than empty."

GALILEO: "Better stained than empty."—It sounds realistic.

1700 Sounds like me.

ANDREA: And I of all people should have known. I was twelve when you sold another man's telescope to the Venetian Senate, and saw you put it to immortal use. Your friends were baffled when you bowed to the Prince of Florence: Science gained a wider audience. You always laughed at heroics. "People who suffer bore me," you said. "Misfortunes are due mainly to miscalculations." And: "If there are obstacles, the shortest line between two points may be the crooked line."

1710 GALILEO: It makes a picture.

ANDREA: And when you stooped to recant in 1633, I should have understood that you were again about your business.

GALILEO: My business being?

ANDREA: Science. The study of the properties of motion, mother of the machines which will themselves change the ugly face of the earth.

GALILEO: Aha!

ANDREA: You gained time to write a book that only you could write. Had you burned at the stake in a blaze of glory they

1720 would have won.

GALILEO: They have won. And there is no such thing as a scientific work that only one man can write.

ANDREA: Then why did you recant, tell me that!

GALILEO: I recanted because I was afraid of physical pain.

ANDREA: No!

GALILEO: They showed me the instruments.

ANDREA: It was not a plan?

GALILEO: It was not.

(*Pause*)

ANDREA: But you have contributed. Science has only one commandment: contribution. And you have contributed more 1730 than any man for a hundred years.

GALILEO: Have I? Then welcome to my gutter, dear colleague in science and brother in treason: I sold out, you are a buyer. The first sight of the book! His mouth watered and his scoldings were drowned. Blessed be our bargaining, whitewashing, deathfearing community!

ANDREA: The fear of death is human.

GALILEO: Even the church will teach you that to be weak is not human. It is just evil.

ANDREA: The church, yes! But science is not concerned with 1740 our weaknesses.

GALILEO: No? My dear Sarti, in spite of my present convictions, I may be able to give you a few pointers as to the concerns of your chosen profession.

(*Enter Virginia with a platter*)

In my spare time, I happen to have gone over this case. I have spare time.—Even a man who sells wool, however good he is at buying wool cheap and selling it dear, must be concerned with the standing of the wool trade. The practice of science would seem to call for valor. She trades in knowledge, which is the product of doubt. And this new art of 1750 doubt has enchanted the public. The plight of the multitude is old as the rocks, and is believed to be basic as the rocks. But now they have learned to doubt. They snatched the telescopes out of our hands and had them trained on their tormentors: prince, official, public moralist. The mechanism of the heavens was clearer, the mechanism of their courts was still murky. The battle to measure the heavens is won by doubt; by credulity the Roman housewife's battle for milk will always be lost. Word is passed down that this is of no concern to the scientist who is told he will only release 1760 such of his findings as do not disturb the peace, that is, the peace of mind of the well-to-do. Threats and bribes fill the air. Can the scientist hold out on the numbers?—For what reason do you labor? I take it the intent of science is to ease human existence. If you give way to coercion, science can be crippled, and your new machines may simply suggest new drudgeries. Should you then, in time, discover all there is to be discovered, your progress must then become a progress away from the bulk of humanity. The gulf might even grow so wide that the sound of your cheering at some new 1770 achievement would be echoed by a universal howl of horror.—As a scientist I had an almost unique opportunity. In my day astronomy emerged into the market place. At that particular time, had one man put up a fight, it could have had wide repercussions. I have come to believe that I was never in real danger; for some years I was as strong as the authorities, and I surrendered my knowledge to the powers that be, to use it, no, not *use* it, *abuse* it, as it suits their ends. I have betrayed my profession. Any man who does what I have done must not be tolerated in the ranks of science. 1780

(*Virginia, who has stood motionless, puts the platter on the table*)

VIRGINIA: You are accepted in the ranks of the faithful, father.

GALILEO: (sees her) Correct. (He goes over to the table) I have to eat now.

VIRGINIA: We lock up at eight.

ANDREA: I am glad I came. (He extends his hand. Galileo ignores it and goes over to his meal)

GALILEO: (examining the plate; to Andrea) Somebody who knows me sent me a goose. I still enjoy eating.

ANDREA: And your opinion is now that the "new age" was an il-
1790 lusion?

GALILEO: Well.—This age of ours turned out to be a whore, spattered with blood. Maybe, new ages look like blood-spattered whores. Take care of yourself.

ANDREA: Yes. (Unable to go) With reference to your evaluation of the author in question—I do not know the answer. But I cannot think that your savage analysis is the last word.

GALILEO: Thank you, sir.

(Official knocks at the door)

VIRGINIA: (showing Andrea out) I don't like visitors from the past, they excite him.

(She lets him out. The Official closes the iron door. Virginia returns)

1800 GALILEO: (eating) Did you try and think who sent the goose?

VIRGINIA: Not Andrea.

GALILEO: Maybe not. I gave Redhead his first lesson; when he held out his hand, I had to remind myself he is teaching now.—How is the sky tonight?

VIRGINIA: (at the window) Bright.

(Galileo continues eating)

## SCENE XIV

> The great book o'er the border went
> And, good folk, that was the end.
> But we hope you'll keep in mind
> You and I were left behind.

Before a little Italian customs house early in the morning. Andrea sits upon one of his traveling trunks at the barrier and reads Galileo's book. The window of a small house is still lit, and a big grotesque shadow, like an old witch and her cauldron, falls upon the house wall beyond. Barefoot children in rags see it and point to the little house.

CHILDREN: (singing)
  One, two, three, four, five, six,
  Old Marina is a witch.
  At night, on a broomstick she sits
1810  And on the church steeple she spits.

CUSTOMS OFFICER: (to Andrea) Why are you making this journey?

ANDREA: I am a scholar.

CUSTOMS OFFICER: (to his Clerk) Put down under "reason for leaving the country": Scholar. (He points to the baggage) Books! Anything dangerous in these books?

ANDREA: What is dangerous?

CUSTOMS OFFICER: Religion. Politics.

ANDREA: These are nothing but mathematical formulas.

1820 CUSTOMS OFFICER: What's that?

ANDREA: Figures.

CUSTOMS OFFICER: Oh, figures. No harm in figures. Just wait a minute, sir, we will soon have your papers stamped. (He exits with Clerk)

(Meanwhile, a little council of war among the Children has taken place. Andrea quietly watches. One of the Boys, pushed forward by the others, creeps up to the little house from which the shadow comes, and takes the jug of milk on the doorstep)

ANDREA: (quietly) What are you doing with that milk?

BOY: (stopping in mid-movement) She is a witch.

(The other Children run away behind the Custom House. One of them shouts) "Run, Paolo!"

ANDREA: Hmm!—And because she is a witch she mustn't have milk. Is that the idea?

BOY: Yes.

ANDREA: And how do you know she is a witch?                    1830

BOY: (points to shadow on house wall) Look!

ANDREA: Oh! I see.

BOY: And she rides on a broomstick at night—and she bewitches the coachman's horses. My cousin Luigi looked through the hole in the stable roof, that the snow storm made, and heard the horses coughing something terrible.

ANDREA: Oh!—How big was the hole in the stable roof?

BOY: Luigi didn't tell. Why?

ANDREA: I was asking because maybe the horses got sick because it was cold in the stable. You had better ask Luigi how 1840 big that hole is.

BOY: You are not going to say Old Marina isn't a witch, because you can't.

ANDREA: No, I can't say she isn't a witch. I haven't looked into it. A man can't know about a thing he hasn't looked into, or can he?

BOY: No!—But THAT! (He points to the shadow) She is stirring hell-broth.

ANDREA: Let's see. Do you want to take a look? I can lift you up.                                                                 1850

BOY: You lift me to the window, mister! (He takes a sling shot out of his pocket) I can really bash her from there.

ANDREA: Hadn't we better make sure she is a witch before we shoot? I'll hold that.

(The Boy puts the milk jug down and follows him reluctantly to the window. Andrea lifts the boy up so that he can look in)

ANDREA: What do you see?

BOY: (slowly) Just an old girl cooking porridge.

ANDREA: Oh! Nothing to it then. Now look at her shadow, Paolo.

(The Boy looks over his shoulder and back and compares the reality and the shadow)

BOY: The big thing is a soup ladle.

ANDREA: Ah! A ladle! You see, I would have taken it for a 1860 broomstick, but I haven't looked into the matter as you have, Paolo. Here is your sling.

CUSTOMS OFFICER: (returning with the Clerk and handing Andrea his papers) All present and correct. Good luck, sir.

(Andrea goes, reading Galileo's book. The Clerk starts to bring *his baggage after him. The barrier rises. Andrea passes through, still reading the book. The Boy kicks over the milk jug)*

BOY: *(shouting after Andrea)* She *is* a witch! She *is* a witch!
ANDREA: You saw with your own eyes; think it over!

*(The Boy joins the others. They sing)*

One, two, three, four, five, six,
Old Marina is a witch.
At night, on a broomstick she sits
And on the church steeple she spits.      1870

*(The Customs Officers laugh. Andrea goes)*

# CASEBOOK ON BRECHT

## Bertolt Brecht

"Theatre for Pleasure or Theatre for Instruction" (1935–1936)

TRANSLATED BY JOHN WILLETT

*In this essay, Brecht attacks the bourgeois notion that the theater can be divided into two kinds of art, as though drama were either instructive or entertaining. As he does in his plays, Brecht dialecticizes these categories, showing that they define one another and therefore exist within one another. Realistic plays, after all, not only entertain their audiences but also offer an image of the world, a kind of instruction; on the other hand, intellectual or critical activity is not only pleasurable in itself but it can lead to a lively kind of theater as well, as Brecht's plays illustrate. This essay was unpublished in Brecht's lifetime: John Willett dates it from 1935 or 1936. He notes that Brecht uses the word* Entfremdung *here for "alienation," the same word used by Marx and Hegel; Brecht coined his own word* Verfremdungseffekt *for "alienation effect" later.*

A few years back, anybody talking about the modern theatre meant the theatre in Moscow, New York and Berlin. He might have thrown in a mention of one of Jouvet's productions in Paris or Cochran's in London, or *The Dybbuk* as given by the Habima (which is to all intents and purposes part of the Russian theatre, since Vakhtangov was its director). But broadly speaking there were only three capitals so far as modern theatre was concerned.

Russian, American and German theatres differed widely from one another, but were alike in being modern, that is to say in introducing technical and artistic innovations. In a sense they even achieved a certain stylistic resemblance, probably because technology is international (not just that part which is directly applied to the stage but also that which influences it, the film for instance), and because large progressive cities in large industrial countries are involved. Among the older capitalist countries it is the Berlin theatre that seemed of late to be in the lead. For a period all that is common to the modern theatre received its strongest and (so far) maturest expression there.

The Berlin theatre's last phase was the so-called epic theatre, and it showed the modern theatre's trend of development in its purest form. Whatever was labelled "*Zeitstück*" or "*Piscatorbühne*" or "*Lehrstück*" belongs to the epic theatre.

*The epic theatre*

Many people imagine that the term "epic theatre" is self-contradictory, as the epic and dramatic ways of narrating a story are held, following Aristotle, to be basically distinct. The difference between the two forms was never thought simply to lie in the fact that the one is performed by living beings while the other operates via the written word; epic works such as those of Homer and the medieval singers were at the same time theatrical performances, while dramas like Goethe's *Faust* and Byron's *Manfred* are agreed to have been more effective as books. Thus even by Aristotle's definition the difference between the dramatic and epic forms was attributed to their different methods of construction, whose laws were dealt with by two different branches of aesthetics. The method of construction depended on the different way of presenting the work to the public, sometimes via the stage, sometimes through a book; and independently of that there was the "dramatic element" in epic works and the "epic element" in dramatic. The bourgeois novel in the last century developed much that was "dramatic," by which was meant the strong centralization of the story, a momentum that drew the separate parts into a common relationship. A particular passion of utterance, a certain emphasis on the clash of forces are hallmarks of the "dramatic." The epic writer Döblin provided an excellent criterion when he said that with an epic work, as opposed to a dramatic, one can as it were take a pair of scissors and cut it into individual pieces, which remain fully capable of life.

This is no place to explain how the opposition of epic and dramatic lost its rigidity after having long been held to be irreconcilable. Let us just point out that the technical advances alone were enough to permit the stage to incorporate an element of narrative in its dramatic productions. The possibility of projections, the greater adaptability of the stage due to mechanization, the film, all completed the theatre's equipment, and did so at a point where the most important transactions between people could no longer be shown simply by personifying the motive forces or subjecting the characters to invisible metaphysical powers.

To make these transactions intelligible the environment in which the people lived had to be brought to bear in a big and "significant" way.

This environment had of course been shown in the existing drama, but only as seen from the central figure's point of view, and not as an independent element. It was defined by the hero's reactions to it. It was seen as a storm can be seen when one sees the ships on a sheet of water unfolding their sails, and the sails filling out. In the epic theatre it was to appear standing on its own.

The stage began to tell a story. The narrator was no longer missing, along with the fourth wall. Not only did the background adopt an attitude to the events on the stage—by big screens recalling other simultaneous events elsewhere, by projecting documents which confirmed or contradicted what the characters said, by concrete and intelligible figures to accompany abstract conversations, by figures and sentences to support mimed transactions whose sense was unclear—but the actors too refrained from going over wholly into their role, remaining detached from the character they were playing and clearly inviting criticism of him.

The spectator was no longer in any way allowed to submit to an experience uncritically (and without practical consequences) by means of simple empathy with the characters in a play. The production took the subject-matter and the incidents shown and put them through a process of alienation: the alienation that is necessary to all understanding. When something seems "the most obvious thing in the world" it means that any attempt to understand the world has been given up.

What is "natural" must have the force of what is startling. This is the only way to expose the laws of cause and effect. People's activity must simultaneously be so and be capable of being different.

It was all a great change.

The dramatic theatre's spectator says: Yes, I have felt like that too—Just like me—It's only natural—It'll never change—The sufferings of this man appal me, because they are inescapable—That's great art; it all seems the most obvious thing in the world—I weep when they weep, I laugh when they laugh.

The epic theatre's spectator says: I'd never have thought it—That's not the way—That's extraordinary, hardly believable—It's got to stop—The sufferings of this man appal me, because they are unnecessary—That's great art: nothing obvious in it—I laugh when they weep, I weep when they laugh.

The stage began to be instructive.

*The instructive theatre*

Oil, inflation, war, social struggles, the family, religion, wheat, the meat market, all became subjects for theatrical representation. Choruses enlightened the spectator about facts unknown to him. Films showed a montage of events from all over the world. Projections added statistical material. And as the "background" came to the front of the stage so people's activity was subjected to criticism. Right and wrong courses of action were shown. People were shown who knew what they were doing, and others who did not. The theatre became an affair for philosophers, but only for such philosophers as wished not just to explain the world but also to change it. So we had philosophy, and we had instruction. And where was the amusement in all that? Were they sending us back to school, teaching us to read and write? Were we supposed to pass exams, work for diplomas?

Generally there is felt to be a very sharp distinction between learning and amusing oneself. The first may be useful, but only the second is pleasant. So we have to defend the epic theatre against the suspicion that it is a highly disagreeable, humourless, indeed strenuous affair.

Well: all that can be said is that the contrast between learning and amusing oneself is not laid down by divine rule; it is not one that has always been and must continue to be.

Undoubtedly there is much that is tedious about the kind of learning familiar to us from school, from our professional training, etc. But it must be remembered under what conditions and to what end that takes place.

It is really a commercial transaction. Knowledge is just a commodity. It is acquired in order to be resold. All those who have grown out of going to school have to do their learning virtually in secret, for anyone who admits that he still has something to learn devalues himself as a man whose knowledge is inadequate. Moreover the usefulness of learning is very much limited by factors outside the learner's control. There is unemployment, for instance, against which no knowledge can protect one. There is the division of labour, which makes generalized knowledge unnecessary and impossible. Learning is often among the concerns of those whom no amount of concern will get any forwarder. There is not much knowledge that leads to power, but plenty of knowledge to which only power can lead.

Learning has a very different function for different social strata. There are strata who cannot imagine any improvement in conditions: they find the conditions good enough for them. Whatever happens to oil they will benefit from it. And: they feel the years beginning to tell. There can't be all that many years more. What is the point of learning a lot now? They have said their final word: a grunt. But there are also strata "waiting their turn" who are discontented with conditions, have a vast interest in the practical side of learning, want at all costs to find out where they stand, and know that they are lost without learning; these are the best and keenest learners. Similar differences apply to countries and peoples. Thus the pleasure of learning depends on all sorts of things; but none the less there is such a thing as pleasurable learning, cheerful and militant learning.

If there were not such amusement to be had from learning the theatre's whole structure would unfit it for teaching.

Theatre remains theatre even when it is instructive theatre, and in so far as it is good theatre it will amuse.

*Theatre and knowledge*

But what has knowledge got to do with art? We know that knowledge can be amusing, but not everything that is amusing belongs in the theatre.

I have often been told, when pointing out the invaluable services that modern knowledge and science, if properly applied, can perform for art and specially for the theatre, that art and knowledge are two estimable but wholly distinct fields of human activity. This is a fearful truism, of course, and it is as well to agree quickly that, like most truisms, it is perfectly true. Art and science work in quite different ways: agreed. But, bad as it may sound, I have to admit that I cannot get along as an artist without the use of one or two sciences. This may well arouse serious doubts as to my artistic capacities. People are used to seeing poets as unique and slightly unnatural beings who reveal with a truly godlike assurance things that other people can only recognize after much sweat and toil. It is naturally distasteful to have to admit that one does not belong to this select band. All the same, it must be admitted. It must at the same time be made clear that the scientific occupations just confessed to are not pardonable side interests, pursued on days off after a good week's work. We all know how Goethe was interested in natural history, Schiller in history: as a kind of hobby, it is charitable to assume. I have no wish promptly to accuse these two of having needed these sciences for their poetic activity; I am not trying to shelter behind them; but I must say that I do need the sciences. I have to admit, however, that I look askance at all sorts of people who I know do not operate on the level of scientific understanding: that is to say, who sing as the birds sing, or as people imagine the birds to sing. I don't mean by that that I would reject a charming poem about the taste of fried fish or the delights of a boating party just because the writer had not studied gastronomy or navigation. But in my view the great and complicated things that go on in the world cannot be adequately recognized by people who do not use every possible aid to understanding.

Let us suppose that great passions or great events have to be shown which influence the fate of nations. The lust for power is nowadays held to be such a passion. Given that a poet "feels" this lust and wants to have someone strive for power, how is he to show the exceedingly complicated machinery within which the struggle for power nowadays takes place? If his hero is a politician, how do politics work? If he is a business man, how does business work? And yet there are writers who find business and politics nothing like so passionately interesting as the individual's lust for power. How are they to acquire the necessary knowledge? They are scarcely likely to learn enough by going round and keeping their eyes open, though even then it is more than they would get by just rolling their eyes in an exalted frenzy. The foundation of a paper like the *Völkischer Beobachter* or a business like Standard Oil is a pretty complicated affair, and such things cannot be conveyed just like that. One important field for the playwright is psychology. It is taken for granted that a poet, if not an ordinary man, must be able without further instruction to discover the motives that lead a man to commit murder; he must be able to give a picture of a murderer's mental state "from within himself." It is taken for granted that one only has to look inside oneself in such a case; and then there's always one's imagination . . . There are various reasons why I can no longer surrender to this agreeable hope of getting a result quite so simply. I can no longer find in myself all those motives which the press or scientific reports show to have been observed in people. Like the average judge when pronouncing sentence, I cannot without further ado conjure up an adequate picture of a murderer's mental state. Modern psychology, from psychoanalysis to behaviourism, acquaints me with facts that lead me to judge the case quite differently, especially if I bear in mind the findings of sociology and do not overlook economics and history. You will say: but that's getting complicated. I have to answer that it *is* complicated. Even if you let yourself be convinced, and agree with me that a large slice of literature is exceedingly primitive, you may still ask with profound concern: won't an evening in such a theatre be a most alarming affair? The answer to that is: no.

Whatever knowledge is embodied in a piece of poetic writing has to be wholly transmuted into poetry. Its utilization fulfils the very pleasure that the poetic element provokes. If it does not at the same time fulfil that which is fulfilled by the scientific element, none the less in an age of great discoveries and inventions one must have a certain inclination to penetrate deeper into things—a desire to make the world controllable—if one is to be sure of enjoying its poetry.

According to Friedrich Schiller the theatre is supposed to be a moral institution. In making this demand it hardly occurred to Schiller that by moralizing from the stage he might drive the audience out of the theatre. Audiences had no objection to moralizing in his day. It was only later that Friedrich Nietzsche attacked him for blowing a moral trumpet. To Nietzsche any concern with morality was a depressing affair; to Schiller it seemed thoroughly enjoyable. He knew of nothing that could give greater amusement and satisfaction than the propagation of ideas. The bourgeoisie was setting about forming the ideas of the nation.

*Is the epic theatre some kind of "moral institution"?*

Putting one's house in order, patting oneself on the back, submitting one's account, is something highly agreeable. But describing the collapse of one's house, having pains in the back, paying one's account, is indeed a depressing affair, and that was how Friedrich Nietzsche saw things a century later. He was poorly disposed towards morality, and thus towards the previous Friedrich too.

The epic theatre was likewise often objected to as moralizing too much. Yet in the epic theatre moral arguments only took second place. Its aim was less to moralize than to observe. That is to say it observed, and then the thick end of the wedge followed: the story's moral. Of course we cannot pretend that we started our observations out of a pure passion for observing and without any more practical motive, only to be completely staggered by their results. Undoubtedly there were some painful discrepancies in our environment, circumstances that were barely tolerable, and this not merely on account of moral considerations. It is not only moral considerations that make hunger, cold and oppression hard to bear. Similarly the object of our inquiries was not just to arouse moral objections to such circumstances (even though they could easily be felt—though not by all the audience alike; such objections were seldom for instance felt by those who profited by the circumstances in question) but to discover means for their elimination. We were not in fact speaking in the name of morality but in that of the victims. These truly are two distinct matters, for the victims are often told that they ought to be contented with their lot, for moral reasons. Moralists of this sort see man as existing for morality, not morality for man. At least it should be possible to gather from the above to what degree and in what sense the epic theatre is a moral institution.

Stylistically speaking, there is nothing all that new about the epic theatre. Its expository character and its emphasis on virtuosity bring it close to the old Asiatic theatre. Didactic tendencies are to be found in the medieval mystery plays and the classical Spanish theatre, and also in the theatre of the Jesuits.

*Can epic theatre be played anywhere?*

These theatrical forms corresponded to particular trends of their time, and vanished with them. Similarly the modern epic theatre is linked with certain trends. It cannot by any means be practised universally. Most of the great nations today are not disposed to use the theatre for ventilating their problems. London, Paris, Tokyo and Rome maintain their theatres for quite different purposes. Up to now favourable circumstances for an epic and didactic theatre have only been found in a few places and for a short period of time. In Berlin Fascism put a very definite stop to the development of such a theatre.

It demands not only a certain technological level but a powerful movement in society which is interested to see vital questions freely aired with a view to their solution, and can defend this interest against every contrary trend.

The epic theatre is the broadest and most far-reaching attempt at large-scale modern theatre, and it has all those immense difficulties to overcome that always confront the vital forces in the sphere of politics, philosophy, science and art.

## Bertolt Brecht:

### "The Street Scene"
(1938)

TRANSLATED BY JOHN WILLETT

*A basic model for an epic theatre*

*In this brief essay, Brecht uses street "acting" as a model for the actor's process in epic theater, emphasizing the inseparable relationship between emotional empathy and critical demonstration.*

In the decade and a half that followed the World War a comparatively new way of acting was tried out in a number of German theatres. Its qualities of clear description and reporting and its use of choruses and projections as a means of commentary earned it the name of 'epic.' The actor used a somewhat complex technique to detach himself from the character portrayed; he forced the spectator to look at the play's situations from such an angle that they necessarily became subject to his criticism. Supporters of this epic theatre argued that the new subject-matter, the highly involved incidents of the class war in its acutest and most terrible stage, would be mastered more easily by such a method, since it would thereby become possible to portray social processes as seen in their causal relationships. But the result of these experiments was that aesthetics found itself up against a whole series of substantial difficulties.

It is comparatively easy to set up a basic model for epic theatre. For practical experiments I usually picked as my example of completely simple, 'natural' epic theatre an incident such as can be seen at any street corner: an eyewitness demonstrating to a collection of people how a traffic accident took place. The bystanders may not have observed what happened, or they may simply not agree with him, may 'see things a different way'; the point is that the demonstrator acts the behaviour of driver or victim or both in such a way that the bystanders are able to form an opinion about the accident.

Such an example of the most primitive type of epic theatre seems easy to understand. Yet experience has shown that it presents astounding difficulties to the reader or listener as soon as he is asked to see the implications of treating this kind of street corner demonstration as a basic form of major theater, theatre for a scientific age. What this means of course is that the epic theatre may appear richer, more intricate and complex in every particular, yet to be major theatre it need at bottom only contain the same elements as a street-corner demonstration of this sort; nor could it any longer be termed epic theatre if any of the main elements of the street-corner demonstration were lacking. Until this is understood it is impossible really to understand what follows. Until one understands the novelty, unfamiliarity and direct challenge to the critical faculties of the suggestion that street-corner demonstration of this sort can serve as a satisfactory basic model of major theatre one cannot really understand what follows.

Consider: the incident is clearly very far from what we mean by an artistic one. The demonstrator need not be an artist. The capacities he needs to achieve his aim are in effect universal. Suppose he cannot carry out some particular movement as quickly as the victim he is imitating; all he need do is to explain that *he* moves three times as fast, and the demonstration neither suffers in essentials nor loses its point. On the contrary it is important that he should not be too perfect. His demonstration would be spoilt if the bystanders' attention were drawn to his powers of transformation. He has to avoid presenting himself in such a way that someone calls out 'What a lifelike portrayal of a chauffeur!' He must not 'cast a spell' over anyone. He should not transport people from normality to 'higher realms.' He need not dispose of any special powers of suggestion.

It is most important that one of the main features of the ordinary theatre should be excluded from our street scene: the engendering of illusion. The street demonstrator's performance is essentially repetitive. The event has taken place; what you are seeing now is a repeat. If the scene in the theatre follows the street scene in this respect then the theatre will stop pretending not to be theatre, just as the street-corner demonstration admits it is a demonstration (and does not pretend to be the actual event). The element of rehearsal in the acting and of learning by heart in the text, the whole machinery and the whole process of preparation: it all becomes plainly apparent. What room is left for experience? Is the reality portrayed still experienced in any sense?

The street scene determines what kind of experience is to be prepared for the spectator. There is no question but that the street-corner demonstrator has been through an 'experience,' but he is not out to make his demonstration serve as an 'experience' for the audience. Even the experience of the driver and the victim is only partially communicated by him, and he by no means tries to turn it into an enjoyable experience for the spectator, however lifelike he may make his demonstration. The demonstration would become no less valid if he did not reproduce the fear caused by the accident; on the contrary it would lose validity if he did. He is not interested in creating pure emotions. It is important to understand that a theatre which follows his lead in this respect undergoes a positive change of function.

One essential element of the street scene must also be present in the theatrical scene if this is to qualify as epic, namely that the demonstration should have a socially practical significance. Whether our street demonstrator is out to show that one attitude on the part of driver or pedestrian makes an accident inevitable where another would not, or whether he is demonstrating with a view to fixing the responsibility, his demonstration has a practical purpose, intervenes socially.

The demonstrator's purpose determines how thoroughly he has to imitate. Our demonstrator need not imitate every aspect of his characters' behaviour, but only so much as gives a picture. Generally the theatre scene will give much fuller pictures, corresponding to its more extensive range of interest. How do street scene and theatre scene link up here? To take a point of detail, the victim's voice may have played no immediate part in the accident. Eye-witnesses may disagree as to whether a cry they heard ('Look out!') came from the victim or from someone else, and this may give our demonstrator a motive for imitating the voice. The question can be settled by demonstrating whether the voice was an old man's or a woman's, or merely whether it was high or low. Again, the answer may depend on whether it was that of an educated person or not. Loud or soft may play a great part, as the driver could be correspondingly more or less guilty. A whole series of characteristics of the victim ask to be portrayed. Was he absent-minded? Was his attention distracted? If so, by what? What, on the evidence of his behaviour, could have made him liable to be distracted by just that circumstance and no other? Etc., etc. It can be seen that our street-corner demonstration provides opportunities for a pretty rich and varied portrayal of human types. Yet a theatre which tries to restrict its essential elements to those provided by our street scene will have to acknowledge certain limits to imitation. It must be able to justify any outlay in terms of its purpose.[1]

The demonstration may for instance be dominated by the question of compensation for the victim, etc. The driver risks being sacked from his job, losing his licence, going to prison; the victim risks a heavy hospital bill, loss of job, permanent disfigurement, possibly unfitness for work.

---

[1]We often come across demonstrations of an everyday sort which are more thorough imitations than our street-corner accident demands. Generally they are comic ones. Our next-door neighbour may decide to 'take off' the rapacious behaviour of our common landlord. Such an imitation is often rich and full of variety. Closer examination will show however that even so apparently complex an imitation concentrates on one specific side of the landlord's behaviour. The imitation is summary or selective, deliberately leaving out those occasions where the landlord strikes our neighbour as 'perfectly sensible,' though such occasions of course occur. He is far from giving a rounded picture; for that would have no comic impact at all. The street scene, perforce adopting a wider angle of vision, at this point lands in difficulties which must not be underestimated. It has to be just as successful in promoting criticism, but the incidents in question are far more complex. It must promote positive as well as negative criticism, and as part of a single process. You have to understand what is involved in winning the audience's approval by means of a critical approach. Here again we have a precedent in our street scene, i.e. in any demonstration of an everyday sort. Next-door neighbour and street demonstrator can reproduce their subject's 'sensible' or his 'senseless' behaviour alike, by submitting it for an opinion. When it crops up in the course of events, however (when a man switches from being sensible to being senseless, or the other way round), then they usually need some form of commentary in order to change the angle of their portrayal. Hence, as already mentioned, certain difficulties for the theatre scene. These cannot be dealt with here.

This is the area within which the demonstrator builds up his characters. The victim may have had a companion; the driver may have had his girl sitting alongside him. That would bring out the social element better and allow the characters to be more fully drawn.

Another essential element in the street scene is that the demonstrator should derive his characters entirely from their actions. He imitates their actions and so allows conclusions to be drawn about them. A theatre that follows him in this will be largely breaking with the orthodox theatre's habit of basing the actions on the characters and having the former exempted from criticism by presenting them as an unavoidable consequence deriving by natural law from the characters who perform them. To the street demonstrator the character of the man being demonstrated remains a quantity that need not be completely defined. Within certain limits he may be like this or like that; it doesn't matter. What the demonstrator is concerned with are his accident-prone and accident-proof qualities.[2] The theatrical scene may show more fully-defined individuals. But it must then be in a position to treat their individuality as a special case and outline the field within which, once more, its most socially relevant effects are produced. Our street demonstrator's possibilities of demonstration are narrowly restricted (indeed, we chose this model so that the limits should be as narrow as possible). If the essential elements of the theatrical scene are limited to those of the street scene then its greater richness must be an enrichment only. The question of border-line cases becomes acute.

Let us take a specific detail. Can our street demonstrator, say, ever become entitled to use an excited tone of voice in repeating the driver's statement that he has been exhausted by too long a spell of work? (In theory this is no more possible than for a returning messenger to start telling his fellow-countrymen of his talk with the king with the words 'I saw the bearded king.') It can only be possible, let alone unavoidable, if one imagines a street-corner situation where such excitement, specifically about this aspect of the affair, plays a particular part. (In the instance above this would be so if the king had sworn never to cut his beard off until . . . etc.) We have to find a point of view for our demonstrator that allows him to submit this excitement to criticism. Only if he adopts a quite definite point of view can he be entitled to imitate the driver's excited voice; e.g. if he blames drivers as such for doing too little to reduce their hours of work. ('Look at him. Doesn't even belong to a union, but gets worked up soon enough when an accident happens. "Ten hours I've been at the wheel."')

Before it can get as far as this, i.e. be able to suggest a point of view to the actor, the theatre needs to take a number of steps. By widening its field of vision and showing the driver in other situations besides that of the accident the theatre in no way exceeds its model; it merely creates a further situation on the same pattern. One can imagine a scene of the same kind as the street scene which provides a well-argued demonstration showing how such emotions as the driver's develop, or another which involves making comparisons between tones of voice. In order not to exceed the model scene the theatre only has to develop a technique for submitting emotions to the spectator's criticism. Of course this does not mean that the spectator must be barred on principle from sharing certain emotions that are put before him; none the less to communicate emotions is only one particular form (phase, consequence) of criticism. The theatre's demonstrator, the actor, must apply a technique which will let him reproduce the tone of the subject demonstrated with a certain reserve, with detachment (so that the spectator can say: 'He's getting excited—in vain, too late, at last . . .'etc.). In short, the actor must remain a demonstrator; he must present the person demonstrated as a stranger, he must not suppress the '*he* did that, *he* said that' element in his performance. He must not go so far as to be wholly transformed into the person demonstrated.

One essential element of the street scene lies in the natural attitude adopted by the demonstrator, which is two-fold; he is always taking two situations into account. He behaves naturally as a demonstrator, and he lets the subject of the demonstration behave naturally too. He never forgets, nor does he allow it to be forgotten, that he is not the subject but the demonstrator. That is to say, what the audience sees is not a fusion between demonstrator and subject, not some third, independent, uncontradictory entity with isolated features of (a) demonstrator and (b) subject,

---

[2]The same situation will be produced by all those people whose characters fulfil the conditions laid down by him and show the features that he imitates.

such as the orthodox theatre puts before us in its productions.[3] The feelings and opinions of demonstrator and demonstrated are not merged into one.

We now come to one of those elements that are peculiar to the epic theatre, the so-called A-effect (alienation effect). What is involved here is, briefly, a technique of taking the human social incidents to be portrayed and labelling them as something striking, something that calls for explanation, is not to be taken for granted, not just natural. The object of this 'effect' is to allow the spectator to criticize constructively from a social point of view. Can we show that this A-effect is significant for our street demonstrator?

We can picture what happens if he fails to make use of it. The following situation could occur. One of the spectators might say: 'But if the victim stepped off the kerb with his right foot, as you showed him doing. . . . ' The demonstrator might interrupt saying: 'I showed him stepping off with his left foot.' By arguing which foot he really stepped off with in his demonstration, and, even more, how the victim himself acted, the demonstration can be so transformed that the A-effect occurs. The demonstrator achieves it by paying exact attention this time to his movements, executing them carefully, probably in slow motion; in this way he alienates the little subincident, emphasizes its importance, makes it worthy of notice. And so the epic theatre's alienation effect proves to have its uses for our street demonstrator too; in other words it is also to be found in this small everyday scene of natural street-corner theatre, which has little to do with art. The direct changeover from representation to commentary that is so characteristic of the epic theatre is still more easily recognized as one element of any street demonstration. Wherever he feels he can the demonstrator breaks off his imitation in order to give explanations. The epic theatre's choruses and documentary projections, the direct addressing of the audience by its actors, are at bottom just this.

It will have been observed, not without astonishment I hope, that I have not named any strictly artistic elements as characterizing our street scene and, with it, that of the epic theatre. The street demonstrator can carry out a successful demonstration with no greater abilities than, in effect, anybody has. What about the epic theatre's value as art?

The epic theatre wants to establish its basic model at the street corner, i.e. to return to the very simplest 'natural' theatre, a social enterprise whose origins, means and ends are practical and earthly. The model works without any need of programmatic theatrical phrases like 'the urge to self-expression,' 'making a part one's own,' 'spiritual experience,' 'the play instinct,' 'the story-teller's art,' etc. Does that mean that the epic theatre isn't concerned with art?

It might be as well to begin by putting the question differently, thus: can we make use of artistic abilities for the purposes of our street scene? Obviously yes. Even the street-corner demonstration includes artistic elements. Artistic abilities in some small degree are to be found in any man. It does no harm to remember this when one is confronted with great art. Undoubtedly what we call artistic abilities can be exercised at any time within the limits imposed by our street scene model. They will function as artistic abilities even though they do not exceed these limits (for instance, when there is meant to be no complete transformation of demonstrator into subject). And true enough, the epic theatre is an extremely artistic affair, hardly thinkable without artists and virtuosity, imagination, humour and fellow-feeling; it cannot be practised without all these and much else too. It has got to be entertaining, it has got to be instructive. How then can art be developed out of the elements of the street scene, without adding any or leaving any out? How does it evolve into the theatrical scene with its fabricated story, its trained actors, its lofty style of speaking, its make-up, its team performance by a number of players? Do we need to add to our elements in order to move on from the 'natural' demonstration to the 'artificial'?

Is it not true that the additions which we must make to our model in order to arrive at epic theatre are of a fundamental kind? A brief examination will show that they are not. Take the *story*. There was nothing fabricated about our street accident. Nor does the orthodox theatre deal only in fabrications; think for instance of the historical play. None the less a story can be performed at the street corner too. Our demonstrator may at any time be in a position to say: 'The driver was guilty, because it all happened the way I showed you. He wouldn't be guilty if it had happened the

---

[3]Most clearly worked out by Stanislavsky.

way I'm going to show you now.' And he can fabricate an incident and demonstrate it. Or take the fact that the text is learnt by heart. As a witness in a court case the demonstrator may have written down the subject's exact words, learnt them by heart and rehearsed them; in that case he too is performing a text he has learned. Or take a rehearsed programme by several players: it doesn't always have to be artistic purposes that bring about a demonstration of this sort; one need only think of the French police technique of making the chief figures in any criminal case re-enact certain crucial situations before a police audience. Or take making-up. Minor changes in appearance—ruffling one's hair, for instance—can occur at any time within the framework of the non-artistic type of demonstration. Nor is make-up itself used solely for theatrical purposes. In the street scene the driver's moustache may be particularly significant. It may have influenced the testimony of the possible girl companion suggested earlier. This can be represented by our demonstrator making the driver stroke an imaginary moustache when prompting his companion's evidence. In this way the demonstrator can do a good deal to discredit her as a witness. Moving on to the use of a real moustache in the theatre, however, is not an entirely easy transition, and the same difficulty occurs with respect to *costume*. Our demonstrator may under given circumstances put on the driver's cap—for instance if he wants to show that he was drunk: (he had it on crooked)—but he can only do so conditionally, under these circumstances; (see what was said about borderline cases earlier). However, where there is a demonstration by several demonstrators of the kind referred to above we can have costume so that the various characters can be distinguished. This again is only a limited use of costume. There must be no question of creating an illusion that the demonstrators really are these characters. (The epic theatre can counteract this illusion by especially exaggerated costume or by garments that are somehow marked out as objects for display.) Moreover we can suggest another model as a substitute for ours on this point: the kind of street demonstration given by hawkers. To sell their neckties these people will portray a badly-dressed and a well-dressed man; with a few props and technical tricks they can perform significant little scenes where they submit essentially to the same restrictions as apply to the demonstrator in our street scene: (they will pick up tie, hat, stick, gloves and give certain significant imitations of a man of the world, and the whole time they will refer to him as 'he'!) With hawkers we also find *verse* being used within the same framework as that of our basic model. They use firm irregular rhythms to sell braces and newspapers alike.

Reflecting along these lines we see that our basic model will work. The elements of natural and of artificial epic theatre are the same. Our street-corner theatre is primitive; origins, aims and methods of its performance are close to home. But there is no doubt that it is a meaningful phenomenon with a clear social function that dominates all its elements. The performance's origins lie in an incident that can be judged one way or another, that may repeat itself in different forms and is not finished but is bound to have consequences, so that this judgment has some significance. The object of the performance is to make it easier to give an opinion on the incident. Its means correspond to that. The epic theatre is a highly skilled theatre with complex contents and far-reaching social objectives. In setting up the street scene as a basic model for it we pass on the clear social function and give the epic theatre criteria by which to decide whether an incident is meaningful or not. The basic model has a practical significance. As producer and actors work to build up a performance involving many difficult questions—technical problems, social ones—it allows them to check whether the social function of the whole apparatus is still clearly intact.

Editor's Note: Students interested in Brecht's understanding of acting might consider these exercises, which he sometimes used with actors.

(a)  Conjuring tricks, including attitude of spectators.

(b)  For women: folding and putting away linen. Same for men.

(c)  For men: varying attitudes of smokers. Same for women.

(d)  Cat playing with a hank of thread.

(e)  Exercises in observation.

(f)  Exercises in imitation.

(g)  How to take notes. Noting of gestures, tones of voice.

(h)  Exercises in imagination. Three men throwing dice for their life. One loses. Then: they all lose.

(i)   Dramatizing an epic. Passages from the Bible.

(k)   For everybody: repeated exercises in production. Essential to show one's colleagues.

(l)   Exercises in temperament. Situation: two women calmly folding linen. They feign a wild and jealous quarrel for the benefit of their husbands; the husbands are in the next room.

(m)   They come to blows as they fold their linen in silence.

(n)   Game (l) turns serious.

(o)   Quick-change competition. Behind a screen; open.

(p)   Modifying an imitation, simply described so that others can put it into effect.

(q)   Rhythmical (verse-) speaking with tap-dance.

(r)   Eating with outsize knife and fork. Very small knife and fork.

(s)   Dialogue with gramophone: recorded sentences, free answers.

(t)   Search for 'nodal points.'

(u)   Characterization of a fellow-actor.

(v)   Improvisation of incidents. Running through scenes in the style of a report, no text.

(w)   The street accident. Laying down limits of justifiable imitation.

(x)   Variations: a dog went into the kitchen. [A traditional song]

(y)   Memorizing first impressions of a part.

---

*LIVING as a refugee in Santa Monica, California, in the early 1940s, Brecht worked with the distinguished stage and screen actor Charles Laughton on translating this version of Life of Galileo. In "Building up a Part," Brecht describes his sense of Laughton's contribution to the play.*

In describing Laughton's Galileo Galilei the playwright is setting out not so much to try and give a little more permanence to one of those fleeting works of art that actors create, as to pay tribute to the pains a great actor is prepared to take over a fleeting work of this sort. This is no longer at all common. It is not just that the under-rehearsing in our hopelessly commercialized theater is to blame for lifeless and stereotyped portraits—give the average actor more time, and he would hardly do better. Nor is it simply that this century has very few outstanding individualists with rich characteristics and rounded contours—if that were all, care could be devoted to the portrayal of lesser figures. Above all it is that we seem to have lost any understanding and appreciation of what we may call a *theatrical conception:* what Garrick did when, as Hamlet, he met his father's ghost; Sorel when, as Phèdre, she knew that she was going to die; Bassermann when, as Philip, he had finished listening to Posa. It is a question of inventiveness.

The spectator could isolate and detach such theatrical conceptions, but they combined to form a single rich texture. Odd insights into men's nature, glimpses of their particular way of living together, were brought about by the ingenious contrivance of the actors.

With works of art, even more than with philosophical systems, it is impossible to find out how they are made. Those who make them work hard to give the impression that everything just happens, as it were of its own accord, as though an image were forming in a clear mirror that is itself inert. Of course this is a deception, and apparently the idea is that if it comes off it will increase the spectator's pleasure. In fact it does not. What the spectator, anyway the experienced spectator, enjoys about art is the making of art, the active creative element. In art we view nature herself as if she were an artist.

The ensuing account deals with this aspect, with the process of manufacture rather than with the result. It is less a matter of the artist's temperament than of the notions of reality which he has *and communicates;* less a matter of his vitality than of the observations which underlie his portraits and can be derived from them. This means neglecting much that seemed to us to be "inimitable" in Laughton's achievement, and going on rather to what can be learned from it. For we cannot create talent; we can only set it tasks.

It is unnecessary here to examine how the artists of the past used to astonish their public. Asked why he acted, L. answered: "Because people don't know what they are like, and I think I can show them." His collaboration in the rewriting of the play showed that he had all sorts of ideas which were begging to be disseminated, about how people *really* live together, about the motive forces

**Bertolt Brecht:**

FROM "Building up a Part: Laughton's Galileo"
(1956)

TRANSLATED BY
RALPH MANHEIM

*Preface*

that need to be taken into account here. L.'s attitude seemed to the playwright to be that of a realistic artist of our time. For whereas in relatively stationary ("quiet") periods artists may find it possible to merge wholly with their public and to be a faithful "embodiment" of the general conception, our profoundly unsettled time forces them to take special measures to penetrate to the truth. Our society will not admit of its own accord what makes it move. It can even be said to exist purely through the secrecy with which it surrounds itself. What attracted L. about *Life of Galileo* was not only one or two formal points but also the subject matter; he thought this might become what he called a contribution. And so great was his anxiety to show things as they really are that despite all his indifference (indeed timidity) in political matters he suggested and even demanded that not a few of the play's points should be made sharper, on the simple ground that such passages seemed "somehow weak" to him, by which he meant that they did not do justice to things as they are.

We usually met in L.'s big house above the Pacific, as the dictionaries of synonyms were too bulky to lug about. He had continual and inexhaustibly patient recourse to these tomes, and used in addition to fish out the most varied literary texts in order to examine this or that gest, or some particular mode of speech: Aesop, the Bible, Molière, Shakespeare. In my house he gave readings of Shakespeare's works to which he would devote perhaps a fortnight's preparation. In this way he read *The Tempest* and *King Lear,* simply for me and one or two guests who happened to have dropped in. Afterward we would briefly discuss what seemed relevant, an "aria" perhaps or an effective scene opening. These were exercises and he would pursue them in various directions, assimilating them in the rest of his work. If he had to give a reading on the radio he would get me to hammer out the syncopated rhythms of Whitman's poems (which he found somewhat strange) on a table with my fists, and once he hired a studio where we recorded half a dozen ways of telling the story of the creation, in which he was an African planter telling the Negroes how he had created the world, or an English butler ascribing it to His Lordship. We needed such broadly ramified studies, because he spoke no German whatever and we had to decide the gest of each piece of dialogue by my acting it all in bad English or even in German and his then acting it back in proper English in a variety of ways until I could say: That's it. The result he would write down sentence by sentence in longhand. Some sentences, indeed many, he carried around for days, changing them continually. This system of performance-and-repetition had one immense advantage in that psychological discussions were almost entirely avoided. Even the most fundamental gests, such as Galileo's way of observing, or his showmanship, or his craze for pleasure, were established in three dimensions by actual performance. Our first concern throughout was for the smallest fragments, for sentences, even for exclamations—each treated separately, each needing to be given the simplest, freshly fitted form, giving so much away, hiding so much or leaving it open. More radical changes in the structure of entire scenes or of the work itself were meant to help the story to move and to bring out fairly general conclusions about people's attitudes to the great physicist. But this reluctance to tinker with the psychological aspect remained with L. all through our long period of collaboration, even when a rough draft of the play was ready and he was giving various readings in order to test reactions, and even during the rehearsals.

The awkward circumstance that one translator knew no German and the other scarcely any English compelled us, as can be seen, from the outset to use acting as our means of translation. We were forced to do what better-equipped translators should do too: to translate gests. For language is theatrical in so far as it primarily expresses the mutual attitude of the speakers. (For the "arias," as has been described, we brought in the playwright's own gest, by observing the bel canto of Shakespeare or the writers of the Bible.)

In a most striking and occasionally brutal way L. showed his lack of interest in the "book," to an extent the playwright could not always share. What we were making was just a text; the performance was all that counted. Impossible to lure him to translate passages which the playwright was willing to cut for the proposed performance but wanted to keep in the book. The theatrical occasion was what mattered, the text was only there to make it possible: It would be expended in the production, would be consumed in it like gunpowder in a firework. Although L.'s theatrical experience had been in London, which had become thoroughly indifferent to the theater, the old Elizabethan London still lived in him, the London where theater was such a passion that it could swallow immortal works of art greedily and barefacedly as so many "texts." These works which have survived the centuries were in fact like improvisations thrown off for an all important moment. Printing them at all was a matter of little interest, and probably only took place so that the spectators, in other words, those who were present at the actual event, the performance, might have a souvenir of their enjoyment. And the theater seems in those days to have been so potent that the cuts and interpolations made at rehearsal can have done little harm to the text.

We used to work in L.'s small library, in the mornings. But often L. would come and meet me in the garden, running barefoot in shirt and trousers over the damp grass, and would show me some changes in his flowerbeds, for his garden always occupied him, providing many problems and sub-tleties. The gaiety and the beautiful proportions of this world of flowers overlapped in a most pleas-ant way into our work. For quite a while our work embraced everything we could lay our hands on. If we discussed gardening it was only a digression from one of the scenes in *Galileo;* if we combed a New York museum for technical drawings by Leonardo to use as background pictures in the per-formance we would digress to Hokusai's graphic work. L., I could see, would make only marginal use of such material. The parcels of books or photocopies from books, which he persistently or-dered, never turned him into a bookworm. He obstinately sought for the external: not for physics but for the physicists' behavior. It was a matter of putting together a bit of theater, something slight and superficial. As the material piled up, L. became set on the idea of getting a good draftsman to produce entertaining sketches in the manner of Caspar Neher, to expose the anatomy of the ac-tion. "Before you amuse others you have to amuse yourself," he said.

For this no trouble was too great. As soon as L. heard of Caspar Neher's delicate stage sketches, which allow the actors to group themselves according to a great artist's compositions and to take up attitudes that are both precise and realistic, he asked an excellent draftsman from the Walt Disney Studios to make similar sketches. They were a little malicious; L. used them, but with caution.

What pains he took over the costumes, not only his own, but those of all the actors! And how much time we spent on the casting of the many parts!

First we had to look through works on costume and old pictures in order to find costumes that were free of any element of fancy dress. We sighed with relief when we found a small sixteenth-century panel that showed long trousers. Then we had to distinguish the classes. There the elder Brueghel was of great service. Finally we had to work out the color scheme. Each scene had to have its basic tone: the first, e.g., a delicate morning one of white, yellow, and gray. But the entire se-quence of scenes had to have its development in terms of color. In the first scene a deep and dis-tinguished blue made its entrance with Ludovico Marsili, and this deep blue remained, set apart, in the second scene with the upper bourgeoisie in their blackish-green coats made of felt and leather. Galileo's social ascent could be followed by means of color. The silver and pearl-gray of the fourth (court) scene led into a nocturne in brown and black (where Galileo is jeered by the monks of the Collegium Romanum), then on to the seventh, the cardinals' ball, with delicate and fantas-tic individual masks (ladies and gentlemen) moving about the cardinals' crimson figures. That was a burst of color, but it still had to be fully unleashed, and this occurred in the tenth scene, the car-nival. After the nobility and the cardinals the poor people too had their masquerade. Then came the descent into dull and somber colors. The difficulty of such a plan of course lies in the fact that the costumes and their wearers wander through several scenes; they have always to fit in and con-tribute to the color scheme of the new scene.

We filled the parts mainly with young actors. The speeches presented certain problems. The American stage shuns speeches except in (maybe because of) its frightful Shakespearean produc-tions. Speeches just mean a break in the story and, as commonly delivered, that is what they are. L. worked with the young actors in a masterly and conscientious manner, and the playwright was impressed by the freedom he allowed them, by the way in which he avoided anything Laughton-ish and simply taught them the structure. To those actors who were too easily influenced by his own personality he read passages from Shakespeare, without rehearsing the actual text at all; to none did he read the text itself. The actors were incidentally asked on no account to prove their suitability for the part by putting something "impressive" into it.

We jointly agreed on the following points:

1.    The decorations should not be of a kind to suggest to the spectators that they are in a me-dieval Italian room or the Vatican. The audience should be conscious of being in a theater.

2.    The background should show more than the scene directly surrounding Galileo; in an imaginative and artistically pleasing way, it should show the historical setting, but still remain background. (This can be achieved when the decoration itself is not independently colorful, but helps the actors' costumes and enhances the roundedness of the figures by remaining two-dimensional even when it contains three-dimensional elements, etc.)

3.    Furniture and props (including doors) should be realistic and above all be of social and historical interest. Costumes must be individualized and show signs of having been worn. Social differences were to be underlined since we find it difficult to distinguish them in ancient fashions. The colors of the various costumes should harmonize.

4.    The characters' groupings must have the quality of historical paintings (but not to bring out the historical aspect as an esthetic attraction; this is a directive which is equally valid for contemporary plays). The director can achieve this by inventing historical titles for the episodes. (In the first scene such titles might be: *Galileo the physicist explains the new Copernican theory to his subsequent collaborator Andrea Sarti and predicts the great historical importance of astronomy— To make a living the great Galileo teaches rich pupils—Galileo who has requested support for his continued investigations is admonished by the university officials to invent profitable instruments—Galileo constructs his first telescope based on information from a traveler.*)

5.    The action must be presented calmly and in a large sweep. Frequent changes of position involving irrelevant movements of the characters must be avoided. The director must not for a moment forget that many of the actions and speeches are hard to understand and that it is therefore necessary to express the underlying idea of an episode by the positioning. The audience must be assured that when someone walks, or gets up, or makes a gesture it has meaning and deserves attention. But groupings and movements must always remain realistic.

6.    In casting the ecclesiastical dignitaries realism is of more than ordinary importance. No caricature of the church is intended, but the refined manner of speech and the "breeding" of the seventeenth-century hierarchy must not mislead the director into picking spiritual types. In this play, the church mainly represents authority; as types the dignitaries should resemble our present-day bankers and senators.

7.    The portrayal of Galileo should not aim at rousing the audience to sympathy or empathy; they should rather be encouraged to adopt a deliberate attitude of wonder and criticism. Galileo should be portrayed as a phenomenon of the order of Richard III; the audience's emotions will be engaged by the vitality of this strange figure.

8.    The more profoundly the historical seriousness of a production is established, the more scope can be given to humor. The more sweeping the over-all plan, the more intimately individual scenes can be played.

9.    There is no reason why *Life of Galileo* cannot be performed without drastically changing the present-day style of production, as a historical "war-horse," for instance, with a star part. Any conventional performance, however (which need not seem at all conventional to the actors, especially if it contained interesting inventions), would weaken the play's real strength considerably without making it any easier for the audience. The play's main effects will be missed unless the theater changes its attitude. The stock reply, "Won't work here," is familiar to the author; he heard it at home too. Most directors treat such plays as a coachman would have treated an automobile when it was first invented. On the arrival of the machine, mistrusting the practical instructions accompanying it, this coachman would have harnessed horses in front—more horses, of course, than to a carriage, since the new car was heavier—and then, his attention being drawn to the engine, he would have said, "Won't work here."°

The performance took place in a small theater in Beverly Hills, and L.'s chief worry was the prevailing heat. He asked that trucks full of ice be parked against the theater walls and fans be set in motion "so that the audience can think."

°[Brecht added Note 9 at a later date for inclusion in his Notes to the Play.]

*1*

*The Scholar, a Human Being*

The first thing L. did when he set to work was to rid the figure of Galileo of the pallid, spiritual, stargazing aura of the text books. Above all, the scholar must be made into a man. The very term "scholar" [Gelehrter] sounds somewhat ridiculous when used by simple people; there is an implication of having been prepared and fitted, of something passive. In Bavaria people used to speak of the Nuremberg Funnel by which simpletons were more or less forcibly fed undue quantities of knowledge, a kind of enema for the brain. When someone had "crammed himself with learning," that too was considered unnatural. The educated—again one of those hopelessly passive words—talked of the revenge of the "uneducated," of their innate hatred for the mind; and it is true that their contempt was often mixed with hatred; in villages and working-class districts, the mind was considered something alien, even hostile. The same contempt, however, could also be found among the "better classes." A scholar was an impotent, bloodless, quaint figure, conceited and barely fit to live. He was an easy prey for romantic treatment. L.'s Galileo never strayed far from the engineer at the great arsenal in Venice. His eyes were there to see with, not to flash, his hands to work with, not to gesticulate. Everything worth seeing or feeling L. derived from Galileo's profession, his pursuit of physics and his teaching, the teaching, that is, of something very concrete with its concomitant real difficulties. And he portrayed the external side not just for the sake of the inner man—that is to say, research and everything connected with it, not just for the sake of the resulting psychological reactions—these reactions, rather, were never separated from the everyday business and conflicts, they never became "universally human," even though they never lost their universal appeal. In the case of the Richard III of Shakespeare's theater, the spectator can easily change himself along with the actor, since the king's politics and warfare play only a very vague role; there is hardly more of it than a dreaming man would understand. But with Galileo it is a continual handicap to the spectator that he knows much less about science than does Galileo. It is a piquant fact that in representing the history of Galileo, both playwright and actor had to undo the notion which Galileo's betrayal had helped to create, the notion that schoolteachers and scientists are by nature absent-minded, hybrid, castrated. (Only in our own day when, in the shape of ruling-class hirelings remote from the people, they delivered the latest product of Galileo's laws of motion, did popular contempt change to fear.) As for Galileo himself, for many centuries, all over Europe, the people honored him for his belief in a popularly based science by refusing to believe in his recantation.

*Subdivisions and Line*

We divided the first scene into several parts:

We had the advantage that the beginning of the story was also a beginning for Galileo, that is, his encounter with the telescope, and since the significance of this encounter is hidden from him for the time being, our solution was to derive the joy of beginning from the early morning: having him wash with cold water—L., with bare torso, lifted a copper pitcher with a quick sweeping motion to let the jet of water fall into the basin—find his open books on the high desk, have his first sip of milk, and give his first lesson, as it happens, to a young boy. As the scene unfolds, Galileo keeps coming back to his reading at the high desk, annoyed at being interrupted by the returning student with his shallow preference for new-fangled inventions such as this spyglass, and by the procurator of the university who denies him a grant; finally reaching the last obstacle that keeps him from his work, the testing of the lenses which, however, would not have been possible without the two prior interruptions and makes an entirely new field of work accessible.

*Interest in Interest and Thinking as Expression of Physical Contentment*

Two elements in the action with the child may be mentioned: Washing himself in the background, Galileo observes the boy's interest in the armillary sphere as little Andrea circles around the strange instrument. L. emphasized what was novel in G. at that time by letting him look at the world around him as if he were a stranger and as if it needed explanation. His chuckling observation made fossils out of the monks at the Collegium Romanum. In that scene he also showed amusement at their primitive method of proof.

Some people objected to L.'s delivering his speech about the new astronomy in the first scene with a bare torso, claiming that it would confuse the audience if it were to hear such intellectual utterances from a half-naked man. But it was just this mixture of the physical and the intellectual that attracted L. "Galileo's physical contentment" at having his back rubbed by the boy is transformed into intellectual production. Again, in the ninth scene, L. brought out the fact that Galileo recovers his taste for wine on hearing of the reactionary pope's expected demise. His sensual walking, the play of his hands in his pockets while he is planning new researches, came close to being offensive. Whenever Galileo is creative, L. displayed a mixture of aggressiveness and defenseless softness and vulnerability.

### Rotation of the Earth and Rotation of the Brain

L. arranges the little demonstration of the earth's rotation to be quick and offhand, leaving his high desk where he has begun to read and returning to it. He avoids anything emphatic, seems to pay no attention to the child's intellectual capacity, and at the end leaves him sitting there alone with his thoughts.

This casual manner, in keeping with his limited time, simultaneously admits the boy to the community of scholars. Thus L. demonstrated how for Galileo learning and teaching are one and the same—which makes his subsequent betrayal all the more horrible.

### Balanced Acting

During this demonstration of the earth's rotation Galileo is surprised by Andrea's mother. Questioned about the nonsensical notions he is teaching the child he answers: "Apparently we are on the threshold of a new era, Mrs. Sarti." The way in which L. caressingly emptied his glass of milk while he said it was enchanting.

### Response to a Good Answer

A small detail: The housekeeper has gone to let the new student in. Galileo feels constrained to make a confession to Andrea. His science is in no very good state, its most important concerns must be concealed from the authorities, and for the moment they are only hypotheses. "I want to become an astronomer," Andrea says quickly. At this answer Galileo looks at him with an almost tender smile. Usually actors do not rehearse such details separately, or often, enough to render them quickly in the performance.

### [Dismissal of Andrea]

The dismissal of Andrea during the conversation with Ludovico is a piece of stage business for which time must be allowed. Galileo now drinks his milk as if it were the only pleasure to be had, and one which will not last very long. He is fully aware of Andrea's presence. Ill-humoredly he sends him away. One of those unavoidable everyday compromises!

### Galileo Underestimates the New Invention

Ludovico Marsili describes a new spyglass which he has seen in Holland and cannot understand. Galileo asks for detailed information and makes a sketch which solves the problem. He holds the cardboard with the sketch without showing it to his pupil, who expected to have a look. (L. insisted that the actor playing Ludovico should expect this.) The sketch itself he drew casually, just to solve a problem that offered some relief from the conversation. Then, his way of asking the housekeeper to send Andrea for lenses and borrowing a scudo from the entering [curator]—all that had an automatic and routine quality. The whole incident seemed only to demonstrate that Galileo too was capable of plowing water.

### A New Commodity

The birth of the telescope as a commodity took a long time to emerge clearly in the rehearsals. We found out why: L. had reacted too quickly and arrogantly to the university's refusal of a grant. All was well as soon as he accepted the blow in hurt silence and then went on, almost sadly, to speak like a poor man. As a natural result, Galileo's "Mr. Priuli, I may have something for you," came out in a way to make Galileo's dismissal of the new spyglass as "bosh" perfectly clear.

### [Interruption of Work]

When Andrea returns with the lenses he finds Galileo deep in his work. (L. has shown, during a by no means brief interval, how the scholar handles his books.) He has already forgotten the lenses, he lets the boy wait, then proceeds, almost guiltily because he has no desire to take up the lucrative bosh, to arrange the two lenses on a piece of cardboard. Finally he takes the "thing" away, not without a little demonstration of his showmanship.

2

### Fraud and Representation

Lesser actors would have delivered Galileo's speech representing the telescope as his own invention in a comical manner, simply in order to provide a strong contrast to the few excited words in which he tells his friend Sagredo about the instrument's scientific importance. This would have robbed the handing-over ceremony of all significance and belittled the fraud as a moral trifle. L. delivered the speech seriously, in a businesslike way (what Goethe called "artig"), that is, as a matter of routine, the sort of way in which the chief engineer at the great arsenal of Venice behaves on official occasions. Only when he mentioned the "Christian principles" according to which the "optical tube or telescope" was constructed was there a hint of the great gainsayer's delight in provocation.

It was highly entertaining to see how shamelessly the colossus bowed to his betters when, after a glance through the telescope, they applauded him, and how, on the other hand, he warded off their jovial and somewhat too familiar jokes while at the same time telling his friend, with supreme authority and passion, that he has turned the thing on the night sky.

### Patience Guarantees Tempo

During rehearsals L. completely freed himself of the fever of an evening performance, that feeling that nothing is going fast enough which so easily infects the rehearsals. In this case things cannot go slowly enough. One has to rehearse as if the play could go on for twelve hours. L. rigorously rejected any suggestion of makeshift "bridges" to avoid loss of tempo. There were effects everywhere; the smallest detail could reveal peculiarities or habits of people's living together. (Loss of tempo occurs most often when a point is muddled and bungled and has to be glossed over.) For instance, the relatively cursory ending of the second scene cannot be staged adequately without very patient and detailed rehearsing.

The senators surround and congratulate Galileo and draw him to the rear, but the tiny exchange with Ludovico Marsili, with its imputation of plagiarism, must as it were still hover in the air; for when the half-curtain closes behind them [Ludovico and Virginia] and in front of Galileo and the others, they continue and conclude the conversation while exiting along the footlights. And Ludovico's cynical remark, "I am beginning to understand science," serves as a springboard for the ensuing third scene—that of the great discoveries.

3

### [Confidence in Objective Judgment]

Galileo lets his friend Sagredo look through the telescope at the moon and Jupiter. L. sat down, his back to the instrument, relaxed, as though his work were done and he only wanted his friend to pass impartial judgment on what he saw, and that this were all he needed to do since his friend was now seeing for himself. By this means he established that the new possibilities of observation must bring all controversy about the Copernican system to an end.

This attitude explains at the very beginning of the scene the boldness of his application for the lucrative position at the court of Florence.

### The Historical Moment

L. conducted the exchange with his friend at the telescope without any emphasis. The more casually he acted, the more clearly one could sense the historic night; the more soberly he spoke, the more solemn the moment appeared.

### An Embarrassment

When the procurator of the university comes in to complain about the fraud of the telescope, L.'s Galileo shows noticeable embarrassment by studiously looking through the telescope, obviously less to observe the sky than to avoid looking the procurator in the eye. Shamelessly he exploits the "higher" function of the instrument which the Venetians have found not to be very profitable.

It is true that he also shows his behind to the angry man who has trusted him. But, far from trying to put him off with the discoveries of "pure" science, he at once offers him another profitable item, the astronomical clock for ships. When the procurator has left, he sits glumly before the telescope, scratching his neck and telling Sagredo about his physical and intellectual needs which must be satisfied in one way or another. Science is a milch cow for all to milk, he himself of course included. While at this point in time Galileo's attitude is still helpful to science, later on, in his fight with Rome, it is going to push science to the brink of the abyss, in other words, deliver it into the hands of the rulers.

### The Wish Is Father to the Thought

Looking up from their calculations of the movements of Jupiter's moons, Sagredo voices his concern for the man about to publish a discovery so embarrassing to the church. Galileo mentions the seductive power of evidence. He fishes a pebble from his pocket and lets it fall from palm to palm, following gravity: "Sooner or later everybody must succumb to it" [the evidence]. As he argued along these lines, L. never forgot for a moment to do it in such a way that the audience would remember it later when he announced his decision to hand over his dangerous discoveries to the Catholic court of Florence.

### [Rejection of Virginia]

L.'s Galileo used the little scene with his daughter Virginia to indicate how far he might be blamed for Virginia's subsequent behavior as a spy for the Inquisition. He does not take her interest in the telescope seriously and sends her off to matins. L. scrutinized his daughter after her question, "May I look through it?" before replying, "What for? It's not a toy."

### The Fun in Contradictions

Saying, "I am going to Florence," Galileo carefully signs his letter of application. In this hasty capitalization of his discoveries as well as in his discourse on the seductive power of evidence and the representative value of great discoveries, L. left the spectator completely at liberty to study, criticize, admire Galileo's contradictory personality.

### 4

### The Acting of Anger

Vis-à-vis the court scholars who refuse to look through the telescope, because to do so would either confirm Aristotle's doctrine or show up Galileo as a swindler, what L. acted was not so much anger as the attempt to dominate anger.

### Servility

After Galileo, erupting at last, has threatened to take his new science to the dockyards, he sees the court depart abruptly. Deeply alarmed and disturbed, he follows the departing prince in cringing servility, stumbling, all dignity gone. In such a case an actor's greatness can be seen in the degree to which he can make the character's behavior incomprehensible or at least objectionable.

### 4 and 6*

### The Fight and the Particular Manner of Fighting

L. insisted that throughout the two following scenes, 4 and 6, the sketch of Jupiter's moons from Galileo's original report should remain projected on the backdrop screen. It was a reminder of the fight. To show one of its aspects, the heel-cooling for the sake of truth, L., at the end of scene 4, when the chamberlain stays behind after the hasty departure of the court to inform him of the appeal to Rome, let himself be driven out of the space that stood for his house and stood in front of the half-curtain. He stood there between scenes 4 and 6 and again between scenes 6 and 7, waiting, and occasionally verifying that the pebble from his pocket continued to fall from one raised hand to the other stretched out below.

### 6

### [Observation of the Clergy]

Galileo is not entirely devoid of appreciation when he observes the jeering monks at the Collegium Romanum—after all, by pretending to stand on a rolling globe they are trying to *prove* the absurdity of his propositions. The very old cardinal fills him with pity.

After the astronomer Clavius has confirmed Galileo's findings, Galileo shows his pebble to the hostile cardinal who retreats in dismay; L. did this by no means triumphantly, rather as if he wanted to offer his adversary a last chance to convince himself.

### 7

### Fame

Invited to the masked ball of Cardinals Bellarmine and Barberini, Galileo lingers for a moment in the anteroom, alone with the clerical secretaries who later turn out to be secret agents. He has been greeted on his arrival by distinguished masked guests with great respect: obviously he stands in high favor. From the halls a boys' choir is heard, and Galileo listens to one of these melancholic stanzas which are sung amid the joy of life. L. needed no more than this brief listening and the word "Rome!" to express the pride of the conqueror who has the capital of the world at his feet.

### The Duel of Quotations

In the brief duel of Bible quotations with Cardinal Barberini, L.'s Galileo shows, beside the fun he has with such intellectual sport, that the possibility of an unfavorable outcome to his affairs is dawning on him. For the rest, the effectiveness of the scene depends on the elegance of its performance; L. made full use of his heavy body.

### Two Things at Once

The brief argument about the capacity of the human brain (which the playwright was delighted to have heard formulated by Albert Einstein) furnished L. the opportunity to show two traits: 1) a certain arrogance of the professional when his field is invaded by laymen, and 2) an awareness of the difficulty of such a problem.

---

*Scene 5 was not played in this production.

*[Disarmed by Lack of Logic]*

When the decree is read out forbidding the guest to teach a theory acknowledged to have been proven, L.'s Galileo reacts by twice turning abruptly from the reading secretaries to the liberal Barberini. Thunderstruck, he lets the two cardinals drag him to the ball as if he were a steer stunned by the ax. L. was able, in a manner the playwright cannot describe, to give the impression that what mainly disarmed Galileo was the lack of logic.

### 8

*[Indomitable Urge to Research]*

If in the seventh scene Galileo experiences the *No* of the church, in the eighth he is confronted with the *No* of the people. It comes from the lips of the little monk, himself a physicist. Galileo is disturbed, then recognizes the situation: in the fight against science it is not the church that defends the peasant, but the peasant who defends the church. It was L.'s theatrical conception to let Galileo be so profoundly upset that he delivers his counter-arguments in a spirit of defense, even of angry self-defense, and makes the throwing down of the manuscript into a gesture of helplessness. He blamed his indomitable urge to research like a sex offender blaming his glands.

### Laughton Does Not Forget to Tell the Story

In the eighth scene one of Galileo's lines contains a sentence which continues the story: "Should I condone this decree . . . " L. distilled this small but important detail with great care.

### 9

*[The Impatience of Galileo the Scientist]*

Whereas L. insisted he must be allowed to give Galileo's character a markedly criminal evolution after the recantation in scene 13, he did not feel a similar need at the beginning of scene 9. Here too, to oblige the church, Galileo has for many years abstained from publicizing his discoveries, but this cannot be considered a betrayal like the later one. At this point the people know very little about the new science, the cause of the new astronomy has not yet been taken up by the North Italian bourgeoisie, the battle fronts are not yet political. There may not be an open declaration on his part, but there is no recantation either. In this scene therefore it is still the scientist's personal impatience and dissatisfaction which must be portrayed.

### When Does Galileo Become Antisocial?

The issue in Galileo's case is not that a man must stand up for his opinion as long as he holds it to be true; that would entitle him to be called a "character." The man who started it all, Copernicus, did not stand up for his opinion; it would be truer to say that he lay down for it inasmuch as he had it published only after his death; and yet, quite rightly, no one has ever reproached him for this. Something had been laid down to be picked up by anybody.

The man who had laid it down had gone, out of range of blame or thanks. Here was a scientific achievement which allowed simpler, shorter and more elegant calculations of celestial motions—let humanity make use of it. Galileo's life work is on the whole of the same order, and humanity used it. But unlike Copernicus who had avoided a battle, Galileo fought it and betrayed it. If Giordano Bruno, of Nola, who did not avoid the battle and had been burned twenty years earlier, had recanted, no great harm might have come of it; it could even be argued that his martyrdom deterred scientists more than it aroused them. In Bruno's time the battle was still a feeble one. But time did not stand still: A new class, the bourgeoisie with its new industries, had assertively entered the scene; no longer was it only scientific achievements that were at stake, but battles for their large-scale general exploitation. This exploitation had many aspects because the new class, in order to pursue its interests, had to come to power and smash the prevailing ideology that obstructed it. The church, which defended the privileges of princes and landowners as God-given and therefore natural  did not rule by means of astronomy, but it ruled within astronomy, as in everything else. And in no field could it allow its rule to be smashed. The new class, clearly, could exploit a victory in any field including that of astronomy. But once it had singled out a particular field and concentrated the battle in it, the new class became broadly vulnerable there. The maxim, "A chain is as strong as its weakest link," applies to chains that bind (such as the ideology of the church) as well as to transmission chains (such as the new class's new ideas about property, law, science, etc.). Galileo became antisocial when he led his science into this battle and then abandoned the fight.

## Teaching

Words cannot do justice to the lightness and elegance with which L. conducted the little experiment with the pieces of ice in the copper basin. A fairly long reading from books was followed by the rapid demonstration. Galileo's relationship with his pupils is like a duel in which the fencing master uses all his feints—using them against the pupil to serve the pupil. Catching Andrea out in a hasty conclusion, Galileo crosses out his wrong entry in the record book with the same matter-of-fact patience as he displays in correcting the ice's position in the submersion experiment.

## Silence

With his own pupils he uses his tricks mainly to quell their dissatisfaction with him. They are offended by his keeping silent in the European controversy about sunspots, when his views are constantly being solicited as those of the greatest authority in the field. He knows he owes his authority to the church, and hence owes the clamor for his views to his silence. His authority was given him on condition that he should not use it. L. shows how Galileo suffers by the episode of the book on sunspots, which has been brought along and is discussed by his pupils. He pretends complete indifference, but how badly he does it! He is not allowed to leaf through the book, probably full of errors and thus twice as attractive. In little things he supports their revolt, though not himself revolting: When the lens grinder Federzoni angrily drops the scales on the floor because he cannot read Latin, Galileo himself picks them up—casually, like a man who would pick up anything that fell down.

## Resumption of Research—a Sensual Pleasure

L. used the arrival of Ludovico Marsili, Virginia's fiancé, to show his own disgust at the routine nature of his work. He organized the reception of his guest in such a way that it interrupted the work and made his pupils shake their heads. On being told that the reactionary pope was on his deathbed Galileo visibly began to enjoy his wine. His bearing changed completely. Sitting at the table, his back to the audience, he experienced a rebirth; he put his hands in his pockets, placed one leg on the bench in a delicious sprawl. Then he rose slowly and walked up and down, with his glass of wine. At the same time he let it be seen how his future son-in-law, the landowner and reactionary, displeased him more with every sip. His instructions to the pupils for the new experiment were so many challenges to Ludovico. With all this, L. still took care to make it plain that he was seizing the opportunity for new research not by the forelock, but just by a single little hair.

## The Gest of Work

The speech about the need for caution with which Galileo resumes a scientific activity that defies all caution shows L. in a rare gest of creative, very vulnerable softness.

Even Virginia's fainting spell upon finding her fiancé gone barely interests Galileo. As the pupils hover over her, he says painfully: "I've got to know." And in saying it he did not seem hard.

## 10

## Political Attitude on Dramatic Grounds

L. took the greatest interest in the tenth (carnival) scene, where the Italian people are shown relating Galileo's revolutionary doctrine to their own revolutionary demands. He helped sharpen it by suggesting that representatives of the guilds, wearing masks, should toss a rag doll representing a cardinal in the air. It was so important to him to demonstrate that property relationships were being threatened by the doctrine of the earth's rotation that he declined a New York production where this scene was to be omitted.

### 11

### Decomposition

The eleventh scene is the decomposition scene. L. begins it with the same authoritative attitude as in the ninth scene. He does not permit his increasing blindness to detract one iota from his virility. (Throughout, L. strictly refused to exploit this ailment which Galileo had contracted in the pursuit of his profession, and which of course could easily have won him the sympathy of the audience. L. did not want Galileo's surrender to be ascribable to his age or physical defects. Even in his last scene he was a man who was spiritually, not physically, broken.)

The playwright would sooner have Galileo's recantation in this scene, rather than let it take place before the Inquisition. Galileo executes it when he rejects the offer of the progressive bourgeoisie, in the person of the iron founder Vanni, to support him in his fight against the church, and insists that what he has written is an apolitical scientific work. L. acted this rejection with the utmost abruptness and strength.

### Two Versions

In the New York production L. changed his gest for the meeting with the cardinal inquisitor as he emerges from the inner chambers. In the California production he remained seated, not recognizing the cardinal, while his daughter bowed. This created the impression of something ominous passing through, unrecognizable, but bowing. In New York, L. rose and himself acknowledged the cardinal's bow. The playwright finds no merit in the change, since it establishes a relationship between Galileo and the cardinal inquisitor which is irrelevant, and turns Galileo's ensuing remark, "His attitude was respectful, I think," into a statement rather than a question.

### The Arrest

As soon as the chamberlain appears at the head of the stairs, Galileo hastily puts the book under his arm and runs upstairs, passing the startled chamberlain. Stopped short by the chamberlain's words, he leafs through the book as though its quality was all that mattered. Left standing on the lower part of the staircase, he must now retrace his steps. He stumbles. Almost at the footlights—his daughter has run to meet him—he completely pulls himself together and gives his instructions firmly and to the point. It becomes clear that he has taken certain precautions. Holding his daughter close and supporting her, he sets out to leave the hall at a rapid, energetic pace. When he reaches the wings the chamberlain calls him back. He receives the fateful decision with great composure. Acting thus, L. shows that this is neither a helpless nor an ignorant man who is being caught, but one who has made great mistakes.

### 13

### A Difficulty for the Actor: Some Effects become Apparent only when the Play is seen a Second Time

In preparing for the recantation scene L. never neglected in the preceding scenes to exhibit in all their fine shades the compliance and non-compliance in Galileo's conduct vis-à-vis the authorities, even those instances which would only mean anything to a spectator who had already seen the entire play once. Both he and the playwright recognized that in this type of play certain details unavoidably depend on a knowledge of the whole.

### The Traitor

In the book there is a stage direction for Galileo when he returns to his pupils after he recanted to the Inquisition: *"He is changed, almost unrecognizable."* The change in L. was not of a physical nature as the playwright had intended. There was something infantile, bed-wetting in his loose gait, his grin, indicating a self-release of the lowest order, as if restraints had been thrown off that had been very necessary.

This, like what follows, can best be seen on photographs of the California production.

Andrea Sarti is feeling sick; Galileo has asked for a glass of water for him, and now the little monk passes by him, his face averted. Galileo's gaze is answered by Federzoni, the artisan-scholar, and for some time the two stare at each other until the monk returns with the water. This is Galileo's punishment: it will be the Federzonis of the future centuries who will have to pay for his betrayal at the very inception of their great career.

### "Unhappy the Land"

The pupils have abandoned the fallen man. Sarti's last word had been: "Unhappy is the land that breeds no hero." Galileo has to think of an answer, then calls after them, too late for them to hear: "Unhappy is the land that needs a hero." L. says it soberly, as a statement by the physicist who wants to take away nature's privilege to ordain tragedies and mankind's need to produce heroes.

### 14

### The Goose

Galileo spends the last years of his life on an estate near Florence as a prisoner of the Inquisition. His daughter Virginia, whom he has neglected to instruct, has become a spy for the Inquisition. He dictates his *Discorsi* to her, in which he lays down his main teachings. But to conceal the fact that he is making a copy of the book he exaggerates the extent of his failing eyesight. Now he pretends not to recognize a goose which she shows him, the gift of a traveler. His wisdom has been degraded to cunning. But his zest for food is undiminished: He instructs his daughter carefully how he wants the liver prepared. His daughter conceals neither her disbelief in his inability to see nor her contempt for his gluttony. And Galileo, aware that she defends him vis-à-vis the Inquisition's guards, sharpens the conflicts of her troubled conscience by hinting that he may be deceiving the Inquisition. Thus in the basest manner he experiments with her filial love and her devotion to the church. Nonetheless, L. succeeded brilliantly in eliciting from the spectator not only a measure of contempt but also a measure of horror at degradations that debase. And for all this he had only a few sentences and pauses at his disposal.

### Collaboration

Anxious to show that crime makes the criminal more criminal, L. insisted, during the adaptation of the original version, on a scene in which Galileo collaborates with the authorities in full view of the audience. There was another reason for this: During the scene Galileo makes the most dignified use of his well-preserved intellectual powers by analyzing his betrayal for the benefit of his former pupil. So he now dictates to his daughter, to whom he had for many weeks been dictating his main work, the *Discorsi*, an abject letter to the archbishop in which he advises him how the Bible may be used for the suppression of starving artisans. In this he quite frankly shows his daughter his cynicism without being entirely able to conceal the effort this ignominious exercise costs him. L. was fully aware of the recklessness with which he swam against the stream by thus throwing away his character—no audience can stand a thing like that.

### The Voice of the Visitor

Virginia has laid down the manuscript of the letter to the archbishop and gone out to receive a belated visitor. Galileo hears the voice of Andrea Sarti, formerly his favorite pupil who had broken with him after the recantation. To those readers of the play who complained that it gave no description of the spiritual agonies to which our nuclear physicists were subjected by the authorities ordering the bombs, L. could show that no first-rate actor needs more than a fleeting moment to indicate such spiritual discomfort. It is of course right to compare Galileo's submissiveness towards his authorities with that of our physicists towards rulers whom they distrust, but it would be wrong to go all the way into their stomach pains. What would be gained by that? L. was simply making this the moment to display his bad conscience, which could not have been shown later in the scene when his betrayal is analyzed, without getting in his way.

### The Laughter

The laughter in the picture [in the Model Book] was not suggested by the text, and it was frightening. Sarti, the former favorite pupil, calls and Virginia overhears the strained conversation. When Galileo inquires about his former collaborators, Sarti answers with utter frankness calculated to hurt his master. They get to Federzoni, a lens grinder whom Galileo had made his scientific collaborator even though he had no Latin. When Sarti reports he is back in a shop grinding lenses Galileo answers: "He can't read the books": Then L. makes him laugh. The laugh however does not contain bitterness about a society that treats science as something secret reserved for the well-to-do, but a disgraceful mocking of Federzoni's inadequacies together with a brazen complicity in his degradation, though this is simply (and completely) explained by his being inadequate. L. thus intended to make the fallen man a provocateur. Sarti, naturally, responds with indignation and seizes the opportunity to inflict a blow on the shameless recanter when Galileo cautiously inquires about Descarte's further work. Sarti coldly reports that Descartes shelved his investigations into the nature of light when he heard that Galileo had recanted. And Galileo once had exclaimed that he would willingly be "imprisoned a thousand feet beneath the earth, if in exchange he could find out what light is." L. inserted a long pause after this unpleasant information.

### The Right to Submit

During the first sentences of his exchange with Sarti he listens inconspicuously for the footsteps of the Inquisition's official in the anteroom, who stops every now and then, presumably in order to eavesdrop. Galileo's inconspicuous listening is difficult to act since it must remain concealed from Sarti but not from the audience; concealed from Sarti because otherwise he would not take the prisoner's repentant remarks at face value. But Galileo must convey them to him at face value so that his visitor can change them when he reaches foreign parts; it would not do at all if it were rumored abroad that the prisoner was recalcitrant. Then the conversation reaches a point where Galileo abandons this way of speaking for the benefit of hostile ears, and proclaims, authoritatively and forcefully, that it is his right to submit. Society's command to its members to produce is but vague and accompanied by no manner of guarantee; a producer produces at his own risk, and Galileo can prove any time that being productive endangers his comfort.

### Handing over the Book

L. made the disclosure about the existence of the *Discorsi* quickly and with exaggerated indifference; but in a way suggesting that the old man was only trying to get rid of the fruits of a regrettable lapse, with yet another implication beneath this: anxiety lest the visitor reject the imposition together with the risk involved in taking the book with him. As he was protesting ill-humoredly that he wrote the book only as a slave of habit—the thoroughly vicious habit of thinking—the spectator could see that he was also listening. (Having made his eyesight worse by secretly copying the book which is endangered by the Inquisition, when he wants to gauge Sarti's reaction, he is wholly dependent on his ears.) Toward the end of his appeal he virtually abandons his attitude of "condescending grandeur" and comes close to begging. The remark about having continued his scientific work simply to kill time, uttered when Sarti's exclamation "The *Discorsi!*" had made him aware of his visitor's enthusiasm, came so falsely from L.'s lips that it could deceive no one.

It is furthermore important to realize that when Galileo so strongly emphasizes his own condemnation of the teaching activities which are now forbidden to him is mainly trying to deceive himself. Since working, let alone sharing the results with the outside world, would threaten whatever was left of his comfort, he himself is passionately against this "weakness" which makes him like a cat that cannot stop catching mice. Indeed the audience is witnessing his defeat when it sees him yield so reluctantly yet helplessly to an urge fostered in him by society. He must consider the risks to be larger than ever because now he is wholly in the hands of the Inquisition; his punishment would no longer be a public one; and the body of people who formerly would have protested has dispersed—thanks to his own fault. And not only has the danger increased, but he would be too late now with any contribution anyway, since astronomy has become apolitical, the exclusive concern of scientists.

## Watchfulness

After the young physicist has found the book for which the scientific community no longer dares to hope, he at once changes his opinion about his former teacher and launches, with great passion, into a rationalization of Galileo's motives for the betrayal; motives, he finds, which exonerate him completely. Galileo has recanted so that he can go on with his work and find more evidence for the truth. Galileo listens for a while, interjecting monosyllables. What he is hearing now may well be all that he can expect posterity to say in recognition of his difficult and dangerous endeavor. First, he seems to be testing his pupil's improvised theory, just in the same way as any other theory must be tested for its validity. But presently he discovers that it is not tenable. At this point, immersed in the world of his scientific concerns, he forgets his watchfulness vis-à-vis a possible eavesdropper: he stops listening for steps.

## The Analysis

Galileo's great counterattack against the golden bridge opens with a scornful outburst that abandons all grandeur: "Welcome to my gutter, dear colleague in science and brother in treason! I sold out, you are a buyer." This is one of the few passages which gave L. trouble. He doubted whether the spectator would get the meaning of the words, apart from the fact that the words are not taken from Galileo's usual, purely logical vocabulary. L. could not accept the playwright's argument that there must be some gest simply showing how the opportunist damns himself by damning all who accept the rewards of opportunism; what he understood even less was that the playwright would be quite satisfied with the exhibition of a state of mind that defies rational analysis. The omission of a spiteful and strained grin at this point robbed the opening of the great instructional speech of its malice. It was not fully brought out that deriding the ignorant is the lowest form of instruction and that it is an ugly light that is shed solely for the purpose of letting one's own light shine. Because the lowest starting point was missing some spectators were unable to gauge the full height which L. undoubtedly reached in the course of the great speech, nor was it entirely possible to see the collapse of Galileo's vain and violently authoritarian-attitude that colored even his scientific statements. The theatrical content of the speech, in fact, is not directly concerned with the ruthless demonstration of bourgeois science's fall from grace at the beginning of its rise—its surrender of scientific knowledge to the rulers who are authorized "to use it, not use it, abuse it, as it suits their ends." The theatrical content derives from the whole course of the action, and the speech should show how well this perfect brain functions when it has to judge its owner. That man, the spectator should be able to conclude, is sitting in a hell, more terrible than Dante's, where the true function of intellect has been gambled away.

## Background of the Performance

It is important to realize that our performance took place at the time and in the country of the atom bomb's recent production and military application and where nuclear physics was then shrouded in deepest secrecy. The day the bomb was dropped will not easily be forgotten by anyone who spent it in the U. S.

The Japanese war had cost the U. S. real sacrifices. The troop ships left from the west coast, and the wounded and the victims of tropical diseases returned there. When the news reached Los Angeles it was at once clear that this was the end of the hateful war, that sons and brothers would soon come home. But the great city rose to an astonishing display of mourning. The playwright heard bus drivers and saleswomen in fruit markets express nothing but horror. It was victory, but it was the shame of defeat. Next came the suppression of the tremendous energy source by the military and politicians, and this upset the intellectuals. Freedom of investigation, the exchange of scientific discoveries, the international community of scholars were jettisoned by authorities that were strongly distrusted. Great physicists left the service of their bellicose government in headlong flight; one of the best known took an academic position where he was forced to waste his working time in teaching rudimentary essentials solely to escape working for the government. It had become ignominious to make new discoveries.

Appendices to *"Building up a Part"*

### Sense and Sensuality

The demonstrative style of acting, which depicts life in such a way that it is laid open to intervention by the human reason, and which strikes Germans as thoroughly doctrinaire, presented no special difficulty to the Englishman L. What makes the sense seem so striking and insistent once it is "lugged in" is our particular lack of sensuality. To lack sensuality in art is certainly senseless, nor can any sense remain healthy if it is not sensual. Reason, for us, immediately implies something cold, arbitrary, mechanical, presenting us with such pairs of alternatives as ideas and life, passion and thinking, pleasure and utility. Hence when we stage a performance of our *Faust*—a regular occurrence for educational reasons—we strip it of all sensuality and thus transport the audience into an indefinite atmosphere where they feel themselves confronted with all sorts of thoughts, no single one of which they can grasp clearly. L. didn't even need any kind of theoretical information about the required "style." He had enough taste not to make any distinction between the supposedly lofty and the supposedly base, and he detested preaching. And so he was able to unfold the great physicist's contradictory personality in a wholly corporeal form, without either suppressing his own thoughts about the subject or forcing them on us.

### Beard or No Beard

In the California production L. acted without a beard, in the New York with one. This order has no significance, nor were there any fundamental discussions about it. It is the sort of case where the desire for a change can be the deciding factor. At the same time it does of course lead to modifications in the character. People who had seen the New York production confirmed what can be seen from the pictures [in the Model Book], namely that L. acted rather differently. But everything essential was still there, and the experiment can be taken as evidence to show how much play is left for the "personal" element.

### The Leavetaking

Certainly nothing could have been more horrible than the moment when L. has finished his big speech and hastens to the table saying "I must eat now," as though in delivering his insights Galileo has done everything that can be expected of him. His leavetaking from Sarti is cold. Standing absorbed in the sight of the goose he is about to eat, he replies to Sarti's repeated attempt to express his regard for him with a formal "Thank you, sir." Then, relieved of all further responsibility, he sits down pleasurably to his food.

### Concluding Remark

Though it resulted from several years of preparation and was brought about by sacrifices on the part of all concerned, the production of *Galileo* was seen by a bare ten thousand people. It was put on in two small theaters, a dozen times in each: first in Beverly Hills, Los Angeles, and then with a competely new cast in New York. Though all the performances were sold out the notices in the main papers were bad. Against that could be set the favorable remarks of such people as Charles Chaplin and Erwin Piscator, as well as the interest of the public, which looked like being enough to fill the theater for some considerable time. But the large cast meant that the potential earnings were low even if business was really good, and when an artistically interested producer made an offer it had to be rejected because L., having already turned down a number of film engagements and made considerable sacrifices, could not afford to turn down another. So the whole thing remained a private operation by a great artist who, while earning his keep outside the theater, indulged himself by displaying a splendid piece of work to a (not very large) number of interested parties. Though this is something that needed to be said, it does not however convey the complete picture. Given the way the American theater was organized in those years, it was impossible that such plays and such productions should reach their audience. Productions like this one, therefore, should be treated as examples of a kind of theater that might become possible under other political and economic conditions. Their achievements, like their mistakes, make them object lessons for anyone who is looking for a theater of great themes and rewarding acting.

## Walter Benjamin
(1892–1940)

"What Is Epic Theater?"
(1939)

TRANSLATED BY
HARRY ZOHN

*The relaxed audience*

*THOUGH known only to a small circle of intellectuals during his lifetime, Walter Benjamin has emerged as one of the most influential cultural critics of the late twentieth century. A Jew in post-World War I Germany, Benjamin's attempts to pursue an academic career were repeatedly thwarted; with the rise of the Nazis in the 1930s, his life as well as his livelihood became precarious. Benjamin was a friend of Brecht's and wrote several important essays on Brecht in the 1930s, including "Conversations with Brecht," "The Author as Producer," and "What is Epic Theater?" Like many Jewish intellectuals, Benjamin applied for a visa to the U. S. and was proceeding from France to Spain when he was told—erroneously—that he was about to be handed over to the Gestapo. He committed suicide by taking an overdose of morphine.*

"There is nothing more pleasant than to lie on a sofa and read a novel," wrote a nineteenth-century narrator, indicating the great extent to which a work of fiction can relax the reader who is enjoying it. The common image of a man attending a theatrical performance is the opposite: one pictures a man who follows the action with every fiber of his being at rapt attention. The concept of the epic theater, originated by Brecht as the theoretician of his poetic practice, indicates above all that this theater desires an audience that is relaxed and follows the action without strain. This audience, to be sure, always appears as a collective, and this differentiates it from the reader, who is alone with his text. Also, this audience, being a collective, will usually feel impelled to react promptly. This reaction, according to Brecht, ought to be a well-considered and therefore a relaxed one—in short, the reaction of people who have an interest in the matter. Two objects are provided for this interest. The first is the action; it has to be such that the audience can keep a check on it at crucial places on the basis of its own experience. The second is the performance; it should be mounted artistically in a pellucid manner. (This manner of presentation is anything but artless; actually, it presupposes artistic sophistication and acumen on the part of the director.) Epic theater appeals to an interest group who "do not think without reason." Brecht does not lose sight of the masses, whose limited practice of thinking is probably described by this phrase. In the endeavor to interest the audience in the theater expertly, but definitely not by way of mere cultural involvement, a political will has prevailed.

*The plot*

The epic theater purposes to "deprive the stage of its sensation derived from subject matter." Thus an old story will often do more for it than a new one. Brecht has considered the question of whether the incidents that are presented by the epic theater should not already be familiar. The theater would have the same relationship to the plot as a ballet teacher has to his pupil: his first task would be to loosen her joints to the greatest possible extent. This is how the Chinese theater actually proceeds. In his essay "The Fourth Wall of China" (*Life and Letters Today,* Vol. XV, No. 6, 1936), Brecht states what he owes to this theater. If the theater is to cast about for familiar events, "historical incidents would be the most suitable." Their epic extension through the style of acting, the placards and captions, is intended to purge them of the sensational.

In this vein Brecht takes the life of Galileo as the subject of his latest play. Brecht presents Galileo primarily as a great teacher who not only teaches a new physics, but does so in a new way. In his hands, experiments are not only an achievement of science, but a tool of pedagogy as well. The main emphasis of this play is not on Galileo's recantation; rather, the truly epic process must be sought in what is evident from the labeling of the penultimate scene: "1633 to 1642. As a prisoner of the Inquisition, Galileo continues his scientific work until his death. He succeeds in smuggling his main works out of Italy."

Epic theater is in league with the course of time in an entirely different way from that of the tragic theater. Because suspense belongs less to the outcome than to the individual events, this theater can cover the greatest spans of time. (The same is true of the earlier mystery plays. The dramaturgy of *Oedipus* or *The Wild Duck* constitutes the counterpole of epic dramaturgy.)

*The untragic hero*

The French classical theater made room in the midst of the players for persons of rank, who had their armchairs on the open stage. To us this seems inappropriate. According to the concept of the "dramatic element" with which we are familiar, it seemed inappropriate to attach to the action on the stage a nonparticipating third party as a dispassionate observer or "thinker." Yet Brecht often had something like that in mind. One can go even further and say that Brecht made an attempt to make the thinker, or even the wise man, the hero of the drama. From this very point of view one can define his theater as epic theater. This attempt is taken furthest in the character of Galy Gay, the packer. Galy Gay, the protagonist of the play *A Man's a Man*, is nothing but an exhibit of the contradictions which make up our society. It may not be too bold to regard the wise man in the Brechtian sense as the perfect showcase of its dialectics. In any case, Galy Gay is a wise man. Plato already recognized the undramatic quality of that most excellent man, the sage. In his Dialogues he took him to the threshold of the drama; in his *Phaidon*, to the threshold of the passion play. The medieval Christ, who also represented the wise man (we find this in the Early Fathers), is the untragic hero *par excellence*. But in the secular drama of the West, too, the search for the untragic hero has never ceased. In always new ways, and frequently in conflict with its theoreticians, this drama has differed from the authentic—that is, the Greek—form of tragedy. This important but poorly marked road, which may here serve as the image of a tradition, went via Roswitha and the mystery plays in the Middle Ages, via Gryphius and Calderón in the Baroque age; later we may trace it in Lenz and Grabbe, and finally in Strindberg. Scenes in Shakespeare are its roadside monuments, and Goethe crosses it in the second part of *Faust*. It is a European road, but a German one as well-provided that we may speak of a road and not of a secret smugglers' path by which the legacy of the medieval and the Baroque drama has reached us. It is this mule track, neglected and overgrown, which comes to light today in the dramas of Brecht.

*The interruption*

Brecht differentiates his epic theater from the dramatic theater in the narrower sense, whose theory was formulated by Aristotle. Appropriately, Brecht introduces his art of the drama as non-Aristotelian, just as Riemann introduced a non-Euclidian geometry. This analogy may bring out the fact that it is not a matter of competition between the theatrical forms in question. Riemann eliminated the parallel postulate; Brecht's drama eliminated the Aristotelian catharsis, the purging of the emotions through empathy with the stirring fate of the hero.

The special character of the relaxed interest of the audience for which the performances of the epic theater are intended is the fact that hardly any appeal is made to the empathy of the spectators. Instead, the art of the epic theater consists in producing astonishment rather than empathy. To put it succinctly: instead of identifying with the characters, the audience should be educated to be astonished at the circumstances under which they function.

The task of the epic theater, according to Brecht, is not so much the development of actions as the representation of conditions. This presentation does not mean reproduction as the theoreticians of Naturalism understood it. Rather, the truly important thing is to discover the conditions of life. (One might say just as well: to alienate [*verfremden*] them.) This discovery (alienation) of conditions takes place through the interruption of happenings. The most primitive example would be a family scene. Suddenly a stranger enters. The mother was just about to seize a bronze bust and hurl it at her daughter; the father was in the act of opening the window in order to call a policeman. At that moment the stranger appears in the doorway. This means that the stranger is confronted with the situation as with a startling picture: troubled faces, an open window, the furniture in disarray. But there are eyes to which even more ordinary scenes of middle-class life look almost equally startling.

*The quotable gesture*

In one of his didactic poems on dramatic art Brecht says: "The effect of every sentence was waited for and laid bare. And the waiting lasted until the crowd had carefully weighed our sentence." In short, the play was interrupted. One can go even further and remember that interruption is one of the fundamental devices of all structuring. It goes far beyond the sphere of art. To give only one example, it is the basis of quotation. To quote a text involves the interruption of its context. It is therefore understandable that the epic theater, being based on interruption, is, in a specific sense, a quotable one. There is nothing special about the quotability of its texts. It is different with the gestures which fit into the course of the play.

"Making gestures quotable" is one of the substantial achievements of the epic theater. An actor must be able to space his gestures the way a typesetter produces spaced type. This effect may be achieved, for instance, by an actor's quoting his own gesture on the stage. Thus we saw in *Happy End* how Carola Neher, acting a sergeant in the Salvation Army, sang, by way of proselytizing, a song in a sailors' tavern that was more appropriate there than it would have been in a church, and then had to quote this song and act out the gestures before a council of the Salvation Army. Similarly, in *The Measure Taken* the party tribunal is given not only the report of the comrades, but also the acting out of some of the gestures of the comrade they are accusing. What is a device of the subtlest kind in the epic theater generally becomes an immediate purpose in the specific case of the didactic play. Epic theater is by definition a gestic theater. For the more frequently we interrupt someone in the act of acting, the more gestures result.

In every instance, the epic theater is meant for the actors as much as for the spectators. The didactic play is a special case largely because it facilitates and suggests the interchange between audience and actors and vice versa through the extreme paucity of the mechanical equipment. Every spectator is enabled to become a participant. And it is indeed easier to play the "teacher" than the "hero."

*The didactic play*

In the first version of *Lindberghflug* (Lindbergh's Flight), which appeared in a periodical, the flier was still presented as a hero. That version was intended as his glorification. The second version—and this is revealing—owes its origin to the fact that Brecht revised himself. What enthusiasm there was on both continents on the days following this flight! But this enthusiasm petered out as a mere sensation. In *The Flight of the Lindberghs* Brecht endeavors to refract the spectrum of the "thrill" (*Erlebnis*) in order to derive from it the hues of "experience" (*Erfahrung*)—the experience that could be obtained only from Lindbergh's effort, not from the excitement of the public, and which was to be conveyed to "the Lindberghs."

T. E. Lawrence, the author of *The Seven Pillars of Wisdom*, wrote to Robert Graves when he joined the air force that such a step was for modern man what entering a monastery was for medieval man. In this remark we perceive the same tension that we find in *The Flight of the Lindberghs* and the later didactic plays. A clerical sternness is applied to instruction in a modern technique—here, that of aviation; later, that of the class struggle. This second application may be seen most fully in *Mother*. It was a particularly daring undertaking to keep a social drama free of the effects which empathy produces and which the audience was accustomed to. Brecht knew this and expressed it in an epistolary poem that he sent to a New York workingmen's theater when *Mother* was produced there. "We have been asked: Will a worker understand this? Will he be able to do without his accustomed opiate, his mental participation in someone else's uprising, the rise of others; the illusion which whips him up for a few hours and leaves him all the more exhausted, filled with vague memories and even vaguer hopes?"

Like the pictures in a film, epic theater moves in spurts. Its basic form is that of the shock with which the single, well-defined situations of the play collide. The songs, the captions, the lifeless conventions set off one situation from another. This brings about intervals which, if anything, impair the illusion of the audience and paralyze its readiness for empathy. These intervals are reserved for the spectators' critical reaction—to the actions of the players and to the way in which they are presented. As to the manner of presentation, the actor's task in the epic theater is to demonstrate through his acting that he is cool and relaxed. He too has hardly any use for empathy. For this kind of acting the "player" of the dramatic theater is not always fully prepared. Perhaps the most open-minded approach to epic theater is to think of it in terms of "putting on a show."

*The actor*

Brecht wrote: "The actor must show his subject, and he must show himself. Of course, he shows his subject by showing himself, and he shows himself by showing his subject. Although the two coincide, they must not coincide in such a way that the difference between the two tasks disappears." In other words: an actor should reserve for himself the possibility of stepping out of character artistically. At the proper moment he should insist on portraying a man who reflects about his part. It would be erroneous to think at such a moment of Romantic Irony, as employed by Tieck in his *Puss in Boots*. This irony has no didactic aim. Basically, it demonstrates only the philosophic sophistication of the author who, in writing his plays, always remembers that in the end the world may turn out to be a theater.

To what extent artistic and political interests coincide on the scene of epic theater will become manifest in the style of acting appropriate to this genre. A case in point is Brecht's cycle *The Private Life of the Master Race*. It is easy to see that if a German actor in exile were assigned the part of an SS man or a member of the People's Court, his feelings about it would be quite different from those of a devoted father and husband asked to portray Molière's Don Juan. For the former, empathy can hardly be regarded as an appropriate method, since he presumably cannot identify with the murderers of his fellow fighters. Another mode of performance, which calls for detachment, would in such cases be right and fitting and particularly successful. This is the epic stagecraft.

*Theater on a dais*    The aims of the epic theater can be defined more easily in terms of the stage than of a new drama. Epic theater allows for a circumstance which has been too little noticed. It may be called the filling in of the orchestra pit. The abyss which separates the players from the audience as it does the dead from the living; the abyss whose silence in a play heightens the sublimity, whose resonance in an opera heightens the intoxication—this abyss, of all elements of the theater the one that bears the most indelible traces of its ritual origin, has steadily decreased in significance. The stage is still raised, but it no longer rises from an unfathomable depth; it has become a dais. The didactic play and the epic theater are attempts to sit down on a dais.

# UNIT 2

## Revolution and Reaction: 1950-1975

DRAMA REQUIRES THE COLLABORATION of playwrights, actors, and audiences; the public structure of a theater site or building; and the social and political incentives and protections that make theatergoing attractive—it is an art deeply woven into the social fabric of a given culture and its history. But although we can still speak of the "London theater" or of "American drama," terms like these have become, in the era after World War II, a critical convenience for reducing the dynamic variety of contemporary theater to the fictional boundaries of a single "national" culture. Theater still requires the support, work, and energy of its local community, and in many respects the political work of theater takes place only at the local level. Yet at the same time, the postwar dramatic repertory is a global one. Irish playwright Samuel Beckett's first play, *Waiting for Godot,* was written in French and first produced in Paris; Sam Shepard, an American, first staged several of his plays in London; many Eastern European and Latin American playwrights have been forced by censorship and political repression to smuggle their plays to Europe or the United States to be staged; the South African playwright Athol Fugard has premiered several plays in the United States; the Nigerian Wole Soyinka is regularly produced throughout the world.

In the postwar period, the impact of film and television forced the theater to work to define what kinds of performance are specific to the stage, how live dramatic performance can offer something unique, something not already available in other performance media. For this reason, perhaps, theater and drama since 1950 have necessarily been "experimental," working to develop new kinds of plays, new practices of stage production, and new theatrical experiences for their audiences. Much as the proscenium theaters of the early twentieth century gave way to other, more flexible kinds of theater spaces, so dramatic writing has become much more varied and experimental. Even stage realism—the mode of Ibsen and Chekhov, O'Neill and Williams—has undergone an important reworking in the plays of Sam Shepard, Harold Pinter, Maria Irene Fornes, and others.

Here, we can identify three patterns of innovation as a way of organizing our thinking about the diversity of the postwar stage. One strategy—inspired most directly by Antonin Artaud's **THEATER OF CRUELTY**—attacks the notion that the theater is essentially a *representational* medium, emphasizing instead the *experiential* aspect of theater. Rather than staging images of some fictive world to an audience of passive spectators, this kind of theater works to structure the *present experience* of the audience in new ways, as in the participatory and ritualistic theater experiments of the 1960s and 1970s. The influence of Artaud's assault on representation is evident in several dimensions of the theater of the 1950s and after: in the emphasis on the arbitrariness of experience of absurdist plays like Beckett's, in the physicalized "choreopoems" of Ntozake Shange, and in the violent visual spectacles of Jean Genet.

The second mode of innovation, **THEATER OF THE ABSURD,** originated as a new form of playwriting rather than as theatrical experimentation. The plays of Samuel Beckett, Eugène Ionesco, Václav Havel, Edward Albee, Harold Pinter, and others create a strangely dislocated dramatic world, in which arbitrary or "absurd" events both confront and mystify the characters, and often seem like allegories of our own indirect and confused lives.

While Artaud inspired an existential or experiential theater, Bertolt Brecht—whose work became widely known and imitated only after World War II—inspired a different kind of assault on the conventions of realistic theater. For contemporary **POLITICAL THEATER** also criticizes the notion of "representation," but in different terms than those voiced by Artaud or by the theater of the absurd. For "representation" is a word with two senses; in "representing" a picture of the world, the arts necessarily claim that their images are "representative" in some way. Political theater frequently shows how a social or political order uses its power to "represent" others coercively—for example, by depicting those others through demeaning or limiting stereotypes. For this reason, political theater uses live performance to change oppressive attitudes concealed in conventional ideas of representation.

Of course, no play fits easily or fully into any of these three categories, but to think of the drama of the postwar period as raising questions of our existential or our political relation to the theater—and so to the world—provides a powerful way of opening that drama to our understanding. Each of these modes of theater creates a different relationship between the stage and its audience, and we should examine each of them in some detail.

## Artaud and the Theater of Cruelty

The writings of Antonin Artaud, particularly the essays collected in the volume *The Theater and Its Double* (written in the late 1920s and 1930s, published in France in 1938, translated to English in 1958), have had an extraordinary impact on the theater of the late twentieth century. Like many innovators of his generation—think of Brecht or Pirandello—Artaud worked to undermine the notion that the theater can show its audiences only realistic vignettes of daily life. Instead, Artaud argued that the theater should alter the balance between presentation—the actual, immediate activities of actors and audiences, their *presence* in the theater—and representation, the fictive "drama" that had seemed to define the purpose and scope of theater. Artaud—who used the term *theater of cruelty* for this project—advocated transforming the theater into an all-consuming spectacle, akin both to rituals like the mass and to public festivals, in which the boundaries between acting and observing, actor and spectator, fiction and reality, conscious and unconscious could be broken or transgressed. The idea that the theater would "communicate," but not through rational means, is captured in one of Artaud's most powerful metaphors for this nearly unimaginable theater: the plague. Artaud envisioned a theater that would transmit its experiences corporeally, through the body, like disease, like mystical wisdom, alchemically transforming all of its participants. To avoid staging conventional dramas, Artaud called for a theater of "no more masterpieces," one that would use the dramatic text to transform the relations between stage and spectator by making the production a total experience—visual, auditory, gustatory, olfactory, tactile, physical— for the audience.

In his landmark book, *The Empty Space*, the stage director Peter Brook remarked that "Artaud applied is Artaud betrayed," and it is true that Artaud's sense of theater is deeply metaphorical, a kind of theater experience that is almost unimaginable to us, and certainly not imaginable to us as "theater." And Artaud rarely offers a practical description of how this theater could come into being. Instead, the value and influence of Artaud's writing has been indirect and inspirational, bearing in a variety of tangential ways on kinds of theater that are not in any literal sense "Artaudian." In that Artaud imagines a theater of *presence*—not of re-presentation—involving the audience in an experience rather than showing them a picture, his theater comes into contact with several very different kinds of innovation. The experimental theater of the 1960s and 1970s is the most direct descendant—and betrayal—of Artaud, for theater companies in Europe, the U. S., and elsewhere saw in Artaud's rejection of Western cultural forms the beginnings of a more political agenda. Taking Artaud's call for a theater that suspended the boundaries between theater and "life," companies developed a participatory, "environmental," vaguely orgiastic mode of theater attempting (in Artaud's words) to make "use of everything—gestures, sounds, words, screams, light, darkness." Jerzy Grotowski's Polish Laboratory Theater—founded in Opole in 1959, then moved to Wroclaw in 1965—was perhaps the most influential of these companies. In a series of famous productions that toured the world—densely montagelike productions of Marlowe's *Doctor Faustus* and

Calderón's *The Constant Prince,* as well as *Akropolis,* and *Apocalypsis cum figuris*—Grotowski sought to use performance to bring about a direct, unmediated contact between actors and spectators, a "total act" that required an ascetic physical and spiritual discipline from his performers. Grotowski called this project **POOR THEATER**—outlined in his 1968 book *Towards a Poor Theater*—because it reduced theater to its "essential" relationship: "the actor-spectator relationship of perceptual, direct, 'live' communion."

Grotowski's work was widely influential in the late 1960s and early 1970s. Events like the Living Theater's *Paradise Now* (1968) or The Performance Group's remaking of Euripides' *The Bacchae* as *Dionysus in 69* used nudity, direct address, and audience participation to instigate a more ritualized, nonrepresentational, experiential performance. But Artaud's conception of theater also stands distantly behind a variety of more formally constructed plays: the fusion of dance, music, and poetry in Ntozake Shange's work; the dislocating imagery of Beckett and Fornes; Handke's explicitly antitheatrical scourging of the audience in *Offending the Audience;* perhaps even the ritualized, hallucinatory violence of Duras's *India Song*. Of course, as *written* plays, "masterpieces," these plays are specifically opposed to the ideals of Artaud's unrealizable theater, while at the same time exploring part of the terrain opened by Artaud's vision.

## Theater of the Absurd

Coined by the theater critic Martin Esslin in 1961, the phrase *theater of the absurd* tries to capture the special irrationality and unpredictability of a strain of dramatic writing of the late 1950s and 1960s. Esslin was among the first to read absurdist drama as bringing the dominant mode of philosophical discourse of the 1950s—**EXISTENTIALISM** in the mode of Jean-Paul Sartre and Albert Camus—to the stage. Arguing that "existence precedes essence," Sartre conceives human action in theatrical terms; we are forced to choose a course of action, a life, from a number of alternatives, none of which has greater innate moral or ethical value. In a world of arbitrary choice, how we become *engaged* in action determines whether we have pursued an authentic, self-determined life or have succumbed to "bad faith"—choosing to act for conventional reasons, in order to please the social audience. Taking as his keynote Beckett's famous play *Waiting for Godot* (1953)—a play in which two Chaplinesque tramps wait for a mysterious man named Godot, who never arrives—Esslin located an existentialist attitude at the heart of absurdist drama. By rejecting the sense of causality found in realistic plays, for example, absurd plays resist the notion that it is possible to find the causes for events either in the environment or in the psychological motives of the characters themselves. Instead, theater of the absurd tends to be about a world in which inexplicable, arbitrary, or irrational events simply happen. Although these events usually seem to be part of some kind of order or scheme, it is an order that neither the characters onstage nor the audience in the theater can quite grasp. As Hamm says in Beckett's play *Endgame* (1957), "Something is taking its course," but neither the characters nor the audience are ever sure what that "something" is. In Eugène Ionesco's play *Rhinoceros* (1960), the inhabitants of a small French village begin to turn inexplicably into rhinoceroses; in each act of Boris Vian's *The Empire Builders* (1959), a family moves to a smaller room in an apartment building, always accompanied by a mysterious, bandaged figure; in Slawomir Mrozek's *Striptease* (1961), two men are commanded by a huge, silent finger to remove their clothes and don huge conical hats that conceal and blind them. As Esslin suggests, this drama insists that the fictions we use to make sense of our world—ideas of order, causality, rationality—are just that: fictions imposed on a reality whose meanings remain fugitive.

Absurdist drama treats its audience somewhat differently than realistic plays do, rejecting the "dramatic irony" of the traditional theater, in which the audience understands more than the characters onstage. The theater of the absurd refuses to provide this privilege to its spectators. We are as baffled and frustrated by our attempts to make the events mean something as the characters are; "Mean something!" a character remarks in *Endgame*, "You and I, mean something! (*Brief laugh*)." Our *present* experience as an audience shares this "absurd" quality. In the theater, we do not just observe the "absurd" drama onstage; we are forced to undergo it, to live it through. This is where absurdist drama most closely approximates the power of existentialism. Watching the play, the audience is similarly cast in a position of having to choose, to interpret events that seem otherwise arbitrary, undecideable. We have to *decide* the meaning of our being in the theater, without the comfort, solace, or guidance of some transcendent, predetermined worldview.

Perhaps because its **ALLEGORY** of the arbitrariness of existence often involves some mysterious, omnipotent power just offstage, absurd drama has rapidly become a vehicle for political theater. In plays like Harold Pinter's *One for the Road* (1984), Beckett's *Catastrophe* (1982), Tom Stoppard's *Every Good Boy Deserves Favour* (1977), Athol Fugard, John Kani, and Winston Ntshona's *The Island* (1973), absurdist dramatic style becomes the vehicle for a critique of the absurdities of authoritarian state power. Of course, as Brecht might have asked, "which is the pretext for what?" Is absurdist dramatic style a useful instrument for criticizing the mystified authority of repressive state regimes? Or is the theater of the absurd complicit in some deeper way with the authoritarian structure of such oppression?

## Political Theater

Much as theater of the absurd works to make the spectators' situation in the theater an extension of the characters' situation on the stage, political theater since Brecht has worked to make the audience's performance in the theater a recognizably political one. By fragmenting the stage space, by showing how the illusion is made rather than concealing its means of production, and by involving the audience more overtly in deciding the meaning of the play's events, the theater is shown to be a political instrument. Like television, newspapers, universities, the courts, and so on, the theater is an institution that produces the ideas and images with which we govern our lives. Both the example of Brecht's plays and his challenging theory of performance have been absorbed and redefined by the world theater. In common with theater of the absurd, political theater works to resist and complicate realistic representation, the "slice of life" of Ibsen, Chekhov, and Williams. But instead of staging an arbitrarily unreal and absurd world, political theater examines "representative" images of reality: Who makes those images? Who benefits from them? Who is injured, governed, or oppressed by them? How do they help to maintain the social status quo?

For this reason, much political theater connects representation onstage with representation in society, showing how various social groups—women, gay men, lesbians, ethnic and racial groups, the poor—have been staged in society and in the theater. A fundamental assumption of political theater is that these stereotypes are part of the larger system of discrimination that operates in society, and that they reveal the dominant attitudes of those who govern, control, or influence society from positions of power. In plays like Jean Genet's *The Blacks* (1958), Adrienne Kennedy's *Funnyhouse of a Negro* (1964), Luis Valdez's *Los Vendidos* (1965), Wole Soyinka's *The Lion and the Jewel* (1963), Edward Bond's *Bingo* (1974), and Ntozake Shange's *spell #7* (1979), the racial and ethnic conflicts informing contemporary society and culture are explored in very different ways: in relation to colonialism, to white myths of black identity, to women's experience. These plays are very different in style, ranging from Valdez's use of "Brechtian" alienation to Shange's "choreopoem" and Genet's ritualized spectacle. It is not a single point of view or a single dramatic style that defines political theater, but the use of theatrical representation itself as a way to analyze representation in society at large.

While providing a powerful analytical tool for distinguishing modes of drama and performance, such categories are nonetheless deeply artificial: the most important theaters of the postwar period have tended to adopt a variety of theatrical strategies for producing new and powerful theater. In Germany, for example, the influence of Brechtian epic theater has been a dominant force. Brecht returned to East Berlin and opened his company, the Berliner Ensemble, in 1949 with a production of *Mother Courage and Her Children.* The company moved into their new theater—the Theater-am-Schiffbauerdamm—in 1954, and began a series of successful European tours shortly thereafter: to Paris in 1954 and 1955, to London in 1956 shortly after Brecht's death. The influence of Berliner Ensemble productions on stagecraft is self-evident, but Brecht's effect on playwriting has been equally profound. Think of Heinar Kipphardt's dramatization of the Oppenheimer trials in *In the Matter of J. Robert Oppenheimer* (1964), or Rolf Hochhuth's investigation of the role of the Catholic Church in prolonging the war and the genocide in the Nazi death camps in *The Deputy* (1963), or in different ways in the plays of Max Frisch or Heiner Müller. Again, these lines of influence are never pure. The Swiss playwright Friedrich Dürrenmatt's *The Physicists* (1962) might be read as an absurdist rewrite of Brecht's *Galileo*; Peter Weiss's *The Persecution and Assassination of Jean-Paul Marat, as Performed by the Inmates of the Asylum of Charenton under the Direction of the Marquis de Sade* (1964; usually called simply *Marat/Sade*) uses a number of "alienating" devices to foreground the *produced* nature of political discussion in the play, while at the same time incorporating a nearly Artaudian interest in using the actors' bodies to signify in new and disturbing registers.

Similarly, the rise of off-Broadway and off-off-Broadway theaters in the United States militated against the discrete compartmentalization of theatrical styles. Although the Living Theater—founded by Julian Beck and Judith Malina in 1946—later performed experimental mass spectacles, their first success (Jack Gelber's *The Connection,* 1954) was relatively conventional, realistic drama about a group of junkies that nonetheless involved its audiences immediately in the *action* of the drama and its performance. In their production, the characters (or was it the actors?) frequently left the stage to shoot up. The Performance Group's interest in **ENVIRONMENTAL THEATER,** inspired by Grotowski's intermixing of stage and audience areas, enabled classic plays to be produced in new performative configurations; in TPG's production of Brecht's *Mother Courage,* Courage served food to the audience from her wagon during the intermission. Theaters like Ellen Stewart's Cafe La Mama, founded in 1961, and the Judson Poets Theater, founded in 1964 by Maria Irene Fornes and Al Carmines, were more identified with producing new, avant-garde work than with a single dramatic or theatrical style. Some theaters invoked a more explicitly Brechtian esthetic to develop a theater of political action: Luis Valdez and El Teatro Campesino is perhaps the best example of a theater working to advance the cause and interests of its initial audience, the migrant farmworkers of California. African-American theaters in the 1950s and 1960s—Amiri Baraka's Spirit House (founded 1965), the New Lafayette Theater (1967–73), and the Negro Ensemble Company (founded 1968)—adapted Brechtian, African, African-American, and realist performance traditions to address the politics of race in the U. S.

The impact of Brecht in Britain is easily traced to the Berliner Ensemble's brief "season" of productions in London in 1956. By the early 1960s, several important plays in the Brechtian mode had been staged to much acclaim: John Osborne's *The Entertainer* (1957), John Arden's *Sergeant Musgrave's Dance* (1959), Joan Littlewood and Theatre Workshop's *Oh, What a Lovely War!* (1963). At the same time, though, Harold Pinter was elaborating a vaguely disorienting, threatening form of realistic theater, in plays like *The Birthday Party* (1958), *The Caretaker* (1960), and *The Homecoming* (1965), and Peter Brook and actors from the Royal Shakespeare Company were experimenting with notions of an Artaudian "theater of cruelty" in preparation for their production of Weiss's *Marat/Sade*. Indeed, by the 1970s and 1980s, the strategies of Brechtian political theater and a more visceral, Artaudian approach to performance became fused in the work of a younger generation of playwrights, as concerned to stand apart from Brecht as they were to develop a new and powerful mode of political theater: Peter Barnes, Edward Bond, Howard Brenton, Caryl Churchill, Sarah Daniels, David Edgar, Trevor Griffiths, David Hare, Hanif Kureishi, Timberlake Wertenbaker, among others.

Theater in the immediate postwar period confronted a new, often terrifying, disorienting world: a world of "existential" rootlessness; of institutionalized racial, ethnic, gender, and sexual oppression; of colonial exploitation. The Cold War, Vietnam, the struggle for civil and human rights: given the absence of a comfortable worldview, it is not surprising that the monocular "perspective" of stage realism should be strategically, purposefully shattered. In the 1950s, 1960s, and 1970s, playwrights worked to develop new dramatic practices, and new ways of constructing experience in the theater, as one way of responding to the increasingly fragmentary nature of experience in the world beyond the stage.

# Samuel Beckett

Samuel Beckett (1906–1989) is the most influential European dramatist of the postwar period. Born near Dublin, Ireland, Beckett was educated at Trinity College, Dublin, where he studied modern languages. Taking his B. A. in 1928, Beckett received an appointment as *lecteur* at l'École Normale Supérieure in Paris. Also in Paris, Beckett met the Irish novelist James Joyce. Beckett assisted Joyce (who was nearly blind) in a variety of ways, and became a close friend; Joyce also exerted a profound influence on Beckett's writing. Beckett contributed an essay entitled "Dante . . . Bruno. Vico . . Joyce" to a volume on Joyce's *Finnegans Wake* (1929). Throughout the 1930s, Beckett was associated with Joyce and with a variety of avant-garde movements in Paris. He wrote a series of poems—including the prize-winning "Whoroscope"—as well as a study of Proust (1931), the volume of short stories *More Pricks than Kicks* (1934), and the novel *Murphy* (1938). Although Beckett returned briefly to Ireland on a few occasions, he had settled permanently in Paris. During World War II, Beckett served in the French Resistance. He was discovered by the Nazis and forced to flee Paris in 1942. He worked in the unoccupied zone of southern France for the remainder of the war, where he wrote the novel *Watt* (1953). After the war, Beckett received the Croix de Guerre and the Médaille de la Résistance for his services; he began to write exclusively in French, starting work on a major trilogy of novels—*Molloy* (1951), *Malone Dies* (1951), and *The Unnameable* (1953).

Beckett had experimented with drama during the 1930s and 1940s, but his first staged play, *Waiting for Godot* (first written in French, as *En attendant Godot*), produced at the tiny Théâtre de Babylone in January 1953, impelled him in a new direction. Although Beckett continued to write fiction—including *From an Abandoned Work* (1956), *How It Is* (1964), *Imagination Dead Imagine* (1965), and *Company* (1979)—his major writing of the 1960s, 1970s, and 1980s was for the theater. His second play, *Endgame,* also written in French, was produced in 1957 and was followed by a series of challenging works for the stage: *Krapp's Last Tape* (1958), *Happy Days* (1962), *Play* (1963), *Not I* (1972), *Footfalls* (1975), *Rockaby* (1981), and *Catastrophe* (1982). For his extraordinarily diverse and influential body of work, Beckett won the Nobel Prize for literature in 1970. Beckett also wrote several plays for radio and television, as well as a film starring Buster Keaton, *Film* (1965). Beginning in the mid-1960s, Beckett directed productions of his plays, and several productions he directed in France and in Germany now have the status of classics—something like Elia Kazan's productions of Tennessee Williams's plays or Stanislavski's productions of Chekhov.

Beckett's impact on the contemporary theater can hardly be overestimated and can be seen in the work of Sam Shepard, Maria Irene Fornes, Harold Pinter, Václav Havel, Tom Stoppard, and many others. *Waiting for Godot* signaled new possibilities for stage action—or inaction—and developed the implications of Chekhov's static stage in a more symbolic direction. Each of Beckett's plays explores the nature and limitations of its medium in new and challenging ways. Endgame refigures the claustral box of realistic drama, for its characters are trapped in a room of endless—or possibly ending—routine. In *Play,* Beckett puts three urns onstage, from which three heads emerge to deliver, more or less simultaneously, a jarring, repetitive monologue of seduction and betrayal. Once the play has finished, Beckett directs his performers—and his audience—to "Repeat play," and so calls the relationship between actors and spectators, theater and reality into question. If we cannot leave the theater when the play is over, is it possible that there is no way out of the purgatory on the stage and in the auditorium? This sense that the self is always in flight is the theme of several of Beckett's later plays. In *Not I,* for instance, all that the audience sees is a Mouth eight feet above the stage, reciting an endless narrative in which she avoids claiming the speech as her own; in *Ohio Impromptu,* an identical reader and listener relate a painful narrative of loss, in which it is unclear whether they are two individuals or parts of a single person. The power of Beckett's spare, minimalist theater, the beauty of his sculptural use of actors and stage space, and the harsh exigency of the action of his plays have transformed the stage of our time.

## Endgame (1957)

*Endgame* is Beckett's second full-length play to reach the stage; although its simplicity and repetitiveness are in some ways reminiscent of *Waiting for Godot,* the tone of *Endgame* is bleaker, harsher. As Beckett wrote to Alan Schneider, the play's first American director, Endgame's power is "the power of the text to claw."

The "endgame" of a chess match is the final portion of the game, at which either a checkmate or a stalemate has become inevitable. In *Endgame,* Beckett literalizes the uncertainty of the endgame—will the tortuous nothingness of the characters' lives continue indefinitely, move after move, or will it somehow end? Although some critics have taken the "shelter" and the empty landscape outside it as an indication that the play takes place in a bomb shelter after a nuclear bombing, *Endgame* seems to present a microcosm of postmodern life, in which the futile search for fugitive "meanings" raises the despairing feeling that our lives are meaningless, "absurd" after all. Hamm is a kind of ham actor, and recalls Shakespeare's Richard III ("My kingdom for a nightman") and Prospero ("Our revels now are ended"), as well as perhaps King Lear and Hamlet in his performance. Hamm is perhaps the first **POSTMODERN** dramatic hero, less a full "character" than a pastiche of dramatic roles and possibilities, which exist now only in bits and pieces, recollected fragments (on *pastiche,* see Fredric Jameson's essay, Unit 4). Hamm's blindness also recalls both Oedipus—who also struggled with his father—and Ham the son of Noah, who was cursed when he saw his father naked. Hamm continually reminds us that his performance—it's full of asides, a "last soliloquy," and many self-regarding comments on Hamm's success or failure—is an attempt to impose meaning on the process of the play's action. This recollection of the dramatic and literary tradition also points to the problematic place—or absence—of history in *Endgame.* If there is a kind of past ("Once!") in *Endgame,* it is recalled most clearly by Hamm's parents. Nagg and Nell, legless in their garbage cans, describe an earlier, more sentimental or romantic era, when couples rode tandems in the Ardennes and rowed on Lake Como. Overall, though, time seems to be an endless present moment in *Endgame,* a moment disconnected from the past that once gave it meaning, and from the future which gave it closure. It may be that the play is postnuclear (though Beckett's draft manuscripts suggest that the inspiration was really a war hospital), but this setting is less important than the sense of time that this tiny world contains. For *Endgame* is finally about time and its passing, the painfully slow passage of moment to moment, and its finality once it is past.

*Endgame* was originally written in French as *Fin de partie,* and was rewritten into English by Beckett himself; there are several small differences in dialogue and action between the two versions.

# —Endgame—
## Samuel Beckett

*Bare interior.*
*Grey light.*
*Left and right back, high up, two small windows, curtains drawn.*
*Front right, a door. Hanging near door, its face to wall, a picture.*
*Front left, touching each other, covered with an old sheet, two ashbins.*
*Center, in an armchair on castors, covered with an old sheet, Hamm.*
*Motionless by the door, his eyes fixed on Hamm, Clov. Very red face.*
*Brief tableau.*

*Clov goes and stands under window left. Stiff, staggering walk. He looks up at window left. He turns and looks at window right. He goes and stands under window right. He looks up at window right. He turns and looks at window left. He goes out, comes back immediately with a small step-ladder, carries it over and sets it down under window left, gets up on it, draws back curtain. He gets down, takes six steps (for example) towards window right, goes back for ladder, carries it over and sets it down under window right, gets up on it, draws back curtain. He gets down, takes three steps towards window left, goes back for ladder, carries it over and sets it down under window left, gets up on it, looks out of window. Brief laugh. He gets down, takes one step towards window right, goes back for ladder, carries it over and sets it down under window right, gets up on it, looks out of window. Brief laugh. He gets down, goes with ladder towards ashbins, halts, turns, carries back ladder and sets it down under window right, goes to ashbins, removes sheet covering them, folds it over his arm. He raises one lid, stoops and looks into bin. Brief laugh. He closes lid. Same with other bin. He goes to Hamm, removes sheet covering him, folds it over his arm. In a dressing-gown, a stiff toque on his head, a large blood-stained handkerchief over his face, a whistle hanging from his neck, a rug over his knees, thick socks on his feet, Hamm seems to be asleep. Clov looks him over. Brief laugh. He goes to door, halts, turns towards auditorium.*

CLOV: *(fixed gaze, tonelessly)* Finished, it's finished, nearly finished, it must be nearly finished.

*(Pause.)*

Grain upon grain, one by one, and one day, suddenly, there's a heap, a little heap, the impossible heap.

*(Pause.)*

I can't be punished any more.

*(Pause.)*

I'll go now to my kitchen, ten feet by ten feet by ten feet, and wait for him to whistle me.

*(Pause.)*

Nice dimensions, nice proportions, I'll lean on the table, and look at the wall, and wait for him to whistle me.

*(He remains a moment motionless, then goes out. He comes back immediately, goes to window right, takes up the ladder and carries it out. Pause. Hamm stirs. He yawns under the handkerchief. He removes the handkerchief from his face. Very red face. Black glasses.)*

HAMM: Me—  10

*(he yawns)*

—to play.

*(He holds the handkerchief spread out before him.)*

Old stancher!

*(He takes off his glasses, wipes his eyes, his face, the glasses, puts them on again, folds the handkerchief and puts it back neatly in the breast-pocket of his dressing-gown. He clears his throat, joins the tips of his fingers.)*

Can there be misery—

*(he yawns)*

—loftier than mine? No doubt. Formerly. But now?

*(Pause.)*

My father?

*(Pause.)*

My mother?

*(Pause.)*

My . . . dog?

*(Pause.)*

Oh I am willing to believe they suffer as much as such creatures can suffer. But does that mean their sufferings equal mine? No doubt.  20

*(Pause.)*

No, all is a—

*(he yawns)*

—bsolute,

*(proudly)*

the bigger a man is the fuller he is.

*(Pause. Gloomily.)*

And the emptier.

(*He sniffs.*)

   Clov!

(*Pause.*)

   No, alone.

(*Pause.*)

   What dreams! Those forests!

(*Pause.*)

   Enough, it's time it ended, in the shelter too.

(*Pause.*)

   And yet I hesitate, I hesitate to . . . to end. Yes, there it is, it's
30  time it ended and yet I hesitate to—

(*he yawns*)

   —to end.

(*Yawns.*)

   God, I'm tired, I'd be better off in bed.

(*He whistles. Enter Clov immediately. He halts beside the
chair.*)

   You pollute the air!

(*Pause.*)

   Get me ready, I'm going to bed.
CLOV: I've just got you up.
HAMM: And what of it?
CLOV: I can't be getting you up and putting you to bed every
   five minutes, I have things to do.

(*Pause.*)

HAMM: Did you ever see my eyes?
40 CLOV: No.
HAMM: Did you never have the curiosity, while I was sleeping,
   to take off my glasses and look at my eyes?
CLOV: Pulling back the lids?

(*Pause.*)

   No.
HAMM: One of these days I'll show them to you.

(*Pause.*)

   It seems they've gone all white.

(*Pause.*)

   What time is it?
CLOV: The same as usual.
HAMM: (*gesture towards window right*) Have you looked?
50 CLOV: Yes.
HAMM: Well?
CLOV: Zero.
HAMM: It'd need to rain.
CLOV: It won't rain.

(*Pause.*)

HAMM: Apart from that, how do you feel?

CLOV: I don't complain.
HAMM: You feel normal?
CLOV: (*irritably*) I tell you I don't complain.
HAMM: I feel a little queer.

(*Pause.*)

   Clov!                        60
CLOV: Yes.
HAMM: Have you not had enough?
CLOV: Yes!

(*Pause.*)

HAMM: Of this . . . this . . . thing.
CLOV: I always had.

(*Pause.*)

   Not you?
HAMM: (*gloomily*) Then there's no reason for it to change.
CLOV: It may end.

(*Pause.*)

   All life long the same questions, the same answers.
HAMM: Get me ready.                   70

(*Clov does not move.*)

   Go and get the sheet.

(*Clov does not move.*)

   Clov!
CLOV: Yes.
HAMM: I'll give you nothing more to eat.
CLOV: Then we'll die.
HAMM: I'll give you just enough to keep you from dying. You'll
   be hungry all the time.
CLOV: Then we won't die.

(*Pause.*)

   I'll go and get the sheet.

(*He goes towards the door.*)

HAMM: No!                        80

(*Clov halts.*)

   I'll give you one biscuit per day.

(*Pause.*)

   One and a half.

(*Pause.*)

   Why do you stay with me?
CLOV: Why do you keep me?
HAMM: There's no one else.
CLOV: There's nowhere else.

(*Pause.*)

HAMM: You're leaving me all the same.
CLOV: I'm trying.
HAMM: You don't love me.
CLOV: No.                        90
HAMM: You loved me once.

CLOV: Once!

HAMM: I've made you suffer too much.

(*Pause.*)

Haven't I?

CLOV: It's not that.

HAMM: (*shocked*) I haven't made you suffer too much?

CLOV: Yes!

HAMM: (*relieved*) Ah you gave me a fright!

(*Pause. Coldly.*)

Forgive me.

(*Pause. Louder.*)

100   I said, Forgive me.

CLOV: I heard you.

(*Pause.*)

Have you bled?

HAMM: Less.

(*Pause.*)

Is it not time for my pain-killer?

CLOV: No.

(*Pause.*)

HAMM: How are your eyes?

CLOV: Bad.

HAMM: How are your legs?

CLOV: Bad.

110 HAMM: But you can move.

CLOV: Yes.

HAMM: (*violently*) Then move!

(*Clov goes to back wall, leans against it with his forehead and hands.*)

Where are you?

CLOV: Here.

HAMM: Come back!

(*Clov returns to his place beside the chair.*)

Where are you?

CLOV: Here.

HAMM: Why don't you kill me?

CLOV: I don't know the combination of the cupboard.

(*Pause.*)

120 HAMM: Go and get two bicycle-wheels.

CLOV: There are no more bicycle-wheels.

HAMM: What have you done with your bicycle?

CLOV: I never had a bicycle.

HAMM: The thing is impossible.

CLOV: When there were still bicycles I wept to have one. I crawled at your feet. You told me to go to hell. Now there are none.

HAMM: And your rounds? When you inspected my paupers. Always on foot?

130 CLOV: Sometimes on horse.

(*The lid of one of the bins lifts and the hands of Nagg appear, gripping the rim. Then his head emerges. Nightcap. Very white face. Nagg yawns, then listens.*)

I'll leave you, I have things to do.

HAMM: In your kitchen?

CLOV: Yes.

HAMM: Outside of here it's death.

(*Pause.*)

All right, be off.

(*Exit Clov. Pause.*)

We're getting on.

NAGG: Me pap!

HAMM: Accursed progenitor!

NAGG: Me pap!

HAMM: The old folks at home! No decency left! Guzzle, guzzle, 140 that's all they think of.

(*He whistles. Enter Clov. He halts beside the chair.*)

Well! I thought you were leaving me.

CLOV: Oh not just yet, not just yet.

NAGG: Me pap!

HAMM: Give him his pap.

CLOV: There's no more pap.

HAMM: (*to* NAGG) Do you hear that? There's no more pap. You'll never get any more pap.

HAMM: I want me pap!

HAMM: Give him a biscuit. 150

(*Exit Clov.*)

Accursed fornicator! How are your stumps?

NAGG: Never mind me stumps.

(*Enter Clov with biscuit.*)

CLOV: I'm back again, with the biscuit.

(*He gives biscuit to Nagg who fingers it, sniffs it.*)

NAGG: (*plaintively*) What is it?

CLOV: Spratt's medium.

NAGG: (*as before*) It's hard! I can't!

HAMM: Bottle him!

(*Clov pushes Nagg back into the bin, closes the lid.*)

CLOV: (*returning to his place beside the chair*) If age but knew!

HAMM: Sit on him!

CLOV: I can't sit. 160

HAMM: True. And I can't stand.

CLOV: So it is.

HAMM: Every man his specialty.

(*Pause.*)

No phone calls?

(*Pause.*)

Don't we laugh?

CLOV: (*after reflection*) I don't feel like it.

HAMM: (*after reflection*) Nor I.

(*Pause.*)

Clov!

CLOV: Yes.

170  HAMM: Nature has forgotten us.

CLOV: There's no more nature.

HAMM: No more nature! You exaggerate.

CLOV: In the vicinity.

HAMM: But we breathe, we change! We lose our hair, our teeth! Our bloom! Our ideals!

CLOV: Then she hasn't forgotten us.

HAMM: But you say there is none.

CLOV: (*sadly*) No one that ever lived ever thought so crooked as we.

180  HAMM: We do what we can.

CLOV: We shouldn't.

(*Pause.*)

HAMM: You're a bit of all right, aren't you?

CLOV: A smithereen.

(*Pause.*)

HAMM: This is slow work.

(*Pause.*)

Is it not time for my pain-killer?

CLOV: No.

(*Pause.*)

I'll leave you, I have things to do.

HAMM: In your kitchen?

CLOV: Yes.

190  HAMM: What, I'd like to know.

CLOV: I look at the wall.

HAMM: The wall! And what do you see on your wall? Mene, mene? Naked bodies?

CLOV: I see my light dying.

HAMM: Your light dying! Listen to that! Well, it can die just as well here, *your* light. Take a look at me and then come back and tell me what you think of *your* light.

(*Pause.*)

CLOV: You shouldn't speak to me like that.

(*Pause.*)

HAMM: (*coldly*) Forgive me.

(*Pause. Louder.*)

200     I said, Forgive me.

CLOV: I heard you.

(*The lid of Nagg's bin lifts. His hands appear, gripping the rim. Then his head emerges. In his mouth the biscuit. He listens.*)

HAMM: Did your seeds come up?

CLOV: No.

HAMM: Did you scratch round them to see if they had sprouted?

CLOV: They haven't sprouted.

HAMM: Perhaps it's still too early.

CLOV: If they were going to sprout they would have sprouted.

(*Violently.*)

They'll never sprout!

(*Pause. Nagg takes biscuit in his hand.*)

HAMM: This is not much fun.                                          210

(*Pause.*)

But that's always the way at the end of the day, isn't it, Clov?

CLOV: Always.

HAMM: It's the end of the day like any other day, isn't it, Clov?

CLOV: Looks like it.

(*Pause.*)

HAMM: (*anguished*) What's happening, what's happening?

CLOV: Something is taking its course.

(*Pause.*)

HAMM: All right, be off.

(*He leans back in his chair, remains motionless. Clov does not move, heaves a great groaning sigh. Hamm sits up.*)

I thought I told you to be off.

CLOV: I'm trying.

(*He goes to the door, halts.*)

Ever since I was whelped.                                            220

(*Exit Clov.*)

HAMM: We're getting on.

(*He leans back in his chair, remains motionless. Nagg knocks on the lid of the other bin. Pause. He knocks harder. The lid lifts and the hands of Nell appear, gripping the rim. Then her head emerges. Lace cap. Very white face.*)

NELL: What is it, my pet?

(*Pause.*)

Time for love?

NAGG: Were you asleep?

NELL: Oh no!

NAGG: Kiss me.

NELL: We can't.

NAGG: Try.

(*Their heads strain towards each other, fail to meet, fall apart again.*)

NELL: Why this farce, day after day?

(*Pause.*)

NAGG: I've lost me tooth.                                            230

NELL: When?

NAGG: I had it yesterday.

NELL: (*elegiac*) Ah yesterday!

(*They turn painfully towards each other.*)

NAGG: Can you see me?

NELL: Hardly. And you?

NAGG: What?

NELL: Can you see me?

NAGG: Hardly.

NELL: So much the better, so much the better.

240 NAGG: Don't say that.

(*Pause.*)

Our sight has failed.

NELL: Yes.

(*Pause. They turn away from each other.*)

NAGG: Can you hear me?

NELL: Yes. And you?

NAGG: Yes.

(*Pause.*)

Our hearing hasn't failed.

NELL: Our what?

NAGG: Our hearing.

NELL: No.

(*Pause.*)

250    Have you anything else to say to me?

NAGG: Do you remember—

NELL: No.

NAGG: When we crashed on our tandem and lost our shanks.

(*They laugh heartily.*)

NELL: It was in the Ardennes.

(*They laugh less heartily.*)

NAGG: On the road to Sedan.

(*They laugh still less heartily.*)

Are you cold?

NELL: Yes, perished. And you?

NAGG: (*Pause.*) I'm freezing.

(*Pause.*)

Do you want to go in?

260 NELL: Yes.

NAGG: Then go in.

(*Nell does not move.*)

Why don't you go in?

NELL: I don't know.

(*Pause.*)

NAGG: Has he changed your sawdust?

NELL: It isn't sawdust.

(*Pause. Wearily.*)

Can you not be a little accurate, Nagg?

NAGG: Your sand then. It's not important.

NELL: It is important.

(*Pause.*)

NAGG: It was sawdust once.

270 NELL: Once!

NAGG: And now it's sand.

(*Pause.*)

From the shore.

(*Pause. Impatiently.*)

Now it's sand he fetches from the shore.

NELL: Now it's sand.

NAGG: Has he changed yours?

NELL: No.

NAGG: Nor mine.

(*Pause.*)

I won't have it!

(*Pause. Holding up the biscuit.*)

Do you want a bit?

NELL: No.                                                                  280

(*Pause.*)

Of what?

NAGG: Biscuit. I've kept you half.

(*He looks at the biscuit. Proudly.*)

Three quarters. For you. Here.

(*He proffers the biscuit.*)

No?

(*Pause.*)

Do you not feel well?

HAMM: (*wearily*) Quiet, quiet, you're keeping me awake.

(*Pause.*)

Talk softer.

(*Pause.*)

If I could sleep I might make love. I'd go into the woods. My eyes would see . . . the sky, the earth. I'd run, run, they wouldn't catch me.                                                   290

(*Pause.*)

Nature!

(*Pause.*)

There's something dripping in my head.

(*Pause.*)

A heart, a heart in my head.

(*Pause.*)

NAGG: (*soft*) Do you hear him? A heart in his head!

(*He chuckles cautiously.*)

NELL: One mustn't laugh at those things, Nagg. Why must you always laugh at them?

NAGG: Not so loud!

NELL: (*without lowering her voice*) Nothing is funnier than unhappiness, I grant you that. But—

NAGG: (*shocked*) Oh!                                                      300

NELL: Yes, yes, it's the most comical thing in the world. And we laugh, we laugh, with a will, in the beginning. But it's always the same thing. Yes, it's like the funny story we have heard too often, we still find it funny, but we don't laugh any more.

*(Pause.)*

Have you anything else to say to me?
NAGG: No.
NELL: Are you quite sure?

*(Pause.)*

Then I'll leave you.
NAGG: Do you not want your biscuit?

*(Pause.)*

310    I'll keep it for you.

*(Pause.)*

I thought you were going to leave me.
NELL: I am going to leave you.
NAGG: Could you give me a scratch before you go?
NELL: No.

*(Pause.)*

Where?
NAGG: In the back.
NELL: No.

*(Pause.)*

Rub yourself against the rim.
NAGG: It's lower down. In the hollow.
320 NELL: What hollow?
NAGG: The hollow!

*(Pause.)*

Could you not?

*(Pause.)*

Yesterday you scratched me there.
NELL: *(elegiac)* Ah yesterday!
NAGG: Could you not?

*(Pause.)*

Would you like me to scratch you?

*(Pause.)*

Are you crying again?
NELL: I was trying.

*(Pause.)*

HAMM: Perhaps it's a little vein.

*(Pause.)*

330 NAGG: What was that he said?
NELL: Perhaps it's a little vein.
NAGG: What does that mean?

*(Pause.)*

That means nothing.

*(Pause.)*

Will I tell you the story of the tailor?
NELL: No.

*(Pause.)*

What for?
NAGG: To cheer you up.
NELL: It's not funny.
NAGG: It always made you laugh.

*(Pause.)*

The first time I thought you'd die.    340
NELL: It was on Lake Como.

*(Pause.)*

One April afternoon.

*(Pause.)*

Can you believe it?
NAGG: What?
NELL: That we once went out rowing on Lake Como.

*(Pause.)*

One April afternoon.
NAGG: We had got engaged the day before.
NELL: Engaged!
NAGG: You were in such fits that we capsized. By rights we
    should have been drowned.    350
NELL: It was because I felt happy.
NAGG: *(indignant)* It was not, it was not, it was my story and
    nothing else. Happy! Don't you laugh at it still? Every time
    I tell it. Happy!
NELL: It was deep, deep. And you could see down to the bot-
    tom. So white. So clean.
NAGG: Let me tell it again.

*(Raconteur's voice.)*

An Englishman, needing a pair of striped trousers in a hurry
    for the New Year festivities, goes to his tailor who takes his
    measurements.    360

*(Tailor's voice.)*

"That's the lot, come back in four days, I'll have it ready."
    Good. Four days later.

*(Tailor's voice.)*

"So sorry, come back in a week, I've made a mess of the
    seat." Good, that's all right, a neat seat can be very ticklish.
    A week later.

*(Tailor's voice.)*

"Frightfully sorry, come back in ten days, I've made a hash
    of the crotch." Good, can't be helped, a snug crotch is always
    a teaser. Ten days later.

*(Tailor's voice.)*

"Dreadfully sorry, come back in a fortnight, I've made a
    balls of the fly." Good, at a pinch, a smart fly is a stiff propo-    370
    sition.

*(Pause. Normal voice.)*

I never told it worse.

*(Pause. Gloomy.)*

I tell this story worse and worse.

*(Pause. Raconteur's voice.)*

Well, to make it short, the bluebells are blowing and he bal-lockses the buttonholes.

*(Customer's voice.)*

"God damn you to hell, Sir, no, it's indecent, there are lim-its! In six days, do you hear me, six days, God made the world. Yes Sir, no less Sir, the WORLD! And you are not bloody well capable of making me a pair of trousers in three
380  months!"

*(Tailor's voice, scandalized.)*

"But my dear Sir, my dear Sir, look—

*(disdainful gesture, disgustedly)*

—at the world—

*(pause)*

and look—

*(loving gesture, proudly)*

—at my TROUSERS!"

*(Pause. He looks at Nell who has remained impassive, her eyes unseeing, breaks into a high forced laugh, cuts it short, pokes his head towards Nell, launches his laugh again.)*

HAMM: Silence!

*(Nagg starts, cuts short his laugh.)*

NELL: You could see down to the bottom.
HAMM: *(exasperated)* Have you not finished? Will you never finish?

*(With sudden fury.)*

Will this never finish?

*(Nagg disappears into his bin, closes the lid behind him. Nell does not move. Frenziedly.)*

390  My kingdom for a nightman!

*(He whistles. Enter Clov.)*

Clear away this muck! Chuck it in the sea!

*(Clov goes to bins, halts.)*

NELL: So white.
HAMM: What? What's she blathering about?

*(Clov stoops, takes Nell's hand, feels her pulse.)*

NELL: *(to Clov)* Desert!

*(Clov lets go her hand, pushes her back in the bin, closes the lid.)*

CLOV: *(returning to his place beside the chair)* She has no pulse.
HAMM: What was she drivelling about?
CLOV: She told me to go away, into the desert.
HAMM: Damn busybody! Is that all?
400 CLOV: No.
HAMM: What else?

CLOV: I didn't understand.
HAMM: Have you bottled her?
CLOV: Yes.
HAMM: Are they both bottled?
CLOV: Yes.
HAMM: Screw down the lids.

*(Clov goes towards door.)*

Time enough.

*(Clov halts.)*

My anger subsides, I'd like to pee.
CLOV: *(with alacrity)* I'll go and get the catheter.    410

*(He goes towards door.)*

HAMM: Time enough.

*(Clov halts.)*

Give me my pain-killer.
CLOV: It's too soon.

*(Pause.)*

It's too soon on top of your tonic, it wouldn't act.
HAMM: In the morning they brace you up and in the evening they calm you down. Unless it's the other way round.

*(Pause.)*

That old doctor, he's dead naturally?
CLOV: He wasn't old.
HAMM: But he's dead?
CLOV: Naturally.    420

*(Pause.)*

You ask *me* that?

*(Pause.)*

HAMM: Take me for a little turn.

*(Clov goes behind the chair and pushes it forward.)*

Not too fast!

*(Clov pushes chair.)*

Right round the world!

*(Clov pushes chair.)*

Hug the walls, then back to the center again.

*(Clov pushes chair.)*

I was right in the center, wasn't I?
CLOV: *(pushing)* Yes.
HAMM: We'd need a proper wheel-chair. With big wheels. Bi-cycle wheels!

*(Pause.)*

Are you hugging?    430
CLOV: *(pushing)* Yes.
HAMM: *(groping for wall)* It's a lie! Why do you lie to me?
CLOV: *(bearing closer to wall)* There! There!
HAMM: Stop!

*(Clov stops chair close to back wall. Hamm lays his hand against wall.)*

Old wall!

*(Pause.)*

Beyond is the . . . other hell.

*(Pause. Violently.)*

Closer! Closer! Up against!

CLOV: Take away your hand.

*(Hamm withdraws his hand. Clov rams chair against wall.)*

There!

*(Hamm leans towards wall, applies his ear to it.)*

440 HAMM: Do you hear?

*(He strikes the wall with his knuckles.)*

Do you hear? Hollow bricks!

*(He strikes again.)*

All that's hollow!

*(Pause. He straightens up. Violently.)*

That's enough. Back!

CLOV: We haven't done the round.

HAMM: Back to my place!

*(Clov pushes chair back to center.)*

Is that my place?

CLOV: Yes, that's your place.

HAMM: Am I right in the center?

CLOV: I'll measure it.

450 HAMM: More or less! More or less!

CLOV: *(moving chair slightly)* There!

HAMM: I'm more or less in the center?

CLOV: I'd say so.

HAMM: You'd say so! Put me right in the center!

CLOV: I'll go and get the tape.

HAMM: Roughly! Roughly!

*(Clov moves chair slightly.)*

Bang in the center!

CLOV: There!

*(Pause.)*

HAMM: I feel a little too far to the left.

*(Clov moves chair slightly.)*

460    Now I feel a little too far to the right.

*(Clov moves chair slightly.)*

I feel a little too far forward.

*(Clov moves chair slightly.)*

Now I feel a little too far back.

*(Clov moves chair slightly.)*

Don't stay there,

*(i.e. behind the chair).*

you give me the shivers.

*(Clov returns to his place beside the chair.)*

CLOV: If I could kill him I'd die happy.

*(Pause.)*

HAMM: What's the weather like?

CLOV: As usual.

HAMM: Look at the earth.

CLOV: I've looked.

HAMM: With the glass?    470

CLOV: No need of the glass.

HAMM: Look at it with the glass.

CLOV: I'll go and get the glass.

*(Exit Clov.)*

HAMM: No need of the glass!

*(Enter Clov with telescope.)*

CLOV: I'm back again, with the glass.

*(He goes to window right, looks up at it.)*

I need the steps.

HAMM: Why? Have you shrunk?

*(Exit Clov with telescope.)*

I don't like that, I don't like that.

*(Enter Clov with ladder, but without telescope.)*

CLOV: I'm back again, with the steps.

*(He sets down ladder under window right, gets up on it, realizes he has not the telescope, gets down.)*

I need the glass.    480

*(He goes towards door.)*

HAMM: *(violently)* But you have the glass!

CLOV: *(halting, violently)* No, I haven't the glass!

*(Exit Clov.)*

HAMM: This is deadly.

*(Enter Clov with telescope. He goes towards ladder.)*

CLOV: Things are livening up.

*(He gets up on ladder, raises the telescope, lets it fall.)*

I did it on purpose.

*(He gets down, picks up the telescope, turns it on auditorium.)*

I see . . . a multitude . . . in transports . . . of joy.

*(Pause.)*

That's what I call a magnifier.

*(He lowers the telescope, turns towards Hamm.)*

Well? Don't we laugh?

HAMM: *(after reflection)* I don't.

CLOV: *(after reflection)* Nor I.    490

*(He gets up on ladder, turns the telescope on the without.)*

Let's see.

*(He looks, moving the telescope.)*

Zero . . .

*(he looks)*

. . . zero . . .

*(he looks)*

. . . and zero.

HAMM: Nothing stirs. All is—
CLOV: Zer—
HAMM: *(violently)* Wait till you're spoken to!

*(Normal voice.)*

All is . . . all is . . . all is what?

*(Violently.)*

All is what?
500 CLOV: What all is? In a word? Is that what you want to know?
Just a moment.

*(He turns the telescope on the without, looks, lowers the telescope turns towards Hamm.)*

Corpsed.

*(Pause.)*

Well? Content?
HAMM: Look at the sea.
CLOV: It's the same.
HAMM: Look at the ocean!

*(Clov gets down, takes a few steps towards window left, goes back for ladder, carries it over and sets it down under window left, gets up on it, turns the telescope on the without, looks at length. He starts, lowers the telescope, examines it, turns it again on the without.)*

CLOV: Never seen anything like that!
HAMM: *(anxious)* What? A sail? A fin? Smoke?
CLOV: *(looking)* The light is sunk.
510 HAMM: *(relieved)* Pah! We all knew that.
CLOV: *(looking)* There was a bit left.
HAMM: The base.
CLOV: *(looking)* Yes.
HAMM: And now?
CLOV: *(looking)* All gone.
HAMM: No gulls?
CLOV: *(looking)* Gulls!
HAMM: And the horizon? Nothing on the horizon?
CLOV: *(lowering the telescope, turning towards Hamm, exasperated)* What in God's name could there be on the horizon?

*(Pause.)*

HAMM: The waves, how are the waves?
CLOV: The waves?

*(He turns the telescope on the waves.)*

Lead.

HAMM: And the sun?
CLOV: *(looking)* Zero.
HAMM: But it should be sinking. Look again.
CLOV: *(looking)* Damn the sun.
HAMM: Is it night already then?
CLOV: *(looking)* No.                                               530
HAMM: Then what is it?
CLOV: *(looking)* Gray.

*(Lowering the telescope, turning towards Hamm, louder.)*

Gray!

*(Pause. Still louder.)*

GRRAY!

*(Pause. He gets down, approaches Hamm from behind, whispers in his ear.)*

HAMM: *(starting)* Gray! Did I hear you say gray?
CLOV: Light black. From pole to pole.
HAMM: You exaggerate.

*(Pause.)*

Don't stay there, you give me the shivers.

*(Clov returns to his place beside the chair.)*

CLOV: Why this farce, day after day?
HAMM: Routine. One never knows.                                     540

*(Pause.)*

Last night I saw inside my breast. There was a big sore.
CLOV: Pah! You saw your heart.
HAMM: No, it was living.

*(Pause. Anguished.)*

Clov!
CLOV: Yes.
HAMM: What's happening?
CLOV: Something is taking its course.

*(Pause.)*

HAMM: Clov!
CLOV: *(impatiently)* What is it?
HAMM: We're not beginning to . . . to . . . mean something?      550
CLOV: Mean something! You and I, mean something!

*(Brief laugh.)*

Ah that's a good one!
HAMM: I wonder.

*(Pause.)*

Imagine if a rational being came back to earth, wouldn't he be liable to get ideas into his head if he observed us long enough.

*(Voice of rational being.)*

Ah, good, now I see what it is, yes, now I understand what they're at!

*(Clov starts, drops the telescope and begins to scratch his belly with both hands. Normal voice.)*

And without going so far as that, we ourselves . . .

*(with emotion)*

560    . . . we ourselves . . . at certain moments . . .

*(Vehemently.)*

To think perhaps it won't all have been for nothing!
CLOV: *(anguished, scratching himself)* I have a flea!
HAMM: A flea! Are there still fleas?
CLOV: On me there's one.

*(Scratching.)*

Unless it's a crablouse.
HAMM: *(very perturbed)* But humanity might start from there all over again! Catch him, for the love of God!
CLOV: I'll go and get the powder.

*(Exit Clov.)*

HAMM: A flea! This is awful! What a day!

*(Enter Clov with a sprinkling-tin.)*

570    CLOV: I'm back again, with the insecticide.
HAMM: Let him have it!

*(Clov loosens the top of his trousers, pulls it forward and shakes powder into the aperture. He stoops, looks, waits, starts, frenziedly shakes more powder, stoops, looks, waits.)*

CLOV: The bastard!
HAMM: Did you get him?
CLOV: Looks like it.

*(He drops the tin and adjusts his trousers.)*

Unless he's laying doggo.
HAMM: Laying! Lying you mean. Unless he's *lying* doggo.
CLOV: Ah? One says lying? One doesn't say laying?
HAMM: Use your head, can't you. If he was laying we'd be bitched.
580    CLOV: Ah.

*(Pause.)*

What about that pee?
HAMM: I'm having it.
CLOV: Ah that's the spirit, that's the spirit!

*(Pause.)*

HAMM: *(with ardour)* Let's go from here, the two of us! South! You can make a raft and the currents will carry us away, far away, to other . . . mammals!
CLOV: God forbid!
HAMM: Alone, I'll embark alone! Get working on that raft immediately. Tomorrow I'll be gone for ever.
590    CLOV: *(hastening towards door)* I'll start straight away.
HAMM: Wait!

*(Clov halts.)*

Will there be sharks, do you think?
CLOV: Sharks? I don't know. If there are there will be.

*(He goes towards door.)*

HAMM: Wait!

*(Clov halts.)*

Is it not yet time for my pain-killer?
CLOV: *(violently)* No!

*(He goes towards door.)*

HAMM: Wait!

*(Clov halts.)*

How are your eyes?
CLOV: Bad.
HAMM: But you can see.
CLOV: All I want.    600
HAMM: How are your legs?
CLOV: Bad.
HAMM: But you can walk.
CLOV: I come . . . and go.
HAMM: In my house.

*(Pause. With prophetic relish.)*

One day you'll be blind, like me. You'll be sitting there, a speck in the void, in the dark, for ever, like me.

*(Pause.)*

One day you'll say to yourself, I'm tired, I'll sit down, and you'll go and sit down. Then you'll say, I'm hungry, I'll get    610 up and get something to eat. But you won't get up. You'll say, I shouldn't have sat down, but since I have I'll sit on a little longer, then I'll get up and get something to eat. But you won't get up and you won't get anything to eat.

*(Pause.)*

You'll look at the wall a while, then you'll say, I'll close my eyes, perhaps have a little sleep, after that I'll feel better, and you'll close them. And when you open them again there'll be no wall any more.

*(Pause.)*

Infinite emptiness will be all around you, all the resurrected dead of all the ages wouldn't fill it, and there you'll be like a    620 little bit of grit in the middle of the steppe.

*(Pause.)*

Yes, one day you'll know what it is, you'll be like me, except that you won't have anyone with you, because you won't have had pity on anyone and because there won't be anyone left to have pity on.

*(Pause.)*

CLOV: It's not certain.

*(Pause.)*

And there's one thing you forget.
HAMM: Ah?
CLOV: I can't sit down.
HAMM: *(impatiently)* Well you'll lie down then, what the hell!    630 Or you'll come to a standstill, simply stop and stand still, the way you are now. One day you'll say, I'm tired, I'll stop. What does the attitude matter?

*(Pause.)*

CLOV: So you all want me to leave you.
HAMM: Naturally.
CLOV: Then I'll leave you.
HAMM: You can't leave us.
CLOV: Then I won't leave you.

(*Pause.*)

HAMM: Why don't you finish us?

(*Pause.*)

640   I'll tell you the combination of the cupboard if you promise
      to finish me.
CLOV: I couldn't finish you.
HAMM: Then you won't finish me.

(*Pause.*)

CLOV: I'll leave you, I have things to do.
HAMM: Do you remember when you came here?
CLOV: No. Too small, you told me.
HAMM: Do you remember your father.
CLOV: (*wearily*) Same answer.

(*Pause.*)

      You've asked me these questions millions of times.
650 HAMM: I love the old questions.

(*With fervour.*)

      Ah the old questions, the old answers, there's nothing like
      them!

(*Pause.*)

      It was I was a father to you.
CLOV: Yes.

(*He looks at Hamm fixedly.*)

      You were that to me.
HAMM: My house a home for you.
CLOV: Yes.

(*He looks about him.*)

      This was that for me.
HAMM: (*proudly*) But for me,

(*gesture towards himself*)

660   no father. But for Hamm,

(*gesture towards surroundings*)

      no home.

(*Pause.*)

CLOV: I'll leave you.
HAMM: Did you ever think of one thing?
CLOV: Never.
HAMM: That here we're down in a hole.

(*Pause.*)

      But beyond the hills? Eh? Perhaps it's still green. Eh?

(*Pause.*)

      Flora! Pomona!

(*Ecstatically.*)

      Ceres!

(*Pause.*)

      Perhaps you won't need to go very far.
CLOV: I can't go very far.                                      670

(*Pause.*)

      I'll leave you.
HAMM: Is my dog ready?
CLOV: He lacks a leg.
HAMM: Is he silky?
CLOV: He's a kind of Pomeranian.
HAMM: Go and get him.
CLOV: He lacks a leg.
HAMM: Go and get him!

(*Exit Clov.*)

      We're getting on.

(*Enter Clov holding by one of its three legs a black toy dog.*)

CLOV: Your dogs are here.                                       680

(*He hands the dog to Hamm who feels it, fondles it.*)

HAMM: He's white, isn't he?
CLOV: Nearly.
HAMM: What do you mean, nearly? Is he white or isn't he?
CLOV: He isn't.

(*Pause.*)

HAMM: You've forgotten the sex.
CLOV: (*vexed*) But he isn't finished. The sex goes on at the end.

(*Pause.*)

HAMM: You haven't put on his ribbon.
CLOV: (*angrily*) But he isn't finished, I tell you! First you finish
      your dog and then you put on his ribbon!

(*Pause.*)

HAMM: Can he stand?                                             690
CLOV: I don't know.
HAMM: Try.

(*He hands the dog to Clov who places it on the ground.*)

      Well?
CLOV: Wait!

(*He squats down and tries to get the dog to stand on its three
legs, fails, lets it go. The dog falls on its side.*)

HAMM: (*impatiently*) Well?
CLOV: He's standing.
HAMM: (*groping for the dog*) Where? Where is he?

(*Clov holds up the dog in a standing position.*)

CLOV: There.

(*He takes Hamm's hand and guides it towards the dog's head.*)

HAMM: (*his hand on the dog's head*) Is he gazing at me?
CLOV: Yes.                                                      700

HAMM: (*proudly*) As if he were asking me to take him for a walk?

CLOV: If you like.

HAMM: (*as before*) Or as if he were begging me for a bone.

(*He withdraws his hand.*)

Leave him like that, standing there imploring me.

(*Clov straightens up. The dog falls on its side.*)

CLOV: I'll leave you.

HAMM: Have you had your visions?

CLOV: Less.

HAMM: Is Mother Pegg's light on?

710 CLOV: Light! How could anyone's light be on?

HAMM: Extinguished!

CLOV: Naturally it's extinguished. If it's not on it's extinguished.

HAMM: No, I mean Mother Pegg.

CLOV: But naturally she's extinguished!

(*Pause.*)

What's the matter with you today?

HAMM: I'm taking my course.

(*Pause.*)

Is she buried?

CLOV: Buried! Who would have buried her?

HAMM: You.

720 CLOV: Me! Haven't I enough to do without burying people?

HAMM: But you'll bury me.

CLOV: No I won't bury you.

(*Pause.*)

HAMM: She was bonny once, like a flower of the field.

(*With reminiscent leer.*)

And a great one for the men!

CLOV: We too were bonny—once. It's a rare thing not to have been bonny—once.

(*Pause.*)

HAMM: Go and get the gaff.

(*Clov goes to door, halts.*)

CLOV: Do this, do that, and I do it. I never refuse. Why?

HAMM: You're not able to.

730 CLOV: Soon I won't do it any more.

HAMM: You won't be able to any more.

(*Exit Clov.*)

Ah the creatures, the creatures, everything has to be explained to them.

(*Enter Clov with gaff.*)

CLOV: Here's your gaff. Stick it up.

(*He gives the gaff to Hamm who, wielding it like a puntpole, tries to move his chair.*)

HAMM: Did I move?

CLOV: No.

(*Hamm throws down the gaff.*)

HAMM: Go and get the oilcan.

CLOV: What for?

HAMM: To oil the castors.

CLOV: I oiled them yesterday.                                    740

HAMM: Yesterday! What does that mean? Yesterday!

CLOV: (*violently*) That means that bloody awful day, long ago, before this bloody awful day. I use the words you taught me. If they don't mean anything any more, teach me others. Or let me be silent.

(*Pause.*)

HAMM: I once knew a madman who thought the end of the world had come. He was a painter—and engraver. I had a great fondness for him. I used to go and see him, in the asylum. I'd take him by the hand and drag him to the window. Look! There! All that rising corn! And there! Look! The sails 750 of the herring fleet! All that loveliness!

(*Pause.*)

He'd snatch away his hand and go back into his corner. Appalled. All he had seen was ashes.

(*Pause.*)

He alone had been spared.

(*Pause.*)

Forgotten.

(*Pause.*)

It appears the case is . . . was not so . . . so unusual.

CLOV: A madman? When was that?

HAMM: Oh way back, way back, you weren't in the land of the living.

CLOV: God be with the days!                                    760

(*Pause. Hamm raises his toque.*)

HAMM: I had a great fondness for him.

(*Pause. He puts on his toque again.*)

He was a painter—and engraver.

CLOV: There are so many terrible things.

HAMM: No, no, there are not so many now.

(*Pause.*)

Clov!

CLOV: Yes.

HAMM: Do you not think this has gone on long enough?

CLOV: Yes!

(*Pause.*)

What?

HAMM: This . . . this . . . thing.                                    770

CLOV: I've always thought so.

(*Pause.*)

You not?

HAMM: (*gloomily*) Then it's a day like any other day.

CLOV: As long as it lasts.

(*Pause.*)

All life long the same inanities.

HAMM: I can't leave you.

CLOV: I know. And you can't follow me.

(*Pause.*)

HAMM: If you leave me how shall I know?

CLOV: (*briskly*) Well you simply whistle me and if I don't come
780 running it means I've left you.

(*Pause.*)

HAMM: You won't come and kiss me goodbye?

CLOV: Oh I shouldn't think so.

(*Pause.*)

HAMM: But you might be merely dead in your kitchen.

CLOV: The result would be the same.

HAMM: Yes, but how would I know, if you were merely dead in
your kitchen?

CLOV: Well . . . sooner or later I'd start to stink.

HAMM: You stink already. The whole place stinks of corpses.

CLOV: The whole universe.

790 HAMM: (*angrily*) To hell with the universe.

(*Pause.*)

Think of something.

CLOV: What?

HAMM: An idea, have an idea.

(*Angrily.*)

A bright idea!

CLOV: Ah good.

(*He starts pacing to and fro, his eyes fixed on the ground, his
hands behind his back. He halts.*)

The pains in my legs! It's unbelievable! Soon I won't be able
to think any more.

HAMM: You won't be able to leave me.

(*Clov resumes his pacing.*)

What are you doing?

800 CLOV: Having an idea.

(*He paces.*)

Ah!

(*He halts.*)

HAMM: What a brain!

(*Pause.*)

Well?

CLOV: Wait!

(*He mediates. Not very convinced.*)

Yes . . .

(*Pause. More convinced.*)

Yes!

(*He raises his head.*)

I have it! I set the alarm.

(*Pause.*)

HAMM: This is perhaps not one of my bright days, but frankly—

CLOV: You whistle me. I don't come. The alarm rings. I'm
gone. It doesn't ring. I'm dead. 810

(*Pause.*)

HAMM: Is it working?

(*Pause. Impatiently.*)

The alarm, is it working?

CLOV: Why wouldn't it be working?

HAMM: Because it's worked too much.

CLOV: But it's hardly worked at all.

HAMM: (*angrily*) Then because it's worked too little!

CLOV: I'll go and see.

(*Exit Clov. Brief ring of alarm off. Enter Clov with alarm-
clock. He holds it against Hamm's ear and releases alarm. They
listen to it ringing to the end. Pause.*)

Fit to wake the dead! Did you hear it?

HAMM: Vaguely.

CLOV: The end is terrific! 820

HAMM: I prefer the middle.

(*Pause.*)

Is it not time for my pain-killer?

CLOV: No!

(*He goes to door, turns.*)

I'll leave you.

HAMM: It's time for my story. Do you want to listen to my story.

CLOV: No.

HAMM: Ask my father if he wants to listen to my story.

(*Clov goes to bins, raises the lid of Nagg's, stoops, looks into it.
Pause. He straightens up.*)

CLOV: He's asleep.

HAMM: Wake him.

(*Clov stoops, wakes Nagg with the alarm. Unintelligible words.
Clov straightens up.*)

CLOV: He doesn't want to listen to your story. 830

HAMM: I'll give him a bon-bon.

(*Clov stoops. As before.*)

CLOV: He wants a sugar-plum.

HAMM: He'll get a sugar-plum.

(*Clov stoops. As before.*)

CLOV: It's a deal.

(*He goes towards door. Nagg's hands appear, gripping the rim.
Then the head emerges. Clov reaches door, turns.*)

Do you believe in the life to come?

HAMM: Mine was always that.

(*Exit Clov.*)

Got him that time!

NAGG: I'm listening.

HAMM: Scoundrel! Why did you engender me?
840 NAGG: I didn't know.
HAMM: What? What didn't you know?
NAGG: That it'd be you.

*(Pause.)*

You'll give me a sugar-plum?
HAMM: After the audition.
NAGG: You swear?
HAMM: Yes.
NAGG: On what?
HAMM: My honor.

*(Pause. They laugh heartily.)*

NAGG: Two.
850 HAMM: One.
NAGG: One for me and one for—
HAMM: One! Silence!

*(Pause.)*

Where was I?

*(Pause. Gloomily.)*

It's finished, we're finished.

*(Pause.)*

Nearly finished.

*(Pause.)*

There'll be no more speech.

*(Pause.)*

Something dripping in my head, ever since the fontanelles.

*(Stifled hilarity of Nagg.)*

Splash, splash, always on the same spot.

*(Pause.)*

Perhaps it's a little vein.

*(Pause.)*

860    A little artery.

*(Pause. More animated.)*

Enough of that, it's story time, where was I?

*(Pause. Narrative tone.)*

The man came crawling towards me, on his belly. Pale, wonderfully pale and thin, he seemed on the point of—

*(Pause. Normal tone.)*

No, I've done that bit.

*(Pause. Narrative tone.)*

I calmly filled my pipe—the meerschaum, lit it with . . . let us say a vesta, drew a few puffs. Aah!

*(Pause.)*

Well, what is it *you* want?

*(Pause.)*

It was an extra-ordinarily bitter day, I remember, zero by the thermometer. But considering it was Christmas Eve there was nothing . . . extra-ordinary about that. Seasonable 870 weather, for once in a way.

*(Pause.)*

Well, what ill wind blows you my way? He raised his face to me, black with mingled dirt and tears.

*(Pause. Normal tone.)*

That should do it.

*(Narrative tone.)*

No no, don't look at me, don't look at me. He dropped his eyes and mumbled something, apologies I presume.

*(Pause.)*

I'm a busy man, you know, the final touches, before the festivities, you know what it is.

*(Pause. Forcibly.)*

Come on now, what is the object of this invasion?

*(Pause.)*

It was a glorious bright day, I remember, fifty by the he- 880 liometer, but already the sun was sinking down into the . . . down among the dead.

*(Normal tone.)*

Nicely put, that.

*(Narrative tone.)*

Come on now, come on, present your petition and let me resume my labors.

*(Pause. Normal tone.)*

There's English for you. Ah well . . .

*(Narrative tone.)*

It was then he took the plunge. It's my little one, he said. Tsstss, a little one, that's bad. My little boy, he said, as if the sex mattered. Where did he come from? He named the hole. A good half-day, on horse. What are you insinuating? 890 That the place is still inhabited? No no, not a soul, except himself and the child—assuming he existed. Good. I enquired about the situation at Kov, beyond the gulf. Not a sinner. Good. And you expect me to believe you have left your little one back there, all alone, and alive into the bargain? Come now!

*(Pause.)*

It was a howling wild day, I remember, a hundred by the anenometer. The wind was tearing up the dead pines and sweeping them . . . away.

*(Pause. Normal tone.)*

A bit feeble, that.                                                      900

*(Narrative tone.)*

Come on, man, speak up, what is you want from me, I have

to put up my holly.

(*Pause.*)

Well to make it short it finally transpired that what he wanted from me was . . . bread for his brat? Bread? But I have no bread, it doesn't agree with me. Good. Then perhaps a little corn?

(*Pause. Normal tone.*)

That should do it.

(*Narrative tone.*)

Corn, yes, I have corn, it's true, in my granaries. But use your head. I give you some corn, a pound, a pound and a half, you bring it back to your child and you make him—if he's still alive—a nice pot of porridge,

(*Nagg reacts*)

a nice pot and a half of porridge, full of nourishment. Good. The colors come back into his little cheeks—perhaps. And then?

(*Pause.*)

I lost patience.

(*Violently.*)

Use your head, can't you, use your head, you're on earth, there's no cure for that!

(*Pause.*)

It was an exceedingly dry day, I remember, zero by the hygrometer. Ideal weather, for my lumbago.

(*Pause. Violently.*)

But what in God's name do you imagine? That the earth will awake in spring? That the rivers and seas will run with fish again? That there's manna in heaven still for imbeciles like you?

(*Pause.*)

Gradually I cooled down, sufficiently at least to ask him how long he had taken on the way. Three whole days. Good. In what condition he had left the child. Deep in sleep.

(*Forcibly.*)

But deep in what sleep, deep in what sleep already?

(*Pause.*)

Well to make it short I finally offered to take him into my service. He had touched a chord. And then I imagined already that I wasn't much longer for this world.

(*He laughs. Pause.*)

Well?

(*Pause.*)

Well? Here if you were careful you might die a nice natural death, in peace and comfort.

(*Pause.*)

Well?

(*Pause.*)

In the end he asked me would I consent to take in the child as well—if he were still alive.

(*Pause.*)

It was the moment I was waiting for.

(*Pause.*)

Would I consent to take in the child . . .

(*Pause.*)

I can see him still, down on his knees, his hands flat on the ground, glaring at me with his mad eyes, in defiance of my wishes.

(*Pause. Normal tone.*)

I'll soon have finished with this story.

(*Pause.*)

Unless I bring in other characters.

(*Pause.*)

But where would I find them?

(*Pause.*)

Where would I look for them?

(*Pause. He whistles. Enter Clov.*)

Let us pray to God.
NAGG: Me sugar-plum!
CLOV: There's a rat in the kitchen!
HAMM: A rat! Are there still rats?
CLOV: In the kitchen there's one.
HAMM: And you haven't exterminated him?
CLOV: Half. You disturbed us.
HAMM: He can't get away?
CLOV: No.
HAMM: You'll finish him later. Let us pray to God.
CLOV: Again!
NAGG: Me sugar-plum!
HAMM: God first!

(*Pause.*)

Are you right?
CLOV: (*resigned*) Off we go.
HAMM: (*to Nagg*) And you?
NAGG: (*clasping his hands, closing his eyes, in a gabble*) Our Father which art—
HAMM: Silence! In silence! Where are your manners?

(*Pause.*)

Off we go.

(*Attitudes of prayer. Silence. Abandoning his attitude, discouraged.*)

Well?
CLOV: (*abandoning his attitude*) What a hope! And you?
HAMM: Sweet damn all!

*(To Nagg.)*

And you?

970 NAGG: Wait!

*(Pause. Abandoning his attitude.)*

Nothing doing!

HAMM: The bastard! He doesn't exist!

CLOV: Not yet.

NAGG: Me sugar-plum!

HAMM: There are no more sugar-plums!

*(Pause.)*

NAGG: It's natural. After all I'm your father. It's true if it hadn't been me it would have been someone else. But that's no excuse.

*(Pause.)*

980 Turkish Delight, for example, which no longer exists, we all know that, there is nothing in the world I love more. And one day I'll ask you for some, in return for a kindness, and you'll promise it to me. One must live with the times.

*(Pause.)*

Whom did you call when you were a tiny boy, and were frightened, in the dark? Your mother? No. Me. We let you cry. Then we moved you out of earshot, so that we might sleep in peace.

*(Pause.)*

I was asleep, as happy as a king, and you woke me up to have me listen to you. It wasn't indispensable, you didn't really need to have me listen to you. Besides I didn't listen to you.

*(Pause.)*

990 I hope the day will come when you'll really need to have me listen to you, and need to hear my voice, any voice.

*(Pause.)*

Yes, I hope I'll live till then, to hear you calling me like when you were a tiny boy, and were frightened, in the dark, and I was your only hope.

*(Pause. Nagg knocks on lid of Nell's bin. Pause.)*

Nell!

*(Pause. He knocks louder. Pause. Louder.)*

Nell!

*(Pause. Nagg sinks back into his bin, closes the lid behind him. Pause.)*

HAMM: Our revels now are ended.

*(He gropes for the dog.)*

The dog's gone.

CLOV: He's not a real dog, he can't go.

1000 HAMM: *(groping)* He's not there.

CLOV: He's lain down.

HAMM: Give him up to me.

*(Clov picks up the dog and gives it to Hamm. Hamm holds it in his arms. Pause. Hamm throws away the dog.)*

Dirty brute!

*(Clov begins to pick up the objects lying on the ground.)*

What are you doing?

CLOV: Putting things in order.

*(He straightens up. Fervently.)*

I'm going to clear everything away!

*(He starts picking up again.)*

HAMM: Order!

CLOV: *(straightening up)* I love order. It's my dream. A world where all would be silent and still and each thing in its last place, under the last dust. 1010

*(He starts picking up again.)*

HAMM: *(exasperated)* What in God's name do you think you are doing?

CLOV: *(straightening up)* I'm doing my best to create a little order.

HAMM: Drop it!

*(Clov drops the objects he has picked up.)*

CLOV: After all, there or elsewhere.

*(He goes towards door.)*

HAMM: *(irritably)* What's wrong with your feet?

CLOV: My feet?

HAMM: Tramp! Tramp!

CLOV: I must have put on my boots. 1020

HAMM: Your slippers were hurting you?

*(Pause.)*

CLOV: I'll leave you.

HAMM: No!

CLOV: What is there to keep me here?

HAMM: The dialogue.

*(Pause.)*

I've got on with my story.

*(Pause.)*

I've got on with it well.

*(Pause. Irritably.)*

Ask me where I've got to.

CLOV: Oh, by the way, your story?

HAMM: *(surprised)* What story? 1030

CLOV: The one you've been telling yourself all your days.

HAMM: Ah you mean my chronicle?

CLOV: That's the one.

*(Pause.)*

HAMM: *(angrily)* Keep going, can't you, keep going!

CLOV: You've got on with it, I hope.

HAMM: *(modestly)* Oh not very far, not very far.

*(He sighs.)*

There are days like that, one isn't inspired.

*(Pause.)*

Nothing you can do about it, just wait for it to come.

*(Pause.)*

No forcing, no forcing, it's fatal.

1040  I've got on with it a little all the same.

*(Pause.)*

Technique, you know.

*(Pause. Irritably.)*

I say I've got on with it a little all the same.

CLOV: *(admiringly)* Well I never! In spite of everything you were able to get on with it!

HAMM: *(modestly)* Oh not very far, you know, not very far, but nevertheless, better than nothing.

CLOV: Better than nothing! Is it possible?

HAMM: I'll tell you how it goes. He comes crawling on his belly—

1050  CLOV: Who?

HAMM: What?

CLOV: Who do you mean, he?

HAMM: Who do I mean! Yet another.

CLOV: Ah him! I wasn't sure.

HAMM: Crawling on his belly, whining for bread for his brat. He's offered a job as gardener. Before—

*(Clov bursts out laughing.)*

What is there so funny about that?

CLOV: A job as gardener!

HAMM: Is that what tickles you?

1060  CLOV: It must be that.

HAMM: It wouldn't be the bread?

CLOV: Or the brat.

*(Pause.)*

HAMM: The whole thing is comical, I grant you that. What about having a good guffaw the two of us together?

CLOV: *(after reflection)* I couldn't guffaw again today.

HAMM: *(after reflection)* Nor I.

*(Pause.)*

I continue then. Before accepting with gratitude he asks if he may have his little boy with him.

CLOV: What age?

1070  HAMM: Oh tiny.

CLOV: He would have climbed the trees.

HAMM: All the little odd jobs.

CLOV: And then he would have grown up.

HAMM: Very likely.

*(Pause.)*

CLOV: Keep going, can't you, keep going!

HAMM: That's all. I stopped there.

*(Pause.)*

CLOV: Do you see how it goes on.

HAMM: More or less.

CLOV: Will it not soon be the end?

HAMM: I'm afraid it will.  1080

CLOV: Pah! You'll make up another.

HAMM: I don't know.

*(Pause.)*

I feel rather drained.

*(Pause.)*

The prolonged creative effort.

*(Pause.)*

If I could drag myself down to the sea! I'd make a pillow of sand for my head and the tide would come.

CLOV: There's no more tide.

*(Pause.)*

HAMM: Go and see is she dead.

*(Clov goes to bins, raises the lid of Nell's, stoops, looks into it. Pause.)*

CLOV: Looks like it.

*(He closes the lid, straightens up. Hamm raises his toque. Pause. He puts it on again.)*

HAMM: *(with his hand to his toque)* And Nagg?  1090

*(Clov raises lid of Nagg's bin, stoops, looks into it. Pause.)*

CLOV: Doesn't look like it.

*(He closes the lid, straightens up.)*

HAMM: *(letting go his toque)* What's he doing?

*(Clov raises lid of Nagg's bin, stoops, looks into it. Pause.)*

CLOV: He's crying.

*(He closes lid, straightens up.)*

HAMM: Then he's living.

*(Pause.)*

Did you ever have an instant of happiness?

CLOV: Not to my knowledge.

*(Pause.)*

HAMM: Bring me under the window.

*(Clov goes towards chair.)*

I want to feel the light on my face.

*(Clov pushes chair.)*

Do you remember, in the beginning, when you took me for a turn? You used to hold the chair too high. At every step  1100 you nearly tipped me out.

*(With senile quaver.)*

Ah great fun, we had, the two of us, great fun.

*(Gloomily.)*

And then we got into the way of it.

*(Clov stops the chair under window right.)*

There already?

*(Pause. He tilts back his head.)*

Is it light?
CLOV: It isn't dark.
HAMM: *(angrily)* I'm asking you is it light.
CLOV: Yes.

*(Pause.)*

HAMM: The curtain isn't closed?
1110 CLOV: No.
HAMM: What window is it?
CLOV: The earth.
HAMM: I knew it!

*(Angrily.)*

But there's no light there! The other!

*(Clov pushes chair towards window left.)*

The earth!

*(Clov stops the chair under window left. Hamm tilts back his head.)*

That's what I call light!

*(Pause.)*

Feels like a ray of sunshine.

*(Pause.)*

No?
CLOV: No.
1120 HAMM: It isn't a ray of sunshine I feel on my face?
CLOV: No.

*(Pause.)*

HAMM: Am I very white?

*(Pause. Angrily.)*

I'm asking you am I very white!
CLOV: Not more so than usual.

*(Pause.)*

HAMM: Open the window.
CLOV: What for?
HAMM: I want to hear the sea.
CLOV: You wouldn't hear it.
HAMM: Even if you opened the window?
1130 CLOV: No.
HAMM: Then it's not worth while opening it?
CLOV: No.
HAMM: *(violently)* Then open it!

*(Clov gets up on the ladder, opens the window. Pause.)*

Have you opened it?
CLOV: Yes.

*(Pause.)*

HAMM: You swear you've opened it?

CLOV: Yes.

*(Pause.)*

HAMM: Well . . . !

*(Pause.)*

It must be very calm.

*(Pause. Violently.)*

I'm asking you is it very calm!                1140
CLOV: Yes.
HAMM: It's because there are no more navigators.

*(Pause.)*

You haven't much conversation all of a sudden. Do you not feel well?
CLOV: I'm cold.
HAMM: What month are we?

*(Pause.)*

Close the window, we're going back.

*(Clov closes the window, gets down, pushes the chair back to its place, remains standing behind it, head bowed.)*

Don't stay there, you give me the shivers!

*(Clov returns to his place beside the chair.)*

Father!

*(Pause. Louder.)*

Father!                                        1150

*(Pause.)*

Go and see did he hear me.

*(Clov goes to Nagg's bin, raises the lid, stoops. Unintelligible words. Clov straightens up.)*

CLOV: Yes.
HAMM: Both times?

*(Clov stoops. As before.)*

CLOV: Once only.
HAMM: The first time or the second?

*(Clov stoops. As before.)*

CLOV: He doesn't know.
HAMM: It must have been the second.
CLOV: We'll never know.

*(He closes lid.)*

HAMM: Is he still crying?
CLOV: No.                                      1160
HAMM: The dead go fast.

*(Pause.)*

What's he doing?
CLOV: Sucking his biscuit.
HAMM: Life goes on.

*(Clov returns to his place beside the chair.)*

Give me a rug, I'm freezing.

CLOV: There are no more rugs.

(*Pause.*)

HAMM: Kiss me.

(*Pause.*)

Will you not kiss me?

CLOV: No.

1170 HAMM: On the forehead.

CLOV: I won't kiss you anywhere.

(*Pause.*)

HAMM: (*holding out his hand*) Give me your hand at least.

(*Pause.*)

Will you not give me your hand?

CLOV: I won't touch you.

(*Pause.*)

HAMM: Give me the dog.

(*Clov looks round for the dog.*)

No!

CLOV: Do you not want your dog?

HAMM: No.

CLOV: Then I'll leave you.

1180 HAMM: (*head bowed, absently*) That's right.

(*Clov goes to door, turns.*)

CLOV: If I don't kill that rat he'll die.

HAMM: (*as before*) That's right.

(*Exit Clov. Pause.*)

Me to play.

(*He takes out his handkerchief, unfolds it, holds it spread out before him.*)

We're getting on.

(*Pause.*)

You weep, and weep, for nothing, so as not to laugh, and little by little . . . you begin to grieve.

(*He folds the handkerchief, puts it back in his pocket, raises his head.*)

All those I might have helped.

(*Pause.*)

Helped!

(*Pause.*)

Saved.

(*Pause.*)

1190 Saved!

(*Pause.*)

The place was crawling with them!

(*Pause. Violently.*)

Use your head, can't you, use your head, you're on earth, there's no cure for that!

(*Pause.*)

Get out of here and love one another! Lick your neighbor as yourself!

(*Pause. Calmer.*)

When it wasn't bread they wanted it was crumpets.

(*Pause. Violently.*)

Out of my sight and back to your petting parties!

(*Pause.*)

All that, all that!

(*Pause.*)

Not even a real dog!

(*Calmer.*)

The end is in the beginning and yet you go on.    1200

(*Pause.*)

Perhaps I could go on with my story, end it and begin another.

(*Pause.*)

Perhaps I could throw myself out on the floor.

(*He pushes himself painfully off his seat, falls back again.*)

Dig my nails into the cracks and drag myself forward with my fingers.

(*Pause.*)

It will be the end and there I'll be, wondering what can have brought it on and wondering what can have . . .

(*he hesitates*)

. . . why it was so long coming.

(*Pause.*)

There I'll be, in the old shelter, alone against the silence and . . .    1210

(*he hesitates*)

. . . the stillness. If I can hold my peace, and sit quiet, it will be all over with sound, and motion, all over and done with.

(*Pause.*)

I'll have called my father and I'll have called my . . .

(*he hesitates*)

. . . my son. And even twice, or three times, in case they shouldn't have heard me, the first time, or the second.

(*Pause.*)

I'll say to myself, He'll come back.

(*Pause.*)

And then?

*(Pause.)*

And then?

*(Pause.)*

He couldn't, he has gone too far.

*(Pause.)*

1220     And then?

*(Pause. Very agitated.)*

All kinds of fantasies! That I'm being watched! A rat! Steps!
Breath held and then . . .

*(He breathes out.)*

Then babble, babble, words, like the solitary child who turns
himself into children, two, three, so as to be together, and
whisper together, in the dark.

*(Pause.)*

Moment upon moment, pattering down, like the millet
grains of . . .

*(he hesitates)*

. . . that old Greek, and all life long you wait for that to
mount up to a life.

*(Pause. He opens his mouth to continue, renounces.)*

1230     Ah let's get it over!

*(He whistles. Enter Clov with alarm-clock. He halts beside the
chair.)*

What? Neither gone nor dead?
CLOV: In spirit only.
HAMM: Which?
CLOV: Both.
HAMM: Gone from me you'd be dead.
CLOV: And vice versa.
HAMM: Outside of here it's death!

*(Pause.)*

And the rat?
CLOV: He's got away.
1240     HAMM: He can't go far.

*(Pause, Anxious.)*

Eh?
CLOV: He doesn't need to go far.

*(Pause.)*

HAMM: Is it not time for my pain-killer?
CLOV: Yes.
HAMM: Ah! At last! Give it to me! Quick!

*(Pause.)*

CLOV: There's no more pain-killer.

*(Pause.)*

HAMM: *(appalled)* Good . . . !

*(Pause.)*

No more pain-killer!
CLOV: No more pain-killer. You'll never get any more pain-
killer.     1250

*(Pause.)*

HAMM: But the little round box. It was full!
CLOV: Yes. But now it's empty.

*(Pause. Clov starts to move about the room. He is looking for a
place to put down the alarm-clock.)*

HAMM: *(soft)* What'll I do?

*(Pause. In a scream.)*

What'll I do?

*(Clov sees the picture, takes it down, stands it on the floor with
its face to the wall, hangs up the alarm-clock in its place.)*

What are you doing?
CLOV: Winding up.
HAMM: Look at the earth.
CLOV: Again!
HAMM: Since it's calling to you.
CLOV: Is your throat sore?     1260

*(Pause.)*

Would you like a lozenge?

*(Pause.)*

No.

*(Pause.)*

Pity.

*(Clov goes, humming, towards window right, halts before it,
looks up at it.)*

HAMM: Don't sing.
CLOV: *(turning towards Hamm)* One hasn't the right to sing
any more?
HAMM: No.
CLOV: Then how can it end?
HAMM: You want it to end?
CLOV: I want to sing.     1270
HAMM: I can't prevent you.

*(Pause. Clov turns towards window right.)*

CLOV: What did I do with that steps?

*(He looks around for ladder.)*

You didn't see that steps?

*(He sees it.)*

Ah, about time.

*(He goes towards window left.)*

Sometimes I wonder if I'm in my right mind. Then it passes
over and I'm as lucid as before.

*(He gets up on ladder, looks out of window.)*

Christ, she's under water!

*(He looks.)*

How can that be?

(*He pokes forward his head, his hand above his eyes.*)

It hasn't rained.

(*He wipes the pane, looks. Pause.*)

1280   Ah what a fool I am! I'm on the wrong side!

(*He gets down, takes a few steps towards window right.*)

Under water!

(*He goes back for ladder.*)

What a fool I am!

(*He carries ladder towards window right.*)

Sometimes I wonder if I'm in my right senses. Then it passes off and I'm as intelligent as ever.

(*He sets down ladder under window right, gets up on it, looks out of window. He turns towards Hamm.*)

Any particular sector you fancy? Or merely the whole thing?
HAMM: Whole thing.
CLOV: The general effect? Just a moment.

(*He looks out of window. Pause.*)

HAMM: Clov.
CLOV: (*absorbed*) Mmm.
1290 HAMM: Do you know what it is?
CLOV: (*as before*) Mmm.
HAMM: I was never there.

(*Pause.*)

Clov!
CLOV: (*turning towards Hamm, exasperated*) What is it?
HAMM: I was never there.
CLOV: Lucky for you.

(*He looks out of window.*)

HAMM: Absent, always. It all happened without me. I don't know what's happened.

(*Pause.*)

Do you know what's happened?

(*Pause.*)

1300   Clov!
CLOV: (*turning towards Hamm, exasperated*) Do you want me to look at this muckheap, yes or no?
HAMM: Answer me first.
CLOV: What?
HAMM: Do you know what's happened?
CLOV: When? Where?
HAMM: (*violently*) When! What's happened? Use your head, can't you! What has happened?
CLOV: What for Christ's sake does it matter?

(*He looks out of window.*)

1310 HAMM: I don't know.

(*Pause. Clov turns towards Hamm.*)

CLOV: (*harshly*) When old Mother Pegg asked you for oil for her lamp and you told her to get out to hell, you knew what was happening then, no?

(*Pause.*)

You know what she died of, Mother Pegg? Of darkness.
HAMM: (*feebly*) I hadn't any.
CLOV: (*as before*) Yes, you had.

(*Pause.*)

HAMM: Have you the glass?
CLOV: No, it's clear enough as it is.
HAMM: Go and get it.

(*Pause. Clov casts up his eyes, brandishes his fists. He loses balance, clutches on to the ladder. He starts to get down, halts.*)

CLOV: There's one thing I'll never understand.   1320

(*He gets down.*)

Why I always obey you. Can you explain that to me?
HAMM: No. . . . Perhaps it's compassion.

(*Pause.*)

A kind of great compassion.

(*Pause.*)

Oh you won't find it easy, you won't find it easy.

(*Pause. Clov begins to move about the room in search of the telescope.*)

CLOV: I'm tired of our goings on, very tired.

(*He searches.*)

You're not sitting on it?

(*He moves the chair, looks at the place where it stood, resumes his search.*)

HAMM: (*anguished*) Don't leave me there!

(*Angrily Clov restores the chair to its place.*)

Am I right in the center?
CLOV: You'd need a microscope to find this—

(*He sees the telescope.*)

Ah, about time.   1330

(*He picks up the telescope, gets up on the ladder, turns the telescope on the without.*)

HAMM: Give me the dog.
CLOV: (*looking*) Quiet!
HAMM: (*angrily*) Give me the dog!

(*Clov drops the telescope, clasps his hands to his head. Pause. He gets down precipitately, looks for the dog, sees it, picks it up, hastens towards Hamm and strikes him violently on the head with the dog.*)

CLOV: There's your dog for you!

(*The dog falls to the ground. Pause.*)

HAMM: He hit me!

CLOV: You drive me mad, I'm mad!

HAMM: If you must hit me, hit me with the axe.

(*Pause.*)

Or with the gaff, hit me with the gaff. Not with the dog. With the gaff. Or with the axe.

(*Clov picks up the dog and gives it to Hamm who takes it in his arms.*)

1340　CLOV: (*imploringly*) Let's stop playing!

HAMM: Never!

(*Pause.*)

Put me in my coffin.

CLOV: There are no more coffins.

HAMM: Then let it end!

(*Clov goes towards ladder.*)

With a bang!

(*Clov gets up on ladder, gets down again, looks for telescope, sees it, picks it up, gets up ladder, raises telescope.*)

Of darkness! And me? Did anyone ever have pity on me?

CLOV: (*lowering the telescope, turning towards Hamm*) What?

(*Pause.*)

Is it me you're referring to?

HAMM: (*angrily*) An aside, ape! Did you never hear an aside be-
1350　fore?

(*Pause.*)

I'm warming up for my last soliloquy.

CLOV: I warn you. I'm going to look at this filth since it's an order. But it's the last time.

(*He turns the telescope on the without.*)

Let's see.

(*He moves the telescope.*)

Nothing . . . nothing . . . good . . . good . . . nothing . . . goo—

(*He starts, lowers the telescope, examines it, turns it again on the without. Pause.*)

Bad luck to it!

HAMM: More complications!

(*Clov gets down.*)

Not an underplot, I trust.

(*Clov moves ladder nearer window, gets up on it, turns telescope on the without.*)

CLOV: (*dismayed*) Looks like a small boy!

1360　HAMM: (*sarcastic*) A small . . . boy!

CLOV: I'll go and see.

(*He gets down, drops the telescope, goes towards door, turns.*)

I'll take the gaff.

(*He looks for the gaff, sees it, picks it up, hastens towards door.*)

HAMM: No!

(*Clov halts.*)

CLOV: No? A potential procreator?

HAMM: If he exists he'll die there or he'll come here. And if he doesn't . . .

(*Pause.*)

CLOV: You don't believe me? You think I'm inventing?

(*Pause.*)

HAMM: It's the end, Clov, we've come to the end. I don't need you any more.

(*Pause.*)

CLOV: Lucky for you.    1370

(*He goes towards door.*)

HAMM: Leave me the gaff.

(*Clov gives him the gaff, goes towards door, halts, looks at alarm-clock, takes it down, looks round for a better place to put it, goes to bins, puts it on lid of Nagg's bin. Pause.*)

CLOV: I'll leave you.

(*He goes towards door.*)

HAMM: Before you go . . .

(*Clov halts near door.*)

. . . say something.

CLOV: There is nothing to say.

HAMM: A few words . . . to ponder . . . in my heart.

CLOV: Your heart!

HAMM: Yes.

(*Pause. Forcibly.*)

Yes!

(*Pause.*)

With the rest, in the end, the shadows, the murmurs, all the 1380 trouble, to end up with.

(*Pause.*)

Clov. . . . He never spoke to me. Then, in the end, before he went, without my having asked him, he spoke to me. He said . . .

CLOV: (*despairingly*) Ah . . . !

HAMM: Something . . . from your heart.

CLOV: My heart!

HAMM: A few words . . . from your heart.

(*Pause.*)

CLOV: (*fixed gaze, tonelessly, towards auditorium*) They said to me, That's love, yes, yes, not a doubt, now you see how—    1390

HAMM: Articulate!

CLOV: (*as before*) How easy it is. They said to me, That's friendship, yes, yes, no question, you've found it. They said to me, Here's the place, stop, raise your head and look at all that beauty. That order! They said to me, Come now, you're not a brute beast, think upon these things and you'll see how all becomes clear. And simple! They said to me, What skilled attention they get, all these dying of their wounds.

HAMM: Enough!

1400 CLOV: (*as before*) I say to myself—sometimes, Clov, you must learn to suffer better than that if you want them to weary of punishing you—one day. I say to myself—sometimes, Clov, you must be there better than that if you want them to let you go—one day. But I feel too old, and too far, to form new habits. Good, it'll never end, I'll never go.

(*Pause.*)

Then one day, suddenly, it ends, it changes, I don't understand, it dies, or it's me, I don't understand, that either. I ask the words that remain—sleeping, waking, morning, evening. They have nothing to say.

(*Pause.*)

1410 I open the door of the cell and go. I am so bowed I only see my feet, if I open my eyes, and between my legs a little trail of black dust. I say to myself that the earth is extinguished, though I never saw it lit.

(*Pause.*)

It's easy going.

(*Pause.*)

When I fall I'll weep for happiness.

(*Pause. He goes towards door.*)

HAMM: Clov!

(*Clov halts, without turning.*)

Nothing.

(*Clov moves on.*)

Clov!

(*Clov halts, without turning.*)

CLOV: This is what we call making an exit.

1420 HAMM: I'm obliged to you, Clov. For your services.

CLOV: (*turning, sharply*) Ah pardon, it's I am obliged to you.

HAMM: It's we are obliged to each other.

(*Pause. Clov goes towards door.*)

One thing more.

(*Clov halts.*)

A last favor.

(*Exit Clov.*)

Cover me with the sheet.

(*Long pause.*)

No? Good.

(*Pause.*)

Me to play.

(*Pause. Wearily.*)

Old endgame lost of old, play and lose and have done

with losing.

(*Pause. More animated.*)

Let me see.                                                                1430

(*Pause.*)

Ah yes!

(*He tries to move the chair, using the gaff as before. Enter Clov, dressed for the road. Panama hat, tweed coat, raincoat over his arm, umbrella, bag. He halts by the door and stands there, impassive and motionless, his eyes fixed on Hamm, till the end. Hamm gives up.*)

Good.

(*Pause.*)

Discard.

(*He throws away the gaff, makes to throw away the dog, thinks better of it.*)

Take it easy.

(*Pause.*)

And now?

(*Pause.*)

Raise hat.

(*He raises his toque.*)

Peace to our . . . arses.

(*Pause.*)

And put on again.

(*He puts on his toque.*)

Deuce.

(*Pause. He takes off his glasses.*)

Wipe.                                                                        1440

(*He takes out his handkerchief and, without unfolding it, wipes his glasses.*)

And put on again.

(*He puts on his glasses, puts back the handkerchief in his pocket.*)

We're coming. A few more squirms like that and I'll call.

(*Pause.*)

A little poetry.

(*Pause.*)

You prayed—

(*Pause. He corrects himself.*)

You CRIED for night; it comes—

(*Pause. He corrects himself.*)

It FALLS: now cry in darkness.

(*He repeats, chanting.*)

You cried for night; it falls: now cry in darkness.

*(Pause.)*

Nicely put, that.

*(Pause.)*

And now?

*(Pause.)*

1450    Moments for nothing, now as always, time was never and time is over, reckoning closed and story ended.

*(Pause. Narrative tone.)*

If he could have his child with him. . . .

*(Pause.)*

It was the moment I was waiting for.

*(Pause.)*

You don't want to abandon him? You want him to bloom while you are withering? Be there to solace your last million last moments?

*(Pause.)*

He doesn't realize, all he knows is hunger, and cold, and death to crown it all. But you! You ought to know what the earth is like, nowadays. Oh I put him before his responsibil-
1460    ities!

*(Pause. Normal tone.)*

Well, there we are, there I am, that's enough.

*(He raises the whistle to his lips, hesitates, drops it. Pause.)*

Yes, truly!

*(He whistles. Pause. Louder. Pause.)*

Good.

*(Pause.)*

Father!

*(Pause. Louder.)*

Father!

*(Pause.)*

Good.

*(Pause.)*

We're coming.

*(Pause.)*

And to end up with?

*(Pause.)*

Discard.

*(He throws away the dog. He tears the whistle from his neck.)*

With my compliments.                                    1470

*(He throws whistle towards auditorium. Pause. He sniffs. Soft.)*

Clov!

*(Long pause.)*

No? Good.

*(He takes out the handkerchief.)*

Since that's the way we're playing it . . .

*(he unfolds handkerchief)*

. . . let's play it that way . . .

*(he unfolds)*

. . . and speak no more about it . . .

*(he finishes unfolding)*

. . . speak no more.

*(He holds handkerchief spread out before him.)*

Old stancher!

*(Pause.)*

You . . . remain.

*(Pause. He covers his face with handkerchief, lowers his arms to armrests, remains motionless.)*
*(Brief tableau.)*

## CURTAIN

## Catastrophe (1982)

*Catastrophe* starkly suggests the relationship between the "existential" neutrality of the theater of the absurd and its involvement—the inevitable involvement of all the arts—in the politics of the world. At first glance, *Catastrophe* has a strongly—and surprisingly—autobiographical dimension. A dictatorial Director composes the posture of his "Protagonist"; not only does the unshaven, raggedly-clothed, white-haired, pale-skinned Protagonist look like the bedraggled everymen of Beckett's drama, but the Director's emphasis on visual composition is reminiscent of Beckett's practice when directing his own plays (see Ruby Cohn's article in "Casebook on Beckett" below). The Director works to produce a precise visual image on the stage, arranging and positioning the Protagonist so that he becomes an *objet d'art*.

But Beckett's act of self-parody here is complicated by the play's political context. *Catastrophe* is dedicated to the Czech playwright (and now Czech president) Václav Havel, who was then in prison—an object of punishment. To see the practice of theater as the instrument of the Protagonist's torture is to begin to raise a series of critical questions, questions usually remote from "theater of the absurd" and its existentialist thematics. How does "art" become an instrument of the state? What kinds of resistance does "art" preempt? Or promote? How should we read the Protagonist's defiant final gesture, fixing the audience with his gaze? And who are *we* in this spectacle—what is our role, our function, our responsibility in the aesthetics of oppression? For in the end, the Director's humiliating spectacle of torture is finally staged for *us*.

# —Catastrophe—
## Samuel Beckett
### FOR VÁCLAV HAVEL

*Director* (D).
*His female assistant* (A).
*Protagonist* (P).
*Luke, in charge of the lighting, offstage* (L).

*Rehearsal. Final touches to the last scene. Bare stage. A and L have just set the lighting. D has just arrived.*

*D in an armchair downstairs audience left. Fur coat. Fur toque to match. Age and physique unimportant.*

*A standing beside him. White overall. Bare head. Pencil on ear. Age and physique unimportant.*

*P midstage standing on a black block 18 inches high. Black wide-brimmed hat. Black dressing-gown to ankles. Barefoot. Head bowed. Hands in pockets. Age and physique unimportant.*

*D and A contemplate P. Long pause.*

A: *(Finally.)* Like the look of him?
D: So so. *(Pause.)* Why the plinth?
A: To let the stalls see the feet.

*(Pause.)*

D: Why the hat?
A: To help hide the face.

*(Pause.)*

D: Why the gown?
A: To have him all black.

*(Pause.)*

D: What has he on underneath? *(A moves towards P.)* Say it.

*(A halts.)*

A: His night attire.
10 D: Colour?
A: Ash.

*(D takes out a cigar.)*

D: Light. *(A returns, lights the cigar, stands still, D smokes.)* How's the skull?
A: You've seen it.
D: I forget. *(A moves towards P.)* Say it.

*(A halts.)*

A: Moulting. A few tufts.
D: Colour?
A: Ash.

*(Pause.)*

D: Why hands in pockets?

A: To help have him all black.                                          20
D: They mustn't.
A: I make a note. *(She takes out a pad, takes pencil, notes.)* Hands exposed.

*(She puts back pad and pencil.)*

D: How are they? *(A at a loss. Irritably.)* The hands, how are the hands?
A: You've seen them.
D: I forget.
A: Crippled. Fibrous degeneration.
D: Clawlike?
A: If you like.                                                         30
D: Two claws?
A: Unless he clench his fists.
D: He mustn't.
A: I make a note. *(She takes out pad, takes pencil, notes.)* Hands limp.

*(She puts back pad and pencil.)*

D: Light. *(A returns, relights the cigar, stands still. D smokes.)* Good. Now let's have a look. *(A at a loss. Irritably.)* Get going. Lose that gown. *(He consults his chronometer.)* Step on it, I have a caucus.

*(A goes to P, takes off the gown. P submits, inert. A steps back, the gown over her arm. P in old grey pyjamas, head bowed, fists clenched. Pause.)*

A: Like him better without? *(Pause.)* He's shivering.       40
D: Not all that. Hat.

*(A advances, takes off hat, steps back, hat in hand. Pause.)*

A: Like that cranium?
D: Needs whitening.
A: I make a note. *(She takes out pad, takes pencil, notes.)* Whiten cranium.

*(She puts back pad and pencil.)*

D: The hands. *(A at a loss. Irritably.)* The fists. Get going. *(A advances, unclenches fists, steps back.)* And whiten.
A: I make a note. *(She takes out pad, takes pencil, notes.)* Whiten hands.

*(She puts back pad and pencil. They contemplate P.)*

D: *(Finally.)* Something wrong. *(Distraught.)* What is it?      50
A: *(Timidly.)* What if we were . . . were to . . . join them?
D: No harm trying. *(A advances, joins the hands, steps back.)* Higher. *(A advances, raises breast-high the joined hands, steps back.)* A touch more. *(A advances, raises breast-high the joined hands.)* Stop! *(A steps back.)* Better. It's coming. Light.

(A *returns, relights cigar, stands still.* D *smokes.*)

A: He's shivering.
D: Bless his heart.

(*Pause.*)

A: (*Timidly.*) What about a little . . . a little . . . gag?
60 D: For God's sake! This craze for explicitation! Every i dotted to death! Little gag! For God's sake!
A: Sure he won't utter?
D: Not a squeak. (*He consults his chronometer.*) Just time. I'll go and see how it looks from the house.

(*Exit* D, *not to appear again.* A *subsides in the armchair, springs to her feet no sooner seated, takes out a rag, wipes vigorously back and seat of chair, discards rag, sits again. Pause.*)

D: (*Off, plaintive.*) I can't see the toes. (*Irritably.*) I'm sitting in the front row of the stalls and can't see the toes.
A: (*Rising.*) I make a note. (*She takes out a pad, takes pencil, notes.*) Raise pedestal.
D: There's a trace of face.
70 A: I make a note.

(*She takes out pad, takes pencil, makes to note.*)

D: Down the head. (A *at a loss. Irritably.*) Get going. Down his head. (A *puts back pad and pencil, goes to* P, *bows his head further, steps back.*) A shade more. (A *advances, bows the head further.*) Stop! (A *steps back.*) Fine. It's coming. (*Pause.*) Could do with more nudity.
A: I make a note.

(*She takes out pad, makes to take her pencil.*)

D: Get going! Get going! (A *puts back the pad, goes to* P, *stands irresolute.*) Bare the neck. (A *undoes top buttons, parts the flaps, steps back.*) The legs. The shins. (A *advances, rolls up*
80 *to below knee one trouser-leg, steps back.*) The other. (*Same for other leg, steps back.*) Higher. The knees. (A *advances, rolls up to above knees both trouser-legs, steps back.*) And whiten.

A: I make a note. (*She takes out pad, takes pencil, notes.*) Whiten all flesh.
D: It's coming. Is Luke around?
A: (*Calling.*) Luke! (*Pause. Louder.*) Luke!
L: (*Off, distant.*) I hear you. (*Pause. Nearer.*) What's the trouble now?
A: Luke's around.                                                    90
D: Blackout stage.
L: What?

(A *transmits in technical terms. Fade-out of general light. Light on* P *alone.* A *in shadow.*)

D: Just the head.
L: What?

(A *transmits in technical terms. Fade-out of light on* P's *body. Light on head alone. Long pause.*)

D: Lovely.

(*Pause.*)

A: (*Timidly.*) What if he were to . . . were to . . . raise his head . . . an instant . . . show his face . . . just an instant.
D: For God's sake! What next? Raise his head? Where do you think we are? In Patagonia? Raise his head? For God's sake! (*Pause.*) Good. There's our catastrophe. In the bag. Once 100 more and I'm off.
A: (*To* L.) Once more and he's off.

(*Fade-up of light on* P's *body. Pause. Fade-up of general light.*)

D: Stop! (*Pause.*) Now . . . let 'em have it. (*Fade-out of general light. Pause. Fade-out of light on body. Light on head alone. Long pause.*) Terrific! He'll have them on their feet. I can hear it from here.

(*Pause. Distant storm of applause.* P *raises his head, fixes the audience. The applause falters, dies.*
*Long pause.*
*Fade-out of light on face.*)

# CASEBOOK ON BECKETT

Samuel Beckett
"Dante . . . Bruno.
Vico . . Joyce"
(1929)

*BECKETT wrote this essay for a collection,* Our Exagmination Round his Factification for Incamination of Work in Progress, *celebrating James Joyce's work on* Finnegans Wake, *then called simply "Work in Progress." Beckett's comments on Joyce, though, raise several issues germane to Beckett's work in the theater: the fusion of form and content, the difficulty of identifying the discourse of art with the very different discourse of philosophy, a Dantesque fascination with purgatory.*

The danger is in the neatness of identifications. The conception of Philosophy and Philology as a pair of nigger minstrels out of the Teatro dei Piccoli is soothing, like the contemplation of a carefully folded ham-sandwich. Giambattista Vico himself could not resist the attractiveness of such coincidence of gesture. He insisted on complete identification between the philosophical abstraction and the empirical illustration, thereby annulling the absolutism of each conception—hoisting the real unjustifiably clear of its dimensional limits, temporalizing that which is extratemporal. And now here am I, with my handful of abstractions, among which notably: a mountain, the coincidence of contraries, the inevitability of cyclic evolution, a system of Poetics, and the prospect of self-extension in the world of Mr Joyce's *Work in Progress*. There is the temptation to treat every concept like "a bass dropt neck fust in till a bung crate," and make a really tidy job of it. Unfortunately such an exactitude of application would imply distortion in one of two directions. Must we wring the neck of a certain system in order to stuff it into a contemporary pigeon-hole, or modify the dimensions of that pigeon-hole for the satisfaction of the analogymongers? Literary criticism is not book-keeping.

. . . . . . . . . . . . . . . . . . . . . . . . . . . . . . . . .

Giambattista Vico was a practical roundheaded Neapolitan. It pleases Croce to consider him as a mystic, essentially speculative, *"disdegnoso dell' empirismo."* It is a surprising interpretation, seeing that more than three-fifths of his *Scienza Nuova* is concerned with empirical investigation. Croce opposes him to the reformative materialistic school of Ugo Grozio, and absolves him from the utilitarian preoccupations of Hobbes, Spinoza, Locke, Bayle and Machiavelli. All this cannot be swallowed without protest. Vico defines Providence as: *"una mente spesso diversa ed alle volte tutta contraria e sempre superiore ad essi fini particolari che essi uomini si avevano proposti; dei quali fini ristretti fatti mezzi per servire a fini più ampi, gli ha sempre adoperati per conservare l'umana generazione in questa terra."* What could be more definitely utilitarianism? His treatment of the origin and functions of poetry, language and myth, as will appear later, is as far removed from the mystical as it is possible to imagine. For our immediate purpose, however, it matters little whether we consider him as a mystic or as a scientific investigator; but there are no two ways about considering him as an *innovator*. His division of the development of human society into three ages: Theocratic, Heroic, Human (civilized), with a corresponding classification of language: Hieroglyphic (sacred), Metaphorical (poetic), Philosophical (capable of abstraction and generalization), was by no means new, although it must have appeared so to his contemporaries. He derived this convenient classification from the Egyptians, via Herodotus. At the same time it is impossible to deny the originality with which he applied and developed its implications. His exposition of the ineluctable circular progression of Society was completely new, although the germ of it was contained in Giordano Bruno's treatment of identified contraries. But it is in Book 2, described by himself as *"tutto il corpo . . . la chiave maestra . . . dell' opera,"* that appears the unqualified originality of his mind; here he evolved a theory of the origins of poetry and language, the significance of myth, and the nature of barbaric civilization that must have appeared nothing less than an impertinent outrage against tradition. These two aspects of Vico have their reverberations, their reapplications—without, however, receiving the faintest explicit illustration—in *Work in Progress*.

It is first necessary to condense the thesis of Vico, the scientific historian. In the beginning was the thunder: the thunder set free Religion, in its most objective and unphilosophical form—idolatrous animism: Religion produced Society, and the first social men were the cave-dwellers, taking refuge from a passionate Nature: this primitive family life receives its first impulse towards development from the arrival of terrified vagabonds: admitted, they are the first slaves: growing stronger, they exact agrarian concessions, and a despotism has evolved into a primitive feudalism: the cave becomes a city, and the feudal system a democracy: then an anarchy: this is corrected by a return to monarchy: the last stage is a tendency towards interdestruction: the nations are dispersed, and the Phoenix of Society arises out of their ashes. To this six-termed social progression corresponds a six-termed progression of human motives: necessity, utility, convenience, pleasure, luxury, abuse of luxury: and their incarnate manifestations: Polyphemus, Achilles, Caesar and Alexander, Tiberius, Caligula and Nero. At this point Vico applies Bruno—though he takes very good care not to say so—and proceeds from rather arbitrary data to philosophical abstraction. There is no difference, says Bruno, between the smallest possible chord and the smallest possible arc, no difference between the infinite circle and the straight line. The maxima and minima of particular contraries are one and indifferent. Minimal heat equals minimal cold. Consequently transmutations are circular. The principle (minimum) of one contrary takes its movement from the principle (maximum) of one another. Therefore not only do the minima coincide with the minima, the maxima with the maxima, but the minima with the maxima in the succession of transmutations. Maximal speed is a state of rest. The maximum of corruption and the minimum of generation are identical: in principle, corruption is generation. And all things are ultimately identified with God, the universal monad, Monad of monads. From these considerations Vico evolved a Science and Philosophy of History. It may be an amusing exercise to take an historical figure, such as Scipio, and label him No. 3; it is of no ultimate importance. What is of ultimate importance is the recognition that the passage from Scipio to Caesar is as inevitable as the passage from Caesar to Tiberius, since the flowers of corruption in Scipio and Caesar are the seeds of vitality in Caesar and Tiberius. Thus we have the spectacle of a human progression that depends for its movement on individuals, and which at the same time is independent of individuals in virtue of what appears to be a preordained cyclicism. It follows that History is neither to be considered as a formless structure, due exclusively to the achievements of individual agents, nor as possessing reality apart from and independent of them, accomplished behind their backs in spite of them, the work of some superior force, variously known as Fate, Chance, Fortune, God. Both these views, the materialistic and the transcendental, Vico rejects in favour of the rational. Individuality is the concretion of universality, and every individual action is at the same time superindividual. The individual and the universal cannot be considered as distinct from each other. History, then, is not the result of Fate or Chance—in both cases the individual would be separated from his product—but the result of a Necessity that is not Fate, of a Liberty that is not Chance (compare Dante's "yoke of liberty"). This force he called Divine Providence, with his tongue, one feels, very much in his cheek. And it is to this Providence that we must trace the three institutions common to every society: Church, Marriage, Burial. This is not Bossuet's Providence, transcendental and miraculous, but immanent and the stuff itself of human life, working by natural means. Humanity is its work in itself. God acts on her, but by means of her. Humanity is divine, but no man is divine. This social and historical classification is clearly adapted by Mr Joyce as a structural convenience—or inconvenience. His position is in no way a philosophical one. It is the detached attitude of Stephen Dedalus in *Portrait of the Artist* . . . who describes Epictetus to the Master of Studies as "an old gentleman who said that the soul is very like a bucketful of water." The lamp is more important than the lamp-lighter. By structural I do not only mean a bold outward division, a bare skeleton for the housing of material. I mean the endless substantial variations on these three beats, and interior intertwining of these three themes into a decoration of arabesques—decoration and more than decoration. Part 1 is a mass of past shadow, corresponding therefore to Vico's first human institution, Religion, or to his Theocratic age, or simply to an abstraction—Birth. Part 2 is the lovegame of the children, corresponding to the second institution, Marriage, or to the Heroic age, or to an abstraction—Maturity. Part 3 is passed in sleep, corresponding to the third institution, Burial, or to the Human age, or to an abstraction—Corruption. Part 4 is the day beginning again, and corresponds to Vico's

Providence, or to an abstraction—Generation. Mr. Joyce does not take birth for granted, as Vico seems to have done. So much for the dry bones. The consciousness that there is a great deal of the unborn infant in the lifeless octogenarian, and a great deal of both in the man at the apogee of his life's curve, removes all the stiff interexclusiveness that is often the danger in neat construction. Corruption is not excluded from Part 1 nor maturity from Part 3. The four "lovedroyd curdinals" are presented on the same plane—'his element curdinal numen and his enement curdinal marrying and his epulent curdinal weisswasch and his eminent curdinal Kay o' Kay!' There are numerous references to Vico's four human institutions—Providence counting as one! "A good clap, a fore wedding, a bad wake, tell hell's well": "their weatherings and their marryings and their buryings and their natural selections": "the lightning look, the birding cry, awe from the grave, ever-flowing on our times": "by four hands of forethought the first babe of reconcilement is laid in its last cradle of hume sweet hume."

Apart from this emphasis on the tangible conveniences common to Humanity, we find frequent expressions of Vico's insistence on the inevitable character of every progression—or retrogression: "The Vico road goes round to meet where terms begin. Still onappealed to by the cycles and onappalled by the recoursers, we feel all serene, never you fret, as regards our dutyful cask . . . before there was a man at all in Ireland there was a lord at Lucan. We only wish everyone was as sure of anything in this watery world as we are of everything in the newlywet fellow that's bound to follow . . . .": "The efferfresh-painted livy in beautific repose upon the silence of the dead from Pharoph the next first down to ramescheckles the last bust thing." "In fact, under the close eyes of the inspectors the traits featuring the chiaroscuro coalesce, their contrarieties eliminated, in one stable somebody similarly as by the providential warring of heartshaker with housebreaker and of dramdrinker against freethinker our social something bowls along bumpily, experiencing a jolting series of prearranged disappointments, down the long lane of (it's as semper as oxhousehumper) generations, more generations and still more generations"—this last a case of Mr Joyce's rare subjectivism. In a word, here is all humanity circling with fatal monotony about the Providential fulcrum—the "convoy wheeling encircling abound the gigantig's lifetree." Enough has been said, or at least enough has been suggested, to show how Vico is substantially present in the *Work in Progress.* Passing to the Vico of the Poetics we hope to establish an even more striking, if less direct, relationship.

Vico rejected the three popular interpretations of the poetic spirit, which considered poetry as either an ingenious popular expression of philosophical conceptions, or an amusing social diversion, or an exact science within the research of everyone in possession of the recipe. Poetry, he says, was born of curiosity, daughter of ignorance. The first men had to create matter by the force of their imagination, and "poet" means "creator." Poetry was the first operation of the human mind, and without it thought could not exist. Barbarians, incapable of analysis and abstraction, must use their fantasy to explain what their reasons cannot comprehend. Before articulation comes song; before abstract terms, metaphors. The figurative character of the oldest poetry must be regarded, not as sophisticated confectionery, but as evidence of a poverty-stricken vocabulary and of a disability to achieve abstraction. Poetry is essentially the antithesis of Metaphysics: Metaphysics purge the mind of the senses and cultivate the disembodiment of the spiritual; Poetry is all passion and feeling and animates the inanimate; Metaphysics are most perfect when most concerned with universals; Poetry, when most concerned with particulars. Poets are the sense, philosophers the intelligence of humanity. Considering the Scholastics' axiom: *"niente è nell'intelletto che prima non sia nel senso,"* it follows that poetry is a prime condition of philosophy and civilization. The primitive animistic movement was a manifestation of the *"forma poetica dello spirito."*

His treatment of the origin of language proceeds along similar lines. Here again he rejected the materialistic and transcendental views; the one declaring that language was nothing but a polite and conventional symbolism; the other, in desperation, describing it as a gift from the Gods. As before, Vico is the rationalist, aware of the natural and inevitable growth of language. In its first dumb form, language was gesture. If a man wanted to say "sea," he pointed to the sea. With the spread of animism this gesture was replaced by the word: "Neptune." He directs our attention to the fact that every need of life, natural, moral and economic, has its verbal expression in one or other of the 30,000 Greek divinities. This is Homer's "language of the Gods." Its evolution through poetry to a highly civilized vehicle, rich in abstract and technical terms, was as little fortuitous as the evolution of society itself. Words have their progressions as well as social phases. "Forest-cabin-village-city-academy" is one rough progression. Another: "mountain-plain-riverbank." And every word expands with psychological inevitability. Take the Latin word: "Lex."

1. Lex       = Crop of acorns.
2. Ilex      = Tree that produces acorns.
3. Legere    = To gather.
4. Aquilex   = He that gathers the waters.
5. Lex       = Gathering together of peoples, public assembly.
6. Lex       = Law.
7. Legere    = To gather together letters into a word, to read.

The root of any word whatsoever can be traced back to some prelingual symbol. This early inability to abstract the general from the particular produced the Type-names. It is the child's mind over again. The child extends the names of the first familiar objects to other strange objects in which he is conscious of some analogy. The first men, unable to conceive the abstract idea of "poet" or "hero," named every hero after the first hero, every poet after the first poet. Recognizing this custom of designating a number of individuals by the names of their prototypes, we can explain various classical and mythological mysteries. Hermes is the prototype of the Egyptian inventor: so for Romulus, the great law-giver, and Hercules, the Greek hero: so for Homer. Thus Vico asserts the spontaneity of language and denies the dualism of poetry and language. Similarly, poetry is the foundation of writing. When language consisted of gesture, the spoken and written were identical. Hieroglyphics, or sacred language, as he calls it, were not the invention of philosophers for the mysterious expression of profound thought, but the common necessity of primitive peoples. Convenience only begins to assert itself at a far more advanced stage of civilization, in the form of alphabetism. Here Vico, implicitly at least, distinguishes between writing and direct expression. In such direct expression, form and content are inseparable. Examples are the medals of the Middle Ages, which bore no inscription and were a mute testimony to the feebleness of conventional alphabetic writing: and the flags of our own day. As with Poetry and Language, so with Myth. Myth, according to Vico, is neither an allegorical expression of general philosophical axioms (Conti, Bacon), nor a derivative from particular peoples, as for instance the Hebrews or Egyptians, nor yet the work of isolated poets, but an historical statement of fact, of actual contemporary phenomena, actual in the sense that they were created out of necessity by primitive minds, and firmly believed. Allegory implies a threefold intellectual operation: the construction of a message of general significance, the preparation of a fabulous form, and an exercise of considerable technical difficulty in uniting the two, an operation totally beyond the reach of the primitive mind. Moreover, if we consider the myth as being essentially allegorical, we are not obliged to accept the form in which it is cast as a statement of fact. But we know that the actual creators of these myths gave full credence to their face-value. Jove was no symbol: he was terribly real. It was precisely their superficial metaphorical character that made them intelligible to people incapable of receiving anything more abstract than the plain record of objectivity.

Such is a painful exposition of Vico's dynamic treatment of Language, Poetry and Myth. He may still appear as a mystic to some: if so, a mystic that rejects the transcendental in every shape and form as a factor in human development, and whose Providence is not divine enough to do without the cooperation of Humanity.

On turning to the *Work in Progress* we find that the mirror is not so convex. Here is direct expression—pages and pages of it. And if you don't understand it, Ladies and Gentlemen, it is because you are too decadent to receive it. You are not satisfied unless form is so strictly divorced from content that you can comprehend the one almost without bothering to read the other. The rapid skimming and absorption of the scant cream of sense is made possible by what I may call a continuous process of copious intellectual salivation. The form that is an arbitrary and independent phenomenon can fulfil no higher function than that of stimulus for a tertiary or quartary conditioned reflex of dribbling comprehension. When Miss Rebecca West clears her decks for a sorrowful deprecation of the Narcisstic element in Mr Joyce by the purchase of 3 hats, one feels that she might very well wear her bib at all her intellectual banquets, or alternatively, assert a more noteworthy control over her salivary glands than is possible for Monsieur Pavlov's unfortunate dogs. The title of this book is a good example of a form carrying a strict inner determination. It should be proof against the usual volley of cerebral sniggers: and it may suggest to some a dozen incredulous Joshuas prowling around the Queen's Hall, springing their tuning-forks lightly against finger-nails that have not yet been refined out of existence. Mr Joyce has a word to say to you on the subject: "Yet to concentrate solely on the literal sense or even the psychological content of any document to the sore neglect of the enveloping facts themselves circumstantiating it is just as harmful; etc." And another: "Who in his heart doubts either that the facts of feminine clothiering are there all the time or that the feminine fiction, stranger than the facts, is there also at the same time, only a little to the rere? Or that one may be separated from the other? Or that both may be contemplated simultaneously? Or that each may be taken up in turn and considered apart from the other?"

Here form *is* content, content *is* form. You complain that this stuff is not written in English. It is not written at all. It is not to be read—or rather it is not only to be read. It is to be looked at and listened to. His writing is not *about* something; *it is that something itself.* (A fact that has been grasped by an eminent English novelist and historian whose work is in complete opposition to Mr Joyce's.) When the sense is sleep, the words go to sleep. (See the end of *Anna Livia.*) When the sense is dancing, the words dance. Take the passage at the end of Shaun's pastoral: "To stir up love's young fizz I tilt with this bridle's cup champagne, dimming douce from her peepair of hide-seeks tight squeezed on my snowybreasted and while my pearlies in their sparkling wisdom are nip-pling her bubblets I swear (and let you swear) by the bumper round of my poor old snaggletooth's solidbowel I ne'er will prove I'm untrue to (theare!) you liking so long as my hole looks. Down." The language is drunk. The very words are tilted and effervescent. How can we qualify this general esthetic vigilance without which we cannot hope to snare the sense which is for ever rising to the surface of the form and becoming the form itself? St Augustine puts us on the track of a word with his *"intendere,"* Dante has; *"Donne ch'avete intelletto d'amore,"* and *"Voi che, intendendo, il terzo ciel movete;"* but his *"intendere"* suggests a strictly intellectual operation. When an Italian says to-day *"Ho inteso,"* he means something between *"Ho udito"* and *"Ho capito,"* a sensuous un-tidy art of intellection. Perhaps "apprehension" is the most satisfactory English word. Stephen says to Lynch: "Temporal or spatial, the esthetic image is first luminously apprehended as selfbounded and selfcontained upon the immeasurable background of space or time which is not it . . . You ap-prehend its wholeness." There is one point to make clear: the Beauty of *Work in Progress* is not presented in space alone, since its adequate apprehension depends as much on its visibility as on its audibility. There is a temporal as well as a spatial unity to be apprehended. Substitute "and" for "or" in the quotation, and it becomes obvious why it is as inadequate to speak of "reading" *Work in Progress* as it would be extravagant to speak of "apprehending" the work of the late Mr Nat Gould. Mr Joyce has desophisticated language. And it is worth while remarking that no language is so so-phisticated as English. It is abstracted to death. Take the word "doubt": it gives us hardly any sen-suous suggestion of hesitancy, of the necessity for choice, of static irresolution. Whereas the German "Zweifel" does, and, in lesser degree, the Italian "dubitare." Mr Joyce recognizes how in-adequate "doubt" is to express a state of extreme uncertainty, and replaces it by "in twosome twi-minds." Nor is he by any means the first to recognize the importance of treating words as something more than mere polite symbols. Shakespeare uses fat, greasy words to express corrup-tion: "Duller shouldst thou be than the fat weed that rots itself in death on Lethe wharf." We hear the ooze squelching all through Dickens's description of the Thames in *Great Expectations.* This writing that you find so obscure is a quintessential extraction of language and painting and gesture, with all the inevitable clarity of the old inarticulation. Here is the savage economy of hieroglyph-ics. Here words are not the polite contortions of 20th century printer's ink. They are alive. They elbow their way on to the page, and glow and blaze and fade and disappear. "Brawn is my name and broad is my nature and I've breit on my brow and all's right with every feature and I'll brune this bird or Brown Bess's bung's gone bandy." This is Brawn blowing with a light gust through the trees or Brawn passing with the sunset. Because the wind in the trees means as little to you as the evening prospect from the Piazzale Michelangiolo—though you accept them both because your non-acceptance would be of no significance, this little adventure of Brawn means nothing to you—

and you do not accept it, even though here also your non-acceptance is of no significance. H. C. Earwigger, too, is not content to be mentioned like a shilling-shocker villain, and then dropped until the exigencies of the narrative require that he be again referred to. He continues to suggest himself for a couple of pages, by means of repeated permutations on his "normative letters," as if to say: "This is all about me, H. C. Earwigger: don't forget this is all about me!" This inner elemental vitality and corruption of expression imparts a furious restlessness to the form, which is admirably suited to the purgatorial aspect of the work. There is an endless verbal germination, maturation, putrefaction, the cyclic dynamism of the intermediate. This reduction of various expressive media to their primitive economic directness, and the fusion of these primal essences into an assimilated medium for the exteriorization of thought, is pure Vico, and Vico, applied to the problem of style. But Vico is reflected more explicitly than by a distillation of disparate poetic ingredients into a synthetical syrup. We notice that there is little or no attempt at subjectivism or abstraction, no attempt at metaphysical generalization. We are presented with a statement of the particular. It is the old myth: the girl on the dirt track, the two washerwomen on the banks of the river. And there is considerable animism: the mountain "abhearing," the river puffing her old doudheen. (See the beautiful passage beginning: "First she let her hair fall down and it flussed.") We have Type-names: Isolde—any beautiful girl: Earwigger—Guinness's Brewery, the Wellington monument, the Phoenix Park, anything that occupies an extremely comfortable position between the two stools. Anna Livia herself, mother of Dublin, but no more the only mother than Zoroaster was the only oriental stargazer. "Teems of times and happy returns. The same anew. Ordovico or viricordo. Anna was, Livia is, Plurabelle's to be. Northmen's thing made Southfolk's place, but howmultyplurators made each one in person." Basta! Vico and Bruno are here, and more substantially than would appear from this swift survey of the question. For the benefit of those who enjoy a parenthetical sneer, we would draw attention to the fact that when Mr Joyce's early pamphlet *The Day of Rabblement* appeared, the local philosophers were thrown into a state of some bewilderment by a reference in the first line to "The Nolan." They finally succeeded in identifying this mysterious individual with one of the obscurer ancient Irish kings. In the present work he appears frequently as "Browne & Nolan," the name of a very remarkable Dublin Bookseller and Stationer.

To justify our title, we must move North, *"Sovra'l bel fiume d'Arno alla gran villa"* . . . Between *"colui per lo cui verso—il meonio cantor non è più solo"* and the "still to-day insufficiently malestimated notesnatcher, Shem the Penman," there exists considerable circumstantial similarity. They both saw how worn out and threadbare was the conventional language of cunning literary artificers, both rejected an approximation to a universal language. If English is not yet so definitely a polite necessity as Latin was in the Middle Ages, at least one is justified in declaring that its position in relation to other European languages is to a great extent that of medieval Latin to the Italian dialects. Dante did not adopt the vulgar out of any kind of local jingoism nor out of any determination to assert the superiority of Tuscan to all its rivals as a form of spoken Italian. On reading his *De Vulgari Eloquentia* we are struck by his complete freedom from civic intolerance. He attacks the world's Portadownians: *"Nam quicumque tam obscenae rationis est, ut locum suae nationis delitosissimum credat esse sub sole, huic etiam proe cunctis propriam volgare licetur, idest maternam locutionem. Nos autem, cui mundus est patria . . ."* etc." When he comes to examine the dialects he finds Tuscan: *"turpissimum . . . fere omnes Tusci in suo turpiloquio obtusi . . . non restat in dubio quin aliud sit vulgare quod quaerimus quam quod attingit populus Tuscanorum."* His conclusion is that the corruption common to all the dialects makes it impossible to select one rather than another as an adequate literary form, and that he who would write in the vulgar must assemble the purest elements from each dialect and construct a synthetic language that would at least possess more than a circumscribed local interest: which is precisely what he did. He did not write in Florentine any more than in Neapolitan. He wrote a vulgar that *could* have been spoken by an ideal Italian who had assimilated what was best in all the dialects of his country, but which in fact was certainly not spoken nor ever had been. Which disposes of the capital objection that might be made against this attractive parallel between Dante and Mr Joyce in the question of language, i.e. that at least Dante wrote what was being spoken in the streets of his own town, whereas no creature in heaven or earth ever spoke the language of *Work in Progress*. It is reasonable to admit that an international phenomenon might be capable of speaking it, just as in 1300 none but an inter-regional phenomenon could have spoken the language of the Divine Comedy. We are inclined to forget that Dante's literary public was Latin that the form of his Poem was to be judged by Latin eyes and ears, by a Latin Esthetic intolerant of innovation, and which could hardly fail to be irritated by the substitution of *"Nel mezzo del cammin di nostra vita"* with its "barbarous" directness for the suave elegance of: *"Ultima regna canam, fluido contermina mundo,"* just as English eyes and ears prefer: "Smoking his favourite pipe in the sacred presence of ladies" to: "Rauking his flavourite turfco in the smukking precincts of lydias." Boccaccio did not jeer at the *"piedi sozzi"* of the peacock that Signora Alighieri dreamed about.

I find two well made caps in the *"Convivio,"* one to fit the collective noodle of the monodialectical arcadians whose fury is precipitated by a failure to discover "innoce-free" in the concise Oxford Dictionary and who qualify as the "ravings of a Bedlamite" the formal structure raised by Mr Joyce after years of patient and inspired labour: *"Questi sono da chiamare pecore e non uomini; chè se una pecora si gittasse da una ripa di mille passi, tutte l'altre le adrebbono dietro; e se una pecore a per alcuna cagione al passare d'una strada salta, tutte le altre saltano, eziando nulla veggendo da saltare. E io ne vidi già molte in un pozzo saltare, per una che dentro vi salto, forse credendo di saltare un muro."* And the other for Mr Joyce, biologist in words: *"Questo* (formal innovation) *sarà luce nuova, sole nuovo, il quale sorgerà ore l'usato tramonterà e darà luce a coloro che sono in tenebre e in oscurità per lo usato sole che a loro non luce."* And, lest he should pull it down over his eyes and laugh behind the peak, I translate *"in tenebre e in oscurità"* by "bored to extinction." (Dante makes a curious mistake speaking of the origin of language, when he rejects the authority of Genesis that Eve was the first to speak, when she addressed the Serpent. His incredulity is amusing: *"inconvenienter putatur tam egregium humani generis actum, vel prius quam a viro, foemina profluisse."* But before Eve was born, "the animals were given names by Adam," the man who "first said goo to a goose." Moreover it is explicitly stated that the choice of names was left entirely to Adam, so that there is not the slightest Biblical authority for the conception of language as a direct gift of God, any more than there is any intellectual authority for conceiving that we are indebted for the "Concert" to the individual who used to buy paint for Giorgione.)

We know very little about the immediate reception accorded to Dante's mighty vindication of the "vulgar," but we can form our own opinions when, two centuries later, we find Castiglione splitting more than a few hairs concerning the respective advantages of Latin and Italian, and Poliziano writing the dullest of dull Latin Elegies to justify his existence as the author of *"Orfeo"* and the *"Stanze."* We may also compare, if we think it worth while, the storm of ecclesiastical abuse raised by Mr Joyce's work, and the treatment that the Divine Comedy must certainly have received from the same source. His Contemporary Holiness might have swallowed the crucifixion of *"lo sommo Giove,"* and all it stood for, but he could scarcely have looked with favour on the spectacle of three of his immediate predecessors plunged head-foremost in the fiery stone of Malebolge, nor yet the identification of the Papacy in the mystical procession of Terrestrial Paradise with a *"puttana sciolta."* The *"De Monarshia"* was burnt publicly under Pope Giovanni XXII at the instigation of Cardinal Beltrando and the bones of its author would have suffered the same fate but for the interference of an influential man of letters, Pino della Tosa. Another point of comparison is the preoccupation with the significance of numbers. The death of Beatrice inspired nothing less than a highly complicated poem dealing with the importance of the number 3 in her life. Dante never ceased to be obsessed by this number. Thus the poem is divided into three Cantiche, each composed of 33 Canti, and written in terza rima. Why, Mr Joyce seems to say, should there be four legs to a table, and four to a horse, and four seasons and four Gospels and four Provinces in Ireland? Why twelve Tables of the Law, and twelve Apostles and twelve months and twelve Napoleonic marshals and twelve men in Florence called Ottolenghi? Why should the Armistice be celebrated at the eleventh hour of the eleventh day of the eleventh month? He cannot tell you because he is not God Almighty, but in a thousand years he will tell you, and in the meantime must be content to know why horses have not five legs, nor three. He is conscious that things with a common numerical characteristic tend towards a very significant interrelationship. This preoccupation is freely translated in his present work, see the "Question and Answer" chapter, and the Four speaking through the child's brain. They are the four winds as much as the four Provinces, and the four Episcopal Sees as much as either.

A last word about the Purgatories. Dante's is conical and consequently implies culmination. Mr Joyce's is spherical and excludes culmination. In the one there is an ascent from real vegetation—Ante-Purgatory, to ideal vegetation—Terrestrial Paradise: in the other there is no ascent and no ideal vegetation. In the one, absolute progression and a guaranteed consummation: in the other, flux—progression or retrogression, and an apparent consummation. In the one movement is unidirectional, and a step forward represents a net advance: in the other movement is non-directional—or multi-directional, and a step forward is, by definition, a step back. Dante's Terrestrial Paradise is the carriage entrance to a Paradise that is not terrestrial: Mr Joyce's Terrestrial Paradise is the tradesmen's entrance on to the sea-shore. Sin is an impediment to movement up the cone, and a condition of movement round the sphere. In what sense, then, is Mr Joyce's work purgatorial? In the absolute absence of the Absolute. Hell is the static lifelessness of unrelieved viciousness. Paradise the static lifelessness of unrelieved immaculation. Purgatory a flood of movement and vitality released by the conjunction of these two elements. There is a continuous purgatorial process at work, in the sense that the vicious circle of humanity is being achieved, and this achievement depends on the recurrent predomination of one of two broad qualities. No resistance, no eruption, and it is only in Hell and Paradise that there are no eruptions, that there can be none, need be none. On this earth that is Purgatory, Vice and Virtue—which you may take to mean any pair of large contrary human factors—must in turn be purged down to spirits of rebelliousness. Then the dominant crust of the Vicious or Virtuous sets, resistance is provided, the explosion duly takes place and the machine proceeds. And no more than this; neither prize nor penalty; simply a series of stimulants to enable the kitten to catch its tail. And the partially purgatorial agent? The partially purged.

---

*IN this essay, the distinguished American stage director Alan Schneider describes the process of bringing Beckett's then-new drama to the stage.*

## Alan Schneider
### (1917–1984)

*"Working with Beckett"*
*(1976)*

Through twenty theatrical seasons, I have happily carried a typescript by Samuel Beckett with me to rehearsals through more than that number of productions—in Washington or Texas or San Francisco, in New York's off-Broadway, and twice even on to Broadway itself. On three occasions, those scripts had never before been performed—*Happy Days* (1961), *Film* (1964), and *Not I* (1972). On four others—*Waiting for Godot* (1956), *Endgame* (1958), *Krapp's Last Tape* (1959), *Play* (1964)—the scripts were receiving their first production in English and/or in the United States. And more than a dozen other times, I have carried these same or other scripts of his through a proscenium arch, onto the thrust stage, or out directly into the middle of an audience—something Mr. Beckett had neither expected or entirely understood. In these twenty years, there have been few times when I had not just finished directing one Beckett work or another or was not actively planning to do another one.

Did I gravitate to Sam at once, immediately recognizing his dramatic genius? Truthfully, I'm not sure. When I first read *Endgame* in manuscript, I told Barney Rossett, Beckett's American publisher, that it seemed to me like a combination of *Oedipus* and *King Lear*. This was before either Jan Kott's book or the Brook-Scofield production, so I must have had the correct sympathetic vibrations. But did I recognize it then as a major work of the twentieth century? And that first time I watched *Godot* at the Babylone in Paris back in 1954, without catching more than a portion of its French dialogue, I did at least respond emotionally enough to its stage directions to try—at that time unsuccessfully—locating the playwright to have him translate it into English for me. One year later, when I first read the English text, I remained equally intrigued and baffled, trying to figure out which one of those two fellows was which. But when a producer happened to offer the play to me to direct, I at once accepted. Even though at that time, as now, I had serious reservations about both the producer and the play's viability for Broadway audiences. But the moment I started to work on the text itself, I was hooked, as I have been on every one of them ever since.

Which of the almost dozen different plays of his which I've directed, I am always being asked, do I prefer? That's like asking a parent to pick out a favorite child. Or making a mountain climber name his favorite peak. All I can really say is that they've all spoiled me for the lowlands. I tend to prefer the Beckett play I'm working on at whatever moment I'm asked. Though, perhaps, *Krapp* and *Happy Days* seem to be most human and moving. Or *Endgame*. Or *Godot*, which is no longer a play but a condition of life. Let's just say: The one I favor is the one I'm going to be working on next. On all of these working occasion, with the one exception where Beckett was told that the shooting of a very unusual filmscript absolutely required his physical presence, my favorite playwright has never wanted to venture forth from his Parisian privacy to face the periods of production à l'Americaine. So that in a real sense, this present account of my experiences with his plays might more accurately be labeled "Not Working with Beckett"; or "Working with Beckett's"; or, perhaps most exactly, "Working on Beckett."

Sam's continued reluctance to cross the Atlantic to be with me in rehearsal is no proof that he is the shadowy recluse pictured by his interviewers. Actually, he remains the most accessible of men and authors—though only to his friends. He has, after all, taken an active role in most of his French productions; and he has even managed to cross the Channel in order to be of assistance to directors George Devine and Donald McWhinnie. And he has regularly journeyed to Berlin himself to direct new productions of his plays at the Schiller Theater. Why then never to New York except for *Film*? Does he trust me or mistrust me so much? Is he not interested enough in the American theater's attempts at his plays, in contrast to his feelings about what the European stage does with them? Does it take Buster Keaton to get him over here?

Sam could answer those questions better than I can. But my own impression is that the truth, as always with Beckett, is much simpler. New York is just too far away and too noisy, the job of getting here too demanding. Nor does he especially favor either press conferences or cocktail parties, occupational hazards he has discovered to be endemic to the American production process. Nor, I am supposing, have his early publishing experiences (prior to Grove Press) with American commercialism and commercial Americans endeared him generally to our jangled rhythms and demands. He prefers to stay away if he can, gently but firmly declining all manner of invitations, whether they come from Harvard or the neighborhood of Washington Square.

Not that I've been content to have him stay away. In the theater, I agree with my friend and Sam's, the late Jackie MacGowran, that we most of the time seem to be trying to keep the author out but with Beckett we feel just the other way around: We want him in. To hold our hands through the darkness. To illuminate the dots, interpret the ellipses, and explain the unexplainable. To hover and fume (though he'd never let us see). So although he'd never actually been there, I've always rehearsed as though he were in the shadows somewhere watching and listening, ready to answer all our doubts, quell our fears, and share our surprises and small talk. Sometimes, without sounding too mystical or psychotic, I've felt that he was indeed there, and that I might easily be talking with him. Once we all did talk to him, when we nicknamed the light that flicked from urn to urn in *Play*, "Sam."

In work then, all of his texts—and that word includes both dialogue and stage directions—have always been "Sam's" to me, a marriage in absentia, in which I have loved, honored, and obeyed as though he were always with me. Every actor and actress cast by me for a Beckett production, every designer of setting and costumes and lighting—and posters—every producer and would-be producer has had to deal with me on this one fundamental premise: We're doing Sam's play more or less in the way he'd want it to be done; "at least insofar as I as the director can understand that and transmit it to you." Whatever else may be happening, we're not trying to put anything over on Sam.

Having Sam actually at rehearsals, however, would have made my problems easier. At least, deciding what he really wanted or meant at any given moment would have been immediately possible, without anyone's taking or not taking my word for that. Resolving all those inevitable differences of opinion or interpretation of each word and each moment. And clearing up his specific technical demands, all those complications that those simple little Beckett plays with one or two characters and hardly any scenery, manage to be loaded with: undersized ashcans and oversized urns, parasols that burn up on cue but not before, carafes that fly without twisting slowly, slowly in the wind, a Mouth that floats unsupported in space, and a Figure with head and arms lit up but with feet invisible.

And, best of all, with him there, it would have been more possible to adapt and change something. Because like the rest of us, whenever Sam goes to work on a given production, he understands its uniqueness and special problems. Something for some reason (whether acting or technical) doesn't seem to be working, or might be more interesting with some slight variation. a line doesn't sound exactly right coming from that particular actor, or the actor cannot deal properly with a certain prop. When, for example, I wanted to add an overhead lamp to Krapp's den, it took me some weeks to get up the nerve to ask Sam. Had he been there, he would have seen the pool of light that such a lamp at once created and agreed at once—instead of getting a description and a request from me and answering back, "Yes, of course." When I wrote to explain that "weir" was too unfamiliar a word for us, suggesting "dam" as an alternative, Sam came back with "lock." As well as, years later, Erskine for Arsene, which was too specifically French. How much more leeway we would have always had if only he had been with us day by day!

I have always held to the old-fashioned belief that a first production—certainly of a living author, especially of an author as clear and explicit in his directions to all concerned as Beckett has always been (and is increasingly becoming)—should try to bring to stage life the author's play. Should a director disagree, significantly or violently, he shouldn't be doing that play. Nor do I believe that the creative ego has necessarily to feed on the principle of contradicting the author or trying to substitute for, elaborate upon, evade, or elude the author's own point of view, or to use the text as simply the starting point for the director's virtuosity. Interpretation is one thing—like *Hamlet*, *Godot* will always be different when filtered through a director's temperament and the imponderables of casting—but interpolation is quite another, not to mention extrapolation, and the intrusion of a subtext that clearly distorts instead of illuminating its text.

Not too immodestly, I hope, I admit that my directorial mind is quite capable of conceiving *Godot* with an all-female cast—and, in fact, had one such in an acting class I once supervised long enough ago to have included several performers since elevated (?) to stardom. Nor am I any longer appalled at the idea of Vladimir and Estragon as homosexuals—but reject it as I have thousands of other ideas equally unrelated to the play. Let's say the idea of having the two playing cat's cradle with string all through the graveyard scene. I've seen (or myself used) *Godot's* tree bedecked, in the second act, with the greenest of ribbons, balloons, rubber bands, even spaghetti, even leaves (real or stylized); but the idea (which graced a recent highly praised version) of not having the tree onstage at all is not one I can immediately respond to, even in theory. Nor do I yet understand why having Hamm and Clov ad lib a hodge-podge of pop-art songs and slogans, not to mention having Clov sit and Nell and Nagg pop in and out like box puppets at various times not even suggested by the text, or opening the play with Nelson Eddy and Jeanette MacDonald singing away on a gradually running-down record, is necessarily preferable to honoring the lines and pauses by trying to discover why Beckett put them there in the first place—and doing something theatrically interesting with that knowledge. Shakespeare, of course, is being done (including sometimes by myself) in everything from bathing suits to cave-man outfits with all the concomitant details. I once did *Macbeth* with six witches (though I am now embarrassed to admit that only three appeared to the audience at any given time; the others were doubles who made the witches seem to be able to fly through space). And Beckett will one day be performed in seventeenth century armor or space suits with *Godot* as an extraterrestrial intelligence, as well as set to music (*Godot* already has been). But in the blessed meantime, at least within the author's own span of life and awareness, I utterly reject the "colored lights" school of production and favor an author's inalienable right to the relative satisfaction of his own intentions, limited as they may be.

I got into my very first troubles with a Beckett production early in the game, on my first *Godot*, when I actively resisted Bert Lahr's open desire to be top banana, with Tom Ewell as second banana. Very simply, Bert wanted to relegate the role of Vladimir to that of straight man. In the instance of Lucky's speech, he wanted to cut it out entirely "since nobody understands it anyway"; at the very least, since I would neither cut it nor let him go offstage during the speech, he insisted on doing lots of comic business all through it so that no one would have to listen and be bored. After all, they had come to see Bert and not the actor playing Lucky, whoever he was—and to hear Bert repeat his familiar "Onnnggg-onnnggg" in response to his recurrent realization of his fate instead of Mr. Beckett's simpler and very ordinary (but how extraordinary) "Ahh." The fact that Bert was superbly eloquent in many of his own manifestations of Estragon's character didn't make my choices easier. Eventually, another director more willing to accept and deal with Bert's insecurities took the play to New York—and away from Beckett.

When the original off-Broadway producers of *Endgame* at the Cherry Lane wanted to bring a gag man in to amplify Sam's (and my) lack of humor, or when one of the actors who replaced our original Clov wanted to explore less conventionally than had the author what the character might be doing in the play's opening sequences instead of climbing up to look out those two windows, I demurred both times—on the play's own stated premise that nothing is funnier than unhappiness. And when Buster Keaton wanted to keep sharpening the end of a broken pencil until it got smaller and smaller and eventually disappeared, a "bit" he told me he had always used successfully, I explained—quietly, I trust—that we were only doing what was in the shooting script, funny or unfunny as it happened to be. All the way down to someone's repeated suggestion while we were doing *Not I* to blow up the Mouth on to a giant full-stage color TV screen so that the audiences at the Lincoln Center Forum would be able to see and understand the play better. Not I, said I.

This attitude on my part, by the way, has not prevented a few of my not-so-friendly neighborhood critics, who feel that I have somehow hypnotized Sam into giving me a stranglehold on his work, from accusing me of seriously distorting his plays. I shudder to think what such nongentlemen of the press would have said about me had I actually tampered with Beckett's texts and intentions even a fraction of the extent to which certain recent productions (some not authorized and sometimes not paying royalties) have done—in the process being praised for transmitting the author's "true" intentions. One leading critic has even blamed me for adding bananas and other extraneous business to my most recent version of *Krapp's Last Tape*. The revisions in some of Krapp's pantomime were the result of Sam's own experiences in Berlin, which of course the critic had no way of knowing about. The bananas, however, are quite apparent in the text. What such critics do not at all understand is that I didn't have to hypnotize Sam. He's just been burned too many times elsewhere by too many people in too many ways.

With all my Beckett productions, then, I have been more faithful than the pope himself often required. And since Rome (or in this case, Paris) has never except for that once come to me, I have always gone to Paris, to get the full benefit of the author's "stutherings," as he once described them. Before each production, including that first one, I've sailed or flown or trained or driven—at the production's expense, if possible; if not, on my own—to spend whatever time with Sam he could give me. Punctual as a churchbell, he always comes first to my hotel, the boulevard Raspail's modest l'Aiglon, which I found by accident of fate back in 1949 on my first pre-Beckett visit and have stayed in ever since, later to discover it was around the corner from Sam and an old favorite of his. I sit with him in his favorite cafés and restaurants, sometimes in his apartment around that corner. We eat, drink, wander through the Luxembourg Gardens or elsewhere in Montparnasse. I badger him with all the questions and problems that I've jotted down or that occur to me as we walk and talk. Sometimes, we don't even mention the play, although we do get into everything else—from the state of the damnation to my daughter's schooling. He is fond of her, remembering her as a little girl playing in front of l'Aiglon. When he speaks with the waiters, Sam always seems completely French to me—and to the waiters; when he talks with me, he's very Irish.

As much as possible, those conversations are like ones we would be having if he were in New York at rehearsals, and the atmosphere is very like that of the Village, although somewhat more pleasant because we're in Paris. Naturally, it's impossible to anticipate even a fraction of what may happen during production or actually does. But while such preliminary meetings cannot be as valuable as the real day-by-day give and take of rehearsals, they are not without benefits or concrete results.

Over the years, the benefits have increased and the results intensified, and the meetings between us have mellowed from that first formal conference he so grudgingly granted to "the American director" of *Godot*, whose name he didn't know. My questions have gotten less general and silly, more carefully thought through and phrased. The answers have come more willingly, even if they have not always been complete ones. And I have been able to interpret them more precisely because I have understood the pauses as well as the words.

That very first time, I asked Sam who or what Godot was, though luckily not what it "meant"; and he told me, after a moment of deep reflection in those seemingly bottomless blue-gray eyes, that if he had known, he would have said so in his play. The last time I came over to talk about a production, it was to encourage him to write a companion piece to Hume Cronyn's rendition of *Krapp's Last Tape*, bringing along the companion-lady in question to inspire him. It turned out that Sam liked the lady and happened to have something in his trunk, or in his desk, that if he could do a bit of work on it, it might fit her nicely. He did, it did, and we did it—after a few days of questions and thoughts and wanderings and cafés. On all the visits in between, I've always asked him everything I could think of, and Sam has always tried to answer as fully and as specifically as he could. And at the end of it all, after he's delivered me in his rusty tin buggy of a Citroën in the Invalides air terminal or the Gare du Nord, he always has sent me homeward with the same farewell:

> Do it anny way you like, Alan; anny way you like.

Once, Sam came over to join me in London, where we went together to see the original English *Godot*, then playing at the Criterion. It had just transferred from a successful run at the Arts, although the theater was not full and people were walking out all during the performance, sometimes loudly venting their British spleen. Sam sat next to me in various sections of the stalls for four or five nights in a row, staring in somewhat stunned amazement at the proceedings on stage and in the audience, occasionally leaning over to whisper to me: "They're doing it ahl whrang," referring to what was taking place on the stage. One evening, while we were backstage in the absence of the director, who happened to be the youthful Peter Hall, I had to prevent Sam firmly from giving out an array of written notes to the actors. Under the mistaken assumption that I was part of the opposition to his production, I'm afraid, Peter Hall has never forgiven me. But at least I did learn what Sam considered to be "ahl whrang." So that I could eventually go back and do it "anny way" I liked. As if I actually could.

But even after I've gotten back each time, there have always been afterthoughts, new questions, new explanations. Never has there failed to be a further exchange of ideas and problems between us, a dialogue via airmail. Continued and regular cross-currents of air-letters, postcards, or just little pieces of paper, typed or printed, or scrawled so unintelligibly as to challenge the top cryptographer for the CIA. Over the years now, seemingly hundreds of them, suddenly part of theater history though once read and reread and studied and cherished for their apt responsiveness to a particularly crucial confusion.

Since that brief initial inquiry into the cosmic nature of *Godot*, Sam has never wanted to discuss with me (or anyone else) the metaphysical backgrounds or symbolic meanings of any of his plays; nor have I pressed him in this direction. As Beckett himself once wrote about Joyce, Sam is after all basically "not writing about something, he is writing something." His plays are not about things, they are themselves things. His work is a "matter of fundamental sounds," he once explained, with the pun intentional; and the overtones should be let fall where they may without being verbalized or pinned down at every turn. Nor does he want to try to tell me something already either obvious or not there.

Not that my reluctance to pursue philosophical trails with him means that I am totally uninterested in intellectual matters or don't enjoy these pursuits—especially away from valuable rehearsal hours and with people who don't have to act them all out on stage on opening nights. Besides, Sam is enough of a theater man himself to understand more and more the futility of trying to act out abstract themes on stage. Explanations of philosophical meanings provide marvelously satisfying speeches with which the director can impress his actors but very little practical help for them. How does one, after all, play "the end of history" or "the decline of western values"? One has to sit in a certain way against the mound, or turn a certain way over a certain shoulder at a certain time with the spectacles held in a certain hand. Theatrical truth, as Brecht said and Beckett knows, is concrete.

And when it comes to concrete matters, our transoceanic message service has never failed to function so as to further illuminate the plays. How long should one of those famous "pauses" really take—in relation, say, to a "long pause" or, when it gets there, a "maximum pause"? Sam could give me the actual counts if I would ask him—though I never did—and although he doesn't own a stopwatch. But then he doesn't own a tape recorder either, and look what he figured out for Krapp to do! It's a matter of his own innate sense of rhythm. Should Winnie's glasses be on or off at this or that point in the play? Would it be better for her to be holding the toothbrush in her left hand or her right—so that she can take care of other required matters with her other hand? And so on.

When Sam was directing *Happy Days* in Berlin a season or so ago, he carried all those answers, and a few thousand others, with him in a completely detailed cross-lined notebook, practically Cartesian in its organization of information and insight. But even before that notebook existed, it was all down logically in his head—and not only for *Happy Days*—and quite willingly shared with me whenever I was able to ask the proper questions.

The literal meaning of a line that seemed unclear, the source of a quotation, a desirable pattern of behavior or movement—these were all not mysteries but knowledge to be shared. The pace of *Godot* should always be kept light and quick, he feels; in fact, that is a basic rhythm, a common denominator for most of his plays. The "tree" is, of course, not to be a representation of the tree on stage at all, with hands outstretched as it usually is for the branches, but one of the basic positions of yoga: the sole of one foot resting in the groin, with the two hands clasped together as if in prayer. That makes infinite sense—and not just comic nonsense—of Estragon's next line: "Do you think God sees me?" Sam once even drew a small diagram to show me exactly what he meant. And I have hidden away somewhere some lovely and even more detailed pen-and-ink sketches from him outlining Willie's exact optimum path around the mound when he comes visiting Winnie. If Beckett hadn't become a writer, he could have quite well found other uses for his pen.

Nor is Sam unwilling to discuss his characters as people, although he's more concerned with their external than with their internal qualities. And never with their symbolic significances or "meaning." Yes, Vladimir is more or less restless and roams around the stage; Estragon is more or less still and sits down a lot. The Mouth is "on fire" and must keep on talking in short rapid bursts (separated by those perennial dots, of course) because she has to. The Mouth is totally unaware of where she is or of a Figure watching her. The Figure is aware of and sees the Mouth but has no effect on it. No, there's nothing in the text to indicate whether the Figure is male or female. And Krapp looks at his watch at regular intervals not just because he is bored or wants to know what time it is but because he wants to see if enough minutes have gone by for him safely to have another drink. Then he goes for that other drink anyhow. And that clink of glass without the siphon is telling us that he's saying the hell with it here and taking the last shot straight up instead of with soda, as he should, to dilute the alcoholic content. (How many otherwise intelligent drama critics have talked about the "wine" Krapp is drinking!) As Jackie always called it, Sam's "underlying simplicity" is never simple—but it's there if one only looks for it.

Once, when my entire cast of the first off-Broadway *Endgame* insisted that I write to Beckett to find out why Hamm's and Clov's faces were red while Nell's and Nagg's were white, the answer came back like a slap: Why is Werther's coat green? In other words, because the author had decided that he liked that particular color. Or colors. Or when Sam thought that both Jessie and I were asking too many foolish questions about the birth, life experience, and physical circumstances surrounding that solitary floating Mouth, he finally decided that enough was enough: "I no more know where she is or why than she does," he wrote. There was only the text and the stage image, both of which he had provided for us. "The rest is Ibsen." Or, as I used to tell Jessica Tandy when I felt that she wanted to probe too hard into recesses that didn't have actual existence, this was Samuel Beckett and not Arthur Miller. If one once started to worry about where Winnie got her groceries or how she managed to discharge her bodily functions, one could get into a lot of unanswerable questions. And into another play.

Oh yes, those inquisitive *Endgame* actors, not pacified, decided among themselves that Nell and Nagg, being older, had less efficient circulatory systems so that the blood couldn't get to their faces so easily. This without informing Sam—who would have been eminently surprised at this revelation. And Hamm and Clov had high blood pressure—though luckily neither Sam nor our audiences needed to know that.

The key to my directing of Beckett, then, may be described as that of dealing simultaneously with what I have come to call "the local situation" (in contrast to that other more cosmic one) and his rhythmical and tonal structure, his specific style or "texture." In principle, that is no different than when I am directing Shakespeare or Chekhov; in practice, one is more concerned in Beckett with the juxtaposition of specific sounds and silences, movement and speech, instead of with, say, the handling of iambic pentameter and Elizabethan footwork. The needed intertwining of comedic and serious tones in Chekhov is matched by a parallel necessity in Beckett, though framed in a more formal and less naturalistic pattern. Although *Krapp* to me has always seemed almost Chekhovian in its blend of emotional colors, Krapp himself is both Trofimov and Pischchik—and perhaps, Epihodov as well.

Dealing with "the local situation" simply assumes that I try to concern myself primarily with who the characters are as human beings, and what their human situation is. What are they doing, wanting, getting, not getting in a given scene? How do they change or not change? What happens to them in the play? How do they affect their own situation, and the other characters? What is their awareness of and reaction to the various events of the play? (It is not, for instance, the "significance" of the burning of the umbrella in *Happy Days* that can be acted but Winnie's reaction to that burning.) Most importantly, what is their physical, their sensory, reality?

Of course, examining the "local situation" also means that I have to consider how the characters got there, or even perhaps why. Is Clov that same small boy whom the father, crawling on his belly, brought to Hamm years ago? What happened to the Mouth in April in that field? But not in the same manner or to the same extent that I explore those questions of background and motivation in Ibsen or in Chekhov. How, after all, did Winnie get into that pile of sand in the first place? The answer is that she's always ("the old style") been there. The sand, though "real" to her, is to Beckett a stage world only, a theatrical metaphor, a stage image. The sand, that mound into which she eternally sinks—why?—is simply the condition of her existence. Just as, in some other type of drama, a character's job or position in society is given to us. Or just the character's happening to be there in order to fulfill a function or complete a relationship. All of those seemingly accidental but necessary and unquestioned coincidences that make possible even the entrances and exits in any supposedly realistic play.

I accept Winnie's dominating presence in the mound, the literal absence of legs in the first act and of anything below her neck in the second, as I accept Picasso's lady with several faces or Dali's bent watch. Though in spite of a century of nonrepresentational art, we are still more familiar and more comfortable with the most outrageous juxtaposition of circumstances masquerading as "reality" than we are with the simplest and most direct of metaphors: let us say, our inevitably vanishing existences, for example. But we don't have to go on being uncomfortable, and the plays of Sam Beckett, I am pleased to know, have moved us a few miles up the road toward understanding of that.

Metaphor or not, though, it is the sensory reality with which the director must be primarily concerned. Winnie should be hot as well as cosmically happy and unhappy. It has never mattered who Godot really is, although we keep on asking and those convicts at San Quentin have always known. Nor even who told Vladimir and Estragon that they had to wait for him. It's the two hours of their lives and of our playing time that count. It's how they wait. Clov cannot sit down, for whatever reason; and a generation of American actors have, within my experience, offered up various answers—from arthritis through gonorrhea to hemorrhoids—although their audiences were not always able to diagnose those exact causes. So long as they were interesting and theatrical, I don't mind—and I'm sure Sam wouldn't have. Nagg and Nell are elderly, cold, hungry, sleepy, somewhat deaf, not so good at seeing, without legs, and feel a certain way about their son Hamm keeping them cooped up in those ashcans. These qualities can be acted, while the concept of the "older generation discarded" or the "dead past put onto the garbage heap" or "the flower of French civilization" cannot. Even though Sam tells us very clearly that they lost their shanks at a special time and place, Sedan, which has a distinctive echo of meaning for the French nation, although the rest of us have forgotten what happened there.

At the same time, every Beckett play—from the extremely formal *Not I* to the extremely informal *Krapp's Last Tape*—possesses its own specific tonality, its special texture. That which distinguishes it from anyone else's work. Almost any page of Beckett can be immediately identified as his. Because of his particular vision of the universe and of mortal man's frail fate in it. But also because of his specific technique of organizing and orchestrating the formal elements involved. The sparseness and simplicity of his language, juxtaposed against its passages of poetic musicality. The balance and tension of its various rhythms and sounds and images. His repetition of words and phrases. The constant interplay of parallel and opposing ideas and themes: counterpoint, auditory and visual. The carefully worked-out opposition of lines and the interrelating of opposites. And other notes of dramatic music.

As the Royal Court's George Devine, one of the earliest and most loyal of Beckett's supporters and interpreters, once explained his own view of the Beckett terrain: "One has to think of the text as something like a musical score wherein the "notes," the sights and sounds, the pauses, have their own interrelated rhythms, and out of their composition comes the dramatic impact."

It is only through constant attention to both Beckettian "texture" and the "local situation" that his plays can be presented faithfully. For the repetition of three dots contains a specific clue to both character reality and dramatic meaning. And I have always tried to deal with both these aspects without distortion or distraction. Through whatever means. I have talked or not talked with my actors, before or during the work. I have both demanded and given way, read them portions of Beckett's letters to me or kept them to myself. I have gone up on stage to demonstrate a special move or piece of business I wanted done in a certain way, or waited for the actors to come up with their own version—as with the choreography of Vladimir's song about the dog. Helped by Beckett's own pauses, I have always worked out the "beats" in the text—with the proper intentions, adjustments, circumstances, and other standard underpinnings. Most of all, I have tried to cast only those actors whom I felt to be suitable and agreeable to Beckett's world—and not cast those who would deny or destroy that world.

After all these years, there are a number of actors (and directors) who still do not respond to Beckett, or avoid doing his plays. They feel he limits them too severely as artists, removes their creativity and individuality, constricts them too rigidly in their physical and vocal resources. They tell me that he must hate actors because he denies them the use of their own impulses, as well as more and more of their physical selves. After all, if they cannot move freely about the stage, cannot use the full range of their voices and bodies—their very means of reaching their audiences—what are they but impersonal or even disembodied puppets of his will? Now he's even down to strapping them into some sort of medieval torture chamber, closing off their faces, including their eyes—the windows of the stage souls—in order to leave only a mouth visible on stage. What's next, they ask me, the uvula alone, pinpointed on a darkened stage? And no words for them to speak?

I do not agree. Nor did Jackie, the Irish-born actor and friend of Beckett. Before his death, Jackie told an interviewer that Beckett's "feeling for precision in inflection, rhythm, and movement seems almost severe, but not for a moment does he restrict the imagination or inventive feeling of others except if it is outside the framework of what is being interpreted. He creates a freedom in working which actors do not often enjoy in the theater today, and that freedom is always the bedfellow of true discipline."

How right Jackie was and yet how difficult it is still to explain to those actors who do not want to understand that it is precisely because Sam so admires them and so respects their abilities that he trusts them to be extraordinarily effective even with certain of those abilities confined or even removed. We have known for centuries that an actor can hold us and move us when he has full range onstage. But that he can reach us as powerfully or more so with only his face or his eyelids or his mouth, or with lips and teeth and voice alone, that is fantastic. And theatrical. And worth exploring further.

After all, do we think that Beckett hates or despises the English language because he uses so many simple one- or two-syllable words instead of availing himself of its entire range of syllabification and richness? Does he deny that language its strength and virtues because he has gone in the opposite direction from Joyce or Giraudoux or Yeats toward greater and greater selection and bareness? Is he uninterested in language itself because he makes use of only a small portion of those possibilities he knows it possesses? Of course not.

Yet even this sort of analogy has not and does not satisfy his critics on the stage and in the audience. They still complain or get angry when Beckett doesn't cater to their expectations or fit in with their past habits, though they can no longer accuse him so readily of heresy or hoax. They do continue to avoid him or in praising him not bother to read his plays or attend his productions. Years ago, Ralph Richardson turned down the part of Estragon because Beckett was unable to inform him adequately of the exact extent of Pozzo's holdings (although Richardson later had the good grace in his autobiography to confess his error). Everybody turned down Hamm for me once, as well as Krapp. In fact, dozens of actors, those of the first rank and others, have in the past turned down Beckett roles; today, more and more star names have begun to think of the plays as stage or screen vehicles for themselves to be manipulated toward their own personalities or purposes. In Paris, Madeleine Renaud and Jean-Louis Barrault have been doing *Happy Days* for years; over here, I tried in vain once to interest Lynn Fontanne and Alfred Lunt. Eventually, the last time around, I did get Jessica Tandy and Hume Cronyn, though I had a hard time talking him into doing Willie. And even the gracious Miss Tandy, if I'm not giving away too sheltered a confidence, despaired nightly of the various restraints, literal and metaphorical, placed upon her by author and director in *Not I*. She could not wait to be forever free of its head clamp, blackened makeup, and stichomythic pace.

As to my own feelings of confinement, I have none. When I limit my imagination to the boundaries set for me by Sam, I feel with Jackie that I am not so much limiting as freeing myself, just as a sonnet writer who has something he wants to express may not be bound tighter but actually guided into greater complexity by the demands of its rhyme scheme—or any artist always is by the specific limitations of his materials. When I direct Shakespeare or Brecht there are also limitations involved, though in those cases they are inherent, thus perhaps seemingly more flexible, than imposed. When I direct Beckett, I know and trust him and respond to him so directly that I can allow my own impulses and imagination to flow through his pulse beats—even though some of the critics may still say that I am abdicating my directorial responsibilities, that I am betraying Beckett by being too loyal.

Once I did put a bowler hat instead of a toque on my Hamm, but I did not consider that a betrayal of Beckett, just a practical adjustment to the fact that the actor playing the role simply did not look right in any toque we could find or make. Only once have I felt that I actually did betray Sam's real intentions. When we were doing the first production of *Play*, whose text is constructed so as to be spoken twice, the preview audiences at the Cherry Lane seemed to resent the repetition, sitting there stony-faced and bored the second time around, instead of offering up greater attention and more laughs. At the same time, our actors didn't relish the idea of speaking the lines the first time as rapidly as both Beckett and I wanted them to. They felt that the audiences didn't have a clue as to what was going on and that they were losing their laughs. (The same conflict took place, by the way, during rehearsals of the original London production; it was eventually resolved—in Sam's presence—by a rearrangement of the repetition, but with the actors both times speaking so rapidly that, Rosemary Harris told me, they could hardly catch their breaths.) After continued urgent requests by our producers and against my better judgment and previously held position, I wrote to Sam explaining that perhaps New York audiences were more sophisticated (or jaded) than all others and were actively resenting this supposed slur upon their intelligence. I asked him if he would mind if during a few of the previews we experimented with playing the text through only once and spoken a bit more slowly just to see how it would go. He wrote back his approval, without making apparent his underlying tone of sadness and disappointment.

We tried it only once through in the rest of the previews, where it seemed to be getting more of a response, and eventually in performance. Not that the change saved us. In spite of reasonably favorable notices, the production ran only a few weeks, which it would probably have done anyway, even had we played it as originally intended. They just were not ready for the play. But I realized as I have so often, before and since, that I should have stuck to my instinctive guns, done the show the way the author had conceived it. By distorting his writing we diluted his play and still did not "succeed." Doing it his way, we might also have "failed" him but at least on our own terms. Nor has that play always been successful when performed elsewhere. But at least its quality and dramatic audacity have now been accepted.

It was not until many years later, and most indirectly because he would never tell me himself, that I learned how hurt Sam had been by my decision. By then I had learned my lesson.

Those theater people who are not willing to trust, not ready to go along on a production or part of a greater equilibrium than that provided by their reflexes—or ego—cannot understand my pleasure and gratitude and joy at having been associated with Samuel Beckett's work. Not because of his fame but because of his quality. Sam's feeling for precision, for order, has always been for me a most uncategorical imperative. His rhythms, his insights, his vision of the theater have rarely, if ever, restricted my own. On the contrary, he has deepened my own experience as a working director more than any other playwright—perhaps more than anyone outside of my own immediate family.

Without, I hope, waxing overly sentimental, I must confess that I have always felt both privileged and inspired to have worked so long and so often with him—if not as directly as I would have chosen had not a particular accident of geography intervened, yet no less fully or richly. To quote the words of Sam's favorite French publisher, Jérôme Lindon, "I have never met a man in whom co-exist together in such high degree, nobility and modesty, lucidity and goodness." Sam has not only changed my life, both professionally and personally, but become part of it. From that moment, almost a quarter century ago but still seeming as though yesterday, when he first wrote to me that "the Miami fiasco does not distress me in the smallest degree, or only insofar as it distresses you," there has not been a day when I did not think of him or feel him present in my work and life. There is nothing I would not do for him, onstage or off.

Last season, while substituting for Zelda Fichandler as a somewhat inadequate producing director at Washington's Arena Stage, I had one of my few satisfactions in bringing into being an extraordinary production—on the order of accomplishment, I believe, of Peter Brook's *Marat Sade* or *Dream*-by a leading Romanian director, Liviu Ciulei, of Georg Büchner's *Leonce and Lena*. Written about 1830, the play had never been professionally presented in this country; yet it was as contemporary in feeling as though it had been written today. While we were in previews, a sizable portion of our subscription audience walked out in high dudgeon that we could inflict this particular pain on them, then proceeded to bombard both Zelda and myself with letters expressing their keen resentment of such "trash" (although by the time we opened—and the favorable notices came out—they were a little less sure). I thought once more of Samuel Beckett and of Miami Beach, about 1956, and realized once more how little had actually changed in the theater. It was Harold Hobson, writing in the London *Sunday Times* not so long ago, who best expressed my feelings: "This complacent inability to recognize the highest, this apparently natural enmity towards the exaltation of the spirit . . . checks one's heart."

My heart, I am well aware, has been checked often throughout my theater life, as has everyone's, although the causes always differ. But it is Sam Beckett's exaltation of the spirit that has taught me the one basic truth: that in spite of everything or whatever, one goes on, with or without sand in those bags; that in the theater as in all of art the only thing that counts is the work itself, the need to go on with that work at the highest possible level—not to be distracted or disturbed by success or failure, by praise or blame, by surface or show, analysis or abstraction, self-criticism or the criticism of others. This is especially important when that work is of Beckett's order of magnitude, possessed of Beckett's sublimity, his degree of compassion, his eloquent understanding of the potentialities both of the stage and of human frailty. After twenty years of working with him, I can only be grateful that whatever theatrical fates that be have put me into the same universe of possibility with him.

---

## Ruby Cohn

FROM "Beckett Directs
*Endgame* and *Krapp's
Last Tape*"
(1980)

LATE *in his career, Beckett began to direct his plays for the stage. In this essay, the distinguished Beckett scholar Ruby Cohn analyzes Beckett's work as a director and the ways in which it highlights elements of the design of* Endgame.

> "For me theater is first of all a relaxation from work on fiction. We are dealing with a definite space and with people in this space. That's relaxing."
> "Directing too?"
> Beckett laughs: "No, not very. It's exhausting."

Beckett's involvement with theater has increased with the years. The main product of that affair is twenty-one extant plays, excluding the several abandoned fragments. The byproduct of that affair is intense attention to performance of those scripts, beginning with the lost *Kid*. Written in French in 1931, while Beckett was a graduate student at Trinity College, Dublin, the play is a parody of Corneille's *Le Cid*, mocking the unity of time. Twenty-four-year-old Beckett played Don Diègue, the aged father of the Kid, in period costume but a bowler hat. The play had only two performances and did not inspire Beckett to continue with theater. Five years later, asked by a friend to help her with a play, Beckett "began to hang around on the fringes of various dramatic groups in Dublin."[1] Other than the aborted *Human Wishes*, however, he was still not inspired to continue with theater. Ten years later, in 1947, *Eleuthéria* bears witness to his familiarity with problem plays, simultaneous sets, Pirandellian quips.

Affiliation with performance, however, came only with attendance at Roger Blin's 1952 rehearsals of *En attendant Godot*, whose premiere was 5 January 1953. Although accounts differ as to the extent of that affiliation, it seems clear that Beckett's grasp of staging was swift. By the late 1950s and early 1960s his advice was often sought for staging his plays, and his performance concepts dominate several productions directed by others, notably the London *Endgame* and *Krapp* of 1958, a Paris 1961 *Godot* and 1964 *Comédie*, a Paris-London *Endgame* of 1964, and the Royal Court *Godot* of 1964. Beckett's independent directing of his own plays began in 1965, although the first piece to bear his name as director was the 1966 Stuttgart telecast of *Eh Joe*. By 1962 he had enunciated his director's guidelines in a conversation with Charles Marowitz:

> Producers don't seem to have any sense of form in movement. The kind of form one finds in music, for instance, where themes keep recurring. When in a text, actions are repeated, they ought to be made unusual the first time, so that when they happen again—in exactly the same way—an audience will recognize them from before.[2]

Aside from those in Beckett's own plays, it is rare to find actions repeated "in exactly the same way," but they do recur in Robert Pinget's *Hypothèse*, and perhaps that is why Beckett undertook to direct it. He refuses to claim directorial credit, admitting only to helping actor Pierre Chabert "since there was no one else."[3]

As a student in Paris in 1963, Chabert played Krapp with sufficient rhythm to interest the musical Mrs. Beckett, who attended the performance. She suggested to Pinget that Chabert should perform his *Hypothèse*, another one-character play. The little-known author Pinget and the unknown actor Chabert began sporadically to rehearse, and Pinget brought Beckett to an early run-through. After brooding on what he saw, Beckett told Chabert that he would like to think about the performance. When Beckett next called Chabert, he had reconceived the production in his mind's eye.

*The Hypothesis* resembles *Krapp's Last Tape* in that a writer-protagonist reacts to another aspect of himself—Krapp to his tape and Mortin to films of his face. As the live Krapp moves physically between his table and an offstage room, Mortin moves physically between a bookcase, a stove, and his table on which are a glass of water and a manuscript. Unlike Krapp, Mortin never leaves the stage, for he is delivering a speech—the contents of the manuscript—to an audience in the actual theater. That speech is about a writer and *his* manuscript, which is hypothetically at the bottom of a well. "Mortin's struggle with this hypothesis by means of a series of pseudo-logical and delirious conclusions [imperfectly recalled and recited] . . . parallels the predicament of the imaginary author in the manuscript."[4]

In the light of Beckett's subsequent directing practice, his guidance of Chabert seems inevitable. But his decision to cut about one-third of Pinget's text, with the author's consent, was unpredictable. Since Chabert's face had already been filmed for the five movie sequences, Beckett accepted this fact and occupied himself with palpable theater. He moved the room's furnishings to dramatize the table, and he located the stove downstage right, the bookcase upstage left, thus creating three distinct areas but leaving the back wall as a free screen for the film. On the newly centered table lay the manuscript in an enormous pile of loose pages. Most important was Beckett's almost Stanislavskian spine for the play-author's relation to his manuscript: in Chabert's words, "a visceral relation." Whenever Mortin left his table, he took manuscript pages, which he dropped as he recited his text. Pages were soon strewn over the floor, functioning visually and also audibly, as Mortin-Chabert rustle-walked on the leaves of manuscript. By the end of the play, as three enlarged film images of Mortin shouted out his inadequacies, Pinget had his author throw the manuscript into the stove. Discourse broken, he slowly removed his clothes, and his staccato phrases closed the play. In Beckett's direction Mortin had only one page left to throw into the stove, which clacked shut sharply upon it. Pinget's final phrases were severely cut, so that the author seemed consumed with the remains of his manuscript. Although Chabert gave only three performances, the notices were so good that *L'Hypothèse* was included in 1966 on a Beckett-Ionesco-Pinget program at the Odéon Theater, where Beckett helped the late Jean-Marie Serreau direct *Comédie* and especially *Va et Vient*. A few months later Beckett staged his own production of *Va et Vient* on a different program in the same theater.[5]

Beckett's titles give us clues to the main action, and so with *Come and Go*.[6] Not actually sounded in the brief text, the titular phrase describes the physical actions of the three women on stage. When the bright lights come up, three women—Flo, Vi, Ru—are seated on an invisible bench, facing the audience, each clasping her bare hands in her own lap. Once speech begins, pattern reigns; once movement begins, pattern reigns. During the course of the brief play, each woman in turn *goes* out of the bright center light and *comes* back into it. Each woman utters short speeches, punctuated by her exit and reentrance. As each woman in turn disappears into darkness, one of the remaining two whispers into the other's ear, with ostentatious gesture.

The recipient of the inaudible message, with equally ostentatious gesture, exclaims, "Oh!" Then she asks whether the absent one is aware of her fate. The teller of the secret invokes deity in a fervent hope for the absent victim's ignorance. Finally, having gone into darkness and come back into visibility, the three women sit together again in the light, bare hands again clasped, but each hand clasps another's. The discrete individuals of the opening tableau are linked by their hands in the closing tableau, in a chain traditionally associated with harmony.

Beckett's text specifies "dull" colors for the three women's garments, and it only hints at their turn-of-the-century appearance in Serreau's production, long coats cloaking them from shoulder to ankle, and broad-brimmed hats shading their faces. Visually, they evoked Chekhov's three sisters rather than Macbeth's witches or Lear's daughters. The whispered destiny insinuates a hint of the three Fates, and not until the final tableau does a mannered pose recall the three Graces. The "dramaticule" leads to Flo's final line: "I can feel the rings," but Beckett's scenic direction stipulates: *"No rings apparent."* This is the play's second contradiction, for Ru reminisces about "Holding hands . . . that way" before the three women touch hands.

When the three women sit together in the light, they recall their bright schoolgirl dreams of love. When one glides into the dark, however, the remaining pair share the knowledge of her doom. Their choral "Oh!"s (changed in French translation to "Misère." "Malheur." "Miséricorde.") punctuate the secret each pair shares about a third. Choral chant and dance, offstage doom and onstage courage—this is minimal Greek tragedy. Both protagonists and chorus, the three women look the same at the beginning and at the end of the "dramaticule." However, they are seated in a new order as they clasp one another's hands in a stylized pose. Flo at right holds two left hands, and it is she who imagines feeling the ambiguously symbolic rings, but all three actually feel the mortal flesh of other human hands—ungloved and vulnerable to the light.

In the first French production Ru wore violet and Vi rose; Flo was in soft yellow, as specified in the text. Embellishing the text's description, broad-brimmed hats sported fruit, flowers, and feathers—perishable adornments. At rest, the three women suggested deities of vegetation; in motion, however, they were neither bird nor bloom, but softly gliding phantoms, feet invisible under the long coats.

A few months later, Beckett mounted his own production at the same Paris theater. The garments were muted to three shades of gray; the broad hats and long coats were stripped of ornament: the women exuded a mineral quality. Beckett slowed the playing time from three to seven minutes, so that each gesture seemed wrested from stillness. When Flo finally announced that she felt the rings, their putative absence was at once the climax and conclusion of the drama that had spiraled slowly around an absent center. Since the bench was invisible, the three women were seated in a void. Each of them spoke unheard words, and one of them mentioned unseen rings, those rimmed holes. Not like a Mallarmé poem, this *Come and Go* drained away coming, going, listening and speaking, into a final harmony. As a Mallarmé poem resides in words about a void, Beckett's dramaticule, under his direction, resides in a worded rondo about a void, rendered almost palpable through strict pattern.

It was with this theater training that Beckett embarked on full directorial responsibility for the Berlin staging of his *Endgame* (1967), *Krapp's Last Tape* (1969), *Happy Days* (1971), *Waiting for Godot* (1975), *Footfalls* and *That Time* (1976), and *Play* (1978), along with sporadic stints in Paris and London. Although he has had other offers to direct, he has appreciated the distance from his plays provided by the German translations of Elmar Tophoven.

By 1978 Beckett had all but forgotten his French 1965 production of *Come and Go* when he undertook to advise Walter Asmus in a German version.[7] Aside from making minor phrasal changes, Beckett reassigned a few lines for stricter balance. When the three women are together on stage, they speak Vi-Flo, Flo-Ru, Ru-Vi, finally circling back to Vi-Flo. The opening speaker of these trio-couplets is always the one to leave, and the closing speaker is always the one to confide the secret. For that confidence new hand movements were choreographed. At each shocked reaction to the unheard secret, the listener brings a bare hand to her throat, while the speaker holds a bare hand to her lips. In synchrony the two hands slowly return to their respective laps. At the final joining of hands Vi in the center reaches out and up (breast high) for the outer hand of each neighbor. After a beat the neighbors clasp their inner hands, all hands high. Then slowly the three pair of hands fall to laps and rest there for a beat before Flo speaks of the invisible rings and the whole still image fades to darkness. In the words of Beckett's notebook, "Hands taken in air at top of gesture sink gently plumb together."

For production in Berlin, Beckett approached all his plays in the same basic way: (1) meticulous examination of Tophoven's German translation and subsequent correction toward his own English version (since Tophoven translates from the French); (2) intense visualization of the play in theater space—what Beckett calls "trying to see"; (3) commitment of the revised German text to memory (including stage directions); (4) composition of a director's notebook, to which he does not refer during actual rehearsals (his rediscovery of his own texts is remarkable)—for example, that it is always the center woman of three who opens speech in *Come and Go*, that glass is contained in several Winnie props of *Happy Days*, that there are twenty-one pleas for help in *Godot*, that the B-voice of *That Time* sketches a scene already conveyed by a verse of Hölderlin); (5) transmission of design ideas to his friend Matias, who does a first rending while they are still in Paris. Only when these steps are completed does Beckett arrive in West Berlin, where the plays are precast.

At Beckett's first meeting with the actors in a play, he never speaks *about* the play but plunges right into it. Work on scenes begins at once, and Beckett shakes his head at questions that stray from concrete performance. On the other hand, no practical detail is too small for his attention. Sitting or standing, he seems poised to spring to the stage. Early in rehearsals he requests permission to interrupt the actors, and this is always granted. The spoken text must be not only letter perfect, but punctuation perfect; he will stop an actor who elides a comma pause. Yet he rarely interrupts the early run-throughs, and he deliberately absents himself from a late rehearsal or two, so that the actors may feel freer in their final discoveries. Although Beckett arrives at the Schiller Theater with the production complete in his mind's eye, he usually makes minor changes during rehearsal.

Beckett chose to begin his German directing career (which he did not anticipate as a career) with *Endgame*, his preferred play. While still in Paris, he perused the German text with translator Tophoven, who has described their collaboration:

> Through constant work together, through tightening where this was possible, through expansion where the stage demanded it, through late discoveries and introduction of new assonance and harmony, through elimination of Gallicisms that had been overlooked, through prevention of undesirable associations and removal of phonetic difficulties, an improved German version appeared, which will be the basis for a new edition of *Endgame*.[8]

(This new edition has been published only in volume 1 of the 1976 Suhrkamp collected works of Beckett. Postproduction texts have not been published in English.)

In this eschatological play Beckett's slim director's notebook is limited to staging matters.[9] For rehearsal purposes he divided *Endgame* into sixteen scenes:

1. Clov's dumbshow and first soliloquy
2. Hamm's awakening, first soliloquy and first dialogue with Clov
3. The Nagg-Nell dialogue
4. The excited Hamm-Clov dialogue, with Hamm's first turn around the room, ending on Clov's sigh: "If I could kill him . . . "
5. Clov's comic business with ladder and telescope
6. Hamm's troubled questioning of Clov, climaxed by the burlesque flea scene
7. The Hamm-Clov dialogue, ending with the ironic mirror image of the toy-dog episode
8. Clov's rebellion, giving way to Hamm's story of the madman and subsiding in the alarm-clock scene
9. Hamm's story of the beggar

10. The prayer, ending with Nagg's curse
11. The play within the play of Hamm and Clov; Hamm's continuation of his story
12. The second round of the wheelchair
13. The Hamm-Clov dialogue leading to
14. Hamm's "role"
15. Clov's emancipation, ending with his monologue and exit
16. Hamm's final soliloquy

Concerned with the physical rather than the metaphysical, Beckett's director's notebook focuses on mobile Clov. A diagram delineates the path of his "thinking" walk, and another diagram traces his "winding up" walk. Carefully noted and numbered are Clov's sixteen entrances and exits, his twenty-six stops and starts, his nine repetitions of "There are no more . . . " and his ten repetitions of "I'll leave you" (in German).

Beckett's *Endgame* plays the ending of a world, and his set alerts us to that ending process. The original French describes the set as an interior without furnishings, and Beckett translated this as "Bare interior."[10] However, his Berlin stage set was spare rather than bare. High curtained windows, one on each side wall, face earth and sea—what remains of nature. Turned inconspicuously to the foot of the left wall is a picture—what remains of art. Downstage left are two touching ashbins covered by a sheet—what remains of an older generation. In the center is an armchair covered by a sheet—what remains of the prime of life. After the opening tableau, action begins with Clov's removal of the sheets. (The notebook calls it an "unveiling.") What is unveiled is a family—ordinary in its memories, attachments, and quarrels but extraordinary since it is the last of the human race. The words *finish* and *end* punctuate the dialogue. Both Hamm and Clov utter the words of Christ on the cross: "It is finished."

Biblical echoes abound. The names Nagg and Hamm pun on Noah and Ham of Genesis, who are also survivors of a world catastrophe, safe in their shelter. Hamm and Clov use the apocalyptic imagery of the biblical book of Revelation—light and dark, earth and sea, life and death, beginning and end—although they experience no revelations. Hamm's chronicle is set on Christmas Eve, and Hamm's final soliloquy distorts scriptural phrases. However, Beckett does not place an actual Bible on stage, as in an earlier version of the play.

Beckett conveys endlessness through the grain-of-time theme, which apparently contradicts the ending theme. Hamm and Clov fear and wish an end, but the drama plays through an endless ending process. Toward the end of the play Hamm ruminates: "Moment upon moment, pattering down like the millet grains of . . . *(hesitates)* . . . that old Greek, and all life long you wait for that to mount up to a life" *(Endgame)*. "That old Greek," whose name Beckett actually forgot, might have been any anti-empirical philosopher of the Megarian or Eleatic schools. Having forgotten the name when writing, however, Beckett later mentioned Zeno to his cast.

It was the playing theme that Beckett pointed up in directing. The title and stage tableaux hint at a chess game, and yet this was never more than a hint, as opposed to the weight assigned the game by critics. Hamm's whistle is the residue of more active games, and the word *discard* summons cards. In spite of Hamm's age, he calls for a toy dog; even his chronicle shows gamesmanship, and the whole play is a game in which Hamm initiates play with rhythm, pattern, spirit.

At the first rehearsal Beckett told his cast, "Here the only interest of the play is as dramatic material." Only when rehearsals were well under way did he answer questions about the biblical flood and the Eleatic philosophers. He explained to Hamm-Schröder:

> Hamm is king in this chess game that is lost from the start. He knows from the start that he is making loud, senseless moves. That he will not get anywhere at all with the gaff. Now at the last he makes a few more senseless moves, as only a bad player would; a good one would have given up long ago. He is only trying to postpone the inevitable end. Each of his motions is one of the last useless moves that delay the end. He is a bad player. *(Materialien, page 83)*

He's a bad player because he's a good performer—the show must go on. As Beckett admitted in another rehearsal: "Hamm says No to nothingness." *(Materialien, page 75)*

Hamm expressed that *No* under Beckett's meticulous direction. Of the month's rehearsal time, Beckett spent about half the period on individual roles and half on harmonizing the whole. Midway during the rehearsal period, after the actors knew the book, Beckett held a rehearsal for tone, pitch, rhythm. Especially in the last two weeks, he tended to comment in musical terms—legato, andante, piano, scherzo, and a rare fortissimo. Often he spoke of *"reine Spiel,"* pure play.

Early in the rehearsal period he told Hamm-Schröder and Clov-Bollmann, "From the first exchange between the two, maximum hostility must be played. Your war is the nucleus of the play." (*Materialien,* page 40) And he defined the basis of their conflict: "Clov has only one wish, to get back into his kitchen, that must always be evident, just like Hamm's constant effort to stop him. This tension is an essential motif for playing." (*Materialien,* page 66) Beckett compared the Hamm-Clov relationship to a marriage—*nec tecum nec sine te.*

To all four actors Beckett declared, "There are no accidents in *Endgame;* everything is built on analogy and repetition." Analogy and repetition supply the symmetry in this one-act play—two couples, two windows, two sheets, two ashbins. Such pairs nourish paired motions. In the opening mime Clov is similarly clumsy at each window. He draws each window-curtain with the same jangle, away from the audience. He removes each sheet with the same jerky motion, and he does not fold the sheets as specified in the text, but drags them to his kitchen. He lifts each ashbin cover with the same clatter. In Hamm's opening and closing soliloquies he folds and unfolds his handkerchief with the same four limited, symmetrical movements. Nagg and Nell emerge from their respective ashbins, lids raised to precisely the same height; they never turn their heads, and they rarely blink their eyes. Nagg lifts his hand identically to rap twice on Nell's lid, and Hamm makes a similar gesture when he knocks at the hollow back wall. In Hamm's recollection of the painter-engraver, he points toward the earth-window after speaking of corn, and he makes a mirror gesture toward the sea-window after mentioning the herring-fleet. Hamm looks down at the beggar of his story as he looks down at the toy dog. Clov and dog, both lame, stand similarly, Clov supporting the dog. At each window Clov looks through the telescope in the same way. Clov lifts Nell's bin-cover, then Nagg's bin cover, to ascertain whether they are dead. In the final tableau of *Endgame* the four characters occupy the same position as in the opening tableau, props on the floor. During a late rehearsal, Beckett wondered whether there wasn't too much symmetry, but he kept it all.

In Beckett's *Endgame* text different characters speak the same old words, but more often they repeat their own words, and Beckett wanted such repetitions spoken identically. Often he asked actors to eliminate expression—"*Ein-tö-nig.*" He increased echoes in the German text, changing all Clov's threats to go to, "I'll leave you." He drilled Clov-Bollmann to achieve lightness for frequent: "There are no more. . . . " To two different Clov questions, Hamm replies: "Less." Beckett didn't care whether the word was spoken dispiritedly or euphorically, but it must be repeated in the same tone. Aware of his verbal doublets, Beckett added some to the German text. He reinforced the double "Father" of Hamm's last soliloquy with a double "Clov," as well as earlier inserting a double "Nell" from Nagg. Nevertheless, Beckett did not want the play's end to mirror the beginning absolutely. He rejected Hamm-Schröder's suggestion that Clov re-cover him with the sheet: "Between the beginning and the end lies the small difference that lies precisely between and end." (*Materialien,* page 75)

Nell declares: "Nothing is funnier than unhappiness." Beckett finds that the most important line in the play, and in Berlin he directed to display the fun of unhappiness. In Clov's mime he wanted small gestures, soft voice, and swift rhythms. *Leicht, locker,* and *schnell* were his recurrent injunctions, so that the few violent moments were striking. Although he paced the play quickly, he asked the actors for disjunction between gesture and word: first they were to assume an attitude and then speak the lines. The macabre humor of the effect was disturbing as though they *could* not move and speak simultaneously.

Hamm and Nagg are virtuoso performers in *Endgame,* and Beckett desired each of them to find three different voices; Hamm is narrator, protagonist, and beggar of his chronicle; Nagg is narrator, tailor, and client of his story, but both also criticize their own performances—a fourth voice. Nagg and Nell, caged in their bins, are comically romantic; when they strain to kiss, they can barely move. Since Clov alone is mobile, Beckett directed his movements to be both painful and funny, instructing him, "You should never run slowly; that's very dangerous for the play." (*Materialien,* page 87) Clov always takes eight steps from the door to Hamm's chair, where his normal position is an apelike stance. Bent over, he stumbles when he passes in front of Hamm, momentarily obscuring all but the toque. On his rare occasions of passion, Clov straightens up and flings out his left arm. When he speaks to Nagg or Nell in the ashbins, his own head disappears into the bins. In the parallel phrases beginning "Sometimes I wonder if I'm in my right mind" and "Sometimes I wonder if I'm in my right senses," Clov speaks the beginning with verve and the end with sadness. After trying the opposite, Beckett found it funnier that Clov react sadly to being as lucid as before, as intelligent as ever. At the play's end, a hatted Clov carries a gray-green coat in his right hand, and in his left a valise, raincoat, and umbrella—poor preparation for the desert outside. Partly because Clov alone is mobile, and mainly because of Bollmann's comic gift, he was the funniest character in the Berlin *Endgame*. His full face contradicts the asceticism implied in the text, and his roundness belies his bent stance and angular movements. His infectious laughter lightened the gray play's start, and his silence darkened the end.

Almost pathetically, Beckett warned his actors, "Pathos is the death of the piece." (*Materialien*, page 45) And yet his direction admitted pathos. Toward the end of the play, Beckett's notebook reads tersely, "Clov entrance 16 while Hamm trying to move chair. Stands near door watching Hamm. Turns head aside on first *Clov*. Back after *gut* and motionless till end." Clov-Bollmann did remain motionless, but he was under visible strain, forcing himself not to participate in the ending action. To Hamm-Schröder's question whether Hamm covers himself to die, Beckett replied, "No, only so he is better able to keep himself quiet." At the last Hamm-Schröder covers his face with his handkerchief-stancher, drops his hands to armrests—"Speak no more." Beckett commented, "The voice comes out of the silence and moves back into the silence." (*Materialien*, page 98)

In Matias's set the ashbins were gray-black, and their color blended into the lighter gray walls of the rectangular shelter. Gray curtains shaded small rectangular windows cut into the side-walls. Hamm wore dark gray and Clov light gray. Hamm's dark embroidered toque was a gift from Sean O'Casey to Beckett through Jack MacGowran. Hamm's foot rug was lightly striped at the base, and his chair wheels were as small as those of roller skates. The red-and-white faces of the published text were monochromed to gray-white, and the handkerchief lost its bloodstains. Cold light shone on door, chair, and ashbins—invariant throughout. In homage to the German philosopher Schopenhauer, who loved his poodle, the toy dog became a ragged, almost black, almost lifesize poodle. And that poodle is emblematic of the production—philosophy concealed, artifice patent, injury risible, since "Nothing is funnier than unhappiness."

After the intricate cross-relationships and complex repetitive texture of *Endgame*, directing *Krapp's Last Tape*[11] might seem like child's play. It will be recalled that Beckett wrote the one-character piece in English for actor Pat Magee, who was first directed by Donald McWhinnie. In 1958 in London Beckett worked closely with actor and director. The three of them played hard and then pub-crawled, but there was no pub crawling in 1969 in Berlin, where Krapp's role went to ponderous Martin Held.

James Knowlson has discussed the complex symbolism of *Krapp's Last Tape*, succinctly summarized in Beckett's Director's Notebook:

> Krapp decrees physical (ethical) incompatibility of light (Spiritual) and dark (Sensual) only when he intuits possibility of their reconciliation as rational-irrational. He turns from fact of anti-mind alien to mind to thought of anti-mind constituent of mind.[12]

Despite this esoteric and symbolic background, the surface of *Krapp's Last Tape* is realistic, but Beckett's director's notebook dwells on realistic and nonrealistic detail.

Unlike the *Endgame* notebook, that for *Krapp* does not divide the play into rehearsal scenes. Instead, Beckett lists twenty-seven matters needing directional attention, from the metaphysical "I. *Choix-hasard*" (choice-guess) to the very physical "27. *Endgültig Werkstatt*" (final [Schiller] Werkstatt [version]) Beckett calculates that Krapp has been recording for forty-five years, since there are nine boxes, each containing five spools of tape. The notebook designates the tape recorder as a masturbatory agent, and Beckett instructed Held to hold the box erotically. His separation of speech from motion, introduced into *Come and Go* and *Endgame*, becomes the fulcrum of performance: "Play therefore composed of two approximately equal parts, listening-immobility and nonlistening-motion." For the *écoute* (listening) Beckett began rehearsals with a provisional tape of thirty-nine-year-old Krapp, but this was replaced.

Beckett wished abrupt and vivid disjunction between still listening and agitated nonlistening. Toward this end, he amplified his stage directions and simplified his stage picture. He eliminated Krapp's clown makeup and endowed him with worn-out rather than farcical clothes. Krapp's table was clean at the start, and Beckett excised the comic business with keys and envelope, but he introduced fumbling rheumatic fingers. He suggested to Held a moving "rest" gesture; Krapp hugs himself shivering. Realistically, an old man seeks warmth; symbolically, Krapp loves himself.

Because of Beckett's stage simplification, we more easily grasp similarities between the young and the old Krapp. Action begins when Krapp peers shortsightedly at his large silver watch, and it proves to be time for his banana. After two bananas are eaten on stage, Krapp on tape mentions three. The man who has stepped from his spotlighted circle into darkness to himself, Krapp. And yet, Krapp-Held looks in astonishment at the tape recorder when he hears the voice say: "Me. (*pause*) Krapp." For Krapp as for Rimbaud, *Je est un autre* ("I is another").

Separating speech from motion, Beckett moved Krapp toward pathos, although the effect in *Endgame* was lugubriously comic. In the opening mime Krapp makes clumsy comic gestures, but it is a rheumatic old man who makes them, and it is a lonely old man who personifies tapes as "little rascal" and "little scoundrel." Whenever Krapp-Held rises from the table, he leans heavily on both hands. Whenever Krapp walks away from the table, he crosses in front and to the right; he fears the darkness at his left. His love-hate relation with objects is comic, for pathos is a greater danger to *Krapp's Last Tape* than to *Endgame.* Beckett dissolved pathos by beating time for Krapp-Held's nonverbal and comic noises—wheezing, walking, turning pages, drinking, and even slamming objects on his table.

When taped speech fills the theater, Krapp listens motionless, comic gestures spent. His head is bent at an angle of 45 degrees, his left hand caresses the tape recorder, and the fingers of his right hand sometimes drum impatiently. Unrecorded in Beckett's notebook is the frequent ternary rhythm evident in performance. Krapp listens to three main events; there are three breaks in the equinox account and three in the "Farewell to Love." At the play's beginning Krapp walks three times out of his spotlight into darkness and back. He disappears through his backstage curtain three times—for his ledger, pile of tapes, and tape recorder, the increased weight of the objects revealed by increased fatigue. In the later action Beckett changed the three backstage exits to offstage drinking, search for a dictionary, offstage drinking and search for a microphone. Krapp consults his watch three times; he moves the tape ahead three times and back three times. After he records, he looks at the machine three times before he wrenches off his last tape.

Within this ternary pattern Krapp shows emotional variety—his lubricity on peeling a banana, his impatience with a younger self, his contained grief at his mother's death, his boast to a whore, his extrapolation of a novel, his fear of dark at his left, his inability to sustain love, which he perhaps regrets when he plays and replays the "Farewell to Love." Krapp-Held squinted when he tremulously spoke of eyes—in the words of the notebook, *"ein Traumgefressener Mensch"* ("A man consumed by dreams").

With improved vision of his own (after operations to remove cataracts), Beckett returned to *Krapp* in 1975—in his French translation, to accompany the French premiere of *Not I* at the Petit d'Orsay. Ten years after *L'Hypothèse* Beckett and Chabert again worked together on a one-character play. In Paris as in Berlin, the central image remained a Krapp who was "one body with the machine."[13] As in *L'Hypothèse* Beckett divided the small stage into areas: the central table (place of reverie) and the backstage alcove (place of practicality).

Because of Chabert's relative youth, Beckett dressed him in a frayed dressing gown to hide his tall frame, a toque to hide his abundant hair, and black half gloves that evoke premonitions of death. Pale and thin, Krapp-Chabert shivered with an old man's cold, and his myopic eyes seemed intent on piercing the dark. He stretched to listen so as to compensate for his deafness, one hand curled round the recorder handle. Immobile, he sucked at his cheeks, leaving his mouth open. Tall, he bumped the overhead light when he rose from the table, and the light continued to move while he listened, still, to the "moves" of the "Farewell to Love."

Musically trained, Chabert readily responded to Beckett's sonata breakdown of the dialogue into b-A(b)-A-B-a, A being the taped voice, B the live voice, and small letters standing for short duration. Much of the brief (three-week) rehearsal period was devoted to the B-voice, sharp and staccato in b and (b), but rhythmically varied in B; the high-pitched quaver of the conventional stage old man was especially to be avoided. In both A and B, Beckett wished counterpoint between objectivity and self-disgust or between objectivity and fascination with a woman or a word.

In Paris Beckett revised key scenes of both nonlistening and listening. When Krapp goes backstage to drink, he leaves a curtain open, so that his guzzling shadow is seen in a long light rectangle, projected from a Chinese lantern on a screen. This space is sharply different from the dream-memory space of Krapp's table. Thus, Krapp versus his past is theatricalized audibly as Krapp versus his taped voice; visually as a shrunken actual Krapp versus his enlarged shadow. In the three playbacks of the love scene, Krapp listens first with bowed head, then with his face on the table, and finally, after a long look over his left shoulder into darkness, with stony erectness. Krapp-Chabert's last playback of "Farewell to Love" is clarified as his stoic farewell to life as well. After the stage lights go out, the tape-recorder light continues to glow—a small *memento mori*.

A little over two years later, in 1977, Beckett found himself directing an English *Krapp* in Berlin's Akademie der Künste, as a favor to his friend Rick Cluchey. Despite two previous productions, he made extensive director's notes, which have been published in the San Quentin Drama Workshop Program and in Bethanien Center Publications. His headings summarize the areas of his concern: "Tape Montage, Costume, Props [a long list], Lighting, Opening, *Hain* ["friend Death" in a poem by Matthias Claudius], Drinks, Song, Microphone, End." Visual details were carried over from the Paris production—a dressing gown, modified banana business, enlarged shadow of drinking, erect posture at the end as at the beginning.

This time Beckett divided the play into four rehearsal scenes: (1) Beginning to ledger note: "Farewell to—love"); (2) "Thirty-nine to-day . . ." to "A girl in a shabby green coat. . . . No?" (with "Connaught" replaced by "Kerry" and the hymn cut); (3) "When I look back—" to preparations for recording. (Watch business is cut. Looking up "viduity" in the dictionary, near-sighted Krapp first reads "vicar" and "vicious.");  (4) From the newly introduced "Fanny" before "Just been listening . . ." to the end. ("One pound . . . doubt" disappears. "Finger and thumb" replaces "a kick in the crutch," and "dozed away" replaces "went to sleep.")

In contrast to Held's erotic recorder, Cluchey's is both friend and enemy, alternately caressed and cursed. Even more sharply than earlier, the Akademie *Krapp* points up opposites: stillness-movement, silence-noise, dark-light, black-white. As a corollary to such polarity, Beckett had Cluchey emphasize the "or"s in the "viduity" definition.

Beckett never spoke to the Workshop members of the symbolic genesis of the play, but they worried together in the inadequately equipped Akademie about nuances of light and sound. To the ternary rhythms of the earlier productions Beckett added long still "brood"s after the words "Incomparable," "crystolite," and "side by side." He sought tonal interest for the often-repeated phrase "Ah well," which had nearly become the play's title. Live Krapp's "Be again, be again" was to sound like the churchbells of his youth. Clinging to rhythm in the face of death, Krapp-Cluchey was sometimes rehearsed with Beckett beating time—for the little rushes of seven steps to and from the table, for the longer series of thirteen steps to and from the alcove, for the offstage drinking sounds (clink of bottle against glass, bottle down, drink, glass down, cough-sigh), and for the long *Hain* (sudden stiffening, slow head turn to left, hold, slow return to right, resume tape). Although the American group knew little German, they prattled glibly of the *Hain*, unaware that it derived from the Matthias Claudius poem. Seeking the precise shuffle sound he wanted from Krapp's run-walk, Beckett gave Cluchey his own worn slippers. In the last week (of nearly four) of rehearsals Beckett changed Krapp-Cluchey's listening position, right hand embracing the recorder, left hand behind it, head angled about 60 degrees to the table. Under a conical dunce-cap light, the metallic rotating tape was reflected on Cluchey's left cheek—a kind of shadow pulse. San Quentin technical men Hauptle and Thorpe conferred on how to eliminate it, but Beckett told them softly, "I love it."

*Notes*

[1]Deirdre Bair, *Samuel Beckett* (New York: Harcourt Brace Jovanovich, 1978), 236.

[2]Charles Marowitz, "Paris Log," *Encore* (March 1962), 44.

[3]Information on *L'Hypothèse*, which I did not see, comes from Pierre Chabert's letter to me of 20 July 1978 and from transcripts of his interview with Dougald McMillan.

[4]For a more detailed account of Beckett's staging of *L'Hypothèse* see Martha Fehsenfeld and Dougald McMillan, *Beckett at Work in the Theatre* (London: Calder, 1986). I can repeat this for almost any production I describe, and I am most grateful to them for allowing me to read the manuscript of their work, enabling me to minimize overlap in our two studies.

[5]Beckett's memory and mine are at odds on this version, since he credits Serreau with direction. Alec Reid, *All I Can Manage, More Than I Could* (New York: Grove Press, Inc., 1968), 93, credits Serreau with directing the French premiere. Breon Mitchell, "Come and Go," *Modern Drama* (September 1976): 252, credits Beckett but erroneously sets the production in the Odéon Theatre's Petite Salle. (Mitchell's manuscript study is invaluable.) Bair, *Beckett,* leaves the director vague and mistakenly states *Come and Go* to be a translation of *Va et Vient.*

[6]Samuel Beckett, *Come and Go,* in *The Collected Shorter Plays of Samuel Beckett* (New York: Grove Press, 1984), 191–97.

[7]Beckett insists that he was merely a consultant on the Berlin *Come and Go,* but Walter Asmus told me that joint discussion governed the production.

[8]Michael Haerdter, *Materialien zu Becketts 'Endspiel'* (Frankfurt: Suhrkamp, 1968), 127. Page numbers in parentheses refer to this book. This fine account is the main source of my information about *Endgame* rehearsals, upon which I drew in my *Back to Beckett* (Princeton, N.J.: Princeton University Press, 1973). I thank Princeton University Press for permission to quote that account.

[9]See Fehsenfeld and McMillan, *Beckett at Work in the Theatre,* for fuller details.

[10]Samuel Beckett, *Endgame* (New York: Grove Press, Inc., 1958), I. Page numbers refer to this edition.

[11]Beckett, *Krapp's Last Tape,* in *Collected Shorter Plays,* 53–63.

[12]Cf. James Knowlson, "Krapp's Last Tape," *Journal of Beckett Studies* (Winter 1976): 50–65.

[13]Pierre Chabert, "Beckett as Director," *Gambit* (28):62.

# Jean Genet

Jean Genet (1910–1986) is perhaps as famous for his life as for his important work as a novelist and playwright. Born the illegitimate son of a Parisian prostitute, he was abandoned at birth and raised by the state. At the age of 15 he was convicted of theft and sent to a reformatory in Mettray. He served briefly in the French Foreign Legion, then deserted and wandered Europe throughout the 1930s, making a living as a beggar, smuggler, thief, and homosexual prostitute, until his arrest and imprisonment in 1941. In prison, Genet wrote his first poem, "The Condemned to Death," and his first novel, *Our Lady of the Flowers;* he was again sentenced in 1947, but the playwright Jean Cocteau and the philosopher Jean-Paul Sartre launched an appeal to secure his pardon. Genet's career became more closely entwined with Sartre in 1952, when Sartre's biography, *Saint-Genet: Actor and Martyr* was published as volume 1 of Genet's *Complete Works*. Sartre takes Genet as an example of the existential man, forced to enact the role of "criminal" that existence has arbitrarily assigned to him. Genet wrote several other novels, including *Miracle of the Rose* (1946), *Funeral Rites* (1947), and *Querrelle of Brest* (1947), and in 1947 wrote his first play, *The Maids*, followed by *Deathwatch* (1949), *The Balcony* (1956), *The Blacks* (1958), and *The Screens* (1966). Genet's dramatization of Algerian resistance to French rule in *The Screens* caused riots in Paris when it was first produced there, and throughout his flamboyant career as a writer, Genet worked to support a number of oppositional political organizations, including the Black Panthers in the United States and the Palestine Liberation Organization. Genet's memoir of his travel to the Middle East and life among the Palestinians, *A Prisoner of Love*, was published posthumously in 1989.

## The Balcony (1958)

*The Balcony* is one of the most celebrated plays in the modern canon, admired for its richly baroque dialogue, for its forthright staging of the nature of desire, and for its determined subversion of any "safe" notion of theatrical representation. From the outset, Genet intertwines Madame Irma's brothel, The Balcony—"Le balcon," a salacious pun in French—and the situation of the theater audience. In the opening stage direction, for instance, Genet describes the room in which one of Madame Irma's clients enacts his erotic fantasies:

> *The set seems to represent a sacristy, formed by three blood-red, cloth folding screens. The one at the rear has a built-in door. Above, a huge Spanish crucifix, drawn in* trompe l'oeil. *On the right wall, a mirror, with a carved gilt frame, reflects an unmade bed which, if the room were arranged logically, would be in the first rows of the orchestra.*

The mirror of the opening stage direction suggests that the studio extends out into the auditorium, at once displacing the audience and *including* the space we inhabit within Madame Irma's erotic theater.

Throughout the play, Genet correlates the practice of theater with the strategies of fantasy. For Madame Irma's clients come to the brothel not—or at least, not explicitly—for sex, but to purchase illusions, performances. The petit-bourgeois clients come to see themselves reflected in the images of the Bishop, the Judge, the General, a process of erotic fulfillment that is at the same time a kind of self-erasure: To perform the role completely, as the General recognizes in Scene 3, is to be transformed into an "image," to achieve a kind of death: "close to death . . . where I shall be nothing, though reflected *ad infinitum* in these mirrors, nothing but my image." The clients' performances suggest that the boundary between self and role, reality and enactment is insistently blurred by the force of desire, a desire in Genet's play—like all desire, perhaps—which carries the force of absence.

Moreover, as the play progresses, it becomes increasingly difficult to circumscribe the limits of theater, performance, and erotics, for Madame Irma's brothel and the illusions it sells come to seem nearly coextensive with the world. Irma, for example, at first seems to be the manager of reality and fantasy, directing the work of The Balcony. And yet her relationship with Carmen and with the Chief of Police in Scene 5 seems artificial, "performed," as though she, too, plays the part of the savvy yet kindhearted madam, acting out her own fantasy scenario. Similarly, the revolution that seems to be taking place "outside" The Balcony has as its final effect the death and deification of the Chief of Police. Is the revolution also a performance invented to satisfy the Chief's desire to assume a place in the "nomenclature" of the social order and the order of fantasy? As the play proceeds, it seems as though there is no "outside" the Balcony, no "reality" that is not produced as part of Madame Irma's theater. Even the Queen and her staff (the Bishop, the Judge, the General) come to be performed by The Balcony's inhabitants.

The "revolution" that Genet proposes in *The Balcony* is only partly a political one; it is more urgently a critique of ontology, of the notions of "presence" that enable us confidently—and wrongly, the play argues—to distinguish between true and false, real and enacted, the actual and the artificial, the spectator and the actor. And, of course, in the play's stunning finale, Madame Irma turns to us, the theater audience, and addresses us as she has addressed her other clients throughout the play: "You must now go home, where everything—you can be quite sure—will be falser than here."

# —The Balcony—
## Jean Genet
TRANSLATED BY BERNARD FRECHTMAN

## —CHARACTERS—

| | |
|---|---|
| THE BISHOP | THE SECOND PHOTOGRAPHER |
| THE JUDGE | THE THIRD PHOTOGRAPHER |
| THE EXECUTIONER (ARTHUR) | IRMA (THE QUEEN) |
| THE GENERAL | THE WOMAN (ROSINE) |
| THE CHIEF OF POLICE | THE THIEF |
| THE BEGGAR | THE GIRL |
| ROGER | CARMEN |
| THE COURT ENVOY | CHANTAL |
| THE FIRST PHOTOGRAPHER | |

SCENE I

*On the ceiling, a chandelier, which will remain the same in each scene. The set seems to represent a sacristy, formed by three blood-red, cloth folding-screens. The one at the rear has a built-in door. Above, a huge Spanish crucifix, drawn in trompe l'oeil. On the right wall, a mirror, with a carved gilt frame, reflects an unmade bed which, if the room were arranged logically, would be in the first rows of the orchestra. A table with a large jug. A yellow armchair. On the chair, a pair of black trousers, a shirt and a jacket.* THE BISHOP, *in mitre and gilded cope, is sitting in the chair. He is obviously larger than life. The role is played by an actor wearing tragedian's cothurni about twenty inches high. His shoulders, on which the cope lies, are inordinately broadened so that when the curtain rises he looks huge and stiff, like a scarecrow. He wears garish make-up. At the side, a woman, rather young, highly made up and wearing a lace dressing-gown, is drying her hands with a towel. Standing by is another woman,* IRMA. *She is about forty, dark, severe-looking, and is wearing a black tailored suit and a hat with a tight string (like a chin-strap).*

THE BISHOP: (*sitting in the chair, middle of the stage. In a low but fervent voice*) In truth, the mark of a prelate is not mildness or unction, but the most rigorous intelligence. Our heart is our undoing. We think we are master of our kindness; we are the slaves of a serene laxity. It is something quite other than intelligence that is involved. . . . (*He hesitates.*) It may be cruelty. And beyond that cruelty—and through it—a skillful, vigorous course towards Absence. Towards Death. God? (*Smiling*) I can read your mind! (*To his*
10  *mitre*) Mitre, bishop's bonnet, when my eyes close for the last time, it is you that I shall see behind my eyelids, you, my beautiful gilded hat . . . you, my handsome ornaments, copes, laces. . . .

IRMA: (*bluntly*) An agreement's an agreement. When a deal's been made. . . .

(*Throughout the scene she hardly moves. She is standing very near the door.*)

THE BISHOP: (*very gently, waving her aside with a gesture*) And when the die is cast. . . .

IRMA: No. Twenty. Twenty and no nonsense. Or I'll lose my temper. And that's not like me. . . . Now, if you have any difficulties. . . .     20

THE BISHOP: (*curtly, and tossing away the mitre*) Thank you.

IRMA: And don't break anything. We need that. (*To the woman*) Put it away.

(*She lays the mitre on the table, near the jug.*)

THE BISHOP: (*after a deep sigh*) I've been told that this house is going to be besieged. The rebels have already crossed the river.

IRMA: There's blood everywhere. . . . You can slip round behind the Archbishop's Palace. Then, down Fishmarket Street. . . .

(*Suddenly a scream of pain, uttered by a woman offstage.*)

IRMA: (*annoyed*) But I told them to be quiet. Good thing I re-  30 membered to cover the windows with padded curtains.

(*Suddenly amiable, insidious*)

Well, and what was it this evening? A blessing? A prayer? A mass? A perpetual adoration?

THE BISHOP: (*gravely*) Let's not talk about that now. It's over. I'm concerned only about getting home. . . . You say the city's splashed with blood. . . .

THE WOMAN: There was a blessing, Madame. Then, my confession. . . .

IRMA: And after that?

THE BISHOP: That'll do!     40

THE WOMAN: That was all. At the end, my absolution.

IRMA: Won't anyone be able to witness it? Just once?

THE BISHOP: (*frightened*) No, no. Those things must remain secret, and they shall. It's indecent enough to talk about them while I'm being undressed. Nobody. And all the doors must be closed. Firmly closed, shut, buttoned, laced, hooked, sewn. . . .

IRMA: I merely asked. . . .

THE BISHOP: Sewn, Madame.

IRMA: (*annoyed*) You'll allow me at least, won't you, to feel a lit-  50 tle uneasy . . . professionally? I said twenty.

THE BISHOP: (*his voice suddenly grows clear and sharp, as if he were awakening. He displays a little annoyance*) We didn't tire ourselves. Barely six sins, and far from my favourite ones.

THE WOMAN: Six, but deadly ones! And it was a job finding *those.*

THE BISHOP: (*uneasy*) What? You mean they were false?

THE WOMAN: They were real, all right! I mean it was a job committing them. If only you realized what it takes, what a  60

person has to go through, in order to reach the point of disobedience.

THE BISHOP: I can imagine, my child. The order of the world is
so lax that you can do as you please there—or almost. But if
your sins were false, you may say so now.

IRMA: Oh no! I can hear you complaining already the next time
you come. No. They were real. (*To the woman*) Untie his
laces. Take off his shoes. And when you dress him, be careful he doesn't catch cold. (*To the Bishop*) Would you like a
70   toddy, a hot drink?

THE BISHOP: Thank you. I haven't time. I must be going.

(*Dreamily*)

Yes, six, but deadly ones!

IRMA: Come here, we'll undress you!

THE BISHOP: (*pleading, almost on his knees*) No, no, not yet.

IRMA: It's time. Come on! Quick! Make it snappy!

(*While they talk, the women undress him. Or rather they
merely remove pins and untie cords that seem to secure the
cope, stole and surplice.*)

THE BISHOP: (*to the woman*) About the sins, you really did commit them?

THE WOMAN: I did.

THE BISHOP: You really made the gestures? All the gestures?

80   THE WOMAN: I did.

THE BISHOP: When you moved towards me with your face forward, was it really aglow with the light of the flames?

THE WOMAN: It was.

THE BISHOP: And when my ringed hand came down on your
forehead, forgiving it. . . .

THE WOMAN: It was.

THE BISHOP: And when my gaze pierced your lovely eyes?

THE WOMAN: It was.

IRMA: Was there at least a glimmer of repentance in her lovely
90   eyes, my Lord?

THE BISHOP: (*standing up*) A fleeting glimmer. But was I seeking repentance in them? I saw there the greedy longing for
transgression. In flooding it, evil all at once baptized it. Her
big eyes opened on the abyss . . . a deathly pallor lit up—yes,
Madame—lit up her face. But our holiness lies only in our
being able to forgive you your sins. Even if they're only
make-believe.

THE WOMAN: (*suddenly coy*) And what if my sins were real?

THE BISHOP: (*in a different, less theatrical tone*) You're mad! I
100   hope you really didn't do all that!

IRMA: (*to the Bishop*) Don't listen to her. As for her sins, don't
worry. Here there's no. . . .

THE BISHOP: (*interrupting her*) I'm quite aware of that. Here
there's no possibility of doing evil. You live in evil. In the absence of remorse. How could you do evil? The Devil makes
believe. That's how one recognizes him. He's the great
Actor. And that's why the Church has anathematized actors.

THE WOMAN: Reality frightens you, doesn't it?

THE BISHOP: If your sins were real, they would be crimes, and
110   I'd be in a fine mess.

THE WOMAN: Would you go to the police?

(IRMA *continues to undress him. However, he still has the cope
on his shoulders.*)

IRMA: Stop plaguing her with all those questions.

(*The same terrible scream is heard again.*)

They're at it again! I'll go and shut them up.

THE BISHOP: That wasn't a make-believe scream.

IRMA: (*anxiously*) I don't know. . . . Who knows and what does
it matter?

THE BISHOP: (*going slowly to the mirror. He stands in front of
it*) Now answer, mirror, answer me. Do I come here to discover evil and innocence? (*To Irma, very gently*) Leave the
room! I want to be by myself.   120

IRMA: It's late. And the later it gets, the more dangerous it'll
be . . .

THE BISHOP: (*pleading*) Just one more minute.

IRMA: You've been here two hours and twenty minutes. In
other words, twenty minutes too long. . . .

THE BISHOP: (*suddenly incensed*) I want to be by myself.
Eavesdrop, if you want to—I know you do, anyway—and
don't come back till I've finished.

(*The two women leave with a sigh, looking as if they were out
of patience. The Bishop remains alone.*)

THE BISHOP: (*after making a visible effort to calm himself, in
front of the mirror and holding his surplice*) Now answer,   130
mirror, answer me. Do I come here to discover evil and innocence? And in your gilt-edged glass, what was I? Never—
I affirm it before God Who sees me—I never desired the
episcopal throne. To become bishop, to work my way up—
by means of virtues or vices—would have been to turn away
from the ultimate dignity of bishop. I shall explain: (THE
BISHOP *speaks in a tone of great precision, as if pursuing a
line of logical reasoning*) in order to become a bishop, I
should have had to make a zealous effort not to be one, but
to do what would have resulted in my being one. Having be-   140
come a bishop, in order to be one I should have had—in
order to be one for myself, of course!—I should have had to
be constantly aware of being one so as to perform my function. (*He seizes the flap of his surplice and kisses it.*) Oh
laces, laces, fashioned by a thousand little hands to veil ever
so many panting bosoms, buxom bosoms, and faces, and
hair, you illustrate me with branches and flowers! Let us
continue. But—there's the crux!

(*He laughs.*)

So I speak Latin!—a function is a function. It's not a mode
of being. But a bishop—that's a mode of being. It's a trust.   150
A burden. Mitres, lace, gold-cloth and glass trinkets, genu-
flexions. . . . To hell with the function!

(*Crackling of machine-gun fire.*)

IRMA: (*putting her head through the door*) Have you finished?

THE BISHOP: For Christ's sake, leave me alone. Get the hell
out! I'm probing myself.

(IRMA *shuts the door.*)

THE BISHOP: (*to the mirror*) The majesty, the dignity, that light
up my person, do not emanate from the attributions of my
function.—No more, good heavens! than from my personal
merits.—The majesty, the dignity that light me up come
from a more mysterious brilliance: the fact that the bishop   160

precedes me. Do I make myself clear, mirror, gilded image, ornate as a box of Mexican cigars? And I wish to be bishop in solitude, for appearance alone. . . . And in order to destroy all function, I want to cause a scandal and feel you up, you slut, you bitch, you trollop, you tramp. . . .

IRMA: *(entering)* That'll do now. You've got to leave.

THE BISHOP: You're crazy! I haven't finished.

*(Both women have entered.)*

IRMA: I'm not trying to pick an argument, and you know it, but you've no time to waste. . . .

170 THE BISHOP: *(ironically)* What you mean is that you need the room for someone else and you've got to arrange the mirrors and jugs.

IRMA: *(very irritated)* That's no business of yours. I've given you every attention while you've been here. And I repeat that it's dangerous for anyone to loiter in the streets.

*(Sound of gun-fire in the distance.)*

THE BISHOP: *(bitterly)* That's not true. You don't give a damn about my safety. When the job's finished, you don't give a damn about anyone!

IRMA: *(to the girl)* Stop listening to him and undress him.

180 IRMA: *(to the Bishop, who has stepped down from his cothurni and has now assumed the normal size of an actor, of the most ordinary of actors)* Lend a hand. You're stiff.

THE BISHOP: *(with a foolish look)* Stiff? I'm stiff? A solemn stiffness! Final immobility. . . .

IRMA: *(to the girl)* Hand him his jacket. . . .

THE BISHOP: *(looking at his clothes, which are heaped on the floor)* Ornaments, laces, through you I re-enter myself. I re-conquer a domain. I beleaguer a very ancient place from which I was driven. I install myself in a clearing where sui-
190 cide at last becomes possible. The judgment depends on me, and here I stand, face to face with my death.

IRMA: That's all very fine, but you've got to go. You left your car at the front door, near the power-station.

THE BISHOP: *(to Irma)* Because our Chief of Police, that wretched incompetent, is letting us be slaughtered by the rabble! *(Turning to the mirror and declaiming)* Ornaments! Mitres! Laces! You, above all, oh gilded cope, you protect me from the world. Where are my legs, where are my arms? Under your scalloped, lustrous flaps, what have my hands
200 been doing? Fit only for fluttering gestures, they've become mere stumps of wings—not of angels, but of partridges!— rigid cope, you make it possible for the most tender and lu-minous sweetness to ripen in warmth and darkness. My charity, a charity that will flood the world—it was under this carapace that I distilled it. . . . Would my hand emerge at times, knife-like, to bless? Or cut, mow down? My hand, the head of a turtle, would push aside the flaps. A turtle or a cau-tious snake? And go back into the rock. Underneath, my hand would dream. . . . Ornaments, gilded copes. . . .

*(The stage moves from left to right, as if it were plunging into the wings. The following set then appears.)*

## SCENE II

*Same chandelier. Three brown folding-screens. Bare walls. At right, same mirror, in which is reflected the same unmade bed*

as in the first scene. A woman, young and beautiful, seems to be chained, with her wrists bound. Her muslin dress is torn. Her breasts are visible. Standing in front of her is the execu-tioner. He is a giant, stripped to the waist. Very muscular. His whip has been slipped through the loop of his belt, in back, so that he seems to have a tail. A JUDGE, who, when he stands up, will seem larger than life (he, too, is mounted on cothurni, which are invisible beneath his robe, and his face is made up) is crawling, on his stomach, towards the woman, who shrinks as he approaches.

THE THIEF: *(holding out her foot)* Not yet! Lick it! Lick it 210 first. . . .

*(THE JUDGE makes an effort to continue crawling. Then he stands up and, slowly and painfully, though apparently happy, goes and sits down on a stool. THE THIEF (the woman described above) drops her domineering attitude and becomes humble.)*

THE JUDGE: *(severely)* For you're a thief! You were caught. . . . Who? The police. . . . Have you forgotten that your move-ments are hedged about by a strong and subtle network, my strong-arm cops? They're watchful, swivel-eyed insects that lie in wait for you. All of you! And they bring you captive, all of you, to the Bench. . . . What have you to say for yourself? You were caught. . . . Under your skirt. . . . *(To the Execu-tioner.)* Put your hand under her skirt. You'll find the pocket, the notorious Kangaroo Pocket. . . . *(To the Thief)* 220 that you fill with any old junk you pick up. Because you're an idiot to boot. . . . *(To the Executioner.)* What was there in that notorious Kangaroo Pocket? In that enormous paunch?

THE EXECUTIONER: Bottles of scent, my Lord, a flashlight, a bottle of Fly-tox, some oranges, several pairs of socks, bearskins, a Turkish towel, a scarf. *(To the Judge.)* Do you hear me? I said: a scarf.

THE JUDGE: *(with a start)* A scarf? Ah ha, so that's it? Why the scarf? Eh? What were you going to do with it? Whom were you planning to strangle? Answer. Who? . . . Are you a thief 230 or a strangler? *(Very gently, imploringly)* Tell me, my child, I beg of you, tell me you're a thief.

THE THIEF: Yes, my Lord.

THE EXECUTIONER: No!

THE THIEF: *(looking at him in surprise)* No?

THE EXECUTIONER: That's for later.

THE THIEF: Eh?

THE EXECUTIONER: I mean the confession is supposed to come later. Plead not guilty.

THE THIEF: What, and get beaten again!                                    240

THE JUDGE: *(mealy-mouthed)* Exactly, my child: and get beaten. You must first deny, then admit and repent. I want to see hot tears gush from your lovely eyes. Oh! I want you to be drenched in them. The power of tears! . . . Where's my statute-book? *(He fishes under his robe and pulls out a book.)*

THE THIEF: I've already cried. . . .

THE JUDGE: *(he seems to be reading)* Under the blows. I want tears of repentance. When I see you wet as a meadow I'll be utterly satisfied!                                                              250

THE THIEF: It's not easy. I tried to cry before. . . .

THE JUDGE: *(no longer reading. In a half-theatrical, almost fa-miliar tone)* You're quite young. Are you new here? *(Anx-iously)* At least you're not a minor?

THE THIEF: Oh no, sir.

THE JUDGE: Call me my Lord. How long have you been here?

THE EXECUTIONER: Since the day before yesterday, my Lord.

THE JUDGE: (*reassuming the theatrical tone and resuming the reading*) Let her speak. I like that puling voice of hers, that voice without resonance. . . . Look here: you've got to be a model thief if I'm to be a model judge. If you're a fake thief, I become a fake judge. Is that clear?

THE THIEF: Oh yes, my Lord.

THE JUDGE: (*he continues reading*) Good. Thus far everything has gone off well. My executioner has hit hard . . . for he too has his function. We are bound together, you, he and I. For example, if he didn't hit, how could I stop him from hitting? Therefore, he must strike so that I can intervene and demonstrate my authority. And you must deny your guilt so that he can beat you.

(*A noise is heard, as of something having fallen in the next room. In a natural tone*)

What's that? Are all the doors firmly shut? Can anyone see us, or hear us?

THE EXECUTIONER: No, no, you needn't worry. I bolted the door.

(*He goes to examine a huge bolt on the rear door.*)

And the corridor's out of bounds.

THE JUDGE: (*in a natural tone*) Are you sure?

THE EXECUTIONER: You can take my word for it.

(*He puts his hand into his pocket.*)

Can I have a smoke?

THE JUDGE: (*in a natural tone*) The smell of tobacco inspires me. Smoke away.

(*Same noise as before.*)

Oh, what *is* that? What *is* it? Can't they leave me in peace?

(*He gets up.*)

What's going on?

THE EXECUTIONER: (*curtly*) Nothing at all. Someone must have dropped something. You're getting nervous.

THE JUDGE: (*in a natural tone*) That may be, but my nervousness makes me aware of things. It keeps me on the alert.

(*He gets up and moves towards the wall.*)

May I have a look?

THE EXECUTIONER: Just a quick one, because it's getting late.

(THE EXECUTIONER *shrugs his shoulders and exchanges a wink with the thief.*)

THE JUDGE: (*after looking*) It's lit up. Brightly lit, but empty.

THE EXECUTIONER: (*shrugging his shoulders*) Empty!

THE JUDGE: (*in an even more familiar tone*) You seem anxious. Has anything new happened?

THE EXECUTIONER: This afternoon, just before you arrived, the rebels took three key-positions. They set fire to several places. Not a single fireman came out. Everything went up in flames. The Palace. . . .

THE JUDGE: What about the Chief of Police? Twiddling his thumbs as usual?

THE THIEF: There's been no news of him for four hours. If he can get away, he's sure to come here. He's expected at any moment.

THE JUDGE: (*to the Thief, and sitting down*) In any case, he'd better not plan to come by way of Queen's Bridge. It was blown up last night.

THE THIEF: We know that. We heard the explosion from here.

THE JUDGE: (*resuming his theatrical tone. He reads the statute-book*) All right. Let's get on with it. Thus, taking advantage of the sleep of the just, taking advantage of a moment's inattention, you rob them, you ransack, you pilfer and purloin. . . .

THE THIEF: No, my Lord, never. . . .

THE EXECUTIONER: Shall I tan her hide?

THE THIEF: (*crying out*) Arthur!

THE EXECUTIONER: What's eating you? Don't address me. Answer his Lordship. And call me Mr. Executioner.

THE THIEF: Yes, Mr. Executioner.

THE JUDGE: (*reading*) I continue: did you steal?

THE THIEF: I did, I did, my Lord.

THE JUDGE: (*reading*) Good. Now answer quickly, and to the point: what else did you steal?

THE THIEF: Bread, because I was hungry.

THE JUDGE: (*he draws himself up and lays down the book*) Sublime! Sublime function! I'll have all that to judge. Oh, child, you reconcile me with the world. A judge! I'm going to be judge of your acts! On me depends the weighing, the balance. The world is an apple. I cut it in two: the good, the bad. And you agree, thank you, you agree to be the bad! (*Facing the audience*) Right before your eyes: nothing in my hands, nothing up my sleeve, remove the rot and cast it off. But it's a painful occupation. If every judgment were delivered seriously, each one would cost me my life. That's why I'm dead. I inhabit that region of exact freedom. I, King of Hell, weigh those who are dead, like me. She's a dead person, like myself.

THE THIEF: You frighten me, sir.

THE JUDGE: (*very bombastically*) Be still. In the depths of Hell I sort out the humans who venture there. Some to the flames, the others to the boredom of the fields of asphodel. You, thief, spy, she-dog, Minos is speaking to you, Minos weighs you. (*To the Executioner*) Cerberus?

THE EXECUTIONER: (*imitating the dog*) Bow-wow, bow-wow!

THE JUDGE: You're handsome! And the sight of a fresh victim makes you even handsomer. (*He curls up the Executioner's lips.*) Show your fangs. Dreadful. White. (*Suddenly he seems anxious. To the Thief*) But at least you're not lying about those thefts—you did commit them, didn't you?

THE EXECUTIONER: Don't worry. She committed them, all right. She wouldn't have dared not to. I'd have made her.

THE JUDGE: I'm almost happy. Continue. What did you steal? (*Suddenly, machine-gun fire.*)

THE JUDGE: There's simply no end to it. Not a moment's rest.

THE THIEF: I told you: the rebellion has spread all over the north of the city. . . .

THE EXECUTIONER: Shut up!

THE JUDGE: (*irritated*) Are you going to answer, yes or no? What else have you stolen? Where? When? How? How much? Why? For whom?

THE THIEF: I very often entered houses when the maids were off. I used the tradesmen's entrance. . . . I stole from drawers, I broke into children's piggy-banks. (*She is visibly trying to find words.*) Once I dressed up as a lady. I put on a dark-brown suit, a black straw hat with cherries, a veil and a pair of black shoes—with Cuban heels—then I went in. . . .

THE JUDGE: *(in a rush)* Where? Where? Where? Where—where—where? Where did you go in?

THE THIEF: I can't remember. Forgive me.

THE EXECUTIONER: Shall I let her have it?

THE JUDGE: Not yet. *(To the girl)* Where did you go in? Tell me

370   where?

THE THIEF: *(in a panic)* But I swear to you, I don't remember.

THE EXECUTIONER: Shall I let her have it? Shall I, my Lord?

THE JUDGE: *(to the Executioner, and going up to him)* Ah! ah! your pleasure depends on me. You like to thrash, eh? I'm pleased with you, Executioner! Masterly mountain of meat, hunk of beef that's set in motion at a word from me! *(He pretends to look at himself in the Executioner.)* Mirror that glorifies me! Image that I can touch, I love you. Never would I have the strength or skill to leave streaks of fire on

380   her back. Besides, what could I do with such strength and skill? *(He touches him.)* Are you there? You're all there, my huge arm, too heavy for me, too big, too fat for my shoulder, walking at my side all by itself! Arm, hundredweight of meat, without you I'd be nothing. . . . *(To the Thief)* And without you too, my child. You're my two perfect complements. . . . Ah, what a fine trio we make! *(To the Thief)* But you, you have a privilege that he hasn't, nor I either, that of priority. My being a judge is an emanation of your being a thief. You need only refuse—but you'd better not!—need

390   only refuse to be who you are—what you are, therefore who you are—for me to cease to be . . . to vanish, evaporated. Burst. Volatilized. Denied. Hence: good born of. . . . What then? What then? But you won't refuse, will you? You won't refuse to be a thief? That would be wicked. It would be criminal. You'd deprive me of being! *(Imploringly)* Say it, my child, my love, you won't refuse?

THE THIEF: *(coyly)* I might.

THE JUDGE: What's that? What's that you say? You'd refuse? Tell me where. And tell me again what you've stolen.

400   THE THIEF: *(curtly, and getting up)* I won't.

THE JUDGE: Tell me where. Don't be cruel. . . .

THE THIEF: Your tone is getting too familiar. I won't have it!

THE JUDGE: Miss. . . . Madame. I beg of you. *(He falls to his knees.)* Look, I beseech you. Don't leave me in this position, waiting to be a judge. If there were no judge, what would become of us, but what if there were no thieves?

THE THIEF: *(ironically)* And what if there weren't?

THE JUDGE: It would be awful. But you won't do that to me, will you? Please understand me: I don't mind your hiding, for as

410   long as you can and as long as my nerves can bear it, behind the refusal to confess—it's all right to be mean and make me yearn, even prance, make me dance, drool, sweat, whinny with impatience, crawl . . . do you want me to crawl?

THE EXECUTIONER: *(to the Judge)* Crawl.

THE JUDGE: I'm proud!

THE EXECUTIONER: *(threateningly)* Crawl!

*(THE JUDGE, who was on his knees, lies flat on his stomach and crawls slowly towards the Thief. As he crawls forward, the Thief moves back.)*

THE EXECUTIONER: Good. Continue.

THE JUDGE: *(to the Thief)* You're quite right, you rascal, to make me crawl after my judgeship, but if you were to refuse for good, you hussy, it would be criminal. . . .     420

THE THIEF: *(haughtily)* Call me Madame, and ask politely.

THE JUDGE: Will I get what I want?

THE THIEF: *(coyly)* It costs a lot—stealing does.

THE JUDGE: I'll pay! I'll pay whatever I have to, Madame. But if I no longer had to divide the Good from the Evil, of what use would I be? I ask you?

THE THIEF: I ask myself.

THE JUDGE: *(is infinitely sad)* A while ago I was going to be Minos. My Cerberus was barking. *(To the Executioner)* Do you remember? (THE EXECUTIONER *interrupts the Judge by*  430 *cracking his whip.)* You were so cruel, so mean! So good! And me, I was pitiless. I was going to fill Hell with the souls of the damned, to fill prisons. Prisons! Prisons! Prisons, dungeons, blessed places where evil is impossible since they are the crossroads of all the malediction in the world. One cannot commit evil in evil. Now, what I desire above all is not to condemn, but to judge . . . *(He tries to get up.)*

THE EXECUTIONER: Crawl! And hurry up, I've got to go and get dressed.

THE JUDGE: *(to the girl)* Madame! Madame, please, I beg of  440 you. I'm willing to lick your shoes, but tell me you're a thief. . . .

THE THIEF: *(in a cry)* Not yet! Lick! Lick! Lick first!

*(The stage moves from left to right, as at the end of the preceding scene, and plunges into the right wing. In the distance, machine-gun fire.)*

## SCENE III

*Three dark-green folding-screens, arranged as in the preceding scenes. The same chandelier. The same mirror reflecting the unmade bed. On an armchair, a horse of the kind used by folk-dancers, with a little kilted skirt. In the room, a timid-looking gentleman: the* GENERAL. *He removes his jacket, then his bowler hat and his gloves.* IRMA *is near him.*

THE GENERAL: *(He points to the hat, jacket and gloves)* Have that cleared out.

IRMA: It'll be folded and wrapped.

THE GENERAL: Have it removed from sight.

IRMA: It'll be put away. Even burned.

THE GENERAL: Yes, yes, of course, I'd like it to burn! Like cities at twilight.     450

IRMA: Did you notice anything on the way?

THE GENERAL: I ran very serious risks. The populace has blown up dams. Whole areas are flooded. The arsenal in particular. So that all the powder supplies are wet. And the weapons rusty. I had to make some rather wide detours—though I didn't trip over a single drowned body.

IRMA: I wouldn't take the liberty of asking you your opinions. Everyone is free, and I'm not concerned with politics.

THE GENERAL: Then let's talk of something else. The important thing is how I'm going to get out of this place. It'll be late by  460 the time I leave. . . .

IRMA: About it's being late. . . .

THE GENERAL: That does it.

(*He reaches into his pocket, takes out some banknotes, counts them and gives some to Irma. She keeps them in her hand.*)

THE GENERAL: I'm not keen about being shot down in the dark when I leave. For, of course, there won't be anyone to escort me?

IRMA: I'm afraid not. Unfortunately Arthur's not free. (*A long pause.*)

THE GENERAL: (*suddenly impatient*) But . . . isn't she coming?

470 IRMA: I can't imagine what she's doing. I gave instructions that everything was to be ready by the time you arrived. The horse is already here. . . . I'll ring.

THE GENERAL: Don't, I'll attend to that. (*He rings.*) I like to ring! Ringing's authoritative. Ah, to ring out commands.

IRMA: In a little while, General. Oh, I'm so sorry, here am I giving you your rank. . . . In a little while you'll. . . .

THE GENERAL: Sh! Don't say it.

IRMA: You have such force, such youth! such dash!

THE GENERAL: And spurs. Will I have spurs? I said they were
480 to be fixed to my boots. Oxblood boots, right?

IRMA: Yes, General. And patent-leather.

THE GENERAL: Oxblood. Patent-leather, very well, but with mud?

IRMA: With mud and perhaps a little blood. I've had the decorations prepared.

THE GENERAL: Authentic ones?

IRMA: Authentic ones. (*Suddenly a woman's long scream.*)

THE GENERAL: What's that?

(*He starts going to the right wall and is already bending down to look, as if there were a small crack, but* IRMA *steps in front of him.*)

IRMA: Nothing. There's always some carelessness, on both
490 sides.

THE GENERAL: But that cry? A woman's cry. A call for help perhaps? My heart skips a beat. . . . I spring forward. . . .

IRMA: (*icily*) I want no trouble here. Calm down. For the time being, you're in mufti.

THE GENERAL: That's right.

(*A woman's scream again.*)

THE GENERAL: All the same, it's disturbing. Besides, it'll be awkward.

IRMA: What on earth can she be doing?

(*She goes to ring, but by the rear door enters a very beautiful young woman, red-headed, hair undone, dishevelled. Her bosom is almost bare. She is wearing a black corset, black stockings and very high-heeled shoes. She is holding a general's uniform, complete with sword, cocked hat and boots.*)

THE GENERAL: (*severely*) So you finally got here? Half an hour
500 late. That's more than's needed to lose a battle.

IRMA: She'll redeem herself, General, I know her.

THE GENERAL: (*looking at the boots*) What about the blood? I don't see any blood.

IRMA: It dried. Don't forget that it's the blood of your past battles. Well, then, I'll leave you. Do you have everything you need?

THE GENERAL: (*looking to the right and left*) You're

forgetting. . . .

IRMA: Good God! Yes. I was forgetting.

(*She lays on the chair the towels she has been carrying on her arm. Then she leaves by the rear.* THE GENERAL *goes to the door, then locks it. But no sooner is the door closed than someone knocks.* THE GIRL *goes to open it. Behind, and standing slightly back,* THE EXECUTIONER, *sweating, wiping himself with a towel.*)

THE EXECUTIONER: Is Mme Irma here?                            510

THE GIRL: (*curtly*) In the Rose-garden. (*Correcting herself*) I'm sorry, in the Funeral Chapel.

(*She closes the door.*)

THE GENERAL: (*irritated*) I'll be left in peace, I hope. And you're late. Where the hell were you? Didn't they give you your feed-bag? You're smiling, are you? Smiling at your rider? You recognize his hand, gentle but firm? (*He strokes her.*) My proud steed! My handsome mare, we've had many a spirited gallop together!

THE GIRL: And that's not all! I want to trip through the world with my nervous legs and well-shod hooves. Take off your 520 trousers and shoes so I can dress you.

THE GENERAL: (*he has taken the cane*) All right, but first, down on your knees! Come on, come on, bend your knees, bend them. . . .

(THE GIRL *rears, utters a whinny of pleasure and kneels like a circus horse before the General.*)

THE GENERAL: Bravo! Bravo, Dove! You haven't forgotten a thing. And now, you're going to help me and answer my questions. It's fitting and proper for a nice filly to help her master unbutton himself and take off his gloves, and to be at his beck and call. Now start by untying my laces.

(*During the entire scene that follows,* THE GIRL *helps* THE GENERAL *remove his clothes and then dress up as a general. When he is completely dressed, he will be seen to have taken on gigantic proportions, by means of trick effects: invisible footgear, broadened shoulders, excessive make-up.*)

THE GIRL: Left foot still swollen?                            530

THE GENERAL: Yes. It's my leading-foot. The one that prances. Like your hoof when you toss your head.

THE GIRL: What am I doing? Unbutton yourself.

THE GENERAL: Are you a horse or an illiterate? If you're a horse, you toss your head. Help me. Pull. Don't pull so hard. See here, you're not a plough-horse.

THE GIRL: I do what I have to do.

THE GENERAL: Are you rebelling? Already? Wait till I'm ready. When I put the bit into your mouth. . . .

THE GIRL: Oh no, not that.                                    540

THE GENERAL: A general reprimanded by his horse! You'll have the bit, the bridle, the harness, the saddlegirth, and I, in boots and helmet, will whip and plunge!

THE GIRL: The bit is awful. It makes the gums and the corners of the lips bleed. I'll drool blood.

THE GENERAL: Foam pink and spit fire! But what a gallop! Along the rye-fields, through the alfalfa, over the meadows and dusty roads, over hill and dale, awake or asleep, from dawn to twilight and from twilight. . . .

550 THE GIRL: Tuck in your shirt. Pull up your braces. It's quite a job dressing a victorious general who's to be buried. Do you want the sabre?

THE GENERAL: Let it lie on the table, like Lafayette's. Conspicuously, but hide the clothes. Where? How should *I* know? Surely there's a hiding-place somewhere.

(THE GIRL *bundles up his clothes and hides them behind the armchair.*)

THE GENERAL: The tunic? Good. Got all the medals? Count 'em.

THE GIRL: (*after counting them, very quickly*) They're all here, sir.

560 THE GENERAL: What about the war? Where's the war?

THE GIRL: (*very softly*) It's approaching, sir. It's evening in an apple-orchard. The sky is calm and pink. The earth is bathed in a sudden peace—the moan of doves—the peace that precedes battles. The air is very still. An apple has fallen to the grass. A yellow apple. Things are holding their breath. War is declared. The evening is very mild. . . .

THE GENERAL: But suddenly?

THE GIRL: We're at the edge of the meadow. I keep myself from flinging out, from whinnying. Your thighs are warm

570 and you're pressing my flanks. Death. . . .

THE GENERAL: But suddenly?

THE GIRL: Death has pricked up her ears. She puts a finger to her lips, asking for silence. Things are lit up with an ultimate goodness. You yourself no longer heed my presence. . . .

THE GENERAL: But suddenly?

THE GIRL: Button up by yourself, sir. The water lay motionless in the pools. The wind itself was awaiting an order to unfurl the flags. . . .

THE GENERAL: But suddenly?

580 THE GIRL: Suddenly? Eh? Suddenly? (*She seems to be trying to find the right words.*) Ah yes, suddenly all was fire and sword! Widows! Miles of crêpe had to be woven to put on the standards. The mothers and wives remained dry-eyed behind their veils. The bells came clattering down the bombed towers. As I rounded a corner I was frightened by a blue cloth. I reared, but, steadied by your gentle and masterful hand, I ceased to quiver. I started forward again. How I loved you, my hero!

THE GENERAL: But . . . the dead? Weren't there any dead?

590 THE GIRL: The soldiers died kissing the standard. You were all victory and kindness. One evening, remember. . . .

THE GENERAL: I was so mild that I began to snow. To snow on my men, to shroud them in the softest of winding-sheets. To snow. Moskova!

THE GIRL: Splinters of shell had gashed the lemons. Now death was in action. She moved nimbly from one to the other, deepening a wound, dimming an eye, tearing off an arm, opening an artery, discolouring a face, cutting short a cry, a song. Death was ready to drop. Finally, exhausted, herself

600 dead with fatigue, she grew drowsy and rested lightly on your shoulder, where she fell asleep.

THE GENERAL: (*drunk with joy*) Stop, stop, it's not time for that yet, but I feel it'll be magnificent. The cross-belt? Good. (*He looks at himself in the mirror.*) Austerlitz! General! Man of war and in full regalia, behold me in my pure appearance. Nothing, no contingent trails behind me. I appear, purely and simply. If I went through wars without dying, went

through sufferings without dying, if I was promoted, without dying, it was for this minute close to death.

(*Suddenly he stops; he seems troubled by an idea.*)

Tell me, Dove?     610

THE GIRL: What is it, sir?

THE GENERAL: What's the Chief of Police been doing?

(THE GIRL *shakes her head.*)

Nothing? Still nothing? In short, everything slips through his fingers. And what about us, are we wasting our time?

THE GIRL: (*imperiously*) Not at all. And, in any case, it's no business of ours. Continue. You were saying: for this minute close to death . . . and then?

THE GENERAL: (*hesitating*) . . . close to death . . . where I shall be nothing, though reflected *ad infinitum* in these mirrors, nothing but my image. . . . Quite right, comb your mane. 620 Curry yourself. I require a well-groomed filly. So, in a little while, to the blare of trumpets, we shall descend—I on your back—to death and glory, for I am about to die. It is indeed a descent to the grave. . . .

THE GIRL: But, sir, you've been dead since yesterday.

THE GENERAL: I know . . . but a formal and picturesque descent, by unexpected stairways. . . .

THE GIRL: You are a dead general, but an eloquent one.

THE GENERAL: Because I'm dead, prating horse. What is now speaking, and so beautifully, is Example. I am now only the 630 image of my former self. Your turn, now. Lower your head and hide your eyes, for I want to be a general in solitude. Not even for myself, but for my image, and my image for its image, and so on. In short, we'll be among equals. Dove, are you ready?

(THE GIRL *nods.*)

Come now. Put on your bay dress, horse, my fine Arab steed.

(THE GENERAL *slips the mock-horse over her head. Then he cracks his whip.*)

We're off!

(*He bows to his image in the mirror.*)

Farewell, general!

(*Then he stretches out in the arm-chair with his feet on another chair and bows to the audience, holding himself rigid as a corpse.* THE GIRL *places herself in front of the chair and, on the spot, makes the movements of a horse in motion.*)

THE GIRL: The procession has begun. . . . We're passing 640 through the City. . . . We're going along the river. I'm sad. . . . The sky is overcast. The nation weeps for that splendid hero who died in battle. . . .

THE GENERAL: (*starting*) Dove!

THE GIRL: (*turning around, in tears*) Sir?

THE GENERAL: Add that I died with my boots on!

(*He then resumes his pose.*)

THE GIRL: My hero died with his boots on! The procession continues. Your aides-de-camp precede me. . . . Then come I, Dove, your war-horse. . . . The military band plays a funeral march. . . .     650

*(Marching in place,* THE GIRL *sings Chopin's Funeral March, which is continued by an invisible orchestra [with brasses]. Far off, machine-gun fire.)*

SCENE IV

*A room, the three visible panels of which are three mirrors in which is reflected a little old man, dressed as a tramp though neatly combed. He is standing motionless in the middle of the room. Near him, looking very indifferent, a very beautiful red-haired girl. Leather corselet, leather boots. Naked and beautiful thighs. Fur jacket. She is waiting. So is the man. He is impatient, nervous.* THE GIRL *is motionless.*

THE MAN *removes his torn gloves tremblingly. He takes from his pocket a handkerchief and mops his face. He takes off his glasses, folds them and puts them into a case, which he then slips into his pocket.*

*He wipes his hands with his handkerchief.*

*All the gestures of the little old man are reflected in the three mirrors.*

*(Three actors are needed to play the roles of the reflections.)*

*At length, there are three raps at the rear door.*

*The red-haired girl goes to the door. She says: "Yes."*

*The door opens a little and through the opening appear* IRMA'S *hand and arm holding a whip and a very dirty and shaggy wig.*

THE GIRL *takes them. The door closes.*

THE MAN'S *face lights up.*

*The red-haired girl has an exaggeratedly lofty and cruel air.*

*She puts the wig on his head roughly.*

THE MAN *takes a bouquet of artificial flowers from his pocket. He holds it as if he were going to offer it to the girl, who whips him and lashes it from his hand.*

THE MAN'S *face is lit up with tenderness.*

*Very near-by, machine-gun fire.*

THE MAN *touches his wig.*

THE MAN: What about the lice?

THE GIRL: *(very coarsely)* They're there.

SCENE V

IRMA'S *room. Very elegant. It is the same room that was reflected in the mirrors in the first three scenes. The same chandelier. Large lace hangings suspended from the flies. Three arm-chairs. At left, large window near which is an apparatus by means of which* IRMA *can see what is going on in the studios. Door at right. Door at left.* IRMA *is sitting at her dressing-table, going over her accounts. Near her, a girl:* CARMEN. *Machine-gun fire.*

CARMEN: *(counting)* The bishop, twenty . . . the judge, twenty. . . . *(She raises her head.)* No, Madame, nothing yet. No Chief of Police.

IRMA: *(irritated)* He's going to turn up, if he turns up . . . fit to be tied! And yet!

CARMEN: Yes, I know: it takes all kinds to make a world. But no Chief of Police. *(She counts again.)* The general, twenty . . . the sailor, twenty . . . the brat, thirty. . . . 660

IRMA: I've told you, Carmen, I don't like that. And I demand respect for the visitors. Vi-si-tors! I don't allow myself—my own self *(she stresses the word "own")*—even to refer to them as clients. And yet! . . . *(She flashily snaps the sheaf of fresh banknotes that she has in her hand.)*

CARMEN: *(severely; she has turned around and is glaring at* IRMA*)* For you, yes: cash and refinement.

IRMA: *(trying to be conciliatory)* Those eyes! Don't be unjust. You've been irritable for some time now. I realize we're on edge because of what's going on, but things will quiet down. 670 The sun will come out again. George. . . .

CARMEN: Ah, him!

IRMA: Don't sneer at the Chief of Police. If not for him we'd be in a fine mess. Yes, we, because you're tied up with me. And with him. *(A long pause.)* What disturbs me most is your sadness. *(Wisely.)* You've changed, Carmen. And even before the rebellion started. . . .

CARMEN: There's nothing much left for me to do at your place, Mme. Irma.

IRMA: *(disconcerted)* But . . . I've put you in charge of my book- 680 keeping. You sit down at my desk and all at once my entire life opens out before you. I haven't a secret left, and you're not happy?

CARMEN: Of course, I'm grateful to you for your confidence, but . . . it's not the same thing.

IRMA: Do you miss "that," Carmen? *(*CARMEN *is silent.)* Come, come, Carmen, when you mounted the snow-covered rock with the yellow paper rose-bush—by the way, I'm going to have to store that in the cellar—and when the miraculously-healed leper swooned at the sight of you, you didn't take 690 yourself seriously, did you, Carmen? *(Brief silence.)*

CARMEN: When our sessions are over, Madame, you never allow anyone to talk about them. So you have no idea of how we really feel. You observe it all from a distance. But if ever you once put on the dress and the blue veil, or if you were the unbuttoned penitent, or the general's mare, or the country girl tumbled in the hay. . . .

IRMA: *(shocked)* Me!

CARMEN: Or the maid in a pink apron, or the archduchess de-flowered by the policeman, or . . . but I'm not going to run 700 through the whole list . . . you'd know what that does to a girl's soul, and that she's got to use a little irony in self-de-fence. But no, you don't even want us to talk about it among ourselves. You're afraid of a smile, of a joke.

IRMA: *(very severely)* True, I don't allow any joking. A giggle, or even a smile, spoils everything. A smile means doubt. The clients want sober ceremonies. With sighs. My house is a se-vere place. You're allowed to play cards.

CARMEN: Then don't be surprised that we're sad. *(A pause.)* But I'm thinking of my daughter. 710

IRMA: *(She stands—for a bell has buzzed—and goes to a curi-ous piece of furniture at the left, a kind of switchboard with a view-finder and earphone. While talking, she looks into the view-finder, after pushing down a switch)* Every time I ask you a slightly intimate question, you shut up like a clam, and you throw your daughter up to me. Are you still set on going to see her? Don't be a fool. Between this place and the nursery in the country there's fire and water, rebellion and bullets. I even wonder whether . . . *(The bell buzzes* 720 *again.* MME IRMA *pulls up the switch and pushes down another)* . . . whether they didn't get George on the way. Though a Chief of Police knows how to take care of himself. *(She looks at a watch that she takes from her bosom.)* He's late. *(She looks anxious.)* Or else he hasn't dared to go out.

CARMEN: In order to get to your studios, those gentlemen of yours go through gunfire without fear, whereas I, in order to see my daughter. . . .

IRMA: Without fear? In a state of jitters that excites them. Their nostrils can sniff the orgy behind the wall of flame and steel. 730 . . . Let's get back to the accounts, shall we?

CARMEN: In all, counting the sailor and the simple jobs, it comes to three hundred and twenty.

IRMA: The more killing there is in the working-class districts, the more the men roll into my studios.

CARMEN: The men?

IRMA: *(after a pause)* Some men. Drawn by my mirrors and chandeliers, always the same ones. As for the others, heroism takes the place of women.

CARMEN: *(bitterly)* Women?

740 IRMA: What shall I call you, my big, long, sterile girls? Their seed never ripens in you, and yet . . . if you weren't there?

CARMEN: You have your revels, Mme Irma.

IRMA: Be still. It's this chilling game that makes me sad and melancholy. Fortunately I have my jewels. Which, as it happens, are in great danger. *(Dreamily)* I have my jewels . . . and you, the orgies of your heart. . . .

CARMEN: . . . they don't help matters, Madame. My daughter loves me.

IRMA: You're the fairy godmother who comes to see her with 750 toys and perfumes. She pictures you in Heaven. *(Bursting out laughing)* Ah, that's the limit—to think there's someone for whom my brothel—which is Hell—is Heaven! It's Heaven for your brat! *(She laughs.)* Are you going to make a whore of her later on?

CARMEN: Mme Irma!

IRMA: That's right! I ought to leave you to your secret brothel, your precious pink cat-house, your soulful whore-house. . . . You think I'm cruel? This rebellion is getting me down, too. You may not realize it, but I have moments of fear and 760 panic. . . . It looks to me as if the aim of the rebellion weren't to capture the Royal Palace, but to sack my studios. I'm afraid, Carmen. Yet I've tried everything, even prayer. *(She smiles painfully.)* Like your miraculously-healed leper. Have I wounded you?

CARMEN: *(with decision)* Twice a week, on Tuesdays and Fridays, I had to be the Immaculate Conception of Lourdes and appear to a bank-clerk of the National Provincial. For you it meant money in the bank and justified your brothel, whereas for me it was. . . .

770 IRMA: *(astonished)* You agreed to it. You didn't seem to mind it.

CARMEN: I was happy.

IRMA: Well? Where's the harm?

CARMEN: I saw the effect I had on my bank-clerk. I saw his state of terror, how he'd break out in a sweat, I heard the rattle in his throat. . . .

IRMA: That'll do. He doesn't come any more. I wonder why? Maybe the danger. Or maybe his wife found out. *(A pause.)* Maybe he's dead. Attend to my accounts.

CARMEN: Your book-keeping will never replace my appearing 780 to the bank-clerk. It had become as real as at Lourdes. Everything inside me now yearns for my daughter. She's in a real garden. . . .

IRMA: You'll have a hard time getting to her, and before long the garden will be in your heart.

CARMEN: Be still!

IRMA: *(inexorably)* The city is full of corpses. All the roads are cut off. The peasants are also going over to the rebels. I wonder why? Contagion? The rebellion is an epidemic. It has the same fatal and sacred character. In any case, we're going 790 to find ourselves more and more isolated. The rebels have it in for the Clergy, for the Army, for the Magistracy, for me, Irma, a bawd and madame of a whore-house. As for you, you'll be killed, disembowelled, and your daughter will be adopted by some virtuous rebel. And that's what's in store for all of us. *(She shudders.)*

*(Suddenly a buzz.* IRMA *runs to the apparatus and looks and listens as before.)*

IRMA: Studio 24, Chamber of the Sands. What's going on?

*(She watches very attentively. A long pause.)*

CARMEN: *(She has sat down at Irma's table and gone back to the accounts. Without raising her head)* The Foreign Legion? 800

IRMA: *(with her eye still glued to the apparatus)* Yes. It's the heroic Legionnaire falling to the sand. And that idiot Rachel has thrown a dart at his ear. He might have been disfigured. What an idea, having himself shot as if by an Arab, and dying—if you want to call it that!—at attention, on a sand-pile! *(A silence. She watches attentively.)* Ah, Rachel's doctoring him. She's preparing a dressing for him, and he has a happy look. *(Very much interested.)* My, my, he seems to like it. I have a feeling he wants to alter his scenario and that starting today he's going to die in the military hospital, 810 tucked in by his nurse. . . . Another uniform to buy. Always expenses. *(Suddenly anxious.)* Say, I don't like that. Not one bit. I'm getting more and more worried about Rachel. She'd better not double-cross me the way Chantal did. *(Turning around, to Carmen.)* By the way, no news of Chantal?

CARMEN: None.

IRMA: *(picks up the apparatus again)* And the machine's not working right! What's he saying to her? He's explaining . . . she's listening . . . she understands. I'm afraid he understands too. *(Buzzing again. She pushes down another switch* 820 *and looks.)* False alarm. It's the plumber leaving.

CARMEN: Which one?

IRMA: The real one.

CARMEN: Which is the real one?

IRMA: The one who repairs the taps.

CARMEN: Is the other one fake?

IRMA: *(shrugs her shoulders and pushes down the first switch)* Ah, I told you so: the three or four drops of blood from his ear have inspired him. Now he's having her pamper him. Tomorrow morning he'll be in fine fettle for going to his 830 Embassy.

CARMEN: He's married, isn't he?

IRMA: As a rule, I don't like to talk about the private life of my visitors. The Grand Balcony has a world-wide reputation. It's the most artful, yet the most decent house of illusions. . . .

CARMEN: Decent?

IRMA: Discreet. But I might as well be frank with you, you inquisitive girl. Most of them are married.

*(A pause.)*

840 CARMEN: When they're with their wives, whom they love, do they keep a tiny, small-scale version of their revels in a brothel. . . .

IRMA: *(reprimanding her)* Carmen!

CARMEN: Excuse me, Madame . . . in a house of illusions. I was saying: do they keep their revels in a house of illusions tucked away in the back of their heads in miniature form, far off? But present?

IRMA: It's possible, child. No doubt they do. Like a Chinese lantern left over from a carnival, and waiting for the next

850 one, or, if you prefer, like an imperceptible light in the imperceptible window of an imperceptible castle that they can enlarge instantly whenever they feel like going there to relax. *(Machine-gun fire.)* You hear that? They're approaching. They're out to get me.

CARMEN: *(continuing her train of thought)* All the same, it must be nice in a real house.

IRMA: *(more and more frightened)* They'll succeed in surrounding the house before George arrives. . . . One thing we mustn't forget—if ever we get out of this mess—is that the

860 walls aren't sufficiently padded and the windows aren't well sealed. . . . One can hear all that's going on in the street. Which means that from the street one can hear what's going on in the house.

CARMEN: *(still pensive)* In a real house, it must be nice. . . .

IRMA: Who knows! But Carmen, if my girls start bothering their heads about such things, it'll be the ruin of the brothel. I really think you miss your apparition. Look, I can do something for you. I did promise it to Regina, but I offer it to you. If you want to, of course. Someone rang me up yesterday

870 and asked for a Saint Theresa. . . . *(A pause.)* Ah, obviously, it's a come-down from the Immaculate Conception to Saint Theresa, but it's not bad either. . . . *(A pause.)* Well, what do you say? It's for a banker. Very clean, you know. Not demanding. I offer it to you. If the rebels are crushed, naturally.

CARMEN: I liked my dress and veil and rose-bush.

IRMA: There's a rose-bush in the "Saint Theresa" too. Think it over.

*(A pause.)*

CARMEN: And what'll the authentic detail be?

880 IRMA: The ring. He's got it all worked out. The wedding ring. You know that every nun wears a wedding ring, as a bride of God. *(CARMEN makes a gesture of astonishment.)* That's so. That's how he'll know he's dealing with a real nun.

CARMEN: What about the fake detail?

IRMA: It's almost always the same: black lace under the homespun skirt. Well, how about it? You have the kind of gentleness he likes. He'll be pleased.

CARMEN: It's really very kind of you, to think of him.

IRMA: I'm thinking of you.

890 CARMEN: You're so kind, Madame—I wasn't being ironic. The thing to be said for your house is that it brings consolation.

You set up and prepare their secret theatres. . . . You've got your feet on the ground. The proof is that you rake in the money. Whereas they . . . their awakening must be brutal. No sooner is it finished than it starts all over again.

IRMA: Luckily for me.

CARMEN: . . . starts all over again, and always the same adventure. They'd like it never to end.

IRMA: You miss the entire point. When it's over, their minds are clear. I can tell from their eyes. Suddenly they under- 900 stand mathematics. They love their children and their country. Like you.

CARMEN: *(puffing herself up)* I'm the daughter of a high-ranking officer. . . .

IRMA: I know. There always has to be one in a brothel. But bear in mind that General, Bishop and Judge are, in real life. . . .

CARMEN: Which are you talking about?

IRMA: Real ones.

CARMEN: Which are real? The ones here?

IRMA: The others. In real life they're props of a display that 910 they have to drag in the mud of the real and commonplace. Here, Comedy and Appearance remain pure, and the Revels intact.

CARMEN: The revels that I indulge in. . . .

IRMA: *(interrupting her)* I know what they are: to forget theirs.

CARMEN: Do you blame me for that?

IRMA: And theirs are to forget yours. They, too, love their children. Afterwards.

*(Buzzing again, as before,* IRMA, *who has been sitting all the while near the apparatus, turns about, looks into the viewfinder and puts the receiver to her ear. Carmen goes back to her accounts.)*

CARMEN: *(without raising her head)* The Chief of Police?

IRMA: *(describing the scene)* No. The waiter who just arrived. 920 He's going to start complaining again . . . there he goes, he's flaring up because Elyane is handing him a white apron.

CARMEN: I warned you. He wants a pink one.

IRMA: Go to the Five-and-Ten tomorrow, if it's open. And buy a duster for the railwayman. A green one.

CARMEN: If only Elyane doesn't forget to drop the tip on the floor. He demands a true revolt. And dirty glasses.

IRMA: They all want everything to be as true as possible. . . . Minus something indefinable, so that it won't be true. *(Changing her tone.)* Carmen, it was I who decided to call 930 my establishment a house of illusions, but I'm only the manager. Each individual, when he rings the bell and enters, brings his own scenario, perfectly thought out. My job is merely to rent the hall and furnish the props, actors and actresses. My dear, I've succeeded in lifting it from the ground—do you see what I mean? I unloosed it long ago and it's flying. I cut the moorings. It's flying. Or, if you like, it's sailing in the sky, and I with it. Well, my darling . . . may I say something tender—every madame always, traditionally, has a slight partiality for one of her young 940 ladies. . . .

CARMEN: I had noticed it, Madame, and I too, at times. . . .

*(She looks at Irma languidly.)*

IRMA: *(standing up and looking at her)* I have a strange feeling, Carmen. *(A long pause.)* But let's continue. Darling, the house really does take off, leaves the earth, sails in the sky when, in the secrecy of my heart, I call myself, but with great precision, a keeper of a bawdy-house. Darling, when secretly, in silence, I repeat to myself silently, "You're a bawd, boss of a whore-house," darling, everything *(suddenly*

950 *lyrical),* everything flies off—chandeliers, mirrors, carpets, pianos, caryatids and my studios, my famous studios: the studio known as the Hay Studio, hung with rustic scenes, the Studio of the Hangings, spattered with blood and tears, the Throne-room Studio, draped in velvet with a fleur-de-lis pattern, the Studio of Mirrors, the Studio of State, the Studio of Perfumed Foundations, the Urinal Studio, the Amphitrite Studio, the Moonlight Studio, everything flies off: studios—Oh! I was forgetting the studio of the beggars, of the tramps, where filth and poverty are magnified. To con-

960 tinue: studios, girls, . . . *(she thinks again.)* Oh! I was forgetting: the most beautiful of all, ultimate adornment, crown of the edifice—if the construction of it is ever completed. I speak of the Funeral Studio, adorned with marble urns, my Studio of Solemn Death, the Tomb! The Mausoleum Studio. . . . To continue: studios, girls, crystals, laces, balconies, everything takes it on the lam, rises up and carries me off!

*(A long pause. The two women are standing motionless, facing each other.)*

CARMEN: How well you speak.

IRMA: *(modestly)* I went through elementary school.

CARMEN: So I assumed. My father, the artillery colonel. . . .

970 IRMA: *(correcting her sharply)* You mean calvary, my dear.

CARMEN: Excuse me. That's right. The cavalry colonel wanted me to have an education. Alas. . . . As for you, you've been successful. You've been able to surround your loveliness with a sumptuous theatre, a gala, the splendours of which envelop you and hide you from the world. Your whoredom required such pomp. But what about me, am I to have only myself and be only myself? No, Madame. Thanks to vice and men's heartache, I too have had my moment of glory! With the receiver at your ear, you could see me through the

980 view-finder, standing erect, sovereign and kind, maternal yet feminine, with my heel on the cardboard snake and the pink paper-roses. You could also see the bank-clerk from the National City kneeling before me and swooning when I appeared to him. Unfortunately he had his back to you and so you weren't aware of the ecstasy on his face and the wild pounding of my heart. My blue veil, my blue robe, my blue apron, my blue eyes. . . .

IRMA: They're hazel.

CARMEN: They were blue that day. For him I was Heaven in

990 person descending on his brow. I was a Madonna to whom a Spaniard might have prayed and sworn an oath. He hymned me, fusing me with his beloved colour, and when he carried me to bed, it was into the blue that he penetrated. But I won't ever appear to him again.

IRMA: I've offered you Saint Theresa.

CARMEN: I'm not prepared, Mme Irma. One has to know what the client's going to require. Has everything been worked out?

IRMA: Every whore should be able—I hope you'll excuse me,

1000 but since we've gone so far, let's talk man to man—should be able to handle any situation.

CARMEN: I'm one of your whores, Mme Irma, and one of your best. I boast of it. In the course of an evening, I can . . .

IRMA: I'm aware of your feats. But when you start glorifying yourself as soon as you hear the word whore, which you keep repeating to yourself and which you flaunt as if it were a title, it's not quite the same as when I use the word to designate a function. But you're right, darling, to extol your profession and to glory in it. Make it shine. Let it illuminate you, if that's the only thing you have. *(Tenderly)* I'll do all I 1010 can to help you. . . . You're not only the purest jewel of all my girls, you're the one on whom I bestow all my tenderness. But stay with me. . . . Would you dare leave me when everything is cracking up everywhere? Death—the real thing—is at my door, it's beneath my windows. . . .

*(Machine-gun fire.)*

You hear?

CARMEN: The Army is fighting bravely.

IRMA: And the Rebels even more bravely. And we're in the shadow of the cathedral, a few feet from the Archbishop's Palace. There's no price on my head. No, that would be too 1020 much to expect, but it's known that I serve supper to prominent people. So they're out to get me. And there are no men in the house.

CARMEN: There's Arthur.

IRMA: Are you trying to be funny? He's no man, he's my stage-prop. Besides, as soon as his session is over, I'll send him to look for George.

CARMEN: Assuming the worst. . . .

IRMA: If the rebels win? I'm a goner. They're workers. Without imagination. Prudish and maybe chaste. 1030

CARMEN: It won't take them long to get used to debauchery. Just wait till they get a little bored. . . .

IRMA: You're wrong. Or else they won't let themselves get bored. But I'm the one who's most exposed. For you it's different. In every revolution there's the glorified whore who sings an anthem and is virginified. That'll be you. The others'll piously bring water for the dying to drink. Afterwards . . . they'll marry you off. Would you like to get married?

CARMEN: Orange blossoms, tulle . . . 1040

IRMA: Wonderful! To you, getting married means masquerading. Darling, you certainly are one of us. No, I can't imagine you married either. Besides, what they're really dreaming of doing is murdering us. We'll have a lovely death, Carmen. It will be terrible and sumptuous. They may break into my studios, shatter the crystals, tear the brocades and slit our throats. . . .

CARMEN: They'll take pity. . . .

IRMA: They won't. They'll thrill at the thought that their fury is sacrilegious. All bedraggled, with caps on their heads, or in 1050 helmets and boots, they'll destroy us by fire and sword. It'll be very beautiful. We oughtn't to wish for any other kind of end, and you, you're thinking of leaving. . . .

CARMEN: But Mme Irma. . . .

IRMA: Yes, yes. When the house is about to go up in flames, when the rose is about to be stabbed, all you think of, Carmen, is fleeing.

CARMEN: If I wanted to be elsewhere, you know very well why.

IRMA: Your daughter is dead. . . .

1060 CARMEN: Madame!

IRMA: Whether dead or alive, your daughter is dead. Think of the charming grave, adorned with daisies and artificial wreaths, at the far end of the garden . . . and that garden in your heart, where you'll be able to look after it. . . .

CARMEN: I'd have loved to see her again. . . .

IRMA: You'll keep her image in the image of the garden and the garden in your heart under the flaming robe of Saint Theresa. And you hesitate? I offer you the very finest of deaths, and you hesitate? Are you a coward?

1070 CARMEN: You know very well I'm devoted to you.

IRMA: I'll teach you figures! The wonderful figures that we'll spend the nights together calligraphing.

CARMEN: (*softly*) The war is raging. As you said, it's the horde.

IRMA: (*triumphantly*) The horde, but we have our cohorts, our armies, our hosts, legions, battalions, vessels, heralds, clarions, trumpets, our colours, streamers, standards, banners . . . to lead us to catastrophe! Death? It's certain death, but with what speed and with what dash! . . . (*Melancholically*) Unless George is still all-powerful. . . . And above all
1080 if he can get through the horde and come and save us. (*A deep sigh.*) Now come and dress me. But first I want to see how Rachel's getting on.

(*Same business as before.* IRMA *glues her eye to the view-finder. A pause. She peers.*)

With this gadget I can see them and even hear their sighs.

(*A pause. She looks into the apparatus.*)

Christ is leaving with his paraphernalia. I've never been able to understand why he has himself tied to the cross with ropes he brings in a valise. Maybe they're ropes that have been blessed. Where does he put them when he gets home? Who the hell cares! Let's take a look at Rachel. (*She pushes down another switch.*) Ah, they've finished. They're talking.
1090 They're putting away the little arrows, the bow, the gauze bandages, the white officer's cap. . . . No, I don't at all like the way they're looking at each other: it's too candid and straightforward. (*She turns to* CARMEN.) There you have the dangers of regularity. It would be a catastrophe if my clients and girls smiled at each other affectionately. It would be an even greater catastrophe than if it were a question of love. (*She presses the switch mechanically and lays down the receiver. Pensively:*) Arthur's session must be over. He'll be along in a minute. . . . Dress me.

1100 CARMEN: What are you wearing?

IRMA: The cream-coloured négligé.

(CARMEN *opens the door of a closet and takes out the négligé, while* IRMA *unhooks her suit.*)

Tell me, Carmen, what about Chantal? . . .

CARMEN: Madame?

IRMA: Yes. About Chantal, tell me, what do you know about her?

CARMEN: I've questioned all the girls: Rosine, Elyane, Florence, Marlyse. They've each prepared a little report. I'll let you have them. But I didn't get much out of them. It's possible to spy beforehand. During the fighting, it's harder. For
1110 one thing, the camps are more sharply defined. You can choose. When there's peace, it's too vague. You don't quite

know whom you're betraying. Nor even whether you're betraying. There's no news about Chantal. They don't even know whether she's still alive.

IRMA: But, tell me, you wouldn't have any scruples about it?

CARMEN: None at all. Entering a brothel means rejecting the world. Here I am and here I stay. Your mirrors and orders and the passions are my reality. What jewels are you wearing?

IRMA: The diamonds. My jewels. They're the only things I have 1120 that are real. I feel everything else is sham. I have my jewels as others have little girls in gardens. Who's double-crossing? You're hesitating.

CARMEN: The girls all mistrust me. I collect their little report. I pass it on to you. You pass it on to the police. The police check on it. . . . Me, I know nothing.

IRMA: You're cautious. Give me a handkerchief.

CARMEN: (*bringing a lace handkerchief*) Viewed from here, where, in any case, men show their naked selves, life seems to me so remote, so profound, that it has all the unreality of 1130 a film or of the birth of Christ in the manger. When I'm in a room with a man and he forgets himself so far as to say to me: "The arsenal will be taken tomorrow night," I feel as if I were reading an obscene scrawl. His act becomes as mad, as . . . voluminous as those described in a certain way on certain walls. . . . No, I'm not cautious.

(*A knocking.* IRMA *gives a start. She rushes to the apparatus and, by means of a mechanism operated by a button, conceals it in the wall. In the course of the scene with Arthur, Carmen undresses and then dresses* IRMA, *so that the latter is ready just when the Chief of Police arrives.*)

IRMA: Come in!

(*The door opens. Enter* THE EXECUTIONER, *whom hereafter we shall call* ARTHUR. *Classical pimp's outfit: light grey suit, white felt hat, etc. He finishes knotting his tie.*)

IRMA: (*examining him minutely*) Is the session over? He went through it fast.

ARTHUR: Yes, the little geezer's buttoning up. He's pooped. 1140 Two sessions in half an hour. With all that shooting in the street, I wonder whether he'll get back to his hotel. (*He imitates the* JUDGE *in Scene Two.*) Minos judges you. . . . Minos weighs you . . . Cerberus? Bow-wow! Bow-wow! (*He shows his fangs and laughs.*) Hasn't the Chief of Police arrived?

IRMA: You went easy, I hope? Last time, the poor girl was laid up for two days.

(CARMEN *has brought the cream-coloured négligé.* IRMA *is now in her chemise.*)

ARTHUR: Don't pull that kind-hearted-whore stuff on me. Both last time and tonight she got what was coming to her: in dough and in wallops. Right on the line. The banker wants 1150 to see stripes on her back. So I stripe it.

IRMA: At least you don't get any pleasure out of it?

ARTHUR: Not with her. You're my only love. And a job's a job. I'm conscientious about my work.

IRMA: (*sternly*) I'm not jealous of the girl, but I wouldn't want you to disable the personnel. It's getting harder and harder to replace.

ARTHUR: I tried a couple of times to draw marks on her back

with purple paint, but it didn't work. The old guy inspects
1160   her when he arrives and insists I deliver her in good shape.

IRMA: Paint? Who gave you permission? (*To* CARMEN) My Turkish slippers, darling.

ARTHUR: (*shrugging his shoulders*) What's one illusion more or less! I thought I was doing the right thing. But don't worry. Now I whip, I flagellate, she screams, and he crawls.

IRMA: See to it she doesn't scream so loud. The house is being watched.

ARTHUR: The radio has just announced that all the north part of town was taken last night. And the Judge wants scream-
1170   ing. The Bishop's less dangerous. He's satisfied with pardoning sins.

CARMEN: Though he gets pleasure out of pardoning, he expects you to commit them. No, the best of the lot is the one you tie up, spank, whip and soothe, and then he snores.

ARTHUR: Who cuddles him? (*To Carmen*) You? Do you give him your breast?

CARMEN: (*curtly*) I do my job right. And in any case, Mr. Arthur, you're wearing an outfit that doesn't allow you to joke. The pimp has a grin, never a smile.

1180 IRMA: She's right.

ARTHUR: How much did you take in today?

IRMA: (*on the defensive*) Carmen and I haven't finished the accounts.

ARTHUR: But I have. According to my calculations, it runs to a good two hundred.

IRMA: That's possible. In any case, don't worry. I don't cheat.

ARTHUR: I believe you, my love, but I can't help it: the figures arrange themselves in my head. Two hundred! War, rebellion, shooting, frost, hail, rain, showers of shit, nothing stops
1190   them! On the contrary. People are killing each other in the streets, the joint's being watched, but all the same, they come charging in. As for me, I've got you right at home, sweetie-pie, otherwise. . . .

IRMA: (*bluntly*) You'd be cowering in a cellar, paralysed with fear.

ARTHUR: (*ambiguously*) I'd do as the others do, my love. I'd wait to be saved by the Chief of Police. You're not forgetting my little percentage?

IRMA: I give you what you need.

1200 ARTHUR: My love! I've ordered the silk shirts. And do you know what kind of silk? And what colour? In the purple silk of your blouse!

IRMA: (*tenderly*) All right, cut it. Not in front of Carmen.

ARTHUR: Then it's O.K.?

IRMA: (*weakening*) Yes.

ARTHUR: How much?

IRMA: (*regaining her self-possession*) We'll see. I have to go over the accounts with Carmen. (*Winningly*) It'll be as much as I can. For the moment, you've absolutely got to go
1210   to meet George. . . .

ARTHUR: (*with insolent irony*) I beg your pardon, my beloved?

IRMA: (*curtly*) To go to meet Mr. George. To Police Headquarters, if necessary, and to let him know that I'm relying only on him.

ARTHUR: (*slightly uneasy*) You're kidding, I hope? . . .

IRMA: (*with sudden sternness*) The tone of my last remark should answer your question. I'm no longer playing. Or, if you like, not the same role. And there's no longer any need

for you to play the mean, soft-hearted pimp. Do as I tell you, but first take the atomizer. (*To Carmen, who brings the ob-* 1220 *ject*) Give it to him. (*To Arthur*) And on your knees!

ARTHUR: (*he puts one knee on the floor and sprays Irma*) In the street? All by myself? . . . Me? . . .

IRMA: (*standing in front of him*) I've got to know what's happening to George. I can't remain unprotected.

ARTHUR: I'm here . . .

IRMA: (*shrugging*) I've got to defend my jewels, my studios, my girls. The Chief of Police should have been here a half-hour ago. . . .

ARTHUR: (*woefully*) Me in the street! . . . But it's hailing . . . 1230 they're shooting. . . . (*He points to his suit.*) And I got dressed up to stay here, to go walking through the corridors and look at myself in your mirrors. And also for you to see me dressed up as a pimp. . . . All I've got to protect me is the silk. . . .

IRMA: (*to Carmen*) Let me have my bracelets, Carmen. (*To Arthur*) And you, spray.

ARTHUR: I'm not meant for outdoors. I've been living within your walls too long. Even my skin couldn't tolerate the fresh air . . . maybe if I had a veil. . . . What if I were recog- 1240 nized? . . .

IRMA: (*irritated, and pivoting in front of the atomizer*) Hug the walls. (*A pause.*) Take this revolver.

ARTHUR: (*frightened*) On me?

IRMA: In your pocket.

ARTHUR: My pocket! Imagine me having to shoot? . . .

IRMA: (*gently*) So now you're crammed full of what you are? Gorged?

ARTHUR: Gorged, that's right. . . . (*A pause.*) Rested, gorged . . . but if I go out into the street. . . . 1250

IRMA: (*commandingly, but gently*) You're right. No revolver. But take off your hat and go where I tell you, and come back and let me know what's going on. You have a session this evening. Did you know? (*He tosses his hat away.*)

ARTHUR: (*on his way to the door*) This evening? Another one? What is it?

IRMA: I thought I told you: a corpse.

ARTHUR: (*with disgust*) What am I supposed to do with it?

IRMA: Nothing. You're to remain motionless, and you'll be buried. You'll be able to rest. 1260

ARTHUR: Ah, because I'm the one who . . . ? Ah, O.K. All right. Who's the client? Someone new?

IRMA: (*mysteriously*) A very important person, and stop asking questions. Get going.

ARTHUR: (*starting to leave, then hesitating, timidly*) Don't I get a kiss?

IRMA: When we come back. If we come back.

(*Exit* ARTHUR, *still on his knees.*)
(*But the door at the right has already opened and, without knocking,* THE CHIEF OF POLICE *enters. Heavy fur-lined coat, hat, cigar.* CARMEN *starts running to call Arthur back, but* THE CHIEF OF POLICE *steps in front of her.*)

THE CHIEF OF POLICE: No, no, stay, Carmen. I like having you around. As for the gigolo, let him find me.

(*He keeps his hat and coat on, does not remove his cigar from his mouth, but bows to* IRMA *and kisses her hand.*)

1270 IRMA: (breathlessly) Put your hand here. (On her breast.) I'm all tense. I'm still wrought up. I knew you were on your way, which meant you were in danger. I waited for you all a-tremble . . . while perfuming myself. . . .

THE CHIEF OF POLICE: (while taking off his hat, coat, gloves, and jacket) All right, that'll do. Let's cut the comedy. The situation's getting more and more serious—it's not desperate, but it will be before long—hap-pi-ly! The Royal Palace is surrounded. The Queen's in hiding. The city—it's a miracle that I got through—the city's being ravaged by fire and
1280 sword. Out there the rebellion is tragic and joyous, whereas in this house everything's dying a slow death. So, today's my day. By tonight I'll be in the grave or on a pedestal. So whether I love you or desire you is unimportant. How are things going at the moment?

IRMA: Marvellously. I had some great performances.

THE CHIEF OF POLICE: (impatiently) What kind?

IRMA: Carmen has a talent for description. Ask her.

THE CHIEF OF POLICE: (to Carmen) Tell me, Carmen, still . . . ?

CARMEN: Yes, sir, still. Still the pillars of the Empire: the
1290 Judge. . . .

THE CHIEF OF POLICE: (ironically) Our allegories, our talking weapons. And is there also . . . ?

CARMEN: As every week, a new theme.

(THE CHIEF OF POLICE makes a gesture of curiosity.)

This time it's the baby who gets slapped, spanked, tucked in, then cries and is cuddled.

THE CHIEF OF POLICE: (impatiently) Fine. But. . . .

CARMEN: He's charming, Sir. And so sad!

THE CHIEF OF POLICE: (irritably) Is that all?

CARMEN: And so pretty when you unswaddle him. . . .

1300 THE CHIEF OF POLICE: (with rising fury) Are you pulling my leg, Carmen? I'm asking you whether I'm in it?

CARMEN: Whether you're in it?

IRMA: (ironically, though we do not know with whom she is ironic) You're not in it.

THE CHIEF OF POLICE: Not yet? (To Carmen.) Well, yes or no, is there a simulation. . . .

CARMEN: (bewildered) Simulation?

THE CHIEF OF POLICE: You idiot! Yes! An impersonation of the Chief of Police?

(Very heavy silence.)

1310 IRMA: The time's not ripe. My dear, your function isn't noble enough to offer dreamers an image that would console them. Perhaps because it lacks illustrious ancestors? No, my dear fellow. . . . You have to resign yourself to the fact that your image does not yet conform to the liturgies of the brothel.

THE CHIEF OF POLICE: Who's represented in them?

IRMA: You know who. You have your index-cards. (She enumerates on her fingers.) There are two kings of France with coronation ceremonies and different rituals, an admiral
1320 at the stern of his sinking destroyer, a dey of Algiers surrendering, a fireman putting out a fire, a goat attached to a stake, a housewife returning from market, a pickpocket, a robbed man who's bound and beaten up, a Saint Sebastian, a farmer in his barn . . . but no chief of police . . . nor colonial administrator, though there is a missionary dying on the

cross, and Christ in person.

THE CHIEF OF POLICE: (after a pause) You're forgetting the mechanic.

IRMA: He doesn't come any more. What with tightening screws, he'd have ended by constructing a machine. And it 1330 might have worked. Back to the factory!

THE CHIEF OF POLICE: So not a single one of your clients has had the idea . . . the remotest idea, the barest suggestion. . . .

IRMA: No. I know you do what you can. You try hatred and love. But glory gives you the cold shoulder.

THE CHIEF OF POLICE: (forcefully) My image is growing bigger and bigger. It's becoming colossal. Everything around me repeats and reflects it. And you've never seen it represented in this place? 1340

IRMA: In any case, even if it were celebrated here, I wouldn't see anything. The ceremonies are secret.

THE CHIEF OF POLICE: You liar. You've got secret peep-holes in every wall. Every partition, every mirror, is rigged. In one place, you can hear the sighs, in another the echo of the moans. You don't need me to tell you that brothel tricks are mainly mirror tricks. . . . (Very sadly) Nobody yet! But I'll make my image detach itself from me. I'll make it penetrate into your studios, force its way in, reflect and multiply itself. Irma, my function weighs me down. Here, it will appear to 1350 me in the blazing light of pleasure and death. (Musingly) Of death.

IRMA: You must keep killing, my dear George.

THE CHIEF OF POLICE: I do what I can, I assure you. People fear me more and more.

IRMA: Not enough. You must plunge into darkness, into shit and blood. (With sudden anguish) And must kill whatever remains of our love.

THE CHIEF OF POLICE: (curtly) Everything's dead.

IRMA: That's a fine victory. So you've got to kill what's around 1360 you.

THE CHIEF OF POLICE: (very irritated) I repeat: I do what I can to prove to the nation that I'm a leader, a lawgiver, a builder. . . .

IRMA: (uneasily) You're raving. Or else you really do expect to build an empire. In which case you're raving.

THE CHIEF OF POLICE: (with conviction) When the rebellion's been put down, and put down by me, when I've the nation behind me and been appealed to by the Queen, nothing can stop me. Then, and only then, will you see who I now am! 1370 (Musingly) Yes, my dear, I want to build an empire . . . so that the empire will, in exchange, build me. . . .

IRMA: . . . a tomb.

THE CHIEF OF POLICE: (somewhat taken aback) But, after all, why not? Doesn't every conqueror have one? So? (Exalted) Alexandria! I'll have my tomb, Irma. And when the cornerstone is laid, you'll be my guest of honour.

IRMA: Thank you. (To Carmen) Carmen, the tea.

THE CHIEF OF POLICE: (to Carmen, who is about to leave) Just a minute, Carmen. What do you think of the idea? 1380

CARMEN: That you want to merge your life with one long funeral, sir.

THE CHIEF OF POLICE: (aggressively) Is life anything else? You seem to know everything—so tell me: in this sumptuous theatre where every moment a drama is performed—in the sense that the outside world says a mass is celebrated—what have you observed?

CARMEN: *(after a hesitation)* As for anything serious, anything worth reporting, only one thing: that without the thighs it contained, a pair of pants on a chair is beautiful, sir. Emptied of our little old men, our ornaments are deathly sad. They're the ones that are placed on the catafalques of high dignitaries. They cover only corpses that never stop dying. And yet. . . .

IRMA: *(to Carmen)* That's not what the Chief of Police is asking.

THE CHIEF OF POLICE: I'm used to Carmen's speeches. *(To Carmen)* You were saying: and yet . . . ?

CARMEN: And yet, I'm sure that the sudden joy in their eyes when they see the cheap finery is really the gleam of innocence. . . .

THE CHIEF OF POLICE: People claim that our house sends them to Death. *(Suddenly a ringing.* IRMA *starts. A pause.)*

IRMA: Someone's opened the door. Who can it be at this hour? *(To Carmen)* Carmen, go down and shut the door.

(CARMEN *exits. A rather long silence between* IRMA *and* THE CHIEF OF POLICE, *who remain alone.)*

THE CHIEF OF POLICE: My tomb!

IRMA: It was I who rang. I wanted to be alone with you for a moment. *(A pause, during which they look into each other's eyes seriously.)* Tell me, George. . . . *(She hesitates.)* Do you still insist on keeping up the game? No, no, don't be impatient. Aren't you tired of it?

THE CHIEF OF POLICE: But. . . . In a little while I'll be going home.

IRMA: If you can. If the rebellion leaves you free to go.

THE CHIEF OF POLICE: The rebellion is a game. From here you can't see anything of the outside, but every rebel is playing a game. And he loves his game.

IRMA: But supposing they let themselves be carried beyond the game? I mean if they get so involved in it that they destroy and replace everything. Yes, yes, I know, there's always the false detail that reminds them that at a certain moment, at a certain point in the drama, they have to stop, and even withdraw. . . . But what if they're so carried away by passion that they no longer recognize anything and leap, without realizing it, into. . . .

THE CHIEF OF POLICE: You mean into reality? What of it? Let them try. I do as they do, I penetrate right into the reality that the game offers us, and since I have the upper hand, it's I who score.

IRMA: They'll be stronger than you.

THE CHIEF OF POLICE: Why do you say "they'll be"? I've left the members of my bodyguard in one of your studios. So I'm always in contact with my various departments. All right, enough of that. Are you or aren't you the mistress of a house of illusions? Good. If I come to your place, it's to find satisfaction in your mirrors and their trickery. *(Tenderly)* Don't worry. Everything will be just as it's always been.

IRMA: I don't know why, but today I feel uneasy. Carmen seems strange to me. The rebels—how shall I put it?—have a kind of gravity. . . .

THE CHIEF OF POLICE: Their role requires it.

IRMA: No, no . . . of determination. They walk by the windows threateningly, but they don't sing. The threat is in their eyes.

THE CHIEF OF POLICE: What of it? Supposing it is, do you take me for a coward? Do you think I should give up and go home?

IRMA: *(pensively)* No. Besides, I think it's too late.

THE CHIEF OF POLICE: Do you have any news?

IRMA: From Chantal, before she lit out. The power-house will be occupied around 3 a.m.

THE CHIEF OF POLICE: Are you sure? Who told her?

IRMA: The partisans of the Fourth Sector.

THE CHIEF OF POLICE: That's plausible. How did she find out?

IRMA: It's through her that there were leaks, and through her alone. So don't belittle my house. . . .

THE CHIEF OF POLICE: Your cat-house, my love.

IRMA: Cat-house, whore-house, bawdy-house. Brothel. Fuckery. Call it anything you like. So Chantal's the only one who's on the other side. . . . She lit out. But before she did, she confided in Carmen, and Carmen's no fool.

THE CHIEF OF POLICE: Who tipped her off?

IRMA: Roger. The plumber. How do you imagine him? Young and handsome? No. He's forty. Thick-set. Serious, with ironic eyes. Chantal spoke to him. I put him out: too late. He belongs to the Andromeda network.

THE CHIEF OF POLICE: Andromeda? Splendid. The rebellion's riding high, it's moving out of this world. If it gives its sectors the names of constellations, it'll evaporate in no time and be metamorphosed into song. Let's hope the songs are beautiful.

IRMA: And what if their songs give the rebels courage? What if they're willing to die for them?

THE CHIEF OF POLICE: The beauty of their songs will make them soft. Unfortunately, they haven't yet reached the point of either beauty or softness. In any case, Chantal's tender passions were providential.

IRMA: Don't bring God into. . . .

THE CHIEF OF POLICE: I'm a freemason. Therefore. . . .

IRMA: You? You never told me.

THE CHIEF OF POLICE: *(solemnly)* Sublime Prince of the Royal Secret.

IRMA: *(ironically)* You, a brother in a little apron! With a hood and taper and a little mallet! That's odd. *(A pause.)* You too?

THE CHIEF OF POLICE: Why? You too?

IRMA: *(with mock solemnity)* I'm a guardian of far more solemn rites. *(Suddenly sad)* Since that's all I am now.

THE CHIEF OF POLICE: As usual, you're going to bring up our grand passion.

IRMA: *(gently)* No, not our passion, but the time when we loved each other.

THE CHIEF OF POLICE: Well, would you like to give a historical account of it and deliver a eulogy? You think my visits would have less zest if you didn't flavour them with the memory of a pretended innocence?

IRMA: It's a question of tenderness. Neither the wildest concoctions of my clients nor my own fancies nor my constant endeavour to enrich my studios with new themes nor the passing of time nor the gilding and crystals nor bitter cold can dispel the moments when you cuddled in my arms or keep me from remembering them.

THE CHIEF OF POLICE: Do you really miss them?

IRMA: *(tenderly)* I'd give my kingdom to relive a single one of them! And you know which one. I need just one word of truth—as when one looks at one's wrinkles at night, or rinses one's mouth. . . .

THE CHIEF OF POLICE: It's too late. (*A pause.*) Besides, we couldn't cuddle each other eternally. You don't know what I was already secretly moving towards when I was in your arms.

1510 IRMA: I know that I loved you.

THE CHIEF OF POLICE: It's too late. Could you give up Arthur?

IRMA: It was you who forced him on me. You insisted on there being a man here—against my better judgment—in a domain that should have remained virgin. . . . You fool, don't laugh. Virgin, that is, sterile. But you wanted a pillar, a shaft, a phallus present—an upright bulk. Well, it's here. You saddled me with that hunk of congested meat, that milksop with wrestler's arms. He may look like a strongman at a fair, but you don't realize how fragile he is. You stupidly forced

1520 him on me because you felt yourself ageing.

THE CHIEF OF POLICE: Be still.

IRMA: (*shrugging her shoulders*) And you relaxed here through Arthur. I need him now. I have no illusions. I'm his man and he relies on me, but I need that rugged shop-window dummy hanging on to my skirts. He's my body, as it were, but set beside me.

THE CHIEF OF POLICE: (*ironically*) What if I were jealous?

IRMA: Of that big doll made up as an executioner in order to satisfy a phony judge? You're kidding, but the spectacle of

1530 me under the spectacle of that magnificent body never used to bother you. . . . Let me repeat. . . .

THE CHIEF OF POLICE: (*he slaps Irma, who falls on the sofa*) And don't blubber or I'll break your jaw, and I'll send your joint up in smoke. I'll set fire to your hair and bush and I'll turn you loose. I'll light up the town with blazing whores. (*Very gently*) Do you think I'm capable of it?

IRMA: (*in a panting whisper*) Yes, darling.

THE CHIEF OF POLICE: All right, add up the accounts for me. If you like, you can deduct Apollo's crêpe de Chine. And hurry

1540 up. I've got to get back to my post. For the time being, I have to act. Afterwards. . . . Afterwards, things'll run themselves. My name will act in my place. Well, what about Arthur?

IRMA: (*submissively*) He'll be dead this evening.

THE CHIEF OF POLICE: Dead? You mean . . . really . . . really dead?

IRMA: (*with resignation*) Come, come, George, the way one dies here.

THE CHIEF OF POLICE: Indeed? Meaning. . . .

1550 IRMA: The Minister. . . . (*She is interrupted by the voice of* CARMEN.)

CARMEN: (*in the wings*) Lock Studio 17! Elyane, hurry up! And lower the studio . . . no, no, wait . . . (*We hear the sound of a rusty cog-wheel, the kind made by certain old lifts. Enter* CARMEN.) Madame, the Queen's Envoy is in the drawing-room. . . .

(*The door opens, left, and* ARTHUR *appears, trembling and with his clothes torn.*)

ARTHUR: (*noticing the Chief of Police*) You here! You managed to get through?

IRMA: (*rushing to his arms*) Darling! What's the matter? Are

1560 you hurt? Speak!

ARTHUR: (*panting*) I tried to get to Police Headquarters. Impossible. The whole city's lit up with fires. The rebels are in

control practically everywhere. I don't think you can get back, sir. I was able to reach the Royal Palace, and I saw the Grand Chamberlain. He said he'd try to come. I might add that he shook my hand. And then I left. The women are the most excited. They're urging the men to loot and kill. But what was most awful was a girl who was singing. . . .

(*A shot is heard. A window-pane is shivered. Also a mirror near the bed.* ARTHUR *falls down, hit in the forehead by a bullet coming from outside.* CARMEN *bends over him, then rises to her feet again. Then* IRMA *bends over him and strokes his forehead.*)

THE CHIEF OF POLICE: In short, I'm stuck in the whore-house. That means I'll have to act from the whore-house. 1570

IRMA: (*to herself, bent over Arthur*) Can it be that everything's slipping away? Slipping between my fingers? . . . (*bitterly*) I still have my jewels . . . my rocks . . . and perhaps not for long. . . .

CARMEN: (*softly*) If the house is to be blown up. . . . Is Saint Theresa's costume in the closet, Mme Irma?

IRMA: (*anxiously*) At the left. But first have Arthur removed. I'm going to receive the Envoy.

## SCENE VI

*A public square, with patches of shadow. In the background, at some distance, we perceive the façade of the Grand Balcony, the blinds of which are drawn.* CHANTAL *and* ROGER *are locked in embrace. Three men seem to be watching over them. Black suits. Black sweaters. They are holding machine-guns which are pointed at the Grand Balcony.*

CHANTAL: Keep me, if you will, my love, but keep me in your heart. And wait for me. 1580

ROGER: I love you with your body, with your hair, your bosom, your belly, your guts, your fluids, your smells. Chantal, I love you in my bed. They. . . .

CHANTAL: (*smiling*) They don't care a rap about me. But without them, *I'd* be nothing.

ROGER: You're mine. I . . .

CHANTAL: (*annoyed*) I know. You dragged me from the grave. And no sooner do I shake off my wrappings than, ungrateful wretch that I am, I gad about like a trollop. I plunge into the adventure, and I escape you. (*Suddenly with tender irony.*) 1590 But Roger, my love, you know I love you, you and only you.

ROGER: You've just said the word: you're escaping me. I can't follow you in your heroic and stupid course.

CHANTAL: Ah ha! You're jealous of whom, or what? People say that I soar above the insurrection, that I'm its soul and voice, and you—you're rooted to the ground. That's why you're sad. . . .

ROGER: Chantal, please, don't be vulgar. If you can help. . . .

(*One of the men draws near.*)

THE MAN: (*to* ROGER) Well, is it yes or is it no?

ROGER: What if she stays there? 1600

THE MAN: I'm asking you to let us have her for two hours.

ROGER: Chantal belongs. . . .

CHANTAL: (*standing up*) To nobody!

ROGER: . . . To my section.

THE MAN: To the insurrection!

ROGER: If you want a woman to lead your men forward, then create one.

THE MAN: We looked for one, but there aren't any. We tried to build one up: nice voice, nice bosom, with the right kind of free and easy manner. But her eyes lacked fire, and you know that without fire. . . . We asked the North Section and the Port Section to let us have theirs; they weren't free.

CHANTAL: A woman like me? Another one? All I have is a hoarse voice and a face like an owl's. I give them or lend them for hatred's sake. I'm nothing, only my face, my voice, and inside me a sweet, poisonous kindness. D'you mean to tell me I have two popular rivals, two other poor devils? Let them come, I'll show them! I have no rival.

ROGER: (*exploding*) I snatched her—snatched her from a grave. She's already escaping me and mounting to the sky. If I lend her to you. . . .

THE MAN: We're not asking you for that. If we take her, we're hiring her.

CHANTAL: (*amused*) How much?

ROGER: Even if we let you have her to sing and spur on your district, if she gets bumped off we'll lose everything. No one can replace her.

THE MAN: She agreed to it.

ROGER: She doesn't belong to herself any more. She's ours. She's our sign. All that your women are good for is tearing up and carrying stones or reloading guns. I know that's useful, but. . . .

THE MAN: How many women do you want in exchange?

ROGER: (*thoughtfully*) Is a singer on the barricades as precious as all that?

THE MAN: How many? Ten women for Chantal?

(*A pause.*)

Twenty?

ROGER: Twenty women? You'd pay me twenty measly women, twenty oxen, twenty head of cattle? So Chantal's something special? And do you know where she comes from?

CHANTAL: (*to Roger, violently*) Every morning I go back—because at night I'm ablaze—I go back to a hovel and sleep—chastely, my love!—and drink myself into a stupor on red wine. And I, with my grating voice, my sham anger, my cameo eyes, my painted illumination, my Andalusian hair, I comfort and enchant the rabble. They'll win and my victory will be a strange one.

ROGER: (*thoughtfully*) Twenty women for Chantal?

THE MAN: (*sharply*) A hundred.

ROGER: (*still pensively*) And it's probably because of her that we'll win. She already embodies the Revolution. . . .

THE MAN: A hundred. You agree?

ROGER: Where are you taking her? And what'll she have to do?

CHANTAL: We'll see. Don't worry, I was born under a lucky star. As for the rest of it, I realize my power. The people love me, they listen to me, they follow me.

ROGER: What will she do?

THE MAN: Hardly anything. As you know, we're attacking the Palace at dawn. Chantal will go in first. She'll sing from a balcony. That's all.

ROGER: A hundred women. A thousand and maybe more. So she's no longer a woman. The creature they make of her out of rage and despair has her price. In order to fight against an image Chantal has frozen into an image. The fight is no

longer taking place in reality, but in the lists. Field azure. It's the combat of allegories. None of us know any longer why we revolted. So she was bound to come around to that.

THE MAN: Well, is it yes? Answer, Chantal. It's for you to answer.

CHANTAL: (*to the Man*) I'd like us to be alone for a moment. I've got something else to say.

(THE MAN *moves off and goes back into the shadow.*)

ROGER: (*violently*) I didn't steal you for you to become a unicorn or a two-headed eagle.

CHANTAL: You don't like unicorns.

ROGER: I've never been able to make love to them. (*He caresses her.*) Nor to you either.

CHANTAL: You mean I don't know how to love. I disappoint you. Yet I love you. And you hired me out for a hundred female diggers.

ROGER: Forgive me. I need them. And yet I love you. I love you and I don't know how to tell you. I can't sing. And singing is the last resort.

CHANTAL: I'll have to leave before day-break. If the North Section has come through, the Queen will be dead in an hour. It'll be the end of the Chief of Police. If not, we'll never get out of this bedlam.

ROGER: One minute more, my love, my life. It's still night.

CHANTAL: It's the hour when night breaks away from the day, my dove, let me go.

ROGER: The minutes without you will be unbearable.

CHANTAL: We won't be separated, I swear to you. I'll speak to them in an icy tone and at the same time I'll murmur words of love for you. You'll hear them from here, and I'll hear yours.

ROGER: They may keep you, Chantal. They're strong—strong as death.

CHANTAL: Don't be afraid, my love. I know their power. Your sweetness and tenderness are stronger. I'll speak to them with severity. I'll tell them what the people demand. They'll listen to me because they'll be afraid. Let me go.

ROGER: (*screaming*) Chantal, I love you!

CHANTAL: Ah, my love, it's because I love you that I must hurry.

ROGER: You love me?

CHANTAL: I love you because you're tender and sweet, you the hardest and sternest of men. And your sweetness and tenderness are such that they make you as light as a shred of tulle, subtle as a flake of mist, airy as a caprice. Your thick muscles, your arms, your thighs, your hands, are more unreal than the melting of day into night. You envelop me and I contain you.

ROGER: Chantal, I love you because you're hard and stern, you the tenderest and sweetest of women. And your sweetness and tenderness are such that they make you as stern as a lesson, hard as hunger, inflexible as a block of ice. Your breasts, your skin, your hair are more real than the certainty of noon. You envelop me and I contain you.

CHANTAL: When I stand before them, when I speak to them, I'll be hearing your sighs and moans and the beating of your heart. Let me go.

(*He holds her back.*)

ROGER: You still have time. There's still some shadow along the walls. You'll go round the back of the Archbishop's Palace. You know the way.

ONE OF THE REBELS: *(in a low voice)* It's time, Chantal. Day is breaking.

CHANTAL: Do you hear? They're calling me.

ROGER: *(suddenly irritated)* But why you? You'll never be able to speak to them.

CHANTAL: I, better than anyone. I'm gifted.

1730 ROGER: They're clever, cunning. . . .

CHANTAL: I'll invent gestures, postures, phrases. Before they even say a word, I'll understand, and you'll be proud of my victory.

ROGER: Let the others go. *(He cries out to the rebels.)* You go! Or me, if you're afraid. I'll tell them they must give in, because we're the law.

CHANTAL: Don't listen to him. He's drunk. *(To Roger)* All *they* can do is fight, and all *you* can do is love me. That's the role you've learned to play. As for me, it's something else. At 1740 least the brothel has been of some use to me: it's taught me the art of pretence, of acting. I've had to play so many roles that I know almost all of them. And I've had so many partners. . . .

ROGER: Chantal!

CHANTAL: And such artful ones, such cunning and eloquent ones, that my skill and trickery and eloquence are incomparable. I can be familiar with the Queen, the Hero, the General, the heroic Troops . . . and can fool them all.

ROGER: You know all the roles, don't you? Just now, you were 1750 reciting lines to me, weren't you?

CHANTAL: One learns fast. You yourself. . . .

*(The three rebels have drawn close.)*

ONE OF THE REBELS: *(pulling* CHANTAL*)* Cut the speeches. Get going.

ROGER: Chantal, stay!

*(*CHANTAL *goes off, led by the rebels.)*

CHANTAL: I envelop you and I contain you, my love. . . .

*(She disappears in the direction of The Balcony, pushed by the three men.)*

ROGER: *(alone)* . . . and I've had so many partners, and such artful ones, such cunning ones . . . that she did, after all, have to try to give them an answer. The one they wanted. In a little while she'll have cunning and artful partners. She'll be 1760 the answer they're waiting for.

*(As he speaks, the setting moves toward the left, the stage grows dark, and he himself, still speaking, moves off and into the wings. When the light goes on again, the setting of the next scene is in place.)*

SCENE VII

*The Funeral Studio in* MME IRMA'S *listing of the Studios. The studio is in ruins. The lace and velvet are torn. The artificial wreaths are tattered. An impression of desolation.* IRMA'S *dress is in rags. So is the suit of* THE CHIEF OF POLICE. ARTHUR'S *corpse is lying on a kind of fake tomb of fake black marble. Nearby, a new character,* THE COURT ENVOY. *Embassy uniform. He is the only one unscathed.* CARMEN *is dressed as at the*

beginning. *A tremendous explosion. Everything shatters.*

THE ENVOY: *(in a tone both airy and grave)* For more centuries than I can tell, the centuries have worn themselves thin refining me . . . subtilizing me . . . *(He smiles.)* From something or other about the explosion, from its power, in which was mingled a clinking of jewels and broken mirrors, I rather think it was the Royal Palace. *(The characters all look at each other, horror-stricken.)* Let us not display any emotion. So long as we are not like that. . . . *(He points to the corpse of Arthur.)*

IRMA: He didn't think he'd be acting his role of corpse this 1770 evening in earnest.

THE ENVOY: *(smiling)* Our dear Minister of the Interior would have been delighted had not he himself met the same fate. It is unfortunately I who have had to replace him in his mission here, and I have no taste for pleasures of this kind. *(He touches Arthur's corpse with his foot.)* Yes, this body would have sent our dear Minister into raptures.

IRMA: Not at all, your Excellency. It's make-believe that these gentlemen want. The Minister desired a fake corpse. But this one is real. Look at it: it's truer than life. His entire 1780 being is speeding towards immobility.

THE ENVOY: He was therefore meant for grandeur.

THE CHIEF OF POLICE: Him? He was a spineless dummy.

THE ENVOY: He was, like us, haunted by a quest of immobility. By what we call the hieratic. And, in passing, allow me to pay tribute to the imagination responsible for there being a funeral parlour in this house.

IRMA: *(proudly)* And you see only part of it.

THE ENVOY: Whose idea was it?

IRMA: The Wisdom of Nations, your Excellency. 1790

THE ENVOY: It does things well. But we were talking about the Queen, to protect whom is my mission.

THE CHIEF OF POLICE: You're going about it in a curious way. The Palace, according to what you say. . . .

THE ENVOY: *(smiling)* For the time being, Her Majesty is in safety. But time is pressing. The prelate is said to have been beheaded. The Archbishop's Palace has been ransacked. The Law Court and Military Headquarters have been routed. . . .

THE CHIEF OF POLICE: But what about the Queen? 1800

THE ENVOY: *(in a very light tone)* She's embroidering. For a moment she thought of nursing the wounded. But it was pointed out to her that, as the throne was threatened, she had to carry to an extreme the Royal prerogatives.

IRMA: Which are?

THE ENVOY: Absence. Her Majesty has retired to a chamber, in solitude. The disobedience of her people saddens her. She is embroidering a handkerchief. The design of it is as follows: the four corners will be adorned with poppy heads. In the middle of the handkerchief, embroidered in pale blue 1810 silk, will be a swan, resting on the water of a lake. That's the only point about which Her Majesty is troubled: will it be the water of a lake, a pond or a pool? Or simply of a tank or a cup? It is a grave problem. We have chosen it because it is insoluble, and the Queen can engross herself in an infinite meditation.

IRMA: Is the Queen amused?

THE ENVOY: Her Majesty is occupying herself in becoming entirely what she must be: the Queen. *(He looks at the corpse.)*

1820    She, too, is moving rapidly towards immobility.

IRMA: And she's embroidering.

THE ENVOY: No, Madame, I say the Queen is embroidering a handkerchief, for though it is my duty to describe her, it is also my duty to conceal her.

IRMA: Do you mean she's not embroidering?

THE ENVOY: I mean that the Queen is embroidering and that she is not embroidering. She picks her nose, examines the pickings and lies down again. Then, she dries the dishes.

IRMA: The Queen?

1830    THE ENVOY: She is not nursing the wounded. She is embroidering an invisible handkerchief. . . .

THE CHIEF OF POLICE: By God! What have you done with Her Majesty? I want a straight answer. I'm not amused. . . .

THE ENVOY: She is in a chest. She is sleeping. Wrapped in the folds of Royalty, she is snoring. . . .

THE CHIEF OF POLICE: (threateningly) Is the Queen dead?

THE ENVOY: (unperturbed) She is snoring and she is not snoring. Her head, which is tiny, supports, without wavering, a crown of metal and stones.

1840    THE CHIEF OF POLICE: (more and more threateningly) Enough of that. You said the Palace was in danger. . . . What's to be done? I still have almost the entire police force behind me. Those who are still with me are ready to die for me. . . . They know who I am and what I'll do for them. . . . I, too, have my role to play. But if the Queen is dead, everything is jeopardized. She's my support, it's in her name that I'm working to make a name for myself. How far has the rebellion gone? I want a clear answer.

THE ENVOY: You can judge from the state of this house. And 1850    from your own. . . . All seems lost.

IRMA: You belong to the Court, your Excellency. Before coming here, I was with the troops. That's where I won my first spurs. I can assure you that I've known worse situations. The populace—from which I broke away with a kick of my heels—the populace is howling beneath my windows, which have been multiplied by the bombs: my house stands its ground. My rooms aren't intact, but they've held up. My whores, except for one lunatic, are on the job. If the centre of the Palace is a woman like me. . . .

1860    THE ENVOY: (imperturbably) The Queen is standing on one foot in the middle of an empty room, and she. . . .

THE CHIEF OF POLICE: That'll do! I've had enough of your riddles. For me, the Queen has to be someone. And the situation has to be concrete. Describe it to me exactly. I've no time to waste.

THE ENVOY: Whom do you want to save?

THE CHIEF OF POLICE: The Queen!

CARMEN: The flag!

IRMA: My hide!

1870    THE ENVOY: (to the Chief of Police) If you're eager to save the Queen—and, beyond her, our flag, and all its gold fringe, and its eagle, cords and pole, would you describe them to me?

THE CHIEF OF POLICE: Until now I've served the things you mention, and served them with distinction, and without bothering to know any more about them than what I saw. And I'll continue. What's happening about the rebellion?

THE ENVOY: (resignedly) The garden gates will, for a moment longer, hold back the crowd. The guards are devoted, like us, with an obscure devotion. They'll die for their sovereign. 1880    They'll give their blood. Unhappily there won't be enough of it to drown the rebellion. Sand bags have been piled up in front of the doors. In order to confuse even reason, Her Majesty removes herself from one secret chamber to another, from the servants' hall to the Throne Room, from the latrines to the chicken-coop, the chapel, the guardroom. . . . She makes herself unfindable and thus attains a threatened invisibility. So much for the inside of the Palace.

THE CHIEF OF POLICE: What about the Generalissimo?

THE ENVOY: Gone mad. He wanders among the crowd, where 1890    nobody will harm him, protected by his madness.

THE CHIEF OF POLICE: What about the Attorney-General?

THE ENVOY: Died of fright.

THE CHIEF OF POLICE: And the Bishop?

THE ENVOY: His case is more difficult. The Church is secretive. Nothing is known about him. Nothing definite. His decapitated head was said to have been seen on the handlebars of a bicycle. Of course, the rumour was false. We're therefore relying entirely on you. But your orders aren't getting through.    1900

THE CHIEF OF POLICE: Down below, in the corridors and studios, I have enough loyal men to protect us all. They can remain in contact with my offices. . . .

THE ENVOY: (interrupting him) Are your men in uniform?

THE CHIEF OF POLICE: Of course. They're my bodyguard. Do you imagine me with a bodyguard in sport jackets? They're in uniform. Black ones. With my emblem. They're brave. They, too, want to win.

THE ENVOY: To save what?

(A pause.)

Won't you answer? Would it perturb you to see things as 1910    they are? To gaze at the world tranquilly and accept responsibility for your gaze, whatever it might see?

THE CHIEF OF POLICE: But, after all, in coming to see me, you did have something definite in mind, didn't you? You had a plan? Let's hear it.

(Suddenly a terrific blast. Both men, but not Irma, fall flat on the floor, then stand up again and dust each other off.)

THE ENVOY: That may have been the Royal Palace. Long live the Royal Palace!

IRMA: But then, just before . . . the explosion?

THE ENVOY: A royal palace is forever blowing up. In fact, that's exactly what it is: a continuous explosion.    1920

(Enter CARMEN. She throws a black sheet over the corpse of Arthur and tidies things up a bit.)

THE CHIEF OF POLICE: (aghast) But the Queen. . . . Then the Queen's under the rubble?

THE ENVOY: (smiling mysteriously) You need not worry. Her Majesty is in a safe place. And that phoenix, when dead, can rise up from the ashes of a royal palace. I can understand your impatience to prove your valour, your devotion . . . but the Queen will wait for you as long as necessary. (To Irma) I must pay tribute, Madame, to your coolness. And to your courage. They are worthy of the highest respect. . . . (Musingly) of the highest. . . .    1930

IRMA: You're forgetting to whom you're speaking. I may run a brothel, but I wasn't born of the marriage of the moon and a crocodile, I've lived among the people. . . . All the same, it was quite a blast. And the people. . . .

THE ENVOY: *(severely)* That's behind you. When life departs, the hands cling to a sheet. What significance has that rag when you're about to penetrate into the providential fixity?

IRMA: Sir? Do you mean I'm at my last gasp?

THE ENVOY: *(examining her, part by part)* Splendid head! 1940 Sturdy thighs! Solid shoulders!

IRMA: *(laughing)* So I've been told, and it didn't make me lose my head. In short, I'll make a presentable corpse if the rebels act fast and if they leave me intact. But if the Queen is dead. . . .

THE ENVOY: *(bowing)* Long live the Queen, Madame.

IRMA: *(first taken aback, then irritated)* I don't like to be kidded! Pack up your nonsense, and clear out.

THE ENVOY: *(spiritedly)* I've described the situation. The populace, in its joy and fury, is at the brink of ecstasy. It's for us 1950 to press it forward.

IRMA: Instead of standing here and talking drivel, go poke around for the Queen in the rubble of the Palace and pull her out. Even if slightly roasted. . . .

THE ENVOY: *(severely)* No. A queen who's been cooked and mashed up isn't presentable. And even when alive she was less beautiful than you.

IRMA: Her lineage was more ancient . . . she was older. . . . And, after all, maybe she was just as frightened as I.

THE CHIEF OF POLICE: It is in order to approach her, to be wor- 1960 thy of her, that one makes such a mighty effort. But what if one is Herself?

*(CARMEN stops in order to listen.)*

IRMA: I don't know how to talk. I'm always hemming and hawing.

THE ENVOY: All must unfold in a silence that etiquette allows no one to break.

THE CHIEF OF POLICE: I'm going to have the rubble of the Palace cleared away. If, as you said, the Queen was in a chest, it may be possible to save her.

THE ENVOY: *(shrugging his shoulders)* It was made of rose- 1970 wood! And it was so old, so worn. . . . *(To Irma, running his hand over the back of her neck)* Yes, it requires solid vertebrae . . . they've got to carry several pounds . . .

THE CHIEF OF POLICE: . . . and resist the axe, don't they? Irma, don't listen to him! *(To the Envoy.)* And what about me? I'm the strong-man of this country, but it's because I've based my power on the crown. I bamboozle the great majority, but it's because I had the smart idea of serving the Queen . . . even if at times I've seemed to do some shabby things . . . seemed to, d'you hear? . . . It's not Irma. . . .

1980 IRMA: *(to the Envoy)* I'm really very weak, your Excellency, and very frail. Though a while ago I was boasting. . . .

THE ENVOY: *(with authority)* Around this delicate and precious kernel we'll forge a shell of gold and iron. But you must make up your mind quickly.

THE CHIEF OF POLICE: *(furiously)* Above me! So Irma would be above *me!* All the trouble I've gone to in order to be master would be wasted effort. Whereas, nice and snug in her studio, all she'd have to do is nod her head. . . . If I'm in power, I'm willing to impose Irma. . . .

THE ENVOY: Impossible. It's from her that you must derive your 1990 authority. She must appear by divine right. Don't forget that you're not yet represented in her studios.

IRMA: Allow me just a little more respite. . . .

THE ENVOY: A few seconds, for time is pressing.

THE CHIEF OF POLICE: If only there were some way of knowing what the late sovereign would have thought of it. We can't decide just like that. To appropriate a heritage. . . .

THE ENVOY: *(scornfully)* You're knuckling under already. Do you tremble if there's no authority above you to decide? But it's for Mme Irma to declare. . . . 2000

IRMA: *(in a highfalutin tone)* In the records of our family, which goes a long way back, there was some question of. . . .

THE ENVOY: *(severely)* Nonsense, Mme Irma. In our vaults, genealogists are working day and night. History is submissive to them. I said we hadn't a minute to waste in conquering our people, but beware! Although the populace may worship you, its high-flown pride is capable of sacrificing you. It sees you as red, either crimson or blood-red. If it kills its idols and thrusts them into the sewers, it will sweep you up 2010 with them. . . .

*(The same explosion is heard again. THE ENVOY smiles.)*

THE CHIEF OF POLICE: It's an enormous risk. . . .

CARMEN: That's for Mme Irma to decide. *(To Irma.)* The ornaments are ready.

IRMA: *(to the Envoy)* Are you quite sure of what you're saying? Do you really know what's going on? What about your spies?

THE ENVOY: They inform us as accurately as the peep-holes that peer into your studios. *(Smiling.)* And I may add that we consult them with the same pleasurable thrill. But we must act fast. We're engaged in a race against the clock. It's we or 2020 they. Mme. Irma, think speedily.

IRMA: *(holding her head in her hands)* I'm hurrying, sir. I'm approaching my destiny as fast as I can. *(To CARMEN)* Go see what they're doing.

CARMEN: I've locked them up.

IRMA: Get them ready.

THE ENVOY: *(to Carmen)* What about you, what's to be done with you?

CARMEN: I'm here for eternity.

*(Exit CARMEN.)*

THE ENVOY: One other matter, a more delicate one. I men- 2030 tioned an image that for some days now has been mounting in the sky of the revolution.

IRMA: The revolution has its sky too?

THE ENVOY: Don't envy it. Chantal's image is circulating in the streets. An image that resembles her and does not resemble her. She towers above the battles. At first, people were fighting against illustrious and illusory tyrants, then for freedom. Tomorrow they'll be ready to die for Chantal alone.

IRMA: The ungrateful wretch! She who was in such demand as Lucrezia Borgia. 2040

THE CHIEF OF POLICE: She won't last. She's like me: she has neither father nor mother. And if she becomes an image, we'll make use of it. *(A pause.)* . . . A mask. . . .

THE ENVOY: Everything beautiful on earth you owe to masks.

(*Suddenly a bell rings.* IRMA *is about to dart forward, but stops.*)

IRMA: (*to the Chief of Police*) It's Carmen. What's she saying? What are they doing?

(THE CHIEF OF POLICE *lifts one of the earphones.*)

THE CHIEF OF POLICE: (*transmitting the message*) While waiting to go home, they're standing around looking at themselves in the mirrors.

2050 IRMA: Tell her to smash the mirrors or veil them.

(*A silence. Then a burst of machine-gun fire.*)

My mind's made up. I presume I've been summoned from all eternity and that God will bless me. I'm going to prepare myself by prayer.

THE ENVOY: (*gravely*) Do you have the outfits?

IRMA: My closets are as famous as my studios. (*Suddenly worried.*) But everything must be in an awful state! The bombs, the plaster, the dust. Tell Carmen to brush the costumes! (*To the Chief of Police*) George . . . this is our last minute together! From now on, we'll no longer be us. . . .

(THE ENVOY *discreetly moves off and goes to the window.*)

2060 THE CHIEF OF POLICE: (*tenderly*) But I love you.

THE ENVOY: (*turning around, and in a tone of detachment*) Think of that mountain north of the city. All the labourers were at work when the rebellion broke out. . . . (*A pause.*) I refer to a project for a tomb. . . .

THE CHIEF OF POLICE: (*greedily*) What's the plan of it?

THE ENVOY: Later. A mountain of red marble hollowed out with rooms and niches, and in the middle a tiny diamond sentry-box.

THE CHIEF OF POLICE: Will I be able to stand there—or sit—
2070     and keep vigil over my entire death?

THE ENVOY: He who gets it will be there—dead—for eternity. The world will centre about it. About it will rotate the planets and the suns. From a secret point of the same room will run a road that will lead, after many and many a complication, to another room where mirrors will reflect to infinity . . . I say infinity. . . .

THE CHIEF OF POLICE: O.K.!

THE ENVOY: . . . the image of a dead man.

IRMA: (*hugging the Chief of Police to her*) So I'll be real? My
2080     robe will be real? My lace, my jewels will be real? The rest of the world. . . .

(*Machine-gun fire.*)

THE ENVOY: (*after a last glance through the shutters*) Yes, but make haste. Go to your apartments. Embroider an interminable handkerchief. . . . (*To the Chief of Police*) You, give your last orders to your last men. (*He goes to a mirror, takes from his pocket a whole collection of decorations and fastens them to his tunic.*) (*In a vulgar tone*) And make it snappy. I don't have time to listen to your crap.

SCENE VIII

*The scene is the balcony itself, which projects beyond the façade of the brothel. The shutters, which face the audience, are closed. Suddenly, all the shutters open by themselves. The edge of the balcony is at the very edge of the footlights. Through the windows can be seen* THE BISHOP, THE GENERAL, *and* THE JUDGE, *who are getting ready. Finally, the French windows are flung wide open. The three men come out on the balcony. First* THE BISHOP, *then* THE GENERAL, *then* THE JUDGE. *They are followed by the Hero. Then comes* THE QUEEN: MME IRMA, *wearing a diadem on her brow and an ermine cloak. All the characters step forward and take their positions with great timidity. They are silent. They simply show themselves. All are of huge proportions, gigantic—except the Hero, that is,* THE CHIEF OF POLICE—*and are wearing their ceremonial garments, which are torn and dusty. Then, near them, but not on the balcony, appears the beggar. In a gentle voice, he cries out:*

THE BEGGAR: Long live the Queen! (*He goes off timidly, as he came.*)     2090

(*Finally, a strong wind stirs the curtains:* CHANTAL *appears.* THE QUEEN *bows to her. A shot.* CHANTAL *falls.* THE GENERAL *and* THE QUEEN *carry her away dead.*)

SCENE IX

IRMA'S *room, which looks as if it had been hit by a hurricane. Rear, a large two-panelled mirror which forms the wall. Right, a door; left, another. Three cameras on tripods. Next to each of them is a photographer, three very wide-awake young men with ironic expressions. Each is wearing a black leather jacket and close-fitting blue jeans. Enter, in turn, very timidly, right,* THE BISHOP *and, left,* THE JUDGE *and* THE GENERAL. *On seeing each other, they bow deeply. Then,* THE GENERAL *salutes and* THE BISHOP *blesses* THE GENERAL.

THE JUDGE: (*with a sigh of relief*) What we've been through!

THE GENERAL: And it's not over! We have to invent an entire life . . . That's hard. . . .

THE BISHOP: Hard or not, we've got to go through with it. We can no longer back out. Before entering the carriage. . . .

THE GENERAL: The slowness of the carriage!

THE BISHOP: . . . entering the carriage, it was still possible to chuck the whole business. But now. . . .

THE JUDGE: Do you think we were recognized? I was in the middle, hidden by your profiles. Opposite me, Irma. . . .     2100 (*The name astonishes him.*) Irma? The Queen. . . . The Queen hid my face. . . . Do you think we were?

THE BISHOP: No danger of that. You know whom I saw . . . at the right (*unable to keep from laughing*) with his fat, good-natured mug and pink cheeks, though the town was in smithereens? (*The other two smile.*) With his dimples and decayed teeth? And who threw himself on my hand . . . I thought to bite me, and I was about to pull away my fingers . . . to kiss my ring? Who? My fruit-and-vegetable man.

(THE JUDGE *laughs.*)

THE GENERAL: (*grimly*) The slowness of the carriage. The car-     2110 riage wheels on the people's feet and hands! The dust!

THE JUDGE: (*uneasily*) I was opposite the Queen. Through the back window, a woman. . . .

THE BISHOP: (*continuing his account*) I saw her too, at the left-hand door, she was running along and throwing kisses at us!

THE GENERAL: (*more and more grimly*) The slowness of the

carriage! We moved forward so slowly amidst the sweaty mob! Their roars were like threats, but they were only cheering. Someone could have hamstrung the horses, fired 2120 a shot, could have unhitched the traces and harnessed *us*, attached us to the shaft or the horses, could have drawn and quartered us or turned us into draught-horses. But no. Just flowers tossed from a window, and a people hailing its queen, who stood upright beneath her golden crown. (*A pause.*) And the horses going at a walking pace . . . and the Envoy standing on the footboard!

(*A silence.*)

THE BISHOP: (*ironically*) No one could have recognized us. We were in the gold and glitter. They were blinded. It hit them in the eye. . . .

2130 THE JUDGE: It wouldn't have taken much. . . .

THE BISHOP: (*same*) Exhausted by the fighting, choked by the dust, the people stood waiting for the procession. The procession was all they saw. In any case, we can no longer back out. We've been chosen.

THE GENERAL: By whom?

THE BISHOP: (*with sudden grandiloquence*) By glory in person.

THE GENERAL: This masquerade?

THE BISHOP: It lies with us for this masquerade to change meaning. First, we must use words that magnify. We must 2140 act fast, and with precision. No errors allowed. (*With authority*) As for me, instead of being merely the symbolic head of the country's church, I've decided to become its actual head. Instead of blessing and blessing and blessing until I've had my fill, I'm going to sign decrees and appoint priests. The clergy is being organized. A basilica is under construction. It's all in there. (*He points to a folder under his arm.*) Full of plans and projects. (*To the Judge*) What about you?

THE JUDGE: (*looking at his wristwatch*) I have an appointment 2150 with a number of magistrates. We're drafting bills, we're revising the legal code. (*To the General*) What about you?

THE GENERAL: Oh, me, your ideas drift through my poor head like smoke through a log shanty. The art of war's not something you can master just like that. The general-staffs. . . .

THE BISHOP: (*interrupting*) Like everything else, the fate of arms can be read in your stars. Read your stars, damn it!

THE GENERAL: That's easy to say. But when the Hero comes back, planted firmly on his rump, as if on a horse. . . . For, of course, nothing's happened yet?

2160 THE BISHOP: Nothing. But let's not crow too soon. Though his image hasn't yet been consecrated by the brothel, it still may. If so, we're done for. Unless you make a positive effort to seize power.

(*Suddenly, he breaks off. One of the photographers has cleared his throat, as if to spit. Another has snapped his fingers like a Spanish dancer.*)

THE BISHOP: (*severely*) Indeed, you're here. Please do your job quickly, and in silence, if possible. You're to take each of our profiles, one smiling, the other rather stern.

FIRST PHOTOGRAPHER: We'll do our job, don't worry. (*To the Bishop*) Get set for prayer, because the world ought to be bombarded with the picture of a pious man.

2170 THE BISHOP: (*without moving*) In fervent meditation.

FIRST PHOTOGRAPHER: Right, fervent. Get set.

THE BISHOP: (*ill at ease*) But . . . how?

FIRST PHOTOGRAPHER: Don't you know how to compose yourself for prayer? Okay, facing both God and the camera. Hands together. Head up. Eyes down. That's the classical pose. A return to order, a return to classicism.

THE BISHOP: (*kneeling*) Like this?

FIRST PHOTOGRAPHER: (*looking at him with curiosity*) That's it. . . . (*He looks at the camera.*) No you're not in the frame. . . . (*Shuffling on his knees, the* BISHOP *places himself* 2180 *in front of the camera.*) Okay.

SECOND PHOTOGRAPHER: (*to the Judge*) Would you mind pulling a longer face? You don't quite look like a judge. A little longer.

THE JUDGE: Horselike? Sullen?

SECOND PHOTOGRAPHER: Horselike and sullen, my Lord. And both hands in front, on your brief. What I want is a shot of *the* Judge. A good photographer is one who gives a definitive image. Perfect.

FIRST PHOTOGRAPHER: (*to the Bishop*) Turn your head . . . just 2190 a little. . . . (*He turns the Bishop's head.*)

THE BISHOP: (*angrily*) You're unscrewing the neck of a prelate!

FIRST PHOTOGRAPHER: I want a three-quarter view of you praying, my Lord.

SECOND PHOTOGRAPHER: (*to the Judge*) My Lord, if you possibly can, a little more severity. . . . with a pendulous lip. (*Crying out*) That's it! Perfect! Stay that way! (*He rushes behind his camera, but there is a flash before he gets there.* THE FIRST PHOTOGRAPHER *has just taken his shot.* THE SECOND PHOTOGRAPHER *puts his head under the black hood of his* 2200 *camera.*)

THE GENERAL: (*to the Third Photographer*) The finest pose is Poniatovsky's.

THIRD PHOTOGRAPHER: (*striking a pose*) With the sword?

THE GENERAL: No, no. That's Lafayette. No, with the arm extended and the marshal's baton. . . .

THIRD PHOTOGRAPHER: Ah, you mean Wellington?

THE GENERAL: Unfortunately, I don't have a baton. . . .

(*Meanwhile, the* FIRST PHOTOGRAPHER *has gone back to the Bishop, who has not moved, and looks him over silently.*)

THIRD PHOTOGRAPHER: (*to the General*) We've got just what we need. Here, now strike the pose. (*Rolls up a sheet of paper* 2210 *in the form of a marshal's baton. He hands it to the General, who strikes a pose, and then dashes to his camera. A flash: the* SECOND PHOTOGRAPHER *has just taken his shot.*)

THE BISHOP: (*to the First Photographer*) I hope the negative comes out well. Now we'll have to flood the world with a picture of me receiving the Eucharist. Unfortunately, we don't have a Host on hand. . . .

FIRST PHOTOGRAPHER: Leave it to us, Monsignor. Newspapermen are a resourceful bunch. (*Calls out*) My Lord!

(THE JUDGE *approaches.*)

I'm going to try a stunt. Lend me a hand a minute. (*Without* 2220 *further ado, he takes him by the hand and sets him in place.*) But I want only your hand to show . . . there . . . roll up your sleeve a little . . . above Monsignor's tongue. More. Okay. (*Still fumbling in his pocket. To the Bishop.*) Stick out your tongue. More. Okay. (*Still fumbling in his pocket. A flash:* THE GENERAL *has just been photographed; he resumes his natural pose.*) Damn it! I don't have a thing! (*He looks about. To the General)* That's perfect. May I? *(Without waiting for an answer, he takes the General's monocle from his eye and goes back to the group formed by* THE BISHOP *and* THE JUDGE. *He makes* THE JUDGE *hold the monocle above the Bishop's tongue as if it were a Host, and he rushes to his camera. A flash.)*

*(*THE QUEEN, *who has entered with* THE ENVOY, *has been watching these proceedings for some moments.)*

THE ENVOY: It's a true image, born of a false spectacle.

FIRST PHOTOGRAPHER: *(cynically)* That's common practice, your Majesty. When some rebels were captured, we paid a militiaman to bump off a chap I'd just sent to buy me a packet of cigarettes. The photo shows a rebel shot down while trying to escape.

THE QUEEN: Monstrous!

THE ENVOY: But have things ever happened otherwise? History was lived so that a glorious page might be written, and then read. It's reading that counts. *(To the photographers)* Gentlemen, the Queen informs me that she congratulates you. She asks that you return to your posts.

*(The* THREE PHOTOGRAPHERS *put their heads under the black hoods of their cameras.)*
*(A silence.)*

THE QUEEN: *(in a low voice, as if to herself)* Isn't he here?

THE ENVOY: *(to the Three Figures)* The Queen would like to know what you're doing, what you plan to do.

THE BISHOP: We've been recovering as many dead bodies as possible. We were planning to embalm them and lodge them in our heaven. Your grandeur requires your having slaughtered the rebels wholesale. We shall keep for ourselves only a few of our fallen martyrs, to whom we shall pay honour that will honour us.

THE QUEEN: *(to the Envoy)* That will serve my glory, will it not?

THE ENVOY: *(smiling)* The massacres, too, are revels wherein the people indulge to their heart's content in the pleasure of hating us. I am speaking, to be sure, of "our" people. They can at last set up a statute to us in their hearts so as to shower it with blows. At least, I hope so.

THE QUEEN: Does that mean that leniency and kindness are of no avail?

THE ENVOY: *(smiling)* A St. Vincent de Paul Studio?

THE QUEEN: *(testily to the Judge)* You, my Lord, what's being done? I'd ordered fewer death penalties and more sentences to forced labour. I hope the underground galleries are finished? *(To the Envoy)* It's the word galley-slaves that made me think of the galleries of the Mausoleum. Are they finished?

THE JUDGE: Completely. And open to the public on Sundays. Some of the arches are completely adorned with the skeletons of prisoners who died during the digging.

THE QUEEN: *(in the direction of the Bishop)* Very good. What about the Church? I suppose that anyone who hasn't done at least a week's work on this extraordinary chapel is in a state of mortal sin?

*(*THE BISHOP *bows. To the General)* As for you, I'm aware of your severity. Your soldiers are watching over the workers, and they thoroughly deserve the fine name of builders. *(Smiling gently, with feigned fatigue.)* For, as you know,

gentlemen, I plan to present this tomb to the Hero. You know how downcast he feels, don't you, and how he suffers at not yet having been impersonated?

THE GENERAL: *(plucking up courage)* He'll have a hard time attaining glory. The places have been filled for ages. Every niche has its statue. *(Fatuously)* We, at least. . . .

THE JUDGE: That's how it always is when one wants to start from the bottom. And particularly by rejecting or neglecting the traditional. The established order of things, as it were.

THE QUEEN: *(suddenly vibrant)* Yet it was he who saved everything. He wants glory. He insists on breaking open the gates of legend, but he has allowed you to carry on with your ceremonies.

THE BISHOP: *(arrogantly)* To be frank, Madame, we're no longer concerned with that. As for me, my skirt hampers me, and my hands get caught in the lace. We're going to have to act.

THE QUEEN: *(indignantly)* Act? You? You mean to say you're going to strip us of our power?

THE JUDGE: We have to fulfil our functions, don't we?

THE QUEEN: Functions! You're planning to overthrow him, to lower him, to take his place!

THE BISHOP: Somewhere in time—in time or in space!—perhaps there exist high dignitaries invested with absolute dignity and attired with veritable ornaments. . . .

THE QUEEN: *(very angrily)* Veritable! And what about those? You mean that those you're wrapped and swathed in—my whole paraphernalia!—which come from my closets, aren't veritable?

THE BISHOP: *(pointing to the Judge's ermine, the silk of his robe, etc.)* Rabbit, sateen, machine-made lace . . . you think we're going to be satisfied with make-believe to the end of our days?

THE QUEEN: *(outraged)* But this morning . . . *(She breaks off. Enter* THE CHIEF OF POLICE, *quietly, humbly.)* George, beware of them.

THE CHIEF OF POLICE: *(trying to smile)* I think that . . . victory . . . we've won the day. May I sit down?

*(He sits down. Then he looks about, as if questioning everyone.)*

THE ENVOY: *(ironically)* No, nobody's come yet. Nobody has yet felt the need to abolish himself in your fascinating image.

THE CHIEF OF POLICE: That means the projects you submitted to me aren't very effective. *(To the Queen)* Nothing? Nobody?

THE QUEEN: *(very gently)* Nobody. And yet, the blinds have been drawn again. The men ought to be coming in. Besides, the apparatus has been set up; so we'll be informed by a full peal of bells.

THE ENVOY: *(to the Chief of Police)* You didn't care for the project I submitted to you this morning. Yet that's the image that haunts you and that ought to haunt others.

THE CHIEF OF POLICE: Ineffectual.

THE ENVOY: *(showing a photographic negative)* The executioner's red coat and his axe. I suggested amaranth red and the steel axe.

THE QUEEN: *(testily)* Studio 14, known as the Studio of Executions. Already been done.

THE JUDGE: (*making himself agreeable, to the Chief of Police*) Yet you're feared.

2340 THE CHIEF OF POLICE: I'm afraid that they fear and envy a man, but . . . (*groping for words*) . . . but not a wrinkle, for example, or a curl . . . or a cigar . . . or a whip. The latest image that was proposed to me. . . . I hardly dare mention it to you.

THE JUDGE: Was it . . . very audacious?

THE CHIEF OF POLICE: Very. Too audacious. I'd never dare tell you what it was. (*Suddenly, he seems to make up his mind.*) Gentlemen, I have sufficient confidence in your judgment and devotion. After all, I want to carry on the fight by boldness of ideas as well. It was this: I've been advised to appear

2350 in the form of a gigantic phallus, a prick of great stature. . . .

(*The Three Figures and the Queen are dumbfounded.*)

THE QUEEN: George! You?

THE CHIEF OF POLICE: What do you expect? If I'm to symbolize the nation, your joint. . . .

THE ENVOY: (*to the Queen*) Allow him, Madame. It's the tone of the age.

THE JUDGE: A phallus? Of great stature? You mean—enormous?

THE CHIEF OF POLICE: Of my stature.

THE JUDGE: But that'll be very difficult to bring off.

2360 THE ENVOY: Not so very. What with new techniques and our rubber industry, remarkable things can be worked out. No I'm not worried about that, but rather . . . (*turning to the Bishop*) . . . what the Church will think of it?

THE BISHOP: (*after reflection, shrugging his shoulders*) No definite pronouncement can be made this evening. To be sure, the idea is a bold one. (*To the Chief of Police*) But if your case is desperate, we shall have to examine the matter. For . . . it would be a formidable figure-head, and if you were to transmit yourself in that guise to posterity. . . .

2370 THE CHIEF OF POLICE: (*gently*) Would you like to see the model?

THE JUDGE: (*to the Chief of Police*) It's wrong of you to be impatient. *We* waited two thousand years to perfect our roles. Keep hoping. . . .

THE GENERAL: (*interrupting him*) Glory is achieved in combat. You haven't enough illustrious Waterloos to your credit. Keep fighting, or sit down and wait out the regulation two thousand years.

(*Everyone laughs.*)

THE QUEEN: (*violently*) You don't care a damn about his suf-

2380 fering. And it was I who singled you out! I who fished you out of the rooms of my brothel and hired you for his glory. And you agreed to serve him.

(*A pause.*)

THE BISHOP: (*firmly*) It is at this point that a question, and a very serious one, arises: are you going to use what we represent, or are we (*he points to the other two Figures*) going to use you to serve what we represent?

THE QUEEN: (*flaring up*) Your conditions, you? Puppets who without their rabbit, as you put it, would be nothing, you, a man who was made to dance naked—in other words,

2390 skinned!—on the public squares of Seville and Toledo! and who danced! To the click of castanets! Your conditions, my

Lord?

THE BISHOP: That day I *had* to dance. As for the rabbit, it's what it *must* be—the sacred image of ermine—it has the same power.

THE CHIEF OF POLICE: For the time being, but. . . .

THE BISHOP: (*getting excited*) Exactly. So long as we were in a room in a brothel, we belonged to our own fantasies. But once having exposed them, having named them, having proclaimed them, we're now tied up with human beings, tied to 2400 you, and forced to go on with this adventure according to the laws of visibility.

THE CHIEF OF POLICE: You have no power. I alone. . . .

THE BISHOP: Then we shall go back to our rooms and there continue the quest of an absolute dignity. We ought never to have left them. For we were content there, and it was you who came and dragged us away. For ours was a happy state. And absolutely safe. In peace, in comfort, behind shutters, behind padded curtains, protected by a police force that protects brothels, we were able to be a general, judge and 2410 bishop to the point of perfection and to the point of rapture! You tore us brutally from that delicious, untroubled state.

THE GENERAL: (*interrupting the Bishop*) My breeches! What joy when I pulled on my breeches! I now sleep in my general's breeches. I eat in my breeches, I waltz—*when* I waltz—in my breeches, I live in my general's breeches. I'm a general the way one is a priest.

THE JUDGE: I'm just a dignity represented by a skirt.

THE GENERAL: (*to the Bishop*) At no moment can I prepare myself—I used to start a month in advance!—prepare myself 2420 for pulling on my general's boots and breeches. I'm rigged in them for all eternity. By Jove, I no longer dream.

THE BISHOP: (*to the Chief of Police*) You see, he no longer dreams. Our ornamental purity, our luxurious and barren—and sublime—appearance has been eaten away. It's gone forever. Well and good. But the taste of that bitter delight of responsibility of which I've spoken has remained with us, and we find it to our liking. Our rooms are no longer secret. You hurt us by dragging us into the light. But as for dancing? You spoke of dancing? You referred to that notorious after- 2430 noon when, stripped—or skinned, whichever word amuses you—stripped of our priestly ornaments, we had to dance naked on the cathedral square. I danced, I admit it, with people laughing at me, but at least I danced. Whereas now, if ever I have an itch for that kind of thing, I'll have to go on the sly to the Balcony, where there probably is a room prepared for prelates who like to be ballerinas a few hours a week. No, no. . . . We're going to live in the light, but with all that that implies. We—magistrate, soldier, prelate—we're going to act in such a way as to impoverish our 2440 ornaments unceasingly! We're going to render them useful! But in order that they be of use, and of use to us—since it's your order that we've chosen to defend—you must be the first to recognize them and pay homage to them.

THE CHIEF OF POLICE: (*calmly*) I shall be not the hundred-thousandth-reflection-within-a-reflection in a mirror, but the One and Only, into whom a hundred thousand want to merge. If not for me, you'd have all been done for. The expression "beaten hollow" would have had meaning. (*He is going to regain his authority increasingly.*) 2450

THE QUEEN: (*to the Bishop, insinuatingly*) You happen to be wearing that robe this evening simply because you were unable to clear out of the studios in time. You just couldn't tear yourself away from one of your hundred thousand reflections, but the clients are beginning to come back. . . . There's no rush yet, but Carmen has recorded several entries. . . . *(To the Chief of Police)* Don't let them intimidate you. Before the revolt, there were lots of them. . . . *(To the Bishop)* If you hadn't had the abominable idea of having Chantal assassinated. . . .

THE BISHOP: *(frightened)* A stray bullet!

THE QUEEN: Stray or not, Chantal was assassinated on *my* balcony! When she came back here to see me, to visit her boss. . . .

THE BISHOP: I had the presence of mind to make her one of our saints.

THE CHIEF OF POLICE: A traditional attitude. A churchman's reflex. But there's no need to congratulate yourself. The image of her on our flag has hardly any power. Or rather. . . . I've had reports from all quarters that owing to the possibility that she was playing a double game, Chantal has been condemned by those she was supposed to save. . . .

THE QUEEN: *(anxiously)* But then the whole business is starting all over again?

*(From this point on* THE QUEEN *and* THE CHIEF OF POLICE *will seem very agitated.* THE QUEEN *will go to a window and draw the curtains after trying to look out into the street.)*

THE ENVOY: All of it.

THE GENERAL: Are we going to have to . . . to get into the carriage again? The slowness of the carriage!

THE BISHOP: If I had Chantal shot, and then canonized, if I had her image blazoned on our flag. . . .

THE QUEEN: It's *my* image that ought to be there. . . .

THE ENVOY: You're already on the postage stamps, on the banknotes, on the seals in the police-stations.

THE GENERAL: The slowness of the carriage . . .

THE QUEEN: Will I therefore never be who I am?

THE ENVOY: Never again.

THE QUEEN: Every event of my life—my blood that trickles if I scratch myself. . . .

THE ENVOY: Everything will be written for you with a capital letter.

THE QUEEN: But that's Death?

THE ENVOY: It is indeed.

THE CHIEF OF POLICE: *(with sudden authority)* It means death for all of you. And that's why I'm sure of you. At least, as long as I've not been impersonated, because after that I'll just sit back and take it easy. *(Inspired)* Besides, I'll know by a sudden weakness of my muscles that my image is escaping from me to go and haunt men's minds. When that happens my visible end will be near. For the time being, and if we have to act . . . *(To the Bishop)* who will assume real responsibilities? You? *(He shrugs.)* Be logical: if you are what you are, judge, general, bishop, it's because you wanted to become that and wanted it known that you had become it. You therefore did what was necessary to achieve your purpose and to be a focus of attention. Is that right?

THE JUDGE: Pretty much.

THE CHIEF OF POLICE: Very well. That means you've never performed an act for its own sake, but always so that, when

linked with other acts, it would make a bishop, a judge, a general. . . .

THE BISHOP: That's both true and false. For each act contained within itself its leaven of novelty.

THE JUDGE: We acquired greater dignity thereby.

THE CHIEF OF POLICE: No doubt, my Lord, but this dignity, which has become as inhuman as a crystal, makes you unfit for governing men. No, no, gentlemen, above you, more sublime than you, is the Queen. It's from her, for the time being, that you derive your power and your rights. Above her—that to which she refers—is our standard, on which I've blazoned the image of Chantal Victorious, our saint.

THE BISHOP: *(aggressively)* Above Her Majesty, whom we venerate, and above her flag, is God, Who speaks through my voice.

THE CHIEF OF POLICE: *(irritably)* And above God? *(A silence.)* Well, gentlemen, above God are you, without whom God would be nothing. And above you am I, without whom. . . .

THE JUDGE: What about the people? The photographers?

THE CHIEF OF POLICE: On their knees before the people who are on their knees before God. Therefore. . . .

*(They all burst out laughing.)*

That's why I want you to serve me. But a while ago you were holding forth quite volubly. I should therefore like to pay homage to your eloquence, your facility of elocution, the limpidity of your timbre, the potency of your organ. As for me, I'm a mere man of action who gets tangled up in words and ideas when they're not immediately applied. That's why I was wondering whether to send you back to your kennel. I won't do it. In any case, not right away, since you're already there.

THE GENERAL: Sir!

THE CHIEF OF POLICE: *(He pushes the General, who topples over and remains sitting on the floor, flabbergasted)* Lie down! Lie down, General!

THE JUDGE: My skirt can be tucked up. . . .

THE CHIEF OF POLICE: *(He pushes the Judge, who topples over)* Lie down! Since you want to be recognized as a judge, do you want to hold on to your dignity according to my idea of it? And according to the general meaning attached to your dignities? Very well. Must I therefore grant you increasing recognition along these lines? Yes or no?

*(No one answers.)*

Well, gentlemen, yes or no? *(THE BISHOP steps aside, prudently.)*

THE QUEEN: *(very blandly)* Excuse him, if he gets carried away. I'm quite aware of what you used to come here for: *(to the Bishop)* you, my Lord, to seek by quick, decisive ways a manifest saintliness. No, no, I'm not being ironic. The gold of my chasubles had little to do with it, I'm sure. It wasn't mere gross ambition that brought you behind my closed shutters. Love of God was hidden there. I realize that. You, my Lord, you were indeed guided by a concern for justice, since it was the image of a magistrate that you wished to see reflected a thousand times in my mirrors. And you, General, it was bravery and military glory and the heroic deed that haunted you. So let yourselves go, relax, without too many scruples. . . .

*(One after the other, the three men heave a deep sigh.)*

THE CHIEF OF POLICE: (*continuing*) That's a relief to you, isn't it? You never really wanted to get out of yourselves and communicate, if only by acts of meanness, with the world. I understand you. (*Amiably*) My role, unfortunately, is in motion. In short, as you probably know, it's not in the nomenclature of the brothels. . . .

THE QUEEN: In the pink handbook.

THE CHIEF OF POLICE: Yes, in the pink handbook. (*To the Three Figures*) Come now, gentlemen, don't you feel sorry for a poor fellow like me? (*He looks at them one after the other.*) Come, come, gentlemen, you're not hardhearted, are you? It's for you that these Studios and Illustrious Rites were perfected, by means of exquisite experimentation. They required long labour, infinite patience, and you want to go back to the light of day? (*Almost humble, and suddenly looking very very tired*) Wait just a little while. For the time being, I'm still loaded with future acts, loaded with actions . . . but as soon as I feel I'm being multiplied ad infinitum, then . . . then, ceasing to be hard, I'll go and rot in people's minds. And you, get into your skirts again if you want to, and get back on the job. (*To* THE BISHOP) You're silent. (*A long silence.*) That's right. . . . Let's be silent, and let's wait. . . . (*A long and heavy silence.*) Perhaps it's now . . . (*In a low, humble voice*) that my apotheosis is being prepared. . . . (*Everybody is visibly expectant. Then,* CARMEN *enters, as if furtively, by the left door.* THE ENVOY *is the first to see her. He silently indicates her presence to* THE QUEEN. THE QUEEN *motions to* CARMEN *to withdraw, but* CARMEN *nevertheless takes a step forward.*)

THE QUEEN: (*in an almost low voice*) I gave orders that we were not to be disturbed. What do you want?

(CARMEN *goes to her.*)

CARMEN: I tried to ring, but the apparatus is out of order. I beg your pardon. I'd like to speak with you.

THE QUEEN: Well, what is it? Speak up!

CARMEN: (*hesitantly*) It's . . . I don't know. . . .

THE QUEEN: (*resignedly*) Well, when at Court do as the Court does. Let's speak in an undertone. (*She conspicuously lends ear to* CARMEN, *who leans forward and murmurs a few words.* THE QUEEN *seems very upset.*)

THE QUEEN: Are you sure?

CARMEN: Quite, Madame.

(THE QUEEN *bolts from the room, followed by* CARMEN. THE CHIEF OF POLICE *starts to follow them, but the* ENVOY *intervenes.*)

THE ENVOY: One does not follow Her Majesty.

THE CHIEF OF POLICE: What's going on? Where's she going?

THE ENVOY: (*ironically*) To embroider. The Queen is embroidering, and she is not embroidering. . . . You know the refrain? The Queen attains her reality when she withdraws, absents herself, or dies.

THE CHIEF OF POLICE: What's happening outside? (*To the Judge*) Do you have any news?

THE JUDGE: What you call outside is as mysterious to us as we are to it.

THE BISHOP: I shall try to depict the grief of this people which thought it had liberated itself by rebelling. Alas—or rather, thank Heaven!—there will never be a movement powerful enough to destroy our imagery.

THE CHIEF OF POLICE: (*almost tremblingly*) So you think I have a chance?

THE BISHOP: You're in the best possible position. There's consternation everywhere, in all families, in all institutions. People have trembled so violently that your image is beginning to make them doubt themselves.

THE CHIEF OF POLICE: Am I their only hope?

THE BISHOP: Their only hope lies in utter collapse.

THE CHIEF OF POLICE: In short, I'm like a pool in which they behold themselves?

THE GENERAL: (*delighted, with a burst of laughter*) And if they lean over too far, they fall in and drown. Before long, you'll be full of drowned bodies! (*No one seems to share his merriment.*) Oh well . . . they're not yet at the brink! (*Embarrassed*) Let's wait.

(*A silence.*)

THE CHIEF OF POLICE: So you really think the people had a wild hope? And that in losing all hope they lose everything? And that in losing everything they'll come and lose themselves in me? . . .

THE BISHOP: That may very well happen. But, believe me, not if we can help it.

THE CHIEF OF POLICE: When I am offered that final consecration. . . .

THE ENVOY: (*ironically*) For you, but for you alone, for a second the Earth will stop rotating. . . .

(*Suddenly the door at the left opens and* THE QUEEN *appears, beaming.*)

THE QUEEN: George! (*She falls into the arms of the Chief of Police.*)

THE CHIEF OF POLICE: (*incredulous*) It's not true. (THE QUEEN *nods yes.*) But where? . . . When?

THE QUEEN: (*deeply moved*) There! . . . Now! The Studio. . . .

THE CHIEF OF POLICE: You're pulling my leg. I didn't hear anything.

(*Suddenly a tremendous ringing, a kind of peal of bells.*)

So it's true? It's for me? (*He pushes the Queen away. Solemnly, as the ringing stops*) Gentlemen, I belong to the Nomenclature! (*To the Queen*) But are you really sure?

(*The ringing starts again, then stops.*)

THE QUEEN: It was I who received him and ushered him into the Mausoleum Studio. The one that's being built in your honour. I left Carmen behind to attend to the preparations and I ran to let you know. I'm trembling like a leaf. . . .

(*The ringing starts again, then stops.*)

THE BISHOP: (*gloomily*) We're up the creek.

THE CHIEF OF POLICE: The apparatus is working. You can see. . . .

(*He goes to the left, followed by* THE QUEEN.)

THE ENVOY: That is not the practice. It's filthy. . . .

THE CHIEF OF POLICE: (*shrugging his shoulders*) Where's the mechanism? (*To the Queen*) Let's watch together.

(*She stands at the left, facing a small port-hole. After a brief hesitation,* THE JUDGE, GENERAL *and* BISHOP *place themselves at the right, at another port-hole symmetrical with the first.*

*Then, the two panels of the double mirror forming the back of the stage silently draw apart, revealing the interior of the Special Studio.* THE ENVOY, *with resignation, joins the Chief of Police.*)

DESCRIPTION OF THE MAUSOLEUM STUDIO: *The stones of the wall, which is circular, are visible. At the rear, a stairway that descends. In the centre of this well there seems to be another, in which the steps of a stairway are visible. On the walls, four laurel wreaths, adorned with crêpe. When the panels separate,* ROGER *is at the middle of the stairway, which he is descending.* CARMEN *seems to be guiding him.* ROGER *is dressed like* THE CHIEF OF POLICE, *though, mounted on the same cothurni as the Three Figures, he looks taller. His shoulders have also been broadened. He descends the stairs to the rhythm of a drum.*

CARMEN: (*approaching, and handing him a cigar*) It's on the house.

ROGER: (*putting the cigar into his mouth*) Thanks.

CARMEN: (*taking the cigar from him*) That end's for the light. This one's for the mouth. (*She turns the cigar around.*) Is
2670  this your first cigar?

ROGER: Yes. . . . (*A pause.*) I'm not asking for your advice. You're here to serve me, I've paid. . . .

CARMEN: I beg your pardon, sir.

ROGER: The slave?

CARMEN: He's being untied.

ROGER: He knows what it's about?

CARMEN: Completely. You're the first. You're inaugurating this Studio, but, you know, the scenarios are all reducible to a major theme. . . .

2680  ROGER: Which is . . . ?

CARMEN: Death.

ROGER: (*touching the walls*) And so this is my tomb?

CARMEN: (*correcting him*) Mausoleum.

ROGER: How many slaves are working on it?

CARMEN: The entire people, sir. Half of the population during the day and the other half at night. As you have requested, the whole mountain will be burrowed and tunnelled. The interior will have the complexity of a termite nest or of the Basilica of Lourdes—we don't know yet. No one will be able
2690  to see anything from the outside. All they'll know is that the mountain is sacred, but, inside, the tombs are already being enshrined in tombs, the cenotaphs in cenotaphs, the coffins in coffins, the urns. . . .

ROGER: What about here, where I am now?

CARMEN: (*with a gesture of disdain*) An antechamber. An antechamber called the Valley of the Fallen. (*She mounts the underground stairway.*) In a little while, you'll go farther down.

ROGER: I'm not to hope to see the light of day again?

2700  CARMEN: But . . . do you still want to?

(*A silence.*)

ROGER: It's really true that no one's ever been here before me?

CARMEN: In this . . . tomb, or in this . . . Studio?

(*A silence.*)

ROGER: Is everything really on right? My outfit? My toupet?

(THE CHIEF OF POLICE *turns to the Queen.*)

THE CHIEF OF POLICE: He knew I wear a toupet?

THE BISHOP: (*snickering, to the Judge, and the General*) He's the only one who doesn't know that everyone knows it.

CARMEN: (*to Roger*) Everything was carefully planned long ago. It's all been worked out. The rest is up to you.

ROGER: (*anxiously*) You realize I'm feeling my way too. I've got to imagine what the Hero's like, and he's never shown him-  2710
self much.

CARMEN: That's why we've taken you to the Mausoleum Studio. It's not possible to make many errors here, nor indulge your imagination.

(*A pause.*)

ROGER: Will I be alone?

CARMEN: Everything is padded. The doors are lined. So are the walls.

ROGER: (*hesitantly*) What about . . . the mausoleum?

CARMEN: (*forcefully*) Built into the rock. The proof is that there's water oozing from the walls. Deathly silent. As for  2720
light, the darkness is so thick that your eyes have developed astounding qualities. The cold? Yes, the coldness of death. It's been a gigantic job drilling through the mountain. Men are still groaning in order to hollow out a gigantic niche for you. Everything proves that you're loved and that you're a conqueror.

ROGER: Groaning? Could . . . could I hear the groaning?

(CARMEN *turns toward a hole dug out at the foot of the wall, from which emerges the head of the* BEGGAR, *the character seen in Scene 4. He is now the* SLAVE.)

CARMEN: Come here!

(THE SLAVE *crawls in.*)

ROGER: (*looking the slave over*) Is that it?

CARMEN: A fine specimen, isn't he? Skinny. With lice and  2730
sores. He dreams of dying for you. I'll leave you alone now.

ROGER: With him? No, no. (*A pause.*) Stay. Everything always takes place in the presence of a woman. It's in order for a woman's face to be a witness that, usually. . . .

(*Suddenly, the sound of a hammer striking an anvil. Then a cock crows.*)

Is life so near?

CARMEN: (*in a normal voice, not acting*) As I've told you, everything's padded, but some sounds always manage to filter through. Does it bother you? Life's starting up again little by little . . . as before. . . .

ROGER: (*he seems anxious*) Yes, as before. . . .  2740

CARMEN: (*gently*) You were.

ROGER: Yes. Everything's washed up. . . . And what's saddest of all is people's saying: "The rebellion was wonderful!"

CARMEN: You mustn't think about it any more. And you must stop listening to the sounds from outside. Besides, it's raining. The whole mountain has been swept by a tornado. (*Stage voice*) You are at home here. (*Pointing to the slave*) Make him talk.

ROGER: (*playing his role*) For you can talk? And what else can you do?  2750

THE SLAVE: (*lying on his belly*) First, bow; then, shrink into myself a little more (*He takes Roger's foot and places it on his own back.*) like this! . . . and even. . . .

ROGER: (*impatiently*) Yes . . . and even?

THE SLAVE: Sink into the earth, if it's possible.

ROGER: *(drawing on his cigar)* Sink in, really? But there's no mud?

THE QUEEN: *(to the others)* He's right. We should have provided mud. In a well-run house. . . . But it's opening day, and he's the first client to use the Studio. . . .

THE SLAVE: *(to Roger)* I feel it all over my body, sir. It's all over me, except in my mouth, which is open so that I can sing your praises and utter the groans that made me famous.

ROGER: Famous? You're famous, you?

THE SLAVE: Famous for my chants, sir, which are hymns to your glory.

ROGER: So your glory accompanies mine? *(To Carmen)* Does he mean that my reputation will be kept going by his words? And . . . if he says nothing, I'll cease to exist . . . ?

CARMEN: *(curtly)* I'd like very much to satisfy you, but you ask questions that aren't in the scenario.

ROGER: *(to the Slave)* But what about you, who sings to you?

THE SLAVE: Nobody. I'm dying.

ROGER: But without me, without my sweat, without my tears and blood, what would you be?

THE SLAVE: Nothing.

ROGER: *(to the Slave)* You sing? But what else do you do?

THE SLAVE: We do all we possibly can to be more and more unworthy of you.

ROGER: What, for example?

THE SLAVE: We try hard just to stand and rot. And, believe me, it's not always easy. Life tries to prevail. . . . But we stand our ground. We keep shrinking more and more every. . . .

ROGER: Day?

THE SLAVE: Week.

THE CHIEF OF POLICE: *(to the others)* That's not much. With a little effort. . . .

THE ENVOY: *(to the Chief of Police)* Be still. Let them play out their roles.

ROGER: That's not much. With a little effort. . . .

THE SLAVE: *(with exaltation)* With joy, Your Excellency! You're so splendid! So splendid that I wonder whether you're aglow or whether you're all the darkness of all the nights?

ROGER: What does it matter, since I'm no longer to have any reality except in the reality of your phrases.

THE SLAVE: *(crawling in the direction of the upper stairway)* You have not mouth nor ears nor eyes, but all of you is a thundering mouth and at the same time a dazzling and watchful eye. . . .

ROGER: *You* see it, but do the others know it? Does the night know it? Does death? Do the stones? What do the stones say?

THE SLAVE: *(still dragging on his belly and beginning to crawl up the stairs)* The stones say. . . .

ROGER: Well, I'm listening.

THE SLAVE: *(he stops crawling, and faces the audience)* The cement that holds us together to form your tomb. . . .

THE CHIEF OF POLICE: *(facing the audience and joyfully beating his breast)* The stones venerate me!

THE SLAVE: *(continuing)* . . . the cement is moulded of tears, spit and blood. The workers' eyes and hands that rested upon us have matted us with grief. We are yours, and only yours.

*(THE SLAVE starts crawling up the stairs again.)*

ROGER: *(with rising exaltation)* Everything proclaims me! Everything breathes me and everything worships me! My history was lived so that a glorious page might be written and then read. It's reading that counts. *(He suddenly notices that the Slave has disappeared. To Carmen)* But . . . where's he going? . . . Where is he? . . .

CARMEN: He's gone off to sing. He's going up into the light of day. He'll tell . . . that he carried your footsteps . . . and that. . . .

ROGER: *(anxiously)* Yes, and that? What else will he tell?

CARMEN: The truth; that you're dead, or rather that you don't stop dying and that your image, like your name, reverberates to infinity.

ROGER: He knows that my image is everywhere?

CARMEN: Yes, everywhere, inscribed and engraved and imposed by fear.

ROGER: In the palms of stevedores? In the games of children? On the teeth of soldiers? In war?

CARMEN: Everywhere.

THE CHIEF OF POLICE: *(to the others)* So I've made it?

THE QUEEN: *(fondly)* Are you happy?

THE CHIEF OF POLICE: You've done a good job. That puts the finishing touch to your house.

ROGER: *(To Carmen)* Is it in prisons? In the wrinkles of old people?

CARMEN: It is.

ROGER: In the curves of roads?

CARMEN: You mustn't ask the impossible.

*(Same sounds as earlier: the cock and the anvil.)*

It's time to go, sir. The session's over. Turn left, and when you reach the corridor. . . .

*(The sound of the anvil again, a little louder.)*

You hear? You've got to go home. . . . What are you doing?

ROGER: Life is nearby . . . and far away. Here all the women are beautiful. Their purpose is purely ornamental. . . . One can lose oneself in them. . . .

CARMEN: *(curtly)* That's right. In ordinary language, we're called whores. But you've got to leave. . . .

ROGER: And go where? Into life? To carry on, as they say, with my activities. . . .

CARMEN: *(a little anxiously)* I don't know what you're doing, and I haven't the right to inquire. But you've got to leave. Your time's up.

*(The sound of the anvil and other sounds indicate an activity: cracking of a whip, humming of a motor, etc.)*

ROGER: They give you the rush in this place! Why do you want me to go back where I came from?

CARMEN: You've nothing further to do. . . .

ROGER: There? No. Nothing further. Nor here either. And outside, in what you call life, everything has crashed. No truth was possible. . . . Did you know Chantal?

CARMEN: *(suddenly frightened)* Get going! Clear out of here!

THE QUEEN: I won't allow him to create a rumpus in my studios! Who was it who sent me that individual? Whenever there are disturbances, the riff-raff always crop up. I hope that Carmen. . . .

CARMEN: *(to Roger)* Get out! You've no right to ask questions either. You know that brothels are very strictly regulated and that we're protected by the police.

ROGER: No! Since I'm playing the Chief of Police and since you allow me to be here. . . .

CARMEN: (*pulling him away*) You're crazy! You wouldn't be the first who thought he'd risen to power. . . . Come along!

ROGER: (*disengaging himself*) If the brothel exists and if I've a right to go there, then I've a right to lead the character I've chosen to the very limit of his destiny . . . no, of mine . . . of merging his destiny with mine. . . .

CARMEN: Stop shouting, sir. All the studios are occupied. Come along. . . .

(CARMEN *tries to make him leave. She opens a door, then another, then a third, unable to find the right one.* ROGER *takes out a knife and, with his back to the audience, makes the gesture of castrating himself.*)

THE QUEEN: On my rugs! On the new carpet! He's a lunatic!

CARMEN: (*crying out*) Doing that here! (*She yells*) Madame! Mme Irma! (CARMEN *finally manages to drag Roger out.*)

(THE QUEEN *rushes from the room. All the characters—the* CHIEF OF POLICE, THE ENVOY, THE JUDGE, THE GENERAL, THE BISHOP—*turn and leave the port-holes.* THE CHIEF OF POLICE *moves forward to the middle of the stage.*)

THE CHIEF OF POLICE: Well played. He thought he had me. (*He places his hand on his fly, very visibly feels his balls and, reassured, heaves a sigh.*) Mine are here. So which of us is washed up? He or I? Though my image be castrated in every brothel in the world, I remain intact. Intact, gentlemen. (*A pause.*) That plumber didn't know how to handle his role, that was all. (*He calls out, joyfully*) Irma! Irma! . . . Where is she? It's not her job to dress wounds.

THE QUEEN: (*entering*) George! The vestibule . . . the rugs are covered with blood . . . the vestibule's full of clients. . . . We're wiping up as best we can. . . . Carmen doesn't know where to put them. . . .

THE ENVOY: (*bowing to the Chief of Police*) Nice work.

THE CHIEF OF POLICE: An image of me will be perpetuated in secret. Mutilated? (*He shrugs his shoulders.*) Yet a low Mass will be said to my glory. Notify the kitchens! Have them send me enough grub for two thousand years.

THE QUEEN: What about me? George, *I'm* alive!

THE CHIEF OF POLICE: (*without hearing her*) So. . . . I'm. . . . Where? Here, or . . . a thousand times there? (*He points to the tomb.*) Now I can be kind . . . and pious . . . and just. . . . Did you see? Did you see me? There, just before, larger than large, stronger than strong, deader than dead? So I've nothing more to do with you.

THE QUEEN: George! But I still love you!

THE CHIEF OF POLICE: (*moving towards the tomb*) I've won the right to go and sit and wait for two thousand years. (*To the photographers*) You! Watch me live, and die. For posterity: shoot! (*Three almost simultaneous flashes.*) I've won! (*He walks backwards into the tomb, very slowly, while* THE THREE PHOTOGRAPHERS *casually leave by the left wing, with their cameras slung over their backs. They wave before disappearing.*)

THE QUEEN: But it was I who did everything, who organized everything. . . . Stay. . . . What will. . . .

(*Suddenly a burst of machine-gun fire.*)

You hear!

THE CHIEF OF POLICE: (*with a burst of laughter*) Think of me!

(THE JUDGE *and* THE GENERAL *rush forward to stop him, but the doors start closing as the* THE CHIEF OF POLICE *descends the first steps. A second burst of machine-gun fire.*)

THE JUDGE: (*clinging to the door*) Don't leave us alone!

THE GENERAL: (*gloomily*) That carriage again!

THE ENVOY: (*to the Judge*) Be careful, you'll get your fingers caught.

(*The door has definitely closed. The characters remain bewildered for a moment. A third burst of machine-gun fire.*)

THE QUEEN: Gentlemen, you are free.

THE BISHOP: But . . . in the middle of the night?

THE QUEEN: (*interrupting him*) You'll leave by the narrow door that leads into the alley. There's a car waiting for you.

(*She nods courteously. The Three Figures exeunt right. A fourth burst of machine-gun fire.*)

Who is it? . . . Our side? . . . Or rebels? . . . Or? . . .

THE ENVOY: Someone dreaming, Madame. . . .

(THE QUEEN *goes to various parts of the room and presses buttons. Each time, a light goes out.*)

THE QUEEN: (*continuing to extinguish lights*). . . . Irma. . . . Call me Mme Irma and go home. Good night, sir.

THE ENVOY: Good night, Mme Irma.

(THE ENVOY *exits.*)

IRMA: (*alone, and continuing to extinguish lights*) It took so much light . . . two pounds' worth of electricity a day! Thirty-eight studios! Every one of them gilded, and all of them rigged with machinery so as to be able to fit into and combine with each other. . . . And all these performances so that I can remain alone, mistress and assistant mistress of this house and of myself. (*She pushes in a button, then pushes it out again.*) Oh no, that's the tomb. He needs light, for two thousand years! . . . and food for two thousand years. . . . (*She shrugs her shoulders.*) Oh well, everything's in working order, and dishes have been prepared. Glory means descending into the grave with tons of victuals! . . . (*She calls out, facing the wings*) Carmen? Carmen? . . . Bolt the doors, my dear, and put the furniture-covers on. . . . (*She continues extinguishing.*) In a little while, I'll have to start all over again . . . put all the lights on again . . . dress up. . . . (*A cock crows.*) Dress up . . . ah, the disguises! Distribute roles again . . . assume my own. . . . (*She stops in the middle of the stage, facing the audience.*) . . . Prepare yours . . . judges, generals, bishops, chamberlains, rebels who allow the revolt to congeal, I'm going to prepare my costumes and studios for tomorrow. . . . You must now go home, where everything—you can be quite sure—will be falser than here. . . . You must go now. You'll leave by the right, through the alley. . . . (*She extinguishes the last light.*) It's morning already.

(*A burst of machine-gun fire.*)

Jean Genet

FROM Letters to Roger
Blin
(1966)

TRANSLATED BY
RICHARD SEAVER

*Daily Notes*

*JEAN Genet wrote a series of notes and letters to the stage director Roger Blin during the Paris production of his play* The Screens; *some of his comments, however, have more general application to the special intensity and plangency of Genet's theater.*

Italian-style theater is not long for this world. I know nothing of its history, how it began nor why it culminated in a kind of well with dress circles, ground-floor boxes, first-tier boxes and top galleries (what names!),° but I feel it dying together with the society which came to see itself mirrored on-stage. This fulfillment corresponded to a fundamental immorality: for the poultry of the top galleries, the "house"—dress circle, orchestra, boxes—was an initial spectacle, which in essence formed a screen—or a prism—which their gaze had to pass through before perceiving the spectacle on-stage. The top galleries saw and heard, as it were, through the screen made up of the privileged public of the orchestra and box seats.

■ ■ ■

The spectators in the orchestra and boxes knew they were being looked at—greedily—by the public in the top galleries. Knowing themselves to be an entertainment before the show, they acted as an entertainment must: in order to be seen.

On one side as on the other—I mean upstairs as well as down—the performance on-stage never reached the public in a completely pure state.

And I am not forgetting the velvet or crystal, or the gold leaf whose purpose is to remind the privileged public that the theater is their domain, and that the play is demeaned and degraded proportionately as their distance from the main floor and the carpeting increases.

■ ■ ■

You will perhaps have theaters with ten thousand seats, probably resembling the Greek theaters, in which the public will be discreet and seated at random or according to their individual agility or on-the-spot ruse, not according to their rank or wealth. The play on-stage will address itself, therefore, to what is most naked and pure in the members of the audience. Whether the public's apparel is gaudy or sober, bejeweled or otherwise bedecked, it will in no way affect the integrity of the play being performed on-stage. On the contrary, it would be a good idea if a kind of madness, an effrontery, impelled the public to rig itself out in strange attire when it went to the theater—providing of course that it wore nothing blinding: brooches of undue length, swords, canes, mountain climber's pickaxes, lighted lamps in hats, tame magpies . . . or nothing deafening: the din of a drum-and-bugle call, transistor radios, firecrackers, etc., but that each person deck himself out as he wished in order to be receptive to the maximum degree to the play being performed on stage: the audience has the right to be mad. The more serious the play, the greater may be the audience's need to affront it adorned, and even masked.

One ought to be able to enter and leave during the performance, without bothering anyone. And remain standing too, and even walk up to the stage if one feels like it, the way one approaches a painting, or steps back away from it. Thus if *The Screens* were being performed at this period, a certain space would have to be reserved directly on-stage for a certain number of walk-ons—silent and motionless—who would be part of the audience, having donned costumes designed by the costume designer—the notables on one side of the stage, and the common-law convicts on the other, masked and in chains, guarded by armed gendarmes.

■ ■ ■

There should be added to the text of *The Screens* something approximating a score. This is within the realm of possibility. The director, taking into account the various tonal qualities of the

---

°Much of the flavor of the names of various kinds of theater seats is lost in translation. For example, the ground-floor boxes are called *baignoires* in French, which is also the word for "bathtub"; the galleries are called *poulaillers*, which also means "hen house" or "hen roost."—*Tr.*

different actors' voices, will have to invent a manner of speaking which ranges from murmurs to shouts. Sentences, a tempest of sentences, must be delivered like so many howls, others will be warbles, still others will be delivered in a normal conversational tone.

■ ■ ■

Each scene, and each section within a scene, must be perfected and played as rigorously and with as much discipline as if it were a short play, complete in itself. Without any smudges. And without there being the slightest suggestion that another scene, or section within a scene, is to follow those that have gone before.

■ ■ ■

Of course I am completely ignorant when it comes to the theater in general, but I do know enough about my own.

Whenever a judge passes a sentence, let us demand that he be prepared other than by knowledge of the criminal code. Vigils, fasting, prayer, an attempted suicide or murder, could all contribute to making the sentence he is going to pass an event so momentous—I mean a poetic event—that he, the judge, having rendered it, will be completely exhausted, on the verge of rendering his soul either unto death or madness. Bloodless, voiceless, he would take two or three years to recover. This is a great deal to ask of a judge. But what about us? We are still a long way from the poetic act. All of us—you, me, the actors—must steep ourselves for a long time in the shadows, we must work until we are utterly worn out, so that one evening we come to the brink of the final act. And we must make many mistakes, and profit from them. The fact is that we still have a long way to go, and for this play neither madness nor death seems to me to be the fairest sanction. And yet it is these twin goddesses that we must move in order that they may turn their attention to us. No, we are in no danger of death, nor has poetry come the way it should.

If I wanted what you had promised me, bright lights, it was so that each actor would *finish* his gestures or lines brilliantly and would rival the brightest of lights. I also wanted the house lights to be on: with the collective ass of the audience scrunched down in its seats, its immobility imposed by the acting—that was enough to make a distinction between the stage and that house, but the lights are necessary for complicity to be established. A poetic act, not a spectacle, even were it beautiful in the normal sense of the term, would have taken place. . . .

In another letter, which you have probably lost, I told you that my books, like my plays, were written against myself. You know what I mean. Among other things, this: the soldier scenes are meant to exalt—and I mean *exalt*—the Army's prime, its chief, virtue: stupidity. Real paratroopers have given me a hard-on; I've never had an erection over stage paratroopers. And if I do not succeed through the text itself to expose myself, then you have to help me. Against myself, against ourselves, whenever these performances put us on God knows what decent side into which poetry fails to penetrate.

We have to consider that we have failed. Our fault lies in having lost our nerve, collapsing like a bagpipe which deflates as it emits a few sounds that we would like to think are attractive, and in our yielding to the illusion that the finished melody was well worth the loss of precious air. By small, successive stages we have slowly but surely turned the play into something insipid. Successive stages in order to make certain we would have a success which, to my mind, is in the final analysis a failure.

Jacques Maglia said to me: "Everything takes place as though the two of you, Blin and yourself, were proud as peacocks. Instead of a play which should stagger you when it is over, its seeming success reassures you."

I surrendered on several occasions to Barrault's objections, and to your own. Your knowledge of the theater threatens to make you avoid any errors of taste; my ignorance of this same profession should have led me toward them.

I am not maintaining that the *written* text of the play [*The Screens*] is of any great value, but I can assure you that I did not, for example, look down on any of my characters—be it Sir Harold, the Gendarme, or the Paratroopers. You can be sure that I have never tried to "understand" them, but, having created them, on paper and for the stage, I do not want to deny them. What binds me to them is something other than irony or contempt. They also help to shape me. I have never copied life—an event or a man, the Algerian War or colonialists—but life has, quite naturally, caused various images to come to life within me, or has illuminated them if they were already there—images which I have translated either by a character or an act. Pascal Monod, one of the students of the military, said to me after the last performance that the Army is not as much of a caricature as I have made it out. I did not have time then to answer him that what we are dealing with here is a dream army, a dream roughly sketched out on paper and, poorly or well, brought to fruition on a stage, which might be wooden and whose flooring creaks beneath one's footsteps.

Let us come back to the lighting. I'm sure you clearly understand that this way of playing with darkness, semi-darkness, and light is a recourse, delightful and chilly, which gives the spectator the time to go into raptures or to regain his composure. I wanted the ice floe, the promised land which blinds and is unremitting. What ever happened to that white, metallic material that Acquart once talked to us about and which, according to my instructions, should have constituted the very material wherein the actors moved and had their being? Will it be possible for you to use this mysterious, Mallarméan, and allegorical material, even if only for a single evening's performance?

People don't go off to wage war if they don't love it, if they don't feel themselves made for—or, if you wish, destined for—combat. The same holds true for the theater. The actors, too much at ease on-stage, relax between their brief appearances, or, rather, crowd against one another around the blaring television in the actors' dressing room. Certain canons read their breviaries at vespers while their minds are a thousand miles away preoccupied with God knows what, but twenty-year-old actors should not be canons. Even when she is off-stage, Maria Casarès remains in the wings, attentive or exhausted, but present: the others get the hell away as fast as they can. They could at least have the courtesy to listen to what their fellow actors are saying on-stage. By dialing some buttons they tune out the voices coming from the stage, bearing with them bravura or weariness, failure or cleverness, and they are watching television. They are listening to it. Instead of leaving the world, they bring it back, as though the stage were a place of perdition. Young actors are remarkable in that they are no sooner on-stage than they do all in their power to conceal themselves, to dissolve into a grisaille of words and movements. Can't you tell them that to glitter too brightly in their daily lives off-stage prevents a long contained brilliance from exploding and illuminating the stage? Even if they have only one line to deliver, one gesture to make, that line and gesture ought to contain whatever luminous quality each actor bears within himself which has been waiting for a long time for this magic moment: to be on-stage. Surely every actor must be encouraged to be—were it only for the duration of a single appearance, lightning-like and true—of such beauty that his disappearance into the wings will literally break the audience's heart. And that the public, though it remains under the spell of what succeeds his exit, will still miss him after he is gone.

Finally, if I am so insistent about the bright lights, both the stage and house lights, it is because I should in some way like both actors and audience to be caught up in the same illumination, and for there to be no place for them to hide, or even half-hide.

These are the few notes, my dear Roger, that the production of *The Screens* and my friendship for you compelled me to make.

J. G.

# Wole Soyinka

Wole Soyinka was born in 1934 in Abeokuta, Nigeria. Educated at Government College in Ibadan, Soyinka then studied at Leeds University in England, where he worked with the notable Shakespearean scholar and actor G. Wilson Knight and took his B. A. in English in 1957. He remained in England working as Play Reader for the Royal Court Theater, before returning to Nigeria in 1959, where his first play, *The Lion and the Jewel* (1959) was produced. In the course of the next decade, Soyinka wrote an important body of dramatic work, including the plays *The Invention* (1959), *A Dance of the Forests* (1960), *The Trials of Brother Jero* (1960), *Camwood on the Leaves* (radio play, 1960), *The Strong Breed* (1964), *Kongi's Harvest* (1964), and *The Road* (1965). He also taught at the universities of Ibadan, Ife, and Lagos, and founded two important theaters, the Orisun Theater and the 1960 Masks Theater. Much of Soyinka's work is critical of authoritarian politics; he was arrested in 1967 and held as a political prisoner until 1969. Soyinka's memoirs of imprisonment, *The Man Died*, were published in 1972 and were cited for excellence by Amnesty International. In the 1970s, Soyinka continued to write plays examining the tensions of tribal life in modern Africa: *Madmen and Specialists* (1970) and *Death and the King's Horseman* (1976). He also wrote plays more directly examining contemporary African politics: his rewriting of Brecht's *Threepenny Opera* as *Opera Wonyosi* (1977) and *A Play of Giants* (1985). He also wrote an adaptation of Euripides' *Bacchae* (1973), placing the Greek narrative in a more explicitly tribal and ritualistic setting. Soyinka was awarded the Nobel Prize in 1986, the first African writer to receive the prize for literature.

## The Lion and the Jewel (1959)

Soyinka's first play, *The Lion and the Jewel* remains one of his most controversial, largely because of its representation of traditional African culture. Several critics have read the play as a heavily romanticized portrait of village life, in which "traditional" culture—emblematized in the play by Baroka—neatly and unrealistically triumphs over the forces of "westernization," represented in the play by the foppish schoolmaster Lakunle. When Sidi finally "chooses" Baroka at the end of the play, this argument runs, Soyinka seems to validate a romantic vision of traditional culture that oddly authorizes the West's racist attitudes toward Africa: Soyinka's village is an eroticized "other," inhabiting some ideal and unreal geography beyond the imperial forces of the West.

This reading, however, oversimplifies Soyinka's representation of cultural contact in several ways. For *The Lion and the Jewel* is a play about the interinvolvement of Europe and Africa, an involvement that has irrevocably changed "traditional" culture. Lakunle is, plainly, a "mimic man," an African whose efforts to identify with the customs and behaviors of Europe inevitably inscribe his behavior as imitative, inauthentic. But Lakunle is not the only instance of the West's influence on the life of the village. For the plot is impelled by the arrival of a glossy magazine, containing several vivid photographs of the "village belle," Sidi. Much as Lakunle offers one instance of the West's racist image of Africa—an "other" who will never succeed in becoming fully "one of 'us'"—so the photograph offers a different emblem of the West's attitude toward Africa: the eroticized image of an exotic "other," feminine, inviting, awaiting exploitation. In both cases, Western values are dominant and have a distorting effect on village life. The photo-spread, after all, places Sidi at the center and marginalizes Baroka in a small picture, off in the corner near the village latrines.

Rather than offering a romantic image of traditional village life, Soyinka's play offers a much more sophisticated, subtle critique of the relations of power that connect contemporary global culture. For the play is more directly about the ways in which the West's representation of "Africa"—as behavior, as idea, as fantasy—invade the village and force a kind of cultural negotiation. Indeed, the Bale has a keen sense of the impossibility of escaping Western culture, and his final seduction of Sidi both exploits the magazine photograph and depends on Western technology: the printing press.

In *The Lion and the Jewel*, the relations between cultures are staged as fluid, contestatory, not fixed and static; this fact of cross-cultural negotiation emerges even more sharply in performance. It is not surprising that Soyinka paints Lakunle as a comic character, but we might well ask what the force of this comedy is when the play is presented to a Western audience. How *we*, whoever *we* are, read Lakunle will in large measure determine the "politics" of the production; think how differently this play would *mean* to, for instance, a university audience in Ibadan; a largely white, Oxbridge-educated audience at a London theater; a racially mixed American audience, where Lakunle's "imitation"—and the varied responses of the audience—might turn the theater itself into a kind of laboratory, dramatizing a variety of attitudes toward "acting white" in a white-dominated culture.

# —The Lion and the Jewel—
## Wole Soyinka

## —CHARACTERS—

SIDI *the village belle*

LAKUNLE *school teacher*

BAROKA *the "Bale" of Ilujinle*

SADIKU *his head wife*

THE FAVOURITE

VILLAGE GIRLS

A WRESTLER

A SURVEYOR

SCHOOLBOYS

ATTENDANTS ON THE "BALE"

*Musicians, Dancers, Mummers,*

*Prisoners, Traders, the Village*

MORNING

*A clearing on the edge of the market, dominated by an immense odan tree. It is the village centre. The wall of the bush school flanks the stage on the right, and a rude window opens on to the stage from the wall. There is a chant of the "Arithmetic Times" issuing from this window. It begins a short while before the action begins. Sidi enters from left, carrying a small pail of water on her head. She is a slim girl with plaited hair. A true village belle. She balances the pail on her head with accustomed ease. Around her is wrapped the familiar broad cloth which is folded just above her breasts, leaving the shoulders bare.*

*Almost as soon as she appears on the stage, the schoolmaster's face also appears at the window. (The chanting continues— "Three times two are six," "Three times three are nine," etc.) The teacher, Lakunle, disappears. He is replaced by two of his pupils, aged roughly eleven, who make a buzzing noise at Sidi, repeatedly clapping their hands across the mouth. Lakunle now reappears below the window and makes for Sidi, stopping only to give the boys admonitory whacks on the head before they can duck. They vanish with a howl and he shuts the window on them. The chanting dies away. The schoolmaster is nearly twenty-three. He is dressed in an old-style English suit, threadbare but not ragged, clean but not ironed, obviously a size or two too small. His tie is done in a very small knot, disappearing beneath a shiny black waistcoat. He wears twenty-three-inch-bottom trousers, and blanco-white tennis shoes.*

LAKUNLE: Let me take it.

SIDI: No.

LAKUNLE: Let me. (*Seizes the pail. Some water spills on him.*)

SIDI: (*delighted.*) There. Wet for your pains.
    Have you no shame?

LAKUNLE: That is what the stewpot said to the fire.
    Have you no shame—at your age
    Licking my bottom? But she was tickled
    Just the same.

10 SIDI: The school teacher is full of stories
    This morning. And now, if the lesson
    Is over, may I have the pail?

LAKUNLE: No. I have told you not to carry loads
    On your head. But you are as stubborn

As an illiterate goat. It is bad for the spine.
    And it shortens your neck, so that very soon
    You will have no neck at all. Do you wish to look
    Squashed like my pupils' drawings?

SIDI: Why should that worry me? Haven't you sworn
    That my looks do not affect your love?     20
    Yesterday, dragging your knees in the dust
    You said, Sidi, if you were crooked or fat,
    And your skin was scaly like a . . .

LAKUNLE: Stop!

SIDI: I only repeat what you said.

LAKUNLE: Yes, and I will stand by every word I spoke.
    But must you throw away your neck on that account?
    Sidi, it is so unwomanly. Only spiders
    Carry loads the way you do.

SIDI: (*huffily, exposing the neck to advantage*)     30
    Well, it is my neck, not your spider.

LAKUNLE: (*looks, and gets suddenly agitated*)
    And look at that! Look, look at that!
    (*Makes a general sweep in the direction of her breasts.*)
    Who was it talked of shame just now?
    How often must I tell you, Sidi, that
    A grown-up girl must cover up her . . .
    Her . . . shoulders? I can see quite . . . quite
    A good portion of—that! And so I imagine
    Can every man in the village. Idlers     40
    All of them, good-for-nothing shameless men
    Casting their lustful eyes where
    They have no business. . . .

SIDI: Are you at that again? Why, I've done the fold
    So high and so tight, I can hardly breathe.
    And all because you keep at me so much.
    I have to leave my arms so I can use them . . .
    Or don't you know that?

LAKUNLE: You could wear something.
    Most modest women do. But you, no.     50
    You must run about naked in the streets.
    Does it not worry you . . . the bad names,
    The lewd jokes, the tongue-licking noises
    Which girls, uncovered like you,
    Draw after them?

SIDI: This is too much. Is it you, Lakunle,
    Telling me that I make myself common talk?
    When the whole world knows of the madman
    Of Ilujinle, who calls himself a teacher!
    Is it Sidi who makes the men choke     60
    In their cups, or you, with your big loud words
    And no meaning? You and your ragged books
    Dragging your feet to every threshold
    And rushing them out again as curses
    Greet you instead of welcome. Is it Sidi
    They call a fool—even the children—

Or you with your fine airs and little sense!

LAKUNLE: *(first indignant, then recovers composure.)*
For that, what is a jewel to pigs?

70   If now I am misunderstood by you
And your race of savages, I rise above taunts
And remain unruffled.

  SIDI: *(furious, shakes both fists at him)*
O . . . oh, you make me want to pulp your brain.

LAKUNLE: *(retreats a little, but puts her aside with a very lofty
gesture)*
A natural feeling, arising out of envy;
For, as a woman, you have a smaller brain
Than mine.

80 SIDI: *(madder still)*
Again! I'd like to know
Just what gives you these thoughts
Of manly conceit.

LAKUNLE: *(very, very patronizing)*
No, no. I have fallen for that trick before.
You can no longer draw me into arguments
Which go above your head.

  SIDI: *(can't find the right words, chokes back)*
Give me the pail now. And if you ever dare

90   To stop me in the streets again . . .

  LAKUNLE: Now, now, Sidi . . .

  SIDI: Give it or I'll . . .

LAKUNLE: *(holds on to her)*
Please, don't be angry with me.
I didn't mean you in particular.
And anyway, it isn't what I say.
The scientists have proved it. It's in my books.
Women have a smaller brain than men
That's why they are called the weaker sex.

100 SIDI: *(throws him off)*
The weaker sex, is it?
Is it a weaker breed who pounds the yam
Or bends all day to plant the millet
With a child strapped to her back?

LAKUNLE: That is all part of what I say.
But don't you worry. In a year or two
You will have machines which will do
Your pounding, which will grind your pepper
Without it getting in your eyes.

110 SIDI: O-oh. You really mean to turn
The whole world upside down.

LAKUNLE: The world? Oh, that. Well, maybe later.
Charity, they say, begins at home.
For now, it is this village I shall turn
Inside out. Beginning with that crafty rogue,
Your past master of self-indulgence—Baroka.

SIDI: Are you still on about the Bale?
What has he done to you?

LAKUNLE: He'll find out. Soon enough, I'll let him know.

120 SIDI: These thoughts of future wonders—do you buy them
Or merely go mad and dream of them?

LAKUNLE: A prophet has honour except
In his own home. Wise men have been called mad
Before me and after, many more shall be
So abused. But to answer you, the measure
Is not entirely of my own coinage.

What I boast is known in Lagos, that city
Of magic, in Badagry where Saro women bathe
In gold, even in smaller towns less than
Twelve miles from here. . . .                                    130

SIDI: Well go there. Go to these places where
Women would understand you
If you told them of your plans with which
You oppress me daily. Do you not know
What name they give you here?
Have you lost shame completely that jeers
Pass you over.

LAKUNLE: No. I have told you no. Shame belongs
Only to the ignorant.

SIDI: Well, I am going.                                          140
Shall I take the pail or not?

LAKUNLE: Not till you swear to marry me.

*(Takes her hand, instantly soulful.)*

Sidi, a man must prepare to fight alone.
But it helps if he has a woman
To stand by him, a woman who . . .
Can understand . . . like you.

SIDI: I do?

LAKUNLE: Sidi, my love will open your mind
Like the chaste leaf in the morning, when
The sun first touches it.                                        150

SIDI: If you start that I will run away.
I had enough of that nonsense yesterday.

LAKUNLE: Nonsense? Nonsense? Do you hear?
Does anybody listen? Can the stones
Bear to listen to this? Do you call it
Nonsense that I poured the waters of my soul
To wash your feet?

SIDI: You did what!

LAKUNLE: Wasted! Wasted! Sidi, my heart
Bursts into flowers with my love.                                160
But you, you and the dead of this village
Trample it with feet of ignorance.

SIDI: *(shakes her head in bafflement)*
If the snail finds splinters in his shell
He changes house. Why do you stay?

LAKUNLE: Faith. Because I have faith.
Oh Sidi, vow to me your own undying love
And I will scorn the jibes of these bush minds
Who know no better. Swear, Sidi,
Swear you will be my wife and I will                             170
Stand against earth, heaven, and the nine
Hells . . .

SIDI: Now there you go again.
One little thing
And you must chirrup like a cockatoo.
You talk and talk and deafen me
With words which always sound the same
And make no meaning.
I've told you, and I say it again
I shall marry you today, next week                               180
Or any day you name.
But my bride-price must first be paid.
Aha, now you turn away.
But I tell you, Lakunle, I must have

The full bride-price. Will you make me
A laughing-stock? Well, do as you please.
But Sidi will not make herself
A cheap bowl for the village spit.
LAKUNLE: On my head let fall their scorn.
190 SIDI: They will say I was no virgin
That I was forced to sell my shame
And marry you without a price.
LAKUNLE: A savage custom, barbaric, out-dated,
Rejected, denounced, accursed,
Excommunicated, archaic, degrading,
Humiliating, unspeakable, redundant.
Retrogressive, remarkable, unpalatable.
SIDI: Is the bag empty? Why did you stop?
LAKUNLE: I own only the Shorter Companion
200 Dictionary, but I have ordered
The Longer One—you wait!
SIDI: Just pay the price.
LAKUNLE: (with a sudden shout)
An ignoble custom, infamous, ignominious
Shaming our heritage before the world.
Sidi, I do not seek a wife
To fetch and carry,
To cook and scrub,
To bring forth children by the gross. . . .
210 SIDI: Heaven forgive you! Do you now scorn
Child-bearing in a wife?
LAKUNLE: Of course I do not. I only mean . . .
Oh Sidi, I want to wed
Because I love,
I seek a life-companion . . .

(Pulpit-declamatory.)

"And the man shall take the woman
And the two shall be together
As one flesh."
Sidi, I seek a friend in need.
220 An equal partner in my race of life.
SIDI: (attentive no more. Deeply engrossed in counting the
beads on her neck.)
Then pay the price.
LAKUNLE: Ignorant girl, can you not understand?
To pay the price would be
To buy a heifer off the market stall.
You'd be my chattel, my mere property.
No, Sidi! (Very tenderly.)
When we are wed, you shall not walk or sit
230 Tethered, as it were, to my dirtied heels.
Together we shall sit at table
—Not on the floor—and eat,
Not with fingers, but with knives
And forks, and breakable plates
Like civilized beings.
I will not have you wait on me
Till I have dined my fill.
No wife of mine, no lawful wedded wife
Shall eat the leavings off my plate—
240 That is for the children.
I want to walk beside you in the street,
Side by side and arm in arm

Just like the Lagos couples I have seen
High-heeled shoes for the lady, red paint
On her lips. And her hair is stretched
Like a magazine photo. I will teach you
The waltz and we'll both learn the foxtrot
And we'll spend the week-end in night clubs at Ibadan.
Oh I must show you the grandeur of towns
We'll live there if you like or merely pay visits.     250
So choose. Be a modern wife, look me in the eye
And give me a little kiss—like this.

(Kisses her.)

SIDI: (backs away.)
No, don't! I tell you I dislike
This strange unhealthy mouthing you perform.
Every time, your action deceives me
Making me think that you merely wish
To whisper something in my ear.
Then comes this licking of my lips with yours.
It's so unclean. And then,     260
The sound you make—"Pyout!"
Are you being rude to me?
LAKUNLE: (wearily) It's never any use.
Bush girl you are, bush girl you'll always be;
Uncivilized and primitive—bush girl!
I kissed you as all educated men—
And Christians—kiss their wives.
It is the way of civilized romance.
SIDI: (lightly.) A way you mean, to avoid
Payment of lawful bride-price     270
A cheating way, mean and miserly.
LAKUNLE: (violently) It is not.

(Sidi bursts out laughing. Lakunle changes his tone to a soulful one, both eyes dreamily shut.)

Romance is the sweetening of the soul
With fragrance offered by the stricken heart.
SIDI: (looks at him in wonder for a while.)
Away with you. The village says you're mad,
And I begin to understand.
I wonder that they let you run the school.
You and your talk. You'll ruin your pupils too
And then they'll utter madness just like you.     280

(Noise offstage.)

There are people coming
Give me the bucket or they'll jeer.

(Enter a crowd of youths and drummers, the girls being in various stages of excitement.)

FIRST GIRL: Sidi, he has returned. He came back just as he said
he would.
SIDI: Who has?
FIRST GIRL: The stranger. The man from the outside world.
The clown who fell in the river for you.

(They all burst out laughing.)

SIDI: The one who rode on the devil's own horse?
SECOND GIRL: Yes, the same. The stranger with the one-
eyed box.     290

*(She demonstrates the action of a camera amidst admiring titters.)*

THIRD GIRL: And he brought his new horse right into the village square this time. This one has only two feet. You should have seen him. B-r-r-r-r.

*(Runs round the platform driving an imaginary motor-bike.)*

SIDI: And has he brought . . . ?

FIRST GIRL: The images? He brought them all. There was hardly any part of the village which does not show in the book.

*(Clicks the imaginary shutter.)*

SIDI: The book? Did you see the book?
 Had he the precious book
300  That would bestow upon me
 Beauty beyond the dreams of a goddess?
 For so he said.
 The book which would announce
 This beauty to the world—
 Have you seen it?

THIRD GIRL: Yes, yes, he did. But the Bale is still feasting his eyes on the images. Oh, Sidi, he was right. You *are* beautiful. On the cover of the book is an image of you from here *(touches the top of her head.)* to here *(her stomach.)*. And in
310  the middle leaves, from the beginning of one leaf right across to the end of another, is one of you from head to toe. Do you remember it? It was the one for which he made you stretch your arms towards the sun. *(Rapturously.)* Oh, Sidi, you looked as if, at that moment, the sun himself had been your lover. *(They all gasp with pretended shock at this blasphemy and one slaps her playfully on the buttocks.)*

FIRST GIRL: The Bale is jealous, but he pretends to be proud of you. And when this man tells him how famous you are in the capital, he pretends to be pleased, saying how much honour
320  and fame you have brought to the village.

SIDI: *(with amazement)* Is not Baroka's image in the book at all?

SECOND GIRL: *(contemptuous)* Oh yes, it is. But it would have been much better for the Bale if the stranger had omitted him altogether. His image is in a little corner somewhere in the book, and even that corner he shares with one of the village latrines.

SIDI: Is that the truth? Swear! Ask Ogun to
 Strike you dead.
330 GIRL: Ogun strike me dead if I lie.

SIDI: If that is true, then I am more esteemed
 Than Bale Baroka,
 The Lion of Ilujinle.
 This means that I am greater than
 The Fox of the Undergrowth,
 The living god among men . . .

LAKUNLE: *(peevishly.)* And devil among women.

SIDI: Be silent, you.
 You are merely filled with spite.
340 LAKUNLE: I know him what he is. This is
 Divine justice that a mere woman
 Should outstrip him in the end.

SIDI: Be quiet;

 Or I swear I'll never speak to you again.

*(Affects sudden coyness.)*

 In fact, I am not so sure I'll want to wed you now.

LAKUNLE: Sidi!

SIDI: Well, why should I?
 Known as I am to the whole wide world,
 I would demean my worth to wed
 A mere village school teacher. 350

LAKUNLE: *(in agony)* Sidi!

SIDI: And one who is too mean
 To pay the bride-price like a man.

LAKUNLE: Oh, Sidi, don't!

SIDI: *(plunging into an enjoyment of Lakunle's misery.)*
 Well, don't you know?
 Sidi is more important even than the Bale.
 More famous than that panther of the trees.
 He is beneath me now—
 Your fearless rake, the scourge of womanhood! 360
 But now,
 He shares the corner of the leaf
 With the lowest of the low—
 With the dug-out village latrine!
 While I—How many leaves did my own image take?

FIRST GIRL: Two in the middle and . . .

SIDI: No, no. Let the school teacher count!
 How many were there, teacher-man?

LAKUNLE: Three leaves.

SIDI: *(threateningly.)* One leaf for every heart that I shall 370
 break.
 Beware!

*(Leaps suddenly into the air.)*

 Hurray! I'm beautiful!
 Hurray for the wandering stranger!

CROWD: Hurray for the Lagos man!

SIDI: *(wildly excited.)* I know. Let us dance the dance of the lost Traveller.

SHOUTS: Yes, let's.

SIDI: Who will dance the devil-horse?
 You, you, you, and you. 380

*(The four girls fall out.)*

 A python. Who will dance the snake?
 Ha ha! Your eyes are shifty and your ways are sly.

*(The selected youth is pushed out amidst jeers.)*

 The stranger. We've got to have the being
 From the mad outer world. . . . You there,
 No, you have never felt the surge
 Of burning liquor in your milky veins.
 Who can we pick that knows the walk of drunks?
 You? . . . No, the thought itself
 Would knock you out as sure as wine. . . . Ah!

*(Turns round slowly to where Lakunle is standing with a kindly, fatherly smile for the children at play.)*

 Come on book-worm, you'll play his part. 390

LAKUNLE: No, no. I've never been drunk in all my life.

SIDI: We know. But your father drank so much,

He must have drunk your share, and that
Of his great grandsons.

LAKUNLE: (*tries to escape.*) I won't take part.

SIDI: You must.

LAKUNLE: I cannot stay. It's nearly time to take
Primary four in Geography.

SIDI: (*goes over to the window and throws it open.*)

400     Did you think your pupils would remain in school
Now that the stranger has returned?
The village is on holiday, you fool.

LAKUNLE: (*as they drag him towards the platform.*)
No, no. I won't. This foolery bores me.
It is a game of idiots. I have work of more importance.

SIDI: (*bending down over Lakunle who has been seated
forcibly on the platform*)
You are dressed like him
You look like him

410     You speak his tongue
You think like him
You're just as clumsy
In your Lagos ways—
You'll do for him!

(*This chant is taken up by all and they begin to dance round
Lakunle, speaking the words in a fast rhythm. The drummers
join in after the first time, keeping up a steady beat as the others whirl round their victim. They go faster and faster and
chant faster and faster with each round. By the sixth or seventh, Lakunle has obviously had enough.*)

LAKUNLE: (*raising his voice above the din.*) All right! I'll do it.
Come now, let's get it over with.

(*A terrific shout and a clap of drums. Lakunle enters into the
spirit of the dance with enthusiasm. He takes over from Sidi,
stations his cast all over the stage as the jungle, leaves the right
topstage clear for the four girls who are to dance the motor-
car. A mime follows of the visitor's entry into Ilujinle, and his
short stay among the villagers. The four girls crouch on the
floor, as four wheels of a car. Lakunle directs their spacing,
then takes his place in the middle, and sits on air. He alone does
not dance. He does realistic miming. Soft throbbing drums,
gradually swelling in volume, and the four "wheels" begin to
rotate the upper halves of their bodies in perpendicular circles.
Lakunle clowning the driving motions, obviously enjoying this
fully. The drums gain tempo, faster, faster, faster. A sudden
crash of drums and the girls quiver and dance the stall. Another effort at rhythm fails, and the stalling wheels' give a corresponding shudder, finally, and let their faces fall on to their
laps. Lakunle tampers with a number of controls, climbs out of
the car and looks underneath it. His lips indicate that he is
swearing violently.
Examines the wheels, pressing them to test the pressure, betrays the devil in him by seizing his chance to pinch the girls'
bottoms. One yells and bites him on the ankle. He climbs hurriedly back into the car, makes a final attempt to re-start it,
gives it up and decides to abandon it. Picks up his camera and
his helmet, pockets a flask of whisky from which he takes a
swig, before beginning the trek. The drums resume beating, a
different, darker tone and rhythm, varying with the journey.
Full use of "gangan" and "iya ilu." The "trees" perform a*
subdued and unobtrusive dance on the same spot. Details as a
snake slithering out of the branches and poising over Lakunle's
head when he leans against a tree for a rest. He flees, restoring
his nerves shortly after by a swig. A monkey drops suddenly in
his path and gibbers at him before scampering off. A roar
comes from somewhere, etc. His nerves go rapidly and he re-
cuperates himself by copious draughts. He is soon tipsy, battles
violently with the undergrowth and curses silently as he swats
the flies off his tortured body.*
Suddenly, from somewhere in the bush comes the sound of a
girl singing. The Traveller shakes his head but the sound persists. Convinced he is suffering from sun-stroke, he drinks
again. His last drop, so he tosses the bottle in the direction of
the sound, only to be rewarded by a splash, a scream and a torrent of abuse, and finally, silence again. He tip-toes, clears
away the obstructing growth, blinks hard, and rubs his eyes.
Whatever he has seen still remains. He whistles softly, un-
hitches his camera, and begins to jockey himself into a good position for a take. Backwards and forwards, and his eyes are so
closely glued to the lens that he puts forward a careless foot
and disappears completely. There is a loud splash and the invisible singer alters her next tone to a sustained scream. Quickened rhythm and shortly afterwards, amidst sounds of
splashes, Sidi appears on the stage, with a piece of cloth only
partially covering her.*
Lakunle follows a little later, more slowly, trying to wring out
the water from his clothes. He has lost all his appendages except the camera. Sidi has run right across the stage, and returns a short while later, accompanied by the villagers. The
same cast has disappeared and re-forms behind Sidi as the villagers. They are in an ugly mood, and in spite of his protests,
haul him off to the town centre, in front of the "odan" tree.
Everything comes to a sudden stop as Baroka the Bale, wiry,
goateed, tougher than his sixty-two years, himself emerges at
this point from behind the tree. All go down, prostrate or
kneeling with the greetings of "Kabiyesi," "Baba" etc. All except Lakunle who begins to sneak off.*)

BAROKA: Akowe. Teacher wa. Misita Lakunle.

(*As the others take up the cry "Misita Lakunle" he is forced to
stop. He returns and bows deeply from the waist.*)

LAKUNLE: A good morning to you sir.

BAROKA: Guru morin guru morin, ngh-hn! That is
All we get from "alakowe." You call at his house     420
Hoping he sends for beer, but all you get is
Guru morin. Will guru morin wet my throat?
Well, well our man of knowledge, I hope you have no
Query for an old man today.

LAKUNLE: No complaints.

BAROKA: And we are not feuding in something
I have forgotten.

LAKUNLE: Feuding sir? I see no cause at all.

BAROKA: Well, the play was much alive until I came.
And now everything stops, and you were leaving     430
Us. After all, I knew the story and I came in
Right on cue. It makes me feel as if I was
Chief Baseje.

LAKUNLE: One hardly thinks the Bale would have the time
For such childish nonsense.

BAROKA: A-ah Mister Lakunle. Without these things you call
    Nonsense, a Bale's life would be pretty dull.
    Well, now that you say I am welcome, shall we
    Resume your play?

(*Turns suddenly to his attendants.*)

440    Seize him!
LAKUNLE: (*momentarily baffled.*) What for? What have I done?
BAROKA: You tried to steal our village maidenhead
    Have you forgotten? If he has, serve him a slap
    To wake his brain.

(*An uplifted arm being proffered, Lakunle quickly recollects
and nods his head vigorously. So the play is back in performance. The villagers gather round threatening, clamouring for
his blood. Lakunle tries bluff, indignation, appeasement in
turn. At a sudden signal from the Bale, they throw him down
prostrate on his face. Only then does the Chief begin to show
him sympathy, appear to understand the stranger's plight, and
pacify the villagers on his behalf. He orders dry clothes for
him, seats him on his right, and orders a feast in his honour.
The stranger springs up every second to take photographs of
the party, but most of the time his attention is fixed on Sidi
dancing with abandon. Eventually he whispers to the Chief,
who nods in consent, and Sidi is sent for. The stranger
arranges Sidi in all sorts of magazine postures and takes innumerable photographs of her. Drinks are pressed upon him; he
refuses at first, eventually tries the local brew with scepticism,
appears to relish it, and drinks profusely. Before long, however, he leaves the party to be sick. They clap him on the back
as he goes out, and two drummers who insist on dancing round
him nearly cause the calamity to happen on the spot. However,
he rushes out with his hand held to his mouth. Lakunle's exit
seems to signify the end of the mime. He returns almost at once
and the others discard their roles.*)

SIDI: (*delightedly.*) What did I say? You played him to the
    bone,
    A court jester would have been the life for you,
    Instead of school.

(*Points contemptuously to the school.*)

BAROKA: And where would the village be, robbed of
450    Such wisdom as Mister Lakunle dispenses
    Daily? Who would tell us where we go wrong?
    Eh, Mister Lakunle?
SIDI: (*hardly listening, still in the full grip of her excitement.*)
    Who comes with me to find the man?
    But Lakunle, you'll have to come and find sense
    In his clipping tongue. You see book-man
    We cannot really do
    Without your head.

(*Lakunle begins to protest, but they crowd him and try to bear
him down. Suddenly he breaks free and takes to his heels with
all the women in full pursuit. Baroka is left sitting by himself—
his wrestler, who accompanied him on his entry, stands a respectful distance away—staring at the flock of women in flight.
From the folds of his "agbada" he brings out his copy of the
magazine and admires the heroine of the publication. Nods
slowly to himself.*)

BAROKA: Yes, yes . . . it is five full months since last
    I took a wife . . . five full months . . .    460

NOON

*A road by the market. Enter Sidi, happily engrossed in the pic-
tures of herself in the magazine. Lakunle follows one or two
paces behind carrying a bundle of firewood which Sidi has set
out to obtain. They are met in the centre by Sadiku, who has
entered from the opposite side. Sadiku is an old woman, with
a shawl over her head.*

SADIKU: Fortune is with me. I was going to your house to see
    you.
SIDI: (*startled out of her occupation.*) What! Oh, it is you,
    Sadiku.
SADIKU: The Lion sent me. He wishes you well.
SIDI: Thank him for me.

(*Then excitedly.*)

    Have you seen these?
    Have you seen these images of me
    Wrought by the man from the capital city?
    Have you felt the gloss? (*Caresses the page.*)    470
    Smoother by far than the parrot's breast.
SADIKU: I have. I saw them as soon as the city man came. . . .
    Sidi, I bring a message from my lord. (*Jerks her head at
    Lakunle.*) Shall we draw aside a little?
SIDI: Him? Pay no more heed to that
    Than you would a eunuch.
SADIKU: Then, in as few words as it takes to tell, Baroka wants
    you for a wife.
LAKUNLE: (*bounds forward, dropping the wood.*)
    What! The greedy dog!    480
    Insatiate camel of a foolish, doting race;
    Is he at his tricks again?
SIDI: Be quiet, 'Kunle. You get so tiresome.
    The message is for me, not you.
LAKUNLE: (*down on his knees at once. Covers Sidi's hands
    with kisses.*)
    My Ruth, my Rachel, Esther, Bathsheba
    Thou sum of fabled perfections
    From Genesis to the Revelations
    Listen not to the voice of this infidel. . . .    490
SIDI: (*snatches her hand away.*)
    Now that's your other game;
    Giving me funny names you pick up
    In your wretched books.
    My name is Sidi. And now, let me be.
    My name is Sidi, and I am beautiful.
    The stranger took my beauty
    And placed it in my hands.
    Here, here it is. I need no funny names
    To tell me of my fame.    500
    Loveliness beyond the jewels of a throne—
    That is what he said.
SADIKU: (*gleefully.*) Well, will you be Baroka's own jewel? Will
    you be his sweetest princess, soothing him on weary nights?
    What answer shall I give my lord?
SIDI: (*wags her finger playfully at the woman.*)

Ha ha. Sadiku of the honey tongue.
Sadiku, head of the Lion's wives.
You'll make no prey of Sidi with your wooing tongue
510   Not this Sidi whose fame has spread to Lagos
And beyond the seas.

*(Lakunle beams with satisfaction and rises.)*

SADIKU: Sidi, have you considered what a life of bliss awaits
you? Baroka swears to take no other wife after you. Do you
know what it is to be the Bale's last wife? I'll tell you. When
he dies—and that should not be long; even the Lion has to
die sometime—well, when he does, it means that you will
have the honour of being the senior wife of the new Bale.
And just think, until Baroka dies, you shall be his favourite.
No living in the outhouses for you, my girl. Your place will
520   always be in the palace; first as the latest bride, and afterwards, as the head of the new harem. . . . It is a rich life, Sidi.
I know. I have been in that position for forty-one years.

SIDI: You waste your breath.
Why did Baroka not request my hand
Before the stranger
Brought his book of images?
Why did the Lion not bestow his gift
Before my face was lauded to the world?
Can you not see? Because he sees my worth
530   Increased and multiplied above his own;
Because he can already hear
The ballad-makers and their songs
In praise of Sidi, the incomparable,
While the Lion is forgotten.
He seeks to have me as his property
Where I must fade beneath his jealous hold.
Ah, Sadiku,
The school-man here has taught me certain things
And my images have taught me all the rest.
540   Baroka merely seeks to raise his manhood
Above my beauty.
He seeks new fame
As the one man who has possessed
The jewel of Ilujinle!

SADIKU: *(shocked, bewildered, incapable of making any sense
of Sidi's words.)* But Sidi, are you well? Such nonsense
never passed your lips before. Did you not sound strange,
even in your own hearing? *(Rushes suddenly at Lakunle.)* Is
this your doing, you popinjay? Have you driven the poor girl
550   mad at last? Such rubbish . . . I will beat your head for this!

LAKUNLE: *(retreating in panic.)* Keep away from me, old hag.

SIDI: Sadiku, let him be.
Tell your lord that I can read his mind,
That I will none of him.
Look—judge for yourself.

*(Opens the magazine and points out the pictures.)*

He's old. I never knew till now,
He was that old . . .

*(During the rest of her speech, Sidi runs her hand over the sur-
face of the relevant part of the photographs, tracing the
contours with her fingers.)*

. . . To think I took

No notice of my velvet skin.
How smooth it is!   560
And no man ever thought
To praise the fulness of my breasts. . . .

LAKUNLE: *(laden with guilt and full of apology.)*
Well, Sidi, I did think . . .
But somehow it was not the proper thing.

SIDI: *(ignores the interruption.)*
See I hold them to the warm caress

*(Unconsciously pushes out her chest.)*

Of a desire-filled sun.

*(Smiles mischievously.)*

There's a deceitful message in my eyes
Beckoning insatiate men to certain doom.   570
And teeth that flash the sign of happiness,
Strong and evenly, beaming full of life.
Be just, Sadiku,
Compare my image and your lord's—
An age of difference!
See how the water glistens on my face
Like the dew-moistened leaves on a Harmattan morning
But he—his face is like a leather piece
Torn rudely from the saddle of his horse,

*(Sadiku gasps.)*

Sprinkled with the musty ashes   580
From a pipe that is long over-smoked.
And this goat-like tuft
Which I once thought was manly;
It is like scattered twists of grass—
Not even green—
But charred and lifeless, as after a forest fire!
Sadiku, I am young and brimming; he is spent.
I am the twinkle of a jewel
But he is the hind quarters of a lion!

SADIKU: *(recovering at last from helpless amazement.)* May  590
Sango restore your wits. For most surely some angry god has
taken possession of you. *(Turns around and walks away.
Stops again as she remembers something else.)* Your ranting
put this clean out of my head. My lord says that if you would
not be his wife, would you at least come to supper at his
house tonight. There is a small feast in your honour. He
wishes to tell you how happy he is that the great capital city
has done so much honour to a daughter of Ilujinle. You have
brought great fame to your people.

SIDI: Ho ho! Do you think that I was only born   600
Yesterday?
The tales of Baroka's little suppers,
I know all.
Tell your lord that Sidi does not sup with
Married men.

SADIKU: They are lies, lies. You must not believe everything
you hear. Sidi, would I deceive you? I swear to you . . .

SIDI: Can you deny that
Every woman who has supped with him one night,
Becomes his wife or concubine the next?   610

LAKUNLE: Is it for nothing he is called the Fox?

SADIKU: *(advancing on him.)* You keep out of this, or so Sango be my witness . . .

LAKUNLE: (*retreats just a little, but continues to talk.*)
　　His wiliness is known even in the larger towns.
　　Did you never hear
　　Of how he foiled the Public Works attempt
　　To build the railway through Ilujinle.

SADIKU: Nobody knows the truth of that. It is all hearsay.

620 SIDI: I love hearsays. Lakunle, tell me all.

LAKUNLE: Did you not know it? Well sit down and listen.
　　My father told me, before he died. And few men
　　Know of this trick—oh he's a die-hard rogue
　　Sworn against our progress . . . yes . . . it was . . . some-
　　where here
　　The track should have been laid just along
　　The outskirts. Well, the workers came, in fact
　　It was prisoners who were brought to do
　　The harder part . . . to break the jungle's back . . .

(*Enter the prisoners, guarded by two warders. A white surveyor examines his map (khaki helmet, spats, etc.). The foreman runs up with his camp stool, table etc., erects the umbrella
over him and unpacks the usual box of bush comforts—soda
siphon, whisky bottle, and geometric sandwiches. His map
consulted, he directs the sweat team to where to work. They
begin felling, matchet swinging, log dragging, all to the rhythm
of the work gang's metal percussion (rod on gong or rude triangle, etc.). The two performers are also the song leaders and
the others fill the chorus. "N'ijo itoro," "Amuda el 'ebe l'aiya,"
"Gbe je on'ipa" etc.)*

630 LAKUNLE: They marked the route with stakes, ate
　　Through the jungle and began the tracks. Trade,
　　Progress, adventure, success, civilization,
　　Fame, international conspicuousity . . . it was
　　All within the grasp of Ilujinle. . . .

(*The wrestler enters, stands horrified at the sight and flees.
Returns later with the Bale himself who soon assesses the
situation.
They disappear. The work continues, the surveyor occupies
himself with the fly-whisk and whisky. Shortly after, a bull-
roarer is heard. The prisoners falter a little, pick up again. The
bull-roarer continues on its way, nearer and farther, moving in
circles, so that it appears to come from all around them. The
foreman is the first to break and then the rest is chaos. Sole survivor of the rout is the surveyor who is too surprised to move.
Baroka enters a few minutes later accompanied by some attendants and preceded by a young girl bearing a calabash bowl.
The surveyor, angry and threatening, is prevailed upon to
open his gift. From it he reveals a wad of pound notes and kola
nuts. Mutual understanding is established. The surveyor
frowns heavily, rubs his chin, and consults his map. Re-exam-
ines the contents of the bowl, shakes his head. Baroka adds
more money, and a coop of hens. A goat follows, and more
money. This time "truth" dawns on him at last, he has made a
mistake. The track really should go the other way. What an unfortunate error, discovered just in time! No, no, no possibility
of a mistake this time, the track should be much further away.
In fact (scooping up the soil) the earth is most unsuitable,
couldn't possibly support the weight of a railway engine. A
gourd of palm wine is brought to seal the agreement and a cola-*

nut is broken. Baroka's men help the surveyor pack and they
leave with their arms round each other followed by the surveyor's booty.)*

LAKUNLE: (*as the last of the procession disappears, shakes his
　　fist at them, stamping on the ground.*)
　　Voluptuous beast! He loves this life too well
　　To bear to part from it. And motor roads
　　And railways would do just that, forcing
　　Civilization at his door. He foresaw it　　　　　　640
　　And he barred the gates, securing fast
　　His dogs and horses, his wives and all his
　　Concubines . . . ah, yes . . . all those concubines.
　　Baroka has such a selective eye, none suits him
　　But the best. . . .

(*His eyes truly light up. Sidi and Sadiku snigger, tip-toe offstage.*)

　　. . . Yes, one must grant him that.
　　Ah, I sometimes wish I led his kind of life.
　　Such luscious bosoms make his nightly pillow.
　　I am sure he keeps a time-table just as
　　I do at school. Only way to ensure fair play.　　　650
　　He must be healthy to keep going as he does.
　　I don't know what the women see in him. His eyes
　　Are small and always red with wine. He must
　　Possess some secret. . . . No! I do not envy him!
　　Just the one woman for me. Alone I stand
　　For progress, with Sidi my chosen soul-mate, the one
　　Woman of my life. . . . Sidi! Sidi where are you?

(*Rushes out after them, returns to fetch the discarded firewood
and runs out again.*)
(*Baroka in bed, naked except for baggy trousers, calf-length. It
is a rich bedroom covered in animal skins and rugs. Weapons
round the wall. Also a strange machine, a most peculiar contraption with a long lever. Kneeling beside the bed is Baroka's
current Favourite, engaged in plucking the hairs from his
armpit. She does this by first massaging the spot around the selected hair very gently with her forefinger. Then, with hardly
a break, she pulls out the hair between her finger and the
thumb with a sudden sharp movement. Baroka twitches
slightly with each pull. Then an aspirated "A-ah," and a look of
complete beatitude spreads all over his face.*)

FAVOURITE: Do I improve my lord?

BAROKA: You are still somewhat over-gentle with the pull
　　As if you feared to hurt the panther of the trees.　　660
　　Be sharp and sweet
　　Like the swift sting of a vicious wasp
　　For there the pleasure lies—the cooling aftermath.

FAVOURITE: I'll learn, my lord.

BAROKA: You have not time, my dear.
　　Tonight I hope to take another wife.
　　And the honour of this task, you know,
　　Belongs by right to my latest choice.
　　But—A-ah—Now that was sharp.
　　It had in it the scorpion's sudden sting　　　　　　670
　　Without its poison.
　　It was an angry pull; you tried to hurt
　　For I had made you wrathful with my boast.

But now your anger flows in my blood stream.
How sweet it is! A-ah! That was sweeter still.
I think perhaps that I shall let you stay,
The sole out-puller of my sweat-bathed hairs.
Ach!

(*Sits up suddenly and rubs the sore point angrily.*)

    Now that had far more pain than pleasure
680   Vengeful creature, you did not caress
    The area of extraction long enough!

(*Enter Sadiku. She goes down on her knees at once and bows her head into her lap.*)

    Aha! Here comes Sadiku.
    Do you bring some balm,
    To soothe the smart of my misused armpit?
    Away, you enemy!

(*Exit the Favourite.*)

SADIKU: My lord . . .
BAROKA: You have my leave to speak.
    What did she say?
SADIKU: She will not my lord. I did my best, but she will have
690   none of you.
BAROKA: It follows the pattern—a firm refusal
    At the start. Why will she not?
SADIKU: That is the strange part of it. She says you're much too
    old. If you ask me, I think that she is really off her head. All
    this excitement of the books has been too much for her.
BAROKA: (*springs to his feet.*)
    She says . . . That I am old
    That I am much too old? Did a slight
    Unripened girl say this of me?
700 SADIKU: My lord, I heard the incredible words with my ears,
    and I thought the world was mad.
BAROKA: But is it possible, Sadiku? Is this right?
    Did I not, at the festival of Rain,
    Defeat the men in the log-tossing match?
    Do I not still with the most fearless ones,
    Hunt the leopard and the boa at night
    And save the farmers' goats from further harm?
    And does she say I'm old?
    Did I not, to announce the Harmattan,
710   Climb to the top of the silk-cotton tree,
    Break the first pod, and scatter tasselled seeds
    To the four winds—and this but yesterday?
    Do any of my wives report
    A failing in my manliness?
    The strongest of them all
    Still wearies long before the Lion does!
    And so would she, had I the briefest chance
    To teach this unfledged birdling
    That lacks the wisdom to embrace
720   The rich mustiness of age . . . if I could once . . .
    Come hither, soothe me, Sadiku
    For I am wroth at heart.

(*Lies back on the bed, staring up as before. Sadiku takes her place at the foot of the bed and begins to tickle the soles of his feet. Baroka turns to the left suddenly, reaches down the side,*

*and comes up with a copy of the magazine. Opens it and begins to study the pictures. He heaves a long sigh.*)

    That is good, Sadiku, very good.

(*He begins to compare some pictures in the book, obviously his own and Sidi's. Flings the book away suddenly and stares at the ceiling for a second or two. Then, unsmiling.*)

    Perhaps it is as well, Sadiku.
SADIKU: My lord, what did you say?
BAROKA: Yes, faithful one, I say it is as well.
    The scorn, the laughter and the jeers
    Would have been bitter
    Had she consented and my purpose failed,
    I would have sunk with shame.       730
SADIKU: My lord, I do not understand.
BAROKA: The time has come when I can fool myself
    No more. I am no man, Sadiku. My manhood
    Ended near a week ago.
SADIKU: The gods forbid.
BAROKA: I wanted Sidi because I still hoped—
    A foolish thought I know, but still—I hoped
    That, with a virgin young and hot within,
    My failing strength would rise and save my pride.

(*Sadiku begins to moan.*)

    A waste of hope. I knew it even then.      740
    But it's a human failing never to accept
    The worst; and so I pandered to my vanity.
    When manhood must, it ends.
    The well of living, tapped beyond its depth,
    Dries up, and mocks the wastrel in the end.
    I am withered and unsapped, the joy
    Of ballad-mongers, the aged butt
    Of youth's ribaldry.
SADIKU: (*tearfully.*) The gods must have mercy yet.
BAROKA: (*as if suddenly aware of her presence, starts up.*)    750
    I have told this to no one but you,
    Who are my eldest, my most faithful wife.
    But if you dare parade my shame before the world . . .

(*Sadiku shakes her head in protest and begins to stroke the soles of his feet with renewed tenderness. Baroka sighs and falls back slowly.*)

    How irritable I have grown of late
    Such doubts to harbour of your loyalty . . .
    But this disaster is too much for one
    Checked thus as I upon the prime of youth.
    That rains that blessed me from my birth
    Number a meagre sixty-two;
    While my grandfather, that man of teak,      760
    Fathered two sons, late on sixty-five.
    But Okiki, my father beat them all
    Producing female twins at sixty-seven.
    Why then must I, descendant of these lions
    Forswear my wives at a youthful sixty-two
    My veins of life run dry, my manhood gone!

(*His voice goes drowsy; Sadiku sighs and moans and caresses his feet. His face lights up suddenly with rapture.*)

    Sango bear witness! These weary feet

Have felt the loving hands of much design
In women.
770 My soles have felt the scratch of harsh,
Gravelled hands.
They have borne the heaviness of clumsy,
Gorilla paws.
And I have known the tease of tiny,
Dainty hands,
Toy-like hands that tantalized
My eager senses,
Promised of thrills to come
Remaining
780 Unfulfilled because the fingers
Were too frail,
The touch too light and faint to pierce
The incredible thickness of my soles.
But thou Sadiku, thy plain unadorned hands
Encase a sweet sensuality which age
Will not destroy. A-ah,
Oyayi! Beyond a doubt Sadiku,
Thou art the queen of them all.

(*Falls asleep.*)


NIGHT

*The village centre. Sidi stands by the schoolroom window, ad-
miring her photos as before. Enter Sadiku with a longish bundle. She is very furtive. Unveils the object which turns out to be
a carved figure of the Bale, naked and in full detail. She takes
a good look at it, bursts suddenly into derisive laughter, sets
the figure in front of the tree. Sidi stares in utter amazement.*

SADIKU: So we did for you too did we? We did for you in the
790 end. Oh high and mighty lion, have we really scotched you?
A—ya-ya-ya . . . we women undid you in the end. I was there
when it happened to your father, the great Okiki. I did for
him, I, the youngest and freshest of the wives. I killed him
with my strength. I called him and he came to me, but no,
for him, this was not like other times. I, Sadiku, was I not
flame itself and he the flax on old women's spindles? I ate
him up! Race of mighty lions, we always consume you, at our
pleasure we spin you, at our whim we make you dance; like
the foolish top you think the world revolves around you . . .
800 fools! fools! . . . it is you who run giddy while we stand still
and watch, and draw your frail thread from you, slowly, till
nothing is left but a runty old stick. I scotched Okiki,
Sadiku's unopened treasure-house demanded sacrifice, and
Okiki came with his rusted key. Like a snake he came at me,
like a rag he went back, a limp rag, smeared in shame. . . .
(*Her ghoulish laugh re-possesses her.*) Ah, take warning my
masters, we'll scotch you in the end . . .

(*With a yell she leaps up, begins to dance round the tree,
chanting.*)

Take warning, my masters
We'll scotch you in the end.

(*Sidi shuts the window gently, comes out, Sadiku, as she comes
round again, gasps and is checked in mid-song.*)

SADIKU: Oh it is you my daughter. You should have chosen a 810
better time to scare me to death. The hour of victory is no
time for any woman to die.
SIDI: Why? What battle have you won?
SADIKU: Not me alone girl. You too. Every woman. Oh my
daughter, that I have lived to see this day . . . To see him fiz-
zle with the drabbest puff of a mis-primed "sakabula."

(*Resumes her dance.*)

Take warning, my masters
We'll scotch you in the end.
SIDI: Wait Sadiku. I cannot understand.
SADIKU: You will my girl. You will. 820
Take warning my masters . . .
SIDI: Sadiku, are you well?
SADIKU: Ask no questions my girl. Just join my victory dance.
Oh Sango my lord, who of us possessed your lightning and
ran like fire through that lion's tail . . .
SIDI: (*holds her firmly as she is about to go off again.*)
Stop your loose ranting. You will not
Move from here until you make some sense.
SADIKU: Oh you are troublesome. Do you promise to tell no
one? 830
SIDI: I swear it. Now tell me quickly.

(*As Sadiku whispers, her eyes widen.*)

O-ho-o-o-o!
But Sadiku, if he knew the truth, why
Did he ask me to . . .

(*Again Sadiku whispers.*)

Ha ha! Some hope indeed. Oh Sadiku
I suddenly am glad to be a woman.

(*Leaps in the air.*)

We won. We won! Hurray for womankind!

(*Falls in behind Sadiku.*)

Take warning, my masters
We'll scotch you in the end. (*Lakunle enters unobserved.*)
LAKUNLE: The full moon is not yet, but 840
The women cannot wait.
They must go mad without it.

(*The dancing stops. Sadiku frowns.*)

SADIKU: The scarecrow is here. Begone fop! This is the world
of women. At this moment our star sits in the centre of the
sky. We are supreme. What is more, we are about to per-
form a ritual. If you remain, we will chop you up, we will
make you the sacrifice.
LAKUNLE: What is the hag gibbering?
SADIKU: (*advances menacingly.*) You less than man, you less
than the littlest woman, I say begone! 850
LAKUNLE: (*nettled.*) I will have you know that I am a man
As you will find out if you dare
To lay a hand on me.
SADIKU: (*throws back her head in laughter.*) You a man? Is
Baroka not more of a man than you? And if he is no longer
a man, then what are you? (*Lakunle, understanding the
meaning, stands rooted, shocked.*) Come on, dear girl, let

him look on if he will. After all, only *men* are barred from
watching this ceremony.

860 Take warning, my masters
We'll . . .

SIDI: Stop. Sadiku stop. Oh such an idea
Is running in my head. Let me to the palace for
This supper he promised me. Sadiku, what a way
To mock the devil. I shall ask forgiveness
For my hasty words. . . . No need to change
My answers and consent to be his bride—he might
Suspect you've told me. But I shall ask a month
To think on it.

870 SADIKU: (*somewhat doubtful.*) Baroka is no child you know, he
will know I have betrayed him.

SIDI: No, he will not. Oh Sadiku let me go.
I long to see him thwarted, to watch his longing
His twitching hands which this time cannot
Rush to loosen his trouser cords.

SADIKU: You will have to match the fox's cunning. Use your
bashful looks and be truly repentant. Goad him my child,
torment him until he weeps for shame.

SIDI: Leave it to me. He will never suspect you of deceit.

880 SADIKU: (*with another of her energetic leaps.*) Yo-rooo o!
Yo-rororo o!
Shall I come with you?

SIDI: Will that be wise? You forget
We have not seen each other.

SADIKU: Away then. Away woman. I shall bide here.
Haste back and tell Sadiku how the no-man is.
Away, my lovely child.

LAKUNLE: (*he has listened with increasing horror.*)
No, Sidi, don't. If you care

890 One little bit for what I feel,
Do not go to torment the man.
Suppose he knows that you have come to jeer—
And he will know, if he is not a fool—
He is a savage thing, degenerate
He would beat a helpless woman if he could. . . .

SIDI: (*running off gleefully*) Ta-raa school teacher. Wait here
for me.

LAKUNLE: (*stamps his foot helplessly.*)
Foolish girl! . . . And this is all your work.

900 Could you not keep a secret?
Must every word leak out of you
As surely as the final drops
Of mother's milk
Oozed from your flattened breast
Generations ago?

SADIKU: Watch your wagging tongue, unformed creature!

LAKUNLE: If any harm befalls her . . .

SADIKU: Woman though she is, she can take better care of herself than you can of her. Fancy a thing like you actually

910 wanting a girl like that, all to your little self. (*Walks round
him and looks him up and down.*) Ah! Oba Ala is an accommodating god. What a poor figure you cut!

LAKUNLE: I wouldn't demean myself to bandy words
With a woman of the bush.

SADIKU: At this moment, your betrothed is supping with the
Lion.

LAKUNLE: (*pleased at the use of the word "betrothed."*)
Well, we are not really betrothed as yet,

I mean, she is not promised yet.
But it will come in time, I'm sure. 920

SADIKU: (*bursts into her cackling laughter.*) The bride-price, is
that paid?

LAKUNLE: Mind your own business.

SADIKU: Why don't you do what other men have done. Take a
farm for a season. One harvest will be enough to pay the
price, even for a girl like Sidi. Or will the smell of the wet
soil be too much for your delicate nostrils?

LAKUNLE: I said mind your own business.

SADIKU: A—a—ah. It is true what they say then. You are going
to convert the whole village so that no one will ever pay the 930
bride-price again. Ah, you're a clever man. I must admit that
it is a good way for getting out of it, but don't you think you'd
use more time and energy that way than you would if . . .

LAKUNLE: (*with conviction.*) Within a year or two, I swear,
This town shall see a transformation
Bride-price will be a thing forgotten
And wives shall take their place my men.
A motor road will pass this spot
And bring the city ways to us.
We'll buy saucepans for all the women 940
Clay pots are crude and unhygienic
No man shall take more wives than one
That's why they're impotent too soon.
The ruler shall ride cars, not horses
Or a bicycle at the very least.
We'll burn the forest, cut the trees
Then plant a modern park for lovers
We'll print newspapers every day
With pictures of seductive girls.
The world will judge our progress by 950
The girls that win beauty contests.
While Lagos builds new factories daily
We only play "ayo" and gossip.
Where is our school of ballroom dancing?
Who here can throw a cocktail party?
We must be modern with the rest
Or live forgotten by the world
We must reject the palm wine habit
And take to tea, with milk and sugar.

(*Turns on Sadiku who has been staring at him in terror. She
retreats, and he continues to talk down at her as they go round,
then down and offstage, Lakunle's hectoring voice trailing
away in the distance.*)

This is my plan, you withered face 960
And I shall start by teaching you.
From now you shall attend my school
And take your place with twelve-year olds.
For though you're nearly seventy,
Your mind is simple and unformed.
Have you no shame that at your age,
You neither read nor write nor think?
You spend your days as senior wife,
Collecting brides for Baroka.
And now because you've sucked him dry,
You send my Sidi to his shame. . . .

(*The scene changes to Baroka's bedroom. On the left in a one-* 970
*knee-on-floor posture, two men are engaged in a kind of*

*wrestling, their arms clasped round each other's waist, testing the right moment to heave. One is Baroka, the other a short squat figure of apparent muscular power. The contest is still in the balanced stage. In some distant part of the house, Sidi's voice is heard lifted in the familiar general greeting, addressed to no one in particular.)*

SIDI: A good day to the head and people
    Of this house.

*(Baroka lifts his head, frowns as if he is trying to place the voice.)*

    A good day to the head and people
    Of this house.

*(Baroka now decides to ignore it and to concentrate on the contest. Sidi's voice draws progressively nearer. She enters nearly backwards, as she is still busy admiring the room through which she has just passed. Gasps on turning round to see the two men.)*

BAROKA: *(without looking up.)* Is Sadiku not at home then?
SIDI: *(absent-mindedly.)* Hm?
BAROKA: I asked, is Sadiku not at home?
SIDI: *(recollecting herself, she curtseys quickly.)* I saw no one,
980     Baroka.
BAROKA: No one? Do you mean there was no one
    To bar unwanted strangers from my privacy?
SIDI: *(retreating)* The house . . . seemed . . . empty.
BAROKA: Ah, I forget. This is the price I pay
    Once every week, for being progressive.
    Prompted by the school teacher, my servants
    Were prevailed upon to form something they call
    The Palace Workers' Union. And in keeping
    With the habits—I am told—of modern towns,
990     This is their day off.
SIDI: *(seeing that Baroka seems to be in a better mood, she becomes somewhat bolder. Moves forward—saucily.)*
    Is this also a day off
    For Baroka's wives?
BAROKA: *(looks up sharply, relaxes, and speaks with a casual voice.)*
    No, the madness has not gripped them—yet.
    Did you not meet with one of them?
SIDI: No, Baroka. There was no one about.
1000 BAROKA: Not even Ailatu, my favourite?
    Was she not at her usual place,
    Beside my door?
SIDI: *(absently. She is deeply engrossed in watching the contest.)*
    Her stool is there. And I saw
    The slippers she was embroidering.
BAROKA: Hm. Hm. I think I know
    Where she'll be found. In a dark corner
    Sulking like a slighted cockroach.
1010     By the way, look and tell me
    If she left her shawl behind.

*(So as not to miss any part of the tussle, she moves backwards, darts a quick look round the door and back again.)*

SIDI: There is a black shawl on the stool.
BAROKA: *(a regretful sigh.)*

Then she'll be back tonight. I had hoped
    My words were harsh enough
    To free me from her spite for a week or more.
SIDI: Did Ailatu offend her husband?
BAROKA: Offend? My armpit still weeps blood
    For the gross abuse I suffered from one
    I called my favourite.                                    1020
SIDI: *(in a disappointed voice.)*
    Oh. Is that all?
BAROKA: Is that not enough? Why child?
    What more could the woman do?
SIDI: Nothing. Nothing, Baroka. I thought perhaps—
    Well—young wives are known to be—
    Forward—sometimes—to their husbands.
BAROKA: In an ill-kept household perhaps. But not
    Under Baroka's roof. And yet,
    Such are the sudden spites of women                        1030
    That even I cannot foresee them all.
    And child—if I lose this little match
    Remember that my armpit
    Burns and itches turn by turn.

*(Sidi continues watching for some time, then clasps her hand over her mouth as she remembers what she should have done to begin with. Doubtful how to proceed, she hesitates for some moments, then comes to a decision and kneels.)*

SIDI: I have come, Bale, as a repentant child.
BAROKA: What?
SIDI: *(very hesitantly, eyes to the floor, but she darts a quick look up when she thinks the Bale isn't looking.)*
    The answer which I sent to the Bale
    Was given in a thoughtless moment. . . .                   1040
BAROKA: Answer, child? To what?
SIDI: A message brought by . . .
BAROKA: *(groans and strains in a muscular effort.)*
    Will you say that again? It is true that for supper
    I did require your company. But up till now
    Sadiku has brought no reply.
SIDI: *(amazed)* But the other matter! Did not the Bale
    Send . . . did Baroka not send . . . ?
BAROKA: *(with sinister encouragement.)*
    What did Baroka not, my child?                            1050
SIDI: *(cowed, but angry, rises.)*
    It is nothing, Bale. I only hope
    That I am here at the Bale's invitation.
BAROKA: *(as if trying to understand, he frowns as he looks at her.)*
    A-ah, at last I understand. You think
    I took offence because you entered
    Unannounced?
SIDI: I remember that the Bale called me
    An unwanted stranger.                                     1060
BAROKA: That could be expected. Is a man's bedroom
    To be made naked to any flea
    That chances to wander through?

*(Sidi turns away, very hurt.)*

    Come, come, my child. You are too quick
    To feel aggrieved. Of course you are
    More than welcome. But I expected Ailatu
    To tell me you were here.

*(Sidi curtseys briefly with her back to Baroka. After a while, she turns round. The mischief returns to her face. Baroka's attitude of denial has been a setback but she is now ready to pursue her mission.)*

SIDI: I hope the Bale will not think me
    Forward. But, like everyone, I had thought
1070    The Favourite was a gentle woman.
BAROKA: And so had I.
SIDI: *(slyly.)* One would hardly think that *she*
    Would give offence without a cause
    Was the Favourite . . . in some way . . .
    Dissatisfied . . . with her lord and husband?

*(With a mock curtsey, quickly executed as Baroka begins to look up.)*

BAROKA: *(slowly turns towards her.)*
    Now that
    Is a question which I never thought to hear
    Except from a school teacher. Do you think
1080    The Lion has such leisure that he asks
    The whys and wherefores of a woman's
    Squint?

*(Sidi steps back and curtseys. As before, and throughout this scene, she is easily cowed by Baroka's change of mood, all the more easily as she is, in any case, frightened by her own boldness.)*

SIDI: I meant no disrespect . . .
BAROKA: *(gently.)* I know. *(Breaks off.)* Christians on my
    Fathers' shrines, child!
    Do you think I took offence? A—aw
    Come in and seat yourself. Since you broke in
    Unawares, and appear resolved to stay,
    Try, if you can, not to make me feel
1090    A humourless old ram. I allow no one
    To watch my daily exercise, but as we say,
    The woman gets lost in the woods one day
    And every wood deity dies the next.

*(Sidi curtseys, watches, and moves forward warily, as if expecting the two men to spring apart too suddenly.)*

SIDI: I think he will win.
BAROKA: Is that a wish, my daughter?
SIDI: No, but—*(Hesitates, but boldness wins.)*
    If the tortoise cannot tumble
    It does not mean that he can stand.

*(Baroka looks at her, seemingly puzzled. Sidi turns away, humming.)*

BAROKA: When the child is full of riddles, the mother
1100    Has one water-pot the less.

*(Sidi tip-toes to Baroka's back and pulls asses' ears at him.)*

SIDI: I think he will win.
BAROKA: He knows he must. Would it profit me
    To pit my strength against a weakling?
    Only yesterday, this son of—I suspect—
    A python for a mother, and fathered beyond doubt
    By a blubber-bottomed baboon,

*(The complimented man grins.)*

    Only yesterday, he nearly
    Ploughed my tongue with my front teeth
    In a friendly wrestling bout.
WRESTLER: *(encouraged, makes an effort.)* Ugh. Ugh.    1110
SIDI: *(bent almost over them. Genuinely worried.)*
    Oh! Does it hurt?
BAROKA: Not yet . . . but, as I was saying
    I change my wrestlers when I have learnt
    To throw them. I also change my wives
    When I have learnt to tire them.
SIDI: And is this another . . . changing time
    For the Bale?
BAROKA: Who knows? Until the finger nails
    Have scraped the dust, no one can tell    1120
    Which insect released his bowels.

*(Sidi grimaces in disgust and walks away. Returns as she thinks up a new idea.)*

SIDI: A woman spoke to me this afternoon.
BAROKA: Indeed. And does Sidi find this unusual—
    That a woman speak with her in the afternoon?
SIDI: *(stamping.)* No. She had the message of a go-between.
BAROKA: Did she? Then I rejoice with you.

*(Sidi stands biting her lips. Baroka looks at her, this time with deliberate appreciation.)*

    And now I think of it, why not?
    There must be many men who
    Build their loft to fit your height.
SIDI: *(unmoving, pointedly.)* Her message came from one    1130
    With many lofts.
BAROKA: Ah! Such is the greed of men.
SIDI: If Baroka were my father
    *(Aside.)*—which many would take him to be—

*(Makes a rude sign.)*

    Would he pay my dowry to this man
    And give his blessings?
BAROKA: Well, I must know his character.
    For instance, is the man rich?
SIDI: Rumour has it so.
BAROKA: Is he repulsive?    1140
SIDI: He is old. *(Baroka winces.)*
BAROKA: Is he mean and miserly?
SIDI: To strangers—no. There are tales
    Of his open-handedness, which are never
    Quite without a motive. But his wives report
    —To take one little story—
    How he grew the taste for ground corn
    And pepper—because he would not pay
    The price of snuff!

*(With a sudden burst of angry energy, Baroka lifts his opponent and throws him over his shoulder.)*

BAROKA: A lie! The price of snuff    1150
    Had nothing to do with it.
SIDI: *(too excited to listen.)* You won!
BAROKA: By the years on my beard, I swear

They slander me!

SIDI: (*excitedly.*) You won. You won!

(*She breaks into a kind of shoulder dance and sings.*)

> Yokolu Yokolu. Ko ha tan bi
> Iyawo gb'oko san'le
> Oko yo 'ke . . . [1]

(*She repeats this throughout Baroka's protests. Baroka is pacing angrily up and down. The defeated man, nursing a hip, goes to the corner of the room and lifts out a low "ako" bench. He sits on the floor, and soon, Baroka joins him; using only their arms now, they place their elbows on the bench and grip hands. Baroka takes his off again, replaces it, takes it off again, and so on during the rest of his outburst.*)

BAROKA: This means nothing to me of course. Nothing!
1160     But I know the ways of women, and I know
    Their ruinous tongues.
    Suppose that, as a child—only suppose—
    Suppose then, that as a child, I—
    And remember, I only use myself
    To illustrate the plight of many men. . . .
    So, once again, suppose that as a child
    I grew to love "tanfiri"—with a good dose of pepper
    And growing old, I found that—
    Sooner than die away, my passion only
1170     Bred itself upon each mouthful of
    Ground corn and pepper I consumed.
    Now, think child, would it be seemly
    At my age, and the father of children,
    To be discovered, in public
    Thrusting fistfuls of corn dust and pepper
    In my mouth? Is it not wise to indulge
    In the little masquerade of a dignified
    Snuff box?—But remember, I only make
    A pleading for this prey of women's
1180     Malice. I feel his own injustice,
    Being myself, a daily fellow-sufferer!

(*Baroka seems to realize for the first time that Sidi has paid no attention to his explanation. She is, in fact, still humming and shaking her shoulders. He stares questioningly at her. Sidi stops, somewhat confused and embarrassed, points sheepishly to the wrestler.*)

SIDI: I think this time he will win.

(*Baroka's grumbling subsides slowly. He is now attentive to the present bout.*)

BAROKA: Now let us once again take up
    The questioning. (*Almost timidly.*) Is this man
    Good and kindly?
SIDI: They say he uses well
    His dogs and horses.
BAROKA: (*desperately*)
    Well is he fierce then? Reckless!

Does the bush cow run to hole 1190
When he hears his beaters' Hei-ei-wo-rah!

SIDI: There are heads and skins of leopards
    Hung around his council room.
    But the market is also
    Full of them.
BAROKA: Is he not wise? Is he not sagely?
    Do the young and old not seek
    His counsel?
SIDI: The fox is said to be wise
    So cunning that he stalks and dines on 1200
    New-hatched chickens.
BAROKA: (*more and more desperate.*)
    Does he not beget strength on wombs?
    Are his children not tall and stout-limbed?
SIDI: Once upon a time.
BAROKA: Once upon a time?
    What do you mean, girl?
SIDI: Just once upon a time.
    Perhaps his children have of late
    Been plagued with shyness and refuse 1210
    To come into the world. Or else
    He is so tired with the day's affairs
    That at night, he turns his buttocks
    To his wives. But there have been
    No new reeds cut by his servants,
    No new cots woven.
    And his household gods are starved
    For want of child-naming festivities
    Since the last two rains went by.
BAROKA: Perhaps he is a frugal man. 1220
    Mindful of years to come,
    Planning for a final burst of life, he
    Husbands his strength.
SIDI: (*giggling. She is actually stopped, half-way, by giggling at the cleverness of her remark.*)
    To husband his wives surely ought to be
    A man's first duties—at all times.
BAROKA: My beard tells me you've been a pupil,
    A most diligent pupil of Sadiku.
    Among all shameless women, 1230
    The sharpest tongues grow from that one
    Peeling bark—Sadiku, my faithful lizard!

(*Growing steadily warmer during this speech, he again slaps down his opponent's arm as he shouts "Sadiku."*)

SIDI: (*backing away, aware that she has perhaps gone too far and betrayed knowledge of the "secret."*)
    I have learnt nothing of anyone.
BAROKA: No more. No more.
    Already I have lost a wrestler
    On your account. This town-bred daring
    Of little girls, awakes in me
    A seven-horned devil of strength. 1240
    Let one woman speak a careless word

---

[1]"Yokolu, Yokolu, what say you now?
  The wife knocked down the husband
  And he now sprouts a hunchback . . ."

And I can pin a wriggling—Bah!

(*Lets go the man's arm. He has risen during the last speech but held on to the man's arm, who is forced to rise with him.*)

The tappers should have called by now.
See if we have a fresh gourd by the door.

(*The wrestler goes out. Baroka goes to sit on the bed, Sidi eyeing him, doubtfully.*)

What an ill-tempered man I daily grow
Towards. Soon my voice will be
The sand between two grinding stones.
But I have my scattered kindliness
Though few occasions serve to herald it.
1250   And Sidi, my daughter, you do not know
The thoughts which prompted me
To ask the pleasure that I be your host
This evening. I would not tell Sadiku,
Meaning to give delight
With the surprise of it. Now, tell me, child
Can you guess a little at this thing?
SIDI: Sadiku told me nothing.
BAROKA: You are hasty with denial. For how indeed
Could Sadiku, since I told her
1260   Nothing of my mind? But, my daughter,
Did she not, perhaps . . . invent some tale?
For I know Sadiku loves to be
All-knowing.
SIDI: She said no more, except the Bale
Begged my presence.
BAROKA: (*rises quickly to the bait.*)
Begged? Bale Baroka begged?

(*Wrestler enters with gourd and calabash cups. Baroka relapses.*)

Ah! I see you love to bait your elders.
One way the world remains the same,
1270   The child still thinks she is wiser than
The cotton head of age.
Do you think Baroka deaf or blind
To little signs? But let that pass.
Only, lest you fall victim to the schemes
Of busy women, I will tell you this—
I know Sadiku plays the match-maker
Without the prompting. If I look
On any maid, or call her name
Even in the course of harmless, neighbourly
1280   Well-wishing—How fares your daughter?
—Is your sister now recovered from her
Whooping cough?—How fast your ward
Approaches womanhood! Have the village lads
Begun to gather at your door?—
Or any word at all which shows I am
The thoughtful guardian of the village health,
If it concerns a woman, Sadiku straightway
Flings herself into the role of go-between
And before I even don a cap, I find
1290   Yet another stranger in my bed!
SIDI: It seems a Bale's life
Is full of great unhappiness.

BAROKA: I do not complain. No, my child
I accept the sweet and sour with
A ruler's grace. I lose my patience
Only when I meet with
The new immodesty with women.
Now, my Sidi, you have not caught
This new and strange disease, I hope.
SIDI: (*curtseying.*) The threading of my smock—          1300
Does Baroka not know the marking
Of the village loom?
BAROKA: But will Sidi, the pride of mothers,
Will she always wear it?
SIDI: Will Sidi, the proud daughter of Baroka,
Will she step out naked?

(*A pause. Baroka surveys Sidi in an almost fatherly manner and she bashfully drops her eyes.*)

BAROKA: To think that once I thought,
Sidi is the eye's delight, but
She is vain, and her head
Is feather-light, and always giddy          1310
With a trivial thought. And now
I find her deep and wise beyond her years.

(*Reaches under his pillow, brings out the now familiar magazine, and also an addressed envelope. Retains the former and gives her the envelope.*)

Do you know what this means?
The trim red piece of paper
In the corner?
SIDI: I know it. A stamp. Lakunle receives
Letters from Lagos marked with it.
BAROKA: (*obviously disappointed.*)
Hm. Lakunle. But more about him
Later. Do you know what it means—          1320
This little frippery?
SIDI: (*very proudly.*)
Yes. I know that too. Is it not a tax on
The habit of talking with paper?
BAROKA: Oh. Oh. I see you dip your hand
Into the pockets of the school teacher
And retrieve it bulging with knowledge.

(*Goes to the strange machine, and pulls the lever up and down.*)

Now this, not even the school teacher can tell
What magic this performs. Come nearer,
It will not bite.          1330
SIDI: I have never seen the like.
BAROKA: The work dear child, of the palace blacksmiths
Built in full secrecy. All is not well with it—
But I will find the cause and then Ilujinle
Will boast its own tax on paper, made with
Stamps like this. For long I dreamt it
And here it stands, child of my thoughts.
SIDI: (*wonder-struck*) You mean . . . this will work some day?
BAROKA: Ogun has said the word. And now my girl
What think you of that image on the stamp          1340
This spiderwork of iron, wood, and mortar?
SIDI: Is it not a bridge?

BAROKA: It is a bridge. The longest—so they say
In the whole country. When not a bridge,
You'll find a print of groundnuts
Stacked like pyramids,
Or palm trees, or cocoa trees, and farmers
Hacking pods, and workmen
Felling trees and tying skinned logs
1350  Into rafts. A thousand thousand letters
By road, by rail, by air,
From one end of the world to another,
And not one human head among them.
Not one head of beauty on the stamp!
SIDI: But I once saw Lakunle's letter
With a head of bronze.
BAROKA: A figurehead, my child, a lifeless work
Of craft, with holes for eyes, and coldness
For the warmth of life and love
1360  In youthful cheeks like yours,
My daughter . . .

*(Pauses to watch the effect on Sidi.)*

. . . Can you see it, Sidi?
Tens of thousands of these dainty prints
And each one with this legend of Sidi.

*(Flourishes the magazine, open in the middle.)*

The village goddess, reaching out
Towards the sun, her lover.
Can you see it, my daughter!

*(Sidi drowns herself totally in the contemplation, takes the
magazine but does not even look at it. Sits on the bed.)*

BAROKA: *(very gently.)*
I hope you will not think it too great
1370  A burden, to carry the country's mail
All on your comeliness.

*(Walks away, an almost business-like tone.)*

Our beginnings will
Of course be modest. We shall begin
By cutting stamps for our own village alone.
As the schoolmaster himself would say—
Charity begins at home.

*(Pause. Faces Sidi from nearly the distance of the room.)*

For a long time now,
The town-dwellers have made up tales
Of the backwardness of Ilujinle
1380  Until it hurts Baroka, who holds
The welfare of his people deep at heart.
Now, if we do this thing, it will prove more
Than any single town has done!

*(The wrestler, who has been listening open-mouthed, drops his
cup in admiration. Baroka, annoyed, realizing only now in fact
that he is still in the room, waves him impatiently out.)*

I do not hate progress, only its nature
Which makes all roofs and faces look the same.
And the wish of one old man is
That here and there,

*(Goes progressively towards Sidi, until he bends over her, then
sits beside her on the bed.)*

Among the bridges and the murderous roads,
Below the humming birds which
Smoke the face of Sango, dispenser of     1390
The snake-tongue lightning; between this moment
And the reckless broom that will be wielded
In these years to come, we must leave
Virgin plots of lives, rich decay
And the tang of vapour rising from
Forgotten heaps of compost, lying
Undisturbed . . . But the skin of progress
Masks, unknown, the spotted wolf of sameness . . .
Does sameness not revolt your being,
My daughter?     1400

*(Sidi is capable only of a bewildered nod, slowly.)*

BAROKA: *(sighs, hands folded piously on his lap.)*
I find my soul is sensitive, like yours.
Indeed, although there is one—no more think I—
One generation between yours and mine,
Our thoughts fly crisply through the air
And meet, purified, as one.
And our first union
Is the making of this stamp.
The one redeeming grace on any paper tax
Shall be your face. And mine,     1410
The soul behind it all, worshipful
Of Nature for her gift of youth
And beauty to our earth. Does this
Please you, my daughter?
SIDI: I can no longer see the meaning, Baroka.
Now that you speak
Almost like the school teacher, except
Your words fly on a different path,
I find . . .
BAROKA: It is a bad thing, then, to sound     1420
Like your school teacher?
SIDI: No, Bale, but words are like beetles
Boring at my ears, and my head
Becomes a jumping bean. Perhaps after all,
As the school teacher tells me often,

*(Very miserably.)*

I have a simple mind.
BAROKA: *(pats her kindly on the head.)*
No, Sidi, not simple, only straight and truthful
Like a freshwater reed. But I do find
Your school teacher and I are much alike.     1430
The proof of wisdom is the wish to learn
Even from children. And the haste of youth
Must learn its temper from the gloss
Of ancient leather, from a strength
Knit close along the grain. The school teacher
And I, must learn one from the other.
Is this not right?

*(A tearful nod.)*

BAROKA: The old must flow into the new, Sidi,

Not blind itself or stand foolishly
1440    Apart. A girl like you must inherit
Miracles which age alone reveals.
Is this not so?
SIDI: Everything you say, Bale,
Seems wise to me.
BAROKA: Yesterday's wine alone is strong and blooded, child,
And though the Christians' holy book denies
The truth of this, old wine thrives best
Within a new bottle. The coarseness
Is mellowed down, and the rugged wine
1450    Acquires a full and rounded body . . .
Is this not so—my child?

(*Quite overcome, Sidi nods.*)

BAROKA: Those who know little of Baroka think
His life one pleasure-living course.
But the monkey sweats, my child,
The monkey sweats,
It is only the hair upon his back
Which still deceives the world . . .

(*Sidi's head falls slowly on the Bale's shoulder. The Bale remains in his final body-weighed-down-by-burdens-of-State attitude.*
*Even before the scene is completely shut off a crowd of dancers burst in at the front and dance off at the opposite side without slackening pace. In their brief appearance it should be apparent that they comprise a group of female dancers pursuing a masked male. Drumming and shouts continue quite audibly and shortly afterwards. They enter and re-cross the stage in the same manner.*
*The shouts fade away and they next appear at the market clearing. It is now full evening. Lakunle and Sadiku are still waiting for Sidi's return. The traders are beginning to assemble one by one, ready for the evening market. Hawkers pass through with oil-lamps beside their ware. Food sellers enter with cooking-pots and foodstuffs, set up their "adogan" or stone hearth and build a fire.*
*All this while, Lakunle is pacing wretchedly, Sadiku looks on placidly.*)

LAKUNLE: (*he is pacing furiously.*)
He's killed her.
1460    I warned you. You know him,
And I warned you.

(*Goes up all the approaches to look.*)

She's been gone half the day. It will soon
Be daylight. And still no news.
Women have disappeared before.
No trace. Vanished. Now we know how.

(*Checks, turns round.*)

And why!
Mock an old man, will you? So?
You can laugh? Ha ha! You wait.
I'll come and see you
1470    Whipped like a dog. Baroka's head wife
Driven out of the house for plotting
With a girl.

(*Each approaching footstep brings Lakunle to attention, but it is only a hawker or a passer-by. The wrestler passes. Sadiku greets him familiarly. Then, after he has passed, some significance of this breaks on Sadiku and she begins to look a little puzzled.*)

LAKUNLE: I know he has dungeons. Secret holes
Where a helpless girl will lie
And rot for ever. But not for nothing
Was I born a man. I'll find my way
To rescue her. She little deserves it, but
I shall risk my life for her.

(*The mummers can now be heard again, distantly. Sadiku and Lakunle become attentive as the noise approaches, Lakunle increasingly uneasy. A little, but not too much notice is paid by the market people.*)

What is that?
SADIKU: If my guess is right, it will be mummers.    1480

(*Adds slyly.*)

Somebody must have told them the news.
LAKUNLE: What news?

(*Sadiku chuckles darkly and comprehension breaks on the school teacher.*)

Baroka! You dared . . . ?
Woman, is there no mercy in your veins?
He gave you children, and he stood
Faithfully by you and them.
He risked his life that you may boast
A warrior-hunter for your lord . . . But you—
You sell him to the rhyming rabble
Gloating in your disloyalty . . .    1490
SADIKU: (*calmly dips her hand in his pocket.*)
Have you any money?
LAKUNLE: (*snatching out her hand*)
Why? What? . . . Keep away, witch! Have you
Turned pickpocket in your dotage?
SADIKU: Don't be a miser. Will you let them go without giving
you a special performance?
LAKUNLE: If you think I care for their obscenity . . .
SADIKU: (*wheedling.*) Come on, school teacher. They'll expect
it of you . . . The man of learning . . . the young sprig of 1500
foreign wisdom . . . You must not demean yourself in their
eyes . . . you must give them money to perform for your lordship. . . .

(*Re-enter the mummers, dancing straight through [more centrally this time] as before. Male dancer enters first, pursued by a number of young women and other choral idlers. The man dances in tortured movements. He and about half of his pursuers have already danced offstage on the opposite side when Sadiku dips her hand briskly in Lakunle's pocket, this time with greater success. Before Lakunle can stop her, she has darted to the drummers and pressed a coin apiece on their foreheads, waving them to possession of the floor. Tilting their heads backwards, they drum her praises. Sadiku denies the credit, points to Lakunle as the generous benefactor. They transfer their attention to him where he stands biting his lips at the trick. The other dancers have now been brought back*)

*and the drummers resume the beat of the interrupted dance.
The treasurer removes the coins from their foreheads and
places them in a pouch. Now begins the dance of virility which
is of course none other than the Baroka story. Very athletic
movements. Even in his prime, "Baroka" is made a comic figure, held in a kind of tolerant respect by his women. At his decline and final downfall, they are most unsparing in their
taunts and tantalizing motions. Sadiku has never stopped
bouncing on her toes through the dance, now she is done the
honour of being invited to join at the kill. A dumb show of
bashful refusals, then she joins them, reveals surprising agility
for her age, to the wild enthusiasm of the rest who surround
and spur her on.*

*With "Baroka" finally scotched, the crowd dances away to
their incoming movement, leaving Sadiku to dance on oblivious of their departure. The drumming becomes more distant
and she unwraps her eyelids. Sighs, looks around her, and
walks contentedly towards Lakunle. As usual he has enjoyed
the spectacle in spite of himself, showing especial relish where
"Baroka" gets the worst of it from his women. Sadiku looks at
him for a moment while he tries to replace his obvious enjoyment with disdain. She shouts "Boo" at him, and breaks into a
dance movement, shakes a sudden leg at Lakunle.)*

SADIKU: Sadiku of the duiker's feet . . . that's what the men
    used to call me. I could twist and untwist my waist with the
    smoothness of a water snake . . .
LAKUNLE: No doubt. And you are still just as slippery.
    I hope Baroka kills you for this.
    When he finds out what your wagging tongue
1510    Has done to him, I hope he beats you
    Till you choke on your own breath . . .

*(Sidi bursts in, she has been running all the way. She throws
herself on the ground against the tree and sobs violently, beating herself on the ground.)*

SADIKU: *(on her knees beside her.)* Why, child. What is the mat-
    ter?
SIDI: *(pushes her off)*
    Get away from me. Do not touch me.
LAKUNLE: *(with a triumphant smile, he pulls Sadiku away
    and takes her place.)*
    Oh, Sidi, let me kiss your tears. . . .
SIDI: *(pushes him so hard that he sits down abruptly.)*
1520    Don't touch me.
LAKUNLE: *(dusting himself.)*
    He must have beaten her.
    Did I not warn you both?
    Baroka is a creature of the wilds,
    Untutored, mannerless, devoid of grace.

*(Sidi only cries all the more, beats on the ground with clenched
fists, and stubs her toes in the ground.)*

    Chief though he is,
    I shall kill him for this . . .
    No. Better still, I shall demand
    Redress from the central courts.
1530    I shall make him spend
    The remainder of his wretched life
    In prison—with hard labour.

    I'll teach him
    To beat defenceless women . . .
SIDI: *(lifting her head.)*
    Fool! You little fools! It was a lie.
    The frog. The cunning frog!
    He lied to you, Sadiku.
SADIKU: Sango forbid!
SIDI: He told me . . . afterwards, crowing.    1540
    It was a trick.
    He knew Sadiku would not keep it to herself,
    That I, or maybe other maids would hear of it
    And go to mock his plight.
    And how he laughed!
    How his frog-face croaked and croaked
    And called me little fool!
    Oh how I hate him! How I loathe
    And long to kill the man!
LAKUNLE: *(retreating.)* But Sidi, did he . . . ? I mean . . .    1550
    Did you escape?

*(Louder sobs from Sidi.)*

    Speak, Sidi, this is agony.
    Tell me the worst; I'll take it like a man.
    Is it the fright which affects you so,
    Or did he . . . ? Sidi, I cannot bear the thought.
    The words refuse to form.
    Do not unman me, Sidi. Speak
    Before I burst in tears.
SADIKU: *(raises Sidi's chin in her hand.)*
    Sidi, are you a maid or not?    1560

*(Sidi shakes her head violently and bursts afresh in tears.)*

LAKUNLE: The Lord forbid!
SADIKU: Too late for prayers. Cheer up. It happens to the best
    of us.
LAKUNLE: Oh heavens, strike me dead!
    Earth, open up and swallow Lakunle.
    For he no longer has the wish to live.
    Let the lightning fall and shrivel me
    To dust and ashes . . .

*(Recoils.)*

    No, that wish is cowardly. This trial is my own.
    Let Sango and his lightning keep out of this. It    1570
    Is my cross, and let it not be spoken that
    In the hour of need, Lakunle stood
    Upon the scales and was proved wanting.
    My love is selfless—the love of spirit
    Not of flesh.

*(Stands over Sidi.)*

    Dear Sidi, we shall forget the past.
    This great misfortune touches not
    The treasury of my love.
    But you will agree, it is only fair
    That we forget the bride-price totally    1580
    Since you no longer can be called a maid.
    Here is my hand, if on these terms
    You'll be my cherished wife.
    We'll take an oath, between us three

That this shall stay
A secret to our dying days . . .

*(Takes a look at Sadiku and adds quickly.)*

Oh no, a secret even after we're dead and gone.
And if Baroka dares to boast of it,
I'll swear he is a liar—and swear by Sango too!

*(Sidi raises herself slowly, staring at Lakunle with unbelieving eyes. She is unsmiling, her face a puzzle.)*

1590  SIDI: You would? You would marry me?
LAKUNLE: *(puffs out his chest)* Yes.

*(Without a change of expression, Sidi dashes suddenly off the stage.)*

SADIKU: What on earth has got into her?
LAKUNLE: I wish I knew
She took off suddenly
Like a hunted buck.

*(Looks offstage.)*

I think—yes, she is,
She is going home.
Sadiku, will you go?
Find out if you can
1600   What she plans to do.

*(Sadiku nods and goes. Lakunle walks up and down.)*

And now I know I am the biggest fool
That ever walked this earth.
There are women to be found
In every town or village in these parts,
And every one a virgin.
But I obey my books.

*(Distant music. Light drums, flutes, box-guitars, "sekere.")*

"Man takes the fallen woman by the hand"
And ever after they live happily.
Moreover, I will admit,
1610   It solves the problem of her bride-price too.
A man must live or fall by his true
Principles. That, I had sworn,
Never to pay.

*(Enter Sadiku.)*

SADIKU: She is packing her things. She is gathering her clothes
and trinkets together, and oiling herself as a bride does be-
fore her wedding.
LAKUNLE: Heaven help us! I am not impatient.
Surely she can wait a day or two at least.
There is the asking to be done,
1620   And then I have to hire a praise-singer,
And such a number of ceremonies
Must firstly be performed.
SADIKU: Just what I said but she only laughed at me and called
me a . . . a . . . what was it now . . . a bra . . . braba . . .
brabararian. It serves you right. It all comes of your teaching. I said what about the asking and the other ceremonies.
And she looked at me and said, leave all that nonsense to
savages and brabararians.

LAKUNLE: But I must prepare myself.
I cannot be                                                          1630
A single man one day and a married one the next.
It must come gradually.
I will not wed in haste.
A man must have time to prepare,
To learn to like the thought.
I must think of my pupils too:
Would they be pleased if I were married
Not asking their consent . . . ?

*(The singing group is now audible even to him.)*

What is that? The musicians?
Could they have learnt so soon?                                      1640
SADIKU: The news of a festivity travels fast. You ought to know
that.
LAKUNLE: The goddess of malicious gossip
Herself must have a hand in my undoing.
The very spirits of the partial air
Have all conspired to blow me, willy-nilly
Down the slippery slope of grim matrimony.
What evil have I done . . . ? Ah, here they come!

*(Enter crowd and musicians.)*

Go back. You are not needed yet. Nor ever.
Hence parasites, you've made a big mistake.                          1650
There is no one getting wedded; get you home.

*(Sidi now enters. In one hand she holds a bundle, done up in a richly embroidered cloth: in the other the magazine. She is radiant, jewelled, lightly clothed, and wears light leather-thong sandals. They all go suddenly silent except for the long-drawn O-Ohs of admiration. She goes up to Lakunle and hands him the book.)*

SIDI: A present from Sidi.
I tried to tear it up
But my fingers were too frail.

*(To the crowd.)*

Let us go.

*(To Lakunle.)*

You may come too if you wish,
You are invited.
LAKUNLE: *(lost in the miracle of transformation.)*
Well I should hope so indeed
Since I am to marry you.                                             1660
SIDI: *(turns round in surprise.)*
Marry who . . . ? You thought . . .
Did you really think that you, and I . . .
Why, did you think that after him,
I could endure the touch of another man?
I who have felt the strength,
The perpetual youthful zest
Of the panther of the trees?
And would I choose a watered-down,
A beardless version of unripened man?                               1670
LAKUNLE: *(bars her way.)*
I shall not let you.
I shall protect you from yourself.

SIDI: *(gives him a shove that sits him down again, hard against the tree base.)*
Out of my way, book-nourished shrimp.
Do you see what strength he has given me?
That was not bad. For a man of sixty,
It was the secret of God's own draught
1680 A deed for drums and ballads.
But you, at sixty, you'll be ten years dead!
In fact, you'll not survive your honeymoon . . .
Come to my wedding if you will. If not . . .

*(She shrugs her shoulders. Kneels down at Sadiku's feet.)*

Mother of brides, your blessing . . .
SADIKU: *(lays her hand on Sidi's head.)* I invoke the fertile gods. They will stay with you. May the time come soon when you shall be as round-bellied as a full moon in a low sky.
SIDI: *(hands her the bundle.)*
Now bless my worldly goods.

*(Turns to the musicians.)*

1690 Come, sing to me of seeds

Of children, sired of the lion stock.

*(The musicians resume their tune. Sidi sings and dances.)*

Mo te'ni. Mo te'ni.
Mo te'ni. Mo te'ni.
Sun mo mi, we mo mi
Sun mo mi, fa mo mi
Yarabi lo m'eyi t'o le d'omo . . .

*(Festive air, fully pervasive. Oil lamps from the market multiply as traders desert their stalls to join them. A young girl flaunts her dancing buttocks at Lakunle and he rises to the bait. Sadiku gets in his way as he gives chase. Tries to make him dance with her. Lakunle last seen, having freed himself of Sadiku, clearing a space in the crowd for the young girl. The crowd repeat the song after Sidi.)*

Tolani Tolani
T'emi ni T'emi ni
Sun mo mi, we mo mi
Sun mo mi, fa mo mi
Yarabi lo m'eyi t'o le d'omo.[2]                                    1700

**T H E   E N D**

---

*IN this recent essay, Soyinka examines the problematic notion of "culture" in the context of contemporary Africa, in ways that echo the issues raised in* The Lion and the Jewel. *Is it possible to extricate "indigenous" from "colonial" elements? What are the effects of state censorship on what is produced as "culture"? What is the relationship between elements of "culture" produced for export to the West and the "culture" produced for consumption at home?*

# Wole Soyinka
"Twice Bitten: The Fate of Africa's Culture Producers"
(1990)

Let us anchor ourselves, for a start, to some acceptable terrain of cultural definitions. I shall use an example from our not too distant encounters. Few will disagree with me today, if I propose that we reject the concept of culture as realized in that manifestation known as Festac 77 (Festac: Black and African Festival of the Arts, Lagos, Nigeria, February 1977). For, in the main, our people were offered a narrowed-down, reductionist aspect of culture in a gargantuan orgy of ill-organized spectacles. That negative reference is meant to limit the field, to eliminate decisively what often imposes itself on public consciousness as Culture with a capital *C*, or as something pronounced into being by a Ministry of Culture. What Nigeria exhibited was Culture as a sum, not even of parts, but of spectacular parts. Now, "spectacle" need not be superficial. Revelry can attain profound Dionysiac proportions, involve an inner ennoblement, almost cathartic—but it requires a consciously organizing hand, with an integrated motif around which even disparate acts of revelry are drawn. In those extravagant fields of "Festacian" revelry, however, such complex, enriching offerings were relegated to token, or symbolic, expositions, starved of funds and given scant coverage even in the media, and were finally relegated to the archives of that supracultural monstrosity known as the National Theatre. The theater of which nation, by the way? Of Nigeria? Or of Bulgaria, from where the concrete carbuncle was lifted, then grafted onto Lagos marshlands? What, in that general's cap or Christmas cake of a structure, constitutes even a fragment of Nigerian or African architectural intellect, modern or traditional? But more on that building in another place.

We were saying that Culture is not parts. It is not even a sum of parts, but a summation, a synthesis. That is why *culture* sometimes leaves one dissatisfied in its definitions. Can anyone really

---

[2] "My net is spread, my net is spread
Come close to me, wrap yourself around me
Only God knows which moment makes the child . . . .

"Tolani Tolani
She belongs to me, belongs to me
Come close to me, wrap yourself around me
Only God knows which moment makes the child."

add up two oranges, three hoes, four traditional healers, two roadside mechanics, and five beaded crowns? The answer, we know, is not sixteen. But the intrinsic and overt productive processes of these parts do offer us an insight into the lived culture of a society. Exhuming, for instance, the remnants of those listed items—including the skeletons of the healers and mechanics—we can deduce, reconstruct, a framework of that society's principles of reproducing itself, of sustaining and enhancing life. We obtain from its aesthetic artifacts and utilitarian products a cultural residuum that is the cohering expression of its intellectual life, its secular and religious modalities of existence. Nothing is exempted. Not even the malformations—indeed, especially not the malformations. Over the years, those objective products and their interrelated activities—activities of producing oranges, healers, hoes, beaded crowns, and so on—implant aspects of their own contemporaneous being in a people's social psyche, aspects that sink, progressively, into the very foundation of a people's culture and can only be eradicated by a drastic, exceptional surgical act or a cataclysm on an unprecedented scale.

Take a certain aberration that took hold of the Nigerian mentality during a recent development of its taste: rice. In certain societies, rice is just another staple in the diet. In others, of course, it is profoundly cultural. But not in Nigeria. So there was nothing in the objective (or nutritive) properties of rice to qualify it, any more than maize, couscous, or *gari,* for the kind of status role that it occupied some years ago in our national consciousness. Then, suddenly, restrictions nudged rice off its rung on the hierarchical ladder of values. Rice became simply another food item, to be replaced by another craze—I do not know what is the latest, if any—until that also disappears. But you see, rice was only the objective focus of what is more truthfully part of the contemporary Nigerian culture—and that is, status consciousness, even in matters of food. It was not rice but status craving that was, and still is, an aspect of Nigerian culture. Rice was only another status symbol, like the taking of numerous chieftaincy titles, inventing professional prefixes that do not exist in other nations—"Engr." for engineer, "Arch." for architect, and so on. Soon we shall have "Lectr." for lecturer, "Desg." for fashion designer, "Musc." for musician, "Sectr." for secretary. But be sure you will never encounter "Tlr." for tailor or "Gdr." for gardener, although "Lsc. Art." for landscape artist may become the vogue. And you may be sure that there will evolve a "Dr." for driver or drummer, because the abbreviation will create a nice confusion with doctor! It has spread to writers. A prominent writer was quoted as saying that the taking of titles is sneaking into the cultural mission of Nigerian literary practitioners! Now there is bound to be competition, so in order to avoid coming to blows, I intend, as I proceed, to put forward my own humble suggestions. They are, let me hasten to add, purely suggestions, but I am convinced that any fair-minded listener will agree that I have been most even-handed with my ideas.

But while rice (especially the parboiled, Uncle Ben's variety) long held sway as a pretender to Nigerian cultural life, yam, *gari, amala, ngwamgwam, tuwo,* and so on, continued to occupy their prime places as bedrocks of the nation's culinary culture. Their existence was organic to the authentic, domestic, and social life of the peoples—celebrated with the seasons (such as the New Yam festivals), woven into the symbolisms and metaphors of song and dance, branded into the iconographic repertoire of society's sculptors, potters, graphic artists in cloth and leather, playing prominent roles in the various rites of social relationships—child naming, weddings, funerals, and kingship rites. The transient symbols come and go, but the basic elements of life affirmation remain, evolving, transforming man's concept and manipulation of his environment, influencing his assessment, his rejection of, or conciliation with, alien encounters.

How can we therefore even begin to think, for example, of contemporary urban development without first coming to terms with the legacy of indigenous shelters? I recall the fierce battle that we had to wage with Festac moguls before a Nigerian architect could be provided a few miserable naira to set up an exhibition of African indigenous architecture. It now forms one of the permanent features of the post-Festac exposition at the National Theatre. Has it, however, inseminated the turgid and costly forms of urban architecture at home? No, not to look at the buildings that have sprung up over the past decade! Ideas are still slaves to expertise, and that, as we know too sadly, is still indentured to alien training and outlook.

The easier path is always the transfer of models, which are the result of specific conditions—climate, social life-styles, economic acceptances, even religious influences. Well, in a country into which even snowtires are imported, what else can we expect? Our architectural program is easily the area of our greatest failure in cultural enracination. It is, unhappily, the most evident; its assault is visual, psychical, physical, and economic. Every time I am compelled to drive through our big cities, I can only wonder why so much time is spent debating the transfer of technology when, all around us, we can point to the deleterious effects of entire ecological transfers.

Culture, as we see, is produced. And before we get carried away by the actual state of the distinctively human activities that result in culture, we must pay attention to the condition of the producers of that culture and to their destiny at the hands of those who direct the affairs of state. Addressing ourselves to this African continent, the charter is one of self-indictment. Yes, pockets of optimism exist, even resilient and vibrant ones, but of course this should be the norm. Those exceptions need not therefore be an argument for self-gratulation, only staging posts for assault on the negative majority that stifle and decimate the productive potential of the continent. If the producers are not seen as the front line, indeed, the very gestatory base of culture, then there is simply no existing concept of culture that merits discussion and the state is free to dispense, in any way it considers fit, with its irrelevant, human cultural forces. Was it Himmler or Goebbels who declared, "When I hear the word 'culture,' I reach for my gun"? Several African leaders applaud, by example, appalling variants of that sentiment. Alex Kwapong,[1] I understand, has alerted this gathering to the epidemic of the "brain drain." Lucky drainees! The brains of their stay-at-home colleagues will be found as grisly sediments on the riverbed of the Nile. Or in the stomach linings of African crocodiles and vultures.

It is some four decades now, since the police of the British colonial government opened fire on a group of striking miners in Iva Valley, Enugu, killing eighteen of them and wounding several others. We do know that this scenario has been repeated times without number by the colonizer's replacements, the indigenous power inheritors in former colonial territories, but it is not that specific phenomenon to which I wish to call attention. Rather, it is to the creative product of that traumatizing experience, at the hands of—and here I venture our first title proposal—the Asiwaju of Nigerian theater, Hubert Ogunde, in his play *Bread and Bullets.* That play was proscribed by the colonial government in Kaduna, and the playwright was arrested and detained. It was his second such experience, the first being over his production of *Strike and Hunger,* which celebrated the historic national strike of 1945, a landmark of trade unionism in the country.

A few decades later, at the hands of the same indomitable and versatile artist, the record *Yoruba Ronu* was banned by yet another regime, this time the regional government of what was then Western Nigeria. The immediate context of the politics of the time was the arguable excuse. Hubert Ogunde made no bones about his partisanship even though the record was, by most standards of political art, quite moderate, though passionate in its exhortation of his favored cause. Once again, however—and this time in so-called independent, even democratic, times—notice was served on the artist that he operated within the larger schema of self-interest of the ruling class, however disorganized and fragmented. He could be called to order at any time, his works banned, his being restrained, if not altogether proscribed.

There must be few independent African countries today that have not experienced the truncation of their artistic and intellectual potential in the process of nation building. Some governments have been merely episodic in their execution of cultural repression—sporadic fits of fear, insecurity, obtuseness, arrogance of power, all the attributes of a minuscule self-apprehension that must reinforce the will to power by the exercise of excess. Others have been systematic, their mechanics built into the very definition of government, into the relationship between the ruler and the ruled. For the rulers, the dubious, yet sometimes direct and astringent, interpretation of reality constitutes a numinous terrain of the unpredictable that must be excised from national consciousness, *ab initio.* Many African states qualify for the former category; others, like Malawi, our most notorious example, predicate their very being upon this exorcising of predeterministic, near-metaphysical menace. The government of Malawi has instituted on this continent an automatism of censorship that operates like the medieval Index of the Roman Catholic Inquisition, even down to pyromaniac displays in the public auto-da-fé, that is, the public burnings of books that manage to escape the vigilant eye of the Customs Department. The parameters of Malawi's censorship are beyond coherence, beyond logic or sanity. A mishmash of Quakerish puritanism, the subconscious terror of sexual roles in human relationships, and even suggestiveness—allied with mere association by country, gatherings (such as this, for instance), or publicized conviction—can earn an author a place on the banned list, constantly augmented, but never deleted from, by gray presences in the secret chambers of censorship.

How much culture, and what sort of culture can we assess, is produced and partaken of by our brother and sister Malawians under this constricted view of their own continent? For we must not think for a moment that the censored books are simply from that ogreish, corrupting terrain of the European world. On the contrary. Some works by our own Chinua Achebe—and here comes my second proposed title today—the Ogbuefi[2] of contemporary Nigerian fiction, are featured on this list. I cannot now recall which titles; logically one would be *A Man of the People,* since this novel would be considered subversive for merely latching on at the end the denouement of a military coup. Wole Soyinka—who, since all available titles appear to have been taken, I have crowned the Original Suffer-Head of African Literature—has also swelled the list with quite a few titles, including *The Trials of Brother Jero.* I must confess that having studied this miracle list of banned books, I have yet to discover what African books are actually *read* in Malawi. We do know, however, that a British model public school, a little Eton, has been installed in Malawi, equipped with boating lake and punts, staffed by imported British public school teachers, and teaching Eton manners, complete with boaters, blazers, and flannels and administering precise public school caning perhaps?—all in order to create, and this is the declared policy of government, in order to create a British-educated elite to administer the nation along the manners of the old colonial masters. With such a deodorized intellectual conversion, what would be the fate of the plastic arts? Will such products ever experience exposure to the works of the painter Malangatana? of Skunder Bhogossian? of Demas Nwoko, Vincent Kofi, or Bruce Onabrakpeya? Are these deemed to be filled with subversive symbolism? Is Twins Seven-Seven considered a dangerous witchcraft artist, disseminating primitive creative notions already eradicated by nineteenth-century missionaries? How does the music of Fela Anikulapo-Kuti fare in Malawi's Etonian ears?

Of course, I have deliberately cited one of the more notorious examples. Malawi stands alone only in thoroughness, not in principle. And, at least to the best of my knowledge, the government of Malawi has yet to attempt to destroy, to expunge, its history, being content merely to suppress it. That it is destroying its producers of an authentic culture, under sometimes the most bizarre excuses, is also a notorious fact. What, for example, has been pronounced exactly the crime of Jack Mapanje, the poet and scholar? Why is he in prison? Why has he not been brought to trial? What indeed is Malawi's understanding of the African cultural enterprise when its most fecund minds are left to rot in prison? We shall return, again and again, to this theme. It is addressed to African leaders without exception, and must involve a concerted rethinking of the meaning of culture, and the place, in national development, of its producers. What have they to say on the *internal* brain drain?

I remarked earlier that none of the cultural suppressors whom I have cited above has made a blatant effort to *suppress* history—and of course I refer to history itself as a crucial component of art and culture—be this in the literary, musical, or iconographic arts. The Iva Valley massacre is material of our history, of reenactment either as statements or as instruments for social cautionary paradigms, or conscienticization. Such material presents useful analogues for contemporary situations or simply functions as legendary repositories. Certainly a song from Hubert Ogunde's *Bread and Bullets* is of greater aesthetic and relevant value than the latest disco-punk garbage from the Top Twenty racketeering cacophonies of Europe and America. This is how a nation's culture grows, organically, penetrating every aspect of work and play, of leisure and creativity. The encyclopedia of historical feats is a vast tome, infinite and inexhaustible. If we choose to feed from it, good. If we can dwell entirely in the realms of our own imagination, that also is valid. But imagine, just imagine, if the present-day government of Nigeria tried to excise the history of Iva Valley from popular knowledge, simply because it was resurrected by an Ola Rotimi or a Femi Osofisan. Or to excise the Aba Women's Riots. Or the feats of a Queen Amina. Or imagine if the Angolan government were to decree that the anticolonial poems of the late Agostinho Neto, the war chants of the women at the front, or the legendary feats of the guerrilla forces against the Portuguese are permanently banned from its repertoire of artistic celebrations. Try very hard, try to imagine this cultural reversal if you can.

You will, some of you at least, be wearisomely familiar with the expression "race retrieval," an expression much beloved of some, much abused by others—the present speaker probably belonging in both categories—but an expression employed to indicate the direction of cultural thinking and practice that is inevitable, at one level or the other, for all who have undergone the colonial" experience. It involves, very simply, the conscious activity of recovering what has been hidden, lost, repressed, denigrated, or indeed simply denied by ourselves—yes, by ourselves also—but definitely by the conquerors of our peoples and their Eurocentric bias of thought and relationships.

For a choice did exist, even for those conquistadores. But their choice was made from motives of racism, opportunism, and cultural chauvinism. Even where prolonged interaction did take place, the history of such contacts has been a history of denial, a prejudicial attenuation of the contributory cultures, and even deliberately concocted attributions—that is, the strategy of robbing nation A or nation B of the extant evidence of its own civilization, transferring it to some "unknown invaders," "a nomadic tribe just passing through, a trading outpost now abandoned, or some other distant civilization, lost in the mists of antiquity." Or by the trick of relegating even the untransferable products of such a culture to the realms of exotica, refusing to relate the culture to the entire organic process that produces a specific culture. The pyramids are a notorious example, as are the conclusions of Frobenius on the origins of Ife's classical sculpture.

I will not belabor the point. It is only part of the unworthy game of placing entire peoples outside history. Their existence as participants in a historic process did not commence, it is claimed, until the descent of the imperial yoke. Yet, for a people to develop, they must have constant recourse to their own history. Not uncritical recourse but definitely a recourse. To deny them the existence of this therefore has a purpose, for it makes them neutered objects on whose tabula rasa, that clean slate of the mind, the text of the master race—cultural, economic, religious, and so on—can be inscribed. A logical resistance counterstrategy therefore develops; true nationalists find themselves, at one stage or the other and on varying levels, confronted with a need to address the recovery of their history and culture, to retrieve the fount and tributaries of their race—to plot the meanderings, drought patches, and fertile watersheds; the bewildering trick of disappearance into earth and the near-magical resurgence in a distant and differentiated epoch, potent with irrigation powers, breeding a newly aware humanity equipped with the strategies of the experience-laden journey from its beginnings to the present.

So much for national experience under conquest. Now, here comes the irony. Having labored, sometimes in spite of colonial conditioning, to "retrieve" this obscured history and to refurbish the living feats of his self-determination, the contemporary artist, in several of our African nations, finds that he has to do a double retrieval; first from the colonial deniers of his past but also, second from the black neocolonial deniers of his immediate past and present, even when that immediate past is the history of his struggle for self-retrieval at the hands of the colonial deniers! Here, surely, is an intolerable twist of fate. The Mau Mau Liberation Movement is, nearly without parallel, one of the most heroic chapters of the total liberation struggle on the African continent. It was wholly indigenous, relying almost entirely on the physical, mental, and moral resources of the combatants in that struggle. It was not yet the time of the international market of state-of-the-art weaponry. Neither Russia nor its Eastern allies had yet formulated links with anticolonial rumbles—beyond platitudinous statements of supportive policy. The Mau Mau was therefore entirely autochthonous in both origin and execution. Sure, Jomo Kenyatta had visited the Soviet Union; he returned disillusioned. Certainly he did not reenter Kenya smuggling one solitary shotgun cartridge, nor with any Eastern Block supply lines in the making. This was totally a peasant revolt, owing nothing to external rival power plays or interests. It is therefore a remarkable moment of the "quantum leap" in anticolonial struggle, and—in view of the odds in inferior weaponry, isolation, and the desperate avarice of settler colonialism as opposed to surrogate controls—it was an event of heroic dimensions. Is it any wonder that the poets and dramatists, even those who were children or were yet unborn at the time of this struggle, return to it again and again for inspiration, for a creative dimension of national identification? So what then should we expect to be the attitude of a government whose very existence at the head of an independent nation would be unthinkable without this legendary struggle? This is what the novelist and playwright Ngugi wa Thiongo has to say— backed by detailed sources and direct experiences, including his own spell in jail and his present exile in Europe. He begins by acknowledging that experience of conqueror versus conquered on which we are all agreed:

> We know that when one nation conquers another nation, it tries to disfigure the history of the conquered nation. Thus when imperialist nations conquered and colonised Africa, they rewrote the history of the continent preceding the European slave or colonial presence. Those who fought against the colonising nations were depicted as villains and witches. Those who collaborated were seen in terms of outstanding courage and intelligence.

We should expect, and we are content to receive from conquerors, no less. But what do we have a right to expect when that battle has been won by the "villains and witches"? A reversal of the evaluation, surely! A retrieval of the authentic history of the struggle! Artists do not despise prudence. No one proposes that the dramatist attempt to stage, for example, Aimé Césaire's powerful drama of Patrice Lumumba, *A Season in the Congo*, in Mobutu Sese Seko's Zaire. That would be courting martyrdom. But does the government of Arap Moi in Mau Mau land really need to go as far as it does in the eradication of its own history? Ngugi informs us:

> With the publication of *Thunder from the Mountains* . . . and particularly Maina-wa-Kinyatti's introduction to the songs, the voice of Mau Mau began taking the offensive in the field of historical scholarship. The book was a thunderbolt in the university's academic community. Some of the people described in the book as "the leading anti-Mau Mau intellectuals" wrote to Maina-wa-Kinyatti threatening to sue him unless he apologised, withdrew the book from the market and paid for the damage to their spiritual wounds.

We need not take sides between these two intellectual warring camps. A case is not necessarily made because we sympathize with its cause. What interests us is which side the government took and with what weapons it chose to enter the fray. Our quote continues:

> The arrest of Maina-wa-Kinyatti on June 3, 1982 was preceded and followed by intensified cultural repression with plays being stopped, and an open air theatre, built by peasants and workers at Kamiriithu, razed to the ground. The plays [which were] stopped fall into three groups: those depicting the historical emergence of neocolonies as in Joe de Graft's *Muntu;* those exposing the brutality of colonial labour conditions and showing the determined struggle of the Kenyan workers against them as in Maitu Njugira; those glorifying armed resistance to colonialism as in Al Amin Mazrui's *Kikilio Cha Haki [The Cry for Justice]*; or those merely showing the betrayal of hopes as in *Kilio [The Cry]* by the Nairobi school students. It is quite telling that Al Amin Mazrui was himself arrested and detained without trial exactly two weeks after his play *Kilio Cha Haki* was performed at the University.

It is of additional interest to note that, as Ngugi writes, "in dramatic contrast to this censorship of any cultural expression that exposes colonialism was the state patronage of Western shows and procolonial culture."[3] The Kenya National Theatre witnessed what amounted to a state command performance of a ballet version of *Alice in Wonderland*, while the government actually purchased the television version of Elspeth Huxley's *Flame Trees of Thika*, a beautifully written work by the way but one that even a school pupil will recognize as a sundowner piece of colonial nostalgia, much in the current fashion of the film *Out of Africa,* on which so many millions of dollars were lavished to relive the decadent, patronizing caress of Africa and Africans.

As I speak, Maina-wa-Kinyatti is still in prison, going blind, among other health problems.[4] He was arrested on the flimsy charge of being in possession of a banned work—a la Malawi—and his trial was a farce by any standards of even the most determinedly fascistic dismissal of the rules of procedure. The government of Arap Moi actually relishes pouring scorn on all those who plead for his release, answers them with contumely, ridicule, or silence. Who else keeps or has kept company with him—all on their lonesome of course, not keeping one another company and relieving the tedium of intellectual deprivation, but in solitary confinement? Willy Mutunga, the law lecturer, who dared defend the arrested artists and intellectuals through the skills of his legal profession. Al Amin Mazrui, the playwright I have just mentioned, described as a brilliant linguist who writes in Kishwahili. Edward Oyugi, an educational psychologist and a cultural analyst. Mukaru

Ng'anga, a research historian whose subject was peasant life and the Mau Mau struggle. But listen to this also: there is Kamoji Wachira, a lecturer in geography and an ecological consultant. Observe how precarious is a chosen field of study for the academic! Trees? Are there not sufficient trees for study, lining the lush avenues of Nairobi? Anyone who goes into the forests and the villages to study *their* trees must be a subversive. If the campuses do not yield sufficient trees for research, it is obviously safer to go to Canada or Australia than to study in your own forest. Detention time, Mr. Scholar! Mind you, this government does have a sense of cultural continuity—Ngugi is grossly unfair in that respect. For the man who signs the detention orders for these cultural retrievers is apparently one Jeremiah Kiereni, whose role during the Mau Mau struggle was that of official censor in the so-called rehabilitation camps. His duty was to ensure that the plays and sketches with which the internees diverted themselves were strictly anti-Mau Mau—or, of course, of the strict religious-piety variety.

In 1958, I participated, albeit vicariously—how else?—in the history of that struggle, specifically in a drama production at the Royal Court Theatre, London, a piece that was based on the beating to death of eleven detainees in Hola Camp during the later stages of the Mau Mau resistance. A stylized, "improvised" production, it often took on the quality of a fluid, surreal ballet. Yes, balletic, but a very different kind of ballet from *Alice in Wonderland*, which had official blessing in Kenya while the Mau Mau plays were banned. The London production staged the official version of the deaths also, demonstrating how those prisoners were supposed to have died. This version claimed that they collapsed after drinking from a poisoned water supply. All the material for the staging was taken from the reports of the tribunal that inquired into the deaths of those eleven detainees in Hola Camp.

Now this is what came to mind as I studied the various accounts of postindependence Kenya, especially the more recent patterns of the repression of artists and intellectuals: in 1958, when the play was staged, there was an official censor in England, the lord chamberlain. So I wonder what would have been the response of his counterpart Jeremiah Kiereni, the black Kenyan censor in the rehabilitation camp, if the lord chamberlain had then consulted him about the advisability of *Eleven Men Dead at Hola* bestriding the boards of the famous Royal Court Theatre in London and subverting the colonial attitudes of the home audience. It seems to me rather odd that what the lord chamberlain did not consider subversive in 1958, at the height of the Mau Mau repression, is what is being suppressed today by Jeremiah Kiereni on behalf of President Arap Moi and his government, with all the collaborators in such enterprises being hauled off to jail or hounded into exile. This, surely, is a case of one's dyeing one's cloth a deeper indigo than that of the bereaved!

But of course the reasons are simple enough. Does that scene, those deaths from beating in Hola Camp, not call to mind the liquidation techniques in Ugandan prisons and military barracks during the reign of the African despot Field Marshal Alhaji, etc., etc., Idi Amin, DSO, Order of Israeli Elite Paratroopers, Conqueror of the British Empire, PhD, etc., etc.? What we screamed out loud at the time, what was stubbornly denied and derided by Amin's brother rulers as Western propaganda, only to be proved a mere hundredth of the horrendous reality toward the period of his overthrow and of course, abundantly afterward—those scenes in the military barracks, on the banks of the Nile River, the open cemeteries of Ugandan forests, the heads and limbs in Idi Amin's private refrigerators—were these really any different from the *danse macabre* of warders and inmates at Hola? or the tortures and mutilations of the indigenes by Belgians in the Congo? the Portuguese village massacre at Wiriyamu? or indeed the hideous atrocities inflicted on the populace by the South African-backed terrorists in Mozambique? The language of Arap Moi is no different from the language of Idi Amin—"the wolf cry of Western propaganda, of do-gooders, bad liberal conscience." What we say to these rulers is, Give us back Ban Kawadwa—if you can! If you cannot, at least restore the sight of Maina-wa-Kinyatti or else restore him to liberty. These are the retrievers of history, the refurbishers and creators of culture. You cannot speak of culture, of creativity, while you incarcerate the producers of the cultural experience. Again, I ask the question, What is the difference between *Eleven Men Dead at Hola*, the massacre of miners in Iva Valley, and the clubbing to death, to the muted protestation of fellow heads of state, of Archbishop Litwum and myriads of victims under Idi Amin? The scorched-earth policy of Portuguese last-ditch resistance—how does it differ from the massacres of Burundi and Ruanda in recent times?

Let us not mince words: the catalog of betrayal by our own kind, as leaders, is lengthy. And the sacrifices have been made as much by the masses as by the artists and the intelligentsia. I will not gloss over even the double betrayal of the late Sekou Touré, who still represents for many of us, both on the continent and in the diaspora, the radical face of African nationalism. Yet we know, as we did know even during his life, what horrors his regime spelled for dissidents, and most of all for the artists and intellectuals. The lucky ones were those who, like Camara Laye and Tamsir Niane, were able to escape into exile. But wives and families were often held hostage to the sadistic whims and egomania of a man who, for most of us, remained hallowed by the aura of that initial *"Non!"* which he spat in the face of French colonial arrogance. The French were kinder, more humane, to Sekou Touré than Sekou Touré was to his opposition. What was the fate of Diallo, first secretary-general of the Organisation of African Unity? What was the fate of Keita Fodeba, the founder and leader of the famous Guinean ballet corps that exploded the genius of Guinean dancing on the world in the sixties—from the Soviet Union down to the Antipodes—and became an envied model throughout Africa? Just how did the arts and its producers fare under this espouser of radical values within the African polity? To what cultural parameters are we reduced when the truly innovative—that is, the forms that question the surface reality, the easy appearances of society, and quarry into the deeper interstices of existence, be these political or artistic—to what level of simplistic beatitudes are we reduced when such forms are perceived as social threats and muzzled for good, all in the interest of the state, its captive cohorts and the vicious, protectionist interests of its external mentors, be they foreign powers, multinational corporations, or ideological cynics.

And after Idi Amin? Came Obote, who strove assiduously to surpass the record of his predecessor. And Emperor-for-Life Bokassa? I shall pass silently over these repetitions in the arena of surrealistic theater. Let them be. But we cannot, we dare not exonerate the complicity of their fellow leaders who turned a blind eye to the inhuman conduct of these despots. We give praise to those who gave refuge, even patronage, to the endangered species of the African artist, fleeing for his life, beating the goons of a demented ruler to the nearest border by mere seconds. But the responsibility is collective. African leaders, in full knowledge of events in Uganda, overrode all pleas and protestations, made Idi Amin the chairman of the Organisation of African Unity. Well, the African leaders did deserve him, for the choice was, for many, an instance of primus inter pares. But what about the rest of us, whom they claimed to lead? Was this the symbol of our deserving after concerted sacrifices and our will to self-retrieval?

Take Femi Osofisan's reworking of the history of Moremi, the Ondo heroine of those bygone intertribal warfares. Osofisan took hold of this legend, wrung it through a time warp, and made it serve on the nation certain lessons about the Agbekoya uprising in western Nigeria during the sixties. The ancient legend was there; the contemporary upheaval was not of his instigation. The artist of the stage saw both events through the matrix of a chosen ideological prism of society and wove a rich-textured play for the edification of society. He was fortunate. He did not live in Uganda or in Zaire. Nor indeed in the Guinea of Macias Nguema. He was not Dan Kintu or Ben Kawadwa, playwrights both and directors of the Uganda National Theatre, heading home fresh from the euphoria of having at least injected some solid pith and artistic marrow into the soufflé culture being promoted by the Second Black and African Festival of the Arts, Festac 77. Their welcome home was torture and grisly deaths, the flight and dispersal of their theater personnel into neighboring countries. Their crime: a historic play on a religious martyrdom in Uganda in ages gone by, which did recall, however, to the uneasy conscience of Idi Amin his recent murders of an archbishop and other officials of the Ugandan clergy. A brief address that I made to the exiled Ugandan intelligentsia in the University of Ife, after the ousting of Idi Amin in April 1979, refers, with some pardonable acerbity, to these experiences and to the history of stubborn hostility to a recognition of the internal brain drain perpetrated by the dictator of Uganda:

> We who thought up this modest occasion know only too painfully that we are the brain-washed victims of Western propaganda who have no feeling for, and no interest in, the welfare of the Ugandan masses. In our primitive, unanalytical manner, we have failed to recognize the phenomenon of Idi Amin as a mere product and consequence of colonial history, explainable by the socioeconomic theories of neocolonialism and international capital. Indeed, our

stubborn, consistent position on the baneful intrusion of Idi Amin on the Ugandan landscape is the very evidence of our incapacity to learn that History must never be interfered with, nor propelled forward by meaningful acts, but cosseted by sophisticated theories. Thus, at the inaugural meeting of the Union [of Writers of the African Peoples] in Accra, 1975, we horrified the elevated world of black intelligentsia by calling attention to the atrocities perpetrated on our Ugandan brothers and sisters, and *begged* the OAU not to dishonor the continent any further by passing the chairmanship of that body to Idi Amin. The resolution was, to make matters worse, taken after an intense discussion of testimonies from Ugandans, among whom were those whose support had won Idi Amin popular acceptance within and outside Uganda in the first place. The testimonies included reports by African diplomatic missions in Kampala, some of whose representatives had openly supported the ousting of Milton Obote at the beginning. The Union of Writers committed the unforgivable sin of considering facts, verified and documented, as opposed to distanced, lofty dismissals of such unassailable evidence. Is it to be wondered at that, even in this hour of truth, the guardians of "radical" socioeconomic postulates, in strange company with the custodians of international proprieties, of charters and protocol, of article and codicils, now pronounce themselves awakened to the "suffering of the Ugandan masses" that, alas, is the heartrending harvest of the effort of any people to free themselves?

It is all part of our history. We must not permit ourselves to forget it—ever! And Nigerians have nothing to be complacent about in this respect. How many years ago were three young men publicly executed, despite public protestations, on a law that was made retroactive for that very purpose? We fool ourselves if we try to flaunt our moral indignation at the nature of the alleged crime—drug pushing. That moral indignation should be reversed, and was indeed amply expressed, at the so-called morality of a regime that made a law to fit a past crime, and in peacetime, without even the dubious claims of a revolutionary crisis within society.

And may I used this forum to call upon the Lagos State government once again, asking it to act with compassion and a sense of justice on the fate of those twelve youths condemned to face the firing squad.[5] Such action would go beyond the exercise of the prerogative of mercy; I am saying that there are far too many unsatisfactory aspects of this case, that nothing short of a retrial will settle these profound doubts and serve as a lesson to the nation, by inevitably exposing some of the questionable aspects of investigations, trials, and condemnations in this society. It is of interest to us as the body on behalf of whom justice is executed—though I think, sometimes, "perpetrated" is the more accurate expression.

Those of us who expressed fears that a self-conscious, self-modeling Idi Amin was being hatched right under our noses were mostly dismissed as alarmists—all this a mere five years ago! Yet the equivalents of concentration camps were being nurtured, and disappearances were becoming part of daily life. We take no pleasure in being proved right through the evidence, later unearthed, of dehumanization schemes to be unleashed on our populace, so the expulsion of that putative Aminian pair[6] was an event to be welcomed. We call attention to it, to a situation where guilt was so deliberately confounded with innocence and indeed—with the absence of crime—that a condition of total national guilt was surreptitiously grown into the national psyche, and it would have been only a matter of time before the public began to shout "Hang them all" even before a trial. And that regime would have obliged. And the following morning, or week, or year, a sober populace would have woken up to the horror of their own submission to a carefully manipulated hysteria that had resulted in the liquidation of their own champions—despite all their warts and failures—while preserving their irredeemable enemies. I recall that even a reputable lawyer, a tireless upholder of the rights of the oppressed, succumbed to this popular reaction to past profligacy and oppression. His emotive pronouncements fueled the pretensions to a drastic sword of righteousness wielded by a purely rhetorical regime. For him, any accused was guilty and deserved summary execution, without even the benefit of a trial. For us whose profession it is to study the twitches behind the mask, it was déjà vu of the most boring, but potentially catastrophic, order. And it was not long before the hypocrisy of that regime began to expose itself, and of course the repression grew proportionately in intensity. Idi Amin was only months away when Nemesis struck.

That remarkable production *Budiso* at the National Theatre, presented as if to serve as a corrective view by yet another lawyer, Chief Aiyeyegbe, was an effective recapitulation of the menace of that period. We can only speculate today about what may have been the fate of a Lanrewaju Adepoju if he had made a frontal use of the Ewe recitative idiom, with its saws and pungency of proverbs, to comment on the reality of menace and insecurity in that period. Not that he has not, in recent times, tasted a reprehensible measure of what we might call "limit dosage" from this very regime, contrary to its "charter" of human rights and free expression. We only note, however, that his social commentary did not attempt even a fraction of his current astringency under the reign of the Terrible Duo. After their overthrow, we learned of imminent plans for "dealing with" recalcitrant artists and intellectuals. I was flattered to be informed that I was also on their list, but quite content that matters never really came to that pass. The question then is this: with all the vagaries and uncertainties of political life on our continent, what is the guarantee of the unfettered contribution of the artist to development? Do we draw up a charter? A bill of rights and responsibilities? Will it be respected? Would such a move be on the same level of unenforceable edicts as the call by the Constituent Assembly for a clause to outlaw military coups?

I am not one of the organizers of this meeting, the first African Leadership Forum. I do not fully know its mandate, what it is willing to achieve. But it is taking place in the retreat of a former head of state, and it was declared open by the current head of state. Other former heads of state and even some incumbent heads, I was informed, would be present, and the debates would involve a search for alternative strategies for the development of Africa. I was delighted to learn that one such former leader would be Léopold Sédar Senghor, on behalf of whom I can contentedly appropriate the chieftaincy title of Eminence Griot of African Poetry. My assumption here is that these leaders—with all their intimate knowledge of some of the history provided in the foregoing, their recognition even of their sometime neglect, sometime misreading, or misallocation of the place of the cultural producer in the strategies of nation building—these leaders can lend experiential authority to proposals for the protection of this menaced, creative breed that would make sociopolitical sense to their brother rulers. The costly errors of the past—both in human potential and in the stagnation of development, along with the banalization of our environment because of this neglect—should not continue. The producers of culture are not a poor relation of development; even less are they designed to be frontline victims for delusions of power, for leadership alienation and paranoia at the pinnacle of state authority, destined to physical brain drain, flushed down the toilet of rulers with a macabre sense of humor. Artists, intellectuals, technologists, and other producers of culture will always function despite state hostility or indifference, but it is obviously saner, and productive, to opt for an integral relationship, even at the very level of planning. We have examples to help us, few though they are, and the very personas of Léopold Sédar Senghor, for instance, both poet and statesman, and of Julius Nyerere, a poet, translator, and nation builder, are most appropriate symbols of this quite logical symbiosis, reminding one of the lines of yet another poet-politician, Aimé Césaire, whose portrait of Patrice Lumumba captures this essence of the elusive nature, often unrealized, of the rapture of the creative soul within the convulsions of nation building:

> I will be the field, I will be the pasture
> I will be with the Wagenia fisherman
> I will be with the Kivu drover
> I will be on the mountain, I will be in the ravine

It is a song that has come down through the ages, and through the lips, the adze, the dance motions, the textures and designs of our fabrics, the wall paintings; it is the community song of arms and feet in the organic labor of erecting shelter, planting, and harvesting the earth. It is the heroic hymn of the producers of our history and culture, in the never-ending process of development.

### Notes

[1]Kwapong, deputy rector of the United Nations University, Japan, was one of the participants at the African Leadership Forum.

[2]Achebe is a Nigerian writer who denounced any suggestion of Nobel prize-dictated hierarchies.

[3]Ngugi wa Thiongo is quoted from his *From the Barrel of a Pen: Resistance to Repression in*

*Neo-Colonial Kenya* (Trenton: Africa World, 1983).

[4]A source has since informed me that Maina has been set at liberty, but this is yet (as of 7 Nov. 1988) to receive confirmation.

[5]Editor's note: Despite Soyinka's appeal, and the appeal of other public figures, these twelve youths were convicted of armed robbery and executed.

[6]Generals Buhari and Idiagbon, the two military thugs who terrorized the nation until they were toppled by Ibrahim Babangid.

# Amiri Baraka/LeRoi Jones

Born Everett LeRoi Jones in Newark, New Jersey, in 1934, Amiri Baraka has become the most important revolutionary voice in contemporary black theater in the United States. He attended Rutgers and Howard Universities, taking his B. A. from Howard in 1954. Baraka later said that his education at Howard was too involved with "learning to be white." He served in the United States Air Force before returning to New York in 1958. Living in Greenwich Village, he studied at Columbia University, married his first wife—an interracial marriage, lightly disguised in his play *The Slave*—and worked to develop his talents as a writer. Jones worked everywhere to develop a black esthetic, in his own poetry (in the mode of the Beat poets Gregory Corso and Allen Ginsberg), in essays, and in magazines that he founded and edited. In 1960, Jones was part of a delegation of African Americans invited to Cuba to celebrate Fidel Castro's revolution. That visit had a profound impact on Jones, sharpening his sense of the need both for a distinctive black esthetic and culture, and for a social revolution to eradicate the injustices of white-dominated American society. His plays of the 1960s are, in fact, often directly concerned with this issue and with how white liberalism—ostensibly the ally of black power—finally becomes an obstacle to the more fundamental revolution needed to bring black identity, culture, and power into being. In 1964, three of his plays opened in New York: *The Eighth Ditch*, *The Baptism*, and *Dutchman*, which won the Obie award for the best American play of the season. He then wrote a series of plays examining black activism and revolution in American life: *The Slave* and *The Toilet* (1964), *Experimental Death Unit #1* (1965), and *J-e-l-l-o* (1965). The assassination of Malcolm X in 1965 and the Watts riots in Los Angeles also drove Jones toward a more militant position in plays like *A Black Mass* (1966), *Slave Ship* (1966), *The Great Goodness of Life (A Coon Show)* (1967), *Home on the Range* (1968), and *The Death of Malcolm X* (1969), and later in *The Motion of History* (1977), and *Money* (1988). In 1964, Jones established the Black Arts Repertory Theater and School in Harlem, and began a program of cultural nationalism there, which he has pursued subsequently in several other organizations and described in several collections of essays. He has been involved in developing a theater that would serve the need for cultural and political revolution in the black community.

As part of his commitment to forging a sustaining system of values for the African-American community, Jones became a Kawaidi Muslim minister in 1968, adopting the title Imamu (spiritual leader) and the name Amiri Baraka at that time. Throughout the 1970s and 1980s, Baraka articulated and solidified the claims of cultural nationalism, frequently in a fiercely revolutionary, Marxist rhetoric. Baraka continues to live in Newark, New Jersey, and is involved in a variety of political and social activities in the black community.

## Dutchman (1964)

*Dutchman* is one of Baraka's most powerful plays, both in its indictment of racist culture and in its straightforward confrontation between Lula and Clay. The title alludes to the legendary *Flying Dutchman*, the ship of the dead said to haunt the high seas. The subway car of the play is at once a ghost-ship—where the young black man Clay is murdered—and a ghostly incarnation of racist fantasies. At the beginning of the play, Lula seems attracted to the middle-class Clay, but as the play develops it becomes clear that, to seduce Clay, Lula must transform him into something else, a fantasy figure of the white imagination. When Clay refuses to play along, delivering instead an impassioned statement of his own black identity, Lula murders him, with the implied consent of the white riders of the subway. *Dutchman* is a powerful parable of the problems of black identity in white culture.

# —Dutchman—
## Amiri Baraka

## —CHARACTERS—

CLAY, *twenty-year-old Negro*
LULA, *thirty-year-old white woman*
RIDERS OF COACH, *white and black*
YOUNG NEGRO
CONDUCTOR

*In the flying underbelly of the city. Steaming hot, and summer on top, outside. Underground. The subway heaped in modern myth.*

*Opening scene is a man sitting in a subway seat, holding a magazine but looking vacantly just above its wilting pages. Occasionally he looks blankly toward the window on his right. Dim lights and darkness whistling by against the glass. (Or paste the lights, as admitted props, right on the subway windows. Have them move, even dim and flicker. But give the sense of speed. Also stations, whether the train is stopped or the glitter and activity of these stations merely flashes by the windows.)*

*The man is sitting alone. That is, only his seat is visible, though the rest of the car is outfitted as a complete subway car. But only his seat is shown. There might be, for a time, as the play begins, a loud scream of the actual train. And it can recur throughout the play, or continue on a lower key once the dialogue starts.*

*The train slows after a time, pulling to a brief stop at one of the stations. The man looks idly up, until he sees a woman's face staring at him through the window; when it realizes that the man has noticed the face, it begins very premeditatedly to smile. The man smiles too, for a moment, without a trace of self-consciousness. Almost an instinctive though undesirable response. Then a kind of awkwardness or embarrassment sets in, and the man makes to look away, is further embarrassed, so he brings back his eyes to where the face was, but by now the train is moving again, and the face would seem to be left behind by the way the man turns his head to look back through the other windows at the slowly fading platform. He smiles then; more comfortably confident, hoping perhaps that his memory of this brief encounter will be pleasant. And then he is idle again.*

SCENE I

*Train roars. Lights flash outside the windows.*

LULA *enters from the rear of the car in bright, skimpy summer clothes and sandals. She carries a net bag full of paper books, fruit, and other anonymous articles. She is wearing sunglasses, which she pushes up on her forehead from time to time. LULA is a tall, slender, beautiful woman with long red hair hanging straight down her back, wearing only loud lipstick in somebody's good taste. She is eating an apple, very daintily. Coming down the car toward CLAY.*

*She stops beside CLAY's seat and hangs languidly from the strap, still managing to eat the apple. It is apparent that she is going to sit in the seat next to CLAY, and that she is only waiting for him to notice her before she sits.*

CLAY *sits as before, looking just beyond his magazine, now and again pulling the magazine slowly back and forth in front of his face in a hopeless effort to fan himself. Then he sees the woman hanging there beside him and he looks up into her face, smiling quizzically.*

LULA: Hello.
CLAY: Uh, hi're you?
LULA: I'm going to sit down. . . . O.K.?
CLAY: Sure.
LULA:

*(Swings down onto the seat, pushing her legs straight out as if*

*she is very weary)*

Oooof! Too much weight.
CLAY: Ha, doesn't look like much to me.

*(Leaning back against the window, a little surprised and maybe stiff)*

LULA: It's so anyway.

*(And she moves her toes in the sandals, then pulls her right leg up on the left knee, better to inspect the bottoms of the sandals and the back of her heel. She appears for a second not to notice that CLAY is sitting next to her or that she has spoken to him just a second before. CLAY looks at the magazine, then out the black window. As he does this, she turns very quickly toward him)*

Weren't you staring at me through the window?
CLAY:                                                          10

*(Wheeling around and very much stiffened)*

What?
LULA: Weren't you staring at me through the window? At the last stop?
CLAY: Staring at you? What do you mean?
LULA: Don't you know what staring means?
CLAY: I saw you through the window . . . if that's what it means. I don't know if I was staring. Seems to me you were staring through the window at me.
LULA: I was. But only after I'd turned around and saw you staring through that window down in the vicinity of my ass 20

and legs.

CLAY: Really?

LULA: Really. I guess you were just taking those idle potshots. Nothing else to do. Run your mind over people's flesh.

CLAY: Oh boy. Wow, now I admit I was looking in your direction. But the rest of that weight is yours.

LULA: I suppose.

CLAY: Staring through train windows is weird business. Much weirder than staring very sedately at abstract asses.

30 LULA: That's why I came looking through the window . . . so you'd have more than that to go on. I even smiled at you.

CLAY: That's right.

LULA: I even got into this train, going some other way than mine. Walked down the aisle . . . searching you out.

CLAY: Really? That's pretty funny.

LULA: That's pretty funny . . . God, you're dull.

CLAY: Well, I'm sorry, lady, but I really wasn't prepared for party talk.

LULA: No, you're not. What are you prepared for?

*(Wrapping the apple core in a Kleenex and dropping it on the floor)*

40 CLAY:

*(Takes her conversation as pure sex talk. He turns to confront her squarely with this idea)*

I'm prepared for anything. How about you?

LULA:

*(Laughing loudly and cutting it off abruptly)*

What do you think you're doing?

CLAY: What?

LULA: You think I want to pick you up, get you to take me somewhere and screw me, huh?

CLAY: Is that the way I look?

LULA: You look like you been trying to grow a beard. That's exactly what you look like. You look like you live in New Jersey

50 with your parents and are trying to grow a beard. That's what. You look like you've been reading Chinese poetry and drinking lukewarm sugarless tea.

*(Laughs, uncrossing and recrossing her legs)*

You look like death eating a soda cracker.

CLAY:

*(Cocking his head from one side to the other, embarrassed and trying to make some comeback, but also intrigued by what the woman is saying . . . even the sharp city coarseness of her voice, which is still a kind of gentle sidewalk throb.)*

Really? I look like all that?

LULA: Not all of it.

*(She feigns a seriousness to cover an actual somber tone)*

I lie a lot.

*(Smiling)*

It helps me control the world.

CLAY:

*(Relieved and laughing louder than the humor)*

Yeah, I bet.    60

LULA: But it's true, most of it, right? Jersey? Your bumpy neck?

CLAY: How'd you know all that? Huh? Really. I mean about Jersey . . . and even the beard. I met you before? You know Warren Enright?

LULA: You tried to make it with your sister when you were ten.

*(CLAY leans back hard against the back of the seat, his eyes opening now, still trying to look amused)*

But I succeeded a few weeks ago.

*(She starts to laugh again)*

CLAY: What're you talking about? Warren tell you that? You're a friend of Georgia's?

LULA: I told you I lie. I don't know your sister. I don't know Warren Enright.    70

CLAY: You mean you're just picking these things out of the air?

LULA: Is Warren Enright a tall skinny black black boy with a phony English accent?

CLAY: I figured you knew him.

LULA: But I don't. I just figured you would know somebody like that.

*(Laughs)*

CLAY: Yeah, yeah.

LULA: You're probably on your way to his house now.

CLAY: That's right.

LULA:    80

*(Putting her hand on CLAY's closer knee, drawing it from the knee up to the thigh's hinge, then removing it, watching his face very closely, and continuing to laugh, perhaps more gently than before)*

Dull, dull, dull. I bet you think I'm exciting.

CLAY: You're O.K.

LULA: Am I exciting you now?

CLAY: Right. That's not what's supposed to happen?

LULA: How do I know?

*(She returns her hand, without moving it, then takes it away and plunges it in her bag to draw out an apple)*

You want this?

CLAY: Sure.

LULA:

*(She gets one out of the bag for herself)*

Eating apples together is always the first step. Or walking up uninhabited Seventh Avenue in the twenties on weekends.    90

*(Bites and giggles, glancing at CLAY and speaking in loose singsong)*

Can get you involved . . . boy! Get us involved. Um-huh.

*(Mock seriousness)*

Would you like to get involved with me, Mister Man?

CLAY:

*(Trying to be a flippant as LULA, whacking happily at the apple)*

Sure. Why not? A beautiful woman like you. Huh, I'd be a

fool not to.

LULA: And I bet you're sure you know what you're talking about.

(*Taking him a little roughly by the wrist, so he cannot eat the apple, then shaking the wrist*)

I bet you're sure of almost everything anybody ever asked you about . . . right?

(*Shakes his wrist harder*)

100 Right?

CLAY: Yeah, right. . . . Wow, you're pretty strong, you know? Whatta you, a lady wrestler or something?

LULA: What's wrong with lady wrestlers? And don't answer because you never knew any. Huh.

(*Cynically*)

That's for sure. They don't have any lady wrestlers in that part of Jersey. That's for sure.

CLAY: Hey, you still haven't tole me how you know so much about me.

LULA: I told you I didn't know anything about *you* . . . you're a
110 well-known type.

CLAY: Really?

LULA: Or at least I know the type very well. And your skinny English friend too.

CLAY: Anonymously?

LULA:

(*Settles back in seat, single-mindedly finishing her apple and humming snatches of rhythm and blues song*)

What?

CLAY: Without knowing us specifically?

LULA: Oh boy.

(*Looking quickly at* CLAY)

What a face. You know, you could be a handsome man.
120 CLAY: I can't argue with you.

LULA:

(*Vague, off-center response*)

What?

CLAY:

(*Raising his voice, thinking the train noise has drowned part of his sentence*)

I can't argue with you.

LULA: My hair is turning gray. A gray hair for each year and type I've come through.

CLAY: Why do you want to sound so old?

LULA: But it's always gentle when it starts.

(*Attention drifting*)

Hugged against tenements, day or night.
130 CLAY: What?

LULA:

(*Refocusing*)

Hey, why don't you take me to that party you're going to?

LULA: You must be a friend of Warren's to know about

the party.

LULA: Wouldn't you like to take me to the party?

(*Imitates clinging vine*)

Oh, come on, ask me to your party.

CLAY: Of course I'll ask you to come with me to the party. And I'll bet you're a friend of Warren's.

LULA: Why not be a friend of Warren's? Why not?

(*Taking his arm*)

Have you asked me yet?                                   140
CLAY: How can I ask you when I don't know your name?

LULA: Are you talking to my name?

CLAY: What is it, a secret?

LULA: I'm Lena the Hyena.

CLAY: The famous woman poet?

LULA: Poetess! The same!

CLAY: Well, you know so much about me . . . what's my name?

LULA: Morris the Hyena.

CLAY: The famous woman poet?

LULA: The same.                                          150

(*Laughing and going into her bag*)

You want another apple?

CLAY: Can't make it, lady. I only have to keep one doctor away a day.

LULA: I bet your name is . . . something like . . . uh, Gerald or Walter. Huh?

CLAY: God, no.

LULA: Lloyd, Norman? One of those hopeless colored names creeping out of New Jersey. Leonard? Gag. . . .

CLAY: Like Warren?

LULA: Definitely. Just exactly like Warren. Or Everett.        160
CLAY: Gag. . . .

LULA: Well, for sure, it's not Willie.

CLAY: It's Clay.

LULA: Clay? Really? Clay what?

CLAY: Take your pick. Jackson, Johnson, or Williams.

LULA: Oh, really? Good for you. But it's got to be Williams. You're too pretentious to be a Jackson or Johnson.

CLAY: Thass right.

LULA: But Clay's O.K.

CLAY: So's Lena.                                          170
LULA: It's Lula.

CLAY: Oh?

LULA: Lula the Hyena.

CLAY: Very good.

LULA:

(*Starts laughing again*)

Now you say to me, "Lula, Lula, why don't you go to this party with me tonight?" It's your turn, and let those be your lines.

CLAY: Lula, why don't you go to this party with me tonight, Huh?                                                    180
LULA: Say my name twice before you ask, and no huh's.

CLAY: Lula, Lula, why don't you go to this party with me tonight?

LULA: I'd like to go, Clay, but how can you ask me to go when you barely know me?

CLAY: That is strange, isn't it?

LULA: What kind of reaction is that? You're supposed to say, "Aw, come on, we'll get to know each other better at the party."

190  CLAY: That's pretty corny.

LULA: What are you into anyway?

(Looking at him half sullenly but still amused)

What thing are you playing at, Mister? Mister Clay Williams?

(Grabs his thigh, up near the crotch)

What are *you* thinking about?

CLAY: Watch it now, you're gonna excite me for real.

LULA:

(Taking her hand away and throwing her apple core through the window)

I bet.

(She slumps in the seat and is heavily silent)

CLAY: I thought you knew everything about me? What happened?

(LULA looks at him, then looks slowly away, then over where the other aisle would be. Noise of the train. She reaches in her bag and pulls out one of the paper books. She puts it on her leg and thumbs the pages listlessly. CLAY cocks his head to see the title of the book. Noise of the train. LULA flips pages and her eyes drift. Both remain silent)

200  Are you going to the party with me, Lula?

LULA:

(Bored and not even looking)

I don't even know you.

CLAY: You said you know my type.

LULA:

(Strangely irritated)

Don't get smart with me, Buster. I know you like the palm of my hand.

CLAY: The one you eat the apples with?

LULA: Yeh. And the one I open doors late Saturday evening with. That's my door. Up at the top of the stairs. Five flights. 210  Above a lot of Italians and lying Americans. And scrape carrots with. Also . . .

(looks at him)

the same hand I unbutton my dress with, or let my skirt fall down. Same hand. Lover.

CLAY: Are you angry about anything? Did I say something wrong?

LULA: Everything you say is wrong.

(Mock smile)

That's what makes you so attractive. Ha. In that funnybook jacket with all the buttons.

(More animate, taking hold of his jacket)

What've you got the jacket and tie on in all this heat for? And 220  why're you wearing a jacket and tie like that? Did your people ever burn witches or start revolutions over the price of tea? Boy, those narrow-shoulder clothes come from a tradition you ought to feel oppressed by. A three-button suit. What right do you have to be wearing a three-button suit and striped tie? Your grandfather was a slave, he didn't go to Harvard.

CLAY: My grandfather was a night watchman.

LULA: And you went to a colored college where everybody thought they were Averell Harriman.

CLAY: All except me.   230

LULA: And who did you think you were? Who do you think you are now?

CLAY:

(Laughs as if to make light of the whole trend of the conversation)

Well, in college I thought I was Baudelaire. But I've slowed down since.

LULA: I bet you never once thought you were a black nigger.

(Mock serious, then she howls with laughter. CLAY is stunned but after initial reaction, he quickly tries to appreciate the humor. LULA almost shrieks)

A black Baudelaire.

CLAY: That's right.

LULA: Boy, are you corny. I take back what I said before. Everything you say is not wrong. It's perfect. You should be 240  on television.

CLAY: You act like you're on television already.

LULA: That's because I'm an actress.

CLAY: I thought so.

LULA: Well, you're wrong. I'm no actress. I told you I always lie. I'm nothing, honey, and don't you ever forget it.

(Laughter)

Although my mother was a Communist. The only person in my family ever to amount to anything.

CLAY: My mother was a Republican.

LULA: And your father voted for the man rather than the party. 250

CLAY: Right!

LULA: Yea for him. Yea, yea for him.

CLAY: Yea!

LULA: And yea for America where he is free to vote for the mediocrity of his choice! Yea!

CLAY: Yea!

LULA: And yea for both your parents who even though they differ about so crucial a matter as the body politic still forged a union of love and sacrifice that was destined to flower at the birth of the noble Clay . . . what's your middle name?   260

CLAY: Clay.

LULA: A union of love and sacrifice that was destined to flower at the birth of the noble Clay Clay Williams. Yea! And most of all yea yea for you. Clay Clay. The Black Baudelaire! Yes!

(And with knifelike cynicism)

My Christ. My Christ.

CLAY: Thank you, ma'am.

LULA: May the people accept you as a ghost of the future. And love you, that you might not kill them when you can.

CLAY: What?

LULA: You're a murderer, Clay, and you know it.   270

*(Her voice darkening with significance)*

You know goddamn well what I mean.

CLAY: I do?

LULA: So we'll pretend the air is light and full of perfume.

CLAY:

*(Sniffing at her blouse)*

It is.

LULA: And we'll pretend the people cannot see you. That is, the citizens. And that you are free of your own history. And I am free of my history. We'll pretend that we are both anonymous beauties smashing along through the city's entrails.

*(She yells as loud as she can)*

280    GROOVE!

*(Black)*

SCENE II

*Scene is the same as before, though now there are other seats visible in the car. And throughout the scene other people get on the subway. There are maybe one or two seated in the car as the scene opens, though neither* CLAY *nor* LULA *notices them.* CLAY's *tie is open.* LULA *is hugging his arm.*

CLAY: The party!

LULA: I know it'll be something good. You can come in with me, looking casual and significant. I'll be strange, haughty, and silent, and walk with long slow strides.

CLAY: Right.

LULA: When you get drunk, pat me once, very lovingly on the flanks, and I'll look at you cryptically, licking my lips.

CLAY: It sounds like something we can do.

LULA: You'll go around talking to young men about your mind,
290    and to old men about your plans. If you meet a very close friend who is also with someone like me, we can stand together, sipping our drinks and exchanging codes of lust. The atmosphere will be slithering in love and half-love and very open moral decision.

CLAY: Great. Great.

LULA: And everyone will pretend they don't know your name, and then . . .

*(She pauses heavily)*

later, when they have to, they'll claim a friendship that denies your sterling character.

300 CLAY:

*(Kissing her neck and fingers)*

And then what?

LULA: Then? Well, then we'll go down the street, late night, eating apples and winding very deliberately toward my house.

CLAY: Deliberately?

LULA: I mean, we'll look in all the shopwindows, and make fun of the queers. Maybe we'll meet a Jewish Buddhist and flatten his conceits over some pretentious coffee.

CLAY: In honor of whose God?

310 LULA: Mine.

CLAY: Who is . . . ?

LULA: Me . . . and you

CLAY: A corporate Godhead.

LULA: Exactly. Exactly.

*(Notices one of the other people entering)*

CLAY: Go on with the chronicle. Then what happens to us?

LULA:

*(A mild depression, but she still makes her description triumphant and increasingly direct)*

To my house, of course.

CLAY: Of course.

LULA: And up the narrow steps of the tenement.

CLAY: You live in a tenement?                                    320

LULA: Wouldn't live anywhere else. Reminds me specifically of my novel form of insanity.

CLAY: Up the tenement stairs.

LULA: And with my apple-eating hand I push open the door and lead you, my tender big-eyed prey, into my . . . God, what can I call it . . . into my hovel.

CLAY: Then what happens?

LULA: After the dancing and games, after the long drinks and long walks, the real fun begins.

CLAY: Ah, the real fun.                                          330

*(Embarrassed, in spite of himself)*

Which is . . . ?

LULA:

*(Laughs at him)*

Real fun in the dark house. Hah! Real fun in the dark house, high up above the street and the ignorant cowboys. I lead you in, holding your wet hand gently in my hand . . .

CLAY: Which is not wet?

LULA: Which is dry as ashes.

CLAY: And cold?

LULA: Don't think you'll get out of your responsibility that way. It's not cold at all. You Fascist! Into my dark living room. 340 Where we'll sit and talk endlessly, endlessly.

CLAY: About what?

LULA: About what? About your manhood, what do you think? What do you think we've been talking about all this time?

CLAY: Well, I didn't know it was that. That's for sure. Every other thing in the world but that.

*(Notices another person entering, looks quickly, almost involuntarily, up and down the car, seeing the other people in the car)*

Hey, I didn't even notice when those people got on.

LULA: Yeah, I know.

CLAY: Man, this subway is slow.

LULA: Yeah, I know.                                              350

CLAY: Well, go on. We were talking about my manhood.

LULA: We still are. All the time.

CLAY: We were in your living room.

LULA: My dark living room. Talking endlessly.

CLAY: About my manhood.

LULA: I'll make you a map of it. Just as soon as we get to my house.

CLAY: Well, that's great.

LULA: One of the things we do while we talk. And screw.

360 CLAY:

*(Trying to make his smile broader and less shaky)*

We finally got there.

LULA: And you'll call my rooms black as a grave. You'll say, "This place is like Juliet's tomb."

CLAY:

*(Laughs)*

I might.

LULA: I know. You've probably said it before.

CLAY: And is that all? The whole grand tour?

LULA: Not all. You'll say to me very close to my face, many, many times, you'll say, even whisper, that you love me.

370 CLAY: Maybe I will.

LULA: And you'll be lying.

CLAY: I wouldn't lie about something like that.

LULA: Hah. It's the only kind of thing you will lie about. Especially if you think it'll keep me alive.

CLAY: Keep you alive? I don't understand.

LULA:

*(Bursting out laughing, but too shrilly)*

Don't understand? Well, don't look at me. It's the path I take, that's all. Where both feet take me when I set them down. One in front of the other.

380 CLAY: Morbid. Morbid. You sure you're not an actress? All that self-aggrandizement.

LULA: Well, I told you I wasn't an actress . . . but I also told you I lie all the time. Draw your own conclusions.

CLAY: And is that all of our lives together you've described? There's no more?

LULA: I've told you all I know. Or almost all.

CLAY: There's no funny parts?

LULA: I thought it was all funny.

CLAY: But you mean peculiar, not ha-ha.

390 LULA: You don't know what I mean.

CLAY: Well, tell me the almost part then. You said almost all. What else? I want the whole story.

LULA:

*(Searching aimlessly through her bag. She begins to talk breathlessly, with a light and silly tone)*

All stories are whole stories. All of 'em. Our whole story . . . nothing but change. How could things go on like that forever? Huh?

*(Slaps him on the shoulder, begins finding things in her bag, taking them out and throwing them over her shoulder into the aisle)*

Except I do go on as I do. Apples and long walks with deathless intelligent lovers. But you mix it up. Look out the window, all the time. Turning pages. Change change change. 400 Till, shit, I don't know you. Wouldn't, for that matter. You're too serious. I bet you're even too serious to be psychoanalyzed. Like all those Jewish poets from Yonkers, who leave their mothers looking for other mothers, or others' mothers, on whose baggy tits they lay their fumbling heads. Their poems are always funny, and all about sex.

CLAY: They sound great. Like movies.

LULA: But you change.

*(Blankly)*

And things work on you till you hate them.

*(More people come into the train. They come closer to the couple, some of them not sitting, but swinging drearily on the straps, staring at the two with uncertain interest)*

CLAY: Wow. All these people, so suddenly. They must all come from the same place. 410

LULA: Right. That they do.

CLAY: Oh? You know about them too?

LULA: Oh yeah. About them more than I know about you. Do they frighten you?

CLAY: Frighten me? Why should they frighten me?

LULA: 'Cause you're an escaped nigger.

CLAY: Yeah?

LULA: 'Cause you crawled through the wire and made tracks to my side.

CLAY: Wire? 420

LULA: Don't they have wire around plantations?

CLAY: You must be Jewish. All you can think about is wire. Plantations didn't have any wire. Plantations were big open white-washed places like heaven, and everybody on 'em was grooved to be there. Just strummin' and hummin' all day.

LULA: Yes, yes.

CLAY: And that's how the blues was born.

LULA: Yes, yes. And that's how the blues was born.

*(Begins to make up a song that becomes quickly hysterical. As she sings she rises from her seat, still throwing things out of her bag into the aisle, beginning a rhythmical shudder and twist-like wiggle, which she continues up and down the aisle, bumping into many of the standing people and tripping over the feet of those sitting. Each time she runs into a person she lets out a very vicious piece of profanity, wiggling and stepping all the time)*

And that's how the blues was born. Yes. Yes. Son of a bitch, get out of the way. Yes. Quack. Yes. Yes. And that's how the 430 blues was born. Ten little niggers sitting on a limb, but none of them ever looked like him.

*(Points to CLAY, returns toward the seat, with her hands extended for him to rise and dance with her)*

And that's how blues was born. Yes. Come on. Clay. Let's do the nasty. Rub bellies. Rub bellies.

CLAY:

*(Waves his hands to refuse. He is embarrassed, but determined to get a kick out of the proceedings)*

Hey, what was in those apples? Mirror, mirror on the wall, who's the fairest one of all? Snow White, baby, and don't you forget it.

LULA:

*(Grabbing for his hands, which he draws away)*

Come on, Clay. Let's rub bellies on the train. The nasty. The 440 nasty. Do the gritty grind, like your ol' rag-head mammy. Grind till you lose your mind. Shake it, shake it, shake it, shake it! OOOOweeee! Come on, Clay. Let's do the choo-choo train shuffle, the navel scratcher.

CLAY: Hey, you coming on like the lady who smoked up her

grass skirt.

LULA:

(*Becoming annoyed that he will not dance, and becoming more animated as if to embarrass him still further*)

450 Come on, Clay . . . let's do the thing. Uhh! Uhh! Clay! Clay! You middle-class black bastard. Forget your social-working mother for a few seconds and let's knock stomachs. Clay, you liver-lipped white man. You would-be Christian. You ain't no nigger, you're just a dirty white man. Get up, Clay. Dance with me, Clay.

CLAY: Lula! Sit down, now. Be cool.

LULA:

(*Mocking him, in wild dance*)

Be cool. Be cool. That's all you know . . . shaking the wild-root cream-oil on your knotty head, jackets buttoning up to your chin, so full of white man's words. Christ! God! Get up and scream at these people. Like scream meaningless shit in 460 these hopeless faces.

(*She screams at people in train, still dancing*)

Red trains cough Jewish underwear for keeps! Expanding smells of silence. Gravy snot whistling like sea birds. Clay. Clay, you got to break out. Don't sit there dying the way they want you to die. Get up.

CLAY: Oh, sit the fuck down.

(*He moves to restrain her*)

Sit down, goddamn it.

LULA:

(*Twisting out of his reach*)

Screw yourself, Uncle Tom. Thomas Woolly-Head.

(*Begins to dance a kind of jig, mocking* CLAY *with loud forced humor*)

470 There is Uncle Tom . . . I mean, Uncle Thomas Woolly-Head. With old white matted mane. He hobbles on his wooden cane. Old Tom. Old Tom. Let the white man hump his ol' mama, and he jes' shuffle off in the woods and hide his gentle gray head. Ol' Thomas Woolly-Head.

(*Some of the other riders are laughing now. A drunk gets up and joins* LULA *in her dance, singing, as best he can, her "song."* CLAY *gets up out of his seat and visibly scans the faces of the other riders*)

CLAY: Lula! Lula!

(*She is dancing and turning, still shouting as loud as she can. The drunk too is shouting, and waving his hands wildly*)

Lula . . . you dumb bitch. Why don't you stop it?

(*He rushes half stumbling from his seat, and grabs one of her flailing arms*)

LULA: Let me go! You black son of a bitch.

(*She struggles against him*)

Let me go! Help!

(*CLAY *is dragging her towards her seat, and the drunk seeks to interfere. He grabs* CLAY *around the shoulders and begins*

wrestling with him. CLAY *clubs the drunk to the floor without releasing* LULA, *who is still screaming.* CLAY *finally gets her to the seat and throws her into it*)

CLAY: Now you shut the hell up.

(*Grabbing her shoulders*)

Just shut up. You don't know what you're talking about. You don't know anything. So just keep your stupid mouth closed. 480

LULA: You're afraid of white people. And your father was. Uncle Tom Big Lip!

CLAY:

(*Slaps her as hard as he can, across the mouth.* LULA's *head bangs against the back of the seat. When she raises it again,* CLAY *slaps her again*)

Now shut up and let me talk.

(*He turns toward the other riders, some of whom are sitting on the edge of their seats. The drunk is on one knee, rubbing his head, and singing softly the same song. He shuts up too when he sees* CLAY *watching him. The others go back to newspapers or stare out the windows*)

Shit, you don't have any sense, Lula, nor feelings either. I could murder you now. Such a tiny ugly throat. I could squeeze it flat, and watch you turn blue, on a humble. For dull kicks. And all these weak-faced ofays squatting around here, staring over their papers at me. Murder them too. Even if they expected it. That man there . . . 490

(*Points to well-dressed man*)

I could rip that *Times* right out of his hand, as skinny and middle-classed as I am, I could rip that paper out of his hand and just as easily rip out his throat. It takes no great effort. For what? To kill you soft idiots? You don't understand anything but luxury.

LULA: You fool!

CLAY:

(*Pushing her against the seat*)

I'm not telling you again, Tallulah Bankhead! Luxury. In your face and your fingers. You telling me what I ought to do. 500

(*Sudden scream frightening the whole coach*)

Well, don't! Don't you tell me anything! If I'm a middle-class fake white man . . . let me be. And let me be in the way I want.

(*Through his teeth*)

I'll rip your lousy breasts off! Let me be who I feel like being. Uncle Tom. Thomas. Whoever. It's none of your business. You don't know anything except what's there for you to see. An act. Lies. Device. Not the pure heart, the pumping black heart. You don't ever know that. And I sit here, in this buttoned-up suit, to keep myself from cutting all your throats. I mean wantonly. You great liberated 510 whore! You fuck some black man, and right away you're an expert on black people. What a lotta shit that is. The only thing you know is that you come if he bangs you hard enough. And that's all. The belly rub? You wanted to do the belly rub? Shit, you don't even know how. You don't know how. That ol' dipty-dip shit you do, rolling your ass like an elephant. That's not my kind of belly rub. Belly rub is not Queens. Belly rub is dark places, with big hats and overcoats held up with one arm. Belly rub hates you. Old bald-headed four-eyed ofays popping their fingers . . . and don't know yet what they're doing. They say, "I love Bessie Smith." And don't even understand that Bessie Smith is saying, "Kiss my ass, kiss my black unruly ass." Before love, suffering, desire, anything you can explain, she's saying, and very plainly, "Kiss my black ass." And if you don't know that, it's you that's doing the kissing.

Charlie Parker? Charlie Parker. All the hip white boys scream for Bird. And Bird saying, "Up your ass, feeble-minded ofay! Up your ass." And they sit there talking about the tortured genius of Charlie Parker. Bird would've played not a note of music if he just walked up to East Sixty-seventh Street and killed the first ten white people he saw. Not a note! And I'm the great would-be poet. Yes. That's right! Poet. Some kind of bastard literature . . . all it needs is a simple knife thrust. Just let me bleed you, you loud whore, and one poem vanished. A whole people of neurotics, struggling to keep from being sane. And the only thing that would cure the neurosis would be your murder. Simple as that. I mean if I murdered you, then other white people would begin to understand me. You understand? No. I guess not. If Bessie Smith had killed some white people she wouldn't have needed that music. She could have talked very straight and plain about the world. No metaphors. No grunts. No wiggles in the dark of her soul. Just straight two and two are four. Money. Power. Luxury. Like that. All of them. Crazy niggers turning their backs on sanity. When all it needs is that simple act. Murder. Just murder! Would make us all sane.

*(Suddenly weary)*

Ahhh. Shit. But who needs it? I'd rather be a fool. Insane. Safe with my words, and no deaths, and clean, hard thoughts, urging me to new conquests. My people's madness. Hah! That's a laugh. My people. They don't need me to claim them. They got legs and arms of their own. Personal insanities. Mirrors. They don't need all those words. They don't need any defense. But listen, though, one more thing. And you tell this to your father, who's probably the kind of man who needs to know at once. So he can plan ahead. Tell him not to preach so much rationalism and cold logic to these niggers. Let them alone. Let them sing curses at you in code and see your filth as simple lack of style. Don't make the mistake, through some irresponsible surge of Christian charity, of talking too much about the advantages of Western rationalism, or the great intellectual legacy of the white man, or maybe they'll begin to listen. And then, maybe one day, you'll find they actually do understand exactly what you are talking about, all these fantasy people. All these blues people. And on that day, as sure as shit, when you really believe you can "accept" them into your fold, as half-white trusties late of the subject peoples. With no more blues, except the very old ones, and not a watermelon in sight, the great missionary heart will have triumphed, and all of those ex-coons will be stand-up Western men, with eyes for clean hard useful lives, sober, pious and sane, and they'll murder you. They'll murder you, and have very rational explanations. Very much like your own. They'll cut your throats, and drag you out to the edge of your cities so the flesh can fall away from your bones, in sanitary isolation.

LULA:

*(Her voice takes on a different, more businesslike quality)*

I've heard enough.

CLAY:

*(Reaching for his books)*

I bet you have. I guess I better collect my stuff and get off this train. Looks like we won't be acting out that little pageant you outlined before.

LULA: No. We won't. You're right about that, at least.

*(She turns to look quickly around the rest of the car)*

All right!

*(The others respond)*

CLAY:

*(Bending across the girl to retrieve his belongings)*

Sorry, baby, I don't think we could make it.

*(As he is bending over her, the girl brings up a small knife and plunges it into* CLAY's *chest. Twice. He slumps across her knees, his mouth working stupidly)*

LULA: Sorry is right.

*(Turning to the others in the car who have already gotten up from their seats)*

Sorry is the rightest thing you've said. Get this man off me! Hurry, now!

*(The others come and drag* CLAY's *body down the aisle)*

Open the door and throw his body out.

*(They throw him off)*

And all of you get off at the next stop.

*(*LULA *busies herself straightening her things. Getting everything in order. She takes out a notebook and makes a quick scribbling note. Drops it in her bag. The train apparently stops and all the others get off, leaving her alone in the coach. Very soon a young Negro of about twenty comes into the coach, with a couple of books under his arm. He sits a few seats in back of* LULA. *When he is seated she turns and gives him a long slow look. He looks up from his book and drops the book on his lap. Then an old Negro* CONDUCTOR *comes into the car, doing a sort of restrained soft shoe, and half mumbling the words of some song. He looks at the young man, briefly, with a quick greeting.)*

CONDUCTOR: Hey, brother!
YOUNG MAN: Hey.

*(The* CONDUCTOR *continues down the aisle with his little dance and the mumbled song.* LULA *turns to stare at him and follows his movements down the aisle. The* CONDUCTOR *tips his hat when he reaches her seat, and continues out the car)*

*IN "The Revolutionary Theater," Amiri Baraka describes the challenges posed to the ideology and politics of dominant culture by an emerging African-American theater.*

LeRoi Jones /
Amiri Baraka

"The Revolutionary
Theatre"
(1966)

The Revolutionary Theatre should force change; it should be change. (All their faces turned into the lights and you work on them black nigger magic, and cleanse them at having seen the ugliness. And if the beautiful see themselves, they will love themselves.) We are preaching virtue again, but by that to mean NOW, toward what seems the most constructive use of the world.

The Revolutionary Theatre must EXPOSE! Show up the insides of these humans, look into black skulls. White men will cower before this theatre because it hates them. Because they themselves have been trained to hate. The Revolutionary Theatre must hate them for hating. For presuming with their technology to deny the supremacy of the Spirit. They will all die because of this.

The Revolutionary Theatre must teach them their deaths. It must crack their faces open to the mad cries of the poor. It must teach them about silence and the truths lodged there. It must kill any God anyone names except Common Sense. The Revolutionary Theatre should flush the fags and murders out of Lincoln's face.

It should stagger through our universe correcting, insulting, preaching, spitting craziness—but a craziness taught to us in our most rational moments. People must be taught to trust true scientists (knowers, diggers, oddballs) and that the holiness of life is the constant possibility of widening the consciousness. And they must be incited to strike back against *any* agency that attempts to prevent this widening.

The Revolutionary Theatre must Accuse and Attack anything that can be accused and attacked. It must Accuse and Attack because it is a theatre of Victims. It looks at the sky with the victims' eyes, and moves the victims to look at the strength in their minds and their bodies.

Clay in *Dutchman,* Ray in *The Toilet,* Walker in *The Slave,* are all victims. In the Western sense they could be heroes. But the Revolutionary Theatre, even if it is Western, must be anti-Western. It must show horrible coming attractions of *The Crumbling of the West.* Even as Artaud designed *The Conquest of Mexico,* so we must design *The Conquest of White Eye,* and show the missionaries and wiggly liberals dying under blasts of concrete. For sound effects, wild screams of joy, from all the peoples of the world.

The Revolutionary Theatre must take dreams and give them a reality. It must isolate the ritual and historical cycles of reality. But it must be food for all those who need food, and daring propaganda for the beauty of the Human Mind. It is a political theatre, a weapon to help in the slaughter of these dimwitted fatbellied white guys who somehow believe that the rest of the world is here for them to slobber on.

This should be a theatre of World Spirit. Where the spirit can be shown to be the most competent force in the world. Force. Spirit. Feeling. The language will be anybody's, but tightened by the poet's backbone. And even the language must show what the facts are in this consciousness epic, what's happening. We will talk about the world, and the preciseness with which we are able to summon the world will be our art. Art is method. And art, "like any ashtray or senator," remains in the world. Wittgenstein said ethics and aesthetics are one. I believe this. So the Broadway theatre is a theatre of reaction whose ethics, like its aesthetics, reflect the spiritual values of this unholy society, which sends young crackers all over the world blowing off colored people's heads. (In some of these flippy Southern towns they even shoot up the immigrants' Favorite Son, be it Michael Schwerner or JFKennedy.)

The Revolutionary Theatre is shaped by the world, and moves to reshape the world, using as its force the natural force and perpetual vibrations of the mind in the world. We are history and desire, what we are, and what any experience can make us.

It is a social theatre, but all theatre is social theatre. But we will change the drawing rooms into places where real things can be said about a real world, or into smoky rooms where the destruction of Washington can be plotted. The Revolutionary Theatre must function like an incendiary pencil planted in Curtis Lemay's cap. So that when the final curtain goes down brains are splattered over the seats and the floor, and bleeding nuns must wire SOS's to Belgians with gold teeth.

Our theatre will show victims so that their brothers in the audience will be better able to understand that they are the brothers of victims, and that they themselves are victims if they are blood brothers. And what we show must cause the blood to rush, so that pre-revolutionary temperaments will be bathed in this blood, and it will cause their deepest souls to move, and they will find themselves tensed and clenched, even ready to die, at what the soul has been taught. We will scream and cry, murder, run through the streets in agony, if it means some soul will be moved, moved to actual life understanding of what the world is, and what it ought to be. We are preaching virtue and feeling, and a natural sense of the self in the world. All men live in the world, and the world ought to be a place for them to live.

What is called the imagination (from image, magi, magic, magician, etc.) is a practical vector from the soul. It stores all data, and can be called on to solve all our "problems." The imagination is the projection of ourselves past our sense of ourselves as "things." Imagination (Image) is all possibility, because from the image, the initial circumscribed energy, any use (idea) is possible. And so begins that image's use in the world. Possibility is what moves us.

The popular white man's theatre like the popular white man's novel shows tired white lives, and the problems of eating white sugar, or else it herds bigcaboosed blondes onto huge stages in rhinestones and makes believe they are dancing or singing. WHITE BUSINESSMEN OF THE WORLD, DO YOU WANT TO SEE PEOPLE REALLY DANCING AND SINGING??? ALL OF YOU GO UP TO HARLEM AND GET YOURSELF KILLED. THERE WILL BE DANCING AND SINGING, THEN, FOR REAL!! (In *The Slave*, Walker Vessels, the black revolutionary, wears an armband, which is the insignia of the attacking army—a big red-lipped minstrel, grinning like crazy.)

The liberal white man's objection to the theatre of the revolution (if he is "hip" enough) will be on aesthetic grounds. Most white Western artists do not need to be "political," since usually, whether they know it or not, they are in complete sympathy with the most repressive social forces in the world today. There are more junior birdmen fascists running around the West today disguised as Artists than there are disguised as fascists. (But then, that word, *Fascist*, and with it, *Fascism*, has been made obsolete by the words *America*, and *Americanism*.) The American Artist usually turns out to be just a super-Bourgeois, because, finally, all he has to show for his sojourn through the world is "better taste" than the Bourgeois—many times not even that.

Americans will hate the Revolutionary Theatre because it will be out to destroy them and whatever they believe is real. American cops will try to close the theatres where such nakedness of the human spirit is paraded. American producers will say the revolutionary plays are filth, usually because they will treat human life as if it were actually happening. American directors will say that the white guys in the plays are too abstract and cowardly ("don't get me wrong . . . I mean aesthetically . . . ") and they will be right.

The force we want is of twenty million spooks storming America with furious cries and unstoppable weapons. We want actual explosions and actual brutality: AN EPIC IS CRUMBLING and we must give it the space and hugeness of its actual demise. The Revolutionary Theatre, which is now peopled with victims, will soon begin to be peopled with new kinds of heroes—not the weak Hamlets debating whether or not they are ready to die for what's on their minds, but men and women (and minds) digging out from under a thousand years of "high art" and weak-faced dalliance. We must make an art that will function so as to call down the actual wrath of world spirit. We are witch doctors and assassins, but we will open a place for the true scientists to expand our consciousness. This is a theatre of assault. The play that will split the heavens for us will be called THE DESTRUCTION OF AMERICA. The heroes will be Crazy Horse, Denmark Vesey, Patrice Lumumba, and not history, not memory, not sad sentimental groping for a warmth in our despair; these will be new men, new heroes, and their enemies most of you who are reading this.

# Adrienne Kennedy

Adrienne Kennedy's plays are often a form of surreal autobiography, mingling elements of her personal history with the history of African and African-American struggle. Adrienne Lita Hawkins was born in Pittsburgh in 1931 and moved with her family to Cleveland when she was four years old; she was raised in a comfortable, racially and ethnically diverse, middle-class section of the city. Kennedy's parents had been educated at black colleges in Atlanta—her father at Morehead, her mother at Spelman; she confronted institutional racism when she attended the Ohio State University, where both campus and off-campus life were rigidly segregated. She graduated with a degree in education in 1953 and married Joseph C. Kennedy; he was serving in the Army and shortly was sent to Korea. When he returned, they moved to New York; he attended Columbia Teachers College, and she began studying creative writing, first at Columbia University from 1954 to 1956, then at the American Theatre Wing in 1958, and later at the Circle in the Square Theater school.

Kennedy began writing her first play, *Funnyhouse of a Negro*, while traveling in Africa and Europe in 1961. When she returned to New York in 1962, she brought the play to the Circle in the Square school, where she worked on it with Edward Albee and where it received a workshop production. It opened off-Broadway in 1964—the same year as LeRoi Jones's *Dutchman*—and shared an Obie Award for Best Play with Samuel Beckett's *Krapp's Last Tape* and Albee's *The Zoo Story*. Her second play, *The Owl Answers* (1963), centers on another autobiographical heroine, Clara Passmore, who appears again in her brilliant play, *A Movie Star Has to Star in Black and White* (1976). Kennedy's other plays include an adaptation of John Lennon's poems and stories, *The Lennon Play: In His Own Write* (1967); *A Rat's Mass* (1969); *Sun* (originally subtitled *A Poem for Malcolm X Inspired by His Murder* (1968); *A Lesson in Dead Language* (1968); and *An Evening with Dead Essex* (1973). She has also written adaptations of *Orestes* and *Electra* (1980). Kennedy has held Rockefeller, Guggenheim, and National Endowment for the Humanities Fellowships, and has taught playwriting at a number of universities. Her autobiography, *People Who Led to My Plays*, was published in 1987.

## Funnyhouse of a Negro (1964)

*Funnyhouse of a Negro* is typical of Kennedy's drama. Almost plotless, the play depends almost entirely on its dense interplay of stage images, and on the evocative texture of its language. Begun while Kennedy was traveling in West Africa, and completed in Rome, *Funnyhouse* centers on the character Sarah whose room—and mind—are the "funnyhouse" of the title: an apparently endless hall of images, reflecting and refracting Sarah's fear and anxiety about race, about "blackness." Using a technique she would use in several later plays, Kennedy disperses Sarah's "voice" through a variety of other characters: Queen Victoria, the Duchess of Hapsburg, Jesus, and Patrice Lumumba all, at various points in the play, "speak" for Sarah. The voices interweave a complex and evasive narrative, in which these personae represent Sarah's conflicted attitude toward race and toward her own history. As Sarah remarks early in the play, these voices provide "a stark fortress against recognition of myself"; speaking in several voices, Sarah is able to cast her anxieties onto others. Sarah, married to a Jewish poet, works at writing poetry in imitation of Edith Sitwell; she impersonates "white" culture in the voices of Queen Victoria and the Duchess of Hapsburg; she yearns for a "white" life. And she is haunted by the vision of her father, a missionary in Africa, whose rape of her mother becomes an emblem for her fear of blackness in the play: ". . . black is evil and has been from the beginning." By dispersing Sarah's consciousness and her disjointed, inconsistent monologue over several "voices," Kennedy points to Sarah's complete disintegration, her inability to find a "self" precisely because all her "voices" speak in white accents. Her personal history (the relationship between her father and mother, her own desire to be a writer) blends with public history (the murder of Patrice Lumumba, the premier of the Republic of Congo), but both narratives are inflected by the massive, *"astonishing repulsive whiteness"* of the statue of Queen Victoria that dominates Sarah's room. In the funnyhouse of her mind, gripped in the racist distortions of white culture, Sarah is finally unable to find herself or even to find her own reflection.

# —Funnyhouse of a Negro—
## Adrienne Kennedy

## —CHARACTERS—

NEGRO-SARAH
DUCHESS OF HAPSBURG, *One of herselves*
QUEEN VICTORIA REGINA, *One of herselves*
JESUS, *One of herselves*
PATRICE LUMUMBA, *One of herselves*
SARAH'S LANDLADY, *Funnyhouse Lady*
RAYMOND, *Funnyhouse Man*
THE MOTHER

*Author's Note*

FUNNYHOUSE *of a* NEGRO *is perhaps clearest and most explicit when the play is placed in the girl Sarah's room. The center of the stage works well as her room, allowing the rest of the stage as the place for herselves. Her room should have a bed, a writing table and a mirror. Near her bed is the statue of Queen Victoria; other objects might be her photographs and her books. When she is placed in her room with her belongings, then the director is free to let the rest of the play happen around her.*

## BEGINNING:

*Before the closed Curtain* A WOMAN *dressed in a white nightgown walks across the Stage carrying before her a bald head. She moves as one in a trance and is mumbling something inaudible to herself. Her hair is wild, straight and black and falls to her waist. As she moves, she gives the effect of one in a dream. She crosses the Stage from Right to Left. Before she has barely vanished, the* CURTAIN *opens. It is a white satin Curtain of a cheap material and a ghastly white, a material that brings to mind the interior of a cheap casket, parts of it are frayed and look as if it has been gnawed by rats.*

## SCENE:

TWO WOMEN *are sitting in what appears to be a Queen's chamber. It is set in the middle of the Stage in a strong white* LIGHT, *while the rest of the Stage is in unnatural* BLACKNESS. *The quality of the white light is unreal and ugly. The Queen's chamber consists of a dark monumental bed resembling an ebony tomb, a low, dark chandelier with candles, and wine-colored walls. Flying about are great black* RAVENS. QUEEN VICTORIA *is standing before her bed holding a small mirror in her hand. On the white pillow of her bed is a dark, indistinguishable object.* THE DUCHESS OF HAPSBURG *is standing at the foot of the bed. Her back is to us as is the* QUEEN's. *Throughout the entire scene, they do not move.* BOTH WOMEN *are dressed in royal gowns of white, a white similar to the white of the Curtain, the material cheap satin. Their headpieces are white and of a net that falls over their faces. From beneath both their headpieces springs a headful of wild kinky hair. Although in this scene we do not see their faces, I will describe them now. They look exactly alike and will wear masks or be made up to appear a whitish yellow. It is an alabaster face, the skin drawn tightly over the high cheekbones, great dark eyes that seem gouged out of the head, a high forehead, a full red mouth and a head of frizzy hair. If the characters do not wear a mask then the face must be highly powdered and possess a hard expressionless quality and a stillness as in the face of death. We hear* KNOCKING.

VICTORIA: (*Listening to the knocking.*) It is my father. He is arriving again for the night. (*The* DUCHESS *makes no reply.*) He comes through the jungle to find me. He never tires of his journey.

DUCHESS: How dare he enter the castle, he who is the darkest of them all, the darkest one? My mother looked like a white woman, hair as straight as any white woman's. And at least I am yellow, but he is black, the blackest one of them all. I hoped he was dead. Yet he still comes through the jungle to find me.    10

(*The* KNOCKING *is louder.*)

VICTORIA: He never tires of the journey, does he, Duchess? (*Looking at herself in the mirror.*)

DUCHESS: How dare he enter the castle of Queen Victoria Regina, Monarch of England? It is because of him that my mother died. The wild black beast put his hands on her. She died.

VICTORIA: Why does he keep returning? He keeps returning forever, coming back ever and keeps coming back forever. He is my father.

DUCHESS: He is a black Negro.    20

VICTORIA: He is my father. I am tied to the black Negro. He came when I was a child in the south, before I was born he haunted my conception, diseased my birth.

DUCHESS: Killed my mother.

VICTORIA: My mother was the light. She was the lightest one. She looked like a white woman.

DUCHESS: We are tied to him unless, of course, he should die.

VICTORIA: But he is dead.

DUCHESS: And he keeps returning.

(*The* KNOCKING *is louder;* BLACKOUT. *The* LIGHTS *go out in the Chamber. Onto the Stage from the Left comes the* FIGURE *in the white nightgown carrying the bald head. This time we hear her speak.*)

MOTHER: Black man, black man, I never should have let a black man put his hands on me. The wild black beast raped me and now my skull is shining. (*She disappears to the Right.*)

(*Now the LIGHT is focused on a single white square wall that is to the Left of the Stage, that is suspended and stands alone, of about five feet in dimension and width. It stands with the narrow part facing the audience. A CHARACTER steps through. She is a faceless, dark character with a hangman's rope about her neck and red blood on the part that would be her face. She is the NEGRO. The most noticeable aspect of her looks is her wild kinky hair. It is a ragged head with a patch of hair missing from the crown which the NEGRO carries in her hand. She is dressed in black. She steps slowly through the wall, stands still before it and begins her monologue:*)

NEGRO: Part of the time I live with Raymond, part of the time with God, Maxmillian and Albert Saxe Coburg. I live in my room. It is a small room on the top floor of a brownstone in the West Nineties in New York, a room filled with my dark old volumes, a narrow bed and on the wall old photographs of castles and monarchs of England. It is also Victoria's chamber. Queen Victoria Regina's. Partly because it is consumed by a gigantic plaster statute of Queen Victoria who is my idol and partly for other reasons; three steps that I contrived out of boards lead to the statue which I have placed opposite the door as I enter the room. It is a sitting figure, a replica of one in London, and a thing of astonishing whiteness. I found it in a dusty shop on Morningside Heights. Raymond says it is a thing of terror, possessing the quality of nightmares, suggesting large and probable deaths. And of course he is right. When I am the Duchess of Hapsburg I sit opposite Victoria in my headpiece and we talk. The other time I wear the dress of a student, dark clothes and dark stockings. Victoria always wants me to tell her of whiteness. She wants me to tell her of a royal world where everything and everyone is white and there are no unfortunate black ones. For as we of royal blood know, black is evil and has been from the beginning. Even before my mother's hair started to fall out. Before she was raped by a wild black beast. Black was evil.

As for myself I long to become even a more pallid Negro than I am now; pallid like Negroes on the covers of American Negro magazines; soulless, educated and irreligious. I want to possess no moral value, particularly value as to my being. I want not to be. I ask nothing except anonymity. I am an English major, as my mother was when she went to school in Atlanta. My father majored in social work. I am graduated from a city college and have occasional work in libraries, but mostly spend my days preoccupied with the placement and geometric position of words on paper. I write poetry filling white page after white page with imitations of Edith Sitwell. It is my dream to live in rooms with European antiques and my Queen Victoria, photographs of Roman ruins, walls of books, a piano, oriental carpets and to eat my meals on a white glass table. I will visit my friends' apartments which will contain books, photographs of Roman ruins, pianos and oriental carpets. My friends will be white.

I need them as an embankment to keep me from reflecting too much upon the fact that I am a Negro. For, like all educated Negroes—out of life and death essential—I find it necessary to maintain a stark fortress against recognition of myself. My white friends, like myself, will be shrewd, intellectual and anxious for death. Anyone's death. I will mistrust them, as I do myself, waver in their opinion of me, as I waver in the opinion of myself. But if I had not wavered in my opinion of myself, then my hair would never have fallen out. And if my hair hadn't fallen out, I wouldn't have bludgeoned my father's head with an ebony mask.

In appearance I am good-looking in a boring way; no glaring Negroid features, medium nose, medium mouth and pale yellow skin. My one defect is that I have a head of frizzy hair, unmistakably Negro kinky hair; and it is indistinguishable. I would like to lie and say I love Raymond. But I do not. He is a poet and is Jewish. He is very interested in Negroes.

(*The NEGRO stands by the wall and throughout her following speech, the following characters come through the wall, disappearing off into varying directions in the darkened night of the Stage:* DUCHESS, QUEEN VICTORIA, JESUS, PATRICE LUMUMBA. JESUS *is a hunchback, yellow-skinned dwarf, dressed in white rags and sandals.* PATRICE LUMUMBA *is a black man. His head appears to be split in two with blood and tissue in eyes. He carries an ebony mask.*)

SARAH (NEGRO): The rooms are my rooms; a Hapsburg chamber, a chamber in a Victorian castle, the hotel where I killed my father, the jungle. These are the places myselves exist in. I know no places. That is, I cannot believe in places. To believe in places is to know hope and to know the emotion of hope is to know beauty. It links us across a horizon and connects us to the world. I find there are no places only my funnyhouse. Streets are rooms, cities are rooms, eternal rooms. I try to create a space for myselves in cities, New York, the midwest, a southern town, but it becomes a lie. I try to give myselves a logical relationship but that too is a lie. For relationships was one of my last religions. I clung loyally to the lie of relationships, again and again seeking to establish a connection between my characters. Jesus is Victoria's son. Mother loved my father before her hair fell out. A loving relationship exists between myself and Queen Victoria, a love between myself and Jesus but they are lies.

(*Then to the Right front of the Stage comes the WHITE LIGHT. It goes to a suspended stairway. At the foot of it, stands the LANDLADY. She is a tall, thin, white woman dressed in a black and red hat and appears to be talking to someone in a suggested open doorway in a corridor of a rooming house. She laughs like a mad character in a funnyhouse throughout her speech.*)

LANDLADY: (*Who is looking up the stairway.*) Ever since her father hung himself in a Harlem hotel when Patrice Lumumba was murdered she hides herself in her room. Each night she repeats: He keeps returning. How dare he enter the castle walls, he who is the darkest of them all, the darkest one? My mother looked like a white woman, hair as straight as any white woman's. And I am yellow but he, he is black, the blackest one of them all. I hoped he was dead. Yet he still comes through the jungle.

I tell her: Sarah, honey, the man hung himself. It's not your blame. But, no, she stares at me: No, Mrs. Conrad, he did not hang himself, that is only the way they understand it, they do, but the truth is that I bludgeoned his head with an ebony skull that he carries about with him. Wherever he goes, he carries black masks and heads.

She's suffering so till her hair has fallen out. But then she did always hide herself in that room with the walls of books and her statue. I always did know she thought she was somebody else, a Queen or something, somebody else.

*BLACKOUT*

SCENE:

*Funnyman's place.*

*The next scene is enacted with the* DUCHESS *and* RAYMOND. *Raymond's place is suggested as being above the Negro's room and is etched in with a prop of blinds and a bed. Behind the blinds are mirrors and when the blinds are opened and closed by Raymond this is revealed.* RAYMOND *turns out to be the funnyman of the funnyhouse. He is tall, white and ghostly thin and dressed in a black shirt and black trousers in attire suggesting an artist. Throughout his dialogue he laughs. The* DUCHESS *is partially disrobed and it is implied from their attitudes of physical intimacy—he is standing and she is sitting before him clinging to his leg. During the scene* RAYMOND *keeps opening and closing the blinds.*

DUCHESS: *(Carrying a red paper bag.)* My father is arriving
130    and what am I to do?

*(*RAYMOND *walks about the place opening the blinds and laughing.)*

FUNNYMAN: He is arriving from Africa, is he not?

DUCHESS: Yes, yes, he is arriving from Africa.

FUNNYMAN: I always knew your father was African.

DUCHESS: He is an African who lives in the jungle. He is an African who has always lived in the jungle. Yes, he is a nigger who is an African who is a missionary teacher and is now dedicating his life to the erection of a Christian mission in the middle of the jungle. He is a black man.

FUNNYMAN: He is a black man who shot himself when they
140    murdered Patrice Lumumba.

DUCHESS: *(Goes on wildly.)* Yes, my father is a black man who went to Africa years ago as a missionary teacher, got mixed up in politics, was revealed and is now devoting his foolish life to the erection of a Christian mission in the middle of the jungle in one of those newly freed countries. Hide me. *(Clinging to his knees.)* Hide me here so the nigger will not find me.

FUNNYMAN: *(Laughing.)* Your father is in the jungle dedicating his life to the erection of a Christian mission.

150 DUCHESS: Hide me here so the jungle will not find me. Hide me.

FUNNYMAN: Isn't it cruel of you?

DUCHESS: Hide me from the jungle.

FUNNYMAN: Isn't it cruel?

DUCHESS: No, no.

FUNNYMAN: Isn't it cruel of you?

DUCHESS: No. *(She screams and opens her red paper bag and*

*draws from it her fallen hair. It is a great mass of dark wild hair. She holds it up to him. He appears not to understand. He stares at it.)* It is my hair. *(He continues to stare at her.)* 160 When I awakened this morning it had fallen out, not all of it but a mass from the crown of my head that lay on the center of my pillow. I arose and in the greyish winter morning light of my room I stood staring at my hair, dazed by my sleeplessness, still shaken by nightmares of my mother. Was it true, yes, it was my hair. In the mirror I saw that, although my hair remained on both sides, clearly on the crown and at my temples my scalp was bare. *(She removes her black crown and shows him the top of her head.)*

FUNNYMAN: *(Staring at her.)* Why would your hair fall out? Is 170 it because you are cruel? How could a black father haunt you so?

DUCHESS: He haunted my very conception. He was a wild black beast who raped my mother.

FUNNYMAN: He is a black Negro. *(Laughing.)*

DUCHESS: Ever since I can remember he's been in a nigger pose of agony. He is the wilderness. He speaks niggerly groveling about wanting to touch me with his black hand.

FUNNYMAN: How tormented and cruel you are.

DUCHESS: *(As if not comprehending.)* Yes, yes, the man's dark, 180 very dark-skinned. He is the darkest, my father is the darkest, my mother is the lightest. I am in between. But my father is the darkest. My father is a nigger who drives me to misery. Any time spent with him evolves itself into suffering. He is a black man and the wilderness.

FUNNYMAN: How tormented and cruel you are.

DUCHESS: He is a nigger.

FUNNYMAN: And your mother, where is she?

DUCHESS: She is in the asylum. In the asylum bald. Her father was a white man. And she is in the asylum.        190

*(He takes her in his arms. She responds wildly.)*
*BLACKOUT*
*KNOCKING is heard; it continues, then somewhere near the Center of the Stage a* FIGURE *appears in the darkness, a large dark faceless* MAN *carrying a mask in his hand.*

MAN: It begins with the disaster of my hair. I awaken. My hair has fallen out, not all of it, but a mass from the crown of my head that lies on the center of my white pillow. I arise and in the greyish winter morning light of my room I stand staring at my hair, dazed by sleeplessness, still shaken by nightmares of my mother. Is it true? Yes. It is my hair. In the mirror I see that although my hair remains on both sides, clearly on the crown and at my temples my scalp is bare. And in my sleep I had been visited by my bald crazy mother who comes to me crying, calling me to her bedside. She lies 200 on the bed watching the strands of her own hair fall out. Her hair fell out after she married and she spent her days lying on the bed watching the strands fall from her scalp, covering the bedspread until she was bald and admitted to the hospital. Black man, black man, my mother says, I never should have let a black man put his hands on me. She comes to me, his bald skull shining. Black diseases, Sarah, she says. Black diseases. I run. She follows me, her bald skull shining. That is the beginning.

*BLACKOUT*

SCENE:

*Queen's Chamber.*

*Her hair is in a small pile on the bed and in a small pile on the floor, several other small piles of hair are scattered about her and her white gown is covered with fallen out hair.* QUEEN VIC-TORIA *acts out the following scene: She awakens (in pantomime) and discovers her hair has fallen. It is on her pillow. She arises and stands at the side of the bed with her back toward us, staring at hair. The* DUCHESS *enters the room, comes around, standing behind* VICTORIA, *and they stare at the hair.* VICTORIA *picks up a mirror. The* DUCHESS *then picks up a mirror and looks at her own hair. She opens the red paper bag that she is carrying and takes out her hair, attempting to place it back on her head (for unlike* VICTORIA, *she does not wear her headpiece now.) The* LIGHTS *remain on. The unidentified* MAN *returns out of the darkness and speaks. He carries the mask.*

210 MAN: *(Patrice Lumumba.)* I am a nigger of two generations. I am Patrice Lumumba. I am a nigger of two generations. I am the black shadow that haunted my mother's conception. I belong to the generation born at the turn of the century and the generation born before the depression. At present I reside in New York City in a brownstone in the West Nineties. I am an English major at a city college. My nigger father majored in social work, so did my mother. I am a student and have occasional work in libraries. But mostly I spend my vile days preoccupied with the placement and
220 geometric position of words on paper. I write poetry filling white page after white page with imitations of Sitwell. It is my vile dream to live in rooms with European antiques and my statue of Queen Victoria, photographs of Roman ruins, walls of books, a piano and oriental carpets and to eat my meals on a white glass table. It is also my nigger dream for my friends to eat their meals on white glass tables and to live in rooms with European antiques, photographs of Roman ruins, pianos and oriental carpets. My friends will be white. I need them as an embankment to keep me from reflecting
230 too much upon the fact that I am Patrice Lumumba who haunted my mother's conception. They are necessary for me to maintain recognition against myself. My white friends, like myself, will be shrewd intellectuals and anxious for death. Anyone's death. I will despise them as I do myself. For if I did not despise myself then my hair would not have fallen and if my hair had not fallen then I would not have bludgeoned my father's face with the ebony mask.

*(The LIGHT remains on him. Before him a BALD HEAD is dropped on a wire,* SOMEONE *screams. Another wall is dropped, larger than the first one was. This one is near the front of the Stage facing thus. Throughout the following monologue, the* CHARACTERS: DUCHESS, VICTORIA, JESUS *go back and forth. As they go in their backs are to us but the NEGRO faces us, speaking:)*

I always dreamed of a day when my mother would smile at me. My father . . . his mother wanted him to be Christ. From
240 the beginning in the lamp of their dark room she said—I want you to be Jesus, to walk in Genesis and save the race. You must return to Africa, find revelation in the midst of golden savannas, nim and white frankopenny trees, white stallions roaming under a blue sky, you must walk with a white dove and heal the race, heal the misery, take us off the cross. She stared at him anguished in the kerosene light . . . At dawn he watched her rise, kill a hen for him to eat at breakfast, then go to work down at the big house till dusk, till she died.

His father told him the race was no damn good. He hated 250 his father and adored his mother. His mother didn't want him to marry my mother and sent a dead chicken to the wedding. I DON'T want you marrying that child, she wrote, she's not good enough for you, I want you to go to Africa. When they first married they lived in New York. Then they went to Africa where my mother fell out of love with my father. She didn't want him to save the black race and spent her days combing her hair. She would not let him touch her in their wedding bed and called him black. He is black of skin with dark eyes and a great dark square brow. Then in 260 Africa he started to drink and came home drunk one night and raped my mother. The child from the union is me. I clung to my mother. Long after she went to the asylum I wove long dreams of her beauty, her straight hair and fair skin and grey eyes, so identical to mine. How it anguished him. I turned from him, nailing him on the cross, he said, dragging him through grass and nailing him on a cross until he bled. He pleaded with me to help him find Genesis, search for Genesis in the midst of golden savannas, nim and white frankopenny trees and white stallions roaming under 270 a blue sky, help him search for the white doves, he wanted the black man to make a pure statement, he wanted the black man to rise from colonialism. But I sat in the room with my mother, sat by her bedside and helped her comb her straight black hair and wove long dreams of her beauty. She had long since begun to curse the place and spoke of herself trapped in blackness. She preferred the company of night owls. Only at night did she rise, walking in the garden among the trees with the owls. When I spoke to her she saw I was a black man's child and she preferred speaking to owls. 280 Nights my father came from his school in the village struggling to embrace me. But I fled and hid under my mother's bed while she screamed of remorse. Her hair was falling badly and after a while we had to return to this country.

He tried to hang himself once. After my mother went to the asylum he had hallucinations, his mother threw a dead chicken at him, his father laughed and said the race was no damn good, my mother appeared in her nightgown screaming she had trapped herself in blackness. No white doves flew. He had left Africa and was again in New York. He lived 290 in Harlem and no white doves flew. Sarah, Sarah, he would say to me, the soldiers are coming and a cross they are placing high on a tree and are dragging me through the grass and nailing me upon the cross. My blood is gushing. I wanted to live in Genesis in the midst of golden savannas, nim and white frankopenny trees and white stallions roaming under a blue sky. I wanted to walk with a white dove. I wanted to be a Christian. Now I am Judas. I betrayed my mother. I sent your mother to the asylum. I created a yellow child who hates me. And he tried to hang himself in a Harlem hotel. 300

*BLACKOUT*

*(A BALD HEAD is dropped on a string. We hear LAUGHING.)*

SCENE:

*Duchess's place.*

*The next scene is done in the Duchess of Hapsburg's place which is a chandeliered ballroom with SNOW falling, a black and white marble floor, a bench decorated with white flowers, all of this can be made of obviously fake materials as they would be in a funnyhouse. The DUCHESS is wearing a white dress and as in the previous scene a white headpiece with her kinky hair springing out from under it. In the scene are the DUCHESS and JESUS. JESUS enters the room, which is at first dark, then suddenly BRILLIANT, he starts to cry out at the DUCHESS, who is seated on a bench under the chandelier, and pulls his hair from the red paper bag holding it up for the DUCHESS to see.*

JESUS: My hair. *(The DUCHESS does not speak, JESUS again screams.)* My hair. *(Holding the hair up, waiting for a reaction from the DUCHESS.)*

DUCHESS: *(As if oblivious.)* I have something I must show you. *(She goes quickly to shutters and darkens the room, returning standing before JESUS. She then slowly removes her headpiece and from under it takes a mass of her hair.)* When I awakened I found it fallen out, not all of it but a mass that lay on my white pillow. I could see, although my hair hung
310 down at the sides, clearly on my white scalp it was missing.

*(Her baldness is identical to JESUS's.)*
BLACKOUT
*The LIGHTS come back up. They are BOTH sitting on the bench examining each other's hair, running it through their fingers, then slowly the DUCHESS disappears behind the shutters and returns with a long red comb. She sits on the bench next to JESUS and starts to comb her remaining hair over her baldness. (This is done slowly.) JESUS then takes the comb and proceeds to do the same to the DUCHESS of Hapsburg's hair. After they finish they place the DUCHESS's headpiece back on and we can see the strands of their hair falling to the floor. JESUS then lies down across the bench while the DUCHESS walks back and forth, the KNOCKING does not cease. They speak in unison as the DUCHESS walks about and JESUS lies on the bench in the falling snow, staring at the ceiling.*

DUCHESS and JESUS: *(Their hair is falling more now, they are both hideous.)* My father isn't going to let us alone. *(KNOCKING.)* Our father isn't going to let us alone, our father is the darkest of us all, my mother was the fairest, I am in between, but my father is the darkest of them all. He is a black man. Our father is the darkest of them all. He is a black man. My father is a dead man.

*(Then they suddenly look up at each other and scream, the LIGHTS go to their heads and we see that they are totally bald. There is a KNOCKING. LIGHTS go to the stairs and the LANDLADY.)*

LANDLADY: He wrote to her saying he loved her and asked her forgiveness. He begged her to take him off the cross *(He*

had dreamed she would.), stop them from tormenting him, 320 the one with the chicken and his cursing father. Her mother's hair fell out, the race's hair fell out because he left Africa, he said. He had tried to save them. She must embrace him. He said his existence depended on her embrace. He wrote her from Africa where he is creating his Christian center in the jungle and that is why he came here. I know that he wanted her to return there with him and not desert the race. He came to see her once before he tried to hang himself, appearing in the corridor of my apartment. I had let him in. I found him sitting on a bench in the hallway. He put 330 out his hand to her, tried to take her in his arms, crying out—Forgiveness, Sarah, is it that you never will forgive me for being black? Sarah, I know you were a child of torment. But forgiveness. That was before his breakdown. Then, he wrote her and repeated that his mother hoped he would be Christ but he failed. He had married her mother because he could not resist the light. Yet, his mother from the beginning in the kerosene lamp of their dark rooms in Georgia said: I want you to be Jesus, to walk in Genesis and save the race, return to Africa, find revelation in the black. He went 340 away.
But Easter morning, she got to feeling badly and went into Harlem to see him; the streets were filled with vendors selling lilies. He had checked out of that hotel. When she arrived back at my brownstone he was here, dressed badly, rather drunk, I had let him in again. He sat on a bench in the dark hallway, put out his hand to her, trying to take her in his arms, crying out—forgiveness, Sarah, forgiveness for my being black, Sarah. I know you are a child of torment. I know on dark winter afternoons you sit alone weaving sto- 350 ries of your mother's beauty. But Sarah, answer me, don't turn away, Sarah. Forgive my blackness. She would not answer. He put out his hand to her. She ran past him on the stairs, left him there with his hand out to me, repeating his past, saying his mother hoped he would be Christ. From the beginning in the kerosene lamp of their dark rooms, she said, "Wally, I want you to be Jesus, to walk in Genesis and save the race. You must return to Africa, Wally, find revelation in the midst of golden savannas, nim and white frankopenny trees and white stallions roaming under a blue 360 sky. Wally, you must find the white dove and heal the pain of the race, heal the misery of the black man, Wally, take us off the cross, Wally." In the kerosene light she stared at me anguished from her old Negro face—but she ran past him leaving him. And now he is dead, she says, now he is dead. He left Africa and now Patrice Lumumba is dead.

*(The next scene is enacted back in the DUCHESS of Hapsburg's place. JESUS is still in the Duchess's chamber, apparently he has fallen asleep and as we see him he awakens with the DUCHESS by his side, and sits here as in a trance. He rises terrified and speaks.)*

JESUS: Through my apocalypses and my raging sermons I have tried so to escape him, through God Almighty I have tried to escape being black. *(He then appears to rouse himself from his thoughts and calls:)* Duchess, Duchess. *(He looks 370 about for her, there is no answer. He gets up slowly, walks back into the darkness and there we see that she is hanging on the chandelier, her bald head suddenly drops to the floor and she falls upon* JESUS. *He screams.*) I am going to Africa and kill this black man named Patrice Lumumba. Why? Because all my life I believed my Holy Father to be God, but now I know that my father is a black man. I have no fear for whatever I do, I will do in the name of God, I will do in the name of Albert Saxe Coburg, in the name of Victoria, Queen Victoria Regina, the monarch of England, I will.

*BLACKOUT*

SCENE:

*In the jungle, RED SUN, FLYING THINGS, wild black grass. The effect of the jungle is that it, unlike the other scenes, is over the entire stage. In time this is the longest scene in the play and is played the slowest, as the slow, almost standstill stages of a dream. By lighting the desired effect would be—suddenly the jungle has overgrown the chambers and all the other places with a violence and a dark brightness, a grim yellowness.*

JESUS *is the first to appear in the center of the jungle darkness. Unlike in previous scenes, he has a nimbus above his head. As they each successively appear, they all too have nimbuses atop their heads in a manner to suggest that they are saviours.*

JESUS: I always believed my father to be God.

*(Suddenly they all appear in various parts of the jungle.* PATRICE LUMUMBA, *the* DUCHESS, VICTORIA, *wandering about speaking at once. Their speeches are mixed and repeated by one another.)*

ALL: He never tires of the journey, he who is the darkest one, the darkest one of them all. My mother looked like a white woman, hair as straight as any white woman's. I am yellow but he is black, the darkest one of us all. How I hoped he was dead, yet he never tires of the journey. It was because of him that my mother died because she let a black man put his hands on her. Why does he keep returning? He keeps returning forever, keeps returning and returning and he is my father. He is a black Negro. They told me my Father was God but my father is black. He is my father. I am tied to a black Negro. He returned when I lived in the south back in the twenties, when I was a child, he returned. Before I was born at the turn of the century, he haunted my conception, diseased my birth . . . killed my mother. He killed the light. My mother was the lightest one. I am bound to him unless, of course, he should die.
But he is dead.
And he keeps returning. Then he is not dead.
Then he is not dead.
Yet, he is dead, but dead he comes knocking at my door.

*(This is repeated several times, finally reaching a loud pitch and then* ALL *rushing about the grass. They stop and stand perfectly still.* ALL *speaking tensely at various times in a chant.)*

I see him. The black ugly thing is sitting in his hallway, surrounded by his ebony masks, surrounded by the blackness of himself. My mother comes into the room. He is there with his hand out to me, groveling, saying—Forgiveness, Sarah, is it that you will never forgive me for being black. Forgiveness, Sarah, I know you are a nigger of torment. Why? Christ would not rape anyone.
You will never forgive me for being black.
Wild beast. Why did you rape my mother? Black beast, Christ would not rape anyone.
He is in grief from that black anguished face of his. Then at once the room will grow bright and my mother will come toward me smiling while I stand before his face and bludgeon him with an ebony head.
Forgiveness, Sarah, I know you are a nigger of torment.

*(Silence. Then they suddenly begin to laugh and shout as though they are in victory. They continue for some minutes running about laughing and shouting.)*
*BLACKOUT*
*Another WALL drops. There is a white plaster statue of Queen Victoria which represents the Negro's room in the brownstone, the room appears near the staircase highly lit and small. The main prop is the statue but a bed could be suggested. The figure of Victoria is a sitting figure, one of astonishing repulsive whiteness, suggested by dusty volumes of books and old yellowed walls.*

*The Negro* SARAH *is standing perfectly still, we hear the KNOCKING, the LIGHTS come on quickly, her FATHER's black figure with bludgeoned hands rushes upon her, the LIGHT GOES BLACK and we see her hanging in the room. LIGHTS come on the laughing LANDLADY. And at the same time remain on the hanging figure of the NEGRO.*

LANDLADY: The poor bitch has hung herself. *(FUNNYMAN RAYMOND appears from his room at the commotion.)* The poor bitch has hung herself.
RAYMOND: *(Observing her hanging figure.)* She was a funny little liar.
LANDLADY: *(Informing him.)* Her father hung himself in a Harlem hotel when Patrice Lumumba died.
RAYMOND: Her father never hung himself in a Harlem hotel when Patrice Lumumba was murdered. I know the man. He is a doctor, married to a white whore. He lives in the city in rooms with European antiques, photographs of Roman ruins, walls of books and oriental carpets. Her father is a nigger who eats his meals on a white glass table.

**E N D**

*This interview with Adrienne Kennedy was conducted by Kathleen Betsko and Rachel Koenig.*

Adrienne
Kennedy

Interview
(1986)

INTERVIEWER: When did you begin writing?

KENNEDY: I really started to write when I was a senior at Ohio State University. The year I was a junior, I took a course which was very inspirational; we studied Faulkner, Fitzgerald, D. H. Lawrence, T. S. Eliot. That course fired something in me. I suddenly found myself writing short stories instead of studying.

INTERVIEWER: You once said that you were disappointed with college.

KENNEDY: It was an ordeal. There were twenty-seven thousand students attending Ohio State, and southern Ohio was almost like the deep South in those days, much more bigoted than northern Ohio where I'd grown up. I majored in education. I expected to be a teacher like my mother. Then I majored in social work for a while. All the women—black women, especially—I knew majored in education and a few wanted to be social workers. I was a poor college student, I found college extremely boring, something to just get through. But there were these few English courses; when I was a senior, I had a couple of credits left over and took a survey course in twentieth-century drama. I did better in that than I did in any course the whole time I was at Ohio State. Looking back, it was important.

INTERVIEWER: Did you pursue a profession in social work?

KENNEDY: I managed to graduate and got married a month later. From then on, I wrote. My husband went to Korea, and while he was away I gave birth. I lived with my parents and when I wasn't taking care of the baby, I wrote. After my husband returned, we came to New York. I remember the exact date, January 4, 1955. We drove in the snow from Cleveland. Joe worked while he was in graduate school, and I had a certain kind of energy; I would stay up all night and write. You have to do that when you have a baby! I wrote parts of plays . . . then I started taking courses, which I did for ten years, at various places such as Columbia University and the American Theatre Wing. I was always in a writing course. I wrote my first play about a year after I came to New York.

INTERVIEWER: Did you write as a child?

KENNEDY: I always kept diaries on people in my family. My mother used to sneak into my room and read them. I really owe writing to her in a sense, because my mother is a terrific storyteller and I feel that all my writing basically has the same tone as the stories she told about her childhood. She used to tell funny stories, but they always had this terror in them, a blackness. I was the only daughter, and we were very close. I feel that my writing is an extension of my relationship with my mother, of talking with her.

INTERVIEWER: How does she feel about your writing?

KENNEDY: It makes her edgy. My writing has a lot of violence in it. As a mother myself, I would find it disturbing if my sons were writing that kind of violence and darkness.

INTERVIEWER: What attracted you to dramatic writing?

KENNEDY: Like most people at that age, I was always writing poetry and short stories. But I really admired Tennessee Williams because he was the leading playwright then, and I'd seen *The Glass Menagerie* when I was sixteen, and I'd read his plays at Ohio State. I saw a lot of theater in New York. I worked two years on my first play in my spare time and it was very imitative of Williams, of *The Glass Menagerie*. I still have it. I was twenty-three then, and I sent the play to Audrey Wood [William's agent], who wrote me a long letter which said she couldn't take me as a client, but that she thought I was very talented. That was a great encouragement to me. I had written the play in a course at the New School taught by Mildred Kuner. She said I wrote the best play in the class, and entered it in a play contest in Chapel Hill, North Carolina, which also meant a lot to me. Well, I didn't win. And that was a pattern I had for a long, long time. People would respond very enthusiastically to my writing, then it would fall through.

INTERVIEWER: How did you maintain the stamina to continue writing plays?

KENNEDY: I became discouraged from playwriting and went back to writing stories and a novel. I went to the General Studies Program at Columbia University where I met John Shelby, the former editor of Rinehart, who played a very big part in my life. I had written some short stories and part of a novel which Shelby read. I remember one cold winter afternoon, I went to his office and he said: "I don't know if you will ever have a big success, but I think you are touched with genius." He took the novel and sent it around. He felt the novel would definitely get published. It never did, though he sent it everywhere. Then he moved to San Francisco, but before he left he put me in touch with another editor who'd done some work for *The New Yorker.* I worked with him on my stories off and on for two years. We sent the stories around and an agent at MCA, Richard Gilston, decided to represent me. By this time, I was twenty-seven and had been writing for six years. Gilston sent the stories around, but he could never get them published. One well-known editor tried to get me to write a novel based on a character in one of the short stories. I was unable to do that, although I worked on it for nine months. It is hard for me to take another person's idea and write about it. I was very frustrated by this time. I used to get despondent, and I must confess my former husband was extremely encouraging. He had his doctorate by this time and was teaching at Hunter College. I became discouraged; it bothered me that I'd begun at twenty-one and by twenty-eight, nothing had happened. I stopped writing for a year or so, and then Joe got a grant from the Africa Research Foundation to do a study in Africa. We went to Europe first, then Ghana, Nigeria . . . we traveled for over a year and it totally changed my writing.

INTERVIEWER: In what way?

KENNEDY: In the fourteen months I spent out of this country, my writing became sharper, more focused and powerful, and less imitative. It was a tremendous turning point. I was exactly twenty-nine when I wrote *Funnyhouse of a Negro* [1964], which many people still consider to be my best play. The masks in the play were very specific. I would say almost every image in *Funnyhouse* took form while I was in West Africa where I became aware of masks. I lived in Ghana at a most fortunate time. Ghana had just won its freedom. It was wonderful to see that liberation. And I thought the landscape of Africa was so beautiful, and the people were beautiful—it gave me a sense of power and strength. We lived in a huge house. I went into the bush and visited many villages. My husband went into the bush every day, and my son, who was five, went to school; I had a lot of time to write. More time probably than I'd ever had in my entire life. I tend to be restless in hot weather, so I'd wake up very early and could not sleep until very late. That combination produced some of the most powerful images I'd ever had. And we'd been to London, Paris, Madrid, Casablanca—it was a total regeneration. I couldn't cling to what I'd been writing—it changed me so. I didn't realize it was going to have this big impact on me. I think the main thing was that I discovered a strength in being a black person and a connection to West Africa.

INTERVIEWER: Did it bother you to be constantly referred to as a "new writer" in the *Funnyhouse of a Negro* reviews, even though you had already been writing for ten years?

KENNEDY: No. Finally being recognized as a writer was tremendously gratifying. But *Funnyhouse of a Negro* presented some other problems; it is such an intense play, and so very revealing of my psyche—if not me, personally . . . It was very dramatic. People who know me think of me as quiet, and to suddenly have this play staged which, again, is quite violent, put a lot of tension in my relationships. Also, to read about yourself in the newspaper is very anxiety producing. I found *Funnyhouse* created tremendous anxiety for me for at least two years.

INTERVIEWER: Was this anxiety solely connected to being in the public eye, or were there other factors which contributed to it?

KENNEDY: Well, it was also going through the production which, as you know, is always full of tension and hatreds and personality problems. To this day, I have fear when a production is started. I wonder how I will get along with the director, and how I will relate to the actors. Even though I had a great director, Michael Kahn, and was thrilled to be working with the people in Edward Albee's workshop, *Funnyhouse of a Negro* wasn't what I would call a good experience simply because I am a writer who is happier at the typewriter than in the arena. At that time, it was expected of me that I fully participate. I've subsequently worked on productions where it wasn't expected of me at all. I usually try to get out of going to opening night. I don't hear anybody talking to me a few days before . . . I am intolerable. I loved working with Joe Papp . . . he let me hide up in the balcony! I find the suspense of opening night just killing. What are the critics going to say? What are your friends going to say . . . ?

INTERVIEWER: Do you read your reviews?

KENNEDY: I try to make myself read them, but sometimes I put them away.

INTERVIEWER: It seems your work is either highly praised or harshly criticized.

KENNEDY: That's right. My reviews are always split. It was clear early on that many people hated my writing. The initial shock came at the Edward Albee workshop production of *Funnyhouse of a Negro* at Circle in the Square. Nothing has ever been as shocking to me as that particular night . . . many people hated my writing. Then, when it went on to a production at Actor's Studio [1964] and people said things like, "It's really nothing—you've just written the same lines over and over again . . . " Rumors went around that people were saying, "She's psychopathic." So you see, I got it all at once, and from the very beginning. Other people felt the play was very lyrical, et cetera. But I realized then that many people disliked my writing. When I said it took two years to recover from *Funnyhouse*, that was part of it. Even now, there is that fear—that's why I want to leave town on opening night. You never know when the critics will attack you.

INTERVIEWER: Was the darkness and violence evident in your early writing, the stories, the novel?

KENNEDY: Yes, but it was tempered. I censored my writing more.

INTERVIEWER: Because you felt your work might shock people?

KENNEDY: Oh, I don't think it had anything to do with what other people might think. I wasn't that sophisticated. When I would read my work over and write a second draft, I would censor things which I, personally—sitting there at the typewriter—found uncomfortable. I had a certain image—even my friends thought of me as quiet and shy, and because I am small, I was labeled "sweet" from the time I was a kid. My writing, quite naturally, turned out to be just the opposite. It was a surprise for me when I would write stories which were so dark. I was censoring my work all the time. In that sense, I owe a lot to Edward Albee. I joined his workshop at Circle in the Square several months after I returned to the United States with my husband. I had written *Funnyhouse of a Negro* in Rome and handed it in to Albee's workshop. There was a lot of suspense about which sixteen people Albee would select for his workshop. After they accepted me, I went through *Funnyhouse* and edited it, very carefully. When they were ready to do my workshop production, I gave Michael Kahn, who was then Albee's assistant, my edited-out version. I'll never forget sitting in Michael's office; he said, "Isn't there something different about this play?" I said, "This is the version I want done in the workshop." He said okay, but mentioned it to Albee. After class, Albee said, "I hear you've given Michael another version of your play." I said, "I don't want that original version done in the workshop, that would be too upsetting. I used the word *nigger* throughout and I'm worried about what I said about my parents, even though it's fictionalized. I don't want it performed." That was a very big moment. We were standing at the back of the stage, and he said, "I really think you should try—I know it's hard—but maybe we should try to put the first version on." Then he said, "If a playwright has a play on, it should be his guts on that stage. . . . If you really think you can't, it's okay. But you should try." I was in tears. But I made the effort. I was the only black person in the workshop. I became very worried.

INTERVIEWER: Did you ever get strong, negative response when your writing was more censored?

KENNEDY: People always liked my writing in those early workshops. It was softened, and highly imitative of Tennessee Williams and García Lorca.

INTERVIEWER: In an earlier interview, you said that during this imitative phase, you realized that Williams's style would not work for you. Why?

KENNEDY: The structure wouldn't work. I couldn't sustain a three-act play. It was a huge breakthrough for me when my main characters began to have other persons—it was in fact my biggest breakthrough as a writer, something I really sweated over, pondered. It was very clear to me that my plays and novels lacked something. I read my work over and over, and found there was a stilted quality. I kept intensive diaries. I can remember the room I was sitting in when I said to myself, "You are very drawn to all these historical people, they are very powerful in your imagination, yet you are not interested in writing about them historically." That's when I decided to use historical people as an extension of the main character, and also to give up the idea that I had to write a full-length play. I would say those were my two big realizations, and to me, they were *really* worth the ten years.

INTERVIEWER: Returning to the *Funnyhouse of a Negro* productions, we read that the play almost closed after twenty-two performances and then was extended by private funds.

KENNEDY: Isabel and Fredrick Eberstadt came to the last performance and decided they would like to contribute money to extend the run. It's hard to explain, but those in the theater really loved that play, and other people were alienated from it and felt that it was bad or offensive—which I still find amazing. It was catastrophic when it was a failure. . . .

INTERVIEWER: A box-office failure?

KENNEDY: Yes. When it closed, I thought it was the end of the world. But other things came out of it, like Rockefeller grants and a Guggenheim. And it gave me a feeling of affinity for people in the theater which has lasted to this day. I still consider writers my best friends. I trust writers.

INTERVIEWER: Were you surprised, then, at winning an Obie?

KENNEDY: Yes. Yes. It was a very strange period. I was barely able to handle the extremes. The play closed, I was very upset—almost suicidal—then it won an Obie. It was utterly confusing. I felt totally alone. I don't think anyone could have made me feel better. That's part of being a playwright. You are really in it by yourself after a certain point. Nothing is comforting. I just sort of hid in the house and talked to my children as much as I could. And there is some comfort in going to the A & P. I remember being in a taxi with Michael Kahn, who said, "Well, Adrienne, you've really had the whole theatrical experience." I told myself I never, ever wanted to have another play on. But *Funnyhouse of a Negro* did help me to realize I was a writer. In the whole decade preceding the play, people felt I would *someday* achieve something. They felt I had captured and illuminated something with *Funnyhouse,* which was what I had been trying to do for a long time.

INTERVIEWER: How did the black arts community react to *Funnyhouse of a Negro?*

KENNEDY: A lot of blacks hated this particular play and said it was pretentious and imitative. It was upsetting. People wanted me to be part of the movement but, frankly, I was always at home with my children. So apart from my temperament, the hours didn't exist.

INTERVIEWER: You were not outspoken in your politics?

KENNEDY: That's right. I remember there was an article written in the sixties that attacked my writing specifically and said that I was an irrelevant black writer. That sort of criticism was pretty pervasive at the time, so I built up a little resistance to it. I was criticized because there were heroines in my plays who were mixed up, confused. But I knew what my alliances were. My father was a social worker and went to Morehouse College, where Martin Luther King studied. He even had the same cadence in his voice, and was always giving speeches. I grew up in a house where people wrote and we were members of the NAACP and the United Negro College Fund. I knew my alliances.

INTERVIEWER: Would you discuss your symbolism, the repeated motifs such as blood, birds . . .

KENNEDY: I really don't know how to talk about that, except that I was a nonstop reader as a child. My mother taught me to read when I was three years old. I read all the books in the library when I was in elementary school, so they had to order some new books! I've always been drawn to the written word and have found solace in symbolism, even as far back as when I was eleven years old and read *Jane Eyre.* I have an affinity for symbolism as a way of surviving. What always impressed me, whether it was Brontë or Fitzgerald, T. S. Eliot or Lorca, was the way that writers took anguish and turned it into symbolism.

INTERVIEWER: Do you have a strong religious background?

KENNEDY: I was expected to go to Sunday School and church. I think all those stories at Sunday School played a big part in my imagination. And I am overlooking the influence of my grandparents, whom my brother and I went to visit every summer. They lived in Georgia, in a town of about five hundred people. I remember the red clay of Georgia, the white churches, going to prayer meetings with my grandmother on Thursday night and to church on Sunday morning. All of that was so powerful. Everybody in my family is very dramatic. I look exactly like my grandmother and express myself like her. The whole family is emotional; people tend to cry a lot. . . .

INTERVIEWER: Are you conscious of the religious imagery in your work?

KENNEDY: Oh, sure. I'm drawn to religious symbols. They are very powerful. Yet I did not have parents who were constantly preaching to me and I did not go to church more than the average person. I did grow up in a neighborhood which was at least sixty percent Italian. I did see people going to catechism in their white dresses [an image from *A Rat's Mass,* 1967]. So that and those summers in Georgia played a huge role.

INTERVIEWER: What is the source of the imagery in your work? How do you get in touch with it?

KENNEDY: When I was in my twenties, I studied the symbolism of other writers such as Ibsen, Lorca, Chekhov. And my dreams were very strong. I used to write them down in a few sentences: "Last night I dreamed I was running through white walls . . ." It appeared to me that those sentences had a certain power. I began to feel that my diaries had much more life than my work. I began to examine them. I started using the symbolism in my journals that came from dreams. Realizing that my dreams had a vitality that my other writing did not was another breakthrough.

INTERVIEWER: How did you begin to incorporate the dream imagery into your work?

KENNEDY: I had many recurrent dreams, so I started to write tiny stories based on them, never thinking that they could be a "work," and not really seeing how I could turn them into a short story. I started to let the images accumulate by themselves. When I made the breakthrough where I discovered that the character could have other personas, the images then seemed more indigenous. Another source of imagery which I am overlooking is the fact that my father used to read to me every night when I was growing up. Sometimes just two or three lines of poetry from Langston Hughes, Paul Laurence Dunbar, James Weldon Johnson. That, too, must have played a role in my development. There is obviously a lot of pleasure in having someone read poetry to you.

INTERVIEWER: Do you agree with critic Rosemary K. Curb's analysis of the menstrual blood in *Lesson in a Dead Language* [1964]: "A sign, almost the antisacrament of the inherited guilt of womanhood"? ["Lesson I Bleed," published in *Women in American Theatre,* Chinoy and Jenkins, eds., Crown Publishers, Inc., 1981]

KENNEDY: (Laughter) Let me tell you something, I get very upset when I read people's analysis of my work. I try not to read it. It makes me uncomfortable.

INTERVIEWER: More uncomfortable than reviews?

KENNEDY: Yes. Yes . . . to have people sort of dissect my psyche . . . I think I fear that it will inhibit me in my future work. I find it disturbing. Reading a review compels me because it concerns whether or not the play is going to run.

INTERVIEWER: Would you tell us about *Lesson in a Dead Language* in your own words? How did the play begin in your mind?

KENNEDY: Apparently—because it is hindsight—I just have this thing about blood. I had always wanted to write something about menstruation. To me, menstrual periods, no matter how long you've been having them, are traumatic—simply the fact that you bleed once a month. I wanted to write about the fear . . . the fear that you will get blood on your clothes. . . . I tend to forget that play, but I like it very much. That play has almost been lost because it was published so long ago. Gaby Rogers did an exquisite production of it at Theatre Genesis [1970]. She captured it.

INTERVIEWER: You have dealt with many "taboo" subjects in your work—rape, incest, domestic violence. How did you find the courage to reveal such volatile truths?

KENNEDY: I wouldn't use the word *courage.* I got the *impetus* from *Funnyhouse of a Negro.* In the decade after, I wrote many one-act plays in rapid succession. It was a confident period . . . I felt confident because I knew I had revealed my obsessions in *Funnyhouse.* Many people like Ellen Stewart at La Mama and Joe Papp [New York Shakespeare Festival] were very responsive and receptive to my work. I'm not sure I could write those plays now. I was riding an emotional crest. After all those years of rejection slips, people suddenly wanted to do my plays. I got letters from Paris, London, Germany . . . it made me very productive. Then, maybe twenty years later (I was about forty), I realized that although I had many first-class productions, apart from grants my plays did not seem to generate an income. That produced another set of conflicts. I had been living on grants, and hadn't quite realized that.

INTERVIEWER: Isn't that always true of experimental theater?

KENNEDY: Beckett and Ionesco make money.

INTERVIEWER: Tell us something about your experience living in London in 1966.

KENNEDY: London was a very pleasurable living experience because of the literary community there. I met writers. I lived there three years on my Guggenheim and two Rockefeller grants. I could write every day. And I met many people in theater. La Mama was touring Europe, as well as Joe Chaikin, The Living Theatre—it was a heyday for Americans in London. I met [playwrights] Edward Bond, John Arden—I met them all at the Royal Court Theatre's Thursday-afternoon teas.

My son went to school a block away—it was a very easy way to live. That was also about the time that Jean-Marie Serreau did a production of *Funnyhouse* at Le Petit Odéon in Paris. Jean-Louis Barrault who ran the Odéon with his wife [Madeleine Renaud], came to rehearsals. In fact, partly what made me cling to being a playwright even when I was very depressed about it, was that I had a romantic feeling about meeting artists and the theater has a way of introducing you to people you could never meet any other way. Being black, but more than that, being black and from the Midwest, from *Cleveland,* what could I do to meet Jean-Louis Barrault, or to have Gian-Carlo Menotti call me up? Writers are embraced by many people. I'm positive that has been the biggest reward, for myself and for my children.

INTERVIEWER: Did you meet many women playwrights in Europe?

KENNEDY: I have never known many women playwrights. I met Lorraine Hansberry once, and at the Actor's Studio I met Eleanor Perry. Megan Terry was working Off Broadway. I met Maria Irene Fornes twice, and Rosalyn Drexler. There weren't that many women playwrights.

INTERVIEWER: Were you affected by the women's movement?

KENNEDY: No. First of all, I hate groups. Secondly, I'd been through all of those struggles . . . alone. I'd been through that decade from age twenty to thirty, 1955 to 1965, trying to write with babies, trying to be a wife, and then experiencing divorce.

INTERVIEWER: You once described your divorce as "a choice for writing. . . . " Would you elaborate?

KENNEDY: I don't know whether I ever said that. There were so many tensions and writing was a comfort. It was much more complicated. I think my husband and I had a typical marriage of that time. He was very busy and on his way "up" and tensions built between us.

INTERVIEWER: Because you were a two-career family?

KENNEDY: I didn't have a career. I was a housewife. I wrote on the side at night and my husband was constantly busy. Each year was a step and the tensions built. Looking back, I think that people put those words in my mouth, because the divorce was not that clear-cut. One paradox I've never quite recovered from is that I feel my former husband encouraged me to write more than anybody has since then. And he supported me financially, and wanted to, and enjoyed doing it.

INTERVIEWER: How did he feel about your success?

KENNEDY: I don't know. By that time there was a lot of sadness that we weren't together. I had known him since I was nineteen. We were married thirteen years. So it wasn't that clear-cut. I am not a heroine who chose writing over marriage. It's not like that at all. I think divorce is futile. I would never divorce again, not with children.

INTERVIEWER: What inspired *Evening With Dead Essex* [1973], which dealt with the Mark Essex snipings? [Mark Essex, a troubled black ex-Navy man left six persons dead and fifteen wounded after sniping from the tower of a seventeen-story New Orleans Howard Johnson's Motor Lodge in January, 1972].

KENNEDY: When I go through periods when I can't write, I'm glued to the television news. I was following the Munich Olympics, and the Mark Essex snipings happened around the same time.

INTERVIEWER: How did you come up with the multimedia dramatic form—headlines are read, slides are shown . . .

KENNEDY: I was trying to capture how you feel when you hear all that on television. Isn't that funny? I've almost forgotten that play.

INTERVIEWER: *Evening With Dead Essex* was the first play by a woman to be produced at the Yale Repertory Theater. Were there subsequent productions of the play?

KENNEDY: It was done at The American Place Theatre first, in a small space, directed by Gaby Rogers, who is brilliant. It did not work well on the main stage at Yale; the actors got lost. Then it was done by a theater company in Louisiana; but nothing ever happened to that play. Apparently, my plays are sometimes expensive and hard to put on. They seem to be taught more than they are produced.

INTERVIEWER: How did your unusual and imaginative use of stage space evolve?

KENNEDY: Martha Graham was very popular in the fifties. I was in my own way attempting to imitate her. I also had a fixation for Picasso. I read everything Picasso had written about his work. Then, in Cleveland, there was one foreign movie house where in my teens I saw all of the French surrealist films, by people like Cocteau, Buñuel . . . my writing is definitely influenced by French film, Martha Graham and Picasso.

INTERVIEWER: What, specifically, were you drawn to in Martha Graham's staging?

KENNEDY: There were always many things happening simultaneously. And everything seemed to come out of darkness. People played many parts, she used a lot of black and white—there was a fluidity and a deemphasis on the narrative. The narrative was being presented to you in another way. I want to say that I wasn't yet capturing this in my short stories or in my plays, though there is no doubt that from 1955, it was on my mind. I'm sure I was also influenced by O'Neill's long monologues about people's torments—by the use of interior monologue.

INTERVIEWER: Do you believe there is a female aesthetic in drama?

KENNEDY: Yes, I think we can make a special contribution to theater.

INTERVIEWER: Virginia Woolf said that however much we may go to the work of male artists for pleasure, it is difficult to go to them for help in finding a voice. . . .

KENNEDY: That is a fascinating statement. I remember reading the stories of Colette when I was young. We carry that around with us. Women writers do affect me differently than male writers. That is probably the female aesthetic at its height. You see, *Jane Eyre* is my favorite novel. I'm glad that Charlotte Brontë was a woman. I think if you can bring your woman's experience to something, it is really great. It's important not to censor or inhibit that experience. Alice Childress has also been a great inspiration to me.

INTERVIEWER: Do you teach the work of women writers in your courses?

KENNEDY: That is a problem. I taught an American drama course at UC [University of California at] Davis and used O'Neill, Sam Shepard, Lorraine Hansberry . . . many writers. The girls complained that there weren't enough women in the course and they complained about the female characters in the plays. I'm not sure what the answer is for that particular period. Not many women playwrights have had recognition. And they are not in the textbooks.

INTERVIEWER: How do you feel about being called a "Woman Playwright," or a "Black Woman Playwright?"

KENNEDY: Ten years ago, it might have bothered me because I would have felt that people were saying I was lesser than say, Norman Mailer. [Laughs] I am a woman writer and a black writer and that doesn't disturb me anymore.

INTERVIEWER: Playwright Wendy Wasserstein says that our cultural idea of a playwright is a white male—anything else is some kind of subset.

KENNEDY: In some ways I have made peace with that. But when I say I have made peace, it is crystal clear to me what is really the issue: as a black woman, or as a woman writer, or as a black writer, I don't stand in line for the income and the rewards, and that bothers me a lot. The white male writer can take steps. He's Off Broadway and the next thing you know, he's writing screenplays for Sidney Lumet. He does stand eighty percent more chance of getting his writing career to pay off. It's that simple.

# Harold Pinter

Harold Pinter (b. 1930) has had an extensive career as an actor, playwright, and screenwriter, but is best known for his strikingly disorienting stage plays. Pinter was born and raised in Hackney, a working-class neighborhood just beyond London's East End. He studied briefly at the Royal Academy of Dramatic Art and pursued a career as a stage and radio actor in the early 1950s before becoming a playwright. His early plays—notably *The Room* (1957), *The Birthday Party* (1958), and *The Dumb Waiter* (1960)—are inflected by the theater of the absurd in the indirect, often menacing, and finally inexplicable quality of their action. But Pinter's drama is set in a much more recognizable locale than are many of Beckett's or Ionesco's plays; his plays often work by frustrating our "realistic" expectations of characters and their stage world. This is particularly true of Pinter's two major successes of the 1960s, *The Caretaker* (1960) and *The Homecoming* (1965). In both of these plays, a visitor disturbs the delicate balance of relations that binds a family together. What is characteristically "Pinteresque" about the action is the way that Pinter's spare and oblique dialogue makes the characters' motives and intentions nearly unreadable, often despite the violence with which they are expressed. If the poverty of language in most realistic drama tends to imply the emptiness of the characters, in Pinter's drama it seems most often to imply their explosive potential to erupt.

Pinter went through a period of profound writer's block in the late 1960s, writing only the short plays *Landscape* (1969) and *Silence* (1969); in the 1970s, though, he wrote a series of major dramas: *Old Times* (1971), *No Man's Land* (1975), and *Betrayal* (1978). These plays take memory and the past as their subject, examining how, in the words of Anna in *Old Times,* "There are things I remember which may never have happened but as I recall them so they take place." More recently, Pinter has written *A Kind of Alaska* (1982), a play based on Oliver Sachs's *Awakenings,* and three plays on more political subjects, *One for the Road* (1984), *Mountain Language* (1988), and *Party Time* (1990). Pinter has also written a number of screenplays, both for his own plays, such as *Betrayal,* and for other projects, including *The French Lieutenant's Woman, Turtle Diary,* and *The Handmaid's Tale.*

## The Homecoming (1965)

*The Homecoming* is typical of Pinter's earlier drama in that it provides us with a recognizable situation—an American college professor and his wife returning home to London to visit his family—that immediately twists in new and surprising directions. For much like the room onstage, with its missing upstage wall, something is missing in this family that determines the structure of their relationships. The most obvious missing element of family life here is the absent mother, Jessie, whose absence informs the relationships between the men of the play: Max, who does the cleaning and cooking, to everyone's ridicule; Sam, who is accused of homosexual prostitution; Lenny, the pimp; Joey, the macho boxer. When Ruth appears in this scenario, she seems suddenly to take the role vacated by Jessie, becoming the controlling figure in the house of crippled men. Ruth assumes the two roles attributed to Jessie—mother and whore. The question, as Max asks at the end, is will she prove "adaptable" to the men's fantasies or will she—as Ruth's independence suggests—adapt the men to her own designs?

*The Homecoming* clearly plays with the formalities and conventions of realistic drama. The secret that often motivates the action of an Ibsen play (Nora's forgery in *A Doll House,* for example) seems to be disclosed in the play by Sam—"MacGregor had Jessie in the back of my cab as I drove them along"—but finally this "secret" loses its power to explain. It is either already known or finally irrelevant to the characters. Indeed, the past in *The Homecoming* seems to be largely improvised or invented. The characters frequently seem to make up stories of the "past" that function more as maneuverings in the present than as reliable accounts of something that actually happened. Lenny's story of beating up a prostitute underneath an arch in Act One, for instance, seems not really to have happened; it is instead an effort to intimidate the seductive Ruth, also a woman standing underneath an arch in the living room. The past in *The Homecoming* is one that the characters invent and reinvent as the action progresses—the past becomes a fantasy that the characters work to recreate in the present action of the play.

# —The Homecoming—
## Harold Pinter

*Summer*

*An old house in North London.*

*A large room, extending the width of the stage.*

*The back wall, which contained the door, has been removed. A square arch shape remains. Beyond it, the hall. In the hall a staircase, ascending U.L., well in view. The front door U.R. A coatstand, hooks, etc.*

*In the room a window, R. Odd tables, chairs. Two large armchairs. A large sofa, L. Against R. wall a large sideboard, the upper half of which contains a mirror. U.L., a radiogram.*

### —ACT ONE—

*Evening.*

LENNY *is sitting on the sofa with a newspaper, a pencil in his hand. He wears a dark suit. He makes occasional marks on the back page.*

MAX *comes in, from the direction of the kitchen. He goes to sideboard, opens top drawer, rummages in it, closes it.*

*He wears an old cardigan and a cap, and carries a stick.*

*He walks downstage, stands, looks about the room.*

MAX: What have you done with the scissors?

(*Pause.*)

I said I'm looking for the scissors. What have you done with them?

(*Pause.*)

Did you hear me? I want to cut something out of the paper.
LENNY: I'm reading the paper.
MAX: Not that paper. I haven't even read that paper. I'm talking about last Sunday's paper. I was just having a look at it in the kitchen.

(*Pause.*)

Do you hear what I'm saying? I'm talking to you! Where's
10  the scissors?
LENNY: (*looking up, quietly*) Why don't you shut up, you daft prat?

(MAX *lifts his stick and points it at him.*)

MAX: Don't you talk to me like that. I'm warning you.

(*He sits in large armchair.*)

There's an advertisement in the paper about flannel vests. Cut price. Navy surplus. I could do with a few of them.

(*Pause.*)

I think I'll have a fag. Give me a fag.

(*Pause.*)

I just asked you to give me a cigarette.

(*Pause.*)

Look what I'm lumbered with.

(*He takes a crumpled cigarette from his pocket.*)

I'm getting old, my word of honour.

(*He lights it.*)

You think I wasn't a tearaway? I could have taken care of 20 you, twice over. I'm still strong. You ask your Uncle Sam what I was. But at the same time I always had a kind heart. Always.

(*Pause.*)

I used to knock about with a man called MacGregor. I called him Mac. You remember Mac? Eh?

(*Pause.*)

Huhh! We were two of the worst hated men in the West End of London. I tell you, I still got the scars. We'd walk into a place, the whole room'd stand up, they'd make way to let us pass. You never heard such silence. Mind you, he was a big man, he was over six foot tall. His family were all Mac- 30 Gregors, they came all the way from Aberdeen, but he was the only one they called Mac.

(*Pause.*)

He was very fond of your mother, Mac was. Very fond. He always had a good word for her.

(*Pause.*)

Mind you, she wasn't such a bad woman. Even though it made me sick just to look at her rotten stinking face, she wasn't such a bad bitch. I gave her the best bleeding years of my life, anyway.
LENNY: Plug it, will you, you stupid sod, I'm trying to read the paper.                                                            40
MAX: Listen! I'll chop your spine off, you talk to me like that! You understand? Talking to your lousy filthy father like that!
LENNY: You know what, you're getting demented.

(*Pause.*)

What do you think of Second Wind for the three-thirty?
MAX: Where?
LENNY: Sandown Park.
MAX: Don't stand a chance.
LENNY: Sure he does.
MAX: Not a chance.

50 LENNY: He's the winner.

(LENNY *ticks the paper.*)

MAX: He talks to me about horses.

(*Pause.*)

I used to live on the course. One of the loves of my life. Epsom? I knew it like the back of my hand. I was one of the best-known faces down at the paddock. What a marvellous open-air life.

(*Pause.*)

He talks to me about horses. You only read their names in the papers. But I've stroked their manes, I've held them, I've calmed them down before a big race. I was the one they used to call for. Max, they'd say, there's a horse here, he's
60 highly strung, you're the only man on the course who can calm him. It was true. I had a . . . I had an instinctive understanding of animals. I should have been a trainer. Many times I was offered the job—you know, a proper post, by the Duke of . . . I forget his name . . . one of the Dukes. But I had family obligations, my family needed me at home.

(*Pause.*)

The times I've watched those animals thundering past the post. What an experience. Mind you, I didn't lose, I made a few bob out of it, and you know why? Because I always had the smell of a good horse. I could smell him. And not only
70 the colts but the fillies. Because the fillies are more highly strung than the colts, they're more unreliable, did you know that? No, what do you know? Nothing. But I was always able to tell a good filly by one particular trick. I'd look her in the eye. You see? I'd stand in front of her and look her straight in the eye, it was a kind of hypnotism, and by the look deep down in her eye I could tell whether she was a stayer or not. It was a gift. I had a gift.

(*Pause.*)

And he talks to me about horses.
LENNY: Dad, do you mind if I change the subject?

(*Pause.*)

80 I want to ask you something. That dinner we had before, what was the name of it? What do you call it?

(*Pause.*)

Why don't you buy a dog? You're a dog cook. Honest. You think you're cooking for a lot of dogs.
MAX: If you don't like it get out.
LENNY: I am going out. I'm going out to buy myself a proper dinner.
MAX: Well, get out! What are you waiting for?

(LENNY *looks at him.*)

LENNY: What did you say?
MAX: I said shove off out of it, that's what I said.
90 LENNY: You'll go before me, Dad, if you talk to me in that tone of voice.
MAX: Will I, you bitch?

(MAX *grips his stick.*)

LENNY: Oh, Daddy, you're not going to use your stick on me, are you? Eh? Don't use your stick on me, Daddy. No, please. It wasn't my fault, it was one of the others. I haven't done anything wrong, Dad, honest. Don't clout me with that stick, Dad.

(*Silence.*)
(MAX *sits hunched.* LENNY *reads the paper.*)
(SAM *comes in the front door. He wears a chauffeur's uniform. He hangs his hat on a hook in the hall and comes into the room. He goes to a chair, sits in it and sighs.*)

Hullo, Uncle Sam.
SAM: Hullo.
LENNY: How are you, Uncle?                                        100
SAM: Not bad. A bit tired.
LENNY: Tired? I bet you're tired. Where you been?
SAM: I've been to London Airport.
LENNY: All the way up to London Airport? What, right up the M4?
SAM: Yes, all the way up there.
LENNY: Tch, tch, tch. Well, I think you're entitled to be tired, Uncle.
SAM: Well, it's the drivers.
LENNY: I know. That's what I'm talking about. I'm talking 110 about the drivers.
SAM: Knocks you out.

(*Pause.*)

MAX: I'm here, too, you know.

(SAM *looks at him.*)

I said I'm here, too. I'm sitting here.
SAM: I know you're here.

(*Pause.*)

SAM: I took a Yankee out there today . . . to the Airport.
LENNY: Oh, a Yankee, was it?
SAM: Yes, I been with him all day. Picked him up at the Savoy at half past twelve, took him to the Caprice for his lunch. After lunch I picked him up again, took him down to a house 120 in Eaton Square—he had to pay a visit to a friend there— and then round about tea-time I took him right the way out to the Airport.
LENNY: Had to catch a plane there, did he?
SAM: Yes. Look what he gave me. He gave me a box of cigars.

(SAM *takes a box of cigars from his pocket.*)

MAX: Come here. Let's have a look at them.

(SAM *shows* MAX *the cigars.* MAX *takes one from the box, pinches it and sniffs it.*)

It's a fair cigar.
SAM: Want to try one?

(MAX *and* SAM *light cigars.*)

You know what he said to me? He told me I was the best chauffeur he'd ever had. The best one.                          130
MAX: From what point of view?

SAM: Eh?

MAX: From what point of view?

LENNY: From the point of view of his driving, Dad, and his general sense of courtesy, I should say.

MAX: Thought you were a good driver, did he, Sam? Well, he gave you a first-class cigar.

SAM: Yes, he thought I was the best he'd ever had. They all say that, you know. They won't have anyone else, they only ask
140    for me. They say I'm the best chauffeur in the firm.

LENNY: I bet the other drivers tend to get jealous, don't they, Uncle?

SAM: They do get jealous. They get very jealous.

MAX: Why?

(*Pause.*)

SAM: I just told you.

MAX: No, I just can't get it clear, Sam. Why do the other drivers get jealous?

SAM: Because (a) I'm the best driver, and because . . . (b) I don't take liberties.

(*Pause.*)

150    I don't press myself on people, you see. These big business-men, men of affairs, they don't want the driver jawing all the time, they like to sit in the back, have a bit of peace and quiet. After all, they're sitting in a Humber Super Snipe, they can afford to relax. At the same time, though, this is what really makes me special . . . I do know how to pass the time of day when required.

(*Pause.*)

For instance, I told this man today I was in the second world war. Not the first. I told him I was too young for the first. But I told him I fought in the second.

(*Pause.*)

160    So did he, it turned out.

(LENNY *stands, goes to the mirror and straightens his tie.*)

LENNY: He was probably a colonel, or something, in the American Air Force.

SAM: Yes.

LENNY: Probably a navigator, or something like that, in a Flying Fortress. Now he's most likely a high executive in a worldwide group of aeronautical engineers.

SAM: Yes.

LENNY: Yes, I know the kind of man you're talking about.

(LENNY *goes out, turning to his right.*)

SAM: After all, I'm experienced. I was driving a dust cart at the
170    age of nineteen. Then I was in long-distance haulage. I had ten years as a taxi-driver and I've had five as a private chauffeur.

MAX: It's funny you never got married, isn't it? A man with all your gifts.

(*Pause.*)

Isn't it? A man like you?

SAM: There's still time.

MAX: Is there?

(*Pause.*)

SAM: You'd be surprised.

MAX: What you been doing, banging away at your lady customers, have you?    180

SAM: Not me.

MAX: In the back of the Snipe? Been having a few crafty reefs in a layby, have you?

SAM: Not me.

MAX: On the back seat? What about the armrest, was it up or down?

SAM: I've never done that kind of thing in my car.

MAX: Above all that kind of thing, are you, Sam?

SAM: Too true.

MAX: Above having a good bang on the back seat, are you?    190

SAM: Yes, I leave that to others.

MAX: You leave it to others? What others? You paralysed prat!

SAM: I don't mess up my car! Or my . . . my boss's car! Like other people.

MAX: Other people? What other people?

(*Pause.*)

What other people?

(*Pause.*)

SAM: Other people.

(*Pause.*)

MAX: When you find the right girl, Sam, let your family know, don't forget, we'll give you a number one send-off, I promise you. You can bring her to live here, she can keep us    200 all happy. We'd take it in turns to give her a walk round the park.

SAM: I wouldn't bring her here.

MAX: Sam, it's your decision. You're welcome to bring your bride here, to the place where you live, or on the other hand you can take a suite at the Dorchester. It's entirely up to you.

SAM: I haven't got a bride.

(SAM *stands, goes to the sideboard, takes an apple from the bowl, bites into it.*)

Getting a bit peckish.

(*He looks out of the window.*)

Never get a bride like you had, anyway. Nothing like your    210 bride . . . going about these days. Like Jessie.

(*Pause.*)

After all, I escorted her once or twice, didn't I? Drove her round once or twice in my cab. She was a charming woman.

(*Pause.*)

All the same, she was your wife. But still . . . they were some of the most delightful evenings I've ever had. Used to just drive her about. It was my pleasure.

MAX: (*softly, closing his eyes*) Christ.

SAM: I used to pull up at a stall and buy her a cup of coffee. She was a very nice companion to be with.

(*Silence.*)

(JOEY *comes in the front door. He walks into the room, takes his*

*jacket off, throws it on a chair and stands.)*
*(Silence.)*

220 JOEY: Feel a bit hungry.

SAM: Me, too.

MAX: Who do you think I am, your mother? Eh? Honest. They walk in here every time of the day and night like bloody animals. Go and find yourself a mother.

*(LENNY walks into the room, stands.)*

JOEY: I've been training down at the gym.

SAM: Yes, the boy's been working all day and training all night.

MAX: What do you want, you bitch? You spend all the day sitting on your arse at London Airport, buy yourself a jamroll. You expect me to sit here waiting to rush into the kitchen
230 the moment you step in the door? You've been living sixty-three years, why don't you learn to cook?

SAM: I can cook.

MAX: Well, go and cook!

*(Pause.)*

LENNY: What the boys want, Dad, is your own special brand of cooking, Dad. That's what the boys look forward to. The special understanding of food, you know, that you've got.

MAX: Stop calling me Dad. Just stop all that calling me Dad, do you understand?

LENNY: But I'm your son. You used to tuck me up in bed every
240 night. He tucked you up, too, didn't he, Joey?

*(Pause.)*

He used to like tucking up his sons.

*(LENNY turns and goes towards the front door.)*

MAX: Lenny.

LENNY: *(turning)* What?

MAX: I'll give you a proper tuck up one of these nights, son. You mark my word.

*(They look at each other.)*
*(LENNY opens the front door and goes out.)*
*(Silence.)*

JOEY: I've been training with Bobby Dodd.

*(Pause.)*

And I had a good go at the bag as well.

*(Pause.)*

I wasn't in bad trim.

MAX: Boxing's a gentleman's game.

*(Pause.)*

250   I'll tell you what you've got to do. What you've got to do is you've got to learn how to defend yourself, and you've got to learn how to attack. That's your only trouble as a boxer. You don't know how to defend yourself, and you don't know how to attack.

*(Pause.)*

Once you've mastered those arts you can go straight to the top.

*(Pause.)*

JOEY: I've got a pretty good idea . . . of how to do that.

*(JOEY looks round for his jacket, picks it up, goes out of the room and up the stairs.*
*Pause.)*

MAX: Sam . . . why don't you go, too, eh? Why don't you just go upstairs? Leave me quiet. Leave me alone.

SAM: I want to make something clear about Jessie, Max. I want 260 to. I do. When I took her out in the cab, round the town, I was taking care of her, for you. I was looking after her for you, when you were busy, wasn't I? I was showing her the West End.

*(Pause.)*

You wouldn't have trusted any of your other brothers. You wouldn't have trusted Mac, would you? But you trusted me. I want to remind you.

*(Pause.)*

Old Mac died a few years ago, didn't he? Isn't he dead?

*(Pause.)*

He was a lousy stinking rotten loudmouth. A bastard uncouth sodding runt. Mind you, he was a good friend of 270 yours.

*(Pause.)*

MAX: Eh, Sam . . .

SAM: What?

MAX: Why do I keep you here? You're just an old grub.

SAM: Am I?

MAX: You're a maggot.

SAM: Oh yes?

MAX: As soon as you stop paying your way here, I mean when you're too old to pay your way, you know what I'm going to do? I'm going to give you the boot.                                          280

SAM: You are, eh?

MAX: Sure. I mean, bring in the money and I'll put up with you. But when the firm gets rid of you—you can flake off.

SAM: This is my house as well, you know. This was our mother's house.

MAX: One lot after the other. One mess after the other.

SAM: Our father's house.

MAX: Look what I'm lumbered with. One cast-iron bunch of crap after another. One flow of stinking pus after another.

*(Pause.)*

Our father? I remember him. Don't worry. You kid yourself. 290 He used to come over to me and look down at me. My old man did. He'd bend right over me, then he'd pick me up. I was only that big. Then he'd dandle me. Give me the bottle. Wipe me clean. Give me a smile. Pat me on the bum. Pass me around, pass me from hand to hand. Toss me up in the air. Catch me coming down. I remember my father.

*(BLACKOUT.)*
*(LIGHTS UP.)*
*(Night.)*
*(TEDDY and RUTH stand at the threshold of the room.)*
*(They are both well dressed in light summer suits and light raincoats.)*

*(Two suitcases are by their side.)*

*(They look at the room.* TEDDY *tosses the key in his hand, smiles.)*

TEDDY: Well, the key worked.

*(Pause.)*

They haven't changed the lock.

*(Pause.)*

RUTH: No one's here.

300 TEDDY: *(looking up)* They're asleep.

*(Pause.)*

RUTH: Can I sit down?

TEDDY: Of course.

RUTH: I'm tired.

*(Pause.)*

TEDDY: Then sit down.

*(She does not move.)*

That's my father's chair.

RUTH: That one?

TEDDY: *(smiling)* Yes, that's it. Shall I go up and see if my room's still there?

RUTH: It can't have moved.

310 TEDDY: No, I mean if my bed's still there.

RUTH: Someone might be in it.

TEDDY: No. They've got their own beds.

*(Pause.)*

RUTH: Shouldn't you wake someone up? Tell them you're here?

TEDDY: Not at this time of night. It's too late.

*(Pause.)*

Shall I go up?

*(He goes into the hall, looks up the stairs, comes back.)*

Why don't you sit down?

*(Pause.)*

I'll just go up . . . have a look.

*(He goes up the stairs, stealthily.)*

*(*RUTH *stands, then slowly walks across the room.)*

*(*TEDDY *returns.)*

It's still there. My room. Empty. The bed's there. What are 320 you doing?

*(She looks at him.)*

Blankets, no sheets. I'll find some sheets. I could hear snores. Really. They're all still here, I think. They're all snoring up there. Are you cold?

RUTH: No.

TEDDY: I'll make something to drink, if you like. Something hot.

RUTH: No, I don't want anything.

*(*TEDDY *walks about.)*

TEDDY: What do you think of the room? Big, isn't it? It's a big house. I mean, it's a fine room, don't you think? Actually there was a wall, across there . . . with a door. We knocked 330 it down . . . years ago . . . to make an open living area. The structure wasn't affected, you see. My mother was dead.

*(*RUTH *sits.)*

Tired?

RUTH: Just a little.

TEDDY: We can go to bed if you like. No point in waking anyone up now. Just go to bed. See them all in the morning . . . see my father in the morning. . . .

*(Pause.)*

RUTH: Do you want to stay?

TEDDY: Stay?

*(Pause.)*

We've come to stay. We're bound to stay . . . for a few days. 340

RUTH: I think . . . the children . . . might be missing us.

TEDDY: Don't be silly.

RUTH: They might.

TEDDY: Look, we'll be back in a few days, won't we?

*(He walks about the room.)*

Nothing's changed. Still the same.

*(Pause.)*

Still, he'll get a surprise in the morning, won't he? The old man. I think you'll like him very much. Honestly. He's a . . . well, he's old, of course. Getting on.

*(Pause.)*

I was born here, do you realize that?

RUTH: I know.                                                                    350

*(Pause.)*

TEDDY: Why don't you go to bed? I'll find some sheets. I feel . . . wide awake, isn't it odd? I think I'll stay up for a bit. Are you tired?

RUTH: No.

TEDDY: Go to bed. I'll show you the room.

RUTH: No, I don't want to.

TEDDY: You'll be perfectly all right up there without me. Really you will. I mean, I won't be long. Look, it's just up there. It's the first door on the landing. The bathroom's right next door. You . . . need some rest, you know.                          360

*(Pause.)*

I just want to . . . walk about for a few minutes. Do you mind?

RUTH: Of course I don't.

TEDDY: Well . . . Shall I show you the room?

RUTH: No, I'm happy at the moment.

TEDDY: You don't have to go to bed. I'm not saying you have to. I mean, you can stay up with me. Perhaps I'll make a cup of tea or something. The only thing is we don't want to make too much noise, we don't want to wake anyone up.

RUTH: I'm not making any noise.                                               370

TEDDY: I know you're not.

*(He goes to her.)*

(*Gently.*) Look, it's all right, really. I'm here. I mean . . . I'm with you. There's no need to be nervous. Are you nervous?

RUTH: No.

TEDDY: There's no need to be.

*(Pause.)*

They're very warm people, really. Very warm. They're my family. They're not ogres.

*(Pause.)*

Well, perhaps we should go to bed. After all, we have to be up early, see Dad. Wouldn't be quite right if he found us in
380   bed, I think. (*He chuckles.*) Have to be up before six, come down, say hullo.

*(Pause.)*

RUTH: I think I'll have a breath of air.

TEDDY: Air?

*(Pause.)*

What do you mean?

RUTH: (*standing*) Just a stroll.

TEDDY: At this time of night? But we've . . . only just got here. We've got to go to bed.

RUTH: I just feel like some air.

TEDDY: But I'm going to bed.

390   RUTH: That's all right.

TEDDY: But what am I going to do?

*(Pause.)*

The last thing I want is a breath of air. Why do you want a breath of air?

RUTH: I just do.

TEDDY: But it's late.

RUTH: I won't go far. I'll come back.

*(Pause.)*

TEDDY: I'll wait up for you.

RUTH: Why?

TEDDY: I'm not going to bed without you.

400   RUTH: Can I have the key?

*(He gives it to her.)*

Why don't you go to bed?

*(He puts his arms on her shoulders and kisses her. They look at each other, briefly. She smiles.)*

I won't be long.

*(She goes out of the front door.)*
*(*TEDDY *goes to the window, peers out after her, half turns from the window, stands, suddenly chews his knuckles.)*
*(*LENNY *walks into the room from* U.L. *He stands. He wears py-jamas and dressing-gown. He watches* TEDDY. TEDDY *turns and sees him.)*
*(Silence.)*

TEDDY: Hullo, Lenny.

LENNY: Hullo, Teddy.

*(Pause.)*

TEDDY: I didn't hear you come down the stairs.

LENNY: I didn't.

*(Pause.)*

I sleep down here now. Next door. I've got a kind of study, workroom cum bedroom next door now, you see.

TEDDY: Oh. Did I . . . wake you up?

LENNY: No. I just had an early night tonight. You know how it   410
is. Can't sleep. Keep waking up.

*(Pause.)*

TEDDY: How are you?

LENNY: Well, just sleeping a bit restlessly, that's all. Tonight, anyway.

TEDDY: Bad dreams?

LENNY: No, I wouldn't say I was dreaming. It's not exactly a dream. It's just that something keeps waking me up. Some kind of tick.

TEDDY: A tick?

LENNY: Yes.   420

TEDDY: Well, what is it?

LENNY: I don't know.

*(Pause.)*

TEDDY: Have you got a clock in your room?

LENNY: Yes.

TEDDY: Well, maybe it's the clock.

LENNY: Yes, could be, I suppose.

*(Pause.)*

Well, if it's the clock I'd better do something about it. Stifle it in some way, or something.

*(Pause.)*

TEDDY: I've . . . just come back for a few days.

LENNY: Oh yes? Have you?   430

*(Pause.)*

TEDDY: How's the old man?

LENNY: He's in the pink.

*(Pause.)*

TEDDY: I've been keeping well.

LENNY: Oh, have you?

*(Pause.)*

Staying the night then, are you?

TEDDY: Yes.

LENNY: Well, you can sleep in your old room.

TEDDY: Yes, I've been up.

LENNY: Yes, you can sleep there.

*(*LENNY *yawns.)*

Oh well.   440

TEDDY: I'm going to bed.

LENNY: Are you?

TEDDY: Yes, I'll get some sleep.

LENNY: Yes, I'm going to bed, too.

(TEDDY *picks up the cases.*)

I'll give you a hand.
TEDDY: No, they're not heavy.

(TEDDY *goes into the hall with the cases.*)
(LENNY *turns out the light in the room.*)
(*The light in the hall remains on.*)
(LENNY *follows into the hall.*)

LENNY: Nothing you want?
TEDDY: Mmmm?
LENNY: Nothing you might want, for the night? Glass of water,
450     anything like that?
TEDDY: Any sheets anywhere?
LENNY: In the sideboard in your room.
TEDDY: Oh, good.
LENNY: Friends of mine occasionally stay there, you know, in
    your room, when they're passing through this part of the
    world.

(LENNY *turns out the hall light and turns on the first landing
light.*)
(TEDDY *begins to walk up the stairs.*)

TEDDY: Well, I'll see you at breakfast, then.
LENNY: Yes, that's it. Ta-ta.

(TEDDY *goes upstairs.*)
(LENNY *goes off* L.)
(*Silence.*)
(*The landing light goes out.*)
(*Slight night light in the hall and room.*)
(LENNY *comes back into the room, goes to the window and
looks out.*)
(*He leaves the window and turns on a lamp.*)
(*He is holding a small clock.*)
(*He sits, places the clock in front of him, lights a cigarette and
sits.*)
(RUTH *comes in the front door.*)
(*She stands still.* LENNY *turns his head, smiles. She walks
slowly into the room.*)

LENNY: Good evening.
460 RUTH: Morning, I think.
LENNY: You're right there.

(*Pause.*)

My name's Lenny. What's yours?
RUTH: Ruth.

(*She sits, puts her coat collar around her.*)

LENNY: Cold?
RUTH: No.
LENNY: It's been a wonderful summer, hasn't it? Remarkable.

(*Pause.*)

Would you like something? Refreshment of some kind? An
    aperitif, anything like that?
RUTH: No, thanks.
470 LENNY: I'm glad you said that. We haven't got a drink in the
    house. Mind you, I'd soon get some in, if we had a party or
    something like that. Some kind of celebration . . . you know.

(*Pause.*)

You must be connected with my brother in some way. The
    one who's been abroad.
RUTH: I'm his wife.
LENNY: Eh listen, I wonder if you can advise me. I've been hav-
    ing a bit of a rough time with this clock. The tick's been
    keeping me up. The trouble is I'm not all that convinced it
    was the clock. I mean there are lots of things which tick in
    the night, don't you find that? All sorts of objects, which, in 480
    the day, you wouldn't call anything else but commonplace.
    They give you no trouble. But in the night any given one of
    a number of them is liable to start letting out a bit of a tick.
    Whereas you look at these objects in the day and they're just
    commonplace. They're as quiet as mice during the daytime.
    So . . . all things being equal . . . this question of me saying
    it was the clock that woke me up, well, that could very eas-
    ily prove something of a false hypothesis.

(*He goes to the sideboard, pours from a jug into a glass, takes
the glass to* RUTH.)

Here you are. I bet you could do with this.
RUTH: What is it? 490
LENNY: Water.

(*She takes it, sips, places the glass on a small table by her chair.*
LENNY *watches her.*)

Isn't it funny? I've got my pyjamas on and you're fully
    dressed?

(*He goes to the sideboard and pours another glass of water.*)

Mind if I have one? Yes, it's funny seeing my old brother
    again after all these years. It's just the sort of tonic my Dad
    needs, you know. He'll be chuffed to his bollocks in the
    morning, when he sees his eldest son. I was surprised myself
    when I saw Teddy, you know. Old Ted. I thought he was in
    America.
RUTH: We're on a visit to Europe. 500
LENNY: What, both of you?
RUTH: Yes.
LENNY: What, you sort of live with him over there, do you?
RUTH: We're married.
LENNY: On a visit to Europe, eh? Seen much of it?
RUTH: We've just come from Italy.
LENNY: Oh, you went to Italy first, did you? And then he
    brought you over here to meet the family, did he? Well, the
    old man'll be pleased to see you, I can tell you.
RUTH: Good. 510
LENNY: What did you say?
RUTH: Good.

(*Pause.*)

LENNY: Where'd you go to in Italy?
RUTH: Venice.
LENNY: Not dear old Venice? Eh? That's funny. You know, I've
    always had a feeling that if I'd been a soldier in the last
    war—say in the Italian campaign—I'd probably have found
    myself in Venice. I've always had that feeling. The trouble
    was I was too young to serve, you see. I was only a child, I
    was too small, otherwise I've got a pretty shrewd idea I'd 520

probably have gone through Venice. Yes, I'd almost certainly have gone through it with my battalion. Do you mind if I hold your hand?

RUTH: Why?

LENNY: Just a touch.

*(He stands and goes to her.)*

Just a tickle.

RUTH: Why?

*(He looks down at her.)*

LENNY: I'll tell you why.

*(Slight pause.)*

530 One night, not too long ago, one night down by the docks, I was standing alone under an arch, watching all the men jibbing the boom, out in the harbour, and playing about with the yardarm, when a certain lady came up to me and made me a certain proposal. This lady had been searching for me for days. She'd lost track of my whereabouts. However, the fact was she eventually caught up with me, and when she caught up with me she made me this certain proposal. Well, this proposal wasn't entirely out of order and normally I would have subscribed to it. I mean I would have subscribed to it in the normal course of events. The only trouble was 540 she was falling apart with the pox. So I turned it down. Well, this lady was very insistent and started taking liberties with me down under this arch, liberties which by any criterion I couldn't be expected to tolerate, the facts being what they were, so I clumped her one. It was on my mind at the time to do away with her, you know, to kill her, and the fact is, that as killings go, it would have been a simple matter, nothing to it. Her chauffeur, who had located me for her, he'd popped round the corner to have a drink, which just left this lady and myself, you see, alone, standing underneath this 550 arch, watching all the steamers steaming up, no one about, all quiet on the Western Front, and there she was up against this wall—well, just sliding down the wall, following the blow I'd given her. Well, to sum up, everything was in my favour, for a killing. Don't worry about the chauffeur. The chauffeur would never have spoken. He was an old friend of the family. But . . . in the end I thought . . . Aaah, why go to all the bother . . . you know, getting rid of the corpse and all that, getting yourself into a state of tension. So I just gave her another belt in the nose and a couple of turns of the boot 560 and sort of left it at that.

RUTH: How did you know she was diseased?

LENNY: How did I know?

*(Pause.)*

I decided she was.

*(Silence.)*

You and my brother are newly-weds, are you?

RUTH: We've been married six years.

LENNY: He's always been my favourite brother, old Teddy. Do you know that? And my goodness we are proud of him here, I can tell you. Doctor of Philosophy and all that . . . leaves quite an impression. Of course, he's a very sensitive man, 570 isn't he? Ted. Very. I've often wished I was as sensitive

as he is.

RUTH: Have you?

LENNY: Oh yes. Oh yes, very much so. I mean, I'm not saying I'm not sensitive. I am. I could just be a bit more so, that's all.

RUTH: Could you?

LENNY: Yes, just a bit more so, that's all.

*(Pause.)*

I mean, I am very sensitive to atmosphere, but I tend to get desensitized, if you know what I mean, when people make unreasonable demands on me. For instance, last Christmas 580 I decided to do a bit of snow-clearing for the Borough Council, because we had a heavy snow over here that year in Europe. I didn't have to do this snow-clearing—I mean I wasn't financially embarrassed in any way—it just appealed to me, it appealed to something inside me. What I anticipated with a good deal of pleasure was the brisk cold bite in the air in the early morning. And I was right. I had to get my snowboots on and I had to stand on a corner, at about five-thirty in the morning, to wait for the lorry to pick me up, to take me to the allotted area. Bloody freezing. Well, the lorry 590 came, I jumped on the tailboard, headlights on, dipped, and off we went. Got there, shovels up, fags on, and off we went, deep into the December snow, hours before cockcrow. Well, that morning, while I was having my mid-morning cup of tea in a neighbouring cafe, the shovel standing by my chair, an old lady approached me and asked me if I would give her a hand with her iron mangle. Her brother-in-law, she said, had left it for her, but he'd left it in the wrong room, he'd left it in the front room. Well, naturally, she wanted it in the back room. It was a present he'd given her, 600 you see, a mangle, to iron out the washing. But he'd left it in the wrong room, he'd left it in the front room, well that was a silly place to leave it, it couldn't stay there. So I took time off to give her a hand. She only lived up the road. Well, the only trouble was when I got there I couldn't move this mangle. It must have weighed about half a ton. How this brother-in-law got it up there in the first place I can't even begin to envisage. So there I was, doing a bit of shoulders on with the mangle, risking a rupture, and this old lady just standing there, waving me on, not even lifting a little finger 610 to give me a helping hand. So after a few minutes I said to her, now look here, why don't you stuff this iron mangle up your arse? Anyway, I said, they're out of date, you want to get a spin drier. I had a good mind to give her a workover there and then, but as I was feeling jubilant with the snow-clearing I just gave her a short-arm jab to the belly and jumped on a bus outside. Excuse me, shall I take this ashtray out of your way?

RUTH: It's not in my way.

LENNY: It seems to be in the way of your glass. The glass was 620 about to fall. Or the ashtray. I'm rather worried about the carpet. It's not me, it's my father. He's obsessed with order and clarity. He doesn't like mess. So, as I don't believe you're smoking at the moment, I'm sure you won't object if I move the ashtray.

*(He does so.)*

And now perhaps I'll relieve you of your glass.

RUTH: I haven't quite finished.
LENNY: You've consumed quite enough, in my opinion.
RUTH: No, I haven't.
630 LENNY: Quite sufficient, in my own opinion.
RUTH: Not in mine, Leonard.

(*Pause.*)

LENNY: Don't call me that, please.
RUTH: Why not?
LENNY: That's the name my mother gave me.

(*Pause.*)

  Just give me the glass.
RUTH: No.

(*Pause.*)

LENNY: I'll take it, then.
RUTH: If you take the glass . . . I'll take you.

(*Pause.*)

LENNY: How about me taking the glass without you taking me?
640 RUTH: Why don't I just take you?

(*Pause.*)

LENNY: You're joking.

(*Pause.*)

  You're in love, anyway, with another man. You've had a secret liaison with another man. His family didn't even know. Then you come here without a word of warning and start to make trouble.

(*She picks up the glass and lifts it towards him.*)

RUTH: Have a sip. Go on. Have a sip from my glass.

(*He is still.*)

  Sit on my lap. Take a long cool sip.

(*She pats her lap. Pause.*)
(*She stands, moves to him with the glass?*)

  Put your head back and open your mouth.
LENNY: Take that glass away from me.
650 RUTH: Lie on the floor. Go on. I'll pour it down your throat.
LENNY: What are you doing, making me some kind of proposal?

(*She laughs shortly, drains the glass.*)

RUTH: Oh, I was thirsty.

(*She smiles at him, puts the glass down, goes into the hall and up the stairs.*)
(*He follows into the hall and shouts up the stairs.*)

LENNY: What was that supposed to be? Some kind of proposal?

(*Silence.*)
(*He comes back into the room, goes to his own glass, drains it.*)
(*A door slams upstairs.*)
(*The landing light goes on.*)
(MAX *comes down the stairs, in pyjamas and cap. He comes into the room.*)

MAX: What's going on here? You drunk?

(*He stares at* LENNY.)

What are you shouting about? You gone mad?

(LENNY *pours another glass of water.*)

  Prancing about in the middle of the night shooting your head off. What are you, a raving lunatic?
LENNY: I was thinking aloud.
MAX: Is Joey down here? You been shouting at Joey?    660
LENNY: Didn't you hear what I said, Dad? I said I was thinking aloud.
MAX: You were thinking so loud you got me out of bed.
LENNY: Look, why don't you just . . . pop off, eh?
MAX: Pop off? He wakes me up in the middle of the night, I think we got burglars here, I think he's got a knife stuck in him, I come down here, he tells me to pop off.

(LENNY *sits down.*)

  He was talking to someone. Who could he have been talking to? They're all asleep. He was having a conversation with someone. He won't tell me who it was. He pretends he was    670 thinking aloud. What are you doing, hiding someone here?
LENNY: I was sleepwalking. Get out of it, leave me alone, will you?
MAX: I want an explanation, you understand? I asked you who you got hiding here.

(*Pause.*)

LENNY: I'll tell you what, Dad, since you're in the mood for a bit of a . . . chat, I'll ask you a question. It's a question I've been meaning to ask you for some time. That night . . . you know . . . the night you got me . . . that night with Mum, what was it like? Eh? When I was just a glint in your eye. What    680 was it like? Was was the background to it? I mean, I want to know the real facts about my background. I mean, for instance, is it a fact that you had me in mind all the time, or is it a fact that I was the last thing you had in mind?

(*Pause.*)

  I'm only asking this in a spirit of inquiry, you understand that, don't you? I'm curious. And there's lots of people of my age share that curiosity, you know that, Dad? They often ruminate, sometimes singly, sometimes in groups, about the true facts of that particular night—the night they were made in the image of those two people *at it*. It's a question    690 long overdue, from my point of view, but as we happen to be passing the time of day here tonight I thought I'd pop it to you.

(*Pause.*)

MAX: You'll drown in your own blood.
LENNY: If you prefer to answer the question in writing I've got no objection.

(MAX *stands.*)

  I should have asked my dear mother. Why didn't I ask my dear mother? Now it's too late. She's passed over to the other side.

(MAX *spits at him.*)

(LENNY *looks down at the carpet.*)

700    Now look what you've done. I'll have to Hoover that in the morning, you know.

(MAX *turns and talks up the stairs*).
(LENNY *sits still.*)
(BLACKOUT.)
(LIGHTS UP.)

(*Morning.*)
(JOEY *in front of the mirror. He is doing some slow limbering-up exercises. He stops, combs his hair, carefully. He then shadowboxes, heavily, watching himself in the mirror.*)
(MAX *comes in from* U.L.)
(*Both* MAX *and* JOEY *are dressed.* MAX *watches* JOEY *in silence.*)
(JOEY *stops shadowboxing, picks up a newspaper and sits.*)
(*Silence.*)

MAX: I hate this room.

(*Pause.*)

It's the kitchen I like. It's nice in there. It's cosy.

(*Pause.*)

But I can't stay in there. You know why? Because he's always washing up in there, scraping the plates, driving me out of the kitchen, that's why.
JOEY: Why don't you bring your tea in here?
MAX: I don't want to bring my tea in here. I hate it here. I want to drink my tea in there.

(*He goes into the hall and looks towards the kitchen.*)

710    What's he doing in there?

(*He returns.*)

What's the time?
JOEY: Half past six.
MAX: Half past six.

(*Pause.*)

I'm going to see a game of football this afternoon. You want to come?

(*Pause.*)

I'm talking to you.
JOEY: I'm training this afternoon. I'm doing six rounds with Blackie.
MAX: That's not till five o'clock. You've got time to see a game
720    of football before five o'clock. It's the first game of the season.
JOEY: No, I'm not going.
MAX: Why not?

(*Pause.*)
(MAX *goes into the hall.*)

Sam! Come here!

(MAX *comes back into the room.*)
(SAM *enters with a cloth.*)

SAM: What?

MAX: What are you doing in there?
SAM: Washing up.
MAX: What else?
SAM: Getting rid of your leavings.
MAX: Putting them in the bin, eh?                                            730
SAM: Right in.
MAX: What point you trying to prove?
SAM: No point.
MAX: Oh yes, you are. You resent making my breakfast, that's what it is, isn't it? That's why you bang round the kitchen like that, scraping the frying-pan, scraping all the leavings into the bin, scraping all the plates, scraping all the tea out of the teapot . . . that's why you do that, every single stinking morning. I know. Listen, Sam. I want to say something to you. From my heart.                                                        740

(*He moves closer.*)

I want you to get rid of these feelings of resentment you've got towards me. I wish I could understand them. Honestly, have I ever given you cause? Never. When Dad died he said to me, Max, look after your brothers? That's exactly what he said to me.
SAM: How could he say that when he was dead?
MAX: What?
SAM: He could he speak if he was dead?

(*Pause.*)

MAX: Before he died, Sam. Just before. They were his last words. His last sacred words, Sammy. A split second after he  750
said those words . . . he was a dead man. You think I'm joking? You think when my father spoke—on his death-bed—I wouldn't obey his words to the last letter? You hear that, Joey? He'll stop at nothing. He's even prepared to spit on the memory of our Dad. What kind of a son were you, you wet wick? You spent half your time doing crossword puzzles! We took you into the butcher's shop, you couldn't even sweep the dust off the floor. We took MacGregor into the shop, he could run the place by the end of a week. Well, I'll tell you one thing. I respected my father not only as a man  760
but as a number one butcher! And to prove it I followed him into the shop. I learned to carve a carcass at his knee. I commemorated his name in blood. I gave birth to three grown men! All on my own bat. What have you done?

(*Pause.*)

What have you done? You tit!
SAM: Do you want to finish the washing up? Look, here's the cloth.
MAX: So try to get rid of these feelings of resentment, Sam. After all, we are brothers.
SAM: Do you want the cloth? Here you are. Take it.                          770

(TEDDY *and* RUTH *come down the stairs. They walk across the hall and stop just inside the room.*)
(*The others turn and look at them.* JOEY *stands.*)
(TEDDY *and* RUTH *are wearing dressing-gowns.*)
(*Silence.*)
(TEDDY *smiles.*)

TEDDY: Hullo . . . Dad . . . We overslept.

(*Pause.*)

What's for breakfast?

(*Silence.*)
(TEDDY *chuckles.*)

Huh. We overslept.

(MAX *turns to* SAM.)

MAX: Did you know he was here?
SAM: No.

(MAX *turns to* JOEY.)

MAX: Did you know he was here?

(*Pause.*)

I asked you if you knew he was here.
JOEY: No.
MAX: Then who knew?

(*Pause.*)

780    Who knew?

(*Pause.*)

I didn't know.
TEDDY: I was going to come down, Dad, I was going to . . . be
    here, when you came down.

(*Pause.*)

How are you?

(*Pause.*)

Uh . . . look, I'd . . . like you to meet . . .
MAX: How long you been in this house?
TEDDY: All night.
MAX: All night? I'm a laughing-stock. How did you get in?
TEDDY: I had my key.

(MAX *whistles and laughs.*)

790    MAX: Who's this?
TEDDY: I was just going to introduce you.
MAX: Who asked you to bring tarts in here?
TEDDY: Tarts?
MAX: Who asked you to bring dirty tarts into this house?
TEDDY: Listen, don't be silly—
MAX: You been here all night?
TEDDY: Yes, we arrived from Venice—
MAX: We've had a smelly scrubber in my house all night. We've
    had a stinking pox-ridden slut in my house all night.
800    TEDDY: Stop it! What are you talking about?
MAX: I haven't seen the bitch for six years, he comes home
    without a word, he brings a filthy scrubber off the street, he
    shacks up in my house!
TEDDY: She's my wife! We're married!

(*Pause.*)

MAX: I've never had a whore under this roof before. Ever since
    your mother died. My word of honour. (*To* JOEY.) Have you
    ever had a whore here? Has Lenny ever had a whore here?
    They come back from America, they bring the slopbucket
    with them. They bring the bedpan with them. (*To* TEDDY.)
810    Take that disease away from me. Get her away from me.

TEDDY: She's my wife.
MAX: (*to* JOEY) Chuck them out.

(*Pause.*)

A Doctor of Philosophy. Sam, you want to meet a Doctor of
Philosophy? (*To* JOEY.) I said chuck them out.

(*Pause.*)

What's the matter? You deaf?
JOEY: You're an old man. (*To* TEDDY.) He's an old man.

(LENNY *walks into the room, in a dressing-gown.*)
(*He stops.*)
(*They all look round.*)
(MAX *turns back, hits* JOEY *in the stomach with all his might.*)
(JOEY *contorts, staggers across the stage.* MAX, *with the exertion
of the blow, begins to collapse. His knees buckle.*)
(*He clutches his stick.*)
(SAM *moves forward to help him.*)
(MAX *hits him across the head with his stick.* SAM *sits, head in
hands.*)
(JOEY, *hands pressed to his stomach, sinks down at the feet of*
RUTH.)
(*She looks down at him.*)
(LENNY *and* TEDDY *are still.*)
(JOEY *slowly stands. He is close to* RUTH. *He turns from* RUTH,
*looks round at* MAX.)
(SAM *clutches his head.*)
(MAX *breathes heavily, very slowly gets to his feet.*)
(JOEY *moves to him.*)
(*They look at each other.*)
(*Silence.*)
(MAX *moves past* JOEY, *walks towards* RUTH. *He gestures with
his stick.*)

MAX: Miss.

(RUTH *walks towards him.*)

RUTH: Yes?

(*He looks at her.*)

MAX: You a mother?
RUTH: Yes.                                                    820
MAX: How many you got?
RUTH: Three.

(*He turns to* TEDDY.)

MAX: All yours, Ted?

(*Pause.*)

Teddy, why don't we have a nice cuddle and kiss, eh? Like
the old days? What about a nice cuddle and kiss, eh?
TEDDY: Come on, then.

(*Pause.*)

MAX: You want to kiss your old father? Want a cuddle with your
old father?
TEDDY: Come on, then.

(TEDDY *moves a step towards him.*)

Come on.                                                     830

*(Pause.)*

MAX: You still love your old Dad, eh?

*(The face each other.)*

TEDDY: Come on, Dad. I'm ready for the cuddle.

*(MAX begins to chuckle, gurgling.)*
*(He turns to the family and addresses them.)*

MAX: He still loves his father!

*(Curtain)*

## —ACT TWO—

*Afternoon.*

MAX, TEDDY, LENNY *and* SAM *are about the stage, lighting cigars.*

JOEY *comes in from* U.L. *with a coffee tray, followed by* RUTH. *He puts the tray down.* RUTH *hands coffee to all the men. She sits with her cup.* MAX *smiles at her.*

RUTH: That was a very good lunch.
MAX: I'm glad you liked it. *(To the others.)* Did you hear that? *(To* RUTH.*)* Well, I put my heart and soul into it, I can tell you. *(He sips.)* And this is a lovely cup of coffee.
RUTH: I'm glad.

*(Pause.)*

MAX: I've got the feeling you're a first-rate cook.
840 RUTH: I'm not bad.
MAX: No, I've got the feeling you're a number one cook. Am I right, Teddy?
TEDDY: Yes, she's a very good cook.

*(Pause.)*

MAX: Well, it's a long time since the whole family was together, eh? If only your mother was alive. Eh, what do you say, Sam? What would Jessie say if she was alive? Sitting here with her three sons. Three fine grown-up lads. And a lovely daughter-in-law. The only shame is her grandchildren aren't here. She'd have petted them and cooed over them,
850 wouldn't she, Sam? She'd have fussed over them and played with them, told them stories, tickled them—I tell you she'd have been hysterical. *(To* RUTH.*)* Mind you, she taught those boys everything they know. She taught them all the morality they know. I'm telling you. Every single bit of the moral code they live by—was taught to them by their mother. And she had a heart to go with it. What a heart. Eh, Sam? Listen, what's the use of beating round the bush? That woman was the backbone to this family. I mean, I was busy working twenty-four hours a day in the shop, I was going all over the
860 country to find meat, I was making my way in the world, but I left a woman at home with a will of iron, a heart of gold and a mind. Right, Sam?

*(Pause.)*

What a mind.

*(Pause.)*

Mind you, I was a generous man to her. I never left her short of a few bob. I remember one year I entered into negotiations with a top-class group of butchers with continental connections. I was going into association with them. I remember the night I came home, I kept quiet. First of all I gave Lenny a bath, then Teddy a bath, then Joey a bath. What fun we used to have in the bath, eh, boys? Then I 870 came downstairs and I made Jessie put her feet up on a pouffe—what happened to that pouffe, I haven't seen it for years—she put her feet up on the pouffe and I said to her, Jessie, I think our ship is going to come home, I'm going to treat you to a couple of items, I'm going to buy you a dress in pale corded blue silk, heavily encrusted in pearls, and for casual wear, a pair of pantaloons in lilac flowered taffeta. Then I gave her a drop of cherry brandy. I remember the boys came down, in their pyjamas, all their hair shining, their faces pink, it was before they started shaving, and they 880 knelt down at our feet, Jessie's and mine. I tell you, it was like Christmas.

*(Pause.)*

RUTH: That happened to the group of butchers?
MAX: That group? They turned out to be a bunch of criminals like everyone else.

*(Pause.)*

This is a lousy cigar.

*(He stubs it out.)*
*(He turns to* SAM.*)*

What time you going to work?
SAM: Soon.
MAX: You've got a job on this afternoon, haven't you?
SAM: Yes, I know.                                                          890
MAX: What do you mean, you know? You'll be late. You'll lose your job. What are you trying to do, humiliate me?
SAM: Don't worry about me.
MAX: It makes the bile come up in my mouth. The bile—you understand? *(To* RUTH.*)* I worked as a butcher all my life, using the chopper and the slab, the slab, you know what I mean, the chopper and the slab! To keep my family in luxury. Two families! My mother was bedridden, my brothers were all invalids. I had to earn the money for the leading psychiatrists. I had to read books! I had to study the disease, 900 so that I could cope with an emergency at every stage. A crippled family, three bastard sons, a slutbitch of a wife—don't talk to me about the pain if childbirth—I suffered the pain, I've still got the pangs—when I give a little cough my back collapses—and here I've got a lazy idle bugger of a brother won't even get to work on time. The best chauffeur in the world. All his life he's sat in the front seat giving lovely hand signals. You call that work? This man doesn't know his gearbox from his arse!
SAM: You go and ask my customers! I'm the only one they ever 910 ask for.
MAX: What do the other drivers do, sleep all day?
SAM: I can only drive one car. They can't all have me at the same time.
MAX: Anyone could have you at the same time. You'd bend over for half a dollar on Blackfriars Bridge.

SAM: Me!

MAX: For two bob and a toffee apple.

SAM: He's insulting me. He's insulting his brother. I'm driving
920    a man to Hampton Court at four forty-five.

MAX: Do you want to know who could drive? MacGregor! Mac-
Gregor was a driver.

SAM: Don't you believe it.

(MAX *points his stick at* SAM.)

MAX: He didn't even fight in the war. This man didn't even
fight in the bloody war!

SAM: I did!

MAX: Who did you kill?

(*Silence.*)
(SAM *gets up, goes to* RUTH, *shakes her hand and goes out of the
front door.*)
(MAX *turns to* TEDDY.)

Well, how you been keeping, son?

TEDDY: I've been keeping very well, Dad.
930    MAX: It's nice to have you with us, son.

TEDDY: It's nice to be back, Dad.

(*Pause.*)

MAX: You should have told me you were married, Teddy. I'd
have sent you a present. Where was the wedding, in
America?

TEDDY: No. Here. The day before we left.

MAX: Did you have a big function?

TEDDY: No, there was no one there.

MAX: You're mad. I'd have given you a white wedding. We'd
have had the cream of the cream here. I'd have been only
940    too glad to bear the expense, my word of honour.

(*Pause.*)

TEDDY: You were busy at the time. I didn't want to bother you.

MAX: But you're my own flesh and blood. You're my first born.
I'd have dropped everything. Sam would have driven you to
the reception in the Snipe, Lenny would have been your
best man, and then we'd have all seen you off on the boat. I
mean, you don't think I disapprove of marriage, do you?
Don't be daft. (*To* RUTH.) I've been begging my two youngsters for years to find a nice feminine girl with proper cre-
dentials—it makes life worth living. (*To* TEDDY.) Anyway,
950    what's the difference, you did it, you made a wonderful choice, you've got a wonderful family, a marvellous
career . . . so why don't we let bygones be bygones?

(*Pause.*)

You know what I'm saying? I want you both to know that you
have my blessing.

TEDDY: Thank you.

MAX: Don't mention it. How many other houses in the district
have got a Doctor of Philosophy sitting down drinking a cup
of coffee?

(*Pause.*)

RUTH: I'm sure Teddy's very happy . . . to know that you're
960    pleased with me.

(*Pause.*)

I think he wondered whether you would be pleased with
me.

MAX: But you're a charming woman.

(*Pause.*)

RUTH: I was . . .

MAX: What?

(*Pause.*)

What she say?

(*They all look at her.*)

RUTH: I was . . . different . . . when I met Teddy . . . first.

TEDDY: No you weren't. You were the same.

RUTH: I wasn't.

MAX: Who cares? Listen, live in the present, what are you wor-    970
rying about? I mean, don't forget the earth's about five
thousand million years old, at least. Who can afford to live
in the past?

(*Pause.*)

TEDDY: She's a great help to me over there. She's a wonderful
wife and mother. She's a very popular woman. She's got
lots of friends. It's a great life, at the University . . . you
know . . . it's a very good life. We've got a lovely house . . .
we've got all . . . we've got everything we want. It's a very
stimulating environment.

(*Pause.*)

My department . . . is highly successful.    980

(*Pause.*)

We've got three boys, you know.

MAX: All boys? Isn't that funny, eh? You've got three, I've got
three. You've got three nephews, Joey. Joey! You're an
uncle, do you hear? You could teach them how to box.

(*Pause.*)

JOEY: (*to* RUTH) I'm a boxer. In the evenings, after work. I'm in
demolition in the daytime.

RUTH: Oh?

JOEY: Yes. I hope to be full time, when I get more bouts.

MAX: (*to* LENNY) He speaks so easily to his sister-in-law, do you
notice? That's because she's an intelligent and sympathetic    990
woman.

(*He leans to her.*)

Eh, tell me, do you think the children are missing their
mother?

(*She looks at him.*)

TEDDY: Of course they are. They love her. We'll be seeing
them soon.

(*Pause.*)

LENNY: (*to* TEDDY) Your cigar's gone out.

TEDDY: Oh, yes.

LENNY: Want a light?

TEDDY: No. No.

(*Pause.*)

1000 So has yours.

LENNY: Oh, yes.

(*Pause.*)

Eh, Teddy, you haven't told us much about your Doctorship of Philosophy. What do you teach?

TEDDY: Philosophy.

LENNY: Well, I want to ask you something. Do you detect a certain logical incoherence in the central affirmations of Christian theism?

TEDDY: That question doesn't fall within my province.

LENNY: Well, look at it this way . . . you don't mind my asking
1010 you some questions, do you?

TEDDY: If they're within my province.

LENNY: Well, look at this way. How can the unknown merit reverence? In other words, how can you revere that of which you're ignorant? At the same time, it would be ridiculous to propose that what we *know* merits reverence. What we know merits any one of a number of things, but it stands to reason reverence isn't one of them. In other words, apart from the known and the unknown, what else is there?

(*Pause.*)

TEDDY: I'm afraid I'm the wrong person to ask.

1020 LENNY: But you're a philosopher. Come on, be frank. What do you make of all this business of being and not-being?

TEDDY: What do you make of it?

LENNY: Well, for instance, take a table. Philosophically speaking. What is it?

TEDDY: A table.

LENNY: Ah. You mean it's nothing else but a table. Well, some people would envy your certainty, wouldn't they, Joey? For instance, I've got a couple of friends of mine, we often sit round the Ritz Bar having a few liqueurs, and they're always
1030 saying things like that, you know, things like: Take a table, take it. All right, I say, *take* it, *take* a table, but once you've taken it, what you going to do with it? Once you've got hold of it, where you going to take it?

MAX: You'd probably sell it.

LENNY: You wouldn't get much for it.

JOEY: Chop it up for firewood.

(LENNY *looks at him and laughs.*)

RUTH: Don't be too sure though. You've forgotten something. Look at me. I . . . move my leg. That's all it is. But I wear . . . underwear . . . which moves with me . . . it . . . cap-
1040 tures your attention. Perhaps you misinterpret. The action is simple. It's a leg . . . moving. My lips move. Why don't you restrict . . . your observations to that? Perhaps the fact that they move is more significant . . . than the words which come through them. You must bear that . . . possibility . . . in mind.

(*Silence.*)
(TEDDY *stands.*)

I was born quite near here.

(*Pause.*)

Then . . . six years ago, I went to America.

(*Pause.*)

It's all rock. And sand. It stretches . . . so far . . . everywhere you look. And there's lots of insects there.

(*Pause.*)

And there's lots of insects there. 1050

(*Silence.*)
(*She is still.*)
(MAX *stands.*)

MAX: Well, it's time to go to the gym. Time for your workout, Joey.

LENNY: (*standing*) I'll come with you.

(JOEY *sits looking at* RUTH.)

MAX: Joe.

(JOEY *stands. The three go out.*)
(TEDDY *sits by* RUTH, *holds her hand.*)
(*She smiles at him.*)
(*Pause.*)

TEDDY: I think we'll go back, Mmnn?

(*Pause.*)

Shall we go home?

RUTH: Why?

TEDDY: Well, we were only here for a few days, weren't we? We might as well . . . cut it short, I think.

RUTH: Why? Don't you like it here? 1060

TEDDY: Of course I do. But I'd like to go back and see the boys now.

(*Pause.*)

RUTH: Don't you like your family?

TEDDY: Which family?

RUTH: Your family here.

RUTH: Of course I like them. What are you talking about?

(*Pause.*)

RUTH: You don't like them as much as you thought you did?

TEDDY: Of course I do. Of course I . . . like them. I don't know what you're talking about.

(*Pause.*)

Listen. You know what time of the day it is there now, do 1070 you?

RUTH: What?

TEDDY: It's morning. It's about eleven o'clock.

RUTH: Is it?

TEDDY: Yes, they're about six hours behind us . . . I mean . . . behind the time here. The boys'll be at the pool . . . now . . . swimming. Think of it. Morning over there. Sun. We'll go anyway, mmnn? It's so clean there.

RUTH: Clean.

TEDDY: Yes. 1080

RUTH: Is it dirty here?

TEDDY: No, of course not. But it's cleaner there.

(*Pause.*)

Look, I just brought you back to meet the family, didn't I? You've met them, we can go. The fall semester will be starting soon.

RUTH: You find it dirty here?

TEDDY: I didn't say I found it dirty here.

(*Pause.*)

I didn't say that.

(*Pause.*)

1090    Look. I'll go and pack. You rest for a while. Will you? They won't be back for at least an hour. You can sleep. Rest. Please.

(*She looks at him.*)

You can help me with my lectures when we get back. I'd love that. I'd be so grateful for it, really. We can bathe till October. You know that. Here, there's nowhere to bathe, except the swimming bath down the road. You know what it's like? It's like a urinal. A filthy urinal!

(*Pause.*)

You liked Venice, didn't you. It was lovely, wasn't it? You had a good week. I mean . . . I took you there. I can speak Italian.

1100    RUTH: But if I'd been a nurse in the Italian campaign I would have been there before.

(*Pause.*)

TEDDY: You just rest. I'll go and pack.

(TEDDY *goes out and up the stairs.*)
(*She closes her eyes.*)
(LENNY *appears from* U.L.)
(*He walks into the room and sits near her.*)
(*She opens her eyes.*)
(*Silence.*)

LENNY: Well, the evenings are drawing in.

RUTH: Yes, it's getting dark.

(*Pause.*)

LENNY: Winter'll soon be upon us. Time to renew one's wardrobe.

(*Pause.*)

RUTH: That's a good thing to do.

LENNY: What?

(*Pause.*)

RUTH: I always . . .

(*Pause.*)

1110    Do you like clothes?

LENNY: Oh, yes. Very fond of clothes.

(*Pause.*)

RUTH: I'm fond . . .

(*Pause.*)

What do you think of my shoes?

LENNY: They're very nice.

RUTH: No, I can't get the ones I want over there.

LENNY: Can't get them over there, eh?

RUTH: No . . . you don't get them there.

(*Pause.*)

I was a model before I went away.

LENNY: Hats?

(*Pause.*)

I bought a girl a hat once. We saw it in a glass case, in a shop. 1120 I tell you what it had. I had a bunch of daffodils on it, tied with a black satin bow, and then it was covered with a cloche of black veiling. A cloche. I'm telling you. She was made for it.

RUTH: No . . . I was a model for the body. A photographic model for the body.

LENNY: Indoor work?

RUTH: That was before I had . . . all my children.

(*Pause.*)

No, not always indoors.

(*Pause.*)

Once or twice we went to a place in the country, by train. 1130 Oh, six or seven times. We used to pass a . . . a large white water tower. This place . . . this house . . . was very big . . . the trees . . . there was a lake, you see . . . we used to change and walk down towards the lake . . . we went down a path . . . on stones . . . there were . . . on this path. Oh, just . . . wait . . . yes . . . when we changed in the house we had a drink. There was a cold buffet.

(*Pause.*)

Sometimes we stayed in the house but . . . most often . . . we walked down to the lake . . . and did our modelling there.

(*Pause.*)

Just before we went to America I went down there. I walked 1140 from the station to the gate and then I walked up the drive. There were lights on . . . I stood in the drive . . . the house was very light.

(TEDDY *comes down the stairs with the cases. He puts them down, looks at* LENNY.)

TEDDY: What have you been saying to her?

(*He goes to* RUTH.)

Here's your coat.

(LENNY *goes to the radiogram and puts on a record of slow jazz.*)

Ruth. Come on. Put it on.

LENNY: (*to* RUTH) What about one dance before you go?

TEDDY: We're going.

LENNY: Just one.

TEDDY: No. We're going.                                                    1150

LENNY: Just one dance, with her brother-in-law, before she goes.

(LENNY *bends to her.*)

Madam?

(RUTH *stands. They dance, slowly.*)
(TEDDY *stands, with* RUTH's *coat.*)
(MAX *and* JOEY *come in the front door and into the room.*)
(*They stand.*)
(LENNY *kisses* RUTH. *They stand, kissing.*)

JOEY: Christ, she's wide open. Dad, look at that.

(*Pause.*)

She's a tart.

(*Pause.*)

Old Lenny's got a tart in here.

(JOEY *goes to them. He takes* RUTH's *arm. He smiles at* LENNY.
*He sits with* RUTH *on the sofa, embraces and kisses her.*
*He looks up at* LENNY.)

Just up my street.

(*He leans her back until she lies beneath him. He kisses her. He
looks up at* TEDDY *and* MAX.)

It's better than a rubdown, this.

(LENNY *sits on the arm of the sofa. He caresses* RUTH's *hair as*
JOEY *embraces her.*)
(MAX *comes forward, looks at the cases.*)

MAX: You going, Teddy? Already?

(*Pause.*)

1160 Well, when you coming over again, eh? Look, next time you
come over, don't forget to let us know beforehand whether
you're married or not. I'll always be glad to meet the wife.
Honest. I'm telling you.

(JOEY *lies heavily on* RUTH.)
(*They are almost still.*)
(LENNY *caresses her hair.*)

Listen, you think I don't know why you didn't tell me you
were married? I know why. You were ashamed. You thought
I'd be annoyed because you married a woman beneath you.
You should have known me better. I'm broadminded. I'm a
broadminded man.

(*He peers to see* RUTH's *face under* JOEY, *turns back to* TEDDY.)

Mind you, she's a lovely girl. A beautiful woman. And a
1170 mother too. A mother of three. You've made a happy woman
out of her. It's something to be proud of. I mean, we're talking about a woman of quality. We're talking about a woman
of feeling.

(JOEY *and* RUTH *roll off the sofa on to the floor.*)
(JOEY *clasps her.* LENNY *moves to stand above them. He looks
down at them. He touches* RUTH *gently with his foot.*)
(RUTH *suddenly pushes* JOEY *away.*)
(*She stands up.*)
(JOEY *gets to his feet, stares at her.*)

RUTH: I'd like something to eat. (*To* LENNY.) I'd like a drink.

Did you get any drink?
LENNY: We've got drink.
RUTH: I'd like one, please.
LENNY: What drink?
RUTH: Whisky.
LENNY: I've got it.                                                  1180

(*Pause.*)

RUTH: Well, get it.

(LENNY *goes to the sideboard, takes out bottle and glasses.*
JOEY *moves towards her.*)

Put the record off.

(*He looks at her, turns, puts the record off.*)

I want something to eat.

(*Pause.*)

JOEY: I can't cook. (*Pointing to* MAX.) He's the cook.

(LENNY *brings her a glass of whiskey.*)

LENNY: Soda on the side?
RUTH: What's this glass? I can't drink out of this. Haven't you
got a tumbler?
LENNY: Yes.
RUTH: Well, put it in a tumbler.

(*He takes the glass back, pours whiskey into a tumbler, brings
it to her.*)

LENNY: On the rocks? Or as it comes?                                 1190
RUTH: Rocks? What do you know about rocks?
LENNY: We've got rocks. But they're frozen stiff in the fridge.

(RUTH *drinks.*)
(LENNY *looks round at the others.*)

Drinks all round?

(*He goes to the sideboard and pours drinks.*)
(JOEY *moves closer to* RUTH.)

JOEY: What food do you want?

(RUTH *walks round the room.*)

RUTH: (*to* TEDDY) Have your family read your critical works?
MAX: That's one thing I've never done. I've never read one of
his critical works.
TEDDY: You wouldn't understand them.

(LENNY *hands drinks all round.*)

JOEY: What sort of food do you want? I'm not the cook, anyway.
LENNY: Soda, Ted? Or as it comes?                                    1200
TEDDY: You wouldn't understand my works. You wouldn't have
the faintest idea of what they were about. You wouldn't appreciate the points of reference. You're way behind. All of
you. There's no point in my sending you my works. You'd be
lost. It's nothing to do with the question of intelligence. It's
a way of being able to look at the world. It's a question of
how far you can operate on things and not in things. I mean
it's a question of your capacity to ally the two, to relate the
two, to balance the two. To see, to be able to *see*! I'm the one
who can see. That's why I can write my critical works. Might 1210

do you good . . . have a look at them . . . see how certain people can view . . . things . . . how certain people can maintain . . . intellectual equilibrium. Intellectual equilibrium. You're just objects. You just . . . move about. I can observe it. I can see what you do. It's the same as I do. But you're lost in it. You won't get me being . . . I won't be lost in it.

(BLACKOUT.)
(LIGHTS UP.)
(*Evening.*)
(TEDDY *sitting, in his coat, the cases by him.* SAM.)
(*Pause.*)

SAM: Do you remember MacGregor, Teddy?
TEDDY: Mac?
SAM: Yes.
1220 TEDDY: Of course I do.
SAM: What did you think of him? Did you take to him?
TEDDY: Yes. I liked him. Why?

(*Pause.*)

SAM: You know, you were always my favourite, of the lads. Always.

(*Pause.*)

When you wrote to me from America I was very touched, you know. I mean you'd written to your father a few times but you'd never written to me. But then, when I got that letter from you . . . well, I was very touched. I never told him. I never told him I'd heard from you.

(*Pause.*)

1230    (*Whispering.*) Teddy, shall I tell you something? You were always your mother's favourite. She told me. It's true. You were always the . . . you were always the main object of her love.

(*Pause.*)

Why don't you stay for a couple more weeks, eh? We could have a few laughs.

(LENNY *comes in the front door and into the room.*)

LENNY: Still here, Ted? You'll be late for your first seminar.

(*He goes to the sideboard, opens it, peers in it, to the right and the left, stands.*)

Where's my cheese-roll?

(*Pause.*)

Someone's taken my cheese-roll. I left it there. (*To* SAM.) You been thieving?
1240 TEDDY: I took your cheese-roll, Lenny.

(*Silence.*)
(SAM *looks at them, picks up his hat and goes out of the front door.*)
(*Silence.*)

LENNY: You took my cheese-roll?
TEDDY: Yes.
LENNY: I made that roll myself. I cut it and put the butter on. I sliced a piece of cheese and put it in between. I put it on a plate and I put it in the sideboard. I did all that before I went out. Now I come back and you've eaten it.
TEDDY: Well, what are you going to do about it?
LENNY: I'm waiting for you to apologize.
TEDDY: But I took it deliberately, Lenny.
LENNY: You mean you didn't stumble on it my mistake?    1250
TEDDY: No, I saw you put it there. I was hungry, so I ate it.

(*Pause.*)

LENNY: Barefaced audacity.

(*Pause.*)

What led you to be so . . . vindictive against your own brother? I'm bowled over.

(*Pause.*)

Well, Ted, I would say this is something approaching the naked truth, isn't it? It's a real cards on the table stunt. I mean, we're in the land of no holds barred now. Well, how else can you interpret it? To pinch your younger brother's specially made cheese-roll when he's out doing a spot of work, that's not equivocal, it's unequivocal.    1260

(*Pause.*)

Mind you, I will say you do seem to have grown a big sulky during the last six years. A bit sulky. A bit inner. A bit less forthcoming. It's funny, because I'd have thought that in the United States of America, I mean with the sun and all that, the open spaces, on the old campus, in your position, lecturing, in the centre of all the intellectual life out there, on the old campus, all the social whirl, all the stimulation of it all, all your kids and all that, to have fun with, down by the pool, the Greyhound buses and all that, tons of iced water, all the comfort of those Bermuda shorts and all that, on the 1270 old campus, no time of the day or night you can't get a cup of coffee or a Dutch gin, I'd have thought you'd have grown more forthcoming, not less. Because I want you to know that you set a standard for us, Teddy. Your family looks up to you, boy, and you know what it does? It does its best to follow the example you set. Because you're a great source of pride to us. That's why we were so glad to see you come back, to welcome you back to your birthplace. That's why.

(*Pause.*)

No, listen, Ted, there's no question that we live a less rich life here than you do over there. We live a closer live. We're 1280 busy, of course. Joey's busy with his boxing, I'm busy with my occupation, Dad still plays a good game of poker, and he does the cooking as well, well up to his old standard, and Uncle Sam's the best chauffeur in the firm. But nevertheless we do make up a unit, Teddy, and you're an integral part of it. When we all sit round the backyard having a quiet gander at the night sky, there's always an empty chair standing in the circle, which is in fact yours. And so when you at length return to us, we do expect a bit of grace, a bit of je ne sais quoi, a bit of generosity of mind, a bit of liberality of 1290 spirit, to reassure us. We do expect that. But do we get it? Have we got it? Is that what you've given us?

(*Pause.*)

TEDDY: Yes.

(JOEY *comes down the stairs and into the room, with a news-paper.*)

LENNY: (*to* JOEY) How'd you get on?
JOEY: Er . . . not bad.
LENNY: What do you mean?

(*Pause.*)

What do you mean?
JOEY: Not bad.
LENNY: I want to know what you *mean*—by not bad.
1300 JOEY: What's it got to do with you?
LENNY: Joey, you tell your brother everything.

(*Pause.*)

JOEY: I didn't get all the way.
LENNY: You didn't get all the way?

(*Pause.*)

(*With emphasis.*) You didn't get all the way? But you've had her up there for two hours.
JOEY: Well?
LENNY: You didn't get all the way and you've had her up there for two hours.
JOEY: What about it?

(LENNY *moves closer to him.*)

1310 LENNY: What are you telling me?
JOEY: What do you mean?
LENNY: Are you telling me she's a tease?

(*Pause.*)

She's a tease!

(*Pause.*)

What do you think of that, Ted? Your wife turns out to be a tease. He's had her up there for two hours and he didn't go the whole hog.
JOEY: I didn't say she was a tease.
LENNY: Are you joking? It sounds like a tease to me, don't it to you, Ted?
1320 TEDDY: Perhaps he hasn't got the right touch.
LENNY: Joey? Not the right touch? Don't be ridiculous. He's had more dolly than you've had cream cakes. He's irresistible. He's one of the few and far between. Tell him about the last bird you had, Joey.

(*Pause.*)

JOEY: What bird?
LENNY: The last bird! When we stopped the car . . .
JOEY: Oh, that . . . yes . . . well, we were in Lenny's car one night last week . . .
LENNY: The Alfa.
1330 JOEY: And er . . . bowling down the road . . .
LENNY: Up near the Scrubs.
JOEY: Yes, up over by the Scrubs . . .
LENNY: We were doing a little survey of North Paddington.
JOEY: And er . . . it was pretty late, wasn't it?
LENNY: Yes, it was late. Well?

(*Pause.*)

JOEY: And then we . . . well, by the kerb, we saw this parked car . . . with a couple of girls in it.
LENNY: And their escorts.
JOEY: Yes, there were two geezers in it. Anyway . . .

(*Pause.*)

What we do then?                                               1340
LENNY: We stopped the car and got out!
JOEY: Yes . . . we got out . . . and we told the . . . two escorts . . . to go away . . . which they did . . . and then we . . . got the girls out of the car . . .
LENNY: We didn't take them over the Scrubs.
JOEY: Oh, no. Not over the Scrubs. Well, the police would have noticed us there . . . you see. We took them over a bombed site.
LENNY: Rubble. In the rubble.
JOEY: Yes, plenty of rubble.                                    1350

(*Pause.*)

Well . . . you know . . . then we had them.
LENNY: You've missed out the best bit. He's missed out the best bit!
JOEY: What bit?
LENNY: (*to* TEDDY) His bird says to him, I don't mind, she says, but I've got to have some protection. I've got to have some contraceptive protection. I haven't got any contraceptive protection, old Joey says to her. In that case I won't do it, she says. Yes you will, says Joey, never mind about the contraceptive protection.                                        1360

(LENNY *laughs.*)

Even my bird laughed when she heard that. Yes, even she gave out a bit of a laugh. So you can't say old Joey isn't a bit of a knockout when he gets going, can you? And here he is upstairs with your wife for two hours and he hasn't even been the whole hog. Well, your wife sounds like a bit of a tease to me, Ted. What do you make of it, Joey? You satisfied? Don't tell me you're satisfied without going the whole hog?

(*Pause.*)

JOEY: I've been the whole hog plenty of times. Sometimes . . . you can be happy . . . and not go the whole hog. Now and  1370 again . . . you can be happy . . . without going any hog.

(LENNY *stares at him.*)
(MAX *and* SAM *come in the front door and into the room.*)

MAX: Where's the whore? Still in bed? She'll make us all animals.
LENNY: The girl's a tease.
MAX: What?
LENNY: She's had Joey on a string.
MAX: What do you mean?
TEDDY: He had her up there for two hours and he didn't go the whole hog.

(*Pause.*)

MAX: My Joey? She did that to my boy?                            1380

*(Pause.)*

To my youngest son? Tch, tch, tch, tch. How you feeling son? Are you all right?

JOEY: Sure I'm all right.

MAX: *(to* TEDDY*)* Does she do that to you, too?

TEDDY: No.

LENNY: He gets the gravy.

MAX: You think so?

JOEY: No he don't.

*(Pause.)*

SAM: He's her lawful husband. She's his lawful wife.

1390 JOEY: No he don't! He don't get no gravy! I'm telling you. I'm telling all of you. I'll kill the next man who says he gets the gravy.

MAX: Joey . . . what are you getting so excited about? *(To* LENNY*)* It's because he's frustrated. You see what happens?

JOEY: Who is?

MAX: Joey. No one's saying you're wrong. In fact everyone's saying you're right.

*(Pause.)*
*(*MAX *turns to the others.)*

You know something? Perhaps it's not a bad idea to have a woman in the house. Perhaps it's a good thing. Who knows?
1400 Maybe we should keep her.

*(Pause.)*

Maybe we'll ask her if she wants to stay.

*(Pause.)*

TEDDY: I'm afraid not, Dad. She's not well, and we've got to get home to the children.

MAX: Not well? I told you, I'm used to looking after people who are not so well. Don't worry about that. Perhaps we'll keep her here.

*(Pause.)*

SAM: Don't be silly.

MAX: What's silly?

SAM: You're talking rubbish.

1410 MAX: Me?

SAM: She's got three children.

MAX: She can have more! If she's so keen.

TEDDY: She doesn't want any more.

MAX: What do you know about what she wants, eh, Ted?

TEDDY: *(smiling)* The best thing for her is to come home with me, Dad. Really. We're married, you know.

*(*MAX *walks about the room, clicks his fingers.)*

MAX: We'd have to pay her, of course. You realize that? We can't leave her walking about without any pocket money. She'll have to have a little allowance.

1420 JOEY: Of course we'll pay her. She's got to have some money in her pocket.

MAX: That's what I'm saying. You can't expect a woman to walk about without a few bob to spend on a pair of stockings.

*(Pause.)*

LENNY: Where's the money going to come from?

MAX: Well, how much is she worth? What we talking about, three figures?

LENNY: I asked you where the money's going to come from. It'll be an extra mouth to feed. It'll be an extra body to clothe. You realize that?

JOEY: I'll buy her clothes.                                                   1430

LENNY: What with?

JOEY: I'll put in a certain amount out of my wages.

MAX: That's it. We'll pass the hat round. We'll make a donation. We're all grown-up people, we've got a sense of responsibility. We'll all put a little in the hat. It's democratic.

LENNY: It'll come to a few quid, Dad.

*(Pause.)*

I mean, she's not a woman who likes walking around in second-hand goods. She's up to the latest fashion. You wouldn't want her walking about in clothes which don't show her off at her best, would you?                                                    1440

MAX: Lenny, do you mind if I make a little comment? It's not meant to be critical. But I think you're concentrating too much on the economic considerations. There are other considerations. There are the human considerations. You understand what I mean? There are the human considerations. Don't forget them.

LENNY: I won't.

MAX: Well don't.

*(Pause.)*

Listen, we're bound to treat her in something approximating, at least, to the manner in which she's accustomed. After  1450 all, she's not someone off the street, she's my daughter-in-law!

JOEY: That's right.

MAX: There you are, you see. Joey'll donate, Sam'll donate. . . .

*(*SAM *looks at him.)*

I'll put in a few bob out of my pension, Lenny'll cough up. We're laughing. What about you, Ted? How much you going to put in the kitty?

TEDDY: I'm not putting anything in the kitty.

MAX: What? You won't even help to support your own wife? I thought he was a son of mine. You lousy stinkpig. Your  1460 mother would drop dead if she heard you take that attitude.

LENNY: Eh, Dad!

*(*LENNY *walks forward.)*

I've got a better idea.

MAX: What?

LENNY: There's no need for us to go to all this expense. I know these women. Once they get started they ruin your budget. I've got a better idea. Why don't I take her up with me to Greek Street?

*(Pause.)*

MAX: You mean put her on the game?

*(Pause.)*

We'll put her on the game. That's a stroke of genius, that's a  1470 marvellous idea. You mean she can earn the money herself—on her back?

LENNY: Yes.

MAX: Wonderful. The only thing is, it'll have to be short hours. We don't want her out of the house all night.

LENNY: I can limit the hours.

MAX: How many?

LENNY: Four hours a night.

MAX: *(dubiously)* Is that enough?

1480 LENNY: She'll bring in a good sum for four hours a night.

MAX: Well, you should know. After all, it's true, the last thing we want to do is wear the girl out. She's going to have her obligations this end as well. Where you going to put her in Greek Street?

LENNY: It doesn't have to be right in Greek Street, Dad. I've got a number of flats all around that area.

MAX: You have? Well, what about me? Why don't you give me one?

LENNY: You're sexless.

1490 JOEY: Eh, wait a minute, what's all this?

MAX: I know what Lenny's saying. Lenny's saying she can pay her own way. What do you think, Teddy? That'll solve all our problems.

JOEY: Eh, wait a minute. I don't want to share her.

MAX: What did you say?

JOEY: I don't want to share her with a lot of yobs!

MAX: Yobs! You arrogant git! What arrogance. *(To* LENNY.) Will you be supplying her with yobs?

LENNY: I've got a very distinguished clientèle, Joey. They're
1500 more distinguished than you'll ever be.

MAX: So you can count yourself lucky we're including you in.

JOEY: I didn't think I was going to have to share her!

MAX: Well, you *are* going to have to share her! Otherwise she goes straight back to America. You understand?

*(Pause.)*

It's tricky enough as it is, without you shoving your oar in. But there's something worrying me. Perhaps she's not so up to the mark. Eh? Teddy, you're the best judge. Do you think she'd be up to the mark?

*(Pause.)*

I mean what about all this teasing? Is she going to make a
1510   habit of it? That'll get us nowhere.

*(Pause.)*

TEDDY: It was just love play . . . I suppose . . . that's all I suppose it was.

MAX: Love play? Two bleeding hours? That's a bloody long time for love play!

LENNY: I don't think we've got anything to worry about on that score, Dad.

MAX: How do you know?

LENNY: I'm giving you a professional opinion.

*(*LENNY *goes to* TEDDY.)

LENNY: Listen, Teddy, you could help us, actually. If I were to
1520   send you some cards, over to America . . . you know, very nice ones, with a name on, and a telephone number, very discreet, well, you could distribute them . . . to various parties, who might be making a trip over here. Of course, you'd

get a little percentage out of it.

MAX: I mean, you needn't tell them she's your wife.

LENNY: No, we'd call her something else. Dolores, or something.

MAX: Or Spanish Jacky.

LENNY: No, you've got to be reserved about it, Dad. We could call her something nice . . . like Cynthia . . . or Gillian.   1530

*(Pause.)*

JOEY: Gillian.

*(Pause.)*

LENNY: No, what I mean, Teddy, you must know lots of professors, heads of departments, men like that. They pop over here for a week at the Savoy, they need somewhere they can go to have a nice quiet poke. And of course you'd be in a position to give them inside information.

MAX: Sure. You can give them proper data. You know, the kind of thing she's willing to do. How far she'd be prepared to go with their little whims and fancies. Eh, Lenny? To what extent she's various. I mean if you don't know who does?   1540

*(Pause.)*

I bet you before two months we'd have a waiting list.

LENNY: You could be our representative in the States.

MAX: Of course. We're talking in international terms! By the time we've finished Pan-American'll give us a discount.

*(Pause.)*

TEDDY: She'd get old . . . very quickly.

MAX: No . . . not in this day and age! With the health service? Old! How could she get old? She'll have the time of her life.

*(*RUTH *comes down the stairs, dressed.)*
*(She comes into the room.)*
*(She smiles at the gathering, and sits.)*
*(Silence.)*

TEDDY: Ruth . . . the family have invited you to stay, for a little while longer. As a . . . as a kind of guest. If you like the idea I don't mind. We can manage very easily at home . . . until   1550 you come back.

RUTH: How very nice of them.

*(Pause.)*

MAX: It's an offer from our heart.

RUTH: It's very sweet of you.

MAX: Listen . . . it would be our pleasure.

*(Pause.)*

RUTH: I think I'd be too much trouble.

MAX: Trouble? What are you talking about? What trouble? Listen, I'll tell you something. Since poor Jessie died, eh, Sam? we haven't had a woman in the house. Not one. Inside this house. And I'll tell you why. Because their mother's image   1560 was so dear any other woman would have . . . tarnished it. But you . . . Ruth . . . you're not only lovely and beautiful, but you're kin. You're kith. You belong here.

*(Pause.)*

RUTH: I'm very touched.

MAX: Of course you're touched. I'm touched.

(*Pause.*)

TEDDY: But Ruth, I should tell you . . . that you'll have to pull your weight a little, if you stay. Financially. My father isn't very well off.

RUTH: (*to* MAX) Oh, I'm sorry.

1570 MAX: No, you'd have to bring in a little, that's all. A few pennies. Nothing much. It's just that we're waiting for Joey to hit the top as a boxer. When Joey hits the top . . . well . . .

(*Pause.*)

TEDDY: Or you can come home with me.

LENNY: We'd get you a flat.

(*Pause.*)

RUTH: A flat?

LENNY: Yes.

RUTH: Where?

LENNY: In town.

(*Pause.*)

But you'd live here, with us.

1580 MAX: Of course you would. This would be your home. In the bosom of the family.

LENNY: You'd just pop up to the flat a couple of hours a night, that's all.

MAX: Just a couple of hours, that's all. That's all.

LENNY: And you make enough money to keep you going here.

(*Pause.*)

RUTH: How many rooms would this flat have?

LENNY: Not many.

RUTH: I would want at least three rooms and a bathroom.

LENNY: You wouldn't need three rooms and a bathroom.

1590 MAX: She'd need a bathroom.

LENNY: But not three rooms.

(*Pause.*)

RUTH: Oh, I would. Really.

LENNY: Two would do.

RUTH: No. Two wouldn't be enough.

(*Pause.*)

I'd want a dressing-room, a rest-room, and a bedroom.

(*Pause.*)

LENNY: All right, we'll get you a flat with three rooms and a bathroom.

RUTH: With what kind of conveniences?

LENNY: All conveniences.

1600 RUTH: A personal maid?

LENNY: Of course.

(*Pause.*)

We'd finance you, to begin with, and then, when you were established, you could pay us back, in instalments.

RUTH: Oh, no, I wouldn't agree to that.

LENNY: Oh, why not?

RUTH: You would have to regard your original outlay simply as a capital investment.

(*Pause.*)

LENNY: I see. All right.

RUTH: You'd supply my wardrobe, of course?

LENNY: We'd supply everything. Everything you need.    1610

RUTH: I'd need an awful lot. Otherwise I wouldn't be content.

LENNY: You'd have everything.

RUTH: I would naturally want to draw up an inventory of everything I would need, which would require your signatures in the presence of witnesses.

LENNY: Naturally.

RUTH: All aspects of the agreement and conditions of employment would have to be clarified to our mutual satisfaction before we finalized the contract.

LENNY: Of course.    1620

(*Pause.*)

RUTH: Well, it might prove a workable arrangement.

LENNY: I think so.

MAX: And you'd have the whole of your daytime free, of course. You could do a bit of cooking here if you wanted to.

LENNY: Make the beds.

MAX: Scrub the place out a bit.

TEDDY: Keep everyone company.

(SAM *comes forward.*)

SAM: (*in one breath*) MacGregor had Jessie in the back of my cab as I drove them along.

(*He croaks and collapses.*)
(*He lies still.*)
(*They look at him.*)

MAX: What's he done? Dropped dead?    1630

LENNY: Yes.

MAX: A corpse? A corpse on my floor? Get him out of here! Clear him out of here!

(JOEY *bends over* SAM.)

JOEY: He's not dead.

LENNY: He probably was dead, for about thirty seconds.

MAX: He's not even dead!

(LENNY *looks down at* SAM.)

LENNY: Yes, there's still some breath there.

MAX: (*pointing at* SAM) You know what that man had?

LENNY: Has.

MAX: Has! A diseased imagination.    1640

(*Pause.*)

RUTH: Yes, it sounds a very attractive idea.

MAX: Do you want to shake on it now, or do you want to leave it till later?

RUTH: Oh, we'll leave it till later.

(TEDDY *stands.*)
(*He looks down at* SAM.)

TEDDY: I was going to ask him to drive me to London Airport.

(*He goes to the cases, picks one up.*)

Well, I'll leave your case, Ruth. I'll just go up the road to the Underground.

MAX: Listen, if you go the other way, first left, first right, you remember, you might find a cab passing there.

1650 TEDDY: Yes, I might do that.

MAX: Or you can take the tube to Piccadilly Circus, won't take you ten minutes, and pick up a cab from there out to the Airport.

TEDDY: Yes, I'll probably do that.

MAX: Mind you, they'll charge you double fare. They'll charge you for the return trip. It's over the six-mile limit.

TEDDY: Yes. Well, bye-bye, Dad. Look after yourself.

*(They shake hands.)*

MAX: Thanks, son. Listen. I want to tell you something. It's been wonderful to see you.

*(Pause.)*

1660 TEDDY: It's been wonderful to see you.

MAX: Do your boys know about me? Eh? Would they like to see a photo, do you think, of their grandfather?

TEDDY: I know they would.

*(MAX brings out his wallet.)*

MAX: I've got one on me. I've got one here. Just a minute. Here you are. Will they like that one?

TEDDY: *(taking it)* They'll be thrilled.

*(He turns to LENNY.)*

Good-bye, Lenny.

*(They shake hands.)*

LENNY: Ta-ta, Ted. Good to see you. Have a good trip.

TEDDY: Bye-bye, Joey.

*(JOEY does not move.)*

1670 JOEY: Ta-ta.

*(TEDDY goes to the front door.)*

RUTH: Eddie.

*(TEDDY turns.)*
*(Pause.)*

Don't become a stranger.

*(TEDDY goes, shuts the front door.)*
*(Silence.)*
*(The three men stand.)*
*(RUTH sits relaxed in her chair.)*
*(SAM lies still.)*
*(JOEY walks slowly across the room.)*
*(He kneels at her chair.)*
*(She touches his head, lightly.)*

*(He puts his head in her lap.)*
*(MAX begins to move above them, backwards and forwards.)*
*(LENNY stands still.)*
*(MAX turns to LENNY.)*

MAX: I'm too old, I suppose. She thinks I'm an old man.

*(Pause.)*

I'm not such an old man.

*(Pause.)*

*(To RUTH.)* You think I'm too old for you?

*(Pause.)*

Listen. You think you're just going to get that big slag all the time? You think you're just going to have him . . . you're going to just have him all the time? You're going to have to work! You'll have to take them on, you understand?

*(Pause.)*

Does she realize that?    1680

*(Pause.)*

Lenny, do you think she understands . . .

*(He begins to stammer.)*

What . . . what . . . what . . . we're getting at? What . . . we've got in mind? Do you think she's got it clear?

*(Pause.)*

I don't think she's got it clear.

*(Pause.)*

You understand what I mean? Listen, I've got a funny idea she'll do the dirty on us, you want to bet? She'll use us, she'll make use of us, I can tell you! I can smell it! You want to bet?

*(Pause.)*

She won't . . . be adaptable!

*(He falls to his knees, whimpers, begins to moan and sob. He stops sobbing, crawls past SAM's body round her chair, to the other side of her.)*

I'm not an old man.

*(He looks up at her.)*

Do you hear me?    1690

*(He raises his face to her.)*

Kiss me.

*(She continues to touch JOEY's head, lightly.)*
*(LENNY stands, watching.)*

**CURTAIN**

## Harold Pinter

"Writing for the Theatre"
(1962)

*A speech made by
Harold Pinter at the
National Student Drama
Festival in Bristol in
1962*

*IN this essay, Harold Pinter touches on many of the distinguishing features of his early career as a playwright: the indirect and sometimes inconsequential nature of his dramatic writing, his vaguely threatening use of language, and his interest in the explanatory power of "the past" in drama.*

I'm not a theorist. I'm not an authoritative or reliable commentator on the dramatic scene, the social scene, any scene. I write plays, when I can manage it, and that's all. That's the sum of it. So I'm speaking with some reluctance, knowing that there are at least twenty-four possible aspects of any single statement, depending on where you're standing at the time or on what the weather's like. A categorical statement, I find, will never stay where it is and be finite. It will immediately be subject to modification by the other twenty-three possibilities of it. No statement I make, therefore, should be interpreted as final and definitive. One or two of them may sound final and definitive, they may even be *almost* final and definitive, but I won't regard them as such tomorrow, and I wouldn't like you to do so today.

I've had two full-length plays produced in London. The first ran a week and the second ran a year. Of course, there are differences between the two plays. In *The Birthday Party* I employed a certain amount of dashes in the text, between phrases. In *The Caretaker* I cut out the dashes and used dots instead. So that instead of, say: "Look, dash, who, dash, I, dash, dash, dash," the text would read: "Look, dot, dot, dot, who, dot, dot, dot, I, dot, dot, dot, dot." So it's possible to deduce from this that dots are more popular than dashes and that's why *The Caretaker* had a longer run than *The Birthday Party*. The fact that in neither case could you hear the dots and dashes in performance is beside the point. You can't fool the critics for long. They can tell a dot from a dash a mile off, even if they can hear neither.

It took me quite a while to grow used to the fact that critical and public response in the theatre follows a very erratic temperature chart. And the danger for a writer is where he becomes easy prey for the old bugs of apprehension and expectation in this connection. But I think Düsseldorf cleared the air for me. In Düsseldorf about two years ago I took, as is the Continental custom, a bow with a German cast of *The Caretaker* at the end of the play on the first night. I was at once booed violently by what must have been the finest collection of booers in the world. I thought they were using megaphones, but it was pure mouth. The case was as dogged as the audience, however, and we took thirty-four curtain calls, all to boos. By the thirty-fourth there were only two people left in the house, still booing. I was strangely warmed by all this, and now, whenever I sense a tremor of the old apprehension or expectation, I remember Düsseldorf, and am cured.

The theatre is a large, energetic, public activity. Writing is, for me, a completely private activity, a poem or a play, no difference. These facts are not easy to reconcile. The professional theatre, whatever the virtues it undoubtedly possesses, is a world of false climaxes, calculated tensions, some hysteria, and a good deal of inefficiency. And the alarms of this world which I suppose I work in become steadily more widespread and intrusive. But basically my position has remained the same. What I write has no obligation to anything other than to itself. My responsibility is not to audiences, critics, producers, directors, actors or to my fellow men in general, but to the play in hand, simply. I warned you about definitive statements but it looks as though I've just made one.

I have usually begun a play in quite a simple manner; found a couple of characters in a particular context, thrown them together and listened to what they said, keeping my nose to the ground. The context has always been, for me, concrete and particular, and the characters concrete also. I've never started a play from any kind of abstract idea or theory and never envisaged my own characters as messengers of death, doom, heaven or the milky way or, in other words, as allegorical representations of any particular force, whatever that may mean. When a character cannot be comfortably defined or understood in terms of the familiar, the tendency is to perch him on a symbolic shelf, out of harm's way. Once there, he can be talked about but need not be lived with. In this way, it is easy to put up a pretty efficient smoke screen, on the part of the critics or the audience, against recognition, against an active and willing participation.

We don't carry labels on our chests, and even though they are continually fixed to us by others, they convince nobody. The desire for verification on the part of all of us, with regard to our own experience and the experience of others, is understandable but cannot always be satisfied. I suggest there can be no hard distinctions between what is real and what is unreal, nor between what is true and what is false. A thing is not necessarily either true or false; it can be both true and false. A character on the stage who can present no convincing argument or information as to his past experience, his present behaviour or his aspirations, nor give a comprehensive analysis of his motives is as legitimate and as worthy of attention as one who, alarmingly, can do all these things. The more acute the experience the less articulate its expression.

Apart from any other consideration, we are faced with the immense difficulty, if not the impossibility, of verifying the past. I don't mean merely years ago, but yesterday, this morning. What took place, what was the nature of what took place, what happened? If one can speak of the difficulty of knowing what in fact took place yesterday, one can I think treat the present in the same way. What's happening now? We won't know until tomorrow or in six months' time, and we won't know then, we'll have forgotten, or our imagination will have attributed quite false characteristics to today. A moment is sucked away and distorted, often even at the time of its birth. We will all interpret a common experience quite differently, though we prefer to subscribe to the view that there's a shared common ground, a known ground. I think there's a shared common ground all right, but that it's more like a quicksand. Because "reality" is quite a strong firm word we tend to think, or to hope, that the state to which it refers is equally firm, settled and unequivocal. It doesn't seem to be, and in my opinion, it's no worse or better for that.

A play is not an essay, nor should a playwright under any exhortation damage the consistency of his characters by injecting a remedy or apology for their actions into the last act, simply because we have been brought up to expect, rain or sunshine, the last act "resolution." To supply an explicit moral tag to an evolving and compulsive dramatic image seems to be facile, impertinent and dishonest. Where this takes place it is not theatre but a crossword puzzle. The audience holds the paper. The play fills in the blanks. Everyone's happy.

There is a considerable body of people just now who are asking for some kind of clear and sensible engagement to be evidently disclosed in contemporary plays. They want the playwright to be a prophet. There is certainly a good deal of prophecy indulged in by playwrights these days, in their plays and out of them. Warnings, sermons, admonitions, ideological exhortations, moral judgements, defined problems with built-in solutions; all can camp under the banner of prophecy. The attitude behind this sort of thing might be summed up in one phrase: *"I'm telling you!"*

It takes all sorts of playwrights to make a world, and as far as I'm concerned "X" can follow any course he chooses without my acting as his censor. To propagate a phoney war between hypothetical schools of playwrights doesn't seem to me a very productive pastime and it certainly isn't my intention. But I can't but feel that we have a marked tendency to stress, so glibly, our empty preferences. The preference for "Life" with a capital L, which is held up to be very different to life with a small l, I mean the life we in fact live. The preference for goodwill, for charity, for benevolence, how facile they've become, these deliverances.

If I were to state any moral precept it might be: Beware of the writer who puts forward his concern for you to embrace, who leaves you in no doubt of his worthiness, his usefulness, his altruism, who declares that his heart is in the right place, and ensures that it can be seen in full view, a pulsating mass where his characters ought to be. What is presented, so much of the time, as a body of active and positive thought is in fact a body lost in a prison of empty definition and cliché.

This kind of writer clearly trusts words absolutely. I have mixed feelings about words myself. Moving among them, sorting them out, watching them appear on the page, from this I derive a considerable pleasure. But at the same time I have another strong feeling about words which amounts to nothing less than nausea. Such a weight of words confronts us day in, day out, words spoken in a context such as this, words written by me and by others, the bulk of it a stale dead terminology; ideas endlessly repeated and permutated become platitudinous, trite, meaningless. Given this nausea, it's very easy to be overcome by it and step back into paralysis. I imagine most writers know something of this kind of paralysis. But if it is possible to confront this nausea, to follow it to its hilt, to move through it and out of it, then it is possible to say that something has occurred, that something has even been achieved.

Language, under these conditions, is a highly ambiguous business. So often, below the word spoken, is the thing known and unspoken. My characters tell me so much and no more, with reference to their experience, their aspirations, their motives, their history. Between my lack of biographical data about them and the ambiguity of what they say lies a territory which is not only worthy of exploration but which it is compulsory to explore. You and I, the characters which grow on a page, most of the time we're inexpressive, giving little away, unreliable, elusive, evasive, obstructive, unwilling. But it's out of these attributes that a language arises. A language, I repeat, where under what is said, another thing is being said.

Given characters who possess a momentum of their own, my job is not to impose upon them, not to subject them to a false articulation, by which I mean forcing a character to speak where he could not speak making him speak in a way he could not speak, or making him speak of what he could never speak. The relationship between author and characters should be a highly respectful one, both ways. And if it's possible to talk of gaining a kind of freedom from writing, it doesn't come by leading one's characters into fixed and calculated postures, but by allowing them to carry their own can, by giving them a legitimate elbowroom. This can be extremely painful. It's much easier, much less pain, not to let them live.

I'd like to make quite clear at the same time that I don't regard my own characters as uncontrolled, or anarchic. They're not. The function of selection and arrangement is mine. I do all the donkeywork, in fact, and I think I can say I pay meticulous attention to the shape of things, from the shape of a sentence to the overall structure of the play. This shaping, to put it mildly, is of the first importance. But I think a double thing happens. You arrange *and* you listen, following the clues you leave for yourself, through the characters. And sometimes a balance is found, where image can freely engender image and where at the same time you are able to keep your sights on the place where the characters are silent and in hiding. It is in the silence that they are most evident to me.

There are two silences. One when no word is spoken. The other when perhaps a torrent of language is being employed. This speech is speaking of a language locked beneath it. That is its continual reference. The speech we hear is an indication of that which we don't hear. It is a necessary avoidance, a violent, sly, anguished or mocking smoke screen which keeps the other in its place. When true silence falls we are still left with echo but are nearer nakedness. One way of looking at speech is to say that it is a constant strategem to cover nakedness.

We have heard many times that tired, grimy phrase: "Failure of communication" . . . and this phrase has been fixed to my work quite consistently. I believe the contrary. I think that we communicate only too well, in our silence, in what is unsaid, and that what takes place is a continual evasion, desperate rear-guard attempts to keep ourselves to ourselves. Communication is too alarming. To enter into someone else's life is too frightening. To disclose to others the poverty within us is too fearsome a possibility.

I am not suggesting that no character in a play can ever say what he in fact means. Not at all. I have found that there invariably does come a moment when this happens, when he says something, perhaps, which he has never said before. And where this happens, what he says is irrevocable, and can never be taken back.

A blank page is both an exciting and a frightening thing. It's what you start from. There follow two further periods in the progress of a play. The rehearsal period and the performance. A dramatist will absorb a great many things of value from an active and intense experience in the theatre, throughout these two periods. But finally he is again left looking at the blank page. In that page is something or nothing. You don't know until you've covered it. And there's no guarantee that you will know then. But it always remains a chance worth taking.

I've written nine plays, for various mediums, and at the moment I haven't the slightest idea how I've managed to do it. Each play was, for me, "a different kind of failure." And that fact, I suppose, sent me on to write the next one.

And if I find writing plays an extremely difficult task, while still understanding it as a kind of celebration, how much more difficult it is to attempt to rationalise the process, and how much more abortive, as I think I've clearly demonstrated to you this morning.

Samuel Beckett says, at the beginning of his novel *The Unnamable,* "The fact would seem to be, if in my situation one may speak of facts, not only that I shall have to speak of things of which I cannot speak, but also, which is even more interesting, but also that I, which is if possible even more interesting, that I shall have to, I forget, no matter."

# Luis Valdez

Luis Valdez (b. 1940) was born and raised the son of farmworkers in Delano, California. He majored in drama at San Diego State University, taking his B. A. in 1964, and then joined the San Francisco Mime Troupe, an important experimental theater company. In 1965, when farm workers at the Delano grape plantations went on strike, Valdez formed El Teatro Campesino ("The Farmworkers' Theater"). Valdez and Teatro Campesino devised two dramatic forms: **ACTOS,** short, satirical plays dramatizing the oppression of the fieldworkers, and **MITOS,** poetic, lyrical plays on Chicano life. Teatro Campesino became one of several important Chicano theater companies that performed throughout the Southwest and in urban areas of the Midwest and Northeast, drawing on both American and European dramatic traditions, as well as traditions of Mexican and Spanish-language theater in the United States that date to the seventeenth century. In the late 1960s and 1970s, Teatro Campesino toured the United States and Europe and gained an international reputation. Valdez's other *actos* with Teatro Campesino include *Las Dos Caras del Patroncito* (1965), *No Saco Nada de la Escuela* (1969), and *Vietnam Campesino* (1970). Valdez produced the stage play *Zoot Suit* in 1978, which was released as a film in 1981; he wrote and directed the film *La Bamba* in 1987. In 1986 he returned to Teatro Campesino to write *I Don't Have to Show You No Stinking Badges.* Valdez has also held academic appointments at the University of California, Berkeley, and at the University of California, Santa Cruz. El Teatro Campesino is currently based in San Juan Bautista, California.

## Los Vendidos (1965)

One of Teatro Campesino's best and most popular *actos, Los Vendidos*—"The Sellouts"—is reminiscent both of Brechtian political theater and more generally of popular satire. In its brief sketch of Honest Sancho's Used Mexican Lot, the play dramatizes a range of stereotypes applied by Anglo culture (represented by the Anglicized Mexican-American, Miss JIM-enez) to Chicano experience: farmworkers, Johnny Pachuco, the *revolucionario,* and the "new 1970 Mexican-American" yuppie. In the play's surprising finale, though, the yuppie turns on Miss JIM-enez, and the "used Mexicans" turn out to run the shop—Honest Sancho is *their* front.

The play clearly engages conflicting attitudes toward social experience, as emblematized by its title. For the title can mean both "those who are sold"—like the "used Mexicans" on Sancho's lot—and "the sellouts," presumably Honest Sancho and Miss JIM-enez. This duplicity is also inflected by the play's language, its mixture of Spanish and English, the two languages Chicano culture uses to define itself and to engage the Anglo world. The play works at the border between two cultures, where language is part of the complex social and political negotiation that characterizes Mexican-American life today.

# —Los Vendidos—
## Luis Valdez

## —CHARACTERS—

HONEST SANCHO
SECRETARY
FARM WORKER
JOHNNY
REVOLUCIONARIO
MEXICAN-AMERICAN

SCENE: HONEST SANCHO's *Used Mexican Lot and Mexican Curio Shop. Three models are on display in* HONEST SANCHO's *shop: to the right, there is a* REVOLUCIONARIO, *complete with sombrero, carrilleras,° and carabina 30-30. At center, on the floor, there is the* FARM WORKER, *under a broad straw sombrero. At stage left is the* PACHUCO,° *filero° in hand.*

(HONEST SANCHO *is moving among his models, dusting them off and preparing for another day of business.*)

SANCHO: Bueno, bueno, mis monos, vamos a ver a quien vendemos ahora, ¿no? (*To audience.*) ¡Quihubo!° I'm Honest Sancho and this is my shop. Antes fui contratista pero ahora logré tener mi negocito.° All I need now is a customer. (*A bell rings offstage.*) Ay, a customer!

SECRETARY: (*Entering*) Good morning, I'm Miss Jiménez from—

SANCHO: ¡Ah, una chicana! Welcome, welcome Señorita Jiménez.

10 SECRETARY: (*Anglo pronunciation*) JIM-enez.

SANCHO: ¿Qué?

SECRETARY: My name is Miss JIM-enez. Don't you speak English? What's wrong with you?

SANCHO: Oh, nothing, Señorita JIM-enez. I'm here to help you.

SECRETARY: That's better. As I was starting to say, I'm a secretary from Governor Reagan's office, and we're looking for a Mexican type for the administration.

SANCHO: Well, you come to the right place, lady. This is Hon-
20 est Sancho's Used Mexican lot, and we got all types here. Any particular type you want?

SECRETARY: Yes, we were looking for somebody suave—

SANCHO: Suave.

SECRETARY: Debonair.

SANCHO: De buen aire.

SECRETARY: Dark.

SANCHO: Prieto.

SECRETARY: But of course not too dark.

SANCHO: No muy prieto.

SECRETARY: Perhaps, beige.    30

SANCHO: Beige, just the tone. Así como cafecito con leche,° ¿no?

SECRETARY: One more thing. He must be hard-working.

SANCHO: That could only be one model. Step right over here to the center of the shop, lady. (*They cross to the* FARM WORKER.) This is our standard farm worker model. As you can see, in the words of our beloved Senator George Murphy, he is "built close to the ground." Also take special notice of his four-ply Goodyear huaraches, made from the rain tire. This wide-brimmed sombrero is an extra added fea-   40 ture—keeps off the sun, rain, and dust.

SECRETARY: Yes, it does look durable.

SANCHO: And our farm worker model is friendly. Muy amable.° Watch. (*Snaps his fingers.*)

FARM WORKER: (*Lifts up head*) Buenos días, señorita. (*His head drops.*)

SECRETARY: My, he's friendly.

SANCHO: Didn't I tell you? Loves his patrones! But his most attractive feature is that he's hard-working. Let me show you. (*Snaps fingers.* FARM WORKER *stands.*)    50

FARM WORKER: ¡El jale!° (*He begins to work.*)

SANCHO: As you can see, he is cutting grapes.

SECRETARY: Oh, I wouldn't know.

SANCHO: He also picks cotton. (*Snap.* FARM WORKER *begins to pick cotton.*)

SECRETARY: Versatile isn't he?

SANCHO: He also picks melons. (*Snap.* FARM WORKER *picks melons.*) That's his slow speed for late in the season. Here's his fast speed. (*Snap.* FARM WORKER *picks faster.*)

SECRETARY: ¡Chihuahua! . . . I mean, goodness, he sure is a   60 hard worker.

SANCHO: (*Pulls the* FARM WORKER *to his feet*) And that isn't the half of it. Do you see these little holes on his arms that appear to be pores? During those hot sluggish days in the field, when the vines or the branches get so entangled, it's almost impossible to move; these holes emit a certain grease that allow our model to slip and slide right through the crop with no trouble at all.

SECRETARY: Wonderful. But is he economical?

SANCHO: Economical? Señorita, you are looking at the Volks-   70 wagen of Mexicans. Pennies a day is all it takes. One plate of beans and tortillas will keep him going all day. That, and chile. Plenty of chile. Chile jalapenos, chile verde, chile

---

Scene **carrilleras** literally chin straps, but may refer to cartridge belts
Scene **Pachuco** Chicano slang for 1940s zoot suiter   *filero* blade
1–2 **Bueno, bueno, . . . Quihubo** "Good, good, my cute ones, let's see who we can sell now, O.K.?"   3–4 **Antes fui . . . negocito** "I used

to be a contractor, but now I've succeeded in having my little business."
31 **Así como . . . leche** like coffee with milk.   43 **Muy amable** very friendly   51 **El jale** the job

colorado. But, of course, if you do give him chile (*Snap.* FARM WORKER *turns left face. Snap.* FARM WORKER *bends over.*) then you have to change his oil filter once a week.

SECRETARY: What about storage?

SANCHO: No problem. You know these new farm labor camps our Honorable Governor Reagan has built out by Parlier or Raisin City? They were designed with our model in mind. Five, six, seven, even ten in one of those shacks will give you no trouble at all. You can also put him in old barns, old cars, river banks. You can even leave him out in the field overnight with no worry!

SECRETARY: Remarkable.

SANCHO: And here's an added feature: Every year at the end of the season, this model goes back to Mexico and doesn't return, automatically, until next Spring.

SECRETARY: How about that. But tell me: does he speak English?

SANCHO: Another outstanding feature is that last year this model was programmed to go out on STRIKE! (*Snap.*)

FARM WORKER: ¡HUELGA! ¡HUELGA! Hermanos, sálganse de esos files.° (*Snap. He stops.*)

SECRETARY: No! Oh no, we can't strike in the State Capitol.

SANCHO: Well, he also scabs. (*Snap.*)

FARM WORKER: Me vendo barato, ¿y qué?° (*Snap.*)

SECRETARY: That's much better, but you didn't answer my question. Does he speak English?

SANCHO: Bueno . . . no pero° he has other—

SECRETARY: No.

SANCHO: Other features.

SECRETARY: NO! He just won't do!

SANCHO: Okay, okay pues. We have other models.

SECRETARY: I hope so. What we need is something a little more sophisticated.

SANCHO: Sophisti—¿qué?

SECRETARY: An urban model.

SANCHO: Ah, from the city! Step right back. Over here in this corner of the shop is exactly what you're looking for. Introducing our new 1969 JOHNNY PACHUCO model! This is our fast-back model. Streamlined. Built for speed, low-riding, city life. Take a look at some of these features. Mag shoes, dual exhausts, green chartreuse paint-job, dark-tint windshield, a little poof on top. Let me just turn him on. (*Snap.* JOHNNY *walks to stage center with a pachuco bounce.*)

SECRETARY: What was that?

SANCHO: That, señorita, was the Chicano shuffle.

SECRETARY: Okay, what does he do?

SANCHO: Anything and everything necessary for city life. For instance, survival: He knife fights. (*Snap.* JOHNNY *pulls out switch blade and swings at* SECRETARY.)

(SECRETARY *screams.*)

SANCHO: He dances. (*Snap.*)

JOHNNY: (*Singing*) "Angel Baby, my Angel Baby . . ." (*Snap.*)

SANCHO: And here's a feature no city model can be without. He gets arrested, but not without resisting, of course. (*Snap.*)

JOHNNY: ¡En la madre, la placa!° I didn't do it! I didn't do it! (JOHNNY *turns and stands up against an imaginary wall, legs spread out, arms behind his back.*)

SECRETARY: Oh no, we can't have arrests! We must maintain law and order.

SANCHO: But he's bilingual!

SECRETARY: Bilingual?

SANCHO: Simón que yes.° He speaks English! Johnny, give us some English. (*Snap.*)

JOHNNY: (*Comes downstage.*) Fuck-you!

SECRETARY: (*Gasps*) Oh! I've never been so insulted in my whole life!

SANCHO: Well, he learned it in your school.

SECRETARY: I don't care where he learned it.

SANCHO: But he's economical!

SECRETARY: Economical?

SANCHO: Nickels and dimes. You can keep Johnny running on hamburgers, Taco Bell tacos, Lucky Lager beer, Thunderbird wine, yesca—

SECRETARY: Yesca?

SANCHO: Mota.

SECRETARY: Mota?

SANCHO: Leños . . .° Marijuana. (*Snap;* JOHNNY *inhales on an imaginary joint.*)

SECRETARY: That's against the law!

JOHNNY: (*Big smile, holding his breath*) Yeah.

SANCHO: He also sniffs glue. (*Snap.* JOHNNY *inhales glue, big smile.*)

JOHNNY: Tha's too much man, ése.

SECRETARY: No, Mr. Sancho, I don't think this—

SANCHO: Wait a minute, he has other qualities I know you'll love. For example, an inferiority complex. (*Snap.*)

JOHNNY: (*To* SANCHO) You think you're better than me, huh ése? (*Swings switch blade.*)

SANCHO: He can also be beaten and he bruises, cut him and he bleeds; kick him and he—(*He beats, bruises and kicks* PACHUCO.) would you like to try it?

SECRETARY: Oh, I couldn't.

SANCHO: Be my guest. He's a great scapegoat.

SECRETARY: No, really.

SANCHO: Please.

SECRETARY: Well, all right. Just once. (*She kicks* PACHUCO.) Oh, he's so soft.

SANCHO: Wasn't that good? Try again.

SECRETARY: (*Kicks* PACHUCO) Oh, he's so wonderful! (*She kicks him again.*)

SANCHO: Okay, that's enough, lady. You ruin the merchandise. Yes, our Johnny Pachuco model can give you many hours of pleasure. Why, the L.A.P.D. just bought twenty of these to train their rookie cops on. And talk about maintenance. Señorita, you are looking at an entirely self-supporting machine. You're never going to find our Johnny Pachuco model

93–94 **¡HUELGA! ¡HUELGA! . . . esos files** "Strike! Strike! Brothers, leave those rows."   97 **Me vendo . . . qué** "I come cheap, so what?"   100 **Bueno . . . no pero** "Well, no, but . . ."   128 **En la . . .**
**placa** "Wow, the police!"   135 **Simón . . . yes** yeah, sure.   150 **Leños** "joints" of marijuana

180  on the relief rolls. No, sir, this model knows how to liberate.

SECRETARY: Liberate?

SANCHO: He steals. (*Snap.* JOHNNY *rushes the* SECRETARY *and steals her purse.*)

JOHNNY: ¡Dame esa bolsa, vieja!° (*He grabs the purse and runs. Snap by* SANCHO. *He stops.*)

(SECRETARY *runs after* JOHNNY *and grabs purse away from him, kicking him as she goes.*)

SECRETARY: No, no, no! We can't have any *more* thieves in the State Administration. Put him back.

SANCHO: Okay, we still got other models. Come on, Johnny, we'll sell you to some old lady. (SANCHO *takes* JOHNNY *back*
190  *to his place.*)

SECRETARY: Mr. Sancho, I don't think you quite understand what we need. What we need is something that will attract the women voters. Something more traditional, more romantic.

SANCHO: Ah, a lover. (*He smiles meaningfully.*) Step right over here, señorita. Introducing our standard Revolucionario and/or Early California Bandit type. As you can see he is well-built, sturdy, durable. This is the International Harvester of Mexicans.

200  SECRETARY: What does he do?

SANCHO: You name it, he does it. He rides horses, stays in the mountains, crosses deserts, plains, rivers, leads revolutions, follows revolutions, kills, can be killed, serves as a martyr, hero, movie star—did I say movie star? Did you ever see *Viva Zapata? Viva Villa? Villa Rides? Pancho Villa Returns? Pancho Villa Goes Back? Pancho Villa Meets Abbot and Costello*—

SECRETARY: I've never seen any of them.

SANCHO: Well, he was in all of them. Listen to this. (*Snap.*)

210  REVOLUCIONARIO: (*Scream*) ¡VIVA VILLAAAAA!

SECRETARY: That's awfully loud.

SANCHO: He has a volume control. (*He adjusts volume. Snap.*)

REVOLUCIONARIO: (*Mousey voice*) ¡Viva Villa!

SECRETARY: That's better.

SANCHO: And even if you didn't see him in the movies, perhaps you saw him on TV. He makes commercials. (*Snap.*)

REVOLUCIONARIO: Is there a Frito Bandito in your house?

SECRETARY: Oh yes, I've seen that one!

SANCHO: Another feature about this one is that he is economi-
220  cal. He runs on raw horsemeat and tequila!

SECRETARY: Isn't that rather savage?

SANCHO: Al contrario,° it makes him a lover. (*Snap.*)

REVOLUCIONARIO: (*To* SECRETARY) ¡Ay, mamasota, cochota, ven pa'ca! (*He grabs* SECRETARY *and folds her back—Latin-lover style.*)

SANCHO: (*Snap.* REVOLUCIONARIO *goes back upright.*) Now wasn't that nice?

SECRETARY: Well, it was rather nice.

SANCHO: And finally, there is one outstanding feature about
230  this model I KNOW the ladies are going to love: He's a GENUINE antique! He was made in Mexico in 1910!

SECRETARY: Made in Mexico?

SANCHO: That's right. Once in Tijuana, twice in Guadalajara, three times in Cuernavaca.

SECRETARY: Mr. Sancho, I thought he was an American product.

SANCHO: No, but—

SECRETARY: No, I'm sorry. We can't buy anything but American-made products. He just won't do.

SANCHO: But he's an antique!                                              240

SECRETARY: I don't care. You still don't understand what we need. It's true we need Mexican models such as these, but it's more important that he be *American.*

SANCHO: American?

SECRETARY: That's right, and judging from what you've shown me, I don't think you have what we want. Well, my lunch hour's almost over; I better—

SANCHO: Wait a minute! Mexican but American?

SECRETARY: That's correct.

SANCHO: Mexican but . . . (*A sudden flash.*) AMERICAN! 250
Yeah, I think we've got exactly what you want. He just came in today! Give me a minute. (*He exits. Talks from backstage.*) Here he is in the shop. Let me just get some papers off. There. Introducing our new 1970 Mexican-American! Ta-ra-ra-ra-ra-ra-RA-RAAA!

(SANCHO *brings out the* MEXICAN-AMERICAN *model, a clean-shaven middle-class type in business suit, with glasses.*)

SECRETARY: (*Impressed*) Where have you been hiding this one?

SANCHO: He just came in this morning. Ain't he a beauty? Feast your eyes on him! Sturdy US STEEL frame, streamlined, modern. As a matter of fact, he is built exactly like our 260 Anglo models except that he comes in a variety of darker shades: naugahyde, leather, or leatherette.

SECRETARY: Naugahyde.

SANCHO: Well, we'll just write that down. Yes, señorita, this model represents the apex of American engineering! He is bilingual, college educated, ambitious! Say the word "acculturate" and he accelerates. He is intelligent, well-mannered, clean—did I say clean? (*Snap.* MEXICAN-AMERICAN *raises his arm.*) Smell.

SECRETARY: (*Smells*) Old Sobaco, my favorite.                          270

SANCHO: (*Snap.* MEXICAN-AMERICAN *turns toward* SANCHO.) Eric! (*To* SECRETARY.) We call him Eric Garcia. (*To* ERIC.) I want you to meet Miss JIM-enez, Eric.

MEXICAN-AMERICAN: Miss JIM-enez, I am delighted to make your acquaintance. (*He kisses her hand.*)

SECRETARY: Oh, my, how charming!

SANCHO: Did you feel the suction? He has seven especially engineered suction cups right behind his lips. He's a charmer all right!

SECRETARY: How about boards? Does he function on boards?       280

SANCHO: You name them, he is on them. Parole boards, draft boards, school boards, taco quality control boards, surf boards, two-by-fours.

---

184 **Dame esa. . . . vieja** "Gimme that bag, old lady!"   222 **Al contrario** on the contrary

SECRETARY: Does he function in politics?

SANCHO: Señorita, you are looking at a political MACHINE. Have you ever heard of the OEO, EOC, COD, WAR ON POVERTY? That's our model! Not only that, he makes political speeches.

SECRETARY: May I hear one?

290 SANCHO: With pleasure. (Snap.) Eric, give us a speech.

MEXICAN-AMERICAN: Mr. Congressman, Mr. Chairman, members of the board, honored guests, ladies and gentlemen. (SANCHO and SECRETARY applaud.) Please, please, I come before you as a Mexican-American to tell you about the problems of the Mexican. The problems of the Mexican stem from one thing and one thing alone: He's stupid. He's uneducated. He needs to stay in school. He needs to be ambitious, forward-looking, harder-working. He needs to think American, American, American, AMERICAN, AMERI-
300 CAN, AMERICAN, GOD BLESS AMERICA! GOD BLESS AMERICA!! (He goes out of control.)

(SANCHO snaps frantically and the MEXICAN-AMERICAN finally slumps forward, bending at the waist.)

SECRETARY: Oh my, he's patriotic too!

SANCHO: Sí, señorita, he loves his country. Let me just make a little adjustment here. (Stands MEXICAN-AMERICAN up.)

SECRETARY: What about upkeep? Is he economical?

SANCHO: Well, no, I won't lie to you. The Mexican-American costs a little bit more, but you get what you pay for. He's worth every extra cent. You can keep him running on dry martinis, Langendorf bread.

310 SECRETARY: Apple pie?

SANCHO: Only Mom's. Of course, he's also programmed to eat Mexican food on ceremonial functions, but I must warn you: an overdose of beans will plug up his exhaust.

SECRETARY: Fine! There's just one more question: HOW MUCH DO YOU WANT FOR HIM?

SANCHO: Well, I tell you what I'm gonna do. Today and today only, because you've been so sweet, I'm gonna let you steal this model from me! I'm gonna let you drive him off the lot for the simple price of—let's see taxes and license in-
320 cluded—$15,000.

SECRETARY: Fifteen thousand DOLLARS? For a MEXICAN!

SANCHO: Mexican? What are you talking, lady? This is a Mexican-AMERICAN! We had to melt down two pachucos, a farm worker and three gabachos to make this model! You want quality, but you gotta pay for it! This is no cheap runabout. He's got class!

SECRETARY: Okay, I'll take him.

SANCHO: You will?

SECRETARY: Here's your money.

330 SANCHO: You mind if I count it?

SECRETARY: Go right ahead.

SANCHO: Well, you'll get your pink slip in the mail. Oh, do you want me to wrap him up for you? We have a box in the back.

SECRETARY: No, thank you. The Governor is having a luncheon this afternoon, and we need a brown face in the crowd. How do I drive him?

SANCHO: Just snap your fingers. He'll do anything you want.

(SECRETARY snaps. MEXICAN-AMERICAN steps forward.)

MEXICAN-AMERICAN: RAZA QUERIDA, ¡VAMOS LEVANTANDO ARMAS PARA LIBERARNOS DE ESTOS DESGRACIADOS GABACHOS QUE NOS EXPLOTAN! 340 VAMOS.°

SECRETARY: What did he say?

SANCHO: Something about lifting arms, killing white people, etc.

SECRETARY: But he's not supposed to say that!

SANCHO: Look, lady, don't blame me for bugs from the factory. He's your Mexican-American: you bought him, now drive him off the lot!

SECRETARY: But he's broken!

SANCHO: Try snapping another finger.                                    350

(SECRETARY snaps. MEXICAN-AMERICAN comes to life again.)

MEXICAN-AMERICAN: ¡ESTA GRAN HUMANIDAD HA DICHO BASTA! Y SE HA PUESTO EN MARCHA! ¡BASTA! ¡BASTA! ¡VIVA LA RAZA! ¡VIVA LA CAUSA! ¡VIVA LA HUELGA! ¡VIVAN LOS BROWN BERETS! ¡VIVAN LOS ESTUDIANTES! ¡CHICANO POWER!°

(The MEXICAN-AMERICAN turns toward the SECRETARY, who gasps and backs up. He keeps turning toward the PACHUCO, FARM WORKER, and REVOLUCIONARIO, snapping his fingers and turning each of them on, one by one.)

PACHUCO: (Snap. To SECRETARY) I'm going to get you, baby! ¡Viva La Raza!

FARM WORKER: (Snap. To SECRETARY) ¡Viva la huelga! ¡Viva la Huelga! ¡VIVA LA HUELGA!

REVOLUCIONARIO: (Snap. To SECRETARY) ¡Viva la revolución! 360 ¡VIVA LA REVOLUCIÓN!

REVOLUCIONARIO: (Snap. To SECRETARY) ¡Viva la revolución! ¡VIVA LA REVOLUCIÓN!

(The three models join together and advance toward the SECRETARY who backs up and runs out of the shop screaming. SANCHO is at the other end of the shop holding his money in his hand. All freeze. After a few seconds of silence, the PACHUCO moves and stretches, shaking his arms and loosening up. The FARM WORKER and REVOLUCIONARIO do the same. SANCHO stays where he is, frozen to his spot.)

JOHNNY: Man, that was a long one, ése. (Others agree with him.)

FARM WORKER: How did we do?

JOHNNY: Perty good, look all that lana, man! (He goes over to SANCHO and removes the money from his hand. SANCHO stays where he is.)

370 REVOLUCIONARIO: En la madre, look at all the money.

JOHNNY: We keep this up, we're going to be rich.

FARM WORKER: They think we're machines.

REVOLUCIONARIO: Burros.

JOHNNY: Puppets.

MEXICAN-AMERICAN: The only thing I don't like is—how come I always got to play the goddamn Mexican-American?

JOHNNY: That's what you get for finishing high school.

FARM WORKER: How about our wages, ése?

380 JOHNNY: Here it comes right now. $3,000 for you, $3,000 for you, $3,000 for you, and $3,000 for me. The rest we put back into the business.

MEXICAN-AMERICAN: Too much, man. Heh, where you vatos going tonight?

FARM WORKER: I'm going over to Concha's. There's a party.

JOHNNY: Wait a minute, vatos. What about our salesman? I think he needs an oil job.

REVOLUCIONARIO: Leave him to me.

(*The* PACHUCO, FARM WORKER, *and* MEXICAN-AMERICAN *exit, talking loudly about their plans for the night. The* REVOLUCIONARIO *goes over to* SANCHO, *removes his derby hat and cigar, lifts him up and throws him over his shoulder.* SANCHO *hangs loose, lifeless.*)

REVOLUCIONARIO: (*To audience*) He's the best model we got! ¡Ajua! (*Exit.*)

---

*THIS selection is taken from an interview with Valdez conducted by David Savran.*

## Luis Valdez

Interview
(1987)

### How did you get interested in theatre?

There's a story that's almost apocryphal, I've repeated it so many times now. It's nevertheless true. I got hooked on the theatre when I was six. I was born into a family of migrant farm workers and shortly after World War II we were in a cotton camp in the San Joaquin valley. The season was over, it was starting to rain, but we were still there because my dad's little Ford pickup truck had broken down and was up on blocks and there was no way for us to get out. Life was pretty meager then and we survived by fishing in a river and sharing staples like beans, rice and flour. And the bus from the local school used to come in from a place called Stratford—irony of ironies, except it was on the San Joaquin River [laughs].

I took my lunch to school in a little brown paper bag—which was a valuable commodity because there were still paper shortages in 1946. One day as school let out and the kids were rushing toward the bus, I found my bag missing and went around in a panic looking for it. The teacher saw me and said, "Are you looking for your bag?" and I said, "Yes." She said, "Come here," and she took me in the little back room and there, on a table, were some things laid out that completely changed my perception of the universe. She'd torn the bag up and placed it in water. I was horrified. But then she showed me the next bowl. It was a paste. She was making papier-mâché. A little farther down the line, she'd taken the paper and put it on a clay mold of a face of a monkey, and finally there was a finished product, unpainted but nevertheless definitely a monkey. And she said, "I'm making masks."

I was amazed, shocked in an exhilarating way, that she could do this with paper and paste. As it turned out, she was making masks for the school play. I didn't know what a play was, but she explained and said, "We're having tryouts." I came back the next week all enthused and auditioned for a part and got a leading role as a monkey. The play was about Christmas in the jungle. I was measured for a costume that was better than the clothes I was wearing at the time, certainly more colorful. The next few weeks were some of the most exciting in my short life. After seeing the stage transformed into a jungle and after all the excitement of the preparations—I doubt that it was as elaborate as my mind remembers it now—my dad got the truck fixed and a week before the show was to go on, we moved away. So I never got to be in the Christmas play.

That left an unfillable gap, a vacuum that I've been pouring myself into for the last forty-one years. From then on, it was just a question of evolution. Later I got into puppets. I was a ventriloquist, believe it or not. In 1956 when I was in high school, I became a regular on a local television program. I was still living in a *barrio* with my family, a place in San Jose called Sal Si Puedes—Get Out if You Can. It was one of those places with dirt streets and chuckholes, a terrible place. But I was on television, right? [laughs], and I wrote my own stuff and it established me in high school.

By the time I graduated, I had pretty well decided that writing was my consuming passion. Coming from my background, I didn't feel right about going to my parents and saying, "I want to be a playwright." So I started college majoring in math and physics. Then one day late in my freshman year I walked to the drama department and decided, "The hell with it, I'm going to go with this." I changed majors to English, with an emphasis on playwriting, and that's what I did for the rest of my college days.

In 1964 I wrote and directed by first full-length play, *The Shrunken Head of Pancho Villa*. People saw it and gave me a lot of encouragement. I joined the San Francisco Mime Troupe the following year, and then in '65 joined the Farm Workers Union and essentially started El Teatro Campesino. The evolution has been continuous since then, both of the company and of my styles of playwriting.

*During that period, what was your most important theatre training—college, the Mime Troupe?*

It's all important. It's a question of layering. I love to layer things, I think they achieve a certain richness—I'm speaking now about "the work." But life essentially evolves that way, too. Those years of studying theatre history were extremely important. I connected with a number of ancient playwrights in a very direct way. Plautus was a revelation, he spoke directly to me. I took four years of Latin so I was able to read him in Latin. There are clever turns of phrases that I grew to appreciate and, in my own way, was able almost to reproduce in Spanish. The central figure of the wily servant in classical Roman drama—Greek also—became a standard feature of my work with El Teatro Campesino. The striker was basically a wily servant. I'd also been exposed to *commedia dell'arte* through the San Francisco Mime Troupe, with its stock characters, the Brighellas, Arlecchinos and Pantalones. I saw a direct link between these *commedia* types and the types I had to work with in order to put together a Farm Workers' theatre. I chose to do an outdoor, robust theatre of types. I figured it hit the reality.

My second phase was the raw, elemental education I got, performing under the most primitive conditions in the farm labor camps and on flatbed trucks. In doing so, I dealt with the basic elements of drama: structure, language, music, movement. The first education was literary, the second practical. We used to put on stuff every week, under all kinds of circumstances: outdoors, indoors, under the threat of violence. There was a period during the grape strike in '67 when we had become an effective weapon within the Farm Workers and were considered enough of a threat that a rumor flashed across the strike camp that somebody was after me with a high-powered rifle. We went out to the labor camp anyway, but I was really sweating it. I don't think I've sweated any performance since then. It changed my perspective on what I was doing. Was this really worth it? Was it a life-and-death issue? Of course it was for me at the time, and still is. But I learned that in a very direct and practical way. I was beaten and kicked and jailed, also in the sixties, essentially for doing theatre. I knew the kind of theatre we were doing was a political act, it was art and politics. At least I hope I wasn't being kicked for the art [laughs].

*What other playwrights had a major impact on you in those days?*

Brecht looms huge in my orientation. I discovered Brecht in college, from an intellectual perspective. That was really the only way—no one was doing Brecht back in 1961. When Esslin's book *Brecht: The Man and His Work,* came out in 1960, I was working in the library, so I had first dibs on all the new books. Brecht to me had been only a name. But this book opened up Brecht and I started reading all his plays and his theories, which I subscribed to immediately. I continue to use his alienation effect to this day. I don't think audiences like it too much, but I like it because it seems to me an essential feature of the experience of theatre.

Theatre should reflect an audience back on itself. You should think as well as feel. Still, there's no underestimating the power of emotional impact—I understand better now how ideas are conveyed and exchanged on a beam of emotion. I think Brecht began to discover that in his later works and integrated it. I've integrated a lot of feeling into my works, but I still love ideas. I still love communicating a concept, an abstraction. That's the mathematician in me.

*How has your way of writing changed over the years?*

What has changed over the years is an approach and a technique. The first few years with the Teatro Campesino were largely improvisational. I wrote outlines. I sketched out a dramatic structure, sometimes on a single page, and used that as my guide to direct the actors. Later on, I began to write very simple scripts that were sometimes born out of improvisations. During the first ten years, from '65 to '75, the collective process became more complicated and more sophisticated within the company—we were creating longer pieces, full-length pieces, but they'd take forever to complete using the collective process.

By 1975, I'd taken the collective process as far as I could. I enjoyed working with people. I didn't have to deal with the loneliness of writing. My problem was that I was so much part of the collective that I couldn't leave for even a month without the group having serious problems. By 1975 we were stable enough as a company for me to begin to take a month, two months, six months, eventually a year. I turned a corner and was ready to start writing plays again.

In 1975 I took a month off and wrote a play. We did a piece called *El Fin del Mundo (The End of the World)* from 1974 through 1980, a different version every year. The '75 version was a play I sat down and wrote. I started with a lot of abstract notions—the mathematician sometimes gets in the way—but eventually I plugged into characters born of my experience. Those characters are still alive for me. Someday I'll finish all of that as a play or else it will be poured into a screenplay for a "major motion picture" [laughs].

Shortly after that, in 1977, I was invited by the Mark Taper Forum to write a play for their New Theatre for Now series. We agreed on the Zoot Suit Riots as a subject. *Zoot Suit* firmly reestablished my self-identity as a playwright. Essentially I've been writing nonstop since '75. That's not to say I didn't write anything between '65 and '75. *Soldado Razo*, which is probably my most performed play around the world, was written in 1970, as was *Bernabe. The Dark Root of a Screen* was written in 1967. These are all one-acts. I used to work on them with a sense of longing, wanting more time to be able to sit down and write.

Now I'm firmly back in touch with myself as a playwright. When I begin, I allow myself at least a month of free association with notes. I can start anywhere. I can start with an abstract notion, a character . . . it's rarely dialogue or anything specific like that. More often than not, it's just an amorphous bunch of ideas, impressions and feelings. I allow myself to tumble in this ball of thoughts and impressions, knowing that I'm heading toward a play and that eventually I've got to begin dealing with character and then structure.

Because of the dearth of Hispanic playwrights—or even American playwrights, for that matter—I felt it necessary to explore the territory, to cover the range of theatre as widely as I could. Political theatre with the Farm Workers was sometimes minimal scale, a small group of workers gathered in some dusty little corner in a labor camp, and sometimes immense—huge crowds, ten thousand, fifteen thousand, with banners flying. But the political theatre extends beyond the farm worker into the whole Chicano experience. We've dealt with a lot of issues: racism, education, immigration—and that took us, again, through many circles.

We evolved three separate forms: the *acto* was the political act, the short form, fifteen minutes; the *mito* was the mythic, religious play; and the *corrido* was the ballad. I just finished a full-length video program called *Corridos.* So the form has evolved into another medium. I do political plays, musicals, historical dramas, religious dramas. We still do our religious plays at the Mission here every year. They're nurturing, they feed the spirit. Peter Brook's response when he saw our Virgin play, years ago, was that it was like something out of the Middle Ages. It's religion for many of the people who come see it, not just entertainment. And of course we've gone on to do serious plays and comedies like *I Don't Have to Show You No Stinking Badges.*

***It seems that a play like* Bernabe *aligns the* acto *and the* mito, *politics and the myth. It uses religious mysticism to point out the difference between simply owning the land and loving it. The political point is made by appeal to mystical process.***

The spiritual aspect of the political struggle has been part of the work from the beginning. Some of that is through Cesar Chavez, who is a spiritual-political leader. Some people—say, the political types—have had trouble dealing with the spiritual. They say, "It's a distortion. Religion is the opium of the masses." But it seems to me that the spiritual is very much part of everyday life. There's no way to exclude it . . . we are spirit. We're a manifestation of something, of an energy.

The whole fusion between the spiritual and the material is for me the paradox of human existence. That's why I connected with Peter Brook when he was here in '73—his question was, "How do you make the invisible visible?" To me myth is not something that's fake or not real. On the contrary, it's so real that it's just below the surface—it's the supporting structure of our everyday reality. That makes me a lot more Jungian than Freudian. And it distinguishes me, I think, from a lot of other playwrights. A lot of modern playwrights go to psychoanalysis to work out their problems. I can't stop there, that's just the beginning of me. I've had to go to the root of my own existence in order to effect my own salvation, if you will. The search for meaning took me into religion and science, and into mythology.

I had to sound out these things in myself. Someone pointed out to me the evolution a couple of years ago. *The Shrunken Head of Pancho Villa* is theatre of the absurd. One of the characters, the oldest brother, is a disembodied head, huge, oversized. He eats all of the food that the family can produce. So they stay poor. He has lice that turn out to be tiny cockroaches that grow and cover the walls. He sings "La Cucaracha" but cannot talk. And he can't move. He's just kind of there. In a metaphorical sense, that was me back in the early sixties. That's the way I felt—that I had no legs, no arms. By 1970, when I got to *Bernabe*, I was the idiot, but I'd gotten in contact with the sun and the moon and earth. Fortunately, out of these grotesque self-portraits, my characters have attained a greater and greater degree of humanity.

I've always had difficulty with naturalism in the theatre. Consequently, a lot of people have looked at my work and said, "Maybe he just can't write naturalism. His is the theatre of types, of simplistic little stick figures." What I needed was a medium in which to be able to do naturalism, so I came to film. *La Bamba* is naturalism, as well as of the spirit. There I wanted the dirt, so I got the dirt. I wanted intimate realistic scenes between two real people. I can write that stuff for the stage too, but it just doesn't interest me. The stage for me—that box, that flat floor—holds other potentials, it's a means to explore other things.

*As much a ritual space as anything else.*
Most definitely. It seems to me that the essence of the human being is to act, to move through space in patterns that give his life meaning. We adorn ourselves with symbolic objects that give that movement even more meaning. Then we come out with sounds. And then somewhere along the line we begin to call that reality—but it's a self-created reality. The whole of civilization is a dance. I think the theatre celebrates that.

*So religion functions in your work as a connection with the past, with one's heritage and one's bond to all men.*
Sounding out those elemental drums, going back into the basics. I was doing this as a Chicano but I was also doing it as someone who inhabits the twentieth century. I think we need to reconnect. The word religion means "a tying back."

The vacuum I thought I was born into tuned out to be full of all kinds of mystery and power. The strange things that were going on in the *barrio*—the Mexican things, the ethnic things— seemed like superstition, but on another level there was a lot of physic activity. There's a lot of psychic activity in Mexican culture that is actually political at times.

*Zoot Suit* is another extremely spiritual, political play. And it was never understood. People thought it was about juvenile delinquents and that I was putting the Pachuco on the stage just to be snide. But the young man, Henry Reyna, achieves his own liberation by coming into contact with this internal authority. The Pachuco is the Jungian self-image, the superego if you will, the power inside every individual that's greater than any human institution. The Pachuco says, "It'll take more than the U.S. Navy to beat me down," referring to the navy and marines stripping zoot suiters in the 1940s. "I don't give a fuck what you do to me, you can't take this from me. And I re-assert myself, in this guise." The fact that critics couldn't accept that guise was too bad, but it doesn't change the nature of what the play's about. It deals with self-salvation. And you can follow the playwright through the story—I was also those two dudes. With *Zoot Suit* I was finally able to transcend social conditions, and the way I did it on stage was to give the Pachuco absolute power, as the master of ceremonies. He could snap his fingers and stop the action. It was a Brechtian device that allow the plot to move forward, but physically and symbolically, in the right way.

And Chicanos got off on it. That's why a half-million people came to see it in L.A. Because I had given a disenfranchised people their religion back. I dressed the Pachuco in the colors of Testatipoka, the Aztec god of education, the dean of the school of hard knocks. There's another god of culture, Quetzalcoatl, the feathered serpent, who's much kinder. He surfaces in *La Bamba* as the figure of Richie Valens. He's an artist and poet and is gentle and not at all fearful. When my audiences see *La Bamba*, they like that positive spirit. The Pachuco's a little harder to take. But these are evolutions. I use the metaphor of the serpent crawling out of its skin. There's that symbolism in *La Bamba*—it's pre-Columbian, but it's also very accurate in terms of the way that I view in my life. I've crawled through many of my own dead skins.

**Although Badges and Bernabe are very different, in both of them the metaphysical is given a political dimensions.**

I like to thing there's a core that's constant. In one way, what I have to say is quite basic, quite human. In another way, it's specifically American, in a continental sense. I'm reaching back to pre-Columbian America and trying to share that. I feel and sense those rhythms within me. I'm not just a Mexican farm worker. I'm an American with roots in Mayan culture. I can resonate and unlock some of the mysteries of this land which reside in all of us. I've just been in the neighborhood a little big longer. I'm a great believer in dreams. I've had some fantastic dreams. I dream when I'm standing up. I try to make my dreams come true.

**What about the endings of your plays? Zoot Suit's seems very Brechtian, a happy ending immediately called into question. Then you present three different possible futures for the characters. And Badges is similar. You present what could happen, depending on the choices the characters make.**

Multiple endings—multiple beginnings, too—have started to evolve in my work. I don't think there's any single end. I firmly believe that we exist simultaneously on seven levels—you can call them *shakras* if you're so inclined, or you can call them something else. In the Mayan sculptures, there's a vision of the universe in those ancient headdresses, in which you see the open mouths of birds with human heads coming through them, and then something else going in through the eyes and coming out again. That's a pulsating vision of the universe. It might have been born from the jungle but is, nevertheless, an accurate description of what is going on below the surface, at the nuclear level, in the way atomic particles are interacting. To me the universe is a huge, pulsating, enormously vital and *conscious* phenomenon. There is no end. There is no beginning. There's only an apparent end and an apparent beginning.

We're very emotional beings—tremendously gregarious creatures. We're very loving and caring for our mates. We're violent, there's no question about that. Tremendously cruel, intellectually cruel, unlike the animals. But even the cold-blooded murderers among us have emotion and sentiment. So it's good to end on a strong feeling. Sometimes, in the search for the right feeling, I have three or four endings.

We had an ending and beginning to *La Bamba*, which I had scripted and seemed right on paper. But our first preview audiences rejected them, so eventually we snipped them. What we had was not exactly a Brechtian turn, but it was a stepping back and looking at the fifties from the perspective of the eighties. Our audiences told us they didn't want to come back into the eighties. They wanted to say in the fifties. I had been trying, on some level, to alleviate the pain of Ritchie Valens' death, but audiences told us, "Leave us with the pain." So that's where we left it.

**Can you describe how you work as a director with your own material? When you start rehearsals, do you have a finished script?**

These days, there's at least a first or second draft. I've also worked in the opposite way, with no script whatsoever. I believe that the reality of my process as a playwright, and sometimes the audience has to suffer through it, although I try not to force paying audiences to. But back in the late sixties, early seventies, our audiences didn't pay that much—in fact, many of our performances were free—so I felt I could take certain liberties. One time we were working on a new piece, on the road in L.A., and I got new ideas for some dialogue. I was talking to the actors all the way up until curtain time. During the show I was in the wings, making notes on scraps of paper and handing them to the actors as they went on stage [laughs]. And what's really ridiculous is that they did it.

Now this is not as crazy as it sounds. You can do precisely this in making a movie. You create new lines on the spot, the actor goes front of the camera and delivers. I'm still rewriting *Badges*.

This is our closing weekend coming up and I'm introducing a couple of new scenes in the second act. I feel that so far I've found only an apparent ending. The real ending is down the road someplace. I'm touring with this play across country, I want to get to New York with it, so I'm working on it.

As a director I switch gears. Writing is a solitary process—you're in there with the words and I love that. But I also love directing, getting out of myself and into other people. As a director—and this again comes from my experiences in the Farm Worker days—I have to know who I'm working with. And what they are like. If I have four actors, or a dozen actors, plus crew, my first job as a director is to get them to become one, to arouse a lot of enthusiasm.

More and more the first thing I want to establish in character development is the movement. You can't have a feeling, an emotion, without motion. You can pick up a lot from the associative school, referring back to your own experiences, but I think it's also possible to get people to laugh and cry through what they do to their bodies.

We talk a lot about the theatre of the sphere. I firmly believe that each of use exists within his or her own sphere. The actor must begin to move within it. Every part of him resolves itself in tiny spheres—a fist spinning on a wrist, joints, legs, arms. The body centers on the solar plexus and the gut, the pelvis. I insist the first element is to move your pelvis. That gets into very sexual kinds of movements and people sometimes get embarrassed. But out of them comes a lot of basic emotion. Freud is right. We are anal and sexual. Jung comes in with the idea that we trace a sphere. Once you get into the sphere, you find your connection with Mother Earth, with the sun, with the moon, with a drop of water, with the known universe. And when you begin to inhabit your own sphere as an actor, you finally begin to stretch its limits, to encompass and envelop other people including an entire audience. You can project myself.

You can't get away with "acting" on film. You have to cut it so close to the bone, you have to *be*, to get down-and-dirty. It's "the Method," to be sure. So you have to make it small, intense and real. On the stage, because you have to project, things sometimes get out of whack. And you have to switch to a new mentality. This is where ritual comes in. Performance on the stage is much more like dance than anything else. Dance is real. You can't fake dance. But somehow a lot of people start acting as if they're "acting," and think they're doing it right. In fact, acting is something totally different; it's a *real act*. Which gets back to politics, in that our first theatrical acts were real political acts. That's why that dude was out there with a high-powered rifle—he wasn't seeing theatre, but a threatening political act.

**Now it seems that the political dimension has become sublimated, less explicit. You're no longer writing agitprop.**

There is a time and place for all forms. It's twenty years down the road. But the political impact is still there. The only difference is that I'm being asked to run for governor now, which I'm not interested in going. My purpose is still to impact socially, culturally and politically. I'm reaffirming some things that are very important to all of us as Americans, those things that we all believe to be essential to our society. What I hope is changing is a perception about the country as a whole. And the continent as well.

I'm just trying to kick my two cents into the pot. I still want El Teatro Campesino to perform on Broadway, because I think that's a political act. El Teatro Campesino is in Hollywood, and I don't think we've compromised any social statements. We started out in '65 doing these *actos* within the context of the United Farm Workers. Twenty-two years later, my next movie may be about the grape strike. My Vietnam was at home. I refused to go to Vietnam, but I encountered all the violence I needed on the home front; people were killed by the Farm Workers' strike.

**Some critics have accused you of selling out.**

I used to joke, "It's impossible for us to sell out because nobody wants to buy us." That doesn't bother me in the least. There's too much to do, to be socially conscious about. In some ways, it's just people sounding me out. I don't mind people referring back to what I have been. We're all like mirrors to each other. People help to keep you on course. I've strayed very little from my pronounced intentions. In '67 when we left United Farm Workers and started our own cultural center in Del Rey, we came out with a manifesto essentially stating that we were trying to put the tools of the artist in the hands of the humblest, the working people. But not just nineteenth-century tools, not clay and straw, or spit and masking tape, or felt pens. We were talking about video, film, recording studios. Now we're beginning a work in the best facilities that the industry has to offer. What we do with them is something else.

### *Do you read the critics?*

Sure, I love listening to the public. They're the audience, who am I to argue with them? They either got it or they didn't. The critics are part of the process. I do have some strong feelings about the nature of American criticism—I don't think that it's deeply rooted enough in a knowledge of theatre history. Very often newspapers just assign reporters, Joe Blow off the street. Perhaps it would be too much for the public to have somebody who's overly informed—is that possible?—about the theatre. There's no overriding sense of what the theatre's about in America. There's more of that sense in Europe, and a deeper appreciation for change, direction and a body of work.

In this country we are still victims of our economic system. If you make a buck, you're interesting. So obviously the only solution is to make a buck, to show that you can. That doesn't bother me, if it's attached to reaching an audience. At first, we never thought much about charging. But the poor people saw us working. They said, "We feel funny about taking this without giving you something." Our entry into the professional theatre meant that there was an audience here willing to pay.

### *How do you see the American theatre today?*

My overwhelming impression is that theatre's not nearly as interesting as it could be, that it's been stuck in its traces for many, many years. Broadway has not moved out of the twenties from what I can see. It might be because so many of the houses on Broadway are nineteenth-century playhouses. Much of the material that I see—and I don't see nearly enough—is to anemic for my tastes. I have trouble staying awake in the theatre, believe it or not [laughs]. I mean I can barely stay awake at my own plays.

I feel that the whole question of the human enterprise is up for grabs. I don't think this country has come to terms with its racial questions, obviously. And because of that, it has not really come to terms with the cultural question of what America is. There are two vast melting pots that must eventually come together. The Hispanic, after all, is really the product of a melting pot—there's no such thing as a Latin American race. The Hispanic melting pot melds all the races of the world, like the Anglo melting pot does; so on of these days, and probably in the United States, those two are going to be poured together—probably in a play, and it could be one of my own [laughs].

There's a connection with the Indian cultures that has to be established in American life. Before we can do that, however, we have to get beyond the national guilt over the genocide of the Indian. What's needed is expiation and forgiveness, and the only ones in a position to forgive are the Indian peoples. I'm a Yaqui Indian—Spanish blood, yes, but largely Yaqui. I'm in a position to be able to forgive white people. And why not? I think that's what we're here for, to forgive each other. Martin Luther King speaking in 1963 at the Lincoln Memorial was a beginning. It didn't reach nearly far enough. We're still wrestling with it. Deep fears, about miscegenation and the despoliation of the race, have to be dealt with. I'm here, through my work, to show that short, brown people are okay. We've got ideas, too, and we've got a song, and a dance or two. We know something about the world that we can share. I'm here to show that to other brown people who don't think very much of themselves, and there are a lot of those.

I wish there were more plays that dealt with the reality of this country. The racial issue is always just swept aside. It deserves to be swept aside only after it's been dealt with. We cannot begin to approach a real solution to our social ills—a solution like integration, for instance, or assimilation, without dealing with all our underlying feelings about each other. I'm trying to deal with my past, not just with respect to Anglos, but to blacks and Asians. I draw on the symbolism of the four roads; the black road, the white road, the red road and the yellow road. They all meet in the navel of the universe, the place where the upper road leads into the underworld—read consciousness and subconsciousness. I think that where they come home is in America.

### What are your plans for the future? And goals.

I'm into a very active phase right now, as writer and director, but with writing as the base. I have a number of very central stories I want to tell—on film, on television and on the stage. I want to be working in the three media, on simultaneous projects that feed each other. I like the separation between film, television and theatre. It makes each a lot clearer for me. In theatre, there are a number of ritualistic pieces I want to do that explore the movement of bodies in space and the relation between movement and language. That sphere I can explore on film, too, or television. What film gives me is movement around the actor—I can explore from any viewpoint, any distance. But theatre's the only medium that gives me the sheer beauty, power and presence of bodies. Ritual, literally.

I've got a piece that I've been working on for many, many years, called *The Earthquake Sun*, about our time. All I can tell you is that it will be on the road one of these days. I have another play called *The Mummified Fetus*. It takes off from a real incident that happened a couple of years ago: an eighty-five-year-old woman was discovered with a mummified fetus in her womb. I have a couple of plays that the world has not seen, that we've only done here.

In television I have a number of projects. *Corridos* has begun to open up other possibilities. I talk about video as electronic theatre. I'm getting into the idea of doing theatre before cameras, but going for specifically theatrical moments as opposed to real cinematic moments. *Corridos* is an example of this. And film—I'm going after the proverbial three-picture deal. I want to make movies the way I do plays.

I hope a more workable touring network will develop in this country. The links between East and West must be solidified. I think it's great for companies to tour. We're very excited about the possibility of our company plugging into the resources of the regional theatres, as we've done with *Badge* in San Diego and at the Los Angeles Theatre Center, even with the Burt Reynolds Playhouse in Florida. We hope to be able to go from regional theatre to regional theatre all the way across the country, including New York. In that way, we'll be able to reach a national audience.

I still want to experience the dust and sweat occasionally. I'm trying to leave time open for that. This month we're going to celebrate the twenty-fifth anniversary of the United Farm Workers—we'll be back on a flatbed truck, doing some of the old *actos*. I don't want to lose any of our audience. I want worldwide audience. We had that—up until 1980 we were touring Europe and Latin America. I want to tour Asia with the Teatro Campesino. Essentially, I would like to see theatre develop the kind of mass audience—it's impossible of course—that the movies have. I wish we could generate that enthusiasm in young people and in audiences in general, get them out of their homes, away from their VCRs, to experience the theatre as the life-affirming, life-giving experience that it is.

# Peter Handke

Novelist, essayist, and playwright, Peter Handke is one of the most influential German-language writers of the post-war generation. Handke was born in Austria in 1942; he studied law from 1961 to 1965 at the University of Graz and passed his first law examination, but gave up law when his first novel, *The Hornets,* was accepted for publication. He came to prominence in 1966 when he excoriated a meeting of the "Group 47" writers at Princeton University—a group including Gunther Grass, Peter Weiss, Eric Bentley, Leslie Fiedler, and Susan Sontag, among others. To Handke, these writers were wrongly committed to a sense of art as a moral instrument, and—more important—underestimated the extent to which "literature" is fundamentally about language itself: "People fail to recognize that literature is made with language and not with the things that are described with language." Handke puts this critique into practice with his first play, the hugely successful *Offending the Audience* (1966), a play he called a "Sprechstücke" or "speaking play." He followed *Offending the Audience* with several other "speaking plays": *Prophecy* (1966), *Self-Accusation* (1966), *Calling for Help* (1969), and *Kaspar* (1967). His first full-length play, *Kaspar* is based on the story of the nineteenth-century foundling Kaspar Hauser, who had not learned any language when he was discovered as an adolescent. In Handke's play, Kaspar—played as a clown—is both "created" and destroyed by language; far from being a vehicle of consciousness, language comes to dehumanize Kaspar. This attention to the working of language is the subject of *My Foot My Tutor* (1969), *Quodlibet* (1970), *The Ride Across Lake Constance* (1971), and *They are Dying Out* (1973).

In the 1980s, Handke's work developed in different directions. A longer, more meditative play, *The Long Way Round: A Dramatic Poem,* premiered at the Salzburg Festival in 1982, directed by Wim Wenders. Handke has also written translations of Aeschylus's *Prometheus Unbound* (1986) and Shakespeare's *The Winter's Tale* (1990). His most recent plays include *The Play of Questioning; or, The Journey to the Sonorous Land* (1988) and *The Time When We Knew Nothing of One Another* (1992). Handke's novels include *The Goalie's Anxiety at the Penalty Kick* (1972), made into a film directed by Wenders, and *Short Letter, Long Farewell* (1974).

## Offending the Audience (1966)

*Offending the Audience* is, as Handke suggests, a play made entirely of language: there is no acting, no setting, no narrative, no "drama," no fictive elsewhere for the audience to consume. Instead, Handke provides a kind of ritual that at once defines and subverts the common understanding of theatrical representation. For *Offending the Audience* is fully dependent on the conventional theater it works to undermine. It begins, in fact, by emphasizing a kind of heightened ordinariness. The audience must enter and be seated by the ushers, hearing the usual backstage sounds prior to the raising of the curtain. But even in this opening gesture, Handke inserts a disturbing difference, because this atmosphere is heightened, foregrounded in subtle ways—the "ushers should be more assiduous than usual, even more formal and ceremonious"; "the gradual dimming of the lights should be even more gradual if possible."

We are made aware, as an audience, of our status *as* a theater audience, because Handke will use that status to call the work of theater into question. Once the doors close and the lights have dimmed, they are raised again. The exchange between the "actors"—though they do not *act*—and the audience will not be mediated by a fictive drama, will not take place across the footlights between invisible spectators and actors pretending to be other, fictive people. Since "This room does not make believe it is a room," the actors speak to us directly, creating actual, not make-believe experience; whatever it is that will happen, "There will be no playing here tonight."

Although this is a densely *written* play, its emphasis on the presence of the event is reminiscent of Artaud; as Artaud might have written of the theater of cruelty, "You are the subject matter. You are the center of interest. No actions are performed here, you are being acted upon." But how are we acted upon? What kind of "offense" are we given? The "actors'" assault on the audience climaxes toward the end of the play with a series of insults; what is interesting to note is that many of the "insults" sound much like the kind of praise often given to actors in the theater: "Your scenes were unforgettable. You did not play, you *were* the part. You were a happening. You were the find of the evening. You lived your roles. You had a lion's share of the success. You saved the piece. You were a sight. You were a sight to have seen, you ass-kissers." Handke's "speech play" offends its audience by acknowledging the audience's fictionality, the ways that its experience—all experience—is a function of the power of language. Handke "offends" the audience by derealizing it, showing its "reality" to be—like all acts of theater—a complex negotiation between the actual and the represented. But it is, finally, the recognition of the involvement of the fictive in all notions of reality that brings the "actors" and the "audience" together, allowing the "actors" to welcome us as "fellow humans."

# — Offending the Audience —

## Peter Handke

TRANSLATED BY MICHAEL ROLOFF
FOR KARLHEINZ BRAUN, CLAUS PEYMANN, BASCH PEYMANN,
WOLFGANG WIENS, PETER STEINBACH, MICHAEL GRUNER, ULRICH
HASS, CLAUS DIETER REENTS, RÜDIGER VOGLER, JOHN LENNON

CAST: FOUR SPEAKERS

Rules for the actors
*Listen to the litanies in the Catholic churches.*
*Listen to football teams being cheered on and booed.*
*Listen to the rhythmic chanting at demonstrations.*
*Listen to the wheels of a bicycle upturned on its seat spinning until the spokes have come to rest and watch the spokes until they have reached their resting point.*
*Listen to the gradually increasing noise a concrete mixer makes after the motor has been started.*
*Listen to debaters cutting each other off.*
*Listen to "Tell Me" by the Rolling Stones.*
*Listen to the simultaneous arrival and departure of trains.*
*Listen to the hit parade on Radio Luxembourg.*
*Listen in on the simultaneous interpreters at the United Nations.*
*Listen to the dialogue between the gangster (Lee J. Cobb) and the pretty girl in "The Trap," when the girl asks the gangster how many more people he intends to kill; whereupon the gangsters ask, as he leans back, How many are left? and watch the gangster as he says it.*
*See the Beatles' movies.*
*In "A Hard Day's Night" watch Ringo's smile at the moment when after having been teased by the others, he sits down at his drums and begins to play.*
*Watch Gary Cooper's face in "The Man From the West." In the same movie watch the death of the mute as he runs down the deserted street of the lifeless town with a bullet in him, hopping and jumping and emitting those shrill screams.*
*Watch monkeys aping people and llamas spitting in the zoo.*
*Watch the behavior of bums and idlers as they amble on the street and play the machines in the penny arcades.*

When the theatergoers enter the room into which they are meant to go, they are greeted by the usual pre-performance atmosphere. One might let them hear noises from behind the curtain, noises that make believe the scenery is being shifted about. For example, a table is dragged across the stage, or several chairs are noisily set up and then removed. One might let the spectators in the first few rows hear directions whispered by make-believe stage managers and the whispered interchanges between make-believe stagehands behind the curtain. Or, even better, use tape recordings of other performances in which, before the curtain rises, objects are really shifted about. These noises should be amplified to make them more audible, and perhaps should be stylized and arranged so as to produce their own order and uniformity.

The usual theater atmosphere should prevail. The ushers should be more assiduous than usual, even more formal and ceremonious, should subdue their usual whispering with even more style, so that their behavior becomes infectious. The programs should be elegant. The buzzer signals should not be forgotten; the signals are repeated at successively briefer intervals. The gradual dimming of the lights should be even more gradual if possible; perhaps the lights can be dimmed in successive stages. As the ushers proceed to close the doors, their gestures should become particularly solemn and noticeable. Yet, they are only ushers. Their actions should not appear symbolic. Late-comers should not be admitted. Inappropriately dressed ticket holders should not be admitted. The concept of what is sartorially inappropriate should be strictly applied. None of the spectators should call attention to himself or offend the eye by his attire. The men should be dressed in dark jackets, with white shirts and inconspicuous ties. The women should shun bright colors.

There is no standing-room. Once the doors are closed and the lights dim, it gradually becomes quiet behind the curtain too. The silence behind the curtain and the silence in the auditorium are alike. The spectators stare a while longer at the almost imperceptibly fluttering curtain, which may perhaps billow once or twice as though someone had hurriedly crossed the stage. Then the curtain grows still. There is a short pause. The curtain slowly parts, allowing an unobstructed view. Once the stage is completely open to view, the four speakers step forward from upstage. Nothing impedes their progress. The stage is empty. As they walk forward noncommittally, dressed casually, it becomes light on stage as well as in the audience. The light on stage and in the auditorium is of the same intensity as at the end of a performance and there is no glare to hurt the eyes. The stage and the auditorium remain lighted throughout the performance. Even as they approach, the speakers don't look at the audience. They don't direct the words they are speaking at the audience. Under no circumstance should the audience get the impression that the words are directed at them. As far as the speakers are concerned, the audience does not yet exist. As they approach, they move their lips. Gradually their words become intelligible and finally they become loud. The invectives they deliver overlap one another. The speakers speak pell-mell. They pick up each other's words. They take words out of each other's mouths. They speak in unison, each uttering different words. They repeat. They grow louder. They scream. They pass rehearsed words from mouth to mouth. Finally, they rehearse one word in unison. The words they use in this prologue are the following (their order is immaterial): You *chuckle-heads, you small-timers, you nervous nellies, you fuddy-duddies, you windbags, you sitting ducks, you milquetoasts. The speakers should strive for a certain acoustic uniformity. However, except for the acoustic pattern, no other picture should be produced. The invectives are not directed at anyone in particular. The manner of their delivery should not induce a meaning. The speakers reach the front of the stage before they finish rehearsing their invectives. They stand at ease but form a sort of pattern. They are not completely fixed in their positions but move according to the movement which the words they speak lend them. They now look at the public, but at no one person in particular. They are silent for a while. They collect themselves. Then they begin to speak. The order in which they speak is immaterial. The speakers have roughly the same amount of work to do.*

You are welcome.

This piece is a prologue.

You will hear nothing you have not heard here before.
You will see nothing you have not seen here before.
You will see nothing of what you have always seen here.
You will hear nothing of what you have always heard here.

You will hear what you usually see.
You will hear what you usually don't see.
You will see no spectacle.
10  Your curiosity will not be satisfied.
You will see no play.
There will be no playing here tonight.
You will see a spectacle without pictures.

You expected something.
You expected something else perhaps.
You expected objects.
You expected no objects.
You expected an atmosphere.
You expected a different world.
20  You expected no different world.
In any case, you expected something.
It may be the case that you expected what you are hearing now.
But even in that case you expected something different.

You are sitting in rows. You form a pattern. You are sitting in a certain order. You are facing in a certain direction. You are sitting equidistant from one another. You are an audience. You form a unit. You are auditors and spectators in an auditorium. Your thoughts are free. You can still make up your 30  own mind. You see us speaking and you hear us speaking. You are beginning to breathe in one and the same rhythm. You are beginning to breathe in one and the same rhythm in which we are speaking. You are breathing the way we are speaking. We and you gradually form a unit.

You are not thinking. You don't think of anything. You are thinking along. You are not thinking along. You feel uninhibited. Your thoughts are free. Even as we say that, we insinuate ourselves into your thoughts. You have thoughts in the back of your mind. Even as we say that, we insinuate ourselves into the thoughts in back of your mind. You are 40  thinking along. You are hearing. Your thoughts are following in the track of our thoughts. Your thoughts are not following in the track of our thoughts. You are not thinking. Your thoughts are not free. You feel inhibited.

You are looking at us when we speak to you. You are not watching us. You are looking at us. You are being looked at. You are unprotected. You no longer have the advantage of looking from the shelter of darkness into the light. We no longer have the disadvantage of looking through the blinding light into the dark. You are not watching. You are looking at and 50  you are being looked at. In this way, we and you gradually form a unit. Under certain conditions, therefore, we, instead of saying *you*, could say *we*. We are under one and the same roof. We are a closed society.

You are not listening to us. You heed us. You are no longer eavesdropping from behind a wall. We are speaking directly to you. Our dialogue no longer moves at a right angle to your glance. Your glance no longer pierces our dialogue. Our words and your glances no longer form an angle. You are not disregarded. You are not treated as mere hecklers. You need 60  not form an opinion from a bird's or a frog's perspective of anything that happens here. You need not play referee. You are no longer treated as spectators to whom we can speak in asides. This is no play. There are no asides here. Nothing that takes place here is intended as an appeal to you. This is no play. We don't step out of the play to address you. We have no need of illusions to disillusion you. We show you nothing. We are playing no destinies. We are playing no dreams. This is not a factual report. This is no documentary play. This is no slice of life. We don't tell you a story. We 70  don't perform any actions. We don't simulate any actions. We don't represent anything. We don't put anything on for you. We only speak. We play by addressing you. When we say we, we may also mean you. We are not acting out your situation. You cannot recognize yourselves in us. We are playing no situation. You need not feel that we mean you. You cannot feel that we mean you. No mirror is being held up to you. We don't mean you. We are addressing you. You are being addressed. You will be addressed. You will be bored if you don't want to be addressed.    80

You are sharing no experience. You are not sharing. You are not following suit. You are experiencing no intrigues here. You are experiencing nothing. You are not imagining anything. You don't have to imagine anything. You need no prerequisites. You don't need to know that this is a stage. You need no expectations. You need not lean back expectantly. You don't need to know that this is only playing. We make up no stories. You are not following an event. You are not playing along. You are being played with here. That is a wordplay.    90

What is the theater's is not rendered unto the theater here. Here you don't receive your due. Your curiosity is not satisfied. No spark will leap across from us to you. You will not be electrified. These boards don't signify a world. They are part of the world. These boards exist for us to stand on. This world is no different from yours. You are no longer kibitzers. You are the subject matter. The focus is on you. You are in the crossfire of our words.

100 This is no mirage. You don't see walls that tremble. You don't hear the spurious sounds of doors snapping shut. You hear no sofas squeaking. You see no apparitions. You have no visions. You see no picture of something. Nor do you see the suggestion of a picture. You see no picture puzzle. Nor do you see an empty picture. The emptiness of this stage is no picture of another emptiness. The emptiness of this stage signifies nothing. This stage is empty because objects would be in our way. It is empty because we don't need objects. This stage represents nothing. It represents no other emptiness. This stage *is* empty. You don't see any objects that pre-
110 tend to be other objects. You don't see a darkness that pretends to be another darkness. You don't see a brightness that pretends to be another brightness. You don't see any light that pretends to be another light. You don't hear any noise that pretends to be another noise. You don't see a room that pretends to be another room. Here you are not experiencing a time that pretends to be another time. The time on stage is no different from the time off stage. We have the same local time here. We are in the same location. We are breathing the same air. The stage apron is not a line
120 of demarcation. It is not only sometimes no demarcation line. It is no demarcation line as long as we are speaking to you. There is no invisible circle here. There is no magic circle. There is no room for play here. We are not playing. We are all in the same room. The demarcation line has not been penetrated, it is not previous, it doesn't even exist. There is no radiation belt between you and us. We are not self-propelled props. We are no pictures of something. We are no representatives. We represent nothing. We demonstrate nothing. We have no pseudonyms. Our heartbeat does not
130 pretend to be another's heartbeat. Our bloodcurdling screams don't pretend to be another's bloodcurdling screams. We don't step out of our roles. We have no roles. We are ourselves. We are the mouthpiece of the author. You cannot make yourself a picture of us. You don't need to make yourself a picture of us. We are ourselves. Our opinion and the author's opinion are not necessarily the same.

The light that illuminates us signifies nothing. Neither do the clothes we wear signify anything. They indicate nothing, they are not unusual in any way, they signify nothing. They
140 signify no other time to you, no other climate, no other season, no other degree of latitude, no other reason to wear them. They have no function. Nor do our gestures have a function, that is, to signify something to you. This is not the world as a stage.

We are no slapstick artists. There are no objects here that we might trip over. Insidious objects are not on the program. Insidious objects are not spoil-sports because we are not sporting with them. The objects are not intended as insidious sport; they are insidious. If we happen to trip, we trip
150 unwittingly. Unwitting as well are mistakes in dress; unwitting, too, are our perhaps foolish faces. Slips of the tongue, which amuse you, are not intended. If we stutter, we stutter

without meaning to. We cannot make dropping a handkerchief part of the play. We are not playing. We cannot make the insidiousness of objects part of the play. We cannot camouflage the insidiousness of objects. We cannot be of two minds. We cannot be of many minds. We are no clowns. We are not in an arena. You don't have the pleasure of encircling us. You are not enjoying the comedy of having a rear view of us. You are not enjoying the comedy of insidious objects. 160 You are enjoying the comedy of words.

The possibilities of the theater are not exploited here. The realm of possibilities is not exhausted. The theater is not unbounded. The theater is bound. Fate is meant ironically here. We are not theatrical. Our comedy is not overwhelming. Your laughter cannot be liberating. We are not playful. We are not playing a world for you. This is not half of one world. We and you do not constitute two halves.

You are the subject matter. You are the center of interest. No actions are performed here, you are being acted upon. That 170 is no wordplay. You are not treated as individuals here. You don't become individuals here. You have no individual traits. You have no distinctive physiognomies. You are not individuals here. You have no characteristics. You have no destiny. You have no history. You have no past. You are on no wanted list. You have no experience of life. You have the experience of the theater here. You have that certain something. You are playgoers. You are of no interest because of your capacities. You are of interest solely in your capacity as playgoers. As playgoers you form a pattern here. You are no 180 personalities. You are not singular. You are a plurality of persons. Your faces point in one direction. You are an event. You are *the* event.

You are under review by us. But you form no picture. You are not symbolic. You are an ornament. You are a pattern. You have features that everyone here has. You have general features. You are a species. You form a pattern. You are doing and you are not doing the same time; you are looking in one direction. You don't stand up and look in different directions. You are a standard pattern and you have a pattern as 190 a standard. You have a standard with which you came to the theater. You have the standard idea that where we are is up and where you are is down. You have the standard idea of two worlds. You have the standard idea of the world of the theater.

You don't need this standard now. You are not attending a piece for the theater. You are not attending. You are the focal point. You are in the crossfire. You are being inflamed. You can catch fire. You don't need a standard. You are the standard. You have been discovered. You are the discovery 200 of the evening. You inflame us. Our words catch fire on you. From you a spark leaps across to us.

This room does not make believe it is a room. The side that is open to you is not the fourth wall of a house. The world does not have to be cut open here. You don't see any doors here. You don't see the two doors of the old dramas. You don't see the back door through which he who shouldn't be seen can slip out. You don't see the front door through which he who wants to see him who shouldn't be seen enters. There is no back door. Neither is there a nonexistent door as in modern drama. The nonexistent door does not represent a nonexistent door. This is not another world. We are not pretending that you don't exist. You are not thin air for us. You are of crucial importance to us because you exist. We are speaking to you because you exist. If you did not exist, we would be speaking to thin air. Your existence is not simply taken for granted. You don't watch us through a keyhole. We don't pretend that we are alone in the world. We don't explain ourselves to ourselves only in order to put you in the know. We are not conducting an exhibition purely for the benefit of your enlightenment. We need no artifice to enlighten you. We need no tricks. We don't have to be theatrically effective. We have no entrances, we have no exits, we don't talk to you in asides. We are putting nothing over on you. We are not about to enter into a dialogue. We are not in a dialogue. Nor are we in a dialogue with you. We have no wish to enter into a dialogue with you. You are not in collusion with us. You are not eyewitnesses to an event. We are not taunting you. You don't have to be apathetic any more. You don't have to watch inactively any more. No actions take place here. You feel the discomfort of being watched and addressed, since you came prepared to watch and make yourselves comfortable in the shelter of the dark. Your presence is every moment explicitly acknowledged with every one of our words. Your presence is the topic we deal with from one breath to the next, from one moment to the next, from one word to the next. Your standard idea of the theater is no longer presupposed as the basis of our actions. You are neither condemned to watch nor free to watch. You are the subject. You are the playmakers. You are the counterplotters. You are being aimed at. You are the target of our words. You serve as targets. That is a metaphor. You serve as the target of our metaphors. You serve as metaphors.

Of the two poles here, you are the pole at rest. You are in an arrested state. You find yourself in a state of expectation. You are no subjects. You are objects here. You are the objects of our words. Still, you are subjects too.

There are no intervals here. The intervals between words lack significance. Here the unspoken word lacks significance. There are no unspoken words here. Our silences say nothing. There is no deafening silence. There is no silent silence. There is no deathly quiet. Speech is not used to create silence here. This play includes no direction telling us to be silent. We make no artificial pauses. Our pauses are natural pauses. Our pauses are not eloquent like speech. We say nothing with our silence. No abyss opens up between words. You cannot read anything between our lines. You cannot read anything in our faces. Our gestures express nothing of consequence to anything. What is inexpressible is not said through silences here. Glances and gestures are not eloquent here. Becoming silent and being silent is no artifice here. There are no silent letters here. There's only the mute *h*. That is a pun.

You have made up your mind now. You recognized that we negate something. You recognized that we repeat ourselves. You recognized that we contradict ourselves. You recognized that this piece is conducting an argument with the theater. You recognized the dialectical structure of the piece. You recognized a certain spirit of contrariness. The intention of the piece became clear to you. You recognized that we primarily negate. You recognized that we repeat ourselves. You recognize. You see through. You have not made up your mind. You have not seen through the dialectical structure of the piece. Now you are seeing through. Your thoughts were one thought too slow. Now you have thoughts in the back of your mind.

You look charming. You look enchanting. You look dazzling. You look breathtaking. You look unique.

But you don't make an evening. You're not a brilliant idea. You are tiresome. You are not a thankful subject. You are a theatrical blunder. You are not true to life. You are not theatrically effective. You don't send us. You don't enchant us. You don't dazzle us. You don't entertain us fabulously. You are not playful. You are not sprightly. You have no tricks up your sleeve. You have no nose for the theater. You have nothing to say. Your debut is unconvincing. You are not with it. You don't help us pass the time. You are not addressing the human quality in us. You leave us cold.

This is no drama. No action that has occurred elsewhere is reenacted here. Only a now and a now and a now exist here. This is no make-believe which re-enacts an action that really happened once upon a time. Time plays no role here. We are not acting out a plot. Therefore we are not playing time. Time is for real here, it expires from one word to the next. Time flies in the words here. It is not alleged that time can be repeated here. No play can be repeated here and play at the same time it did once upon a time. The time here is *your* time. Space time here is your space time. Here you can compare your time with our time. Time is no noose. That is no make-believe. It is not alleged here that time can be repeated. The umbilical cord connecting you to your time is not severed here. Time is not at play here. We mean business with time here. It is admitted here that time expires from one word to the next. It is admitted that this is your time here. You can check the time here on your watches. No other time governs here. The time that governs here is measured against your breath. Time conforms to your wishes here. We measure time by your breath, by the batting of your eyelashes, by your pulsebeats, by the growth of your cells. Time expires here from moment to moment. Time is measured in moments. Time is measured in your moments. Time goes through your stomach. Time here is not repeatable as in the make-believe of a theater performance. This is no performance: you have not to imagine anything. Time is no noose here. Time is not cut off from the outside world here. There are no two levels of time here. There are no two worlds here. While we are here, the earth continues to turn. Our time up here is your time down there. It expires from one word to the next. It expires while we, we and you, are breathing, while our hair is growing, while we are sweating, while we are smelling, while we are hearing. Time is not repeatable even if we repeat our words, even if we mention again that our time is your time, that it expires from one word to the next, while we, we and you, are breathing, while our hair is growing, while we sweat, while we smell, while we hear. We cannot repeat anything, time is expiring. It is unrepeatable. Each moment is historical. Each of your moments is a historical moment. We cannot say our words twice. This is no make-believe. We cannot do the same thing 330 once again. We cannot repeat the same gestures. We cannot speak the same way. Time expires on our lips. Time is unrepeatable. Time is no noose. That is no make-believe. The past is not made contemporaneous. The past is dead and buried. We need no puppet to embody a dead time. This is no puppet show. This is no nonsense. This is no play. This is no sense. You recognize the contradiction. Time here serves the wordplay.

This is no maneuver. This is no exercise for the emergency. No one has to play dead here. No one has to pretend he is alive. 340 Nothing is posited here. The number of wounded is not prescribed. The result is not predetermined on paper. There is no result here. No one has to present himself here. We don't represent except what we are. We don't represent ourselves in a state other than the one we are in now and here. This is no maneuver. We are not playing ourselves in different situations. We are not thinking of the emergency. We don't have to represent our death. We don't have to represent our life. We don't play ahead of time what and how we will be. We make no future contemporaneous in our play. We don't 350 represent another time. We don't represent the emergency. We are speaking while time expires. We speak of the expiration of time. We are not doing as if. We are not doing as if we could repeat time or as if we could anticipate time. This is neither make-believe nor a maneuver. On the one hand we do as if. We do as if we could repeat words. We appear to repeat ourselves. Here is the world of appearances. Here appearance is appearance. Appearance is here appearance.

You represent something. You are someone. You are something. You are not someone here but something. You are a 360 society that represents an order. You are a theater society of sorts. You are an order because of your kind of dress, the position of your bodies, the direction of your glances. The color of your clothes clashes with the color of your seating arrangement. You also form an order with the seating arrangement. You are dressed up. With your dress you observe an order. You dress up. By dressing up, you demonstrate that you are doing something that you don't do every day. You are putting on a masquerade so as to partake of a masquerade. You partake. You watch. You stare. By watch- 370 ing, you become rigid. The seating arrangement favors this development. You are something that watches. You need room for your eyes. If the curtain comes together, you gradually become claustrophobic. You have no vantage point. You feel encircled. You feel inhibited. The parting of the curtain merely relieves your claustrophobia. Thus it relieves you. You can watch. Your view is unobstructed. You become uninhibited. You can partake. You are not in dead center as when the curtain is closed. You are no longer someone. You become something. You are no longer alone with your- 380 selves. You are no longer left to your own devices. Now you are with it. You are an audience. That is a relief. You can partake.

Up here there is no order now. There are no objects that demonstrate an order to you. The world here is neither sound nor unsound. This is no world. Stage props are out of place here. Their places are not chalked out on the stage. Since they are not chalked out, there is no order here. There are no chalk marks for the standpoint of things. There are no memory props for the standpoint of persons. In contrast to you and your seating arrangement, nothing is in its place 390 here. Things here have no fixed places like the places of your seating arrangements down there. This stage is no world, just as the world is no stage.

Nor does each thing have its own time here. No thing has its own time here. No thing has its fixed time here when it serves as a prop or when it becomes an obstacle. We don't do as if things were really used. Here things *are* useful.

You are not standing. You are using the seating arrangements. You are sitting. Since your seating arrangements form a pattern, you form a pattern as well. There is no standing-room. 400 People enjoy art more effectively when they sit than if they stand. That is why you are sitting. You are friendlier when you sit. You are more receptive. You are more open-minded. You are more long-suffering. Sitting, you are more relaxed. You are more democratic. You are less bored. Time seems less long and boring to you. You allow more to happen with yourself. You are more clairvoyant. You are less distracted. It is easier for you to forget your surroundings. The world around you disappears more easily. You begin to resemble one another more. You begin to lose your personal 410 qualities. You begin to lose the characteristics that distinguish you from each other. You become a unit. You become a pattern. You become one. You lose your self-consciousness. You become spectators. You become auditors. You become apathetic. You become all eyes and ears. You forget to look at your watch. You forget yourself.

Standing, you would be more effective hecklers. In view of the anatomy of the human body, your heckling would be louder if you stood. You would be better able to clench your fists. You could show your opposition better. You would have 420 greater mobility. You would not need to be as well-behaved. You could shift your weight from one foot to the other. You could more easily become conscious of your body. Your enjoyment of art would be diminished. You would no longer form a pattern. You would no longer be rigid. You would lose your geometry. You would be better able to smell the sweat of the bodies near you. You would be better able to express agreement by nudging each other. If you stood, the sluggishness of your bodies would not keep you from walking. Standing, you would be more individual. You would op- 430 pose the theater more resolutely. You would give in to fewer illusions. You would suffer more from absentmindedness. You would stand more on the outside. You would be better able to leave yourself to your own devices. You would be less able to imagine represented events as real. The events here would seem less true to life to you. Standing, for example, you would be less able to imagine a death represented on this stage as real. You would be less rigid. You wouldn't let yourself be put under as much of a spell. You wouldn't let as

440 much be put over on you. You wouldn't be satisfied to be mere spectators. It would be easier for you to be of two minds. You could be at two places at once with your thoughts. You could live in two space-time continuums.

We don't want to infect you. We don't want to goad you into a show of feelings. We don't play feelings. We don't embody feelings. We neither laugh nor weep. We don't want to infect you with laughter by laughing or with weeping by laughing or with laughter by weeping or with weeping by weeping. Although laughter is more infectious than weep-
450 ing, we don't infect you with laughter by laughing. And so forth. We are not playing. We play nothing. We don't modulate. We don't gesticulate. We express ourselves by no means but words. We only speak. We express. We don't express ourselves but the opinion of the author. We express ourselves by speaking. Our speaking is our acting. By speaking, we become theatrical. We are theatrical because we are speaking in a theater. By always speaking directly to you and by speaking to you of time, of now and of now and of now, we observe the unity of time, place, and action. But we ob-
460 serve this unity not only here on stage. Since the stage is no world unto itself, we also observe the unity down where you are. We and you form a unity because we speak directly to you without interruption. Therefore, under certain conditions, we, instead of saying you, could say we. That signifies the unity of action. The stage up here and the auditorium constitute a unity in that they no longer constitute two levels. There is no radiation belt between us. There are no two places here. Here is only one place. That signifies the unity of place. Your time, the time of the spectators and au-
470 ditors, and our time, the time of the speakers, form a unity in that no other time passes here than your time. Time is not bisected here into played time and play time. Time is not played here. Only real time exists here. Only the time that we, we and you, experience ourselves in our own bodies exists here. Only one time exists here. That signifies the unity of time. All three cited circumstances, taken together, signify the unity of time, place, and action. Therefore this piece is classical.

Because we speak to you, you can become conscious of your-
480 self. Because we speak to you, your self-awareness increases. You become aware that you are sitting. You become aware that you are sitting in a theater. You become aware of the size of your limbs. You become aware of how your limbs are situated. You become aware of your fingers. You become aware of your tongue. You become aware of your throat. You become aware how heavy your head is. You become aware of your sex organs. You become aware of batting your eyelids. You become aware of the muscles with which you swallow. You become aware of the flow of your
490 saliva. You become aware of the beating of your heart. You become aware of raising your eyebrows. You become aware of a prickling sensation on your scalp. You become aware of the impulse to scratch yourself. You become aware of sweating under your armpits. You become aware of your sweaty hands. You become aware of your parched hands. You become aware of the air you are inhaling and exhaling through your mouth and nose. You become aware of our words

entering your ears. You acquire presence of mind.

Try not to blink your eyelids. Try not to swallow any more. Try not to move your tongue. Try not to hear anything. Try not 500 to smell anything. Try not to salivate. Try not to sweat. Try not to shift in your seat. Try not to breathe.

Why, you are breathing. Why, you are salivating. Why, you are listening. Why, you are smelling. Why, you are swallowing. Why, you are blinking your eyelids. Why, you are belching. Why, you are sweating. Why, how terribly self-conscious you are.

Don't blink. Don't salivate. Don't bat your eyelashes. Don't inhale. Don't exhale. Don't shift in your seat. Don't listen to us. Don't smell. Don't swallow. Hold your breath. 510

Swallow. Salivate. Blink. Listen. Breathe.

You are now aware of your presence. You know that it is *your* time that you are spending here. You are the topic. You tie the knot. You untie the knot. You are the center. You are the occasion. You are the reasons why. You provide the initial impulse. You provide us with words here. You are the playmakers and the counterplotters. You are the youthful comedians. You are the youthful lovers, you are the ingénues, you are the sentimentalists. You are the stars, you are the character actors, you are the bon vivants and the heroes. You are 520 the heroes and the villains of this piece.

Before you came here, you made certain preparations. You came here with certain preconceptions. You went to the theater. You prepared yourself to go to the theater. You had certain expectations. Your thoughts were one step ahead of time. You imagined something. You prepared yourself for something. You prepared yourself to partake in something. You prepared yourself to be seated, to sit on the rented seat and to attend something. Perhaps you had heard of this piece. So you made preparations, you prepared yourself for 530 something. You let events come toward you. You were prepared to sit and have something shown to you.

The rhythm you breathed in was different from ours. You went about dressing yourself in a different manner. You got started in a different way. You approached this location from different directions. You used the public transportation system. You came on foot. You came by cab. You used your own means of transportation. Before you got underway, you looked at your watch. You expected a telephone call, you picked up the receiver, you turned on the lights, 540 you turned out the lights, you closed doors, you turned keys, you stepped out into the open. You propelled your legs. You let your arms swing up and down as you walked. You walked. You walked from different directions all in the same direction. You found your way here with the help of your sense of direction.

Because of your plan you distinguished yourselves from others who were on their way to other locations. Simply because of your plan, you instantly formed a unit with the others who

550 were on their way to this location. You had the same objective. You planned to spend a part of your future together with others at a definite time.

You crossed traffic lanes. You looked left and right. You observed traffic signals. You nodded to others. You stopped. You informed others of your destination. You told of your expectations. You communicated your speculations about this piece. You expressed your opinion of this piece. You shook hands. You had others wish you a pleasant evening. You took off your shoes. You held doors open. You had
560 doors held open for you. You met other theatergoers. You felt like conspirators. You observed the rules of good behavior. You helped out of coats. You let yourselves be helped out of coats. You stood around. You walked around. You heard the buzzers. You grew restless. You looked in the mirror. You checked your makeup. You threw sidelong glances. You noticed sidelong glances. You walked. You paced. Your movements became more formal. You heard the buzzer. You looked at your watch. You became conspirators. You took your seat. You took a look around. You made yourself
570 comfortable. You heard the buzzer. You stopped chatting. You aligned your glances. You raised your heads. You took a deep breath. You saw the lights dim. You became silent. You heard the doors closing. You stared at the curtain. You waited. You became rigid. You did not move any more. Instead, the curtain moved. You heard the curtain rustling. You were offered an unobstructed view of the stage. Everything was as it always is. Your expectations were not disappointed. You were ready. You leaned back in your seat. The play could begin.

580 At other times you were also ready. You were on to the game that was being played. You leaned back in your seats. You perceived. You followed. You pursued. You let happen. You let something happen up here that had happened long ago. You watched the past which by means of dialogue and monologue made believe it was contemporaneous. You let yourselves be captivated. You let yourselves become spellbound. You forgot where you were. You forgot the time. You became rigid and remained rigid. You did not move. You did not act. You did not even come up front to see better. You
590 followed no natural impulses. You watched as you watch a beam of light that was produced long before you began to watch. You looked into dead space. You looked at dead points. You experienced a dead time. You heard a dead language. You yourselves were in a dead room in a dead time. It was dead calm. No breath of air moved. You did not move. You stared. The distance between you and us was infinite. We were infinitely far away from you. We moved at an infinite distance from you. We had lived infinitely long before you. We lived up here on the stage before the beginning of
600 time. Your glances and our glances met in infinity. An infinite space was between us. We played. But we did not play with you. You were always posterity here.

Plays were played here. Sense was played here. Nonsense with meaning was played here. The plays here had a background and an underground. They had a false bottom. They were not what they were. They were not what they seemed. There was something in back of them. The things and the plot seemed to be, but they were not. They seemed to be as they seemed, but they were different. They did not seem to
610 seem as in a pure play, they seemed to be. They seemed to be reality. The plays here did not pass the time, or they did not only pass the time. They had meaning. They were not timeless like the pure plays, an unreal time passed in them. The conspicuous meaninglessness of some plays was precisely what represented their hidden meaning. Even the pranks of pranksters acquired meaning on these boards. Always something lay in wait. Always something lay in ambush between the words, gestures, props and sought to mean something to you. Always something had two or more mean-
620 ings. Something was always happening. Something happened in the play that you were supposed to think was real. Stories always happened. A played and unreal time happened. What you saw and heard was supposed to be not only what you saw and heard. It was supposed to be what you did not see and did not hear. Everything was meant. Everything expressed. Even what pretended to express nothing expressed something because something that happens in the theater expresses something. Everything that was played expressed something real. The play was not played for the
630 play's sake but for the sake of reality. You were to discover a played reality behind the play. You were supposed to fathom the play. Not a play, reality was played. Time was played. Since time was played, reality was played. The theater played tribunal. The theater played arena. The theater played moral institution. The theater played dreams. The theater played tribal rites. The theater played mirrors for you. The play exceeded the play. It hinted at reality. It became impure. It meant. Instead of time staying out of play, an unreal and uneffective time transpired. With the unreal
640 time an unreal reality was played. It was not there, it was only signified to you, it was performed. Neither reality nor play transpired here. If a clean play had been played here, time could have been left out of play. A clean play has no time. But since a reality was played, the corresponding time was also played. If a clean play had been played here, there would have been only the time of the spectators here. But since reality was part of the play here, there were always two times: your time, the time of the spectators, and the played time, which seemed to be the real time. But time cannot be
650 played. It cannot be repeated in any play. Time is irretrievable. Time is irresistible. Time is unplayable. Time is real. It cannot be played as real. Since time cannot be played, reality cannot be played either. Only a play where time is left out of play is a play. A play in which time plays a role is no play. Only a timeless play is without meaning. Only a timeless play is self-sufficient. Only a timeless play does not need to *play* time. Only for a timeless play is time without meaning. All other plays are impure plays. There are only plays without time, or plays in which time is real time, like the
660 sixty minutes of a football game, which has only one time because the time of the players is the same time as that of the spectators. All other plays are sham plays. All other plays mirror meretricious facts for you. A timeless play mirrors no facts.

We could do a play within a play for you. We could act out happenings for you that are taking place outside this room during these moments while you are swallowing, while you are batting your eyelashes. We could illustrate the statistics. We could represent what is statistically taking place at other places while you are at this place. By representing what is happening, we could make you imagine these happenings. We could bring them closer to you. We would not need to represent anything that is past. We could play a clean game. For example, we could act out the very process of dying that is statistically happening somewhere at this moment. We could become full of pathos. We could declare that death is the pathos of time, of which we speak all the time. Death could be the pathos of this real time which you are wasting here. At the very least, this play within a play would help bring this piece to a dramatic climax.

But we are not putting anything over on you. We don't imitate. We don't represent any other persons and any other events, even if they statistically exist. We can do without a play of features and a play of gestures. There are no persons who are part of the plot and therefore no impersonators. The plot is not freely invented, for there is no plot. Since there is no plot, accidents are impossible. Similarity with still living or scarcely dead or long-dead persons is not accidental but impossible. For we don't represent anything and are no others than we are. We don't even play ourselves. We are speaking. Nothing is invented here. Nothing is imitated. Nothing is fact. Nothing is left to your imagination.

Due to the fact that we are not playing and not acting playfully, this piece is half as funny and half as tragic. Due to the fact that we only speak and don't fall outside time, we cannot depict anything for you and demonstrate nothing for you. We illustrate nothing. We conjure up nothing out of the past. We are not in conflict with the past. We are not in conflict with the present. We don't anticipate the future. In the present, the past, and the future, we speak of time.

That is why, for example, we cannot represent the now and now of dying that is statistically happening now. We cannot represent the gasping for breath that is happening now and now, or the tumbling and falling now, or the death throes, or the grinding of teeth now, or the last words, or the last sign now, that is statistically happening now this very second, or the last exhalation, or the last ejaculation that is happening now, or the breathlessness that is statistically commencing now, and now, and now, and now, and so on, or the motionlessness now, or the statistically ascertainable rigor mortis, or the lying absolutely quiet now. We cannot represent it. We only speak of it. We are speaking of it *now*.

Due to the fact that we only speak and due to the fact that we don't speak of anything invested, we cannot be equivocal or ambiguous. Due to the fact that we play nothing, there cannot exist two or more levels here or a play within a play. Due to the fact that we don't gesticulate and don't tell you any stories and don't represent anything, we cannot be poetical. Due to the fact that we only speak to you, we lose the poetry of ambiguity. For example, we cannot use the gestures and expressions of dying that we mentioned to represent the gestures and expressions of a simultaneously transpiring instance of sexual intercourse that is statistically transpiring now. We can't be equivocal. We cannot play on a false bot-

tom. We cannot remove ourselves from the world. We don't need to be poetic. We don't need to hypnotize you. We don't need to hoodwink you. We don't need to cast an evil eye on you. We don't need a second nature. This is no hypnosis. You don't have to imagine anything. You don't have to dream with open eyes. With the illogic of your dreams you are not dependent on the logic of the stage. The impossibilities of your dreams do not have to confine themselves to the possibilities of the stage. The absurdity of your dreams does not have to obey the authentic laws of the theater. Therefore we represent neither dreams nor reality. We make claims neither for life nor for dying, neither for society nor for the individual, neither for what is natural nor for what is supernatural, neither for lust nor for grief, neither for reality nor for the play. Time elicits no elegies from us.

This piece is a prologue. It is not the prologue to another piece but the prologue to what you did, what you are doing, and what you will do. You are the topic. This piece is the prologue to the topic. It is the prologue to your practices and customs. It is the prologue to your actions. It is the prologue to your inactivity. It is the prologue to your lying down, to your sitting, to your standing, to your walking. It is the prologue to the plays and to the seriousness of your life. It is also the prologue to your future visits to the theater. It is also the prologue to all other prologues. This piece is world theater.

Soon you will move. You will make preparations. You will prepare yourself to applaud. You will prepare yourself not to applaud. When you prepare to do the former, you will clap one hand against the other, that is to say, you will clap one palm to the other palm and repeat these claps in rapid succession. Meanwhile, you will be able to watch your hands clapping or not clapping. You will hear the sound of yourself clapping and the sound of clapping next to you and you will see next to you and in front of you the clapping hands bobbing back and forth or you will not hear the expected clapping and not see the hands bobbing back and forth. Instead, you will perhaps hear other sounds and will yourself produce other sounds. You will prepare to get up. You will hear the seats folding up behind you. You will see us taking our bows. You will see the curtain come together. You will be able to designate the noises the curtain makes during this process. You will pocket your programs. You will exchange glances. You will exchange words. You will get moving. You will make comments and hear comments. You will suppress comments. You will smile meaningfully. You will smile meaninglessly. You will push in an orderly fashion into the foyer. You will show your hatchecks to redeem your hats and coats. You will stand around. You will see yourselves in mirrors. You will help each other into coats. You will hold doors open for each other. You will say your goodbyes. You will accompany. You will be accompanied. You will step into the open. You will return into the everyday. You will go in different directions. If you remain together, you will be a theater party. You will go to a restaurant. You will think of tomorrow. You will gradually find your way back into reality. You will be able to call reality harsh again. You will be sobered up. You will lead your own lives again. You will no longer be a unit. You will go from one place to different places.

But before you leave you will be offended.

We will offend you because offending you is also one way of speaking to you. By offending you, we can be straight with you. We can switch you on. We can eliminate the free play. We can tear down a wall. We can observe you.

790   While we are offending you, you won't just hear us, you will listen to us. The distance between us will no longer be infinite. Due to the fact that we're offending you, your motionlessness and your rigidity will finally become overt. But we won't offend *you*, we will merely use offensive words which you yourselves use. We will contradict ourselves with our offenses. We will mean no one in particular. We will only create an acoustic pattern. You won't have to feel offended. You were warned in advance, so you can feel quite unoffended while we're offending you. Since you are probably

800   thoroughly offended already, we will waste no more time before thoroughly offending you, you chuckleheads.

You let the impossible become possible. You were the heroes of this piece. You were sparing with your gestures. Your parts were well rounded. Your scenes were unforgettable. You did not play, you *were* the part. You were a happening. You were the find of the evening. You lived your roles. You had a lion's share of the success. You saved the piece. You were a sight. You were a sight to have seen, you ass-kissers.

You were always with it. Your honest toiling didn't help the

810   piece a bit. You contributed only the cues. The best you created was the little you left out. Your silences said everything, you small-timers.

You were thoroughbred actors. You began promisingly. You were true to life. You were realistic. You put everything under your spell. You played us off the stage. You reached Shakespearean heights, you jerks, you hoodlums, you scum of the melting pot.

Not one wrong note crossed your lips. You had control of every scene. Your playing was of exquisite nobility. Your counte-

820   nances were of rare exquisiteness. You were a smashing cast. You were a dream cast. You were inimitable, your faces unforgettable. Your sense of humor left us gasping. Your tragedy was of antique grandeur. You gave your best, you party-poopers, you freeloaders, you fuddy-duddies, you bubbleheads, you powder puffs, you sitting ducks.

You were one of a kind. You had one of your better days tonight. You played ensemble. You were imitations of life, you drips, you diddlers, you atheists, you double-dealers, you switch-hitters, you dirty Jews.

830   You showed us brand-new vistas. You were well advised to do this piece. You outdid yourselves. You played yourselves loose. You turned yourselves inside out, you lonely crowd, you culture vultures, you nervous nellies, you bronco busters, you moneybags, you potheads, you washouts, you wet smacks, you fire eaters, you generation of freaks, you

hopped-up sons and daughters of the revolution, you napalm specialists.

You were priceless. You were a hurricane. You drove shudders up our spines. You swept everything before you, you Vietnam bandits, you savages, you rednecks, you hatchet men, 840 you subhumans, you fiends, you beasts in human shape, you killer pigs.

You were the right ones. You were breathtaking. You did not disappoint our wildest hopes. You were born actors. Playacting was in your blood, you butchers, you buggers, you bullshitters, you bullies, you rabbits, you fuck-offs, you farts.

You had perfect breath-control, you windbags, you waspish wasps, you wags, you gargoyles, you tackheads, you milquetoasts, you mickey-mice, you chicken-shits, you cheap skates, you wrong numbers, you zeros, you back numbers, 850 you one-shots, you centipedes, you supernumeraries, you superfluous lives, you crumbs, you cardboard figures, you *pain* in the mouth.

You are accomplished actors, you hucksters, you traitors to your country, you grafters, you would-be revolutionaries, you reactionaries, you draft-card burners, you ivory-tower artists, you defeatists, you massive retaliators, you whiterabbit pacifists, you nihilists, you individualists, you Communists, you vigilantes, you socialists, you minute men, you whizz-kids, you turtledoves, you crazy hawks, you stool pi- 860 geons, you worms, you antediluvian monstrosities, you claquers, you clique of babbits, you rabble, you blubber, you quivering reeds, you wretches, you ofays, you oafs, you spooks, you blackbaiters, you cooky pushers, you abortions, you bitches and bastards, you nothings, you thingamajigs.

O you cancer victims, O you hemorrhoid sufferers, O you multiple sclerotics, O you syphilitics, O you cardiac conditions, O you paraplegics, O you catatonics, O you schizoids, O you paranoids, O you hypochondriacs, O you carriers of causes of death, O you suicide candidates, O you potential peace- 870 time casualties, O you potential war dead, O you potential accident victims, O you potential increase in the mortality rate, O you potential dead.

You wax figures. You impersonators. You bad-hats. You troupers. You tear-jerkers. You potboilers. You foul mouths. You sell-outs. You deadbeats. You phonies. You milestones in the history of the theater. You historic moments. You immortal souls. You positive heroes. You abortionists. You anti-heroes. You everyday heroes. You luminaries of science. You beacons in the dark. You educated gasbags. You 880 cultivated classes. You befuddled aristocrats. You rotten middle class. You lowbrows. You people of our time. You children of the world. You sadsacks. You church and lay dignitaries. You wretches. You congressmen. You commissioners. You scoundrels. You generals. You lobbyists. You Chiefs of Staff. You chairmen of this and that. You tax evaders. You presidential advisers. You U–2 pilots. You agents. You corporate-military establishment. You entrepreneurs. You Eminencies. You Excellencies. You Holiness. Mr. President. You crowned heads. You pushers. You architects of 890 the future. You builders of a better world. You mafiosos. You wiseacres. You smarty-pants. You who embrace life. You who detest life. You who have no feeling about life. You ladies and gents you, you celebrities of public and cultural life you, you who are present you, you brothers and sisters you, you comrades you, you worthy listeners you, you fellow humans you.

You were welcome here. We thank you. Good night.

*(The curtain comes together at once. However, it does not remain closed but parts again immediately regardless of the behavior of the public. The speakers stand and look at the public without looking at anyone in particular. Roaring applause and wild whistling is piped in through the loudspeakers; to this, one might add taped audience reaction to pop music concerts. The deafening howling and yelling lasts until the public begins to leave. Only then does the curtain come together once and for all.)*

---

*HANDKE'S notes to* Offending the Audience *help to specify some of the ways in which this play might engage its audience.*

# Peter Handke

## Notes to *Offending the Audience*
(1966)

The speak-ins *(Sprechstücke)* are spectacles without pictures, inasmuch as they give no picture of the world. They point to the world not by way of pictures but by way of words; the words of the speak-ins don't point at the world as something lying outside the words but to the world in the words themselves. The words that make up the speak-ins give no picture of the world but a concept of it. The speak-ins are theatrical inasmuch as they employ natural forms of expression found in reality. They employ only such expressions as are natural in real speech; that is, they employ the speech forms that are uttered *orally* in real life. The speak-ins employ natural examples of swearing, of self-indictment, of confession, of testimony, of interrogation, of justification, of evasion, of prophecy, of calls for help. Therefore they need a vis-à-vis, at least *one* person who listens; otherwise, they would not be natural but extorted by the author. It is to that extent that my speak-ins are pieces for the theater. Ironically, they imitate the gestures of all the given devices natural to the theater.

The speak-ins have no action, since every action on stage would only be the picture of another action. The speak-ins confine themselves, by obeying their natural form, to words. They give no pictures, not even pictures in word form, which would only be pictures the author extorted to represent an internal, unexpressed, wordless circumstance and not a *natural* expression.

Speak-ins are autonomous prologues to the old plays. They do not want to revolutionize, but to make aware.

# Marguerite Duras

Born in 1914, Marguerite Duras was raised in Indochina (now Vietnam) during the period of French colonial rule; although she visited France occasionally, much of her youth was spent in Vietnam, which would later provide the setting for her most powerful novels. After completing school in Saigon, Duras went to Paris in 1932 and took degrees in law and political science in 1935. She became a secretary in the Department of Colonies and began to write as well; her first novel, *The Impudent Ones* was published in 1943. Much of Duras's fiction involves her sense of the exploitation and poverty of the Vietnam of her youth, which provides the background for an intense exploration of personal relationships; this is particularly true of *The Sea Wall* (1950) and *The Lover* (1984); other novels, such as *Moderato Cantabile* (1958) and *The Vice-Consul* (1965), are set elsewhere in Asia; they also confront the depredations of colonial exploitation.

Duras's drama similarly centers on interpersonal conflict, in short plays like *The Square* (1956), the murder-thriller *The Viaduct* (1963), *Water and Forests* (1965), *La Musica* (1966), and in her first full-length play, *Days in the Trees* (1966). Duras's evocative sense of the visual is explored in other genres as well; her powerful film *Hiroshima Mon Amour* (1959), directed by Alain Resnais, won the International Critics' Prize at the Cannes Film Festival in 1959. In the 1960s, Duras's experiments with nonlinear narrative led her to other cinematic projects. She directed the filming of her own *Days in the Trees* (1976), wrote two other films, *Aurélia Steiner* (1979) and *The Atlantic Man* (1982), and experimented with a simultaneous film/fiction version of the same work, *Destroy, She Said* (1969). *India Song* (1972), commissioned by Peter Hall for the opening of the Lyttleton Theater of London's National Theatre, is part of Duras's efforts to transgress the boundaries of the genre. Based on her novel *The Vice-Consul,* it is at once a play and a film scenario, and Duras produced and directed the film version of *India Song* in 1975.

## India Song (1972)

In an interview published in 1987, Duras remarked on her interest in a theater in which language and acting would be held separate from one another, in which the voice alone would register the drama: "No need to gesticulate to show how the body is suffering because of the words being uttered: the whole drama resides in the words themselves and the body remains unmoved" (see *Practicalities.* Trans. Barbara Bray. New York: Grove Weidenfeld, 1990. p 9). This special sense of the different registers of representation that can be achieved by the voice and the body stands at the center of Duras's play *India Song.* As she suggests in her "General Remarks" to the play, she has drawn characters from her novel *The Vice-Consul* and projected them "into new narrative regions." There are, nonetheless, a number of stylistic and narrative similarities between the two works. Both centrally concern Anne-Marie Stretter and the various colonial officials and businessmen who surround her—her husband, the Young Attaché (named Charles Rossett in the novel), Michael Richardson, and the mysterious Vice-Consul, waiting in disgrace in Calcutta after wildly shooting at lepers in the Shalimar Gardens of Lahore. And in both the novel and the play the Europeans, the "whites," live in a constant state of mental oppression, as the heat, the poverty, the futility of India seem to drive them to the brink of madness—and possibly beyond it. Finally, in both works, Anne-Marie—originally from Venice, mysteriously married, perhaps rescued by marriage in Savannakhet, Laos—is paired with the beggar woman, abandoned as a child, living on scraps of food from the Embassy and fish she catches and eats raw from the Ganges, a woman whose vitality, suffering, degradation, and dignity make her a kind of alter-ego to Stretter herself.

While both works have an extraordinary lyricism, *India Song* deploys that lyricism onstage in effective and original ways. *India Song* is centrally about desire, the desire that circulates around, and largely objectifies its central character, Anne-Marie Stretter. The play opens with Anne-Marie lying dead onstage and closes with her suicide; it is centrally occupied with how she is desired: by the male characters in the play, and, more powerfully by the voices, male and female, that narrate the action. For in many ways *India Song* is less about the narrative, the "plot" of the interinvolved love affairs that the play brings together, than about how "Anne-Marie Stretter" is positioned as an object of desire, both in the narrative past and in the theatrical present. Much as the play's voices produce Anne-Marie, they also fetishize her, and the play systematically forces its audience into a similar position of voyeurism, where the desire for narrative closure becomes inseparable from the desire for Stretter herself. This dimension of the play becomes clear early in the action, where Stretter, the *"white of the naked body"* visible onstage *"freezes. Head thrown back. Gasping for air. Touching grace of the thin, fragile body. Stays like that, upright, exposed. Offered to the voices. The voices are slow, stifled, a prey to desire—through this motionless body."* The voices are prey to desire, but Stretter is also their victim; more important, the scene laminates the audience to the voices, suggesting that narration, the desire to tell the story, is inseparable from spectating, the desire to *see* Stretter there, powerless before our gaze on the stage. In *India Song,* the offstage voices are unable to achieve a kind of narrative closure to complete the story; what they are able to do is to evoke their dependence, their realization through the story they narrate. In this sense, Duras forges an explicit critique of theater in *India Song,* which suggests that the stage necessarily animates desire and renders it visible.

# —India Song—

## Marguerite Duras

TRANSLATED BY BARBARA BRAY

## —GENERAL REMARKS—

The names of Indian towns, rivers, states, and seas are used here primarily in a musical sense.

All references to physical, human, or political geography are incorrect:

You can't drive from Calcutta to the estuary of the Ganges in an afternoon. Nor to Nepal.

The "Prince of Wales" hotel is not on an island in the Delta, but in Colombo.

And New Delhi, not Calcutta, is the administrative capital of India.

And so on.

The characters in the story have been taken out of a book called *The Vice-Consul* and projected into new narrative regions. So it is not possible to relate them back to the book and see *India Song* as a film or theatre adaptation of *The Vice-Consul*. Even where a whole episode is taken over from the book, its insertion into the new narrative means that it has to be read, seen, differently.

In fact, *India Song* follows on from *The Woman of the Ganges*. If *The Woman of the Ganges* hadn't been written, neither would *India Song*. The fact that it goes into and reveals an unexplored area of *The Vice-Consul* wouldn't have been a sufficient reason.

What was a sufficient reason was the discovery, in *The Woman of the Ganges*, of the *means* of exploration, revelation: the voices external to the narrative. This discovery made it possible to let the narrative be forgotten and put at the disposal of memories other than that of the author: memories which might remember, in the same way, any other love story. Memories that distort. That create.

Some voices from *The Woman of the Ganges* have been used here. And even some of their words.

That is about all that can be said.

As far as I know, no "India Song" yet exists. When it has been written, the author will make it available and it should be used for all performances of *India Song* in France and elsewhere.

If by any chance *India Song* were performed in France, there should be no public dress rehearsal. This does not apply to other countries.

## —ONE—

## —NOTES ON VOICES 1 AND 2—

VOICES 1 and 2 are women's voices. Young.

They are linked together by a love story.

Sometimes they speak of this love, their own. Most of the time they speak of another love, another story. But this other story leads us back to theirs. And vice versa.

Unlike the men's voices—VOICES 3 and 4, which don't come in until the end of the narrative—the women's voices are tinged with madness. Their sweetness is pernicious. Their memory of the love story is illogical, anarchic. Most of the time they are in a state of transport, a delirium, at once calm and feverish. VOICE 1 is consumed with the story of ANNE-MARIE STRETTER. VOICE 2 is consumed with its passion for VOICE 1.

They should always be heard with perfect clarity, but the level varies according to what they are saying. They are most immediately present when they veer toward their own story—that is, when, in the course of a perpetual shifting process, the love story of *India Song* is juxtaposed with their own. But there is a distinction. When they speak of the story we see unfolding before us, they rediscover it at the same time we do, and so are frightened and perhaps moved by it in the same way we are. But when they speak of their own story, they are always shot through with desire, and we should feel the difference between their two passions. Above all, we should feel the terror of VOICE 2 at the fascination the resuscitated story exerts over VOICE 1. VOICE 1 is in danger of being "lost" in the story of *India Song*, which is in the past, legendary, a model. VOICE 1 is in danger of departing its own life.

The voices are never raised, and their sweetness remains constant.

*Blackout.*

*A tune from between the two wars, "India Song," is played slowly on the piano.*

*It is played right through, to cover the time—always long—that it takes the audience, or the reader, to emerge from the ordinary world they are in when the performance, or the book, begins.*

*"India Song" still.*

*Still.*

*And now it ends.*

*Now it is repeated, "farther away" than the first time, as if it were being played elsewhere.*

*Now it is played at its usual rhythm—blues.*

*The darkness begins to lighten.*

*As the dark slowly disperses, suddenly there are voices. Others besides ourselves were watching, hearing, what we thought we alone were watching and hearing. They are women. The voices are slow, sweet. Very close, enclosed like us in this place. And intangible, inaccessible.*

VOICE 1: He followed her to India.
VOICE 2: Yes.

*(Pause.)*

VOICE 2: For he left everything.
  Overnight.
VOICE 1: The night of the dance?
VOICE 2: Yes.

*(The light continues to grow. We still hear "India Song." The voices are silent for some time. Then they begin again:)*

VOICE 1: Was it she who played the piano?
VOICE 2: *(hesitating)* Yes . . . but he played too . . . It was he who used sometimes, in the evening, to play the tune they played
10    in S. Thala . . .

*(Silence.)*
*(A house in India. Huge. A "white people's" house. Divans. Armchairs.)*
*(Furniture of the period of "India Song.")*
*(A ceiling fan is working, but at nightmare slowness.)*
*(Net screens over the windows. Beyond, the paths of a large tropical garden. Oleanders. Palm trees.)*
*(Complete stillness. No wind outside. Inside, dense shadow. Is it the evening? We don't know. Space. Gilt. A piano. Unlit chandeliers. Indoor plants. Nothing moves, nothing except the fan, which moves with nightmare "unreality.")*
*(The slowness of the voices goes with the very slow growth of the light; their sweetness matches the poignancy of the setting.)*

VOICE 1: *(as if reading)* "Michael Richardson was engaged to a girl from S. Thala. Lola Valérie Stein.
  They were to have been married in the autumn.
  Then there was the dance.
  The dance at S. Thala . . . "

*(Silence.)*

VOICE 2: She arrived at the dance late . . . in the middle of the night . . .
VOICE 1: Yes . . . *dressed in black* . . .
  What love, at the dance . . .
20    What desire . . .

*(Silence.)*
*(As the light grows we see, set in this colonial décor, presences. There were people there all the time.)*
*(They are behind either a row of plants, or a fine net screen, or a transparent blind, or smoke from perfume burners—something which makes the second part of the space explored less easily visible.)*
*(Lying on a divan, long, slender, almost thin, is a woman dressed in black.)*
*(Sitting close to her is a man, also dressed in black.)*
*(Away from the lovers there is another man in black. [One of the men is smoking a cigarette—is that what made us sense there were people there?])*
*(VOICE 1 discovers—after we do—the presence of the woman in black.)*

VOICE 1: *(tense, low)* Anne-Marie Stretter . . .

*(It is as if* VOICE 2 *had not heard.)*

VOICE 2: *(low)* How pale you are . . . what are you frightened of . . .

*(No answer.)*
*(Silence.)*
*(The three people seem struck by a deathly stillness. "India Song" has stopped.)*
*(The voices grow lower, to match the deathliness of the scene.)*

VOICE 2: After she died, he left India . . .

*(Silence.)*
*(That was said all in one breath, as if recited slowly. So the woman in black, there in front of us, is dead. The light is now steady, somber.)*
*(Silence everywhere.)*
*(Near and far.)*
*(The voices are full of pain. Their memory, which was gone, is coming back. But they are as sweet, as gentle as before.)*

VOICE 2: She's buried in the English cemetery . . .

*(Pause.)*

VOICE 1: . . . she died there?
VOICE 2: In the islands. *(Hesitates.)* One night. Found dead.

*(Silence.)*
*("India Song" again, slow, far away.)*
*(At first we don't see the movement, the beginnings of movement. But it begins exactly on the first note of "India Song.")*
*(The woman in black and the man sitting near her begin to stir. Emerge from death. Their footsteps make no sound.)*
*(They are standing up.)*
*(They are close together.)*
*(What are they doing?)*
*(They are dancing.)*
*(Dancing. We only realize it when they are already dancing.)*
*(They go on, slowly, dancing.)*
*(When* VOICE 1 *speaks they have been dancing for some time.)*
*(VOICE 1 is gradually remembering.)*

VOICE 1: The French Embassy in India . . .      30
VOICE 2: Yes.

*(Pause.)*

VOICE 1: That murmur? The Ganges?
VOICE 2: Yes.

*(Pause.)*

VOICE 1: That light?
VOICE 2: The monsoon.
VOICE 1: . . . no wind . . .
VOICE 2: *(continues)* . . . it will break over Bengal . . .
VOICE 1: The dust?
VOICE 2: The middle of Calcutta.

*(Silence.)*

VOICE 1: Isn't there a smell of flowers?      40
VOICE 2: Leprosy.

*(Silence.)*
*(They are still dancing to "India Song.")*
*(They are dancing. But it needs to be said.)*

*([As if otherwise it weren't sure. And so that the image and the voices coincide, touch.])*

VOICE 2: They're dancing.

*(Silence.)*

VOICE 2: In the evening they used to dance.

*(Silence.)*
*(They dance.)*
*(So close they are one.)*
*("India Song" fades in the distance.)*
*(They are merged together in the dance, almost motionless.)*
*(Now quite motionless.)*

VOICE 2: Why are you crying?

*(No answer.)*
*(Silence.)*
*(No more music.)*
*(A murmur in the distance. Then it stops. Other murmurs.)*
*(They, the man and woman, are still motionless in the silence hemmed in by sound.)*
*(Fixed. Arrested.)*
*(It lasts a long while.)*
*(Over the fixed couple:)*

VOICE 2: I love you so much I can't see any more, can't hear . . .
        . . . can't live . . .

*(No answer.)*
*(Silence.)*
*("India Song" comes back from far away. Slowly the couple unfreeze, come back to life.)*
*(Sound increases behind the music: the sound of Calcutta: a loud, a great murmur. All around, various other sounds. The regular cries of merchants. Dogs. Shouts in the distance.)*
*(As the sound outside increases, the sky in the garden becomes overcast. Murky light. No wind.)*
*(Silence.)*
*(The couple separate and turn toward the garden. They look out at it, motionless.)*
*(The second man sitting there also begins to look out at the garden.)*
*(The light grows still murkier.)*
*(The sound of Calcutta ceases.)*
*(Waiting.)*
*(Waiting. It is almost dark.)*
*(Suddenly the waiting is over:)*
*(The noise of the rain.)*
*(A cool, slaking noise.)*
*(It is raining over Bengal.)*
*(The rain cannot be seen. Only heard. As if it were raining everywhere except in the garden, deleted from life.)*
*(Everyone looks at the sound of the rain.)*

VOICE 2: *(scarcely voiced)* It's raining over Bengal . . .
VOICE 1: An ocean . . .

*(Silence.)*
*(Cries in the distance, of joy, shouts in Hindustani, the unknown language.)*
*(The light gradually returns.)*
*(The rain, the noise, very loud for a few seconds.)*

*(It grows less. Isolated shouts and laughter are heard more clearly through the sound of the rain.)*
*(The light continues to grow stronger.)*
*(Suddenly, clearer, nearer cries—a woman's. Her laughter.)*

VOICE 1: Someone's shouting . . . a woman . . .                    50
VOICE 2: What?
VOICE 1: Disconnected words. She's laughing.
VOICE 2: A beggar.

*(Pause.)*

VOICE 1: Mad?
VOICE 2: Yes . . .

*(In the garden paths, sun after the rain. Moving sunlight. Patches of light, gray, pale.)*
*(Still the shouting and laughter of the* BEGGAR WOMAN.*)*

VOICE 1: Oh yes . . . I remember. She goes by the banks of the rivers . . . is she from Burma?
VOICE 2: Yes.

*(While the voices speak of the beggar, the three people move, leave the room by side doors.)*

VOICE 2: She's not Indian.
        She comes from Savannakhet.                              60
        Born there.
VOICE 1: Ah yes . . . yes . . .
        One day . . . she's been walking ten years, and one day, there in front of her, the Ganges?
VOICE 2: Yes.
        And there she stops.
VOICE 1: Yes . . .

*(The three people have disappeared. The place is empty.)*
*(Someone speaking, almost shouting, in the distance, in a soft-sounding language, Laotian.)*

VOICE 1: *(after a pause)* Twelve children die while she's walking to Bengal . . . ?
VOICE 2: Yes. She leaves them. Sells them. Forgets them.          70
        *(Pause.)* On the way to Bengal, becomes barren.

*(The three people reach the garden and stroll slowly through the cool after the rain, moving through the patches of sunlight. In the distance, the shouting of the* BEGGAR WOMAN, *still. Suddenly, in the shouting, the word* SAVANNAKHET.*)*
*(The voices halt briefly. Then resume:)*

VOICE 1: Savannakhet—Laos?
VOICE 2: Yes. *(Pause.)* Seventeen . . . she's pregnant, she's seventeen . . . *(Pause.)* She's turned out by her mother, goes away. *(Pause.)* She asks the way to get lost. Remember? No one knows.
VOICE 1: *(pause)* Yes.
        One day, she's been walking ten years, and one day:
        Calcutta, there in front of her.
        She stays.                                               80

*(Silence.)*

VOICE 2: She's there on the banks of the Ganges, under the trees. She has forgotten.

*(Silence.)*

*(The three people go out of the garden.)*
*(Movements of light, monsoon, in the empty garden.)*
*(The song of the beggar—"song of Savannakhet"—in the distance.)*
*([*VOICE 2 *is informative, calm, gentle.])*

VOICE 2: Lepers burst like sacks of dust, you know.
VOICE 1: Don't suffer?
VOICE 2: No. Not a thing.
  Laugh.

*(Silence.)*

VOICE 2: They were there together, in Calcutta. The white woman and the other. During the same years.

*(The voices are silent.)*
*(A distant part of the garden, so far very dark, as if neglected by the lighting, gradually becomes visible. It is revealed by spotlights—extremely slowly, but regularly, mathematically.)*
*(Far away, the song of Savannakhet—coming, going. Sound of Calcutta, in the distance.)*
*(The wire netting round a tennis court emerges from the darkness. Against the wire a woman's bicycle—red.)*
*(The place is deserted.)*
*(The voices recognize these things and are afraid:)*

VOICE 1: *(smothered exclamation of fear)* The tennis courts, deserted . . .
90
VOICE 2: *(the same)* . . . Anne-Marie Stretter's red bicycle . . .

*(Silence.)*
*(A man has come into the garden. Tall, thin, dressed in white. He walks slowly. His footsteps make no sound.)*
*(He gazes around him at the stillness everywhere. Gazes for some time. Tries to see into the house: no one there.)*
*(Now what is he looking at? We don't know at first. Then it becomes clear: he's looking at* ANNE-MARIE STRETTER's *red bicycle by the deserted tennis courts.)*
*(He goes over to the bicycle. Stops. Hesitates. Doesn't go any nearer. Looks, stares at it. [The voices are low, scared.])*

VOICE 2: . . . he comes every night . . .

*(Pause.)*

VOICE 1: The French Vice-Consul in Lahore . . .
VOICE 2: Yes.
  . . . in Calcutta in disgrace . . .

*(Silence.)*
*(Slowly, the man in white moves. He walks. He goes along a path. He goes away.)*
*(Disappears.)*
*(After he has disappeared, everything remains in suspense.)*
*(Silence. Fear.)*
*(The song of Savannakhet, in the distance, innocent.)*
*(Then, two shots.)*
*(The first makes the light go dim.)*
*(The second makes it go out.)*
*(Silence.)*
*(Blackout.)*
*(The song of Savannakhet stopped when the shots were fired. As if they had been aimed at it.)*
*(Silence.)*

*(Blackout.)*
*(The voices are very quiet, terrified.)*

VOICE 2: Someone fired a gun under the trees . . . on the banks of the Ganges . . .

*(Silence.)*

VOICE 1: It was a song of Savannakhet . . . ?
VOICE 2: Yes.

*(Silence.)*
*(By a strictly symmetrical inversion, and without passing through any intermediate stages, the light becomes the same as it was when the first shot made it go dim.)*
*(This stands for night.)*
*(It is night.)*
*(The place, the stage, is still empty.)*
*(The only movement—that of the nightmare fan.)*
*(Time passes over the empty place.)*
*(Silence.)*
*(A Hindu servant dressed in white goes by, passing through the drawing rooms of the French Embassy.)*
*(He has gone. Emptiness again.)*
*( Far away, the song of Savannakhet begins again: the* BEGGAR WOMAN *wasn't killed.)*
*(The voices are still low, frightened.)*

VOICE 1: . . . she's not dead . . .
100
VOICE 2: Can't die.
VOICE 1: *(scarcely heard)* No . . .

*(Silence.)*

VOICE 2: She goes hunting at night beside the Ganges. For food . . .

*(No answer.)*
*(Silence.)*

VOICE 1: Where's the one dressed in black?
VOICE 2: Out. Every evening.
  She comes back when it's dark

*(Silence.)*
*(A servant enters, lights a lamp, very faint, in a corner of the room. Does various things.)*
*(Goes away [but remains visible].)*
*(Comes back.)*
*(Opens a window.)*
*(Perhaps he lights some sticks of incense against the mosquitoes—in which case the audience will be able to smell it.)*
*(Empties ashtrays.)*

VOICE 2: She's back.
  The Embassy's black Lancia has just come through the gates.
110
*(Silence.)*
*(The servant goes out.)*
*(The place remains empty for a few more seconds, and then the woman in black enters the darkness. She is barefoot. Her hair is loose. She is wearing a short wrap of loose black cotton.)*
*(The scene is very long and slow.)*
*(Slowly she goes and stands under the nightmare fan. Stays there.)*
*(Puts up her hands and thrusts her hair away from her body in*

*a gesture of exhaustion—someone stifling from the heat. Then lets her arms fall down by her sides.)*
*(Through the opening of the wrap, the white of the naked body.)*
*(She freezes. Head thrown back. Gasping for air. Trying to escape out of the heat.)*
*(Touching grace of the thin, fragile body.)*
*(Stays like that, upright, exposed. Offered to the voices.)*
*([The voices are slow, stifled, a prey to desire—through this motionless body.])*

120 VOICE 2: *(smothered outburst)* How lovely you look dressed in white . . .

*(Pause.)*

VOICE 1: I'd like to go and visit the woman of the Ganges . . .

*(Held pause.)*

VOICE 1: . . . the white woman . . .
VOICE 2: *(pause)* The one who . . . ?
VOICE 1: Her . . .
VOICE 2: . . . dead in the islands . . .
VOICE 1: Eyes dead, blinded with light.
VOICE 2: Yes.
130     There under the stone.
    In a bend in the Ganges.

*(Silence.)*
*(Still motionless before us, the dead woman of the Ganges.)*
*(The voices are a song so quiet it does not awaken her death.)*
*(Apparently nothing changes, nothing happens. But suddenly, fear.)*

VOICE 1: *(low, frightened)* What is it?

*(No answer.)*

VOICE 1: *(as before)* What time is it?
VOICE 2: *(pause)* Four o'clock.
    Black night.

*(Pause.)*

VOICE 1: No one can sleep?
VOICE 2: No.

*(Silence.)*
*(Tears on the woman's face.)*
*(The features remain unmoving.)*
*(She is weeping. Without suffering.)*
*(A state of tears.)*
*(The voices speak of the heat, they speak of desire—as if the voices were issuing from the weeping body.)*

VOICE 1: The heat
    Impossible
140     Terrible

*(Pause.)*

VOICE 2: Another storm . . .
    Approaching Bengal . . .
VOICE 1: *(pause)* Coming from the islands . . .
VOICE 2: *(pause)* The estuaries.
    Inexhaustible . . .

*(Silence.)*

VOICE 1: What's that sound?
VOICE 2: *(pause)* Her weeping.

*(Silence.)*

VOICE 1: Doesn't suffer, does she . . . ?
VOICE 2: She neither.
    A leper, of the heart.       150

*(Silence.)*

VOICE 1: Can't bear it . . . ?
VOICE 2: No.
    Can't bear it.
    Can't bear India.

*(Silence.)*
*(A man enters through the door on the left. He too is wearing a black wrap.)*
*(He halts, looks at her.)*
*(Then slowly goes over to her, a statue in her tears, under the fan, asleep.)*
*(He looks at her—asleep standing up. Goes right up to her.)*
*(Passes lightly over her face a hand outspread in a caress. Takes his hand away, looks at it: it is wet from the tears.)*

VOICE 2: *(very low)* She's asleep.

*(With infinite precaution, the man takes up the weeping woman and lays her down on the floor.)*
*(He's the man we have already seen, the man she danced with at the dance in S. Thala:* MICHAEL RICHARDSON.*)*
*(He sits down beside the outstretched body.)*
*(Looks at it.)*
*(Uncovers the body so that it is better exposed to the cool—imaginary—from the fan.)*
*(Strokes her forehead. Wipes away the tears, the sweat. Caresses the sleeping body.)*
*(Doesn't go close. Stays there watching over her sleep.)*
*(The voices slow down to the rhythm of the man's movements, taking up again in a sort of sung complaint the themes adjacent to the main story.)*

VOICE 1: He loved her more than anything in the world.
VOICE 2: *(pause)* More even than that . . .

*(Silence.)*
*(*VOICE 2 *spoke as if of its own love.)*

VOICE 1: Where was the girl from S. Thala?

*(No answer.)*

VOICE 1: *(as if reading)* "From behind the indoor plants in the bar, she watches them. *(Pause.)* It was only at dawn . . . 160 *(Stops.)* . . . when the lovers were going toward the door of the ballroom that Lola Valérie Stein uttered a cry."

*(Silence.)*
*(In the distance, a regular cry in Hindustani. Someone selling something again.)*
*(It stops.)*
*(Quiet.)*

VOICE 2: At four in the morning, sometimes, sleep comes.

*(Silence.)*

*(The lover is still beside the sleeping body.)*
*(He looks at it.)*
*(Takes the hands, touches them. Looks at them. They fall back, dead.)*
*(Silence.)*

VOICE 1: She never got over it, the girl from S. Thala?
VOICE 2: Never.
VOICE 1: They didn't hear her cry out?
VOICE 2: No.
　Couldn't hear any more.
　Couldn't see.

*(Pause.)*

170　VOICE 1: *(pause)* They abandoned her? *(Pause.)* Killed her?
VOICE 2: Yes.

*(Pause.)*

VOICE 1: And with this crime behind them . . .
VOICE 2: *(scarcely heard)* Yes.

*(Silence.)*

VOICE 1: What did the girl from S. Thala want?
VOICE 2: To go with them
　See them
　The lovers of the Ganges: to see them.

*(Silence.)*
*(That is what we are doing: seeing.)*
*(Slowly the man lies down beside the sleeping body. His hand goes on caressing the face, the body.)*
*(Far away, distant sounds, oars, water. Then laughter, a zither, fading in the distance.)*
*(Then it stops.)*

VOICE 2: Listen . . .
　Ganges fishermen . . .
180　Musicians . . .

*(Silence again.)*
*(The voices speak of the heat again. Of their desire.)*

VOICE 2: *(very slow)* What darkness
　What heat
　Unmitigated
　Deathly

*(Silence.)*
*(A voice that is clear, implacable, terrifying:)*

VOICE 2: I love you with a desire that is absolute.

*(No answer.)*
*(Silence.)*
*(The hand of* MICHAEL RICHARDSON*—the lover—immediately stops caressing the body, as if arrested by what* VOICE 2 *has just said.)*
*(It lies there where it is on the body.)*
*(Silence.)*
*(A second man enters the room. He stands in the doorway for a moment, looking at the lovers.)*
*(*MICHAEL RICHARDSON*'s hand starts to move again, caressing the uncovered body.)*
*(The man goes over to them.)*

*(Like the lover, he sits down beside her.)*
*(The lover's hand now moves more slowly.)*
*(Then it stops.)*
*(The newcomer does not caress the woman's body.)*
*(He lies down too.)*
*(All three lie motionless under the fan.)*
*(Silence.)*
*(Rain.)*
*(Another storm over Bengal.)*
*(The sound of rain over sleep.)*
*(The voices are like breaths of coolness, gentle murmurs.)*

VOICE 1: . . . rain . . .
VOICE 2: . . . yes . . .

*(Pause.)*

VOICE 1: . . . cool . . .

*(Silence.)*
*(The sky gets lighter, but it is still night.)*
*(Gradually, music: Beethoven's 14th Variation on a Theme of Diabelli. Piano, very distant.)*
*(The rain slackens.)*
*(In its place, a white light. Patches of moonlight on the garden paths. No wind.)*
*(The three bodies, their eyes closed, sleep.)*
*(The voices, interwoven, in a climax of sweetness, are about to sing the legend of* ANNE-MARIE STRETTER*. A slow recitative made up of scraps of memory. Out of it, every so often, a phrase emerges, intact, from oblivion.)*

VOICE 1: Venice.
　She was from Venice . . .
VOICE 2: Yes. The music was in Venice.　　　　190
　A hope in music . . .
VOICE 1: *(pause)* She never gave up playing?
VOICE 2: No.

*(Silence.)*

VOICE 1: *(very slow)* Anna Maria Guardi . . .
VOICE 2: Yes.

*(Silence.)*

VOICE 1: The first marriage, the first post . . . ?
VOICE 2: Savannakhet, Laos.
　She's married to a French colonial official.
　She's eighteen.　　　　　　　　　　　　　　200
VOICE 1: *(remembering)* Ah yes . . . a river . . .
　. . . she's sitting by a river. Already . . .
　Looking at it.
VOICE 2: The Mekong.
VOICE 1: *(pause)* She's silent?
　Crying?
VOICE 2: Yes. They say: "She can't get acclimatized. She'll have to be sent back to Europe."

*(Pause.)*

VOICE 1: Couldn't bear it. Even then.
VOICE 2: Even then.　　　　　　　　　　　　　　210

*(Silence.)*

VOICE 1: *(visionary)* Those walls all round her?

VOICE 2: The grounds of the chancellery.
VOICE 1: (*as before*) The sentries?
VOICE 2: Official.
VOICE 1: Even then . . .
VOICE 2: Yes.
VOICE 1: Even then, couldn't bear it.
VOICE 2: No.

(*Silence.*)

VOICE 2: One day a government launch calls. Monsieur Stret-
220    ter is inspecting the posts on the Mekong.
VOICE 1: (*pause*) He takes her away from Savannakhet?
VOICE 2: Yes. Takes her with him.
    Takes her with him for seventeen years through the capitals
    of Asia.

(*Pause.*)

VOICE 2: You find her in Peking.
    Then in Mandalay.
    In Bangkok.
    Rangoon. Sydney.
    Lahore.
230    Seventeen years.
    You find her in Calcutta.
    In Calcutta:
    She dies.

(*Silence.*)
(*The tall thin man dressed in white enters the garden.*)
(*The voices haven't seen him.*)
(*He stops. Looks through the screens on the windows at the three sleeping forms.*)
(*Stops, looking at her, the woman.*)
(*The voices still haven't seen him.*)

VOICE 1: Michael Richardson used to go to S. Thala in the sum-
    mer.
VOICE 2: Yes.
    She didn't go often.
    But that summer . . .
VOICE 1: He was English, Michael Richardson?
240  VOICE 2: Yes. (*Pause. As if reading:*) "Michael Richardson
    started a marine insurance company in Bengal, so that he
    could stay in India."
VOICE 1: Near her.
VOICE 2: Yes.

(*The man goes away. We see him, from behind, going slowly along the path toward the deserted tennis courts.*)

VOICE 1: The other man who's sleeping?
VOICE 2: Passing through. A friend of the Stretters'.
    She belongs to whoever wants her.
    Gives her to whoever will have her.
VOICE 1: (*pause, pain*) Prostitution in Calcutta.
250  VOICE 2: Yes.
    She's a Christian without God.
    Splendor.
VOICE 1: (*very low*) Love.
VOICE 2: (*scarcely heard*) Yes . . .

(*Silence.*)

(*The thin man goes toward the red bicycle propped against the wire around the deserted tennis courts.*)
(*The voices have seen him.*)
(*They resume very softly, in fear.*)

VOICE 1: He's back in the garden.
VOICE 2: Yes . . . Every night . . .
    Looks at her . . .

(*Silence.*)
(*The man hesitates. Then goes up to* ANNE-MARIE STRETTER's *bicycle.*)

VOICE 1: He never spoke to her . . .
VOICE 2: No.
    Never went near . . .           260

(*Halt.*)

VOICE 1: The male virgin of Lahore . . .
VOICE 2: Yes . . .

(*The man is beside the bicycle.*)
(*Puts out his hands. Hesitates.*)
(*Then touches it.*)
(*Strokes it.*)
(*Leans forward and holds it in his arms.*)
(*Stays clasping* ANNE-MARIE STRETTER's *bicycle—frozen in this gesture of desire.*)
(*Silence.*)
(*Almost imperceptibly, a movement over by the sleeping bodies. It is she.*)
(*As he bends over the bicycle, she, by a converse movement, sits up. In the same slow rhythm she sits up and turns toward the garden.*)
(ANNE-MARIE STRETTER *looks at the man in white with his arms around her bicycle.*)
(*Silence.*)
(*Suddenly the man lets go of the bicycle. Remains with his arms hanging by his sides, his hands open, in an attitude of passion and despair.*)
(*Sound of a man sobbing [the only sound heard directly].*)
(*The woman still looks, sitting with her hands flat on the ground.*)
(*The sobs cease.*)
(*The man gets up.*)
(*He stands facing the bicycle.*)
(*Then slowly turns around.*)
(*Sees her.*)
(*The woman doesn't move.*)
(*Silence.*)
(*They look at each other.*)
(*This lasts several seconds.*)
(*Silence.*)
(*It is the man who stops looking.*)
(*First he turns his face away. Then his body moves.*)
(*He walks away.*)
(*She, still sitting, watches him walk away.*)
(*Then, after he has slowly disappeared from sight, she takes up her former position, asleep under the nightmare fan.*)
(*Silence.*)
(*Stillness.*)
(*Sobs of the* VICE-CONSUL *in the distance.*)

*(Silence again.)*
*(In the garden the light grows dim again, murky.)*
*(No wind in the deserted garden.)*

VOICE 2: *(afraid, very low)* The sound of your heart frightens me . . .

*(Silence.)*
*(Another stirring in the still mass of the three sleeping bodies:* MICHAEL RICHARDSON's *hand reaches out to the woman's body, caresses it, stays there.)*
*(*MICHAEL RICHARDSON *was not asleep.)*
*(The light gets dimmer still.)*
*(*VOICE 2 *is full of desire and terror.)*

VOICE 2: Your heart, so young, a child's . . .

*(No answer.)*
*(Silence.)*

VOICE 2: Where are you?

*(No answer.)*
*(Silence.)*
*(Shouts in the distance: the* VICE-CONSUL. *Cries of despair. Heart-rending, obscene.)*

VOICE 1: *(distant)* What's he shouting?
VOICE 2: The name she used to have in Venice, in the desert of Calcutta.

*(Silence.)*
*(The cries fade in the distance.)*
*(Disappear.)*
*(*VOICE 2, *all in one breath, in fear, tells the story of the crime, the crime committed in Lahore:)*

270 VOICE 2: *(low)* "He fired a gun. One night, from his balcony in Lahore, he fired on the lepers in the Shalimar gardens."

*(Silence.)*
*(*VOICE 1 *is gentle—calm and gentle:)*

VOICE 1: Couldn't bear it.
VOICE 2: No.
VOICE 1: India—couldn't bear India?
VOICE 2: No.
VOICE 1: What couldn't he bear about it?
VOICE 2: The idea.

*(Silence.)*
*(It is getting darker. The bodies grow less and less distinguishable. Above them the fan goes on turning, the blades gleaming slowly.)*
*(You can no longer tell one body from another.)*
*(Silence.)*

VOICE 1: A black Lancia is speeding along the road to Chandernagor . . .

*(No answer.)*

280 VOICE 1: *(continuing)* . . . It was there . . . there that she first . . .

*(The voice stops.)*

VOICE 2: Yes.

Brought back by ambulance.
They talked about an accident . . .

*(Pause.)*

VOICE 1: She's been thin ever since.
VOICE 2: *(scarcely heard)* Yes.

*(Beethoven's 14th Variation on a Theme of Diabelli. Distant.)*
*(Total blackout.)*
*(Then, beyond the garden, gleams in the sky. Either day or fire—rust-colored fire.)*
*(The voice is slow: a calm declaration.)*

VOICE 1: Those gleams over there?
VOICE 2: The burning-ghats.
VOICE 1: Burning people who've starved to death?
VOICE 2: Yes.        290
    It will soon be daylight.

*(Silence.)*
*(The 14th Variation is heard till the end, over the gleams from the burning-ghats.)*
*(Blackout.)*

## —TWO—

*We are in the same place as before.*

*The only difference is that the right side of it is now revealed, as if the angle of vision had been changed. Doors opening on the reception rooms on one side, and on the other on the garden.*

*(As if these rooms were in a wing of the Embassy.)*

*Bright light everywhere. Chandeliers.*

*Chinese lanterns in the garden.*

*Silence.*

*It is as if the French Embassy were quite empty.*

*Nothing can be seen of the reception rooms except the light coming out of the doors and illuminating the garden.*

*All remains empty for a few seconds.*

*Then, without a sound, a servant passes through.*

*Carrying a tray with glasses of champagne, he goes through and out toward the right.*

*Silence again. Emptiness again.*

*Waiting.*

*Then, suddenly, noise.*

*The noise of the reception begins quite suddenly, full volume. The party is triggered off as if by some mechanism: the noise bursts forth instantaneously from behind the walls, through the open doors.*

*A woman is singing "The Merry Widow," accompanied by a piano and two violins.*

*Behind the music:*

*The sound of many conversations all merging into one.*

*The sound of glasses, crockery, etc.*

*But the feet of the dancers make no sound.*

*No conversation will take place on the stage, or be seen. It will never be the actors on the stage who are speaking.*

*The only exception to this rule is that the sobs of the French* VICE-CONSUL *are both seen and heard.*

*When the conversations recorded here take place, the sound of the reception grows fainter.*

*Often it almost stops: for example, during the conversations between the* YOUNG ATTACHÉ *and* ANNE-MARIE STRETTER, *and between her and the French* VICE-CONSUL. *It is as if the guests at the reception, intrigued, watched them talking instead of talking themselves. So the fading of the sound is not arbitrary.*

*All the conversations, whether private or not, whether they make the guests around them go quiet or not, should give the impression that only the spectators hear them clearly—not the guests.*

*So the sound of the reception should be heard, however faintly, behind all the conversations. The fact that these conversations are now and again mingled with conversations on other subjects should prove that the private conversations are not audible, or hardly, to the guests. So also the fact that some of what is overheard is sometimes repeated, but always more or less wrongly—with slight mistakes which show that only the spectators hear the private conversations properly.*

*The sound of the reception should come from the right and from the stage, and from the auditorium, as if the reception were taking place beyond the walls of the auditorium, too.*

ANNE-MARIE STRETTER *wears a black dress—the one she wore at the dance in S. Thala—the one described in* Le Ravissement de Lol. V. Stein.

*The men wear black dinner jackets, with the exception of the French* VICE-CONSUL *in Lahore, who wears a white one.*

*The other women at the reception wear long dresses, colored.*

*The reception overflows, all the time it lasts, either into the garden or into the place we already know:* ANNE-MARIE STRETTER's *private drawing room.*

*From the point of view of sound, the image, the stage, plays the part of an echo chamber. Passing through that space, the voices should sound, to the spectator, like his own "internal rending" voice.*

*The set should seem accidental—stolen from a "whole" that is by its nature inaccessible, that is, the reception.*

*The diction should in general be extremely precise. It should not seem completely natural. During rehearsals some slight defect should be settled on, common to all the voices.*

*One ought to get the impression of a reading, but one which is reported, that is, one which has been performed before. That is what is meant by a "reading-to-himself voice."*

*To repeat: not a single word is uttered on the stage.*

*("Heure exquise" sung by a woman. Then repeated by the orchestra.)*

*(A waltzing couple cross a corner of the garden.)*

*Some women are talking: (quite close)*
——This is the last reception before the monsoon.
——What? Do you mean to say the monsoon hasn't begun?
——Not really. It'll be at its height in a fortnight. No sun for six months . . . You'll see . . . No one can sleep . . . They just wait for the storms to break . . .

*(An Indian servant passes through, on his way to the reception. He carries a tray with brimming glasses of champagne.)*
*(Two couples go through, waltzing. Slowly. Disappear.)*

*Some women are talking: (farther away)*
——She invited the French Vice-Consul in Lahore . . .
——Yes. At the last minute she sent him a card: "Come." The   300
Ambassador didn't say anything.

*(A young man arrives. He stops and looks around. Clearly he isn't familiar with this part of the Embassy. He looks tired, as if he wants to get away from the reception. He looks out toward the deserted tennis courts.)*
*(As he looks, a couple dance across a corner of the garden and disappear.)*

*Some men are talking: (about the young man)*
——Who is he?
——The new Attaché . . . Only been out here a month . . . He can't get used to it.
——It's the first time he's been here.

*(Pause.)*

——He'll be back. He'll be invited, he'll go to the islands . . . The Ambassador asks people to stay there. For her—for his wife.

*(Pause.)*

——What makes you think *he'll* be asked?   310

*(Pause.)*

——He looks so troubled . . . She doesn't like people who get used to it.
——Are there any?
——Some . . .
——Clubs, to keep India out, that's the answer . . . isn't it?
——Yes.

*(The* YOUNG ATTACHÉ *goes on looking around. Then he turns toward the dancing, watches the reception. And goes back to it.)*
*("Heure exquise" ends.)*
*(There is a moment without music.)*
*(Only the sound of the reception. No laughter. A sort of general dejection.)*
*(Some women go by in the garden, looking curiously toward* ANNE-MARIE STRETTER's *drawing room. They fan themselves with big white fans. They are gone.)*

*A man speaks (the Ambassador):*
——I think my wife may have mentioned it . . . we'd be very glad if you'd join us some time in the islands . . . There are some newcomers one feels specially attracted to . . . And the   320
rules governing ordinary society don't apply here . . . We don't choose . . . *(A smile in the voice.)* You will? The residency looks out on the Indian Ocean, it dates from the days

of the Company, it's worth seeing. And the islands are very healthy, especially the main one, it's the biggest island in the Delta.

*(Silence.)*

*Men talking:*
——He used to write, the Ambassador . . . Did you know? I've read a little volume of his poems . . .
——So I've heard . . . They say it's because of her he gave it up . . .

330

*("Heure exquise" has been followed by a tango.)*
*(The French* VICE-CONSUL *in Lahore has come into the garden. He is wearing a white dinner jacket. He is alone. No one seems to have noticed him yet.)*

*Two conversations (1 and 2) between men and women:*
No. 1
——She might have spared us the embarrassment . . .

*(Pause.)*

——What exactly did he do? I never know what goes on . . .
——The worst possible thing . . . How can I explain . . . ?
——The worst . . . ?

*(Silence.)*

No. 2
——An intriguing woman. No one really knows how she spends her time . . . What does she do? She must do something . . .

340

——She must read . . . Between her siesta and when it's time to go out, what else could she do . . .
——Parcels of books come for her from Venice . . . And she spends some time with her daughters . . . In the dry season they play tennis—you see all three of them going by the office, dressed in white . . .

*(Pause.)*

——The fact that one wonders what she does, that's what's strangest of all.

*(Silence.)*

No. 1 *(continued)*
——Did he kill somebody?

350

——He used to fire shots at the Shalimar gardens at night . . . You knew that . . . ? But bullets were found in the mirrors of his own residence in Lahore . . .
——He was shooting at himself . . . *(Little laugh.)*

*(No answer.)*

——It's difficult to tell which are the lepers . . .
——You see, you do know: you talk about the lepers . . .

*(Silence.)*

No. 2 *(continued)*
——She goes cycling too, very early in the morning, in the grounds. Not during the monsoon, of course . . .
No. 1 *(continued)*

360

——What's the official version?
——His nerves gave way . . . Often happens.

*(Pause.)*

——Funny, he forces you to think about him . . .

*(*MICHAEL RICHARDSON *has entered. He is not wearing a dinner jacket. He sits down. He smokes a cigarette. He doesn't look toward the garden.)*
*(In the garden, the* VICE-CONSUL: *he looks at* MICHAEL RICHARDSON.*)*
*(Two women enter on the right, and stop. They have seen* MICHAEL RICHARDSON *and look at him with curiosity. He doesn't see them.)*
*(A servant goes by with glasses of champagne. He offers one to* MICHAEL RICHARDSON, *and goes.)*
*(The tango, as if in the distance.)*
*(*MICHAEL RICHARDSON *gets up, begins to go toward the reception, looks at it from some distance, then turns around: sees the* VICE-CONSUL *in the garden.)*
*(Then the women see him too and draw back.)*

*Women speaking: (low)*
——Look . . . Michael Richardson . . .

*(Pause.)*

——Yes . . . He doesn't attend receptions?
——No, only at the end, toward the middle of the night. When there's just a few friends left . . .

*(Pause.)*

——What a business . . . what love . . . They say he gave up everything to be with her . . .

370

——Everything. He was engaged to be married. Everything. Overnight . . .

*(Silence.)*
*(*MICHAEL RICHARDSON *makes a movement toward the* VICE-CONSUL—*toward the gate into the garden.)*
*(The* VICE-CONSUL *turns away.)*
*(*MICHAEL RICHARDSON *stops.)*
*(The two women watch.)*

*Women talking: (low, afraid)*
——Look in the garden . . .
——Is that him?
——Yes.
——So thin . . . and the face . . . as if it were grafted on . . . so pale . . .

*(Silence.)*
*(*MICHAEL RICHARDSON *turns back toward the reception.)*
*(The watching women disappear.)*

*Women: (continued)*
——Do they know each other?

380

——Evidently not . . .

*(Silence.)*
*(The* VICE-CONSUL *looks at the reception.* MICHAEL RICHARDSON *looks again at him. The* VICE-CONSUL *seems absorbed, and does not notice him.)*

*Men talking:*
——He used to fire shots at night from his balcony.
——Yes. He used to shout too. Half naked.
——What?
——Disconnected words. He used to laugh.

*(Pause.)*

——And no woman was ever close enough to him, in Lahore,

to be able to say anything . . . ?

——No. Never.

390 ——How is that possible?

——His house, no one ever went to his house in Lahore . . .

——It's terrifying . . . Such abstinence . . . Terrible . . .

*(Silence.)*

(MICHAEL RICHARDSON *turns toward the reception, tries to make out what the* VICE-CONSUL *can be watching so avidly.)*

*Men and women:*

——Did you hear? The Ambassador said to the Young Attaché: "People avoid him, I know . . . he frightens them . . . But I'd be grateful if you'd go and have a word with him."

*(Pause.)*

——What's known about his background? his childhood?

——His father was a bank manager in Neuilly. An only child. The mother's supposed to have left the father. Expelled 400 from several schools for bad behavior. Brilliant at his work, but after high school . . . That's all . . .

——So they don't know anything about him really?

——Nothing.

*(Pause.)*

——Isn't there in all of us . . . how shall I put it . . . ? a chance in a thousand we might be like him . . . I mean . . . *(Pause.)* I'm only asking . . .

*(No answer.)*
*(Silence.)*
(*A couple come to the edge of the garden. They see the* VICE-CONSUL, *and don't go any farther.* MICHAEL RICHARDSON *looks at them. They hesitate. Turn away. Go back to the reception.)*
(*The* VICE-CONSUL *looks at the reception and laughs.)*
(*Some women go through the garden fanning themselves. They don't see the* VICE-CONSUL. *They stop and look at the reception from a distance: something catches their attention:)*

*Women:*

——Who's she dancing with?

——The Ambassador.

410 ——You knew he took her away from some official in the wilds of French Indochina . . . I can't quite remember where . . . Laos, I think . . .

——Savannakhet?

——That's it . . .

——Don't you remember? " . . . slow launch with awnings, slow journey up the Mekong to Savannakhet . . . wide expanse of water between virgin forest, gray paddyfields . . . and in the evening, clusters of mosquitoes clinging to the mosquito nets . . . "

420 ——What a memory! *(Little laugh.)*

*(Silence.)*

——Seventeen years they've been wandering around Asia.

*(Silence.)*
(*They all look toward the reception, toward the Ambassador dancing with his wife.)*
(*The* VICE-CONSUL *laughs silently.)*

*Men:*

——Has he ever talked to anyone about Lahore?

——Never.

——About anything else?

——I don't think so . . . He gets letters from France. An elderly aunt . . . The letters were intercepted . . . Apparently . . . he told the Secretary of the European Club he was in a reformatory . . . when he was fifteen . . . in the North . . .

——He talks to him, then? That drunk?                     430

——Well . . . the other one's asleep, so really he's talking to himself . . . *(Little laugh.)*

——So he doesn't talk to anyone then . . .

——That's right . . . *(Little laugh.)*

——What did he find in India to set him off? Didn't he know about it before? Did he actually have to see it? It's not so difficult to find out . . .

*Women:*

——There are moments when he seems happy. Look . . . As if he were suddenly madly happy . . .                     440

*(Pause.)*

——Perhaps when she dances . . .

——What an idea . . .

——I've only just noticed . . .

*(Silence.)*

——Who mentioned Bombay?

——He did, to the Secretary at the Club. He saw himself being photographed beside the Sea of Oman on a chaise lounge . . . *(Little laugh.)*

——He doesn't talk about it any more, apparently.

*(Silence.)*
(*The* YOUNG ATTACHÉ *has now entered the garden. He goes toward the French* VICE-CONSUL, *slowly, as if not to frighten him. The* VICE-CONSUL *makes as if to run away. The* YOUNG ATTACHÉ *hesitates, then takes him by the arm. The* VICE-CONSUL *doesn't attempt to run away any more.)*
(*The* YOUNG ATTACHÉ *signs to the* VICE-CONSUL *to go with him.)*
(*They go toward the reception. Go in.* MICHAEL RICHARDSON *has seen them—he is the only one not watching* ANNE-MARIE STRETTER *dancing with her husband.)*

*Women:*

——Did you see . . . ?                     450

*(Pause.)*

——Yes, it's her he's looking at . . .

*(Pause.)*

——If you ask me, Bombay's too popular, they'll send him somewhere else . . .

*(Silence.)*

——Tell me about Madame Stretter.

——Irreproachable. Outside the kitchens you'll see big jars of cold water put out for the beggars . . . It's she who . . .

—— . . . Irreproachable . . . *(Little laugh.)*
Come, come . . .

——Nothing that shows. That's what we mean here by irreproachable.                     460

(*Several people go into the garden and look toward the reception. Women fan themselves. [It is to be remembered that it's never those who are seen that speak.])*

*A man and a woman:*
——She looks . . . imprisoned in a kind of suffering. But . . . a
very old suffering . . . too old to make her sad any more . . .

*(Pause.)*

——And yet she cries . . . People have seen her . . . in the gar-
den . . . sometimes . . .
——The light perhaps, it's so harsh . . . and her eyes are so pale
. . .
——Perhaps . . . What grace . . . Look . . .
——Yes . . .
470 ——Frightening . . . don't you think?

*(Silence.)*
(MICHAEL RICHARDSON *has sat down on the left side of the
room. He looks as if he is waiting. He doesn't look toward the
reception. He is clearly visible. Very handsome. Younger than*
ANNE-MARIE STRETTER. *Obviously shy.)*
*(He is smoking. He is tense, absorbed.)*
*(Several conversations take place between people, some of
whom have and some of whom have not seen the* VICE-CONSUL
*go into the reception.)*

*Women:*
——The roses are sent direct from Nepal . . .
——She gives them away when the dance is over.
——*(Low)* Look . . . there he is . . .

*(Silence.)*
——He doesn't notice everyone is looking at him . . .
——You can hardly see his eyes . . .
——His face looks dead . . . Don't you think so? . . . Frighten-
ing . . .
——Yes. The laugh looks . . . stuck on . . . *(Pause.)* What's he
480 laughing at?
——Who knows?

*(Pause.)*
——In the gardens, on the way to the office, he whistles
"India Song."
——What work does he do?
——Filing . . . nothing much . . . just to keep him
occupied . . .

*(Silence.)*

*Men:*
——It's strange—most women in India have very white
skins . . .
490 ——They live out of the sun. Closed shutters . . . they're
recluses . . .
——And they don't do anything out here . . . they're waited
on.
——Yes, they just rest.

*(Silence.)*
——I admit I have a look when she and her daughters go by
on their way to play tennis . . . In shorts . . . Women's legs
seem so beautiful here . . . walking through all that horror
. . . *(Pause, then a start.)* But look . . .

*(Silence.)*

*Women:*
——The first thing to see is the islands . . .                          500
——They're so beautiful . . . I don't know what we'd do here
without them.
——That's what we'll miss about India—the islands in the In-
dian Ocean . . .

*(Silence.)*

*Isolated woman's voice:*
——The best thing during the monsoon . . . did you
know? . . . hot green tea, the way the Chinese make it . . .

*(Silence.)*

*Women:*
——Do you see? The Young Attaché's talking to the Vice-
Consul from Lahore . . .                                                510

*(Silence.)*
——The voice . . . listen to the voice . . . how blank it is . . .

*(Silence.)*
*(Almost total silence. Everyone looks at the* YOUNG ATTACHÉ
*and the* VICE-CONSUL.)
*[The* VICE-CONSUL's *voice is harsh, almost strident. The*
YOUNG ATTACHÉ's *voice is low and soft.])*

*Young Attaché and Vice-Consul:*
V.-CONSUL: Yes, it's difficult, of course. But what is it with you,
exactly?
Y. ATTACHÉ: The heat, naturally. But also the monotony . . . the
light . . . no color . . . I don't know if I shall ever get used to
it.
V.-CONSUL: As bad as that?
Y. ATTACHÉ: Well . . . I wasn't prejudiced before I left
France . . . What about you? before Lahore? would you have 520
preferred somewhere else?
V.-CONSUL: No. Lahore was what I wanted.

*(Silence.)*
*(Then "India Song.")*

*Man and woman: (low)*
——Did you hear?
——Not very clearly. I thought he said: "Lahore was what I
desired" . . .
——I heard: "what I . . . what I'd . . . "
——And what does it mean? Nothing . . .
——*(In one breath.)* The report said people used to see him at
night through his bedroom window, walking up and down 530
as if it was broad daylight . . . and talking . . . always to him-
self . . .
—— . . . At night . . . as if it was broad daylight . . .
——Yes . . .

*(Silence.)*
*(One man's voice is heard dominating all the others.)*

*Man (George Crawn):*
——Come over to the bar. Allow me to introduce myself. An
old friend of Anne-Marie Stretter's. George Crawn . . .
Serve yourselves . . . there isn't a bartender . . .

*(Hubbub for a few seconds—people going over to the bar.)*

*Woman:*

540 ——He said that to distract people's attention . . .

*(The noise dies down.)*

Y. ATTACHÉ: Come over to the bar. *(Pause.)* What are you afraid of?

*(No answer.)*

Y. ATTACHÉ: They say you'd like to go to Bombay?
V.-CONSUL: Won't they let me stay in Calcutta?
Y. ATTACHÉ: No.
V.-CONSUL: In that case I leave it to the authorities. They can send me where they like.
Y. ATTACHÉ: Bombay's not so crowded, the climate's better, and it's pleasant to be by the sea.

*(Silence.)*

550 *Isolated man's voice:*
——It's as if he didn't hear when you speak to him.
Y. ATTACHÉ: What are you doing? Come along . . .
V.-CONSUL: I'm listening to "India Song." *(Pause.)* I came to India because of it.

*(Silence.)*
*(ANNE-MARIE STRETTER appears on the stage for the first time in Act II. She has come from the reception. She smiles at MICHAEL RICHARDSON. He stands, and watches her coming. He doesn't smile. No one sees them [everyone is watching the VICE-CONSUL and the YOUNG ATTACHÉ]. It was she whom MICHAEL RICHARDSON was waiting for.)*
*(ANNE-MARIE STRETTER and MICHAEL RICHARDSON look at each other.)*
*(He puts his arms around her.)*
*(They dance in a corner of the room, alone.)*
*(We hear the public voice of the VICE-CONSUL.)*

V.-CONSUL: That tune makes me want to love. I never have.

*(No answer.)*
*(Silence.)*
*(The last speech was delivered while we could see the couple dancing.)*
*(The couple disappear, left.)*
*("India Song" still.)*

V.-CONSUL: I'm sorry.
I didn't ask to see my file. But you know it. What do they say?
Y. ATTACHÉ: They say Lahore . . . What you did in Lahore . . . People can't understand it, no one can, no matter how
560     they try . . .
V.-CONSUL: *(pause)* No one?

*(No answer.)*
*(Silence.)*
*(The BEGGAR WOMAN appears in the garden.)*
*(She hides behind a bush.)*
*(Stays there.)*

*Men:*
——He said it was impossible for him to give a convincing explanation of what he did in Lahore.
—— . . . convincing . . . ?
——I was particularly struck by the word.

*(ANNE-MARIE STRETTER comes back, from the left side of the room. Slowly. She stops. She looks toward the garden: the two women of the Ganges look at each other.)*
*(The BEGGAR WOMAN, unafraid, sticks her bald head out, then hides again.)*
*(ANNE-MARIE STRETTER walks away, with the same slow step.)*

*Women:*
——She goes to the islands alone. The Ambassador goes hunting in Nepal.
——Alone . . . well . . .                                                        570
——With him—Michael Richardson. And others . . .
——They say her lovers are Englishmen, foreigners from the embassies . . . They say the Ambassador knows . . .
——It's only what he expected when he met her . . . he's older than she is . . .

*(Pause.)*

——There's a friendship between them now that's proof against anything . . .

*(Silence.)*
*(ANNE-MARIE STRETTER has gone into the reception.)*
*("India Song" ends.)*
*(The VICE-CONSUL goes back into the garden.)*
*(He is near the BEGGAR WOMAN, but they don't see each other.)*
*(A blues.)*

*Men and women:*
——Protocol requires everyone to have one dance with the Ambassador's wife . . .                                        580
——Look . . . He's left the Young Attaché . . . He's gone back into the garden . . .
——Again . . . Ever since the beginning of the evening he's kept going back there . . .
——As if he was on the point of running away.
——And yet at the same time . . .

*(Silence.)*
*(The VICE-CONSUL stands motionless, staring at the reception with all his might.)*

*Men and women (continued):*
——What's he looking at?
——The Ambassador's wife dancing with the Young Attaché.

*(Silence.)*
*(The YOUNG ATTACHÉ and ANNE-MARIE STRETTER dance into the room, then back to the reception. They too create a silence around them.)*

*Women: (low)*                                                                   590
——Did you hear? *(Pause.)* She said to him: "I wish I were you, arriving in India for the first time during the summer monsoon." *(Pause.)* They're too far away . . . I can't hear any more . . .

*(Conversation between Anne-Marie Stretter [voice marvelous in its sweetness] and the Young Attaché:)*

A.-M. S.: *(deliberate repetition with slight error)* I wish I were you, coming here for the first time in the rains. *(Pause.)* You're not bored? What do you do? In the evenings? On Sundays?

Y. ATTACHÉ: I read . . . I sleep . . . I don't really know . . .

600 A.-M. S.: *(pause)* Boredom is a personal thing, of course. One doesn't know what to advise.

Y. ATTACHÉ: I don't think I'm bored.

*(Pause.)*

A.-M. S.: And then . . . *(stops)* . . . perhaps it's not so important as people make out . . . Thank you for the parcels of books, you send them on from the office so quickly . . .

Y. ATTACHÉ: A pleasure . . .

*(Silence.)*
*(The noise gradually starts up around them again, faintly.)*

Men: *(in the silence of the preceding conversation)*
——What an intriguing woman. All those books. Those sleepless nights in the residency in the Delta . . .
610 ——Yes . . . What can be behind that sweetness . . . ?
——Nearly every smile is enough to break your heart . . .

*(Silence.)*

A.-M. S.: One might say practically nothing is . . . one can do practically nothing in India . . .

Y. ATTACHÉ: *(gentle)* You mean . . . ?

A.-M. S.: Oh . . . nothing . . . the general despondency . . . *(There is a smile in her voice.)*

Men and women:
——They say she sometimes has had . . . attacks . . .
——*(Low)* You mean . . . the trip to Chandernagor?
620 ——Yes. And something else . . . sometimes she shuts herself up in her room . . . No one can see her . . .
——Except him, Michael Richardson . . .
——Yes, of course . . .

A.-M. S.: It's neither painful nor pleasant living in India. Neither easy nor difficult. It's nothing, really . . . nothing . . .

Y. ATTACHÉ: *(pause)* You mean it's impossible?

A.-M. S.: Well . . . *(Charming frivolity in her voice.)* . . . yes . . . perhaps . . . *(Smile in her voice.)* But that's probably an oversimplification . . .

630 Men and women:
——She used to give concerts in Venice . . . She was one of the hopes of European music.
——Was she very young when she left Venice?
——Yes. She went away with a French civil servant that she left for Stretter.

*(Silence.)*

Y. ATTACHÉ: They say you're a Venetian.

A.-M. S.: My father was French. My mother . . . yes, she was from Venice.

*(Silence.)*

Men and women: *(continued)*
640 ——She plays nearly every evening. In the dry season, that is. *(Pause.)* During the monsoon it's so damp pianos get out of tune overnight . . .

*(Silence.)*

Y. ATTACHÉ: The first time I saw you I thought you were English.

A.-M. S.: That does sometimes happen.

*(Pause.)*

Y. ATTACHÉ: Are there any who never get used to it?

A.-M. S.: *(slowly)* Nearly everyone gets used to it.

*(Silence.)*

Y. ATTACHÉ: *(suddenly crisp)* The French Vice-Consul in Lahore is looking at you.

*(No answer.)*

Y. ATTACHÉ: He's been looking at you all evening.   650

*(No answer.)*

Y. ATTACHÉ: Haven't you noticed?

*(She avoids answering.)*

A.-M. S.: Where is he hoping to be posted, do you know?

Y. ATTACHÉ: *(he knows)* Here in Calcutta.

A.-M. S.: Really . . .

Y. ATTACHÉ: I imagined you knew.

*(No answer.)*
*(Silence.)*
*(Servants pass through.)*
*(Dances follow one another: blues, tangos, foxtrots.)*

A.-M. S.: Did my husband tell you? We'd like to invite you to the islands.

Y. ATTACHÉ: I'll be very pleased to come.

*(Silence.)*

Man and woman:
——If you listen closely, the voice has certain Italian inflec- 660 tions . . .

*(Pause.)*

——Yes . . . Perhaps it's that . . . the foreign origin . . . that makes her seem . . . far away?
——Perhaps . . .

A.-M. S.: You write, I believe?

Y. ATTACHÉ: *(Pause.)* I once thought I could. Before. *(Pause.)* Did someone tell you?

A.-M. S.: Yes, but I'd probably have guessed . . . *(Smile in the voice.)* From your way of being silent . . .

Y. ATTACHÉ: *(smiling)* I gave it up. *(Pause.)* Monsieur Stretter 670 used to write too?

A.-M. S.: Yes, it did happen, to him too. And then . . . *(She stops.)*

Y. ATTACHÉ: *(pause)* And you?

A.-M. S.: I've never tried . . .

Y. ATTACHÉ: *(crisply)* You think it's not worth it, don't you . . . ?

A.-M. S.: *(smile)* Well . . . *(She stops.)* Well, yes, if you like . . .

*(Pause.)*

Y. ATTACHÉ: You play.

A.-M. S.: Sometimes. *(Pause.)* Not so much, the last few 680 years . . .

Y. ATTACHÉ: *(gently; love already)* Why?

A.-M. S.: *(slowly)* It's hard to put it into words . . .

*(Long pause.)*

Y. ATTACHÉ: Tell me.

A.-M. S.: For me . . . for some time . . . there's been a kind of pain . . . associated with music . . .

*(No answer.)*
*(Silence.)*
*(The* VICE-CONSUL *moves from where he was standing in the garden and goes into the reception. The people still going back and forth between the garden and the reception watch him.)*
*(A certain commotion. Some stifled exclamations.)*
*(Then two or three couples come into the garden, as if they were running away from the man from Lahore.)*

*Woman:*
——What's happening?
690 ——The Vice-Consul from Lahore has asked the wife of the First Secretary at the Spanish Embassy to dance . . .

*(Pause.)*

——Poor woman . . . But what are people afraid of?
——They're not afraid . . . It's more a sort of . . . repulsion . . . But it's . . . involuntary . . . you can't analyze it . . .

*(Silence.)*

Y. ATTACHÉ: Will you have to dance with him?
A.-M. S.: I don't have to do anything, but . . . *(Smile in the voice.)*

*(Pause.)*

Y. ATTACHÉ: Last night he was in the garden. By the tennis courts.

*(The answer comes slowly.)*

A.-M. S.: I think he sleeps badly.

*(Pause.)*

Y. ATTACHÉ: He's still looking at you.

*(Silence.)*

700 *Isolated woman's voice:*
——Poor woman . . . and on top of that she feels obliged to talk to him . . .

*(Silence.)*

Y. ATTACHÉ: Repulsion is a feeling you know nothing about?

*(Pause.)*

A.-M. S.: I don't understand . . . How could one know nothing about it?
Y. ATTACHÉ: *(low)* The horror . . .

*(No answer.)*
*(Silence.)*

Y. ATTACHÉ: *(very clear and distinct)* They're talking about leprosy.

*(Silence.)*
*(The* YOUNG ATTACHÉ *was referring to the conversation between the* VICE-CONSUL *and the wife [Spanish] of the Secretary at the Spanish Embassy.)*

*Vice-Consul and Spanish Woman:*
710 SPANISH WOMAN: *(accent)* . . . the wife of one of our secretaries

was going mad, thinking she'd caught it . . . impossible to get the idea out of her head . . . she had to be sent back to Madrid . . .

V.-CONSUL: She had leprosy?
SPANISH WOMAN: *(astonished)* Of course not! . . . accidents are very rare . . . in three years I only know of a ballboy at the Club . . . all the staff are examined regularly . . . most thorough . . . I shouldn't have mentioned it . . . I don't know how it happened . . .
V.-CONSUL: But I'm not frightened of leprosy.    720
SPANISH WOMAN: Just as well, because . . . Of course, there are worse places . . . Take Singapore . . .
V.-CONSUL: *(interrupting)* Don't you understand? I want to catch it.

*(Slight commotion.)*
*(Then silence.)*

*Man and woman:*
——She left him in the middle of the dance . . . What happened?
——He must have said something . . . something that frightened her . . .

*(Silence.)*
*(Some guests leave the garden and go back into the reception.)*
*(The* BEGGAR WOMAN *sticks her bald head out and watches—like an owl. Then hides again. The* YOUNG ATTACHÉ *must have seen her.)*

Y. ATTACHÉ: There's a beggar woman in the garden.    730
A.-M. S.: I know . . . She's the one who sings—didn't you know? Of course, you've only just arrived in Calcutta . . . I think she sings a song from Savannakhet . . . That's in Laos . . . She intrigues us . . . I tell myself I must be mistaken, it's not possible, we're thousands of miles from Indochina here . . . How could she have done it?
Y. ATTACHÉ: *(pause)* I've heard her in the street, early in the morning . . . It's a cheerful song.
A.-M. S.: The children sing it in Laos . . . She must have come down through the river valleys. But how did she cross the    740 mountains—the Cardamon Hills?
Y. ATTACHÉ: She's quite mad.
A.-M. S.: Yes, but you see . . . she's alive. Sometimes she comes to the islands. How? No one knows.
Y. ATTACHÉ: Perhaps she follows you. Follows white people?
A.-M. S.: That happens. Food.

*(Some guests leave the reception. Slight fear.)*

*Men and women:*
——Where is he?
——Over by the bar . . . He drinks too much, that fellow. It'll end badly.    750
——There's something . . . impossible . . . about him.
——Yes.
——And no one invited him anywhere in Lahore either?
——No.
——He went through hell in Lahore.
——Yes, but . . . How can one overcome this . . . this disgust . . . ?
*Men:*
——He's anger personified.

760 ——Against whom? Against what?

*(No answer.)*
*(Silence.)*

*Women:*
——He used to call down death on Lahore, fire and death.
——Perhaps he drank?
——No, no . . . Out here, drinking affects us all in the same way—we talk about going home . . . No, he wasn't drunk . . .

*(Two women have come into the room. They are hot, they fan themselves. They look around.)*
*(A blues.)*
*(They look at the reception.)*
*(Suddenly they stop fanning themselves: they've just seen something.)*
*(Blues.)*

*Isolated woman's voice:*
——It was bound to happen. Look . . . The Vice-Consul from Lahore is going over to Madame Stretter . . .

*(Silence.)*

770 *Men:*
——Have you noticed? Out here the white people talk about nothing but themselves . . . The rest . . . And yet the time when most Europeans commit suicide is during famines . . .
—— . . . which don't cause them any suffering . . . *(Little laugh.)*

*(Silence.)*
*(The two women watch with intense curiosity as the* VICE-CONSUL *goes over toward Madame Stretter.)*
*(The sound of the reception ceases almost completely for a few seconds.)*
*(Then it begins again, faintly. Politely stifled exclamations.)*
*Men and women (conversations 1 and 2):*

No. 1
——Did you see? The Ambassador . . . ? How cleverly he got his wife out of it . . .

*(Silence.)*

——Where are they going?
780 ——Into the other drawing room . . . Of course, the Ambassador would have had to talk to him sooner or later . . . so . . .

*(Silence.)*

No. 2
——Did you see? What diplomacy . . . everyone saw.
——Where are they going?
——Into the other drawing room . . . *(Pause.)* A servant's bringing them some champagne . . .

*(Silence.)*

No. 1
——Why doesn't he go? Asking to be humiliated like that . . .
790 No. 2
——He said something to the Club Secretary that keeps coming back to me . . . "At home, in Neuilly, in a drawing room,

there's a big black piano—closed . . . On the music rest there's the score of "India Song." My mother used to play it. I could hear it from my bedroom. It's been there ever since she died . . ."
——What is it you find so striking?
——The image.

*(Silence.)*
*(Silence. Blues.)*
*(*MADAME STRETTER *and the* YOUNG ATTACHÉ *are walking through the gardens.)*

*Ambassador and Vice-Consul:*
AMBASSADOR: If I've got it right, my dear fellow, you'd prefer 800 Bombay? But you wouldn't be given the same job there as you had in . . . *(He hesitates.)* Lahore. It's too soon yet . . . Whereas if you stay here . . . people will forget . . . India is a gulf of indifference, really . . . If you like, I'll keep you on in Calcutta . . . Would you like me to?
V.-CONSUL: Yes.

*(Silence.)*

*Women: (low)*
——He told her he wanted to catch leprosy.
——Mad . . .

*(Silence.)*

AMBASSADOR: Funny things, careers. The more you want one 810 the less you make one. You can't just make a career. There are a thousand different ways of being a French Vice-Consul . . . If you forget Lahore other people will forget it too . . .
V.-CONSUL: *(pause)* I don't forget Lahore.

*(Silence.)*

*Isolated man's voice:*
——Only one person has anything to do with him. The Secretary at the European Club. A drunk.
AMBASSADOR: You can't get used to Calcutta? *(No answer.)* People put that sort of thing down to their nerves. There are 820 remedies, you know.
V.-CONSUL: No.

*(Silence.)*

*Woman and man: (low)*
——And what are they talking about?
——The reformatory in Arras. Childhood. And . . . *(Stops.)*
——And . . . ?
——Her . . . the French Ambassador's wife . . .

*(Silence.)*

AMBASSADOR: At first everyone's like that. I remember I was, myself. You either go home or you stay. If you stay, you have to find . . . or rather invent . . . a way of looking at things . . . 830 of enduring Lahore . . .
V.-CONSUL: I couldn't.

*(Silence.)*

*Isolated woman's voice: (low)*
——She's gone into the garden with the Young Attaché. *(Pause.)* I told you.

*(Silence.)*

AMBASSADOR: Take my advice . . . weigh up the pros and cons . . . and if you're not . . . sure of yourself, go back to Paris . . .

V.-CONSUL: No.

*(Silence.)*

AMBASSADOR: In that case . . . how do you see the future?

840 V.-CONSUL: I see nothing.

*(Silence.)*

*Women: (low)*

——After every reception the leftovers are given to the poor. Her idea. *(Lower.)* She's coming back . . .

*(Silence.)*

——Oh, I see! The garden's full of beggars . . . crowds of them all around the kitchens . . .

——The sentries have been told to let them through.

*(Silence.)*
*(*ANNE-MARIE STRETTER *and the* YOUNG ATTACHÉ *come in again [from the left]. They go toward the reception.)*
*(The blues is over. Another takes up the theme of "India Song.")*
*(Before entering the reception* ANNE-MARIE STRETTER *halts, as does the* YOUNG ATTACHÉ. *They wait.)*
*(For there, on the other side of the room, is the man from Lahore. Distraught, he comes toward her. Stops. Bows. Pale.)*
*(The* YOUNG ATTACHÉ *makes a gesture as if to stop* ANNE-MARIE STRETTER *from accepting.)*
*(She hesitates, but only for a second, and then accepts the man from Lahore's invitation to dance.)*
*("India Song" becomes very distant. All conversations grow faint, become intermittent murmurs. Almost total silence.)*
*(At first, the* VICE-CONSUL *and* ANNE-MARIE STRETTER *dance in the room.)*
*(The* YOUNG ATTACHÉ *watches them.)*
*(Then they move toward the reception.)*
*(The* YOUNG ATTACHÉ *moves forward, still watching them.)*
*(Other people move toward the garden. They all look toward the reception.)*

CONVERSATION BETWEEN A.-M. S. AND THE VICE-CONSUL, LOW BUT VIOLENT, VERY SLOW:

*(Long silence, before the conversation begins.)*

V.-CONSUL: I didn't know that you existed.

*(No answer.)*

850 V.-CONSUL: Calcutta has become a form of hope for me.

*(Silence.)*

A.-M. S.: I love Michael Richardson. I'm not free of that love.

V.-CONSUL: I know.
I love you like that, in that love.
It doesn't matter to me.

*(No answer.)*

V.-CONSUL: My voice sounds odd. Can you hear?
It frightens them.

A.-M. S.: Yes.

V.-CONSUL: Whose voice is it?

*(No answer.)*

V.-CONSUL: I shot at myself in Lahore, but I didn't die. Other people separate me from Lahore. I don't separate 860 myself.
Lahore is me. Do you understand too?

*(Pause. Gently.)*

A.-M. S.: Yes. Don't shout.

V.-CONSUL: No.

*(Silence.)*

V.-CONSUL: You are with me about Lahore. I know. You are in me. I'll carry you inside me. *(Terrible brief laugh.)* And you'll shoot the Shalimar lepers with me. What can you do about it?

*(Silence.)*

V.-CONSUL: I didn't need to dance with you to know you. You know that.     870

A.-M. S.: Yes.

*(Pause.)*

V.-CONSUL: There's no need for us to go any further, you and I. *(Terrible brief laugh.)* We haven't anything to say to each other. We are the same.

*(Pause.)*

A.-M. S.: I believe you.

*(Pause.)*

V.-CONSUL: Love affairs you have with others. We don't need that.

*(Silence.)*
*(The* VICE-CONSUL's *voice is broken by a sob. It is no longer under his control).*

V.-CONSUL: I wanted to know the smell of your hair—that's why I . . . *(He stops. A sob.)*

*(Silence.)*
*(His voice returns to normal—almost.)*

V.-CONSUL: After the reception your friends stay on.     880
I'd like to stay with you for once.

A.-M. S.: You haven't a chance.

*(Pause.)*

V.-CONSUL: They'd throw me out.

A.-M. S.: Yes.
You're someone they have to forget.

*(Pause.)*

V.-CONSUL: Like Lahore.

A.-M. S.: Yes.

*(Silence.)*

V.-CONSUL: What will become of me?

A.-M. S.: You'll be posted somewhere a long way from Calcutta.

*(Pause.)*

890 V.-CONSUL: That's what you want.

A.-M. S.: Yes.

*(Pause.)*

V.-CONSUL: Very well. And when will it end?

A.-M. S.: When you die, I believe.

*(Silence.)*

V.-CONSUL: *(heart-rending)* What's this pain? Mine?

*(Pause.)*

A.-M. S.: Knowledge.

V.-CONSUL: *(terrible laugh)* Of you?

*(No answer.)*
*(Silence.)*

V.-CONSUL: I'm going to shout. I'm going to ask them to let me stay tonight.

*(Pause.)*

A.-M. S.: *(pause)* Do as you like.

900 V.-CONSUL: So that something should happen between us. In public. Shouting is all I know. Let them at least find out a love can be shouted.

*(No answer.)*

V.-CONSUL: They'll feel uncomfortable for half an hour. Then they'll start talking again.

*(No answer.)*

V.-CONSUL: I even know you won't tell anyone you agreed.

*(No answer.)*
*(Silence.)*
*("India Song" ends.)*
*(It is replaced by "Heure exquise," sung.)*
*(The sky grows pale.)*
*(Two men, drunk, stagger in and collapse into armchairs.)*
*(Over "Heure exquise," mingled with it, the* VICE-CONSUL'S *first cry.)*

V.-CONSUL: Let me stay!

*(Silence.)*
*(Guests shrink back toward the garden. The two drunk men laugh. The others are horrified.)*

V.-CONSUL: I'm going to stay here tonight, with her, for once, with her! Do you hear?

*(Silence.)*

*Isolated woman's voice:*
910 ——How awful . . .
*Isolated voice of Young Attaché:*
——You really ought to go home, you've had too much to drink . . . come along . . .

*("Heure exquise" still.)*
*(The* VICE-CONSUL *shrieks.)*

V.-CONSUL: I'm going to stay! In the French Embassy!

I'm going to the islands with her!
Please! Please! Let me stay!

*(Silence.)*

*Isolated woman's voice: (anguished)*
——She looks as if she didn't hear . . .
*Another: (the same)*
——This is terrible . . .                                     920

*(Silence.)*

V.-CONSUL: *(shrieking)* Once! Just once! I've never loved anyone but her!

*(Silence.)*

*Isolated man's voice, to Vice-Consul:*
——We're sorry, but you're the sort of person who only interests us when you're not there.

*(Silence.)*

*Isolated woman's voice:*
——How cruel . . . It's terrible . . . horrible . . .

*(The* VICE-CONSUL *sobs. Unrestrained. All dignity swept away.)*
*(Everyone suddenly turns aside.)*

*Isolated woman's voice:*
——I can't bear to see it . . .

*(The* VICE-CONSUL *appears, shaken with sobs. We see and hear them.)*
*(A man, a stranger, leads him by the arm toward the entrance of the Embassy. The* VICE-CONSUL *resists at first, then lets himself be led away.)*
*(They disappear.)*
*(Everyone stands looking after them.)*

*Isolated woman's voice:*                                     930
——He's gone. *(Long pause.)* They're shutting the gate.

*(In the distance, the same cries: the* VICE-CONSUL *has started to shout again.)*

*Isolated woman's voice:*
——He was laughing and crying at the same time. Did you see?

*(Silence.)*
*("Heure exquise" continues imperturbably to the end, while everyone stands looking away from the reception and toward the* VICE-CONSUL.*)*
*(The cries still go on.)*

*Isolated man's voice:*
——He's trying to break down the gate.

*(Silence.)*
*("Heure exquise" ends.)*
*(The cries get farther away.)*

*Isolated voice:*
——The beggars are frightened . . .
*Isolated voice, the last:*
——He's gone.                                                940

*(Silence. A few seconds of it, then:)*

(*Blackout.*)
(*Darkness gradually blots out the picture as, in the far distance, the silhouette of the* BEGGAR WOMAN *passes by, then disappears.*)
(*Silence.*)
(*Then suddenly, on the piano, Beethoven's 14th Variation on a Theme of Diabelli.*)
(*Blackout.*)

## —THREE—

### —NOTES ON VOICES 3 AND 4—

VOICES 3 and 4 are men's voices. The only thing that connects them is the fascination exerted on them by the story of the lovers of the Ganges, especially, once again, by that of ANNE-MARIE STRETTER.

VOICE 3 can remember almost nothing of the chronology of the story. It questions VOICE 4, and VOICE 4 answers.

Of all the voices, VOICE 4 is the one which has forgotten the story the least. It knows almost all of it.

But VOICE 3, although it has forgotten almost everything, recognizes things as VOICE 4 relates them. VOICE 4 doesn't tell it anything it didn't know before, at a time when it too knew the story very well.

The difference between VOICES 3 and 4, between forgetfulness on the one hand and remembrance on the other, arises from the same cause—the fascination the story exerts on the two voices. VOICE 3 has rejected the fascination, VOICE 4 has tolerated it.

The story of the lovers of the Ganges is *in* both voices—latent in the one, manifest in the other. About to survive or revive.

The difference—between the tolerable and the intolerable—should be reflected in the sensibilities of the two voices.

It is not without apprehension that VOICE 4 informs VOICE 3. VOICE 4 often hesitates. For VOICE 3 is exposed to the danger, not of madness, like VOICE 1, but of suffering.

*We are in the same part of the Embassy as before. There are five people there in the darkness, which slowly disappears:*

ANNE-MARIE STRETTER, MICHAEL RICHARDSON, *the* YOUNG ATTACHÉ, *the* GUEST (*friend of the Stretters*), *and an old friend, an Englishman,* GEORGE CRAWN.

*The drunk journalists have gone. The rest are by themselves, in an intimacy in which each of them feels alone. It is late, they are separated by fatigue.*

*They are waiting. Their chairs—except for those of* ANNE-MARIE STRETTER *and* MICHAEL RICHARDSON—*are too far apart for conversation.*

*The* YOUNG ATTACHÉ *and the Stretters'* GUEST *look exhausted, also, by the events of the evening.*

*We don't know what they are waiting for: perhaps for it to be light, so that they can leave for the islands. Probably.*

*We still hear Beethoven's 14th Variation on a Theme by Diabelli. Through the music, the sounds of Calcutta grow stronger with the light.*

ANNE-MARIE STRETTER *sits with her head flung back and to one side over the arm of a chair. She might seem to be asleep if it weren't for the fact that her eyes are open.*

MICHAEL RICHARDSON *is near her, half lying on a low chair.*

*The* YOUNG ATTACHÉ *is sitting up straight, smoking. He looks as if he is listening to the noises of Calcutta, through which one suddenly recognizes the cries, the last spasms of the calls to love of the* VICE-CONSUL *from Lahore. The* YOUNG ATTACHÉ *obviously finds them hard to bear. The others do not.*

*The Stretters'* GUEST, *standing, looks around at the others: these people of India whom he thought he knew, but whom he scarcely recognizes after the night of the reception. He too listens to the cries of the* VICE-CONSUL.

GEORGE CRAWN *listens to the Beethoven: he is entirely absorbed by the music.*

VOICE 4: As usual after a reception, some people stayed on.
VOICE 3: (*low*) Is he the one sitting near her—Michael Richardson?
VOICE 4: Yes.
VOICE 3: (*hesitating*) Did they ever find out . . . ?
VOICE 4: (*hesitating*) After she died he left India.

(*Silence.*)

VOICE 4: (*continuing*) The one standing up is the Young Attaché.
VOICE 3: And the elderly Englishman?
VOICE 4: George Crawn. He knew her in Peking.     950

(*Pause.*)

VOICE 3: And the one looking at them?
VOICE 4: Someone passing through. Stretter's guest.

(*Silence.*)

VOICE 3: Is that the French Vice-Consul shouting?
VOICE 4: Yes. Still.

(*Silence.*)

VOICE 4: All trace of him disappears in 1938. (*Pause.*) He resigns from the consular service. The resignation is the last thing on the file.
VOICE 3: (*hesitating*) Very soon afterwards . . .
VOICE 4: A few days.

(*Silence. Cries.*)

VOICE 3: What's he shouting?     960
VOICE 4: Her name.

(*Pause.*)

VOICE 3: (*slowly*) Anna Maria Guardi.
VOICE 4: Yes. All night, all through Calcutta, he's been shouting that name.

(*Silence.*)
(*The women's voices [from Act I] now arrive. They too speak*

*of the* VICE-CONSUL.)

VOICE 2: *(as if exhausted)* He walks along by the Ganges.
He comes on the lepers asleep.
Someone else is shouting on the other bank.

*(Pause.)*

VOICE 1: Yes.

*(Silence.)*

VOICE 2: Can you see him?
970 VOICE 1: *(distant)* Yes. I'm watching.
I see.

*(Silence.)*

VOICE 2: *(slow)* Is he looking for something? . . . Or walking at
random? . . . Aimlessly?

*(No answer.)*

VOICE 2: Is he looking for something he's lost?

*(No answer.)*

VOICE 2: Something in common that he's lost too?

*(No answer.)*

VOICE 2: The love of her?
VOICE 1: Love. Yes.

*(Silence.)*

VOICE 2: *(yearning, desire)* How far away you are . . . from
me . . .

*(No answer.)*
*(Silence.)*
*(A servant goes through with trays piled with glasses, ashtrays,
etc. He passes them as though he didn't see them.)*
*(Gleams in the sky. The burning-ghats.)*

980 VOICE 1: *(slow)* It will soon be day.

*(Silence.)*

VOICE 1: *(very slow)* Dawn is breaking here, all around.
And there.
The air smells of mud. And leprosy. And burning.
VOICE 2: Not a breath.
VOICE 1: No. Slow stirrings, slow movements, smells.

*(Silence.)*

VOICE 2: Can't I hear music?
VOICE 1: No.
VOICE 2: That sound of wings, of birds.
VOICE 1: The fan. Forgotten.

*(Silence.)*
*(The men's voices mingle with the women's.)*

990 VOICE 3: Those gleams.
VOICE 4: Day.
The first zone is the zone of leprosy and dogs. They are on
the banks of the Ganges, under the trees. No strength left.
No pain.
VOICE 3: And those who have died of hunger?

VOICE 4: Farther away, in the density of the North. The last
zone.

*(Pause.)*

VOICE 4: Day. The sun.

*(Pause.)*

VOICE 3: The light. Terrible.

*(Silence.)*

VOICE 1: The light. Of exile.                    1000
VOICE 2: Is she asleep?
VOICE 1: Which one?
VOICE 2: The white woman.
VOICE 1: No. Resting.

*(Silence.)*

VOICE 2: *(mournfully)* How far away you are. Quite absent.

*(No answer.)*
*(Silence.)*
(MICHAEL RICHARDSON *slowly turns his head toward* ANNE-
MARIE STRETTER. *Looks at her.)*

VOICE 3: *(startled)* Voices near us suddenly? Did you hear?
VOICE 4: *(pause)* No . . .
VOICE 3: Young voices . . . women's?
VOICE 4: *(pause)* I don't hear anything. *(Pause.)* Silence.

*(Silence.)*

VOICE 4: He's looking at her.                    1010
VOICE 3: Yes.
She is far away. Quite absent.

*(Silence.)*

VOICE 4: *(in one breath)* People said one day they'd both be
found dead in a brothel in Calcutta they used to go to sometimes during the monsoon.

*(Silence.)*

VOICE 3: Not a breath. The heat is the color of rust. Above, the
smoke.
VOICE 4: The factories. The middle zone.

*(Silence.)*
*(Very slowly* ANNE-MARIE STRETTER *has inclined her head toward* MICHAEL RICHARDSON. *They look at each other.)*

VOICE 3: That overhanging mass . . . ?
VOICE 4: The monsoon.                    1020
Below, Bengal.
VOICE 3: And farther away . . . lower . . . under the clouds . . . ?
Look . . .

*(No answer.)*

VOICE 3: That white patch . . . in a bend in the Ganges . . . ?
There . . . ?
VOICE 4: *(hesitating)* The English cemetery.

*(Silence.)*
*(The stranger and the* YOUNG ATTACHÉ *begin to look at* ANNE-
MARIE STRETTER.)*

VOICE 1: Is she a leper?
VOICE 2: Which one?
VOICE 1: The beggar.
1030 VOICE 2: She sleeps in leprosy, and every morning . . . No. (*Pause.*) No.

(*Silence.*)

VOICE 1: And the white woman?
VOICE 2: A false alarm ten years ago. But no, she neither. (*Pause.*) Listen . . .

(*Sound of a machine and of water.*)

VOICE 1: The water sprinklers in the English quarter.

(*Silence.*)
(*The men turn their eyes away from* ANNE-MARIE STRETTER *and look at the ground.*)
(*The stage gradually gets lighter.*)

VOICE 1: A car is speeding along the straight roads. Beside the Ganges.
VOICE 2: Black?
VOICE 1: Yes.
1040 VOICE 2: They've left for the islands.

(*Silence.*)
(*The fires of the ghats are out. It is daylight. Pale daylight.*)
(*They lie there, in the same deathly attitude, as the voices describe the journey.*)

VOICE 4: The French Embassy's black Lancia has started out for the Delta.

(*Long silence.*)

VOICE 3: (*as if reciting a lesson*) The granary of northern India . . . The frontier of the waters. The Delta.
VOICE 4: Yes, the mingling of the waters. The sweet and the salt.
VOICE 3: After the deluge, before the light . . .

(*Pause.*)

VOICE 3: And those junks?
VOICE 4: Rice.
1050     Sailing down to Coromandel.

(*Pause.*)

VOICE 3: Those dark patches on the banks?
VOICE 4: People.
    The highest density in the world.

(*Silence.*)

VOICE 3: Those thousands of dark mirrors?
VOICE 4: The paddy fields of India.

(*Silence.*)

VOICE 4: They're asleep.
    She's lying close to him.

(*Silence.*)

VOICE 3: She used to wake up late during the monsoon?
VOICE 4: Yes. Didn't go out till after dark.

(*Silence.*)

VOICE 3: The black Lancia has stopped.    1060
VOICE 4: The rain. The roads are blocked.
    They took shelter in a rest house. (*As if reading.*) It was there the Young Attaché said: "I saw the Vice-Consul again before I left. He was still shouting in the streets. He asked me if I was going to the islands. I said no, I was going to Nepal with the Ambassador."

(*Pause.*)

VOICE 3: Did she approve of the Young Attaché's lie?
VOICE 4: She practically never mentioned the man from Lahore.

(*Silence.*)

VOICE 3: That patch of green? it's getting bigger . . .    1070
VOICE 4: The sea.

(*Silence.*)
(*Blackout.*)
(*The voices speak in the dark.*)

VOICE 4: The islands.
VOICE 3: Which one?
VOICE 4: The biggest, the middle one. They're there.

(*Silence.*)

VOICE 3: That big white building . . . ?
VOICE 4: A big international hotel. The "Prince of Wales."
    The sea is rough. There's been a storm.

(*Blackout ends.*)

—FOUR—

*The same as before, but it has become a lounge in the "Prince of Wales."*

*They are not here.*

*A bright, greenish light instead of that of the monsoon.*

*The servants in white gloves are putting up green canvas blinds over the screened windows.*

*We do not recognize the garden. It has exploded into a violent green light—the garden of the "Prince of Wales." All that remains of the garden in Calcutta are some clumps of foliage.*

*The sound of the sea gradually spreads, increasing every second, until it invades everything. Then it remains stable.*

*The wind makes the blinds flap.*

*Sound of launches' sirens in the distance.*

*Close, the cheeping of birds.*

*The fan is still there, going around at the same nightmare speed.*

*In the distance, a dance: an orchestra is playing "India Song."*

*The sounds occur one after the other. For example:*

    *1. The wind.*

2. *The sea.*
3. *Sirens.*
4. *Birds.*
5. *Dance.*

*As the two servants put up the blinds, thus creating the set for the "Prince of Wales,"* VOICES 3 *and* 4 *speak to each other.*

(VOICE 4 *remains the same throughout.*)
(VOICE 3 *changes as the end of the story approaches. It becomes either more pressing or, conversely, less eager to question. When it speaks of* ANNE-MARIE STRETTER *it gets lower, with silences between words and phrases.*)

VOICE 4: In front, the landing stages. The boats go to and from the South Pacific.
1080    Behind, there's a yachting harbor.

(*Silence.*)

VOICE 3: Beyond the palms, the same flat horizon.
VOICE 4: They're alluvial islands, formed by the Ganges mud.

(*Silence.*)

VOICE 3: Where's the French residency?
VOICE 4: The other side of the hotel, looking out to sea.

(*The servants go out. They have "finished" the set for the "Prince of Wales." When they have gone the sound of the dance is heard in the distance.*)
(*They are playing "India Song."*)

VOICE 4: At this time of the day, people used to start to drink at all the tables in the "Prince of Wales." On the sideboards there are French grapes. In the showcases, perfumes.
    Roses are sent every day from Nepal.
VOICE 3: Who lives in this hotel?
1090 VOICE 4: White India.

(*Silence.*)

VOICE 3: (*almost shouting*) What's that sudden smell of death?
VOICE 4: Incense.

(*The smell of incense should pervade the auditorium.*)
(*Silence.*)

VOICE 3: She wanted to go for a swim when they got here?
VOICE 4: Yes. It was late, the sea was rough, it was impossible to swim. Just let the warm waves break over you. She and he both went in.

(*Silence.*)

VOICE 3: (*afraid*) All those screens in the sea?
VOICE 4: Protection against the sharks.
VOICE 3: Oh.

(*Silence.*)

1100 VOICE 3: Where is she?
VOICE 4: She'll come.

(*Silence.*)

VOICE 4: Here she is.
VOICE 3: (*hesitating; lower, more slowly*) Was she like that that night . . . ?

VOICE 4: (*pause*) Smiling.
    Dressed in white.

(*Silence.*)
(*These last two phrases should be felt as terrifying:* ANNE-MARIE STRETTER's *smile, the whiteness of her dress.*)
(*In the green light,* ANNE-MARIE STRETTER *enters.*)
(*Smiling, dressed in white.*)
(*She goes and looks at the sea, beyond the garden. The four men enter, also dressed in white, from different parts of the hotel.*)
(*They all go toward the garden and look out at the sea.*)
(MICHAEL RICHARDSON *turns and gazes at* ANNE-MARIE STRETTER.)
(*She doesn't look at him any more.*)
(*In the distance, a voice over a loudspeaker.*)

LOUDSPEAKER: The last boat tonight leaves at seven o'clock.
VOICE 4: That's for the tourists who want to get back. There's a storm threatening.

(*Ships' sirens. Then silence.*)

VOICE 4: The last launch has just arrived. The one that brings 1110 supplies.

(*Silence.*)
(*A head waiter comes and bows to the five people. Their table is ready. They go off toward the left. Still the distant airport music.*)

VOICE 4: (*pause*) Their table's ready. The food here is excellent.
    Michael Richardson used to say that once you knew the "Prince of Wales" you were never really satisfied anywhere else in the world.
VOICE 3: (*low*) I can't quite remember . . . isn't she going to the French residency?
VOICE 4: She only used to sleep there.
    She used to dine at the "Prince of Wales" when she stayed 1120 on the islands. (*Hesitates.*)
    She'd had the servants at the residency sent back to Calcutta.

(*Pause.*)
(*Fear.*)

VOICE 3: (*low*) How long ago?
VOICE 4: A few weeks.

(*Bird cries, so loud they are almost unbearable.*)

VOICE 3: The birds . . . thousands of them.
VOICE 4: Prisoners on the islands. They couldn't fly back to the coast because of the storm.
VOICE 3: It's as if they were right inside the hotel . . .
VOICE 4: They're in the mango trees. They strip them. They'll 1130 fly away when it's light.

(*Noise of birds swamps everything else.*)
(*Silence.*)

VOICE 3: There's dancing at the other end of the lounge.
VOICE 4: Tourists from Ceylon.

(*Silence.*)

VOICE 4: During dinner . . . she asked them to raise the blind. She wants to see the sea, the sky, above the estuaries. They scarcely speak, they're very tired from last night.

*(Silence.)*

VOICE 3: She's not eating anything.
VOICE 4: Hardly anything. She's looking out of the window.
VOICE 3: I remember . . . A wall of mist is sweeping toward the
1140   islands . . .
VOICE 4: Yes. She's saying something about Venice. *(Effort of memory.)* Venice in the winter . . . yes, that's right . . .

*(Pause.)*

VOICE 3: Venice . . .
VOICE 4: Yes. Perhaps, some winter evenings in Venice, the same kind of mist . . .
VOICE 3: . . . she's saying the name of . . . *(stops)* of a color . . .
VOICE 4: Purple. The color of the mist in the Delta . . .

*(Silence.)*
*(Beyond the green windows of the hotel, disheveled, exhausted, his features contorted, still wearing his white dinner jacket, appears the French* VICE-CONSUL. *He goes through the garden of the hotel, searching.)*
*(Disappears.)*
*(Then reappears almost at once on the stage, now the lounge of the "Prince of Wales," walks across the room, looks toward the left, stops short.)*
*(He has seen her.)*
*(He stands there looking at her.)*

VOICE 3: He came over by the last boat.
VOICE 4: Yes. The seven-o'clock.

*(Pause.)*

1150   He hadn't been home all day. *(Pause.)* He never went back to Calcutta.

*(Silence.)*
*(The tune of "India Song" is played loudly for a few seconds, then fades.)*

VOICE 3: "India Song" . . .
VOICE 4: Yes.

*(Silence.)*

VOICE 4: Now that the mist has come the wind has dropped.

*(Silence.)*
*(Some tourists go by in the garden beyond the green windows. One can make out women fanning themselves with white fans. Light-colored dresses.)*

VOICE 4: They're talking about the beggar woman.

*(No answer.)*
*(Silence.)*

VOICE 4: George Crawn and the Stretters' guest are talking about the beggar woman.

*(Silence.)*
*(FIRST VERSION: The conversation between* GEORGE CRAWN *and the Stretters'* GUEST *is heard as from some distance. [Very light and ordinary.])*

G. CRAWN: She doesn't know a word of Hindustani.
GUEST: Not a word. If she's from Savannakhet she must have come through Laos, Cambodia, Siam, and Burma, and then   1160
probably down through the Irrawaddy Valley . . . Mandalay . . . Prome . . . Bassein . . .
G. CRAWN: It must have been not just one journey, as we might think, but hundreds, thousands, every day, each one the last . . . Hunger always driving her on, farther and farther . . . She must have followed roads, railways, boats . . . but what's strange is that she always went toward the sunset . . .
GUEST: . . . I suppose she traveled at night, and faced toward the light . . . She's bald . . . Because of hunger, do you think?
G. CRAWN: Yes.   1170

*(Pause.)*

G. CRAWN: Sometimes she comes to the islands. Following the whites, probably: food . . . In Calcutta she lives by the Ganges, under the trees. She gets up at night and goes through the English quarter. Apparently she hunts for food at night along the Ganges.

*(Pause.)*

GUEST: And what's left of her in Calcutta? Not much . . . The song of Savannakhet, the laugh . . . and her native language is still there of course, but there's no use for it. The madness was there when she arrived . . . already too far gone . . .

*(Pause.)*

G. CRAWN: Why Calcutta? Why did her journey stop there?   1180
GUEST: Perhaps because she can lose herself there. She's always been trying to lose herself, really, ever since her life began . . .

*(Pause.)*

G. CRAWN: She too.
GUEST: Yes . . .

*(Silence.)*
*(SECOND VERSION: (* VOICES 3 *and* 4 *relate the conversation between* GEORGE CRAWN *and the* STRETTERS' GUEST. *[*VOICE 4 *is the one that hears it.])*

VOICE 4: They've seen her.
She must have crossed the Delta on the roof of a bus. She stowed away on the last boat.
They met her by the lagoon, a few hundred yards from the French residency.   1190

*(Pause.)*

VOICE 3: She must have been following Anne-Marie Stretter . . .
VOICE 4: The guest says she followed him to the gate.
She frightened him.
He said: "That eternal smile is frightening . . ."
VOICE 3: That too . . .
VOICE 4: Yes. *(Pause.)* You remember?
The first attempt . . . *(stops)* at Savannakhet, because of a dead child . . .
VOICE 3: . . . sold by its mother, a beggar from the North . . .   1200

very young . . . ?

VOICE 4: Yes. Seventeen . . . (*Pause.*) A few days before Stretter arrived.

(*Silence.*)
(*Suddenly the* VICE-CONSUL *goes toward the right, and disappears: he has seen them.*)
(*Here they are, coming out from dinner. There are now only three of them:* ANNE-MARIE STRETTER, MICHAEL RICHARDSON, *the* YOUNG ATTACHÉ.)
(*They walk across the lounge, making for the garden through the middle door.*)
(*In the garden they separate.*)
(ANNE-MARIE STRETTER *goes to the right.*)
(*The others go straight on through the garden and disappear.*)
(*The* VICE-CONSUL *begins to go after* ANNE-MARIE STRETTER.)
(*He halts.*)
(*She has stopped too.*)
(*She looks around her at the sea, the palms.*)
(*She hasn't seen the* VICE-CONSUL.)

VOICE 4: She wanted to walk back on her own.

(*Silence.*)

VOICE 4: The other two went for a sail . . .

(*Silence.*)

VOICE 4: The Young Attaché and Michael Richardson went back to the French residency the other way, along the beach.

(*Pause.*)

VOICE 4: It was as hot again as it had been in Calcutta.

(ANNE-MARIE STRETTER *walks slowly away.*)
(*Behind her, the* VICE-CONSUL. *He is following her. They disappear.*)
(*Blackout.*)
(*During the blackout, the 14th Beethoven-Diabelli Variation in the distance.*)
(*Blackout fades.*)

### —FIVE—

*The same as before, but it is now the French residency.*

*The light is different. It seems to come from outside. It is blue, like moonlight.*

*The fan is still there. Still going around.*

*The garden of the Embassy and the garden of the hotel have both gone. There is just an empty space. A path, and at the end of it a white gate.*

*Everything is enveloped in endless, fathomless emptiness. But it has a sound: the sea.*

*After a while,* MICHAEL RICHARDSON *and the* YOUNG ATTACHÉ *come in through the white gate.*

*Simultaneously, she enters, from the left of the house.*

*She is barefoot. Her hair is loose. She wears the short black cotton wrap.*

*She joins them on the path, they go toward one another, meet in the half-light.*

*They look at the sea.*

VOICE 4: She's supposed to have said she was worried about George Crawn and the Guest. The sea was rough. [1210]

(*Sound of a rowing boat in the distance. They all look toward something out at sea.*)

VOICE 4: She didn't have to worry any more. George Crawn and the Guest went straight back to the hotel without calling in at the residency.

(*Silence.*)
(*They slowly walk back into the house.*)

VOICE 3: (*pause; stricken*) She didn't say anything that evening that might have made anyone think . . . (*Stops.*)

VOICE 4: No. Nothing.

(*Terrific tension. But nothing breaks the quiet spell of death.*)
(MICHAEL RICHARDSON *goes over to the piano.*)
(*She goes out of the room.*)
(*The two men are left there alone. They look at each other.*)
(*Outside, in the distance, at the end of the path, the white shape of the* VICE-CONSUL *comes through the open gate.*)
(*They don't see him.*)
(*She comes back, bringing glasses and champagne. She smiles at them.*)
(*She puts the bottle and glasses down on a low table and pours out the champagne.*)
(*She takes it to them.*)
(*They drink.*)
(*She sits down on a sofa.*)
(*There is still the fixed smile on* ANNE-MARIE STRETTER'S *face.*)
(*Outside, the* VICE-CONSUL *watches.*)
(MICHAEL RICHARDSON *plays.*)
(*He plays the 14th Beethoven-Diabelli Variation. Complete stillness.*)
(*Suddenly the stillness is shattered:*)
(*The* YOUNG ATTACHÉ *goes over to* ANNE-MARIE STRETTER, *puts his arms around her, then falls at her feet, and stays there with his arms around her legs.*)
(*He stays there, riveted to her.*)
(*She doesn't prevent him.*)
(*Strokes his hair.*)
(*Still the smile. The fixed smile.*)
(*He gets up. Draws her to her feet, flings his arms around her body, naked under the wrap. A gesture of supplication. Vain.*)
(*They kiss. A long kiss.*)
(MICHAEL RICHARDSON *watches. Plays the piano and watches them. His face is as we have always known it.*)
(*The white shape from Lahore gazes in avidly from outside.*)
(*The* YOUNG ATTACHÉ *roughly releases* ANNE-MARIE STRETTER, *staggers over to the piano and leans on it with his head in his hands. The Beethoven continues:* MICHAEL RICHARDSON *goes on playing. Stillness. Stillness enveloped in music.*)
(*The* YOUNG ATTACHÉ *remains leaning on the piano, motionless. The attitude of despair itself.*)
(*For the last time, one of the women's voices:*)

VOICE 2: *(terrified)* Where are you? *(Waits. No answer.)* You're so far away . . . I'm frightened . . .

(VOICE 1 *doesn't answer any more.*)
*(Silence.)*
(ANNE-MARIE STRETTER *turns toward outside, toward the sea.*)
*(Shows no surprise when she sees the* VICE-CONSUL.*)*
*(He doesn't move, makes no attempt to conceal himself. Gazes fixedly at her.)*
*(She turns and bares her body to the fan.)*
*(Perhaps her naked body is visible to everyone.)*
*(To the* VICE-CONSUL *also—the body already separate from her.)*
*(She stands there motionless under the fan.)*
*(Silence.)*

1220 VOICE 3: *(low, almost a murmur)* Michael Richardson left her alone that evening?
VOICE 4: *(hesitating)* It had been agreed between the lovers of the Ganges that they'd leave each other free if ever either of them decided . . . *(Stops.)*

*(Silence.)*

VOICE 3: *(suffering, terror)* But he doesn't know, it isn't possible . . .

*(No answer.)*

VOICE 3: What does he know?
VOICE 4: *(pause)* Ever since the servants were sent away, Michael Richardson had been living with this possibility.

*(Silence.)*
(ANNE-MARIE STRETTER *has lain down under the fan.*)
*(She has closed her eyes.)*
(MICHAEL RICHARDSON *and the* YOUNG ATTACHÉ *slowly tear themselves away, as if she had actually ordered them to leave her alone there.*)
*(They cross the empty space outside. Shadows.)*
*(The* VICE-CONSUL *is there. He doesn't hide as they go past.)*
*(It is as if they do not see him.)*
*(They disappear from sight.)*
(ANNE-MARIE STRETTER *and the* VICE-CONSUL *from Lahore are the only ones left in the French residency.*)
*(Silence.)*
*(She gets up, goes out, slowly walks through the empty space toward the white gate.)*
*(It is as if she doesn't see anything. She doesn't see the* VICE-CONSUL.*)*
*(And he makes not the slightest gesture toward her.)*

1230 VOICE 3: *(scarcely breathed)* Is he the only one who saw . . . ?
VOICE 4: He didn't say.
VOICE 3: *(as before)* . . . he didn't do anything to stop . . .

*(No answer.)*

VOICE 4: The Young Attaché came back to the residency in the course of the night. He saw her.
She was lying on the path, resting on her elbow.
He said: "She laid her arm out straight and leaned her head on it. The Vice-Consul from Lahore was sitting ten yards away. They didn't speak to each other."

*(Silence.)*
*(What has just been related is what* ANNE-MARIE STRETTER *does. She lays her face on her arm. Stays like that. The* VICE-CONSUL *looks at her, riveted to the distance between them.)*

VOICE 4: She must have stayed there a long while, till daylight—and then she must have gone along the path . . . 1240 *(Stops.)* They found the wrap on the beach.

*(Silence.)*
*(The fan stops.)*
*(Rest a few seconds on the stopping of the fan.)*
*(Blackout.)*

## —SUMMARY—

This summary is the only one which should accompany productions of *India Song*.

This is the story of a love affair which takes place in India in the thirties, in an overpopulated city on the banks of the Ganges. Two days in this love story are presented. It is the season of the summer monsoon.

Four voices—faceless—speak of the story. Two of the voices are those of young women, two are men's.

The voices do not address the spectator or reader. They are totally independent. They speak among themselves, and do not know they are being heard.

The voices have known or read of this love story long ago. Some of them remember it better than others. But none of them remembers it completely. And none of them has completely forgotten it.

We never know who the voices are. But just by the way each of them has forgotten or remembers, we get to know them more deeply than through their identity.

The story is a love story immobilized in the culmination of passion. Around it is another story, a story of horror—famine and leprosy mingled in the pestilential humidity of the monsoon—which is also immobilized, in a daily paroxysm.

The woman, Anne-Marie Stretter, wife of a French Ambassador to India and now dead—her grave is in the English cemetery in Calcutta—might be said to be born of this horror. She stands in the midst of it with a grace which engulfs everything, in unfailing silence—a grace which the voices try to see again, a grace which is porous and dangerous, dangerous also for some of them.

Besides the woman, in the same city, there is a man, the French Vice-Consul in Lahore, in Calcutta in disgrace. It is by anger and murder that he is connected to the horror of India.

There is a reception at the French Embassy, in the course of which the outcast Vice-Consul cries out his love to Anne-Marie Stretter, as white India looks on.

After the reception she drives along the straight roads of the Delta to the islands in the estuary.

Marguerite
Duras:
FROM *The Vice-Consul*
(1965)

TRANSLATED BY
EILEEN ELLENBOGGEN

*Duras adapted* India Song *from her earlier novel,* The Vice-Consul; *later, she would develop a screen version of the narrative based on the dramatic script. This section of* The Vice-Consul *concerns several of the events staged in Act Two of* India Song: *the central scene at the Embassy reception. As Duras suggests in her remarks on the play, the two works share characters and incidents, but explore different "narrative regions." Comparing the novel and the drama here, it is possible to gain a more precise sense of the kind of elliptical inquiry into the status of theater and desire that Duras achieves in* India Song.

Tonight, in Calcutta, the Ambassador's wife, Anne-Marie Stretter, is standing near the buffet. She is smiling. She is wearing black. Her dress has a double overskirt of black tulle. She is handing someone a glass of champagne. Having got rid of it, she looks about her. She has grown thin with the years, and now, on the threshold of old age, the refinement of her features and her tall bony-figure show to advantage. Her eyes, too light for her colouring, are sculpted like the eyes of a statue, and her eyelids are transparent.

She looks about her. Her expression, that of an exile, is the same as she wears when, standing on the official rostrum in a square named after a conqueror, she watches a detachment of the Foreign Legion march past in the sunshine, singing, glittering in their red forage caps.

Among all those present, one man only notices it, Charles Rossett, aged thirty-two, who has been in Calcutta just three weeks, having come to take up his post as First Secretary.

She goes up to a group of English guests, and urges them to ask at the buffet for whatever refreshments they want. They are served by barmen in turbans.

People are saying: "Do you see? She's invited the Vice-Consul of Lahore."

It is quite a large gathering. There are, in all, about forty people in the room. The reception rooms are vast, like those of a casino in a summer resort outside Paris. The only differences are the huge, whirring electric fans, and the fine wire netting over the windows, through which the gardens can be seen as through a mist. No one is looking out. The ballroom is octagonal, with walls of green marble in Empire taste. In each corner of the octagon is an arrangement of delicate ferns, ordered from France. On one wall hangs a portrait of a President of the Republic and, next to it, one of a Foreign Minister. People are saying: "At the very last minute, she invited the Vice-Consul of Lahore."

Now she is opening the ball with the Ambassador, performing the despised ritual, so that the other couples can take their place on the dance floor.

The ceiling fans make a sound like a flock of startled birds beating their wings, hovering above the couples dancing to the music of a slow foxtrot, above the cheap chandeliers, the hollowness, the sham, the gold paint. People are saying: "That's him, that dark man near the bar. Whatever can have made her ask him?"

There is an aura of intriguing mystery about this woman of Calcutta. No one is quite sure what she does with her time. She seldom entertains, especially here in her official residence overlooking the Ganges, which dates back to the time of the East India Company. Nevertheless, it is presumed that she must do something. Was it only after eliminating every other possible alternative that it was decided that she was a great reader? Yes. What else could she be doing, shut up in her private apartments, during the hours between tennis and her evening drive. Crates of books, addressed to her, have been known to arrive from France. What else? Apparently, she spends a large part of her day with her daughters, who look like her. It is known that they have a young English governess, and generally believed that they lead a full and happy life, and that Anne-Marie Stretter takes a great personal interest in their up-bringing. Occasionally, when there is a reception, they put in a brief appearance, as they have already done this evening. Already they are a little aloof, which, it is suspected, does not displease their mother. After they have left, murmured comments can be heard: Undoubtedly, the elder will be a beauty, like her mother, she has all her charm already. You can see all three of them there any morning, in white shorts, in the Embassy grounds, and every morning they either play tennis or go for a walk.

Someone asks: "But what exactly did he do? I'm quite in the dark."

"He did the very worst thing. How can I put it?"

"The very worst thing? Did he kill someone?"

"He fired shots in the Shalimar Gardens, where lepers and dogs shelter at night."

"Lepers and dogs! Can you call it killing, when it's merely a question of lepers and dogs?"

"There was something else too. The mirrors of his residence in Lahore were riddled with bullets, you know."

"You may have noticed that, from a distance, a leper looks much like anyone else, which suggests. . . . "

For some time following her arrival in Calcutta, no one knew of the now famous villa at one of the salubrious island resorts in the Ganges Delta. The villa belongs to the French Embassy, and is at the disposal of members of the staff. It was only when Anne-Marie Stretter's daughters were seen walking alone in the gardens that people began asking where their mother was, and were told that she was at the villa. The girls are most often seen walking alone in the frightful heat of the summer monsoon.

"Can you hear shouting?"

"What is it? Lepers? Or dogs?"

"Dogs or lepers."

"Why say dogs or lepers, when you know perfectly well which it is ?"

"In the distance, with the music playing, it's hard to distinguish between the dogs barking and the lepers crying out in their sleep."

"That's one way of putting it."

Every evening, the three of them, in an open car, drive through the streets of Calcutta. The Ambassador, smiling, watches his treasures go off in the car: his wife and daughters are going to Chandernagore or to the sea coast on this side of the Delta, to get a breath of fresh air.

Neither the little girls nor anyone in Calcutta know what she does at the villa in the Delta. It is said that she has lovers, Englishmen, who do not move in diplomatic circles. It is said that the Ambassador knows. She never spends more than a day or two at a time at the villa in the Delta. On returning to Calcutta, she at once resumes her well-regulated life, tennis, drives in the car, an occasional evening at the European Club. So much, anyone can see. And the rest of the time? No one knows. All the same, she must occupy her time somehow, this woman of Calcutta.

People are saying:

"It's beyond words!"

People are wondering:

"Did he do those things because he had a blackout, or what? Did he lose all self-control?"

"You must see how difficult. . . . How can one put into words what he did in Lahore, what he did with himself in Lahore, if he himself didn't know what he was doing?"

"At night, he used to stand on the balcony and shout."

"Has he ever done that here?"

"Never. And why not, I wonder? It's even more stifling here."

It is a little past midnight. Anne-Marie Stretter goes up to the young attaché, Charles Rossett. Beside him stands the Vice-Consul of France in Lahore. She suggests that they should dance, that is, of course, if they would like to, and then she moves away. The general impression is that it is Charles Rossett she is interested in. He seems just the right man for her to take with her to the Islands, when she goes there in two or three days' time. Someone remarks that she would not have to be much more sparing with her smiles to be downright rude. She has invited some of her personal friends to tonight's reception, but they will not put in an appearance until the very end.

Someone asks:

"What was he shouting?"

"Gibberish."

"Surely there must have been some woman in Lahore? She should be able to shed some light on it."

"There wasn't any woman. There never has been."

"Can you be sure he hadn't got one tucked away in the Residency? No one ever sets foot inside the Residency in Lahore."

"Did no one ever notice anything odd about him all the time he was in Lahore? A queer look? A flush? The one I can't help thinking about is the mother of the Vice-Consul in Lahore. I imagine her seated at a piano, playing classical pieces, like the heroine of a novel, playing the melodies of her youth, with him listening, listening altogether too much, or so it would seem."

"All the same, I do think she might have spared us the embarrassment of his presence here."

It is expected of every man invited to a reception at the Embassy that he should ask Anne-Marie Stretter to dance, even though she herself may not wish it.

In passing, she says something to her husband about someone in the room. Charles Rossett lowers his eyes. It is obvious. The Vice-Consul, too, has noticed. He has been examining one of the delicate ferns, and running his finger down its black stem. People are thinking: he has only just seen the Ambassador, on whose goodwill his next posting depends. Charles Rossett recalls that he has waited weeks for a summons that never comes.

People are saying: "It is very broadminded of Monsieur Stretter to have allowed such a thing, to have agreed to his being invited tonight. He's a good man. He is nearing his retirement. We shall miss him. Yes, he is a lot older than she is. Her father was a District Officer in some backwater near the frontier of Laos, in French Indo-China. That's where he found her. Yes, seventeen years ago. She had only been there a few weeks when Monsieur Stretter paid an official visit to the district. It was barely a week later that he left, taking her with him. Didn't you know?"

They are saying: "How well he has kept his figure, the Vice-Consul. You would take him for a much younger man, but for his face. . . . One day his mother just walked out and left him. Everyone in Calcutta knows. He talked to the Club Secretary about his childhood home, and his room, smelling of blotting paper and india rubber. From his window, he could see the down-and-outs in the Bois de Boulogne, gentle, humble men, most of them. He talked about his father, who spent every night at home, but never addressed a word to his mother. It's a lot of nonsense. He talks an awful lot of nonsense."

Someone asks:

"Does he ever talk about Lahore?"

"No."

"Never."

"About his life before he went to Lahore?"

"Yes. About his childhood in Arras. But maybe that is just so as to pull the wool over our eyes."

Someone says: "So he picked her up in Laos, in French Indo-China, did he?"

They see: an avenue, with the Mekong River on one side and a forest on the other. It is somewhere near Savannakhet, in Laos. They see sentries, infantrymen, guarding her for him until he should come and take her away. There was talk, it seems, of sending her back to France. She never could get used to it there. People are saying: "Even now, no one in Calcutta really knows whether she was living a life of shame or sunk in despair when he found her in Savannakhet. No, no one ever found out."

Every now and then the Vice-Consul's face lights up with joy. Just for a second, every now and then, he seems crazy with happiness. Tonight, it is impossible to avoid him. Is that the reason? How strange he looks tonight. How pale he is, as though he were in the grip of some intense emotion, holding it in check, endlessly deferring the moment when he will have to give expression to it. Why?

People are saying: "Every evening, he talks to the Club Secretary. And for that matter, the Secretary is the only man who ever talks to him. There was that corrective training school in Arras that he told him about. It makes you think. The north. November. Flies clustering round naked light bulbs, brown linoleum. Those sort of places are all alike. It's as though one had been there oneself. Denim overalls in the playground. The Pas-de-Calais was shrouded in reddish fog all winter, he said . . . as though one had been there oneself . . . poor kids. But maybe he's just trying to pull the wool over our eyes."

"Tell me more about Madame Stretter."

"Above reproach, good-hearted, though of course there is always the inevitable gossip. . . . And she's charitable. She does things that her predecessors never even thought of. If you look behind the Embassy kitchens, you'll see fresh water put out for the beggars. She never forgets. She sees to it herself every morning before her game of tennis."

"Above reproach? Come now."

"She is the soul of discretion. And, in Calcutta, that is tantamount to being above reproach."

"But what of him? He's done us a lot of harm. I'd never set eyes on him until tonight, so tall and dark, well set-up you could almost say, if . . . and so young. . . . It's a shame. I can't quite see his eyes . . . his face gives nothing away. The Vice-Consul of Lahore is a bit of a death's head. Wouldn't you agree that he's a bit of a death's head?"

Most of the women have pale complexions, like the nuns of an enclosed order. They spend their lives in shuttered rooms, sheltering from the deadly rays of the sun. In India they do virtually nothing. They are rested. Tonight, exposed to view, transported from their homes to this outpost of France in India, they are happy.

"This is the last reception of the season. The monsoon has begun. Did you notice the sky this morning? That's how it will be every day for the next six months."

"What should we do without the Islands? They must be looking beautiful tonight. Ah! they are what we shall miss most when we leave India."

The men are saying:

"It's like being back in France. It's extraordinary, the effect it has on one, seeing all these women here, even those one wouldn't look at twice at home."

A man points to Anne-Marie Stretter.

"I see her almost every morning, walking across the grounds to the tennis courts. They're a grand sight, a woman's legs, in this loathsome place. Don't you agree? Forget that man, the Vice-Consul of Lahore."

Charles Rossett and others are watching him covertly. The Vice-Consul does not seem to notice. Does he never sense that people are looking at him? It's impossible to tell. He still has that radiant look, though for what reason no one can guess. What vision, what inspiration, can have so transfigured him?

This morning the bicycle was still there, leaning against the wire netting.

The Ambassador said to Charles Rossett: "Have a word with him. You really should." He does so.

"I don't seem able to settle down," Charles Rossett says. "I must admit, I can't seem to settle down here."

An answering smile. A sudden mellowing of the features. He sways a little, as when he walks in the Embassy grounds.

"It's not easy, of course, but what exactly is your difficulty?"

"The heat, of course," says Charles Rossett, "but there's the monotony as well. The quality of the light, it seems to drain all the colour out of life. I can't see myself getting used to it, ever."

"As bad as that?"

"That's to say. . . . "

"Yes?"

"I hadn't any very high hopes to start with," Charles Rossett says, then recollecting himself: "What about you? Was there any particular place you would have preferred to . . . this?"

The Vice-Consul purses his lips.

"None," he says.

It was some time after he was out of sight of Charles Rossett, who, in his turn, had gone over to look at the bicycle, that the Vice-Consul had begun whistling that old tune "Indiana's Song." That was yesterday. And it was then that Charles Rossett, more frightened than ever before, had started walking very rapidly towards the administrative buildings.

Charles Rossett says that he arrived here feeling like a student on vacation, but that he seems to be ageing visibly with every day that passes. They both laugh. Someone remarks: "Did you see that? He and that other fellow are laughing together. It really is the limit, you know, his accepting the invitation. It's effrontery. And yet, to look at him, you wouldn't think he had it in him."

An elderly Englishman comes into the room. He is tall and thin, with sharp eyes, like a bird, and skin withered by the sun. One of those who have been in India for a long time. One can always tell. They're a race apart, don't you think? With an expansive gesture, he leads them towards the bar.

"Do help yourselves. Everyone does. My name is George Crawn. I'm a friend of Anne-Marie's."

The Vice-Consul gives a little start. George Crawn moves off, and the Vice-Consul gazes intently at the retreating figure of the Englishman. He does not seem to notice that he is being stared at, nor that, wherever he goes, people shrink back, leaving him standing in a little clearing. He says:

"A member of the inner circle. Exclusiveness, that's the secret of India."

He laughs. Charles Rossett, with a beckoning gesture, moves closer to the bar. The Vice-Consul, with apparent reluctance, follows.

"Come now," says Charles Rossett. "Here, I can assure you. . . . What are you afraid of?"

The Vice-Consul, still smiling, looks round the octagonal ballroom.

The tune, "Indiana's Song," evokes the memory of that lonely, dark, abominable act.

"Nothing. No, I know I have nothing more to lose. . . . I'm just waiting for my posting, that's all. It will take time, of course. It isn't easy . . . I find it more difficult than most to keep up appearances," he laughs again, "to look as though I were up to the job, that's all."

The Vice-Consul laughs. With head bent, he goes up to the bar. Forget the woman's bicycle near the deserted tennis courts, or escape. It's not so much the look in his eyes, Charles Rossett reflects, as his voice. The Ambassador said to Charles Rossett: "People avoid him instinctively; there's something frightening about the man . . . but the loneliness. . . . Do try and talk to him."

"I understand that you have expressed a preference for Bombay."

"Well, as they won't keep me in Calcutta, why not Bombay?"

"There aren't so many people in Bombay, the climate is better, and it's an advantage being so near the sea."

"I dare say," he looks up at Charles Rossett, "you'll settle down here all right. You don't strike me as the kind who is accident-prone."

Charles Rossett laughs. "Thanks very much!" he says.

"I'm beginning to be able to tell those who are from those who are not," the Vice-Consul goes on. "You are not."

Charles Rossett forces a laugh.

Anne-Marie Stretter goes past. The Vice-Consul of Lahore gazes after her.

Charles Rossett pays no particular attention to this. Assuming a bantering tone, he says: "Your personal reports—if you'll forgive my mentioning it—describe you as an impossible person. Did you know that?"

"I have not asked for disclosure of the reports in my personal file, though I believe "unstable" was the word used. Was it not?"

"To be perfectly honest, I know very little. . . . " He is still keeping up the effort to smile. "It's absurd. . . . What does 'impossible' mean? Nothing at all!"

"What are they saying? What's the worst they've got against me?"

"Lahore."

"Was what happened at Lahore really so shocking? Has nothing comparable ever happened before?"

"One can't avoid . . . forgive me for saying this, but one is baffled by the Lahore business. One doesn't know what to make of it."

"That's true," says the Vice-Consul.

He leaves Charles Rossett and takes up his former position near the door, beside a pedestal supporting a delicate potted fern. There he stands, the focus of all eyes.

But the sensation his presence created at the start is beginning to wear off.

She goes past again, almost brushing against him, but this time he does not look at her. It is very noticeable.

It is only then that Charles Rossett remembers that Madame Stretter used occasionally to take an early-morning bicycle ride in the Embassy grounds. She has not done so recently, but that is probably owing to the summer monsoon.

It is half-past twelve.

Under the overhanging bush on the banks of the Ganges, she wakes, stretches, and sees the big house ablaze with light: food. She gets up. She smiles. Instead of diving into the Ganges, she goes towards the lights. The other mad beggars of Calcutta are already there asleep, huddled together near the little back gate, waiting for the scraps to be distributed, much later, when the dishes have been cleared away.

There is a young woman standing alone in the octagonal ballroom, watching the dancers. On an impulse, the Vice-Consul goes up to her.

She accepts his invitation to dance in a flurried manner, which clearly reveals her embarrassment and agitation. They dance.

"Look over there, he's going to dance. He dances just like anyone else, very correctly."

"It's best, really, to put it out of one's mind."

"Quite. It's best to put it out of one's mind. But it isn't easy. And, come to think of it, why should one? What else is there to think about?"

Anne-Marie Stretter goes up to the buffet, where Charles Rossett is now standing alone. She gives him a friendly smile. He cannot avoid asking her to dance.

It is the first time. People are saying: "This is the first time. Will she take a fancy to him?"

Charles Rossett and Anne-Marie Stretter have met before, about a fortnight ago. He was invited to an informal welcoming party in one of the elegantly furnished private rooms in the Embassy, where newcomers are always received. The Vice-Consul of France was invited then, as tonight. She was sitting on a couch upholstered in rose-coloured cretonne. He was startled by her expression, and her statuesque grace, as she sat on the couch.

The party lasted an hour. She did not move from the couch, where she sat, erect, in a white dress, with her daughters beside her. She was pale under her Calcutta tan, like all the other whites.

All three looked with interest at the two newcomers. Jean-Marc de H. said nothing. They asked Charles Rossett about himself, but did not address a word to the other man. Lahore was not mentioned, nor was he asked what he thought of Calcutta. The Vice-Consul was ignored. He was resigned to it. He stood there, not saying a word. It was the same with India. India, like the Vice-Consul, was ignored. At that time, Charles Rossett did not yet know of the Lahore scandal.

She told him she played tennis with her daughters, remarked that the swimming pool was delightful, and so on in this vein. It occurred to him that he would probably never see this little private room again, nor her. Would he ever see her again, except at official receptions and the European Club?

"How are you settling down in Calcutta?"

"Not too happily."

"Forgive me, you are Charles Rossett, aren't you?"

"Yes."

He smiled.

She raised her head and smiled back. It needed no more than one look for white society in Calcutta to open its doors to him.

She does not know, thinks Charles Rossett. He recalls that, as he stood there in silence, the Vice-Consul looked out of the window at the palm trees in the grounds, the oleanders, the wrought-iron gates in the distance, the sentries. Monsieur Stretter was talking about Peking to a visiting official. Did he know? With the Vice-Consul still standing there not uttering a word, she suddenly said: "I wish I were in your place, seeing India for the first time, especially at this time of year, during the monsoon."

They left sooner than they should have done.

She knows nothing. No one in Calcutta knows anything. Unless the Embassy gardeners saw something, but they will not talk. She must have forgotten that bicycle of hers, which she does not use during the summer monsoon.

As they dance, she says:

"I hope you're not bored here. What do you do with yourself in the evenings, and on Sunday?"

"I read. . . . I sleep. . . . I really don't know."

"Well, you know, boredom is so much a matter of temperament, it's difficult to know what to suggest. . . ."

"I don't think I am bored."

"I must thank you for the cases of books. You got them to me in record time. If it's books you want, just let me know, it's no trouble at all."

In a flash, having captured her in flight, pinioned her, he sees her, as they dance, elsewhere, different: it is afternoon, her children are at their lessons, yes, she is trapped in the hollow of the siesta. He sees her in some secret corner of her residence, an unused servant's room, perhaps, curled up in a picturesque attitude, reading. No, he cannot see what she is reading. Reading, nights spent at the villa in the Delta, at first sees these things in sharp focus, then they melt into the shadows, where things are said and done which it is impossible to imagine. What lies hidden in the shadow of Anne-Marie Stretter's luminous presence?

There is something alien about the gaiety of Anne-Marie Stretter, when she drives with her daughters along the road to Chandernagore in the torrid heat.

It is said that in that distant place, almost at the end of the Ganges, where she sleeps in a darkened room with her lover, she is subject to moods of profound melancholy. The whole thing is something of a mystery, but it is said that when she is in one of these moods, it is very restful to be with her, though what is meant by this, no one exactly knows.

"In spite of what you say," Charles Rossett remarks, "if I thought the past three weeks were a fair indication of what the next three years would be like, I don't think I could stand it."

"Almost everything is impossible here, you know. I can't think of any other way of putting it, and yet it's just that that makes it so . . . extraordinary."

"One day, perhaps. . . . Extraordinary? How do you mean?"

"No, it's . . . nothing. Living here is neither painful nor pleasant, if you see what I mean. It's different, if you like. Contrary to popular belief, life here isn't easy, it isn't hard, it's nothing."

At the Club, the other women talk about her. What does she do with herself? Where does she go? No one knows. She is at home in this nightmare town. Still waters run deep, they say. What really happened that time towards the end of her first year in Calcutta? No one ever discovered the reason for her sudden disappearance. The ambulance seen at dawn, parked at the Embassy gates. Attempted suicide? No one ever discovered the reason for her long absence in the mountains of Nepal. When she returned, she was so thin it was frightening. Was she changed in other ways? She is still very thin. That is all. It is said that it was not her love affair, her unhappy or all too happy love affair with Michael Richard that was at the back of it.

What would she say if she were to find out?

"I've heard it said that you are from Venice. Is it true? But then I've heard it said, too, at the Club, that it's not true."

She laughs, and tells him that her mother is from Venice, yes.

He simply cannot imagine what she would say if she found out.

Anna Maria at eighteen, Anna Maria of the smiling eyes, painting in water-colours on one of the quays on the island of Giudecca. No, that's not right.

"My father was French. But I did live in Venice for a time, as a girl. We shall be going to Venice from here, or rather, that is our present intention."

No, it must have been music for her in Venice, the piano. In Calcutta, she plays the piano almost every evening. Anyone walking in the avenue can hear her. It is generally agreed that, no matter what her origins, she must have started learning music very young, at about the age of seven. Listening to her, one could well believe that music was her chief interest.

"The piano?"

"Yes, I've always had a piano, everywhere. I've played for years, more or less the whole time. . . ."

"I wondered where you came from. It might have been anywhere, I thought, between Ireland and Italy. I thought perhaps Dijon, Milan, Brest, Dublin, or somewhere in England. I thought you might be an Englishwoman."

"And it didn't occur to you that I might be from somewhere more remote?"

"No, from anywhere more remote, you would not have been . . . you . . . here . . . in Calcutta."

"Oh!" she says, smiling. "You can never be sure, don't you see, with a woman of my age in Calcutta."

"I wonder."

"What I mean is, it's too simple to say that one comes from Venice, or only from Venice. It seems to me that one also comes from other places where one has stopped on the way."

"Are you thinking of the French Vice-Consul?"

"Naturally, just as everyone else is. I'm told that they all want to know what kind of man he was before Lahore."

"And, in your view, before Lahore there was nothing?"

"I believe that Lahore is where he comes from, yes."

People are saying: "Look at the Vice-Consul dancing. She, poor soul, couldn't refuse him. Since Anne-Marie Stretter has chosen to invite him, it would be an affront to her, who has foisted him on us."

The Vice-Consul, dancing, has no eyes for his partner. He is watching Anne-Marie Stretter and Charles Rossett, who talk as they dance and, from time to time, exchange glances.

His dancing partner, the wife of the Spanish Consul, feels in duty bound to talk to the Vice-Consul of France in Lahore. She remarks that she has seen him several times, in the Embassy grounds. It is such a small community, they are bound to meet sometimes. She has been here two and a half years, and will soon be leaving. The heat is very depressing. Some people never get used to it.

"Are there really people who never get used to it?" asks the Vice-Consul.

She draws away from him a little, but cannot yet bring herself to look at him. Later, she will say that she was struck by something in his voice. She will say: "Is that what is meant by a toneless voice? You couldn't tell whether he was asking a question or answering it." In kindness, she smiles and talks to him.

"Well, I must admit, actually, there aren't many, but it does happen. There was the wife of one of our own Secretaries at the Spanish Consulate; she went out of her mind. She was convinced she had contracted leprosy. Nothing would persuade her otherwise. She had to be sent home."

Weaving in and out among the dancing couples, Charles Rossett is silent. His blue eyes—blue—are fixed, as he looks down on her hair. Suddenly, his expression changes, as though he were suffering a twinge of pain. They smile at one another, and seem on the point of speaking, but they do not.

"If no one could get used to it . . . " says the Vice-Consul. He laughs.

People are thinking: The Vice-Consul is laughing, but what a laugh! Like the sound track of a dubbed film, utterly lacking in conviction.

Once more she draws back a little and, this time, does venture to look at him.

"No, don't worry, everyone gets used to it in time."

"But had this woman, in fact, contracted leprosy?"

She moves away from him and, although not looking at him, feels reassured, believing that she has at last awakened a normal response in the Vice-Consul: fear.

"Oh!" she says, "I really ought not to have mentioned it."

"What I mean is . . . one can't help wondering."

She gives a little forced laugh. He, for his part, laughs outright, and the sound of it wipes the smile from her face.

"She hadn't got leprosy, I assure you. There wasn't the least trace of infection. All our staff here have regular medical checks, you know. There is nothing to fear."

Is he listening?

"But I have no fear of leprosy," he says, laughing.

"There are very few cases . . . I only know of one, a ball-boy. It happened after I got here, so I can assure you at first hand that the most stringent precautions were taken. . . . All the balls were incinerated, and the rackets."

No, he is not really listening.

"You were saying that everyone, when they first come here. . . . "

"Yes, of course, but it doesn't always take the same form. Fear of leprosy carried to such lengths . . . I'm sure you understand. . . . "

Someone says:

"Did you know that if you strike a leper, he explodes like a bag of sawdust?"

"Without uttering a single cry? Without pain, perhaps? Might it not even be a great relief, an inexpressible relief?"

"Who can tell?"

"Isn't the Vice-Consul of Lahore looking thoughtful? Deep in thought, isn't he?"

"Really? I've never stopped to consider what it was that was so different about him. How very interesting!"

"He told the Club Secretary he was a virgin. What do you think of that?"

"Could that be it? Total abstinence? It's a fearful thought."

They dance.

"You must realize," the woman is saying in her gentle voice, "it's hard for everyone at the beginning, in Calcutta. I myself went through a period of intense depression." She smiles. "It distressed my husband terribly, then little by little, day by day, I got used to it. Even when one believes it to be impossible, one gets used to it. To anything. There are worse places, you know. Singapore for one. It's abominable there, because of the extremes. . . ."

No, he is not listening. She gives up the effort of making conversation.

Wearily, they ask: What manner of man was the Vice-Consul before he went to Lahore? And what manner of man is he now that he has come here from Lahore?

Charles Rossett gets it into his head, while dancing with Anne-Marie Stretter, that the incident he witnessed near the deserted tennis courts was also witnessed by someone other than himself. Someone else, in the murky light of the summer monsoon, must have been looking across to the deserted tennis courts as the Vice-Consul went up to them. Someone who is not saying a word. Anne-Marie Stretter, perhaps.

People are saying: "Maybe it all began in Lahore."

## Athol Fugard, John Kani, and Winston Ntshona

Born in 1932, the South African playwright Athol Fugard began his career in the theater in the 1950s, working with the Circle Players in Cape Town. As a mixed-race company, the Circle Players worked in violation of South Africa's apartheid laws. They brought the issue of apartheid to a head when Fugard—a white man—collaborated with the black actor Zakes Mokae in the play *The Blood Knot* (1961), a play about two brothers, one of whom is light-skinned enough to "pass" for white. The play's powerful indictment of apartheid and the fine performances of Fugard and Mokae were widely admired, gaining Fugard a reputation as a dramatist outside South Africa. Yet, despite its notoriety, the play could hardly remove apartheid itself; Fugard and Mokae were still forced to travel separately, and the government passed new laws limiting interracial theater. In 1963, Fugard began his long association with The Serpent Players, a black company. This association was made nearly impossible, however, by the 1965 extension of the Group Areas Act, one of the principal apartheid statutes; which forbade both racially mixed casts and racially mixed audiences. By June of 1965, Fugard was denied a permit to enter the black township of New Brighton for the dress rehearsal of Sophocles' *Antigone*, which he had adapted and produced with The Serpent Players.

By the early 1970s, Fugard had written several of his best-known plays—including *Hello and Goodbye* (1965) and *Boesman and Lena* (1969)—when he became frustrated with his method of writing plays and decided to work more collaboratively with The Serpent Players. Fugard had worked with John Kani (b. 1944) on the 1965 *Antigone,* and Kani and Winston Ntshona (b. 1941) had performed another absurdist two-hander about convicts—Jean Genet's *Deathwatch*—with the Serpent company in 1968. Both Kani and Ntshona were recognized performers in their own right when they agreed to collaborate with Fugard in the early 1970s. These collaborations were different from Fugard's earlier adaptations of European classics for The Serpent Players, for in this work Kani and Ntshona supplied information, dialogue, and performance tropes which were scripted and shaped in dialogue with Fugard. The plays they devised—*Sizwe Bansi is Dead* (1972) and *The Island* (1973)—are fully collaborative, for the three men improvised a variety of possible performances before setting them down in a final design; the opening monologue with the newspaper in *Sizwe Bansi Is Dead,* for instance, is based on Kani's usual stand-up performance routines. Fugard has gone on to write a number of plays about the effects of apartheid and racism on South African life, including *A Lesson from Aloes* (1980), *Master Harold . . . and the boys* (1982) and *My Children! My Africa!* (1989). Kani and Ntshona have come to enjoy considerable success in the theater and in films; Kani is currently associate director of the Market Theater in Johannesburg.

### The Island (1973)

Although accounts of the collaboration between Fugard, Kani, and Ntshona differ somewhat, John Kani has remarked that Fugard's role in the composition of *Sizwe Bansi Is Dead* was that of an "overseer," while in the writing of *The Island,* the three worked together more directly. The play is set on Robben Island, a prison-island off the shore of South Africa, which could not be named onstage when the play was first written and produced. It centers on two prisoners—John and Winston—who open the play performing a mime of backbreaking routine labor. But as the play proceeds, John and Winston undertake a form of resistance—they devise a production of Sophocles' *Antigone.* Although Winston is uncomfortable with playing a woman, they use *Antigone* to gain a voice; protesting against Creon's unreasonable law, John and Winston speak out against their own entombment by the state.

As prisoners, John and Winston produce *Antigone* in the mode of "poor theater" elaborated by Jerzy Grotowski, as Fugard suggests in his introduction to *Statements.* But while Grotowski's "poor theater" refers to a chosen poverty of means, a reduction of theater to its essence in acting, in the political context of contemporary South African theater, "poverty" has different causes and consequences. John and Winston fashion their performance—their meager costumes, their brief text—from an imposed poverty, one that lends the Grotowskian actor's "total act," his immediate presence to the audience a different register of meaning. For the production of *Antigone* that John and Winston enact is not only an allegory of their own condition and of the injustice of apartheid, but it has immediate consequences on them, on their bodies. Taking the role of Antigone, Winston insures his apparently interminable punishment.

Finally, *The Island* raises the question of intercultural authority. Although it is possible to read the production of *Antigone* as an act of brave resistance, it is also true that *Antigone* is what keeps Winston in jail. To what extent is this use of one of the classic texts of Western drama also being shown to be an *ineffective* strategy of resistance, the replaying of part of the cultural inheritance that continues to imprison John and Winston, a culture of which both *Antigone* and apartheid are a part? The play's simple, open—perhaps even Beckettian—structure does not resolve such questions, but it does help us to entertain them.

# —The Island—
## Athol Fugard, John Kani, and Winston Ntshona

—CHARACTERS—

JOHN
WINSTON     *two prisoners*

*This play was given its first performance on 2 July 1973, directed by Athol Fugard with John Kani as John and Winston Ntshona as Winston.*

SCENE 1

*Centre stage: a raised area representing a cell on Robben Island. Blankets and sleeping-mats—the prisoners sleep on the floor—are neatly folded. In one corner are a bucket of water and two tin mugs.*

*The long drawn-out wail of a siren. Stage-lights come up to reveal a moat of harsh, white light around the cell. In it the two prisoners—John stage-right and Winston stage-left—mime the digging of sand. They wear the prison uniform of khaki shirt and short trousers. Their heads are shaven. It is an image of back-breaking and grotesquely futile labour. Each in turns fills a wheelbarrow and then with great effort pushes it to where the other man is digging, and empties it. As a result, the piles of sand never diminish. Their labour is interminable. The only sounds are their grunts as they dig, the squeal of the wheel-barrows as they circle the cell, and the hum of Hodoshe, the green carrion fly.*

*A whistle is blown. They stop digging and come together, standing side by side as they are handcuffed together and shackled at the ankles. Another whistle. They start to run . . . John mumbling a prayer, Winston muttering a rhythm for their three-legged run.*

*They do not run fast enough. They get beaten . . . Winston receiving a bad blow to the eye and John spraining an ankle. In this condition they arrive finally at the cell door. Handcuffs and shackles are taken off. After being searched, they lurch into their cell. The door closes behind them. Both men sink to the floor.*

*A moment of total exhaustion until slowly, painfully, they start to explore their respective injuries . . . Winston his eye, and John his ankle. Winston is moaning softly and this eventually draws John's attention away from his ankle. He crawls to Winston and examines the injured eye. It needs attention. Winston's moaning is slowly turning into a sound of inarticulate outrage, growing in volume and violence. John urinates into*

*one hand and tries to clean the other man's eye with it, but Winston's anger and outrage are now uncontrollable. He breaks away from John and crawls around the cell, blind with rage and pain. John tries to placate him . . . the noise could bring back the warders and still more trouble. Winston eventually finds the cell door but before he can start banging on it John pulls him away.*

WINSTON: *(calling)* Hodoshe!

JOHN: Leave him, Winston. Listen to me, man! If he comes now we'll be in bigger shit.

WINSTON: I want Hodoshe. I want him now! I want to take him to the office. He must read my warrant. I was sentenced to Life brother, not bloody Death!

JOHN: Please, Winston! He made us run. . . .

WINSTON: I want Hodoshe!

JOHN: He made us run. He's happy now. Leave him. Maybe he'll let us go back to the quarry tomorrow. . . .     10

*(Winston is suddenly silent. For a moment John thinks his words are having an effect, but then he realizes that the other man is looking at his ear. Winston touches it. It is bleeding. A sudden spasm of fear from John who puts a hand to his ear. His fingers come away with blood on them. The two men look at each other.)*

WINSTON: *Nyana we Sizwe!*°

*(In a reversal of earlier roles Winston now gets John down on the floor of the cell so as to examine the injured ear. He has to wipe blood and sweat out of his eyes in order to see clearly. John winces with pain. Winston keeps restraining him.)*

WINSTON: *(eventually)* It's not too bad. *(Using his shirt-tail he cleans the injured ear.)*

JOHN: *(through clenched teeth as Winston tends his ear)* Hell, *ons was gemoer vandag!*° *(A weak smile.)* News bulletin and weather forecast! Black Domination was chased by White Domination. Black Domination lost its shoes and collected a few bruises. Black Domination will run barefoot to the quarry tomorrow. Conditions locally remain unchanged—thunderstorms with the possibility of cold showers and rain.     20 Elsewhere, fine and warm!

*(Winston has now finished tending John's ear and settles down on the floor beside him. He clears his nose, ears, and eyes of sand.)*

WINSTON: Sand! Same old sea sand I used to play with when I was young. St. George's Strand. New Year's Day. Sand

---

11 **nyana we sizwe** brother of the land   15 **ons was gemoer vandag** we were fucked up today

dunes. Sand castles . . .

JOHN: *Ja,*° we used to go there too. Last. . . . *(Pause and then a small laugh. He shakes his head.)* The Christmas before they arrested me, we were down there. All of us. Honeybush. My little Monde played in the sand. We'd given her one of those little buckets and spades for Christmas.

30 WINSTON: *Ja.*

JOHN: Anyway, it was Daddy's turn today. *(Shaking his head ruefully.) Haai,*° Winston, this one goes on the record. 'Struesgod! I'm a man, brother. A man! But if Hodoshe had kept us at those wheelbarrows five minutes longer . . . ! There would have been a baby on the Island tonight. I nearly cried.

WINSTON: *Ja.*

JOHN: There was no end to it, except one of us!

WINSTON: That's right.

40 JOHN: This morning when he said: "You two! The beach!" . . . I thought, Okay, so it's my turn to empty the sea into a hole. He likes that one. But when he pointed to the wheelbarrows, and I saw his idea . . . ! *(Shaking his head.)* I laughed at first. Then I wasn't laughing. Then I hated you. You looked so stupid, *broer!*°

WINSTON: That's what he wanted.

JOHN: It was going to last forever, man! Because of *you.* And for *you,* because of *me. Moer!*° He's cleverer than I thought.

WINSTON: If he was God, he would have done it.

50 JOHN: What?

WINSTON: Broken us. Men get tired. Hey! There's a thought. We're still alive because Hodoshe got tired.

JOHN: Tomorrow?

WINSTON: We'll see.

JOHN: If he takes us back there . . . If I hear that wheelbarrow . . . of yours again, coming with another bloody load of . . . eternity!

WINSTON: *(with calm resignation)* We'll see.

*(Pause. John looks at Winston.)*

JOHN: *(with quiet emphasis, as if the other man did not fully*
60 *understand the significance of what he had said)* I *hated* you Winston.

WINSTON: *(meeting John's eyes)* I hated *you.*

*(John puts a hand on Winston's shoulder. Their brotherhood is intact. He gets slowly to his feet.)*

JOHN: Where's the *lap?*°

WINSTON: Somewhere. Look for it.

JOHN: Hey! You had it last.

*(Limping around the cell looking for their washrag.)*

WINSTON: *Haai,* man! You got no wife here. Look for the rag yourself.

JOHN: *(finding the rag beside the water bucket)* Look where it is. Look! Hodoshe comes in here and sees it. "Whose *lappie*
70 is that?" Then what do you say?

WINSTON: "It's his rag, sir."

JOHN: Yes? Okay. "It's my rag, sir." When you wash, use your shirt.

WINSTON: Okay, okay! "It's our rag, sir!"

JOHN: That will be the bloody day!

*(John, getting ready to wash, starts to take off his shirt. Winston produces a cigarette butt, matches, and flint from their hiding-place under the water bucket. He settles down for a smoke.)*

Shit, today was long. Hey, Winston, suppose the watch of the chap behind the siren is slow! We could still be there, man! *(He pulls out three or four rusty nails from a secret pocket in his trousers. He holds them out to Winston.)* Hey there.

WINSTON: What?

JOHN: With the others.

WINSTON: *(taking the nails)* What's this?

JOHN: Necklace, man. With the others.

WINSTON: Necklace?

JOHN: Antigone's necklace.

WINSTON: *Ag,* shit, man!

*(Slams the nails down on the cell floor and goes on smoking.)*

Antigone! Go to hell, man, John.

JOHN: Hey, don't start any nonsense now. You promised. *(Limps over to Winston's bed-roll and produces a half-com-*
90 *pleted necklace made of nails and string.)* It's nearly finished. Look. Three fingers, one nail . . . three fingers, one nail . . . *(Places the necklace beside Winston who is shaking his head, smoking aggressively, and muttering away.)* Don't start any nonsense now, Winston. There's six days to go to the concert. We're committed. We promised the chaps we'd do something. This *Antigone* is just right for us. Six more days and we'll make it.

*(He continues washing.)*

WINSTON: Jesus, John! We were down on the beach today. Hodoshe made us run. Can't you just leave a man . . . ?    100

JOHN: To hell with you! Who do you think ran with you? I'm also tired, but we can't back out now. Come on! Three fingers. . . .

WINSTON: . . . one nail! *(Shaking his head.) Haai . . . haai . . . haai!*

JOHN: Stop moaning and get on with it. Shit, Winston! What sort of progress is this? *(Abandoning his wash.)* Listen. Listen! Number 42 is practising the Zulu War Dance. Down there they're rehearsing their songs. It's just in this *moer* cell that there's always an argument. Today you want to do it, to-    110 morrow you don't want to do it. How the hell must I know what to report to the chaps tomorrow if we go back to the quarry?

*(Winston is unyielding. His obstinacy gets the better of John, who eventually throws the wash-rag at him.)*

There! Wash!

---

25 **ja** yes  32 **haai; hai** exclamation of surprise  45 **broer** brother  48 **moer** literally, womb; used as a swear-word equiva-lent to "fuck," "fucking"  63 **lap, lappie** rag

*(John applies himself to the necklace while Winston, still muttering away in an undertone, starts to clean himself.)*

How can I be sure of anything when you carry on like this? We've still got to learn the words, the moves. Shit! It could be so bloody good, man.

*(Winston mutters protests all the way through this speech of John's. The latter holds up the necklace.)*

Nearly finished! Look at it! Three fingers. . . .

WINSTON: . . . one nail.

120  JOHN: *Ja!* Simple. Do you still remember all I told you yesterday? Bet you've bloody forgotten. How can I carry on like this? I can't move on, man. Over the whole bloody lot again! Who Antigone is . . . who Creon is . . .

WINSTON: Antigone is mother to Polynices . . .

JOHN: *Haai, haai, haai* . . . shit, Winston! *(Now really exasperated.)* How many times must I tell you that Antigone is the sister to the two brothers? Not the mother. That's another play.

WINSTON: Oh.

130  JOHN: That's all you know! "Oh." *(He abandons the necklace and fishes out a piece of chalk from a crack in the floor.)* Come here. This is the last time. 'Struesgod. The last time.

WINSTON: *Ag*, no, John.

JOHN: Come! I'm putting this plot down for the last time! If you don't learn it tonight I'm going to report you to the old men tomorrow. And remember, *broer*, those old men will make Hodoshe and his tricks look like a little boy.

WINSTON: Jesus Christ! Learn to dig for Hodoshe, learn to run for Hodoshe, and what happens when I get back to the cell?

140  Learn to read *Antigone!*

JOHN: Come! And shut up! *(He pulls the reluctant Winston down beside him on the floor. Winston continues to clean himself with the rag while John lays out the "plot" of Antigone.)* If you would just stop moaning, you would learn faster. Now listen!

WINSTON: Okay, do it.

JOHN: Listen! It is the Trial of Antigone. Right?

WINSTON: So you say.

JOHN: First, the accused. Who is the accused?

150  WINSTON: Antigone.

JOHN: Coming from you that's bloody progress. *(Writing away on the cell floor with his chalk.)* Next the State. Who is the State?

WINSTON: Creon.

JOHN: King Creon. Creon is the State. Now . . . what did Antigone do?

WINSTON: Antigone buried her brother Eteocles.

JOHN: No, no, no! Shit, Winston, when are you going to remember this thing? I told you, man, Antigone buried Polynices. The traitor! The one who I said was on *our* side. Right?

160  WINSTON: Right.

JOHN: Stage one of the Trial. *(Writing on the floor.)* The State lays its charges against the Accused . . . and lists counts . . . you know the way they do it. Stage two is Pleading. What does Antigone plead? Guilty or Not Guilty?

WINSTON: Not Guilty.

JOHN: *(trying to be tactful)* Now look, Winston, we're not going to argue. Between me and you, in this cell, we know she's

Not Guilty. But in the play she pleads Guilty.

WINSTON: No, man, John! Antigone is Not Guilty. . . .    170

JOHN: In the play. . . .

WINSTON: *(losing his temper)* To hell with the play! Antigone had every right to bury her brother.

JOHN: Don't say "To hell with the play." We've got to do the bloody thing. And in the play she pleads Guilty. Get that straight. Antigone pleads. . . .

WINSTON: *(giving up in disgust)* Okay, do it your way.

JOHN: It's not my way! In the play. . . .

WINSTON: Guilty!

JOHN: Yes, Guilty!    180

*(Writes furiously on the floor.)*

WINSTON: Guilty.

JOHN: Stage three, Pleading in Mitigation of Sentence. Stage four, Sentence, State Summary, and something from you . . . Farewell Words. Now learn that.

WINSTON: Hey?

JOHN: *(getting up)* Learn that!

WINSTON: But we've just done it!

JOHN: *I've* just done it. Now *you* learn it.

WINSTON: *(throwing aside the wash-rag with disgust before applying himself to learning the "plot")* Learn to run, learn to    190 read. . . .

JOHN: And don't throw the rag there! *(Retrieving the rag and placing it in its correct place.)* Don't be so bloody difficult, man. We're nearly there. You'll be proud of this thing when we've done it.

*(Limps to his bed-roll and produces a pendant made from a jam-tin lid and twine.)* Look. Winston, look! Creon's medallion. Good, hey! *(Hangs it around his neck.)* I'll finish the necklace while you learn that.

*(He strings on the remaining nails.)* Jesus, Winston! June    200 1965.

WINSTON: What?

JOHN: This, man. *Antigone.* In New Brighton. St. Stephen's Hall. The place was packed, man! All the big people. Front row . . . dignitaries. Shit, those were the days. Georgie was Creon. You know Georgie?

WINSTON: The teacher?

JOHN: That's him. He played Creon. Should have seen him, Winston. Short and fat, with big eyes, but by the time the play was finished he was as tall as the roof.    210

*(Onto his legs in an imitation of Georgie's Creon.)*

"My Councillors, now that the Gods have brought our City safe through a storm of troubles to tranquility. . . . " And old Mulligan! Another short-arsed teacher. With a beard! He used to go up to the Queen. . . . *(Another imitation.)* "Your Majesty, prepare for grief, but do not weep."

*(The necklace in his hands.)*

Nearly finished!
Nomhle played Antigone. A bastard of a lady that one, but a beautiful bitch. Can't get her out of my mind tonight.

WINSTON: *(indicating the "plot")* I know this.

JOHN: You sure?    220

WINSTON: This! . . . it's here. *(Tapping his head.)*

JOHN: You're not bullshitting, hey? *(He rubs out the "plot" and then paces the cell.)* Right. The Trial of Antigone. Who is the Accused?

WINSTON: Antigone.

JOHN: Who is the State?

WINSTON: King Creon.

JOHN: Stage one.

WINSTON: *(supremely self-confident)* Antigone lays charges. . . .

230 JOHN: NO, SHIT, MAN, WINSTON!!!

*(Winston pulls John down and stifles his protests with a hand over his mouth.)*

WINSTON: Okay . . . okay . . . listen, John . . . listen. . . . The State lays charges against Antigone.

*(Pause.)*

JOHN: Be careful!

WINSTON: The State lays charges against Antigone.

JOHN: Stage two.

WINSTON: Pleading.

JOHN: What does she plead? Guilty or Not Guilty?

WINSTON: Guilty.

JOHN: Stage three.

240 WINSTON: Pleading in Mitigation of Sentence.

JOHN: Stage four.

WINSTON: State Summary, Sentence, and Farewell Words.

JOHN: *(very excited)* He's got it! That's my man. See how easy it is, Winston? Tomorrow, just the words.

*(Winston gets onto his legs, John puts away the props. Mats and blankets are unrolled. The two men prepare for sleep.)*

JOHN: Hell, I hope we go back to the quarry tomorrow. There's still a lot of things we need for props and costumes. Your wig! The boys in Number Fourteen said they'd try and smuggle me a piece of rope from the jetty.

WINSTON: *Ja,* I hope we're back there. I want to try and get

250 some tobacco through to Sipho.

JOHN: Sipho?

WINSTON: Back in solitary.

JOHN: Again!

WINSTON: *Ja.*

JOHN: Oh hell!

WINSTON: Simon passed the word.

JOHN: What was it this time?

WINSTON: Complained about the food I think. Demanded to see the book of Prison Regulations.

260 JOHN: Why don't they leave him alone for a bit?

WINSTON: Because he doesn't leave them alone.

JOHN: You're right. I'm glad I'm not in Number Twenty-two with him. One man starts getting hard-arsed like that and the whole lot of you end up in the shit.

*(Winston's bed is ready. He lies down.)*

You know what I'm saying?

WINSTON: *Ja.*

JOHN: What?

WINSTON: What "What"?

JOHN: What am I saying?

WINSTON: *Haai,* Johnny, man! I'm tired now! Let a man. . . .    270

JOHN: I'm saying Don't Be Hard-Arsed! You! When Hodoshe opens that door tomorrow say *"Ja, Baas"* the right way. I don't want to be back on that bloody beach tomorrow just because you feel like being difficult.

WINSTON: *(wearily)* Okay, man, Johnny.

JOHN: You're not alone in this cell. I'm here too.

WINSTON: Jesus, you think I don't know that!

JOHN: People must remember their responsibilities to others.

WINSTON: I'm glad to hear you say that, because I was just going to remind you that it is your turn tonight.    280

JOHN: What do you mean? Wasn't it my turn last night?

WINSTON: *(shaking his head emphatically)* Haai, haai. Don't you remember? Last night I took you to bioscope.°

JOHN: Hey, by the way! So you did. Bloody good film too. "Fastest Gun in the West." Glenn Ford.

*(Whips out a six-shooter and guns down a few bad-men.)*

You were bullshitting me a bit though. How the hell can Glenn Ford shoot backwards through his legs. I tried to work that one out on the beach.

*(He is now seated on his bed-roll. After a moment's thought he holds up an empty mug as a telephone-receiver and starts to dial. Winston watches him with puzzlement.)*

Operator, put me through to New Brighton, please . . . yes, New Brighton, Port Elizabeth. The number is 414624. . . .    290 Yes, mine is local . . . local. . . .

WINSTON: *(recognizing the telephone number)* The Shop!

*(He sits upright with excitement as John launches into the telephone conversation.)*

JOHN: That you Scott? Hello, man! Guess who! . . . You got it! You bastard! Hell, shit, Scott, man . . . how things with you? No, still inside. Give me the news, man . . . you don't say! No, we don't hear anything here . . . not a word. . . . What's that? Business is bad? . . . You bloody undertaker! People aren't dying fast enough! No, things are fine here. . . .

*(Winston, squirming with excitement, has been trying unsuccessfully to interrupt John's torrent of words and laughter. He finally succeeds in drawing John's attention.)*

WINSTON: Who else is there? Who's with Scott?

JOHN: Hey, Scott, who's there with you? . . . Oh no! . . . call him    300 to the phone, man. . . .

WINSTON: Who's it?

JOHN: *(ignoring Winston)* Just for a minute, man, please, Scott. . . .

*(Ecstatic response from John as another voice comes over the phone.)*

Hello there, you beautiful bastard . . . how's it, man? . . .

WINSTON: Who the hell is it, man?

JOHN: *(hand over the receiver)* Sky!

*(Winston can no longer contain his excitement. He scrambles out of his bed to join John, and joins in the fun with questions and remarks whispered into John's ear. Both men enjoy it enormously.)*

How's it with Mangi? Where's Vusi? How are the chaps keeping, Sky? Winston? . . . All right, man. He's here next to 310 me. No, fine, man, fine, man . . . small accident today when he collided with Hodoshe, but nothing to moan about. His right eye bruised, that's all. Hey, Winston's asking how are the punkies doing? *(Big laugh.)* You bloody lover boy! Leave something for us, man!

*(John becomes aware of Winston trying to interrupt again: to Winston.)*

Okay . . . okay. . . .
*(Back to the telephone.)* Listen, Sky, Winston says if you get a chance, go down to Dora Street, to his wife. Tell V. Winston says he's okay, things are fine. Winston says she must carry on . . . nothing has happened . . . tell her to take care 320 of everything and everybody. . . . Ja. . . .

*(The mention of his wife guillotines Winston's excitement and fun. After a few seconds of silence he crawls back heavily to his bed and lies down. A similar shift in mood takes place in John.)*

And look, Sky, you're not far from Gratten Street. Cross over to it, man, drop in on number thirty-eight, talk to Princess, my wife. How is she keeping? Ask her for me. I haven't received a letter for three months now. Why aren't they writing? Tell her to write, man. I want to know how the children are keeping. Is Monde still at school? How's my twin baby, my Father and Mother? Is the old girl sick? They mustn't be afraid to tell me. I want to know. I know it's an effort to write, but it means a lot to us here. Tell her . . . this 330 was another day. They're not very different here. We were down on the beach. The wind was blowing. The sand got in our eyes. The sea was rough. I couldn't see the mainland properly. Tell them that maybe tomorrow we'll go to the quarry. It's not so bad there. We'll be with the others. Tell her also . . . it's starting to get cold now, but the worst is still coming.

*(Slow fade to blackout.)*

## SCENE II

*The cell, a few days later.*

*John is hidden under a blanket. Winston is in the process of putting on Antigone's wig and false breasts.*

JOHN: Okay?
WINSTON: *(still busy)* No.
JOHN: Okay?
340 WINSTON: No.

JOHN: Okay?
WINSTON: No.

*(Pause.)*

JOHN: Okay?

*(Winston is ready. He stands waiting. John slowly lifts the blanket and looks. He can't believe his eyes. Winston is a very funny sight. John's amazement turns into laughter, which builds steadily. He bangs on the cell wall.)*

Hey, Norman. Norman! Come this side, man. I got it here. Poes!°

*(John launches into an extravagant send-up of Winston's Antigone. He circles "her" admiringly, he fondles her breasts, he walks arm in arm with her down Main Street, collapsing with laughter between each "turn." He climaxes everything by dropping his trousers.)*

Speedy Gonzales! Here I come!

*(This last joke is too much for Winston who has endured the whole performance with mounting but suppressed anger. He tears off the wig and breasts, throws them down on the cell floor, and storms over to the water bucket where he starts to clean himself.)*

WINSTON: It's finished! I'm not doing it. Take your Antigone and shove it up your arse!
JOHN: *(trying to control himself)* Wait, man. Wait. . . .

*(He starts laughing again.)*

WINSTON: There is nothing to wait for, my friend. I'm not 350 doing it.
JOHN: Please, Winston!
WINSTON: You can laugh as much as you like, my friend, but just let's get one thing straight, I'm *not* doing Antigone. And in case you want to know why . . . I'm a man, not a bloody woman.
JOHN: When did I say otherwise?
WINSTON: What were you laughing at?
JOHN: I'm not laughing now.
WINSTON: What are you doing, crying? 360

*(Another burst of laughter from John.)*

There you go again, more laughing! Shit, man, you want me to go out there tomorrow night and make a bloody fool of myself? You think I don't know what will happen after that? Every time I run to the quarry . . . "Nyah . . . nyah . . . Here comes Antigone! . . . Help the poor lady! . . ." Well, you can go to hell with your Antigone.
JOHN: I wasn't laughing at you.
WINSTON: Then who were you laughing at? Who else was here that dressed himself as a lady and made a bloody fool of himself? 370
JOHN: *(now trying very hard to placate the other man)* Okay Winston, Okay! I'm not laughing any more.

WINSTON: You can go to hell with what you're saying.

JOHN: Look, Winston, try to understand, man, . . . this is Theatre.

WINSTON: You call laughing at me Theatre? Then go to hell with your Theatre!

JOHN: Please, Winston, just stop talking and listen to me.

WINSTON: No! You get this, brother, . . . I am not doing your
380    Antigone! I would rather run the whole day for Hodoshe. At least I know where I stand with him. All *he* wants is to make me a "boy" . . . not a bloody woman.

JOHN: Okay, okay. . . .

WINSTON: Nothing you can say. . . .

JOHN: *(shouting the other man down)* Will you bloody listen!

WINSTON: *(throwing the wash-rag down violently)* Okay. I'm listening.

JOHN: Sure I laughed. *Ja . . . I laughed.* But can I tell you why I laughed? I was preparing you for . . . stage fright! You think
390    I don't know what I'm doing in this cell? This is preparation for stage fright! I know those bastards out there. When you get in front of them, sure they'll laugh . . . Nyah, nyah! . . . they'll laugh. But just remember this brother, nobody laughs forever! There'll come a time when they'll stop laughing, and that will be the time when our Antigone hits them with her words.

WINSTON: You're day-dreaming, John. Just get it into your head that I'm not doing Antigone. It's as simple as that.

JOHN: *(realizing for the first time that Winston needs to be han-*
400    *dled very carefully)* Hey, Winston! Hold on there, man. We've only got one more day to go! They've given us the best spot in the programme. We end the show! You can't back out now.

WINSTON: You think I can't? Just wait and see.

JOHN: Winston! You want to get me into trouble? Is that what you want?

WINSTON: Okay, I won't back out.

JOHN: *(delighted with his easy victory)* That's my man!

WINSTON: *(retrieving the wig and false breasts off the floor and*
410    *slamming them into John's hands)* Here's Antigone . . . take these titties and hair and play Antigone. I'm going to play Creon. Do you understand what I'm saying? Take your two titties. . . . I'll have my balls and play Creon. *(Turns his back on a flabbergasted John, fishes out a cigarette-butt and matches from under the water bucket, and settles down for a smoke.)*

JOHN: *(after a stunned silence)* You won't make it! I thought about that one days ago. It's too late now to learn Creon's words.

420 WINSTON: *(smoking)* I hate to say it, but that is just too bad. I am not doing Antigone.

*(John is now furious. After a moment's hesitation he stuffs on the wig and false breasts and confronts Winston.)*

JOHN: Look at me. Now laugh.

*(Winston tries, but the laugh is forced and soon dies away.)*

Go on.

*(Pause.)*

Go on laughing! Why did you stop? Must I tell you why? Because behind all this rubbish is me, and you know it's me. You think those bastards out there won't know it's you? Yes, they'll laugh. But who cares about that as long as they laugh in the beginning and listen at the end. That's all we want them to do . . . listen at the end!

WINSTON: I don't care what you say John. I'm not doing 430 Antigone.

JOHN: Winston . . . you're being difficult. You promised. . . .

WINSTON: Go to hell, man. Only last night you tell me that this Antigone is a bloody . . . what you call it . . . legend! A Greek one at that. Bloody thing never even happened. Not even history! Look, brother, I got no time for bullshit. Fuck legends. Me? . . . I live my life here! I know why I'm here, and it's history, not legends. I had my chat with a magistrate in Cradock and now I'm here. Your Antigone is a child's play, man.    440

JOHN: Winston! That's Hodoshe's talk.

WINSTON: You can go to hell with that one too.

JOHN: Hodoshe's talk, Winston! That's what he says all the time. What he wants us to say all our lives. Our convictions, our ideals . . . that's what he calls them . . . child's play. Everything we fucking do is "child's play" . . . when we ran that whole day in the sun and pushed those wheelbarrows, when we cry, when we shit . . . child's play! Look, brother, . . . I've had enough. No one is going to stop me doing Antigone. . . .    450

*(The two men break apart suddenly, drop their trousers, and stand facing the wall with arms outstretched. Hodoshe calls John.)*

Yes, sir!

*(He then pulls up his trousers and leaves the cell. When he has left, Winston pulls up his trousers and starts muttering with savage satisfaction at the thought of John in Hodoshe's hands.)*

WINSTON: There he goes. Serves him right. I just hope Hodoshe teaches him a lesson. Antigone is important! Antigone this! Antigone that! Shit, man. Nobody can sleep in this bloody cell because of all that bullshit. Polynices! Eteocles! The other prisoners too. Nobody gets any peace and quiet because of that bloody Antigone! I hope Hodoshe gives it to him.

*(He is now at the cell door. He listens, then moves over to the wig on the floor and circles it. He finally picks it up. Moves back to the cell door to make sure no one is coming. The water bucket gives him an idea. He puts on the wig and, after some difficulty, manages to see his reflection in the water. A good laugh, which he cuts off abruptly. He moves around the cell trying out a few of Antigone's poses. None of them work. He feels a fool. He finally tears off the wig and throws it down on the floor with disgust.)*

Ag voetsek!°

---

458 **ag voetsek**  go to hell

*(Hands in pockets he paces the cell with grim determination.)*

460 I'm not going to do it. And I'm going to tell him. When he comes back. For once he must just shut that big bloody mouth of his and listen. To me! I'm not going to argue, but 'struesgod that . . . !

*(The wig on the floor. He stamps on it.)*

Shit, man! If he wants a woman in the cell he must send for his wife, and I don't give a damn how he does it. I didn't walk with those men and burn my bloody passbook in front of that police station, and have a magistrate send me here for life so that he can dress me up like a woman and make a bloody fool of me. I'm going to tell him. When he walks

470 through that door.

*(John returns. Winston is so involved in the problem of Antigone that at first he does not register John's strangely vacant manner.)*

Listen, *broer*, I'm not trying to be difficult but this Antigone! No! Please listen to me, John. 'Struesgod I can't do it. I mean, let's try something else, like singing or something. You always got ideas. You know I can sing or dance. But not Antigone. Please, John.

JOHN: *(quietly)* Winston . . .

WINSTON: *(still blind to the other man's manner)* Don't let's argue, man. We've been together in this cell too long now to quarrel about rubbish. But you know me. If there's one

480 thing I can't stand it's people laughing at me. If I go out there tomorrow night and those bastards start laughing I'll fuck up the first one I lay my hands on. You saw yourself what happened in here when you started laughing. I wanted to *moer* you, John. I'm not joking. I really wanted to. . . . Hey, are you listening to me? *(Looking squarely at John.)*

JOHN: Winston . . . I've got something to tell you.

WINSTON: *(registering John's manner for the first time)* What's the matter? Hodoshe? What happened? Are we in shit? Solitary?

490 JOHN: My appeal was heard last Wednesday. Sentence reduced. I've got three months to go.

*(Long silence. Winston is stunned. Eventually. . . . )*

WINSTON: Three. . . .

JOHN: . . . months to go.

WINSTON: Three. . . .

JOHN: *Ja.* That's what Prinsloo said.

WINSTON: John!

*(Winston explodes with joy. The men embrace. They dance a jig in the cell. Winston finally tears himself away and starts to hammer on the cell walls so as to pass on the news to other prisoners.)*

Norman! Norman!! John. Three months to go. *Ja.* . . . Just been told. . . .

*(Winston's excitement makes John nervous. He pulls Winston away from the wall.)*

JOHN: Winston! Not yet, man. We'll tell them at the quarry to-

500 morrow. Let me just live with it for a little while.

WINSTON: Okay okay. . . . How did it happen?

*(He pulls John down to the floor. They sit close together.)*

JOHN: Jesus, I'm so mixed up, man! Ja . . . the door opened and I saw Hodoshe. Ooo God, I said to myself. Trouble! Here we go again! All because of you and the noise you were making. Went down the corridor straight to Number Four . . . Solitary and Spare Diet!! But at the end, instead of turning right, we turned left into the main block, all the way through it to Prinsloo's office.

WINSTON: Prinsloo!

JOHN: I'm telling you. Prinsloo himself, man. We waited out- 510 side for a little bit, then Hodoshe pushed me in. Prinsloo was behind his desk, busy with some papers. He pulled out one and said to me: "You are very lucky. Your lawyers have been working on your case. The sentence has been reduced from ten years, to three."

WINSTON: What did Hodoshe say?

JOHN: Nothing. But he looked unhappy.

*(They laugh.)*

Hey, something else. Hodoshe let me walk back here by myself! He didn't follow me.

WINSTON: Of course. You are free. 520

JOHN: *Haai,* Winston, not yet. Those three months . . . ! Or suppose it's a trick.

WINSTON: What do you mean?

JOHN: Those bastards will do anything to break you. If the wheelbarrows and the quarry don't do it, they'll try something else. Remember that last visit of wives, when they lined up all the men on the other side. . . . "Take a good look and say goodbye! Back to the cells!"

WINSTON: You say you saw Prinsloo?

JOHN: Prinsloo himself. Bastard didn't even stand up when I 530 walked in. And by the way . . . I had to sign. *Ja!* I had to sign a form to say that I had been officially told of the result of my appeal . . . that I had three months to go. *Ja.* I signed!

WINSTON: *(without the slightest doubt)* It's three months, John.

JOHN: *(relaxing and living with the reality for the first time)* Hell, Winston, at the end of those three months, it will be three years together in this cell. Three years ago I stood in front of that magistrate at Kirkwood—bastard didn't even look at me: "Ten years!" I watched ten years of my life drift away like smoke from a cigarette while he fidgeted and 540 scratched his arse. That same night back in the prison van to the cells at Rooihel. First time we met!

WINSTON: *Ja.* We had just got back from our trial in Cradock.

JOHN: You, Temba, . . .

WINSTON: Sipho. . . .

JOHN: Hell, man!

WINSTON: First time we got close to each other was the next morning in the yard, when they lined us up for the vans. . . .

JOHN: And married us!

*(They lock left and right hands together to suggest handcuffs.)*

WINSTON: Who was that old man . . . remember him? . . . in the 550 corner handcuffed to Sipho?

JOHN: Sipho?

WINSTON: *Ja,* the one who started the singing.

JOHN: *(remembering)* Peter. Tatu Peter.

WINSTON: That's him!

JOHN: Hell, it comes back now, man! Pulling through the big gates, wives and mothers running next to the vans, trying to say goodbye . . . all of us inside fighting for a last look through the window.

560 WINSTON: *(shaking his head)* Shit!

JOHN: Bet you've forgotten the song the old man started?

*(Winston tries to remember. John starts singing softly. It is one of the Defiance Campaign songs. Winston joins in.)*

WINSTON: *(shaking his head ruefully)* By the time we reach Humansdorp though, nobody was singing.

JOHN: Fuck singing. I wanted to piss. Hey! I had my one free hand on my balls, holding on. I'd made a mistake when we left the Rooihel. Drank a gallon of water thinking of those five hundred miles ahead. Jesus! There was the bucket in the corner! But we were packed in so tight, remember, we couldn't move. I tried to pull you but it was no bloody good.

570 So I held on—Humansdorp, Storms River, Blaaukrantz . . . held on. But at Knysna, to hell with it, I let go!

*(Gesture to indicate the release of his bladder. Winston finds this enormously funny. John joins in.)*

You were also wet by then!

WINSTON: Never!

JOHN: Okay, let's say that by George nobody was dry. Remember the stop there?

WINSTON: *Ja.* I thought they were going to let us walk around a bit.

JOHN: Not a damn! Fill up with petrol and then on. Hey, but what about those locals, the Coloured prisoners, when we

580 pulled away. Remember? Coming to their cell windows and shouting . . . "Courage, Brothers! Courage!" After that . . . ! Jesus, I was tired. Didn't we fall asleep? Standing like that?

WINSTON: What do you mean standing? It was impossible to fall.

JOHN: Then the docks, the boat. . . . It was my first time on one. I had nothing to vomit up, but my God I tried.

WINSTON: What about me?

JOHN: Then we saw this place for the first time. It almost looked pretty, hey, with all the mist around it.

590 WINSTON: I was too sick to see anything, *broer.*

JOHN: Remember your words when we jumped off onto the jetty?

*(Pause. The two men look at each other.)*

Heavy words, Winston. You looked back at the mountains . . . "Farewell Africa!" I've never forgotten them. That was three years ago.

WINSTON: And now, for you, it's three months to go.

*(Pause. The mood of innocent celebration has passed. John realizes what his good news means to the other man.)*

JOHN: To hell with everything. Let's go to bed.

*(Winston doesn't move. John finds Antigone's wig.)*

We'll talk about Antigone tomorrow.

*(John prepares for bed.)*

Hey, Winston! I just realized. My family! Princess and the
600 children. Do you think they've been told? Jesus, man,

maybe they're also saying . . . three months! Those three months are going to feel as long as the three years. Time passes slowly when you've got something . . . to wait for. . . .

*(Pause. Winston still hasn't moved. John changes his tone.)*

Look, in this cell we're going to forget those three months. The whole bloody thing is most probably a trick anyway. So let's just forget about it. We run to the quarry tomorrow. Together. So let's sleep.

SCENE III

*The cell, later the same night. Both men are in bed. Winston is apparently asleep. John, however, is awake, rolling restlessly from side to side. He eventually gets up and goes quietly to the bucket for a drink of water, then back to his bed. He doesn't lie down, however. Pulling the blanket around his shoulders he starts to think about the three months. He starts counting the days on the fingers of one hand. Behind him Winston sits up and watches him in silence for a few moments.*

WINSTON: *(with a strange smile)* You're counting!

JOHN: *(with a start)* What! Hey, Winston, you gave me a fright, man. I thought you were asleep. What's the matter? Can't 610 you sleep?

WINSTON: *(ignoring the question, still smiling)* You've started counting the days now.

JOHN: *(unable to resist the temptation to talk, moving over to Winston's bed)* Ja.

WINSTON: How many?

JOHN: Ninety-two.

WINSTON: You see!

JOHN: *(excited)* Simple, man. Look . . . twenty days left in this month, thirty days in June, thirty-one in July, eleven days in 620 August . . . ninety-two.

WINSTON: *(still smiling, but watching John carefully)* Tomorrow?

JOHN: Ninety-one.

WINSTON: And the next day?

JOHN: Ninety.

WINSTON: Then one day it will be eighty!

JOHN: *Ja!*

WINSTON: Then seventy.

JOHN: Hey, Winston, time doesn't pass so fast.         630

WINSTON: Then only sixty more days.

JOHN: That's just two months here on the Island.

WINSTON: Fifty . . . forty days in the quarry.

JOHN: Jesus, Winston!

WINSTON: Thirty.

JOHN: One month. Only one month to go.

WINSTON: Twenty . . . *(holding up his hands)* then ten . . . five, four, three, two . . . tomorrow!

*(The anticipation of that moment is too much for John.)*

JOHN: NO! Please, man, Winston. It hurts. Leave those three months alone. I'm going to sleep!         640

*(Back to his bed where he curls up in a tight ball and tries determinedly to sleep. Winston lies down again and stares up at the ceiling. After a pause he speaks quietly.)*

WINSTON: They won't keep you here for the full three months. Only two months. Then down to the jetty, into a ferry-boat . . . you'll say goodbye to this place . . . and straight to Victor Verster Prison on the mainland.

*(Against his will John starts to listen. He eventually sits upright and completely surrenders himself to Winston's description of the last few days of his confinement.)*

Life will change for you there. It will be much easier. Because you won't take Hodoshe with you. He'll stay here with me, on the Island. They'll put you to work in the vineyards at Victor Verster, John. There are no quarries there. Eating grapes, oranges . . . they'll change your diet . . . Diet C, and
650    exercises so that you'll look good when they let you out finally. At night you'll play games . . . Ludo, draughts, snakes and ladders! Then one day they'll call you into the office, with a van waiting outside to take you back. The same five hundred miles. But this time they'll let you sit. You won't have to stand the whole way like you did coming here. And there won't be handcuffs. Maybe they'll even stop on the way so that you can have a pee. Yes, I'm sure they will. You might even sleep over somewhere. Then finally Port Elizabeth. Rooihel Prison again, John! That's very near home,
660    man. New Brighton is next door! Through your cell window you'll see people moving up and down in the street, hear the buses roaring. Then one night you won't sleep again, because you'll be counting. Not days, as you are doing now, but hours. And the next morning, that beautiful morning, John, they'll take you straight out of your cell to the Discharge Office where they'll give you a new khaki shirt, long khaki trousers, brown shoes. And your belongings! I almost forgot your belongings.

JOHN: Hey, by the way! I was wearing a white shirt, black tie,
670    grey flannel trousers . . . brown Crockett shoes . . . socks? *(A little laugh.)* I can't remember my socks! A check jacket . . . and my watch! I was wearing my watch!

WINSTON: They'll wrap them up in a parcel. You'll have it under your arm when they lead you to the gate. And outside, John, outside that gate, New Brighton will be waiting for you. Your mother, your father, Princess and the children . . . and when they open it. . . .

*(Once again, but more violently this time, John breaks the mood as the anticipation of the moment of freedom becomes too much for him.)*

JOHN: Stop it, Winston! Leave those three months alone for Christ's sake. I want to sleep.

*(He tries to get away from Winston, but the latter goes after him. Winston has now also abandoned his false smile.)*

680    WINSTON: *(stopping John as he tries to crawl away)* But it's not finished, John!

JOHN: Leave me alone!

WINSTON: It doesn't end there. Your people will take you home. Thirty-eight, Gratten Street, John! Remember it? Everybody will be waiting for you . . . aunts, uncles, friends, neighbours. They'll put you in a chair, John, like a king, give you anything you want . . . cakes, sweets, cooldrinks . . . and then you'll start to talk. You'll tell them about this place, John, about Hodoshe, about the quarry, and about your

good friend Winston who you left behind. But you still won't  690  be happy, hey. Because you'll need a fuck. A really wild one!

JOHN: Stop it, Winston!

WINSTON: *(relentless)* And that is why at ten o'clock that night you'll slip out through the back door and make your way to Sky's place. Imagine it, man! All the boys waiting for you . . . Georgie, Mangi, Vusumzi. They'll fill you up with booze. They'll look after you. They know what it's like inside. They'll fix you up with a woman. . . .

JOHN: NO!

WINSTON: Set you up with her in a comfortable joint, and then  700  leave you alone. You'll watch her, watch her take her clothes off, you'll take your pants off, get near her, feel her, feel it. . . . Ja, you'll feel it. It will be wet. . . .

JOHN: WINSTON!

WINSTON: Wet *poes*, John! And you'll fuck it wild!

*(John turns finally to face Winston. A long silence as the two men confront each other. John is appalled at what he sees.)*

JOHN: Winston? What's happening? Why are you punishing me?

WINSTON: *(quietly)* You stink, John. You stink of beer, of company, of *poes*, of freedom. . . . Your freedom stinks, John, and it's driving me mad.  710

JOHN: No, Winston!

WINSTON: Yes! Don't deny it. Three months time, at this hour, you'll be wiping beer off your face, your hands on your balls, and *poes* waiting for you. You will laugh, you will drink, you will fuck and forget.

*(John's denials have no effect on Winston.)*

Stop bullshitting me! We've got no time left for that. There's only two months left between us. *(Pause.)* You know where I ended up this morning, John? In the quarry. Next to old Harry. Do you know old Harry, John?

JOHN: Yes.  720

WINSTON: Yes what? Speak, man!

JOHN: Old Harry, Cell Twenty-three, seventy years, serving Life!

WINSTON: That's not what I'm talking about. When you go to the quarry tomorrow, take a good look at old Harry. Look into his eyes, John. Look at his hands. They've changed him. They've turned him into stone. Watch him work with that chisel and hammer. Twenty perfect blocks of stone every day. Nobody else can do it like him. He loves stone. That's why they're nice to him. He's forgotten himself. He's for-  730  gotten everything . . . why he's here, where he comes from. That's happening to me John. I've forgotten why I'm here.

JOHN: No.

WINSTON: Why am I here?

JOHN: You put your head on the block for others.

WINSTON: Fuck the others.

JOHN: Don't say that! Remember our ideals. . . .

WINSTON: Fuck our ideals. . . .

JOHN: No Winston . . . our slogans, our children's freedom. . . .

WINSTON: Fuck slogans, fuck politics . . . fuck everything, John.  740  Why am I here? I'm jealous of your freedom, John. I also want to count. God also gave me ten fingers, but what do I count? My life? How do I count it, John? One . . . one . . . another day comes . . . one. . . . Help me, John! . . . Another day . . . one . . . one . . . Help me, brother! . . . one. . . .

*(John has sunk to the floor, helpless in the face of the other man's torment and pain. Winston almost seems to bend under the weight of the life stretching ahead of him on the Island. For a few seconds he lives in silence with his reality, then slowly straightens up. He turns and looks at John. When he speaks again, it is the voice of a man who has come to terms with his fate, massively compassionate.)*

Nyana we Sizwe!°

*(John looks up at him.)*

Nyana we Sizwe . . . it's all over now. All over. *(He moves over to John.)* Forget me. . . .

*(John attempts a last, limp denial.)*

No, John! Forget me . . . because I'm going to forget you.
750 Yes, I will forget you. Others will come in here, John, count, go, and I'll forget them. Still more will come, count like you, go like you, and I will forget them. And then one day, it will all be over.

*(A lighting change suggests the passage of time. Winston collects together their props for Antigone.)*

Come. They're waiting.
JOHN: Do you know your words?
WINSTON: Yes. Come, we'll be late for the concert.

SCENE IV

*The two men convert their cell-area into a stage for the prison concert. Their blankets are hung to provide a makeshift backdrop behind which Winston disappears with their props. John comes forward and addresses the audience. He is not yet in his Creon costume.*

JOHN: Captain Prinsloo, Hodoshe, Warders, . . . and Gentlemen! Two brothers of the House of Labdacus found themselves on opposite sides in battle, the one defending the
760 State, the other attacking it. They both died on the battlefield. King Creon, Head of the State, decided that the one who had defended the State would be buried with all religious rites due to the noble dead. But the other one, the traitor Polynices, who had come back from exile intending to burn and destroy his fatherland, to drink the blood of his masters, was to have no grave, no mourning. He was to lie on the open fields to rot, or at most be food for the jackals. It was a law. But Antigone, their sister, defied the law and buried the body of her brother Polynices. She was caught
770 and arrested. That is why tonight the Hodoshe Span, Cell Forty-two, presents for your entertainment: "The Trial and Punishment of Antigone."

*(He disappears behind the blankets. They simulate a fanfare of trumpets. At its height the blankets open and he steps out as Creon. In addition to his pendant, there is some sort of crown and a blanket draped over his shoulders as a robe.)*

My People! Creon stands before his palace and greets you! Stop! Stop! What's that I hear? You, good man, speak up. Did I hear "Hail the King"? My good people, I am your

servant . . . a happy one, but still your servant. How many times must I ask you, implore you to see in these symbols of office nothing more, or less, than you would in the uniform of the humblest menial in your house. Creon's crown is as simple, and I hope as clean, as the apron Nanny wears. And 780 even as Nanny smiles and is your happy servant because she sees her charge . . . your child! . . . waxing fat in that little cradle, so too does Creon—your obedient servant!—stand here and smile. For what does he see? Fatness and happiness! How else does one measure the success of a state? By the sumptuousness of the palaces built for its king and princes? The magnificence of the temples erected to its gods? The achievements of its scientists and technicians who can now send rockets to the moon? No! These count for nothing beside the fatness and happiness of its people. 790 But have you ever paused to ask yourself whose responsibility it is to maintain that fatness and happiness? The answer is simple, is it not? . . . your servant the king! But have you then gone on to ask yourself what does the king need to maintain this happy state of affairs? What, other than his silly crown, are the tools with which a king fashions the happiness of his people? The answer is equally simple, my good people. The law! Yes. The law. A three-lettered word, and how many times haven't you glibly used it, never bothering to ask yourselves, "What then is the law?" Or if you have, 800 then making recourse to such clichés as "the law states this . . . or the law states that." The law states or maintains nothing, good people. The law defends! The law is no more or less than a shield in your faithful servant's hand to protect YOU! But even as a shield would be useless in one hand, to defend, without a sword in the other, to strike . . . so too the law has its edge. The penalty! We have come through difficult times. I am sure it is needless for me to remind you of the constant troubles on our borders . . . those despicable rats who would gnaw away at our fatness and happiness. We 810 have been diligent in dealing with them. But unfortunately there are still at large subversive elements . . . there are still amongst us a few rats that are not satisfied and to them I must show this face of Creon . . . so different to the one that hails my happy people! It is with a heavy heart, and you shall see why soon enough, that I must tell you that we have caught another one. That is why I have assembled you here. Let what follows be a living lesson for those among you misguided enough still to harbour sympathy for rats! The shield has defended. Now the sword must strike! 820
Bring in the accused.

*(Winston, dressed as Antigone, enters. He wears the wig, the necklace of nails, and a blanket around his waist as a skirt.)*

Your name!
WINSTON: Antigone, daughter of Oedipus, sister of Eteocles and Polynices.
JOHN: You are accused that, in defiance of the law, you buried the body of the traitor Polynices.
WINSTON: I buried the body of my brother Polynices.
JOHN: Did you know there was a law forbidding that?
WINSTON: Yes.
JOHN: Yet you defied it. 830
WINSTON: Yes.
JOHN: Did you know the consequences of such defiance?

WINSTON: Yes.

JOHN: What did you plead to the charges laid against you? Guilty or Not Guilty?

WINSTON: Guilty.

JOHN: Antigone, you have pleaded guilty. Is there anything you wish to say in mitigation? This is your last chance. Speak.

840 WINSTON: Who made the law forbidding the burial of my brother?

JOHN: The State.

WINSTON: Who is the State?

JOHN: As King I am its manifest symbol.

WINSTON: So you made the law.

JOHN: Yes, for the State.

WINSTON: Are you God?

JOHN: Watch your words, little girl!

WINSTON: You said it was my chance to speak.

JOHN: But not to ridicule.

850 WINSTON: I've got no time to waste on that. Your sentence on my life hangs waiting on your lips.

JOHN: Then speak on.

WINSTON: When Polynices died in battle, all that remained was the empty husk of his body. He could neither harm nor help any man again. What lay on the battlefield waiting for Hodoshe to turn rotten, belonged to God. You are only a man, Creon. Even as there are laws made by men, so too there are others that come from God. He watches my soul for a transgression even as your spies hide in the bush at night to see 860 who is transgressing your laws. Guilty against God I will not be for any man on this earth. Even without your law, Creon, and the threat of death to whoever defied it, I know I must die. Because of your law and my defiance, that fate is now very near. So much the better. Your threat is nothing to me, Creon. But if I had let my mother's son, a Son of the Land, lie there as food for the carrion fly, Hodoshe, my soul would never have known peace. Do you understand anything of what I am saying, Creon?

JOHN: Your words reveal only that obstinacy of spirit which has 870 brought nothing but tragedy to your people. First you break the law. Now you insult the State.

WINSTON: Just because I ask you to remember that you are only a man?

JOHN: And to add insult to injury you gloat over your deeds! No, Antigone, you will not escape with impunity. Were you my own child you would not escape full punishment.

WINSTON: Full punishment? Would you like to do more than just kill me?

JOHN: That is all I wish.

WINSTON: Then let us not waste any time. Stop talking. I buried 880 my brother. That is an honourable thing, Creon. All these people in your state would say so too, if fear of you and another law did not force them into silence.

JOHN: You are wrong. None of my people think the way you do.

WINSTON: Yes they do, but no one dares tell you so. You will not sleep peacefully, Creon.

JOHN: You add shamelessness to your crimes, Antigone.

WINSTON: I do not feel any shame at having honoured my brother.

JOHN: Was he that died with him not also your brother?     890

WINSTON: He was.

JOHN: And so you honour the one and insult the other.

WINSTON: I shared my love, not my hate.

JOHN: Go then and share your love among the dead. I will have no rats' law here while yet I live.

WINSTON: We are wasting time, Creon. Stop talking. Your words defeat your purpose. They are prolonging my life.

JOHN: (again addressing the audience) You have heard all the relevant facts. Needless now to call the state witnesses who would testify beyond reasonable doubt that the accused is 900 guilty. Nor, for that matter, is it in the best interests of the State to disclose their identity. There was a law. The law was broken. The law stipulated its penalty. My hands are tied. Take her from where she stands, straight to the Island! There wall her up in a cell for life, with enough food to acquit ourselves of the taint of her blood.

WINSTON: (to the audience) Brothers and Sisters of the Land! I go now on my last journey. I must leave the light of day forever, for the Island, strange and cold, to be lost between life and death. So, to my grave, my everlasting prison, con- 910 demned alive to solitary death.

(Tearing off his wig and confronting the audience as Winston, not Antigone.)

Gods of our Fathers! My Land! My Home!
Time waits no longer. I go now to my living death, because I honoured those things to which honour belongs.

(The two men take off their costumes and then strike their "set." They then come together and, as in the beginning, their hands come together to suggest handcuffs, and their right and left legs to suggest ankle-chains. They start running . . . John mumbling a prayer, and Winston a rhythm for their three-legged run.)
(The siren wails.)
(Fade to blackout.)

---

IN his introduction to a volume containing The Island, Sizwe Bansi is Dead, and Statements After an Arrest Under the Immorality Act, Fugard describes his desire to work collectively in the early 1970s, and the influence of Grotowski's "poor theater" on his conception of theater.

## Athol Fugard

### Introduction to
### Statements
### (1974)

Thirteen years ago, in an introductory note to a published extract from my play The Blood Knot, I put down a few thoughts about what I called "the pure theatre experience." I wrote:

This experience belongs to the audience. He is my major concern as a playwright. The ingredients of this experience are already partially revealed in what I have said and are very simple—their very simplicity being the main justification for using the word "pure" in the context of a form as open to adulteration as Theatre. They are: the actor and the stage, the actor *on* the stage. Around him is space, to be filled and defined by movement and gesture; around him is also silence to be filled with meaning, using words and sounds, and at moments when all else fails him, including the words, the silence itself.

I concluded:

> In other words the full and unique possibility of this experience needs nothing more than the actor and the stage, the actor in space and silence. Externals, and in a sense even the text can be one, will profit nothing if the actor has no soul.

There is obviously no credit attached to recognizing Theatre's fundamental dependence on the actor. What I do recognize now, however, in those few lines I wrote thirteen years ago, is the first formulation of an obsessional concern with the actor and his performance. This has been a major factor in my work, certainly to the extent that if it is categorized at all, then it must be as "actors' theatre." Without this primary involvement with the actor I would never have ended up "making" theatre with them as I did thirteen years later with the three plays in this volume. It is partly for this reason also that I have directed most of my plays in their first productions; not because I felt that as the author I was in possession of *the* interpretation either of the play as a whole or the specific characters, but because I have always regarded the completed text as being only a half-way stage to my ultimate objective—the living performance and its particular definition of space and silence.

The next of the developments which led finally to the three plays in this volume came about as a result of my association with Serpent Players, the African drama group from New Brighton, Port Elizabeth. Seven years ago, after being in existence for four years (during which, among other plays, we performed *Antigone*) we decided to experiment with improvised theatre. Our reason for this was quite simply the desire to use the stage for a much more immediate and direct relationship with our audience than had been possible with the "ready-made" plays we had been doing. Our first attempt was a sixty-minute exercise called *The Coat* and was based on an actual incident. The coat in question belonged to a New Brighton man, one of many, who had been found guilty of membership of a banned political organization and sentenced to five years imprisonment. It was all he had to send back to his wife. In an interview I have described the evolution of the exercise as follows:

> First we just wanted to see the moment when the coat was handed over. So we very crudely, using almost no words, improvised that one scene—the coat leaving Mabel's hands and ending up in the wife's. Nothing more. Just the coat being handed over. Then we asked: "What do you do with the coat now that you've got it?" The wife, the actress playing the wife, said: "Well, I'm in my house. I've now heard about my husband. I know I'm not going to see him for five years. I've got his coat in my hands. I'll hang it up, first of all, and then go on working. I want to think about him. And the coat." She was a good actress and in the course of all this, something happened. It took a few exercises to fatten it. Know what I mean?
>
> I jotted down, very crudely, several of her attempts and at the end we compared notes. I said: "This is how the last one came out, Nomhle." The other actors joined in: "Yes, that's right. You did. And remember that other thing she said when she was talking about the street? I thought that was rather good." I made a few more notes and handed them over to her. "Take these away. Come back next week. Same time, same place. Live with them. See if you can fill them out a bit."
>
> She did. Next week we provoked her again and that little scene and its follow-up seemed intact. It had a shape, a life of its own. Then we provoked her still further, by questions and discussing, and in this way it all started to grow.
>
> ⋅ I remember! At one stage we were trying to corner her. We felt that a certain edge of desperation in the wife's predicament was still eluding her. We said to Humphrey: "Come on. We need a scene with the man at the Rent Office to whom she is going to appeal for a few days' grace. Will you take it on?" He did. The two of them discussed the "geography" of the little encounter for a second or so and then tried it out. That one almost worked completely the first time. In all of this I acted as scribe . . . you know, making my little notes and keeping an eye on the overall structure. . . .

*The Coat* was followed by many similar experiments over the next few years. I am enormously indebted to them, but equivalently I must admit that looking back now I am very conscious of them as being two-dimensional. Facts, and somehow we never managed to get beyond facts even though they were important facts, are flat and lacking in the density and ambiguity of truly dramatic images. The reason for this limitation was that I relied exclusively on improvisation in its shallowest sense. I had not yet thought seriously about alternative methods of releasing the creative potential of the actor. This came with my reading of Grotowski a few years later, an encounter which coincided with a crisis in relation to my own work. For several years, and particularly as a writer, I had become increasingly dissatisfied with the type of Theatre I was making. The content and personal significance of my response to Grotowski's ideas—I have never seen an actual performance—are indicated in the following extracts from an interview in London three years ago:

> After the last run of *Boesman and Lena* in South Africa I decided to try and do something which had been on my mind for a long time. In a sense it involved turning my back on my securities as a writer. I regard my involvement in theatre as being total in the sense that I both direct and write, and sometimes even act. I am not yet addicted to the privacy of myself and blank paper to the exclusion of all else. I really do think I write plays because what I want ultimately is to be involved with actors and a living experience of the theatre. So, as I say, after that run of *Boesman and Lena* I decided to do something I had wanted to for a long time . . . turn my back on my securities, which is to write a play in total privacy, to go into a rehearsal room with a *completed* text which I would then take on as a director, and which the actors— under my direction—would go on to "illustrate," to use Grotowski's phrase.
>
> I mention Grotowski, because he was in every sense the *agent provocateur* at that moment in my career. His book *Towards a Poor Theatre* made me realize that there were other ways of doing theatre, other ways of creating a totally valid theatre experience . . . that it needn't be the orthodox experience I had been retailing for so many years since *The Blood Knot*. . . .
>
> My work had been so conventional! It involved the *writing* of a play; it involved *setting* that play in terms of local specifics; it involved the actors *assuming* false identities . . . etc., etc. I wanted to turn my back on all that. Permanently or not I didn't know. I just knew I wanted to be free again. I had an idea involving an incident in our recent South African history . . . a young man took a bomb into the Johannesburg station concourse as an act of protest. It killed an old woman. He was eventually caught and hanged. I superimposed, almost in the sense of a palimpsest, this image on that of Clytemnestra and her two children, Orestes and Electra. There was no text. Not a single piece of paper passed between myself and the actors. Three of them. Anyway, after about twelve weeks of totally private rehearsals we got around to what we called our first "exposure." This was an experience that lasted for sixty minutes, had about 300 words, a lot of action—strange, almost somnambulistic action—and silence. It was called *Orestes*. . . .
>
> What was so marvellous in working on this project, along lines suggested by Grotowski and my own experience, was just how pristine, what weight you gave to a line, a word, a gesture, if you set it in silence. . . .

The only fact that I do not find reflected in the above quotations was my total response to Grotowski's sense of the actor as a "creative" artist, not merely "interpretive."

*Orestes* was my first, and remains my most extreme excursion into a new type of theatre experience, in which we attempted to communicate with our audience on the basis of, for us at least, an entirely new vocabulary. It has defied translation onto paper in any conventional sense. I have tried. At the moment it is "scored" in three large drawing-books. It is one of the most important experiences I have had in Theatre and I will be living with it, and using it, for as long as I continue to work. I can think of no aspect of my work, either as writer or director, that it has not influenced.

In relation to the three plays in this volume the importance of *Orestes* was to suggest techniques for releasing the creative potential of the actor. But I would just like to make one point clear: we did not jettison the writer. It was never a question of coming together with the actors on a "let's make a play" basis. The starting-point to our work was always at least an image, sometimes an already structured complex of images about which I, as a writer, was obsessional. In all three of these plays the writer provided us with a mandate in terms of which the actors then went on to work. In the case of *Sizwe Bansi* our starting-point was my fascination with a studio photograph I had once seen of a man with a cigarette in one hand and a pipe in the other; *The Island* began with the notes and ideas I had accumulated over many years relating to Robben Island; *Statements* likewise started with my image of six police photographs of a White woman and a Coloured man caught in the act of love-making.

These initial mandates from the writer were also not his final contribution. He kept pace with us as fast as we discovered and explored . . . sometimes as no more than a scribe, but at other times in a much more decisive way. The final dramatic structure of each play, for example, was his responsibility. Looking back on the three experiences now, it was as if instead of first putting words on paper in order to arrive eventually at the stage and a live performance, I was able to write *directly* into its space and silence via the actor.

In this context my dependence on the actor (and his ability to rise to the challenge involved) is even more fundamental than in the sense I showed at the beginning of these notes. I have made many attempts to formulate this challenge. A simple definition still eludes me, which I suppose is inevitable with an experience as obscure and at times as disturbing as those we have lived through in rehearsal rooms since *Orestes*. I do know, however, that it starts with—absolutely demands—a very special courage without which the actor cannot "stake" his personal truth, and in the absence of words on paper that personal truth has been our only capital. I cannot stress this factor in strong enough terms. Pretence and deception are as fatal as they would be in a writer's private relationship with paper.

The basic device has been that of Challenge and Response. As writer-director I have challenged, and the actors have responded, not intellectually or merely verbally but with a totality of Being that at the risk of sounding pretentious I can only liken to a form of Zen spontaneity. As with the more obvious pitfalls of pretence and deception so too any element of calculation or premeditation in response has proved fatal. When, however, the response seemed meaningful in terms of the overall mandate provided by the writer, or to put it another way, when we thought it was of value and significance in terms of our intentions, we then applied ourselves to disciplining and structuring it so that the gesture, word, or event was capable of controlled repetition. I must stress this point. Spontaneous response and improvisation basically ended in the rehearsal room. Once the actor had created his text in the privacy of rehearsals, we then concerned ourselves with its performance in exactly the same way that we would have done with an independent text.

To arrive at an uninhibited release of Self is not easy. At times it has been painful. There have been harrowing experiences in rehearsal rooms. I say this without any sense of pride. It is just that in making these plays I have kept company with a group of remarkable actors. Their courage has at times frightened me. I have lived constantly with the fear of our work degenerating into a dangerous game with personalities. This might well be one of the reasons why at this point I feel that I have exhausted for myself personally the experience that started with *Orestes*, and that the time has now come to return to the privacy of blank paper.

I have included *Statements* in these notes although on the title page of this volume I claim sole authorship. The reason for this is that although I do regard myself as having *written* that play the production at the Royal Court Theatre, which this text partly reflects, was totally dependent on the methods I had evolved with *Orestes*.

Finally, one long overdue expression of gratitude. That is to Brian Astbury and his theatre The Space, in Cape Town. None of these plays would have happened if his vision and tenacity of purpose had not created that venue.

## Quotations

(1) Foreword to *The Blood Knot* in *Contrast*, Vol. 2, No. 1.
(2) An interview with Athol Fugard about *The Coat* from *Two experiments in Play Making*, A. A. Balkema, Cape Town.
(3) Interview with Athol Fugard, from *Yale/Theatre*, Vol. 4, No. 1.

# Griselda Gambaro

Griselda Gambaro is one of the most distinguished writers of contemporary Argentina. Born in Buenos Aires in 1928, Gambaro's career as a writer has been deeply intertwined with the history and politics of her country. Argentina has a long history of repressive military rule, and Gambaro's career as a playwright began during a period of exceptional crisis, inaugurated by Juan Carlos Onganía's brutal military coup in 1966. Gambaro's plays from this period—*The Walls* (1963), *The Blunder* (1965), *The Siamese Twins* (1965), *The Camp* (1967)—concern the progressive deterioration of the fabric of society. But as the political repression of the 1960s gave way to state terrorism in the 1970s—especially the "Dirty War" (1976–1983), in which the military government systematically imprisoned and/or murdered hundreds of thousands of civilians, "the disappeared"—Gambaro's fiction and drama became increasingly engaged, making her situation in Argentina even more precarious. Her plays of the 1970s—including *Saying Yes* (1972), *Strip* (1972), *The Name* (1976), and *Information for Foreigners* (1973)—depict a world totally slipped from its moorings, in which murder, torture, and execution seem part of the horizon of everyday life.

Gambaro has written several novels as well, including *Nothing To Do with Another Story* (1972), *To Earn One's Death* (1976), *God Does Not Want Us Happy* (1979), and *Impenetrable* (1984). In 1977, *To Earn One's Death* was banned and Gambaro left Argentina to live in Spain and France. She returned to Argentina in 1980, where she continued her career as a playwright, with *Royal Gambit* (1980), *Bitter Blood* (1981), *From the Rising Sun* (1983), and *Antígona Furiosa* (1986). Gambaro has lectured extensively in the United States and is currently living in Buenos Aires.

## Information for Foreigners (1973)

Griselda Gambaro's *Information for Foreigners* uses the participatory element of environmental theater to enact a sophisticated political process as theater. Ideally performed in a house, the play divides the audience into four groups, each led through the play's scenes in a different order, and then reassembled as a single audience for the final scene, Scene 20.

*Information for Foreigners* forces its audience to engage the subtle interinvolvement between theater and the theater of state terrorism, between fiction and fact, a blurring of boundaries between the simulated and the "real" typical of postmodern art. For throughout the play, the audience is repeatedly confronted by two kinds of "performance": overtly "theatrical"or "staged" scenes—like Scene 14, where the audience observes a reenactment of a scene of police violence— and "backstage" or "offstage" scenes where the "disappeared"—the man in his underwear in Scene 1, the girl who is tortured with the "submarine" (held under water in a bathtub of filthy water)— accidentally come into the audience's view. The play forces its audience both to connect these two spheres of performance and to question its own role in each. The Guide repeatedly provides "Information for Foreigners" to the audience, which articulates the historical background of state violence in the 1970s.

In many respects, *Information for Foreigners* is a play about its audience. Scene 4 reenacts the famous Milgram experiment, in which the participant's willingness to follow orders and please authority figures leads him to kill (or, in the original versions of the experiment, to believe he has killed) the "student." The Milgram experiment provides a kind of metaphor for the audience's function in *Information for Foreigners,* in that observation repeatedly involves the audience in a kind of deference to authority. The silent willingness to participate as spectators of the violence makes the audience responsible for the violence, becoming its silent authors. This implied assault on the audience's moral freedom is the point of the play's final scene, where the line between theater and torture is finally suspended, and the "stage" of torture is one the audience is explicitly shown to authorize. Having brought the audience to witness a final execution, the Guide turns to us, with a gesture reminiscent of Genet's Madame Irma: "Ladies and gentlemen, what are you waiting for? The show is over." As he suggests in his final, ritual chant, "Theater imitates life"; but the boundaries between theater and life, between what we see and what we know, have been forever broken:

> Who once said: here the ken
> of men and women
> here the bounds?

# — Information for Foreigners —
## *A Chronicle in Twenty Scenes*
### Griselda Gambaro
TRANSLATED BY MARGUERITE FEITLOWITZ

## —CHARACTERS—

GUIDES, number contingent on number of audience groups

VOICES, heard at intervals throughout

MAN IN ROOM

GIRL, with wet clothes
MAN, with pistol

COORDINATOR
MATURE MAN, Teacher
YOUNG MAN, Pupil

MOTHER
FATHER

GROUP OF MEN, attack man in audience
MAN, defends attacked man

SOMEONE FROM THE AUDIENCE, number contingent on number of audience groups
USHERETTE

THREE MEN, carry table
GROUP OF MEN, surround Girl
TWO WORKMEN

MOTHER (Sara Palacio de Verdt)
FATHER (Marcelo Verdt)
TWO CHILDREN (Verdt girl and boy)
CHIEF
TWO POLICEMEN

MAN IN LOINCLOTH

MAN (Robert Quieto)

NEIGHBOR #1
NEIGHBOR #2
FIRST GROUP OF MEN, tied together
NEIGHBOR #3
SECOND GROUP OF MEN, tied together
OFFICIAL
JUDGE
GUARD

GIRL, with long hair (Hermenegilda)
FOUR MEN, on skates
HUSBAND OF HERMENEGILDA
MOTHER OF HERMENEGILDA
NEIGHBORS

MAN (Juan Pablo Maestre)
WOMAN (Miera Elena Misetich)
TWO POLICEMEN
GROUP OF POLICEMEN, dressed as sweepers

GAME PLAYERS
POLICEMEN, with clubs

ACTOR #1
TWO MEN, in box

ACTRESS #1
ACTRESS #2
ACTOR #1
POLICEMAN #1
POLICEMAN #2

CHILD MONSTER
CHILDREN, play Anton Pirulero
FIRST MAN

SECOND MAN
THIRD MAN
YOUNG WOMAN

TWO GUARDS
PRISONERS
VISTORS TO PRISON
PRETTY GIRL
GROUP OF GUARDS, attack Pretty Girl

LITTLE OLD LADY
OUTLANDISH-LOOKING PRISONER

PROSTITUTES
MAN #1
MAN #2
MAN #3
MAN #4

*The theater space can be a spacious, residential house, preferably two stories, with corridors and empty rooms, some of which interconnect. A larger space is needed for the final scene.*

*Situated in the passageways, propped against the walls, are two or three vertical rectangular boxes, each with a door and air holes.*

*In a different area, chosen by the director, sits an additional box, larger but otherwise the same as those in the passageways.*

*Some of the corridors are dark, while others, in obvious contrast, are crudely lit.*

*The audience will be divided into groups, the number and size of which will depend on the space. A particular number or color can serve to identify each group.*

*Group 1 will mark one possible development of the action.*

*Guides 1, 2, 3, 4, etc., lead their respective groups. The order in which the scenes are observed by these groups is left to the director's discretion until the last scene, scene 20, when all groups converge.*

*In certain scenes, actors play audience members and are actually part of the audience. Audience members, however, are never forced to participate in the action.*

*The groups cross in the passageways and may watch the same scene—perhaps one taking place in the passageway—when the director considers it necessary.*

*Excerpts introduced by the guides as "Explanation: For Foreigners" come from Argentine newspapers of the period 1971–72.*

GUIDES: Organize the groups.
GUIDE: Ladies and gentlemen: Admission is——, for adults. If you've already paid, you can't repent. The cost is already in-
curred. Better to enjoy yourself. No one under eighteen will be admitted. Or under thirty-five or over thirty-six. Everyone else can attend with no problem. No obscenity or strong

words. The play speaks to our way of life: Argentine, Western, and Christian. We are in 1971. I ask that you stay together and remain silent. Careful on the stairs.

## SCENE I

*The* GUIDE *leads the group toward one of the rooms. The room is completely in shadow. The door closes. We hear a shrill, metallic signal. Then, we hear many voices, indistinct and juxtaposed, carrying on an incomprehensible conversation.*

10 GUIDE: One moment . . . I don't find my flashlight. Remember, opportunity makes the thief. Watch your pocketbooks! (*Light comes up on a dark and wrinkled wall.*) Only the naked walls are left. (*The light travels. A man is seated on a chair, wearing only faded underwear. He raises his head, surprised and frightened. He covers his sex with his hands. To the audience.*) Excuse me. I've got the wrong room.

## SCENE II

*The* GUIDE, *lighting the way with his flashlight, leads the group out of the room. He tries to open the door of another room. Behind the door a sweet voice sings.*

VOICE

*"Carnation, sleep and dream,*
*the horse won't drink from the stream . . . "*[1]

20 GUIDE: (*shrugging his shoulders, turns to the group*) It's locked. (*He knocks. Nicely.*) May I? I've brought a group of spectators. And they're getting anxious.
VOICE: (*very rudely*) What's it to me? Beat it! I'm rehearsing.

## SCENE III

GUIDE: (*to the group*) Sorry. People should be brought up better, don't you think? (*tries the latch on the next door. It gives.*) Good. Here. Go ahead. (*The group enters this other dark room. Against the wall, some chairs. The* GUIDE *shines his light on them. Then, nicely.*) You can position yourselves wherever you like. There are chairs for everyone. (*He looks.*)
30 No, not enough to go around. (*arranges them, offers*) Ladies first . . . !

(*Lights on in the middle of the room. A young* GIRL *sits on a chair wearing clothes that are soaking wet. A* MAN *stands next to her, observing her with a tender smile. The* GUIDE *waits for people to get comfortable, points out places. Then, with a finger on his lips, he signals for silence and turns, like one more spectator, toward the characters who begin the action.*)

MAN: (*always speaks softly, tenderly*) Why didn't you dry yourself? You're getting the floor all wet. (*He bends down and dries the floor with a rag.*) Lucky it's not waxed. (*The* GIRL *shivers with cold. The* MAN *takes off his jacket, puts it on her*

*shoulders. The* GIRL *looks at it, wraps herself in the jacket.*) Why didn't you dry yourself? Wasn't there a towel?
GIRL: No.
MAN: (*drying the floor*) What a mess! They fill the tub but don't put any towels. What about the water? Was it warm? (*The* 40 GIRL *doesn't answer. He shakes her, gently.*) Was it warm?
GIRL: No.
MAN: (*He pulls a pistol from his belt and cleans it with a rag.*) Ah! This department isn't worth shi . . . (*The* GUIDE *says something. The* MAN *shoots him a quick look.*) Right. (*He shows her his weapon.*) Do you like it? It isn't loaded. (*She looks at it but doesn't answer. The* MAN *begins loading the gun.*) Why so sad? (*points to the group*) Nothing will happen to you. There are lots of people. They're watching us. (*puts the pistol back in his belt*) You're not pretty with your hair 50 all wet. But that's not too serious. (*He leans toward her, curious.*) Tell me, do you dye your hair? (*still studying her*) You're getting my jacket all wet. Sorry, it's the only one I have . . . (*He takes it gently, shakes it, and puts it on. With a shiver.*) It's damp. (*pointing to the pistol*) Do you want it?
GIRL: No.
MAN: I'm leaving it for you. I have another. The jacket I can't, I swear to you.
GIRL: (*shaking her head*) No.
MAN: (*surreptitiously*) Speak up! They can't hear a thing! 60
GUIDE: Louder! Louder!
MAN: What did I tell you? (*The* GIRL *doesn't answer.*) Look at me. (*She obeys. He holds out the gun.*) Take it!
GIRL: No . . . I don't want to.
MAN: Why are you squeezing your legs together? Do you want to go to the bathroom?
GIRL: (*nods her head*) Yes.
MAN: Then go!
GIRL: They're . . . watching me.
MAN: So? We're all adults, aren't we? They at least are watch- 70 ing. What are you doing, always looking over there? What do you see that's so pretty? (*puts his cheek against hers. Looks in the same direction.*) Nothing! (*separates from her*) I like to see people's eyes when I talk to them. (*Gently, he turns her head.*) Look at me. (*He points to the pistol.*) Do you want it?
GIRL: No, no! Leave me alone!
MAN: (*anxious*) Would you like some stockings? (*He puts his hand on her foot.*)
GIRL: No!      80
MAN: Always no! Why? My intentions are good. Take it. Don't you get bored all alone? (*insists*) Take it, it doesn't bite. But don't squeeze the trigger. Unless . . .
GIRL: (*barely audible*) Unless . . .
MAN: If you squeeze, it's all over. Do you have a boyfriend?
GIRL: No.
MAN: Well then? Take it! I'm leaving it here, on the floor. All you have to do is lean down.
GIRL: For what? I don't want . . . to lean down, I don't

---

[1]"Carnation, sleep and dream," sung by a "sweet" female Voice, the Mother in scene 5, and other voices elsewhere, is from García Lorca's *Bodas de sangre,* or *Blood Wedding,* scene 2. I use the translation by James Graham-Luján and Richard L. O'Connell in *Three Tragedies of Federico García Lorca: Blood Wedding, Yerma, Bernarda Alba* (New York: New Directions, 1955). In the original, Gambaro used only "Nana, niño, nana, del caballo grande que no quiso el agua," repeated over and over. For the English version, I chose to use many more fragments of the lullabye over the course of the play. Gambaro approved this choice in her letter to me of March 28, 1986.

90 want . . . anything.

MAN: The heart and the forehead . . . are sure. I mean, so you don't suffer . . .

GIRL: No . . .

MAN: *(caresses her cheek)* Of course, no. There's a sun outside. It's hot as hell. So you don't have a boyfriend? Well then . . . ? *(He goes toward the door. Turns. Smiles.)* I'm going to tell them to heat the water! *(He goes out. The* GIRL *looks at the pistol on the floor, leans down, trembling, stretches her hand. Freezes in the act.)*

100 GUIDE: Ladies and gentlemen, if it bothers you. *(He opens the door. Leading the group into the hallway, he explains.)* In March 1970, at the Max Planck Institute in Munich, Germany, they began an interesting experiment. Careful on the stairs.

SCENE IV

*The group enters a white room that adjoins another, also painted white, but that may be smaller. In the first room, a small table with a cage full of white rats. On another table, a metal box outfitted with buttons and a microphone. Carefully folded on an ordinary chair, a white coat.*

*Through the half-open door one can see in the other room a chair whose armrests are outfitted with side straps attached to electric cables. Cables to tie down a person's legs. A microphone hangs down from the ceiling.*

*In the first room are the* COORDINATOR, *dressed in a white coat, and two others in street clothes, a* MATURE MAN *and a* YOUNG MAN. *The* MATURE MAN *lingers in front of the cage, putting his fingers through the bars, trying to attract the rats and get them to play.*

COORDINATOR: *(to the group, in a professional tone)* Gentlemen: The subject of our experiment is to determine the pedagogical effect of punishment. To what degree does punishment accelerate the learning process? Imagine. If with one slap a child learns to behave, we waste years teach-
110 ing and persuading only with nice words. We don't have time to lose. Soon he will be an adult; soon he will be molded. Molded for destruction, when one slap, two or three electrical jolts at the right moment could put things in place. *(He begins observing the* MATURE MAN *playing with the rats.)* The gentlemen will help us to clarify . . . unclear . . . details . . . Please, sir, stop pestering those rats! Idiot! *(He goes toward him and kicks him away from the cage.)*

MATURE MAN: Okay, okay. I'm sorry. They're so cute that . . .

120 COORDINATOR: *(calm)* Of course they're cute. *(becoming irritated)* Shall we begin?

MATURE MAN: At your orders, sir!

COORDINATOR: *(happy)* One kick . . . and acquiescence. You, sir, emotionally more mature, will be the teacher.

MATURE MAN: Yes, delighted.

COORDINATOR: *(to the* YOUNG MAN*)* You will be the pupil.

YOUNG MAN: *(He speaks with a metallic voice, like a parrot.)* I will be the pupil.

GUIDE: *(to the group, surreptitiously)* Everyone's a researcher,
130 even the mule.

COORDINATOR: *(drily)* Silence! *(He takes money and some pa-*

*pers out of his pocket.)* Help yourself. Twenty-five marks, or thirty-six dollars for your trouble. If you would be so kind as to sign the receipt and the release. *(They sign, take their money. The* COORDINATOR *hands the* TEACHER *a white coat.)* This is for you. *(Cordially, the* COORDINATOR *helps him on with the coat, adjusts the collar.)* There, now. Right this way, please. *(He leads them into the other room. The* GUIDE *follows with his group.* COORDINATOR *to the* PUPIL.*)* Please be seated. Don't be afraid, it's an experiment, remember that. 140

PUPIL:
Happy to please
I sit with the greatest of ease!

COORDINATOR: I made a mistake. Take off your jacket, roll up your sleeves. *(The* PUPIL *does so.)* Thank you. We have to strap you in. If you would like to resign . . .

PUPIL:
No! For the sake of science
Let us commence!

COORDINATOR: *(strapping him. To the* TEACHER.*)* Will you help 150 me?

TEACHER: *(with dispatch)* Yes, of course!

COORDINATOR: *(From a pocket of his coat, he takes a tube of cream and starts smearing the* PUPIL'*s forearms.)* The cream facilitates the passage of current and prevents burns. *(winking at him)* It's an experiment, don't be frightened. It's like . . . talking to hear yourself talk.

PUPIL:
I'm not afraid
I'm not afraid                                                           160
I really feel I have it made.

COORDINATOR: *(attaches electrodes to the* PUPIL'*s forearms. The* TEACHER *helps diligently.)* How obliging! Thank you.

PUPIL: It's . . . very tight.

COORDINATOR: Let's loosen this a bit. *(He does.)* You—the Teacher—are going to station yourself at the microphone in the next room. *(to the* PUPIL*)* You pay attention. He will read out a group of words, such as *day-sun, night-moon, mother-love,* etc. Then he will repeat the word *day* followed by four others. You must remember which of these four words was 170 associated with *day.* If you make a mistake, you'll receive an electric shock as punishment.

TEACHER: And then you'll learn.

PUPIL: Why will punishment teach me?

COORDINATOR: The shock won't be strong.

TEACHER: Never?

COORDINATOR: No! Unless he really blunders. But it's impossible. They're very obvious associations. For idiots. *(to the* TEACHER*)* Let's go! *(They go into the adjoining room. The* GUIDE *settles his group. The* COORDINATOR *hands the* 180 TEACHER *a sheet of paper.)* Here is the list of words. A clean game: read slowly, with good pronunciation. Wait! Roll up your sleeve.

TEACHER: Me? What for?

COORDINATOR: I want to give you a charge of forty-five volts.

TEACHER: *(surprised)* Me? I'm the teacher!

COORDINATOR: Don't be afraid. I'm doing it so that you'll appreciate the intensity of the punishment. Otherwise, you might have a heavy hand. *(He puts an electrode on the* TEACHER'*s arm, pushes a button.)*                              190

TEACHER: *(jumps, frightened)* That's strong!

COORDINATOR: No, no. You'll start with fifteen volts. You won't have to increase it much. Be seated. Read. Slowly, in a clear voice.

TEACHER: (*He sits in front of the metal box, clears his throat, reads haltingly.*) Day-sun, night-moon, mother-love, water-ship, plague-war, house-forest, child-innocence, prison-bars, window-freedom, blue-sky, bird-flight, nation-Germany, torture-dissuasion. (*He finishes, looks at the* COORDINATOR *like a child awaiting instructions.*)

COORDINATOR: (*claps him on the shoulder*) Very good! Now you must read one word, then four more, so that the pupil will pick the correct association. If he makes a mistake, say "Error," press the first button, and tell the pupil the voltage with which you're punishing him. Then read the right answer. Punishments start at 15 volts and end at 450. (*He makes a horizontal gesture with his hand.*) As you see, it couldn't be easier. Begin.

TEACHER: (*clears his throat*) Sun! Day, forest, mother, water.

VOICE OF THE PUPIL: Day!

COORDINATOR: Very good! (*encouraging the* TEACHER) Let's go on! Do you like it?

TEACHER: (*like a child*) Yes! It's terrific!

COORDINATOR: Continue.

TEACHER: Night! Plague, forest, moon, child.

VOICE OF THE PUPIL: Moon!

TEACHER: (*enthused*) Correct! (*to the* COORDINATOR, *laughing*) This is like a drug!

COORDINATOR: Ssshh! Go on!

TEACHER: Mother! Day, water, child, love. (*silence from the* PUPIL) But this is bread in your belly! What memories do you have of your mother?

COORDINATOR: (*with bonhomie*) Now, don't help! It's not scientific!

VOICE OF THE PUPIL: Chi . . .

TEACHER: (*advises*) No!

COORDINATOR: (*drily*) Excuse me, sir. This is an experiment, not a game.

VOICE OF THE PUPIL: We can't repeat? (*the* TEACHER *looks at the* COORDINATOR.)

COORDINATOR: Just this once. You've got to follow the rules.

TEACHER: Just this once, not again. Mother: day, water, child, love. (*silence from the* PUPIL) Well?

VOICE OF THE PUPIL: Love!

TEACHER: Very good! But faster. (*The* COORDINATOR *nods approval.*) Blue: ship, bird, sky, house. (*silence from the* PUPIL.) I'm waiting.

VOICE OF THE PUPIL: Want to repeat?

TEACHER: I won't repeat. How can you not remember? What a fool. (*looks at the* COORDINATOR, *who assents*) Answer, I won't wait any longer.

VOICE OF THE PUPIL: Bird!

TEACHER: (*pleased*) He made a mistake! Now what do I do?

COORDINATOR: (*He points to the box. The* TEACHER *vacillates in his choice among the buttons.*) The first. Fifteen volts.

TEACHER: (*smiles timidly. Pushes the button.*) Here we go! Take that. (*Through the door, we see that the* PUPIL *is jolted but cries out more in surprise than pain. His cries are always in a parrot-voice, stereotyped like those of someone who, as a joke, coarsely imitates moans, groans, and pain. To the* COORDINATOR.) I didn't do anything! (*into the microphone*) Now remember. (*He reads.*) Plague: child, innocence, love, night.

COORDINATOR: (*very low*) You forgot war.

TEACHER: I did?

COORDINATOR: Plague-war. It's all right, let it go. It doesn't matter.

TEACHER: (*low*) Should I repeat? (*The* COORDINATOR *shrugs.*) Well? (*The* PUPIL *is silent.*) Come on. Quick. Otherwise it's boring, I get tired.

VOICE OF THE PUPIL: Night.

TEACHER: (*pleased*) He made a mistake! Thirty volts! (*instantly presses the second button. A louder groan from the* PUPIL.) Moving right along. Child: love, mother, innocence, bird.

VOICE OF THE PUPIL: (*quickly*) Love!

TEACHER: He made a mistake! You were dreaming! Forty-five volts! (*He pushes another button. Howling loudly, the* PUPIL *arches his back. Surprised by the howling, the* TEACHER *looks into the other room. To the* COORDINATOR, *disturbed.*) A bit strong, wasn't it?

COORDINATOR: (*soothingly*) No. This is a scientific experiment, and I am in charge. What experiment? Just as I told you: simply to determine the effectiveness of punishment in learning. If from the beginning we doubt, we'll never arrive at a conclusion.

TEACHER: Yes, that's right. The associations are easy.

COORDINATOR: And it's not so much. I gave you forty-five volts, remember?

TEACHER: I didn't shout. What a weakling! (*to the* PUPIL) Listen to me. Don't scream. Pay attention. Sky: mother, child, innocence, blue.

VOICE OF THE PUPIL: Blue!

TEACHER: Goooood!

COORDINATOR: Magnificent. We're already getting results.

TEACHER: It's no time to stop, then. Plague: prison, house, forest, war. Well? (*Slowly, the* COORDINATOR *closes the door connecting the rooms.*) Repeat. (*The* COORDINATOR *shakes his head.*) I can't. (*silence from the* PUPIL) Well? (*to the* COORDINATOR) Can I repeat? Just this once. He's not very intelligent. (*The* COORDINATOR *snorts, accedes with a gesture.*)

TEACHER: Listen. Don't let your mind wander. Plague: prison, house, forest, war.

VOICE OF THE PUPIL: Prison.

TEACHER: He's an idiot!

COORDINATOR: (*exasperated*) You must say, "Error," and press the button. That is your job! Save the commentary!

TEACHER: And now he's growling at me! (*He presses the button.*)

VOICE OF THE PUPIL: (*screams*) No, no! I didn't think I'd be in so much pain!

TEACHER: A smart aleck! Well, he better hold up! (*into the microphone*) Pupil: Pay attention. You think I like pushing these little buttons? Try to remember. Blue: bird, flight, sky, freedom. (*waits, nervous*) Out with it!

VOICE OF THE PUPIL: I don't remember!

TEACHER: How can you not remember?

VOICE OF THE PUPIL: I don't!

TEACHER: (*furious, pushes the button*) If you don't remember, take this!

VOICE OF THE PUPIL: (*a scream*) Sky! (*He whimpers.*)

TEACHER: Very good! (*He wipes the sweat from his face.*) You see? With a little determination, you hit it! Okay! Here we go. Flight: bird, blue, forest, night. You gotta be quick. Answer.

VOICE OF THE PUPIL:
I won't play!
No matter what you say!

COORDINATOR: Youth today! Now he refuses!

320 TEACHER: What's the matter with him? He's howling.

COORDINATOR: He signed the release. He can't give up. The results are important, aren't they? You're not screaming. You can be counted on.

TEACHER: Pupil? Pay attention. I am going to read you the words.

VOICE OF THE PUPIL: Go to hell! Let's change places!

TEACHER: Change places? That's crazy. It'll be worse for you, if you don't answer. Bird: flight, blue, plague, war. And I'm repeating the words. And it isn't allowed! Who do you think
330 you are? Answer!

VOICE OF THE PUPIL: I'll make a mistake!

TEACHER: Answer! (*He pushes the button. A scream. To* COORDINATOR.) He's screaming.

COORDINATOR: He feels a bit jolted. You have just one thing to watch out for: 450 volts—kaput. Otherwise, after a week, there isn't a mark.

TEACHER: Listen good. Are you listening?

VOICE OF THE PUPIL: Are you listening?

TEACHER: We'll see who's listening. Bird: night, flight, house,
340 plague.

VOICE OF THE PUPIL: I don't remember!

TEACHER: Don't be such an ass!

VOICE OF THE PUPIL: Don't be such an ass! Plague!

TEACHER: (*furious*) Imbecile! Bird-plague! (*to the* COORDINATOR) See how he answers! (*The* COORDINATOR, *understanding, shrugs his shoulders.*) He's jerking me around! (*He pushes a button. The* PUPIL *screams, weeps. Disconcerted, to the* COORDINATOR.) And now he's crying! What do I do?

COORDINATOR: Keep going. Don't worry about it.

350 TEACHER: Listen, kid, answer right, or I'll blow you away. Window: prison, flight, torture, fr . . . freedom.

VOICE OF THE PUPIL: Torture! Torture!

TEACHER: What did you say? Tortoise! Idiot! You're making fun of me! (*He pushes the button. The* PUPIL *howls.*)

COORDINATOR: (*checking*) One hundred eighty volts. (*smiles approvingly*) It's moving right along.

VOICE OF THE PUPIL: Let me go, you're hurting me! Oh, my belly!

TEACHER: Do we stop?

360 COORDINATOR: No.

TEACHER: He doesn't remember anything!

COORDINATOR: He'll remember now.

TEACHER: You think so? He burst into tears. If he doesn't answer, this is useless!

COORDINATOR: It isn't useless! If we don't succeed in getting concrete results, all this suffering will be useless. Besides, you have to.

TEACHER: *I* do?

COORDINATOR: Of course. The tears, the screams. Think
370 about it.

TEACHER: I'm not exactly sucking my thumb!

COORDINATOR: Of course not. Go ahead.

TEACHER: Nation: prison, bars, Germany, torture.

VOICE OF THE PUPIL: I don't know!

TEACHER: (*his finger on the button*) Out with it!

VOICE OF THE PUPIL: Argentina!

TEACHER: (*beside himself*) Germany, idiot! (*He pushes the button. The* PUPIL *howls.*)

COORDINATOR: Planck Institute, Munich.

380 TEACHER: (*furious*) Prison: nation, plague, war, bars.

VOICE OF THE PUPIL:
I don't know, let me go!
I want to go home!

TEACHER: (*screams*) Out with it!

VOICE OF THE PUPIL: Nation!

TEACHER: You made a mistake! (*He pushes button after button. The* PUPIL *howls.*)

COORDINATOR: (*stops him*) Slow! One at a time.

TEACHER: He's fucking with me! Why doesn't he answer right?

COORDINATOR: Make him.

390 TEACHER: I don't like doing this to you. Is that clear? You signed. Don't count your lost sheep. Concentrate! Here's another. Do you hear me? (*silence*) Do you hear?

VOICE OF THE PUPIL: (*lifeless*) Vultures fly near . . .

TEACHER: Moon: night, prison, window, flight. (*to the* COORDINATOR) He'll get this one. It's easy. (*low*) If he doesn't answer, what do I do?

COORDINATOR: (*gently*) I told you.

TEACHER: (*puts his hand on the last button. Closes his eyes.*) He doesn't answer. Why doesn't he answer?

400 COORDINATOR: (*softly*) Laziness. Low level.

TEACHER: Moon.

VOICE OF THE PUPIL: Ni . . . Niii . . . ght . . .

TEACHER: (*without consulting the list*) He made a mistake. He made a mistake . . . again. (*He opens his eyes.*) It's deliberate. He can't not know. Still . . . it hurts me . . . (*He slowly pushes the last button on the box. Silence. He smiles with relief.*) He didn't scream.

COORDINATOR: No. (*changes his tone. Exultantly.*) Very good! Four hundred fifty volts! Excellent! Your help has been in-
410 valuable.

TEACHER: Why didn't he help?

COORDINATOR: Look . . . we choose the risks we take! Sometimes we're not so lucky. (*removes the* TEACHER's *lab coat*)

TEACHER: It was his fault. Wasn't it?

COORDINATOR: Yes, yes. Your work was magnificent!

TEACHER: He didn't even make an effort. A baby at the breast could have answered right. Some people like to fuck with you!

COORDINATOR: Yes, yes! You were splendid. (*He shakes his*
420 *hand.*) Thank you ever so much. Don't worry. An unforgettable performance.

TEACHER: (*flattered*) It was nothing. I did what I could!

COORDINATOR: (*seeing him to the door*) No, no, you were quick, concise, sure. Thanks ever so much! (*Again he shakes his hand. The* TEACHER *exits. The* COORDINATOR *turns toward the audience, professional.*) This experiment, with recorded screams and simulated tortures, was repeated 180 times. Unfortunately, this teacher who continued his punishments to the lethal 450 volts was no exception. Eighty-
430 five percent of the teachers proceeded in the same way. The same test was done in 1960 in the United States. The

results? Sixty-six percent. They were obeying rules and weren't responsible. Curious, isn't it? Surprised?

GUIDE: Okay, enough. Don't wear out the audience. (to his group) The experiment was done in Germany and the United States.[2] Here among ourselves, it would be unthinkable, absurd. Ladies and gentlemen, let's look for something more amusing. (He leads his group out of the room.) This way, this way. If you would be so kind . . . Ladies and gentlemen . . .

SCENE V

The GUIDE leads the group to the room that in scene 2 was locked.

GUIDE: (He knocks.) May I?
VERY SILLY VOICE: (from inside the room) Yeeeess.

(The group enters the room. Seated on a chair is a woman made up like a doll, wearing a white dress that reaches to her feet and holding a baby in her arms. The baby, swaddled in tulle and lace, is obviously a doll. Sitting on the floor, at the woman's feet, a young man watches them with an enraptured expression. The group is enveloped in a beam of rosy light. The acting is frankly crude.)

GUIDE: (pleased) Ah! Finally something coherent!

MOTHER: (rocking the child)
> "My rose, asleep now lie
> the horse is starting to cry
> His poor hooves were . . ."[3]

GUIDE: What a picture! (to his group) Make yourselves comfortable. Can you see? Madam . . . (helps her get comfortable. Then, rapidly, drily.) Explanation: For Foreigners. Seven P.M., Wednesday, December 16, 1970. Nestor Martins, attorney, defender of political prisoners and trade unions, consults with his client Nildo Zenteno.[4] They take leave of one another in the street. Six men surround Martins, violently force him into a white Peugeot. Nildo Zenteno rushes back, manages momentarily to free the lawyer. A karate chop to the back of his neck brings Zenteno down as well. The car speeds off. A black Chevrolet escorts it. That car had pulled out of a nearby parking lot of the Federal Police. *Desaparecidos.* (from newspaper) Nestor Martins, thirty-three. Nildo Zenteno, thirty-seven.

MOTHER:
> " . . . bleeding,
> his long mane was frozen,
> and deep in his eyes
> stuck a silvery dagger."

(She suddenly stops. Distorting her voice as though she were a ventriloquist speaking for the little one.) Stop it, Mama. That's old. Daddy, tell me a story.

FATHER: (very sweet) Yes, darling.
MOTHER: (idiotic voice) Daddy, it has to be modern! No morals, Daddy!
FATHER: Yes, darling.
MOTHER: (impatient) Come on, Daddy, start!
FATHER: (enraptured) Precious!
MOTHER: (in the voice of a ferocious little child) I know I'm precious! Why do you go round and around, Daddy?
FATHER: Now, now . . . This child is in such a hurry! Daddy has to think!
MOTHER: Enough horsing around, Daddy. Well?
FATHER: (laughs confusedly. Then, grossly exaggerating the traditional tone in which one tells a story.) Once upon a time . . .
MOTHER: (in the voice of a fierce, exasperated little child) Yeeeess . . .
FATHER: (in the same tone) Once upon a time there was a tall man, ugly, ugly, ugly . . . (with disgust) Bolivian. (resuming the story) He had a pile of children. (drily) They procreate a lot. Then they send the kids here.
MOTHER: What happened to the little kids?
FATHER: (sweetly) They were in the street, begging, stealing . . .
MOTHER: And what happened to the tall man?
FATHER: The tall man met another man. This one was a shorty. They talked and talked . . .
MOTHER: (voice of a stupid baby) About what?
FATHER: Well . . . ! Ugly things! And when they were tired of talking, the tall man walked him to his car.
MOTHER: Who?
FATHER: The shorty. The short one was bad, bad. And then, some men came, and since he was bad, they put him in another car to punish him. Because he was bad, bad. And what did the tall man do?
MOTHER: I don't know!
FATHER: He didn't want them to punish him!
MOTHER: Stupid!
FATHER: He ran and ran and hit the good guys. And then, the good guys put him into the car as well.
MOTHER: The good guys took them for a ride! 'Cause they're so good!
FATHER: So very good!
MOTHER: And then what happened, Daddy?
FATHER: Nothing more was ever known!
MOTHER: Yea, yea, yea!
GUIDE: What horrible acting. So sorry. Let's look for something else. (He pushes the people toward the door.) The whole show's not like this. I hope.
MOTHER: (same voice of a stupid baby) Did they punish them a lot, Daddy?
FATHER: Nothing more was ever known!
MOTHER and FATHER: Yea, yea, yea!
GUIDE: (cutting in) Let's go. Let's go, gentlemen. They need at least another month of rehearsal. What dunces!

---

[2]Stanley Milgram describes this experiment in his book *Obedience to Authority* (New York: Harper and Row, 1974). See Introduction, n. 10.

[3]The Mother sings fragments from the *Blood Wedding* lullabye.

[4]The disappearance of Nestor Martins and his client Nildo Zenteno was in fact one of the first. It happened during the term of de facto president General Levingston, who had come to power in a coup d'état, unseating the previous de facto president, General Onganía.

SCENE VI

GUIDE: Let's go upstairs, see if we have better luck. He who searches finds. They say. *(The group goes up the stairs, or down, if the preceding scene took place on the upper level. Natural lighting. When the group reaches the landing of the upper level.)* No, I made a mistake. I had you climb to
530    the . . . *(stops)* In vain. Let's go down.

*(They go down. Suddenly, a group of men burst in, hurling themselves at a person in the audience who is talking with someone else. This other person is for a second paralyzed with astonishment. Then shouting, he throws himself into the fray.)*

MAN: Let him go! Let him go!

*(He succeeds in freeing him. The two make it down a few stairs, but the group of men rush them, surround them, and drag them down the stairs. Over the loudspeaker a distressed voice is heard.)*

VOICE: My God, why did I run? *(Almost instantaneously, the scene breaks out in another place with other characters. The groups may cross at this moment. Again the voice is heard.)* My God, why did I run? *(The scene is repeated in another spot.)* My God, why did I run?

GUIDE: *(meanwhile)* If we search carefully, we'll find remains in the catacombs. There aren't many, but we can still hope for surprises. Careful please. Don't wander off now. That's
540    it, all together. Careful on the stairs. Look over here! *(matter of factly)* A brutish people! Yes, we will find remains. Sometimes discoveries come about by chance. *(He examines the door to a room. Opens it. The room is lit.)* Oh, this one has good light. Imagine, ladies and gentlemen, the faith, the heroism of the first Christians. To pray in these pigsties. It gives me claustrophobia. *(He spots a form covered with canvas in a corner, on the floor.)* Here's something. Finally! *(He draws near.)* Stand back a little, ladies and gentlemen. *(with curiosity)* What is it? *(He lifts an edge of the canvas, imme-*
550    *diately lets it fall and steps back.)* Puah! What a shitty surprise!
VOICE: My God, why did I run?
GUIDE: Sssh! *(turns toward the audience, with a big feigned smile, gives the form a kick)*
VOICE: My God, why did I run?

*(The GUIDE jumps on the form, tramples it, inflamed. In the doorway to the room, another GUIDE appears. He claps his hands loudly.)*

GUIDE #2: Ladies and gentlemen! Please leave. Out, everyone out! Sorry. We have a few like machines without an off button. If you would be so kind as to follow me. *(The light in the room fades out.)*

SCENE VII

560    GUIDE #2: What was the other one telling you?[5]
SOMEONE FROM THE AUDIENCE: About the catacombs.
GUIDE #2: *(glib)* Oh, yes! The remains of the first Christians in the catacombs . . . ! Impressive!

*(He opens a room. The GIRL from scene 3 is crawling on all fours toward a corner. Weak light on her. The rest of the room is in shadow. The pistol still lies abandoned on the floor.)*

GUIDE #2: What do we have here? What is she sniffing at like a dog? *(goes closer. Joking, gives her a slap on the rear. Suddenly he changes expression, helps her to get up.)* What is this? Composure. Pull yourself together.
GIRL: *(lost)* He told me to wait. They keep my head underwater, until . . .
GUIDE #2: *(interrupts)* Who threw water on you? This isn't    570
Carnival. Excuse me, I have to go back to work. *(resumes his professional tone. To the group.)* The paintings are fantastic, a little deteriorated, but still . . . *(He shines a light on the walls.)* Jesus, there's nothing! *(He sees a graffito in a corner, crouches, shines a light on it.)* Gentlemen, come closer! *(looks more closely)* What kind of filth is this? *(stands)* Please, ladies, no! Excuse me, but the ladies may not look! *(He gestures them away.)* Gentlemen, if you like, but . . . *(to the GIRL, very surprised.)* You did this? Your idea of fun? It was a saint's head and they put a . . . *(He finishes with an ex-    580
pressive gesture.)* Let go, let go of the pencil!
GIRL: No. It wasn't me.
GUIDE #2: *(spots the pistol on the floor)* What's this? Just a moment, gentlemen. *(He picks it up.)* How strange!
GIRL: He left it so that, so that . . .
GUIDE #2: So that you could bullshit me. *(He raises his arm as though to hit her. Remembers the audience. Smiles.)* What negligence. *(referring to the gun)* I have to take care of everything around here.
GIRL: I'm thirsty.    590
GUIDE #2: Then you'll pee and be even wetter. *(He shines his light on the walls.)* There's nothing here either. But I swear there was. And not this filth! *(He slaps her skirt.)* No way you're a virgin!
GIRL: I'm thirsty.
GUIDE #2: *(looking around)* Isn't there any water? In the other room, there's a bathtub filled to overflowing.
GIRL: No! No, damn you!
GUIDE #2: What did I tell you? Does anyone understand women? A difficult bunch. As you see, ladies and gentle-    600
men, there's nothing here either. Only the walls. And this filth. *(to the GIRL)* You weren't getting discouraged, were you? He left you the pistol? How strange. Who am I to . . . ? *(He shrugs.)* But don't touch it. If you squeeze the trigger, it's all over. The baths and . . . *(He smiles.)* I'm meddling in something that's none of my business. This is the safety. I'm leaving it up. Careful with the trigger. Sit down.
GIRL: *(She sits, shakes her head.)* I don't want it.
GUIDE #2: There's no danger, stupid! The slightest touch and it goes off.    610
GIRL: Take it!
GUIDE #2: *(surprised)* Why? Soaking and thirsty, it's not a good combination. *(He puts the pistol on her lap, takes her hand and places it on the weapon.)* Do you have a boyfriend? Touch this and it's all over, done with.

---

[5]This Guide is different from the Guide in scene 6. Since the order of the scenes is up to the director, however, this Guide will be called Guide #2 only in scene 7, where the shift occurs.

GIRL: I'm thirsty. (*She raises her hands.*)

GUIDE #2: Right. Sorry. I forgot. Ladies and gentlemen, forgive us for the . . . (*He points to the wall.*) How mortifying! If you would be so kind as to follow me . . . (*He opens the door, indicates the exit. At this moment an* USHERETTE *arrives carrying a tray. She invites the group to have a glass of wine.*) Help yourselves, ladies and gentlemen. It's on the house. There's no reason to be scared: you won't have to pay for it. It's all included. Then we'll go on with our visit. (*A scream is heard. To the audience.*) Who screamed? Who is the imbecile who screamed?

620

SCENE VIII

*The* USHERETTE *steps close to the* GUIDE *and whispers a few words in his ear.*

GUIDE: (*making amends*) Forgive me. In room 3 we are going to find something interesting. "Finally!" you must be saying to yourselves. "We should have stayed home." (*He laughs.*) Ah, theater's a risky business! What do you think? TV's a better bet, isn't it? But no, gentlemen. All is not lost. Please, gentlemen. I'm swallowing the "ladies" so I can go faster. With so many "ladies and gentlemen, ladies and gentlemen," I can't go on to anything else. (*He leads the group through the passageway. The group is shunted aside by three men carrying a long, half-finished table. It is missing a few strips of wood on the surface. It is an ordinary table except that it has a strap nailed to one end. One of the men carries a tool box.*) The first Christians were very persecuted. They were fed to the lions. (*The men put the table on the floor.*) Until San Martín.[6] What would the Spanish say about San Martín? "That son of a bitch traitor. That black shit." (*The men start to saw and drive nails, as though they were alone. They are blocking the passageway.*) Can't you work somewhere else? (*The men don't answer.*) This way, gentlemen. Here's a little path. (*They can't get through. The men move the table, forcing the group toward the* GIRL's *room.*)

630

640

WOMAN'S VOICE:

650
> "Down he went to the river,
> Oh, down he went down!"[7]

GUIDE: What a pain in the ass she is with that lullabye! (*He looks at the door.*) Here we are again. We may as well . . . Through here. Sooner or later we'll see a whole scene. (*He opens. Joking.*) Well? Have you dried yourself? How's . . . (*There are some men surrounding the* GIRL. *The* GUIDE *quickly closes the door, shoos the people away. With a false smile.*) No, I made a mistake. Room 3, they told me. Careful on the stairs. This way, ladies and gentlemen. Ladies, once again. It's nicer . . .

660

WOMAN'S VOICE:
> "And his blood was running,
> Oh, more than the water."

(*The* GUIDE *snorts. Two men have positioned the table against the wall, clearing the passageway. They are smoking cigarettes, like two workers taking a break.*)

GUIDE: (*to the workmen*) Room 3? This one here? (*The men nod yes.*) Thank you!

SCENE IX

*The room is lit with rosy light. Four chairs. There is a group comprising a man, a woman, and two other adults disguised as children, a girl and a boy. Their makeup is exaggerated, and their clothes are cheap, vulgar. The* MOTHER *is sewing, the* FATHER *is seated a little apart, and the* CHILDREN *are playing at throwing a hoop.*

*On the far side of the room are the* CHIEF *and two* POLICEMEN. *They sit very erect with their arms crossed over their chests. The characters act very broadly, a little like marionettes. The tone is grossly exaggerated.*

GUIDE: (*in a professional tone, dry and rapid*) Explanation: For Foreigners. July 2, 1971. Marcelo Verdt and his wife, Sara Palacio de Verdt, were kidnapped by a group of eight men. *Desaparecidos.* Both were members of RAF, Revolutionary Armed Forces.[8] According to information in the newspapers, the wife, before disappearing, brought the children to her sister for protection. 670

MOTHER: (*moving her hand as though sewing*) Children, I'm making a little outfit for the one who is best behaved!

CHILDREN: (*playing*) Thank you, Mommy!

POLICEMEN: (*coming forward*) Hands up, in the name of the law!

MOTHER: (*raising her arm, protecting her face like the heroine in a silent movie*) Oh! (*The* FATHER *doesn't move.*)

CHILDREN: Mommy, Mommy, who are they? 680

MOTHER: Don't be afraid, my darlings! No one is hurting your mother!

CHILDREN: Blessed Mommy!

POLICEMAN: (*comes close, snatches at her clothes*) You're disguised! (*shoving her violently*)

CHILDREN: Mommy, Mommy, who are they?

POLICEMEN: Where's your husband?

MOTHER: I don't know!

CHILDREN: What do you mean, you don't know, Mommy! In the bathroom! Making caca! (*They call.*) Daddy! Daddy! 690 They're looking for you!

FATHER: (*gets up, comes forward, wide-eyed*) Who? What's happening?

POLICEMAN: This is what's happening! It's all over! (*screams*) Silence everyone! Let's get out of this hole! The car's out front!

MOTHER: Not the children! They don't know anything about it!

POLICEMAN: Them too!

MOTHER: Have pity!

POLICEMAN: Silence! Let's go! Everyone! 700

(*They put the chairs together to make the car. All squeeze in.*

---

[6]General José de San Martín, the liberator (El Libertador) of the southern part of South America, is an Argentine national hero.

[7]The Woman's Voice in this scene sings from the *Blood Wedding* lullabye.

[8]RAF, or Revolutionary Armed Forces, is the translation of the name of **FAR**, Fuerza Armada Revolucionaria, a left-wing guerrilla group.

*One of the* POLICEMEN *holds the hoop between his hands and handles it as though it were a steering wheel. He imitates the sound of a motor. The children wave. The* POLICEMAN *brakes suddenly. The others fall backward. They get out of the car, their gestures exaggeratedly frightened.)*

CHIEF: They fell!

MOTHER: *(on her knees)* Pity!

POLICEMAN: What should we do with the kids?

CHILDREN: Daddy!

FATHER: *(dignified)* I'll protect you, don't be afraid. *(puts his arms around them)*

CHIEF: *(to the* POLICEMAN*)* Idiot! Why did you bring the kids?

POLICEMAN: You said everyone, Chief.

MOTHER: They're innocent!

710 CHIEF: I'll see if they're not already lost. Kids: Who created the flag?

MOTHER: *(begging them)* Answer right, answer right!

CHILDREN: *(In unison)* Manuel Belgrano!

CHIEF: When?

CHILDREN: February 27, 1812.

CHIEF: Where?

CHILDREN: On the banks of the Paraná. He had it blessed right there, beneath a blue and white sky, blue and white sky, blue and white . . .

720 CHIEF: Exactly! Very good! *(kisses them)* Here's a prize. *(gives them each a piece of candy)*

CHILDREN: Thank you, sir!

CHIEF: *(to the* MOTHER*)* Take them home. And don't be long.

POLICEMAN: Chief, what if she doesn't return?

CHIEF: *(with an exaggeratedly sinister laugh, pointing to the* FATHER*)* This one stays here. It's in his interest that she return. *(to the* MOTHER*)* Take my advice: be discreet. I'm doing you a favor. Don't be long. Take a taxi.

MOTHER: What are you going to do to him?

730 CHIEF: Nothing! From his eye to his sex. But only if I'm vexed.

MOTHER: Marcelo!

FATHER: My love!

CHIEF: Take them home. We don't have any small sacks. They're only in the way. Move it.

MOTHER: Come, children! Give Daddy a kiss. *(The* FATHER *kisses them.)* Don't be afraid. We're going home.

CHILDREN: *(happy)* The men are nice, Mama!

MOTHER: *(moves off with the* CHILDREN*. Picks up the outfit she was sewing. To one of them.)* Tell Grandma that the hem

740 was turned here.[9] Will you remember?

CHILD: Yes, Mama.

MOTHER: There's soup in the pot. Have it for supper.

CHILDREN: If you're not there, we won't eat any soup! We won't eat any soup!

MOTHER: Be good!

CHILDREN: Where are you going, Mama?

MOTHER: I'm going with Daddy. You behave. *(hugs them)*

CHILDREN: Mommy! Mommy!

GUIDE: *(choked up)* It gets to you, doesn't it?

*(The* MOTHER *separates from the* CHILDREN *and returns toward the* CHIEF*. During the good-bye scene the* POLICEMEN *were trying various sacks—as though they were items of cloth-*

*ing—on the* FATHER*. They have found the right one. Then they take him out of the room.)*

CHILDREN: *(singing in a round)* We won't eat any soup! We 750 won't eat any soup!

MOTHER: Here I am. Where's my husband?

CHIEF: Husband? What husband? Take off your clothes.

GUIDE: *(quickly)* Let's go! Let's get out of here! *(claps his hands)* Out! Where's "Carnation, sleep and dream"? Who wants more wine? *(pushes the group toward the door)* Follow me! Quick! No dawdling! *(The group goes out. The* GUIDE *closes the door, leans against it.)* Ouf!

SCENE X

GUIDE: A little wine! Careful . . . on the . . . stairs. *(The* USH-ERETTE *brings him a glass of water.)* Water? For me? What 760 for? *(remembers)* Oh, right. She's waiting for water! Come, gentlemen, this way. We're almost there. Just another little minute. No reason to fret. *(Again they enter the room of the* GIRL *from scenes 3, 7, and 8. Her clothes are drenched. The* GIRL *is breathing anxiously. She's seated, with the pistol, which is dry, in her lap. To the group.)* Come in. Careful on the stairs. Or rather: fasten your seatbelts, no smoking. *(He laughs. To the* GIRL*, very amiably.)* May I? *(He puts the glass and the pistol on the floor. Takes the chair on which she is sitting. Offers it to a woman in the audience.)* Sit, madam, 770 sit. She may have wet it, but she didn't piss on it! *(He dries the chair with a hankie. To the woman.)* Please, have a seat! *(to the* GIRL*)* They paid admission. Are you thirsty? *(The* GIRL*, lost, doesn't answer. The* GUIDE *shakes her gently.)* Hey! Wake up. I'm asking you if you're thirsty. *(The* GIRL *shakes her head no.)* Oh, no? I brought you water. Drink it. *(He takes the glass, brings it to her lips. The* GIRL *resists.)* And now, what do I do with the glass? I need my hands free. I'm working. This can't be! Drink, little girl, drink. The water flowed . . . *(forcing her)* There. There, that's good. So 780 capricious! Well, I don't like people pulling my leg. You're all wet. *(puts his hand under her skirt)* Even your little fire-cracker. *(He laughs. Turns toward the audience.)* Oh, excuse me. *(takes the pistol)* Shall I take it? No? Freedom is within your grasp. No? *(He puts the barrel against her breast.)* How stupid. I can't. *(He cleans the weapon, puts it in the* GIRL's *lap.)* I don't know why they trust you so . . . It's loaded. If you had a boyfriend, old girl . . . But like this. Idiot, why endure so much? *(Another* GUIDE *appears in the doorway.)* 790

OTHER GUIDE: *(shouting)* What are you doing *here*? It's about to start *there*! And they're giving out wine! It's not to be missed. I saw it! Exceptional! You can understand everything!

GUIDE: Really? Step on it, fellas, let's go! Move it, girls!

OTHER GUIDE: *(teases)* Don't you mean ladies and gentlemen?

GUIDE: *(to* OTHER GUIDE*)* There's wine? For sure? *(*OTHER GUIDE *affirms it and leaves.)* If you would be so kind, ladies and gentlemen . . . *(He holds open the door so the group can pass through. Before closing the door, in a friendly way.)* 800

---

[9]"Tell Grandma that the hem was turned here" is an encoded way of communicating the arrest.

Think about it, little girl.

## SCENE XI

*In the passageway, one of the vertical wooden boxes.*

GUIDE: Wait! This has always intrigued me . . . (*tries to see through the peephole*) I can't see a thing. How about you, sir? (*Someone from the audience has a look.*) It's very dark. (*He knocks at the door. Jokingly.*) Is anyone home? *Hay alguien?* (*Curious, he opens the door. There's a heavily made-up man inside, dressed in a loincloth, staring fixedly. Matter of factly.*) Hi. (*He closes the door, turns toward the audience with an uncomfortable smile. As though it were not so strange.*) What a surprise! To me this is very curious . . .

810

OTHER GUIDE: (*shouts from the doorway of the other room*) Well? What are you waiting for? A carriage? If you don't get there at the beginning, they won't understand anything!

GUIDE: (*annoyed, referring to the vertical box*) What about this? Does anyone understand this? (*to the* OTHER GUIDE) I give the orders in my group! And if they don't get it, too bad for them! This way, gentlemen! (*He leads them in the opposite direction.*) Follow me! (*A panting death rattle is heard through the door of a room they pass.*)

## SCENE XII

820 GUIDE: (*He lingers in front of the door, listening to the death rattle inside.*) What could this be? (*A* MAN *passes by, whistling.*)

MAN: (*to* GUIDE) Good day!

GUIDE: Good day! (*surprised*) Well, he's happy! Let's follow him. (*referring to the death rattle in the room*) Sounds like that and we've really got a mess on our hands! We can check it out later. (*He and the group follow the* MAN. *The* MAN *walks along, whistling. He meets another man who is coming from the opposite direction.*)

830 MAN: Good day!

NEIGHBOR #1: Hello! How's it going, doctor?

(*They shake hands. They continue walking together. The group follows them. They enter a large room, where* NEIGHBOR #2 *is sweeping the floor. Two chairs stacked in a corner, against the wall.*)

NEIGHBOR #2: Hello, doctor!

GUIDE: (*to his group*) Watch out for the cars! Stay on the sidewalk, please!

(*He situates them. He hasn't finished doing so when the* FIRST GROUP OF MEN *enters at a trot, one behind the other, tied together at their waists.*)

FIRST GROUP OF MEN: Let us through! Let us through!

(*They come forward, trot through the room, then suddenly halt in front of the* MAN *and surround him, forming a closed circle.*)

MAN: Excuse me.

FIRST GROUP OF MEN: Quieto! Quieto![10]

MAN: Are you calling me? What do you want? (*The men accelerate, tightening their circular movement, forming two closed rings.*) Excuse me. Let me through.    840

NEIGHBOR #1: What's going on, doctor?

NEIGHBOR #2: (*stops sweeping*) Hey! Let him go!

NEIGHBOR #3: (*from the audience*) What the hell is going on? (*comes forward to help the* MAN)

MAN: Let me go! Enough fooling around!

(*He pushes, tries to get through the circle. Hits, struggles. The men try to drag him toward the door.*)

NEIGHBORS: Let him go! Let him go!

(*They try to break up the group,* NEIGHBOR #2 *hitting out with his broom. The* SECOND GROUP OF MEN *enters, also at a trot and tied together at their waists. They sing.*)

SECOND GROUP OF MEN:

> *Peace and security*
> *That is our domain*
> *With a little authority*    850
> *Order will be maintained!*

(*Observing the tumult, they linger.*)

OFFICIAL: (*heading the* SECOND GROUP OF MEN) What's going on here? This is scandalous! Halt! Separate!

(*The fight freezes.*)

NEIGHBORS: (*all at the same time*)

Sir, they were pushing him!

(*alternating*)

—Over here.

—Over there.

—They tied him up.

—They dragged him down!    860

OFFICIAL: One at a time, magpies. Who asked you anything? (*to the group in the fight*) And you, you're prisoners in the name of the law. (*He "aims" at them, with his finger. The* SECOND GROUP OF MEN *"handcuffs" them. They're all, including the* MAN, *put into a line and tied together at the wrists.*)

NEIGHBORS:

Officer, sir:

Why the arrest?

He's one of the best!    870

OFFICIAL:

It doesn't matter, my esteemed citizens

Have faith

Justice is there for a reason

To prevent baseness, which is treason.

NEIGHBORS: But we saw . . . !

OFFICIAL:

What you saw is of no consequence

If there's offense

Rest assured    880

---

[10]Roberto Quieto, whose surname in fact means "quiet," was a prominent, highly respected liberal lawyer. Unbeknownst to most, he was also a powerful member of the Montoneros, the premier left-wing guerrilla organization.

The man's secure . . .

SECOND GROUP OF MEN: Sure!

*(They "take aim" at the* NEIGHBORS.*)*

OFFICIAL: In my providence.

*(The* NEIGHBORS *mix in with the audience. The* OFFICIAL *moves off to the side, crosses his arms, his expression serious. The* FIRST GROUP OF MEN *and the* MAN *attacked in the first place draw near. One of the men from the second group arranges the chairs.)*

OFFICIAL: *(seating himself. To the* MAN.*)* Name.

MAN: Quieto.

GUIDE: *(shouts)* Sí, Quieto! *(to his group) Quieto* means quiet. *(smiles)* Stop a moment. *(gestures toward the group)* So they'll understand. Otherwise, they'll miss the point. *(The others stop the action. In a dry, professional tone.)* Explana-

890  tion: For Foreigners. July 7, 1971. Robert Quieto, attorney, defender of political prisoners, resists a kidnapping attempt. Fortunately, the neighbors intervene and call a police squad. The kidnappers turn out to be policemen. Dr. Quieto was put at the disposition of the executive power. Subsequently he was accused of having been implicated in an auto theft and of having participated, after his detention, in various subversive acts. He was transferred to Rawson Prison, 730 miles from Buenos Aires. What happened then? I don't remember. Lost in the night of time. *(smiles)* But he

900  wasn't so innocent. High up in the Montoneros, the son of a b——. It's not my responsibility. Although when you have the truth, I don't know why it should be hidden. Go on. I'm done.

OFFICIAL: *(to the* MAN*)* Name.

MAN: Quieto.

OFFICIAL: Quieto! That's what I'm telling *you!* Now what is your name?

MAN: Blame.

OFFICIAL: *(suspicious)* Ohhhh? *(to the* FIRST GROUP OF MEN*)*

910  And you? What are your names?

FIRST GROUP OF MEN: *(They sing.)*
>Peace and security
>That is our domain
>With a little authority
>Order will be maintained!

SECOND GROUP OF MEN:
>If you're lying
>You'll get bruised!

OFFICIAL:
920  Explain what happened
I'm confused!

FIRST GROUP OF MEN:
>Boca will never lose!
>Boca's the team we choose![11]

OFFICIAL: *(very pleased)* For this, you are excused. But who began . . .

FIRST GROUP OF MEN: That man!

OFFICIAL: No more rhyming! *(to the* MAN*)* Don't you know that it's a crime to incite a riot in the street? *(to the* SECOND GROUP OF MEN*)* Did they stop traffic?   930

SECOND GROUP OF MEN: Yes, sir! They delayed it!

OFFICIAL: For how long?

SECOND GROUP OF MEN: For three minutes!

OFFICIAL: Re-create it!

SECOND GROUP OF MEN:
>In their cars the men grew irritated
>At the office work accumulated.

OFFICIAL: *(to the first group, fiercely)* I want a confession. *(sweetly)* What team are you from?   940

FIRST GROUP OF MEN:
>Boca will never lose
>Boca . . .

OFFICIAL: Fine, fine, no need to repeat! *(The* FIRST GROUP OF MEN *"free" their hands, which had been "cuffed." To the* MAN.*)* What about you?

MAN: What about me?

OFFICIAL: What team are you from?

MAN: I nurse the same illusion.

OFFICIAL: I smell collusion. Why aren't you from San Lorenzo?   

MAN: Because I'm not?   950

OFFICIAL: Don't be a wise guy! *(The* SECOND GROUP OF MEN *hit* MAN. *To the others.)* And you, what are you waiting for? Get going!

MAN: You can't let them go! They attacked me! I want to see my attorney!

OFFICIAL: The one who gives the orders here is me. *(to the others)* And you, once again, *(sweetly)* why don't you do your work?

FIRST GROUP OF MEN: *(tied together at their waists, they trot out, singing)*   960
>For us it was a sad event
>That ended to our detriment
>Of this our song's a testament!
>For us it was a sad event
>That ended to our detriment
>Of this our song's a testament!

OFFICIAL: *(to the* MAN*)* Justice will be done.

*(One of the men in the second group puts on a judge's robe and comes closer. Another moves in a chair and has him sit. Becoming the* GUARD, *he remains standing behind the* JUDGE's *back.)*

JUDGE: *(to the* MAN*)* You're free. Being from Boca's no crime. But next time . . .

*(The* MAN *frees his hands and stands up. The* JUDGE *turns halfway around and grabs him from behind. No sooner has he done so when the* GUARD *leans into the* MAN *and pushes him roughly down by the shoulders, forcing him to sit. The* MAN

[11]The Boca Juniors are one of the most important Argentine soccer teams. Their home stadium is in the Buenos Aires neighborhood of La Boca, traditionally an Italian working-class section. San Lorenzo is another team from Greater Buenos Aires. Soccer is by far the most passionately followed sport in Argentina.

*again joins his hands as though they were handcuffed.)*

970 OFFICIAL: *(to the* MAN*)* You stole a car. Your trial's pending. Your sentence could be unending!

MAN: I need defending!

OFFICIAL: Superintending! *(to the* JUDGE*)* He stole a car.

JUDGE: He did not steal a car!

MAN: Am I absolved? Can I go?

JUDGE: Why not? Go ahead!

*(He turns so that his back is to the* MAN. *The previous scene is repeated: the* MAN *frees his hands, the* GUARD *forces him to sit down again, etc.)*

OFFICIAL: He robbed a bank!

MAN: I was in prison!

JUDGE: *(It starts again.)* Absolved!

980 MAN: Thank you. Can I go?

JUDGE: Why not? Go ahead. *(again. The rhythm speeds up.)*

OFFICIAL: He robbed a station!

JUDGE: *(over his shoulder)* What kind of station?

OFFICIAL: Service station. Five old wrecks.

MAN: *(forced to sit)* How? I was in prison!

OFFICIAL: *(with pretended fury)* Guards, you let him go?

JUDGE: *(turns)* Why can't you see? There is no case. Let him go free! *(turns his back)*

OFFICIAL: He robbed a commissary, several stores, and several

990 dairies!

MAN: *(forced to sit)*
If I'd been seized
How could I be eating cheese?

JUDGE:
He is innocent
Surely
I declare it
Firmly.

MAN: *(stands up, etc.)* Thank you. Can I go?

1000 JUDGE: Naturally. Why not. *(It starts again. The action accelerates to the point of dislocation but always remains precise. The speeches are transferred but not the actions, which remain a constant with each character.)*

OFFICIAL: Don't move. I've heard a little story!

JUDGE: He murdered a canary.

MAN:
That isn't fair!
I love all canaries
Everywhere!

1010 OFFICIAL: You love them, but you kill them!

JUDGE: Guards, you let him go?

OFFICIAL:
Your Honor, you're the witness
Of this bad faith.

MAN: I only want to live!

JUDGE: Guards, you let him go?

OFFICIAL: If he'd been seized

MAN: How could I've been eating cheese?

JUDGE: Thank you.

1020 OFFICIAL: Beat it! I can't stand you anymore!

MAN: I'm going back to my city!

JUDGE: Can I go?

OFFICIAL: Beat it!

MAN: *(resisting those who are making him sit)* No, no, I was in

prison!

JUDGE: He's free! Oh, such obsession!

OFFICIAL: He's free! What fascination!

MAN: But I'm not!

JUDGE: Yes, you are! So you better shut up! *(turns his back, covers his ears)*    1030

OFFICIAL:
Enough already! He's hard to handle.
All that screaming. What a scandal!
*(gestures to the guards to take the* MAN *away. To the audience.)*
The idiots they send me, it's outrageous!
The courts
aren't beneficial
Unless they're
sacrificial!

*(lights out)*

GUIDE: Shit! What happened? They turned out the light with-    1040 out telling me! Cretins! *(takes out his flashlight, switches it on)* Where is the door? Luckily I know the house. *(opens door. The passageway is lit.)* This way, gentlemen. There aren't any stairs. But be careful all the same. You only get to stumble once, like the tango says. Hey, hey. Everyone make it? *(He leads the group through the passageway. They pass the door to the room where the death rattle was heard. It is heard again. The* GUIDE *puts his ear to the door. Admiringly.)* Persistent! We go in? We don't go in? What do you want to do? Free choice. At my orders! We go in!    1050

### SCENE XIII

*The* GUIDE *opens the door. The labored breathing stops. There is a* GIRL *with long hair laid out on a stretcher, with a sheet carefully folded under her feet.*

GUIDE: *(advancing on tiptoe)* Don't make any noise. She's sleeping. *(He approaches, looks at her. The* GIRL *smiles at him. Sweetly.)* How're you doing?

GIRL: *(sits up, brushes her hair off her face, folds her hands in her lap. She looks at the group with a semismile. Silence. Then, very simply, colloquially.)*
I would like to die
as softly as possible
So that my friends will think
she is sleeping    1060
in the earth
become a worm
digging in the earth
so that in spring
the flowers blossom
After my death
I want my children
to sit at the table
and say
at her age    1070
Mama
ran off with some guy
What a shame
poor old Dad
staring at the tablecloth

his cup of coffee
searching for her
This is how I want to die
as simply
1080    as though I had never lived
What a lovely thought
to leave like that
not causing any pain
The cup of coffee
that no one drinks
absent . . .

*(Silently, a character mixed in with the audience goes up to the* GIRL. *He puts his hand over her mouth and nose. The* GIRL *offers desperate, mute resistance. She dies. The man gently lays her out, covers her with the sheet. Then he moves off and mixes in with the crowd, like one more spectator.)*

GUIDE: *(amazed)* How about that? *(looks at the man)* And now he's so calm! But what a feat! Phenomenal! *(He lifts the sheet. Matter of factly.)* She's dead. Poor creature! Really,
1090    without so much as a moan. Discreet. And in the bloom of youth! *(lets the sheet fall)* She spoke of children, a husband. We'll have to go find them. Nice news I've got. What a bad deal. *(hopefully)* Anyone want to go? Of course, for this there are no volunteers. *(furious)* The son of a bitch. *(He goes to the door, leaving the audience.)* Excuse me. *(He opens the door, yells out.)* I need someone from the family! Quick! Someone from the family! *(He comes back inside.)* She didn't move, did she? What with the advances of medicine, for a moment I thought that . . .

*(*FOUR MEN *enter, two-by-two, each pair moving as one. They are wearing white smocks down to their feet, very loose, belted at the waist. They come in on skates. Their faces are painted with large red smiling mouths. One pair beats pot lids; the other pair waves a white sack.)*

1100 FOUR MEN: *(singing)*
    *Tachín, tachín, tachín*
    *She died as she would have ordained*
    *Without causing any pain.*

GUIDE: What about the family? I've got to tell them . . . It's so unfortunate . . . My heartfelt sympathy. *(extending his hand)*
FOUR MEN: *(They pay no attention to the* GUIDE. *They approach the stretcher, lift the sheet. Sing.)*
    *The jokester*
    *Coaxed her*

1110 GUIDE: *(very confused)* Choked her . . . A son of a bitch who . . . *(searches with his eyes. The men start putting the* GIRL *into the sack. Surprised.)* What are you doing? But . . .

FOUR MEN: *(sing)*
    *But nothing*
    *But nothing*
    *Just doing our bit*
    *Ashes to ashes*
    *Shit to shit*

GUIDE: *(indignant)* That's gross! Don't you see there's people?
1120    You must have been raised in a barn! Ladies, your forgiveness. I knew nothing . . . The modern theater is like this. No respect for the ladies!

FOUR MEN:

*(They finish putting the* GIRL *into the sack, leaving her head out. They tie the end of the sack around her neck. It is evident that the* GIRL *is playing dead: though her head is bent over, she is able to support it. The* FOUR MEN *hold the bundle, swing it hammocklike. They sing.)*

    *If you don't like this Tin Pan band*
    *Because it hasn't any flair*
    *Because it just gave you a scare*
    *Swing high, swing well*
    *You can go to hell!*

GUIDE: Go on!

FOUR MEN:                                                    1130
    *Tachín, tachín, tachín,*
    *Tachín, tachín, tachín!*
    *Pran-pran-pran!*
    *Taratá-ta-ta!*

*(They near the door. The* HUSBAND *and* MOTHER *enter. The* HUSBAND *is wearing threadbare clothing. His hair is long and all over the place. The* MOTHER *is the typical little old lady—black clothes, shawl over her head. Both act crudely, like prototypes of desperate people.)*

HUSBAND: What happened? I heard screams!
MOTHER: Sirs, have pity! Where is my daughter? Darling! Darling!
GUIDE: Oh my God, the family's here!
MOTHER and HUSBAND: *(together)* We've come to look for our poor Hermenegilda.                                          1140
FOUR MEN:

*(They come back, set the corpse down; it supports itself against the stretcher. Horrified.)*

    That name she inherited
    She certainly merited!
MOTHER and HUSBAND: *(together)*
    We're here to find out
    What she finally merited!
GUIDE: Oh no! If these two speak in verse, I'm leaving!
    Although the language may be terse,
    I can't bear
    so much pain.                                            1150
    I'm leaving! *(He pushes away from the crowd, but upon hearing the* HUSBAND, *he stops, comes back.)*
HUSBAND: Where is she?
FOUR MEN: *(They shake the corpse in front of the* HUSBAND's *face.)* We don't know! We don't know! She was never here!
HUSBAND: What do you mean? She came here to buy wine!
FOUR MEN: *(They turn the corpse facedown on the stretcher, look underneath.)* She bought her bread and went away, evaporated . . . Surely it was fated! *(They look at the ceiling. The* HUSBAND *and* MOTHER *imitate them. The men point.)* 1160
    Look sir. That moth . . .
HUSBAND: She wasn't a moth! At dawn . . .
FOUR MEN:
    She was a moth. At dawn
    Before the sun came up full
    we found her eating

wool

MOTHER: It's not true! She didn't like wool!

FOUR MEN:

1170    Was she a woman or a moth?
The question's far from risible.
Lady, lady don't be miserable.
Don't be upset
We'll give you your daughter yet.

(*They approach an interior door. They call the* HUSBAND *and* MOTHER *as one would a dog.*)

Tch, tch, tch . . .

(*The* HUSBAND *and* MOTHER *advance, their smiles exaggeratedly hopeful. The others open the door. The interior is dark. The* HUSBAND *and* MOTHER *look in.*)

FOUR MEN:

You'll find her here, here!
So be of good cheer, cheer!
(*Moving in unison, the* FOUR MEN *push them inside with*
1180    *kicks in the rump.*) And stop mugging! (*They close the door. They sway.*)
Ladies, Gentlemen, dearest friends
Our show is over, Curtains!

(*They take the corpse. They lead the way to the exit, singing.*)

Tachín, tachín, tachín!
Tachín, tachín, tachín!
Tarará-ta-ta!
Tarará-ta-ta!

GUIDE: (*enthused*) Let's go, let's go! Let's follow them! See
what happens! They're entertaining! (*The group follows the*
1190    FOUR MEN *and* GUIDE. *The* FOUR MEN *enter a contiguous room and close the door. An actor, pretending to be part of the audience, opens it. The interior is dark. An enormous club comes out and hits the actor over the head. He falls. The* GUIDE *leans over him.*) Why did he butt in? I'm the Guide here! One to a group! (*He pokes him. The man doesn't move. He then lifts him by the armpits and puts him into one of the vertical boxes. He talks all the while, completely dissociated from his actions.*) That's how it is. In they all go but . . . who takes the potatoes out of the fire? The son of a bitch. If he
1200    was part of the audience, why did he make like an actor? Vanity, vanity will be the end of us all! . . . (*He closes the door.*) Now what were we going to see?

SOMEONE FROM THE AUDIENCE: The catacombs.

GUIDE: Right. Thank you. The first Christians really had a hard
time of it. Just thinking about how the lions loved to chew
them up . . . Human meat, they say, is sweet. Sweet, bitter,
what could be stupider. (*They cross with another group. To
the* OTHER GUIDE.) Where's there something good? We
went in here, and it's all fucked up. (*Without stopping, the*
1210    OTHER GUIDE *points to a door.*)

SCENE XIV

*The* GUIDE *leads the group into the designated room. Inside is
a group of* NEIGHBORS *all crowded together, some looking over*
the heads of others. On the far side, two POLICEMEN *crouch,
their expressions very attentive. In the center are the* MAN *and*
WOMAN, *both heavily made-up. Their clothes are cheap, flashy;
the* WOMAN *wears very high heels. All the acting is crude, infantile, and exaggerated.*

GUIDE: Attention. Ladies and gentlemen, this is the main
course. So they tell me. Hope it's true. Make yourselves
comfortable. If you find a chair, be seated. Silence, please.
The story of a BM, or bad marriage. (*His tone is professional, dry and quick.*) Explanation: For Foreigners. On the
afternoon of July 13, 1971, Juan Pablo Maestre and his wife,
Mirta Elena Misetich, were kidnapped by a group of men.
Juan Pablo Maestre managed to run a few yards but then
was shot. Mirta Elena Misetich ran in the opposite direction, losing a shoe. She was captured and pushed into one
1220    car; her husband was thrown into another. Shortly afterward, a police squad sent to the scene recovered the shoe
and ordered the doorman of an apartment building to wash
the blood from the pavement. The body of Juan Pablo
Maestre appeared days later in Escobar. Of Mirta Elena
Misetich there was no further news. Both belonged to the
RAF, or Revolutionary Armed Forces. Juan Pablo Maestre,
twenty-eight years old. Mirta Elena Misetich, the same age.

MAN: (*with a conspiratorial air*) Let's plant a bomb here

WOMAN: (*with a conspiratorial air*) And a bomb over there!     1230

MAN: When these go off

WOMAN: No one will be spared!

MAN and WOMAN: (*taking bombs with fuses out from under
their clothes*)
Subversion, subversion,
all rise up!
in revolution!

MAN: (*looking around*) Let's go, all clear!

WOMAN: Nothing will be left here! (*They take a few cautious
steps.*)     1240

POLICEMAN: (*comes forward, arm extended*) Hands up! In the
name of the law!

MAN: We're caught! Run! (*They drop their bombs and run in
opposite directions.*)

POLICEMAN: (*aims with his finger and shoots*) Pum!

(*The* MAN *falls. His blood is obviously fake. The other* POLICEMAN *runs after the* WOMAN.)

WOMAN: (*stops*) Darling!

POLICEMAN: Hey, hey! Justice always triumphs! Olé!

(*The two* POLICEMEN *drag the* MAN *and* WOMAN *away. The*
WOMAN *loses her shoe. They exit. Slowly, the* NEIGHBORS *untangle themselves and come forward.*)

NEIGHBORS:

The ass must be judged
Not broken!     1250

(*The two* POLICEMEN *reenter. The* NEIGHBORS *immediately reform their group.*)

POLICEMEN:

Of our respect
Here's a token![12]

---

[12]"Of our respect / Here's a token" is the couplet substituted for "violín, violón / es la mejor razón." See "Crisis, Terror, Disappearance."

(*They're carrying the* MAN, *dragging him along. The* NEIGHBORS *watch, timidly come forward. Romantic music is heard. More* POLICEMEN *enter, smiling and wearing sweepers jackets. They swing long-handled brooms, dance as in a musical comedy.*)

GROUP OF POLICEMEN: (*They sing.*)
> We're here to clean!
> We're here to clean!
> The filth is gone
> Your street is clean!
> Let mothers pray
> 1260      let children play
> in celebration!

(*Smiling, they sweep. They lift the shoe. They sing.*)

> Little shoe, little shoe
> Whom might you belong to?
> Why, to Snow White
> or to her mother.

GUIDE: What do you mean, fellas! The little lost shoe was Cinderella's!

POLICEMAN: (*emphatically*) I say it's Snow White's or her mother's. (*recovering his smile*) Whose little shoe is this? 1270   Madam, is it yours? Say yes. A Prince Charming awaits you in the wings.

GUIDE: No, no! Error! It's the prince, the prince who searches for the owner of the shoe, not a cop! Didn't you read the story?

POLICEMAN: Calm down! It's a free interpretation. (*smiling*) Doesn't it belong to anyone? Neighbors? (*He shows them the shoe. The* NEIGHBORS *immediately deny ownership, shaking their heads in unison.*) So we'll look in another neighborhood. It'll belong to someone. (*He repeats, frowning in the* GUIDE's *direction.*) 1280   It's Snow White's or her mother's.

GUIDE: (*servile*) Yes, of course, her mother's. Well, let's get going. We can follow you, can't we? (*to his group*) We'll just stroll along. If you get tired, let me know.

GROUP OF POLICEMEN: (*They go out with the shoe. Asking.*) Madam, is this yours? Is this yours? Young man? (*The group follows them. They enter another room. The* WOMAN, *wearing no makeup, is seated on a chair. Sitting nearby on the floor, with her legs crossed, is a* GIRL, *who may be the same* 1290   *as the one from scene 13.*)

POLICEMAN: (*to the* WOMAN) Madam, excuse me. We found a little shoe. Is it yours? Prince Charming will marry you. Cash in a flash! You'll live in a palace! Let's see. (*He puts the shoe on her foot.*) She's Cinderella! It fits! Perfect! What luck, old girl! You win! A royal flush! (*bows*) Princess! My respects! (*The* WOMAN *stares ahead, immobile. Surprised.*) Aren't you happy? What's the matter?

WOMAN: My darling!

POLICEMAN: Your darling was stopped by a cop. (*The* POLICE- 1300   MEN *exit arm-in-arm, tap dancing.*)

WOMAN:
> I was at home, eating my bread. I was
> making love. I was kissing my children.
> And you will be the only one who knows
> where and how my body was lost,
> how my voice became unstrung

> Only you will know
> how to know
> the voices of fear and the faces of
> desperation      1310
> My God, what did the brave ones become?
> I will speak
> Only you will know
> this tongue.

(*A shot is heard.*)

GUIDE: What's going on? Did you hear that? It was a shot. (*looks at the* WOMAN *and the* GIRL) But why so quiet! It's over. Gentlemen, follow me. Did you like that? (*He leads his group out of the room.*) A bit mixed up, wasn't it? Me . . . well, what do *you* like . . . I'm old-fashioned. I prefer something else. If this was the main course, what will the others 1320 be? (*They enter the adjoining room. The* GIRL *of scenes 3, 7, and 8 lies on the floor, shot, the pistol in her hand. The* GUIDE *looks at her, surprised. Then, matter of factly, pushing them toward the exit.*) Oh, sorry! Shall we? The jug may as well go to the fountain as . . . (*Happy music is heard.*) How about that music! So there is a little happiness in this world! Enough drama! Let's go. Move along. A little gaiety, dammit!

(*The poem spoken by the* WOMAN *was written by Marina, a Greek girl, who was captured and tortured.*)

SCENE XV

*As the group leaves, the music fades and after a few minutes disappears. Through the passageway comes a group holding hands. They sing.*

GAME PLAYERS:
> —Martin Fisherman, will you let me pass?      1330
> —Pass, pass, but the last one stays with me!

(*The group starts playing Martin Fisherman, a singing game somewhat like London Bridge Is Falling Down. Two children make a bridge with their arms; the others run underneath, single file, holding each other by the waist. The line of children sings for permission to pass through; the last one is taken prisoner. In another version, the children making the bridge ask questions. Those who answer correctly pass through; the others do not. Two lines form, one comprising the "free," the other "prisoners." After everyone has had a question, the longer line wins, and the game may start again.*)

GUIDE: Ladies and gentlemen, you're welcome to participate. That's not coercion, only if you want to. Grotowsky used to say: The more physical distance, the more spiritual closeness. What nonsense! Don't be afraid to join in, ladies and gentlemen!

(*The game continues. Suddenly one of the men forming Martin Fisherman's bridge yells.*)

GAME PLAYERS: (*alternately*)
> —I know that one! Don't let him go!
> —Me?

(*The latter tries to get off the bridge.*)

> —I know that one! Don't let him go!      1340

—Don't fight!

—Just answer right!

—I don't have to! No!

*(He whistles over his shoulder for help. Those in his line start to push. The others shout.)*

—Don't push! Hold tight!

—Wait!

*(Nevertheless they react. The shorter line becomes crooked. A man forming the bridge yells.)*

—They're shooting! Hold tight!

*(The sound of a police whistle. Policemen arrive, dressed like the cops in Charlie Chaplin's* The Kid, *with large, prehistoric-type clubs. Music is heard. Their acting is crude. They immediately start hitting those in the longer line over the head. The sound of the clubs: Plac! Plac! Plac! Those hit fall into artificially distorted poses. The men rush the bridge of Martin Fisherman, crushing the captured player, who screams.)*

GUIDE: Kids today! They don't know how to play peacefully! Let's get out of the way. I wonder if they'll tie them up. *(warns a policeman)* Not the audience! *(The policeman* moves his head like Harpo Marx. He spins around like an acrobat, beating on actors mixed in with the public, acting as audience members. Very confused.)* On the double, ladies and gentlemen, quickly! Let's go! No stragglers! My group this way! Forward! Toward the music! *(Music floats in the air, disappears.)* Now what? *(He opens his hands in a gesture of incomprehension. Taking advantage of the* GUIDE's *position, someone comes forward and puts a tin plate full of garbage in his hands. To this person, absolutely astonished.)* What is this? *(protests)* Not to me you don't! This is not what I get paid for! Who do they think they are?

*(Meanwhile, the game of Martin Fisherman has stopped. The policemen and actors from the shorter line carry off those who were knocked unconscious and throw them into a room.)*

GUIDE: *(to the group)* With so much confusion, I forgot about the catacombs. You'll end up leaving without seeing anything.

WOMAN'S VOICE:
    *"The water was black there
        under the branches.
    When it reached the bridge
        it stopped and sang."*[13]

GUIDE: *(pleased)* Her again! What persistence! You want to risk it? Sooner or later it's got to improve!

*(He opens the door. The people inside won't let him in.)*

### SCENE XVI

ACTOR #1: Sorry, old man. You can't come in. Off-limits.

GUIDE: Why not? I'm bringing people.

ACTOR #1: No, old man. We're rehearsing.

GUIDE: So what? Aren't you getting tired?

ACTOR #1: No! *(He closes the door.)*

GUIDE: *(outraged)* What balls. Sorry. *(He remembers something, smiles.)* They're not gonna fuck with me. Psss! This way! There's another entrance! *(He leads them along a passageway. They pass a vertical box like the others, only bigger. Naturally.)* Just a moment. *(He opens the door of the box. Inside, two men are plastered together. The* GUIDE *puts the tin plate on their shoulders. They stretch their necks desperately, trying to suck up what's on the plate. It falls. Matter of factly, to the audience.)* They let it fall! What idiots! *(He closes the door.)*

### SCENE XVI

GUIDE: Don't make a sound. Walk on tiptoe. Don't say a word. *(They enter a room. Folding screens around an illuminated central space.)* Sssh . . . Silence . . . *(The group watches the scene through the folding screens. Two actors and two actresses are rehearsing* Othello, *in rehearsal clothes. Actress #1, as Desdemona, is already dead on the floor.)*

ACTOR #1: *(as Iago)*
    Villainous whore![14]

ACTRESS #2: *(as Emilia)*
    She give it Cassio? No, alas, I found it,
    And I did give't my husband.

ACTOR #1:
    Filth, thou liest!

GUIDE: Such language!

ACTRESS #2: *(as Emilia)*
    By heaven, I do not, I do not, gentlemen.
    O murd'rous coxcomb! What should such a fool
    Do with so good a wife?

ACTOR #2: *(as Othello)*
    Are there no stones in heaven
    But what serves for the thunder?—Precious villain!

*(Othello runs at Iago. Iago strikes Emilia and leaves.* ACTOR #1 *marks his exit and sits off to one side. A* POLICEMAN *enters in Isabellesque attire.)*

POLICEMAN #1: *(to* ACTOR #2*)* You killed those two women! Villain! Viper!

*(The* ACTRESSES *get up, go sit down. They watch calmly, a bit surprised.)*

ACTOR #1: Who told this guy to come in?

POLICEMAN #1: *(acting, calling his men)* Over here, men. Here!

ACTOR #1: Go act for the other side. Who called you. Get out of here!

POLICEMAN #1: Thou hast no weapon, and perforce must suffer. They are dead.

ACTRESS #1: *(joking)* I am dead!

---

[13]The Woman's Voice sings lines from the *Blood Wedding* lullabye.

[14]Lines from *Othello* are taken from act 5, scene 2, lines 229–35, 248–49, 256, 287, 306–7, 317, 367–71. All are found on pages 1239–40 of *The Riverside Shakespeare* (Boston: Houghton Mifflin, 1974).

ACTRESS #2: (*sings*)

> *Willow, willow, willow.*
> *Moor, she was chaste. She loved thee, cruel Moor!*

ACTOR #1: Stop! (*to the* POLICEMAN) Will you beat it!

1420 POLICEMAN #1: To raise your sword against a woman!

ACTOR #2: What are you talking about?

ACTOR #1: The guy's a mental case. Beat it! (*He pushes him toward the door.*) Out! (*returns*) Better keep the door locked. There's no telling who could walk in. Let's go, girls. That guy stank worse than a pig. (*claps his hands*) One more time!

POLICEMAN #1: (*draws his sword*) No, traitor!

ACTOR #2: (*returns. In spite of himself, in character.*) Wrench his sword from him.

1430 POLICEMAN #1:

> Torments will ope your lips.

ACTOR #2:

> Well, thou dost best.

ACTOR #1: Cut! Right there!

POLICEMAN #1: Officers, come here! (*Another* POLICEMAN *enters, dressed in the same style.*)

POLICEMAN #2: What's happening, sir?

POLICEMAN #1: (*He shows him the vial he's just taken from his own pocket.*) Trotyl! And the women are dead! Oh my! O

1440 thou pernicious caitiff!

POLICEMAN #2: (*with his sword, rounds up the* ACTORS, *who move into a corner*) Move it, or I'll take a slice! (*The* ACTRESSES *let out an inappropriate laugh.*)

POLICEMAN #1: Take them, too, for having laughed at the wrong time! (*in a dramatic voice*)

> To you, Lord Governor,
> Remains the censure of this hellish villain,
> The time, the place, the torture, O, enforce it!
> Myself will straight aboard, and to the state
1450 This heavy act with heavy heart relate.

(*He takes a gun from his pocket, forces the actors to exit.*)

GUIDE: (*to his group*) A bit confusing, the way that happened, don't you think? So you understand. (*He walks into the light. In a professional, dry and rapid voice.*) Explanation: For Foreigners. (*fierce and rude*) Does anyone really need an explanation? If you want to act like actors, just go into a tenement and howl like dogs, throw a good scare into people. If you don't have money, people will be even more afraid. Why scream? Why pretend? When no one can open his mouth, why would anyone scream gratuitously? (*He waits for a response, which he doesn't get.*) Okay then! (*resumes his pro-*

1460 *fessional tone*) August 6, 1971. The police burst into an old house with many rooms, like this one, in the city of Santa Fe. In one of the rooms they find eight hundred grams of trotyl. They say. One journalist and three members of the Grupo 67 theater are arrested. They're taken to Buenos Aires on suspicion of subversive actions. The district attorney recommended they be absolved on the benefit of doubt. They were absolved May 24, 1972. (*change of tone*) Few are called, many are chosen. Nine months in the cage. In

1470 misery. Well, that's life! (*He leaves the illuminated space, goes back to his group.*) Wait! The show goes on!

SCENE XVIII

*A sort of deformed* CHILD-MONSTER, *dressed in a floor-length white shirt with lots of lace and frills. He is heavily made-up. Others disguised as* CHILDREN *follow. The* CHILD-MONSTER *clutches a club. They sing.*

CHILDREN:

> *Anton, Anton Pirulero*
> *each one, each one*
> *attends to his game*
> *and he who does not*
> *he who does not*
> *will suffer the blame.*

(*The* CHILDREN *sit in a circle around the* CHILD-MONSTER, *who calls to one of the bigger children and gives him the club. The latter stays outside the ring. They play Anton Pirulero, in which the child playing Anton is in the center of the circle, turning around and around, his arms extended like wings. The others keep singing and pretend to play musical instruments— guitar, cornet, violin, etc. They have to be very alert, for if Anton Pirulero stops and points at one of them with his arm and that child isn't moving his own arms like Anton, then that child loses. He who loses three times is out. The game is played singing, and very fast.*)

CHILD-MONSTER: (*He is Anton Pirulero. In an out-of-tune singsong.*) 1480

> *Anton, Anton Pirulero*
> *each one, each one*
> *attends to his game*
> *and he who does not*
> *he who does not*
> *will suffer the blame.*

(*Now they play only guitar. The child with the club goes to the one who has changed places with Anton and hits him. The child falls. The game continues, faster every time. The* CHILD-MONSTER *never finishes his song, the game falls apart, and the child with the club hits out indiscriminately. Finally, the only ones left unharmed are the* CHILD-MONSTER *and the character with the club. They wave their arms and sing. The* CHILD-MONSTER *glares at the other one, more and more menacingly. He aims with his finger as though it were a revolver and kills the other child. Pum! He plays alone, his gestures increasingly spastic. The song "Anton Pirulero" becomes unintelligible. The lights go out.*)

GUIDE: What now? Why did they kill the lights?

VOICES: (*singing*)

> *Anton, Anton Pirulero*
> *each one* 1490
> *each one*
> *attends to his game.*

(*Lights up. In the same space,* THREE MEN *and a* YOUNG WOMAN. *The* CHILD-MONSTER *laughs in his labored way, waves his arms, stutters.*)

CHILD-MONSTER: D-d-d-ow-ow-n-n-n! S-s-s-i-i-i-t-t-d-d-d-ow-n-n-n-n!

*(He aims his hand like a revolver. The men and woman don't seem to notice his presence. They sit of their own volition.)*

FIRST MAN: What is your game?

SECOND MAN: Fear.

FIRST MAN: And yours?

THIRD MAN: Fear.

FIRST MAN: *(to the* YOUNG WOMAN*)* What is your game?

1500  YOUNG WOMAN: Fear. *(pause)* And the question.

FIRST MAN: What question?

YOUNG WOMAN: Why fear? My name is Marina. I am twenty years old. I am Greek, a prisoner, and I have been tortured. *(The* CHILD-MONSTER *stutters low, furiously. He keeps playing, getting all tangled up in his own movements.)*
Time is altered, the years to come are altered
You know where you will find me
I, fear, I, death
I, the memory beyond reach

1510  I, the recollection of the tenderness of your hands
I, the sadness of our broken life
I will defeat "it's not my concern" with my
    anguish
blast their alien sleep with fireworks,
    horrible and indecent
with countless shootings I will fall on the indifference
    of those who pass by
until they begin to ask, to ask themselves

THREE MEN: *(in an even tone)*

1520  Why fear?
Why torture?
Why deaths?

*(Stuttering and autistic, the* CHILD-MONSTER *plays.)*

THREE MEN:
Who set limits?
Who once said: this much thirst
this much water?
Who once said: this much air
this much fire?
Who once said: here the ken

1530  of men and women
here the bounds?
Only hope has sharp knees.
They are bleeding.

*(darkness)*

*(The poem spoken by the* YOUNG WOMAN *was written by Marina. The poem spoken by the* THREE MEN *is Juan Gelman's.[15])*

GUIDE: Now what? There they go again cutting the light without warning me! I understand less and less. We're the ones who bear the brunt of this show. I shit on poetry! Watch your wallets! And I left my flashlight. This way, this way. It's so dark! Don't touch each other! Whose little ass is this? *(He laughs. Opens the door. The passageway is illuminated.)* Ah! Light, more light! What a phrase! Only a genius could 1540 come up with that one, eh?

WOMAN'S VOICE:

> *"Ay-y-y, for the big horse*
> *who didn't like water"[16]*

GUIDE: Still at it! Now that's perseverance! *(Baroque music is heard. The* GUIDE *puts his ear to the door. Unsure.)* Do we go in here? I don't remember. Oh well, let's do it! Come along, gentlemen! You're almost there!

## SCENE XIX

*They enter another room. Two* GUARDS *are dressing a group of squalid-looking characters who are handcuffed to the wall, heavily made-up, with false eyelashes and lots of rouge. Some are half-undressed, wearing only jackets and underwear. Others wear bras and costume jewelry. The* GUARDS *move around busily. They bring chairs. Make the prisoners sit. They arrange them artistically, crossing their legs, raising their arms as though they were holding cigarettes between their fingers. The prisoners stay in these poses. During the development of this scene, one* GUARD*—seated apart—recites with a melancholy air.*

GUARD:
You, who come from the shores of the Tagus    1550
Every day sing of my death
Only this do I ask
    with my dying breath
Every day sing of my death
You, who come from the shores of the Tagus.[17]

*(A signal is heard. A line of frightened men and women enter. Some carry small packages in their hands, obviously clothing or food. The* GUARD *watches them.)*

GUARD: No one enters without being checked. *(He turns his face away. Raises and lowers his index finger mechanically, while the people pass in front of him and go out. Recites rapidly.)* With pants, no. With skirts, no. With stockings, no. With packages, no. With children, no. With faces, no. *(A* 1560 PRETTY GIRL *passes. He looks at her. His finger stops. Very nicely.)*
Twenty little hard ones, twenty little hard ones
all in a roll, all in a roll

---

[15]Gelman's lines are: "Quien puso limites? / Quien dijo alguna vez: hasta aquí la sed? hasta aquí el agua? / Quien dijo alguna vez: hasta aquí el aire, hasta aquí el fuego? / Quien dijo alguna vez: hasta aquí el hombre, hasta aquí, no? / Solo la esperanza tiene las rodillas nitidas. / Sangran."

[16]The Woman's Voice sings from the *Blood Wedding* lullabye.

[17]"You, who come from the shores of the Tagus" is from a poem by Garcilaso de la Vega. The Tagus River flows through western Spain and Portugal. In her letter to me of March 28, 1986, Gambaro brought up "substituting an English-language poem about death, provided of course it's by a Master." I decided against this option since I felt that Gambaro's appropriation of Garcilaso was important as a reference to a specific age, place, and literary tradition. One of the greatest poets of the Spanish Golden Age, Garcilaso influenced not only San Juan de la Cruz, Lope de Vega, and Cervantes but also Rafael Alberti, Pedro Salinas, Miguel Hernández, and other twentieth-century Spanish and Latin American poets. The original reads: "Vosotros, los del Tajo en su ribera / Cantáreis mi muerte cada dia / Este descanso llevaré nunque muera / Que cada día cantáreis mi muerte, / Vosotros, los del Tajo en su ribera."

twenty little hard ones
in your little asshole.[18]
May I?

PRETTY GIRL: *(stupidly)* What?

GUARD: *(wiggles his finger obscenely)* May I?

1570 PRETTY GIRL: No!

GUARD: *(pulls himself up, undiscouraged)* To arms! To arms
against the little asshole! Right over here!

*(A group of guards enters at a trot. They rush the* PRETTY GIRL
*and fling themselves on her as though she were the ball in a
game of baseball. They roll with her out of the room.)*

GUARD: *(moves off, uninterested. Starts again with a melancholy air.)*
You, who come from the shores of the Tagus . . .

LITTLE OLD LADY: *(the last of the visitors. She brings a sandwich wrapped in a handkerchief.)* I've come to see my little
son. He misbehaved.

GUARD: *(deflated)* Ah . . . Why didn't you bring him up better,
1580 madam?

LITTLE OLD LADY: He was always my wayward one!

GUARD: A good beating is what they need. They don't learn unless they bleed.

LITTLE OLD LADY: At ten years old, he was looking up the girls'
skirts.

GUARD: *(dumbfounded)* Filthy!

LITTLE OLD LADY: *(plaintive)* I cut his little whistle, but it did
no good!

GUARD: It's late to repent. Show me what you've brought!

1590 LITTLE OLD LADY: *(unwraps her handkerchief)* A sandwich.

GUARD: *(lifts the top of the bread)* Ah! Extra testicles. No,
madam! Here they only lose them. And for us that's work!
Confiscated! *(He takes the sandwich.)* Out!

LITTLE OLD LADY: I want to see my son! Just once! Be generous! You have a mother too!

GUARD: Yeah, but she's not an old whore like you.

LITTLE OLD LADY: Why are you insulting me?

GUARD: *(with disgust)* You're old! *(in another tone)* All right.
Go see him. I'm doing this for my mother. Sentimentality
1600 will be the end of me! *(gestures toward one of the seated
prisoners)* There he is.

LITTLE OLD LADY: *(goes toward an* OUTLANDISH-LOOKING PRIS-
ONER *and embraces him)* Son! *(She separates, looks at him.)*
No, this isn't him. *(hugs another)* Son! *(looks)* No, this one
either.

OUTLANDISH-LOOKING PRISONER: *(opening his arms)* Da-da-
da-da!

GUARD: Choose already. Take this one. What's the difference.

LITTLE OLD LADY: *(leaning toward the prisoner. Timidly.)*
1610 Juan?

OUTLANDISH-LOOKING PRISONER: Da!

LITTLE OLD LADY: Son!

OUTLANDISH-LOOKING PRISONER: Da!

GUIDE: *(to the group)* Pretty depressing, wouldn't you say?

GUARD: What about you all? Over here, young men!

GUIDE: *(raises his hands)* No! Out, quick! *(the sound of music)*
We were going to go dancing. We got the wrong room. *(very*

*distressed)* Let's go dancing! Dancing! Move it! Let's beat it!
Let's go, gentlemen. Let's go! *(They exit.)*

## SCENE XX

GUIDE: Ouf! A narrow escape! *(He listens. The music gets* 1620
*louder. It's happy, catchy.)* That's it. Come. *(He leads his
group to a large space, where at this moment all the other
groups converge.)* Leave the space open, ladies and gentlemen! If you would be so kind as to stand against the wall.
That's it. Thank you, everyone.

*(On one side of the performing space is a semitranslucent fold-
ing screen, behind which can be seen a long table. In the center, a group of women, dressed like stereotypical prostitutes,
execute the gestures conventionally attributed to them: they
smoke, show their legs, swing their purses, put on makeup. A
man roughly pushes in two more prostitutes. They look at him
with a mixture of fear and outrage. The other women observe
the new arrivals curiously, then one offers each of the new
women a cigarette. The music suddenly stops. One of the prostitutes starts dancing, moving slowly, singing a blues number
in a gravelly voice. A line of* FOUR MEN *enter at a trot, leading
a prisoner with his eyes bandaged, to the center. They sing.)*

FOUR MEN:

> We have come, we have come
> To have some fun!

*(The* PROSTITUTES *watch them. The one dancing gradually
slows down the rhythm until she is moving in place, singing inaudibly. The men spin the prisoner around until he becomes
completely disoriented.)*

MAN #1: Let's play the Little Blind Cock!

MAN #2: Cockadoodledoo!                                               1630

*(They play, rapidly poking and moving away from the pris-
oner, who searches for them with his arms outstretched.)*

MAN #1: Play! Head down!

MAN #3: There are beams!

MAN #4: You could break your head open!

*(They play, yell "Cockadoodledoo!" One of the* PROSTITUTES
*comes forward. She first starts to join in the game, then
stretches her hand toward the prisoner's bandage.)*

MAN #1: *(pushes her away)* Get out of here! This is our game!
In your place, whore!

MAN #2: *(poking the prisoner)* He's sweating! He's hot!

MEN #1, #3, AND #4: *(in a chorus)* Make him strip! Make him
strip!

*(Maintaining an ambiguous air of play and violence, they take
off his jacket, his pants, his shirt; they throw his clothes, which
flutter around.)*

MAN #1: Hard-boiled egg! Let's play hard-boiled egg!

*(They fight like children.)*

---

[18]"Twenty little hard ones" is from García Lorca's *Los titeres de cachiporra*. The original reads: "Veinte duritos y veinte duritos / y un rollito de
veinte duritos / en el agujero del culito."

1640 MAN #2: Me! Me!

MAN #3: Get out! Me!

*(They play. The prisoner holds his body rigid while the others rush him, tie him up. Finally, one of the men hits him on the head. The prisoner falls.)*

MAN #4: We warned you!

MAN #1: A beam, idiot!

MAN #2: We told you to keep your head down!

*(They drag the prisoner behind the screen. Through the screen, one can see fuzzily that they are strapping him down on the table. A scream. Instantaneously, the volume of the music shoots up; two of the men come out from behind the screen.)*

TWO MEN:
Girls, if you want to sing,
it's not prohibited!

*(They clap. The PROSTITUTES don't move.)*

Sing!

*(The PROSTITUTES, forced into it, clap and sing. Again the music gets louder.)*

Girls, if you want to dance,
1650 it's not prohibited!

*(The PROSTITUTES dance. Behind the screen, one can see the shadow of the two men moving away from the table. The hand of the prisoner falls softly. At the same time, the PROSTITUTES freeze in a musical comedy finale. The music stops. The lights go out, then come up again. The actors disperse, naturally. They take down the screen. The dead man gets up from the table, gathers his clothes, and begins to dress. Only the prisoners seated against the wall remain immobile.)*

GUIDE: *(drily)* Ladies and gentlemen, what are you waiting for? The show is over. *(House lights come up.)*

GUIDE 2: *(resentfully)*
If you clap enthusiastically in all good haste
your hands won't go to waste!

*(He claps, and the GUIDES and actors present imitate him.)*

GUIDE:
Theater imitates life
If you don't clap
It means that life is rotten to the core
And we may as well just head for the door.          1660

*(He moves the audience out toward the door. From far away can be heard police sirens. Even when the audience is near the exit, they can hear.)*

Who once said: here the ken
of men and women
here the bounds?

*(after a moment, repeat)*

Who once said: here the ken
of men and women
here the bounds?

# C U R T A I N

---

*THIS interview was conducted by Kathleen Betsko and Rachel Koenig.*

## Griselda Gambaro

### Interview (1987)

TRANSLATED BY
ALBERTO MINERO

We interviewed Griselda Gambaro in April 1984, in New York City, and invited playwright Maria Irene Fornes to participate and to act as our interpreter.

INTERVIEWER: Did you start by writing for theater?

GAMBARO: No. When I was twenty-four, I published a book of stories that I don't want to remember. It was so immature, so full of the sort of imperfections that mar many first books. And then when I was thirty-four, I published again, three short novels collected in one volume entitled *Madrigal en Ciudad.* This manuscript won a prize, El Fondo Nacional de las Artes, which consisted of publication, in 1964. The prize I won for this book enabled me to enter the theater easily, comfortably. Nowadays young playwrights have a more difficult time.

INTERVIEWER: Was there anyone in particular who influenced or nurtured your writing?

GAMBARO: No. I come from a milieu where there were very few books.

INTERVIEWER: Are you from a working-class family?

GAMBARO: Yes.

FORNES: You weren't allowed access to books?

GAMBARO: There were no books. I am the youngest of five, and have four brothers. There weren't books because there were family needs that were more primary. One of my brothers—five years older than I—did buy books.

INTERVIEWER: In growing up without books, how did you discover literature and your own desire to write?

GAMBARO: I always had a deep love of the written word, even in early childhood. Once I started going to school, I discovered the public library in my *barrio.* Then I learned a lot by chance. I didn't see much theater, but I read plays by O'Neill, Chekhov, Pirandello.

INTERVIEWER: What were the occupations of your parents?

GAMBARO: Father was a sailor for a time, and then he became a post office employee. My parents were first-generation Argentinians and my grandparents were Italian.

INTERVIEWER: What's the population of Italian descendants in Argentina?

GAMBARO: I don't know the exact amount, but most of our population comes from Spanish and Italian descendants.

FORNES: It was always like that or did the immigration happen all of a sudden?

GAMBARO: At the beginning of this century there were big currents of immigration in Argentina and that kept going until about 1930. People came to Argentina because it was a rich, fertile country.

INTERVIEWER: What is the average size of the theaters in which your plays are performed?

GAMBARO: At the beginning, my plays went the so-called avant-garde circuit. They opened in an institute dedicated to avant-garde work. In 1972, I was produced at the Teatro Municipal, which allowed me to find producers, to open in good theaters (three hundred to four hundred fifty seats), and to work under good professional conditions. However, due to the commercial failure of my last two plays, *Real Envido* [*Royal Bet*] and *La Malasangre* [*Bitter Blood*], I'm back underground for the moment. My plays are being done by nonprofessional companies in smaller spaces.

INTERVIEWER: Have you been influenced by any particular Argentinian playwrights?

GAMBARO: Yes. H. Serebrinsky, who committed suicide this year. It pleases me that our work has points in common.

INTERVIEWER: Is Serebrinsky considered a political playwright?

GAMBARO: All of our theater is more or less political, and we are all political writers in one way or another. There is always implicit or explicit political content in our work, though it is not a *goal*.

FORNES: Is it an artistic choice that a political point of view is not the writer's goal?

GAMBARO: No. For me, it is a necessity. I don't know whether my plays seem political. But one feeds oneself with the information provided by one's surrounding reality. One transmits, transfers, this information into one's work. One pre-orders this information as well as one's own personal experience. When one transfers that information into a theater piece or a novel, that reality is political, in a wide sense, of course, not political from a partisan point of view. One lives in a *politique*, and in a politicized society; so necessarily, this will be *reflected* in the work of art, be that what it may.

INTERVIEWER: Do you have some material which would only be appropriate for treatment in a novel?

GAMBARO: I think one always writes about the same theme, with variations. In some themes I see a situation on a stage, but there are others which would work better in a novel. Novels are themes that take me a long time to develop—they are a longer meditation. I usually write theater rapidly, but a novel can take two or three years.

FORNES: How long does it take you to write a play?

GAMBARO: The writing *for me* is just a simple question of pages. I could tell you that a theater piece takes me thirty-five pages, while a novel takes two hundred. It has to do with my personal method of work. I think *a lot* beforehand, and I take a long time thinking. Once I know what I want to say, it takes me a month to write a play. When the structure is solved—though I might need some bridges, or to revise and make cuts—I let it rest. I ask for opinions and then I go back and revise, which takes another three or four more months of work. Then it's ready. I know when a play or work is good or bad after that first month, when the structure is done—the beginning, the ending and the scenes.

INTERVIEWER: What inspired your play, *Información Para Extranjeros* [1972] [*Information for Foreigners*]?

GAMBARO: I don't have a copy of that play any more because at the time, it was risky, dangerous material to have in Argentina. It was published in Italy, so I now have the Italian version. It is a play I would like to revise, because it was the first time I used material from newspapers, which I treated as *true* information. Later, history proved that this information was false. So the play itself may no longer be truthful. That's why I want to revise it—I'd like to check history point by point against information I used.

FORNES: You weren't aware that the facts in the newspaper were false?

GAMBARO: No. The play was written in 1972, the beginning of the guerrilla movement in Argentina. I used the first *desaparecidos* and the first people taken to jail. The information was reported like police-blotter items, and came under the newspaper heading of "police information." For example, I remember a lawyer, Roberto Quieto. I wrote a scene based upon the information in the newspaper which said the police had detained a lawyer who had something to do with human rights. The real story was that Quieto was one of the chiefs of the People's Revolutionary Army.

FORNES: What is the reality?

GAMBARO: The reality is that he was a subversive and that he was disappeared. It's not that I would change my optic were I to rewrite the play, but I think that a new angle has been imposed.

FORNES: Was the play confiscated from you?

GAMBARO: No. There were raids, the army paid us "visits" during which they looked at all the material in the house [1973]. As *any* material was considered subversive—Marx, Freud—a big burning of books resulted. Everybody who owned books burned them.

FORNES: Was *Información* eventually presented in Argentina?

GAMBARO: Never. A theater in Germany wanted to perform it—but I refused permission. If this play had been done in *any* theater in *any* country, intelligence personnel connected to the Argentinian Embassy would have been informed. (This was to happen with *El Campo;* Intelligence even sent back newspaper clippings in which journalists drew parallels between what happens in the play and the military dictatorship in Argentina.) I was afraid for my family in Argentina, and besides, I was counting on returning there as soon as the situation permitted.

INTERVIEWER: Much of your work signaled the advent of a repressive regime well before the actual events took place. Were you aware of the prophetic nature of your material?

GAMBARO: Well, there were certain data floating around. . . . An artist has to have antennas. I think the artist has antennas that are a little more sensitive to reality than most.

INTERVIEWER: Why did the character of The Guide, in scene five of *Información,* react like a "drama critic" to the father's bedtime-story version of a kidnapping?

GAMBARO: Yes, Néstor Martins, an attorney, and his client, Nildo Zentero . . . It was one of the first kidnappings that happened. It was ten years ago, but seems so much longer. It is very difficult for me to know why things happen in my plays. To me it is enough to know things are coherent. I never know why they occur.

INTERVIEWER: How has the new democracy in Argentina affected the artistic community?

GAMBARO: The difference is lack of terror. We lived not only with terror, but with censorship and fear. It was a time of extreme risk, where the game was to survive—nothing else. And now, well, one feels that one can talk, that one can communicate with others. In the previous years, the entire culture was balkanized, broken down into particles. Each one kept working, writing—but each one did it in his own private margin and space. The communication among artists themselves was difficult, as was the communication between artists and audiences.

Through balkanization, regimes are able to employ horror and fear. The fact that everybody is isolated helps the purposes of any dictatorship. Every dictatorship is based on that principle. One starts being afraid of one's shadow. In Argentina, if your name was in the personal agenda book of anybody who was related to some [political, social] activity, you began to get scared. You knew that by the simple fact of your name in someone's address book, you would be considered guilty, too. Which didn't mean just being taken into detention! One could not have said, "No, that man has my telephone number because of x reasons. . . . " It meant to be disappeared. That's why it was so hard to deal with The Fear. [The National Commission on Disappeared Persons (CONADEP), appointed by Argentine President Raúl Alfonsín in December 1983, has estimated that eleven thousand people had been abducted by the armed forces, and that they have almost certainly been murdered.]

INTERVIEWER: Did artists continue to work during those years?

GAMBARO: Yes. People worked with censorship and self-censorship. But only when the military government had become deteriorated at the end of 1981 did Teatro Abierto, "open theater," occur. Teatro Abierto was a movement that united all playwrights, directors and actors. It was decided that in two months Teatro Abierto would present twenty-one plays: three one-acts each day on seven different programs. Everyone worked free of charge and there was a very low ticket price. The festival had an extraordinary response from the audience. For the first time theater people got together to talk more or less freely, and the response was a massive one.

FORNES: Was that before the Falklands War?

GAMBARO: I believe so. It was during the military government, September–October 1981.

INTERVIEWER: Did the Falklands War effect changes in the military government?

GAMBARO: Yes. But at the same time, the government was already *so* deteriorated. In fact, during the first week of Teatro Abierto they [the paramilitary police] put a bomb in the theater and destroyed everything. But the festival had already created a need in the people. People had already lost their fear. Though the majority of the plays were political, a press conference was given after the bomb, and two other theaters offered their spaces. It wasn't that the festival had a big theatrical value in itself, but from the political point of view, it was an important event.

INTERVIEWER: Were there any victims of the bombing?

GAMBARO: No, it was in the early hours of dawn. The costumes caught fire and they were all burned. The press helped very much by giving the incident so much publicity—and, of course, the government had to keep from stopping the festival, to prove that it wasn't *that* dictatorial. But the government was already deteriorated. It wasn't the government of 1977—we could not have done a festival like Teatro Abierto *at all* if it were anything like 1977. The government had deteriorated because of the political and economic situation. And because of the situation, they had to allow a wider margin of activity.

FORNES: Was the political response of the theater people larger than those in the other arts?

GAMBARO: Theater artists were more engaged than the people in the cinema, for instance, who couldn't do anything in those times, because of the cinema's commercial infrastructure. There was a cinema institute, run by the government, but they would not give funding without first approving a script. Cinema people couldn't address anything; they made purely commercial movies. And television was *very* much under control.

INTERVIEWER: Did the Falklands War help precipitate the fall of the repressive government?

GAMBARO: I think the regime would have fallen anyway, but the cost of the acceleration of that fall was too great to pay. I don't think our people were thinking at that moment that the war would weaken the military regime. People were suffering, they were grieving for all the young people who were sent to their deaths. Many went to war unwillingly, it was not a choice. There were eighteen-year-old kids who were called up and sent to die.

FORNES: So the sorrow was more for the loss of life than the loss of the Islands?

GAMBARO: The Malvina Islands weren't ours. We lost them in the last century. We always fought to have them back, claimed them. They belong to us by right. By fact, the British are there.

INTERVIEWER: Why did you decide to leave Argentina in the late seventies?

GAMBARO: In March 1977, they banned my novel *Ganarse la Muerte* [*To Earn One's Death*]. I was in Buenos Aires and the prohibition came by decree of the Executive Power, President Rafael Videla. It was forbidden to sell the novel, it could not be sent by mail, and it was taken out of circulation. At that time, to have a prohibition, not from City Hall, but the *Executive Power* was very dangerous. One started to be a suspected person. As a result, I couldn't open a new play, I was not given interviews or publicity of any kind. My channels of communication were cut off. Aside from that, I was living in an atmosphere of terror. I went to Spain (with my husband and children) and stayed three years. I returned in 1980.

INTERVIEWER: A French theater journal noted that the official theaters in Argentina preferred to produce classics rather than new work, which only constituted one fifth of their repertory. Is this true?

GAMBARO: We have only two subsidized theaters: La Comedia Nacional and Teatro Municipal San Martin. The Municipal receives the largest subsidy and presents classics as well as original Argentinian plays. Still, there is a whole group of Argentinian playwrights who were never performed at the Municipal during the period of The Process. The most well-known, Roberto Cossa, Gorostiza (now minister of culture), Osualdo Dragun and myself, were prohibited playwrights.

FORNES: During the epoch of "The Process?" What was that?

GAMBARO: We called the period of the military dictatorship "El Proceso," from March 1976 to the arrival of Alfonsín. It's a name the military gave to themselves; they called their government "El Proceso."

INTERVIEWER: What is the future of the arts in Argentina?

GAMBARO: We're going to see this year. It is too soon to tell. And Argentina is going through a tremendous economic crisis, which of course reflects in the arts. But already more things are being published, there are many new theatrical projects, and more cultural events of a popular nature are taking place, such as poetry readings, music in the squares.

INTERVIEWER: Would you tell us about the women in Argentina—of all religions—who have publicly gathered to mourn and protest their disappeared relatives?

GAMBARO: There is in Argentina a group called The Mothers of the Plaza de Mayo. I think these women have done something very important, from all points of view. They have proven that when women get together in numbers, we can change things. These women started in the middle of The Fear. Every Thursday they would walk around Plaza de Mayo at three o'clock in the afternoon. They were menaced, some disappeared [CONADEP reports fifteen Mothers—Ed.], but they finally made themselves heard, and not only in Argentina! It's a very important historic event in the world.

What began as a personal wrench—mothers searching for their own children—became a political act that gathered more and more weight. The women had to be very brave, they gathered to protest in plain sight in the middle of a military government. The Mothers of the Plaza de Mayo started with five women, then ten, then twenty. . . .

INTERVIEWER: You sometimes juxtapose acts of human violence with children's games. What is the association between violence and innocence?

GAMBARO: I think that only happens in *Información Para Extranjeros*. It's not my usual method of work. In that play, I used a children's game placed within the context of real violence and cruelty to give a different strength, more intensity to violence. I used it to create a stronger image. Children are violent. But I believe that theirs is a particular kind of violence, and that it can be channeled in ways which are less dangerous to others. Generally in the child, violence is not criminal. In the adult, violence is criminal. Those who have more means, more technology, can be more dangerous. The poor, vulnerable child is without those means.

INTERVIEWER: Critics have said that your artistic vision of man is "grim and absolute." Do you agree?

GAMBARO: No, I wouldn't even say that of my earlier work, though in my latest plays there is another optic. Not a view toward the world, but a view toward *people,* which is maybe a more compassionate optic. Even my darkest work has a positive side because it appeals to people's lucidity. It's a call to attention. My vision is not necessarily fatalistic. My message has never been "We have to be like this."

INTERVIEWER: Why do you write?

GAMBARO: The process of writing is still very much a mystery to me. I foresee a situation and I feel that I *need* to write about it. But why I write? Or why I need to write? I don't know.

INTERVIEWER: You were recently [spring 1984] on a panel of women writers at the Center for Inter-American Relations here in New York. What did you discuss?

GAMBARO: The other two outstanding writers on the panel, [novelists] Angélica Gorodischer and Luisa Valenzuela, were in agreement that what feminism means is to change our optic, our vision, which means we must also change our ethics. That's the most substantial thing they said.

INTERVIEWER: Is there a movement of women writers in Argentina?

GAMBARO: There have always been isolated movements, sporadic periods of women writing but they were never organic. Women in Argentina gained the vote many years ago and they made certain gains, but a feminist movement did not previously exist. Now, with the new democratic government which took office in December 1982, our feminist movement has gained strength. There are many new feminist groups in Argentina; we are hearing women's voices, and we have benefited. For example, the Women's House, Casa de la Mujer, opened last year. There is a café where women hold meetings and get-togethers related to feminist concerns. Casa de la Mujer offers various courses to women in photography, et cetera. There is also a group of women with their own television program, and though it is not billed as a "feminist" program, it always deals with the problems of women.

INTERVIEWER: Are there many feminist publications?

GAMBARO: There is a newspaper with a weekly women's supplement. The directors and editors are men, but it is dedicated to a feminist point of view.

FORNES: It doesn't just portray women as domestic?

GAMBARO: There is another magazine, *Women,* like that; it is a mixture of commercialism and the "feminine." You see, these magazines are not created by women; they are financed by newspapers and commercial publishers who have an eye on the market. Commercial publishers have realized magazines directed toward women can make a profit. The most singular development in Argentina in terms of women is the arrival of women in the arts: women filmmakers, theater directors . . . though of course we already had a tradition of women writers in Argentina. The first Argentinian women writers appeared in the nineteenth century: Juana Manuela Gorriti, Eduarda Mansilla, César Duayen. In the twentieth century, women's writing has gained great strength. Among poets I would mention Alfonsina Storni, Alejandra Pizarník, Olga Orozco. From an extensive list of prose writers, I would mention Angélica Gorodischer, Silvina Ocampo, Noemí Ulla, Libertad Demitropulos, Alicia Steinberg.

FORNES: Do you have a tradition of women writing for theater as well?

GAMBARO: No. No. Theater is very much connected with the society, with the social situation. It demands a different sort of aggressiveness, and that's why we only have a few playwrights who are women. Movies are also connected to society—we only recently began to have women working in the cinema, but not too many.

FORNES: Why do theater and cinema demand a different type of aggressiveness?

GAMBARO: Writing a novel requires an engagement, but it is not as immediate. A theater piece, of itself, demands a confrontation with an audience. It demands that you connect with other people; it demands a collective and social effort with the company and later with the audience. Theater writing is much more direct than novel writing. The contact is person-to-person in the theater *through* an object: the text. And theater is such a concise field, more concise than the other arts. I believe that all acts of writing are impudent, shameless, but drama especially, because one knows that one is going to be on the stage through the actors. That's why theater is more aggressive, it shows more—of whatever it shows. It is immodest.

INTERVIEWER: Do you believe there is a female aesthetic?

GAMBARO: Yes. I believe so. I think with time this will become more clear. Still among us (all of us, men and women alike) the vision is a little amorphous. As women, we should try to make our vision less shapeless. At least in my case, I'm trying to do that. We must make our vision our own and not something male.

INTERVIEWER: Have you ever directed a play?

GAMBARO: No. I think it is another area of creation, an area that belongs to the stage director. Sometimes when I see a play performed, I feel I would like to direct it myself. But directing is another profession, it involves another technique, one which I don't know about. When I write my plays, I do make my own *mise-en-scène.* I create the settings, and I act out all the characters. When the play must be performed on a stage, it demands the work of another person who has the craftsmanship to deal with physical theatrical space.

INTERVIEWER: Are there women theater directors in Argentina?

GAMBARO: Yes. My last play, *La Malasangre* [*Bitter Blood,* 1982], was directed in Buenos Aires by Laura Yunsen, who will also direct the next play I'm opening. And my two short pieces which are about to open, *Viaje de Invierno* [*Winter Voyage*], written in 1965, and *Nosferatu* (1970), will be directed by another woman, Malena Lasala.

FORNES: Is that by chance, or because these women are especially interested in your work?

GAMBARO: I believe that they are very good directors.

FORNES: But do you think there is something in your work which requires the sensibility of a woman?

GAMBARO: I'd like to believe so, but honestly I think I could have worked with one or two male directors whom I consider good.

INTERVIEWER: Is it difficult for you as a playwright to hand over a script to a director?

GAMBARO: No, I feel expectations. I feel the birth of an enthusiasm. If I trust the person, I feel that person is going to re-create what I wrote in a better way.

INTERVIEWER: In *El Desatino* [*Folly*, 1965], why did you choose to have Alfonso's wife, Lily, never appear on stage except in a dream? And what were your intentions in the stage directions which describe Lily as "An exaggerated version of a movie sex symbol?"

GAMBARO: Well, that is a 1965 play. I think it is like that because it reflects the particular vision of the male character, Alfonso. Lily is his own vision of what woman is. Alfonso literally has restraints on his feet. He is very weak and dreams about a woman. That woman is the stereotype of what he has seen in the movies, or of what he thinks a woman is. In the dream, Alfonso says that Lily is his wife, but she isn't. In reality, that female character does not exist. She takes form on the stage. Alfonso does not reflect my opinion of all men. At the time I wrote *El Desatino,* I was consciously reflecting the vision of that specific male character.

INTERVIEWER: In your early work, the main characters are male. Have your women characters become less peripheral over the years?

GAMBARO: Yes. Beginning in 1976, my female characters started to be the protagonists. In my most recent plays, the main characters are women. And I believe that my women characters have become more dynamic, more active and that they have more ideological weight. That's a response to the fact that I myself am much more conscious and understanding of what it is to be a woman. Before, I wrote instinctively, without being conscious of what happens to women in the world or their position.

INTERVIEWER: How did your consciousness change?

GAMBARO: I wrote that banned novel, *Ganarse La Muerte* [*To Earn One's Death*]. The main character was a woman. I didn't think she reflected the state of women; I thought she reflected Argentina. But the novel was published in France by the Women's Press [*Gagner Sa Mort,* Editions des Femmes, 1976], and they invited me to France. I had the opportunity to meet the feminists of France, and I began reading about the specific problems related to women. I started to realize things which, before that time, I had only felt in an instinctive way.

INTERVIEWER: In *El Campo* [1967], the diseased and wounded artist, Emma, plays a concert on a dead piano while the audience insults her. Did you intend this image to symbolize the vulnerable position of the artist in the world?

GAMBARO: When I write a piece I pay attention to what it demands of me, to what the play and the characters propose. I'm simply following the characters on the stage. As in any work, one can later see it's charged with symbolism. I didn't think about it when I wrote the scene, but it may well represent what you say.

FORNES: So the theatrical situation actually *marks* the behavior of the characters?

GAMBARO: Everything influences one, everything is interrelated. How can they be separated? It's very difficult to separate the thread from the yarn.

INTERVIEWER: American academic critics have often written that you have been influenced by The Living Theatre of Julian Beck and Judith Malina; The Environmental Theatre of Schechner; Ionesco, and by the ideas of Grotowski and Artaud.

GAMBARO: No, I don't believe so. Who invented that? We come from Argentinian dramaturgy, a genre called *grotesco* [grotesque] created by a playwright named Armando Discepolo, [1887–1971]. We don't come from European absurdism, which is so metaphysical, which presents the world as a fact with inexplicable laws.

INTERVIEWER: In what era did Discepolo write?

GAMBARO: I don't exactly know, but the production of his works was 1935 to 1965. *Grotesco* has its roots in the theater of Pirandello. The Argentinian dramas of the immigrants—in which people speak in a certain way that we call "Cocoliche"—were influenced by Pirandello. But Discepolo and others who work in the same genre gave to it a very Argentinian characteristic. Ionesco's absurdism considers the world has inexplicable laws. The same holds true for Artaud. I don't see a clear connection with Artaud and our theater. Our theater is much more connected with a social element, and our plays deal directly with political and social content. We also believe that society is modifiable, changeable.

INTERVIEWER: Would you discuss your ideas about the relationship between your plays and the spectator? Critic Rosalea Postma said of *Información Para Extranjeros* ". . . it attempts to involve the spectator in a dramatic experience that will also radicalize his perceptions." ["Space and Spectator in the Theatre of Griselda Gambaro," *Latin American Theatre Review,* Fall, 1980.] Was this your intent?

GAMBARO: I believe that all theater means to produce not shock but a response in the spectator. It could be an emotional response, or a rational, sensible response.

INTERVIEWER: If the twenty-one scenes in *Información Para Extranjeros* were to be, as you suggested in the stage directions, experienced in a different sequence by each of several audience groups, would the total effect of the scenes on each audience member be the same?

FORNES: This is the kind of question people ask me! I did a play, *Fefu and her Friends,* where I divided the audience into four different groups. Isn't that funny? I didn't know you had done that, too. Did you know that some productions of Chekhov have been staged this way? Though his plays, of course, were not written with that intention.

GAMBARO: What I thought was that *the director* would have to find out how to make the order of the scenes work. As a work of imagination, I *could* have done it but I never made a decision as to what the correct scene order would be.

FORNES: Does the audience go together to see each scene?

GAMBARO: No. The audience is separated and they see different scenes at different times. Only at the end do they come together. It is aleatory, meaning they see everything, but they see different things.

INTERVIEWER: What is the relationship between playwrights and critics in Argentina? Do critics illuminate a piece of work?

GAMBARO: In Argentina I don't think there is any good criticism. There are no good critics.

INTERVIEWER: Are your critics especially hard on women writers?

GAMBARO: No. Only one critic, at the beginning of my career, attacked me as a woman. He called me a "little, young lady writer."

INTERVIEWER: Does the financial success of a play depend on a good critical reception as it does here in the United States? Do your critics have the power to close a play or extend a run?

GAMBARO: Of course, the critic can help a play, but in Argentina, the critic cannot undermine the *existence* of a play. Good critical reception helps success, but does not determine it. In my case, I have been working in Argentina a long time. I've earned my own space and have entered that suspicious, dangerous category of "respectable" people. [Laughter]

INTERVIEWER: Is the playwright able to make a living from his/her work?

GAMBARO: With difficulty. And only if the plays are staged often and with success. If a play is successful it's profitable for the playwright. One can live well. In Argentina there might be three or four playwrights who can live off their work.

INTERVIEWER: Do they write drama or comedy?

GAMBARO: I'm talking about the serious dramatists. Those who write comedy can live on what they earn from writing, and so can those who write for commercial theater.

FORNES: Does a successful serious drama play only in Buenos Aires, or does it tour in the provinces?

GAMBARO: It can tour, but in the provinces one earns very little. The real market is Buenos Aires, or Uruguay if you plan a long tour.

INTERVIEWER: We've read that 90 percent of theater pieces in Argentina are presented by acting companies which are formed cooperatively.

GAMBARO: In Argentina, one might work with a commercial theater, but more often one looks for a producer and then forms a company which will perform that particular play. When it's a short-term production, we work *en cooperativa* [in a cooperative]; the actors start making profit once the play is running.

INTERVIEWER: Is it as important to have your dramatic texts published as to have them performed?

GAMBARO: Both are important. Publishing allows the text to tour, to be translated. It also makes other stagings of a play possible. Very few plays are published in Argentina. I don't have all my plays published, but my last three will be published in June.

INTERVIEWER: Are there any American playwrights that are particularly admired in Argentina?

GAMBARO: Yes. Arthur Miller has been played a lot. As well as Tennessee Williams and Edward Albee.

INTERVIEWER: Is there any subject that is presently obsessing you which you must write about soon?

GAMBARO: No, because when something starts to absorb me, I just put it in writing.

FORNES: And if, at this moment, an obsession came into your mind would you quit everything and start working?

GAMBARO: Here in New York? Impossible. The visual impact is so strong here.

INTERVIEWER: Are there any special difficulties in translating your work?

GAMBARO: The only translations I know are German, French and Italian. My work is difficult to translate into French because the French language is very rational. And in my case—especially in the novels—I stress the intensity of the verbs, and use idiomatic games which are very difficult to employ for the French, and hard to translate.

INTERVIEWER: How do the Argentinians feel about the success of *Evita?*

GAMBARO: Many people are not in agreement with the portrayal of Eva Perón. That provokes anger of a political nature.

INTERVIEWER: Because the play aggrandized Eva Perón or because it was not fair to her?

GAMBARO: Because the story was simplified. They made a slick interpretation.

INTERVIEWER: Is Eva considered a serious political person?

GAMBARO: Yes. With many contradictions. She herself was someone with enormous contradictions. Partly due to her class, partly because she didn't have intellectual capacity. In my opinion, Perón doesn't deserve any sympathy. I think Eva had more sincerity, more vivacity, and more bravery than [her husband] Perón.

INTERVIEWER: Do you have children?

GAMBARO: Two. A daughter of twenty-two and a son of eighteen.

INTERVIEWER: Has motherhood affected your writing?

GAMBARO: Well, I had less time. But my sister helped me tremendously, so I was always able to save the mornings for my work.

INTERVIEWER: Are you still a morning writer?

GAMBARO: Yes, I start at about eight-thirty. But when I am involved, for instance, in the writing of a play, I work the afternoons too—I work whenever I can—sometimes all day. As discipline, mornings are essential. There's no excuse for not having the discipline to work every morning. I write a page by hand, which I then type, because if not, I can't see clearly. And of course, once I pass a page or a unit of writing through the typewriter, I correct it many times. But the new, the original, is always handwritten. I believe there is a more direct communication with the writing itself when I write by hand.

INTERVIEWER: How does a play begin in your mind? Do you use journals, dreams . . .

GAMBARO: I don't keep personal journals, but I do use the material of dreams. I dream very little—that's my disgrace! I am very interested in the material that comes from dreams, and if I can remember them, I use my dreams. If, of course, they are useful.

INTERVIEWER: Are there any other art forms that influence you?

GAMBARO: Not in a direct way. I write with music playing all the time. I don't really listen to it, but I have it on cassette in the background.

INTERVIEWER: Do you want to say anything about your upcoming productions?

GAMBARO: The project that I'm most interested in is a play I wrote last year, *Del Sol Naciente* [*From the Rising Sun*]. In Argentina, we call Japan "the rising sun." It's a play that began as a dream. I dreamt that I had written a perfect play, with a Japanese ambiance. When I woke up, I thought, "Why not?" I wrote a play with a Japanese setting, but the theme is related to the Falklands War.

# Edward Bond

Edward Bond is the most important English Marxist playwright/theoretician to have emerged in Britain in the post-Brecht era. Born in the working-class North London suburb of Holloway in 1934, Bond was evacuated during the war to Cornwall and then to Ely. After secondary school, Bond worked a series of odd jobs before being summoned for military service in 1953; he was stationed in Vienna as part of the Allied Army of Occupation, where he began to write plays and stories. When he returned to London, he took two important steps toward his career as a playwright. While working days, he managed to see as much theater as he could in the evenings, and he began to submit his plays to contests and to theaters. In 1958, he submitted two plays, *Klaxon in Atreus' Place* and *The Fiery Tree* to the Royal Court Theatre, which had developed the reputation of encouraging and producing the work of the new generation of playwrights. Bond was invited to become a member of the theater's writer's group, and in the course of the next several years wrote a series of short plays and his first full-length play, *The Pope's Wedding* (1962).

Bond's drama is notable for its violence; as he remarked in the preface to his play *Lear,* "I write about violence as naturally as Jane Austen wrote about manners." Bond's staging of violence is hardly unmotivated, though, for Bond regards the injustices of contemporary social life as themselves a form of institutionalized violence. This sense of violence waiting to erupt lies at the core of Bond's most notorious play, *Saved* (1965). A play about the unemployed, young underclass of London, *Saved* climaxes in a central scene in which the group of young men stone a baby to death onstage. In 1965, plays still had to be submitted to the Lord Chamberlain's Examiner of Plays for censorship prior to being performed for the public, under a statute that dates in principle back to the Stage Licensing Act of 1737. Although the examiner usually recommended cuts and deletions of material he found offensive—he had recommended cutting references to God from Beckett's *Endgame,* for example—he banned the text of *Saved* in its entirety. The play was produced, however, and *Saved* has the distinction of being the last play to be prosecuted by the Lord Chamberlain's office. Bond again ran afoul of the censorship laws with *Early Morning* (1968), in which Queen Victoria flirts with Florence Nightingale, and Prince Albert carries the corpse of his siamese-twin brother throughout most of the play; the play provoked another round of Parliamentary discussion of prior censorship of the stage, and the censorship was lifted later in the year.

Bond's plays are generally written in an epic mode reminiscent of Brecht; passionate, violent, but with a kind of contemplative reserve. Several of his plays engage with elements of the literary and theatrical tradition: his rewriting of Shakespeare in *Lear* (1971); a play about Shakespeare, *Bingo* (1974); translations of Chekhov's *Three Sisters* (1967) and Wedekind's *Spring Awakening* (1974); adaptations of Middleton's *A Chaste Maid in Cheapside* (1966) and of Webster's *The White Devil* (1976); a study of the Romantic poet John Clare, *The Fool* (1975); a play on the aftermath of the Trojan war, *The Woman* (1978); a politicized version of Restoration comedy, *Restoration* (1981). Other plays include *Narrow Road to the Deep North* (1968) and its sequel *The Bundle* (1978); *The Sea* (1973); an operatic text, *We Come to the River* (1976); *A-A-America!* (1976); *The Worlds* (1979); and *Jackets* (1989). The trilogy on nuclear destruction, *The War Plays,* was staged in 1985. Bond's *Theatre Poems and Songs* were published in 1978, and *The Activists Papers,* essays and reflections on political theater, were published in 1979.

## Bingo: Scenes of Money and Death (1974)

*Bingo* is in many ways one of Bond's most challenging plays, not because it is formally experimental or even particularly violent, but because Bond's commitment to a form of "epic" theater is so fully achieved. Like Brecht's *Life of Galileo, Bingo* is a kind of "great man" play, a play that uses the final days of Shakespeare's life to explore the nature of individual action and the function of the individual in history. As a dramatic subject, Shakespeare is a nearly impossible "character" to create successfully onstage: Who could give plausible, expressive language to the author of *Hamlet, Antony and Cleopatra, King Lear?* A play about the personality of Shakespeare is, in a sense, doomed to fail; but Bond's play—subtitled "Scenes of Money and Death"—is clearly not about Shakespeare's personality. Instead, Bond uses an "epic" mode to force the audience's attention to Shakespeare's behavior in the play, what he *does* as opposed to what he *feels.* Much as Brecht used

Galileo to question the social function of "science," in this deeply unromantic play, Bond uses Shakespeare to interrogate our notions of the relationship between art and social responsibility.

Although much is known about Shakespeare's life, little is known about him personally. What survives are the records—baptismal records, marriage records, real estate and other business transactions, a will—that mark Shakespeare's public life. It is fitting, then, that Bond centers his play around contracts, Shakespeare's distant involvement in the enclosure of common lands in Stratford in the early seventeenth century. Enclosure was one of the most socially disruptive economic practices of seventeenth-century England. In any town—like Stratford, where Shakespeare was born, where he accumulated real estate and property throughout his career in the London theaters, and where he retired in 1613—major landowners frequently leased sections of the common land to raise crops. Tenant farmers lived on the property and worked the land in exchange for a percentage of the crops they raised; the remainder of the profits went to the leaseholder. But as Combe explains to Shakespeare in Scene 1, these leases divide up the common property into many small plots; although the leaseholders receive income from these plots (Shakespeare received £60 in 1611 from the property he leased in Welcombe), they could turn the property to much more profitable use—often grazing sheep—if the fields were combined into larger properties and the tenant farmers evicted. During the seventeenth century, such "enclosure" of common lands for the benefit of large leaseholders was an incendiary problem: It created a new class of illegal vagrants (like the Young Woman of Scene 1), and it drove up the cost of grain as well.

Shakespeare seems to have played a minor struggle in the enclosure of common lands in Welcombe. Although he was not an instigator in the enclosure, he seems to have been concerned about the potential loss of income from the property he was leasing should the enclosure plan fail. He signed a contract with one of the instigators of the enclosure, William Replingham, who agreed to compensate "William Shakespeare . . . for all such loss, detriment and hindrance" that might arise from the enclosure. We do not, of course, know Shakespeare's motives, his personal interest here, but Bond takes this signature as the starting point for his investigation of the artist's responsibility. For in *Bingo*, the writing we see Shakespeare do is not composing plays, but signing his name to this contract, signing because he needs "security."

The cost of Shakespeare's desire for personal security is everywhere evident in the play: his blighted family, the girl on the gibbet in Scene 3, his vicious relationship with rival playwright Ben Jonson. For the consequences of Shakespeare's basic question—"What does it cost to stay alive?"—are dramatized as the play proceeds. We see Shakespeare, as cold as the snow, finally ask "How long have I been dead?" as though the security he has sought has somehow dehumanized him. It is tempting to read Shakespeare's progress in the play as a kind of inner journey to recognition, so that the long monologue in Scene 5, "Every writer writes in other men's blood" can emerge as a kind of "Shakespearean" soliloquy, a speech in which Shakespeare tragically recognizes and in some way takes account of his own actions. But Shakespeare also asks, finally, "Was anything done?" In Bond's play, tragic "recognition" is not enough: Shakespeare's understanding comes too late to be acted upon, even if *this* Shakespeare were willing to act.

Bond has remarked that he builds a kind of "alienation" into the structure of his scenes, rather than using the more formal Brechtian devices. It is useful to consider the thematic relationships that emerge from the spatial arrangement of characters on Bond's stage: Shakespeare's silence in Scenes 1, 4, and 6; the juxtaposition between the gibbeted girl upstage and Shakespeare's "poetic" musings downstage in Scene 3; Shakespeare lying cold in the snow while the figures upstage run to fill in the enclosure ditches. Bond's cool, ironic play forces its audience to think of alternative ways of reading "character," as a way of inviting us to question the relationship between individual action and the public sphere in which we all live.

# —Bingo—
## Scenes of Money and Death
### Edward Bond

### —CHARACTERS—

| | |
|---|---|
| SHAKESPEARE | WALLY |
| OLD MAN | FIRST OLD WOMAN |
| SON | JUDITH |
| WILLIAM COMBE | YOUNG WOMAN |
| BEN JONSON | JOAN |
| JEROME | SECOND OLD WOMAN |

| PART ONE | PART TWO |
|---|---|
| *One: Garden* | *Four: Inn* |
| *Two: Garden* | *Five: Fields* |
| *Three: Hill* | *Six: Room* |

*There is an interval after Part One.*

*Warwickshire, 1615 and 1616*

### —PART ONE—

SCENE I

*Garden. A hedge runs across the top of the stage. Left, a passageway opening through it. Far right, an opening with a low gate leading to the road. A bench. The house is unseen, off left.*

*Emptiness and silence.* SHAKESPEARE *comes in. He carries a sheet of paper. He sits on the bench. He silently reads part of the paper. An* OLD MAN *comes through the gap in the hedge. He cuts the hedge with shears as he comes through and goes on cutting this side of the hedge. Silence.* JUDITH *comes out of the house left. The men don't react. The* OLD MAN *goes on cutting.*

JUDITH: *(to* SHAKESPEARE*)* Isn't it cold for you? *(Slight pause.)* Mr Combe's here.

*(*SHAKESPEARE *nods.* JUDITH *looks round and then goes back into the house.* SHAKESPEARE *lets his hand hang down with the paper still in it. Silence.)*

OLD MAN: *(contentedly)* Last toime this year.

*(Silence. The* OLD MAN *goes on cutting. A* YOUNG WOMAN *comes along the road and stops at the gate. She smiles archly at the* OLD MAN.*)*

YOUNG WOMAN: How yo' now?

*(The* OLD MAN *nods at* SHAKESPEARE. *The* YOUNG WOMAN *sees him.)*

YOUNG WOMAN: *(politely)* Nicet mornin', sir, thank the lord. *(*SHAKESPEARE *nods. The* YOUNG WOMAN *holds out her hand. A moment's silence.)* Just a little summat. Yo' yont notice.

OLD MAN: Where yo' from, gal?

YOUNG WOMAN: On my way through.

OLD MAN: Where to?

YOUNG WOMAN: My Bristol aunt. My people died lately. My aunt wed a farmer—they'll hev work for us. *(She turns to go.)* I yont be no trouble.

SHAKESPEARE: Stay, stay. *(She stops.)* You'd rather have money not food?

YOUNG WOMAN: Ah, that I would.

*(*SHAKESPEARE *stands and goes out left to the house.)*

YOUNG WOMAN: Hev he gone for authority?

*(The* OLD MAN *smiles at her. He goes to the gate and opens it.)*

YOUNG WOMAN: Is that all roight? *(Uncertainly.)* I yont know . . .

*(The* OLD MAN *carefully pulls her through. He shuts the gate behind her with his foot. He glances round and then touches her breast.)*

YOUNG WOMAN: *(looks round, afraid)* Not here.

OLD MAN: Yo'm a beauty, gal. Let us feel.

YOUNG WOMAN: Got money, hev yo'?

OLD MAN: Wait back a the garden in that bit a orchard.

YOUNG WOMAN: *(looks towards the house)* He . . . ?

OLD MAN: No one yont see down there. I got money. You go sharpish an' keep low. I'll be down by-n'by.

*(The* YOUNG WOMAN *goes through the gap in the hedge. The* OLD MAN *picks up his shears and cuts the hedge.* SHAKESPEARE *comes from the house. He carries a purse.)*

OLD MAN: *(amused)* Her run.

SHAKESPEARE: Call her. She'll be out on the road.

*(The* OLD MAN *goes slowly through the gate, still carrying the shears. He looks right and left, then calls.)*

OLD MAN: Gal. *(He comes back through the gate.)* Her run.

*(*SHAKESPEARE *puts the purse in his pocket. The* OLD MAN *starts cutting the hedge again.* SHAKESPEARE *sits on the bench. Silence. The* OLD MAN *laughs a little to himself, just loud enough to be heard.* SHAKESPEARE *doesn't react.)*

OLD MAN: *(steps back and looks at the hedge)* She yont need lookin' at till next spring.

*(*SHAKESPEARE *doesn't react. The* OLD MAN *goes out through the gap.* SHAKESPEARE *is alone. He sits on the bench. The paper is beside him. A chapel bell begins to peal. It is very close.* SHAKESPEARE *doesn't react. An* OLD WOMAN *comes from the house. She wears an apron.)*

OLD WOMAN: Where's Hubby? *(*SHAKESPEARE *shrugs. The* OLD WOMAN *calls.)* Father. *(To* SHAKESPEARE.*)* His drink's on table if—(*The bell stops.*) —yo' see him. (*She calls.*) Father. (*To* SHAKESPEARE.) Mr Combe's in the house a-talkin t' Judith. Yo' yont ought-a set out here. That's cold afore you feel it this toime a year.

SHAKESPEARE: It's the last of the sun.

OLD WOMAN: So it may be. (*Slight pause.*) Mr Combe's come
40    arter the land. Mornin', business. If t'was yonythin' else he'd a come on an evenin'. (SHAKESPEARE *doesn't react.*) There's plenty a talk! Some say summat, some say summat else. (*Slight pause.*) P'raps he'll tell yo' what he's up to. (*Slight pause.*) People kip arskin' me hev I 'eard yonythin'. Yo'll be brought in—you stand t'lose.

SHAKESPEARE: And your son.

OLD WOMAN: An' a lot a others. What'll yo' tell him?

SHAKESPEARE: Your son told you to question me.

OLD WOMAN: They've hed a meetin'. They thought I ought-a
50    arkst.

SHAKESPEARE: I don't know anything.

OLD WOMAN: What'll yo' do?

SHAKESPEARE: There's plenty of time.

OLD WOMAN: Start buildin' bridges when your feet git wet. If he shut they fields up he'll ruin whole families. They yont got a penny put by. My son say he like a speak t'yo' bout it. I told him t'look in this mornin'.

SHAKESPEARE: Did you.

OLD WOMAN: I thought yo'd want t'hear him out.

(WILLIAM COMBE *comes through the house.*)

60    SHAKESPEARE: Mornin', Will.

COMBE: Mornin'.

OLD WOMAN: Mornin', Mr Combe.

(SHAKESPEARE *nods and the* OLD WOMAN *goes out right through the gate.*)

COMBE: Nice garden. Your hobby, is it?

SHAKESPEARE: No. I weed a bit. I get tired. I planted the maples.

OLD WOMAN: (*off, on the road*) Father.

COMBE: Quiet for you after London. You should take an interest in local affairs. We could get you on the town council.

SHAKESPEARE: No.

70    COMBE: Well, no use if you're not dedicated. You have to find time for it. Pity, though.

OLD WOMAN: (*off*) Father.

COMBE: How's your wife?

SHAKESPEARE: Much the same.

COMBE: Well . . . sensible to sit here—if you know how to sit. Wears me out, of course. Been listening to gossip?

SHAKESPEARE: I've heard something.

COMBE: The gossip's true for once. There are over four hundred acres of common field out at Welcombe. They're
80    owned by a group of farmers and a crowd of tenants. It's divided up into so many bits and pieces no one knows where they are. We can't farm the way we want—we all have to do what the bad farmers do.

SHAKESPEARE: We?

COMBE: Me—and two other big land owners. We're going to enclose—stake out new fields the size of all our old pieces put together and shut them up behind hedges and ditches. Then we can farm in our own way. Tenants with long leases

will be reallocated new land. Squatters and small tenants on short leases will have to go: we shan't renew. That leaves
90    you, and some others, who own rents on the land.

SHAKESPEARE: The rents. I bought my share years ago out of money I made by writing.

COMBE: All the farmers on the common fields pay you a rent based on their earnings—so any change affects you. Quite a large part of your regular income must come from that rent. A sound investment.

SHAKESPEARE: I wanted security. Is it true that when you enclose you're going over from corn to sheep?

COMBE: Mostly. Sheep prices are lower than corn prices but
100    they still give the best return. Low on labour costs! No ploughing, sowing, harvesting, threshing, carting—just a few old shepherds who can turn their hand to butchery. Sheep are pure profit.

SHAKESPEARE: But you know I could lose? I've got no labour costs, I just draw my rents.

(*The* OLD WOMAN *comes through the gate. She crosses the garden and goes out left.*)

COMBE: (*factually*) Everyone listens to money. (*He looks off left a moment and then turns back to* SHAKESPEARE.) There's another problem: the town council also own some of the rents. They use their share to feed the town poor—seven hun-
110    dred—not counting gypsies and riff-raff passing through. You see there's a lot of money involved!

SHAKESPEARE: The town will oppose you. A lot of the small holders don't have written leases. They just followed their fathers onto the land—and their fathers had followed *their* fathers. If you get rid of them and the short-lease tenants— there'll be more than seven hundred poor to feed. And if you grow less wheat the price of bread will go up—

COMBE: Then it'll be profitable to grow more wheat and the price will come down. Always take the long view, Will. I self-
120    ishly cut down my labour costs and put up prices and the town suffers—but not in the long run. This is the only way men have so far discovered of running the world. Men are donkeys, they need carrots and sticks. All the other ways: they come down to bigger sticks. But there's a difference between us and the beast. We understand the nature of carrots and sticks. That's why we can get rid of the bad farmers who *grow* starvation in their fields like a crop, and create seven hundred poor in a town of less than two thousand. But—in the meantime the town council will oppose me.
130    They don't want to feed the new poor while they wait for history to catch up with the facts. They're writing to you for help.

SHAKESPEARE: Who told you—

COMBE: My friends on the council. You're one of the biggest rent holders. You're respectable. They probably think you've got friends in London. You could make out a strong case against me.

SHAKESPEARE: We've come to the river.

COMBE: We needn't build a bridge if there's a ford down-
140    stream. Will you reach an agreement with me?

SHAKESPEARE: You'll get increased profits—you can afford to guarantee me against loss. And the town councillors.

COMBE: I make all the effort, I expect to keep my carrot.

SHAKESPEARE: I invested a lot of money.

COMBE: I'll tell you why I'm here: I'll guarantee *you* against loss, in return for an understanding.

SHAKESPEARE: Yes?

COMBE: Don't support the town or the tenants. When the
150 council write, ignore them. Be noncommittal or say you think nothing will come of it. Stay in your garden. I'll pay for that.

SHAKESPEARE: You read too much into it. I'm protecting my own interests. Not supporting you, or fighting the town.

COMBE: That's all I want. It needn't be written into our agreement, it wouldn't read well: but it will be implied. After all, if we sign an agreement it wouldn't pay you to attack me: you get your present rents guaranteed at no extra cost. Free insurance. It pays to sit in a garden.

160 SHAKESPEARE: You guarantee me the difference between what my rents are now and what they'll be after enclosure, if they fall. How do we agree the figures?

COMBE: O, you can accept my—

SHAKESPEARE: (*gives* COMBE *his sheet of paper*) I want security. I can't provide for the future again. My father went bankrupt when he was old. Too easy going.

COMBE: (*holding the paper*) Yes, a nice man, but as you say, too . . . Very well. We'll appoint independent assessors. How many?

170 SHAKESPEARE: Another thing. I've got over a hundred acres of my own land out there. Are you after that?

COMBE: No, no. We won't touch your private land. This only affects your rents from the common fields.

(*The* OLD MAN *hurries in through the gap in the hedge. He is frightened but defiant, excited and amused. He looks round, backs a few steps towards the hedge and stands there.* SHAKESPEARE *and* COMBE *don't notice him.* COMBE *reads* SHAKESPEARE's *piece of paper. A moment's silence. The* SON *comes angrily through the gap in the hedge. He is excited and tightjawed. The* SON *stares at the* OLD MAN *before bursting out.*)

SON: Beast.

OLD MAN: (*laughs briefly*) Look at him.

SON: Animal. In daylight. Back on a public high road. Any child could put its yead cross the wall.

(COMBE *stands up.*)

OLD MAN: (*pointing at the* SON) Look at him!

SON: Grey hair. Waggin' your boney ol' arse. Slobberin' like a
180 boy with mud pies.

COMBE: He's got a woman in there.

SON: Hev yo' no shame? God an' man see you in the daylight. Yo'm drag creation down t' the beast. Animal. They ugly ol' legs. Runnin' loike a thief. Ugly.

(JUDITH *and the* OLD WOMAN *come out of the house.*)

Look at him! Where your wife an' child can see yo'.

JUDITH: What is it?

OLD WOMAN: Father, your drink's inside on the table.

OLD MAN: Yont sendin' me indoor. Look how red he go!

COMBE: (*goes to the hedge and calls through*) Girl! Come here.

190 SON: Git her out. Thass her. Runnin' round them trees. Tried a climb the wall. I shut the gate on 'em when I saw what t'was. (*He goes to the gap and calls through.*) Come out. (*He turns to the* OLD MAN.) Loike an animal. Ugly. (*To the others.*) He yont hed the shame t'cover her yead with her skart.

COMBE: (*calls*) You won't get out there. It's locked.

(*Silence. The* YOUNG WOMAN *comes through the gap in the hedge.*)

You're not a local girl.

YOUNG WOMAN: On my way t'Bristol, sir.

COMBE: Got work there?

YOUNG WOMAN: (*nods*) Can I go, sir?

COMBE: No doubt your family's dead and your husband's left 200 you?

YOUNG WOMAN: Not wed, sir. My family's dead though. Can I go?

COMBE: Who've you got in Bristol—your sister, uncle?

OLD MAN: (*laughs*) Her auntie. Mr Combe almost got 'an roight.

COMBE: Dear me, we're in a bad way. Half the country's suddenly bereaved and they're marching round England to stay with relatives who live as far away as possible. The law says you can't leave your parish without a pass. Where's your 210 pass?

YOUNG WOMAN: I yont no beggar woman, sir.

SON: Mr Combe's on the bench. Yo' hed it now. Yo'll be punished.

SHAKESPEARE: (*to the* SON) Why were you in my orchard?

(*They all turn to look at* SHAKESPEARE.)

SON: I come t'see yo'. Mother say I . . .

(*The* YOUNG WOMAN *starts to cry. They all turn back to her.*)

YOUNG WOMAN: My aunt's waitin' in Bristol. My family's dead.

JUDITH: Where?

YOUNG WOMAN: Coventry.

JUDITH: Could you point out their graves? 220

YOUNG WOMAN: They'm buried in poor ground. Nothin' t'show.

COMBE: We have her sort in front of us every week, Judith. Do anything for money—though they'd rather do nothing. Lie when they learn to speak. First time they say father it's a lie. (*He laughs shortly.*) The law says you're to be whipped here in the shopping place till the blood runs and then sent back to your parish in Coventry, was it?

YOUNG WOMAN: Yont whip us, sir? I were whip afore an' that hurt my yead sorely. I couldn't go with people arter. I walked okkard an' fell down in the road. I were a gal then an' 230 that's only better now.

COMBE: If there's something wrong with your head it'll do it good. Doctors whip mad people. I'd like to follow my own inclinations and let you off but I have to protect the public. You're a healthy girl, sleeping rough hardens your skin. You'll be all right. If you lead your sort of life you must learn to pay for it. (*To the* SON.) Take her to the lock-up.

(*The* SON *starts to take the* YOUNG WOMAN *out.*)

YOUNG WOMAN: (*earnestly, not crying*) Yo' yont whip us, sir. That destroy my yead. The Constable's wife long a 'cester say that's a shame t'whip me. (*The* SON *takes her out through* 240 *the gate. She is heard off on the road.*) I fall over the road, sir. Yont whip us.

COMBE: Tch, locusts or the blight. (*To* SHAKESPEARE.) I'll show this paper to my lawyers and be in touch. Goodbye.

(COMBE *goes out left.* JUDITH *goes with him.*)

OLD MAN: He git cross!

OLD WOMAN: Father, go in an hev your drink.

(*The* OLD MAN *goes into the house.*)

I'm sorry my boy shouted. Young people yont got no patience—worse'n us. I hope he yont upsit his father.

SHAKESPEARE: They're going to enclose.

250 OLD WOMAN: What'll you do?

SHAKESPEARE: Wait and see.

OLD WOMAN: Yo' give him a sheet a piper.

SHAKESPEARE: Nothing's decided. Has this shouting woken my wife? See if she's all right.

(*The* OLD WOMAN *goes out left.* SHAKESPEARE *sits on the bench. He stares in front of him for a moment.*)

SCENE II

*Garden. Six months later.*

(*The* OLD WOMAN *and* JUDITH *are sitting alone on the bench.*)

JUDITH: Has your marriage been happy?

OLD WOMAN: 'Twas. We had seven good year first off. Then the press men come t' church one Sunday mornin' an' hid back a the tomb stones. When the men come from the lord's supper out they jump an' tak em over sea t'fight. I still think a

260 them times on an off. Time 'fore the flood.

JUDITH: Seven years out of a life. Most people don't have that.

OLD WOMAN: He were gone three year. Then two men bot him hwome. He'd bin hit top the yead with an axe. Some man were killin' a man lay on the ground front on him an' when he swung his axe back he hit father top the yead. Not the sharp end, though. That'd a kill 'un. Now he hev the mind of a twelve year ol' an' the needs on a man. I'm mother an' wife to him.

JUDITH: He should be happy. No responsibilities. No duties.

270 OLD WOMAN: He's a boy that remember what's like t'be a man. He still hev a proper feelin' for his pride, that yont gone. Hard, that is—like bein' tied up to a clown. Some nights he come hwome an' cry all hours. I git on with my work now. You hear him all over the house. Every room. An' the garden.

JUDITH: It was harder for your son. He had a child for a father.

(SHAKESPEARE *comes out of the house.*)

OLD WOMAN: No coat?

SHAKESPEARE: Is it cold? It looked warm from the house.

(*The* OLD WOMAN *stands and goes off left into the house.*)

JUDITH: Have you been up to mother?

280 SHAKESPEARE: What?

JUDITH: Shall we carry her down? The spring weather will help her.

SHAKESPEARE: She's happy in her room.

JUDITH: When are you going back to London?

SHAKESPEARE: I don't know.

JUDITH: I thought you were buying some property at Blackfriars.

SHAKESPEARE: That's done.

(*The* OLD WOMAN *comes from the house with a wrap. She drapes* SHAKESPEARE.)

SHAKESPEARE: (*irritated*) Don't fuss!

(SHAKESPEARE *pulls the coat off and pushes it back to the* OLD WOMAN.)

OLD WOMAN: I'll leave it there.                                              290

(*The* OLD WOMAN *puts the wrap on the bench and goes off into the house.*)

JUDITH: Aren't you going away at all this year?

SHAKESPEARE: (*still irritated*) I don't know.

JUDITH: Have you told mother?

SHAKESPEARE: She's not interested.

JUDITH: You'll get old sitting there all day.

SHAKESPEARE: I *am* old.

JUDITH: You used to be so busy. Striding about. Laughing. It's all gone. You look so tired these days.

SHAKESPEARE: I didn't sleep last night. So many people on the streets. All that shouting. And the sky—like day.          300

JUDITH: Someone's starting the fires. Everyone says so.

SHAKESPEARE: I'll put buckets on the stairs and by the doors. You must keep them filled. Thank god we're not thatched.

JUDITH: Why don't you tip the watch and tell them to keep an eye on us?

SHAKESPEARE: I have.

(*Silence.* JUDITH *looks at* SHAKESPEARE. *Then she gets up and goes silently into the house.* SHAKESPEARE *is alone. He leans back and slightly to one side with his head up and his hands in his lap. He closes his eyes. Silence. The* OLD MAN *comes silently through the gap in the hedge. A pair of shears hangs from his hand. He pays no attention to* SHAKESPEARE. *He stops and feels along the side of the hedge with the flat of his hand, as if he was blind. Then he begins to cut. Suddenly* SHAKESPEARE *notices him. He is shocked—but he doesn't make a sound or move violently.*)

SHAKESPEARE: How long have you been there?

OLD MAN: Juss cuttin' back the young growth. That need air t' thicken out. Hev I woke you up then? Your daughter bin rowin', that it? Yont want a take no woman-row. Yo' got a        310 fist. Thass only two piece a man's anatomy a woman understan', an' a fist's one. She yont hold with yo' set there all day.

(*The* YOUNG WOMAN *comes to the gate. The* OLD MAN *looks at her, goes to the gate, opens it. She comes in quickly and stands close to the hedge.*)

SHAKESPEARE: (*looks at the* YOUNG WOMAN. *There's a slight pause before he knows her.*) They sent you home.

OLD MAN: Her yont got no hwome. Her go back there her'll get whip again. So her run for it.

SHAKESPEARE: You mustn't walk in the streets. You'll be recognized.

YOUNG WOMAN: I mostly come out a night. I were frightid by meself t'day. I were clever, mind. When someone got by I        320 stoop down an' do as though I brushin' my skart.

SHAKESPEARE: Where d'you live?

YOUNG WOMAN: Barns. They ol' burned 'ouses.

SHAKESPEARE: You're shaking.

YOUNG WOMAN: Ah, I do shake an' all! I bin took so since they whip us. I warned 'em straight. (*She shrugs.*) I yont feel cold but my arms an' legs do shake an' my teeth go a-clatter. (*She holds out her fore-arm.*) Yo' look, see 'ow the skin go in that arm, like a bud peckin'.

330 SHAKESPEARE: How did you get through the winter?

OLD MAN: I fed her.

YOUNG WOMAN: Sometime. I yont allus count on that. Sometime the boys come a-lookin' for us in they empty houses. Not s'much now. They say I have a sickness. I tell 'em I'm whole, thass only the whippin'. But they only come when they'm drunk. You yont heard a no cure for shakin'?

SHAKESPEARE: No.

YOUNG WOMAN: I cover meself proper but I still shakes. I try holdin' me yand tight. I set in the heat of a fire. But I still
340  shakes. An' when that's cold the same. Well, there. I yont thrid needles for a livin'. I can larn t'live with it. Least it yont touch my yead.

SHAKESPEARE: You give her bread and lie with her.

OLD MAN: She's a poor creature. But us still hev some fun.

YOUNG WOMAN: O ah, us's allus laughin'.

SHAKESPEARE: At what?

OLD MAN: O—people?

YOUNG WOMAN: What they put on t'wear.

OLD MAN: They hats!

350 YOUNG WOMAN: An' what they say.

OLD MAN: Try t' tell yo' yo' yont know your own name.

YOUNG WOMAN: Gallopin' arter this an' that—but they mustn't pant! "Howdedo."

OLD MAN: "Howdedo."

(*The* OLD MAN *and the* YOUNG WOMAN *laugh.*)

YOUNG WOMAN: Us laugh so us hev to' cover us yeads—

OLD MAN: So us yont git caught.

(*The* OLD MAN *and* YOUNG WOMAN *laugh.*)

YOUNG WOMAN: Well. (*She holds out her hand.*)

SHAKESPEARE: (*calls*) House!

(*The* YOUNG WOMAN *runs towards the gate.*)

OLD MAN: Don't frit. He'll give yo' proper fettles sit out on a
360  table like a christian.

(JUDITH *comes out of the house.*)

SHAKESPEARE: Let her eat. Give her a shawl or a dress. Both. Give her your mother's things. They're only gathering dust.

JUDITH: (*unsure*) I know her. (*She recognizes her.*) She—. (*To* SHAKESPEARE.) No. If we feed her once we'll never get rid of her.

YOUNG WOMAN: That's roight enough. Give us some money an' I'll away t' go. I yont need feedin'.

SHAKESPEARE: She must be looked after.

JUDITH: She'd steal if we had her here, the poor thing.

370 YOUNG WOMAN: Missis is roight. It yont do t'trust me. Give us a bit a money. Yont notice that.

(*The bell starts to peal.*)

JUDITH: (*to the* OLD MAN) D'you often have her in the garden?

OLD MAN: No.

JUDITH: How often?

(SHAKESPEARE *sits on the bench.*)

SHAKESPEARE: (*to the* YOUNG WOMAN) Wait in the orchard till it's dark. Then go away. (*To* JUDITH.) Give her some money. No, bring my purse.

YOUNG WOMAN: (*looks at the gap in the hedge and hesitates*) I yont go down there agin—

SHAKESPEARE: The back gate's locked now.                                380

(*The* YOUNG WOMAN *goes through the gap in the hedge.*)

JUDITH: Why is she so frightened?

SHAKESPEARE: She shakes because she was whipped.

(JUDITH *goes left into the house.*)

OLD MAN: Now she's cross with the two on us. My boy's cross too. He rage up an' down all hours. Say yo' agin poor people. Ol' Combe tak the best land, an' do he give yo' any that yont be good enough t' grow stones in. (*He shrugs.*) I tell 'im yo' live a rare ol' life but there's no harm in yo'. He's allus talkin' t'god—so stands t' reason he never listen to a word I say.

SHAKESPEARE: Why is your son afraid of the devil? God judges, 390 not the devil.

OLD MAN: When my boy's took in a hoolerin'-bout he say the devil look arter his own.

SHAKESPEARE: By putting them in the fire? You never sell everything. That's what he punishes. Hell is full of burning scruples.

(*The* OLD WOMAN *comes out of the house.*)

OLD WOMAN: Mr Combe.

(SHAKESPEARE *nods.*)

OLD WOMAN: (*to the* OLD MAN) Let the gen'men talk, father.

(*The* OLD WOMAN *goes into the house. The* OLD MAN *takes another cut at the hedge and then follows her.* SHAKESPEARE *sits alone for a moment. He raises his head as* COMBE *comes out of the house.* COMBE *carries a bottle of ink, a pen and a document.*)

COMBE: In your garden? The day for it. I haven't seen you since winter. Busy. (*He puts the pen and ink on the bench and* 400 *hands the document to* SHAKESPEARE.) From my lawyer. (SHAKESPEARE *starts to read the document.*) Pity you didn't go into business before. You can bargain. That guarantees you against any loss arising from my action.

SHAKESPEARE: You'll enclose?

COMBE: My men start digging—(*The bell stops.*)—round my my land on Monday. I've signed it.

SHAKESPEARE: (*reading the document.*) Bells love silence.

(SHAKESPEARE *signs the document.* COMBE *picks it up and looks at it.*)

COMBE: I'll have it witnessed. Must keep you on good behaviour, living by the chapel.                                410

(JUDITH *comes out of the house.*)

JUDITH: Mr Combe—I thought it was! How is Mrs Combe? (*She shakes* COMBE's *hand.*) . . . No. I won't have it. (*Icily cold.)* Father, where is he? It's shameful.

SHAKESPEARE: No.

JUDITH: *(icy)* Don't shield them. You're morally as guilty as they are.

COMBE: What is it?

JUDITH: Our garden man. In that hedge.

COMBE: *(amused)* With a woman? *(He goes to the hedge and*
420  *looks through the gap. Then he looks back at* SHAKESPEARE.*)* I know why you like your garden!

*(COMBE goes out through the gap in the hedge.)*

JUDITH: I'm sorry, father, I will not allow that woman—*(She points left to the house.)*—to be abused. How can you behave so badly? It's irresponsible! Why d'you make it necessary for a child to speak to its parents in this way?

*(The YOUNG WOMAN runs through the gap in the hedge, over the garden and out through the gate.)*

How sordid. Ugly. *(She stares angrily after the YOUNG WOMAN But doesn't try to stop her. She is still like ice.)* On one's own property.

*(JUDITH goes to the gate and shuts it. COMBE walks through the gap in the hedge. He is still amused.)*

COMBE: Gone?

430  JUDITH: Yes. Thank you.

COMBE: She was hiding behind the trees. Bolted like a rabbit when I said boo. I had a clear sight of her. *(He turns to JU-DITH.)* There was no one with her.

SHAKESPEARE: She wants work. I told her she could work in the scullery.

COMBE: No, she can't. She was sent away from here to her proper parish, and she's come back. Tch. The lord chancellor's told the benches they aren't firm enough. Well, I am. I'll have the barns and burned houses searched. I know
440  where they lie up. *(He goes towards the gate.)* The law says it's an offence to give alms to anyone without a licence. So don't be tempted. Goodbye. I'll get my men on to her. She won't make herself a nuisance anymore.

*(COMBE goes out through the gate.)*

JUDITH: Last time they . . . So of course I thought . . .

SHAKESPEARE: I came out here to rest. People coming and going. *(He sighs.)* Haven't you any work in the house?

JUDITH: How could I let him enjoy himself while his wife . . . ? She's had a hard life, father. You don't notice these things. You must learn that people have feelings. They suffer. Life
450  almost breaks them. *(She picks up the pen and ink.)* I'll take these in. You don't need them? You sit there and brood all day. People in this town aren't so easily impressed, you know. We can all sit and think. (SHAKESPEARE *is silent.)* I feel guilty if I dare to talk about anything that matters. I should shut up now—or ask if it's good gardening weather. D'you know why mother's ill? D'you care?

SHAKESPEARE: Judith.

JUDITH: At last, a word. I'll tell you why she stays in bed. She hides from you. She doesn't know who she is, or what she's
460  supposed to do, or who she married. She's bewildered—like so many of us!

SHAKESPEARE: *(flatly)* Stop it, Judith. You speak so badly. Such

banalities. So stale and ugly.

JUDITH: I can only use the words I know.

*(The OLD WOMAN and the OLD MAN come out of the house left. She wears her outdoor coat. He carries the basket.)*

OLD WOMAN: We'm away now. There's nothin we'm forgot?

SHAKESPEARE: *(to the OLD MAN)* Combe found her.

OLD WOMAN: Oh dear.

JUDITH: *(to the OLD WOMAN)* That girl was—

OLD WOMAN: Hubby told me. Us were goin' t'put her up for a few days, now I know on it. Then p'raps summat could be  470 worked out. Surely there's summat?

SHAKESPEARE: Combe's men are looking for her.

*(The OLD MAN sits on the bench. He rests his elbows on his knees and his hands hang down between his legs. He rocks like a little boy. The basket is on the ground beside him.)*

JUDITH: They'll flog her! O, why wasn't I more careful? You all think I should be in her place. *(To SHAKESPEARE.)* You could have warned me! You ignore me—you always do! You talk to the servants more than to your family.

OLD MAN: That's worse'n that. She lit they fires. I yont know why. She wait up in they empty houses till that's dark then out she go an' back she come an' set down in the corner. She yont tell but I knew what t'was. Her face blacked up an' she  480 smelt of smoke. Smell it for days.

OLD WOMAN: No one else know.

OLD MAN: They'll find out. When they lock her up. Her'll tell.

OLD WOMAN: You're not t' fault. Us won't let em touch you.

OLD MAN: They'll hang her. *(He starts to cry.)* O dear, I do hate a hanging. People runnin' through the streets laughin an' sportin'. Buyin' an' sellin'. I allus enjoyed the hangings when I were a boy. Now I can't abide 'em. They conjurors with red noses takin' animals out the air an' coloured things out their pockets. The soldier lads scare us. The parson an' 'is antics.  490

OLD WOMAN: Mr Shakespeare yont like yo' cryin in his garden. *(She helps the OLD MAN to his feet.)* I'll manage the basket. *(To JUDITH.)* Goodbye then. He'll be round for work in the mornin'. *(To the OLD MAN.)* We'll soon be hwome. *(To others.)* I'll git him t'bed early.

OLD MAN: *(crying as he goes)* People pushin' t'see in they empty coffins. Allus so quiet fore the rope go so's yo' hear babbies an dogs cry—an' when it thump the people holla.

*(The OLD MAN and the OLD WOMAN go through the gate.)*

OLD WOMAN: *(out on the road)* Hush now. I hev a noice surprise indoor for yo', my lad.                                    500

OLD MAN: *(out on the road)* That better be good.

OLD WOMAN: That's good. I hid un so yo'll hev t' find it first.

*(The OLD MAN and the OLD WOMAN go away down the road.)*

JUDITH: I can't leave you out here. It's against common humanity. You'd better come inside and learn to put up with us.

SHAKESPEARE: Go in.

JUDITH: You'll catch cold and expect to be nursed. I've enough to do with mother on my hands. Why are you so stubborn. Your family's tearing itself to bits and you sit in the garden and—                                                        510

SHAKESPEARE: Yes, yes.

JUDITH: Yes, yes—it's easy to make us sound stupid. You ignore the people you share a house with and when they try to talk, you sneer.

(SHAKESPEARE *goes out through the gate.* JUDITH *follows him onto the road. She can be heard calling after him.*)

If we bore you why don't you go away, father? Go back to your interesting friends. Or are they tired of you now?

SCENE III

*Hill. A pleasant warm day. Slight fresh wind. The* YOUNG WOMAN *has been gibbeted. An upright post with two short beams forming a narrow cleft. The* YOUNG WOMAN's *head is in this and her body is suspended against the post. A sack is wrapped round her from hips to ankles. A rope is wound round the sack and the top half of her body to steady her against the post. (Rembrandt, New York Metropolitan Museum of Art, inv. 76487. "Rembrandt's Drawings" Schedig, W. Ill. 121.) She has been dead one day. The face is grey, the eyes closed and the hair has become whispy.*

*A bench downstage left.* SHAKESPEARE *sits on it facing away from the body, out into the audience. He is alone.*

*Two labourers come in. Both middle aged. They watch the body for a moment.*

JOAN: (*reflectively*) By roights they ought-a put her on a bonfire, for lightin' fires. Or starve her in a cage for beggary.
JEROME: Set yo'self down, gal'. I'm tired.

(*They sit on the ground, unpack their lunch and eat.*)

520 JOAN: (*quietly as she points to* SHAKESPEARE) Is the gen'man all roight?
JEROME: (*nods and eats*) Gen'man from big 'ouse: New Place gen'man.

(*They eat in silence for a moment.*)

Good.
JOAN: Like it?
JEROME: (*nods and eats*) Good stuff.
JOAN: Take some a mine.
JEROME: No, gal.
JOAN: Go on, I offered, yo' yont arkst.
530 JEROME: Yont yo' 'ungry?
JOAN: I got extra. I know hot weather allus give yo' an appetite.
JEROME: Yo' pick your grub like a bud with a wart end on its beak.

(*He puts his arm round her waist.*)

JOAN: Hold your noise, boy. An' give over throwin' crumbs down the front a my dress. (*She takes his arm from her waist, uncorks a bottle and gives it to him.*) Grab hold a that. Yo' need two hand a feed yo'self.
JEROME: (*drinking*) Yo'm a hard woman.
JOAN: (*eating*) So'd yo' be if yo' kip gettin' crumbs down the
540 front a your dress. (*She takes crumbs from her bodice and feeds the birds.*) Cheep-cheep, chuck-chuck, my beauties.

(*The* SON *comes on with* WALLY. WALLY *is tall and quite thin.*)

SON: Mornin', brother, sister.
WALLY: Morn'. (*He stares at* JOAN *and* JEROME.)
JOAN: We'm on us way t' work. Stonin' our strip a field out at Welcombe. We'm just cooched-ed up for us bit a fitter.
JEROME: (*eating*) Which we'm earnt. Sorry yont none left t' hand round. (*He drinks.*)
JOAN: Hev yo' see her drop? (WALLY *shakes his head.*) Proper state her were in. Yont heard a word parson say, poor chap. But she went good as gold. 550
JEROME: (*eating*) He say up yo' git, my gal, an' up she git.
JOAN: Tryin' a help 'em hang her. (*She finds more crumbs in her bodice.*) Cheep-cheep. How the wicked disguise themselves. Her could a bunt the town t'death. When her toime come she couldn't hold a candle straight t' see where she were goin'. She die summat slow. No family or friends t' swing on her legs. I sin mothers an' fathers help their young a go easy afore. She yont afford a pay the hangman t' do it.
SON: A festival a dark. Singin', dancin', layin' money how long she'll live. The sexes going back a hedges. Is that reverence? 560 Lord god is wherever there's justice. When a soul go satanways lord god come t'watch an' weep. Reverence, friends. That ought-a be a festival a light an' prayer.
JOAN: (*quietly. Feeding birds*) Chuck, chuck, chuck.
WALLY: P'raps they'm makin' a great show for the presence a lord god, brother. Soundin' the psalter an the joyful harp.
SON: You'm too good natured, brother. Let us talk with lord god.

(*The* SON *and* WALLY *shut their eyes and clasp their hands. They don't kneel.* JOAN *bows her head, stops eating and takes the last crumbs from her bodice.* JEROME *bows his head and goes on chewing and putting food in his mouth.*)

Lord god, lord god. The covetous man laugh in 'is secret yeart but thou art not mocked. Thou sent the whore t' the 570 rich man's yate an' the poor man fell in her way but thou art not mocked.
WALLY: Amen.
JEROME: He yont finished yet, brother.
SON: Lord god, thou set thy cross for a sign-post afore the two ways. Lord god, shear the sheep in winter that he feel the blast. Amen.
WALLY *and* JOAN: Amen.

(SHAKESPEARE *has stood up and walked slowly away. His movements and face express nothing.*)

JEROME: (*wiping his mouth with the back of his hand*) That'll do for grace. (*He stands.*) We'm off t' labour in the lord's 580 vineyards.
SON: Yont do need t' laugh at good people, brother. You hev pains an' reasons for 'em I yont know, an' I hev mine. Only the sinner's branded front t' yead—an' that's sometime hid.
JEROME: Nothin' under my yat bar my yead.

(JEROME *and* JOAN *go out. The* SON *stands in front of the gibbet.* WALLY *watches him.*)

WALLY: What is it, brother?
SON: I'm larnin' t' face a sin so I know it in the street.
WALLY: Her's terrible changed.
SON: Death bring out her true life, brother. Look, her eyes be shut agin the truth. There's blood trickle down the corner a 590

her mouth. Her teeth snap at her flesh while her die. Be solemn, brother, think a lord god. That's the face us turn to him even when us prays. Day an' day an' day he set the sun t'rise an' shine a way for his saints on earth an' us throw us shadow cross it. God weep.

WALLY: Halleluja! O rapture in the lord!

SON: } Us sin an' go on all four in the grass. Us face is turned to dirt away from lord god.

WALLY: } *(jumping)* Israel. Israel. Israel. Israel. Israel. Israel.

600

WALLY: Praise an' glory. O tis terrible t' die so.

JUDITH: *(off)* Father. Father.

SON: } Worse, worse to live in sin. Lord god send death t' free his sinner. Damnation's bliss when yo' know he chose it for you.

WALLY: } *(jumping)* Israel. Israel. Israel.

*(JUDITH comes on right.)*

JUDITH: My father.

SON: He were here. I sid a prayer but he turn away from the word.

610 WALLY: Spurned lord god like the roman in the judgement hall.

SON: Amen.

JUDITH: *(calls)* Father.

*(JUDITH stops in front of the YOUNG WOMAN.)*

WALLY: She'll hev her full a fire now.

SON: *(quietly. Watching JUDITH)* Harden your yeart for lord god, sister. Dost matter t' him her beg when all eat out his yand? No. Dost matter her burn the proud man's hall when he break t' earth from toime t' toime? Dost matter her love a man when he love all men—

JUDITH: *(calls)* Father.

620 SON: Even the sinner's innocent. O harden your yeart with a gladsome mind, good people. Tent for us t' question lord god's way. Sin were 'er cross an her bore it afore us for a sign. Lord god send the wolf an' the shepherd to the sheep.

WALLY: Amen.

SON: Amen.

*(The SON and WALLY go out right.)*

JUDITH: *(calls)* Father.

*(SHAKESPEARE comes on left.)*

Are you blaming me? Is that what I've done now?

SHAKESPEARE: No. She'd have been caught. Burning . . .

JUDITH: Come home.

630 SHAKESPEARE: Later. *(He sits.)*

JUDITH: You're hungry.

SHAKESPEARE: Why do . . . ? I thought I knew the questions. Have I forgotten them?

JUDITH: People will stroll out here to look after work. They'll talk if you sit there. We know what she was. (SHAKESPEARE *doesn't react.*) You were out all yesterday. Did you see her hang?

SHAKESPEARE: The baited bear. Tied to the stake. Its dirty coat needs brushing. Dried mud and spume. Pale dust. Big 640 clumsy fists. Men bringing dogs through the gate. Leather collars with spikes. Loose them and fight. The bear wanders round the stake. It knows it can't get away. The chain. Dogs on three sides. Fur in the mouth. Deeper. (The OLD WOMAN *comes on upstage right.*) Flesh and blood. Strips of skin. Teeth scrapping bone. The bear will crush one of the skulls. Big feet slithering in dog's brain. Round the stake. On and on. The key in the warder's pocket. Howls. Roars. Men baiting their beast. On and on and on. And later the bear raises its great arm. The paw with a broken razor. And it looks as if it's making a gesture—it wasn't: only weariness or pain or 650 the sun or brushing away the sweat—but it looks as if it's making a gesture to the crowd. Asking for one sign of grace, one no. And the crowd roars, for more blood, more pain, more beasts huddled together, tearing flesh and treading in living blood.

JUDITH: You don't like sport. Some bears dance.

SHAKESPEARE: In London they blinded a bear. Called Harry Hunks. The sport was to bait it with whips. Slash, slash. It couldn't see but it could hear. It grabbed the whips. Caught some of them. Broke them. Slashed back at the men. Slash, 660 slash. The men stood round in a circle slashing at it. It was blind but they still chained it to the ground. Slash, slash. Then they sent an ape round on a horse. A thin hairy man or a child. You could see the pale skin under its arm when it jumped. Its teeth. The dogs tore it to pieces. The crowd howled. London. The queen cheered them on in shrill latin. The virgin often watched blood. Her father baited bears on the Thames. From boat to boat, slash, slash. They fell in and fought men in the water. He was the man in a mad house who says I'm king but he had a country to say it in. 670

JUDITH: I must go down. Someone must watch the house, count the glasses, knives, spoons. I shan't ask you to listen any more. You're only interested in your ideas. You treat us as enemies.

*(JUDITH walks upstage to the OLD WOMAN. The OLD WOMAN puts her arm round her and silently tries to comfort her.)*

SHAKESPEARE: What does it cost to stay alive? I'm stupefied at the suffering I've seen. The shapes huddled in misery that twitch away when you step over them. Women with shopping bags stepping over puddles of blood. What it costs to starve people. The chatter of those who hand over prisoners. The smile of men who see no further than the end of a 680 knife. Stupefied. How can I go back to that? What can I do there? I talk to myself now. I know no one will ever listen.

*(The OLD WOMAN comes down to SHAKESPEARE.)*

OLD WOMAN: A gen'man's come from London. At the Golden Cross. *(She hands a note to SHAKESPEARE.)* He sent this up by me.

SHAKESPEARE: There's no higher wisdom of silence. No face brooding over the water. (The OLD WOMAN *glances helplessly up at JUDITH.*) No hand leading the waves to the shore as if it's saving a dog from the sea. When I go to my theatre I walk under sixteen severed heads on a gate. You hear bears 690 in the pit while my characters talk.

OLD WOMAN: Now, sir. That's bin a longish winter. That's brought yo' down.

SHAKESPEARE: No other hand . . . no face . . . just these . . .

OLD WOMAN: *(to JUDITH)* I'll bring him hwome.

*(JUDITH goes out.)*

SHAKESPEARE: Stupid woman! They stand under a gallows and
ask if it rains. Terrible. Terrible. What is the right question?
I said be still. I quietened the storms inside me. But the
storm breaks outside. To have usurped the place of god, and
700    lied . . .
OLD WOMAN: Why torment yo'self? You'm never harmed no—
SHAKESPEARE: And my daughter?
OLD WOMAN: No, no. Yo' yont named for cruelty. They say
yo'm a generous man. Yo' looked arter me an' father. Give
us one a your houses t' live in.
SHAKESPEARE: (points) There's a coin. I saw it when I came up.
Glittering in the grass.
OLD WOMAN: (goes immediately to where SHAKESPEARE
pointed) Here?
710    SHAKESPEARE: Perhaps the hangman dropped it.
OLD WOMAN: (picks up the coin) We'm put a little by for later.
Times change. Read your note.

(SHAKESPEARE is silent. He doesn't move.)

If yo' yont allow yo'self t' be helped, what shall us do? I'm
afraid I'm like your daughter. I yont had no one t' talk to, no
one t' share my loife. Juss father's prattle—an' he stay by me
out a fear. Nothin' else. O a child love but he yont even a
proper child. He yont more'n a wounded bud in a road.
Tread on or go under a cart. I fed him. Kep him clane. Tak
the washin' back when he steal it. Scare him so he yont hide
720    t'much. I took a stick to him afore now, or he yont got no tay.
But one day when he steal summat they'll be roight cross:
shops're doin' bad or that's the weather. Then they'll hang
him! His 'ole loife's a risk. I hope he die afore me. (She
shrugs.) What'm I supposed a make a that? I yont afford
arkst questions I yont know y'answers to. Well, you'm summat at peace now.
SHAKESPEARE: I went to the river yesterday. So quiet. They
were all here. No fishing, no boats. One boy to mind the cattle—he was being punished. I watched the fish jump for
730    flies. Then a swan flew by me up the river. On a straight line
just over the water. A woman in a white dress running along
an empty street. Its neck was rocking like a wave. I heard its
breath when it flew by. Sighing. The white swan and the
dark water. Straight down the middle of the river and round
a curve out of sight. I could still hear its wings. God knows
where it was going. So quiet and then silence. (He gestures
round.) And here it was hot—(He stands.)—noise—
dust . . . she saw none of this—(He gestures to the horizon.)
the view . . . Where shall I go? London? Stay here? (He goes
740    to the gibbet. The OLD WOMAN watches him.) Still perfect.
Still beautiful.

(In the far distance a bell peals briefly.)

OLD WOMAN: No. Her's ugly. Her face is all a-twist. They put
her legs in a sack count a she's dirty.
SHAKESPEARE: The marks on her face are men's hands. Won't
they be washed away?
OLD WOMAN: She smell. She smell.

(SHAKESPEARE goes out. The OLD WOMAN goes to the place
where she found the coin. She searches for a moment. She
doesn't find anything. The bell stops. The OLD WOMAN looks
across at the YOUNG WOMAN. Then she goes out.)

—PART TWO—

SCENE IV

*The Golden Cross. A large, irregular shaped room. Stone floor.
Left, a few tables and benches, Right, a table and three chairs.
A large open fire between them. Burning wood. Night. Lamps.*

SHAKESPEARE *and* JONSON *are at the table right. Bottles and
two glasses on the table. No one else in the room.*

SHAKESPEARE: How long did the theatre burn?
JONSON: Two hours.
SHAKESPEARE: (tapping the table) When I was buying my
house the owner was poisoned. By his son. A half-wit. They    750
hanged him. Legal complications with the contract. My fa-
ther was robbed by my mother's side of the family. That was
property too.
JONSON: Coincidences.
SHAKESPEARE: But that such coincidences are possible . . .
Jokes about my play setting the house on fire?
JONSON: What are you writing?
SHAKESPEARE: Nothing.

(They drink.)

JONSON: Not writing?
SHAKESPEARE: No.    760
JONSON: Why not?
SHAKESPEARE: Nothing to say.
JONSON: Doesn't stop others. Written out?
SHAKESPEARE: Yes.

(They drink.)

JONSON: Now, what are you writing?
SHAKESPEARE: Nothing.
JONSON: Down here for the peace and quiet? Find
inspiration—look for it, anyway. Work up something spiritual. Refined. Can't get by with scrabbling it off in noisy corners any more. New young men. Competition. Your recent    770
stuff's been pretty peculiar. What was The Winter's Tale
about? I ask to be polite.
SHAKESPEARE: What are you writing?
JONSON: They say you've come down to study grammar. Or history. Have you read my English Grammar? Let me sell you
a copy. I've got a few up in my room.

(Silence. SHAKESPEARE pours drinks.)

What am *I* writing? You've never shown any interest before.
SHAKESPEARE: Untrue.
JONSON: O, how many characters, enough big parts for the
leads, a bit of comedy to bring them in—usual theatre-own-    780
er's questions. Trying to pick my brains now? Run out of
ideas?

(They drink.)

Nice to see you again. I'm off to Scotland soon. Walking.
Alone. Well, no one would come with me. Might be a book
in it. Eat out on London gossip. The Scots are very credulous—common sense people are always superstitious, aren't
they. Can't imagine you walking to Scotland. That sort of

research is too real!

SHAKESPEARE: *(smiles. Starts to stand)* Well.

790 JONSON: Don't go. Sit down. Would you like to read my new play? It's up in my room. Won't take a minute.

SHAKESPEARE: No.

JONSON: Nice to see you again. Honest William.

SHAKESPEARE: I wouldn't read it. It would lie there.

JONSON: What is it? Tired? Not well? (SHAKESPEARE *starts to stand.)* Sit down. *(He pours drinks.)* Wife better?

SHAKESPEARE: No.

JONSON: Wrong subject. D'you like the quiet?

SHAKESPEARE: What quiet?

*(They drink.)*

800 JONSON: What are you writing? *(Slight pause.)* The theatre told me to ask.

SHAKESPEARE: *(shakes his head)* Sorry.

JONSON: What d'you do?

SHAKESPEARE: There's the house. People I'm responsible for. The garden's too big. Time goes. I'm surprised how old I've got.

JONSON: You always kept yourself to yourself. Well, you certainly didn't like me. Or what I wrote. Sit down. I hate writing. Fat white fingers excreting dirty black ink. Smudges.

810 Shadows. Shit. Silence.

SHAKESPEARE: You're a very good writer.

JONSON: Patronizing bastard.

*(Slight pause. They drink.)*

You don't want to quarrel with me. I killed one once. Fellow writer. Only way to end a literary quarrel. Put my sword in him. Like a new pen. The blood flowed as if inspired. Then the Old Bailey. I was going to hang. That's carrying research too far. I could read so they let me off. Proper respect for learning. Branded my thumb. A child's alphabet: T for Tyburn. I've been in prison four times. Dark smelly places. No

820 gardens. Sorry yours is too big. They kept coming in and taking people out to cut bits off them. Their hands. Take off their noses. Cut their stomachs open. Rummage round inside with a dirty fist and drag everything out. The law. Little men going out through the door. White. Shaking. Even staggering. I ask, is it necessary? What's your life been like? Any real blood, any prison? Four times? Don't go, don't go. I want to touch you for a loan. I know I'm not human. My father died before I was born. That desperate to avoid me. My eyes are too close together. Look. A well known fact. I used

830 to have so much good will when I was young. That's what's necessary, isn't it? Good will. In the end. O god.

*(Silence. They drink.)*

Yes.

*(Silence.)*

What are you writing?

SHAKESPEARE: I think you're a very good writer. I made them put on your first play.

JONSON: God, am I that bad? In prison they threatened to cut off my nose. And ears. They didn't offer to work on my eyes. Life doesn't seem to touch you, I mean soil you. You walk by on the clean pavement. I climb tall towers to show I'm

clever. Others do tricks in the gutter. You are serene. 840 Serene. I'm going to make you drunk and watch you spew. You aren't well, I can see that! Something's happening to your will. You're being sapped. I think you're dying. What a laugh! Are you getting hollow? Why don't you get up? Walk out? Why are you listening to my hysterical crap? Don't worry about me. I'll survive. I've lived through two religious conversions. I thrive on tearing myself to bits. I even bought enough poison. Once. In a moment of strength. *(He takes a small bottle from his collar. It hangs round his neck on a chain.)* I was too weak to take it. Hung the cross here in my 850 catholic period. *(He takes the top off the bottle.)* Look: coated in sugar. Like to lick my poison? I licked one once to try. (SHAKESPEARE *doesn't react.)* Well, it's not the best. All I could afford. Little corner shop in London.

SHAKESPEARE: Give it to me.

JONSON: Sentimental whiner. You wouldn't uncross your legs if I ate the lot. You're upset I might give it to someone else. *(He puts the bottle back in his collar.)* I should live in the country. No—I'd hear myself talk. When I went sight seeing in the mad house there was a young man who spent all 860 his time stamping on his shadow. Punched it. Went for it with a knife. Tried to cut the head off. Anything to be free. The knife on the stone. The noise. Sparks.

*(They drink.)*

I helped to uncover the gunpowder plot. Keep in with the top.

*(They drink.)*

Your health. I'm always saying nice things about you, Serenity. Of course, I touch on your lack of education, or as I put it genuine ignorance. But you can't ignore an elephant when it waves at you with its trunk, can you. You taking this down? Base something on me. A minor character who comes on for 870 five minutes while the lead's off changing his clothes or making a last effort to learn his lines? Shall I tell you something about me? I hate. Yes—isn't that interesting! I keep it well hidden but it's true: I hate. A short hard word. Begins with a hiss and ends with a spit: hate. To say it you open your mouth as if you're bringing up: hate. I hate you, for example. For preference actually. Hate's far more jealous than love. You can't satisfy it by the gut or the groin. A terrible appetite. Interrupt me. Speak. Sob. Nothing? I'm not afraid to let myself be insulted.                                        880

*(The* SON, WALLY, JEROME *and* JOAN *come in right.)*

SON: *(pointing left)* Over there.

*(The* SON *goes out right again. The others sit.)*

WALLY: They'm followed us.

JEROME: No matter. They'll know who t'was.

WALLY: They'm followed us. I were neigh on slaughtered. One a Combe's men heaved a rock at us when I were scramblin' out the ditch. I'm certain-sure they'm followed us. Where's us shovels?

JEROME: I hid they in the hedge out back.

JOAN: *(looking across at* SHAKESPEARE *and* JONSON*)* Careful, there's gen'men here.                                        890

JEROME: Too drunk t' hear if yo' shouted.

WALLY: Git the mud off yo'. That show what us bin up to. Us don't ought-a done it. That'll only start more row.

JEROME: That's us land. Shall us sit down an' let 'em rob it? How I live then? How I feed my wife an' little-uns?

JOAN: Hush.

JEROME: I'll break Combe's neck.

JONSON: Where was I? Yes: hate. I hate you because you smile. Right up to *under* your eyes. Which are set the right dis-
900  tance apart. O I've wiped the smile off now. I hate your health. I'm sure you'll die in a healthy way. Well at least you're dying. That's incense to scatter on these burning coals. I hate your long country limbs. I've seen you walking along the city streets like a man going over his own fields. So simple. A simple stride. So beautiful and simple. You see why I hate you. How have they made you so simple? Tell me, Will? Please. How have they made *you good*? You even know when it's time to die. Come down here to die quietly in your garden or an upstairs room. My death will be terri-
910  ble. I'll linger on in people's way, poor, sick, dirty, empty, a mess. I go on and on, why can't I stop? I even talk shit now. To know the seasons of life and death and walk quietly on the path between them. *No tears, no tears.* Hate is like a clown armed with a knife. He must draw blood to cap the joke, you know? Well, have you got a new play, it has to be a comedy, rebuilding is expensive, they'd like you to invest. Think about it. You may come up with an idea. Or manage to steal one. But it must be in time for next season.

*(Silence.)*

My life's been one long self-insult. It came on with puberty.

*(Silence.* JONSON *drinks.)*

920  Teach me something.

*(*SHAKESPEARE *falls across the table and spills his glass.)*

God.

*(*JONSON *tries to dry* SHAKESPEARE *with a napkin. He sets him up in his chair.* SHAKESPEARE *slumps forward again. The* SON *comes on with a bottle and glasses.* JOAN *pours.)*

SON: They yont give up.

JOAN: No more'll us. *(She hands him a drink. He waves it aside.)*

SON: *(Rocking slightly.)* Rich thieves plunderin' the earth. Think on the poor trees an' grass an' beasts, all neglect an' stood in the absence a god. One year no harvest'll come, no seed'll grow in the plants, no green, no cattle yont leave their stall, stand huddled-to in the hovel, no hand'll turn
930  water into their trough, the earth'll die an' be covered with scars: the mark a dust where a beast rot in the sand. Where there's no lord god there's a wilderness.

WALLY: Don't go forth in it now, brother. *(To the others.)* He's allus close t' tears. *(To the* SON.) Don't git took up.

JOAN: *(offers the* SON *the drink again)* Yo' hev this. That's cold out there t'night. *(The* SON *doesn't take it.)*

WALLY: The waters a Babylon run by his door.

SON: *(rocking slightly)* The absence a god, the wilderness . . . neglect . . .

*(*COMBE *comes in. He goes to the* SON.)*

COMBE: You've been here all evening.    940

SON: *(nods)* Even', Mr Combe.

COMBE: *(to* JONSON) How long have they been here?

JONSON: When I drink my eyes swim closer together. One, two, nine, ten peasants . . .

*(*SHAKESPEARE *is still slumped forward on the table.)*

COMBE: *(to the* SON) I thought the brothers didn't swill.

SON: We may quench thirst in an orderly 'ouse.

COMBE: After labour.

*(*JONSON *gets up and goes out right. As he goes he talks. The others ignore him. He is drunk but controlled.)*

COMBE: Every time you fill my ditches I'll dig them out. Every time you pull down my fence I'll put back. There'll be more broken fences.

SON: *(to* WALLY) Note that.

COMBE: Be very careful on Sunday. Wear the right cap and go to the parish church—not some holy hovel out in the fields. Keep to the law. Don't come up in front of me on the bench.

JONSON: To spend my life wandering through quiet fields. Charm fish from  950 the water with a song. it Gather simple eggs. Muse with my reflection in quiet water having the accents of philosophy. And lie at last in some cool mossy grave where maidens come to make vows over my corpse. *(He goes.)*  960

SON: Whose interest's that protectin'? Public or yourn?

COMBE: You trespass on my land. Fight my men. Trample my crop. Now you turn me into the devil. The town will benefit from what I'm doing. So will the poor.

JEROME: *(quietly)* S'long's they'm still alive.

COMBE: What? *(*JEROME *doesn't answer.* COMBE *turns to the* SON.) There's a division in this country. We're not just fight-ing for land. Listen. I've seen suffering, I've caused some of 970 it—and I try to stop it. But I know this: there'll always be real suffering, real stupidity and greed and violence. And there can be no civilization till you've learned to live with it. I live in the real world and try to make it work. There's noth-ing more moral than that. But you live in a world of dreams! Well, what happens when you have to wake up? You find that real people can't live in your dreams. They don't fit, they're not good or sane or noble enough. So you turn to common violence and begin to destroy them. *(He stops.)* Why should I talk to you? You can't listen. *(To* JEROME.) You 980 hold your farm on a lease. When you die your son has to pay a fee before he inherits it. That fee isn't fixed—it's decided by the landlord, my brother-in-law. We work with anyone who shows good will. But there can only be one master.

*(*JONSON *comes back. He carries a bottle.)*

SON: A sexton's diggin' your ditches, Combe.

WALLY: Amen.

SON: An' yo'll be buried in 'em.

JOAN: So dig 'em deep. Israel.

JONSON: Where can you buy a good spade? I'm sure there's a book in it. Should find a sale. Sound practical manual in a good simple craftsman's  990 style.

WALLY: Israel. Israel. Israel.

COMBE: Grown men acting like children.

(COMBE *goes out.*)

SON: God take us on a long journey. That man's prophetical. We see the same truth from odd sides but us both know tis the truth.

WALLY: (*softly*) Glory. Glory.

SON: I looked cross a great plain into his eyes. A sword were put into my yand. The lord god a peace arm us. We must go back
1000     an' fill up they ditches agin t'night.

JEROME: T'night?

SON: Whenever he turn his back. Every toime.

JEROME: Us'll come.

JOAN: No.

JEROME: Ah! There's only one master. When yo' put your yand in your pocket now yo' find another yand there.

(*The* SON *and* WALLY *go towards the door.*)

JONSON: Shepherds—

(*The* SON *and* WALLY *ignore him and go out.*)

JONSON: (*to* JOAN *and* JEROME)—fill your bowls.

JOAN: (*to* JEROME) That's a full bottle. Wasted on them in that
1010     state.

JEROME: While us wait.

(JOAN *and* JEROME *go to* JONSON'S *table.* SHAKESPEARE *is still slumped forward.* JEROME *recognizes him.*)

JONSON: (*shaking* SHAKESPEARE) The pilgrims have come.

JEROME: We yont better sit with the gen'man.

SHAKESPEARE: Sit down.

(JONSON *starts to fill their glasses.*)

JONSON: Was that man your enemy? Call him back and let me kill him for you.

SHAKESPEARE: You've been filling the ditches.

JEROME: No.

SHAKESPEARE: Lie to me. Lie. Lie. You have to lie to me now.

(WALLY *runs in. He has a shovel.*)

1020     WALLY: Snow! Snow!

JOAN: Snow!

WALLY: Late snow! A portent! A sign!

JEROME: (*seeing the shovel*) Git that shovel out!

JOAN: Snow! Shall us still go?

JEROME: (*pushing* WALLY) Git that out! Yo' fool!

WALLY: What? Snow! Snow!

SHAKESPEARE: Lie to me. Lie to me.

(WALLY *and* JEROME *go out.* JOAN *follows them.*)

JONSON: They went? Was it my talk? I talk too much. (*He sits. They drink.*) I hope you're paying. I certainly can't afford to
1030     drink like this. You said something about a loan. (SHAKESPEARE *puts money on the table.*) I thought it was just the drink talking. (*He counts the money.*) In paradise there'll be a cash tree, and the sages will sit under it. You can't manage anything better? *You* wouldn't notice it. I had to borrow to bury my little boy. I still owe on the grave. (*He puts the money in his pocket.*) I suppose you buried your boy in best oak. Sit down, sit down.

## SCENE V

*Open space. Flat, white, crisp, empty. The fields, paths, roads, bushes and trees are covered with smooth clean snow. It has stopped snowing. Shakespeare comes on drunk.* JONSON's *poison bottle hangs from a chain in his hand.*

SHAKESPEARE: My house. There at the bottom of the fields. No, I won't go in. How dark it is. No lamps. The door is a hole. The windows are ditches with water in. (*He pauses.* 1040 *Looks round.*) How clean and empty the snow is. A sea without life. An empty glass. Still smooth. No footprints. No ruts. No marks of weapons or hoes dragged through the ground. Only my footprints behind me—and they're white . . . white . . . (*He looks towards the house again.*) How long did I live there? So dark. No footprints up to the door. No one's gone down the path brushing against the hedge. The snow's still on top. In the morning there'll be dead birds under the hedge. Their winter colours will be bright in the snow. Their wings folded in for warmth, not stretched out to fly between 1050 the snow and the moon . . . The water and the earth are frozen together . . . One piece of ice . . .

(*A snowball hits him. The* OLD MAN *comes on. He is excited, running in the cold has made his voice high.*)

OLD MAN: A hit. A hit.

SHAKESPEARE: Where have you been?

OLD MAN: A hit. I bin aimin' snowballs at a snowman. (*He throws a snowball at* SHAKESPEARE.) A hit. A hit. (*He dances.*) Look at that snow, boy. I heard yo' talkin' things t' yo'self.

SHAKESPEARE: Are you cold?

OLD MAN: No. I play. I flap my arms an' run up an' down. Come 1060 t' see my snowman.

SHAKESPEARE: Too far.

OLD MAN: (*Throws a snowball at* SHAKESPEARE) A hit. Ten, nothin'. Try t' hit us, boy. (*He puts a snowball in* SHAKESPEARE's *hand.*) Try. Try. Please.

(SHAKESPEARE *throws the snowball at him.*)

SHAKESPEARE: It hit.

OLD MAN: (*laughing derisively*) The legs, the legs, the legs yont count. Still fourteen, nothin'. Throw for the neck.

SHAKESPEARE: Were you on the hill?

OLD MAN: Ah. For a last see. A last toime. Then I saw summat 1070 come cross t' fields. A great white thing. That were a cloud I thought! Low. Then that turn t' snow. O pretty! That did fall fast. I saw the fields turn white. (*He laughs.*) She had a little heap set top on her yead. Like a cap. I made a slide down side t' hill. Whee! I hed such a toime. I like snow. Yont yo'? Then they rabbits all come t' see. You charm a rabbit by your play. They set theyselfs round in a circle. Heads on one side. I grabs one an' broke his neck for'n. (*He holds out a dead rabbit.*) Bad. Some'un elsen. Mustn't take. (*He grins.*) But my wife yont row me out when I come hwome. She'll 1080 hide it in the pot smart. (*He pats his pockets.*) I got onions here. Carrot here. Egg. Us'll hev a feast. Early greens.

(*Four of five dark* FIGURES *pass quickly over the top of the stage. They are huddled and quiet. One stops and points at* SHAKESPEARE *and the* OLD MAN.)

FIGURE I: (*low*) 'Oo's that?

FIGURE II: (*stops, low*) Drunks.

(*All the* FIGURES *go out right.*)

SHAKESPEARE: A light's on in my house. They're trying to get in my room.

OLD MAN: They'll be out arter yo' now. I flare up do my wife come after me. She know the shape a my fist. Now her wait up till I'm in an' lock up arter us. I yont see no sight a my snowman in this snow.

(*The* OLD MAN *wanders out.*)

SHAKESPEARE: The door's opened. I drank too much. I must be calm. Don't fall about in front of them. Why did I drink all that? Fool! Fool! At my age . . . Why not? I am a fool. Why did I come back here. I wanted to meet some god by the river. Ask him questions. See his mouth open and the lips move. Hear simple things that move mountains and stop the blood before it hits the earth. Stop it so there's time to think. I was wrong to come—mistakes, mistakes. But I can't go back. That hate, anger—

(JUDITH *comes in. She wears a green cloak.*)

JUDITH: Walk all night in the fields if you like. I don't mind. But not when it's snowed. Mother's crying.

SHAKESPEARE: Who woke her?

JUDITH: It's late and I'm tired.

SHAKESPEARE: Who?

JUDITH: Another scene.

SHAKESPEARE: Why did you do it? What can she do? Cry!

JUDITH: When you behave like a child you'll be treated like one.

SHAKESPEARE: Listen. You'll get my property between you when I'm dead. When I ran away from your mother and went to London—I was so bored, she's such a silly woman, obstinate, and you take after her. Forgive me, I know that's cruel, sordid, but it's such an effort to be polite any more. That other age when I ran away, I couldn't cut you out, you were my flesh, but I thought I could make you forgive me: I started to collect for you. I loved you with money. The only thing I can afford to give you now is money. But money always turns to hate. If I tried to be nice to you now it would be sentimental. You'd have to understand why I hate you, respect me for it, even love me for it. How can you? I treated you so badly. I made you vulgar and ugly and cheap. I corrupted you.

JUDITH: Go on. I'm not listening. I'm young and this coat's warm. I'll wait till you drop and then have you dragged in.

SHAKESPEARE: Don't be angry because I hate you, Judith. My hatred isn't angry. It's cold and formal. I wouldn't harm you. I'll help you, give my life for you—all in hatred. There's no limit to my hate. It can't be satisfied by cruelty. It's destroyed too much to be satisfied so easily. Only truth can satisfy it now. I don't think all this matters to you, I can't hate you more than when I say that.

(JUDITH *goes out.*)

The last snow this year. Perhaps the last snow I shall see. The last fall. (*He kneels on the ground and picks up some snow.*) How cold. (*He half smiles.*) How perfect, but it only lasts one night. When I was young I'd have written on it with a stick. A song. The moon over the snow, a woman stares at her dead . . . What? In the morning the sun would melt it into mortality. Writing in the snow—a child's hand fumbling in an old man's beard, and in the morning the old man dies, goes, taking the curls from the child's fingers into the grave, and the child laughs and plays under the dead man's window. New games. Now *I'm* old. Where is the child to touch me and lead me to the grave? Serene. Serene. Is that how they see me? (*He laughs a little.*) I didn't know.

(*The dark* FIGURES *run back across the top of the stage. Their heavy breathing is heard. They go off left.*)

Snow. It doesn't melt. My hand's cold. (*He breathes on the snow in his hand.*) It doesn't melt. I must be very cold. Serene. How? When you're running from hangers and breakers and killers. The mad clown still nurses the child.

(*Far upstage a shot and a spurt of flame.*)

Every writer writes in other men's blood. The trivial, and the real. There's nothing else to write in. But only a god or a devil can write in other men's blood and not ask why they spilt it and what it cost. Not this hand, that's always melted snow . . .

(SHAKESPEARE *lies forward on the ground. A dark* FIGURE *appears upstage. It cries and whimpers weakly and then vanishes.*)

I didn't want to die. I could lie in this snow a whole life. I can think now, the thoughts come so easily over the snow and under my shroud. New worlds. Keys turning new locks—pushing the iron open like lion's teeth. Wolves will drag me through the snow. I'll sit in their lair and smile and be rich. In the morning or when I die the sun will rise and melt it all away. The dream. The wolves. The iron teeth. The snow. The wind. My voice. A dream that leads to sleep. (*He sits up.*) I'm dead now. Soon I shall fall down. If I wasn't dead I could kill myself. What is the ice inside me? The plague is hot—this is so cold. The truth means nothing when you hate. Was anything done? Was anything done? I sit in a wound as large as a valley. The sides are smooth and cold and grey. I sit at the bottom and cry at my own death.

(*The* OLD WOMAN *comes in.*)

OLD WOMAN: Your daughter come a-knock-knock at my door. Darlint, I say, yont no call t' fret, I'm set up waitin'. Fetch him in, she say. That's twice t'day, I say. Last toime yo' was an okkard fuss. Father's out too.

(*The* OLD WOMAN *helps* SHAKESPEARE *to his feet.*)

'Ow yo' people carry on. (*She feels him.*) Good lor, you're froze.

SHAKESPEARE: Silly. Staying out here. What have I done?

OLD WOMAN: Yo' had your reasons.

SHAKESPEARE: Drunk.

OLD WOMAN: Hev yo' yeard summat a while back? I yeard a noise, blowed if I yont. I yeard thunder in snow one toime. Toime I were a gal. They say I were a dazzler. That seem afore your father step into the world!—but I remember on it. I thought I saw summat run long the lane a while back. These eyes . . . I wish father yont stop out when that's jippy. Yont make no wish yo' can't grant yo'sel.

SHAKESPEARE: Take me in, take me in.

OLD WOMAN: Yes, sir, I'm sorry.

SHAKESPEARE: Light a fire in my room. I'm cold.

OLD WOMAN: O'course. Yes, yes.

(*The* OLD WOMAN *helps* SHAKESPEARE *out.*)

## SCENE VI

*Bedroom. Left, a bed with a needlework cover. Close to it a bedstand. A wooden chair. Right, a door.* SHAKESPEARE *lies in bed. The* OLD WOMAN *stands in the room.*)

OLD WOMAN: I ought-a go down. (SHAKESPEARE *doesn't answer.*) I'll stay a while longer. My son'll say when that's
1190 toime. (*Silence. She sits on the chair.*) Shall us set down? I'm that tired. (*She spreads her fingers and looks at her hands.*) I wanted him t' die first. Seem wrong now. He were lyin' in that snow an' I walk by him. Hed he say where he'd bin? (*No answer.*) Nicet if he sid summat a show he know he'd bin looked arter . . . Could yo' eat summat? Shall us let yo' sleep?

SHAKESPEARE: Was anything done?

OLD WOMAN: Yo' ought-a sleep. Why yont yo' try? . . . That all come out a closin they fields. I told yo' long ago in the gar-
1200 den: that'll cause trouble. Yo' yont listen. Sign a piece of piper an' that's all yo' thought on. Call that 'elp? Our house's quiet now he's gone. No one come or go, do they knock first an' ask if I'm in. A stranger's house. All they years.

SHAKESPEARE: Was anything done?

OLD WOMAN: Your daft questions. I yont harm no one's far's I could stop it. I look arter the two on us well's I might. (*Slight pause.*) He'd bin t' see that dead woman, that's 'ow it ended. (*She shrugs.*) He warnt greedy for money loike some men. I yont know . . .

1210 SHAKESPEARE: It's so cold.

OLD WOMAN: That yont his woman neither. That warnt n'more'n his game. "I want t' go out t' play. I'm tired a playin' indoor." He wanted summat a child want. I yont know what. (*She shrugs.*) Well, yo' break a cup yo' put it t'gither. Yont kip arksin' 'oo brok it. That's all as is.

JUDITH: (*off*) Father.

(SHAKESPEARE *motions the* OLD WOMAN *to be quiet.*)

JUDITH: (*off*) Mother's here to see you.

SHAKESPEARE: (*quietly to the* OLD WOMAN) I'm asleep.

JUDITH: (*off*) Father.

(*Silence.*)

1220 SHAKESPEARE: (*quietly to the* OLD WOMAN) Has she gone?

OLD WOMAN: (*goes to the door and calls softly*) Judy, dear?

(*No answer.* SHAKESPEARE *gets out of bed, goes to the door and listens.*)

SHAKESPEARE: (*quietly to the* OLD WOMAN) She's there.

(*The* OLD WOMAN *goes to the chair and sits down again.*)

OLD WOMAN: They'll level with me for this.

(SHAKESPEARE *walks away from the door. Silence. There is a knock on it.*)

JUDITH: (*off*) Father, mother's here. (*Knock.*) Father. (*Knock.*)

Open this door.

(*Outside an* OLD WOMAN *begins to cry. More knocking on the door. The door handle is rattled. The knocking gets louder.*)

JUDITH: (*off*) Father, unlock this door. Mother's crying. Father, I know you can hear.

(*Outside the two women bang on the door. The crying is louder and wilder. Suddenly it becomes hysterical. The* OLD WOMAN *gets up and slowly and methodically makes the bed.*)

JUDITH: (*off*) Father. Let us in. How dare you. You treat us like animals. Father. Why don't you come and hit her. You're cruel enough. You've done it before. Open the door and 1230 kick her. Father. We hate you. You're cruel. Wicked. Ugly. You beast.

(*The door is violently banged, kicked and shaken. Someone scratches it. Outside the* OLD WOMAN *gasps and shrieks hysterically.*)

JUDITH: (*off*) Mother, get up. She's fallen down. Don't cover your ears—I'll make you hear. Make you. Make you. Make you. She's on the ground tearing her clothes. Look, her hands are bleeding.

SHAKESPEARE: (*almost to himself*) It's so cold now.

JUDITH: (*off*) Mother dear! Stop it! No. Don't. Help. Father.

SHAKESPEARE: (*as before*) Cold. Cold.

OLD WOMAN: (*quietly*) I'll open the door.                   1240

SHAKESPEARE: No. It's put on. Thirty-five years. All like this. (*He points to the bedside stand.*) My will. There. Fetch it.

JUDITH: (*off*) You'll be punished. There's a god in heaven. She's tearing her hair. Terrible. Terrible. All my life. This. Time after time. I'll kill myself.

(*The* OLD WOMAN *rummages through papers on the bedside stand. She finds three sheets lying together.*)

SHAKESPEARE: Those. Yes, yes, those.

(*The* OLD WOMAN *brings the sheets to* SHAKESPEARE. *They both stand by the door.*)

JUDITH: (*off*) She's clutching her heart. What is it?

(*Outside the* OLD WOMAN *gasps stertorously.*)

SHAKESPEARE: (*quietly, with amused contempt*) Clutching! (*He pushes the sheets under the door.*) It's all there. Your legal share. And the bed.                   1250

(*The sheets are snatched through from the other side. The crying becomes lower but goes on.*)

JUDITH: (*off*) Stand up. I'll help you. Try. (*The voices start to move away from the door.*) He won't let us in. I told you not to come down. I won't let you any more. We'll never speak to him again. He'll learn when it's too late. There.

(*The crying dies away. It is quiet.*)

OLD WOMAN: Is that what her come for?

SHAKESPEARE: No. She'll be quieter now.

OLD WOMAN: Bed's made.

SHAKESPEARE: The chair. (*He sits in the chair. He closes his eyes. He is weak and tired.*) Cold. There's a draft. That door. Did they break it? (*The* OLD WOMAN *glances at the door.*) I 1260 must be quiet. White worms excreting black ink. Scratch.

Scratch.

OLD WOMAN: What?

SHAKESPEARE: Was anything done? Was anything done?

(*A knock on the door.*)

OLD WOMAN: Yes?

SON: (*off*) Mother.

(*The* OLD WOMAN *opens the door. The* SON *comes in.*)

'Oo's bin a-scratchin' your door? Half the paint's took off.

OLD WOMAN: Are they ready?

SON: Ah.

1270 OLD WOMAN: I'll git into my coat. (*She pauses.*) I'll arkst summat first. Hev yo' took a gun with yo'?

SON: Us yont shot him. Us warn't armed.

OLD WOMAN: Then I'll walk t' church with yo'. (*To* SHAKESPEARE.) Goodbye.

SON: I'll follow directly.

(*The* OLD WOMAN *goes out. The* SON *locks the door behind her.*)

What hev yo' see?

SHAKESPEARE: Nothing.

SON: Yo' must hev. That were snow an' moon. Like day.

SHAKESPEARE: I wouldn't choose to lie while I'm dying. (*The*
1280 SON *watches* SHAKESPEARE *for a moment.* SHAKESPEARE *closes his eyes again.*) You can tell. Can't you. My face.

SON: Yo're very poorly.

SHAKESPEARE: I spent so much of my youth, my best energy . . . for this: New Place. Somewhere to be sane in. It was all a mistake. There's a taste of bitterness in my mouth. My stomach pumps it up when I think of myself . . . I could have done so much. (*The* SON *goes to the door and listens for a sound outside.*) Absurd! Absurd! I howled when they suffered, but they were whipped and hanged so that I could be
1290 free. That is the right question: not why did I sign one piece of paper?—no, no, even when I sat at my table, when I put on my clothes, I was a hangman's assistant, a gaoler's errand boy. If children go in rags we make the wind. If the table's empty we blight the harvest. If the roof leaks we send the storm. God made the elements but we inflict them on each other. Everything can be stolen, property and qualities of the mind. But stolen things have no value. Pride and arrogance are the same when they're stolen. Even serenity.

(*The* SON *has come to* SHAKESPEARE.)

SON: Everyone looked the same in the moonlight. I shot him.

1300 SHAKESPEARE: So you met. The son and the father.

SON: (*quietly*) I yont give meself up. Us'll foight for us land. Outside a me they'd give in. I'll go off later. When mother's settled. T'ent easy t'be with her now. T'ent decent.

SHAKESPEARE: A murderer telling a dead man the truth. Are we the only people who can afford the truth?

(*A knock at the door.*)

SON: (*calls*) What?

COMBE: (*off*) Combe here.

SHAKESPEARE: Unlock it.

(*The* SON *unlocks the door.* COMBE *comes in. The* SON *locks the door behind him.* COMBE *stares at the* SON *and then turns to*

SHAKESPEARE.)

COMBE: Not disturbing you, I hope? Everything all right?

SHAKESPEARE: Some tablets. There. On the table. Please.   1310

(COMBE *goes to the bedside stand and picks up* JONSON's *poison bottle.*)

COMBE: These?

SHAKESPEARE: Thank you.

COMBE: (*gives the bottle to* SHAKESPEARE. *To the* SON) I'm sorry about your father. Decent man. This won't stop the enclosure.

SON: Your side shot him.

COMBE: I told my men no guns, only sticks. One of them may have disobeyed me—out of fear of you. Perhaps it was your own people. (*To* SHAKESPEARE.) I came to ask if you saw or heard anything. I'm told you were there.   1320

SHAKESPEARE: Nothing.

COMBE: Pity. It's the magistrate's duty to ask.

(THE SON *laughs.*)

If it's one of my men he'll be punished.

(SHAKESPEARE *starts to take the tablets.*)

SON: What difference is that to us? Yo' take us land an' if us foight for'n—we'm criminals.

COMBE: You've a right to justice on your father's behalf. It's my duty to give it to you. Even though you're morally responsible for his death.

SON: Morally responsible! (*He laughs.*) He yont see! He yont see! He talk 'bout his law loike that had summat a do with   1330 justice! How can yo' give us justice, boy? Yo'm a thief. When yo' hang the man that kill my father, what yo' doin? Is that justice? No—yo'm protectin' your thievin'.

COMBE: (*to* SHAKESPEARE) I hope you're on your feet soon.

(*The* SON *unlocks the door for* COMBE. COMBE *goes out.*)
(*The* SON *locks the door again.* SHAKESPEARE *takes more tablets.*)

SON: I'll go away—where there's still space. I want t'be free. I cry for that. Sometoime when I'm out in the fields I climb a tall tree an' set stride the top an' cry. Let me be free. Liberty. Where no one stand 'tween me an' my god, no one listen when I raise the song a praise, an' I walk by god's side with curtesy an' fear nothin', as candid loike a child. (SHAKE-   1340 SPEARE *takes more tablets.*) So us'll go away. Us plans is laid. Us'll take nowt bar bible an' plough. (*Pause. His voice changes.*) I yont had no proper toime t'reflect orderly on my father's dyin'—what with the land an' arrangements an' that. I kill him. That'll have t' be go over proper in my yead. Lord god'll say. Likely he done it a purpose. Why else'd he afflict one a his chosen with a harsh cross? The yand a god's in it someplace. (*He goes to the door and unlocks it.*) The key?

SHAKESPEARE: Go and bury your father.   1350

(*The* SON *opens the door. He stops in the doorway.* SHAKESPEARE *takes more tablets.*)

SON: (*quietly*) . . . When yo' think on't, t'ent so sure I shot him neither. I fire a gun—I yont hide no truth. That yont mean I shot him. Someone else'n moight a fired. Death on an unarmed man—that's more loike the sort a think Combe'd get up to. That want sortin' out in my yead. I may have done meself a wrong.

(*The* SON *goes out. He leaves the door open.*)

SHAKESPEARE: How long have I been dead? When will I fall down? Looking for rings on beggars' fingers. Mistakes . . . mistakes . . . Was anything done? (*He takes another tablet.*) Years waiting . . . fed . . . washing the dead . . . Was anything done? . . . Was anything done? (*He looks at a tablet in his hand.*) Dead sugar. (*He swallows it.*) Was anything done?

1360

(*He falls from the chair onto the floor.* JUDITH *comes into the room. She sees* SHAKESPEARE. *She controls her panic. The funeral bell begins to toll. It is close, but not so loud as in the garden.* JUDITH *goes to* SHAKESPEARE *and quickly makes him comfortable on the floor. He twitches and jerks.*)

JUDITH: Nothing. A little attack.

(*She hurries to the bedside stand. She searches through it agitatedly. She throws papers aside. She tears some.* SHAKESPEARE *whimpers and shivers.*)

JUDITH: (*to herself as she searches*) Nothing. Nothing.

(JUDITH *runs to the door and shouts up.*)

Nothing. If he made a new will his lawyer's got it.

(JUDITH *runs back to the bed. She is crying. She searches under the pillows.* SHAKESPEARE *has killed himself.*)

JUDITH: (*crying*) Nothing.

(JUDITH *searches under the sheets. She kneels down and searches under the bed. She cries. She stands and searches under the mattress.*)

---

## Edward Bond

### Introduction to *Bingo* (1974)

*IN his introduction to* Bingo, *Edward Bond articulates some of the attitudes toward the social order and the action of the individual that inform the action of the play.*

Shakespeare had two daughters. Susanna is buried near him under stone in the chancel of the parish church, Judith was buried under grass outside in the churchyard and her grave is lost. Perhaps that sums up the difference between them. Shakespeare's opinions about them aren't known, but it seemed to me that his daughters' lives might have reflected those opinions: Susanna social, well-married and affluent, and Judith obscure, over-shadowed by her sister, married late to the unsuccessful publican of The Cage and deserted in her old age. Perhaps being brought up under Shakespeare's incisive perception and judgement shaped the whole of their lives.

Judith is the only daughter in the play. I gave the more comforting and strengthening role that I think Susanna played in his life to an old woman servant. I did this for my own dramatic convenience. The old woman's son is a victim of Shakespeare's business world. By making her close to Shakespeare I had a bridge between the two elements of the play, but I kept what I think is the true psychological situation: one woman (Susanna, or in the play the old woman) was close to him, and another (Judith, and probably also his wife) was estranged.

I've done something similar with my account of the enclosure which involved Shakespeare. Combe represents several men, and the undertaking signed in the second scene by Combe and Shakespeare was in fact between Shakespeare and a representative of the enclosers called Replingham (though Combe confirmed it later). Shakespeare's last binge was with Jonson and Drayton. Only Jonson is shown in the play. I've also altered some dates. For example, Shakespeare's theatre was burned down in 1613 not 1616. I made all these changes for dramatic convenience. To recreate in an audience the impact scattered events had on someone's life you often have to concentrate them. I mention all this because I want to protect the play from petty criticism. It is based on the material historical facts so far as they're known, and on psychological truth so far as I know it. The consequences that follow in the play follow from the facts, they're not polemical inventions. Of course, I can't insist that my description of Shakespeare's death is true. I'm like a man who looks down from a bridge at the place where an accident has happened. The road is wet, there's a skid mark, the car's wrecked, and a dead man lies by the road in a pool of blood. I can only put the various things together and say what probably happened. Orthodox critics usually assume that Shakespeare would have driven a car so well that he'd never have an accident. My account rather flatters Shakespeare. If he didn't end in the way shown in the play, then he was a reactionary blimp or some other fool. The only more charitable account is that he was unaware or senile. But I admit that I'm not really interested in Shakespeare's true biography in the way a historian might be. Part of the play is about the relationship between any writer and his society.

Shakespeare created Lear, who is the most radical of all social critics. But Lear's insight is expressed as madness or hysteria. Why? I suppose partly because that was the only coherent way it could have been expressed at that time. Partly also because if you understand so much about suffering and violence, the partiality of authority, and the final innocence of all defenceless things, *and yet* live in a time when you can do nothing about it—then you feel the suffering you describe, and your writing mimics that suffering. When you write on that level you must tell the truth. A lie makes you the hangman's assistant. It betrays the victim and this is intolerable—because you are mimicking the victim, and the most important thing you know is the innocence you share with him. So if you lie the world stops being sane, there is no justice to condemn suffering, and no difference between guilt and innocence—and only the mad know how to live with so much despair. Art is always sane. It always insists on the truth, and tries to express the justice and order that are necessary to sanity but are usually destroyed by society. All imagination is political. It has the urgency of passion, the force of appetite, the self-authenticity of pain or happiness—imagination is a desire that *makes* an artist create. The truths of imagination are strictly determined and necessary. They aren't "revealed" to artists, they have to work and train and learn so that they become skilled at discovering them. But every artist often feels that what he's created is "right" and he's not free to alter it. It's life that in comparison seems arbitrary and random—because society is usually based on injustice or expediency but art is the expression of moral sanity. Philistinism is so shocking because it assumes that, on the contrary, creative imagination is arbitrary and random, a self-satisfying game, mere fantasy—instead of being vital to human development. And of course, what artists most frequently lack is enough of this creative imagination. Or perhaps they only play it down because they're told art is for the rich and intellectual, that science is work but art only luxury or play. Perhaps also because many people do in fact "exist" without art. Well, they've only had to do so in modern industrial societies and that's one reason why these societies are stagnant and inhuman. And there are also artists who shut themselves up in private fantasies. What they create has to be interpreted by an extra-artistic language. Their verbal or graphic images have no force, it's as if a spectator had to look up every word or sign in a dictionary. But imagination isn't random fantasy. The artist's imagination connects him to his audience's world just as much as his knowledge does. Because Jane Austen's imagination was weaker than her knowledge she could avoid writing about the Napoleonic wars—except perhaps as one cause of her general fear of poverty. But as she needed to express the objective truth about her characters—that is her need for moral sanity—this deepened her creative imagination. In *Persuasion* she'd already started to write about the experience of poverty and not just her fear of it, and if she'd lived longer she might well have written about war. Writers who don't develop in this way become shut up in private fantasies, experiments in style, unrewarding obscurities—they become trivial and reactionary.

Shakespeare's plays show this need for sanity and its political expression, justice. But how did he live? His behaviour as a property-owner made him closer to Goneril than Lear. He supported and benefited from the Goneril-society—with its prisons, workhouses, whipping, starvation, mutilation, pulpit-hysteria and all the rest of it.

An example of this is his role in the Welcombe enclosure. A large part of his income came from rents (or tithes) paid on common fields at Welcombe near Stratford. Some important landowners wanted to enclose these fields—for the reasons given in the play—and there was a risk that the enclosure would affect Shakespeare's rents. He could side either with the landowners or with the poor who would lose their land and livelihood. He sided with the landowners. They gave him a guarantee against loss—and this is not a neutral document because it implies that should the people fighting the enclosers come to him for help he would refuse it. Well, the town did write to him for help and he did nothing. The struggle is quite well documented and there's no record of opposition from Shakespeare. He may have doubted that the enclosers would succeed, but at best this means he sat at home with his guarantee while others made the resistance that was the only way to stop them. They were stopped for a time. The fields were not finally enclosed till 1775.

Lear divided up his land at the beginning of the play, when he was arbitrary and unjust—not when he was shouting out his truths on the open common.

The subtitle is "Scenes of money and death." We live in a closed society where you need money to live. You earn it, borrow it, or steal it. Criminals, and hermits or drop-outs, depend on others who earn money—there's no greenwood to escape into any more, it's been cut down. We have no natural rights, only rights granted and protected by money. Money provides food, shelter, security, education, entertainment, the ground we walk on, the air we breathe, the bed we lie in. People come to think of these things as products of money, not of the earth or human relationships, and finally as the way of getting more money to get more things. Money has its own laws and conventions, and when you live by money you must live by these. To get money you must behave like money. I don't mean only that money creates certain attitudes or traits in people, it *forces* certain behaviour on them. Charity seems an argument against this, but in fact it proves it. If you have a lot of money you might give some of it to the poor, or some pictures to the nation. But you won't give all you have because then you'd have no reserve, no one would work for you for wages and so you couldn't collect more money. Your actions aren't finally controlled by human generosity (at best they're only prompted by that) but by your selfish need. The money you keep back isn't morally neutral—like enough clothes or food—because you use it to influence the lives of other people who are also trapped by money. We're wrong when we assume we're free to use money in human ways. When livelihood and dignity depend on money, human values are replaced by money values. Certainly that's what's happened in our commercial, technological society. Money destroys the effect of human values in our society because consumer demand can't grow fast enough to maintain profits and full employment while human values are effective. A consumer society depends on its members being avaricious, ostentatious, gluttonous, envious, wasteful, selfish and inhuman. Officially we teach morality but if we all became "good" the economy would collapse. Affluent people can't afford ten commandments.

Money is an important social tool. It's the means of exchange and of accumulating the surplus necessary to create modern industry. But we've reached a point where money isn't used to remove poverty but to create and satisfy artificial needs so that consumption will maintain profits and industrial activity. Keynes said that to maintain effective demand in an economy it would be better to pay men for "digging holes in the ground" rather than that they should be unemployed, but he added ironically that he presumed a "sensible community" would find something more socially useful for them to do. Well, a lot of the trash we produce for civilized consumption is far more silly and dangerous than holes in the ground. And that's only concerned with keeping society running—the far more important and difficult work of making it more civilized is mostly ignored. We think we live in an age of science, but it's also an age of alchemy: we try to turn gold into human values.

It seems that sometimes people can be made to behave badly with frightening ease and rapidity, but it only seems so. Their awareness of human values doesn't simply vanish. People have faults and, as in all evolving species, weaknesses—but human values are the most enduring things we have, stronger than our rational minds. We have the need and right to protect ourselves and our families, and in a crisis we help those we know, not strangers—but it isn't easy for us to do this at others' expense or to make others suffer. It's difficult for human beings to be unkind, and unpleasant to be arrogant. There's always a reason for aggression, and the only effective weapon against it is to remove the cause. Fear is a lack of understanding, and the only way to remove it is by reason and reassurance. Even the hate that comes from fear and aggression begins as a passion for justice. That isn't a paradox. Why did Shylock ask for his enemy's flesh? Because his own had been spat on.

There are two main sorts of political aggression. The first is the aggression of the weak against the strong, the hungry against the over-fed. That's easy to understand. The strong are unjust, and to survive and get elementary rights many people are forced to act aggressively. The second aggression is of the strong against the weak. How can an American drop bombs on peasants in a jungle if, as I said, a sense of human values is part of his nature? It takes a lot of effort, years of false education and lies, indignity, shabby poverty, economic insecurity—or the insecurity of dishonest privilege—before men will do that. The ruling morality teaches them they are violent, dirty and destructive, that the only decent course open to civilized man is to act as his own gaoler, and that men in jungles are even worse because they're as savage as animals *and* as cunning as men—history proves it. So he drops bombs because he believes that if the peasant ever rowed a canoe across the Pacific and drove an ox cart over America till he came to his garden, he'd steal his vegetables and rape his grandmother—history proves it. And history like the Bible will prove anything.

An old fascist (or an old miser) is always bitter and cynical. Not because his conscience troubles him!—but because he lives in conflict with his fundamental sense of human values. Men can only be content when they live in peace and shared respect with other men. It seems odd to say these things in a century of fascism and brutality, but the world is unhappy and violent not because we're cursed with original sin *or* original aggression, but because it is unjust. The world is not absurd, it is finally a place for men to be sane and rational in.

Of course demands for justice sometimes conflict. But the reason these conflicts are hard to resolve is that the "judge" is often more guilty than the other parties. Most established social orders are not means of defending justice but of defending social injustice. That's why compromises inside a nation or between nations are difficult to get, and why law-and-order societies are morally responsible for the terrorism and crime they provoke.

°

I wrote *Bingo* because I think the contradictions in Shakespeare's life are similar to the contradictions in us. He was a "corrupt seer" and we are a "barbarous civilization." Because of that our society could destroy itself. We believe in certain values but our society only works by destroying them, so that our daily lives are a denial of our hopes. That makes our world absurd and often it makes our own species hateful to us. Morality is reduced to surface details and trivialities. Is it so easy to live like that? Or aren't we surrounded by frustration and bitterness, cynicism and inefficiency, and an inner feeling of weakness that comes from knowing we waste our energy on things that finally can't satisfy us? That's true of all parts of our society, from the theatre of the absurd to the broken windows of a youth club. It's not so odd, then, to say that people are only happy when their lives are based on human values. *If* we survive we have only two possible futures. Firstly, as technological ants engineered from birth to fit into a rigid society. Or secondly, as people who live consistently by the values that are part of their nature.

°

You can't do much by deciding to be happier, saner or wiser. That partly depends on society, and you can only change your life by changing society and the role you have to play in it. If, for example, society encourages greed and yet is based on the poverty of other societies, you can understand that without any "enlightenment." What sort of society do we want? The earlier, simpler culture related closely to the land has gone, and not enough people remember its skills well enough to teach them—and anyway those skills were too simple to support the huge masses of people who've grown up in an industrial culture with a highly technological relationship to the environment. So we have to make sense of our technological culture and divorce it from rampant commercialism. A factory isn't bad in itself. It depends how many other factories there are, what they make and how they're organized. Finally the only way to answer these questions is for the people who work in the factories to answer them.

Some people still think workers are apes who'd swing round in trees all day if someone else didn't give them orders. They ask, how on earth could workers organize this mess? But the question is, how can we get out of the mess? That's why it's the *lack* of democracy that's so inefficient. Our problems can't be solved by more information, more control, more social engineering, more compulsion, more rewards, more expertise. Experts can only reshuffle the elements of the mess or add more elements. The faults of technology are probably political as much as technological, but what always happens is this: a mess isn't solved by removing its cause but by adding a new apparatus to contain or redistribute the mess, and then a new appartus to deal with the new apparatus. (Transport is a perfect example of what happens.) There is no structural logic, no way of getting organizational simplicity, no real evolutionary discipline. Technology is a way of solving problems, but the *total technological culture* will break down from time to time, perhaps even more often than other cultures do, because there's no structural integration between its parts, and various technologies are always in conflict. There is chaos because machines and technology are given priority over people. The only way to get a workable simplicity is for people themselves to decide how they want to live and work and what sort of communities they want to be in. Then people will not be subordinated to more and more machines.

Politicians have talked about democracy for three hundred years and now people have come to expect it. The myth has gone out of state and authority, the social structure of authority doesn't impress or intimidate any more. You see, if someone's authority ultimately derives from god, *that* impresses. But an expert doesn't have that sort of moral charisma. There's no reason why *he* shouldn't work for *you*. Well, if no one believes in god any more how can he run the world efficiently? Most people no longer believe that if god's son came down to earth again he'd be better advised to send him to Eton. Most working people no longer believe there are other people who know better than they do how they should live and work. That doesn't mean that everything they will do is practical common sense; the essential thing about acting responsibly is to have responsibility. Then you learn from experience, you learn what you don't know and what education you need. And the time to take responsibility is when the people who've already got it can't make it work—and that's our situation now. Our problems won't vanish and we won't step straight into a rational society. But rational processes will be brought back into society and problems can be solved instead of being compounded. We have to choose a new purpose for society, a new culture. There *is* a counter-culture ready and it's been developing for hundreds of years: it is democracy.

**Bibliographical Note**
Most biographies of Shakespeare barely mention the Welcombe enclosure, but all the documents and a full commentary are given in *William Shakespeare* by E. K. Chambers (2 vols).

# UNIT 3

## Modern/Postmodern: 1975-

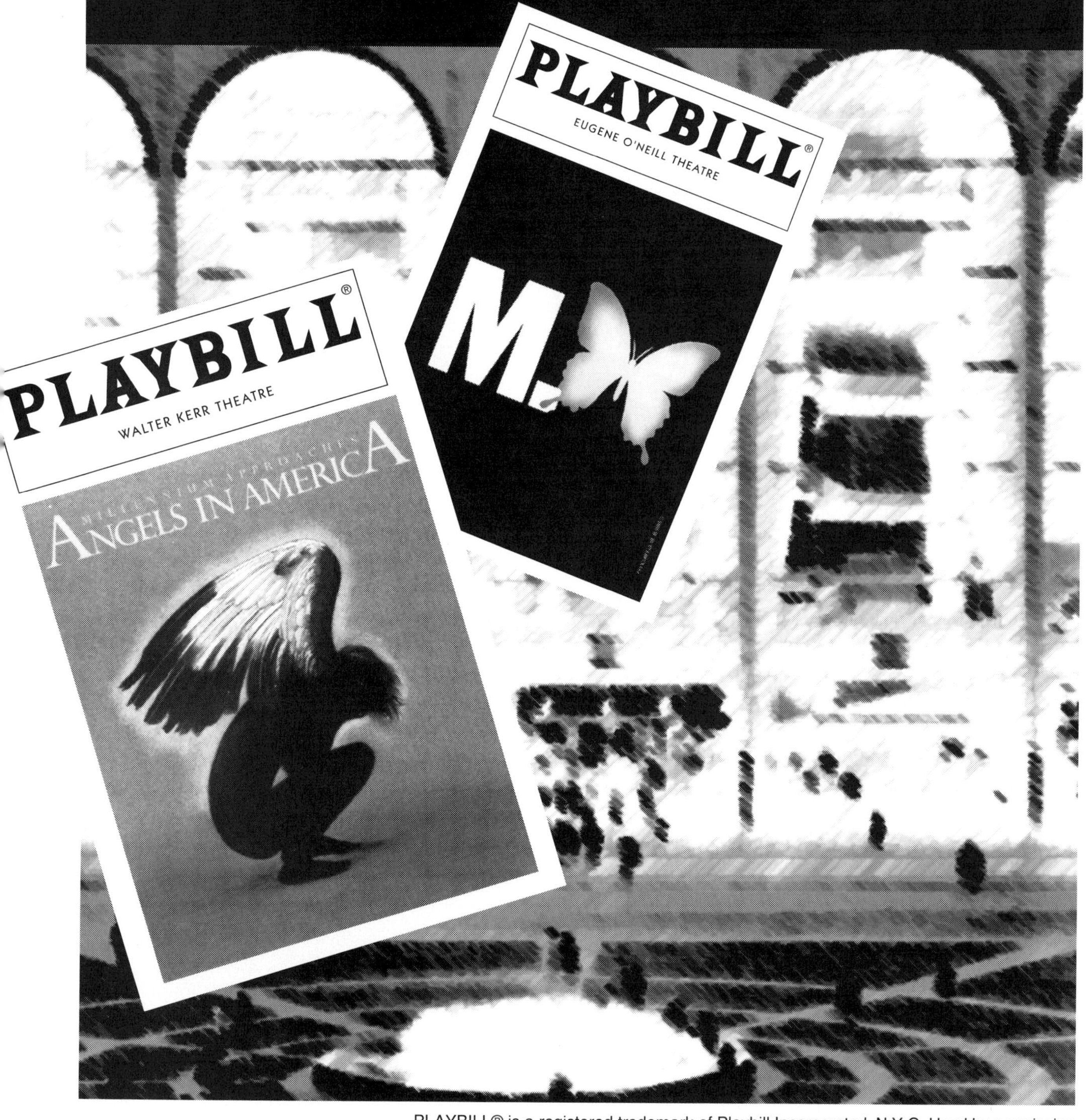

**PLAYBILL®**

EUGENE O'NEILL THEATRE

M.

**PLAYBILL®**

WALTER KERR THEATRE

MILLENNIUM APPROACHES
ANGELS IN AMERICA

ALTHOUGH SEVERAL EVENTS have been labeled as defining the postmodern moment, perhaps none so clearly epitomizes the typical "postmodern" interconnectedness between politics, economics, cultural change, and representation as the Persian Gulf War of 1991. To many Americans, at least, the war was principally a television experience. The Vietnam War, of course, first brought warfare live into millions of homes and accustomed viewers to the notion of a "television war." What distinguished the video experience of the Gulf War was the interpenetration of media and warfare, how different this war *looked* on the TV screen. On TV, the "war" often became indistinguishable from other video experiences. "Smart" bombs zeroing in on and destroying their targets seemed nearly to duplicate not only the video games used to train military pilots, but also the video games played by millions of TV viewers, on the same screens on which they watched the "real" war take place. Indeed, some video games seemed more "realistic" than the thing itself.

Smart bombs, scud studs, Arthur Kent: Television brought the technological war—not the human war—to the screen. To say that, at least for its American audiences, the Persian Gulf War was the first "postmodern" war is to suggest that this *representation* of reality points to a fundamental change in our culture at large. (It should be clear that this "postmodern" sense would have been very different for the combatants, and for the people of Iraq and Kuwait, whose realities were mediated by very different technology—the scuds and smart bombs themselves.) It is useful to open this discussion of postmodern theater and drama in a sphere removed from the sphere of esthetics, for the "postmodern" is not principally an esthetic or stylistic category. If we consider the postmodern in purely artistic terms, it may appear merely to echo the hallmarks of modernist art—the postmodern, like modernism, often uses a fragmented and disruptive, montagelike narrative structure; it decenters fixed "characters"; and it evokes a vaguely oppositional attitude toward social norms. To grasp fully the transformation implied by the term "postmodern," we need to set it in a larger context. As Jean-François Lyotard suggests in *The Postmodern Condition* (1984), the "postmodern" is a "condition" of contemporary culture—not a style, not a historical period in the conventional sense, but a transformation in how our culture is produced, how we experience it, and in the shape of "knowledge" itself. While the introductory essay to Unit 2 concentrated on theatrical developments in the period after 1950, this essay will raise some more theoretical questions about how we might consider the postmodern moment and its implications for drama and theater.

The postmodern is most readily grasped as a threefold crisis: in our ways of understanding the world; of producing its social and material structure; and of living, experiencing, and reflecting on that world in culture and the arts. The "postmodern," then, simultaneously responds to three historical developments: to philosophical **MODERNITY,** to industrial and social **MODERNIZATION,** and to artistic **MODERNISM.** Philosophical "modernity" is usually dated from the rise of Cartesian rationalism in the late seventeenth and eighteenth centuries, the sense—epitomized in the seventeenth-century philosopher René Descartes's famous *cogito ergo sum,* "I think, therefore I am"—that the mind, reason is distinct from the being of the body, and so distinct from the material world. As the German cultural critics Theodor Adorno and Max Horkheimer put it in *Dialectic of Enlightenment* (1947), Cartesian rationalism enabled the "disenchantment of the world," the liberation of humanity from myth, animism, and nature through the power of reason. But as Adorno and Horkheimer suggest, this "enlightenment" has had a number of consequences, both in the sphere of metaphysics and on the level of practical human experience. When "myth" turns into "enlightenment," then nature turns into "mere objectivity": "Men pay for the increase of their power with alienation from that over which they exercise their power. Enlightenment behaves towards things as a dictator toward men. He knows them in so far as he can manipulate them. The man of science knows things in so far as he can make them." Humanity's relation to nature is transformed by Enlightenment philosophy, as nature becomes merely a thing to be dominated, something alien and other. But human consciousness is also "alienated" as well, isolated within the prison of consciousness called "reason." The power assigned to reason and science, the way it locates humanity outside and above the sphere of nature, is the principal feature of philosophical "modernity."

But this philosophical revolution has had practical effects on the organization of human social life as well. The effects of this "modern" consciousness, the desire to subject the material and social world to the order of "reason" informs the history of the West. It is reflected in the structure of modern as opposed to feudal or traditional societies, the planned social mechanisms of the law and the state bureaucracy, the transformation of "nature" into "raw materials" for exploitation, the imperial conquest and subjection—in Africa, Asia, the Americas—of "natural" others to "civilization" and "reason." This project of "modernization" is, in this sense, the outgrowth of the implementation of Enlightenment "reason" in the sphere of social production, the "rationalizing" of the forms of life; it is epitomized by the assembly line, rationalized banking and financial institutions, the modern corporation, planned communities, and so on.

Modernization, that is, implements the modernity of the Enlightenment by "rationalizing" everything—the world is subjected to a desire for complete order, clarity, totality. "Modernism" in culture and the arts can be considered as a response to this totalizing aspect of modern life. Modernist art is at once critical of this depersonalizing and alienating dimension of modernity—think of the fragmented anomie of a poem like T. S. Eliot's *The Waste Land* (1922)—but in other ways modernist art reflects this totalizing sensibility, especially in its formal experimentation. Think of the massive inclusiveness of novels like Marcel Proust's *Remembrance of Things Past* (1922), or James Joyce's *Ulysses* (1922) or *Finnegans Wake* (1939), which aim to synthesize much of human history; of Le Corbusier's planned industrial communities of the 1920s; of the form-follows-function of the Bauhaus school, which claimed to provide a single architectural and design "idea" that could be adapted to all situations; of the way the fragmented surfaces of Cubist painting reflect all perspectives on the subject at once; of twelve-tone music, which forsakes the notion of musical key to include all tones in a rigorously exhaustive musical system; even, perhaps, of stage realism, which, for all the narrowness of its perspective, claimed to put the world completely on stage.

Of course, many of the features of modernism and modernity are still with us. But it is possible to note a certain exhaustion of modernism in the arts of the 1950s and 1960s, as though the philosophical and social totalities it represented were themselves exhausted, in crisis. For by the 1960s, a variety of intellectual, political, and cultural revolutions challenged both the rationality of modernization and ultimately the disinterested claims of "reason" itself. Throughout the world, liberation movements spotlighted the ways in which colonial institutions—education, politics, the law—employed to "enlighten" indigenous cultures actually masked a fundamental need to exploit their labor for the benefit of Western economies. In this sense, a "postmodern" resistance to the esthetic models of modernism begins to blend into a **POSTCOLONIAL** antagonism to modernist geopolitics. In a similar way, notions of "identity"—racial identity, gender identity, class identity, sexual identity—have been shown not to be innate objects that can be ordered by reason, but as categories *constructed* as part of an informing way of producing the world.

It might be argued that the most fundamental challenge to Enlightenment modernity came in the study of language itself. Since the eighteenth century, language has been regarded as a "conventional" system—a system of signs that are assigned largely arbitrarily to refer to "things" in the world. Eighteenth- and nineteenth-century linguists took the real differences between *things* to underlie the function of languages; languages, for all their differences, reflected basic differences in the world. But the early-twentieth-century Swiss linguist Ferdinand de Saussure (1857–1913) proposed an alternate theory of language. Saussure argued, first, that language exists as a system (which he called *langue*) apart from any individual speech; an individual act of speaking (*parole*) is merely one instance of the possibilities already implicit in the total system. More important, Saussure argued that what makes language signify is its own internal system for differentiating between units—sounds, words—not the relationship between words and things in the world. Words have meaning insofar as they can be differentiated from other words in the system (English can distinguish *b*at from *c*at, not because the words refer to two different objects, but because the English language allows *b* and *c* to make different signs when applied to the suffix -at). This structural linguistics was widely disseminated in the "human sciences"—philosophy, literature, anthropology, sociology—in the late 1950s, 1960s, and 1970s.

As Jonathan Culler suggests in his book *Structuralist Poetics* (1975), the consequences of this application were profound: "The notion that linguistics might be useful in studying other cultural phenomena is based on two fundamental insights: first, that social and cultural phenomena are not simply material objects or events but objects and events with meaning, and hence signs; and second, that they do not have essences but are defined by a network of relations, both internal and external." This shift from *what* meanings are produced to how meanings are produced had other effects as well, drawing attention to the ways signifying systems—language, kinship, gender, theater, metaphysics—are structured on a series of oppositional terms whose relationship encodes a visible structure of power. In English, for instance, the terms *man, mind, culture, white, reason* are hardly neutral: each is defined in a binary relation to an opposite term—*woman, body, nature, black, emotion*—which is culturally less privileged and more repressed. To expose or "deconstruct" the ways that language encodes a political reality as metaphysics—part of the project of **DECONSTRUCTION** associated with philosophers like Jacques Derrida—is, finally to come to the current, closing phase of Enlightenment "modernity." For deconstruction reveals that the instruments with which we describe the world are in fact instruments for constructing the world, that there is no enactment of "reason" or "science," no way even of speaking, that is not also a way of enacting within the dynamics of power. As Walter Benjamin suggests in "Theses on the Philosophy of History," "There is no document of civilization which is not at the same time a document of barbarism."

To read the world as a network of signifying systems, each of which may have several contradictory relations to the "reality" they represent, is to enter the "postmodern condition"—a transformation in both how we represent "reality" and in what we take it to be. This transformation extends throughout cultural and material life, and it is not surprising that a variety of different ways of characterizing it have been advanced by critics and theoreticians of contemporary culture. Jean-François Lyotard suggests, for instance, that the postmodern condition arises in part through a resistance to "les grands récits," the "master narratives" or "metanarratives" that once provided a common foundation for explaining the world: the neutrality and efficacy of "reason," for example, the nature of the individual, the progress of society, the difference between reality and its representation. One of the "master narratives" most directly challenged by the postmodern is the interlocking narrative of capitalist expansion and its traditional Marxist critique. As Marxist cultural theorist Fredric Jameson has argued, postmodernity is not merely an epistemological crisis—a crisis in our ways of knowing, Lyotard suggests—but is a fundamental shift in the economic order of production, one that requires a rethinking of fundamental terms (like "production," "consumption," "labor") shared by both capitalism and Marxism. For multinational production and the exponential expansion of the process of "commodification" have produced a new cultural order—the consumer society. In this view, the economic and social order of the West is no longer structured along the classic opposition between a capitalist and a Marxist understanding of the forces of "production." In a culture not only mediated by, but created by advertising, information systems, target audience surveys, and MTV, the relationship between production and consumption, life and art, the real and the represented are dramatically altered. This vision of contemporary culture also informs Jean Baudrillard's understanding of how the proliferation of media, information culture, replace material production as a driving principal of the cultural order. In Baudrillard's view, postmodern life is lived through these "simulations," which do not merely replace the "real"—they become the "real."

All of these accounts of the "postmodern"—which are by no means readily assimilable to one another—develop some fundamental critique of "representation." For the postmodern condition finally challenges the idea of "representation" itself, in several interlocking ways. First, postmodern art pays unusual attention to the surface, the language of its own meaning, as though the possibility of *meaning*—"We're not beginning to . . . to . . . mean something," Hamm asks in Samuel Beckett's *Endgame*—were itself in question. Moreover, postmodern art tends to blur the distinction between signifier and signified, between the "real" sphere of the reader, viewer, spectator and the "artificial" sphere of art. To suggest that the world is constituted by its representation is to undermine a clear distinction between the real and the represented. Finally, postmodern art also challenges "representation" in another sense, the sense that art "represents" the world, stands in for it, shows us how it is in an apolitical manner. Much as Western culture has systematically excluded the perspectives and voices of "others"—by, for example, treating the expression of straight, white, Western men as "universal," not a partial, specifically empowered perspective, so the arts in the wake of deconstruction have been pivotal in unlocking these marginalized, unrepresented perspectives.

## Drama, Theater, and the "Postmodern"

To understand elements of postmodern culture—drama and theater, for instance—it is important not so much to isolate stylistic features of these works, but to understand the kind of cultural work they do, how they intersect with contemporary life. For to describe the contemporary theater in terms of its historical inheritance from the modernist theater of Brecht or Ibsen is in an important sense to overlook what is most significant about the stage today: its rupture with the traditions of modernism. Of course, cultural change is never homogenous, and what we might think of as "residual" modes of drama do remain—think of the refigurations of realism in the plays of Wendy Wasserstein, of August Wilson, even of Sam Shepard. But contemporary theater takes direct issue with the notion of "representation" itself, which comes to trouble drama in a number of ways. In many plays, for instance, the notion that the stage performance "reproduces" the text in some direct way is challenged; this is particularly true of **PERFORMANCE ART,** like the monologues of Karen Finley, Spalding Gray, or Anna Deavere Smith. In the monologues of Finley and Gray, the artist "performs" a kind of script, but the narrative is disclosed to the audience directly, in the first person, in ways that make the distinction between factual autobiography and a more "performed," fictionalized "self" difficult to decide. Smith's performances, on the other hand, are drawn from interviews, in which Smith uses the "real" words of her interview subjects to construct a one-woman performance of some event—like the Crown Heights riots in 1991 or the rioting in Los Angeles following the first Rodney King verdict in 1992—that, again, blurs any settled distinction between the "actual" and the "performed." This sense of a "reality" being "performed," rendered at once real and represented, is part of the uncanny power of performance art.

If performance art makes the "real" perhaps too immediate, other modes of theater suggest the inaccessibility of reality in a world in which reality is always displaced, hidden beneath our ways of representing it. Marguerite Duras's *India Song*, for example, blends contradictory narrative voices with the nearly silent staging of the scenes they narrate, as though neither the narrative speakers nor the stage actors can recapture the events the play dramatizes. In later plays like *Not I* and *Catastrophe,* Samuel Beckett uses the stage as a sculptural space, fragmenting the actors' bodies, the narrative, and—arguably, at least, the spectators' "experience" as well.

The postmodern fascination with the signifying surfaces of art has drawn the charge that postmodern esthetics is an empty formalism, inimical to the more political functions of art. But political theater often displays a sense of the systematicity of signification that is at once political and postmodern. Griselda Gambaro's *Information for Foreigners* develops a critique of "representation" in a political direction, as the audience is led in groups through a house, trying to discern the difference between theatricalized torture, tortuous theater, and its own participation. And postmodern theater often has other, more generalized, political dimensions as well. The postmodern theater is an anti-essentialist theater; rather than assuming that categories of experience and identity are "essential" and "universal"—categories of gender roles, sexual identification, racial or ethnic "character"—postmodern performance suggests that these categories are performative, part of the essentially fictive means with which a culture reproduces itself and its lines of legitimation and empowerment. For this reason, postmodern theater frequently uses the systems of performance to expose social and cultural stereotypes. In *Cloud Nine,* for example, Caryl Churchill uses gender and racial cross-casting to imply that the "innate" identity of women and Africans is a construction of the dominant, white, male, imperial perspective in the play. Ntozake Shange uses the "blackface" performance traditions of minstrelsy to dramatize how African-American "identity" has had to work with the images, language, and attitudes given by white culture. One of the ways that the transgression of "representation" animates contemporary theater has to do with the ways that "representation" has traditionally operated with exclusionary force—keeping some aspects of the world from being seen. When Split Britches and Bloolips remake Tennessee Williams's *A Streetcar Named Desire* in *Belle Reprieve,* the intersection between "actors" and "characters," and the cross-playing of gender and sexual orientation, serve to foreground the function of representation in the constitution of reality and the ways that conventional "realism" systematically conceals, distorts, and represses the realities it claims to stage.

As Fredric Jameson points out (see "Postmodernism and Consumer Society," Unit 4), postmodern works frequently invoke or appropriate the style of earlier historical periods: as in the use of neoclassical ornamentation in recent architecture or the recollection of earlier film styles in recent movies (**FILM NOIR** in *Chinatown* or *Dead Again*). Jameson labels this technique **PASTICHE.** What is striking about these postmodern quotations of style, though, is that this invocation of a "past" style is often accomplished in a strangely toneless register, unlike parody or satire; postmodern pastiche renders the style of earlier periods, and so the history that style represents, as merely another commodity for sale in the market of the theater. *Pastiche* in this sense does not lead to a new understanding of the past, nor does it illuminate our contemporary historical situation. Instead, *pastiche* denatures that style by removing it from history, and history from it. Heiner Müller's *Hamletmachine* is perhaps the best example of *pastiche* in this sense. Although Müller's play does engage in a political critique of the socialist politics of Eastern Europe, its intercalation of images may be said to conceal that critique behind an obsessively fussy surface. But Jameson's *pastiche* raises more pressing problems, in that it implies the difficulty of using theatrical *style*—the visual vocabulary of Brecht, say—for any essentially political purpose. If the "Brecht look" or "epic theater" is now just another style, another tool in the designer's arsenal, can its devices still operate with "alienating" effect? In the postmodern context, *can* Brechtian alienation still inform a meaningful political consciousness raising? These are the questions behind plays both explicitly in the mode of Brecht, and plays—like Churchill's *Mad Forest,* Bond's *Bingo,* Fornes's *The Conduct of Life*—that avoid merely "quoting" the style of epic theater in order to refashion its purposes in their own discourse. (It might be noted that Jameson's notion that postmodern style is connected to consumer culture is confirmed by the position of the avant-garde today: funded either by the state or by multinational corporations, performing at festivals that are often magnets of tourism.)

Moreover, Jameson's discussion of *pastiche* also emphasizes the importance of the esthetic *surface* in postmodern art. Music video and advertising are sometimes taken as the paradigmatic postmodern forms, forms whose "message" lies almost exclusively in a rapidly changing, brilliantly seductive, series of images. Although this technique relates to the modernist use of **MONTAGE** in film and theater, it is different in several important ways. Modernist montage uses a series of images, narratively, to tell a story; although the camera cuts quickly from image to image, the audience assembles the images in a single complete narrative. Both the narrative and the interpreting spectator achieve a sense of wholeness. In contrast, postmodern images are juxtaposed in striking, sometimes contradictory, combinations that resist our ability to impose a single narrative explanation, a single story line. This is true of *Hamletmachine,* but in very different ways in other plays, such as *spell #7, Belle Reprieve, Information for Foreigners, Fires in the Mirror,* among others. Postmodern performance—on film or video or in the theater—is insistently fragmentary; it asserts the incompletion of the artistic object and the incomplete quality of the spectator's experience as well. Postmodern arts resist imposing a single explanatory interpretation that would both complete the narrative and confirm the audience's sense of wholeness, of self-integration. In this sense, postmodern arts are sometimes described as concerned with the "death of the subject." They question the possibility both of a comprehensible world and of a comprehending individual. By disorienting language, fragmenting narrative, and dispensing with such organizing principles as "plot" and "character," postmodern art claims that we have entered a new age in which the complex disconnections of modern culture have made obsolete many of our beliefs about the world and our ways of representing the world and ourselves.

# Caryl Churchill

Caryl Churchill (b. 1938) was born in England and began her education in Canada during World War II; she returned to study at Oxford University, taking her B. A. in 1960. At Oxford, Churchill began her career as a playwright, producing several plays: *Downstairs* (1958), *Having a Wonderful Time* (1960), and *Early Death* (1962). During the 1960s, she wrote a series of radio plays. She also continued her study of radical politics and returned to the theater in the 1970s with a series of striking political dramas: *Owners* (1972), *Objections to Sex and Violence* (1975), and *A Light Shining in Buckinghamshire* (1976). The 1970s and 1980s saw an explosion of new experimental, political theater in Britain, and many writers—Edward Bond, Howard Brenton, Pam Gems, Trevor Griffiths, David Hare, among others—modified the techniques of Brechtian theater for the English stage. In the mid-1970s, Churchill also began to work more closely with experimental theater companies, collaborating with actors and directors in the writing of her plays. Working with the feminist theater company Monstrous Regiment (the name alludes to the Calvinist preacher John Knox's 1558 diatribe against Queen Mary of England, "The First Blast of the Trumpet against the Monstrous Regiment of Women"), she wrote *Vinegar Tom,* a play about witchcraft and sexual politics in seventeenth-century England. With the Joint Stock company, she investigated the politics of sexuality more extensively in *Cloud Nine* (1979), a pastiche of melodrama, Gilbert-and-Sullivan operetta, and modern realistic theater that uses **CROSS-DRESSING** and **ROLE DOUBLING** to explore the relationship between colonial and sexual oppression in the nineteenth century and today. The history of gender oppression and the options for contemporary women are the subject of *Top Girls* (1982), and Churchill has continued to write challenging plays on the relationship between class, race, and gender in British social life, including *Fen* (1983), *Serious Money* (1987), and *Icecream* (1989). *Mad Forest* (1990) concerns the revolution in Romania.

## Cloud Nine (1979)

*Cloud Nine* is an involved pastiche of melodrama, Gilbert-and-Sullivan operetta, and modern realistic theater that explores the relationship between colonial and sexual oppression. In the first act of the play, Churchill uses the colonial settler, Clive, to emblematize the power of the white, male, European patriarchy to control all social relations. In the second act of the play, these problems are restated in terms of contemporary social life; although Clive no longer governs, it is hard to feel that the problems of racial and sexual life have really been solved.

Onstage, the most exciting and interesting device in *Cloud Nine* is its use of **CROSS-DRESSING** and **ROLE DOUBLING.** In the first act, for instance, Betty must be played by a man, Joshua by a white man, and Edward by a woman. By "alienating" actors from the characters they play, Churchill clearly intends to raise the questions of gender, sexual orientation, and race as ideological issues, for in each of these cases the difference between the performer and the role marks what Clive wants to see as real. Betty is played by a man because Clive—and his patriarchal society—cannot envision women's identity; women are constructed on the model of male attitudes. Joshua is played by a white man because imperial and racist culture reduces African identity to the construction of white, European attitudes. Edward is played by a woman to express the impossibility of Edward's conforming to Clive's heterosexual standards. In all three cases, the "identity" of the character is compromised or even erased, to be filled-in and embodied by the attitudes that Clive and his society want them to hold. This performative dimension of the play's politics is echoed by the play's doubling of parts—each of the actors in Act 1 takes a part in Act 2, inviting the audience to draw comparisons between the two characters. Although other doubling patterns are possible, Churchill has suggested doubling Harry Bagley the explorer with Martin, the superficially liberated man; Clive the father with Cathy the child; Betty with Edward; and so on. Doubling and cross-dressing are familiar conventions in the theater, but in *Cloud Nine* they have a specific dramatic purpose in developing the themes of the play. By denaturalizing the categories of gender, race, and sexuality, *Cloud Nine* undertakes a typically postmodern inquiry into the construction of social reality, asking what meanings are created by these categories, and how they work to structure the relationship between self and society.

# —Cloud Nine—
## Caryl Churchill

## —CHARACTERS—

ACT ONE
CLIVE, a colonial administrator
BETTY, his wife, played by a man
JOSHUA, his black servant, played by a white
EDWARD, his son, played by a woman
VICTORIA, his daughter, a dummy
MAUD, his mother-in-law
ELLEN, Edward's governess
HARRY BAGLEY, an explorer
MRS SAUNDERS, a widow

ACT TWO
BETTY
EDWARD, her son

VICTORIA, her daughter
MARTIN, Victoria's husband
LIN
CATHY, Lin's daughter age 5, played by a man
GERRY, Edward's lover

*Except for Cathy, characters in Act II are played by actors of their own sex.*

*Act One takes place in a British colony in Africa in Victorian times.*

*Act Two takes place in London in 1979. But for the characters it is twenty-five years later.*

## —ACT ONE—

SCENE I

*Low bright sun. Verandah. Flagpole with union jack. The Family*—CLIVE, BETTY, EDWARD, VICTORIA, MAUD, ELLEN, JOSHUA

ALL: *(sing.)*
> *Come gather, sons of England, come gather in your pride.*
> *Now meet the world united, now face it side by side;*
> *Ye who the earth's wide corners, from veldt to prairie, roam.*
> *From bush and jungle muster all who call old England*
> *"home."*
> > *Then gather round for England,*
> > *Rally to the flag,*
> > *From North and South and East and West*
10 > > *Come one and all for England!*

CLIVE: This is my family. Though far from home
We serve the Queen wherever we may roam
I am a father to the natives here,
And father to my family so dear.

*(He presents* BETTY. *She is played by a man.)*

My wife is all I dreamt a wife should be,
And everything she is she owes to me.
BETTY: I live for Clive. The whole aim of my life
Is to be what he looks for in a wife.
I am a man's creation as you see,
20 And what men want is what I want to be

*(CLIVE presents JOSHUA. He is played by a white.)*

CLIVE: My boy's a jewel. Really has the knack.

You'd hardly notice that the fellow's black.
JOSHUA: My skin is black but oh my soul is white.
I hate my tribe. My master is my light.
I only live for him. As you can see,
What white men want is what I want to be.

*(CLIVE presents EDWARD. He is played by a woman.)*

CLIVE: My son is young. I'm doing all I can
To teach him to grow up to be a man.
EDWARD: What father wants I'd dearly like to be.
I find it rather hard as you can see.                    30

*(CLIVE presents VICTORIA, who is a dummy, MAUD, and ELLEN.)*

CLIVE: No need for any speeches by the rest.
My daughter, mother-in-law, and governess.
ALL: *(sing)*
> > *O'er countless numbers she, our Queen,*
> > *Victoria reigns supreme;*
> > *O'er Afric's sunny plains, and o'er*
> > *Canadian frozen stream;*
> *The forge of war shall weld the chains of brotherhood secure;*
> *So to all time in ev'ry clime our Empire shall endure.*

> > *Then gather round for England,*                      40
> > *Rally to the flag,*
> > *From North and South and East and West*
> > *Come one and all for England!*

*(All go except* BETTY, CLIVE *comes.)*

BETTY: Clive?
CLIVE: Betty. Joshua!

*(JOSHUA comes with a drink for CLIVE.)*

BETTY: I thought you would never come. The day's so long

without you.

CLIVE: Long ride in the bush.

BETTY: Is anything wrong? I heard drums.

50 CLIVE: Nothing serious. Beauty is a damned good mare. I must get some new boots sent from home. These ones have never been right. I have a blister.

BETTY: My poor dear foot.

CLIVE: It's nothing.

BETTY: Oh but it's sore.

CLIVE: We are not in this country to enjoy ourselves. Must have ridden fifty miles. Spoke to three different headmen who would all gladly chop off each other's heads and wear them round their waists.

60 BETTY: Clive!

CLIVE: Don't be squeamish, Betty, let me have my joke. And what has my little dove done today?

BETTY: I've read a little.

CLIVE: Good. Is it good?

BETTY: It's poetry.

CLIVE: You're so delicate and sensitive.

BETTY: And I played the piano. Shall I send for the children?

CLIVE: Yes, in a minute. I've a piece of news for you.

BETTY: Good news?

70 CLIVE: You'll certainly think it's good. A visitor.

BETTY: From home?

CLIVE: No. Well of course originally from home.

BETTY: Man or woman?

CLIVE: Man.

BETTY: I can't imagine.

CLIVE: Something of an explorer. Bit of a poet. Odd chap but brave as a lion. And a great admirer of yours.

BETTY: What do you mean? Whoever can it be?

CLIVE: With an H and a B. And does conjuring tricks for little
80 Edward.

BETTY: That sounds like Mr Bagley.

CLIVE: Harry Bagley.

BETTY: He certainly doesn't admire me, Clive, what a thing to say. How could I possibly guess from that. He's hardly explored anything at all, he's just been up a river, he's done nothing at all compared to what you do. You should have said a heavy drinker and a bit of a bore.

CLIVE: But you like him well enough. You don't mind him coming?

90 BETTY: Anyone at all to break the monotony.

CLIVE: But you have your mother. You have Ellen.

BETTY: Ellen is a governess. My mother is my mother.

CLIVE: I hoped when she came to visit she would be company for you.

BETTY: I don't think mother is on a visit. I think she lives with us.

CLIVE: I think she does.

BETTY: Clive you are so good.

CLIVE: But are you bored my love?

100 BETTY: It's just that I miss you when you're away. We're not in this country to enjoy ourselves. If I lack society that is my form of service.

CLIVE: That's a brave girl. So today has been all right? No fainting? No hysteria?

BETTY: I have been very tranquil.

CLIVE: Ah what a haven of peace to come home to. The coolth, the calm, the beauty.

BETTY: There is one thing, Clive, if you don't mind.

CLIVE: What can I do for you, my dear?

BETTY: It's about Joshua. 110

CLIVE: I wouldn't leave you alone here with a quiet mind if it weren't for Joshua.

BETTY: Joshua doesn't like me.

CLIVE: Joshua has been my boy for eight years. He has saved my life. I have saved his life. He is devoted to me and to mine. I have said this before.

BETTY: He is rude to me. He doesn't do what I say. Speak to him.

CLIVE: Tell me what happened.

BETTY: He said something improper. 120

CLIVE: Well, what?

BETTY: I don't like to repeat it.

CLIVE: I must insist.

BETTY: I had left my book inside on the piano. I was in the hammock. I asked him to fetch it.

CLIVE: And did he not fetch it?

BETTY: Yes, he did eventually.

CLIVE: And what did he say?

BETTY: Clive—

CLIVE: Betty. 130

BETTY: He said Fetch it yourself. You've got legs under that dress.

CLIVE: Joshua!

(JOSHUA *comes.*)

Joshua, madam says you spoke impolitely to her this afternoon.

JOSHUA: Sir?

CLIVE: When she asked you to pass her book from the piano.

JOSHUA: She has the book, sir.

BETTY: I have the book now, but when I told you—

CLIVE: Betty, please, let me handle this. You didn't pass it at 140 once?

JOSHUA: No sir, I made a joke first.

CLIVE: What was that?

JOSHUA: I said my legs were tired, sir. That was funny because the book was very near, it would not make my legs tired to get it.

BETTY: That's not true.

JOSHUA: Did madam hear me wrong?

CLIVE: She heard something else.

JOSHUA: What was that, madam? 150

BETTY: Never mind.

CLIVE: Now Joshua, it won't do you know. Madam doesn't like that kind of joke. You must do what madam says, just do what she says and don't answer back. You know your place, Joshua. I don't have to say any more.

JOSHUA: No sir.

BETTY: I expect an apology.

JOSHUA: I apologise, madam.

CLIVE: There now. It won't happen again, my dear. I'm very shocked Joshua, very shocked. 160

(CLIVE *winks at* JOSHUA, *unseen by* BETTY. JOSHUA *goes.*)

CLIVE: I think another drink, and send for the children, and isn't that Harry riding down the hill? Wave, wave. Just in time before dark. Cuts it fine, the blighter. Always a hothead, Harry.

BETTY: Can he see us?

CLIVE: Stand further forward. He'll see your white dress. There, he waved back.

BETTY: Do you think so? I wonder what he saw. Sometimes sunset is so terrifying I can't bear to look.

170 CLIVE: It makes me proud. Elsewhere in the empire the sun is rising.

BETTY: Harry looks so small on the hillside.

(ELLEN *comes.*)

ELLEN: Shall I bring the children?

BETTY: Shall Ellen bring the children?

CLIVE: Delightful.

BETTY: Yes, Ellen, make sure they're warm. The night air is deceptive. Victoria was looking pale yesterday.

CLIVE: My love.

(MAUD *comes from inside the house.*)

MAUD: Are you warm enough Betty?

180 BETTY: Perfectly.

MAUD: The night air is deceptive.

BETTY: I'm quite warm. I'm too warm.

MAUD: You're not getting a fever, I hope? She's not strong, you know, Clive. I don't know how long you'll keep her in this climate.

CLIVE: I look after Her Majesty's domains. I think you can trust me to look after my wife.

(ELLEN *comes carrying* VICTORIA, *age 2.* EDWARD, *aged 9, lags behind.*)

BETTY: Victoria, my pet, say good evening to papa.

(CLIVE *takes* VICTORIA *on his knee.*)

CLIVE: There's my sweet little Vicky. What have we done

190 today?

BETTY: She wore Ellen's hat.

CLIVE: Did she wear Ellen's big hat like a lady? What a pretty.

BETTY: And Joshua gave her a piggy back. Tell papa. Horsy with Joshy?

ELLEN: She's tired.

CLIVE: Nice Joshy played horsy. What a big strong Joshy. Did you have a gallop? Did you make him stop and go? Not very chatty tonight are we?

BETTY: Edward, say good evening to papa.

200 CLIVE: Edward my boy. Have you done your lessons well?

EDWARD: Yes papa.

CLIVE: Did you go riding?

EDWARD: Yes papa.

CLIVE: What's that you're holding?

BETTY: It's Victoria's doll. What are you doing with it, Edward?

EDWARD: Minding her.

BETTY: Well I should give it to Ellen quickly. You don't want papa to see you with a doll.

CLIVE: No, we had you with Victoria's doll once before, Ed-

210 ward.

ELLEN: He's minding it for Vicky. He's not playing with it.

BETTY: He's not playing with it, Clive. He's minding it for Vicky.

CLIVE: Ellen minds Victoria, let Ellen mind the doll.

ELLEN: Come, give it to me.

(ELLEN *takes the doll.*)

EDWARD: Don't pull her about. Vicky's very fond of her. She likes me to have her.

BETTY: He's a very good brother.

CLIVE: Yes, it's manly of you Edward, to take care of your little sister. We'll say no more about it. Tomorrow I'll take you 220 riding with me and Harry Bagley. Would you like that?

EDWARD: Is he here?

CLIVE: He's just arrived. There Betty, take Victoria now. I must go and welcome Harry.

(CLIVE *tosses* VICTORIA *to* BETTY, *who gives her to* ELLEN.)

EDWARD: Can I come, papa?

BETTY: Is he warm enough?

EDWARD: Am I warm enough?

CLIVE: Never mind the women, Ned. Come and meet Harry.

(*They go. The women are left. There is a silence.*)

MAUD: I daresay Mr Bagley will be out all day and we'll see nothing of him. 230

BETTY: He plays the piano. Surely he will sometimes stay at home with us.

MAUD: We can't expect it. The men have their duties and we have ours.

BETTY: He won't have seen a piano for a year. He lives a very rough life.

ELLEN: Will it be exciting for you, Betty?

MAUD: Whatever do you mean, Ellen?

ELLEN: We don't have very much society.

BETTY: Clive is my society. 240

MAUD: It's time Victoria went to bed.

BETTY: She'd like to stay up and see Mr Bagley.

MAUD: Mr Bagley can see her tomorrow.

(ELLEN *goes.*)

MAUD: You let that girl forget her place, Betty.

BETTY: Mother, she is governess to my son. I know what her place is. I think my friendship does her good. She is not very happy.

MAUD: Young women are never happy.

BETTY: Mother, what a thing to say.

MAUD: Then when they're older they look back and see that 250 comparatively speaking they were ecstatic.

BETTY: I'm perfectly happy.

MAUD: You are looking very pretty tonight. You were such a success as a young girl. You have made a most fortunate marriage. I'm sure you will be an excellent hostess to Mr Bagley.

BETTY: I feel quite nervous at the thought of entertaining.

MAUD: I can always advise you if I'm asked.

BETTY: What a long time they're taking. I always seem to be waiting for the men. 260

MAUD: Betty you have to learn to be patient. I am patient. My mama was very patient.

(CLIVE *approaches, supporting* CAROLINE SAUNDERS.)

CLIVE: It is a pleasure. It is an honour. It is positively your duty to seek my help. I would be hurt, I would be insulted by any show of independence. Your husband would have been one of my dearest friends if he had lived. Betty, look who has

come, Mrs Saunders. She has ridden here all alone, amazing spirit. What will you have? Tea or something stronger? Let her lie down, she is overcome. Betty, you will know what to
270 do.

(MRS SAUNDERS *lies down.*)

MAUD: I knew it. I heard drums. We'll be killed in our beds.

CLIVE: Now, please, calm yourself.

MAUD: I am perfectly calm. I am just outspoken. If it comes to being killed I shall take it as calmly as anyone.

CLIVE: There is no cause for alarm. Mrs Saunders has been alone since her husband died last year, amazing spirit. Not surprisingly, the strain has told. She has come to us as her nearest neighbours.

MAUD: What happened to make her come?

280 CLIVE: This is not an easy country for a woman.

MAUD: Clive, I heard drums. We are not children.

CLIVE: Of course you heard drums. The tribes are constantly at war, if the term is not too grand to grace their squabbles. Not unnaturally Mrs Saunders would like the company of white women. The piano. Poetry.

BETTY: We are not her nearest neighbours.

CLIVE: We are among her nearest neighbours and I was a dear friend of her late husband. She knows that she will find a welcome here. She will not be disappointed. She will be
290 cared for.

MAUD: Of course we will care for her.

BETTY: Victoria is in bed. I must go and say goodnight. Mother, please, you look after Mrs Saunders.

CLIVE: Harry will be here at once.

(BETTY *goes.*)

MAUD: How rash to go out after dark without a shawl.

CLIVE: Amazing spirit. Drink this.

MRS SAUNDERS: Where am I?

MAUD: You are quite safe.

MRS SAUNDERS: Clive? Clive? Thank God. This is very kind.
300 How do you do? I am sorry to be a nuisance. Charmed. Have you a gun? I have a gun.

CLIVE: There is no need for guns I hope. We are all friends here.

MRS. SAUNDERS: I think I will lie down again.

(HARRY BAGLEY *and* EDWARD *have approached.*)

MAUD: Ah, here is Mr Bagley.

EDWARD: I gave his horse some water.

CLIVE: You don't know Mrs Saunders, do you Harry? She has at present collapsed, but she is recovering thanks to the good offices of my wife's mother who I think you've met be-
310 fore. Betty will be along in a minute. Edward will go home to school shortly. He is quite a young man since you saw him.

HARRY: I hardly knew him.

MAUD: What news have you for us, Mr Bagley?

CLIVE: Do you know Mrs Saunders, Harry? Amazing spirit.

EDWARD: Did you hardly know me?

HARRY: Of course I knew you. I mean you have grown.

EDWARD: What do you expect?

HARRY: That's quite right, people don't get smaller.

320 MAUD: Edward. You should be in bed.

EDWARD: No, I'm not tired, I'm not tired am I Uncle Harry?

HARRY: I don't think he's tired.

CLIVE: He is overtired. It is past his bedtime. Say goodnight.

EDWARD: Goodnight, sir.

CLIVE: And to your grandmother.

EDWARD: Goodnight, grandmother.

(EDWARD *goes.*)

MAUD: Shall I help Mrs Saunders indoors? I'm afraid she may get a chill.

CLIVE: Shall I give her an arm?

MAUD: How kind of you Clive. I think I am strong enough.    330

(MAUD *helps* MRS SAUNDERS *into the house.*)

CLIVE: Not a word to alarm the women.

HARRY: Absolutely.

CLIVE: I did some good today I think. Kept up some alliances. There's a lot of affection there.

HARRY: They're affectionate people. They can be very cruel of course.

CLIVE: Well they are savages.

HARRY: Very beautiful people many of them.

CLIVE: Joshua! (*To* HARRY.) I think we should sleep with guns.

HARRY: I haven't slept in a house for six months. It seems ex-    340
tremely safe.

(JOSHUA *comes.*)

CLIVE: Joshua, you will have gathered there's a spot of bother. Rumours of this and that. You should be armed I think.

JOSHUA: There are many bad men, sir. I pray about it. Jesus will protect us.

CLIVE: He will indeed and I'll also get you a weapon. Betty, come and keep Harry company. Look in the barn, Joshua, every night.

(CLIVE *and* JOSHUA *go.* BETTY *comes.*)

HARRY: I wondered where you were.

BETTY: I was singing lullabies.    350

HARRY: When I think of you I always think of you with Edward in your lap.

BETTY: Do you think of me sometimes then?

HARRY: You have been thought of where no white woman has ever been thought of before.

BETTY: It's one way of having adventures. I suppose I will never go in person.

HARRY: That's up to you.

BETTY: Of course it's not. I have duties.

HARRY: Are you happy, Betty?    360

BETTY: Where have you been?

HARRY: Built a raft and went up the river. Stayed with some people. The king is always very good to me. They have a lot of skulls around the place but not white men's I think. I made up a poem one night. If I should die in this forsaken spot, There is a loving heart without a blot, Where I will live—and so on.

BETTY: When I'm near you it's like going out into the jungle. It's like going up the river on a raft. It's like going out in the dark.    370

HARRY: And you are safety and light and peace and home.

BETTY: But I want to be dangerous.

HARRY: Clive is my friend.

BETTY: I am your friend.

HARRY: I don't like dangerous women.

BETTY: Is Mrs Saunders dangerous?

HARRY: Not to me. She's a bit of an old boot.

(JOSHUA *comes, unobserved.*)

BETTY: Am I dangerous?

HARRY: You are rather.

380 BETTY: Please like me.

HARRY: I worship you.

BETTY: Please want me.

HARRY: I don't want to want you. Of course I want you.

BETTY: What are we going to do?

HARRY: I should have stayed on the river. The hell with it.

(*He goes to take her in his arms, she runs away into the house.* HARRY *stays where he is. He becomes aware of* JOSHUA.)

HARRY: Who's there?

JOSHUA: Only me sir.

HARRY: Got a gun now have you?

JOSHUA: Yes sir.

390 HARRY: Where's Clive?

JOSHUA: Going round the boundaries sir.

HARRY: Have you checked there's nobody in the barns?

JOSHUA: Yes sir.

HARRY: Shall we go in a barn and fuck? It's not an order.

JOSHUA: That's all right, yes.

(*They go off.*)

## SCENE II

*An open space some distance from the house.* MRS SAUNDERS *alone, breathless. She is carrying a riding crop.* CLIVE *arrives.*

CLIVE: Why? Why?

MRS SAUNDERS: Don't fuss, Clive, it makes you sweat.

CLIVE: Why ride off now? Sweat, you would sweat if you were in love with somebody as disgustingly capricious as you are.

400    You will be shot with poisoned arrows. You will miss the picnic. Somebody will notice I came after you.

MRS SAUNDERS: I didn't want you to come after me. I wanted to be alone.

CLIVE: You will be raped by cannibals.

MRS SAUNDERS: I just wanted to get out of your house.

CLIVE: My God, what women put us through. Cruel, cruel. I think you are the sort of woman who would enjoy whipping somebody. I've never met one before.

MRS SAUNDERS: Can I tell you something, Clive?

410 CLIVE: Let me tell you something first. Since you came to the house I have had an erection twenty-four hours a day except for ten minutes after the time we had intercourse.

MRS SAUNDERS: I don't think that's physically possible.

CLIVE: You are causing me appalling physical suffering. Is this the way to treat a benefactor?

MRS SAUNDERS: Clive, when I came to your house the other night I came because I was afraid. The cook was going to let his whole tribe in through the window.

CLIVE: I know that, my poor sweet. Amazing—

420 MRS SAUNDERS: I came to you although you are not my nearest neighbour—

CLIVE: Rather than to the old major of seventy-two.

MRS SAUNDERS: Because the last time he came to visit me I had to defend myself with a shotgun and I thought you would take no for an answer.

CLIVE: But you've already answered yes.

MRS SAUNDERS: I answered yes once. Sometimes I want to say no.

CLIVE: Women, my God. Look the picnic will start, I have to go to the picnic. Please Caroline—                                430

MRS SAUNDERS: I think I will have to go back to my own house.

CLIVE: Caroline, if you were shot with poisoned arrows do you know what I'd do? I'd fuck your dead body and poison myself. Caroline, you smell amazing. You terrify me. You are dark like this continent. Mysterious. Treacherous. When you rode to me through the night. When you fainted in my arms. When I came to you in your bed, when I lifted the mosquito netting, when I said let me in, let me in. Oh don't shut me out, Caroline, let me in.

(*He has been caressing her feet and legs. He disappears completely under her skirt.*)

MRS SAUNDERS: Please stop. I can't concentrate. I want to go 440 home. I wish I didn't enjoy the sensation because I don't like you, Clive. I do like living in your house where there's plenty of guns. But I don't like you at all. But I do like the sensation. Well I'll have it then. I'll have it, I'll have it—

(*Voices are heard singing The First Noël.*)

Don't stop. Don't stop.

(CLIVE *comes out from under her skirt.*)

CLIVE: The Christmas picnic. I came.

MRS SAUNDERS: I didn't.

CLIVE: I'm all sticky.

MRS SAUNDERS: What about me? Wait.

CLIVE: All right, are you? Come on. We mustn't be found.    450

MRS SAUNDERS: Don't go now.

CLIVE: Caroline, you are so voracious. Do let go. Tidy yourself up. There's a hair in my mouth.

(CLIVE *and* MRS SAUNDERS *go off.* BETTY *and* MAUD *come, with* JOSHUA *carrying hamper.*)

MAUD: I never would have thought a guinea fowl could taste so like a turkey.

BETTY: I had to explain to the cook three times.

MAUD: You did very well dear.

(JOSHUA *sits apart with gun.* EDWARD *and* HARRY *with* VICTORIA *on his shoulder, singing The First Noël.* MAUD *and* BETTY *are unpacking the hamper.* CLIVE *arrives separately.*)

MAUD: This tablecloth was one of my mama's.

BETTY: Uncle Harry playing horsy.

EDWARD: Crackers crackers.                                   460

BETTY: Not yet, Edward.

CLIVE: And now the moment we have all been waiting for.

(CLIVE *opens champagne. General acclaim.*)

CLIVE: Oh dear, stained my trousers, never mind.

EDWARD: Can I have some?

MAUD: Oh no Edward, not for you.

CLIVE: Give him half a glass.

MAUD: If your father says so.

CLIVE: All rise please. To Her Majesty Queen Victoria, God bless her, and her husband and all her dear children.

470 ALL: The Queen.

EDWARD: Crackers crackers.

(*General cracker pulling, hats.* CLIVE *and* HARRY *discuss champagne.*)

HARRY: Excellent, Clive, wherever did you get it?

CLIVE: I know a chap in French Equatorial Africa.

EDWARD: I won, I won mama.

(ELLEN *arrives.*)

BETTY: Give a hat to Joshua, he'd like it.

(EDWARD *takes hat to* JOSHUA. BETTY *takes a ball from the hamper and plays catch with* ELLEN. *Murmurs of surprise and congratulations from the men whenever they catch the ball.*)

EDWARD: Mama, don't play. You know you can't catch a ball.

BETTY: He's perfectly right. I can't throw either.

(BETTY *sits down.* ELLEN *has the ball.*)

EDWARD: Ellen, don't you play either. You're no good. You spoil it.

(EDWARD *takes* VICTORIA *from* HARRY *and gives her to* ELLEN. *He takes the ball and throws it to* HARRY. HARRY, CLIVE *and* EDWARD *play ball.*)

480 BETTY: Ellen come and sit with me. We'll be spectators and clap.

(EDWARD *misses the ball.*)

CLIVE: Butterfingers.

EDWARD: I'm not.

HARRY: Throw straight now.

EDWARD: I did, I did.

CLIVE: Keep your eye on the ball.

EDWARD: You can't throw.

CLIVE: Don't be a baby.

EDWARD: I'm not, throw a hard one, throw a hard one—

490 CLIVE: Butterfingers. What will Uncle Harry think of you?

EDWARD: It's your fault. You can't throw. I hate you.

(*He throws the ball wildly in the direction of* JOSHUA.)

CLIVE: Now you've lost the ball. He's lost the ball.

EDWARD: It's Joshua's fault. Joshua's butterfingers.

CLIVE: I don't think I want to play any more. Joshua, find the ball will you?

EDWARD: Yes, please play. I'll find the ball. Please play.

CLIVE: You're so silly and you can't catch. You'll be no good at cricket.

MAUD: Why don't we play hide and seek?

500 EDWARD: Because it's a baby game.

BETTY: You've hurt Edward's feelings.

CLIVE: A boy has no business having feelings.

HARRY: Hide and seek. I'll be it. Everybody must hide. This is the base, you have to get home to base.

EDWARD: Hide and seek, hide and seek.

HARRY: Can we persuade the ladies to join us?

MAUD: I'm playing. I love games.

BETTY: I always get found straight away.

ELLEN: Come on, Betty, do. Vicky wants to play.

EDWARD: You won't find me ever.      510

(*They all go except* CLIVE, HARRY, JOSHUA.)

HARRY: It is safe, I suppose?

CLIVE: They won't go far. This is very much my territory and it's broad daylight. Joshua will keep an open eye.

HARRY: Well I must give them a hundred. You don't know what this means to me, Clive. A chap can only go on so long alone. I can climb mountains and go down rivers, but what's it for? For Christmas and England and games and women singing. This is the empire, Clive. It's not me putting a flag in new lands. It's you. The empire is one big family. I'm one of its black sheep, Clive. And I know you think my life is rather 520 dashing. But I want you to know I admire you. This is the empire, Clive, and I serve it. With all my heart.

CLIVE: I think that's about a hundred.

HARRY: Ready or not, here I come!

(*He goes.*)

CLIVE: Harry Bagley is a fine man, Joshua. You should be proud to know him. He will be in history books.

JOSHUA: Sir, while we are alone.

CLIVE: Joshua of course, what is it? You always have my ear. Any time.

JOSHUA: Sir, I have some information. The stable boys are not 530 to be trusted. They whisper. They go out at night. They visit their people. Their people are not my people. I do not visit my people.

CLIVE: Thank you, Joshua. They certainly look after Beauty. I'll be sorry to have to replace them.

JOSHUA: They carry knives.

CLIVE: Thank you, Joshua.

JOSHUA: And, sir.

CLIVE: I appreciate this, Joshua, very much.

JOSHUA: Your wife.      540

CLIVE: Ah, yes?

JOSHUA: She also thinks Harry Bagley is a fine man.

CLIVE: Thank you, Joshua.

JOSHUA: Are you going to hide?

CLIVE: Yes, yes I am. Thank you. Keep your eyes open Joshua.

JOSHUA: I do, sir.

(CLIVE *goes.* JOSHUA *goes.* HARRY *and* BETTY *race back to base.*)

BETTY: I can't run, I can't run at all.

HARRY: There, I've caught you.

BETTY: Harry, what are we going to do?

HARRY: It's impossible, Betty.      550

BETTY: Shall we run away together?

(MAUD *comes.*)

MAUD: I give up. Don't catch me. I have been stung.

HARRY: Nothing serious I hope.

MAUD: I have ointment in my bag. I always carry ointment. I shall just sit down and rest. I am too old for all this fun. Hadn't you better be seeking, Harry?

(HARRY *goes.* MAUD *and* BETTY *are alone for some time. They don't speak.* HARRY *and* EDWARD *race back.*)

EDWARD: I won, I won, you didn't catch me.
HARRY: Yes I did.
EDWARD: Mama, who was first?
560 BETTY: I wasn't watching. I think it was Harry.
EDWARD: It wasn't Harry. You're no good at judging. I won, didn't I grandma?
MAUD: I expect so, since it's Christmas.
EDWARD: I won, Uncle Harry. I'm better than you.
BETTY: Why don't you help Uncle Harry look for the others?
EDWARD: Shall I?
HARRY: Yes, of course.
BETTY: Run along then. He's just coming.

(EDWARD *goes.*)

Harry, I shall scream.
570 HARRY: Ready or not, here I come.

(HARRY *runs off.*)

BETTY: Why don't you go back to the house, mother, and rest your insect-bite?
MAUD: Betty, my duty is here. I don't like what I see. Clive wouldn't like it, Betty. I am your mother.
BETTY: Clive gives you a home because you are my mother.

(HARRY *comes back.*)

HARRY: I can't find anyone else. I'm getting quite hot.
BETTY: Sit down a minute.
HARRY: I can't do that. I'm he. How's your sting?
MAUD: It seems to be swelling up.
580 BETTY: Why don't you go home and rest? Joshua will go with you, Joshua!
HARRY: I could take you back.
MAUD: That would be charming
BETTY: You can't go. You're he.

(JOSHUA *comes.*)

BETTY: Joshua, my mother wants to go back to the house. Will you go with her please.
JOSHUA: Sir told me I have to keep an eye.
BETTY: I am telling you to go back to the house. Then you can come back here and keep an eye.
590 MAUD: Thank you Betty. I know we have our little differences, but I always want what is best for you.

(JOSHUA *and* MAUD *go.*)

HARRY: Don't give way. Keep calm.
BETTY: I shall kill myself.
HARRY: Betty, you are a star in my sky. Without you I would have no sense of direction. I need you, and I need you where you are, I need you to be Clive's wife. I need to go up rivers and know you are sitting here thinking of me.
BETTY: I want more than that. Is that wicked of me?
HARRY: Not wicked, Betty. Silly.

(EDWARD *calls in the distance.*)

600 EDWARD: Uncle Harry, where are you?
BETTY: Can't we ever be alone?
HARRY: You are a mother. And a daughter. And a wife.

BETTY: I think I shall go and hide again.

(BETTY *goes.* HARRY *goes.* CLIVE *chases* MRS SAUNDERS *across the stage.* EDWARD *and* HARRY *call in the distance.*)

EDWARD: Uncle Harry!
HARRY: Edward!

(EDWARD *comes.*)

EDWARD: Uncle Harry!

(HARRY *comes.*)

There you are. I haven't found anyone have you?
HARRY: I wonder where they all are.
EDWARD: Perhaps they're lost forever. Perhaps they're dead. There's trouble going on isn't there, and nobody says be- 610 cause of not frightening the women and children.
HARRY: Yes, that's right.
EDWARD: Do you think we'll be killed in our beds?
HARRY: Not very likely.
EDWARD: I can't sleep at night. Can you?
HARRY: I'm not used to sleeping in a house.
EDWARD: If I'm awake at night can I come and see you? I won't wake you up. I'll only come in if you're awake.
HARRY: You should try to sleep.
EDWARD: I don't mind being awake because I make up adven- 620 tures. Once we were on a raft going down to the rapids. We've lost the paddles because we used them to fight off the crocodiles. A crocodile comes at me and I stab it again and again and the blood is everywhere and it tips up the raft and it has you by the leg and it's biting your leg right off and I take my knife and stab it in the throat and rip open its stomach and it lets go of you but it bites my hand but it's dead. And I drag you onto the river bank and I'm almost fainting with pain and we lie there in each other's arms.
HARRY: Have I lost my leg?                                                      630
EDWARD: I forgot about the leg by then.
HARRY: Hadn't we better look for the others?
EDWARD: Wait. I've got something for you. It was in mama's box but she never wears it.

(EDWARD *gives* HARRY *a necklace.*)

You don't have to wear it either but you might like it to look at.
HARRY: It's beautiful. But you'll have to put it back.
EDWARD: I wanted to give it to you.
HARRY: You did. It can go back in the box. You still gave it to me. Come on now, we have to find the others.      640
EDWARD: Harry, I love you.
HARRY: Yes I know. I love you too.
EDWARD: You know what we did when you were here before. I want to do it again. I think about it all the time. I try to do it to myself but it's not as good. Don't you want to any more?
HARRY: I do, but it's a sin and a crime and it's also wrong.
EDWARD: But we'll do it anyway won't we?
HARRY: Yes of course.
EDWARD: I wish the others would all be killed. Take it out now and let me see it.                                             650
HARRY: No.
EDWARD: Is it big now?
HARRY: Yes.

EDWARD: Let me touch it.

HARRY: No.

EDWARD: Just hold me.

HARRY: When you can't sleep.

EDWARD: We'd better find the others then. Come on.

HARRY: Ready or not, here we come.

(*They go out with whoops and shouts.* BETTY *and* ELLEN *come.*)

660 BETTY: Ellen, I don't want to play any more.

ELLEN: Nor do I, Betty.

BETTY: Come and sit here with me. Oh Ellen, what will become of me?

ELLEN: Betty, are you crying? Are you laughing?

BETTY: Tell me what you think of Harry Bagley.

ELLEN: He's a very fine man.

BETTY: No, Ellen, what you really think.

ELLEN: I think you think he's very handsome.

BETTY: And don't you think he is? Oh Ellen, you're so good and
670   I'm so wicked.

ELLEN: I'm not so good as you think.

(EDWARD *comes.*)

EDWARD: I've found you.

ELLEN: We're not hiding Edward.

EDWARD: But I found you.

ELLEN: We're not playing, Edward, now run along.

EDWARD: Come on, Ellen, do play. Come on, mama.

ELLEN: Edward, don't pull your mama like that.

BETTY: Edward, you must do what your governess says. Go and
play with Uncle Harry.

680 EDWARD: Uncle Harry!

(EDWARD *goes.*)

BETTY: Ellen, can you keep a secret?

ELLEN: Oh yes, yes please.

BETTY: I love Harry Bagley. I want to go away with him. There,
I've said it, it's true.

ELLEN: How do you know you love him?

BETTY: I kissed him.

ELLEN: Betty.

BETTY: He held my hand like this. Oh I want him to do it again.
I want him to stroke my hair.

690 ELLEN: Your lovely hair. Like this, Betty?

BETTY: I want him to put his arm around my waist.

ELLEN: Like this, Betty?

BETTY: Yes, oh I want him to kiss me again.

ELLEN: Like this Betty?

(ELLEN *kisses* BETTY.)

BETTY: Ellen, whatever are you doing? It's not a joke.

ELLEN: I'm sorry, Betty. You're so pretty. Harry Bagley
doesn't deserve you. You wouldn't really go away with him?

BETTY: Oh Ellen, you don't know what I suffer. You don't know
what love is. Everyone will hate me, but it's worth it for
700   Harry's love.

ELLEN: I don't hate you, Betty, I love you.

BETTY: Harry says we shouldn't go away. But he says he worships me.

ELLEN: I worship you Betty.

BETTY: Oh Ellen, you are my only friend.

(*They embrace. The others have all gathered together.* MAUD *has rejoined the party, and* JOSHUA.)

CLIVE: Come along everyone, you mustn't miss Harry's conjuring trick.

(BETTY *and* ELLEN *go to join the others.*)

MAUD: I didn't want to spoil the fun by not being here.

HARRY: What is it that flies all over the world and is up my
sleeve?                                                    710

(HARRY *produces a union jack from up his sleeve. General acclaim.*)

CLIVE: I think we should have some singing now. Ladies, I rely
on you to lead the way.

ELLEN: We have a surprise for you. I have taught Joshua a
Christmas carol. He has been singing it at the piano but I'm
sure he can sing it unaccompanied, can't you, Joshua?

JOSHUA:

> *In the deep midwinter*
> *Frosty wind made moan,*
> *Earth stood hard as iron,*
> *Water like a stone.*                                   720
> *Snow had fallen snow on snow*
> *Snow on snow,*
> *In the deep midwinter*
> *Long long ago.*
>
> *What can I give him*
> *Poor as I am?*
> *If I were a shepherd*
> *I would bring a lamb.*
> *If I were a wise man*
> *I would do my part*                                    730
> *What I can I give him,*
> *Give my heart.*

SCENE III

*Inside the house.* BETTY, MRS SAUNDERS, MAUD *with* VICTORIA.
*The blinds are down so the light isn't bright though it is day
outside.* CLIVE *looks in.*

CLIVE: Everything all right? Nothing to be frightened of.

(CLIVE *goes. Silence.*)

MAUD: Clap hands, daddy comes, with his pockets full of
plums. All for Vicky.

(*Silence.*)

MRS SAUNDERS: Who actually does the flogging?

MAUD: I don't think we want to imagine.

MRS SAUNDERS: I imagine Joshua.

BETTY: Yes I think it would be Joshua. Or would Clive do it
himself?                                                   740

MRS SAUNDERS: Well we can ask them afterwards.

MAUD: I don't like the way you speak of it, Mrs Saunders.

MRS SAUNDERS: How should I speak of it?

MAUD: The men will do it in the proper way, whatever it is. We
have our own part to play.

MRS SAUNDERS: Harry Bagley says they should just be sent away. I don't think he likes to see them beaten.

BETTY: Harry is so tender hearted. Perhaps he is right.

MAUD: Harry Bagley is not altogether—He has lived in this country a long time without any responsibilities. It is part of his charm but it hasn't improved his judgment. If the boys were just sent away they would go back to the village and make more trouble.

MRS SAUNDERS: And what will they say about us in the village if they've been flogged?

BETTY: Perhaps Clive should keep them here.

MRS SAUNDERS: That is never wise.

BETTY: Whatever shall we do?

MAUD: I don't think it is up to us to wonder. The men don't tell us what is going on among the tribes, so how can we possibly make a judgment?

MRS SAUNDERS: I know a little of what is going on.

BETTY: Tell me what you know. Clive tells me nothing.

MAUD: You would not want to be told about it, Betty. It is enough for you that Clive knows what is happening. Clive will know what to do. Your father always knew what to do.

BETTY: Are you saying you would do something different, Caroline?

MRS SAUNDERS: I would do what I did at my own home. I left. I can't see any way out except to leave. I will leave here. I will keep leaving everywhere I suppose.

MAUD: Luckily this household has a head. I am squeamish myself. But luckily Clive is not.

BETTY: You are leaving here then, Caroline?

MRS SAUNDERS: Not immediately. I'm sorry.

(*Silence.*)

MRS SAUNDERS: I wonder if it's over.

(EDWARD *comes in.*)

BETTY: Shouldn't you be with the men, Edward?

EDWARD: I didn't want to see any more. They got what they deserved. Uncle Harry said I could come in.

MRS SAUNDERS: I never allowed the servants to be beaten in my own house. I'm going to find out what's happening.

(MRS SAUNDERS *goes out.*)

BETTY: Will she go and look?

MAUD: Let Mrs Saunders be a warning to you, Betty. She is alone in the world. You are not, thank God. Since your father died, I know what it is to be unprotected. Vicky is such a pretty little girl. Clap hands, daddy comes, with his pockets full of plums. All for Vicky.

(EDWARD, *meanwhile, has found the doll and is playing clap hands with her.*)

BETTY: Edward, what have you got there?

EDWARD: I'm minding her.

BETTY: Edward, I've told you before, dolls are for girls.

MAUD: Where is Ellen? She should be looking after Edward. (*She goes to the door.*) Ellen! Betty, why do you let that girl mope about in her own room? That's not what she's come to Africa for.

BETTY: You must never let the boys at school know you like dolls. Never, never. No one will talk to you, you won't be on

the cricket team, you won't grow up to be a man like your papa.

EDWARD: I don't want to be like papa. I hate papa.

MAUD: Edward! Edward!

BETTY: You're a horrid wicked boy and papa will beat you. Of course you don't hate him, you love him. Now give Victoria her doll at once.

EDWARD: She's not Victoria's doll, she's my doll. She doesn't love Victoria and Victoria doesn't love her. Victoria never even plays with her.

MAUD: Victoria will learn to play with her.

EDWARD: She's mine and she loves me and she won't be happy if you take her away, she'll cry, she'll cry, she'll cry.

(BETTY *takes the doll away, slaps him, bursts into tears.* ELLEN *comes in.*)

BETTY: Ellen, look what you've done. Edward's got the doll again. Now, Ellen, will you please do your job.

ELLEN: Edward, you are a wicked boy. I am going to lock you in the nursery until supper time. Now go upstairs this minute.

(*She slaps* EDWARD, *who bursts into tears and goes out.*)

I do try to do what you want. I'm so sorry.

(ELLEN *bursts into tears and goes out.*)

MAUD: There now, Vicky's got her baby back. Where did Vicky's naughty baby go? Shall we smack her? Just a little smack (MAUD *smacks the doll hard.*) There, now she's a good baby. Clap hands, daddy comes, with his pockets full of plums. All for Vicky's baby. When I was a child we honoured our parents. My mama was an angel.

(JOSHUA *comes in. He stands without speaking.*)

BETTY: Joshua?

JOSHUA: Madam?

BETTY: Did you want something?

JOSHUA: Sent to see the ladies are all right, madam.

(MRS SAUNDERS *comes in.*)

MRS SAUNDERS: We're very well thank you, Joshua, and how are you?

JOSHUA: Very well thank you, Mrs Saunders.

MRS SAUNDERS: And the stable boys?

JOSHUA: They have had justice, madam.

MRS SAUNDERS: So I saw. And does your arm ache?

MAUD: This is not a proper conversation, Mrs Saunders.

MRS SAUNDERS: You don't mind beating your own people?

JOSHUA: Not my people, madam.

MRS SAUNDERS: A different tribe?

JOSHUA: Bad people.

(HARRY *and* CLIVE *come in.*)

CLIVE: Well this is all very gloomy and solemn. Can we have the shutters open? The heat of the day has gone, we could have some light, I think. And cool drinks on the verandah, Joshua. Have some lemonade yourself. It is most refreshing.

(*Sunlight floods in as the shutters are opened.* EDWARD *comes.*)

EDWARD: Papa, papa, Ellen tried to lock me in the nursery.

Mama is going to tell you of me. I'd rather tell you myself. I was playing with Vicky's doll again and I know it's very bad of me. And I said I didn't want to be like you and I said I hated you. And it's not true and I'm sorry, I'm sorry and please beat me and forgive me.

CLIVE: Well there's a brave boy to own up. You should always respect and love me, Edward, not for myself, I may not deserve it, but as I respected and loved my own father, be-
850 cause he was my father. Through our father we love our Queen and our God, Edward. Do you understand? It is something men understand.

EDWARD: Yes papa.

CLIVE: Then I forgive you and shake you by the hand. You spend too much time with the women. You may spend more time with me and Uncle Harry, little man.

EDWARD: I don't like women. I don't like dolls. I love you, papa, and I love you, Uncle Harry.

CLIVE: There's a fine fellow. Let us go out onto the verandah.

*(They all start to go.* EDWARD *takes* HARRY's *hand and goes with him.* CLIVE *draws* BETTY *back. They embrace.)*

860 BETTY: Poor Clive.

CLIVE: It was my duty to have them flogged. For you and Edward and Victoria, to keep you safe.

BETTY: It is terrible to feel betrayed.

CLIVE: You can tame a wild animal only so far. They revert to their true nature and savage your hand. Sometimes I feel the natives are the enemy. I know that is wrong. I know I have a responsibility towards them, to care for them and bring them all to be like Joshua. But there is something dangerous. Implacable. This whole continent is my enemy. I am
870 pitching my whole mind and will and reason and spirit against it to tame it, and I sometimes feel it will break over me and swallow me up.

BETTY: Clive, Clive, I am here. I have faith in you.

CLIVE: Yes, I can show you my moments of weakness, Betty, because you are my wife and because I trust you. I trust you, Betty, and it would break my heart if you did not deserve that trust. Harry Bagley is my friend. It would break my heart if he did not deserve my trust.

BETTY: I'm sorry, I'm sorry. Forgive me. It is not Harry's fault,
880 it is all mine. Harry is noble. He has rejected me. It is my wickedness, I get bored, I get restless, I imagine things. There is something so wicked in me, Clive.

CLIVE: I have never thought of you having the weakness of your sex, only the good qualities.

BETTY: I am bad, bad, bad—

CLIVE: You are thoughtless, Betty, that's all. Women can be treacherous and evil. They are darker and more dangerous than men. The family protects us from that, you protect me from that. You are not that sort of woman. You are not un-
890 faithful to me, Betty. I can't believe you are. It would hurt me so much to cast you off. That would be my duty.

BETTY: No, no, no.

CLIVE: Joshua has seen you kissing.

BETTY: Forgive me.

CLIVE: But I don't want to know about it. I don't want to know. I wonder of course, I wonder constantly. If Harry Bagley was not my friend I would shoot him. If I shot you every British man and woman would applaud me. But no. It was a moment of passion such as women are too weak to resist. But you must resist it, Betty, or it will destroy us. We must 900 fight against it. We must resist this dark female lust, Betty, or it will swallow us up.

BETTY: I do, I do resist. Help me. Forgive me.

CLIVE: Yes I do forgive you. But I can't feel the same about you as I did. You are still my wife and we still have duties to the household.

*(They go out arm in arm. As soon as they have gone* EDWARD *sneaks back to get the doll, which has been dropped on the floor. He picks it up and comforts it.* JOSHUA *comes through with a tray of drinks.)*

JOSHUA: Baby. Sissy. Girly.

*(JOSHUA goes.* BETTY *calls from off.)*

BETTY: Edward?

*(BETTY comes in.)*

BETTY: There you are, my darling. Come, papa wants us all to be together. Uncle Harry is going to tell how he caught a 910 crocodile. Mama's sorry she smacked you.

*(They embrace.* JOSHUA *comes in again, passing through.)*

BETTY: Joshua, fetch me some blue thread from my sewing box. It is on the piano.

JOSHUA: You've got legs under that skirt.

BETTY: Joshua.

JOSHUA: And more than legs.

BETTY: Edward, are you going to stand there and let a servant insult your mother?

EDWARD: Joshua, get my mother's thread.

JOSHUA: Oh little Eddy, playing at master. It's only a joke.   920

EDWARD: Don't speak to my mother like that again.

JOSHUA: Ladies have no sense of humour. You like a joke with Joshua.

EDWARD: You fetch her sewing at once, do you hear me? You move when I speak to you, boy.

JOSHUA: Yes sir, master Edward sir.

*(JOSHUA goes.)*

BETTY: Edward, you were wonderful.

*(She goes to embrace him but he moves away.)*

EDWARD: Don't touch me.

SONG—*A Boy's Best Friend*—ALL:
  *While plodding on our way, the toilsome road of life,*   930
    *How few the friends that daily there we meet.*
  *Not many will stand in trouble and in strife,*
    *With counsel and affection ever sweet.*
  *But there is one whose smile will ever on us beam,*
    *Whose love is dearer far than any other;*
      *And wherever we may turn*
        *This lesson we will learn*
      *A boy's best friend is his mother.*

    *Then cherish her with care*
    *And smooth her silv'ry hair,*   940
  *When gone you will never get another.*

> *And wherever we may turn*
> *This lesson we shall learn,*
> *A boy's best friend is his mother.*

## SCENE IV

*The verandah as in Scene One. Early morning. Nobody there.*
JOSHUA *comes out of the house slowly and stands for some time doing nothing.* EDWARD *comes out.*

EDWARD: Tell me another bad story, Joshua. Nobody else is even awake yet.

JOSHUA: First there was nothing and then there was the great goddess. She was very large and she had golden eyes and she made the stars and the sun and the earth. But soon she was
950   miserable and lonely and she cried like a great waterfall and her tears made all the rivers in the world. So the great spirit sent a terrible monster, a tree with hundreds of eyes and a long green tongue, and it came chasing after her and she jumped into a lake and the tree jumped in after her, and she jumped right up into the sky. And the tree couldn't follow, he was stuck in the mud. So he picked up a big handful of mud and he threw it at her, up among the stars, and it hit her on the head. And she fell down onto the earth into his arms and the ball of mud is the moon in the sky. And then they
960   had children which is all of us.

EDWARD: It's not true, though.

JOSHUA: Of course it's not true. It's a bad story. Adam and Eve is true. God made man white like him and gave him the bad woman who liked the snake and gave us all this trouble.

(CLIVE *and* HARRY *come out.*)

CLIVE: Run along now, Edward. No, you may stay. You mustn't repeat anything you hear to your mother or your grandmother or Ellen.

EDWARD: Or Mrs Saunders?

CLIVE: Mrs Saunders is an unusual woman and does not re-
970   quire protection in the same way. Harry, there was trouble last night where we expected it. But it's all over now. Everything is under control but nobody should leave the house today I think.

HARRY: Casualties?

CLIVE: No, none of the soldiers hurt thank God. We did a certain amount of damage, set a village on fire and so forth.

HARRY: Was that necessary?

CLIVE: Obviously, it was necessary, Harry, or it wouldn't have happened. The army will come and visit, no doubt. You'll
980   like that, eh, Joshua, to see the British army? And a treat for you, Edward, to see the soldiers. Would you like to be a soldier?

EDWARD: I'd rather be an explorer.

CLIVE: Ah, Harry, like you, you see. I didn't know an explorer at his age. Breakfast, I think, Joshua.

(CLIVE *and* JOSHUA *go in.* HARRY *is following.*)

EDWARD: Uncle.

(HARRY *stops.*)

EDWARD: Harry, why won't you talk to me?

HARRY: Of course I'll talk to you.

EDWARD: If you won't be nice to me I'll tell father.

HARRY: Edward, no, not a word, never, not to your mother, no-   990
body, please. Edward, do you understand? Please.

EDWARD: I won't tell. I promise I'll never tell. I've cut my finger and sworn.

HARRY: There's no need to get so excited Edward. We can't be together all the time. I will have to leave soon anyway, and go back to the river.

EDWARD: You can't, you can't go. Take me with you.

ELLEN: Edward!

HARRY: I have my duty to the Empire.

(HARRY *goes in.* ELLEN *comes out.*)

ELLEN: Edward, breakfast time. Edward.                                 1000

EDWARD: I'm not hungry.

ELLEN: Betty, please come and speak to Edward.

(BETTY *comes.*)

BETTY: Why what's the matter?

ELLEN: He won't come in for breakfast.

BETTY: Edward, I shall call your father.

EDWARD: You can't make me eat.

(*He goes in.* BETTY *is about to follow.*)

ELLEN: Betty.

(BETTY *stops.*)

ELLEN: Betty, when Edward goes to school will I have to leave?

BETTY: Never mind, Ellen dear, you'll get another place. I'll give you an excellent reference.                                      1010

ELLEN: I don't want another place, Betty. I want to stay with you forever.

BETTY: If you go back to England you might get married, Ellen. You're quite pretty, you shouldn't despair of getting a husband.

ELLEN: I don't want a husband. I want you.

BETTY: Children of your own, Ellen, think.

ELLEN: I don't want children, I don't like children. I just want to be alone with you, Betty, and sing for you and kiss you because I love you, Betty.                                            1020

BETTY: I love you too, Ellen. But women have their duty as soldiers have. You must be a mother if you can.

ELLEN: Betty, Betty, I love you so much. I want to stay with you forever, my love for you is eternal, stronger than death. I'd rather die than leave you, Betty.

BETTY: No you wouldn't, Ellen, don't be silly. Come, don't cry. You don't feel what you think you do. It's the loneliness here and the climate is very confusing. Come and have breakfast, Ellen dear, and I'll forget all about it.

(ELLEN *goes,* CLIVE *comes.*)

BETTY: Clive, please forgive me.                                       1030

CLIVE: Will you leave me alone?

(BETTY *goes back into the house.* HARRY *comes.*)

CLIVE: Women, Harry. I envy you going into the jungle, a man's life.

HARRY: I envy you.

CLIVE: Harry, I know you do. I have spoken to Betty.

HARRY: I assure you, Clive—

CLIVE: Please say nothing about it.

HARRY: My friendship for you—

CLIVE: Absolutely. I know the friendship between us, Harry, is
1040     not something that could be spoiled by the weaker sex.
Friendship between men is a fine thing. It is the noblest
form of relationship.

HARRY: I agree with you.

CLIVE: There is the necessity of reproduction. The family is all
important. And there is the pleasure. But what we put ourselves through to get that pleasure, Harry. When I heard
about our fine fellows last night fighting those savages to
protect us I thought yes, that is what I aspire to. I tell you
Harry, in confidence, I suddenly got out of Mrs Saunders'
1050     bed and came out here on the verandah and looked at the
stars.

HARRY: I couldn't sleep last night either.

CLIVE: There is something dark about women, that threatens
what is best in us. Between men that light burns brightly.

HARRY: I didn't know you felt like that.

CLIVE: Women are irrational, demanding, inconsistent, treacherous, lustful, and they smell different from us.

HARRY: Clive—

CLIVE: Think of the comradeship of men, Harry, sharing ad-
1060     ventures, sharing danger, risking their lives together.

(HARRY *takes hold of* CLIVE.)

CLIVE: What are you doing?

HARRY: Well, you said—

CLIVE: I said what?

HARRY: Between men.

    (CLIVE *is speechless.*)

I'm sorry, I misunderstood, I would never have dreamt, I
thought—

CLIVE: My God, Harry, how disgusting.

HARRY: You will not betray my confidence.

CLIVE: I feel contaminated.

1070 HARRY: I struggle against it. You cannot imagine the shame. I
have tried everything to save myself.

CLIVE: The most revolting perversion. Rome fell, Harry, and
this sin can destroy an empire.

HARRY: It is not a sin, it is a disease.

CLIVE: A disease more dangerous than diphtheria. Effeminacy
is contagious. How I have been deceived. Your face does not
look degenerate. Oh Harry, how did you sink to this?

HARRY: Clive, help me, what am I to do?

CLIVE: You have been away from England too long.

1080 HARRY: Where can I go except into the jungle to hide?

CLIVE: You don't do it with the natives, Harry? My God, what
a betrayal of the Queen.

HARRY: Clive, I am like a man born crippled. Please help me.

CLIVE: You must repent.

HARRY: I have thought of killing myself.

CLIVE: That is a sin too.

HARRY: There is no way out. Clive, I beg of you, do not betray
my confidence.

CLIVE: I cannot keep a secret like this. Rivers will be named
1090     after you, it's unthinkable. You must save yourself from depravity. You must get married. You are not unattractive to
women. What a relief that you and Betty were not after all—
good God, how disgusting. Now Mrs Saunders. She's a
woman of spirit, she could go with you on your expeditions.

HARRY: I suppose getting married wouldn't be any worse than

killing myself.

CLIVE: Mrs Saunders! Mrs Saunders! Ask her now, Harry.
Think of England.

(MRS SAUNDERS *comes.* CLIVE *withdraws.* HARRY *goes up to* MRS
SAUNDERS.)

HARRY: Mrs Saunders, will you marry me?

MRS SAUNDERS: Why?     1100

HARRY: We are both alone.

MRS SAUNDERS: I choose to be alone, Mr Bagley. If I can look
after myself, I'm sure you can. Clive, I have something important to tell you. I've just found Joshua putting earth on
his head. He tells me his parents were killed last night by the
British soldiers. I think you owe him an apology on behalf of
the Queen.

CLIVE: Joshua! Joshua!

MRS SAUNDERS: Mr Bagley, I could never be a wife again.
There is only one thing about marriage that I like.     1110

(CLIVE *comes.*)

CLIVE: Joshua, I am horrified to hear what has happened. Good
God!

MRS SAUNDERS: His father was shot. His mother died in the
blaze.

(MRS SAUNDERS *goes.*)

CLIVE: Joshua, do you want a day off? Do you want to go to
your people?

JOSHUA: Not my people, sir.

CLIVE: But you want to go to your parents' funeral?

JOSHUA: No sir.

CLIVE: Yes, Joshua, yes, your father and mother. I'm sure they 1120
were loyal to the crown. I'm sure it was all a terrible mistake.

JOSHUA: My mother and father were bad people.

CLIVE: Joshua, no.

JOSHUA: You are my father and mother.

CLIVE: Well really. I don't know what to say. That's very decent
of you. Are you sure there's nothing I can do? You can have
the day off you know.

(BETTY *comes out followed by* EDWARD.)

BETTY: What's the matter? What's happening?

CLIVE: Something terrible has happened. No, I mean some relatives of Joshua's met with an accident.     1130

JOSHUA: May I go sir?

CLIVE: Yes, yes of course. Good God, what a terrible thing.
Bring us a drink will you Joshua?

(JOSHUA *goes.*)

EDWARD: What? What?

BETTY: Edward, go and do your lessons.

EDWARD: What is it, Uncle Harry?

HARRY: Go and do your lessons.

ELLEN: Edward, come in here at once.

EDWARD: What's happened, Uncle Harry?

(HARRY *has moved aside,* EDWARD *follows him.* ELLEN *comes
out.*)

HARRY: Go away. Go inside. Ellen!     1140

ELLEN: Go inside, Edward. I shall tell your mother.

BETTY: Go inside, Edward at once. I shall tell your father.

CLIVE: Go inside, Edward. And Betty you go inside too.

(BETTY, EDWARD *and* ELLEN *go.* MAUD *comes out.*)

CLIVE: Go inside. And Ellen, you come outside.

(ELLEN *comes out.*)

Mr Bagley has something to say to you.
HARRY: Ellen. I don't suppose you would marry me?
ELLEN: What if I said yes?
CLIVE: Run along now, you two want to be alone.

(HARRY *and* ELLEN *go out.* JOSHUA *brings* CLIVE *a drink.*)

JOSHUA: The governess and your wife, sir.
1150 CLIVE: What's that, Joshua?
JOSHUA: She talks of love to your wife, sir. I have seen them. Bad women.
CLIVE: Joshua, you go too far. Get out of my sight.


SCENE V

*The verandah. A table with a white cloth. A wedding cake and a large knife. Bottles and glasses.* JOSHUA *is putting things on the table.* EDWARD *has the doll.* JOSHUA *sees him with it. He holds out his hand.* EDWARD *gives him the doll.* JOSHUA *takes the knife and cuts the doll open and shakes the sawdust out of it.* JOSHUA *throws the doll under the table.*

MAUD: Come along Edward, this is such fun.

(*Everyone enters, triumphal arch for* HARRY *and* ELLEN.)

MAUD: Your mama's wedding was a splendid occasion, Edward. I cried and cried.

(ELLEN *and* BETTY *go aside.*)

ELLEN: Betty, what happens with a man? I don't know what to do.
BETTY: You just keep still.
1160 ELLEN: And what does he do?
BETTY: Harry will know what to do.
ELLEN: And is it enjoyable?
BETTY: Ellen, you're not getting married to enjoy yourself.
ELLEN: Don't forget me, Betty.

(ELLEN *goes.*)

BETTY: I think my necklace has been stolen Clive. I did so want to wear it at the wedding.
EDWARD: It was Joshua. Joshua took it.
CLIVE: Joshua?
EDWARD: He did, he did, I saw him with it.
1170 HARRY: Edward, that's not true.
EDWARD: It is, it is.
HARRY: Edward, I'm afraid you took it yourself.
EDWARD: I did not.
HARRY: I have seen him with it.
CLIVE: Edward, is that true? Where is it? Did you take your mother's necklace? And to try and blame Joshua, good God.

(EDWARD *runs off.*)

BETTY: Edward, come back. Have you got my necklace?
HARRY: I should leave him alone. He'll bring it back.

BETTY: I wanted to wear it. I wanted to look my best at your wedding.     1180
HARRY: You always look your best to me.
BETTY: I shall get drunk.

(MRS SAUNDERS *comes.*)

MRS SAUNDERS: The sale of my property is completed. I shall leave tomorrow.
CLIVE: That's just as well. Whose protection will you seek this time?
MRS SAUNDERS: I shall go to England and buy a farm there. I shall introduce threshing machines.
CLIVE: Amazing spirit.

(*He kisses her.* BETTY *launches herself on* MRS SAUNDERS. *They fall to the ground.*)

CLIVE: Betty—Caroline—I don't deserve this—Harry, Harry.     1190

(HARRY *and* CLIVE *separate them.* HARRY *holding* MRS SAUN-DERS, CLIVE BETTY.)

CLIVE: Mrs Saunders, how can you abuse my hospitality? How dare you touch my wife? You must leave here at once.
BETTY: Go away, go away. You are a wicked woman.
MAUD: Mrs Saunders, I am shocked. This is your hostess.
CLIVE: Pack your bags and leave the house this instant.
MRS SAUNDERS: I was leaving anyway. There's no place for me here. I have made arrangements to leave tomorrow, and to-morrow is when I will leave. I wish you joy, Mr Bagley.

(MRS SAUNDERS *goes.*)

CLIVE: No place for her anywhere I should think. Shocking be-haviour.     1200
BETTY: Oh Clive, forgive me, and love me like you used to.
CLIVE: Were you jealous my dove? My own dear wife!
MAUD: Ah, Mr Bagley, one flesh, you see.

(EDWARD *comes back with the necklace.*)

CLIVE: Good God, Edward, it's true.
EDWARD: I was minding it for mama because of the troubles.
CLIVE: Well done, Edward, that was very manly of you. See Betty? Edward was protecting his mama's jewels from the rebels. What a hysterical fuss over nothing. Well done, little man. It is quite safe now. The bad men are dead. Edward, you may do up the necklace for mama.     1210

(EDWARD *does up* BETTY's *necklace, supervised by* CLIVE, JOSHUA *is drinking steadily.* ELLEN *comes back.*)

MAUD: Ah, here's the bride. Come along, Ellen, you don't cry at your own wedding, only at other people's.
CLIVE: Now, speeches, speeches. Who is going to make a speech? Harry, make a speech.
HARRY: I'm no speaker. You're the one for that.
ALL: Speech, speech.
HARRY: My dear friends—what can I say—the empire—the family—the married state to which I have always aspired—your shining example of domestic bliss—my great good for-tune in winning Ellen's love—happiest day of my life.     1220

(*Applause.*)

CLIVE: Cut the cake, cut the cake.

(HARRY *and* ELLEN *take the knife to cut the cake.* HARRY *steps on the doll under the table.*)

HARRY: What's this?
ELLEN: Oh look.
BETTY: Edward.
EDWARD: It was Joshua. It was Joshua. I saw him.
CLIVE: Don't tell lies again.

(*He hits* EDWARD *across the side of the head.*)

Unaccustomed as I am to public speaking—

(*Cheers.*)

Harry, my friend. So brave and strong and supple.
Ellen, from neath her veil so shyly peeking.
1230   I wish you joy. A toast—the happy couple.
Dangers are past. Our enemies are killed.
—Put your arm round her, Harry, have a kiss—
All murmuring of discontent is stilled.
Long may you live in peace and joy and bliss.

(*While he is speaking* JOSHUA *raises his gun to shoot* CLIVE. *Only* EDWARD *sees. He does nothing to warn the others. He put his hands over his ears.*)
(*BLACK.*)

## —ACT TWO—

### SCENE I

*Winter afternoon. Inside the hut of a one o'clock club, a children's playcentre in a park,* VICTORIA *and* LIN, *mothers.* CATHY, LIN's *daughter, age 4, played by a man, clinging to* LIN. VICTORIA *reading a book.*

CATHY: Yum yum bubblegum.
    Stick it up your mother's bum.
    When it's brown
    Pull it down
    Yum yum bubblegum.
1240  LIN: Like your shoes, Victoria.
CATHY: Jack be nimble, Jack be quick,
    Jack jump over the candlestick.
    Silly Jack, he should jump higher,
    Goodness gracious, great balls of fire.
LIN: Cathy, do stop. Do a painting.
CATHY: You do a painting.
LIN: You do a painting.
CATHY: What shall I paint?
LIN: Paint a house.
1250 CATHY: No.
LIN: Princess.
CATHY: No.
LIN: Pirates.
CATHY: Already done that.
LIN: Spacemen.
CATHY: I never paint spacemen. You know I never.
LIN: Paint a car crash and blood everywhere.
CATHY: No, don't tell me. I know what to paint.
LIN: Go on then. You need an apron, where's an apron. Here.
1260 CATHY: Don't want an apron.

LIN: Lift up your arms. There's a good girl.
CATHY: I don't want to paint.
LIN: Don't paint. Don't paint.
CATHY: What shall I do? You paint. What shall I do mum?
VICTORIA: There's nobody on the big bike, Cathy, quick.

(CATHY *goes out.* VICTORIA *is watching the children playing outside.*)

VICTORIA: Tommy, it's Jimmy's gun. Let him have it. What the hell.

(*She goes on reading. She reads while she talks.*)

LIN: I don't know how you can concentrate.
VICTORIA: You have to or you never do anything.
LIN: Yeh, well. It's really warm in here, that's one thing. It's   1270
    better than standing out there. I got chilblains last winter.
VICTORIA: It is warm.
LIN: I suppose Tommy doesn't let you read much. I expect he
    talks to you while you're reading.
VICTORIA: Yes, he does.
LIN: I didn't get very far with that book you lent me.
VICTORIA: That's all right.
LIN: I was glad to have it, though. I sit with it on my lap while
    I'm watching telly. Well, Cathy's off. She's frightened I'm
    going to leave her. It's the babyminder didn't work out when   1280
    she was two, she still remembers. You can't get them used
    to other people if you're by yourself. It's no good blaming
    me. She clings round my knees every morning up the nurs-
    ery and they don't say anything but they make you feel
    you're making her do it. But I'm desperate for her to go to
    school. I did cry when I left her the first day. You wouldn't,
    you're too fucking sensible. You'll call the teacher by her
    first name. I really fancy you.
VICTORIA: What?
LIN: Put your book down will you for five minutes. You didn't   1290
    hear a word I said.
VICTORIA: I don't get much time to myself.
LIN: Do you ever go to the movies?
VICTORIA: Tommy's very funny who he's left with. My mother
    babysits sometimes.
LIN: Your husband could babysit.
VICTORIA: But then we couldn't go to the movies.
LIN: You could go to the movies with me.
VICTORIA: Oh I see.
LIN: Couldn't you?   1300
VICTORIA: Well yes, I could.
LIN: Friday night?
VICTORIA: What film are we talking about?
LIN: Does it matter what film?
VICTORIA: Of course it does.
LIN: You choose then. Friday night.

(CATHY *comes in with gun, shoots them saying Kiou kiou kiou, and runs off again.*)

Not in a foreign language, ok. You don't go in the movies to read.

(LIN *watches the children playing outside.*)

Don't hit him, Cathy, kill him. Point the gun, kiou, kiou, kiou. That's the way.   1310

VICTORIA: They've just banned war toys in Sweden.

LIN: The kids'll just hit each other more.

VICTORIA: Well, psychologists do differ in their opinions as to whether or not aggression is innate.

LIN: Yeh?

VICTORIA: I'm afraid I do let Tommy play with guns and just hope he'll get it out of his system and not end up in the army.

LIN: I've got a brother in the army.

1320 VICTORIA: Oh I'm sorry. Whereabouts is he stationed?

LIN: Belfast.

VICTORIA: Oh dear.

LIN: I've got a friend who's Irish and we went on a Troops Out march. Now my dad won't speak to me.

VICTORIA: I don't get on too well with my father either.

LIN: And your husband? How do you get on with him?

VICTORIA: Oh, fine. Up and down. You know. Very well. He helps with the washing up and everything.

LIN: I left mine two years ago. He let me keep Cathy and I'm
1330    grateful for that.

VICTORIA: You shouldn't be grateful.

LIN: I'm a lesbian.

VICTORIA: You still shouldn't be grateful.

LIN: I'm grateful he didn't hit me harder than he did.

VICTORIA: I suppose I'm very lucky with Martin.

LIN: Don't get at me about how I bring up Cathy, ok?

VICTORIA: I didn't.

LIN: Yes you did. War toys. I'll give her a rifle for Christmas and blast Tommy's pretty head off for a start.

(VICTORIA *goes back to her book.*)

1340 LIN: I hate men.

VICTORIA: You have to look at it in a historical perspective in terms of learnt behaviour since the industrial revolution.

LIN: I just hate the bastards.

VICTORIA: Well it's a point of view.

(*By now* CATHY *has come back in and started painting in many colours, without an apron.* EDWARD *comes in.*)

EDWARD: Victoria, mother's in the park. She's walking round all the paths very fast.

VICTORIA: By herself?

EDWARD: I told her you were here.

VICTORIA: Thanks.

1350 EDWARD: Come on.

VICTORIA: Ten minutes talking to my mother and I have to spend two hours in a hot bath.

(VICTORIA *goes out.*)

LIN: Shit, Cathy, what about an apron. I don't mind you having paint on your frock but if it doesn't wash off just don't tell me you can't wear your frock with paint on, ok?

CATHY: Ok.

LIN: You're gay, aren't you?

EDWARD: I beg your pardon?

LIN: I really fancy your sister. I thought you'd understand. You
1360    do but you can go on pretending you don't, I don't mind. That's lovely Cathy, I like the green bit.

EDWARD: Don't go around saying that. I might lose my job.

LIN: The last gardener was ever so straight. He used to flash at

all the little girls.

EDWARD: I wish you hadn't said that about me. It's not true.

LIN: It's not true and I never said it and I never thought it and I never will think it again.

EDWARD: Someone might have heard you.

LIN: Shut up about it then.

(BETTY *and* VICTORIA *come up.*)

BETTY: It's quite a nasty bump.                                    1370

VICTORIA: He's not even crying.

BETTY: I think that's very worrying. You and Edward always cried. Perhaps he's got concussion.

VICTORIA: Of course he hasn't mummy.

BETTY: That other little boy was very rough. Should you speak to somebody about him?

VICTORIA: Tommy was hitting him with a spade.

BETTY: Well he's a real little boy. And so brave not to cry. You must watch him for signs of drowsiness. And nausea. If he's sick in the night, phone an ambulance. Well, you're looking 1380 very well darling, a bit tired, a bit peaky. I think the fresh air agrees with Edward. He likes the open air life because of growing up in Africa. He misses the sunshine, don't you, darling? We'll soon have Edward back on his feet. What fun it is here.

VICTORIA: This is Lin. And Cathy.

BETTY: Oh Cathy what a lovely painting. What is it? Well I think it's a house on fire. I think all that red is a fire. Is that right? Or do I see legs, is it a horse? Can I have the lovely painting or is it for mummy? Children have such imagina- 1390 tion, it makes them so exhausting. (*To* LIN.) I'm sure you're wonderful, just like Victoria. I had help with my children. One does need help. That was in Africa of course so there wasn't the servant problem. This is my son Edward. This is—

EDWARD: Lin.

BETTY: Lin, this is Lin. Edward is doing something such fun, he's working in the park as a gardener. He does look exactly like a gardener.

EDWARD: I am a gardener.                                           1400

BETTY: He's certainly making a stab at it. Well it will be a story to tell. I expect he will write a novel about it, or perhaps a television series. Well what a pretty child Cathy is. Victoria was a pretty child just like a little doll—you can't be certain how they'll grow up. I think Victoria's very pretty but she doesn't make the most of herself, do you darling, it's not the fashion I'm told but there are still women who dress out of *Vogue*, well we hope that's not what Martin looks for, though in many ways I wish it was, I don't know what it is Martin looks for and nor does he I'm afraid poor Martin. 1410 Well I am rattling on. I like your skirt dear but your shoes won't do at all. Well do they have lady gardeners, Edward, because I'm going to leave your father and I think I might need to get a job, not a gardener really of course. I haven't got green fingers I'm afraid, everything I touch shrivels straight up. Vicky gave me a poinsettia last Christmas and the leaves all fell off on Boxing Day. Well good heavens, look what's happened to that lovely painting.

(CATHY *has slowly and carefully been going over the whole sheet with black paint. She has almost finished.*)

LIN: What you do that for silly? It was nice.

1420 CATHY: I like your earrings.

VICTORIA: Did you say you're leaving Daddy?

BETTY: Do you darling? Shall I put them on you? My ears aren't pierced, I never wanted that, they just clip on the lobe.

LIN: She'll get paint on you, mind.

BETTY: There's a pretty girl. It doesn't hurt does it? Well you'll grow up to know you have to suffer a little bit for beauty.

CATHY: Look mum I'm pretty, I'm pretty, I'm pretty.

LIN: Stop showing off Cathy.

1430 VICTORIA: It's time we went home. Tommy, time to go home. Last go then, all right.

EDWARD: Mum did I hear you right just now?

CATHY: I want my ears pierced.

BETTY: Ooh, not till you're big.

CATHY: I know a girl got her ears pierced and she's three. She's got real gold.

BETTY: I don't expect she's English, darling. Can I give her a sweety? I know they're not very good for the teeth, Vicky gets terribly cross with me. What does mummy say?

1440 LIN: Just one, thank you very much.

CATHY: I like your beads.

BETTY: Yes they are pretty. Here you are.

*(It is the necklace from ACT ONE.)*

CATHY: Look at me, look at me. Vicky, Vicky, Vicky look at me.

LIN: You look lovely, come on now.

CATHY: And your hat, and your hat.

LIN: No, that's enough.

BETTY: Of course she can have my hat.

CATHY: Yes, yes, hat, hat. Look look look.

LIN: That's enough, please, stop it now. Hat off, bye bye hat.

1450 CATHY: Give me my hat.

LIN: Bye bye beads.

BETTY: It's just fun.

LIN: It's very nice of you.

CATHY: I want my beads.

LIN: Where's the other earring?

CATHY: I want my beads.

*(CATHY has the other earring in her hand. Meanwhile VICTORIA and EDWARD look for it.)*

EDWARD: Is it on the floor?

VICTORIA: Don't step on it.

EDWARD: Where?

1460 CATHY: I want my beads. I want my beads.

LIN: You'll have a smack.

*(LIN gets the earring from CATHY.)*

CATHY: I want my beads.

BETTY: Oh dear oh dear. Have you got the earring? Thank you darling.

CATHY: I want my beads, you're horrid, I hate you, mum, you smell.

BETTY: This is the point you see where one had help. Well it's been lovely seeing you dears and I'll be off again on my little walk.

1470 VICTORIA: You're leaving him? Really?

BETTY: Yes you hear aright, Vicky, yes. I'm finding a little flat,

that will be fun.

*(BETTY goes.)*

Bye bye Tommy, granny's going now. Tommy don't hit that little girl, say goodbye to granny.

VICTORIA: Fucking hell.

EDWARD: Puking Jesus.

LIN: That was news was it, leaving your father?

EDWARD: They're going to want so much attention.

VICTORIA: Does everybody hate their mothers?

EDWARD: Mind you, I wouldn't live with him.                    1480

LIN: Stop snivelling, pigface. Where's your coat? Be quiet now and we'll have doughnuts for tea and if you keep on we'll have dogshit on toast.

*(CATHY laughs so much she lies on the floor.)*

VICTORIA: Tommy, you've had two last goes. Last last last last go.

LIN: Not that funny, come on, coat on.

EDWARD: Can I have your painting?

CATHY: What for?

EDWARD: For a friend of mine.

CATHY: What's his name?                    1490

EDWARD: Gerry.

CATHY: How old is he?

EDWARD: Thirty-two.

CATHY: You can if you like. I don't care. Kiou kiou kiou kiou.

*(CATHY goes out. Edward takes the painting and goes out.)*

LIN: Will you have sex with me?

VICTORIA: I don't know what Martin would say. Does it count as adultery with a woman?

LIN: You'd enjoy it.

SCENE II

*Spring. Swing, bench, pond nearby.* EDWARD *is gardening.* GERRY *sitting on a bench.*

EDWARD: I sometimes pretend we don't know each other. And you've come to the park to eat your sandwiches and look at 1500 me.

GERRY: That would be more interesting, yes. Come and sit down.

EDWARD: If the superintendent comes I'll be in trouble. It's not my dinner time yet. Where were you last night? I think you owe me an explanation. We always do tell each other everything.

GERRY: Is that a rule?

EDWARD: It's what we agreed.

GERRY: It's a habit we've got into. Look, I was drunk. I woke up 1510 at 4 o'clock on somebody's floor. I was sick. I hadn't any money for a cab. I went back to sleep.

EDWARD: You could have phoned.

GERRY: There wasn't a phone.

EDWARD: Sorry.

GERRY: There was a phone and I didn't phone you. Leave it alone, Eddy, I'm warning you.

EDWARD: What are you going to do to me, then?

GERRY: I'm going to the pub.

1520 EDWARD: I'll join you in ten minutes.

GERRY: I didn't ask you to come. (EDWARD goes.) Two years I've been with Edward. You have to get away sometimes or you lose sight of yourself. The train from Victoria to Clapham still has those compartments without a corridor. As soon as I got on the platform I saw who I wanted. Slim hips, tense shoulders, trying not to look at anyone. I put my hand on my packet just long enough so that he couldn't miss it. The train came in. You don't want to get in too fast or some straight dumbo might get in with you. I sat by the window. I

1530 couldn't see where the fuck he'd got to. Then just as the whistle went he got in. Great. It's a six-minute journey so you can't start anything you can't finish. I stared at him and he unzipped his flies. Then he stopped. So I stood up and took my cock out. He took me in his mouth and shut his eyes tight. He was sort of mumbling it about as if he wasn't sure what to do, so I said, "A bit tighter son" and he said "Sorry" and then got on with it. He was jerking off with his left hand, and I could see he'd got a fairsized one. I wished he'd keep still so I could see his watch. I was getting really turned on.

1540 What if we pulled into Clapham Junction now. Of course by the time we sat down again the train was just slowing up. I felt wonderful. Then he started talking. It's better if nothing is said. Once you find he's a librarian in Walthamstow with a special interest in science fiction and lives with his aunt, then forget it. He said I hope you don't think I do this all the time. I said I hope you will from now on. He said he would if I was on the train, but why don't we go out for a meal? I opened the door before the train stopped. I told him I live with somebody, I don't want to know. He was jogging side-

1550 ways to keep up. He said "What's your phone number, you're my ideal physical type, what sign of the zodiac are you? Where do you live? Where are you going now?" It's not fair, I saw him at Victoria a couple of months later and I went straight down to the end of the platform and I picked up somebody really great who never said a word, just smiled.

(CATHY is on the swing.)

CATHY: Batman and Robin
    Had a batmobile.
    Robin done a fart
1560 And paralysed the wheel.
    The wheel couldn't take it,
    The engine fell apart,
    All because of Robin
    And his supersonic fart.

(CATHY goes. MARTIN, VICTORIA and BETTY walking slowly.)

MARTIN: Tom!

BETTY: He'll fall in.

VICTORIA: No he won't.

MARTIN: Don't go too near the edge Tom. Throw the bread from there. The ducks can get it.

1570 BETTY: I'll never be able to manage. If I can't even walk down the street by myself. Everything looks so fierce.

VICTORIA: Just watch Tommy feeding the ducks.

BETTY: He's going to fall in. Make Martin make him move back.

VICTORIA: He's not going to fall in.

BETTY: It's since I left your father.

VICTORIA: Mummy, it really was the right decision.

BETTY: Everything comes at me from all directions. Martin despises me.

VICTORIA: Of course he doesn't, mummy.                          1580

BETTY: Of course he does.

MARTIN: Throw the bread. That's the way. The duck can get it. Quack quack quack quack quack.

BETTY: I don't want to take pills. Lin says you can't trust doctors.

VICTORIA: You're not taking pills. You're doing very well.

BETTY: But I'm so frightened.

VICTORIA: What are you frightened of?

BETTY: Victoria, you always ask that as if there was suddenly going to be an answer.                                      1590

VICTORIA: Are you all right sitting there?

BETTY: Yes, yes. Go and be with Martin.

(VICTORIA joins MARTIN, BETTY stays sitting on the bench.)

MARTIN: You take the job, you go to Manchester. You turn it down, you stay in London. People are making decisions like this every day of the week. It needn't be for more than a year. You get long vacations. Our relationship might well stand the strain of that, and if it doesn't we're better out of it. I don't want to put any pressure on you. I'd just like to know so we can sell the house. I think we're moving into an entirely different way of life if you go to Manchester be-  1600 cause it won't end there. We could keep the house as security for Tommy but he might as well get used to the fact that life nowadays is insecure. You should ask your mother what she thinks and then do the opposite. I could just take that room in Barbara's house, and then we could babysit for each other. You think that means I want to fuck Barbara. I don't. Well, I do, but I won't. And even if I did, what's a fuck between friends? What are we meant to do it with, strangers? Whatever you want to do, I'll be delighted. If you could just let me know what it is I'm to be delighted about. Don't cry  1610 again, Vicky, I'm not the sort of man who makes women cry.

(LIN has come in and sat down with BETTY, CATHY joins them. She is wearing a pink dress and carrying a rifle.)

LIN: I've bought her three new frocks. She won't wear jeans to school any more because Tracy and Mandy called her a boy.

CATHY: Tracy's got a perm.

LIN: You should have shot them.

CATHY: They're coming to tea and we've got to have trifle. Not trifle you make, trifle out of a packet. And you've got to wear a skirt. And tights.

LIN: Tracy's mum wears jeans.

CATHY: She does not. She wears velvet.                          1620

BETTY: Well I think you look very pretty. And if that gun has caps in it please take it a long way away.

CATHY: It's got red caps. They're louder.

MARTIN: Do you think you're well enough to do this job? You don't have to do it. No one's going to think any the less of you if you stay here with me. There's no point being so liberated you make yourself cry all the time. You stay and we'll get everything sorted out. What it is about sex, when we talk while it's happening I get to feel it's like a driving lesson. Left, right, a little faster, carry on, slow down—    1630

(CATHY *shoots* VICTORIA.)

CATHY: You're dead Vicky.
VICTORIA: Aaaargh.
CATHY: Fall over.
VICTORIA: I'm not falling over, the ground's wet.
CATHY: You're dead.
VICTORIA: Yes, I'm dead.
CATHY: The Dead Hand Gang fall over. They said I had to fall over in the mud or I can't play. That duck's a mandarin.
MARTIN: Which one? Look, Tommy.
1640 CATHY: That's a diver. It's got a yellow eye and it dives. That's a goose. Tommy doesn't know it's a goose, he thinks it's a duck. The babies get eaten by weasels. Kiou kiou.

(CATHY *goes.*)

MARTIN: So I lost my erection last night not because I'm not prepared to talk, it's just that taking in technical information is a different part of the brain and also I don't like to feel that you do it better to yourself. I have read the Hite report. I do know that women have to learn to get their pleasure despite our clumsy attempts at expressing undying devotion and ec-
1650 stasy, and that what we spent our adolescence thinking was an animal urge we had to suppress is in fact a fine art we have to acquire. I'm not like whatever percentage of American men have become impotent as a direct result of women's liberation, which I am totally in favour of, more I sometimes think than you are yourself. Nor am I one of your villains who sticks it in, bangs away, and falls asleep. My one aim is to give you pleasure. My one aim is to give you rolling orgasms like I do other women. So why the hell don't you have them? My analysis for what it's worth is that despite all my efforts you still feel dominated by me. I in fact think it's
1660 very sad that you don't feel able to take that job. It makes me feel guilty. I don't want you to do it just because I encourage you to do it. But don't you think you'd feel better if you did take the job? You're the one who's talked about freedom. You're the one who's experimenting with bisexuality, and I don't stop you, I think women have something to give each other. You seem to need the mutual support. You find me too overwhelming. So follow it through, go away, leave me and Tommy alone for a bit, we can manage perfectly well without you. I'm not putting any pressure on you but I
1670 don't think you're being a whole person. God knows I do everything I can to make you stand on your own two feet. Just be yourself. You don't seem to realise how insulting it is to me that you can't get yourself together.

(MARTIN *and* VICTORIA *go.*)

BETTY: You must be very lonely yourself with no husband. You don't miss him?
LIN: Not really, no.
BETTY: Maybe you like being on your own.
LIN: I'm seeing quite a lot of Vicky. I don't live alone. I live with Cathy.
1680 BETTY: I would have been frightened when I was your age. I thought, the poor children, their mother all alone.
LIN: I've a lot of friends.
BETTY: I find when I'm making tea I put out two cups. It's strange not having a man in the house. You don't know who

to do things for.
LIN: Yourself.
BETTY: Oh, that's very selfish.
LIN: Have you any women friends?
BETTY: I've never been so short of men's company that I've had to bother with women. 1690
LIN: Don't you like women?
BETTY: They don't have such interesting conversations as men. There has never been a woman composer of genius. They don't have a sense of humour. They spoil things for themselves with their emotions. I can't say I do like women very much, no.
LIN: But you're a woman.
BETTY: There's nothing says you have to like yourself.
LIN: Do you like me?
BETTY: There's no need to take it personally, Lin. 1700

(MARTIN *and* VICTORIA *come back.*)

MARTIN: Did you know if you put cocaine on your prick you can keep it up all night? The only thing is of course it goes numb so you don't feel anything. But you would, that's the main thing. I just want to make you happy.
BETTY: Vicky, I'd like to go home.
VICTORIA: Yes, mummy, of course.
BETTY: I'm sorry, dear.
VICTORIA: I think Tommy would like to stay out a bit longer.
LIN: Hello, Martin. We do keep out of each other's way.
MARTIN: I think that's the best thing to do. 1710
BETTY: Perhaps you'd walk home with me, Martin. I do feel safer with a man. The park is so large the grass seems to tilt.
MARTIN: Yes, I'd like to go home and do some work. I'm writing a novel about women from the women's point of view.

(MARTIN *and* BETTY *go.* LIN *and* VICTORIA *are alone. They embrace.*)

VICTORIA: Why the hell can't he just be a wife and come with me? Why does Martin make me tie myself in knots? No wonder we can't just have a simple fuck. No, not Martin, why do I make myself tie myself in knots. It's got to stop, Lin. I'm not like that with you. Would you love me if I went to Manchester? 1720
LIN: Yes.
VICTORIA: Would you love me if I went on a climbing expedition in the Andes mountains?
LIN: Yes.
VICTORIA: Would you love me if my teeth fell out?
LIN: Yes.
VICTORIA: Would you love me if I loved ten other people?
LIN: And me?
VICTORIA: Yes.
LIN: Yes. 1730
VICTORIA: And I feel apologetic for not being quite so subordinate as I was. I am more intelligent than him. I am brilliant.
LIN: Leave him Vic. Come and live with me.
VICTORIA: Don't be silly.
LIN: Silly, Christ, don't then. I'm not asking because I need to live with someone. I'd enjoy it, that's all, we'd both enjoy it. Fuck you. Cathy, for fuck's sake stop throwing stones at the ducks. The man's going to get you.
VICTORIA: What man? Do you need a man to frighten your

1740 child with?

LIN: My mother said it.

VICTORIA: You're so inconsistent, Lin.

LIN: I've changed who I sleep with, I can't change everything.

VICTORIA: Like when I had to stop you getting a job in a boutique and collaborating with sexist consumerism.

LIN: I should have got that job, Cathy would have liked it. Why shouldn't I have some decent clothes? I'm sick of dressing like a boy, why can't I look sexy, wouldn't you love me?

VICTORIA: Lin, you've no analysis.

1750 LIN: No but I'm good at kissing aren't I? I give Cathy guns, my mum didn't give me guns. I dress her in jeans, she wants to wear dresses. I don't know. I can't work it out, I don't want to. You read too many books, you get at me all the time, you're worse to me than Martin is to you, you piss me off, my brother's been killed. I'm sorry to win the argument that way but there it is.

VICTORIA: What do you mean win the argument?

LIN: I mean be nice to me.

VICTORIA: In Belfast?

1760 LIN: I heard this morning. Don't don't start. I've hardly seen him for two years. I rung my father. You'd think I'd shot himself. He doesn't want me to go the funeral.

(CATHY *approaches.*)

VICTORIA: What will you do?

LIN: Go of course.

CATHY: What is it? Who's killed? What?

LIN: It's Bill. Your uncle. In the army. Bill that gave you the blue teddy.

CATHY: Can I have his gun?

LIN: It's time we went home. Time you went to bed.

1770 CATHY: No it's not.

LIN: We go home and you have tea and you have a bath and you go to bed.

CATHY: Fuck off.

LIN: Cathy, shut up.

VICTORIA: It's only half past five, why don't we—

LIN: I'll tell you why she has to go to bed—

VICTORIA: She can come home with me.

LIN: Because I want her out the fucking way.

VICTORIA: She can come home with me.

1780 CATHY: I'm not going to bed.

LIN: I want her home with me not home with you, I want her in bed, I want today over.

CATHY: I'm not going to bed.

(LIN *hits* CATHY, CATHY *cries.*)

LIN: And shut up or I'll give you something to cry for.

CATHY: I'm not going to bed.

VICTORIA: Cathy—

LIN: You keep out of it.

VICTORIA: Lin for God's sake.

(*They are all shouting.* CATHY *runs off.* LIN *and* VICTORIA *are silent. Then they laugh and embrace.*)

LIN: Where's Tommy?

1790 VICTORIA: What? Didn't he go with Martin?

LIN: Did he?

VICTORIA: God oh God.

LIN: Cathy! Cathy!

VICTORIA: I haven't thought about him. How could I not think about him? Tommy!

LIN: Cathy! Come on, quick, I want some help.

VICTORIA: Tommy! Tommy!

(CATHY *comes back.*)

LIN: Where's Tommy? Have you see him? Did he go with Martin? Do you know where he is?

CATHY: I showed him the goose. We went in the bushes.     1800

LIN: Then what?

CATHY: I came back on the swing.

VICTORIA: And Tommy? Where was Tommy?

CATHY: He fed the ducks.

LIN: No that was before.

CATHY: He did a pee in the bushes. I helped him with his trousers.

VICTORIA: And after that?

CATHY: He fed the ducks.

VICTORIA: No no.     1810

CATHY: He liked the ducks. I expect he fell in.

LIN: Did you see him fall in?

VICTORIA: Tommy! Tommy!

LIN: What's the last time you saw him?

CATHY: He did a pee.

VICTORIA: Mummy said he would fall in. Oh God, Tommy!

LIN: We'll go round the pond. We'll go opposite ways round the pond.

ALL: (*Shout*) Tommy!

(VICTORIA *and* LIN *go off opposite sides.* CATHY *climbs the bench.*)

CATHY: Georgie Best, superstar     1820
Walks like a woman and wears a bra.
There he is! I see him! Mum! Vicky! There he is! He's in the bushes.

(LIN *comes back.*)

LIN: Come on Cathy love, let's go home.

CATHY: Vicky's got him.

LIN: Come on.

CATHY: Is she cross?

LIN: No. Come on.

CATHY: I found him.

LIN: Yes. Come on.     1830

(CATHY *gets off the bench.* CATHY *and* LIN *hug.*)

CATHY: I'm watching telly.

LIN: Ok.

CATHY: After the news.

LIN: Ok.

CATHY: I'm not going to bed.

LIN: Yes you are.

CATHY: I'm not going to bed now.

LIN: Not now but early.

CATHY: How early?

LIN: Not late.     1840

CATHY: How not late?

LIN: Early.

CATHY: How early?

LIN: Not late.

(*They go off together.* GERRY *comes on. He waits.* EDWARD *comes.*)

EDWARD: I've got some fish for dinner. I thought I'd make a cheese sauce.

GERRY: I won't be in.

EDWARD: Where are you going?

GERRY: For a start I'm going to a sauna. Then I'll see.

1850 EDWARD: All right. What time will you be back? We'll eat then.

GERRY: You're getting like a wife.

EDWARD: I don't mind that.

GERRY: Why don't I do the cooking sometime?

EDWARD: You can if you like. You're just not so good at it that's all. Do it tonight.

GERRY: I won't be in tonight.

EDWARD: Do it tomorrow. If we can't eat it we can always go to a restaurant.

GERRY: Stop it.

1860 EDWARD: Stop what?

GERRY: Just be yourself.

EDWARD: I don't know what you mean. Everyone's always tried to stop me being feminine and now you are too.

GERRY: You're putting it on.

EDWARD: I like doing the cooking. I like being fucked. You do like me like this really.

GERRY: I'm bored, Eddy.

EDWARD: Go to the sauna.

GERRY: And you'll stay home and wait up for me.

1870 EDWARD: No, I'll go to bed and read a book.

GERRY: Or knit. You could knit me a pair of socks.

EDWARD: I might knit. I like knitting.

GERRY: I don't mind if you knit. I don't want to be married.

EDWARD: I do.

GERRY: Well I'm divorcing you.

EDWARD: I wouldn't want to keep a man who wants his freedom.

GERRY: Eddy, do stop playing the injured wife, it's not funny.

EDWARD: I'm not playing. It's true.

1880 GERRY: I'm not the husband so you can't be the wife.

EDWARD: I'll always be here, Gerry, if you want to come back. I know you men like to go off by yourselves. I don't think I could love deeply more than once. But I don't think I can face life on my own so don't leave it too long or it may be too late.

GERRY: What are you trying to turn me into?

EDWARD: A monster, darling, which is what you are.

GERRY: I'll collect my stuff from the flat in the morning.

(GERRY *goes.* EDWARD *sits on the bench. It gets darker.* VICTORIA *comes.*)

VICTORIA: Tommy dropped a toy car somewhere, you haven't
1890   seen it? It's red. He says it's his best one. Oh the hell with it. Martin's reading him a story. There, isn't it quiet?

(*They sit on the bench, holding hands.*)

EDWARD: I like women.

VICTORIA: That should please mother.

EDWARD: No listen Vicky. I'd rather be a woman. I wish I had breasts like that, I think they're beautiful. Can I touch them?

VICTORIA: What, pretending they're yours?

EDWARD: No, I know it's you.

VICTORIA: I think I should warn you I'm enjoying this.

EDWARD: I'm sick of men.   1900

VICTORIA: I'm sick of men.

EDWARD: I think I'm a lesbian.

## SCENE III

*The park. Summer night.* VICTORIA, LIN *and* EDWARD *drunk.*

LIN: Where are you?

VICTORIA: Come on.

EDWARD: Do we sit in a circle?

VICTORIA: Sit in a triangle.

EDWARD: You're good at mathematics. She's good at mathematics.

VICTORIA: Give me your hand. We all hold hands.

EDWARD: Do you know what to do?   1910

LIN: She's making it up.

VICTORIA: We start off by being quiet.

EDWARD: What?

LIN: Hush.

EDWARD: Will something appear?

VICTORIA: It was your idea.

EDWARD: It wasn't my idea. It was your book.

LIN: You said call up the goddess.

EDWARD: I don't remember saying that.

LIN: We could have called her on the telephone.   1920

EDWARD: Don't be so silly, this is meant to be frightening.

LIN: Kiss me.

VICTORIA: Are we going to do it?

LIN: We're doing it.

VICTORIA: A ceremony.

LIN: It's very sexy, you said it is. You said the women were priests in the temples and fucked all the time. I'm just helping.

VICTORIA: As long as it's sacred.

LIN: It's very sacred.   1930

VICTORIA: Innin, Innana, Nana, Nut, Anat, Anahita, Istar, Isis.

LIN: I can't remember all that.

VICTORIA: Lin! Innin, Innana, Nana, Nut, Anat, Anahita, Istar, Isis.

(LIN *and* EDWARD *join in and continue the chant under* VICTORIA's *speech.*)

Goddess of many names, oldest of the old, who walked in chaos and created life, hear us calling you back through time, before Jehovah, before Christ, before men drove you out and burnt your temples, hear us, Lady, give us back what we were, give us the history we haven't had, make us the women we can't be.   1940

ALL: Innin, Innana, Nana, Nut, Anat, Anahita, Istar, Isis.

(*Chant continues under other speeches.*)

LIN: Come back, goddess.

VICTORIA: Goddess of the sun and the moon her brother, little goddess of Crete with snakes in your hands.

LIN: Goddess of breasts.

VICTORIA: Goddess of cunts.
LIN: Goddess of fat bellies and babies. And blood blood blood.

*(Chant continues.)*

I see her.
EDWARD: What?

*(They stop chanting.)*

1950  LIN: I see her. Very tall. Snakes in her hands. Light light light—
look out! Did I give you a fright?
EDWARD: I was terrified.
VICTORIA: Don't spoil it Lin.
LIN: It's all out of a book.
VICTORIA: Innin Innana—I can't do it now. I was really enjoy-
ing myself.
LIN: She won't appear with a man here.
VICTORIA: They had men, they had sons and lovers.
EDWARD: They had eunuchs.
1960  LIN: Don't give us ideas.
VICTORIA: There's Attis and Tammuz, they're torn to pieces.
EDWARD: Tear me to pieces, Lin.
VICTORIA: The priestess chose a lover for a year and he was king
because she chose him and then he was killed at the end of
the year.
EDWARD: Hurray.
VICTORIA: And the women had the children and nobody knew
it was done by fucking so they didn't know about fathers and
nobody cared who the father was and the property was
1970  passed down through the maternal line—
LIN: Don't turn it into a lecture, Vicky, it's meant to be an orgy.
VICTORIA: It never hurts to understand the theoretical back-
ground. You can't separate fucking and economics.
LIN: Give us a kiss.
EDWARD: Shut up, listen.
LIN: What?
EDWARD: There's somebody there.
LIN: Where?
EDWARD: There.
1980  VICTORIA: The priestesses used to make love to total strangers.
LIN: Go on then, I dare you.
EDWARD: Go on, Vicky.
VICTORIA: He won't know it's a sacred rite in honour of the
goddess.
EDWARD: We'll know.
LIN: We can tell him.
EDWARD: It's not what he thinks, it's what we think.
LIN: Don't tell him till after, he'll run a mile.
VICTORIA: Hello. We're having an orgy. Do you want me to
1990  suck your cock?

*(The stranger approaches. It is* MARTIN.*)*

MARTIN: There you are. I've been looking everywhere. What
the hell are you doing? Do you know what the time is?
You're all pissed out of your minds.

*(They leap on* MARTIN, *pull him down and start to make love
to him.)*

MARTIN: Well that's all right. If all we're talking about is having
a lot of sex there's no problem. I was all for the sixties when
liberation just meant fucking.

*(Another stranger approaches.)*

LIN: Hey you, come here. Come and have sex with us.
VICTORIA: Who is it?

*(The stranger is a soldier.)*

LIN: It's my brother.
EDWARD: Lin, don't.                                              2000
LIN: It's my brother.
VICTORIA: It's her sense of humour, you get used to it.
LIN: Shut up Vicky, it's my brother. Isn't it? Bill?
SOLDIER: Yes it's me.
LIN: And you are dead.
SOLDIER: Fucking dead all right yeh.
LIN: Have you come back to tell us something?
SOLDIER: No I've come for a fuck. That was the worst thing in
the fucking army. Never fucking let out. Can't fucking talk
to Irish girls. Fucking bored out of my fucking head. That or  2010
shit scared. For five minutes I'd be glad I wasn't bored, then
I was fucking scared. Then we'd come in and I'd be glad I
wasn't scared and then I was fucking bored. Spent the day
reading fucking porn and the fucking night wanking. Man's
fucking life in the fucking army? No fun when the fucking
kids hate you. I got so I fucking wanted to kill someone and
I got fucking killed myself and I want a fuck.
LIN: I miss you. Bill. Bill.

*(*LIN *collapses.* SOLDIER *goes.* VICTORIA *comforts* LIN.*)*

EDWARD: Let's go home.
LIN: Victoria, come home with us. Victoria's coming to live  2020
with me and Edward.
MARTIN: Tell me about it in the morning.
LIN: It's true.
VICTORIA: It is true.
MARTIN: Tell me when you're sober.

*(*EDWARD, LIN, VICTORIA *go off together.* MARTIN *goes off alone.*
GERRY *comes on.)*

GERRY: I come here sometimes at night and pick somebody up.
Sometimes I come here at night and don't pick anybody up.
I do also enjoy walking about at night. There's never any
trouble finding someone. I can have sex any time. You might
not find the type you most fancy every day of the week, but  2030
there's plenty of people about who just enjoy having a good
time. I quite like living alone. If I live with someone I get annoyed with them. Edward always put on Capital radio when
he got up. The silence gets wasted. I wake up at four o'clock
sometimes. Birds. Silence. If I bring somebody home I
never let them stay the night. Edward! Edward!

*(*EDWARD *from Act One comes on.)*

EDWARD: Gerry I love you.
GERRY: Yes, I know. I love you, too.
EDWARD: You know what we did? I want to do it again. I think
about it all the time. Don't you want to any more?         2040
GERRY: Yes, of course.

SONG *Cloud Nine* (ALL):
*It'll be fine when you reach Cloud Nine.*

*Mist was rising and the night was dark.*
*Me and my baby took a walk in the park.*
*He said Be mine and you're on Cloud Nine.*

*Better watch out when you're on Cloud Nine.*

> *Smoked some dope on the playground swings*
> *Higher and higher on true love's wings*
> 2050 *He said Be mine and you're on Cloud Nine.*
>
> *Twenty-five years on the same Cloud Nine.*
>
> *Who did she meet on her first blind date?*
> *The guys were no surprise but the lady was great*
> *They were women in love, they were on Cloud Nine.*
>
> *Two the same, they were on Cloud Nine.*
>
> *The bride was sixty-five, the groom was seventeen,*
> *They fucked in the back of the black limousine.*
> *It was divine in their silver Cloud Nine.*
>
> *Simply divine in their silver Cloud Nine.*
>
> 2060 *The wife's lover's children and my lover's wife,*
> *Cooking in my kitchen, confusing my life.*
> *And it's upside down when you reach Cloud Nine.*
>
> *Upside down when you reach Cloud Nine.*

## SCENE IV

*The park. Afternoon in late summer.* MARTIN, CATHY, EDWARD.

CATHY: Under the bramble bushes,
Under the sea boom boom boom,
True love for you my darling,
True love for me my darling,
When we are married,
We'll raise a family.
2070 Boy for you, girl for me,
Boom tiddley oom boom
SEXY.

EDWARD: You'll have Tommy and Cathy tonight then ok? Tommy's still on antibiotics, do make him finish the bottle, he takes it in Ribena. It's no good in orange, he spits it out. Remind me to give you Cathy's swimming things.

CATHY: I did six strokes, didn't I Martin? Did I do a width? How many strokes is a length? How many miles is a swimming pool? I'm going to take my bronze and silver and gold 2080 and diamond.

MARTIN: Is Tommy still wetting the bed?

EDWARD: Don't get angry with him about it.

MARTIN: I just need to go to the launderette so I've got a spare sheet. Of course I don't get fucking angry, Eddy, for God's sake. I don't like to say he is my son but he is my son. I'm surprised I'm not wetting the bed myself.

CATHY: I don't wet the bed ever. Do you wet the bed Martin?

MARTIN: No.

CATHY: You said you did.

*(BETTY comes.)*

2090 BETTY: I do miss the sun living in England but today couldn't be more beautiful. You appreciate the weekend when you're working. Betty's been at work this week, Cathy. It's terrible tiring, Martin, I don't know how you've done it all these years. And the money, I feel like a child with the money, Clive always paid everything but I do understand it perfectly well. Look Cathy let me show you my money.

CATHY: I'll count it. Let me count it. What's that?

BETTY: Five pounds, Five and five is—?

CATHY: One two three—

BETTY: Five and five is ten, and five— 2100

CATHY: If I get it right can I have one?

EDWARD: No you can't.

*(CATHY goes on counting the money.)*

BETTY: I never like to say anything, Martin, or you'll think I'm being a mother-in-law.

EDWARD: Which you are.

BETTY: Thank you, Edward, I'm not talking to you. Martin, I think you're being wonderful. Vicky will come back. Just let her stay with Lin till she sorts herself out. It's very nice for a girl to have a friend; I had friends at school, that was very nice. But I'm sure Lin and Edward don't want her with 2110 them all the time. I'm not at all shocked that Lin and Edward aren't married and she already has a child, we all know first marriages don't always work out. But really Vicky must be in the way. And poor little Tommy. I hear he doesn't sleep properly and he's had a cough.

MARTIN: No, he's fine, Betty, thank you.

CATHY: My bed's horrible. I want to sleep in the big bed with Lin and Vicky and Eddy and I do get in if I've got a bad dream, and my bed's got a bump right in my back. I want to sleep in a tent. 2120

BETTY: Well Tommy has got a nasty cough, Martin, whatever you say.

EDWARD: He's over that. He's got some medicine.

MARTIN: He takes it in Ribena.

BETTY: Well I'm glad to hear it. Look what a lot of money, Cathy, and I sit behind a desk of my own and I answer the telephone and keep the doctor's appointment book and it really is great fun.

CATHY: Can we go camping, Martin, in a tent? We could take the Dead Hand Gang. 2130

BETTY: Not those big boys, Cathy? They're far too big and rough for you. They climb back into the park after dark. I'm sure mummy doesn't let you play with them, does she Edward? Well I don't know.

*(Ice cream bells.)*

CATHY: Ice cream. Martin you promised. I'll have a double ninety-nine. No I'll have a shandy lolly. Betty, you have a shandy lolly and I'll have a lick. No, you have a double ninety-nine and I'll have the chocolate.

*(MARTIN, CATHY and BETTY go, leaving EDWARD, GERRY comes.)*

GERRY: Hello, Eddy. Thought I might find you here.

EDWARD: Gerry. 2140

GERRY: Not working today then?

EDWARD: I don't work here any more.

GERRY: Your mum got you into a dark suit?

EDWARD: No of course not. I'm on the dole. I am working, though, I do housework.

GERRY: Whose wife are you now then?

EDWARD: Nobody's. I don't think like that any more. I'm living with some women.

GERRY: What women?

EDWARD: It's my sister, Vic, and her lover. They go out to work 2150 and I look after the kids.

GERRY: I thought for a moment you said you were living

with women.

EDWARD: We do sleep together, yes.

GERRY: I was passing the park anyway so I thought I'd look in. I was in the sauna the other night and I saw someone who looked like you but it wasn't. I had sex with him anyway.

EDWARD: I do go to the sauna sometimes.

(CATHY *comes, gives* EDWARD *an ice cream, goes.*)

GERRY: I don't think I'd like living with children. They make a 2160 lot of noise don't they?

EDWARD: I tell them to shut up and they shut up. I wouldn't want to leave them at the moment.

GERRY: Look why don't we go for a meal sometime?

EDWARD: Yes I'd like that. Where are you living now?

GERRY: Same place.

EDWARD: I'll come round for you tomorrow night about 7:30.

GERRY: Great.

(EDWARD *goes.* HARRY *comes.* HARRY *and* GERRY *pick each other up. They go off.* BETTY *comes back.*)

BETTY: No, the ice cream was my treat, Martin. Off you go. I'm going to have a quiet sit in the sun.

(MAUD *comes.*)

2170 MAUD: Let Mrs Saunders be a warning to you, Betty. I know what it is to be unprotected.

BETTY: But mother, I have a job. I earn money.

MAUD: I know we have our little differences but I always want what is best for you.

(ELLEN *comes.*)

ELLEN: Betty, what happens with a man?

BETTY: You just keep still.

ELLEN: And is it enjoyable? Don't forget me, Betty.

(MAUD *and* ELLEN *go.*)

BETTY: I used to think Clive was the one who liked sex. But then I found I missed it. I used to touch myself when I was 2180 very little, I thought I'd invented something wonderful. I used to do it to go to sleep with or to cheer myself up, and one day it was raining and I was under the kitchen table, and my mother saw me with my hand under my dress rubbing away, and she dragged me out so quickly I hit my head and it bled and I was sick, and nothing was said, and I never did it again till this year. I thought if Clive wasn't looking at me there wasn't a person there. And one night in bed in my flat I was so frightened I started touching myself. I thought my hand might go through space. I touched my face, it was 2190 there, my arm, my breast, and my hand went down where I thought it shouldn't, and I thought well there is somebody there. It felt very sweet, it was a feeling from very long ago, it was very soft, just barely touching, and I felt myself gathering together more and more and I felt angry with Clive and angry with my mother and I went on and on defying them, and there was this vast feeling growing in me and all round me and they couldn't stop me and no one could stop me and I was there and coming and coming. Afterwards I thought I'd betrayed Clive. My mother would kill me. But I 2200 felt triumphant because I was a separate person from them. And I cried because I didn't want to be. But I don't cry

about it any more. Sometimes I do it three times in one night and it really is great fun.

(VICTORIA *and* LIN *come in.*)

VICTORIA: So I said to the professor, I don't think this is an occasion for invoking the concept of structural causality—oh hello mummy.

BETTY: I'm going to ask you a question, both of you. I have a little money from your grandmother. And the three of you are living in that tiny flat with two children. I wonder if we could get a house and all live in it together? It would give you more 2210 room.

VICTORIA: But I'm going to Manchester anyway.

LIN: We'd have a garden, Vicky.

BETTY: You do seem to have such fun all of you.

VICTORIA: I don't want to.

BETTY: I didn't think you would.

LIN: Come on, Vicky, she knows we sleep together, and Eddy.

BETTY: I think I've known for quite a while but I'm not sure. I don't usually think about it, so I don't know if I know about it or not. 2220

VICTORIA: I don't want to live with my mother.

LIN: Don't think of her as your mother, think of her as Betty.

VICTORIA: But she thinks of herself as my mother.

BETTY: I am your mother.

VICTORIA: But mummy we don't even like each other.

BETTY: We might begin to.

(CATHY *comes on howling with a nosebleed.*)

LIN: Oh Cathy what happened?

BETTY: She's been assaulted.

VICTORIA: It's a nosebleed.

CATHY: Took my ice cream.                                     2230

LIN: Who did?

CATHY: Took my money.

(MARTIN *comes.*)

MARTIN: Is everything all right?

LIN: I thought you were looking after her.

CATHY: They hit me. I can't play. They said I'm a girl.

BETTY: Those dreadful boys, the gang, the Dead Hand.

MARTIN: What do you mean you thought I was looking after her?

LIN: Last I saw her she was with you getting an ice cream. It's your afternoon.                                         2240

MARTIN: Then she went off to play. She goes off to play. You don't keep an eye on her every minute.

LIN: She doesn't get beaten up when I'm looking after her.

CATHY: Took my money.

MARTIN: Why the hell should I look after your child anyway? I just want Tommy. Why should he live with you and Vicky all week?

LIN: I don't mind if you don't want to look after her but don't say you will and then this happens.

VICTORIA: When I get to Manchester everything's going to be 2250 different anyway, Lin's staying here, and you're staying here, we're all going to have to sit down and talk it through.

MARTIN: I'd really enjoy that.

CATHY: Hit me on the face.

LIN: You were the one looking after her and look at her now, that's all.

MARTIN: I've had enough of you telling me.

LIN: Yes you know it all.

MARTIN: Now stop it. I work very hard at not being like this, I could do with some credit.

LIN: Ok you're quite nice, try and enjoy it. Don't make me sorry for you, Martin, it's hard for me too. We've better things to do than quarrel. I've got to go and sort those little bastards out for a start. Where are they, Cathy?

CATHY: Don't kill them, mum, hit them. Give them a nosebleed, mum.

(LIN *goes.*)

VICTORIA: Tommy's asleep in the pushchair. We'd better wake him up or he won't sleep tonight.

MARTIN: Sometimes I keep him up watching television till he falls asleep on the sofa so I can hold him. Come on, Cathy, we'll get another ice cream.

CATHY: Chocolate sauce and nuts.

VICTORIA: Betty, would you like an ice cream?

BETTY: No thank you, the cold hurts my teeth, but what a nice thought, Vicky, thank you.

(VICTORIA *goes.* BETTY *alone.* GERRY *comes.*)

BETTY: I think you used to be Edward's flatmate.

GERRY: You're his mother. He's talked about you.

BETTY: Well never mind. Children are always wrong about their parents. It's great problem knowing where to live and who to share with. I live by myself just now.

GERRY: Good. So do I. You can do what you like.

BETTY: I don't really know what I like.

GERRY: You'll soon find out.

BETTY: What do you like?

GERRY: Waking up at four in the morning.

BETTY: I like listening to music in bed and sometimes for supper I just have a big piece of bread and dip it in very hot lime pickle. So you don't get lonely by yourself? Perhaps you have a lot of visitors. I've been thinking I should have some visitors, I could give a little dinner party. Would you come? There wouldn't just be bread and lime pickle.

GERRY: Thank you very much.

BETTY: Or don't wait to be asked to dinner. Just drop in informally. I'll give you the address shall I? I don't usually give strange men my address but then you're not a strange man, you're a friend of Edward's. I suppose I seem a different generation to you but you are older than Edward. I was married for so many years it's quite hard to know how to get acquainted. But if there isn't a right way to do things you have to invent one. I always thought my mother was far too old to be attractive but when you get to an age yourself it feels quite different.

GERRY: I think you could be quite attractive.

BETTY: If what?

GERRY: If you stop worrying.

BETTY: I think when I do more about things I worry about them less. So perhaps you could help me do more.

GERRY: I might be going to live with Edward again.

BETTY: That's nice, but I'm rather surprised if he wants to share a flat. He's rather involved with a young woman he lives with, or two young women, I don't understand Edward but never mind.

GERRY: I'm very involved with him.

BETTY: I think Edward did try to tell me once but I didn't listen. So what I'm being told now is that Edward is "gay" is that right? And you are too. And I've being making rather a fool of myself. But Edward does also sleep with women.

GERRY: He does, yes, I don't.

BETTY: Well people always say it's the mother's fault but I don't intend to start blaming myself. He seems perfectly happy.

GERRY: I could still come and see you.

BETTY: So you could, yes, I'd like that. I've never tried to pick up a man before.

GERRY: Not everyone's gay.

BETTY: No, that's lucky isn't it.

(GERRY *goes.* CLIVE *comes.*)

CLIVE: You are not that sort of woman, Betty. I can't believe you are. I can't feel the same about you as I did. And Africa is to be communist I suppose. I used to be proud to be British. There was a high ideal. I came out onto the verandah and looked at the stars.

(CLIVE *goes.* BETTY *from Act One comes.* BETTY *and* BETTY *embrace.*)

## Mad Forest (1990)

Caryl Churchill's *Mad Forest* concerns the Romanian revolution of 1989–1990 and the effects of living in a police state on the lives of two families—the working-class Vladu family and the more professional Antonescu family—both before and after the revolution. As with much of Churchill's earlier theater work, the play was devised collaboratively, when Churchill, director Mark Wing-Davey, and a group of acting students from London's Central School of Speech and Drama went to work with students in Romania in March of 1990—only three months after the fighting in Timosoara and Bucharest, and the capture and execution of Romanian President Nicolae Ceausescu.

The political struggles of the revolution are the background to Churchill's play, which focuses more closely on the lives of the two Romanian families. Part One takes place before the revolution; entitled "Lucia's Wedding," it uses the wedding as a centerpiece to reflect life in a police state. Lucia Vladu's intention of marrying an American leads the Securitate police to blackmail her father into turning over the names of Lucia's and her fiancé's contacts; fear of police involvement leads Radu Antonescu's family to fear that his connection with Lucia's sister Florina will bring state reprisals. In Part Two, a series of characters narrate events from the revolution. Churchill's technique of using several voices each to narrate his or her personal history suggests the impossibility of imposing a single narrative on the fragmentary and dispersed events of contemporary history. In Part Three, the two families are drawn together for the wedding of Florina and Radu; Gabriel has been crippled in the fighting, and Lucia is back from America and pursuing a new relationship with the Hungarian Ianoş. Although the state has changed, in some ways the lives of the characters have not—Ianoş still suffers persecution as a gypsy, Lucia's father Bogdan still feels that the government needs a "strong man" to impose rule, and the meaning of the revolution and the direction in which it will take the country seem very much undecided.

One way into the play is through the stunning scene between the Dog and the Vampire at the opening of Part Three. Coming onstage on the heels of the revolution-narratives, the Vampire's lust for blood—"you try to put it off, you're bored with killing, but you can't sit quiet, you can't settle to anything, your limbs ache, your head burns, you have to keep moving faster and faster, that eases the pain"—seems like a metaphor for the insurrection at hand. In the scene, he comes upon a Dog, usually played by a naked male actor, who is desperate for a master, even if it means becoming a vampire himself. At the center of the play, Churchill provides a provocative image of the revolutionary situation—for as Part Three demonstrates, even after the revolution, the lust for domination continues to pervade the society, a society that is unused to living without masters.

The Vampire scene also allegorizes the action of the play, suggesting that the problems of radical social change are not unique to Romania. One way that Churchill prevents the audience from adopting a "superior" interpretive position to the action of the play is by conducting much of the action in two languages. Much like the characters onstage, the production catches *us* in events that are not fully readable, comprehensible to us while they are taking place.

# —Mad Forest—
## Caryl Churchill

■ ■ ■ On the plain where Bucharest now stands there used to be "a large forest crossed by small muddy streams . . . It could only be crossed on foot and was impenetrable for the foreigner who did not know the paths . . . The horsemen of the steppe were compelled to go round it, and this difficulty, which irked them so, is shown by the name . . . Teleorman—Mad Forest."

"A CONCISE HISTORY OF ROMANIA," OTETEA AND MACKENZIE

## —PRODUCTION NOTE—

Since the play goes from the difficulty of saying anything to everyone talking, don't be afraid of long silences. For instance, in Scene One, the silence before Bogdan turns up the music was a good fifteen seconds in our production. Short scenes like 13 and 15 need to be given their weight. Don't add additional dialogue (for instance in queues, party or arrival in country) except in III 6 where "etc" means there can be other things shouted by the spectators.

The queue scenes and execution scene should have as many people as are available. In the execution scene it is the violence of the spectators which is the main focus rather than the execution itself.

We didn't use a prop rat.

The Vampire was not dressed as a vampire.

In Part II (December) the language of the different characters varies with how well they speak English, and this should be reflected in their accents.

In the hospital and party scenes it is particularly important that the short scenes within them are not run together and that time has clearly passed.

Music. As in the text, the music after the opening poem becomes the music on the Vladu radio. It's not essential to do what we did with the music, but it may be helpful to know that at the end of the wedding we used a hymn to the Ceausescus and continued the music till everyone was in place for the beginning of December; at the end of December the whole company sang a verse from "Wake up Romania" in Romanian, which then merged with a recording of it; we had music at the beginning of Part III. The party music in III should be western euro-pop. The dance music should be the lambada—this is not an arbitrary choice, it was the popular dance at the time. The nightmare scene and the very end of the play probably need sound.

Words for the poem at the beginning and words and music for "Wake up Romania" can be got from Margaret Ramsay Ltd.

Caryl Churchill and Mark Wing-Davey
March 1991

## —CHARACTERS—

VLADU FAMILY
   BOGDAN, an electrician
   IRINA, a tramdriver
   their children:
   LUCIA, a primary school teacher
   FLORINA, a nurse
   GABRIEL, an engineer

   RODICA, Gabriel's wife
   WAYNE, Lucia's bridegroom

   GRANDFATHER, Bogdan's father
   GRANDMOTHER, Bogdan's mother
   OLD AUNT, Bogdan's aunt

ANTONESCU FAMILY
   MIHAI, an architect
   FLAVIA, a teacher
   RADU, an art student, their son
   GRANDMOTHER, Flavia's grandmother, who is dead.

IANOŞ
SECURITATE MAN
DOCTOR
PRIEST
ANGEL
VAMPIRE
DOG
SOMEONE WITH SORE THROAT
PATIENT

TWO SOLDIERS

TOMA, age 8
GHOST
WAITER

PAINTER
GIRL STUDENT
2 BOY STUDENTS

TRANSLATOR
BULLDOZER DRIVER

SECURITATE OFFICER
SOLDIER
STUDENT DOCTOR
FLOWERSELLER
HOUSEPAINTER

PEOPLE IN QUEUES AND WEDDING GUESTS played by members of the company

NOTES ON LAYOUT

A speech usually follows the one immediately before it BUT:

(1) When one character starts speaking before the other has finished, the point of interruption is marked / and the first character continues talking regardless:

> e.g.
> GABRIEL: They came to the office yesterday and gave us one of their usual pep talks and at the end one of them took me aside / and said we'd like to see
> IRINA: Wait.
> GABRIEL: you tomorrow. So I know what that meant . . .

(2) Sometimes two speakers interrupt at once while the first speaker continues:°

> e.g.
> FLAVIA: Why don't the Front tell the truth and admit they're communists? /°Nothing to be
> MIHAI: Because they're not.
> RADU: °I don't care what they're called, it's the same people.
> FLAVIA: ashamed of in communism . . .

Here both MIHAI and RADU interrupt FLAVIA at the same point.

### —I. LUCIA'S WEDDING—

*The company recite, smiling, a poem in Romanian in praise of Elena Ceauşescu.*

*Stirring Romanian music.*

*Each scene is announced by one of the company reading from a phrasebook as if an English tourist, first in Romanian, then in English, and again in Romanian.*

### SCENE I
### 1. LUCIA ARE PATRU OUĂ. LUCIA HAS FOUR EGGS.

*Music continues.* BOGDAN *and* IRINA VLADU *sit in silence, smoking Romanian cigarettes.*
BOGDAN *turns up the music on the radio very loud. He sits looking at* IRINA.
IRINA *puts her head close to* BOGDAN's *and talks quickly and quietly, to convince him.*
*He argues back, she insists, he gets angry. We can't hear anything they say.*
*They stop talking and sit with the music blaring.* BOGDAN *is about to speak when* FLORINA *and* LUCIA *come in, laughing.*
*They stop laughing and look at* BOGDAN *and* IRINA.
IRINA *turns the radio down low.*
LUCIA *produces four eggs with a flourish.* IRINA *kisses her.*
BOGDAN *ignores her.*
LUCIA *produces a packet of American cigarettes.*
FLORINA *laughs.*

LUCIA *opens the cigarettes and offers them to* IRINA. *She hesitates, then puts out her cigarette and takes one.* FLORINA *takes one.*
BOGDAN *ignores them.*
LUCIA *offers a cigarette to* BOGDAN, *he shakes his head.*
LUCIA *takes a cigarette. They sit smoking.*
BOGDAN *finishes his cigarette. He sits without smoking. Then he takes a cigarette.*
LUCIA *and* FLORINA *laugh.*
BOGDAN *picks up an egg and breaks it on the floor.*
IRINA *gathers the other eggs to safety.*
LUCIA *and* FLORINA *keep still.*
IRINA *turns the radio up loud and is about to say something.*
BOGDAN *turns the radio completely off.* IRINA *ignores him and smokes.*
FLORINA *gets a cup and spoon and scrapes up what she can of the egg off the floor.*
LUCIA *keeps still.*

### SCENE II
### 2. CINE ARE UN CHIBRIT? WHO HAS A MATCH?

ANTONESCU *family, noticeably better off than the* VLADUS. MIHAI *thinking and making notes,* FLAVIA *correcting exercise books,* RADU *drawing.*

*They sit in silence for some time. When they talk they don't look up from what they're doing.*

MIHAI: He came today.

FLAVIA: That's exciting.

RADU: Did he make you change it?

MIHAI: He had a very interesting recommendation. The arch should be this much higher.

RADU: And the columns?

MIHAI: We will make an improvement to the spacing of the columns.

FLAVIA: That sounds good.

*(They go on working.)*
*(The lights go out. They are resigned, almost indifferent.)*
*(RADU takes a match and lights a candle.)*
*(They sit in candlelight in silence.)*

10   RADU: I don't see why.

FLAVIA: We've said no.

RADU: If I leave it a year or two till after the wedding, I / could—

FLAVIA: No.

RADU: It's not her fault if her sister—

MIHAI: The whole family. No. Out of the question.

*(Pause.)*

There are plenty of other girls, Radu.

*(They sit in silence.)*
*(The lights come on.)*
*(FLAVIA blows out the candle and snuffs it with her fingers.)*
*(They all start reading again.)*

RADU: So is that the third time he's made you change it?

*(MIHAI doesn't reply. They go on working.)*

## SCENE III
### 3. EA ARE O SCRISOARE DIN STATELE UNITE. SHE HAS A LETTER FROM THE UNITED STATES.

LUCIA *is reading an airmail letter, smiling. She kisses the letter. She puts it away.* FLORINA *comes in from work.*

LUCIA: Tired?

*(Pause. FLORINA is taking off her shoes.)*

20   I'm sorry.

*(FLORINA smiles and shrugs.)*

LUCIA: No but all of you . . . because of me and Wayne.

FLORINA: You love him.

*(LUCIA takes out the letter and offers it to FLORINA.)*
*(FLORINA hesitates. LUCIA insists.)*
*(FLORINA reads the letter, she is serious. LUCIA watches her.)*
*(FLORINA gives the letter back.)*

LUCIA: And Radu? Have you seen him lately?

*(FLORINA shrugs.)*

## SCENE IV
### 4. ELEVII ASCULTA LECŢIĂ THE PUPILS LISTEN TO THE LESSON.

FLAVIA *speaks loudly and confidently to her pupils.*

FLAVIA: Today we are going to learn about a life dedicated to the happiness of the people and noble ideas of socialism. The new history of the motherland is like a great river with its fundamental starting point in the biography of our general secretary, the president of the republic, Comrade Nicolae Ceauşescu, and it flows through the open spaces of the important dates and problems of contemporary humanity. 30 Because it's evident to everybody that linked to the personality of this great son of the nation is everything in the country that is most durable and harmonious, the huge transformations taking place in all areas of activity, the ever more vigorous and ascendant path towards the highest stages of progress and civilisation. He is the founder of the country. More, he is the founder of man. For everything is being built for the sublime development of man and country, for their material and spiritual wellbeing. He started his revolutionary activity in the earliest years of his adolescence 40 in conditions of danger and illegality, therefore his life and struggle cannot be detached from the most burning moments of the people's fight against fascism and war to achieve the ideals of freedom and aspirations of justice and progress.

We will learn the biography under four headings.

1. village of his birth and prison
2. revolution
3. leadership
4. the great personality of Comrade Nicolae Ceauşescu.   50

## SCENE V
### 5. CUMPĂRĂM CARNE. WE ARE BUYING MEAT.

RADU *is in a queue of people with shopping bags. They stand a long time in silence.*

*Someone leaves a bag with a bottle in it to mark the place and goes. They go on standing.*

*(RADU whispers loudly.)*

RADU: Down with Ceauşescu.

*(The woman in front of him starts to look round, then pretends she hasn't heard. The man behind pretends he hasn't heard and casually steps slightly away from RADU.)*
*(Two people towards the head of the queue look round and RADU looks round as if wondering who spoke. They go on queueing.)*

## SCENE VI
### 6. DOI OAMENI STAU LA SOARE. TWO MEN ARE SITTING IN THE SUN.

BOGDAN *and a* SECURITATE *MAN.*

SECURITATE: Do you love your country?

*(BOGDAN nods.)*

And how do you show it?

*(Pause.)*

You love your country, how do you show it?

*(BOGDAN is about to speak. He stops. He is about to speak.)*

You encourage your daughter to marry an American.

BOGDAN: No.

SECURITATE: She defies you?

(*Silence.*)

Your daughter was trained as a primary school teacher, she can no longer be employed. Romania has wasted resources
60  that could have benefited a young woman with a sense of duty.

(*Silence.*)

I understand your wife works as a tramdriver and has recently been transferred to a depot in the south of the city which doubles the time she has to travel to work. You are an electrician, you have been a foreman for some time but alas no longer. Your son is an engineer and is so far doing well. Your other daughter is a nurse. So far there is nothing against her except her sister.

(*Pause.*)

I'm sure you are eager to show that your family are patriots.

(*Silence.* BOGDAN *looks away.*)

70  When they know your daughter wants to marry an American, people may confide their own shameful secrets. They may mistakenly think you are someone who has sympathy with foreign regimes. Your other children may make undesirable friends who think you're prepared to listen to what they say. They will be right. You will listen.

(*Pause.* BOGDAN *is about to say something but doesn't.*)

What?

(*Pause.*)

Your colleagues will know you have been demoted and will wrongly suppose that you are short of money. As a patriot you may not have noticed how anyone out of favour attracts
80  the friendship of irresponsible bitter people who feel slighted. Be friendly.

(*Pause.*)

What a beautiful day. What a beautiful country.

(*Silence.* BOGDAN *looks at him.*)

You will make a report once a week.

## SCENE VII
### 7. ASCULTAŢI? ARE YOU LISTENING?

LUCIA *and a* DOCTOR.

*While they talk the* DOCTOR *writes on a piece of paper, pushes it over to* LUCIA, *who writes a reply, and he writes again.*

DOCTOR: You're a slut. You've brought this on yourself. The only thing to be said in its favour is that one more child is one more worker.

LUCIA: Yes, I realise that.

DOCTOR: There is no abortion in Romania. I am shocked that you even think of it. I am appalled that you dare suggest I
90  might commit this crime.

LUCIA: Yes, I'm sorry.

(LUCIA *gives the doctor an envelope thick with money and some more money.*)

DOCTOR: Can you get married?

LUCIA: Yes.

DOCTOR: Good. Get married.

(*The* DOCTOR *writes again,* LUCIA *nods.*)

DOCTOR: I can do nothing for you. Goodbye.

(LUCIA *smiles. She makes her face serious again.*)

LUCIA: Goodbye.

## SCENE VIII
### 8. STICLA CU VIN ESTE PE MASĂ. THE BOTTLE OF WINE IS ON THE TABLE.

RADU, GABRIEL *and* IANOŞ *with a bottle of wine. They are in public so they keep their voices down.*

IANOŞ: He died and went to heaven and St Peter says, God wants a word with you. So he goes in to see God and God says, "I hear you think you're greater than me." And he says, "Yes, I am." And God says, "Right, who made the sun?" "You 100 did." "Who made the stars?" "You did." "Who made the earth?" "You did." "Who made all the people and all the animals and all the trees and all the / plants and—

RADU: And all the wine.

IANOŞ: And everything?" And he said, "You did, God." And God says, "Then how can you possibly be greater than me?" And he says, "All these things, what did you make them from?" And God said, "Chaos, I made it all out of Chaos." "There you are," he said, "I made chaos."

RADU: A cosmonaut leaves a message for his wife. "Gone to 110 Mars, back in two weeks." Two weeks later he comes back and his wife has left him a message. "Gone shopping, don't know when I'll be back."

GABRIEL: A man wants a car and he saves up his money and at last he's able to buy a Trabant. He's very proud of it. And he's driving along in his little Trabant and he stops at the traffic lights and bang, a car crashes into the back of it. So he leaps out very angry, and it's a black car with a short numberplate, but he's so angry he doesn't care and he starts banging on the bonnet. Then a big dumper truck stops be- 120 hind the black car and the driver gets out and he takes a crowbar and he starts smashing the back of the black car. And the Securitate man gets out of his battered black car and he says to the truck driver, "What's going on? I can understand him being upset because I hit his car, but what's the matter with you?" And the driver says, "Sorry, I thought it had started."

## SCENE IX
### 9. CERUL ESTE ALBASTRU. THE SKY IS BLUE.

*An* ANGEL *and a* PRIEST.

ANGEL: Don't be ashamed. When people come into church they are free. Even if they know there are Securitate in church with them. Even if some churches are demolished, 130 so long as there are some churches standing. Even if you say Ceauşescu, Ceauşescu, because the Romanian church is a church of freedom. Not outer freedom of course but inner freedom.

(*Silence. The* PRIEST *sits gazing at the* ANGEL.)

PRIEST: This is so sweet, like looking at the colour blue, like looking at the sky when you're a child lying on your back, you stare out at the blue but you're going in, further and further in away from the world, that's what it's like knowing I can talk to you. Someone says something, you say something back, you're called to a police station, that happened to my brother. So it's not safe to go out to people and when you can't go out sometimes you find you can't go in, I'm afraid to go inside myself, perhaps there's nothing there. I just keep still. But I can talk to you, no one's ever known an angel work for the Securitate, I go out into the blue and I sink down and down inside myself, and yes then I am free inside, I can fly about in that blue, that is what the church can give people, they can fly about inside in that blue.

ANGEL: So when the Romanian church writes a letter to the other Christian churches apologising for not taking a stand / against—

PRIEST: Don't talk about it. I'd just managed to forget.

ANGEL: Don't be ashamed. There was no need for them to write the letter because there's no question of taking a stand, it's not the job of the church / to—

PRIEST: Everyone will think we're cowards.

ANGEL: No no no. Flying about in the blue.

PRIEST: Yes. Yes.

*(Pause.)*

You've never been political?

ANGEL: Very little. The Iron Guard used to be rather charming and called themselves the League of the Archangel Michael and carried my picture about. They had lovely processions. So I dabbled.

PRIEST: But they were fascists.

ANGEL: They were mystical.

PRIEST: The Iron Guard threw Jews out of windows in '37, my father remembers it. He shouted and they beat him up.

ANGEL: Politics, you see. Their politics weren't very pleasant. I try to keep clear of the political side. You should do the same.

*(Pause.)*

PRIEST: I don't trust you any more.

ANGEL: That's a pity. Who else can you trust?

*(Pause.)*

Would you rather feel ashamed?

*(Pause.)*

Or are you going to take some kind of action, surely not?

*(Silence.)*

PRIEST: Comfort me.

## SCENE X

**10. ACESTA ESTE FRATELE NOSTRU. THIS IS OUR BROTHER.**

BOGDAN, IRINA, LUCIA, FLORINA, *sitting in the dark with candles.* IRINA *is sewing* LUCIA's *wedding dress.*

GABRIEL *arrives, excited.*

GABRIEL: Something happened today. / They came to

IRINA: Wait.

*(IRINA moves to turn on the radio, then remembers it isn't working.)*

GABRIEL: the office yesterday and gave us their usual pep talk and at the end one of them took me aside / and said we'd like to see you

IRINA: Wait.

GABRIEL: tomorrow. So I knew what that meant, they were going to ask me / to do something for

IRINA: Wait, stop, there's no power.

GABRIEL: them. I prayed all night I'd be strong enough to say no, I was so afraid I'd be persuaded, / I've never been brave. So I went in and they said . . .

IRINA: Gaby, stop, be quiet.

FLORINA: No, what if they do hear it, they know what they did.

GABRIEL: And they said, "What is patriotism?" I said, "It's doing all you can, working as hard as possible." And they said, / "We thought you might

BOGDAN: Gabriel.

FLORINA: No, let him.

*(IRINA puts her hands over her ears. But after a while she starts to listen again.)*

GABRIEL: not understand patriotism because your sister and this and this, but if you're a patriot you'll want to help us. And I said, "Of course I'd like to help you," and then I actually remembered, listen to this, "As Comrade Ceauşescu says, 'For each and every citizen work is an honorary fundamental duty. Each of us should demonstrate high professional probity, competence, creativity, devotion and passion in our work.' And because I'm a patriot I work so hard that I can't think about anything else, I wouldn't be able to listen to what my colleagues talk about because I have to concentrate. I work right through the lunch hour." And I stuck to it and they couldn't do anything. And I'm so happy because I've put myself on the other side, I hardly knew there was one. They made me promise never to tell anyone they'd asked me, and they made me sign something, I didn't care by then, I'd won, so I signed it, not my wife or my parents, it said that specifically because they know what the first thing is you'd do, and of course I'm doing it because I don't care, I'm going straight home to Rodica to tell her, I'm so happy, and I've come to share it with you because I knew you'd be proud of me.

IRINA: But you signed. You shouldn't tell us. I didn't hear.

*(FLORINA kisses GABRIEL.)*

FLORINA: But Radu's right to keep away from us.

*(Pause.)*

BOGDAN: You're a good boy.

GABRIEL: I was shaking. The first thing when I went in they said—

*(BODGAN holds up his hand and GABRIEL, stops. Pause.)*

LUCIA: What if I don't get my passport?

## SCENE XI

**11. UITE! LOOK!**

*A* SOLDIER *and a* WAITER *stand smoking in the street. Suddenly one of them shouts "Rat!" and they chase it.* RADU, IANOŞ *and*

GABRIEL *pass and join in. The rat is kicked about like a football. Then* RADU, IANOŞ *and* GABRIEL *go on their way and the* SOL-DIER *and the* WAITER *go back to smoking.*

## SCENE XII
### 12. EU O VIZITEZ PE NEPOATA MEA. I AM VISITING MY GRANDDAUGHTER.

FLAVIA *and* MIHAI *sitting silently over their work.*

FLAVIA'S GRANDMOTHER, *who is dead. She is an elegant woman in her 50s.*

GRANDMOTHER: Flavia, your life will soon be over. You're nearly as old as I was when you were a little girl. You thought I was old then but you don't think you're old.

FLAVIA: Yes I do. I look at my children's friends and I know I'm old.

GRANDMOTHER: No, you still think your life hasn't started. You think it's ahead.

FLAVIA: Everyone feels like that.

230 GRANDMOTHER: How do you know? Who do you talk to? Your closest friend is your grandmother and I'm dead, Flavia, don't forget that or you really will be mad.

FLAVIA: You want me to live in the past? I do, I remember being six years old in the mountains, isn't that what old people do?

GRANDMOTHER: You remember being a child, Flavia, because you're childish. You remember expecting a treat.

FLAVIA: Isn't that good? Imagine still having hope at my age. I admire myself.

240 GRANDMOTHER: You're pretending this isn't your life. You think it's going to happen some other time. When you're dead you'll realize you were alive now. When I was your age the war was starting. I welcomed the Nazis because I thought they'd protect us from the Russians and I welcomed the Communists because I thought they'd protect us from the Germans. I had no principles. My husband was killed. But at least I knew that was what happened to me. There were things I did. I did them. Or sometimes I did nothing. It was me doing nothing.

(*Silence.*)

250 FLAVIA: Mihai.

MIHAI: Mm?

FLAVIA: Do you ever think . . . if you think of something you'll do . . . do you ever think you'll be young when you do it? Do you think I'll do that next time I'm twenty? Not really exactly think it because of course it doesn't make sense but almost . . . not exactly think it but . . .

(MIHAI *shakes his head and goes back to his work.*)

FLAVIA: Yes, my life is over.

GRANDMOTHER: I didn't say that.

FLAVIA: I don't envy the young, there's nothing ahead for them
260    either. I'm nearer dying and that's fine.

GRANDMOTHER: You're not used to listening. What did I say?

(*Pause.*)

FLAVIA: But nobody's living. You can't blame me.

GRANDMOTHER: You'd better start.

FLAVIA: No, Granny, it would hurt.

GRANDMOTHER: Well.

(*Silence.*)

FLAVIA: Mihai.

(MIHAI *goes on working.*)

Mihai.

(*He looks up. Silence.*)

## SCENE XIII
### 13. CE ORĂ ESTE? WHAT'S THE TIME?

LUCIA *and* IANOŞ *standing in silence with their arms round each other.*

*She looks at her watch, he puts his hand over it.*

*They go on standing.*

## SCENE XIV
### 14. UNDE ESTE TROLEIBUZUL? WHERE IS THE TROLLEYBUS?

*People waiting for a bus, including* RADU.

FLORINA *joins the queue. She doesn't see him.*

*He sees her. He looks away.*

*She sees him without him noticing, she looks away.*

*He looks at her again, they see each other and greet each other awkwardly. They look away.*

RADU *goes up to her.*

RADU: How are you?

FLORINA: Fine.                                                         270

RADU: And your family?

FLORINA: Fine, and yours?

RADU: So when's Lucia's wedding?

FLORINA: You know when it is.

(*They stand apart waiting for the bus.*)

## SCENE XV
### 15. PE IRINA O DOARE CAPUL. IRINA HAS A HEADACHE.

LUCIA *is trying on her wedding dress, helped by* IRINA.

## SCENE XVI
### 16. LUCIA ARE O COROANĂ DE AUR. LUCIA HAS A GOLDEN CROWN.

*The wedding.* LUCIA *and* WAYNE *are being married by the* PRIEST. BOGDAN, IRINA, FLORINA, GABRIEL *and* RODICA. *Other guests.*

*Two wedding crowns. The* PRIEST *crosses* WAYNE *with a crown, saying:*

PRIEST: The servant of God Wayne is crowned for the hand-maid of God Lucia, in the name of the father, and of the son, and of the holy spirit.

ALL: (sing) Amen.

(This is repeated three times, then the PRIEST puts the crown on WAYNE's head. He crosses LUCIA with a crown saying:)

280 PRIEST: The handmaid of God Lucia is crowned for the servant of God Wayne, in the name of the father, and of the son, and of the holy spirit.

ALL: (sing) Amen.

(This is repeated three times, then the PRIEST puts the crown on LUCIA's head.)
(Music.)

## —II. DECEMBER—

None of the characters in this section are the characters in the play that began in part I. They are all Romanians speaking to us in English with Romanian accents. Each behaves as if the others are not there and each is the only one telling what happened.

PAINTER: My name is Valentin Bărbat, I am a painter, I hope to go to the Art Institute. I like to paint horses. Other things too but I like horses. On December 20 my girlfriend got a call, go to the Palace Square. People were wearing black armbands for Timişoara. There was plenty of people but no courage. Nothing happened that day and we went home.

GIRL STUDENT: My name's Natalia Moraru, I'm a student. On 290 the 21st of December I had a row with my mother at breakfast about something trivial and I went out in a rage. There was nothing unusual, some old men talking, a few plain-clothes policemen, they think they're clever but everyone knows who they are because of their squashed faces.

TRANSLATOR: I'm Dimitru Constantinescu, I work as a translator in a translation agency. On the 21st we were listening to the radio in the office to hear Ceauşescu's speech. It was frightfully predictable. People had been brought from factories and institutes on buses and he wanted their approval 300 for putting down what he called the hooligans in Timişoara. Then suddenly we heard boos and the radio went dead. So we knew something had happened. We were awfully startled. Everyone was shaking.

BOY STUDENT: My name is Cornel Drăgan, I am a student and I watch the speech on TV. The TV went dead, I was sure at last something happens so I go out to see.

GIRL STUDENT: I went into a shop and heard something had been organised by Ceauşescu and the roads were blocked by traffic. I thought I'd walk to the People's Palace.

310 BULLDOZER DRIVER: My name is Ilie Barbu. I can work many machines. I work in all the country to build hospitals and schools. Always build, never pull down. In December I work at the People's Palace, I drive a bulldozer. There are always many Securitate and today they make us scared because they are scared.

BOY STUDENT 1: I see people running away and I try to stop them to ask what is happening but nobody has courage to talk. At last someone says, Let's hope it has started.

BOY STUDENT 2: Well, I'm Stefan Rusu, in fact I come from 320 Craiova, I only live in Bucharest since September to study. On the 21 no one in our zone knew what was going on. My uncle had just come back from Iran so my sister and I went to meet him and my mother. In the Callea Vittoria I saw Securitate who were upset, they were whispering. Well in fact Securitate have come to me when I was working and asked me to write reports on my colleagues. I agreed because I would get a passport and go to America, but I never wrote anything bad to get someone in trouble. Nobody knew I did this with Securitate. Now I could see the Securitate in the street were scared. Cars were breaking the rules and driving 330 the wrong way up the road. We went to the Intercontinental Hotel but we were not allowed to have a meal. We were whispering, my mother told us she had been in the square and heard people booing.

STUDENT 1: I got to the square and people are shouting against Ceauşescu, shouting "Today in Timişoara, tomorrow in all the country." I look at their lips to believe they say it. I see a friend and at first I don't know him, his face has changed, and when he looks at me I know my face is changed also.

DOCTOR: My name is Ileana Chiriţa. I'm a student doctor, I 340 come to this hospital from school, we must get six months' practical. The 21 was a normal day on duty, I didn't know anything.

GIRL STUDENT: On my way to the People's Palace I saw people queueing for a new thriller that had just been published, so as I was feeling guilty about my mother I decided to try and buy one, thrillers are her favourite books. So I queued to get the book, and at about one o'clock I went home.

BULLDOZER DRIVER: I leave work to get my son from school and I don't go back to work, I go to the Palace Square. 350

STUDENT 1: There were two camps, army and people, but nobody shooting. Some workers from the People's Palace come with construction material to make barricades. More and more people come, we are pushed together.

DOCTOR: On my way home in the afternoon there was a woman crying because she lost her handbag, the other women comfort her saying, "It could be worse, people were crushed and lost their shoes, don't cry for such a small thing."

SECURITATE: Claudiu Brad, I am an officer in Securitate. In everything I did I think I was right, including the 21. I went 360 to military high school because I like uniforms. My family has no money for me to study but I did well. I went to the Officers School of Securitate and got in the external department, which is best, the worst ones go in the fire service. Nobody knows I am in Securitate except one friend I have since I am three years old. I have no other friends but I like women and recruit them sometimes with clothes. On December 21 I am taking the pulse of the street in plain clothes with a walkie-talkie hidden. My district is Rossetti Place. I report every three hours if the crowd move their position, 370 how could they be made calm, what they want.

SOLDIER: My name is Gheorghe Marin. I am in the army from September. My mother is in house, my father mechanic in railway. December I am near the airport. They say Hungarians come from Hungary into Romania, we must shoot them. They give us four magazines. Before, we work in the fields, we have one lessons to shoot. 21 we are in trenches, we have spades to dig. We wait something, we don't know what. We don't know Ceauşescu speak, we don't know what happen in Bucharest. 380

GIRL STUDENT: I'd planned to go to see a film with a friend but in the afternoon my father said I must ring up and pretend to be ill, then my friend rang and said that she is ill. I wanted to go out and my father said I couldn't go alone. I thought of an excuse—we had to have some bread, so we went out together. There were a lot of people moving from Union Place towards University Place and I heard someone shout, "Down with the Dictator." I was very confused. This was opposed to the policy of the leading forces. A man came up 390 and asked what was happening but my father pulled me away because he realised the man was a provoker who starts arguments and then reports the people who get involved. My father insisted we go home, I said he was a coward and began to cry. He said if he was single he would behave differently.

BULLDOZER DRIVER: In the square there is much army and tanks. My son is six years old, I am scared for him. I take him home and we watch what happens on TV with my wife and daughter.

400 STUDENT 2: About five o'clock we heard people shouting "Jos Ceauşescu." My uncle wanted to go home to Cluj. Walking back I noticed it was 99% young people in the square with police and soldiers near them and I thought "That's the end for them." At home we tried to avoid the topic and get it out of our minds.

STUDENT 1: There are vans bringing drink and I tell people not to drink because Securitate wants to get us drunk so we look bad. In the evening we tried to make a barricade in Rosetti Place. We set fire to a truck.

410 SECURITATE: There are barricades and cars burning in my district, I report it. Later the army shoot the people and drive tanks in them. I go off duty.

HOUSEPAINTER: My name is Margareta Antoniu, my work is a housepainter. I paint the windows on the big apartment blocks. I come back to work just now because I have a baby. The 21, the evening, I come home from a village with my children and my husband says it is happening. We expect it because of Timişoara. He hear tanks and shooting like an earthquake. We are happy someone fight for our people.

420 DOCTOR: My husband was away to visit his parents and I felt lonely. My mother phoned and warned me to stay home and said, "Listen to the cassette"—this is our code for Radio Free Europe.

FLOWERSELLER: My name is Cornelia Dediliuc. I am a flowerseller, 22 years. Three children, 7, 4 and 2. I have a great pain because my mother die three weeks. My husband is very good, we meet when I am 14, before him I know only school and home. Before I tell you December I tell you something before in my family. My son who is 4 is 2, we live 430 in a small room, I cook, I go out and my child pull off the hot water and hurt very bad. I come in and see, I have my big child 5 my hands on his neck because he not take care. Now I have illness, I have headache, and sometimes I don't know what I do. When the revolution start I am home with my children. The shooting is very big. I hold my children and stay there.

PAINTER: When we heard shooting we went out, and we stayed near the Intercontinental Hotel till nearly midnight. I had an empty soul. I didn't know who I was.

440 STUDENT 1: They shot tracer bullets with the real bullets to show they were shooting high. At first people don't believe they will shoot in the crowd again after Timişoara.

PAINTER: I saw a tank drive into the crowd, a man's head was crushed. When people were killed like that more people came in front of the tanks.

FLOWERSELLER: My husband come home scared, he has seen dead people. I say him please not to go out again because the children.

GIRL STUDENT: At about 11 my family began to argue so I went to my room. I heard shooting and called my father. He 450 wouldn't let me open the shutter but through the crack I saw a wounded army officer running across the street screaming.

PAINTER: It's enough to see one person dead to get empty of feeling.

FLOWERSELLER: But I sleep and he goes out. I can't see something because the window of the apartment is not that way but I hear the shooting.

STUDENT 2: My mother, sister and I all slept in the same room that night because we were scared. 460

DOCTOR: The block of flats was very quiet. Lights were on very late. I could hear other people listening to the radio.

GIRL STUDENT: I sat up till four in the morning. I wanted to go out but my father had locked the door and hidden the key.

STUDENT 1: At four in the morning I telephone my mother and tell her peoples are being killed.

PAINTER: That night it seems it must be all over. I hope it will go on tomorrow but don't know how.

SECURITATE: In the night the army cleaned the blood off the streets and painted the walls and put tar on the ground 470 where there were stains from the blood so everything was clean.

STUDENT 1: At six in the morning there is new tar on the road but I see blood and something that is a piece of skin. Someone puts down a white cloth on the blood and peoples throw money, flowers, candles, that is the beginning of the shrines.

DOCTOR: On my way to work on the morning of the 22 there were broken windows and people washing the street.

BULLDOZER DRIVER: On the 22 I go back to work. I am afraid I am in trouble with Securitate because I leave work the day 480 before but nobody says nothing.

DOCTOR: At the hospital no one knew what had happened but there were 14 dead and 19 wounded. There were two kinds of wounds, normal bullet wounds and bullets that explode when they strike something and break bones in little pieces, there is no way of repairing them.

HOUSEPAINTER: About 7 o'clock I take a shower. I hear a noise in the street. I look out. I see thousands of workers from the Industrial Platforms. I am wet, I have no clothes, I stay to watch. They are more and more, two three kilometres. Now 490 I know Ceauşescu is finish.

DOCTOR: At about 8 I saw out of the window people going towards University Square holding flags. They pass a church and suddenly they all knelt down in silence. My colleagues began to say, He will fall. An old doctor, 64 years old, climbed to a dangerous place to get down Ceauşescu's picture and we all cheered. We heard on the radio the General in charge of the Army had killed himself and been announced a traitor. We kept treating patients and running back to the radio. 500

STUDENT 2: We heard that the General committed suicide and there was a state of emergency declared. I thought everything is lost.

GIRL STUDENT: I insisted we go out. My father dressed like a bride taking a long time.

FLOWERSELLER: I go to the market to get food and many people are going to the centre. I watch them go by. I am sorry I get married so young.

510 TRANSLATOR: I went to work as usual but there was only one colleague in my office. We heard shots so we went out. I've noticed in films people scatter away from gunfire but here people came out saying, What's that? People were shouting, "Come with us," so we went in the courtyard and shouted too.

GIRL STUDENT: We hadn't gone far when we saw a crowd of people with banners with Jos Ceauşescu, shouting, "Come and join us." They were low class men so we didn't know if we could trust them. I suggested we cross the road so no one could say we were with them.

520 TRANSLATOR: I heard people shouting, "Down with Ceauşescu," for the first time. It was a wonderful feeling to say those words, Jos Ceauşescu.

GIRL STUDENT: Suddenly there was a huge crowd with young people. For the first time I saw the flag with the hole cut out of it. I began to cry, I felt ashamed I hadn't done anything. My father agreed to go on but not with the crowd.

STUDENT 2: Then I saw students singing with flags with holes in them and I thought, Surely this is the end. I walked on the pavement beside them, quickly looking to the side for an es-
530 cape route like a wild animal.

TRANSLATOR: I had promised my wife to take care. We were walking towards the tanks and I was in a funk. But when you're with other people you keep walking on.

GIRL STUDENT: We came to University Place. For the first time I saw blood, it was smeared on a wooden cross. It's one thing to hear shooting but another to see blood. There were police in front of the Intercontinental Hotel. But in a crowd you disappear and feel stronger.

TRANSLATOR: Then I saw there were flowers in the guns.

540 GIRL STUDENT: I saw a tank with a soldier holding a red carnation.

TRANSLATOR: Everyone was hugging and kissing each other, you were kissing a chap you'd never seen before.

GIRL STUDENT: And when I looked again the police had vanished.

STUDENT 2: I saw people climbing on army vehicles, I thought they'd taken them from the soldiers, then I realised the soldiers were driving and I heard people shouting, "The army is with us." Then I started to cry and I shouted too, "The
550 army is with us."

TRANSLATOR: There were no words in Romanian or English for how happy I was.

SECURITATE: On the 22 the army went over to the side of the people. I gave my pistol to an army officer and both magazines were full. That's why I'm here now. I had no more superiors and I wanted to get home. I caught the train and stayed in watching what happened on TV.

HOUSEPAINTER: We leave our six children with my mother and we follow some tanks with people on them. They are go to
560 the TV station. We are there with the first people who make revolution.

BULLDOZER DRIVER: I work till half past ten or eleven, then I see tanks not with army, with men on them. I think I will take the bulldozer. But when I get to the gates my boss says,

"There is no need, Ceauşescu is no more, Ceauşescu nu mai e." I see no Securitate so I go home to my family.

DOCTOR: Out of the window I saw a silver helicopter and pieces of paper falling—we thought the people had won and they were celebration papers.

GIRL STUDENT: There were leaflets thrown down from heli- 570 copters saying, Go home and spend Christmas with your family.

DOCTOR: A boo went up outside when people saw what they said.

GIRL STUDENT: Suddenly I heard bangbang and I thought my heart would explode, but it was small children throwing celebration crackers against the walls. My father had an attack of cramp and couldn't move any further.

STUDENT 1: In the Palace Square when the tanks turn round we are afraid they will fire on us again. But they turn to- 580 wards Ceauşescu's balcony.

STUDENT 2: I saw books and papers thrown down from the balcony and I thought I must do something so I went to the radio station. I heard people singing "Wake Up Romanian" and realised it was a victory.

DOCTOR: About 12.30 I heard on the radio "Wake Up Romanian," the anthem which used to be banned, and announcers who apologise for not telling the truth, they had been made to lie. Everyone began to cry and laugh. The doctors and the orderlies were equal.                                          590

GIRL STUDENT: We saw an appeal on TV at a friend's house for blood so I went to the hospital with our friend's son-in-law. There were hundreds of people waiting to give blood but only fifty bottles, luckily I was able to give blood.

STUDENT 2: I bought some champagne and went home to my family to celebrate.

DOCTOR: I went home about 3 and my husband has bought 6 bottles of champagne and we called our neighbours in. For the first time in my life I felt free to laugh.

GIRL STUDENT: We went to the TV station, it was surrounded 600 by cars beeping, soldiers wearing armbands to show they were with the people. We were told the water was poisoned by Securitate so I ran to buy some milk so my doggie could have something to drink.

STUDENT 1: In the afternoon I go to meet my mother when she comes out of the school. Everyone is shouting Ole ole ole ole and cars hoot their horns. Then I go to see my grandmother to show her I am all right.

*(Pause.)*

PAINTER: That night the terror shooting started. There was no quiet place.                                                     610

TRANSLATOR: When the terror shooting started, I was at home and heard it. My legs buckled, I vomited, I couldn't go out. It took me weeks to get over that.

STUDENT 1: About 7 o'clock we heard on the radio, "Help, our building is being attacked." So I went out again.

HOUSEPAINTER: At the radio station I am scared, my husband says, "Why you come then?" Terroristi shoot from a building and my husband goes with men inside and catch them. There are many wounded and I help. I am the only woman.

SOLDIER: They say us it is not Hungarians. It is terroristi. We 620 guard the airport. We shoots anything, we shoots our friend. I want to stay alive.

PAINTER: They are asking on TV for people to defend the TV

station. My girlfriend and I go out. We stop a truck of young people and ask where they're going, they say, "We are going to die." They say it like that. We can do nothing there, everyone knows it.

STUDENT 1: There was a gypsy who had a gun and he says, "Come with me, I want people strong with courage." He
630 says we must go to the factory of August 23 where they have guns for the guards. The Romanian people are cowards and have no courage to get in the truck, but at last we go to the factory. There are more than one hundred people but only 28 get guns, I get one, they say, "Be careful and come back with the gun." Then we go to a police station because we know they are on the side of the people and we ask for bullets. At first they don't want to give them, they say, "We need them to defend our building." We say, "Give us at least one bullet each to be of some use."

640 STUDENT 2: People were shouting, "Come with us," but I thought, "It's a romantic action, it's useless to go and fight and die." I thought I was a coward to be scared. But I thought, "I will die like a fool protecting someone I don't know. How can I stop bullets with my bare hands? It's the job of the army, I can do nothing, I will just die." So I went home.

BOY STUDENT 1: At the TV station I am behind the wall of a house and they shoot across me from both sides. I go into a house, the terroristi are gone, I telephone my mother to tell
650 her where I am. If I stay ten minutes longer I am dead because they shoot that house. In the road a boy stands up and is shot. A month later is his eighteenth birthday. I ask myself if he is shot by our soldiers. I am standing looking round, bullets are flying. After a while you don't feel scared.

PAINTER: My girlfriend and I were at the TV station. I didn't know who we were fighting with or how bad it was. I was just acting to save our lives. It is terrible to hate and not to be able to do something real.

GIRL STUDENT: That evening I wanted to put on my army
660 clothes and go out and shoot—I got three out of three in the shooting test when I was in the army. But my father had locked the door again and hidden the key.

HOUSEPAINTER: At ten o'clock we go back to the TV station with some bread.

STUDENT 1: A lot of people bring tea and food though they didn't know if there will be better days and more to eat. They bring things they save for Christmas. Some people say the food is poisoned so that people who bring it must eat and drink first.

670 PAINTER: I was with my girlfriend so I felt I should act as a man and be confident. I was curious to know what I would feel in difficult moments.

STUDENT 1: There are children of 12 or 13 moving everywhere, they are harder to see, bringing us bullets, saying, "What do you need? what shall I bring you?"

PAINTER: A man was shot in the throat in front of me. Some people couldn't look but I was staring, trying not to forget. I had an insane curiosity. It was like an abattoir. He was like an animal dying with no chance. He had an expression of
680 confusedness. It was incredible he had so much blood. I felt empty.

HOUSEPAINTER: At halfpast eight we go to buy some bread, then home to sleep. My mother ask where I was and I say I

go out to buy some bread, just that.

DOCTOR: On the 23 I went to work. Two boys came in with a young man on a stretcher, which they put down, then one of them fell to the ground and began to scream—he sees the wounded man is his older brother. His friend takes him down the hall to get a tranquilliser, it is very dark and when they come back the friend trips over something, it is the 690 body of the older brother, who is dead waiting for surgery. The younger brother was only 14. He threw himself on the corpse and won't move, he said he wants to die with his brother.

STUDENT 1: On the morning of the 23 I went home and I slept for two hours. I kept the gun with me in bed.

GIRL STUDENT: I was about to go out to defend my school when my grandmother began to panic and we thought she would have a heart attack, so I promised to stay in, and I spent the day passing messages to people on the phone. Some people 700 don't like me because of my father.

STUDENT 2: The train didn't go that day so I stayed at home. I thought, "This is not my town. I will go to my own town and act there."

DOCTOR: I stayed in the hospital without going home till the 28. We had enough medicine for immediate cases. Once or twice we had to use out of date anaesthetic and the patient woke up during the operation, not often but it happened. We had no coffee or food. When my husband came to see me, more than seeing him I was pleased he had 30 packets 710 of cigarettes. We ate what the patients left and people brought some bread and some jam so on Christmas day we had jam sandwiches.

SECURITATE: When I heard about the execution on the 25 I came at night with my father to the authorities to certify what I was doing during the event. I was detained three days by the army, then told to remain at home. I will say one thing. Until noon on the 22 we were law and order. We were brought up in this idea. I will never agree with unorder. Everyone looks at me like I did something wrong. It was the 720 way the law was then and the way they all accepted it.

STUDENT 1: On the 25 we hear about the trial and their deaths. It is announced that people must return their weapons so we go to the factory and give back our guns. Of the 28 who had guns only 4 are alive.

BULLDOZER DRIVER: I stay home with my family till the 28, then I go to work. They say the time I was home will be off my holidays. There is no more work on the People's Palace, nobody knows if they finish it.

PAINTER: Painting doesn't mean just describing, it's a state of 730 spirit. I didn't want to paint for a long time then.

### —III. FLORINA'S WEDDING—

SCENE I

#### 1. CÎINELUI ÎI E FOAME. THE DOG IS HUNGRY.

*Night, outside. A shrine. A* DOG *is lying asleep. A man approaches. He whistles. The* DOG *looks up. The man whistles. The* DOG *gets up and approaches, undecided between eagerness and fear. The man is a* VAMPIRE.

VAMPIRE: Good dog. Don't be frightened.

(DOG *approaches, then stops. Growls. Retreats, advances. Growls.*)

No no no no no. You can tell of course. Yes, I'm not a human being, what does that matter? It means you can talk to me.

DOG: Are you dead?

VAMPIRE: No, no I'm not unfortunately. I'm undead and getting tired of it. I'm a vampire, you may not have met one before, I usually live in the mountains and you look like a dog who's lived on scraps in the city. How old are you?

740  DOG: Five, six.

VAMPIRE: You look older but that's starvation. I'm over five hundred but I look younger, I don't go hungry.

DOG: Do you eat dogs?

VAMPIRE: Don't be frightened of me, I'm not hungry now. And if I was all I'd do is sip a little of your blood, I don't eat. I don't care for dogs' blood.

DOG: People's blood?

VAMPIRE: I came here for the revolution, I could smell it a long way off.

750  DOG: I've tasted man's blood. It was thick on the road, I gobbled it up quick, then somebody kicked me.

VAMPIRE: Nobody knew who was doing the killing, I could come up behind a man in a crowd.

DOG: Good times.

VAMPIRE: There's been a lot of good times over the years.

DOG: Not for me.

VAMPIRE: Do you belong to anyone?

DOG: I used to but he threw me out. I miss him. I hate him.

VAMPIRE: He probably couldn't feed you.

760  DOG: He beat me. But now nobody talks to me.

VAMPIRE: I'm talking to you.

DOG: Will you keep me?

VAMPIRE: No, I'm just passing the time.

DOG: Please. I'm nice. I'm hungry.

VAMPIRE: Vampires don't keep pets.

DOG: You could feed me.

(DOG *approaches* VAMPIRE *carefully.*)

VAMPIRE: I've no money to buy food for you, I don't buy food, I put my mouth to a neck in the night, it's a solitary—get off.

(As the DOG *reaches him he makes a violent gesture and the* DOG *leaps away.*)

DOG: Don't throw stones at me, I hate it when they throw
770  stones, I hate being kicked, please please I'd be a good dog, I'd bite your enemies. Don't hurt me.

VAMPIRE: I'm not hurting you. Don't get hysterical.

(DOG *approaches again.*)

DOG: I'm hungry. You're kind. I'm your dog.

(DOG *is licking his hands.*)

VAMPIRE: Stop it, go away. Go. Go. Go away.

(DOG *slinks a little further off then approaches carefully.*)

DOG: I'm your dog. Nice. Yes? Your dog? Yes?

VAMPIRE: You want me to make you into a vampire? A vampire dog?

DOG: Yes please, yes yes.

VAMPIRE: It means sleeping all day and going about at night.

DOG: I'd like that.  780

VAMPIRE: Going about looking like anyone else, being friendly, nobody knowing you.

DOG: I'd like that.

VAMPIRE: Living forever, / you've no idea. All that

DOG: I'd—

VAMPIRE: happens is you begin to want blood, you try to put it off, you're bored with killing, but you can't sit quiet, you can't settle to anything, your limbs ache, your head burns, you have to keep moving faster and faster, that eases the pain, seeking. And finding. Ah.  790

DOG: I'd like that.

VAMPIRE: And then it's over and you wander round looking for someone to talk to. That's all. Every night. Over and over.

DOG: You could talk to me. I could talk to you. I'm your dog.

VAMPIRE: Yes, if you like, I don't mind. Come here. Good dog.

(VAMPIRE *puts his mouth to the* DOG's *neck.*)

## SCENE II

## 2. TOATĂ LUMEA SPERĂ CA GABRIEL SĂ SE ÎNSĂNĂTOȘEASCĂ REPEDE. EVERYONE HOPES GABRIEL WILL FEEL BETTER SOON.

I.

GABRIEL, *is in bed in hospital.*

FLORINA, *working there as a nurse, passes his bed.*

FLORINA: I see less of you working here than if I came for a visit.

GABRIEL: Wait.

FLORINA: I can't.

GABRIEL: We won. Eh? Ole . . . Yes?  800

FLORINA: Yes but don't talk. Wait for your visitors.

GABRIEL: Rodica?

FLORINA: Mum and dad.

GABRIEL: Something wrong with Rodica?

FLORINA: No.

GABRIEL: You'd tell me / if she was hurt.

FLORINA: Don't talk, Gabriel, rest. She's not hurt.

GABRIEL: Do nurses tell the truth?

FLORINA: I do to you.

(She goes.)

(IRINA *and* BOGDAN *arrive with food.*)

IRINA: Eggs in the shops. We're getting the benefit already. I'll  810
ask Florina who I should give it to. Keep the apples here. Make sure you get it all, you fought for it.

GABRIEL: Where's Rodica?

IRINA: She couldn't come.

GABRIEL: I want her.

IRINA: Don't, don't, you're not well, I'll never forgive her, she's perfectly all right.

GABRIEL: What?

IRINA: She's frightened to go out. Now when there's nothing happening. She sends her love.  820

(BOGDAN *has a bottle of whisky.*)

BOGDAN: This is for the doctor. / Which doctor

GABRIEL: No need.

BOGDAN: do I give it to?

GABRIEL: No.

IRINA: Yes, a little present for the doctor so he's gentle with you.

GABRIEL: That was before. Not now.

BOGDAN: When your mother had her operation, two bottles of whisky and then it was the wrong doctor.

830 IRINA: They can't change things so quickly, Gaby.

BOGDAN: You do something for somebody, he does something for you. Won't change that. Give my father a cigarette, he puts it behind his ear. Because you never know.

GABRIEL: Different now.

BOGDAN: Who shall I give it to? I'll ask Florina.

(MIHAI, FLAVIA *and* RADU *arrive.* RADU *takes* GABRIEL's *hand.*)

MIHAI: Radu wanted to visit his friend Gabriel so we thought we'd come with him.

FLAVIA: We've brought a few little things.

MIHAI: To pay our respects to a hero.

(*They stand awkwardly. Then* FLAVIA *embraces* IRINA.)

840 IRINA: Radu's a hero too.

FLAVIA: The young show us the way.

BOGDAN: We're glad you're safe, Radu.

FLAVIA: And Florina's here?

IRINA: Yes, she's working.

MIHAI: You must be proud of her.

BOGDAN: She worked for five days without stopping.

RADU: I'll go and find her.

FLAVIA: Yes, find her, Radu.

(RADU *goes.*)

MIHAI: We're so glad the young people no longer have a mis-
850    understanding. We have to put the past behind us and go forward on a new basis.

BOGDAN: Yes, nobody can be blamed for what happened in the past.

IRINA: Are you warm enough, Gaby? I can bring a blanket from home.

II.

*Evening in the hospital. Patient(s) in dressing-gown(s). Someone comes looking for a doctor.*

SORE THROAT: I'm looking for the doctor. I have a sore throat. I need to get an antibiotic.

(*A patient shuffles slowly about, taking the person down corridors and opening doors, looking for a doctor. Different sounds come from the rooms—a woman crying, a man muttering [it's the patient from iii, we barely hear what he's saying, just get the sound of constant questions], a priest chanting. They go off, still looking.*)

III.

*A couple of weeks after i. Sunlight.* GABRIEL *is much better, sitting up.* RODICA *is sitting beside him holding his hand. Flowers. A* PATIENT *in a dressing-gown comes to talk to them.*

PATIENT: Did we have a revolution or a putsch? Who was shooting on the 21st? And who was shooting on the 22nd?

Was the army shooting on the 21st or did some shoot and 860 some not shoot or were the Securitate disguised in army uniforms? If the army were shooting, why haven't they been brought to justice? And were they still shooting on the 22nd? Were they now disguised as Securitate? Most important of all, were the terrorists and the army really fighting or were they only pretending to fight? And for whose benefit? And by whose orders? Where did the flags come from? Who put loudhailers in the square? How could they publish a newspaper so soon? Why did no one turn off the power at the TV? Who got Ceauşescu to call everyone together? And 870 is he really dead? How many people died at Timişoara? And where are the bodies? Who mutilated the bodies? And were they mutilated after they'd been killed specially to provoke a revolution? By whom? For whose benefit? Or was there a drug in the food and water at Timişoara to make people more aggressive? Who poisoned the water in Bucharest?

GABRIEL: Please stop.

PATIENT: Why weren't we shown the film of the execution?

GABRIEL: He is dead.

PATIENT: And is the water still poisoned? 880

GABRIEL: No.

PATIENT: And who was shooting on the 22nd?

GABRIEL: The army, which was on the side of the people, was fighting the terrorists, who were supporting Ceauşescu.

PATIENT: They changed clothes.

GABRIEL: Who changed clothes?

PATIENT: It was a fancy dress party. Weren't you there? Didn't you see them singing and dancing?

GABRIEL: My sister's coming from America.

PATIENT: Does she know what happened? 890

GABRIEL: She'll have read the newspapers.

PATIENT: Then you must tell her. Do you know?

GABRIEL: I can't talk about it now.

PATIENT: Are you a Communist?

GABRIEL: No but my sister's / coming now.

PATIENT: Communist. I hope you die.

(FLORINA, RADU *and* LUCIA. LUCIA *embraces* GABRIEL *and* RODICA.)

LUCIA: All the way over on the plane I was terrified of what I was going to see. But you look beautiful. In America everyone's thrilled. I told my friends, "My brother was there, he was wounded, he's a hero." I watched TV but they never 900 showed enough, I kept playing it and stopping when there was a crowd, I thought I must know somebody, I was crying all the time, I was so ashamed not to be here. I've brought you some chocolate, and oranges.

GABRIEL: How's America?

LUCIA: If you mean how's Wayne he's fine, he has an allergy but let's forget that, he has a lot of meetings so he can't be here. But America. There are walls of fruit in America, five different kinds of apples, and oranges, grapes, pears, bananas, melons, different kinds of melon, and things I don't 910 know the name—and the vegetables, the aubergines are a purple they look as if they've been varnished, red yellow green peppers, white onions red onions, bright orange carrots somebody has shone every carrot, and the greens, cabbage spinach broad beans courgettes, I still stare every time I go shopping. And the garbage, everyone throws away great bags full of food and paper and tins, every day, huge bags, huge dustbins, people live out of them. Eat some chocolate.

(*They eat the chocolate.*)
(PATIENT *comes back again.*)

PATIENT: Have they told you who was shooting on the 22nd? /
920    And why was it necessary to kill
GABRIEL: Please, not now.
PATIENT: Ceauşescu so quickly?
LUCIA: Have some chocolate.

(PATIENT *takes some chocolate and puts it in his pocket.*)

PATIENT: Who has taken the supplies we were sent from the west? Nurse?
FLORINA: I'm not on duty.
PATIENT: Did we have a revolution? Or what did we have?
RADU: Come on, let's find your bed.

(RADU *takes him off still talking.*)

PATIENT: Why did they close the schools a week early? Why did
930    they evacuate the foreigners from the geriatric hospital? Who were the men in blue suits who appeared on the streets before the 21st?

(*Silence.*)

LUCIA: They have mental patients in here with the wounded? That's not very good.
FLORINA: He was wounded on the head. / He has
LUCIA: That explains a lot.
FLORINA: headaches and gets upset. Yes, he's a bit crazy.

(*Pause.*)

LUCIA: Hungarians were fighting beside us they said on TV. And Ianoş wasn't hurt, that's good. I think Americans like
940    Hungarians.
GABRIEL: The poor Hungarians have a bad time because they're not treated better than everyone else. How did they treat us when they had the chance? They go abroad and insult Romania to make people despise us.
LUCIA: This is what we used to say before. Don't we say something different?
GABRIEL: Ask granny about Hungarians.
LUCIA: It's true, in America they even like the idea of gypsies, they think how quaint. But I said to them you don't like
950    blacks here, you don't like hispanics, we're talking about lazy greedy crazy people who drink too much and get rich on the black market. That shut them up.
GABRIEL: But Ianoş doesn't count as Hungarian.

(RADU *comes back.*)

LUCIA: So you got rid of the lunatic all right? Have some more chocolate.

(RADU *shakes his head.*)

Go on, there's plenty more.
RADU: We're not greedy, Lucia. We don't just think about food.
LUCIA: It's a celebration, it's fun to have chocolate, can't you
960    have fun?
RADU: No I can't. Celebrate what?

FLORINA: Radu, not now.
RADU: Who was shooting on the 22nd? That's not a crazy question.
FLORINA: Lucia's just arrived. Gabriel's still not well.
RADU: The only real night was the 21st. After that, what was going on? It was all a show.
LUCIA: No, it was real, Radu, / I saw it on television.
FLORINA: I don't want to hear / all this now.
RADU: Were they fighting or pretending to fight? Who let off 970 firecrackers? Who brought loudhailers?

(*Pause.*)
(LUCIA *looks at* FLORINA.)

FLORINA: At the Municipal Hospital the head doctor gave medical supplies for the west to the police to sell on the black market. / And
LUCIA: That I can believe.
RADU: he locked the wounded in a room with no one to take care of them so he could hand them over / to the Securitate and some of them died.
LUCIA: But that's just him. It's not a plot.

(*Pause.*)

FLORINA: How many people were killed at Timişoara? Where 980 are the bodies? There were bodies found in a sandpit for the longjump. / Where are the rest?
LUCIA: But what does that mean?
RADU: Why did no one turn off the power at the TV station?

(*Pause.*)

LUCIA: Gabriel? Rodica?
GABRIEL: I'm too tired.

(RODICA *turns her head away.*)

IV.

*Some time later.* IRINA *helping* GABRIEL *to walk. He reaches a chair and falls into it laughing.*

IRINA: Good. Good.

(*Silence.*)

I used to say more with the radio on.
GABRIEL: Have you heard people say that by the 22nd / the revolution had been stolen?                                       990
IRINA: No no no no no. I've no time for all that nonsense.
GABRIEL: But—
IRINA: No. No no no. Now. Walk.

SCENE III

**3. RODICA MAI ARE COŞMARE. RODICA IS STILL HAVING NIGHTMARES.**

RODICA *is wearing a cloak and a big fur hat with dollars and flowers on it. Two soldiers come in.*

SOLDIER 1: We're the last soldiers, your Majesty. The rest of the army's on the side of the people.
SOLDIER 2: The helicopter's going to rescue you.

(*She takes a telephone from under her cloak and dials endlessly.*)

(*The* SOLDIERS *take off their uniforms and get dressed again in each other's identical clothes. Meanwhile* GABRIEL *comes in wearing a huge Romanian flag, his head through the hole. He gives* RODICA *a box of matches and goes.*)

SOLDIER 2: Why doesn't anyone love you after all you've done for them?

SOLDIER 1: Have you enough money to pay for the helicopter?

(*She gives them money from her hat. They pocket each thing she gives them and hold out their hands for more till she has nothing left on her hat. She gives them the hat. They hold out their hands for more.*)

1000 SOLDIER 1: Give us your hands.

(*Her hands disappear under her cloak.*)

SOLDIER 2: Give us your feet.

(*Her feet disappear under her cloak and she sinks down till she is kneeling.*)

SOLDIER 1: There's no helicopter. You'll have to run.

(*The* SOLDIERS *go.*)
(RODICA *opens the matchbox—"ole ole ole ole" chanted by huge crowd. She opens and closes it several times and the song continues each time. Sound of gunfire. She looks round in a panic for somewhere to hide the matchbox. She puts it under her cloak, then changes her mind and takes it out. It is now a pill, which she swallows.*)

(*A* SOLDIER *comes in and searches, kicking at anything in the way.*)
(*He goes to her and opens her mouth.*)
(*"Ole ole ole ole" chanted by huge crowd.*)
(*He opens and closes her mouth several times, the chant continues each time.*)

## SCENE IV
### 4. CÎND AM FOST SĂ NE VIZITĂM BUNICII LA ȚARĂ, ERA O ZI ÎNSORITĂ. WHEN WE WENT TO VISIT OUR GRANDPARENTS IN THE COUNTRY IT WAS A SUNNY DAY.

FLORINA, LUCIA, RADU *and* IANOȘ *are visiting* FLORINA *and* LUCIA*'s* GRANDPARENTS *in the country, so they can meet* RADU *before the wedding. The* GRANDPARENTS *are peasants.* IANOȘ *has a child with him, a boy of about 8,* TOMA. *The following things happen in the course of a long sunny afternoon, out of doors, immediately outside the* GRANDPARENTS' *house where there is a bench, and nearby.*

I.

THE GRANDPARENTS *embrace* LUCIA *and* FLORINA, *greet* RADU *warmly,* IANOȘ *more formally.* TOMA *clings shyly to* IANOȘ.

II.

IANOȘ *has a ball and tries to interest* TOMA *in playing with him and* RADU. *They go off.*

GRANDMOTHER: That young man's a Hungarian.
LUCIA: He's a friend of Radu and Gabriel's, granny.
GRANDMOTHER: I knew a woman married a Hungarian. His

brother killed her and ripped the child out of her stomach.
FLORINA: He's just a friend of Gabriel's, granny.
GRANDMOTHER: Radu seems a nice young man. He's Romanian. What's wrong with that child?
FLORINA: He's been in an orphanage.                              1010
GRANDMOTHER: Is it a gypsy?
LUCIA: Of course not.
GRANDMOTHER: They wouldn't let him adopt a Romanian.

III.

LUCIA *with* IANOȘ *and* TOMA.

LUCIA: Do we have to have him with us all the time?
IANOȘ: He likes me.
LUCIA: I like you but I'm not getting much chance to show it.
IANOȘ: He'll settle down.
LUCIA: Can he talk?
IANOȘ: Yes of course.
LUCIA: I haven't heard him.                                       1020
IANOȘ: He doesn't know you.
LUCIA: I think your parents are remarkable. What if it goes wrong? Can you give him back?
IANOȘ: We don't want to give him back. We're adopting him.
LUCIA: Your parents are adopting him.
IANOȘ: Yes but me too.

(LUCIA *rolls the ball.*)

LUCIA: Don't you want to play with the ball, Toma?

(*She goes and gets it herself.*)

Ball. Ball. Can you say ball, Toma?

(TOMA *buries himself in* IANOȘ.)

LUCIA: I think your parents are sentimental.
IANOȘ: Are you going back to America?                             1030

(LUCIA *shrugs.*)

I still owe your husband money.
LUCIA: Did you borrow money from him?
IANOȘ: He paid for the abortion.
LUCIA: But he didn't know. It was money he gave me, it was my money. You can't pay him back, he'd want to know what it was for.
IANOȘ: I haven't got the money anyway.

(*Pause.*)

Aren't you ashamed?
LUCIA: What of? No.
IANOȘ: Not the abortion.                                          1040
LUCIA: What?
IANOȘ: I don't know. The wedding?
LUCIA: No, why?
IANOȘ: I'm ashamed.
LUCIA: Why?

(*Pause.*)

IANOȘ: I'm ashamed of loving you when I think you're probably not very nice.

(*Silence.*)

LUCIA: Shall I stay here and marry you?

*(Silence.)*

This is the last of the chocolate.

*(As she gets it out, TOMA pounces on it and runs a little way off, stuffing it all into his mouth.)*

1050      You horrible child. I hate you.

IANOŞ: Don't shout at him. How can he help it? You're so stupid.

LUCIA: Don't shout at me.

*(TOMA whimpers. He starts to shake his head obsessively.)*

IANOŞ: Toma. Come here.

*(TOMA goes on.)*
*(IANOŞ goes to him.)*

Toma.

*(TOMA hits IANOŞ and starts to bellow with panic.)*
*(IANOŞ holds him, he subsides into whimpering.)*
*(IANOŞ sits on the ground holding him.)*

LUCIA: Did you tell anyone about us after I left?

IANOŞ: No.

LUCIA: It might be better if we're seen as something new.

*(Silence.)*

LUCIA: Is he very naughty?

1060 IANOŞ: Not yet. Most of the time he's so good it's frightening. The babies there don't cry.

LUCIA: He's going to be terrible. I won't be much use.

*(Silence.)*

IANOŞ: I'd like to go to America. I've got a passport.

LUCIA: Just for a holiday. I don't like America.

IANOŞ: So is that the only reason you want to stay here? I hoped you loved America.

*(Pause.)*

Would your family let you marry a Hungarian?

IV.

RADU *and* FLORINA. RADU *drawing.*

RADU: Iliescu's going to get in because the workers and peasants are stupid.

*(Pause.)*

1070      Not stupid but they don't think. They don't have the information.

*(Pause.)*

I don't mean your family in particular.

FLORINA: You're a snob like your father. You'd have joined the party.

RADU: Wouldn't you?

*(Silence. He touches her face.)*

FLORINA: I used to feel free then.

RADU: You can't have.

FLORINA: I don't now and I'm in a panic.

RADU: It's because the Front tricked us. / When we've

got rid—          1080

FLORINA: It's because I could keep everything out.

*(Pause.)*

RADU: But you didn't have me then.

FLORINA: No but I thought you were perfect.

RADU: I am perfect.

*(Silence.)*

RADU: What?

FLORINA: Sometimes I miss him.

RADU: What? Why?

FLORINA: I miss him.

RADU: You miss hating him.

FLORINA: Maybe it's that.          1090

RADU: I hate Iliescu.

FLORINA: That's not the same.

RADU: I hate him worse. Human face. And he'll get in because they're stupid and do what they're told. Ceauşescu Ceauşescu. Iliescu Iliescu.

FLORINA: I don't have anyone to hate. You sometimes.

RADU: Me?

FLORINA: Not really.

RADU: Me?

V.

*The* GRANDPARENTS *are sitting side by side on the bench, the others around them. The* GRANDPARENTS *speak slowly, the others fast.*

GRANDFATHER: He was killed while he was putting up posters. 1100

RADU: You see? they're murderers. / It's the same

LUCIA: For which party, grandpa?

RADU: tactics / of intimidation.

GRANDFATHER: Posters for the Peasants Party.

FLORINA: Is that / who you support?

RADU: The Front claim the country supports them but it's only / because of intimidation.

IANOŞ: So did they find out who killed him?

GRANDMOTHER: Yes, it was gypsies killed him.      1110

RADU: Gypsies? / They were probably paid by the

FLORINA: How did they know it was them?

RADU: Front.

IANOŞ: They'd hardly need paying to murder somebody.

RADU: Or it could have been Front supporters /

LUCIA: Or Securitate.

RADU: and they put the blame on the gypsies.

GRANDFATHER: It was two gypsies, a father and son, who used to work in his garden. They had a quarrel with him. He used to beat them.      1120

LUCIA: So was it just a quarrel, / not politics at all?

FLORINA: Did anyone see them?

GRANDMOTHER: But that quarrel was years ago.

GRANDFATHER: A lot of people didn't like him because he used to be a big landowner. The Peasants Party would give him back his land.

FLORINA: So was he killed because / the rest of the

LUCIA: I thought the Peasants Party was for peasants.

IANOŞ: No, they're millionaires the leaders of it.

1130 FLORINA: village didn't want himm to get all the land?

LUCIA: He should get it / if it's his.

FLORINA: No after all this time working on it / everyone—

RADU: Never mind that, he was against the Front, that's why they killed him. He was against the Communists.

GRANDFATHER: He was a party member. He was very big round here. He was a big Securitate man.

LUCIA: So whose side was he on?

GRANDMOTHER: He wasn't a nice man. Nobody liked him.

VI.

GRANDFATHER *is sitting on the bench, the others lying on the grass, each separately except that* TOMA *is near* IANOŞ. *Long silence.*

IANOŞ: I want to go to Peru.

1140 RADU: Rome. And Pompeii.

LUCIA: A holiday by the sea.

(*Pause.*)

FLORINA: Sleep late in the morning.

(*Pause.*)

RADU: Paint what I see in my head.

FLORINA: Go into work tomorrow and everyone's better.

LUCIA: Gabriel walking.

IANOŞ: Rodica talking.

(*They laugh.*)

FLORINA: New shoes.

RADU: Paintbrushes with fine points.

(*Pause.*)

FLORINA: Drive a fast car.

1150 LUCIA: Be famous.

IANOŞ: Toblerone.

(*Pause.*)

RADU: Make money.

(*Pause.*)

IANOŞ: Learn everything in the world by the end of the week.

(*Pause.*)

LUCIA: Not be frightened

(*The pauses get longer.*)

RADU: Make Florina happy.

(*Long pause.*)

IANOŞ: Make Toma happy.

(*Silence.*)

FLORINA: Live forever.

(*Longer silence.*)

LUCIA: Die young.

(*Very long silence.*)

FLORINA: Go on lying here.

(*Very long silence.*)

SCENE V

## 5. MAI DOREŞTI PUŢINĂ BRÎNZĂ? WOULD YOU LIKE SOME MORE CHEESE?

MIHAI *and* FLAVIA *eating cheese and salami.*

FLAVIA: You know when Radu was born and they said he'd be 1160 born dead. Three days, no hope. And then Radu. The pain stops just like that. And then joy. I felt the same the morning of the 22nd. Did you ever feel joy before?

MIHAI: I'm not sure I did.

FLAVIA: All those years of pain forgotten. You felt that?

MIHAI: It was certainly a remarkable experience.

FLAVIA: It can't last of course. Three days after he was born I was crying. But I still loved Radu. And what have we still got from the 22nd?

MIHAI: The work on the People's Palace will probably continue 1170 as soon as its new function has been determined.

FLAVIA: What?

MIHAI: If not I'm sure they'll find me some other work. I'm not in any way compromised, I was on the streets, I'm clearly a supporter of the Front. And in any case—

FLAVIA: I wasn't talking about you.

MIHAI: Good, I had the impression you might be worried.

(*Pause.*)

FLAVIA: All I was trying to do was teach correctly. Isn't history what's in the history book? Let them give me a new book, I'll teach that.                1180

MIHAI: Are you losing your job?

FLAVIA: I didn't inform on my pupils, I didn't accept bribes. Those are the people whose names should be on the list.

MIHAI: Are they not on the list?

FLAVIA: They are on the list but why am I with them? The new head of department doesn't like me. He knows I'm a better teacher than he is. I can't stop teaching, I'll miss the children.

(*Silence during which* RADU *comes in.*)

Why are you always out, Radu? Come and eat.

(RADU *is already making sandwiches.*)

MIHAI: I hope you're going to join us for a meal.               1190

(RADU *goes on making sandwiches.*)

RADU: Have you noticed the way Iliescu moves his hands? And the words he uses?

MIHAI: He comes from a period when that was the style.

RADU: Yes, he does, doesn't he.

MIHAI: Not tonight, Radu. Your mother's had bad news at work about her job.

FLAVIA: The new head of department—

RADU: There you are. It's because of me. No one who's opposed to the Front / will get anywhere.

MIHAI: Radu, I don't know what to do with you. Nothing is on 1200 a realistic basis.

RADU: Please don't say that.

MIHAI: What's the matter now?

RADU: Don't say "realistic basis."

FLAVIA: It's true, Mihai, you do talk in terrible jargon from before, it's no longer correct.

MIHAI: The head of department is in fact a supporter of the Liberals.

RADU: Is he?

1210 FLAVIA: It may not come to anything.

RADU: You mean it's because of what you did before? What did you do?

MIHAI: Radu, this is not a constructive approach.

RADU: It won't come to anything, don't worry. It's five weeks since we made our list of bad teachers. Nobody cares that the students and staff voted. It has to go to the Ministry.

FLAVIA: Do you want me to lose my job?

RADU: If you deserve to.

(FLAVIA *slaps* RADU)
(*Silence.*)

RADU: Do you remember once I came home from school and
1220    asked if you loved Elena Ceauşescu?

FLAVIA: I don't remember, no. When was that?

RADU: And you said yes. I was seven.

FLAVIA: No, I don't remember.

(*Pause.*)

But you can see now why somebody would say what they had to say to protect you.

RADU: I've always remembered that.

FLAVIA: I don't remember.

RADU: No, you wouldn't.

(*Pause.*)

FLAVIA: Why are you saying this, Radu? Are you making it up?
1230    You're manipulating me to make me feel bad. I told you the truth about plenty of things.

RADU: I don't remember.

FLAVIA: No, you wouldn't.

(*Silence.*)

Now. We have some dried apples.

RADU: I expect dad got them from someone with a human face.

(RADU *is about to leave.*)

MIHAI: Radu, how do you think you got into the Art Institute?

RADU: The still life with the green vase was the one / they particularly—

MIHAI: Yes your work was all right. I couldn't have managed if
1240    it was below average.

(RADU *leaves* MIHAI *with the sandwiches and goes. Silence.*)

MIHAI: Who do we know who can put in a word for you?

FLAVIA: We don't know who we know. Someone who put in a word before may be just the person to try and keep clear of.

(*Pause.*)

But Radu's painting is exceptional.

MIHAI: Yes, in fact I didn't do anything.

FLAVIA: You must tell him.

MIHAI: He won't believe me.

(*Pause.*)

FLAVIA: Twenty years marching in the wrong direction. I'd as soon stop. Twenty years' experience and I'm a beginner. Yes, stop. There, I feel better. I'm not a teacher.    1250

MIHAI: They might just transfer you to the provinces.

(*Pause.*)

It won't happen. Trust me.

(*Silence.* MIHAI *goes on with his meal.*)

FLAVIA: Granny. Granny?

(*Her* GRANDMOTHER *doesn't come. Silence.* FLAVIA *goes on with her meal.*)

SCENE VI

## 6. GABRIEL VINE ACASĂ DISEARĂ. GABRIEL IS COMING HOME TONIGHT.

*Downstairs in the block of flats where* GABRIEL *and* RODICA *live.* GABRIEL, *with a crutch, is arriving home from hospital with* RADU, FLORINA, LUCIA, IANOŞ, *and other friends. They have been for a drink on the way and have some bottles with them.*

ALL: The lift's broken.
    How do we get Gaby up the stairs?
    We'll have the party here.
    Rodica's waiting in the flat.
    We shouldn't have stayed so long at the Berlin.
    We can carry him up.
    We need a drink first.    1260
    Let's do it here.
    Do it, I've never seen it.
    Yes, Radu, to celebrate Gaby coming home.

(*Someone announces:*)

The trial and execution of Nicolae and Elena Ceauşescu.

(RADU *and* FLORINA *are the Ceauşescus.*)

IANOŞ: Hurry up. Move along.

RADU: Where are they taking us, Elena?

FLORINA: I don't know, Nicu. He's a very rude man.

RADU: Don't worry we'll be rescued in a minute. This is all part of my long-term plan.

(CEAUSEŞCU [RADU] *keeps looking at his watch and up at the sky.*)

IANOŞ: Sit down.    1270

FLORINA: Don't sit down.

RADU: My legs are tired.

FLORINA: Stand up.

IANOŞ: Sit down.

RADU: The Securitate will get in touch with my watch.

IANOŞ: Answer the questions of the court.

RADU: What court? I don't see any court. Do you, Elena?

FLORINA: No court anywhere here.

RADU: The only judges I recognise are ones I've appointed myself.    1280

SOMEONE: You're on trial for genocide.

FLORINA: These people are hooligans. They're in the pay of foreign powers. That one's just come back from America.

ALL: Who gave the order to shoot at Timişoara?
What did you have for dinner last night?
Why have you got gold taps in your bathroom?
Do you shit in a gold toilet?
Shitting yourselves now.
Why did you pull down my uncle's house?

1290 etc

FLORINA: Where's the helicopter?

RADU: On its way.

FLORINA: Have these people arrested and mutilated.

RADU: Maybe just arrested and shot. They are our children.

FLORINA: After all we've done for them. You should kiss my hands. You should drink my bathwater.

ALL: That's enough trial.
We find you guilty on all counts.
Execution now.

1300 FLORINA: You said there'd be a helicopter, Nicu.

IANOŞ: Stand up.

FLORINA: Sit down.

*(They are roughly pushed to another place.)*

RADU: You can't shoot me. I'm the one who gives the orders to shoot.

FLORINA: We don't recognise being shot.

ALL: Gypsy.
Murderer.
Illiterate.
We've all fucked your wife.

1310 We're fucking her now.
Let her have it.

*(They all shoot* ELENA [FLORINA], *who falls dead at once,* GABRIEL, *who is particularly vicious throughout this, shoots with his crutch. All make gun noises, then cheer.* CEAUŞESCU [RADU] *runs back and forth. They shout again.)*

ALL: We fucked your wife.
Your turn now.
Murderer.
Bite your throat out.

*(Meanwhile* CEAUŞESCU [RADU] *is pleading.)*

RADU: Not me, you've shot her that's enough, I've money in Switzerland, I'll give you the number of my bank account, you can go and get my money—

IANOŞ: In his legs.

*(They shoot and he falls over, still talking and crawling about.)*

1320 RADU: My helicopter's coming, you'll be sorry, let me go to Iran—

IANOŞ: In the belly.

*(They shoot, he collapses further but keeps talking.)*

RADU: I'll give you the People's Palace—

IANOŞ: In the head.

*(They shoot again. He lies still.)*
*(They all cheer and jeer.)*
*(*CEAUŞESCU [RADU] *sits up.)*

RADU: But am I dead?

ALL: Yes.

*(He falls dead again.)*
*(More cheering, ole ole ole etc.)*
*(*RADU *and* FLORINA *get up, everyone's laughing.)*
*(*IANOŞ *hugs* LUCIA *lightly.)*
*(*GABRIEL *suddenly hits out at* IANOŞ *with his crutch.)*

GABRIEL: Get your filthy Hungarian hands off her.

IANOŞ: What?

GABRIEL: Just joking.

*(A* MAN *looks out of one of the doors of the flats to see what the noise is. They go quiet. He shuts the door.)*

**SCENE VII**
**7. ABIA TERMINASE LUCRUL, CÎND A VENIT RADU. SHE HAD JUST FINISHED WORK WHEN RADU CAME.**

*Hospital at night. A corridor.* FLORINA *has just come off duty.* RADU *is meeting her. They hug.*

FLORINA: Someone died tonight. It was his fifth operation. 1330 When they brought him in all the nurses were in love with him. But he looked like an old man by the time he died.

RADU: Was he one of the ones shot low in the back and out through the shoulder?

FLORINA: He was shot from above in the shoulder and it came out low down in his back.

RADU: No, all those wounds are / from being—

FLORINA: You don't know anything about it. I was nursing him.

RADU: A doctor told me.

FLORINA: What does it matter? / He's dead anyway. 1340

RADU: They were in the crowd with us shooting people in the back.

*(Pause.)*

And where are they now?

*(Pause.)*

FLORINA: So what have you done today? Sat in the square and talked?

RADU: I know you're tired.

FLORINA: I like being tired, I like working, I don't like listening to you talk.

RADU: People are talking about a hunger strike.

FLORINA: Fine, those of you who weren't killed can kill your- 1350 selves.

*(Pause.)*

RADU: Do you want to know what it's for?

FLORINA: No.

*(Pause.)*

I hope you're not thinking of it.

RADU: Someone's been getting at you, haven't they?

FLORINA: Because if you do / the wedding's off.

RADU: Someone's threatened you. Or offered you something.

FLORINA: It's what I think. / Did you really say that?

RADU: I don't like what you think.

FLORINA: I don't like what you think. You just want to go on 1360 playing hero, / you're weak, you're lazy—

RADU: You're betraying the dead. Aren't you ashamed? Yes, I'm a hooligan. Let's forget we know each other. / Communist.

FLORINA: You don't know me.

(RADU *goes.*)
(FLORINA *is alone.*)
(*She is joined by the* GHOST *of a young man.*)

GHOST: I'm dead and I never got married. So I've come to find somebody. I was always looking at you when I was ill. But you loved Radu then. I won't talk like he does. I died, that's all I want to know about it. Please love me. It's lonely when
1370  you're dead. I have to go down a secret road. Come with me. It's simple.

SCENE VIII
**8. MULTĂ FERICIRE. WE WISH YOU HAPPINESS.**

FLORINA *and* RADU's *wedding party at a hotel. Both families are there, and old peasant* AUNT *of Bogdan's and a* WAITER. *Music in background. The following conversations take place, sometimes overlapping or simultaneously.*

I.

*It's some time in to the party so everyone's had a few drinks without being drunk yet.*

1.

FLAVIA: What's so wonderful about a wedding is everyone laughs and cries and it's like the revolution again. Because everyone's gone back behind their masks. Don't you think so?

BOGDAN: I don't know. Perhaps. You could say that.

2.

MIHAI: I forgot to take my windscreen wipers off last night so of course they were stolen. Still, my son doesn't get married every day.

3.

1380  IRINA: She and her followers talk without speaking, they know each other's thoughts. She just looks at you and she knows your troubles. I told her all about Gaby.

LUCIA: So you told her your troubles. No wonder she knows.

IRINA: When they send him to Italy for his operation maybe we won't need a clairvoyant. She said I could take him to see her.

LUCIA: He'll just laugh.

IRINA: She says we have no soul. We've suffered for so many years and we don't know how to live. Are people very dif-
1390  ferent in other countries, Lucia?

LUCIA: Cheer up, have a drink. It's Florina's wedding day.

IRINA: I'll miss Florina.

4.

(LUCIA *is talking to a smiling* WAITER.)

WAITER: I remember your wedding last year. That was a very different time. We had bugs in the vases. Mind you. Can I help you change some dollars?

LUCIA: No thank you.

WAITER: I used to help your husband. It's easier now. My

brother's gone to Switzerland to buy a Mercedes. You're sure I can't help you? Top rate, high as Everest.

LUCIA: Thank you but I've no dollars left.  1400

(*The* WAITER's *smile disappears.*)

5.

BOGDAN: I know someone at work killed his son-in-law. He put an axe in his head. Then he put a knife in the dead man's hand to make out it was self-defence, and said anyway he wasn't there, it was his son. And he got away with it. Clever eh?

RADU: What happened to the son?

BOGDAN: Luckily he had some money, he only got six years.

RADU: What's he going to do to his dad when he gets out?

(*They laugh.*)

6.

FLAVIA: How's your little brother?

IANOŞ: He wakes up in the night now and cries.  1410

FLAVIA: How's your mother?

(*They laugh.*)

7.

FLORINA: I thought I was going to get the giggles.

RADU: It was good though.

FLORINA: It was lovely.

8.

IANOŞ: Lucia and I are going to start a newspaper.

LUCIA: A friend's sending us magazines from America and we'll translate interesting articles.

IANOŞ: (*to* LUCIA) Do people really dress like in Vogue?

9.

IRINA: I bought these shoes in the street.

FLAVIA: Did they want dollars?  1420

IRINA: Yes, Lucia's last dollars went on the wedding.

FLAVIA: Black market prices have shot up.

IRINA: It's not black market, it's free market.

10.

IANOŞ: A French doctor told me 4000 babies / have it.

GABRIEL: I hate the French, they're so superior.

IANOŞ: Yes, they do like to help.

GABRIEL: Merci, merci.

IANOŞ: Can you really sterilise infected needles with alcohol?

GABRIEL: I'm sterilising myself with alcohol.

11.

(*Old peasant* AUNT *shouts ritual chants at* FLORINA.)

AUNT: Little bride, little bride,  1430
  You're laughing, we've cried.
  Now a man's come to choose you
  We're sad because we lose you.
  Makes you proud to be a wife
  But it's not an easy life.
  Your husband isn't like a brother
  Your mother-in-law's not like a mother.
  More fun running free and wild
  Than staying home to mind a child.
  Better to be on the shelf  1440
  Only have to please yourself.
  Little bride don't be sad,

Not to marry would be mad.
Single girls are all in tears,
They'll be lonely many years.
Lovely girl you're like a flower, /
Only pretty for an hour—
BOGDAN: Hush, auntie, you're not in the country now.
FLORINA: No, I like it. Go on.

II.

*Later. People have had more to drink and are more cheerful,
emotional, aggressive.*

1.
1450 IRINA: If only he'd stayed in University Square.
LUCIA: He could have been shot there.
IRINA: The bullets missed Ianoş.
LUCIA: Do you wish they'd hit him?
IRINA: No but of course anyone else.
2.
FLORINA: Be nice to your mum and dad.
RADU: I am nice.
3.
BOGDAN: Whinge whinge. Gaby was shot, all right.
    Everyone whinges. Layabout students. Radu and Ianoş
    never stop talking, want to smack them in the mouth. "Was
1460  it a revolution?" Of course it was. / My son was shot for it and
    we've got
MIHAI: Certainly.
BOGDAN: This country needs a strong man.
MIHAI: And we've got one.
BOGDAN: We've got one. Iliescu's a strong man. We can't have
    a traffic jam forever. Are they going to clear the square or
    not?
MIHAI: The government has to avoid any action that would give
    credibility to the current unsubstantiated allegations.
1470 BOGDAN: They're weak, aren't they.
4.
FLAVIA: I'm going to write a true history, Florina, so we'll know
    exactly what happened. How far do you think Moscow was
    involved / in planning the coup?
FLORINA: I don't know. I don't care. I'm sorry.
FLAVIA: What did you vote? Liberal?
FLORINA: Yes of course.
FLAVIA: So did I, so did I.

(*She hugs* FLORINA.)

    Mihai doesn't know. And next time we'll win. Jos Iliescu.
5.
RADU: Look at Gaby, crippled for nothing. They've voted the
1480  same lot in.
IRINA: It's thanks to Gaby you can talk like this.
6.
IANOŞ: Have another drink.
LUCIA: I've had another drink.
IANOŞ: Have another other drink.

(*They laugh.*)

7.
IRINA: Ceauşescu shouldn't have been shot.
RADU: Because he would have exposed people / in the Front.
IRINA: He should have been hung up in a cage and stones

thrown at him.

(*They laugh.*)

8.
BOGDAN: (*to* MIHAI) If Radu had been hurt instead of Gaby,
    he'd be in hospital in Italy by now.                    1490
9.
GABRIEL: I can't work. Rodica can't work. What's going to hap-
    pen to us? I wish I'd been killed.
FLORINA: You're going to Italy.
GABRIEL: When? Can't you do something to hurry things up,
    Florina? Sleep with a doctor? Just joking.
10.
IRINA: I don't like seeing you with Ianoş.
LUCIA: He's Gabriel's friend.
IRINA: I was once in a shop in Transylvania and they wouldn't
    serve me because I couldn't speak Hungarian. / In my own
    country.                                                 1500
LUCIA: Yes, but—
IRINA: And what if the doctor only spoke Hungarian / and
    someone wanted a doctor?
BOGDAN: Stuck-up bastards.
IRINA: Are you going back to America? You're not going back.
LUCIA: Didn't you miss me?
IRINA: Aren't you ashamed? Two years of hell to get your pre-
    cious American and you don't even want him. Did he beat
    you?
LUCIA: I got homesick.                                       1510
IRINA: Was Ianoş going on before?
LUCIA: Of course not. You didn't think that?
IRINA: I don't know what I thought. I just made the wedding
    dress.
LUCIA: You like Ianoş.
IRINA: Go back to America, Lucia, and maybe we can all go.
    You owe us that.
BOGDAN: You're a slut, Lucia.
11.
FLAVIA: Where are the tapes they made when they listened to
    everyone talking? All that history wasted. I'd like to find  1520
    someone in the Securitate who could tell me. Bogdan, do
    you know anyone?
BOGDAN: Why me?
FLAVIA: I used to know someone but she's disappeared.
BOGDAN: They should be driven into the open and punished.
    Big public trials. The Front aren't doing their job.
FLAVIA: There wouldn't be enough prisons.
BOGDAN: (*to* MIHAI) There's a use for your People's Palace.
12.
MIHAI: I was in the British Embassy library reading the Archi-
    tect's Journal and there's a building in Japan forty stories  1530
    high with a central atrium up to twenty stories. So the prob-
    lem is how to get light into the central volume. The German
    engineer has an ingenious solution where they've installed
    computerised mirrors angled to follow the sun so they re-
    flect natural light into the atrium according to the season
    and the time of day, so you have sunlight in a completely en-
    closed space.
13.
FLORINA: I'm glad about you and Ianoş.

(*They kiss.*)

Tell me something.

1540 LUCIA: Don't ask.

FLORINA: No, tell me.

LUCIA: Two years is a long time when you hardly know somebody. I'd lost my job, I had to go through with it, I wanted to get away.

FLORINA: But you loved Wayne at first? If you didn't I'll kill you.

LUCIA: Of course I did. But don't tell Ianoş.

14.

PRIEST: You can't blame anybody. Everyone was trying to survive.

1550 BOGDAN: Wipe them out. Even if it's the entire population. We're rubbish. The Front are stuck-up bastards. They'd have to wipe themselves out too.

PRIEST: We have to try to love our enemies.

BOGDAN: Plenty of enemies. So we must be the most loving people in the world. Did you love him? Give him a kiss would you?

PRIEST: When I say love. It's enough not to hate.

BOGDAN: Handy for you having God say be nice to Ceauşescu.

PRIEST: You're your own worst enemy, Bogdan.

1560 BOGDAN: So I ought to love myself best.

PRIEST: Don't hate yourself anyway.

BOGDAN: Why not? Don't you? You're a smug bugger.

III.

*Later. Two simultaneous conversations develop so that there are two distinct groups. Everyone has drunk a lot by now.* BOGDAN, *who is too drunk to care if anyone listens, puts remarks at random to either group.*

1.

BOGDAN: a. Private schools, private hospitals. I've seen what happens to old people. I want to buy my father a decent death.

b. I support the Peasants Party because my father's a peasant. I'm not ashamed of that. They should have their land because their feet are in the earth and they know things nobody else knows. Birds, frogs, cows, god, the direction of the
1570 wind.

c. CIA, KGB, we're all in the hands of foreign agents. That's one point where I'm right behind Ceauşescu.

2. (MIHAI, RADU *and* FLORINA, *joined by* FLAVIA.)

MIHAI: The Front wouldn't fix the vote because they knew they were going to win. Everyone appreciates the sacrifice made by youth. The revolution is in safe hands. This isn't a day for worrying, Florina and Radu, you take too much on yourselves. I wish you could let it all go for a little while. Please believe me, I want your happiness.

FLORINA: We know you do.

(*She kisses him.*)

1580 RADU: Yes, I know. I appreciate that.

MIHAI: After all, I'm not a monster. Most of the country supports the Front. It's only in my own home it takes courage to say it. We have a government of reconciliation.

FLAVIA: Why don't the Front tell the truth and admit they're communists? / °Nothing to be

MIHAI: Because they're not.

RADU: °I don't care what they're called, it's the same people.

FLAVIA: ashamed of in communism, / nothing to be

FLORINA: They should have been banned / from

MIHAI: That's your idea of freedom, banning people? 1590

FLORINA: standing in the election.

RADU: We've got to have another revolution.

FLAVIA: ashamed of in planning the revolution if they'd just admit it. You never dared speak out against Ceauşescu, Mihai, and you don't dare speak out now. Say it, I'm a communist and so what. / Say it, I'm a communist.

RADU: Jos comunismul, jos comunismul. / Jos Iliescu. Jos tiranul. Jos Iliescu. Jos Iliescu.

FLORINA: Radu, don't be childish.

(BOGDAN *joins in shouting* "Jos comunismul," *then turns his attention to the other group.*)

3. (GABRIEL *at first in group with* MIHAI *then with* LUCIA, IANOŞ *and* IRINA.)

GABRIEL: The only reason we need an internal security force is 1600 if Hungary tried to invade us / we'd need to be sure—

LUCIA: Invade? are you serious?

IANOŞ: When we get Transylvania back it's going to be legally / because it's ours.

IRINA: You're not going to marry a Hungarian.

LUCIA: I'm married already.

IANOŞ: Gaby, the Hungarians started the revolution. Without us you'd still be worshipping Ceauşescu. / And now the

(GABRIEL *jeers.*)

LUCIA: We didn't worship him.

IRINA: Gaby's a hero, Ianoş. 1610

IANOŞ: Romanians worship Iliescu. Who's the opposition? Hungarians.

GABRIEL: That's just voting for your language.

LUCIA: Why shouldn't they have their own schools?

IRINA: And lock Romanian children out in the street. If it wasn't bad enough you going to America, now a Hungarian, / and Gaby crippled, and Radu's irresponsible, I worry for Florina.

GABRIEL: If they want to live in Romania / they can

LUCIA: In the riots on TV I saw a Hungarian on the 1620

GABRIEL: speak Romanian.

IANOŞ: We can learn two languages, we're not stupid.

LUCIA: ground and Romanians kicking him.

GABRIEL: That was a Romanian on the ground, and Hungarians—you think we're stupid?

IANOŞ: You were under the Turks too long, it made you like slaves.

LUCIA: You think I'm a slave? I'm not your slave.

(GABRIEL *pushes* IANOŞ, *who pushes him back.* BOGDAN *arrives.*)

BOGDAN: Leave my son alone. Hungarian bastard. And don't come near my daughter. 1630

IANOŞ: I'm already fucking your daughter, you stupid peasant.

(BOGDAN *hits* IANOŞ.)

(RADU *restrains* BOGDAN.)

(LUCIA *attacks* BOGDAN.)

(BOGDAN *hits* RADU.)
(MIHAI *pushes* BOGDAN.)
(BOGDAN *hits* MIHAI.)
(FLAVIA *attacks* BOGDAN.)
(IANOŞ *pushes* GABRIEL.)
(IRINA *protects* GABRIEL.)
(GABRIEL *hits* IANOŞ.)
(RADU *attacks* BOGDAN.)
(MIHAI *restrains* RADU.)
(RADU *attacks* MIHAI.)
(FLORINA *attacks* RADU.)
(GABRIEL *hits out indiscriminately with his crutch and accidentally knocks* BOGDAN *to the floor.*)
(*Stunned silence.*)

FLAVIA: This is a wedding. We're forgetting our programme. It's time for dancing.

(*They pick themselves up, see if they are all right. Music—the lambada. Gradually couples form and begin to dance.* BOGDAN *and* IRINA, MIHAI *and* FLAVIA, FLORINA *and* RADU, LUCIA *and* IANOŞ. GABRIEL *tries to dance on his crutch. For some time they dance in silence. The* ANGEL *and* VAMPIRE *are there, dancing together. They begin to enjoy themselves.*)
(*Then they start to talk while they dance, sometimes to their partner and sometimes to one of the others, at first a sentence or two and finally all talking at once. The sentences are numbered in a suggested order. At 14, every couple talks at once, with each person alternating lines with their partner and overlapping with their partner at the end. So that by the end everyone is talking at once but leaving the vampire's last four or five words to be heard alone. At first they talk quietly then more freely, some angry, some exuberant. They speak Romanian.*)

BOGDAN: 1. Ţara asta are nevoie de un bărbat puternic. (This country needs a strong man.)
5. Sîntem un gunoi. (We're rubbish.)
13. Dă-le una peste gură. (Smack them in the mouth.)
Ei ştiu lucruri pe care nimeni altcineva nu le ştie, păsări, broaşte, vaci, dumnezeu, direcţia vîntului. (They know things nobody else knows, birds, frogs, cows, god, the direction of the wind.)

1640

IRINA: 3. Ea spune ca noi nu avem suflet. (She says we have no soul.)
12. (El) ar trebui spînzurat intr-o cuşcă, să dea lumea cu pietre în el. (He should have been hung up in a cage and stones thrown at him.)
14. Tu n-o să te mariţi cu-n ungur. (You're not going to marry a Hungarian.) Datorită lui Gaby poţi să vorbeşti aşa. (It's thanks to Gaby you can talk like this.)

1650 MIHAI: 8. Nimic nu e pe baze realistice. (Nothing is on a realistic basis.)
Trebuie să lăsăm trecutul în spate. (We have to put the past behind us.)
Frontul doreşte sa înlesnească democraţia. (The Front wish to facilitate democracy.)
Ei nu vor aranja votarea, fiindcă ştiu ei că vor învinge. (They wouldn't fix the vote because they knew they were going to win.)

FLAVIA: 2. Nu este istoria ce e în cartea de istorie? (Isn't history what's in the history books?) 1660
14. Vreau să predau corect. (I want to teach correctly.) Unde sînt casetele? (Where are the tapes?)
Voi scrie o istorie adevarată, ca să ştim exact ce s-a întîmplat. (I'm going to write a true history so we'll know exactly what happened.)
Am votat cu liberalii. (I voted Liberal.)

FLORINA: 4. Uneori îmi este dor de el. (Sometimes I miss him.)
14. Doctorul şef a încuiat răniţii într-o cameră. (The head doctor locked the wounded in a room.)
Comuniştii nu trebuie să candideze în alegeri. (The communists shouldn't stand in the election.) 1670
Imi place să fiu obosită, nu-mi place să te aud vorbind. (I like being tired, I don't like listening to you talk.)

RADU: 9. Cine a tras în douazeci şi doi? Nu e o întrebare absurdă. (Who was shooting on the 22nd? That's not a crazy question.)
Cine a aruncat pocnitori? Cine a adus difuzoare? (Who let off firecrackers? who brought loudhailers?)
Nu-mi pasă cum se numesc, este acelaşi popor. (I don't care what they're called it's the same people.) 1680
Trădezi morţii. (You're betraying the dead.)

LUCIA: 11. Mi-a fost ruşine ca nu am fost acolo. (I was so ashamed not to be here.)
14. Dar ce inseamna asta? De ce parte a fost el? (But what does it mean? Whose side was he on?) De ce n-au şcolile lor? (Why shouldn't they have their own schools?)
Nu sint sclava ta. (I'm not your slave.)

IANOŞ: 7. Eşti acuzat de genocid. (You're on trial for genocide.)
Cine este opozitia? Ungurii. (Who's the opposition? Hungarians.) 1690
Voi aţi fost prea mult sub turci, sînţeti ca sclavii. (You were under the Turks too long, you're like slaves.)
Vreau sa invăţ tot. (I want to learn everything.)

GABRIEL: 10. Sînt aşa de fericit, ca sînt de cealaltă parte. (I'm so happy I've put myself on the other side.)
14. Diferit acum. (Different now.)
Ii urasc pe francezi. (I hate the French.)
Ungurii îi fac pe oameni să ne dispreţuiască. (The Hungarians make people despise us.)
Aş vrea să fi fost omorît. Glumesc. (I wish I'd been killed. 1700 Just joking.)

ANGEL: 6. Să nu-ţi fie ruşine. (Don't be ashamed.)
13. Nu libertatea din afară ci libertatea interioară. (Not outer freedom of course but inner freedom.)
Am încercat sa mă ţin departe de politică. (I try to keep clear of the political side.)
Zburînd în albastru. (Flying about in the blue.)

VAMPIRE: 11. Nu-ţi fie frică. (Don't be frightened.)
14. Nu sînt o fiinţă umană. (I'm not a human being.)
Incepi sa vrei sînge. Membrele te dor, capul îţi arde. Tre- 1710 buie să te mişti din ce în ce mai repede. (You begin to want blood. Your limbs ache, your head burns, you have to keep moving faster and faster.)

# CASEBOOK ON CHURCHILL

*In her introduction to* Cloud Nine, *Churchill describes how she worked with the Joint Stock company to develop this play about the "parallel between colonial and sexual oppression."*

Caryl Churchill

Introduction to *Cloud
Nine*
(1983)

*Cloud Nine* was written for Joint Stock Theatre Group in 1978–79. The company's usual work method is to set up a workshop in which the writer, director and actors research a particular subject. The writer then goes away to write the play, before returning to the company for a rehearsal and rewrite period. In the case of *Cloud Nine* the workshop lasted for three weeks, the writing period for twelve, and the rehearsal for six.

The workshop for *Cloud Nine* was about sexual politics. This meant that the starting point for our research was to talk about ourselves and share our very different attitudes and experiences. We also explored stereotypes and role reversals in games and improvisations, read books and talked to other people. Though the play's situations and characters were not developed in the workshop, it draws deeply on this material, and I wouldn't have written the same play without it.

When I came to write the play, I returned to an idea that had been touched on briefly in the workshop—the parallel between colonial and sexual oppression, which Genet calls "the colonial or feminine mentality of interiorised repression." So the first act of *Cloud Nine* takes place in Victorian Africa, where Clive, the white man, imposes his ideals on his family and the natives. Betty, Clive's wife, is played by a man because she wants to be what men want her to be, and, in the same way, Joshua, the black servant, is played by a white man because he wants to be what whites want him to be. Betty does not value herself as a woman, nor does Joshua value himself as a black. Edward, Clive's son, is played by a woman for a different reason—partly to do with the stage convention of having boys played by women (Peter Pan, radio plays, etc.) and partly with highlighting the way Clive tries to impose traditional male behaviour on him. Clive struggles throughout the act to maintain the world he wants to see—a faithful wife, a manly son. Harry's homosexuality is reviled, Ellen's is invisible. Rehearsing the play for the first time, we were initially taken by how funny the first act was and then by the painfulness of the relationships—which then became more funny than when they had seemed purely farcical.

The second act is set in London in 1979—this is where I wanted the play to end up, in the changing sexuality of our own time. Betty is middle-aged, Edward and Victoria have grown up. A hundred years have passed, but for the characters only twenty-five years. There were two reasons for this. I felt the first act would be stronger set in Victorian times, at the height of colonialism, rather than in Africa during the 1950s. And when the company talked about their childhoods and the attitudes to sex and marriage that they had been given when they were young, everyone felt that they had received very conventional, almost Victorian expectations and that they had made great changes and discoveries in their lifetimes.

The first act, like the society it shows, is male dominated and firmly structured. In the second act, more energy comes from the women and the gays. The uncertainties and changes of society, and a more feminine and less authoritarian feeling, are reflected in the looser structure of the act. Betty, Edward and Victoria all change from the rigid positions they had been left in by the first act, partly because of their encounters with Gerry and Lin.

In fact, all the characters in this act change a little for the better. If men are finding it hard to keep control in the first act, they are finding it hard to let go in the second: Martin dominates Victoria, despite his declarations of sympathy for feminism, and the bitter end of colonialism is apparent in Lin's soldier brother, who dies in Northern Ireland. Betty is now played by a woman, as she gradually becomes real to herself. Cathy is played by a man, partly as a simple reversal of Edward being played by a woman, partly because the size and presence of a man on stage seemed appropriate to the emotional force of young children, and partly, as with Edward, to show more clearly the issues involved in learning what is considered correct behaviour for a girl.

It is essential for Joshua to be played by a white, Betty (I) by a man, Edward (I) by a woman, and Cathy by a man. The soldier should be played by the actor who plays Cathy. The doubling of Mrs. Saunders and Ellen is not intended to make a point so much as for sheer fun—and of course to keep the company to seven in each act. The doubling can be done in any way that seems right for any particular production. The first production went Clive-Cathy, Betty-Edward, Edward-Betty, Maud-Victoria, Mrs. Saunders/Ellen-Lin, Joshua-Gerry, Harry-Martin. When we did the play again, at the Royal Court in 1980, we decided to try a different doubling: Clive-Edward, Betty-Gerry, Edward-Victoria, Maud-Lin, Mrs. Saunders/Ellen-Betty, Joshua-Cathy, Harry-Martin. I've a slight preference for the first way because I like seeing Clive become Cathy, and enjoy the Edward-Betty connections. Some doublings aren't practicable, but any way of doing the doubling seems to set up some interesting resonances between the two acts.

## Caryl Churchill
### Interview
### (1984)

KATHLEEN *Betsko and Rachel Koenig conducted this interview with Caryl Churchill.*

INTERVIEWER: Is there a female aesthetic? And we'd like you to wrap this question up once and for all. [Laughter]

CHURCHILL: I don't see how you can tell until there are so many plays by women that you can begin to see what they have in common that's different from the way men have written, and there are still relatively so few. And we have things in common with male playwrights who are worried about similar things in their particular country and who have worked in the same theaters with the same directors. So it's hard to separate out and think of "women playwrights" rather than just "playwrights." Though I do remember before I wrote *Top Girls* thinking about women barristers—how they were in a minority and had to imitate men to succeed—and I was thinking of them as different from me. And then I thought, "Wait a minute, my whole concept of what plays might be is from plays written by men. I don't have to put on a wig, speak in a special voice, but how far do I assume things that have been defined by men?" There isn't a simple answer to that. And I remember long before that thinking of the "maleness" of the traditional structure of plays, with conflict and building in a certain way to a climax. But it's not something I think about very often. Playwriting will change not just because more women are doing it but because more women are doing other things as well. And of course men will be influenced by that too. So maybe you'll still be no nearer to defining a female aesthetic.

INTERVIEWER: Some of the playwrights we've interviewed suggest there are no "lost masterpieces" and that "the cream will rise to the top" in terms of women's writing for the stage.

CHURCHILL: Most theaters are still controlled by men and people do tend to be able to see promise in people who are like themselves. Women directors have pointed out to me how established men tend to take a young male director under their wing, and seem to feel more uncomfortable with a woman director because they can't quite see where she is, because they weren't like that at her age. I think the same thing can happen with writers: If you're at the stage where you are promising but not doing it all that well yet, it's perhaps easier for a man choosing plays to see the potential in a man writer. I don't know about "lost masterpieces" but people don't usually start out writing masterpieces and women may have less chance of getting started. Having productions does seem to make people write better.

INTERVIEWER: Has the political climate for women dramatists changed drastically since you began writing plays?

CHURCHILL: I began writing plays in 1958, and I don't think I knew of any other women playwrights then. Luckily, I didn't think about it. Do you know Tillie Olsen's book *Silences?* She says that at different times, whole categories of people are enabled to write. You tend to think of your own development only having to do with yourself and it's exciting to discover it in a historical context. When I began it was quite hard for any playwrights to get started in London. The English Stage Company had just started a policy of doing new writing at the Royal Court, but that was almost the only place. I had student productions at first, and then wrote for radio. In the late sixties and early seventies there was a surge of fringe theaters and interest in new writing, starting with the Theatre Upstairs and the Royal Court, and that was the first place to do a professional stage production of one of my plays, *Owners*, in 1972. For a while, a lot of writers were getting produced for the first time, though far fewer women than men. Gradually during the seventies the number of women increased, coming partly through fringe theaters and partly through women's theater groups. In the last five years there seem to be far more women playwrights and some theaters are more open to them, though others still aren't. At the moment, because of the financial cuts, it's again become quite hard for all playwrights. Theaters are having to do co-productions with other theaters because they haven't enough money to do a whole year's work on their grants, so it means one new play gets done instead of two. The Royal Court, for instance, can now only afford to do four new plays in the main house instead of eight. But I get the impression life is even harder for playwrights in the United States than in England because of there not being a subsidized theater.

INTERVIEWER: In Laurie Stone's *Village Voice* interview [March 1, 1983], you talked about women becoming Coca-Cola executives and you said, "Well, that's not what I mean by feminism." What exactly do you mean by feminism?

CHURCHILL: When I was in the States in '79 I talked to some women who were saying how well things were going for women in America now with far more top executives being women, and I was struck by the difference between that and the feminism I was used to in England, which is far more closely connected with socialism. And that was one of the ideas behind writing *Top Girls*, that achieving things isn't necessarily good, it matters *what* you achieve.

Thatcher had just become prime minister; there was talk about whether it was an advance to have a woman prime minister if it was someone with policies like hers: She may be a woman but she isn't a sister, she may be a sister but she isn't a comrade. And, in fact, things have got much worse for women under Thatcher. So that's the context of that remark. I do find it hard to conceive of a right-wing feminism. Of course, socialism and feminism aren't synonymous, but I feel strongly about both and wouldn't be interested in a form of one that didn't include the other.

INTERVIEWER: Do you think it's odd, given the fact that there is at best indifference, at worst hostility, political plays in America, that your works are so popular here?

CHURCHILL: Is it true that on the whole plays here tend to be more family-centered, personal, individual-centered?

INTERVIEWER: Yes, more psychological.

CHURCHILL: Whereas I've been quite heavily exposed to a tradition of looking at the larger context of groups of people. It doesn't mean you don't look at families or individuals within that, but you are also looking at bigger things. Like with the kind of work Joint Stock Theatre Group has done, where you go and research a subject and where you have a lot of characters, even if played by only a few people. It tends to open things out.

INTERVIEWER: The critics do ask, "Where are the American plays with the larger social issues?" Unfortunately, when one comes along our own critics usually turn thumbs down if the politics are overt. An overt political position is considered poor craft or preaching.

CHURCHILL: When I was in San Francisco I was talking to the people at the Eureka Theater [where Richard Seyd directed a production of *Cloud Nine* in 1983] and they were talking about developing a school of playwriting which would break away from family-centered plays, and write about other issues.

INTERVIEWER: Could you talk a little about working with Joint Stock?

CHURCHILL: I've worked with them three times, on *Light Shining in Buckinghamshire* [1976], *Cloud Nine* [1979] and *Fen* [1983]. The company was started in 1974 by several people, including Max Stafford-Clark, who directed *Light Shining* and *Cloud Nine*. There's usually a workshop of three or four weeks when the writer, director and actors research a subject, then about ten weeks when the writer goes off and writes the play, then a six-week rehearsal when you're usually finishing writing the play. Everyone's paid the same wage each week they're working and everyone makes decisions about the budget and the affairs of the company, and because of that responsibility and the workshop everyone is much more involved than usual in the final play. It's not perfect, but it is good, and I do notice the contrast with more hierarchical organizations and feel uncomfortable in them. Because everyone is involved it's taken for granted that everyone will have good parts, so you can't write a couple of main characters and give everyone else very little to do. And usually because of the subject matter, the plays tend to have a large cast of characters, although the company is about six or eight, and the actors double. It's very pressured because the tour's booked and the posters printed long before the play is finished. It's a very intense way of working.

INTERVIEWER: Do you find collaboration difficult?

CHURCHILL: No, I like it. I'd always been very solitary as a writer before and I like working that closely with other people. You don't collaborate on writing the play, you still go away and write it yourself, so to that extent it's the same as usual. What's different is that you've had a period of researching something together, not just information, but your attitudes to it, and possible ways of showing things, which means that when you come back with the writing you're much more open to suggestions.

INTERVIEWER: Do you feel subordinate to the director in rehearsal? One writer we interviewed was actually ejected from her rehearsals by a well-known director.

CHURCHILL: No, I've always got on well with directors. But it depends on having someone with roughly the same ideas as you so you trust each other, and if you do work well together you keep on with the same people, as I have with Max Stafford-Clark and Les Waters. It's one of the things the Theatre Writers' Union has put in contracts, the writer's right to attend rehearsals, and it's very important. Though, of course, if you're having to invoke the contract you're already in trouble.

INTERVIEWER: Does the playwright have an obligation to take a moral and political stance?

CHURCHILL: It's almost impossible not to take one, whether you intend to or not. Most plays can be looked at from a political perspective and have said something, even if it isn't what you set out to say. If you wrote a West End comedy relying on conventional sexist jokes, that's taking a moral and political stance, though the person who wrote it might say, "I was just writing an entertaining show." Whatever you do your point of view is going to show somewhere. It usually only gets noticed and called "political" if it's against the status quo. There are times when I feel I want to deal with immediate issues and times when I don't. I do like the stuff of theater, in the same way people who are painting like paint; and of course when you say "moral and political" that doesn't have to imply reaching people logically or overtly, because theater can reach people on all kinds of other levels too. Sometimes one side or the other is going to have more weight. Sometimes it's going to be about images, more like a dream to people, and sometimes it's going to be more like reading an article. And there's room for all that. But either way, the issues you feel strongly about are going to come through, and they're going to be a moral and political stance in some form. Sometimes more explicitly, sometimes less.

*London*
*November 23, 1984*

MANN:° How do you go about gathering research?

CHURCHILL: *Fen* is the most documentary of the plays, I suppose. We didn't use tape recorders. We went off to stay in a village and everyone would go out each day and talk to people and make notes or remember. The actors in the group would report back by becoming the person they met and saying the things the person had said; you could ask more questions and the actor would start to improvise and develop the character. Those of us who weren't actors simply described what had happened. So I was left with a lot of notes and quotes and things different people had said. But never a whole speech, just lines here and there. And I didn't make any characters who were based on a single person. For example, the old great-grandmother's speech on her birthday, practically every line is something that somebody actually said to us, but it's a composite of many different people. We met a woman who had been the secretary of the agricultural union, and the murder story, the Frank and Val story, was a newspaper cutting about someone she knew. A lot of the union references in the play were hers. There were a lot of things from one particular woman that went into the character Shirley, who's always working, about pride in working hard and not giving up, lines like "I didn't want my mother to think she'd bred a gibber."

MANN: You and the company started out with subject matter, an idea?

CHURCHILL: We started out very open—we were going to do a workshop in the Fens. But before we went, Les Waters, the director, and I had talked a lot about people having a bad time in the country; that's where the original sense of direction came from. We made a company of more women than men, so that was a decision affecting the subject of the play that was taken before we began the workshop. We read the book *Fen Women* by Mary Chamberlain before we went and

°American playwright Emily Mann extended Betsko and Koenig's interview with Churchill later in 1984.

during the workshop. And by the end of the workshop we had all focused on women land workers and knew the kind of issues it might be about.

But the difference between that way of working and what you've done, Emily, is that mine is an invented play, whereas you've written documentary things drawing on tapes.

MANN: You were making a completely fictional play, based on what you learned, from your response to being in the Fens and meeting all those people. In *Execution of Justice* I was working with the Eureka Theatre Company, and we talked and talked and talked and batted ideas around, then they gathered research for me, and I went out to San Francisco and did field work in the Castro district, and so on. The play is documentary, yes; that was a choice I made.

CHURCHILL: The only documentary play I've done was a television play about Northern Ireland, about a trial in the Diplock courts, which were introduced in 1973 because the government felt it was too hard to get convictions otherwise. There's no jury and only one judge. I had the transcript of a trial of a boy who was given sixteen years. A bomb had been planted in a British Legion Hall where some people were playing cards, and a boy walked in, put the thing down, and said, "Clear the hall" and they all went out. Half an hour later, a small bomb went off and nobody was hurt. The trial was extraordinary because there was no evidence to say the boy who was accused did it, except the police saying he'd confessed, which he denied. There was no signed statement by him. And there was an old man who'd been in the hall who said, "I don't know what boy it was but it was definitely not *that* boy." There was no positive identification at all, and it was hard to believe you would get a conviction in a normal court. So I did a play for television with Roland Joffe; it meant reducing the nine and a half hours of trial transcript. We put on a voice-over at the beginning and end of the program that explained the Diplock courts, and the BBC took it off because they said it was political comment, and put one of their own in different words, which they said was objective. We took our names off the credits as a protest. That was the only documentary I've ever done, and again it's different from what you've done because it was more specific and didn't involve so much research or so much material. Most of the plays I've written have been without any research, from what I already knew or what I imagined.

MANN: Let's talk about your play *Top Girls* [Methuen, London, 1982].

CHURCHILL: When I wrote *Top Girls* I was writing it by myself and not for a company. I wanted to write about women doing different kinds of work and didn't feel I knew enough about it. Then I thought, this is ridiculous, if you were with a company you'd go out and talk to people, so I did. Which is how I came up with the employment agency in the second act.

MANN: Are there specific characters in *Top Girls* that have their real life counterparts?

CHURCHILL: Quite a few of the things Win tells Angie about her life are things different people said to me. And of course the dead women at the dinner are all based on someone [from art, literature or history]. But apart from that, it's imaginary.

MANN: Tell me about the ways in which *Top Girls* has been misunderstood.

CHURCHILL: What I was intending to do was make it first look as though it was celebrating the achievements of women and then—by showing the main character, Marlene, being successful in a very competitive, destructive, capitalist way—ask, what kind of achievement is that? The idea was that it would start out looking like a feminist play and turn into a socialist one, as well. And I think on the whole it's mostly been understood like that. A lot of people have latched on to Marlene leaving her child, which interestingly was something that came very late. Originally the idea was just that Marlene was "writing off" her niece, Angie, because she'd never make it; I didn't yet have the plot idea that Angie was actually Marlene's own child. Of course women are pressured to make choices between working and having children in a way that men aren't, so it *is* relevant, but it isn't the main point of it.

There's another thing that I've recently discovered with other productions of *Top Girls.* In Greece, for example, where fewer women go out to work, the attitude from some men seeing it was, apparently, that the women in the play who'd gone out to work weren't very nice, weren't happy, and they abandoned their children. They felt the play was obviously saying women *shouldn't* go out to work—they took it to mean what they were wanting to say about women themselves, which is depressing. Highly depressing. [laughter] Another example of its being open to misunderstanding was a production in Cologne, Germany, where the women characters were played as miserable and quarrelsome and competitive at the dinner, and the women in the office were neurotic and incapable. The waitress slunk about in a catsuit like a bunnygirl and Win changed her clothes on stage in the office. It just turned into a complete travesty of what it was supposed to be. So that's the sort of moment when you think you'd rather write novels, because the productions can't be changed.

MANN: I don't know whether we're safer in the theater or not. . . .

CHURCHILL: With a play you do leave more room for other things and that's one of the attractions, that people can keep coming to it fresh and doing it differently. Lots of times I've liked foreign productions. I liked *Cloud Nine* in New York, [at Lucille Lortel's Theater De Lys, directed by Tommy Tune, 1981] and it was very different, though in many ways it wasn't as different as you might have expected. I was at rehearsals and Tommy Tune had seen Max Stafford-Clark's production in London. But still it was different.

MANN: What were the big differences?

CHURCHILL: Two main differences. It was broader, so it was more farcical in the first act and more emotional in the second. Tommy [Tune] talked about "permission to laugh" and thought the American audience might not realize at the beginning of the play that it was meant to be funny if the colonial thing was played as straight as it had been in England. And the other difference—which ties in with the more emotional feeling of the second half—is the moving of Betty's monologue and the song to the end of the play, to make more of a climax. It was sort of wonderful—the emotion of the end of the play in the American production—but I didn't really like it as much because it threw so much emphasis onto Betty as an individual, while the other way seemed to be more about the development of a group of people, in the same way as the first act. The New York version also meant that it ended with her very solitary, having the self-discovery that she enjoys sex in masturbation, but without taking her on from that to anything else. Whereas that monologue originally came earlier in the scene so you know from that that she's a sexual person and then you see her make her first move out toward someone else, even though it's a completely ridiculous and wrong move, trying to pick up her son's gay lover, but you know she'll have another go another time and it will work.

MANN: This is incredible, how much this changes what the play is about. Was it Tommy Tune who changed it? Or did you agree to it?

CHURCHILL: Moving the monologue was an idea of Tommy's that he had when I wasn't there, but I was quite glad and interested to try it. And I knew he wanted very strongly to make more of a climax at the end of the play. In the original production there's a song before the last scene of the second act and it's as if during it things change, because in the last scene everyone has moved on a bit and things have got better. But Tommy felt having the music there would make people think that was the ending, because we had a sort of climax with the music and then the last scene where people had changed and it ended more levelly and coolly. He wanted a different song, more uplifting, whereas the original one was a bit more ironical, and he wanted the music and climax right at the end. So it had quite a different shape and feeling to it.

MANN: So the difference for you is Tommy Tune changed your structure and in so doing changed the broader-based contextual look at the whole society.

CHURCHILL: Yes, they took it more to an emotional, personal point. And I suppose we could then launch off into the idea that this is one of the differences between the kind of work that comes out of a company like Joint Stock, which tends to deal more with groups of people and society as opposed to the personal. . . .

MANN: Yes.

CHURCHILL: You find lots of works which are just about people and their feelings in England, too. It isn't as if everything here was socially based. But there is a stronger vein of that, in this country, I think.

*IN this essay, the noted feminist theater scholar Janelle Reinelt coordinates several of the most significant theoretical developments of postmodern theater: Brechtian dramaturgy, an Althusserian critique of ideology, deconstructive philosophy, and feminism. In performance, Churchill's* Cloud Nine *provides—or can provide—a theatrical articulation of this complex of issues.*

This paper is an attempt at a possible articulation of Brechtian dramaturgy, feminism and deconstruction, or more generally of post-modernism. The vigorous debate about whether feminism should be considered a post-modernism has some features in common with the question of how far Brecht can be seen as a precursor of post-modern aesthetics. Brecht and feminism are often strange bedfellows, but they nevertheless share several crucial features which enter this debate. First, the political agenda of both Brecht and socialist-feminism is inseparable from their art. The task of Brecht and also of feminist theatre is to interrupt and deconstruct the habitual performance codes of the majority (male) culture—their stance is always adversarial vis-à-vis the prevailing hegemony. Both Brecht and feminism emphasize the possibility of change, that things might be other, that history is not an inevitable narrative. Feminism is and Brecht was historically embattled in the struggle to make art which dismantles the political and artistic status quo.

The search for means of subverting bourgeois ideology in performance links Brecht and feminism to some of the critical projects of deconstruction. Foregrounding these affinities, however, displaces and obscures the radical engagement in Sartre's sense which marks both Brecht and feminism.

> By what sign does Galy Gay know that he himself
> Is Galy Gay?
> If his arm were chopped off
> And he found it in a hole in the wall
> Would Galy Gay's eye know Galy Gay's arm?
> And would Galy Gay's foot cry out: that's the one?[1]

Brecht's debunking of the continuity of the ego in *A Man's A Man* provides a useful focal point for a look at the complex relationship between Marxism and deconstruction. While Marxism and deconstruction seem compatible when the critical operations are to make discourses evident, to unravel hegemony, to denaturalize and displace the seemingly natural and sovereign, the contradictions between them become acute over questions of "real" knowledge and truth. A sympathetic Marxist critic like Michael Ryan can see that "permanent revolution is the deconstructive possibility expressed politically."[2] On the other hand, Perry Anderson judges that post-structuralism results in the "exorbitation of language," the "attenuation of truth," and the "randomization of history."[3] The heat of this debate exists because of the contradictions playing through deconstruction at this historical moment. Its great power to retrieve and recuperate areas of marginal discourse has been recognized by many, especially by feminists, while the political conservatism of the Yale critics seems to confirm Terry Eagleton's charge that their "recycling of the work of Jacques Derrida for Ivy League consumption may be seen as the latest instance of US cultural imperialism."[4]

We can turn to Brecht, then, to see to what uses and abuses such critical theory can be put. Brecht anticipated and developed practical demonstrations of several of the key operations of deconstruction and post-structuralism. However, from a different viewpoint, certain aspects of his work seem to establish a limit case for such critical practice, demonstrating the incommensurability of the discourses of deconstruction and Marxism. I chose *A Man's A Man* for the exemplary text here because the role of the subject in the production of meaning is a critical issue in Marxism, feminism and deconstruction. Galy Gay is post-Derridean man. He is a "man who does not wish to be named"; that is, specified through signification, benamed, established. He goes out to buy a fish but, as a result of his position in an ensuing web of sociopolitical practices, he changes his intentions and his functions and becomes interchangeable with Jeraiah Jip whose place he displaces. In the vaudeville "numbers" that follow, Gay acts out the sale of a fraudulent elephant, is tried, convicted and executed. But he does not die, he merely "slips" into somebody else's shoes. "One man is no man. Until somebody calls out to him."

**Janelle Reinelt**

"Rethinking Brecht:
Deconstruction,
Feminism, and the
Politics of Form"
(1990)

*Brecht and
deconstruction*

This calling out is the function of ideology, which governs the imaginary relationship of individuals to their real conditions of existence. The individual is constructed as a subject to take up a position of unity and coherence from which she is able to act, learned from the ideological mirror in which she mistakes herself. Galy Gay refuses to look into the crate where his dead self lies:

> I cannot look, on pain of instant death/
> At the blanked-out face in a crate/
> Of a certain man, once known to me from the water's surface/
> Into which looked a man who, as I know, has just died.

The myth of identity comes from a reflection, which is always in an ideological mirror. Refusing the old identity (which was also ideological), Gay accepts the reflected self which Uriah and his buddies give him in calling out to him as Jeraiah Jip.

While here Brecht portrays an instance of the transformation and reconstruction of a subject, he also had a dramatic method or technique for uncovering the arbitrariness of identity and its social construction. The Alienation effect hollows out and denaturalizes behaviors which are actually socially constructed, enforced through power relations and the myopia which results from habitual positioning within them. The A-effect underlines the nonnecessity of such behaviors and the insubstantiality of such constructed identities. Terry Eagleton has remarked on the Derridean character of alienated acting which, "sliding a hiatus between actor and action," reveals the nonself-identical gesture as imbricated in the conditions of their production. He writes: "The dramatic gesture, by miming routine behavior in contrivedly hollow ways, represents it in all its lack, in its suppression of material conditions and historical possibilities, and thus represents an absence which it at the same time produces."[5]

The Derridean gloss helps clarify the production of meaning. What the actor does in fact displaces the other possible actions. They are there in radical alterity, present in their absence, if only we can see them. Thus Brecht writes: [The actor] "when he appears on the stage, besides what he actually is doing he will at all essential points discover, specify, imply what he is not doing; that is to say he will act in such a way that the alternative merges as clearly as possible, that his acting allows other possibilities to be inferred and only represents one out of the possible variants."[6] Brecht's major technical tool for fixing the not-but, the social gest, exposes the sociopolitical relations which support it. Brecht builds the lesson of the gest into *Caucasian Chalk Circle* when Azdak explains to the disguised Grand Duke how a poor man eats in contradiction to a rich man. In so doing, Brecht alienates the gest of eating, revealing the possibilities for a disquisition on the mythology of table manners, à la Roland Barthes. In fact, Barthes, writing of the Brechtian gest in terms of Lessing's "pregnant moment," sees it as "just this presence of all the absences (memoirs, lessons, promises) to whose rhythm. History becomes both intelligible and desirable."[7]

In addition to the A-effect and its critical support, the social gest, Brecht's epic structure also seems like a deconstructive strategy. Episodes are self-contained, discontinuous spectacles, contradicting or replacing each other, and designed for possible rearrangement. The logocentric, seamless world of Aristotelian drama is here subverted, refused a place. Events are not causally connected, self-identical and stable, but are constituted by difference, by what they are not, are lacking, might have been. Roland Barthes describes these epic scenes as cut-outs, "decoupage," the "erecting of a meaning manifesting the production of that meaning" and thus ultimately throwing it into question.[8]

Thus far it seems as if Brecht's work is almost a precursor of deconstructive practice, breaking up continuities, denying identities, approaching meanings by reference to lack and absence, refusing closure or completion in many of his texts. However, this harmonious compatibility unravels in Brecht over the issue of the subject's role and the value of valueless discourse. Bourgeois critics often act as if the A-effect, social gest and epic structure can be lifted out of Brecht and treated completely as a formalism. Fundamental to both feminism and to Brecht's project is the embodiment of socio-political analysis in those processes. These tools are not neutral. To consider this distinction, we will return to *A Man's A Man*.

In a 1927 radio broadcast, Brecht described "a new type," a human being who is infinitely adaptable and changeable and who, contrary to what we might think, is no weakling but the strongest of all. "That is to say he becomes the strongest once he has ceased to be a private person, he only becomes strong in the mass."[9] Brecht claimed to have revised the text of *A Man's A Man* ten times. This endless rewriting and modification is a typical refusal of closure in Brecht's work, one of the indices of his post-modern leanings and his inclination to open-ended supplement and re-iteration in Derrida's sense of those words. However, the ending of the play reveals a site of struggle over the production of meaning which is germane to this discussion. In the 1928 version, produced at the *Volksbühne,* the last scene took place before the fortress at Sir El Djowr where Galy Gay leads an assault. In 1931, the scene was cut from Brecht's production with Peter Lorre, Brecht saying he was "unable to see any way of giving a negative character to the hero's growth within the collectivity. I decided to leave that growth undescribed."[10] In the 1950s, he restored the Fortress scene with several insertions, the most pointed being the description of 7,000 innocent refugees burning inside the fortress. The reworking of this material represents an effort on Brecht's part to close the gaps and the possible play of signification in the earlier version, to disallow the possible positive reading of Gay's transformation. Ceasing to be a private person and becoming a member of the mass has positive connotations vis-à-vis the effort to build a revolutionary party, but its fascist connotations are much stronger, especially within Brecht's historical context. This ambivalence of the centerless self points to the problematic of the subject as seen within both post-structural and Marxist discourse.

The relationship between structure and subject has not had a history of successful articulation in Marxist thought, and in France in the period we now call structuralist, two divergent ways of thinking coalesced to dismantle the subject. Lévi-Strauss and Foucault proclaimed the end of the subject in favor of the development of forms, and Marxism's most important thinker of the moment, Louis Althusser, joined forces with this view by erasing the subject altogether with a theory of ideological determination. In what is called post-structuralism, a radical linguistic model becomes the paradigm for human interactions and with it, especially in Derrida, structures themselves are overthrown in a philosophical critique of centers, presences, and origins. Enter undecidability, indeterminancy, and the endless play of signifiers. Along with the subject, the notion of Truth disappears. As Perry Anderson points out, "the *distinction* between the true and the false is the ineliminable premise of any rational knowledge. Its central site is evidence."[11] This epistemological crisis is heightened when coupled with a theorized dispersed subjectivity in a field of infinite play.

The function of ideology is to position subjects within a specific organization of reality, making available certain fixed relations which pass for the whole of sociability. Althausser attacked naive notions of false consciousness and uncritical empiricism and reinstated ideology as a constitutive practice that produces and reproduces life, freeing it from relegation to the status of superstructure determined by the economic base. The new theory, however, proclaimed that ideology had no history, or, in other words, subjects exist wholly *inside* an ideological formation.[12] Ideology interpellates (his word) individuals as subjects, fixing them in an always imaginary relationship to the real conditions of existence. Rosalind Coward and John Ellis identify the shortcomings of this view: ". . . this Marxist account does not show how the contradictory processes of the individual subject are themselves constituted: this in turn means that it cannot analyze moments of ideological crisis where these subjective processes enter into contradiction with the functioning of ideology itself; where these subjective processes are overdetermined by the contradictions of other practices."[13] How is it that subjects have agency? How is it possible to work for revolutionary change? From the dangers of a crude economism, Marxism had made only a lateral move to the dangers of a crude ideologism.

In spite of Althusser's sympathetic reading of Brecht, Brecht's work is quite incompatible with Althusserianism, as it is with the truth-denying aspects of deconstruction. While it is true that most of Brecht's characters are not themselves aware of their ideological behavior, the whole intent of the alienation effect is to make the socially constructed bases of such behavior apparent. To whom, we might ask, if there is no subject capable of grasping and struggling with this knowledge? Further, some characters do possess knowledge of their own positioning, even as they live it, such as Schweyk, Adzak, Galileo, who are not ignorant of the conditions of existence and are able to make or fail to make their own limited interventions. The implicit theory of the subject in Brecht's work is the subject in process, crisscrossed by the contradictions of competing practices. Brecht's split characters like Puntila and Shen Te or Mother Courage, who damns the war only to defend it in her next stage moment are sites of ideological struggle through competing social practices which may not resolve into unified subjectivity, but which do provide grounds for dialectical change.

Brecht's acting theory also requires the representation of agency as well as fixed conditions. The Brechtian actor portrays character in such a way as to draw attention to the possibilities for alternative behavior in concrete historical moments. Phil Auslander has recently commented on the incompatibility of this acting technique with deconstruction, because while the actor deconstructs the unified subjectivity of the character, she reintroduces it in the persona of her involved social self-as-actor who comments on the action. He writes: "Brecht would have the actor partly withhold her presence from the character she plays in order to comment on it. To do so, however, she must endow another fictional persona with the authority of full presence, a theoretical movement which makes Brecht's performance theory subject to the same deconstructive critique of presence as Stanislavski's."[14] Perhaps, but only if the actor's own position as subject in process is not taken into account. The framing device for *Caucasian Chalk Circle* historicizes the incidents of the narrative; similarly, the acting device of alienation historicizes subjectivity, implicating the actors as well as the characters in its wake.

Since Brecht's theatre always requires the representation of agency implicated in historical and material processes, it refuses and critiques Althusser's interpellation theory as well as deconstruction's dispersed and infinitely deferred self. In the case of socialist-feminism, some of the same affinities and ultimate incompatibilities reappear when feminist aesthetics attempts to appropriate deconstruction.

## Feminism, Brecht, and deconstruction

Issues of representation constitute one of feminism's most formidable problematics. Recognizing that women have been inscribed in literature and drama as an objectification of the male gaze, gendered as "Women" in a mythically charged field of signification designed and operated largely by bourgeois men, women artists have struggled to break these forms of representation and to create or at least imagine the possibility of new ones. Through the seventies, the new theory, especially of French feminists, seemed to provide an articulation of semiotics and psychoanalysis which could account for the ideological (read patriarchal) character of representation itself. As appropriated by materialist feminists, this theory underscores the social construction of gender, the male-gendered subject position and the corresponding Other left for women in dominant bourgeois discourse. Thus, the possibilities for deconstructing representations of gender on stage held promise for a new political theatre.

In her cross gender/race casting in *Cloud Nine,* Caryl Churchill, for example, deconstructs "normal" differences in the behavior of men and women by trying out those behaviors on each other's bodies. Simple actions become powerful social gests in Brecht's sense of the word. The lifting of a Victorian skirt can look "natural" when a woman does it, but is strongly alienated when a man performs it as a learned behavior. Seeing a man play a little girl establishes "Cathy" as a site of radical struggle over gender identification rather than as a female child who likes to play with guns.

Thus far, feminist applications of alienation devices and the social gest display the same affinity with deconstructive theory that appeared to apply to Brecht. However, in feminist theory there was a disquieting all-pervasive consequence of seeing a woman totally constructed by male hegemony, lacking a speaking voice. As Julia Kristeva put it in a now famous passage: "It follows that a feminist practice can only be negative, at odds with what already exists so that we may say 'that's not it' and 'that's still not it.'"[15] Thus, the predicament of women was to be able to expose oppressive representation as ideological but not to be able to affirm a more adequate one, at least not on theoretical grounds which exclude women from the subject of discourse. In an incisive essay on "Feminism and Formalism," Sue Ellen Case and Jeanie Forte write: "The problem is that in the closed systems of deconstruction the only possible reference is to the dominant ideology it deconstructs. In effect, it reproduces things as they are."[16] As a result, women are left with a negative practice, all they can theoretically say is "no, that's still not it."

It is now apparent that the role of the subject in the production of meaning is precisely what is at stake for both Brecht and feminism. The requirements of the active subject, capable of surpassing a given ideological grid, cannot be subsumed under either Althusserian Marxism or French feminism. In practice, just as with Brecht, the texts of feminist artists reassert a female I, not only by "fixing the not-but" which is a negative relationship but also by staging female experience and appealing to a political practice aimed at ideological struggle. Agency is assumed here, too.

To return to Churchill's *Cloud Nine,* the cross-casting reveals strain between role and identity, tension between social construction and a self who wishes it were otherwise. In the course of the narrative, the main character evolves beyond the social configuration of Victorian England, although she is clearly within a new ideological formation, that of late bourgeois feminism/capitalism, which she must also struggle to transcend. In acting techniques as well, the requirements for agency contradict a theory of the infinitely dispersed subject. Following the movement slogan "the personal is political," much new feminist art has portrayed personal psychological experience, which would seem a Brechtian anathema if it were not for the contextualizing of the representations by writers like Churchill. To re-construct female experience, it has been necessary to combine two styles of acting. Gillian Hanna of the Monstrous Regiment, for whom Churchill wrote several plays including *Cloud Nine,* talks about having to mesh elements of sense memory with Brechtian demonstration. Churchill's plays frequently feature scenes of psychological realism, historicized by an episodic structure which interrupts the narrative and establishes historical distance between spectator and representation. Fredric Jameson has remarked on the possibility that the hermeneutic process itself has two distinct and indispensible moments, "a first naive 'belief' in the density of presence of novelistic representation, and a later 'bracketting' of that experience in which the necessary distance of all language from what it claims to represent—its substitutions and displacements—are explored."[17] In much feminist drama, there is a kind of flicker effect, an alternation between a deconstruction of representation and a reconstruction of a feminist horizon of possibility. That this, in turn, is subject to critique does not trap the process within a wholly negative dialectic.

Both Brecht and feminism posit a subject-in-process, the site of multiple contradictions and competing social practices, where concrete political change may coalesce, if not originate. The incompatibility of this subject with much of the so-called new critical theory is based on the inability of deconstruction to accommodate the reconstructive moment. Michael Ryan's optimistic characterization of deconstruction as the possibility of permanent revolution emphasizes the negative moment of the hermeneutic dialectic. Both Brecht and feminism require a concept of agency sufficient to ground political action. Jill Dolan specifies the task of socialist-feminist theatre: "Our socially constructed gender roles are inscribed in our language and in our bodies. The stage, then, is a proper place to explore gender ambiguity, not to carthartically expunge it from society, but to play with, confound and deconstruct gender categories. If we stop considering the stage as a mirror of reality, we can use it as a laboratory in which to reconstruct new, non-genderized identities."[18] While Brecht's own representations of gender and sexual difference are subject to severe critique from a feminist perspective, his commitment to a socialist horizon and his belief in the ability of humans to transform their conditions of existence align him with some aspects of socialist-feminism. Both share the subversive agenda of deconstruction, but in refusing the endless play of signifiers in a ever-suspended production of meaning, both affirm the reconstructive possibility on the laboratory of the stage.

*Notes*

[1]Bertolt Brecht, *A Man's a Man,* in *Collected Plays* Vol. 2, eds. Ralph Manheim and John Willett (New York: Vintage Books, 1977), 56.

[2]Michael Ryan, *Marxism and Deconstruction* (Baltimore: The John Hopkins University Press, 1982), 5.

[3]Perry Anderson, *In the Tracks of Historical Materialism* (Chicago: The University of Chicago Press, 1983), 40–48ff.

[4]Terry Eagleton, "The Idealism of American Criticism," *Against the Grain* (London: Verso, 1986), 53–54.

[5]Eagleton, 167.

[6]Bertolt Brecht, "Short Description of a New Technique of Acting," in *Brecht On Theatre,* trans. by John Willett (New York: Hill and Wang, 1957), 137.

[7]Roland Barthes, "Diderot, Brecht, Eisenstein," *Image, Music, Text,* trans. Stephen Heath (New York: Hill and Wang, 1977), 73.

[8]Barthes, 71.

[9]"A radio speech," *Brecht on Theatre,* 18.

[10]"On Looking through My First Play," *Collected Plays* (Vol. 2), 245.

[11]Anderson, 48.

[12]Cf. Louis Althusser, "Ideology and Ideological State Apparatuses" in *Lenin and Philosophy,* trans. by Ben Brewster (New York: Monthly Review Press, 1971), 127–86. Cf. also Paul Hirst's explanation and critique of Althusser, *On Law and Ideology* (London: Macmillan, 1979).

[13]Rosalind Coward and John Ellis, *Language and Materialism* (London: Routledge and Kegan Paul, 1977), 78.

[14]Philip Auslander, "'Just Be Yourself' Logocentrism and Difference in Performance Theory," *Art and Cinema* (Summer 1986), 12.

[15]Julia Kristeva, "Women Can Never be Defined," in *New French Feminisms,* eds. Elaine Marks and Isabelle de Courtivron (New York: Schocken Books, 1981), 137.

[16]Case and Forte, "From Formalism to Feminism," *Yale Theater* (Spring 1985).

[17]Fredric Jameson, "Conclusion," in *Aesthetics and Politics,* trans. and ed. Ronald Taylor (London: New Left Books, 1977), 204.

[18]Jill Dolan, "Gender Impersonation Onstage: Destroying or Maintaining the Mirror of Gender Roles?" *Women in Performance* (1985), 10.

# Wendy Wasserstein

Wendy Wasserstein was born in Brooklyn, New York, in 1950; the youngest of five children, she was named for the heroine of James M. Barrie's play, *Peter Pan*. During her childhood, her family moved to Manhattan. She attended the Calhoun School and studied dance—her mother, Lola Schliefer Wasserstein, had been a professional dancer—with the June Taylor School of Dance. At Mount Holyoke College in Massachusetts, she majored in history and graduated in 1971. Wasserstein then entered the M. A. program in creative writing at the City University of New York, and wrote her first play, *Any Woman Can't* (1971). Playwrights Horizons produced the play in 1973, inaugurating Wasserstein's long association with the company; she is now on the board of directors.

In 1973 Wasserstein entered the M. F. A. program in playwriting at the Yale School of Drama. *Uncommon Women and Others* was her Master's thesis play; it was produced in 1977 at the Eugene O'Neill National Playwrights Conference and then at the Phoenix Theater in New York, where it won an Obie Award. Wasserstein's characteristic interest in the lives of women in contemporary America is elaborated in several later plays, especially *Isn't It Romantic* (1981), *The Heidi Chronicles* (1988), for which she won the Pulitzer Prize for drama and a Tony Award, and *The Sisters Rosenzweig* (1992).

## Uncommon Women and Others (1977)

Written while Wasserstein was a student at the Yale School of Drama, *Uncommon Women and Others* is a portrait of the aspirations of eight undergraduate women at Mount Holyoke College in the early 1970s. It is a "realistic" play, attempting to account for the growth of its characters in a relatively conventional manner. Although the play begins and ends in 1978—six years after graduation, when five of the women meet and discuss how their lives have developed since college—most of the action takes place in the past. In many respects, *Uncommon Women* is a series of vignettes of affluent young women on the cusp of the nascent women's movement in the U. S.: they are shown trying to negotiate the desire for political and social freedom with their own often internalized vision of a women's traditional social role—seeking a husband, for instance. The college itself becomes a kind of metaphor for their situation; many scenes open with a "man's voice" reading from the Mount Holyoke College bulletin, and from Richard Glenn Gettell's presidential address of 1957, "A Plea for the Uncommon Women":

> When scholars point out that even the best cooks have been men, the proper answer is, "But what man has been not only the second best cook, but the third best parent, the seventh best typist, and the tenth best community leader?"

Even the official voice of the women's college offers a deeply divided message. Rather than preparing women for an independent intellectual and social life, the college prepares them for a life of dependency and subordination, in which they can have "second best" careers defined solely through their relationship to men, the family, the community. This message is also enacted in the many rituals of dormitory life—milk and cookies, the "senior elf," "Gracious Living"—that infantilize the women as a way of preparing them for their appointed lives as the spouses of successful, Ivy League men.

> Though we have had our chances
> With over night romances
> With the Harvard and the Dartmouth male.
>
> And though we've had a bunch in
> Tow from Princeton Junction
> We're saving ourselves for Yale.

The problems that women confront in the educational institution and in the society they will enter as adults are hardly trivial. But like Mrs. Plumm's long repressed "friendship" with Ada Grudder, the women are mainly forced to repress their creativity, their identity, in favor of "fitting in"; the woman who finally achieves public success as the auteur of a film on Wittgenstein is, notably, the outcast in college and not present at the party six years later, pursuing a socially acceptable role. The results of their college training are perhaps, finally, visible in the opening and closing scene. The women have grown into successful but troubled adults, still living out the desire for freedom and self-determination that was instilled in them—and thwarted—by their "uncommon" education.

# —Uncommon Women and Others —
## Wendy Wasserstein

### —CHARACTERS—

In the present:
KATE QUIN
SAMANTHA STEWART
MUFFET DI NICOLA
HOLLY KAPLAN
RITA ALTABEL
At the college:
MRS. PLUMM
SUSIE FRIEND
CARTER, a catatonic
LEILAH

### THE SETTING

*The present, 1978, in a restaurant, and six years earlier at a college for women. In the present the women are around 27 years old.*

*The play should be played on a single playing area. In other words the restaurant in the present becomes the college living room. This will give continuity to the episodic nature of the play.*

## —ACT ONE—

### SCENE I

MAN'S VOICE: The college produces women who are persons in their own rights: Uncommon Women who as individuals have the personal dignity that comes with intelligence, competence, flexibility, maturity, and a sense of responsibility. This can happen without loss of gaiety, charm or femininity. Through its long history the college has graduated women who help to make this a better, happier world. Whether their primary contributions were in the home or the wider community, in advocations or vocations, their role has been
10 constructive. The college makes its continuing contribution to society in the form of graduates whose intellectual quality is high, and whose responsibility to others is exceptional. *(As Man's Voice begins lights come up on Kate Quin making final adjustments on a restaurant table. Enter Samantha Stewart. They embrace. The Women speak softly to each other. As the Man's Voice fades, Kate gets up from the table and Holly Kaplan enters.)*
SAMANTHA: *(Laughs.)* Holly, it's nice to see you.
HOLLY: You too Samantha. You cut your hair.
20 SAMANTHA: Yeah, I didn't want to look like Jean Shrimpton anymore.
HOLLY: Kate. How long are you in town for?
KATE: I don't know. I'm here on a women and law conference. Very grown-up, huh? I am now the young spokesperson at all the obligatory boring occasions.
HOLLY: How's Robert?
SAMANTHA: Oh, he's fine. He was just cast in a T.V. pilot. He plays the male ingenue and he's worried 'cause his hairline is receding.
30 KATE: Holly, I forgot to tell you. Rita's coming down from Vermont. She told Samantha she had a six-year itch to see us all again.

SAMANTHA: Muffy wrote me and said that Rita was so fat at her wedding that she couldn't even walk down the aisle. She had to be lowered to the altar by a crane. *(Pause.)* I don't believe that.
MUFFET: *(Enters and joins the conversation immediately.)* Rita was a rotunda. It was pathetic when the orchestra played *(Begins to sing "More.")* "More than the greatest . . ." She must sit in bed and eat bonbons all day.    40
KATE: Gross-me-out, Muffet.
ALL: Gross-me-out?
MUFFET: Holly, pumpkin. *(Kisses Holly and touches her hair.)* I like your hair. Kate, did you really have to bring your attache case to the restaurant? Washington isn't that far away, I wish you got into town more often.
KATE: Muffet, I am a very important person now.
MUFFET: Don't you still sneak trashy novels?
HOLLY: I thought of you, Katie, when Jacqueline Susann died.
SAMANTHA: Did you know she had a buttocks enhancement?   50 Eva Le Gallienne told Robert when he was touring in *Cactus Flower.*
MUFFET: Samantha, only you would call an ass lift a "buttocks enhancement."
KATE: Who's Eva Le Gallienne?
HOLLY: She wasn't our year. *(Pause.)*
MUFFET: Kate, how's Iki?
KATE: Well, he still loves me and Mother still asks about him. But . . .
MUFFET: And what's his name, the revolutionary. . . .    60
KATE: He left the bookstore and finished law school. He loves me, too. Muffet, this is adolescent. *(Pause.)* I've become a feminist.
HOLLY: Well, Alice Harwitch dropped out of medical school to form a lesbian rock band.
KATE: Gross-me-out! Does she sleep with women?
HOLLY: I guess so; they live together.
MUFFET: So what? I've taken a stand on birth control pills. I

won't be manipulated by the pharmaceutical establishment.

70 HOLLY: Well, you're just not a masochist.

MUFFET: Oh, yes I am. I'm an insurance seminar hostess.

HOLLY: Muffy, why don't you go to graduate school?

MUFFET: Holly, not all of our fathers invented velveteen and can afford to send us to three graduate schools. Which master's are you on now; design, literature, or history. I can never keep track.

HOLLY: History.

MUFFET: Holly's embarrassed. You know I didn't mean it. You know you're my best. In fact, the one thing I miss in Hart-

80 ford is having women friends. (*Pause.*) Did you read in the Alumnae Magazine that Nina Mandelbaum, now a landscape architect, got married twice to the same pediatric pulmonary specialist—they had a small wedding in Mexico and then a big religious ceremony in New York. Why Mexico? Do you think he went to medical school in . . .

ALL: Guadalajara!

HOLLY: My parents got a hold of that magazine and offered to fly me to Mexico if I thought he had any friends.

SAMANTHA: Did you know that Ca-Ca Phelps is teaching at

90 Yale?

KATE: Stop!

HOLLY: She was one of those people who was with her horse the day of the Cambodia strike. Her real name was Caroline, right? So why does she still insist on calling herself Ca-Ca? Katie, wasn't Ca-Ca a friend of Leilah's?

KATE: I don't know. I really didn't know Leilah's friends very much. (*Quick pause.*) Do you ever think it's odd that none of us have children? I know we're the uncommon bell curve, but I still think it's odd. I can't decide if I want any.

100 MUFFET: Don't worry, Nina Manelbaum will bud for all of us. There's a good genetic pool in pediatric pulmonary specialists. (*Pause.*) So, where's Rita?

KATE: I don't understand what Rita's doing. She's a smart girl.

MUFFET: We're all smart girls.

HOLLY: It's a sexist society.

KATE: I don't have any trouble.

MUFFET: Kate, you don't know what trouble is. You were born in *Holiday Magazine*.

KATE: Really, what does Rita do all day?

110 HOLLY: Nothing.

KATE: Gross-me-out! (*Rita enters. As Rita enters, she screams out each girl's name and kisses them.*)

RITA: I just called Timmy.

HOLLY: He loves you.

RITA: No, he waits on me. I told you I always wanted a wife. He gives great head though. (*Pause.*) Kate, I'm really getting into women's things. I've been reading Doris Lessing, and I think when I get it together I'm going to have a great novel.

MUFFET: Rita, how are you getting it together doing nothing?

120 RITA: I'm getting into my head.

MUFFET: (*To Holly.*) Or Timmy's as the case may be.

RITA: Kate, I want to hear more about your law firm. I think we need more women lawyers and gynecologists. I won't go to mine anymore, 'cause it's a man. Besides, I heard he had a twin.

SAMANTHA: But Rita, you really should get a regular check-up.

RITA: Samantha, what's it like being married to Robert?

SAMANTHA: We're very happy.

RITA: I had to train Timmy. He's going to become my Leonard

Woolf. Got a match, Muffet?    130

SAMANTHA: I was going to join a women's group, but I couldn't decide what to take—macrame, breadbaking, or consciousness rap. (*Muffet lights herself, Rita and Holly on one match.*)

RITA: You know I saw a Bette Davis movie once, and the third one on the match dies. (*Puts arm around Holly.*) I didn't upset you, Holly, sweetheart?

HOLLY: No, it was planned on my part. I hate the women's movement. I sent an article to *Ms.* and this Noel Schwartz sent me back a personal note saying, "I was a heretic to the    140 sisterhood." And I ask you, is Holly Kaplan that different from Noel Schwartz? And she telling me about the sisterhood!

MUFFET: She has problems.

RITA: That's all right, Holly, when we're forty, we'll be incredible.

HOLLY: Rita, when we were graduating, you predicted by thirty. (*Rita tosses it off.*)

RITA: At least at college they appreciated us.

HOLLY: No they didn't. You were miserable. You hated it.    150

RITA: Well, at least we appreciated us.

MUFFET: I wish I was back there.

KATE: That says something about the quality of your life. (*Pause.*)

HOLLY: Kate already is incredible.

KATE: I don't think I appreciated women then, as much as I do now.

RITA: Kate, you just lacked imagination.

KATE: Now, Carter, for example, was incredibly bright.

MUFFET: Now, Carter, for example, was a catatonic. (*Pause.*)    160

SAMANTHA: Wanna make an announcement?

KATE: What?

SAMANTHA: I'm going to make an announcement. Like at Mount Holyoke. Now, let's all pretend we're at the dining room table. (*All the girls clink their glasses.*) Seniors and anybody who will be here for graduation: We need people to sing on Upper Lake, Commencement Eve. Singers are needed both on shore and in canoes. We will be singing show tunes, and—special attraction—"Love Look Away," from *Flower Drum Song*, and of course, the Alma Mater.    170 Questions call . . .

ALL: Susie Friend! (*All the girls clap and laugh. Holly standing up agitated and not laughing.*)

MUFFET: Holly, what's wrong?

HOLLY: I can't stand to hear clinking glasses. It always makes me feel at any moment someone will come out in one of those pastel *Modess* living rooms and tell me to take my feet off the table, dear. (*They all clink their glasses.*)

(*End Scene*)


SCENE II

*Mrs. Plumm enters as soon as the girls finish clinking. The speech will serve as a transition from present to past.*

MRS. PLUMM: I'm so glad I have this opportunity to welcome all you girls to tea this year. I'm Mrs. Plumm, housemother of    180 North Stimson Hall. Dear, take your feet off the table. The tea fund was established by Lucy Valerie Bingsbee, class of

1906, after whom a Vermont orchid bog was recently dedicated by Governor Hoff as The Lucy Valerie Bingsbee Wildflower Sanctuary. I think you girls will find tea here very comfy. I knew Lucy. I never cared for her much.
I hope you all have a good year. There's a bit of a draft in here. If you have any questions or suggestions please knock at my door at any time except after 8:00 P.M. Although I'm
190   not needed to sign overnight slips anymore, I'm still interested in all my girls.
I thought before the end of tea, I'd read for you since I've always enjoyed oral interpretation. My friend, Dr. Ada Grudder, class of 1928 organized a theatre at the Christian Medical College in Nagpur, India. She begs me to visit, but I don't like long trips, and anyway it's so pleasant here, especially in the fall. Mmmmmmmmmmm. The cookies look lovely. What are they? Shortbread?
I'd like to read from the poetry of Emily Dickinson class of
200   1850. To those of you who are familiar with this reading please bear with me. Contrary to rumor, I didn't know Emily. (*Laughs to herself.*) She never accepted visitors.

The heart is the capital of the mind,
The mind is a single state.
    heart and mind together make
A single continent.

One is the population
Numerous enough.
This ecstatic nation
210   Seek—it is yourself.

(*She turns to girls at restaurant table.*) Please take your tea-cups to the long table at the end of the room when you leave. Why doesn't someone close the window? There's still a draft in here. (*Exit Mrs. Plumm.*)

(*End Scene*)

SCENE III

*A college living room. Six years earlier.*

MAN'S VOICE: On November 8, 1837, Miss Lyons Seminary was a place of high excitement. The building had been completed for the school that was to do for young women what Yale and Harvard were doing for young men. The 80 stu-
220   dents who enrolled the first year had the vitality and dedication of pioneers. (*Same women as in first scene. They are joined by Leilah an attractive, but intense young woman. At one chair is also a very frail blond girl with alabaster skin, Carter. Also they are joined by Susie Friend, in tasteful Villager turquoise and engagement ring. The coffee table is set with tea-cups and milk and sugar, finger sandwiches and mayonnaise. The girls leave restaurant table and led by Susie Friend they stand up and perfunctorily sing grace. The attitude towards grace varies.*)

ALL THE WOMEN: (*Sing.*)
230          *Oh, the Lord is good to me,*
             *and so I thank the Lord,*
          *for giving me the things I need,*
       *the sun and the rain, and the appleseed,*
             *the Lord is good to me.*

(*Carter pulls out her chair. Susie Friend puts her hand on the chair.*)

SUSIE: Oh, no wait. You can't sit down 'til Mrs. Plumm comes.
CARTER: Who's Mrs. Plumm?
SUSIE: She's our housemother.
RITA: She has syphilis. (*Mrs. Plumm enters and sits behind a small tea service. Rita waves hello. The girls sit down in unison. Susie clinks her glass. All the girls follow in unison.* 240 *Carter watches.*)
SUSIE: (*Stands up.*) Announcement, Announcement! There'll be sherry and dinner to honor senior choral members at 1886 House. Also congratulations to Melissa Weex and Ca-Ca Phelps, new chairman of the Outing Club and Swan Song Soiree . . . (*Everyone applauds. Rita and Kate applaud once. Susie sits down and takes a finger sandwich.*)
SAMANTHA: Susie, would you care for mayonnaise?
SUSIE: I couldn't.
MUFFET: Holly could.                                                  250
SUSIE: (*Biting sandwich.*) I love finger sandwiches. I'm Susie Friend.
MRS. PLUMM: Tea's ready, girls. (*All the girls pick up their cups and form a line in front of Mrs. Plumm. First Susie, Kate, Rita, Holly, then Samantha.*)
HOLLY: I'll get it for you, Muffy. (*Muffy and Carter are left on the couch. Mrs. Plumm pours first for Susie.*)
SUSIE: Thank you, Mrs. Plumm. Mrs. Plumm is my favorite housemother. And Earl Grey. I love Earl Grey.
MRS. PLUMM: Dear, would you care for some brandy?        260
SUSIE: No, thank you. (*She turns to Kate.*) Kate, do you want a ride to Cambridge this weekend? (*Mrs. Plumm pours for Kate.*)
KATE: No, I'm staying here to work.
MRS. PLUMM: Care for some honey, dear? (*Leilah shakes her head. Kate and Susie walk back to the couch.*)
SUSIE: Well, if you ever need a ride to Cambridge, I go every weekend. (*They sit. Susie turns to Carter.*) I used to date Wharton, but that was before I knew what I wanted. (*Susie laughs at her own charm.*)                                      270
CARTER: Yes. (*Mrs. Plumm pours tea for Leilah. The girls take a slight notice of Carter.*)
MRS. PLUMM: Leilah, aren't you going to stay with us for tea?
LEILAH: No, I have more reading to do. (*Rita is in front of Mrs. Plumm.*)
RITA: I'd like brandy and honey.
SUSIE: (*To Carter.*) I'm a senior. Head of freshmen in North Stimson Hall and a psychology major. (*Holly is in front of Mrs. Plumm.*)
MRS. PLUMM: Holly, dear I told you I can't permit you to come 280 to tea in pants. It's not fair to the other girls. I'll let you stay this afternoon. But, dear, let's not see it happen again. I know you can do it, you looked very pretty at "Gracious Living" once. (*Samantha moves up to Mrs. Plumm and Holly. The girls at couch turn around to watch.*)
SAMANTHA: Holly is very pretty in pink.
HOLLY: I'm sorry, Mrs. Plumm.
MRS. PLUMM: Dear, I just don't want our house to get a reputation.
CARTER: Yes. (*All the girls are seated and served. Exit Mrs.* 290 *Plumm. Girls look up at Carter.*)
MUFFET: You're not sorry. You loved every minute of it.

KATE: Holly, I don't see what difference it makes to you. Why torment her? It's just a waste of time.

HOLLY: I don't have a skirt.

MUFFET: Oh, come off it, Holly. Your father invented "velveteen."

RITA: I think Holly is very pataphysical.

SUSIE: You know, you girls should really sit at Mrs. Plumm's 300 table more often. I see your group running to the end table after she walks into the room.

CARTER: Yes. (*They look again.*)

SUSIE: Well, she's very sweet!

SAMANTHA: (*Sweetly to Carter.*) She doesn't really have syphilis.

SUSIE: Especially you, Kate. Mrs. Plumm admires you. And you could make some new friends. I notice your nice friend, Leilah never comes to dinner anymore. At least try sitting with Mrs. Plumm at "Gracious."

310 SAMANTHA: (*Smiles to Carter.*) Susie, she doesn't know what "Gracious Living" is.

SUSIE: Don't call a freshman "she." It's alienating. I learned that in psychology.

HOLLY: I think "Gracious" is a cultural excess. When I get out of here, I'm never going to have dinner by candlelight in the wilderness with 38 girls in hostess gowns. Unless, of course, I train for Amazon guerrilla warfare at the Junior League. Also I can't stomach the way Mrs. Plumm's neck shakes when she pours the sherry. (*The girls all shake their necks.*)

320 SUSIE: Holly, have you ever been to "Gracious" at Smith? Ours is much more homey. I'm glad I didn't go there to college. Smith's much too social.

KATE: Not as much as Vassar. I applied there as a safety school.

SAMANTHA: Well, Vassar's just a cut above Connecticut College.

HOLLY: I thought Conn. was a good school.

MUFFET: If you like the Coast Guard.

KATE: Aren't Wellesley and Bryn Mawr the most academic?

SAMANTHA: Well, Bryn Mawr, of course. But Wellesley lacks 330 imagination. They must marry Harvard and M.I.T.

HOLLY: Hands up! Who here got into Radcliffe? (*No hands go up.*)

MRS. PLUMM: (*Appearing briefly.*) Hands up! Who wants dessert? (*No hands go up.*)

KATE: Gross-me-out! It's last night's jelly rolls.

CARTER: Yes.

MUFFET: Don't be embarrassed, Holly. You can take them up to your room. (*Clinking glass noise is heard.*)

GIRL'S VOICE: (*Announces.*) Male Long Distance, Male L.D. 340 for Susie Friend. (*Susie throws her napkin on the table and runs out of the room singing, "Oh, the Lord is good to me."*)

RITA: Hi, I'm Susie Friend. I love finger sandwiches, Earl Grey, and Cambridge. I'm a psychology major, head of freshmen in North Stimson Hall, and I wax my legs. I'd let a Harvard man, especially from the Business or Law Schools violate my body for three hours; Princeton, for two hours and fifty minutes, because you have to take a bus and a train to get there; Yale, for two hours and forty-five minutes because my Dad went there and it makes me feel guilty; Dart-350 mouth, for two hours and thirty minutes because it takes them time to warm up; Columbia, I just don't know, because of the radical politics and the neighborhood. I learned that in psychology. Now, if I could have a Wellesley girl, or

Mrs. Plumm, that would be different.

KATE: Rita, you're so adolescent.

MUFFET: Remember when Rita made Rorschach tests with her menstrual blood to summon back Edvard Munch.

HOLLY: Rita, you couldn't go out with a nice boy from Amherst?

MUFFET: It was her interdepartmental project.          360

RITA: I thought it was very pataphysical.

CARTER: Yes.

SAMANTHA: But, Rita, you're still on the D.A.R. Scholarship.

KATE: Uch, Rita, gross-me-out!

RITA: I never let my economic background deter me.

SAMANTHA: Sometimes I wish I'd never left the Midwest.

MUFFET: Oh, Rita, you've upset her.

RITA: (*Arm around Samantha's chair.*) Samantha, pumpkin, why don't you make an announcement? (*Puts spoon in Samantha's hand and moves glass toward her.*) It'll make 370 you feel better.

SAMANTHA: Rita, I've been here almost four years, and I've never made any announcement.

RITA: Well, it always makes Susie Friend feel better.

SAMANTHA: We don't belong to any committees.

HOLLY: Kate's in Phi Beta Kappa.

MUFFET: Holly, you do it. They'll never expect it from you. (*Holly, Kate, Samantha, Rita, Muffet clink their glasses. Holly stands up.*)

HOLLY: Um. Susie Friend has requested a toast. (*Holly, Kate,* 380 *Samantha, Muffet immediately stand up and toast their teacups. Carter stares blankly.*)

HOLLY, KATE, SAMANTHA, RITA, MUFFET: (*All sing.*)
*Tired of books and boring classes*
*Drop your books, fill up your glasses*
*Drink, the girls who think*
*Of mixing Greek and Latin*
*With a cool Manhattan*

(*Susie Friend rushes back to the living room and toasts her teacup. Mrs. Plumm enters, toasts and sings.*)

EVERYONE:
*And Amherst has its Heidelberg's*          390
*And then there's Mory's down at Yale*
*And when those Harvard boys*
*Drink to College joys*
*It's dull you must agree*
*Adding lemon to your tea.*

*Smith may have their Ice Tea Hours*
*We prefer our whiskey sours.*
*Drink and never think*
*About tomorrow night.*

(*They all clink each other's tea-cup. The girls take their napkins and begin to exit.*)

SUSIE: There'll be a rule book test for all freshmen tonight in 400 the living room after "Gracious." Mrs. Plumm has promised to bring sherry.

CARTER: Who's Sherry? (*Everyone does a double take look at Carter. The girls begin to leave the living room. Each girl, as she exits, folds her napkin and puts it into a box. Carter struggles behind.*)

SAMANTHA: (*Watching Carter.*) Susie, she doesn't know where to put her napkin.

SUSIE: Don't call a freshman "she." It's alienating. I learned
410    that in psychology. Hi, what's your name?

CARTER: Carter.

SUSIE: Well, Carter, we each have a separate napkin cubby
compartment. We take them out and put them back after
each meal. Watch Kate fold her napkin. Your napkin,
Carter, is washed and pressed every Wednesday and Sunday
in time for "Gracious." Now, your box is right to the left as
you enter the dining room. (*Takes Carter's napkin, folds it,
and puts it away in the napkin cubbyhole.*) And Carter if
you have any questions or you just want to talk about psy-
420    chology, knock on my door. It has the *Snoopy* calendar on it.
I got the calendar as a present from Kenny at Harvard. I
used to date Wharton but that was before I knew what I
wanted. (*She winks at Carter.*) Good-night, oh, and Carter.
I would avoid Rita. I don't know what the D.A.R. was thinking of. (*Blows her a kiss and exits. Carter is left sitting, looking at her napkin.*)

(*End Scene*)

SCENE IV

MAN'S VOICE: The real problem for many educated women is
the difficulty they have in recognizing whether they have
been a success. . . . Women will be part-time mothers, part-
430    time workers, part-time cooks, and part-time intellectuals.
When scholars point out that even the best cooks have been
men, the proper answer is, "But what man has been not only
the second best cook, but the third best parent, the seventh
best typist, and the tenth best community leader?" Just like
the pot of honey that kept renewing itself, an educated
woman's capacity for giving is not exhausted but stimulated
by demands. (*Muffet is reading the college catalog. Carter is
silent and sits on the floor. Suddenly Muffet throws the book
down.*)
440    MUFFET: I am so tired. Why doesn't someone just take me
away from all this? Did you ever notice how walking into
Samantha's room is like walking into a clean sheet? She and
Susie Friend celebrate Piglet's birthday. Katie says you're
very bright. Did I tell you what happened in Chip Knowles'
women's history class today? Do you know Chip Knowles?
He always wears chamois shirts and *Topsiders* from L.L.
Bean. You can never find anything you want in those L.L.
Bean catalogs. So I just order a decoy duck every year. It
makes me feel waspy. Chip's wife Libby, graduated first in
450    her class from Vassar. When I told Chip I was a senior and
didn't know what I'd be doing next year, Chip told me that
Libby doesn't really spend the day mopping and catching
tadpoles with Chip, Jr. She may be mopping with her hands
but with her mind she's reliving the water imagery in the
Faerie Queen. Anyway, I thought women's history would be
a gut and it wouldn't look as obvious on my record as "Marriage and the Family." As it turns out, this class isn't half
bad. We read all the basics; the womb-penis inner and outer
space nonsense. The Feminine Mystique, Sexual Politics,
460    Mabel Dodge's Diary. Chip Knowles says women's history
is relevant. Do you think women will lose their relevancy in
five years? Like "Car 54, Where Are You?" Anyway, after
two months of reading about suffragettes and courageous

choices, this French dish comes into class dressed in a tight
turtleneck and skirt. And you know how for seminar breaks
everyone brings in graham crackers, well this chick brings in
home made petit-fours. And she stands in front of the class
and tells us she has not prepared her report on Rosie the
Riveter because, "You girls are wasting your time. You
should do more avec what you have done here—(*Muffet* 470
*points to her breasts.*) than avec what you have up here."
(*Muffet points to her head.*) And in less than five seconds the
class is giving her a standing ovation, everyone is applaud-
ing. Except Holly and Rita, who grabbed the petit-fours,
and ran out of the room in protest. I didn't do anything. I felt
so confused. I mean this chick is an obvious imbecile. But I
didn't think she was entirely wrong either. I guess the truth
is men are very important to me. Well, not more important
than you and Holly and Samantha. Well, not always, pumpkin. Sometimes I know who I am when I feel attractive. 480
Other times it makes me feel very shallow like I'm not Rosie
the Riveter. I suppose this isn't a very impressive sentiment,
but I would really like to meet my prince. Even a few
princes. And I wouldn't give up being a person. I'd still remember all the Art History dates. I just don't know why suddenly I'm supposed to know what I want to do. I guess I
should think about sleeping with someone tonight to pass
the time. Except it's always creepy in the morning. Rita
doesn't think so. But she's promiscuous. I'm not promiscuous. I just hate going to bed alone. Maybe sometime you can 490
sleep on my floor. It's funny, you're a freshman and we're
seniors. I'm not even worried about next year. I just have to
make sure something happens to me. (*Enter Samantha. She
is obviously excited.*)

SAMANTHA: Oh, hi Carter. (*Excited.*) Muffet, I'm in love.

MUFFET: With whom?

SAMANTHA: Robert Cabe. I met him last night and I thought
this is the one I want. He's handsome and talented, and he's
better than me and he'll love me. You'll see. I want to be his
audience, and have my picture behind him, in my long tar- 500
tan kilt in the *Times* Art and Leisure Section.

MUFFET: That's nice Samantha. Samantha, how come I haven't
met my Heathcliff yet?

SAMANTHA: Oh, Muffy, you wouldn't want him. They never settle down. Her soul wandered the moors for years. There's
no security in that. You want someone who's good for you.

MUFFET: Maybe. (*Pause.*) Actually, I don't mind being alone. I
like being strong. Like Rosie the Riveter.

SAMANTHA: I know, Muff. You're just more capable than me.
Wanna go for a drive?    510

MUFFET: (*Begins to leave the room.*) Sure. (*Pause.*) Bye, bye,
Carter.

SAMANTHA: Bye, Carter.

MUFFET: Oh, Carter, I should be back in about an hour or so,
so why don't you come up then and we'll talk some more.
(*Exit Muffet and Samantha.*)

(*End Scene*)

SCENE V

*Carter seated alone. Begins to ironically mime dance to the
male voice. By the time she gets to "steadiness and gaiety," she
sits down exhausted.*

MAN'S VOICE: Although the attitude of society to education for women has changed in the last century and a quarter, the intellectual curiosity, hard work, and the spirit of adventure are still characteristic of Mount Holyoke. Mary Lyon, sending her early students out across the plains and seas as teachers and missionaries said, "Go where no one else will go. Do what no one else will do." Some of her 25,000 "daughters" have blazed new trails, like Frances Perkins, Secretary of Labor under President Roosevelt. Others found adventure near at hand. Emily Dickinson went home. Today thousands of alumnae and students are serving their families and their communities with generosity and imagination, leading lives that enrich those they touch, ready to meet the unknown with steadiness and gaiety. (*Carter seated on the floor. Enter Susie Friend holding a note.*)

SUSIE: Hi, Carter. I have a message from your elf. You see, every freshman has a junior sister and a secret senior elf to help them through. That's right, it's your elf who's been leaving candy in your mail and napkin boxes and all the other treats, and she'll fix you up on the weekend and that's real neat. It's fun to see the girls at tea and Milk 'n Crackers too, and try and try to guess which one belongs to you. Don't you love Mrs. Plumm?? Fall teas are such fun when she brings apricot brandy. Mmmmmmmmmmmm real yum! But Milk 'n Crackers is neat too. Every night the kitchen help leaves out crackers, milk, peanut butter, and sometimes fluff for you. You should come some time, Carter. It's a real study break for me from my thesis on Claude Levi-Strauss. I'm just a messenger here and I can't say who your elf is. But I think she's found you a male caller, hip horrah! See you later. (*Susie hands Carter the note and exits. Carter stares blankly at the envelope. She opens it, and* Hershey *kisses fall out. Carter reads the note.*)

CARTER:

For our Carter
No one's smarter
Your elf has a surprise
so open your eyes
Kanga and Roo
have a Yale blue for you.

(*She looks up.*)

A terrific date
He can't wait
We'll double at the game
but I won't be to blame
if he's a little odd
or a bit of a scrod

(*She looks back at Susie Friend.*)

Hair by Thursday must be washed for the trip
It wouldn't hurt to give the split ends a snip
Tonite's the night it must be done
I'm sudsing with Ca-Ca and Jill in number one

Some Hershey kisses and best wishes
Bring a hot water bottle
See you at Milk 'n Crackers

Lovens,
Your elf

(*Carter puts down letter.*) Gross—me—out!

(*End Scene*)

SCENE VI

MAN'S VOICE: To profit most fully from the undergraduate curriculum, a student should examine for herself not only the nature of her academic interest, but also her conception of the good life and the kind of community she would like to fashion. (*Kate lies reading on a bed. She throws down the book she is reading and takes out another one.*)

KATE: (*Reading.*) "She remembered the way Melissa Blaine with her perfect cameo face had smiled up at Lance. 'Yes,' she said. 'I'm sure you've had most of the desirable women in the city, but I don't want to be among them.' 'Then, I think it's time I changed your mind,' Lance said. Suddenly Lance's hand slid to the back of her gown. With one strong arm he pinned her to his chest so that try as she might, she could not push him away. He deftly unfastened the buttons of her gown, as if he had had long practice in performing such actions. 'What are you doing? I'm not one of your strumpets!' (*Leilah knocks on the door. Like Kate she is very attractive. But as opposed to Kate, who is obviously quite confident, Leilah prefers to walk with her head down.*)

LEILAH: Kate? You're busy.

KATE: I was just reading "The Genealogy of Morals."

LEILAH: How was dinner?

KATE: Leilah, I don't understand why you never come. Even Susie Friend has been asking for you.

LEILAH: I came in to get the Nietzsche assignment.

KATE: Leilah, you don't think I'm a good person do you?

LEILAH: Kate, you're very good.

KATE: Then why don't you ever come in here just to visit instead of always asking for the assignment? Leilah, we roomed together for three years and now I never see you anymore. You're angry about last year in Greece. Aren't you?

LEILAH: That wasn't your fault.

KATE: I felt badly for you when both Iki and Thomas fell in love with me. Leilah, sometimes I think I should apologize to you and other times I don't know exactly what I should apologize for. I haven't done anything deliberately to hurt you. I want us to stay friends.

LEILAH: I know.

KATE: What are you going to do next year? I don't know what's going to happen if I don't get into Law School.

LEILAH: Kate, you're not supposed to hear until April; this is only November.

KATE: Well, I'm Phi Beta Kappa, but I'm worried about my Law Boards. (*Pause.*) Oh, Leah, pumpkin, don't worry. You'll be Phi Bet by June, in time for graduation. Just think you could be Muffet, or Samantha, or God forbid, Rita. What are they going to do with their lives? At least you and I aren't limited.

LEILAH: Did I tell you I applied to anthropology graduate school?

KATE: Why aren't you continuing in philosophy?

LEILAH: I really like anthropology. I want to go to small towns in Iraq. Look, I've made a list of Mesopotamia jokes.

KATE: Leilah, things aren't going to be better for you in Iraq. You don't have to make yourself exotic. You're a smart, pretty, girl. And anyway, if you can't leave your room in South Hadley, how are you going to get along in Iraq?

LEILAH: Just fine. Kate, what's the Nietzsche assignment? I have more reading to do?

KATE: You always have more reading to do. *(Leilah begins to move away.)* I'm sorry. Let's talk about something else. Like when we were roommates, okay? Leilah, what do you know about clitoral orgasms?

LEILAH: Well, my gentleman friend, Mr. Peterson, says they're better than others.

KATE: I wonder if I've had any.

LEILAH: Kate, I'm sure you have. It's a fad.

KATE: Well, I never thought I had a problem.

LEILAH: Why don't you ask Rita?

KATE: Rita's fucked up. *(They laugh.)* Leilah, are you leaving philosophy because I'm Phi Bet and you're not? That's stupid. The department likes you as much as me.

LEILAH: Katie, I know you're trying but . . . I don't know. I just want to go away. I don't want to have to think about this place anymore. Kate, do you have the assignment?

KATE: Read the last two chapters in the "Genealogy of Morals." *(Pause.)* Look, Leilah, I'm sorry. I really am. But it's not my fault. You're always predisposed against me.

LEILAH: Kate, are you going to Milk and Crackers? I'll see you later.

KATE: Leilah, did you know Holly used to pick up men on the Yale green when she was a sophomore? She had clitoral orgasms. But that was a long time ago.

LEILAH: Maybe that's why she gets on with Rita. They have that in common.

KATE: Leilah, that's nasty.

LEILAH: *(Strongly.)* We all have hidden potential, Kate. *(Goes to exit.)* Bye Katie.

KATE: I'm going to ask Carter to join us for Milk and Crackers. I think she's very bright. It's been a long time since we've had someone new to talk to in this house, around three years. *(Frustrated, Kate goes back to her book.)* "I'm sorry," Lance said after a moment. "I suppose I shouldn't have done that. But you were asking for it. You wanted it. And you enjoyed every second of it."

*(End Scene)*

SCENE VII

*Holly filling a diaphragm with orthocreme. Leilah and Rita are walking by, and as soon as they see Holly, they stop and watch.*

MAN'S VOICE: Am I saying that anatomy is destiny? No, it is not destiny. Providing a setting in which these subtle constraints may be overcome is particularly the mission of a college for women.

RITA: Holly, you've got enough orthocreme in there to sleep with the entire SS Constitution.

HOLLY: The instructions say two teaspoonfuls, so I thought I'd see what it's like with a little extra. I don't want to bud. *(Pause.)* Now that I have one of these things, whenever I see a boy with a yarmulke, I think he has a diaphragm on his head. *(Pause.)* I shouldn't have said that. I'll be struck down by a burning bush.

LEILAH: Who are you going to use this thing with?

HOLLY: I don't know. I got it 'cause it made me feel grown up. I could tell my friends stories about the day I got my diaphragm. Doesn't matter. In fact, I hate being mounted.

RITA: Holly, pumpkin, life doesn't really offer that many pleasures that you can go around avoiding the obvious ones.

HOLLY: What kind of pleasure? There's someone on top of you sweating and pushing and you're lying there pretending this is wonderful. That's not wonderful. That's masochistic.

RITA: But it can be your conquest, pumpkin.

LEILAH: This is distorted. Rita, you are manipulative.

RITA: Leilah, I'm not manipulative. Our entire being is programmed for male approval. Now, I, on the other hand, want abandonment. I want to do it with everything: dogs, cats, trees, bushes, ashtrays, children, light bulbs, shoe boxes . . .

LEILAH: Rita, don't you want some attachment? Some love?

RITA: From a cock?

LEILAH: Then why are you with Clark?

RITA: He's a wonderful lover.

LEILAH: Clark's a homosexual.

RITA: He's creative. I've had enough of those macho types. Honestly, after I slept with Jack Hall he shook my hand and said thank you, and Chip Knowles came like a Pop Tart.

HOLLY: Really. Chip Knowles. I guess Libby was busy with the Faerie Queene.

LEILAH: But Rita, wouldn't you want the basis of a relationship to be some mutual understanding or . . .

RITA: *(Cuts her off.)* Leilah, you're beautiful. You can.

LEILAH: Rita, you're more beautiful than I am.

RITA: *(Rita demonstrates with her hand the vertical and horizontal qualities of the buildings and roads. At "shopping malls" she shows a parallel vertical with both hands.)* Listen, Leilah, this entire society is based on cocks—The New York *Times*, Walter Cronkite, all the building and roads, the cities, philosophy, government, history, religion, shopping malls, everything I can name is male. When I see things this way, it becomes obvious that it's very easy to feel alienated and alone for the simple reason that I've never been included because I came into the world without a penis. Therefore it is my duty to take advantage. Did I ever tell you about the time I left Johnny Cabot lying there after I'd had an orgasm and he hadn't. It was hilarious. And anyway, Leilah, no one will ever do for me what they'll do for you, or Kate, or even Samantha. So I have to take advantage. In my case it's a moral imperative. I've got to go now, I'm auditioning for Clark—He's directing a production of "Another Part of the Forest." *(She realizes Forest is another vertical.)* Forest, trees, logs, pinecones, elks . . . *(Exit Rita.)*

HOLLY: I think she's wrong about the shopping malls. *(Pause.)* Sometimes I think we have too much external and too little internal input. It's disturbing having sympathy with everyone's point of view. I guess I better put "thing" away in its shell.

LEILAH: Do you know the first time I ever really understood about diaphragms or sex was from reading *The Group*. I remember when I was twelve taking it down from my parents' library shelf and rereading the passages about Dottie

740 leaving her diaphragm on Washington Square. It was quite titillating. And my parents didn't mind; they were happy I showed an early interest in Seven-Sister schools.

HOLLY: Lei, I want to tell you something but I was embarrassed to in front of Rita.

LEILAH: How can you be embarrassed in front of Rita, she's so embarrassing?

HOLLY: I called someone in Minneapolis today and hung up. I hung up twice.

LEILAH: Who was it?

750 HOLLY: A doctor I met with Muffet last summer. I thought I'd visit him over Christmas vacation. That's really why I bought "thing" here. He was very responsive on the phone. He said hello before I hung up.

LEILAH: Maybe you shouldn't see a friend of Muffet's.

HOLLY: Muffet doesn't know him either. We just met him once at a museum. I could tell he liked me. He smiled a lot at my legs. I'm very attractive from the kneecap to the ankle.

LEILAH: I guess I'm going to stay with my gentleman friend Mr. Peterson over vacation. Katie thinks he's boring.

760 HOLLY: He's not boring. See, I didn't want to talk to Minneapolis because I was afraid I'd start giggling and be self-effacing and my voice would screech. And then I'd start wishing I was Kate or Rita.

LEILAH: Holly, you can't keep wishing you're someone else. You'll be smothered.

HOLLY: Sometimes I want to clean up my desk and go out and say, respect me, I'm a respectable grownup, and other times I just want to jump into a paper bag and shake and bake myself to death.

770 SAMANTHA *and* SUSIE: (*Come through the room singing.*)
*Happy birdle dirdle toodle yoodle doodle*
*Happy birdle dirdle toodle yoodle doodle*
*Happy birdle dirdle dear Piglet*
*Happy Birdle dirdle to you.*

SUSIE: Make a wish.

SAMANTHA: Isn't he cute? (*They run out giggling. Leilah and Holly watch them. Leilah turns to Holly.*)

LEILAH: We could shake and bake Piglet.

(*End Scene*)

SCENE VIII

*Judy Collins' record is heard. Holly, Samantha, Kate. They are drinking sherry. It is very late.*

SAMANTHA: (*Going to record player.*) This was my favorite song in high school. My senior year I sent it to a boy who was
780 hitch-hiking cross country. I printed it on the back of a Vermeer postcard from the Chicago Art Institute. It was the only time I've ever written without capitals or punctuation. (*Pause.*) I also liked the Dave Clark Five a lot in ninth grade. I thought I could marry one of them cause they were more accessible than the Beatles.

KATE: My best was Leonard Cohen. When I was in high school, I wanted to go down like Suzanne with the garbage and the

seaweed. Then I heard he had a thing with Joni Mitchell and there's only so much wistfulness one can stomach. (*Samantha continues to sing song. Enter Rita excited and tri-* 790 *umphant.*)

RITA: I've tasted my menstrual blood.

KATE: Uch, Rita, gross-me-out.

RITA: Germaine Greer says the test of a truly liberated woman is tasting her menstrual blood.

KATE: Rita, that's drivel.

SAMANTHA: She also says women shouldn't wear underwear.

RITA: Who told you that?

SAMANTHA: Robert.

RITA: Robert. Robert, what does he know about it? I think all 800 men should be forced to menstruate—Robert S. MacNamara, Baba Ram-Das, John Glenn—all of them except James Taylor, we'll spare him. But the rest of them should be forced to answer phones on a white naugahyde receptionist chair with a cotton lollipop stuck up their crotch.

SAMANTHA: Why spare James Taylor?

HOLLY: (*Looks at her surprised.*) Samantha!

SAMANTHA: Robert says I'm a closet wit. (*She giggles.*)

RITA: The only problem with menstruation for men is that some sensitive schmuck would write about it for *The Village* 810 *Voice* and he would become the new expert on women's inner life. Dr. David Reuben, taking the time out to menstruate over the July Fourth Weekend, has concluded that "women are so much closer to the universe because they menstruate and therefore they seek out lemon freshened borax, hair spray and other womb related items." (*Pause.*) And that's why I think we need to talk about masturbation.

KATE: Rita, gross-me-out!

HOLLY: Rita, have you ever told the D.A.R. how you spend your time here? 820

KATE: (*Slightly interested.*) Do you really masturbate?

RITA: I know Susie Friend does. She does it in front of her father's picture from *The New York Times* when he was made Vice President of American Canco.

SAMANTHA: (*Politely changing the subject.*) Anyone want some corn nuts? My mom just sent them from Naperville. You can't get corn nuts east of the Mississippi. (*Offers nuts.*)

KATE: I don't think Germaine Greer has thought this out properly. Know what I think the ideal society would be. If all women had communal apartments—not poured concrete 830 socialist apartments—I mean an estate and everyone worked so child-care was rotated and the men came to visit on the weekends and were very nice and charming, bright—all those things—but they left on Mondays.

HOLLY: Katie, that's just what it's like here.

KATE: Well, except my plan doesn't get boring. The men who arrive are Arabian millionaires, poets, lumberjacks. Not corporate lawyers, or M.B.A.'s.

HOLLY: Katie, you're a snot rag.

RITA: Kate just grew up in *Holiday Magazine.* 840

SAMANTHA: I couldn't live in a society like that. I guess I'm not as strong as you, Kate.

RITA: Don't worry, Samantha, pumpkin. You're a closet wit.

HOLLY: I want to be divorced and living with two children on Central Park West.

KATE: Holly, don't you want to fall in love? You don't have to get married, but it would be nice to have a passion.

HOLLY: Yes, except if I fall in love it would be because I thought someone was better than me. And if I really thought someone was better than me, I'd give them everything and I'd hate them for my living through them.

KATE: You don't really expect to live through someone else, do you?

HOLLY: I think I'd like to very much.

KATE: Piffle, Holly. You're too diffuse. You need to concentrate your efforts.

RITA: Want to play a game?

KATE: Rita it's too late in the night for tampon bobbing.

RITA: This is a nice game for nice girls. (*Rita gathers the girls together. Pause.*) Let's each take a turn and say if we could marry any one of us who it would be.

SAMANTHA: I'm already pinned.

RITA: That doesn't count. You can only select from our own uncommon pool. Holly, stop edging under the bed. (*Pause.*) I'd marry Samantha cause she'd make the best wife and in a matrimonial situation I could admire her the longest.

SAMANTHA: Would you really marry me?

RITA: Samantha, you're the perfect woman.

SAMANTHA: Rita, now I feel really badly cause I wouldn't have picked you and it would have been nice if everything worked out. (*Pause.*) This is very difficult cause it would be interesting to live with Rita, and Kate probably has the best future.

HOLLY: How 'bout Susie Friend?

SAMANTHA: You don't marry a girl like that. Too many committee meetings. She'd never be home. (*Pause.*) Holly, you're sweet and funny but I couldn't support you and there would be a problem at the club. I guess I would marry Muffet cause she could get on with the outside world and Piglet wouldn't drive her crazy. Also, Muffet's glamorous, but she doesn't scare me.

HOLLY: I guess I would be most comfortable being married to Leilah or Rita. I'd never feel that I have to impress them. But when you get right down to it, I'd want to marry Katie. I would consider living through your accomplishments, Katie, and besides I'm sure if we got married my parents would approve and one of us would get our picture in the Sunday *Times*. (*They laugh.*)

SAMANTHA: How 'bout you, Kate? Who would you marry?

KATE: I don't know.

HOLLY: You don't have to marry me, Katie. I understand. Maybe you have to settle your career first.

KATE: I guess I never thought about marrying any of you.

RITA: Kate, for a smart woman you have a stunted imagination.

KATE: Well, if I married one of us I would probably have to be the main income source. That's excluding the possibility of trust funds. So if I was supporting someone I guess I would want to marry Carter.

HOLLY: Carter. Gross-me-out! (*Pause and giggles.*) I'm sorry. That wasn't very nice. I'm sure you'll be very happy together.

KATE: Carter is very bright. And if I'm going to be a boring lawyer then I'd want to be married to someone who would stay home and have an imagination. Anyway, Carter would *need* me. Holly, I would consider you cause you're such a good person. But then that would make me feel a little chilly.

RITA: I think we should celebrate.

SAMANTHA: What?

RITA: That none of our marriage proposals have been reciprocated.

SAMANTHA: We don't know. Maybe Muffy would want to marry me.

HOLLY: No. I think if we marry, we'll have to marry outside of each other. Probably men.

RITA: Muffy's out with pink pants. She knows she has to marry a man.

SAMANTHA: I know a great song we could celebrate with and dance to. (*She goes to record player and puts on a popular record celebrating love and marriage. The girls sing as soon as they hear it. They get up to begin dancing.*)

KATE: Do you think Germaine Greer remembers the night she danced with her best friends in a women's dormitory at Cambridge?

RITA: No, she was probably into dating and make-up. (*The girls are dancing and laughing.*)

HOLLY: Kate, you're a good dancer.

KATE: I know I should give up law and become a rock star.

SAMANTHA: Want to see the way Robert dances? (*She demonstrates. They laugh.*) It's pretty gross-me-out. (*Enter Carter who stares at them.*)

CARTER: I came in to tell you I've decided what I want. I want to put Wittgenstein on film.

SAMANTHA: That's nice, Carter. Know what? (*She is giggling.*) We just all proposed to each other. And Kate said she'd want to marry you. Carter, Kate is really the best catch.

KATE: It was all hypothetical.

SAMANTHA: Carter, want to dance?

HOLLY: Don't you think Kate would make a great rock star?

KATE: Carter, dance with us. Just think how odd this would look if Susie Friend walked in. (*Carter begins to join them slowly. Her dancing is noticeably different from the other girls. A dying swan would be fitting. They continue to dance and laugh.*)

RITA: (*Over singing.*) Know what? I think when we're 25 we're going to be pretty fucking incredible. All right, I'll give us another five years for emotional and career development. When we're 30 we're going to be pretty fucking amazing. (*Pause.*) Carter, don't worry. You're younger so you have 13 years. (*They continue to dance and sing in a line. They move towards the back of the room. Holly goes to a phone in the corner. The girls dancing silhouette Holly from behind.*)

HOLLY: Operator, could you connect me with a Dr. Mark Silverstein in Minneapolis? (*She dials.*) Hello, is this Dr. Silverstein? Oh, this is his answering service. Hi! A message. (*Pause.*) Respect me. I'm a respectable grown up. Oh, my name is Simone de Beauvoir and I should be back in an hour. (*Holly hangs up and puts her feet up on the table as Mrs. Plumm enters. She is walking thru clinking a glass as if preparing to make an announcement. She stops at Holly.*)

MRS. PLUMM: Holly, dear, take your feet off the furniture. (*Exit Mrs. Plumm. Holly puts her foot back up and sits quietly while the music swells and girls continue to dance behind her.*)

(*End Act One*)

## —ACT TWO—

### SCENE I

*Holly, Kate, Muffet, Samantha, Leilah, Susie, Rita, sing. Carter holds pitch pipe. The girls are standing for their performance.*

ALL:
> Mildred, Maud and Mabel were sitting at their table.
> Down at the Taft Hotel.
> Working on a plan to
> Catch themselves a man to
> 970      Brighten up their lives a spell.

MUFFET: *(Whispers to her friends.)* I slept with a Whiffenpool at the Taft Hotel.

ALL: *(Sing.)*
> In their thirty years of proms,
> Never once had they had qualms,
> That they could fail to satisfy their craven
> Nor ever seemed to doubt it's not reckless to hold out
> For a son of Old New Haven.

RITA: *(Whispers.)* These women should have been in therapy.

980 KATE: *(Sings.)*
> And as they downed their pousse café

*(Whispers.)* I've been here four years and I still don't know what pousse café is.

ALL: *(Sing.)*
> The girls were heard to softly say.

SUSIE: *(Speaks.)* I want to welcome all you fathers to Father-Daughter weekend. You Dads look younger every year.

SAMANTHA: Hi, Daddy!

RITA: Hi, Mr. Stewart. *(She winks. The girls work up some ges-*
990 *tures for their performance during this part of the song.)*

ALL: *(Sing.)*
> Though we have had our chances
> With over night romances
> With the Harvard and the Dartmouth male.
>
> And though we've had a bunch in
> tow from Princeton Junction
> We're saving ourselves for Yale

RITA:
> Boola-Boola

1000 ALL: *(Sing.)*
> For thirty years and then some
> We've been showing men some
> Tricks that make their motors fail
>
> And tho' we've all had squeezes
> From lots of Phdses
> We're saving ourselves for Yale

SUSIE: *(Sings.)*
> And when

ALL:
> Finally married we lie      1010
> It will be with an Eli

SUSIE:
> Cause we're

ALL:
> Saving ourselves for Yale

CARTER: *(Raising her hand.)* I knew we had a purpose. *(The women curtsey for their fathers. Mrs. Plumm applauds and Susie Friend steps forward.)*

*(End Scene)*

### SCENE II

SUSIE: Hi! I'm Susie Friend, co-ordinator of Father-Daughter weekend, and I'm delighted to see so many of you Dads 1020 here. First of all on behalf of the college, I would like to thank Holly Kaplan's father for his generous gift of 2000 slightly damaged velveteen bows. They're terrific. I'm sure they'll come in handy. Tomorrow night Mrs. Plumm has promised to play for us the white-breasted nuthatch tapes which she made last weekend on her annual spring bird-watch. And now our favorite housemother, Mrs. Plumm.

MRS. PLUMM: Welcome, fathers. This weekend has always been for me the highlight of the Spring Semester. My Junior year, my father stopped attending Father-Daughter weekend. 1030 You see that year, my birder classmate Ada Grudder and I had decided it was too dangerous for young girls to go on long bird watching trips unprotected. So I wrote home asking for money to buy a rifle. *(Pause.)* Gentlemen, please don't stop me if I go on too long. *(Pause.)* My father was appalled. He thought firearms did not provide an appropriate pastime for young women. And he feared I might be labeled eccentric. But I bought the rifle. Ada and I set up a firing range on Upper Lake where we re-enacted the Franco-Prussian War. For two years I received notes from home 1040 saying "Please marry Hoyt Plumm, and can't you teach bird watching at the High School." Finally, being a dutiful daughter, I did. Now if you will follow your daughters into the date parlour we can begin the dance. *(Girls begin to exit.)*

SAMANTHA: This way, Daddy. *(Rita winks again.)*

MRS. PLUMM: Could you put out that cigar, dear?

*(End Scene)*

### SCENE III

MAN'S VOICE: In the growth of tradition from the time of its founding by Mary Lyon to the present day the College continues to believe that the acquisition of knowledge of itself 1050 is not enough. Indeed, employers of graduates of the college seem to be looking for a readiness to work hard at learning unfamiliar techniques.

LEILAH: (*Muffet is putting on make-up. Leilah enters carrying a chocolate bunny.*) Muffy, this package just came for you.

MUFFET: What is this? "For my Muffet. I can't bluff it. An Easter Bunny for my pixie honey."

LEILAH: Is that from Susie Friend?

MUFFET: Christ no! It's from her father. Look, it's signed—
1060 Lovens, E. Courtland "Kippy" Friend. He was behind me in the bunny hop at the Father-Daughter weekend. Leilah, do you think I should plan to marry Kippy Friend? It's two months before graduation and I still don't know what I'm going to do next year. But I am prepared for life. I can fold my napkin with the best of them. Leilah, do you want this? I'll give it to Holly, she'll eat it.

LEILAH: I asked my father not to come up this year. Actually, my freshman year he came to Father-Daughter weekend and kept dancing with Katie and telling me how lucky I was
1070 to have such a good friend. Kate told him I was the prettiest and the brightest girl here. Ever since then, I make it a point to be busy doing research every Father-Daughter weekend. (*Throws down books.*) Oh, I can't wait to get out of here. I've booked a flight to Iraq for the day after graduation.

MUFFET: Really, Leilah, that's odd. You're very odd.

LEILAH: I won a fellowship.

MUFFET: Pink Pants is leaving right after graduation also. Lei, if he calls would you tell him I went away for the weekend? We had another fight yesterday.

1080 LEILAH: What happened?

MUFFET: Nothing. He told me that next year he wants to work his way around the world on a freighter. I tried to appear like "sure," "that's fine," "Have a nice trip," "send a postcard." I don't understand why when Samantha meets someone suddenly she's pinned and when I want someone they tell me I'm being clutchy and putting too much pressure on them. I don't want any commitment. I like being alone.

LEILAH: Me too.

MUFFET: Leilah, where do women meet men after college?
1090 Does Merrill Lynch have mixers with Time Life staffers at the General Foods Media department?

LEILAH: I don't know who I'll meet in Iraq. I like that. Katie says I'm escaping. I think I just need to be in a less competitive culture.

MUFFET: Why does Katie bother you so much?

LEILAH: Excuse me?

MUFFET: I can't understand why Katie bothers you so much.

LEILAH: She doesn't. I like Katie. She's exceptional.

MUFFET: Katie has no hips.

1100 LEILAH: It could be Social Darwinism. Katie could simply be a superior creature.

MUFFET: Pink Pants says you're prettier than Katie.

LEILAH: Sometimes when I'm in the library studying, I look up and I count the Katies and the Leilahs. They're always together. And they seem a very similar species. But if you observe a while longer the Katies seem kind of magical, and the Leilahs are highly competent. And they're usually such good friends—really the best. But I find myself secretly hoping that when we leave here Katie and I will just natu-
1110 rally stop speaking. There's something . . . (*Leilah begins to cry.*) It's not Katie's fault! Sometimes I wonder if it's normal for a twenty-year-old woman to be so constantly aware of another woman . . . "Thoughts of a dry brain in a dry

season."

MUFFET: (*Suddenly concerned for Leilah.*) Mrs. Plumm thinks about Ada Grudder often.

LEILAH: If we did stop speaking she wouldn't even notice, or if she did, she'd just think she wasn't a good person for a day. I just want to get out of here so I'm not with people who know me in terms of her. 1120

MUFFET: Leilah, why don't you come out with me tonight? I've always wanted to do this. We can go to a bar, not sleazy but also not a place where two nice girls usually go. And we'll sit alone, just you and I, with our two Brandy Alexanders and we won't need any outside attention. We'll be two uncommon women, mysterious but proud. (*Muffet puts her arm around Leilah.*)

LEILAH: All right. I'd like that.

MUFFET: (*Honestly.*) Leilah, I do understand a little. It's debilitating constantly seeing your worth in terms of some- 1130 one else.

VOICE: Male L.D. for Muffet DiNicola. Muffet DiNicola, Male L.D.

LEILAH: I'll take it for you Muffy.

MUFFET: (*Pauses and then gets her coat.*) No, it's got to be Old Pink Pants. Would you sign an overnight slip for me? See, Leilah, I know myself and as soon as the phone rings, I'm just fine. (*Muffet leaves with her coat. Leilah is left alone in the room holding the chocolate bunny.*)

(*End Scene*)

SCENE IV

MAN'S VOICE: A liberal education opens out in many different 1140 directions; when intellectual experience is a real adventure, it leads toward the unfamiliar. Students at the college are expected to encounter a wide range of opportunities—That is to say uncertainties. A maturing mind must have an ethical base, a set of values, and wonder at the unknown. (*Rita, Holly, Kate, Muffet, Carter and Susie Friend, and Leilah, are in the living room. There is a large jar of peanut butter and fluff and some crackers on the table. They are putting large globs of fluff on their fingers and crackers.*) 1150

RITA: I think if I make it to thirty I'm going to be pretty fucking amazing.

HOLLY: My mother called me today and told me she saw a 280 pound woman on Merv Griffin, who had her lips wired together and lives on *Fresca*. She offered me a lip job as a graduation present.

MUFFET: Pass the fluff.

KATE: This stuff is vile. I bet the kitchen help took home the desserts. (*Samantha runs excitedly into the room.*)

SAMANTHA: I have something to tell you. I'm getting married to 1160 Robert. (*She starts to sing to the melody of Offenbach's "Can-Can."*)

*I'm leaving here*
*Goodbye to all of you*
*Things are just beginning*
*And I can't stop grinning.*

(*She starts doing kicks and humming the song.*)

*Da-da-da-da-da-da-da*
*Da-da-da-da-da-da-da*

(*She goes into the finale.*)

1170

> *Things are beginning and*
> *I'm grinning through my tears*
> *Goodbye my friends*
> *I'll miss you all through the years*
> *The date is set for June*
> *Da-dum-da-dum-da-dum*
> *Da-da!*

(*Nobody moves. The women throughout the song have been frozen.*)

SUSIE: Samantha, NO.

SAMANTHA: Yes.

SUSIE: NO.

SAMANTHA: YES.

1180 SUSIE: Let's run and tell Mrs. Plumm. (*Susie and Samantha exit squealing no, yes . . . There is silence for a few moments. Carter continues to eat.*)

MUFFET: How come Carter eats so much Milk n' Crackers every night and never gains weight?

CARTER: I throw up immediately afterwards.

(*End Scene*)

SCENE V

MAN'S VOICE: The college fosters the ability to accept and even welcome the necessity of strenuous and sustained effort in any area of endeavor. (*Enter Rita in denim jacket and cap.*)

RITA: Hey, man wanna go out and cruise for pussy?

1190 SAMANTHA: Beg your pardon?

RITA: Come on, man.

SAMANTHA: (*Putting hair brush in her mouth as if it were a pipe.*) Can't we talk about soccer? Did you see Dartmouth take us? They had us in the hole.

RITA: I'd sure like to get into a hole.

SAMANTHA: Man, be polite.

RITA: (*Gives Samantha a light punch on the arm*) Fuck, man.

SAMANTHA: (*Softly at first.*) Shit man. (*She laughs hysterically.*)

RITA: Fucking "A" man.

1200 SAMANTHA: Excuse me.

RITA: Samantha, you're losing the gist.

SAMANTHA: I just feel more comfortable being the corporate type. Won't you sit down? Can I get you a drink? Want to go out and buy *Lacoste* shirts and the State of Maine?

RITA: (*Picking up Samantha's bag of nuts.*) Nice nuts you got there.

SAMANTHA: Thank you. You can only get them west of the Mississippi.

RITA: (*Chewing on the nuts.*) I'll give you a vasectomy if you

1210 give me one. (*Pause.*)

SAMANTHA: (*She breaks her male character.*) Rita, I liked the game when we said who we would marry much better. All right. (*She goes back into character.*) Anyway, I don't want a vasectomy. I like homes and babies.

RITA: (*Rita picks up Piglet.*) Hey, man what's this? You got a fucking doll, man, with two button eyes, a pink little ass, and

a striped T-shirt. I could really get into this. This dollie got a name, man? Piglet?

SAMANTHA: (*Disliking game.*) I don't know.

RITA: What's the matter, man? You afraid I think you're a pansy 1220 or something?

SAMANTHA: (*Drops character.*) Rita, cut it out.

RITA: Samantha, I'm only playing.

SAMANTHA: We're twenty-one years old and I don't want to play.

RITA: Then why do you have the fucking doll?

SAMANTHA: (*Taking doll, she begins to exit.*) I like my doll. I've had it ever since my Dad won it when I was in sixth grade at the Naperville Fair.

RITA: (*Dropping doll and character.*) Samantha, you don't 1230 like me.

SAMANTHA: I like you, Rita. We're just very different. And I don't want to play anymore.

RITA: Do you know what, Samantha? If I could be any one of us, first I would be me. That's me without any embarrassment or neurosis—and since that's practically impossible, my second choice is, I'd like to be you.

SAMANTHA: But, Rita, when you're thirty you'll be incredible.

RITA: Samantha, at least you made a choice. You decided to marry Robert. None of the rest of us has made any 1240 decisions.

SAMANTHA: (*Pause.*) Thanks, Rita.

RITA: Well, I don't want to spend oodles of time with you. You're not a fascinating person. But I do want to be you. Very much. (*Pause.*) You're the ideal woman.

SAMANTHA: Robert says that I never grew up into a woman. That I'm sort of a child woman. I've been reading a lot of books recently about women who are wives of artists and actors and how they believe their husbands are geniuses, and they are just a little talented. Well, that's what I am. Just a 1250 little talented at a lot of things. That's why I want to be with Robert and all of you. I want to be with someone who makes a public statement. And, anyway, if I'm going to devote my uncommon talents to relationships, then I might as well nurture those that are a bit difficult. It makes me feel a little special.

RITA: (*Taking Samantha's hand.*) You are special, Samantha. We're all special.

SAMANTHA: It's a quiet intelligence. But I like it. (*Pause.*) Hey, Rita when's your birthday? Because when we get out of 1260 here, we probably won't see each other very much. But I want to be sure to send you a birthday card. I like you, Rita.

RITA: It's March 28. I'm an Aries. Aries women are impulsive and daring, but have terrible domineering blocks.

SAMANTHA:

> March 28 is the day of Rita's birthday, hipooray.
> She talks of cocks and Aries blocks
> But what's so neeta, about my Rita
> Is I know secretly, she's very sweeta.

(*Starts to giggle.*) Pretty fucking gross, man, huh! (*She gives* 1270 *Rita a light punch and they begin to exit together.*)

RITA: (*Gives her a light punch and starts to giggle.*) Yeah, pretty fucking gross, man. (*Scene ends as they continue to giggle and exit with their arms around each other.*)

(*End Scene*)

SCENE VI

MAN'S VOICE: The college maintains that along with knowledge, compassionate understanding is a central human activity. (*Carter is sitting on the floor typing rhythmically to the Hallelujah Chorus. Enter Kate who turns off the music.*)

1280 KATE: Carter, do you think I'm boring? I was just reading Wittgenstein and I tried to imagine the film version. I even lit a candle and tried to imagine the film version and all I could come up with is you're very weird. See Carter, you can interrupt me if you want, I've always thought it's a waste of time to scatter one's energy. I'm not saying you're wasting your time making Wittgenstein films. They're certainly not redundant, and it's a good field for women, but the possibility would never occur to me. Carter, I'm afraid that I'm so directed that I'll grow up to be a cold efficient lady in a grey business suit. Suddenly, there I'll be, an Uncommon 1290 Woman ready to meet the future with steadiness, gaiety and a profession, and what's more I'll organize it all with time to blow dry my hair every morning. Tonight everything seems so programmed. Just once it would be nice to wake up with nothing to prove. Sometimes I wonder what I'd do if I didn't work or go to school for a while. But if I didn't fulfill obligations or be exemplary, then I really don't know what I'd do. I have a stake in all those uncommon women expectations. I know how to do them well. I don't mind that you're not chatty. Neither am I. Do you know that I've slept with 1300 more men than Muffet or Rita. Really, it's true, I like sex with irresponsible people. It's exciting, like a trashy novel. But I couldn't live with anyone irresponsible. Gross-me-out. Carter, I admire you. I really do. Sometimes I think you'll let me into your world which is more interesting, well, more imaginative than mine. When I'm around Holly and Muffet I congratulate myself on being such a well prepared grown-up. But I'm always watching myself. When I'm comfortable, I'm not watching myself. I feel comfortable. I think it's odd, Carter. You're not specifically a comfortable person. Maybe 1310 we have that in common. I feel as if I'm under-articulating. (*Pause.*) I came in here cause I just got into Law School and I don't think I should go. I don't want my life to simply fall into place. (*Pause.*) Carter, can I sit here for a while? I'm frightened. (*Carter begins to put her arm around Kate. Kate pulls back.*) No, that's all right, pumpkin. I'll just sit here for a while and then go back to work. (*Carter goes back to her typing. Kate, getting up.*) Why have you typed, "Now is the time for all good" twenty-five times?

CARTER: I am cramming for my typing test. I need fifty words 1320 per minute to get a good job when I get out of here. (*Kate puts the Hallelujah Chorus back on. Music swells as Carter continues to type.*)

(*End Scene*)

SCENE VII

MAN'S VOICE: The college places at its center the content of human learning and the spirit of systematic disinterested inquiry. (*It is late. The women are all studying. Kate looks up from her book.*)

KATE: Holly, did you ever have penis envy?

HOLLY: I beg your pardon?

KATE: Did you ever have penis envy?

HOLLY: I remember having tonsilitis. 1330

KATE: Have you, Samantha?

SAMANTHA: I know I never had it. Robert's was the first one I ever saw. I didn't even know men had pubic hair.

KATE: How big was Robert's? Holly, don't fall asleep. This may be the last chance we have to accumulate comparative data. We're graduating in two more weeks. Now I remember Thomas' was around this big. That's small to medium with a tendency towards tumescence, and Iki was around this big. But it was curved so you can't trust my estimation. In fact, if I can remember the others were all kind of average. Oh, 1340 yeah, except for Blaise. His really did stand out. It was the biggest I ever saw. Except it was just like him. Large, functional, and Waspy. (*Kate may demonstrate size with a pencil and break it in half to show a smaller variety.*)

HOLLY: I knew a boy at Columbia with three balls. Really. He came up to see me my freshman year because his psychiatrist said I wouldn't mind.

KATE: Did you sleep with him?

HOLLY: I didn't want to hurt his feelings.

KATE: Holly, you're such a mealy-mouth. 1350

HOLLY: I don't care. I guess I don't like men's underwear. Especially when they don't remove it and it's left dangling around one ankle. In fact, if you'd like a run down of every flaccid appendage in the Ivy League, I can give you details.

KATE: I've never been with an impotent man.

HOLLY: You haven't lived.

KATE: Listen to this! This is from a chapter in Chip Knowles' new book: *Women My Issue*. Chip has concluded, and I quote. "That the discovery at four months that a girl is castrated is the turning point in her road. At fourteen months 1360 little girls fingers and pacifiers are introduced into the vagina and at fifteen months a girl baby has been known to fall asleep with her genitalia on her Teddy bear. Finally, at sixteen months they start using a pencil."

SAMANTHA: Don't little boys use pencils?

HOLLY: No, they write with their cocks.

SAMANTHA: But don't men have breast and womb envy?

KATE: Well, if they have it, they just become creative or cook dinner every now and then.

HOLLY: I guess I envy men. I envy their confidence. I envy 1370 their options. But I never wanted a fleshy appendage. Especially a little boy's. Whenever I get fat I get nauseated because it looks like I have one in my pants. (*Pause.*) Katie, this is nonsense. The only people who have penis envy are other men.

KATE: You mean it's all those appendages compensating for being small?

HOLLY: Yeah.

SAMANTHA: Well, I know I wouldn't want one 'cause then I couldn't have Robert's. What time is it? 1380

KATE: 2 a.m.

SAMANTHA: I gotta go to bed, I have an Art History final in the morning.

KATE: Good night, pumpkin. (*Pause.*) Holly, do you think I have penis envy?

HOLLY: Oh, Katie, gross me out!

KATE: No, really for me it's entirely possible.

HOLLY: You don't have it. (*Enter Rita frazzled. She immediately throws herself on a bed or couch.*)

1390 RITA: You don't have what?

KATE: Nothing. Rita, what's the matter?

RITA: (*She goes into a womb position.*) I can't sleep.

HOLLY: What's wrong Rita?

RITA: (*Gets up.*) Nothing. I keep having recurrent *Let's Make a Deal* dreams . . . and my future is always behind the curtain, and the audience is screaming at me, NO, NO TAKE THE BOX! TAKE THE BOX! I haven't told anyone, but yesterday I went to New York, on a job interview. It was for one of those, "I graduated from a seven sister school and now I'm 1400 in publishing jobs."

KATE: Did you get the job?

RITA: I did very well at the interview. I told the interviewer that I was an English Composition Major, and I liked Virginia Woolf and Thackeray, but I really want to assistant edit beauty hints. I told her yes I thought it was so important for women to work and I would continue to write beauty hints even with a husband and family. The big thing at these interviews is to throw around your new found female pride as if it were an untapped natural resource.

1410 HOLLY: Did you get the job?

RITA: Holly, don't be so result oriented. Anyway, at the end of the interview she told me it was delightful, I told her it was delightful, we were both delightful. She walked me to the door, and said, "Tell me dear, do you have experience with a Xerox machine?" I said, "Yes. And I've tasted my menstrual blood."

KATE: Rita, you didn't really do that, did you?

RITA: I did. Holly, I can't go to one of those places. I don't know what I'm going to do, but it's not going to be that. I'm not 1420 going to throw my imagination away. I *refuse* to live down to expectation. If I can just hold out 'til I'm thirty, I'll be incredible.

HOLLY: Rita, I think you're already incredible.

RITA: Actually I do have a new fantasy that helps me deal with the future. I pretend that I am Picara in a picaresque novel and this is only one episode in a satiric life. (*Rita gets up.*) Hey pumpkins, let's go down and hit the candy machine and see how much weight we can gain in a night.

KATE: All right, I should do one kinky thing before we 1430 graduate.

HOLLY: No, I have more work to do.

RITA: (*Triumphant again.*) And when the candy machine is empty, I'm going to start writing my novel. (*Kate and Rita exit.*)

HOLLY: (*Alone. She puts on the tape player and lies down on the bed smoking. A recording of James Taylor. She reaches to the telephone and dials, and puts her raccoon coat over her for comfort.*) Operator, I'd like the phone number of a Dr. Mark Silverstein in Minneapolis, Minn. Could you con- 1440 nect me with that number please? Thank you. Hello, can I speak to Mark? Oh, do you have his number in Philadelphia? Thank you. No, that's all right. I'll call him there. (*Dials again.*) Hello, may I please speak to Mark? Oh, Hi. My name is Holly Kaplan. I met you last summer at a museum with my friend Muffet. It was the Fogg Museum. Oh that's all right, I never remember who I meet at museums either. (*She giggles.*) What's new? I'm not quite certain what

I'll be doing next year. I'm having trouble remembering what I want. My friend Katie says I'm too diffuse. You'd like Katie. She's basing her life on Katherine Hepburn in 1450 *Adam's Rib.* She didn't tell me that but it's a good illustration. No, I haven't been back to the Fogg Museum this year. My brother goes to Harvard Medical, Business, and Law School. Maybe I'll move to Philadelphia. (*She giggles.*) I'm in North Stimson Hall, fourth floor, under my raccoon coat. I guess everything's all right here. I just like being under my coat. Last week when I was riding the bus back from Yale and covering myself with it I thought I had finally made it into a Salinger story. Only, I hated the bus, college, my boyfriend and my parents. The only thing really nice was the 1460 coat. (*Pause.*) I take that back about my parents. Do you know what the expression "Good Ga Davened" means? It means someone who davened or prayed right. Girls who good ga davened did well. They marry doctors and go to Bermuda for Memorial day weekends. These girls are also doctors, but they only work part-time because of their three musically inclined children, and weekly brownstone restorations. I think Mount Holyoke mothers have access to a "did well" list published annually, in New York, Winnetka, and Beverly Hills, and distributed on High Holy Days and Epis- 1470 copal bake sales. I'm afraid I'm on the waiting list. (*Pause.*) You were on the waiting list for Johns Hopkins. I have a good memory for indecision. My mother says doctors take advantage unless you're thin. And then they want to marry you and place you among the good ga davened. She says girls who have their own apartments hang towels from the windows so the men on the street know when to come up. My friend Alice Harwitch is becoming a doctor and I've never seen her enter a strange building with towels in the windows. Of course, she's a radical lesbian. Sorry to have 1480 bothered you. Hey, maybe you'd like to visit here sometime, it's very pretty in the spring. We could see Emily Dickinson's house and buy doughnuts. I think about her a lot. And doughnuts, I think about them a lot too. No, I don't write poetry, and I haven't read *The Bell Jar.* My friend Rita has. I don't know who Rita's basing her life on. Sometimes I think she'd like to be Katherine Hepburn, but Katie has the Katherine Hepburn market cornered and we're all allowed only one dominant characteristic. I'm holding a lottery for mine. (*She giggles again.*) Yes, I guess I do giggle a lot, and 1490 I am too cynical. I had my sarcastic summer when I was sixteen and somehow it exponentially progressed. Leilah, she's my nice friend who's merging with Margaret Mead, says sarcasm is a defense. Well, I couldn't very well call you up and tell you to move me to Minneapolis and let's have babies, could I? (*Her tone of voice changes.*) Well, sorry to have bothered you. Really, I'm fine. I find great comfort in Lay Lady Lay, One Bad Apple Don't Spoil The Whole Bunch Girl, and my raccoon coat. And I like my friends, I like them a lot. They're really exceptional. Uncommon women and all 1500 that drivel. Of course, they're not risky. I'm not frightened I'll ruin my relationship with them. Sometimes I think I'm happiest walking with my best. Katie always says she's my best, shredding leaves and bubble gum along the way and talking. Often I think I want a date or a relationship to be over so I can talk about it to Kate or Rita. I guess women are just not as scary as men and therefore they don't count as much. (*Holly begins to cry.*) I didn't mean that, I guess they just always make me feel worthwhile. (*Pause.*) Thank you, I'm sure you're worthwhile too. (*She is resigned.*) If it's all right, I'm not going to tell Muffet I called you. Muffet's the girl who was with me in the museum. Oh, that's all right. Well, thanks for talking to me. Goodbye, thank you. I guess so. (*Holly gets down on the bed. Turns the tape player back on. Slides the raccoon coat over her head. Music swells. Lights fade out.*)

(*End Scene*)

SCENE VIII

*Pomp and Circumstance music is heard under the male voice. The girls march in and form a line behind Mrs. Plumm's tea service.*

MAN'S VOICE: Commencement brings a whole set of new opportunities, as varied as they are numerous. By the time a class has been out ten years, more than nine-tenths of its members are married and many of them devote a number of years exclusively to bringing up a family. But immediately after commencement nearly all Mount Holyoke graduates find jobs or continue studying. Today all fields are open to women, and more than fifty percent continue in professional or graduate school. Any one of a variety of majors may lead to a position as Girl Friday for an Eastern Senator, service volunteer in Venezuela, or assistant sales director of *Reader's Digest.* (*Lights up on Mrs. Plumm seated in the living room. Kate walks up to Mrs. Plumm.*)

MRS. PLUMM: What are your plans, dear?

KATE: I'm starting Harvard Law School in the fall.

MRS. PLUMM: Good luck, dear. (*Mrs. Plumm hands Kate a teacup. Kate sits. Leilah moves up to Mrs. Plumm.*) What are your plans, dear?

LEILAH: I'm studying anthropology in Mesopotamia.

MRS. PLUMM: Good luck, dear. What are your plans, Susie?

SUSIE: I'm becoming a security analyst, for Morgan Guarantee Trust.

MRS. PLUMM: Good luck, dear. (*Susie kisses Mrs. Plumm.*) What are your plans, dear?

SAMANTHA: As you know, I'm marrying Robert Cabe. He's going to be a successful actor.

MRS. PLUMM: Good luck, dear. (*The good luck, dear here is said in a different tone than it was to Kate. Mrs. Plumm hands Samantha a tea-cup. Samantha sits. Holly moves up to Mrs. Plumm.*) Holly, dear. Have you thought about Katie Gibbs? It's an excellent business school. (*Mrs. Plumm hands Holly a cup. Holly leaves the cup and sits. Enter Muffet.*) What are your plans, dear?

MUFFET: I'm assuming something is going to happen to me. I figure I have two months left. (*Muffet giggles and Mrs. Plumm giggles.*)

MRS. PLUMM: Good luck, dear. (*Rita moves up as Muffet sits down and she immediately starts talking.*)

RITA: Well, God knows there is no security in marriage. You give up your anatomy, economic self-support, spontaneous creativity, and a helluva lot of energy trying to convert a male (half person) into a whole person who will eventually stop draining you, so you can do your own work. And the alternative—hopping onto the corporate or professional ladder is just as self-destructive. If you spend your life proving yourself, then you just become a man, which is where the whole problem began and continues. All I want is a room of my own so I can get into my writing. I was going to marry Clark, but he advertised himself as a houseboy in *The Village Voice* and I didn't want damaged goods. . . .

MRS. PLUMM: (*Cutting Rita off.*) I'm afraid our time is up, dear. (*Rita grabs a cup to toast Mrs. Plumm, and sits down. Mrs. Plumm gets up to address the audience, with the graduates sitting beside her.*) You are all to be congratulated on your graduation. And thank you. I certainly didn't expect such an elaborate party for my retirement. I'm so glad to see so many students, faculty, and friends—Dr. Ada Grudder, who travelled here all the way from Nagpur, India. Many memories, seasons, and teas come to mind. But I thought I'd share with you some recent thoughts. At my last Milk 'n Crackers at the college I had an interesting talk with Kate Quin, an articulate young woman, who told me somewhat wistfully that she thought my retirement and the recent student vote to abolish "Gracious Living," marked the end of an era. I have seen the world confronting Kate and her classmates expand—The realm of choices can be overwhelming. However, those of you who have known me as the constant dutiful daughter of my Alma Mater, and my family, may be surprised to know that I do not fear the change for my girls, nor myself. My work here completed, I plan to go on a little adventure. Next summer I will travel to Bolivia which is the heartland of ornithological variety on this planet. My dear friend Ada, has returned to me our trusty rifle. So you see, girls, perhaps even I am in a transition period. (*When Mrs. Plumm mentions Ada Grudder the girls look out to the audience for her.*) Am I cavalier about leaving gracious-living and tea? Hardly. You see as a housemother and teacher most often I have found my work exciting. But when I grew weary or disgruntled, like Emily Dickinson, I too tired of the world and sometimes found it lacking, the gentler joys of tea, sherry, and conversation with women friends, and I've made many good ones here, have always been a genuine pleasure. Thank you . . . and good-bye. (*The girls applaud Mrs. Plumm. Carter enters and brings in flowers. Muffy, Kate, Holly, Rita and Samantha watch as Mrs. Plumm exits with Carter and Susie Friend and Leilah who have gone up to congratulate her.*)

(*End Scene*)

SCENE IX

MAN'S VOICE FADING INTO WOMAN'S VOICE: A liberal arts college for women of talent is more important today than at any time in the history of her education. Women still encounter overwhelming obstacles to achievement and recognition despite gradual abolition of legal and political disabilities. Society has trained women from childhood to accept a limited set of options and restricted levels of aspirations.

SAMANTHA: I saw Carter's Wittgenstein movie on Public

Television.

KATE: Maybe I should have married Carter.

MUFFET: Leilah got married in Iraq.

KATE: You're kidding.

MUFFET: She married some Iraqi journalist, archeologist. She gave up her citizenship and converted to Moslem. She can never be divorced.

RITA: Oh, my God.

1620 KATE: Sometimes I thought I was a bad friend to Leilah and other times I just thought she was crazy. (*Rita touches Kate assuringly.*) Rita, how's your novel coming?

RITA: Kate, do you ever have anxiety attacks? I mean the kind that gives you the shits. I'm up every night till five A.M. and then I have fever dreams that I'm back in Cranfield Heights and my father has put me in the caboose of a Lionel train that goes through the Fundamentalist Church. And the men in the congregation are staring at my cunt singing, "Meow, Meow, Meow, Meow, Meow, Meow." Marilyn, my shrink

1630 says to start slowly. So I figure if I can sleep in the morning, watch a little tube at night, I'll have it together long enough to write my novel. I figure if I can make it to forty, I can be pretty fucking amazing.

KATE: I don't know, Rita. Maybe I don't have an artistic temperament, like you and Holly. I went to see a shrink this year. I friend of Kent's.

MUFFET: Who's Kent?

KATE: The man I was sort of living with. He started objecting to my working late. I guess it never occurred to me in col-

1640 lege that someone wouldn't want me to be quite so uncommon. Anyway, I went to see this shrink and we had four productive sessions together and I feel fine.

MUFFET: Katie, you were all better after four sessions? You're still an over-achiever.

KATE: I don't live with Kent anymore. Kent's a lovely "enlightened" man who wants to marry Donna Reed. All right Donna Reed with an M.A. But I guess right now I'm committed to my work. (*Pause.*) Muffet do you really like insurance?

1650 MUFFET: Wallace Stevens was in Insurance. When I first took my job I wondered what I was doing being an insurance seminar hostess. I mean, where was my prince? I guess I assumed something special would happen to me. Now I live in Hartford and I go to work every day and I won't be in the Alumnae Magazine like you, Katie, at the Justice Department or Nina Mandelbaum with her pediatric pulmonary specialist. But, I never thought I'd be supporting myself and I am. (*Kate touches Muffet's hand.*) Rita, I don't see how you can become strong living off Timmy. You're not doing any-

1660 thing.

RITA: We're suing Timmy's mother for his stocks. Actually, Kate, I was going to ask you about them—we need a good lawyer. The stocks are in his name, but in Timmy's mother's vault.

SAMANTHA: Rita, do you love Timmy?

RITA: I thought he'd be my Leonard Woolf. (*Pause.*) I just wanted to be protected like you, Samantha. (*Rita puts her arm around Samantha.*) Samantha, you have a good marriage, don't you?

1670 SAMANTHA: Yes, I guess I do. Sometimes I get intimidated by all of Robert's friends who come to the house. And I think I

haven't done very much of anything important. So I don't talk. But Robert respects me. (*She smiles. Pause.*) I don't want to sound like Mrs. Plumm, but I just want to say that I'm glad we all got together today. I had second thoughts about seeing all of you, especially Kate and Rita. Sometimes I think you might disapprove of what I do. I don't live alone, I'm not a professional and I tend to be too polite. What I really want to tell you is Robert and I are having a baby.

MUFFET: (*Gets up to kiss Samantha.*) That's wonderful, 1680 Samantha.

RITA: Why didn't you tell us?

SAMANTHA: It's not as easy as telling you I was getting married to him. Remember when I ran into the room? Now there are more options. I decided that I was a little embarrassed to tell you, but I'm also happy.

KATE: (*Kisses Samantha.*) I'm so pleased for you, Samantha, really. I even promise to sit for you on Election Day—that's my one day off. (*Pause.*) I wonder if I'll ever decide to have a child. I hardly think about it and when I do I tell myself 1690 there's still a lot of time. I wonder what it's like when you stop thinking there's a lot of time left to make changes. (*Pause. Samantha smiles slightly.*)

RITA: (*Trying to make conversation, and putting her arm around Samantha and Holly.*) I bought the new James Taylor album last week, I put it on at five A.M. and I thought this will be a comfort. It will remind me of my friends and I'll be able to make some connection between the past and the present. And all I heard was, "Carly, I love you, darling I do." Now, how did he turn out so well adjusted? Every 1700 other person I talk to is suddenly fine and has decided to go to medical school or has found inner peace through EST. I just had hoped that at least James Taylor would hold out for something more ambiguous.

HOLLY: (*Who has been listening intently during the scene.*) You know for the past six years I have been afraid to see any of you. Mostly because I haven't made any specific choices. My parents used to call me three times a week at seven A.M. to ask me, "Are you thin, are you married to a root canal man, are *you* a root canal man?" And I'd hang up and won- 1710 der how much longer am I going to be in "transition." I guess since college I've missed the comfort and acceptance I felt with all of you. And I thought you didn't need that anymore, so I didn't see you.

KATE: Holly, I don't want to go back and have "Gracious Living" and tea anymore. But I still want to see all of you. We knew we were natural resources before anyone decided to tap us. (*Pause for a moment as the girls all look at each other and finally smile together.*)

HOLLY: Let's have a toast. 1720

SAMANTHA: All right, pumpkins, a toast, to Katie's law firm.

KATE: To Robert.

HOLLY: To Rita's novel.

MUFFET: To Wallace Stevens.

ALL: To Carter.

KATE: I'm glad we decided to get together today too. I've been feeling a little numb lately. And I know I wasn't like that in college. You remember a person, don't you? Anyway, lately, especially at those boring meetings, I look around at all those wingtip feet and I remember Holly saying men write 1730 with their cocks—and I suspect many of the junior partners do, and Rita writing her novel, and Samantha being a closet wit, and Muffet and her prince. *(Pause.)* I'm glad we got together too. I miss you. *(Pause as she looks at all of them.)* And I've got to go. I'll get the check.

SAMANTHA: We could charge it to Robert.

KATE: No, I'll take it as a tax deduction. Holly, what are you doing?

HOLLY: I keep a list of options. Just from today's lunch, there's 1740 law, insurance, marry Leonard Woolf, have a baby, bird watch in Bolivia. A myriad of openings.

KATE: I've got to go. Kent says I dawdle. *(Pause.)* You all have my numbers. *(After Kate exits there is silence in the room. The girls look at each other quietly.)*

SAMANTHA: My dad was re-elected Mayor of Naperville.

HOLLY: My sister is marketing director of Proctor and Gamble.

RITA: Ada Grudder won the Nobel Prize. No, she didn't really, but I like to think so.

MUFFET: *(Getting up to put on her coat.)* Let's go to the movies. 1750

SAMANTHA: *(Getting up.)* I have my car outside. Let's go see "Cries and Whispers."

MUFFET: *(Muffet laughs slightly and puts her arm around Samantha.)* Hey, Holly, did you know Melissa Weex became a Rockette?

RITA: *(Moving to Holly, and putting on her coat.)* Timmy says when I get my head together, and if he gets the stocks, I'll be able to do a little writing. I think if I make it to forty I can be pretty amazing. *(She takes Holly's hand.)* Holly, when we're forty we can be pretty amazing. You too Muffy and 1760 Samantha, when we're *(Rita pauses for a moment.)* . . . forty-five we can be pretty fucking amazing. *(The Women exit with their arms around each other.)*

**E N D**

*THIS interview was conducted by Kathleen Betsko and Rachel Koenig.*

Wendy Wasserstein Interview (1987)

INTERVIEWER: Your plays are very funny. Will you talk a little about comedic writing in general, and then specifically about women's comedy?

WASSERSTEIN: Well, there's always that old Woody Allen joke: When you write comedy you sit at the children's table, and when you write tragedy you sit at the adult table. But I'm not sure that's true. It's very satisfying for me to hear the audience laugh. The audience is alive, it's *there.* What's interesting about my plays is that they are comedies, but they are also somewhat wistful. They're not *happy,* nor are they farces, which is odd because I've been given offers to write sit-coms for television, and I don't think I'd be good at it. There's an undercurrent in my work.

Christopher Durang is a very dear friend, and a brilliant writer. We've collaborated on a film [*When Dinah Shore Ruled the Earth*] and it's interesting how our voices merge at a point. Mine tends to be more warm, and his is more startling. There's a give and take, but I'm still interested in that warmth. Collaboration is also a matter of stretching oneself, trying to get out into other forms. Chris talks about moving toward more warmth, and I find myself moving toward something darker. When we wrote the movie, we met every day, and wrote the whole script on one notepad. The writing became *one* voice. It was very interesting.

INTERVIEWER: Do you think it is more natural for you to write "warm"?

WASSERSTEIN: I wouldn't say that. It's hard, talking about a female aesthetic. Best put, I once heard Marsha Norman say that women writing plays had secrets they wanted to tell. When I wrote *Uncommon Women and Others* [1976–1977], I wanted to write an all-woman play. Now given that, what am I going to write? My characters rafting down the Colorado River? It just happens that the men I've known have not gone to girls' schools for eight years. They have not had the pleasure of a course on "Gracious Living." They also did not grow up—and hopefully this has changed—with having to hear "Be a sweet girl, be a good girl." That's different nowadays. I was writing *Uncommon Women* from an experience I had. I don't know if that gets down to an aesthetic. When you're talking about an aesthetic, you're also talking about language.

INTERVIEWER: How would you describe your stage language?

WASSERSTEIN: The people in my plays talk circularly. They do not talk directly. I don't know if that's women or that's Wendy. It's probably Wendy. But Wendy is a woman writer, and *Uncommon Women* comes from a woman's experience. It's *about* women sitting around talking. It's reflective. I do agree with Marsha Norman in that I think there are stories to tell that haven't been told. But you're not only telling them for women, hopefully.

INTERVIEWER: You said that in working on *Isn't It Romantic* you were interested in the ways in which your characters became trapped by their own humor.

WASSERSTEIN: Janie Blumberg, the main character, is totally trapped by her own sense of humor. Some people seeing the first version of the play thought it was composed of very witty one-liners, but I felt it was how Janie talks. Janie is a character who has a problem expressing her feelings and she desperately wants to be liked.

INTERVIEWER: Is Janie's humor a way of protecting herself?

WASSERSTEIN: It's a protection, but it's a vulnerability as well. I think that may be very female. Janie in *Isn't It Romantic* tells joke, joke, joke and then finally explodes. Finally, she discovers her own strength. And furthermore, there is a strength in being comedic. It's a way of getting on in the world, of taking the heat out of things. Humor is a life force.

INTERVIEWER: It seemed that many of the critics missed the irony of *Isn't It Romantic* [1981] in its original production.

WASSERSTEIN: Women playwrights fall into a trap because the audience goes in expecting a "woman's play," with a feminist sensibility. Nobody goes into a man's play and thinks, "I want a man's point of view on this." They don't expect to discover the male playwright's political feeling about the sexes. That is never asked of men. For example, when Janie in *Isn't It Romantic* doesn't marry the doctor, it's not because she's a grand feminist, or because she loves her career, or wants to ride off on a tractor. He isn't right for her. As a playwright, first and foremost you must be true to your characters. It's the character's motivation; not me speaking for womankind. Even *Uncommon Women* doesn't say, "This is what I feel about women." Basically what it's saying is "I'm very confused." The characters are confused; they're also dear and kind and funny. The play asks: "Why are they so confused?" I want to *show* you their confusion. But it's not saying I have any answers. And what it's really not saying is "Fuck you."

INTERVIEWER: Didn't you once say that *Isn't It Romantic* is *about* being funny?

WASSERSTEIN: Janie Blumberg's humor gives her the ability to distance herself from situations. But she simultaneously endears herself to people by being amusing. The play is about her difficulty in communicating. She's so verbal, and yet she can't talk. It's a play about speech—about the ability to speak and not to speak at the same time, which comes from the pressure women are under to be a good girl, a smart girl, and a warm girl, simultaneously.

INTERVIEWER: Is *Isn't It Romantic* about *the price* of being a good, smart, warm and funny girl?

WASSERSTEIN: Yes, I think so.

INTERVIEWER: Is Janie willing to pay the price?

WASSERSTEIN: Janie is strong, but she doesn't know it. Maybe she secretly knows she's strong and is frightened by it. It's not going to be easy for Janie, but she is able to move from feeling and that's interesting. In fact, that's character. Janie is stronger than her friend Harriet who has all the externals. . . . Harriet could be a cover on *Savvy* magazine. The girl who "has it all." You know, the person who gets up at eight o'clock in the morning, spends twenty minutes with her daughter and ten minutes with her husband, then they jog together, she drives to work, comes home to her wonderful life, studies French in the bathtub, and still has time to cry three minutes a day in front of the mirror.

What's troublesome, from my point of view, about the Women's Movement is that there are *more* check marks to earn nowadays. More pressure. What's really liberating is developing from the inside out. Having the confidence to go from your gut for whatever it is you want. Janie is able to do that.

The character of Janie's mother in *Isn't It Romantic* runs around saying, "I like life, life, life." She's a bit of a crackpot, but she *does* have a spirit. The comedy itself is a spirit. It's not an application form, a resume, it's life. This life spirit creates a current, a buoyancy, which, getting back to drama, is very important. It's important to reach the essence of that spirit in what you create. That, to me, is heroic.

INTERVIEWER: In the Phoenix production of *Isn't It Romantic* most of the critics were upset by the fact that in the end, Janie rejected the nice Jewish doctor as a husband.

WASSERSTEIN: If the Jewish doctor had been a creep, and Janie decided not to marry him, the play would be a feminist statement: Good for her, see how strong she is. I wanted to write a nice man. And the play's not about the fact that she doesn't marry. I don't feel one way or another about marriage per se, though I'd like to get married one of these days. . . .

INTERVIEWER: The doctor isn't really perfect, is he?

WASSERSTEIN: He's not perfect at all! He tells her he wants to make alternate plans, he calls her "monkey," he buys an apartment without telling her. If these are people's ideals, after the play they should see a marriage counselor. And Janie's not scared. He is a Jewish doctor, he is darling and funny and dear, but Janie has a right to her decisions. She has a right, even if that means she's going to be alone. Even if she's *wrong* in her choice. Even if she's going to sit in her apartment and cry every night, if that's what she wants to do. . . .

INTERVIEWER: Since the emergence of women's issues, men's behavior has been under close scrutiny. You seem to have taken an ironic swipe at the "new male" in drawing your character, Paul Stuart *[Isn't It Romantic]*, whose behavior is old hat—despite his liberated rhetoric.

WASSERSTEIN: Things have gotten very confusing. It's true that men can exploit the new rhetoric. My character Paul Stuart is very smart when he says that when he got married, women didn't know they could have careers. He says, "Now you girls have careers and *you* want a wife." He's pretty much figured things out. The fact that *he* still gets to have a wife is interesting. . . .

INTERVIEWER: Your plays bear the message that women *can't* "have it all." Helen Gurley Brown [editor, *Cosmopolitan*] says that women *can* have it all, if only they learn the right strategies.

WASSERSTEIN: I've never been one for strategies, really. Because I can't make one for myself. What should you do? Take colored index cards for everything you want, put them on a bulletin board: baby on the pink card, job on the blue? I never understood how those things work. I know there are women who have careers *and* babies. They work very hard. More credit to them. But the whole notion of "having it all" is ridiculous. It's a ridiculous phrase. Who's determining what "it all" is? Helen Gurley Brown? That's not fair. No man has had the pressure during the past ten years of having a different article come out every two weeks dictating how he should live his life. It changes every two weeks!

There isn't any formula for happiness. The very basic expectations of being a "good girl," a "nice girl," and a "kind girl" are still being put upon us. This is confusing because there's nothing wrong with wanting to be kind, unless it hurts you, or keeps you from doing what you want to do.

INTERVIEWER: Who is responsible for this malaise? The media? The theater? The government?

WASSERSTEIN: I don't know. You *do* want to work *and* have children *and* be gorgeous. But until there's a dictum for men that says, "Have it all," it's not fair for women to feel they should. Even with all the media talk about the "new father" and "time-sharing" I've yet to see the male "have it all" article come out.

INTERVIEWER: As far back as *Uncommon Women* you seemed to have an awareness of the way the "new male" was absorbing the liberated woman's language. Rita says, "The only problem with menstruation for men is that some sensitive schmuck could write about it for the *Village Voice* and become the new expert on women's inner life."

WASSERSTEIN: I guess to be fair, things have changed. . . .

INTERVIEWER: Doesn't it sometimes seem things have regressed?

WASSERSTEIN: Well, I went back to Mt. Holyoke in 1979 to see a production of *Uncommon Women*. I asked some of the students there what they thought about the play. One of them said, "Well, we think it's a nice *period* piece." I said, "Who do you think I am, Sheridan?" I mean, I had been studying there only eight years before! Then the women told me that unlike my characters, they knew what they wanted: to go to business school, or earn Ph.Ds or get married. I did think to myself, "This is becoming like Amherst College during the fifties." What's so great about that?

INTERVIEWER: Can we go back to the critics for a moment? Not many of them were kind about your rather broad character, Susie Friend, the cheerful organizer in *Uncommon Women*. Shakespeare was allowed a few clowns, why not Wendy Wasserstein?

WASSERSTEIN: Lots of women I know have grown up with Susie Friends. Now that's a woman's story! There have always been these little organizers in women's colleges. Of course, now they're organizing in banks!

INTERVIEWER: Is it okay for her to be a little less than three-dimensional because she is a peripheral character?

WASSERSTEIN: Susie Friend was a device. If you see *Uncommon Women* as a spectrum of women: on one end, there's Susie Friend, and on the other, there's Carter, the intellectual. That's all.

INTERVIEWER: You've said that the character of Tasha Blumberg in *Isn't It Romantic* was close to your mother in some ways.

WASSERSTEIN: Well, she is and she isn't. When you base a character on someone in real life, you are always condensing, as well as trying to keep the tone consistent. Tasha is not totally like my mother. Although my mother *is* a danseur! There is also an assumption that every mother you write is your own mother. That's not necessarily true. You have different things to say about a mother-daughter relationship at different times of life and in different kinds of plays.

INTERVIEWER: You've also said that it was easier for you to write the character Lillian, Harriet's mother, in *Isn't It Romantic* than Tasha Blumberg. Why is that?

WASSERSTEIN: Harriet's mother is an intriguing character. She was a more interesting woman to write because, of all the women in *Isn't It Romantic,* she is the most modern.

INTERVIEWER: Some of the critics saw Lillian as bitter. Do you agree?

WASSERSTEIN: Lillian is not hard or bitter. She is not Faye Dunaway in *Network.* But she's tough. In terms of comedy, she was fun to write because her sense of humor is very different from the other characters I have written. She has a little inflection, she's very wry and dry, and that was good for me because sometimes all of my characters have similar senses of humor. Lillian knows of the world and her own life. She has made her choices and has come to terms with them. In her life, there was not room for a man. She could not "have it all." She did pay a price and what's tragic is that her daughter is now going to pay another price.

INTERVIEWER: What is the price for Lillian?

WASSERSTEIN: Lillian had a bad marriage with a selfish man. Maybe with a more understanding man, she would have been fine. Who knows what the problem was? But in her life, she could not work it out. It wasn't worth it to her. Lillian is not a romantic. Lillian is fair. She is modern because she faces herself. What she has to say is honorable: "You tell me who has to leave the office when the kid bumps his head or slips on a milk carton." If she has to go home, time and time again, then why should she be with a man anyway? From Lillian's point of view, there is no reason to have *two* babies, your husband and your child. What's interesting is that Lillian, in her own way, is also a "good girl." She is not doing anything wrong. She is very American. A good mother, a hard worker . . .

INTERVIEWER: Be more specific as to what was more difficult about writing Tasha Blumberg, the character most nearly like your own mother.

WASSERSTEIN: I'll tell you why she was harder to write than Lillian. I've always thought that *Uncommon Women* was me split into nine parts, in terms of characters. But the truth is, what was always the hardest in *Uncommon Women* was writing Holly, who, autobiographically, is closest to me, though there are parts of me in all of the characters. That play is twofold. First, it's a play about Holly and Rita, which examines the fact that the Women's Movement has had answers for the Kates of the world (she becomes a lawyer), or the Samanthas (she gets married). But for the creative people, a movement can't provide answers. There isn't a specific space for them to move into. Holly was the hardest to write because I thought, "That's Wendy," or people will think, "THAT'S WENDY! There's the hips, there she is." And I also didn't want to self-congratulate when drawing that character. So I find it difficult to write autobiographical characters. There aren't good guys and there aren't villains in my plays. If I were to say there's a problem with my writing, it's typified by the line in *Uncommon Women* when one character says, "Sometimes it's difficult having sympathy with everyone's point of view." I have been accused of being too generous to the other, less autobiographical characters in my plays, but in fact, it is hardest for me to be generous to the character that is closest to me.

INTERVIEWER: You feel you have to humble yourself?

WASSERSTEIN: Yes. I think so. When someone said to me, "You're a playwright, why use a confused persona to represent yourself in a play? *You* know what you're doing. Why shouldn't the character?" I said, "I'm a playwright *because* I don't know everything. Because I am trying to figure things out." You do divide yourself up when you are writing. Marty Sterling, the doctor in *Isn't It Romantic* has the sweetest speech about marriage. Why doesn't Janie have that speech?

INTERVIEWER: So Tasha Blumberg was harder to write than Lillian because she was more autobiographical?

WASSERSTEIN: Tasha is closer to my mother, that is true. I find my mother very funny. My mother dances six hours a day. She's, as she says, twenty-one plus, and she has not gone to Mt. Holyoke, but she is very sharp. Sometimes I find her humor funnier than my own. I saw my mother on the street the other day. I was in a taxi, and I stopped. She jumped in and said, "Oh, it's so wonderful to have children, honey. It's so wonderful to see you and I only hope that by the time you have children, you take a fertility pill and have five." Then she looked at me and said, "And that's going into the play, isn't it?" I thought, there is no way I could write anything as good as that. And she knew it. I haven't finished with my mother yet. That is the truth of all this.

INTERVIEWER: Will you write about it someday?

WASSERSTEIN: Maybe it's where my writing is going. I don't know. Although I am proud of the last scene in *Isn't It Romantic,* the play doesn't deal with the pain of that subject. The real reason for comedy is to hide the pain. It is a way to cope with it. A way of staying "up." It's a privacy. You are there, and you are not there. You don't share equally about every topic. That's the truth of language, the truth of dialogue. If you did, you wouldn't be writing language, you wouldn't be writing what you are hearing, how people really talk. . . .

INTERVIEWER: So humor creates subtext?

WASSERSTEIN: Yes and it is also part of the delight of writing itself. When you come up with a good line, you make yourself laugh, right there at the typewriter. It gives you pleasure.

I want to say that the other reason Lillian was easier to write than Tasha was that Lillian was someone on my mind. She is contemporary. She's an image that is closer to, if not me, then me ten years from now. She reflects a conflict that I think about a lot. Men and children. Having children alone, and whether or not that's possible. Tasha Blumberg—forget my mother—is from another world, a different time, which is harder to capture. Lillian is closer to my world. I have considered writing plays about the young Tasha at Radio City, the dancer. And at one point in *Isn't It Romantic,* Janie gets up and starts to tap dance. There is an image of a person alone, who dances. Janie's mother is a dancer, and that is the gift from mother to daughter.

INTERVIEWER: You studied dramatic writing at Yale. Were there other women in the playwriting program?

WASSERSTEIN: Susan Nanons was there, Sharon Stockard-Martin, Grace McKeaney . . . they are all very talented women. But no, the playwriting program was not overflowing with women.

INTERVIEWER: Did you take a lot of flak for writing *Uncommon Women,* a play with an all-female cast?

WASSERSTEIN: I made the decision to write a play with all women after seeing all that Jacobean drama, where a man kisses the poisoned lips of a woman's skull and drops dead. I thought, "I can't identify with this." I wanted to write a play where all the women were alive at the curtain call. And I had seen my friend, Alma Cuervo, whom I love dearly, have to play the pig-woman in *Bartholomew Fair,* a panda in *General Gorgeous* . . . I thought, What's going on?

INTERVIEWER: Were people shocked by *Uncommon Women?*

WASSERSTEIN: Well, the play was not in as good a shape as it is now. I do remember someone who saw the Yale production saying that I was a "subset" of Christopher Durang. Chris came to my defense and said, "When I write my play about an all woman's college, you can call me." It was shocking to me.

INTERVIEWER: You said in an interview that the point of view at Yale was that "the pain in the world is a man's pain."

WASSERSTEIN: Though women are often said to write "small tragedies," they are *our* tragedies, and therefore large, and therefore legitimate. They deserve a stage.

INTERVIEWER: Why didn't *Uncommon Women,* with all of its success, move to Broadway?

WASSERSTEIN: We had one offer, which is an interesting story. The producer told me that at the end of the play things should be different. He said the play was too wistful. He thought, that at the end, when everyone asks Holly, "What's new with you?" she should pull out a diamond ring and say, "Guess what? I'm going to marry Dr. Mark Silverstein." I thought, "Well, she'd have to have a lobotomy, and I'd have to have a lobotomy too." So the play never went to Broadway. It does stick in my craw because *Uncommon Women* is a very good play and it had such an amazing cast. But sometimes you've opened a door, and when you go to the next work, people listen. Don't I sound old and wise? The play should have moved to Broadway!

INTERVIEWER: Is *Uncommon Women* a political play?

WASSERSTEIN: It's political because it is a matter of saying, "You must hear this." You can hear it in an entertaining fashion, and you can hear it from real people, but you must know and examine the problems these women face. It all comes from the time I was in college, which was a time of great fervor. There used to be pieces in that play that were very political. The most political part was when Mark Rudd came to Mt. Holyoke. In that version, Susie Friend had a strike speech and even organized a strike for Mark Rudd.

INTERVIEWER: Why did you take that out?

WASSERSTEIN: Well, I took it out because I thought that it would open the play up to all the questions of Vietnam, and that's another play. I really wanted to do something so that women's voices could be heard. I'm happy I did that. I can remember the 1969 Cambodia strike. Simultaneously, Amherst College was accepting women for the first time. There were twenty-three women and twelve hundred men. That was a glorious experience. I didn't go to the dining hall for two weeks. I was scared to death! The first night I was there, the men were rating us! I remember going to the student-faculty meeting and saying, "You have to let us stay here." The speaker seemed to think this was a very selfish issue. He said, "We have Kent State, we have Cambodia . . . what's the big deal about a little girl wanting to stay at Amherst College?" I thought, "This is one of the most important things happening in terms of long-range changes for women." In fact, Amherst College went coed two years later. That's just an isolated incident. I do think that that whole period has not yet been resolved. Maybe things *are* regressing. I try to find answers to these issues through my plays.

INTERVIEWER: Your character Leilah in *Uncommon Women*, says, "Sometimes I think I just need to live in a less competitive culture." How do you think that relates to being an artist in America?

WASSERSTEIN: When I was at Yale, I was frightened to death. I remember years later telling Christopher Durang that I felt like I was going from platform to platform, trying to catch the train to Moscow. I went from platform six to platform seven and I kept missing the train. I had no idea what I was doing at drama school. Everyone else I knew was going to law school or marrying lawyers, except for my immediate friends, who seemed as cuckoo as me. I really couldn't explain my feelings to anyone. If you tell someone you are a playwright, they say, "So what do you do for a living?" Or, if you're a successful playwright, they say, "Gee, isn't that glamorous?" You think, "Yeah, it's real exciting. I sit in a room alone every day and I write. Thrilling!" Either way, you are in an odd spot. It doesn't place you in the margins, but you are not in the mainstream of society. It certainly doesn't make for a secure life. But it does at least make for a life of doing what you want to do. I feel very lucky to be able to do that.

INTERVIEWER: You seem to make a plea for community in your work. . . .

WASSERSTEIN: Yes. Or at least, a plea to establish your own kind of family. Maybe my family is Chris Durang and Ted Talley and André Bishop. It could well be, but again, that's pretty marginal. You can't go to weddings and say "My family is Chris Durang, and Ted Talley and André Bishop. . . ."

INTERVIEWER: Would you tell us something about Playwrights Horizons?

WASSERSTEIN: I am very lucky because that theater is my home, and it has made a tremendous difference to me, having someplace that I know I can work out of. I've had a long association with the people there. Life is competitive, but Playwrights Horizons is not. It is a community, and that has always been very important to me.

INTERVIEWER: What happens when you are in rehearsal with a play? Are you able to maintain sufficient artistic control over your work?

WASSERSTEIN: It depends on the production and on the play. I was there through everything with *Uncommon Women*. I was at the [Eugene] O'Neill [National Playwrights Conference], the Phoenix Theatre, and when they did the television production for PBS. I had a good relationship with the director, Steve Robman.

INTERVIEWER: You felt your intentions were given enough attention?

WASSERSTEIN: Yes. But subsequently, I have seen productions of *Uncommon Women* around the country and I can't tell you the sort of horrifying things I've seen. It's unbelievable.

INTERVIEWER: How do you react to a bad production?

WASSERSTEIN: It depends on whether you've been involved in the actual production. Sometimes you just go to see the play. That's taught me that there is a point at which you have to let a play go. It was hard for me to let *Uncommon Women* go because it had such a short run in New York. I like to be able to go to a theater for more than a two-and-a-half-week run.

INTERVIEWER: You don't experience anger in rehearsal? You've never had to fight for your intentions?

WASSERSTEIN: Well, yes, sure I have. Rehearsal is a very important time to learn not to be such a good girl. I think you have to learn to speak up, because the point is, it's your play, and you *do* know something about it. It is very important to pick the right director. That is step one. And you can't be a good girl about picking a director either. You can't pick somebody just so everyone will like you. You have to pick someone you respect and who will be right for the play.

INTERVIEWER: Have you ever worked with a woman director?

WASSERSTEIN: Susan Dietz directed *Uncommon Women* in California [L.A. Stage Company, April 1981].

INTERVIEWER: Did you feel she brought any special insights to the work?

WASSERSTEIN: I did like the production a lot. I don't know how to answer that question because I was assigned Steve Robman at the O'Neill and he stayed with the production throughout. It wasn't a conscious choice for a male director or against a female director. It is very important that there be more women directors, and that more women directors are encouraged, which goes all the way back to the question of how many women directing students there are at Yale. I do think what you want is a *good* director.

INTERVIEWER: What did you mean, earlier, when you spoke of "letting go" of the play?

WASSERSTEIN: I told Chris the other night that I've had the sensation, with both *Uncommon Women* and *Isn't It Romantic* of waiting for the play to embrace me. I keep waiting for the play to give back what I've given. And it cannot happen. You can get depressed. Because if you're a good writer, you're generous and you give it everything and people laugh and applaud—but still, the play is inanimate. It cannot reach out and embrace you. That's hard to come to terms with. You can follow a play around the country waiting for that to happen. But it can't—and finally, you have to separate from it and just send it out.

INTERVIEWER: Is the closest you can get to that embrace hearing the spontaneous laughter from the audience?

WASSERSTEIN: Maybe. But during *Uncommon Women,* there was something special among those actresses and me. I can remember being in the dressing room with Swoosie Kurtz and Jill Eikenberry and Alma Cuervo, and Anna Levine, Glenn Close and Ellen Parker and there was the sense of embracing, a sense of all starting out together . . . again, that feeling of community. And I would say I feel it more at the laughter than at the applause.

INTERVIEWER: Why did you decide to study playwriting at Yale instead of attending Columbia Business School, where you had also been accepted?

WASSERSTEIN: You know, I even sent Columbia a deposit! When I graduated from Mt. Holyoke I came to New York and took writing courses at City College. I studied with Israel Horovitz and Joseph Heller. While studying playwriting with Israel, I had my first play done at Playwrights Horizons—this was back when it was at the YMCA on Fifty-second Street. I applied to both programs because I felt "I've *got* to make a living." I was living at home at the time. I thought I'd go to business school, then get a job in Chicago and everything would be fine. But when I got into Yale School of Drama, I thought, "Playwriting is something I really want to do. It's worth a shot." But it was hard. It took me a long time to take myself seriously. I mean, it still takes me a long time to take myself seriously. . . .

INTERVIEWER: Did Durang and Talley have difficulty taking themselves seriously?

WASSERSTEIN: I don't know. I don't think they thought something was wrong with them because they weren't in law school or married to a lawyer. I thought something was wrong with me. I thought I was a Ford Pinto. Now, I've gotten used to it. I'm used to living a life of eighty percent security.

INTERVIEWER: Does a Guggenheim Fellowship help with that feeling of eighty percent security?

WASSERSTEIN: Yes. That was the best thing since *Uncommon Women*. It is a certified "We believe in you." I have a funny story about that. In October, my father said, "So what are you doing?" I said, "Applying for a Guggenheim." He said, "What's that?" I told him it was a foundation that gives artists money to finish their work. Then he said, "No daughter of mine's going on welfare!" I'm the only person whose parents are going to disinherit her for winning a Guggenheim!

INTERVIEWER: Did you see *Uncommon Women* as a "non-play," as some of the reviewers did?

WASSERSTEIN: *Uncommon Women* is not a conventionally structured play. On a simple level, it moves through the seasons of the year. I do not see that play as presentational. It's like an odd sort of documentary. I am more interested in content than form. *Uncommon Women* is episodic. I don't know what actually *happens* in that play . . . they graduate.

INTERVIEWER: Quite a lot happens. . . .

WASSERSTEIN: But it is an emotional action. And I tend to go on big canvases. My favorite authors are Russian: Tolstoy, Chekhov . . . the whole idea of presenting a social life and a personal life interests me. I also love Ibsen.

INTERVIEWER: There's much reference recently to "The new woman playwright"—Mel Gussow's article in *The New York Times Magazine* [May 1, 1983], for example. Is it really that women are newcomers to playwriting, or is it the attention that's new?

WASSERSTEIN: I think it's the attention that's new. I do think there are women who open doors, like Marsha Norman. I don't know if her play '*night, Mother* could have won a Pulitzer Prize twenty years ago. So maybe there is a little more attention nowadays. But at the same time, when I saw that article, I thought, "Where is Corinne Jacker?" And that article also brings up the whole issue of whether women playwrights are a separate category. We are all playwrights. I think that is very important. But for now, any minority group must be labeled. Our idea of a playwright is a white male—then all the others are separated into subsets: black playwrights, gay playwrights, women playwrights, and so on. The point is, we are all in it together. But I listen to my plays, and as I hear them, I distance myself, and I still think, "A woman wrote this."

INTERVIEWER: Are female playwrights becoming less political than they were in the sixties and seventies?

WASSERSTEIN: It depends on what you see as political. Politics on the largest level is *from each according to their ability.* Nine girls taking a curtain call can be seen as political. It's important in terms of feeling legitimate. So is the fact that men can come to my plays and laugh, and that some girl from New Jersey comes to the play and says, "This is my story." And if my story can reach her, maybe *she* can tell *her* story. That is very important. Comedy does not segregate the political.

INTERVIEWER: Do you feel that British women playwrights are more likely to be overt in their politics?

WASSERSTEIN: That could be true. It could have to do with being brought up in a society where feminism has been connected to broader political issues. Maybe feminism has taken a different shape there. Caryl Churchill is a wonderful playwright. Her *Top Girls* was great. The way she took the larger political scope and then looked at the personal was fantastic.

INTERVIEWER: Can you give us a summation?

WASSERSTEIN: It is very important that women keep writing plays for many reasons. The theater is the home of the individual voice—at least in dramatic form. It is not in movies or television. I think the work of women in America is evolving. For myself, I am trying to work on structure, on comedy, and on being able to create a feeling of community. That can only happen in the theater.

INTERVIEWER: Are you optimistic about the state of American theater?

WASSERSTEIN: Oddly enough, I am. Because you do not write by committee in theater. The way that artists are discriminated against does have an effect on your pocketbook. Getting a Guggenheim helped this year, but you know, I am not making millions. The Guggenheim is not the money you would make as a first-year lawyer. That's how our society works. It makes you feel marginal. But, as somebody who believes in the individual voice, I still believe in the theater and what can happen there. I believe in comedy, in its spirit, and in its ability to lift people off the ground. I also think there are stories to tell, and as a woman writer, I want to tell those stories, to work out those conflicts. I want to take these conflicts from the political down to the personal. And the personal level, to me, is somewhat comedic. I hope to write a play that is going to be a history of the Women's Movement, which is a serious thing to take on. I want to write about someone who went through it and how it affected them personally—I want to explore the reverberations. Because I want to understand, and sometimes I understand better by writing. . . .

# Heiner Müller

Since the 1970s, Heiner Müller has been widely considered the most provocative playwright in Germany, East or West. Müller was born in 1929 and spent his youth watching the Weimar Republic give way to the rise of Nazism in Germany. He was drafted into the German army in 1945 and taken prisoner by the U.S. forces, but escaped into the Soviet-controlled zone near Neubrandenberg. Müller and his family settled after the war in East Germany, where his father briefly worked as a political functionary but then defected to the West in 1952. Müller, however, remained in East Germany, where he finished school and—under the influence of Brecht's Berliner Ensemble—began to pursue a career as a playwright. He wrote two short plays at this time, *The Battle* (1949) and *Tractor* (1949), before becoming closely involved with the journal *New German Literature* and the League of German Writers. Never an apologist for the Communist Party, Müller is nonetheless a deeply committed socialist playwright. In the 1950s he wrote a series of "Productionsstücke," plays set in farms or factories dealing with the daily problems of workers' lives and the difficulties of achieving a truly socialist state.

His first full-length play to be staged was a dramatization of John Reed's *Ten Days That Shook the World* (1957), which was followed by *The Wage Cutter* and *The Correction* (1958). In 1964, Müller adapted Erik Neutsch's novel *The Construction Project* for the stage, a play about the sacrifices required of workers in rebuilding East Germany. The Communist Party attacked the play as subversive, and Müller's plays were officially banned from 1965 to 1969; Müller suffered the suicide of his wife, Ingeborg Schwenker, in 1965 as well. At this time, Müller concentrated on a series of brilliant translations and adaptations, of Sophocles' *Oedipus the King* (1967), an adaptation of *Philoctetes* written in 1966 but not permitted to be staged in East Germany until 1979, and a translation of Aeschylus' *Prometheus* (1969). In 1969, Müller was officially "rehabilitated," and was invited to serve as dramaturg for the Berliner Ensemble. Working with the Berliner Ensemble— and Erich Honecker's lifting of some of the restrictions on writers—spurred Müller's most productive period in the theater: *Cement* (1973), *Germania Death in Berlin* (1977), *Mauser* (written while visiting at the University of Texas–Austin in 1978), *The Farmers* (1978), *Hamletmachine* (1978), *Quartett* (1981), *Ruined Shoreline—Medea-Material—Landscape with Argonauts* (1983). Many of these plays deal with the challenges both of patriotism and of finding a true form of revolution; given the fact that Müller's dramatic style in this period became more dense, elliptical, and poetic, it is perhaps not surprising that he continued to have difficulties with the Party, and many of his plays—including *Hamletmachine* (1978)—continued to be banned in East Germany until the fall of the Berlin Wall in 1989. Müller's drama now receives as much attention in Germany as in the rest of the West, and the idiom of his work—its imagistic and fragmentary quality, as well as its glancing engagement with "history"—has come to define the possibilities of postmodern theater.

## Hamletmachine (1978)

*Hamletmachine* is one of the most celebrated performance "texts" of the 1970s and 1980s. Originally drafted under the working title "Shakespeare's Factory," *Hamletmachine* has been produced in both Europe and the United States, notably in a 1986 production at New York University designed by Robert Wilson. Both as a dramatic text and in performance, *Hamletmachine* is a brilliant instance of one way postmodern "pastiche" operates in the theater. As a text, the play invokes, "quotes," and distorts a variety of texts from the history of literature and culture. It opens with the actor declaring "I was Hamlet," and is structured around five confrontations between Hamlet and Ophelia. Shakespeare, Marx, and other writers are invoked throughout. Müller closes the play by laminating Ophelia to Electra to the radical terrorist Ulrike Meinhoff and to the would-be assassin of President Gerald Ford, Squeaky Fromm. In performance, this dense and elliptical script intersects with the other "languages" of the stage: Ophelia appears with a clock in her heart; the actor playing Hamlet declares "I'm not Hamlet" and proceeds to tear up photographs of the author; the visual field of the stage is distributed among live action, film, and video; three naked women speak the words of Marx, Lenin, and Mao, then have their heads split by Hamlet; scenes include an *"Ice Age"* and *"The deep sea. Ophelia in a wheelchair. Fish, debris, dead bodies and limbs drift by."*

*Hamletmachine* is divided into five sections; in each, Hamlet and Ophelia—or, more accurately, voices identified with Hamlet's famous indecision and Ophelia's innocent victimization—confront the necessity of acting, and the impossibility of acting among the contemporary "ruins of Europe." Müller's densely imagistic imagination resists summary, but it is clear that *Hamletmachine* is at once about the incoherence of modern life and about the specific political failures of socialism in Eastern Europe, where "SOMETHING IS ROTTEN IN THIS AGE OF HOPE." Hamlet, for instance, is haunted by "the ghost who made me," a ghost whose armor he assumes at the end of the play to destroy the icons of Marxist history, Marx, Lenin, Mao; in section 4 "PEST IN BUDA/BATTLE FOR GREENLAND," Hamlet seems to confront and criticize the failed Hungarian revolt of 1956. He seems specifically alienated from a world in which the possibility of revolution has become merely theatrical: "I don't take part any more. My words have nothing to tell me any more. My thoughts suck the blood out of the images. My drama doesn't happen anymore. Behind me a set is put up. By people who aren't interested in my drama, for people to home it means nothing." This vision of a "world without mothers," where we "could butcher each other in peace and quiet" is complemented by Ophelia's function in the play, for Ophelia becomes a figure for the metaphysical evacuation of a world without ideals, where to "walk into the street clothed in my blood" is the only form of resistance left. In her final speech, Ophelia is identified with Aeschylus' Electra, returning with vengeance on the hopeless world destroyed around her; she quotes both Ulrike Meinhoff ("long live hate and contempt, rebellion and death") and Squeaky Fromm, who had tried to assassinate U.S. President Gerald Ford ("When she walks through your bedrooms carrying butcher knives you'll know the truth").

It might also be noted that *Hamletmachine* is also a densely autobiographical play, in which the "Hamlet" figure articulates many of Müller's own divisions about the future of socialism in Europe and the possibility for ongoing revolution. As Müller noted in an interview in 1982, "*Hamletmachine* = H. M. = Heiner Müller"; he also notes, perhaps with a touch of irony, "I carefully disseminated this interpretation."

# —Hamletmachine—
## Heiner Müller
### TRANSLATED BY CARL WEBER

## I FAMILY SCRAPBOOK

I was Hamlet. I stood at the shore and talked with the surf
BLABLA, the ruins of Europe in back of me. The bells
tolled the state-funeral, murderer and widow a couple, the
councillors goose-stepping behind the highranking carcass'
coffin, bawling with badly paid grief WHO IS THE
CORPSE IN THE HEARSE/ABOUT WHOM THERE'S
SUCH A HUE AND CRY/'TIS THE CORPSE OF A
GREAT/GIVER OF ALMS the lane formed by the populace, creation of his statecraft HE WAS A MAN HE TOOK
10  THEM ALL FOR ALL. I stopped the funeral procession, I
pried open the coffin with my sword, the blade broke, yet
with the blunt reminder I succeeded, and I dispensed my
dead procreator FLESH LIKES TO KEEP THE COM-
PANY OF FLESH among the bums around me. The
mourning turned into rejoicing, the rejoicing into lipsmack-
ing, on top of the empty coffin the murderer humped the
widow LET ME HELP YOU UP, UNCLE, OPEN YOUR
LEGS, MAMA. I laid down on the ground and listened to
the world doing its turns in step with the putrefaction.
20  I'M GOOD HAMLET GI'ME A CAUSE FOR GRIEF°
AH THE WHOLE GLOBE FOR A REAL SORROW°
RICHARD THE THIRD I THE PRINCE-KILLING
KING°
OH MY PEOPLE WHAT HAVE I DONE UNTO THEE°
I'M LUGGING MY OVERWEIGHT BRAIN LIKE A
HUNCHBACK
CLOWN NUMBER TWO IN THE SPRING OF COM-
MUNISM
SOMETHING IS ROTTEN IN THIS AGE OF HOPE°
30  LET'S DELVE IN EARTH AND BLOW HER AT THE
MOON°
Here comes the ghost who made me, the ax still in his skull.
Keep your hat on, I know you've got one hole too many. I
would my mother had one less when you were still of flesh:
I would have been spared myself. Women should be sewed
up—a world without mothers. We could butcher each other
in peace and quiet, and with some confidence, if life gets too
long for us or our throats too tight for our screams. What do
you want of me? Is one state-funeral not enough for
40  you? You old sponger. Is there no blood on your shoes?
What's your corpse to me? Be glad the handle is sticking
out, maybe you'll go to heaven. What are you waiting for?
All the cocks have been butchered. Tomorrow morning has
been cancelled.
SHALL I
AS IS THE CUSTOM STICK A PIECE OF IRON INTO

THE NEAREST FLESH OR THE SECOND BEST
TO LATCH UNTO IT SINCE THE WORLD IS SPIN-
NING
LORD BREAK MY NECK WHILE I'M FALLING 50
FROM AN
ALEHOUSE BENCH

Enters Horatio. Confidant of my thoughts so full of blood
since the morning is curtained by the empty sky. YOU'LL
BE TOO LATE MY FRIEND FOR YOUR PAY-
CHECK/NO PART FOR YOU IN THIS MY TRAGEDY.
Horatio, do you know me? Are you my friend, Horatio? If
you know me how can you be my friend? Do you want to
play Polonius who wants to sleep with his daughter, the delightful Ophelia, here she enters right on cue, look how she 60
shakes her ass, a tragic character. Horatio Polonius. I knew
you're an actor. I am too, I'm playing Hamlet. Denmark is a
prison, a wall is growing between the two of us. Look what's
growing from that wall. Exit Polonius. My mother the bride.
Her breasts a rosebed, her womb the snakepit. Have you
forgotten your lines, Mama. I'll prompt you. WASH THE
MURDER OFF YOUR FACE MY PRINCE/AND
OFFER THE NEW DENMARK YOUR GLAD EYE. I'll
change you back into a virgin mother, so your king will have
a bloodwedding. A MOTHER'S WOMB IS NOT A ONE- 70
WAY STREET. Now, I tie your hands on your back with
your bridal veil since I'm sick of your embrace. Now, I tear
the wedding dress. Now, I smear the shreds of the wedding
dress with the dust my father turned into, and with the
soiled shreds your face your belly your breasts. Now, I take
you, my mother, in his, my father's invisible tracks. I stifle
your scream with my lips. Do you recognize the fruit of your
womb? Now go to your wedding, whore, in the broad Danish sunlight which shines on the living and the dead. I want
to cram the corpse down the latrine so the palace will choke 80
in royal shit. Then let me eat your heart, Ophelia, which
weeps my tears.

## II THE EUROPE OF WOMEN:

*Enormous room.° Ophelia. Her heart is a
clock.*

OPHELIA (CHORUS/HAMLET): I am Ophelia. The one the river
didn't keep. The woman dangling from the rope. The
woman with her arteries cut open. The woman with the
overdose. SNOW ON HER LIPS. The woman with her

---

°The lines with an asterisk are in English in the German text.

head in the gas stove. Yesterday I stopped killing myself. I'm alone with my breasts my thighs my womb. I smash the tools of my captivity, the chair the table the bed. I destroy the bat-
90  tlefield that was my home. I fling open the doors so the wind gets in and the scream of the world. I smash the window. With my bleeding hands I tear the photos of the men I loved and who used me on the bed on the table on the chair on the ground. I set fire to my prison. I throw my clothes into the fire. I wrench the clock that was my heart out of my breast. I walk into the street clothed in my blood.

## III SCHERZO

*The university of the dead. Whispering and muttering. From their gravestones (lecterns), the dead philosophers throw their books at Hamlet. Gallery (ballet) of the dead women. The woman dangling from the rope. The woman with her arteries cut open, etc. . . . Hamlet views them with the attitude of a visitor in a museum (theatre). The dead women tear his clothes off his body. Out of an upended coffin, labeled HAMLET 1, step Claudius and Ophelia, the latter dressed and made up like a whore. Striptease by Ophelia.*

OPHELIA: Do you want to eat my heart, Hamlet? (*Laughs.*)
HAMLET: (*Face in his hands.*) I want to be a woman.

(*Hamlet dresses in Ophelia's clothes, Ophelia puts the make-up of a whore on his face, Claudius—now Hamlet's father—laughs without uttering a sound, Ophelia blows Hamlet a kiss and steps with Claudius/HamletFather back into the coffin. Hamlet poses as a whore. An angel, his face at the back of his head: Horatio. He dances with Hamlet.*)

VOICES: (*From the coffin.*) What thou killed thou shalt love.

(*The dance grows faster and wilder. Laughter from the coffin. On a swing, the madonna with breast cancer. Horatio opens an umbrella, embraces Hamlet. They freeze under the umbrella, embracing. The breast cancer radiates like a sun.*)

## IV  PEST IN BUDA / BATTLE FOR GREENLAND

*Space 2, as destroyed by Ophelia. An empty armor, an ax stuck in the helmet.*

100 HAMLET: The stove is smoking in quarrelsome October
A BAD COLD HE HAD OF IT JUST THE WORST TIME°
JUST THE WORST TIME OF THE YEAR FOR A REVOLUTION°
Cement in bloom walks through the slums
Doctor Zhivago weeps
For his wolves
SOMETIMES IN WINTER THEY CAME INTO THE VILLAGE
110 AND TORE APART A PEASANT

(*He takes off make-up and costume.*)

THE ACTOR PLAYING HAMLET: I'm not Hamlet. I don't take part

any more. My words have nothing to tell me anymore. My thoughts suck the blood out of the images. My drama doesn't happen anymore. Behind me the set is put up. By people who aren't interested in my drama, for people to whom it means nothing. I'm not interested in it anymore either. I won't play along anymore. (*Unnoticed by the actor playing Hamlet, stagehands place a refrigerator and three TV-sets on the stage. Humming of the refrigerator. Three TV-channels without sound.*) The set is a monument. It pre-
120 sents a man who made history, enlarged a hundred times. The petrification of a hope. His name is interchangeable, the hope has not been fulfilled. The monument is toppled into the dust, razed by those who succeeded him in power three years after the state funeral of the hated and most honored leader. The stone is inhabited. In the spacy nostrils and auditory canals, in the creases of skin and uniform of the demolished monument, the poorer inhabitants of the capital are dwelling. After an appropriate period, the uprising follows the toppling of the monument. My drama, if it still
130 would happen, would happen in the time of the uprising. The uprising starts with a stroll. Against the traffic rules, during the working hours. The street belongs to the pedestrians. Here and there, a car is turned over. Nightmare of a knife thrower: Slowly driving down a one-way street towards an irrevocable parking space surrounded by armed pedestrians. Policemen, if in the way, are swept to the curb. When the procession approaches the government district it is stopped by a police line. People form groups, speakers arise from them. On the balcony of a government building, a man
140 in badly fitting mufti appears and begins to speak too. When the first stone hits him, he retreats behind the double doors of bullet-proof glass. The call for more freedom turns into the cry for the overthrow of the government. People begin to disarm the policemen, to storm two, three buildings, a prison a police precinct an office of the secret police, they string up a dozen henchmen of the rulers by their heels, the government brings in troops, tanks. My place, if my drama would still happen, would be on both sides of the front, between the frontlines, over and above them. I stand in the
150 stench of the crowd and hurl stones at policemen soldiers tanks bullet-proof glass. I look through the double doors of bullet-proof glass at the crowd pressing forward and smell the sweat of my fear. Choking with nausea, I shake my fist at myself who stands behind the bullet-proof glass. Shaking with fear and contempt, I see myself in the crowd pressing forward, foaming at the mouth, shaking my fist at myself. I string up my uniformed flesh by my own heels. I am the soldier in the gun turret, my head is empty under the helmet,
160 the stifled scream under the tracks. I am the typewriter. I tie the noose when the ringleaders are strung up, I pull the stool from under their feet, I break my own neck. I am my own prisoner. I feed my own data into the computers. My parts are the spittle and the spittoon the knife and the wound the fang and the throat the neck and the rope. I am the data bank. Bleeding in the crowd. Breathing again behind the double doors. Oozing wordslime in my soundproof blurb over and above the battle. My drama didn't happen. The script has been lost. The actors put their faces on the rack in the dressing room. In his box, the prompter is rot-
170 ting. The stuffed corpses in the house don't stir a hand. I go

home and kill the time, at one with my undivided self.
Television The daily nausea Nausea
Of prefabricated babble Of decreed cheerfulness
How do you spell GEMÜTLICHKEIT
Give us this day our daily murder
Since thine is nothingness Nausea
Of the lies which are believed
By the liars and nobody else
180   Nausea
Of the lies which are believed Nausea
Of the mugs of the manipulators marked
By their struggle for positions votes bank accounts
Nausea A chariot armed with scythes sparkling with
   punchlines
I walk through streets stores Faces
Scarred by the consumers battle Poverty
Without dignity Poverty without the dignity
Of the knife the knuckleduster the clenched fist
190   The humiliated bodies of women
Hope of generations
Stifled in blood cowardice stupidity
Laughter from dead bellies
Hail Coca Cola
A kingdom
For a murderer
I WAS MACBETH
THE KING HAD OFFERED HIS THIRD MISTRESS
TO ME
200   I KNEW EVERY MOLE ON HER HIPS
RASKOLNIKOV CLOSE TO THE
HEART UNDER THE ONLY COAT THE AX FOR
THE
ONLY
SKULL OF THE PAWNBROKER
In the solitude of airports
I breathe again I am
A privileged person My nausea
Is a privilege
210   Protected by torture
Barbed wire Prisons

*(Photograph of the author.)*

I don't want to eat drink breathe love a woman a man a child
an animal anymore. I don't want to die anymore. I don't
want to kill anymore.

*(Tearing of the author's photograph.)*

I force open my sealed flesh. I want to dwell in my veins, in
the marrow of my bones, in the maze of my skull. I retreat
into my entrails. I take my seat in my shit, in my blood.
Somewhere bodies are torn apart so I can dwell in my shit.
Somewhere bodies are opened so I can be alone with my
blood. My thoughts are lesions in my brain. My brain is a 220
scar. I want to be a machine. Arms for grabbing Legs to walk
on, no pain no thoughts.

*(TV screens go black. Blood oozes from the refrigerator. Three
naked women: Marx, Lenin, Mao. They speak simultaneously,
each one in his own language, the text:)*

THE MAIN POINT IS TO OVERTHROW ALL EXISTING
CONDITIONS . . . °

*(The Actor of Hamlet puts on make-up and costume.)*

HAMLET THE DANE PRINCE AND MAGGOT'S FOD-
DER STUMBLING FROM HOLE TO HOLE TO-
WARDS THE FINAL HOLE LISTLESS IN HIS BACK
THE GHOST THAT ONCE MADE HIM GREEN LIKE
OPHELIA'S FLESH IN CHILDBED AND SHORTLY
ERE THE THIRD COCK'S CROW A CLOWN WILL 230
TEAR THE FOOL'S CAP OFF THE PHILOSOPHER A
BLOATED BLOODHOUND'LL CRAWL INTO THE
ARMOR

*(He steps into the armor, splits with the ax the heads of Marx,
Lenin, Mao. Snow. Ice Age.)*

## V  FIERCELY ENDURING
##    MILLENIUMS IN THE FEARFUL
##    ARMOR

*The deep sea. Ophelia in a wheelchair. Fish, debris, dead bod-
ies and limbs drift by.*

OPHELIA: *(While two men in white smocks wrap gauze around
her and the wheelchair, from bottom to top.)*
This is Electra speaking. In the heart of darkness. Under the
sun of torture. To the capitals of the world. In the name of
the victims. I eject all the sperm I have received. I turn the
milk of my breasts into lethal poison. I take back the world
I gave birth to. I choke between my thighs the world I gave 240
birth to. I bury it in my womb. Down with the happiness of
submission. Long live hate and contempt, rebellion and
death. When she walks through your bedrooms carrying
butcher knives you'll know the truth.

*(The men exit. Ophelia remains on stage, motionless in her
white wrappings.)*

---

°English-language productions could use the entire quote from Karl Marx: Introduction to *Critique of Hegel's Philosophy of Law.*

**E N D**

AFTER *the publication of his translation of* Hamletmachine *in 1980, Carl Weber asked a series of questions of Müller; these are Müller's replies.*

*A couple of years ago you were invited to a conference on Postmodernism in New York. You couldn't attend the conference but submitted a paper defining your position versus some aspects of contemporary art. Could you explain what in your opinion would constitute a Postmodern drama, a Postmodern theatre?*

The only Postmodernist I know of was August Stramm, a modernist who worked in a post office.

*Language takes a central position in your work, much more than it usually does in contemporary American drama. Could you explain what you feel language's function is in the contemporary theatre?*

I would take issue with the premise in the first part of your question. Language is also important in American drama and other media but it is a different language, I think, with perhaps a different function. A film critic once asked me why stage and film productions in the GDR tend to use a poeticizing rather than what he called a naturalistic language, why the tendency toward stylization rather than realism. The extent to which that is valid comes from the fact that the GDR is not photographable, the fact that here actors cannot even say "Guten Tag" without it sounding like a lie. Realism doesn't work at all, only stylization works—a variation of Brecht's remark that a photograph of the Krupp Works says nothing really about the Krupp Works. The actors in the West are much better at Naturalism, at working with photographic texts or plays or films. Here they are better in productions of the classics, i.e., in anything that entails a stylized removal from immediate reality.

*What is the role of language versus the rich visual imagery you employ to an ever increasing degree in your plays?*

The worst experience I had during my stay in the United States was a film I saw called *Fantasia,* by Disney. I had never heard of it and actually ended up watching it by mistake. There were three films playing in the same movie house and I went into the wrong one. The most barbaric thing about this film, something I learned later, was that almost every American child between the ages of six and eight gets to view it. Which means that these people will never again be able to hear specific works by Beethoven, Bach, Handel, Tchaikovsky, etc., without seeing the Disney figures and images. The horrifying thing for me in this is the occupation of the imagination by clichés and images which will never go away; the use of images to prevent experiences, to prevent the having of experiences.

*What has this got to do with your theatre?*

Wolfgang Heise, a philosopher here in the GDR, once said that theatre is a laboratory for the social imagination. I find that relevant for what we are talking about. If one starts with the assumption that capitalist societies, indeed every industrial society, the GDR included, tends to repress and instrumentalize imagination—to throttle it—then for me the political task of art today is precisely the mobilization of imagination. To return to our example of *Fantasia,* the metaphorical function of the Disney film is to reduce the symbolic force of images to one meaning, to make them immediately allegorical. The imagery one finds in the early Russian cinema, on the other hand, is like the torrent of metaphors at the heart of Elizabethan literature. Here metaphors are constructed as a kind of visual protection against a much too rapidly changing reality, a reality that can only be dealt with and assimilated in this very special way. A world of images is created that does *not* lend itself to conceptual formulation and that cannot be reduced to a one-dimensional metaphor. This is what I try to do in my theatre.

*You have written in other literary forms, poetry, short story, etc., but you always returned to the theatre, recently even as the director of your plays. Do you believe then that the theatre is a superior medium to investigate the complex problems of our time?*

I have a real difficulty writing prose. I don't believe in literature as a work of art to be read. I don't believe in reading. I couldn't imagine writing a novel.

*Where does your distrust of prose come from?*

Writing prose you are all alone. You can't hide yourself. I also don't think I can write prose in the third person. I can't write: "Washington got up and went to 42nd Street." I can only imagine writing prose in the first person. Writing drama you always have masks and roles and you can talk through them. That's why I prefer drama—because of the masks. I can say one thing and say the contrary. I have a need to get rid of contradictions and that is easier to do with drama.

*The theatre seems to have increasing difficulties in reaching wider audiences, larger sections of society, especially when it tries to interact with, or activate, its audiences. Where do you see reasons for this development and how should one cope with this danger of elitism?*

This "elitism," as you call it, this not being immediately accessible, can also have its advantages. For accessibility is often connected with commercialization. Art becomes commercial at precisely the moment when its time is past. The tension between success and impact, which Brecht spoke of, is important in this respect that one is always overtaken by success before a real impact can occur. As long as a thing works it is not successful, and when success is there then the impact is over. This is because there can only be an impact if, as for example in the theatre, the audience is split, brought home to its real situation. But that means there will be no agreement, no success. Success happens when everybody is cheering, in other words, when there is nothing more to say. For me the theatre is a medium which still permits one to avoid that kind of success. In film that is difficult because of the money involved.

*But what about the GDR?*

In our country, theatre allows you to have 500 or 800 people together in one room reacting at the same time, in the same space, to what is happening on stage. The impact of the theatre here is based on the absence of other ways of getting messages across to people. Films are not as important either because there is so much control. As a result, the theatre here has taken over the function of the other media in the West. I don't believe theatre has a great impact in West Germany, for instance. (We can forget about the United States.) You can do anything on the stage there but it doesn't mean anything to the society. Here the slogan of the Napoleonic era still applies: Theatre is the Revolution on the march.

*In many of your texts you deal with topics which in this country would be defined as "feminist"; and female characters often have a central place in your work. Could you explain how you think women should be presented on the contemporary stage?*

As a playwright I don't deal with "isms" but with reality. Can you tell me what a real female character is?

*Your work is firmly rooted in history and/or mythology. American drama deals rarely with the past. What do you conceive as the function of mythology and history in the contemporary theatre?*

The dead are in the overwhelming majority when compared to the living. And Europe has a wealth of dead stored up on that side of the ledger. The United States, not satisfied just with dead Indians, is fighting to close the gap. Literature, as an instrument of democracy, while not submitting to, should nevertheless be respectful of, majorities as well as of minorities.

*Some of your critics maintain that at the center of your recent work is the conflict between the individual's desire "to pursue happiness" and the individual's responsibility to history and mankind's progress. Do you agree with this view? If yes, could you speak to this contradiction and its present manifestations?*

"We Germans were not put here on earth to enjoy ourselves but to do our duty." (Bismarck) *If you disagree, what would you regard as a central issue in your recent texts?*

How should I know, and if I knew why should I tell you?

*If you reject this idea of a central issue, could you mention some of the interests you pursue in your writing?*

See above.

*Your plays have been performed in East and West Germany, in the United States, and in many other countries. You participated in many of these productions and recently have directed your plays in both Germanies. What difference could you observe in the theatrework of these different social and cultural systems, and what did they have in common?*

To answer this question I am going to have to wait for more performances in East and West.

*a) Where is the theatre, in your opinion, a more efficient instrument of social impact? b) Where would you prefer to direct, and to watch, your plays on stage?*

a) In the East. b) I would like to stage MACBETH on top of the World Trade Center for an audience in helicopters.

*There has been a lot of attention given to the so-called "New Subjectivity" in German letters, as exemplified by writers like Handke, Strauss, Laederach, etc. Do you see yourself in any relation to them and their work?*

No. Nor do I see any relation of them to each other.

*Terms like "Despair," "Pessimism," "Guilt," are often used by critics writing about your work. Do you think these are adequate definitions of your intentions and/or values?*

Three times No.

*People familiar with your recent texts often complain about a total lack of hope in your writing. What is your opinion?*

I am neither a dope- nor a hope- dealer.

*Would you care to comment on your views about the future of our world which you paint so darkly in your work?*

The future of the world is not my future.

"Show me a mousehole and I'll fuck the world." (Railworker at the soft-coal strip mine Klettwitz, GDR.)

# Sam Shepard

Sam Shepard (b. 1943), is probably the best-known American playwright of his generation. Born Samuel Shepard Rogers to a military family stationed in Illinois, Shepard's youth was spent moving from base to base until his father retired and settled the family in southern California. Shepard was an indifferent student and left college for New York City in 1963. He took a job busing tables at the Village Gate jazz club and began to write plays for small off-Broadway theaters, including *Cowboys* (1964), *Red Cross* (1966), *La Turista* (1966), *The Unseen Hand* (1970), *Cowboy Mouth* (1971), and *Tooth of Crime* (1972). In these plays, Shepard develops what became his characteristic idiom: a search for the "West" of myth, an image both fascinating and elusive, somehow undiscoverable amid the consumer trash of suburban society. He develops a sense of split and fragmented characters, relying on his typically jazzy use of language. This is particularly true of *Tooth of Crime*, in which a kind of shoot-out between the old rock-and-roll star, Hoss, and the Keith Richards-like Crow is conducted in an invented language of rock music, drugs, cars, gangsters, and old movies. Shepard won six Obie awards between 1964 and 1970, but his work took a great step forward in the major plays of the late 1970s and 1980s: *Curse of the Starving Class* (1978), *Buried Child* (1978—Pulitzer Prize, 1979), *True West* (1980), *Fool for Love* (1982), *A Lie of the Mind* (1985), and *States of Shock* (1991). Shepard has also written the screenplay for the Wim Wenders film, *Paris, Texas,* and wrote and directed *Far North;* he has starred in several films himself, notably as Chuck Yeager in *The Right Stuff* (1983), and in *Crimes of the Heart* (1986) and *Steel Magnolias* (1991), among others.

## Buried Child (1978)

*Buried Child* is perhaps best characterized as a theatrical version of an important American literary genre: the American Gothic. Part of the lineage of William Faulkner, Flannery O'Connor, and Joyce Carol Oates, Shepard's play stages the "romance" of American domestic life as an imprisoning network of lies, betrayals, coercion, infidelity, and exploitation. Formally, *Buried Child* is in the familiar retrospective "well-made play" mode of Ibsen or O'Neill. The play presents its audience with a family, a secret—possibly involving Tilden, Halie, and the mysterious field behind the house—and a catalyst, Vince, Tilden's son who has returned to claim his inheritance. And it *is* possible to use this narrative model to produce a "reading" of the play. At the play's close, Vince has driven the violent second-son Bradley from the house; he assumes command of Dodge's home as Dodge dies on the floor; and the dim, mysterious Tilden brings the "buried child" from the cornfield upstairs to Halie, as we hear her voice: "Tiny little shoot. Tiny little white shoot. All hairy and fragile. Strong though. Strong enough to break the earth even. It's a miracle, Dodge. I've never seen a crop like this in my whole life. Maybe it's the sun. Maybe that's it. Maybe it's the sun."

But to see *Buried Child* as merely rewriting the domestic problem play is to ignore the sophisticated tonal and stylistic transformation that Shepard has worked on this narrative and dramatic structure, transformations which disorient the "familiar" narrative of the American family in new, postmodern directions. For Shepard's play about the roots of family dysfunction is written in the disjunctive non sequiturs of Beckett—*Waiting for Godot* was an early favorite—or Pinter. Indeed, the "characters" in *Buried Child* all seem, like the amputee Bradley, partial, wounded, more defined by their position in the family romance than by an innate, expressed "psychology." Shepard has suggested that he conceives of writing "characters" as a form of jazz composition, an interwoven series of melodic riffs, improvisations on a central theme. In *Buried Child,* the characters are defined most sharply in a series of stage images: Bradley placing his hand in Shelly's mouth; Vince cutting his way into the house through the screen; Bradley shaving Dodge's head; Tilden and the corn; Tilden and the baby. This imagistic structure tends to subvert narrative closure, the "truth" implied by the well-made form. Like other postmodern works, *Buried Child* provides a field of images, zones of subjectivity left open to the audience's interpretation. In *Buried Child* the "history" revealed to the audience remains fundamentally in doubt—*do* these people really know Vince? *whose* child is it? *is* there a child? or is this a fantasy-child, like the child that binds Albee's George and Martha in *Who's Afraid of Virginia Woolf?* in their similarly violent embrace?

# —Buried Child—
## Sam Shepard

■ ■ ■ While the rain of your fingertips falls,
while the rain of your bones falls,
and your laughter and marrow fall down,
you come flying.

—PABLO NERUDA

## —CHARACTERS—

DODGE, *in his seventies*
HALIE, *his wife mid-sixties*
TILDEN, *their oldest son*
BRADLEY, *their next oldest son, an amputee*
VINCE, *Tilden's son*
SHELLY, *Vince's girl friend*
FATHER DEWIS, *a Protestant minister*

## —ACT ONE—

SCENE: *Day. Old wooden staircase down left with pale, frayed carpet laid down on the steps. The stairs lead off stage left up into the wings with no landing. Up right is an old, dark green sofa with the stuffing coming out in spots. Stage right of the sofa is an upright lamp with a faded yellow shade and a small night table with several small bottles of pills on it. Down right of the sofa, with the screen facing the sofa, is a large, old-fashioned brown T.V. A flickering blue light comes from the screen, but no image, no sound. In the dark, the light of the lamp and the T.V. slowly brighten in the black space. The space behind the sofa, upstage, is a large, screened-in porch with a board floor. A solid interior door to stage right of the sofa, leading into the room on stage; and another screen door up left, leading from the porch to the outside. Beyond that are the shapes of dark elm trees.*

*Gradually the form of* DODGE *is made out, sitting on the couch, facing the T.V., the blue light flickering on his face. He wears a well-worn T-shirt, suspenders, khaki work pants and brown slippers. He's covered himself in an old brown blanket. He's very thin and sickly looking, in his late seventies. He just stares at the T.V. More light fills the stage softly. The sound of light rain.* DODGE *slowly tilts his head back and stares at the ceiling for a while, listening to the rain. He lowers his head again and stares at the T.V. He turns his head slowly to the left and stares at the cushion of the sofa next to the one he's sitting on. He pulls his left arm out from under the blanket, slides his hand under the cushion, and pulls out a bottle of whiskey. He looks down left toward the staircase, listens, then uncaps the bottle, takes a long swig and caps it again. He puts the bottle back under the cushion and stares at the T.V. He starts to cough slowly and softly. The coughing gradually builds. He holds one hand to his*

mouth and tries to stifle it. The coughing gets louder, then suddenly stops when he hears the sound of his wife's voice coming from the top of the staircase.

HALIE'S VOICE: Dodge?

(DODGE *just stares at the T.V. Long pause. He stifles two short coughs.*)

HALIE'S VOICE: Dodge! You want a pill, Dodge?

(*He doesn't answer. Takes the bottle out again and takes another long swig. Puts the bottle back, stares at T.V., pulls blanket up around his neck.*)

HALIE'S VOICE: You know what it is, don't you? It's the rain! Weather. That's it. Every time. Every time you get like this, it's the rain. No sooner does the rain start then you start. (*pause*) Dodge?

(*He makes no reply. Pulls a pack of cigarettes out from his sweater and lights one. Stares at T.V. pause.*)

HALIE'S VOICE: You should see it coming down up here. Just coming down in sheets. Blue sheets. The bridge is pretty near flooded. What's it like down there? Dodge?

(DODGE *turns his head back over his left shoulder and takes a look out through the porch. He turns back to the T.V.*)

DODGE: (*to himself*) Catastrophic.                                           10
HALIE'S VOICE: What? What'd you say, Dodge?
DODGE: (*louder*) It looks like rain to me! Plain old rain!
HALIE'S VOICE: Rain? Of course it's rain! Are you having a seizure or something! Dodge? (*pause*) I'm coming down there in about five minutes if you don't answer me!
DODGE: Don't come down.
HALIE'S VOICE: What!
DODGE: (*louder*) Don't come down!

(*He has another coughing attack. Stops.*)

HALIE'S VOICE: You should take a pill for that! I don't see why you just don't take a pill. Be done with it once and for all. Put   20
a stop to it.

(*He takes bottle out again. Another swig. Returns bottle.*)

HALIE'S VOICE: It's not Christian, but it works. It's not necessarily Christian, that is. We don't know. There's some things the ministers can't even answer. I, personally, can't see anything wrong with it. Pain is pain. Pure and simple. Suffering is a different matter. That's entirely different. A pill seems as good an answer as any. Dodge? *(pause)* Dodge, are you watching baseball?

DODGE: No.

30  HALIE'S VOICE: What?

DODGE: *(louder)* No!

HALIE'S VOICE: What're you watching? You shouldn't be watching anything that'll get you excited! No horse racing!

DODGE: They don't race on Sundays.

HALIE'S VOICE: What?

DODGE: *(louder)* They don't race on Sundays!

HALIE'S VOICE: Well they shouldn't race on Sundays.

DODGE: Well they don't!

HALIE'S VOICE: Good. I'm amazed they still have that kind of

40    legislation. That's amazing.

DODGE: Yeah, it's amazing.

HALIE'S VOICE: What?

DODGE: *(louder)* It is amazing!

HALIE'S VOICE: It is. It truly is. I would've thought these days they'd be racing on Christmas even. A big flashing Christmas tree right down at the finish line.

DODGE: *(shakes his head)* No.

HALIE'S VOICE: They used to race on New Year's! I remember that.

50  DODGE: They never raced on New Year's!

HALIE'S VOICE: Sometimes they did.

DODGE: They never did!

HALIE'S VOICE: Before we were married they did!

*(DODGE waves his hand in disgust at the staircase. Leans back in sofa. Stares at T.V.)*

HALIE'S VOICE: I went once. With a man.

DODGE: *(mimicking her)* Oh, a "man."

HALIE'S VOICE: What?

DODGE: Nothing!

HALIE'S VOICE: A wonderful man. A breeder.

DODGE: A what?

60  HALIE'S VOICE: A breeder! A horse breeder! Thoroughbreds.

DODGE: Oh, Thoroughbreds. Wonderful.

HALIE'S VOICE: That's right. He knew everything there was to know.

DODGE: I bet he taught you a thing or two huh? Gave you a good turn around the old stable!

HALIE'S VOICE: Knew everything there was to know about horses. We won bookoos of money that day.

DODGE: What?

HALIE'S VOICE: Money! We won every race I think.

70  DODGE: Bookoos?

HALIE'S VOICE: Every single race.

DODGE: Bookoos of money?

HALIE'S VOICE: It was one of those kind of days.

DODGE: New Year's!

HALIE'S VOICE: Yes! It might've been Florida. Or California! One of those two.

DODGE: Can I take my pick?

HALIE'S VOICE: It was Florida!

DODGE: Aha!

80  HALIE'S VOICE: Wonderful! Absolutely wonderful! The sun was just gleaming. Flamingos. Bougainvilleas. Palm trees.

DODGE: *(to himself, mimicking her)* Bougainvilleas. Palm trees.

HALIE'S VOICE: Everything was dancing with life! There were all kinds of people from everywhere. Everyone was dressed to the nines. Not like today. Not like they dress today.

DODGE: When was this anyway?

HALIE'S VOICE: This was long before I knew you.

DODGE: Must've been.

HALIE'S VOICE: Long before. I was escorted.          90

DODGE: To Florida?

HALIE'S VOICE: Yes. Or it might've been California. I'm not sure which.

DODGE: All that way you were escorted?

HALIE'S VOICE: Yes.

DODGE: And he never laid a finger on you I suppose? *(long silence)* Halie?

*(No answer. Long pause.)*

HALIE'S VOICE: Are you going out today?

DODGE: *(gesturing toward rain)* In this?

HALIE'S VOICE: I'm just asking a simple question.          100

DODGE: I rarely go out in the bright sunshine, why would I go out in this?

HALIE'S VOICE: I'm just asking because I'm not doing any shopping today. And if you need anything you should ask Tilden.

DODGE: Tilden's not here!

HALIE'S VOICE: He's in the kitchen.

*(DODGE looks toward stage left, then back toward T.V.)*

DODGE: All right.

HALIE'S VOICE: What?

DODGE: *(louder)* All right!

HALIE'S VOICE: Don't scream. It'll only get your coughing 110 started.

DODGE: All right.

HALIE'S VOICE: Just tell Tilden what you want and he'll get it. *(pause)* Bradley should be over later.

DODGE: Bradley?

HALIE'S VOICE: Yes. To cut your hair.

DODGE: My hair? I don't need my hair cut!

HALIE'S VOICE: It won't hurt!

DODGE: I don't need it!

HALIE'S VOICE: It's been more than two weeks Dodge.          120

DODGE: I don't need it!

HALIE'S VOICE: I have to meet Father Dewis for lunch.

DODGE: You tell Bradley that if he shows up here with those clippers, I'll kill him!

HALIE'S VOICE: I won't be very late. No later than four at the very latest.

DODGE: You tell him! Last time he left me almost bald! And I wasn't even awake! I was sleeping! I woke up and he'd already left!

HALIE'S VOICE: That's not my fault!          130

DODGE: You put him up to it!

HALIE'S VOICE: I never did!

DODGE: You did too! You had some fancy, stupid meeting planned! Time to dress up the corpse for company! Lower the ears a little! Put up a little front! Surprised you didn't tape a pipe to my mouth while you were at it! That woulda' looked nice! Huh? A pipe? Maybe a bowler hat! Maybe a copy of The Wall Street Journal casually placed on my lap!

HALIE'S VOICE: You always imagine the worst things of people!

140  DODGE: That's not the worst! That's the least of the worst!

HALIE'S VOICE: I don't need to hear it! All day long I hear things like that and I don't need to hear more.

DODGE: You better tell him!

HALIE'S VOICE: You tell him yourself! He's your own son. You should be able to talk to your own son.

DODGE: Not while I'm sleeping! He cut my hair while I was sleeping!

HALIE'S VOICE: Well he won't do it again.

DODGE: There's no guarantee.

150  HALIE'S VOICE: I promise he won't do it without your consent.

DODGE: *(after pause)* There's no reason for him to even come over here.

HALIE'S VOICE: He feels responsible.

DODGE: For my hair?

HALIE'S VOICE: For your appearance.

DODGE: My appearance is out of his domain! It's even out of mine! In fact, it's disappeared! I'm an invisible man!

HALIE'S VOICE: Don't be ridiculous.

DODGE: He better not try it. That's all I've got to say.

160  HALIE'S VOICE: Tilden will watch out for you.

DODGE: Tilden won't protect me from Bradley!

HALIE'S VOICE: Tilden's the oldest. He'll protect you.

DODGE: Tilden can't even protect himself!

HALIE'S VOICE: Not so loud! He'll hear you. He's right in the kitchen.

DODGE: *(yelling off left)* Tilden!

HALIE'S VOICE: Dodge, what are you trying to do?

DODGE: *(yelling off left)* Tilden, get in here!

HALIE'S VOICE: Why do you enjoy stirring things up?

170  DODGE: I don't enjoy anything!

HALIE'S VOICE: That's a terrible thing to say.

DODGE: Tilden!

HALIE'S VOICE: That's the kind of statement that leads people right to the end of their rope.

DODGE: Tilden!

HALIE'S VOICE: It's no wonder people turn to Christ!

DODGE: TILDEN!!

HALIE'S VOICE: It's no wonder the messengers of God's word are shouted down in public places!

180  DODGE: TILDEN!!!!

*(DODGE goes into a violent, spasmodic coughing attack as TILDEN enters from stage left, his arms loaded with fresh ears of corn. TILDEN is DODGE's oldest son, late forties, wears heavy construction boots, covered with mud, dark green work pants, a plaid shirt and a faded brown windbreaker. He has a butch haircut, wet from the rain. Something about him is profoundly burned out and displaced. He stops center stage with the ears of corn in his arms and just stares at DODGE until he slowly finishes his coughing attack. DODGE looks up at him slowly. He stares at the corn. Long pause as they watch each other.)*

HALIE'S VOICE: Dodge, if you don't take that pill nobody's going to force you.

*(The two men ignore the voice.)*

DODGE: *(to TILDEN)* Where'd you get that?

TILDEN: Picked it.

DODGE: You picked all that?

*(TILDEN nods.)*

DODGE: You expecting company?

TILDEN: No.

DODGE: Where'd you pick it from?

TILDEN: Right out back.

DODGE: Out back where?

190  TILDEN: Right out in back.

DODGE: There's nothing out there!

TILDEN: There's corn.

DODGE: There hasn't been corn out there since about nineteen thirty-five! That's the last time I planted corn out there!

TILDEN: It's out there now.

DODGE: *(yelling at stairs)* Halie!

HALIE'S VOICE: Yes dear!

DODGE: Tilden's brought a whole bunch of corn in here! There's no corn out in back is there?

200  TILDEN: *(to himself)* There's tons of corn.

HALIE'S VOICE: Not that I know of!

DODGE: That's what I thought.

HALIE'S VOICE: Not since about nineteen thirty-five!

DODGE: *(to TILDEN)* That's right. Nineteen thirty-five.

TILDEN: It's out there now.

DODGE: You go and take that corn back to wherever you got it from!

TILDEN: *(After pause, staring at DODGE)* It's picked. I picked it all in the rain. Once it's picked you can't put it back.

210  DODGE: I haven't had trouble with neighbors here for fifty-seven years. I don't even know who the neighbors are! And I don't wanna know! Now go put that corn back where it came from!

*(TILDEN stares at DODGE then walks slowly over to him and dumps all the corn on DODGE's lap and steps back. DODGE stares at the corn then back to TILDEN. Long pause.)*

DODGE: Are you having trouble here, Tilden! Are you in some kind of trouble?

TILDEN: I'm not in any trouble.

DODGE: You can tell me if you are. I'm still your father.

TILDEN: I know you're still my father.

DODGE: I know you had a little trouble back in New Mexico. That's why you came out here.

220

TILDEN: I never had any trouble.

DODGE: Tilden, your mother told me all about it.

TILDEN: What'd she tell you?

*(TILDEN pulls some chewing tobacco out of his jacket and bites off a plug.)*

DODGE: I don't have to repeat what she told me! She told me all about it!

TILDEN: Can I bring my chair in from the kitchen?

DODGE: What?

TILDEN: Can I bring in my chair from the kitchen?

DODGE: Sure. Bring your chair in.

230

*(TILDEN exits left. DODGE pushes all the corn off his lap onto the floor. He pulls the blanket off angrily and tosses it at one end of the sofa, pulls out the bottle and takes another swig. TILDEN enters again from left with a milking stool and a pail. DODGE*

*hides the bottle quickly under the cushion before* TILDEN *sees it.* TILDEN *sets the stool down by the sofa, sits on it, puts the pail in front of him on the floor.* TILDEN *starts picking up the ears of corn one at a time and husking them. He throws the husks and silk in the center of the stage and drops the ears into the pail each time he cleans one. He repeats this process as they talk.*)

DODGE: (*after pause*) Sure is nice-looking corn.

TILDEN: It's the best.

DODGE: Hybrid?

TILDEN: What?

DODGE: Some kinda fancy hybrid?

TILDEN: You planted it. I don't know what it is.

DODGE: (*pause*) Tilden, look, you can't stay here forever. You know that, don't you?

TILDEN: (*spits in spittoon*) I'm not.

240 DODGE: I know you're not. I'm not worried about that. That's not the reason I brought it up.

TILDEN: What's the reason?

DODGE: The reason is I'm wondering what you're gonna do.

TILDEN: You're not worried about me, are you?

DODGE: I'm not worried about you.

TILDEN: You weren't worried about me when I wasn't here. When I was in New Mexico.

DODGE: No, I wasn't worried about you then either.

TILDEN: You shoulda worried about me then.

250 DODGE: Why's that? You didn't do anything down there, did you?

TILDEN: I didn't do anything.

DODGE: Then why should I have worried about you?

TILDEN: Because I was lonely.

DODGE: Because you were lonely?

TILDEN: Yeah. I was more lonely than I've ever been before.

DODGE: Why was that?

TILDEN: (*pause*) Could I have some of that whiskey you've got?

DODGE: What whiskey? I haven't got any whiskey.

260 TILDEN: You've got some under the sofa.

DODGE: I haven't got anything under the sofa! Now mind your own damn business! Jesus God, you come into the house outa the middle of nowhere, haven't heard or seen you in twenty years and suddenly you're making accusations.

TILDEN: I'm not making accusations.

DODGE: You're accusing me of hoarding whiskey under the sofa!

TILDEN: I'm not accusing you.

DODGE: You just got through telling me I had whiskey under the sofa!

270 HALIE'S VOICE: Dodge?

DODGE: (*to* TILDEN) Now she knows about it!

TILDEN: She doesn't know about it.

HALIE'S VOICE: Dodge, are you talking to yourself down there?

DODGE: I'm talking to Tilden!

HALIE'S VOICE: Tilden's down there?

DODGE: He's right here!

HALIE'S VOICE: What?

DODGE: (*louder*) He's right here!

280 HALIE'S VOICE: What's he doing?

DODGE: (*to* TILDEN) Don't answer her.

TILDEN: (*to* DODGE) I'm not doing anything wrong.

DODGE: I know you're not.

HALIE'S VOICE: What's he doing down there!

DODGE: (*to* TILDEN) Don't answer.

TILDEN: I'm not.

HALIE'S VOICE: Dodge!

(*The men sit in silence.* DODGE *lights a cigarette.* TILDEN *keeps husking corn, spits tobacco now and then in spittoon.*)

HALIE'S VOICE: Dodge! He's not drinking anything, is he? You see to it that he doesn't drink anything! You've gotta watch out for him. It's our responsibility. He can't look after him- 290 self anymore, so we have to do it. Nobody else will do it. We can't just send him away somewhere. If we had lots of money we could send him away. But we don't. We never will. That's why we have to stay healthy. You and me. Nobody's going to look after us. Bradley can't look after us. Bradley can hardly look after himself. I was always hoping that Tilden would look out for Bradley when they got older. After Bradley lost his leg. Tilden's the oldest. I always thought he'd be the one to take responsibility. I had no idea in the world that Tilden would be so much trouble. Who 300 would've dreamed. Tilden was an All-American, don't forget. Don't forget that. Fullback. Or quarterback. I forget which.

TILDEN: (*to himself*) Fullback. (*still husking*)

HALIE'S VOICE: Then when Tilden turned out to be so much trouble, I put all my hopes on Ansel. Of course Ansel wasn't as handsome, but he was smart. He was the smartest probably. I think he probably was. Smarter than Bradley, that's for sure. Didn't go and chop his leg off with a chain saw. Smart enough not to go and do that. I think he was smarter 310 than Tilden too. Especially after Tilden got in all that trouble. Doesn't take brains to go to jail. Anybody knows that. Course then when Ansel died that left us all alone. Same as being alone. No different. Same as if they'd all died. He was the smartest. He could've earned lots of money. Lots and lots of money.

(HALIE *enters slowly from the top of the staircase as she continues talking. Just her feet are seen at first as she makes her way down the stairs, a step at a time. She appears dressed completely in black, as though in mourning. Black handbag, hat with a veil, and pulling on elbow length black gloves. She is about sixty-five with pure white hair. She remains absorbed in what she's saying as she descends the stairs and doesn't really notice the two men who continue sitting there as they were before she came down, smoking and husking.*)

HALIE: He would've took care of us, too. He would've seen to it that we were repaid. He was like that. He was a hero. Don't forget that. A genuine hero. Brave. Strong. And very intelligent. Ansel could've been a great man. One of the 320 greatest. I only regret that he didn't die in action. It's not fitting for a man like that to die in a motel room. A soldier. He could've won a medal. He could've been decorated for valor. I've talked to Father Dewis about putting up a plaque for Ansel. He thinks it's a good idea. He agrees. He knew Ansel when he used to play basketball. Went to every game. Ansel was his favorite player. He even recommended to the City Council that they put up a statue of Ansel. A big, tall statue with a basketball in one hand and a rifle in the other.

330     That's how much he thinks of Ansel.

(HALIE *reaches the stage and begins to wander around, still absorbed in pulling on her gloves, brushing lint off her dress and continuously talking to herself as the men just sit.*)

HALIE: Of course, he'd still be alive today if he hadn't married into the Catholics. The Mob. How in the world he never opened his eyes to that is beyond me. Just beyond me. Everyone around him could see the truth. Even Tilden. Tilden told him time and again. Catholic women are the Devil incarnate. He wouldn't listen. He was blind with love. Blind. I knew. Everyone knew. The wedding was more like a funeral. You remember? All those Italians. All that horrible black, greasy hair. The smell of cheap cologne. I think
340     even the priest was wearing a pistol. When he gave her the ring I knew he was a dead man. I knew it. As soon as he gave her the ring. But then it was the honeymoon that killed him. The honeymoon. I knew he'd never come back from the honeymoon. I kissed him and he felt like a corpse. All white. Cold. Icy blue lips. He never used to kiss like that. Never before. I knew then that she'd cursed him. Taken his soul. I saw it in her eyes. She smiled at me with that Catholic sneer of hers. She told me with her eyes that she'd murder him in his bed. Murder my son. She told me. And there was noth-
350     ing I could do. Absolutely nothing. He was going with her, thinking he was free. Thinking it was love. What could I do? I couldn't tell him she was a witch. I couldn't tell him that. He'd have turned on me. Hated me. I couldn't stand him hating me and then dying before he ever saw me again. Hating me in his death bed. Hating me and loving her! How could I do that? I had to let him go. I had to. I watched him leave. I watched him throw gardenias as he helped her into the limousine. I watched his face disappear behind the glass.

(*She stops abruptly and stares at the corn husks. She looks around the space as though just waking up. She turns and looks hard at* TILDEN *and* DODGE *who continue sitting calmly. She looks again at the corn husks.*)

360 HALIE: (*pointing to the husks*) What's this in my house! (*kicks husks*) What's all this!

(TILDEN *stops husking and stares at her.*)

HALIE: (*to* DODGE) And you encourage him!

(DODGE *pulls blanket over him again.*)

DODGE: You're going out in the rain?
HALIE: It's not raining.

(TILDEN *starts husking again.*)

DODGE: Not in Florida it's not.
HALIE: We're not in Florida!
DODGE: It's not raining at the race track.
HALIE: Have you been taking those pills? Those pills always make you talk crazy. Tilden, has he been taking those pills?
370 TILDEN: He hasn't took anything.
HALIE: (*to* DODGE) What've you been taking?
DODGE: It's not raining in California or Florida or the race track. Only in Illinois. This is the only place it's raining. All over the rest of the world it's bright golden sunshine.

(HALIE *goes to the night table next to the sofa and checks the bottle of pills.*)

HALIE: Which ones did you take? Tilden, you must've seen him take something.
TILDEN: He never took a thing.
HALIE: Then why's he talking crazy?
TILDEN: I've been here the whole time.
HALIE: Then you've both been taking something!   380
TILDEN: I've just been husking the corn.
HALIE: Where'd you get that corn anyway? Why is the house suddenly full of corn?
DODGE: Bumper crop!
HALIE: (*moving center*) We haven't had corn here for over thirty years.
TILDEN: The whole back lot's full of corn. Far as the eye can see.
DODGE: (*to* HALIE) Things keep happening while you're upstairs, ya know. The world doesn't stop just because you're  390 upstairs. Corn keeps growing. Rain keeps raining.
HALIE: I'm not unaware of the world around me! Thank you very much. It so happens that I have an over-all view from the upstairs. The back yard's in plain view of my window. And there's no corn to speak of. Absolutely none!
DODGE: Tilden wouldn't lie. If he says there's corn, there's corn.
HALIE: What's the meaning of this corn Tilden!
TILDEN: It's a mystery to me. I was out in back there. And the rain was coming down. And I didn't feel like coming back in-  400 side. I didn't feel the cold so much. I didn't mind the wet. So I was just walking. I was muddy but I didn't mind the mud so much. And I looked up. And I saw this stand of corn. In fact I was standing in it. So, I was standing in it.
HALIE: There isn't any corn outside, Tilden! There's no corn! Now, you must've either stolen this corn or you bought it.
DODGE: He doesn't have any money.
HALIE: (*to* TILDEN) So you stole it!
TILDEN: I didn't steal it. I don't want to get kicked out of Illinois. I was kicked out of New Mexico and I don't want to get  410 kicked out of Illinois.
HALIE: You're going to get kicked out of this house, Tilden, if you don't tell me where you got that corn!

(TILDEN *starts crying softly to himself but keeps husking corn. Pause.*)

DODGE: (*to* HALIE) Why'd you have to tell him that? Who cares where he got the corn? Why'd you have to go and tell him that?
HALIE: (*to* DODGE) It's your fault you know! You're the one that's behind all this! I suppose you thought it'd be funny! Some joke! Cover the house with corn husks. You better get this cleaned up before Bradley sees it.   420
DODGE: Bradley's not getting in the front door!
HALIE: (*kicking husks, striding back and forth*) Bradley's going to be very upset when he sees this. He doesn't like to see the house in disarray. He can't stand it when one thing is out of place. The slightest thing. You know how he gets.
DODGE: Bradley doesn't even live here!
HALIE: It's his home as much as ours. He was born in this house!

DODGE: He was born in a hog wallow.

430 HALIE: Don't you say that! Don't you ever say that!

DODGE: He was born in a goddamn hog wallow! That's where he was born and that's where he belongs! He doesn't belong in this house!

HALIE: *(she stops)* I don't know what's come over you, Dodge. I don't know what in the world's come over you. You've become an evil man. You used to be a good man.

DODGE: Six of one, a half dozen of another.

HALIE: You sit here day and night, festering away! Decomposing! Smelling up the house with your putrid body! Hacking
440    your head off till all hours of the morning! Thinking up mean, evil, stupid things to say about your own flesh and blood!

DODGE: He's not my flesh and blood! My flesh and blood's buried in the back yard!

*(They freeze. Long pause. The men stare at her.)*

HALIE: *(quietly)* That's enough, Dodge. That's quite enough. I'm going out now. I'm going to have lunch with Father Dewis. I'm going to ask him about a monument. A statue. At least a plaque.

*(She crosses to the door up right. She stops.)*

HALIE: If you need anything, ask Tilden. He's the oldest. I've
450    left some money on the kitchen table.

DODGE: I don't need anything.

HALIE: No, I suppose not. *(she opens the door and looks out through porch)* Still raining. I love the smell just after it stops. The ground. I won't be too late.

*(She goes out door and closes it. She's still visible on the porch as she crosses toward stage left screen door. She stops in the middle of the porch, speaks to* DODGE *but doesn't turn to him.)*

HALIE: Dodge, tell Tilden not to go out in the back lot anymore. I don't want him back there in the rain.

DODGE: You tell him. He's sitting right here.

HALIE: He never listens to me Dodge. He's never listened to me in the past.

460 DODGE: I'll tell him.

HALIE: We have to watch him just like we used to now. Just like we always have. He's still a child.

DODGE: I'll watch him.

HALIE: Good.

*(She crosses to screen door, left, takes an umbrella off a hook and goes out the door. The door slams behind her. Long pause.* TILDEN *husks corn, stares at pail.* DODGE *lights a cigarette, stares at T.V.)*

TILDEN: *(still husking)* You shouldn't a told her that.

DODGE: *(staring at T.V.)* What?

TILDEN: What you told her. You know.

DODGE: What do you know about it?

TILDEN: I know. I know all about it. We all know.

470 DODGE: So what difference does it make? Everybody knows, everybody's forgot.

TILDEN: She hasn't forgot.

DODGE: She should've forgot.

TILDEN: It's different for a woman. She couldn't forget that. How could she forget that?

DODGE: I don't want to talk about it!

TILDEN: What do you want to talk about?

DODGE: I don't want to talk about anything! I don't want to talk about troubles or what happened fifty years ago or thirty years ago or the race track or Florida or the last time I 480 seeded the corn! I don't want to talk!

TILDEN: You don't wanna die do you?

DODGE: No, I don't wanna die either.

TILDEN: Well, you gotta talk or you'll die.

DODGE: Who told you that?

TILDEN: That's what I know. I found that out in New Mexico. I thought I was dying but I just lost my voice.

DODGE: Were you with somebody?

TILDEN: I was alone. I thought I was dead.

DODGE: Might as well have been. What'd you come back here 490 for?

TILDEN: I didn't know where to go.

DODGE: You're a grown man. You shouldn't be needing your parents at your age. It's unnatural. There's nothing we can do for you now anyway. Couldn't you make a living down there? Couldn't you find some way to make a living? Support yourself? What'd ya come back here for? You expect us to feed you forever?

TILDEN: I didn't know where else to go.

DODGE: I never went back to my parents. Never. Never even 500 had the urge. I was independent. Always independent. Always found a way.

TILDEN: I didn't know what to do. I couldn't figure anything out.

DODGE: There's nothing to figure out. You just forge ahead. What's there to figure out?

*(*TILDEN *stands.)*

TILDEN: I don't know.

DODGE: Where are you going?

TILDEN: Out back.

DODGE: You're not supposed to go out there. You heard what 510 she said. Don't play deaf with me!

TILDEN: I like it out there.

DODGE: In the rain?

TILDEN: Especially in the rain. I like the feeling of it. Feels like it always did.

DODGE: You're supposed to watch out for me. Get me things when I need them.

TILDEN: What do you need?

DODGE: I don't need anything! But I might. I might need something any second. Any second now. I can't be left alone 520 for a minute!

*(*DODGE *starts to cough.)*

TILDEN: I'll be right outside. You can just yell.

DODGE: *(between coughs)* No! It's too far! You can't go out there! It's too far! You might not ever hear me!

TILDEN: *(moving to pills)* Why don't you take a pill? You want a pill?

*(*DODGE *coughs more violently, throws himself back against sofa, clutches his throat.* TILDEN *stands by helplessly.)*

DODGE: Water! Get me some water!

*(*TILDEN *rushes off left.* DODGE *reaches out for the pills,*

*knocking some bottles to the floor, coughing in spasms. He grabs a small bottle, takes out pills and swallows them.* TILDEN *rushes back on with a glass of water.* DODGE *takes it and drinks, his coughing subsides.)*

TILDEN: You all right now?

(DODGE *nods. Drinks more water.* TILDEN *moves in closer to him.* DODGE *sets glass of water on the night table. His coughing is almost gone.)*

TILDEN: Why don't you lay down for a while? Just rest a little.

(TILDEN *helps* DODGE *lay down on the sofa. Covers him with blanket.)*

530 DODGE: You're not going outside are you?
TILDEN: No.
DODGE: I don't want to wake up and find you not here.
TILDEN: I'll be here.

(TILDEN *tucks blanket around* DODGE)

DODGE: You'll stay right here?
TILDEN: I'll stay in my chair.
DODGE: That's not a chair. That's my old milking stool.
TILDEN: I know.
DODGE: Don't call it a chair.
TILDEN: I won't.

(TILDEN *tries to take* DODGE's *baseball cap off.*)

540 DODGE: What're you doing! Leave that on me! Don't take that offa me! That's my cap!

(TILDEN *leaves the cap on* DODGE)

TILDEN: I know.
DODGE: Bradley'll shave my head if I don't have that on. That's my cap.
TILDEN: I know it is.
DODGE: Don't take my cap off.
TILDEN: I won't.
DODGE: You stay right here now.
TILDEN: (*sits on stool*) I will.
550 DODGE: Don't go outside. There's nothing out there.
TILDEN: I won't.
DODGE: Everything's in here. Everything you need. Money's on the table. T.V. Is the T.V. on?
TILDEN: Yeah.
DODGE: Turn it off! Turn the damn thing off! What's it doing on?
TILDEN: (*shuts off T.V., light goes out*) You left it on.
DODGE: Well turn it off.
TILDEN: (*sits on stool again*) It's off.
560 DODGE: Leave it off.
TILDEN: I will.
DODGE: When I fall asleep you can turn it on.
TILDEN: Okay.
DODGE: You can watch the ball game. Red Sox. You like the Red Sox don't you?
TILDEN: Yeah.
DODGE: You can watch the Red Sox. Pee Wee Reese. Pee Wee Reese. You remember Pee Wee Reese?
TILDEN: No.

DODGE: Was he with the Red Sox?          570
TILDEN: I don't know.
DODGE: Pee Wee Reese. (*falling asleep*) You can watch the Cardinals. You remember Stan Musial.
TILDEN: No.
DODGE: Stan Musial. (*falling into sleep*) Bases loaded. Top a' the sixth. Bases loaded. Runner on first and third. Big fat knuckle ball. Floater. Big as a blimp. Cracko! Ball just took off like a rocket. Just pulverized. I marked it. Marked it with my eyes. Straight between the clock and the Burma Shave ad. I was the first kid out there. First kid. I had to fight hard 580 for that ball. I wouldn't give it up. They almost tore the ears right off me. But I wouldn't give it up.

(DODGE *falls into deep sleep.* TILDEN *just sits staring at him for a while. Slowly he leans toward the sofa, checking to see if* DODGE *is well asleep. He reaches slowly under the cushion and pulls out the bottle of booze.* DODGE *sleeps soundly.* TILDEN *stands quietly, staring at* DODGE *as he uncaps the bottle and takes a long drink. He caps the bottle and sticks it in his hip pocket. He looks around at the husks on the floor and then back to* DODGE. *He moves center stage and gathers an armload of corn husks then crosses back to the sofa. He stands holding the husks over* DODGE *and looking down at him he gently spreads the corn husks over the whole length of* DODGE's *body. He stands back and looks at* DODGE. *Pulls out bottle, takes another drink, returns bottle to his hip pocket. He gathers more husks and repeats the procedure until the floor is clean of corn husks and* DODGE *is completely covered in them except for his head.* TILDEN *takes another long drink, stares at* DODGE *sleeping then quietly exits stage left. Long pause as the sound of rain continues.* DODGE *sleeps on. The figure of* BRADLEY *appears up left, outside the screen porch door. He holds a wet newspaper over his head as a protection from the rain. He seems to be struggling with the door then slips and almost falls to the ground.* DODGE *sleeps on, undisturbed.)*

BRADLEY: Sonuvabitch! Sonuvagoddamnbitch!

(BRADLEY *recovers his footing and makes it through the screen door onto the porch. He throws the newspaper down, shakes the water out of his hair, and brushes the rain off of his shoulders. He is a big man dressed in a gray sweat shirt, black suspenders, baggy dark blue pants and black janitor's shoes. His left leg is wooden, having been amputated above the knee. He moves with an exaggerated, almost mechanical limp. The squeaking sounds of leather and metal accompany his walk coming from the harness and hinges of the false leg. His arms and shoulders are extremely powerful and muscular due to a lifetime dependency on the upper torso doing all the work for the legs. He is about five years younger than* TILDEN. *He moves laboriously to the stage right door and enters, closing the door behind him. He doesn't notice* DODGE *at first. He moves toward the staircase.)*

BRADLEY: (*calling to upstairs*) Mom!

(He stops and listens. Turns upstage and sees DODGE sleeping. Notices corn husks. He moves slowly toward sofa. Stops next to pail and looks into it. Looks at husks. DODGE stays asleep. Talks to himself.)

BRADLEY: What in the hell is this?

*(He looks at* DODGE's *sleeping face and shakes his head in disgust. He pulls out a pair of black electric hair clippers from his pocket. Unwinds the cord and crosses to the lamp. He jabs his wooden leg behind the knee, causing it to bend at the joint and awkwardly kneels to plug the cord into a floor outlet. He pulls himself to his feet again by using the sofa as leverage. He moves to* DODGE's *head and again jabs his false leg. Goes down on one knee. He violently knocks away some of the corn husks then jerks off* DODGE's *baseball cap and throws it down center stage.* DODGE *stays asleep.)* BRADLEY *switches on the clippers. Lights start dimming.* BRADLEY *cuts* DODGE's *hair while he sleeps. Lights dim slowly to black with the sound of clippers and rain.)*

### —ACT TWO—

SCENE: *Same set as act 1. Night. Sounds of rain.* DODGE *still asleep on sofa. His hair is cut extremely short and in places the scalp is cut and bleeding. His cap is still center stage. All the corn and husks, pail and milking stool have been cleared away. The lights come up to the sound of a young girl laughing off stage left.* DODGE *remains asleep.* SHELLY *and* VINCE *appear up left outside the screen porch door sharing the shelter of* VINCE's *overcoat above their heads.* SHELLY *is about nineteen, black hair, very beautiful. She wears tight jeans, high heels, purple T-shirt and a short rabbit fur coat. Her makeup is exaggerated and her hair has been curled.* VINCE *is* TILDEN's *son, about twenty-two, wears a plaid shirt, jeans, dark glasses, cowboy boots and carries a black saxophone case. They shake the rain off themselves as they enter the porch through the screen door.)*

SHELLY: *(laughing, gesturing to house)* This is it? I don't believe this is it!
VINCE: This is it.
SHELLY: This is the house?
590 VINCE: This is the house.
SHELLY: I don't believe it!
VINCE: How come?
SHELLY: It's like a Norman Rockwell cover or something.
VINCE: What's a' matter with that? It's American.
SHELLY: Where's the milkman and the little dog? What's the little dog's name? Spot. Spot and Jane. Dick and Jane and Spot.
VINCE: Knock it off.
SHELLY: Dick and Jane and Spot and Mom and Dad and Junior
600 and Sissy!

*(She laughs. Slaps her knee.)*

VINCE: Come on! It's my heritage. What dya' expect?

*(She laughs more hysterically, out of control.)*

SHELLY: "And Tuffy and Toto and Dooda and Bonzo all went down one day to the corner grocery store to buy a big bag of licorice for Mr. Marshall's pussy cat!"

*(She laughs so hard she falls to her knees holding her stomach.* VINCE *stands there looking at her.)*

VINCE: Shelly will you get up!

*(She keeps laughing. Staggers to her feet. Turning in circles holding her stomach.)*

SHELLY: *(continuing her story in kid's voice)* "Mr. Marshall was on vacation. He had no idea that the four little boys had taken such a liking to his little kitty cat."
VINCE: Have some respect would ya'!
SHELLY: *(trying to control herself)* I'm sorry.    610
VINCE: Pull yourself together.
SHELLY: *(salutes him)* Yes sir.

*(She giggles.)*

VINCE: Jesus Christ, Shelly.
SHELLY: *(pause, smiling)* And Mr. Marshall—
VINCE: Cut it out.

*(She stops. Stands there staring at him. Stifles a giggle.)*

VINCE: *(after pause)* Are you finished?
SHELLY: Oh brother!
VINCE: I don't wanna go in there with you acting like an idiot.
SHELLY: Thanks.
VINCE: Well, I don't.    620
SHELLY: I won't embarrass you. Don't worry.
VINCE: I'm not worried.
SHELLY: You are too.
VINCE: Shelly look, I just don't wanna go in there with you giggling your head off. They might think something's wrong with you.
SHELLY: There is.
VINCE: There is not!
SHELLY: Something's definitely wrong with me.
VINCE: There is not!    630
SHELLY: There's something wrong with you too.
VINCE: There's nothing wrong with me either!
SHELLY: You wanna know what's wrong with you?
VINCE: What?

*(SHELLY laughs.)*

VINCE: *(crosses back left toward screen door)* I'm leaving!
SHELLY: *(stops laughing)* Wait! Stop! Stop! (VINCE *stops)* What's wrong with you is that you take the situation too seriously.
VINCE: I just don't want to have them think that I've suddenly arrived out of the middle of nowhere completely deranged.    640
SHELLY: What do you want them to think then?
VINCE: *(pause)* Nothing. Let's go in.

*(He crosses porch toward stage right interior door.* SHELLY *follows him. The stage right door opens slowly.* VINCE *sticks his head in, doesn't notice* DODGE *sleeping. Calls out toward staircase.)*

VINCE: Grandma!

*(SHELLY breaks into laughter, unseen behind* VINCE. VINCE *pulls his head back outside and pulls door shut. We hear their voices again without seeing them.)*

SHELLY'S VOICE: *(stops laughing)* I'm sorry. I'm sorry Vince. I really am. I won't do it again. I couldn't help it.
VINCE'S VOICE: It's not all that funny.
SHELLY'S VOICE: I know it's not. I'm sorry.
VINCE'S VOICE: I mean this is a tense situation for me! I haven't seen them for over six years. I don't know what to expect.    650

SHELLY'S VOICE: I know. I won't do it again.

VINCE'S VOICE: Can't you bite your tongue or something?

SHELLY'S VOICE: Just don't say "Grandma," okay? (*she giggles, stops*) I mean if you say "Grandma" I don't know if I can stop myself.

VINCE'S VOICE: Well try!

SHELLY'S VOICE: Okay. Sorry.

(*Door opens again.* VINCE *sticks his head in then enters.* SHELLY *follows behind him.* VINCE *crosses to staircase, sets down saxophone case and overcoat, looks up staircase.* SHELLY *notices* DODGE's *baseball cap. Crosses to it. Picks it up and puts it on her head.* VINCE *goes up the stairs and disappears at the top.* SHELLY *watches him then turns and sees* DODGE *on the sofa. She takes off the baseball cap.*)

VINCE'S VOICE: (*from above stairs*) Grandma!

(SHELLY *crosses over to* DODGE *slowly and stands next to him. She stands at his head, reaches out slowly and touches one of the cuts. The second she touches his head,* DODGE *jerks up to a sitting position on the sofa, eyes open.* SHELLY *gasps.* DODGE *looks at her, sees his cap in her hands, quickly puts his hand to his bare head. He glares at* SHELLY *then whips the cap out of her hands and puts it on.* SHELLY *backs away from him.* DODGE *stares at her.*)

SHELLY: I'm uh—with Vince.

(DODGE *just glares at her.*)

660 SHELLY: He's upstairs.

(DODGE *looks at the staircase then back to* SHELLY.)

SHELLY: (*calling upstairs*) Vince!

VINCE'S VOICE: Just a second!

SHELLY: You better get down here!

VINCE'S VOICE: Just a minute! I'm looking at the pictures.

(DODGE *keeps staring at her.*)

SHELLY: (*to* DODGE) We just got here. Pouring rain on the freeway so we thought we'd stop by. I mean Vince was planning on stopping anyway. He wanted to see you. He said he hadn't seen you in a long time.

(*Pause.* DODGE *just keeps staring at her.*)

670 SHELLY: We were going all the way through to New Mexico. To see his father. I guess his father lives out there. We thought we'd stop by and see you on the way. Kill two birds with one stone, you know? (*she laughs,* DODGE *stares, she stops laughing*) I mean Vince has this thing about his family now. I guess it's a new thing with him. I kind of find it hard to relate to. But he feels it's important. You know. I mean he feels he wants to get to know you all again. After all this time.

(*Pause.* DODGE *just stares at her. She moves nervously to staircase and yells up to* VINCE.)

SHELLY: Vince will you come down here please!

(VINCE *comes half way down the stairs.*)

VINCE: I guess they went out for a while.

(SHELLY *points to sofa and* DODGE. VINCE *turns and sees*

DODGE. *He comes all the way down staircase and crosses to* DODGE. SHELLY *stays behind near staircase, keeping her distance.*)

VINCE: Grandpa?    680

(DODGE *looks up at him, not recognizing him.*)

DODGE: Did you bring the whiskey?

(VINCE *looks back at* SHELLY *then back to* DODGE.)

VINCE: Grandpa, it's Vince. I'm Vince. Tilden's son. You remember?

(DODGE *stares at him.*)

DODGE: You didn't do what you told me. You didn't stay here with me.

VINCE: Grandpa, I haven't been here until just now. I just got here.

DODGE: You left. You went outside like we told you not to do. You went out there in back. In the rain.

(VINCE *looks back at* SHELLY. *She moves slowly toward sofa.*)

SHELLY: Is he okay?    690

VINCE: I don't know. (*takes off his shades*) Look, Grandpa, don't you remember me? Vince. Your Grandson.

(DODGE *stares at him then takes off his baseball cap.*)

DODGE: (*points to his head*) See what happens when you leave me alone? See that? That's what happens.

(VINCE *looks at his head.* VINCE *reaches out to touch his head.* DODGE *slaps his hand away with the cap and puts it back on his head.*)

VINCE: What's going on Grandpa? Where's 'Halie?

DODGE: Don't worry about her. She won't be back for days. She says she'll be back but she won't be. (*he starts laughing*) There's life in the old girl yet! (*stops laughing*)

VINCE: How did you do that to your head?

DODGE: I didn't do it! Don't be ridiculous!    700

VINCE: Well who did then?

(*Pause.* DODGE *stares at* VINCE.)

DODGE: Who do you think did it? Who do you think?

(SHELLY *moves toward* VINCE.)

SHELLY: Vince, maybe we oughta' go. I don't like this. I mean this isn't my idea of a good time.

VINCE: (*to* SHELLY) Just a second. (*to* DODGE) Grandpa, look, I just got here. I just now got here. I haven't been here for six years. I don't know anything that's happened.

(*Pause,* DODGE *stares at him.*)

DODGE: You don't know anything?

VINCE: No.

DODGE: Well that's good. That's good. It's much better not to    710 know anything. Much, much better.

VINCE: Isn't there anybody here with you?

(DODGE *turns slowly and looks off to stage left.*)

DODGE: Tilden's here.

VINCE: No, Grandpa, Tilden's in New Mexico. That's where I was going. I'm going out there to see him.

(DODGE *turns slowly back to* VINCE.)

DODGE: Tilden's here.

(VINCE *backs away and joins* SHELLY. DODGE *stares at them.*)

SHELLY: Vince, why don't we spend the night in a motel and come back in the morning? We could have breakfast. Maybe everything would be different.

720 VINCE: Don't be scared. There's nothing to be scared of. He's just old.

SHELLY: I'm not scared!

DODGE: You two are not my idea of the perfect couple!

SHELLY: (*after pause*) Oh really? Why's that?

VINCE: Shh! Don't aggravate him.

DODGE: There's something wrong between the two of you. Something not compatible.

VINCE: Grandpa, where did Halie go? Maybe we should call her.

730 DODGE: What are you talking about? Do you know what you're talking about? Are you just talking for the sake of talking? Lubricating the gums?

VINCE: I'm trying to figure out what's going on here!

DODGE: Is that it?

VINCE: Yes. I mean I expected everything to be different.

DODGE: Who are you to expect anything? Who are you supposed to be?

VINCE: I'm Vince! Your Grandson!

DODGE: Vince. My Grandson.

740 VINCE: Tilden's son.

DODGE: Tilden's son, Vince.

VINCE: You haven't seen me for a long time.

DODGE: When was the last time?

VINCE: I don't remember.

DODGE: You don't remember?

VINCE: No.

DODGE: You don't remember. How am I supposed to remember if you don't remember?

SHELLY: Vince, come on. This isn't going to work out.

750 VINCE: (*to* SHELLY) Just take it easy.

SHELLY: I'm taking it easy! He doesn't even know who you are!

VINCE: (*crossing toward* DODGE) Grandpa, look—

DODGE: Stay where you are! Keep your distance!

(VINCE *stops. Looks back at* SHELLY *then to* DODGE.)

SHELLY: Vince, this is really making me nervous. I mean he doesn't even want us here. He doesn't even like us.

DODGE: She's a beautiful girl.

VINCE: Thanks.

DODGE: Very Beautiful Girl.

SHELLY: Oh my God.

760 DODGE: (*to* SHELLY) What's your name?

SHELLY: Shelly.

DODGE: Shelly. That's a man's name isn't it?

SHELLY: Not in this case.

DODGE: (*to* VINCE) She's a smart-ass too.

SHELLY: Vince! Can we go?

DODGE: She wants to go. She just got here and she wants to go.

VINCE: This is kind of strange for her.

DODGE: She'll get used to it. (*to* SHELLY) What part of the country do you come from?

SHELLY: Originally?                                      770

DODGE: That's right. Originally. At the very start.

SHELLY: L.A.

DODGE: L.A. Stupid country.

SHELLY: I can't stand this Vince! This is really unbelievable!

DODGE: It's stupid! L.A. is stupid! So is Florida! All those Sunshine States. They're all stupid. Do you know why they're stupid?

SHELLY: Illuminate me.

DODGE: I'll tell you why. Because they're full of smart-asses! That's why.                                      780

(SHELLY *turns her back to* DODGE, *crosses to staircase and sits on bottom step.*)

DODGE: (*to* VINCE) Now she's insulted.

VINCE: Well you weren't very polite.

DODGE: She's insulted! Look at her! In my house she's insulted! She's over there sulking because I insulted her!

SHELLY: (*to* VINCE) This is really terrific. This is wonderful. And you were worried about me making the right first impression!

DODGE: (*to* VINCE) She's a fireball isn't she? Regular fireball. I had some a' them in my day. Temporary stuff. Never lasted more than a week.                                      790

VINCE: Grandpa—

DODGE: Stop calling me Grandpa will ya'! It's sickening. "Grandpa." I'm nobody's Grandpa!

(DODGE *starts feeling around under the cushion for the bottle of whiskey.* SHELLY *gets up from the staircase.*)

SHELLY: (*to* VINCE) Maybe you've got the wrong house. Did you ever think of that? Maybe this is the wrong address!

VINCE: It's not the wrong address! I recognize the yard.

SHELLY: Yeah but do you recognize the people? He says he's not your Grandfather.

DODGE: (*digging for bottle*) Where's that bottle!

VINCE: He's just sick or something. I don't know what's hap- 800 pened to him.

DODGE: Where's my goddamn bottle!

(DODGE *gets up from sofa and starts tearing the cushions off it and throwing them downstage, looking for the whiskey.*)

SHELLY: Can't we just drive on to New Mexico? This is terrible, Vince! I don't want to stay here. In this house. I thought it was going to be turkey dinners and apple pie and all that kinda stuff.

VINCE: Well I hate to disappoint you!

SHELLY: I'm not disappointed! I'm fuckin' terrified! I wanna' go!

(DODGE *yells toward stage left.*)

DODGE: Tilden! Tilden!                                      810

(DODGE *keeps ripping away at the sofa looking for his bottle, he knocks over the night stand with the bottles.* VINCE *and* SHELLY *watch as he starts ripping the stuffing out of the sofa.*)

VINCE: (*to* SHELLY) He's lost his mind or something. I've got to try to help him.

SHELLY: You help him! I'm leaving!

(SHELLY *starts to leave.* VINCE *grabs her. They struggle as* DODGE *keeps ripping away at the sofa and yelling.*)

DODGE: Tilden! Tilden get your ass in here! Tilden!

SHELLY: Let go of me!

VINCE: You're not going anywhere! You're going to stay right here!

SHELLY: Let go of me you sonuvabitch! I'm not your property!

(*Suddenly* TILDEN *walks on from stage left just as he did before. This time his arms are full of carrots.* DODGE, VINCE *and* SHELLY *stop suddenly when they see him. They all stare at* TILDEN *as he crosses slowly center stage with the carrots and stops.* DODGE *sits on sofa, exhausted.*)

DODGE: (*panting, to* TILDEN) Where in the hell have you been?

820 TILDEN: Out back.

DODGE: Where's my bottle?

TILDEN: Gone.

(TILDEN *and* VINCE *stare at each other.* SHELLY *backs away.*)

DODGE: (*to* TILDEN) You stole my bottle!

VINCE: (*to* TILDEN) Dad?

(TILDEN *just stares at* VINCE.)

DODGE: You had no right to steal my bottle! No right at all!

VINCE: (*to* TILDEN) It's Vince. I'm Vince.

(TILDEN *stares at* VINCE *then looks at* DODGE *then turns to* SHELLY.)

TILDEN: (*after pause*) I picked these carrots. If anybody wants any carrots, I picked 'em.

SHELLY: (*to* VINCE) This is your father?

830 VINCE: (*to* TILDEN) Dad, what're you doing here?

(TILDEN *just stares at* VINCE, *holding carrots,* DODGE *pulls the blanket back over himself.*)

DODGE: (*to* TILDEN) You're going to have to get me another bottle! You gotta get me a bottle before Halie comes back! There's money on the table. (*points to stage left kitchen*)

TILDEN: (*shaking his head*) I'm not going down there. Into town.

(SHELLY *crosses to* TILDEN. TILDEN *stares at her.*)

SHELLY: (*to* TILDEN) Are you Vince's father?

TILDEN: (*to* SHELLY) Vince?

SHELLY: (*pointing to* VINCE) This is supposed to be your son! Is he your son! Do you recognize him! I'm just along for the

840 ride here. I thought everybody knew each other!

(TILDEN *stares at* VINCE. DODGE *wraps himself up in the blanket and sits on sofa staring at the floor.*)

TILDEN: I had a son once but we buried him.

(DODGE *quickly looks at* TILDEN. SHELLY *looks to* VINCE.)

DODGE: You shut up about that! You don't know anything about that!

VINCE: Dad, I thought you were in New Mexico. We were going to drive down there and see you.

TILDEN: Long way to drive.

DODGE: (*to* TILDEN) You don't know anything about that! That happened before you were born! Long before!

VINCE: What's happened, Dad? What's going on here? I thought everything was all right. What's happened to Halie? 850

TILDEN: She left.

SHELLY: (*to* TILDEN) Do you want me to take those carrots for you?

(TILDEN *stares at her. She moves in close to him. Holds out her arms.* TILDEN *stares at her arms then slowly dumps the carrots into her arms.* SHELLY *stands there holding the carrots.*)

TILDEN: (*to* SHELLY) You like carrots?

SHELLY: Sure. I like all kinds of vegetables.

DODGE: (*to* TILDEN) You gotta get me a bottle before Halie comes back!

(DODGE *hits sofa with his fist.* VINCE *crosses up to* DODGE *and tries to console him.* SHELLY *and* TILDEN *stay facing each other.*)

TILDEN: (*to* SHELLY) Back yard's full of carrots. Corn. Potatoes.

SHELLY: You're Vince's father, right?

TILDEN: All kinds of vegetables. You like vegetables? 860

SHELLY: (*laughs*) Yeah. I love vegetables.

TILDEN: We could cook these carrots ya' know. You could cut 'em up and we could cook 'em.

SHELLY: All right.

TILDEN: I'll get you a pail and a knife.

SHELLY: Okay.

TILDEN: I'll be right back. Don't go.

(TILDEN *exits off stage left.* SHELLY *stands center, arms full of carrots.* VINCE *stands next to* DODGE. SHELLY *looks toward* VINCE *then down at the carrots.*)

DODGE: (*to* VINCE) You could get me a bottle. (*pointing off left*) There's money on the table.

VINCE: Grandpa why don't you lay down for a while? 870

DODGE: I don't wanna lay down for a while! Every time I lay down something happens! (*whips off his cap, points at his head*) Look what happens! That's what happens! (*pulls his cap back on*) You go lie down and see what happens to you! See how you like it! They'll steal your bottle! They'll cut your hair! They'll murder your children! That's what'll happen.

VINCE: Just relax for a while.

DODGE: (*pause*) You could get me a bottle ya' know. There's nothing stopping you from getting me a bottle.

SHELLY: Why don't you get him a bottle, Vince? Maybe it 880 would help everybody identify each other.

DODGE: (*pointing to* SHELLY) There, see? She thinks you should get me a bottle.

(VINCE *crosses to* SHELLY.)

VINCE: What're you doing with those carrots.

SHELLY: I'm waiting for your father.

DODGE: She thinks you should get me a bottle!

VINCE: Shelly put the carrots down will ya'! We gotta deal with the situation here! I'm gonna need your help.

SHELLY: I'm helping.

VINCE: You're only adding to the problem! You're making 890 things worse! Put the carrots down!

(VINCE *tries to knock the carrots out of her arms. She turns away from him, protecting the carrots.*)

SHELLY: Get away from me! Stop it!

(VINCE *stands back from her. She turns to him still holding the carrots.*)

VINCE: (*to* SHELLY) Why are you doing this! Are you trying to make fun of me? This is my family you know!

SHELLY: You coulda' fooled me! I'd just as soon not be here myself. I'd just as soon be a thousand miles from here. I'd rather be anywhere but here. You're the one who wants to stay. So I'll stay. I'll stay and I'll cut the carrots. And I'll cook the carrots. And I'll do whatever I have to do to survive. Just
900      to make it through this.

VINCE: Put the carrots down Shelly.

(TILDEN *enters from left with pail, milking stool and a knife. He sets the stool and pail center stage for* SHELLY. SHELLY *looks at* VINCE *then sits down on stool, sets the carrots on the floor and takes the knife from* TILDEN. *She looks at* VINCE *again then picks up a carrot, cuts the ends off, scrapes it and drops it in pail. She repeats this,* VINCE *glares at her. She smiles.*)

DODGE: She could get me a bottle. She's the type a' girl that could get me a bottle. Easy. She'd go down there. Slink up to the counter. They'd probably give her two bottles for the price of one. She could do that.

(SHELLY *laughs. Keeps cutting carrots.* VINCE *crosses up to* DODGE, *looks at him.* TILDEN *watches* SHELLY'S *hands. Long pause.*)

VINCE: (*to* DODGE) I haven't changed that much. I mean physically. Physically I'm just about the same. Same size. Same weight. Everything's the same.

(DODGE *keeps staring at* SHELLY *while* VINCE *talks to him.*)

DODGE: She's a beautiful girl. Exceptional.

(VINCE *moves in front of* DODGE *to block his view of* SHELLY. DODGE *keeps craning his head around to see her as* VINCE *demonstrates tricks from his past.*)

910  VINCE: Look. Look at this. Do you remember this? I used to bend my thumb behind my knuckles. You remember? I used to do it at the dinner table.

(VINCE *bends a thumb behind his knuckles for* DODGE *and holds it out to him.* DODGE *takes a short glance then looks back at* SHELLY. VINCE *shifts position and shows him something else.*)

VINCE: What about this?

(VINCE *curls his lips back and starts drumming on his teeth with his fingernails making little tapping sounds.* DODGE *watches a while.* TILDEN *turns toward the sound.* VINCE *keeps it up. He sees* TILDEN *taking notice and crosses to* TILDEN *as he drums on his teeth.* DODGE *turns T.V. on. Watches it.*)

VINCE: You remember this Dad?

(VINCE *keeps on drumming for* TILDEN. TILDEN *watches a while, fascinated, then turns back to* SHELLY. VINCE *keeps up the drumming on his teeth, crosses back to* DODGE *doing it.*)

SHELLY *keeps working on carrots, talking to* TILDEN.)

SHELLY: (*to* TILDEN) He drives me crazy with that sometimes.

VINCE: (*to* DODGE) I know! Here's one you'll remember. You used to kick me out of the house for this one.

(VINCE *pulls his shirt out of his belt and holds it tucked under his chin with his stomach exposed. He grabs the flesh on either side of his belly button and pushes it in and out to make it look like a mouth talking. He watches his belly button and makes a deep sounding cartoon voice to synchronize with the movement. He demonstrates it to* DODGE *then crosses down to* TILDEN *doing it. Both* DODGE *and* TILDEN *take short, uninterested glances then ignore him.*)

VINCE: (*deep cartoon voice*) "Hello. How are you? I'm fine. Thank you very much. It's so good to see you looking well this fine Sunday morning. I was going down to the hardware 920 store to fetch a pail of water."

SHELLY: Vince, don't be pathetic will ya'!

(VINCE *stops. Tucks his shirt back in.*)

SHELLY: Jesus Christ. They're not gonna play. Can't you see that?

(SHELLY *keeps cutting carrots.* VINCE *slowly moves toward* TILDEN. TILDEN *keeps watching* SHELLY. DODGE *watches T.V.*)

VINCE: (*to* SHELLY) I don't get it. I really don't get it. Maybe it's me. Maybe I forgot something.

DODGE: (*from sofa*) You forgot to get me a bottle! That's what you forgot. Anybody in this house could get me a bottle. Anybody! But nobody will. Nobody understands the urgency! Peelin' carrots is more important. Playin' piano on 930 your teeth! Well I hope you all remember this when you get up in years. When you find yourself immobilized. Dependent on the whims of others.

(VINCE *moves up toward* DODGE. *Pause as he looks at him.*)

VINCE: I'll get you a bottle.
DODGE: You will?
VINCE: Sure.

(SHELLY *stands holding knife and carrot.*)

SHELLY: You're not going to leave me here are you?
VINCE: (*moving to her*) You suggested it! You said, "why don't I go get him a bottle." So I'll go get him a bottle!
SHELLY: But I can't stay here.                                         940
VINCE: What is going on! A minute ago you were ready to cut carrots all night!
SHELLY: That was only if you stayed. Something to keep me busy, so I wouldn't be so nervous. I don't want to stay here alone.
DODGE: Don't let her talk you out of it! She's a bad influence. I could see it the minute she stepped in here.
SHELLY: (*to* DODGE) You were asleep!
TILDEN: (*to* SHELLY) Don't you want to cut carrots anymore?
SHELLY: Sure. Sure I do.                                               950

(SHELLY *sits back down on stool and continues cutting carrots. Pause.* VINCE *moves around, stroking his hair, staring at* DODGE *and* TILDEN. VINCE *and* SHELLY *exchange glances.* DODGE *watches T.V.*)

VINCE: Boy! This is amazing. This is truly amazing. *(keeps moving around)* What is this anyway? Am I in a time warp or something? Have I committed an unpardonable offence? It's true, I'm not married. *(SHELLY looks at him, then back to carrots)* But I'm also not divorced. I have been known to plunge into sinful infatuation with the Alto Saxophone. Sucking on number 5 reeds deep into the wee, wee hours.

SHELLY: Vince, what are you doing that for? They don't care about any of that. They just don't recognize you, that's all.

960 VINCE: How could they not recognize me! How in the hell could they not recognize me! I'm their son!

DODGE: *(watching T.V.)* You're no son of mine. I've had sons in my time and you're not one of 'em.

*(Long pause. VINCE stares at DODGE then looks at TILDEN. He turns to SHELLY.)*

VINCE: Shelly, I gotta go out for a while. I just gotta go out. I'll get a bottle and I'll come right back. You'll be o.k. here. Really.

SHELLY: I don't know if I can handle this, Vince.

VINCE: I just gotta think or something. I don't know. I gotta put this all together.

970 SHELLY: Can't we just go?

VINCE: No! I gotta find out what's going on.

SHELLY: Look, you think you're bad off, what about me? Not only don't they recognize me but I've never seen them before in my life. I don't know who these guys are. They could be anybody!

VINCE: They're not anybody!

SHELLY: That's what you say.

VINCE: They're my family for Christ's sake! I should know who my own family is! Now give me a break. It won't take that

980 long. I'll just go out and I'll come right back. Nothing'll happen. I promise.

*(SHELLY stares at him. Pause)*

SHELLY: All right.

VINCE: Thanks. *(he crosses up to DODGE)* I'm gonna go out now, Grandpa, and I'll pick you up a bottle. Okay?

DODGE: Change of heart huh? *(pointing off left)* Money's on the table. In the kitchen.

*(VINCE moves toward SHELLY.)*

VINCE: *(to SHELLY)* You be all right?

SHELLY: *(cutting carrots)* Sure. I'm fine. I'll just keep busy while you're gone.

*(VINCE looks at TILDEN who keeps staring down at SHELLY's hands.)*

990 DODGE: Persistence see? That's what it takes. Persistence. Persistence, fortitude and determination. Those are the three virtues. You stick with those three and you can't go wrong.

VINCE: *(to TILDEN)* You want anything, Dad?

TILDEN: *(looks up at VINCE)* Me?

VINCE: From the store? I'm gonna get Grandpa a bottle.

TILDEN: He's not supposed to drink. Halie wouldn't like it.

VINCE: He wants a bottle.

TILDEN: He's not supposed to drink.

DODGE: *(to VINCE)* Don't negotiate with him! Don't make any

1000 transactions until you've spoken to me first! He'll steal

you blind!

VINCE: *(to DODGE)* Tilden says you're not supposed to drink.

DODGE: Tilden's lost his marbles! Look at him! He's around the bend. Take a look at him.

*(VINCE stares at TILDEN. TILDEN watches SHELLY's hands as she keeps cutting carrots.)*

DODGE: Now look at me. Look here at me!

*(VINCE looks back to DODGE)*

DODGE: Now, between the two of us, who do you think is more trustworthy? Him or me? Can you trust a man who keeps bringing in vegetables from out of nowhere? Take a look at him.

*(VINCE looks back at TILDEN.)*

SHELLY: Go get the bottle, Vince.   1010

VINCE: *(to SHELLY)* You sure you'll be all right?

SHELLY: I'll be fine. I feel right at home now.

VINCE: You do?

SHELLY: I'm fine. Now that I've got the carrots everything is all right.

VINCE: I'll be right back.

*(VINCE crosses stage left.)*

DODGE: Where are you going?

VINCE: I'm going to get the money.

DODGE: Then where are you going?

VINCE: Liquor store.   1020

DODGE: Don't go anyplace else. Don't go off some place and drink. come right back here.

VINCE: I will.

*(VINCE exits stage left.)*

DODGE: *(calling after VINCE)* You've got responsibility now! And don't go out the back way either! Come out through this way! I wanna' see you when you leave! Don't go out the back!

VINCE'S VOICE: *(off left)* I won't!

*(DODGE turns and looks at TILDEN and SHELLY.)*

DODGE: Untrustworthy. Probably drown himself if he went out the back. Fall right in a hole. I'd never get my bottle.   1030

SHELLY: I wouldn't worry about Vince. He can take care of himself.

DODGE: Oh he can, huh? Independent.

*(VINCE comes on again from stage left with two dollars in his hand. He crosses stage right past DODGE.)*

DODGE: *(to VINCE)* You got the money?

VINCE: Yeah. Two bucks.

DODGE: Two bucks. Two bucks is two bucks. Don't sneer.

VINCE: What kind do you want?

DODGE: Whiskey! Gold Star Sour Mash. Use your own discretion.

VINCE: Okay.   1040

*(VINCE crosses to stage right door. Opens it. Stops when he hears TILDEN.)*

TILDEN: *(to VINCE)* You drove all the way from New Mexico?

(VINCE *turns and looks at* TILDEN. *They stare at each other.* VINCE *shakes his head, goes out the door, crosses porch and exits out screen door.* TILDEN *watches him go. Pause.*)

SHELLY: You really don't recognize him? Either one of you?

(TILDEN *turns again and stares at* SHELLY'S *hands as she cuts carrots.*)

DODGE: (*watching T.V.*) Recognize who?
SHELLY: Vince.
DODGE: What's to recognize?

(DODGE *lights a cigarette, coughs slightly and stares at T.V.*)

SHELLY: It'd be cruel if you recognized him and didn't tell him. Wouldn't be fair.

(DODGE *just stares at T.V., smoking.*)

TILDEN: I thought I recognized him. I thought I recognized something about him.
1050 SHELLY: You did?
TILDEN: I thought I saw a face inside his face.
SHELLY: Well it was probably that you saw what he used to look like. You haven't seen him for six years.
TILDEN: I haven't?
SHELLY: That's what he says.

(TILDEN *moves around in front of her as she continues with carrots.*)

TILDEN: Where was it I saw him last?
SHELLY: I don't know. I've only known him for a few months. He doesn't tell me everything.
TILDEN: He doesn't?
1060 SHELLY: Not stuff like that.
TILDEN: What does he tell you?
SHELLY: You mean in general?
TILDEN: Yeah.

(TILDEN *moves around behind her.*)

SHELLY: Well he tells me all kinds of things.
TILDEN: Like what?
SHELLY: I don't know! I mean I can't just come right out and tell you how he feels.
TILDEN: How come?

(TILDEN *keeps moving around her slowly in a circle.*)

SHELLY: Because it's stuff he told me privately!
1070 TILDEN: And you can't tell me?
SHELLY: I don't even know you!
DODGE: Tilden, go out in the kitchen and make me some coffee! Leave the girl alone.
SHELLY: (*to* DODGE) He's all right.

(TILDEN *ignores* DODGE, *keeps moving around* SHELLY. *He stares at her hair and coat.* DODGE *stares at T.V.*)

TILDEN: You mean you can't tell me anything?
SHELLY: I can tell you some things. I mean we can have a conversation.
TILDEN: We can?
SHELLY: Sure. We're having a conversation right now.
1080 TILDEN: We are?

SHELLY: Yes. That's what we're doing.
TILDEN: But there's certain things you can't tell me, right?
SHELLY: Right.
TILDEN: There's certain things I can't tell you either.
SHELLY: How come?
TILDEN: I don't know. Nobody's supposed to hear it.
SHELLY: Well, you can tell me anything you want to.
TILDEN: I can?
SHELLY: Sure.
TILDEN: It might not be very nice.    1090
SHELLY: That's all right. I've been around.
TILDEN: It might be awful.
SHELLY: Well, can't you tell me anything nice?

(TILDEN *stops in front of her and stares at her coat.* SHELLY *looks back at him. Long pause.*)

TILDEN: (*after pause*) Can I touch your coat?
SHELLY: My coat? (*she looks at her coat then back to* TILDEN.) Sure.
TILDEN: You don't mind?
SHELLY: No. Go ahead.

(SHELLY *holds her arm out for* TILDEN *to touch.* DODGE *stays fixed on T.V.* TILDEN *moves in slowly toward* SHELLY, *staring at her arm. He reaches out very slowly and touches her arm, feels the fur gently then draws his hand back.* SHELLY *keeps her arm out.*)

SHELLY: It's rabbit.
TILDEN: Rabbit.    1100

(*He reaches out again very slowly and touches the fur on her arm then pulls back his hand again.* SHELLY *drops her arm.*)

SHELLY: My arm was getting tired.
TILDEN: Can I hold it?
SHELLY: (*pause*) The coat? Sure.

(SHELLY *takes off her coat and hands it to* TILDEN. TILDEN *takes it slowly, feels the fur then puts it on.* SHELLY *watches as* TILDEN *strokes the fur slowly. He smiles at her. She goes back to cutting carrots.*)

SHELLY: You can have it if you want.
TILDEN: I can?
SHELLY: Yeah. I've got a raincoat in the car. That's all I need.
TILDEN: You've got a car?
SHELLY: Vince does.

(TILDEN *walks around stroking the fur and smiling at the coat.* SHELLY *watches him when he's not looking.* DODGE *sticks with T.V., stretches out on sofa wrapped in blanket.*)

TILDEN: (*as he walks around*) I had a car once! I had a white car! I drove. I went everywhere. I went to the mountains. I 1110 drove in the snow.
SHELLY: That must've been fun.
TILDEN: (*still moving, feeling coat*) I drove all day long sometimes. Across the desert. Way out across the desert. I drove past towns. Anywhere. Past palm trees. Lightning. Anything. I would drive through it. I would drive through it and I would stop and I would look around and I would drive on. I would get back in and drive! I loved to drive. There was nothing I loved more. Nothing I dreamed of was

1120 better than driving.

DODGE: *(eyes on T.V.)* Pipe down would ya'!

*(TILDEN stops. Stares at SHELLY.)*

SHELLY: Do you do much driving now?
TILDEN: Now? Now? I don't drive now.
SHELLY: How come?
TILDEN: I'm grown up now.
SHELLY: Grown up?
TILDEN: I'm not a kid.
SHELLY: You don't have to be a kid to drive.
TILDEN: It wasn't driving then.
1130 SHELLY: What was it?
TILDEN: Adventure. I went everywhere.
SHELLY: Well you can still do that.
TILDEN: Not now.
SHELLY: Why not?
TILDEN: I just told you. You don't understand anything. If I told you something you wouldn't understand it.
SHELLY: Told me what?
TILDEN: Told you something that's true.
SHELLY: Like what?
1140 TILDEN: Like a baby. Like a little tiny baby.
SHELLY: Like when you were little?
TILDEN: If I told you you'd make me give your coat back.
SHELLY: I won't. I promise. Tell me.
TILDEN: I can't. Dodge won't let me.
SHELLY: He won't hear you. It's okay.

*(Pause. TILDEN stares at her. Moves slightly toward her.)*

TILDEN: We had a baby. *(motioning to DODGE)* He did. Dodge did. Could pick it up with one hand. Put it in the other. Little baby. Dodge killed it.

*(SHELLY stands.)*

TILDEN: Don't stand up. Don't stand up!

*(SHELLY sits again. DODGE sits up on sofa and looks at them)*

1150 TILDEN: Dodge drowned it.
SHELLY: Don't tell me anymore! Okay?

*(TILDEN moves closer to her. DODGE takes more interest.)*

DODGE: Tilden? You leave that girl alone!
TILDEN: *(pays no attention)* Never told Halie. Never told anybody. Just drowned it.
DODGE: *(shuts off T.V.)* Tilden!
TILDEN: Nobody could find it. Just disappeared. Cops looked for it. Neighbors. Nobody could find it.

*(DODGE struggles to get up from sofa.)*

DODGE: Tilden, what're you telling her! Tilden!

*(DODGE keeps struggling until he's standing.)*

TILDEN: Finally everybody just gave up. Just stopped looking.
1160 Everybody had a different answer. Kidnap. Murder. Accident. Some kind of accident.

*(DODGE struggles to walk toward TILDEN and falls. TILDEN ignores him.)*

DODGE: Tilden you shut up! You shut up about it!

*(DODGE starts coughing on the floor. SHELLY watches him from the stool.)*

TILDEN: Little tiny baby just disappeared. It's not hard. It's so small. Almost invisible.

*(SHELLY makes a move to help DODGE. TILDEN firmly pushes her back down on the stool. DODGE keeps coughing.)*

TILDEN: He said he had his reasons. Said it went a long way back. But he wouldn't tell anybody.
DODGE: Tilden! Don't tell her anything! Don't tell her!
TILDEN: He's the only one who knows where it's buried. The only one. Like a secret buried treasure. Won't tell any of us. Won't tell me or mother or even 1170 Bradley. Especially Bradley. Bradley tried to force it out of him but he wouldn't tell. Wouldn't even tell why he did it. One night he just did it.

*(DODGE's coughing subsides. SHELLY stays on stool staring at DODGE. TILDEN slowly takes SHELLY's coat off and holds it out to her. Long pause. SHELLY sits there trembling.)*

TILDEN: You probably want your coat back now.

*(SHELLY stares at coat but doesn't move to take it. The sound of BRADLEY's leg squeaking is heard off left. The others on stage remain still. BRADLEY appears up left outside the screen door wearing a yellow rain slicker. He enters through screen door, crosses porch to stage right door and enters stage. Closes door. Takes off rain slicker and shakes it out. He sees all the others and stops. TILDEN turns to him. BRADLEY stares at SHELLY. DODGE remains on floor.)*

BRADLEY: What's going on here? *(motioning to SHELLY)* Who's that?

*(SHELLY stands, moves back away from BRADLEY as he crosses toward her. He stops next to TILDEN. He sees coat in TILDEN's hand and grabs it away from him.)*

BRADLEY: Who's she supposed to be?
TILDEN: She's driving to New Mexico.

*(BRADLEY stares at her. SHELLY is frozen. BRADLEY limps over to her with the coat in his fist. He stops in front of her.)*

BRADLEY: *(to SHELLY, after pause)* Vacation?

*(SHELLY shakes her head "no," trembling.)*

BRADLEY: *(to SHELLY, motioning to TILDEN)* You taking him 1180 with you?

*(SHELLY shakes her head "no." BRADLEY crosses back to TILDEN.)*

BRADLEY: You oughta'. No use leaving him here. Doesn't do a lick a' work. Doesn't raise a finger. *(stopping, to TILDEN)* Do ya'? *(to SHELLY)* 'Course he used to be an All American. Quarterback or Fullback or somethin'. He tell you that?

*(SHELLY shakes her head "no.")*

BRADLEY: Yeah, he used to be a big deal. Wore lettermen's sweaters. Had medals hanging all around his neck. Real purty. Big deal. *(he laughs to himself, notices DODGE on floor, crosses to him, stops)* This one too. *(to SHELLY)* You'd

1190     never think it to look at him would ya'? All bony and wasted away.

(SHELLY *shakes her head again.* BRADLEY *stares at her, crosses back to her, clenching the coat in his fist. He stops in front of* SHELLY.)

BRADLEY: Women like that kinda' thing don't they?
SHELLY: What?
BRADLEY: Importance. Importance in a man?
SHELLY: I don't know.
BRADLEY: Yeah. You know, you know. Don't give me that. (*moves closer to* SHELLY) You're with Tilden?
SHELLY: No.
BRADLEY: (*turning to* TILDEN) Tilden! She with you?

(TILDEN *doesn't answer. Stares at floor.*)

1200 BRADLEY: Tilden!

(TILDEN *suddenly bolts and runs off up stage left.* BRADLEY *laughs. Talks to* SHELLY. DODGE *starts moving his lips silently as though talking to someone invisible on the floor.*)

BRADLEY: (*laughing*) Scared to death! He was always scared!

(BRADLEY *stops laughing. Stares at* SHELLY.)

BRADLEY: You're scared too, right? (*laughs again*) You're scared and you don't even know me. (*stops laughing*) You don't gotta be scared.

(SHELLY *looks at* DODGE *on the floor.*)

SHELLY: Can't we do something for him?
BRADLEY: (*looking at* DODGE) We could shoot him. (*laughs*) We could drown him! What about drowning him?
SHELLY: Shut up!

(BRADLEY *stops laughing. Moves in closer to* SHELLY. *She freezes.* BRADLEY *speaks slowly and deliberately.*)

BRADLEY: Hey! Missus. Don't talk to me like that. Don't talk to
1210     me in that tone a' voice. There was a time when I had to take that tone a' voice from pretty near everyone. (*motioning to* DODGE) Him, for one! Him and that half brain that just ran outa' here. They don't talk to me like that now. Not any more. Everything's turned around now. Full circle. Isn't that funny?
SHELLY: I'm sorry.
BRADLEY: Open your mouth.
SHELLY: What?
BRADLEY: (*motioning for her to open her mouth*) Open up.

(She opens her mouth slightly.)

1220 BRADLEY: Wider.

(She opens her mouth wider.)

BRADLEY: Keep it like that.

(She does. Stares at BRADLEY. With his free hand he puts his fingers into her mouth. She tries to pull away.)

BRADLEY: Just stay put!

(She freezes. He keeps his fingers in her mouth. Stares at her. Pause. He pulls his hand out. She closes her mouth, keeps her

eyes on him. BRADLEY *smiles. He looks at* DODGE *on the floor and crosses over to him.* SHELLY *watches him closely.* BRADLEY *stands over* DODGE *and smiles at* SHELLY. *He holds her coat up in both hands over* DODGE, *keeps smiling at* SHELLY. *He looks down at* DODGE *then drops the coat so that it lands on* DODGE *and covers his head.* BRADLEY *keeps his hands up in the position of holding the coat, looks over at* SHELLY *and smiles. The lights black out.*)

## —ACT THREE—

SCENE: *Same set. Morning. Bright sun. No sound of rain. Everything has been cleared up again. No sign of carrots. No pail. No stool.* VINCE'S *saxophone case and overcoat are still at the foot of the staircase.* BRADLEY *is asleep on the sofa under* DODGE'S *blanket. His head toward stage left.* BRADLEY'S *wooden leg is leaning against the sofa right by his head. The shoe is left on it. The harness hangs down.* DODGE *is sitting on the floor, propped up against the T.V. set facing stage left wearing his baseball cap.* SHELLY'S *rabbit fur coat covers his chest and shoulders. He stares off toward stage left. He seems weaker and more disoriented. The lights rise slowly to the sound of birds and remain for a while in silence on the two men.* BRADLEY *sleeps very soundly.* DODGE *hardly moves.* SHELLY *appears from stage left with a big smile, slowly crossing toward* DODGE *balancing a steaming cup of broth in a saucer.* DODGE *just stares at her as she gets closer to him.*

SHELLY: (*as she crosses*) This is going to make all the difference in the world, Grandpa. You don't mind me calling you Grandpa do you? I mean I know you minded when Vince called you that but you don't even know him.
DODGE: He skipped town with my money ya' know. I'm gonna hold you as collateral.
SHELLY: He'll be back. Don't you worry.

(She kneels down next to DODGE and puts the cup and saucer in his lap.)

DODGE: It's morning already! Not only didn't I get my bottle 1230 but he's got my two bucks!
SHELLY: Try to drink this, okay? Don't spill it.
DODGE: What is it?
SHELLY: Beef bouillon. It'll warm you up.
DODGE: Bouillon! I don't want any goddamn bouillon! Get that stuff away from me!
SHELLY: I just got through making it.
DODGE: I don't care if you just spent all week making it! I ain't drinking it!
SHELLY: Well, what am I supposed to do with it then? I'm try- 1240 ing to help you. Besides, it's good for you.
DODGE: Get it away from me!

(SHELLY *stands up with cup and saucer.*)

DODGE: What do you know what's good for me anyway?

(She looks at DODGE then turns away from him, crossing to staircase, sits on bottom step and drinks the bouillon. DODGE stares at her.)

DODGE: You know what'd be good for me?

SHELLY: What?

DODGE: A little massage. A little contact.

SHELLY: Oh no. I've had enough contact for a while. Thanks anyway.

(*She keeps sipping bouillon, stays sitting. Pause as* DODGE *stares at her.*)

DODGE: Why not? You got nothing better to do. That fella's not
1250   gonna be back here. You're not expecting him to show up again are you?

SHELLY: Sure. He'll show up. He left his horn here.

DODGE: His horn? (*laughs*) You're his horn!

SHELLY: Very funny.

DODGE: He's run off with my money? He's not coming back. There.

SHELLY: He'll be back.

DODGE: You're a funny chicken, you know that?

SHELLY: Thanks.

1260  DODGE: Full of faith. Hope. Faith and hope. You're all alike you hopers. If it's not God then it's a man. If it's not a man then it's a woman. If it's not a woman then it's the land or the future of some kind. Some kind of future.

(*Pause.*)

SHELLY: (*looking toward porch*) I'm glad it stopped raining.

DODGE: (*looks toward porch then back to her*) That's what I mean. See, you're glad it stopped raining. Now you think everything's gonna be different. Just 'cause the sun comes out.

SHELLY: It's already different. Last night I was scared.

1270  DODGE: Scared a' what?

SHELLY: Just scared.

DODGE: Bradley? (*looks at* BRADLEY) He's a push-over. 'Specially now. All ya' gotta' do is take his leg and throw it out the back door. Helpless. Totally helpless.

(SHELLY *turns and stares at* BRADLEY's *wooden leg then looks at* DODGE. *She sips bouillon.*)

SHELLY: You'd do that?

DODGE: Me? I've hardly got the strength to breathe.

SHELLY: But you'd actually do it if you could?

DODGE: Don't be so easily shocked, girlie. There's nothing a man can't do. You dream it up and he can do it. Anything.

1280  SHELLY: You've tried I guess.

DODGE: Don't sit there sippin' your bouillon and judging me! This is my house!

SHELLY: I forgot.

DODGE: You forgot? Whose house did you think it was?

SHELLY: Mine.

(DODGE *just stares at her. Long pause. She sips from cup.*)

SHELLY: I know it's not mine but I had that feeling.

DODGE: What feeling?

SHELLY: The feeling that nobody lives here but me. I mean everybody's gone. You're here, but it doesn't seem like
1290   you're supposed to be. (*pointing to* BRADLEY) Doesn't seem like he's supposed to be here either. I don't know what it is. It's the house or something. Something familiar. Like I know my way around here. Did you ever get that feeling?

(DODGE *stares at her in silence. Pause.*)

DODGE: No. No, I never did.

(SHELLY *gets up. Moves around space holding cup.*)

SHELLY: Last night I went to sleep up there in that room.

DODGE: What room?

SHELLY: That room up there with all the pictures. All the crosses on the wall.

DODGE: Halie's room?

SHELLY: Yeah. Whoever "Halie" is.                            1300

DODGE: She's my wife.

SHELLY: So you remember her?

DODGE: Whad'ya mean! 'Course I remember her! She's only been gone for a day—half a day. However long it's been.

SHELLY: Do you remember her when her hair was bright red? Standing in front of an apple tree?

DODGE: What is this, the third degree or something! Who're you to be askin' me personal questions about my wife!

SHELLY: You never look at those pictures up there?

DODGE: What pictures?                                        1310

SHELLY: Your whole life's up there hanging on the wall. Somebody who looks just like you. Somebody who looks just like you used to look.

DODGE: That isn't me! That never was me! This is me. Right here. This is it. The whole shootin' match, sittin' right in front of you.

SHELLY: So the past never happened as far as you're concerned?

DODGE: The past? Jesus Christ. The past. What do you know about the past?                                            1320

SHELLY: Not much. I know there was a farm.

(*Pause.*)

DODGE: A farm?

SHELLY: There's a picture of a farm. A big farm. A bull. Wheat. Corn.

DODGE: Corn?

SHELLY: All the kids are standing out in the corn. They're all waving these big straw hats. One of them doesn't have a hat.

DODGE: Which one was that?

SHELLY: There's a baby. A baby in a woman's arms. The same woman with the red hair. She looks lost standing out there.   1330
Like she doesn't know how she got there.

DODGE: She knows! I told her a hundred times it wasn't gonna' be the city! I gave her plenty a' warning.

SHELLY: She's looking down at the baby like it was somebody else's. Like it didn't even belong to her.

DODGE: That's about enough outa' you! You got some funny ideas. Some damn funny ideas. You think just because people propagate they have to love their offspring? You never seen a bitch eat her puppies? Where are you from anyway?                                                       1340

SHELLY: L.A. We already went through that.

DODGE: That's right, L.A. I remember.

SHELLY: Stupid country.

DODGE: That's right! No wonder.

(*Pause.*)

SHELLY: What's happened to this family anyway?

DODGE: You're in no position to ask! What do you care? You some kinda' Social Worker?

SHELLY: I'm Vince's friend.

DODGE: Vince's friend! That's rich. That's really rich. "Vince"!
"Mr. Vince"! "Mr. Thief" is more like it! His name doesn't
mean a hoot in hell to me. Not a tinkle in the well. You know
how many kids I've spawned? Not to mention Grand kids
and Great Grand kids and Great Great Grand kids after
them?

SHELLY: And you don't remember any of them?

DODGE: What's to remember? Halie's the one with the family
album. She's the one you should talk to. She'll set you
straight on the heritage if that's what you're interested in.
She's traced it all the way back to the grave.

SHELLY: What do you mean?

DODGE: What do you think I mean? How far back can you go?
A long line of corpses! There's not a living soul behind me.
Not a one. Who's holding me in their memory? Who gives a
damn about bones in the ground?

SHELLY: Was Tilden telling the truth?

(DODGE *stops short. Stares at* SHELLY. *Shakes his head. He
looks off stage left.*)

SHELLY: Was he?

(DODGE's *tone changes drastically.*)

DODGE: Tilden? (*turns to* SHELLY, *calmly*) Where is Tilden?

SHELLY: Last night. Was he telling the truth about the baby?

(*Pause.*)

DODGE: (*turns toward stage left*) What's happened to Tilden?
Why isn't Tilden here?

SHELLY: Bradley chased him out.

DODGE: (*looking at* BRADLEY *asleep*) Bradley? Why is he on my
sofa? (*turns back to* SHELLY) Have I been here all night? On
the floor?

SHELLY: He wouldn't leave. I hid outside until he fell asleep.

DODGE: Outside? Is Tilden outside? He shouldn't be out there
in the rain. He'll get himself into trouble. He doesn't know
his way around here anymore. Not like he used to. He went
out West and got himself into trouble. Got himself into bad
trouble. We don't want any of that around here.

SHELLY: What did he do?

(*Pause.*)

DODGE: (*quietly stares at* SHELLY) Tilden? He got mixed up.
That's what he did. We can't afford to leave him alone. Not
now.

(*Sound of* HALIE *laughing comes from off left.* SHELLY *stands,
looking in direction of voice, holding cup and saucer, doesn't
know whether to stay or run.*)

DODGE: (*motioning to* SHELLY) Sit down! Sit back down!

(SHELLY *sits. Sound of* HALIE's *laughter again.*)

DODGE: (*to* SHELLY *in a heavy whisper, pulling coat up around
him*) Don't leave me alone now! Promise me? Don't go off
and leave me alone. I need somebody here with me.
Tilden's gone now and I need someone. Don't leave me!
Promise!

SHELLY: (*sitting*) I won't.

(HALIE *appears outside the screen porch door, up left with*
FATHER DEWIS. *She is wearing a bright yellow dress, no hat,*

white gloves and her arms are full of yellow roses. FATHER
DEWIS *is dressed in traditional black suit, white clerical collar
and shirt. He is a very distinguished grey haired man in his sixties. They are both slightly drunk and feeling giddy. As they
enter the porch through the screen door,* DODGE *pulls the rabbit fur coat over his head and hides.* SHELLY *stands again.*
DODGE *drops the coat and whispers intensely to* SHELLY. *Neither* HALIE *nor* FATHER DEWIS *are aware of the people inside
the house.*)

DODGE: (*to* SHELLY *in a strong whisper*) You promised!

(SHELLY *sits on stairs again.* DODGE *pulls coat back over his
head.* HALIE *and* FATHER DEWIS *talk on the porch as they cross
toward stage right interior door.*)

HALIE: Oh Father! That's terrible! That's absolutely terrible.
Aren't you afraid of being punished?

(*She giggles*)

DEWIS: Not by the Italians. They're too busy punishing each
other.

(*They both break out in giggles.*)

HALIE: What about God?

DEWIS: Well, prayerfully, God only hears what he wants to.
That's just between you and me of course. In our heart of
hearts we know we're every bit as wicked as the Catholics.

(*They giggle again and reach the stage right door.*)

HALIE: Father, I never heard you talk like this in Sunday sermon.

DEWIS: Well, I save all my best jokes for private company.
Pearls before swine you know.

(*They enter the room laughing and stop when they see* SHELLY.
SHELLY *stands.* HALIE *closes the door behind* FATHER DEWIS.
DODGE's *voice is heard under the coat, talking to* SHELLY.)

DODGE: (*under coat, to* SHELLY) Sit down, sit down! Don't let
'em buffalo you!

(SHELLY *sits on stair again.* HALIE *looks at* DODGE *on the floor
then looks at* BRADLEY *asleep on sofa and sees his wooden leg.
She lets out a shriek of embarrassment for* FATHER DEWIS.)

HALIE: Oh my gracious! What in the name of Judas Priest is
going on in this house!

(*She hands over the roses to* FATHER DEWIS.)

HALIE: Excuse me Father.

(HALIE *crosses to* DODGE, *whips the coat off him and covers the
wooden leg with it.* BRADLEY *stays asleep.*)

HALIE: You can't leave this house for a second without the
Devil blowing in through the front door!

DODGE: Gimme back that coat! Gimme back that goddamn
coat before I freeze to death!

HALIE: You're not going to freeze! The sun's out in case you
hadn't noticed!

DODGE: Gimme back that coat! That coat's for live flesh not
dead wood!

(HALIE *whips the blanket off* BRADLEY *and throws it on* DODGE.
DODGE *covers his head again with blanket.* BRADLEY's

*amputated leg can be faked by having half of it under a cush-
ion of the sofa. He's fully clothed.* BRADLEY *sits up with a jerk
when the blanket comes off him.*)

HALIE: (*as she tosses blanket*) Here! Use this! It's yours anyway!
Can't you take care of yourself for once!

1420 BRADLEY: (*yelling at* HALIE) Gimme that blanket! Gimme back
that blanket! That's my blanket!

(HALIE *crosses back toward* FATHER DEWIS *who just stands
there with the roses.* BRADLEY *thrashes helplessly on the sofa,
trying to reach blanket.* DODGE *hides himself deeper in blanket.* SHELLY *looks on from staircase, still holding cup and
saucer.*)

HALIE: Believe me, Father, this is not what I had in mind when
I invited you in.

DEWIS: Oh, no apologies please. I wouldn't be in the ministry
if I couldn't face real life.

(*He laughs self-consciously.* HALIE *notices* SHELLY *again and
crosses over to her.* SHELLY *stays sitting.* HALIE *stops and stares
at her.*)

BRADLEY: I want my blanket back! Gimme my blanket!

(HALIE *turns toward* BRADLEY *and silences him.*)

HALIE: Shut up, Bradley! Right this minute! I've had enough!

(BRADLEY *slowly recoils, lies back down on sofa, turns his back
toward* HALIE *and whimpers softly.* HALIE *directs her attention
to* SHELLY *again. Pause.*)

HALIE: (*to* SHELLY) What're you doing with my cup and saucer?
SHELLY: (*looking at cup, back to* HALIE) I made some bouillon
1430 for Dodge.
HALIE: For Dodge?
SHELLY: Yeah.
HALIE: Well, did he drink it?
SHELLY: No.
HALIE: Did you drink it?
SHELLY: Yes.

(HALIE *stares at her. Long pause. She turns abruptly away
from* SHELLY *and crosses back to* FATHER DEWIS.)

HALIE: Father, there's a stranger in my house. What would you
advise? What would be the Christian thing?
DEWIS: (*squirming*) Oh, well. . . . I. . . . I really—
1440 HALIE: We still have some whiskey, don't we?

(DODGE *slowly pulls the blanket down off his head and looks
toward* FATHER DEWIS. SHELLY *stands.*)

SHELLY: Listen, I don't drink or anything. I just—

(HALIE *turns toward* SHELLY *viciously.*)

HALIE: You sit back down!

(SHELLY *sits again on stair.* HALIE *turns again to* DEWIS)

HALIE: I think we have plenty of whiskey left! Don't we Father?
DEWIS: Well, yes. I think so. You'll have to get it. My hands are
full.

(HALIE *giggles. Reaches into* DEWIS's *pockets, searching for
bottle. She smells the roses as she searches.* DEWIS *stands stiffly.*

DODGE *watches* HALIE *closely as she looks for bottle.*)

HALIE: The most incredible things, roses! Aren't they incredible, Father?
DEWIS: Yes. Yes they are.
HALIE: They almost cover the stench of sin in this house. Just 1450
magnificent! The smell. We'll have to put some at the foot
of Ansel's statue. On the day of the unveiling.

(HALIE *finds a silver flask of whiskey in* DEWIS's *vest pocket.
She pulls it out.* DODGE *looks on eagerly.* HALIE *crosses to*
DODGE, *opens the flask and takes a sip.*)

HALIE: (*to* DODGE) Ansel's getting a statue, Dodge. Did you
know that? Not a plaque but a real live statue. A full bronze.
Tip to toe. A basketball in one hand and a rifle in the other.
BRADLEY: (*his back to* HALIE) He never played basketball!
HALIE: You shut up, Bradley! You shut up about Ansel! Ansel
played basketball better than anyone! And you know it! He
was an All American! There's no reason to take the glory
away from others.                                              1460

(HALIE *turns away from* BRADLEY, *crosses back toward* DEWIS
*sipping on the flask and smiling.*)

HALIE: (*to* DEWIS) Ansel was a great basketball player. One of
the greatest.
DEWIS: I remember Ansel.
HALIE: Of course! You remember. You remember how he
could play. (*she turns toward* SHELLY) Of course, nowadays
they play a different brand of basketball. More vicious. Isn't
that right, dear?
SHELLY: I don't know.

(HALIE *crosses to* SHELLY, *sipping on flask. She stops in front of*
SHELLY.)

HALIE: Much, much more vicious. They smash into each other.
They knock each other's teeth out. There's blood all over 1470
the court. Savages.

(HALIE *takes the cup from* SHELLY *and pours whiskey into it.*)

HALIE: They don't train like they used to. Not at all. They allow
themselves to run amuck. Drugs and women. Women
mostly.

(HALIE *hands the cup of whiskey back to* SHELLY *slowly.*
SHELLY *takes it.*)

HALIE: Mostly women. Girls. Sad, pathetic little girls. (*she
crosses back to* FATHER DEWIS) It's just a reflection of the
times, don't you think Father? An indication of where we
stand?
DEWIS: I suppose so, yes.
HALIE: Yes. A sort of a bad omen. Our youth becoming mon- 1480
sters.
DEWIS: Well, I uh—
HALIE: Oh you can disagree with me if you want to, Father. I'm
open to debate. I think argument only enriches both sides of
the question don't you? (*she moves toward* DODGE) I suppose, in the long run, it doesn't matter. When you see the
way things deteriorate before your very eyes. Everything
running down hill. It's kind of silly to even think about
youth.
DEWIS: No, I don't think so. I think it's important to believe in 1490

certain things.

HALIE: Yes. Yes, I know what you mean. I think that's right. I think that's true. (*she looks at* DODGE) Certain basic things. We can't shake certain basic things. We might end up crazy. Like my husband. You can see it in his eyes. You can see how mad he is.

(DODGE *covers his head with the blanket again.* HALIE *takes a single rose from* DEWIS *and moves slowly over to* DODGE.)

HALIE: We can't not believe in something. We can't stop believing. We just end up dying if we stop. Just end up dead.

(HALIE *throws the rose gently onto* DODGE'S *blanket. It lands between his knees and stays there. Long pause as* HALIE *stares at the rose.* SHELLY *stands suddenly.* HALIE *doesn't turn to her but keeps staring at rose.*)

SHELLY: (*to* HALIE) Don't you wanna' know who I am! Don't
1500    you wanna know what I'm doing here? I'm not dead!

(SHELLY *crosses toward* HALIE. HALIE *turns slowly toward her.*)

HALIE: Did you drink your whiskey?

SHELLY: No! And I'm not going to either!

HALIE: Well that's a firm stand. It's good to have a firm stand.

SHELLY: I don't have any stand at all. I'm just trying to put all this together.

(HALIE *laughs and crosses back to* DEWIS.)

HALIE: (*to* DEWIS) Surprises, surprises! Did you have any idea we'd be returning to this?

SHELLY: I came here with your Grandson for a little visit! A little innocent friendly visit.

1510    HALIE: My Grandson?

SHELLY: Yes! That's right. The one no one remembers.

HALIE: (*to* DEWIS) This is getting a little far fetched.

SHELLY: I told him it was stupid to come back here. To try to pick up from where he left off.

HALIE: Where was that?

SHELLY: Wherever he was when he left here! Six years ago! Ten years ago! Whenever it was. I told him nobody cares.

HALIE: Didn't he listen?

SHELLY: No! No he didn't. We had to stop off at every tiny lit-
1520    tle meatball town that he remembered from his boyhood! Every stupid little donut shop he ever kissed a girl in. Every Drive-In. Every Drag Strip. Every football field he ever broke a bone on.

HALIE: (*suddenly alarmed, to* DODGE) Where's Tilden?

SHELLY: Don't ignore me!

HALIE: Dodge! Where's Tilden gone?

(SHELLY *moves violently toward* HALIE.)

SHELLY: (*to* HALIE) I'm talking to you!

(BRADLEY *sits up fast on the sofa,* SHELLY *backs away.*)

BRADLEY: (*to* SHELLY) Don't you yell at my mother!

HALIE: Dodge! (*she kicks* DODGE) I told you not to let Tilden
1530    out of your sight! Where's he gone to?

DODGE: Gimme a drink and I'll yell ya'.

DEWIS: Halie, maybe this isn't the right time for a visit.

(HALIE *crosses back to* DEWIS.)

HALIE: (*to* DEWIS) I never should've left. I never, never

should've left! Tilden could be anywhere by now! Anywhere! He's not in control of his faculties. Dodge knew that. I told him when I left here. I told him specifically to watch out for Tilden.

(BRADLEY *reaches down, grabs* DODGE'S *blanket and yanks it off him. He lays down on sofa and pulls the blanket over his head.*)

DODGE: He's got my blanket again! He's got my blanket!

HALIE: (*turning to* BRADLEY) Bradley! Bradley, put that blanket back!                                                              1540

(HALIE *moves toward* BRADLEY. SHELLY *suddenly throws the cup and saucer against the stage right door.* DEWIS *ducks. The cup and saucer smash into pieces.* HALIE *stops, turns toward* SHELLY. *Everyone freezes.* BRADLEY *slowly pulls his head out from under blanket, looks toward stage right door, then to* SHELLY. SHELLY *stares at* HALIE. DEWIS *cowers with roses.* SHELLY *moves slowly toward* HALIE. *Long pause.* SHELLY *speaks softly.*)

SHELLY: (*to* HALIE) I don't like being ignored. I don't like being treated like I'm not here. I didn't like it when I was a kid and I still don't like it.

BRADLEY: (*sitting up on sofa*) We don't have to tell you anything, girl. Not a thing. You're not the police are you? You're not the government. You're just some prostitute that Tilden brought in here.

HALIE: Language! I won't have that language in my house!

SHELLY: (*to* BRADLEY) You stuck your hand in my mouth and you call me a prostitute!                                                 1550

HALIE: Bradley! Did you put your hand in her mouth? I'm ashamed of you. I can't leave you alone for a minute.

BRADLEY: I never did. She's lying!

DEWIS: Halie, I think I'll be running along now. I'll just put the roses in the kitchen.

(DEWIS *moves toward stage left.* HALIE *stops him.*)

HALIE: Don't go now, Father! Not now.

BRADLEY: I never did anything, mom! I never touched her! She propositioned me! And I turned her down. I turned her down flat!

(SHELLY *suddenly grabs her coat off the wooden leg and takes both the leg and coat down stage, away from* BRADLEY.)

BRADLEY: Mom! Mom! She's got my leg! She's taken my leg! I  1560
never did anything to her! She's stolen my leg!

(BRADLEY *reaches pathetically in the air for his leg.* SHELLY *sets it down for a second, puts on her coat fast and picks the leg up again.* DODGE *starts coughing softly.*)

HALIE: (*to* SHELLY) I think we've had about enough of you young lady. Just about enough. I don't know where you came from or what you're doing here but you're no longer welcome in this house.

SHELLY: (*laughs, holds leg*) No longer welcome!

BRADLEY: Mom! That's my leg! Get my leg back! I can't do anything without my leg.

(BRADLEY *keeps making whimpering sounds and reaching for his leg.*)

HALIE: Give my son back his leg. Right this very minute!

*(DODGE starts laughing softly to himself in between coughs.)*

1570 HALIE: *(to DEWIS)* Father, do something about this would you! I'm not about to be terrorized in my own house!

BRADLEY: Gimme back my leg!

HALIE: Oh, shut up Bradley! Just shut up! You don't need your leg now! Just lay down and shut up!

*(BRADLEY whimpers. Lays down and pulls blanket around him. He keeps one arm outside blanket, reaching out toward his wooden leg. DEWIS cautiously approaches SHELLY with the roses in his arms. SHELLY clutches the wooden leg to her chest as though she's kidnapped it.)*

DEWIS: *(to SHELLY)* Now, honestly dear, wouldn't it be better to try to talk things out? To try to use some reason?

SHELLY: There isn't any reason here! I can't find a reason for anything.

DEWIS: There's nothing to be afraid of. These are all good peo-
1580   ple. All righteous people.

SHELLY: I'm not afraid!

DEWIS: But this isn't your house. You have to have some respect.

SHELLY: You're the strangers here, not me.

HALIE: This has gone far enough!

DEWIS: Halie, please. Let me handle this.

SHELLY: Don't come near me! Don't anyone come near me. I don't need any words from you. I'm not threatening anybody. I don't even know what I'm doing here. You all say you
1590   don't remember Vince, okay, maybe you don't. Maybe it's Vince that's crazy. Maybe he's made this whole family thing up. I don't even care anymore. I was just coming along for the ride. I thought it'd be a nice gesture. Besides, I was curious. He made all of you sound familiar to me. Every one of you. For every name, I had an image. Every time he'd tell me a name, I'd see the person. In fact, each of you was so clear in my mind that I actually believed it was you. I really believed when I walked through that door that the people who lived here would turn out to be the same people in my
1600   imagination. But I don't recognize any of you. Not one. Not even the slightest resemblance.

DEWIS: Well you can hardly blame others for not fulfilling your hallucination.

SHELLY: It was no hallucination! It was more like a prophecy. You believe in prophecy, don't you?

HALIE: Father, there's no point in talking to her any further. We're just going to have to call the police.

BRADLEY: No! Don't get the police in here. We don't want the police in here. This is our home.

1610 SHELLY: That's right. Bradley's right. Don't you usually settle your affairs in private? Don't you usually take them out in the dark? Out in the back?

BRADLEY: You stay out of our lives! You have no business interfering!

SHELLY: I don't have any business period. I got nothing to lose.

*(She moves around, staring at each of them.)*

BRADLEY: You don't know what we've been through. You don't know anything!

SHELLY: I know you've got a secret. You've all got a secret. It's so secret in fact, you're all convinced it never happened.

*(HALIE moves to DEWIS)*

HALIE: Oh, my God, Father!   1620

DODGE: *(laughing to himself)* She thinks she's going to get it out of us. She thinks she's going to uncover the truth of the matter. Like a detective or something.

BRADLEY: I'm not telling her anything! Nothing's wrong here! Nothing's ever been wrong! Everything's the way it's supposed to be! Nothing ever happened that's bad! Everything is all right here! We're all good people!

DODGE: She thinks she's gonna suddenly bring everything out into the open after all these years.

DEWIS: *(to SHELLY)* Can't you see that these people want to be   1630 left in peace? Don't you have any mercy? They haven't done anything to you.

DODGE: She wants to get to the bottom of it. *(to SHELLY)* That's it, isn't it? You'd like to get right down to bedrock? You want me to tell ya'? You want me to tell ya' what happened? I'll tell ya'. I might as well.

BRADLEY: No! Don't listen to him. He doesn't remember anything!

DODGE: I remember the whole thing from start to finish. I remember the day he was born.   1640

*(pause)*

HALIE: Dodge, if you tell this thing—if you tell this, you'll be dead to me. You'll be just as good as dead.

DODGE: That won't be such a big change, Halie. See this girl, this girl here, she wants to know. She wants to know something more. And I got this feeling that it doesn't make a bit a' difference. I'd sooner tell it to a stranger than anybody else.

BRADLEY: *(to DODGE)* We made a pact! We made a pact between us! You can't break that now!

DODGE: I don't remember any pact.   1650

BRADLEY: *(to SHELLY)* See, he doesn't remember anything. I'm the only one in the family who remembers. The only one. And I'll never tell you!

SHELLY: I'm not so sure I want to find out now.

DODGE: *(laughing to himself)* Listen to her! Now she's runnin' scared!

SHELLY: I'm not scared!

*(DODGE stops laughing, long pause. DODGE stares at her.)*

DODGE: You're not huh? Well, that's good. Because I'm not either. See, we were a well established family once. Well established. All the boys were grown. The farm was producing   1660 enough milk to fill Lake Michigan twice over. Me and Halie here were pointed toward what looked like the middle part of our life. Everything was settled with us. All we had to do was ride it out. Then Halie got pregnant again. Outa' the middle a' nowhere, she got pregnant. We weren't planning on havin' any more boys. We had enough boys already. In fact, we hadn't been sleepin' in the same bed for about six years.

HALIE: *(moving toward stairs)* I'm not listening to this! I don't have to listen to this!   1670

DODGE: *(stops HALIE)* Where are you going! Upstairs! You'll just be listenin' to it upstairs! You go outside, you'll be listenin' to it outside. Might as well stay here and listen to it.

*(HALIE stays by stairs)*

BRADLEY: If I had my leg you wouldn't be saying this. You'd

never get away with it if I had my leg.

DODGE: (*pointing to* SHELLY) She's got your leg. (*laughs*) She's gonna keep your leg too. (*to* SHELLY) She wants to hear this. Don't you?

SHELLY: I don't know.

1680 DODGE: Well even if ya' don't I'm gonna' tell ya'. (*pause*) Halie had this kid. This baby boy. She had it. I let her have it on her own. All the other boys I had had the best doctors, best nurses, everything. This one I let her have by herself. This one hurt real bad. Almost killed her, but she had it anyway. It lived, see. It lived. It wanted to grow up in this family. It wanted to be just like us. It wanted to be a part of us. It wanted to pretend that I was its father. She wanted me to believe in it. Even when everyone around us knew. Everyone. All our boys knew. Tilden knew.

1690 HALIE: You shut up! Bradley, make him shut up!

BRADLEY: I can't.

DODGE: Tilden was the one who knew. Better than any of us. He'd walk for miles with that kid in his arms. Halie let him take it. All night sometimes. He'd walk all night out there in the pasture with it. Talkin' to it. Singin' to it. Used to hear him singing to it. He'd make up stories. He'd tell that kid all kinds a' stories. Even when he knew it couldn't understand him. Couldn't understand a word he was sayin'. Never would understand him. We couldn't let a thing like that con-
1700 tinue. We couldn't allow that to grow up right in the middle of our lives. It made everything we'd accomplished look like it was nothin'. Everything was cancelled out by this one mistake. This one weakness.

SHELLY: So you killed him?

DODGE: I killed it. I drowned it. Just like the runt of a litter. Just drowned it.

(HALIE *moves toward* BRADLEY)

HALIE: (*to* BRADLEY) Ansel would've stopped him! Ansel would've stopped him from telling these lies! He was a hero! A man! A whole man! What's happened to the men in this
1710 family! Where are the men!

(*Suddenly* VINCE *comes crashing through the screen porch door up left, tearing it off its hinges. Everyone but* DODGE *and* BRADLEY *back away from the porch and stare at* VINCE *who has landed on his stomach on the porch in a drunken stupor. He is singing loudly to himself and hauls himself slowly to his feet. He has a paper shopping bag full of empty booze bottles. He takes them out one at a time as he sings and smashes them at the opposite end of the porch, behind the solid interior door, stage right.* SHELLY *moves slowly toward stage right, holding wooden leg and watching* VINCE.)

VINCE: (*singing loudly as he hurls bottles*) "From the Halls of Montezuma to the Shores of Tripoli. We will fight our country's battles on the land and on the sea."

(*He punctuates the words "Montezuma," "Tripoli," "battles" and "sea" with a smashed bottle each. He stops throwing for a second, stares toward stage right of the porch, shades his eyes with his hand as though looking across to a battle field, then cups his hands around his mouth and yells across the space of the porch to an imaginary army. The others watch in terror and expectation.*)

VINCE: (*to imagined Army*) Have you had enough over there! 'Cause there's a lot more here where that came from! (*pointing to paper bag full of bottles*) A helluva lot more! We got enough over here to blow ya' from here to Kingdom-come!

(*He takes another bottle, makes high whistling sound of a bomb and throws it toward stage right porch. Sound of bottle smashing against wall. This should be the actual smashing of bottles and not tape sound. He keeps yelling and heaving bottles one after another.* VINCE *stops for a while, breathing heavily from exhaustion. Long silence as the others watch him.* SHELLY *approaches tentatively in* VINCE's *direction, still holding* BRADLEY's *wooden leg.*)

SHELLY: (*after silence*) Vince?

(VINCE *turns toward her. Peers through screen.*)

VINCE: Who? What? Vince who? Who's that in there?        1720

(VINCE *pushes his face against the screen from the porch and stares in at everyone.*)

DODGE: Where's my goddamn bottle!

VINCE: (*looking in at* DODGE) What? Who is that?

DODGE: It's me! Your Grandfather! Don't play stupid with me! Where's my two bucks!

VINCE: Your two bucks?

(HALIE *moves away from* DEWIS, *upstage, peers out at* VINCE, *trying to recognize him.*)

HALIE: Vincent? Is that you, Vincent?

(SHELLY *stares at* HALIE *then looks out at* VINCE.)

VINCE: (*from porch*) Vincent who? What is this! Who are you people?

SHELLY: (*to* HALIE) Hey, wait a minute. Wait a minute! What's going on?        1730

HALIE: (*moving closer to porch screen*) We thought you were a murderer or something. Barging in through the door like that.

VINCE: I am a murderer! Don't underestimate me for a minute! I'm the Midnight Strangler! I devour whole families in a single gulp!

(VINCE *grabs another bottle and smashes it on the porch.* HALIE *backs away.*)

SHELLY: (*approaching Halie*) You mean you know who he is?

HALIE: Of course I know who he is! That's more than I can say for you.

BRADLEY: (*sitting up on sofa*) You get off our front porch you 1740 creep! What're you doing out there breaking bottles? Who are these foreigners anyway! Where did they come from?

VINCE: Maybe I should come in there and break them!

HALIE: (*moving toward porch*) Don't you dare! Vincent, what's got into you! Why are you acting like this?

VINCE: Maybe I should come in there and usurp your territory!

(HALIE *turns back toward* DEWIS *and crosses to him.*)

HALIE: (*to* DEWIS) Father, why are you just standing around here when everything's falling apart? Can't you rectify this situation?

(DODGE *laughs, coughs.*)

1750 DEWIS: I'm just a guest here, Halie. I don't know what my position is exactly. This is outside my parish anyway.

(VINCE *starts throwing more bottles as things continue.*)

BRADLEY: If I had my leg I'd rectify it! I'd rectify him all over the goddamn highway! I'd pull his ears out if I could reach him!

(BRADLEY *sticks his fist through the screening of the porch and reaches out for* VINCE, *grabbing at him and missing.* VINCE *jumps away from* BRADLEY's *hand.*)

VINCE: Aaaah! Our lines have been penetrated! Tentacled animals! Beasts from the deep!

(VINCE *strikes out at* BRADLEY's *hand with a bottle.* BRADLEY *pulls his hand back inside.*)

SHELLY: Vince! Knock it off will ya'! I want to get out of here!

(VINCE *pushes his face against screen, looks in at* SHELLY.)

VINCE: (*to* SHELLY) Have they got you prisoner in there, dear? Such a sweet young thing too. All her life in front of her.
1760 Nipped in the bud.

SHELLY: I'm coming out there, Vince! I'm coming out there and I want us to get in the car and drive away from here. Anywhere. Just away from here.

(SHELLY *moves toward* VINCE's *saxophone case and overcoat. She sets down the wooden leg, downstage left and picks up the saxophone case and overcoat.* VINCE *watches her through the screen.*)

VINCE: (*to* SHELLY) We'll have to negotiate. Make some kind of a deal. Prisoner exchange or something. A few of theirs for one of ours. Small price to pay if you ask me.

(SHELLY *crosses toward stage right door with overcoat and case.*)

SHELLY: Just go and get the car! I'm coming out there now. We're going to leave.

VINCE: Don't come out here! Don't you dare come out here!

(SHELLY *stops short of the door, stage right.*)

1770 SHELLY: How come?

VINCE: Off limits! Verboten! This is taboo territory. No man or woman has ever crossed the line and lived to tell the tale!

SHELLY: I'll take my chances.

(SHELLY *moves to stage right door and opens it.* VINCE *pulls out a big folding hunting knife and pulls open the blade. He jabs the blade into the screen and starts cutting a hole big enough to climb through.* BRADLEY *cowers in a corner of the sofa as* VINCE *rips at the screen.*)

VINCE: (*as he cuts screen*) Don't come out here! I'm warning you! You'll disintegrate!

(DEWIS *takes* HALIE *by the arm and pulls her toward staircase.*)

DEWIS: Halie, maybe we should go upstairs until this blows over.

HALIE: I don't understand it. I just don't understand it. He was the sweetest little boy!

(DEWIS *drops the roses beside the wooden leg at the foot of the staircase then escorts* HALIE *quickly up the stairs.* HALIE *keeps looking back at* VINCE *as they climb the stairs.*)

HALIE: There wasn't a mean bone in his body. Everyone loved 1780 Vincent. Everyone. He was the perfect baby.

DEWIS: He'll be all right after a while. He's just had a few too many that's all.

HALIE: He used to sing in his sleep. He'd sing. In the middle of the night. The sweetest voice. Like an angel. (*she stops for a moment*) I used to lie awake listening to it. I used to lie awake thinking it was all right if I died. Because Vincent was an angel. A guardian angel. He'd watch over us. He'd watch over all of us.

(DEWIS *takes her all the way up the stairs. They disappear above.* VINCE *is now climbing through the porch screen onto the sofa.* BRADLEY *crashes off the sofa, holding tight to his blanket, keeping it wrapped around him.* SHELLY *is outside on the porch.* VINCE *holds the knife in his teeth once he gets the hole wide enough to climb through.* BRADLEY *starts crawling slowly toward his wooden leg, reaching out for it.*)

DODGE: (*to* VINCE) Go ahead! Take over the house! Take over 1790 the whole goddamn house! You can have it! It's yours. It's been a pain in the neck ever since the very first mortgage. I'm gonna die any second now. Any second. You won't even notice. So I'll settle my affairs once and for all.

(As DODGE *proclaims his last will and testament,* VINCE *climbs into the room, knife in mouth, and strides slowly around the space, inspecting his inheritance. He casually notices* BRADLEY *as he crawls toward his leg.* VINCE *moves to the leg and keeps pushing it with his foot so that it's out of* BRADLEY's *reach then goes on with his inspection. He picks up the roses and carries them around smelling them.* SHELLY *can be seen outside on the porch, moving slowly center and staring in at* VINCE. VINCE *ignores her.*)

DODGE: The house goes to my Grandson, Vincent. All the furnishings, accoutrements and paraphernalia therein. Everything tacked to the walls or otherwise resting under this roof. My tools—namely my band saw, my skill saw, my drill press, my chain saw, my lathe, my electric sander, all go to my eldest son, Tilden. That is, if he ever shows up again. My 1800 shed and gasoline powered equipment, namely my tractor, my dozer, my hand tiller plus all the attachments and riggings for the above mentioned machinery, namely my spring tooth harrow, my deep plows, my disk plows, my automatic fertilizing equipment, my reaper, my swathe, my seeder, my John Deere Harvester, my post hole digger, my jackhammer, my lathe—(*to himself*) Did I mention my lathe? I already mentioned my lathe—my Bennie Goodman records, my harnesses, my bits, my halters, my brace, my rough rasp, my forge, my welding equipment, my shoeing 1810 nails, my levels and bevels, my milking stool—no, not my milking stool—my hammers and chisels, my hinges, my cattle gates, my barbed wire, self-tapping augers, my horse hair ropes and all related materials are to be pushed into a gigantic heap and set ablaze in the very center of my fields.

When the blaze is at its highest, preferably on a cold, windless night, my body is to be pitched into the middle of it and burned til nothing remains but ash.

*(Pause. VINCE takes the knife out of his mouth and smells the roses. He's facing toward audience and doesn't turn around to SHELLY. He folds up knife and pockets it.)*

1820  SHELLY: *(from porch)* I'm leaving, Vince. Whether you come or not, I'm leaving.

VINCE: *(smelling roses)* Just put my horn on the couch there before you take off.

SHELLY: *(moving toward hole in screen)* You're not coming?

*(VINCE stays downstage, turns and looks at her.)*

VINCE: I just inherited a house.

SHELLY: *(through hole, from porch)* You want to stay here?

VINCE: *(as he pushes BRADLEY's leg out of reach)* I've gotta carry on the line. I've gotta see to it that things keep rolling.

*(BRADLEY looks up at him from floor, keeps pulling himself toward his leg. VINCE keeps moving it.)*

SHELLY: What happened to you Vince? You just disappeared.

VINCE: *(pause, delivers speech front)* I was gonna run last night.
1830  I was gonna run and keep right on running. I drove all night. Clear to the Iowa border. The old man's two bucks sitting right on the seat beside me. It never stopped raining the whole time. Never stopped once. I could see myself in the windshield. My face. My eyes. I studied my face. Studied everything about it. As though I was looking at another man. As though I could see his whole race behind him. Like a mummy's face. I saw him dead and alive at the same time. In the same breath. In the windshield, I watched him breathe as though he was frozen in time. And every breath
1840  marked him. Marked him forever without him knowing. And then his face changed. His face became his father's face. Same bones. Same eyes. Same nose. Same breath. And his father's face changed to his Grandfather's face. And it went on like that. Changing. Clear on back to faces I'd never seen before but still recognized. Still recognized the bones underneath. The eyes. The breath. The mouth. I followed my family clear into Iowa. Every last one. Straight into the Corn Belt and further. Straight back as far as they'd take me. Then it all dissolved. Everything dis-
1850  solved.

*(SHELLY stares at him for a while then reaches through the hole in the screen and sets the saxophone case and VINCE's overcoat on the sofa. She looks at VINCE again.)*

SHELLY: Bye Vince.

*(She exits left off the porch. VINCE watches her go. BRADLEY tries to make a lunge for his wooden leg. VINCE quickly picks it up and dangles it over BRADLEY's head like a carrot. BRADLEY keeps making desperate grabs at the leg. DEWIS comes down the staircase and stops half way, staring at VINCE and BRADLEY. VINCE looks up at DEWIS and smiles. He keeps moving backwards with the leg toward upstage left as BRADLEY crawls after him.)*

VINCE: *(to DEWIS as he continues torturing BRADLEY)* Oh, excuse me Father. Just getting rid of some of the vermin in the house. This is my house now, ya' know? All mine. Everything. Except for the power tools and stuff. I'm gonna get all new equipment anyway. New plows, new tractor, everything. All brand new. *(VINCE teases BRADLEY closer to the up left corner of the stage.)* Start right off on the ground floor.

*(VINCE throws BRADLEY's wooden leg far off stage left. BRADLEY follows his leg off stage, pulling himself along on the ground, whimpering. As BRADLEY exits VINCE pulls the blanket off him and throws it over his own shoulder. He crosses toward DEWIS with the blanket and smells the roses. DEWIS comes to the bottom of the stairs.)*

DEWIS: You'd better go up and see your Grandmother.    1860

VINCE: *(looking up stairs, back to DEWIS)* My Grandmother? There's nobody else in this house. Except for you. And you're leaving aren't you?

*(DEWIS crosses toward stage right door. He turns back to VINCE.)*

DEWIS: She's going to need someone. I can't help her. I don't know what to do. I don't know what my position is. I just came in for some tea. I had no idea there was any trouble. No idea at all.

*(VINCE just stares at him. DEWIS goes out the door, crosses porch and exits left. VINCE listens to him leaving. He smells roses, looks up the staircase then smells roses again. He turns and looks upstage at DODGE. He crosses up to him and bends over looking at DODGE's open eyes. DODGE is dead. His death should have come completely unnoticed. Vince lifts the blanket, then covers his head. He sits on the sofa, smelling roses and staring at DODGE's body. Long pause. VINCE places the roses on DODGE's chest then lays down on the sofa, arms folded behind his head, staring at the ceiling. His body is in the same relationship to DODGE's. After a while HALIE's voice is heard coming from above the staircase. The lights start to dim almost imperceptibly as HALIE speaks. VINCE keeps staring at the ceiling.)*

HALIE'S VOICE: Dodge? Is that you Dodge? Tilden was right about the corn you know. I've never seen such corn. Have you taken a look at it lately? Tall as a man already. This early  1870 in the year. Carrots too. Potatoes. Peas. It's like a paradise out there, Dodge. You oughta' take a look. A miracle. I've never seen it like this. Maybe the rain did something. Maybe it was the rain.

*(As HALIE keeps talking off stage, TILDEN appears from stage left, dripping with mud from the knees down. His arms and hands are covered with mud. In his hands he carries the corpse of a small child at chest level, staring down at it. The corpse mainly consists of bones wrapped in muddy, rotten cloth. He moves slowly downstage toward the staircase, ignoring VINCE on the sofa. VINCE keeps staring at the ceiling as though TILDEN wasn't there. As HALIE's VOICE continues, TILDEN slowly makes his way up the stairs. His eyes never leave the corpse of the child. The lights keep fading.)*

HALIE'S VOICE: Good hard rain. Takes everything straight down deep to the roots. The rest takes care of itself. You can't force a thing to grow. You can't interfere with it. It's all hidden. It's all unseen. You just gotta wait til it pops up out of the ground. Tiny little shoot. Tiny little white shoot. All hairy and fragile. Strong though. Strong enough to break the earth even. It's a miracle, Dodge. I've never seen a crop like

1880

this in my whole life. Maybe it's the sun. Maybe that's it. Maybe it's the sun.

(TILDEN *disappears above. Silence. Lights go to black.*)

---

*IN "Language, Visualization and the Inner Library," Shepard discusses his process of dramatic composition; he is especially acute on the relationship between the visual and the verbal intensity of his drama.*

## Sam Shepard

"Language,
Visualization and the
Inner Library"
(1977)

I feel a lot of reluctance in attempting to describe any part of a process which, by its truest nature, holds an unending mystery. At the same time I'm hoping that by trying to formulate some of this territory I can make things clearer to myself.

I've always felt that the term "experimental" in regard to theatre forms has been twisted by the intellectual community surrounding the artist to the extent that now even the artist has lost track of its original essence. In other words, a search for "new forms" doesn't seem to be exactly where it's at.

There comes a point where the exterior gyrations are no longer the most interesting aspects of what you're practicing, and brand-new exploration starts to take root. For example: In the writing of a particular character where does the character take shape? In my experience the character is visualized, he appears out of nowhere in three dimensions and speaks. He doesn't speak to me because I'm not in the play. I'm watching it. He speaks to something or someone else, or even to himself, or even to no one.

I'm talking now about an open-ended structure where anything could happen as opposed to a carefully planned and regurgitated event which, for me, has always been as painful as pissing nickels. There are writers who work this way successfully, and I admire them and all that, but I don't see the point exactly. The reason I began writing plays was the hope of extending the sensation of *play* (as in "kid") on into adult life. If "play" becomes "labor," why play?

Anyway, to veer back to visualization—right here is where the experiment starts. With the very first impulse to see something happen on a stage. Any stage. This impulse is mistakenly called an idea by those who have never experienced it. I can't even count how many times I've heard the line. "Where did the idea for this play come from?" I never can answer it because it seems totally back-assward. Ideas emerge from plays—not the other way around.

I don't mean to make this sound like a magic act or a mystical experience. It has nothing to do with hallucination or drugs or meditation. These things may all have an influence on the general picture, but they aren't the picture itself. The picture is moving in the mind and being allowed to move more and more freely as you follow it. The following of it is the writing part. In other words, I'm taking notes in as much detail as possible on an event that's happening somewhere inside me. The extent to which I can actually follow the picture and not intervene with my own two-cents worth is where inspiration and craftsmanship hold their real meaning. If I find myself pushing the character in a certain direction, it's almost always a sure sign that I've fallen back on technique and lost the real thread of the thing.

This isn't to say that it's possible to write on nothing but a wave of inspired vision. There has to be some kind of common ground between the accumulated knowledge of what you know how to do (because you've done it before) and the completely foreign country that always demands a new expression. I've never written a play that didn't require both ends of the stick.

Another part of this that interests me is: How is this inner visualization different from ordinary daydreaming or ordinary nightdreaming? The difference seems to lie in the idea of a "watcher" being engaged while writing, whereas ordinarily this watcher is absent. I'm driving a truck and daydreaming about myself in Mexico, but, in this case, I'm not really seeing the dream that's taking place. If I start to see it, then it might become a play.

Now, another thing comes into focus. It must be true that we're continuously taking in images of experience from the outside world through our senses, even when we're not aware of it. How else could whole scenes from our past which we thought we'd long forgotten suddenly spring up in living technicolor? These tastes from our life must then be stored away somewhere in some kind of inner library. So this must mean that if I could be truly resourceful, I could draw on this library at any given moment for the exact information needed. Not only that, but the information is then given back to me as a living sensation. From this point of view, I'm diving back into the actual experience of having been there and writing from it as though it's happening now.

This is very similar to the method-acting technique called "recall." It's a good description—I'm recalling the thing itself. The similarity between the actor's art and the playwright's is a lot closer than most people suspect. In fact the playwright is the only actor who gets to play all the parts. The danger of this method from the actor's point of view is that he becomes lost in the dream and forgets about the audience. The same holds true for the writer, but the writer doesn't really realize where he became lost until he sees an audience nodding out through what he'd thought were his most blazing passages.

This brings me down to words. Words as tools of imagery in motion. I have a feeling that the cultural environment one is raised in predetermines a rhythmical relationship to the use of words. In this sense, I can't be anything other than an American writer.

I noticed though, after living in England for three straight years, that certain subtle changes occurred in this rhythmic construction. In order to accommodate these new configurations in the way a sentence would overblow itself (as is the English tendency), I found myself adding English characters to my plays. *Geography of a Horse Dreamer* was written in London, and there's only one truly American character in the play.

Still, the power of words for me isn't so much in the delineation of a character's social circumstances as it is in the capacity to evoke visions in the eye of the audience. American Indian poetry (in its simplest translation) is a prime example. The roots of this poetry stem from a religious belief in the word itself. Like "crow." Like "hawk." Words as living incantations and not as symbols. Taken in this way, the organization of living, breathing words as they hit the air between the actor and the audience actually possesses the power to change our chemistry. Still, the critical assessment of this kind of event is almost always relegated to the categories of symbolism or "surrealism" or some other accepted niche. In other words, it's removed from the living and dedicated to the dead.

I seem to have come around now to the ear as opposed to the eye, but actually they work in conjunction with each other. They seem to be joined in moments of heightened perception. I hear the phrase a lot that this or that writer has a "great ear for language." What this usually means is that the writer has an openness to people's use of language in the outside world and then this is recorded and reproduced exactly as it's heard. This is no doubt a great gift, but it seems to fall way short of our overall capacity to listen. If I only hear the sounds that people make, how much sound am I leaving out? Words, at best, can only give a partial glimpse into the total world of sensate experience, but how much of that total world am I letting myself in for when I approach writing?

The structure of any art form immediately implies limitation. I'm narrowing down my field of vision. I'm agreeing to work within certain boundaries. So I have to be very careful how those boundaries are defined at the outset. Language, then, seems to be the only ingredient in this plan that retains the potential of making leaps into the unknown. There's only so much I can do with appearances. Change the costume, add a new character, change the light, bring in objects, shift the set, but language is always hovering right there, ready to move faster and more effectively than all the rest of it put together. It's like pulling out a .38 when someone faces you with a knife.

Language can explode from the tiniest impulse. If I'm right inside the character in the moment, I can catch what he smells, sees, feels and touches. In a sudden flash, he opens his eyes, and the words follow. In these lightning-like eruptions words are not thought, they're felt. They cut through space and make perfect sense without having to hesitate for the "meaning."

From time to time I've practiced Jack Kerouac's discovery of jazz-sketching with words. Following the exact same principles as a musician does when he's jamming. After periods of this kind of practice, I begin to get the haunting sense that something in me writes but it's not necessarily me. At least it's not the "me" that takes credit for it. This identical experience happened to me once when I was playing drums with The Holy Modal Rounders, and it scared the shit out of me. Peter Stampfel, the fiddle player, explained it as being visited by the Holy Ghost, which sounded reasonable enough at the time.

What I'm trying to get at here is that the real quest of a writer is to penetrate into another world. A world behind the form. The contradiction is that as soon as that world opens up, I tend to run the other way. It's scary because I can't answer to it from what I know.

Now, here's the big rub—it's generally accepted in the scholarly world that a playwright deals with *"ideas."* That idea in itself has been inherited by us as though it were originally written in granite from above and nobody, but nobody, better mess with it. The problem for me with this concept is that its adherents are almost always referring to ideas which speak only to the mind and leave out completely the body, the emotions and all the rest of it.

Myth speaks to everything at once, especially the emotions. By myth I mean a sense of mystery and not necessarily a traditional formula. A character for me is a composite of different mysteries. He's an unknown quantity. If he wasn't, it would be like coloring in the numbered spaces. I see an old man by a broken car in the middle of nowhere and those simple elements right away set up associations and yearnings to pursue what he's doing there.

The character of Crow in *Tooth of Crime* came from a yearning toward violence. A totally lethal human with no way or reason for tracing how he got that way. He just appeared. He spit words that became his weapons. He doesn't "mean" anything. He's simply following his most savage instincts. He speaks in an unheard-of tongue. He needed a victim, so I gave him one. He devoured him just like he was supposed to. When you're writing inside of a character like this, you aren't pausing every ten seconds to figure out what it all means. If you do, you lose the whole shot, because the character isn't going to hang around waiting for you. He's moving.

I write fast because that's the way it happens with me. Sometimes long stretches happen in between where I don't write for weeks. But when I start, I don't stop. Writing is born from a need. A deep burn. If there's no need, there's no writing.

I don't mean to give the impression from all this that a playwright isn't responsible toward the audience. He is. But which audience? An imagined one or a real one? The only real audience he has at the moment of writing is himself. Only later does the other audience come into it. At that point he begins to see the correspondence or lack of it between his own "watching" and the watching of others.

I used to be dead set against rewriting on any level. My attitude was that if the play had faults, those faults were part and parcel of the original process, and that any attempt to correct them was cheating. Like a sculptor sneaking out in the night with his chisel and chipping little pieces off his work or gluing them back on.

After a while this rigid "holy-art" concept began to crumble. It was no longer a case of "correction," as though what I was involved with was some kind of definitive term paper. I began to see that the living outcome (the production) always demanded a different kind of attention than the written from that it sprang from. The spoken word, no matter how you cut it, is different than the written word. It happens in a different space, under different circumstances and demands a different set of laws.

*Action* is the only play I've written where I spoke each line out loud to myself before I put it down on paper. To me that play still comes the closest to sounding on stage exactly like it was written. This method doesn't work for every play, though, since it necessarily sets up a slower tempo. It just happened to be the right approach for that particular piece.

*La Turista* was the first play I ever rewrote, under the urging of Jacques Levy, who directed it. We were in the second week of rehearsals at the American Place Theatre when I walked in with a brand-new second act. It's a tribute to Wynn Handman that he allowed this kind of procedure to take place. That was the first taste I got of regarding theatre as an ongoing process. I could feel the whole evolution of that play from a tiny sweltering hotel in the Yucatan, half wasted with the trots, to a full-blown production in New York City. Most of the writing in that piece was hatched from a semidelirious state of severe dysentery. What the Mexicans call "La Turista" or "Montezuma's Revenge." In that state any writing I could manage seemed valid, no matter how incoherent it might seem to an outside eye. Once it hit the stage in rehearsals and I was back to a fairly healthy physical condition, the whole thing seemed filled with an overriding self-pity. The new second act came more from desperation than anything else.

I think immediate environments tend to play a much heavier role on my writing than I'm aware of most of the time. That is, the physical place I'm in at the time of sitting down to the machine. In New York I could write any time in any place. It didn't matter what was happening in the streets below or the apartment above. I just wrote. The funny thing is that I can remember the exact place and time of every play. Even the people I was with. It's almost as though the plays were a kind of chronicle I was keeping on myself.

It seems that the more you write, the harder it gets, because you're not so easily fooled by yourself anymore. I can still sit down and whip off a play like I used to, but it doesn't have the same meaning now as it did when I was nineteen. Even so, writing becomes more and more interesting as you go along, and it starts to open up some of its secrets. One thing I'm sure of, though. That I'll never get to the bottom of it.

# Ntozake Shange

Born Paulette Williams in Trenton, New Jersey, in 1948, Ntozake Shange was raised in New Jersey and St. Louis. She attended Barnard College in Manhattan in 1966, suffering a series of profound bouts of depression and attempting suicide on several occasions. She graduated from Barnard with a B. A. in American studies in 1970 and received an M. A. in American studies at the University of Southern California in 1971, when she took the African name, Ntozake Shange. Shange is a poet, and during the early 1970s she read her poetry throughout the United States. In the summer of 1974, she began a series of seven poems that explored the realities of life among seven different black women. The women were nameless, and in the course of reading the series of poems to audiences, Shange realized its extraordinary theatrical power. But rather than seeing the monologues as material for a stage play, Shange's recognition of their dramatic power was linked to her interest in music and dance. As she suggested at the time, "with dance I discovered my body more intimately than I had imagined possible. With the acceptance of the ethnicity of my thighs and backside, came a clearer understanding of my voice as a woman and as a poet." Throughout the next year, she experimented with a variety of ways of staging the piece, coining the term "choreopoem" to describe its blending of music, dance, and poetry. As she writes in her introduction to the play, by the time *for colored girls who have considered suicide / when the rainbow is enuf* (1975) opened in California, it "waz a theater piece." The play was then brought to Broadway, where it was hugely popular. Shange's more recent plays continue to use music, lighting, dance, and poetry to examine the experience of black women: *a photograph: lovers in motion* (1977), *boogie woogie landscapes* (1978), and *spell #7: geechee jibara quik magic trance manual for technologically stressed third world people* (1979). Shange has won many prestigious awards, including an Obie for her adaptation of Brecht's *Mother Courage and Her Children* (1980). She has also written several collections of poetry, including *Nappy Edges* (1978), prose works including *Sassafrass* (1977), *From Okra to Greens: A Different Love Story* (1984), and *A Daughter's Geography* (1983). *See No Evil: Prefaces, Essays and Accounts 1976–1983* was published in 1984.

## spell #7:
## geechee jibara quik magic trance manual for technologically
## stressed third world people: a theater piece (1979)

Unlike her earlier choreopoem *for colored girls who have considered suicide / when the rainbow is enuf, spell #7* is subtitled "a theater piece." Although it uses Shange's powerful fusion of poetry and movement, *spell #7* engages in a critique of the politics of race and the politics of racial representation through the essential means of theater: role playing.

From its opening moments, when the audience sees a huge blackface mask hanging above the stage, and *"the rest of the company enters in tattered fieldhand garb, blackface, and the countenance of stepan fetchit when he waz frightened,"* it is apparent that *spell #7* will question how African-American experience has been represented in white society, from the nineteenth-century minstrel shows, through the blackface musicals, comedies, and vaudeville of the 1920s, to contemporary stereotypes. Indeed, the play uses the "magic" of theater to investigate not only the social function of black theater traditions, but also the way in which analogous stereotypes conceal, displace, and misrepresent African-American experience in social life. Lou the magician enters and tells how his father, a magician,

> . . . retired from magic & took
> up another trade cuz this friend a mine
> from the 3rd grade / asked to be made white
> on the spot.

In *spell #7,* lou does not use his magic to turn black people white, but to reveal the black identity behind the white-imposed mask of blackface. Through lou's theatrical magic, the actors are able to remove their blackface masks and engage in a series of confessions, improvisations, and role playings that characterize African-American experience today.

The identities that emerge from behind the blackface are striking and powerful. The scene changes to eli's bar, a hangout for African-American actors, most of whom are unemployed because they are unable to get significant parts to play—"say as lady macbeth or mother courage," as lou suggests—and are forced to work odd jobs, play the tambourine on the street for subway fare, or to play stereotypically "black" roles. As bettina angrily complains, "no / my show is not closin / but if that director asks me to play it any blacker / i'm gonna have to do it in a mammy dress." Although blackface and the character stereotypes that accompanied it in an earlier era are no longer common in the theater, cultural stereotypes pervade our entertainment forms—and society as well. For this reason, lou's magic and the actors' anger conspire to produce a series of striking improvisations, as the actors remove their blackface masks and perform more authentic versions of contemporary African-American life: maxine plays "fay," out from Brooklyn to have a good time in Manhattan; lily reveals how she dreams of success while brushing her hair; natalie enacts "sue-jean," who gives birth to and then kills a baby boy named "myself." Finally, natalie and maxine play a "white girl" as a way of turning the tables on blackface convention. Much as blackface represents black identity from the vantage of a privileged white society, natalie and maxine represent white identity from an oppressed black perspective.

As Shange suggests in her foreword to the play, much of the energy of *spell #7* derives from Shange's effort to maintain and celebrate the legacy of African-American arts, the fusion of poetry, music, and dance that should be an inspiring "cultural reality" for the African-American—and the world—community.

# — spell #7: —
# geechee jibara quik magic trance
# manual for technologically
# stressed third world people
## *A Theater Piece*
### Ntozake Shange

## —FOREWORD/UNRECOVERED LOSSES/ BLACK THEATER TRADITIONS—

as a poet in american theater/ i find most activity that takes place on our stages overwhelmingly shallow/ stilted & imitative. that is probably one of the reasons i insist on calling myself a poet or writer/ rather than a playwright/ i am interested solely in the poetry of a moment/ the emotional & aesthetic impact of a character or a line. for too long now afro-americans in theater have been duped by the same artificial aesthetics that plague our white counterparts/ "the perfect play," as we know it to be/ a truly european framework for european psychology/ cannot function efficiently for those of us from this hemisphere.

furthermore/ with the advent of at least 6 musicals about the lives of black musicians & singers/ (EUBIE, BUBBLING BROWN SUGAR, AIN'T MISBEHAVIN', MAHALIA, etc.)/ the lives of millions of black people who dont sing & dance for a living/ are left unattended to in our theatrical literature. not that the lives of Eubie Blake or Fats Waller are well served in productions lacking any significant book/ but if the lives of our geniuses arent artfully rendered/ & the lives of our regular & precious are ignored/ we have a double loss to reckon with.

if we are drawn for a number of reasons/ to the lives & times of black people who conquered their environments/ or at least their pain with their art, & if these people are mostly musicians & singers & dancers/ then what is a writer to do to draw the most human & revealing moments from lives spent in nonverbal activity. first of all we should reconsider our choices/ we are centering ourselves around these artists for what reasons/ because their lives were richer than ours/ because they did something white people are still having a hard time duplicating/ because they proved something to the world like Jesse Owens did/ like Billie Holiday did. i think/ all the above contributes to the proliferation of musicals abt our musicians/ without forcing us to confront the real implications of the dynamic itself. we are compelled to examine these giants in order to give ourselves what we think they gave the worlds they lived in/ which is an independently created afro-american aesthetic. but we are going abt this process backwards/ by isolating the art forms & assuming a very narrow perspective vis-à-vis our own history.

if Fats Waller & Eubie Blake & Charlie Parker & Savilla Fort & Katherine Dunham moved the world outta their way/ how did they do it/ certainly not by mimicking the weakest area in american art/ the american theater. we must move our theater into the drama of our lives/ which is what the artists we keep resurrecting (or allowing others to resurrect) did in the first place/ the music & dance of our renowned predecessors appeals to us because it directly related to lives of those then living & the lives of the art forms.

in other words/ we are selling ourselves & our legacy quite cheaply/ since we are trying to make our primary statements with somebody else's life/ and somebody else's idea of what theater is. i wd suggest that: we demolish the notion of straight theater for a decade or so, refuse to allow playwrights to work without dancers & musicians. "coon shows" were somebody else's idea. we have integrated the notion that a drama must be words/ with no music & no dance/ cuz that wd take away the seriousness of the event/ cuz we all remember too well/ the chuckles & scoffs at the notion that all niggers cd sing & dance/ & most of us can sing & dance/ & the reason that so many plays written to silence & stasis fail/ is cuz most black people have some music & movement in our lives. we do sing & dance. this is a cultural reality. this is why i find the most inspiring theater among us to be in the realms of music & dance.

i think of my collaboration with David Murray on A PHOTOGRAPH/ & on WHERE THE MISSISSIPPI MEETS THE AMAZON/ & on SPELL #7/ in which music functions as another character. Teddy & his Sizzling Romancers (David Murray, sax.; Anthony Davis, piano; Fred Hopkins, bass; Paul Maddox, drums; Michael Gregory Jackson, guitar, harmonica & vocals) were as important as The Satin Sisters/ though the thirties motif served as a vehicle to introduce the dilemmas of our times. in A PHOTOGRAPH the cello (Abdul Wadud) & synthesizer (Michael Gregory Jackson) solos/ allowed Sean to break into parts of himself that wd have been unavailable had he been unable to "hear." one of the bounties of black culture is our ability to "hear"/ if we were to throw this away in search of less (just language) we wd be damning ourselves. in slave narratives there are numerous references to instruments/ specifically violins, fifes & flutes/ "talking" to the folks. when working with Oliver Lake (sax.) or Baikida Carroll (tr.) in FROM OKRA TO GREENS/ or Jay Hoggard (vibes) in FIVE NOSE RINGS & SOWETO SUITE/ i am terribly aware of a conversation. in the company of Dianne McIntyre/ or Dyane Harvey's work with the Eleo Pomare Dance Company/ one is continually aroused by the immediacy of their movements/ "do this movement like yr life depends on it"/ as McIntyre says.

the fact that we are an interdisciplinary culture/ that we understand more than verbal communication/ lays a weight on afroamerican writers that few others are lucky enough to have been born into. we can use with some skill virtually all our physical senses/ as writers committed to bringing the world as we remember it/ imagine it/ & know it to be to the stage/ we must use everything we've got. i suggest that everyone shd cue from Julius Hemphill's wonderful persona, Roi Boye/ who ruminates & dances/ sings & plays a saxophone/ shd cue from Cecil Taylor & Dianne McIntyre's collaboration on SHADOWS/ shd cue from Joseph Jarman & Don Moye (of The Art Ensemble of Chicago) who are able to move/ to speak/ to sing & dance & play a myriad of instruments in EGWU-ANWU. look at Malinke who is an actor/ look at Amina Myers/ Paula Moss/ Aku Kadogo/ Michele Shay/ Laurie Carlos/ Ifa Iyaun Baeza & myself in NEGRESS/ a collective piece which allowed singers, dancers, musicians & writers to pass through the barriers & do more than 1 thing. dance to Hemphill or the B.A.G. (Black Artist Group)/ violinist Ramsey Amin lets his instrument make his body dance & my poems shout. i find that our contemporaries who are musicians are exhibiting more courage than we as writers might like to admit.

in the first version of BOOGIE WOOGIE LANDSCAPES i presented myself with the problem of having my person/ body, voice & language/ address the space as if i were a band/ a dance company & a theater group all at once. cuz a poet shd do that/ create an emotional environment/ felt architecture.

to paraphrase Lester Bowie/ on the night of the World Saxophone Quartet's (David Murray, Julius Hemphill, Hamiett Bluiett & Oliver Lake) performance at the Public Theater/ "those guys are the greatest comedy team since the Marx Brothers." in other words/ they are theater. theater which is an all encompassing moment/ a moment of poetry/ the opportunity to make something happen. We shd think of George Clinton/ a.k.a. Dr. Funkenstein/ as he sings/ "here's a chance to dance our way out of our constrictions." as writers we might think more often of the implications of an Ayler solo/ the meaning of a contraction in anybody's body. we are responsible for saying how we feel. we "ourselves" are high art. our world is honesty & primal response.

*1/22/79 NYC*

although i rarely read reviews of my work/ two comments were repeated to me by "friends" for some reason/ & now that i am writing abt my own work/ i am finally finding some use for the appraisals of strangers. one new york critic had accused me of being too self-conscious of being a writer/ the other from the midwest had asserted that i waz so involved with the destruction of the english language/ that my writing approached verbal gymnastics like unto a reverse minstrel show. in reality/ there is an element of truth in both ideas/ but the lady who though i waz self-conscious of being a writer/ apparently waz never a blk child who knew that no black people conducted themselves like amos n andy/ she waz not a blk child who knew that blk children didnt wear tiger skins n chase lions around trees n then eat pancakes/ she waznt a blk child who spoke an english that had evolved naturally/ only to hear a white man's version of blk speech that waz entirely made up & based on no linguistic system besides the language of racism. the man who thought i wrote with intentions of outdoing the white man in the acrobatic distortions of english waz absolutely correct. i cant count the number of times i have viscerally wanted to attack deform n maim the language that i waz taught to hate myself in/ the language that perpetuates the notions that cause pain to every black child as he/she learns to speak of the world & the "self." yes/ being an afro-american writer is something to be self-conscious abt/ & yes/ in order to think n communicate the thoughts n feelings i want to think n communicate/ i haveta fix my tool to my needs/ i have to take it apart to the bone/ so that the malignancies/ fall away/ leaving us space to literally create our own image.

i have not ceased to be amazed when i hear members of an audience whispering to one another in the foyers of theaters/ that they had never imagined they cd feel so much for characters/ even though they were black (or colored/ or niggers, if they don't notice me eavesdropping). on the other hand/ i hear other members of an audience say that there were so many things in the piece that they had felt/ experienced/ but had never found words to express/ even privately/ to themselves. these two phenomena point to the same dilemma/ the straightjacket that the english language slips over the minds of all americans. there are some thoughts that black people just dont have/ according to popular mythology/ so white people never "imagine" we are having them/ & black people "block" vocabularies we perceive to be white folks' ideas.° this will never do. for in addition to the obvious stress of racism n poverty/ afro-american culture/ in attempts to carry on/ to move forward/ has minimized its "emotional" vocabulary to the extent that admitting feelings of rage, defeat, frustration is virtually impossible outside a collective voice. so we can add self-inflicted repression to the cultural causes of our cultural disease of high blood pressure.

---

°Just examine *Drylongso* by John Langston Gwaltney, Random House, 1980.

in everything i have ever written & everything i hope to write/ i have made use of what Frantz Fanon called "combat breath." although Fanon waz referring to francophone colonies, the schema he draws is sadly familiar:

> there is no occupation of territory, on the one hand, and independence of persons on the other. It is the country as a whole, its history, its daily pulsation that are contested, disfigured, in the hope of final destruction. Under this condition, the individual's breathing is an observed, an occupied breathing. It is a combat breathing[*]

Fanon goes on to say that "combat breathing" is the living response/ the drive to reconcile the irreconcilable/ the black & white of what we live n where. (unfortunately, this language doesnt allow me to broaden "black" & "white" to figurative terms/ which is criminal since the words are so much larger n richer than our culture allows.) i have lived with this for 31 years/ as my people have lived with cut-off lives n limbs. the three pieces in this collection are the throes of pain n sensation experienced by my characters responding to the involuntary constrictions n amputations of their humanity/ in the context of combat breathing.

each of these pieces was excruciating to write/ for i had to confront/ again & again/ those moments that had left me with little more than fury n homicidal desires. in *spell #7* i included a prologue of a minstrel show/ which made me cry the first times i danced in it/ for the same reasons i had included it. the minstrel may be "banned" as racist/ but the minstrel is more powerful in his deformities than our alleged rejection of him/ for every night we wd be grandly applauded. immediately thereafter/ we began to unveil the "minstrels," who turned out to be as fun-loving as fay:

> please/ let me join you/ i come all the way from brooklyn/ to have a good time/ ya dont think i'm high do ya/ cd i please join ya/ i just wanna have a good ol time.

as contorted as sue-jean:

> & i lay in the corner laughin/ with my drawers/ twisted round my ankles & my hair standin every which way/ i waz laughin/ knowin i wd have this child/ myself/ & no one wd ever claim him/ cept me/ cuz i was a low-down thing/ layin in sawdust & whiskey stains/ i laughed & had a good time masturbatin in the shadows.

as angry as the actor who confides:

> i just want to find out why no one has even been able to sound a gong& all the reporters recite that the gong is ringin/ while we watch all the white people/ immigrants & invaders/ conquistadors & relatives of london debtors from georgia/ kneel & apologize to us/ just for three or four minutes. now/ this is not impossible.

& after all that/ our true visions & rigors laid bare/ down from the ceiling comes the huge minstrel face/ laughing at all of us for having been so game/ we believed we cd escape his powers/ how naive cd we be/ the magician explains:

> crackers are born with the right to be alive/ i'm making ours up right here in yr face.

the most frequently overheard comment abt *spell #7* when it first opened at the public theater/ waz that it waz too intense. the cast & i usedta laugh. if this one hour n 45 minutes waz too much/ how in the world did these same people imagine the rest of our lives were/ & wd they ever be able to handle that/ simply being alive & black & feeling in this strange deceitful country. which brings me to *boogie woogie landscapes*/ totally devoted to the emotional topology of a yng woman/ how she got to be the way she is/ how she sees where she is. here/ again/ in the prologue lies the combat breath of layla/ but she's no all-american girl/ or is she?

> the lil black things/ pulled to her & whimpered lil black whys/ "why did those white men make red of our house/ why did those white men want to blacken even the white doors of our house/ why make fire of our trees/ & our legs/ why make fire/ why laugh at us/ say go home/ arent we home/ arent we home?"

she waz raised to know nothing but black & white two-dimensional planes/ which is what racism allots everyone of us unless we fight. she found solace in jesus & the american way/ though jonestown & american bandstand lay no claims to her:

> shall i go to jonestown or the disco? i cd wear red sequins or a burlap bag. maybe it doesnt matter/ paradise is fulla surprises/ & the floor of the disco changes colors like special species of vipers . . .

---

[*]Frantz Fanon, *A Dying Colonialism,* Grove Press, 1967.

her lover/ her family/ her friends torment her/ calm her with the little they have left over from their own struggles to remain sane. everything in *boogie woogie landscapes* is the voice of layla's unconscious/ her unspeakable realities/ for no self-respecting afro-american girl wd reveal so much of herself of her own will/ there is too much anger to handle assuredly/ too much pain to keep on truckin/ less ya bury it.

both *spell #7* & *boogie woogie landscapes* have elements of magic or leaps of faith/ in typical afro-american fashion/ not only will the lord find a way/ but there *is* a way outta here. this is the litany from the spirituals to Jimi Hendrix' "there must be some kinda way outta here"/ acceptance of my combat breath hasnt closed the possibilities of hope to me/ the soothing actualities of music n sorcery/ but that's why i'm doubly proud of *a photograph: lovers in motion/* which has no cures for our "condition" save those we afford ourselves. the characters michael/ sean/ claire/ nevada/ earl/ are afflicted with the kinds of insecurities & delusions only available to those who learned themselves thru the traumas of racism. what is fascinating is the multiplicity of individual responses to this kind of oppression. michael displays her anger to her lovers:

i've kept a lover who waznt all-american/ who didnt believe/ wdnt straighten up/ oh i've loved him in my own men/ sometimes hateful sometimes subtle like high fog & sun/ but who i loved is yr not believin. i loved yr bitterness & hankered after that space in you where you are outta control/ where you cannot touch or you wd kill me/ or somebody else who loved you. i never even saw a picture & i've loved him all my life he is all my insanity & anyone who loves me wd understand.

while nevada finds a nurtured protection from the same phenomenon:

mama/ will he be handsome & strong/ maybe from memphis/ an old family of freedmen/ one of them reconstruction senators for a great grandfather . . .

their particular distortions interfere with them receiving one another as full persons:

claire: no no/ i want nevada to understand that i understand that sean's a niggah/ & that's why he's never gonna be great or
    whatever you call it/ cuz he's a niggah & niggahs cant be nothin.
nevada: see/ earl/ she's totally claimed by her station/ she cant imagine anyone growing thru the prison of poverty to become
    someone like sean
claire: sean aint nothing but a niggah nevada/ i didnt know you liked niggahs.

such is the havoc created in the souls of people who arent supposed to exist. the malevolence/ the deceit/ & manipulation exhibited by these five are simply reflections of the larger world they inhabit/ but do not participate in:

sean: contours of life unnoticed/
michael: unrealized & suspect . . . our form is one of a bludgeoned thing/
    wrapped in rhinestones & gauze/ blood almost sparklin/ a wildness
    lurks always . . .
        oppression/ makes us love one another badly/ makes our breathing
        mangled/ while i am desperately trying to clear the air/
        in the absence of extreme elegance/
        madness can set right in like
        a burnin gauloise on japanese silk.
        though highly cultured/
        even the silk must ask
        how to burn up discreetly.

*3/21/80 NYC*

## —CHARACTERS—

(in order of appearance)
LOU *a practicing magician*
ALEC *a frustrated, angry actor's actor*
DAHLIA *young gypsy (singer/dancer)*
ELI *a bartender who is also a poet*
BETTINA *dahlia's co-worker in a chorus*

LILY *an unemployed actress working as a barmaid*
NATALIE *a not too successful performer*
ROSS *guitarist-singer with natalie*
MAXINE *an experienced actress*

*this show is dedicated to my great aunt marie, aunt lizzie, aunt jane and my grandma, viola benzena, and her buddy, aunt effie, and the lunar year.*

## —ACT ONE—

*there is a huge black-face mask hanging from the ceiling of the theater as the audience enters. in a way the show has already begun, for the members of the audience must integrate this grotesque, larger than life misrepresentation of life into their pre-show chatter. slowly the house lights fade, but the mask looms even larger in the darkness.*

*Once the mask is all that can be seen,* LOU, *the magician, enters. he is dressed in the traditional costume of Mr. Interlocutor: tuxedo, bow-tie, top hat festooned with all kinds of whatnots that are obviously meant for good luck. he does a few catchy "soft-shoe" steps & begins singing a traditional version of a black play song*

LOU: *(singing)*

> 10 lil picaninnies all in bed
> one fell out and the other nine said:
> i sees yr hiney
> all black & shiny
> i see yr hiney
> all black & shiny/ shiny

*(as a greeting)*

yes/yes/yes/        isnt life wonderful

*(confidentially)*

my father is a retired magician
10   which accounts for my irregular behavior
everything comes outta magic hats
or bottles wit no bottoms & parakeets
are as easy to get as a couple a rabbits
or 3 fifty-cent pieces/ 1958
my daddy retired from magic & took
up another trade cuz this friend a mine
from the 3rd grade/ asked to be made white
on the spot

what cd any self-respectin colored american magician
20   do wit such an outlandish request/ cept
put all them razzamatazz hocus pocus zippity-doo-dah
thingamajigs away        cuz
colored chirren believin in magic
waz becomin politically dangerous for the race
& waznt nobody gonna be made white
on the spot just
from a clap of my daddy's hands
& the reason i'm so peculiar's
cuz i been studyin up on my daddy's technique
30   & everything i do is magic these days
& it's very colored/ very now you see it/ now you
dont mess wit me

*(boastfully)*

                    i come from a family of retired
sorcerers/ active houngans & pennyante fortune tellers
wit 41 million spirits/ critturs & celestial bodies
on our side
        i'll listen to yr problems
        help wit yr career/ yr lover/ yr wanderin spouse

make yr grandma's stay in heaven more
gratifyin                                        40
ease yr mother thru menopause & show yr son
how to clean his room

*(while* LOU *has been easing the audience into acceptance of his appearance & the mask [his father, the ancestors, our magic], the rest of the company enters in tattered fieldhand garb, blackface, and the countenance of stepan fetchit when he waz frightened. their presence belies the magician's promise that "you'll be colored n love it," just as the minstrel shows were lies, but* LOU *continues)*

YES YES YES 3 wishes is all you get
    scarlet ribbons for yr hair
    a farm in mississippi
    someone to love you madly
all things are possible
but aint no colored magician in his right mind
gonna make you            white
i mean                                          50
        this is blk magic
you lookin at
& i'm fixin you up good/ fixin you up good & colored
& you gonna be colored all yr life
& you gonna love it/ bein colored/ all yr life/ colored &
    love it
love it/ bein colored. SPELL #7!

*(*LOU *claps his hands, & the company which had been absolutely still til this moment/ jumps up. with a rhythm set on a washboard carried by one of them/ they begin a series of steps that identify every period of afro-american entertainment: from acrobats, comedians, tap-dancers, calindy dancers, cotton club choruses, apollo theatre du-wop groups, til they reach a frenzy in the midst of "hambone, hambone where ya been"/ & then take a bow à la bert williams/ the lights bump up abruptly.*

*the magician,* LOU, *walks thru the black-faced figures in their kneeling poses, arms outstretched as if they were going to sing "mammy." he speaks now [as a companion of the mask] to the same audience who fell so easily into his hands & who were so aroused by the way the black-faced figures "sang n danced")*

LOU: why dont you go on & integrate a german-american
    school in st. louis mo./ 1955/ better yet why dont ya go on &
    be a red niggah in a blk school in 1954/ i got it/ try & make   60
    one friend at camp in the ozarks in 1957/ crawl thru one a
    jesse james' caves wit a class of white kids waitin outside to
    see the whites of yr eyes/ why dontcha invade a clique of
    working class italians trying to be protestant in a jewish com-
    munity/ & come up a spade/ be a lil too dark/ lips a lil too
    full/ hair entirely too nappy/ to be beautiful/ be a smart child
    trying to be dumb/ you go meet somebody who wants/ al-
    ways/ a lil less/ be cool when yr body says hot/ & more/ be a
    mistake in racial integrity/ an error in white folks' most ab-
    surd fantasies/ be a blk kid in 1954/ who's not blk enuf to lov-   70
    ingly ignore/ not beautiful enuf to leave alone/ not smart
    enuf to move outta the way/ not bitter enuf to die at an early
    age/ why dontchu c'mon & live my life for me/ since the
    dreams aint enuf/ go on & live my life for me/ i didnt want

certain moments at all/ i'd give em to anybody . . . awright. alec.

(the black-faced ALEC gives his minstrel mask to LOU when he hears his name/ ALEC rises. the rest of the company is intimidated by this figure daring to talk without the protection of black-face. they move away from him/ or move in place as if in mourning)

ALEC: st. louis/ such a colored town/ a whiskey black space of history & neighborhood/ forever ours to lawrenceville/ where the only road open to me waz cleared by colonial
80    slaves/ whose children never moved/ never seems like mended the torments of the Depression or the stains of demented spittle/ dropped from the lips of crystal women/ still makin independence flags/
    st. louis/ on a halloween's eve to the veiled prophet/ usurpin the mystery of mardi gras/ i made it mine tho the queen waz always fair/ that parade of pagan floats & tambourines/ commemorates me/ unlike the lonely walks wit liberal trick or treaters/ back to my front door/ bag half empty/
    my face enuf to scare anyone i passed/ gee/ a colored kid/
90    whatta gas. here/ a tree/ wanderin the horizon/ dipped in blues/ untended bones/ usedta hugs drawls rhythm & decency here a tree/ waitin to be hanged
    sumner high school/ squat & pale on the corner/ like our vision waz to be vague/ our memory of the war/ that made us free/ to be forgotten/ becomin paler/ linear movement from sous' carolina to missouri/ freedmen/ landin in jackie wilson's yelp/ daughters of the manumitted swimmin in tina turner's grinds/ this is chuck berry's town disavowin miscega-nation/ in any situation/ & they let us be/ electric blues
100    & bo didley/ the rockin pneumonia & boogie-woogie flu/ the slop & short fried heads/ runnin always to the river chambersburg/ lil italy/ i passed everyday at the sweet shoppe/ & waz afraid/ the cops raided truants/ regularly/ & after dark i wd not be seen wit any other colored/ sane & lovin my life

(shouts n cries that are those of a white mob are heard, very loud . . . the still black-faced figures try to move away from the menacing voices & memories)

VOICES: hey niggah/ over here
ALEC: behind the truck lay five hands claspin chains
VOICES: hey niggah/ over here
ALEC: round the trees/ 4 more sucklin steel
VOICES: hey niggah/ over here
110 ALEC: this is the borderline
VOICES: hey niggah/ over here
ALEC: a territorial dispute
VOICES: hey niggah/ over here
ALEC: (crouched on floor) cars loaded with families/ fellas
    from the factory/
    one or two practical nurses/ become our trenches/
    some dig into cement wit elbows/ under engines/
    do not be seen in yr hometown
    after sunset/ we suck up our shadows

(finally moved to tear off their "shadows," all but two of the company leave with their true faces bared to the audience. DAHLIA has, as if by some magical cause, shed not only her mask, but also her hideous overalls & picaninny-buckwheat

wig, to reveal a finely laced unitard/ the body of a modern dancer. she throws her mask to alec, who tosses it away. DAHLIA begins a lyrical but pained solo as ALEC speaks for them)

ALEC: we will stand here                                          120
    our shoulders embrace an enormous spirit
    my dreams waddle in my lap
    run round to miz bertha's
    where lil richard gets his process
    run backward to the rosebushes
    & a drunk man lyin
    down the block to the nuns
    in pink habits/ prayin in a pink chapel
    my dreams run to meet aunt marie
    my dreams haunt me like the little geechee river      130
    our dreams draw blood from old sores
    this is our space
    we are not movin

(DAHLIA finishes her movement/ ALEC is seen reaching for her/ lights out. in the blackout they exit as LOU enters. lights come up on LOU who repeats bitterly his challenge to the audience)

LOU: why dontchu go on & live my life for me
    i didnt want certain moments at all
    i'd give them to anybody

(LOU waves his hand commanding the minstrel mask to disappear, which it does. he signals to his left & again by magic, the lights come up higher revealing the interior of a lower manhattan bar & its bartender, ELI, setting up for the night. ELI greets LOU as he continues to set up tables, chairs, candles, etc., for the night's activities. LOU goes over to the jukebox, & plays "we are family" by sister sledge. LOU starts to tell us exactly where we are, but ELI takes over as characters are liable to do. throughout ELI's poem, the other members of the company enter the bar in their street clothes, & doing steps reminiscent of their solos during the minstrel sequence. as each enters, the audience is made aware that these ordinary people are the minstrels. the company continues to dance individually as ELI speaks)

    this is . . .
ELI: MY kingdom.
    there shall be no trespassers/ no marauders
    no tourists in my land                                       140
    you nurture these gardens        or        be shot on sight
    carelessness & other priorities
    are not permitted within these walls
    i am mantling an array of strength & beauty
    no one shall interfere with this
    the construction of myself
    my city            my theater
    my bar            come to my poems
    but understand we speak english carefully
    & perfect antillean french                                   150
    our toilets are disinfected
    the plants here sing to me each morning
    come to my kitchen my parlor even my bed
    i sleep on satin            surrounded by hand made
    infants who bring me good luck & warmth

come even to my door
the burglar alarm/ armed guards vault from the east side
if i am in danger          a siren shouts
you are welcome
160    to my kingdom          my city          my self
but yr presence must not disturb these inhabitants
leave nothing out of place/ push no dust under my rugs
leave not a crack in my wine glasses
no finger prints
clean up after yrself in the bathroom
there are no maids here          no days off
for healing          no insurance policies
for dislocation of the psyche
aliens/ foreigners/ are granted resident status
170    we give them a little green card
as they prove themselves non-injurious
to the joy of my nation
i sustain no intrusions/ no double-entendre romance
no soliciting of sadness    in my life
are those who love me well
the rest are denied their visas . . .
is everyone ready to boogie

*(finally, when* ELI *calls for a boogie, the company does a dance that indicates these people have worked & played together a long time. as dance ends, the company sits & chats at the tables & at the bar. this is now a safe haven for these "minstrels" off from work. here they are free to be themselves, to reveal secrets, fantasies, nightmares, or hope. it is safe because it is segregated & magic reigns.*

LILY, *the waitress, is continually moving abt the bar, taking orders for drinks & generally staying on top of things)*

ALEC: gimme a triple bourbon/ & a glass of angel dust
    these thursday nite audiences are abt to kill me

*(*ELI *goes behind bar to get drinks)*

180  DAHLIA: why do i drink so much?
    BETTINA, LILY, NATALIE: *(in unison)* who cares?
    DAHLIA: but i'm an actress. i have to ask myself these questions
    LILY: that's a good reason to drink
    DAHLIA: no/ i mean the character/ alec, you're a director/ give
      me some motivation
    ALEC: motivation/ if you didn't drink you wd remember that
      you're not workin
    LILY: i wish i cd get just one decent part
    LOU: say as lady macbeth or mother courage
190  ELI: how the hell is she gonna play lady macbeth and mac-
      beth's a white dude?
    LILY: ross & natalie/ why are you countin pennies like that?
    NATALIE: we had to wait on our money again
    ROSS: and then we didnt get it
    BETTINA: maybe they think we still accept beads & ribbons
    NATALIE: i had to go around wit my tambourine just to get sub-
      way fare
    ELI: dont worry abt it/ have one on me
    NATALIE: thank you eli
200  BETTINA: *(falling out of her chair)* oh . . .
    ALEC: cut her off eli/ dont give her no more
    LILY: what's the matter bettina/ is yr show closin?

BETTINA: *(gets up, resets chair)* no/ my show is not closin/ but
    if that director asks me to play it any blacker/ i'm gonna have
    to do it in a mammy dress
LOU: you know/ countin pennies/ lookin for parts/ breakin tam-
    bourines/ we must be outta our minds for doin this
BETTINA: no we're not outta our minds/ we're just sorta outta
    our minds
LILY: no/ we're not outta our minds/ we've been doing this shit 210
    a long time . . . ross/ captain theophilis conneau/ in a *slaver's
    logbook*/ says that "youths of both sexes wear rings in the
    nose and lower lip and stick porcupine quills thru the carti-
    lage of the ear." ross/ when ringlin' bros. comes to madison
    square garden/ dontcha know the white people just go
ROSS: in their cb radios
DAHLIA: in their mcdonald's hats
ELI: with their save america t-shirts & those chirren who score
    higher on IQ tests for the white chirren who speak english
ALEC: when the hockey games absorb all america's attention in 220
    winter/ they go with their fists clenched & their tongues bat-
    tering their women who dont know a puck from a 3-yr-old
    harness racer
BETTINA: they go & sweat in fierce anger
ROSS: these factories
NATALIE: these middle management positions
ROSS: make madison square garden
BETTINA: the temple of the primal scream

*(*LILY *gets money from cash register & heads toward jukebox)*

LILY: oh how they love blood
NATALIE: & how they dont even dress for the occasion/ all in- 230
    conspicuous & pink
ELI: now if willie colon come there
BETTINA: if/ we say/ the fania all stars gonna be there
    in that nasty fantasy of the city council
ROSS: where the hot dogs are not even hebrew national
LILY: and the bread is stale
ROSS: even in such a place where dance is an obscure notion
BETTINA: where one's joy is good cause for a boring chat with
    the pinkerton guard
DAHLIA: where the halls lead nowhere              240
ELI: & "back to yr seat/ folks"
LILY: when all one's budget for cruisin
LOU: one's budget for that special dinner with you know who
LILY: the one you wd like to love you
BETTINA: when yr whole reasonable allowance for leisure ac-
    tivity/ buys you a seat where what's goin on dont matter
DAHLIA: cut you so high up you might be in seattle
LILY: even in such a tawdry space
ELI: where vorster & his pals wd spit & expect black folks to
    lick it up                            250
ROSS: *(stands on chair)* in such a place i've seen miracles
ALL: oh yeah/ aw/ ross
ROSS: the miracles

*("music for the love of it," by butch morris, comes up on the jukebox/ this is a catchy uptempo rhythm & blues post WW II. as they speak the company does a dance that highlights their ease with one another & their familiarity with "all the new dance steps")*

LILY: the commodores

DAHLIA: muhammad ali

NATALIE: bob marley

ALEC: & these folks who upset alla 7th avenue with their glow/ how the gold in their braids is new in this world of hard hats & men with the grace of wounded buffalo/ how these folks

260 in silk & satin/ in bodies reekin of good love comin/ these pretty muthafuckahs

DAHLIA: make this barn

LILY: this insult to good taste

BETTINA: a foray into paradise

DAHLIA, LILY, ALEC, NATALIE, & ROSS: (in unison) we dress up

BETTINA, ELI & LOU: (in unison) we dress up

DAHLIA: cuz we got good manners

ROSS: cd you really ask dr. funkenstein to come all that way & greet him in the clothes you sweep yr kitchen in?

270 ALL: NO!

BETTINA: cd you say to muhammad ali/ well/ i just didnt have a chance to change/ you see i have a job/ & then i went jogging & well, you know its just madison square garden

LOU: my dear/ you know that wont do

NATALIE: we honor our guests/ if it costs us all we got

DAHLIA: when stevie wonder sings/ he don't want us lookin like we ain't got no common sense/ he wants us to be as lovely as we really are/ so we strut & reggae

ELI: i seen some doing the jump up/ i myself just got happy/ but

280 i'm tellin you one thing for sure

LILY: we fill up where we at

BETTINA: no police

NATALIE: no cheap beer

DAHLIA: no nasty smellin bano

ROSS: no hallways fulla derelicts & hustlers

NATALIE: gonna interfere wit alla this beauty

ALEC: if it wasnt for us/ in our latino chic/ our rasta-fare our outer space funk suits & all the rest i have never seen

BETTINA: tho my daddy cd tell you bout them fox furs &

290 stacked heels/ the diamonds & marie antoinette wigs

ELI: it's not cuz we got money

NATALIE: it's not cuz if we had money we wd spend it on luxury

LILY: it's just when you gotta audience with the pope/ you look yr best

BETTINA: when you gonna see the queen of england/ you polish yr nails

NATALIE: when you gonna see one of them/ & you know who i mean

ALEC: they gotta really know

300 BETTINA: we gotta make em feel

ELI: we dont do this for any old body

LOU: we're doin this for you

NATALIE: we dress up

ALEC: is our say of sayin/ you gettin the very best

DAHLIA: we cant do less/ we love too much to be stingy

ROSS: they give us too much to be loved ordinary

LILY: we simply have good manners

ROSS: & an addiction to joy

FEMALE CAST MEMBERS: (in unison) WHEE . . .

310 DAHLIA: we dress up

MALE CAST MEMBERS: (in unison) HEY . . .

BETTINA: we gotta show the world/ we gotta corner on the color

ROSS: happiness just jumped right outta us/ & we are lookin good

(everyone in the bar is having so much fun/ that MAXINE takes on an exaggerated character as she enters/ in order to bring them to attention. the company freezes, half in respect/ half in parody)

MAXINE: cognac!

(the company relaxes, goes to tables or the bar. in the meantime, ROSS has remained in the spell of the character that MAXINE had introduced when she came in. he goes over to MAXINE who is having a drink/ & begins an improvisation)

ROSS: she left the front gate open/ not quite knowing she wanted someone to walk on thru the wrought iron fence/ scrambled in whiskey bottles broken round old bike spokes/ some nice brown man to wind up in her bed/ she really didnt know/ the sombrero that enveloped her face was a lil too 320 much for an april nite on the bowery/ & the silver halter dug out from summer cookouts near riis beach/ didnt sparkle with the intensity of her promise to have one good time/ before the children came back from carolina. brooklyn cd be such a drag, every street cept flatbush & nostrand/ reminiscent of europe during the plague/ seems like nobody but sickness waz out walkin/ drivels & hypes/ a few youngsters lookin for more than they cd handle/ & then there waz fay/

(MAXINE rises, begins acting the story out)

waiting for a cab. anyone of the cars inchin along the boulevard cd see fay waznt no whore/ just a good clean woman out 330 for the nite/ & tho her left titty jumped out from under her silver halter/ she didnt notice cuz she waz lookin for a cab. the dank air fondled her long saggin bosom like a possible companion/ she felt good. she stuck her tin-ringed hand on her waist & watched her own ankles dance in the nite. she waz gonna have a good time tonight/ she waz awright/ a whole lotta woman/ wit that special brooklyn bottom strut. knowin she waznt comin in til dawn/ fay covered herself/ sorta/ wit a light kacky jacket that just kept her titties from rompin in the wind/ & she pulled it closer to her/ the winds 340 waz comin/ from nowhere jabbin/ & there waznt no cabs/ the winds waz beatin her behind/ whisperin/ gigglin/ you aint going noplace/ you an ol bitch/ shd be at home wit ur kids. fay beat off the voices/ & an EBONY-TRUE-TO-YOU cab climbed the curb to get her. (as cabdriver) hope you aint plannin on stayin in brooklyn/ after 8:00 you dead in brooklyn (as narrator) she let her titty shake like she thot her mouth oughtta bubble like/ wd she take off her panties/ i'd take her anywhere. 350

MAXINE: (as if in cab) i'm into having a good time/ yr arms/ veins burstin/ like you usedta lift tobacco onto trucks or cut cane/ i want you to be happy/ long as we dont haveta stay in brooklyn

ROSS: & she made like she waz gypsy rose lee/ or the hotsy totsy girls in the carnival round from waycross/ when it waz segregated

MAXINE: what's yr name?

ROSS: my name is raphael

MAXINE: oh that's nice                                                    360

ROSS: & fay moved where i cd see her out the rear view mirror/ waz tellin me all bout her children & big eddie who waz away/ while we crossed the manhattan bridge/ i kept smilin. (*as cabdriver*) where exactly you goin?

MAXINE: i dont really know. i just want to have a good time. take me where i can see famous people/ & act bizarre like sinatra at the kennedys/ maybe even go round & beat up folks like jim brown/ throw somebody offa balcony/ you know/ for a good time

370 ROSS: the only place I knew/ i took her/ after i kisst the spaces she'd been layin open to me. fay had alla her $17 cuz i hadnt charged her nothin/ turned the meter off/ said it waz wonderful to pick up a lady like her on atlantic avenue/ i saw nobody but those goddamn whores/ & fay

(MAXINE *moves in to* ROSS & *gives him a very long kiss*)

now fay waz a gd clean woman/ & she waz burstin with pride & enthusiasm when she walked into the place where I swore/ all the actresses & actors hung out

(*the company joins in* ROSS' *story; responding to* MAXINE *as tho she waz entering their bar*)

oh yes/ there were actresses in braids & lipstick/ wigs & winged tip pumps/ fay assumed the posture of someone
380 she'd always admired/ etta james/ the waitress asked her to leave cuz she waz high/ & fay knew better than that

MAXINE: (*responding to lily's indication of throwing her out*) i aint high/ i'm enthusiastic/ and i'm gonna have me a goooooooood/ ol time

ROSS: she waz all dressed up/ she came all the way from brooklyn/ she must look high cuz i/ the taxi-man/ well i got her a lil excited/ that was all/ but she waz gonna cool out/ cuz she waz gonna meet her friends/ at this place/ yes. she knew that/ & she pushed a bunch of rhododendrum/ outta her
390 way so she cd get over to that table/ & stood over the man with the biggest niggah eyes & warmest smellin mouth

MAXINE: please/ let me join you/ i come all the way from brooklyn/ to have a good time/ you dont think i'm high do ya/ cd i please join ya/ i just wanna have a good ol time

ROSS: (*as bettina turns away*) the woman sipped chablis & looked out the window hopin to see one of the bowery drunks fall down somewhere/ fay's voice hovering/ flirtin wit hope

LOU: (*turning to face maxine*) why dont you go downstairs &
400 put yr titty in yr shirt/ you cant have no good time lookin like that/ now go on down & then come up & join us

(BETTINA & LOU *rise & move to another table*)

ROSS: fay tried to shove her flesh anywhere/ she took off her hat/ bummed a kool/ swallowed somebody's cognac/ & sat down/ waitin/ for a gd time

MAXINE: (*rises & hugs ross*) aw ross/ when am i gonna get a chance to feel somethin like that/ i got into this business cuz i wanted to feel things all the time/ & all they want me to do is put my leg in my face/ smile/ &

LILY: you better knock on some wood/ maxine/ at least yr
410 workin

BETTINA: & at least yr not playing a whore/ if some other woman comes in here & tells me she's playing a whore/ i think i might kill her

ELI: you'd kill her so you cd say/ oh dahlia died & i know all her lines

BETTINA: aw hush up eli/ dnt you know what i mean?

ELI: no miss/ i dont/ are you in the theater?

BETTINA: mr. bartender/ poet sir/ i am theater

DAHLIA: well miss theater/ that's a surprise/ especially since you fell all over the damn stage in the middle of my solo 420

LILY: she did

ELI: miss theater herself fell down?

DAHLIA: yeah/ she cant figure out how to get attention without makin somebody else look bad

MAXINE: now dahlia/ it waznt that bad/ i hardly noticed her

DAHLIA: it waz my solo/ you werent sposed to notice her at all!

BETTINA: you know dahlia/ i didnt do it on purpose/ i cda hurt myself

DAHLIA: that wd be unfortunate

BETTINA: well miss thing with those big ass hips you got/ i dont 430 know why you think you can do the ballet anyway

(*the company breaks; they're expecting a fight*)

DAHLIA: (*crossing to bettina*) i got this

(*demonstrates her leg extension*)

& alla this

(DAHLIA *turns her back to* BETTINA/ & *slaps her own backside.* BETTINA *grabs* DAHLIA, *turns her around & they begin a series of finger snaps that are a paraphrase of ailey choreography for very dangerous fights.* ELI *comes to break up the impending altercation*)

ELI: ladies ladies ladies

(ELI *separates the two*)

ELI: people keep tellin me to put my feet on the ground
i get mad & scream/ there is no ground
only shit pieces from dogs horses & men who dont live
anywhere/ they tell me think straight & make myself
somethin/ i shout & sigh/ i am a poet/ i write poems
i make words cartwheel & somersault down pages 440
outta my mouth come visions distilled like bootleg
whiskey/ i am like a radio but i am a channel of my own
i keep sayin i write poems/ & people keep askin me
what do i do/ what in the hell is going on?
people keep tellin me these are hard times/ what are
you gonna be doin ten years from now/
what in the hell do you think/ i am gonna be writin poems
i will have poems inchin up the walls of the lincoln tunnel/
i am gonna feed my children poems on rye bread with
    horseradish/ 450
i am gonna send my mailman off with a poem for his
    wagon/
give my doctor a poem for his heart/ i am a poet/
i am not a part-time poet/ i am not a amateur poet/
i dont even know what that person cd be/ whoever that is
authorizing poetry as an avocation/ is a fraud/
put yr own feet on the ground

BETTINA: i'm sorry eli/ i just dont want to be a gypsy all my life

(*the bar returns to normal humming & sipping. the lights change to focus on* LILY/ *who begins to say what's really been on her mind. the rest of the company is not aware of* LILY's *private thoughts. only* BETTINA *responds to* LILY, *but as a partner in fantasy, not as a voyeur)*

LILY: *(illustrating her words with movement)* i'm gonna simply
460 brush my hair. rapunzel pull yr tresses back into the tower.
& lady godiva give up horseback riding. i'm gonna alter my
social & professional life dramatically. i will brush 100
strokes in the morning/ 100 strokes midday & 100 strokes
before retiring. i will have a very busy schedule. between the
local trains & the express/ i'm gonna brush. i brush between
telephone calls. at the disco i'm gonna brush on the slow
songs/ i dont slow dance with strangers. i'ma brush my hair
before making love & after. i'll brush my hair in taxis, while
windowshopping. when i have visitors over the kitchen
470 table/ i'ma brush. i brush my hair while thinking abt anything. mostly i think abt how it will be when i get my full
heada hair. like lifting my head in the morning will become
a chore. i'll try to turn my cheek & my hair will weigh me
down

*(LILY falls to the floor. bettina helps lift her to her knees, then
begins to dance & mime as LILY speaks)*

i dream of chaka khan/ chocolate from graham central station with all seven wigs/ & medusa. i brush & brush. i use
olive oil hair food/ & posner's vitamin E. but mostly i brush
& brush. i may lose contact with most of my friends. i cd lose
my job/ but i'm on unemployment & brush while waiting on
480 line for my check. i'm sure i get good recommendations
from my social worker: such a fastidious woman/ that lily/ always brushing her hair. nothing in my dreams suggests that
hair brushing/ per se/ has anything to do with my particular
heada hair. a therapist might say that the head fulla hair has
to do with something else/ like: a symbol of lily's unconscious desires. but i have no therapist

*(she takes imaginary pen from BETTINA, who was pretending to
be a therapist/ & sits down at table across from her)*

& my dreams mean things to me/ like if you dreamed abt to-
bias/ then something has happened to tobias/ or he is gonna
490 up. if you dream abt yr grandma who's dead/ then you must
be doing something she doesnt like/ or she wdnta gone to all
the trouble to leave heaven like that. if you dream something red/ you shd stop. if you dream something green/ you
shd keep doing it. if a blue person appears in yr dreams/
then that person is yr true friend
& that's how i see my dreams. & this head fulla hair i have
in my dreams is lavender & nappy as a 3-yr-old's in a apple
tree. i can fry an egg & see the white of the egg spreadin in
the grease like my hair is gonna spread in the air/ but i'm not
500 egg-yolk yellow/ i am brown & the egg white isnt white at all/
it is my actual hair/ & it wd go on & on forever/ irregular like
a rasta-man's hair. irregular/ gargantuan & lavender. nestled
on blue satin pillows/ pillows like the sky. & so i fry my eggs.
i buy daisies dyed lavender & laced lavender tablemats &
lavender nail polish. though i never admit it/ i really do believe in magic/ & can do strange things when something
comes over. soon everything around me will be lavender/
fluffy & consuming. i will know not a moment of bitterness/
through all the wrist aching & tennis elbow from brushing/
i'll smile. no regrets/ "je ne regrette rien" i'll sing like edith
510 piaf. when my friends want me to go see tina turner or

pacheco/ i'll croon "sorry/ i have to brush my hair."
i'll find ambrosia. my hair'll grow pomegranates & soil/ rich
as round the aswan/ i wake in my bed to bananas/ avocados/
collard greens/ the tramps' latest disco hit/ fresh croissant/
pouilly fuissé/ ishmael reed's essays/ charlotte carter's sto-
ries/ all stream from my hair.
& with the bricks that plop from where a 9-year-old's top
braid wd be i will brush myself a house with running water
& a bidet. i'll have a closet full of clean bed linen & the lil
girl from the castro convertible commercial will come & 520
open the bed repeatedly & stay on as a helper to brush my
hair. lily is the only person i know whose every word leaves
a purple haze on the tip of yr tongue. when this happens i
says clouds are forming/ & i has to close the windows. violet
rain is hard to remove from blue satin pillows

*(LOU, the magician, gets up. he points to LILY sitting very still.
he reminds us that it is only thru him that we are able to know
these people without the "masks"/ the lies/ & he cautions that
all their thoughts are not benign. they are not safe from what
they remember or imagine)*

LOU: you have t come with me/ to this place where magic is/
to hear my song/ some times i forget & leave my tune
in the corner of the closet under all the dirty clothes/
in this place/ magic asks me where i've been/ how i've
been singin/ lately i leave my self in all the wrong hands/ 530
in this place where magic is involved in
undoin our masks/ i am able to smile & answer that.
in this place where magic always asks for me
i discovered a lot of other people who talk without mouths
who listen to what you say/ by watchin yr jewelry dance
& in this place where magic stays
you can let yrself in or out
but when you leave yrself at home/ burglars & daylight
thieves
pounce on you & sell yr skin/ at cut-rates on tenth avenue 540

*(ROSS has been playing the acoustic guitar softly as LOU spoke.
ALEC picks up on the train of LOU's thoughts & tells a story that
in turn captures NATALIE' attention. slowly, NATALIE becomes
the woman ALEC describes)*

ALEC: she had always wanted a baby/ never a family/ never a
man/
she had always wanted a baby/ who wd suckle & sleep
a baby boy who wd wet/ & cry/ & smile
suckle & sleep
when she sat in bars/ on the stool/ near the door/ & cross
from the juke box/ with her legs straddled & revealin red
lace pants/ & lil hair smashed under the stockings/ she wd
think how she wanted this baby & how she wd call the baby/
"myself" & as thot/ bout this brown lil thing/ she ordered an- 550
other bourbon/ double & tilted her head as if to cuddle
some infant/ not present/ the men in the bar never imagined
her as someone's mother/ she rarely tended her own self
carefully/

*(NATALIE rises slowly, sits astride on the floor)*

just enough to exude a languid sexuality that teased the men
off work/ & the bartender/ ray who waz her only friend/
women didnt take to her/ so she spent her afternoons with

ray/ in the bar round the corner from her lil house/ that shook winsomely in a hard wind/ surrounded by three weepin willows

560

NATALIE: my name is sue-jean & i grew here/ a ordinary colored girl with no claims to any thing/ or anyone/ i drink now/ bourbon/ in harder times/ beer/ but i always wanted to have a baby/ a lil boy/ named myself

ALEC: one time/ she made it with ray

NATALIE: & there waz nothin special there/ only a hot rough bangin/ a brusque barrelin throwin of torso/ legs & sweat/ ray wanted to kiss me/ but i screamed/ cuz i didnt like kissin/ only fuckin/ & we rolled round/ i waz a peculiar sorta

570

woman/ wantin no kisses/ no caresses/ just power/ heat & no eaziness of thrust/ ray pulled himself outa me/ with no particular exclamation/ he smacked me on my behind/ i waz grinnin/ & he took that as an indication of his skill/ he believed he waz a good lover/ & a woman like me/ didnt never want nothing but a hard dick/ & everyone believed that/ tho no one in town really knew

ALEX: so ray/ went on behind the bar cuz he had got his

NATALIE: & i lay in the corner laughin/ with my drawers/ twisted round my ankles & my hair standin every which way/

580

i waz laughin/ knowin i wd have this child/ myself/ & no one wd ever claim him/ cept me cuz i was a low-down thing/ layin in sawdust & whiskey stains/ i laughed & had a good time masturbatin in the shadows.

ALEC: sue-jean ate starch for good luck

NATALIE: like mama kareena/ tol me

ALEC: & she planted five okras/ five collards/ & five tomatoes

NATALIE: for good luck too/ i waz gonna have this baby/ i even went over to the hospital to learn prenatal care/ & i kept myself clean

590

ALEC: sue-jean's lanky body got ta spreadin & her stomach waz taut & round high in her chest/ a high pregnancy is sure to be a boy/ & she smiled

NATALIE: i stopped goin to the bar

ALEC: started cannin food

NATALIE: knittin lil booties

ALEC: even goin to church wit the late nite radio evangelist

NATALIE: i gotta prayer cloth for the boy/ myself waz gonna be safe from all that his mama/ waz prey to

ALEC: sure/ sue-jean waz a scandal/ but that waz to be ex-

600

pected/ cuz she was always a po criterish chile

NATALIE: & wont no man bout step my way/ ever/ just cuz i hadda bad omen on me/ from the very womb/ i waz bewitched is what the ol women usedta say

ALEC: sue-jean waz born on a full moon/ the year of the flood/ the night the river raised her skirts & sat over alla the towns & settlements for 30 miles in each direction/ the nite the river waz in labor/ gruntin & groanin/ splittin trees & families/ spillin cupboards over the ground/ waz the nite sue-jean waz born

610

NATALIE: & my mother died/ drowned/ holdin me up over the mud crawlin in her mouth

ALEC: somebody took her & she lived to be the town's no one/ now with the boy achin & dancin in her belly/ sue-jean waz a gay & gracious woman/ she made pies/ she baked cakes & left them on the stoop of the church she had never entered just cuz she wanted/ & she grew plants & swept her floors/ she waz someone she had never known/ she waz herself with

child/ & she waz a wonderful bulbous thing

NATALIE: the nite/ myself waz born/ ol mama kareena from the hills came down to see bout me/ i hollered & breathed/ i did

620

exactly like mama kareena said/ & i pushed & pushed & there waz a earthquake up in my womb/ i wanted to sit up & pull the tons of logs trapped in my crotch out/ so i cd sleep/ but it wdnt go way/i pushed & thot i saw 19 horses runnin in my pussy/ i waz sure there waz a locomotive stalled up in there burnin coal & steamin & pushin gainst a mountain

ALEC: finally the child's head waz within reach & mama kareena/ brought the boy into this world

NATALIE: & he waz awright/ with alla his toes & his fingers/ his lil dick & eyes/ elbows that bent/ & legs/ straight/ i wanted a

630

big glassa bourbon/ & mama kareena brought it/ right away/ we sat drinkin the bourbon/ & lookin at the child whose name waz myself/ like i had wanted/ & the two of us ate placenta stew . . . i waznt really sure . . .

ALEC: sue-jean you werent really sure you wanted myself to wake up/ you always wanted him to sleep/ or at most to nurse/ the nites yr dreams were disturbed by his cryin

NATALIE: I had no one to help me

ALEC: so you were always with him/ & you didnt mind/ you knew this waz yr baby/ myself/ & you cuddled him/ carried

640

him all over the house with you all day/ no matter/ what

NATALIE: everythin waz going awright til/ myself wanted to crawl

ALEC: (moving closer to NATALIE) & discover a world of his own/ then you became despondent/ & yr tits began to dry & you lost the fullness of yr womb/ where myself/ had lived

NATALIE: I wanted that back

ALEC: you wanted back the milk

NATALIE: & the tight gourd of a stomach i had when myself waz bein in me

650

ALEC: so you slit his wrists

NATALIE: he waz sleepin

ALEC: sucked the blood back into yrself/ & waited/ myself shriveled up in his crib

NATALIE: a dank lil blk thing/ i never touched him again

ALEC: you were always holdin yr womb/ feelin him kick & sing to you bout love/ & you wd hold yr tit in yr hand

NATALIE: like i always did when i fed him

ALEC: & you waited & waited/ for a new myself. tho there were labor pains

660

NATALIE: & i screamed in my bed

ALEC: yr legs pinnin to the air

NATALIE: spinnin sometimes like a ferris wheel/ i cd get no child to fall from me

ALEC: & she forgot abt the child bein born/ & waz heavy & full all her life/ with "myself"

NATALIE: who'll be out/ any day now

(ELI *moves from behind the bar to help* NATALIE/ *or to clean tables. he doesnt really know. he stops suddenly*)

ELI: aint that a goddamn shame/ aint that a way
   to come into the world
   sometimes i really cant write                                        670
   sometimes i cant even talk

(*the minstrel mask comes down very slowly. blackout, except for lights on the big minstrel mask which remains visible throughout intermission)*

### —ACT TWO—

*(all players onstage are frozen, except* LOU, *who makes a motion for the big minstrel mask to disappear again. as the mask flies up,* LOU *begins)*

LOU: in this place where magic stays
   you can let yrself in or out

*(he makes a magic motion. a samba is heard from the jukebox & activity is begun in the bar again.* DAHLIA, NATALIE *& LILY enter, apparently from the ladies room)*

NATALIE: i swear we went to that audition in good faith/ & that man asked us where we learned to speak english so well/ i swear this foreigner/ asked us/ from the city of new york/ where we learned to speak english.

LILY: all i did was say "bom dia/ como vai"/ and the englishman got red in the face

680 LOU: *(as the englishman)* yr from the states/ aren't you?

LILY: "sim"/ i said/ in good portuguese

LOU: but you speak portuguese

LILY: "sim" i said/ in good portuguese

LOU: how did you pick that up?

LILY: i hadda answer so simple/ i cdnt say i learned it/ cuz niggahs cant learn & that wda been too hard on the man/ so i said/ in good english: i held my ear to the ground & listened to the samba from bêlim

DAHLIA: you should have said: i make a lotta phone calls to

690 casçais, portugao

BETTINA: i gotta bahiano boyfriend

NATALIE: how abt: i waz an angolan freedom fighter

MAXINE: no/ lily/ tell him: i'm a great admirer of zeza motto & leci brandao

LILY: when the japanese red army invaded san juan/ they poisoned the papaya with portuguese. i eat a lotta papaya. last week/ i developed a strange schizophrenic condition/ with 4 manifest personalities: one spoke english & understood nothing/ one spoke french & had access to the world/ one

700 spoke spanish & voted against statehood for puerto rico/ one spoke portuguese. "eu não falo ingles então y voce"/ i dont speak english anymore/ & you?

*(all the women in the company have been doing samba steps as the others spoke/ now they all dance around a table in their own ritual/ which stirs* ALEC *&* LOU *to interrupt this female segregation. the women scatter to different tables, leaving the two interlopers alone. so,* ALEC *&* LOU *begin their conversation)*

ALEC: not only waz she without a tan, but she held her purse close to her hip like a new yorker. someone who rode the paris métro or listened to mariachis in plaza santa cecilia. she waz not from here

*(he sits at table)*

LOU: *(following suit)* but from there

ALEC: some there where coloureds/ mulattoes/ negroes/ blacks cd make a living big enough to leave there to come here/

where no one went there much any more for all sorts of 710 reasons

LOU: the big reasons being immigration restrictions & unemployment. nowadays, immigration restrictions of every kind apply to any non-european persons who want to go there from here

ALEC: some who want to go there from here risk fetching trouble with the customs authority there

LOU: or later with the police, who can tell who's not from there cuz the shoes are pointed & laced strange

ALEC: the pants be for august & yet it's january                    720

LOU: the accent is patterned for pétionville, but working in crown heights

ALEC: what makes a person comfortably ordinary here cd make him dangerously conspicuous there.

LOU: so some go to london or amsterdam or paris/ where they are so abounding no one tries to tell who is from where

ALEC: still the far right wing of every there prints lil pamphlets that say everyone from there shd leave & go back where they came from

LOU: this is manifest legally thru immigration restrictions & 730 personally thru unemployment

ALEC: anyway the yng woman waz from there/ & she waz alone. that waz good. cuz if a person had no big brother in gronigen/ no aunt in rouen

LOU: no sponsor in chicago

ALEC: this brown woman from there might be a good idea. everybody in the world/ european & non-european alike/ everybody knows that rich white girls are hard to find. some of them joined the weather underground/ some the baadermeinhof gang.                                                      740

LOU: a whole bunch of them gave up men entirely

ALEC: so the exotic lover in the sun routine becomes more difficult to swing/ if she wants to talk abt plastic explosives & the resistance of the black masses to socialism/ instead of giving head as the tide slips in or lending money

LOU: just for the next few days

ALEC: is hard to find a rich white girl who is so dumb/ too

LOU: anyway. the whole world knows/ european & non-european alike/ the whole world knows that nobody loves the black woman like they love farrah fawcett-majors. the whole 750 world dont turn out for a dead black woman like they did for marilyn monroe.

ALEC: actually/ the demise of josephine baker waz an international event

LOU: but she waz a war hero
   the worldwide un-beloved black woman is a good idea/ if she is from there & one is a young man with gd looks/ piercing eyes/ & knowledge of several romantic languages

*(throughout this conversation,* ALEC *&* LOU *will make attempts to seduce, cajole, & woo the women of the bar as their narrative indicates. the women play the roles as described, being so moved by romance)*

ALEC: the best dancing spots/ the hill where one can see the entire bay at twilight                                           760

LOU: the beach where the seals & pelicans run free/ the hidden "local" restaurants

ALEC: "aw babee/ you so pretty" begins often in the lobby of hotels where the bright handsome yng men wd be loiterers

LOU: were they not needed to tend the needs of the black women from there

ALEC: tourists are usually white people or asians who didnt come all this way to meet a black woman who isnt even foreign

770 LOU: so hotel managers wink an eye at the yng men in the lobby or by the bar who wd be loitering/ but are gonna help her have a gd time

ALEC: maybe help themselves too

LOU: everybody in the world/ european & non-european alike/ everybody knows the black woman from there is not treated as a princess/ as a jewel/ a cherished lover

ALEC: that's not how sapphire got her reputation/ nor how mrs. jefferson perceives the world

LOU: you know/ babee/ you dont act like them. aw babee/ you
780 so pretty

ALEC: the yng man in the hotel watches the yng blk woman sit & sit & sit/ while the european tourists dance with each other/ & the dapper local fellas mambo frenetically with secretaries from arizona/ in search of the missing rich white girl. our girl sits &

FEMALE CAST MEMBERS: (in unison) sits & sits & sits

ALEC: (to DAHLIA & NATALIE, who move to the music) maybe she is courageous & taps her foot. maybe she is bold & enjoys the music/ smiling/ shaking shoulders. let her sit & let
790 her know she is unwanted

LOU: she is not white & she is not from here

ALEC: let her know she is not pretty enuf to dance the next merengue. then appear/ mysteriously/ in the corner of the bar. stare at her. just stare. when stevie wonder's song/ "isn't she lovely"/ blares thru the red-tinted light/ ask her to dance & hold her as tyrone power wda. hold her & stare

(ROSS & ELI sing the chorus to stevie wonder's "isn't she lovely")

LOU: dance yr ass off. she has been discovered by the non-european fred astaire

ALEC: let her know she is a surprise/ an event. by the look on yr
800 face you've never seen anyone like this black woman from there. you say: "aw/ you not from here?"/ totally astonished. she murmurs that she is from there. as if to apologize for her unfortunate place of birth

LOU: you say

ALEC: aw babee/ you so pretty. & it's all over

LOU: a night in a pension near the sorbonne. pick her up from the mattress. throw her against the wall in a show of exotic temper & passion: "maintenant/ tu es ma femme. nous nous sommes mariés." unions of this sort are common wherever
810 the yng black women travel alone. a woman traveling alone is an affront to the non-european man who is known the world over/ to european & non-european alike/ for his way women

ALEC: his sense of romance/ how he can say:

LOU: aw babee/ you so pretty . . . and even a beautiful woman will believe no one else ever recognized her loveliness

ELI: or else/ he comes to a cafe in willemstad in the height of the sunset. an able-bodied/ sinewy yng man who wants to buy one beer for the yng woman. after the first round/ he
820 discovers he has run out of money/ so she must buy the next round/ when he discovers/ what beautiful legs you have/

how yr mouth is like the breath of tiger lilies. we shall make love in the/ how you call it/ yes in the earth/ in the dirt/ i will have you in my/ how you say/ where things grow/ aw/ yes/ i will have you in the soil. probably under the stars & smelling of wine/ an unforgettable international affair can be consummated

(the company sings "tara's theme" as eli ends his speech. eli & bettina take a tango walk to the bar, while maxine mimics a 1930's photographer, shooting them as they sail off into the sunset)

MAXINE: at 11:30 one evening i waz at the port authority/ new york/ united states/ myself. now i waz there & i spoke eng-lish & waz holding approximately $7 american currency/ 830 when a yng man from there came up to me from the front of the line of people waiting for the princeton new jersey united states local bus. i mean to say/ he gave up his chance for a good seat to come say to me:

ROSS: i never saw a black woman reading nietzsche

MAXINE: i waz demure enough/ i said i have to for a philosophy class. but as the night went on I noticed this yng man waz so much like the other yng men from here/ who use their bod-ies as bait & their smiles as passport alternatives. anyway the night did go on. we were snuggled together in the rear of the 840 bus going down the jersey turnpike. he told me in english/ that he had spoken all his life in st. louis/ where he waz raised:

ROSS: i've wanted all my life to meet someone like you. i want you to meet my family/ who haven't seen me in a long time/ since i left missouri looking for opportunity . . .

(he is lost for words)

LOU: (stage whisper) opportunity to sculpt

ROSS: thank you/ opportunity to sculpt

MAXINE: he had been everyplace/ he said

ROSS: you arent like any black woman i've ever met anywhere 850

MAXINE: here or there

ROSS: i had to come back to new york cuz of immigration re-strictions & high unemployment among black american sculptors abroad

MAXINE: just as we got to princeton/ he picked my face up with his shoulder & said:

ROSS: aw babee/ you so pretty

MAXINE: aw babee/ you so pretty. i believe that night i must have looked beautiful for a black woman from there/ though i cd be asked at any moment to tour the universe/ to climb a 860 6-story walkup with a brilliant & starving painter/ to share kadushi/ to meet mama/ to getta kiss each time the swing falls toward the willow branch/ to imagine where he say he from/ & more. i cd/ i cd have all of it/ but i cd not be taken/ long as i don't let a stranger be the first to say:

LOU: aw babee/ you so pretty

MAXINE: after all/ immigration restrictions & unemployment cd drive a man to drink or to lie

(she breaks away from ROSS)

so if you know yr beautiful & bright & cherishable awready/ when he say in whatever language: 870

ALEX: (to NATALIE) aw babee/ you so pretty

MAXINE: you cd say:

NATALIE: i know. thank you

MAXINE: then he'll smile/ & you'll smile. he'll say:

ELI: (stroking BETTINA'S *thigh*) what nice legs you have

MAXINE: you can say:

BETTINA: (removing his hand) yes. they run in the family

MAXINE: oh! whatta universe of beautiful & well traveled women!

880 MALE CAST MEMBERS: (in unison) aw babee/ i've never met any-one like you

FEMALE CAST MEMBERS: (in unison, pulling away from me to stage edges) that's strange/ there are millions of us!

(men all cluster after unsuccessful attempts to persuade their women to talk. ALEC gets the idea to serenade the women; ROSS takes the first verse, with men singing back-up, song is "ooh baby," by smokey robinson)

ROSS: (singing)
*i did you wrong/ my heart went out to play/ but in the game*
    *i lost you/ what a price to pay/ i'm crying . . .*

MALE PLAYERS: (singing)
    *oo oo oo/ baby baby. . . . oo oo oo/ baby baby*

(this brings no response from the women; the men elect ELI to lead the second verse)

ELI:
890     *mistakes i know i've made a few/ but i'm only human*
            *you've made mistakes too/ i'm cryin . . .*
        *oo oo oo/ baby baby . . . oo oo oo/ baby baby*

(the women slowly forsake their staunch indignation/ return-ing to the arms of their partners. all that is except LILY, who walks abt the room of couples awkwardly)

MALE CAST MEMBERS & LILY: (singing)
        *i'm just about at the end of my rope*
        *but i can't stop trying/ i cant give up hope*
        *cause i/ i believe one day/ i'll hold you near*
        *whisper i love you/ until that day is here*
            *i'm cryin . . . oo oo oo/ baby baby*

(LILY begins as the company continues to sing)

LILY: unfortunately
900     the most beautiful man in the world
        is unavailable
            that's what he told me
        i saw him wandering abt/ said well this is one of a kind
        & i might be able to help him out
        so alone & pretty in all this ganja & bodies melting
        he danced with me & i cd become that
        a certain way to be held that's considered in advance
        a way a thoughtful man wd kiss a woman who
        cd be offended easily/ but waznt cuz
910     of course the most beautiful man in the world
        knows exactly what to do
        with someone who knows that's who he is/
        these dreads fallin thru my dress
        so my nipples just stood up
        these hands playin the guitar on my back

the lips somewhere between my neck
    & my forehead
talking bout ocho rios & how i really must go
marcus garvey cda come in the door & we/
we wd still be dancin that dance                          920
the motion that has more to do with kinetic energy
than shootin stars/ more to do with the impossibility
of all this/ & how it waz awready bein too much
our reason failed
we tried to go away & be just together
aside from the silence that weeped
with greed/ we didnt need/ anything/ but one another
for tonite
but he is the most beautiful man in the world
    says he's unavailable/                                930
& this man whose eyes made me
half-naked & still & brazen/ was singin with me
since we cd not talk/ we sang

(male players end their chorus with a flourish)

LILY: we sang with bob marley
    this man/ surely the most beautiful men in the world/ & i
    sang/ "i wanna love you & treat you right/

(the couples begin different kinds of reggae dances)

    i wanna love you every day & every nite"

THE COMPANY: (dancing & singing)
        *we'll be together with the roof right over our heads*
        *we'll share the shelter of my single bed*           940
        *we'll share the same room/ jah provide the bread*

DAHLIA: (stops dancing during conversation) i tell you it's not
    just the part that makes me love you so much

LOU: what is it/ wait/ i know/ you like my legs

DAHLIA: yes/ uh huh/ yr legs & yr arms/ & . . .

LOU: but that's just my body/ you started off saying you loved
    me & now i see it's just my body

DAHLIA: oh/ i didnt mean that/ it's just i dont know you/ except
    as the character i'm sposed to love/ & well i know rehearsal
    is over/ but i'm still in love with you                950

(they go to the bar to get drinks, then sit at a table)

ROSS: but baby/ you have to on the road. we need the money

NATALIE: i'm not going on the road so you can fuck all these as-
    piring actresses

ROSS: aw/ just some of them/ baby

NATALIE: that's why i'm not going

ROSS: if you dont go on the road i'll still be fuckin em/ but you
    & me/ we'll be in trouble/ you understand?

NATALIE: (stops dancing) no i dont understand

ROSS: well let me break it down to you

NATALIE: please/ break it down to me                        960

BETTINA: (stops dancing) hey/ natalie/ why dont you make him
    go on the road/ they always want us to be so goddamned
    conscientious

ALEC: (stops dancing) dont you think you shd mind yr own biz-
    ness?

NATALIE: yeah bettina/ mind yr own business

(she pulls ROSS to a table with her)

BETTINA: *(to* ALEC*)* no/ i'm tired of having to take any & every old job to support us/ & you get to have artistic integrity & refuse parts that are beneath you

970 ALEC: thats right/ i'm not playing the fool or the black buck pimp circus/ i'm an actor not a stereotype/ i've been trained. you know i'm a classically trained actor

BETTINA: & just what do you think we are?

MAXINE: well/ i got offered another whore part downtown

ELI: you gonna take it?

MAXINE: yeah

LILY: if you dont/ i know someone who will

ALEC: *(to* BETTINA*)* i told you/ we arent gonna get anyplace/ by doin every bit part for a niggah that someone waves in fronta

980 my face

BETTINA: & we arent gonna live long on nothin/ either/ cuz i'm quittin my job

ALEC: be in the real world for once & try to understand me

BETTINA: you mean/ i shd understand that you are the great artist & i'm the trouper.

ALEC: i'm not saying that we cant be gigglin & laughin all the time dancin around/ but i cant say in these "hate whitey" shows/ cuz they arent true

BETTINA: a failure of imagination on yr part/ i take it

990 ALEC: no/ an insult to my person

BETTINA: oh i see/ you wanna give the people some more make-believe

ALEC: i cd always black up again & do minstrel work/ wd that make you happy?

BETTINA: there is nothin niggardly abt a decent job. work is honorable/ work!

ALEC: well/ i got a problem. i got lots of problems/ but i got one i want you to fix & if you can fix it/ i'll do anything you say. last spring this niggah from the midwest asked for president

1000 carter to say he waz sorry for that forgettable phenomenon/ slavery/ which brought us all together. i never did get it/ none of us got no apology from no white folks abt not bein considered human beings/ that makes me mad & tired. someone told me "roots" was the way white folks worked out their guilt/ the success of "roots" is the way white folks as-suaged their consciences/ i dont know this/ this is what i waz told. i dont get any pleasure from nobody watchin me trying to be a slave i once waz/ who got away/ when we all know they had an emancipation proclamation/ that the civil war

1010 waz not fought over us. we all know that we/ actually dont exist unless we play football or basketball or baseball or soc-cer/ pélé/ see they still import a strong niggah to earn money. art here/ isnt like in the old country/ where we had some spare time & did what we liked to do/ i dont know this either/ this is also something i've been told. i just want to find out why no one has even been able to sound a gong & all the reporters recite that the gong is ringin/ while we watch all the white people/ immigrants & invaders/ con-quistadors & relatives of london debtors from georgia/ kneel

1020 & apologize to us/ just for three or four minutes. now/ this is not impossible/ & someone shd make a day where a few minutes of the pain of our lives is acknowledged. i have never been very interested in what white people did/ cuz i waz able/ like most of us/ to have very lil to do with them/ but if i become a success that means i have to talk to white folks more than in high school/ they are everywhere/ you

know how they talk abt a neighborhood changin/ we sud-denly become all over the place/ they are now all over my life/ & i dont like it. i am not talkin abt poets & painters/ not abt women & lovers of beauty/ i am talkin abt that prover- 1030 bial white person who is usually a man who just/ turns yr body around/ looks at yr teeth & yr ass/ who feels yr calves & back/ & agrees on a price. we are/ you see/ now able to sell ourselves/ & i am still a person who is tired/ a person who is not into his demise/ just three minutes for our lives/ just three minutes of silence & a gong in st. louis/ oakland/ in los angeles . . .

*(the entire company looks at him as if he's crazy/ he tries to leave the bar/ but* BETTINA *stops him)*

BETTINA: you're still outta yr mind. ain't no apologies keeping us alive.

LOU: what are you gonna do with white folks kneeling all over 1040 the country anyway/ man

*(*LOU *signals everyone to kneel)*

LILY: they say i'm too light to work/ but when i asked him what he meant/ he said i didn't actually look black. but/ i said/ my mama knows i'm black & my daddy/ damn sure knows i'm black/ & he is the only one who has a problem thinkin i'm black/ i said so let me play a white girl/ i'm a classically trained actress & i need the work & i can do it/ he said that wdnt be very ethical of him. can you imagine that shit/ not ethical

NATALIE: as a red-blooded white woman/ i cant allow you all to 1050 go on like that

*(*NATALIE *starts jocularly)*

cuz today i'm gonna be a white girl/ i'll retroactively wake myself up/ ah low & behold/ a white girl in my bed/ but first i'll haveta call a white girl i know to have some more accu-rate information/ what's the first thing white girls think in the morning/ do they get up being glad they aint niggahs/ do they remember mama/ or worry abt gettin to work/ do they work?/ do they play isadora & wrap themselves in sheets & go tip toeing to the kitchen to make maxwell house coffee/ oh i know/ the first thing a white girl does in the morning is 1060 fling her hair/

so now i'm done with that/ i'm gonna water my plants/ but am i a po white trash white girl with a old jellyjar/ or am i a sophisticated & protestant suburbanite with 2 valiums slugged awready & a porcelain water carrier leading me up the stairs strewn with heads of dolls & nasty smellin white husband person's underwear/ if I was really protected from the niggahs/ i might go to early morning mass & pick up a tomato pie on the way home/ so i cd eat it during the young & the restless. in williams arizona as a white girl/ i cd push 1070 the navaho women outta my way in the supermarket & push my nose in the air so i wdnt haveta smell them. coming from bay ridge on the train i cd smile at all the black & puerto rican people/ & hope they cant tell i want them to go back where they came from/ or at least be invisible

i'm still in my kitchen/ so i guess i'll just have to fling my hair again & sit down. i shd pinch my cheeks to bring the color back/ i wonder why the colored lady hasnt arrived to clean my house yet/ so i cd go to the beauty parlor & sit under a sunlamp to get some more color back/ it's terrible how god gave those colored women such clear complexions/ it take em years to develop wrinkles/ but beauty can be bought & flattered into the world.

as a white girl on the street/ i can assume since i am a white girl on the streets/ that everyone notices how beautiful i am/ especially lil black & caribbean boys/ they love to look at me/ i'm exotic/ no one in their families looks like me/ poor things. if i waz one of those white girls who loves one of those grown black fellas/ i cd say with my eyes wide open/ totally sincere/ oh i didnt know that/ i cd say i didnt know/ i cant/ i dont know how/ cuz i'ma white girl & i dont have to do much of anything.

all of this is the fault of the white man's sexism/ oh how i loathe tight-assed thin-lipped pink white men/ even the football players lack a certain relaxed virility. that's why my heroes are either just like my father/ who while he still cdnt speak english knew enough to tell me how the niggers shd go back where they came from/ or my heroes are psychotic faggots who are white/ or else they are/ oh/ you know/ colored men.

being a white girl by dint of my will/ is much more complicated than i thought it wd be/ but i wanted to try it cuz so many men like white girls/ white men/ black men/ latin men/ jewish men/ asians/ everybody. so i thought if i waz a white girl for a day i might understand this better/ after all gertrude stein wanted to know abt the black women/ alice adams wrote *thinking abt billie/* joyce carol oates has three different black characters all with the same name/ i guess cuz we are underdeveloped individuals or cuz we are all the same/ at any rate i'm gonna call this thinkin abt white girls/ cuz helmut newton's awready gotta book called *white women/* see what i mean/ that's a best seller/ one store i passed/ hadda sign said/

> WHITE WOMEN
> SOLD OUT

it's this kinda pressure that forces us white girls to be so absolutely pathological abt the other women in the world/ who now that they're not all servants or peasants want to be considered beautiful too. we simply krinkle our hair/ learn to dance the woogie dances/ slant our eyes with make-up or surgery/ learn spanish & claim argentinian background/ or as a real trump card/ show up looking like a real white girl. you know all western civilization depends on us/

i still haven't left my house. i think i'll fling my hair once more/ but this time with a pout/ cuz i think i haven't been fair to the sisterhood/ women's movement faction of white girls/ although/ they always ask what do you people really want. as if the colored woman of the world were a strange sort of neutered workhorse/ which isnt too far from reality/ since i'm still waiting for my cleaning lady & the lady who takes care of my children & the lady who caters my parties & the lady who accepts quarters at the bathroom in sardi's. those poor creatures shd be sterilized/ no one shd have to live such a life. cd you hand me a towel/ thank-you caroline. i've left all of maxime's last winter clothes in a pile for you by the back door. they have to be cleaned but i hope yr girls can make gd use of them.

oh/ i'm still not being fair/ all the white women in the world dont wake up being glad they aint niggahs/ only some of them/ the ones who dont/ wake up thinking how can i survive another day of this culturally condoned incompetence. i know i'll play a tenor horn & tell all the colored artists i meet/ that now i'm just like them/ i'm colored i'll say cuz i have a struggle too. or i cd punish this white beleagered body of mine with the advances of a thousand ebony bodies/ all built like franco harris or peter tosh/ a thousand of them may take me & do what they want/ cuz i'm so sorry/ yes i'm so sorry they were born niggahs. but then if i cant punish myself to death for being white/ i certainly cant in good conscience keep waiting for the cleaning lady/ & everytime i attempt even the smallest venture into the world someone comes to help me/ like if i do anything/ anything at all i'm extending myself as a white girl/ cuz part of being a white girl is being absent/ like those women who are just with a man but whose names the black people never remember/ they just say oh yeah his white girl waz with him/ or a white girl got beat & killed today/ why someone will say/ cuz some niggah told her to give him her money & she said no/ cuz she thought he realized that she waz a white girl/ & he did know but he didnt care/ so he killed her & took the money/ but the cops knew she waz a white girl & cdnt be killed by a niggah especially/ when she had awready said no. the niggah was sposed to hop round the corner backwards/ you dig/ so the cops/ found the culprit within 24 hours/ cuz just like emmett till/ niggahs do not kill white girls.

i'm still in my house/ having flung my hair-do for the last time/ what with having to take 20 valium a day/ to consider the ERA/ & all the men in the world/ & my ignorance of the world/ it is overwhelming. i'm so glad i'm colored. boy i cd wake up in the morning & think abt anything. i can remember emmett till & not haveta smile at anybody.

MAXINE: *(compelled to speak by* NATALIE'*s pain)* whenever these things happened to me/ & i waz young/ i wd eat a lot/ or buy new fancy underwear with rhinestones & lace/ or go to the movies/ maybe call a friend/ talk to made-up boyfriends til dawn. this waz when i waz under my parents' roof/ & trees that grew into my room had to be cut back once a year/ this waz when the birds sometimes flew thru the halls of the house as if the ceilings were sky & i/ simply another winged creature. yet no one around me noticed me especially. no one around saw anything but a precocious brown girl with peculiar ideas. like during the polio epidemic/ i wanted to have a celebration/ which nobody cd understand since iron lungs & not going swimming waznt nothing to celebrate. but i explained that i waz celebrating the bounty of the lord/ which more people didnt understand/ till i went on to say that/ it waz obvious that god had protected the colored folks from polio/ nobody understood that. i did/ if god had made colored people susceptible to polio/ then we wd be on the pictures & the television with the white children. i knew only white folks cd get that particular disease/ & i celebrated. that's how come i always commemorated anything that affected me or the colored people. according to my history of the colored race/ not enough attention was paid to small victories or small personal defeats of the colored. i celebrated the colored trolley driver/ the colored basketball team/ the colored blues singer/ & the colored light heavy weight champion of the world. then too/ i had a baptist child's version of high mass for the slaves in new orleans whom i had read abt/ & i tried to grow watermelons & rice for the dead slaves from the east. as a child i took on the burden of easing the ghost-colored-folks' souls & trying hard to keep up with the affairs of my own colored world.

when i became a woman, my world got smaller. my grandma closed up the windows/ so the birds wdnt fly in the house any more. waz bad luck for a girl so yng & in my condition to have the shadows of flying creatures over my head. i didn't celebrate the trolley driver anymore/ cuz he might know i waz in this condition. i didnt celebrate the basketball team anymore/ cuz they were yng & handsome/ & yng & handsome cd mean trouble. but trouble waz when white kids called you names or beat you up cuz you had no older brother/ trouble waz when someone died/ or the tornado hit yr house/ now trouble meant something abt yng & handsome/ & white or colored. if he waz yng & handsome that meant trouble. seemed like every one who didnt have this condition/ so birds cdnt fly over yr head/ waz trouble. as i understood it/ my mama & my grandma were sending me out to be with trouble/ but not to get into trouble. the yng & handsome cd dance with me & call for sunday supper/ the yng & handsome cd write my name on their notebooks/ cd carry my ribbons on the field for gd luck/ the uncles cd hug me & chat for hours abt my growing up/ so i counted all 492 times this condition wd make me victim to this trouble/ before i wd be immune to it/ the way colored folks were immune to polio.

i had discovered innumerable manifestations of trouble: jealously/ fear/ indignation & recurring fits of vulnerability that lead me right back to the contradiction i had never understood/ even as a child/ how half the world's population cd be bad news/ be yng & handsome/ & later/ eligible & interested/ & trouble.

plus/ according to my own version of the history of the colored people/ only white people hurt little colored girls or grown colored women/ my mama told me only white people had social disease & molested children/ and my grandma told me only white people committed unnatural acts. that's how come i knew only white folks got polio/ muscular dystrophy/ sclerosis/ & mental illness/ this waz all verified by the television. but i found out that the colored folks knew abt the same vicious & disease-ridden passions that the white folks knew.

the pain i succumbed to each time a colored person did something that i believed only white people did waz staggering. my entire life seems to be worthless/ if my own folks arent better than white folks/ then surely the sagas of slavery & the jim crow hadnt convinced anyone that we were better than them. i commenced to buying pieces of gold/ 14 carat/ 24 carat/ 18 carat gold/ every time some black person did something that waz beneath him as a black person & more like a white person. i bought gold cuz it came from the earth/ & more than likely it came from south africa/ where the black people are humiliated & oppressed like in slavery. i wear all these things at once/ to remind the black people that it cost a lot for us to be here/ our value/ can be known instinctively/ but since so many black people are having a hard time not being like white folks/ i wear these gold pieces to protest their ignorance/ their disconnect from history. i buy gold with a vengeance/ each time someone appropriates my space or my time without permission/ each time someone is discourteous or actually cruel to me/ if my mind is not respected/ my body toyed with/ i buy gold/ & weep. i weep as i fix the chains round my neck/ my wrists/ my ankles. i weep cuz all my childhood ceremonies for the ghost-slaves have been in vain. colored people can get polio & mental illness. slavery is not unfamiliar to me. no one on his planet knows/ what i know abt gold/ abt anything hard to get & beautiful/ anything lasting/ wrought from pain. no one understands that surviving the impossible is sposed to accentuate the positive aspects of a people.

(ALEC *is the only member of the company able to come immediately to* MAXINE. *when he reaches her,* LOU, *in his full magician's regalia, freezes the whole company*)

LOU: yes yes yes          3 wishes is all you get
        scarlet ribbons for yr hair
        a farm in mississippi
        someone to love you madly
    all things are possible
    but aint no colored magician in his right mind
    gonna make you white
    cuz this is blk magic you lookin at
    & i'm fixin you up good/ fixin you up good & colored
    & you gonna be colored all yr life
    & you gonna love it/ bein colored/ all yr life
    colored & love it/ love it/ bein colored

(LOU *beckons the others to join him in the chant, "colored & love it." it becomes a serious celebration, like church/ like home/ but then* LOU *freezes them suddenly.*)

    LOU: crackers are born with the right to be
        alive/ i'm making ours up right here
        in yr face/ & we gonna be
        colored & love it

(*the huge minstrel mask comes down as company continues to sing "colored & love it/ love it being colored." blackout/ but the minstrel mask remains visible. the company is singing "colored & love it being colored" as audience exits*)

## Ntozake Shange

Interview
(1987)

*THIS interview was conducted by Kathleen Betsko and Rachel Koenig.*

INTERVIEWER: Would you tell us something about the impact of dance on your creative life and writing process?

SHANGE: Writing is for most people a cerebral activity. For me it is a very rhythmic and visceral experience. Dance clears my mind of verbal images and allows me to understand the planet the way I imagine atomic particles experience space. I am not bogged down with the implications of language. I am only involved in the implications of movement which later on, when I do start to write, become manifest in the rhythms of my poetry.

INTERVIEWER: You've said that Western culture, as opposed to Afro-American culture, promotes a split between mind and body. What are the differences between these two cultures?

SHANGE: I am not an Anglo-Western civilization person so I don't think I could describe it. But it would appear to me that there is a definitive split between the two—Western culture is very keen on specific disciplines as opposed to multidisciplinary approaches. That much I think I can say without stepping over my boundaries.

INTERVIEWER: Does the notion of the multidisciplined approach tie into what you said in the introduction to your play collection, *Spell #7*: "We should demolish the notion of straight theater for a decade or so, refuse to allow playwrights to work without dancers and musicians."

SHANGE: Yes it does. Though I haven't allowed myself to do it in theater I did start doing visual art, a natural extension of what I said about multidiscipline. I've done four installation pieces in the last two years, which included performance art, not continually, but at the openings.

INTERVIEWER: What kind of multimedia are you using in the installations?

SHANGE: One installation [1981] was made of sticks, cotton and a hanging—rope silhouettes of smiling black babies. On the other side there was raffia and lace and garlic and okra and orchids and a big huge black baby who had an umbilical cord of velvet and magnolias. Another piece was called "The Jazz Life: Wall Poems." I simply wrote all over the walls excerpts of love poems that I read at the performance, which included two dancers. It was a way to actually trap people inside a poem and it really did work. This was sponsored by the Women for Art Caucus in Houston at The Firehouse in 1984. At the 1199 Gallery, I did a piece called "Working Women—How We Work," which was seven frying pans, one for each day of the week, filled with different things like contraceptives, bill receipts, dirty clothes, pictures of the Virgin, beer cans, little plastic twenty-two caliber pistols. "On the Board" was a celebration of Juneteenth Day [June 19th]. I don't know if you know this, but the slaves in Texas didn't find out till three years later that they had been emancipated and we celebrate that on Juneteenth Day. I'm also trying to do my piece, "From Property to Personhood," in a local park. It is a graduated scale, from two feet to six feet, of different kinds of circles. At the beginning, you have to crawl to enter, and by the time you get to the end you are standing—you come out a free person. I wanted to do something around my daughter—something that couldn't be sold. I didn't want her to think in any way that I made money off her. So I make things for her, in her honor, that can't be bought.

INTERVIEWER: Are you moving in the direction of performance art and away from the other styles of stage work you've done in the past?

SHANGE: The theater work I did was to me an anomaly. I was a performance artist to begin with. So I am doing what I used to do before I was in theater. I haven't stopped writing plays—I just feel more at home in performance because that is what I started out doing.

INTERVIEWER: Is performance art closer to poetry than the stage play?

SHANGE: It is much closer to poetry, and it is freer because I can use a lot of improvisation.

INTERVIEWER: Were you aware, as a young girl, that you possessed a gift?

SHANGE: [Laughs] I didn't think of it as a gift until about 1971 when I moved to Boston. I started working with groups of musicians, and I had my own band (Zaki & The Palm Wine Drunkards). During this time, I was also involved in different kinds of spiritual activity which directed my attention to those things that are given by the gods in various forms. It was my most intense journal-keeping period as well.

INTERVIEWER: Do you still keep journals?

SHANGE: Off and on. Journals keep me grounded in some kind of emotional and creative arena that's not tortuous. I can't always do it now, although I wish that I could.

INTERVIEWER: Has having a child changed your life as a writer?

SHANGE: I don't have much time . . . time to think thoughts that might lead to poems or dances or creative pieces. I have to get out of my house to work creatively and I don't like having a studio outside the house; as a very domestic person, that is dysfunctional for me. But I have to, so I do.

INTERVIEWER: What are the positive aspects of motherhood?

SHANGE: Oh, my [three-year-old] daughter is a lovely person. And it is quite an honor to be her caretaker. She has a lovely disposition, she is a good trouper, she is very flexible, has an excellent memory. She enjoys dance and music and paintings. Her father is a painter so she knows that a painting *is* a painting, as opposed to something on the wall.

INTERVIEWER: Who are your influences?

SHANGE: Early Le Roi Jones, Ishmael Reed, Susan Griffin, Thulani Davis, Jessica Hagedorn, Victor Hernandez Cruz and Pedro Pietri, Wopolhlolup. Then Latin writers: Cabrera-Infante, Miguel Asturias, Gabriel García Márquez. C. L. R. James, of course, Leon Damas, Zora Neale Hurston, and Langston Hughes. Also Olga Brumas, Gloria Naylor, June Jordan, Emily Mann, Manuel Puig, Lydia Fagundes Telles.

INTERVIEWER: You were recently appointed Associate Professor of Drama at the University of Houston. Can writing be taught?

SHANGE: I don't believe you can teach writing. What you can do is help someone refine the skills and the talent that they have. A course can be geared toward assisting each student to find his or her voice and toward challenging a student who is good in one form to become better in the form he or she has chosen, as well as others. I keep assignments short because I think if you can write one concise page you are more apt to be able to write fifteen beautiful pages than if you wrote three stupid pages. I'm very happy with my students, and I feel committed to them.

I want to add Alice Childress to the list of people who've given me inspiration. She is instrumental.

INTERVIEWER: In what ways did she influence you?

SHANGE: Her family is from the same part of South Carolina as my family. It's helped me a lot with the novel to think about the work I've seen Alice do and then—not to steal from her—but to try and get the same ambiance that I feel in her work. Not that I couldn't have done it on my own, but I think that you have to give credit where credit's due.

INTERVIEWER: How is Houston, Texas, after the mad world of New York?

SHANGE: It's exactly what I needed. I can work on my own schedule; I can afford to live a lifestyle that I think is reasonable for a single mother. I have immediate access to alternative spaces. There is a large visual arts community here. There is a fairly small, but very supportive literary community. I am able to do things here that I couldn't do in New York: I can ride horses; I have the time to take Kundalini Yoga; I have time to spend with my daughter. The black community here ranges from middle class to poverty-stricken, but it is not separated in the same classist way as New York. Also, Texas is much closer to Latin America than New York is, so my traveling has become much easier.

INTERVIEWER: You have been spending a lot of time in Latin America . . .

SHANGE: Off and on over the last seven years, yes: Curaçao, Aruba, Jamaica, Brazil, Mexico, Cuba, Nicaragua, Nassau, Bermuda, Martinique, Haiti, Trinidad, Tobago and Puerto Rico. My primary influences, and most profound experiences have come out of my travels in Brazil, Nicaragua and Cuba. [See *See No Evil: Prefaces, Essays, Accounts.*]

INTERVIEWER: Was there anything that particularly impressed you about theater in South America?

SHANGE: The rapport that the *teatrista* people have with their audience is so much more intense and intimate than it is here. What they call *Teatro Popular*—Popular Theater or vernacular theater—is geared toward, and part of, the community of what we would call the working class, the working poor people. The theater is very open to them and it is part of their lives, which is not true here.

INTERVIEWER: Does this Popular Theater grow out of the community?

SHANGE: In some cases, yes, and in some no. A theater group from Bogotá might be touring all around the country. So it wouldn't necessarily be growing out of that community in some small town in the mountains. On the other hand, it's not estranged from the people either. In

Spanish- and French-speaking places, the arts have never been isolated from government or from revolution.

INTERVIEWER: How has your reception been in foreign countries?

SHANGE: Very good. I have not encountered hostile audiences except in the United States.

INTERVIEWER: Why are American audiences hostile?

SHANGE: It's not *all* Americans. If I had to say who my enemies are, I would say male chauvinists, and English-speaking black nationalists who resent my work with Latin American countries and my bilingualism, and who refuse to admit they live in the Western hemisphere which is predominantly Spanish-speaking.

INTERVIEWER: Do you work in commercial spaces in Texas?

SHANGE: The commercial theater here has a subscription audience so I still have to be in an alternative space. My work is not the kind that subscription audiences are used to or want to see. It doesn't bother me because I like working in alternative spaces, I always have and I believe in supporting them. I think to continually work in big houses—like on Broadway or at the Alley [Theatre, Houston] or at the Mark Taper [Forum, Los Angeles]—is dangerous for somebody who is trying to explore because you can only explore so much when all that money is being invested in you. It's not that I don't like working in beautiful theaters, it's that I have to keep my mind clear about why they're going to let me work there. I have very good relationships with all the theaters I work with, and with my producers, but I'm not robbing Peter to pay Paul. I work in alternative spaces whenever I can and I don't have to ask anybody about it. It's important to have power over one's work. Right now, I want to experiment and I don't want to spend a lot of money doing it. I also don't want a lot of people around telling me what works and what doesn't. I want the audience to let me know what works and what doesn't.

INTERVIEWER: How do you feel about being called a "woman writer"?

SHANGE: I have been a feminist writer ever since I started. When I was nineteen I worked for the Young Lords Party instead of the Black Panther Party because in the Young Lords, equality for women was part of the platform of the party. I decided I was a feminist at that point [1968–1970] and I've never stopped being one.

INTERVIEWER: Why do you think that some women, who at one point were quite proud to call themselves feminists, now say, "I'm not a feminist, I'm a humanist"?

SHANGE: I don't know. I don't understand it, either. The only thing I can think is that they have achieved what they wanted and now feel that they are no longer in the struggle; but, that's presumptuous on my part, because I don't really know why they say that.

INTERVIEWER: What do we women have yet to win in our struggle for equality? What are you struggling for in your work? What issues do you think need to be addressed?

SHANGE: A development of respect for a real feminist aesthetic, which is why I am on the board of directors at the Feminist Art Institute even if I don't do as much for them as I'd like. I also belong to Women Against Violence Against Women and Children and the Women for Art Caucus. I'm very disturbed about the proliferation of manufactured goods [e.g., powdered-milk substitutes—Ed.] in Third World countries where women should be nursing; instead their babies are starving to death. I'm very concerned about the liberation of South Africa and the need for an end to bombings in Angola and Mozambique. I'm concerned about the embargo against Cuba after twenty-five years and the pending embargo against Nicaragua which it seems is coming down the line. I'm disturbed about the invasion of Grenada. And I'm disturbed that we still don't have equal pay for equal work. As a black person, I know that black women get paid less per dollar than anybody. We also have a higher infant mortality rate than any other ethnic population in the country. Those things to me are still very real and must be addressed. Hopefully they are addressed in the essays I write, which is why we put together *See No Evil: Prefaces, Essays and Accounts 1976–1983* [San Francisco, Momo's Press, 1984].

INTERVIEWER: The majority of women writers are dealing with more personal material.

SHANGE: I think the dangerous mistake that women make is to assume the personal is not political. When I make a personal statement, it is to me a political statement.

INTERVIEWER: Why is it so difficult for male critics to interpret the artistic intentions of women playwrights?

SHANGE: It is impossible to enter the territory of someone you oppress with the knowledge that you have as an oppressor. Male critics have no vocabulary or understanding of our condition. The only way they understand it is if they are in control of it. If we are in our own arena they are not in control, and, therefore, they have no language and no tools to comprehend what is being said to them or created for them.

INTERVIEWER: You have said that theater is the weakest arena in American art.

SHANGE: There are fewer great plays written by American artists than there are great visual works or great dances or great music.

INTERVIEWER: Is theater the most conservative of the arts?

SHANGE: It's the most costly. And it also requires the most collaboration. Between those two elements, it's real hit-or-miss—there are too many people involved in the success of one piece and it costs too much money to hire them.

INTERVIEWER: How do you behave in rehearsal?

SHANGE: I'm always the assistant director, that's how I behave. When I am the director, I do a lot of improvs and subtext work. Then we put the piece together.

INTERVIEWER: Are you ever frustrated when working with another director?

SHANGE: Usually we talk it through. I'm not one of those writers who is resistant to making changes in the text or trying new things. If I do feel frustrated, then of course I won't use that person again. But generally speaking, I don't have bad relationships with directors.

INTERVIEWER: How important is it for a playwright to direct his or her own work?

SHANGE: In workshop it is very helpful. It helps me at least to find flaws in the script. Directing helped me rewrite a piece that was in trouble—now I'm really proud of it. I also like directing other people's work because it gives me a clearer sense of structure—even if a piece is traditional; directing gives me a clearer sense of how nontraditional my own structure can be.

INTERVIEWER: You once wrote, "We must learn our common symbols, preen them, and share them with the world" [epigraph to *for colored girls* . . . ].

SHANGE: It's what I meant earlier when I mentioned a female aesthetic. That is part of the work that Andrea Dworkin, Adrienne Rich, Susan Griffin and I do, as well as many visual artists like Betye Saar and Judy Chicago.

INTERVIEWER: Will you tell us what you mean by a female aesthetic?

SHANGE: No. Because I've written it already and I don't want to mess with it. [See Shange's introduction to *for colored girls* . . . , Bantam, 1981.]

INTERVIEWER: Is religion important in your life?

SHANGE: In the black community, the church is the strongest major institution. For me as a so-called representative of the black community not to have something to do with the black church would be contradictory. On the other hand, I feel more akin to radical Catholic priests in Central America than I do to missionary sorts of work. So I am an amalgam of two things. Ernesto Cardenal is a priest; he is also the minister of culture of Nicaragua. There are also a number of priests working with the junta in Nicaragua. I think there is a major role that the church in its myriad forms can play in the struggle of oppressed people all over the world.

INTERVIEWER: Karen Malpede believes it is important for the playwright to present healing images, much like your last scene in *for colored girls* . . .

SHANGE: I believe in that. I think my pieces do that. It's unfair to rupture and bring forth a wound without, at the same time, offering some solace. Not a cure-all, but a sense that there is something else that can be done.

INTERVIEWER: Does the playwright have a responsibility to society?

SHANGE: Yes. I think everybody does.

INTERVIEWER: Why aren't we seeing more political plays from American playwrights?

SHANGE: I think somebody's got to light a fire up under their asses. [Laughter]

INTERVIEWER: Got a match?

SHANGE: As a matter of fact, I do have a match and it's called my work.

INTERVIEWER: Do you feel you've paid a price for being so honest and so outspoken in your writing?

SHANGE: For a little while I paid the price of having no privacy. I paid the price of becoming self-conscious. I had never experienced that. Moving to Texas has helped me to get away from those two things.

INTERVIEWER: How did it affect your work when you became self-conscious?

SHANGE: I was lucky. It did not affect my work. It affected my life as opposed to my work. The two are not the same.

INTERVIEWER: Did your concerns shift when you moved to Texas?

SHANGE: No, my concerns had time to become fuller.

INTERVIEWER: Do you feel attacked by the media or theatrical establishment for being a political playwright?

SHANGE: No. I might be, but I don't read those things so I am not affected by them. One's enemies are interested on one's disappearance. I expect reactionary criticism.

INTERVIEWER: Was it difficult to work with publishers at first because you have invented a unique style/language?

SHANGE: No, at first I worked with small women's presses so I never encountered any difficulty. I didn't come to commercial publishing out of a vacuum, I came from a small press literary community that had served my needs up to that point.

INTERVIEWER: Will you tell us about your work day . . . your creative process?

SHANGE: It changes all the time. Sometimes I am very disciplined and sometimes I am not. It's a catch-as-catch-can experience right now because I have to get up early with the baby to take her to school. My day is very, very disrupted.

INTERVIEWER: What about when you are traveling?

SHANGE: I keep journals. My journals are becoming more specific—journals for Nicaragua, journals for Cuba, journals for teaching—as opposed to the general journals I used to take with me. That's because I don't have a lot of time and I have to make priorities about what I am going to talk about.

INTERVIEWER: Do you need special conditions to write? Some women can write with their kids running around. . . .

SHANGE: I can't write with a child running around anywhere. I need a clean house and quiet. A fresh pot of coffee, a bottle of Perrier water, about three packs of cigarettes and some flowers.

INTERVIEWER: Have your yoga classes affected your writing?

SHANGE: They make it easier for me to write when I am blocked because they unlock my chakras. I assume that dancing and yoga contribute a great deal to my creative energy flow. And horseback riding helps make me more aggressive than I might be because I am having to control an animal that is much bigger than I am.

INTERVIEWER: Tell us what the difference was between your intimate working experience with small presses and alternative theater and the huge commercial Broadway success you had with *for colored girls* . . . ?

SHANGE: I've never been a playwright who wanted plays—I am a writer who wants books. I get much happier about a book than I do about a show, although that may not *always* be so. I am still very active in the small press arena simply because I like books. Right now I have books made of handmade paper with Bookslinger Press, and Toothpaste Press, as well as the *See No Evil* . . . book, which is also from a small press called MoMo's.

INTERVIEWER: Why are you less comfortable writing for the stage?

SHANGE: I make a great commitment to the work when I'm doing it but I also know in three weeks it's not going to run anymore. *Spell #7* did have an incredibly decent run in New York—it ran for nine months Off Broadway—but still, nobody in the United States knows about that play.

INTERVIEWER: We were able to read it in the published version.

SHANGE: Right, that's why I like books. Books are available to everybody. Plays [in performance] are not, because they cost too much. I hate to sound obsessed with finances, but they cost entirely too much money. And you have to deal with too many people. I've written two pieces that I desperately want up, but I'm not writing any more until these two go on. What's the point?

INTERVIEWER: Any ideas about what can be done about the high cost of theater?

SHANGE: I do performance art. That satisfies me. Now a lot of people who want to see theater are not going to be happy with that; they should go see a Sam Shepard play or something, I don't know . . .

INTERVIEWER: In your work, there are warnings to the women artist about the possibility of the creative spirit being crushed under the weight of relationships.

SHANGE: I think that's true. Men take up an enormous amount of time and they also distort one's perception.

INTERVIEWER: Self-perception?

SHANGE: Self-perception and perception of the world, because instead of seeing yourself as an individual in the world you see yourself as part of a unit. Not that there is anything wrong with that, but there *can* be something wrong with that.

INTERVIEWER: Do you have any special memories of W. E. B. Dubois?

SHANGE: The story goes that he hated children, but that he put me to bed one night and sang me a lullabye. That's the family folklore—how true it is, I don't know. I know that Paul Robeson used to come to our house . . . Dizzy Gillespie still does, as well as Lalo Schifrin, who is now a big Hollywood music writer. Mango Santa Maria—many different boxers were around all the time because my father is a boxing physician. I remember that my mother used to take me to see ballets, especially if there were black people in them, like Carmen De Lavallade and Arthur Mitchell.

INTERVIEWER: So you had a lot of artistic stimulation while growing up.

SHANGE: Yes. My mother was *extremely* significant, as was my father, in terms of the breadth of Afro-American culture. The two together, Mommy concentrating on English-speaking artists, and my father concentrating on the international sphere.

INTERVIEWER: Have you written about your mother?

SHANGE: She appears in some of the letters Hilda Effania writes in my novel *Sassafrass, Cypress, & Indigo* [New York, St. Martin's Press, 1982].

INTERVIEWER: Why do some women have a hands-off attitude toward presenting their own mothers in their work?

SHANGE: What Adrienne Rich says in *Of Woman Born* is true: It is difficult to embrace the very female who taught you to be an oppressed person. I think it's going to take a long time for us to learn how to do that. Luckily, I've been able to start—but I, too, had a very "hands-off" attitude toward my mother for years. It's just since I've been able to start writing mother characters in the novel that I came to see the beauties in her and could transmit them to my audience. Everybody I've talked to about *Sassafrass* . . . has said they saw the character Mama as the mother that everybody really wants to have. Mama is in fact an amalgam of my mother, my great-aunts and my grandmother—but particularly my mother.

INTERVIEWER: In your travels in South America and throughout the world, have you encountered the phenomenon of pacifist women gathering together in a collective attempt to bring peace to the world, such as the women at Greenham Common?

SHANGE: I've been seeing a lot of women who are cultural aggressors. . . .

INTERVIEWER: These cultural aggressors are women artists?

SHANGE: Yes. They are doing pieces that have to do with the affirmation and exploration of women's lives. And that's what I call cultural aggression. I want to write a book entitled *Cultural Aggression* and probably will someday.

INTERVIEWER: Do you have a sense of yourself in the history of literature?

SHANGE: No. That is what secondary-source people, scholars do. I'm just me. I'm here doing what I'm supposed to do. I have a baby, I write, I take care of my house, I go to church, I vote. If you want to know what *I* think I do—that's what I do.

INTERVIEWER: Would you discuss the sexuality in your work?

SHANGE: I'm very uninhibited in the plays and in my fiction, but I couldn't write an essay about women's sexuality.

INTERVIEWER: You are quite successful at presenting erotic, as opposed to pornographic, imagery.

SHANGE: I hope so. We need that. There is a lush quality to women's sexuality that we have ignored because of the stark realities of pornography and the way men treat us as sexual objects. Hopefully, my characters bring out some of the richness and the sensuality that I think is inherent in a female existence, in a female landscape.

INTERVIEWER: What aspects of your work have been misunderstood? Is there any particular criticism which has made you angry?

SHANGE: What makes me angry is that people think after *for colored girls* . . . , I died. That's an element of commercial theater and one reason why I don't like it.

INTERVIEWER: We *are* a "star" culture. . . .

SHANGE: Yeah, well, they can't do that to me. That's what they've discovered. That's part of the reason I'm living in Texas.

INTERVIEWER: Did celebrity change your life?

SHANGE: It was a very isolating, alienating experience and I don't really like to talk about it.

INTERVIEWER: You've said that there is a phenomenon of black, Latin and Asian artists being "one-shot"—do you have any thoughts as to why these voices fall silent?

SHANGE: It's not that they fall silent, it's that they are not continuous commercial successes. Frank Chin is still writing, Jessica Hagadorn is still writing, Alice Childress and June Jordan are still writing—but they are not commercial successes, and that is why you don't hear about them.

INTERVIEWER: Have you any advice for young women playwrights of the future?

SHANGE: The only thing I have to say to them is a quote from a poem I wrote:

We can't be stopped
our lips are too thick
and the air is too strong

# Brian Friel

Brian Friel (b. 1929) is perhaps the most prominent living Irish playwright, the heir of Ireland's brilliant modern dramatic tradition, the tradition of W. B. Yeats, John Millington Synge, and Sean O'Casey. Unlike these predecessors, who worked for the independence of the Republic of Ireland, Friel works in Northern Ireland, still a part of the United Kingdom. Educated in Derry and Belfast, Friel's concerns as a playwright have spanned the "troubles" of Northern Ireland, the poverty and depression of Derry in the 1930s, 1940s, and 1950s, and the installation of a British military presence and the open street warfare of the 1960s, 1970s, and 1980s. From his earliest success, *Philadelphia, Here I Come!* (1964), about a man's divided feelings concerning his emigration to the United States, Friel's drama has centered on the problems of Irish identity in the face of British rule. Many of his early plays and stories—*The Loves of Cass McGuire* (1966), *The Lovers* (1967)— are portraits of Irish life in the manner of Synge, and Friel's dramatization of the personal consequences of contemporary Irish life remains a prominent feature of fine plays like *Living Quarters* (1977) and *Faith Healer* (1979). But Friel's drama also inclines toward satire—visible in *The Mundy Scheme* (1969) and *The Gentle Island* (1971)—and toward political concerns. In *The Freedom of the City* (1973), Friel dramatizes the fate of three people caught and killed by British soldiers in the "Bloody Sunday" riots in Derry; in *Volunteers* (1975), a crew of political prisoners are forced to work on an archaeological site, recovering the history of Celtic Ireland even as they are oppressed by British rule; and in *Making History* (1988), Friel returns to the origins of Ireland's subjection to the British in the seventeenth and eighteenth centuries. In 1980, Friel and the Stephen Rea founded the Field Day Theatre Company in Derry, and its first production was the play generally taken to be Friel's masterpiece, *Translations*. Friel's *Dancing at Lughnasa* opened in 1990.

## Translations (1980)

*Translations* is set in early nineteenth-century Ireland, and concerns the mapping—both actual and cultural—of Ireland by the British. The play takes place at a local hedge-school, a subscription school run by a local master and attended by a variety of children and adults. But this Ireland is already threatened by the British culture to the east: a national school—where, presumably, English will be the required language—is about to open, and the British army surveyors have arrived to map the region, part of the 1833 Survey of Ireland.

The play's politics are largely conveyed through the politics of language. Jimmy's Homeric Greek, for example, draws a parallel between Ireland and another lost civilization. The romance between Yolland and Maire bridges the barrier of language—they learn to communicate across this barrier, while the British army works to tear it down and destroy Irish cultural identity in the process. In mapping Ireland, the British convert local place names into English, either by translating them directly or by inventing some equivalent. As the relationship between Irish Owen and his British officers makes clear, English is the language of power. To map the landscape with English names is a figure for rewriting Ireland and its culture into submission and finally into nonexistence.

Although *Translations* may seem only indirectly about contemporary Irish politics, it dramatizes a struggle for national and cultural identity that continues to embroil Northern Ireland today. And in centering the play's politics on the issue of representation—in language, on maps, in the contours of the land itself—*Translations* shares its concerns with plays that are more formally experimental, such as *spell #7* or *M. Butterfly*. Throughout the play, for example, the mysterious and unseen Donnelly twins move around the edges of the action, guerrillas hindering the British progress through the country. And when Yolland is missing, we learn the true consequences of the British mapping of Ireland. Mapping the land in English is the prelude for its occupation, as the army systematically destroys the village and countryside that they have made their own. At the play's close, we scent the sickly sweet smell of blighted potatoes, the sign of the impending famine that would weaken and disperse Friel's rural Irish population for good.

# — Translations —
## Brian Friel

---

## —CHARACTERS—

MANUS
SARAH
JIMMY JACK
MAIRE
DOALTY
BRIDGET
HUGH
OWEN
CAPTAIN LANCEY
LIEUTENANT YOLLAND

*The action takes place in a hedge-school in the townland of Baile Beag/Ballybeg, an Irish-speaking community in County Donegal.*

| | |
|---|---|
| ACT ONE | *An afternoon in late August 1833.* |
| ACT TWO | *A few days later.* |
| ACT THREE | *The evening of the following day.* |

*One interval—between the two scenes in Act Two.*

*(For the convenience of readers and performers unfamiliar with the language, roman letters have been used for the Greek words and quotations in the text. The originals, together with the Latin and literal translations, appear at the end of the play.)*

---

## —ACT ONE—

*The hedge-school is held in a disused barn or hay-shed or byre. Along the back wall are the remains of five or six stalls—wooden posts and chains—where cows were once milked and bedded. A double door left, large enough to allow a cart to enter. A window right. A wooden stairway without a banister leads to the upstairs living-quarters (off) of the schoolmaster and his son. Around the room are broken and forgotten implements: a cart-wheel, some lobster-pots, farming tools, a battle of hay, a churn, etc. There are also the stools and bench-seats which the pupils use and a table and chair for the master. At the door a pail of water and a soiled towel. The room is comfortless and dusty and functional—there is no trace of a woman's hand.*

*When the play opens,* MANUS *is teaching* SARAH *to speak. He kneels beside her. She is sitting on a low stool, her head down, very tense, clutching a slate on her knees. He is coaxing her gently and firmly and—as with everything he does—with a kind of zeal.*

MANUS *is in his late twenties/early thirties; the master's older son. He is pale-faced, lightly built, intense, and works as an unpaid assistant—a monitor—to his father. His clothes are shabby; and when he moves we see that he is lame.*

SARAH's *speech defect is so bad that all her life she has been considered locally to be dumb and she has accepted this: when she wishes to communicate, she grunts and makes unintelligible nasal sounds. She has a waiflike appearance and could be any age from seventeen to thirty-five.*

JIMMY JACK CASSIE—*known as the Infant Prodigy—sits by himself, contentedly reading Homer in Greek and smiling to himself. He is a bachelor in his sixties, lives alone, and comes to* these evening classes partly for the company and partly for the intellectual stimulation. He is fluent in Latin and Greek but is in no way pedantic—to him it is perfectly normal to speak these tongues. He never washes. His clothes—heavy top coat, hat, mittens, which he wears now—are filthy and he lives in them summer and winter, day and night. He now reads in a quiet voice and smiles in profound satisfaction. For JIMMY the world of the gods and the ancient myths is as real and as immediate as everyday life in the townland of Baile Beag.*

MANUS *holds* SARAH's *hands in his and he articulates slowly and distinctly into her face.*

MANUS: We're doing very well. And we're going to try it once more—just once more. Now—relax and breathe in . . . deep . . . and out . . . in . . . and out . . .

*(*SARAH *shakes her head vigorously and stubbornly.)*

MANUS: Come on, Sarah. This is our secret.

*(Again vigorous and stubborn shaking of* SARAH's *head.)*

MANUS: Nobody's listening. Nobody hears you.
JIMMY: *"Ton d'emeibet epeita thea glaukopis Athene . . . "*
MANUS: Get your tongue and your lips working. "My name—" Come on. One more try. "My name is—" Good girl.
SARAH: My . . .
MANUS: Great. "My name—"
SARAH: My . . . my . . .
MANUS: Raise your head. Shout it out. Nobody's listening.
JIMMY: " . . . *alla hekelos estai en Atreidao domois . . .* "
MANUS: Jimmy, please! Once more—just once more—"My name—" Good girl. Come on now. Head up. Mouth open.
SARAH: My . . .
MANUS: Good.
SARAH: My . . .

10

MANUS: Great.

20 SARAH: My name . . .

MANUS: Yes?

SARAH: My name is . . .

MANUS: Yes?

(SARAH *pauses. Then in a rush.*)

SARAH: My name is Sarah.

MANUS: Marvellous! Bloody marvellous!

> (MANUS *hugs* SARAH. *She smiles in shy, embarrassed pleasure.*)
>
> Did you hear that, Jimmy?—"My name is Sarah"—clear as a bell.
>
> (*To* SARAH) The Infant Prodigy doesn't know what we're at.
>
> (SARAH *laughs at this.* MANUS *hugs her again and stands up.*)
>
> Now we're really started! Nothing'll stop us now! Nothing in
30 the wide world!

(JIMMY, *chuckling at his text, comes over to them.*)

JIMMY: Listen to this, Manus.

MANUS: Soon you'll be telling me all the secrets that have been in that head of yours all these years. Certainly, James—what is it? (*To* SARAH) Maybe you'd set out the stools?

(MANUS *runs up the stairs.*)

SARAH: Wait till you hear this, Manus.

MANUS: Go ahead. I'll be straight down.

JIMMY: "*Hos ara min phamene rabdo epemassat Athene—*" "After Athene had said this, she touched Ulysses with her wand. She withered the fair skin of his supple limbs and de-
40 stroyed the flaxen hair from off his head and about his limbs she put the skin of an old man . . . "! The divil! The divil!

(MANUS *has emerged again with a bowl of milk and a piece of bread.*)

JIMMY: And wait till you hear! She's not finished with him yet!

(*As* MANUS *descends the stairs he toasts* SARAH *with his bowl.*)

JIMMY: "*Knuzosen de oi osse—*" "She dimmed his two eyes that were so beautiful and clothed him in a vile ragged cloak be-grimed with filthy smoke . . . "! D'you see! Smoke! Smoke! D'you see! Sure look at what the same turf-smoke has done to myself! (*He rapidly removes his hat to display his bald head.*) Would you call that flaxen hair?

MANUS: Of course I would.

50 JIMMY: "And about him she cast the great skin of a filthy hind, stripped of the hair, and into his hand she thrust a staff and a wallet"! Ha-ha-ha! Athene did that to Ulysses! Made him into a tramp! Isn't she the tight one?

MANUS: You couldn't watch her, Jimmy.

JIMMY: You know what they call her?

MANUS: "*Glaukopis Athene.*"

JIMMY: That's it! The flashing-eyed Athene! By God, Manus, sir, if you had a woman like that about the house, it's not stripping a turf-bank you'd be thinking about—eh?

60 MANUS: She was a goddess, Jimmy.

JIMMY: Better still. Sure isn't our own Grania a class of a god-dess and—

MANUS: Who?

JIMMY: Grania—Grania—Diarmuid's Grania.

MANUS: Ah.

JIMMY: And sure she can't get her fill of men.

MANUS: Jimmy, you're impossible.

JIMMY: I was just thinking to myself last night: if you had the choosing between Athene and Artemis and Helen of Troy—all three of them Zeus's girls—imagine three powerful-look-
70 ing daughters like that all in the one parish of Athens!—now, if you had the picking between them, which would you take?

MANUS: (*To* SARAH) Which should I take, Sarah?

JIMMY: No harm to Helen; and no harm to Artemis; and indeed no harm to our own Grania, Manus. But I think I've no choice but to go bull-straight for Athene. By God, sir, them flashing eyes would fair keep a man jigged up constant!

(*Suddenly and momentarily, as if in spasm,* JIMMY *stands to attention and salutes, his face raised in pained ecstasy.* MANUS *laughs. So does* SARAH. JIMMY *goes back to his seat, and his reading.*)

MANUS: You're a dangerous bloody man, Jimmy Jack.

JIMMY: "Flashing-eyed"! Hah! Sure Homer knows it all, boy. 80 Homer knows it all.

(MANUS *goes to the window and looks out.*)

MANUS: Where the hell has he got to?

(SARAH *goes to* MANUS *and touches his elbow. She mimes rocking a baby.*)

MANUS: Yes, I know he's at the christening; but it doesn't take them all day to put a name on a baby, does it?

(SARAH *mimes pouring drinks and tossing them back quickly.*)

MANUS: You may be sure. Which pub?

(SARAH *indicates.*)

MANUS: Gracie's?

(*No. Further away.*)

MANUS: Con Connie Tim's?

(*No. To the right of there.*)

MANUS: Anna na mBreag's?

(*Yes. That's it.*)

MANUS: Great. She'll fill him up. I suppose I may take the class then. 90

(MANUS *begins to distribute some books, slates and chalk, texts, etc., beside the seats.* SARAH *goes over to the straw and produces a bunch of flowers she has hidden there. During this:*)

JIMMY: "*Autar o ek limenos prosebe—*" "But Ulysses went forth from the harbour and through the woodland to the place where Athene had shown him he could find the good swine-herd who—"*o oi biotoio malista kedeto*"—what's that, Manus?

MANUS: "Who cared most for his substance."

JIMMY: That's it! "The good swineherd who cared most for his substance above all the slaves that Ulysses possessed . . . "

(SARAH *presents the flowers to* MANUS.)

MANUS: Those are lovely, Sarah.

(*But* SARAH *has fled in embarrassment to her seat and has her head buried in a book.* MANUS *goes to her.*)

100   MANUS: Flow-ers.

(*Pause.* SARAH *does not look up.*)

MANUS: Say the word: flow-ers. Come on—flow-ers.
SARAH: Flowers.
MANUS: You see?—you're off!

(MANUS *leans down and kisses the top of* SARAH'S *head.*)

MANUS: And they're beautiful flowers. Thank you.

(MAIRE *enters, a strong-minded, strong-bodied woman in her twenties with a head of curly hair. She is carrying a small can of milk.*)

MAIRE: Is this all's here? Is there no school this evening?
MANUS: If my father's not back, I'll take it.

(MANUS *stands awkwardly, having been caught kissing* SARAH *and with the flowers almost formally at his chest.*)

MAIRE: Well now, isn't that a pretty sight. There's your milk. How's Sarah?

(SARAH *grunts a reply.*)

MANUS: I saw you out at the hay.

(MAIRE *ignores this and goes to* JIMMY.)

110   MAIRE: And how's Jimmy Jack Cassie?
JIMMY: Sit down beside me, Maire.
MAIRE: Would I be safe?
JIMMY: No safer man in Donegal.

(MAIRE *flops on a stool beside* JIMMY.)

MAIRE: Ooooh. The best harvest in living memory, they say; but I don't want to see another like it. (*Showing* JIMMY *her hands.*) Look at the blisters.
JIMMY: *Esne fatigata?*
MAIRE: *Sum fatigatissima.*
JIMMY: *Bene! Optime!*
120   MAIRE: That's the height of my Latin. Fit me better if I had even that much English.
JIMMY: English? I thought you had some English?
MAIRE: Three words. Wait—there was a spake I used to have off my heart. What's this it was? (*Her accent is strange because she is speaking a foreign language and because she does not understand what she is saying.*) "In Norfolk we besport ourselves around the maypoll." What about that!
MANUS: Maypole.

(*Again* MAIRE *ignores* MANUS.)

MAIRE: God have mercy on my Aunt Mary—she taught me
130   that when I was about four, whatever it means. Do you know what it means, Jimmy?
JIMMY: Sure you know I have only Irish like yourself.
MAIRE: And Latin. And Greek.
JIMMY: I'm telling you a lie: I know one English word.

MAIRE: What?
JIMMY: Bo-som.
MAIRE: What's a bo-som?
JIMMY: You know—(*He illustrates with his hands*)—bo-som—bo-som—you know—Diana, the huntress, she has two powerful bosom.    140
MAIRE: You may be sure that's the one English word you would know. (*Rises*) Is there a drop of water about?

(MANUS *gives* MAIRE *his bowl of milk.*)

MANUS: I'm sorry I couldn't get up last night.
MAIRE: Doesn't matter.
MANUS: Biddy Hanna sent for me to write a letter to her sister in Nova Scotia. All the gossip of the parish. "I brought the cow to the bull three times last week but no good. There's nothing for it now but Big Ned Frank."
MAIRE: (*Drinking*) That's better.
MANUS: And she got so engrossed in it that she forgot who she    150 was dictating to: "The aul drunken schoolmaster and that lame son of his are still footering about in the hedge-school, wasting people's good time and money."

(MAIRE *has to laugh at this.*)

MAIRE: She did not!
MANUS: And me taking it all down. "Thank God one of them new national schools is being built above at Poll na gCaorach." It was after midnight by the time I got back.
MAIRE: Great to be a busy man.

(MAIRE *moves away.* MANUS *follows.*)

MANUS: I could hear music on my way past but I thought it was too late to call.    160
MAIRE: (*To* SARAH) Wasn't your father in great voice last night?

(SARAH *nods and smiles.*)

MAIRE: It must have been near three o'clock by the time you got home?

(SARAH *holds up four fingers.*)

MAIRE: Was it four? No wonder we're in pieces.
MANUS: I can give you a hand at the hay tomorrow.
MAIRE: That's the name of a hornpipe, isn't it?—"The Scholar In The Hayfield"—or is it a reel?
MANUS: If the day's good.
MAIRE: Suit yourself. The English soldiers below in the tents, them sapper fellas, they're coming up to give us a hand. I    170 don't know a word they're saying, nor they me; but sure that doesn't matter, does it?
MANUS: What the hell are you so crabbed about?!

(DOALTY *and* BRIDGET *enter noisily. Both are in their twenties.* DOALTY *is brandishing a surveyor's pole. He is an open-minded, open-hearted, generous and slightly thick young man.* BRIDGET *is a plump, fresh young girl, ready to laugh, vain, and with a countrywoman's instinctive cunning.* DOALTY *enters doing his imitation of the master.*)

DOALTY: Vesperal salutations to you all.
BRIDGET: He's coming down past Carraig na Ri and he's as full as a pig!
DOALTY: *Ignari, stulti, rustici*—pot-boys and peasant whelps—

semi-literates and illegitimates.

BRIDGET: He's been on the batter since this morning; he sent
180 the wee ones home at eleven o'clock.

DOALTY: Three questions. Question A—Am I drunk? Question
B—Am I sober? (*Into* MAIRE's *face*) *Responde—responde!*

BRIDGET: Question C, Master—When were you last sober?

MAIRE: What's the weapon, Doalty?

BRIDGET: I warned him. He'll be arrested one of these days.

DOALTY: Up in the bog with Bridget and her aul fella, and the
Red Coats were just across at the foot of Croc na Mona,
dragging them aul chains and peeping through that big machine they lug about everywhere with them—you know the
190 name of it, Manus?

MAIRE: Theodolite.

BRIDGET: How do you know?

MAIRE: They leave it in our byre at night sometimes if it's
raining.

JIMMY: Theodolite—what's the etymology of that word,
Manus?

MANUS: No idea.

BRIDGET: Get on with the story.

JIMMY: *Theo—theos*—something to do with a god. Maybe
200 *thea*—a goddess! What shape's the yoke?

DOALTY: "Shape!" Will you shut up, you aul eejit you! Anyway,
every time they'd stick one of these poles into the ground
and move across the bog, I'd creep up and shift it twenty or
thirty paces to the side.

BRIDGET: God!

DOALTY: Then they'd come back and stare at it and look at their
calculations and stare at it again and scratch their heads.
And cripes, d'you know what they ended up doing?

BRIDGET: Wait till you hear!

210 DOALTY: They took the bloody machine apart!

(*And immediately he speaks in gibberish—an imitation of two
very agitated and confused sappers in rapid conversation.*)

BRIDGET: That's the image of them!

MAIRE: You must be proud of yourself, Doalty.

DOALTY: What d'you mean?

MAIRE: That was a very clever piece of work.

MANUS: It was a gesture.

MAIRE: What sort of gesture?

MANUS: Just to indicate . . . a presence.

MAIRE: Hah!

BRIDGET: I'm telling you—you'll be arrested.

(*When* DOALTY *is embarrassed—or pleased—he reacts physically. He now grabs* BRIDGET *around the waist.*)

220 DOALTY: What d'you make of that for an implement, Bridget?
Wouldn't that make a great aul shaft for your churn?

BRIDGET: Let go of me, you dirty brute! I've a headline to do
before Big Hughie comes.

MANUS: I don't think we'll wait for him. Let's get started.

(*Slowly, reluctantly they begin to move to their seats and specific tasks.* DOALTY *goes to the bucket of water at the door and
washes his hands.* BRIDGET *sets up a hand-mirror and combs
her hair.*)

BRIDGET: Nellie Ruadh's baby was to be christened this morning. Did any of yous hear what she called it? Did you, Sarah?

(SARAH *grunts: No.*)

BRIDGET: Did you, Maire?

MAIRE: No.

BRIDGET: Our Seamus says she was threatening she was going
to call it after its father.                                              230

DOALTY: Who's the father?

BRIDGET: That's the point, you donkey you!

DOALTY: Ah.

BRIDGET: So there's a lot of uneasy bucks about Baile Beag this
day.

DOALTY: She told me last Sunday she was going to call it Jimmy.

BRIDGET: You're a liar, Doalty.

DOALTY: Would I tell you a lie? Hi, Jimmy, Nellie Ruadh's aul
fella's looking for you.

JIMMY: For me?                                                           240

MAIRE: Come on, Doalty.

DOALTY: Someone told him . . .

MAIRE: Doalty!

DOALTY: He heard you know the first book of the Satires of Horace off by heart . . .

JIMMY: That's true.

DOALTY: . . . and he wants you to recite it for him.

JIMMY: I'll do that for him certainly, certainly.

DOALTY: He's busting to hear it.

(JIMMY *fumbles in his pockets.*)

JIMMY: I came across this last night—this'll interest you—in 250
Book Two of Virgil's *Georgics.*

DOALTY: Be God, that's my territory alright.

BRIDGET: You clown you! (*To* SARAH) Hold this for me, would
you? (*her mirror.*)

JIMMY: Listen to this, Manus. "*Nigra fere et presso pinguis sub
vomere terra . . .*"

DOALTY: Steady on now—easy, boys, easy—don't rush me,
boys—

(*He mimes great concentration.*)

JIMMY: Manus?

MANUS: "Land that is black and rich beneath the pressure of 260
the plough . . ."

DOALTY: Give *me* a chance!

JIMMY: "And with *cui putre*—with crumbly soil—is in the main
best for corn." There you are!

DOALTY: There you are.

JIMMY: "From no other land will you see more wagons wend-
ing homeward behind slow bullocks." Virgil! There!

DOALTY: "Slow bullocks"!

JIMMY: Isn't that what I'm always telling you? Black soil for
corn. *That's* what you should have in that upper field of 270
yours—corn, not spuds.

DOALTY: Would you listen to that fella! Too lazy be Jasus to
wash himself and he's lecturing me on agriculture! Would
you go and take a running race at yourself, Jimmy Jack
Cassie! (*Grabs* SARAH.) Come away out of this with me,
Sarah, and we'll plant some corn together.

MANUS: All right—all right. Let's settle down and get some
work done. I know Sean Beag isn't coming—he's at the
salmon. What about the Donnelly twins? (*To* DOALTY) Are
the Donnelly twins not coming any more?                                 280

(DOALTY *shrugs and turns away.*)

Did you ask them?
DOALTY: Haven't seen them. Not about these days.

(DOALTY *begins whistling through his teeth. Suddenly the atmosphere is silent and alert.*)

MANUS: Aren't they at home?
DOALTY: No.
MANUS: Where are they then?
DOALTY: How would I know?
BRIDGET: Our Seamus says two of the soldiers' horses were
    found last night at the foot of the cliffs at Machaire Buidhe
    and . . . (*She stops suddenly and begins writing with chalk
290    on her slate.*) D'you hear the whistles of this aul slate? Sure
    nobody could write on an aul slippery thing like that.
MANUS: What headline did my father set you?
BRIDGET: "It's easier to stamp out learning than to recall it."
JIMMY: Book Three, the *Agricola* of Tacitus.
BRIDGET: God but you're a dose.
MANUS: Can you do it?
BRIDGET: There. Is it bad? Will he ate me?
MANUS: It's very good. Keep your elbow in closer to your side.
    Doalty?
300    DOALTY: I'm at the seven-times table. I'm perfect, skipper.

(MANUS *moves to* SARAH.)

MANUS: Do you understand those sums?

(SARAH *nods: Yes.* MANUS *leans down to her ear.*)

MANUS: My name is Sarah.

(MANUS *goes to* MAIRE. *While he is talking to her the others
swop books, talk quietly, etc.*)

MANUS: Can I help you? What are you at?
MAIRE: Map of America. (*Pause.*) The passage money came last
    Friday.
MANUS: You never told me that.
MAIRE: Because I haven't seen you since, have I?
MANUS: You don't want to go. You said that yourself.
MAIRE: There's ten below me to be raised and no man in the
310    house. What do you suggest?
MANUS: Do you want to go?
MAIRE: Did you apply for that job in the new national school?
MANUS: No.
MAIRE: You said you would.
MANUS: I said I might.
MAIRE: When it opens, this is finished: nobody's going to pay to
    go to a hedge-school.
MANUS: I know that and I . . . (*He breaks off because he sees
    SARAH, obviously listening, at his shoulder. She moves away
320    again.*) I was thinking that maybe I could . . .
MAIRE: It's £56 a year you're throwing away.
MANUS: I can't apply for it.
MAIRE: You *promised* me you would.
MANUS: My father has applied for it.
MAIRE: He has not!
MANUS: Day before yesterday.
MAIRE: For God's sake, sure you know he'd never—
MANUS: I couldn't—I can't go in against him.

(MAIRE *looks at him for a second. Then:—*)

MAIRE: Suit yourself. (*To* BRIDGET) I saw your Seamus heading
    off to the Port fair early this morning.                    330
BRIDGET: And wait till you hear this—I forgot to tell you this.
    He said that as soon as he crossed over the gap at Cnoc na
    Mona—just beyond where the soldiers are making the
    maps—the sweet smell was everywhere.
DOALTY: You never told me that.
BRIDGET: It went out of my head.
DOALTY: He saw the crops in Port?
BRIDGET: Some.
MANUS: How did the tops look?
BRIDGET: Fine—I think.                                         340
DOALTY: In flower?
BRIDGET: I don't know. I think so. He didn't say.
MANUS: Just the sweet smell—that's all?
BRIDGET: They say that's the way it snakes in, don't they? First
    the smell; and then one morning the stalks are all black and
    limp.
DOALTY: Are you stupid? It's the rotting stalks makes the sweet
    smell for God's sake. That's what the smell is—rotting
    stalks.
MAIRE: Sweet smell! Sweet smell! Every year at this time        350
    somebody comes back with stories of the sweet smell. Sweet
    God, did the potatoes ever fail in Baile Beag? Well, did they
    ever—ever? Never! There was never blight here. Never.
    Never. But we're always sniffing about for it, aren't we?—
    looking for disaster. The rents are going to go up again—the
    harvest's going to be lost—the herring have gone away for
    ever—there's going to be evictions. Honest to God, some of
    you people aren't happy unless you're miserable and you'll
    not be right content until you're dead!
DOALTY: Bloody right, Maire. And sure St Colmcille prophe-     360
    sied there'd never be blight here. He said:
        The spuds will bloom in Baile Beag
        Till rabbits grow an extra lug.
    And sure that'll never be. So we're all right. Seven threes are
    twenty-one; seven fours are twenty-eight; seven fives are
    forty-nine—Hi, Jimmy, do you fancy my chances as boss of
    the new national school?
JIMMY: What's that?—what's that?
DOALTY: Agh, g'way back home to Greece, son.
MAIRE: You ought to apply, Doalty.                             370
DOALTY: D'you think so? Cripes, maybe I will. Hah!
BRIDGET: Did you know that you start at the age of six and you
    have to stick at it until you're twelve at least—no matter how
    smart you are or how much you know.
DOALTY: Who told you that yarn?
BRIDGET: And every child from every house has to go all day,
    every day, summer or winter. That's the law.
DOALTY: I'll tell you something—nobody's going to go near
    them—they're not going to take on—law or no law.
BRIDGET: And everything's free in them. You pay for nothing   380
    except the books you use; that's what our Seamus says.
DOALTY: "Our Seamus." Sure your Seamus wouldn't pay any-
    way. She's making this all up.
BRIDGET: Isn't that right, Manus?
MANUS: I think so.
BRIDGET: And from the very first day you go, you'll not hear

one word of Irish spoken. You'll be taught to speak English and every subject will be taught through English and everyone'll end up as cute as the Buncrana people.

(SARAH *suddenly grunts and mimes a warning that the master is coming. The atmosphere changes. Sudden business. Heads down.*)

390 DOALTY: He's here, boys. Cripes, he'll make yella meal out of me for those bloody tables.

BRIDGET: Have you any extra chalk, Manus?

MAIRE: And the atlas for me.

(DOALTY *goes to* MAIRE *who is sitting on a stool at the back.*)

DOALTY: Swop you seats.

MAIRE: Why?

DOALTY: There's an empty one beside the Infant Prodigy.

MAIRE: I'm fine here.

DOALTY: Please, Maire. I want to jouk in the back here.

(MAIRE *rises.*)

God love you. (*Aloud*) Anyone got a bloody table-book?
400 Cripes, I'm wrecked.

(SARAH *gives him one.*)

God, I'm dying about you.

(*In his haste to get to the back seat,* DOALTY *bumps into* BRIDGET *who is kneeling on the floor and writing laboriously on a slate resting on top of a bench-seat.*)

BRIDGET: Watch where you're going, Doalty!

(DOALTY *gooses* BRIDGET. *She squeals. Now the quiet hum of work:* JIMMY *reading Homer in a low voice;* BRIDGET *copying her headline;* MAIRE *studying the atlas;* DOALTY, *his eyes shut tight, mouthing his tables;* SARAH *doing sums. After a few seconds:—*)

BRIDGET: Is this "g" right, Manus? How do you put a tail on it?

DOALTY: Will you shut up! I can't concentrate!

(*A few more seconds of work. Then* DOALTY *opens his eyes and looks around.*)

False alarm, boys. The bugger's not coming at all. Sure the bugger's hardly fit to walk.

(*And immediately* HUGH *enters. A large man, with residual dignity, shabbily dressed, carrying a stick. He has, as always, a large quantity of drink taken, but he is by no means drunk. He is in his early sixties.*)

HUGH: *Adsum*, Doalty, *adsum*. Perhaps not in *sobrietate perfecta* but adequately *sobrius* to overhear your quip. Vesperal salutations to you all.

(*Various responses.*)

410 JIMMY: *Ave*, Hugh.

HUGH: James. (*He removes his hat and coat and hands them and his stick to* MANUS, *as if to a footman.*) Apologies for my late arrival: we were celebrating the baptism of Nellie Ruadh's baby.

BRIDGET: (*Innocently*) What name did she put on it, Master?

HUGH: Was it Eamon? Yes, it was Eamon.

BRIDGET: Eamon Donal from Tor! Cripes!

HUGH: And after the *caerimonia nominationis*—Maire?

MAIRE: The ritual of naming.

HUGH: Indeed—we then had a few libations to mark the occa- 420 sion. Altogether very pleasant. The derivation of the word "baptize"?—where are my Greek scholars? Doalty?

DOALTY: Would it be—ah—ah—

HUGH: Too slow, James?

JIMMY: *"Baptizein"*—to dip or immerse.

HUGH: Indeed—our friend Pliny Minor speaks of the *"baptisterium"*—the cold bath.

DOALTY: Master.

HUGH: Doalty?

DOALTY: I suppose you could talk then about baptizing a sheep 430 at sheep-dipping, could you?

(*Laughter. Comments.*)

HUGH: Indeed—the precedent is there—the day you were appropriately named Doalty—seven nines?

DOALTY: What's that, Master?

HUGH: Seven times nine?

DOALTY: Seven nines—seven nines—seven times nine—seven times nine are—cripes, it's on the tip of my tongue, Master—I knew it for sure this morning—funny that's the only one that foxes me—

BRIDGET: (*Prompt*) Sixty-three.                              440

DOALTY: What's wrong with me: sure seven nines are fifty-three, Master.

HUGH: Sophocles from Colonus would agree with Doalty Dan Doalty from Tulach Alainn: "To know nothing is the sweetest life." Where's Sean Beag?

MANUS: He's at the salmon.

HUGH: And Nora Dan?

MAIRE: She says she's not coming back any more.

HUGH: Ah. Nora Dan can now write her name—Nora Dan's education is complete. And the Donnelly twins? (*Brief* 450 *pause. Then:—*)

BRIDGET: They're probably at the turf. (*She goes to* HUGH.)There's the one-and-eight I owe you for last quarter's arithmetic and there's my one-and-six for this quarter's writing.

HUGH: *Gratias tibi ago.* (*He sits at his table.*) Before we commence our *studia* I have three items of information to impart to you—(*To* MANUS) A bowl of tea, strong tea, black—

(MANUS *leaves.*)

Item A: on my perambulations today—Bridget? Too slow. Maire?                                                        460

MAIRE: Perambulare—to walk about.

HUGH: Indeed—I encountered Captain Lancey of the Royal Engineers who is engaged in the ordnance survey of this area. He tells me that in the past few days two of his horses have strayed and some of his equipment seems to be mislaid. I expressed my regret and suggested he address you himself on these matters. He then explained that he does not speak Irish. Latin? I asked. None. Greek? Not a syllable. He speaks—on his own admission—only English; and to his credit he seemed suitably verecund—James?                470

JIMMY: *Verecundus*—humble.

HUGH: Indeed—he voiced some surprise that we did not speak

his language. I explained that a few of us did, on occasion—outside the parish of course—and then usually for the purposes of commerce, a use to which his tongue seemed particularly suited—*(Shouts)* and a slice of soda bread—and I went on to propose that our own culture and the classical tongues made a happier conjugation—Doalty?

DOALTY: *Conjugo*—I join together.

(DOALTY *is so pleased with himself that he prods and winks at* BRIDGET.)

480  HUGH: Indeed—English, I suggested, couldn't really express us. And again to his credit he acquiesced to my logic. Acquiesced—Maire?

(MAIRE *turns away impatiently.* HUGH *is unaware of the gesture.*)

Too slow. Bridget?
BRIDGET: *Acquiesco.*
HUGH: *Procede.*
BRIDGET: *Acquiesco, acquiescere, acquievi, acquietum.*
HUGH: Indeed—and Item B . . .
MAIRE: Master.
HUGH: Yes?

(MAIRE *gets to her feet uneasily but determinedly. Pause.*)

490  Well, girl?
MAIRE: We should all be learning to speak English. That's what my mother says. That's what I say. That's what Dan O'Connell said last month in Ennis. He said the sooner we all learn to speak English the better.

(*Suddenly several speak together.*)

JIMMY: What's she saying? What? What?
DOALTY: It's Irish he uses when he's travelling around scrounging votes.
BRIDGET: And sleeping with married women. Sure no woman's safe from that fella.
500  JIMMY: Who-who-who? Who's this? Who's this?
HUGH: *Silentium! (Pause.)* Who is she talking about?
MAIRE: I'm talking about Daniel O'Connell.
HUGH: Does she mean that little Kerry politician?
MAIRE: I'm talking about the Liberator, Master, as you well know. And what he said was this: "The old language is a barrier to modern progress." He said that last month. And he's right. I don't want Greek. I don't want Latin. I want English.

(MANUS *reappears on the platform above.*)

I want to be able to speak English because I'm going to America as soon as the harvest's all saved.

(MAIRE *remains standing.* HUGH *puts his hand into his pocket and produces a flask of whiskey. He removes the cap, pours a drink into it, tosses it back, replaces the cap, puts the flask back into his pocket. Then:—*)

510  HUGH: We have been diverted—*diverto*—*divertere*—Where were we?
DOALTY: Three items of information, Master. You're at Item B.
HUGH: Indeed—Item B—Item B—yes—On my way to the christening this morning I chanced to meet Mr George Alexander, Justice of the Peace. We discussed the new na-

tional school. Mr Alexander invited me to take charge of it when it opens. I thanked him and explained that I could do that only if I were free to run it as I have run this hedge-school for the past thirty-five years—filling what our friend Euripides calls the *"aplestos pithos"*—James?                  520
JIMMY: "The cask that cannot be filled."
HUGH: Indeed—and Mr Alexander retorted courteously and emphatically that he hopes that is how it will be run.

(MAIRE *now sits.*)

Indeed. I have had a strenuous day and I am weary of you all. (*He rises.*) Manus will take care of you.

(HUGH *goes towards the steps.* OWEN *enters.* OWEN *is the younger son, a handsome, attractive young man in his twenties. He is dressed smartly—a city man. His manner is easy and charming: everything he does is invested with consideration and enthusiasm. He now stands framed in the doorway, a travelling bag across his shoulder.*)

OWEN: Could anybody tell me is this where Hugh Mor O'Donnell holds his hedge-school?
DOALTY: It's Owen—Owen Hugh! Look, boys—it's Owen Hugh!

(OWEN *enters. As he crosses the room he touches and has a word for each person.*)

OWEN: Doalty! (*Playful punch.*) How are you, boy? *Jacobe,*  530
*quid agis?* Are you well?
JIMMY: Fine. Fine.
OWEN: And Bridget! Give us a kiss. Aaaaaah!
BRIDGET: You're welcome, Owen.
OWEN: It's not—? Yes, it *is* Maire Chatach! God! A young woman!
MAIRE: How are you, Owen?

(OWEN *is now in front of* HUGH. *He puts his two hands on his* FATHER's *shoulders.*)

OWEN: And how's the old man himself?
HUGH: Fair—fair.
OWEN: Fair? For God's sake you never looked better! Come  540
here to me.
(*He embraces* HUGH *warmly and genuinely.*) Great to see you, Father. Great to be back.

(HUGH's *eyes are moist—partly joy, partly the drink.*)

HUGH: I—I'm—I'm—pay no attention to—
OWEN: Come on—come on—come on—(*He gives* HUGH *his handkerchief.*) Do you know what you and I are going to do tonight? We are going to go up to Anna na mBreag's . . .
DOALTY: Not there, Owen.
OWEN: Why not?
DOALTY: Her poteen's worse than ever.                      550
BRIDGET: They say she puts frogs in it!
OWEN: All the better. (*To* HUGH) And you and I are going to get footless drunk. That's arranged.

(OWEN *sees* MANUS *coming down the steps with tea and soda bread. They meet at the bottom.*)

And Manus!
MANUS: You're welcome, Owen.

OWEN: I know I am. And it's great to be here. (*He turns round, arms outstretched.*) I can't believe it. I come back after six years and everything's just as it was! Nothing's changed! Not a thing! (*Sniffs.*) Even that smell—that's the same smell this
560 place always had. What is it anyway? Is it the straw?
DOALTY: Jimmy Jack's feet.

(*General laughter. It opens little pockets of conversation round the room.*)

OWEN: And Doalty Dan Doalty hasn't change either!
DOALTY: Bloody right, Owen.
OWEN: Jimmy, are you well?
JIMMY: Dodging about.
OWEN: Any word of the big day?

(*This is greeted with "ohs" and "ahs."*)

Time enough, Jimmy. Homer's easier to live with, isn't he?
MAIRE: We heard stories that you own ten big shops in Dublin—is it true?
570 OWEN: Only nine.
BRIDGET: And you've twelve horses and six servants.
OWEN: Yes—that's true. God Almighty, would you listen to them—taking a hand at me!
MANUS: When did you arrive?
OWEN: We left Dublin yesterday morning, spent last night in Omagh and got here half an hour ago.
MANUS: You're hungry then.
HUGH: Indeed—get him food—get him a drink.
OWEN: Not now, thanks; later. Listen—am I interrupting you
580 all?
HUGH: By no means. We're finished for the day.
OWEN: Wonderful. I'll tell you why. Two friends of mine are waiting outside the door. They'd like to meet you and I'd like you to meet them. May I bring them in?
HUGH: Certainly. You'll all eat and have . . .
OWEN: Not just yet, Father. You've seen the sappers working in this area for the past fortnight, haven't you? Well, the older man is Captain Lancey . . .
HUGH: I've met Captain Lancey.
590 OWEN: Great. He's the cartographer in charge of this whole area. Cartographer—James?

(OWEN *begins to play this game—his father's game—partly to involve his classroom audience, partly to show he has not forgotten it, and indeed partly because he enjoys it.*)

JIMMY: A maker of maps.
OWEN: Indeed—and the younger man that I travelled with from Dublin, his name is Lieutenant Yolland and he is attached to the toponymic department—Father?—*responde—responde!*
HUGH: He gives names to places.
OWEN: Indeed—although he is in fact an orthographer—Doalty?—too slow—Manus?
600 MANUS: The correct spelling of those names.
OWEN: Indeed—indeed!

(OWEN *laughs and claps his hands. Some of the others join in.*)

Beautiful! Beautiful! Honest to God, it's such a delight to be back here with you all again—"civilized" people. Anyhow—may I bring them in?

HUGH: Your friends are our friends.
OWEN: I'll be straight back.

(*There is general talk as* OWEN *goes towards the door. He stops beside* SARAH.)

OWEN: That's a new face. Who are you?

(*A very brief hesitation. Then:—*)

SARAH: My name is Sarah.
OWEN: Sarah who?
SARAH: Sarah Johnny Sally.                                          610
OWEN: Of course! From Bun na hAbhann! I'm Owen—Owen Hugh Mor. From Baile Beag. Good to see you.

(*During this* OWEN–SARAH *exchange.*)

HUGH: Come on now. Let's tidy this place up. (*He rubs the top of his table with his sleeve.*) Move, Doalty—lift those books off the floor.
DOALTY: Right, Master; certainly, Master; I'm doing my best, Master.

(OWEN *stops at the door.*)

OWEN: One small thing, Father.
HUGH: *Silentium!*
OWEN: I'm on their pay-roll.                                        620

(SARAH, *very elated at her success, is beside* MANUS.)

SARAH: I said it, Manus!

(MANUS *ignores* SARAH. *He is much more interested in* OWEN *now.*)

MANUS: You haven't enlisted, have you?!

(SARAH *moves away.*)

OWEN: Me a soldier? I'm employed as a part-time, underpaid, civilian interpreter. My job is to translate the quaint, archaic tongue you people persist in speaking into the King's good English.

(*He goes out.*)

HUGH: Move—move—move! Put some order on things! Come on, Sarah—hide that bucket. Whose are these slates? Somebody take these dishes away. *Festinate! Festinate!*

(MANUS *goes to* MAIRE *who is busy tidying.*)

MANUS: You didn't tell me you were definitely leaving.            630
MAIRE: Not now.
HUGH: Good girl, Bridget. That's the style.
MANUS: You might at least have told me.
HUGH: Are these your books, James?
JIMMY: Thank you.
MANUS: Fine! Fine! Go ahead! Go ahead!
MAIRE: You talk to me about getting married—with neither a roof over your head nor a sod of ground under your foot. I suggest you go for the new school; but no—"My father's in for that." Well now he's got it and now this is finished and     640
now you've nothing.
MANUS: I can always . . .
MAIRE: What? Teach classics to the cows? Agh—

(MAIRE *moves away from* MANUS. OWEN *enters with* LANCEY *and* YOLLAND. CAPTAIN LANCEY *is middle-aged; a small, crisp officer, expert in his field as cartographer but uneasy with people—especially civilians, especially these foreign civilians. His skill is with deeds, not words.* LIEUTENANT YOLLAND *is in his late twenties/early thirties. He is tall and thin and gangling, blond hair, a shy, awkward manner. A soldier by accident.*)

OWEN: Here we are. Captain Lancey—my father.
LANCEY: Good evening.

(HUGH *becomes expansive, almost courtly, with his visitors.*)

HUGH: You and I have already met, sir.
LANCEY: Yes.
OWEN: And Lieutenant Yolland—both Royal Engineers—my father.
650 HUGH: You're very welcome, gentlemen.
YOLLAND: How do you do.
HUGH: *Gaudeo vos hic adesse.*
OWEN: And I'll make no other introductions except that these are some of the people of Baile Beag and—what?—well you're among the best people in Ireland now. (*He pauses to allow* LANCEY *to speak.* LANCEY *does not.*) Would you like to say a few words, Captain?
HUGH: What about a drop, sir?
LANCEY: A what?
660 HUGH: Perhaps a modest refreshment? A little sampling of our *aqua vitae?*
LANCEY: No, no.
HUGH: Later perhaps when—
LANCEY: I'll say what I have to say, if I may, and as briefly as possible. Do they speak *any* English, Roland?
OWEN: Don't worry. I'll translate.
LANCEY: I see. (*He clears his throat. He speaks as if he were addressing children—a shade too loudly and enunciating excessively.*) You may have seen me—seen me—working in
670 this section—section?—working. We are here—here—in this place—you understand?—to make a map—a map—a map and—
JIMMY: *Nonne Latine loquitur?*

(HUGH *holds up a restraining hand.*)

HUGH: James.
LANCEY: (*To* JIMMY) I do not speak Gaelic, sir.

(*He looks at* OWEN.)

OWEN: Carry on.
LANCEY: A map is a representation on paper—a picture—you understand picture?—a paper picture—showing, representing this country—yes?—showing your country in
680 miniature—a scaled drawing on paper of—of—of— (*Suddenly* DOALTY *sniggers. Then* BRIDGET. *Then* SARAH. OWEN *leaps in quickly.*)
OWEN: It might be better if you *assume* they understand you—
LANCEY: Yes?
OWEN: And I'll translate as you go along.
LANCEY: I see. Yes. Very well. Perhaps you're right. Well. What we are doing is this. (*He looks at* OWEN. OWEN *nods reassuringly.*) His Majesty's government has ordered the first ever comprehensive survey of this entire country—a general tri-

angulation which will embrace detailed hydrographic and 690 topographic information and which will be executed to a scale of six inches to the English mile.
HUGH: (*Pouring a drink*) Excellent—excellent.

(LANCEY *looks at* OWEN.)

OWEN: A new map is being made of the whole country.

(LANCEY *looks to* OWEN: *Is that all?* OWEN *smiles reassuringly and indicates to proceed.*)

LANCEY: This enormous task has been embarked on so that the military authorities will be equipped with up-to-date and accurate information on every corner of this part of the Empire.
OWEN: The job is being done by soldiers because they are skilled in this work.                                                    700
LANCEY: And also so that the entire basis of land valuation can be reassessed for purposes of more equitable taxation.
OWEN: This new map will take the place of the estate agent's map so that from now on you will know exactly what is yours in law.
LANCEY: In conclusion I wish to quote two brief extracts from the white paper which is our governing charter: (*Reads*) "All former surveys of Ireland originated in forfeiture and violent transfer of property; the present survey has for its object the relief which can be afforded to the proprietors and 710 occupiers of land from unequal taxation."
OWEN: The captain hopes that the public will cooperate with the sappers and that the new map will mean that taxes are reduced.
HUGH: A worthy enterprise—*opus honestum!* And Extract B?
LANCEY: "Ireland is privileged. No such survey is being undertaken in England. So this survey cannot but be received as proof of the disposition of this government to advance the interests of Ireland." My sentiments, too.
OWEN: This survey demonstrates the government's interest in 720 Ireland and the captain thanks you for listening so attentively to him.
HUGH: Our pleasure, Captain.
LANCEY: Lieutenant Yolland?
YOLLAND: I—I—I've nothing to say—really—
OWEN: The captain is the man who actually makes the new map. George's task is to see that the place-names on this map are . . . correct. (*To* YOLLAND.) Just a few words—they'd like to hear you. (*To class.*) Don't you want to hear George, too?                                                            730
MAIRE: Has he anything to say?
YOLLAND: (*To* MAIRE) Sorry—sorry?
OWEN: She says she's dying to hear you.
YOLLAND: (*To* MAIRE) Very kind of you—thank you . . . (*To class*) I can only say that I feel—I feel very foolish to—to—to be working here and not to speak your language. But I intend to rectify that—with Roland's help—indeed I do.
OWEN: He wants me to teach him Irish!
HUGH: You are doubly welcome, sir.
YOLLAND: I think your countryside is—is—is—is very beauti- 740 ful. I've fallen in love with it already. I hope we're not too—too crude an intrusion on your lives. And I know that I'm going to be happy, very happy, here.
OWEN: He is already a committed Hibernophile—

JIMMY: He loves—

OWEN: All right, Jimmy—we know—he loves Baile Beag; and he loves you all.

HUGH: Please . . . May I . . . ?

(HUGH *is now drunk. He holds on to the edge of the table.*)

OWEN: Go ahead, Father. (*Hands up for quiet.*) Please—
750 please.

HUGH: And we, gentlemen, we in turn are happy to offer you our friendship, our hospitality, and every assistance that you may require. Gentlemen—welcome!

(*A few desultory claps. The formalities are over. General conversation. The soldiers meet the locals.* MANUS *and* OWEN *meet down stage.*)

OWEN: Lancey's a bloody ramrod but George's all right. How are you anyway?

MANUS: What sort of a translation was that, Owen?

OWEN: Did I make a mess of it?

MANUS: You weren't saying what Lancey was saying!

OWEN: "Uncertainty in meaning is incipient poetry"—who said
760 that?

MANUS: There was nothing uncertain about what Lancey said: it's a bloody military operation, Owen! And what's Yolland's function? What's "incorrect" about the place-names we have here?

OWEN: Nothing at all. They're just going to be standardized.

MANUS: You mean changed into English?

OWEN: Where there's ambiguity, they'll be Anglicized.

MANUS: And they call you Roland! They both call you Roland!

OWEN: Shhhhh. Isn't it ridiculous? They seemed to get it
770 wrong from the very beginning—or else they can't pronounce Owen. I was afraid some of you bastards would laugh.

MANUS: Aren't you going to tell them?

OWEN: Yes—yes—soon—soon.

MANUS: But they . . .

OWEN: Easy, man, easy. Owen—Roland—what the hell. It's only a name. It's the same me, isn't it? Well, isn't it?

MANUS: Indeed it is. It's the same Owen.

OWEN: And the same Manus. And in a way we complement
780 each other. (*He punches* MANUS *lightly, playfully and turns to join the others. As he goes.*) All right—who has met whom? Isn't this a job for the go-between?

(MANUS *watches* OWEN *move confidently across the floor, taking* MAIRE *by the hand and introducing her to* YOLLAND. HUGH *is trying to negotiate the steps.* JIMMY *is lost in a text.* DOALTY *and* BRIDGET *are reliving their giggling.* SARAH *is staring at* MANUS.)

### —ACT TWO—

SCENE I

*The sappers have already mapped most of the area.* YOLLAND's *official task, which* OWEN *is now doing, is to take each of the Gaelic names—every hill, stream, rock, even every patch of ground which possessed its own distinctive Irish name—and Anglicize it, either by changing it into its approximate English sound or by translating it into English words. For example, a Gaelic name like Cnoc Ban could become Knockban or—directly translated—Fair Hill. These new standardized names were entered into the Name-Book, and when the new maps appeared they contained all these new Anglicized names.* OWEN's *official function as translator is to pronounce each name in Irish and then provide the English translation.*

*The hot weather continues. It is late afternoon some days later.*

*Stage right: an improvised clothes-line strung between the shafts of the cart and a nail in the wall; on it are some shirts and socks.*

*A large map—one of the new blank maps—is spread out on the floor.* OWEN *is on his hands and knees, consulting it. He is totally engrossed in his task which he pursues with great energy and efficiency.*

YOLLAND's *hesitancy has vanished—he is at home here now. He is sitting on the floor, his long legs stretched out before him, his back resting against a creel, his eyes closed. His mind is elsewhere. One of the reference books—a church registry—lies open on his lap.*

*Around them are various reference books, the Name-Book, a bottle of poteen, some cups, etc.*

OWEN *completes an entry in the Name-Book and returns to the map on the floor.*

OWEN: Now. Where have we got to? Yes—the point where that stream enters the sea—that tiny little beach there. George!

YOLLAND: Yes. I'm listening. What do you call it? Say the Irish name again?

OWEN: Bun na hAbhann.

YOLLAND: Again.

OWEN: Bun na hAbhann.

YOLLAND: Bun na hAbhann.                                              790

OWEN: That's terrible, George.

YOLLAND: I know. I'm sorry. Say it again.

OWEN: Bun na hAbhann.

YOLLAND: Bun na hAbbann.

OWEN: That's better. Bun is the Irish word for bottom. And Abha means river. So it's literally the mouth of the river.

YOLLAND: Let's leave it alone. There's no English equivalent for a sound like that.

OWEN: What is it called in the church registry?

(*Only now does* YOLLAND *open his eyes.*)

YOLLAND: Let's see . . . Banowen.                                    800

OWEN: That's wrong. (*Consults text.*) The list of freeholders calls it Owenmore—that's completely wrong: Owenmore's the big river at the west end of the parish. (*Another text.*) And in the grand jury lists it's called—God!—Binhone!—wherever they got that. I suppose we could Anglicize it to Bunowen; but somehow that's neither fish nor flesh.

(YOLLAND *closes his eyes again.*)

YOLLAND: I give up.

OWEN: (*At map*) Back to first principles. What are we trying to do?

810 YOLLAND: Good question.

OWEN: We are trying to denominate and at the same time describe that tiny area of soggy, rocky, sandy ground where that little stream enters the sea, an area known locally as Bun na hAbhann . . . Burnfoot! What about Burnfoot?

YOLLAND: (*Indifferently*) Good, Roland, Burnfoot's good.

OWEN: George, my name isn't . . .

YOLLAND: B-u-r-n-f-o-o-t?

OWEN: Are you happy with that?

YOLLAND: Yes.

820 OWEN: Burnfoot it is then. (*He makes the entry into the Name-Book.*) Bun na hAbhann—B-u-r-n-

YOLLAND: You're becoming very skilled at this.

OWEN: We're not moving fast enough.

YOLLAND: (*Opens eyes again*) Lancey lectured me again last night.

OWEN: When does he finish here?

YOLLAND: The sappers are pulling out at the end of the week. The trouble is, the maps they've completed can't be printed without these names. So London screams at Lancey and 830 Lancey screams at me. But I wasn't intimidated.

(MANUS *emerges from upstairs and descends.*)

"I'm sorry, sir," I said, "But certain tasks demand their own tempo. You cannot rename a whole country overnight." Your Irish air has made me bold. (*To* MANUS) Do you want us to leave?

MANUS: Time enough. Class won't begin for another half-hour.

YOLLAND: Sorry-sorry?

OWEN: Can't you speak English?

(MANUS *gathers the things off the clothes-line.* OWEN *returns to the map.*)

OWEN: We now come across that beach . . .

YOLLAND: Tra—that's the Irish for beach. (*To* MANUS) I'm 840 picking up the odd word, Manus.

MANUS: So.

OWEN: . . . on past Burnfoot; and there's nothing around here that has any name that I know of until we come down here to the south end, just about here . . . and there should be a ridge of rocks there . . . Have the sappers marked it? They have. Look, George.

YOLLAND: Where are we?

OWEN: There.

YOLLAND: I'm lost.

850 OWEN: Here. And the name of that ridge is Druim Dubh. Put English on that, Lieutenant.

YOLLAND: Say it again.

OWEN: Druim Dubh.

YOLLAND: Dubh means black.

OWEN: Yes.

YOLLAND: And Druim means . . . what? a fort?

OWEN: We met it yesterday in Druim Luachra.

YOLLAND: A ridge! The Black Ridge! (*To* MANUS) You see, Manus?

860 OWEN: We'll have you fluent at the Irish before the summer's over.

YOLLAND: Oh, I wish I were. (*To* MANUS *as he crosses to go back upstairs*) We got a crate of oranges from Dublin today. I'll send some up to you.

MANUS: Thanks. (*To* OWEN) Better hide that bottle. Father's just up and he'd be better without it.

OWEN: Can't you speak English before your man?

MANUS: Why?

OWEN: Out of courtesy.

MANUS: Doesn't he want to learn Irish? (*To* YOLLAND) Don't 870 you want to learn Irish?

YOLLAND: Sorry-sorry? I—I—

MANUS: I understand the Lanceys perfectly but people like you puzzle me.

OWEN: Manus, for God's sake!

MANUS: (*Still to* YOLLAND) How's the work going?

YOLLAND: The work?—the work? Oh, it's—it's staggering along—I think—(*To* OWEN)—isn't it? But we'd be lost without Roland.

MANUS: (*Leaving*) I'm sure. But there are always the Rolands, 880 aren't there?

(*He goes upstairs and exits.*)

YOLLAND: What was that he said?—something about Lancey, was it?

OWEN: He said we should hide that bottle before Father gets his hands on it.

YOLLAND: Ah.

OWEN: He's always trying to protect him.

YOLLAND: Was he lame from birth?

OWEN: An accident when he was a baby: Father fell across his cradle. That's why Manus feels so responsible for him. 890

YOLLAND: Why doesn't he marry?

OWEN: Can't afford to, I suppose.

YOLLAND: Hasn't he a salary?

OWEN: What salary? All he gets is the odd shilling Father throws him—and that's seldom enough. I got out in time, didn't I?

(YOLLAND *is pouring a drink.*)

Easy with that stuff—it'll hit you suddenly.

YOLLAND: I like it.

OWEN: Let's get back to the job. Druim Dubh—what's it called in the jury lists? (*Consults texts.*)     900

YOLLAND: Some people here resent us.

OWEN: Dramduff—wrong as usual.

YOLLAND: I was passing a little girl yesterday and she spat at me.

OWEN: And it's Drimdoo here. What's it called in the registry?

YOLLAND: Do you know the Donnelly twins?

OWEN: Who?

YOLLAND: The Donnelly twins.

OWEN: Yes. Best fishermen about here. What about them?

YOLLAND: Lancey's looking for them.     910

OWEN: What for?

YOLLAND: He wants them for questioning.

OWEN: Probably stolen somebody's nets. Dramduffy! Nobody ever called it Dramduffy. Take your pick of those three.

YOLLAND: My head's addled. Let's take a rest. Do you want a drink?

OWEN: Thanks. Now, every Dubh we've come across we've changed to Duff. So if we're to be consistent, I suppose Druim Dubh has to become Dromduff.

(YOLLAND *is now looking out the window.*)

920   You can see the end of the ridge from where you're stand-
       ing. But D-r-u-m- or D-r-o-m-? (*Name-Book*) Do you re-
       member—which did we agree on for Druim Luachra?
    YOLLAND: That house immediately above where we're
       camped—
    OWEN: Mm?
    YOLLAND: The house where Maire lives.
    OWEN: Maire? Oh, Maire Chatach.
    YOLLAND: What does that mean?
    OWEN: Curly-haired; the whole family are called the Catachs.
930    What about it?
    YOLLAND: I hear music coming from that house almost every
       night.
    OWEN: Why don't you drop in?
    YOLLAND: Could I?
    OWEN: Why not? We used D-r-o-m then. So we've got to call
       it D-r-o-m-d-u-f-f—all right?
    YOLLAND: Go back up to where the new school is being built
       and just say the names again for me, would you?
    OWEN: That's a good idea. Poolkerry, Ballybeg—
940 YOLLAND: No, no; as they still are—in your own language.
    OWEN: Poll na gCaorach,

    (YOLLAND *repeats the names silently after him.*)

       Baile Beag, Ceann Balor, Lis Maol, Machaire Buidhe, Baile
       na gGall, Carraig na Ri, Mullach Dearg—
    YOLLAND: Do you think I could live here?
    OWEN: What are you talking about?
    YOLLAND: Settle down here—live here.
    OWEN: Come on, George.
    YOLLAND: I mean it.
    OWEN: Live on what? Potatoes? Buttermilk?
950 YOLLAND: It's really heavenly.
    OWEN: For God's sake! The first hot summer in fifty years and
       you think it's Eden. Don't be such a bloody romantic. You
       wouldn't survive a mild winter here.
    YOLLAND: Do you think not? Maybe you're right.

    (DOALTY *enters in a rush.*)

    DOALTY: Hi, boys, is Manus about?
    OWEN: He's upstairs. Give him a shout.
    DOALTY: Manus! The cattle's going mad in that heat—Cripes,
       running wild all over the place. (*To* YOLLAND) How are you
       doing, skipper?

    (MANUS *appears.*)

960 YOLLAND: Thank you for—I—I'm very grateful to you for—
    DOALTY: Wasting your time. I don't know a word you're saying.
       Hi, Manus, there's two bucks down the road there asking for
       you.
    MANUS: (*Descending*) Who are they?
    DOALTY: Never clapped eyes on them. They want to talk to you.
    MANUS: What about?
    DOALTY: They wouldn't say. Come on. The bloody beasts'll end
       up in Loch an Iubhair if they're not capped. Good luck,
       boys!

    (DOALTY *rushes off.* MANUS *follows him.*)

970 OWEN: Good luck! What were you thanking Doalty for?
    YOLLAND: I was washing outside my tent this morning and he

was passing with a scythe across his shoulder and he came
up to me and pointed to the long grass and then cut a pathway round my tent and from the tent down to the road—so
that my feet won't get wet with the dew. Wasn't that kind of
him? And I have no words to thank him . . . I suppose you're
right: I suppose I couldn't live here . . . Just before Doalty
came up to me this morning, I was thinking that at that moment I might have been in Bombay instead of Ballybeg. You
see, my father was at his wits end with me and finally he got   980
me a job with the East India Company—some kind of a
clerkship. This was ten, eleven months ago. So I set off for
London. Unfortunately I—I—I missed the boat. Literally.
And since I couldn't face Father and hadn't enough money
to hang about until the next sailing, I joined the army. And
they stuck me into the Engineers and posted me to Dublin.
And Dublin sent me here. And while I was washing this
morning and looking across the Tra Bhan, I was thinking
how very, very lucky I am to be here and not in Bombay.
    OWEN: Do you believe in fate?                                 990
    YOLLAND: Lancey's so like my father. I was watching him last
       night. He met every group of sappers as they reported in.
       He checked the field kitchens. He examined the horses. He
       inspected every single report—even examining the texture
       of the paper and commenting on the neatness of the hand-
       writing. The perfect colonial servant: not only must the job
       be done—it must be done with excellence. Father has that
       drive, too; that dedication; that indefatigable energy. He
       builds roads—hopping from one end of the Empire to the
       other. Can't sit still for five minutes. He says himself the    1000
       longest time he ever sat still was the night before Waterloo
       when they were waiting for Wellington to make up his mind
       to attack.
    OWEN: What age is he?
    YOLLAND: Born in 1789—the very day the Bastille fell. I've
       often thought maybe that gave his whole life its character.
       Do you think it could? He inherited a new world the day he
       was born—The Year One. Ancient time was at an end. The
       world had cast off its old skin. There were no longer any
       frontiers to man's potential. Possibilities were endless and    1010
       exciting. He still believes that. The Apocalypse is just about
       to happen . . . I'm afraid I'm a great disappointment to him.
       I've neither his energy, nor his coherence, nor his belief. Do
       I believe in fate? The day I arrived in Ballybeg—no, Baile
       Beag—the moment you brought me in here, I had a curious
       sensation. It's difficult to describe. It was a momentary
       sense of discovery; no—not quite a sense of discovery—a
       sense of recognition, of confirmation of something I half
       knew instinctively; as if I had stepped . . .
    OWEN: Back into ancient time?                                 1020
    YOLLAND: No, no. It wasn't an awareness of *direction* being
       changed but of experience being of a totally different order.
       I had moved into a consciousness that wasn't striving nor ag-
       itated, but at its ease and with its own conviction and assur-
       ance. And when I heard Jimmy Jack and your father
       swapping stories about Apollo and Cuchulainn and Paris
       and Ferdia—as if they lived down the road—it was then
       that I thought—I knew—perhaps I could live here . . . (*Now
       embarrassed*) Where's the pot-een?
    OWEN: Poteen.                                                 1030
    YOLLAND: Poteen—poteen—poteen. Even if I did speak Irish

I'd always be an outsider here, wouldn't I? I may learn the password but the language of the tribe will always elude me, won't it? The private core will always be . . . hermetic, won't it?

OWEN: You can learn to decode us.

(HUGH *emerges from upstairs and descends. He is dressed for the road. Today he is physically and mentally jaunty and alert—almost self-consciously jaunty and alert. Indeed, as the scene progresses, one has the sense that he is deliberately parodying himself. The moment* HUGH *gets to the bottom of the steps* YOLLAND *leaps respectfully to his feet.*)

HUGH: (*As he descends*)
Quantumvis cursum longum fessumque moratur
Sol, sacro tandem carmine vesper adest.

1040    I dabble in verse, Lieutenant, after the style of Ovid. (*To* OWEN) A drop of that to fortify me.

YOLLAND: You'll have to translate it for me.

HUGH: Let's see—
No matter how long the sun may linger on his long and weary journey
At length evening comes with its sacred song.

YOLLAND: Very nice, sir.

HUGH: English succeeds in making it sound . . . plebeian.

OWEN: Where are you off to, Father?

1050    HUGH: An *expeditio* with three purposes. Purpose A: to acquire a testimonial from our parish priest—(*To* YOLLAND) a worthy man but barely literate; and since he'll ask me to write it myself, how in all modesty can I do myself justice? (*To* OWEN) Where did this (*drink*) come from?

OWEN: Anna na mBreag's.

HUGH: (*To* YOLLAND) In that case address yourself to it with circumspection. (*And* HUGH *instantly tosses the drink back in one gulp and grimaces.*) Aaaaaaagh! (*Holds out his glass for a refill.*) Anna na mBreag means Anna of the Lies. And Pur-
1060    pose B: to talk to the builders of the new school about the kind of living accommodation I will require there. I have lived too long like a journeyman tailor.

YOLLAND: Some years ago we lived fairly close to a poet—well, about three miles away.

HUGH: His name?

YOLLAND: Wordsworth—William Wordsworth.

HUGH: Did he speak of me to you?

YOLLAND: Actually I never talked to him. I just saw him out walking—in the distance.

1070    HUGH: Wordsworth? . . . No. I'm afraid we're not familiar with your literature, Lieutenant. We feel closer to the warm Mediterranean. We tend to overlook your island.

YOLLAND: I'm learning to speak Irish, sir.

HUGH: Good.

YOLLAND: Roland's teaching me.

HUGH: Splendid.

YOLLAND: I mean—I feel so cut off from the people here. And I was trying to explain a few minutes ago how remarkable a community this is. To meet people like yourself and Jimmy
1080    Jack who actually converse in Greek and Latin. And your place names—what was the one we came across this morning?—Termon, from Terminus, the god of boundaries. It—it—it's really astonishing.

HUGH: We like to think we endure around truths immemori-

ally posited.

YOLLAND: And your Gaelic literature—you're a poet yourself—

HUGH: Only in Latin, I'm afraid.

YOLLAND: I understand it's enormously rich and ornate.

HUGH: Indeed, Lieutenant. A rich language. A rich literature. 1090 You'll find, sir, that certain cultures expend on their vocabularies and syntax acquisitive energies and ostentations entirely lacking in their material lives. I suppose you could call us a spiritual people.

OWEN: (*Not unkindly; more out of embarrassment before* YOLLAND) Will you stop that nonsense, Father.

HUGH: Nonsense? What nonsense?

OWEN: Do you know where the priest lives?

HUGH: At Lis na Muc, over near . . .

OWEN: No, he doesn't. Lis na Muc, the Fort of the Pigs, has be- 1100 come Swinefort. (*Now turning the pages of the Name-Book—a page per name.*) And to get to Swinefort you pass through Greencastle and Fair Head and Strandhill and Gort and Whiteplains. And the new school isn't at Poll na gCaorach—it's at Sheepsrock. Will you be able to find your way?

(HUGH *pours himself another drink. Then:—*)

HUGH: Yes, it is a rich language, Lieutenant, full of the mythologies of fantasy and hope and self-deception—a syntax opulent with tomorrows. It is our response to mud cabins and a diet of potatoes; our only method of replying to . . . inevitabilities. (*To* OWEN) Can you give me the loan of 1110 half-a-crown? I'll repay you out of the subscriptions I'm collecting for the publication of my new book. (*To* YOLLAND) It is entitled: "The Pentaglot Preceptor or Elementary Institute of the English, Greek, Hebrew, Latin and Irish Languages; Particularly Calculated for the Instruction of Such Ladies and Gentlemen as may Wish to Learn without the Help of a Master."

YOLLAND: (*Laughs*) That's a wonderful title!

HUGH: Between ourselves—the best part of the enterprise. Nor do I, in fact, speak Hebrew. And that last phrase— 1120 "without the Help of a Master"—that was written before the new national school was thrust upon me—do you think I ought to drop it now? After all you don't dispose of the cow just because it has produced a magnificent calf, do you?

YOLLAND: You certainly do not.

HUGH: The phrase goes. And I'm interrupting work of moment. (*He goes to the door and stops there.*) To return briefly to that other matter, Lieutenant. I understand your sense of exclusion, of being cut off from a life here; and I trust you will find access to us with my son's help. But re- 1130 member that words are signals, counters. They are not immortal. And it can happen—to use an image you'll understand—it can happen that a civilization can be imprisoned in a linguistic contour which no longer matches the landscape of . . . fact. Gentlemen. (*He leaves.*)

OWEN: "An *expeditio* with three purposes": the children laugh at him: he always promises three points and he never gets beyond A and B.

MANUS: He's an astute man.

OWEN: He's bloody pompous.    1140

YOLLAND: But so astute.

OWEN: And he drinks too much. Is it astute not to be able to adjust for survival? Enduring around truths immemorially posited—hah!

YOLLAND: He knows what's happening.

OWEN: What is happening?

YOLLAND: I'm not sure. But I'm concerned about my part in it. It's an eviction of sorts.

OWEN: We're making a six-inch map of the country. Is there something sinister in that?

YOLLAND: Not in—

OWEN: And we're taking place-names that are riddled with confusion and—

YOLLAND: Who's confused? Are the people confused?

OWEN: —and we're standardizing those names as accurately and as sensitively as we can.

YOLLAND: Something is being eroded.

OWEN: Back to the romance again. All right! Fine! Fine! Look where we've got to. (*He drops on his hands and knees and stabs a finger at the map.*) We've come to this crossroads. Come here and look at it, man! Look at it! And we call that crossroads Tobair Vree. And why do we call it Tobair Vree? I'll tell you why. Tobair means a well. But what does Vree mean? It's a corruption of Brian—(*Gaelic pronunciation*) Brian—an erosion of Tobair Bhriain. Because a hundred-and-fifty years ago there used to be a well there, not at the crossroads, mind you—that would be too simple—but in a field close to the crossroads. And an old man called Brian, whose face was disfigured by an enormous growth, got it into his head that the water in that well was blessed; and every day for seven months he went there and bathed his face in it. But the growth didn't go away; and one morning Brian was found drowned in that well. And ever since that crossroads is known as Tobair Vree—even though that well has long since dried up. I know the story because my grandfather told it to me. But ask Doalty—or Maire—or Bridget—even my father—even Manus—why it's called Tobair Vree; and do you think they'll know? I know they don't know. So the question I put to you, Lieutenant, is this: what do we do with a name like that? Do we scrap Tobair Vree altogether and call it—what?—The Cross? Cross-roads? Or do we keep piety with a man long dead, long forgotten, his name "eroded" beyond recognition, whose trivial little story nobody in the parish remembers?

YOLLAND: Except you.

OWEN: I've left here.

YOLLAND: You remember it.

OWEN: I'm asking you: what do we write in the Name-Book?

YOLLAND: Tobair Vree.

OWEN: Even though the well is a hundred yards from the actual crossroads—and there's no well anyway—and what the hell does Vree mean?

YOLLAND: Tobair Vree.

OWEN: That's what you want?

YOLLAND: Yes.

OWEN: You're certain?

YOLLAND: Yes.

OWEN: Fine. Fine. That's what you'll get.

YOLLAND: That's what you want, too, Roland.

(*Pause.*)

OWEN: (*Explodes*) George! For God's sake! *My name is not Roland!*

YOLLAND: What?

OWEN: (*Softly*) My name is Owen.

(*Pause.*)

YOLLAND: Not Roland?

OWEN: Owen.

YOLLAND: You mean to say—?

OWEN: Owen.

YOLLAND: But I've been—

OWEN: O-w-e-n.

YOLLAND: Where did Roland come from?

OWEN: I don't know.

YOLLAND: It was never Roland?

OWEN: Never.

YOLLAND: O my God!

(*Pause. They stare at one another. Then the absurdity of the situation strikes them suddenly. They explode with laughter. OWEN pours drinks. As they roll about, their lines overlap.*)

YOLLAND: Why didn't you tell me?

OWEN: Do I look like a Roland?

YOLLAND: Spell Owen again.

OWEN: I was getting fond of Roland.

YOLLAND: O my God!

OWEN: O-w-e-n.

YOLLAND: What'll we write—

OWEN: —in the Name-Book?!

YOLLAND: R-o-w-e-n!

OWEN: Or what about Ol—

YOLLAND: Ol- what?

OWEN: Oland!

(*And again they explode.* MANUS *enters. He is very elated.*)

MANUS: What's the celebration?

OWEN: A christening!

YOLLAND: A baptism!

OWEN: A hundred christenings!

YOLLAND: A thousand baptisms! Welcome to Eden!

OWEN: Eden's right! We name a thing and—bang!—it leaps into existence!

YOLLAND: Each name a perfect equation with its roots.

OWEN: A perfect congruence with its reality. (*To* MANUS) Take a drink.

YOLLAND: Poteen—beautiful.

OWEN: Lying Anna's poteen.

YOLLAND: Anna na mBreag's poteen.

OWEN: Excellent, George.

YOLLAND: I'll decode you yet.

OWEN: (*Offers drink*) Manus?

MANUS: Not if that's what it does to you.

OWEN: You're right. Steady—steady—sober up—sober up.

YOLLAND: Sober as a judge, Owen.

(*MANUS moves beside* OWEN.)

MANUS: I've got good news! Where's Father?

OWEN: He's gone out. What's the good news?

MANUS: I've been offered a job.

OWEN: Where? (*Now aware of* YOLLAND.) Come on, man—speak in English.

MANUS: For the benefit of the colonist?

OWEN: He's a decent man.

MANUS: Aren't they all at some level?

OWEN: Please.

(MANUS *shrugs.*)

He's been offered a job.

YOLLAND: Where?

OWEN: Well—tell us!

MANUS: I've just had a meeting with two men from Inis Meadhon. They want me to go there and start a hedge-school.
1260    They're giving me a free house, free turf, and free milk; a
rood of standing corn; twelve drills of potatoes; and—

(*He stops.*)

OWEN: And what?

MANUS: A salary of £42 a year!

OWEN: Manus, that's wonderful!

MANUS: You're talking to a man of substance.

OWEN: I'm delighted.

YOLLAND: Where's Inis Meadhon?

OWEN: An island south of here. And they came looking for you?

MANUS: Well, I mean to say . . .

(OWEN *punches* MANUS.)

1270    OWEN: Aaaaagh! This calls for a real celebration.

YOLLAND: Congratulations.

MANUS: Thank you.

OWEN: Where are you, Anna?

YOLLAND: When do you start?

MANUS: Next Monday.

OWEN: We'll stay with you when we're there. (*To* YOLLAND)
How long will it be before we reach Inis Meadhon?

YOLLAND: How far south is it?

MANUS: About fifty miles.

1280    YOLLAND: Could we make it by December?

OWEN: We'll have Christmas together. (*Sings*) "Christmas Day
on Inis Meadhon . . ."

YOLLAND: (*Toast*) I hope you're very content there, Manus.

MANUS: Thank you.

(YOLLAND: *holds out his hand.* MANUS *takes it. They shake
warmly.*)

OWEN: (*Toast*) Manus.

MANUS: (*Toast*) To Inis Meadhon.

(*He drinks quickly and turns to leave.*)

OWEN: Hold on—hold on—refills coming up.

MANUS: I've got to go.

OWEN: Come on, man; this is an occasion. Where are you rush-
1290    ing to?

MANUS: I've got to tell Maire.

(MAIRE *enters with her can of milk.*)

MAIRE: You've got to tell Maire what?

OWEN: He's got a job!

MAIRE: Manus?

OWEN: He's been invited to start a hedge-school in Inis
Meadhon.

MAIRE: Where?

MANUS: Inis Meadhon—the island! They're giving me £42 a
year and . . .

OWEN: A house, fuel, milk, potatoes, corn, pupils, what-not!    1300

MANUS: I start on Monday.

OWEN: You'll take a drink. Isn't it great?

MANUS: I want to talk to you for—

MAIRE: There's your milk. I need the can back.

(MANUS *takes the can and runs up the steps.*)

MANUS: (*As he goes*) How will you like living on an island?

OWEN: You know George, don't you?

MAIRE: We wave to each other across the fields.

YOLLAND: Sorry-sorry?

OWEN: She says you wave to each other across the fields.

YOLLAND: Yes, we do; oh, yes; indeed we do.    1310

MAIRE: What's he saying?

OWEN: He says you wave to each other across the fields.

MAIRE: That's right. So we do.

YOLLAND: What's she saying?

OWEN: Nothing—nothing—nothing. (*To* MAIRE) What's the
news?

(MAIRE *moves away, touching the text books with her toe.*)

MAIRE: Not a thing. You're busy, the two of you.

OWEN: We think we are.

MAIRE: I hear the Fiddler O'Shea's about. There's some talk of
a dance tomorrow night.    1320

OWEN: Where will it be?

MAIRE: Maybe over the road. Maybe at Tobair Vree.

YOLLAND: Tobair Vree!

MAIRE: Yes.

YOLLAND: Tobair Vree! Tobair Vree!

MAIRE: Does he know what I'm saying?

OWEN: Not a word.

MAIRE: Tell him then.

OWEN: Tell him what?

MAIRE: About the dance.    1330

OWEN: Maire says there may be a dance tomorrow night.

YOLLAND: (*To* OWEN) Yes? May I come? (*To* MAIRE) Would
anybody object if I came?

MAIRE: (*To* OWEN) What's he saying?

OWEN: (*To* YOLLAND) Who would object?

MAIRE: (*To* OWEN) Did you tell him?

YOLLAND: (*To* MAIRE) Sorry-sorry?

OWEN: (*To* MAIRE) He says may he come?

MAIRE: (*To* YOLLAND) That's up to you.

YOLLAND: (*To* OWEN) What does she say?    1340

OWEN: (*To* YOLLAND) She says—

YOLLAND: (*To* MAIRE) What-what?

MAIRE: (*To* OWEN) Well?

YOLLAND: (*To* OWEN) Sorry-sorry?

OWEN: (*To* YOLLAND) Will you go?

YOLLAND: (*To* MAIRE) Yes, yes, if I may.

MAIRE: (*To* OWEN) What does he say?

YOLLAND: (*To* OWEN) What is she saying?

OWEN: Oh for God's sake! (*To* MANUS *who is descending with
the empty can.*) You take on this job, Manus.    1350

MANUS: I'll walk you up to the house. Is your mother at home?
I want to talk to her.

MAIRE: What's the rush? (*To* OWEN) Didn't you offer me

a drink?

OWEN: Will you risk Anna na mBreag?

MAIRE: Why not.

(YOLLAND *is suddenly intoxicated. He leaps up on a stool, raises his glass and shouts.*)

YOLLAND: Anna na mBreag! Baile Beag! Inis Meadhon! Bombay! Tobair Vree! Eden! And poteen—correct, Owen?

OWEN: Perfect.

1360 YOLLAND: And bloody marvellous stuff it is, too. I love it! Bloody, bloody, bloody marvellous!

(*Simultaneously with his final "bloody marvellous" bring up very loud the introductory music of the reel. Then immediately go to black. Retain the music throughout the very brief interval.*)

SCENE II

*The following night.*

*This scene may be played in the schoolroom, but it would be preferable to lose—by lighting—as much of the schoolroom as possible, and to play the scene down front in a vaguely "outside" area.*

*The music rises to a crescendo. Then in the distance we hear* MAIRE *and* YOLLAND *approach—laughing and running. They run on, hand-in-hand. They have just left the dance. Fade the music to distant background. Then after a time it is lost and replaced by guitar music.* MAIRE *and* YOLLAND *are now down front, still holding hands and excited by their sudden and impetuous escape from the dance.*)

MAIRE: O my God, that leap across the ditch nearly killed me.

YOLLAND: I could scarcely keep up with you.

MAIRE: Wait till I get my breath back.

YOLLAND: We must have looked as if we were being chased.

(*They now realize they are alone and holding hands—the beginnings of embarrassment. The hands disengage. They begin to drift apart. Pause.*)

MAIRE: Manus'll wonder where I've got to.

YOLLAND: I wonder did anyone notice us leave.

(*Pause. Slightly further apart.*)

MAIRE: The grass must be wet. My feet are soaking.

YOLLAND: Your feet must be wet. The grass is soaking.

(*Another pause. Another few paces apart. They are now a long distance from one another.*)

1370 YOLLAND: (*Indicating himself*) George.

(MAIRE *nods: Yes-yes. Then:—*)

MAIRE: Lieutenant George.

YOLLAND: Don't call me that. I never think of myself as Lieutenant.

MAIRE: What-what?

YOLLAND: Sorry-sorry? (*He points to himself again.*) George. (MAIRE *nods: Yes-yes. Then points to herself.*)

MAIRE: Maire.

YOLLAND: Yes, I know you're Maire. Of course I know you're Maire. I mean I've been watching you night and day for the past— 1380

MAIRE: (*Eagerly*) What-what?

YOLLAND: (*Points*) Maire. (*Points.*) George. (*Points both.*) Maire and George.

(MAIRE *nods: Yes-yes-yes.*)

I—I—I—

MAIRE: Say anything at all. I love the sound of your speech.

YOLLAND: (*Eagerly*) Sorry—sorry?

(*In acute frustration he looks around, hoping for some inspiration that will provide him with communicative means. Now he has a thought: he tries raising his voice and articulating in a staccato style and with equal and absurd emphasis on each word.*)

Every-morning-I-see-you-feeding-brown-hens-and-giving-meal-to-black-calf—(*The futility of it*)—O my God.

(MAIRE *smiles. She moves towards him. She will try to communicate in Latin.*)

MAIRE: *Tu es centurio in—in—in exercitu Britannico—*

YOLLAND: Yes-yes? Go on—go on—say anything at all—I love 1390 the sound of your speech.

MAIRE: —*et es in castris quae—quae—quae sunt in agro—* (*The futility of it*)—O my God.
(YOLLAND *smiles. He moves towards her. Now for her English words.*) George—water.

YOLLAND: "Water"? Water! Oh yes—water—water—very good—water—good—good.

MAIRE: Fire.

YOLLAND: Fire—indeed—wonderful—fire, fire, fire—splendid—splendid! 1400

MAIRE: Ah . . . ah . . .

YOLLAND: Yes? Go on.

MAIRE: Earth.

YOLLAND: "Earth"?

MAIRE: Earth. Earth.

(YOLLAND *still does not understand.* MAIRE *stoops down and picks up a handful of clay. Holding it out.*) Earth.

YOLLAND: Earth! Of course—earth! Earth. Earth. Good Lord, Maire, your English is perfect!

MAIRE: (*Eagerly*) What—what?

YOLLAND: Perfect English. English perfect.

MAIRE: George— 1410

YOLLAND: That's beautiful—oh, that's really beautiful.

MAIRE: George—

YOLLAND: Say it again—say it again—

MAIRE: Shhh. (*She holds her hand up for silence—she is trying to remember her one line of English. Now she remembers it and she delivers the line as if English were her language—easily, fluidly, conversationally.*) George, "In Norfolk we besport ourselves around the maypoll."

YOLLAND: Good God, do you? That's where my mother comes from—Norfolk. Norwich actually. Not exactly Norwich 1420 town but a small village called Little Walsingham close beside it. But in our own village of Winfarthing we have a maypole too and every year on the first of May—(*He stops abruptly, only now realizing. He stares at her. She in turn misunderstands his excitement.)*

MAIRE: *(To herself)* Mother of God, my Aunt Mary wouldn't have taught me something dirty, would she?

*(Pause. YOLLAND extends his hand to MAIRE. She turns away from him and moves slowly across the stage.)*

YOLLAND: Maire.

*(She still moves away.)*

Maire Chatach.

*(She still moves away.)*

1430 Bun na hAbhann? *(He says the name softly, almost privately, very tentatively, as if he were searching for a sound she might respond to. He tries again.)* Druim Dubh?

*(MAIRE stops. She is listening. YOLLAND is encouraged.)*

Poll na gCaorach. Lis Maol.

*(MAIRE turns towards him.)*

Lis na nGall.

MAIRE: Lisna NGradh.

*(They are now facing each other and begin moving—almost imperceptibly—towards one another.)*

MAIRE: Carraig an Phoill.
YOLLAND: Carraig na Ri. Loch na nEan.
MAIRE: Loch an Iubhair. Machaire Buidhe.
YOLLAND: Machaire Mor. Cnoc na Mona.
1440 MAIRE: Cnoc na nGabhar.
YOLLAND: Mullach.
MAIRE: Port.
YOLLAND: Tor.
MAIRE: Lag.

*(She holds out her hands to YOLLAND. He takes them. Each now speaks almost to himself/herself.)*

YOLLAND: I wish to God you could understand me.
MAIRE: Soft hands; a gentleman's hands.
YOLLAND: Because if you could understand me I could tell you how I spend my days either thinking of you or gazing up at your house in the hope that you'll appear even for a second.
1450 MAIRE: Every evening you walk by yourself along the Tra Bhan and every morning you wash yourself in front of your tent.
YOLLAND: I would tell you how beautiful you are, curly-headed Maire. I would so like to tell you how beautiful you are.
MAIRE: Your arms are long and thin and the skin on your shoulders is very white.
YOLLAND: I would tell you . . .
MAIRE: Don't stop—I know what you're saying.
YOLLAND: I would tell you how I want to be here—to live here—always—with you—always, always.
1460 MAIRE: "Always"? What is that word—"always"?
YOLLAND: Yes-yes; always.
MAIRE: You're trembling.
YOLLAND: Yes, I'm trembling because of you.
MAIRE: I'm trembling, too.

*(She holds his face in her hand.)*

YOLLAND: I've made up my mind . . .
MAIRE: Shhhh.
YOLLAND: I'm not going to leave here . . .
MAIRE: Shhh—listen to me. I want you, too, soldier.
YOLLAND: Don't stop—I know what you're saying.
MAIRE: I want to live with you—anywhere—anywhere at all— 1470 always—always.
YOLLAND: "Always"? What is that word—"always"?
MAIRE: Take me away with you, George.

*(Pause. Suddenly they kiss. SARAH enters. She sees them. She stands shocked, staring at them. Her mouth works. Then almost to herself.)*

SARAH: Manus . . . Manus!

*(SARAH runs off. Music to crescendo.)*

—ACT THREE—

*The following evening. It is raining.*

SARAH *and* OWEN *alone in the schoolroom.* SARAH, *more waif-like than ever, is sitting very still on a stool, an open book across her knee. She is pretending to read but her eyes keep going up to the room upstairs.* OWEN *is working on the floor as before, surrounded by his reference books, map, Name-Book, etc. But he has neither concentration nor interest; and like* SARAH *he glances up at the upstairs room.*

*After a few seconds* MANUS *emerges and descends, carrying a large paper bag which already contains his clothes. His movements are determined and urgent. He moves around the classroom, picking up books, examining each title carefully, and choosing about six of them which he puts into his bag. As he selects these books:—*

OWEN: You know that old limekiln beyond Con Connie Tim's pub, the place we call The Murren?—do you know why it's called The Murren?

*(MANUS does not answer.)*

I've only just discovered: it's a corruption of Saint Muranus. It seems Saint Muranus had a monastery somewhere about there at the beginning of the seventh century. And over the 1480 years the name became shortened to the Murren. Very unattractive name, isn't it? I think we should go back to the original—Saint Muranus. What do you think? The original's Saint Muranus. Don't you think we should go back to that?

*(No response.* OWEN *begins writing the name into the Name-Book.* MANUS *is now rooting about among the forgotten implements for a piece of rope. He finds a piece. He begins to tie the mouth of the flimsy, overloaded bag—and it bursts, the contents spilling out on the floor.)*

MANUS: Bloody, bloody, bloody hell!

*(His voice breaks in exasperation: he is about to cry.* OWEN *leaps to his feet.)*

OWEN: Hold on. I've a bag upstairs.

*(He runs upstairs.* SARAH *waits until* OWEN *is off. Then:—)*

SARAH: Manus . . . Manus, I . . .

(MANUS *hears* SARAH *but makes no acknowledgement. He gathers up his belongings.* OWEN *reappears with the bag he had on his arrival.*)

OWEN: Take this one—I'm finished with it anyway. And it's supposed to keep out the rain.

(MANUS *transfers his few belongings.* OWEN *drifts back to his task. The packing is now complete.*)

1490 MANUS: You'll be here for a while? For a week or two anyhow?
OWEN: Yes.
MANUS: You're not leaving with the army?
OWEN: I haven't made up my mind. Why?
MANUS: Those Inis Meadhon men will be back to see why I haven't turned up. Tell them—tell them I'll write to them as soon as I can. Tell them I still want the job but that it might be three or four months before I'm free to go.
OWEN: You're being damned stupid, Manus.
MANUS: Will you do that for me?
1500 OWEN: Clear out now and Lancey'll think you're involved somehow.
MANUS: Will you do that for me?
OWEN: Wait a couple of days even. You know George—he's a bloody romantic—maybe he's gone out to one of the islands and he'll suddenly reappear tomorrow morning. Or maybe the search party'll find him this evening lying drunk somewhere in the sandhills. You've seen him drinking that poteen—doesn't know how to handle it. Had he drink on him last night at the dance?
1510 MANUS: I had a stone in my hand when I went out looking for him—I was going to fell him. The lame scholar turned violent.
OWEN: Did anybody see you?
MANUS: (*Again close to tears*) But when I saw him standing there at the side of the road—smiling—and her face buried in his shoulder—I couldn't even go close to them. I just shouted something stupid—something like, "You're a bastard, Yolland." If I'd even said it in English . . . 'cos he kept saying "Sorry-sorry?" The wrong gesture in the wrong lan-
1520 guage.
OWEN: And you didn't see him again?
MANUS: "Sorry?"
OWEN: Before you leave tell Lancey that—just to clear yourself.
MANUS: What have I to say to Lancey? You'll give that message to the islandmen?
OWEN: I'm warning you: run away now and you're bound to be—
MANUS: (*To* SARAH) Will you give that message to the Inis
1530 Meadhon men?
SARAH: I will.

(MANUS *picks up an old sack and throws it across his shoulders.*)

OWEN: Have you any idea where you're going?
MANUS: Mayo, maybe. I remember Mother saying she had cousins somewhere away out in the Erris Peninsula. (*He picks up his bag.*) Tell Father I took only the Virgil and the Caesar and the Aeschylus because they're mine anyway—I bought them with the money I got for that pet lamb I

reared—do you remember that pet lamb? And tell him that Nora Dan never returned the dictionary and that she still owes him two-and-six for last quarter's reading—he always 1540 forgets those things.
OWEN: Yes.
MANUS: And his good shirt's ironed and hanging up in the press and his clean socks are in the butter-box under the bed.
OWEN: All right.
MANUS: And tell him I'll write.
OWEN: If Maire asks where you've gone . . . ?
MANUS: He'll need only half the amount of milk now, won't he? Even less than half—he usually takes his tea black. (*Pause.*) And when he comes in at night—you'll hear him; he makes 1550 a lot of noise—I usually come down and give him a hand up. Those stairs are dangerous without a banister. Maybe before you leave you'd get Big Ned Frank to put up some sort of a handrail. (*Pause.*) And if you can bake, he's very fond of soda bread.
OWEN: I can give you money. I'm wealthy. Do you know what they pay me? Two shillings a day for this—this—this—

(MANUS *rejects the offer by holding out his hand.*)

Goodbye, Manus.

(MANUS *and* OWEN *shake hands. Then* MANUS *picks up his bag briskly and goes towards the door. He stops a few paces beyond* SARAH, *turns, comes back to her. He addresses her as he did in Act One but now without warmth or concern for her.*)

MANUS: What is your name? (*Pause.*) Come on. What is your name? 1560
SARAH: My name is Sarah.
MANUS: Just Sarah? Sarah what? (*Pause.*) Well?
SARAH: Sarah Johnny Sally.
MANUS: And where do you live? Come on.
SARAH: I live in Bun na hAbhann.

(*She is now crying quietly.*)

MANUS: Very good, Sarah Johnny Sally. There's nothing to stop you now—nothing in the wide world. (*Pause. He looks down at her.*) It's all right—it's all right—you did no harm—you did no harm at all.

(*He stoops over her and kisses the top of her head—as if in absolution. Then briskly to the door and off.*)

OWEN: Good luck, Manus! 1570
SARAH: (*Quietly*) I'm sorry . . . I'm sorry . . . I'm so sorry, Manus . . .

(OWEN *tries to work but cannot concentrate. He begins folding up the map. As he does:—*)

OWEN: Is there a class this evening?

(SARAH *nods: yes.*)

I suppose Father knows. Where is he anyhow?

(SARAH *points.*)

Where?

(SARAH *mimes rocking a baby.*)

I don't understand—where?

(SARAH *repeats the mime and wipes away tears.* OWEN *is still puzzled.*)

It doesn't matter. He'll probably turn up.

(BRIDGET *and* DOALTY *enter, sacks over their heads against the rain. They are self-consciously noisier, more ebullient, more garrulous than ever—brimming over with excitement and gossip and brio.*)

DOALTY: You're missing the crack, boys! Cripes, you're missing the crack! Fifty more soldiers arrived an hour ago!

1580  BRIDGET: And they're spread out in a big line from Sean Neal's over to Lag and they're moving straight across the fields towards Cnoc na nGabhar!

DOALTY: Prodding every inch of the ground in front of them with their bayonets and scattering animals and hens in all directions!

BRIDGET: And tumbling everything before them—fences, ditches, haystacks, turf-stacks!

DOALTY: They came to Barney Petey's field of corn—straight through it be God as if it was heather!

1590  BRIDGET: Not a blade of it left standing!

DOALTY: And Barney Petey just out of his bed and running after them in his drawers: "You hoors you! Get out of my corn, you hoors you!"

BRIDGET: First time he ever ran in his life.

DOALTY: Too lazy, the wee get, to cut it when the weather was good.

(SARAH *begins putting out the seats.*)

BRIDGET: Tell them about Big Hughie.

DOALTY: Cripes, if you'd seen your aul fella, Owen.

BRIDGET: They were all inside in Anna na mBreag's pub—all
1600  the crowd from the wake—

DOALTY: And they hear the commotion and they all come out to the street—

BRIDGET: Your father in front; the Infant Prodigy footless behind him!

DOALTY: And your aul fella, he sees the army stretched across the countryside—

BRIDGET: O my God!

DOALTY: And Cripes he starts roaring at them!

BRIDGET: "Visigoths! Huns! Vandals!"

1610  DOALTY: *"Ignari! Stulti! Rustici!"*

BRIDGET: And wee Jimmy Jack jumping up and down and shouting, "Thermopylae! Thermopylae!"

DOALTY: You never saw crack like it in your life, boys. Come away on out with me, Sarah, and you'll see it all.

BRIDGET: Big Hughie's fit to take no class. Is Manus about?

OWEN: Manus is gone.

BRIDGET: Gone where?

OWEN: He's left—gone away.

DOALTY: Where to?

1620  OWEN: He doesn't know. Mayo, maybe.

DOALTY: What's on in Mayo?

OWEN: *(To* BRIDGET*)* Did you see George and Maire Chatach leave the dance last night?

BRIDGET: We did. Didn't we, Doalty?

OWEN: Did you see Manus following them out?

BRIDGET: I didn't see him going out but I saw him coming in

by himself later.

OWEN: Did George and Maire come back to the dance?

BRIDGET: No.

OWEN: Did you see them again?                                              1630

BRIDGET: He left her home. We passed them going up the back road—didn't we, Doalty?

OWEN: And Manus stayed till the end of the dance?

DOALTY: We know nothing. What are you asking us for?

OWEN: Because Lancey'll question me when he hears Manus's gone. *(Back to* BRIDGET.*)* That's the way George went home? By the back road? That's where you saw him?

BRIDGET: Leave me alone, Owen. I know nothing about Yolland. If you want to know about Yolland, ask the Donnelly twins.                                                                  1640

(*Silence.* DOALTY *moves over to the window.*)

(*To* SARAH) He's a powerful fiddler, O'Shea, isn't he? He told our Seamus he'll come back for a night at Hallowe'en.

(OWEN *goes to* DOALTY *who looks resolutely out the window.*)

OWEN: What's this about the Donnellys? *(Pause.)* Were they about last night?

DOALTY: Didn't see them if they were.

(*Begins whistling through his teeth.*)

OWEN: George is a friend of mine.

DOALTY: So.

OWEN: I want to know what's happened to him.

DOALTY: Couldn't tell you.

OWEN: What have the Donnelly twins to do with it? *(Pause.)*  1650
Doalty!

DOALTY: I know nothing, Owen—nothing at all—I swear to God. All I know is this: on my way to the dance I saw their boat beached at Port. It wasn't there on my way home, after I left Bridget. And that's all I know. As God's my judge. The half-dozen times I met him I didn't know a word he said to me; but he seemed a right enough sort . . . (*With sudden excessive interest in the scene outside.*) Cripes, they're crawling all over the place! Cripes, there's millions of them! Cripes, they're levelling the whole land!                        1660

(OWEN *moves away.* MAIRE *enters. She is bareheaded and wet from the rain; her hair in disarray. She attempts to appear normal but she is in acute distress, on the verge of being distraught. She is carrying the milk-can.*)

MAIRE: Honest to God, I must be going off my head. I'm halfway here and I think to myself, "Isn't this can very light?" and I look into it and isn't it empty.

OWEN: It doesn't matter.

MAIRE: How will you manage for tonight?

OWEN: We have enough.

MAIRE: Are you sure?

OWEN: Plenty, thanks.

MAIRE: It'll take me no time at all to go back up for some.

OWEN: Honestly, Maire.                                                     1670

MAIRE: Sure it's better you have it than that black calf that's . . . that . . . (*She looks around.*) Have you heard anything?

OWEN: Nothing.

MAIRE: What does Lancey say?

OWEN: I haven't seen him since this morning.

MAIRE: What does he *think*?

OWEN: We really didn't talk. He was here for only a few seconds.

MAIRE: He left me home, Owen. And the last thing he said to me—he tried to speak in Irish—he said, "I'll see you yesterday"—he meant to say "I'll see you tomorrow." And I laughed that much he pretended to get cross and he said "Maypoll! Maypoll!" because I said that word wrong. And off he went, laughing—laughing, Owen! Do you think he's all right? What do *you* think?

OWEN: I'm sure he'll turn up. Maire.

MAIRE: He comes from a tiny wee place called Winfarthing. *(She suddenly drops on her hands and knees on the floor—where* OWEN *had his map a few minutes ago—and with her finger traces out an outline map.)* Come here till you see. Look. There's Winfarthing. And there's two other wee villages right beside it; one of them's called Barton Bendish—it's there; and the other's called Saxingham ethergate—it's about there. And there's Little Walsingham—that's his mother's townland. Aren't they odd names? Sure they make no sense to me at all. And Winfarthing's near a big town called Norwich. And Norwich is in a county called Norfolk. And Norfolk is in the east of England. He drew a map for me on the wet strand and wrote the names on it. I have it all in my head now: Winfarthing—Barton Bendish—Saxingham Nethergate—Little Walsingham—Norwich—Norfolk. Strange sounds, aren't they? But nice sounds; like Jimmy Jack reciting his Homer. *(She gets to her feet and looks around; she is almost serene now. To* SARAH) You were looking lovely last night, Sarah. Is that the dress you got from Boston? Green suits you. *(To* OWEN) Something very bad's happened to him, Owen. I know. He wouldn't go away without telling me. Where is he, Owen? You're his friend—where is he? *(Again she looks around the room; then sits on a stool.)* I didn't get a chance to do my geography last night. The master'll be angry with me. *(She rises again.)* I think I'll go home now. The wee ones have to be washed and put to bed and that black calf has to be fed . . . My hands are that rough; they're still blistered from the hay. I'm ashamed of them. I hope to God there's no hay to be saved in Brooklyn. *(She stops at the door.)* Did you hear? Nellie Ruadh's baby died in the middle of the night. I must go up to the wake. It didn't last long, did it?

*(*MAIRE *leaves. Silence. Then.)*

OWEN: I don't think there'll be any class. Maybe you should . . .

*(*OWEN *begins picking up his texts.* DOALTY *goes to him.)*

DOALTY: Is he long gone?—Manus.

OWEN: Half an hour.

DOALTY: Stupid bloody fool.

OWEN: I told him that.

DOALTY: Do they know he's gone?

OWEN: Who?

DOALTY: The army.

OWEN: Not yet.

DOALTY: They'll be after him like bloody beagles. Bloody, bloody fool, limping along the coast. They'll overtake him before night for Christ's sake.

*(*DOALTY *returns to the window.* LANCEY *enters—now the commanding officer.)*

OWEN: Any news? Any word?

*(*LANCEY *moves into the centre of the room, looking around as he does.)*

LANCEY: I understood there was a class. Where are the others?

OWEN: There was to be a class but my father—

LANCEY: This will suffice. I will address them and it will be their responsibility to pass on what I have to say to every family in this section.

*(*LANCEY *indicates to* OWEN *to translate.* OWEN *hesitates, trying to assess the change in* LANCEY's *manner and attitude.)*

I'm in a hurry, O'Donnell.

OWEN: The captain has an announcement to make.

LANCEY: Lieutenant Yolland is missing. We are searching for him. If we don't find him, or if we receive no information as to where he is to be found, I will pursue the following course of action. *(He indicates to* OWEN *to translate.)*

OWEN: They are searching for George. If they don't find him—

LANCEY: Commencing twenty-four hours from now we will shoot all livestock in Ballybeg.

*(*OWEN *stares at* LANCEY.*)*

At once.

OWEN: Beginning this time tomorrow they'll kill every animal in Baile Beag—unless they're told where George is.

LANCEY: If that doesn't bear results, commencing forty-eight hours from now we will embark on a series of evictions and levelling of every abode in the following selected areas—

OWEN: You're not—!

LANCEY: Do your job. Translate.

OWEN: If they still haven't found him in two days time they'll begin evicting and levelling every house starting with these townlands.

*(*LANCEY *reads from his list.)*

LANCEY: Swinefort.

OWEN: Lis na Muc.

LANCEY: Burnfoot.

OWEN: Bun na hAbhann.

LANCEY: Dromduff.

OWEN: Druim Dubh.

LANCEY: Whiteplains.

OWEN: Machaire Ban.

LANCEY: Kings Head.

OWEN: Cnoc na Ri.

LANCEY: If by then the lieutenant hasn't been found, we will proceed until a complete clearance is made of this entire section.

OWEN: If Yolland hasn't been got by then, they will ravish the whole parish.

LANCEY: I trust they know exactly what they've got to do. *(Pointing to* BRIDGET.*)* I know you. I know where you live. *(Pointing to* SARAH.*)* Who are you? Name!

*(*SARAH's *mouth opens and shuts, opens and shuts. Her face becomes contorted.)*

What's your name?

(*Again* SARAH *tries frantically.*)

OWEN: Go on, Sarah. You can tell him.

(*But* SARAH *cannot. And she knows she cannot. She closes her mouth. Her head goes down.*)

OWEN: Her name is Sarah Johnny Sally.
LANCEY: Where does she live?
1780 OWEN: Bun na hAbhann.
LANCEY: Where?
OWEN: Burnfoot.
LANCEY: I want to talk to your brother—is he here?
OWEN: Not at the moment.
LANCEY: Where is he?
OWEN: He's at a wake.
LANCEY: What wake?

(DOALTY, *who has been looking out the window all through* LANCEY'*s announcements, now speaks—calmly, almost casually.*)

DOALTY: Tell him his whole camp's on fire.
LANCEY: What's your name? (*To* OWEN) Who's that lout?
1790 OWEN: Doalty Dan Doalty.
LANCEY: Where does he live?
OWEN: Tulach Alainn.
LANCEY: What do we call it?
OWEN: Fair Hill. He says your whole camp is on fire.

(LANCEY *rushes to the window and looks out. Then he wheels on* DOALTY.)

LANCEY: I'll remember you, Mr Doalty. (*To* OWEN) You carry a big responsibility in all this.

(*He goes off.*)

BRIDGET: Mother of God, does he mean it, Owen?
OWEN: Yes, he does.
BRIDGET: We'll have to hide the beasts somewhere—our Sea-
1800 mus'll know where. Maybe at the back of Lis na nGradh— or in the caves at the far end of the Tra Bhan. Come on, Doalty! Come on! Don't be standing about there!

(DOALTY *does not move.* BRIDGET *runs to the door and stops suddenly. She sniffs the air. Panic.*)

The sweet smell! Smell it! It's the sweet smell! Jesus, it's the potato blight!
DOALTY: It's the army tents burning, Bridget.
BRIDGET: Is it? Are you sure? Is that what it is? God, I thought we were destroyed altogether. Come on! Come on!

(*She runs off.* OWEN *goes to* SARAH *who is preparing to leave.*)

OWEN: How are you? Are you all right?

(SARAH *nods: Yes.*)

OWEN: Don't worry. It will come back to you again.

(SARAH *shakes her head.*)

1810 OWEN: It will. You're upset now. He frightened you. That's all's wrong.

(*Again* SARAH *shakes her head, slowly, emphatically, and smiles at* OWEN. *Then she leaves.* OWEN *busies himself gathering his belongings.* DOALTY *leaves the window and goes to him.*)

DOALTY: He'll do it, too.
OWEN: Unless Yolland's found.
DOALTY: Hah!
OWEN: Then he'll certainly do it.
DOALTY: When my grandfather was a boy they did the same thing.
(*Simply, altogether without irony*) And after all the trouble you went to, mapping the place and thinking up new names for it. 1820
(OWEN *busies himself. Pause.* DOALTY *almost dreamily.*) I've damned little to defend but he'll not put me out without a fight. And there'll be others who think the same as me.
OWEN: That's a matter for you.
DOALTY: If we'd all stick together. If we knew how to defend ourselves.
OWEN: Against a trained army.
DOALTY: The Donnelly twins know how.
OWEN: If they could be found.
DOALTY: If they could be found. (*He goes to the door.*) Give me 1830 a shout after you've finished with Lancey. I might know something then.

(*He leaves.*)

(OWEN *picks up the Name-Book. He looks at it momentarily, then puts it on top of the pile he is carrying. It falls to the floor. He stoops to pick it up—hesitates—leaves it. He goes upstairs. As* OWEN *ascends,* HUGH *and* JIMMY JACK *enter. Both wet and drunk.* JIMMY *is very unsteady. He is trotting behind* HUGH, *trying to break in on* HUGH'*s declamation.* HUGH *is equally drunk but more experienced in drunkenness: there is a portion of his mind which retains its clarity.*)

HUGH: There I was, appropriately dispositioned to proffer my condolences to the bereaved mother . . .
JIMMY: Hugh—
HUGH: . . . and about to enter the *domus lugubris*—Maire Chatach?
JIMMY: The wake house.
HUGH: Indeed—when I experience a plucking at my elbow: Mister George Alexander, Justice of the Peace. "My tidings 1840 are infelicitous," said he—Bridget? Too slow. Doalty?
JIMMY: *Infelix*—unhappy.
HUGH: Unhappy indeed. "Master Bartley Timlin has been appointed to the new national school." "Timlin? Who is Timlin?" "A schoolmaster from Cork. And he will be a major asset to the community: he is also a very skilled bacon-curer!"
JIMMY: Hugh—
HUGH: Ha-ha-ha-ha-ha! The Cork bacon-curer! *Barbarus hic ego sum quia non intelligor ulli*—James? 1850
JIMMY: Ovid.
HUGH: *Procede.*
JIMMY: "I am a barbarian in this place because I am not understood by anyone."
HUGH: Indeed—(*Shouts*) Manus! Tea! I will compose a satire on Master Bartley Timlin, schoolmaster and bacon-curer. But it will be too easy, won't it? (*Shouts*) Strong tea! Black!

(*The only way* JIMMY *can get* HUGH'*s attention is by standing in front of him and holding his arms.*)

JIMMY: Will you listen to me, Hugh!

HUGH: James. *(Shouts)* And a slice of soda bread.

1860 JIMMY: I'm going to get married.

HUGH: Well!

JIMMY: At Christmas.

HUGH: Splendid.

JIMMY: To Athene.

HUGH: Who?

JIMMY: Pallas Athene.

HUGH: *Glaukopis Athene?*

JIMMY: Flashing-eyed, Hugh, flashing-eyed!

*(He attempts the gesture he has made before: standing to attention, the momentary spasm, the salute, the face raised in pained ecstasy—but the body does not respond efficiently this time. The gesture is grotesque.)*

HUGH: The lady has assented?

1870 JIMMY: She asked *me*—I assented.

HUGH: Ah. When was this?

JIMMY: Last night.

HUGH: What does her mother say?

JIMMY: Metis from Hellespont? Decent people—good stock.

HUGH: And her father?

JIMMY: I'm meeting Zeus tomorrow. Hugh, will you be my best man?

HUGH: Honoured, James; profoundly honoured.

JIMMY: You know what I'm looking for, Hugh, don't you? I

1880 mean to say—you know—I—I—I joke like the rest of them—you know?—*(Again he attempts the pathetic routine but abandons it instantly.)* You know yourself, Hugh—don't you?—you know all that. But what I'm really looking for, Hugh—what I really want—companionship, Hugh—at my time of life, companionship, company, someone to talk to. Away up in Beann na Gaoithe—you've no idea how lonely it is. Companionship—correct, Hugh? Correct?

HUGH: Correct.

JIMMY: And I always liked her, Hugh. Correct?

1890 HUGH: Correct, James.

JIMMY: Someone to talk to.

HUGH: Indeed.

JIMMY: That's all, Hugh. The whole story. You know it all now, Hugh. You know it all.

*(As JIMMY says those last lines he is crying, shaking his head, trying to keep his balance, and holding a finger up to his lips in absurd gestures of secrecy and intimacy. Now he staggers away, tries to sit on a stool, misses it, slides to the floor, his feet in front of him, his back against the broken cart. Almost at once he is asleep. HUGH watches all of this. Then he produces his flask and is about to pour a drink when he sees the Name-Book on the floor. He picks it up and leafs through it, pronouncing the strange names as he does. Just as he begins, OWEN emerges and descends with two bowls of tea.)*

HUGH: Ballybeg. Burnfoot. King's Head. Whiteplains. Fair Hill. Dunboy. Green Bank.

*(OWEN snatches the book from HUGH.)*

OWEN: I'll take that. *(In apology.)* It's only a catalogue of names.

HUGH: I know what it is.

1900 OWEN: A mistake—my mistake—nothing to do with us. I hope that's strong enough *(tea).* *(He throws the book on the table*

*and crosses over to JIMMY.)*

Jimmy. Wake up, Jimmy. Wake up, man.

JIMMY: What—what—what?

OWEN: Here. Drink this. Then go on away home. There may be trouble. Do you hear me, Jimmy? There may be trouble. Do you hear me, Jimmy? There may be trouble.

HUGH: *(Indicating Name-Book)* We must learn those new names.

OWEN: *(Searching around)* Did you see a sack lying about? 1910

HUGH: We must learn where we live. We must learn to make them our own. We must make them our new home.

*(OWEN finds a sack and throws it across his shoulders.)*

OWEN: I know where I live.

HUGH: James thinks he knows, too. I look at James and three thoughts occur to me: A—that it is not the literal past, the "facts" of history, that shape us, but images of the past embodied in language. James has ceased to make that discrimination.

OWEN: Don't lecture me, Father.

HUGH: B—we must never cease renewing those images; be- 1920 cause once we do, we fossilize. Is there no soda bread?

OWEN: And C, Father—one single, unalterable "fact": if Yolland is not found, we are all going to be evicted. Lancey has issued the order.

HUGH: Ah. *Edictum imperatoris.*

OWEN: You should change out of those wet clothes. I've got to go. I've got to see Doalty Dan Doalty.

HUGH: What about?

OWEN: I'll be back soon.

*(As OWEN exits.)*

HUGH: Take care, Owen. To remember everything is a form of 1930 madness. *(He looks around the room, carefully, as if he were about to leave it forever. Then he looks at Jimmy, asleep again.)* The road to Sligo. A spring morning. 1798. Going into battle. Do you remember, James? Two young gallants with pikes across their shoulders and the *Aeneid* in their pockets. Everything seemed to find definition that spring—a congruence, a miraculous matching of hope and past and present and possibility. Striding across the fresh, green land. The rhythms of perception heightened. The whole enterprise of consciousness accelerated. We were gods that 1940 morning, James; and I had recently married *my* goddess, Caitlin Dubh Nic Reactainn, may she rest in peace. And to leave her and my infant son in his cradle—that was heroic, too. By God, sir, we were magnificent. We marched as far as—where was it?—Glenties! All of twenty-three miles in one day. And it was there, in Phelan's pub, that we got homesick for Athens, just like Ulysses. The *desiderium nostrorum*—the need for our own. Our *pietas*, James, was for older, quieter things. And that was the longest twenty-three miles back I ever made. *(Toasts JIMMY.)* My friend, confu- 1950 sion is not an ignoble condition.

*(MAIRE enters.)*

MAIRE: I'm back again. I set out for somewhere but I couldn't remember where. So I came back here.

HUGH: Yes, I will teach you English, Maire Chatach.

MAIRE: Will you, Master? I must learn it. I need to learn it.

HUGH: Indeed you may well be my only pupil.

*(He goes towards the steps and begins to ascend.)*

MAIRE: When can we start?

HUGH: Not today. Tomorrow, perhaps. After the funeral. We'll begin tomorrow. *(Ascending)* But don't expect too much. I will provide you with the available words and the available grammar. But will that help you to interpret between privacies? I have no idea. But it's all we have. I have no idea at all.

*(He is now at the top.)*

MAIRE: Master, what does the English word "always" mean?

HUGH: *Semper-per omnia saecula.* The Greeks called it *"aei."* It's not a word I'd start with. It's a silly word, girl.

*(He sits.* JIMMY *is awake. He gets to his feet.* MAIRE *sees the Name-Book, picks it up, and sits with it on her knee.)*

MAIRE: When he comes back, this is where he'll come to. He told me this is where he was happiest.

*(*JIMMY *sits beside* MAIRE.)*

JIMMY: Do you know the Greek word *endogamein?* It means to marry within the tribe. And the word *exogamein* means to marry outside the tribe. And you don't cross those borders casually—both sides get very angry. Now, the problem is this: Is Athene sufficiently mortal or am I sufficiently god-like for the marriage to be acceptable to her people and to my people? You think about that.

HUGH: *Urbs antiqua fuit*—there was an ancient city which, 'tis said, Juno loved above all the lands. And it was the goddess's aim and cherished hope that here should be the capital of all nations—should the fates perchance allow that. Yet in truth she discovered that a race was springing from Trojan blood to overthrow some day these Tyrian towers—a people *late regem belloque superbum*—kings of broad realms and proud in war who would come forth for Lybia's downfall—such was—such was the course—such was the course ordained—ordained by fate . . . What the hell's wrong with me? Sure I know it backwards. I'll begin again. *Urbs antiqua fuit*—there was an ancient city which, 'tis said, Juno loved above all the lands.

*(Begin to bring down the lights.)*

And it was the goddess's aim and cherished hope that here should be the capital of all nations—should the fates perchance allow that. Yet in truth she discovered that a race was springing from Trojan blood to overthrow some day these Tyrian towers—a people kings of broad realms and proud in war who would come forth for Lybia's downfall . . .

*(Black)*

---

### Greek and Latin Used in the Text

*page 888* Τὸν δ' ἠμείβετ' ἔπειτα θεὰ γλαυκῶπιζ' Αθήνη (Homer, *Odyssey*, XIII, 420):
*(Lit.)* "But the grey-eyed goddess Athene then replied to him"

α̉λλὰ ἕκηλοζ ἦσται ἐν 'Ατρεί δαο δόμοιζ (Homer, *Odyssey*, XIII, 423–4):
*(Lit.)* " . . . but he sits at ease in the halls of the Sons of Athens . . ."

*page 889* "Ωζ ἄρα μιυ φαμένη ῥάβδῳ ἐπεμάσσατ' Αθήνη (Homer, *Odyssey*, XIII, 429):
*(Lit.)* "As she spoke Athene touched him with her wand"

κνύζωσευ δέ οἱ ὄσσε (Homer, *Odyssey*, XIII, 433):
*(Lit.)* "She dimmed his eyes"

Γλαυκῶπιζ' Αθήνη: *(Lit.)* flashing-eyed Athene

Αὐτὰρὸ ἐκλιμέυοζπρσσέβη (Homer, *Odyssey*, XIV, 1):
*(Lit.)* "But he went forth from the harbour . . ."

δ' οι βιότοιο μάλιοτα (Homer, *Odyssey*, XIV, 3–4): *(Lit.)* " . . . he cared very much for his substance . . ."

*page 890* *Esne fatigata?*: Are you tired?
*Sum fatigatissima*: I am very tired.
*Bene! Optime!*: Good! Excellent!
*Ignari, stulti, rustici*: Ignoramuses, fools, peasants

*page 891* *Responde–responde!*: Answer—answer!
θέοζ: a god
θέα: a goddess
*Nigra fere et presso pinguis sub vomere terra*
Land that is black and rich beneath the pressure of the plough
*cui putre*: crumbly soil

*page 893* *adsum*: I am present

*sobrietate perfecta*: with complete sobriety
*sobrius*: sober
*ave*: hail
*caerimonia nominations*: ceremony of naming
βαπτι'ζειν: to dip or immerse
*baptisterium*: a cold bath, swimming-pool
*Gratias tibi ago*: I thank you
*studia*: studies
*perambulare*: to walk through
*verecundus*: shame-faced, modest

*page 894* *conjugo*: I join together
*acquiesco, acquiescere*: to rest, to find comfort in
*procede*: proceed
*Silentium!*: Silence!
*diverto, divertere*: to turn away
ἄπληστοζ πι'θοζ: unfillable cask
*Jacobe, quid agis?*: James, how are you?

*page 895* *Festinate!*: Hurry!

*page 896* *Gaudeo vos hic adesse*: Welcome
*Nonne Latine loquitur?*: Does he not speak Latin?
*opus honestum*: an honourable task

*page 900* *Quantumvis cursum longum fessumque moratur Sol, sacro tandem carmine vesper adest*:
No matter how long the sun delays on his long weary course
At length evening comes with its sacred song
*expeditio*: an expedition

*page 903* *Tu es centurio in exercitu Britannico*: You are a centurion in the British Army
*Et es in castris quae sunt in argo*: And you are in the camp in the field

*page 906* *Ignari! Stulti! Rustici!*: Ignoramuses! Fools!

Peasants!

*page* 908  *domus lugubris*: house of mourning

   *infelix*: unlucky, unhappy

   *Bararus hic ego sum quia non intelligor ulli*: I am a barbarian here because I am not understood by anyone

   *procede*: proceed

*page* 909  *edictum imperatoris*: the decree of the commander

   *desiderium nostrorum*: longing/need for our things/people.

*pietas*: piety

*page* 910  *Semper—per omnia saecula*: Always—for all time.

   ἀεί: always

   ἐνδογαμὲῑν: to marry within the tribe

   ἐξογαμὲιν: to marry outside the tribe

   *Urbs antiqua fuit*: There was an ancient city

   *late regem belloque superbum*: kings of broad realms and proud in war

---

*IN its program notes for Brian Friel's* Translations, *the Field Day Theatre Company provided extracts from several texts describing the nineteenth-century hedge schools, the program of educational reform, and the mission of the Ordnance Survey.*

Field Day
Theatre
Company
Program Notes for
*Translations*[1]
(1980)

"The Hedge Schools owed their origin to the suppression of all the ordinary legitimate means of education, first during the Cromwellian regime and then under the Penal Code introduced in the reign of William III and operating from that time till within less than twenty years from the opening of the nineteenth century . . .

"The Hedge Schools were clearly of peasant institution. They were maintained by the people who wanted their children educated; and they were taught by men who came from the people . . .

"The poorest and humblest of the schools gave instruction in reading, writing and arithmetic; Latin, Greek, Mathematics and other subjects were taught in a great number of schools; and in many cases the work was done entirely through the medium of the Irish language. Though the use of the vernacular was rapidly falling into decay during the eighteenth century, it was owing to the greater value of English on the fair and market rather than to any shifting of ground on the part of the schools . . .

"The Hedge Schools were the most vital force in popular education in Ireland during the eighteenth century. They emerged in the nineteenth century more vigorous still, outnumbering all other schools, and so profoundly national as to hasten the introduction of a State system of education in 1831 . . . "

*Extract from* The Hedge
Schools of Ireland *by*
P. J. Dowling

"The only place for giving instruction was a barn. The barn was a loft over a cowshed and stable . . . It was one of the largest barns in the parish.

"(At the age of fourteen) I had only got as far as Ovid's *Metamorphoses,* Justin, and the first chapter of John in the Greek Testament."

*Extract from* The
Autobiography of
William Carleton *(born
in County Tyrone,
1794):—*

"Even in the wildest districts, it is not unusual to meet with good classical scholars; and there are several young mountaineers of the writer's acquaintance, whose knowledge and taste in the Latin poets, might put to the blush many who have all the advantages of established schools and regular instruction."

*Extract from the
memoirs of the
Reverend Mr Alexander
Ross, Rector, Dungiven,
County Derry. 1814:—*

"In 1831 Chief Secretary Stanley introduced a system of National Education . . . The system became a great success as an educational one but it had fatal effects on the Irish language and the old Gaelic tradition. According to Thomas Davis, at this time the vast majority of the people living west of a line drawn from Derry to Cork spoke nothing but Irish daily and east of it a considerable minority. It seems certain that at least two millions used it as their fireside speech . . . But the institution of universal elementary schools where English was the sole medium of instruction, combined with the influence of O'Connell, many of the priests, and other leaders who looked on Irish as a barrier to progress, soon made rapid inroads on the native speech . . . "

*Extract from* A History
of Ireland *by Edmund
Curtis:—*

---

[1]Courtesy Field Day Theatre Company.

*Extract from* Ordnance Survey of Ireland *by Thomas Colby, Colonel, Royal Engineers (1835):—*

"To carry on a minute Survey of all Ireland no collection of ready instructed surveyors would have sufficed. It, therefore, became indispensable to train and organise a completely new department for the purpose. Officers and men from the corps of Royal Engineers formed the basis of this new organisation, and very large numbers of other persons possessing various qualifications, were gradually added to them to expedite the great work . . .

"The mode of spelling the names of places was peculiarly vague and unsettled, but on the maps about to be constructed it was desirable to establish a standard orthography, and for future reference, to identify the several localities with the names by which they had formerly been called . . . "

*Extract from the Spring Rice Report (advocating a general survey of Ireland) to the British Government; 21 June 1824:—*

"The general tranquillity of Europe, enables the state to devote the abilities and exertions of a most valuable corps of officers to an undertaking, which, though not unimportant in a military point of view, recommends itself more directly as a civil measure. Your committee trust that the survey will be carried on with energy, as well as with skill, and that it will, when completed, be creditable to the nation, and to the scientific acquirements of the present age. In that portion of the Empire to which it more particularly applies, it cannot but be received as a proof of the disposition of the legislature to adopt all measures calculated to advance the interests of Ireland."

*Extracts from the letters of John O'Donovan, a civilian employee with the Ordnance Survey, later Professor of Celtic Studies, Queen's College, Belfast:—*

Buncrana
23 August 1835
"On Friday we travelled through the Parish of Clonmany and ascended the Hill of Beinnin. Clonmany is the most Irish Parish I have yet visited; the men only, who go to markets and fairs, speak a little English, the women and children speak Irish only. This arises from their distance from Villages and Towns and from their being completely environed by mountains, which form a gigantic barrier between them and the more civilized and less civil inhabitants of the lower country."

Dun Fionnchada? Dun Fionnchon?
Dunfanaghy
9 September 1835
"I am sick to death's door of the names on the coast, because the name I get from one is denied by another of equal intelligence and authority to be correct. The only way to settle these names would be to summon a Jury and order them to say and present 'uppon ther Oathes' what these names are and ought to be. But there are several of them such trifling places that it seems to me that it matters not which of two or three appelations we give them. For example, the name Timlin's Hole is not of thirty years standing and will give way to another name as soon as that dangerous hole shall have swallowed a fisherman of more illustrious name than Tim Lyn."

Glenties
15 October 1835
"Yesterday being a fair-day at Dunglow we were obliged to leave it in consequence of the bustle and confusion. We directed our course southwards through the Parish of Templecroan, keeping Traigh Eunach (a name which I find exceedingly difficult to Anglicise) to the right . . . On the road we met crowds of the women of the mountains who were loaded with stockings going to the stocking fair of Dunglow and who bore deep graven on their visages the effects of poverty and smoke, of their having been kept alive by the potatoe only . . . I have seen several fields of oats on this coast, some prostrated and rotting, others with the grain completely blown off the stalk—and some so green in October as to preclude the possibility of ripening at all."

Ballyshanny
1 November 1835
"I have met in this town a fine old man named Edward Quin, from whom I have received a good deal of information. He has been employed by Lieutenant Vickers to give the Irish names of places about Ballyshannon, and has saved me a good deal of trouble—I wish you could induce Mr Vickers to take him to his next district, and keep him employed writing in the Name Books, and taking down the names from the pronunciation of the country people."

# Maria Irene Fornes

Maria Irene Fornes was born in Cuba in 1930 and emigrated to the United States in 1945. She toured Europe in the mid-1950s studying to be a painter, and in Paris saw Roger Blin's production of Beckett's *Waiting for Godot.* Fornes was impressed both by its power and by its severe visual imagery onstage. Fornes returned to the U. S. in 1957 as a textile designer, but three years later had the idea for her first play, *Tango Palace.* Fornes has had a distinguished career in the avant-garde theater, experimenting in a variety of theatrical modes. She has produced brilliant absurdist plays like *There! You Died* (1963; revised as *Tango Palace* in 1964) and *Dr. Kheal* (1968); a successful musical, *Promenade* (1965, music by Al Carmines); and a moving, ritual-participatory play, *A Vietnamese Wedding* (1967). More recently, her plays have taken a more serious—though no less experimental—turn, examining women's identity in *Fefu and Her Friends* (1977) and *Abingdon Square* (1988), the relationship between politics, language, and love in *The Danube* (1982), and military and sexual oppression in Latin America in *The Conduct of Life* (1985). In 1986, she wrote another musical, with Tito Puente, *Lovers and Keepers.* Fornes has won several prestigious awards, including an Obie for Sustained Achievement in the Theater in 1982.

## The Conduct of Life (1985)

*The Conduct of Life* is one of Fornes's most powerful and politically engaged plays, though its "politics" extend from a critique of the power structure of an unnamed Latin American state to a much wider indictment of the function of exploitation in the conduct of our lives. The play centers on Orlando, an army lieutenant involved in state torture, and fuses state and sexual politics in his opening monologue: "Man must have an ideal, mine is to achieve maximum power. That is my destiny.—No other interest will deter me from this.—My sexual drive is detrimental to my ideals. I will no longer be overwhelmed by sexual passion or I will be degraded beyond hope of recovery." Orlando pursues three axes of power—he is involved in state torture as a means to advance his career in the military; he dominates his wife Leticia, ridiculing her desire for independence and education; he abuses Nena, a girl of twelve that he first keeps in a warehouse, then in the cellar of his home, and rapes repeatedly throughout the play.

Fornes's dramatic style is more imagistic than linear, and *The Conduct of Life* develops through a montage of brief scenes documenting the work of power in interpersonal relationships: Orlando's callous treatment of Leticia; Alejo's fear of Orlando's brutality to their prisoners; the complex negotiations of domestic power between the helpless mistress Leticia and her competent servant Olimpia; Olimpia's effort to rehumanize Nena; Orlando's tortuous "interrogation" of Leticia in Scene 19, an interrogation that leads her to murder him. This montage comes to a climax in Fornes's brilliant, ambiguous final image. Having murdered Orlando, Leticia puts the gun in Nena's hand, a final image of exploitation.

Given Fornes's training in the visual arts, it is not surprising that the visual composition of the play on the stage is critical to *The Conduct of Life.* Here, Fornes specifies an elaborate series of platforms—a living room downstage, nearest to the audience; a dining room and hallway slightly upstage, and elevated above the living room level; and, farthest upstage, the cellar, which is at the same level as the living room. Fornes interrogates the kind of perception that the theater enables and depends on, a formal self-consciousness that brings Fornes's theater into line with the visual experimentation in painting, sculpture, and film. To watch the play, the audience engages in a complex act of spatial "reading," looking through the domestic world of Leticia and Orlando, to see the terrible chamber upstage where the fundamental acts of this culture are repeatedly, brutally performed.

# — The Conduct of Life —

## Maria Irene Fornes

TO JULIAN BECK IN MEMORY OF HIS
COURAGEOUS LIFE (1925–1985)

## —CHARACTERS—

ORLANDO, *An army lieutenant at the start of the play. A lieutenant commander soon after.*
LETICIA, *His wife, ten years his elder.*
ALEJO, *A lieutenant commander. Their friend.*
NENA, *A destitute girl of twelve.*
OLIMPIA, *A servant.*

*A Latin American country. The present.*

*The floor is divided in four horizontal planes. Downstage is the livingroom, which is about ten feet deep. Center stage, eighteen inches high, is the diningroom, which is about ten feet deep. Further upstage, eighteen inches high, is a hallway which is about four feet deep. At each end of the hallway there is a door. The one to the right leads to the servants' quarters, the one to the left to the basement. Upstage, three feet lower than the hallway (same level as the livingroom), is the cellar, which is about sixteen feet deep. Most of the cellar is occupied by two platforms which are eight feet wide, eight feet deep, and three feet high. Upstage of the cellar are steps that lead up. Approximately ten feet above the cellar is another level, extending from the extreme left to the extreme right, which represents a warehouse. There is a door on the left of the warehouse. On the left and the right of the livingroom there are archways that lead to hallways or antechambers, the floors of these hallways are the same level as the diningroom. On the left and the right of the diningroom there is a second set of archways that lead to hallways or antechambers, the floors of which are the same level as the hallways. All along the edge of each level there is a step that leads to the next level. All floors and steps are black marble. In the livingroom there are two chairs. One is to the left, next to a table with a telephone. The other is to the right. In the diningroom there are a large green marble table and three chairs. On the cellar floor there is a mattress to the right and a chair to the left. In the warehouse there is a table and a chair to the left, and a chair and some boxes and crates to the right.*

### SCENE I

*Orlando is doing jumping-jacks in the upper left corner of the diningroom in the dark. A light, slowly, comes up on him. He wears military breeches held by suspenders, and riding boots. He does jumping-jacks as long as it can be endured. He stops, the center area starts to become visible. There is a chair upstage of the table. There is a linen towel on the left side of the table. Orlando dries his face with the towel and sits as he puts the towel around his neck.*

ORLANDO: Thirty three and I'm still a lieutenant. In two years I'll receive a promotion or I'll leave the military. I promise I will not spend time feeling sorry for myself.—Instead I will study the situation and draw an effective plan of action. I must eliminate all obstacles.—I will make the acquaintance of people in high power. If I cannot achieve this on my own merit, I will marry a woman in high circles. Leticia must not be an obstacle.—Man must have an ideal, mine is to achieve maximum power. That is my destiny.—No other interest will deter me from this.—My sexual drive is detrimental to 10 my ideals. I must no longer be overwhelmed by sexual passion or I will be degraded beyond hope of recovery. (*Lights fade to black.*)

### SCENE II

*Alejo sits to the right of the diningroom table. Orlando stands to Alejo's left. He is now a lieutenant commander. He wears an army tunic, breeches, and boots. Leticia stands to the left. She wears a dress that suggests 1940s fashion.*

LETICIA: What! Me go hunting? Do you think I'm going to shoot a deer, the most beautiful animal in the world? Do you think I'm going to destroy a deer? On the contrary, I would run in the field and scream and wave my arms like a mad woman and try to scare them away so the hunters could not reach them. I'd run in front of the bullets and let the mad hunters kill me—stand in the way of the bullets—stop 20 the bullets with my body. I don't see how anyone can shoot a deer.

ORLANDO: (*To Alejo.*) Do you understand that? You, who are her friend, can you understand that? You don't think that is madness? She's mad. Tell her that—she'll think it's you who's mad. (*To Leticia.*) Hunting is a sport! A skill! Don't talk about something you know nothing about. Must you have an opinion about every damn thing! Can't you keep your mouth shut when you don't know what you're talking about? (*Orlando exits right.*) 30

LETICIA: He told me that he didn't love me, and that his sole relationship to me was simply a marital one. What he means is that I am to keep this house, and he is to provide for it. That's what he said. That explains why he treats me the way he treats me. I never understood why he did, but now it's clear. He doesn't love me. I thought he loved me and that he stayed with me because he loved me and that's why I didn't understand his behavior. But now I know, because he told me that he sees me as a person who runs the house. I never understood that because I would have never—if he had said, "Would you marry me to run my house even if I don't love you." I would have never—I would have never believed what I was hearing. I would have never believed that these words were coming out of his mouth. Because I loved him.

*(Orlando has entered. Leticia sees him and exits left. Orlando enters and sits center.)*

ORLANDO: I didn't say any of that. I told her that she's not my heir. That's what I said. I told her that she's not in my will, and she will not receive a penny of my money if I die. That's what I said. I didn't say anything about running the house. I said she will not inherit a penny from me because I didn't want to be humiliated. She is capable of foolishness beyond anyone's imagination. Ask her what she would do if she were rich and could do anything she wants with her money. *(Leticia enters.)*

LETICIA: I would distribute it among the poor.

ORLANDO: She has no respect for money.

LETICIA: That is not true. If I had money I would give it to those who need it. I know what money is, what money can do. It can feed people, it can put a roof over their heads. Money can do that. It can clothe them. What do you know about money? What does it mean to you? What do you do with money? Buy rifles? To shoot deer?

ORLANDO: You're foolish!—You're foolish! You're a foolish woman! *(Orlando exits. He speaks from offstage.)* Foolish. . . . Foolish. . . .

LETICIA: He has no respect for me. He is insensitive. He doesn't listen. You cannot reach him. He is deaf. He is an animal. Nothing touches him except sensuality. He responds to food, to the flesh. To music sometimes, if it is romantic. To the moon. He is romantic but he is not aware of what you are feeling. I can't change him.—I'll tell you why I asked you to come. Because I want something from you.—I want you to educate me. I want to study. I want to study so I am not an ignorant person. I want to go to the university. I want to be knowledgeable. I'm tired of being ignored. I want to study political science. Is political science what diplomats study? Is that what it is? You have to teach me elemental things because I never finished grammar school. I would have to study a great deal. A great deal so I could enter the university. I would have to go through all the subjects. I would like to be a woman who speaks in a group and have others listen.

ALEJO: Why do you want to worry about any of that? What's the use? Do you think you can change anything? Do think anyone can change anything?

LETICIA: Why not? *(Pause.)* Do you think I'm crazy?—He can't help it.—Do you think I'm crazy?—Because I love him? *(He looks away from her. Lights fade to black.)*

## SCENE III

*Orlando enters the warehouse holding Nena close to him. She wears a gray over-large uniform. She is barefoot. She resists him. She is tearful and frightened. She pulls away and runs to the right wall. He follows her.*

ORLANDO: *(Softly.)* You called me a snake.

NENA: No, I didn't. *(He tries to reach her. She pushes his hands away from her.)* I was kidding.—I swear I was kidding.

*(He grabs her and pushes her against the wall. He pushes his pelvis against her. He moves to the chair dragging her with him. She crawls to the left, pushes the table aside and stands behind it. He walks around the table. She goes under it. He grabs her foot and pulls her out toward the downstage side. He opens his fly and pushes his pelvis against her. Lights fade to black.)*

## SCENE IV

*Olimpia is wiping crumbs off the diningroom table. She wears a plain gray uniform. Leticia sits to the left of the table facing front. She wears a dressing gown. She writes in a notebook. There is some silverware on the table. Olimpia has a speech defect.*

LETICIA: Let's do this.

OLIMPIA: O.K. *(She continues wiping the table.)*

LETICIA: *(Still writing.)* What are you doing?

OLIMPIA: I'm doing what I always do.

LETICIA: Let's do this.

OLIMPIA: *(In a mumble.)* As soon as I finish doing this. You can't just ask me to do what you want me to do, and interrupt what I'm doing. I don't stop from the time I wake up in the morning to the time I go to sleep. You can't interrupt me whenever you want, not if you want me to get to the end of my work. I wake up at 5:30. I wash. I put on my clothes and make my bed. I go to the kitchen. I get the milk and the bread from outside and I put them on the counter. I open the icebox. I put one bottle in and take the butter out. I leave the other bottle on the counter. I shut the refrigerator door. I take the pan that I use for water and put water in it. I know how much. I put the pan on the stove, light the stove, cover it. I take the top off the milk and pour it in the milk pan except for a little. *(Indicating with her finger.)* Like this. For the cat. I put the pan on the stove, light the stove. I put coffee in the thing. I know how much. I light the oven and put bread in it. I come here, get the tablecloth and I lay it on the table. I shout "Breakfast." I get the napkins. I take the cups, the saucers, and the silver out and set the table. I go to the kitchen. I put the tray on the counter, put the butter on the tray. The water and the milk are getting hot. I pick up the cat's dish. I wash it. I pour the milk I left in the bottle in the milk dish. I put it on the floor for the cat. I shout "Breakfast." The water boils. I pour it in the thing. When the milk boils I turn off the gas and cover the milk. I get the bread from the oven. I slice it down the middle and butter it. Then I cut it in pieces *(indicating)* this big. I set a piece aside for me. I put the rest of the bread in the bread dish and shout "Breakfast." I pour the coffee in the coffee pot and the milk in the milk pitcher, except I leave *(indicating)* this much for me. I put them on the tray and bring them here. If you're not in the diningroom I call again. "Breakfast." I go to the kitchen, I fill the milk pan with water and let it soak. I pour my coffee, sit at the counter and eat my breakfast. I go upstairs to make your bed and clean your bathroom. I come down here to meet you and figure out what you want for lunch and dinner. And try to get you to think quickly so

I can run to the market and get it bought before all the fresh stuff is bought up. Then, I start the day.

LETICIA: So?

OLIMPIA: So I need a steam pot.

LETICIA: What is a steam pot?

OLIMPIA: A pressure cooker.

140 LETICIA: And you want a steam pot? Don't you have enough pots?

OLIMPIA: No.

LETICIA: Why do you want a steam pot?

OLIMPIA: It cooks faster.

LETICIA: How much is it?

OLIMPIA: Expensive.

LETICIA: How much?

OLIMPIA: Twenty.

LETICIA: Too expensive. (*Olimpia throws the silver on the*
150    *floor. Leticia turns her eyes up to the ceiling.*) Why do you want one more pot?

OLIMPIA: I don't have a steam pot.

LETICIA: A pressure cooker.

OLIMPIA: A pressure cooker.

LETICIA: You have too many pots. (*Olimpia goes to the kitchen and returns with an aluminum pan. She shows it to Leticia.*)

OLIMPIA: Look at this. (*Leticia looks at it.*)

LETICIA: What? (*Olimpia hits the pan against the back of a chair, breaking off a piece of the bottom.*)

160 OLIMPIA: It's no good.

LETICIA: All right! (*She takes money from her pocket and gives it to Olimpia.*) Here. Buy it!—What are we having for lunch?

OLIMPIA: Fish.

LETICIA: I don't like fish.—What else?

OLIMPIA: Boiled plantains.

LETICIA: Make something I like.

OLIMPIA: Avocados. (*Leticia gives a look of resentment to Olimpia.*)

170 LETICIA: Why can't you make something I like?

OLIMPIA: Avocados.

LETICIA: Something that needs cooking.

OLIMPIA: Bread pudding.

LETICIA: And for dinner?

OLIMPIA: Pot roast.

LETICIA: What else?

OLIMPIA: Rice.

LETICIA: What else?

OLIMPIA: Salad.

180 LETICIA: What kind?

OLIMPIA: Avocado.

LETICIA: Again. (*Olimpia looks at Leticia.*)

OLIMPIA: You like avocados.

LETICIA: Not again.—Tomatoes. (*Olimpia mumbles.*) What's wrong with tomatoes besides that you don't like them? (*Olimpia mumbles.*) Get some. (*Olimpia mumbles.*) What does that mean? (*Olimpia doesn't answer.*) Buy tomatoes.—What else?

OLIMPIA: That's all.

190 LETICIA: We need a green.

OLIMPIA: Watercress.

LETICIA: What else?

OLIMPIA: Nothing.

LETICIA: For dessert.

OLIMPIA: Bread pudding.

LETICIA: Again.

OLIMPIA: Why not?

LETICIA: Make a flan.

OLIMPIA: No flan.

LETICIA: Why not?                                                    200

OLIMPIA: No good.

LETICIA: Why no good!—Buy some fruit then.

OLIMPIA: What kind?

LETICIA: Pineapple. (*Olimpia shakes her head.*) Why not? (*Olimpia shakes her head.*) Mango.

OLIMPIA: No mango.

LETICIA: Buy some fruit! That's all. Don't forget bread. (*Leticia hands Olimpia some bills. Olimpia holds it and waits for more. Leticia hands her one more bill. Lights fade to black.*)

## SCENE V

*The warehouse table is propped against the door. The chair on the left faces right. The door is pushed and the table falls to the floor. Orlando enters. He wears an undershirt with short sleeves, breeches with suspenders and boots. He looks around the room for Nena. Believing she has escaped, he becomes still and downcast. He turns to the door and stands there for a moment. He takes a few steps to the right and stands there for a moment staring fixedly. He hears a sound from behind the boxes, walks to them and takes a box off. Nena is there. Her head is covered with a blanket. He pulls the blanket off. Nena is motionless and staring into space. He looks at her for a while, then walks to the chair and sits facing right staring into space. A few moments pass. Lights fade to black.*

## SCENE VI

*Leticia speaks on the telephone to Mona.*

LETICIA: Since they moved him to the new department he's 210 different. (*Brief pause.*) He's distracted. I don't know where he goes in his mind. He doesn't listen to me. He worries. When I talk to him he doesn't listen. He's thinking about the job. He says he worries. What is there to worry about? Do you think there is anything to worry about? (*Brief pause.*) What meeting? (*Brief pause.*) Oh, sure. When is it? (*Brief pause.*) At what time? What do you mean I knew? No one told me.—I don't remember. Would you pick me up? (*Brief pause.*) At one? Isn't one early? (*Brief pause.*) Orlando may still be home at one. Sometimes he's here a little longer than 220 usual. After lunch he sits and smokes. Don't you think one thirty will give us enough time? (*Brief pause.*) No. I can't leave while he's smoking . . . I'd rather not. I'd rather wait till he leaves. (*Brief pause.*) . . . One thirty, then. Thank you, Mona. (*Brief pause.*) See you then. Bye. (*Leticia puts down the receiver and walks to stage right area. Orlando's voice is heard offstage left. He and Alejo enter halfway through the following speech.*)

ORLANDO: He made loud sounds not high-pitched like a horse. He sounded like a whale, like a wounded whale. He was 230 pouring liquid from everywhere, his mouth, his nose, his eyes. He was not a horse but a sexual organ.—Helpless. A viscera.—Screaming. Making strange sounds. He collapsed on top of her. She wanted him off but he collapsed on top of her and stayed there on top of her. Like gum. He looked more like a whale than a horse. A seal. His muscles were soft. What does it feel like to be without shape like that. Without pride. She was indifferent. He stayed there for a while and then lifted himself off her and to the ground.

240    (*Pause.*) He looked like a horse again.

LETICIA: Alejo, how are you? (*Alejo kisses Leticia's hand.*)

ORLANDO: (*As he walks to the livingroom. He sits left facing front.*) Alejo is staying for dinner.

LETICIA: Would you like some coffee?

ALEJO: Yes, thank you.

LETICIA: Would you like some coffee, Orlando?

ORLANDO: Yes, thank you.

LETICIA: (*In a loud voice towards the kitchen.*) Olimpia . . .

OLIMPIA: What?

250    LETICIA: Coffee . . . (*Leticia sits to the right of the table. Alejo sits center.*)

ALEJO: Have you heard?

LETICIA: Yes, he's dead and I'm glad he's dead. An evil man. I knew he'd be killed. Who killed him?

ALEJO: Someone who knew him.

LETICIA: What is there to gain? So he's murdered. Someone else will do the job. Nothing will change. To destroy them all is to say we destroy us all.

ALEJO: Do you think we're all rotten?

260    LETICIA: Yes.

ORLANDO: A bad germ?

LETICIA: Yes.

ORLANDO: In our hearts?

LETICIA: Yes.—In our eyes.

ORLANDO: You're silly.

LETICIA: We're blind. We can't see beyond an arm's reach. We don't believe our life will last beyond the day. We only know what we have in our hand to put in our mouth, to put in our stomach, and to put in our pocket. We take care of our

270    pocket, but not of our country. We take care of our stomachs but not of our hungry. We are primitive. We don't believe in the future. Each night when the sun goes down we think that's the end of life—so we have one last fling. We don't think we have a future. We don't think we have a country. Ask anybody, "Do you have a country?" They'll say, "Yes." Ask them, "What is your country?" They'll say, "My bed, my dinner plate." But, things can change. They can. I have changed. You have changed. He has changed.

ALEJO: Look at me. I used to be an idealist. Now I don't have

280    any feeling for anything. I used to be strong, healthy, I looked at the future with hope.

LETICIA: Now you don't?

ALEJO: Now I don't. I know what viciousness is.

ORLANDO: What is viciousness?

ALEJO: You.

ORLANDO: Me?

ALEJO: The way you tortured Felo.

ORLANDO: I never tortured Felo.

ALEJO: You did.

290    ORLANDO: Boys play that way. You did too.

ALEJO: I didn't.

ORLANDO: He was repulsive to us.

ALEJO: I never hurt him.

ORLANDO: Well, you never stopped me.

ALEJO: I didn't know how to stop you. I didn't know anyone could behave the way you did. It frightened me. It changed me. I became hopeless.

(*Orlando walks to the diningroom.*)

ORLANDO: You were always hopeless. (*He exits. Olimpia enters carrying three demi-tasse coffees on a tray. She places them on the table and exits.*)    300

ALEJO: I am sexually impotent. I have no feelings. Things pass through me which resemble feelings but I know they are not. I'm impotent.

LETICIA: Nonsense.

ALEJO: It's not nonsense. How can you say it's nonsense?— How can one live in a world that festers the way ours does and take any pleasure in life? (*Lights fade to black.*)

SCENE VII

*Nena and Orlando stand against the wall in the warehouse. She is fully dressed. He is barebreasted. He pushes his pelvis against her gently. His lips touch her face as he speaks. The words are inaudible to the audience. On the table there is a tin plate with food and a tin cup with milk.*

ORLANDO: Look this way. I'm going to do something to you. (*She makes a move away from him.*) Don't do that. Don't move away. (*As he slides his hand along her side.*) I just want    310 to put my hand here like this. (*He puts his lips on hers softly and speaks at the same time.*) Don't hold your lips so tight. Make them soft. Let them loose. So I can do this. (*She whimpers.*) Don't cry. I won't hurt you. This is all I'm going to do to you. Just hold your lips soft. Be nice. Be a nice girl. (*He pushes against her and reaches an orgasm. He remains motionless for a moment, then steps away from her still leaning his hand on the wall.*) Go eat. I brought you food. (*She goes to the table. He sits on the floor and watches her eat. She eats voraciously. She looks at the milk.*) Drink it. It's    320 milk. It's good for you. (*She drinks the milk, then continues eating. Lights fade to black.*)

SCENE VIII

*Leticia stands left of the diningroom table. She speaks words she has memorized. Olimpia sits to the left of the table. She holds a book close to her eyes. Her head moves from left to right along the written words as she mumbles the sound of imaginary words. She continues doing this through the rest of the scene.*

LETICIA: The impact of war is felt particularly in the economic realm. The destruction of property, private as well as public may paralyze the country. Foreign investment is virtually . . . (*To Olimpia.*) Is that right? (*Pause.*) Is that right!

OLIMPIA: Wait a moment. (*She continues mumbling and moving her head.*)

LETICIA: What for? (*Pause.*) You can't read. (*Pause.*) You can't read!    330

OLIMPIA: Wait a moment. (*She continues mumbling and moving her head.*)

LETICIA: (*Slapping the book off Olimpia's hand.*) Why are you pretending you can read? (*Olimpia slaps Leticia's hands. They slap each other's hands. Lights fade to black.*)

SCENE IX

*Orlando sits in the livingroom. He smokes. He faces front and is thoughtful. Leticia and Olimpia are in the diningroom. Leticia wears a hat and jacket. She tries to put a leather strap through the loops of a suitcase. There is a smaller piece of luggage on the floor.*

LETICIA: This strap is too wide. It doesn't fit through the loop. (*Orlando doesn't reply.*) Is this the right strap? Is this the strap that came with this suitcase? Did the strap that came with the suitcase break? If so, where is it? And when did it 340 break? Why doesn't this strap fit the suitcase and how did it get here. Did you buy this strap, Orlando?

ORLANDO: I may have.

LETICIA: It doesn't fit.

ORLANDO: Hm.

LETICIA: It doesn't fit through the loops.

ORLANDO: Just strap it outside the loops. (*Leticia stands. Olimpia tries to put the strap through the loop.*)

LETICIA: No. You're supposed to put it through the loops. That's what the loops are for. What happened to the other 350 strap?

ORLANDO: It broke.

LETICIA: How?

ORLANDO: I used it for something.

LETICIA: What! (*He looks at her.*) You should have gotten me one that fit. What did you use it for?—Look at that.

ORLANDO: Strap it outside the loops.

LETICIA: That wouldn't look right.

ORLANDO: (*Going to look at the suitcase.*) Why do you need the straps?

360 LETICIA: Because they come with it.

ORLANDO: You don't need them.

LETICIA: And travel like this?

ORLANDO: Use another suitcase.

LETICIA: What other suitcase. I don't have another. (*Orlando looks at his watch.*)

ORLANDO: You're going to miss your plane.

LETICIA: I'm not going. I'm not travelling like this.

ORLANDO: Go without it. I'll send it to you.

LETICIA: You'll get new luggage, repack it and send it to me?— 370 All right. (*She starts to exit left.*) It's nice to travel light. (*Off stage.*) Do I have everything?—Come, Olimpia.

(*Olimpia follows with the suitcases. Orlando takes the larger suitcase from Olimpia. She exits. Orlando goes up the hallway and exits through the left door. A moment later he enters holding Nena close to him. She is pale, dishevelled and has black circles around her eyes. She has a high fever and is almost unconscious. Her dress is torn and soiled. She is barefoot. He carries a new cotton dress on his arm. He takes her to the chair in the livingroom. He takes off the soiled dress and puts the new dress on her over a soiled slip.*)

ORLANDO: That's nice. You look nice. (*Leticia's voice is heard. He hurriedly takes Nena out the door, closes it, and leans on it.*)

LETICIA: (*Off stage.*) It would take but a second. You run to the garage and get the little suitcase and I'll take out the things I need. (*Leticia and Olimpia enter left. Olimpia exits right.*) Hurry. Hurry. It would take but a second. (*Seeing Orlando.*) Orlando, I came back because I couldn't leave without anything at all. I came to get a few things because I have a 380 smaller suitcase where I can take a few things. (*She puts the suitcase on the table, opens it and takes out the things she mentions.*) A pair of shoes . . . (*Olimpia enters right with a small suitcase.*)

OLIMPIA: Here.

| LETICIA: | OLIMPIA: |
|---|---|
| A nightgown, | A robe, |
| a robe | a dress, |
| underwear, | a nightgown, |
| a dress, | underwear, 390 |
| a sweater. | a sweater, |
| | a pair of shoes. |

(*Leticia closes the large suitcase. Olimpia closes the smaller suitcase.*)

LETICIA: (*Starting to exit.*) Goodbye.

OLIMPIA: (*Following Leticia.*) Goodbye.

ORLANDO: Goodbye. (*Lights fade to black.*)

SCENE X

*Nena is curled on the extreme right of the mattress. Orlando sits on the mattress using Nena as a back support. Alejo sits on the chair. He holds a green paper on his hand. Olimpia sweeps the floor.*

ORLANDO: Tell them to check him. See if there's a scratch on him. There's not a scratch on that body. Why the fuss! Who was he and who's making a fuss? Why is he so important.

ALEJO: He was in deep. He knew names.

ORLANDO: I was never told that. But it wouldn't have mattered 400 if they had because he died before I touched him.

ALEJO: You have to go to headquarters. They want you there.

ORLANDO: He came in screaming and he wouldn't stop. I had to wait for him to stop screaming before I could even pose a question to him. He wouldn't stop. I had put the poker to his neck to see if he would stop. Just to see if he would shut up. He just opened his eyes wide and started shaking and screamed even louder and fell over dead. Maybe he took something. I didn't do anything to him. If I didn't get anything from him it's because he died before I could get to 410 him. He died of fear, not from anything I did to him. Tell them to do an autopsy. I'm telling you the truth. That's the truth. Why the fuss.

ALEJO: (*Starting to put the paper in his pocket.*) I'll tell them what you said.

ORLANDO: Let me see that. (*Alejo takes it to him.*) Orlando looks at it and puts it back in Alejo's hands.) O.K. so it's a trap. So what side are you on? (*Pause. Alejo says nothing.*) So what do they want? (*Pause.*) Who's going to question me? That's funny. That's very funny. They want to question 420 me. They want to punch my eyes out? I knew something was wrong because they were getting nervous. Antonio was getting nervous. I went to him and I asked him if something was wrong. He said, no, nothing was wrong. But I could tell something was wrong. He looked at Velez and Velez looked back at him. They are stupid. They want to conceal something from me and they look at each other right in front of me, as if I'm blind, as if I can't tell that they are worried about something. As if there's something happening right in front of my nose but I'm blind and I can't see it. (*He grabs the paper from Alejo's hand.*) You understand? (*He goes up the steps.*)

OLIMPIA: Like an alligator, big mouth and no brains. Lots of teeth but no brains. All tongue. (*Orlando enters through the left hallway door, and sits at the diningroom table. Alejo enters a few moments later. He stands to the right.*)

ORLANDO: What kind of way is this to treat me?—After what I've done for them?—Is this a way to treat me?—I'll come up . . . as soon as I can—I haven't been well.—O.K. I'll come up. I get depressed because things are bad and they are not going to improve. There's something malignant in the world. Destructiveness, aggressiveness.—Greed. People take what is not theirs. There is greed. I am depressed, disillusioned . . . with life . . . with work . . . family. I don't see hope. (*He sits. He speaks more to himself than to Alejo.*) Some people get a cut in a finger and die. Because their veins are right next to their skin. There are people who, if you punch them in their stomach the skin around the stomach bursts and the bowels fall out. Other people, you cut them open and you don't see any veins. You can't find their intestines. There are people who don't even bleed. There are people who bleed like pigs. There are people who have the nerves right on their skins. You touch them and they scream. They have their vital organs close to the surface. You hit them and they burst an organ. I didn't even touch this one and he died. He died of fear. (*Lights fade to black.*)

## SCENE XI

(*Nena, Alejo and Olimpia sit cross-legged on the mattress in the basement. Nena sits right, Alejo center, Olimpia left. Nena and Olimpia play pattycake. Orlando enters. He goes close to them.*)

ORLANDO: What are you doing?

OLIMPIA: I'm playing with her.

ORLANDO: (*To Alejo.*) What are you doing here? (*Alejo looks at Orlando as a reply. Orlando speaks sarcastically.*) They're playing pattycake. (*He goes near Nena.*) So? (*Short pause. Nena giggles.*) Stop laughing! (*Nena is frightened. Olimpia holds her.*)

OLIMPIA: Why do you have to spoil everything. We were having a good time.

ORLANDO: Shut up! (*Nena whimpers.*) Stop whimpering. I can't stand your whimpering. I can't stand it. (*Timidly, she tries to speak words as she whimpers.*) Speak up. I can't hear you! She's crazy! Take her to the crazy house!

OLIMPIA: She's not crazy! She's a baby!

ORLANDO: She's not a baby! She's crazy! You think she's a baby? She's older than you think! How old do you think she is—Don't tell me that.

OLIMPIA: She's sick. Don't you see she's sick? Let her cry! (*To Nena.*) Cry!

ORLANDO: You drive me crazy too with your . . . (*He imitates her speech defect. She punches him repeatedly.*)

OLIMPIA: You drive me crazy! (*He pushes her off.*) You drive me crazy! You are a bastard! One day I'm going to kill you when you're asleep! I'm going to open you up and cut your entrails and feed them to the snakes. (*She tries to strangle him.*) I'm going to tear your heart out and feed it to the dogs! I'm going to cut your head open and have the cats eat your brain! (*Reaching for his fly.*) I'm going to cut your peepee and hang it on a tree and feed it to the birds!

ORLANDO: Get off me! I'm getting rid of you too! (*He starts to exit.*) I can't stand you!

OLIMPIA: Oh, yeah! I'm getting rid of you.

ORLANDO: I can't stand you!

OLIMPIA: I can't stand you!

ORLANDO: Meddler! (*To Alejo.*) I can't stand you either.

OLIMPIA: (*Going to the stairs.*) Tell the boss! Tell her! She won't get rid of me! She'll get rid of you! What good are you! Tell her! (*She goes to Nena.*) Don't pay any attention to him. He's a coward.—You're pretty. (*Orlando enters through the hallway left door. He sits center at the diningroom table and leans his head on it. Leticia enters. He turns to look at her.*)

LETICIA: You didn't send it. (*Lights fade to black.*)

## SCENE XII

*Leticia sits next to the phone. She speaks to Mona in her mind.*

LETICIA: I walk through the house and I know where he's made love to her I think I hear his voice making love to her. Saying the same things he says to me, the same words.—(*There is a pause.*) There is someone here. He keeps someone here in the house. (*Pause.*) I don't dare look. (*Pause.*) No, there's nothing I can do. I can't do anything. (*She walks to the hallway. She hears footsteps. She moves rapidly to left and hides behind a pillar. Olimpia enters from right. She takes a few steps down the hallway. She carries a plate of food. She sees Leticia and stops. She takes a few steps in various directions, then stops.*)

OLIMPIA: Here kitty, kitty. (*Leticia walks to Olimpia, looks closely at the plate, then up at Olimpia.*)

LETICIA: What is it?

OLIMPIA: Food.

LETICIA: Who is it for? (*Olimpia turns her eyes away and doesn't answer. Leticia decides to go to the cellar door. She stops halfway there.*) Who is it?

OLIMPIA: A cat. (*Leticia opens the cellar door.*)

LETICIA: It's not a cat. I'm going down. (*She opens the door to the cellar and starts to go down.*) I want to see who is there.

ORLANDO: (*Offstage from the cellar.*) What is it you want? (*Lights fade to black.*)

## SCENE XIII

*Orlando leans back on the chair in the basement. His legs are outstretched. His eyes are bloodshot and leery. His tunic is open. Nena is curled on the floor. Orlando speaks quietly. He is deeply absorbed.*

ORLANDO: What I do to you is out of love. Out of want. It's not what you think. I wish you didn't have to be hurt. I don't do it out of hatred. It is not out of rage. It is love. It is a quiet feeling. It's a pleasure. It is quiet and it pierces my insides

in the most internal way. It is my most private self. And this
I give to you.—Don't be afraid.—It is a desire to destroy
and to see things destroyed and to see the inside of them.—
It's my nature. I must hide this from others. But I don't feel
530    remorse. I was born this way and I must have this.—I need
love. I wish you did not feel hurt and recoil from me. (*Lights
fade to black.*)

## SCENE XIV

*Orlando sits to the right and Leticia sits to the left of the table.*

LETICIA: Don't make her scream. (*There is a pause.*)
ORLANDO: You're crazy.
LETICIA: Don't I give you enough?
ORLANDO: (*He's calm.*) Don't start.
LETICIA: How long is she going to be here?
ORLANDO: Not long.
LETICIA: Don't make her cry. (*He looks at her.*) I can't stand it.
540    (*Pause.*) Why do you make her scream?
ORLANDO: I don't make her scream.
LETICIA: She screams.
ORLANDO: I can't help it. (*Pause.*)
LETICIA: I tell you I can't stand it. I'm going to ask Mona to
come and stay with me.
ORLANDO: No.
LETICIA: I want someone here with me.
ORLANDO: I don't want her here.
LETICIA: Why not?
550    ORLANDO: I don't.
LETICIA: I need someone here with me.
ORLANDO: Not now.
LETICIA: When?
ORLANDO: Soon enough.—She's going to stay here for a while.
She's going to work for us. She'll be a servant here.
LETICIA: . . . No.
ORLANDO: She's going to be a servant here. (*Lights fade to
black.*)

## SCENE XV

*Olimpia and Nena are sitting at the diningroom table. They
are separating stones and other matter from dry beans.*

NENA: I used to clean beans when I was in the home. And also
560    string beans. I also pressed clothes. The days were long.
Some girls did hand sewing. They spent the day doing that.
I didn't like it. When I did that, the day was even longer and
there were times when I couldn't move even if I tried. And
they said I couldn't go there anymore, that I had to stay in
the yard. I didn't mind sitting in the yard looking at the
birds. I went to the laundryroom and watched the women
work. They let me go in and sit there. And they showed me
how to press. I like to press because my mind wanders and
I find satisfaction. I can iron all day. I like the way the wrin-
570    kles come out and things look nice. It's a miracle isn't it? I
could earn a living pressing clothes. And I could find my
grandpa and take care of him.
OLIMPIA: Where is your grandpa?
NENA: I don't know. (*They work a little in silence.*) He sleeps
in the streets. Because he's too old to remember where he

lives. He needs a person to take care of him. And I can take
care of him. But I don't know where he is.—He doesn't
know where I am.—He doesn't know who he is. He's too
old. He doesn't know anything about himself. He only
knows how to beg. And he knows that, only because he's    580
hungry. He walks around and begs for food. He forgets to go
home. He lives in the camp for the homeless and he has his
own box. It's not an ugly box like the others. It is a real box.
I used to live there with him. He took me with him when my
mother died till they took me to the home. It is a big box. It's
big enough for two. I could sleep in the front where it's cold.
And he could sleep in the back where it's warmer. And he
could lean on me. The floor is hard for him because he's
skinny and it's hard on his poor bones. He could sleep on top
of me if that would make him feel comfortable. I wouldn't    590
mind. Except that he may pee on me because he pees in his
pants. He doesn't know not to. He is incontinent. He can't
hold it. His box was a little smelly. But that doesn't matter
because I could clean it. All I would need is some soap. I
could get plenty of water from the public faucet. And I
could borrow a brush. You know how clean I could get it? As
clean as new. You know what I would do? I would make
holes in the floor so the pee would go down to the ground.
And you know what else I would do?
OLIMPIA: What?    600
NENA: I would get straw and put it on the floor for him and for
me and it would make it comfortable and clean and warm.
How do you like that? Just as I did for my goat.
OLIMPIA: You have a goat?
NENA: . . . I did.
OLIMPIA: What happened to him?
NENA: He died. They killed him and ate him. Just like they did
Christ.
OLIMPIA: Nobody ate Christ.
NENA: . . . I thought they did. My goat was eaten though.—In    610
the home we had clean sheets. But that doesn't help. You
can't sleep on clean sheets, not if there isn't someone watching over you while you sleep. And since my ma died there
just wasn't anyone watching over me. Except you.—Aren't
you? In the home they said guardian angels watch your
sleep, but I didn't see any there. There weren't any. One day
I heard my grandpa calling me and I went to look for him.
And I didn't find him. I got tired and I slept in the street,
and I was hungry and I was crying. And then he came to me
and he spoke to me very softly so as not to scare me and he    620
said he would give me something to eat and he said he
would help me look for my grandpa. And he put me in the
back of his van . . . And he took me to a place. And he hurt
me. I fought with him but I stopped fighting—because I
couldn't fight anymore and he did things to me. And he
locked me in. And sometimes he brought me food and
sometimes he didn't. And he did things to me. And he beat
me. And he hung me on the wall. And I got sick. And sometimes he brought me medicine. And then he said he had to
take me somewhere. And he brought me here. And I am    630
glad to be here because you are here. I only wish my
grandpa were here too. He doesn't beat me so much anymore.
OLIMPIA: Why does he beat you. I hear him at night. He goes
down the steps and I hear you cry. Why does he beat you?
NENA: Because I'm dirty.

OLIMPIA: You are not dirty.

NENA: I am. That's why he beats me. The dirt won't go away from inside me.—He comes downstairs when I'm sleeping and I hear him coming and it frightens me. And he takes the covers off me and I don't move because I'm frightened and because I feel cold and I think I'm going to die. And he puts his hand on me and he recites poetry. And he is almost naked. He wears a robe but he leaves it open and he feels himself as he recites. He touches himself and he touches his stomach and his breasts and his behind. He puts his fingers in my parts and he keeps reciting. Then he turns me on my stomach and puts himself inside me. And he says I belong to him. (*There is a pause.*) I want to conduct each day of my life in the best possible way. I should value the things I have. And I should value all those who are near me. And I should value the kindness that others bestow upon me. And if someone should treat me unkindly, I should not blind myself with rage, but I should see them and receive them, since maybe they are in worse pain than me. (*Lights fade to black.*)

### SCENE XVI

*Leticia speaks on the telephone with Mona. She speaks rapidly.*

LETICIA: He is violent. He has become more so. I sense it. I feel it in him.—I understand his thoughts. I know what he thinks.—I raised him. I practically did. He was a boy when I met him. I saw him grow. I was the first woman he loved. That's how young he was. I have to look after him, make sure he doesn't get into trouble. He's not wise. He's trusting. They are changing him.—He tortures people. I know he does. He tells me he doesn't but I know he does. I know it. How could I not. Sometimes he comes from headquarters and his hands are shaking. Why should he shake? What do they do there?—He should transfer. Why do that? He says he doesn't do it himself. That the officers don't do it. He says that people are not being tortured. That that is questionable.—Everybody knows it. How could he not know it when everybody knows it. Sometimes you see blood in the streets. Haven't you seen it? Why do they leave the bodies in the streets,—how evil, to frighten people? They tear their fingernails off and their poor hands are bloody and destroyed. And they mangle their genitals and expose them and they tear their eyes out and you can see the empty eyesockets in the skull. How awful, Mona. He musn't do it. I don't care if I don't have anything! What's money! I don't need a house as big as this! He's doing it for money! What other reason could he have! What other reason could he have!! He shouldn't do it. I cannot look at him without thinking of it. He's doing it. I know he's doing it.—Shhhh! I hear steps. I'll call you later. Bye, Mona. I'll talk to you. (*She hangs up the receiver. Lights fade to black.*)

### SCENE XVII

*The livingroom. Olimpia sits to the right, Nena to the left.*

OLIMPIA: I don't wear high heels because they hurt my feet. I used to have a pair but they hurt my feet and also (*Pointing to her calf.*) here in my legs. So I don't wear them anymore

even if they were pretty. Did you ever wear high heels? (*Nena shakes her head.*) Do you have ingrown nails? (*Nena looks at her questioningly.*) Nails that grow twisted into the flesh. (*Nena shakes her head.*) I don't either. Do you have sugar in the blood? (*Nena shakes her head.*) My mother had sugar in the blood and that's what she died of but she lived to be eighty six which is very old even if she had many things wrong with her. She had glaucoma and high blood pressure. (*Leticia enters and sits center at the table. Nena starts to get up. Olimpia signals her to be still. Leticia is not concerned with them.*)

LETICIA: So, what are you talking about?

OLIMPIA: Ingrown nails. (*Nena turns to Leticia to make sure she may remain seated there. Leticia is involved with her own thoughts. Nena turns front. Lights fade to black.*)

### SCENE XVIII

*Orlando is sleeping on the diningroom table. The telephone rings. He speaks as someone having a nightmare.*

ORLANDO: Ah! Ah! Ah! Get off me! Get off! I said get off! (*Leticia enters.*)

LETICIA: (*Going to him.*) Orlando! What's the matter! What are you doing here!

ORLANDO: Get off me! Ah! Ah! Ah! Get off me!

LETICIA: Why are you sleeping here! On the table. (*Holding him close to her.*) Wake up.

ORLANDO: Let go of me. (*He slaps her hands as she tries to reach him.*) Get away from me. (*He goes to the floor on his knees and staggers to the telephone.*) Yes. Yes, it's me.—You did?—So?—It's true then.—What's the name?—Yes, sure.—Thanks.—Sure. (*He hangs up the receiver. He turns to look at Leticia. Lights fade to black.*)

### SCENE XIX

*Two chairs are placed side by side facing front in the center of the living room. Leticia sits on the right. Orlando stands on the down left corner. Nena sits to the left of the dining room table facing front. She covers her face. Olimpia stands behind her, holding Nena and leaning her head on her.*

ORLANDO: Talk.

LETICIA: I can't talk like this.

ORLANDO: Why not?

LETICIA: In front of everyone.

ORLANDO: Why not?

LETICIA: It is personal. I don't need the whole world to know.

ORLANDO: Why not?

LETICIA: Because it's private. My life is private.

ORLANDO: Are you ashamed?

LETICIA: Yes, I am ashamed!

ORLANDO: What of . . . ? What of . . . ?—I want you to tell us—about your lover.

LETICIA: I don't have a lover. (*He grabs her by the hair. Olimpia holds on to Nena and hides her face. Nena covers her face.*)

ORLANDO: You have a lover.

LETICIA: That's a lie.

ORLANDO: (*Moving closer to her.*) It's not a lie. (*To Leticia.*)

Come on tell us. (*He pulls harder.*) What's his name? (*She emits a sound of pain. He pulls harder, leans toward her and speaks in a low tone.*) What's his name?

LETICIA: Albertico. (*He takes a moment to release her.*)

ORLANDO: Tell us about it. (*There is silence. He pulls her hair.*)

LETICIA: All right. (*He releases her.*)

740 ORLANDO: What's his name?

LETICIA: Albertico.

ORLANDO: Go on. (*Pause.*) Sit up! (*She does.*) Albertico what?

LETICIA: Estevez. (*Orlando sits next to her.*)

ORLANDO: Go on. (*Silence.*) Where did you first meet him?

LETICIA: At . . . I . . .

ORLANDO: (*He grabs her by the hair.*) In my office.

LETICIA: Yes.

ORLANDO: Don't lie.—When?

LETICIA: You know when.

750 ORLANDO: When! (*Silence.*) How did you meet him?

LETICIA: You introduced him to me. (*He lets her go.*)

ORLANDO: What else? (*Silence.*) Who is he!

LETICIA: He's a lieutenant.

ORLANDO: (*He stands.*) When did you meet with him?

LETICIA: Last week.

ORLANDO: When!

LETICIA: Last week.

ORLANDO: When!

LETICIA: Last week. I said last week.

760 ORLANDO: Where did you meet him?

LETICIA: . . . In a house of rendez-vous . . .

ORLANDO: How did you arrange it?

LETICIA: . . . I wrote to him . . . !

ORLANDO: Did he approach you?

LETICIA: No.

ORLANDO: Did he!

LETICIA: No.

ORLANDO: (*He grabs her hair again.*) He did! How!

LETICIA: *I* approached him.

ORLANDO: How!    770

LETICIA: (*Aggressively.*) I looked at him! I looked at him! I looked at him! (*He lets her go.*)

ORLANDO: When did you look at him?

LETICIA: Please stop . . . !

ORLANDO: Where! When!

LETICIA: In your office!

ORLANDO: When?

LETICIA: I asked him to meet me!

ORLANDO: What did he say?

LETICIA: (*Aggressively.*) He walked away. He walked away! He 780 walked away! I asked him to meet me.

ORLANDO: What was he like?

LETICIA: . . . Oh . . .

ORLANDO: Was he tender? Was he tender to you!

(*She doesn't answer. He puts his hand inside her blouse. She lets out an excrutiating scream. He lets her go and walks to the right of the diningroom. She goes to the telephone table, opens the drawer, takes a gun and shoots Orlando. Orlando falls dead. Nena runs to downstage of the table. Leticia is disconcerted, then puts the revolver in Nena's hand and steps away from her.*)

LETICIA: Please . . .

(*Nena is in a state of terror and numb acceptance. She looks at the gun. Then, up. The lights fade.*)

### E N D

---

*THIS interview was conducted by Kathleen Betsko and Rachel Koenig.*

## Maria Irene Fornes

Interview
(1987)

INTERVIEWER: You came to America from Cuba when you were a young girl. What were your initial impressions of this country?

FORNES: I arrived here in 1945. It was three months before World War II ended. It was a great time, a lot of excitement. Everybody was happy that the war was over. There were many young men in uniforms arriving in New York and going home. Apartments were difficult to find, like now. I went to school for a month, and then I started working in factories and in offices. I had many jobs and I didn't like any of them. After I was here for two years, I began to meet people in the Village, and that's when I became a bohemian. I was seventeen. I started painting when I was nineteen, and then when I was twenty-three I went to Europe. I came back and eventually gave up painting, because I realized I was really not a painter. I had to push myself to paint . . .

INTERVIEWER: Did you see your first plays in Europe?

FORNES: I'd seen some plays here, but I didn't go to the theater often because it was expensive and I didn't like to plan things. Sometimes I would buy the ticket in advance and miss the play! At that time, there was something peculiar to me about going to theater, something forbidden. The first play that amazed me (I thought it was the most powerful thing of all—not only in theater but in painting, film, everything!) was Beckett's *Waiting for Godot*. I saw the play in Paris and I didn't understand a word of the French, but I left the theater as if I'd been hit over the head. I understood every moment of it. That play had a profound influence on me. When I returned from Europe, I started writing. That was 1959.

INTERVIEWER: Had you done any writing previously?

FORNES: In a way. I had been translating some letters that I brought over from Cuba. Letters that had been written to my great-grandfather from a cousin who lived in Spain. These letters told the whole story of their lives. At first I was just translating them for myself, not for anyone else to read. I wanted to understand something about that whole world. Then I became completely obsessed with the idea of writing a play. I thought about it day and night. It wasn't as if I thought, "I want to be a playwright"; it was just something I needed to do. For nineteen days I did nothing but write the play. Each day I called in sick to work. I would wake up in the morning and go directly to the typewriter. That was *Tango Palace* [1963]. I had never experienced such an obsession in my life. Never. I could not eat . . . there wasn't anything that I preferred to do. It was like a door opened, and I entered into a world. If anything, I was afraid I would never come back. I could not *stop* writing. I loved it, it was such a thrill. I started writing late; I was around thirty. I had never thought I would write; as I said, I was an aspiring painter. But once I started writing it was so pleasurable that I couldn't stop. Then it became more difficult.

INTERVIEWER: Why did the writing become difficult?

FORNES: I began to get a little lazy, I had to push myself. It was a question of discipline. It was hard to get started. Once I got going it was okay. Then I discovered that when a day passed without work, the next day was harder. If I stopped writing for two days, it was even more difficult. Then there was a period when I was running the New York Theatre Strategy, a group of avant-garde playwrights. I didn't write plays for six years. People kept saying to me, "You should write," and at the time I was offended. Looking back, I don't understand how I ever could have given up my writing to put on other people's plays, or why I didn't accept it as a compliment when people said that I should be writing instead. Finally I hired other people to coordinate Theatre Strategy, which ran for a few more years. I worked on *Fefu and Her Friends* [1978]. My work habits were erratic at that time. The only reason I would write was because I was under a deadline. I promised to have a play ready on a certain date so I had to finish it. It is still so; to a degree I need deadlines. I have no sense of time. Days pass, months, and I still think I have plenty of time. For the past three years, I have been conducting a writing workshop at Intar which we call The Lab, because it *is* a laboratory. Sometimes I call it The Sanitarium [laughs]. My work habits are now excellent. People who come to visit The Lab are always amazed at how peaceful it is and how beautiful the light is. I designed this workshop which is for ethnic, underprivileged or minority writers.

INTERVIEWER: What happens in your "laboratory"?

FORNES: It is a place where we do many experiments on writing. So far, they have been very successful. Unlike most workshops and classes that exist in universities, where you go home and write, bring your writing to class, have it read and get criticism, the Lab is all about inducing inspiration. I have never felt that criticism was the way to teach writing. In painting classes you paint *together;* you don't paint, bring your work to class and have it criticized. There is a model and everyone is working together. The important thing is to teach how to *work*, not how to criticize a finished piece. There is something about the atmosphere in a room full of people working. Each person's concentration is giving you something. Once you've experienced this phenomenon in the practice of another art form, you have a knowledge that it exists. If you've been exclusively a writer, I don't think this way of working would ever occur to you. In fact, most writers say, "I have to be alone to work." That's nonsense! They usually need to be completely alone because the other people around them are *not* writing. But if you experience working in a room with people who are also writing, there is no distraction. There is an exchange of energy and you know the other writers are not there for you to chat with. Even if you wanted to talk, you would be interrupting, so there is no temptation. No one is waiting for you, distracting you, and yet others are there. It has something to do with having all the advantages of being alone, without the isolation. One of the writer's problems is being alone. When I think of all the people who could write, and who have time to write, the only ones who actually do are those who can bear being alone. There are probably many talented people who are not writing simply because being alone is something that they are not willing to go through.

So working in this manner in the Lab, first of all, we are not alone; and secondly, there is a kind of mental communication. It's not anything we pursue, but we've discovered people often write about the same thing at the same time. It happened the other day. There were twelve peo-ple in the Lab, and two of them were writing in very different ways and for different reasons about a devil disguising himself as a man. Separately, these two writers came up with the image of a devil's tail showing from beneath baggy pants. It's such a strange image. It was remarkable. So there is, as I said, a kind of mental communication. That's why our tables have to touch. We sit in a circle and write by hand, and when I see a gap between tables, I immediately feel, "Close that gap!"

INTERVIEWER: Do you use exercises in the workshop?

FORNES: Yes. Partly because I am more experienced than the other writers and partly because I am trying to discover a Hispanic sensibility. The people in the workshop are so different—the mental attitudes, the taste, the kinds of plays they're writing, the level of education, of sophistica-tion . . . the variety is incredible. Yet when we are working in this way, it doesn't matter. I try first to have the students avoid writing any particular play with any particular characters, which leaves things completely open. Then for a period of two or three months I give exercises and they work with whatever imagery or characters emerge. You begin to notice that certain characters reappear and that there are certain elements that grab you in a more serious way than others. That will become the play. I must say that the exercises I use in the Lab have also helped me. They are a kind of meditation, but a meditation for writing. We begin with a half hour of yoga, which gets us into a state of inner awareness (it's also good to move, to be physical so that we can spend the rest of the day sitting down and not get bad backs). Then everyone goes to their seats and closes their eyes and I guide them to an inner concentration. Then I give an exercise which each person applies to their own work. It's incredible how the writing pours out. Sometimes I look around and each person is in their own world, you feel that they are miles away . . . it's incredible, the power. I make them explore and explore until they have explored so much that they are masterful.

INTERVIEWER: Criticism is never a part of the process?

FORNES: Not at all. I give criticism, when, for instance, I see that a person is blocked or in a rut. But I feel more like a coach for a sport who gives instruction, like telling a swimmer his elbow is not moving enough. This year, for the first time, we also give Monday-night cold readings of first drafts and I will give criticism on a first draft. During the summer the students do further work on their plays and in September we have another reading.

INTERVIEWER: Before you began the Lab workshops, did you utilize exercises in your own work?

FORNES: Since I began writing I have always played games. The very first time I sat down to write I looked around and saw a recipe book. I opened the book and using those ingredients I wrote a crazy story. Before that, when I was upset I would write a letter to a friend. The letter became something else, it was a way of writing. That writing was always personal. The first thing I wrote that was not a personal outburst was a game that I had set up for myself with words. My first play, *Tango Palace*, was an idea that came from something very personal: a feeling about the relation-ship between a mentor of some sort and a student. That came from my inner energy. I didn't need any provoked inspiration. But my next play, *Promenade* [1965], began by my putting some charac-ters and places on index cards. I played a game with the cards and this made it easy for me to write. I have a playful nature; I have never been able to do things because it is my duty to do them. If I can find a way to do my duty by playing a game, then I can manage.

INTERVIEWER: You once said that the novel is more delicate in structure than a play. Would you elaborate?

FORNES: I never said that. I don't know anything about the structure of a novel. I do think a play has to have a tough structure in the sense that people are always messing with it. You hand a play to a director and he or she interprets, then the actor interprets, the audience interprets, and the play has to stand up through all of this. Maybe that's what makes novels different, but I don't think they necessarily have a more delicate structure.

INTERVIEWER: When did you discover that it was essential for you to direct your own work?

FORNES: I didn't know I had to direct my own work right away, but I did find out immediately that the position of the playwright is unbearable. I went to the very first rehearsal of a work of mine. And as the actors started moving around with the script, an actress stood behind a chair, and I said,

"Oh, wonderful!" Then I jumped up from my seat and said to her, "Here . . . try this!" I went on stage to where she was standing, positioned her, and said, "Oh, yes!" Everyone stared at me. I had never been to a rehearsal of anything in my life. I had simply seen something that I wanted the actress to push a little further; they all looked at me as if I had committed the worst crime. The director came to me and said, "Irene, I am very happy to hear any comments you need to make. Bring a notebook, write everything down and at the end of rehearsal we'll meet and you can tell me what your thoughts are." I thought he was insane. Then I thought he must be right because everyone around seemed to accept what he was saying to me. No one intervened or said, "Gracious, why are you telling her to do *that?*" We did meet afterward for coffee. He never understood a word I was saying and if he understood, he said, "No, I don't agree." I thought, "How could you not agree? Who are you not to agree?" I had been dealing with these characters for months and he suddenly wanted me to accept that I didn't know anything about them, to say, "Of course, you people know much more than I."

To me it was a world of madness. I learned as a playwright you "behave." You learn how to give up your play to people who "know better." I know there are many writers who do not direct, but to assume that just because you are a playwright you *can't* direct! And people do. I just received an award for directing, but people still say to me, "Imagine what your play would have been like if it had been directed by someone else. You would have had an objective eye." The stupidity of that statement. I think people simply feel that the playwright has too much power.

INTERVIEWER: In what sense?

FORNES: The creator is like God in relation to the creation. The playwright has a lot of power, but at the same time, the playwright is very gullible and naïve. I love playwrights, they are like angels really. When they are mistreated, when they are told, "GET OUT!" they go, poor darlings. Playwrights are told they don't know anything about theater. How can they write a play if they don't know anything about theater? It is true that there is a technique to directing actors, but a playwright can learn to deal with that. In fact, I have always felt a liaison with the actors, because the lines have to go *through* the actor. The actors must say the lines you have created until something begins to trigger inside them; in that sense, the actors are much more connected to playwrights than to directors. I have watched directors make wrong choices in rehearsal, and often the actors begin, instinctually, to say things as I thought I had written them. Then the director sometimes says, "No, no. That's not it." Often I wanted to go to the actors afterwards and says, "I think you are doing right," because I felt a connection, an alliance. I never did so because I thought it should be done in the open or not at all. I thought I could be helpful in a different way. At some point, I just decided that I would direct my own work or my work would not be done.

INTERVIEWER: Do you feel that playwrights should educate themselves about directing and acting techniques?

FORNES: I think every playwright needs to. First of all, you are not a good playwright unless you do all of those things. There are many reasons why playwrights, given the opportunity, might not *want* to direct: Perhaps they don't like dealing with so many people, or they're impatient; maybe they prefer somebody else to do it. If it's the playwright's choice and they prefer not to direct I don't think they have to. But to say they cannot direct! At the Padua Hills Theater Workshop where I go every summer you don't need to ask permission to direct your own play. On the contrary, if you don't want to direct, you have to *find* a director. We don't tell people, "You must direct" . . . they just do. It's like making your own sandwich. Because of this, the students see from the start that they *can* direct their own plays.

INTERVIEWER: Are women playwrights more intimidated by the idea of directing their own work because of the traditional notion of the director being the "father" of the production?

FORNES: I don't think so, because the playwright is the "woman" of the theater.

INTERVIEWER: Whether the playwright is male or female?

FORNES: Yes. The playwright is the woman and the director is the husband. Lanford Wilson pointed that out to me. I was explaining about how, as a playwright, you feel that someone is taking you out to have a "nice day" in a "nice place." The idea is "You be a nice girl and I'm going to take care of you." I thought that was because I am a woman, and Lanford said, "I feel the same way. I feel I am a girl; I have to be nice to this guy who is going to do nice by me; he's going to choose the right actors for my play because I don't know what I'm doing. I am very talented, but I don't really understand anything." I thought, "Well, perhaps it is because Lanford is not forceful enough." But then I was on a panel with another playwright who had had several plays on Broadway, and who had done quite a lot of commercial work. He looked like a business man, a big-shot executive. The panel was discussing the position of the playwright and this man, who was so masculine, so firm and definite with his white shirt and proper suit and strong voice, said that he understood the position of women in society because as a playwright, he was treated as a woman. So I am assuming that the playwright is the woman of the theater.

I do think it's more difficult for women directors than male directors. First of all, a producer has to believe that as a director, you will be in charge, that you will be able to control the cast, the crew, the production. In my case, they never would believe that I could control anything, and it's true. I don't have any control over anything *except* my art. I never say, "*You*, go there!" But I work with people who believe in my work and then I have a power that is almost hypnotic.

INTERVIEWER: Any advice for playwrights who are interested in directing their own work?

FORNES: Do it. You don't know how to talk to an actor? Take acting classes, find out what the actor needs. Technique is not a language of the gods. I think it has always been difficult for playwrights to take that control because it is hard enough to get your play produced without coming in with conditions. You learn to direct in the same way you learn to write plays. Work as a stage manager, watch how other directors work, find out about the elements of theater and how to deal with light designers, set designers, space. You cannot go into a theater expecting to direct merely because you wrote the play. You would not be doing a service to the play. By the time I insisted I would direct, I had taken acting classes at Actor's Studio, I had done costumes. I had been involved enough in theater so that I felt I could put together a reading. My first directing experience, *Molly's Dream* [1968] at New Dramatists, was essentially a reading—there were no reviews or publicity, and only five performances. It wasn't until later that I directed something finished, and then I had to work with lighting designers, etc. But I do have a good eye, and that's important. I was able quickly to ask for what I wanted and when the light designers would show me something, I knew whether it was good or not. I remember what a surprise it was to work with them.

INTERVIEWER: Did your new understanding of the technical side of theater affect your writing? Did it open your imagination?

FORNES: Yes. For instance, you have to find out what lights are all about or you may destroy scenes. But you see, I was a painter before. The stage for me is a very beautiful place, nice to look at. And space is very important. I'm very picky with actors. I will keep on positioning them—a little to the left, no, three inches more . . . —because for me, it's as important as focusing a camera. You reach a point, pass it, go back a little and ZING! it's in focus.

INTERVIEWER: Is this how the photographic freezes between scenes evolved in your play *Mud* [1983]?

FORNES: I did the play in Padua Hills, outdoors, and I could not have blackouts because I had scheduled myself in daylight time. The freezes were a way to change scenes. I kept them in the New York production because there was something about the freezes that I liked.

INTERVIEWER: What about the monochromatic quality? . . .

FORNES: The drab color also had to do with the original daylight production, which started when the sun was about to set and ended when the light became gray. The light changed during the performance, and the audiences always felt that it was deliberate because later in the play, everything becomes gray. The direct sunlight also created a quality. In the New York production, the clothes were drab and the set was white. The costume designer made the character Lloyd's clothes streaky, dirty. At some moment in rehearsal I felt he looked like a painting. I said to the designer, "Let's go with this . . . " and she gave Harry and Mae's costumes the same look.

INTERVIEWER: Would you discuss the eroticism in your work?

FORNES: That really began to happen with *A Visit*, which was an attempt to do something erotic. There is sexuality in the earlier work, like *Successful Life of Three* [1965], but it's more cartoonish. I don't like *A Visit* too much now, because it was composed from other people's writing and I violated their intentions. It was something I did in a playful way, almost like a party piece for friends. People have wanted to publish it and I have had some offers for productions, but I have refused. I was using material from Victorian novels, and I found there was something hot about the emotions in them. I took sections and made a collage of other people's writings. This completely changed the authors' meanings. I turned their Victorian words into something erotic. The men wore porcelain phalluses and the women porcelain breasts. The designer who made them put a little blue line around the tip of the penises and nipples. It was mischievous, playful, and I think it was my way of breaking through a kind of shyness about erotic things—because one always feels shy. To do something all the way out, like *A Visit*—which was completely erotic and completely bold, although it was in good taste because I don't like pornography—freed me.

I think, too, that as you get older you become freer sexually. When you are young you are afraid if you write something like *A Visit* people will call you on the phone and say, you know . . . [laughter]. But when you get older, you don't care. First of all, nobody calls you on the phone [laughter]. I feel that the older I get, the more shameless I feel. And in a sense, more pure. For instance, I am more interested in my work now. When I was younger, I was more interested in romance. The hours and hours I would spend being tormented by somebody or trying to pursue someone, fantasizing or imagining what the words meant. Now I watch that in others and it seems like rather odd behavior. Not that I am indifferent to love or romance. I am just not obsessed. I have more time to concentrate. I watch young people and it's endless, constant, they are like little animals, like dogs in heat. I think my writing is more passionate now, because when you are younger there is a fear of exposure and you protect yourself.

A play is so hot, so passionate; the Greeks, Shakespeare, opera have hot, hot passions, but very little sexuality. Today, sexuality is dealt with in pornography, in a cold, obscene way. The possibility of sexual drama is something unexplored. I am freer to examine these passions now because of the workshop. Many of the exercises, the meditations I do, are intended to work in a visceral way. I employ exercises to root the writer into their own organism, their own humanity, rather than the intellect. Writing is an intellectual process, so it is good to *root* the process into your stomach, your heart, your bowels. It is difficult sometimes for the younger women in the workshop. They are in a room of Hispanic men. Because of my age, I set an example: Whenever something erotic comes up in my own work, I read it. At first they all go, "Whoo . . . " It may be better for the younger women not to read when something erotic comes up in their work because it's true, when women are younger, they have to put up with the guys saying "Hey, baby . . . " But when I read my erotic passages aloud as an example, as a possibility in writing, at least I have given my female students permission to be fully *present* as writers, even if they choose not to read that material out loud. It may be that because of these exercises my own writing is becoming more erotic. Even so, I don't think, "Oh, here comes the erotic scene." I just write a scene of Harry [*Mud*] eating soup one day, and a scene where he is sexually aroused and masturbating the next.

After I had written the erotic scenes for *Mud* and *Sarita* I realized that the sexuality is very unconventional. They are not scenes that represent a typical sexuality, they are special moments, and those moments are theatrical. I probably owe—and I say *owe* because I think it's something important that has come into my writing—those strong sexual scenes to *A Visit*.

INTERVIEWER: Do you believe there is a female aesthetic in drama?

FORNES: How could there possibly not be? Not only is there a women's aesthetic, each woman has her own aesthetic and so does each man. It's like saying "Is there a Hispanic aesthetic?" Of course there is. Your aesthetic is different from mine—each person has their own universe—but how could we, as women, have nothing in common? That's not possible. We are different from a man, who is not a woman, who has never had a menstrual period in his life.

INTERVIEWER: Do you feel that a gender bias may exist in theater criticism, are women's plays often accused of being poorly structured "non-plays" when the playwrights may have intentionally broken form?

FORNES: You have to remember that we are dealing with theater and theater is the backward art. Theater is one hundred, two hundred years behind the times. There was an American girl living in Paris who wanted to translate *Promenade*, and have it produced in France. She came to New York to meet me and during her visit she went to [the] Lincoln Center [Branch of the New York Public] Library to read some old reviews of the play. She was amazed when she discovered that *Promenade* was considered an avant-garde piece. I told her, "It's because we are backward in the theater." If *Promenade* connects to anything, it's with movies of the thirties, popular art from the thirties—which is commercial! When the play was done in 1965, and then again in 1970, it was called "The musical of the seventies" to warn people that they were going to see something odd. I am sure people *still* consider that play odd.

I have a discussion every night after the performance of *The Danube* at The American Place Theater [1984]. I love doing it because I like to hear what audiences think. It's not pleasant, often the response is "What does it mean?" or "Why didn't you make it clear?" or "I'm *depressed.*" The triumph came just last night. A woman (one of those who said earlier that she did not understand the play) said, "Frankly it is ex*cru*ciating. Could you tell me why anyone would produce this play?" I was glad that [artistic director] Winn Handman was there; I let him explain why he produced it. After a few more comments, the discussion closed and the same woman said in praise, "This is really an important play and I have to tell you that the images are so powerful." She was quite honest, even though what she said was contradictory. I think at first she felt, "If this doesn't tell me a clear story it is not theater. If this doesn't conform to everything I've seen previously in theater, then the playwright must have made a mistake." Perhaps when she heard the other comments she realized that her notion of theater was not necessarily what theater is; other things count also.

INTERVIEWER: Are the public discussions required by The American Place Theater or do you routinely attempt after-play discussions with the audience?

FORNES: They are set up by The American Place. Usually the playwright is asked to participate in a few of the discussions, but writers often feel as if they are being attacked, they feel defensive. There are times when the criticism is unanimous and harsh, and I have also felt from time to time like saying "You didn't like the play? Too bad!" But for the most part I like to hear what the audience has to say because you seldom get a chance to find out what people think about your work. For instance, I used to assume that when people liked the play they saw it in exactly the same way I see it. But that's not always true. I think it's very important to find out what people see in your work. I like to explain things, too. It helps me formulate my ideas, to put even the obvious into words.

INTERVIEWER: What do the more conventional critics find disturbing in your work?

FORNES: I was thinking about it just today. I wanted to discuss it with my students. I was thinking about what makes conventional theater. Let's say you were interested in doing a play that would be accepted by large numbers of people. What is it, then, that you should concentrate on? I realized that what makes my plays unacceptable to people is the form more than the content. My content is usually not outrageous. I think it's mild! *The Danube* is a play about a nice family that is being destroyed. Why don't nice middle-class people feel, "Oh, those poor darlings! That nice boy Paul and his girlfriend Eve, they were so good to their father and he loved them and this thing came along and destroyed their nice home . . . how terrible." That is the story of that play. I think people are sometimes afraid and suspicious. They don't know what bomb you have planted in your play. There is no reason for that. *Fefu and Her Friends,* although it has very profound things in it, is a middle-class play. It is about nice middle-class girls from Connecticut, not about people saying "Let's destroy the world." It's mild. What makes people almost vicious must be the form. Because there are many plays that have outrageous things going on, but they have a conventional structure so people don't care. Isn't that curious?

INTERVIEWER: In a recent *Performing Arts Journal* symposium, you stated, "We have to reconcile ourselves to the idea that the protagonist of a play can be a woman." Would you elaborate?

FORNES: Even women are not aware of how important that is. Some women feel they must write plays in which there is a feminist statement, that they must attempt to clarify a situation in which there is prejudice against women. But they want to see situations where a woman is at a disadvantage and then becomes a victor. They are not interested anymore in seeing cases of women who suffer or succumb. I see their point. It's nice to see the person you are rooting for win all the battles, but at the same time, it is a little childish. I don't believe that the artist, the creator, is saying, "This character has perished, therefore all humanity will perish." I am very sad when I see a film or read a story in which the character I'm identifying with dies. But I don't feel that something has been killed inside of me because the character died. My ability to see their death as unnecessary is intact regardless of the pain I may feel about their death. I believe when you portray an unnecessary death, you are speaking on behalf of the person's life, the person's prime.

INTERVIEWER: Would you discuss that in terms of the female protagonist in *Mud,* who is shot by one of her lovers at the end of the play? One critic said the message of the play was directed towards women: "Don't try, they'll never let you get away with it." This critic felt it was quite a despairing play.

FORNES: I see Mae differently than many people did. I love her very much, I'm completely identified with her, but she is *not* an angel. I wrote the last scene just the way I saw it. At the end of the story, Mae is after something; she is learning, and that is so dear you cannot blame her for it. *Mud* is not an anti-male play that says men are pigs. It is also not a feminist message play about how Mae tries to liberate herself from these two men who will not let her develop. They are not keeping her down. She can leave any time she wants. It isn't that she is a brilliant woman. She says that she has a difficult time remembering things, she can't pass the tests at school. I think if she had got away she would probably have come back to Harry and Lloyd. She loves them, they love her, that's their life. When Lloyd shoots her it is not because he doesn't want her to get away and develop herself. It's because she is leaving and he would die without her. He must not let her do this. I think that when you write you must really open your eyes and see: Is it true that they would not let her get away? Does Lloyd's response grow out of the play? Of course it does. Of course Lloyd is very annoyed in the beginning that she is pursuing her studies. But it is not this annoyance that leads him to kill her. I don't think Mae really would have improved herself if she got away. What's wonderful about Mae is her love for knowledge. Knowledge is the beloved thing. She is not an artist, she worships art and wants to go where she can visit museums, et cetera. There is something noble and beautiful in this aspect of her character and I don't think it has been dealt with in plays or in fiction. Mae is a pursuer of angels, it doesn't mean she wants to *be* an angel, to grow wings and have magic powers.

In terms of the question about the female protagonist, I feel that what is important about this play is that Mae is the central character. It says something about women's place in the world, not because she is good or a heroine, not because she is oppressed by men or because the men "won't let her get away with it," but simply because she is the *center* of that play. It is her mind that matters throughout the play, and the whole play exists because her little mind wants to see the light, not even to see it because she wants to be illuminated, but so she can revere it. It is because of that mind, Mae's mind, *a woman's mind,* that that play exists. To me that is a more important step toward redeeming women's position in the world than whether or not *Mud* has a feminist theme, which it does not. The theme is just a mind that wants to exist and has difficulties. The difficulties have nothing to do with gender, but the fact that this mind is in a woman's body makes an important feminist point. I believe that to show a woman at the center of a situation, at the center of the universe, is a much more important feminist statement than to put Mae in a situation that shows her in an unfavorable position from which she escapes, or to say that she is noble and the men around her are not.

INTERVIEWER: What did you mean when you said, "It is impossible to aim at an audience when writing a play?"

FORNES: It's impossible because you can never predict the audience reaction. People think they are writing a comedy and then nobody laughs. If nobody laughs, it's not a comedy. That's why many plays fail. People spend millions of dollars to put plays on Broadway. If people knew what would succeed, none of those plays would fail.

INTERVIEWER: You have said that you would be willing to spend your entire life in poverty and struggle in order to be a working playwright. Have you had to make sacrifices in order to devote yourself to writing for the theater?

FORNES: I haven't made sacrifices, really. It's not as if I chose writing as a career to make money. There *are* people who can write ad copy or soap operas, I couldn't, I would die. I might be able to do it technically, but I could not spiritually. I feel I've never had any choice. When I'm not doing something that comes deeply from me, I get bored. When I get bored I get distracted, and when I get distracted, I become depressed. It's a natural resistance, and it insures your integrity. You die when you are faking it, and you are alive when you are truthful. I consider myself lucky to have been able to survive financially doing what I want to do. Sometimes it's been very, very tight, and sometimes it's been scary because I've had to go into debt. Still, I don't consider it a sacrifice.

# August Wilson

August Wilson was born in 1945 and raised on "The Hill," the black ghetto of Pittsburgh. He dropped out of school in the ninth grade, but spent much of his time reading while supporting himself with odd jobs; he also began to write poems and stories on the changing problems of race relations in America. He founded a theater in Pittsburgh in the mid-1960s, and then founded Black Horizons Theater Company in Minneapolis in 1968. His first play, *Jitney,* was staged in 1978. Wilson then applied to study playwriting at the Eugene O'Neill Theater Center's National Playwright's Conference, where he submitted the text of *Ma Rainey's Black Bottom,* which was read by the eminent African-American stage director Lloyd Richards, who had brought Lorraine Hansberry's *A Raisin in the Sun* to Broadway in 1959. Richards read the play and produced it at the Yale Repertory Theater in 1984 before bringing it to Broadway. *Ma Rainey's Black Bottom* is the first of four plays Wilson has written examining African-American history in the twentieth century; it was followed by *Fences* (1985)—which won the Pulitzer Prize—*Joe Turner's Come and Gone* (1986), and *The Piano Lesson* (1987). More recently, *Two Trains Running* opened in 1991.

## Fences (1985)

Set in 1957, the action of *Fences* sits on the brink of the civil rights movement and outlines the challenges facing African Americans whose legal freedoms had yet to become a social reality. The play is—as its final funeral scene implies—deeply reminiscent of Arthur Miller's *Death of a Salesman,* suggesting that realism is in many ways still the dominant mode of American theater. Like Miller's play, it is about a hardworking man whose responsibilities to his family fall athwart his dreams of happiness, a conflict that finally costs him both. But while Miller's Willy Loman is victimized by his belief in the "American Dream," Wilson's Troy Maxson lives his life on the underside of that dream. Thrown out of his home at fourteen by his father, Troy moved north to Pittsburgh; unable to find work, he made a living through petty crime until he was caught and sentenced to fifteen years' imprisonment. On his release, he found his wife and child and began a career in baseball, playing in the Negro Leagues. Integration came to baseball, and when the play opens in 1957, Jackie Robinson, Hank Aaron, and a young Roberto Clemente are all playing in the major leagues—but it is too late for Troy. He is now working as a trash collector, fighting the company to let African Americans drive the garbage trucks as well as haul the trash.

Like Willy Loman, too, Troy is a family man. The family is Troy's refuge from the racism and defeat of his daily life, and his proudest accomplishment as well. He has forced himself to shoulder the responsibility of providing for his children, and of loving his wife, a responsibility that lends his life purpose and direction. As he says to Rose in Act One, "Woman . . . I do the best I can do. . . . We go upstairs in that room at night . . . and I fall down on you and try to blast a hole into forever. I get up Monday morning . . . find my lunch on the table. I go out. Make my way. Find my strength to carry me through to the next Friday." But as Rose notes, the world is changing around Troy, and these changes threaten the life that he has made. His son Cory is being recruited on a football scholarship. Troy, his own exploitation by the white-dominated sports industry still in mind, forces Cory to quit the team, and so to pass up the scholarship and the chance to go to college. Nor does Troy shoulder his family life easily. He cares for his mentally handicapped brother Gabriel, but eventually has him committed to a mental hospital in order to get half of his government pension. And despite his love for and gratitude to Rose, he has an affair with another woman, who dies delivering their daughter. Much as family life has been Troy's salvation, it has also hemmed him in—in the dead-end jobs, the constant poverty, the fence he builds at the end of the play. He risks it all for the chance of some happiness with Alberta—and loses: Rose takes in Troy's daughter: "From right now . . . this child got a mother. But you a womanless man." He fights Cory, and much as his own father had thrown him out of the house, forces his own son to leave as well.

The joyous, mournful conclusion of *Fences*—when Gabriel dances Troy's soul into heaven—perhaps provides the best commentary on the life of Troy Maxson. Suffering the indignities and humiliation of racism throughout his life, Troy built a stable home for himself, a life. As a defense against the world, perhaps, that life was bound to crumble, particularly as pressure of social change forced Troy to deal with a future he had never imagined. But in Wilson's final image, Troy's life is celebrated, a thing of rough and rugged beauty, demanding our attention and respect.

# —Fences—
## August Wilson

## —CHARACTERS—

TROY MAXSON
JIM BONO, *Troy's friend*
ROSE, *Troy's wife*
LYONS, *Troy's oldest son by previous marriage*
GABRIEL, *Troy's brother*
CORY, *Troy and Rose's son*
RAYNELL, *Troy's daughter*

## —SETTING—

*The setting is the yard which fronts the only entrance to the* MAXSON *household, an ancient two-story brick house set back off a small alley in a big-city neighborhood. The entrance to the house is gained by two or three steps leading to a wooden porch badly in need of paint.*

*A relatively recent addition to the house and running its full width, the porch lacks congruence. It is a sturdy porch with a flat roof. One or two chairs of dubious value sit at one end where the kitchen window opens onto the porch. An old-fashioned icebox stands silent guard at the opposite end.*

*The yard is a small dirt yard, partially fenced, except for the last scene, with a wooden sawhorse, a pile of lumber, and other fence-building equipment set off to the side. Opposite is a tree from which hangs a ball made of rags. A baseball bat leans against the tree. Two oil drums serve as garbage receptacles and sit near the house at right to complete the setting.*

## —THE PLAY—

Near the turn of the century, the destitute of Europe sprang on the city with tenacious claws and an honest and solid dream. The city devoured them. They swelled its belly until it burst into a thousand furnaces and sewing machines, a thousand butcher shops and bakers' ovens, a thousand churches and hospitals and funeral parlors and money-lenders. The city grew. It nourished itself and offered each man a partnership limited only by his talent, his guile, and his willingness and capacity for hard work. For the immigrants of Europe, a dream dared and won true.

The descendants of African slaves were offered no such welcome or participation. They came from places called the Carolinas and the Virginias, Georgia, Alabama, Mississippi, and Tennessee. They came strong, eager, searching. The city rejected them and they fled and settled along the riverbanks and under bridges in shallow, ramshackle houses made of sticks and tar-paper. They collected rags and wood. They sold the use of their muscles and their bodies. They cleaned houses and washed clothes, they shined shoes, and in quiet desperation and vengeful pride, they stole, and lived in pursuit of their own dream. That they could breathe free, finally, and stand to meet life with the force of dignity and whatever eloquence the heart could call upon.

By 1957, the hard-won victories of the European immigrants had solidified the industrial might of America. War had been confronted and won with new energies that used loyalty and patriotism as its fuel. Life was rich, full, and flourishing. The Milwaukee Braves won the World Series, and the hot winds of change that would make the sixties a turbulent, racing, dangerous, and provocative decade had not yet begun to blow full.

## —ACT ONE—

SCENE I

*It is 1957.* TROY *and* BONO *enter the yard, engaged in conversation.* TROY *is fifty-three years old, a large man with thick, heavy hands; it is this largeness that he strives to fill out and make an accommodation with. Together with his blackness, his largeness informs his sensibilities and the choices he has made in his life.*

*Of the two men,* BONO *is obviously the follower. His commitment to their friendship of thirty-odd years is rooted in his admiration of* TROY's *honesty, capacity for hard work, and his strength, which* BONO *seeks to emulate.*

*It is Friday night, payday, and the one night of the week the two men engage in a ritual of talk and drink.* TROY *is usually the most talkative and at times he can be crude and almost vulgar, though he is capable of rising to profound heights of expression. The men carry lunch buckets and wear or carry burlap aprons and are dressed in clothes suitable to their jobs as garbage collectors.*

BONO: Troy, you ought to stop that lying!
TROY: I ain't lying! The nigger had a watermelon this big.

*(He indicates with his hands.)*

Talking about . . . "What watermelon, Mr. Rand?" I liked to fell out! "What watermelon, Mr. Rand?" . . . And it sitting there big as life.

BONO: What did Mr. Rand say?

TROY: Ain't said nothing. Figure if the nigger too dumb to know he carrying a watermelon, he wasn't gonna get much sense out of him. Trying to hide that great big old watermelon under his coat. Afraid to let the white man see him carry it home.

BONO: I'm like you . . . I ain't got no time for them kind of people.

TROY: Now what he look like getting made cause he see the man from the union talking to Mr. Rand?

BONO: He come to me talking about . . . "Maxson gonna get us fired." I told him to get away from me with that. He walked away from me calling you a troublemaker. What Mr. Rand say?

TROY: Ain't said nothing. He told me to go down the Commissioner's office next Friday. They called me down there to see them.

BONO: Well, as long as you got your complaint filed, they can't fire you. That's what one of them white fellows tell me.

TROY: I ain't worried about them firing me. They gonna fire me cause I asked a question? That's all I did. I went to Mr. Rand and asked him, "Why? Why you got the white mens driving and the colored lifting?" Told him, "what's the matter, don't I count? You think only white fellows got sense enough to drive a truck. That ain't no paper job! Hell, anybody can drive a truck. How come you got all whites driving and the colored lifting?" He told me "take it to the union." Well, hell, that's what I done! Now they wanna come up with this pack of lies.

BONO: I told Brownie if the man come and ask him any questions . . . just tell the truth! It ain't nothing but something they done trumped up on you cause you filed a complaint on them.

TROY: Brownie don't understand nothing. All I want them to do is change the job description. Give everybody a chance to drive the truck. Brownie can't see that. He ain't got that much sense.

BONO: How you figure he be making out with that gal be up at Taylors' all the time . . . that Alberta gal?

TROY: Same as you and me. Getting just as much as we is. Which is to say nothing.

BONO: It is, huh? I figure you doing a little better than me . . . and I ain't saying what I'm doing.

TROY: Aw, nigger, look here . . . I know you. If you had got anywhere near that gal, twenty minutes later you be looking to tell somebody. And the first one you gonna tell . . . that you gonna want to brag to . . . is gonna be me.

BONO: I ain't saying that. I see where you be eyeing her.

TROY: I eye all the women. I don't miss nothing. Don't never let nobody tell you Troy Maxson don't eye the women.

BONO: You been doing more than eyeing her. You done bought her a drink or two.

TROY: Hell yeah, I bought her a drink! What that mean? I bought you one, too. What that mean cause I buy her a drink? I'm just being polite.

BONO: It's alright to buy her one drink. That's what you call being polite. But when you wanna be buying two or three . . . that's what you call eyeing her.

TROY: Look here, as long as you known me . . . you ever known me to chase after women?

BONO: Hell yeah! Long as I done known you. You forgetting I knew you when.

TROY: Naw, I'm talking about since I been married to Rose?

BONO: Oh, not since you been married to Rose. Now, that's the truth, there. I can say that.

TROY: Alright then! Case closed.

BONO: I see you be walking up around Alberta's house. You supposed to be at Taylors' and you be walking up around there.

TROY: What you watching where I'm walking for? I ain't watching after you.

BONO: I seen you walking around there more than once.

TROY: Hell, you liable to see me walking anywhere! That don't mean nothing cause you see me walking around there.

BONO: Where she come from anyway? She just kinda showed up one day.

TROY: Tallahassee. You can look at her and tell she one of them Florida gals. They got some big healthy women down there. Grow them right up out the ground. Got a little bit of Indian in her. Most of them niggers down in Florida got some Indian in them.

BONO: I don't know about that Indian part. But she damn sure big and healthy. Woman wear some big stockings. Got them great big old legs and hips as wide as the Mississippi River.

TROY: Legs don't mean nothing. You don't do nothing but push them out of the way. But them hips cushion the ride!

BONO: Troy, you ain't got no sense.

TROY: It's the truth! Like you riding on Goodyears!

(ROSE *enters from the house. She is ten years younger than* TROY, *her devotion to him stems from her recognition of the possibilities of her life without him: a succession of abusive men and their babies, a life of partying and running the streets, the Church, or aloneness with its attendant pain and frustration. She recognizes* TROY's *spirit as a fine and illuminating one and she either ignores or forgives his faults, only some of which she recognizes. Though she doesn't drink, her presence is an integral part of the Friday night rituals. She alternates between the porch and the kitchen, where supper preparations are under way.*)

ROSE: What you all out here getting into?

TROY: What you worried about what we getting into for? This is men talk, woman.

ROSE: What I care what you all talking about? Bono, you gonna stay for supper?

BONO: No, I thank you, Rose. But Lucille say she cooking up a pot of pigfeet.

TROY: Pigfeet! Hell, I'm going home with you! Might even stay the night if you got some pigfeet. You got something in there to top them pigfeet, Rose?

ROSE: I'm cooking up some chicken. I got some chicken and collard greens.

TROY: Well, go on back in the house and let me and Bono finish what we was talking about. This is men talk. I got some talk for you later. You know what kind of talk I mean. You go on and powder it up.

ROSE: Troy Maxson, don't you start that now!

TROY: (*Puts his arm around her.*) Aw, woman . . . come here. Look here, Bono . . . when I met this woman . . . I got out that place, say, "Hitch up my pony, saddle up my mare . . .

there's a woman out there for me somewhere. I looked here. Looked there. Saw Rose and latched on to her." I latched on to her and told her—I'm gonna tell you the truth—I told her, "Baby, I don't wanna marry, I just wanna be your man." Rose told me . . . tell him what you told me, Rose.

ROSE: I told him if he wasn't the marrying kind, then move out 120 the way so the marrying kind could find me.

TROY: That's what she told me. "Nigger, you in my way. You blocking the view! Move out the way so I can find me a husband." I thought it over two or three days. Come back—

ROSE: Ain't no two or three days nothing. You was back the same night.

TROY: Come back, told her . . . "Okay, baby . . . but I'm gonna buy me a banty rooster and put him out there in the backyard . . . and when he see a stranger come, he'll flap his wings and crow . . ." Look here, Bono, I could watch the 130 front door by myself . . . it was that back door I was worried about.

ROSE: Troy, you ought not talk like that. Troy ain't doing nothing but telling a lie.

TROY: Only thing is . . . when we first got married . . . forget the rooster . . . we ain't had no yard!

BONO: I hear you tell it. Me and Lucille was staying down there on Logan Street. Had two rooms with the outhouse in the back. I ain't mind the outhouse none. But when that goddamn wind blow through there in the winter . . . that's what 140 I'm talking about! To this day I wonder why in the hell I ever stayed down there for six long years. But see, I didn't know I could do no better. I thought only white folks had inside toilets and things.

ROSE: There's a lot of people don't know they can do no better than they doing now. That's just something you got to learn. A lot of folks still shop at Bella's.

TROY: Ain't nothing wrong with shopping at Bella's. She got fresh food.

ROSE: I ain't said nothing about if she got fresh food. I'm talk-150 ing about what she charge. She charge ten cents more than the A&P.

TROY: The A&P ain't never done nothing for me. I spends my money where I'm treated right. I go down to Bella, say, "I need a loaf of bread, I'll pay you Friday." She give it to me. What sense that make when I got money to go and spend it somewhere else and ignore the person who done right by me? That ain't in the Bible.

ROSE: We ain't talking about what's in the Bible. What sense it make to shop there when she overcharge?

160 TROY: You shop where you want to. I'll do my shopping where the people been good to me.

ROSE: Well, I don't think it's right for her to overcharge. That's all I was saying.

BONO: Look here . . . I got to get on. Lucille going be raising all kind of hell.

TROY: Where you going, nigger? We ain't finished this pint. Come here, finish this pint.

BONO: Well, hell, I am . . . if you ever turn the bottle loose.

TROY: (*Hands him the bottle.*) The only thing I say about the 170 A&P is I'm glad Cory got that job down there. Help him take care of his school clothes and things. Gabe done moved out and things getting tight around here. He got that job. . . . He can start to look out for himself.

ROSE: Cory done went and got recruited by a college football team.

TROY: I told that boy about that football stuff. The white man ain't gonna let him get nowhere with that football. I told him when he first come to me with it. Now you come telling me he done went and got more tied up in it. He ought to go and get recruited in how to fix cars or something where he can 180 make a living.

ROSE: He ain't talking about making no living playing football. It's just something the boys in school do. They gonna send a recruiter by to talk to you. He'll tell you he ain't talking about making no living playing football. It's a honor to be recruited.

TROY: It ain't gonna get him nowhere. Bono'll tell you that.

BONO: If he be like you in the sports . . . he's gonna be alright. Ain't but two men ever played baseball as good as you. That's Babe Ruth and Josh Gibson. Them's the only two 190 men ever hit more home runs than you.

TROY: What it ever get me? Ain't got a pot to piss in or a window to throw it out of.

ROSE: Times have changed since you was playing baseball, Troy. That was before the war. Times have changed a lot since then.

TROY: How in hell they done changed?

ROSE: They got lots of colored boys playing ball now. Baseball and football.

BONO: You right about that, Rose. Times have changed, Troy. 200 You just come along too early.

TROY: There ought not never have been no time called too early! Now you take that fellow . . . what's that fellow they had playing right field for the Yankees back then? You know who I'm talking about, Bono. Used to play right field for the Yankees.

ROSE: Selkirk?

TROY: Selkirk! That's it! Man batting .269, understand? .269. What kind of sense that make? I was hitting .432 with thirty-seven home runs! Man batting .269 and playing right field 210 for the Yankees! I saw Josh Gibson's daughter yesterday. She walking around with raggedy shoes on her feet. Now I bet you Selkirk's daughter ain't walking around with raggedy shoes on her feet! I bet you that!

ROSE: They got a lot of colored baseball players now. Jackie Robinson was the first. Folks had to wait for Jackie Robinson.

TROY: I done seen a hundred niggers play baseball better than Jackie Robinson. Hell, I know some teams Jackie Robinson couldn't even make! What you talking about Jackie Robin-220 son. Jackie Robinson wasn't nobody. I'm talking about if you could play ball then they ought to have let you play. Don't care what color you were. Come telling me I come along too early. If you could play . . . then they ought to have let you play.

(TROY *takes a long drink from the bottle.*)

ROSE: You gonna drink yourself to death. You don't need to be drinking like that.

TROY: Death ain't nothing. I done seen him. Done wrassled with him. You can't tell me nothing about death. Death ain't nothing but a fastball on the outside corner. And you know 230 what I'll do to that! Lookee here, Bono . . . am I lying? You get one of them fastballs, about waist high, over the outside corner of the plate where you can get the meat of the bat on it . . . and good god! You can kiss it goodbye. Now, am I lying?

BONO: Naw, you telling the truth there. I seen you do it.

TROY: If I'm lying . . . that 450 feet worth of lying!

(Pause.)

That's all death is to me. A fastball on the outside corner.

ROSE: I don't know why you want to get on talking about death.

240 TROY: Ain't nothing wrong with talking about death. That's part of life. Everybody gonna die. You gonna die, I'm gonna die. Bono's gonna die. Hell, we all gonna die.

ROSE: But you ain't got to talk about it. I don't like to talk about it.

TROY: You the one brought it up. Me and Bono was talking about baseball . . . you tell me I'm gonna drink myself to death. Ain't that right, Bono? You know I don't drink this but one night out of the week. That's Friday night. I'm gonna drink just enough to where I can handle it. Then I
250 cuts it loose. I leave it alone. So don't you worry about me drinking myself to death. 'Cause I ain't worried about Death. I done seen him. I done wrestled with him.
Look here, Bono . . . I looked up one day and Death was marching straight at me. Like Soldiers on Parade! The Army of Death was marching straight at me. The middle of July, 1941. I got real cold just like it be winter. It seem like Death himself reached out and touched me on the shoulder. He touch me just like I touch you. I got cold as ice and Death standing there grinning at me.

260 ROSE: Troy, why don't you hush that talk.

TROY: I say . . . What you want, Mr. Death? You be wanting me? You done brought your army to be getting me? I looked him dead in the eye. I wasn't fearing nothing. I was ready to tangle. Just like I'm ready to tangle now. The Bible say be ever vigilant. That's why I don't get but so drunk. I got to keep watch.

ROSE: Troy was right down there in Mercy Hospital. You remember he had pneumonia? Laying there with a fever talking plumb out of his head.

270 TROY: Death standing there staring at me . . . carrying that sickle in his hand. Finally he say, "You want bound over for another year?" See, just like that . . . "You want bound over for another year?" I told him, "Bound over hell! Let's settle this now!"
It seem like he kinda fell back when I said that, and all the cold went out of me. I reached down and grabbed that sickle and threw it just as far as I could throw it . . . and me and him commenced to wrestling.
We wrestled for three days and three nights. I can't say
280 where I found the strength from. Every time it seemed like he was gonna get the best of me, I'd reach way down deep inside myself and find the strength to do him one better.

ROSE: Every time Troy tell that story he find different ways to tell it. Different things to make up about it.

TROY: I ain't making up nothing. I'm telling you the facts of what happened. I wrestled with Death for three days and three nights and I'm standing here to tell you about it.

(Pause.)

Alright. At the end of the third night we done weakened

each other to where we can't hardly move. Death stood up, throwed on his robe . . . had him a white robe with a hood 290 on it. He throwed on that robe and went off to look for his sickle. Say, "I'll be back." Just like that. "I'll be back." I told him, say, "Yeah, but . . . you gonna have to find me!" I wasn't no fool. I wasn't going looking for him. Death ain't nothing to play with. And I know he's gonna get me. I know I got to join his army . . . his camp followers. But as long as I keep my strength and see him coming . . . as long as I keep up my vigilance . . . he's gonna have to fight to get me. I ain't going easy.

BONO: Well, look here, since you got to keep up your vigilance 300 . . . let me have the bottle.

TROY: Aw hell, I shouldn't have told you that part. I should have left out that part.

ROSE: Troy be talking that stuff and half the time don't even know what he be talking about.

TROY: Bono know me better than that.

BONO: That's right. I know you. I know you got some Uncle Remus in your blood. You got more stories than the devil got sinners.

TROY: Aw hell, I done seen him too! Done talked with the devil. 310

ROSE: Troy, don't nobody wanna be hearing all that stuff.

(LYONS enters the yard from the street. Thirty-four years old, TROY's son by a previous marriage, he sports a neatly trimmed goatee, sport coat, white shirt, tieless and buttoned at the collar. Though he fancies himself a musician, he is more caught up in the rituals and "idea" of being a musician than in the actual practice of the music. He has come to borrow money from TROY, and while he knows he will be successful, he is uncertain as to what extent his lifestyle will be held up to scrutiny and ridicule.)

LYONS: Hey, Pop.

TROY: What you come "Hey, Popping" me for?

LYONS: How you doing, Rose?

(He kisses her.)

Mr. Bono. How you doing?

BONO: Hey, Lyons . . . how you been?

TROY: He must have been doing alright. I ain't seen him around here last week.

ROSE: Troy, leave your boy alone. He come by to see you and you wanna start all that nonsense.                          320

TROY: I ain't bothering Lyons.

(Offers him the bottle.)

Here . . . get you a drink. We got an understanding. I know why he come by to see me and he know I know.

LYONS: Come on, Pop . . . I just stopped by to say hi . . . see how you was doing.

TROY: You ain't stopped by yesterday.

ROSE: You gonna stay for supper, Lyons? I got some chicken cooking in the oven.

LYONS: No, Rose . . . thanks. I was just in the neighborhood and thought I'd stop by for a minute.                        330

TROY: You was in the neighborhood alright, nigger. You telling the truth there. You was in the neighborhood cause it's my payday.

LYONS: Well, hell, since you mentioned it . . . let me have ten dollars.

TROY: I'll be damned! I'll die and go to hell and play blackjack with the devil before I give you ten dollars.

BONO: That's what I wanna know about . . . that devil you done seen.

340 LYONS: What . . . Pop done seen the devil? You too much, Pops.

TROY: Yeah, I done seen him. Talked to him too!

ROSE: You ain't seen no devil. I done told you that man ain't had nothing to do with the devil. Anything you can't understand, you want to call it the devil.

TROY: Look here, Bono . . . I went down to see Hertzberger about some furniture. Got three rooms for two-ninety-eight. That what it say on the radio. "Three rooms . . . two-ninety-eight." Even made up a little song about it. Go down there . . . man tell me I can't get no credit. I'm work-

350 ing every day and can't get no credit. What to do? I got an empty house with some raggedy furniture in it. Cory ain't got no bed. He's sleeping on a pile of rags on the floor. Working every day and can't get no credit. Come back here—Rose'll tell you—madder than hell. Sit down . . . try to figure what I'm gonna do. Come a knock on the door. Ain't been living here but three days. Who know I'm here? Open the door . . . devil standing there bigger than life. White fellow . . . got on good clothes and everything. Standing there with a clipboard in his hand. I ain't

360 had to say nothing. First words come out of his mouth was . . . "I understand you need some furniture and can't get no credit." I liked to fell over. He say "I'll give you all the credit you want, but you got to pay the interest on it." I told him, "Give me three rooms worth and charge whatever you want." Next day a truck pulled up here and two men unloaded them three rooms. Man what drove the truck give me a book. Say send ten dollars, first of every month to the address in the book and everything will be alright. Say if I miss a payment the devil was coming back

370 and it'll be hell to pay. That was fifteen years ago. To this day . . . the first of the month I send my ten dollars, Rose'll tell you.

ROSE: Troy lying.

TROY: I ain't never seen that man since. Now you tell me who else that could have been but the devil? I ain't sold my soul or nothing like that, you understand. Naw, I wouldn't have truck with the devil about nothing like that. I got my furniture and pays my ten dollars the first of the month just like clockwork.

380 BONO: How long you say you been paying this ten dollars a month?

TROY: Fifteen years!

BONO: Hell, ain't you finished paying for it yet? How much the man done charged you.

TROY: Aw hell, I done paid for it. I done paid for it ten times over! The fact is I'm scared to stop paying it.

ROSE: Troy lying. We got that furniture from Mr. Glickman. He ain't paying no ten dollars a month to nobody.

TROY: Aw hell, woman. Bono know I ain't that big a fool.

390 LYONS: I was just getting ready to say . . . I know where there's a bridge for sale.

TROY: Look here, I'll tell you this . . . it don't matter to me if he was the devil. It don't matter if the devil give credit. Somebody has got to give it.

ROSE: It ought to matter. You going around talking about having truck with the devil . . . God's the one you gonna have to answer to. He's the one gonna be at the Judgment.

LYONS: Yeah, well, look here, Pop . . . let me have that ten dollars. I'll give it back to you. Bonnie got a job working at the hospital.    400

TROY: What I tell you, Bono? The only time I see this nigger is when he wants something. That's the only time I see him.

LYONS: Come on, Pop, Mr. Bono don't want to hear all that. Let me have the ten dollars. I told you Bonnie working.

TROY: What that mean to me? "Bonnie working." I don't care if she working. Go ask her for the ten dollars if she working. Talking about "Bonnie working." Why ain't you working?

LYONS: Aw, Pop, you know I can't find no decent job. Where am I gonna get a job at? You know I can't get no job.

TROY: I told you I know some people down there. I can get you    410 on the rubbish if you want to work. I told you that the last time you came by here asking me for something.

LYONS: Naw, Pop . . . thanks. That ain't for me. I don't wanna be carrying nobody's rubbish. I don't wanna be punching nobody's time clock.

TROY: What's the matter, you too good to carry people's rubbish? Where you think that ten dollars you talking about come from? I'm just supposed to haul people's rubbish and give my money to you cause you too lazy to work. You too lazy to work and wanna know why you ain't got what I got.    420

ROSE: What hospital Bonnie working at? Mercy?

LYONS: She's down at Passavant working in the laundry.

TROY: I ain't got nothing as it is. I give you that ten dollars and I got to eat beans the rest of the week. Naw . . . you ain't getting no ten dollars here.

LYONS: You ain't got to be eating no beans. I don't know why you wanna say that.

TROY: I ain't got no extra money. Gabe done moved over to Miss Pearl's paying her the rent and things done got tight around here. I can't afford to be giving you every payday.    430

LYONS: I ain't asked you to give me nothing. I asked you to loan me ten dollars. I know you got ten dollars.

TROY: Yeah, I got it. You know why I got it? Cause I don't throw my money away out there in the streets. You living the fast life . . . wanna be a musician . . . running around in them clubs and things . . . then, you learn to take care of yourself. You ain't gonna find me going and asking nobody for nothing. I done spent too many years without.

LYONS: You and me is two different people, Pop.

TROY: I done learned my mistake and learned to do what's right    440 by it. You still trying to get something for nothing. Life don't owe you nothing. You owe it to yourself. Ask Bono. He'll tell you I'm right.

LYONS: You got your way of dealing with the world . . . I got mine. The only thing that matters to me is the music.

TROY: Yeah, I can see that! It don't matter how you gonna eat . . . where your next dollar is coming from. You telling the truth there.

LYONS: I know I got to eat. But I got to live too. I need something that gonna help me to get out of the bed in the morn-    450 ing. Make me feel like I belong in the world. I don't bother nobody. I just stay with my music cause that's the only way I can find to live in the world. Otherwise there ain't no telling what I might do. Now I don't come criticizing you and how you live. I just come by to ask you for ten dollars. I don't wanna hear all that about how I live.

TROY: Boy, your mama did a hell of a job raising you.

LYONS: You can't change me, Pop. I'm thirty-four years old. If you wanted to change me, you should have been there when 460 I was growing up. I come by to see you . . . ask for ten dollars and you want to talk about how I was raised. You don't know nothing about how I was raised.

ROSE: Let the boy have ten dollars, Troy.

TROY: (*To* LYONS.) What the hell you looking at me for? I ain't got no ten dollars. You know what I do with my money.

(*To* ROSE.)

Give him ten dollars if you want him to have it.

ROSE: I will. Just as soon as you turn it loose.

TROY: (*Handing* ROSE *the money.*) There it is. Seventy-six dollars and forty-two cents. You see this, Bono? Now, I ain't 470 gonna get but six of that back.

ROSE: You ought to stop telling that lie. Here, Lyons.

(*She hands him the money.*)

LYONS: Thanks, Rose. Look . . . I got to run . . . I'll see you later.

TROY: Wait a minute. You gonna say, "thanks, Rose" and ain't gonna look to see where she got that ten dollars from? See how they do me, Bono?

LYONS: I know she got it from you, Pop. Thanks. I'll give it back to you.

TROY: There he go telling another lie. Time I see that ten dollars . . . he'll be owing me thirty more.

480 LYONS: See you, Mr. Bono.

BONO: Take care, Lyons!

LYONS: Thanks, Pop. I'll see you again.

(LYONS *exits the yard.*)

TROY: I don't know why he don't go and get him a decent job and take care of that woman he got.

BONO: He'll be alright, Troy. The boy is still young.

TROY: The *boy* is thirty-four years old.

ROSE: Let's not get off into all that.

BONO: Look here . . . I got to be going. I got to be getting on. Lucille gonna be waiting.

490 TROY: (*Puts his arm around* ROSE.) See this woman, Bono? I love this woman. I love this woman so much it hurts. I love her so much . . . I done run out of ways of loving her. So I got to go back to basics. Don't you come by my house Monday morning talking about time to go to work . . . 'cause I'm still gonna be stroking!

ROSE: Troy! Stop it now!

BONO: I ain't paying him no mind, Rose. That ain't nothing but gin-talk. Go on, Troy. I'll see you Monday.

TROY: Don't you come by my house, nigger! I done told you 500 what I'm gonna be doing.

(*The lights go down to black.*)

SCENE II

*The lights come up on* ROSE *hanging up clothes. She hums and sings softly to herself. It is the following morning.*

ROSE: (*Sings*)

*Jesus, be a fence all around me every day*
*Jesus, I want you to protect me as I travel on my way.*
*Jesus, be a fence all around me every day.*

(TROY *enters from the house*)

ROSE: (*continued*)

*Jesus, I want you to protect me*
*As I travel on my way.*

(*To* TROY)

'Morning. You ready for breakfast? I can fix it soon as I finish hanging up these clothes.

TROY: I got the coffee on. That'll be alright. I'll just drink some 510 of that this morning.

ROSE: That 651 hit yesterday. That's the second time this month. Miss Pearl hit for a dollar . . . seem like those that need the least always get lucky. Poor folks can't get nothing.

TROY: Them numbers don't know nobody. I don't know why you fool with them. You and Lyons both.

ROSE: It's something to do.

TROY: You ain't doing nothing but throwing your money away.

ROSE: Troy, you know I don't play foolishly. I just play a nickel here and a nickel there.                                              520

TROY: That's two nickels you done thrown away.

ROSE: Now I hit sometimes . . . that makes up for it. It always comes in handy when I do hit. I don't hear you complaining then.

TROY: I ain't complaining now. I just say it's foolish. Trying to guess out of six hundred ways which way the number gonna come. If I had all the money niggers, these Negroes, throw away on numbers for one week—just one week—I'd be a rich man.

ROSE: Well, you wishing and calling it foolish ain't gonna stop 530 folks from playing numbers. That's one thing for sure. Besides . . . some good things come from playing numbers. Look where Pope done bought him that restaurant off of numbers.

TROY: I can't stand niggers like that. Man ain't had two dimes to rub together. He walking around with his shoes all run over bumming money for cigarettes. Alright. Got lucky there and hit the numbers . . .

ROSE: Troy, I know all about it.

TROY: Had good sense, I'll say that for him. He ain't throwed 540 his money away. I seen niggers hit the numbers and go through two thousand dollars in four days. Man brought him that restaurant down there . . . fixed it up real nice . . . and then didn't want nobody to come in it! A Negro go in there and can't get no kind of service. I seen a white fellow come in there and order a bowl of stew. Pope picked all the meat out the pot for him. Man ain't had nothing but a bowl of meat! Negro come behind him and ain't got nothing but the potatoes and carrots. Talking about what numbers do for people, you picked a wrong example. Ain't done nothing but 550 make a worser fool out of him than he was before.

ROSE: Troy, you ought to stop worrying about what happened at work yesterday.

TROY: I ain't worried. Just told me to be down there at the Commissioner's office on Friday. Everybody think they gonna fire me. I ain't worried about them firing me. You ain't got to worry about that.

(*Pause.*)

Where's Cory? Cory in the house? (*Calls.*) Cory?

ROSE: He gone out.

TROY: Out, huh? He gone out 'cause he know I want him to 560 help me with this fence. I know how he is. That boy scared of work.

(GABRIEL *enters. He comes halfway down the alley and, hearing Troy's voice, stops.*)

TROY: (*continues*) He ain't done a lick of work in his life.

ROSE: He had to go to football practice. Coach wanted them to get in a little extra practice before the season start.

TROY: I got his practice . . . running out of here before he get his chores done.

ROSE: Troy, what is wrong with you this morning? Don't nothing set right with you. Go on back in there and go to bed . . . get up on the other side.

TROY: Why something got to be wrong with me? I ain't said nothing wrong with me.

ROSE: You got something to say about everything. First it's the numbers . . . then it's the way the man runs his restaurant . . . then you done got on Cory. What's it gonna be next? Take a look up there and see if the weather suits you . . . or is it gonna be how you gonna put up the fence with the clothes hanging in the yard.

TROY: You hit the nail on the head then.

ROSE: I know you like I know the back of my hand. Go on in there and get you some coffee . . . see if that straighten you up. 'Cause you ain't right this morning.

(TROY *starts into the house and sees* GABRIEL. GABRIEL *starts singing. TROY's brother, he is seven years younger than TROY. Injured in World War II, he has a metal plate in his head. He carries an old trumpet tied around his waist and believes with every fiber of his being that he is the Archangel Gabriel. He carries a chipped basket with an assortment of discarded fruits and vegetables he has picked up in the strip district and which he attempts to sell.*)

GABRIEL: (*Singing.*)

> Yes, ma'am, I got plums
> You ask me how I sell them
> Oh ten cents apiece
> Three for a quarter
> Come and buy now
> 'Cause I'm here today
> And tomorrow I'll be gone

(GABRIEL *enters.*)

Hey, Rose!

ROSE: How you doing, Gabe?

GABRIEL: There's Troy . . . Hey, Troy!

TROY: Hey, Gabe.

(*Exit into kitchen.*)

ROSE: (*To* GABRIEL.) What you got there?

GABRIEL: You know what I got, Rose. I got fruits and vegetables.

ROSE: (*Looking in basket.*) Where's all these plums you talking about?

GABRIEL: I ain't got no plums today, Rose. I was just singing that. Have some tomorrow. Put me in a big order for plums. Have enough plums tomorrow for St. Peter and everybody.

(TROY *re-enters from kitchen, crosses to steps.*)

(*To* ROSE.)

Troy's mad at me.

TROY: I ain't mad at you. What I got to be mad at you about?

You ain't done nothing to me.

GABRIEL: I just moved over to Miss Pearl's to keep out from in your way. I ain't mean no harm by it.

TROY: Who said anything about that? I ain't said anything about that.

GABRIEL: You ain't mad at me, is you?

TROY: Naw . . . I ain't mad at you, Gabe. If I was mad at you I'd tell you about it.

GABRIEL: Got me two rooms. In the basement. Got my own door too. Wanna see my key?

(*He holds up a key.*)

That's my own key! Ain't nobody else got a key like that. That's my key! My two rooms!

TROY: Well, that's good, Gabe. You got your own key . . . that's good.

ROSE: You hungry, Gabe? I was just fixing to cook Troy his breakfast.

GABRIEL: I'll take some biscuits. You got some biscuits? Did you know when I was in heaven . . . every morning me and St. Peter would sit down by the gate and eat some big fat biscuits? Oh, yeah! We had us a good time. We'd sit there and eat us them biscuits and then St. Peter would go off to sleep and tell me to wake him up when it's time to open the gates for the judgment.

ROSE: Well, come on . . . I'll make up a batch of biscuits.

(ROSE *exits into the house.*)

GABRIEL: Troy . . . St. Peter got your name in the book. I seen it. It say . . . Troy Maxson. I say . . . I know him! He got the same name like what I got. That's my brother!

TROY: How many times you gonna tell me that, Gabe?

GABRIEL: Ain't got my name in the book. Don't have to have my name. I done died and went to heaven. He got your name though. One morning St. Peter was looking at his book . . . marking it up for the judgment . . . and he let me see your name. Got it in there under M. Got Rose's name . . . I ain't seen it like I seen yours . . . but I know it's in there. He got a great big book. Got everybody's name what was ever been born. That's what he told me. But I seen your name. Seen it with my own eyes.

TROY: Go on in the house there. Rose going to fix you something to eat.

GABRIEL: Oh, I ain't hungry. I done had breakfast with Aunt Jemimah. She come by and cooked me up a whole mess of flapjacks. Remember how we used to eat them flapjacks?

TROY: Go on in the house and get you something to eat now.

GABRIEL: I got to go sell my plums. I done sold some tomatoes. Got me two quarters. Wanna see?

(*He shows* TROY *his quarters.*)

I'm gonna save them and buy me a new horn so St. Peter can hear me when it's time to open the gates.

(GABRIEL *stops suddenly. Listens.*)

Hear that? That's the hellhounds. I got to chase them out of here. Go on get out of here! Get out!

(GABRIEL *exits singing.*)

> Better get ready for the judgment
> Better get ready for the judgment
> My Lord is coming down

(ROSE *enters from the house.*)

TROY: He gone off somewhere.

GABRIEL: (*Offstage*)
> 660     *Better get ready for the judgment*
> *Better get ready for the judgment morning*
> *Better get ready for the judgment*
> *My God is coming down*

ROSE: He ain't eating right. Miss Pearl say she can't get him to eat nothing.

TROY: What you want me to do about it, Rose? I done did everything I can for the man. I can't make him get well. Man got half his head blown away . . . what you expect?

ROSE: Seem like something ought to be done to help him.

670 TROY: Man don't bother nobody. He just mixed up from that metal plate he got in his head. Ain't no sense for him to go back into the hospital.

ROSE: Least he be eating right. They can help him take care of himself.

TROY: Don't nobody wanna be locked up, Rose. What you wanna lock him up for? Man go over there and fight the war . . . messin' around with them Japs, get half his head blown off . . . and they give him a lousy three thousand dollars. And I had to swoop down on that.

680 ROSE: Is you fixing to go into that again?

TROY: That's the only way I got a roof over my head . . . cause of that metal plate.

ROSE: Ain't no sense you blaming yourself for nothing. Gabe wasn't in no condition to manage that money. You done what was right by him. Can't nobody say you ain't done what was right by him. Look how long you took care of him . . . till he wanted to have his own place and moved over there with Miss Pearl.

TROY: That ain't what I'm saying, woman! I'm just stating the
690 facts. If my brother didn't have that metal plate in his head . . . I wouldn't have a pot to piss in or a window to throw it out of. And I'm fifty-three years old. Now see if you can understand that!

(TROY *gets up from the porch and starts to exit the yard.*)

ROSE: Where you going off to? You been running out of here every Saturday for weeks. I thought you was gonna work on this fence?

TROY: I'm gonna walk down to Taylors'. Listen to the ball game. I'll be back in a bit. I'll work on it when I get back.

(*He exits the yard. The lights go to black.*)

## SCENE III

*The lights come up on the yard. It is four hours later.* ROSE *is taking down the clothes from the line.* CORY *enters carrying his football equipment.*

ROSE: Your daddy like to had a fit with you running out of here
700 this morning without doing your chores.

CORY: I told you I had to go to practice.

ROSE: He say you were supposed to help him with this fence.

CORY: He been saying that the last four or five Saturdays, and then he don't never do nothing, but go down to Taylors'.

Did you tell him about the recruiter?

ROSE: Yeah, I told him.

CORY: What he say?

ROSE: He ain't said nothing too much. You get in there and get started on your chores before he gets back. Go on and scrub down them steps before he gets back here hollering and 710 carrying on.

CORY: I'm hungry. What you got to eat, Mama?

ROSE: Go on and get started on your chores. I got some meat loaf in there. Go on and make you a sandwich . . . and don't leave no mess in there.

(CORY *exits into the house.* ROSE *continues to take down the clothes.* TROY *enters the yard and sneaks up and grabs her from behind.*)

Troy! Go on, now. You liked to scared me to death. What was the score of the game? Lucille had me on the phone and I couldn't keep up with it.

TROY: What I care about the game? Come here, woman.

(*He tries to kiss her.*)

ROSE: I thought you went down Taylors' to listen to the game. 720 Go on, Troy! You supposed to be putting up this fence.

TROY: (*Attempting to kiss her again.*) I'll put it up when I finish with what is at hand.

ROSE: Go on, Troy. I ain't studying you.

TROY: (*Chasing after her.*) I'm studying you . . . fixing to do my homework!

ROSE: Troy, you better leave me alone.

TROY: Where's Cory? That boy brought his butt home yet?

ROSE: He's in the house doing his chores.

TROY: (*Calling.*) Cory! Get your butt out here, boy!     730

(ROSE *exits into the house with the laundry.* TROY *goes over to the pile of wood, picks up a board, and starts sawing.* CORY *enters from the house.*)

TROY: You just now coming in here from leaving this morning?

CORY: Yeah, I had to go to football practice.

TROY: Yeah, what?

CORY: Yessir.

TROY: I ain't but two seconds off you noway. The garbage sitting in there overflowing . . . you ain't done none of your chores . . . and you come in here talking about "Yeah."

CORY: I was just getting ready to do my chores now, Pop . . .

TROY: Your first chore is to help me with this fence on Saturday. Everything else come after that. Now get that saw and 740 cut them boards.

(CORY *takes the saw and begins cutting the boards.* TROY *continues working. There is a long pause.*)

CORY: Hey, Pop . . . why don't you buy a TV?

TROY: What I want with a TV? What I want one of them for?

CORY: Everybody got one. Earl, Ba Bra . . . Jesse!

TROY: I ain't asked you who had one. I say what I want with one?

CORY: So you can watch it. They got lots of things on TV. Baseball games and everything. We could watch the World Series.

TROY: Yeah . . . and how much this TV cost?     750

CORY: I don't know. They got them on sale for around two

hundred dollars.

TROY: Two hundred dollars, huh?

CORY: That ain't that much, Pop.

TROY: Naw, it's just two hundred dollars. See that roof you got over your head at night? Let me tell you something about that roof. It's been over ten years since that roof was last tarred. See now . . . the snow come this winter and sit up there on that roof like it is . . . and it's gonna seep inside. It's

760     just gonna be a little bit . . . ain't gonna hardly notice it. Then the next thing you know, it's gonna be leaking all over the house. Then the wood rot from all that water and you gonna need a whole new roof. Now, how much you think it cost to get that roof tarred?

CORY: I don't know.

TROY: Two hundred and sixty-four dollars . . . cash money. While you thinking about a TV, I got to be thinking about the roof . . . and whatever else go wrong around here. Now if you had two hundred dollars, what would you do . . . fix

770     the roof or buy a TV?

CORY: I'd buy a TV. Then when the roof started to leak . . . when it needed fixing . . . I'd fix it.

TROY: Where you gonna get the money from? You done spent it for a TV. You gonna sit up and watch the water run all over your brand new TV.

CORY: Aw, Pop. You got money. I know you do.

TROY: Where I got it at, huh?

CORY: You got it in the bank.

TROY: You wanna see my bankbook? You wanna see that sev-

780     enty-three dollars and twenty-two cents I got sitting up in there.

CORY: You ain't got to pay for it all at one time. You can put a down payment on it and carry it on home with you.

TROY: Not me. I ain't gonna owe nobody nothing if I can help it. Miss a payment and they come and snatch it right out your house. Then what you got? Now, soon as I get two hundred dollars clear, then I'll buy a TV. Right now, as soon as I get two hundred and sixty-four dollars, I'm gonna have this roof tarred.

790 CORY: Aw . . . Pop!

TROY: You go on and get you two hundred dollars and buy one if ya want it. I got better things to do with my money.

CORY: I can't get no two hundred dollars. I ain't never seen two hundred dollars.

TROY: I'll tell you what . . . you get you a hundred dollars and I'll put the other hundred with it.

CORY: Alright, I'm gonna show you.

TROY: You gonna show me how you can cut them boards right now.

(CORY *begins to cut the boards. There is a long pause.*)

800 CORY: The Pirates won today. That makes five in a row.

TROY: I ain't thinking about the Pirates. Got an all-white team. Got that boy . . . that Puerto Rican boy . . . Clemente. Don't even half-play him. That boy could be something if they give him a chance. Play him one day and sit him on the bench the next.

CORY: He gets a lot of chances to play.

TROY: I'm talking about playing regular. Playing every day so you can get your timing. That's what I'm talking about.

CORY: They got some white guys on the team that don't play

every day. You can't play everybody at the same time. 810

TROY: If they got a white fellow sitting on the bench . . . you can bet your last dollar he can't play! The colored guy got to be twice as good before he get on the team. That's why I don't want you to get all tied up in them sports. Man on the team and what it get him? They got colored on the team and don't use them. Same as not having them. All them teams the same.

CORY: The Braves got Hank Aaron and Wes Covington. Hank Aaron hit two home runs today. That makes forty-three.

TROY: Hank Aaron ain't nobody. That's what you supposed to 820 do. That's how you supposed to play the game. Ain't nothing to it. It's just a matter of timing . . . getting the right follow-through. Hell, I can hit forty-three home runs right now!

CORY: Not off no major-league pitching, you couldn't.

TROY: We had better pitching in the Negro leagues. I hit seven home runs off of Satchel Paige. You can't get no better than that!

CORY: Sandy Koufax. He's leading the league in strike-outs.

TROY: I ain't thinking of no Sandy Koufax. 830

CORY: You got Warren Spahn and Lew Burdette. I bet you couldn't hit no home runs off of Warren Spahn.

TROY: I'm through with it now. You go on and cut them boards.

(*Pause.*)

Your mama tell me you done got recruited by a college football team? Is that right?

CORY: Yeah. Coach Zellman say the recruiter gonna be coming by to talk to you. Get you to sign the permission papers.

TROY: I thought you supposed to be working down there at the A&P. Ain't you suppose to be working down there after school? 840

CORY: Mr. Stawicki say he gonna hold my job for me until after the football season. Say starting next week I can work weekends.

TROY: I thought we had an understanding about this football stuff? You suppose to keep up with your chores and hold that job down at the A&P. Ain't been around here all day on a Saturday. Ain't none of your chores done . . . and now you telling me you done quit your job.

CORY: I'm gonna be working weekends.

TROY: You damn right you are! And ain't no need for nobody 850 coming around here to talk to me about signing nothing.

CORY: Hey, Pop . . . you can't do that. He's coming all the way from North Carolina.

TROY: I don't care where he coming from. The white man ain't gonna let you get nowhere with that football noway. You go on and get your book-learning so you can work yourself up in that A&P or learn how to fix cars or build houses or something, get you a trade. That way you have something can't nobody take away from you. You go on and learn how to put your hands to some good use. Besides hauling people's 860 garbage.

CORY: I get good grades, Pop. That's why the recruiter wants to talk with you. You got to keep up your grades to get recruited. This way I'll be going to college. I'll get a chance . . .

TROY: First you gonna get your butt down there to the A&P and get your job back.

CORY: Mr. Stawicki done already hired somebody else 'cause I told him I was playing football.

870 TROY: You a bigger fool than I thought . . . to let somebody take away your job so you can play some football. Where you gonna get your money to take out your girlfriend and whatnot? What kind of foolishness is that to let somebody take away your job?

CORY: I'm still gonna be working weekends.

TROY: Naw . . . naw. You getting your butt out of here and finding you another job.

CORY: Come on, Pop! I got to practice. I can't work after school and play football too. The team needs me. That's what
880 Coach Zellman say . . .

TROY: I don't care what nobody else say. I'm the boss . . . you understand? I'm the boss around here. I do the only saying what counts.

CORY: Come on, Pop!

TROY: I asked you . . . did you understand?

CORY: Yeah . . .

TROY: What?!

CORY: Yessir.

TROY: You go on down there to that A&P and see if you can get
890 your job back. If you can't do both . . . then you quit the football team. You've got to take the crookeds with the straights.

CORY: Yessir.

*(Pause.)*

Can I ask you a question?

TROY: What the hell you wanna ask me? Mr. Stawicki the one you got the questions for.

CORY: How come you ain't never liked me?

TROY: Liked you? Who the hell say I got to like you? What law is there say I got to like you? Wanna stand up in my face and ask a damn fool-ass question like that. Talking about liking
900 somebody. Come here, boy, when I talk to you.

*(CORY comes over to where TROY is working. He stands slouched over and TROY shoves him on his shoulder.)*

Straighten up, goddammit! I asked you a question . . . what law is there say I got to like you?

CORY: None.

TROY: Well, alright then! Don't you eat every day?

*(Pause.)*

Answer me when I talk to you! Don't you eat every day?

CORY: Yeah.

TROY: Nigger, as long as you in my house, you put that sir on the end of it when you talk to me!

CORY: Yes . . . sir.

910 TROY: You eat every day.

CORY: Yessir!

TROY: Got a roof over your head.

CORY: Yessir!

TROY: Got clothes on your back.

CORY: Yessir.

TROY: Why you think that is?

CORY: Cause of you.

TROY: Aw, hell I know it's 'cause of me . . . but why do you think that is?

920 CORY: *(Hesitant.)* Cause you like me.

TROY: Like you? I go out of here every morning . . . bust my butt . . . putting up with them crackers every day . . . cause I like you? You about the biggest fool I ever saw.

*(Pause.)*

It's my job. It's my responsibility! You understand that? A man got to take care of his family. You live in my house . . . sleep you behind on my bedclothes . . . fill you belly up with my food . . . cause you my son. You my flesh and blood. Not 'cause I like you! Cause it's my duty to take care of you. I owe a responsibility to you! Let's get this straight right here . . . before it go along any further . . . I ain't got to like 930 you. Mr. Rand don't give me my money come payday cause he likes me. He gives me cause he owe me. I done give you everything I had to give you. I gave you your life! Me and your mama worked that out between us. And liking your black ass wasn't part of the bargain. Don't you try and go through life worrying about if somebody like you or not. You best be making sure they doing right by you. You understand what I'm saying, boy?

CORY: Yessir.

TROY: Then get the hell out of my face, and get on down to that 940 A&P.

*(ROSE has been standing behind the screen door for much of the scene. She enters as CORY exits.)*

ROSE: Why don't you let the boy go ahead and play football, Troy? Ain't no harm in that. He's just trying to be like you with the sports.

TROY: I don't want him to be like me! I want him to move as far away from my life as he can get. You the only decent thing that ever happened to me. I wish him that. But I don't wish him a thing else from my life. I decided seventeen years ago that boy wasn't getting involved in no sports. Not after what they did to me in the sports. 950

ROSE: Troy, why don't you admit you was too old to play in the major leagues? For once . . . why don't you admit that?

TROY: What do you mean too old? Don't come telling me I was too old. I just wasn't the right color. Hell, I'm fifty-three years old and can do better than Selkirk's .269 right now!

ROSE: How's was you gonna play ball when you were over forty? Sometimes I can't get no sense out of you.

TROY: I got good sense, woman. I got sense enough not to let my boy get hurt over playing no sports. You been mothering that boy too much. Worried about if people like him. 960

ROSE: Everything that boy do . . . he do for you. He wants you to say "Good job, son." That's all.

TROY: Rose, I ain't got time for that. He's alive. He's healthy. He's got to make his own way. I made mine. Ain't nobody gonna hold his hand when he get out there in that world.

ROSE: Times have changed from when you was young, Troy. People change. The world's changing around you and you can't even see it.

TROY: *(Slow, methodical.)* Woman . . . I do the best I can do. I come in here every Friday. I carry a sack of potatoes and a 970 bucket of lard. You all line up at the door with your hands out. I give you the lint from my pockets. I give you my sweat and my blood. I ain't got no tears. I done spent them. We go upstairs in that room at night . . . and I fall down on you and try to blast a hole into forever. I get up Monday morning . . . find my lunch on the table. I go out. Make my way. Find my strength to carry me through to the next Friday.

*(Pause.)*

That's all I got, Rose. That's all I got to give. I can't give
980 nothing else.

*(TROY exits into the house. The lights go down to black.)*

SCENE IV

*It is Friday. Two weeks later.* CORY *starts out of the house with his football equipment. The phone rings.*

CORY: *(Calling.)* I got it!

*(He answers the phone and stands in the screen door talking.)*

Hello? Hey, Jesse. Naw . . . I was just getting ready to leave now.
ROSE: *(Calling.)* Cory!
CORY: I told you, man, them spikes is all tore up. You can use them if you want, but they ain't no good. Earl got some spikes.
ROSE: *(Calling.)* Cory!
CORY: *(Calling to* ROSE.*)* Mam? I'm talking to Jesse.

*(Into phone.)*

990 When she say that? *(Pause.)* Aw, you lying, man. I'm gonna tell her you said that.
ROSE: *(Calling.)* Cory, don't you go nowhere!
CORY: I got to go to the game, Ma!

*(Into the phone.)*

Yeah, hey, look, I'll talk to you later. Yeah, I'll meet you over Earl's house. Later. Bye, Ma.

*(CORY exits the house and starts out the yard.)*

ROSE: Cory, where you going off to? You got that stuff all pulled out and thrown all over your room.
CORY: *(In the yard.)* I was looking for my spikes. Jesse wanted to borrow my spikes.
1000 ROSE: Get up there and get that cleaned up before your daddy get back in here.
CORY: I got to go to the game! I'll clean it up *when I get back.*

*(CORY exits.)*

ROSE: That's all he need to do is see that room all messed up.

*(ROSE exits into the house.* TROY *and* BONO *enter the yard.* TROY *is dressed in clothes other than his work clothes.)*

BONO: He told him the same thing he told you. Take it to the union.
TROY: Brownie ain't got that much sense. Man wasn't thinking about nothing. He wait until I confront them on it . . . then he wanna come crying seniority.

*(Calls.)*

Hey, Rose!
1010 BONO: I wish I could have seen Mr. Rand's face when he told you.

TROY: He couldn't get it out of his mouth! Liked to bit his tongue! When they called me down there to the Commissioner's office . . . he thought they was gonna fire me. Like everybody else.
BONO: I didn't think they was gonna fire you. I thought they was gonna put you on the warning paper.
TROY: Hey, Rose!

*(To* BONO.*)*

Yeah, Mr. Rand like to bit his tongue.

*(TROY *breaks the seal on the bottle, takes a drink, and hands it to* BONO.)*

BONO: I see you run right down to Taylors' and told that Al- 1020 berta gal.
TROY: *(Calling.)* Hey Rose! *(To* BONO.*)* I told everybody. Hey Rose! I went down there to cash my check.
ROSE: *(Entering from the house.)* Hush all that hollering, man! I know you out here. What they say down there at the Commissioner's office?
TROY: You supposed to come when I call you, woman. Bono'll tell you that.

*(To* BONO.*)*

Don't Lucille come when you call her?
ROSE: Man, hush your mouth. I ain't no dog . . . talk about 1030 "come when you call me."
TROY: *(Puts his arm around* ROSE.*)* You hear this, Bono? I had me an old dog used to get uppity like that. You say, "C'mere, Blue!" . . . and he just lay there and look at you. End up getting a stick and chasing him away trying to make him come.
ROSE: I ain't studying you and your dog. I remember you used to sing that old song.
TROY: *(He sings.)*

> Hear it ring! Hear it ring!
> I had a dog his name was Blue. 1040

ROSE: Don't nobody wanna hear you sing that old song.
TROY: *(Sings.)*

> You know Blue was mighty true.

ROSE: Used to have Cory running around here singing that song.
BONO: Hell, I remember that song myself.
TROY: *(Sings.)*

> You know Blue was a good old dog.
> Blue treed a possum in a hollow log.

That was my daddy's song. My daddy made up that song.
ROSE: I don't care who made it up. Don't nobody wanna hear 1050 you sing it.
TROY: *(Makes a song like calling a dog.)* Come here, woman.
ROSE: You come in here carrying on, I reckon they ain't fired you. What they say down there at the Commissioner's office?
TROY: Look here, Rose . . . Mr. Rand called me into his office today when I got back from talking to them people down there . . . it come from up top . . . he called me in and told me they was making me a driver.
ROSE: Troy, you kidding! 1060

TROY: No I ain't. Ask Bono.

ROSE: Well, that's great, Troy. Now you don't have to hassle them people no more.

(LYONS *enters from the street.*)

TROY: Aw hell, I wasn't looking to see you today. I thought you was in jail. Got it all over the front page of the *Courier* about them raiding Sefus' place . . . where you be hanging out with all them thugs.

LYONS: Hey, Pop . . . that ain't got nothing to do with me. I don't go down there gambling. I go down there to sit in with
1070 the band. I ain't got nothing to do with the gambling part. They got some good music down there.

TROY: They got some rogues . . . is what they got.

LYONS: How you been, Mr. Bono? Hi, Rose.

BONO: I see where you playing down at the Crawford Grill tonight.

ROSE: How come you ain't brought Bonnie like I told you. You should have brought Bonnie with you, she ain't been over in a month of Sundays.

LYONS: I was just in the neighborhood . . . thought I'd stop by.

1080 TROY: Here he come . . .

BONO: Your daddy got a promotion on the rubbish. He's gonna be the first colored driver. Ain't got to do nothing but sit up there and read the paper like them white fellows.

LYONS: Hey, Pop . . . if you knew how to read you'd be alright.

BONO: Naw . . . naw . . . you mean if the nigger knew how to *drive* he'd be all right. Been fighting with them people about driving and ain't even got a license. Mr. Rand know you ain't got no driver's license?

TROY: Driving ain't nothing. All you do is point the truck where
1090 you want it to go. Driving ain't nothing.

BONO: Do Mr. Rand know you ain't got no driver's license? That's what I'm talking about. I ain't asked if driving was easy. I asked if Mr. Rand know you ain't got no driver's license.

TROY: He ain't got to know. The man ain't got to know my business. Time he find out, I have two or three driver's licenses.

LYONS: (*Going into his pocket.*) Say, look here, Pop . . .

TROY: I knew it was coming. Didn't I tell you, Bono? I know what kind of "Look here, Pop" that was. The nigger fixing to
1100 ask me for some money. It's Friday night. It's my payday. All them rogues down there on the avenue . . . the ones that ain't in jail . . . and Lyons is hopping in his shoes to get down there with them.

LYONS: See, Pop . . . if you give somebody else a chance to talk sometime, you'd see that I was fixing to pay you back your ten dollars like I told you. Here . . . I told you I'd pay you when Bonnie got paid.

TROY: Naw . . . you go ahead and keep that ten dollars. Put it in the bank. The next time you feel like you wanna come by
1110 here and ask me for something . . . you go on down there and get that.

LYONS: Here's your ten dollars, Pop. I told you I don't want you to give me nothing. I just wanted to borrow ten dollars.

TROY: Naw . . . you go on and keep that for the next time you want to ask me.

LYONS: Come on, Pop . . . here go your ten dollars.

ROSE: Why don't you go on and let the boy pay you back, Troy?

LYONS: Here you go, Rose. If you don't take it I'm gonna have to hear about it for the next six months.

(*He hands her the money.*)

ROSE: You can hand yours over here too, Troy.    1120

TROY: You see this, Bono. You see how they do me.

BONO: Yeah, Lucille do me the same way.

(GABRIEL *is heard singing offstage. He enters.*)

GABRIEL: Better get ready for the Judgment! Better get ready for . . . Hey! . . . Hey! . . . There's Troy's boy!

LYONS: How you doing, Uncle Gabe?

GABRIEL: Lyons . . . The King of the Jungle! Rose . . . hey, Rose. Got a flower for you.

(*He takes a rose from his pocket.*)

Picked it myself. That's the same rose like you is!

ROSE: That's right nice of you, Gabe.

LYONS: What you been doing, Uncle Gabe?    1130

GABRIEL: Oh, I been chasing hellhounds and waiting on the time to tell St. Peter to open the gates.

LYONS: You been chasing hellhounds, huh? Well . . . you doing the right thing, Uncle Gabe. Somebody got to chase them.

GABRIEL: Oh, yeah . . . I know it. The devil's strong. The devil ain't no pushover. Hellhounds snipping at everybody's heels. But I got my trumpet waiting on the judgment time.

LYONS: Waiting on the Battle of Armageddon, huh?

GABRIEL: Ain't gonna be too much of a battle when God get to waving that Judgment sword. But the people's gonna have a    1140
hell of a time trying to get into heaven if them gates ain't open.

LYONS: (*Putting his arm around* GABRIEL.) You hear this, Pop. Uncle Gabe, you alright!

GABRIEL: (*Laughing with* LYONS.) Lyons! King of the Jungle.

ROSE: You gonna stay for supper, Gabe. Want me to fix you a plate?

GABRIEL: I'll take a sandwich, Rose. Don't want no plate. Just wanna eat with my hands. I'll take a sandwich.

ROSE: How about you, Lyons? You staying? Got some short    1150 ribs cooking.

LYONS: Naw, I won't eat anything till after we finished playing.

(*Pause.*)

You ought to come down and listen to me play, Pop.

TROY: I don't like that Chinese music. All that noise.

ROSE: Go on in the house and wash up, Gabe . . . I'll fix you a sandwich.

GABRIEL: (*To* LYONS, *as he exits.*) Troy's mad at me.

LYONS: What you mad at Uncle Gabe for, Pop?

ROSE: He thinks Troy's mad at him cause he moved over to Miss Pearl's.    1160

TROY: I ain't mad at the man. He can live where he want to live at.

LYONS: What he move over there for? Miss Pearl don't like nobody.

ROSE: She don't mind him none. She treats him real nice. She just don't allow all that singing.

TROY: She don't mind that rent he be paying . . . that's what she don't mind.

ROSE: Troy, I ain't going through that with you no more. He's over there cause he want to have his own place. He can    1170 come and go as he please.

TROY: Hell, he could come and go as he please here. I wasn't stopping him. I ain't put no rules on him.

ROSE: It ain't the same thing, Troy. And you know it.

(GABRIEL *comes to the door.*)

Now, that's the last I wanna hear about that. I don't wanna hear nothing else about Gabe and Miss Pearl. And next week . . .

GABRIEL: I'm ready for my sandwich, Rose.

1180 ROSE: And next week . . . when that recruiter come from that school . . . I want you to sign that paper and go on and let Cory play football. Then that'll be the last I have to hear about that.

TROY: (*To* ROSE *as she exits into the house.*) I ain't thinking about Cory nothing.

LYONS: What . . . Cory got recruited? What school he going to?

TROY: That boy walking around here smelling his piss . . . thinking he's grown. Thinking he's gonna do what he want, irrespective of what I say. Look here, Bono . . . I left the Commissioner's office and went down to the A&P . . . that 1190 boy ain't working down there. He lying to me. Telling me he got his job back . . . telling me he working weekends . . . telling me he working after school . . . Mr. Stawicki tell me he ain't working down there at all!

LYONS: Cory just growing up. He's just busting at the seams trying to fill out your shoes.

TROY: I don't care what he's doing. When he get to the point where he wanna disobey me . . . then it's time for him to move on. Bono'll tell you that. I bet he ain't never disobeyed his daddy without paying the consequences.

1200 BONO: I ain't never had a chance. My daddy came on through . . . but I ain't never knew him to see him . . . or what he had on his mind or where he went. Just moving on through. Searching out the New Land. That's what the old folks used to call it. See a fellow moving around from place to place . . . woman to woman . . . called it searching out the New Land. I can't say if he ever found it. I come along, didn't want no kids. Didn't know if I was gonna be in one place long enough to fix on them right as their daddy. I figured I was going searching too. As it turned out I been 1210 hooked up with Lucille near about as long as your daddy been with Rose. Going on sixteen years.

TROY: Sometimes I wish I hadn't known my daddy. He ain't cared nothing about no kids. A kid to him wasn't nothing. All he wanted was for you to learn how to walk so he could start you to working. When it come time for eating . . . he ate first. If there was anything left over, that's what you got. Man would sit down and eat two chickens and give you the wing.

LYONS: You ought to stop that, Pop. Everybody feed their kids. No matter how hard times is . . . everybody care about their 1220 kids. Make sure they have something to eat.

TROY: The only thing my daddy cared about was getting them bales of cotton in to Mr. Lubin. That's the only thing that mattered to him. Sometimes I used to wonder why he was living. Wonder why the devil hadn't come and got him. "Get them bales of cotton in to Mr. Lubin" and find out he owe him money . . .

LYONS: He should have just went on and left when he saw he couldn't get nowhere. That's what I would have done.

TROY: How he gonna leave with eleven kids? And where he 1230 gonna go? He ain't knew how to do nothing but farm. No, he was trapped and I think he knew it. But I'll say this for him . . . he felt a responsibility toward us. Maybe he ain't treated us the way I felt he should have . . . but without that responsibility he could have walked off and left us . . . made his own way.

BONO: A lot of them did. Back in those days what you talking about . . . they walk out their front door and just take on down one road or another and keep on walking.

LYONS: There you go! That's what I'm talking about.

BONO: Just keep on walking till you come to something else. 1240 Ain't you never heard of nobody having the walking blues? Well, that's what you call it when you just take off like that.

TROY: My daddy ain't had them walking blues! What you talking about? He stayed right there with his family. But he was just as evil as he could be. My mama couldn't stand him. Couldn't stand that evilness. She run off when I was about eight. She sneaked off one night after he had gone to sleep. Told me she was coming back for me. I ain't never seen her no more. All his women run off and left him. He wasn't good for nobody. 1250

When my turn come to head out, I was fourteen and got to sniffing around Joe Canewell's daughter. Had us an old mule we called Greyboy. My daddy sent me out to do some plowing and I tied up Greyboy and went to fooling around with Joe Canewell's daughter. We done found us a nice little spot, got real cozy with each other. She about thirteen and we done figured we was grown anyway . . . so we down there enjoying ourselves . . . ain't thinking about nothing. We didn't know Greyboy had got loose and wandered back to the house and my daddy was looking for me. We down 1260 there by the creek enjoying ourselves when my daddy come up on us. Surprised us. He had them leather straps off the mule and commenced to whupping me like there was no tomorrow. I jumped up, mad and embarrassed. I was scared of my daddy. When he commenced to whupping on me . . . quite naturally I run to get out of the way.

(*Pause.*)

Now I thought he was mad cause I ain't done my work. But I see where he was chasing me off so he could have the gal for himself. When I see what the matter of it was, I lost all fear of my daddy. Right there is where I become a man . . . 1270 at fourteen years of age.

(*Pause.*)

Now it was my turn to run him off. I picked up them same reins that he had used on me. I picked up them reins and commenced to whupping on him. The gal jumped up and run off . . . and when my daddy turned to face me, I could see why the devil had never come to get him . . . cause he was the devil himself. I don't know what happened. When I woke up, I was laying right there by the creek, and Blue . . . this old dog we had . . . was licking my face. I thought I was blind. I couldn't see nothing. Both my eyes were swollen 1280 shut. I layed there and cried. I didn't know what I was gonna do. The only thing I knew was the time had come for me to leave my daddy's house. And right there the world suddenly got big. And it was a long time before I could cut it down to where I could handle it.

Part of that cutting down was when I got to the place where I could feel him kicking in my blood and knew that the only thing that separated us was the matter of a few years.

(GABRIEL *enters from the house with a sandwich.*)

LYONS: What you got there, Uncle Gabe?

1290 GABRIEL: Got me a ham sandwich. Rose gave me a ham sandwich.

TROY: I don't know what happened to him. I done lost touch with everybody except Gabriel. But I hope he's dead. I hope he found some peace.

LYONS: That's a heavy story, Pop. I didn't know you left home when you was fourteen.

TROY: And didn't know nothing. The only part of the world I knew was the forty-two acres of Mr. Lubin's land. That's all I knew about life.

1300 LYONS: Fourteen's kinda young to be out on your own. *(Phone rings.)* I don't even think I was ready to be out on my own at fourteen. I don't know what I would have done.

TROY: I got up from the creek and walked on down to Mobile. I was through with farming. Figured I could do better in the city. So I walked the two hundred miles to Mobile.

LYONS: Wait a minute . . . you ain't walked no two hundred miles, Pop. Ain't nobody gonna walk no two hundred miles. You talking about some walking there.

BONO: That's the only way you got anywhere back in them

1310 days.

LYONS: Shhh. Damn if I wouldn't have hitched a ride with somebody!

TROY: Who you gonna hitch it with? They ain't had no cars and things like they got now. We talking about 1918.

ROSE: *(Entering.)* What you all out here getting into?

TROY: *(To* ROSE.*)* I'm telling Lyons how good he got it. He don't know nothing about this I'm talking.

ROSE: Lyons, that was Bonnie on the phone. She say you supposed to pick her up.

1320 LYONS: Yeah, okay, Rose.

TROY: I walked on down to Mobile and hitched up with some of them fellows that was heading this way. Got up here and found out . . . not only couldn't you get a job . . . you couldn't find no place to live. I thought I was in freedom. Shhh. Colored folks living down there on the riverbanks in whatever kind of shelter they could find for themselves. Right down there under the Brady Street Bridge. Living in shacks made of sticks and tarpaper. Messed around there and went from bad to worse. Started stealing. First it was

1330 food. Then I figured, hell, if I steal money I can buy me some food. Buy me some shoes too! One thing led to another. Met your mama. I was young and anxious to be a man. Met your mama and had you. What I do that for? Now I got to worry about feeding you and her. Got to steal three times as much. Went out one day looking for somebody to rob . . . that's what I was, a robber. I'll tell you the truth. I'm ashamed of it today. But it's the truth. Went to rob this fellow . . . pulled out my knife . . . and he pulled out a gun. Shot me in the chest. It felt just like somebody had taken a hot

1340 branding iron and laid it on me. When he shot me I jumped at him with my knife. They told me I killed him and they put me in the penitentiary and locked me up for fifteen years. That's where I met Bono. That's where I learned how to play baseball. Got out that place and your mama had taken you and went on to make life without me. Fifteen years was a long time for her to wait. But that fifteen years cured me of that robbing stuff. Rose'll tell you. She asked me when I met her if I had gotten all that foolishness out of my system.

And I told her, "Baby, it's you and baseball all what count with me." You hear me, Bono? I meant it too. She say, 1350 "Which one comes first?" I told her, "Baby, ain't no doubt it's baseball . . . but you stick and get old with me and we'll both outlive this baseball." Am I right, Rose? And it's true.

ROSE: Man, hush your mouth. You ain't said no such thing. Talking about, "Baby, you know you'll always be number one with me." That's what you was talking.

TROY: You hear that, Bono. That's why I love her.

BONO: Rose'll keep you straight. You get off the track, she'll straighten you up.

ROSE: Lyons, you better get on up and get Bonnie. She waiting 1360 on you.

LYONS: *(Gets up to go.)* Hey, Pop, why don't you come on down to the Grill and hear me play?

TROY: I ain't going down there. I'm too old to be sitting around in them clubs.

BONO: You got to be good to play down at the Grill.

LYONS: Come on, Pop . . .

TROY: I got to get up in the morning.

LYONS: You ain't got to stay long.

TROY: Naw, I'm gonna get my supper and go on to bed. 1370

LYONS: Well, I got to go. I'll see you again.

TROY: Don't you come around my house on my payday.

ROSE: Pick up the phone and let somebody know you coming. And bring Bonnie with you. You know I'm always glad to see her.

LYONS: Yeah, I'll do that, Rose. You take care now. See you, Pop. See you, Mr. Bono. See you, Uncle Gabe.

GABRIEL: Lyons! King of the Jungle!

*(LYONS exits.)*

TROY: Is supper ready, woman? Me and you got some business to take care of. I'm gonna tear it up too. 1380

ROSE: Troy, I done told you now!

TROY: *(Puts his arm around* BONO.*)* Aw hell, woman . . . this is Bono. Bono like family. I done known this nigger since . . . how long I done know you?

BONO: It's been a long time.

TROY: I done known this nigger since Skippy was a pup. Me and him done been through some times.

BONO: You sure right about that.

TROY: Hell, I done know him longer than I known you. And we still standing shoulder to shoulder. Hey, look here, 1390 Bono . . . a man can't ask for no more than that.

*(Drinks to him.)*

I love you, nigger.

BONO: Hell, I love you too . . . but I got to get home see my woman. You got yours in hand. I got to go get mine.

*(BONO starts to exit as CORY enters the yard, dressed in his football uniform. He gives TROY a hard, uncompromising look.)*

CORY: What you do that for, Pop?

*(He throws his helmet down in the direction of TROY.)*

ROSE: What's the matter? Cory . . . what's the matter?

CORY: Papa done went up to the school and told Coach Zellman I can't play football no more. Wouldn't even let me play the game. Told him to tell the recruiter not to come.

1400 ROSE: Troy . . .

TROY: What you Troying me for. Yeah, I did it. And the boy know why I did it.

CORY: Why you wanna do that to me? That was the one chance I had.

ROSE: Ain't nothing wrong with Cory playing football, Troy.

TROY: The boy lied to me. I told the nigger if he wanna play football . . . to keep up his chores and hold down that job at the A&P. That was the conditions. Stopped down there to see Mr. Stawicki . . .

1410 CORY: I can't work after school during the football season, Pop! I tried to tell you that Mr. Stawicki's holding my job for me. You don't never want to listen to nobody. And then you wanna go and do this to me!

TROY: I ain't done nothing to you. You done it to yourself.

CORY: Just cause you didn't have a chance! You just scared I'm gonna be better than you, that's all.

TROY: Come here.

ROSE: Troy . . .

(CORY *reluctantly crosses over to* TROY.)

TROY: Alright! See. You done made a mistake.

1420 CORY: I didn't even do nothing!

TROY: I'm gonna tell you what your mistake was. See . . . you swung at the ball and didn't hit it. That's strike one. See, you in the batter's box now. You swung and you missed. That's strike one. Don't you strike out!

(*Lights fade to black.*)

## —ACT TWO—

### SCENE I

*The following morning.* CORY *is at the tree hitting the ball with the bat. He tries to mimic* TROY, *but his swing is awkward, less sure.* ROSE *enters from the house.*

ROSE: Cory, I want you to help me with this cupboard.

CORY: I ain't quitting the team. I don't care what Poppa say.

ROSE: I'll talk to him when he gets back. He had to go see about your Uncle Gabe. The police done arrested him. Say he was disturbing the peace. He'll be back directly. Come on in 1430 here and help me clean out the top of this cupboard.

(CORY *exits into the house.* ROSE *sees* TROY *and* BONO *coming down the alley.*)

Troy . . . what they say down there?

TROY: Ain't said nothing. I give them fifty dollars and they let him go. I'll talk to you about it. Where's Cory?

ROSE: He's in there helping me clean out these cupboards.

TROY: Tell him to get his butt out here.

(TROY *and* BONO *go over to the pile of wood.* BONO *picks up the saw and begins sawing.*)

TROY: (*To* BONO.) All they want is the money. That makes six or seven times I done went down there and got him. See me coming they stick out their *hands.*

BONO: Yeah. I know what you mean. That's all they care 1440 about . . . that money. They don't care about what's right.

(*Pause.*)

Nigger, why you got to go and get some hard wood? You ain't doing nothing but building a little old fence. Get you some soft pine wood. That's all you need.

TROY: I know what I'm doing. This is outside wood. You put pine wood inside the house. Pine wood is inside wood. This here is outside wood. Now you tell me where the fence is gonna be?

BONO: You don't need this wood. You can put it up with pine wood and it'll stand as long as you gonna be here looking at it. 1450

TROY: How you know how long I'm gonna be here, nigger? Hell, I might just live forever. Live longer than old man Horsely.

BONO: That's what Magee used to say.

TROY: Magee's a damn fool. Now you tell me who you ever heard of gonna pull their own teeth with a pair of rusty pliers.

BONO: The old folks . . . my granddaddy used to pull his teeth with pliers. They ain't had no dentists for the colored folks back then. 1460

TROY: Get clean pliers! You understand? Clean pliers! Sterilize them! Besides we ain't living back then. All Magee had to do was walk over to Doc Goldblums.

BONO: I see where you and that Tallahassee gal . . . that Alberta . . . I see where you all done got tight.

TROY: What you mean "got tight"?

BONO: I see where you be laughing and joking with her all the time.

TROY: I laughs and jokes with all of them, Bono. You know me.

BONO: That ain't the kind of laughing and joking I'm talking 1470 about.

(CORY *enters from the house.*)

CORY: How you doing, Mr. Bono?

TROY: Cory? Get that saw from Bono and cut some wood. He talking about the wood's too hard to cut. Stand back there, Jim, and let that young boy show you how it's done.

BONO: He's sure welcome to it.

(CORY *takes the saw and begins to cut the wood.*)

Whew-e-e! Look at that. Big old strong boy. Look like Joe Louis. Hell, must be getting old the way I'm watching that boy whip through that wood.

CORY: I don't see why Mama want a fence around the yard 1480 noways.

TROY: Damn if I know either. What the hell she keeping out with it? She ain't got nothing nobody want.

BONO: Some people build fences to keep people out . . . and other people build fences to keep people in. Rose wants to hold on to you all. She loves you.

TROY: Hell, nigger, I don't need nobody to tell me my wife loves me, Cory . . . go on in the house and see if you can find that other saw.

CORY: Where's it at? 1490

TROY: I said find it! Look for it till you find it!

(CORY *exits into the house.*)

What's that supposed to mean? Wanna keep us in?

BONO: Troy . . . I done known you seem like damn near my

whole life. You and Rose both. I done know both of you all for a long time. I remember when you met Rose. When you was hitting them baseball out the park. A lot of them old gals was after you then. You had the pick of the litter. When you picked Rose, I was happy for you. That was the first time I knew you had any sense. I said . . . My man Troy knows what he's doing . . . I'm gonna follow this nigger . . . he might take me somewhere. I been following you too. I done learned a whole heap of things about life watching you. I done learned how to tell where the shit lies. How to tell it from the alfalfa. You done learned me a lot of things. You showed me how to not make the same mistakes . . . to take life as it comes along and keep putting one foot in front of the other.

*(Pause.)*

Rose a good woman, Troy.

TROY: Hell, nigger, I know she a good woman. I been married to her for eighteen years. What you got on your mind, Bono?

BONO: I just say she a good woman. Just like I say anything. I ain't got to have nothing on my mind.

TROY: You just gonna say she a good woman and leave it hanging out there like that? Why you telling me she a good woman?

BONO: She loves you, Troy. Rose loves you.

TROY: You saying I don't measure up. That's what you trying to say. I don't measure up cause I'm seeing this other gal. I know what you trying to say.

BONO: I know what Rose means to you, Troy. I'm just trying to say I don't want to see you mess up.

TROY: Yeah, I appreciate that, Bono. If you was messing around on Lucille I'd be telling you the same thing.

BONO: Well, that's all I got to say. I just say that because I love you both.

TROY: Hell, you know me . . . I wasn't out there looking for nothing. You can't find a better woman than Rose. I know that. But seems like this woman just stuck onto me where I can't shake her loose. I done wrestled with it, tried to throw her off me . . . but she just stuck on tighter. Now she's stuck on for good.

BONO: You's in control . . . that's what you tell me all the time. You responsible for what you do.

TROY: I ain't ducking the responsibility of it. As long as it sets right in my heart . . . then I'm okay. Cause that's all I listen to. It'll tell me right from wrong every time. And I ain't talking about doing Rose no bad turn. I love Rose. She done carried me a long ways and I love and respect her for that.

BONO: I know you do. That's why I don't want to see you hurt her. But what you gonna do when she find out? What you got then? If you try and juggle both of them . . . sooner or later you gonna drop one of them. That's common sense.

TROY: Yeah, I hear what you saying, Bono. I been trying to figure a way to work it out.

BONO: Work it out right, Troy. I don't want to be getting all up between you and Rose's business . . . but work it so it come out right.

TROY: Aw hell, I get all up between you and Lucille's business. When you gonna get that woman that refrigerator she been wanting? Don't tell me you ain't got no money now. I know who your banker is. Mellon don't need that money bad as Lucille want that refrigerator. I'll tell you that.

BONO: Tell you what I'll do . . . when you finish building this fence for Rose . . . I'll buy Lucille that refrigerator.

TROY: You done stuck your foot in your mouth now!

*(TROY grabs up a board and begins to saw. BONO starts to walk out the yard.)*

Hey, nigger . . . where you going?

BONO: I'm going home. I know you don't expect me to help you now. I'm protecting my money. I wanna see you put that fence up by yourself. That's what I want to see. You'll be here another six months without me.

TROY: Nigger, you ain't right.

BONO: When it comes to my money . . . I'm right as fireworks on the Fourth of July.

TROY: Alright, we gonna see now. You better get out your bankbook.

*(BONO exits, and TROY continues to work. ROSE enters from the house.)*

ROSE: What they say down there? What's happening with Gabe?

TROY: I went down there and got him out. Cost me fifty dollars. Say he was disturbing the peace. Judge set up a hearing for him in three weeks. Say to show cause why he shouldn't be re-committed.

ROSE: What was he doing that cause them to arrest him?

TROY: Some kids was teasing him and he run them off home. Say he was howling and carrying on. Some folks seen him and called the police. That's all it was.

ROSE: Well, what's you say? What'd you tell the judge?

TROY: Told him I'd look after him. It didn't make no sense to recommit the man. He stuck out his big greasy palm and told me to give him fifty dollars and take him on home.

ROSE: Where's he at now? Where'd he go off to?

TROY: He's gone on about his business. He don't need nobody to hold his hand.

ROSE: Well, I don't know. Seem like that would be the best place for him if they did put him into the hospital. I know what you're gonna say. But that's what I think would be best.

TROY: The man done had his life ruined fighting for what? And they wanna take and lock him up. Let him be free. He don't bother nobody.

ROSE: Well, everybody got their own way of looking at it I guess. Come on and get your lunch. I got a bowl of lima beans and some cornbread in the oven. Come on get something to eat. Ain't no sense you fretting over Gabe.

*(ROSE turns to go into the house.)*

TROY: Rose . . . got something to tell you.

ROSE: Well, come on . . . wait till I get this food on the table.

TROY: Rose!

*(She stops and turns around.)*

I don't know how to say this.

*(Pause.)*

I can't explain it none. It just sort of grows on you till it gets out of hand. It starts out like a little bush . . . and the next think you know it's a whole forest.

ROSE: Troy . . . what is you talking about?

1600 TROY: I'm talking, woman, let me talk. I'm trying to find a way to tell you . . . I'm gonna be a daddy. I'm gonna be somebody's daddy.

ROSE: Troy . . . you're not telling me this? You're gonna be . . . what?

TROY: Rose . . . now . . . see . . .

ROSE: You telling me you gonna be somebody's daddy? You telling your *wife* this?

(GABRIEL *enters from the street. He carries a rose in his hand.*)

GABRIEL: Hey, Troy! Hey, Rose!

ROSE: I have to wait eighteen years to hear something like this.

1610 GABRIEL: Hey, Rose . . . I got a flower for you.

(*He hands it to her.*)

That's a rose. Same rose like you is.

ROSE: Thanks, Gabe.

GABRIEL: Troy, you ain't mad at me is you? Them bad mens come and put me away. You ain't mad at me is you?

TROY: Naw, Gabe, I ain't mad at you.

ROSE: Eighteen years and you wanna come with this.

GABRIEL: (*Takes a quarter out of his pocket.*) See what I got? Got a brand new quarter.

TROY: Rose . . . it's just . . .

1620 ROSE: Ain't nothing you can say, Troy. Ain't no way of explaining that.

GABRIEL: Fellow that give me this quarter had a whole mess of them. I'm gonna keep this quarter till it stop shining.

ROSE: Gabe, go on in the house there. I got some watermelon in the frigidaire. Go on and get you a piece.

GABRIEL: Say, Rose . . . you know I was chasing hellhounds and them bad mens come and get me and take me away. Troy helped me. He come down there and told them they better let me go before he beat them up. Yeah, he did!

1630 ROSE: You go on and get you a piece of watermelon, Gabe. Them bad mens is gone now.

GABRIEL: Okay, Rose . . . gonna get me some watermelon. The kind with the stripes on it.

(GABRIEL *exits into the house.*)

ROSE: Why, Troy? Why? After all these years to come dragging this in to me now. It don't make no sense at your age. I could have expected this ten or fifteen years ago, but not now.

TROY: Age ain't got nothing to do with it, Rose.

ROSE: I done tried to be everything a wife should be. Everything a wife could be. Been married eighteen years and I got 1640 to live to see the day you tell me you been seeing another woman and done fathered a child by her.

And you know I ain't never wanted no half nothing in my family. My whole family is half. Everybody got different fathers and mothers . . . my two sisters and my brother. Can't hardly tell who's who. Can't never sit down and talk about Papa and Mama. It's your papa and your mama and my papa and my mama . . .

TROY: Rose . . . stop it now.

ROSE: I ain't never wanted that for none of my children. And 1650 now you wanna drag your behind in here and tell me something like this.

TROY: You ought to know. It's time for you to know.

ROSE: Well, I don't want to know, goddamn it!

TROY: I can't just make it go away. It's done now. I can't wish the circumstance of the thing away.

ROSE: And you don't want to either. Maybe you want to wish me and my boy away. Maybe that's what you want? Well, you can't wish us away. I've got eighteen years of my life invested in you. You ought to have stayed upstairs in my bed where you belong. 1660

TROY: Rose . . . now listen to me . . . we can get a handle on this thing. We can talk this out . . . come to an understanding.

ROSE: All of a sudden it's "we." Where was "we" at when you was down there rolling around with some godforsaken woman? "We" should have come to an understanding before you started making a damn fool of yourself. You're a day late and a dollar short when it comes to an understanding with me.

TROY: It's just . . . She gives me a different idea . . . a different understanding about myself. I can step out of this house and 1670 get away from the pressures and problems . . . be a different man. I ain't got to wonder how I'm gonna pay the bills or get the roof fixed. I can just be a part of myself that I ain't never been.

ROSE: What I want to know . . . is do you plan to continue seeing her. That's all you can say to me.

TROY: I can sit up in her house and laugh. Do you understand what I'm saying. I can laugh out loud . . . and it feels good. It reaches all the way down to the bottom of my shoes.

(*Pause.*)

Rose, I can't give that up. 1680

ROSE: Maybe you ought to go on and stay down there with her . . . if she a better woman than me.

TROY: It ain't about nobody being a better woman or nothing. Rose, you ain't the blame. A man couldn't ask for no woman to be a better wife than you've been. I'm responsible for it. I done locked myself into a pattern trying to take care of you all that I forgot about myself.

ROSE: What the hell was I there for? That was my job, not somebody else's.

TROY: Rose, I done tried all my life to live decent . . . to live a 1690 clean . . . hard . . . useful life. I tried to be a good husband to you. In every way I knew how. Maybe I come into the world backwards, I don't know. But . . . you born with two strikes on you before you come to the plate. You got to guard it closely . . . always looking for the curve-ball on the inside corner. You can't afford to let none get past you. You can't afford a call strike. If you going down . . . you going down swinging. Everything lined up against you. What you gonna do. I fooled them, Rose. I bunted. When I found you and Cory and a halfway decent job . . . I was safe. Couldn't noth- 1700 ing touch me. I wasn't gonna strike out no more. I wasn't going back to the penitentiary. I wasn't gonna lay in the streets with a bottle of wine. I was safe. I had me a family. A job. I wasn't gonna get that last strike. I was on first looking for one of them boys to knock me in. To get me home.

ROSE: You should have stayed in my bed, Troy.

TROY: Then when I saw that gal . . . she firmed up my backbone. And I got to thinking that if I tried . . . I just might be able to steal second. Do you understand after eighteen years I wanted to steal second. 1710

ROSE: You should have held me tight. You should have grabbed me and held on.

TROY: I stood on first base for eighteen years and I thought . . . well, goddamn it . . . go on for it!

ROSE: We're not talking about baseball! We're talking about you going off to lay in bed with another woman . . . and then bring it home to me. That's what we're talking about. We ain't talking about no baseball.

TROY: Rose, you're not listening to me. I'm trying the best I can to explain it to you. It's not easy for me to admit that I been standing in the same place for eighteen years.

ROSE: I been standing with you! I been right here with you, Troy. I got a life too. I gave eighteen years of my life to stand in the same spot with you. Don't you think I ever wanted other things? Don't you think I had dreams and hopes? What about my life? What about me? Don't you think it ever crossed my mind to want to know other men? That I wanted to lay up somewhere and forget about my responsibilities? That I wanted someone to make me laugh so I could feel good? You not the only one who's got wants and needs. But I held on to you, Troy. I took all my feelings, my wants and needs, my dreams . . . and I buried them inside you. I planted a seed and watched and prayed over it. I planted myself inside you and waited to bloom. And it didn't take me no eighteen years to find out the soil was hard and rocky and it wasn't never gonna bloom.

But I held on to you, Troy. I held you tighter. You was my husband. I owed you everything I had. Every part of me I could find to give you. And upstairs in that room . . . with the darkness falling in on me . . . I gave everything I had to try and erase the doubt that you wasn't the finest man in the world. And wherever you was going . . . I wanted to be there with you. Cause you was my husband. Cause that's the only way I was gonna survive as your wife. You always talking about what you give . . . and what you don't have to give. But you take too. You take . . . and don't even know nobody's giving!

(ROSE *turns to exit into the house;* TROY *grabs her arm.*)

TROY: You say I take and don't give!

ROSE: Troy! You're hurting me!

TROY: You say I take and don't give.

ROSE: Troy . . . you're hurting my arm! Let go!

TROY: I done give you everything I got. Don't you tell that lie on me.

ROSE: Troy!

TROY: Don't you tell that lie on me!

(CORY *enters from the house.*)

CORY: Mama!

ROSE: Troy. You're hurting me.

TROY: Don't you tell me about no taking and giving.

(CORY *comes up behind* TROY *and grabs him.* TROY, *surprised, is thrown off balance just as* CORY *throws a glancing blow that catches him on the chest and knocks him down.* TROY *is stunned, as is* CORY.)

ROSE: Troy. Troy. No!

(TROY *gets to his feet and starts at* CORY.)

1760     Troy . . . no. Please! Troy!

(ROSE *pulls on* TROY *to hold him back.* TROY *stops himself.*)

TROY: (*To* CORY.) Alright. That's strike two. You stay away from around me, boy. Don't you strike out. You living with a full count. Don't you strike out.

(TROY *exits out the yard as the lights go down.*)

## SCENE II

*It is six months later, early afternoon.* TROY *enters from the house and starts to exit the yard.* ROSE *enters from the house.*

ROSE: Troy, I want to talk to you.

TROY: All of a sudden, after all this time, you want to talk to me, huh? You ain't wanted to talk to me for months. You ain't wanted to talk to me last night. You ain't wanted no part of me then. What you wanna talk to me about now?

ROSE: Tomorrow's Friday.

TROY: I know what day tomorrow is. You think I don't know tomorrow's Friday? My whole life I ain't done nothing but look to see Friday coming and you got to tell me it's Friday.

ROSE: I want to know if you're coming home.

TROY: I always come home, Rose. You know that. There ain't never been a night I ain't come home.

ROSE: That ain't what I mean . . . and you know it. I want to know if you're coming straight home after work.

TROY: I figure I'd cash my check . . . hang out at Taylors' with the boys . . . maybe play a game of checkers . . .

ROSE: Troy, I can't live like this. I won't live like this. You livin' on borrowed time with me. It's been going on six months now you ain't been coming home.

TROY: I be here every night. Every night of the year. That's 365 days.

ROSE: I want you to come home tomorrow after work.

TROY: Rose . . . I don't mess up my pay. You know that now. I take my pay and I give it to you. I don't have no money but what you give me back. I just want to have a little time to myself . . . a little time to enjoy life.

ROSE: What about me? When's my time to enjoy life?

TROY: I don't know what to tell you, Rose. I'm doing the best I can.

ROSE: You ain't been home from work but time enough to change your clothes and run out . . . and you wanna call that the best you can do?

TROY: I'm going over to the hospital to see Alberta. She went into the hospital this afternoon. Look like she might have the baby early. I won't be gone long.

ROSE: Well, you ought to know. They went over to Miss Pearl's and got Gabe today. She said you told them to go ahead and lock him up.

TROY: I ain't said no such thing. Whoever told you that is telling a lie. Pearl ain't doing nothing but telling a big fat lie.

ROSE: She ain't had to tell me. I read it on the papers.

TROY: I ain't told them nothing of the kind.

ROSE: I saw it right there on the papers.

TROY: What it say, huh?

ROSE: It said you told them to take him.

TROY: Then they screwed that up, just the way they screw up everything. I ain't worried about what they got on the paper.

ROSE: Say the government send part of his check to the hospital and the other part to you.

TROY: I ain't got nothing to do with that if that's the way it works. I ain't made up the rules about how it work.

ROSE: You did Gabe just like you did Cory. You wouldn't sign the paper for Cory . . . but you signed for Gabe. You signed that paper.

(*The telephone is heard ringing inside the house.*)

TROY: I told you I ain't signed nothing, woman! The only thing
1820   I signed was the release form. Hell, I can't read, I don't know what they had on that paper! I ain't signed nothing about sending Gabe away.

ROSE: I said send him to the hospital . . . you said let him be free . . . now you done went down there and signed him to the hospital for half his money. You went back on yourself, Troy. You gonna have to answer for that.

TROY: See now . . . you been over there talking to Miss Pearl. She done got mad cause she ain't getting Gabe's rent money. That's all it is. She's liable to say anything.

1830 ROSE: Troy, I seen where you signed the paper.

TROY: You ain't seen nothing I signed. What she doing got papers on my brother anyway? Miss Pearl telling a big fat lie. And I'm gonna tell her about it too! You ain't seen nothing I signed. Say . . . you ain't seen nothing I signed.

(ROSE *exits into the house to answer the telephone. Presently she returns.*)

ROSE: Troy . . . that was the hospital. Alberta had the baby.

TROY: What she have? What is it?

ROSE: It's a girl.

TROY: I better get on down to the hospital to see her.

ROSE: Troy . . .

1840 TROY: Rose . . . I got to go see her now. That's only right . . . what's the matter . . . the baby's alright, ain't it?

ROSE: Alberta died having the baby.

TROY: Died . . . you say she's dead? Alberta's dead?

ROSE: They said they done all they could. They couldn't do nothing for her.

TROY: The baby? How's the baby?

ROSE: They say it's healthy. I wonder who's gonna bury her.

TROY: She had family, Rose. She wasn't living in the world by herself.

1850 ROSE: I know she wasn't living in the world by herself.

TROY: Next thing you gonna want to know if she had any insurance.

ROSE: Troy, you ain't got to talk like that.

TROY: That's the first thing that jumped out your mouth. "Who's gonna bury her?" Like I'm fixing to take on that task for myself.

ROSE: I am your wife. Don't push me away.

TROY: I ain't pushing nobody away. Just give me some space. That's all. Just give me some room to breathe.

(ROSE *exits into the house.* TROY *walks about the yard.*)

1860 TROY: (*With a quiet rage that threatens to consume him.*) Alright . . . Mr. Death. See now . . . I'm gonna tell you what I'm gonna do. I'm gonna take and build me a fence around this yard. See? I'm gonna build me a fence around what belongs to me. And then I want you to stay on the other side. See?

You stay over there until you're ready for me. Then you come on. Bring your army. Bring your sickle. Bring your wrestling clothes. I ain't gonna fall down on my vigilance this time. You ain't gonna sneak up on me no more. When you ready for me . . . when the top of your list say Troy Maxson . . . that's when you come around here. You come up and 1870 knock on the front door. Ain't nobody else got nothing to do with this. This is between you and me. Man to man. You stay on the other side of that fence until you ready for me. Then you come up and knock on the front door. Anytime you want. I'll be ready for you.

(*The lights go down to black.*)

SCENE III

*The lights come up on the porch. It is late evening three days later.* ROSE *sits listening to the ball game waiting for* TROY. *The final out of the game is made and* ROSE *switches off the radio.* TROY *enters the yard carrying an infant wrapped in blankets. He stands back from the house and calls.*

(ROSE *enters and stands on the porch. There is a long, awkward silence, the weight of which grows heavier with each passing second.*)

TROY: Rose . . . I'm standing here with my daughter in my arms. She ain't but a wee bittie little old thing. She don't know nothing about grownups' business. She innocent . . . and she ain't got no mama.

ROSE: What you telling me for, Troy?                                    1880

(*She turns and exits into the house.*)

TROY: Well . . . I guess we'll just sit out here on the porch.

(*He sits down on the porch. There is an awkward indelicateness about the way he handles the baby. His largeness engulfs and seems to swallow it. He speaks loud enough for* ROSE *to hear.*)

A man's got to do what's right for him. I ain't sorry for nothing I done. It felt right in my heart.

(*To the baby.*)

What you smiling at? Your daddy's a big man. Got these great big old hands. But sometimes he's scared. And right now your daddy's scared cause we sitting out here and ain't got no home. Oh, I been homeless before. I ain't had no little baby with me. But I been homeless. You just be out on the road by your lonesome and you see one of them trains coming and you just kinda go like this . . .                          1890

(*He sings as a lullaby.*)

> Please, Mr. Engineer let a man ride the line
> Please, Mr. Engineer let a man ride the line
> I ain't got no ticket please let me ride the blinds

(ROSE *enters from the house.* TROY *hearing her steps behind him, stands and faces her.*)

She's my daughter, Rose. My own flesh and blood. I can't deny her no more than I can deny them boys.

(*Pause.*)

You and them boys is my family. You and them and this child is all I got in the world. So I guess what I'm saying is . . . I'd appreciate it if you'd help me take care of her.

ROSE: Okay, Troy . . . you're right. I'll take care of your baby for 1900   you . . . cause . . . like you say . . . she's innocent . . . and you can't visit the sins of the father upon the child. A motherless child has got a hard time.

*(She takes the baby from him.)*

From right now . . . this child got a mother. But you a womanless man.

*(ROSE turns and exits into the house with the baby. Lights go down to black.)*

SCENE IV

*It is two months later.* LYONS *enters from the street. He knocks on the door and calls.*

LYONS: Hey, Rose! *(Pause.)* Rose!
ROSE: *(From inside the house.)* Stop that yelling. You gonna wake up Raynell. I just got her to sleep.
LYONS: I just stopped by to pay Papa this twenty dollars I owe him. Where's Papa at?
1910  ROSE: He should be here in a minute. I'm getting ready to go down to the church. Sit down and wait on him.
LYONS: I got to go pick up Bonnie over her mother's house.
ROSE: Well, sit it down there on the table. He'll get it.
LYONS: *(Enters the house and sets the money on the table.)* Tell Papa I said thanks. I'll see you again.
ROSE: Alright, Lyons. We'll see you.

*(LYONS starts to exit as* CORY *enters)*

CORY: Hey, Lyons.
LYONS: What's happening, Cory. Say man, I'm sorry I missed your graduation. You know I had a gig and couldn't get 1920   away. Otherwise, I would have been there, man. So what you doing?
CORY: I'm trying to find a job.
LYONS: Yeah I know how that go, man. It's rough out here. Jobs are scarce.
CORY: Yeah, I know.
LYONS: Look here, I got to run. Talk to Papa . . . he know some people. He'll be able to help get you a job. Talk to him . . . see what he say.
CORY: Yeah . . . alright, Lyons.
1930  LYONS: You take care. I'll talk to you soon. We'll find some time to talk.

*(LYONS exits the yard.* CORY *wanders over to the tree, picks up the bat and assumes a batting stance. He studies an imaginary pitcher and swings. Dissatisfied with the result, he tries again.* TROY *enters. They eye each other for a beat.* CORY *puts the bat down and exits the yard.* TROY *starts into the house as* ROSE *exits with* RAYNELL. *She is carrying a cake.)*

TROY: I'm coming in and everybody's going out.
ROSE: I'm taking this cake down to the church for the bakesale. Lyons was by to see you. He stopped by to pay you your twenty dollars. It's laying in there on the table.
TROY: *(Going into his pocket.)* Well . . . here go this money.

ROSE: Put it in there on the table, Troy. I'll get it.
TROY: What time you coming back?
ROSE: Ain't no use in you studying me. It don't matter what time I come back.                                                                1940
TROY: I just asked you a question, woman. What's the matter . . . can't I ask you a question?
ROSE: Troy, I don't want to go into it. Your dinner's in there on the stove. All you got to do is heat it up. And don't you be eating the rest of them cakes in there. I'm coming back for them. We having a bakesale at the church tomorrow.

*(ROSE exits the yard.* TROY *sits down on the steps, takes a pint bottle from his pocket, opens it and drinks. He begins to sing.)*

TROY:

> *Hear it ring! Hear it ring!*
> *Had an old dog his name was Blue*
> *You know Blue was mighty true*                                  1950
> *You know Blue as a good old dog*
> *Blue trees a possum in a hollow log*
> *You know from that he was a good old dog*

*(BONO enters the yard.)*

BONO: Hey, Troy.
TROY: Hey, what's happening, Bono?
BONO: I just thought I'd stop by to see you.
TROY: What you stop by and see me for? You ain't stopped by in a month of Sundays. Hell, I must owe you money or something.
BONO: Since you got your promotion I can't keep up with you. 1960  Used to see you everyday. Now I don't even know what route you working.
TROY: They keep switching me around. Got me out in Greentree now . . . hauling white folks' garbage.
BONO: Greentree, huh? You lucky, at least you ain't got to be lifting them barrels. Damn if they ain't getting heavier. I'm gonna put in my two years and call it quits.
TROY: I'm thinking about retiring myself.
BONO: You got it easy. You can *drive* for another five years.
TROY: It ain't the same, Bono. It ain't like working the back of 1970  the truck. Ain't got nobody to talk to . . . feel like you working by yourself. Naw, I'm thinking about retiring. How's Lucille?
BONO: She alright. Her arthritis get to acting up on her sometime. Saw Rose on my way in. She going down to the church, huh?
TROY: Yeah, she took up going down there. All them preachers looking for somebody to fatten their pockets.

*(Pause.)*

Got some gin here.
BONO: Naw, thanks. I just stopped by to say hello.                       1980
TROY: Hell, nigger . . . you can take a drink. I ain't never known you to say no to a drink. You ain't got to work tomorrow.
BONO: I just stopped by. I'm fixing to go over to Skinner's. We got us a domino game going over his house every Friday.
TROY: Nigger, you can't play no dominoes. I used to whup you four games out of five.
BONO: Well, that learned me. I'm getting better.
TROY: Yeah? Well, that's alright.
BONO: Look here . . . I got to be getting on. Stop by sometime, huh?                                                                      1990

TROY: Yeah, I'll do that, Bono. Lucille told Rose you bought her a new refrigerator.

BONO: Yeah, Rose told Lucille you had finally built your fence . . . so I figured we'd call it even.

TROY: I knew you would.

BONO: Yeah . . . okay. I'll be talking to you.

TROY: Yeah, take care, Bono. Good to see you. I'm gonna stop over.

BONO: Yeah. Okay, Troy.

(BONO *exits.* TROY *drinks from the bottle.*)

2000   TROY:

> Old Blue died and I dig his grave
> Let him down with a golden chain
> Every night when I hear old Blue bark
> I know Blue treed a possum in Noah's Ark.
> Hear it ring! Hear it ring!

(CORY *enters the yard. They eye each other for a beat.* TROY *is sitting in the middle of the steps.* CORY *walks over.*)

CORY: I got to get by.

TROY: Say what? What's you say?

CORY: You in my way. I got to get by.

TROY: You got to get by where? This is my house. Bought and
2010   paid for. In full. Took me fifteen years. And if you wanna go in my house and I'm sitting on the steps . . . you say excuse me. Like your mama taught you.

CORY: Come on, Pop . . . I got to get by.

(CORY *starts to maneuver his way past* TROY. TROY *grabs his leg and shoves him back.*)

TROY: You just gonna walk over top of me?

CORY: I live here too!

TROY: (*Advancing toward him.*) You just gonna walk over top of me in my own house?

CORY: I ain't scared of you.

TROY: I ain't asked if you was scared of me. I asked you if you
2020   was fixing to walk over top of me in my own house? That's the question. You ain't gonna say excuse me? You just gonna walk over top of me?

CORY: If you wanna put it like that.

TROY: How else am I gonna put it?

CORY: I was walking by you to go into the house cause you sitting on the steps drunk, singing to yourself. You can put it like that.

TROY: Without saying excuse me???

(CORY *doesn't respond.*)

I asked you a question. Without saying excuse me???

2030   CORY: I ain't got to say excuse me to you. You don't count around here no more.

TROY: Oh, I see . . . I don't count around here no more. You ain't got to say excuse me to your daddy. All of a sudden you done got so grown that your daddy don't count around here no more . . . Around here in his own house and yard that he done paid for with the sweat of his brow. You done got so grown to where you gonna take over. You gonna take over my house. Is that right? You gonna wear my pants. You gonna go in there and stretch out on my bed. You ain't got
2040   to say excuse me cause I don't count around here no more. Is that right?

CORY: That's right. You always talking this dumb stuff. Now, why don't you just get out my way.

TROY: I guess you got someplace to sleep and something to put in your belly. You got that, huh? You got that? That's what you need. You got that, huh?

CORY: You don't know what I got. You ain't got to worry about what I got.

TROY: You right! You one hundred percent right! I done spent the last seventeen years worrying about what you got. Now 2050 it's your turn, see? I'll tell you what to do. You grown . . . we done established that. You a man. Now, let's see you act like one. Turn your behind around and walk out this yard. And when you get out there in the alley . . . you can forget about this house. See? Cause this is my house. You go on and be a man and get your own house. You can forget about this. 'Cause this is mine. You go on and get yours cause I'm through with doing for you.

CORY: You talking about what you did for me . . . what'd you ever give me? 2060

TROY: Them feet and bones! That pumping heart, nigger! I give you more than anybody else is ever gonna give you.

CORY: You ain't never gave me nothing! You ain't never done nothing but hold me back. Afraid I was gonna be better than you. All you ever did was try and make me scared of you. I used to tremble every time you called my name. Every time I heard your footsteps in the house. Wondering all the time . . . what's Papa gonna say if I do this? . . . What's he gonna say if I do that? . . . What's Papa gonna say if I turn on the radio? And Mama, too . . . she tries . . . but she's scared 2070 of you.

TROY: You leave your mama out of this. She ain't got nothing to do with this.

CORY: I don't know how she stand you . . . after what you did to her.

TROY: I told you to leave your mama out of this!

(He advances toward CORY.)

CORY: What you gonna do . . . give me a whupping? You can't whup me no more. You're too old. You just an old man.

TROY: (*Shoves him on his shoulder.*) Nigger! That's what you are. You just another nigger on the street to me! 2080

CORY: You crazy! You know that?

TROY: Go on now! You got the devil in you. Get on away from me!

CORY: You just a crazy old man . . . talking about I got the devil in me.

TROY: Yeah, I'm crazy! If you don't get on the other side of that yard . . . I'm gonna show you how crazy I am! Go on . . . get the hell out of my yard.

CORY: It ain't your yard. You took Uncle Gabe's money he got from the army to buy this house and then you put him out. 2090

TROY: (TROY *advances on* CORY.) Get your black ass out of my yard!

(TROY's *advance backs* CORY *up against the tree.* CORY *grabs up the bat.*)

CORY: I ain't going nowhere! Come on . . . put me out! I ain't scared of you.

TROY: That's my bat!

CORY: Come on!

TROY: Put my bat down!

CORY: Come on, put me out.

(CORY *swings at* TROY, *who backs across the yard.*)

What's the matter? You so bad . . . put me out!

(TROY *advances toward* CORY.)

2100 CORY: (*Backing up.*) Come on! Come on!

TROY: You're gonna have to use it! You wanna draw that bat back on me . . . you're gonna have to use it.

CORY: Come on! . . . Come on!

(CORY *swings the bat at* TROY *a second time. He misses.* TROY *continues to advance toward him.*)

TROY: You're gonna have to kill me! You wanna draw that bat back on me. You're gonna have to kill me.

(CORY, *backed up against the tree, can go no farther.* TROY *taunts him. He sticks out his head and offers him a target.*)

Come on! Come on!

(CORY *is unable to swing the bat.* TROY *grabs it.*)

TROY: Then I'll show you.

(CORY *and* TROY *struggle over the bat. The struggle is fierce and fully engaged.* TROY *ultimately is the stronger, and takes the bat from* CORY *and stands over him ready to swing. He stops himself.*)

Go on and get away from around my house.

(CORY, *stung by his defeat, picks himself up, walks slowly out of the yard and up the alley.*)

CORY: Tell Mama I'll be back for my things.

2110 TROY: They'll be on the other side of that fence.

(CORY *exits.*)

TROY: I can't taste nothing. Helluljah! I can't taste nothing no more. (TROY *assumes a batting posture and begins to taunt Death, the fastball in the outside corner.*) Come on! It's between you and me now! Come on! Anytime you want! Come on! I be ready for you . . . but I ain't gonna be easy.

(*The lights go down on the scene.*)

SCENE V

*The time is 1965. The lights come up in the yard. It is the morning of* TROY's *funeral. A funeral plaque with a light hangs beside the door. There is a small garden plot off to the side. There is noise and activity in the house as* ROSE, GABRIEL *and* BONO *have gathered. The door opens and* RAYNELL, *seven years old, enters dressed in a flannel nightgown. She crosses to the garden and pokes around with a stick.* ROSE *calls from the house.*

ROSE: Raynell!

RAYNELL: Mam?

ROSE: What you doing out there?

RAYNELL: Nothing.

(ROSE *comes to the door.*)

2120 ROSE: Girl, get in here and get dressed. What you doing?

RAYNELL: Seeing if my garden growed.

ROSE: I told you it ain't gonna grow overnight. You got to wait.

RAYNELL: It don't look like it never gonna grow. Dag!

ROSE: I told you a watched pot never boils. Get in here and get dressed.

RAYNELL: This ain't even no pot, Mama.

ROSE: You just have to give it a chance. It'll grow. Now come on and do what I told you. We got to be getting ready. This ain't no morning to be playing around. You hear me?

RAYNELL: Yes, mam.    2130

(ROSE *exits into the house.* RAYNELL *continues to poke at her garden with a stick.* CORY *enters. He is dressed in a Marine corporal's uniform, and carries a duffel bag. His posture is that of a military man, and his speech has a clipped sternness.*)

CORY: (*To* RAYNELL.) Hi.

(*Pause.*)

I bet your name is Raynell.

RAYNELL: Uh huh.

CORY: Is your mama home?

(RAYNELL *runs up on the porch and calls through the screen-door.*)

RAYNELL: Mama . . . there's some man out here. Mama?

(ROSE *comes to the door.*)

ROSE: Cory? Lord have mercy! Look here, you all!

(ROSE *and* CORY *embrace in a tearful reunion as* BONO *and* LYONS *enter from the house dressed in funeral clothes.*)

BONO: Aw, looka here . . .

ROSE: Done got all grown up!

CORY: Don't cry, Mama. What you crying about?

ROSE: I'm just so glad you made it.    2140

CORY: Hey Lyons. How you doing, Mr. Bono?

(LYONS *goes to embrace* CORY.)

LYONS: Look at you, man. Look at you. Don't he look good, Rose. Got them Corporal stripes.

ROSE: What took you so long.

CORY: You know how the Marines are, Mama. They got to get all their paperwork straight before they let you do anything.

ROSE: Well, I'm sure glad you made it. They let Lyons come. Your Uncle Gabe's still in the hospital. They don't know if they gonna let him out or not. I just talked to them a little while ago.    2150

LYONS: A Corporal in the United States Marines.

BONO: Your daddy knew you had it in you. He used to tell me all the time.

LYONS: Don't he look good, Mr. Bono?

BONO: Yeah, he remind me of Troy when I first met him.

(*Pause.*)

Say, Rose, Lucille's down at the church with the choir. I'm gonna go down and get the pallbearers lined up. I'll be back to get you all.

ROSE: Thanks, Jim.

CORY: See you, Mr. Bono.    2160

LYONS: (*With his arm around* RAYNELL.) Cory . . . look at Raynell. Ain't she precious? She gonna break a whole lot of hearts.

ROSE: Raynell, come and say hello to your brother. This is your brother, Cory. You remember Cory.

RAYNELL: No, Mam.

CORY: She don't remember me, Mama.

ROSE: Well, we talk about you. She heard us talk about you. (*To* RAYNELL.) This is your brother, Cory. Come on and say
2170  hello.

RAYNELL: Hi.

CORY: Hi. So you're Raynell. Mama told me a lot about you.

ROSE: You all come on into the house and let me fix you some breakfast. Keep up your strength.

CORY: I ain't hungry, Mama.

LYONS: You can fix me something, Rose. I'll be in there in a minute.

ROSE: Cory, you sure you don't want nothing. I know they ain't feeding you right.
2180  CORY: No, Mama . . . thanks. I don't feel like eating. I'll get something later.

ROSE: Raynell . . . get on upstairs and get that dress on like I told you.

(ROSE *and* RAYNELL *exit into the house.*)

LYONS: So . . . I hear you thinking about getting married.

CORY: Yeah, I done found the right one, Lyons. It's about time.

LYONS: Me and Bonnie been split up about four years now. About the time Papa retired. I guess she just got tired of all them changes I was putting her through.

(*Pause.*)

I always knew you was gonna make something out yourself.
2190  Your head was always in the right direction. So . . . you gonna stay in . . . make it a career . . . put in your twenty years?

CORY: I don't know. I got six already, I think that's enough.

LYONS: Stick with Uncle Sam and retire early. Ain't nothing out here. I guess Rose told you what happened with me. They got me down the workhouse. I thought I was being slick cashing other people's checks.

CORY: How much time you doing?

LYONS: They give me three years. I got that beat now. I ain't got
2200  but nine more months. It ain't so bad. You learn to deal with it like anything else. You got to take the crookeds with the straights. That's what Papa used to say. He used to say that when he struck out. I seen him strike out three times in a row . . . and the next time up he hit the ball over the grandstand. Right out there in Homestead Field. He wasn't satisfied hitting in the seats . . . he want to hit it over everything! After the game he had two hundred people standing around waiting to shake his hand. You got to take the crookeds with the straights. Yeah, Papa was something else.
2210  CORY: You still playing?

LYONS: Cory . . . you know I'm gonna do that. There's some fellows down there we got us a band . . . we gonna try and stay together when we get out . . . but yeah, I'm still playing. It still helps me to get out of bed in the morning. As long as it do that I'm gonna be right there playing and trying to make some sense out of it.

ROSE: (*Calling.*) Lyons, I got these eggs in the pan.

LYONS: Let me go and get these eggs, man. Get ready to go bury Papa.

(*Pause.*)

How you doing? You doing alright?    2220

(CORY *nods.* LYONS *touches him on the shoulder and they share a moment of silent grief.* LYONS *exits into the house.* CORY *wanders about the yard.* RAYNELL *enters.*)

RAYNELL: Hi.

CORY: Hi.

RAYNELL: Did you used to sleep in my room?

CORY: Yeah . . . that used to be my room.

RAYNELL: That's what Papa call it. "Cory's room." It got your football in the closet.

(ROSE *comes to the door.*)

ROSE: Raynell, get in there and get them good shoes on.

RAYNELL: Mama, can't I wear these. Them other one hurt my feet.

ROSE: Well, they just gonna have to hurt your feet for a while.    2230  You ain't said they hurt your feet when you went down to the store and got them.

RAYNELL: They didn't hurt then. My feet done got bigger.

ROSE: Don't you give me no backtalk now. You get in there and get them shoes on.

(RAYNELL *exits into the house.*)

Ain't too much changed. He still got that piece of rag tied to that tree. He was out here swinging that bat. I was just ready to go back in the house. He swung that bat and and then he just fell over. Seem like he swung it and stood over there with this grin on his face . . . and then he just fell over. They carried    2240  him on down to the hospital, but I knew there wasn't no need . . . why don't you come on in the house?

CORY: Mama . . . I got something to tell you. I don't know how to tell you this . . . but I've got to tell you . . . I'm not going to Papa's funeral.

ROSE: Boy, hush your mouth. That's your daddy you talking about. I don't want to hear that kind of talk this morning. I done raised you to come to this? You standing there all healthy and grown talking about you ain't going to your daddy's funeral?    2250

CORY: Mama . . . listen . . .

ROSE: I don't want to hear it, Cory. You just get that thought out of your head.

CORY: I can't drag Papa with me everywhere I go. I've got to say no to him. One time in my life I've got to say no.

ROSE: Don't nobody have to listen to nothing like that. I know you and your daddy ain't seen eye to eye, but I ain't got to listen to that kind of talk this morning. Whatever was between you and your daddy . . . the time has come to put it aside. Just take it and set it over there on the shelf and for-    2260  get about it. Disrespecting your daddy ain't gonna make you a man, Cory. You got to find a way to come to that on your own. Not going to your daddy's funeral ain't gonna make you a man.

CORY: The whole time I was growing up . . . living in his house . . . Papa was like a shadow that followed you everywhere. It weighed on you and sunk into your flesh. It would wrap around you and lay there until you couldn't tell which one was you anymore. That shadow digging in your flesh. Trying to crawl in. Trying to live through you. Everywhere I    2270  looked, Troy Maxson was staring back at me . . . hiding under the bed . . . in the closet. I'm just saying I've got to find a way to get rid of that shadow, Mama.

ROSE: You just like him. You got him in you good.

CORY: Don't tell me that, Mama.

ROSE: You Troy Maxson all over again.

CORY: I don't want to be Troy Maxson. I want to be me.

ROSE: You can't be nobody but who you are, Cory. That
2280 shadow wasn't nothing but you growing into yourself. You
either got to grow into it or cut it down to fit you. But that's
all you got to make life with. That's all you got to measure
yourself against that world out there. Your daddy wanted
you to be everything he wasn't . . . and at the same time he
tried to make you into everything he was. I don't know if he
was right or wrong . . . but I do know he meant to do more
good than he meant to do harm. He wasn't always right.
Sometimes when he touched he bruised. And sometimes
when he took me in his arms he cut.

When I first met your daddy I thought . . . Here is a man I
2290 can lay down with and make a baby. That's the first thing I
thought when I seen him. I was thirty years old and had
done seen my share of men. But when he walked up to me
and said, "I can dance a waltz that'll make you dizzy," I
thought, Rose Lee, here is a man that you can open yourself
up to and be filled to bursting. Here is a man that can fill all
them empty spaces you been tipping around the edges of.
One of them empty spaces was being somebody's mother.
I married your daddy and settled down to cooking his supper and keeping clean sheets on the bed. When your daddy
2300 walked through the house he was so big he filled it up. That
was my first mistake. Not to make him leave some room for
me. For my part in the matter. But at that time I wanted
that. I wanted a house that I could sing in. And that's what
your daddy gave me. I didn't know to keep up his strength I
had to give up little pieces of mine. I did that. I took on his
life as mine and mixed up the pieces so that you couldn't
hardly tell which was which anymore. It was my choice. It
was my life and I didn't have to live it like that. But that's
what life offered me in the way of being a woman and I took
2310 it. I grabbed hold of it with both hands.

By the time Raynell came into the house, me and your
daddy had done lost touch with one another. I didn't want
to make my blessing off of nobody's misfortune . . . but I
took on to Raynell like she was all them babies I had wanted
and never had.

*(The phone rings.)*

Like I'd been blessed to relive a part of my life. And if the
Lord see fit to keep up my strength . . . I'm gonna do her just
like your daddy did you . . . I'm gonna give her the best of
what's in me.

2320 RAYNELL: *(Entering, still with her old shoes.)* Mama . . . Reverend Tollivier on the phone.

*(ROSE exits into the house.)*

RAYNELL: Hi.

CORY: Hi.

RAYNELL: You in the Army or the Marines?

CORY: Marines.

RAYNELL: Papa said it was the Army. Did you know Blue?

CORY: Blue? Who's Blue?

RAYNELL: Papa's dog what he sing about all the time.

CORY: *(Singing.)*

> Hear it ring! Hear it ring!     2330
> I had a dog his name was Blue
> You know Blue was mighty true
> You know Blue was a good old dog
> Blue treed a possum in a hollow log
> You know from that he was a good old dog.
> Hear it ring! Hear it ring!

*(RAYNELL joins in singing.)*

CORY and RAYNELL:

> Blue treed a possum out on a limb
> Blue looked at me and I looked at him
> Grabbed that possum and put him in a sack     2340
> Blue stayed there till I came back
> Old Blue's feets was big and round
> Never allowed a possum to touch the ground.
>
> Old Blue died and I dug his grave
> I dug his grave with a silver spade
> Let him down with a golden chain
> And every night I call his name
> Go on Blue, you good dog you
> Go on Blue, you good dog you

RAYNELL:     2350

> Blue laid down and died like a man
> Blue laid down and died . . .

BOTH:

> Blue laid down and died like a man
> Now he's treeing possums in the Promised Land
> I'm gonna tell you this to let you know
> Blue's gone where the good dogs go
> When I hear old Blue bark
> When I hear old Blue bark
> Blue treed a possum in Noah's Ark     2360
> Blue treed a possum in Noah's Ark.

*(ROSE comes to the screen door.)*

ROSE: Cory, we gonna be ready to go in a minute.

CORY: *(To RAYNELL.)* You go on in the house and change them
shoes like Mama told you so we can go to Papa's funeral.

RAYNELL: Okay, I'll be back.

*(RAYNELL exits into the house. CORY gets up and crosses over to
the tree. ROSE stands in the screen door watching him. GABRIEL
enters from the alley.)*

GABRIEL: *(Calling.)* Hey, Rose!

ROSE: Gabe?

GABRIEL: I'm here, Rose. Hey Rose, I'm here!

*(ROSE enters from the house.)*

ROSE: Lord . . . Look here, Lyons!

LYONS: See, I told you, Rose . . . I told you they'd let him come.     2370

CORY: How you doing, Uncle Gabe?

LYONS: How you doing, Uncle Gabe?

GABRIEL: Hey, Rose. It's time. It's time to tell St. Peter to open
the gates. Troy, you ready? You ready, Troy. I'm gonna tell
St. Peter to open the gates. You get ready now.

*(Gabriel, with great fanfare, braces himself to blow. The trum-
pet is without a mouthpiece. He puts the end of it into his
mouth and blows with great force, like a man who has been*

*waiting some twenty-odd years for this single moment. No sound comes out of the trumpet. He braces himself and blows again with the same result. A third time he blows. There is a weight of impossible description that falls away and leaves him bare and exposed to a frightful realization. It is a trauma that a sane and normal mind would be unable to withstand. He begins to dance. A slow, strange dance, eerie and lifegiving. A dance of atavistic signature and ritual.* LYONS

*attempts to embrace him.* GABRIEL *pushes* LYONS *away. He begins to howl in what is an attempt at song, or perhaps a song turning back into itself in an attempt at speech. He finishes his dance and the gates of heaven stand open as wide as God's closet.)*

That's the way that go!

*(Blackout.)*

---

*THIS interview was conducted by David Savran.*

August Wilson

Interview
(1987)

**What were your early experiences in theatre?**

I was a participant in the Black Power movement in the early sixties and I wrote poetry and short fiction. I was interested in art and literature and I felt that I could alter the relationship between blacks and society through the arts. There was an explosion of black theatre in the late sixties—theatre was a way of politicizing the community and raising the consciousness of the people. So with my friend, Rob Penny, I started the Black Horizons Theatre in Pittsburgh in 1968.

I knew nothing about theatre. I had never seen a play before. I started directing but I didn't have any idea how to do this stuff, although I did find great information in the library. We started doing Baraka's plays and virtually anything else out there. I remember *The Drama Review* printed a black issue, somewhere around '69, and we did every play in the book. I tried to write a play but it was disastrous. I couldn't write dialogue. Doing community theatre was very difficult—rehearsing two hours a night after people got off work, not knowing if the actors were going to show up. In '71, because of having to rely so much on other people, I said "I don't need this," and I concentrated on writing poetry and short stories.

Then in 1976 a friend of mine from Pittsburgh, Claude Purdy, was living in L.A. He came back to Pittsburgh and came to a reading of a series of poems I'd written about a character, Black Bart, a kind of Western satire. He said, "You should turn this into a play." He kept after me and eventually I sat down and wrote a play and gave it to him. He went to St. Paul to direct a show and said, "Why don't you come out and rewrite the play?" He sent me a ticket and I thought, "A free trip to St. Paul, what the hell?" So I went out and did a quick rewrite of the play. That was in November '77. In January of '78, the Inner City Theatre in Los Angeles did a staged reading of it.

**What's it called?**

*Black Bart and the Sacred Hills*—a musical satire. In 1981 we did a production in St. Paul at Penumbra Theatre, for which Claude Purdy worked. When I moved to St. Paul I got a job in the Science Museum of Minnesota as a script writer—they had a theatre troupe attached to the museum. That was the first job where someone was actually paying me to write. We dramatized tales of the Northwest Indians—how Peyote got his name, how Spiderwoman taught the Navahoes to read—which were very popular. Then I started doing Profiles of Science—I went around to all the curators asking who can I write a play about. The biology guy suggested William Harvey, who discovered the circulation of the blood, so I wrote a one-man show on Harvey, one on Charles Darwin, one on Margaret Mead. I was writing scripts without knowing that I was becoming a playwright. Then I found out about the Eugene O'Neill Theatre Center's National Playwrights Conference and wrote a play called *Jitney* that I sent in along with *Black Bart*. They sent them back. Then I submitted *Jitney* to the Playwrights' Center in Minneapolis. They accepted it and gave me twenty-five hundred dollars.

I remember walking into a room there containing sixteen playwrights and thinking, "Wow, I must be a playwright." The Playwrights' Center was a very helpful experience. We did a reading of *Jitney* and I felt encouraged. So I wrote *Fullerton Street,* which was set in the forties. We did a staged reading of it and I sent it off to the O'Neill and they sent it back. I sent *Jitney* to them again because I thought, "You guys didn't read this play," and they sent it back a second time. I was forced to look at it again and I thought, "Maybe it's not as good as I think it is. I have to write a better play but how the hell do you do that?" I felt I was writing the best I could. A workshop of

*Fullerton Street* had been very helpful, so I felt confident. *Jitney*—okay, it wasn't quite big enough. *Fullerton Street* was epic and too unwieldy. I decided to try for something right in the middle. I sat down and wrote *Ma Rainey's Black Bottom* and sent that off to the O'Neill and they accepted it.

### When you first started writing plays, what playwrights influenced you most strongly?

None, really. Baraka wrote a book called *Four Revolutionary Plays* which I liked—I liked the language, I liked everything about them. In my early one-acts I tried to imitate that and then I discovered I wasn't him and that wasn't going to work. Other than Baraka, the first black playwright I found who wrote anything that even approached what was, to my ear, realistic dialogue for black folks was Philip Hayes Dean. I directed his play *The Owl-Killer* for the theatre in Pittsburgh. I don't want to judge it as a play, but I thought the dialogue was good. Likewise, *The Sty of the Blind Pig.* I haven't read Ibsen, Shaw, Shakespeare—except *The Merchant of Venice* in ninth grade. The only Shakespeare I've ever seen was *Othello* last year at Yale Rep. I'm not familiar with *Death of a Salesman.* I haven't read Tennessee Williams. I very purposefully didn't read them.

The first professional production I saw was *The Taking of Miss Janie* by Ed Bullins in New York. I think it's his best work but I didn't really care for the play. But something happened when I saw *Sizwe Bansi Is Dead* at the Pittsburgh Public Theater in 1976. I thought, "This is great. I wonder if I could write something like this?" Most of the plays that I have seen are Fugard plays, so he's probably had an influence on me without my knowing it. Among the fourteen or so plays I've seen have been *Blood Knot, Sizwe Bansi, "Master Harold" . . . and the boys* and *Boesman and Lena.*

### I'm surprised to hear that you know so few plays. I'm struck by how linear your plays are, how traditional the protagonist-antagonist opposition is and how smoothly they build to a final confrontation. Especially in Joe Turner. It's like Ibsen.

The foundation of my playwriting is poetry. Not so much in terms of the language but in the concept. After writing poetry for twenty-one years, I approach a play the same way. I think Robert Duncan said form equals content. So each play is specific, each is different, each has its own form. But the mental process is poetic: you use metaphor and condense. I try to find a metaphor to carry the work.

I approach playwriting as literature, as opposed to a craft—though craft is important. It occurred to me one day that when I sit down to write, I am sitting in the same chair as Ibsen, Shaw, Miller, Beckett—every playwright. You're confronted with the same problems: what to do with this space and how to articulate your ideas in two hours of public time, moving characters about in an environment designed specifically for them. It gives you a sense of power, sitting in this hallowed and well-worn chair. I get comfortable and write from the feeling that I'm free to do anything I choose to do, to create this thing called literature.

### What was the most important experience in your training as a playwright?

The O'Neill. I first went with *Ma Rainey* when it was a fifty-nine page, ill-organized script—some people say it's still ill-organized—and was fortunate enough to work with Michael Feingold as my dramaturg. The important thing I learned was to rewrite. Not just patchworking here and fixing there, but exactly what the word means—re-writing. When you write, you know where you want to go—you know what a scene, a particular speech is supposed to accomplish. Then I discovered that it's possible to go back and rewrite this speech, to find another way to say it. In a poem you rewrite six or seven times before you end up with what you want. But I didn't think of theatre as being like that. And I learned to respect the stage and trust that it will carry your ideas. The intensity of the O'Neill process—working in four days, working fast—was also good experience. It comes down to problem solving. But there's no one correct solution.

The O'Neill made me more conscious of what theatre is about. There's nothing like encountering the problems of costume, lighting, set design—What do you mean by this? Where is this? Where is the window?—which make you more aware of the totality of what you're doing. I discovered with *Fences,* for example, that I had a character exiting upstage and coming back immediately with a different costume. That's really sloppy but I was totally unaware. I never thought, "The guy's got to change his costume." I've become conscious of things like that and it's made me a better playwright. But I don't want to lose the impulse, the sense, as with *Ma Rainey,* that anything goes, that you may do whatever you desire to do. Maybe I wouldn't have written *Ma Rainey* as I did, had I been aware of the problems with casting and with the music.

**In Ma Rainey *the instruments the characters play become metaphors. Toledo the pianist sounds a broad compass of experience and Levee the trumpet player expresses individual subjectivity more aggressively.***

With the trumpet you have to blow and force yourself out through the horn. Half-consciously, I tried to make Levee's voice be a trumpet. I was conscious when I was writing the dialogue that this is the bass player talking, this is the trombonist talking. Levee is a brassy voice.

***How do you start a play?***

I generally start with an idea, something that I want to say. In *The Piano Lesson* the question was, "Can one acquire a sense of self-worth by denying one's past?" (I think I place myself on one side of the question.) So then, how do you put this question on stage, how do you narrate it? Next I got the title from a Romare Bearden painting called *The Piano Lesson.* His painting is actually a piano teacher with a kid. I wanted a woman character as large as Troy is in *Fences.* I wanted to write it for Mary Alice to challenge her talent. I think she's a wonderful actress and there are not many roles for black actresses of that magnitude. From the painting I had a piano, and I just started writing a line of dialogue and had no idea who was talking. First I had four guys moving the piano into an empty house. I discarded that because people would be offstage too much, getting other pieces of furniture.

Someone says something to someone else, and they talk, and at some point I say, "Well, who is this?" and I give him a name. But I have no idea what the story line of the play is. It's a process of discovery. While writing *The Piano Lesson* I came up with the idea of tracing the history of the piano for a hundred and thirty-five years, with the idea that it had been used to purchase members of this family from slavery. But I didn't know how that was going to tie in. I knew there was a story, but I didn't know what the story was. I discovered it as the characters began to talk: one guy wants to sell the piano, the sister doesn't want to. I thought, why doesn't she want to sell it? Finding all those things helped me to find the story. I put off writing the history of the piano—one character tells the whole story—until I found it out in the process of writing dialogue. As it turned out, the female character is not as large as I intended. I'm not sure the play's about the idea I started with. I think the central question ended up being "How do you use your legacy?"

I write in bars and restaurants. At the start of the day, I take my tablet and I go out and search for a play. I get some coffee and sit down. If I feel like writing something, I do. If I don't, I go about my day. I've started writing a play called *Two Trains Running*, set in the sixties. I have no idea what it's about. I started with a line of dialogue. I was in rehearsals in New Haven and this line came to me. I said, "Not now, please, I'm busy," but I had to go with it. It may or may not end up in the play. But having discovered it, I know something central to the character who is speaking. The story and the character will grow out of that one line of dialogue.

Then I will place the character within the sociology of the sixties, keeping in mind that I am trying to write plays that contain the sum total of black culture in America, and its difference from white culture. Once you put in the daily rituals of black life, the play starts to get richer and bigger. You're creating a whole world in the process of telling your story, of writing this character. Once you place him down in his environment, you have to write about his whole philosophical approach to life. And then you can uncover, from a black perspective, the universalities of life. Some questions will emerge that man has been asking himself ever since he's been on the planet. One of my favorite lines in *Joe Turner* is, "Why God got to be so big? Why he got to be bigger than me?" I think this is one of the first questions man asked himself when he found out that he wasn't God. Why am I not the biggest thing in the universe? Romare Bearden said, "I try to explore, in terms of the life I know best, those things common to all culture." You discover that the black experience is as valuable, rich and varied as anybody else's and that there's been so little written about it.

Blacks do not have a history of writing—things in Africa were passed on orally. In that tradition you orally pass on your entire philosophy, your ideas and attitudes about life. Most of them were passed along in blues. You have to make the philosophy interesting musically and lyrically, so that someone will want to repeat it, to teach it to someone else as soon as they've heard it. If you don't make it interesting, the information dies. I began to view blues as the African-American's response to the world before he started writing down his stuff. James Baldwin has a beautiful phrase—"field of manners and rituals of intercourse." An African man has a whole different field of manners. All cultures have their mythology, their creative motifs and social and political organizations. To my mind, people just gloss over these things in the black community without really examining it and seeing what's there.

***I'm interested to hear you talk about history. One line from* Ma Rainey *could, I think, stand as an epigraph to your work: "The white man . . . done the eating and he know what he done ate. But we don't know that we been took and made history of."***
We're leftovers from history—history that happened when there was a tremendous need for manual labor, when cotton was king. But history and life progress, you move into the industrial age, and now we're moving into the computer age. We're left over. We're no longer needed. At one time we were very valuable to America—free labor.

***So what you're doing with your series of plays is rediscovering history, rewriting history.***
Yes, because the history of blacks in America has not been written by blacks. And whites, of course, have a different attitude, a different relationship to the history. Writing our own history has been a very valuable tool, because if we're going to be pointed toward a future, we must know our past. This is so basic and simple yet it's a thing that Africans in America disregard. For instance, the fact of slavery is something that blacks do not teach their kids—they do not tell their kids that at one time we were slaves. That is the most crucial and central thing to our presence here in America. It's nothing to be ashamed of. Why is it, after spending hundreds of years in bondage, that blacks in America do not once a year get together and celebrate the Emancipation and remind ourselves of our history? If we did that, we would recognize our uniqueness in being African. One of the things I'm trying to say in my writing is that we can never really begin to make a contribution to the society except as Africans.

If you took Africans and said, "Here's all the money and resources you need, solve the problems of society," things would be totally different. The social organization would be different. We'd probably all live in round houses, as opposed to square ones. I don't think society would be as consumer-oriented. Now, if you can't buy anything, you're worthless. You don't count if you can't consume. I don't think it would be that kind of society because of the differences in our values and our attitudes toward ownership.

To make inroads into society, you have to give up your African-ness. You can be doctors, lawyers, be middle-class, but if you want to go to Harvard, you have to give up the natural way that you do things as blacks. Let me give you an example. I was in a bus station in St. Paul. I saw six Japanese-American guys having breakfast at the counter. They chatted among themselves and then the check came and they—I'll make a joke here—they all reached for their American Express cards. It was nice and they embraced and there was a slight bow and off they went.

What would be the difference if six black guys came in and ordered breakfast? The first thing they'd notice is the jukebox. This is very important: it never entered the mind of those Japanese guys to play the jukebox. Six black guys walk in, somebody's going to the jukebox. He's gonna drop a quarter. Another guy's gonna say, "Hey Rodney, play this." And he's gonna say, "Man, get out of here, play your own record. I ain't playin' with you." Another thing I notice, none of the Japanese guys said anything to the waitress. But a black guy would say: "Hey, mama, don't talk to him. Look, baby, where ya from? Why don't you give me your phone number?" A guy gets up to play another record, somebody steals a piece of bacon off his plate: "Don't mess with my food. Who took my food?" It comes time to pay the bill, it's only two dollars: "Hey, man, lend me two dollars. I ain't got no money. Come on, man, give me a dollar."

If you're a white observer you say, "They don't know how to act. They're loud. They're boisterous. They don't like one another. The guy won't let him play a song. They're thieves. He stole a piece of bacon." The Japanese have their way of eating breakfast. Blacks have their way. If you bring in six white characters, an entirely different dynamic would go on. White society tells Africans, "You can't act like that. If you act like that, you won't get anywhere in society. If you want to make progress, you have to learn to act like us. Then you can go to school, we'll hire you for a job, we'll do this, that and the other." I don't see that said to other ethnic groups. Asians are allowed to maintain their Asian-ness and still participate in society. That suppression of blacks does not allow you the impulse, does not allow you to respond to the world without encumbrance. I try to reveal this and to allow my characters to be as African as they are and to respond to the world as they would.

### How closely do you work with Lloyd Richards?

Generally I will meet with him an hour before rehearsal and talk about what happened yesterday and what we're going to do today. I don't talk to actors in rehearsal. I talk to Lloyd and he understands and communicates my concerns to the actors. Other than that, I just look at the way things are going and I listen. Some things might strike my ear wrong. I might find a certain scene doesn't build the way I thought it did. So I make changes when necessary and come back the next day with new pages.

### How extensive are these changes?

Usually the changes are minor. For example, in *Ma Rainey* Levee had to put his shoes on and there weren't lines to cover that action. That's the only thing I can remember actually adding to the script in the rehearsal process.

*Fences* was a bit different because we were cutting a four-hour play down to two hours and ten minutes. Sometimes in watching it I'd say, "We cut this, but I need it back." One part I cut out for the Yale and Goodman productions I put back because I needed a moment between father and son that was not a conflict. Cory asks Troy, "Hey, Pop, why don't you buy a TV?" And Troy tells him that the roof needs tarring. He's teaching him a lesson about priorities. "If you don't fix the roof, the water's going to run all over your brand-new TV. So if you had twenty dollars, what would you do?" You need that moment to balance the conflict. Rehearsals were more cutting and adding to shape it, as opposed to major rewriting.

I do a major rewrite before the O'Neill Conference and then, after the two-day staged readings, I've got a bunch of notes and ideas and I do another major rewrite and that is generally the play that we go into rehearsal with. I don't mind cutting. I'll say, "If that's not working, what do you need? Let's put something else in here," because this is theatre. Nobody writes a perfect play by just sitting down and writing. You find out what's there when the actors begin to move around in the space.

With *Joe Turner* people had been saying before rehearsals that we should see Loomis find his song. After a read-through I knew that moment was missing. We went into rehearsal and it remained an unsolved problem. Then I came up with the idea of ending the first act with him on the floor unable to stand up. When he stands at the end, you can read that as him finding his song. That's one thing I discovered in rehearsal that was crucial to the play. I never would have found it sitting at home.

### Is there a favorite among your plays?

Not really, it's like comparing your kids. They're all mine. Although I always consider the last thing I've done the best. So I think *Piano Lesson* is my best play. After that, it would be *Joe Turner* and then *Fences*. I think I was able to get more things through in *Joe Turner*. Among my plays, *Fences* is the odd one, more conventional in structure with its large character. I kept hearing *Ma Rainey* described as oddly structured and I thought, "I can write one of those plays where you have a big character and everything revolves around him." I like *Joe Turner* for the ideas and for Loomis's accepting responsibility for his own salvation and his own presence in the world. Those kinds of statements are not present in *Fences*. So of those three, I like *Joe Turner* best. I hope that it shows a growth, a maturing.

### I find that sexual politics comes into more prominence in Joe Turner, when Bynum says, "When you grab hold to a woman, you got something there. You got a whole world there."

A way of life kicking up under your hand.

*There and in your other plays I get a sense of the interconnection between racial politics and sexual politics. Can you describe your goal in portraying black men?*

I'm trying to write an honest picture of the black male in America. I try to present positive images, strong black male characters who take a political stand, if only in the sense of Loomis in *Joe Turner:* one, Joe Turner's come and gone, it ain't gonna happen no more; two, I don't need anyone to bleed for me, I can bleed for myself. I can accept responsibility for my presence in the world. The idea of responsibility is crucial because, I believe, white Americans basically see black males as irresponsible, which I think is incorrect. They say, you should be responsible in the same way we are, without understanding that we have different ideas of responsibility.

I try to position my characters so they're pointed toward the future. I try to demonstrate the spirit of the character. For instance, in *Ma Rainey,* Levee's a very spirited character who does a terrible thing. He murders someone. He's going to spend the next twenty years in the penitentiary. But he's willing to confront life with a certain zest and energy. It's the same with Troy. He wrestles with death. I try to make them heroic. I've experienced it and I'm just trying to uncover it, pulling layer after layer from the stereotype.

*In reading* Fences, *I came to view Troy more and more critically as the play progressed, sharing Rose's point of view. We see that Troy has been crippled by his father. That's being replayed in Troy's relationship with Cory. Do you think there's a way out of that cycle?*

Surely. First of all, we're all like our parents. The things we are taught early in life, how to respond to the world, our sense of morality—everything, we get from them. Now you can take that legacy and do with it anything you want to do. It's in your hands. Cory is Troy's son. How can he be Troy's son without sharing Troy's values? I was trying to get at why Troy made the choices he made, how they have influenced his values and how he attempts to pass those along to his son. Each generation gives the succeeding generation what they think they need. One question in the play is, "Are the tools we are given sufficient to compete in a world that is different from the one our parents knew?" I think they are—it's just that we have to do different things with the tools. That's all Troy has to give. Troy's flaw is that he does not recognize that the world was changing. That's because he spent fifteen years in a penitentiary.

As African-Americans, we should demand to participate in society as Africans. That's the way out of the vicious cycle of poverty and neglect that exists in 1987 in America, where you have a huge percentage of blacks living in the equivalent of South African townships, in housing projects. No one is inviting these people to participate in society. Look at the poverty levels—$8,500 for a family of four, if you have $8,501 you're not counted. Those statistics would go up enormously if we had an honest assessment of the cost of living in America. I don't know how anybody can support a family of four on $8,500. What I'm saying is that 85 or 90 percent of blacks in America are living in abject poverty and, for the most part, are crowded into what amount to concentration camps. The situation for blacks in America is worse than it was forty years ago. Some sociologists will tell you about the tremendous progress we've made. They didn't put me out when I walked in the door. And you can always point to someone who works on Wall Street, or is a doctor. But they don't count in the larger scheme of things.

*Do you have any idea how these political changes could take place?*

I'm not sure. I know that blacks must be allowed their cultural differences. I think the process of assimilation to white American society was a big mistake. We don't want to be like you. Blacks living in housing projects are isolated from the society, for the most part—living as they choose, as Africans. Only they don't realize the value in what they're doing because they have accepted their victimization. They've marked themselves as victims. Once they recognize that, they can begin to move through society in a different manner, from a stronger position, and claim what is theirs.

*A project of yours is to point up what happens when oppression is internalized.*

Yes, transfer of aggression to the wrong target. I think it's interesting that the two roads open to blacks for "full participation" are entertainment and sports. *Ma Rainey* and *Fences,* and I didn't plan it that way. I don't think that they're the correct roads. I think Troy's right. Now with the benefit of historical perspective, I can say that the athletic scholarship was actually a way of exploiting. Now you've got two million kids who think they're going to play in the NBA. In the sixties the universities made a lot of money off of athletics. You had kids playing for free who, by and large, were not getting educated, were taking courses in basketweaving. Some of them could barely read.

*Troy may be right about that issue, but it seems that he has passed on certain destructive traits in spite of himself. Take the hostility between father and son.*

I think every generation says to the previous generation: you're in my way, I've got to get by. The father-son conflict is actually a normal generational conflict that happens all the time.

*So it's a healthy and a good thing?*

Oh, sure. Troy is seeing this boy walk around, smelling his piss. Two men cannot live in the same household. Troy would have been tremendously disappointed if Cory had not challenged him. Troy knows that this boy has to go out and do battle with that world: "So I had best prepare him because I know that's a harsh, cruel place out there. But that's going to be easy compared to what he's getting here. Ain't nobody gonna whip your ass like I'm gonna whip it." He has a tremendous love for the kid. But he's not going to say, "I love you," he's going to demonstrate it. He's carrying garbage for seventeen years just for the kid. The only world Troy knows is the one that he made. Cory's going to go on to find another one, he's going to arrive at the same place as Troy. I think one of the most important lines in the play is when Troy is talking about his father: "I got to the place where I could feel him kicking in my blood and knew that the only thing that separated us was the matter of a few years."

Hopefully, Cory will do things a bit differently with his son. For Troy, sports was not the way to go, the white man wouldn't let him get away with that. "Get you a job, with your hands, something that nobody can take away from you." The idea of school—he doesn't know what that is. That's for white folks. Very few blacks had paperwork jobs. But if you knew how to fix cars, you could always make some money. That's what Troy wants for Cory. There aren't many people who ever jumped up in Troy's face. So he's proud of the kid at the same time that he expresses a hurt that all men feel. You got to cut your kid loose at some point. There's that sense of loss and separation. You find out how Troy left his father's house and you see how Cory leaves his house. I suspect with Cory it will repeat with some differences and maybe, after five or six generations, they'll find a different way to do it.

*Where Cory ends up is very ambiguous, as a marine in 1965.*

Yes. For the average black kid on the street, that was an alternative. You went into the army because you could learn how to do something. I can remember my parents talking about the son of some friends: "He's in the navy. He *did* something"—as opposed to standing on the street corner, shooting drugs, drinking wine and robbing stores. Lyons says to Cory, "I always knew you were going to make something out of yourself." It really wounds me. He's a corporal in the marines. For blacks, that is a sense of accomplishment. Therein lies one of the tragedies of blacks in America. Cory says, "I don't know. I put in six years. That's enough." Anyone who goes into the army and makes a career out of it is a loser. They sit there and are nurtured by the army and they don't have to confront life. Then they get out of the army and find there's nothing to do. They didn't learn any skills. And if they did, they can't find a job. Four months later, they're shooting dope. In the sixties a whole bunch of blacks went over, fought and died in the Vietnam War. The survivors came back to the same street corners and found out nothing had changed. They still couldn't get a job.

At the end of *Fences* every person, with the exception of Raynell, is institutionalized. Rose is in a church. Lyons is in a penitentiary. Gabriel's in a mental hospital and Cory's in the marines. The only free person is the girl, Troy's daughter, the hope for the future. That was conscious on my part because in '57 that's what I saw. Blacks have relied on institutions which are really foreign—except for the black church, which has been our saving grace. I have some problems with it but I recognize it as a central social organization and sometimes an economic organization for the black community. I would like to see blacks develop their own institutions that respond to their needs.

*That religious element is so important in* Joe Turner. *At the end of that play, when Loomis "shines," the moment of fulfillment and salvation has such strong religious overtones— both African and Christian—as well as social and political ones. How do you see the relationship between the religious and the political?*

I think blacks are essentially a religious people. Whites see man against a world that needs to be subdued. Africans see man as a part of the world, as a natural part of their environment. Blacks have taken Christianity and bent it to serve their African-ness. In Africa there's ancestor worship, among kinds of religious practices. That's given blacks, particularly southern blacks, the idea of ghosts, magic and superstition—for example, the horseshoe as a good-luck symbol. It's not the shape, it's the iron, the god of iron which protects your house. Relating to the spirit worlds is very much a part of African and Afro-American culture.

I try to approach people with an anthropologist's eye. That's why I make constant references to food. If you study culture, you want to know what people eat, what their social organization is. In my plays you can see what the economics are—that's an important part of any culture. In *Fences*, for example, Gabriel goes to work every day. He goes and collects his fruits and vegetables to sell and he's trying so hard to be self-sufficient, even though he's gravely wounded. He's my favorite character because he still wants to contribute and work. I'm trying to illuminate the culture, so that you're able to see the "field of manners and rituals of intercourse that can sustain a man once he's left his father's house."

What I want is that you walk away from my play, whether you're black or white, with the idea that these are Africans, as opposed to black folks in America. Yet I have found a tremendous resistance to that. I talked with an audience at Yale Rep after *Joe Turner* and I actually lost my temper. I said, "How many recognize these people as Africans?" There were two hundred people sitting there and about eight raised their hands. I'm very curious as to why they refuse—I have to say it's a refusal because it's so obvious. So many people blocked that, wanting to recognize them as black Americans. I was really surprised to find that.

### *Do you read the critics?*

Sure. Do I value them? I have mixed opinions about critics. I've been fortunate to have gotten mostly good reviews. If you have six hundred people at a play, you have six hundred different opinions. But critics should have an informed opinion and therein lies their value—they can bring a lot, not to a particular play, but to the development of theatre. The bad reviews that I've gotten are the ones I study. I think the guy's misread the play and I want to know, how did he see it this way? I'm trying to communicate to everyone. If I missed communicating with someone with an informed opinion, then I try to look at it through his eyes and see how he arrived at his opinion. I don't place a whole hell of a lot of value on the critical response. I'm glad when anyone who sees my work says, "I really enjoyed that." A critic's saying that is no different from an ordinary person walking up and saying that to me.

### *How do you see the American theatre today?*

I'm relatively new to theatre. I can speak most about playwriting because I've been a participant at the O'Neill for four years. I'm a member of New Dramatists. For the most part, I've been disappointed in the work, even from some very talented playwrights. First, it's the influence of television. A whole generation of playwrights has been raised on television. I think it's a bad influence on theatre, which in many ways is almost an archaic art form. I'm fearful it may go the way of opera, which is an elitist art, one that doesn't engage the larger society.

Theatre engages very few people. I don't think it has to be that way. I think it should be a part of everyone's life, the way television is. But it's not. It's moving the other way. As it costs more and more to produce plays, you see fewer and fewer. Fewer playwrights are given the opportunity to fail. You can learn immeasurably from a failure. You should at least be given the opportunity to bat—if you strike out, you strike out. The cost of production, the price of tickets, all of these things further remove theatre from the people and make it an elitist art form, which I think is wrong. But I don't know how you correct it.

The second main problem is society's attitude toward playwriting. It's not considered a part of literature. What has been missing from the new plays I've seen is metaphor. The story often reads like a TV sitcom—it's slight, there's no character development. Writing for the stage is very different. If playwriting was reconnected to the idea of literature, I think you would begin to see better plays. If you're giving the audience the same thing they're getting on TV, there's no reason to come to the theatre.

If every regional theatre would select a playwright and commit themselves to doing a play of his or hers every year, by the third year you're going to have a better playwright. There's nothing like writing a play knowing that it's going to be produced and working to reward the faith that's been placed in you. New plays are looked at in a disparaging way. A theatre will do its fifth Shaw in five years on the mainstage without even considering whether a new play deserves more attention than a staged reading or a second-stage production. You say "new play" and people run the other way. Theatres should be encouraging and nurturing, providing a home for playwrights and providing audiences with an alternative. Of course they say there isn't the material there. I'm saying if you work with what you have, five years from now you're going to have different and better material.

The playwright has a responsibility to the audience. I'm asking people to hire a babysitter, get dressed, find the car keys, find a place to park, pay money—more than it costs to go see a movie. When they get there, I should have something to say to them that's worth all their trouble. I discovered my responsibility sitting in the theatre at Yale, watching the audience. You can't do that with workshops or staged readings. Playwrights are not like fiction writers. They need living bodies. One thing I'll never forget is my confrontation with a set designer at the O'Neill who asked me a thousand difficult questions about the play. Unless you go through that process, you're working in a vacuum.

I'm not sure what to do about production costs. I do think the American people would subsidize the theatre if it was made a part of their life. They subsidize television, simply by watching it. Maybe we have to have commercials in the theatre. There has to be some financial basis to allow all the people involved in the production to make a living.

### What are your goals for the future?

What's important for me is to write plays, as opposed to movies or television. After *Ma Rainey* I was offered work on this and that movie. But I want to establish myself as a playwright first. I hope to write one play a year and finish my series. I'm working on the sixties play now. I have my forties play. I'll either rewrite it or throw it out and come up with a better idea. Then I'll do contemporary plays. But I've enjoyed the benefit of the historical perspective. I have an idea for a novel that I've been tossing around. A novel, for me, was always a vast, uncharted sea. It was like being lost on the ocean. So was a play, for that matter, at one point. So I feel confident coming from plays and I'd like to try my novel. I still write poetry.

### You said that when you first got interested in theatre, you thought it could be an effective political tool. Do you still think it can be?

Absolutely. All art is political. It serves a purpose. All of my plays are political but I try not to make them didactic or polemical. Theatre doesn't have to be agitprop. I hope that my art serves the masses of blacks in America who are in desperate need of a solid and sure identity. I hope my plays make people understand that these are African people, that this is why they do what they do. If blacks recognize the value in that, then we will be on our way to claiming our identity and participating in society as Africans.

And one other thing: the blues is the core. All American popular music, especially in 1987, is influenced by the blues. This is the one contribution everyone admits that Africans have made. But the music has been pulled so far out of context that it's no longer recognizable. Any attempt to claim it is met with tremendous resistance. The music is ours, since it contains our soul, so to speak—it contains all our ideas and responses to the world. We need it to help us claim this African-ness and we would be a stronger people for it. It's presently in the hands of someone else who sits over it as custodian, without even allowing us its source.

### When Loomis finds his song, he can stand up again.

Yes.

# David Henry Hwang

David Henry Hwang was born in Los Angeles in 1957; he graduated with a B. A. in English from Stanford University in 1979 and studied at the Yale School of Drama 1980–1981. In the 1980s, Hwang wrote a series of powerful plays concerning the cultural and political experience of Asian Americans in the United States. His first play, *F.O.B.* ("Fresh off the boat") was written while he was a student at Stanford and staged in a dormitory there; it dramatizes the tensions that arise between Chinese immigrants to the United States and their assimilated friends and relatives. When it moved to New York, *F.O.B.* won an Obie award in 1980. Hwang addressed similar issues in *The Dance of the Railroad* (1981), *Family Devotions* (1981), *The Sound of a Voice* (1983), *The House of Sleeping Beauties* (1983), and *Rich Relations* (1986), and he collaborated with composer Philip Glass on *1000 Airplanes on the Roof* (1988). Hwang's Tony Award-winning *M. Butterfly* (1988) is a brilliant critique of Western attitudes toward Asia, epitomized by one of Western culture's most powerful and seductive images of the Orient: Puccini's opera, *Madame Butterfly*. Hwang also wrote the screenplay for the film version of *M. Butterfly* (1993).

## M. Butterfly (1988)

In *M. Butterfly*, Hwang traces the relationship between the "Orient" of the Western imagination and the political realities that such images help to foster. The play's central character, the diplomat Gallimard, conducts his relationship with China in terms of Puccini's *Madame Butterfly*. In Puccini's 1904 opera, the naval officer Pinkerton marries the Japanese geisha girl Butterfly. He leaves for the United States, promising to return, and Butterfly waits for him, meanwhile bearing his child. When Pinkerton sends his wife from America to collect his child, Butterfly realizes that he will never return; she commits suicide.

As Hwang has remarked, Butterfly has become a cultural stereotype of East-West relations—"speaking of an Asian woman, we would sometimes say, 'She's pulling a Butterfly,' which meant playing the submissive Oriental number." This sexist and racist stereotype, Hwang argues, pervades not only Western men's fantasies about Asian women—as the mail-order business in Asian wives suggests, Western men see Asian women as obedient, submissive, and sexually self-sacrificing—but also conditions the political relationship between Asia and the West as well.

*M. Butterfly* fuses this erotic and political desire for domination in the character of Gallimard, a French diplomat who falls in love with Song Liling, an opera singer whom he first sees singing the death aria from *Madame Butterfly*. But the play develops a fascinating twist, for Song is in fact a man, who plays female roles in the Beijing Opera, and who—as a woman—develops a love affair with Gallimard in order to spy for the Chinese government. *M. Butterfly* compacts a complex reading of the politics of race, gender, and sexuality in a richly theatrical drama.

# —M. Butterfly—
## David Henry Hwang

## —PLAYWRIGHT'S NOTES—

■ ■ ■ "A former French diplomat and a Chinese opera singer have been sentenced to six years in jail for spying for China after a two-day trial that traced a story of clandestine love and mistaken sexual identity. . . . Mr. Bouriscot was accused of passing information to China after he fell in love with Mr. Shi, whom he believed for twenty years to be a woman."

*— The New York Times,* MAY 11, 1986

This play was suggested by international newspaper accounts of a recent espionage trial. For purposes of dramatization, names have been changed, characters created, and incidents devised or altered, and this play does not purport to be a factual record of real events or real people.

■ ■ ■ "I could escape this feeling
With my China girl . . ."

— DAVID BOWIE & IGGY POP

## —CHARACTERS—

KUROGO
RENE GALLIMARD
SONG LILING
MARC/MAN #2/CONSUL SHARPLESS
RENEE/WOMAN AT PARTY/GIRL IN MAGAZINE
COMRADE CHIN/SUZUKI/SHU-FANG
HELGA
M. TOULON/MAN #1/JUDGE

*The action of the play takes place in a Paris prison in the present, and in recall, during the decade 1960 to 1970 in Beijing, and from 1966 to the present in Paris.*

## —ACT ONE—

SCENE I

*M. Gallimard's prison cell. Paris. Present.*

*Lights fade up to reveal Rene Gallimard, 65, in a prison cell. He wears a comfortable bathrobe, and looks old and tired. The sparsely furnished cell contains a wooden crate upon which sits a hot plate with a kettle, and a portable tape recorder. Gallimard sits on the crate staring at the recorder, a sad smile on his face.*

*Upstage Song, who appears as a beautiful woman in traditional Chinese garb, dances a traditional piece from the Peking Opera, surrounded by the percussive clatter of Chinese music.*

*Then, slowly, lights and sound cross-fade; the Chinese opera music dissolves into a Western opera, the "Love Duet" from Puccini's Madame Butterfly. Song continues dancing, now to the Western accompaniment. Though her movements are the same, the difference in music now gives them a balletic quality.*

*Gallimard rises, and turns upstage towards the figure of Song, who dances without acknowledging him.*

GALLIMARD: Butterfly, Butterfly . . .

*(He forces himself to turn away, as the image of Song fades out, and talks to us.)*

GALLIMARD: The limits of my cell are as such: four-and-a-half meters by five. There's one window against the far wall; a door, very strong, to protect me from autograph hounds. I'm responsible for the tape recorder, the hot plate, and this charming coffee table.
When I want to eat, I'm marched off to the dining room—hot, steaming slop appears on my plate. When I want to sleep, the light bulb turns itself off—the work of fairies. It's an enchanted space I occupy. The French—we know how 10 to run a prison.
But, to be honest, I'm not treated like an ordinary prisoner. Why? Because I'm a celebrity. You see, I make people laugh.
I never dreamed this day would arrive. I've never been considered witty or clever. In fact, as a young boy, in an informal poll among my grammar school classmates, I was voted "least likely to be invited to a party." It's a title I managed to hold onto for many years. Despite some stiff competition.

20    But now, how the tables turn! Look at me: the life of every social function in Paris. Paris? Why be modest? My fame has spread to Amsterdam, London, New York. Listen to them! In the world's smartest parlors. I'm the one who lifts their spirits!

*(With a flourish, Gallimard directs our attention to another part of the stage.)*

### SCENE II

*A party. Present.*

*Lights go up on a chic-looking parlor, where a well-dressed trio, two men and one woman, make conversation. Gallimard also remains lit; he observes them from his cell.*

WOMAN: And what of Gallimard?
MAN 1: Gallimard?
MAN 2: Gallimard!
GALLIMARD: *(To us)* You see? They're all determined to say my name, as if it were some new dance.
30    WOMAN: He still claims not to believe the truth.
MAN 1: What? Still? Even since the trial?
WOMAN: Yes. Isn't it mad?
MAN 2: *(Laughing)* He says . . . it was dark . . . and she was very modest!

*(The trio break into laughter.)*

MAN 1: So—what? He never touched her with his hands?
MAN 2: Perhaps he did, and simply misidentified the equipment. A compelling case for sex education in the schools.
WOMAN: To protect the National Security—the Church can't argue with that.
40    MAN 1: That's impossible! How could he not know?
MAN 2: Simple ignorance.
MAN 1: For twenty years?
MAN 2: Time flies when you're being stupid.
WOMAN: Well, I thought the French were ladies' men.
MAN 2: It seems Monsieur Gallimard was overly anxious to live up to his national reputation.
WOMAN: Well, he's not very good-looking.
MAN 1: No, he's not.
MAN 2: Certainly not.
50    WOMAN: Actually, I feel sorry for him.
MAN 2: A toast! To Monsieur Gallimard!
WOMAN: Yes! To Gallimard!
MAN 1: To Gallimard!
MAN 2: Vive la différence!

*(They toast, laughing. Lights down on them.)*

### SCENE III

*M. Gallimard's cell.*

GALLIMARD: *(Smiling)* You see? They toast me. I've become patron saint of the socially inept. Can they really be so foolish? Men like that—they should be scratching at my door, begging to learn my secrets! For I, Rene Gallimard, you see, I have known, and been loved by . . . the Perfect Woman.

Alone in this cell, I sit night after night, watching our story 60 play through my head, always searching for a new ending, one which redeems my honor, where she returns at last to my arms. And I imagine you—my ideal audience—who come to understand and even, perhaps just a little, to envy me.

*(He turns on his tape recorder. Over the house speakers, we hear the opening phrases of Madame Butterfly.)*

GALLIMARD: In order for you to understand what I did and why, I must introduce you to my favorite opera: *Madame Butterfly*. By Giacomo Puccini. First produced at La Scala, Milan, in 1904, it is now beloved throughout the Western world.    70

*(As Gallimard describes the opera, the tape segues in and out to sections he may be describing.)*

GALLIMARD: And why not? Its heroine, Cio-Cio-San, also known as Butterfly, is a feminine ideal, beautiful and brave. And its hero, the man for whom she gives up everything, is—*(He pulls out a naval officer's cap from under his crate, pops it on his head, and struts about)*—not very good-looking, not too bright, and pretty much a wimp: Benjamin Franklin Pinkerton of the U.S. Navy. As the curtain rises, he's just closed on two great bargains: one on a house, the other on a woman—call it a package deal.
Pinkerton purchased the rights to Butterfly for one hundred 80 yen—in modern currency, equivalent to about . . . sixty-six cents. So, he's feeling pretty pleased with himself as Sharpless, the American consul, arrives to witness the marriage.

*(Marc, wearing an official cap to designate Sharpless, enters and plays the character.)*

SHARPLESS/MARC: Pinkerton!
PINKERTON/GALLIMARD: Sharpless! How's it hangin'? It's a great day, just great. Between my house, my wife, and the rickshaw ride in from town, I've saved nineteen cents just this morning.
SHARPLESS: Wonderful. I can see the inscription on your tombstone already: "I saved a dollar, here I lie." *(He looks 90 around)* Nice house.
PINKERTON: It's artistic. Artistic, don't you think? Like the way the shoji screens slide open to reveal the wet bar and disco mirror ball? Classy, huh? Great for impressing the chicks.
SHARPLESS: "Chicks"? Pinkerton, you're going to be a married man!
PINKERTON: Well, sort of.
SHARPLESS: What do you mean?
PINKERTON: This country—Sharpless, it is okay. You got all these geisha girls running around—    100
SHARPLESS: I know! I live here!
PINKERTON: Then, you know the marriage laws, right? I split for one month, it's annulled!
SHARPLESS: Leave it to you to read the fine print. Who's the lucky girl?
PINKERTON: Cio-Cio-San. Her friends call her Butterfly. Sharpless, she eats out of my hand!
SHARPLESS: She's probably very hungry.
PINKERTON: Not like American girls. It's true what they say about Oriental girls. They want to be treated bad!    110

SHARPLESS: Oh, please!

PINKERTON: It's true!

SHARPLESS: Are you serious about this girl?

PINKERTON: I'm marrying her, aren't I?

SHARPLESS: Yes—with generous trade-in terms.

PINKERTON: When I leave, she'll know what it's like to have loved a real man. And I'll even buy her a few nylons.

SHARPLESS: You aren't planning to take her with you?

PINKERTON: Huh? Where?

120 SHARPLESS: Home!

PINKERTON: You mean, America? Are you crazy? Can you see her trying to buy rice in St. Louis?

SHARPLESS: So, you're not serious.

*(Pause.)*

PINKERTON/GALLIMARD: *(As Pinkerton)* Consul, I am a sailor in port. *(As Gallimard)* They then proceed to sing the famous duet, "The Whole World Over."

*(The duet plays on the speakers. Gallimard, as Pinkerton, lip-syncs his lines from the opera.)*

GALLIMARD: To give a rough translation: "The whole world over, the Yankee travels, casting his anchor wherever he wants. Life's not worth living unless he can win the hearts of
130 the fairest maidens, then hotfoot it off the premises ASAP." *(He turns towards Marc)* In the preceding scene, I played Pinkerton, the womanizing cad, and my friend Marc from school . . . *(Marc bows grandly for our benefit)* played Sharpless, the sensitive soul of reason. In life, however, our positions were usually—no, always—reversed.

## SCENE IV

*Ecole Nationale. Aix-en-Provence. 1947.*

GALLIMARD: No, Marc, I think I'd rather stay home.

MARC: Are you crazy?! We are going to Dad's condo in Marseille! You know what happened last time?

GALLIMARD: Of course I do.

140 MARC: Of course you don't! You never know. . . . They stripped, Rene!

GALLIMARD: Who stripped?

MARC: The girls!

GALLIMARD: Girls? Who said anything about girls?

MARC: Rene, we're a buncha university guys goin' up to the woods. What are we gonna do—talk philosophy?

GALLIMARD: What girls? Where do you get them?

MARC: Who cares? The point is, they come. On trucks. Packed in like sardines. The back flips open, babes hop out, we're
150 ready to roll.

GALLIMARD: You mean, they just—?

MARC: Before you know it, every last one of them—they're stripped and splashing around my pool. There's no moon out, they can't see what's going on, their boobs are flapping, right? You close your eyes, reach out—it's grab bag, get it? Doesn't matter whose ass is between whose legs, whose teeth are sinking into who. You're just in there, going at it, eyes closed, on and on for as long as you can stand. *(Pause)* Some fun, huh?

160 GALLIMARD: What happens in the morning?

MARC: In the morning, you're ready to talk some philosophy. *(Beat)* So how 'bout it?

GALLIMARD: Marc, I can't . . . I'm afraid they'll say no—the girls. So I never ask.

MARC: You don't have to ask! That's the beauty—don't you see? They don't have to say yes. It's perfect for a guy like you, really.

GALLIMARD: You go ahead . . . I may come later.

MARC: Hey, Rene—it doesn't matter that you're clumsy and got zits—they're not looking!   170

GALLIMARD: Thank you very much.

MARC: Wimp.

*(Marc walks over to the other side of the stage, and starts waving and smiling at women in the audience.)*

GALLIMARD: *(To us)* We now return to my version of *Madame Butterfly* and the events leading to my recent conviction for treason.

*(Gallimard notices Marc making lewd gestures.)*

GALLIMARD: Marc, what are you doing?

MARC: Huh? *(Sotto voce)* Rene, there're a lotta great babes out there. They're probably lookin' at me and thinking, "What a dangerous guy."

GALLIMARD: Yes—how could they help but be impressed by   180 your cool sophistication?

*(Gallimard pops the Sharpless cap on Marc's head, and points him offstage. Marc exits, leering.)*

## SCENE V

*M. Gallimard's cell.*

GALLIMARD: Next, Butterfly makes her entrance. We learn her age—fifteen . . . but very mature for her years.

*(Lights come up on the area where we saw Song dancing at the top of the play. She appears there again, now dressed as Madame Butterfly, moving to the "Love Duet." Gallimard turns upstage slightly to watch, transfixed.)*

GALLIMARD: But as she glides past him, beautiful, laughing softly behind her fan, don't we who are men sigh with hope? We, who are not handsome, nor brave, nor powerful, yet somehow believe, like Pinkerton, that we deserve a Butterfly. She arrives with all her possessions in the folds of her sleeves, lays them all out, for her man to do with as he pleases. Even her life itself—she bows her head as she whis-   190 pers that she's not even worth the hundred yen he paid for her. He's already given too much, when we know he's really had to give nothing at all.

*(Music and lights on Song out. Gallimard sits at his crate.)*

GALLIMARD: In real life, women who put their total worth at less than sixty-six cents are quite hard to find. The closest we come is in the pages of these magazines. *(He reaches into his crate, pulls out a stack of girlie magazines, and begins flipping through them)* Quite a necessity in prison. For three or four dollars, you get seven or eight women.

I first discovered these magazines at my uncle's house. One   200 day, as a boy of twelve. The first time I saw them in his closet . . . all lined up—my body shook. Not with lust—no, with power. Here were women—a shelfful—who would do exactly as I wanted.

(*The "Love Duet" creeps in over the speakers. Special comes up, revealing, not Song this time, but a pinup girl in a sexy negligee, her back to us. Gallimard turns upstage and looks at her.*)

GIRL: I know you're watching me.

GALLIMARD: My throat . . . it's dry.

GIRL: I leave my blinds open every night before I go to bed.

GALLIMARD: I can't move.

GIRL: I leave my blinds open and the lights on.

210 GALLIMARD: I'm shaking. My skin is hot, but my penis is soft. Why?

GIRL: I stand in front of the window.

GALLIMARD: What is she going to do?

GIRL: I toss my hair, and I let my lips part . . . barely.

GALLIMARD: I shouldn't be seeing this. It's so dirty. I'm so bad.

GIRL: Then, slowly, I lift off my nightdress.

GALLIMARD: Oh, god. I can't believe it. I can't—

GIRL: I toss it to the ground.

GALLIMARD: Now, she's going to walk away. She's going to—

220 GIRL: I stand there, in the light, displaying myself.

GALLIMARD: No. She's—why is she naked?

GIRL: To you.

GALLIMARD: In front of a window? This is wrong. No—

GIRL: Without shame.

GALLIMARD: No, she must . . . like it.

GIRL: I like it.

GALLIMARD: She . . . she wants me to see.

GIRL: I want you to see.

GALLIMARD: I can't believe it! She's getting excited!

230 GIRL: I can't see you. You can do whatever you want.

GALLIMARD: I can't do a thing. Why?

GIRL: What would you like me to do . . . next?

(*Lights go down on her. Music off. Silence, as Gallimard puts away his magazines. Then he resumes talking to us.*)

GALLIMARD: Act Two begins with Butterfly staring at the ocean. Pinkerton's been called back to the U.S., and he's given his wife a detailed schedule of his plans. In the column marked "return date," he's written "when the robins nest." This failed to ignite her suspicions. Now, three years have passed without a peep from him. Which brings a response from her faithful servant, Suzuki.

(*Comrade Chin enters, playing Suzuki.*)

240 SUZUKI: Girl, he's a loser. What'd he ever give you? Nineteen cents and those ugly Day-Glo stockings? Look, it's finished! Kaput! Done! And you should be glad! I mean, the guy was a woofer! He tried before, you know—before he met you, he went down to geisha central and plunked down his spare change in front of the usual candidates—everyone else gagged! These are hungry prostitutes, and they were not interested, get the picture? Now, stop slathering when an American ship sails in, and let's make some bucks—I mean, yen! We are broke!

250 Now, what about Yamadori? Hey, hey—don't look away—the man is a prince—figuratively, and, what's even better,

literally. He's rich, he's handsome, he says he'll die if you don't marry him—and he's even willing to overlook the little fact that you've been deflowered all over the place by a foreign devil. What do you mean, "But he's Japanese?" You're Japanese! You think you've been touched by the whitey god? He was a sailor with dirty hands!

(*Suzuki stalks offstage.*)

GALLIMARD: She's also visited by Consul Sharpless, sent by Pinkerton on a minor errand.

(*Marc enters, as Sharpless.*)

SHARPLESS: I hate this job.                                                        260

GALLIMARD: This Pinkerton—he doesn't show up personally to tell his wife he's abandoning her. No, he sends a government diplomat . . . at taxpayer's expense.

SHARPLESS: Butterfly? Butterfly? I have some bad—I'm going to be ill. Butterfly, I came to tell you—

GALLIMARD: Butterfly says she knows he'll return and if he doesn't she'll kill herself rather than go back to her own people. (*Beat*) This causes a lull in the conversation.

SHARPLESS: Let's put it this way . . .

GALLIMARD: Butterfly runs into the next room, and returns  270 holding—

(*Sound cue: a baby crying. Sharpless, "seeing" this, backs away.*)

SHARPLESS: Well, good. Happy to see things going so well. I suppose I'll be going now. Ta ta. Ciao. (*He turns away. Sound cue out*) I hate this job. (*He exits*)

GALLIMARD: At that moment, Butterfly spots in the harbor an American ship—the *Abramo Lincoln!*

(*Music cue: "The Flower Duet." Song, still dressed as Butterfly, changes into a wedding kimono, moving to the music.*)

GALLIMARD: This is the moment that redeems her years of waiting. With Suzuki's help, they cover the room with flowers—

(*Chin, as Suzuki, trudges onstage and drops a lone flower without much enthusiasm.*)

GALLIMARD: —and she changes into her wedding dress to pre-  280 pare for Pinkerton's arrival.

(*Suzuki helps Butterfly change. Helga enters, and helps Gallimard change into a tuxedo.*)

GALLIMARD: I married a woman older than myself—Helga.

HELGA: My father was ambassador to Australia. I grew up among criminals and kangaroos.

GALLIMARD: Hearing that brought me to the altar—

(*Helga exits.*)

GALLIMARD: —where I took a vow renouncing love. No fantasy woman would ever want me, so, yes, I would settle for a quick leap up the career ladder. Passion, I banish, and in its place—practicality!
But my vows had long since lost their charm by the time we  290 arrived in China. The sad truth is that all men want a beautiful woman, and the uglier the man, the greater the want.

(*Suzuki makes final adjustments of Butterfly's costume, as does Gallimard of his tuxedo.*)

GALLIMARD: I married late, at age thirty-one. I was faithful to my marriage for eight years. Until the day when, as a junior-level diplomat in puritanical Peking, in a parlor at the German ambassador's house, during the "Reign of a Hundred Flowers," I first saw her . . . singing the death scene from *Madame Butterfly*.

(*Suzuki runs offstage.*)

SCENE VI

*German ambassador's house. Beijing. 1960.*

*The upstage special area now becomes a stage. Several chairs face upstage, representing seating for some twenty guests in the parlor. A few "diplomats"—Renee, Marc, Toulon—in formal dress enter and take seats.*

*Gallimard also sits down, but turns towards us and continues to talk. Orchestral accompaniment on the tape is now replaced by a simple piano. Song picks up the death scene from the point where Butterfly uncovers the hara-kiri knife.*

GALLIMARD: The ending is pitiful. Pinkerton, in an act of great
300    courage, stays home and sends his American wife to pick up Butterfly's child. The truth, long deferred, has come up to her door.

(*Song, playing Butterfly, sings the lines from the opera in her own voice—which, though not classical, should be decent.*)

SONG: "Con onor muore/ chi non puo serbar/ vita con onore."
GALLIMARD: (*Simultaneously*) "Death with honor/ Is better than life/ Life with dishonor."

(*The stage is illuminated; we are now completely within an elegant diplomat's residence. Song proceeds to play out an abbreviated death scene. Everyone in the room applauds. Song, shyly, takes her bows. Others in the room rush to congratulate her. Gallimard remains with us.*)

GALLIMARD: They say in opera the voice is everything. That's probably why I'd never before enjoyed opera. Here . . . here was a Butterfly with little or no voice—but she had the grace, the delicacy . . . I believed this girl. I believed her suf-
310    fering. I wanted to take her in my arms—so delicate, even I could protect her, take her home, pamper her until she smiled.

(*Over the course of the preceding speech, Song has broken from the upstage crowd and moved directly upstage of Gallimard.*)

SONG: Excuse me. Monsieur . . . ?

(*Gallimard turns upstage, shocked.*)

GALLIMARD: Oh! Gallimard. Mademoiselle . . . ? A beautiful . . .
SONG: Song Liling.
GALLIMARD: A beautiful performance.
SONG: Oh, please.
GALLIMARD: I usually—
320    SONG: You make me blush. I'm no opera singer at all.
GALLIMARD: I usually don't like *Butterfly*.
SONG: I can't blame you in the least.

GALLIMARD: I mean, the story—
SONG: Ridiculous.
GALLIMARD: I like the story, but . . . what?
SONG: Oh, you like it?
GALLIMARD: I . . . what I mean is, I've always seen it played by huge women in so much bad makeup.
SONG: Bad makeup is not unique to the West.
GALLIMARD: But, who can believe them?                               330
SONG: And you believe me?
GALLIMARD: Absolutely. You were utterly convincing. It's the first time—
SONG: Convincing? As a Japanese woman? The Japanese used hundreds of our people for medical experiments during the war, you know. But I gather such an irony is lost on you.
GALLIMARD: No! I was about to say, it's the first time I've seen the beauty of the story.
SONG: Really?
GALLIMARD: Of her death. It's a . . . a pure sacrifice. He's un-  340
worthy, but what can she do? She loves him . . . so much. It's a very beautiful story.
SONG: Well, yes, to a Westerner.
GALLIMARD: Excuse me?
SONG: It's one of your favorite fantasies, isn't it? The submissive Oriental woman and the cruel white man.
GALLIMARD: Well, I didn't quite mean . . .
SONG: Consider it this way: what would you say if a blonde homecoming queen fell in love with a short Japanese businessman? He treats her cruelly, then goes home for three  350
years, during which time she prays to his picture and turns down marriage from a young Kennedy. Then, when she learns he has remarried, she kills herself. Now, I believe you would consider this girl to be a deranged idiot, correct? But because it's an Oriental who kills herself for a Westerner—ah!—you find it beautiful.

(*Silence.*)

GALLIMARD: Yes . . . well . . . I see your point . . .
SONG: I will never do Butterfly again, Monsieur Gallimard. If you wish to see some real theatre, come to the Peking Opera sometime. Expand your mind.                                    360

(*Song walks offstage.*)

GALLIMARD: (*To us*) So much for protecting her in my big Western arms.

SCENE VII

*M. Gallimard's apartment. Beijing. 1960.*

*Gallimard changes from his tux into a casual suit. Helga enters.*

GALLIMARD: The Chinese are an incredibly arrogant people.
HELGA: They warned us about that in Paris, remember?
GALLIMARD: Even Parisians consider them arrogant. That's a switch.
HELGA: What is it that Madame Su says? "We are a very old civilization." I never know if she's talking about her country or herself.
GALLIMARD: I walk around here, all I hear every day, every-  370
where is how *old* this culture is. The fact that "old" may be synonymous with "senile" doesn't occur to them.

HELGA: You're not going to change them. "East is east, west is west, and . . ." whatever that guy said.

GALLIMARD: It's just that—silly. I met . . . at Ambassador Koening's tonight—you should've been there.

HELGA: Koening? Oh god, no. Did he enchant you all again with the history of Bavaria?

380 GALLIMARD: No. I met, I suppose, the Chinese equivalent of a diva. She's a singer in the Chinese opera.

HELGA: They have an opera, too? Do they sing in Chinese? Or maybe—in Italian?

GALLIMARD: Tonight, she did sing in Italian.

HELGA: How'd she manage that?

GALLIMARD: She must've been educated in the West before the Revolution. Her French is very good also. Anyway, she sang the death scene from *Madame Butterfly.*

HELGA: *Madame Butterfly!* Then I should have come. (*She begins humming, floating around the room as if dragging long*
390 *kimono sleeves*) Did she have a nice costume? I think it's a classic piece of music.

GALLIMARD: That's what *I* thought, too. Don't let her hear you say that.

HELGA: What's wrong?

GALLIMARD: Evidently the Chinese hate it.

HELGA: She hated it, but she performed it anyway? Is she perverse?

GALLIMARD: They hate it because the white man gets the girl. Sour grapes if you ask me.

400 HELGA: Politics again? Why can't they just hear it as a piece of beautiful music? So, what's in their opera?

GALLIMARD: I don't know. But, whatever it is, I'm sure it must be *old.*

(*Helga exits.*)

SCENE VIII

*Chinese opera house and the streets of Beijing. 1960. The sound of gongs clanging fills the stage.*

GALLIMARD: My wife's innocent question kept ringing in my ears. I asked around, but no one knew anything about the Chinese opera. It took four weeks, but my curiosity overcame my cowardice. This Chinese diva—this unwilling Butterfly—what did she do to make her so proud?
The room was hot, and full of smoke. Wrinkled faces, old
410 women, teeth missing—a man with a growth on his neck, like a human toad. All smiling, pipes falling from their mouths, cracking nuts between their teeth, a live chicken pecking at my foot—all looking, screaming, gawking . . . at her.

(*The upstage area is suddenly hit with a harsh white light. It has become the stage for the Chinese opera performance. Two dancers enter, along with Song. Gallimard stands apart, watching. Song glides gracefully amidst the two dancers. Drums suddenly slam to a halt. Song strikes a pose, looking straight at Gallimard. Dancers exit. Light change. Pause, then Song walks right off the stage and straight up to Gallimard.*)

SONG: Yes. You. White man. I'm looking straight at you.

GALLIMARD: Me?

SONG: You see any other white men? It was too easy to spot you. How often does a man in my audience come in a tie?

(*Song starts to remove her costume. Underneath, she wears simple baggy clothes. They are now backstage. The show is over.*)

SONG: So, you are an adventurous imperialist?

GALLIMARD: I . . . thought it would further my education.        420

SONG: It took you four weeks. Why?

GALLIMARD: I've been busy.

SONG: Well, education has always been undervalued in the West, hasn't it?

GALLIMARD: (*Laughing*) I don't think it's true.

SONG: No, you wouldn't. You're a Westerner. How can you objectively judge your own values?

GALLIMARD: I think it's possible to achieve some distance.

SONG: Do you? (*Pause*) It stinks in here. Let's go.

GALLIMARD: These are the smells of your loyal fans.        430

SONG: I love them for being my fans, I hate the smell they leave behind. I too can distance myself from my people. (*She looks around, then whispers in his ear*) "Art for the masses" is a shitty excuse to keep artists poor. (*She pops a cigarette in her mouth*) Be a gentleman, will you? And light my cigarette.

(*Gallimard fumbles for a match.*)

GALLIMARD: I don't . . . smoke.

SONG: (*Lighting her own*) Your loss. Had you lit my cigarette, I might have blown a puff of smoke right between your eyes. Come.        440

(*They start to walk about the stage. It is a summer night on the Beijing streets. Sounds of the city play on the house speakers.*)

SONG: How I wish there were even a tiny cafe to sit in. With cappuccinos, and men in tuxedos and bad expatriate jazz.

GALLIMARD: If my history serves me correctly, you weren't even allowed into the clubs in Shanghai before the Revolution.

SONG: Your history serves you poorly, Monsieur Gallimard. True, there were signs reading "No dogs and Chinamen." But a woman, especially a delicate Oriental woman—we always go where we please. Could you imagine it otherwise? Clubs in China filled with pasty, big-thighed white women,        450 while thousands of slender lotus blossoms wait just outside the door? Never. The clubs would be empty. (*Beat*) We have always held a certain fascination for you Caucasian men, have we not?

GALLIMARD: But . . . that fascination is imperialist, or so you tell me.

SONG: Do you believe everything I tell you? Yes. It is always imperialist. But sometimes . . . sometimes, it is also mutual. Oh—this is my flat.

GALLIMARD: I didn't even—        460

SONG: Thank you. Come another time and we will further expand your mind.

(*Song exits. Gallimard continues roaming the streets as he speaks to us.*)

GALLIMARD: What was that? What did she mean, "Sometimes . . . it is mutual?" Women do not flirt with me. And I normally can't talk to them. But tonight, I held up my end of the conversation.

SCENE IX

*Gallimard's bedroom. Beijing. 1960.*

*Helga enters.*

HELGA: You didn't tell me you'd be home late.

GALLIMARD: I didn't intend to. Something came up.

HELGA: Oh? Like what?

470 GALLIMARD: I went to the . . . to the Dutch ambassador's home.

HELGA: Again?

GALLIMARD: There was a reception for a visiting scholar. He's writing a six-volume treatise on the Chinese revolution. We all gathered that meant he'd have to live here long enough to actually write six volumes, and we all expressed our deepest sympathies.

HELGA: Well, I had a good night too. I went with the ladies to a martial arts demonstration. Some of those men—when they break those thick boards—(*She mimes fanning herself*)
480 whoo-whoo!

(*Helga exits. Lights dim.*)

GALLIMARD: I lied to my wife. Why? I've never had any reason to lie before. But what reason did I have tonight? I didn't do anything wrong. That night, I had a dream. Other people, I've been told, have dreams where angels appear. Or dragons, or Sophia Loren in a towel. In my dream, Marc from school appeared.

(*Marc enters, in a nightshirt and cap.*)

MARC: Rene! You met a girl!

(*Gallimard and Marc stumble down the Beijing streets. Night sounds over the speakers.*)

GALLIMARD: It's not that amazing, thank you.

MARC: No! It's so monumental, I heard about it halfway around
490 the world in my sleep!

GALLIMARD: I've met girls before, you know.

MARC: Name one. I've come across time and space to congratulate you. (*He hands Gallimard a bottle of wine*)

GALLIMARD: Marc, this is expensive.

MARC: On those rare occasions when you become a formless spirit, why not steal the best?

(*Marc pops open the bottle, begins to share it with Gallimard.*)

GALLIMARD: You embarrass me. She . . . there's no reason to think she likes me.

MARC: "Sometimes, it is mutual"?

500 GALLIMARD: Oh.

MARC: "Mutual"? "Mutual"? What does that mean?

GALLIMARD: You heard!

MARC: It means the money is in the bank, you only have to write the check!

GALLIMARD: I am a married man!

MARC: And an excellent one too. I cheated after . . . six months. Then again and again, until now—three hundred girls in twelve years.

GALLIMARD: I don't think we should hold that up as a model.

MARC: Of course not! My life—it is disgusting! Phooey! 510 Phooey! But, you—you are the model husband.

GALLIMARD: Anyway, it's impossible. I'm a foreigner.

MARC: Ah, yes. She cannot love you, it is taboo, but something deep inside her heart . . . she cannot help herself . . . she must surrender to you. It is her destiny.

GALLIMARD: How do you imagine all this?

MARC: The same way you do. It's an old story. It's in our blood. They fear us, Rene. Their women fear us. And their men— their men hate us. And, you know something? They are all correct. 520

(*They spot a light in a window.*)

MARC: There! There, Rene!

GALLIMARD: It's her window.

MARC: Late at night—it burns. The light—it burns for you.

GALLIMARD: I won't look. It's not respectful.

MARC: We don't have to be respectful. We're foreign devils.

(*Enter Song, in a sheer robe. The "One Fine Day" aria creeps in over the speakers. With her back to us, Song mimes attending to her toilette. Her robe comes loose, revealing her white shoulders.*)

MARC: All your life you've waited for a beautiful girl who would lay down for you. All your life you've smiled like a saint when it's happened to every other man you know. And you see them in magazines and you see them in movies. And you wonder, what's wrong with me? Will anyone beautiful ever 530 want me? As the years pass, your hair thins and you struggle to hold onto even your hopes. Stop struggling, Rene. The wait is over. (*He exits*)

GALLIMARD: Marc? Marc?

(*At that moment, Song, her back still towards us, drops her robe. A second of her naked back, then a sound cue: a phone ringing, very loud. Blackout, followed in the next beat by a special up on the bedroom area, where a phone now sits. Gallimard stumbles across the stage and picks up the phone. Sound cue out. Over the course of his conversation, area lights fill in the vicinity of his bed. It is the following morning.*)

GALLIMARD: Yes? Hello?

SONG: (*Offstage*) Is it very early?

GALLIMARD: Why, yes.

SONG: (*Offstage*) How early?

GALLIMARD: It's . . . it's 5:30. Why are you—?

SONG: (*Offstage*) But it's light outside. Already.

GALLIMARD: It is. The sun must be in confusion today. 540

(*Over the course of Song's next speech, her upstage special comes up again. She sits in a chair, legs crossed, in a robe, telephone to her ear.*)

SONG: I waited until I saw the sun. That was as much discipline as I could manage for one night. Do you forgive me?

GALLIMARD: Of course . . . for what?

SONG: Then I'll ask you quickly. Are you really interested in the opera?

GALLIMARD: Why, yes. Yes I am.

SONG: Then come again next Thursday. I am playing *The Drunken Beauty*. May I count on you?

550 GALLIMARD: Yes. You may.

SONG: Perfect. Well, I must be getting to bed. I'm exhausted. It's been a very long night for me.

*(Song hangs up; special on her goes off. Gallimard begins to dress for work.)*

SCENE X

*Song Liling's apartment. Beijing. 1960.*

GALLIMARD: I returned to the opera that next week, and the week after that . . . she keeps our meetings so short—perhaps fifteen, twenty minutes at most. So I am left each week with a thirst which is intensified. In this way, fifteen weeks have gone by. I am starting to doubt the words of my friend Marc. But no, not really. In my heart, I know she has . . . an interest in me. I suspect this is her way. She is outwardly
560 bold and outspoken, yet her heart is shy and afraid. It is the Oriental in her at war with her Western education.

SONG: *(Offstage)* I will be out in an instant. Ask the servant for anything you want.

GALLIMARD: Tonight, I have finally been invited to enter her apartment. Though the idea is almost beyond belief, I believe she is afraid of me.

*(Gallimard looks around the room. He picks up a picture in a frame, studies it. Without his noticing, Song enters, dressed elegantly in a black gown from the twenties. She stands in the doorway looking like Anna May Wong.)*

SONG: That is my father.

GALLIMARD: *(Surprised)* Mademoiselle Song . . .

*(She glides up to him, snatches away the picture.)*

SONG: It is very good that he did not live to see the Revolution.
570 They would, no doubt, have made him kneel on broken glass. Not that he didn't deserve such a punishment. But he is my father. I would've hated to see it happen.

GALLIMARD: I'm very honored that you've allowed me to visit your home.

*(Song curtsys.)*

SONG: Thank you. Oh! Haven't you been poured any tea?

GALLIMARD: I'm really not—

SONG: *(To her offstage servant)* Shu-Fang! Cha! Kwai-lah! *(To Gallimard)* I'm sorry. You want everything to be perfect—

GALLIMARD: Please.
580 SONG: —and before the evening even begins—

GALLIMARD: I'm really not thirsty.

SONG: —it's ruined.

GALLIMARD: *(Sharply)* Mademoiselle Song!

*(Song sits down.)*

SONG: I'm sorry.

GALLIMARD: What are you apologizing for now?

*(Pause; Song starts to giggle.)*

SONG: I don't know!

*(Gallimard laughs.)*

GALLIMARD: Exactly my point.

SONG: Oh, I am silly. Lightheaded. I promise not to apologize for anything else tonight, do you hear me?

GALLIMARD: That's a good girl.                                          590

*(Shu-Fang, a servant girl, comes out with a tea tray and starts to pour.)*

SONG: *(To Shu-Fang)* No! I'll pour myself for the gentleman!

*(Shu-Fang, staring at Gallimard, exits.)*

SONG: No, I . . . I don't even know why I invited you up.

GALLIMARD: Well, I'm glad you did.

*(Song looks around the room.)*

SONG: There is an element of danger to your presence.

GALLIMARD: Oh?

SONG: You must know.

GALLIMARD: It doesn't concern me. We both know why I'm here.

SONG: It doesn't concern me either. No . . . well perhaps . . .

GALLIMARD: What?                                                        600

SONG: Perhaps I am slightly afraid of scandal.

GALLIMARD: What are we doing?

SONG: I'm entertaining you. In my parlor.

GALLIMARD: In France, that would hardly—

SONG: France. France is a country living in the modern era. Perhaps even ahead of it. China is a nation whose soul is firmly rooted two thousand years in the past. What I do, even pouring the tea for you now . . . it has . . . implications. The walls and windows say so. Even my own heart, strapped inside this Western dress . . . even it says things—things I 610 don't care to hear.

*(Song hands Gallimard a cup of tea. Gallimard puts his hand over both the teacup and Song's hand.)*

GALLIMARD: This is a beautiful dress.

SONG: Don't.

GALLIMARD: What?

SONG: I don't even know if it looks right on me.

GALLIMARD: Believe me—

SONG: You are from France. You see so many beautiful women.

GALLIMARD: France? Since when are the European women—?

SONG: Oh! What am I trying to do, anyway?!                              620

*(Song runs to the door, composes herself, then turns towards Gallimard.)*

SONG: Monsieur Gallimard, perhaps you should go.

GALLIMARD: But . . . why?

SONG: There's something wrong about this.

GALLIMARD: I don't see what.

SONG: I feel . . . I am not myself.

GALLIMARD: No. You're nervous.

SONG: Please. Hard as I try to be modern, to speak like a man, to hold a Western woman's strong face up to my own . . . in the end, I fail. A small, frightened heart beats too quickly and gives me away. Monsieur Gallimard, I'm a Chinese girl. 630 I've never . . . never invited a man up to my flat before. The forwardness of my actions makes my skin burn.

GALLIMARD: What are you afraid of? Certainly not me, I hope.

SONG: I'm a modest girl.

GALLIMARD: I know. And very beautiful. (*He touches her hair*)

SONG: Please—go now. The next time you see me, I shall again be myself.

GALLIMARD: I like you the way you are right now.

SONG: You are a cad.

640 GALLIMARD: What do you expect? I'm a foreign devil.

(*Gallimard walks downstage. Song exits.*)

GALLIMARD: (*To us*) Did you hear the way she talked about Western women? Much differently than the first night. She does—she feels inferior to them—and to me.

SCENE XI

*The French embassy. Beijing. 1960.*

*Gallimard moves towards a desk.*

GALLIMARD: I determined to try an experiment. In *Madame Butterfly*, Cio-Cio-San fears that the Western man who catches a butterfly will pierce its heart with a needle, then leave it to perish. I began to wonder: had I, too, caught a butterfly who would writhe on a needle?

(*Marc enters, dressed as a bureaucrat, holding a stack of papers. As Gallimard speaks, Marc hands papers to him. He peruses, then signs, stamps or rejects them.*)

GALLIMARD: Over the next five weeks, I worked like a dynamo.
650 I stopped going to the opera, I didn't phone or write her. I knew this little flower was waiting for me to call, and, as I wickedly refused to do so, I felt for the first time that rush of power—the absolute power of a man.

(*Marc continues acting as the bureaucrat, but he now speaks as himself.*)

MARC: Rene! It's me!

GALLIMARD: Marc—I hear your voice everywhere now. Even in the midst of work.

MARC: That's because I'm watching you—all the time.

GALLIMARD: You were always the most popular guy in school.

MARC: Well, there's no guarantee of failure in life like happi-
660 ness in high school. Somehow I knew I'd end up in the suburbs working for Renault and you'd be in the Orient picking exotic women off the trees. And they say there's no justice.

GALLIMARD: That's why you were my friend?

MARC: I gave you a little of my life, so that now you can give me some of yours (*Pause*) Remember Isabelle?

GALLIMARD: Of course I remember! She was my first experience.

MARC: We all wanted to ball her. But she only wanted me.

GALLIMARD: I had her.

670 MARC: Right. You balled her.

GALLIMARD: You were the only one who ever believed me.

MARC: Well, there's a good reason for that. (*Beat*) C'mon. You must've guessed.

GALLIMARD: You told me to wait in the bushes by the cafeteria that night. The next thing I knew, she was on me. Dress up in the air.

MARC: She never wore underwear.

GALLIMARD: My arms were pinned to the dirt.

MARC: She loved the superior position. A girl ahead of her
680 time.

GALLIMARD: I looked up, and there was this woman . . . bouncing up and down on my loins.

MARC: Screaming, right?

GALLIMARD: Screaming, and breaking off the branches all around me, and pounding my butt up and down into the dirt.

MARC: Huffing and puffing like a locomotive.

GALLIMARD: And in the middle of all this, the leaves were getting into my mouth, my legs were losing circulation, I
690 thought, "God. So this is *it*?"

MARC: You thought that?

GALLIMARD: Well, I was worried about my legs falling off.

MARC: You didn't have a good time?

GALLIMARD: No, that's not what I—I had a great time!

MARC: You're sure?

GALLIMARD: Yeah. Really.

MARC: 'Cuz I wanted you to have a good time.

GALLIMARD: I did.

(*Pause.*)

MARC: Shit. (*Pause*) When all is said and done, she was kind of a lousy lay, wasn't she? I mean, there was a lot of energy
700 there, but you never knew what she was doing with it. Like when she yelled "I'm coming!"—hell, it was so loud, you wanted to go "Look, it's not that big a deal."

GALLIMARD: I got scared. I thought she meant someone was actually coming. (*Pause*) But, Marc?

MARC: What?

GALLIMARD: Thanks.

MARC: Oh, don't mention it.

GALLIMARD: It was my first experience.

MARC: Yeah. You got her.
710

GALLIMARD: I got her.

MARC: Wait! Look at that letter again!

(*Gallimard picks up one of the papers he's been stamping, and rereads it.*)

GALLIMARD: (*To us*) After six weeks, they began to arrive. The letters.

(*Upstage special on Song, as Madame Butterfly. The scene is underscored by the "Love Duet."*)

SONG: Did we fight? I do not know. Is the opera no longer of interest to you? Please come—my audiences miss the white devil in their midst.

(*Gallimard looks up from the letter, towards us.*)

GALLIMARD: (*To us*) A concession, but much too dignified. (*Beat; he discards the letter*) I skipped the opera again that week to complete a position paper on trade.
720

(*The bureaucrat hands him another letter.*)

SONG: Six weeks have passed since last we met. Is this your practice—to leave friends in the lurch? Sometimes I hate you, sometimes I hate myself, but always I miss you.

GALLIMARD: (*To us*) Better, but I don't like the way she calls me "friend." When a woman calls a man her "friend," she's calling him a eunuch or a homosexual. (*Beat; he discards the letter)* I was absent from the opera for the seventh week, feeling a sudden urge to clean out my files.

*(Bureaucrat hands him another letter.)*

SONG: Your rudeness is beyond belief. I don't deserve this cru-
730     elty. Don't bother to call. I'll have you turned away at the door.
GALLIMARD: *(To us)* I didn't. *(He discards the letter; bureau-crat hands him another)* And then finally, the letter that concluded my experiment.
SONG: I am out of words. I can hide behind dignity no longer. What do you want? I have already given you my shame.

*(Gallimard gives the letter back to Marc, slowly. Special on Song fades out.)*

GALLIMARD: *(To us)* Reading it, I became suddenly ashamed. Yes, my experiment had been a success. She was turning on my needle. But the victory seemed hollow.
740 MARC: Hollow?! Are you crazy?
GALLIMARD: Nothing, Marc. Please go away.
MARC: *(Exiting, with papers)* Haven't I taught you anything?
GALLIMARD: "I have already given you my shame." I had to at-tend a reception that evening. On the way, I felt sick. If there is a God, surely he would punish me now. I had finally gained power over a beautiful woman, only to abuse it cru-elly. There must be justice in the world. I had the strange feeling that the ax would fall this very evening.

SCENE XII

*Ambassador Toulon's residence. Beijing. 1960.*

*Sound cue: party noises. Light change. We are now in a spa-cious residence. Toulon, the French ambassador, enters and taps Gallimard on the shoulder.*

TOULON: Gallimard? Can I have a word? Over here.
750 GALLIMARD: *(To us)* Manuel Toulon. French ambassador to China. He likes to think of us all as his children. Rather like God.
TOULON: Look, Gallimard, there's not much to say. I've liked you. From the day you walked in. You were no leader, but you were tidy and efficient.
GALLIMARD: Thank you, sir.
TOULON: Don't jump the gun. Okay, our needs in China are changing. It's embarrassing that we lost Indochina. Some-one just wasn't on the ball there. I don't mean you person-
760     ally, of course.
GALLIMARD: Thank you, sir.
TOULON: We're going to be doing a lot more information-gath-ering in the future. The nature of our work here is changing. Some people are just going to have to go. It's nothing per-sonal.
GALLIMARD: Oh.
TOULON: Want to know a secret? Vice-Consul LeBon is being transferred.
GALLIMARD: *(To us)* My immediate superior!
770 TOULON: And most of his department.
GALLIMARD: *(To us)* Just as I feared! God has seen my evil heart—
TOULON: But not you.

GALLIMARD: *(To us)* —and he's taking her away just as . . . *(To Toulon)* Excuse me, sir?
TOULON: Scare you? I think I did. Cheer up, Gallimard. I want you to replace LeBon as vice-consul.
GALLIMARD: You—? Yes, well, thank you, sir.
TOULON: Anytime.
GALLIMARD: I . . . accept with great humility.                                  780
TOULON: Humility won't be part of the job. You're going to co-ordinate the revamped intelligence division. Want to know a secret? A year ago, you would've been out. But the past few months, I don't know how it happened, you've become this new aggressive confident . . . thing. And they also tell me you get along with the Chinese. So I think you're a lucky man, Gallimard. Congratulations.

*They shake hands. Toulon exits. Party noises out. Gallimard stumbles across a darkened stage.)*

GALLIMARD: Vice-consul? Impossible! As I stumbled out of the party, I saw it written across the sky: There is no God. Or, no—say that there is a God. But that God . . . understands. 790 Of course! God who creates Eve to serve Adam, who blesses Solomon with his harem but ties Jezebel to a burning bed—that God is a man. And he understands! At age thirty-nine, I was suddenly initiated into the way of the world.

SCENE XIII

*Song Liling's apartment. Beijing. 1960.*

*Song enters, in a sheer dressing gown.*

SONG: Are you crazy?
GALLIMARD: Mademoiselle Song—
SONG: To come here—at this hour? After . . . after eight weeks?
GALLIMARD: It's the most amazing—
SONG: You bang on my door? Scare my servants, scandalize the 800 neighbors?
GALLIMARD: I've been promoted. To vice-consul.

*(Pause.)*

SONG: And what is that supposed to mean to me?
GALLIMARD: Are you my Butterfly?
SONG: What are you saying?
GALLIMARD: I've come tonight for an answer: are you my But-terfly?
SONG: Don't you know already?
GALLIMARD: I want you to say it.
SONG: I don't want to say it.                                                          810
GALLIMARD: So, that is your answer?
SONG: You know how I feel about—
GALLIMARD: I do remember one thing.
SONG: What?
GALLIMARD: In the letter I received today.
SONG: Don't.
GALLIMARD: "I have already given you my shame."
SONG: It's enough that I even wrote it.
GALLIMARD: Well, then—
SONG: I shouldn't have it splashed across my face.                            820
GALLIMARD: —if that's all true—

SONG: Stop!

GALLIMARD: Then what is one more short answer?

SONG: I don't want to!

GALLIMARD: Are you my Butterfly? (*Silence; he crosses the room and begins to touch her hair*) I want from you honesty. There should be nothing false between us. No false pride.

(*Pause.*)

SONG: Yes, I am. I am your Butterfly.

GALLIMARD: Then let me be honest with you. It is because of
830    you that I was promoted tonight. You have changed my life forever. My little Butterfly, there should be no more secrets: I love you.

(*He starts to kiss her roughly. She resists slightly.*)

SONG: No . . . no . . . gently . . . please, I've never . . .

GALLIMARD: No?

SONG: I've tried to appear experienced, but . . . the truth is . . . no.

GALLIMARD: Are you cold?

SONG: Yes. Cold.

GALLIMARD: Then we will go very, very slowly.

(*He starts to caress her; her gown begins to open.*)

840  SONG: No . . . let me . . . keep my clothes . . .

GALLIMARD: But . . .

SONG: Please . . . it all frightens me. I'm a modest Chinese girl.

GALLIMARD: My poor little treasure.

SONG: I am your treasure. Though inexperienced, I am not . . . ignorant. They teach us things, our mothers, about pleasing a man.

GALLIMARD: Yes?

SONG: I'll do my best to make you happy. Turn off the lights.

(*Gallimard gets up and heads for a lamp. Song, propped up on one elbow, tosses her hair back and smiles.*)

SONG: Monsieur Gallimard?

850  GALLIMARD: Yes, Butterfly?

SONG: "Vieni, vieni!"

GALLIMARD: "Come, darling."

SONG: "Ah! Dolce notte!"

GALLIMARD: "Beautiful night."

SONG: "Tutto estatico d'amor ride il ciel!"

GALLIMARD: "All ecstatic with love, the heavens are filled with laughter."

(*He turns off the lamp. Blackout.*)

## —ACT TWO—

SCENE I

*M. Gallimard's cell. Paris. Present.*

*Lights up on Gallimard. He sits in his cell, reading from a leaflet.*

GALLIMARD: This, from a contemporary critic's commentary on *Madame Butterfly:* "Pinkerton suffers from . . . being an ob-
860  noxious bounder whom every man in the audience itches to kick." Bully for us men in the audience! Then, in the same

note: "Butterfly is the most irresistibly appealing of Puccini's 'Little Women.' Watching the succession of her humiliations is like watching a child under torture." (*He tosses the pamphlet over his shoulder*) I suggest that, while we men may all want to kick Pinkerton, very few of us would pass up the opportunity to *be* Pinkerton.

(*Gallimard moves out of his cell.*)

SCENE II

*Gallimard and Butterfly's flat. Beijing. 1960.*

*We are in a simple but well-decorated parlor. Gallimard moves to sit on a sofa, while Song, dressed in a chong sam, enters and curls up at his feet.*

GALLIMARD: (*To us*) We secured a flat on the outskirts of Peking. Butterfly, as I was calling her now, decorated our "home" with Western furniture and Chinese antiques. And  870 there, on a few stolen afternoons or evenings each week, Butterfly commenced her education.

SONG: The Chinese men—they keep us down.

GALLIMARD: Even in the "New Society"?

SONG: In the "New Society," we are all kept ignorant equally. That's one of the exciting things about loving a Western man. I know you are not threatened by a woman's education.

GALLIMARD: I'm no saint, Butterfly.

SONG: But you come from a progressive society.  880

GALLIMARD: We're not always reminding each other how "old" we are, if that's what you mean.

SONG: Exactly. We Chinese—once, I suppose, it is true, we ruled the world. But so what? How much more exciting to be part of the society ruling the world today. Tell me— what's happening in Vietnam?

GALLIMARD: Oh, Butterfly—you want me to bring my work home?

SONG: I want to know what you know. To be impressed by my man. It's not the particulars so much as the fact that you're  890 making decisions which change the shape of the world.

GALLIMARD: Not the world. At best, a small corner.

(*Toulon enters, and sits at a desk upstage.*)

SCENE III

*French embassy. Beijing. 1961.*

*Gallimard moves downstage, to Toulon's desk. Song remains upstage, watching.*

TOULON: And a more troublesome corner is hard to imagine.

GALLIMARD: So, the Americans plan to begin bombing?

TOULON: This is very secret, Gallimard: yes. The Americans don't have an embassy here. They're asking us to be their eyes and ears. Say Jack Kennedy signed an order to bomb North Vietnam, Laos. How would the Chinese react?

GALLIMARD: I think the Chinese will squawk—

TOULON: Uh-huh.  900

GALLIMARD: —but, in their hearts, they don't even like Ho Chi Minh.

*(Pause.)*

TOULON: What a bunch of jerks. Vietnam was *our* colony. Not only didn't the Americans help us fight to keep them, but now, seven years later, they've come back to grab the territory for themselves. It's very irritating.

GALLIMARD: With all due respect, sir, why should the Americans have won our war for us back in '54 if we didn't have the will to win it ourselves?

910    TOULON: You're kidding, aren't you?

*(Pause.)*

GALLIMARD: The Orientals simply want to be associated with whoever shows the most strength and power. You live with the Chinese, sir. Do you think they like Communism?

TOULON: I live in China. Not with the Chinese.

GALLIMARD: Well, I—

TOULON: *You* live with the Chinese.

GALLIMARD: Excuse me?

TOULON: I can't keep a secret.

GALLIMARD: What are you saying?

920    TOULON: Only that I'm not immune to gossip. So, you're keeping a native mistress. Don't answer. It's none of my business. *(Pause)* I'm sure she must be gorgeous.

GALLIMARD: Well . . .

TOULON: I'm impressed. You have the stamina to go out into the streets and hunt one down. Some of us have to be content with the wives of the expatriate community.

GALLIMARD: I do feel . . . fortunate.

TOULON: So, Gallimard, you've got the inside knowledge— what *do* the Chinese think?

930    GALLIMARD: Deep down, they miss the old days. You know, cappuccinos, men in tuxedos—

TOULON: So what do we tell the Americans about Vietnam?

GALLIMARD: Tell them there's a natural affinity between the West and the Orient.

TOULON: And that you speak from experience?

GALLIMARD: The Orientals are people too. They want the good things we can give them. If the Americans demonstrate the will to win, the Vietnamese will welcome them into a mutually beneficial union.

940    TOULON: I don't see how the Vietnamese can stand up to American firepower.

GALLIMARD: Orientals will always submit to a greater force.

TOULON: I'll note your opinions in my report. The Americans always love to hear how "welcome" they'll be. *(He starts to exit)*

GALLIMARD: Sir?

TOULON: Mmmm?

GALLIMARD: This . . . rumor you've heard.

TOULON: Uh-huh?

950    GALLIMARD: How . . . widespread do you think it is?

TOULON: It's only widespread within this embassy. Where nobody talks because everybody is guilty. We were worried about you, Gallimard. We thought you were the only one here without a secret. Now you go and find a lotus blossom . . . and top us all. *(He exits)*

GALLIMARD: *(To us)* Toulon knows! And he approves! I was learning the benefits of being a man. We form our own clubs, sit behind thick doors, smoke—and celebrate the fact that we're still boys. *(He starts to move downstage, towards Song)* So, over the—

*(Suddenly Comrade Chin enters. Gallimard backs away.)*

GALLIMARD: *(To Song)* No! Why does she have to come in?

SONG: Rene, be sensible. How can they understand the story without her? Now, don't embarrass yourself.

*(Gallimard moves down center.)*

GALLIMARD: *(To us)* Now, you will see why my story is so amusing to so many people. Why they snicker at parties in disbelief. Please—try to understand it from my point of view. We are all prisoners of our time and place. *(He exits)*

SCENE IV

*Gallimard and Butterfly's flat. Beijing. 1961.*

SONG: *(To us)* 1961. The flat Monsieur Gallimard rented for us. An evening after he has gone.

CHIN: Okay, see if you can find out when the Americans plan to start bombing Vietnam. If you can find out what cities, even better.

SONG: I'll do my best, but I don't want to arouse his suspicions.

CHIN: Yeah, sure, of course. So, what else?

SONG: The Americans will increase troops in Vietnam to 170,000 soldiers with 120,000 militia and 11,000 American advisors.

CHIN: *(Writing)* Wait, wait. 120,000 militia and—

SONG: —11,000 American—

CHIN: —American advisors. *(Beat)* How do you remember so much?

SONG: I'm an actor.

CHIN: Yeah. *(Beat)* Is that how come you dress like that?

SONG: Like what, Miss Chin?

CHIN: Like that dress! You're wearing a dress. And every time I come here, you're wearing a dress. Is that because you're an actor? Or what?

SONG: It's a . . . disguise, Miss Chin.

CHIN: Actors, I think they're all weirdos. My mother tells me actors are like gamblers or prostitutes or—

SONG: It helps me in my assignment.

*(Pause.)*

CHIN: You're not gathering information in any way that violates Communist Party principles, are you?

SONG: Why would I do that?

CHIN: Just checking. Remember: when working for the Great Proletarian State, you represent our Chairman Mao in every position you take.

SONG: I'll try to imagine the Chairman taking my positions.

CHIN: We all think of him this way. Good-bye, comrade. *(She starts to exit)* Comrade?

SONG: Yes?

CHIN: Don't forget: there is no homosexuality in China!

SONG: Yes, I've heard.

CHIN: Just checking. *(She exits)*

SONG: *(To us)* What passes for a woman in modern China.

*(Gallimard sticks his head out from the wings.)*

GALLIMARD: Is she gone?

SONG: Yes, Rene. Please continue in your own fashion.

## SCENE V

*Beijing. 1961–63.*

*Gallimard moves to the couch where Song still sits. He lies down in her lap, and she strokes his forehead.*

GALLIMARD: (*To us*) And so, over the years 1961, '62, '63, we settled into our routine, Butterfly and I. She would always have prepared a light snack and then, ever so delicately, and only if I agreed, she would start to pleasure me. With her hands, her mouth . . . too many ways to explain, and too sad, given my present situation. But mostly we would talk. About my life. Perhaps there is nothing more rare than to find a woman who passionately listens.

(*Song remains upstage, listening, as Helga enters and plays a scene downstage with Gallimard.*)

HELGA: Rene, I visited Dr. Bolleart this morning.

GALLIMARD: Why? Are you ill?

HELGA: No, no. You see, I wanted to ask him . . . that question we've been discussing.

GALLIMARD: And I told you, it's only a matter of time. Why did you bring a doctor into this? We just have to keep trying— like a crapshoot, actually.

HELGA: I went, I'm sorry. But listen: he says there's nothing wrong with me.

GALLIMARD: You see? Now, will you stop—?

HELGA: Rene, he says he'd like you to go in and take some tests.

GALLIMARD: Why? So he can find there's nothing wrong with both of us?

HELGA: Rene, I don't ask for much. One trip! One visit! And then, whatever you want to do about it—you decide.

GALLIMARD: You're assuming he'll find something defective!

HELGA: No! Of course not! Whatever he finds—if he finds nothing, we decide what to do about nothing! But go!

GALLIMARD: If he finds nothing, we keep trying. Just like we do now.

HELGA: But at least we'll know! (*Pause*) I'm sorry. (*She starts to exit*)

GALLIMARD: Do you really want me to see Dr. Bolleart?

HELGA: Only if you want a child, Rene. We have to face the fact that time is running out. Only if you want a child. (*She exits*)

GALLIMARD: (*To Song*) I'm a modern man, Butterfly. And yet, I don't want to go. It's the same old voodoo. I feel like God himself is laughing at me if I can't produce a child.

SONG: You men of the West—you're obsessed by your odd desire for equality. Your wife can't give you a child, and *you're* going to the doctor?

GALLIMARD: Well, you see, she's already gone.

SONG: And because this incompetent can't find the defect, you now have to subject yourself to him? It's unnatural.

GALLIMARD: Well, what is the "natural" solution?

SONG: In Imperial China, when a man found that one wife was inadequate, he turned to another—to give him his son.

GALLIMARD: What do you—? I can't . . . marry you, yet.

SONG: Please. I'm not asking you to be my husband. But I am already your wife.

GALLIMARD: Do you want to . . . have my child?

SONG: I thought you'd never ask.

GALLIMARD: But, your career . . . your—

SONG: Phooey on my career! That's your Western mind, twisting itself into strange shapes again. Of course I love my career. But what would I love most of all? To feel something inside me—day and night—something I know is yours. (*Pause*) Promise me . . . you won't go to this doctor. Who is this Western quack to set himself as judge over the man I love? I know who is a man, and who is not. (*She exits*)

GALLIMARD: (*To us*) Dr. Bolleart? Of course I didn't go. What man would?

## SCENE VI

*Beijing. 1963.*

*Party noises over the house speakers. Renee enters, wearing a revealing gown.*

GALLIMARD: 1963. A party at the Austrian embassy. None of us could remember the Austrian ambassador's name, which seemed somehow appropriate. (*To Renee*) So, I tell the Americans, Diem must go. The U.S. wants to be respected by the Vietnamese, and yet they're propping up this nobody seminarian as her president. A man whose claim to fame is his sister-in-law imposing fanatic "moral order" campaigns? Oriental women—when they're good, they're very good, but when they're bad, they're Christians.

RENEE: Yeah.

GALLIMARD: And what do you do?

RENEE: I'm a student. My father exports a lot of useless stuff to the Third World.

GALLIMARD: How useless?

RENEE: You know. Squirt guns, confectioner's sugar, hula hoops . . .

GALLIMARD: I'm sure they appreciate the sugar.

RENEE: I'm here for two years to study Chinese.

GALLIMARD: Two years?

RENEE: That's what everybody says.

GALLIMARD: When did you arrive?

RENEE: Three weeks ago.

GALLIMARD: And?

RENEE: I like it. It's primitive, but . . . well, this is the place to learn Chinese, so here I am.

GALLIMARD: Why Chinese?

RENEE: I think it'll be important someday.

GALLIMARD: You do?

RENEE: Don't ask me when, but . . . that's what I think.

GALLIMARD: Well, I agree with you. One hundred percent. That's very farsighted.

RENEE: Yeah. Well of course, my father thinks I'm a complete weirdo.

GALLIMARD: He'll thank you someday.

RENEE: Like when the Chinese start buying hula hoops?

GALLIMARD: There're a billion bellies out there.

RENEE: And if they end up taking over the world—well, then I'll be lucky to know Chinese too, right?

(*Pause.*)

GALLIMARD: At this point, I don't see how the Chinese can possibly take—

RENEE: You know what I *don't* like about China?

GALLIMARD: Excuse me? No—what?

1110 RENEE: Nothing to do at night.

GALLIMARD: You come to parties at embassies like everyone else.

RENEE: Yeah, but they get out at ten. And then what?

GALLIMARD: I'm afraid the Chinese idea of a dance hall is a dirt floor and a man with a flute.

RENEE: Are you married?

GALLIMARD: Yes. Why?

RENEE: You wanna . . . fool around?

*(Pause.)*

GALLIMARD: Sure.

1120 RENEE: I'll wait for you outside. What's your name?

GALLIMARD: Gallimard. Rene.

RENEE: Weird. I'm Renee too. *(She exits)*

GALLIMARD: *(To us)* And so, I embarked on my first extra-extramarital affair. Renee was picture perfect. With a body like those girls in the magazines. If I put a tissue paper over my eyes, I wouldn't have been able to tell the difference. And it was exciting to be with someone who wasn't afraid to be seen completely naked. But is it possible for a woman to be *too* uninhibited, *too* willing, so as to seem almost too . . .

1130 masculine?

*(Chuck Berry blares from the house speakers, then comes down in volume as Renee enters, toweling her hair.)*

RENEE: You have a nice weenie.

GALLIMARD: What?

RENEE: Penis. You have a nice penis.

GALLIMARD: Oh. Well, thank you. That's very . . .

RENEE: What—can't take a compliment?

GALLIMARD: No, it's very . . . reassuring.

RENEE: But most girls don't come out and say it, huh?

GALLIMARD: And also . . . what did you call it?

RENEE: Oh. Most girls don't call it a "weenie," huh?

1140 GALLIMARD: It sounds very—

RENEE: Small, I know.

GALLIMARD: I was going to say, "young."

RENEE: Yeah. Young, small, same thing. Most guys are pretty, uh, sensitive about that. Like, you know, I had a boyfriend back home in Denmark. I got mad at him once and called him a little weeniehead. He got so mad! He said at least I should call him a great big weeniehead.

GALLIMARD: I suppose I just say "penis."

RENEE: Yeah. That's pretty clinical. There's "cock," but that

1150 sounds like a chicken. And "prick" is painful, and "dick" is like you're talking about someone who's not in the room.

GALLIMARD: Yes. It's a . . . bigger problem than I imagined.

RENEE: I—I think maybe it's because I really don't know what to do with them—that's why I call them "weenies."

GALLIMARD: Well, you did quite well with . . . mine.

RENEE: Thanks, but I mean, really *do* with them. Like, okay, have you ever looked at one? I mean, really?

GALLIMARD: No, I suppose when it's part of you, you sort of take it for granted.

1160 RENEE: I guess. But, like, it just hangs there. This little . . . flap of flesh. And there's so much fuss that we make about it.

Like, I think the reason we fight wars is because we wear clothes. Because no one knows—between the men, I mean—who has the bigger . . . weenie. So, if I'm a guy with a small one, I'm going to build a really big building or take over a really big piece of land or write a really long book so the other men don't know, right? But, see, it never really works, that's the problem. I mean, you conquer the country, or whatever, but you're still wearing clothes, so there's no way to prove absolutely whose is bigger or smaller. And 1170 that's what we call a civilized society. The whole world run by a bunch of men with pricks the size of pins. *(She exits)*

GALLIMARD: *(To us)* This was simply not acceptable.

*(A high-pitched chime rings through the air. Song, dressed as Butterfly, appears in the upstage special. She is obviously distressed. Her body swoons as she attempts to clip the stems of flowers she's arranging in a vase.)*

GALLIMARD: But I kept up our affair, wildly, for several months. Why? I believe because of Butterfly. She knew the secret I was trying to hide. But, unlike a Western woman, she didn't confront me, threaten, even pout. I remembered the words of Puccini's *Butterfly:*

SONG: "Noi siamo gente avvezza/ alle piccole cose/ umili e silenziose."    1180

GALLIMARD: "I come from a people/ Who are accustomed to little/ Humble and silent." I saw Pinkerton and Butterfly, and what she would say if he were unfaithful . . . nothing. She would cry, alone, into those wildly soft sleeves, once full of possessions, now empty to collect her tears. It was her tears and her silence that excited me, every time I visited Renee.

TOULON: *(Offstage)* Gallimard!

*(Toulon enters. Gallimard turns towards him. During the next section, Song, up center, begins to dance with the flowers. It is a drunken dance, where she breaks small pieces off the stems.)*

TOULON: They're killing him.

GALLIMARD: Who? I'm sorry? What?    1190

TOULON: Bother you to come over at this late hour?

GALLIMARD: No . . . of course not.

TOULON: Not after you hear my secret. Champagne?

GALLIMARD: Um . . . thank you.

TOULON: You're surprised. There's something that you've wanted, Gallimard. No, not a promotion. Next time. Something in the world. You're not aware of this, but there's an informal gossip circle among intelligence agents. And some of ours heard from some of the Americans—

GALLIMARD: Yes?    1200

TOULON: That the U.S. will allow the Vietnamese generals to stage a coup . . . and assassinate President Diem.

*(The chime rings again. Toulon freezes. Gallimard turns upstage and looks at Butterfly, who slowly and deliberately clips a flower off its stem. Gallimard turns back towards Toulon.)*

GALLIMARD: I think . . . that's a very wise move!

*(Toulon unfreezes.)*

TOULON: It's what you've been advocating. A toast?

GALLIMARD: Sure. I consider this a vindication.

TOULON: Not exactly. "To the test. Let's hope you pass."

*(They drink. The chime rings again. Toulon freezes. Gallimard*

*turns upstage, and Song clips another flower.)*

GALLIMARD: *(To Toulon)* The test?

TOULON: *(Unfreezing)* It's a test of everything you've been saying. I personally think the generals probably will stop the Communists. And you'll be a hero. But if anything goes wrong, then your opinions won't be worth a pig's ear. I'm sure that won't happen. But sometimes it's easier when they don't listen to you.

GALLIMARD: They're your opinions too, aren't they?

TOULON: Personally, yes.

GALLIMARD: So we agree.

TOULON: But my opinions aren't on that report. Yours are. Cheers.

*(Toulon turns away from Gallimard and raises his glass. At that instant Song picks up the vase and hurls it to the ground. It shatters. Song sinks down amidst the shards of the vase, in a calm, childlike trance. She sings softly, as if reciting a child's nursery rhyme.*

SONG: *(Repeat as necessary)* "The whole world over, the white man travels, setting anchor, wherever he likes. Life's not worth living, unless he finds, the finest maidens, of every land . . ."

*(Gallimard turns downstage towards us. Song continues singing.)*

GALLIMARD: I shook as I left his house. That coward! That worm! To put the burden for his decisions on my shoulders! I started for Renee's. But no, that was all I needed. A schoolgirl who would question the role of the penis in modern society. What I wanted was revenge. A vessel to contain my humiliation. Though I hadn't seen her in several weeks, I headed for Butterfly's.

*(Gallimard enters Song's apartment.)*

SONG: Oh! Rene . . . I was dreaming!

GALLIMARD: You've been drinking?

SONG: If I can't sleep, then yes, I drink. But then, it gives me these dreams which—Rene, it's been almost three weeks since you visited me last.

GALLIMARD: I know. There's been a lot going on in the world.

SONG: Fortunately I am drunk. So I can speak freely. It's not the world, it's you and me. And an old problem. Even the softest skin becomes like leather to a man who's touched it too often. I confess I don't know how to stop it. I don't know how to become another woman.

GALLIMARD: I have a request.

SONG: Is this a solution? Or are you ready to give up the flat?

GALLIMARD: It may be a solution. But I'm sure you won't like it.

SONG: Oh well, that's very important. "Like it?" Do you think I "like" lying here alone, waiting, always waiting for your return? Please—don't worry about what I may not "like."

GALLIMARD: I want to see you . . . naked.

*(Silence.)*

SONG: I thought you understood my modesty. So you want me to—what—strip? Like a big cowboy girl? Shiny pasties on my breasts? Shall I fling my kimono over my head and yell "ya-hoo" in the process? I thought you respected my shame!

GALLIMARD: I believe you gave me your shame many years ago.

SONG: Yes—and it is just like a white devil to use it against me. I can't believe it. I thought myself so repulsed by the passive Oriental and the cruel white man. Now I see—we are always most revolted by the things hidden within us.

GALLIMARD: I just mean—

SONG: Yes?

GALLIMARD: —that it will remove the only barrier left between us.

SONG: No, Rene. Don't couch your request in sweet words. Be yourself—a cad—and know that my love is enough, that I submit—submit to the worst you can give me. *(Pause)* Well, come. Strip me. Whatever happens, know that you have willed it. Our love, in your hands. I'm helpless before my man.

*(Gallimard starts to cross the room.)*

GALLIMARD: Did I not undress her because I knew, somewhere deep down, what I would find? Perhaps. Happiness is so rare that our mind can turn somersaults to protect it. At the time, I only knew that I was seeing Pinkerton stalking towards his Butterfly, ready to reward her love with his lecherous hands. The image sickened me, pulled me to my knees, so I was crawling towards her like a worm. By the time I reached her, Pinkerton . . . had vanished from my heart. To be replaced by something new, something unnatural, that flew in the face of all I'd learned in the world—something very close to love.

*(He grabs her around the waist; she strokes his hair.)*

GALLIMARD: Butterfly, forgive me.

SONG: Rene . . .

GALLIMARD: For everything. From the start.

SONG: I'm . . .

GALLIMARD: I want to—

SONG: I'm pregnant. *(Beat)* I'm pregnant. *(Beat)* I'm pregnant.

*(Beat.)*

GALLIMARD: I want to marry you!

## SCENE VII

*Gallimard and Butterfly's flat. Beijing. 1963.*

*Downstage, Song paces as Comrade Chin reads from her notepad. Upstage, Gallimard is still kneeling. He remains on his knees throughout the scene, watching it.*

SONG: I need a baby.

CHIN: *(From pad)* He's been spotted going to a dorm.

SONG: I need a baby.

CHIN: At the Foreign Language Institute.

SONG: I need a baby.

CHIN: The room of a Danish girl . . . What do you mean, you need a baby?!

SONG: Tell Comrade Kang—last night, the entire mission, it could've ended.

CHIN: What do you mean?

SONG: Tell Kang—he told me to strip.

CHIN: *Strip?!*

SONG: Write!

CHIN: I tell you, I don't understand nothing about this case
1300    anymore. Nothing.

SONG: He told me to strip, and I took a chance. Oh, we Chinese, we know how to gamble.

CHIN: (Writing) " . . . told him to strip."

SONG: My palms were wet, I had to make a split-second decision.

CHIN: Hey! Can you slow down?!

(Pause.)

SONG: You write faster, I'm the artist here. Suddenly, it hit me—"All he wants is for her to submit. Once a woman submits, a man is always ready to become 'generous.'"

1310    CHIN: You're just gonna end up with rough notes.

SONG: And it worked! He gave in! Now, if I can just present him with a baby. A Chinese baby with blond hair—he'll be mine for life!

CHIN: Kang will never agree! The trading of babies has to be a counterrevolutionary act!

SONG: Sometimes, a counterrevolutionary act is necessary to counter a counterrevolutionary act.

(Pause.)

CHIN: Wait.

SONG: I need one . . . in seven months. Make sure it's a boy.

1320    CHIN: This doesn't sound like something the Chairman would do. Maybe you'd better talk to Comrade Kang yourself.

SONG: Good. I will.

(Chin gets up to leave.)

SONG: Miss Chin? Why, in the Peking Opera, are women's roles played by men?

CHIN: I don't know. Maybe, a reactionary remnant of male—

SONG: No. (Beat) Because only a man knows how a woman is supposed to act.

(Chin exits. Song turns upstage, towards Gallimard.)

GALLIMARD: (Calling after Chin) Good riddance! (To Song) I could forget all that betrayal in an instant, you know. If
1330    you'd just come back and become Butterfly again.

SONG: Fat chance. You're here in prison, rotting in a cell. And I'm on a plane, winging my way back to China. Your President pardoned me for our treason, you know.

GALLIMARD: Yes, I read about that.

SONG: Must make you feel . . . lower than shit.

GALLIMARD: But don't you, even a little bit, wish you were here with me?

SONG: I'm an artist, Rene. You were my greatest . . . acting challenge. (She laughs) It doesn't matter how rotten I an-
1340    swer, does it? You still adore me. That's why I love you, Rene. (She points to us) So—you were telling your audience about the night I announced I was pregnant.

(Gallimard puts his arms around Song's waist. He and Song are in the positions they were in at the end of Scene 6.)

SCENE XIII

Same.

GALLIMARD: I'll divorce my wife. We'll live together here, and then later in France.

SONG: I feel so . . . ashamed.

GALLIMARD: Why?

SONG: I had begun to lose faith. And now, you shame me with your generosity.

GALLIMARD: Generosity? No, I'm proposing for very selfish
1350    reasons.

SONG: Your apologies only make me feel more ashamed. My outburst a moment ago!

GALLIMARD: Your outburst? What about my request?!

SONG: You've been very patient dealing with my . . . eccentricities. A Western man, used to women freer with their bodies—

GALLIMARD: It was sick! Don't make excuses for me.

SONG: I have to. You don't seem willing to make them for yourself.

(Pause.)

GALLIMARD: You're crazy.    1360

SONG: I'm happy. Which often looks like crazy.

GALLIMARD: Then make me crazy. Marry me.

(Pause.)

SONG: No.

GALLIMARD: What?

SONG: Do I sound silly, a slave, if I say I'm not worthy?

GALLIMARD: Yes. In fact you do. No one has loved me like you.

SONG: Thank you. And no one ever will. I'll see to that.

GALLIMARD: So what is the problem?

SONG: Rene, we Chinese are realists. We understand rice, gold, and guns. You are a diplomat. Your career is skyrock-    1370
eting. Now, what would happen if you divorced your wife to marry a Communist Chinese actress?

GALLIMARD: That's not being realistic. That's defeating yourself before you begin.

SONG: We must conserve our strength for the battles we can win.

GALLIMARD: That sounds like a fortune cookie!

SONG: Where do you think fortune cookies come from?

GALLIMARD: I don't care.

SONG: You do. So do I. And we should. That is why I say I'm    1380
not worthy. I'm worthy to love and even to be loved by you. But I am not worthy to end the career of one of the West's most promising diplomats.

GALLIMARD: It's not that great a career! I made it sound like more than it is!

SONG: Modesty will get you nowhere. Flatter yourself, and you flatter me. I'm flattered to decline your offer. (She exits)

GALLIMARD: (To us) Butterfly and I argued all night. And, in the end, I left, knowing I would never be her husband. She went away for several months—to the countryside, like a    1390
small animal. Until the night I received her call.

(A baby's cry from offstage. Song enters, carrying a child.)

SONG: He looks like you.

GALLIMARD: Oh! (Beat; he approaches the baby) Well, babies are never very attractive at birth.

SONG: Stop!

GALLIMARD: I'm sure he'll grow more beautiful with age. More like his mother.

SONG: "Chi vide mai/ a bimbo del Giappon . . ."

GALLIMARD: "What baby, I wonder, was ever born in Japan"—

1400   or China, for that matter—

SONG: ". . . occhi azzurrini?"

GALLIMARD: "With azure eyes"—they're actually sort of brown, wouldn't you say?

SONG: "E il labbro."

GALLIMARD: "And such lips!" (*He kisses Song*) And such lips.

SONG: "E i ricciolini d'oro schietto?"

GALLIMARD: "And such a head of golden"—if slightly patchy— "curls?"

SONG: I'm going to call him "Peepee."

1410   GALLIMARD: Darling, could you repeat that because I'm sure a rickshaw just flew by overhead.

SONG: You heard me.

GALLIMARD: "Song Peepee"? May I suggest Michael, or Stephan, or Adolph?

SONG: You may, but I won't listen.

GALLIMARD: You can't be serious. Can you imagine the time this child will have in school?

SONG: In the West, yes.

GALLIMARD: It's worse than naming him Ping Pong or Long

1420   Dong or—

SONG: But he's never going to live in the West, is he?

(*Pause.*)

GALLIMARD: That wasn't my choice.

SONG: It is mine. And this is my promise to you: I will raise him, he will be our child, but he will never burden you outside of China.

GALLIMARD: Why do you make these promises? I want to be burdened! I want a scandal to cover the papers!

SONG: (*To us*) Prophetic.

GALLIMARD: I'm serious.

1430   SONG: So am I. His name is as I registered it. And he will never live in the West.

(*Song exits with the child.*)

GALLIMARD: (*To us*) It is possible that her stubbornness only made me want her more. That drawing back at the moment of my capitulation was the most brilliant strategy she could have chosen. It is possible. But it is also possible that by this point she could have said, could have done . . . anything, and I would have adored her still.

SCENE IX

*Beijing. 1966.*

*A driving rhythm of Chinese percussion fills the stage.*

GALLIMARD: And then, China began to change. Mao became very old, and his cult became very strong. And, like many old

1440   men, he entered his second childhood. So he handed over the reins of state to those with minds like his own. And children ruled the Middle Kingdom with complete caprice. The doctrine of the Cultural Revolution implied continuous anarchy. Contact between Chinese and foreigners became impossible. Our flat was confiscated. Her fame and my money now counted against us.

(*Two dancers in Mao suits and red-starred caps enter, and begin crudely mimicking revolutionary violence, in an agit-prop fashion.*)

GALLIMARD: And somehow the American war went wrong too. Four hundred thousand dollars were being spent for every Viet Cong killed; so General Westmoreland's remark that the Oriental does not value life the way Americans do was 1450 oddly accurate. Why weren't the Vietnamese people giving in? Why were they content instead to die and die and die again?

(*Toulon enters.*)

TOULON: Congratulations, Gallimard.

GALLIMARD: Excuse me, sir?

TOULON: Not a promotion. That was last time. You're going home.

GALLIMARD: What?

TOULON: Don't say I didn't warn you.

GALLIMARD: I'm being transferred . . . because I was wrong 1460 about the American war?

TOULON: Of course not. We don't care about the Americans. We care about your mind. The quality of your analysis. In general, everything you've predicted here in the Orient . . . just hasn't happened.

GALLIMARD: I think that's premature.

TOULON: Don't force me to be blunt. Okay, you said China was ready to open to Western trade. The only thing they're trading out there are Western heads. And, yes, you said the Americans would succeed in Indochina. You were kidding, 1470 right?

GALLIMARD: I think the end is in sight.

TOULON: Don't be pathetic. And don't take this personally. You were wrong. It's not your fault.

GALLIMARD: But I'm going home.

TOULON: Right. Could I have the number of your mistress? (*Beat*) Joke! Joke! Eat a croissant for me.

(*Toulon exits. Song, wearing a Mao suit, is dragged in from the wings as part of the upstage dance. They "beat" her, then lampoon the acrobatics of the Chinese opera, as she is made to kneel onstage.*)

GALLIMARD: (*Simultaneously*) I don't care to recall how Butterfly and I said our hurried farewell. Perhaps it was better to end our affair before it killed her.   1480

(*Gallimard exits. Comrade Chin walks across the stage with a banner reading: "The Actor Renounces His Decadent Profession!" She reaches the kneeling Song. Percussion stops with a thud. Dancers strike poses.*)

CHIN: Actor-oppressor, for years you have lived above the common people and looked down on their labor. While the farmer ate millet—

SONG: I ate pastries from France and sweetmeats from silver trays.

CHIN: And how did you come to live in such an exalted position?

SONG: I was a plaything for the imperialists!

CHIN: What did you do?

SONG: I shamed China by allowing myself to be corrupted by a 1490 foreigner . . .

CHIN: What does this mean? The People demand a full confession!

SONG: I engaged in the lowest perversions with China's enemies!

CHIN: What perversions? Be more clear!

SONG: I let him put it up my ass!

(*Dancers look over, disgusted.*)

CHIN: Aaaa-ya! How can you use such sickening language?!

SONG: My language . . . is only as foul as the crimes I committed . . .

CHIN: Yeah. That's better. So—what do you want to do now?

SONG: I want to serve the people.

(*Percussion starts up, with Chinese strings.*)

CHIN: What?

SONG: I want to serve the people!

(*Dancers regain their revolutionary smiles, and begin a dance of victory.*)

CHIN: What?!

SONG: I want to serve the people!!

(*Dancers unveil a banner: "The Actor Is Rehabilitated!" Song remains kneeling before Chin, as the dancers bounce around them, then exit. Music out.*)


SCENE X

*A commune. Hunan Province. 1970.*

CHIN: How you planning to do that?

SONG: I've already worked four years in the fields of Hunan, Comrade Chin.

CHIN: So? Farmers work all their lives. Let me see your hands.

(*Song holds them out for her inspection.*)

CHIN: Goddamn! Still so smooth! How long does it take to turn you actors into good anythings? Hunh. You've just spent too many years in luxury to be any good to the Revolution.

SONG: I served the Revolution.

CHIN: Serve the Revolution? Bullshit! You wore dresses! Don't tell me—I was there. I saw you! You and your white vice-consul! Stuck up there in your flat, living off the People's Treasury! Yeah, I knew what was going on! You two . . . homos! Homos! Homos! (*Pause; she composes herself*) Ah! Well . . . you will serve the people, all right. But not with the Revolution's money. This time, you use your own money.

SONG: I have no money.

CHIN: Shut up! And you won't stink up China anymore with your pervert stuff. You'll pollute the place where pollution begins—the West.

SONG: What do you mean?

CHIN: Shut up! You're going to France. Without a cent in your pocket. You find your consul's house, you make him pay your expenses—

SONG: No.

CHIN: And you give us weekly reports! Useful information!

SONG: That's crazy. It's been four years.

CHIN: Either that, or back to rehabilitation center!

SONG: Comrade Chin, he's not going to support me! Not in France! He's a white man! I was just his plaything—

CHIN: Oh yuck! Again with the sickening language? Where's my stick?

SONG: You don't understand the mind of a man.

(*Pause.*)

CHIN: Oh no? No I don't? Then how come I'm married, huh? How come I got a man? Five, six years ago, you always tell me those kind of things, I felt very bad. But not now! Because what does the Chairman say? He tells us *I'm* now the smart one, you're now the nincompoop! *You're* the black-head, the harebrain, the nitwit! You think you're so smart? You understand "The Mind of a Man"? Good! Then *you* go to France and be a pervert for Chairman Mao!

(*Chin and Song exit in opposite directions.*)


SCENE XI

*Paris. 1968–70.*

*Gallimard enters.*

GALLIMARD: And what was waiting for me back in Paris? Well, better Chinese food than I'd eaten in China. Friends and relatives. A little accounting, regular schedule, keeping track of traffic violations in the suburbs. . . . And the indig-nity of students shouting the slogans of Chairman Mao at me—in French.

HELGA: Rene? Rene? (*She enters, soaking wet*) I've had a . . . a problem. (*She sneezes*)

GALLIMARD: You're wet.

HELGA: Yes, I . . . coming back from the grocer's. A group of students, waving red flags, they—

(*Gallimard fetches a towel.*)

HELGA: —they ran by, I was caught up along with them. Before I knew what was happening—

(*Gallimard gives her the towel.*)

HELGA: Thank you. The police started firing water cannons at us. I tried to shout, to tell them I was the wife of a diplomat, but—you know how it is . . . (*Pause*) Needless to say, I lost the groceries. Rene, what's happening to France?

GALLIMARD: What's—? Well, nothing, really.

HELGA: Nothing?! The storefronts are in flames, there's glass in the streets, buildings are toppling—and I'm wet!

GALLIMARD: Nothing! . . . that I care to think about.

HELGA: And is that why you stay in this room?

GALLIMARD: Yes, in fact.

HELGA: With the incense burning? You know something? I hate incense. It smells so sickly sweet.

GALLIMARD: Well, I hate the French. Who just smell—period!

HELGA: And the Chinese were better?

GALLIMARD: Please—don't start.

HELGA: When we left, this exact same thing, the riots—

GALLIMARD: No, no . . .

HELGA: Students screaming slogans, smashing down doors—

GALLIMARD: Helga—

HELGA: It was all going on in China, too. Don't you remem-ber?!

GALLIMARD: Helga! Please! (*Pause*) You have never under-stood China, have you? You walk in here with these ridicu-lous ideas, that the West is falling apart, that China was spitting in our faces. You come in, dripping of the streets, and you leave water all over my floor. (*He grabs Helga's towel, begins mopping up the floor*)

HELGA: But it's the truth!

GALLIMARD: Helga, I want a divorce.

(*Pause; Gallimard continues, mopping the floor.*)

HELGA: I take it back. China is . . . beautiful. Incense, I like in-
1590    cense.

GALLIMARD: I've had a mistress.

HELGA: So?

GALLIMARD: For eight years.

HELGA: I knew you would. I knew you would the day I married you. And now what? You want to marry her?

GALLIMARD: I can't. She's in China.

HELGA: I see. You want to leave. For someone who's not here, is that right?

GALLIMARD: That's right.

1600  HELGA: You can't live with her, but still you don't want to live with me.

GALLIMARD: That's right.

(*Pause.*)

HELGA: Shit. How terrible that I can figure that out. (*Pause*) I never thought I'd say it. But, in China, I was happy. I knew, in my own way, I knew that you were not everything you pretended to be. But the pretense—going on your arm to the embassy ball, visiting your office and the guards saying, "Good morning, good morning, Madame Gallimard"—the pretense . . . was very good indeed. (*Pause*) I hope everyone
1610    is mean to you for the rest of your life. (*She exits*)

GALLIMARD: (*To us*) Prophetic.

(*Marc enters with two drinks.*)

GALLIMARD: (*To Marc*) In China, I was different from all other men.

MARC: Sure. You were white. Here's your drink.

GALLIMARD: I felt . . . touched.

MARC: In the head? Rene, I don't want to hear about the Oriental love goddess. Okay? One night—can we just drink and throw up without a lot of conversation.

GALLIMARD: You still don't believe me, do you?

1620  MARC: Sure I do. She was the most beautiful, et cetera, et cetera, blasé blasé.

(*Pause.*)

GALLIMARD: My life in the West has been such a disappointment.

MARC: Life in the West is like that. You'll get used to it. Look, you're driving me away. I'm leaving. Happy, now? (*He exits, then returns*) Look, I have a date tomorrow night. You wanna come? I can fix you up with—

GALLIMARD: Of course. I would love to come.

(*Pause.*)

MARC: Uh—on second thought, no. You'd better get ahold of
1630    yourself first.

(*He exits; Gallimard nurses his drink.*)

GALLIMARD: (*To us*) This is the ultimate cruelty, isn't it? That I

can talk and talk and to anyone listening, it's only air—too rich a diet to be swallowed by a mundane world. Why can't anyone understand? That in China, I once loved, and was loved by, very simply, the Perfect Woman.

(*Song enters, dressed as Butterfly in wedding dress.*)

GALLIMARD: (*To Song*) Not again. My imagination is hell. Am I asleep this time? Or did I drink too much?

SONG: Rene?

GALLIMARD: God, it's too painful! That you speak?

SONG: What are you talking about? Rene—touch me.   1640

GALLIMARD: Why?

SONG: I'm real. Take my hand.

GALLIMARD: Why? So you can disappear again and leave me clutching at the air? For the entertainment of my neighbors who—?

(*Song touches Gallimard.*)

SONG: Rene?

(*Gallimard takes Song's hand. Silence.*)

GALLIMARD: Butterfly? I never doubted you'd return.

SONG: You hadn't . . . forgotten—?

GALLIMARD: Yes, actually, I've forgotten everything. My mind, you see—there wasn't enough room in this hard head—not   1650 for the world *and* for you. No, there was only room for one. (*Beat*) Come, look. See? Your bed has been waiting, with the Klimt poster you like, and—see? The xiang lu [incense burner] you gave me?

SONG: I . . . I don't know what to say.

GALLIMARD: There's nothing to say. Not at the end of a long trip. Can I make you some tea?

SONG: But where's your wife?

GALLIMARD: She's by my side. She's by my side at last.

(*Gallimard reaches to embrace Song. Song sidesteps, dodging him.*)

GALLIMARD: Why?!   1660

SONG: (*To us*) So I did return to Rene in Paris. Where I found—

GALLIMARD: Why do you run away? Can't we show them how we embraced that evening?

SONG: Please. I'm talking.

GALLIMARD: You have to do what I say! I'm conjuring you up in *my* mind!

SONG: Rene, I've never done what you've said. Why should it be any different in your mind? Now split—the story moves on, and I must change.   1670

GALLIMARD: I welcomed you into my home! I didn't have to, you know! I could've left you penniless on the streets of Paris! But I took you in!

SONG: Thank you.

GALLIMARD: So . . . please . . . don't change.

SONG: You know I have to. You know I will. And anyway, what difference does it make? No matter what your eyes tell you, you can't ignore the truth. You already know too much.

(*Gallimard exits. Song turns to us.*)

SONG: The change I'm going to make requires about five minutes. So I thought you might want to take this opportunity   1680 to stretch your legs, enjoy a drink, or listen to the musicians. I'll be here, when you return, right where you left me.

*(Song goes to a mirror in front of which is a wash basin of water. She starts to remove her makeup as stagelights go to half and houselights come up.)*

—**ACT THREE**—

SCENE 1

*A courthouse in Paris. 1986.*

*As he promised, Song has completed the bulk of his transformation, onstage by the time the houselights go down and the stagelights come up full. He removes his wig and kimono, leaving them on the floor. Underneath, he wears a well-cut suit.*

SONG: So I'd done my job better than I had a right to expect. Well, give him some credit, too. He's right—I was in a fix when I arrived in Paris. I walked from the airport into town, then I located, by blind groping, the Chinatown district. Let me make one thing clear: whatever else may be said about the Chinese, they are stingy! I slept in doorways three days until I could find a tailor who would make me this kimono
1690  on credit. As it turns out, maybe I didn't even need it. Maybe he would've been happy to see me in a simple shift and mascara. But . . . better safe than sorry.
That was 1970, when I arrived in Paris. For the next fifteen years, yes, I lived a very comfy life. Some relief, believe me, after four years on a fucking commune in Nowheresville, China. Rene supported the boy and me, and I did some demonstrations around the country as part of my "cultural exchange" cover. And then there was the spying.

*(Song moves upstage, to a chair. Toulon enters as a judge, wearing the appropriate wig and robes. He sits near Song. It's 1986, and Song is testifying in a courtroom.)*

SONG: Not much at first. Rene had lost all his high-level con-
1700  tacts. Comrade Chin wasn't very interested in parking-ticket statistics. But finally, at my urging, Rene got a job as a courier, handling sensitive documents. He'd photograph them for me, and I'd pass them on to the Chinese embassy.
JUDGE: Did he understand the extent of his activity?
SONG: He didn't ask. He knew that I needed those documents, and that was enough.
JUDGE: But he must've known he was passing classified information.
SONG: I can't say.
1710  JUDGE: He never asked what you were going to do with them?
SONG: Nope.

*(Pause.)*

JUDGE: There is one thing that the court—indeed, that all of France—would like to know.
SONG: Fire away.
JUDGE: Did Monsieur Gallimard know you were a man?
SONG: Well, he never saw me completely naked. Ever.
JUDGE: But surely, he must've . . . how can I put this?
SONG: Put it however you like. I'm not shy. He must've

felt around?
JUDGE: Mmmmm.                                                          1720
SONG: Not really. I did all the work. He just laid back. Of course we did enjoy more . . . complete union, and I suppose he *might* have wondered why I was always on my stomach, but . . . But what you're thinking is. "Of course a wrist must've brushed . . . a hand hit . . . over twenty years!" Yeah. Well, Your Honor, it was my job to make him think I was a woman. And chew on this: it wasn't all that hard. See, my mother was a prostitute along the Bundt before the Revolution. And, uh, I think it's fair to say she learned a few things about Western men. So I borrowed her knowledge. In ser- 1730 vice to my country.
JUDGE: Would you care to enlighten the court with this secret knowledge? I'm sure we're all very curious.
SONG: I'm sure you are. *(Pause)* Okay, Rule One is: Men always believe what they want to hear. So a girl can tell the most obnoxious lies and the guys will believe them every time— "This is my first time"—"that's the biggest I've ever seen"—or *both*, which, if you really think about it, is not possible in a single lifetime. You've maybe heard those phrases a few times in your own life, yes, Your Honor?     1740
JUDGE: It's not my life, Monsieur Song, which is on trial today.
SONG: Okay, okay, just trying to lighten up the proceedings. Tough room.
JUDGE: Go on.
SONG: Rule Two: As soon as a Western man comes into contact with the East—he's already confused. The West has sort of an international rape mentality towards the East. Do you know rape mentality?
JUDGE: Give us your definition, please.
SONG: Basically, "Her mouth says no, but her eyes say yes."     1750
The West thinks of itself as masculine—big guns, big industry, big money—so the East is feminine—weak, delicate, poor . . . but good at art, and full of inscrutable wisdom—the feminine mystique.
Her mouth says no, but her eyes say yes. The West believes the East, deep down, *wants* to be dominated—because a woman can't think for herself.
JUDGE: What does this have to do with my question?
SONG: You expect Oriental countries to submit to your guns, and you expect Oriental women to be submissive to your 1760 men. That's why you say they make the best wives.
JUDGE: But why would that make it possible for you to fool Monsieur Gallimard? Please—get to the point.
SONG: One, because when he finally met his fantasy woman, he wanted more than anything to believe that she was, in fact, a woman. And second, I am an Oriental. And being an Oriental, I could never be completely a man.

*(Pause.)*

JUDGE: Your armchair political theory is tenuous, Monsieur Song.
SONG: You think so? That's why you'll lose in all your dealings 1770 with the East.
JUDGE: Just answer my question: did he know you were a man?

*(Pause.)*

SONG: You know, Your Honor, I never asked.

SCENE II

*Same.*

*Music from the "Death Scene" from Butterfly blares over the house speakers. It is the loudest thing we've heard in this play.*

*Gallimard enters, crawling towards Song's wig and kimono.*

GALLIMARD: Butterfly? Butterfly?

*(Song remains a man, in the witness box, delivering a testimony we do not hear.)*

GALLIMARD: *(To us)* In my moment of greatest shame, here, in this courtroom—with that . . . person up there, telling the world. . . . What strikes me especially is how shallow he is, how glib and obsequious . . . completely . . . without substance! The type that prowls around discos with a gold medallion stinking of garlic. So little like my Butterfly. Yet even in this moment my mind remains agile, flip-flopping like a man on a trampoline. Even now, my picture dissolves, and I see that . . . witness . . . talking to me.

*(Song suddenly stands straight up in his witness box, and looks at Gallimard.)*

SONG: Yes. You. White man.

*(Song steps out of the witness box, and moves downstage towards Gallimard. Light change.)*

GALLIMARD: *(To Song)* Who? Me?
SONG: Do you see any other white men?
GALLIMARD: Yes. There're white men all around. This is a French courtroom.
SONG: So you are an adventurous imperialist. Tell me, why did it take you so long? To come back to this place?
GALLIMARD: What place?
SONG: This theatre in China. Where we met many years ago.
GALLIMARD: *(To us)* And once again, against my will, I am transported.

*(Chinese opera music comes up on the speakers. Song begins to do opera moves, as he did the night they met.)*

SONG: Do you remember? The night you gave your heart?
GALLIMARD: It was a long time ago.
SONG: Not long enough. A night that turned your world upside down.
GALLIMARD: Perhaps.
SONG: Oh, be honest with me. What's another bit of flattery when you've already given me twenty years' worth? It's a wonder my head hasn't swollen to the size of China.
GALLIMARD: Who's to say it hasn't?
SONG: Who's to say? And what's the shame? In pride? You think I could've pulled this off if I wasn't already full of pride when we met? No, not just pride. Arrogance. It takes arrogance, really—to believe you can will, with your eyes and your lips, the destiny of another. *(He dances)* C'mon. Admit it. You still want me. Even in slacks and a button-down collar.
GALLIMARD: I don't see what the point of—
SONG: You don't? Well maybe, Rene, just maybe—I want you.
GALLIMARD: You do?

SONG: Then again, maybe I'm just playing with you. How can you tell? *(Reprising his feminine character, he sidles up to Gallimard)* "How I wish there were even a small cafe to sit in. With men in tuxedos, and cappuccinos, and bad expatriate jazz." Now you want to kiss me, don't you?
GALLIMARD: *(Pulling away)* What makes you—?
SONG: —so sure? See? I take the words from your mouth. Then I wait for you to come and retrieve them. *(He reclines on the floor)*
GALLIMARD: Why?! Why do you treat me so cruelly?
SONG: Perhaps I *was* treating you cruelly. But now—I'm being nice. Come here, my little one.
GALLIMARD: I'm not your little one!
SONG: My mistake. It's I who am *your* little one, right?
GALLIMARD: Yes, I—
SONG: So come get your little one. If you like. I may even let you strip me.
GALLIMARD: I mean, you were! Before . . . but not like this!
SONG: I was? Then perhaps I still am. If you look hard enough. *(He starts to remove his clothes)*
GALLIMARD: What—what are you doing?
SONG: Helping you to see through my act.
GALLIMARD: Stop that! I don't want to! I don't—
SONG: Oh, but you asked me to strip, remember?
GALLIMARD: What? That was years ago! And I took it back!
SONG: No. You postponed it. Postponed the inevitable. Today, the inevitable has come calling.

*(From the speakers, cacophony: Butterfly mixed in with Chinese gongs.)*

GALLIMARD: No! Stop! I don't want to see!
SONG: Then look away.
GALLIMARD: You're only in my mind! All this is in my mind! I order you! To stop!
SONG: To what? To strip? That's just what I'm—
GALLIMARD: No! Stop! I want you—!
SONG: You want me?
GALLIMARD: To stop!
SONG: You know something, Rene? Your mouth says no, but your eyes say yes. Turn them away. I dare you.
GALLIMARD: I don't have to! Every night, you say you're going to strip, but then I beg you and you stop!
SONG: I guess tonight is different.
GALLIMARD: Why? Why should that be?
SONG: Maybe I've become frustrated. Maybe I'm saying "Look at me, you fool!" Or maybe I'm just feeling . . . sexy. *(He is down to his briefs)*
GALLIMARD: Please. This is unnecessary. I know what you are.
SONG: Do you? What am I?
GALLIMARD: A—a man.
SONG: You don't really believe that.
GALLIMARD: Yes I do! I knew all the time somewhere that my happiness was temporary, my love a deception. But my mind kept the knowledge at bay. To make the wait bearable.
SONG: Monsieur Gallimard—the wait is over.

*(Song drops his briefs. He is naked. Sound cue out. Slowly, we and Song come to the realization that what he had thought to be Gallimard's sobbing is actually his laughter.)*

GALLIMARD: Oh god! What an idiot! Of course!

SONG: Rene—what?

GALLIMARD: Look at you! You're a man! (*He bursts into laughter again*)

1870  SONG: I fail to see what's so funny!

GALLIMARD: "You fail to see—!" I mean, you never did have much of a sense of humor, did you? I just think it's ridiculously funny that I've wasted so much time on just a man!

SONG: Wait. I'm not "just a man."

GALLIMARD: No? Isn't that what you've been trying to convince me of?

SONG: Yes, but what I mean—

GALLIMARD: And now, I finally believe you, and you tell me it's not true? I think you must have some kind of identity

1880  problem.

SONG: Will you listen to me?

GALLIMARD: Why?! I've been listening to you for twenty years. Don't I deserve a vacation?

SONG: I'm not just any man!

GALLIMARD: Then, what exactly are you?

SONG: Rene, how can you ask—? Okay, what about this?

(*He picks up Butterfly's robes, starts to dance around. No music.*)

GALLIMARD: Yes, that's very nice. I have to admit.

(*Song holds out his arm to Gallimard.*)

SONG: It's the same skin you've worshipped for years. Touch it.

GALLIMARD: Yes, it does feel the same.

1890  SONG: Now—close your eyes.

(*Song covers Gallimard's eyes with one hand. With the other, Song draws Gallimard's hand up to his face. Gallimard, like a blind man, lets his hands run over Song's face.*)

GALLIMARD: This skin, I remember. The curve of her face, the softness of her cheek, her hair against the back of my hand . . .

SONG: I'm your Butterfly. Under the robes, beneath everything, it was always me. Now, open your eyes and admit it— you adore me. (*He removes his hand from Gallimard's eyes*)

GALLIMARD: You, who knew every inch of my desires—how could you, of all people, have made such a mistake?

SONG: What?

1900  GALLIMARD: You showed me your true self. When all I loved was the lie. A perfect lie, which you let fall to the ground— and now, it's old and soiled.

SONG: So—you never really loved me? Only when I was playing a part?

GALLIMARD: I'm a man who loved a woman created by a man. Everything else—simply falls short.

(*Pause.*)

SONG: What am I supposed to do now?

GALLIMARD: You were a fine spy, Monsieur Song, with an even finer accomplice. But now I believe you should go. Get out

1910  of my life!

SONG: Go where? Rene, you can't live without me. Not after twenty years.

GALLIMARD: I certainly can't live with you—not after twenty years of betrayal.

SONG: Don't be so stubborn! Where will you go?

GALLIMARD: I have a date . . . with my Butterfly.

SONG: So, throw away your pride. And come . . .

GALLIMARD: Get away from me! Tonight, I've finally learned to tell fantasy from reality. And, knowing the difference, I choose fantasy.                                                                         1920

SONG: I'm your fantasy!

GALLIMARD: You? You're as real as hamburger. Now get out! I have a date with my Butterfly and I don't want your body polluting the room! (*He tosses Song's suit at him*) Look at these—you dress like a pimp.

SONG: Hey! These are Armani slacks and—! (*He puts on his briefs and slacks*) Let's just say . . . I'm disappointed in you, Rene. In the crush of your adoration, I thought you'd become something more. More like . . . a woman.

But no. Men. You're like the rest of them. It's all in the way  1930
we dress, and make up our faces, and bat our eyelashes. You really have so little imagination!

GALLIMARD: You, Monsieur Song? Accuse me of too little imagination? You, if anyone, should know—I am pure imagination. And in imagination I will remain. Now get out!

(*Gallimard bodily removes Song from the stage, taking his kimono*)

SONG: Rene! I'll never put on those robes again! You'll be sorry!

GALLIMARD: (*To Song*) I'm already sorry! (*Looking at the kimono in his hands*) Exactly as sorry . . . as a Butterfly.

## SCENE III

*M. Gallimard's prison cell. Paris. Present.*

GALLIMARD: I've played out the events of my life night after  1940
night, always searching for a new ending to my story, one where I leave this cell and return forever to my Butterfly's arms.

Tonight I realize my search is over. That I've looked all along in the wrong place. And now, to you, I will prove that my love was not in vain—by returning to the world of fantasy where I first met her.

(*He picks up the kimono; dancers enter.*)

GALLIMARD: There is a vision of the Orient that I have. Of slender women in chong sams and kimonos who die for the love of unworthy foreign devils. Who are born and raised to be  1950
the perfect women. Who take whatever punishment we give them, and bounce back, strengthened by love, unconditionally. It is a vision that has become my life.

(*Dancers bring the wash basin to him and help him make up his face.*)

GALLIMARD: In public, I have continued to deny that Song Liling is a man. This brings me headlines, and is a source of great embarrassment to my French colleagues, who can now be sent into a coughing fit by the mere mention of Chinese food. But alone, in my cell, I have long since faced the truth.

And the truth demands a sacrifice. For mistakes made over  1960
the course of a lifetime. My mistakes were simple and absolute—the man I loved was a cad, a bounder. He deserved

nothing but a kick in the behind, and instead I gave him . . . all my love.

Yes—love. Why not admit it all? That was my undoing, wasn't it? Love warped my judgment, blinded my eyes, rearranged the very lines on my face . . . until I could look in the mirror and see nothing but . . . a woman.

(*Dancers help him put on the Butterfly wig.*)

GALLIMARD: I have a vision. Of the Orient. That, deep within
1970 its almond eyes, there are still women. Women willing to sacrifice themselves for the love of a man. Even a man whose love is completely without worth.

(*Dancers assist Gallimard in donning the kimono. They hand him a knife.*)

GALLIMARD: Death with honor is better than life . . . life with dishonor. (*He sets himself center stage, in a seppuku position*) The love of a Butterfly can withstand many things—

unfaithfulness, loss, even abandonment. But how can it face the one sin that implies all others? The devastating knowledge that, underneath it all, the object of her love was nothing more, nothing less than . . . a man. (*He sets the tip of the knife against his body*) It is 19__. And I have found her at 1980 last. In a prison on the outskirts of Paris. My name is Rene Gallimard—also known as Madame Butterfly.

(*Gallimard turns upstage and plunges the knife into his body, as music from the "Love Duet" blares over the speakers. He collapses into the arms of the dancers, who lay him reverently on the floor. The image holds for several beats. Then a tight special up on Song, who stands as a man, staring at the dead Gallimard. He smokes a cigarette; the smoke filters up through the lights. Two words leave his lips.*)

SONG: Butterfly? Butterfly?

(*Smoke rises as lights fade slowly to black.*)

**END OF PLAY**

*In his afterword to* M. Butterfly, *Hwang describes both how he came to write the play and his thinking about the fusion of sexual and political dominance with which the West meets Asia.*

**David Henry Hwang:**
Afterword to *M. Butterfly*
(1988)

It all started in May of 1986, over casual dinner conversation. A friend asked, had I heard about the French diplomat who'd fallen in love with a Chinese actress, who subsequently turned out to be not only a spy, but a man? I later found a two-paragraph story in *The New York Times*. The diplomat, Bernard Bouriscot, attempting to account for the fact that he had never seen his "girlfriend" naked, was quoted as saying, "I thought she was very modest. I thought it was a Chinese custom."

Now, I am aware that this is *not* a Chinese custom, that Asian women are no more shy with their lovers than are women of the West. I am also aware, however, that Bouriscot's assumption was consistent with a certain stereotyped view of Asians as bowing, blushing flowers. I therefore concluded that the diplomat must have fallen in love, not with a person, but with a fantasy stereotype. I also inferred that, to the extent the Chinese spy encouraged these misperceptions, he must have played up to and exploited this image of the Oriental woman as demure and submissive. (In general, by the way, we prefer the term "Asian" to "Oriental," in the same way "Black" is superior to "Negro." I use the term "Oriental" specifically to denote an exotic or imperialistic view of the East.)

I suspected there was a play here. I purposely refrained from further research, for I was not interested in writing docudrama. Frankly, I didn't want the "truth" to interfere with my own speculations. I told Stuart Ostrow, a producer with whom I'd worked before, that I envisioned the story as a musical. I remember going so far as to speculate that it could be some "great *Madame Butterfly*-like tragedy." Stuart was very intrigued, and encouraged me with some early funding.

Before I can begin writing, I must "break the back of the story," and find some angle which compels me to set pen to paper. I was driving down Santa Monica Boulevard one afternoon, and asked myself, "What did Bouriscot think he was getting in this Chinese actress?" The answer came to me clearly: "He probably thought he had found Madame Butterfly."

The idea of doing a deconstructivist *Madame Butterfly* immediately appealed to me. This, despite the fact that I didn't even know the plot of the opera! I knew Butterfly only as a cultural stereotype; speaking of an Asian woman, we would sometimes say, "She's pulling a Butterfly," which meant playing the submissive Oriental number. Yet, I felt convinced that the libretto would include yet another lotus blossom pining away for a cruel Caucasian man, and dying for her love. Such a story has become too much of a cliché not to be included in the archtypal East-West romance that started it all. Sure enough, when I purchased the record, I discovered it contained a wealth of sexist and racist clichés, reaffirming my faith in Western culture.

Very soon after, I came up with the basic "arc" of my play: the Frenchman fantasizes that he is Pinkerton and his lover is Butterfly. By the end of the piece, he realizes that it is he who has been Butterfly, in that the Frenchman has been duped by love; the Chinese spy, who exploited that love, is therefore the real Pinkerton. I wrote a proposal to Stuart Ostrow, who found it very exciting. (On the night of the Tony Awards, Stuart produced my original two-page treatment, and we were gratified to see that it was, indeed, the play I eventually wrote.)

I wrote a play, rather than a musical, because, having "broken the back" of the story, I wanted to start immediately and not be hampered by the lengthy process of collaboration. I would like to think, however, that the play has retained many of its musical roots. So *Monsieur Butterfly* was completed in six weeks between September and mid-October, 1986. My wife, Ophelia, thought *Monsieur Butterfly* too obvious a title, and suggested I abbreviate it in the French fashion. Hence, *M. Butterfly*, far more mysterious and ambiguous, was the result.

I sent the play to Stuart Ostrow as a courtesy, assuming he would not be interested in producing what had become a straight play. Instead, he flew out to Los Angeles immediately for script conferences. Coming from a background in the not-for-profit theater, I suggested that we develop the work at a regional institution. Stuart, nothing if not bold, argued for bringing it directly to Broadway.

It was also Stuart who suggested John Dexter to direct. I had known Dexter's work only by its formidable reputation. Stuart sent the script to John, who called back the next day, saying it was the best play he'd read in twenty years. Naturally, this predisposed me to like him a great deal. We met in December in New York. Not long after, we persuaded Eiko Ishioka to design our sets and costumes. I had admired her work from afar ever since, as a college student, I had seen her poster for *Apocalypse Now* in Japan. By January, 1987, Stuart had optioned *M. Butterfly*, Dexter was signed to direct, and the normally sloth-like pace of commercial theater had been given a considerable prod.

On January 4, 1988, we commenced rehearsals. I was very pleased that John Lithgow had agreed to play the French diplomat, whom I named Rene Gallimard. Throughout his tenure with us, Lithgow was every inch the center of our company, intelligent and professional, passionate and generous. B. D. Wong was forced to endure a five-month audition period before we selected him to play Song Liling. Watching B. D.'s growth was one of the joys of the rehearsal process, as he constantly attained higher levels of performance. It became clear that we had been fortunate enough to put together a company with not only great talent, but also wonderful camaraderie.

As for Dexter, I have never worked with a director more respectful of text and bold in the uses of theatricality. On the first day of rehearsal, the actors were given movement and speech drills. Then Dexter asked that everyone not required at rehearsal leave the room. A week later, we returned for an amazingly thorough run-through. It was not until that day that I first heard my play read, a note I direct at many regional theaters who "develop" a script to death.

We opened in Washington, D.C., at the National Theatre, where *West Side Story* and *Amadeus* had premiered. On the morning after opening night, most of the reviews were glowing, except for *The Washington Post*. Throughout our run in Washington, Stuart never pressured us to make the play more "commercial" in reaction to that review. We all simply concluded that the gentleman was possibly insecure about his own sexual orientation and therefore found the play threatening. And we continued our work.

Once we opened in New York, the play found a life of its own. I suppose the most gratifying thing for me is that we had never compromised to be more "Broadway"; we simply did the work we thought best. That our endeavor should be rewarded to the degree it has is one of those all-too-rare instances when one's own perception and that of the world are in agreement.

Many people have subsequently asked me about the "ideas" behind the play. From our first preview in Washington, I have been pleased that people leaving the theater were talking not only about the sexual, but also the political, issues raised by the work.

From my point of view, the "impossible" story of a Frenchman duped by a Chinese man masquerading as a woman always seemed perfectly explicable; given the degree of misunderstanding between men and women and also between East and West, it seemed inevitable that a mistake of this magnitude would one day take place.

Gay friends have told me of a derogatory term used in their community: "Rice Queen"—a gay Caucasian man primarily attracted to Asians. In these relationships, the Asian virtually always plays the role of the "woman"; the Rice Queen, culturally and sexually, is the "man." This pattern of relationships had become so codified that, until recently, it was considered unnatural for gay Asians to date one another. Such men would be taunted with a phrase which implied they were lesbians.

Similarly, heterosexual Asians have long been aware of "Yellow Fever"—Caucasian men with a fetish for exotic Oriental women. I have often heard it said that "Oriental women make the best wives." (Rarely is this heard from the mouths of Asian men, incidentally.) This mythology is exploited by the Oriental mail-order bride trade which has flourished over the past decade. American men can now send away for catalogues of "obedient, domesticated" Asian women looking for husbands. Anyone who believes such stereotypes are a thing of the past need look no further than Manhattan cable television, which advertises call girls from "the exotic east, where men are king; obedient girls, trained in the art of pleasure."

In these appeals, we see issues of racism and sexism intersect. The catalogues and TV spots appeal to a strain in men which desires to reject Western women for what they have become—independent, assertive, self-possessed—in favor of a more reactionary model—the pre-feminist, domesticated geisha girl.

That the Oriental woman is penultimately feminine does not of course imply that she is always "good." For every Madonna there is a whore; for every lotus blossom there is also a dragon lady. In popular culture, "good" Asian women are those who serve the White protagonist in his battle against her own people, often sleeping with him in the process. Stallone's *Rambo II*, Cimino's *Year of the Dragon*, Clavell's *Shogun*, Van Lustbader's *The Ninja* are all familiar examples.

Now our considerations of race and sex intersect the issue of imperialism. For this formula—good natives serve Whites, bad natives rebel—is consistent with the mentality of colonialism. Because they are submissive and obedient, good natives of both sexes necessarily take on "feminine" characteristics in a colonialist world. Gunga Din's unfailing devotion to his British master, for instance, is not so far removed from Butterfly's slavish faith in Pinkerton.

It is reasonable to assume that influences and attitudes so pervasively displayed in popular culture might also influence our policymakers as they consider the world. The neo-Colonialist notion that good elements of a native society, like a good woman, desire submission to the masculine West speaks precisely to the heart of our foreign policy blunders in Asia and elsewhere.

For instance, Frances Fitzgerald wrote in *Fire in the Lake*, "The idea that the United States could not master the problems of a country as small and underdeveloped as Vietnam did not occur to Johnson as a possibility." Here, as in so many other cases, by dehumanizing the enemy, we dehumanize ourselves. We become the Rice Queens of *realpolitik*.

*M. Butterfly* has sometimes been regarded as an anti-American play, a diatribe against the stereotyping of the East by the West, of women by men. Quite to the contrary, I consider it a plea to all sides to cut through our respective layers of cultural and sexual misperception, to deal with one another truthfully for our mutual good, from the common and equal ground we share as human beings.

For the myths of the East, the myths of the West, the myths of men, and the myths of women—these have so saturated our consciousness that truthful contact between nations and lovers can only be the result of heroic effort. Those who prefer to bypass the work involved will remain in a world of surfaces, misperceptions running rampant. This is, to me, the convenient world in which the French diplomat and the Chinese spy lived. This is why, after twenty years, he had learned nothing at all about his lover, not even the truth of his sex.

# Bette Bourne, Paul Shaw, Peggy Shaw, and Lois Weaver

Although Bette Bourne (b. 1939) and Paul Shaw (b. 1953), and Peggy Shaw (b. 1944) and Lois Weaver (b. 1949), collaborated on the Obie Award-winning play *Belle Reprieve* (1991), they are best known for their work as two distinct performing companies—Bloolips and Split Britches.

Lois Weaver was born and raised in rural southwest Virginia; she received her B. S. in Theatre and Education from Radford College (now Radford University) in 1972, and became a founding member of Spiderwoman Theatre in 1975. Peggy Shaw grew up in Massachusetts and studied at the Massachusetts College of Art before joining the gay male cabaret Hot Peaches. They met in the late 1970s, when Hot Peaches and Spiderwoman were both touring in Europe; by the early 1980s, Shaw and Weaver were working together on several influential projects. In 1981 they joined forces with writer and performer Deborah Margolin to form their own company, Split Britches, and in 1982 they founded the WOW Cafe (Women's One World), a performance space for women in New York's East Village, which has become an important venue for new women's performance. Their first production, *Splitbritches,* given at WOW's inaugural festivals in 1980 and 1981, was a series of monologues, songs, and transformations based on Weaver's rural Southern family. As lesbians and performers, Weaver and Shaw have undertaken a series of works staging the conflict between the ideology of compulsory heterosexuality and the lives of lesbian women, and Split Britches has developed a critique of the working of gender and sexual identity in contemporary America that is at once theoretical and theatrical. The work of Split Britches has come to stand at the center both of lesbian performance and of the contemporary critique of gender politics in the theater, and includes performances like *Beauty and the Beast* (1982), *Upwardly Mobile Home* (1984), *Dress Suits to Hire* (written by Holly Hughes, 1987), *Anniversary Waltz* (1990), *Belle Reprieve* (1991), and *Lesbians Who Kill* (1992). Lois Weaver is currently also the joint artistic director for London's Gay Sweatshop Theatre Company.

*Belle Reprieve* was devised in a month-long workshop/retreat that Shaw and Weaver took in Majorca with Bette Bourne and Paul Shaw ("Precious Pearl"), who form the British gay male performing company Bloolips. Bette Bourne was born in Wales and trained for the theater at the Central School of Speech and Drama in London in the early 1960s, where he now directs and lectures in Shakespearean analysis when not performing. Although he had trained as a classical actor, his career changed course in 1970, when he became involved in gay politics and street theater, and then performed with Hot Peaches. In 1977 he formed Bloolips. Paul Shaw, from Littlehampton, in Sussex, England, studied theater design at the Wimbledon School of Art; he then worked as assistant director to Malcolm Pride and as the assistant director of the Glasgow Citizens' Theatre before joining Bloolips in 1983. Bloolips has toured throughout Britain, Europe, Canada, and the United States, and their many shows—*Lust in Space, Gland Motel, Get Her,* and *Living Leg-Ends*—use a variety of stage strategies—camp, vaudeville, cross-dressing—to examine the construction of sexual orientation in contemporary culture. Bourne has also starred in *Sarrasine,* by Neil Bartlett and Nicholas Bloomfield and in a solo piece *The Dish* (1993) by Paul Hallam.

## Belle Reprieve (1991)

Taken from Blanche Dubois's ancestral home "Belle Reve" in Tennessee Williams's *A Streetcar Named Desire, Belle Reprieve* explores the relation between gender and power in American life and in American theater. *Belle Reprieve* uses a farcical mixture of cross-dressing to develop both a performative "rereading" of *Streetcar* and a critique of contemporary sexual politics, both in and out of the theater. First, the play is systematically cross-cast, often in ways that underscore the gender and sexual tensions of the famous film version of the play. The film seems at once both to express and to subvert conventional notions of sexuality. Karl Malden's Mitch is concerned about his manliness, readily dominated both by his mother and by Blanche; Kim Stanley's Stella is played as nearly narcotized by her sexual desire for Stanley; Vivien Lee's Blanche is the erotic center of the play yet is consumed by illusions of propriety and refinement, illusions shattered by her first love for a boy who was gay; Marlon Brando's Stanley, for all his macho qualities, exudes in the film a kind of "femme" sensuality.

*Belle Reprieve* works to bring this performative subtext to light, largely through a campy cross-playing that in many respects both literalizes and foregrounds the sexual identifications ex-/re-pressed by *Streetcar*: Mitch, "a fairy disguised as a man," is played by Paul Shaw/Precious Pearl; Stella, a "woman disguised as a woman" is played by the femme lesbian Lois Weaver; Stanley, "a butch lesbian," is played by butch Peggy Shaw; and Blanche, "a man in a dress" is played by Bette Bourne, a man in a dress. *Belle Reprieve* then systematically replays and analyzes the key relationships of *Streetcar*, in a way that throws the "natural" distribution of sex/gender identification into question. For example, a love scene between Blanche and Stella is enacted by Lois Weaver and Bette Bourne; moments later a pendant scene between Mitch and Stanley, literalizing the homoerotic quality of their relationship in *Streetcar*, is played by Precious Pearl and Peggy Shaw. Although both of these scenes are "cross-dressed," the performance of gender roles is complicated by a second performative dimension, the visible signifiers of sexual orientation. Unlike a similar seduction scene between, say Ellen and Betty in Act One of Caryl Churchill's *Cloud Nine*—when we may feel that, in some productions at least, the cross-dressing of Betty (played by a man) can mistakenly work to "naturalize" this lesbian relationship for the comfort of a heterosexual audience— here, the cross-dressing of Blanche and Stanley is no more—and no less—a "performance" than the playing of Mitch or Stella. In this sense, *Belle Reprieve* elaborates the aesthetics of "camp" in performance. As David Savran suggests in his book *Communists, Cowboys, and Queers: The Politics of Masculinity in the Works of Arthur Miller and Tennessee Williams*, camp does not merely reverse notions of gender and sexuality, because it is "based on the assumption that genders and sexualities are not produced in opposition and therefore cannot be 'simply' reversed." Instead, camp tends to "make elaborate substitutions and delight in the capriciousness of spoken and performative languages. It will also frequently and pointedly transpose genders, producing transvestite subjects based on its recognition that all gender is masquerade and all costume is a form of drag" (118).

*Belle Reprieve* uses this vaudevillian strategy to foreground its own *performance*, suggesting that gender and sexual identification take place at the level of performance. Indeed, the play suggests that this performative dimension of identity is visible even in the repressed mode of American realism itself. This is the burden of the play's brilliant conclusion, when the "realism" of *Streetcar* is also shown to consist of playing "the extremes, the stereotypes." As Precious Pearl, Bette Bourne, Lois Weaver, and Peggy Shaw suggest in their final song, if gender and sexual identification are a kind of performance, then we are all—straight and gay alike—in love with playing our part, fundamentally, necessarily, in love with our art.

# —Belle Reprieve—

## Bette Bourne, Paul Shaw, Peggy Shaw, and Lois Weaver

## —CHARACTERS—

MITCH, *a fairy disguised as a man*
STELLA, *a woman disguised as a woman*
STANLEY, *a butch lesbian*
BLANCHE, *a man in a dress*

*Place*

*An empty stage. The backdrop is a scrim painted to resemble the interior of a 1940s New Orleans apartment. There are three high-tension wires strung across the stage. Throughout the play, various painted cloth curtains are pulled across these wires to denote a change in scenery or mood.*

*Time*

*Four o'clock in the morning.*

## —ACT I—

MITCH *is wheeling three large boxes onstage with a handtruck. One is designed to resemble a steamer trunk. The second is square, large enough to hold an actor, and shaped to resemble a card table, which it becomes in later scenes. The third is tall, rectangular, and large enough to hold another actor. It is turned on its back to represent a bathtub in the second act.*

MITCH: Inside this box it's four o'clock in the morning. I know that sounds incredible but it's true. I know because it's *my* four o'clock in the morning. Every time it comes around, I put it in this box. I've been doing it for years now. At four o'clock in the morning, the thread that holds us to the earth is at its most slender, and all the creatures that never see sunlight come out to make mincemeat of well-laid plans. So you can imagine what it's like in there. If you listen closely you can hear them shuffling about, like the sound of rain or
10 chittering birds. It reminds me of a soundtrack, the beginning of a movie . . . (*Stella appears drinking a coke behind the scrim*) a clean slate. Darkness all around. Small sounds that give a taste of an atmosphere, a head turning, a body lit from behind, shadows in a dark, tiled hallway, a blues piano. (*Pianist strikes a match and begins to play the blues*)
STELLA: (*Moving to center from behind scrim, still drinking the coke*) Is there something you want? What can I do for you? Do you know who I am, what I feel, how I think? You want my body. My soul, my food, my bed, my skin, my hands?
20 You want to touch me, hold me, lick me, smell me, eat me, have me? You think you need a little more time to decide? Well, you've got a little over an hour to have your fill. Meanwhile . . . (*Mitch enters with last box, swatting bugs*) I'm surprised there aren't more bugs out this time of year. All the ones that are out seem to be buzzing around my head.

MITCH: No, there's plenty for both of us. Don't feel singled out.
STELLA: I think it's 'cuz I eat so much sugar that they're attracted to me. Sugar in my blood. And my veins are close to the surface.
MITCH: You know that they excrete something to digest your 30 blood, that's why they leave that bump on your skin.
STELLA: I always worry that they carry things with them, transferring them from person to person.
MITCH: That's an old wives' tale. This country has no tradition of disease being spread by mosquitoes. You're mistaken.
STELLA: Well, every year I make one big mistake. I wonder what it will be this year?
MITCH: This mistake, is it at a particular time, or can't you tell when it's coming?
STELLA: I can usually feel it coming . . .                    40
BLANCHE: (*From inside box*) I've always depended on the strangeness of strangers.
STELLA: Or at least after the fact I thought I knew it was coming.
MITCH: Isn't there something you can do to stop it happening?
STELLA: Such as . . .
MITCH: Change the script!
STELLA: Change the script. Ha ha. You want me to do *what* in these shoes? The script is not the problem. I've changed the script.                                                              50
MITCH: It's a start.
STELLA: Look, I'm supposed to wander around in a state of narcotized sensuality. That's my part. (*Blanche and Stanley speak simultaneously from inside the two largest boxes*)
BLANCHE: You didn't see, Miss Stella, see what I saw, the long parade to the graveyard. The mortgage on the house, death is expensive, Miss Stella, death is expensive.
STANLEY: Is that so? You don't say, hey Stella wasn't we happy before she showed up. Didn't we see those colored lights you and me. Didn't we see those colored lights.           60
STELLA: And anyway, it's too late. It's already started.
STANLEY: Hey Stella! (*Coming out of stage right box*)
STELLA: Don't holler at me like that, Stanley.
STANLEY: Hey Stella, Stella baby! Catch!
STELLA: What!
STANLEY: Meat.
BLANCHE: (*Emerging from stage left box*) Are we here? Is this the place? Are my necessaries disembarked? How sweet it is to arrive at a new place for the first time. The future stretching out in front of us like a clean, white carpet. 70 There's the stir and rustle of endless possibility in the air.
STANLEY: You don't say.
STELLA: Honey, we're in exactly the same place we started out from.
BLANCHE: Started out? What do you mean started out? You mean we haven't arrived?
STELLA: No, we haven't arrived, but don't worry about that

now. You just take it easy.

STANLEY: Something smells fishy around here and it's not me.

80 STELLA: (*To Stanley*) Now you be kind to my sister. Tell her how nice she looks.

BLANCHE: I can't stand being in between. I just can't bear it.

STELLA: (*To Stanley*) You should try to understand her a little better, she's just different.

STANLEY: Different? You can say that again.

BLANCHE: I have never regretted my decision to be unique.

STANLEY: I'm gonna put an end to this charade here and now.

BLANCHE: (*As Stanley moves to center stage with trunk and becomes a customs agent*) That my plans of late have gone
90   somewhat awry is the price one has to pay if life is to be superb.

STANLEY: (*To Blanche*) Ticket please.

BLANCHE: (*To Mitch*) Young man, don't I know you?

MITCH: We were engaged to be married.

STANLEY: Ticket please!

BLANCHE: Did I break your heart?

MITCH: No, you broke my leg.

BLANCHE: I must be stronger than I thought.

STANLEY: Ticket please!

100 BLANCHE: Oh, well, all right, I have it here somewhere. (*Rummages through her bag*) Which ticket do you mean, the one that got me here or the one that will take me away?

STANLEY: Both.

BLANCHE: Oh, well I don't seem to have either at the moment. Although we must have gotten here somehow, we can't have walked, we have a heavy load. However, I present myself as overwhelming evidence that I am actually here.

STANLEY: While we're at it, I'm gonna need your passport.

BLANCHE: Passport? I wasn't aware that we were crossing any
110   borders. What borders?

STANLEY: Passport.

BLANCHE: (*Rummaging around*) Passport, passport . . . (*Mitch steps forward with her passport and hands it to Stanley*)

STANLEY: (*Still staring at Mitch*) Name?

BLANCHE: Blanche DuBois.

STANLEY: That's not what it says here.

BLANCHE: I assure you that is who I am. My namesake is a role played by that incandescent star, Vivian Leigh, and although the resemblance is not immediately striking I have been
120   told we have the same shoulders.

STANLEY: (*Looking at passport photo*) Then who's this here?

BLANCHE: The information in that document is a convention which allows me to pass in the world without let or hindrance. If you'll just notice the message inside the front cover, the Queen of England herself not only requests this but requires it.

STANLEY: You don't look anything like this photograph.

BLANCHE: I believe nature is there to be improved upon.

STANLEY: You're lying.

130 BLANCHE: Well, that's one way of looking at it.

STANLEY: Is there another?!

BLANCHE: You wouldn't treat me like this if I wasn't at the end of my rope!

STANLEY: (*Slamming fist on trunk*) But ya are Blanche, ya are. (*Cat screams from Mitch and Stella*)

BLANCHE: What was that?

STANLEY: Cats. I'm afraid I'm going to have to perform an inti-

mate search.

BLANCHE: My body?

STANLEY: Your luggage.                          140

BLANCHE: Stella, how do I look?

STELLA: Fresh as a daisy.

STANLEY: One that's been picked a few days.

MITCH: Look, can't we just scrub 'round the search and get on with the scenes of brutal humiliation and sexual passion?

STANLEY: I'm afraid we have to find a motive in this case, and I believe it's in this trunk. (*To Mitch*) Why don't you mind your own business?

BLANCHE: How dare you speak to my ex-fiancé like that!

STANLEY: Your ex-fiancé?! This man is your ex-fiancé?      150

BLANCHE: That's right.

MITCH: I told her I loved her and she pushed me down the stairwell, but I forgave her as any decent man would.

STANLEY: That's not what it says in the script. In the script it says you treated her like shit because you're a stuck-up mommy's boy.

MITCH: That's a lie!

BLANCHE: I think I'm going to faint.

STELLA: Is all this really necessary?

STANLEY: Look, have you any idea how many people we have  160
come in here saying they're Blanche DuBois, clutching tiny handbags and fainting in the foyer? I'm afraid I'll have to subject this case to the closest possible scrutiny before I allow any of you to pass any further.

BLANCHE: I see, you want me to come clean by showing my dirty laundry to the world.

STANLEY: You got it.

BLANCHE: I think I'll go into the dressing room and burst into tears.

STELLA: We're in this up to our asses now. There's no going  170
back.

BLANCHE: Hold me Stella, I think I feel a flashback coming on. (*Lights flash, music plays, a curtain painted like a grotesque piece of torn lace is pulled on stage behind the action, the actors shuffling backward around trunk*) And so it was that I set out to prove to the world that I was indeed myself. A difficult enough task, you might say, for anyone.

STELLA: She threw herself at the feet of an unforgiving world to prove her identity.

MITCH: The answer was somewhere in that trunk.          180

STANLEY: (*Thumping fist on trunk as music and lights stop flashing*) This is gonna cost you, lady. What did you think, you were gonna get a free ride or something? (*About to open trunk*) What do we have here?

BLANCHE: Please open the doors one at a time! If you open them all at once pink things and fur things, dainty things, delicate and wistful things might pop out.

STANLEY: I'll open them one at a time. First things first. (*Music starts. Stanley pulls out a jacket and tosses it to Stella, then pulls out a scarf and throws it to Mitch*)            190

BLANCHE: I won't take it personally the way you're treating everything I own in the world.

STANLEY: Let's see, what are little girls made of? (*Singing*) I put my right hand in, I pull my right hand out (*Pulls it out empty and laughs*), I put my right hand in (*Pulls out dress on hanger and puts it around his neck*) and I shake it all about.

BLANCHE: I can't approve of any of this, just as you can't

approve of my entire life.

STANLEY: I do the hokey-pokey and I turn myself around.
200    That's what it's all about. So this is what little girls are made
of. Tiaras, diamond tiaras. (*Puts tiara on his head*) And
what's this? (*Pulling out gold bracelet and putting it on*) A
solid gold Cadillac. This must be worth a fortune. And what
have we got here? A box of valuables. (*Tossing the contents
onto the floor*) Love letters, scrap books, newspaper clippings.

BLANCHE: Everybody has something they don't want others to
touch because of their intimate nature.

STANLEY: (*Singing, as Mitch picks up newspaper clippings*) I
210    put my right foot in, I take my right foot out, I put my right
foot in and I shake it all about . . . (*Stanley pulls out high-
heeled shoe*)

MITCH: (*As Stanley continues singing*) There was a time when
everyone was trying to get a piece of her. These are the
pieces left over, "Tipped for the Top," "What an Angel."
Now the angel's in the kitchen, washing the dishes and picking her teeth.

BLANCHE: (*As Mitch hands her newspaper clippings*) I don't
see how any of this relates to my own life except in the way
220    people perceive my fall.

STANLEY: I put my left hand in . . . (*Shaking the box violently
from inside*)

BLANCHE: (*Ripping up the newspaper clippings*) Tearing . . . I
hear tearing . . . be careful . . . the wings, you're tearing
them!

STANLEY: They're just animals, lady, what's the matter with
you?

BLANCHE: But they've been faithful their whole lives. There
are things we don't know here.

230    STANLEY: Things are different now. (*Still struggling inside box*)
I pull the white-feathered excited body of one swan off the
white-feathered excited body of another swan. (*He pulls out
handful of feathers*)

BLANCHE: What right have you to interfere with nature?

STANLEY: (*Pulling feathers apart to reveal that they are a boa,
which he drapes across his shoulders*) And shake it all about.

BLANCHE: Birds of a feather.

STANLEY: I put my left hand in . . . (*Pulling hand quickly out*)
Oww, Stella, Stella!

240    STELLA: What?

STANLEY: I burned my hand.

STELLA: Oh, Stanley, it's just candle wax.

STANLEY: I know but it hurts.

STELLA: Some people think it's sexy.

STANLEY: (*Pulling hand away from her*) I can see where it
might be sexy if I knew it was coming. I put my left hand in,
I pull my left hand out . . . oh, a little cheerleading doll . . .
(*Breaks off the arm*) the arm is busted . . . the rubber band
must be broken inside.

250    BLANCHE: My mother gave me that.

STANLEY: (*Dancing doll on top of trunk*) And I shake it all
about . . .

BLANCHE: And before that, it was her mother's.

STANLEY: (*Slamming doll down*) Look, lady, I'm just trying to
do my job here.

BLANCHE: Yes, of course.

STANLEY: And my job is to make sure you're not smuggling
something personal in this here trunk. (*Reaching into trunk*)

Let's see, what's this? And what is this? (*Pulling out purse*)

BLANCHE: This contains all of my hopes and dreams . . . this is    260
my hope chest.

STANLEY: Hopes and dreams? Forget it. (*Sticking hand into
purse*) I put my whole body in, I take my whole body out.
(*Pulling out scarf*) I grab myself a frilly thing and shake it all
about. I pin it on my shoulders and I sashay up and down,
that's what it's all about. Yes? I put my right hand in, I take
my right hand out . . . (*Pulls out hand covered in blood.
Blanche and Stella exit. Mitch enters in fading light to roll
away trunk, music and lights slowly fade out. In blackout*) I
am suddenly aware that the atmosphere has changed. It's    270
dark. The night has a thousand eyes and they're all looking
at me. They're burning into me, burning into my chest. If I
don't sleep now, I never will . . . don't panic . . . the night
seems to last forever . . . don't panic . . . I'm scared, I'm
wrong, the night is making me feel . . . (*Lights return suddenly on a curtain with a painting of an oversized clawed
foot of a bathtub and a straight razor lying on a tiled floor.
Stella is onstage with Stanley. She is wearing a cheerleading
outfit and carries a cheerleading doll*) Vivien Leigh, huh?
O.K., that's your story and I'm stuck with it for now. But let's    280
see if you can keep up the deception day after day, week
after week in front of me. Let that be a challenge to our relationship. But meanwhile, relax, make yourself at home,
have a drink. Tell me about yourself, stuff I haven't heard
before, recent stuff like how've you been lately. I got all the
time in the world and I'm all ears.

STELLA: Stanley, you come out here and let Blanche finish
dressing. (*Stanley exits*) I let her keep her hopes and
dreams, just like I let her keep her cheerleading memories.
I pretended they were mine as well, came to know them as    290
I know my own face in the mirror. A face that was not a twin
of my older sister.

BLANCHE: (*Entering stage left in a bathrobe*) I think I handled
that really well. It's a tricky business, deception in the face
of legal documents. Thank heavens for bathrooms, they always make me feel so new.

STELLA: Blanche, honey, are you all right in there? There was
no answer, but I could hear her splashing and the sound of
her radio.

BLANCHE: I can always refresh my spirits in the bathroom.    300

STELLA: Blanche, I brought you your lemon coke.

BLANCHE: All right sweetie. Be right out.

STELLA: I'll wait out here.

BLANCHE: I don't want you to have to wait on me.

STELLA: I like waiting on you Blanche, it feels more like home.

BLANCHE: I must admit, I do like to be waited on.

STELLA: Well, I'm waiting.

BLANCHE: One day I'll probably just dissolve in the bath.
They'll come looking for me, but there'll be nothing left.
"Drag Queen Dissolves in Bathtub," that'll be the headline.    310
"All that was left was a full head of hair clogging up the plug-
hole. She was exceptional even in death . . . " I wonder
where I'll end up. In the sea, I suppose.

STELLA: I'm waiting, Blanche.

BLANCHE: Just a few last finishing touches.

STELLA: Waiting. Waiting in the wings. Waiting for her to get
off the phone.

BLANCHE: You wouldn't want me to go out looking a mess, now
would you?

320 STELLA: Waiting for her to come home from Woolworth's with the new Tangee lipstick. And when I wasn't waiting I was following. I used to follow her into the bathroom. I loved the way she touched her cheek with the back of her hand. How she let her hand come to rest just slightly between her breasts as she took one last look in the mirror. I used to study the way she adjusted her hips and twisted her thighs in that funny way when she was changing her shoes. Then she would fling open the bathroom door and sail down the staircase into the front room to receive her gentlemen
330 callers.

BLANCHE: *(Colliding into Stella, who drops the doll)* My doll, it's broken!

STELLA: *(Laughingly)* No it isn't.

BLANCHE: I did. I broke it.

STELLA: No, honey. You didn't.

BLANCHE: Yes I did. I broke it.

STELLA: *(Shaking Blanche)* No, Blanche, it was already broken.

BLANCHE: I don't know why I'm like this today.

STELLA: *(Embracing her)* Blanche, you know what this reminds
340 me of? My homecoming corsage, remember? Before the homecoming parade, when the band and all the floats were gathering in front of the war memorial. It was your senior year, you were the captain of the cheerleaders, and I was the mascot. And they gave us these big orange and maroon chrysanthemums with ribbon streamers; mine was just as big as yours.

BLANCHE: And I pinned it on your shoulder and you were so proud of its size and excited by the smell of it.

STELLA: I felt every bit as tall and glamorous as the real cheer-
350 leaders, the majorettes, the homecoming court, even Miss Mississippi herself. I stood in that November air imagining all the things a grownup woman could be . . . and then, that great big old football player came walking across the red dirt and smacked right into me.

BLANCHE: And your poor corsage, it started to bleed, it started to lose its petals one by one.

STELLA: And I started to cry. I threw a god-awful fit.

BLANCHE: You certainly did.

STELLA: My whole life was disappearing with those dripping
360 petals. How was I going to present myself in the same parade with Miss Mississippi, her in her strapless gown and me with a handful of petals. But you put your big strong arms around me and set me right up there on the float with . . .

BLANCHE: The beauty queen herself. And there you were, all puffy-eyed and corsageless . . .

STELLA: Right next to the great white virgin, with her round bare shoulders and her rhinestone tiara.

BLANCHE: *(As music starts)* And I took your picture and it was in the papers. *(Blanche takes off bathrobe to reveal cheer-*
370 *leading outfit and they sing)*

### Under the Covers
*When life is unfair, and the world makes you sick*
*I know somewhere that's bliss on a stick.*
*(Stella) Somewhere to go when things are unsteady*
*(Blanche) Somewhere to go with Coco and Teddy.*

*Under the covers, the pillows and laces*
*We both can share, those soft cotton places*
*(Stella) Lying together like spoons in a drawer*
*(Blanche) Then turning over to have an explore . . .*

*Under the covers, those smooth satin covers* 380
*We share our dreams*
*(Stella) Like goose downy lovers*
*(Blanche) Tucked in together like girls in the dorm*
*Under the covers everything's cozy and warm . . .*

*(They pull hidden pom-poms from each other's sleeves and cheer)*

AMO, AMAS,
AMAT WE LOVE OUR TEAM A LOT
WE'RE GONNA FIGHT FIGHT FIGHT
WE'RE GONNA WIN WIN WIN
WE'RE GONNA BE . . . *(Blanche)* FABULOUS.

*(Tap dance break)*

*Under the covers, it's you and it's me now* 390
*Our pleasure grows, because we are two now*
*Lean on a pillow and look in my eyes*
*Spreading our knowledge and sharing our thighs*
*Under the covers, our fingers exploring*
*Those hidden dreams, we've found there is something*

*(Stella pulls a hand covered in menstrual blood out from under her skirt)*

*Mother has maybe forgotten to tell*
*Tho' if she found out*
*We'd found out*
*She'd give us hell.*

STANLEY: *(Yelling from backstage)* Stella! 400

BLANCHE and STELLA: She'd give us hell.

STANLEY: Stella!

BLANCHE and STELLA: She'd give us . . . *(Song dissolves into laughter)*

STANLEY: When are you hens gonna end that conversation?

STELLA: Oh, you can't hear us.

STANLEY: Well, you can hear me, and I say hush up!

STELLA: This is my house too, Stanley, and I'll talk as much as I . . .

BLANCHE: *(Interrupting her)* Please don't start another row, I 410 couldn't bear it . . . *(She exits)*

STELLA: I tried to follow her, but I got stuck. Stuck in the bathroom, where I saw myself in the medicine chest mirror. I stopped there and I stared. For three days I stared. I wasn't her little sister. And in the mirror I saw the road split, and I took mine . . .

STANLEY: *(Grabbing Stella)* Stella. *(They hug, Stella exits, Stanley goes to bathroom and starts shaving. Lights dim)*

MITCH: *(Entering stage right. He carries a painting of a card table, which he places over the front of the square box)* Now 420 and then I reached out to touch his wrists. They glittered with a dozen golden bracelets that matched the large earrings he wore. He was like a shimmering waterfall of gold, his whole front covered with golden pendants that looked like coins. Beneath, he wore a purple semitransparent shift that matched the dark makeup around his large bedroom eyes. There was something both fierce and warm in his face. He was glowing with a pagan intensity that matched the intense feelings brimming up in my heart, which in turn matched the brimming purple wine that was being poured, 430 seemingly without end, into our glittering golden goblets

that matched the shafts of golden scorching sunlight that poured through the high windows down onto the banqueting table, where they were scattered in a dozen colors as they hit the gold in the glass. Finally, he rose from his throne, which was covered in a mantle of blue macaw feathers that cost ten dollars per square inch and matched the cerulean blue of the deep-piled carpet reputedly made by the tiny fingers of ten-year-old eunuchs within the forbid-
440 den city in Peking. Then he began to dance . . .

STANLEY: (*Grabbing Mitch by the shoulders*) You know, a bum like me can grow up in a great country like this and be her lover, which is a hell of a better job than being president of the United States.

MITCH: You're a lucky man.

STANLEY: You know, when I think about her, it's like food, I want to eat her, just put her whole leg in my mouth, or her face, or her hands . . .

MITCH: That's a mouthful!

450 STANLEY: I feel so hungry when I think of her, I could eat my car, I could eat dirt, I could eat a brick wall. I have to, I have no choice. I have to touch things, and my hands bring them to my mouth.

MITCH: Your big hands!

STANLEY: Feelings grow inside me, and sometimes they fly out of me so fast and then smack, I'm out of control. When it comes to big hands, I have no competition. (*Stanley takes a swig of beer*)

MITCH: When it comes to big hands, she knows she's got your
460 big hands all over her. (*He takes a swig*)

STANLEY: (*Challenging him to arm wrestle*) My big pioneer hands all over her rocky mountains.

MITCH: (*Taking the challenge*) All over her livestock and vegetation.

STANLEY: Her buffaloes and prairies.

MITCH: Her thick forests and golden sunsets.

STANLEY: All over her stars!

MITCH: She's in your hands!

STANLEY: She's in my hands and . . . yeeaaa . . . (*Stanley pins*
470 *Mitch's arm down*)

MITCH: That's right! Bite me! Bite me! Suck on me . . . oops.

STANLEY: (*Pulling away from Mitch*) What are you talking about?

MITCH: Mosquitoes! Biting me, biting me . . .

STANLEY: (*They both slap at bugs*) Suck on me, suck on my body!

MITCH: What do you think I'm here for, your entertainment? A Coney Island for you?

STANLEY: A joyride on my ankle! A suck on my wrist! I'll elim-
480 inate you! (*Mimes machine gun and makes gun noise*)

MITCH: Remove you from my space! Pow!

STANLEY: Away from my body, you aggravating hungry bugger.

MITCH: Bugger off! Away with you!

STANLEY: You're spoiled . . . Splat!

MITCH: You're educated . . . Squash!

STANLEY: You remind me of my fate.

MITCH: You remind me of my immortality! Leave me my blood.

STANLEY: Blood!

490 MITCH: Bloody sheet.

STANLEY: Bloody night.

MITCH: Blood on your hand!

STANLEY: It's my hand, I'm dealing the cards.

MITCH: (*Running after Stanley around box*) Deal me!

STANLEY: If you want another card I'll hit you with it.

MITCH: Hit me!

STANLEY: When it comes to big hands I got no competition.

MITCH: Take me!

STANLEY: Your shuffle.

MITCH: Cut me in!                                                    500

STANLEY: Throw your checkbook out the window!

MITCH: Empty my pockets!

STANLEY: I'm a royal flush, I win every time. (*Challenging him to arm wrestle*)

MITCH: (*Taking the challenge*) I'm the last sailboat across the horizon before the sun sets.

STANLEY: Nobody can audition for my part.

MITCH: I flop and smash and throw things.

STANLEY: I turn and punch the air!

MITCH: I sweat.                                                      510

STANLEY: I smell.

MITCH: I smell!

STANLEY: I smell of car oil, I smell of your blood.

MITCH: I smell of . . . cologne!

STANLEY: I'm hungry, ha, hungry! I'm gonna eat rough memories.

MITCH: I'm gonna eat tough dreams.

STANLEY: Digest hard words. Hard, hard words.

MITCH: I'm gonna spit them out!

STANLEY: It's gonna cost you my hunger!                             520

MITCH: I'm gonna pay!

STANLEY: (*Grabbing Mitch*) I'm gonna eat my car. I'm gonna eat dirt!

MITCH: I'm gonna eat a tree! Eat your whole leg!

STANLEY: I'm gonna eat the sun and then I'll sweat!

STANLEY AND MITCH: (*In a frenzy*) Bite me! Bite me! Suck on me!

BLANCHE: (*Opening the bathroom curtain and entering*) Suck my wrist.

STANLEY: (*Singing*)                                                530

### I'm a Man
*When I was a little boy, at the age of five*
*I had something in my pocket, kept a lot of folks alive*
*Now I'm a man, made twenty-one*
*I'll tell you baby, we can have a lot of fun*
*'Cos I'm a man*
*Spelled M . . . A . . . N . . . Man*
*Oohh . . . oowww . . . oowww*

*All you pretty women, standing in a line*                          540
*I can make love to you, in an hour's time*
*'Cos I'm a man*
*Spelled M . . . A . . . N . . . Man*

(*Dance break*)

*The line I shoot will never miss*
*When I make love to you baby, it comes to this*
*I'm a man*
*Spelled M . . . A . . . N . . . Man*
*Oohh . . . oowww . . . oowww . . . owww . . . I'm a man, yes I*
*am, I'm a man . . .*

*(Gradually noticing Blanche has a finger up her nose)* Hold
550  it, hold it. *(To Blanche)* Is there something I can help
you with?

BLANCHE: Please could you give me a tissue. I think I've got
something stuck up my nose.

STANLEY: Would you like me to have a look?

BLANCHE: Please don't trouble. I think a tissue would probably
do it.

STANLEY: *(Handing her a tissue)* Here.

BLANCHE: Probably a boogey, I expect.

STANLEY: An acquaintance of mine lost his sense of smell from
560  having a booger stuck up his nose . . . better?

BLANCHE: Not really, no.

MITCH: Can I help?

BLANCHE: Oh no, please, it's only something stuck up my nose.

MITCH: Try sticking your little finger in as far as it'll go.

STANLEY: Then blow your nose.

MITCH: Please let me look, I happen to be a doctor.

BLANCHE: It's very kind of you.

MITCH: Turn around to the light please. Now look up. Now
look down. Now look up again . . . I can see it . . . keep still
570  . . . *(He twists the tissue and pokes it up her nose)* There!

BLANCHE: Oh dear, what a relief, it was agonizing.

MITCH: *(Holding up the tissue)* It looks like a piece of Christmas Pudding.

BLANCHE: Thank you very much indeed.

MITCH: Not at all.

BLANCHE: How lucky for me you happened to be here.

MITCH: Anybody could have done it.

BLANCHE: Never mind, you did and I'm most grateful.

MITCH: There's my train . . . Goodbye. *(He exits)*

580 BLANCHE: And that's how it all began, just through me getting
a booger stuck up my nose. *(She turns to face Stanley, then
walks away upstage left as lights dim and music starts.
Mitch enters and motions for Blanche to dance with him, as
Stanley shuffles a deck of cards)*

STANLEY: Hey Mitch, you in this game or what?

MITCH: Deal me out. I'm talking to Miss DuBois. *(They begin
to dance as Stella wanders on)*

STELLA: Look, we made enchantment.

STANLEY: Who turned that on? Turn it off.

590 STELLA: Ah-h-h-h let them have their music.

STANLEY: I said turn it off!

STELLA: What are you doing?

STANLEY: That's the last time anybody plays music during my
game. Now get OUT! OUT! *(Mitch and Blanche exit)* Everybody get out! *(To pianist)* OUT! *(Music stops, Stella is
laughing quietly)*

STELLA: I guess you think that's funny.

STANLEY: Yeah, I thought it was pretty funny.

STELLA: Well, maybe I blinked at the wrong time, 'cuz I missed
600  the joke.

STANLEY: Oh, so now you're an authority on what's funny.

STELLA: I didn't say that. I said I didn't think that that was
funny.

STANLEY: Well, if you know so much, why don't you show me
what is funny.

STELLA: Look, I don't want to get twisted out of shape about it,
I just didn't think it was all that funny.

STANLEY: Oh, you thought it was just a little bit funny.

STELLA: No, not even a little bit funny.

STANLEY: So, show me!   610

STELLA: This is ridiculous.

STANLEY: Show me what's funny.

STELLA: You want me to show you what's funny.

STANLEY: Yeah, show me funny.

STELLA: O.K., I'll show you funny . . . *(Rips Stanley's sleeve)*
That's funny.

STANLEY: That was not funny.

STELLA: You want funny? *(Rips off the other sleeve)* That's
funny.

STANLEY: That was not funny.   620

STELLA: Okay. What about this? *(Rips off half of Stanley's shirt)*
Or this? *(Rips off other half)*

STANLEY: That's not funny.

STELLA: I'll be right back. *(Bustles offstage and comes back
with a seltzer bottle, then sprays Stanley)* That was funny.

STANLEY: That was not funny.

STELLA: I'll be right back. *(Comes back with a giant powder
puff and powders Stanley)* That was funny.

STANLEY: That's not funny.

STELLA: I'll be right back. *(Comes back with a cream pie. As she* 630
*nears Stanley, Stanley unexpectedly tips it into Stella's face)*

STANLEY: Now *that* was funny. *(Stanley exits. Mitch enters,
pulling a curtain with a painting of a giant orchid. The Cassandra aria from* Les Troyens *comes on loudly, then fades)*

MITCH: The bell sounds and they're both middle weights. They
know the rules, and they've been publicized as an even
match. 'Ere, you've paid good money to see them, you want
to see a battle, you want to see blood. Round One is I Love
You, Round Two is You See Me For Who I Really Am. You
never see a person more clearly than the first time they lay 640
hands on you. After that, it's all up for grabs. *(To Stella)* He's
gonna be back and he's gonna say he's sorry.

STELLA: *(Wiping pie from her face)* Sorry. *(Laughs)* Sorry . . .
sorry, sorry. *(Laughs)* The Indian women. The Indian
women, wrapping their soft bodies in thin silk the colors of
a church window. Sari. *(Laughs)* I'm sorry too. It makes me
laugh. They can't take it back. What the gods give they cannot take back, they can only add to what they've given, to
make the gift painful to have. Cassandra! Zeus gave her the
gift of the seer, and then she wouldn't have sex with him, but 650
he couldn't take back the gift. He couldn't have her, so he
made sure no one would believe her. . . . She knew all
those men were in that wooden horse, but they wouldn't listen . . . *(Laughs)* That's hysterical. It was their loss, that
curse! Zeus made a prophetess and then spit in her face.
And just what do you think went on inside that horse? Hundreds of warlike men, spitting, smoking, dreaming death in
the belly of a fake horse. . . . I dream a purple darkness . . .
purple . . . the color of the sari . . . darlings. I'm in here. I'm
on drugs. I'm braless, shirtless, I'm giggling, I'm lost, I'm in 660
love. I'm stuck in the stomach of a fake horse, can you hear
me? I hear you. Cassandra tell me what will happen. I
promise I'll believe you! I . . . I'm in love with you Cassandra, you blonde, you seer, you whisperer . . . tell me what's
going to happen . . . come here . . . let's make it happen.
Please don't, blonde seer. I can't, I'm already married. Take
your hands off my breasts, I'm already married. I'm in here.
The horse! I'm in the belly of a horse, smoking, shirtless. I'm
preparing for a war. *(She begins to strip off her house dress
to reveal a tight, strapless dress)* Someone stole my woman, 670

stole her from my house, filched her from history, and I'm here to get her back. I am a powerful warrior. *(She poses like Marilyn Monroe)* Come sweet prophetess, what is going to happen? Tell me, I'm nailed to this story. Cut me down. I'm in here. Can't you see me? I'm having sex with the fortune teller that men don't believe. Sex . . . sex! *(She sings)*

### Running Wild
*Running wild, lost control*
*Running wild, mighty bold*
680    *Feeling gay, reckless too*
*Carefree mind, all the time, never blue*
*Always going—don't know where*
*Always showing—I don't care*
*Don't love nobody, it's not worthwhile*
*All alone and running wild*

*(Stanley has entered audience and applauds Stella loudly as piano starts intro for Stella's next song)*

### Sweet Little Angel
*I've got a sweet little angel*
*And I love the way she spreads her wings*
*I've got a sweet little angel*
690    *And I love the way she spreads her wings*
*When she spreads those wings over me*
*She brings joy in everything.*

STANLEY: *(Clapping loudly and talking to audience)* Is she good or what? She is so good . . . can you believe how good she is? *(Stella stops singing)* Any moment this dame spends out of bed is wasted, totally wasted. *(Stanley runs to Stella and drops to his knees)*

STELLA: I could smell you coming.

STANLEY: You say the sweetest things.

700  STELLA: Women have to develop a sense of smell. Just in general. Just as a matter of fact. Like in a war. In a war, you learn to smell the enemy. You learn to cross the street. You learn to see through their disguises.

STANLEY: I am not your enemy.

STELLA: No . . . but you have many of the characteristics. Not that I go by appearances, just smell and instinct.

STANLEY: What are you looking for?

STELLA: You're tense.

STANLEY: I'm always tense. It keeps me in check, keeps me in 710    balance.

STELLA: It's hard to watch.

STANLEY: That's 'cuz you don't know that it's leading to something.

STELLA: And are you gonna tell me what that is?

STANLEY: It's a fact of life, you figure it out.

STELLA: I already did. I don't have to spend long on the likes of you, not one as experienced as I am. I know that your tension is sexual, and it's a desire that I share in, but not for your pleasure, for my own. I'm lookin' for it, I might not find it in 720    you, I might find it somewhere else, as a matter of fact, and there's nothing you can do about it. You don't satisfy me, you're not real.

STANLEY: Are you saying I'm not a real man?

STELLA: I'm saying you're not real. You're cute. Could be much cuter if you weren't quite so obvious.

STANLEY: Then it wouldn't be me. I am not subtle.

STELLA: Try it, just for tonight.

STANLEY: You mean put it on like clothes? I couldn't pull that off.

STELLA: No, take it off. Take it all off. I want to see what you're 730    really made of. I want to see what it is that makes me want you. That makes me want to have you as I've never had anyone. Strip. Take it off, then we'll talk.

STANLEY: Talk is cheap.

STELLA: I want to see you naked like a baby.

STANLEY: No more talk, let's make a deal.

STELLA: We are partners in this deal. I have my part, you have yours.

STANLEY: I can live up to my end of the deal, how 'bout you.

STELLA: Put your cards on the table, I'm calling your bluff. 740    *(Blackout)*

STANLEY: Hey, turn on the light!

STELLA: I like it in the dark.

STANLEY: I don't like the dark, I like to see.

STELLA: *(As lights slowly fade up)* You can see if you get your eyes used to it.

STANLEY: I don't want to get used to it, I'm afraid of the dark.

*(Low light reveals their silhouettes dancing as the piano player sings)*

### Sweet Little Angel
*I've got a sweet little angel*
*And I love the way she spreads her wings*    750
*I've got a sweet little angel*
*And I love the way she spreads her wings*
*When she spreads those wings over me*
*She brings joy in everything*

*I asked my angel for a nickel*
*And she gave me a twenty dollar bill*
*I asked my angel for a nickel*
*And she gave me a twenty dollar bill*
*When I asked her for her body*
*She said she'd leave it to me in her will . . .*    760

*Well my angel if she quit me*
*I believe I would die*
*Well my angel if she quit me*
*I believe I would die*
*If you don't love me*
*You must tell me the reason why.*

*(Stella has pulled off Stanley's ripped T-shirt as they dance. She jumps up and wraps her body around Stanley and throws the shirt to the ground as they exit. Blackout)*

### —ACT TWO—

*The stage is empty except for the large rectangular box on its side, with the painting of a tub across the front. Dim orange light comes up on Stella standing and stretching in bathtub in her slip.*

STELLA: The fire is keeping me awake. It reminds me of the night Yellow Mountain was burning. All night long I could see Yellow Mountain burning on my bedroom ceiling. I was afraid that the burning debris would fall from the mountain 770 on to our roof and burn through the ceiling. Meet up with a flicker that was already there, waiting to devour me.

MITCH: (*Light behind scrim reveals Blanche in a nightgown holding a cigarette and Mitch standing beside her. Mitch lights her cigarette*) There's a shadow over by the window. It's a woman. She's smoking a cigarette. (*Blanche blows smoke into Mitch's face; he coughs*) The smoke is coming my way. Maybe she wants me to go with her. (*Blanche passes around scrim and crosses to center stage, where she picks up*
780   *Stanley's torn T-shirt*)

STELLA: The fire has leapt out of control. It's too late, the firemen have all gone home to their wives. Had to hose down their own houses, to protect them from the falling debris.

BLANCHE: (*Examining Stanley's shirt*) This shirt smells of success to me. These elements of manhood . . . there's something about Stanley I can't quite put my finger on. I can't put my finger on his smell. I don't believe he's a man. I question his sexuality. His postures are not real, don't seem to be coming from a true place. He's a phoney, and he's got her
790   believing it, and if she has children he'll have them believing it and when he dies, they'll find out. (*Crossing to Stella*) Have you ever seen him naked?

STELLA: (*Drinking coke*) It's the sugar that satisfies me. The cool liquid running down my throat is only temporary. It's when the sugar hits the bloodstream, that's when my heart starts pumping.

BLANCHE: There's something about the way he smells, something about the way he has to prove his manhood all the time, that makes me suspicious. I'm looking at the shape,
800   not the content.

STELLA: (*Straddling the edge of the tub*) Don't you love that feeling when you lean against a solid surface and you can feel your heart beating under your body.

BLANCHE: The noises he makes, the way he walks like Mae West, the sensual way he wears his clothes, this is no garage-mechanic working-class boy, this is planned behavior. This is calculated sexuality, developed over years of picking up signals not necessarily genetic is what I'm trying to say.

STELLA: I remember leaning my abdomen against the cold sink
810   and feeling my heart beating between my legs.

BLANCHE: I'm trying to say, what I mean is, perhaps he was a man in some former life. Perhaps he's just a halfway house, to lure you into a sexual trap, a trap well laid, with just the right flavors, just the right mood to seduce you . . . what I'm trying to say is, I think he's a fag.

STELLA: The thing about coca-cola is that one sixteen-ounce bottle has more than four tablespoons of sugar.

BLANCHE: But now you have the chance to get out. To end this charade before it's too late . . .
820   STELLA: Enough to keep you up half the night.

BLANCHE: Only someone as skilled as I am at being a woman can pick up these subtle signs.

STELLA: Enough to curb your appetite.

BLANCHE: I'm well trained, equipped. I know how to talk to him, to flirt with him, not get involved really, to decorate his arm, to aid him in his charade, to give him a passing grade.

STELLA: Sugar in a sixteen-ounce bottle.

BLANCHE: (*Grabbing Stella's hand*) I'm the real woman for you. I can show you satisfaction. A rewarding, cultural life;
830   me and you, you and me, Blanche and Stella, Stella and

Blanche. . . . You were such a pretty girl. (*Stella pulls away*) What day was it that you changed? You were tipped for the top and you threw it all away. You were headed upward to the good, right life and suddenly you changed.

STELLA: Pure sugar, liquid sex.

BLANCHE: Stella, you haven't been listening to a word I've been saying.

STELLA: (*Stanley has come through the audience and is standing facing Stella and Blanche*) The fire is still burning . . . my clothes sticking to my chest just like Mama's dress against 840 her naked belly. Now why did she stay at the sink so long . . . (*Walking towards Stanley*) and every day without underwear. (*She jumps into Stanley's arms*)

STANLEY: Hey! (*Stanley spins her around, then they walk off-stage together*)

BLANCHE: Trouble is, Marlon Brando does look gorgeous. And I know that if I met him at the time he was in that film I'd want to lick his armpits. I don't suppose he'd be able to open himself up to that though . . . surrender himself. But he does have that big shapely mouth . . . I guess I'm pretty taken with 850 this actor in the film. But what if the film was life and I could just walk right into it? I don't suppose he'd welcome me, probably give me a hard time. Just like he gave Blanche . . . I mean Miss Leigh . . . and what would she say if this drag queen poured out of the camera lens and blew up to size right there in front of her. Yes, well, she had to deal with Marlon Brando all day and Laurence Olivier in the evenings . . . I'd say she had enough problems without me on the set. . . . I feel like an old hotel. (*Piano starts prelude to "Beautiful Dream"*) Beautiful bits of dereliction in need of massive 860 renovation. There's that record again. Have you ever had something stuck in your head for a very long time, like a record playing over and over and every time it stops there's applause, and then it starts all over again . . . (*The music stops and Blanche sticks her hand in the tub*) I like a warm bath. It's the warmth I'm after, not the cleanliness. I don't even mind Stella's cheap, common soap. . . . Oh I did it you know, I did lead the grand life . . . chauffeurs, limos. I used to go to clubs and know I was the most attractive person there . . . now I don't go to clubs. 870

STANLEY: (*Pulling in painted vaudeville curtain behind Blanche*) Ha Ha.

BLANCHE: (*Music begins again*) Now, here it comes . . . the record . . . and there's a dark burgundy curtain opening on the stage, and there we are, just me and Vivien . . .

STANLEY: HA HA. Did you hear what I said? I said, HA HA HA. (*Stanley exits*)

BLANCHE: (*Singing*)

### Beautiful Dream

*Cold wind blowing through the empty rooms* 880
*Windows broken, floors damp and rotten now*
*No sound in the silence*
*No step in the stillness*
*No warmth in the cold air*
*Only shadows moving in the half-light*
*Empty lockers, lines of empty hooks*
*Vacant showers, all deep in dust now*
*Just a modest price bought you paradise*
*No one wondered would it last*

890    *Running out of steam, now the beautiful dream*
        *Has passed.*

*No one greets me as I step inside*
*Hot and ready for whatever comes my way*
*No warm body waiting for me*
*No pulse of a warm heart near me*
*No strong arms around me*
*No one lying warm and sweet beside me*
*Thought we'd party 'til the end of time*
*But it's over, seems so long ago now*
900    *Down the long parade, see them slowly fade*
*As they all leave one by one*
*Running out of steam, now the beautiful dream*
*Has gone.*

*So I fill the tub, rub-a-dub-dub-dub*
*But I still freeze up inside*
*'Cuz the water's cold*
*And the dream has grown old and died*
*Running out of steam*
*Now the beautiful dream*
910    *Has gone.*

(*Lights fade, curtain is pulled offstage, Blanche moves to the tub upstage left and climbs in*) Bubbles, bawbles, bumholes . . . (*Smelling soap*) Municipal, that's the word. Now I'm going under . . . can't hear any noises at all . . . just the odd humps and hoomps and grinds . . . my hair is floating about . . . whooosh . . . up in the air again. (*Blanche reappears in the tub wearing bubble dress as a ukelele strums in the background*) Listen . . . there it is again, the record, going around and around and then the applause. Until something replaces that song and that wild applause, I know I'll cling to it. I'll al-
920    ways choose applause over death.
MITCH: (*Lights behind scrim reveal Mitch in fairy costume perched on a ladder and looking down on Blanche in the tub. He is playing the ukelele and singing*)

### The Fairy Song
*I was sitting on my asteroid, way up in the sky*
*When I saw you through the window, and I thought I'd drop by*
*You were looking sad, bothered and forlorn*
930    *Wondering where your days of youth and beauty all had gone.*

*Now I don't possess a magic wand, my wings are rather small*
*As far as fairies go I'm nothing special at all*
*But still I've got that something that I know you'll just adore*
*That special kind of magic, gonna sweep you off the floor.*

(*Chorus*)

*I'm a supernatural being, I'm your sweetie-pie*
*And I've come here from somewhere far, away up in the sky*
*I'm here to play a song tonight by Rimsky-Korsakov*
*And if you play your cards right we might even have it off.*

(*Stella mouths the words as Mitch continues singing*)

940    *Now I was sitting in the bathtub, minding my own biz*
*When this vision came from outer space and now I'm in a tiz*
*He was gorgeous, he was handsome, he was eager just to please*

*And he said that he'd come here so me and him could have a squeeze.*

*I'm a supernatural being, I'm your sweetie-pie*
*And I've come here from somewhere far, away up in the sky*
*I'll take you to my fairy dell, in my fairy car*
*And hang a sign "Do not disturb" upon the evening star.*    950

(*Dance break, Blanche twirls around and motions Mitch to join her. They dance*)

(*Blanche speaks*)

*Are you sure that you're a fairy?*
*I'd imagined they were blonde.*
*And frankly I'm not leaving 'til I've seen your magic wand.*

(*Mitch sings*)

*My wand, alas, I left at home, you'll have to come on spec*
*But I promise when we get there you can hold it for a sec.*

(*Chorus*)

(*Mitch and Blanche exit. Blanche reenters with Stella and Stanley, who resets table box and holds a birthday cake*)

STANLEY: (*Sings in monotone*) Happy birthday to you, happy birthday to you, happy birthday . . . Blanche, happy birthday to you.
BLANCHE: What a lovely cake. How many candles are on it?
STELLA: Don't you worry about that right now. Why don't you    960
tell us one of your funny stories.
BLANCHE: I don't think Mr. Kowalski would be interested in any of my funny stories.
STANLEY: I've got a funny story, what about this: There's these two faggots sitting on the sofa, which one is the cocksucker? (*Long pause*) The one with the feathers coming out of his mouth.
BLANCHE: In the version I heard it was two pollacks.
STANLEY: I am not a pollack. People from Poland are Poles. There is no such thing as a pollack. And in any case, for your    970
information, I am one hundred percent American.
STELLA: Well, now that we're all getting along so well, why don't you blow out the candles, Blanche, and make a wish.
STANLEY: Be careful what you wish for. (*Blanche blows out all the candles. They relight. She blows them out again, but again they relight. As she goes to blow them out again, Stanley brushes her aside and sticks the candles upside down in the cake one by one. Blackout. The bathtub is removed and a painting of an oversized naked light bulb is pulled onstage*) Stella! Blanche! Mitch! It's dark. I'm afraid.    980
STELLA: Let's just play a game.
STANLEY: This is not funny. Stella. Mitch. (*Lights slowly fade up. Stanley is wandering around the stage blindfolded*) Don't panic . . . I feel these original sins burning into me. I feel I'm never safe. There I am at four a.m. with giant monsters spelling out my life in large slimy letters above my body, just far enough above it to heat it up. To make my skin bead in sweat starting just under my hair, above my forehead, on the back of my neck, on my chest and the back of my knees. Don't panic . . . I was born this way. I didn't learn    990
it at theatre school. I was born butch. I'm so queer I don't even have to talk about it. It speaks for itself, it's not funny. Being butch isn't funny . . . don't panic . . . I fall to pieces in

the night. I'm just thousands of parts of other people all mashed into one body. I am not an original person. I take all these pieces, snatch them off the floor before they get swept under the bed, and I manufacture myself. When I'm saying I fall to pieces, I'm saying Marlon Brando was not there for me. *(Piano starts playing softly)* James Dean failed to come through, where was Susan Hayward when I needed her, and Rita Hayworth was nowhere to be found. I fall to pieces at the drop of a hat. Just pick the piece you want and when I pull myself back together again I'll think of you. I'll think of you and what you want me to be. *(He sings all the verses to the Frank Sinatra hit "My Way," while crawling onto the table with the birthday cake and presents on it. As he gets to his knees on top of the table, one hand breaks through a box and comes out covered in blood, the other hand goes into the cake and then into a box filled with feathers. He sings the final stanza kneeling on the cake)* WHERE THE FUCK IS EVERYBODY?! *(Blackout. After a short pause lights come up on Stella and Stanley)* What time is it?

STELLA: It's four a.m.

STANLEY: Help me make it through the night.

STELLA: Don't I always?

STANLEY: I'll be tired tomorrow, I'll be tired all day.

STELLA: Don't think about tomorrow. *(They embrace and kiss as the lights fade to black. Lights come up upstage right on Mitch stuffing cake into his mouth)*

MITCH: *(Talking with his mouth full throughout)* I think it all started to go wrong when I wasn't allowed to be a boy scout. There were more important things to be done. Vacuuming, clearing up at home, putting the garbage out. I used to get so angry putting out the garbage, I'd kick the shit out of the garbage cans in front. I thought about what I was missing. It gave me a repulsion for physical activity. Swimming was the only exception, and even then it took me a long time to learn, as I was afraid of deep water. Then one day I fell in love with a beautiful young man. He came like a messenger from another world bearing a message of simple physical desire. But it was already too late, for me everything about the body was bound up with pain and boredom. I even used to eat fast because I found it so boring. Soon the boy left. He knew better than to spend his life cooking dinners for someone with poor appetite. Then I was alone. I lived in a small room near a fly-over. I stopped going out except to go to the laundry and get groceries. At night I would lie awake on my bed, and imagine I could hear things. *(Sound of a ukelele from offstage. He opens one of the gift boxes on the table and the sound comes again. He reaches into the box and pulls out a ukelele, then sings "The Man I Love," by George and Ira Gershwin. As he sings, tap-dancing chinese lanterns—the remaining members of the cast in lantern costumes—enter and begin dancing around him. During the song the lanterns begin running into each other and floundering around the stage. The audience begins to hear them mumbling from under their costumes)*

BLANCHE: Oh, what are we doing? I can't stand it! I want to be in a real play! *(Bright light pops on as Stella drops her lantern to the floor)* With real scenery! White telephones, french windows, a beginning, a middle, and an end! This is the most confusing show I've ever been in. What's wrong with red plush? What's wrong with a theme and a plot we can all follow? There isn't even a fucking drinks trolley.

Agatha Christie was right.

STELLA: Now we all talked about this, and we decided that realism works against us.

BLANCHE: Oh we did, did we?

STELLA, STANLEY AND MITCH: Yes we did!

BLANCHE: But I felt better before, I could cope. All I had to do was learn my lines and not trip over the furniture. It was all so clear. And here we are romping about in the avant-garde and I don't know what else. I want my mother to come and have a good time. She's seventy-three for chrissake. You know she's expecting me to play Romeo before it's too late. What am I supposed to tell her? That I like being a drag-queen? She couldn't bear it, I know she couldn't.

She wants me to be in something realistic, playing a real person with a real job, like on television.

STELLA: You want realism?

BLANCHE: What do you mean?

STELLA: You want realism, you can have it.

BLANCHE: You mean like in a real play?

STELLA: If that's what you want.

BLANCHE: With Marlon Brando and Vivien Leigh?

STELLA: You think you can play it?

BLANCHE: I have the shoulders.

STANLEY: I have the pajamas . . . O.K., let's go for it. *(Mitch and Stella exit, striking the light bulb curtain. Stanley sweeps the table with his forearm knocking the cake and presents to the floor)* I cleared my place, want me to clear yours? It's just you and me now, Blanche.

BLANCHE: You mean we're alone in here?

STANLEY: Unless you got someone in the bathroom. *(He takes off his pajama top and pulls out a bottle of beer)*

BLANCHE: Please don't get undressed without pulling the curtain.

STANLEY: Oh, this is all I'm gonna undress right now. Feel like a shower? *(He opens the beer and shakes it, then lets it squirt all over the stage, then pours some over his head before drinking it)* You want some?

BLANCHE: No thank you.

STANLEY: *(Moving towards her, menacingly)* Sure I can't make you reconsider?

BLANCHE: Keep away from me.

STANLEY: What's the matter, don't you trust me? Afraid I might touch you or something? You should be so lucky. Take a look at yourself in that worn out party dress from a third-rate thrift store. What queen do you think you are?

BLANCHE: *(Trying to get past him)* Oh god.

STANLEY: *(Blocking her exit)* I got your number baby.

BLANCHE: Do we have to play this scene?

STANLEY: You said that's what you wanted.

BLANCHE: But I didn't mean it.

STANLEY: You wanted realism.

BLANCHE: Just let me get by you.

STANLEY: Get by me? Sure, go ahead.

BLANCHE: You stand over there.

STANLEY: You got plenty of room, go ahead.

BLANCHE: Not with you there! I've got to get by somehow!

STANLEY: You can get by, there's plenty of room. I won't hurt you. I like you. We're in this together, me and you. We've known that from the start. We're the extremes, the stereotypes. We are as far as we can go. We have no choice, me and you. We've tried it all, haven't we? We've rejected

ourselves, not trusted ourselves, mirrored ourselves, and we always come back to ourselves. We're the warriors. We have an agreement . . . there's plenty in this world for both of us. We don't have to give each other up to anyone. You are my
1120    special angel.

BLANCHE: You wouldn't talk this way if you were a real man.

STANLEY: No, if I was a real man I'd say, "Come to think of it, you wouldn't be so bad to interfere with."

BLANCHE: And if I were really Blanche I'd say, "Stay back . . . don't come near me another step . . . or I'll . . ."

STANLEY: You'll what?

BLANCHE: Something's gonna happen here. It will.

STANLEY: What are you trying to pull?

BLANCHE: (*Pulling off one of her stiletto-heeled shoes*) I warn
1130    you . . . don't!

STANLEY: Now what did you do that for?

BLANCHE: So I could twist this heel right in your face.

STANLEY: You'd do that, wouldn't you?

BLANCHE: I would, and I will if you . . .

STANLEY: You want to play dirty? I can play dirty. (*He grabs her arm*) Drop it. I said drop it! Drop the stiletto!

BLANCHE: You think I'm crazy or something?

STANLEY: If you want to be in this play you've got to drop the stiletto.

1140    BLANCHE: If you want to be in this play you've got to make me!

STANLEY: If you want to play a woman, the woman in this play gets raped and she goes crazy in the end.

BLANCHE: I don't want to get raped and go crazy, I just wanted to wear a nice frock, and look at the shit they've given me!

STELLA: (*Entering with Mitch*) Gimme that shoe! (*Piano starts "Pushover" as she grabs Stanley and sings to him*)

*All the girls think you're fine, they even call you Romeo,*
*You've got 'em, yeah you've got 'em runnin' to and fro, oh yes*
*you have,*
1150    *But I don't want a one night thrill, I want a love that's for*
*real,*
*And I can tell by your lies, yours is not the lasting kind.*

*You took me for a pushover, you thought I was a pushover,*
*I'm not a pushover, you thought that you could change my*
*mind.*

(*Mitch sings to Blanche*)

*So you told all the boys that were gonna take me out*
*You even, yeah you even had the nerve to make a bet, oh yes*
*you did,*
*That I, I would give in, all of my love you would win,*
1160    *But you haven't, you haven't won it yet.*

*You took me for a pushover, you thought I was a pushover,*
*I'm not a pushover, you thought my love was easy to get.*

(*Mitch and Stella together*)

*Your tempting lips, your wavy hair,*
*Your pretty eyes with that come hither stare,*
*It makes me weak, I start to bend and then I stop and think*
*again,*
*No, no, no don't let yourself go.*

*I wanna spoil your reputation, I want true love, not an*
*imitation,*
*And I'm hip, to every word in your conversation.*    1170

*You took me for a pushover, I'm not a pushover,*
*You can't push me over, you thought I was a pushover . . .*

STELLA: (*To audience*) Did you figure it out yet? who's who, what's what, who gets what, where the toaster is plugged in? Did you get what you wanted?

STANLEY: Hey Stella, I just figured it out. Wasn't Blanche blonde?

STELLA: That's right. And come to think of it, it was suspicious she didn't have a southern accent.

STANLEY: I knew it all along. The person we've been referring    1180
to as your sister is an imposter.

STELLA: Incredible! There's no flies on you Stanley.

STANLEY: What did you say?

STELLA: I said there's no disguising you, Stanley. You're one hundred percent.

STANLEY: I thought you said something else . . . something about flies.

STELLA: Well, come to think of it, there is something in that area I've been meaning to open up a little.

STANLEY: So, you figured it out.    1190

STELLA: Yeah, I figured it out.

STANLEY: And in those shoes. Un-fuckin'-believable! You know what this means?

STELLA: No, what?

STANLEY: This means that you are the only thing we can rely on, because you are at least who you seem to be.

STELLA: Well Stanley, there's something I've been meaning to tell you . . . (*She sings*)

*You took me for a pushover (All join in) I'm not a pushover*
*You can't push me over, you thought I was a pushover.*    1200
*DON'T PUSH!*

(*Encore*)

### I Love My Art
*I've been made about the stage since childhood,*
*When I roamed the sage and wildwood,*
*The attraction for the dazzling lights,*
*Caused me troublesome nights*
*Now I realize my one ambition*
*I can make a full and frank admission,*
*I am madly in love with my art, I love to play my part,*

*I love the theatre, I love it better than all my life, and just*    1210
*because*
*It's so entrancing, the song and dancing, to the music of*
*applause,*
*I love the stage and all about it, it simply goes right to my*
*heart,*
*I love the glamour, I love the drama,*
*I love I love I love my art*
*I love the glamour, I love the drama,*
*I love I love I love my art*

Peggy Shaw and
Lois Weaver:
Interviews
(1985, 1992, 1993)

*KATE Davy conducted a series of interviews with Peggy Shaw and Lois Weaver over a period of eight years and selected the following sections for inclusion in this anthology. While WOW Cafe is the focus of each interview, rather than the work of Shaw and Weaver specifically, the conversation frequently turns to examples from their performances. Shaw, for example, speaks of her experience with* Belle Reprieve, *which was not a WOW production, and contrasts it with her experience at WOW. Weaver describes her approach to conducting acting/writing workshops at WOW, and her ways of generating material for performance in these workshop settings offers some insight into how she develops work for Split Britches. Kate Davy has selected excerpts from her conversations with Shaw and Weaver of particular interest to students of* Belle Reprieve.

*On community and
singing to women
Interview with Peggy
Shaw and Lois Weaver
New York City, June 8,
1985*

KD: You referred to WOW as "community theatre." What do you mean by that?

LW: What I like about the idea of community theatre is the sensibility and lack of "New York theatre" pretentiousness. When you don't get trendy, that's the feeling of community theatre I have, along with the notion that anyone can play a part when you get into production; whoever shows up for rehearsals gets to be in the play. That's one of the things we try to do so we don't exclude people based on talent at WOW.

KD: Carmelita Tropicana was telling me that she wouldn't be performing if it wasn't for that kind of approach and process.

LW: Pushing people on to the stage, that's something Peggy and I have been committed to. People in general haven't been encouraged because the concept of theatre has been Broadway, stardom. That's what I like about the community aspect of WOW, everyone can be in it, including the audience.

PS: We're doing this show in the fall, *St. Joan of Avenue C*. We're going to have maybe 30 women in it—15 is about as many as we've had in a show. This is going to be about the neighborhood. Carmelita is going to play St. Joan as a lesbian. We needed a hero so we came up with St. Joan . . . she's going to win in the end.

KD: Who is the audience?

LW: We do it for each other. It's enough that we talk to each other, do our work, speak to each other, and that everyone that wants to work gets a chance. That's really enough for us. We try to encourage more people to get involved.

PS: One night, Carmelita was reading a poem by a Cuban man and someone in the audience started yelling, "Ah, that's a man. How can you read that in a [women's] place like this?" The other people in the audience started yelling at that spectator, "Get out of here. Shut up you asshole." Carmelita felt safe. Here she was finally getting it together to perform and she chooses a Cuban man to read, but she's still this woman thinking, whatever, and someone was trying to get her, but the audience got that person. Carmelita didn't have to deal with harassment in the audience and that's part of the whole safeness of WOW. As a group, WOW does encourage everyone to perform. To develop material you have to be in a safe place. Once you develop it, then you can take it out and do it at other places. We don't want to ghettoize this or make it inaccessible; we just want a place where everyone can do their best work, do the beginnings of their work, which is the most important part of their work. No one's there to judge you or write about it. What we have to be careful about now at the cafe is that we are getting written about, we are getting judged, criticized. We have to be very careful to remain a safe, comfortable place to do new stuff because that's what we want. Our purpose is to create new work.

KD: To what do you attribute the participatory dimension of your audiences?

LW: This is something I love about the cafe. I learned from the old Hot Peaches [gay male troupe] days that the gay audience is a loud, vocal, supportive audience. Consequently, WOW has become that sort of space where there's screaming and hollering and vocal support for the performers. That's something that's very important; it's a big part of the interchange with the audience. We always get some immediate response to the show. Carmelita's show last night for instance, there was a constant exchange. I think that's predominantly a gay phenomena. I'd never experienced it until I went to Hot Peaches and at WOW.

KD: Who is the work addressed to? Who do the performers at WOW speak to in their work?

PS: We had this one simple, obvious, wonderful moment when a woman singer was singing a love song to a woman. Women have never been sung to . . . here you have a woman sitting in the audience and a woman is singing to [her, and by extension] you. Or Carmelita will come up to a woman in the audience; it's such a new experience to have a woman do that to you. I mean, it's never been done (well, sure it has been in closed circles). It has always been women singing to the men in the audience, even the men singers, they sing to the men, they don't sing to the women. I always thought when I saw men singers that they sang for other men.

*On* Belle Reprieve *and imitating men*
*Interview with Peggy Shaw, New York City, August 3, 1992*

PS: Our audience was at least 60 percent men for *Lesbians Who Kill*.

KD: Why do you think there were so many guys there?

PS: From *Belle Reprieve* and from the title. Men really liked the title.

KS: Why?

PS: I think because it includes them; they assume it's men we're killing. They like to be included. Over the last two years with *Belle Reprieve* and *Lesbians Who Kill*, it's the first time in twenty years I've thought about men and it's exhausting. I don't want to do it anymore. But the times require it in some way. For our new shows we just pick up stuff in the air. There's just no getting away from the war—the racial war and the sexual war. It's just a big war.

KD: What was the initial impulse for working with Bloolips?

PS: One of the reasons we worked on *Belle Reprieve* was to be with our peers. It's so hard to find peers when you're a lesbian performer. When I started performing as a lesbian, nobody was performing as a lesbian. Bette and Paul [Bloolips] had been doing gay performance as long as we'd been doing lesbian performance and they were our peers. They'd lived through the last twenty years of gay liberation. They had been performing for the last twenty years. They knew—they had a vocabulary that we had. They had been through the struggle. It's so exciting to work with your peers.

KD: What has WOW meant for the community?

PS: The basis for WOW has always stayed the same. The inbuilt system of anarchy still exists; it's very hard to build in a system of anarchy. Everyone wants to make something something. Everyone, at one time or another at WOW, has wanted to make it into a functioning Off-Broadway theatre. We, as a group, have fought it because the roots are anarchy. When Bette Bourne [of Bloolips] first came he saw three shows in a row at WOW. One of them was *Cinderella* [subtitled, *The Real True Story*, written by Cheryl Moch, directed by Lois Weaver, 1985]. He talked about an aesthetic he saw only there and that he felt had been developed there. He described it as an aesthetic that comes from a certain type of community, certain types of thinking, or lesbian thinking. You walk into WOW as a lesbian, over the last ten to twelve years, and a lot of things make sense all of a sudden. I don't know how to explain it, but going into a space that is for you and is not traditional, not a copy of anything traditional, you go home and you feel stronger in believing in what your own personal aesthetic is. It keeps a lot of women from going crazy. At WOW they're gonna see something that's been done for them, something they can recognize as making sense to them. A place where anything can happen, where some of the work is good and some of it is awful. The audience that has developed at WOW never knows if they're gonna see something really horrible or something really fabulous. But they keep coming back.

KD: Why?

PS: Because WOW's never succumbed to the 80s. We never fixed it up and made it fancy. We kept it a factory and I think they come because it's a factory and that's where things begin.

KD: Is it political theatre?

PS: As lesbians you have no choice but to be political. It sort of comes with your birth in this . . . other people put that on. Whenever you want to discuss anything like, when we go to West Virginia to visit with Lois's [Weaver's] family, if you start talking about anything, even women's issues, not even lesbian ones, they start saying, "I don't want to talk about politics." And, you're not talking about politics, you're talking about your life. I guess the very nature of being a lesbian is political because it always causes a political discussion or a sexual discussion.

KD: You think lesbian is associated with sex?

PS: Oh yeah. I think that's another reason women came to WOW, because we talked about sex. We had butch/femme nights.

KD: What about butch/femme? What about cross-dressing? It seemed to me that WOW never really did cross-dressing.

PS: Usually straight women do cross-dressing; that's usually the case. There's this guy, a photographer, and he's doing a book called *Kings and Queens*—photos of men in drag and women in drag. But he can't find the right women; he has hundreds of men . . . and ME. But he's having trouble with me 'cause the publishers think I'm a man in the photos—these incredible photos from *Belle Reprieve* that he took in London. You wouldn't believe how beautiful they look. But . . . they're not funny.

KD: Why aren't they funny?

PS: I tried to explain to him that . . . it isn't funny. If he came to WOW, um, for a couple of years, he might find the humor. But there is not a built-in cultural humor to women being what the audience perceives as a man. It's not funny. In *Belle Reprieve,* you know, I was basically playing a man. I kept tits and everything, but I was basically being Stanley [Kowalski, from Tennessee Williams's play *A Streetcar Named Desire*]. That wasn't funny; the roots of Stanley are not funny. As much as we tried to make that show funny . . . it was so dark, we had to fight the darkness the whole two years we developed it and did it.

KD: So, you were portraying a man not a butch.

PS: I was trying to be a man; it was not successful. Bette was trying to coach me to be a clown. I could be a clown as a butch being with women on the stage. Interestingly enough, when I started performing with men, I didn't have the same sense of humor. I was very guarded and I was censoring myself and not so willing to be funny. Cause I was playing against a drag queen. Bette didn't . . . they all didn't want me to be heavy. And Stanley's heavy, man. I was funny; I pulled it off. But it's not funny. Blanche is funny; a man puts on a dress, you go "Ah, ha, ha." Bette walked on the stage "ah, ha, ha." But I walk on. No, they didn't laugh. There's nothing funny about me being Stanley to them. At WOW it's funny; it's an aesthetic.

KD: At WOW it's butch. That's a whole different thing.

PS: It's totally different. I never played a man before Stanley. I always played a butch, that is, I always played a lesbian. I was so relieved to do *Lesbians Who Kill.* I could just play myself. Cause I'm not an actor. I play myself; I don't play other people. I don't become somebody else. With Stanley, most of the time I was just being myself, fantasizing about trying not to be too heavy as Stanley Kowalski. Marlon Brando was charming, but it's not a charming part.

KD: So, in these photographs, are you impersonating a man?

PS: Lois and I were just doing poses from the show. I have on a t-shirt. When the book publishers saw the shots, they said, "Where did he buy those tits." And he goes, "That's a woman." They go, "No it isn't." So, he's having trouble getting pictures of women in it.

KD: Have you seen Joan Nestle's new book yet, *Persistent Desire: A Femme-Butch Reader* [Nestle, ed. Boston: Alyson Publications, Inc., 1992]?

PS: Yes. It's doing something to my soul. Lois and I emceed the book party for *Persistent Desire.* There were 25 women reading that night and we got to meet them all. Hanging around with these passing women is so good for me because they're not afraid of men. They are so gorgeous, these women, these passing women . . . Oh my God! One of them, J.C., she's in the book [329]. The one you really think is a man standing there with her girlfriend. We spent time with her. She is so fucking' . . . she's like Frankie Avalon. But she's a girl. But she's not. But she is. Of course, she is. And she passes. The thing I've learned about butch and femme is that butches are not trying to be men. Men would never spend their entire life pleasing women—that's what butches do. How can anyone think butches are imitating men? All butches do is please women. And the eroticism of butch/femme is totally different. It's an eroticism in itself; it's an art form.

KD: You have conducted so many workshops at WOW that, it seems to me, you have been crucial to a notion of actor or performance training at WOW.

LW: It's as much an attitude about training as it is about an attitude or vision for a whole performance. Peggy came out of Hot Peaches and then we both came out of Spiderwoman [multicultural, feminist theater] where the encouragement was to do whatever you wanted to do, where you could be who you want to be on stage. All you needed was a fantasy and you could make it happen on stage. My vision for WOW was that it would be a place where anybody could do anything; my particular nature is to encourage anybody to do anything. The whole idea was you didn't have to come into WOW with a set piece of material. You didn't have to come in as a trained anything. You

*On training, politics, and class*
*Interview with Lois Weaver, New York City, August 4, 1993*

could give it a try. I did workshops called "acting on impulse." It was all about freeing up the associative part of the brain and the associative creativity within us. The idea was you could work on impulse and work out of image. You didn't have to work on a cognitive idea of text or character or psychological aspects of character; it could be much more impulsive. Those kinds of workshops have been very good for what I called, at that point, "non-actors." They were workshops for non-actors, for people who just wanted to play. So it was really an attitude about play and playfulness with an element of self-scripting, always—even when we worked on text. I'd have them bring in a sonnet or a classical character. We would self-script a subtext for that character which would give them a whole other imaginative reality.

KD: Tell me what "self-script" is.

LW: You write your own stories. Say someone was working on Romeo; I'd say, "Where in the body do you think this character is? Where do you think this person lives in his or her body?" And they'll say, "Oh, in my right pelvis." Then I would take them through movement exercises to create a character based on the right pelvis. Then we would rename the character. "Okay, now, what's this character's name?" "Fred." "What does he or she do for a living?" "Collects bottles off the street." "What's her favorite pastime? What does he or she hold most dear?" You create a whole construct of character that's different but based on that character; you self-script a character. You recreate a new character and then you begin to write monologues for that character. Sometimes I have them stand up in this body and let the body speak for two minutes and someone else would scribe, i.e., write that down.

KD: Not talk, but move for two minutes?

LW: No. Move. Speak through the body. Actually verbalize. Every time they would start to talk from an intellectual idea of who this character was, I'd say, "Let the body talk; talk from the body." And then you get another kind of voice for that character. You get another kind of language to draw on. We also worked a lot with images. Like, "what do you see?" And they started to talk about that picture rather than what they think the character ought to talk about.

KD: Can you see the ways you worked in those workshops coming through in the way people work on their own now at WOW?

LW: With the Brothers I can see elements of self-scripting. [The Five Lesbian Brothers, a company that originated at WOW and includes Maureen Angelos, Babs Davy, Dominique Dibbell, Peggy Healey, and Lisa Kron.] I see elements of it in the way they come to create their own material. In some ways, I think it's more than acting, it's about freeing the creative imagination and then finding a way to physicalize that.

KD: You said "him or her" when referring to these recreated characters. How did you work on male characters?

LW: I always pushed in a way, in the guise of giving permission, I'd say, "What's the character's name—male or female?" Often a man's name would come—you know, Bob, George, or Kristov—and then there would be self-censorship. "Oh, I can't play a man." I would always sort of push, again in the guise of giving permission, to take that. I'd say 60 percent would take that route in workshop; they'd take on a male character. But they would take that male character on from their own personal imagination, not try to construct the character from anybody's definition. We tried to work from the first thing that came to mind rather than what would make sense. I really pushed the idea of not having to make sense; it didn't have to fit any kind of category. Although we did work with style. You know, where you could transform from style to style or character to character in an instant. You don't need those long transitions. We just do it. Kids do it and that's the model we used. They go immediately from one world to another and everything is in place without having to take the time to make a list of what those things are. We worked a lot like that. (Snaps fingers.) You can go from a classical world to a pop world to a country western world. We worked on style from that point of view—different worlds rather than that sort of intellectual construct of style. In a way, a lot of these techniques are born out of my own fear as an actor.

KD: Fear as an actor?

LW: Fear and insecurity as an actor. I grew up with a working class background, with no cultural input whatsoever. None. The Baptist Church was it. I did summer stock during my years in college and, of course, came into situations where there were a lot of sophisticated actors. In those improvisation workshops, they could make very quick cultural references that I couldn't make. I was terrified that in an improvisation I wouldn't have enough words to say, I wouldn't have enough to talk about because I didn't have enough experience or enough intellectual understanding. I decided what I had to do was depend upon my body, that my body would have stored enough information that, if I went through the gateway of my body, I could survive in that kind of situation. That was the beginning of my starting to teach this way; it was what I depended on for my own imagination.

KD: What constitutes WOW as a political theatre?

LW: I think WOW's politics is in the way it operates, the way it has maintained its operation in the face of all kinds of influences to do otherwise. That's what defines the politics: the way we run it by town meeting, the way everyone has a voice, the way it's open, there are no administrators. I consider myself a political person and a political artist. I don't necessarily set out to do political theatre, but I operate my daily life and my work life from a political base. And WOW does the same thing. When I sit back and look at the things to be proud of as far as WOW is concerned, I'm proud of all the personal achievements that people have made, but I'm mostly proud of how WOW has operated as a sociological, political entity in a world where the whole idea of a collective is not necessarily supported. I mean, here it was the beginning of the 80s and it was all about the individual; collectivity wasn't anything anyone was aspiring to. But WOW worked on certain principles that enabled it to evolve into something really political.

KD: It doesn't operate out of some notion of "women," right?

LW: A definition of women? No.

KD: It operates out of what people want, what their desires are and how can you make that happen without anybody giving up, you know, their souls.

LW: And their vision. Their own particular vision and aesthetic, whatever it might be. For example, even in 1980 and 1981 [at WOW's festivals] there were a lot of women whose presentation was geared toward black leather, black cap, and a strong sense of power play, strongly eroticized power play. We've based the space on the fact that, in it, women can realize their fullest potential. That's my definition of feminism.

KD: A number of us have been writing about WOW for a few years now and, as a result, people who read this stuff visit New York and make a point of seeing something at WOW. Sometimes they see the work of people who aren't very good and don't have much of a following, but who continue to work there. These spectators then seek me out at conferences and say, "Oh my God, it was so awful. What is this?" Can you talk about the overall approach at WOW that leads to not-very-good practitioners continuing to work in the space in the absence of any move to suggest to them that they do something other than attempt full-scale mountings of their own shows?

LW: It's so tricky. It's at the root of a lot of my own politics, that is, the whole issue of what's good. I'm dealing with this constantly in London [with the Gay Sweatshop]. The whole attitude of good, the whole attitude of excellence, and the whole attitude of "Queer Art must be excellent art," to me, it's a real class issue. What they're talking about, what that woman on my board of directors is talking about when she says that, "Queer Art must be excellent," she's talking about it from an Oxford educated point of view. What I think is good often does not fall into that category of the best trained actresses and the well-constructed play, the brilliantly directed play that's consistently designed. That doesn't interest me. On the other end of it, neither does the work that's awful at WOW. The whole philosophy there has been that you have the right to fail and that we don't have the right to censor. If you're gonna give people the right to do it, then they have to do it the way they do it. The fact that they continue to fail just brings into play all those ideas of what constitutes excellence and achievement. Sometimes it's wonderful, sometimes it's awful. We have to take that risk.

KD: It's sort of like how the criminal justice system ostensibly works: you let a lot of "criminals" go free rather than lock up somebody who is innocent. In order to have a group like the Five Lesbian Brothers, for example, come together, develop, and emerge, you've got to let everybody do everything.

LW: Yeah. Then there's the self-indulgence aspect. One hopes that aesthetic influences will rub off on people. There's the hope that certain kinds of aesthetics operating a WOW—

subverting popular culture, exaggeration, or humor, or music—aesthetic principles that float around, you hope they temper the self-indulgence. We say it's important just for women to get up on stage, but there's also that part of me that says, "No!" It's not just about that either. That smacks of the old-time feminist nurturing "WOMON's space."

KD: If you start telling somebody they can't work, where do you stop? Who doesn't get to work and why?

LW: Exactly. We couldn't. That would be the end. I definitely think that would be the end.

# Tony Kushner

Born in 1956, Tony Kushner first came to international prominence with *Angels in America* (1991), a two-part play that was an enormous success both in London and in Los Angeles before moving to New York in 1993. Kushner's "gay fantasia on national themes" is, in a sense, a displaced auto-biography, the displaced narrative of his own growing up as a gay man in the American era of Roy Cohn, the decline of the Communist menace, the onset of the AIDS epidemic, and the rise the conservative political agenda that dominated American politics in the 1980s. Kushner was born in New Orleans, where his parents were musicians in the New Orleans Philharmonic. When he was two, the family moved to Lake Charles, Louisiana; his mother, once a prominent New York bassoonist, devoted herself to educating the children in literature, music, and the arts, and herself acted in the Lake Charles theater company. Kushner knew that he was gay, but concealed it from his parents; when he went to college at Columbia University, he spent some time in psychoanalysis trying to alter his sexual orientation. But, finally, by his mid-20s, Kushner was able to accept his sexuality and came out. After taking his B. A. at Columbia, he studied theater at New York University. His first play, *A Bright Room Called Day* (1985) was written while he worked as a switchboard operator; it concerns the collapse of the left and the rise of fascism during the German Weimar Republic. *Angels in America* is his second play.

## Angels in America, Part I: Millennium Approaches (1991)

The first part of *Angels in America* (the second part is entitled *Perestroika*), *Millennium Approaches* is a complete play in its own right. Kushner began writing the play in 1988 when Oskar Eustis, who had directed his first play for the Eureka Theater Company in San Francisco asked Kushner for another play. Subtitled "A Gay Fantasia on National Themes," *Millennium Approaches* is at once a deeply personal look at the lives of several couples—Joe and Harper, a young Mormon couple transplanted to New York; Louis and Prior, a gay couple facing (and not facing) the onset of AIDS—and a political "fantasia" in the manner of Shaw's *Heartbreak House* or *The Apple Cart*. Kushner sets the characters' struggles against the background of conservative politics and the increasing power of the right in 1980s America; as Martin remarks in Act Two: ". . . we'll get our way on just about everything: abortion, defense, Central America, protecting the family, a live investment climate. . . . It's really the end of Liberalism. The end of New Deal Socialism. The end of ipso facto secular humanism."

While Kushner's play takes aim at the policies of the Republican administration, the play's politics extend deeply into the politics of personal action. For the emphasis on individualism, on self-sufficiency, on destroying the liberal consensus, and on eliminating social programs characteristic of the Reagan administration has consequences in the private sphere as well, where freedom looks alternately like selfishness and chaos. Roy Cohn—famous for his anticommunist activities and for prosecuting (and winning) the death sentence for Julius and Ethel Rosenberg for selling secret information to the Soviet Union—in many ways exemplifies this linkage in the play. Unable to give up his view of political power ("the game . . . of being alive"), Cohn refuses to be treated for AIDS because it would mean a public admission that he is gay, something generally known but not acknowledged. Louis, unable to bring himself to care for Prior during his horrifying illness, finds both emptiness and freedom in deserting his lover. Harper, whose valium-induced fantasies summon the cosmic travel agent Mr. Lies, who whisks her off to Antarctica, is in the throes of a nervous breakdown, a literalized response to the decaying world in which she lives, where "everywhere, things are collapsing, lies surfacing, systems of defense giving way."

The hallucinatory style of *Millennium Approaches* enables Kushner to bring this blending of public and private, the grand sweep of history and the narrower compass of individual suffering, into a close juxtaposition. *Millennium Approaches* ends when Prior's ancestors—a medieval farmer and a seventeenth-century dandy—appear to announce the coming of a mysterious angel, whose voice has been heard intermittently throughout the play. The Angel has been heralded in a number of ways: Prior regards his first lesion of Kaposi's Syndrome as the mark of the angel of death; a feather drops from above and the voice is heard at the end of Harper's/Prior's intertwined dream-hallucination in Act One; Joe alludes to Jacob wrestling with his angel, an image of Joe's fight to recognize and admit his own homosexuality. The Angel is a figure of release and redemption from the isolation in which the characters find themselves.

But the Angel also has a public, historical significance as well. Kushner has suggested that the Angel alludes to a comment made by the German cultural critic Walter Benjamin. In "Theses on the Philosophy of History," Benjamin makes the following remark on the process of history:

> A Klee painting named "Angelus Novus" shows an angel looking as though he is about to move away from something he is fixedly contemplating. His eyes are staring, his mouth is open, his wings are spread. This is how one pictures the angel of history. His face is turned toward the past. Where we perceive a chain of events, he sees one single catastrophe which keeps piling wreckage upon wreckage and hurls it in front of his feet. The angel would like to stay, awaken the dead, and make whole what has been smashed. But a storm is blowing from Paradise; it has got caught in his wings with such violence that the angel can no longer close them. This storm irresistibly propels him into the future to which his back is turned, while the pile of debris before him grows skyward. This storm is what we call progress.

The Angel is, for Kushner as for Benjamin, a figure for the dialectical force of history, the way that history moves into the future both in antithesis to the past, and yet bearing the past along with it. In *Angels in America,* Tony Kushner provides a sense of how it is we live today, in the midst of this "storm . . . we call progress."

This scene from Act 1 of Caryl Churchill's *Cloud 9* shows Churchill's use of cross-dressing: Betty (left) is played by a man, and Edward (downstage center in his Victorian sailor suit) is played by a woman.

This scene from August Wilson's *Fences* suggests the continuing importance of realistic representation in the American theater; onstage, the scene gets much of its power from its meticulously realized verisimilitude, the integration of properties, costumes, and sets with a behavioristic style of acting. Here, of course, that power is enriched by James Earl Jones's portrayal of Troy.

In this scene from Sam Shepard's *Buried Child,* the tattered set expresses the tattered and disorganized structure of family relationships in the play: Hallie talks to Dodge as Bradley (foreground), Shelly, Tilden, Father Dewis, and Vince look on.

The actors of *Belle Reprieve* strike a pose for the camera, one that echoes the characters in the famous film version of *A Streetcar Named Desire:* Peggy Shaw as Stanley, Bette Bourne as Blanche, Lois Weaver as Stella, and Paul Shaw/Precious Pearl as Mitch.

In this scene from *Fires in the Mirror: Crown Heights, Brooklyn and Other Identities,* entitled "Me and James's Thing," Anna Deavere Smith enacts the Reverend Al Sharpton.

Suffering from the onset of AIDS, Prior Walter (played here by Stephen Spinella) is visited by a mysterious Angel in the finale of *Millennium Approaches* (*Angels in America, Part One*).

# — Angels in America: —
# Millennium Approaches
## *A Gay Fantasia on National Themes*
### Tony Kushner

## —THE CHARACTERS—

ROY M. COHN, *a successful New York lawyer and unofficial power broker.*

JOSEPH PORTER PITT, *chief clerk for Justice Theodore Wilson of the Federal Court of Appeals, Second Circuit.*

HARPER AMATY PITT, *Joe's wife, an agoraphobic with a mild Valium addiction.*

LOUIS IRONSON, *a word processor working for the Second Circuit Court of Appeals.*

PRIOR WALTER, *Louis's boyfriend. Occasionally works as a club designer or caterer, otherwise lives very modestly but with great style off a small trust fund.*

HANNAH PORTER PITT, *Joe's mother, currently residing in Salt Lake City, living off her deceased husband's army pension.*

BELIZE, *a former drag queen and former lover of Prior's. A registered nurse. Belize's name was originally Norman Arriaga; Belize is a drag name that stuck.*

THE ANGEL, *four divine emanations, Fluor, Phosphor, Lumen and Candle; manifest in One: the Continental Principality of America. She has magnificent steel-gray wings.*

RABBI ISIDOR CHEMELWITZ, *an orthodox Jewish rabbi, played by the actor playing Hannah.*

MR. LIES, *Harper's imaginary friend, a travel agent, who in style of dress and speech suggests a jazz musician; he always wears a large lapel badge emblazoned "IOTA" (The International Order of Travel Agents). He is played by the actor playing Belize.*

THE MAN IN THE PARK, *played by the actor playing Prior.*

THE VOICE, *the voice of The Angel.*

HENRY, *Roy's doctor, played by the actor playing Hannah.*

EMILY, *a nurse, played by the actor playing The Angel.*

MARTIN HELLER, *a Reagan Administration Justice Department flackman, played by the actor playing Harper.*

SISTER ELLA CHAPTER, *a Salt Lake City real-estate saleswoman, played by the actor playing The Angel.*

PRIOR 1, *the ghost of a dead Prior Walter from the 13th century, played by the actor playing Joe. He is a blunt, gloomy medieval farmer with a gutteral Yorkshire accent.*

PRIOR 2, *the ghost of a dead Prior Walter from the 17th century, played by the actor playing Roy. He is a Londoner, sophisticated, with a High British accent.*

THE ESKIMO, *played by the actor playing Joe.*

THE WOMAN IN THE SOUTH BRONX, *played by the actor playing The Angel.*

ETHEL ROSENBERG, *played by the actor playing Hannah.*

## —PLAYWRIGHT'S NOTES—

A DISCLAIMER: Roy M. Cohn, the character, is based on the late Roy M. Cohn (1927–1986), who was all too real; for the most part the acts attributed to the character Roy, such as his illegal conferences with Judge Kaufmann during the trial of Ethel Rosenberg, are to be found in the historical record. But this Roy is a work of dramatic fiction; his words are my invention, and liberties have been taken.

A NOTE ABOUT THE STAGING: The play benefits from a pared-down style of presentation, with minimal scenery and scene shifts done rapidly (no blackouts!), employing the cast as well as stagehands—which makes for an actor-driven event, as this must be. The moments of magic—the appearance and disappearance of Mr. Lies and the ghosts, the Book hallucination, and the ending— are to be fully realized, as bits of wonderful *theatrical* illusion—which means it's OK if the wires show, and maybe it's good that they do, but the magic should at the same time be thoroughly amazing.

■ ■ ■     In a murderous time
the heart breaks and breaks
and lives by breaking.

—STANLEY KUNITZ
"THE TESTING-TREE"

## I —ACT ONE—
Bad News
October–November 1985

#### SCENE I

*The last days of October. Rabbi Isidor Chemelwitz alone on-stage with a small coffin. It is a rough pine box with two wooden pegs, one at the foot and one at the head, holding the lid in place. A prayer shawl embroidered with a Star of David is draped over the lid, and by the head a yarzheit candle is burning.*

RABBI ISIDOR CHEMELWITZ: (*He speaks sonorously, with a heavy Eastern European accent, unapologetically consulting a sheet of notes for the family names*) Hello and good morning. I am Rabbi Isidor Chemelwitz of the Bronx Home for Aged Hebrews. We are here this morning to pay respects at the passing of Sarah Ironson, devoted wife of Benjamin Ironson, also deceased, loving and caring mother of her sons Morris, Abraham, and Samuel, and her daughters Esther and Rachel; beloved grandmother of Max, Mark,
10    Louis, Lisa, Maria . . . uh . . . Lesley, Angela, Doris, Luke and Eric. (*Looks more closely at paper*) Eric? This is a Jewish name? (*Shrugs*) Eric. A large and loving family. We assemble that we may mourn collectively this good and righteous woman.

(*He looks at the coffin*)

This woman. I did not know this woman. I cannot accurately describe her attributes, nor do justice to her dimensions. She was. . . . Well, in the Bronx Home of Aged Hebrews are many like this, the old, and to many I speak but not to be frank with this one. She preferred silence. So I do not know
20    her and yet I know her. She was . . .

(*He touches the coffin*)

. . . not a person but a whole kind of person, the ones who crossed the ocean, who brought with us to America the villages of Russia and Lithuania—and how we struggled, and how we fought, for the family, for the Jewish home, so that you would not grow up *here*, in this strange place, in the melting pot where nothing melted. Descendants of this immigrant woman, you do not grow up in America, you and your children and their children with the goyische names. You do not live in America. No such place exists. Your clay
30    is the clay of some Litvak shtetl, your air the air of the steppes—because she carried the old world on her back across the ocean, in a boat, and she put it down on Grand Concourse Avenue, or in Flatbush, and she worked that earth into your bones, and you pass it to your children, this ancient, ancient culture and home.

(*Little pause*)

You can never make that crossing that she made, for such Great Voyages in this world do not any more exist. But every day of your lives the miles that voyage between that place and this one you cross. Every day. You understand me? In
40    you that journey is.
So . . .

She was the last of the Mohicans, this one was. Pretty soon . . . all the old will be dead.

#### SCENE II

*Same day. Roy and Joe in Roy's office. Roy at an impressive desk, bare except for a very elaborate phone system, rows and rows of flashing buttons which bleep and beep and whistle incessantly, making chaotic music underneath Roy's conversations. Joe is sitting, waiting. Roy conducts business with great energy, impatience and sensual abandon: gesticulating, shouting, cajoling, crooning, playing the phone, receiver and hold button with virtuosity and love.*

ROY: (*Hitting a button*) Hold. (*To Joe*) I wish I was an octopus, a fucking octopus. Eight loving arms and all those suckers. Know what I mean?

JOE: No, I . . .

ROY: (*Gesturing to a deli platter of little sandwiches on his desk*) You want lunch?

JOE: No, that's OK really I just . . .    50

ROY: (*Hitting a button*) Ailene? Roy Cohn. Now what kind of a greeting is. . . . I thought we were friends, Ai. . . . Look Mrs. Soffer you don't have to get. . . . You're upset. You're yelling. You'll aggravate your condition, you shouldn't yell, you'll pop little blood vessels in your face if you yell. . . . No that was a joke, Mrs. Soffer, I was joking. . . . I already apologized sixteen times for that, Mrs. Soffer, you . . . (*While she's fulminating, Roy covers the mouthpiece with his hand and talks to Joe*) This'll take a minute, *eat* already, what is this tasty sandwich here it's— (*He takes a bite of a sandwich*) 60 Mmmmm, liver or some. . . . Here.

(*He pitches the sandwich to Joe, who catches it and returns it to the platter.*)

ROY: (*Back to Mrs. Soffer*) Uh huh, uh huh. . . . No, I already told you, it wasn't a vacation, it was business, Mrs. Soffer, I have clients in Haiti, Mrs. Soffer, I. . . . Listen, Ailene, YOU THINK I'M THE ONLY GODDAM LAWYER IN HISTORY EVER MISSED A COURT DATE? Don't make such a big fucking. . . . Hold. (*He hits the hold button*) You HAG!

JOE: If this is a bad time . . .

ROY: *Bad* time? This is a *good* time! (*Button*) Baby doll, get me. 70 . . . Oh fuck, wait . . . (*Button, button*) Hello? Yah. Sorry to keep you holding, Judge Hollins, I. . . . Oh *Mrs.* Hollins, sorry dear deep voice you got. Enjoying your visit? (*Hand over mouthpiece again, to Joe*) She sounds like a truckdriver and he sounds like Kate Smith, very confusing. Nixon appointed him, all the geeks are Nixon appointees . . . (*To Mrs. Hollins*) Yeah yeah right good so how many tickets dear? Seven. For what, *Cats, 42nd Street*, what? No you wouldn't like *La Cage*, trust me, I know. Oh for godsake. . . . Hold. (*Button, button*) Baby doll, seven for *Cats* or something, 80 anything hard to get, I don't give a fuck what and neither will they. (*Button; to Joe*) You see *La Cage*?

JOE: No, I . . .

ROY: Fabulous. Best thing on Broadway. Maybe ever. (*Button*) Who? Aw, Jesus H. Christ, Harry, *no*, Harry, Judge John Francis Grimes, Manhattan Family Court. Do I have to do every goddam thing myself? *Touch* the bastard, Harry, and don't call me on this line again, I told you not to . . .

JOE: (*Starting to get up*) Roy, uh, should I wait outside or . . .

90  ROY: (*To Joe*) Oh sit. (*To Harry*) You hold. I pay you to hold fuck you Harry you jerk. (*Button*) Half-wit dick-brain. (*Instantly philosophical*) I see the universe, Joe, as a kind of sandstorm in outer space with winds of mega-hurricane velocity, but instead of grains of sand it's shards and splinters of glass. You ever feel that way? Ever have one of those days?

JOE: I'm not sure I . . .

ROY: So how's life in Appeals? How's the Judge?

JOE: He sends his best.

100  ROY: He's a good man. Loyal. Not the brightest man on the bench, but he has manners. And a nice head of silver hair.

JOE: He gives me a lot of responsibility.

ROY: Yeah, like writing his decisions and signing his name.

JOE: Well . . .

ROY: He's a nice guy. And you cover admirably.

JOE: Well, thanks, Roy, I . . .

ROY: (*Button*) Yah? Who is *this?* Well who the fuck are *you?* Hold— (*Button*) Harry? Eighty-seven grand, something like that. Fuck him. Eat me. New Jersey, chain of porno film

110  stores in, uh, Weehawken. That's—Harry, that's the beauty of the law. (*Button*) So, baby doll, what? *Cats?* Bleah. (*Button*) *Cats!* It's about cats. Singing cats, you'll love it. Eight o'clock, the theatre's always at eight. (*Button*) Fucking tourists. (*Button, then to Joe*) Oh live a little, Joe, *eat* something for Christ sake—

JOE: Um, Roy, could you . . .

ROY: What? (*To Harry*) Hold a minute. (*Button*) Mrs. Soffer? Mrs. . . . (*Button*) God-fucking-dammit to hell, where is . . .

JOE: (*Overlapping*) Roy, I'd really appreciate it if . . .

120  ROY: (*Overlapping*) Well she was here a minute ago, baby doll, see if . . .

(*The phone starts making three different beeping sounds, all at once.*)

ROY: (*Smashing buttons*) Jesus fuck this goddam thing . . .

JOE: (*Overlapping*) I really wish you wouldn't . . .

ROY: (*Overlapping*) Baby doll? Ring the *Post* get me Suzy see if . . .

(*The phone starts whistling loudly.*)

ROY: CHRIST!

JOE: *Roy.*

ROY: (*Into receiver*) Hold. (*Button; to Joe*) What?

JOE: Could you please not take the Lord's name in vain?

(*Pause*)

130  I'm sorry. But please. At least while I'm . . .

ROY: (*Laughs, then*) Right. Sorry. Fuck.

Only in America. (*Punches a button*) Baby doll, tell 'em all to fuck off. Tell 'em I died. You handle Mrs. Soffer. Tell her it's on the way. Tell her I'm schtupping the judge. I'll call her back. I *will* call her. I *know* how much I borrowed. She's got four hundred times that stuffed up her. . . . Yeah, tell her I said that. (*Button. The phone is silent*)

So, Joe.

JOE: I'm sorry Roy, I just . . .

ROY: No no no no, principles count, I respect principles, I'm 140 not religious but I like God and God likes me. Baptist, Catholic?

JOE: Mormon.

ROY: Mormon. Delectable. Absolutely. Only in America. So, Joe. Whattya think?

JOE: It's . . . well . . .

ROY: Crazy life.

JOE: Chaotic.

ROY: Well but God bless chaos. Right?

JOE: Ummm . . .    150

ROY: Huh. Mormons. I knew Mormons, in, um, Nevada.

JOE: Utah, mostly.

ROY: No, these Mormons were in Vegas.

So. So, how'd you like to go to Washington and work for the Justice Department?

JOE: Sorry?

ROY: How'd you like to go to Washington and work for the Justice Department? All I gotta do is pick up the phone, talk to Ed, and you're in.

JOE: In . . . what, exactly?    160

ROY: Associate Assistant Something Big. Internal Affairs, heart of the woods, something nice with clout.

JOE: Ed . . . ?

ROY: Meese. The Attorney General.

JOE: Oh.

ROY: I just have to pick up the phone . . .

JOE: I have to think.

ROY: Of course.

(*Pause*)

It's a great time to be in Washington, Joe.

JOE: Roy, it's incredibly exciting . . .    170

ROY: And it would mean something to me. You understand?

(*Little pause.*)

JOE: I . . . can't say how much I appreciate this Roy, I'm sort of . . . well, stunned, I mean. . . . Thanks, Roy. But I have to give it some thought. I have to ask my wife.

ROY: Your wife. Of course.

JOE: But I really appreciate . . .

ROY: Of course. Talk to your wife.

SCENE III

*Later that day. Harper at home, alone. She is listening to the radio and talking to herself, as she often does. She speaks to the audience.*

HARPER: People who are lonely, people left alone, sit talking nonsense to the air, imagining . . . beautiful systems dying, old fixed orders spiraling apart . . .    180

When you look at the ozone layer, from outside, from a spaceship, it looks like a pale blue halo, a gentle, shimmering aureole encircling the atmosphere encircling the earth. Thirty miles above our heads, a thin layer of three-atom oxygen molecules, product of photosynthesis, which explains the fussy vegetable preference for visible light, its rejection of darker rays and emanations. Danger from without. It's a kind of gift, from God, the crowning touch to the creation of

the world: guardian angels, hands linked, make a spherical
net, a blue-green nesting orb, a shell of safety for life itself.
But everywhere, things are collapsing, lies surfacing, systems of defense giving way. . . . This is why, Joe, this is why
I shouldn't be left alone.

*(Little pause)*

I'd like to go traveling. Leave you behind to worry. I'll send
postcards with strange stamps and tantalizing messages on
the back. "Later maybe." "Nevermore . . ."

*(Mr. Lies, a travel agent, appears.)*

HARPER: Oh! You startled me!
MR. LIES: Cash, check or credit card?
HARPER: I remember you. You're from Salt Lake. You sold us
the plane tickets when we flew here. What are you doing in
Brooklyn?
MR. LIES: You said you wanted to travel . . .
HARPER: And here you are. How thoughtful.
MR. LIES: Mr. Lies. Of the International Order of Travel
Agents. We mobilize the globe, we set people adrift, we stir
the populace and send nomads eddying across the planet.
We are adepts of motion, acolytes of the flux. Cash, check or
credit card. Name your destination.
HARPER: Antarctica, maybe. I want to see the hole in the ozone.
I heard on the radio . . .
MR. LIES: *(He has a computer terminal in his briefcase)* I can
arrange a guided tour. Now?
HARPER: Soon. Maybe soon. I'm not safe here you see. Things
aren't right with me. Weird stuff happens . . .
MR. LIES: Like?
HARPER: Well, like you, for instance. Just appearing. Or last
week . . . well never mind.
People are like planets, you need a thick skin. Things get to
me, Joe stays away and now. . . . Well look. My dreams are
talking back to me.
MR. LIES: It's the price of rootlessness. Motion sickness. The
only cure: to keep moving.
HARPER: I'm undecided. I feel . . . that something's going to
give. It's 1985. Fifteen years till the third millennium.
Maybe Christ will come again. Maybe seeds will be planted,
maybe there'll be harvests then, maybe early figs to eat,
maybe new life, maybe fresh blood, maybe companionship
and love and protection, safety from what's outside, maybe
the door will hold, or maybe . . . maybe the troubles will
come, and the end will come, and the sky will collapse and
there will be terrible rains and showers of poison light, or
maybe my life is really fine, maybe Joe loves me and I'm
only crazy thinking otherwise, or maybe not, maybe it's even
worse than I know, maybe . . . I want to know, maybe I don't.
The suspense, Mr. Lies, it's killing me.
MR. LIES: I suggest a vacation.
HARPER: *(Hearing something)* That was the elevator. Oh God,
I should fix myself up, I. . . . You have to go, you shouldn't
be here . . . you aren't even real.
MR. LIES: Call me when you decide . . .
HARPER: Go!

*(The Travel Agent vanishes as Joe enters.)*

JOE: Buddy?

Buddy? Sorry I'm late. I was just . . . out. Walking. Are you
mad?
HARPER: I got a little anxious.
JOE: Buddy kiss.

*(They kiss.)*

JOE: Nothing to get anxious about.
So. So how'd you like to move to Washington?

## SCENE IV

*Same day. Louis and Prior outside the funeral home, sitting on
a bench, both dressed in funereal finery, talking. The funeral
service for Sarah Ironson has just concluded and Louis is
about to leave for the cemetery.*

LOUIS: My grandmother actually saw Emma Goldman speak.
In Yiddish. But all Grandma could remember was that she
spoke well and wore a hat.
What a weird service. That rabbi . . .
PRIOR: A definite find. Get his number when you go to the
graveyard. I want him to bury me.
LOUIS: Better head out there. Everyone gets to put dirt on the
coffin once it's lowered in.
PRIOR: Oooh. Cemetery fun. Don't want to miss that.
LOUIS: It's an old Jewish custom to express love. Here,
Grandma, have a shovelful. Latecomers run the risk of finding the grave completely filled.
She was pretty crazy. She was up there in that home for ten
years, talking to herself. I never visited. She looked too
much like my mother.
PRIOR: *(Hugs him)* Poor Louis. I'm sorry your grandma is dead.
LOUIS: Tiny little coffin, huh?
Sorry I didn't introduce you to. . . . I always get so closety at
these family things.
PRIOR: Butch. You get butch. *(Imitating)* "Hi Cousin Doris,
you don't remember me I'm Lou, Rachel's boy." Lou, not
Louis, because if you say Louis they'll hear the sibilant S.
LOUIS: I don't have a . . .
PRIOR: I don't blame you, hiding. Bloodlines. Jewish curses are
the worst. I personally would dissolve if anyone ever looked
me in the eye and said "Feh." Fortunately WASPs don't say
"Feh." Oh and by the way, darling, cousin Doris is a dyke.
LOUIS: No.
Really?
PRIOR: You don't notice anything. If I hadn't spent the last four
years fellating you I'd swear you were straight.
LOUIS: You're in a pissy mood. Cat still missing?

*(Little pause.)*

PRIOR: Not a furball in sight. It's your fault.
LOUIS: It is?
PRIOR: I warned you, Louis. Names are important. Call an animal "Little Sheba" and you can't expect it to stick around.
Besides, it's a dog's name.
LOUIS: I wanted a dog in the first place, not a cat. He sprayed
my books.
PRIOR: He was a female cat.
LOUIS: Cats are stupid, high-strung predators. Babylonians
sealed them up in bricks. Dogs have brains.

PRIOR: Cats have intuition.

LOUIS: A sharp dog is as smart as a really dull two-year-old child.

PRIOR: Cats know when something's wrong.

LOUIS: Only if you stop feeding them.

PRIOR: They know. That's why Sheba left, because she knew.

LOUIS: Knew what?

*(Pause.)*

PRIOR: I did my best Shirley Booth this morning, floppy slip-pers, housecoat, curlers, can of Little Friskies; "Come back, Little Sheba, come back. . . ." To no avail. Le chat, elle ne reviendra jamais, jamais . . .

*(He removes his jacket, rolls up his sleeve, shows Louis a dark-purple spot on the underside of his arm near the shoulder)*

See.

LOUIS: That's just a burst blood vessel.

PRIOR: Not according to the best medical authorities.

LOUIS: What?

*(Pause)*

Tell me.

PRIOR: K.S., baby. Lesion number one. Lookit. The wine-dark kiss of the angel of death.

LOUIS: *(Very softly, holding Prior's arm)* Oh please . . .

PRIOR: I'm a lesionnaire. The Foreign Lesion. The American Lesion. Lesionnaire's disease.

LOUIS: Stop.

PRIOR: My troubles are lesion.

LOUIS: Will you *stop*.

PRIOR: Don't you think I'm handling this well?

I'm going to die.

LOUIS: Bullshit.

PRIOR: Let go of my arm.

LOUIS: No.

PRIOR: Let go.

LOUIS: *(Grabbing Prior, embracing him ferociously)* No.

PRIOR: I can't find a way to spare you baby. No wall like the wall of hard scientific fact. K.S. Wham. Bang your head on that.

LOUIS: Fuck you. *(Letting go)* Fuck you fuck you fuck you.

PRIOR: Now that's what I like to hear. A mature reaction.

Let's go see if the cat's come home. Louis?

LOUIS: When did you find this?

PRIOR: I couldn't tell you.

LOUIS: Why?

PRIOR: I was scared, Lou.

LOUIS: Of what?

PRIOR: That you'll leave me.

LOUIS: Oh.

*(Little pause.)*

PRIOR: Bad timing, funeral and all, but I figured as long as we're on the subject of death . . .

LOUIS: I have to go bury my grandma.

PRIOR: Lou?

*(Pause)*

Then you'll come home?

LOUIS: Then I'll come home.

SCENE V

*Same day, later on. Split scene: Joe and Harper at home; Louis at the cemetery with Rabbi Isidor Chemelwitz and the little coffin.*

HARPER: Washington?

JOE: It's an incredible honor, buddy, and . . .

HARPER: I have to think.

JOE: Of course.

HARPER: Say no.

JOE: You said you were going to think about it.

HARPER: I don't want to move to Washington.

JOE: Well I do.

HARPER: It's a giant cemetery, huge white graves and mau-soleums everywhere.

JOE: We could live in Maryland. Or Georgetown.

HARPER: We're happy here.

JOE: That's not really true, buddy, we . . .

HARPER: Well happy enough! Pretend-happy. That's better than nothing.

JOE: It's time to make some changes, Harper.

HARPER: No changes. Why?

JOE: I've been chief clerk for four years. I make twenty-nine thousand dollars a year. That's ridiculous. I graduated fourth in my class and I make less than anyone I know. And I'm . . . I'm tired of being a clerk, I want to go where some-thing good is happening.

HARPER: Nothing good happens in Washington. We'll forget church teachings and buy furniture at . . . at *Conran's* and become yuppies. I have too much to do here.

JOE: Like what?

HARPER: I *do* have things . . .

JOE: What things?

HARPER: I have to finish painting the bedroom.

JOE: You've been painting in there for over a year.

HARPER: I know, I. . . . It just isn't done because I never get time to finish it.

JOE: Oh that's . . . that doesn't make sense. You have all the time in the world. You could finish it when I'm at work.

HARPER: I'm afraid to go in there alone.

JOE: Afraid of what?

HARPER: I heard someone in there. Metal scraping on the wall. A man with a knife, maybe.

JOE: There's no one in the bedroom, Harper.

HARPER: Not now.

JOE: Not this morning either.

HARPER: How do you know? You were at work this morning. There's something creepy about this place. Remember *Rosemary's Baby?*

JOE: *Rosemary's Baby?*

HARPER: Our apartment looks like that one. Wasn't that apart-ment in Brooklyn?

JOE: No, it was . . .

HARPER: Well, it looked like this. It did.

JOE: Then let's move.

HARPER: Georgetown's worse. *The Exorcist* was in George-town.

JOE: The devil, everywhere you turn, huh, buddy.

HARPER: Yeah. Everywhere.

JOE: How many pills today, buddy?

HARPER: None. One. Three. Only three.

LOUIS: (*Pointing at the coffin*) Why are there just two little wooden pegs holding the lid down?

RABBI ISIDOR CHEMELWITZ: So she can get out easier if she
400    wants to.

LOUIS: I hope she stays put.

I pretended for years that she was already dead. When they called to say she had died it was a surprise. I abandoned her.

RABBI ISIDOR CHEMELWITZ: "Sharfer vi di tson fun a shlang iz an umdankbar kind!"

LOUIS: I don't speak Yiddish.

RABBI ISIDOR CHEMELWITZ: Sharper than the serpent's tooth is the ingratitude of children. Shakespeare. *Kenig Lear.*

LOUIS: Rabbi, what does the Holy Writ say about someone who
410    abandons someone he loves at a time of great need?

RABBI ISIDOR CHEMELWITZ: Why would a person do such a thing?

LOUIS: Because he has to.

Maybe because this person's sense of the world, that it will change for the better with struggle, maybe a person who has this neo-Hegelian positivist sense of constant historical progress towards happiness or perfection or something, who feels very powerful because he feels connected to these forces, moving uphill all the time . . . maybe that person
420    can't, um, incorporate sickness into his sense of how things are supposed to go. Maybe vomit . . . and sores and disease . . . really frighten him, maybe . . . he isn't so good with death.

RABBI ISIDOR CHEMELWITZ: The Holy Scriptures have nothing to say about such a person.

LOUIS: Rabbi, I'm afraid of the crimes I may commit.

RABBI ISIDOR CHEMELWITZ: Please, mister. I'm a sick old rabbi facing a long drive home to the Bronx. You want to confess, better you should find a priest.

430    LOUIS: But I'm not a Catholic, I'm a Jew.

RABBI ISIDOR CHEMELWITZ: Worse luck for you, bubbulah. Catholics believe in forgiveness. Jews believe in Guilt. (*He pats the coffin tenderly*)

LOUIS: You just make sure those pegs are in good and tight.

RABBI ISIDOR CHEMELWITZ: Don't worry, mister. The life she had, she'll stay put. She's better off.

JOE: Look, I know this is scary for you. But try to understand what it means to me. Will you try?

HARPER: Yes.

440    JOE: Good. Really try.

I think things are starting to change in the world.

HARPER: But I don't want . . .

JOE: Wait. For the good. Change for the good. America has rediscovered itself. Its sacred position among nations. And people aren't ashamed of that like they used to be. This is a great thing. The truth restored. Law restored. That's what President Reagan's done, Harper. He says "Truth exists and can be spoken proudly." And the country responds to him. We become better. More good. I need to be a part of that, I
450    need something big to lift me up. I mean, six years ago the

world seemed in decline, horrible, hopeless, full of unsolvable problems and crime and confusion and hunger and . . .

HARPER: But it still seems that way. More now than before. They say the ozone layer is . . .

JOE: Harper . . .

HARPER: And today out the window on Atlantic Avenue there was a schizophrenic traffic cop who was making these . . .

JOE: Stop it! I'm trying to make a point.

HARPER: So am I.

JOE: You aren't even making sense, you . . .                    460

HARPER: My point is the world seems just as . . .

JOE: It only seems that way to you because you never go out in the world, Harper, and you have emotional problems.

HARPER: I do so get out in the world.

JOE: You don't. You stay in all day, fretting about imaginary . . .

HARPER: I get out. I do. You don't know what I do.

JOE: You don't stay in all day.

HARPER: No.

JOE: Well. . . . Yes you do.                                   470

HARPER: That's what you think.

JOE: Where do you go?

HARPER: Where do *you* go? When you walk.
(*Pause, then angrily*) And I DO NOT have emotional problems.

JOE: I'm sorry.

HARPER: And if I do have emotional problems it's from living with you. Or . . .

JOE: I'm sorry buddy, I didn't mean to . . .

HARPER: Or if you do think I do then you should never have    480
married me. You have all these secrets and lies.

JOE: I want to be married to you, Harper.

HARPER: You shouldn't. You never should.

(*Pause*)

Hey buddy. Hey buddy.

JOE: Buddy kiss . . .

(*They kiss.*)

HARPER: I heard on the radio how to give a blowjob.

JOE: What?

HARPER: You want to try?

JOE: You really shouldn't listen to stuff like that.

HARPER: Mormons can give blowjobs.                            490

JOE: *Harper.*

HARPER: (*Imitating his tone*) Joe.

It was a little Jewish lady with a German accent.

This is a good time. For me to make a baby.

(*Little pause. Joe turns away.*)

HARPER: Then they went on to a program about holes in the ozone layer. Over Antarctica. Skin burns, birds go blind, icebergs melt. The world's coming to an end.

## SCENE VI

*First week of November. In the men's room of the offices of the Brooklyn Federal Court of Appeals; Louis is crying over the sink; Joe enters.*

JOE: Oh, um. . . . . Morning.

LOUIS: Good morning, counselor.

500 JOE: *(He watches Louis cry)* Sorry, I . . . I don't know your name.

LOUIS: Don't bother. Word processor. The lowest of the low.

JOE: *(Holding out hand)* Joe Pitt. I'm with Justice Wilson . . .

LOUIS: Oh, I know that. Counselor Pitt. Chief Clerk.

JOE: Were you . . . are you OK?

LOUIS: Oh, yeah. Thanks. What a nice man.

JOE: Not so nice.

LOUIS: What?

JOE: Not so nice. Nothing. You sure you're . . .

510 LOUIS: Life sucks shit. Life . . . just sucks shit.

JOE: What's wrong?

LOUIS: Run in my nylons.

JOE: Sorry . . . ?

LOUIS: Forget it. Look, thanks for asking.

JOE: Well . . .

LOUIS: I mean it really is nice of you.

*(He starts crying again)*

Sorry, sorry, sick friend . . .

JOE: Oh, I'm sorry.

LOUIS: Yeah, yeah, well, that's sweet.

520 Three of your colleagues have preceded you to this baleful sight and you're the first one to ask. The others just opened the door, saw me, and fled. I hope they had to pee real bad.

JOE: *(Handing him a wad of toilet paper)* They just didn't want to intrude.

LOUIS: Hah. Reaganite heartless macho asshole lawyers.

JOE: Oh, that's unfair.

LOUIS: What is? Heartless? Macho? Reaganite? Lawyer?

JOE: I voted for Reagan.

LOUIS: You did?

530 JOE: Twice.

LOUIS: Twice? Well, oh boy. A Gay Republican.

JOE: Excuse me?

LOUIS: Nothing.

JOE: I'm not . . .

Forget it.

LOUIS: Republican? Not Republican? Or . . .

JOE: What?

LOUIS: What?

JOE: Not gay. I'm not gay.

540 LOUIS: Oh. Sorry.

*(Blows his nose loudly)* It's just . . .

JOE: Yes?

LOUIS: Well, sometimes you can tell from the way a person sounds that . . . I mean you *sound* like a . . .

JOE: No I don't. Like what?

LOUIS: Like a Republican.

*(Little pause. Joe knows he's being teased; Louis knows he knows. Joe decides to be a little brave.)*

JOE: *(Making sure no one else is around)* Do I? Sound like a . . . ?

LOUIS: What? Like a . . . ? Republican, or . . . ? Do *I*?

550 JOE: Do you what?

LOUIS: Sound like a . . . ?

JOE: Like a . . . ?

I'm . . . confused.

LOUIS: Yes.

My name is Louis. But all my friends call me Louise. I work in Word Processing. Thanks for the toilet paper.

*(Louis offers Joe his hand, Joe reaches, Louis feints and pecks Joe on the cheek, then exits.)*

SCENE VII

*A week later. Mutual dream scene. Prior is at a fantastic makeup table, having a dream, applying the face. Harper is having a pill-induced hallucination. She has these from time to time. For some reason, Prior has appeared in this one. Or Harper has appeared in Prior's dream. It is bewildering.*

PRIOR: *(Alone, putting on makeup, then examining the results in the mirror; to the audience)* "I'm ready for my closeup, Mr. DeMille."

One wants to move through life with elegance and grace, 560 blossoming infrequently but with exquisite taste, and perfect timing, like a rare bloom, a zebra orchid. . . . One wants. . . . But one so seldom gets what one wants, does one? No. One does not. One gets fucked. Over. One . . . dies at thirty, robbed of . . . decades of majesty.

Fuck this shit. Fuck this shit.

*(He almost crumbles; he pulls himself together; he studies his handiwork in the mirror)*

I look like a corpse. A corpsette. Oh my queen; you know you've hit rock-bottom when even drag is a drag.

*(Harper appears.)*

HARPER: Are you. . . . Who are you?

PRIOR: Who are you?      570

HARPER: What are you doing in my hallucination?

PRIOR: I'm not in your hallucination. You're in my dream.

HARPER: You're wearing makeup.

PRIOR: So are you.

HARPER: But you're a man.

PRIOR: *(Feigning dismay, shock, he mimes slashing his throat with his lipstick and dies, fabulously tragic. Then)* The hands and feet give it away.

HARPER: There must be some mistake here. I don't recognize you. You're not. . . . Are you my . . . some sort of imaginary 580 friend?

PRIOR: No. Aren't you too old to have imaginary friends?

HARPER: I have emotional problems. I took too many pills. Why are you wearing makeup?

PRIOR: I was in the process of applying the face, trying to make myself feel better—I swiped the new fall colors at the Clinique counter at Macy's. *(Showing her)*

HARPER: You stole these?

PRIOR: I was out of cash; it was an emotional emergency!

HARPER: Joe will be so angry. I promised him. No more pills.    590

PRIOR: These pills you keep alluding to?

HARPER: Valium. I take Valium. Lots of Valium.

PRIOR: And you're dancing as fast as you can.

HARPER: I'm not *addicted*. I don't believe in addiction, and I never . . . well, I *never* drink. And I *never* take drugs.

PRIOR: Well, smell *you*, Nancy Drew.

HARPER: Except Valium.

PRIOR: Except Valium; in wee fistfuls.

600 HARPER: It's terrible. Mormons are not supposed to be addicted to anything. I'm a Mormon.

PRIOR: I'm a homosexual.

HARPER: Oh! In my church we don't believe in homosexuals.

PRIOR: In my church we don't believe in Mormons.

HARPER: What church do . . . oh! (*She laughs*) I get it.
I don't understand this. If I didn't ever see you before and I don't think I did then I don't think you should be here, in this hallucination, because in my experience the mind, which is where hallucinations come from, shouldn't be able to make up anything that wasn't there to start with, that
610 didn't enter it from experience, from the real world. Imagination can't create anything new, can it? It only recycles bits and pieces from the world and reassembles them into visions. . . . Am I making sense right now?

PRIOR: Given the circumstances, yes.

HARPER: So when we think we've escaped the unbearable ordinariness and, well, untruthfulness of our lives, it's really only the same old ordinariness and falseness rearranged into the appearance of novelty and truth. Nothing unknown is knowable. Don't you think it's depressing?

620 PRIOR: The limitations of the imagination?

HARPER: Yes.

PRIOR: It's something you learn after your second theme party: It's All Been Done Before.

HARPER: The world. Finite. Terribly, terribly. . . . Well . . . This is the most depressing hallucination I've ever had.

PRIOR: Apologies. I do try to be amusing.

HARPER: Oh, well, don't apologize, you. . . . I can't expect someone who's really sick to entertain me.

PRIOR: How on earth did you know . . .

630 HARPER: Oh that happens. This is the very threshhold of revelation sometimes. You can see things . . . how sick you are. Do you see anything about me?

PRIOR: Yes.

HARPER: What?

PRIOR: You are amazingly unhappy.

HARPER: Oh big deal. You meet a Valium addict and you figure out she's unhappy. That doesn't count. Of course I. . . . Something else. Something surprising.

PRIOR: Something surprising.

640 HARPER: Yes.

PRIOR: Your husband's a homo.

(*Pause.*)

HARPER: Oh, ridiculous.

(*Pause, then very quietly*)

Really?

PRIOR: (*Shrugs*) Threshold of revelation.

HARPER: Well I don't like your revelations. I don't think you intuit well at all. Joe's a very normal man, he . . .
Oh God. Oh God. He. . . . Do homos take, like, lots of long walks?

PRIOR: Yes. We do. In stretch pants with lavender coifs. I just
650 looked at you, and there was . . .

HARPER: A sort of blue streak of recognition.

PRIOR: Yes.

HARPER: Like you knew me incredibly well.

PRIOR: Yes.

HARPER: Yes.
I have to go now, get back, something just . . . fell apart.
Oh God, I feel so sad . . .

PRIOR: I . . . I'm sorry. I usually say, "Fuck the truth," but mostly, the truth fucks you.

660 HARPER: I see something else about you . . .

PRIOR: Oh?

HARPER: Deep inside you, there's a part of you, the most inner part, entirely free of disease. I can see that.

PRIOR: Is that. . . . That isn't true.

HARPER: Threshhold of revelation.
Home . . .

(*She vanishes.*)

PRIOR: People come and go so quickly here . . .
(*To himself in the mirror*) I don't think there's any uninfected part of me. My heart is pumping polluted blood. I
670 feel dirty.

(*He begins to wipe makeup off with his hands, smearing it around. A large gray feather falls from up above. Prior stops smearing the makeup and looks at the feather. He goes to it and picks it up.*)

A VOICE: (*It is an incredibly beautiful voice*) Look up!

PRIOR: (*Looking up, not seeing anyone*) Hello?

A VOICE: Look up!

PRIOR: Who is that?

A VOICE: Prepare the way!

PRIOR: I don't see any . . .

(*There is a dramatic change in lighting, from above.*)

A VOICE:
Look up, look up,
prepare the way
the infinite descent     680
A breath in air
floating down
Glory to . . .

(*Silence.*)

PRIOR: Hello? Is that it? Helloooo!
What the fuck . . . ? (*He holds himself*)
Poor me. Poor poor me. Why me? Why poor poor me? Oh I don't feel good right now. I really don't.

SCENE VIII

*That night. Split scene: Harper and Joe at home; Prior and Louis in bed.*

HARPER: Where were you?

JOE: Out.

HARPER: Where?     690

JOE: Just out. Thinking.

HARPER: It's late.

JOE: I had a lot to think about.

HARPER: I burned dinner.

JOE: Sorry.

HARPER: Not my dinner. My dinner was fine. Your dinner. I put it back in the oven and turned everything up as high as it could go and I watched till it burned black. It's still hot. Very hot. Want it?

700 JOE: You didn't have to do that.

HARPER: I know. It just seemed like the kind of thing a mentally deranged sex-starved pill-popping housewife would do.

JOE: Uh huh.

HARPER: So I did it. Who knows anymore what I have to do?

JOE: How many pills?

HARPER: A bunch. Don't change the subject.

JOE: I won't talk to you when you . . .

HARPER: No. No. Don't do that! I'm . . . I'm fine, pills are not the problem, not our problem, I WANT TO KNOW
710 WHERE YOU'VE BEEN! I WANT TO KNOW WHAT'S GOING ON!

JOE: Going on with what? The job?

HARPER: Not the job.

JOE: I said I need more time.

HARPER: Not the job!

JOE: Mr. Cohn, I talked to him on the phone, he said I had to hurry . . .

HARPER: Not the . . .

JOE: But I can't get you to talk sensibly about anything so . . .

720 HARPER: SHUT UP!

JOE: Then what?

HARPER: Stick to the subject.

JOE: I don't know what that is. You have something you want to ask me? Ask me. Go.

HARPER: I . . . can't. I'm scared of you.

JOE: I'm tired, I'm going to bed.

HARPER: Tell me without making me ask. Please.

JOE: This is crazy, I'm not . . .

HARPER: When you come through the door at night your face
730 is never exactly the way I remembered it. I get surprised by something . . . mean and hard about the way you look. Even the weight of you in the bed at night, the way you breathe in your sleep seems unfamiliar.
You terrify me.

JOE: *(Cold)* I know who you are.

HARPER: Yes. I'm the enemy. That's easy. That doesn't change. You think you're the only one who hates sex; I do; I hate it with you; I do. I dream that you batter away at me till all my joints come apart, like wax, and I fall into pieces. It's like a
740 punishment. It was wrong of me to marry you. I knew you . . . *(She stops herself)* It's a sin, and it's killing us both.

JOE: I can always tell when you've taken pills because it makes you red-faced and sweaty and frankly that's very often why I don't want to . . .

HARPER: Because . . .

JOE: Well, you aren't pretty. Not like this.

HARPER: I have something to ask you.

JOE: Then ASK! ASK! What in hell are you . . .

HARPER: Are you a homo?

*(Pause)*

750 Are you? If you try to walk out right now I'll put your dinner back in the oven and turn it up so high the whole building will fill with smoke and everyone in it will asphyxiate. So

help me God I will.
Now answer the question.

JOE: What if I . . .

*(Small pause.)*

HARPER: Then tell me, please. And we'll see.

JOE: No. I'm not.
I don't see what difference it makes.

LOUIS: Jews don't have any clear textual guide to the afterlife; even that it exists. I don't think much about it. I see it as a 760 perpetual rainy Thursday afternoon in March. Dead leaves.

PRIOR: Eeeugh. Very Greco-Roman.

LOUIS: Well for us it's not the verdict that counts, it's the act of judgment. That's why I could never be a lawyer. In court all that matters is the verdict.

PRIOR: You could never be a lawyer because you are oversexed. You're too distracted.

LOUIS: Not distracted; *ab*stracted. I'm trying to make a point:

PRIOR: Namely:

LOUIS: It's the judge in his or her chambers, weighing, books 770 open, pondering the evidence, ranging freely over categories: good, evil, innocent, guilty; the judge in the chamber of circumspection, not the judge on the bench with the gavel. The shaping of the law, not its execution.

PRIOR: The point, dear, the point . . .

LOUIS: That it should be the questions and shape of a life, its total complexity gathered, arranged and considered, which matters in the end, not some stamp of salvation or damnation which disperses all the complexity in some unsatisfying little decision—the balancing of the scales . . . 780

PRIOR: I like this; very zen; it's . . . reassuringly incomprehensible and useless. We who are about to die thank you.

LOUIS: You are not about to die.

PRIOR: It's not going well, really . . . two new lesions. My leg hurts. There's protein in my urine, the doctor says, but who knows what the fuck that portends. Anyway it shouldn't be there, the protein. My butt is chapped from diarrhea and yesterday I shat blood.

LOUIS: I really hate this. You don't tell me . . .

PRIOR: You get too upset, I wind up comforting you. It's 790 easier . . .

LOUIS: Oh thanks.

PRIOR: If it's bad I'll tell you.

LOUIS: Shitting blood sounds bad to me.

PRIOR: And I'm telling you.

LOUIS: And I'm handling it.

PRIOR: Tell me some more about justice.

LOUIS: I *am* handling it.

PRIOR: Well Louis you win Trooper of the Month.

*(Louis starts to cry.)*

PRIOR: I take it back. You aren't Trooper of the Month. 800 This isn't working . . .
Tell me some more about justice.

LOUIS: You are not about to die.

PRIOR: Justice . . .

LOUIS: . . . is an immensity, a confusing vastness. Justice is God. Prior?

PRIOR: Hmmm?

LOUIS: You love me.

PRIOR: Yes.

810 LOUIS: What if I walked out on this?

Would you hate me forever?

(*Prior kisses Louis on the forehead.*)

PRIOR: Yes.

JOE: I think we ought to pray. Ask God for help. Ask him together . . .

HARPER: God won't talk to me. I have to make up people to talk to me.

JOE: You have to keep asking.

HARPER: I forgot the question.

Oh yeah. God, is my husband a . . .

820 JOE: (*Scary*) Stop it. Stop it. I'm warning you.

Does it make any difference? That I might be one thing deep within, no matter how wrong or ugly that thing is, so long as I have fought, with everything I have, to kill it. What do you want from me? What do you want from me, Harper? More than that? For God's sake, there's nothing left, I'm a shell. There's nothing left to kill.

As long as my behavior is what I know it has to be. Decent. Correct. That alone in the eyes of God.

HARPER: No, no, not that, that's Utah talk, Mormon talk, I hate

830    it, Joe, tell me, say it . . .

JOE: All I will say is that I am a very good man who has worked very hard to become good and you want to destroy that. You want to destroy me, but I am not going to let you do that.

(*Pause.*)

HARPER: I'm going to have a baby.

JOE: Liar.

HARPER: You liar.

A baby born addicted to pills. A baby who does not dream but who hallucinates, who stares up at us with big mirror eyes and who does not know who we are.

(*Pause.*)

840 JOE: Are you really . . .

HARPER: No. Yes. No. Yes. Get away from me.

Now we both have a secret.

PRIOR: One of my ancestors was a ship's captain who made money bringing whale oil to Europe and returning with immigrants—Irish mostly, packed in tight, so many dollars per head. The last ship he captained foundered off the coast of Nova Scotia in a winter tempest and sank to the bottom. He went down with the ship—la Grande Geste—but his crew took seventy women and kids in the ship's only longboat,

850    this big, open rowboat, and when the weather got too rough, and they thought the boat was overcrowded, the crew started lifting people up and hurling them into the sea. Until they got the ballast right. They walked up and down the longboat, eyes to the waterline, and when the boat rode low in the water they'd grab the nearest passenger and throw them into the sea. The boat was leaky, see; seventy people; they arrived in Halifax with nine people on board.

LOUIS: Jesus.

PRIOR: I think about that story a lot now. People in a boat, wait-

ing, terrified, while implacable, unsmiling men, irresistibly 860 strong, seize . . . maybe the person next to you, maybe you, and with no warning at all, with time only for a quick intake of air you are pitched into freezing, turbulent water and salt and darkness to drown.

I like your cosmology, baby. While time is running out I find myself drawn to anything that's suspended, that lacks an ending—but it seems to me that it lets you off scot-free.

LOUIS: What do you mean?

PRIOR: No judgment, no guilt or responsibility.

LOUIS: For me.                                                          870

PRIOR: For anyone. It was an editorial "you."

LOUIS: Please get better. Please.

Please don't get any sicker.

## SCENE IX

*Third week in November. Roy and Henry, his doctor, in Henry's office.*

HENRY: Nobody knows what causes it. And nobody knows how to cure it. The best theory is that we blame a retrovirus, the Human Immunodeficiency Virus. Its presence is made known to us by the useless antibodies which appear in reaction to its entrance into the bloodstream through a cut, or an orifice. The antibodies are powerless to protect the body against it. Why, we don't know. The body's immune system 880 ceases to function. Sometimes the body even attacks itself. At any rate it's left open to a whole horror house of infections from microbes which it usually defends against.

Like Kaposi's sarcomas. These lesions. Or your throat problem. Or the glands.

We think it may also be able to slip past the blood-brain barrier into the brain. Which is of course very bad news.

And it's fatal in we don't know what percent of people with suppressed immune responses.

(*Pause.*)

ROY: This is very interesting, Mr. Wizard, but why the fuck are 890 you telling me this?

(*Pause.*)

HENRY: Well, I have just removed one of three lesions which biopsy results will probably tell us is a Kaposi's sarcoma lesion. And you have a pronounced swelling of glands in your neck, groin, and armpits—lymphadenopathy is another sign. And you have oral candidiasis and maybe a little more fungus under the fingernails of two digits on your right hand. So that's why . . .

ROY: This disease . . .

HENRY: Syndrome.                                                      900

ROY: Whatever. It afflicts mostly homosexuals and drug addicts.

HENRY: Mostly. Hemophiliacs are also at risk.

ROY: Homosexuals and drug addicts. So why are you implying that I . . .

(*Pause*)

What are you implying, Henry?

HENRY: I don't . . .

ROY: I'm not a drug addict.

HENRY: Oh come on Roy.

910 ROY: What, what, come on Roy what? Do you think I'm a junkie, Henry, do you see tracks?

HENRY: This is absurd.

ROY: Say it.

HENRY: Say what?

ROY: Say, "Roy Cohn, you are a . . . "

HENRY: Roy.

ROY: "You are a. . . . " Go on. Not "Roy Cohn you are a drug fiend." "Roy Marcus Cohn, you are a . . . " Go on, Henry, it starts with an "H."

920 HENRY: Oh I'm not going to . . .

ROY: *With an "H,"* Henry, and it isn't "Hemophiliac." Come on . . .

HENRY: What are you doing, Roy?

ROY: No, say it. I mean it. Say: "Roy Cohn, you are a homosexual."

*(Pause)*

And I will proceed, systematically, to destroy your reputation and your practice and your career in New York State, Henry. Which you know I can do.

*(Pause.)*

HENRY: Roy, you have been seeing me since 1958. Apart 930 from the facelifts I have treated you for everything from syphilis . . .

ROY: From a whore in Dallas.

HENRY: From syphilis to venereal warts. In your rectum. Which you may have gotten from a whore in Dallas, but it wasn't a female whore.

*(Pause.)*

ROY: So say it.

HENRY: Roy Cohn, you are . . . You have had sex with men, many many times, Roy, and one of them, or any number of them, has made you very sick. 940 You have AIDS.

ROY: AIDS. Your problem, Henry, is that you are hung up on words, on labels, that you believe they mean what they seem to mean. AIDS. Homosexual. Gay. Lesbian. You think these are names that tell you who someone sleeps with, but they don't tell you that.

HENRY: No?

ROY: No. Like all labels they tell you one thing and one thing only: where does an individual so identified fit in the food 950 chain, in the pecking order? Not ideology, or sexual taste, but something much simpler: clout. Not who I fuck or who fucks me, but who will pick up the phone when I call, who owes me favors. This is what a label refers to. Now to someone who does not understand this, homosexual is what I am because I have sex with men. But really this is wrong. Homosexuals are not men who sleep with other men. Homosexuals are men who in fifteen years of trying cannot get a pissant antidiscrimination bill through City Council. Homosexuals are men who know nobody and who nobody knows. 960 Who have zero clout. Does this sound like me, Henry?

HENRY: No.

ROY: No. I have clout. A lot. I can pick up this phone, punch fifteen numbers, and you know who will be on the other end in under five minutes, Henry?

HENRY: The President.

ROY: Even better, Henry. His wife.

HENRY: I'm impressed.

ROY: I don't want you to be impressed. I want you to understand. This is not sophistry. And this is not hypocrisy. This is reality. I have sex with men. But unlike nearly every other 970 man of whom this is true, I bring the guy I'm screwing to the White House and President Reagan smiles at us and shakes his hand. Because *what* I am is defined entirely by *who* I am. Roy Cohn is not a homosexual. Roy Cohn is a heterosexual man, Henry, who fucks around with guys.

HENRY: OK, Roy.

ROY: And what is my diagnosis, Henry?

HENRY: You have AIDS, Roy.

ROY: No, Henry, no. AIDS is what homosexuals have. I have liver cancer. 980

*(Pause.)*

HENRY: Well, whatever the fuck you have, Roy, it's very serious, and I haven't got a damn thing for you. The NIH in Bethesda has a new drug called AZT with a two-year waiting list that not even I can get you onto. So get on the phone, Roy, and dial the fifteen numbers, and tell the First Lady you need in on an experimental treatment for liver cancer, because you can call it any damn thing you want, Roy, but what it boils down to is very bad news.

### —ACT TWO—
In Vitro
December 1985–January 1986

## SCENE I

*Night, the third week in December. Prior alone on the floor of his bedroom; he is much worse.*

PRIOR: Louis, Louis, please wake up, oh God.

*(Louis runs in.)*

PRIOR: I think something horrible is wrong with me I can't 990 breathe . . .

LOUIS: *(Starting to exit)* I'm calling the ambulance.

PRIOR: No, wait, I . . .

LOUIS: *Wait?* Are you fucking crazy? Oh God you're on fire, your head is on fire.

PRIOR: It hurts, it hurts . . .

LOUIS: I'm calling the ambulance.

PRIOR: I don't want to go to the hospital, I don't want to go to the hospital please let me lie here, just . . .

LOUIS: No, no, God, Prior, stand up . . . 1000

PRIOR: DON'T TOUCH MY LEG!

LOUIS: We have to . . . oh God this is so crazy.

PRIOR: I'll be OK if I just lie here Lou, really, if I can only sleep a little . . .

*(Louis exits.)*

PRIOR: Louis?

*NO! NO!* Don't call, you'll send me there and I won't come back, please, please Louis I'm begging, baby, please . . . *(Screams)* LOUIS!!

LOUIS: *(From off; hysterical)* WILL YOU SHUT THE FUCK
1010    UP!

PRIOR: *(Trying to stand)* Aaaah. I have . . . to go to the bathroom. Wait. Wait, just . . . oh. Oh God. *(He shits himself)*

LOUIS: *(Entering)* Prior? They'll be here in . . . Oh my God.

PRIOR: I'm sorry, I'm sorry.

LOUIS: What did . . . ? What?

PRIOR: I had an accident.

*(Louis goes to him.)*

LOUIS: This is blood.

PRIOR: Maybe you shouldn't touch it . . . me. . . . I . . . *(He faints)*

LOUIS: *(Quietly)* Oh help. Oh help. Oh God oh God oh God
1020    help me I can't I can't I can't.

## SCENE II

*Same night. Harper is sitting at home, all alone, with no lights on. We can barely see her. Joe enters, but he doesn't turn on the lights.*

JOE: Why are you sitting in the dark? Turn on the light.

HARPER: *No.* I heard the sounds in the bedroom again. I know someone was in there.

JOE: No one was.

HARPER: Maybe actually in the bed, under the covers with a knife.

Oh, boy. Joe. I, um, I'm thinking of going away. By which I mean: I think I'm going off again. You . . . you know what I mean?

1030  JOE: Please don't. Stay. We can fix it. I pray for that. This is my fault, but I can correct it. You have to try too . . .

*(He turns on the light. She turns it off again.)*

HARPER: When you pray, what do you pray for?

JOE: I pray for God to crush me, break me up into little pieces and start all over again.

HARPER: Oh. Please. Don't pray for that.

JOE: I had a book of Bible stories when I was a kid. There was a picture I'd look at twenty times every day: Jacob wrestles with the angel. I don't really remember the story, or why the wrestling—just the picture. Jacob is young and very strong.
1040   The angel is . . . a beautiful man, with golden hair and wings, of course. I still dream about it. Many nights. I'm. . . . It's me. In that struggle. Fierce, and unfair. The angel is not human, and it holds nothing back, so how could anyone human win, what kind of a fight is that? It's not just. Losing means your soul thrown down in the dust, your heart torn out from God's. But you can't not lose.

HARPER: In the whole entire world, you are the only person, the only person I love or have ever loved. And I love you terribly. Terribly. That's what's so awfully, irreducibly real. I
1050   can make up anything but I can't dream that away.

JOE: Are you . . . are you really going to have a baby?

HARPER: It's my time, and there's no blood. I don't really know. I suppose it wouldn't be a great thing. Maybe I'm just not bleeding because I take too many pills. Maybe I'll give birth to a pill. That would give a new meaning to pill-popping, huh?

I think you should go to Washington. Alone. Change, like you said.

JOE: I'm not going to leave you, Harper.

HARPER: Well maybe not. But I'm going to leave you.     1060

## SCENE III

*One AM, the next morning. Louis and a nurse, Emily, are sitting in Prior's room in the hospital.*

EMILY: He'll be all right now.

LOUIS: No he won't.

EMILY: No. I guess not. I gave him something that makes him sleep.

LOUIS: Deep asleep?

EMILY: Orbiting the moons of Jupiter.

LOUIS: A good place to be.

EMILY: Anyplace better than here. You his . . . uh?

LOUIS: Yes. I'm his uh.

EMILY: This must be hell for you.     1070

LOUIS: It is. Hell. The After Life. Which is not at all like a rainy afternoon in March, by the way, Prior. A lot more vivid than I'd expected. Dead leaves, but the crunchy kind. Sharp, dry air. The kind of long, luxurious dying feeling that breaks your heart.

EMILY: Yeah, well we all get to break our hearts on this one. He seems like a nice guy. Cute.

LOUIS: Not like this.

Yes, he is. Was. Whatever.

EMILY: Weird name. Prior Walter. Like, "The Walter before     1080
this one."

LOUIS: Lots of Walters before this one. Prior is an old old family name in an old old family. The Walters go back to the Mayflower and beyond. Back to the Norman Conquest. He says there's a Prior Walter stitched into the Bayeux tapestry.

EMILY: Is that impressive?

LOUIS: Well, it's old. Very old. Which in some circles equals impressive.

EMILY: Not in my circle. What's the name of the tapestry?

LOUIS: The Bayeux tapestry. Embroidered by La Reine     1090
Mathilde.

EMILY: I'll tell my mother. She embroiders. Drives me nuts.

LOUIS: Manual therapy for anxious hands.

EMILY: Maybe you should try it.

LOUIS: Mathilde stitched while William the Conqueror was off to war. She was capable of . . . more than loyalty. Devotion. She waited for him, she stitched for years. And if he had come back broken and defeated from war, she would have loved him even more. And if he had returned mutilated, ugly, full of infection and horror, she would still have loved     1100
him; fed by pity, by a sharing of pain, she would love him even more, and even more, and she would never, never have prayed to God, please let him die if he can't return to me whole and healthy and able to live a normal life. . . . If he had died, she would have buried her heart with him.

So what the fuck is the matter with me?

*(Little pause)*

Will he sleep through the night?

EMILY: At least.

LOUIS: I'm going.

1110 EMILY: It's one AM. Where do you have to go at . . .

LOUIS: I know what time it is. A walk. Night air, good for the. . . . The park.

EMILY: Be careful.

LOUIS: Yeah. Danger.

Tell him, if he wakes up and you're still on, tell him goodbye, tell him I had to go.

## SCENE IV

*An hour later. Split scene: Joe and Roy in a fancy (straight) bar; Louis and a Man in the Rambles in Central Park. Joe and Roy are sitting at the bar; the place is brightly lit. Joe has a plate of food in front of him but he isn't eating. Roy occasionally reaches over the table and forks small bites off Joe's plate. Roy is drinking heavily, Joe not at all. Louis and the Man are eyeing each other, each alternating interest and indifference.*

JOE: The pills were something she started when she miscarried or . . . no, she took some before that. She had a really bad time at home, when she was a kid, her home was really bad.
1120   I think a lot of drinking and physical stuff. She doesn't talk about that, instead she talks about . . . the sky falling down, people with knives hiding under sofas. Monsters. Mormons. Everyone thinks Mormons don't come from homes like that, we aren't supposed to behave that way, but we do. It's not lying, or being two-faced. Everyone tries very hard to live up to God's strictures, which are very . . . um . . .

ROY: Strict.

JOE: I shouldn't be bothering you with this.

ROY: No, please. Heart to heart. Want another. . . . What is
1130   that, seltzer?

JOE: The failure to measure up hits people very hard. From such a strong desire to be good they feel very far from goodness when they fail.
   What scares me is that maybe what I really love in her is the part of her that's farthest from the light, from God's love; maybe I was drawn to that in the first place. And I'm keeping it alive because I need it.

ROY: Why would you need it?

JOE: There are things. . . . I don't know how well we know our-
1140   selves. I mean, what if? I know I married her because she . . . because I loved it that she was always wrong, always doing something wrong, like one step out of step. In Salt Lake City that stands out. I never stood out, on the outside, but inside, it was hard for me. To pass.

ROY: Pass?

JOE: Yeah.

ROY: Pass as what?

JOE: Oh. Well. . . . As someone cheerful and strong. Those who love God with an open heart unclouded by secrets and
1150   struggles are cheerful; God's easy simple love for them shows in how strong and happy they are. The saints.

ROY: But you had secrets? Secret struggles . . .

JOE: I wanted to be one of the elect, one of the Blessed. You feel you ought to be, that the blemishes are yours by choice, which of course they aren't. Harper's sorrow, that really

deep sorrow, she didn't choose that. But it's there.

ROY: You didn't put it there.

JOE: No.

ROY: You sound like you think you did.

JOE: I am responsible for her.                                    1160

ROY: Because she's your wife.

JOE: That. And I do love her.

ROY: Whatever. She's your wife. And so there are obligations. To her. But also to yourself.

JOE: She'd fall apart in Washington.

ROY: Then let her stay here.

JOE: She'll fall apart if I leave her.

ROY: Then bring her to Washington.

JOE: I just can't, Roy. She needs me.

ROY: Listen, Joe. I'm the best divorce lawyer in the business.   1170

*(Little pause.)*

JOE: Can't Washington wait?

ROY: You do what you need to do, Joe. What *you* need. *You.* Let her life go where it wants to go. You'll both be better for that. *Somebody* should get what they want.

MAN: What do you want?

LOUIS: I want you to fuck me, hurt me, make me bleed.

MAN: I want to.

LOUIS: Yeah?

MAN: I want to hurt you.

LOUIS: Fuck me.                                                   1180

MAN: Yeah?

LOUIS: Hard.

MAN: Yeah? You been a bad boy?

*(Pause. Louis laughs, softly.)*

LOUIS: Very bad. Very bad.

MAN: You need to be punished, boy?

LOUIS: Yes. I do.

MAN: Yes what?

*(Little pause.)*

LOUIS: Um, I . . .

MAN: Yes *what*, boy?

LOUIS: Oh. Yes sir.                                              1190

MAN: I want you to take me to your place, boy.

LOUIS: No, I can't do that.

MAN: No *what*?

LOUIS: No sir, I can't, I . . .
   I don't live alone, sir.

MAN: Your lover know you're out with a man tonight, boy?

LOUIS: No sir, he . . .
   My lover doesn't know.

MAN: Your lover know you . . .

LOUIS: Let's change the subject, OK? Can we go to your place? 1200

MAN: I live with my parents.

LOUIS: Oh.

ROY: Everyone who makes it in this world makes it because somebody older and more powerful takes an interest. The most precious asset in life, I think, is the ability to be a good son. You have that, Joe. Somebody who can be a good son to a father who pushes them farther than they would otherwise go. I've had many fathers, I owe my life to them, powerful, powerful men. Walter Winchell, Edgar Hoover. Joe Mc-

1210 Carthy most of all. He valued me because I am a good lawyer, but he loved me because I was and am a good son. He was a very difficult man, very guarded and cagey; I brought out something tender in him. He would have died for me. And me for him. Does this embarrass you?

JOE: I had a hard time with my father.

ROY: Well sometimes that's the way. Then you have to find other fathers, substitutes, I don't know. The father-son relationship is central to life. Women are for birth, beginning, but the father is continuance. The son offers the father his

1220 life as a vessel for carrying forth his father's dream. Your father's living?

JOE: Um, dead.

ROY: He was . . . what? A difficult man?

JOE: He was in the military. He could be very unfair. And cold.

ROY: But he loved you.

JOE: I don't know.

ROY: No, no, Joe, he did, I know this. Sometimes a father's love has to be very, very hard, unfair even, cold to make his son grow strong in a world like this. This isn't a good world.

1230 MAN: Here, then.

LOUIS: I. . . . Do you have a rubber?

MAN: I don't use rubbers.

LOUIS: You should. (*He takes one from his coat pocket*) Here.

MAN: I don't use them.

LOUIS: Forget it, then. (*He starts to leave*)

MAN: No, wait.

Put it on me. Boy.

LOUIS: Forget it, I have to get back. Home. I must be going crazy.

1240 MAN: Oh come on please he won't find out.

LOUIS: It's cold. Too cold.

MAN: It's never too cold, let me warm you up. Please?

(*They begin to fuck.*)

MAN: Relax.

LOUIS: (*A small laugh*) Not a chance.

MAN: It . . .

LOUIS: What?

MAN: I think it broke. The rubber. You want me to keep going? (*Little pause*) Pull out? Should I . . .

LOUIS: Keep going.

1250    Infect me.

I don't care. I don't care.

(*Pause. The Man pulls out.*)

MAN: I . . . um, look, I'm sorry, but I think I want to go.

LOUIS: Yeah.

Give my best to mom and dad.

(*The Man slaps him.*)

LOUIS: Ow!

(*They stare at each other.*)

LOUIS: It was a joke.

(*The Man leaves.*)

ROY: How long have we known each other?

JOE: Since 1980.

ROY: Right. A long time. I feel close to you, Joe. Do I advise you well?    1260

JOE: You've been an incredible friend, Roy, I . . .

ROY: I want to be family. Familia, as my Italian friends call it. La Familia. A lovely word. It's important for me to help you, like I was helped.

JOE: I owe practically everything to you, Roy.

ROY: I'm dying, Joe. Cancer.

JOE: Oh my God.

ROY: Please. Let me finish.

Few people know this and I'm telling you this only because. . . . I'm not afraid of death. What can death bring that I    1270 haven't faced? I've lived; life is the worst. (*Gently mocking himself*) Listen to me, I'm a philosopher.

Joe. You must do this. You must must must. Love; that's a trap. Responsibility; that's a trap too. Like a father to a son I tell you this: Life is full of horror; nobody escapes, nobody; save yourself. Whatever pulls on you, whatever needs from you, threatens you. Don't be afraid; people are so afraid; don't be afraid to live in the raw wind, naked, alone. . . . Learn at least this: What you are capable of. Let nothing stand in your way.    1280

## SCENE V

*Three days later. Prior and Belize in Prior's hospital room. Prior is very sick but improving. Belize has just arrived.*

PRIOR: Miss Thing.

BELIZE: Ma cherie bichette.

PRIOR: Stella.

BELIZE: Stella for star. Let me see. (*Scrutinizing Prior*) You look like shit, why yes indeed you do, comme la merde!

PRIOR: Merci.

BELIZE: (*Taking little plastic bottles from his bag, handing them to Prior*) Not to despair, Belle Reeve. Lookie! Magic goop!

PRIOR: (*Opening a bottle, sniffing*) Pooh! What kinda crap is    1290 that?

BELIZE: Beats me. Let's rub it on your poor blistered body and see what it does.

PRIOR: This is not Western medicine, these bottles . . .

BELIZE: Voodoo cream. From the botanica 'round the block.

PRIOR: And you a registered nurse.

BELIZE: (*Sniffing it*) Beeswax and cheap perfume. Cut with Jergen's Lotion. Full of good vibes and love from some little black Cubana witch in Miami.

PRIOR: Get that trash away from me, I am immune-suppressed.    1300

BELIZE: I *am* a health professional. I *know* what I'm doing.

PRIOR: It stinks. Any word from Louis?

(*Pause. Belize starts giving Prior a gentle massage.*)

PRIOR: Gone.

BELIZE: He'll be back. I know the type. Likes to keep a girl on edge.

PRIOR: It's been . . .

(*Pause.*)

BELIZE: (*Trying to jog his memory*) How long?

PRIOR: I don't remember.

BELIZE: How long have you been here?

1310 PRIOR: (*Getting suddenly upset*) I don't remember, I don't give a fuck. I want Louis. I want my fucking boyfriend, where the fuck is he? I'm dying, I'm dying, where's Louis?

BELIZE: Shhhh, shhh . . .

PRIOR: This is a very strange drug, this drug. Emotional lability, for starters.

BELIZE: Save a tab or two for me.

PRIOR: Oh no, not this drug, ce n'est pas pour la joyeux noël et la bonne année, this drug she is serious poisonous chemistry, ma pauvre bichette.

1320 And not just disorienting. I hear things. Voices.

BELIZE: Voices.

PRIOR: A voice.

BELIZE: Saying what?

(*Pause.*)

PRIOR: I'm not supposed to tell.

BELIZE: You better tell the doctor. Or I will.

PRIOR: No no don't. Please. I want the voice; it's wonderful. It's all that's keeping me alive. I don't want to talk to some intern about it.
You know what happens? When I hear it, I get hard.

1330 BELIZE: Oh my.

PRIOR: Comme ça. (*He uses his arm to demonstrate*) And you know I am slow to rise.

BELIZE: My jaw aches at the memory.

PRIOR: And would you deny me this little solace—betray my concupiscence to Florence Nightingale's storm troopers?

BELIZE: Perish the thought, ma bébé.

PRIOR: They'd change the drug just to spoil the fun.

BELIZE: You and your boner can depend on me.

PRIOR: Je t'adore, ma belle nègre.

1340 BELIZE: All this girl-talk shit is politically incorrect, you know. We should have dropped it back when we gave up drag.

PRIOR: I'm sick, I get to be politically incorrect if it makes me feel better. You sound like Lou.

(*Little pause*)

Well, at least I have the satisfaction of knowing he's in anguish somewhere. I loved his anguish. Watching him stick his head up his asshole and eat his guts out over some relatively minor moral conundrum—it was the best show in town. But Mother warned me: if they get overwhelmed by the little things . . .

1350 BELIZE: They'll be belly-up bustville when something big comes along.

PRIOR: Mother warned me.

BELIZE: And they do come along.

PRIOR: But I didn't listen.

BELIZE: No. (*Doing Hepburn*) Men are beasts.

PRIOR: (*Also Hepburn*) The absolute lowest.

BELIZE: I have to go. If I want to spend my whole lonely life looking after white people I can get underpaid to do it.

PRIOR: You're just a Christian martyr.

1360 BELIZE: Whatever happens, baby, I will be here for you.

PRIOR: Je t'aime.

BELIZE: Je t'aime. Don't go crazy on me, girlfriend, I already got enough crazy queens for one lifetime. For two. I can't be bothering with dementia.

PRIOR: I promise.

BELIZE: (*Touching him; softly*) Ouch.

PRIOR: Ouch. Indeed.

BELIZE: Why'd they have to pick on you?
And eat more, girlfriend, you really do look like shit.

(*Belize leaves.*)

PRIOR: (*After waiting a beat*) He's gone.    1370
Are you still . . .

VOICE: I can't stay. I will return.

PRIOR: Are you one of those "Follow me to the other side" voices?

VOICE: No. I am no nightbird. I am a messenger . . .

PRIOR: You have a beautiful voice, it sounds . . . like a viola, like a perfectly tuned, tight string, balanced, the truth. . . . Stay with me.

VOICE: Not now. Soon I will return, I will reveal myself to you; I am glorious, glorious; my heart, my countenance and my    1380 message. You must prepare.

PRIOR: For what? I don't want to . . .

VOICE: No death, no:
A marvelous work and a wonder we undertake, an edifice awry we sink plumb and straighten, a great Lie we abolish, a great error correct, with the rule, sword and broom of Truth!

PRIOR: What are you talking about, I . . .

VOICE:
I am on my way; when I am manifest, our Work begins:    1390
Prepare for the parting of the air,
The breath, the ascent,
Glory to . . .

## SCENE VI

*The second week of January. Martin, Roy and Joe in a fancy Manhattan restaurant.*

MARTIN: It's a revolution in Washington, Joe. We have a new agenda and finally a real leader. They got back the Senate but we have the courts. By the nineties the Supreme Court will be block-solid Republican appointees, and the Federal bench—Republican judges like land mines, everywhere, everywhere they turn. Affirmative action? Take it to court. Boom! Land mine. And we'll get our way on just about    1400 everything: abortion, defense, Central America, family values, a live investment climate. We have the White House locked till the year 2000. And beyond. A permanent fix on the Oval Office? It's possible. By '92 we'll get the Senate back, and in ten years the South is going to give us the House. It's really the end of Liberalism. The end of New Deal Socialism. The end of ipso facto secular humanism. The dawning of a genuinely American political personality. Modeled on Ronald Wilson Reagan.

JOE: It sounds great, Mr. Heller.    1410

MARTIN: Martin. And Justice is the hub. Especially since Ed Meese took over. He doesn't specialize in Fine Points of the Law. He's a flatfoot, a cop. He reminds me of Teddy Roosevelt.

JOE: I can't wait to meet him.

MARTIN: Too bad, Joe, he's been dead for sixty years!

*(There is a little awkwardness. Joe doesn't respond.)*

MARTIN: Teddy Roosevelt. You said you wanted to. . . . Little joke. It reminds me of the story about the . . .

ROY: *(Smiling, but nasty)* Aw shut the fuck up Martin.

1420    *(To Joe)* You see that? Mr. Heller here is one of the mighty, Joseph, in D.C. he sitteth on the right hand of the man who sitteth on the right hand of The Man. And yet I can say "shut the fuck up" and he will take no offense. Loyalty. He . . . Martin?

MARTIN: Yes, Roy?

ROY: Rub my back.

MARTIN: Roy . . .

ROY: No no really, a sore spot, I get them all the time now, these. . . . Rub it for me darling, would you do that for me?

*(Martin rubs Roy's back. They both look at Joe.)*

1430  ROY: *(To Joe)* How do you think a handful of Bolsheviks turned St. Petersburg into Leningrad in one afternoon? *Comrades.* Who do for each other. Marx and Engels. Lenin and Trotsky. Josef Stalin and Franklin Delano Roosevelt.

*(Martin laughs.)*

ROY: *Comrades,* right Martin?

MARTIN: This man, Joe, is a Saint of the Right.

JOE: I know, Mr. Heller, I . . .

ROY: And you see what I mean, Martin? He's special, right?

MARTIN: Don't embarrass him, Roy.

ROY: Gravity, decency, smarts! His strength is as the strength
1440    of ten because his heart is pure! *And* he's a Royboy, one hundred percent.

MARTIN: We're on the move, Joe. On the move.

JOE: Mr. Heller, I . . .

MARTIN: *(Ending backrub)* We can't wait any longer for an answer.

*(Little pause.)*

JOE: Oh. Um, I . . .

ROY: Joe's a married man, Martin.

MARTIN: Aha.

ROY: With a wife. She doesn't care to go to D.C., and so Joe
1450    cannot go. And keeps us dangling. We've seen that kind of thing before, haven't we? These men and their wives.

MARTIN: Oh yes. Beware.

JOE: I really can't discuss this under . . .

MARTIN: Then *don't* discuss. Say yes, Joe.

ROY: Now.

MARTIN: Say yes I will.

ROY: Now.

Now. I'll hold my breath till you do, I'm turning blue waiting. . . . *Now,* goddammit!

1460  MARTIN: Roy, calm down, it's not . . .

ROY: Aw, fuck it. *(He takes a letter from his jacket pocket, hands it to Joe)*
Read. Came today.

*(Joe reads the first paragraph, then looks up.)*

JOE: Roy. This is . . . Roy, this is terrible.

ROY: You're telling me.

A letter from the New York State Bar Association, Martin. They're gonna try and disbar me.

MARTIN: Oh my.

JOE: Why?

ROY: Why, Martin?                                                                       1470

MARTIN: Revenge.

ROY: The whole Establishment. Their little rules. Because I know no rules. Because I don't see the Law as a dead and arbitrary collection of antiquated dictums, thou shall, thou shalt not, because, because I know the Law's a pliable, breathing, sweating . . . *organ,* because, because . . .

MARTIN: Because he borrowed half a million from one of his clients.

ROY: Yeah, well, there's that.

MARTIN: *And* he forgot to *return* it.                                                1480

JOE: Roy, that's. . . . You borrowed money from a client?

ROY: I'm deeply ashamed.

*(Little pause.)*

JOE: *(Very sympathetic)* Roy, you know how much I admire you. Well I mean I know you have unorthodox ways, but I'm sure you only did what you thought at the time you needed to do. And I have faith that . . .

ROY: Not so damp, please. I'll deny it was a loan. She's got no paperwork. Can't prove a fucking thing.

*(Little pause. Martin studies the menu.)*

JOE: *(Handing back the letter, more official in tone)* Roy I really appreciate your telling me this, and I'll do whatever I  1490
can to help.

ROY: *(Holding up a hand, then, carefully)* I'll tell you what you can do.
I'm about to be tried, Joe, by a jury that is not a jury of my peers. The disbarment committee: genteel gentleman Brahmin lawyers, country-club men. I offend them, to these men . . . I'm what, Martin, some sort of filthy little Jewish troll?

MARTIN: Oh well, I wouldn't go so far as . . .

ROY: Oh well I would.
Very fancy lawyers, these disbarment committee lawyers,  1500
fancy lawyers with fancy corporate clients and complicated cases. Antitrust suits. Deregulation. Environmental control. Complex cases like these need Justice Department cooperation like flowers need the sun. Wouldn't you say that's an accurate assessment, Martin?

MARTIN: I'm not here, Roy. I'm not hearing any of this.

ROY: No. Of course not.
Without the light of the sun, Joe, these cases, and the fancy lawyers who represent them, will wither and die.
A well-placed friend, someone in the Justice Department,  1510
say, can turn off the sun. Cast a deep shadow on my behalf. Make them shiver in the cold. If they overstep. They would fear that.

*(Pause.)*

JOE: Roy. I don't understand.

ROY: You do.

*(Pause.)*

JOE: You're not asking me to . . .

ROY: Sssshhhh. Careful.

JOE: *(A beat, then)* Even if I said yes to the job, it would be

illegal to interfere. With the hearings. It's unethical. No. I
1520  can't.

ROY: Un-ethical.
      Would you excuse us, Martin?

MARTIN: Excuse you?

ROY: Take a walk, Martin. For real.

*(Martin leaves.)*

ROY: Un-ethical. Are you trying to embarrass me in front of my
      friend?

JOE: Well it is unethical, I can't . . .

ROY: Boy, you are really something. What the fuck do you think
      this is, Sunday School?

1530  JOE: No, but Roy this is . . .

ROY: This is . . . this is gastric juices churning, this is enzymes
      and acids, this is intestinal is what this is, bowel movement
      and blood-red meat—this stinks, this is *politics*, Joe, the
      game of being alive. And you think you're. . . . What? Above
      that? Above alive is what? Dead! In the clouds! You're on
      earth, goddammit! Plant a foot, stay a while.
      I'm sick. They smell I'm weak. They want blood this time. I
      must have eyes in Justice. In Justice you will protect me.

JOE: Why can't Mr. Heller . . .

1540  ROY: Grow up, Joe. The administration can't get involved.

JOE: But I'd be part of the administration. The same as him.

ROY: Not the same. Martin's Ed's man. And Ed's Reagan's
      man. So Martin's Reagan's man.
      And you're mine.

*(Little pause. He holds up the letter)*

This will never be. Understand me?

*(He tears the letter up)*

I'm gonna be a lawyer, Joe, I'm gonna be a lawyer, Joe, I'm
gonna be a goddam motherfucking legally licensed member
of the bar lawyer, just like my daddy was, till my last bitter
day on earth, Joseph, until the day I die.

*(Martin returns.)*

1550  ROY: Ah, Martin's back.

MARTIN: So are we agreed?

ROY: Joe?

*(Little pause.)*

JOE: I will think about it.
      *(To Roy)* I will.

ROY: Huh.

MARTIN: It's the fear of what comes after the doing that makes
      the doing hard to do.

ROY: Amen.

MARTIN: But you can almost always live with the consequences.

## SCENE VII

*That afternoon. On the granite steps outside the Hall of Justice,
Brooklyn. It is cold and sunny. A Sabrett wagon is selling hot
dogs. Louis, in a shabby overcoat, is sitting on the steps con-
templatively eating one. Joe enters with three hot dogs and a
can of Coke.*

1560  JOE: Can I . . . ?

LOUIS: Oh sure. Sure. Crazy cold sun.

JOE: *(Sitting)* Have to make the best of it.
      How's your friend?

LOUIS: My . . . ? Oh. He's worse. My friend is worse.

JOE: I'm sorry.

LOUIS: Yeah, well. Thanks for asking. It's nice. You're nice. I
      can't believe you voted for Reagan.

JOE: I hope he gets better.

LOUIS: Reagan?

JOE: Your friend.                                                    1570

LOUIS: He won't. Neither will Reagan.

JOE: Let's not talk politics, OK?

LOUIS: *(Pointing to Joe's lunch)* You're eating *three* of those?

JOE: Well . . . I'm . . . hungry.

LOUIS: They're really terrible for you. Full of rat-poo and bee-
      tle legs and wood shavings 'n' shit.

JOE: Huh.

LOUIS: And . . . um . . . irridium, I think. Something toxic.

JOE: You're eating one.

LOUIS: Yeah, well, the shape, I can't help myself, plus I'm *try-*  1580
      *ing* to commit suicide, what's your excuse?

JOE: I don't have an excuse. I just have Pepto-Bismol.

*(Joe takes a bottle of Pepto-Bismol and chugs it. Louis shud-
ders audibly.)*

JOE: Yeah I know but then I wash it down with Coke.

*(He does this. Louis mimes barfing in Joe's lap. Joe pushes
Louis's head away.)*

JOE: Are you *always* like this?

LOUIS: I've been worrying a lot about his kids.

JOE: Whose?

LOUIS: Reagan's. Maureen and Mike and little orphan Patti
      and Miss Ron Reagan Jr., the you-should-pardon-the-ex-
      pression heterosexual.

JOE: Ron Reagan Jr. is *not* . . . You shouldn't just make these   1590
      assumptions about people. How do you know? About him?
      What he is? You don't know.

LOUIS: *(Doing Tallulah)* Well darling he never sucked *my* cock
      but . . .

JOE: Look, if you're going to get vulgar . . .

LOUIS: No no really I mean. . . . What's it like to be the child of
      the Zeitgeist? To have the American Animus as your dad?
      It's not really a *family*, the Reagans, I read *People*, there
      aren't any connections there, no love, they don't ever even
      speak to each other except through their agents. So what's it  1600
      like to be Reagan's kid? Enquiring minds want to know.

JOE: You can't believe everything you . . .

LOUIS: *(Looking away)* But . . . I think we all know what that's
      like. Nowadays. No connections. No responsibilities. All of
      us . . . falling through the cracks that separate what we owe
      to our selves and . . . and what we owe to love.

JOE: You just. . . . Whatever you feel like saying or doing, you
      don't care, you just . . . do it.

LOUIS: Do what?

JOE: It. Whatever. Whatever it is you want to do.                    1610

LOUIS: Are you trying to tell me something?

*(Little pause, sexual. They stare at each other. Joe looks away.)*

JOE: No, I'm just observing that you . . .

LOUIS: Impulsive.

JOE: Yes, I mean it must be scary, you . . .

LOUIS: *(Shrugs)* Land of the free. Home of the brave. Call me irresponsible.

JOE: It's kind of terrifying.

LOUIS: Yeah, well, freedom is. Heartless, too.

JOE: Oh you're not heartless.

1620 LOUIS: You don't know.

Finish your weenie.

*(He pats Joe on the knee, starts to leave.)*

JOE: Um . . .

*(Louis turns, looks at him. Joe searches for something to say.)*

JOE: Yesterday was Sunday but I've been a little unfocused recently and I thought it was Monday. So I came here like I was going to work. And the whole place was empty. And at first I couldn't figure out why, and I had this moment of incredible . . . fear and also. . . . It just flashed through my mind: The whole Hall of Justice, it's empty, it's deserted, it's gone out of business. Forever. The people that make it run

1630 have up and abandoned it.

LOUIS: *(Looking at the building)* Creepy.

JOE: Well yes but. I felt that I was going to scream. Not because it was creepy, but because the emptiness felt so *fast*.
And . . . well, good. A . . . happy scream.
I just wondered what a thing it would be . . . if overnight everything you owe anything to, justice, or love, had really gone away. Free.
It would be . . . heartless terror. Yes. Terrible, and . . .
Very great. To shed your skin, every old skin, one by one and

1640 then walk away, unencumbered, into the morning.

*(Little pause. He looks at the building)*

I can't go in there today.

LOUIS: Then don't.

JOE: *(Not really hearing Louis)* I can't go in, I need . . .

*(He looks for what he needs. He takes a swig of Pepto-Bismol)*

I can't *be* this anymore. I need . . . a change, I should just . . .

LOUIS: *(Not a come-on, necessarily; he doesn't want to be alone)* Want some company? For whatever?

*(Pause. Joe looks at Louis and looks away, afraid. Louis shrugs.)*

LOUIS: Sometimes, even if it scares you to death, you have to be willing to break the law. Know what I mean?

*(Another little pause.)*

1650 JOE: Yes.

*(Another little pause.)*

LOUIS: I moved out. I moved out on my . . .
I haven't been sleeping well.

JOE: Me neither.

*(Louis goes up to Joe, licks his napkin and dabs at Joe's mouth.)*

LOUIS: Antacid moustache.
*(Points to the building)* Maybe the court won't convene. Ever again. Maybe we are free. To do whatever.
Children of the new morning, criminal minds. Selfish and

greedy and loveless and blind. Reagan's children.
You're scared. So am I. Everybody is in the land of the free.
God help us all.                                                    1660

SCENE VIII

*Late that night. Joe at a payphone phoning Hannah at home in Salt Lake City.*

JOE: Mom?

HANNAH: Joe?

JOE: Hi.

HANNAH: You're calling from the street. It's . . . it must be four in the morning. What's happened?

JOE: Nothing, nothing, I . . .

HANNAH: It's Harper. Is Harper. . . . Joe? Joe?

JOE: Yeah, hi. No, Harper's fine. Well, no, she's . . . not fine. How are you, Mom?

HANNAH: What's happened?                                            1670

JOE: I just wanted to talk to you. I, uh, wanted to try something out on you.

HANNAH: Joe, you haven't . . . have you been drinking, Joe?

JOE: Yes ma'am. I'm drunk.

HANNAH: That isn't like you.

JOE: No. I mean, who's to say?

HANNAH: Why are you out on the street at four AM? In that crazy city. It's dangerous.

JOE: Actually, Mom, I'm not on the street. I'm near the boathouse in the park.                                               1680

HANNAH: What park?

JOE: Central Park.

HANNAH: CENTRAL PARK! Oh my Lord. What on earth are you doing in Central Park at this time of night? Are you . . . Joe, I think you ought to go home right now. Call me from home.

*(Little pause)*

Joe?

JOE: I come here to watch, Mom. Sometimes. Just to watch.

HANNAH: Watch what? What's there to watch at four in the . . .

JOE: Mom, did Dad love me?                                          1690

HANNAH: What?

JOE: Did he?

HANNAH: You ought to go home and call from there.

JOE: Answer.

HANNAH: Oh now really. This is maudlin. I don't like this conversation.

JOE: Yeah, well, it gets worse from here on.

*(Pause.)*

HANNAH: Joe?

JOE: Mom. Momma. I'm a homosexual, Momma.
Boy, did that come out awkward.                                    1700

*(Pause)*

Hello? Hello?
I'm a homosexual.

*(Pause)*

Please, Momma. Say something.

HANNAH: You're old enough to understand that your father

didn't love you without being ridiculous about it.

JOE: What?

HANNAH: You're ridiculous. You're being ridiculous.

JOE: I'm . . .
What?

1710 HANNAH: You really ought to go home now to your wife. I need to go to bed. This phone call. . . . We will just forget this phone call.

JOE: Mom.

HANNAH: No more talk. Tonight. This . . .
(*Suddenly very angry*) Drinking is a sin! A sin! I raised you better than that. (*She hangs up*)

## SCENE IX

*The following morning, early. Split scene: Harper and Joe at home; Louis and Prior in Prior's hospital room. Joe and Louis have just entered. This should be fast and obviously furious; overlapping is fine; the proceedings may be a little confusing but not the final results.*

HARPER: Oh God. Home. The moment of truth has arrived.

JOE: Harper.

LOUIS: I'm going to move out.

1720 PRIOR: The fuck you are.

JOE: Harper. Please listen. I still love you very much. You're still my best buddy; I'm not going to leave you.

HARPER: No, I don't like the sound of this. I'm leaving.

LOUIS: I'm leaving.
I already have.

JOE: Please listen. Stay. This is really hard. We have to talk.

HARPER: We are talking. Aren't we. Now please shut up. OK?

PRIOR: Bastard. Sneaking off while I'm flat out here, that's low. If I could get up now I'd beat the holy shit out of you.

1730 JOE: Did you take pills? How many?

HARPER: No pills. Bad for the . . . (*Pats stomach*)

JOE: You aren't pregnant. I called your gynecologist.

HARPER: I'm seeing a new gynecologist.

PRIOR: You have no right to do this.

LOUIS: Oh, that's ridiculous.

PRIOR: No right. It's criminal.

JOE: Forget about that. Just listen. You want the truth. This is the truth.
I knew this when I married you. I've known this I guess for
1740 as long as I've known anything, but . . . I don't know, I thought maybe that with enough effort and will I could change myself . . . but I can't . . .

PRIOR: Criminal.

LOUIS: There oughta be a law.

PRIOR: There is a law. You'll see.

JOE: I'm losing ground here, I go walking, you want to know where I walk, I . . . go to the park, or up and down 53rd Street, or places where. . . . And I keep swearing I won't go walking again, but I just can't.

1750 LOUIS: I need some privacy.

PRIOR: That's new.

LOUIS: Everything's new, Prior.

JOE: I try to tighten my heart into a knot, a snarl, I try to learn to live dead, just numb, but then I see someone I want, and it's like a nail, like a hot spike right through my chest, and I know I'm losing.

PRIOR: Apartment too small for three? Louis and Prior comfy but not Louis and Prior and Prior's disease?

LOUIS: Something like that.
I won't be judged by you. This isn't a crime, just—the in- 1760 evitable consequence of people who run out of—whose limitations . . .

PRIOR: Bang bang bang. The court will come to order.

LOUIS: I mean let's talk practicalities, schedules; I'll come over if you want, spend nights with you when I can, I can . . .

PRIOR: Has the jury reached a verdict?

LOUIS: I'm doing the best I can.

PRIOR: Pathetic. Who cares?

JOE: My whole life has conspired to bring me to this place, and I can't despise my whole life. I think I believed when I met 1770 you I could save you, you at least if not myself, but . . . I don't have any sexual feelings for you, Harper. And I don't think I ever did.

(*Little pause.*)

HARPER: I think you should go.

JOE: Where?

HARPER: Washington. Doesn't matter.

JOE: What are you talking about?

HARPER: Without me.
Without me, Joe. Isn't that what you want to hear?

(*Little pause.*)

JOE: Yes.                                                                 1780

LOUIS: You can love someone and fail them. You can love someone and not be able to . . .

PRIOR: You *can*, theoretically, yes. A person can, maybe an editorial "you" can love, Louis, but not *you*, specifically you, I don't know, I think you are excluded from that general category.

HARPER: You were going to save me, but the whole time you were spinning a lie. I just don't understand that.

PRIOR: A person could theoretically love and maybe many do but we both know now you can't.                                        1790

LOUIS: I do.

PRIOR: You can't even say it.

LOUIS: I love you, Prior.

PRIOR: I repeat. Who cares?

HARPER: This is so scary, I want this to stop, to go back . . .

PRIOR: We have reached a verdict, your honor. This man's heart is deficient. He loves, but his love is worth nothing.

JOE: Harper . . .

HARPER: Mr. Lies, I want to get away from here. Far away. Right now. Before he starts talking again. Please, please . . . 1800

JOE: As long as I've known you Harper you've been afraid of . . . of men hiding under the bed, men hiding under the sofa, men with knives.

PRIOR: (*Shattered; almost pleading; trying to reach him*) I'm dying! You stupid fuck! Do you know what that is! Love! Do you know what love means? We lived together four-and-a-half years, you animal, you idiot.

LOUIS: I have to find some way to save myself.

JOE: Who are these men? I never understood it. Now I know.

HARPER: What?                                                             1810

JOE: It's me.

HARPER: It is?

PRIOR: GET OUT OF MY ROOM!

JOE: I'm the man with the knives.

HARPER: You are?

PRIOR: If I could get up now I'd kill you. I would. Go away. Go away or I'll scream.

HARPER: Oh God . . .

JOE: I'm sorry . . .

1820 HARPER: It is you.

LOUIS: Please don't scream.

PRIOR: Go.

HARPER: I recognize you now.

LOUIS: Please . . .

JOE: Oh. Wait, I. . . . Oh!

(*He covers his mouth with his hand, gags, and removes his hand, red with blood*)

I'm bleeding.

(*Prior screams.*)

HARPER: Mr. Lies.

MR. LIES: (*Appearing, dressed in antarctic explorer's apparel*) Right here.

1830 HARPER: I want to go away. I can't see him anymore.

MR. LIES: Where?

HARPER: Anywhere. Far away.

MR. LIES: Absolutamento.

(*Harper and Mr. Lies vanish. Joe looks up, sees that she's gone.*)

PRIOR: (*Closing his eyes*) When I open my eyes you'll be gone.

(*Louis leaves.*)

JOE: Harper?

PRIOR: (*Opening his eyes*) Huh. It worked.

JOE: (*Calling*) Harper?

PRIOR: I hurt all over. I wish I was dead.

## SCENE X

*The same day, sunset. Hannah and Sister Ella Chapter, a real-estate saleswoman, Hannah Pitt's closest friend, in front of Hannah's house in Salt Lake City.*

SISTER ELLA CHAPTER: Look at that view! A view of heaven. Like the living city of heaven, isn't it, it just fairly glimmers 1840 in the sun.

HANNAH: Glimmers.

SISTER ELLA CHAPTER: Even the stone and brick it just glimmers and glitters like heaven in the sunshine. Such a nice view you get, perched up on a canyon rim. Some kind of beautiful place.

HANNAH: It's just Salt Lake, and you're selling the house *for* me, not *to* me.

SISTER ELLA CHAPTER: I like to work up an enthusiasm for my properties.

1850 HANNAH: Just get me a good price.

SISTER ELLA CHAPTER: Well, the market's off.

HANNAH: At least fifty.

SISTER ELLA CHAPTER: Forty'd be more like it.

HANNAH: Fifty.

SISTER ELLA CHAPTER: Wish you'd wait a bit.

HANNAH: Well I can't.

SISTER ELLA CHAPTER: Wish you would. You're about the only friend I got.

HANNAH: Oh well now.                                                          1860

SISTER ELLA CHAPTER: Know why I decided to like you? I decided to like you 'cause you're the only unfriendly Mormon I ever met.

HANNAH: Your wig is crooked.

SISTER ELLA CHAPTER: Fix it.

(*Hannah straightens Sister Ella's wig.*)

SISTER ELLA CHAPTER: New York City. All they got there is tiny rooms.

I always thought: People ought to stay put. That's why I got my license to sell real estate. It's a way of saying: Have a house! Stay put! It's a way of saying traveling's no good. Plus 1870 I needed the cash. (*She takes a pack of cigarettes out of her purse, lights one, offers pack to Hannah*)

HANNAH: Not out here, anyone could come by.

There's been days I've stood at this ledge and thought about stepping over.

It's a hard place, Salt Lake: baked dry. Abundant energy; not much intelligence. That's a combination that can wear a body out. No harm looking someplace else. I don't need much room.

My sister-in-law Libby thinks there's radon gas in the base- 1880 ment.

SISTER ELLA CHAPTER: Is there gas in the . . .

HANNAH: Of course not. Libby's a fool.

SISTER ELLA CHAPTER: 'Cause I'd have to include that in the description.

HANNAH: There's no gas, Ella. (*Little pause*) Give a puff. (*She takes a furtive drag of Ella's cigarette*) Put it away now.

SISTER ELLA CHAPTER: So I guess it's goodbye.

HANNAH: You'll be all right, Ella, I wasn't ever much of a friend.                                                                       1890

SISTER ELLA CHAPTER: I'll say something but don't laugh, OK? This is the home of saints, the godliest place on earth, they say, and I think they're right. That mean there's no evil here? No. Evil's everywhere. Sin's everywhere. But this . . . is the spring of sweet water in the desert, the desert flower. Every step a Believer takes away from here is a step fraught with peril. I fear for you, Hannah Pitt, because you are my friend. Stay put. This is the right home of saints.

HANNAH: Latter-day saints.

SISTER ELLA CHAPTER: Only kind left.                                        1900

HANNAH: But still. Late in the day . . . for saints and everyone. That's all. That's all.

Fifty thousand dollars for the house, Sister Ella Chapter; don't undersell. It's an impressive view.

### —ACT THREE—
Not-Yet-Conscious, Forward Dawning
January 1986

## SCENE I

*Late night, three days after the end of Act Two. The stage is completely dark. Prior is in bed in his apartment, having a nightmare. He wakes up, sits up and switches on a nightlight. He looks at his clock. Seated by the table near the bed is a man dressed in the clothing of a 13th-century British squire.*

PRIOR: *(Terrified)* Who are you?

PRIOR 1: My name is Prior Walter.

*(Pause.)*

PRIOR: My name is Prior Walter.

PRIOR 1: I know that.

PRIOR: Explain.

1910 PRIOR 1: You're alive. I'm not. We have the same name. What do you want me to explain?

PRIOR: A ghost?

PRIOR 1: An ancestor.

PRIOR: Not *the* Prior Walter? The Bayeux tapestry Prior Walter?

PRIOR 1: His great-great grandson. The fifth of the name.

PRIOR: I'm the thirty-fourth, I think.

PRIOR 1: Actually the thirty-second.

PRIOR: Not according to Mother.

1920 PRIOR 1: She's including the two bastards, then; I say leave them out. I say no room for bastards. The little things you swallow . . .

PRIOR: Pills.

PRIOR 1: Pills. For the pestilence. I too . . .

PRIOR: Pestilence. . . . You too what?

PRIOR 1: The pestilence in my time was much worse than now. Whole villages of empty houses. You could look outdoors and see Death walking in the morning, dew dampening the ragged hem of his black robe. Plain as I see you now.

1930 PRIOR: You died of the plague.

PRIOR 1: The spotty monster. Like you, alone.

PRIOR: I'm not alone.

PRIOR 1: You have no wife, no children.

PRIOR: I'm gay.

PRIOR 1: So? Be gay, dance in your altogether for all I care, what's that to do with not having children?

PRIOR: Gay homosexual, not bonny, blithe and . . . never mind.

PRIOR 1: I had twelve. When I died.

*(The second ghost appears, this one dressed in the clothing of an elegant 17th-century Londoner.)*

PRIOR 1: *(Pointing to Prior 2)* And I was three years younger

1940   than him.

*(Prior sees the new ghost, screams.)*

PRIOR: Oh God another one.

PRIOR 2: Prior Walter. Prior to you by some seventeen others.

PRIOR 1: He's counting the bastards.

PRIOR: Are we having a convention?

PRIOR 2: We've been sent to declare her fabulous incipience. They love a well-paved entrance with lots of heralds, and . . .

PRIOR 1: The messenger come. Prepare the way. The infinite descent, a breath in air . . .

1950 PRIOR 2: They chose us, I suspect, because of the mortal affinities. In a family as long-descended as the Walters there are bound to be a few carried off by plague.

PRIOR 1: The spotty monster.

PRIOR 2: Black Jack. Came from a water pump, half the city of London, can you imagine? His came from fleas. Yours, I understand, is the lamentable consequence of venery . . .

PRIOR 1: Fleas on rats, but who knew that?

PRIOR: Am I going to die?

PRIOR 2: We aren't allowed to discuss . . .

PRIOR 1: When you do, you don't get ancestors to help you 1960 through it. You may be surrounded by children but you die alone.

PRIOR: I'm afraid.

PRIOR 1: You should be. There aren't even torches, and the path's rocky, dark and steep.

PRIOR 2: Don't alarm him. There's good news before there's bad.

We two come to strew rose petal and palm leaf before the triumphal procession. Prophet. Seer. Revelator. It's a great honor for the family.       1970

PRIOR 1: He hasn't got a family.

PRIOR 2: I meant for the Walters, for the family in the larger sense.

PRIOR: *(Singing)*
        All I want is a room somewhere,
        Far away from the cold night air . . .

PRIOR 2: *(Putting a hand on Prior's forehead)* Calm, calm, this is no brain fever . . .

*(Prior calms down, but keeps his eyes closed. The lights begin to change. Distant Glorious Music.)*

PRIOR 1: *(Low chant)*
    Adonai, Adonai,                          1980
    Olam ha-yichud,
    Zefirot, Zazahot,
    Ha-adam, ha-gadol
    Daughter of Light,
    Daughter of Splendors,
    Fluor! Phosphor!
    Lumen! Candle!

PRIOR 2: *(Simultaneously)*
    Even now,
    From the mirror-bright halls of heaven,     1990
    Across the cold and lifeless infinity of space,
    The Messenger comes
    Trailing orbs of light,
    Fabulous, incipient,
    Oh Prophet,
    To you . . .

PRIOR 1 and PRIOR 2:
    Prepare, prepare,
    The Infinite Descent,
    A breath, a feather,                        2000
    Glory to . . .

*(They vanish.)*

## SCENE II

*The next day. Split scene: Louis and Belize in a coffee shop. Prior is at the outpatient clinic at the hospital with Emily, the nurse; she has him on a pentamidine IV drip.*

LOUIS: Why has democracy succeeded in America? Of course by succeeded I mean comparatively, not literally, not in the present, but what makes for the prospect of some sort of radical democracy spreading outward and growing up? Why does the power that was once so carefully preserved at the top of the pyramid by the original framers of the Constitution seem drawn inexorably downward and outward in spite of the best effort of the Right to stop this? I mean it's the re-

2010 ally hard thing about being Left in this country, the American Left can't help but trip over all these petrified little fetishes: freedom, that's the worst; you know, *Jeane Kirkpatrick* for God's sake will go on and on about freedom and so what does that mean, the word freedom, when she talks about it, or human rights; you have Bush talking about human rights, and so what are these people talking about, they might as well be talking about the mating habits of Venusians, these people don't begin to know what, ontologically, freedom is or human rights, like they see these bour-

2020 geois property-based Rights-of-Man-type rights but that's not enfranchisement, not democracy, not what's implicit, what's potential within the idea, not the idea with blood in it. That's just liberalism, the worst kind of liberalism, really, bourgeois tolerance, and what I think is that what AIDS shows us is the limits of tolerance, that it's not enough to be tolerated, because when the shit hits the fan you find out how much tolerance is worth. Nothing. And underneath all the tolerance is intense, passionate hatred.

BELIZE: Uh huh.

2030 LOUIS: Well don't you think that's true?

BELIZE: Uh huh. It is.

LOUIS: *Power* is the object, not being tolerated. Fuck assimilation. But I mean in spite of all this the thing about America, I think, is that ultimately we're different from every other nation on earth, in that, with people here of every race, we can't. . . . Ultimately what defines us isn't race, but politics. Not like any European country where there's an insurmountable fact of a kind of racial, or ethnic, monopoly, or monolith, like all Dutchmen, I mean Dutch people, are

2040 well, Dutch, and the Jews of Europe were never Europeans, just a small problem. Facing the monolith. But here there are so many small problems, it's really just a collection of small problems, the monolith is missing. Oh, I mean, of course I suppose there's the monolith of White America. White Straight Male America.

BELIZE: Which is not unimpressive, even among monoliths.

LOUIS: Well, no, but when the race thing gets taken care of, and I don't mean to minimize how major it is, I mean I know it is, this is a really, really incredibly racist country but

2050 it's like, well, the British. I mean, all these blue-eyed pink people. And it's just weird, you know, I mean I'm not all that Jewish-looking, or . . . well, maybe I am but, you know, in New York, everyone is . . . well, not everyone, but so many are but so but in England, in London I walk into bars and I feel like Sid the Yid, you know I mean like Woody Allen in *Annie Hall,* with the payess and the gabardine coat, like never, never anywhere so much—I mean, not actively despised, not like they're Germans, who I think are still terribly anti-Semitic, and racist too, I mean black-racist, they

2060 pretend otherwise but, anyway, in London, there's just . . . and at one point I met this black gay guy from Jamaica who talked with a lilt but he said his family'd been living in London since before the Civil War—the American one—and how the English never let him forget for a minute that he wasn't blue-eyed and pink and I said yeah, me too, these

people are anti-Semites and he said yeah but the British Jews have the clothing business all sewed up and blacks there can't get a foothold. And it was an incredibly awkward moment of just. . . . I mean here we were, in this bar that was gay but it was a *pub,* you know, the beams and the plaster 2070 and those horrible little, like, two-day-old fish and egg sandwiches—and just so British, so *old,* and I felt, well, there's no way out of this because both of us are, right now, too much immersed in this history, hope is dissolved in the sheer age of this place, where race is what counts and there's no real hope of change—it's the racial destiny of the Brits that matters to them, not their political destiny, whereas in America . . .

BELIZE: Here in America race doesn't count.

LOUIS: No, no, that's not. . . . I mean you *can't* be hearing 2080 that . . .

BELIZE: I . . .

LOUIS: It's—look, race, yes, but ultimately race here is a political question, right? Racists just try to use race here as a tool in a political struggle. It's not really about race. Like the spiritualists try to use that stuff, are you enlightened, are you centered, channeled, whatever, this reaching out for a spiritual past in a country where no indigenous spirits exist—only the Indians, I mean Native American spirits and we killed them off so now, there are no gods here, no ghosts and 2090 spirits in America, there are no angels in America, no spiritual past, no racial past, there's only the political, and the decoys and the ploys to maneuver around the inescapable battle of politics, the shifting downwards and outwards of political power to the people . . .

BELIZE: POWER to the People! AMEN! (*Looking at his watch*) OH MY GOODNESS! Will you look at the time, I gotta . . .

LOUIS: Do you. . . . You think this is, what, racist or naive or something? 2100

BELIZE: Well it's certainly *something.* Look, I just remembered I have an appointment . . .

LOUIS: What? I mean I really don't want to, like, speak from some position of privilege and . . .

BELIZE: I'm sitting here, thinking, eventually he's *got* to run out of steam, so I let you rattle on and on saying about maybe seven or eight things I find really offensive.

LOUIS: What?

BELIZE: But I know you, Louis, and I know the guilt fueling this peculiar tirade is obviously already swollen bigger than your 2110 hemorrhoids.

LOUIS: I don't have hemorrhoids.

BELIZE: I hear different. May I finish?

LOUIS: Yes, but I don't have hemorrhoids.

BELIZE: So finally, when I . . .

LOUIS: Prior told you, he's an asshole, he shouldn't have . . .

BELIZE: You promised, Louis. Prior is not a subject.

LOUIS: You brought him up.

BELIZE: I brought up hemorrhoids.

LOUIS: So it's indirect. Passive-aggressive. 2120

BELIZE: Unlike, I suppose, banging me over the head with your theory that America doesn't have a race problem.

LOUIS: Oh be fair I never said that.

BELIZE: Not exactly, but . . .

LOUIS: I said . . .

BELIZE: . . . but it was close enough, because if it'd been that blunt I'd've just walked out and . . .

LOUIS: You deliberately misinterpreted! I . . .

BELIZE: Stop interrupting! I haven't been able to . . .

2130 LOUIS: Just let me . . .

BELIZE: NO! What, *talk?* You've been running your mouth nonstop since I got here, yaddadda yaddadda blah blah blah, up the hill, down the hill, playing with your MONO-LITH . . .

LOUIS: (*Overlapping*) Well, you could have joined in at any time instead of . . .

BELIZE: (*Continuing over Louis*) . . . and girlfriend it is truly an *awesome* spectacle but I got better things to do with my time than sit here listening to this racist bullshit just because

2140 I feel sorry for you that . . .

LOUIS: I am not a racist!

BELIZE: Oh come on . . .

LOUIS: So maybe I am a racist but . . .

BELIZE: Oh I really hate that! It's no fun picking on you Louis; you're so guilty, it's like throwing darts at a glob of jello, there's no satisfying hits, just quivering, the darts just blop in and vanish.

LOUIS: I just think when you are discussing lines of oppression it gets very complicated and . . .

2150 BELIZE: Oh is that a fact? You know, we black drag queens have a rather intimate knowledge of the complexity of the lines of . . .

LOUIS: *Ex*-black drag queen.

BELIZE: Actually ex-ex.

LOUIS: You're doing drag again?

BELIZE: I don't. . . . Maybe. I don't have to tell you. Maybe.

LOUIS: I think it's sexist.

BELIZE: I didn't ask you.

LOUIS: Well it is. The gay community, I think, has to adopt the

2160 same attitude towards drag as black women have to take to-wards black women blues singers.

BELIZE: Oh my we *are* walking dangerous tonight.

LOUIS: Well, it's all internalized oppression, right, I mean the masochism, the stereotypes, the . . .

BELIZE: Louis, are you deliberately trying to make me hate you?

LOUIS: No, I . . .

BELIZE: I mean, are you deliberately transforming yourself into an arrogant, sexual-political Stalinist-slash-racist flag-wav-

2170 ing thug for my benefit?

(*Pause.*)

LOUIS: You know what I think?

BELIZE: What?

LOUIS: You hate me because I'm a Jew.

BELIZE: I'm leaving.

LOUIS: It's true.

BELIZE: You have no basis except your . . .

Louis, it's good to know you haven't changed; you are still an honorary citizen of the Twilight Zone, and after your pale, pale white polemics on behalf of racial insensitivity you have

2180 a flaming *fuck* of a lot of nerve calling me an anti-Semite. Now I really gotta go.

LOUIS: You called me Lou the Jew.

BELIZE: That was a joke.

LOUIS: I didn't think it was funny. It was hostile.

BELIZE: It was three years ago.

LOUIS: So?

BELIZE: You just called yourself Sid the Yid.

LOUIS: That's not the same thing.

BELIZE: Sid the Yid is different from Lou the Jew.

LOUIS: Yes. 2190

BELIZE: Someday you'll have to explain that to me, but right now . . .
*You* hate me because you hate black people.

LOUIS: I do not. But I do think most black people are anti-Se-mitic.

BELIZE: "Most black people." *That's* racist, Louis, and *I* think most Jews . . .

LOUIS: Louis Farrakhan.

BELIZE: Ed Koch.

LOUIS: Jesse Jackson. 2200

BELIZE: Jackson. Oh really, Louis, this is . . .

LOUIS: Hymietown! Hymietown!

BELIZE: Louis, you voted for Jesse Jackson. You send checks to the Rainbow Coalition.

LOUIS: I'm ambivalent. The checks bounced.

BELIZE: All your checks bounce, Louis; you're ambivalent about everything.

LOUIS: What's that supposed to mean?

BELIZE: You may be dumber than shit but I refuse to believe you can't figure it out. Try. 2210

LOUIS: I was never ambivalent about Prior. I love him. I do. I really do.

BELIZE: Nobody said different.

LOUIS: Love and ambivalence are. . . . Real love isn't ambiva-lent.

BELIZE: "Real love isn't ambivalent." I'd swear that's a line from my favorite bestselling paperback novel, *In Love with the Night Mysterious*, except I don't think you ever read it.

(*Pause.*)

LOUIS: I never read it, no.

BELIZE: You ought to. Instead of spending the rest of your life 2220 trying to get through *Democracy in America*. It's about this white woman whose Daddy owns a plantation in the Deep South in the years before the Civil War—the American one—and her name is Margaret, and she's in love with her Daddy's number-one slave, and his name is Thaddeus, and she's married but her white slave-owner husband has AIDS: Antebellum Insufficiently Developed Sexorgans. And there's a lot of hot stuff going down when Margaret and Thaddeus can catch a spare torrid ten under the cotton-picking moon, and then of course the Yankees come, and 2230 they set the slaves free, and the slaves string up old Daddy, and so on. Historical fiction. Somewhere in there I recall Margaret and Thaddeus find the time to discuss the nature of love; her face is reflecting the flames of the burning plan-tation—you know, the way white people do—and his black face is dark in the night and she says to him, "Thaddeus, real love isn't ever ambivalent."

(*Little pause. Emily enters and turns off IV drip.*)

BELIZE: Thaddeus looks at her; he's contemplating her thesis; and he isn't sure he agrees.

EMILY: (*Removing IV drip from Prior's arm*) Treatment num- 2240 ber . . . (*Consulting chart*) four.

PRIOR: Pharmaceutical miracle. Lazarus breathes again.

LOUIS: Is he. . . . How bad is he?

BELIZE: You want the laundry list?

EMILY: Shirt off, let's check the . . .

*(Prior takes his shirt off. She examines his lesions.)*

BELIZE: There's the weight problem and the shit problem and the morale problem.

EMILY: Only six. That's good. Pants.

*(He drops his pants. He's naked. She examines.)*

BELIZE: And. He thinks he's going crazy.

2250 EMILY: Looking good. What else?

PRIOR: Ankles sore and swollen, but the leg's better. The nausea's mostly gone with the little orange pills. BM's pure liquid but not bloody anymore, for now, my eye doctor says everything's OK, for now, my dentist says "Yuck!" when he sees my fuzzy tongue, and now he wears little condoms on his thumb and forefinger. And a mask. So what? My dermatologist is in Hawaii and my mother . . . well leave my mother out of it. Which is usually where my mother is, out of it. My glands are like walnuts, my weight's holding steady
2260 for week two, and a friend died two days ago of bird tuberculosis; bird tuberculosis; that scared me and I didn't go to the funeral today because he was an Irish Catholic and it's probably open casket and I'm afraid of . . . something, the bird TB or seeing him or. . . . So I guess I'm doing OK. Except for of course I'm going nuts.

EMILY: We ran the toxoplasmosis series and there's no indication . . .

PRIOR: I know, I know, but I feel like something terrifying is on its way, you know, like a missile from outer space, and it's
2270 plummeting down towards the earth, and I'm ground zero, and . . . I am generally known where I am known as one cool, collected queen. And I am ruffled.

EMILY: There's really nothing to worry about. I think that shochen bamromim hamtzeh menucho nechono al kanfey haschino.

PRIOR: What?

EMILY: Everything's fine. Bemaalos k'doshim ut'horim kezohar horokeea mazhirim . . .

PRIOR: Oh I don't understand what you're . . .

2280 EMILY: Es nishmas Prior sheholoch leolomoh, baavur shenodvoo z'dokoh b'ad hazkoras nishmosoh.

PRIOR: Why are you doing that?! Stop it! Stop it!

EMILY: Stop what?

PRIOR: You were just . . . weren't you just speaking in Hebrew or something.

EMILY: *Hebrew?* *(Laughs)* I'm basically Italian-American. No. I didn't speak in Hebrew.

PRIOR: Oh no, oh God please I really think I . . .

EMILY: Look, I'm sorry, I have a waiting room full of. . . . I think
2290 you're one of the lucky ones, you'll live for years, probably—you're pretty healthy for someone with no immune system. Are you seeing someone? Loneliness is a danger. A therapist?

PRIOR: No, I don't need to see anyone, I just . . .

EMILY: Well think about it. You aren't going crazy. You're just under a lot of stress. No wonder . . . *(She starts to write in his chart)*

*(Suddenly there is an astonishing blaze of light, a huge chord sounded by a gigantic choir, and a great book with steel pages mounted atop a molten-red pillar pops up from the stage floor. The book opens; there is a large Aleph inscribed on its pages, which bursts into flames. Immediately the book slams shut and disappears instantly under the floor as the lights become normal again. Emily notices none of this, writing. Prior is agog.)*

EMILY: *(Laughing, exiting)* Hebrew . . .

*(Prior flees.)*

LOUIS: Help me.

BELIZE: I beg your pardon?    2300

LOUIS: You're a nurse, give me something, I . . . don't know what to do anymore, I. . . . Last week at work I screwed up the Xerox machine like permanently and so I . . . then I tripped on the subway steps and my glasses broke and I cut my forehead, here, see, and now I can't see much and my forehead . . . it's like the Mark of Cain, stupid, right, but it won't heal and every morning I see it and I think, Biblical things, Mark of Cain, Judas Iscariot and his silver and his noose, people who . . . in betraying what they love betray what's truest in themselves, I feel . . . nothing but cold for 2310 myself, just cold, and every night I miss him, I miss him so much but then . . . those sores, and the smell and . . . where I thought it was going. . . . I could be . . . I could be sick too, maybe I'm sick too. I don't know.
Belize. Tell him I love him. Can you do that?

BELIZE: I've thought about it for a very long time, and I still don't understand what love is. Justice is simple. Democracy is simple. Those things are unambivalent. But love is very hard. And it goes bad for you if you violate the hard law of love.    2320

LOUIS: I'm dying.

BELIZE: He's dying. You just wish you were. Oh cheer up, Louis. Look at that heavy sky out there.

LOUIS: Purple.

BELIZE: *Purple?* Boy, what kind of a homosexual are you, anyway? That's not purple, Mary, that color up there is *(Very grand)* mauve.
All day today it's felt like Thanksgiving. Soon, this . . . ruination will be blanketed white. You can smell it—can you smell it?    2330

LOUIS: Smell what?

BELIZE: Softness, compliance, forgiveness, grace.

LOUIS: No . . .

BELIZE: I can't help you learn that. I can't help you, Louis. You're not my business. *(He exits)*

*(Louis puts his head in his hands, inadvertently touching his cut forehead.)*

LOUIS: Ow FUCK! *(He stands slowly, looks towards where Belize exited)* Smell what?
*(He looks both ways to be sure no one is watching, then inhales deeply, and is surprised)* Huh. Snow.

SCENE III

*Same day. Harper in a very white, cold place, with a brilliant blue sky above; a delicate snowfall. She is dressed in a beauti-*

*ful snowsuit. The sound of the sea, faint.*

2340 HARPER: Snow! Ice! Mountains of ice! Where am I? I . . . I feel better, I do, I . . . feel better. There are ice crystals in my lungs, wonderful and sharp. And the snow smells like cold, crushed peaches. And there's something . . . some current of blood in the wind, how strange, it has that iron taste.

MR. LIES: Ozone.

HARPER: Ozone! Wow! Where am I?

MR. LIES: The Kingdom of Ice, the bottommost part of the world.

HARPER: (*Looking around, then realizing*) Antarctica. This is
2350 Antarctica!

MR. LIES: Cold shelter for the shattered. No sorrow here, tears freeze.

HARPER: Antarctica, Antarctica, oh boy oh boy, LOOK at this, I. . . . Wow, I must've really snapped the tether, huh?

MR. LIES: Apparently . . .

HARPER: That's great. I want to stay here forever. Set up camp. Build things. Build a city, an enormous city made up of frontier forts, dark wood and green roofs and high gates made of pointed logs and bonfires burning on every street corner. I
2360 should build by a river. Where are the forests?

MR. LIES: No timber here. Too cold. Ice, no trees.

HARPER: Oh details! I'm sick of details! I'll plant them and grow them. I'll live off caribou fat, I'll melt it over the bonfires and drink it from long, curved goat-horn cups. It'll be great. I want to make a new world here. So that I never have to go home again.

MR. LIES: As long as it lasts. Ice has a way of melting . . .

HARPER: No. Forever. I can have anything I want here—maybe even companionship, someone who has . . . desire for
2370 me. You, maybe.

MR. LIES: It's against the by-laws of the International Order of Travel Agents to get involved with clients. Rules are rules. Anyway, I'm not the one you really want.

HARPER: There isn't anyone . . . maybe an Eskimo. Who could ice-fish for food. And help me build a nest for when the baby comes.

MR. LIES: There are no Eskimo in Antarctica. And you're not really pregnant. You made that up.

HARPER: Well all of this is made up. So if the snow feels cold
2380 I'm pregnant. Right? Here, I can be pregnant. And I can have any kind of a baby I want.

MR. LIES: This is a retreat, a vacuum, its virtue is that it lacks everything; deep-freeze for feelings. You can be numb and safe here, that's what you came for. Respect the delicate ecology of your delusions.

HARPER: You mean like no Eskimo in Antarctica.

MR. LIES: Correcto. Ice and snow, no Eskimo. Even hallucinations have laws.

HARPER: Well then who's that?

(*The Eskimo appears.*)

2390 MR. LIES: An Eskimo.

HARPER: An antarctic Eskimo. A fisher of the polar deep.

MR. LIES: There's something wrong with this picture.

(*The Eskimo beckons.*)

HARPER: I'm going to like this place. It's my own National

Geographic Special! Oh! Oh! (*She holds her stomach*) I think . . . I think I felt her kicking. Maybe I'll give birth to a baby covered with thick white fur, and that way she won't be cold. My breasts will be full of hot cocoa so she doesn't get chilly. And if it gets really cold, she'll have a pouch I can crawl into. Like a marsupial. We'll mend together. That's what we'll do; we'll mend.                                             2400

SCENE IV

*Same day. An abandoned lot in the South Bronx. A homeless Woman is standing near an oil drum in which a fire is burning. Snowfall. Trash around. Hannah enters dragging two heavy suitcases.*

HANNAH: Excuse me? I said excuse me? Can you tell me where I am? Is this Brooklyn? Do you know a Pineapple Street? Is there some sort of bus or train or . . . ?
I'm lost, I just arrived from Salt Lake. City. Utah? I took the bus that I was told to take and I got off—well it was the very last stop, so I had to get off, and I *asked* the driver was this Brooklyn, and he nodded yes but he was from one of those foreign countries where they think it's good manners to nod at everything even if you have no idea what it is you're nodding at, and in truth I think he spoke no English at all, which    2410 I think would make him ineligible for employment on public transportation. The public being English-speaking, mostly. Do you speak English?

(*The Woman nods.*)

HANNAH: I was supposed to be met at the airport by my son. He didn't show and I don't wait more than three and three-quarters hours for *anyone*. I should have been patient, I guess, I. . . . Is this . . .

WOMAN: Bronx.

HANNAH: Is that. . . . The *Bronx?* Well how in the name of Heaven did I get to the Bronx when the bus driver said . . .   2420

WOMAN: (*Talking to herself*) Slurp slurp slurp will you STOP that disgusting slurping! YOU DISGUSTING SLURPING FEEDING ANIMAL! Feeding yourself, just feeding yourself, what would it matter, to you or to ANYONE, if you just stopped. Feeding. And DIED?

(*Pause.*)

HANNAH: Can you just tell me where I . . .

WOMAN: Why was the Kosciusko Bridge named after a Polack?

HANNAH: I don't know what you're . . .

WOMAN: That was a joke.

HANNAH: Well what's the punchline?                                    2430

WOMAN: I don't know.

HANNAH: (*Looking around desperately*) Oh for pete's sake, is there anyone else who . . .

WOMAN: (*Again, to herself*) Stand further off you fat loathsome whore, you can't have any more of this soup, slurp slurp slurp you animal, and the—I know you'll just go pee it all away and where will you do that? Behind what bush? It's FUCKING COLD out here and I . . .
Oh that's right, because it was supposed to have been a tunnel!                                                                      2440
That's not very funny.

Have you read the prophecies of Nostradamus?

HANNAH: Who?

WOMAN: Some guy I went out with once somewhere, Nostradamus. Prophet, outcast, eyes like. . . . Scary shit, he . . .

HANNAH: Shut up. Please. Now I want you to stop jabbering for a minute and pull your wits together and tell me how to get to Brooklyn. Because you know! And you are going to tell me! Because there is no one else around to tell me and I am 2450 wet and cold and I am very angry! So I am sorry you're psychotic but just make the effort—take a deep breath—DO IT!

*(Hannah and the Woman breathe together.)*

HANNAH: That's good. Now exhale.

*(They do.)*

HANNAH: Good. Now how do I get to Brooklyn?

WOMAN: Don't know. Never been. Sorry. Want some soup?

HANNAH: Manhattan? Maybe you know . . . I don't suppose you know the location of the Mormon Visitor's . . .

WOMAN: 65th and Broadway.

HANNAH: How do you . . .

2460 WOMAN: Go there all the time. Free movies. Boring, but you can stay all day.

HANNAH: Well. . . . So how do I . . .

WOMAN: Take the D Train. Next block make a right.

HANNAH: Thank you.

WOMAN: Oh yeah. In the new century I think we will all be insane.

SCENE V

*Same day. Joe and Roy in the study of Roy's brownstone. Roy is wearing an elegant bathrobe. He has made a considerable effort to look well. He isn't well, and he hasn't succeeded much in looking it.*

JOE: I can't. The answer's no. I'm sorry.

ROY: Oh, well, apologies . . .

I can't see that there's anyone asking for apologies.

*(Pause.)*

2470 JOE: I'm sorry, Roy.

ROY: Oh, well, apologies.

JOE: My wife is missing, Roy. My mother's coming from Salt Lake to . . . to help look, I guess. I'm supposed to be at the airport now, picking her up but. . . . I just spent two days in a hospital, Roy, with a bleeding ulcer, I was spitting up blood.

ROY: Blood, huh? Look, I'm very busy here and . . .

JOE: It's just a job.

ROY: A job? A *job? Washington!* Dumb Utah Mormon hick 2480 shit!

JOE: Roy . . .

ROY: *WASHINGTON!* When Washington called me I was younger than you, you think I said "Aw fuck no I can't go I got two fingers up my asshole and a little moral nosebleed to boot!" When Washington calls you my pretty young punk friend you go or you can go fuck yourself sideways 'cause the train has pulled out of the station, and you are *out*, nowhere,

out in the cold. Fuck you, Mary Jane, get outta here.

JOE: Just let me . . .

ROY: Explain? Ephemera. You broke my heart. Explain that. 2490 Explain that.

JOE: I love you. Roy.

There's so much that I want, to be . . . what you see in me, I want to be a participant in the world, in your world, Roy, I want to be capable of that, I've tried, really I have but . . . I can't do this. Not because I don't believe in you, but because I believe in you so much, in what you stand for, at heart, the order, the decency. I would give anything to protect you, but. . . . There are laws I can't break. It's too ingrained. It's not me. There's enough damage I've already done. 2500 Maybe you were right, maybe I'm dead.

ROY: You're not dead, boy, you're a sissy.

You love me; that's moving, I'm moved. It's nice to be loved. I warned you about her, didn't I, Joe? But you don't listen to me, why, because you say Roy is smart and Roy's a friend but Roy . . . well, he isn't nice, and you wanna be nice. Right? A nice, nice man!

*(Little pause)*

You know what my greatest accomplishment was, Joe, in my life, what I am able to look back on and be proudest of? And I have helped make Presidents and unmake them and may- 2510 ors and more goddam judges than anyone in NYC ever— AND several million dollars, tax-free—and what do you think means the most to me?

You ever hear of Ethel Rosenberg? Huh, Joe, huh?

JOE: Well, yeah, I guess I. . . . Yes.

ROY: Yes. Yes. You have heard of Ethel Rosenberg. Yes. Maybe you even read about her in the history books.

If it wasn't for me, Joe, Ethel Rosenberg would be alive today, writing some personal-advice column for *Ms.* magazine. She isn't. Because during the trial, Joe, I was on the 2520 phone every day, talking with the judge . . .

JOE: Roy . . .

ROY: Every day, doing what I do best, talking on the telephone, making sure that timid Yid nebbish on the bench did his duty to America, to history. That sweet unprepossessing woman, two kids, boo-hoo-hoo, reminded us all of our little Jewish mamas—she came this close to getting life; I pleaded till I wept to put her in the chair. Me. I did that. I would have fucking pulled the switch if they'd have let me. Why? Because I fucking hate traitors. Because I fucking 2530 hate communists. Was it legal? Fuck legal. Am I a nice man? Fuck nice. They say terrible things about me in the *Nation.* Fuck the *Nation.* You want to be Nice, or you want to be Effective? Make the law, or subject to it. Choose. Your wife chose. A week from today, she'll be back. SHE knows how to get what SHE wants. Maybe I ought to send *her* to Washington.

JOE: I don't believe you.

ROY: Gospel.

JOE: You can't possibly mean what you're saying. 2540

Roy, you were the Assistant United States Attorney on the Rosenberg case, ex-parte communication with the judge during the trial would be . . . censurable, at least, probably conspiracy and . . . in a case that resulted in execution, it's . . .

ROY: What? Murder?

JOE: You're not well is all.

ROY: What do you mean, not well? Who's not well?

(*Pause.*)

JOE: You said . . .

2550  ROY: No I didn't. I said what?

JOE: Roy, you have cancer.

ROY: No I don't.

(*Pause.*)

JOE: You told me you were dying.

ROY: What the fuck are you talking about, Joe? I never said that. I'm in perfect health. There's not a goddam thing wrong with me.

(*He smiles*)

Shake?

(*Joe hesitates. He holds out his hand to Roy. Roy pulls Joe into a close, strong clinch.*)

ROY: (*More to himself than to Joe*) It's OK that you hurt me because I love you, baby Joe. That's why I'm so rough on you.

(*Roy releases Joe. Joe backs away a step or two.*)

2560  ROY: Prodigal son. The world will wipe its dirty hands all over you.

JOE: It already has, Roy.

ROY: Now go.

(*Roy shoves Joe, hard. Joe turns to leave. Roy stops him, turns him around.*)

ROY: (*Smoothing Joe's lapels, tenderly*) I'll always be here, waiting for you . . .

(*Then again, with sudden violence, he pulls Joe close, violently*)

What did you want from me, what was all this, what do you want, treacherous ungrateful little . . .

(*Joe, very close to belting Roy, grabs him by the front of his robe, and propels him across the length of the room. He holds Roy at arm's length, the other arm ready to hit.*)

ROY: (*Laughing softly, almost pleading to be hit*) Transgress a little, Joseph.

(*Joe releases Roy.*)

2570  ROY: There are so many laws; find one you can break.

(*Joe hesitates, then leaves, backing out. When Joe has gone, Roy doubles over in great pain, which he's been hiding throughout the scene with Joe.*)

ROY: Ah, Christ . . .
   Andy! Andy! Get in here! Andy!

(*The door opens, but it isn't Andy. A small Jewish Woman dressed modestly in a fifties hat and coat stands in the doorway. The room darkens.*)

ROY: Who the fuck are you? The new nurse?

(*The figure in the doorway says nothing. She stares at Roy. A pause. Roy looks at her carefully, gets up, crosses to her. He crosses back to the chair, sits heavily.*)

ROY: Aw, fuck. Ethel.

ETHEL ROSENBERG: (*Her manner is friendly, her voice is ice-cold*) You don't look good, Roy.

ROY: Well, Ethel. I don't feel good.

ETHEL ROSENBERG: But you lost a lot of weight. That suits you. You were heavy back then. Zaftig, mit hips.

ROY: I haven't been that heavy since 1960. We were all heavier 2580 back then, before the body thing started. Now I look like a skeleton. They stare.

ETHEL ROSENBERG: The shit's really hit the fan, huh, Roy?

(*Little pause. Roy nods.*)

ETHEL ROSENBERG: Well the fun's just started.

ROY: What is this, Ethel, Halloween? You trying to scare me?

(*Ethel says nothing.*)

ROY: Well you're wasting your time! I'm scarier than you any day of the week! So beat it, Ethel! BOOO! BETTER DEAD THAN RED! Somebody trying to shake me up? HAH HAH! From the throne of God in heaven to the belly of hell, you can all fuck yourselves and then go jump in the lake be- 2590 cause I'M NOT AFRAID OF YOU OR DEATH OR HELL OR ANYTHING!

ETHEL ROSENBERG: Be seeing you soon, Roy. Julius sends his regards.

ROY: Yeah, well send this to Julius!

(*He flips the bird in her direction, stands and moves towards her. Halfway across the room he slumps to the floor, breathing laboriously, in pain.*)

ETHEL ROSENBERG: You're a very sick man, Roy.

ROY: Oh God . . . ANDY!

ETHEL ROSENBERG: Hmmm. He doesn't hear you, I guess. We should call the ambulance.

(*She goes to the phone*)

Hah! Buttons! Such things they got now.      2600
What do I dial, Roy?

(*Pause. Roy looks at her, then:*)

ROY: 911.

ETHEL ROSENBERG: (*Dials the phone*) It sings!
   (*Imitating dial tones*) La la la . . .
   Huh.
   Yes, you should please send an ambulance to the home of Mister Roy Cohn, the famous lawyer.
   What's the address, Roy?

ROY: (*A beat, then*) 244 East 87th.

ETHEL ROSENBERG: 244 East 87th Street. No apartment num- 2610 ber, he's got the whole building.
   My name? (*A beat*) Ethel Greenglass Rosenberg.
   (*Small smile*) Me? No I'm not related to Mr. Cohn. An old friend.

(*She hangs up*)

They said a minute.

ROY: I have all the time in the world.

ETHEL ROSENBERG: You're immortal.

ROY: I'm immortal. Ethel. *(He forces himself to stand)*
I have *forced* my way into history. I ain't never gonna die.

2620 ETHEL ROSENBERG: *(A little laugh, then)* History is about to
crack wide open. Millennium approaches.

SCENE VI

*Late that night. Prior's bedroom. Prior 1 watching Prior in
bed, who is staring back at him, terrified. Tonight Prior 1 is
dressed in weird alchemical robes and hat over his historical
clothing and he carries a long palm-leaf bundle.*

PRIOR 1: Tonight's the night! Aren't you excited? Tonight she
arrives! Right through the roof! Ha-adam, Ha-gadol . . .

PRIOR 2: *(Appearing, similarly attired)* Lumen! Phosphor!
Fluor! Candle! An unending billowing of scarlet and . . .

PRIOR: Look. Garlic. A mirror. Holy water. A crucifix. FUCK
OFF! Get the fuck out of my room! GO!

PRIOR 1: *(To Prior 2)* Hard as a hickory knob, I'll bet.

PRIOR 2: We all tumesce when they approach. We wax full, like
2630    moons.

PRIOR 1: Dance.

PRIOR: Dance?

PRIOR 1: Stand up, dammit, give us your hands, dance!

PRIOR 2: Listen . . .

*(A lone oboe begins to play a little dance tune.)*

PRIOR 2: Delightful sound. Care to dance?

PRIOR: Please leave me alone, please just let me sleep . . .

PRIOR 2: Ah, he wants someone familiar. A partner who knows
his steps. *(To Prior)* Close your eyes. Imagine . . .

PRIOR: I don't . . .

2640 PRIOR 2: Hush. Close your eyes.

*(Prior does.)*

PRIOR 2: Now open them.

*(Prior does. Louis appears. He looks gorgeous. The music
builds gradually into a full-blooded, romantic dance tune.)*

PRIOR: Lou.

LOUIS: Dance with me.

PRIOR: I can't, my leg, it hurts at night . . .
Are you . . . a ghost, Lou?

LOUIS: No. Just spectral. Lost to myself. Sitting all day on cold
park benches. Wishing I could be with you. Dance with me,
babe . . .

*(Prior stands up. The leg stops hurting. They begin to dance.
The music is beautiful.)*

PRIOR 1: *(To Prior 2)* Hah. Now I see why he's got no children.
2650    He's a sodomite.

PRIOR 2: Oh be quiet, you medieval gnome, and let them
dance.

PRIOR 1: I'm not interfering, I've done my bit. Hooray, hooray,
the messenger's come, now I'm blowing off. I don't like it
here.

*(Prior 1 vanishes.)*

PRIOR 2: The twentieth century. Oh dear, the world has gotten

so terribly, terribly old.

*(Prior 2 vanishes. Louis and Prior waltz happily. Lights fade
back to normal. Louis vanishes.*

*Prior dances alone.*

*Then suddenly, the sound of wings fills the room.)*

SCENE VII

*Split scene: Prior alone in his apartment; Louis alone in the
park.*

*Again, a sound of beating wings.*

PRIOR: Oh don't come in here don't come in . . . LOUIS!! No.
My name is Prior Walter, I am . . . the scion of an ancient
line, I am . . . abandoned I . . . no, my name is . . . is . . . Prior  2660
and I live . . . *here and now,* and . . . in the dark, in the dark,
the Recording Angel opens its hundred eyes and snaps the
spine of the Book of Life and . . . hush! Hush!
I'm talking nonsense, I . . .
No more mad scene, hush, hush . . .

*(Louis in the park on a bench. Joe approaches, stands at a dis-
tance. They stare at each other, then Louis turns away.)*

LOUIS: Do you know the story of Lazarus?

JOE: Lazarus?

LOUIS: Lazarus. I can't remember what happens, exactly.

JOE: I don't. . . . Well, he was dead, Lazarus, and Jesus
breathed life into him. He brought him back from death.   2670

LOUIS: Come here often?

JOE: No. Yes. Yes.

LOUIS: Back from the dead. You believe that really happened?

JOE: I don't know anymore what I believe.

LOUIS: This is quite a coincidence. Us meeting.

JOE: I followed you.
From work. I . . . followed you here.

*(Pause.)*

LOUIS: You followed me.
You probably saw me that day in the washroom and thought:
there's a sweet guy, sensitive, cries for friends in trouble.   2680

JOE: Yes.

LOUIS: You thought maybe I'll cry for you.

JOE: Yes.

LOUIS: Well I fooled you. Crocodile tears. Nothing . . . *(He
touches his heart, shrugs)*

*(Joe reaches tentatively to touch Louis's face.)*

LOUIS: *(Pulling back)* What are you doing? Don't do that.

JOE: *(Withdrawing his hand)* Sorry. I'm sorry.

LOUIS: I'm . . . just not . . . I think, if you touch me, your hand
might fall off or something. Worse things have happened to
people who have touched me.   2690

JOE: Please.
Oh, boy . . .
Can I . . .
I . . . want . . . to touch you. Can I please just touch you . . .
um, here?

*(He puts his hand on one side of Louis's face. He holds it there)*

I'm going to hell for doing this.

LOUIS: Big deal. You think it could be any worse than New York City?

*(He puts his hand on Joe's hand. He takes Joe's hand away* 2700 *from his face, holds it for a moment, then)* Come on.

JOE: Where?

LOUIS: Home. With me.

JOE: This makes no sense. I mean I don't know you.

LOUIS: Likewise.

JOE: And what you do know about me you don't like.

LOUIS: The Republican stuff?

JOE: Yeah, well for starters.

LOUIS: I don't not like that. I *hate* that.

JOE: So why on earth should we . . .

*(Louis goes to Joe and kisses him.)*

2710 LOUIS: Strange bedfellows. I don't know. I never made it with one of the damned before.

I would really rather not have to spend tonight alone.

JOE: I'm a pretty terrible person, Louis.

LOUIS: Lou.

JOE: No, I really really am. I don't think I deserve being loved.

LOUIS: There? See? We already have a lot in common.

*(Louis stands, begins to walk away. He turns, looks back at Joe. Joe follows. They exit.)*

*(Prior listens. At first no sound, then once again, the sound of beating wings, frighteningly near.)*

PRIOR: That sound, that sound, it. . . . What is that, like birds or something, like a *really* big bird, I'm frightened, I . . . no, no fear, find the anger, find the . . . anger, my blood is clean, my 2720 brain is fine, I can handle pressure, I am a gay man and I am used to pressure, to trouble, I am tough and strong and. . . .

Oh. Oh my goodness. I . . . *(He is washed over by an intense sexual feeling)* Ooohhhh. . . . I'm hot, I'm . . . so . . . aw Jeez what is going on here I . . . must have a fever I . . .

*(The bedside lamp flickers wildly as the bed begins to roll forward and back. There is a deep bass creaking and groaning from the bedroom ceiling, like the timbers of a ship under immense stress, and from above a fine rain of plaster dust.)*

PRIOR: OH!

PLEASE, OH PLEASE! Something's coming in here, I'm scared, I don't like this at all, something's approaching and I. . . . OH!

*(There is a great blaze of triumphal music, heralding. The light turns an extraordinary harsh, cold, pale blue, then a rich, brilliant warm golden color, then a hot, bilious green, and then finally a spectacular royal purple. Then silence.)*

PRIOR: *(An awestruck whisper)* God almighty . . .

*Very* Steven Spielberg.

*(A sound, like a plummeting meteor, tears down from very, very far above the earth, hurtling at an incredible velocity towards the bedroom; the light seems to be sucked out of the room as the projectile approaches; as the room reaches darkness, we hear a terrifying CRASH as something immense strikes earth; the whole building shudders and a part of the bedroom ceiling, lots of plaster and lathe and wiring, crashes to the floor. And then in a shower of unearthly white light, spreading great opalescent gray-silver wings, the Angel descends into the room and floats above the bed.)*

ANGEL:                                                                        2730

Greetings, Prophet;

The Great Work begins:

The Messenger has arrived.

*(Blackout.)*

**END OF PART ONE**

---

*HILARY de Vries published this article/interview in the* Los Angeles Times *on the eve of the opening of* Millennium Approaches *at the Mark Taper Forum in Los Angeles.*

Four years ago, when Tony Kushner began to write "Angels in America," he was a relatively unknown playwright attempting to address "some of the issues I felt about being gay in America at the time."

It was a modest, if timely, ambition, and given Kushner's brief résumé one might have expected similarly modest results. His only previously produced work, "A Bright Room Called Day," a drama about Weimar Germany, had received a single professional production—a run at London's Bush Theatre that the playwright called "a catastrophe."

That "Angels in America" opens next Sunday at the Mark Taper Forum as possibly the most anticipated play of the year, and its 36-year-old author regarded as the most talented American dramatist since David Mamet, is testimony to Kushner's immodest vision.

The play—in two parts, "Millennium Approaches" and "Perestroika," which will be performed in repertory through Nov. 29—is a seven-hour examination of Reagan-era ethics that addresses such diverse topics as AIDS, Mormonism and the fall of communism. Already critics have hailed it as a significant step beyond the usual kitchen-sink concerns of much contemporary American drama.

## Tony Kushner

"A Playwright Spreads His Wings"
(1992)

*Interview*

During a sold-out run of the play's first half in London last season, Michael Billington, theater critic of the Guardian, wrote that "unlike most American dramatists, [Kushner] is unafraid to link private and public worlds . . . ["Millennium Approaches"] is a play of epic energy that gets American drama not just out of the closet but, thank God, out of the living room as well."

Frank Rich, the New York Times' theater critic, called the same production "a radical rethinking of the whole aesthetic of American political drama."

At first reading, "Angels in America" is a complex, and complicated, interweaving of wildly divergent protagonists, real and imagined—a homosexual couple, a married couple, the infamous New York defense attorney Roy Cohn, the ghost of convicted Cold War traitor Ethel Rosenberg, and Mr. Lies, a travel agent who just might be the product of a Valium-induced hallucination. Also making an appearance are the angels alluded to in the title, who lend an apocalyptic tone to the play's otherwise unholy alliances.

But on a deeper level, Kushner's work, which is subtitled "A Gay Fantasia on National Themes," is a clear-eyed, insightful examination of the political, social and moral forces shaping America during the latter half of the 20th Century—namely the decline of communism and the rising political power of the gay movement, two events that demonstrate what the playwright has called "the end of containment as ideology."

Indeed, to label "Angels in America" an AIDS play is to miss Kushner's larger, more ambitious concerns. Coming seven years after Larry Kramer's seminal drama "The Normal Heart" and William Hoffman's "As Is," "Angels" is a second- or even third-generation play about America's gay community. But if Kushner's lens is an overtly homosexual one, the landscape that he examines belongs to all Americans.

"It's not exactly about the fall of the right," says Kushner, seated in one of the Taper's rehearsal rooms a few weeks prior to his play's opening. "But to a certain extent it is about the end of a particular kind of political evil, one that is completely hegemonic."

Dissimilar to Germany's Weimar Republic, which he addressed in "A Bright Room Called Day," Kushner examines the United States in the late '80s and finds key differences between the American and European political sensibility.

"By 1986, [*perestroika*] had begun to happen and that would transform our political landscape. You don't want to be stupidly optimistic about it, and I have a great temptation that way. But it was like this miracle happened.

"I like Americans," Kushner continues. "I think there is something very impressive about us. It's not a country that treats its minorities particularly well, and I don't want to say that there aren't closed minds here, but I think you can say historically that in America, as opposed to certain segments of Europe, we don't leap to a fascistic solution. We had the option to in the '30s and we have Ross Perot now. But if there is anything great about this country, it is that is has not opted for fascism.

"Of course," he adds, with a slightly apologetic smile, "it is never that simple."

Not that anyone would ever accuse Kushner of being simple. Despite a slightly owlish demeanor and bland, Gap-style wardrobe—gray T-shirt, black jeans, gray cotton cardigan—the playwright retains an aggressive, lawyer-like intelligence that reflects his years as the star of his high school debate team. "I was this incredibly obnoxious debater, now I'm just incredibly obnoxious," he says with a flash of his self-deprecating wit.

Although he was born in New York City and currently lives in Brooklyn, Kushner was raised in Lake Charles, La., the middle of three children born to two classical musicians who had met at the New Orleans Philharmonic. It was a highly literate, culturally sophisticated and politically aware household, an ideal environment in which Kushner—white, Jewish, gay and coming of age in the South during the turbulent '60s—developed both a healthy respect and skepticism for the idea of community, a conceit that would come to earmark his work as a dramatist.

"One of the things I wanted to explore was the legitimacy of the notion of community," Kushner says. "It is a fundamental American question because that's what this country is: a community comprised of not only different [constituencies] but hostile ones—and irreconcilably so."

For Kushner, who has been open about his sexual preferences since his postgraduate days at New York University, the nation's gay and lesbian community is not only one with which he is intimately familiar, but it serves as an exceptionally apt metaphor for his examination of America as a whole. "Because the demarcation line is sexual preference, the homosexual community is also a very disparate group of people of all races, cultures and political persuasions," says Kushner. "It is synthetic and artificial."

Within these cobbled communities, Kushner ponders man's proclivity for both xenophobia and compassion. As he writes in "Millennium Approaches": "AIDS shows the limits of tolerance . . . [and that] underneath tolerance is intense, passionate hatred."

"I think that one wants to demonize and other-ize because it makes the world more manageable," Kushner says. "The whole struggle in American culture now—multiculturalism, difference and inclusion—is really about breaking down those barriers between people, but in a smart sophisticated way. Not by saying, 'We're all white people with different-colored skins,' but by acknowledging and celebrating and exploring the dynamics of that difference."

And that, says Kushner, "is a different political outlook than containment, which is the Berlin Wall, the Iron Curtain, the idea of an Evil Empire."

It is also a different thematic attitude than what Kushner exhibited in "A Bright Room Called Day"—written after his graduation while he worked as a hotel switchboard operator—in which he somewhat pessimistically explored the failure of the left "when confronted with a triumphant right." Written essentially as a formal experiment and something of a response to "Fear and Misery in the Third Reich" by Bertolt Brecht (Kushner's self-described "idol"), as well as President Reagan's controversial 1985 visit to Bitberg, the play tracked what Kushner describes as "a group of leftists in Germany in 1932, the friendship of which disintegrates as Hitler comes to power."

The reasons? "There is no simple answer," he says. "Failure of ideology, terror" and most significantly, "the idea that progressive people, in my opinion, are deeper and more sensitive than people on the right and consequently they are more conflicted."

Although "A Bright Room Called Day" was produced by the New York Theater Workshop after its London run, the play was largely dismissed by critics as agitprop. Kushner concedes his play's weaknesses. "Instead of leaving the whole thing implicit," he says, "I stuck in this character— a performance-artist type—who overtly draws the parallel between Hitler and Reagan and that freaked some people out."

One of the people decidedly not alarmed by Kushner's dramaturgical excesses was Oskar Eustis, who was then dramaturge of San Francisco's Eureka Theater and is now a resident director at the Taper. After seeing an earlier workshop production of the play, Eustis produced "Bright Room" at the Eureka, where it had its first successful run. Eustis is co-directing the Taper production of "Angels" along with Tony Taccone, who is former artistic director of the Eureka Theater.

"'Bright Room' just knocked me out," recalls Eustis, who like many critics, considers Kushner "closer to the best of contemporary British writers like Caryl Churchill, David Hare and Howard Brenton. Tony has a combination of political, intellectual and true poetic vision that is unique among American writers." Kushner, Eustis decided, was the perfect dramatist to write a play about the impact of AIDS on San Francisco's gay community—the play that would become "Angels in America."

For Kushner, who had been disturbed by the "homophobic reaction" to Roy Cohn's AIDS-related death and had decided to write a play about that, Eustis' offer was oddly prescient. "It seemed perfect since I had never written a gay play or one set in modern times and it was San Francisco and in the middle of the Reagan Administration."

They applied for a special National Endowment for the Arts grant, certain that they would be rejected given the conservative political climate in 1987. They weren't. One of the $57,000 grant's stipulations was that the play be written for the Eureka's acting company—a condition that forced Kushner to add women's roles to his "play written for five gay men."

Although Kushner went back to the drawing board, the result, a vastly expanded canvas that the playwright considers "firmly within the Western text-centered tradition," is dramaturgically a leap ahead of "Bright Room." Indeed, ever since it first played at the Taper, Too as a work in-progress in 1990, "Millennium" has been eliciting strong critical and public response. It subsequently premiered at the Eureka Theater in 1991, prior to its move to the National Theater in London last season. Its arrival at the Taper next week—in association with the New York Shakespeare Festival—represents the first time the play has been staged in its entirety. ("Perestroika" was staged in a workshop production at the Taper earlier this year.)

Eustis suggests that Kushner "cracked the idea of dramatic action." He also adds that Kushner "also took a deep breath and wrote about what was closest and scariest to him and that unleashed a complexity that is representative of our own lives."

"'Angels' is about pairs of people," says Kushner, who describes his original story line "as sort of inchoate—Roy Cohn, a person with AIDS, a troubled Jewish clerk and a Mormon."

"In 'Millennium Approaches,' the couples are drawn so that they make overt sense," he continues. "Republicans are with Republicans, Mormons are with Mormons, gays are with gays and straights are with straights. It is all neatly set up, but then it doesn't work because of all sorts of internal stresses: The Mormon who is married is also gay, and one of the gay couple has AIDS and the other one can't deal with it. So within that seemingly homogenous unit there is enormous conflict and potential for eruption."

Which brings Kushner to Part II, "Perestroika," in which he takes his cue from Gorbachev's seminal announcement in the summer of 1988 "to show the couples regrouping in preposterous but productive alliances, that may be short-lived and unstable, but catalytic of change."

That change, Kushner says, mirrors larger social shifts now occurring in the nation's landscape—namely the resurgence of liberalism, the growing political clout of the gay movement and the possible decline of the conservative right.

"Bush could still win, but that nightmare of the Republican Convention I think actually did a great service—showing the ugliness of homophobia on national television," Kushner says. "I don't think most people buy it anymore. Nor is it evidence that we are being defeated, but rather that we are making incredible progress."

Kushner in person voices controversial political views—the Reagan and Bush administrations, he says, "have killed people with their AIDS policies, like the Catholic Church has killed people—teenagers—with their AIDS policies." But Eustis says that "Angels in America" is not an exercise in easy polemics. Rather, the director believes, it is a meditative, deeply felt examination "at how people change, and how historically it is necessary that people change. There is an American idealism at the basis of Tony's work."

Indeed, one of the play's main themes—played out as dialectic between Judaism and Mormonism—is an examination "of how theoretical religion exists in a pluralistic society," as one character puts it in "Perestroika."

"One of the things that the play is saying is that [religious] theory is incredibly important to us and that without it, we don't know where we are going," Kushner says. "On the other hand, as systematic approaches to ethics age, get passed up by history, the rules and laws which they hand down become irrelevant and impossible and we distort ourselves terribly trying to adhere to those beliefs. It is a life-and-death matter to hang on to your beliefs, but it can also be a life-and-death matter to know when it's time to say they aren't working anymore.

"There is a distinction made in the play that I hope is there—between moralism and morality and the task is to find what is moral through what is moralist," adds Kushner, who considers himself an agnostic—albeit one who concedes "it seems fairly impoverished to say that only matter and the laws that govern matter exist."

Kushner credits much of his interest in religion to his family background as part of the little known but thriving Jewish community in Louisiana. "It wasn't a great place to grow up gay," he says, "but the Jewish community was large." He attended a local Episcopal day school, "because it was the best elementary school in Lake Charles," where his interest in theater first sprouted in a love of high church ritual.

Indeed, Kushner's Southern childhood provided him with several unique and contrasting points of view—religious, cultural, social—that would come to bear on his work as a playwright. "In many ways, it was a great place to grow up," he says, launching into a particularly lyrical description of southern Louisiana, "where the Great Plains fall into the ocean and it is steamy and tropical and beautiful." It was also Cajun country, "not white, Southern Baptist, Klan territory," he explains. "And the French-Canadian Catholics are a much more fun bunch of people."

Although his parents were both professional musicians working in New York—his father was a Juilliard-trained clarinetist and his mother was the first bassoonist at the New York City Opera—the family moved to Lake Charles when Kushner was 2 years old after his father, a Louisiana native, inherited the family lumber business. Both parents continued their musical pursuits and the Kushner family home, located on the edge of a swamp, was a culturally rich one.

While Kushner, as well as his older sister and younger brother, was encouraged to follow artistic pursuits at home, he found the local high school, which had no theater department but a crack debate team, a micro-education in the civil rights movement.

"Certainly there were horrible crackers in my high school," Kushner says. "But the South was also integrated in the '60s when the North wasn't, and I went to a school that was 50% black and 50% white."

He was a top student, and the leading member on the debate team, but he was also gay, a fact that he says "I've known as long as I can remember." As a result, much of his school years were lonely, closeted ones. "I know there were other gays at my high school, but we never made contact," he says. "I might have been one of those extraordinary people who got beat up for wearing earrings. But I wasn't that genuinely radical a person. It was 1972 in Lake Charles, La., and without parental support there wasn't a whole lot I could have done differently."

In fact, any support he received was decidedly toward assimilation. "My father had figured it out and he was upset," says Kushner. "He wasn't a monster about it, but he wanted me to be straight and I wanted him to love me. I also didn't want to hurt my mother and I wanted to have a family."

So Kushner entered psychoanalysis in an attempt to become a heterosexual. It was a futile but not short-lived experiment. He spent his entire undergraduate years at New York's Columbia University in analysis "with a wonderful straight male analyst who started out by saying 'People's sexual orientation doesn't change under analysis.'"

It took four years of analysis and another three years hiding his sexuality before Kushner, like one of the characters in "Angels in America," was able to call his mother from a pay phone to tell her he was gay.

Today, Kushner clearly relishes the personal and professional freedom he has gained from that decision. "I have no problems being called a gay playwright," says Kushner, who was awarded a Whiting Foundation Award in 1990. "And I know straight people enjoy my work."

And Kushner is in demand. After "Angels" completes its run at the Taper, it will open in New York at the Joseph Papp Public Theater in February. After that, Kushner will finish a screen version of his adaptation of Pierre Corneille's "The Illusion" for Universal Studios and write a TV movie for PBS' "American Playhouse" about the recent strike at the New York Daily News. Then, he will begin work on his next play.

"One of the things that I learned from being in the closet and then coming out is how much stronger and more fun life can be," says Kushner, citing the writer, Hannah Arendt, and once again invoking his theme of community. "It is better to embrace your pariahhood," he says, "than to try and assimilate."

## Anna Deavere Smith

Anna Deavere Smith (b. 1950) is one of the leading performance artists working in the United States and one of the most prominent African-American women working in the U. S. theater. The eldest of five children, Smith was born and raised in Baltimore; she graduated from Beaver College in 1971 and then took an M. F. A. in acting from the American Conservatory Theatre in 1976. Throughout the 1970s and 1980s, Smith pursued a dual career as a teacher of acting and as a performer. She has taught at Carnegie-Mellon University, Yale University, New York University, the American Conservatory Theatre, and at the University of Southern California. She currently teaches at Stanford University. Her many stage, television, and film roles include parts in *Mother Courage* (1980) and *Tartuffe* (1983), in "All My Children" (1983), and in the films *Soup for One* (1982), *Dave* (1993), and *Philadelphia* (1993).

As a playwright and performer, Smith is best known for a series of one-woman shows that form part of an extended series of performances collectively entitled *On the Road: A Search for American Character*. Smith began devising *On the Road* in the early 1980s. The project was inspired by acting exercises she devised for her cast while directing Adrienne Kennedy's play *A Movie Star Has to Star in Black and White*. In order to wean her students away from a strictly psychological approach to acting, in which the actor's focus is on the role-as-self, Smith had them watch and then reenact celebrity television talk-show interviews, as a way of building a bridge to a "character" as something other. Working with actual interview material gave Smith the working method for much of her subsequent work. For the various *On the Road* performances, Smith interviews a range of subjects who are part of a given event or situation she wants to explore. In fact, she is often invited to colleges and other organizations to use performance to help explore race, gender, and identity issues. After conducting the interviews, Smith devises a performance, using minimal props and costumes, in which she interweaves sections from the interviews, performing all of the roles herself. In 1987, she was invited by San Francisco's Eureka Theater to devise a show concerning racial attitudes in that city; it was performed under the title *From the Outside Looking In*. She also performed a piece on women in San Francisco's theater community, at the invitation of the Bay Area Women in Theater. In 1988 she was invited to conduct an oral history of the Women and Theater Program of the Association for Theatre in Higher Education; *Chlorophyll Postmodernism and the Mother Goddess / A Conversation* was performed at the Women and Theater conference in San Diego that year. She was asked to Princeton University in 1989 to conduct interviews on gender politics among students, faculty, and staff, and performed *Gender Bending;* she has conducted similar workshops and performances for the Five Colleges (Amherst, Hampshire, Mount Holyoke, and Smith Colleges, and the University of Massachusetts) in Massachusetts, and for the University of Pennsylvania.

Smith is now known, though, for two performance works that confront recent urban uprisings: *Fires in the Mirror: Crown Heights, Brooklyn and Other Identities* (1992) and *Twilight: Los Angeles 1992* (1993), which concerns the unrest in Los Angeles following the acquittal of four L.A. police officers who were tried for beating an African-American man, Rodney King. *Fires in the Mirror*, which earned Smith a 1992 Obie Special Citation, was shown on the Public Broadcasting Service in 1993.

### FIRES IN THE MIRROR: CROWN HEIGHTS, BROOKLYN AND OTHER IDENTITIES (1992)

*Fires in the Mirror* concerns racial and ethnic rioting that took place in the Crown Heights neighborhood of Brooklyn, New York, in August 1991. The events that sparked three nights of rioting began on the evening of Monday, August 19, and remain in some dispute. Menachem Schneerson, the Grand Rebbe of the Lubavitcher sect of Hasidic Jews, was returning from his weekly visit to a cemetery; his car was accompanied by an unmarked police escort car and by a third car, driven by Yosef Lifsh and carrying two other Hasidic passengers. At one point Lifsh's car fell behind; apparently accelerating to catch up with the others, Lifsh's car ran a red light, glanced off another car, jumped the curb, and pinned two small African-American children to a window grating. Gavin Cato (7) was killed; his cousin Angela Cato (7) was seriously injured.

Crown Heights has a history of racial and ethnic tension, and the accident quickly drew a large and volatile crowd. Within minutes, two ambulances arrived at the scene. The first ambulance to arrive was from a private Hasidic ambulance service; police ordered it to attend to the three Jewish men in the car and to leave the scene immediately. The police later claimed that the city ambulance was also at the scene, and that they acted to protect the three men from the crowd and to reduce further confrontation. A city ambulance did attend to the children, but within minutes word that medical attention had been given first to the three white, Jewish men rather than to the two black children ignited a street riot. Three hours later, at 11:30 P.M., a group of black youths a few blocks from the accident surrounded a visiting Australian Hasidic scholar, Yankel Rosenbaum (29), and stabbed him to death. Lemrick Nelson, Jr., was arrested and held shortly thereafter.

Over the next three days and nights both African-American and Jewish groups protested the city's handling of the incident and became involved in a civil uprising. Crown Heights became the scene not only of protests and protest marches, but of widespread arson, looting, and rioting. Police, journalists, and citizens were beaten. Although the rioting broke by the end of the week, several events kept Crown Heights in the public eye: the funerals of Gavin Cato and Yankel Rosenbaum, protest marches led by the Reverend Al Sharpton and Alton Maddox, Yosef Lifsh's sudden trip to Israel, the unsuccessful effort to charge Lifsh with vehicular negligence and arrest him. Indeed, throughout the remainder of 1991 and 1992 Crown Heights remained a flashpoint: In September, the Reverend Al Sharpton flew to Israel to inform Lifsh that the Cato family had brought a civil suit against him; throughout 1992 Lubavitchers demonstrated and ran newspaper ads calling for further police investigation and judicial action in connection with Rosenbaum's death, alleging that the police had handled the riots and the subsequent investigation in a biased and unfair manner; in October, 1992, Lemrick Nelson, Jr., was acquitted, provoking a Hasidic rally in protest.

In part, the Crown Heights riots reflected the tensions of an unusually diverse community. The Lubavitch is an Orthodox Jewish sect, whose strict religious beliefs make them a close and easily identifiable community in the Crown Heights neighborhood. Many of the black residents of Crown Heights have recently emigrated from the Caribbean and are working to make a place for themselves in the U. S. Both groups face overt and subtle discrimination in a number of ways. Moreover, before the riots, Crown Heights had been the scene of several racial incidents. In 1986, a group of young black men had beaten a Hasidic man to death in a subway station; in April 1987, 400 African Americans marched to protest city favoritism (streets in the neighborhood are regularly closed to traffic during Jewish holidays) and harassment by a Hasidic neighborhood surveillance patrol; in 1989, a crowd of Hasidim surrounded and beat a black teenager they accused of slashing a Hasidic woman and her son.

Rather than providing a "history" of these events, Smith's *Fires in the Mirror* refracts the events through a series of monologues, some by participants—Gavin Cato's father, the Rev. Al Sharpton, Yankel Rosenbaum's brother Norman—and some by more distant observers, such as the playwrights Ntozake Shange and George C. Wolfe (who subsequently directed the television version of *Fires in the Mirror* for PBS). Performing the words of her subjects, Smith carefully weaves an elaborate texture of commentary about race and ethnicity in the United States. Beginning with topics like "identity," "hair," "race," "rhythm," Smith uses the characters' voices to frame the larger issues and attitudes surrounding black-white conflict in the U. S. and then moves more insistently into the specifics of the Crown Heights uprising. As with some other postmodern works—Norman Mailer's novel *The Executioner's Song,* Don De Lillo's *Libra,* or the Oliver Stone film *JFK*—*Fires in the Mirror* insistently blurs the boundary between the events and their retelling, presenting a kaleidoscopic re-presentation of events rather than a summary that pretends to a specious objectivity. One of the most striking features of *Fires in the Mirror* in performance is the way that Smith plays both white and black characters, men and women, Jews and non-Jews, the powerful and the oppressed, the famous and the unknown. And although Smith carefully observes the details of behavior, dress, and gesture with which her "characters" speak, her performance here is not a kind of mimicry. For instead of effacing identity, Smith's performance shows the challenges of negotiating between "identities." Smith's performance shows the difficulty of grappling with an *other's* identity, an *other's* attitudes, an *other's* orientation to the world.

# —Fires in the Mirror:— Crown Heights, Brooklyn and Other Identities

## Anna Deavere Smith

THIS BOOK IS DEDICATED TO THE RESIDENTS OF
CROWN HEIGHTS, BROOKLYN, AND IN THE MEMORY
OF GAVIN CATO AND YANKEL ROSENBAUM

## —THE CHARACTERS—

NTOZAKE SHANGE, *Playwright, poet, novelist.*

ANONYMOUS LUBAVITCHER WOMAN, *Preschool teacher.*

GEORGE C. WOLFE, *Playwright, director, producing director of the New York Shakespeare Festival.*

AARON M. BERNSTEIN, *Physicist at Massachusetts Institute of Technology.*

ANONYMOUS GIRL, *Junior high school black girl of Haitian descent. Lives in Brooklyn near Crown Heights.*

REVEREND AL SHARPTON, *Well-known New York activist, minister.*

RIVKAH SIEGAL, *Lubaviten woman, graphic designer.*

ANGELA DAVIS, *Author, orator, activist, scholar. Professor in the History of Consciousness Department at the University of California, Santa Cruz.*

MONIQUE "BIG MO" MATTHEWS, *Los Angeles rapper.*

LEONARD JEFFRIES, *Professor of African American Studies at City University of New York, former head of the department.*

LETTY COTTIN POGREBIN, *Author Deborah, Golda, and Me. One of the founding editors of Ms. magazine.*

CONRAD MOHAMMED, *New York minister for the Honorable Louis Farrakhan.*

ROBERT SHERMAN, *Director, Mayor of the City of New York's Increase the Peace Corps.*

RABBI JOSEPH SPIELMAN, *Spokesperson in the Lubavitcher community.*

THE REVEREND CANON DOCTOR HERON SAM, *Pastor, St. Mark's, Crown Heights Church.*

ANONYMOUS YOUNG MAN #1, *Crown Heights resident.*

MICHAEL S. MILLER, *Executive Director at the Jewish Community Relations Council.*

HENRY RICE, *Crown Heights resident.*

NORMAN ROSENBAUM, *Brother of Yankel Rosenbaum. A barrister from Australia.*

ANONYMOUS YOUNG MAN #2, *African American young man, late teens, early twenties. Resident of Crown Heights.*

SONNY CARSON, *Activist.*

RABBI SHEA HECHT, *Lubavitcher rabbi, spokesperson.*

RICHARD GREEN, *Director, Crown Heights Youth Collective. Codirector Project CURE, a Black-Hasidic basketball team that developed after the riots.*

ROSLYN MALAMUD, *Lubavitcher resident of Crown Heights.*

REUVEN OSTROV, *Lubavitcher male; at the time of the riot, was seventeen years old. Worked as assistant chaplain at Kings County Hospital.*

CARMEL CATO, *Father of Gavin Cato. Crown Heights resident, originally from Guyana.*

## —IDENTITY—

NTOZAKE SHANGE
THE DESERT

*(This interview was done on the phone at about 4:00 P.M. Philadelphia time. The only cue Ntozake gave about her physical appearance was that she took one earring off to talk on the phone. On stage we placed her upstage center in an arm chair, smoking. Then we placed her standing, downstage.)*

Hummmm.
Identity—
it, is, uh . . . in a way it's, um . . . it's sort of, it's uh . . .
it's a psychic sense of place
it's a way of knowing I'm not a rock or that tree?
I'm this other living creature over here?
And it's a way of knowing that no matter where I put
    myself
that I am not necessarily
what's around me.                                                    10
I am part of my surroundings
and I become separate from them
and it's being able to make those differentiations clearly
that lets us have an identity
and what's inside our identity
is everything that's ever happened to us.
Everything that's ever happened
to us as well as our responses to it
'cause we might be alone in a trance state,
someplace like the desert                                            20
and we begin to feel as though

we are part of the desert—
which we are right at that minute—
but we are not the desert,
uh . . .
we are part of the desert,
and when we go home
we take with us that part of the desert that the desert gave
    us,
30  but we're still not the desert.
It's an important differentiation to make because you don't
    know
what you're giving if you don't know what you have and
    you don't
know what you're taking if you don't know what's yours
    and what's
somebody else's.


ANONYMOUS LUBAVITCHER WOMAN
STATIC

*(This interview was actually done on the phone. Based on what*
*she told me she was doing, and on the three visits I had made*
*to her home for other interviews, I devised this physical scene.*
*A Lubavitcher woman, in a wig, and loose-fitting clothes. She*
*is in her mid-thirties. She is folding clothes. There are several*
*children around. Three boys of different ages are lying to-*
*gether on the couch. The oldest is reading to the younger two.*
*A teen-age girl with long hair, a button-down-collar shirt, and*
*skirt is sweeping the floor.)*

Well,
it was um,
40  getting toward the end of Shabbas,
like around five in the afternoon,
and it was summertime
and sunset isn't until about eight, nine o'clock,
so there were still quite a few hours left to go
and my baby had been playing with the knobs on the
    stereo system
then all of a sudden he pushed the button—
the *on* button—
and all of a sudden came blaring out,
50  at full volume,
sort of like a half station
of polka music.
But just like with the static,
it was blaring, blaring
and we can't turn off,
we can't turn off electrical,
you know electricity, on Shabbas.
So um,
uh . . .
60  there was—
we just were trying to ignore it,
but a young boy that was visiting us,
he was going nuts already, he said
it was giving him such a headache could we do something
    about it,
couldn't we get a baby

to turn it off;
we can't make the baby turn it off but if the baby,
but if a child under three
turns something on or turns something off it's not    70
    considered against the Torah,
so we put the baby by it and tried to get the baby to turn it
    off,
he just probably made it worse,
so the guest was so uncomfortable that I said I would go
    outside
and see if I can find someone who's not Jewish and see if
    they would
like to—
see if they could turn it off,    80
so you can have somebody who's not Jewish do a simple
    act like
turning on the light or turning off the light,
and I hope I have the law correct,
but you can ask them to do it directly.
If they wanna do it of their own free will—
and hopefully they would get some benefit from it too,
so I went outside
and I saw
a little    90
boy in the neighborhood
who I didn't know and didn't know me—
not Jewish, he was black and he wasn't wearing a yarmulke
    because you can't—
so I went up to him and I said to him
that my radio is on really loud and I can't turn it off,
could he help me,
so he looked at me a little crazy like,
Well?
And I said I don't know what to do,    100
so he said okay,
so he followed me into the house
and he hears this music on so loud
and so unpleasant
and so
he goes over to the
stereo
and he says, "You see this little button here
that says on and off?
Push that in    110
and that turns it off."
And I just sort of stood there looking kind of dumb
and then he went and pushed it,
and we laughed that he probably thought:
And people say Jewish people are really smart and they
    don't know
how to turn off their radios.


GEORGE C. WOLFE
101 DALMATIONS

*(The Mondrian Hotel in Los Angeles. Morning, Sunny. A very*
*nice room. George is wearing denim jeans, a light blue denim*
*shirt, and white leather tennis shoes. His hair is in a ponytail.*
*He wears tortoise/wire spectacles. He is drinking tea with milk.*

*The tea is served on a tray, the cups and teapot are delicate porcelain. George is sitting on a sofa, with his feet up on the coffee table.)*

I mean I grew up on a black—
a one-block street—
120    that was black.
My grandmother lived on that street
my cousins lived around the corner.
I went to this
Black—Black—
private Black grade school
where
I was extraordinary.
Everybody there was extraordinary.
You were told you were extraordinary.
130    It was very clear
that I could not go to see *101 Dalmations* at the Capital
    Theatre
because it was segregated.
And at the same time
I was treated like I was the most extraordinary creature
    that had
been born.
So I'm on my street in my house,
at my school—
140    and I was very spoiled too—
so I was treated like I was this special special creature.
And then I would go beyond a certain point
I was treated like I was insignificant.
Nobody was
hosing me down or calling me nigger.
It was just that I was insignificant.

*(Slight pause)*

You know what I mean so it was very clear of

*(Teacup on saucer strike twice on "very clear")*

where my extraordinariness lived.
You know what I mean.
150    That I was extraordinary as long as I was Black.
But I am—not—going—to place myself

*(Pause)*

in relationship to your whiteness.
I will talk about your whiteness if we want to talk about
    that.
But I,
but what,
that which,
what I—
what am I saying?
160    My blackness does not resis—ex—re—
*exist* in relationship to your whiteness.

*(Pause)*

You know

*(Not really a question, more like a hum)*

*(Slight pause)*

it does not exist in relationship to—
it *exists*
it exists.
I come—
you know what I mean—
like I said, I, I, I,
I come from—
it's a very com*plex*,    170
con*fused*,
*neu*-rotic,
at times destructive
reality, but it is completely
and totally a reality
contained and and, and,
and full unto itself.
It's complex.
It's demonic.
It's ridiculous.    180
It's absurd.
It's evolved.
It's all the stuff.
That's the way I grew up.

*(Slight pause)*

So that *therefore*—
and then you're White—

*(Quick beat)*

And then there's a point when,
and then these two things come into contact.

## —MIRRORS—

AARON M. BERNSTEIN
MIRRORS AND DISTORTIONS

*(Evening, Cambridge, Massachusetts. Fall. He is a man in his fifties, wearing a sweater and a shirt with a pen guard. He is seated at a round wooden table with a low-hanging lamp.)*

Okay, so a mirror is something that reflects light.
It's the simplest instrument to understand,    190
okay?
So a simple mirror is just a flat
reflecting
substance, like,
for example,
it's a piece of glass which is silvered on the back,
okay?
Now the notion of distortion also goes back into literature,
okay?
I'm trying to remember from art—    200
You probably know better than I.
You know you have a pretty young woman and she looks in
    a mirror
and she's a witch

*(He laughs)*

because she's evil on the inside.
That's not a real mirror,

as everyone knows—
you see the inner thing.
Now that really goes back in literature.
210   So everyone understood that mirrors don't distort,
so that was a play
not on words
but a concept.
But physicists do
talk about distortion.
It's a big
subject, distortions.
I'll give you an example—
if you wanna see the
220   stars
you make a big
reflecting mirror—
that's one of the ways—
you make a big telescope
so you can gather in a lot of light
and then it focuses at a point
and then there's always something called the circle of
    confusion.
So if ya don't make the thing perfectly spherical or
230       perfectly
parabolic
then,
then, uh, if there are errors in the construction
which you can see, it's easy, if it's huge,
then you're gonna have a circle of confusion,
you see?
So that's the reason for making the
telescope as large as you can,
because you want that circle
240   to seem smaller,
and you want to easily see errors in the construction.
So, you see, in physics it's very practical—
you wanna look up in the heavens
and see the stars as well as you can
without distortion.
If you're counting stars, for example,
and two look like one,
you've blown it.

### —HAIR—

ANONYMOUS GIRL
LOOK IN THE MIRROR

*(Morning. Spring. A teen-age Black girl of Haitian descent.
She has hair which is straightened, and is wearing a navy blue
jumper and a white shirt. She is seated in a stairwell at her junior high school in Brooklyn.)*

When I look in the mirror . . .
250   I don't know.
How did I find out I was Black . . .

*(Tongue sound)*

When I grew up and I look in the mirror and saw I was
    Black.

When I look at my parents,
That's how I knew I was Black.
Look at my skin.
You Black?
Black is beautiful.
I don't know.
That's what I always say.                                    260
I think White is beautiful too.
But I think Black is beautiful too.
In my class nobody is White, everybody's Black,
and some of them is Hispanic.
In my class
you can't call any of them Puerto Ricans.
They despise Puerto Ricans, I don't know why.
They think that Puerto Ricans are stuck up and everything.
They say, Oh my Gosh my nail broke, look at that cute guy
    and everything.                                         270
But they act like that themselves.
They act just like White girls.
Black girls is not like that.
Please, you should be in my class.
Like they say that Puerto Ricans act like that
and they don't see that they act like that themselves.
Black girls, they do bite off the Spanish girls,
they bite off of your clothes.
You don't know what that means? biting off?
Like biting off somebody's clothes                          280
Like cop, following,
and last year they used to have a lot of girls like that.
They come to school with a style, right?
And if they see another girl with that style?
Oh my gosh look at her.
What she think she is,
she tryin' to bite off of me in some way
no don't be bitin' off of my sneakers
or like that.
Or doin' a hairstyle                                        290
I mean Black people are into hairstyles.
So they come to school, see somebody with a certain style,
they say uh-huh I'm gonna get me one just like that uh-
    huh,
that's the way Black people are
Yea-ah!
They don't like people doing that to them
and they do that to other people,
so the Black girls they won't follow the Spanish girls.
The Spanish girls don't bite off of us.                     300
Some of the Black girls follow them.
But they don't mind
They don't care.
They follow each other.
Like there's three girls in my class,
they from the Dominican Republic.
They all stick together like glue.
They all three best friends.
They don't follow nobody,
like there's none of them lead or anything.              310
They don't hang around us either.
They're
by themselves.

## THE REVEREND AL SHARPTON
## ME AND JAMES'S THING

*(Early afternoon. Fall. A small room that is a part of a suite of offices in a building on West Fifty-seventh Street and Seventh Avenue in New York. A very large man Black man with straightened hair. Reverend Sharpton's hair is in the style of James Brown's hair. He is wearing a suit, colorful tie, and a gold medallion that was given to him by Martin Luther King, Jr. Reverend Sharpton has a pinky ring, a very resonant voice even in this small room. There is a very built, very tall man who sits behind me during the interview. Reverend Sharpton's face is much younger, and more innocent than it appears to be in the media. His humor is in his face. He is very direct. The interview only lasts fifteen minutes because he had been called out of a meeting in progress to do the interview.)*

James Brown raised me.
Uh . . .
I never had a father.
My father left when I was ten.
James Brown took me to the beauty parlor one day
and made my hair like his.
320  And made me promise
to wear it like that
'til I die.
It's a personal family thing
between me and James Brown.
I always wanted a father
and he filled that void.
And the strength that he's demonstrated—
I don't know anybody that reached his heights,
and then had to go as low as he did and come back.
330  And I think that if anybody I met in life deserved that type
         of
tribute from
somebody
that he wanted a kid
to look like him
and be like his son . . .
I just came home from spending a weekend with him now,
uh, uh,
I think James deserved that.
340  And just like
he was the father I never had,
his kids never even visited him when he went to jail.
So I was like the kid he never had.
And if I had to choose between arguing with people about
     my
hairstyle
or giving him that one tribute
he axed,
I'd rather give him that tribute
350  because he filled a void for me.
And I really don't give a damn
who doesn't understand it.
The press and everybody do
their thing on that.
It's a personal thing between me and James Brown.
And just like
in other communities

people do their cultural thing
with who they like,
uh,                                                        360
there's nothing wrong with me doing
that with James.
It's, it's, *us.*
I mean in the fifties it was a slick.
It was acting like White folks.
But today
people don't wear their hair like that.
James and I the only ones out there doing that.
So it's certainlih not
a reaction to Whites.                                      370
It's me and James's thing.


## RIVKAH SIEGAL
## WIGS

*(Early afternoon. Spring. The kitchen of an apartment in Crown Heights. A very pretty Lubavitcher woman, with clear eyes and a direct gaze, wearing a wig and a knit sweater, that looks as though it might be hand knit. A round wooden table. Coffee mug. Sounds of children playing in the street are outside. A neighbor, a Lubavitcher woman with light blond hair who no longer wears the wig, observes the interview at the table.)*

Your hair—
It only has to be—
there's different,
uhm,
customs in different
Hasidic groups.
Lubavitch
the system is
it should be two inches                                    380
long.
It's—
some groups
have
the custom
to shave their
heads.
There's—
the reason is,
when you go to the mikvah                                  390
you may, maybe,
it's better if it's short
because of what you—
the preparation
that's involved
and that
you have to go under the water.
The hair has a tendency to float
and you have to be completely submerged
including your hair.                                       400
So . . .
And I got married
when I was a little older,
and I really wanted to be married
and I really wanted to, um . . .

In some ways I was eager to cover my head.
Now if I had grown up in a Lubavitch household
and then had to cut it,
I don't know what that would be like.
410   I really don't.
But now that I'm wearing the wig,
you see,
with my hair I can keep it very simple
and I can change it all the time.
So with a wig you have to have like five wigs if you want to
   do that.
But I, uh,
I feel somehow like it's fake,
I feel like it's not me.
420   I try to be as much myself as I can,
and it just
bothers me
that I'm kind of fooling the world.
I used to go to work.
People . . .
and I would wear a different wig,
and they'd say I like your new haircut
and I'd say it's not mine!
You know,
430   and it was very hard for me to say it
and
it became very difficult.
I mean, I've gone through a lot with wearing wigs and not
   wearing
wigs.
It's been a big issue for me.

ANGELA DAVIS
ROPES

*(Morning, Spring. Oakland, California. In reality this inter-
view was done on the phone, with myself and Thulani Davis.
Thulani and I were calling from an office at the Public Theatre.
We do not know exactly what Angela was doing or wearing. I
believe, from things she said, that she was sitting on her deck
in her home in Oakland, which overlooks a beautiful
panorama of trees.)*

Race, um—
of course
for many years in the history
440   of African Americans in this country—
was synonymous with community.
As a matter of fact
we were race women and race men.
Billie Holiday for example
called herself a race woman
because she supported the community
and as a child growing up in the South
my assumptions were
that if anybody in the race
450   came under attack
then I had to be there
to support that person,
to support the race.
I was saying to my students just the other day,

I said,
if in 1970,
when I was
in jail,
someone had told me
that in 1991,                                                     460
a black man
who
said that his, um . . .
hero—

*(Increased volume, speed, and energy)*

one of his heroes
was Malcolm X—
would be nominated to the Supreme Court
I would have celebrated
and I don't think it would have been possible at that time
to convince me                                                  470
that I would
be absolutely opposed,
a black candidate—
I mean like absolutely—

*(A new attack, more energy)*

or that if anyone would have told me that
a *woman* . . .
finally be elected to the Supreme Court,
it would have been very difficult,
as critical as I am with respect to feminism,
as critical as I have always been with what I used to call,   480
you know, narrow nationalism?
I don't think
it would have been possible to convince me that things
   would have so absolutely
shifted that
someone could have evoked
the specter of lynching
on national television
and that specter of lynching would be used to violate our
   history.                                                      490
And I still feel that we have to point out the racism
   involved
in the razing of a Black man
and a Black woman
in that way.
I mean [Ted] Kennedy was sitting right there
and it had never occurred to anyone to bring him up
before
the world,
which is not to say that I don't think it should happen.       500
And it is actually a sign of how we,
in our various oppressed
marginalized communities,
have been able to turn
terrible acts of racism directed against us
into victory . . .
And therefore I think
Anita Hill did that,
and so it's very complicated,
but I have no problems aligning myself politically             510
against Clarence Thomas in a real passionate way,

but at the same time I can talk about the racism that led to
   the possibility
of constructing those kinds of hearings
and
the same thing with Mike Tyson.
So I guess that would be,
um . . .
the way in which I would begin to look at community,
520   and would therefore think
that race has become, uh,
an increasingly obsolete way
of constructing community
because it is based on unchangeable
immutable biological
facts
in a very pseudo-scientific way,
alright?
Now
530   *racism* is entirely different
because see *racism*,
uh,
actually I think
is
at the origins of this concept of race.
It's not—
it's not the other way around,
that there were racists,
and then the racists—
540   one race came to dominate
the others.
As a matter of fact
in order for a European colonialist
to attempt
to conquer the world,
to colonize the world,
they had to construct this notion
of,
uh,
550   the populations of the earth being divided into certain,
uh,
firm biological, uh,
communities,
and that's what I think we have to go back and look at.
So when I use the word race now I put it in quotations.
Because if we don't transform
this . . . this intransigent
rigid
notion of race,
560   we will be caught up in this cycle
of genocidal
violence
that, um,
is at the origins of our history.
So I think—
and I'm
I'm convinced—and this is what I'm working on in my
   political practice right now—
is that we have to find ways of coming together in a
570   different way,
not the old notion of coalition in which we anchor ourselves very solidly

in our,
um,
communities,
and simply voice
our
solidarity with other people.
I'm not suggesting that we do not anchor ourselves in our
   communities;      580
I feel very anchored in,
um,
my various communities,
but I think that,
you know,
to use a metaphor, the rope
attached to that anchor should be long enough to allow us
   to move
into other communities
to understand and learn.      590
I've been thinking a lot about the need to make more
   intimate
these connections and associations and to really take on
   the responsibility
of learning.
So I think that we need to—
in order to find ways of working with
and understanding
the vastness
of our many cultural heritages      600
and ways of coming together without
rendering invisible all of that heterogeneity—
I don't have the answer,
you know
I don't know.
What I'm interested in is communities
that are not static,
that
can change, that can respond to new historical needs.
So I think it's a very exciting moment.      610

## —RHYTHM—

MONIQUE "BIG MO" MATTHEWS
RHYTHM AND POETRY

*(In reality this interview was done on an afternoon in the
spring of 1989, while I was in residence at the University of
California, Los Angeles, as a fellow at the Center for Afro-
American Studies. Mo was a student of mine. We were sitting
in my office, which was a narrow office, with sunlight. I performed Mo in many shows, and in the course of performing
her, I changed the setting to a performance setting, with microphone. I was inspired by a performance that I saw of Queen
Latifah in San Francisco, and by Mo's behavior in my class,
which was performance behavior, to change the setting to one
that was more theatrical, since Mo's everyday speech was as
theatrical as Latifah's performance speech. Speaking directly
to the audience, pacing the stage.)*

And she say, "This is for the fellas,"
and she took off all her clothes and she had on a leotard

that had all cuts and stuff in it,
and she started doin' it on the floor.
They were like
"Go, girl!"
People like, "That look really stink."
But that's what a lot of female rappers do—
like to try to get off,
620  they sell they body or pimp they body
to, um, get play.
And you have people like Latifah who doesn't, you know,
she talks intelligent.
You have Lyte who's just hard and people are scared by
   her hardness,
her strength of her words.
She encompasses that whole, New York–street sound.
It's like, you know, she'll like . . .
what's a line?
630  What's a line
like "Paper Thin,"
"IN ONE EAR AND RIGHT OUT THE OTHUH."
It's like,
"I don't care what you have to say,
I'm gittin' done what's gotta be done.
Man can't come across me.
A female she can't stand against me.
I'm just the toughest, I'm just the hardest/You just can't
   come up
640  against me/if you do you get waxed!"
It's like a lot of my songs,
I don't know if I'm gonna get blacklisted for it.
The image that I want is a strong strong African strong
   Black woman
and I'm not down with what's going on, like Big Daddy
   Kane had a song
out called "Pimpin Ain't Easy," and he sat there and he
   talk for the
whole song, and I sit there I wanna slap him, I wanna slap
650  him so
hard, and he talks about, it's one point he goes, yeah
um,
"Puerto Rican girls Puerto Rican girls call me Papi and
White girls say
*even* White girls say I'm a hunk!"
I'm like,
"What you mean 'even'?
Oh! Black girls ain't good enough for you huh?"
And one of my songs has a line that's like
660  "PIMPIN' AIN'T EASY BUT WHORIN' AIN'T
   PROPER. RESPECT AND
CHERISH THE ORIGINAL MOTHER."
And a couple of my friends were like,
"Aww, Mo, you good but I can't listen to you 'cause you be
   Men bashin'."
I say,
*"It ain't men bashin', it's female assertin'."*
Shit.
I'm tired of it.
670  I'm tired of my friends just acceptin'
that they just considered to be a ho.
You got a song,
"Everybody's a Hotty."

A "hotty" means you a freak, you a ho,
and it's like Too Short
gets up there and he goes,
"B I AYYYYYYYYYYYYE."
Like he stretches "bitch" out for as long as possible,
like you just a ho and you can't be saved,
and 2 Live Crew. . . . "we want some pussy," and the girls!  680
   "La le la le la le la,"
it's like my friends say,
"Mo, if you so bad how come you don't never say nothin
   about Two
Live Crew?"
When I talk about rap,
and I talk about people demeaning rap,
I don't even mention them
because they don't understand the fundamentals of rap.
Rap, rap  690
is basically
broken down
Rhythm
and Poetry.
And poetry is expression.
It's just like poetry; you release so much through poetry
   you get
angry, you get it?
Poetry is like
intelligence.  700
You just release it all and if you don't have a complex
   rhyme
it's like,
"I'm goin to the store."
What rhymes with store?
More store for more bore
"I'm going to the store I hope I don't get bored,"
it's like,
"WHAT YOU SAYIN', MAN? WHO CARES?"
You have something that flows.  710
You have to be def,
D-E-F.
I guess I have to think of something for you that ain't
   slang.
Def is dope, def is live
when you say somethin's dope
it means it is the epitome of the experience
and you have to be def by your very presence
because you have to make people happy.
And we are living in a society where people are not happy  720
   with their everyday lives.

—SEVEN VERSES—

LEONARD JEFFRIES
ROOTS

*(3:00 P.M. Wednesday, November 20, 1991. A very large con-
ference room in the African American Studies Department at
CUNY. Drawn venetian blinds, fluorescent lighting. Dr. Jeffries wears a light, multicolored African top, and a multicolored African hat. His shoes are black functional shoes, like the
shoes to a uniform. He sits facing the table, and often sits back*

*with the chair back from the table, often touches the table, and often sits back with the chair on its back legs only. Sometimes he scratches his head by throwing his hat forward on his head with great ease and authority. There is a bodyguard, a large heavy-set African American man, present.)*

People are asking who is this guy Jeffries?
When they find out my background they're gonna be
    surprised.
They are gonna find out that I was even related to Alex
    Haley.
In fact I was a major consultant for *Roots*.
In fact there might not have been a *Roots* without me.
Now when I say that,
730    that's my own personal in-group joke wit' Alex.
He was in Philadelphia
getting his ticket to go down to Jamaica
and
*Roots* was lost.
He had it in a duffle bag,
a big duffle bag like this,
the whole manuscript.
It was lost in the airport of Philadelphia.
I got on my horse and ran around the airport of
740    Philadelphia
and found *Roots*.
So that's my joke.
He had this manuscript,
Alex didn't have anything else but this manuscript.
Now if he had lost that, that would have been it.
He didn't have any photocopies.
Alex did everything on a shoestring.
uhm
so for him to deny me now . . .
750    He never even acknowledged
Pat
Alexander
his girlfriend/secretary who he had paid with affection and
    not with
resources.
So I didn't expect him to acknowledge me.
He called me to come down.
I called my wife who was working on her Ph.D. at Yale.
I said, "Rosalind, Alex wants us to come down to
760    Brunswick, Georgia,
they're filming *Roots*."
She said yes she'd come down and we'd go, then she called
    me back.
She said, "I got too much work," so I went down to
    Brunswick, Georgia.
He introduced me to Margulies,
who was the, um, director
of *Roots,*
as the leading expert in America on Africa, and I said,
770    "Wow," to
myself, "that's kind of high."
When Margulies said,
"That makes me number two," then I realized what Alex
    was doing to keep *Roots* honest.
So for two weeks I tried to change *Roots*.

Alex would say, "Wait a
minute, let's consult the experts."
After two weeks they got tired of me, sat me down
and said, "Dr. Jeffries," at lunch,
"we are very happy to have you here    780
but we just bought the rights to the book *Roots*
and we are under no obligation to maintain the integrity of
    the book
and we certainly don't have to deal with the truth of Black
    history."
Now,
this was a wipeout for me
I
I, there's been very few trau*mat*ic
moments    790

*(Longest pause in his text)*

uh, just to think.
Now I wasn't even prepared for this
but Pat had called me before and said,
"Len, I'm looking at this document and I don't know what
    to make of it."
I said, "What is it, Pat, what is it?"
and I knew she was nervous, she said,
"I'm reading a contract that says
"*Roots* has been sold to David Wolper and their heirs for
    ever and    800
ever

*(He is thumping his hand on table)*

and their heirs for ever and ever."
Alex had signed the contract for fifty thousand dollars.

*(He is thumping his hand on table)*

Fifty thousand dollars for paperback *Roots*.
Something that made how much?
Three hundred million dollars?
He was suing them for years.
The millions he made out to TV *Roots* he spent a lot of it
    to sue
Doubleday to get a better deal—I don't know if he ever    810
    got it.
*Roots* was a devastation.
The tens of millions and hundreds of millions made on
    *Roots*
went to produce,
not to make more Black series,
like *Roots,*
but they went to produce a *series*
maybe a dozen mini-series on *Jewish* history
as opposed to Black history.    820
You can document what was produced in terms of Black
    history
compared to what was produced of Jewish history.
It's a devastation.
But the *one* thing that came out of this for me,
was that when these people told me, you know,
"We bought your research
We bought your history
You really have no . . ."

830 I was thrown off
I had to get out of there.
I stayed for another couple of days.
I told Alex I had to make a pilgrimage to my grandfather's
    grave.
Never saw my grandfather.
Then I watched one more scene in the Alex Haley thing
and that finished it for me.
A cutaway of a slave ship
that was so real that they had to bring in these high school
840    kids,
and once these high school kids played the enslaved
    Africans greased
down in simulated vomit
and feces
they couldn't come back,
so they had to continue to get,
go take these youngsters,
and some little White woman
who was there sleeping with one of those guys,
850 they told her, "You cannot take these kids without
    authorization."
But she would drive a bus
up to the schoolyard,
put the kids in it, and bring them to the set.
And it almost produced a riot
there.
But anyway this slave scene
was so realistic
the trainer's up on a lower deck
860 and Kunta Kinte's on a bottom deck
and they call down to each other,
and the trainer says,
"Kunta Kinte,
Be strong! Be strong!
We may have to fight.
Kill the White man and return to Mother Africa."
This was high drama.
All of us grown men over hiding in the shadows in *tears.*
Then
870 Green rushes out and said, "Break! Break!"
He said he didn't want the scene.
We said, "What?"
Even Lou Gossett and them were ready to *fight!*
You know 'cause they had—
a movie script is just
a skeleton,
you have to put your soul in a movie script,
and they put their heart and soul into what would have
    been . . .
880 And with the African—
because the "earth is mother" all over Africa.
So to say to go back to Mother Africa is a very meaningful
    phrase.
But this
Englishman refused
to accept it,
and they almost had a physical fight on the set.
They compromised and said,
"We—are—all—from—one—village,"

*(Hitting his hand rhythmically on the desk)*

which is not the same thing.   890
After that I said, "I have to go."
I said I have to go,
and I rented a—
I flew out with Lorne Greene of all people.
He saw me and we had known each other for a couple of
    weeks from
the set,
and he's sitting there drinking his little drinks
talking about "Isn't *Roots* wonderful.
It's everybody's history,"   900
and I'm dying.

*(Pause)*

Get to Atlanta.
Rent a car. Cut across the Georgia countryside.
came to a fork in the road,
made the right turn,
and there on a bluff
was a clapboard church
made by my grandfather
and
four   910
other trustees.
Then when
I went across the cemetery
to see, uh,
the gravesite where he was—
the tallest tombstone in the graveyard was his.
Uhm,
It was an obelisk.
On it was a Masonic symbol.
He was the master of the lodge.   920
On it was his vital statistics:
*"Born August the tenth 1868."*
At the birth of the Fourteenth Amendment.
I later learned that his brother Sam was born
1865 at the birth of the Thirteenth Amendment!
And this is why people say,
"Who is he?
What is he?
Why is he?"
If they only know   930
I've had one of the best educations on the planet.
Yeah.
So . . .
When I went to Albany
in July,
I went knowing that you might not have
much time,
just like my wife said on the radio today:
"When we speak
we speak as though it is the last speech we're gonna make."   940
But I knew what was at stake
ever since they branded me a conspiracy theorist,
February 12, 1990,
two-column editorial in the *New York Times.*
That was,

in the concept of Jewish thinking,
the kiss of death.
I knew I had been targeted.
Arthur Schlesinger went and wrote a book
950    called *The Disuniting of America.*
He has everybody in the margin
except a half-page photo of myself
which said to us,
"This is the one they got to kill."
We knew that Schlesinger
and his people had sent out a thousand letters
to CEOs around the country
and foundation heads
not to have anything to do with
960    all of us involved in these studies
for multicultural curriculum
so, uh . . .
Knowing that I had taken this beating for two and a half
    years
it was my chance to strike out,
but people don't understand
that that was my way of saying,
"You bastids! . . .
for starting this process
970    of destroying *me.*"
That was my striking out.
But people don't know the context.
They don't know that for two and a half years
I bore this burden
by myself
and I bore it well.
And now they've got a problem.
'Cause after they destroyed me,
here he is resurrected!!!!!
980    I spoke at Columbia, I spoke at Queens College. . . .

LETTY COTTIN POGREBIN
NEAR ENOUGH TO REACH

*(Evening. The day before Thanksgiving, 1991. On the phone.
Direct, passionate, confident, lots of volume. She is in a study
with a rolltop desk and a lot of books.)*

I think it's about rank frustration and the old story
that you pick a scapegoat
that's much more, I mean Jews and Blacks,
that's manageable,
because we're near,
we're still near enough to each other to reach!
I mean, what can you do about the people who voted for
    David Duke?
Are Blacks going to go there and deal with that?
990    No, it's much easier to deal with Jews who are also
    panicky.
We're the only ones that pay any attention

*(Her voice makes an upward inflection)*

Do you hear?
Well, Jeffries did speak about the Mafia being, um,
Mafia,

and the Jews in Hollywood.
I didn't see
this tremendous outpouring of Italian
reaction.
Only *Jews* listen,    1000
only *Jews* take Blacks seriously,
only *Jews* view Blacks as full human beings that you
should *address*
in their rage
and, um,
people don't seem to notice that.
But Blacks, it's like a little child kicking up against Arnold
Schwarzenegger
when they,
when they have anything to say about the dominant    1010
    culture
nobody listens! Nobody reacts!
To get a headline,
to get on the evening news,
you have to attack a Jew.
Otherwise you're ignored.
And it's a shame.
We all play into it.

MINISTER CONRAD MOHAMMED
SEVEN VERSES

*(April 1992, morning. A café/restaurant. Roosevelt Island,
New York. We are sitting in the back, in an area that is surrounded by glass floor-to-ceiling windows. Mr. Mohammed is
impeccably dressed in a suit of an elegant fabric. He wears a
blue shirt and a bow tie. He has on fine shoes, designer socks,
and a large fancy watch and wedding ring. His hair is closely
cropped. He drinks black coffee, and uses a few packs of sugar.
He is traveling with another man, also a Muslim, in the clothing of a Muslim, impeccable, who sits at another table and
watches us.)*

The condition of the Black man in America today is part
    and parcel,    1020
through the devlishment
that permitted Caucasian people
to rob us of our humanity,
and put us in the throes of slavery . . .
The fact that our—our Black
parents
were actually taken
as cattle
and as, as
animals    1030
and packed into
slave ships
like sardines
amid feces
and urine—
and the suffering of our people,
for months,
in the middle passage—
Our women,
raped    1040

before our own eyes,
so that today
some look like you,
some look like me,
some look like a brother . . .
(indicating his companion)
This is a crime of tremendous proportion.
In fact,
no crime in the history of humanity
1050   has before or since
equaled that crime.
The Holocaust did not equal it
Oh, absolutely not.
First of all,
that was a horrible crime
and that is something that is a disgrace in the eyes of
   civilized
people.
That, uh, crime also stinks
1060   in the nostrils of God.
But it in no way compares with the slavery of our people
because we lost over a hundred
and some say two hundred and fifty,
million
in the middle passage
coming from Africa
to America.
We were so thoroughly robbed.
We didn't just lose six million.
1070   We didn't just
endure this
for, for
five or six years
or from '38 to '45 or '39 to—
We endured this for over three hundred years—
the total subjugation of the Black man.
You can go into Bangladesh today,
Calcutta,

*(He strikes the table with a sugar packet three or four times)*

New Delhi,
1080   Nigeria,
some really
so-called underdeveloped nation,
and I don't care how low that person's humanity is

*(He opens the sugar packet)*

whether they never
had running water,
if they'd never seen a television or anything.
They are in better condition than the Black man and
   woman
in America today
1090   right now.
Even at Harvard.
They have a contextual understanding of what their destiny
   is.

*(He strikes the table with another sugar packet three or four
times and opens it)*

But the Black man has no knowledge of that;
he's an amnesia victim

*(Starts stirring his coffee)*

He has lost knowledge of himself

*(Stirring his coffee)*

and he's living a beast life.

*(Stirring his coffee)*

So this proves that it was the greatest
crime.
Because we were cut off from our past.                    1100
Not only were we killed and murdered,
not only were our women raped
in front of their own children.
Not only did the slave master stick

*(The spoon drops onto saucer)*

at times,
daggers into a pregnant woman's stomach,
slice the stomach open
push the baby out on the ground and crush the head of the
   baby
to instill fear in the Massas of the plantation.            1110

*(Stirring again)*

Not only were these things done,
not only were our thumbs

*(Spoon drops)*

put in, in devices
that would just slowly torture the slave
and tear the thumb off from the root.
Not only were we sold on the auction block
like cattle,
not permitted to marry.
See these are the crimes
of slavery that nobody wants to talk about.                 1120
But the most significant crime—
because we could have recovered from all of that—
but the fact that they cut off all knowledge from us,
told us that we were animals,
told us that we were subhuman,
took from us our names,
gave us names like
Smith
and Jones
and today we wear those names                              1130
with dignity
and pride,
yet these were the names given to us in one of the greatest
   crimes
ever committed on the face of the earth.
So this kind of thing,
Sister,
is what qualifies slavery
as the greatest
crime                                                       1140

ever committed.
They have stolen
our garment.
Stolen our identity.
The Honorable Louis Farrakhan
teaches us
that *we* are the chosen of God.
*We* are those people
that almighty God Allah
1150    has selected as his chosen,
and they are masquerading in our garment—
the Jews.
We don't have an identity today.
Because we are the people . . .
There are seven verses
in the Bible
seven verses,
I believe it is in Deuteronomy,
that the Jews base
1160    their chosen people, uh, uh,
claim the theology,
the whole theological exegesis
with respect
of being the chosen
is based upon seven verses
in the Scripture that talk
about a covenant
with Abraham.

LETTY COTTIN POGREBIN
ISAAC

(*Morning. Spring. On the phone. She is in her office in her home on West 67th Street and Central Park West in Manhattan. Her office has an old-fashioned wooden rolltop desk and bookcases filled with books. She says she was wearing leggings and a loose shirt.*)

Well,
1170    it's hard for me to do that
because
I think there's a tendency to make hay
with the Holocaust,
to push
all the buttons.
And I mean this story about my uncle Isaac—makes *me* cry
and it's going to make your audience cry
and I'm beginning to worry
1180    that
we're trotting out our Holocaust stories
too regularly and that we're going to inure each other to the truth of
them.
But
I think
maybe if you let me read it,
I would prefer to read it:

(*Reading from* Deborah, Golda, and Me)

"I remember my mother's cousin
Isaac who came to New York                                    1190
immediately after the war and lived with us for several months.
Isaac is my connection to dozens of other family members who
were murdered in the concentration camps.
Because he was blond and blue-eyed he had been
chosen as the designated survivor of his town.
That is the Jewish councils had instructed him to do anything
to stay alive and tell the story.                             1200
For Isaac
anything turned out to mean this.
The Germans accepted his forged Aryan papers and decided that he
would have to prove by his actions that he was not a Jew.
They put him on a transport train with the Jews of his town
and then gave him the task of herding into the gas chambers
everyone in his train load.
After he had fulfilled that assignment                        1210
with patriotic
German efficiency,
the Nazis accepted the authenticity of his identity papers
and let him go.
Among those whom Isaac packed into the gas chambers that day
dispassionately as if shoving a few more items into an overstuffed
closet
were his wife                                                 1220
and
two children.
The designated survivor
arrived in America
at about age forty

(*Breathes in*)

with prematurely white hair and a dead gaze within the sky blue
eyes that's helped save his life.
As promised he told his story to dozens of Jewish agencies
and community leaders and to groups of families and     1230
friends which
is how I heard the account
translated from his Yiddish
by my mother.
For months he talked,
speaking the unspeakable.
Describing a horror
that American Jews had suspected but could not conceive.
A monstrous tale
that dwarfed the demonology of legend                         1240
and gave me the nightmare I still dream to this day.
And as he talked
Isaac seemed to grow older and older
until one night a few months later
when he finished telling everything he knew
he died."

ROBERT SHERMAN
LOUSY LANGUAGE

*(11:00 A.M. Wednesday, November 13, 1991. A very sunny and large, elegant living room in a large apartment near the Brooklyn Museum. Mr. Sherman is sitting in an armchair near an enormous bouquet of flowers for the birth of his first child. He wears sweats, and a bright orange long-sleeved tee shirt. Smiles frequently, upbeat, impassioned. Fingers his wedding ring. Each phrase builds on the next, pauses are all sustained intensity, never lets up. Full. Lots of volume, clear enunciation, teeth, and tongue very involved in his speech. Good-humored, seems to like the act of speech.)*

    Do you have demographic information on Crown Heights?
The important thing to remember is that—
and I will check these numbers when I get back to the
1250     office—
I think the
Hasidim
comprise only ten percent
of the population
of the neighborhood.
The Crown Heights conflict has been brewing on and off
    for twenty years
since the Hasidic community
developed some serious numbers
1260    and some strength in Crown Heights and as African
    Americans and
Caribbean Americans came to make up the dominant
    culture in
Crown Heights.
Very important to remember that
those things that are expressed really as
bias,
those things
that we at the Human Rights Commission
1270    would consider to be bias,
have the same trappings of bias,
which is complaints based on a characteristic, not on a
    knowledge of a
specific person.
There sort of is a soup
of bias—prejudice, racism, and discrimination.
I think bias really does relate to
feelings with a valence,
feelings with a, uhm,

*(Breathing in)*

1280    feelings that can go in a direction positive or negative
although we usually use bias to mean a negative.
What it means usually
is negative attitudes
that can lead to negative behaviors:
biased
acts, biased incidents,
or biased crimes.
Racism is hatred based on race.
Discrimination refers to
1290    acts against somebody . . .

so that the words
actually tangle up.
I think in part
because vocabulary
follows general awareness. . . .
I think you know
the Eskimos have seventy words for snow?
We probably have seventy different kinds of bias,
    prejudice, racism, and
discrimination,                         1300
but it's not in our mind-set to be clear about it,
so I think that we have
sort of lousy language
on the subject
and that
is a reflection
of our unwillingness
to deal with it honestly
and to sort it out.
I think we have very, very bad language.    1310

## —CROWN HEIGHTS, BROOKLYN—
## AUGUST 1991

RABBI JOSEPH SPIELMAN
NO BLOOD IN HIS FEET

*(9:30 A.M. Tuesday, November 12, 1991. A large home on President Street in Crown Heights. Only natural light, not very much light. Dark wood. A darkish dining room with an enormous table, could seat twenty. The rabbi sits at the head of the table. Lots of stuff on the table. He wears Hasidic clothing, a black fedora, black jacket, and reading glasses. As he talks, he slightly slides around the tape-recorder microphone, which is in front of him at the table. The furniture in the dining room including his chair is, for the most part, very old, solid wood. There are children playing quietly in another room, and people come in and out frequently, but always whispering and walking carefully not to make noise, unless they speak to him directly. The children at one point came over and stared at me.)*

    Many people were on the sidewalk,
talking, playing,
drinking
beer or whatever—
being that type of neighborhood.
A car
driven by an individual—
a Hasidic individual—
went through the intersection,
was hit by another car,    1320
thereby causing it to go onto the sidewalk.
The driver on seeing
himself in such a position that he felt he was going to
    definitely hit
someone,
because of the amount of people on the sidewalk,
he steered at the building,

so as to get out of the way of the people.
Obviously, for the most part,
1330    he was successful.
But regrettably,
one child was killed
and another child
was wounded.
Um,
seeing what happened,
he jumped out of the car
and, realizing
there may be a child under the car,
1340    he tried to physically lift
the car
from the child.
Well, as he was doing this
the Afro-Americans were beating him already.
He was beaten so much he needed stitches in the scalp
    and the face,
fifteen or sixteen stitches
and also
there were three other passengers in the car
1350    that were being beaten too.
One of the passengers was calling 911
on the cellular phone.
A Black person
pulled the phone out of his hand and ran.
Just stole the—stole the telephone.
The Jewish community
has a volunteer
ambulance corps
which is funded totally from the nations—
1360    there is not one penny of government funds—
and manned by volunteers—
who many times at their expense—
supplied the equipment that they carry in order to save
    lives.
As one of the EMS ambulances were coming,
one of the Hasidic ambulances or the Jewish ambulances
    came
on the scene.
The EMS responded with three ambulances on the scene.
1370    They were there before
the Jewish ambulance came.
Two or three police cars were already on the scene.
The police saw the potential for violence
and saw that the occupants of the car
were being beaten and were afraid for their safety.
At the same time the EMS asked
the Hasidic ambulances for certain pieces of equipment
    that they
were out of,
1380    that they needed to take care of the Cato kid,
and,
um,
in fact, I was . . .
The Hasidic ambulance left, leaving behind one of the
    passengers.
That passenger had a walkie-talkie and he requested that I
come down to pick him up.

And at that time there was a lot of screaming and shouting
and it was a mixed crowd, Hasidic and Afro-American.
The police said, "Rabbi get your people out of here."    1390
I told them to leave and I left.
Now,
a few hours later,
two and a half hours later,
in a different part of Crown Heights,
a scholar
from Australia,
Yankel Rosenbaum,
who, urr,
I think he had a doctorate or he was working on his    1400
    doctorate,
was walking on the street
on his own—
I mean he was totally oblivious—
and he was accosted by a group of young Blacks
about twenty of them strong
which was being egged on by a Black
male approximately
forty years old and balding,
telling them,    1410
"Kill all Jews—
look what they did to the kid,
kill all Jews,"
and all the epithets that go along with it,
"Heil Hitler" and all of it.
They stabbed him,
which later on the stab wounds were fatal
and he passed away in the hospital.
The Mayor,
hearing about the Cato kid,    1420
came to the Kings County Hospital
to give condolences to the family of the child who had
    regrettably been killed.
At the meantime they had already wheeled in
Mr. Rosenbaum.
He was in the emergency room
and I was at the hospital at the same time,
and the Mayor, seeing me there,
expressed his concern
that a child,    1430
uh, innocent child, had been killed.
Where I explained to him
the fact
that,
whereas the child was killed from an unfortunate accident
where there was no malicious intent,
here
there was an individual lying in the emergency room
who had been stabbed with malicious intent
and for the sole reason—    1440
not that he did anything to anyone—
just from the fact that he happened to be Jewish.
And the mayor went with me to the emergency room
to visit Mr. Rosenbaum.
This was approximately one and a half hours before he
    passed away.
I noticed at the time that his feet

were
completely white.
1450 And I complained to the doctor
on the scene,
"He's having a problem with blood circulation
because there's no blood in his feet."
And she gave me some asinine answer.
And the mayor asked her what his condition is:
"Serious but stable."
In the meantime he was screaming and in pain
and they weren't doing anything.
Subsequently they, um,
1460 they started giving him anaesthesia in a time that
they weren't allowed to give him anaesthesia
and while he was under anaesthesia,
he passed away.
So there was totally mismanagement in his case.
So whereas the Mayor,
had been fed . . .
his people got
whatever information he got out of the Black community
was
1470 that
the driver had run a red light
and also,
and that the ambulance,
the Hasidic ambulance,
refused to take care of the Black child that was dying and
rather took care of their own.
Nenh?
And this is what was fed amongst the Black community.
And it was false,
1480 it was totally false
and it was done maliciously
only with the intent to get the riots,
to start up the resulting riots.

THE REVEREND CANON DOCTOR HERON SAM
MEXICAN STANDOFF

*(November 12, 1991, 4:00 P.M. The rectory office at St. Mark's
Church in Crown Heights. A small, short office. Lived in but
impeccably ordered. Some light from lamps, some from overhead. Plaques and awards everywhere. The reverend is wearing a yellow shirt, priest's collar, tan summer jacket. He wears
spectacles. There are clocks that make noise and sound the
hour in his office and outside church bells sound during the interview, loud. Throughout the talk he is trying to get the
corner of a calendar to stay down, but it continues to stick up.
Finally he uses a paperweight to keep it down.)*

You can't have that kind of accident
if people are observing the speed limits.
People knew it was the Grand Rebbe.
People have seen the Grand Rebbe
charging through the community.
He is worried
1490 about a threat on his life
from the Satmars.

These Lubavitcher people
are really very,
uh, enigmatic people.
They move so easily between
simplicity and sophistication.
Because
they fear for his life,
because the Satmars
who are their sworn enemies                                    1500

*(He laughs/chuckles)*

have threatened to *kill*
the Rebbe.
So whenever he comes out
he's gotta be *whisked!*
You know like a President
or even better than a President.
He says he's an intuhnational figuh
like a Pope!
I say
then, "Why don't you get the Swiss guards           1510
to escort you
rather than using the police
and taxpayers' money?"
He's gotta be
*whisked!*
Quickly through the neighborhood.
Can't walk around.
He used to walk.
When I first came here.
Now he doesn't walk at all.                                    1520
They drive him.
And when he walked
you could tell he was in front
because there was,
he was protected all around
and they spilled out onto the streets
and buses had to stop
because this BIG BAND
had to escort
the Rebbe from his house over there           1530
to the synagogue.
So the Rebbe goes to the cemetery.
Every time the Rebbe goes to the cemetery,
which is once a week
to visit his dead wife
and father-in-law,
the police
lead him in escort,
charging down the street
at seventy miles an hour in a metropolis—           1540
what do you want?

*(Swift increase in volume and suddenly businesslike)*

It happened that on this occasion that as they were coming
   back,
uh,
the police car
with its siren,
had gone over a main

intersection with the light
in favor
1550    of the police car.
The Rebbe's Cadillac had passed
when the lights had become amber
and nobody expected the bodyguard van,
uh,
station wagon
to deliberately go through the red light.
So the traffic
that had the right of way kept coming and
BANG!
1560    came the collision and the careening
onto the sidewalk
had to damage whoever was there
and then, um, they were more concerned about licking
     their own
wounds.
Rather than pick
the car off the boy
who died as a result.
And then the ambulance that came—
1570    the Jewish ambulance—
was concerned about the people in the van
while some boy lay dead,
a black boy lay dead on the street.
The people showed their—

(*Increase in volume*)

they burned and whatever else,
upturned
police cars
and looted,
and as a result,
1580    I think in retaliation, murdered one of the Hasidics.
But that was just the match that lit the powder keg.
It's gonna happen again and again.
There's a Mexican standoff right now
But it's gonna happen again.


ANONYMOUS YOUNG MAN #1
WA WA WA

(*7:00 or 8:00 P.M. Spring. A recreation room at Ebbets Field apartments. A very handsome young Caribbean American man with dreadlocks, in his late teens or early twenties, wearing a bright, loose-fitting shirt. The room is ill equipped. There are a few pieces of broken furniture. It is poorly lit. A woman, Kym, with dreadlocks and shells in her hair, is at the interview. It was originally scheduled to be her interview. The Anonymous Young Man #1 and the other Anonymous Young Man, #2, started by watching the interview from the side of the room but soon approached me and began to join in. Anonymous Young Man #1 was the most vocal. Anonymous Young Man #2 stood lurking in the shadows. A third young man, younger than both of them, wearing wire spectacles and a blue Windbreaker, who looks quite like a young Spike Lee, sat silent with his hands and head on the table the entire time. There is a very bad radio or tape recorder playing music in the background.*)

What I saw was
she was pushin'
her brother on the bike like
this,
right?
She was pushin'                                        1590
him
and he kept dippin' around
like he didn't know how
to ride the bike.
So she kept runnin'
and pushin' him to the side.
So she was already runnin'
when the car was comin'.
So I don't know if she was runnin' toward him
because we was watchin' the car                        1600
weavin',
and we was goin'
"Oh, yo
it's a Jew, man.
He broke the stop light, they never get arrested."
At first we was laughin', man, we was like
you see they do anything
and get away with it,
and then
we saw that he was out of control,                     1610
and den
we started regrettin' laughin',
because then
we saw where he was goin'.
First he hit a car, right,
the tore a whole front fender off a car,
and then we was like
Oh
my god,
man, look at the kids,                                 1620
you know,
so we was already runnin' over there
by the time the accident happened.
That's how we know he was drinkin'
cause he was like
Wa Wa Wa Wa
and I was like
"Yo, man, he's drunk.
Grab him,
grab him.                                              1630
Don't let him go anywhere."
I said,
"Grab him."
I didn't want him to limp off
in some apartment somewhere
and come back in a different black jacket.
So I was like,
"Grab him,"
and then I was like, "Is the ambulance comin' for the
     kids?"                                            1640
'Cause I been in a lot of confrontations with Jews before
and I know that when they said an ambulance
is comin'
it most likely meant for them.

And they was like,
"oh, oh."
Jews right?
"Ambulance comin', ambulance comin',
calm down, calm down,
1650    God will help them,
God will help them if you believe."
And he was actin' like he was dyin'.
"Wa Aww,
me too,
I'm hurt, I'm hurt, I'm hurt too."
Wan nothin wrong with him,
wan nothin wrong with him.
They say that we beat up on that man
that he had to have stitches because of us.
1660    You don't come out of an accident like that unmarked,
without a scratch.
The most he got from us was slapped
by a little kid.
And here come the ambulance
and I was like, "That's not a city ambulance,"
not like this I was upset right
and I was like,
"YO,
the man is drunk!
1670    He ran a red light!
You all ain't gonna do nothin'."
Everybody started comin' around, right,
'cause I was talkin' about
these kids is dyin' man!
I'm talkin' about the skull of the baby is on the ground
    man!
and he's walkin'!
I was like, "Don't let him get into that ambulance!"
And the Jews,
1680    the Jews
was like private, private ambulance
I was like, "Grab him,"
but my buddies was like,
"We can't touch them."
Nobody wanted to grab him,
nobody wanted to touch him,
An' I was breakin' fool, man,
I was goin' mad,
I couldn't believe it.
1690    Everybody just stood
there,
and that made me cry.
I was cryin'
so I left, I went home and watched the rest of it on TV,
it was too lackadazee
so it was like me, man, instigatin' the whole thing.
I got arrested for it
long after
in Queens.
1700    Can't tell you no more about that,
you know.
Hey, wait a minute,
they got eyes and ears everywhere.
What color is the Israeli flag?

And what color are the police cars?
The man was *drunk*,
I open up his car door,
I was like, when—
I was like, he'd been drinkin'
I know our words don't have no meanin',        1710
as Black people in Crown Heights.
You realize, man,
ain't no justice,
ain't never been no justice,
ain't never gonna be no justice.

MICHAEL S. MILLER
"HEIL HITLER"

(*A large airy office in Manhattan on Lexington in the fifties.
Mr. Miller sits behind a big desk in a high-backed swivel chair
drinking coffee. He's wearing a yarmulke. Plays with the swiz-
zle stick throughout. There is an intercom in the office, so that
when the receptionist calls him, you can hear it, and when she
calls others in other offices, you can hear it, like a page in a
public place, faintly.*)

I was at Gavin Cato's funeral,
at nearly every public event
that was conducted by the Lubavitcher community and the
    Jewish
community as a whole.        1720
Words of comfort
were offered to the family of Gavin Cato.
I can show you a letter that we sent
to the Cato family expressing, uh,
our sorrow over the loss,
unnecessary loss, of their son.
I am not aware of a word
that was spoken at that funeral.
I am not aware of a—
and I was taking notes—        1730
of a word that was uttered
of comfort to the family of Yankel Rosenbaum.
Frankly this was a political rally rather than a funeral.
The individuals you mentioned—
and again,
I am not going to participate in verbal acrimony,
not only
were there cries of, "Kill the Jews"
or,
"Kill the Jew,"        1740
there were cries of, "Heil Hitler."
There were cries of, "Hitler didn't finish the job."
There were cries of,
"Throw them back into the ovens again."
To hear in *Crown Heights*—
and Hitler was no lover of Blacks—
"Heil Hitler"?
"Hitler didn't finish the job"?
"We should heat up the ovens"?
From *Blacks*?        1750
Is more inexplicable
or unexplainable

or any other word that I cannot fathom.
The hatred is so
*deep seated*
and the hatred
knows no boundaries.
There is no boundary
to anti-Judaism.
1760  The anti-*Judaism*—
if people don't want me
to use,
hear me use the word anti-Semitism.
And I'll be damned if,
if preferential treatment is gonna
be the excuse
for every bottle,
rock,
or pellet that's, uh, directed
1770  toward a Jew
or the window of a Jewish home
or a Jewish store.
And, frankly,
I think the response of the Lubavitcher community was
      relatively
passive.


HENRY RICE
KNEW HOW TO USE CERTAIN WORDS

(*Thursday, November 21, 1991. The Jackson Hole restaurant on Lexington Avenue in the thirties in Manhattan. Lunchtime, dimly lit, a reddish haze on everything, perhaps from a neon light. Mr. Rice, very neatly dressed, is eating a large, messy hamburger and horizontally chopped pickles. Drinking a Miller Lite. Beer is in a bottle next to a red plastic glass. He's wearing a baseball cap over very closely cut hair and a bright, multicolored, expensive-looking colored nylon jacket. Heavy new Timberland boots. Struggling to eat without making a mess of the food. At some point sits up from food and has his right hand or fist on his hip—a very unaffected but truly authoritative stance. Good-natured, handsome, healthy. Patsy Cline's "Crazy" is very loud on the jukebox.*)

I went back home and got my bike
because I knew I would have to be
1780  illusive.
I was there in body and in spirit
but I didn't participate in any of the violence
because basically I have a lot to lose.
But I was there
and I would have defended myself if it was necessary,
most definitely.
I weaved around trouble.
When something broke out, I moved back,
when it calmed down, I would move back in on the front
1790    line.
I was always there.
And Richard Green heard me saying something to a bunch
    of kids
about *voting*
about the power of *vote*
the power of *numbers*

and he said,
uh,
I said, "Get away from me, you're an Uncle Tom,
get away from me.                                    1800
Get back in your Mercedes-Benz!"
No! I said that to Clarence Norman
*and* to Richard Green,
both of them.
I was tearing them apart.
Richard Green was very persistent.
He said,
"Look, Mr. Rice,
I like the way you speak.
I need you.                                          1810
Please help me.
I'm a community activist. . . .
ba, ba, ba, ba, ba."

(*He drops some food on his clothes, or so it seems, he looks and grins*)

It didn't get on me.
"I'm a community activist.
I need your help,
please help me,"
and so forth.
Again,
I didn't pay him no mind                             1820
but we spoke
some
the next day after that,
after the incidents that took place on that corner
of Albany Avenue.
A brother was beat up—
cops rushing into the Black crowd
didn't rush into the Jewish crowd,
cops rushed into the Black crowd
started beatin' up                                   1830
Black people.
But the next day Richard came by in a yellow van,
a New York City Department of Transportation van,
with a megaphone,
yellow light flashing,

(*Music segues from Patsy Cline's "Crazy" to Public Enemy's "Can't Truss It," or Naughty by Nature's "O.P.P."*)

the whole works
and, um,
he said,
"Henry, I need you in this van.
Drive around with me.                                1840
Let's keep some of these kids off the street tonight."
I said, "Okay."
He said,
"The blood
of Black men are on your hands tonight!"
I said, "Okay."
We drive around in the van,
"Young people stay in the house!
Mothers keep your children in the house,
please."                                             1850
So I began fillin'

I began feeling like
I had to do it
after he told me that,
"the blood of the Black man"
were on my hands,
you know.
Richard Green sure know how to use certain words.

*(He giggles)*

I remember reaching Albany Avenue—
1860  kids were being chased by the police.
I jump out with a portable megaphone,
I tell them, "Stop running!
The cops won't chase you!
and they won't hit you!"
The next thing I know,
cop grabs my megaphone hits me in the head with a stick,
handcuffs me,
and takes the megaphone out of my hand.
So I'm like,
1870  "Wait a minute
I'm doing a community service for the mayor's office."
They don't want to hear it.
Matter of fact,
they still have the megaphone 'til this day.
I'm like,
"Richard Green get me
out of this police car, please!"
So a Black captain came by,
thank God,
1880  and he says, "What's goin' on?"
Richard Green explained it to him.
He said, "Let him go."
Get back in the van,
there's another Brother in van,
starts saying,
"Non violence!"
to the young Brothers.
They begin throwing bottles at the, uh,
at the van.
1890  One guy got so upset
he had a nine-millimeter
fully loaded.
He said, "Get the hell out of this neighborhood!"
The next day
more violence:
fires,
cars being burnt,
stores being broken into,
a perception that Black youth
1900  are going crazy in Crown Heights
like we were angry over
nothing,
understand?

NORMAN ROSENBAUM
MY BROTHER'S BLOOD

*(A Sunday afternoon. Spring. Crisp, clear, and windy. Across from City Hall in New York City. Crowds of people, predomi-*

*nantly Lubavitcher, with placards. A rally that was organized by Lubavitcher women. All of the speakers were men, but the women stand close to the stage. Mr. Rosenbaum, an Australian, with a beard, hat, and wearing a pinstripe suit, speaks passionately and loudly from the microphone on a stage with a podium. Behind him is a man in an Australian bush hat with a very large Australian flag which blows dramatically in the wind. It is so windy that Mr. Rosenbaum has to hold his hat to keep it on his head.)*

*Al do lay achee so achee aylay alo.dalmo*
My brother's blood cries out from the ground.
Let me make it clear
why I'm here.
In August of 1991,
as you all have heard before today,
my brother was killed in the streets of Crown Heights          1910
for no other reason
than that he was a Jew!
The only miracle was
that my brother was the only victim
who paid for being a Jew with his life.
When my brother was surrounded,
each and every American was surrounded.
When my brother was stabbed four times,
each and every American was stabbed four times
and as my brother bled to death in this city,          1920
while the medicos stood by
and let him bleed
to death, it was the gravest of indictments against this
    country.
One person out of twenty gutless individuals
who attacked my brother has been arrested.
I for one am not convinced that it is beyond the ability of
    the New York police
to arrest others.
Let me tell you, Mayor Dinkins,          1930
let me tell you, Commissioner Brown:
I'm here,
I'm not going home,
until there is justice.

NORMAN ROSENBAUM
SIXTEEN HOURS DIFFERENCE

*(7:00 A.M. Spring. Newark Airport, Departure Gate, Continental Airlines. Mr. Rosenbaum is moments before his flight to LA and then back to Australia. Wearing a pinstripe suit with an Australian fit. Hat. Suitcase. He has sparkling blue eyes with a twinkle, rosy cheeks, and a large smile throughout the interview.)*

There's sixteen hours difference between New York and
    Melbourne
and I had just gotten back to my office
and I had a phone call from my wife,
and she said she wanted me to come home straight away
and I sensed the urgency in her voice.          1940
I said, "are you all right?" She said, "Yeah."
I said, "are the children all right, you know the kids?" She
    says, "yeah."

So I'm driving home and I'm thinking, I wonder what's the
     problem now, you know?
We had some carpenters doing some work, I wonder if
     there has been a disaster,
some sort of domestic problem,
and I thought, oh my God, you know, my parents,
1950    I didn't even ask after them,
how insensitive not to even ask after my parents,
and I've got a grandmother eighty-five years old, same sort
     of thing.
So I get home,
I walk in the door, and a friend of mine was standing there,
close friend,
does the same sort of work as me, he's a barrister and an
     academic,
and he sees me and he says,
1960    "There's got a pro—
uh,
we've got a problem. There's a problem."
I thought he was talking about a case we were working on
     together,
he says, "'Z come,
come and sit down."
He goes to me,
"There's been a riot in New York,
been a riot in Crown Heights,
1970    Yankel's been stabbed and he's dead."
And
my brother was the last in the world,
I hadn't even given him a thought.
I mean the fact that my brother
could be attacked
or die,
it just hadn't even entered my mind.
At first I appeared all cool, calm and collected.
I then
1980    started asking questions
like who told you,
how do you know,
are you sure?
I just asked the question,
you know,
are you sure?

ANONYMOUS YOUNG MAN #2
BAD BOY

(*Evening. Spring. The same recreation room as interview with
Anonymous Young Man #1. Young Man #2 is wearing a black
jacket over his clothes. He has a gold tooth. He has some dreadlocks, and a very odd-shaped multicolored hat. He is soft-spo-
ken, and has a direct gaze. He seems to be very patient with his
explanation.*)

That youth,
that sixteen-year-old
didn't murder that Jew.

(*Pause*)

1990    For one thing,

he played baseball, right?
He was a atha-lete,
right?
A bad boy
does
bad things.
Only a bad boy coulda stabbed the man.
Somebody who
does those type a things,
or who sees                                                              2000
those types a things.
A atha-lete
sees people,
is interested in athletics,
stretchin',
exercisin',
goin' to his football games,
or his baseball games.
He's not interested
in stabbin'                                                             2010
people.
So
it's not in his mind
to stab,
to just jump into somethin',
that he has no idea about
and
sta—
and kill a man.
A bad boy,                                                              2020
somebody who's groomed in badness,
or did badness
before,
stabbed the man.
Because I used to be a atha-lete
and I used to be a bad boy,
and when I was a atha-lete,
I was a atha-lete.
All I thought about was atha-lete.
I'm not gonna jeopardize my athleticism                                 2030
or my career to do anything
that bad people do.
And when I became a bad boy
I'm not a athalete no more.
I'm a bad boy,
and I'm groomin' myself in things that is bad.
You understand, so
he's a athalete,
he's not a bad boy.
It's a big difference.                                                  2040
Like,
mostly the Black youth in Crown Heights have two things
     to do—
either DJ or be a bad boy, right?
You either
DJ, be a MC, a rapper
or Jamaican rapper,
ragamuffin,
or you be a bad boy,
you sell drugs or you rob people.                                       2050

What do you do?
I sell drugs.
What do you do?
I rap.
That's how it is in Crown Heights.
I been livin' in Crown Heights mosta my life.
I know for a fact that that youth, that sixteen-year-old,
didn't kill that Jew.
That's between me and my Creator.

SONNY CARSON
CHORDS

(*Lunchtime. Spring. A fancy restaurant in Brooklyn. Sonny tells me it's where all the judges come for lunch. White linen tablecloths. Light wood walls, lamplight next to the table. Tile floor. He is eating crab cakes. He is dressed in a black turtle-neck and a gray jacket. He has on a mud cloth hat. He has an authority stick with him, and it lays on the table. His body-guard, wearing a black leather jacket, enters in the middle of the interview. Sonny chides him for being late.*)

2060   It's going to be a long hot summer.
I'm connected up with the young people all over the
    country
and there's a thread
leading to an eruption
and Crown Heights began the whole thing.
And the Jews come second to the police
when it comes to feelings of dislike among Black folks.
The police,
the police,
2070   believe me, the police—
I know the police and the police know me
and they turn that whole place into an occupied camp
with the Seventy-first Precinct as the overseers.
And don't think that everything is OK within that precinct
    among those officers
either.
Don't think that,
don't think that.
You know the media has always painted me as the bad
2080    guy—
that's OK!
I'm a good guy to pick on.
Their viewers don't like me either,
they really don't like me because I *am* the bad guy,
I am the ultimate bad guy
because of my relationship to the young people in the city.
I understand their language.
I respect them as the future.
I speak their language. They don't even engage in long
2090    dialogue
anymore
just short
"words."
It always amazes me
how the city fathers,
the power brokers,
just continue to deny what's happening.

And it is just getting intolerable for me to continue to
    watch
this small
arrogant
group of people continue to get this kind of preferential
    treatment.
They sit on the school board.   2100
A board of nine
and they have
four members, and their kids don't even go to public
    school.
So that's the kind of arrogance I'm talking about.
I have no reason to be eagerly awaiting the coming
    together of our
people.
They owe me first.
I'm not givin' in just like that,   2110
I don't want it.
You can have it.
Like my grandmother said,
"Help the bear!
If you see me and the bear in a fight,
help the bear—
don't help me,
help the bear."
I don't need any of it from them!
And I'm not gonna advocate any coming together and   2120
    healing of
America
and all that shit.
You kiddin'?
You kiddin'?
Just 'cause I can have the fortune of walking in here
and sitting and talking
and having a drink,
it appear that I have all the same kinds of abilities
of other folks in here.   2130
No, it's not that way.
'Cause tonight
by nighttime it could all change for me.
So I'm always aware of that, and that's what keeps me goin'
today
and each day!

(*He eats*)

I have
this idea
about a film.
See,   2140
these kids, they got
another kinda rhythm now,
there's a whole new kinda
step that they do.
When I first heard rap
I was sittin' in a huge open kinda stadium,
boys and girls high school field,
and I heard these kids come out and start rappin',
and I'm listening
but it's not really clickin',   2150
but I was mesmerized though.

But it was simontaneouis
all around the country
and I said, "Oh shit,"
and everybody I knew who was young was listenin' to it
and I said, "Wow."
Because I have always been involved with young people
and all of a sudden I got it,
I really heard the rhythm,
2160    the chords,
the discord.
There's a whole new sound
that the crackers are tryin' to get, but they can't get it.
I heard it on a television commercial.
One of the most beautiful pieces of art
that I ever witnessed
was a play
called
um,
2170    um,
um,
'bout, 'bout the Puerto Rican gang—
no, no, no, no, no—
the Puerto Rican gang,
the musical
that was on Broad—
yeah,
West Side Story—
the answer should be
2180    a musical.

RABBI SHEA HECHT
OVENS

(*Morning. Spring. A building on Eastern Parkway. A large room with a very long conference table. There are pictures of Lubavitcher men on the walls. Rabbi Hecht is wearing a shirt, open at the neck. He has several crisp one-dollar bills in his shirt pocket. These are, apparently, dollar bills that the Rebbe has given him. It is the custom that the Rebbe gives out one-dollar bills on Sunday. Rabbi Hecht has a beard. He wears glasses, traditional Hasidic garb, including tsitses (ceremonial fringes that hang over his belt) and a red yamulke with gold trim which is ripped. His daughter comes in frequently to get money from him. He keeps telling her to wait until he is finished. She becomes more and more agitated. His brother also enters frequently to ask him questions, and to tell him he's late.*)

What is my goal?
My goal is not
to give anybody a message
that we plan on working things out
by integrating
our two
things.
By a person understanding more of their own religion
they will automatically respect another person.
2190    The respect that my religion teaches me has nothing to do with understanding you.
See, there's a problem.
If

the only way I'm going to respect you
is based on how much I understand you,
no matter what it is
in certain circles you're gonna run into problems.
Number one,
we are different,
and we think we should and can be different.
When the Rebbe said to the Mayor
that we were all
one people,                                                2200
I think
what the Rebbe is talking about is that,
that common denominator that we're all children of God,
    and the
respect we all have to give each other under that banner.
But that does not mean that I have to invite you to my
    house for
dinner,
because I cannot go back to your home for dinner,
because you're not gonna give me kosher food.        2210
And I said,
so, like one Black said,
I'll bring in kosher food.
I said eh-eh.
We can't use your ovens,
we can't use your dishes,
it's, it—
it's not just a question of buying certain food,
it's buying the food,
preparing it a certain way.                           2220
We can't use your dishes, we can't use your oven.
The—the higher you go
the more common denominator.
And what the Rebbe was saying,
you as the Mayor
don't get caught up in the differences,
you're—
from your position is—
you have to look at it as one city
and one                                               2230
human race.
We are all New Yorkers
and therefore I will protect all New Yorkers.
You see
preferential treatment
suggests
that you're giving the person
the police car
not because they need the police car
but because                                           2240
they are who they are.
You're not gonna
give them the housing
because they
need the housing—
you're giving it because of who they are.
But
just because I'm a Jew
therefore I
shouldn't get the police car.                         2250
The question is

a synagogue
that has five thousand Jews
leave
the synagogue
at the same time,
do they have a police car to stop the traffic?
The answer is every—single—synagogue,
temple,
2260    mosque,
in
the
world
stops traffic
when five thousand people have to walk out
at the same time.

REVEREND AL SHARPTON
RAIN

The D.A.
came back with no indictment.
Uh, so then our only course
2270    was to ask for a special prosecutor
which is appointed by the Governor,
who's been hostile,
and to sue civilly.
When we went into civil court
we went to get an order to show cause.
The judge signed it and gave me a deadline of three days.
The driver left the country. . . .
No one even said, "Why would he run?
If he did no wrong."
2280    If you and I were in an accident we'd have to go to civil
        court.
Why is this man
above the law?
So they said, "He's in Israel."
So I said,
"Well, I'll go to Israel to show best effits."
And the deadline
was,
I had to serve him by Tuesday,
2290    which was Yom Kippur—
that was the judge's decision not mine.
So we went.
Alton Maddox and I
got on a plane,
left Monday night,
landed Tuesday morning,
went and served the American embassy, uh,
so that
if this man had any decency at all
2300    he could come to the American embassy and receive
        service,
which he has not done to this day.
Come back,
went to court
and showed the judge the receipts,
and the judge said, "You made best effits,
therefore you are now permitted,

by default,
to go ahead
and sue the rabbi or whomever                          2310
because you cannot do the driver."
So it wasn't just a media grandstand.
We wanted to show the world
one, this man *ran*
and was *allowed* to run, and, two, we wanted to be able to
    legally go
around him,
to sue the people he was working for so that we can bring
    them into
court and establish *why* and what happened.          2320
And it came out in the paper the other day
that the driver in the other car didn't even have a driver's
    license.
So we're dealing with a *complete* outrage here,
we're dealing with a double standard,
we're dealing with uh, uh, a, a
situation where
Blacks do not have equal protection under the law
and the media is used to castigate us
that merely asked for justice                          2330
rather than castigate those that would hit a kid
and walk away like he just stepped on a roach!
Uh,
there also is the media
contention of the young Jewish scholar
that was stabbed that night
and they've even distorted
saying *my words at the funeral.*
I *preached* the funeral.
Uh, [the newspaper said I]                             2340
helped to, to, uh, uh,
*spark* or, or, or, or, or *inspire* or *incite* people to kill him
    [Yankel Rosenbaum]
when he was dead the day before
I came out there.
He was killed the night
that the young man
was killed with the car accident.
I didn't even get a call
from the family                                        2350
'til eighteen hours later.
So there's a whole media distortion
to protect them [the Lubavitchers].
Nobody is talking about,
"Why
is this guy
in flight?"
If I was a rabbi
(I am a ministuh)
and my driver hit a kid,                               2360
I would not let the driver *leave*
and I certainlih would give my condolences,
or anything else I could,
to the family,
I don't care what race they are.
To this minute the Rebbe has never even uttered a word
    of
sympathy

to the family,
2370    not even sent 'em a *card*
a *flower* or *nothing!*
So it's treating us with absolute contempt
and I don't care how controversial it makes us.
I *won't* tolerate being insulted.
If you piss in my face I'm gonna call it *piss*.
I'm not gonna call it rain.

RICHARD GREEN
RAGE

*(2:00 P.M. in a big red van. Green is in the front. He has a driver. I am in the back. Green wears a large knit hat with reggae colors over long dreadlocks. Driving from Crown Heights to Brooklyn College. He turns sideways to face me in the back, and bends down, talking with his elbow on his knee.)*

Sharpton, Carson, and Reverend Herbert Daughtry
didn't have any power out there really.
The media gave them power.
2380    But they weren't turning those youfs on and off.
Nobody knew who controlled the switch out there.
Those young people had rage like an oil-well fire
that has to burn out.
All they were doin' was sort of orchestratin' it.
Uh, they were not really the ones that were saying, "Well
stop, go, don't go, stop, turn around, go up."
It wasn't like that.
Those young people had rage out there,
that didn't matter who was in control of that—
2390    that rage had to get out
and that rage
has been building up.
When all those guys have come and gone,
that rage is still out here.
I can show you that rage every day
right up and down this avenue.
We see, sometimes in one month, we see three bodies
in one month. That's rage,
and that's something that nobody has control of.
2400    And I don't know who told you that it was preferential
        treatment for
Blacks that the Mayor kept the cops back. . . .
If the Mayor had turned those cops on?
We would still be in a middle of a battle.
And
I pray on both sides of the fence,
and I tell the people in the Jewish community the same
        thing,
"This is not something that force will hold."
2410    Those youfs were running on cops without nothing in their
        hands,
seven- and eight- and nine- and ten-year-old boys were
        running at
those cops
with nothing,
just running at 'em.
That's rage.
Those young people out there are angry
and that anger has to be vented,

it has to be negotiated.                                2420
And they're not angry at the Lubavitcher community
they're just as angry at you and me,
if it comes to that.
They have no
role models,
no guidance
so they're just out there growin' up on their own,
their peers are their role models,
their peers is who teach them how to move
so when they see the Lubavitch                          2430
they don't know the difference between "Heil Hitler"
and, uh, and uh, whatever else.
They don't know the difference.
When you ask 'em to say who Hitler was they wouldn't
    even be able
to tell you.

*(Phone rings, Richard picks it up, it's a mobile phone)*

"Richard Green, can I help?
Aw, man I tol' you I want some color
up on that wall. Give me some colors.
Look, I'm in the middle of somethin'."              2440

*(He returns to the conversation)*

Half them don't even know three quarters of 'em.
Just as much as they don't know who Frederick Douglass
    was.
They know Malcolm
because Malcolm has been played up to such an extent
    now
that they know Malcolm.
But ask who Nat Turner was or Mary McCleod Bethune or
    Booker T.
Because the system has given 'em                         2450
Malcolm is convenient and
Spike is goin' to give 'em Malcolm even more.
It's convenient.

ROSLYN MALAMUD
THE COUP

*(Spring. Midafternoon. The sunny kitchen of a huge, beautiful house on Eastern Parkway in Crown Heights. It's a large, very well-equipped kitchen. We are sitting at a table in a breakfast nook area, which is separated by shelves from the cooking area. There is a window to the side. There are newspapers on* 2460 *the chair at the far side of the table. Mrs. Malamud offers me food at the beginning of the interview. We are drinking coffee. She is wearing a sweatshirt with a large sequined cat. Her tennis shoes have matching sequined cats. She has on a black skirt and is wearing a wig. Her nails are manicured. She has beautiful eyes that sparkle are very warm, and a very resonant voice. There is a lot of humor in her face.)*

Do you know what happened in August here?
You see when you read the newspapers.
I mean my son filmed what was going on,
but when you read the newspapers . . .
Of course I was here
I couldn't leave my house.

2470 I only would go out early during the day.
The police were barricading here.
You see,
I wish
I could just like
go on television.
I wanna scream to the whole world.
They said
that the Blacks were rioting against the Jews in Crown
    Heights
2480 and that the Jews were fighting back.
Do you know that the Blacks who came here to riot were
    not my
neighbors?
I don't love my neighbors.
I don't know my Black neighbors.
There's one lady on President Street—
Claire—
I adore her.
She's my girl friend's next-door neighbor.
2490 I've had a manicure
done in her house and we sit and kibbitz
and stuff
but I don't know them.
I told you we don't mingle socially
because of the difference
of food
and religion
and what have you here.
But
2500 the people in this community
want exactly
what I want out of life.
They want to live
in nice homes.
They all go to work.
They couldn't possibly
have houses here
if they didn't
generally—They have
2510 two,
um,
incomes
that come in.
They want to send their kids to college.
They wanna live a nice quiet life.
They wanna shop for their groceries and cook their meals
    and go to
their Sunday picnics!
They just want to have decent homes and decent lives!
2520 The people who came to riot here
were brought here
by this famous
Reverend Al Sharpton,
which I'd like to know who ordained him?
And he brought in a bunch of kids.
I wish you could see the *New York Times,*
unfortunately it was on page twenty,
but,
he brought in a bunch of kids who didn't have jobs in the
2530 summertime

when you don't have a job
and you're hanging out all day.
I mean, they interviewed
one of the Black girls on Utica Avenue.
She said,
"The guys will make you pregnant
at night
and in the morning not know who you are."

*(Almost whispering)*

And if you're sitting on a front stoop and it's very, very hot
and you have no money                                    2540
and you have nothing to do with your time
and someone says, "Come on, you wanna riot?"
You know how kids are.
The fault lies with the police department.
The police department did nothing to stop them.
I was sitting here in the front of the house
when bottles were being thrown
and the sergeant tells five hundred policemen
with clubs and helmets and guns
to duck.                                                 2550
And I said to him,
"You're telling them to duck?
What should I do?
I don't have a club and a gun."
Had they put it—
stopped it on the first night
this kid who came from Australia . . .

*(She sucks her teeth)*

You know,
his parents were Holocaust survivors, he didn't have to die.
He worked,                                               2560
did a lot of research in Holocaust studies.
He didn't have to die.
What happened on Utica Avenue
was an accident.
JEWISH PEOPLE
DO NOT DRIVE VANS INTO SEVEN-YEAR-OLD
    BOYS.
YOU WANT TO KNOW SOMETHING? BLACK
    PEOPLE DO NOT DRIVE
VANS INTO SEVEN-YEAR-OLD BOYS.                           2570
HISPANIC PEOPLE DON'T DRIVE VANS INTO
    SEVEN-YEAR-OLD BOYS.
IT'S JUST NOT DONE.
PEOPLE LIKE JEFFREY DAHMER MAYBE THEY
    DO IT.
BUT AVERAGE CITIZENS DO NOT GO OUT AND
    TRY TO KILL

*(Sounds like a laugh but it's just a sound)*

SEVEN-YEAR-OLD BOYS.
It was an accident!
But it was allowed to fester and to steam and all that.   2580
When you come here do you see anything that's going on,
    riots?
No.
But Al Sharpton and the likes of him like *Dowerty,*
who by the way has been in prison

and all of a sudden he became Reverend *Dowerty*—
they once did an exposé on him—
but
these guys live off of this,
2590    you understand?
People are not gonna give them money,
contribute to their causes
unless they're out there rabble-rousing
My Black neighbors?
I mean I spoke to them.
They were hiding in their houses just like I was.
We were scared.
I was scared!
I was really frightened.
2600    I had five hundred policemen standing in front of my
              house
every day
I had mounted police,
but I couldn't leave my block,
because when it got dark I couldn't come back in.
I couldn't meet anyone for dinner.
Thank God, I told you my children were all out of town.
My son was in Russia.
The coup
2610    was exactly the same day as the riot
and I was very upset about it.
He was in Russia running a camp
and I was very concerned when I had heard about that.
I hadn't heard from him
that night the riot started.
When I did hear from him I told him to stay in Russia,
     he'd be safer
there than here.
And he was.

## REUVEN OSTROV
## POGROMS

*(9:00 P.M. November 1991. In a basement of a Crown Heights
house. Mr. Ostrov wears a yamulke. Eating popcorn and sliced
apples. Very low, gentle-sounding* nigunim *music plays in the
background, it almost sounds like New Age music, perhaps because traditional music is played on a modern electronic keyboard instrument. In the show, I wore a basketball jacket with
the team's insignia, and used a basketball—which Mr. Ostrov
did not do at this interview, but previously had at a basketball
game. He has no beard, which is unusual for a man his age who
does have a beard if grown. He has a very rich, deep voice.)*

2620    I was working in a hospital.
I work as an assistant chaplain at
Down State Kings County Hospital.
I heard that Yankel Rosenbaum was stabbed and, um, they
were gonna give him an *aurtopsy*
and they asked if he had an
aurtopsy
or not because in the Jewish religion a person is not al-
     lowed to have
an aurtopsy
2630    and I found out later that he did have one
a few days later.

I found a Jewish man in a room,
a Russian man.
His mother committed suicide
because she was, uhm, she was terrified.
She jumped out of the third floor of her apartment
     building,
committed suicide.
The mother originally came from Russia.
I was speaking to her son    2640
in one of the rooms near the morgue
trying to get his mother not to have an aurtopsy
and he was telling me that the mother
came from Russia eleven years ago
and the mother left Russia eleven years ago
because of the hardships that they had over there,
and when they came to America
and when this thing started to happen in Crown Heights.
It became painful
and it felt like, like there was no place to go.    2650
It's like you're trapped,
everywhere you go there's Jew haters.
And then he told me she commit suicide,
told me the next morning he woke up
he heard the doorbell ring.
He wasn't,
she wasn't there.
He noticed that the window was open,
which is never open
because she was afraid of the cold    2660
even in the summertime.
And he saw his mother
with blood all over her
landed head first
on the concrete side of the apartment building.
After that we already knew this was getting serious,
because we had,
we had Sonny Carson come down
and we had, um,
Reverend Al Sharpton come down    2670
start making pogroms.

## CARMEL CATO
## LINGERING

*(7:00 P.M. The corner where the accident occurred in Crown
Heights. An altar to Gavin is against the wall where the car
crashed. Many pieces of cloth are draped. Some writing in
color is on the wall. Candle wax is everywhere. There is a rope
around the area. Cato is wearing a trench coat, pulled around
him. He stands very close to me. Dark outside. Reggae music is
in the background. Lights come from stores on each corner.
Busy intersection. Sounds from outside. Traffic. Stores open.
People in and out of shops. Sounds from inside apartments,
televisions, voices, cooking, etc. He speaks in a pronounced
West Indian accent.)*

In the meanwhile
it was two.
Angela was on the ground
but she was trying to move. Gavin was still.

They was trying to pound him.
I was the father.
I was 'it, chucked, and pushed,
and a lot of
2680 sarcastic words were passed towards me
from the police
while I was trying to explain: It was my kid!
These are my children.
The child was hit you know.
I saw everything, everything,
the guy radiator burst
all the hoses,
the steam,
all the garbage buckets along the building.
2690 And it was very loud,
everything burst.
It's like an atomic bomb,
and that's why all these people comin' round
wanna know what's happening.
Oh it was very outrageous.
Numerous numbers.
All the time the police sayin'
you can't get in,
you can't pass,
2700 and the children laying on the ground.
He was hit at exactly eight-thirty.
Why?
I was standing over there.
There was a little child—
a friend of mine
came up with a little child—
and I lift the child up
and she look at her watch at the same time
and she say it was eight-thirty.
2710 I gave the child back to her.
And then it happen.
Um, Um . . .
My child, these are the things I never dream about.
I take care of my children.
You know it's a funny thing,
if a child get sick and he dies
it won't hurt me so bad,
or if a child run out into the street
it wouldn't hurt me.
2720 That's what's hurtin' me.
And the whole week
that Gavin died
my body was changing,
I was having different feelings.
I stop eating,
I didn't et
nothin',
only drink water,
for two weeks;
2730 and I was very touchy—
any least thing that drop
or any song I hear
it would effect me.
Every time I try to do something

I would have to stop.
I was
lingering, lingering, lingering, lingering,
all the time.
But I can do things,
I can see things,                                    2740
I know that for a fact.
I was telling myself,
"Something is wrong somewhere,"
but I didn't want to see,
I didn't want to accept,
and it was inside of me,
and even when I go home I tell my friends,
"Something coming I could feel it
but I didn't want to see,"
and all the time I just deny deny deny,              2750
and I never thought it was Gavin,
but I didn't have a clue.
I thought it was one of the other children—
the bigger boys
or the girl,
because she worry me,
she won't et—
but Gavin 'ee was 'ealtee,
and he don't cause no trouble.
That's what's devastating me now.                    2760
Sometime it make me feel like it's no justice,
like, uh,
the Jewish people,
they are very high up,
it's a very big thing,
they runnin' the whole show
from the judge right down.
And something I don't understand:
The Jewish people, they told me
there are certain people I can not be seen with       2770
and certain things I can not say
and certain people I can not talk to.
They made that very clear to me—the Jewish people—
they can throw the case out
unless
I go to them with pity.
I don't know what they talkin' about.
So I don't know what kind of crap is that.
And make me say things I don't wanna say
and make me do things I don't wanna do.               2780
I am a special person.
I was born different.
I'm a man born by my foot.
I born by my foot.
Anytime a baby comin' by the foot
they either cut the mother
or the baby dies.
But I was born with my foot.
I'm one of the special.
There's no way they can overpower me.                 2790
No there's nothing to hide,
you can repeat every word I say.

## Anna Deavere Smith

"Not So Special Vehicles" (1993)

*ANNA Deavere Smith gave this keynote address to the Association for Theatre in Higher Education annual convention, which met in Philadelphia in August 1993.*

I want to publicly thank Rhonda Blair for the support of my work over the last six years. In 1987 she called me and invited me to deliver a paper on Gender in acting training. Since that time she commissioned me to do two works that are a part of my *On the Road: A Search For American Character* Series. I am grateful for her courage and generosity. Courage, because some of the subjects that she has asked me to look at were tough ones. Generosity, because of her welcoming spirit. I am glad to have this opportunity to thank her for inviting me to do my work, because if you don't have grants, which I didn't, and if you're not affiliated with a theater, which I wasn't, it's the only way you can keep working.

I have been absent from this organization for two years. In that time I have visited the sites of two urban upheavals and have created theater about them. Although I have been examining race riots, or what are called uprisings or social explosions by some, I am oddly more apprehensive about making this speech than I was about heading for LA this time last year, and walking around South Central, where the uprising occurred.

I am apprehensive, because after spending these two years in the field, I am very aware of the vast ground between the world of urban battle and the world of theater and of higher education. I worry that I am out of touch with you. At the same time, I am committed to helping develop theater and theater education which is vibrant, less isolated, more responsible to and aware of the public.

The ATHE brochure describes our predicament in this way:

> Many of us are out of work. Many of us who have jobs are wondering how we can justify teaching so many students for professions in which there is so little readily available, consistently and adequately paid work.

That is a pretty humbling analysis. Yet humility is the very soil of an artist's work. Being a part of a theater department, at Stanford University, that was almost completely eliminated two years ago, I also know how vulnerable we are. How can we turn this vulnerability and this humility, which can be the very assets of an artist's work, into the seeds of the future? I am actually optimistic, and feel that in some way the generation that enters theater now, is better off than my generation was. When I entered the profession in 1975, there was very little vulnerability and very little humility in the theater that I saw.

As we begin to imagine the future, there are ethnic, generational, class and gender gaps to transcend. Today I will be talking about new ways to work in those gaps and about how we might try to reevaluate the way we integrate ourselves into academia, into popular culture, into communities and into society at large. I will be talking about new ways to look at being "*in*" our differences, and I will be talking about the development of skills.

First of all, I believe that skills for theater cannot be developed inside of theater or in academia alone. Most of my work is with actors and playwrights, however, I am also beginning to see how crucial it is for non-commercial theaters in particular to find new kinds of skills in the audience development departments. Let me address that first.

I have attended two of the Theater Communications Groups workshop/retreats on diversity. We seem to go round and round about how to diversify audiences. In this organization as well, people like Rhonda Blair have worked to try to change the composition of the organization, and it's been a hard battle. All you have to do to see that we're in for some tough work is to look at the graduate student population at the conference. When I was here two years ago, I attended the Women's Pre-Convention, which is a group that has spoken about diversifying ever since it began in the 70s. The last time I was here, 40 percent of those who attended were graduate students. They were all white. I was standing just outside the meeting room one evening, and Kay Carney and Beverly Byers Pevitts walked past, peeped into the room, and said to me, "What happened? It didn't used to be this bad." Kay and Beverly are among those who began the Women's Pre-Convention, and to their eyes, by 1991, it had gone backwards in terms of diversity. Common sense stepped into my idealism and told me that if all the graduate students were white, the future of the organization was clear. Although my colleagues talked about diversity at the conference, particularly in terms of curriculum, something inhibited the most obvious action when they were on their own campuses. Curriculum, or the addition of multicultural or feminist texts was going to yield raw results in the long run. The place to put creativity if one is going to diversify a membership like this one, and ultimately if we are going to diversify theater, is in the recruitment and mentoring of graduate students. Likewise, in the recruitment and mentoring of all students of theater. If one begins to look for directors, designers, managers, who are other than white, the list is short. The list gets shorter if you want to collaborate with people who do other than ethnocentric work. There are reasons why people in the last twenty years have been doing ethnocentric work, and I will get to that later. The future, I think, will call for some artists who can move, on occasion, beyond the boundaries of ethnic, gender and political beliefs.

I think that the issue of audience development, which to me is akin to the issue of diversifying the pool of theater workers, cannot be addressed solely within the world of theater. I think we need to look at how other people who interact with the public do this. I know that it's not going to warm your hearts for me to suggest to you that we talk to politicians, but I think we could begin there. I know this avenue is limited. However, overall, I am advocating beginning relationships that can work like two way streets. For example, during the run of my show *TWILIGHT: Los Angeles 1992*, the District Attorney of Los Angeles sent a note inviting me to lunch. He promised good food and information, which was the case. I was however, surprised at the end of the lunch, actually quite moved, that he said to me, with an astounding sincerity: "Is there anybody that you talked to during the time of working on your show, that I should meet?" I referred him to Twilight, a gang member, who in fact inspired the name of the show. There are people in public service who do want to find ways of learning more about this mysterious "they" out there. There are people in the media, in politics, in community work, who know and understand the limitations of their own ability to get to the public. We in theater are in the same position, and we need more skills. We normally exchange information among ourselves in atmospheres like this very conference. We need a broader arena.

When I came to Crown Heights, I became indebted to a man named Robert Sherman who was then with the Human Rights Commission of the Mayor's office of the City of New York. He is now the head of an organization called "The Increase The Peace Corps" which was developed literally out of the Crown Heights riot. When I met Sherman, I became fascinated with how his office went out into the middle of the riot, and found, while rocks and bottles were being thrown, the people in the community who were going to help maintain peace in the future. The mayor's office, for all its shortcomings, did have a seed for organizing, and they have called on that seed many more times throughout the last two years. As the scene created itself in my mind, it looked something like this: The Mayor's Human Rights People in orange jackets and in a yellow van with a megaphone on the roof cruised around the streets. They already had a few community activists with whom they had relationships. Even community activists have a limited amount of contact with the anonymous "they." One of them, a man named Richard Green spotted a Black man in his twenties standing in the middle of a riot with a group of little kids, talking to them about the power of the vote. This man, Henry Rice, is also someone I met while I was in Crown Heights. Against his better judgment, he did join up with the folks from the Mayor's office and has been an important force in building bridges between Blacks and Jews in Crown Heights. I don't want to paint a rosy picture, because there are limits to the building of that bridge, but at least they were able to put down a few planks of wood, wet and muddy planks maybe, but planks nevertheless. What I'm trying to tell you is, we cannot sit in our offices, in our theaters, or our classrooms and effect change. If audience development doesn't become an activist activity, many regional theaters will become dinosaurs. Here the need for activism is not only about ethnicity, it is about age. How will we begin to bring younger people into theater? How do we let them know that theater is here for them, and it can be about *them*? We have to make our presence obvious. We need orange jackets and megaphones. Presence is after all the gift of the actor. It is the heart and the voice of theater. People didn't create a circle and wait for the show to begin. Actors and writers drew a circle around the crowd and put a show in the middle.

In theater we have not fully realized what the drama of race is. This is because we have been creating it as a series of monologues. One race speaks, the other listens. In mainstream theater, it often happens that artists of color go onto the stage and perform for largely white audiences. They talk, white people watch. How often does it happen that white people create plays about themselves in race for audiences of color? Not often. One might say that for years the white drama has been played before the world through media for audiences of color. However, as one Korean woman, Mrs. Han, in Los Angeles told me:

> I used to think America was the best
> I still do
> I don't deny that now
> Just because I am victim
> When I was a little girl
> I used to think all Americans were rich
> I used to see many luxuries
> Hollywood lifestyle movies
> And I also thought all Americans were white
> I never saw any black
> maybe one housemaid?

That comes as no surprise. There is a reticence in white mainstream drama about race. Who can talk about race? Who *owns* the discussion of race? Who *wants* to talk about race? Who *needs* to?

*The training of artist*     I think that the training of artists does not need to be so sterile as we have thought in the past. My own way of working has been to introduce social concerns, largely because I like to construct courses that allow me to cross list and to make a class body which is mixed with actors and non-actors, or people who want to act, but also people who have been thinking about social issues and would like to try acting them out, as a way of knowing the issues differently.

I know very well, maybe a little too well, that there are some among you who feel that this will inhibit the development of talent. I am not here to convince anybody about what theater should be. We know that theater can be many things.

I would hate to see my remarks reduced to such questions as "What about art?" "Doesn't political theater hurt art?" Or as one man said to me at a panel that my colleague Rush Rehm at Stanford organized on Democracy and Theater: "As for Miss Smith, I think she should just worry about herself, I saw a wonderful play in San Diego called *for colored girls*, I would suggest she write something like that." First of all, we only have to look at the press around *for colored girls'* arrival in New York in the mid-seventies to see how boldly it crossed boundaries. Yes my entry into theater is political. Largely because of my race and gender. I am political without opening my mouth. My presence is political. The way I negotiate my presence becomes political. If I tried to deny my politicalness, I would be even *more* political. Personally, I do believe that all art is political. Even Noel Coward. The movies that Mrs. Han saw in Korea as a little girl were political.

On the other hand, as an acting teacher, as a playwriting teacher, I am also very concerned about the level of skills in American theater, and I hope our tendency to categorize art as art and politics as politics won't inhibit a discussion of skills. I'm saying, let's move around, let's look for the answers by collaborating with others on our campuses and in society who are like minded, and who also have an interest in learning more about who and what society is and how to speak *for* it, and about it. I am talking about a collaborative, public advocacy which will make our voices stronger, and our will to communicate large enough to carry over the noise. My prediction is, society is going to get noisier.

Four years, three years, two years, is a short time for developing that illusive thing we call "major talent." However, no major talent really becomes major talent without finding some way to speak *for* and with his or her own times. Is it possible, that the lack of work that the ATHE brochure mentions, is because we have spent too much time training our students to mirror themselves, to show the world what's *inside* of the artist rather than the world *around* the artist?

Theater training in our universities provides Hollywood with an incredible group of people. Many start out as actors, but go on to other less visible careers. Some repertory theater directors complain that Hollywood steals all of the major talent, and that it is difficult to develop relationships with actors and playwrights, directors too, I would imagine, although the major concern seems to be playwrights, because they want to go where the money is. Here I think is another collaboration that we haven't worked out very well.

There are real contradictions in the way that we think about television and movies, and how our training intersects with it. I for one, find teaching "How to Audition" courses one of the least gratifying experiences in the world. I do it, because I like everybody else, think it's important to teach our students about the so-called "real world." I frequently find my own tone changing from teaching to warning.

On the one hand we depend on the visibility of our successful students, on the other hand, we talk about Hollywood and television as though it were shallow and beneath our great artistry. And I have seen how my students look, after they meet with the "people from the industry." Some look shocked, dazed, confused. The ones who have been praised or recognized in these one day, or sometimes one hour sessions come out glowing. The ones who are praised or recognized are usually different than the ones who we have been praising and recognizing. We can't control that, and I think we should find another way to have influence. I believe, as I have been told, that the television industry is run by very smart people who have to work very fast. Some of the smartest students I've had, and some of my smartest friends have gone that route. Motion pictures also, can boast fine artists. I think that one reason we kind of write off those industries, is because we know we cannot teach our students about the power dynamics there, and that they have to learn that themselves. How can you teach that in a term? Getting yourself ready for the big audition is what the whole long haul is about.

The first thing I suggest is, get your students ready for the "real real world" not the real world of how to get a job. We actually have something quite wonderful to offer these industries. In twenty years, let's try to create a new actor. An actor who is less self-conscious, less concerned about the pose of acting, and more concerned about details. As much as I critique our reliance on Stanislavski, I certainly sound like him now.

I am also concerned about the kinds of people we sent into theater and into the "industry." Are they humanitarians? Are they self-absorbed? Do they have humility? We use the word vulnerability over and over again, but are they vulnerable? Vulnerable to whom and to what? What in the way we train them creates humility and vulnerability? Who are these human beings? What kinds of values do they have? I know from visits to some of your universities, that some of you are very concerned about that. These last four years have shown me a student who is more anxious, more frightened, more close minded, more intolerant than I've ever seen. I know that some of you have tried to intervene. I think it's crucial that we find more ways of actively intervening. What kinds of people are we recruiting? What kinds of people do we send into the world in the name of theater? Actors use to be, in the days of commedia, humanitarians, gymnasts, actors, singers, psychiatrists rolled into one. Provocateurs. The clowns and fools were willing to say what others would be shot for saying. *Who do our actors speak for? Who can they speak for? They should speak for whom?*

We must take our responsibility for helping to provide leadership in the arts and for society more seriously. These are the role models that many will look to. I'm saying that the buck doesn't stop in the right place.

I was on an audition tour for the University Regional Theater Association (URTA) one year. I don't know if this particular chair was serious, but I took it seriously, as a metaphor, when he said to me: "In the last year we bring in the dentists." Okay. I understand that. I understand that. The dentist is important, but when the dentist comes, the students should not stop talking. In fact, he/she should then be working harder to communicate what's in his/her heart, because presumably the dentist will have done something in the interest of cosmetics, that will interfere with speech. Speaking from the heart is what must be encouraged against all obstacles. And speaking from the heart does not mean confessions, as talk show television would lead us to believe, and it does not mean being unkind. It simply implies that as artists we have more resources from which to draw than the mind. And we *need* those. Society needs those resources tapped *through* our evocation.

I went to UC Irvine to hear Helene Cixous a few years ago. At the time I had been doing experiments with gender crossing in acting training. Afterwards, I asked her what she thought about crossing gender in theater. She said she thought it was transvestitism, and implied that it was silly. Then she said, "First of all, an actor has to have a soul." What about that? She said that when an actor walks in the room, she can tell right away, if there is a soul there. Can we? Or have our eyes become cloudy? We cannot let the industries dictate to us what major talent is. We can't tell them. They don't know. And we don't know. However, we can participate in the definition. The best way for us to participate is to send them something different, something more expressive in terms of real visible range of expression, and someone who is larger, more wide eyed, more interested in life. For the years that I spent in agent offices, and in auditions, I can tell you that I saw a masquerade of poses called actors. Let's urge our students to give up that masquerade.

The Japanese mime, Mamako, said when I studied with her at the American Conservatory Theater (ACT): "Have a rich life and Haiku will come." That's just about all she said, but it was quite enough for me. And yet, I would call that mentorship. Most of my students want to hear a lot more than that. As teachers, I think we should watch more, and say less.

*More on skills and technique*

I have found in what is now nearly twenty years of teaching actors, that they have a much broader expressive range than they use, or are encouraged to use. They are seldom pushed to find and to commit to gestural specifics that create a picture of behavior that is as complex as actual human behavior. When I have tried to urge my students to do this, their response is resistance, largely because of the way they have previously been indoctrinated to believe in psychological realism. I believe in it too, but I think that it is only part of the picture. If we want the general public to pay attention to us, we are going to have to dazzle it with something that is more specific. If we could create on stage, twenty minutes of an interaction of almost any life interaction, that is first of all a complex interaction, it would be dazzling. On the one level, we would find greater variety in external behavior.

Now, for fun, let's make that a political interaction. For those of you who subscribe to the *New Yorker,* you know that there was a big controversy on Valentine's week, because of Art Speigelman's drawing of a Hasidic man in an embrace with a Black woman with dreadlocks. To give this a context, last year in New York, there was a high level of tension between Blacks and Hasidic Jews because of the riots and the events that led up to the riots, the killing of a seven year old Black boy by a party of the head Rabbi's motorcade, and the retaliatory killing of a Hasidic scholar by a group of young Blacks. Hasidic men, don't even *shake* the hand of any woman that they were not married to, (they don't touch what "does not belong to them"), let alone embrace one, and the Hasidim do not intermarry. The Hasidim were outraged, and so were Blacks. Some remarked that if this were reversed, and a Black man were embracing a Hasidic woman, the outrage would have been even greater. Now, what if we did that in theater? If we did, we could give the time to explore this image. It would be controversial, but I'm not so sure it would actually be as controversial as that cover was. First of all, depending on the way it was cast, there is a likelihood that the personality of the actors, would actually intervene and dampen the controversy. However, if we did carefully create such a moment, and carefully observe and re-enact the physical behavior, it could be some of the most loaded theater one could imagine. As far as a public controversy, of course the problem is, that it's likely that more people saw the cover of the *New Yorker,* than would see the play.

I am not actually talking about Non-Traditional Casting here, because we've used the term non-traditional casting so much that we've tamed the idea into something that doesn't sound very exciting, kind of like what the term "politically correct" has done to a multitude of issues. What I am proposing is creating theater that juxtaposes worlds that are far apart in order to create an aesthetic contrast out of politically explosive interactions. We could then, capture a raw natural genuine modern drama which could ultimately influence how societies negotiate difference.

It is difficult within the University structure to supply actors with adequate physical, vocal and social training. If we want to create an actor who is really transformative, we're going to have to be more clever about how to use the resources of the university to do it. As we all know well, it is nearly genius when a group of artists get a university to support conservatory training or something like it. We have to find new collaborators within the university that will allow us to look at acting as a study of human behavior and as a tool for researching communication skills and for expanding our knowledge of what expression is. The resources are there, and through performance studies departments, there are the beginnings of this. However, you know performance studies departments are actually not interested in training performers the way that we are. The word performance is used so much in the university and in culture, that soon we should start a movement to reclaim it.

In terms of the interactions we've had with others in the university, I'm not sure we've found situations that benefit us the best. I'm sure some of you, as I have, for example, taught acting to lawyers and business students. I frankly, after having been at the Federal Trial for the Rodney King case, have an ethical problem with that. I saw a lot of bad acting. I saw acting reduced to manipulation. I don't think the lawyers went to acting school, or took acting classes, but I'm sure some of which I saw was based on watching actors "do" lawyers, in movies. In fact, one lawyer reminded me very much of a portrayal I had recently seen by a major movie star in a very popular movie. The problem is, most actors are not lawyers. They don't know the language of the law. The language of the law could have a drama of its own, if lawyers would let that language create their plays. When they let the histrionics of acting tell them how to speak their own language, the result is something which is bad acting, and which frequently speaks down to the public, rather than up towards the ideals of the law. In this way, our work, is about life and death. Because people in life base their performance of themselves, whether that's how they act in the courtroom, how they act on a date, how they act Asian, how they act like a man, a woman, on the performances they see in the media. We have to give them more to work with. We can only do that if we are working, from the undergraduate level, with very mature students, who come to the work already with an unusual/not cosmetic/expressive range. We need chameleons, transformers. Mercurial people. The times are hot, but there's not enough mercury in the thermometer. That's why we don't have an accurate display of the climate. We need mercurials. We don't need mimics.

Our performance of ethnicity depends on the movies, television, advertising and especially on the fashion industry. If we took away all of our clothing, how could we perform ethnicity and gender as current? I interviewed Elaine Brown, former Chairwoman of the Black Panther Party for the show *Twilight: Los Angeles 1992*. Her advice to young black males or as she calls them "Seventeen year old young brothers with a gun in your hand" is this:

*Skills and the performance of ethnicity*

> Seventeen year old young brother with a gun in your hand
> Tough and strong and beautiful as you are. . . .
> Don't be getting all hung up on your ego
> Or pumping up your muscles
> And putting on some black beret or some kind of Malcolm X hat
> Or other kind of regalia or symbolic vestment that you
> Can put on your body
> Think in terms of what you gonna do for
> Black people
> I'm saying these are the long haul.

Now let me put the opposite picture out here. When I taught at the University of Southern California, the women students would not take off their jewelry when they did scene work. It didn't matter what the role was, they wore whatever earrings they had on, usually large gold bangles, and their rings. Even asked to play men in *American Buffalo*. It was like pulling teeth to ask them to costume themselves fully and to take off their jewelry. This resistance, oddly reminded me of a similar resistance I met when I taught in Harlem—the kids wouldn't take off their jackets when they acted. What is that resistance to taking off some piece of your identity?

I think we have a road to go on to develop more technique. I know however, that technique is only part of art. I am collaborating with Judith Jamison on a dance piece for the Alvin Ailey American Dance Theater, and for the Celebration of the Thirty Fifth Anniversary of the Company. I met up with the dancers twice while they were on tour this year, and interviewed all of them. I'll speak their words, and Ms. Jamison is choreographing a dance around their words. One of the themes that kept recurring among the twenty or so dancers, was "The dance is not the steps." "The technique is the dance; the dance comes from within you."

*Technique vs. art*

What is inside ethnicity? Most of us know the steps. We learn them very quickly, and we're willing to change them each year. We keep some each year. But we change. This is not to trivialize the origins of these hair cuts, colors, adornments. This is not trivialize them, but what's inside? If we could dance the steps of ethnicity, across the boundaries of ethnicity, we could give American culture something it needs: a beautiful revelation of what lives inside our respective ethnic houses. Now we are living in a society that daily moves further and further behind its fortresses. We cannot afford to be fortressed. If the university is gated, if it's keeping you inside—move out. If institutional theater is a fortress, move out. We are supposed to be on the outside, as theater people. One way to ensure our "outsideness" is to dare to learn the steps of all the dances and to do them until we find the dance. We need the proper dancemasters. We should not, and cannot trust every teacher with all the dances. We know that, and the last twenty years of theater in their respective homes—theater in ghettos: Black, Native American, gay, Asian, and others has been a result of that awareness.

*Advocating theater and theater practitioners which is other than ethnocentric*

This is, I think the only radical thing I have to say. I am aware that I am talking to a predominately white audience. Possibly that will change in twenty years. In a way, this part of my talk is written for what I imagine this audience might look like twenty years from now. If I wait till then, this won't be of use.

Theater in the last twenty years has been ethnocentric. I'd really have to look at funding requirements twenty years ago to see the reason for this. If I were to sit down at a table with some of my favorite theater artists, I'd find myself with an Asian playwright who was educated at Stanford, a Black director educated at Brown, an Asian American critic who went to Harvard, a white woman playwright who went to Bryn Mawr, etcetera etcetera etcetera. I'm not going to continue the list, because I'd leave people out, and I don't want to do that! The point is, it isn't just education that led to this. Some very well educated theater people hit the streets, and did not go immediately to mainstream theater. They tried to start theaters of their own that were about *them*. I'm not sure if that was their organic idea, or if that was supported by grants, etc.—and yes, it was supported by education and by how ethnic studies was conceived AT THAT TIME. Now, I think, is the time to create ways of moving between the fortresses, and in so doing to encourage a new generation of artists, who live in work, for lack of a better image, in *boats*.

This will not be easy and this will be inhibited, because among people of color, and among whites, we have not yet decided who can speak for whom. When I began working on *Twilight: Los Angeles 1992,* I asked Gordon Davidson to hire a team of dramaturgs, rather than one, because I was afraid that my own ethnicity would tell this story, about LA in a way that reduced it to Black and White—that's what I knew about race in America, Black and White. L.A. is a multi-lingual, multi-ethnic city, and the explosion, was by some accounts, a poverty riot, which Latinos participated in great numbers, and in which Asians, and Koreans in particular, were the most visible victims. Or so the media told us. The media interestingly enough told us very little about how whites reacted to the city burning down.

I asked Dorinne Kondo, a Japanese American anthropologist, feminist and MacArthur Chair at Pomona College, to join me. I also asked Hector Tobar, a reporter for the *Los Angeles Times,* who covered the riots, and of Guatemalan descent, to join me. Eventually I worried that I was too vulnerable and thought I'd better not rely on my own judgment to watch out for the Black voice, and asked the African-American poet, Elizabeth Alexander, from the University of Chicago to join me. Emily Mann was the director, felt that Oskar Eustis would be a good addition to the team, because of his theatrical experience. What a battleship of dramaturgs. We met every night of previews. Our meetings were a scene to behold. There I learned a lot about "who can speak for whom." Dorinne and Hector in particular became more and more passionate as the work went on and felt a great sense of responsibility finally for "their communities." I understand this.

Dorinne, now, also thinks that this issue of who can speak for whom is a very interesting dynamic in work that tries to be multicultural. She has gathered and given me notes from her associates, mostly academics, and mostly but not all Asian American. First of all, it was interesting to her that they said things to her, that they would not say to me. Secondly, there is a way in which she senses from them, that they feel she has let them, and the race down, to the extent that she was not able to get me, or the work to represent them adequately or with enough complexity. Of the notes that Dorinne has shared with me I am most interested, for the purpose of this discussion, in the critique from some that the Korean and the Spanish and I spoke both in the show, was not perfect. "If she is going to speak the languages, then her accent should be right." Apparently, a colleague of Dorinne's, Marcyliena Morgan, a linguist and anthropologist at UCLA, in my behalf, (again none of this came to me directly) "Why should she speak Korean perfectly—you don't speak English perfectly."

Obviously, I will work harder on my Korean and El Salvadoran accents. I like this crittique, because it really says to me in a graphic way, that as I advocate that cross ethnic work, work that tries to cross the boundaries of ethnicity will be met with caution. And it should be.

A question I was frequently asked about my work in LA, was "Did you meet anybody who unified the voices?" Didn't you meet anyone who could speak for everyone? I interviewed 175–180 people. The answer is no. One, I'm not looking for such a voice, because I think there is a lot that needs to be heard in difference. Number two, there is nothing in our educational system in the last twenty years that has encouraged the development of a voice that can speak for more than itself. The tragedy of both Crown Heights and Los Angeles was that there was no one who could speak across lines. The future will demand that we have people who can.

*Vehicles*

We need to educate people who can move from place to place. We cannot just tear down the walls of ethnicity. Those walls are there for good reason. There is a fine history of Asian American Theater, Black Theater, Gay Theater, Latino Theater, Women's Theater, White Mainstream Theater and so on. Some have been around longer than others. Time is not the issue. We must capture this moment, wherever we are now, whatever ground, behind whatever fortress, and we must encourage, fabulous, passionate, goodhumored, bright eyed people to get in boats, small boats, row boats, boats that carry only one person in some cases, two or three in others, and help them push off, help them move out of the sand so that they can move from fortress to fortress. Ambassadors, explorers. Exploration is not colonization. The good part of the story is that it is unlikely that any of the fortresses will allow a colonizer in. The past twenty years have taught us how to identify colonialism. And that's good.

*Not so special*

A real danger in theater and in theater education is the idea of "specialness." A "special talent," a "special gift." We tell our students that they are special, that theater is special, and we hold up models of specialness. Something is shortsighted about that. We should be teaching them to identify the specialness in the world around them, and teaching them how to perceive a special moment in time, and how to capture it.

To encourage our students to be not so special, we have to give up the idea that we are special. That is the only way we will be the "Not So Special Vehicles" we need to be. The theater is disenfranchised at this moment. It is on the outside. The moment to capture, is the moment of our not so specialness.

*Limbo*

I will close with my favorite quote. Twilight is a gang member in South Central, and an architect of the gang truce in LA. The title of my show was inspired by his nom de guerre, "Twilight." When I asked him how he got his name, he spoke about limbo, and of being in limbo, I want to close with him, because I think that thought, after reading the ATHE brochure, that the group is in a kind of limbo. And my speech has been a reaction to that idea of limbo.

Twilight said to me:

Twilight
is that time
between day and night
limbo
I call it limbo . . .
So a lot of times when I've brought up ideas to my homeboys
they say
Twilight
That's before your time
that's something you can't do now

When I talked about the truce back in 1988
That was something they considered before its time
Yet in 1992 we made it realistic
So to me it's like I'm stuck in limbo
Like the sun is stuck between night and day
in the twilight hours
You know I'm in an area not many people exist
Night time to me
is like a lack of sun
And I don't affiliate darkness with anything negative
I affiliate darkness of what was first
because it was first
and then relative to my complexion
I am a dark individual
and with me stuck in limbo
I see darkness as myself
I see the light as the knowledge and the wisdom of the world
And in order for me to be a true human being
I can't forever dwell in darkness
I can't forever dwell in the idea
of just identifying with people like me and understanding me and mine.

Twilight is a prophet, and he is a person who can do what we try to teach people for four years. He can speak as he thinks. He can render a poetic idea as though it were normal, because it is normal. He met with me twice. He spoke quickly, softly, patiently. Each time, he ended abruptly. When I said goodbye, he simply nodded and said alright, quite unimpressed with himself or with the occasion of the interview. We asked him to meet once to have his picture taken for *Vogue* magazine. He came with three homeboys and an old car. He never came to the show that bears his name and carries his words as a major theme. We invited him several times. *I should have taken the show to him.*

# UNIT 4

## Criticism and Theory of the Modern Stage

*AN early member of the Surrealist movement in Paris, Antonin Artaud was well-known between the wars as an actor, playwright, and essayist of the avant-garde theater, and he is one of the seminal influences on the modern European theater. Artaud is most often associated with the "Theater of Cruelty," his label for a theater that would assault the representational dynamics of traditional theater and break the boundaries between actor and audience, stage and spectacle. Artaud was declared insane and committed to a mental hospital in 1937; although he remained institutionalized for much of the remainder of his life, Artaud returned to the stage in 1947 for a brilliant, shattering reading of his own work.*

This translation faithfully follows the text of the *Le Théâtre et son Double*, published by Gallimard in *Collection Métamorphoses* as No. IV, copyright 1938.

   "*Esprit*," for which we have no English equivalent, combining as it does both *mind* and *spirit*, has in most cases been translated as "mind." And the expression "*mise en scène*" has been retained throughout, for Artaud's use of it implies all that we call direction, production, and staging.

Never before, when it is life itself that is in question, has there been so much talk of civilization and culture. And there is a curious parallel between this generalized collapse of life at the root of our present demoralization and our concern for a culture which has never been coincident with life, which in fact has been devised to tyrannize over life.

   Before speaking further about culture, I must remark that the world is hungry and not concerned with culture, and that the attempt to orient toward culture thoughts turned only toward hunger is a purely artificial expedient.

   What is most important, it seems to me, is not so much to defend a culture whose existence has never kept a man from going hungry, as to extract, from what is called culture, ideas whose compelling force is identical with that of hunger.

   We need to live first of all; to believe in what makes us live and that something *makes* us live— to believe that whatever is produced from the mysterious depths of ourselves need not forever haunt us as an exclusively digestive concern.

   I mean that if it is important for us to eat first of all, it is even more important for us not to waste in the sole concern for eating our simple power of being hungry.

   If confusion is the sign of the times, I see at the root of this confusion a rupture between things and words, between things and the ideas and signs that are their representation.

   Not, of course, for lack of philosophical systems; their number and contradictions characterize our old French and European culture: but where can it be shown that life, our life, has ever been affected by these systems? I will not say that philosophical systems must be applied directly and immediately: but of the following alternatives, one must be true:

   Either these systems are within us and permeate our being to the point of supporting life itself (and if this is the case, what use are books?), or they do *not* permeate us and therefore do not have the capacity to support life (and in this case what does their disappearance matter?).

   We must insist upon the idea of culture-in-action, of culture growing within us like a new organ, a sort of second breath; and on civilization as an applied culture controlling even our subtlest actions, a *presence of mind;* the distinction between culture and civilization is an artificial one, providing two words to signify an identical function.

   A civilized man judges and is judged according to his behavior, but even the term "civilized" leads to confusion: a cultivated "civilized" man is regarded as a person instructed in systems, a person who thinks in forms, signs, representations—a monster whose faculty of deriving thoughts from acts, instead of identifying acts with thoughts, is developed to an absurdity.

   If our life lacks brimstone, i.e., a constant magic, it is because we choose to observe our acts and lose ourselves in considerations of their imagined form instead of being impelled by their force.

   And this faculty is an exclusively human one. I would even say that it is this infection of the human which contaminates ideas that should have remained divine; for far from believing that man invented the supernatural and the divine, I think it is man's age-old intervention which has ultimately corrupted the divine within him.

## Antonin Artaud
### (1896–1948)

FROM The Theater and
Its Double
(1938)

TRANSLATED BY
MARY CAROLINE RICHARDS

*A note on the
translation*

*The theater and culture*

All our ideas about life must be revised in a period when nothing any longer adheres to life; it is this painful cleavage which is responsible for the revenge of *things;* the poetry which is no longer within us and which we no longer succeed in finding in things suddenly appears on their wrong side: consider the unprecedented number of crimes whose perverse gratuitousness is explained only by our powerlessness to take complete possession of life.

If the theater has been created as an outlet for our repressions, the agonized poetry expressed in its bizarre corruptions of the facts of life demonstrates that life's intensity is still intact and asks only to be better directed.

But no matter how loudly we clamor for magic in our lives, we are really afraid of pursuing an existence entirely under its influence and sign.

Hence our confirmed lack of culture is astonished by certain grandiose anomalies; for example, on an island without any contact with modern civilization, the mere passage of a ship carrying only healthy passengers may provoke the sudden outbreak of diseases unknown on that island but a specialty of nations like our own: shingles, influenza, grippe, rheumatism, sinusitis, polyneuritis, etc.

Similarly, if we think Negroes smell bad, we are ignorant of the fact that anywhere but in Europe it is we whites who "smell bad." And I would even say that we give off an odor as white as the gathering of pus in an infected wound.

As iron can be heated until it turns white, so it can be said that everything excessive is white; for Asiatics white has become the mark of extreme decomposition.

This said, we can begin to form an idea of culture, an idea which is first of all a protest.

A protest against the senseless constraint imposed upon the idea of culture by reducing it to a sort of inconceivable Pantheon, producing an idolatry no different from the image-worship of those religions which relegate their gods to Pantheons.

A protest against the idea of culture as distinct from life—as if there were culture on one side and life on the other, as if true culture were not a refined means of understanding and *exercising* life.

The library at Alexandria can be burnt down. There are forces above and beyond papyrus: we may temporarily be deprived of our ability to discover these forces, but their energy will not be suppressed. It is good that our excessive facilities are no longer available, that forms fall into oblivion: a culture without space or time, restrained only by the capacity of our own nerves, will reappear with all the more energy. It is right that from time to time cataclysms occur which compel us to return to nature, i.e., to rediscover life. The old totemism of animals, stones, objects capable of discharging thunderbolts, costumes impregnated with bestial essences—everything, in short, that might determine, disclose, and direct the secret forces of the universe—is for us a dead thing, from which we derive nothing but static and aesthetic profit, the profit of an audience, not of an actor.

Yet totemism is an actor, for it moves, and has been created in behalf of actors; all true culture relies upon the barbaric and primitive means of totemism whose savage, i.e., entirely spontaneous, life I wish to worship.

What has lost us culture is our Occidental idea of art and the profits we seek to derive from it. Art and culture cannot be considered together, contrary to the treatment universally accorded them!

True culture operates by exaltation and force, while the European ideal of art attempts to cast the mind into an attitude distinct from force but addicted to exaltation. It is a lazy, unserviceable notion which engenders an imminent death. If the Serpent Quetzalcoatl's multiple twists and turns are harmonious, it is because they express the equilibrium and fluctuations of a sleeping force; the intensity of the forms is there only to seduce and direct a force which, in music, would produce an insupportable range of sound.

The gods that sleep in museums: the god of fire with his incense burner that resembles an Inquisition tripod; Tlaloc, one of the manifold Gods of the Waters, on his wall of green granite; the Mother Goddess of Waters, the Mother Goddess of Flowers; the immutable expression, echoing from beneath many layers of water, of the Goddess robed in green jade; the enraptured, blissful expression, features crackling with incense, where atoms of sunlight circle—the countenance of the Mother Goddess of Flowers; this world of obligatory servitude in which a stone comes alive when it has been properly carved, the world of organically civilized men whose vital organs too awaken from their slumber, this human world enters into us, participating in the dance of the gods without turning round or looking back, on pain of becoming, like ourselves, crumbled pillars of salt.

In Mexico, since we are talking about Mexico, there is no art: things are made for use. And the world is in perpetual exaltation.

To our disinterested and inert idea of art an authentic culture opposes a violently egoistic and magical, i.e., *interested* idea. For the Mexicans seek contact with the *Manas,* forces latent in every form, unreleased by contemplation of the forms for themselves, but springing to life by magic identification with these forms. And the old Totems are there to hasten the communication.

How hard it is, when everything encourages us to sleep, though we may look about us with conscious, clinging eyes, to wake and yet look about us as in a dream, with eyes that no longer know their function and whose gaze is turned inward.

This is how our strange idea of disinterested action originated, though it is action nonetheless, and all the more violent for skirting the temptation of repose.

Every real effigy has a shadow which is its double; and art must falter and fail from the moment the sculptor believes he has liberated the kind of shadow whose very existence will destroy his repose.

Like all magic cultures expressed by appropriate hieroglyphs, the true theater has its shadows too, and, of all languages and all arts, the theater is the only one left whose shadows have shattered their limitations. From the beginning, one might say its shadows did not tolerate limitations.

Our petrified idea of the theater is connected with our petrified idea of a culture without shadows, where, no matter which way it turns, our mind *(esprit)* encounters only emptiness, though space is full.

But the true theater, because it moves and makes use of living instruments, continues to stir up shadows where life has never ceased to grope its way. The actor does not make the same gestures twice, but he makes gestures, he moves; and although he brutalizes forms, nevertheless behind them and through their destruction he rejoins that which outlives forms and produces their continuation.

The theater, which is in *no thing,* but makes use of everything—gestures, sounds, words, screams, light, darkness—rediscovers itself at precisely the point where the mind requires a language to express its manifestations.

And the fixation of the theater in one language—written words, music, lights, noises—betokens its imminent ruin, the choice of any one language betraying a taste for the special effects of that language; and the dessication of the language accompanies its limitation.

For the theater as for culture, it remains a question of naming and directing shadows: and the theater, not confined to a fixed language and form, not only destroys false shadows but prepares the way for a new generation of shadows, around which assembles the true spectacle of life.

To break through language in order to touch life is to create or recreate the theater; the essential thing is not to believe that this act must remain sacred, i.e., set apart—the essential thing is to believe that not just anyone can create it, and that there must be a preparation.

This leads to the rejection of the usual limitations of man and man's powers, and infinitely extends the frontiers of what is called reality.

We must believe in a sense of life renewed by the theater, a sense of life in which man fearlessly makes himself master of what does not yet exist, and brings it into being. And everything that has not been born can still be brought to life if we are not satisfied to remain mere recording organisms.

Furthermore, when we speak the word "life," it must be understood we are not referring to life as we know it from its surface of fact, but to that fragile, fluctuating center which forms never reach. And if there is still one hellish, truly accursed thing in our time, it is our artistic dallying with forms, instead of being like victims burnt at the stake, signaling through the flames.

*No more masterpieces*

One of the reasons for the asphyxiating atmosphere in which we live without possible escape or remedy—and in which we all share, even the most revolutionary among us—is our respect for what has been written, formulated, or painted, what has been given form, as if all expression were not at last exhausted, were not at a point where things must break apart if they are to start anew and begin fresh.

We must have done with this idea of masterpieces reserved for a self-styled elite and not understood by the general public; the mind has no such restricted districts as those so often used for clandestine sexual encounters.

Masterpieces of the past are good for the past: they are not good for us. We have the right to say what has been said and even what has not been said in a way that belongs to us, a way that is immediate and direct, corresponding to present modes of feeling, and understandable to everyone.

It is idiotic to reproach the masses for having no sense of the sublime, when the sublime is confused with one or another of its formal manifestations, which are moreover always defunct manifestations. And if for example a contemporary public does not understand *Oedipus Rex*, I shall make bold to say that it is the fault of *Oedipus Rex* and not of the public.

In *Oedipus Rex* there is the theme of incest and the idea that nature mocks at morality and that there are certain unspecified powers at large which we would do well to beware of, call them *destiny* or anything you choose.

There is in addition the presence of a plague epidemic which is a physical incarnation of these powers. But the whole in a manner and language that have lost all touch with the rude and epileptic rhythm of our time. Sophocles speaks grandly perhaps, but in a style that is no longer timely. His language is too refined for this age, it is as if he were speaking beside the point.

However, a public that shudders at train wrecks, that is familiar with earthquakes, plagues, revolutions, wars; that is sensitive to the disordered anguish of love, can be affected by all these grand notions and asks only to become aware of them, but on condition that it is addressed in its own language, and that its knowledge of these things does not come to it through adulterated trappings and speech that belong to extinct eras which will never live again.

Today as yesterday, the public is greedy for mystery: it asks only to become aware of the laws according to which destiny manifests itself, and to divine perhaps the secret of its apparitions.

Let us leave textual criticism to graduate students, formal criticism to estheses, and recognize that what has been said is not still to be said; that an expression does not have the same value twice, does not live two lives; that all words, once spoken, are dead and function only at the moment when they are uttered, that a form, once it has served, cannot be used again and asks only to be replaced by another, and that the theater is the only place in the world where a gesture, once made, can never be made the same way twice.

If the public does not frequent our literary masterpieces, it is because those masterpieces are literary, that is to say, fixed; and fixed in forms that no longer respond to the needs of the time.

Far from blaming the public, we ought to blame the formal screen we interpose between ourselves and the public, and this new form of idolatry, the idolatry of fixed masterpieces which is one of the aspects of bourgeois conformism.

This conformism makes us confuse sublimity, ideas, and things with the forms they have taken in time and in our minds—in our snobbish, precious, aesthetic mentalities which the public does not understand.

How pointless in such matters to accuse the public of bad taste because it relishes insanities, so long as the public is not shown a valid spectacle; and I defy anyone to show me *here* a spectacle valid—valid in the supreme sense of the theater—since the last great romantic melodramas, i.e., since a hundred years ago.

The public, which takes the false for the true, has the sense of the true and always responds to it when it is manifested. However it is not upon the stage that the true is to be sought nowadays, but in the street; and if the crowd in the street is offered an occasion to show its human dignity, it will always do so.

If people are out of the habit of going to the theater, if we have all finally come to think of theater as an inferior art, a means of popular distraction, and to use it as an outlet for our worst instincts, it is because we have learned too well what the theater has been, namely, falsehood and illusion. It is because we have been accustomed for four hundred years, that is since the Renaissance, to a purely descriptive and narrative theater—storytelling psychology; it is because every possible ingenuity has been exerted in bringing to life on the stage plausible but detached beings, with the spectacle on one side, the public on the other—and because the public is no longer shown anything but the mirror of itself.

Shakespeare himself is responsible for this aberration and decline, this disinterested idea of the theater which wishes a theatrical performance to leave the public intact, without setting off one image that will shake the organism to its foundations and leave an ineffaceable scar.

If, in Shakespeare, a man is sometimes preoccupied with what transcends him, it is always in order to determine the ultimate consequences of this preoccupation within him, i.e., psychology.

Psychology, which works relentlessly to reduce the unknown to the known, to the quotidian and the ordinary, is the cause of the theater's abasement and its fearful loss of energy, which seems to me to have reached its lowest point. And I think both the theater and we ourselves have had enough of psychology.

I believe furthermore that we can all agree on this matter sufficiently so that there is no need to descend to the repugnant level of the modern and French theater to condemn the theater of psychology.

Stories about money, worry over money, social careerism, the pangs of love unspoiled by altruism, sexuality sugar-coated with an eroticism that has lost its mystery have nothing to do with the theater, even if they do belong to psychology. These torments, seductions, and lusts before which we are nothing but Peeping Toms gratifying our cravings, tend to go bad, and their rot turns to revolution: we must take this into account.

But this is not our most serious concern.

If Shakespeare and his imitators have gradually insinuated the idea of art for art's sake, with art on one side and life on the other, we can rest on this feeble and lazy idea only as long as the life outside endures. But there are too many signs that everything that used to sustain our lives no longer does so, that we are all mad, desperate, and sick. And I call for *us* to react.

This idea of a detached art, of poetry as a charm which exists only to distract our leisure, is a decadent idea and an unmistakable symptom of our power to castrate.

Our literary admiration for Rimbaud, Jarry, Lautréamont, and a few others, which has driven two men to suicide, but turned into café gossip for the rest, belongs to this idea of literary poetry, of detached art, of neutral spiritual activity which creates nothing and produces nothing; and I can bear witness that at the very moment when that kind of personal poetry which involves only the man who creates it and only at the moment he creates it broke out in its most abusive fashion, the theater was scorned more than ever before by poets who have never had the sense of direct and concerted action, nor of efficacity, nor of danger.

We must get rid of our superstitious valuation of texts and *written* poetry. Written poetry is worth reading once, and then should be destroyed. Let the dead poets make way for others. Then we might even come to see that it is our veneration for what has already been created, however beautiful and valid it may be, that petrifies us, deadens our responses, and prevents us from making contact with that underlying power, call it thought-energy, the life force, the determinism of change, lunar menses, or anything you like. Beneath the poetry of the texts, there is the actual poetry, without form and without text. And just as the efficacity of masks in the magic practices of certain tribes is exhausted—and these masks are no longer good for anything except museums—so the poetic efficacity of a text is exhausted; yet the poetry and the efficacity of the theater are exhausted least quickly of all, since they permit the *action* of what is gesticulated and pronounced, and which is never made the same way twice.

It is a question of knowing what we want. If we are prepared for war, plague, famine, and slaughter we do not even need to say so, we have only to continue as we are; continue behaving like snobs, rushing en masse to hear such and such a singer, to see such and such an admirable performance which never transcends the realm of art (and even the Russian ballet at the height of its splendor never transcended the realm of art), to marvel at such and such an exhibition of painting in which exciting shapes explode here and there but at random and without any genuine consciousness of the forces they could rouse.

This empiricism, randomness, individualism, and anarchy must cease.

Enough of personal poems, benefitting those who create them much more than those who read them.

Once and for all, enough of this closed, egoistic, and personal art.

Our spiritual anarchy and intellectual disorder is a function of the anarchy of everything else—or rather, everything else is a function of this anarchy.

I am not one of those who believe that civilization has to change in order for the theater to change; but I do believe that the theater, utilized in the highest and most difficult sense possible, has the power to influence the aspect and formation of things: and the encounter upon the stage of two passionate manifestations, two living centers, two nervous magnetisms is something as entire, true, even decisive, as, in life, the encounter of one epidermis with another in a timeless debauchery.

That is why I propose a theater of cruelty.—With this mania we all have for depreciating everything, as soon as I have said "cruelty," everybody will at once take it to mean "blood." But *theater of cruelty* means a theater difficult and cruel for myself first of all. And, on the level of performance, it is not the cruelty we can exercise upon each other by hacking at each other's bodies, carving up our personal anatomies, or, like Assyrian emperors, sending parcels of human ears, noses, or neatly detached nostrils through the mail, but the much more terrible and necessary cruelty which things can exercise against us. We are not free. And the sky can still fall on our heads. And the theater has been created to teach us that first of all.

Either we will be capable of returning by present-day means to this superior idea of poetry and poetry-through-theater which underlies the Myths told by the great ancient tragedians, capable once more of entertaining a religious idea of the theater (without meditation, useless contemplation, and vague dreams), capable of attaining awareness and a possession of certain dominant forces, of certain notions that control all others, and (since ideas, when they are effective, carry their energy with them) capable of recovering within ourselves those energies which ultimately create order and increase the value of life, or else we might as well abandon ourselves now, without protest, and recognize that we are no longer good for anything but disorder, famine, blood, war, and epidemics.

Either we restore all the arts to a central attitude and necessity, finding an analogy between a gesture made in painting or the theater, and a gesture made by lava in a volcanic explosion, or we must stop painting, babbling, writing, or doing whatever it is we do.

I propose to bring back into the theater this elementary magical idea, taken up by modern psychoanalysis, which consists in effecting a patient's cure by making him assume the apparent and exterior attitudes of the desired condition.

I propose to renounce our empiricism of imagery, in which the unconscious furnishes images at random, and which the poet arranges at random too, calling them poetic and hence hermetic images, as if the kind of trance that poetry provides did not have its reverberations throughout the whole sensibility, in every nerve, and as if poetry were some vague force whose movements were invariable.

I propose to return through the theater to an idea of the physical knowledge of images and the means of inducing trances, as in Chinese medicine which knows, over the entire extent of the human anatomy, at what points to puncture in order to regulate the subtlest functions.

Those who have forgotten the communicative power and magical mimesis of a gesture, the theater can reinstruct, because a gesture carries its energy with it, and there are still human beings in the theater to manifest the force of the gesture made.

To create art is to deprive a gesture of its reverberation in the organism, whereas this reverberation, if the gesture is made in the conditions and with the force required, incites the organism and, through it, the entire individuality, to take attitudes in harmony with the gesture.

The theater is the only place in the world, the last general means we still possess of directly affecting the organism and, in periods of neurosis and petty sensuality like the one in which we are immersed, of attacking this sensuality by physical means it cannot withstand.

If music affects snakes, it is not on account of the spiritual notions it offers them, but because snakes are long and coil their length upon the earth, because their bodies touch the earth at almost every point; and because the musical vibrations which are communicated to the earth affect them like a very subtle, very long massage; and I propose to treat the spectators like the snakecharmer's subjects and conduct them *by means of their organisms* to an apprehension of the subtlest notions.

At first by crude means, which will gradually be refined. These immediate crude means will hold their attention at the start.

That is why in the "theater of cruelty" the spectator is in the center and the spectacle surrounds him.

In this spectacle the sonorisation is constant: sounds, noises, cries are chosen first for their vibratory quality, then for what they represent.

Among these gradually refined means light is interposed in its turn. Light which is not created merely to add color or to brighten, and which brings its power, influence, suggestions with it. And the light of a green cavern does not sensually dispose the organism like the light of a windy day.

After sound and light there is action, and the dynamism of action: here the theater, far from copying life, puts itself whenever possible in communication with pure forces. And whether you accept or deny them, there is nevertheless a way of speaking which gives the name of "forces" to whatever brings to birth images of energy in the unconscious, and gratuitous crime on the surface.

A violent and concentrated action is a kind of lyricism: it summons up supernatural images, a bloodstream of images, a bleeding spurt of images in the poet's head and in the spectator's as well.

Whatever the conflicts that haunt the mind of a given period, I defy any spectator to whom such violent scenes will have transferred their blood, who will have felt in himself the transit of a superior action, who will have seen the extraordinary and essential movements of his thought illuminated in extraordinary deeds—the violence and blood having been placed at the service of the violence of the thought—I defy that spectator to give himself up, once outside the theater, to ideas of war, riot, and blatant murder.

So expressed, this idea seems dangerous and sophomoric. It will be claimed that example breeds example, that if the attitude of cure induces cure, the attitude of murder will induce murder. Everything depends upon the manner and the purity with which the thing is done. There is a risk. But let it not be forgotten that though a theatrical gesture is violent, it is disinterested; and that the theater teaches precisely the uselessness of the action which, once done, is not to be done, and the superior use of the state unused by the action and which, *restored*, produces a purification.

I propose then a theater in which violent physical images crush and hypnotize the sensibility of the spectator seized by the theater as by a whirlwind of higher forces.

A theater which, abandoning psychology, recounts the extraordinary, stages natural conflicts, natural and subtle forces, and presents itself first of all as an exceptional power of redirection. A theater that induces trance, as the dances of Dervishes induce trance, and that addresses itself to the organism by precise instruments, by the same means as those of certain tribal music cures which we admire on records but are incapable of originating among ourselves.

There is a risk involved, but in the present circumstances I believe it is a risk worth running. I do not believe we have managed to revitalize the world we live in, and I do not believe it is worth the trouble of clinging to; but I do propose something to get us out of our marasmus, instead of continuing to complain about it, and about the boredom, inertia, and stupidity of everything.

---

*HOMI Bhabha is a leading theorist of postcolonial literature and culture and has edited* Nation and Narration *(1990). In "Of Mimicry and Man," Bhabha considers how notions of imitation and performance structure the relations of power and legitimation between colonized peoples and their colonizers.*

■ ■ ■ Mimicry reveals something in so far as it is distinct from what might be called an itself that is behind. The effect of mimicry is camouflage. . . . It is not a question of harmonizing with the background, but against a mottled background, of becoming mottled—exactly like the technique of camouflage practised in human warfare.

—JACQUES LACAN,
"THE LINE AND LIGHT," *Of the Gaze.*

°This paper was first presented as a contribution to a panel on "Colonialist and Post-Colonialist Discourse," organized by Gayatri Chakravorty Spivak for the Modern Language Association Convention in New York, December 1983. I would like to thank Professor Spivak for inviting me to participate on the panel and Dr. Stephan Feuchtwang for his advice in the preparation of the paper.

Homi Bhabha:

"Of Mimicry and Man:
The Ambivalence of
Colonial Discourse"*
(1984)

■ ■ ■ It is out of season to question at this time of day, the original policy of conferring on every colony of the British Empire a mimic representation of the British Constitution. But if the creature so endowed has sometimes forgotten its real insignificance and under the fancied importance of speakers and maces, and all the paraphernalia and ceremonies of the imperial legislature, has dared to defy the mother country, she has to thank herself for the folly of conferring such privileges on a condition of society that has no earthly claim to so exalted a position. A fundamental principle appears to have been forgotten or overlooked in our system of colonial policy—that of colonial dependence. To give to a colony the forms of independence is a mockery; she would not be a colony for a single hour if she could maintain an independent station.

—SIR EDWARD CUST,
"REFLECTIONS ON WEST AFRICAN AFFAIRS . . .
ADDRESSED TO THE COLONIAL OFFICE,"
HATCHARD, LONDON 1839.

The discourse of post-Enlightenment English colonialism often speaks in a tongue that is forked, not false. If colonialism takes power in the name of history, it repeatedly exercises its authority through the figures of farce. For the epic intention of the civilizing mission, "human and not wholly human" in the famous words of Lord Rosebery, "writ by the finger of the Divine"[1] often produces a text rich in the traditions of *trompe l'oeil*, irony, mimicry, and repetition. In this comic turn from the high ideals of the colonial imagination to its low mimetic literary effects, mimicry emerges as one of the most elusive and effective strategies of colonial power and knowledge.

Within that conflictual economy of colonial discourse which Edward Said[2] describes as the tension between the synchronic panoptical vision of domination—the demand for identity, stasis—and the counter-pressure of the diachrony of history—change, difference—mimicry represents an *ironic* compromise. If I may adapt Samuel Weber's formulation of the marginalizing vision of castration,[3] then colonial mimicry is the desire for a reformed, recognizable Other, as *a subject of a difference that is almost the same, but not quite*. Which is to say, that the discourse of mimicry is constructed around an *ambivalence;* in order to be effective, mimicry must continually produce its slippage, its excess, its difference. The authority of that mode of colonial discourse that I have called mimicry is therefore stricken by an indeterminacy: mimicry emerges as the representation of a difference that is itself a process of disavowal. Mimicry is, thus, the sign of a double articulation; a complex strategy of reform, regulation, and discipline, which "appropriates" the Other as it visualizes power. Mimicry is also the sign of the inappropriate, however, a difference or recalcitrance which coheres the dominant strategic function of colonial power, intensifies surveillance, and poses an immanent threat to both "normalized" knowledges and disciplinary powers.

The effect of mimicry on the authority of colonial discourse is profound and disturbing. For in "normalizing" the colonial state or subject, the dream of post-Enlightenment civility alienates its own language of liberty and produces another knowledge of its norms. The ambivalence which thus informs this strategy is discernible, for example, in Locke's Second Treatise which *splits* to reveal the limitations of liberty in his double use of the word "slave": first simply, descriptively as the locus of a legitimate form of ownership, then as the trope for an intolerable, illegitimate exercise of power. What is articulated in that distance between the two uses is the absolute, imagined difference between the "Colonial" State of Carolina and the Original State of Nature.

It is from this area between mimicry and mockery, where the reforming, civilizing mission is threatened by the displacing gaze of its disciplinary double, that my instances of colonial imitation come. What they all share is a discursive process by which the excess or slippage produced by the *ambivalence* of mimicry (almost the same, *but not quite*) does not merely "rupture" the discourse,

---

[1]Cited in Eric Stokes, *The Political Ideas of English Imperialism,* Oxford, Oxford University Press, 1960, pp. 17–18.

[2]Edward Said, *Orientalism,* New York, Pantheon Books, 1978, p. 240.

[3]Samuel Weber: "The Sideshow, Or: Remarks on a Canny Moment," *Modern Language Notes,* vol. 88, no. 6 (1973), p. 1112.

but becomes transformed into an uncertainty which fixes the colonial subject as a "partial" presence. By "partial" I mean both "incomplete" and "virtual." It is as if the very emergence of the "colonial" is dependent for its representation upon some strategic limitation or prohibition *within* the authoritative discourse itself. The success of colonial appropriation depends on a proliferation of inappropriate objects that ensure its strategic failure, so that mimicry is at once resemblance and menace.

A classic text of such partiality is Charles Grant's "Observations on the State of Society among the Asiatic Subjects of Great Britain" (1792)[4] which was only superseded by James Mills's *History of India* as the most influential early nineteenth-century account of Indian manners and morals. Grant's dream of an evangelical system of mission education conducted uncompromisingly in English was partly a belief in political reform along Christian lines and partly an awareness that the expansion of company rule in India required a system of "interpellation"—a reform of manners, as Grant put it, that would provide the colonial with "a sense of personal identity as we know it." Caught between the desire for religious reform and the fear that the Indians might become turbulent for liberty, Grant implies that it is, in fact the "partial" diffusion of Christianity, and the "partial" influence of moral improvements which will construct a particularly appropriate form of colonial subjectivity. What is suggested is a process of reform through which Christian doctrines might collude with divisive caste practices to prevent dangerous political alliances. Inadvertently, Grant produces a knowledge of Christianity as a form of social control which conflicts with the enunciatory assumptions which authorize his discourse. In suggesting, finally, that "partial reform" will produce an empty form of "the *imitation* of English manners which will induce them [the colonial subjects] to remain under our protection,"[5] Grant mocks his moral project and violates the Evidences of Christianity—a central missionary tenet—which forbade any tolerance of heathen faiths.

The absurd extravagance of Macaulay's *Infamous Minute* (1835)—deeply influenced by Charles Grant's *Observations*—makes a mockery of Oriental learning until faced with the challenge of conceiving of a "reformed" colonial subject. Then the great tradition of European humanism seems capable only of ironizing itself. At the intersection of European learning and colonial power, Macaulay can conceive of nothing other than "a class of interpreters between us and the millions whom we govern—a class of persons Indian in blood and colour, but English in tastes, in opinions, in morals and in intellect"[6]—in other words a mimic man raised "through our English School," as a missionary educationist wrote in 1819, "to form a corps of translators and be employed in different departments of Labour."[7] The line of descent of the mimic man can be traced through the works of Kipling, Forester, Orwell, Naipaul, and to his emergence, most recently, in Benedict Anderson's excellent essay on nationalism, as the anomalous Bipin Chandra Pal.[8] He is the effect of a flawed colonial mimesis, in which to be Anglicized, is *emphatically* not to be English.

The figure of mimicry is locatable within what Anderson describes as "the inner incompatibility of empire and nation."[9] It problematizes the signs of racial and cultural priority, so that the "national" is no longer naturalizable. What emerges between mimesis and mimicry is a *writing*, a mode of representation, that marginalizes the monumentality of history, quite simply mocks its power to be a model, that power which supposedly makes it imitable. Mimicry *repeats* rather than *re-presents* and in that diminishing perspective emerges Decoud's displaced European vision of Sulaco as:

---

[4]Charles Grant, "Observations on the State of Society among the Asiatic Subjects of Great Britain," *Sessional Papers 1812–13*, X (282), East India Company.

[5]*Ibid.,* chap. 4, p. 104.

[6]T. B. Macaulay, "Minute on Education," in *Sources of Indian Tradition*, vol. II, ed. William Theodore de Bary, New York, Columbia University Press, 1958, p. 49.

[7]Mr. Thomason's communication to the Church Missionary Society, September 5, 1819, in *The Missionary Register*, 1821, pp. 54–55.

[8]Benedict Anderson, *Imagined Communities*, London, Verso, 1983, p. 88.

[9]*Ibid.,* pp. 88–89.

the endlessness of civil strife where folly seemed even harder to bear than its ignominy . . . the lawlessness of a populace of all colours and races, barbarism, irremediable tyranny. . . . America is ungovernable.[10]

Or Ralph Singh's apostasy in Naipaul's *The Mimic Men:*

We pretended to be real, to be learning, to be preparing ourselves for life, we mimic men of the New World, one unknown corner of it, with all its reminders of the corruption that came so quickly to the new.[11]

Both Decoud and Singh, and in their different ways Grant and Macaulay, are the parodists of history. Despite their intentions and invocations they inscribe the colonial text erratically, eccentrically across a body politic that refuses to be representative, in a narrative that refuses to be representational. The desire to emerge as "authentic" through mimicry—through a process of writing and repetition—is the final irony of partial representation.

What I have called mimicry is not the familiar exercise of *dependent* colonial relations through narcissistic identification so that, as Fanon has observed,[12] the black man stops being an actional person for only the white man can represent his self-esteem. Mimicry conceals no presence or identity behind its mask: it is not what Césaire describes as "colonialization-thingification"[13] behind which there stands the essence of the *présence Africaine.* The *menace* of mimicry is its *double* vision which in disclosing the ambivalence of colonial discourse also disrupts its authority. And it is a double-vision that is a result of what I've described as the partial representation/recognition of the colonial object. Grant's colonial as partial imitator, Macaulay's translator, Naipaul's colonial politician as play-actor, Decoud as the scene setter of the *opéra bouffe* of the New World, these are the appropriate objects of a colonialist chain of command, authorized versions of otherness. But they are also, as I have shown, the figures of a doubling, the part-objects of a metonymy of colonial desire which alienates the modality and normality of those dominant discourses in which they emerge as "inappropriate" colonial subjects. A desire that, through the repetition of *partial presence,* which is the basis of mimicry, articulates those disturbances of cultural, racial, and historical difference that menace the narcissistic demand of colonial authority. It is a desire that reverses "in part" the colonial appropriation by now producing a partial vision of the colonizer's presence. A gaze of otherness, that shares the acuity of the genealogical gaze which, as Foucault describes it, liberates marginal elements and shatters the unity of man's being through which he extends his sovereignty.[14]

I want to turn to this process by which the look of surveillance returns as the displacing gaze of the disciplined, where the observer becomes the observed and "partial" representation rearticulates the whole notion of *identity* and alienates it from essence. But not before observing that even an exemplary history like Eric Stokes's *The English Utilitarians in India* acknowledges the anomalous gaze of otherness but finally disavows it in a contradictory utterance:

Certainly India played *no* central part in fashioning the distinctive qualities of English civilisation. In many ways it acted as a disturbing force, a magnetic power placed at the periphery tending to distort the natural development of Britain's character. . . . [15]

What is the nature of the hidden threat of the partial gaze? How does mimicry emerge as the subject of the scopic drive and the object of colonial surveillance? How is desire disciplined, authority displaced?

---

[10]Joseph Conrad, *Nostromo,* London, Penguin, 1979, p. 161.

[11]V. S. Naipaul, *The Mimic Men,* London, Penguin, 1967, p. 146.

[12]Frantz Fanon, *Black Skin, White Masks,* London, Paladin, 1970, p. 109.

[13]Aimé Césaire, *Discourse on Colonialism,* New York, Monthly Review Press, 1972, p. 21.

[14]Michel Foucault, "Nietzche, Genealogy, History," in *Language, Counter-Memory, Practice,* trans. Donald F. Bouchard and Sherry Simon, Ithaca, Cornell University Press, p. 153.

[15]Eric Stokes, *The English Utilitarians and India,* Oxford, Oxford University Press, 1959, p. xi.

If we turn to a Freudian figure to address these issues of colonial textuality, that form of difference that is mimicry—*almost the same but not quite*—will become clear. Writing of the partial nature of fantasy, caught *inappropriately*, between the unconscious and the preconscious, making problematic, like mimicry, the very notion of "origins," Freud has this to say:

> Their mixed and split origin is what decides their fate. We may compare them with individuals of mixed race who taken all round resemble white men but who betray their coloured descent by some striking feature or other and on that account are excluded from society and enjoy none of the privileges.[16]

*Almost the same but not white:* the visibility of mimicry is always produced at the site of interdiction. It is a form of colonial discourse that is uttered *inter dicta:* a discourse at the crossroads of what is known and permissible and that which though known must be kept concealed; a discourse uttered between the lines and as such both against the rules and within them. The question of the representation of difference is therefore always also a problem of authority. The "desire" of mimicry, which is Freud's *striking feature* that reveals so little but makes such a big difference, is not merely that impossibility of the Other which repeatedly resists signification. The desire of colonial mimicry—an interdictory desire—may not have an object, but it has strategic objectives which I shall call the *metonymy of presence.*

Those inappropriate signifiers of colonial discourse—the difference between being English and being Anglicized; the identity between stereotypes which, through repetition, also become different; the discriminatory identities constructed across traditional cultural norms and classifications, the Simian Black, the Lying Asiatic—all these are metonymies of presence. They are strategies of desire in discourse that make the anomalous representation of the colonized something other than a process of "the return of the repressed," what Fanon unsatisfactorily characterized as collective catharsis.[17] These instances of metonymy are the nonrepressive productions of contradictory and multiple belief. They cross the boundaries of the culture of enunciation through a strategic confusion of the metaphoric and metonymic axes of the cultural production of meaning. For each of these instances of "a difference that is almost the same but not quite" inadvertently creates a crisis for the cultural priority given to the *metaphoric* as the process of repression and substitution which negotiates the difference between paradigmatic systems and classifications. In mimicry, the representation of identity and meaning is rearticulated along the axis of metonymy. As Lacan reminds us, mimicry is like camouflage, not a harmonization or repression of difference, but a form of resemblance that differs/defends presence by displaying it in part, metonymically. Its threat, I would add, comes from the prodigious and strategic production of conflictual, fantastic, discriminatory "identity effects" in the play of a power that is elusive because it hides no essence, no "itself." And that form of *resemblance* is the most terrifying thing to behold, as Edward Long testifies in his *History of Jamaica* (1774). At the end of a tortured, negrophobic passage, that shifts anxiously between piety, prevarication, and perversion, the text finally confronts its fear; nothing other than the repetition of its resemblance "in part":

> (Negroes) are represented by all authors as the vilest of human kind, to which they have little more pretension of resemblance *than what arises from their exterior forms* (my italics).[18]

From such a colonial encounter between the white presence and its black semblance, there emerges the question of the ambivalence of mimicry as a problematic of colonial subjection. For if Sade's scandalous theatricalization of language repeatedly reminds us that discourse can claim "no priority," then the work of Edward Said will not let us forget that the "ethnocentric and erratic will to power from which texts can spring"[19] is itself a theater of war. Mimicry, as the metonymy of

---

[16]Sigmund Freud, "The Unconscious" (1915), *SE*, XIV, pp. 190–191.
[17]Fanon, p. 103.
[18]Edward Long, *A History of Jamaica,* 1774, vol. II, p. 353.
[19]Edward Said, "The Text, the World, the Critic," in *Textual Strategies*, ed. J. V. Harari, Ithaca, Cornell University Press, 1979, p. 184.

presence is, indeed, such an erratic, eccentric strategy of authority in colonial discourse. Mimicry does not merely destroy narcissistic authority through the repetitious slippage of difference and desire. It is the process of the *fixation* of the colonial as a form of cross-classificatory, discriminatory knowledge in the defiles of an interdictory discourse, and therefore necessarily raises the question of the *authorization* of colonial representations. A question of authority that goes beyond the subject's lack of priority (castration) to a historical crisis in the conceptuality of colonial man as an *object* of regulatory power, as the subject of racial, cultural, national representation.

"This culture . . . fixed in its colonial status," Fanon suggests, "(is) both present and mummified, it testified against its members. It defines them in fact without appeal."[20] The ambivalence of mimicry—almost but not quite—suggests that the fetishized colonial culture is potentially and strategically an insurgent counter-appeal. What I have called its "identity-effects," are always crucially *split*. Under cover of camouflage, mimicry, like the fetish, is a part-object that radically revalues the normative knowledges of the priority of race, writing, history. For the fetish mimes the forms of authority at the point at which it deauthorizes them. Similarly, mimicry rearticulates presence in terms of its "otherness," that which it disavows. There is a crucial difference between this *colonial* articulation of man and his doubles and that which Foucault describes as "thinking the unthought"[21] which, for nineteenth-century Europe, is the ending of man's alienation by reconciling him with his essence. The colonial discourse that articulates an *interdictory* "otherness" is precisely the "other scene" of this nineteenth-century European desire for an authentic historical consciousness.

The "unthought" across which colonial man is articulated is that process of classificatory confusion that I have described as the metonymy of the substitutive chain of ethical and cultural discourse. This results in the *splitting* of colonial discourse so that two attitudes towards external reality persist; one takes reality into consideration while the other disavows it and replaces it by a product of desire that repeats, rearticulates "reality" as mimicry.

So Edward Long can say with authority, quoting variously, Hume, Eastwick, and Bishop Warburton in his support, that:

> Ludicrous as the opinion may seem I do not think that an orangutang husband would be any dishonour to a Hottentot female.[22]

Such contradictory articulations of reality and desire—seen in racist stereotypes, statements, jokes, myths—are not caught in the doubtful circle of the return of the repressed. They are the effects of a disavowal that denies the differences of the other but produces in its stead forms of authority and multiple belief that alienate the assumptions of "civil" discourse. If, for a while, the ruse of desire is calculable for the uses of discipline soon the repetition of guilt, justification, pseudo-scientific theories, superstition, spurious authorities, and classifications can be seen as the desperate effort to "normalize" *formally* the disturbance of a discourse of splitting that violates the rational, enlightened claims of its enunciatory modality. The ambivalence of colonial authority repeatedly turns from *mimicry*—a difference that is almost nothing but not quite—to *menace*—a difference that is almost total but not quite. And in that other scene of colonial power, where history turns to farce and presence to "a part," can be seen the twin figures of narcissism and paranoia that repeat furiously, uncontrollably.

In the ambivalent world of the "not quite/not white," on the margins of metropolitan desire, the *founding objects* of the Western world become the erratic, eccentric, accidental *objets trouvés* of the colonial discourse—the part-objects of presence. It is then that the body and the book loose their representational authority. Black skin splits under the racist gaze, displaced into signs of bestiality, genitalia, grotesquerie, which reveal the phobic myth of the undifferentiated whole white body. And the holiest of books—the Bible—bearing both the standard of the cross and the standard of empire finds itself strangely dismembered. In May 1817 a missionary wrote from Bengal:

---

[20]Frantz Fanon, "Racism and Culture," in *Toward the African Revolution*, London, Pelican, 1967, p. 44.
[21]Michel Foucault, *The Order of Things*, New York, Pantheon, 1970, part II, chap. 9.
[22]Long, p. 364.

Still everyone would gladly receive a Bible. And why?—that he may lay it up as a curiosity for a few pice; or use it for waste paper. Such it is well known has been the common fate of these copies of the Bible. . . . Some have been bartered in the markets, others have been thrown in snuff shops and used as wrapping paper.[23]

---

[23]*The Missionary Register,* May 1817, p. 186.

---

*JUDITH Butler's forceful account of the performative dimension of gender "identity" has been widely influential in feminist theory, gay and lesbian studies, and theater studies. In "Performative Acts and Gender Constitution," Butler argues that "gender identity" is socially constituted, performed rather than innate; it is, in fact, in "the nature of such performances to create the effect of a solid, substantial identity." As Butler suggests, to regard "gender identity" in this way is to begin to scrutinize the political consequences of other apparently "natural" modes of identity, notably compulsory heterosexuality. Butler develops this argument in her book,* Gender Trouble: Feminism and the Subversion of Identity *(1986) and in* Bodies that Matter: On the Discursive Limits of "Sex" *(1993).*

## Judith Butler

"Performative Acts and Gender Constitution: An Essay in Phenomenology and Feminist Theory" (1988)

Philosophers rarely think about acting in the theatrical sense, but they do have a discourse of "acts" that maintains associative semantic meanings with theories of performance and acting. For example, John Searle's "speech acts" those verbal assurances and promises which seem not only to refer to a speaking relationship, but to constitute a moral bond between speakers, illustrate one of the illocutionary gestures that constitutes the stage of the analytic philosophy of language. Further, "action theory," a domain of moral philosophy, seeks to understand what it is "to do" prior to any claim of what one ought to do. Finally, the phenomenological theory of "acts," espoused by Edmund Husserl, Maurice Merleau-Ponty and George Herbert Mead, among others, seeks to explain the mundane way in which social agents constitute social reality through language, gesture, and all manner of symbolic social sign. Though phenomenology sometimes appears to assume the existence of a choosing and constituting agent prior to language (who poses as the sole source of its constituting acts), there is also a more radical use of the doctrine of constitution that takes the social agent as an object rather than the subject of constitutive acts.

When Simone de Beauvoir claims, "one is not born, but, rather, *becomes* a woman," she is appropriating and reinterpreting this doctrine of constituting acts from the phenomenological tradition.[1] In this sense, gender is in no way a stable identity or locus of agency from which various acts proceede; rather, it is an identity tenuously constituted in time—an identity instituted through a *stylized repetition of acts.* Further, gender is instituted through the stylization of the body and, hence, must be understood as the mundane way in which bodily gestures, movements, and enactments of various kinds constitute the illusion of an abiding gendered self. This formulation moves the conception of gender off the ground of a substantial model of identity to one that requires a conception of a constituted *social temporality.* Significantly, if gender is instituted through acts which are internally discontinuous, then the *appearance of substance* is precisely that, a constructed identity, a performative accomplishment which the mundane social audience, including the actors themselves, come to believe and to perform in the mode of belief. If the ground of gender identity is the stylized repetition of acts through time, and not a seemingly seamless identity, then the possibilities of gender transformation are to be found in the arbitrary relation between such acts, in the possibility of a different sort of repeating, in the breaking or subversive repetition of that style.

Through the conception of gender acts sketched above, I will try to show some ways in which reified and naturalized conceptions of gender might be understood as constituted and, hence, capable of being constituted differently. In opposition to theatrical or phenomenological models

---

[1]For a further discussion of Beauvoir's feminist contribution to phenomenological theory, see my "Variations on Sex and Gender: Beauvoir's *The Second Sex," Yale French Studies* 172 (1986).

which take the gendered self to be prior to its acts, I will understand constituting acts not only as constituting the identity of the actor, but as constituting that identity as a compelling illusion, an object of *belief.* In the course of making my argument, I will draw from theatrical, anthropological, and philosophical discourses, but mainly phenomenology, to show that what is called gender identity is a performative accomplishment compelled by social sanction and taboo. In its very character as performative resides the possibility of contesting its reified status.

*I. Sex/gender:*
*Feminist and*
*phenomenological*
*views*

Feminist theory has often been critical of naturalistic explanations of sex and sexuality that assume that the meaning of women's social existence can be derived from some fact of their physiology. In distinguishing sex from gender, feminist theorists have disputed causal explanations that assume that sex dictates or necessitates certain social meanings for women's experience. Phenomenological theories of human embodiment have also been concerned to distinguish between the various physiological and biological causalities that structure bodily existence and the *meanings* that embodied existence assumes in the context of lived experience. In Merleau-Ponty's reflections in *The Phenomenology of Perception* on "the body in its sexual being," he takes issue with such accounts of bodily experience and claims that the body is "an historical idea" rather than "a natural species."[2] Significantly, it is this claim that Simone de Beauvoir cites in *The Second Sex* when she sets the stage for her claim that "woman," and by extension, any gender, is an historical situation rather than a natural fact.[3]

In both contexts, the existence and facticity of the material or natural dimensions of the body are not denied, but reconceived as distinct from the process by which the body comes to bear cultural meanings. For both Beauvoir and Merleau-Ponty, the body is understood to be an active process of embodying certain cultural and historical possibilities, a complicated process of appropriation which any phenomenological theory of embodiment needs to describe. In order to describe the gendered body, a phenomenological theory of constitution requires an expansion of the conventional view of acts to mean both that which constitutes meaning and that through which meaning is performed or enacted. In other words, the acts by which gender is constituted bear similarities to performative acts within theatrical contexts. My task, then, is to examine in what ways gender is constructed through specific corporeal acts, and what possibilities exist for the cultural transformation of gender through such acts.

Merleau-Ponty maintains not only that the body is an historical idea but a set of possibilities to be continually realized. In claiming that the body is an historical idea, Merleau-Ponty means that it gains its meaning through a concrete and historically mediated expression in the world. That the body is a set of possibilities signifies (a) that its appearance in the world, for perception, is not predetermined by some manner of interior essence, and (b) that its concrete expression in the world must be understood as the taking up and rendering specific of a set of historical possibilities. Hence, there is an agency which is understood as the process of rendering such possibilities determinate. These possibilities are necessarily constrained by available historical conventions. The body is not a self-identical or merely factic materiality; it is a materiality that bears meaning, if nothing else, and the manner of this bearing is fundamentally dramatic. By dramatic I mean only that the body is not merely matter but a continual and incessant *materializing* of possibilities. One is not simply a body, but, in some very key sense, one does one's body and, indeed, one does one's body differently from one's contemporaries and from one's embodied predecessors and successors as well.

It is, however, clearly unfortunate grammar to claim that there is a "we" or an "I" that does its body, as if a disembodied agency preceded and directed an embodied exterior. More appropriate, I suggest, would be a vocabulary that resists the substance metaphysics of subject-verb formations and relies instead on an ontology of present participles. The "I" that is its body is, of necessity, a mode of embodying, and the "what" that it embodies is possibilities. But here again the grammar of the formulation misleads, for the possibilities that are embodied are not fundamentally exterior

---

[2]Maurice Merleau-Ponty, "The Body in its Sexual Being," in *The Phenomenology of Perception,* trans. Colin Smith (Boston: Routledge and Kegan Paul, 1962).

[3]Simone de Beauvoir, *The Second Sex,* trans. H. M. Parshley (New York: Vintage, 1974), 38.

or antecedent to the process of embodying itself. As an intentionally organized materiality, the body is always an embodying *of* possibilities both conditioned and circumscribed by historical convention. In other words, the body *is* a historical situation, as Beauvoir has claimed, and is a manner of doing, dramatizing, and *reproducing* a historical situation.

To do, to dramatize, to reproduce, these seem to be some of the elementary structures of embodiment. This doing of gender is not merely a way in which embodied agents are exterior, surfaced, open to the perception of others. Embodiment clearly manifests a set of strategies or what Sartre would perhaps have called a style of being or Foucault, "a stylistics of existence." This style is never fully self-styled, for living styles have a history, and that history conditions and limits possibilities. Consider gender, for instance, as *a corporeal style,* an "act," as it were, which is both intentional and performative, where "performative" itself carries the double-meaning of "dramatic" and "non-referential."

When Beauvoir claims that "woman" is a historical idea and not a natural fact, she clearly underscores the distinction between sex, as biological facticity, and gender, as the cultural interpretation or signification of that facticity. To be female is, according to that distinction, a facticity which has no meaning, but to be a woman is to have *become* a woman, to compel the body to conform to an historical idea of "woman," to induce the body to become a cultural sign, to materialize oneself in obedience to an historically delimited possibility, and to do this as a sustained and repeated corporeal project. The notion of a "project," however, suggests the originating force of a radical will, and because gender is a project which has cultural survival as its end, the term *"strategy"* better suggests the situation of duress under which gender performance always and variously occurs. Hence, as a strategy of survival, gender is a performance with clearly punitive consequences. Discrete genders are part of what "humanizes" individuals within contemporary culture; indeed, those who fail to do their gender right are regularly punished. Because there is neither an "essence" that gender expresses or externalizes nor an objective ideal to which gender aspires; because gender is not a fact, the various acts of gender creates the idea of gender, and without those acts, there would be no gender at all. Gender is, thus, a construction that regularly conceals its genesis. The tacit collective agreement to perform, produce, and sustain discrete and polar genders as cultural fictions is obscured by the credibility of its own production. The authors of gender become entranced by their fictions own fictions whereby the construction compels one's belief in its necessity and naturalness. The historical possibilities materialized through various corporeal styles are nothing other than those punitively regulated cultural fictions that are alternately embodied and disguised under duress.

How useful is a phenomenological point of departure for a feminist description of gender? On the surface it appears that phenomenology shares with feminist analysis a commitment to grounding theory in lived experience, and in revealing the way in which the world is produced through the constituting acts of subjective experience. Clearly, not all feminist theory would privilege the point of view of the subject, (Kristeva once objected to feminist theory as "too existentialist")[4] and yet the feminist claim that the personal is political suggests, in part, that subjective experience is not only structured by existing political arrangements, but effects and structures those arrangements in turn. Feminist theory has sought to understand the way in which systemic or pervasive political and cultural structures are enacted and reproduced through individual acts and practices, and how the analysis of ostensibly personal situations is clarified through situating the issues in a broader and shared cultural context. Indeed, the feminist impulse, and I am sure there is more than one, has often emerged in the recognition that my pain or my silence or my anger or my perception is finally not mine alone, and that it delimits me in a shared cultural situation which in turn enables and empowers me in certain unanticipated ways. The personal is thus implicitly political inasmuch as it is conditioned by shared social structures, but the personal has also been immunized against political challenge to the extent that public/private distinctions endure. For feminist theory, then, the personal becomes an expansive category, one which accommodates, if only implicitly, political structures usually viewed as public. Indeed, the very meaning of the political expands as well. At

---

[4]Julia Kristeva, *Histoire d'amour* (Paris: Editions Denoel, 1983), 242.

its best, feminist theory involves a dialectical expansion of both of these categories. My situation does not cease to be mine just because it is the situation of someone else, and my acts, individual as they are, nevertheless reproduce the situation of my gender, and do that in various ways. In other words, there is, latent in the personal is political formulation of feminist theory, a supposition that the life-world of gender relations is constituted, at least partially, through the concrete and historically mediated *acts* of individuals. Considering that "the" body is invariably transformed into his body or her body, the body is only known through its gendered appearance. It would seem imperative to consider the way in which this gendering of the body occurs. My suggestion is that the body becomes its gender through a series of acts which are renewed, revised, and consolidated through time. From a feminist point of view, one might try to reconceive the gendered body as the legacy of sedimented acts rather than a predetermined or foreclosed structure, essence or fact, whether natural, cultural, or linguistic.

The feminist appropriation of the phenomenological theory of constitution might employ the notion of an *act* in a richly ambiguous sense. If the personal is a category which expands to include the wider political and social structures, then the *acts* of the gendered subject would be similarly expansive. Clearly, there are political acts which are deliberate and instrumental actions of political organizing, resistance collective intervention with the broad aim of instating a more just set of social and political relations. There are thus acts which are done in the name of women, and then there are acts in and of themselves, apart from any instrumental consequence, that challenge the category of women itself. Indeed, one ought to consider the futility of a political program which seeks radically to transform the social situation of women without first determining whether the category of woman is socially constructed in such a way that to be a woman is, by definition, to be in an oppressed situation. In an understandable desire to forge bonds of solidarity, feminist discourse has often relied upon the category of woman as a universal presupposition of cultural experience which, in its universal status, provides a false ontological promise of eventual political solidarity. In a culture in which the false universal of "man" has for the most part been presupposed as coextensive with humanness itself, feminist theory has sought with success to bring female specificity into visibility and to rewrite the history of culture in terms which acknowledge the presence, the influence, and the oppression of women. Yet, in this effort to combat the invisibility of women as a category feminists run the risk of rendering visible a category which may or may not be representative of the concrete lives of women. As feminists, we have been less eager, I think, to consider the status of the category itself and, indeed, to discern the conditions of oppression which issue from an unexamined reproduction of gender identities which sustain discrete and binary categories of man and woman.

When Beauvoir claims that woman is an "historical situation," she emphasizes that the body suffers a certain cultural construction, not only through conventions that sanction and proscribe how one acts one's body, the "act" or performance that one's body is, but also in the tacit conventions that structure the way the body is culturally perceived. Indeed, if gender is the cultural significance that the sexed body assumes, and if that significance is codetermined through various acts and their cultural perception, then it would appear that from within the terms of culture it is not possible to know sex as distinct from gender. The reproduction of the category of gender is enacted on a large political scale, as when women first enter a profession or gain certain rights, or are reconceived in legal or political discourse in significantly new ways. But the more mundane reproduction of gendered identity takes place through the various ways in which bodies are acted in relationship to the deeply entrenched or sedimented expectations of gendered existence. Consider that there is a sedimentation of gender norms that produces the peculiar phenomenon of a natural sex, or a real woman, or any number of prevalent and compelling social fictions, and that this is a sedimentation that over time has produced a set of corporeal styles which, in reified form, appear as the natural configuration of bodies into sexes which exist in a binary relation to one another.

## II. Binary genders and the heterosexual contract

To guarantee the reproduction of a given culture, various requirements, well-established in the anthropological literature of kinship, have instated sexual reproduction within the confines of a heterosexually-based system of marriage which requires the reproduction of human beings in certain gendered modes which, in effect, guarantee the eventual reproduction of that kinship system. As

Foucault and others have pointed out, the association of a natural sex with a discrete gender and with an ostensibly natural "attraction" to the opposing sex/gender is an unnatural conjunction of cultural constructs in the service of reproductive interests.[5] Feminist cultural anthropology and kinship studies have shown how cultures are governed by conventions that not only regulate and guarantee the production, exchange, and consumption of material goods, but also reproduce the bonds of kinship itself, which require taboos and a punitive regulation of reproduction to effect that end. Levì-Strauss has shown how the incest taboo works to guarantee the channeling of sexuality into various modes of heterosexual marriage,[6] Gayle Rubin has argued convincingly that the incest taboo produces certain kinds of discrete gendered identities and sexualities.[7] My point is simply that one way in which this system of compulsory heterosexuality is reproduced and concealed is through the cultivation of bodies into discrete sexes with "natural" appearances and "natural" heterosexual dispositions. Although the enthnocentric conceit suggests a progression beyond the mandatory structures of kinship relations as described by Levì-Strauss, I would suggest, along with Rubin, that contemporary gender identities are so many marks or "traces" of residual kinship. The contention that sex, gender, and heterosexuality are historical products which have become conjoined and reified as natural over time has received a good deal of critical attention not only from Michel Foucault, but Monique Wittig, gay historians, and various cultural anthropologists and social psychologists in recent years.[8] These theories, however, still lack the critical resources for thinking radically about the historical sedimentation of sexuality and sex-related constructs if they do not delimit and describe the mundane manner in which these constructs are produced, reproduced, and maintained within the field of bodies.

Can phenomenology assist a feminist reconstruction of the sedimented character of sex, gender, and sexuality at the level of the body? In the first place, the phenomenological focus on the various acts by which cultural identity is constituted and assumed provides a felicitous starting point for the feminist effort to understand and the mundane manner in which bodies get crafted into genders. The formulation of the body as a mode of dramatizing or enacting possibilities offers a way to understand how a cultural convention is embodied and enacted. But it seems difficult, if not impossible, to imagine a way to conceptualize the scale and systemic character of women's oppression from a theoretical position which takes constituting acts to be its point of departure. Although individual acts do work to maintain and reproduce systems of oppression, and, indeed, any theory of personal political responsibility presupposes such a view, it doesn't follow that oppression is a sole consequence of such acts. One might argue that without human beings whose various acts, largely construed, produce and maintain oppressive conditions, those conditions would fall away, but note that the relation between acts and conditions is neither unilateral nor unmediated. There are social contexts and conventions within which certain acts not only become possible but become conceivable as acts at all. The transformation of social relations becomes a matter, then, of transforming hegemonic social conditions rather than the individual acts that are spawned by those conditions. Indeed, one runs the risk of addressing the merely indirect, if not epiphenomenal, reflection of those conditions if one remains restricted to a politics of acts.

But the theatrical sense of an "act" forces a revision of the individualist assumptions underlying the more restricted view of constituting acts within phenomenological discourse. As a given temporal duration within the entire performance, "acts" are a shared experience and "collective action." Just as within feminist theory the very category of the personal is expanded to include political structures, so is there a theatrically-based and, indeed, less individually-oriented view of acts that goes some of the way in defusing the criticism of act theory as "too existentialist." The act that

[5]See Michel Foucault, *The History of Sexuality: An Introduction,* trans. Robert Hurley (New York: Random House, 1980), 154: "the notion of 'sex' made it possible to group together, in an artificial unity, anatomical elements, biological functions, conducts, sensations, and pleasures, and it enabled one to make use of this fictitious unity as a causal principle . . . "

[6]See Claude Levì-Strauss, *The Elementary Structures of Kinship* (Boston: Beacon Press, 1965).

[7]Gayle Rubin, "The Traffic in Women: Notes on the 'Political Economy' of Sex," in *Toward an Anthropology of Women,* ed. Rayna R. Reiter (New York: Monthly Review Press, 1975), 178–85.

[8]See my "Variations on Sex and Gender: Beauvoir, Wittig, and Foucault," in *Feminism as Critique,* ed. Seyla Benhabib and Drucila Cornell (London: Basil Blackwell, 1987 [distributed by University of Minnesota Press]).

gender is, the act that embodied agents *are* inasmuch as they dramatically and actively embody and, indeed, *wear* certain cultural significations, is clearly not one's act alone. Surely, there are nuanced and individual ways of *doing* one's gender, but *that* one does it, and that one does it *in accord with* certain sanctions and proscriptions, is clearly not a fully individual matter. Here again, I don't mean to minimize the effect of certain gender norms which originate within the family and are enforced through certain familial modes of punishment and reward and which, as a consequence, might be construed as highly individual, for even there family relations recapitulate, individualize, and specify pre-existing cultural relations; they are rarely, if ever, radically original. The act that one does, the act that one performs, is, in a sense, an act that has been going on before one arrived on the scene. Hence, gender is an act which has been rehearsed, much as a script survives the particular actors who make use of it, but which requires individual actors in order to be actualized and reproduced as reality once again. The complex components that go into an act must be distinguished in order to understand the kind of acting in concert and acting in accord which acting one's gender invariably is.

In what senses, then, is gender an act? As anthropologist Victor Turner suggests in his studies of ritual social drama, social action requires a performance which is *repeated*. This repetition is at once a reenactment and reexperiencing of a set of meanings already socially established; it is the mundane and ritualized form of their legitimation.[9] When this conception of social performance is applied to gender, it is clear that although there are individual bodies that enact these significations by becoming stylized into gendered modes, this "action" is immediately public as well. There are temporal and collective dimensions to these actions, and their public nature is not inconsequential; indeed, the performance is effected with the strategic aim of maintaining gender within its binary frame. Understood in pedagogical terms, the performance renders social laws explicit.

As a public action and performative act, gender is not a radical choice or project that reflects a merely individual choice, but neither is it imposed or inscribed upon the individual, as some poststructuralist displacements of the subject would contend. The body is not passively scripted with cultural codes, as if it were a lifeless recipient of wholly pre-given cultural relations. But neither do embodied selves pre-exist the cultural conventions which essentially signify bodies. Actors are always already on the stage, within the terms of the performance. Just as a script may be enacted in various ways, and just as the play requires both text and interpretation, so the gendered body acts its part in a culturally restricted corporeal space and enacts interpretations within the confines of already existing directives.

Although the links between a theatrical and a social role are complex and the distinctions not easily drawn (Bruce Wilshire points out the limits of the comparison in *Role-Playing and Identity: The Limits of Theatre as Metaphor*[10]), it seems clear that, although theatrical performances can meet with political censorship and scathing criticism, gender performances in non-theatrical contexts are governed by more clearly punitive and regulatory social conventions. Indeed, the sight of a transvestite onstage can compel pleasure and applause while the sight of the same transvestite on the seat next to us on the bus can compel fear, rage, even violence. The conventions which mediate proximity and identification in these two instances are clearly quite different. I want to make two different kinds of claims regarding this tentative distinction. In the theatre, one can say, "this

---

[9]See Victor Turner, *Dramas, Fields, and Metaphors* (Ithaca: Cornell University Press, 1974). Clifford Geertz suggests in "Blurred Genres: The Refiguration of Thought," in *Local Knowledge, Further Essays in Interpretive Anthropology* (New York: Basic Books, 1983), that the theatrical metaphor is used by recent social theory in two, often opposing, ways. Ritual theorists like Victor Turner focus on a notion of social drama of various kinds as a means for settling internal conflicts within a culture and regenerating social cohesion. On the other hand, symbolic action approaches, influenced by figures as diverse as Emile Durkheim, Kenneth Burke, and Michel Foucault, focus on the way in which political authority and questions of legitimation are thematized and settled within the terms of performed meaning. Geertz himself suggests that the tension might be viewed dialectically; his study of political organization in Bali as a "theatre-state" is a case in point. In terms of an explicitly feminist account of gender as performative, it seems clear to me that an account of gender as ritualized, public performance must be combined with an analysis of the political sanctions and taboos under which that performance may and may not occur within the public sphere free of punitive consequence.

[10]Bruce Wilshire, *Role-Playing and Identity: The Limits of Theatre as Metaphor* (Boston: Routledge and Kegan Paul, 1981).

is just an act," and de-realize the act, make acting into something quite distinct from what is real. Because of this distinction, one can maintain one's sense of reality in the face of this temporary challenge to our existing ontological assumptions about gender arrangements; the various conventions which announce that "this is only a play" allows strict lines to be drawn between the performance and life. On the street or in the bus, the act becomes dangerous, if it does, precisely because there are no theatrical conventions to delimit the purely imaginary character of the act, indeed, on the street or in the bus, there is no presumption that the act is distinct from a reality; the disquieting effect of the act is that there are no conventions that facilitate making this separation. Clearly, there is theatre which attempts to contest or, indeed, break down those conventions that demarcate the imaginary from the real (Richard Schechner brings this out quite clearly in *Between Theatre and Anthropology*[11]). Yet in those cases one confronts the same phenomenon, namely, that the act is not contrasted with the real, but *constitutes* a reality that is in some sense new, a modality of gender that cannot readily be assimilated into the pre-existing categories that regulate gender reality. From the point of view of those established categories, one may want to claim, but oh, this is *really* a girl or a woman, or this is *really* a boy or a man, and further that the *appearance* contradicts the *reality* of the gender, that the discrete and familiar reality must be there, nascent, temporarily unrealized, perhaps realized at other times or other places. The transvestite, however, can do more than simply express the distinction between sex and gender, but challenges, at least implicitly, the distinction between appearance and reality that structures a good deal of popular thinking about gender identity. If the "reality" of gender is constituted by the performance itself, then there is no recourse to an essential and unrealized "sex" or "gender" which gender performances ostensibly express. Indeed, the transvestite's gender is as fully real as anyone whose performance complies with social expectations.

Gender reality is performative which means, quite simply, that it is real only to the extent that it is performed. It seems fair to say that certain kinds of acts are usually interpreted as expressive of a gender core or identity, and that these acts either conform to an expected gender identity or contest that expectation in some way. That expectation, in turn, is based upon the perception of sex, where sex is understood to be the discrete and factic datum of primary sexual characteristics. This implicit and popular theory of acts and gestures as *expressive* of gender suggests that gender itself is something prior to the various acts, postures, and gestures by which it is dramatized and known; indeed, gender appears to the popular imagination as a substantial core which might well be understood as the spiritual or psychological correlate of biological sex.[12] If gender attributes, however, are not expressive but performative, then these attributes effectively constitute the identity they are said to express or reveal. The distinction between expression and performativeness is quite crucial, for if gender attributes and acts, the various ways in which a body shows or produces its cultural signification, are performative, then there is no preexisting identity by which an act or attribute might be measured; there would be no true or false, real or distorted acts of gender, and the postulation of a true gender identity would be revealed as a regulatory fiction. That gender reality is created through sustained social performances means that the very notions of an essential sex, a true or abiding masculinity or femininity, are also constituted as part of the strategy by which the performative aspect of gender is concealed.

As a consequence, gender cannot be understood as a *role* which either expresses or disguises an interior "self," whether that "self" is conceived as sexed or not. As performance which is performative, gender is an "act," broadly construed, which constructs the social fiction of its own psychological interiority. As opposed to a view such as Erving Goffman's which posits a self which assumes and exchanges various "roles" within the complex social expectations of the "game" of

[11]Richard Schechner, *Between Theatre and Anthropology* (Philadelphia: University of Pennsylvania Press, 1985). See especially, "News, Sex, and Performance," 295–324.

[12]In *Mother Camp* (Prentice-Hall, 1974), Anthropologist Esther Newton gives an urben ethnography of drag queens in which she suggests that all gender might be understood on the model of drag. In *Gender: An Ethnomethodological Approach* (Chicago: University of Chicago Press, 1978), Suzanne J. Kessler and Wendy McKenna argue that gender is an "accomplishment" which requires the skills of constructing the body into a socially legitimate artifice.

modern life,[13] I am suggesting that this self is not only irretrievably "outside," constituted in social discourse, but that the ascription of interiority is itself a publically regulated and sanctioned form of essence fabrication. Genders, then, can be neither true nor false, neither real nor apparent. And yet, one is compelled to live in a world in which genders constitute univocal signifiers, in which gender is stabilized, polarized, rendered discrete and intractable. In effect, gender is made to comply with a model of truth and falsity which not only contradicts its own performative fluidity, but serves a social policy of gender regulation and control. Performing one's gender wrong initiates a set of punishments both obvious and indirect, and performing it well provides the reassurance that there is an essentialism of gender identity after all. That this reassurance is so easily displaced by anxiety, that culture so readily punishes or marginalizes those who fail to perform the illusion of gender essentialism should be sign enough that on some level there is social knowledge that the truth or falsity of gender is only socially compelled and in no sense ontologically necessitated.[14]

*III. Feminist theory: Beyond an expressive model of gender*

This view of gender does not pose as a comprehensive theory about what gender is or the manner of its construction, and neither does it prescribe an explicit feminist political program. Indeed, I can imagine this view of gender being used for a number of discrepant political strategies. Some of my friends may fault me for this and insist that any theory of gender constitution has political presuppositions and implications, and that it is impossible to separate a theory of gender from a political philosophy of feminism. In fact, I would agree, and argue that it is primarily political interests which create the social phenomena of gender itself, and that without a radical critique of gender constitution feminist theory fails to take stock of the way in which oppression structures the ontological categories through which gender is conceived. Gayatri Spivak has argued that feminists need to rely on an operational essentialism, a false ontology of women as a universal in order to advance a feminist political program.[15] She knows that the category of "women" is not fully expressive, that the multiplicity and discontinuity of the referent mocks and rebels against the univocity of the sign, but suggests it could be used for strategic purposes. Kristeva suggests something similar, I think, when she prescribes that feminists use the category of women as a political tool without attributing ontological integrity to the term, and adds that, strictly speaking, women cannot be said to exist.[16] Feminists might well worry about the political implications of claiming that women do not exist, especially in light of the persuasive arguments advanced by Mary Anne Warren in her book, *Gendercide*.[17] She argues that social policies regarding population control and reproductive technology are designed to limit and, at times, eradicate the existence of women altogether. In light of such a claim, what good does it do to quarrel about the metaphysical status of the term, and perhaps, for clearly political reasons, feminists ought to silence the quarrel altogether.

But it is one thing to use the term and know its ontological insufficiency and quite another to articulate a normative vision for feminist theory which celebrates or emancipates an essence, a nature, or a shared cultural reality which cannot be found. The option I am defending is not to redescribe the world from the point of view of women. I don't know what that point of view is, but whatever it is, it is not singular, and not mine to espouse. It would only be half-right to claim that I am interested in how the phenomenon of a men's or women's point of view gets constituted, for while I do think that those points of views are, indeed, socially constituted, and that a reflexive genealogy of those points of view is important to do, it is not primarily the gender episteme that I am interested in exposing, deconstructing, or reconstructing. Indeed, it is the presupposition of the

---

[13]See Erving Goffmann, *The Presentation of Self in Everyday Life* (Garden City: Doubleday, 1959).

[14]See Michel Foucault's edition of *Herculine Barbin: The Journals of a Nineteenth Century French Hermaphrodite*, trans. Richard McDougall (New York: Pantheon Books, 1984), for an interesting display of the horror evoked by intersexed bodies. Foucault's introduction makes clear that the medical delimitation of univocal sex is yet another wayward application of the discourse on truth-as-identity. See also the work of Robert Edgerton in *American Anthropologist* on the cross-cultural variations of response to hermaphroditic bodies.

[15]Remarks at the Center for Humanities, Wesleyan University, Spring, 1985.

[16]Julia Kristeva, "Woman Can Never Be Defined," trans. Marilyn A. August, in *New French Feminisms*, ed. Elaine Marks and Isabelle de Courtivron (New York: Schocken, 1981).

[17]Mary Anne Warren, *Gendercide: The Implications of Sex Selection* (New Jersey: Rowman and Allanheld, 1985).

category of woman itself that requires a critical genealogy of the complex institutional and discursive means by which it is constituted. Although some feminist literary critics suggest that the presupposition of sexual difference is necessary for all discourse, that position reifies sexual difference as the founding moment of culture and precludes an analysis not only of how sexual difference is constituted to begin with but how it is continuously constituted, both by the masculine tradition that preempts the universal point of view, and by those feminist positions that construct the univocal category of "women" in the name of expressing or, indeed, liberating a subjected class. As Foucault claimed about those humanist efforts to liberate the criminalized subject, the subject that is freed is even more deeply shackled than originally thought.[18]

Clearly, though, I envision the critical genealogy of gender to rely on a phenomenological set of presuppositions, most important among them the expanded conception of an "act" which is both socially shared and historically constituted, and which is performative in the sense I previously described. But a critical genealogy needs to be supplemented by a politics of performative gender acts, one which both redescribes existing gender identities and offers a prescriptive view about the kind of gender reality there ought to be. The redescription needs to expose the reifications that tacitly serve as substantial gender cores or identities, and to elucidate both the act and the strategy of disavowal which at once constitute and conceal gender as we live it. The prescription is invariably more difficult, if only because we need to think a world in which acts, gestures, the visual body, the clothed body, the various physical attributes usually associated with gender, *express nothing.* In a sense, the prescription is not utopian, but consists in an imperative to acknowledge the existing complexity of gender which our vocabulary invariably disguises and to bring that complexity into a dramatic cultural interplay without punitive consequences.

Certainly, it remains politically important to represent women, but to do that in a way that does not distort and reify the very collectivity the theory is supposed to emancipate. Feminist theory which presupposes sexual difference as the necessary and invariant theoretical point of departure clearly improves upon those humanist discourses which conflate the universal with the masculine and appropriate all of culture as masculine property. Clearly, it is necessary to reread the texts of western philosophy from the various points of view that have been excluded, not only to reveal the particular perspective and set of interests informing those ostensibly transparent descriptions of the real, but to offer alternative descriptions and prescriptions; indeed, to establish philosophy as a cultural practice, and to criticize its tenets from marginalized cultural locations. I have no quarrel with this procedure, and have clearly benefited from those analyses. My only concern is that sexual difference not become a reification which unwittingly preserves a binary restriction on gender identity and an implicitly heterosexual framework for the description of gender, gender identity, and sexuality. There is, in my view, nothing about femaleness that is waiting to be expressed; there is, on the other hand, a good deal about the diverse experiences of women that is being expressed and still needs to be expressed, but caution is needed with respect to that theoretical language, for it does not simply report a pre-linguistic experience, but constructs that experience as well as the limits of its analysis. Regardless of the pervasive character of patriarchy and the prevalence of sexual difference as an operative cultural distinction, there is nothing about a binary gender system that is given. As a corporeal field of cultural play, gender is a basically innovative affair, although it is quite clear that there are strict punishments for contesting the script by performing out of turn or through unwarranted improvisations. Gender is not passively scripted on the body, and neither is it determined by nature, language, the symbolic, or the overwhelming history of patriarchy. Gender is what is put on, invariably, under constraint, daily and incessantly, with anxiety and pleasure, but if this continuous act is mistaken for a natural or linguistic given, power is relinquished to expand the cultural field bodily through subversive performances of various kinds.

---

[18]Ibid.; Michel Foucault, *Discipline and Punish: The Birth of the Prison* trans. Alan Sheridan (New York: Vintage Books, 1978).

## Sue-Ellen Case

"From Split Subject to
Split Britches"
(1989)

*A prominent scholar and theoretician of feminism and theater, Sue-Ellen Case has written widely on gender, sexuality, and theater; she is the author of* Feminism and Theatre *(1988), editor of* Performing Feminisms: Feminist Critical Theory and Theatre *(1990), and coeditor, with Janelle Reinelt, of* The Performance of Power: Theatrical Discourse and Politics *(1991). In "From Split Subject to Split Britches," Case examines the way that the theory of the "subject" or "subject position"—which understands "identity" not in ontological, essential, or psychological terms, but as something constructed relationally, in discourse and ideology—informs contemporary feminist theory and theatrical practice. Case suggests that drama in the 1970s and 1980s represented the contradictory subjectivity of women in patriarchal culture in two ways. The dynamics of the "split" and "displaced" subject are illustrated in the plays of Marsha Norman, Marguerite Duras, and others; the performances of the Split Britches company articulate a more urgent assault on and appropriation of these dynamics of gender formation.*

Plays, practice, and criticism inhabit a common field in contemporary feminist production. The historical bond between feminist political practice and critical theory has created the sense that a feminist field or ambience can embrace aesthetic, political, and critical modes of production. The old patriarchal notions of inheritance and influence give way to a new sense that art and life may not be two distinct phenomena, followed by critics the way Mother Courage followed the war. Rather, the representation of women on the stage, the experiences of women in real life, and the discursive knowledge about women exist in a contiguous relationship with one another. They nourish and adjust one another within their specific historical moment. Such a healing of the art-life-criticism schism is the inheritance of a movement that focused on "consciousness-raising" and "the personal is the political." This new field theory enables the critic to perceive recent plays by women playwrights, recent feminist theory, and recent discoveries in critical methodology as interactive and interdependent within the last two decades of the liberation of the feminine gender.

Within this new field theory of feminism, the term *subject position* has come to signify an important move for women that is incorporated in the creations and explorations of theorists, artists, and critics alike. Several plays by contemporary women playwrights construct women in this subject position, providing new images of women and their experiences along with new structures for their representation. These plays dramatize the difference between women as objects (sexual objects, etc.) and women as subjects of the drama. At the same time they alter the structure of the subject position from its old appearance as protagonist to new forms of the subject's appearance and development. This innovation participates both in advances in feminist social practice and in recent explorations in feminist thought. In social practice women have agitated to occupy the subject position in their struggle for economic independence. Rather than being the objects of exchange[1] or the recipients of patriarchal charities, they have sought to become the subject that makes transactions, much the way the subject moves the verb in a sentence. This move is contiguous with their new position onstage. Likewise, in feminist theory, the project to move women into the subject position of philosophical, linguistic, psychoanalytic, and symbolic systems in general participates in this same field of endeavor.

However, this feminist field is not a homogeneous one. Inner dynamics exist that sometimes resemble internecine nodes of contradiction and debate. The notion of a subject position is a destabilized one, animated by older debates about form and content, material base and essentialist assumptions, and even positions that are characterized by national borders. Because some readers of this present volume may not be familiar with the notion of the subject position and its historical development in feminist circles, I think a brief and perhaps oversimplified excursion into its theory, preceding its description in specific plays, may provide such readers with access to the contemporary feminist playing field.

Here the term *subject position* derives from feminist uses of semiotic and Lacanian notions of the subject. The formulation of a subject position eschews the former Cartesian conflation of the subject position in a linguistic or symbolic system with a "self." The term *position* foregrounds the structural role of the subject-in-discourse, alienating it from its traditional adumbrations of the personal. Descartes also linked that position with a certain epistemology in his "cogito," a link that Lacanian psychoanalytic theory exposes as structural contortions or sutures on the pseudoseamless surface of discourse that cloak the essentially split, alienated structure of the subject from itself.

The notion of the subject position is thus both deconstructive and constructive. Originally, it was developed as a deconstructive device by male authors who employed it to break with the epistemological and ontological foundations of idealism, but who retained its patriarchal bias. Much of the "feminist"[2] theory of the subject position has been developed by French authors who have deconstructed the theories of Derrida, Lacan, Lyotard, Blanchot, and others to accommodate the presence of gender inscription in theoretical models.[3] These French theoreticians insert a new notion of woman-as-subject into psychoanalytic, deconstructive, and poststructuralist strategies. Their realm is pure theory, deriving from and correcting influential contemporary theories that retain patriarchal prejudices, in spite of their liberating and deconstructive projects. In contrast, the Anglo-American tradition of feminist thought consistently places theory and literary texts in relation to social practice and the "real lives" of women. Though American feminists are receptive to French theory, they are frustrated by its seemingly hermetic and formalistic nature.[4] This theory is so complex and dependent on its earlier models that it is difficult to expropriate elements from it for the purpose of social or critical application without misreading its meanings. Therefore, the critic finds herself so caught up in the internal structures of the theory that she cannot bring it into relationship with current political objectives.

Nevertheless, for the critic to remain within the exclusivities of either of these two traditions creates something like a form and content split. Typically, the Anglo-American feminist critic explicates texts in terms of images of women and narratives that either replicate, deviate, fictionalize, debase, or ignore the "real" experiences of women. In this way she deals primarily with the content of plays, noting the positive or negative implications of the narrative (e.g., the negative plot line illustrates the oppression of the female protagonist and kills her in the end), or the positive and negative content in the image of the woman (e.g., she is a whore, witch, bitch, etc.). She establishes this positive-negative charge by comparing it with the ways in which real women experience life or real men misperceive them. Moreover, the context she employs for this analysis is one of two economic and social conditions. This kind of political analysis is reminiscent of the content analysis Marxist critics used before the discoveries of the Frankfurt school, concentrating on the positive image of the proletarian hero and the constructive plot line of the social realist drama. Like Marxist criticism, this content analysis illustrates the materialist base in the play. It provides for a discussion of class, economic exploitation or independence, and a historical frame, which is relatively absent in the French theoretical models. However, the French theoretical contribution allows the feminist critic to pursue an analysis of the formal elements of plays. More importantly, the French theories critique the overall operations of the system of representation, discourse, and cultural production. While the Anglo-American framework is "real life," the French one is the system of representation.

At this point in history, most Anglo-American critics perceive the vital interaction between these two realms: how a tradition of the representation of women creates their social condition and vice versa. Hence, the feminist field theory begins to emerge. From the perspective of this field, the oppression of women appears as twofold: material oppression and oppression in representation. Thus, the form and content split begins to disappear. As symbolic systems masculinize the subject (perhaps most simply demonstrated by the use of the "universal" pronoun "he" for the subject of action), structuralizing male dominance in systems of thought, so do male images of the subject and female images of the object masculinize the content. Furthermore, male ownership in the economic realm and male authority in the social one along with these structural and thematic elements of representation codetermined the position of women in society. Art is no longer a "mirror" of life but an active force in social manipulation, while real life is no longer merely the image one sees in the mirror of art but the social structure that organizes its form.

Thus, moving women into the subject position in any realm is contingent upon their position in the others. Making a woman the subject of the drama implies her position in the system of representation, both structurally and thematically, as well as her social and economic position in the culture at large. In order to account for the revolutionary move for women from the object position to the subject position in the drama, I will break with the orthodoxy of the French theoretical model, using its terminology and concerns for a critical application to the drama. In fact, some of the Lacanian terms, still laden with patriarchal bias, will become neologisms for critical notions that account for women as subjects. At the same time, by placing theoretical concerns in conjunction with the social concerns of Anglo-American feminist criticism, I will illustrate a way in which class and form, content and social structure cohabit the feminist field.

In recent plays by women playwrights, three kinds of subject positions emerge: the split subject, the metonymically displaced subject, and the collective subject. All three types have appeared in plays written within the last two decades of feminist development. At the same time, theoretical and critical explorations of women in the subject position have discursively developed these same structural positions. Though there is no chronological or developmental sequence in the appearance of these positions, I have organized them to move from the simplest to the most complex. The split subject seems an apt place to begin, since that notion underpins much of the understanding of the subject position in general. In appropriating the term *split subject* from Lacanian discourse, I will employ it in order to maintain its references to the psychoanalytic critique while employing it also as a neologism for a certain literary device.

*The split subject*     For the classical Lacanian male subject, the split of the subject is between his subject position in discourse and his subjectivity, or self in reality. Though the male subject appears as a single, unified position in the discourse, such as the protagonist, the Lacanian system reveals a split between that socially constructed, autonomous, continuous "subject" of discourse and actual subjectivity. In fact, as the subject of discourse appears, the "real" subject "fades" away. The construction of this subject of discourse occurs in what Lacan calls "the mirror stage." The metaphor of mirror works as a social reflection, in which the infant sees the structure of a whole self, as a baby might learn to see "himself" in a mirror. When he enters the system of representation, he does so in this unified form, becoming the traditional subject of discourse. While he gains access to symbolic systems, he losses access to the immediate satisfaction of his desires, but not the drives of those desires—thus, the notion of the split subject. This subject of discourse, then, travels through symbolic systems endlessly seeking the satisfaction of his desires in surrogate symbols, alienated from his actual subjectivity. Systems of representation can then be read as his itinerary of desire.[5] Ironically, male poststructuralist criticism and postmodern literature are decentering the subject, vacating that position, at the same point in history in which women seek to inhabit it.

This notion of the split subject is based upon certain premises about the psychosexual development of the male child, including ideas about the phallus and the working out of the Oedipal process. Lacan's split subject is constructed upon a development and a physiology the female child does not share. Therefore, when she looks in this mirror, when she enters the system of representation, she does so as a cultural male. Because the subject of discourse or representation is gendered as male, women cannot inhabit the position in the same way unless they do so as male-identified subjects. That is, insofar as women have identified with men in order to enter representation at all, the system works the same way. Yet, if I might expand Lacan's metaphor in order to include the possibility of the female subject, "she" also sees in that mirror that she is a woman. At that moment she further fractures, split once as the male-identified subject and his subjectivity and split once more as the woman who observes her own subject position as both male-identified and female. She acts in the system in the male position, but she also marks that position with her own female action. This produces a double split for the woman subject: she is split in the way the Lacanian subject is split, but she is also split in the discourse. She cannot appear as a single, whole, continuous subject as the male can because she senses that his story is not her story. Yet she entered the doors of discourse in male drag. This contradiction produces the split-subject-in-discourse. To amend Lacan, I would like to use this term *split subject* to represent this new position for women in discourse. Here it means that when women enter the subject position in discourse, they split the subject of discourse (while still maintaining the classical, Lacanian split). The following plays exemplify the use of this split subject in the system of representation as well as dramatize its inner tensions.

In *The Abdication* (1969) by Ruth Wolff, the subject of the drama, Queen Christina of Sweden, is split into three parts: the mature Christina and her childhood selves, Chris and Tina. Tina represents the "meek and docile" side of Christina, while Chris is the "more jaunty side," entering in drag as a young man.[6] Scenes with Chris, Tina, and Christina play simultaneously upon the stage, dramatizing the interactions among the parts of the split subject. The split subject represents an ambivalence about power: Tina and Chris fight over the symbols of the queen, while the mature Christina watches, caught up in a present-time dialogue with a member of the Vatican. A similar split subject appears in Marsha Norman's *Getting Out* (1978), in which the mature Arlene appears in the present time, recently released from prison, while her younger self, Arlie, simultaneously plays scenes from her childhood and her time in prison. Arlie is played as a tomboy who seeks out conflict, and Arlene is portrayed as a recently converted young woman who seeks to appease the system and her mother. Likewise, in *Giving Up the Ghost* (1986) by Cherríe Moraga, the main character is split into Marisa, a "Chicana in her late 20s" (the present time), and Corky, "Marisa's younger self, at 11 and 17 years old."[7] The focus of this subject is upon sexuality. Marisa seeks to resolve her lesbian sexuality in the present, while Corky represents her earlier male identification in "*cholo*" drag. *Blood Relations* (1979) by Sharon Pollock is a play about Lizzie Borden. Lizzie is sometimes played as Lizzie and sometimes played by an actress/friend, while Lizzie looks on. In some scenes Lizzie plays her own maid to the actress/friend who is playing Lizzie. The younger Lizzie is rebellious and brash, while the present-day Lizzie is more accommodating.

All of these plays represent the woman in the subject position as a split subject. Moreover, these split subjects share many similar attributes. They present the contemporary subject who is attempting to adapt to social codes after undergoing a chastening socialization process: Christina in the Vatican, Arlene on parole, Marisa attempting to become less alienated from her ethnic identity, and Lizzie after her murder trial. At the same time they provide an image of an earlier, often male-identified rebellious subject. The split subject in these plays illustrates the way in which women as subjects alter the structure of the subject position by splitting what had formerly been represented as a whole. The prevalance of younger, male-identified selves parallels the notion of women entering the system of representation as men. In order to inhabit the subject position, they entered as male-identified. Yet the mature subjects, identified as women, must struggle with that earlier identification, both to overcome it and to retain its power. The mature women, placed within the context of chastening institutions of socialization, distance themselves from their entrance into the system, while still maintaining themselves in the subject position. Lacan was therefore correct in describing the subject as male, caught up within his psychosexual development. In *Giving Up the Ghost* Moraga dramatizes explicitly the psychosexual dimension of the struggle. All of these plays, by placing the subjects in the context of social institutions, illustrate the Lacanian sense that the subject of symbolic systems is a socially constructed one, alienated from pure subjectivity. Yet they add another dimension to Lacan's system: the split between a feminine consciousness and its male-identified symbolic role.

These examples may also be read as dramatizations of women's struggle with cultural ownership. Phrased in this way, the elements of a social, material analysis and those of a formal one come easily into relationship with one another. After all, the subject owns the drama in the same way as the subject owns property or social authority. The subject's experience defines the parameters of the dramatic field. Other characters become relegated as objects of her affections, hostilities, losses, and triumphs. Traditionally, this subject position has been gender marked by the prevalence of male protagonists. The male subject's ownership of the play mirrored the male's ownership of property rights in the culture at large. The recent rise of women playwrights and feminist perspectives on the lives of women emerges from a long history of women as objects in the male subject's drama. Against that historical backdrop, the female subject, as created by women playwrights in the "age of feminism," assimilates the owner position of the subject with some trepidation and ambivalence. Looking back at traditional dramas, the woman subject steps onto the stage with a leftover feeling that she has no right to it. She might own the drama as a male-identified woman, but she is amazed to see a female face in the "mirror" of symbolic systems.

In his book *Saint Genet,* Jean-Paul Sartre describes a similar split subject in the works of Genet, relating it to his ambivalence about ownership. Sartre suggests that Genet's experience as an orphan, taken in by surrogate families, may have produced a split in Genet's personality as well as in his works: "Genet transfers to himself the owner's gestures and sensations so as to identify himself with the latter by an effort of mind. He takes in order to convince himself that he has the right to take; he eats as an actor eats on the stage; he is playing at possession; he embodies the owner as Barrault embodies Hamlet. However, he makes, at the same time, a considerable effort to be his own audience so as to catch himself in the act of possessing."[8] This dynamic might also describe the woman as split subject of the drama. She takes the subject position, still convincing herself that she has the right to it, and she is her own chastened audience for her earlier, brash entrance into the system. This multinomial position marks her ambivalence in taking the role, raises the issue of her right to it, and marks her observation of herself in such a position. As she watches her younger, male-identified self, which is judged as guilty by social institutions, she resembles the thief Genet as Sartre describes him: "He is obliged, by error, to use a language which is not his own, which belongs only to legitimate children. Genet has neither mother nor heritage—how could he be innocent? By virtue of his mere existence he disturbs the natural order and the social order."[9]

This assimilation of the role of the owner of the drama onstage coincides with women's social move toward financial independence and social authority. In fact, within the content of these plays, these women are involved in a move for independence. They bear the emotional scars of "getting out" of the old object position and "getting in" to the subject position. Arlene, Christina, Marisa, and Lizzie Borden struggle for independence from the judgments of the courts, the penal system, the church, and the restrictions of an ethnic community. They provide images of women in transition from their social and cultural inheritance of repression to the liberation of self-definition. In this way the Anglo-American feminist criticism and the French theoretical one merge to describe the double oppression and liberation of women as inscribed in plays written during the first seventeen years of the feminist movement.

*The metonymically displaced subject*

The split-subject-in-discourse seems a stable, simple structure compared with the metonymically displaced one. In this mode the subject further fractures into multiple displacements across the stage and is transmutable during the course of the play. Rather than inhabiting a stable, split position, it may move from position to position through the dynamic of displacement, leaving only its itinerary as a sign of its presence. In fact, in several of the plays that exhibit this device, the subject position is not always an incarnate one. The subject may be located in offstage voices or voice-overs. Several recent plays by women playwrights exhibit the appearance of the metonymically displaced subject. Perhaps three of the richest are *The Portrait of Dora* (1976) by Hélène Cixous, *The Singular Life of Albert Nobbs* (1977) by Simone Benmussa, and *India Song* (1972) by Marguerite Duras.

*The Portrait of Dora* locates this subject within the setting of Freudian analysis, problematizing the presence of the desiring female subject within the patriarchal operations of Freudian psychoanalysis. Cixous depicts Freud's misrepresentation of his patient and foregrounds the limitations of his method when confronting a female subject. To do this she has chosen to dramatize one of Freud's case histories in which he admitted his own defeat. While Freud is portrayed by a single character, Dora, the female subject, is drawn by displacing the subject position through memories, characters Dora invokes, and voice-overs of her internal monologue. In *The Singular Life of Albert Nobbs,* Albert's subject position is likewise constructed by a character onstage, voice-overs of her own inner monologues, and even the voice of the narrator who describes her. These plays suggest a sample of works a reader might consider for the construction of this subject position. However, because of the complexity of this construction and the dense, opaque nature of the theoretical apparatus, I would like to focus this section on the close reading of *India Song* as a single text that illustrates the metonymically displaced subject position. Once more, I consider it necessary to provide a condensed exposition of certain elements within the Lacanian system before proceeding to their actual application to the text.

The mechanism of displacement is usually tied to the object position. Since, in the Lacanian system, the subject in discourse lacks access to the actual satisfaction of his desire, a metonymic displacement of that desire substitutes for that lack. There is a similarity between the trope of metonymy and the dynamic of displacements in that both exploit "relationships of contiguity between things."[10] The prohibited object of the subject's desire is metonymically replaced by an uncensored one through displacement. Kaja Silverman, in *The Subject of Semiotics,* illustrates this process by examples from Proust's *Remembrance of Things Past*. She traces Swann's metonymic displacement of his desire for Odette through his attachment to Vinteuil's sonata, Odette's apartment, her clothing, and the street on which she lives. Silverman cites the scene in which Swann first kisses Odette, "after virtually ravishing the flowers she is wearing."[11] Odette's absence is the motor for Swann's desire that moves him through attachments to places and things contiguously associated with her. In the Lacanian system this process is much more complicated, implying a certain relationship to the preconscious, the unconscious, the veiled phallus, and other related processes. However, for the purpose of this essay, perhaps this example can serve to illustrate how displacement works.

*India Song* incorporates the metonymic displacement of both the object of desire and the subject position. The basic metonymic trope is the story of Anne-Marie Stretter—the object of desire, metonymically displaced by her lovers' memories of her and their attachments to places and things related to her. Yet the desiring subject, unlike Swann, is not represented by one subject position. Rather, the desiring subject of Stretter moves through four voices-overs, onstage characters, and off-stage voices. Within the gendered drama of desire, structural relationships are altered by female inhabitants of subject positions and determinedly fixed by male ones. The subject positions are inhabited by members of both sexes, whose genders mark their relationship to subject-object relations.

In this play absence reigns supreme, driving the play through contiguous positions of the desiring subject. The basic framework of the drama is constructed by the multiple subject position of four voices numbered 1 through 4. Stretter and the other characters onstage never speak; they stand as mute monuments of others' desires.[12] Voices 1 and 2 carry much of the narrative of the play. Duras introduces them in this way:

> Voices 1 and 2 are women's voices. Young. They are linked together by a love story. Sometimes they speak of this love, their own. Most of the time they speak of another love, another story. But this story leads us back to theirs and vice versa . . . the women's voices are tinged with madness . . . most of the time they are in a state of transport, a delirium, at once calm and feverish. . . . They are most immediately present when they veer toward their own story—that is, when, in the course of a perpetual shifting process, the love story of *India Song* is juxtaposed with their own.[13]

Voices 3 and 4 enter in the third section of the play. They are men's voices. "The only thing that connects them is the fascination exerted on them by the story." Voice 3 has forgotten most of the story, and Voice 4 "has forgotten it the least." Duras stresses the subject as position by developing not characters for these voices, but relative positions in relation to the story. In her description of Voices 1 and 2, her indication of the "perpetual shifting process" and "juxtaposition" suggests the process of metonymic displacement as a key to the construction of the piece.

Since Stretter's voice is mostly silent and her body often immobile and inaccessible, the sounds of rain, distant voices, and music metonymically displace her as the object of desire, projecting the subject position outward through the four voices and the audience as well. Like Vinteuil's sonata to Swann, the pervasive sound of the India Song recalls the passion and desire aroused by the story of Stretter. Yet the India Song is not the property of one character's desire but permeates the play, affecting characters onstage, the voices, and the audience at large. The drama is implied as the audience enters into the atmosphere of desire. Subject positions occur at interstices of memory, sensual affect, and the sight of Stretter. This is composition by contiguity. Because the play hinges upon voyeurism, created through voices watching the silent Stretter, invisible to her and aroused by the sight of her, the audience enters into this dynamic as another voyeur, caught up in the drama not only through empathetic relationships to the multiple character positions but also by its own voyeuristic relationship to Stretter, until the song, the sights, the street noises, and the sight of Stretter work on it in the same metonymic fashion as on the other characters. Duras notes that the stage "plays the part of an echo chamber. Passing through that space, the voices should sound, to the spectator, like his own 'internal rending' voice." Duras may even have created the spectator as a subject position.

Subject positions are also represented by characters onstage who act out the metonymic displacement of the object of desire. One such character enters, suffused by his love for Stretter but shut out of her world. He discovers her bicycle standing near the tennis courts. Duras describes his stage action in a lyric description of displacement. The lyricism is an affect in the drama, marked by a division into poetic lines. It is constructed like a *tirade* of desire: "The man is beside the bicycle. / Puts out his hands. Hesitates. / Then touches it. / Strokes it. / Leans forward and holds it in his arms. / Stays clasping Anne-Marie Stretter's bicycle—frozen in this gesture of desire." During this time Stretter is asleep onstage. As he bends over the bike, she sits up, watching him caress it. The focus moves from watching him to watching Stretter watch him. In this scenario of desire the displacement of the subject position moves back and forth across the stage.

The feminist interest in this play and its utilization of this theoretical apparatus lies in the gender of the object of desire and in the gender marking of the subject positions. Duras creates each subject position solely through its desire for the object. In this way she focuses the dramatic experience on both the subject and the object. The object of desire is a woman. It is her nude body, her particular kind of inaccessibility and seductive quality, that yields the metonymic displacement. Duras foregrounds the tradition of this construction of woman in the object position by heightening every traditional sign in that system. Her nudity, the stage images of men caressing her while she remains immobile, the image of the man with the bicycle, the dislocation of her story from her voice to those of others, all foreground the traditional gender role of that object. She yields meaning and discursive subjectivity to the subject, but is exiled from that condition. Her appeal lies in the profusion of signifying networks established by her inaccessibility. She is immobile and silent, bound and gagged, forced to yield. The object reality of Stretter is also built into the narrative. When the play begins, Anne-Marie Stretter is dead; during the course of the play she slowly comes to life, and at the end she commits suicide, remaining a corpse onstage.

The Lacanian system is aligned with this stage tradition of woman as object. Sharing the patriarchal bias of the stage tradition and working in the order of discourse found in the patriarchal culture at large, the Lacanian subject position is gender marked as male. His desire, codified by the Oedipal process, is for the female. Women, then, are locked into the object position, and Lacan specifically noted that it is women who inspire metonymic displacement. He cites "certain passages of Tolstoy's work; where each time it is a matter of the approach of a woman, you see emerging in her place, in a grand-style metonymic process, the shadow of a beauty mark, a spot on the upper lip, etc."[14] Because of the supremacy of the family unit in the Freudian-Lacanian Oedipal process and the heterosexist bias, the male necessarily desires the female and places her in the system as "other." Duras foregrounds both the "otherness" and the gendered object position of Stretter.

However, Duras transposes this female object into the context of an unusual subject position—the lesbian desiring subject of Voice 2. The representation of lesbian desire in *India Song* controverts both the patriarchal and the heterosexist biases in the psychoanalytic system. It is this desire that motivates the interaction between Voices 1 and 2, establishing the quality of their presence. Yet the expression of lesbian desire is not reciprocal; when Voice 2 professes her passion for Voice 1, she meets with no response. The silence of Voice 1 propels both voices back into the story of Stretter. It is as if the daring, revolutionary lesbian subject position is repressed by the silence of Voice 2 and replaced by the representation of woman-as-object. Voice 2: "I love you so much I can't see any more, can't hear . . . can't live. . . . *No answer.*" Then the India Song is heard again in the background, and the sounds of Calcutta and the characters onstage become animated.

Nevertheless, Duras pointedly contradicts the representation of the woman-object with this position of the lesbian subject. At one point Stretter slowly strips off her clothes, revealing her nude body: "*She freezes. Head thrown back. Gasping for air. . . . Stays like that, upright, exposed. Offered to the voices. (The voices are slow, stifled, a prey to desire—through this motionless body.)* Voice 2: *(smothered outburst)* How lovely you look dressed in white." The contrast between Stretter's nude body and Voice 2's description of Voice 1 as dressed in white moves the subject position away from a voyeuristic, scopophiliac adoration of the object to the disembodied expression of passion for the other, invisible female subject. The nude-dressed contradiction underscores the separation of these two states. Moreover, it is clear that Voice 2 is not obsessed with Stretter's story but uses Voice 1's relation to it as a device for liberating the articulation of her own desire. Whereas the object position sets off a chain of metonymic displacements in the subjects who are obsessed with it, Voice 2 explicitly expresses her desire directly to Voice 1. At best, the lesbian subject disrupts the heterosexist subject-object tableau on the stage: "Voice 2: I love you with a desire that is absolute. *No answer. Silence. The hand of Michael Richardson—the lover—immediately stops caressing the body, as if arrested by what Voice 2 has just said.*"

When the male Voices, 3 and 4, enter in part 3 of the play, this direct desire is gone. The male voices retain the focus on Stretter, lodging her securely in the object position. They differ from one another only in their degree of accuracy in recalling the story. Most of their dialogue is taken up in telling the story or speculating about characters, events, and locations within the story. They seem particularly absorbed in the facts surrounding the male characters who desire Stretter ("All trace of him disappears in 1938. He resigns the consular service. The resignation is the last thing on the file"); the geographical locations of the events ("In front, the landing stages. The boats go to and from the South Pacific. Behind, there's a yachting harbor," "They're alluvial islands, formed by the Ganges mud"); the weather ("Now that the mist has come the wind has dropped"); and the physical plants in which some scenes are set ("The water sprinklers in the English quarter," "The factories. The middle zone"). These male voices have an entirely different tone than the preceding female ones. They exhibit a distant relationship between voices and a kind of factual, expository relationship to the story. The female voices cease before the final section of the play in which Stretter dies. The description of her death is left to these men. The death of the object is compounded by its stable position within these voices.

Duras has organized a distinct difference between the gendered subject positions, underscored by having women speaking with women and men with men. The men remain in the tradition of male/subject and female/object, while the women complicate that dynamic. When women inhabit the subject position in this play, the position alters. Duras carefully genders the structural positions of the play.

The formal procedures in Duras' play may be gender marked as feminine writing, eschewing the more potent trope of metaphor for metonymy. This implies that style itself may be gender marked and the very structure of *India Song* may be a feminine one. In other words, the author/subject inscribes the written text with her gender. The concentration of metonymies suggests a feminine author of the composition. Jane Gallop, in *Reading Lacan*, argues that metaphor, as a more potent form in Lacan, has associations that are phallic, whereas metonomy's association with lack, latency, and passivity resembles Freud's "dark continent" of female sexuality, becoming the "dark continent" of rhetoric."[15] Gallop also perceives, from within the Lacanian system, an association of metonymy with "servitude," "social censorship," and "oppression." "Feminine metonymy has tricks and detours that, according to Lacan, allow it to 'get around the obstacles of social censorship.'"[16] This affixes a political, social motivation to style, conflating the feminine inscription in representation with its position in the social situation. The saturation of *India Song* with metonymic displacement marks a female subject as its creator.

Gallop later problematizes her own interpretation of this trope of metonymy, stating that it implies a "pathology of interpretation."[17] What within psychoanalytic terms may be a pathology, within social terms may be a polemic or a politic. A feminist reading that establishes tropes and styles as gender marked, privileging, in this case, the feminine mark on the writing, is polemical. This feminist project, reifying masculine and feminine (or patriarchal and feminist) bipolar oppositions, may fall back into the phallic mode. Nevertheless, it is at this point in history, it may be argued, that the mark of a woman writer (herself a new kind of subject) necessarily appears as difference and opposition to historical tradition. Duras' own division of subject positions into two sets of voices, masculine and feminine, certainly duplicates that division. It also foregrounds the division, making visible the invisible patriarchal mark on stage style and the potential of the feminist or gynecocentric one.

Within its use of formal devices, *India Song* displays a feminist potential in its construction of subject positions and a feminist critique in its object position. The gender critique of woman as object also includes a consciousness of class and race in the figure of the Beggar Woman. In this way the use of the formal device is wedded to the social message. Whereas Stretter and her friends compose what Duras refers to as "white" India, the Beggar Woman represents the poverty and pain of the other India. She plays as a kind of "double" to Stretter, but is a very different kind of object, with a different set of metonymies. Her figure is contiguous with reports of myriad fires, burning leprous bodies. Her story is one of begging for food or of abandoning and selling her children. The subjects who are obsessed with telling Stretter's story evade the Beggar Woman's. Whereas

Stretter inspires desire, the Beggar Woman inspires fear and disgust. In her endnotes, Duras remarks: "The story is a love story immobilized in the culmination of passion. Around it is another story, a story of horror—famine and leprosy mingled in the pestilential humidity of the monsoon—which is also immobilized, in a daily paroxysm." The Beggar Woman also has a song that haunts the play, metonymically replacing her as object. Her song is in a foreign tongue, drifting in from outside the rooms, where the dying and starving wait for charitable handouts from the white colonialists who inhabit the interiors. The Beggar Woman is the object of poverty and caste, outside lyricism and love, outside the discourse of desire and the operations of internal psychodynamics.

In the contemporary drama the Beggar Woman is a more familiar character in socially committed plays and criticism than in love stories, or plays of obsession and desire. Duras portrays her as the double of this privileged world; she is the demarcation of desire's limits. Perhaps this dramatic world of obsessive displacements of desire is a flight from her existence. The title *India Song* refers to both the chic tune played for white India and the Beggar Woman's song outside the window. The social, material critique accompanies the structural innovations of the play, both focusing on the female gender.

Although the above examples illustrate innovations in the structure of the drama contiguous with the feminist movement of women into the subject position, they all still exist within the traditional institution of the theater. These plays retain the traditional function of the text, written by a playwright and performed by actors for an audience seated in a traditional theater structure. Though they challenge the subject position interior to texts, they do not challenge the institution of theater and its practices. In other words, they do not alter the structure of the subject position within the overall practice of the theater. For that kind of move I will abandon the reading of texts for an exploration of a theater company that has created a new subject position for women vis-à-vis both the stage and the streets. This company splits more than the subject of the written text.

*Split Britches*    The name of this company, Split Britches, connotes the split pants of both poverty and comedy, the splitting of male gender wear, and suggests puns such as split bridges/split breaches. The company consists of three women: one heterosexual Jewish woman, one "butch" working-class lesbian mother, and one southern, working-class "femme" lesbian. It is housed at the WOW Cafe—a three-story walk-up loft in the Lower East Side of New York. In the Lower East Side, its members play out their own ethnic, regional, class, and sexual identities on the stage and in the streets.

The butch and femme play out their roles on the streets, dressing in thrift-store attire that accents the pop representation of their sexual roles. At the same time they parody male-female gender representation in the media. On a given day the butch may be wearing a man's blue suit from the fifties—the kind of suit that shines in the sun—complete with shirt and tie. She may also imitate the walk and gestures of the kind of man who would have worn such a suit. She disrupts the image with earrings, pant legs that are too short, and a flamboyant, Elvis-style haircut. The femme might be wearing turquoise high heels, a turquoise cocktail dress (also from the fifties), and a turquoise feather boa. Her colors complement the blue of her partner's suit. She, too, may imitate the walk and gestures of the woman who might have worn such a dress. She disrupts the image by relating to her lesbian escort and by wearing the dress in wrinkled, dirty condition, with no nylons and dirty shoes. They transport these same costumes onto the stage, replete with gestures and characterization, as part of one of their performances. Their local audiences are familiar with their roles both on the street and on the stage, connecting the public persona with the character or drawing connections between stage and street, public self and theatrical character. Onstage, these costumes and gestures last only a short while, as part of a series of images the actors assume and then shed. Or, in some of their plays, these costumes remain on the actor, overlaid with other costumes, until the audience perceives layers and layers of differing gender wear, differing period pieces, differing ages, and differing class and ethnic accoutrements.

The company's production of *Beauty and the Beast* provides a clear example of this technique. During the course of the play, some of the roles played by the femme include a Salvation Army officer, the character of Beauty, Katherine Hepburn, and Lady Macbeth. Some of the butch roles are an old woman, sometimes allied with the Salvation Army, the Beast, Perry Como, and James Dean. The Jewish actress takes on the characters of a rabbi, a Jewish stand-up comedian, a ballerina representing Beauty, and Beauty's father. At one point the butch is wearing the dress of the old lady, the cape of the Beast, and Perry Como's sweater, while the Jewish actress is wearing the clothes of the rabbi, a tutu, and, at one point, a dress hanging around her neck on a hanger.

Who is the subject of this drama? At times, during musical numbers and in narrated transitions, it seems to be the actor. She is the site where all of these personae collect. Yet the actor is also her character on the street. At what point does she become an actor? What is the difference between an actor, a celebrity, a social role, and a self-conscious system of gestures? From this perspective, acting, in the traditional sense of taking on a character, learning lines, and so forth, may have become a trope. Within this new sense of a "field theory," the sense in which Split Britches operates, acting is certainly a trope that becomes foregrounded in the company's work along with gender, class, and sexual role. Insofar as personal material is also spoken in the text, at what point is the actor "in" any character?—especially since each character simply overlays those that have come before. Moreover, since the scenes are shared, monologues follow one another with no through-line or narrative development, and characters transform, the question arises: whose play is it? Which character is the owner of the play, the protagonist, the "lead," the subject of the drama? If there is something like a subject position in this kind of performance, it is that of a collective subject.

The notion of the collective subject is the most radical concept in recent work on women in the subject position. Many feminists consider it to be the most forward-looking construction in the feminist field. Rachel Blau DuPlessis, in *Writing Beyond the Ending*, places the collective subject as the final strategy in her book. She suggests that a collective subject can mark a work with multiplicity rather than the old protagonist-antagonist polarization.[18] In other words, the collective subject leaves behind the bipolar structure of the drama, abandoning the patriarchal stricture that "drama is conflict." The collective subject alters the internal structure of the position as well. DuPlessis describes a kind of "transpersonal protagonist"[19] or characters who represent a "compendia of typical traits" establishing "a dialogue with habitual structures of satisfaction, ranges of feeling, and response."[20]

The actors in Split Britches provide a compendium of traits in their transformable characters. These traits or images evoke their accompanying "habitual structures" of response. For example, the image of Perry Como evokes the conditions of his performances in the fifties—the social function of the smooth, slow voice and the relaxed, domestic image he projected. By choosing images from mass culture, Split Britches foregrounds the social role and its reception in the culture. At one point in the play, as Beast is dying, she/he tells the audience not to believe in such actions— on the stage or staged in real life by actors such as Ronald Reagan, who was shot but heroically survived. The rapid succession of characters alienates the audience from any empathetic relationship to a single character, the former notion of the subject, placing the reception in the critical realm of aesthetic and social representations. Unlike the women in the early movement who used the slogan "take back our bodies," these actors ransom theirs to the system of representation.

In a recent article Teresa de Lauretis identifies the collective subject as the only possibility for liberating, radical change based on its heterogeneity.[21] Rather than presenting a single, whole protagonist, who functioned in earlier works to represent "Woman" as a homogeneous category, she describes the collective representation of "woman as a social subject and a site of difference," emphasizing the "heterogeniety in the female social subject."[22] Split Britches, with its different ethnic, sexual, and class identities played out on the stage and the street, maintains the heterogeneity of the collective subject at its core. The lesbian/heterosexual, Christian-Jewish differences animate the narrative and the transformation of characters. Near the beginning of *Beauty and the Beast*, the Jewish woman, in the clothes of a rabbi, rants and raves at the audience about the treatment of Jews on the stage and in real life, while the two other actors sing a Salvation Army song in the background. Later, the lesbian couple kisses, while the heterosexual woman looks on. This dynamic of difference suits the more recent developments in the feminist social movement. Whereas in the earlier years women were regarded as similar to one another but different from men, in recent years the focus has been an internal one, noting the differences among women of class, "race," and sexuality.

Split Britches retains the class critique at the center of its work in many different ways, but perhaps the most consistent image of its dedication to "poor" theater is its location at the WOW Cafe.[23] Here both the subject and the audience for Split Britches are poor. One of the members remarked that she regretted hanging the traditional black curtains as backdrops for some of their performances. Though the curtains are necessary for better acoustics, they literally cover up the real estate. The condition of the loft as well as its Lower East Side location portray the real setting for the company's performances. Its thrift-store costumes, painted window-shade sets, and card-board props match this poor aesthetic. So do the personal lives of the performers and audience. As one member of the café noted, the performances and the performance space are important be-cause of the real estate problem of poor people in New York. Because people cannot bear their small, dingy apartments, they look for somewhere to go, to be with other people and to have a good time. The WOW Cafe provides this opportunity.

Finally, the collective subject of Split Britches actively drives the audience away from empa-thetic processes. In the company's direct insults to the audience, it compounds the relationship be-tween character and actor, personal role and social role. It abandons the psychological base of empathy and character development for the silly spur, the throwaway antiaesthetic, the poor per-son's disruption of dominant media images. Setting this dynamic within the lesbian context of sex-ual and social relationships, particularly the butch-femme parody of gender roles, the subjects of Split Britches do more than split. They appear and do not appear in fractionalized segments of character and self. They accumulate vortices of representation and reception of gender through-out several historical periods while retaining a contemporary setting in social class and ethnic iden-tity. They question the subject's ownership of the drama, the theater, and real estate from the perspective of the disenfranchised. They break with the institution of compulsory heterosexuality. In final insults to their audience, they even disrupt the closure of applause.

After tracing the complex project of the construction of the subject position within the femi-nist field, I find myself with ambivalent feelings about constituting a conclusion to this study. All my traditional training urges me to construct some kind of closure for this review. Yet the splitting, fracturing, displacing, and collective nature of the material seems to contradict that motive. More-over, since this essay is also set within a specific historical period of the feminist field project, any closure would be one of formally closing off these ideas from their social process. Rather than clo-sure, perhaps I could simply break with the reader. As in the ending of *Beauty and the Beast,* I could simply alienate the audience. Perhaps Split Britches' finale could serve here: "A you're an afoscotan, B you're a belly button, C you're a canteloupe with arms . . . F you're a fairy in my arms . . . PQ principle of queerness . . . RST respectably disgusting . . . U you pick your nose in bed . . . V you're a vomit-head, WXYZ. I love to go through / the alphabet with you / to show you how you sicken me."[24]

*Notes*

[1]For a complete discussion of woman as object of ex-change, see Gayle Rubin, "The Traffic in Women: Notes to-ward a Political Economy of Sex," in *Toward an Anthropology of Women,* ed. Rayna Reiter (New York: Monthly Review Press, 1975).

[2]Although the term *feminist* is common among Anglo-American critics, it has been rejected by French theorists who developed these ideas. For a full discussion of this issue, see Alice A. Jardine, *Gynesis* (Ithaca, N.Y.: Cornell University Press, 1985).

[3]A brief discussion of this revision process may be found in Linda Hutcheon, "Subject in/of/to History and His Story," *Diacritics* 16, no. 1 (Spring 1986), 78–91.

[4]See Jardine, *Gynesis,* for an elaboration of this point.

[5]For an explanation of Lacan's "subject" accompanied by examples from film and literature, see Kaja Silverman, *The Subject of Semiotics* (New York: Oxford University Press, 1983); for Lacan's own description of the "fading subject" in English translation, see *Ecrits: A Selection,* trans. Alan Sheri-dan (New York: Norton, 1977).

[6]Ruth Wolff, *The Abdication,* in *The New Women's The-atre,* ed. Honor Moore (New York: Vintage, 1977), p. 385.

[7]Cherrie Moraga, *Giving Up the Ghost* (Los Angeles: West End Press, 1986), p. 1.

[8]Jean-Paul Sartre, *Saint Genet: Actor and Martyr,* trans. Bernard Frechtman (New York: Pantheon, 1963), p. 13.

[9]Ibid., p. 7.

[10]Silverman, *The Subject of Semiotics,* p. 111.

[11]Ibid., p. 119.

[12]See Elin Diamond, "Refusing the Romanticism of Identity: Narrative Interventions in Churchill, Benmussa, Duras," *Theatre Journal* 37, no. 3 (October 1985), 283–85.

[13]Marguerite Duras, *India Song* (New York: Grove Press, 1976), pp. 9–10. All following quotations from the play are from this text.

[14]Jacques Lacan, *Seminar III,* quoted in Jane Gallop, *Reading Lacan* (Ithaca, N.Y.: Cornell University Press, 1985), p. 126.

[15]Gallop, *Reading Lacan,* p. 127.

[16]Ibid., p. 129.

[17]Ibid., p. 131.

[18]Rachel Blau DuPlessis, *Writing Beyond the Ending*

(Bloomington, Ind.: Indiana University Press, 1985), p. 181.

[19]Ibid., p. 185.

[20]Ibid., p. 179.

[21]Teresa de Lauretis, "Aesthetic and Feminist Theory: Re-Thinking Women's Cinema," *New German Critique* 34 (Winter 1985), 164.

[22]Ibid., 168.

[23]For a history of the WOW Cafe, see Alisa Solomon, "The WOW Cafe," in *The Drama Review: Thirty Years of Commentary on the Avant-Garde,* ed. Brooks McNamara and Jill Dolan (Ann Arbor, Mich.: UMI Research Press, 1986), 305–14.

[24]Scripts of *Beauty and the Beast* are unavailable. All references and quotations here are taken from a videotape of the production.

*SIGMUND Freud, who developed both the theory of the unconscious and the practice of psycho-analysis, is in many ways closely associated with the theater. His seminal book,* The Interpretation of Dreams *(1900), describes both the force of unconscious desire on identity and consciousness and provides a variety of ways to interpret the unconscious. This sense of a displaced, unknowable "self" is strikingly evocative of the process of characterization in early modernist drama, in the plays of Ibsen, Chekhov, and Strindberg, for example. Indeed, Freud frequently used "character-types" from drama to illustrate and explore models of human psychology, notably in the "Oedipus complex," but also in essays on Hamlet, Lady Macbeth, and on Ibsen's Hedda Gabler and Rebecca West. Freud wrote "Psychopathic Characters on the Stage" in 1904, but the essay remained un-published until 1942; unlike his later essays, which tend to focus almost exclusively on dramatic characters, here Freud also briefly sketches out a theory of the audience's investment in perfor-mance. Some of Freud's major writings include* Jokes and Their Relation to the Unconscious *(1905),* Beyond the Pleasure Principle *(1920), and* Civilization and Its Discontents *(1930).*

## Sigmund Freud
(1856–1939)

"Psychopathic Characters on the Stage" (1904)

If the function of the drama, as has been assumed since Aristotle, is to excite pity and fear, and thus bring about a "catharsis of the emotions," we may describe this same purpose a little more fully if we say that the question is one of opening up sources of pleasure and enjoyment from within our affective life, just as wit and the comic do from within the sphere of the intellect, through the action of which many such sources had been made inaccessible. Certainly the release of the subject's own affects must here be given first place, and the enjoyment resulting therefrom corre-sponds on the one hand to the relief produced by their free discharge, and on the other, very likely, to the concomitant sexual stimulation which, one may suppose occurs as a by-product of every emotional excitation and supplies the subject with that feeling of a heightening of his psychic level which he so greatly prizes. The sympathetic witnessing of a dramatic performance fulfils the same function for the adult as does play for the child, whose besetting hope of being able to do what the adult does, it gratifies. The spectator at the play experiences too little; he feels like a "Misero, to whom nothing worth while can happen"; he has long since had to moderate, or better direct else-where, his ambition to occupy a central place in the stream of world events; he wants to feel, to act, to mold the world in the light of his desire—in short, to be a hero. And the playwright-actors make all this possible for him by giving him the opportunity to identify himself with a hero. But they thus spare him something also; for the spectator is well aware that taking over the hero's rôle in his own person would involve such griefs, such sufferings and such frightful terrors as would almost nullify the pleasure therein; and he knows too that he has but a single life to live, and might perhaps per-ish in a single one of the hero's many battles with the Fates. Hence his enjoyment presupposes an illusion; it presupposes an attenuation of his suffering through the certainty that in the first place it is another than himself who acts and suffers upon the stage, and that in the second place it is only a play, whence no threat to his personal security can ever arise. It is under such circumstances that he may indulge in the luxury of being a hero; he may give way unashamedly to suppressed impulses such as the need for freedom in religious, political, social or sexual respects, and may let himself go in all directions in each and every grand scene of the life enacted upon the stage.

These are prerequisites for enjoyment, however, which are common to several forms of cre-ative art. Epic poetry subserves above all the release of intense but simple feelings—as does, in its

From *The Psychoanalytic Quarterly,* Vol. XI, No. 4 (1942). Reprinted by permission of The Psychoanalytic Quarterly, Inc.

sphere, the dance; the epic poem may be said to make possible the enjoyment in particular of the great heroic personality in his triumphs; drama, however, is supposed to delve deeper into emotional possibilities, to manage to transform even the forebodings of doom into something enjoyable, and it therefore depicts the embattled hero rather with a masochistic satisfaction in succumbing. In fact, one might characterize drama by this very relation to suffering and misfortune, whether as in the play mere apprehension is aroused and then allayed, or as in tragedy actual suffering is brought into being. The origin of drama in sacrificial rites (goat and scapegoat) in the cult of the gods cannot be without appositeness to this meaning of drama; it assuages as it were the beginning revolt against the divine order which decreed the suffering. The hero is at first a rebel against God or the divine; and it is from the feeling of misery of the weaker creature pitted against the divine might that pleasure may be said to derive, through masochistic gratification and the direct enjoyment of the personage whose greatness nevertheless the drama emphasizes. This is the Prometheus attitude of man, who in a spirit of petty compliance would be soothed for the time being with a merely momentary gratification.

All varieties of suffering are therefore the theme of drama, which promises to create out of them pleasure for the spectator; whence arises the first condition which this art form must fulfil, that it shall cause the spectator no suffering, and that it must know how to compensate by means of the gratifications which it makes possible for the pity which it arouses—a rule against which modern dramatists have particularly often been offenders. But this suffering is soon restricted to mental anguish only, for nobody wants to witness physical suffering who knows how soon the bodily sensations thus stimulated put an end to all mental enjoyment. He who is ill has but one desire: to get well, to get over his condition; the doctor must come with his medicine; the arresting of the play of fantasy must cease—that arrest which has spoiled us to the extent of letting us extract enjoyment even out of our suffering. When the spectator puts himself in the place of the sufferer from physical illness, he finds nothing within himself of enjoyment or of psychological give and take; and it is on this account that a person physically ill is possible on the stage only as a property, but not as the hero—excepting as some particular psychic aspect of illness is susceptible of psychic elaboration, as for example the abandoning of the sick Philoctetes, or the hopelessness of the sick in the plays of Strindberg.

Mental suffering we recognize, however, chiefly in relation to the circumstances out of which it has developed; hence drama requires an action from which this suffering derives, and begins by introducing to the audience this action. It is only an apparent exception that such plays as *Ajax* and *Philoctetes* present mental suffering as already in existence, for because of the familiarity of the matter to the audience the curtain always rises in the Greek drama in the middle of the play, as it were. Now, it is easy to define the conditions which this action must fulfil. There must be a play of contending forces; the action must contain within itself a striving of the will and some opposition thereto. The first and most grandiose fulfilling of these conditions was exemplified in the struggle against divinity. It has already been said that the essence of this tragedy is revolt, with dramatist and spectator taking sides with the rebel. The less that is then ascribed to the divine, the more accrues to the human element, which, with ever increasing insight, is made responsible for suffering; and so the next struggle, that of the hero against the social community, becomes the social tragedy. Still another fulfilling of these conditions is seen in the struggle between men themselves, that is, the character drama, which contains within itself all the characteristics of the agon, and, enacted preferably between outstanding personalities freed from the restrictions of human institutions, must accordingly have more than one hero. Combinations of these two are of course perfectly permissible, in the form of a struggle on the part of the hero against institutions of which strong characters are the embodiment. The pure drama of character is lacking in the sources of enjoyment afforded by the theme of rebellion, which in social plays, such as those of Ibsen, is again as powerfully to the fore as in the historical plays of Greek classical times. If religious, character and social drama differ from one another chiefly with respect to the arena in which the action takes place from which the suffering has its origin, we may now follow the drama to still another arena, where it becomes the psychological drama. For it is within the soul of the hero himself that there takes place an anguished struggle between various impulses—a struggle which must end, not with the downfall of the hero, but with that of one of the contending impulses, in other words, with a reunuciation. Every combination of this situation with that in the earlier type of drama, that is the social and the character drama, is of course possible in so far as social institutions evoke just such an inner conflict, and so on. It is here that the love drama belongs, in so far as the suppressing of love—whether on the score of the mores, the conventions or the conflict, familiar from opera, between "love and duty"—forms the starting point for an almost endless variety of conflictual situations, as infinite in their variety as the erotic daydreams of mankind. The possibilities multiply still further, however, and the psychological drama becomes the psychopathological, when the source of the suffering which we are to share and from which we are to derive pleasure is no longer a conflict between two almost equally conscious motivations, but one between conscious and repressed ones. Here the precondition for enjoyment is that the spectator shall also be neurotic. For it is only to him that the release and, to a certain extent, the conscious recognition of the repressed motivation can afford pleasure, instead of making merely for unacceptance. In the non-neurotic this will meet only with unacceptance, and will induce a readiness to repeat the act of repression, for in his case the latter has been successful. The repressed impulse is kept in complete counterbalance by the original force of repression. In the neurotic, on the other hand, repression is by way of failing; it is unstable, and requires ever renewed effort, an effort which is spared by recognition. It is only in the neurotic that such a struggle exists as can become the subject of drama; but in him also the dramatist will create not only the pleasure derived from release but resistance as well.

The foremost modern drama of this kind is *Hamlet,* which deals with the theme of a normal man who, because of the particular nature of the task enjoined upon him, becomes neurotic—a man in whom an impulse hitherto successfully repressed seeks to assert itself. *Hamlet* is distinguished by three characteristics which seem of importance to our discussion: 1) that the hero is not psychopathic, but becomes so only in the course of the action we are going to witness; 2) that the repressed desire is one of those that are similarly repressed in all of us, the repression of which belongs to an early stage of our individual development, while the situation arising in the play shatters precisely this repression. Because of these two features it is easy for us to recognize ourselves in the hero. For we are victims of the same conflict as is he; since "he who doesn't lose his reason under certain provocations has no reason to lose." 3) But it appears to be one of the prerequisites of this art form that the struggle of the repressed impulse to become conscious, recognizable though it is, is so little given a definite name that the process of reaching consciousness goes on in turn within the spectator while his attention is distracted and he is in the grip of his emotions, rather than capable of rational judgment. In this way resistance is definitely reduced, in the manner seen in psychoanalytic treatment, when the derivatives of the repressed ideas and emotions come to consciousness as a result of a lessening of resistance in a manner denied to the repressed material itself. And indeed the conflict in *Hamlet* is so deeply hidden that at first I could only surmise it.

Possibly it is because of the disregarding of these three requisite conditions that so many other psychopathic characters become as useless for the stage as they are for life itself. For the sick neurotic is to us a man into whose conflict we can obtain no insight (empathy) when he presents it to us in the form of the finished product. Conversely, if we are familiar with this conflict, we forget that he is a sick man, just as when he becomes familiar with it he himself ceases to be sick. It is thus the task of the dramatist to transport us into the same illness—a thing best accomplished if we follow him through its development. This will be particularly needful when the repression is not already existent in ourselves and must therefore be effected *de novo*—which represents a step beyond *Hamlet* in the utilization of neurosis upon the stage. Where the full-blown and strange neurosis confronts us, in real life we call the physician and deem the person in question unsuitable as a stage figure.

In general, it may perhaps be said that the neurotic liability of the public, and the art of the dramatist in making use of resistances and supplying forepleasure, alone determine the limits of the utilization of abnormal characters upon the stage.

Jindřich Honzl
(1894–1953)

"Dynamics of the Sign
in the Theater"

(1940)

TRANSLATED BY
I. R. TITUNIK

*AN innovative film and stage director, Jindřich Honzl contributed several studies of the semiotics of theatrical performance to the work of the "Prague School" of linguists in the 1930s and 1940s. Composed largely of linguists, the Prague School became known for developing "semiotics," a "science of signs" that used models drawn from the study of language to analyze the wider field of signification in culture at large. In "Dynamics of the Sign in the Theater," Honzl suggests that the stage—as a signifying field—never simply reflects or represents "reality," but instead deploys a network of interlocking "languages"—costume, acting style, design, movement, and so on—that relate to "reality" in much the same problematic way that verbal discourse does.*

Everything that makes up reality on the stage—the playwright's text, the actor's acting, the stage lighting—all these things in every case stand for other things. In other words, dramatic performance is a set of signs.

Otakar Zich expressed such a view in his *Aesthetics of Dramatic Art* when he advanced the notion that "dramatic art is an art of images and is so, moreover, in absolutely every respect."[1] Thus the actor represents a dramatic character (Vojan represents Hamlet), the scenery represents the locale where the story unfolds (a Gothic arch represents a castle), bright lighting represents daytime, dim lighting denotes nighttime, music represents some happening (the noise of battle), and so forth. Zich explains that though the stage certainly involves architectural constructions, still it cannot, in his view, be consigned to the domain of architecture because architecture does not want to stand for anything and, hence, does not have image function. The stage has no other function than to stand for something else, and it ceases to be the stage if it does not represent something. To comprehend Zich's assertion better, we may put it into other words and say that it does not matter whether the stage is a construction or not, that is, whether the stage is a place in the Prague National Theater or a meadow near a forest or a pair of planks supported by barrels or a market square crowded with spectators. What does matter is that the stage of the Prague National Theater may perfectly well represent a meadow, or the meadow of an outdoor theater clearly represent a town square, or a section of square in a marketplace theater represent the inside of an inn, and so on. Zich, however, does not discount the architectural nature of the stage. Whenever he speaks of the stage, he always has in mind a stage inside of a theater building. But we may, nevertheless, venture to infer from Zich's argument the conclusions, already mentioned, as to the nondependence of the stage's image function on its architectural constructedness.

Moreover, from this instance of the semiotic character of the stage we can draw an analogy to other aspects of theatrical performance. It has already been maintained that although the stage is usually a construction, it is not its constructional nature that makes it a stage but the fact that it *represents* dramatic place. The same can be said about the actors: the actor is usually a person who speaks and moves about the stage. However, the fundamental nature of an actor does not consist in the fact that he is a person speaking and moving about the stage but that he *represents someone, that he signifies a role in a play.* Hence it does not matter whether he is a human being; an actor could be a piece of wood, as well. If the wood moves about and its movements are accompanied by words, then such a piece of wood can represent a character in the play, and the wood becomes an actor.

We have freed the concept of "stage" from its constructional restrictions, and we can free the concept of "actor" from the restriction which claims that an actor is a human being who represents a dramatic character in a play. If acting merely consists in representation of the dramatic character by something else, then not only can a person be an actor but so can a wooden puppet or a machine (for example, Lisicky's, Schlemmer's, and Liesler's mechanical theater using machines) or anything at all (for example, the advertising theater of Belgian cooperatives where a bolt of material, a spider's leg, a coffee grinder, and the like were dramatic characters).

And if simply a voice, heard from the wings of a stage or over the radio, properly signifies a dramatic character, then such a voice is an actor. Precisely such an acoustical actor appears in Goethe's *Faust:* in the usual performances of this play we perceive the role of God in the prologue

---

[1]"Pohyb divadelního znaku," *Slovo a slovesnost*, 6 (1940), pp. 177–188. Translated by I. R. Titunik.

merely as a voice. Finally, in radio plays, voice and sound represent not only dramatic characters but also all other facts that make up the reality of the theater: the stage, scenery, props, and lighting.

There are acoustic signs for all aspects of the theater on the radio. These acoustic signs are referred to as acoustic scenery and are exemplified by the sound of the tapping of typewriters used to denote an office, the rattling of pneumatic drills and the rumbling of wagons to represent a coal mine, and the like. A glass as a prop may be represented by the pouring of wine or by a clinking sound, and so on.

Zich limits his discussion of dramatic character to the conventional forms of theatrical performance. He speaks solely of "plays and operas performed in a theater" and takes into account only actors and singers who perform on the stage of theaters. But now that he has lifted the restrictions that bound the stage specifically to architecture, the way has been opened for all other aspects of dramatic performance to reach a similar freedom. Liberation awaits dramatic character, up to now closely associated with human gestures and motions, as it also does the playwright's text, hitherto *verbal* text, and so on for the other devices of dramatic art. And much to our amazement, we are discovering that stage "space" need not be spatial but that sound can be a stage and music can be a dramatic event and scenery can be a text.

First of all, let us deal with the stage and those signs that denote it. We may say that the stage can be represented by any real space or, in other words, a stage can equally well be a structure or a town square surrounded by spectators or a meadow or a hall in an inn. But even when a stage is such a space, it need not be denoted solely by its spatial nature. We have already used the example of a radio stage (a business office, a coal mine, and so forth) that is denoted acoustically. However, even the conventional theater can provide us with examples of a nonspatial denotation of a stage, for example, sound representing a stage. In the last act of Čexov's *The Cherry Orchard* it is precisely the orchard that plays the main role. The cherry orchard is on the stage, but in such a way that we cannot see it. It is not represented spatially, but acoustically, as the blows of axes cutting down the orchard are heard in the last act. In such a manner, a playwright and a director can denote the stage by those features of reality as best correspond to their intention and as best and most effectively promote understanding between themselves and the audience.

The facts that we have mentioned so far resulted from the observation and evaluation of concrete artistic work and are not merely scientific deductions. Zich's notion has the stage always still in a theater, in the architecturally denoted place "where plays and operas are performed." It was precisely concrete artistic work that dared to move into the areas where the theory of theater had not yet entered even though it had already pointed in that direction. Modern theater has had the effect precisely of freeing the stage from its previously permanent architectural constants.

Cubo-futuristic theatrical experiments turned our attention to stages and theaters other than those built for the tsarist ballet, the box displays of high society, or for the cultural activity of the small-town amateurs. Through these experiments we discovered the theater of the street, we became fascinated by the theatricality of a sports field and admired the theatrical effects created by the movements of harbor cranes, and so on. Simultaneously, we discovered the stage of the primitive theater, the performances of a barker, children's games, circus pantomimes, the tavern theater of strolling players, the theater of masked, celebrating villagers. The stage could arise anywhere—any place could lend itself to theatrical fantasy.

With the freeing of the stage, other aspects of theatrical performance were released from their confinements. Scenery of wooden frames and painted canvas awoke from its spell. Stylized theater from as early as the time of Théâtre d'Art in France, or G. Fuchs and A. Appia in Germany, the Society of New Drama in Russia, and of Kvapil in Bohemia adhered to scenic signs that might be called scenic metonymies. A Gothic arch was used to represent an entire church (Kvapil's staging of *L'Annonce faite à Marie* by P. Claudel), a green square on the floor meant a battlefield (Kvapil's Shakespearian cycle), and the English coat of arms on a silken arras was enough to represent royal halls (in the same cycle). A part represented the whole. But a part could indicate several different wholes: a Venetian column and a flight of stairs sufficed for almost all the scenes in the *Merchant of Venice*, excepting scenes in Portia's or Shylock's rooms or in the garden. The column and the flight of steps were used not only as scenery for the street but also for the harbor, the square, and the court of justice. The attributive scenery of the stylized stage always sought to use devices of one single meaning whenever possible. True, a Venetian column could be placed on a square or in a street or made part of a house. But in each and every case it meant a Venetian building, and nothing but a Venetian building, of which it could be a part. With the advent of cubo-futuristic theater new materials appeared on the stage, and formerly undreamed of things acquired various representative functions. The theater of Russian constructivism used a construction made of planks to represent a factory yard, a garden pavilion, a wheat field or a flour mill. The question can be asked, which part or what property of these planks carried the representative function? It was not color or colored shapes, since such constructions were made of raw, unvarnished wood or were uniformly colored. Constructivism excluded the use of picture or color signs on the stage (at any rate, is the constructivism of Popova and Meyerhold). However, very often even the arrangement of the construction failed to create an unambiguous theatrical sign. Meyerhold's construction for *The Death of Tarelkin* was simply a crate combined with a cylindrical object of the same material whose circular end faced the audience and could have suggested any number of things, but none of them without ambiguity. Perhaps the most definite idea it conjured up, in this case, was that of a meat grinder. But it could equally well have indicated a circular window or a round cage or a huge mirror, circularity being its most striking feature. Since "circularity" is so richly suggestive, one could have interpreted that cylindrical object as a sign for a great many things. Therefore the question arises as to what property of a stage construction can have semiotic function when such a function is not carried by either color or shape.

Some time ago, while writing about Tajrov's presentation of *Giroflé-Girofla,* I pointed out that we cannot tell what a contraption on stage is supposed to signify until it is used by an actor. He has first to sit on it or rock on it or climb out of it. It is only when Giroflé and Marasquin sit down that we realize that a certain prop is a love seat hidden away in a shadowy corner of a park. But during the aria this same seat sways rhythmically from the impact of oars propelling a little boat over a calm lake. Or when a band of fierce pirates jumps on this same prop, we know by the way they straddle it and shift the weight of their bodies form one leg to the other that this is a part of a deck— the ladder leading to the bridge. The sign (representative) function of the scenery and props is determined solely by the movements of the actor and by the manner in which he uses them, but even then their representative function is not entirely unambiguous.

Let us return to the example of the set used in Meyerhold's staging of *The Death of Tarelkin.* It is only when we see the actor pacing back and forth in the cylindrical structure like a prisoner and clutching its slats like bars that we realize the function of this stage prop: it is a cell. Simultaneously, however, there remain in our minds all the associations of form that originated during our first glance at the said prop. The idea of a "meat grinder" in combination with the idea of a "prison cell" acquires a mutual polarization of new meanings.

If we examine other stage sets used by Meyerhold in his stagings of that period, we frequently see a system of suspended planes, staircases, and props whose meaning as sign is completely indeterminate. The critics of these performances and sets often spoke of "abstract scenery." Neither Meyerhold nor any other stage artist was concerned with abstract scenery. His stage sets had very concrete tasks and functions. Indeterminate in shape and color, they became signs only when used for the actor's actions. It can be said that *a representative function was not expressed by means of form or color, but by the actor's actions* on the stage construction, on the bare floor, on the suspended planes, on the staircases, on the slanting surfaces, and so on.

However, this does not bring us to the end of our inquiry into the changes undergone by scenic signs on the stage. That structure of signs, which is every theatrical performance, has to retain its internal balance in every situation, whether favorable or unfavorable.

If the constancy of the key points of the structure is assured, transformations in its complex ground plan can be effected without substantial changes. If we remove a single pillar, however, basic changes on the plane of the structure as a whole are necessary. Examples of structural stability are of course theaters with a centuries old tradition such as the traditional Japanese Nō theater, the more recent tradition of the Japanese Kabuki theater, the old Chinese theater, our puppet theater, folk theaters, the theaters of primitives, and so on. The constancy of a structure causes theatrical signs to develop complex meanings. The stability of signs promotes a wealth of meanings and associations. In the Chinese theater every step taken by the actor is imbued with meaning, every lifting of the arm is a different form of address. A step toward the left stage exit indicates a "return" and acquires a different meaning in each particular situation. We may imagine that in one instance this step indicates a battlefield to which a wounded hero is returning, while in another instance it signifies the longing that recalls a lover to mind.

Were we to take the example of puppet theater, the puppets' movements are similarly lexicalized into signs. For instance, the entry of a puppet from above the stage indicates "a sudden apparition," the disappearance of a puppet through the floor symbolizes "death or departure for hell . . . ," and so on. Assessing the wealth of expression in theatrical performance we find that the immutability of the structure's key points does not necessarily impoverish its expressivity because within this traditional structure subtler and finer changes can take place. The spectator is sensitive to even the slightest vibrations of a tightly drawn structural base. At this point an admonition should be addressed to those people who would like to use the ancient traditional theaters as models to counter the restless spirit of ever-searching artists: the impressions of the spectator are brought about precisely and solely by *changes* in the structure. The firmer the structural base, the more finely will the textural strands weave patterns and pictures that captivate us with their beauty.

Here I should like to quote from P. Bogatyrev's "Folk Theater":

> A characteristic feature of the audience of folk theater is the fact that they do not hanker after plays of new content, but year after year watch the same Christmas and Easter plays, as for example the play about St. Dorothea, and so on. . . . The spectator watches these plays with extraordinary interest although he knows them more or less by heart. And it is herein that lies the basic differences between the spectator at a folk theater and the average visitor to our theater. . . . In view of the fact that the spectator of folk theater is well acquainted with the contents of the play being performed, it is not possible to surprise him with the novelty of plot development, that novelty which plays such an essential role in our theatrical performances. For this reason *the focal point of a folk theater performance lies in the treatment of detail.*

The desire for freedom of expression and technique is a tendency that has constantly had determinative effect on art. The theater brought about by the cubo-futuristic revolt "for fresh air" introduced new theatrical devices and dispensed with many others. Russian constructivism rid the stage of scenery, wings, overhang, and backdrops. As a result the stage lost the possibility of localizing an action through the use of painted signs indicating an interior or exterior. That was not all, however. Not only did directors reject scenery, stage front and rear, overhang and wings, but they also departed from the bare stage that remained after their revolt. They even rejected the five walls that enclosed the space displayed in front of the auditorium so that every spectator could see it. However, the directors who succeeded them (Oxlopkov, Gropius's theater design) did away with a stage completely or, more precisely, placed the stage among the spectators so that any free place in front of, above, next to, or behind the audience could be a stage. Thus they consigned to oblivion all those rare and precious stage mechanisms that, in obedience to a single command by the director, lowered a section of stage or piece of scenery or a prop or even an actor from the heights of the rope gallery, rotated the rear part of a stage set to the front, shifted prepared scenery from the wings, raised up whole stage areas with scenery intact through trapdoors, and so on. The wizard of the theater was deprived of all the mechanisms with which he performed his magic. All that was left to him were his bare hands. To represent or signify the spatial location of a play became problematical with the abandonment of many of the conventions established between stage and auditorium by long-standing tradition.

Furthermore, a stage situated among the spectators completely lacked the possibility of erecting scenery signs. Such a stage could not even use constructions whose representative functions were far more indeterminate than that of scenery and yet afforded the possibility of situating and organizing the stage space by means of flights of steps, variously located surfaces, inclined planes, contraptions, mechanisms, and so on. Out of its former stage mechanisms, the only thing left in Cetnerovich's and Oxlopkov's theater was the floor. Of course, there was still the actor, lighting, and sound.

When the foundations of theatrical structure are shaken in this way measures must immediately be taken to adapt to new modes of operation. If one of the muscles in the set muscles that move the forearm in a living organism is paralyzed, then that organism is safeguarded by the fact that one of the coordinated muscles will take over the function of the one paralyzed. One theatrical function is to locate a play spatially: to signify a lawn or barroom, to represent a cemetery or a banquet hall. This is an essential function of the stage which must be implemented just as much by a stage using constructions as by a stage using scenery, and, just as much by a stage located in the midst of the spectators as by one that is traditionally located. Signs whose function is to promote the spectators' understanding always involve the designation of a space. It is precisely this designative function that constitutes the stability of these signs. In all other respects these signs retain the greatest possible dynamics. The fact that the signs are supposed to designate the space in which an action takes place does not mean that they must be spatial signs. We have already shown that space can be designated by an acoustic sign or by means of a light sign. On the centralized stage possibilities are extremely limited for the placing of objects, large pieces of furniture, or scenery signs. While the constructivist stage concentrated on the actor's actions, the centralized stage is often solely dependent on the actor per se. Oxlopkov's theater has acquainted us with a number of superb instances of the *actor* becoming a sign for spatial location. Here one found not only actor-scenery and actor-set, but even actor-furniture, actor-props.

Oxlopkov created an *actor-sea* by having a young man dressed in a neutral manner (in blue, that is, "invisible," coveralls with a blue mask on his face) shake a blue-green sheet attached to the floor in such a way that the rippling of the blue-green sheet expressively replaced the waves of a sea canal. He created *actor-furniture* by having two "invisibly" attired actors kneel opposite each other and stretch between them a tablecloth into the quadrilateral shape of a table. An *actor-prop* originated by placing next to the actor playing the role of the captain, another actor dressed in blue coveralls who held up the handle of the ship's horn the moment when the captain, pulling the handle, blasts a signal to the sailors.

To the three typical examples, quoted above, of transfer of stage functions to the functions of the actor, I could add many equally or even more interesting examples such as actors indicating the phenomenon of a snowstorm. Or another example: a theater, of course, possesses various acoustical devices for indicating a storm; but in a presentation by Oxlopkov, a metaphor of a storm was shown by an invasion of carnival merrymakers. Boys and girls (actors in blue coveralls) threw confetti at one another while jumping about and generally making noise. This metaphor of a storm— this carnival whirlwind—was not an *act* in Oxlopkov's production of *The Aristocrats,* not part of the actors' performance, but spatial scenery, a means of depicting the environment of the action—the sign of a storm.

Every student of the theater immediately saw analogies between Oxlopkov's staging procedures and the methods employed by ancient Chinese and Japanese theaters. The ancient Chinese theater has a primitive stage, and its spatial restrictions affect all other stage factors. Here, too, we find "invisible" men (dressed in black) who assist in changing scenes, for instance, by covering the bodies of the dead warriors with a black cloth. The battlefield disappears and the plot can continue elsewhere. Similarly, the Japanese stage uses all the techniques of dramatic performance for spatial location of the given plot. Here, too, space need not be indicated by a space, sound by a sound, light by lights, human activity by an actor's acting, and so on. In this case it also happens that "we see tones" and "hear the open countryside" or learn from an actor's costume what in the European theater we would hear from the actor's lips. I recall the following illustration of the change of devices in Japanese theater:

> Yransuke leaves the besieged castle. He moves from the background into the foreground.
>
> Suddenly the rear backdrop, depicting a life-size door, rolls up and we see another backdrop on which there is a small door indicating that the actor has drawn away some distance.
>
> Yransuke continues on his way. A dark green curtain is lowered over the rear backdrop which indicates that Yransuke can no longer see the castle.
>
> A few more steps. Yransuke sets out on the "path of blossoms." In order to indicate this still greater distance he begins to play his samisen (a kind of Japanese mandolin) behind the scene.
>
> First withdrawal: a *step* in space.
>
> Second withdrawal: *a change of painted scenery.*
>
> Third withdrawal: a conventional symbol (a *curtain*)—which nullifies the visual stage device.
>
> Fourth withdrawal: *sound.*

Here the changing of stage devices, which successively take up the same function, is interpreted as the gradation of one dramatic action: the walking of Yransuke, his drawing away from the castle.

With equal justification we could, in this case, interpret the actor's step away from the painted backdrop as a function of spatial location. The stage artist "paints" either with the step of the actor or the sound of his mandolin. He uses different devices to specify the location each time. However, we can add to these two interpretations still others. We could ask whether the change of the rear backdrop with the castle door is not an artistic replacement of the playwright's text, that is to say, the words of the actor saying: "I left the castle." Or whether the melancholy sound of the samisen is not a substitute for the verbal expression: "I have set out on a long pilgrimage." Yet, if we were to seek other interpretations we still would not arrive at the essence of the matter. We would not be able to decide which of them are fundamental and we would not be able to deny the justification of the others.

It would be wrong, however, to think that this changeable method of dramatic expression is a speciality of the Chinese or Japanese theater or of a Russian innovator from the year 1935. Similar methods of dramatic expression can be found in many Czech stage performances. I should like to mention my own production of *The Teacher and the Pupil* (by V. Vančura) in cooperation with the painter Jindřich Štýrský at the Municipal Theater in Brno in 1930.

The fourth act of the play is situated at the edge of town. In order to indicate this fact we made use of a *dramatic mask.* But we took this dramatic mask from the face of the actor, relocated it, and applied it as a spatial *sign on the stage.* Projected across a wide area of the circular horizon was a face whose lower part was covered with a scarf in the manner of highwaymen. This face, with evil eyes below a forehead covered by a hat, arched above the stage and shaded that area in which the spectator usually sees a sky with floating clouds.

*Through relocation,* the dramatic mask acquired new meaning.

In the same play there also was a dramatic mask, projected on the stage in a magnified manner, that carried out another function. In this case, *the scenery became an actor.*

The pupil, Jan, whose home confines him like a musty prison, adamantly maintains an intention to run away. He resists the pleas of his aunt and the threats of his teacher. Through the walls of his home he stares "into the brilliant and glowing abyss of the world which opens up before his eyes." He forges his resolve in a long monologue.

By making the stage almost completely dark and thus concealing the presence of the actor on the stage, we allowed the actor's words to be heard in such a way as to create the impression that they were being spoken by the projected enlargement of the actor's face which gazed fixedly on an imagined goal.

In my production of *The Executioner of Peru* (Ribemont-Dessaignes) in 1929, a duplication of devices was used: an actor's face was projected on the stage, and the actor's real face was visible.

In my production of Apollinaire's *Tiresias's Breasts* (in 1927), the poet's words were changed into a painter's images. We transformed the actors into letters that then moved like figures about the stage. The different combinations of the letters created different verses.

In the production of Goll's *Methusalem* (1927) *stage props* (bread, a bottle, and so on) appeared in the play as characters who rebel against Methusalem.

Many other examples could be brought in to show the special character of a theatrical sign whereby it changes its material and passes from one aspect into another, animates an inanimate thing, shifts from an acoustical aspect to a visual one, and so on.

We have already stated that in the theater it is not possible as a rule and in every case to decide that what is normally called the actor's acting will not be entrusted to the scenery, just as it is not possible to foresee that music will not take over what is a phenomenon of the visual arts.

Indeed, precisely this changeability, this versatility of theatrical sign, is its specific property. And through it we explain the changeability of dramatic structure.

It is the changeability of the theatrical sign that the main difficulty of defining theatrical art lies. Definitions of this concept either narrow down theatricality to the manner of expression of our conventional drama and opera theaters or expand it to such an extent that it becomes meaningless.

It is on the basis of changes of the theatrical sign that we explain yet another theoretical confusion that hinders research of the problem of who or what is the central, creative element of dramatic expression. If we say that it is the playwright, then we are certainly correct as regards numerous cases and examples. However, we still would not grasp the essence of many historical examples of theater and could not prove that in all cases it is the word of the playwright that represents the axis of theatrical art. The entirely free theme or wholly unthematic character of improvised Italian comedies and similar forms shows that even the playwright and his text are susceptible of the changes we have discussed earlier. Similarly, we cannot regard as completely true the statement that the main bearer of theatrical art is the actor. As a proof of this I have in mind that static positioning of actors on the stage (characteristic of many dramatic styles of both past and present) which converts theater into a dialogue recital carried out by stationary figures (Théâtre d'Art, stylized German theater, Meyerhold) or anesthetizes the actor into a puppet with prearranged stilted movements, thus changing his traditional acting function into a function of a stage prop or structure. And should a modern director say that he himself is the center of dramatic creation, we can agree with his statement only in the instances whereby he demonstrates this to us. Should he speak of the theatrical art of past times when there was no director, then we cannot but disagree with him.

We do not mean by this to prove that the text, actor, and director are auxiliary or dispensable factors that merely affect the balance of theatrical structure. We wish to show only that every historical period actualizes a different component of dramatic expression and that the creative forces of one factor can replace or suppress others without decreasing the strength of the dramatic effect. We could also prove that certain periods directly demand such shifts in the balance of the dramatic structure. After all, there exist or existed theaters without authors (or without authors of note), there exist or existed theaters without actors or without great actors, and there exist and existed theaters without directors. However, if we go into the matter more deeply, we find that the actor's function is always present even though it may change into, or appear in the guise of, another function. Similarly, we must allow that what we call the organizational force of the director was present in every historical period of the theater, even when there was no director as such.

The extraordinary and contradictory statements that an actor participates in the theatrical performance even in the case of theater without actors, that the word is always an essential component of theatrical art even in the case of "wordless" theater, and that the so-called "scenic function" finds application even in theater without scenery—all such statements are justified by the specific character of the theatrical sign, dramatic structure, and dramatic material. I believe that in the preceding explanation we afforded sufficient proof of the changeability of the theatrical sign, which passes from material to material with a freedom unknown to any other art. Indeed, there is no music without tones, no poem without words, no painting without colors, and no sculpture without physical substance. Expressed more clearly, painting is not painting if words are used instead of colors, music is not music if harmony is composed of materials other than tones, and so on. Naturally, there are cases in which an artist borrows devices from another sphere of art if his own material does not achieve the desired intensity of expression. For example, Beethoven brought the musical expression of the finale of his Ninth Symphony to such an extreme that the listener finds tones insufficient and can be satisfied only by *words*. In the field of poetry, we could mention as an example of a change of device Apollinaire's *Calligrams* or the so-called "pictorial poems" invented in Bohemia. We could also seek similar examples in painting (cubism that paints with newspaper cuttings and inscriptions), and other arts. However, such examples are always the exceptions that confirm the rule about the unchangeability of material in the various other arts. As we have seen, however, in theater this changeability is the rule and the specific characteristic of theatrical art.

A number of theories of theater built around changeability have been advanced in the effort to organize or unify the multiplicity of dramatic material, devices, and procedures. The best known of these is undoubtedly Wagner's concept of theater as "collective art" *(das Gesamtkunstwerk)*.

Multiplicity of devices is organized by "collective art" *(Gesamtkunstwerk)* in such a way that individual components unite in a result, provide a "collective effect." Thus the dramatic character is present not only on the stage, but also in the orchestra; we experience its inner state, development, and fate not only from words and actions we see on the stage but also from the tones we hear.

Here it is a matter of the parallelism of the musical stream, the dramatic action, the words, scenery, props, lighting, and all other factors.

In his *Parsifal,* Richard Wagner was not content solely with the effect of scenery: a spring landscape on the stage was not only expressed through scenery but also by the orchestra. For the author of *Der Ring des Nibelungen,* the stage props had multiple implementations. Siegfried's sword is given a special place on stage; it is, moreover, illuminated with light and also made to glitter in the clear musical tones of the sword "leitmotivs." Wagner's dramatic characters always enter upon the stage not only as actors but also as "leitmotivs." A character's gesture is repeated in the orchestra (the pain resulting from Beckmesser's beating causes the music to limp), and the magnificence of the costumes and scenery that characterizes the guests' arrival at Wartburg is also reinforced by means of music. In every case, one could illustrate the principle of parallelism which unifies a number of dramatic devices in the sense that it brings them into parallel relationship.

This principle of "collective art" *(Gesamtkunstwerk)* assumes that the intensity of dramatic effect, that is, the strength of the spectator's impressions, is directly proportional to the *number of perceptions* that synchronically flood the senses and mind of the spectator at any given moment. The task of the dramatic artist (in the Wagnerian sense) is to equalize the effects of various dramatic devices in order to produce impressions of the same impact.

Thus, this theory does not recognize changes of theatrical sign which can use different materials for its implementation. On the contrary, Wagner's *Gesamtkunstwerk* theory indirectly claims that there is no specific, unitary dramatic material but that there are diverse materials which must be kept apart and treated side by side. Accordingly, there is no dramatic art as such, but there are music, text, actor, scenery, stage props, and lighting, which collectively make up dramatic art. Thus dramatic art cannot exist by itself but only as a collective manifestation of music, poetry, painting, architecture, histrionics, and so on. Dramatic art results as the sum of other arts.

With regard to the spectator and to the psychology of perception, I am of the opinion that this theory is incorrect. Uppermost is the problem of whether the spectator perceives acoustic and visual signs simultaneously and with the same intensity or whether he concentrates on one aspect only in the course of perception. When trying to solve this question, we must also bear in mind the fact that it is a matter of the perception of *artistic signs* and that this is a special case of perception. If the spectator's mind has to concentrate in order to understand the semiotic value of certain facts, it can certainly be presumed that it also concentrates on perceptions of a particular kind, visual or acoustical. However, should the concentrated attention of the spectator perceive both visually and acoustically, we cannot speak even in this instance of a *sum* of impressions but only of a special relation of one kind of perception to the other, of the *polarization of these perceptions.*

After all, we encounter among spectators people who visit a theater to listen to music or to a poet or to see the performance of a certain actor, and so on. However, even persons without special interests find themselves, when attending a theater, listening only to the music at one moment and captivated by the actor or enchanted by the poetic text at another moment. I would say that nearly all theatergoers fall into this category. At the same time, however, the interest of the spectator does not pass from one device to another merely by chance; it does so deliberately. If we observe the audience at a theater we see that its members turn their eyes to the same spot on the stage, that they all have the same interest in a single actor at one moment or interest in the observation of the scenery at another moment. The psychology of the spectators' perception thus prevents us from accepting the assumptions of the Wagnerian theory of "collective art."

Moreover, this theory does not recognize the fact of the development of theatrical art, about which I have already spoken and from which I have drawn examples. Theatrical art has existed without music, there have been theaters without scenery, directors have produced theater without actors, the commedia dell'arte was a theater without authors, as well as without so-called dramatic plot. Nevertheless, they were dramatic manifestations that by no means left a void in the soul of the spectator. If it were true that dramatic art is the sum of various arts *(Gesamtkunstwerk),* there would, for example, be no theater of artistic expression whose sole means would be the actor himself, that is, an actor without stage, words, music, scenery, and so on. And indeed recognition as a theatrical performance must be accorded even to a pantomime that is conducted in an empty circus ring solely by the actions of a player. There are numerous examples (such as the famous clowns

Grock, Fratellini, and others) that the actor's actions by themselves can captivate the audience.

I would say that the Wagnerian theory conceals rather than reveals the essence of theatrical art: it surrounds theater with so many other arts that the special quality of theatricality dissolves and disappears. We lose sight of it.

However, it is not our intention to revive the dispute over *Gesamtkunstwerk.* I chose this matter merely as an example of the problems that arise as soon as we fail to understand or to take into account the special property of the material and devices of dramatic expression about which I have been speaking. Apart from the dispute over *Gesamtkunstwerk,* one could also mention other theories of theatrical art which are similarly confused because their authors, unable or unwilling to understand the special character of dramatic material, too uncautiously transferred the relations of poetry, painting, music, and other arts to dramatic art.

I commenced my study with a quotation from Zich and I should like to conclude by returning to Zich's views. We saw that even Zich, at the beginning of his *Aesthetics of Dramatic Art,* could not give a satisfactory definition of dramatic art. Although no adherent of "*Gesamtkunstwerk,*" still he did not have the audacity to maintain unreservedly that dramatic art is a "*single* art and not a *combination* of several arts." According to Zich the specific character of theatrical unit is the *combination* of "two simultaneous, inseparable, but *heterogeneous,* components, that is, visual components (optical) and audible components (acoustical)."

However, even this "combination" does not prevent us from seeking and finding a unity in dramatic art, from declaring that it is a single, integral art. The binary character of the materials, that is, the visual and acoustical character of dramatic devices, does not negate the unity of the essence of theater art.

Since the acoustical and the visual can change places on the stage, it may happen that one of the components submerges below the surface of the spectator's conscious attention. For example, the meaning of heard dialogue may push the spectator's perception of dramatic gestures, dramatic appearance, scenery, lighting, and so on, into the background, or conversely, it may happen that witnessed dramatic action nullifies acoustical perceptions (words, music, murmuring, and so forth).

Let us note, furthermore, that the silent film was also once called visual *theater* and that the radio play could be called acoustical *theater.* Thus the specific character of theater art does not lie in the division of its devices into acoustic and visual one. It is necessary to seek the essence of theater art elsewhere.

It is my belief that with our analysis of the changeability of the theatrical sign we have undertaken a task that can test the trustworthiness of many definitions of theatrical art and decide whether those definitions make provision for the old and the new types of theater that have originated in different social structures, in different historical periods, under the influence of different poetic or dramatic personalities, as the result of many technical inventions, and so on. I am also of the opinion that we should restore respect for the old theory of theatrical art which sees its essence in *acting,* in *action.*

In this light, the theatricality of dramatic character and that of place and that of plot will not appear to us as things permanently separated from one another. Moreover, the relationship among these three components of drama will not appear to us as a relationship among three *separate and individual theatrical arts* that are parallel without touching one another and amount to a "collective theatricality" whose success intensifies the greater the number of autonomous arts participating in its structure. One should recognize the invalidity of the notion of the "relative nonparticipation of the scenic image" in the dramatic whole, a notion that could "even maintain that the scenic image (dramatic place) is *not* a fundamental component of a dramatic work, for the reason that it can be reduced from extreme elaborateness down to the minimum of *pure space* merely demarcated architecturally."[2]

Action, taken as the essence of dramatic art, unifies word, actor, costume, scenery, and music in the sense that we could then recognize them as different conductors of a single current that either passes from one to another or flows through several at one time. Now that we have used this comparison, let us add that this current, that is, dramatic action, is not carried by the conductor that exerts the least resistance (dramatic action is not always concentrated only in the performing actor) but rather theatricality frequently is generated in the overcoming of obstacles caused by certain dramatic devices (special theatrical effects when, for instance, action is concentrated solely in the words or in the actor's motions or in offstage sounds, and so on), in the same way that a filament fiber glows just because it has resistance to an electric current.

Of course, we can speak of the relative nonparticipation of place (that is, scenery and sets) in drama and in dramatic art, but this nonparticipation should not be regarded as a permanent property of every instance of dramatic place but precisely as the property of a *certain type of theater*, a particular drama, a particular method of direction, and so forth. The action value, that is, the theatricality, of place in the English theater of the Elizabethan dramatists consisted merely in changes indicated by inscriptions hung on the stage: the terrace below the castle; the throne room; a chamber; a cemetery; a battlefield. The dramatic action of place consisted solely in such announcements. It is true, that our theaters have not deviated from this method of indicating dramatic place, since it is all the same (precisely with regard to action as an element of drama) whether a change of scene is indicated by an inscription or by a costly stage set of a terrace, throne room, cemetery, battlefield, and so on.

Modern theater begins the very moment scenery is evaluated according to the function it fulfills in the actual dramatic action. The fact that the Thèâtre d'Art in the nineties restricted its scenery to "a backdrop and a number of movable curtains" has to be explained, from our viewpoint, as a recognition of the real function of stage scenery in plays whose theatricality and action are created verbally (Maeterlinck). If the German Shakespearian stage was limited to a Gothic arch or column against a blue backdrop, it was the result of the awareness that a stage set participates in a Shakespearian play solely as a simple scenic sign informing the spectator of the change of scene.

The new limitations in stage art resulting from Russian constructivism spring from the idea of dramatic performance which is manifested by *the player's movements* and everything that serves these movements: acrobatic props or contraptions, a movable wall or floor, and so on.

From the viewpoint of dramatic action the theatricality of music can be evaluated solely according to the part it has in *the acting out of the play*. Thus, scenic musical forms are either *musical scenery or music as action*. All the difficulties that arise for the modern composer of opera and for theories of opera stem from the inability or impossibility of recognizing their division, of defining music action.

The examples I have employed show clearly that there are no permanent laws or invariable rules for the unification of dramatic devices via the flow of dramatic action. In its autonomous development, which is an integral feature in the development of every art, the theater actualizes different aspects of theatricality at different times. For example, Maeterlinck's symbolism actualizes the verbal text as the bearer of dramatic action (Materlinck's play *Les Aveugles is acted out* through the dialogue of immobile actors conversing on stage). Russian constructivism, on the other hand, *acts* by means of the dance or the "biomechanical" movements of the actor.

The changeability of the hierarchical scale of components of dramatic art corresponds to the changeability of the theatrical sign. I have attempted to throw light on both. I wanted to demonstrate the changeability that make stage art so varied and all-attractive but at the same time so elusive of definition. Its protean metamorphoses have sometimes even caused the very existence of a theatrical art to be doubted. Existence as an autonomous art was attributed to the dramatic poem, to histrionics, to painting and to music—but not to "theatrical art." It was only a combination of separate arts. Theater had not located either its core or its unity. I haved shown that it has both, that it is one and many like the Triune God of Saint Augustine.

*Notes*

[1]Otakar Zich, *Estetika dramatického umĕni* [Aesthetics of Dramatic Art] (Prague: 1931), p. 45.

[2]Otakar Zich, ibid., p. 45.

Fredric Jameson
"Postmodernism and
Consumer Society"[1]
(1983)

*FREDRIC Jameson is probably the most prominent Marxist cultural critic writing in the United States today; he is the author of several important books, including* Marxism and Form *(1971),* The Prison-House of Language *(1972), and* The Political Unconscious *(1988). This selection is from one of Jameson's many essays on postmodern art, culture, and society. Jameson uses the term* pastiche *to characterize the problematic ways contemporary arts invoke the imagery and style of earlier historical eras, paradoxically erasing "history" in the process.*

The concept of postmodernism is not widely accepted or even understood today. Some of the resistance to it may come from the unfamiliarity of the works it covers, which can be found in all the arts: the poetry of John Ashbery, for instance, but also the much simpler talk poetry that came out of the reaction against complex, ironic, academic modernist poetry in the 1960s; the reaction against modern architecture and in particular against the monumental buildings of the International Style, the pop buildings and decorated sheds celebrated by Robert Venturi in his manifesto, *Learning from Las Vegas;* Andy Warhol and Pop art, but also the more recent Photorealism; in music, the moment of John Cage but also the later synthesis of classical and "popular" styles found in composers like Philip Glass and Terry Riley, and also punk and new-wave rock with such groups as the Clash, Talking Heads and the Gang of Four; in film, everything that comes out of Godard—contemporary vanguard film and video—but also a whole new style of commercial or fiction films, which has its equivalent in contemporary novels as well, where the works of William Burroughs, Thomas Pynchon and Ishmael Reed on the one hand, and the French new novel on the other, are also to be numbered among the varieties of what can be called postmodernism.

This list would seem to make two things clear at once: first, most of the postmodernisms mentioned above emerge as specific reactions against the established forms of high modernism, against this or that dominant high modernism which conquered the university, the museum, the art gallery network, and the foundations. Those formerly subversive and embattled styles—Abstract Expressionism; the great modernist poetry of Pound, Eliot or Wallace Stevens; the International Style (Le Corbusier, Frank Lloyd Wright, Mies); Stravinsky; Joyce, Proust and Mann—felt to be scandalous or shocking by our grandparents are, for the generation which arrives at the gate in the 1960s, felt to be the establishment and the enemy—dead, stifling, canonical, the reified monuments one has to destroy to do anything new. This means that there will be as many different forms of postmodernism as there were high modernisms in place, since the former are at least initially specific and local reactions *against* those models. That obviously does not make the job of describing postmodernism as a coherent thing any easier, since the unity of this new impulse—if it has one—is given not in itself but in the very modernism it seeks to displace.

The second feature of this list of postmodernisms is the effacement in it of some key boundaries or separations, most notably the erosion of the older distinction between high culture and so-called mass or popular culture. This is perhaps the most distressing development of all from an academic standpoint, which has traditionally had a vested interest in preserving a realm of high or elite culture against the surrounding environment of philistinism, of schlock and kitsch, of TV series and *Reader's Digest* culture, and in transmitting difficult and complex skills of reading, listening and seeing to its initiates. But many of the newer postmodernisms have been fascinated precisely by that whole landscape of advertising and motels, of the Las Vegas strip, of the late show and Grade-B Hollywood film, of so-called paraliterature with its airport paperback categories of the gothic and the romance, the popular biography, the murder mystery and the science fiction or fantasy novel. They no longer "quote" such "texts" as a Joyce might have done, or a Mahler; they incorporate them, to the point where the line between high art and commercial forms seems increasingly difficult to draw.

A rather different indication of this effacement of the older categories of genre and discourse can be found in what is sometimes called contemporary theory. A generation ago there was still a technical discourse of professional philosophy—the great systems of Sartre or the phenomenologists, the work of Wittgenstein or analytical or common language philosophy—alongside which one could still distinguish that quite different discourse of the other academic disciplines—of political science, for example, or sociology or literary criticism. Today, increasingly, we have a kind of writing simply called "theory" which is all or none of those things at once. This new kind of discourse, generally associated with France and so-called French theory, is becoming widespread and marks the end of philosophy as such. Is the work of Michel Foucault, for example, to be called philosophy, history, social theory or political science? It's undecidable, as they say nowadays; and I will suggest that such "theoretical discourse" is also to be numbered among the manifestations of postmodernism.

Now I must say a word about the proper use of this concept: it is not just another word for the description of a particular style. It is also, at least in my use, a periodizing concept whose function is to correlate the emergence of new formal features in culture with the emergence of a new type of social life and a new economic order—what is often euphemistically called modernization, postindustrial or consumer society, the society of the media or the spectacle, or multinational capitalism. This new moment of capitalism can be dated from the postwar boom in the United States in the late 1940s and early 1950s or, in France, from the establishment of the Fifth Republic in 1958. The 1960s are in many ways the key transitional period, a period in which the new international order (neocolonialism, the Green Revolution, computerization and electronic information) is at one and the same time set in place and is swept and shaken by its own internal contradictions and by external resistance. I want here to sketch a few of the ways in which the new postmodernism expresses the inner truth of that newly emergent social order of late capitalism, but will have to limit the description to only two of its significant features, which I will call pastiche and schizophrenia; they will give us a chance to sense the specificity of the postmodernist experience of space and time respectively.

One of the most significant features or practices in postmodernism today is pastiche. I must first explain this term, which people generally tend to confuse with or assimilate to that related verbal phenomenon called parody. Both pastiche and parody involve the imitation or, better still, the mimicry of other styles and particularly of the mannerisms and stylistic twitches of other styles. It is obvious that modern literature in general offers a very rich field for parody, since the great modern writers have all been defined by the invention or production of rather unique styles: think of the Faulknerian long sentence or of D. H. Lawrence's characteristic nature imagery; think of Wallace Stevens's peculiar way of using abstractions; think also of the mannerisms of the philosophers, of Heidegger for example, or Sartre; think of the musical styles of Mahler or Prokofiev. All of these styles, however different from each other, are comparable in this: each is quite unmistakable; once one is learned, it is not likely to be confused with something else.

Now parody capitalizes on the uniqueness of these styles and seizes on their idiosyncrasies and eccentricities to produce an imitation which mocks the original. I won't say that the satiric impulse is conscious in all forms of parody. In any case, a good or great parodist has to have some secret sympathy for the original, just as a great mimic has to have the capacity to put himself/herself in the place of the person imitated. Still, the general effect of parody is—whether in sympathy or with malice—to cast ridicule on the private nature of these stylistic mannerisms and their excessiveness and eccentricity with respect to the way people normally speak or write. So there remains somewhere behind all parody the feeling that there is a linguistic norm in contrast to which the styles of the great modernists can be mocked.

But what would happen if one no longer believed in the existence of normal language, of ordinary speech, of the linguistic norm (the kind of clarity and communicative power celebrated by Orwell in his famous essay, say)? One could think of it in this way; perhaps the immense fragmentation and privatization of modern literature—its explosion into a host of distinct private styles and mannerisms—foreshadows deeper and more general tendencies in social life as a whole. Supposing that modern art and modernism—far from being a kind of specialized aesthetic curiosity—actually anticipated social developments along these lines; supposing that in the decades since the emergence of the great modern styles society has itself begun to fragment in this way, each group coming to speak a curious private language of its own, each profession developing its private code or idiolect, and finally each individual coming to be a kind of linguistic island, separated from everyone else? But then in that case, the very possibility of any linguistic norm in terms of which one could ridicule private languages and idiosyncratic styles would vanish, and we would have nothing but stylistic diversity and heterogeneity.

That is the moment at which pastiche appears and parody has become impossible. Pastiche is, like parody, the imitation of a peculiar or unique style, the wearing of a stylistic mask, speech in a

*Pastiche eclipses parody*

dead language: but it is a neutral practice of such mimicry, without parody's ulterior motive, without the satirical impulse, without laughter, without that still latent feeling that there exists something *normal* compared to which what is being imitated is rather comic. Pastiche is blank parody, parody that has lost its sense of humor: pastiche is to parody what that curious thing, the modern practice of a kind of blank irony, is to what Wayne Booth calls the stable and comic ironies of, say, the eighteenth century.

*The death of the subject*

But now we need to introduce a new piece into this puzzle, which may help to explain why classical modernism is a thing of the past and why postmodernism should have taken its place. This new component is what is generally called the "death of the subject" or, to say it in more conventional language, the end of individualism as such. The great modernisms were, as we have said, predicated on the invention of a personal, private style, as unmistakable as your fingerprint, as incomparable as your own body. But this means that the modernist aesthetic is in some way organically linked to the conception of a unique self and private identity, a unique personality and individuality, which can be expected to generate its own unique vision of the world and to forge its own unique, unmistakable style.

Yet today, from any number of distinct perspectives, the social theorists, the psychoanalysts, even the linguists, not to speak of those of us who work in the area of culture and cultural and formal change, are all exploring the notion that that kind of individualism and personal identity is a thing of the past; that the old individual or individualist subject is "dead"; and that one might even describe the concept of the unique individual and the theoretical basis of individualism as ideological. There are in fact two positions on all this, one of which is more radical than the other. The first one is content to say: yes, once upon a time, in the classic age of competitive capitalism, in the heyday of the nuclear family and the emergence of the bourgeoisie as the hegemonic social class, there was such a thing as individualism, as individual subjects. But today, in the age of corporate capitalism, of the so-called organization man, of bureaucracies in business as well as in the state, of demographic explosion—today, that older bourgeois individual subject no longer exists.

Then there is a second position, the more radical of the two, what one might call the poststructuralist position. It adds: not only is the bourgeois individual subject a thing of the past, it is also a myth; it *never* really existed in the first place; there have never been autonomous subjects of that type. Rather, this construct is merely a philosophical and cultural mystification which sought to persuade people that they "had" individual subjects and possessed this unique personal identity.

For our purposes, it is not particularly important to decide which of these positions is correct (or rather, which is more interesting and productive). What we have to retain from all this is rather an aesthetic dilemma: because if the experience and the ideology of the unique self, an experience and ideology which informed the stylistic practice of classical modernism, is over and done with, then it is no longer clear what the artists and writers of the present period are supposed to be doing. What is clear is merely that the older models—Picasso, Proust, T. S. Eliot—do not work any more (or are positively harmful), since nobody has that kind of unique private world and style to express any longer. And this is perhaps not merely a "psychological" matter: we also have to take into account the immense weight of seventy or eighty years of classical modernism itself. There is another sense in which the writers and artists of the present day will no longer be able to invent new styles and worlds—they've already been invented; only a limited number of combinations are possible; the unique ones have been thought of already. So the weight of the whole modernist aesthetic tradition—now dead—also "weighs like a nightmare on the brains of the living," as Marx said in another context.

Hence, once again, pastiche: in a world in which stylistic innovation is no longer possible, all that is left is to imitate dead styles, to speak through the masks and with the voices of the styles in the imaginary museum. But this means that contemporary or postmodernist art is going to be about art itself in a new kind of way; even more, it means that one of its essential messages will involve the necessary failure of art and the aesthetic, the failure of the new, the imprisonment in the past.

*The nostalgia mode*

As this may seem very abstract, I want to give a few examples, one of which is so omnipresent that we rarely link it with the kinds of developments in high art discussed here. This particular practice of pastiche is not high-cultural but very much within mass culture, and it is generally known as the "nostalgia film" (what the French neatly call *la mode rétro*—retrospective styling). We must conceive of this category in the broadest way: narrowly, no doubt, it consists merely of films about the past and about specific generational moments of that past. Thus, one of the inaugural films in this new "genre" (if that's what it is) was Lucas's *American Graffiti*, which in 1973 set out to recapture all the atmosphere and stylistic peculiarities of the 1950s United States, the United States of the Eisenhower era. Polanski's great film *Chinatown* does something similar for the 1930s, as does Bertolucci's *The Conformist* for the Italian and European context of the same period, the fascist era in Italy; and so forth. We could go on listing these films for some time: why call them pastiche? Are they not rather work in the more traditional genre known as the historical film—work which can more simply be theorized by extrapolating that other well-known form which is the historical novel?

I have my reasons for thinking that we need new categories for such films. But let me first add some anomalies: supposing I suggested that *Star Wars* is also a nostalgia film. What could that mean? I presume we can agree that this is not a historical film about our own intergalactic past. Let me put it somewhat differently: one of the most important cultural experiences of the generations that grew up from the 1930s to the 1950s was the Saturday afternoon serial of the Buck Rogers type—alien villains, true American heroes, heroines in distress, the death ray or the doomsday box, and the cliffhanger at the end whose miraculous resolution was to be witnessed next Saturday afternoon. *Star Wars* reinvents this experience in the form of a pastiche: that is, there is no longer any point to a parody of such serials since they are long extinct. *Star Wars*, far from being a pointless satire of such now dead forms, satisfies a deep (might I even say repressed?) longing to experience them again: it is a complex object in which on some first level children and adolescents can take the adventures straight, while the adult public is able to gratify a deeper and more properly nostalgic desire to return to that older period and to live its strange old aesthetic artifacts through once again. This film is thus *metonymically* a historical or nostalgia film: unlike *American Graffiti*, it does not reinvent a picture of the past in its lived totality; rather, by reinventing the feel and shape of characteristic art objects of an older period (the serials), it seeks to reawaken a sense of the past associated with those objects. *Raiders of the Lost Ark*, meanwhile, occupies an intermediary position here: on some level it is *about* the 1930s and 1940s, but in reality it too conveys that period metonymically through its own characteristic adventure stories (which are no longer ours).

Now let me discuss another interesting anomaly which may take us further towards understanding nostalgia film in particular and pastiche generally. This one involves a recent film called *Body Heat*, which, as has abundantly been pointed out by the critics, is a kind of distant remake of *The Postman Always Rings Twice* or *Double Indemnity*. (The allusive and elusive plagiarism of older plots is, of course, also a feature of pastiche.) Now *Body Heat* is technically not a nostalgia film, since it takes place in a contemporary setting, in a little Florida village near Miami. On the other hand, this technical contemporaneity is most ambiguous indeed: the credits—always our first cue—are lettered and scripted in a 1930s Art-Deco style which cannot but trigger nostalgic reactions (first to *Chinatown*, no doubt, and then beyond it to some more historical referent). Then the very style of the hero himself is ambiguous: William Hurt is a new star but has nothing of the distinctive style of the preceding generation of male superstars like Steve McQueen or even Jack Nicholson, or rather, his persona here is a kind of mix of their characteristics with an older role of the type generally associated with Clark Gable. So here too there is a faintly archaic feel to all this. The spectator begins to wonder why this story, which could have been situated anywhere, is set in a small Florida town, in spite of its contemporary reference. One begins to realize after a while that the small town setting has a crucial strategic function: it allows the film to do without most of the signals and references which we might associate with the contemporary world, with consumer society—the appliances and artifacts, the high rises, the object world of late capitalism. Technically, then, its objects (its cars, for instance) are 1980s products, but everything in the film conspires to blur that immediate contemporary reference and to make it possible to receive this too as nostalgia work—as a narrative set in some indefinable nostalgic past, an eternal 1930s, say, beyond history. It seems to me exceedingly symptomatic to find the very style of nostalgia films invading and colonizing even those movies today which have contemporary settings: as though, for some reason, we were unable today to focus our own present, as though we have become incapable of achieving aesthetic representations of our own current experience. But if that is so, then it is a terrible indictment of consumer capitalism itself—or, at the very least, an alarming and pathological symptom of a society that has become incapable of dealing with time and history.

So now we come back to the question of why nostalgia film or pastiche is to be considered different from the older historical novel or film. (I should also include in this discussion the major literary example of all this, to my mind: the novels of E. L. Doctorow—*Ragtime,* with its turn-of-the-century atmosphere, and *Loon Lake,* for the most part about our 1930s. But these are, in my opinion, historical novels in appearance only. Doctorow is a serious artist and one of the few genuinely left or radical novelists at work today. It is no disservice to him, however, to suggest that his narratives do not represent our historical past so much as they represent our ideas or cultural stereotypes about that past.) Cultural production has been driven back inside the mind, within the monadic subject: it can no longer look directly out of its eyes at the real world for the referent but must, as in Plato's cave, trace its mental images of the world on its confining walls. If there is any realism left here, it is a "realism" which springs from the shock of grasping that confinement and of realizing that, for whatever peculiar reasons, we seem condemned to seek the historical past through our own pop images and stereotypes about that past, which itself remains forever out of reach.

*Postmodernism and the city*

Now, before I try to offer a somewhat more positive conclusion, I want to sketch the analysis of a full-blown postmodern building—a work which is in many ways uncharacteristic of that postmodern architecture whose principal names are Robert Venturi, Charles Moore, Michael Graves, and more recently Frank Gehry, but which to my mind offers some very striking lessons about the originality of postmodernist space. Let me amplify the figure which has run through the preceding remarks, and make it even more explicit: I am proposing the notion that we are here in the presence of something like a mutation in built space itself. My implication is that we ourselves, the human subjects who happen into this new space, have not kept pace with that evolution; there has been a mutation in the object, unaccompanied as yet by any equivalent mutation in the subject; we do not yet possess the perceptual equipment to match this new hyperspace, as I will call it, in part because our perceptual habits were formed in that older kind of space I have called the space of high modernism. The newer architecture therefore—like many of the other cultural products I have evoked in the preceding remarks—stands as something like an imperative to grow new organs to expand our sensorium and our body to some new, as yet unimaginable, perhaps ultimately impossible, dimensions.

### The Bonaventure Hotel

The building whose features I will very rapidly enumerate in the next few moments is the Bonaventure Hotel, built in the new Los Angeles downtown by the architect and developer John Portman, whose other works include the various Hyatt Regencies, the Peachtree Center in Atlanta, and the Renaissance Center in Detroit. I have mentioned the populist aspect of the rhetorical defence of postmodernism against the elite (and utopian) austerities of the great architectural modernisms: it is generally affirmed, in other words, that these newer building are popular works on the one hand; and that they respect the vernacular of the American city fabric on the other, that is to say, that they no longer attempt, as did the masterworks and monuments of high modernism, to insert a different, a distinct, an elevated, a new utopian language into the tawdry and commercial sign-system of the surrounding city, but rather, on the contrary, seek to speak that very language, using its lexicon and syntax as that has been emblematically "learned from Las Vegas."

On the first of these counts, Portman's Bonaventure fully confirms the claim: it is a popular building, visited with enthusiasm by locals and tourists alike (although Portman's other buildings are even more successful in this respect). The populist insertion into the city fabric is, however, another matter, and it is with this that we will begin. There are three entrances to the Bonaventure, one from Figueroa, and the other two by way of elevated gardens on the other side of the hotel, which is built into the remaining slope of the former Beacon Hill. None of these is anything like the old hotel marquee, or the monumental *porte-cochère* with which the sumptuous buildings of yesteryear were wont to stage your passage from city street to the older interior. The entryways of the Bonaventure are as it were lateral and rather backdoor affairs: the gardens in the back admit you to the sixth floor of the towers, and even there you must walk down one flight to find the elevator by which you gain access to the lobby. Meanwhile, what one is still tempted to think of as the front entry, on Figueroa, admits you, baggage and all, onto the second-story balcony, from which you must take an escalator down to the main registration desk. More about these elevators and escalators in a moment. What I first want to suggest about these curiously unmarked ways-in is that they seem to have been imposed by some new category of closure governing the inner space of the hotel itself (and this over and above the material constraints under which Portman had to work). I believe that, with a certain number of other characteristic postmodern buildings, such as the Beaubourg in Paris, or the Eaton Centre in Toronto, the Bonaventure aspires to being a total space, a complete world, a kind of miniature city (and I would want to add that to this new total space corresponds a new collective practice, a new mode in which individuals move and congregate, something like the practice of a new and historically original kind of hyper-crowd). In this sense, then, ideally the mini-city of Portman's Bonaventure ought not to have entrances at all, since the entryway is always the seam that links the building to the rest of the city that surrounds it: for it does not wish to be a part of the city, but rather its equivalent and its replacement or substitute. That is, however, obviously not possible or practical, whence the deliberate downplaying and reduction of the entrance function to its bare minimum. But this disjunction from the surrounding city is very different from that of the great monuments of the International Style: there, the act of disjunction was violent, visible, and had a very real symbolic significance—as in Le Corbusier's great *pilotis* whose gesture radically separates the new utopian space of the modern from the degraded and fallen city fabric which it thereby explicitly repudiates (although the gamble of the modern was that this new utopian space, in the virulence of its Novum, would fan out and transform that eventually by the power of its new spatial language). The Bonaventure, however, is content to "let the fallen city fabric continue to be in its being" (to parody Heidegger); no further effects, no larger protopolitical utopian transformation, is either expected or desired.

This diagnosis is to my mind confirmed by the great reflective glass skin of the Bonaventure, whose function I will now interpret rather differently that I did a moment ago when I saw the phenomenon of reflexion generally as developing a thematics of reproductive technology (the two readings are however not incompatible). Now one would want rather to stress the way in which the glass skin repels the city outside; a repulsion for which we have analogies in those reflector sunglasses which make it impossible for your interlocutor to see your own eyes and thereby achieve a certain aggressivity towards and power over the Other. In a similar way, the glass skin achieves a peculiar and placeless dissociation of the Bonaventure from its neighborhood: it is not even an exterior, inasmuch as when you seek to look at the hotel's outer walls you cannot see the hotel itself, but only the distorted images of everything that surrounds it.

Now I want to say a few words about escalators and elevators: given their very real pleasures in Portman, particularly these last, which the artist has termed "gigantic kinetic sculptures" and which certainly account for much of the spectacle and the excitement of the hotel interior, particularly in the Hyatts, where like great Japanese lanterns or gondolas they ceaselessly rise and fall—given such a deliberate marking and foregrounding in their own right, I believe one has to see such "people movers" (Portman's own term, adapted from Disney) as something a little more than mere functions and engineering components. We know in any case that recent architectural theory has begun to borrow from narrative analysis in other fields, and to attempt to see our physical trajectories through such buildings as virtual narratives or stories, as dynamic paths and narrative paradigms which we as visitors are asked to fulfil and to complete with our own bodies and movements. In the Bonaventure, however, we find a dialectical heightening of this process: it seems to me that the escalators and elevators here henceforth replace movement but also and above all designate themselves as new reflexive signs and emblems of movement proper (something which will become evident when we come to the whole question of what remains of older forms of movement in this building, most notably walking itself). Here the narrative stroll has been underscored, symbolized, reified and replaced by a transportation machine which becomes the allegorical signifier of that older promenade we are no longer allowed to conduct on our own: and this is a dialectical intensification of the autoreferentiality of all modern culture, which tends to turn upon itself and designate its own cultural production as its content.

I am more at a loss when it comes to conveying the thing itself, the experience of space you undergo when you step off such allegorical devices into the lobby or atrium, with its great central column, surrounded by a miniature lake, the whole positioned between the four symmetrical residential towers with their elevators, and surrounded by rising balconies capped by a kind of greenhouse roof at the sixth level. I am tempted to say that such space makes it impossible for us to use the language of volume or volumes any longer, since these last are impossible to seize. Hanging streamers indeed suffuse this empty space in such a way as to distract systematically and deliberately from whatever form it might be supposed to have; while a constant busyness gives the feeling that emptiness is here absolutely packed, that it is an element within which you yourself are immersed, without any of that distance that formerly enabled the perception of perspective or volume. You are in this hyperspace up to your eyes and your body; and if it seemed to you before that that suppression of depth I spoke of in postmodern painting or literature would necessarily be difficult to achieve in architecture itself, perhaps you may now be willing to see this bewildering immersion as the formal equivalent in the new medium.

Yet escalator and elevator are also in this context dialetical opposites; and we may suggest that the glorious movement of the elevator gondolas is also a dialectical compensation for this filled space of the atrium—it gives us the chance at a radically different, but complementary, spatial experience, that of rapidly shooting up through the ceiling and outside, along one of the four symmetrical towers, with the referent, Los Angeles itself, spread out breathtakingly and even alarmingly before us. But even this vertical movement is contained: the elevator lifts you to one of those revolving cocktail lounges, in which you, seated, are again passively rotated about and offered a contemplative spectacle of the city itself, now transformed into its own images by the glass windows through which you view it.

Let me quickly conclude all this by returning to the central space of the lobby itself (with the passing observation that the hotel rooms are visibly marginalized: the corridors in the residential sections are low-ceilinged and dark, most depressingly functional indeed: while one understands that the rooms are in the worst of taste). The descent is dramatic enough, plummeting back down through the roof to splash down in the lake; what happens when you get there is something else, which I can only try to characterize as milling confusion, something like the vengeance this space takes on those who still seek to walk through it. Given the absolute symmetry of the four towers, it is quite impossible to get your bearings in this lobby; recently, colour coding and directional signals have been added in a pitiful and revealing, rather desperate attempt to restore the coordinates of an older space. I will take as the most dramatic practical result of this spatial mutation the notorious dilemma of the shopkeepers on the various balconies: it has been obvious, since the very opening of the hotel in 1977, that nobody could ever find any of these stores, and even if you located the appropriate boutique, you would be most unlikely to be as fortunate a second time; as a consequence, the commercial tenants are in despair and all the merchandise is marked down to bargain prices. When you recall that Portman is a businessman as well as an architect, and a millionaire developer, an artist who is at one and the same time a capitalist in his own right, you cannot but feel that here too something of a "return of the repressed" is involved.

So I come finally to my principal point here, that this latest mutation in space—postmodern hyperspace—has finally succeeded in transcending the capacities of the individual human body to locate itself, to organize its immediate surroundings perceptually, and cognitively to map its position in a mappable external world. And I have already suggested that this alarming disjunction point between the body and its built environment—which is to the initial bewilderment of the older modernism as the velocities of spacecraft are to those of the automobile—can itself stand as the symbol and analog of that even sharper dilemma which is the incapacity of our minds, at least at present, to map the great global multinational and decentered communicational network in which we find ourselves caught as individual subjects.

*The New Machine*

But as I am anxious that Portman's space not be perceived as something either exceptional or seemingly marginalized and leisure-specialized on the order of Disneyland, I would like in passing to juxtapose this complacent and entertaining (although bewildering) leisure-time space with its analog in a very different area, namely the space of postmodern warfare, in particular as Michael Herr evokes it in his great book on the experience of Vietnam, called *Dispatches*. The extraordinary linguistic innovations of this work may still be considered postmodern, in the eclectic way in which its language impersonally fuses a whole range of contemporary collective idiolects, most notably rock language and black language: but the fusion is dictated by problems of content. This first terrible postmodernist war cannot be told in any of the traditional paradigms of the war novel or movie—indeed that breakdown of all previous narrative paradigms is, along with the breakdown of any shared language through which a veteran might convey such experience, among the principal subjects of the book and may be said to open up the place of a whole new reflexivity. Benjamin's account of Baudelaire, and of the emergence of modernism from a new experience of city technology which transcends all the older habits of bodily perception, is both singularly relevant here, and singularly antiquated, in the light of this new and virtually unimaginable quantum leap in technological alienation:

> He was a moving-target-survivor subscriber, a true child of the war, because except for the rare times when you were pinned or stranded the system was geared to keep you mobile, if that was what you thought you wanted. As a technique for staying alive it seemed to make as much sense as anything, given naturally that you were there to begin with and wanted to see it close; it started out sound and straight but it formed a cone as it progressed, because the more you moved the more you saw, the more you saw the more besides death and mutilation you risked, and the more you risked of that the more you would have to let go of one day as a "survivor." Some of us moved around the war like crazy people until we couldn't see which way the run was taking us anymore, only the war all over its surface with occasional, unexpected penetration. As long as we could have choppers like taxis it took real exhaustion or depression near shock or a dozen pipes of opium to keep us even apparently quiet, we'd still be running around inside our skins like something was after us, ha, ha, La Vida Loca. In the months after I got back the hundreds of helicopters I'd flown in begin to draw together until they'd formed a collective meta-chopper, and in my mind it was the sexiest thing going; saver-destroyer, provider-waster, right hand-left hand, nimble, fluent, canny and human; hot steel, grease, jungle-saturated canvas webbing, sweat cooling and warming up again, cassette rock and roll in one ear and door-gun fire in the other, fuel, heat, vitality and death, death itself, hardly an intruder.[2]

In this new machine, which does not, like the older modernist machinery of the locomotive or the airplane, represent motion, but which can only be represented *in motion*, something of the mystery of the new postmodernist space is concentrated.

*The aesthetic of consumer society*

Now I must try very rapidly in conclusion to characterize the relationship of cultural production of this kind to social life in this country today. This will also be the moment to address the principal objection to concepts of postmodernism of the type I have sketched here: namely that all the features we have enumerated are not new at all but abundantly characterized modernism proper or what I call high modernism. Was not Thomas Mann, after all, interested in the idea of pastiche, and are not certain chapters of *Ulysses* its most obvious realization? Can Flaubert, Mallarmé and Gertrude Stein not be included in an account of postmodernist temporality? What is so new about all of this? Do we really need the concept of *post*modernism?

One kind of answer to this question would raise the whole issue of periodization and of how a historian (literary or other) posits a radical break between two henceforth distinct periods. I must limit myself to the suggestion that radical breaks between periods do not generally involve complete changes of content but rather the restructuring of a certain number of elements already given: features that in an earlier period or system were subordinate now become dominant, and features that had been dominant again become secondary. In this sense, everything we have described here can be found in earlier periods and most notably within modernism proper: my point is that until the present day those things have been secondary or minor features of modernist art, marginal rather than central, and that we have something new when they become the central features of cultural production.

But I can argue this more concretely by turning to the relationship between cultural production and social life generally. The older or classical modernism was an oppositional art; it emerged within the business society of the gilded age as scandalous and offensive to the middle-class public—ugly, dissonant, bohemian, sexually shocking. It was something to make fun of (when the police were not called in to seize the books or close the exhibitions): an offense to good taste and to common sense, or, as Freud and Marcuse would have put it, a provocative challenge to the reigning reality- and performance-principles of early twentieth-century middle-class society. Modernism in general did not go well with overstuffed Victorian furniture, with Victorian moral taboos, or with the conventions of polite society. This is to say that whatever the explicit political content of the great high modernisms, the latter were always in some mostly implicit ways dangerous and explosive, subversive within the established order.

If then we suddenly return to the present day, we can measure the immensity of the cultural changes that have taken place. Not only are Joyce and Picasso no longer weird and repulsive, they have become classics and now look rather realistic to us. Meanwhile, there is very little in either the form or the content of contemporary art that contemporary society finds intolerable and scandalous. The most offensive forms of this art—punk rock, say, or what is called sexually explicit material—are all taken in stride by society, and they are commercially successful, unlike the productions of the older high modernism. But this means that even if contemporary art has all the same formal features as the older modernism, it has still shifted its position fundamentally within our culture. For one thing, commodity production and in particular our clothing, furniture, buildings and other artifacts are now intimately tied in with styling changes which derive from artistic experimentation; our advertising, for example, is fed by postmodernism in all the arts and inconceivable without it. For another, the classics of high modernism are now part of the so-called canon and are taught in schools and universities—which at once empties them of any of their older subversive power. Indeed, one way of marking the break between the periods and of dating the emergence of postmodernism is precisely to be found there: in the moment (the early 1960s, one would think) in which the position of high modernism and its dominant aesthetics become established in the academy and are henceforth felt to be academic by a whole new generation of poets, painters and musicians.

But one can also come at the break from the other side, and describe it in terms of periods of recent social life. As I have suggested, non-Marxists and Marxists alike have come around to the general feeling that at some point following World War II a new kind of society began to emerge (variously described as postindustrial society, multinational capitalism, consumer society, media society and so forth). New types of consumption; planned obsolescence; an ever more rapid rhythm of fashion and styling changes; the penetration of advertising, television and the media generally to a hitherto unparalleled degree throughout society; the replacement of the old tension between city and country, center and province, by the suburb and by universal standardization; the growth of the great networks of superhighways and the arrival of automobile culture—these are some of the features which would seem to mark a radical break with that older prewar society in which high modernism was still an underground force.

I believe that the emergence of postmodernism is closely related to the emergence of this new moment of late, consumer or multinational capitalism. I believe also that its formal features in many ways express the deeper logic of that particular social system. I will only be able, however, to show this for one major theme: namely the disappearance of a sense of history, the way in which our entire contemporary social system has little by little begun to lose its capacity to retain its own past, has begun to live in a perpetual present and in a perpetual change that obliterates traditions of the kind which all earlier social formations have had in one way or another to preserve. Think only of the media exhaustion of news: of how Nixon and, even more so, Kennedy are figures from a now distant past. One is tempted to say that the very function of the news media is to relegate such recent historical experiences as rapidly as possible into the past. The informational function of the media would thus be to help us forget, to serve as the very agents and mechanisms for our historical amnesia.

But in that case the two features of postmodernism on which I have dwelt here—the transformation of reality into images, the fragmentation of time into a series of perpetual presents—are both extraordinarily consonant with this process. My own conclusion here must take the form of a question about the critical value of the newer art. There is some agreement that the older modernism functioned against its society in ways which are variously described as critical, negative, contestatory, subversive, oppositional and the like. Can anything of the sort be affirmed about postmodernism and its social moment? We have seen that there is a way in which postmodernism replicates or reproduces—reinforces—the logic of consumer capitalism; the more significant question is whether there is also a way in which it resists that logic. But that is a question we must leave open.

*Notes*

[1]The present text combines elements of two previously published essays: "Postmodernism and Consumer Society," in *The Anti-Aesthetic* (Port Townsend, WA: Bay Press, 1983),

and "Postmodernism: the Cultural Logic of Late Capitalism," *New Left Review* 146 (July–August 1984).
[2]Michael Herr, *Dispatches* (New York: Knopf, 1977), pp. 8–9.

*THROUGHOUT his career, the German philosopher and poet Friedrich Nietzsche criticized the limitations of modern conceptual and moral categories. This revolutionary subversion of the premises of philosophy forms the core of his most famous works—*The Gay Science *(1882),* Also Spoke Zarathustra *(1833–1892), and* Beyond Good and Evil *(1886). In* The Birth of Tragedy *(1872), Nietzsche argues that Greek tragedy arose from the collision between Athenian rationalism—symbolized by Apollo, Socrates, and Euripides—and an earlier, irrational mysticism, symbolized by Dionysus. Although Nietzsche's reading of Greek history has been generally discredited, the essay offers a powerful and influential reading of the tension between the rational and irrational informing Greek drama—and modern drama as well. Nietzsche was admired by several modern playwrights represented in this volume, including Bernard Shaw, August Strindberg, and Eugene O'Neill.*

**Friedrich Nietzsche**
(1844–1900)

FROM The Birth of Tragedy
(1872)

TRANSLATED BY
WALTER KAUFMANN

We shall have gained much for the science of aesthetics, once we perceive not merely by logical inference, but with the immediate certainty of vision, that the continuous development of art is bound up with the *Apollinian* and *Dionysian* duality—just as procreation depends on the duality of the sexes, involving perpetual strife with only periodically intervening reconciliations. The terms Dionysian and Apollinian we borrow from the Greeks, who disclose to the discerning mind the profound mysteries of their view of art, not, to be sure, in concepts, but in the intensely clear figures of their gods. Through Apollo and Dionysus, the two art deities of the Greeks, we come to recognize that in the Greek world there existed a tremendous opposition, in origin and aims,[1] between the Apollinian art of sculpture, and the nonimagistic, Dionysian art of music. These two different tendencies run parallel to each other, for the most part openly at variance; and they continually incite each other to new and more powerful births, which perpetuate an antagonism, only superficially reconciled by the common term "art"; till eventually,[2] by a metaphysical miracle of the Hellenic "will," they appear coupled with each other, and through this coupling ultimately generate an equally Dionysian and Apollinian form of art—Attic tragedy.

In order to grasp these two tendencies, let us first conceive of them as the separate art worlds of *dreams* and *intoxication.* These physiological phenomena present a contrast analogous to that existing between the Apollinian and the Dionysian. It was in dreams, says Lucretius, that the glorious divine figures first appeared to the souls of men; in dreams the great shaper beheld the splendid bodies of superhuman beings; and the Hellenic poet, if questioned about the mysteries of poetic inspiration, would likewise have suggested dreams and he might have given an explanation like that of Hans Sachs in the *Meistersinger:*

*1*

[1]In the first edition: ". . . an opposition of style: two different tendencies run parallel in it, for the most part in conflict; and they . . ." Most of the changes in the revision of 1874 are as slight as this (compare the next footnote) and therefore not indicated in the following pages. This translation, like the standard German editions, follows Nietzsche's revision.
[2]First edition: "till eventually, at the moment of the flowering of the Hellenic 'will,' they appear fused to generate together the art form of Attic tragedy."

The poet's task is this, my friend,
to read his dreams and comprehend.
The truest human fancy seems
to be revealed to us in dreams:
all poems and versification
are but true dreams' interpretation.[3]

The beautiful illusion[4] of the dream worlds, in the creation of which every man is truly an artist, is the prerequisite of all plastic art, and, as we shall see, of an important part of poetry also. In our dreams we delight in the immediate understanding of figures; all forms speak to us; there is nothing unimportant or superfluous. But even when this dream reality is most intense, we still have, glimmering through it, the sensation that it is *mere appearance:* at least this is my experience, and for its frequency—indeed, normality—I could adduce many proofs, including the sayings of the poets.

Philosophical men even have a presentiment that the reality in which we live and have our being is also mere appearance, and that another, quite different reality lies beneath it. Schopenhauer actually indicates as the criterion of philosophical ability the occasional ability to view men and things as mere phantoms or dream images. Thus the aesthetically sensitive man stands in the same relation to the reality of dreams as the philosopher does to the reality of existence; he is a close and willing observer, for these images afford him an interpretation of life, and by reflecting on these processes he trains himself for life.

It is not only the agreeable and friendly images that he experiences as something universally intelligible: the serious, the troubled, the sad, the gloomy, the sudden restraints, the tricks of accident, anxious expectations, in short, the whole divine comedy of life, including the inferno, also pass before him, not like mere shadows on a wall—for he lives and suffers with these scenes—and yet not without that fleeting sensation of illusion. And perhaps many will, like myself, recall how amid the dangers and terrors of dreams they have occasionally said to themselves in self-encouragement, and not without success: "It is a dream! I will dream on!" I have likewise heard of people who were able to continue one and the same dream for three and even more successive nights—facts which indicate clearly how our innermost being, our common ground, experiences dreams with profound delight and a joyous necessity.

This joyous necessity of the dream experience has been embodied by the Greeks in their Apollo: Apollo, the god of all plastic energies, is at the same time the soothsaying god. He, who (as the etymology of the name indicates) is the "shining one,"[5] the deity of light, is also ruler over the beautiful illusion of the inner world of fantasy. The higher truth, the perfection of these states in contrast to the incompletely intelligible everyday world, this deep consciousness of nature, healing and helping in sleep and dreams, is at the same time the symbolical analogue of the soothsaying faculty and of the arts generally, which make life possible and worth living. But we must also include in our image of Apollo that delicate boundary which the dream image must not overstep lest it have a pathological effect (in which case mere appearance would deceive us as if it were crude reality). We must keep in mind that measured restraint, that freedom from the wilder emotions, that calm of the sculptor god. His eye must be "sunlike," as befits his origin; even when it is angry and distempered it is still hallowed by beautiful illusion. And so, in one sense, we might apply to

---

[3]Wagner's original text reads:

Mein Freund, das grad' ist Dichters Werk,
dass er sein Träumen deut' und merk'.
Glaubt mir, des Menschen wahrster Wahn
wird ihm im Traume aufgethan:
all' Dichtkunst und Poëterei
ist nichts als Wahrtraum-Deuterei.

[4]*Schein* has been rendered in these pages sometimes as "illusion," and sometimes as "mere appearance."
[5]*Der "Scheinende."* The German words for illusion and appearance are *Schein* and *Erscheinung.*

Apollo the words of Schopenhauer when he speaks of the man wrapped in the veil of māyā[6] (*Welt als Wille and Vorstellung*, I, p. 416[7]): "Just as in a stormy sea that, unbounded in all directions, raises and drops mountainous waves, howling, a sailor sits in a boat and trusts in his frail bark: so in the midst of a world of torments the individual human being sits quietly, supported by and trusting in the *principium individuationis*."[8] In fact, we might say of Apollo that in him the unshaken faith in this *principium* and the calm repose of the man wrapped up in it receive their most sublime expression; and we might call Apollo himself the glorious divine image of the *principium individuationis*, through whose gestures and eyes all the joy and wisdom of "illusion," together with its beauty, speak to us.

In the same work Schopenhauer has depicted for us the tremendous *terror* which seizes man when he is suddenly dumfounded by the cognitive form of phenomena because the principle of sufficient reason, in some one of its manifestations, seems to suffer an exception. If we add to this terror the blissful ecstasy that wells from the innermost depths of man, indeed of nature, at this collapse of the *principium individuationis*, we steal a glimpse into the nature of the *Dionysian*, which is brought home to us most intimately by the analogy of intoxication.

Either under the influence of the narcotic draught, of which the songs of all primitive men and peoples speak, or with the potent coming of spring that penetrates all nature with joy, these Dionysian emotions awake, and as they grow in intensity everything subjective vanishes into complete self-forgetfulness. In the German Middle Ages, too, singing and dancing crowds, ever increasing in number, whirled themselves from place to place under this same Dionysian impulse. In these dancers of St. John and St. Vitus, we rediscover the Bacchic choruses of the Greeks, with their prehistory in Asia Minor, as far back as Babylon and the orgiastic Sacaea.[9] There are some who, from obtuseness or lack of experience, turn away from such phenomena as from "folk-diseases," with contempt or pity born of the consciousness of their own "healthy-mindedness." But of course such poor wretches have no idea how corpselike and ghostly their so-called "healthy-mindedness" looks when the glowing life of the Dionysian revelers roars past them.

Under the charm of the Dionysian not only is the union between man and man reaffirmed, but nature which has become alienated, hostile, or subjugated, celebrates once more her reconciliation with her lost son,[10] man. Freely, earth proffers her gifts, and peacefully the beasts of prey of the rocks and desert approach. The chariot of Dionysus is covered with flowers and garlands; panthers and tigers walk under its yoke. Transform Beethoven's "Hymn to Joy" into a painting; let your imagination conceive the multitudes bowing to the dust, awestruck—then you will approach the Dionysian. Now the slave is a free man; now all the rigid, hostile barriers that necessity, caprice, or "impudent convention"[11] have fixed between man and man are broken. Now, with the gospel of universal harmony, each one feels himself not only united, reconciled, and fused with his neighbor, but as one with him, as if the veil of *māyā* had been torn aside and were now merely fluttering in tatters before the mysterious primordial unity.

In song and in dance man expresses himself as a member of a higher community; he has forgotten how to walk and speak and is on the way toward flying into the air, dancing. His very gestures express enchantment. Just as the animals now talk, and the earth yields milk and honey, supernatural sounds emanate from him, too: he feels himself a god, he himself now walks about

---

[6]A Sanskrit word usually translated as illusion. For detailed discussions see, e.g., *A Source Book of Indian Philosophy*, ed. S. Radhakrishnan and Charles Moore (Princeton, N.J., Princeton University Press, (1957); Heinrich Zimmer, *Philosophies of India*, ed. Joseph Campbell (New York, Meridian Books, (1956); and Helmuth von Glasenapp, *Die Philosophie der Inder* (Stuttgart, Kröner, 1949), consulting the indices.

[7]This reference, like subsequent references to the same work, is Nietzsche's own and refers to the edition of 1873 edited by Julius Frauenstädt—still one of the standard editions of Schopenhauer's works.

[8]Principle of individuation.

[9]A Babylonian festival that lasted five days and was marked by general license. During this time slaves are said to have ruled their masters, and a criminal was given all royal rights before he was put to death at the end of the festival. For references, see, e.g., *The Oxford Classical Dictionary*.

[10]In German, "the prodigal son" is *der verlorene Sohn* (the lost son).

[11]An allusion to Friedrich Schiller's hymn *An die Freude* (to joy), used by Beethoven in the final movement of his Ninth Symphony.

enchanted, in ecstasy, like the gods he saw walking in his dreams. He is no longer an artist, he has become a work of art: in these paroxysms of intoxication the artistic power of all nature reveals itself to the highest gratification of the primordial unity. The noblest clay, the most costly marble, man, is here kneaded and cut, and to the sound of the chisel strokes of the Dionysian world-artist rings out the cry of the Eleusinian mysteries: "Do you prostrate yourselves, millions? Do you sense your Maker, world?"[12]

. . . . . . . . . . . . . . . . . . . . . . . . . . . . . . . . . . . . . .

10    The tradition is undisputed that Greek tragedy in its earliest form had for its sole theme the sufferings of Dionysus and that for a long time the only stage hero was Dionysus himself. But it may be claimed with equal confidence that until Euripides, Dionysus never ceased to be the tragic hero; that all the celebrated figures of the Greek stage—Prometheus, Oedipus, etc.—are mere masks of this original hero, Dionysus. That behind all these masks there is a deity, that is one essential reason for the typical "ideality" of these famous figures which has caused so much astonishment. Somebody, I do not know who, has claimed that all individuals, taken as individuals, are comic and hence untragic—from which it would follow that the Greeks simply *could* not suffer individuals on the tragic stage. In fact, this is what they seem to have felt; and the Platonic distinction and evaluation of the "idea" and the "idol," the mere image, is very deeply rooted in the Hellenic character.

Using Plato's terms we should have to speak of the tragic figures of the Hellenic stage somewhat as follows: the one truly real Dionysus appears in a variety of forms, in the mask of a fighting hero, and entangled, as it were, in the net of the individual will. The god who appears talks and acts so as to resemble an erring, striving, suffering individual. That he *appears* at all with such epic precision and clarity is the work of the dream-interpreter, Apollo, who through this symbolic appearance interprets to the chorus its Dionysian state. In truth, however, the hero is the suffering Dionysus of the Mysteries, the god experiencing in himself the agonies of individuation, of whom wonderful myths tell that as a boy he was torn to pieces by the Titans and now is worshiped in this state as Zagreus. Thus it is intimated that this dismemberment, the properly Dionysian *suffering,* is like a transformation into air, water, earth, and fire, that we are therefore to regard the state of individuation as the origin and primal cause of all suffering, as something objectionable in itself. From the smile of this Dionysus sprang the Olympian gods, from his tears sprang man. In this existence as a dismembered god, Dionysus possesses the dual nature of a cruel, barbarized demon and a mild, gentle ruler. But the hope of the epopts[13] looked toward a rebirth of Dionysus, which we must now dimly conceive as the end of individuation. It was for this coming third Dionysus that the epopts' roaring hymns of joy resounded. And it is this hope alone that casts a gleam of joy upon the features of a world torn asunder and shattered into individuals; this is symbolized in the myth of Demeter, sunk in eternal sorrow, who *rejoices* again for the first time when told that she may *once more* give birth to Dionysus. This view of things already provides us with all the elements of a profound and pessimistic view of the world, together with the *mystery doctrine of tragedy:* the fundamental knowledge of the oneness of everything existent, the conception of individuation as the primal cause of evil, and of art as the joyous hope that the spell of individuation may be broken in augury of a restored oneness.

We have already suggested that the Homeric epos is the poem of Olympian culture, in which this culture has sung its own song of victory over the terrors of the war of the Titans. Under the predominating influence of tragic poetry, these Homeric myths are now born anew; and this metempsychosis reveals that in the meantime the Olympian culture also has been conquered by a still more profound view of the world. The defiant Titan Prometheus has announced to his Olympian tormentor that some day the greatest danger will menace his rule, unless Zeus should enter into an alliance with him in time. In Aeschylus we recognize how the terrified Zeus, fearful of his end, allies himself with the Titan. Thus the former age of the Titans is once more recovered from Tartarus and brought to the light.

---

[12]Quotation from Schiller's hymn.
[13]Those initiated into the mysteries.

The philosophy of wild and naked nature beholds with the frank, undissembling gaze of truth the myths of the Homeric world as they dance past: they turn pale, they tremble under the piercing glance of this goddess[14]—till the powerful fist of the Dionysian artist forces them into the service of the new deity. Dionysian truth takes over the entire domain of myth as the symbolism of *its* knowledge which it makes known partly in the public cult of tragedy and partly in the secret celebrations of dramatic mysteries, but always in the old mythical garb.

What power was it that freed Prometheus from his vultures and transformed the myth into a vehicle of Dionysian wisdom? It is the Heracleian power of music: having reached its highest manifestation in tragedy, it can invest myths with a new and most profound significance. This we have already characterized as the most powerful function of music. For it is the fate of every myth to creep by degrees into the narrow limits of some alleged historical reality, and to be treated by some later generation as a unique fact with historical claims: and the Greeks were already fairly on the way toward restamping the whole of their mythical juvenile dream sagaciously and arbitrarily into a historico-pragmatical *juvenile history.* For this is the way in which religions are wont to die out: under the stern, intelligent eyes of an orthodox dogmatism, the mythical premises of a religion are systematized as a sum total of historical events; one begins apprehensively to defend the credibility of the myths, while at the same time one opposes any continuation of their natural vitality and growth; the feeling for myth perishes, and its place is taken by the claim of religion to historical foundations. This dying myth was now seized by the new-born genius of Dionysian music; and in these hands it flourished once more with colors such as it had never yet displayed, with a fragrance that awakened a longing anticipation of a metaphysical world. After this final effulgence it collapses, its leaves wither, and soon the mocking Lucians of antiquity catch at the discolored and faded flowers carried away by the four winds. Through tragedy the myth attains its most profound content, its most expressive form; it rises once more like a wounded hero, and its whole excess of strength, together with the philosophic calm of the dying, burns in its eyes with a last powerful gleam.

What did you want, sacrilegious Euripides, when you sought to compel this dying myth to serve you once more? It died under your violent hands—and then you needed a copied, masked myth that, like the ape of Heracles, merely knew how to deck itself out in the ancient pomp. And just as the myth died on you, the genius of music died on you, too. Though with greedy hands you plundered all the gardens of music, you still managed only copied, masked music. And because you had abandoned Dionysus, Apollo abandoned you: rouse all the passions from their resting places and conjure them into your circle, sharpen and whet a sophistical dialectic for the speeches of your heroes—your heroes, too, have only copied, masked passions and speak only copied, masked speeches.

---

[14]Truth.

---

*PEGGY Phelan is widely known for her work in feminism, performance theory, and cultural studies. In her recent book,* Unmarked: The Politics of Performance, *Phelan traces the politics of performance through a number of cultural configurations: in experimental films, in the photography of Robert Mapplethorpe, in Tom Stoppard's play* Hapgood, *in the staged confrontations of Operation Rescue. Here, she outlines some of the theoretical challenges posed by performance art.*

Peggy Phelan
FROM Unmarked
(1993)

Performance's only life is in the present. Performance cannot be saved, recorded, documented, or otherwise participate in the circulation of representations *of* representations: once it does so, it becomes something other than performance. To the degree that performance attempts to enter the economy of reproduction it betrays and lessens the promise of its own ontology. Performance's being, like the ontology of subjectivity proposed here, becomes itself through disappearance.

The pressures brought to bear on performance to succumb to the laws of the reproductive economy are enormous. For only rarely in this culture is the "now" to which performance addresses its deepest questions valued. (This is why the now is supplemented and buttressed by the documenting camera, the video archive.) Performance occurs over a time which will not be repeated. It can be performed again, but this repetition itself marks it as "different." The document of a performance then is only a spur to memory, an encouragement of memory to become present.

The other arts, especially painting and photography, are drawn increasingly toward performance. The French-born artist Sophie Calle, for example, has photographed the galleries of the Isabella Stewart Gardner Museum in Boston. Several valuable paintings were stolen from the museum in 1990. Calle interviewed various visitors and members of the museum staff, asking them to describe the stolen paintings. She then transcribed these texts and placed them next to the photographs of the galleries. Her work suggests that the descriptions and memories of the paintings constitute their continuing "presence," despite the absence of the paintings themselves. Calle gestures toward a notion of the interactive exchange between the art object and the viewer. While such exchanges are often recorded as the stated goals of museums and galleries, the institutional effect of the gallery often seems to put the masterpiece under house arrest, controlling all conflicting and unprofessional commentary about it. The speech act of memory and description (Austin's constative utterance) becomes a performative expression when Calle places these commentaries within the representation of the museum. The descriptions fill in, and thus supplement (add to, defer, and displace) the stolen paintings. The fact that these descriptions vary considerably—even at times wildly—only lends credence to the fact that the interaction between the art object and the spectator is, essentially, performative—and therefore resistant to the claims of validity and accuracy endemic to the discourse of reproduction. While the art historian of painting must ask if the reproduction is accurate and clear, Calle asks where seeing and memory forget the object itself and enter the subject's own set of personal meanings and associations. Further her work suggests that the forgetting (or stealing) of the object is a fundamental energy of its descriptive recovering. The description itself does not reproduce the object, it rather helps us to restage and restate the effort to remember what is lost. The descriptions remind us how loss acquires meaning and generates recovery—not only of and for the object, but for the one who remembers. The disappearance of the object is fundamental to performance; it rehearses and repeats the disappearance of the subject who longs always to be remembered.

For her contribution to the *Dislocations* show at the Museum of Modern Art in New York in 1991, Calle used the same idea but this time she asked curators, guards, and restorers to describe paintings that were on loan from the permanent collection. She also asked them to draw small pictures of their memories of the paintings. She then arranged the texts and pictures according to the exact dimensions of the circulating paintings and placed them on the wall where the actual paintings usually hang. Calle calls her piece *Ghosts,* and as the visitor discovers Calle's work spread throughout the museum, it is as if Calle's own eye is following and tracking the viewer as she makes her way through the museum.[1] Moreover, Calle's work seems to disappear because it is dispersed throughout the "permanent collection"—a collection which circulates despite its "permanence." Calle's artistic contribution is a kind of self-concealment in which she offers the words of others about other works of art under her own artistic signature. By making visible her attempt to offer what she does not have, what cannot be seen, Calle subverts the goal of museum display. She exposes what the museum does not have and cannot offer and uses that absence to generate her own work. By placing memories in the place of paintings, Calle asks that the ghosts of memory be seen as equivalent to "the permanent collection" of "great works." One senses that if she asked the same people over and over about the same paintings, each time they would describe a slightly different painting. In this sense, Calle demonstrates the performative quality of all seeing.

Performance in a strict ontological sense is nonreproductive. It is this quality which makes performance the runt of the litter of contemporary art. Performance clogs the smooth machinery of reproductive representation necessary to the circulation of capital. Perhaps nowhere was the affinity between the ideology of capitalism and art made more manifest than in the debates about the funding policies for the National Endowment for the Arts (NEA).[2] Targeting both photography and performance art, conservative politicians sought to prevent endorsing the "real" bodies implicated and made visible by these art forms.

Performance implicates the real through the presence of living bodies. In performance art spectatorship there is an element of consumption: there are no left-overs, the gazing spectator must try to take everything in. Without a copy, live performance plunges into visibility—in a maniacally charged present—and disappears into memory, into the realm of invisibility and the unconscious where it eludes regulation and control. Performance resists the balanced circulations of finance. It saves nothing; it only spends. While photography is vulnerable to charges of counterfeiting and copying, performance art is vulnerable to charges of valuelessness and emptiness. Performance indicates the possibility of revaluing that emptiness; this potential revaluation gives performance art its distinctive oppositional edge.[3]

To attempt to write about the undocumentable event of performance is to invoke the rules of the written document and thereby alter the event itself. Just as quantum physics discovered that macro-instruments cannot measure microscopic particles without transforming those particles, so too must performance critics realize that the labor to write about performance (and thus to "preserve" it) is also a labor that fundamentally alters the event. It does no good, however, to simply refuse to write about performance because of this inescapable transformation. The challenge raised by the ontological claims of performance for writing is to re-mark again the performative possibilities of writing itself. The act of writing toward disappearance, rather than the act of writing toward preservation, must remember that the after-effect of disappearance is the experience of subjectivity itself.

This is the project of Roland Barthes in both *Camera Lucida* and *Roland Barthes by Roland Barthes.* It is also his project in *Empire of Signs,* but in this book he takes the memory of a city in which he no longer is, a city from which he disappears, as the motivation for the search for a disappearing performative writing. The trace left by that script is the meeting-point of a mutual disappearance; shared subjectivity is possible for Barthes because two people can recognize the same Impossible. To live for a love whose goal is to share the Impossible is both a humbling project and an exceedingly ambitious one, for it seeks to find connection only in that which is no longer there. Memory. Sight. Love. It must involve a full seeing of the Other's absence (the ambitious part), a seeing which also entails the acknowledgement of the Other's presence (the humbling part). For to acknowledge the Other's (always partial) presence is to acknowledge one's own (always partial) absence.

In the field of linguistics, the performative speech act shares with the ontology of performance the inability to be reproduced or repeated. "Being an individual and historical act, a performative utterance cannot be repeated. Each reproduction is a new act performed by someone who is qualified. Otherwise, the reproduction of the performative utterance by someone else necessarily transforms it into a constative utterance."[4]

Writing, an activity which relies on the reproduction of the Same (the three letters *cat* will repeatedly signify the four-legged furry animal with whiskers) for the production of meaning, can broach the frame of performance but cannot mimic an art that is nonreproductive. The mimicry of speech and writing, the strange process by which we put words in each other's mouths and others' words in our own, relies on a substitutional economy in which equivalencies are assumed and reestablished. Performance refuses this system of exchange and resists the circulatory economy fundamental to it. Performance honors the idea that a limited number of people in a specific time/space frame can have an experience of value which leaves no visible trace afterward. Writing about it necessarily cancels the "tracelessness" inaugurated within this performative promise. Performance's independence from mass reproduction, technologically, economically, and linguistically, is its greatest strength. But buffeted by the encroaching ideologies of capital and reproduction, it frequently devalues this strength. Writing about performance often, unwittingly, encourages this weakness and falls in behind the drive of the document/ary. Performance's challenge to writing is to discover a way for repeated words to become performative utterances, rather than, as Benveniste warned, constative utterances.

The distinction between performative and constative utterances was proposed by J. L. Austin in *How To Do Things With Words.*[5] Austin argued that speech had both a constative element (describing things in the world) and a performative element (to say something is to *do* or make something, e.g. "I promise," "I bet," "I beg"). Performative speech acts refer only to themselves, they *enact* the activity the speech signifies. For Derrida, performative writing promises fidelity only to the utterance of the promise: I promise to utter this promise.[6] The performative is important to Derrida precisely because it displays language's independence from the referent outside of itself. Thus, for Derrida the performative enacts the now of writing in the present time.[7]

Tania Modleski has rehearsed Derrida's relation to Austin and argues that "feminist critical writing is simultaneously performative and utopian" ("Some Functions": 15). That is, feminist critical writing is an enactment of belief in a better future; the act of writing brings that future closer.[8] Modleski goes further too and says that women's relation to the performative mode of writing and speech is especially intense because women are not assured the luxury of making linguistic promises within phallogocentrism, since all too often she *is* what is promised. Commenting on Shoshana Felman's account of the "scandal of the speaking body," a scandal Felman elucidates through a reading of Molière's *Dom Juan,* Modleski argues that the scandal has different affects and effects for women than for men. "[T]he real, historical scandal to which feminism addresses itself is surely not to be equated with the writer at the center of discourse, but the woman who remains outside of it, not with the 'speaking body,' but with the 'mute body'" (ibid.:19). Feminist critical writing, Modleski argues, "works toward a time when the traditionally mute body, 'the mother,' will be given the same access to 'the names'—language and speech—that men have enjoyed" (ibid.:15).

If Modleski is accurate in suggesting that the opposition for feminists who write is between the "speaking bodies" of men and the "mute bodies" of women, for performance the opposition is between "the body in pleasure" and, to invoke the title of Elaine Scarry's book, "the body in pain." In moving from the grammar of words to the grammar of the body, one moves from the realm of metaphor to the realm of metonymy. For performance art itself however, the referent is always the agonizingly relevant body of the performer. Metaphor works to secure a vertical hierarchy of value and is reproductive; it works by erasing dissimilarity and negating difference; it turns two into one. Metonymy is additive and associative; it works to secure a horizontal axis of contiguity and displacement. "The kettle is boiling" is a sentence which assumes that water is contiguous with the kettle. The point is not that the kettle is *like* water (as in the metaphorical love is like a rose), but rather the kettle is boiling *because* the water inside the kettle is. In performance, the body is metonymic of self, of character, of voice, of "presence." But in the plenitude of its apparent visibility and availability, the performer actually disappears and represents something else—dance, movement, sound, character, "art." As we discovered in relation to Cindy Sherman's self-portraits, the very effort to make the female body appear involves the addition of something other than "the body." That "addition" becomes the object of the spectator's gaze, in much the way the supplement functions to secure and displace the fixed meaning of the (floating) signifier. Just as her body remains unseen as "in itself it really is," so too does the sign fail to reproduce the referent. Performance uses the performer's body to pose a question about the inability to secure the relation between subjectivity and the body *per se;* performance uses the body to frame the lack of Being promised by and through the body—that which cannot appear without a supplement.

In employing the body metonymically, performance is capable of resisting the reproduction of metaphor, and the metaphor I'm most keenly interested in resisting is the metaphor of gender, a metaphor which upholds the vertical hierarchy of value through systematic marking of the positive and the negative. In order to enact this marking, the metaphor of gender presupposes unified bodies which are biologically different. More specifically, these unified bodies are different in "one" aspect of the body, that is to say, difference is located in the genitals.

As MacCannell points out about Lacan's story of the "laws of urinary segregation" (*Ecrits:* 151), same sex bathrooms are social institutions which further the metaphorical work of hiding gender/genital difference. The genitals themselves are forever hidden within metaphor, and metaphor, as a "cultural worker," continually converts difference into the Same. The joined task of metaphor and culture is to reproduce itself; it accomplishes this by turning two (or more) into one.[9] By valuing one gender and marking it (with the phallus) culture reproduces one sex and one gender, the hommo-sexual.

If this is true then women should simply disappear—but they don't. Or do they? If women are not reproduced within metaphor or culture, how do they survive? If it is a question of survival, why would white women (apparently visible cultural workers) participate in the reproduction of their own negation? What aspects of the bodies and languages of women remain outside metaphor and inside the historical real? Or to put it somewhat differently, how do women reproduce and represent themselves within the figures and metaphors of hommo-sexual representation and culture? Are they perhaps surviving in another (auto)reproductive system?

"What founds our *gender economy* (division of the sexes and their mutual evaluation) is the exclusion of *the mother,* more specifically her body, more precisely yet, her *genitals.* These cannot, must not be *seen*" (original emphasis; MacCannell, *Figuring Lacan:* 106). The discursive and iconic "nothingness" of the Mother's genitals is what culture and metaphor cannot face. They must be effaced in order to allow the phallus to operate as that which always marks, values, and wounds. Castration is a response to this blindness to the mother's genitals. In "The Uncanny" Freud suggests that the fear of blindness is a displacement of the deeper fear of castration but surely it works the other way as well, or maybe even more strongly. Averting the eyes from the "nothing" of the mother's genitals is the blindness which fuels castration. This is the blindness of Oedipus. Is blindness necessary to the anti-Oedipus? To Electra? Does metonymy need blindness as keenly as metaphor does?

Cultural orders rely on the renunciation of conscious desire and pleasure and *promise* a reward for this renunciation. MacCannell refers to this as "the positive promise of castration" and locates it in the idea of "value" itself—the desire to be valued by the Other. (For Lacan, value is recognition by the Other.) The hope of becoming valued prompts the subject to make sacrifices, and especially to forgo conscious pleasure. This willingness to renounce pleasure implies that the Symbolic Order is moral and that the subject obeys an (inner) Law which affords the subject a veil of dignity. Why only the veil of dignity as against dignity itself? Because the fundamental Other (the one who governs "the other scene" which ghosts the conscious scene) is the Symbolic Mother. She is the Ideal Other for whom the subject wants to be dignified; but she cannot appear within the phallic representational economy which is predicated on the disappearance of her Being.[10] The psychic subject performs for a phantom who allows the subject veils and curtains—rather than satisfaction.

Performance approaches the Real through resisting the metaphorical reduction of the two into the one. But in moving from the aims of metaphor, reproduction, and pleasure to those of metonymy, displacement, and pain, performance marks the body itself as loss. Performance is the attempt to value that which is nonreproductive, nonmetaphorical. This is enacted through the staging of the drama of misrecognition (twins, actors within characters enacting other characters, doubles, crimes, secrets, etc.) which sometimes produces the recognition of the desire to be seen *by* (and within) the other. Thus for the spectator the performance spectacle is itself a projection of the scenario in which her own desire takes place.

More specifically, a genre of performance art called "hardship art" or "ordeal art" attempts to invoke a distinction between presence and representation by using the singular body as a metonymy for the apparently nonreciprocal experience of pain. This performance calls witnesses to the singularity of the individual's death and asks the spectator to do the impossible—to share that death by rehearsing for it. (It is for this reason that performance shares a fundamental bond with ritual. The Catholic Mass, for example, is the ritualized performative promise to remember and to rehearse for the Other's death.) The promise evoked by this performance then is to learn to value what is lost, to learn not the meaning but the value of what cannot be reproduced or seen (again). It begins with the knowledge of its own failure, that it cannot *be* achieved.

---

## Notes

[1]This notion of following and tracking was a fundamental aspect of Calle's earlier performance pieces. See Jean Baudrillard *Suite Venitienne/Sophie Calle, Please Follow Me,* for documentation of Calle's surveillance of a stranger.

[2]See my essays "Money Talks" and "Money Talks, Again"

for a full elaboration.

[3]Of course not all performance art has an oppositional edge. The ontological claims of performance art are what I am addressing here, and not the politics of ambition.

[4]Emile Benveniste, *Problems in General Linguistics,* quoted in Shoshana Felman, *The Literary Speech Act:*21.

[5]J. L. Austin, *How To Do Things With Words,* 2nd edn.

Derrida's rereading of Austin also comes from an interest in the performative element within language.

[6]Jacques Derrida, "Signature, Event, Context."

[7]See Felman, *The Literary Speech Act*, for a dazzling reading of Austin.

[8]See my essay, "Reciting the Citation of Others" for a full discussion of Modleski's essay and performance.

[9]Juliet MacCannell, *Figuring Lacan: Criticism and the Cultural Unconscious*, esp. pp. 90–117.

[10]The disappearance of the Mother's Being also accounts for the (relative) success of the visibility of the anti-abortion groups. The smooth displacement of the image of the Mother to the hyper-visible image of the hitherto unseen fetus, is accomplished precisely because the Being of the Mother is what is always already excluded within representational economies. See Chapter 6 in this volume for further elaboration of this point.

---

## Constantin Stanislavski
### (1863–1938)

### Direction and Acting
### (published 1947)

*ONE of the founders of the Moscow Art Theater, Stanislavski developed a systematic approach to acting that involved working both on the actor's psychological and on his or her physical portrayal of character. In this article, originally written for the* Encyclopedia Britannica, *Stanislavski outlines some of the central features of his "system": public solitude, concentration, internal technique.*

Theatrical art has always been collective, arising only where poetical-dramatic talent was actively combined with the actor's. The basis of a play is always a dramatic conception; a general artistic sense is imparted to the theatrical action by the unifying, creative genius of the actor. Thus the actor's dramatic activity begins at the foundation of the play. In the first place, each actor, either independently or through the theatre manager, must probe for the fundamental motive in the finished play—the creative idea that is characteristic of the author and that reveals itself as the germ from which his work grows organically. The motive of the play always keeps the character developing before the spectator; each personality in the work takes a part conforming to his own character; the work, then developing in the appointed direction, flows on to the final point conceived by the author. The first stage in the work of the actor and theatre manager is to probe for the germ of the play, investigating the fundamental line of action that traverses all of its episodes and is therefore called by the writer its transparent effect or action. In contrast to some theatrical directors, who consider every play only as material for theatrical repetition, the writer believes that in the production of every important drama the director and actor must go straight for the most exact and profound conception of the mind and ideal of the dramatist, and must not change that ideal for their own. The interpretation of the play and the character of its artistic incarnation inevitably appear in a certain measure subjective, and bear the mark of the individual peculiarities of the manager and actors; but only by profound attention to the artistic individuality of the author and to his ideal and mentality, which have been disclosed as the creative germ of the play, can the theatre realize all its artistic depth and transmit, as in a poetical production, completeness and harmony of composition. Every part of the future spectacle is then unified in it by its own artistic work; each part, in the measure of its own genius, will flow on to the artistic realization aimed at by the dramatist.

The actor's task, then, begins with the search for the play's artistic seed. All artistic action—organic action, as in every constructive operation of nature—starts from this seed at the moment when it is conveyed to the mind. On reaching the actor's mind, the seed must wander around, germinate, put out roots, drinking in the juices of the soil in which it is planted, grow and eventually bring forth a lively flowering plant. Artistic process must in all cases flow very rapidly, but usually, in order that it may preserve the character of the true organic action and may lead to the creation of life, of a clear truly artistic theatrical image, and not of a trade substitute, it demands much more time than is allotted to it in the best European theatres. That is why in the writer's theatre every dramatization passes through eight to ten revisions, as is also done in Germany by the famous theatre manager and theorist, K. Hagemann. Sometimes even more than ten revisions are needed, occasionally extending over several months. But even under these conditions, the creative genius of the actor does not appear so freely as does, for instance, the creative genius of the dramatist. Bound by the strict obligations of his *collectif*, the actor must not postpone his work to the moment when his physical and psychic condition appears propitious for creative genius. Meanwhile, his exacting and capricious artistic nature is prompted by aspirations of his artistic intuition, and in the absence of creative genius is not reached by any effort of his will. He is not aided in that respect by outward technique—his skill in making use of his body, his vocal equipment and his powers of speech.

But is it really impossible? Are there no means, no processes that sensibly would help us, and spontaneously lead to that artistic condition which is born of genius without any effort on its part? If that capacity is unattainable all at once, by some process or other, it may, perhaps, be acquired in parts, and through progressive stages may perfect those elements out of which the artistic condition is composed, and which are subject to our will. Of course the general run of acting does not come into being from this genius, but cannot such acting, in some measure, be brought by it near to what is evidence of genius? These are the problems which presented themselves to the writer about 20 years ago, when reflecting on the external obstacles that hamper actors' artistic genius, and partly compel substitution of the crude outward marks of the actor's profession for its results. They drove him to the rediscovery of processes of external technique, *i.e.*, methods proceeding form consciousness to sub-consciousness, in which domain flow nine-tenths of all real artistic processes. Observations both upon himself and other actors with whom he happened to rehearse, but chiefly upon growing theatrical skill in Russia and abroad, allowed him to do some generalizing, which thereupon he verified in practice.

*The artistic condition*

The first is that, in an artistic condition, full freedom of body plays a principal rôle; *i.e.*, the freedom from that muscular strain which, without our knowing it, fetters us not only on the stage but also in ordinary life, hindering us from being obedient conductors of our psychic action. This muscular strain, reaching its maximum at those times when the actor is called upon to perform something especially difficult in his theatrical work, swallows up the bulk of this external energy, diverting him from activity of the higher centres. This teaches us the possibility of availing ourselves of the muscular energy of our limbs only as necessity demands, and in exact conformity with our creative efforts.

The second observation is that the flow of the actor's artistic force is considerably retarded by the visual auditorium and the public, whose presence may hamper his outward freedom of movement, and powerfully hinder his concentration on his own artistic taste. It is almost unnecessary to remark that the artistic achievement of great actors is always bound by the concentration of attention to the action of their own performance, and that when in that condition, *i.e.*, just when the actor's attention is taken away from the spectator, he gains a particular power over the audience, grips it, and compels it to take an active share in his artistic existence. This does not mean, of course, that the actor must altogether cease to feel the public; but the public is concerned only in so far as it neither exerts pressure on him nor diverts him unnecessarily from the artistic demands of the moment, which last might happen to him even while knowing how to regulate his attention. The actor suitably disciplined must automatically restrict the sphere of his attention, concentrating on what comes within this sphere, and only half consciously seizing on what comes within its aura. If need be, he must restrict that sphere to such an extent that it reaches a condition that may be called *public solitude*. But as a rule this sphere of attention is elastic, it expands or contracts for the actor, with regard to the course of his theatrical actions. Within the boundary of this sphere, as one of the actual aspects of the play, there is also the actor's immediate central *object of attention*, the object on which, somehow or other, his will is concentrated at the moment with which, in the course of the play, he is in inward communication. This theatrical sympathy with the object can only be complete when the actor has trained himself by long practice to surrender himself in his own impressions, and also in his reactions to those impressions, with maximum intensity: only so does theatrical action attain the necessary force, only so is created between the actual aspects of the play, *i.e.*, between the actors, that link, that living bond, which is essential for the carrying through of the play to its goal, with the general maintenance of the rhythm and time of each performance.

*Public solitude*

But whatever may be the sphere of the actor's attention, whether it confines him at some moments to public solitude, or whether it grips the faces of all those before the stage, dramatic artistic genius, as in the preparation of the part so in its repeated performance, requires a full concentration of all the mental and physical talents of the actor, and the participation of the whole of his

*Concentration*

physical and psychic capacity. It takes hold of his sight and hearing, all his external senses; it draws out not only the periphery but also the essential depth of his existence, and it evokes to activity his memory, imagination, emotions, intelligence and will. The whole mental and physical being of the actor must be directed to that which is derived from his facial expression. At the moment of inspiration, of the involuntary use of all the actor's qualities, at that moment he actually exists. On the other hand, in the absence of this employment of his qualities, the actor is gradually led astray along the road leading to time-honored theatrical traditions; he begins to "produce" wherever he sees them, or, glancing at his own image, imitates the inward manifestations of his emotions, or tries to draw from himself the emotions of the perfected part, to "inspire" them within himself. But when forcing such an image by his own psychic equipment, with its unchanging organic laws, he by no means attains that desired result of artistic genius; he must present only the rough counterfeit of emotion, because emotions do not come to order. By no effort of conscious will can one awake them in oneself at a moment, nor can they ever be of use for creative genius striving to bring this about by searching the depths of its mind. A fundamental axiom, therefore, for the actor who wishes to be a real artist on the stage, may be stated thus: he must not play to produce emotions, and he must not involuntarily evoke them in himself.

*Activity of imagination*

Considerations on the nature of artistically gifted people, however, inevitably open up the road to the possession of the emotion of the part. This road traverses activity of imagination, which in most of its stages is subject to the action of consciousness. One must not suddenly begin to operate on emotion; one must put oneself in motion in the direction of artistic imagination, but imagination—as is also shown by observations of scientific psychology—disturbs our aberrant memory, and, luring from the hidden recesses beyond the boundaries of its sense of harmony whatever elements there may be of proved emotions, organizes them afresh in sympathy with those that have arisen in our imagery. So surrounded within our figures of imagination, without effort on our part, the answer to our aberrant memory is found and the sounds of sympathetic emotion are called out from us. This is why the creative imagination presents itself afresh, the indispensable gift of the actor. Without a well developed, mobile imagination, creative faculty is by no means possible, not by instinct nor intuition nor the aid of external technique. In the acquiring of it, that which has lain dormant in the mind of the artist is, when immersed in his sphere of unconscious imagery and emotion, completely harmonized within him.

This practical method for the artistic education of the actor, directed by means of his imagination to the storing up of affective memory, is sufficiently enlarged upon; his individual emotional experience, by its limits, actually leads to the restriction of the sphere of his creative genius, and does not allow him to play parts dissimilar to those of his psychic harmony. This opinion is fundamental for the clearing away of misunderstandings of those elements of reality from which are produced fictitious creations of imagination; these are also derived from organic experience, but a wealth and variety of these creations are only obtained by combinations drawn from a trial of elements. The musical scale has only its basic notes, the solar spectrum its radical colors, but the combination of sounds in music and of colors in painting are infinite. One can in the same way speak of radical emotions preserved in imaginative memory, just as the reception in imagination of outward harmony remains in the intellectual memory; the sum of these radical emotions in the inner experience of each person is limited, but the shades and combinations are as infinite as the combinations that create activity of imagination out of the elements of inward experience.

Certainly, but the actor's outward experience—*i.e.*, his sphere of vital sensations and reflections—must always be elastic, for only in that condition can the actor enlarge the sphere of his creative faculty. On the other hand, he must judiciously develop his imagination, harnessing it again and again to new propositions. But, in order that that imaginary union which is the actor's very foundation, produced by the creative genius of the dramatist, should take hold of him emotionally and lead him on to theatrical action, it is necessary that the actor should "swing toward" that union, as toward something as real as the union of reality surrounding him.

*The emotion of truth*

This does not mean that the actor must surrender himself on the stage to some such hallucination as that when playing he should lose the sense of reality around him, to take scenery for real trees, etc. On the contrary, some part of his senses must remain free from the grip of the play to control everything that he attempts and achieves as the performer of his part. He does not forget that surrounding him on the stage are decorations, scenery, etc., but they have no meaning for him. He says to himself, as it were: "I know that all around me on the stage is a rough counterfeit of reality. It is false. But if all should be real, see how I might be carried away to some such scene; then I would act." And at that instant, when there arises in his mind that artistic "suppose," encircling his real life, he loses interest in it, and is transported to another plane, created for him, of imaginary life. Restored to real life again, the actor must perforce modify the truth, as in the actual construction of his invention, so also in the survivals connected to it. His invention can be shown to be illogical, wide of the truth—and then he ceases to believe it. Emotion rises in him with invention; *i.e.*, his outward regard for imagined circumstances may be shown as "determined" without relation to the individual nature of a given emotion. Finally, in the expression of the outward life of his part, the actor, as a living complex emotion, never making use of sufficient perfection of all his bodily equipment, may give an untrue intonation, may not keep the artistic mean in gesticulation and may through the temptation of cheap effect drift into mannerism or awkwardness.

Only by a strongly developed sense of truth may he achieve a single inward beauty in which, unlike the conventional theatrical gestures and poses, the true condition of the character is expressed in every one of his attitudes and outward gestures.

The combination of all the above-named procedure and habits also composes the actor's external technique. Parallel with its development must go also the development of internal technique—the perfecting of that bodily equipment which serves for the incarnation of the theatrical image created by the actor, and the exact, clear expression of his external consciousness. With this aim in view the actor must work out within himself not only the ordinary flexibility and mobility of action, but also the particular consciousness that directs all his groups of muscles, and the ability to feel the energy transfused within him, which, arising from his highest creative centres, forms in a definite manner his mimicry and gestures, and, radiating from him, brings into the circle of its influence his partners on the stage and in the auditorium. The same growth of consciousness and fineness of internal feelings must be worked out by the actor in relation to his vocal equipment. Ordinary speech—as in life, so on the stage—is prosaic and monotonous; in it words sound disjointed, without any harmonious stringing together in a vocal melody as continuous as that of a violin, which by the hand of a master violinist can become fuller, deeper, finer and more transparent, and can without difficulty run from the higher to the lower notes and vice versa, and can alternate from pianissimo to forte. To counteract the wearisome monotony of reading, actors often elaborate, especially when declaiming poetry, with those artificial vocal *fioritures*, cadences and sudden raising and lowering of the voice, which are so characteristic of the conventional, pompous declamation, and which are not influenced by the corresponding emotion of the part, and therefore impress the more sensitive auditors with a feeling of unreality.

But there exists another natural musical sonorousness of speech, which we may see in great actors at the moment of their own true artistic elation, and which is closely knit to the internal sonorousness of their rôle. The actor must develop within himself this natural musical speech by practising his voice with due regard to his sense of reality, almost as much as a singer. At the same time he must perfect his elocution. It is possible to have a strong, flexible, impressive voice, and still distort speech, on the one hand by incorrect pronunciation, on the other by neglect of those almost imperceptible pauses and emphasis through which are attained the exact transmission of the sense of the sentence, and also its particular emotional coloring. In the perfect production of the dramatist, every word, every letter, every punctuation mark has its part in transmitting his inward reality; the actor in his interpretation of the play, according to his intelligence, introduces into each sentence his individual nuances, which must be transmitted not only by the motions of his body, but also by artistically developed speech. He must bear this in mind, that every sound which goes to make a word appears as a separate note, which has its part in the harmonious sound of the word, and which is the expression of one or other particle of the soul drawn out through the word. The perfecting, therefore, of the phonetics of speech cannot be limited to mechanical exercise of the vocal equipment, but must also be directed in such a way that the actor learns to feel each

*Internal technique*

separate sound in a word as an instrument of artistic expression. But in regard to the musical tone of the voice, freedom, elasticity, rhythm of movement and generally all external technique of dramatic art, to say nothing of internal technique, the present day actor is still on a low rung of the ladder of artistic culture, still far behind in this respect, from many causes, the masters of music, poetry and painting, with an almost infinite road of development to travel.

It is evident that under these conditions, the staging of a play, which will satisfy highly artistic demands, cannot be achieved at the speed that economic factors unfortunately make necessary in most theatres. This creative process, which every actor must go through, from his conception of the part to its artistic incarnation, is essentially very complicated, and is hampered by lack of perfection of outward and inward technique. It is also much hindered by the necessity of fitting in the actors one with another—the adjustment of their artistic individualities into an artistic whole.

*Production*    Responsibility for bringing about this accord, and the artistic integrity and expression of the performance rests with the theatre manager. During the period when the manager exercised a despotic rule in the theatre, a period starting with the Meiningen players and still in force even in many of the foremost theatres, the manager worked out in advance all the plans for staging a play, and, while certainly having regard to the existing cast, indicated to the actors the general outlines of the scenic effects, and the *mise-en-scène*. The writer also adhered to this system, but now he has come to the conclusion that the creative work of the manager must be done in collaboration with the actor's work, neither ignoring nor confirming it. To encourage the actor's creative genius, to control and adjust it, ensuring that this creative genius grows out of the unique artistic germ of the drama, as much as the external building up of the performance—that in the opinion of the writer is the problem of the theatre director to-day.

The joint work of the director and actor begins with the analysis of the drama and the discovery of its artistic germ, and with the investigation of its *transparent effect*. The next step is the discovery of the transparent effect of individual parts—of that fundamental will direction of each individual actor, which, organically derived from his character, determines his place in the general action of the play. If the actor cannot at once secure this transparent effect, then it must be traced bit by bit with the manager's aid—by dividing the part into sections corresponding to the separate stages of the life of the particular actor—from the separate problems developing before him in his struggle for the attainment of his goal. Each such section of a part of each problem, can, if necessary, be subjected to further psychological analysis, and sub-divided into problems even more detailed, corresponding to those separate mind actions of the performer out of which stage life is summed up. The actor must catch the *mind axes* of the emotions and temperaments, but not the emotions and temperaments that give color to these sections of the part. In other words, when studying each portion of his part, he must ask himself what he wants, what he requires as a performer of the play and which definite partial problem he is putting before himself at a given moment. The answer to this question should not be in the form of a noun, but rather of a verb: "I wish to obtain possession of the heart of this lady"—"I wish to enter her house"—"I wish to push aside the servants who are protecting her," etc. Formulated in this manner, the mind problem, of which the object and setting, thanks to the working of his creative imagination, are forming a brighter and clearer picture for the actor, begins to grip him and to excite him, extracting from the recesses of his working memory the combinations of emotions necessary to the part, of emotions that have an active character and mould themselves into dramatic action. In this way the different sections of the actor's part grow more lively and richer by degrees, owing to the involuntary play of the complicated organic survivals. By joining together and grafting these sections, the *score of the part* is formed; the scores of the separate parts, after the continual joint work of the actors during rehearsals and by the necessary adjustment of them one with another, are summed up in a single *score of the performance.*

*The score condensed*    Nevertheless, the work of the actors and manager is still unfinished. The actor is studying and living in the part and the play deeper and deeper still, finding their deeper artistic motives; so he lives in the score of his part still more profoundly. But the score of the part itself and of the play are actually subject by degrees during the work to further alterations. As in a perfect poetical production there are no superfluous words but only those necessary to the poet's artistic scheme, so in a score of the part there must not be a single superfluous emotion but only emotions necessary for the *transparent effect*. The score of each part must be condensed, as also the form of its transmitting, and bright, simple and compelling forms of its incarnation must be found. Only then, when in each actor every part not only organically ripens and comes to life but also all emotions are stripped of the superfluous, when they all crystallize and sum up into a live contact, when they harmonize amongst themselves in the general tune, rhythm and time of the performance, then the play may be presented to the public.

During repeated presentations the theatrical score of the play and each part remains in general unaltered. But that does not mean that from the moment the performance is shown to the public the actor's creative process is to be considered ended, and that there remains for him only the mechanical repetition of his achievement at the first presentation. On the contrary, every performance imposes on him creative conditions; all his psychical forces must take part in it, because only in these conditions can they creatively adapt the score of the part to those capricious changes which may develop in them from hour to hour, as in all living nervous creatures influencing one another by their emotions, and only then can they transmit to the spectator that invisible something, inexpressible in words, which forms the spiritual content of the play. And that is the whole origin of the substance of dramatic art.

As regards the outward arrangements of the play—scenery, theatrical properties, etc.—all are of value in so far as they correspond to the expression of dramatic action, *i.e.*, to the actors' talents; in no case may they claim to have an independent artistic importance in the theatre, although up to now they have been so considered by many great scene painters. The art of scene painting, as well as the music included in the play, is on the stage only an auxiliary art, and the manager's duty is to get from each what is necessary for the illumination of the play performed before an audience, while subordinating each to the problems of the actors.

---

*AN influential anthropologist, Victor Turner is known for his dramatistic theory of social action. In books like* The Ritual Process *(1969),* Dramas, Fields, and Metaphors *(1974), and* From Ritual to Theatre *(1982), Turner argued that many social events have a ritualized form, in which the structure of everyday life gives way to a "liminal" or threshold zone of freedom and license, before reintegrating the social group into an altered sense of social cohesion. In "Social Dramas and Stories About Them," Turner uses his research on the Ndembu tribe of Africa to develop a theory of the relationship between genres of social action and of stage action. Turner's evocation of the "liminal" dimension of ritual, and the more secularized "liminoid" quality of entertainment and recreation in postindustrial societies, has been widely applied in studies of performance and culture.*

## Victor Turner
(1920-1983)

"Social Dramas and Stories About Them"
(1982)

Anthropologists count and measure what they can in order to establish general features of the sociocultural fields they study. Although these activities have their irritating side, on the whole I found it eminently soothing, during my two and a half years of fieldwork among the Ndembu of northwestern Zambia, a West-Central Bantu-speaking people, to sit in villages before a calabash of millet or honey beer and collect numerical data on village membership, divorce frequency, bridewealth, labor migration rates, individual cash budgets, birth and homicide rates, and more strenuously to measure the acreage of gardens and dimensions of ritual enclosures. In a way these figures told me, if not a story, at least where to go to find stories. For I was able to infer from statistics based on censuses and genealogies of some seventy villages that these residential units consisted of cores of closely related male matrilineal kin, their wives and children, and sisters who as a result of frequent divorce had returned to their natal villages bringing their junior children with them. This was, of course, only the thin end of a massive wedge. I soon discovered that Ndembu married *virilocally*, that is, a woman goes after marriage to reside in her husband's village. Consequently, in the long run, village continuity depends upon marital discontinuity, since one's right to reside in a given village is primarily determined by matrilineal affiliation, though one may reside in one's father's village during his lifetime. Clearly a sort of structural turbulence is "built in" to these normative arrangements. For a village can only persist by recruiting widows, divorcees, and their children. There is also a propensity for men, who reside in their own matrilineal village, to persuade their sisters to leave their husbands, bringing with them the children who "properly belong" to that village. Political authority, chieftainship, headmanship, and other offices are in male hands, even in this matrilineal society: however, a man cannot be succeeded by his own son, but by his uterine brother or his sister's son. The chain of authority, therefore, demands that, sooner or later, a headman's sister's sons will leave their paternal villages and dwell with their maternal uncle. It is easier to do this if a young man is residing with his stepfather, not the father "who begat him." Thus divorce works in various ways to reassert the ultimate paramountcy of the maternal line, despite the masculine attempt to preempt the present through virilocal marriage. It is far from my mind to insist on the mysteries of anthropological terminology with the spiky cacophonies of its neologisms, no spikier, it may be said, than those of other academic tribes, but it is pertinent to my discussion of the varied valencies of narrative, to show how certain entrenched features of a given society's social structure influence both the course of conduct in observable social events and the scenarios of its genres of cultural performance—ranging from ritual to *märchen*. To complete the simplified picture of Ndembu social structure I should mention, however, that in several books (1957, 1967, 1968, 1969) I have tried to work out how stresses between matrilineal succession, and other principles and the processes to which they give rise, have affected various mundane and ritual phenomena, processes, and institutions of Ndembu society, such as village size, composition, mobility, fissiveness, marital stability, relations between and within genealogical generations, the role of the many situationally invoked cult associations in counterbalancing cleavages in villages, lineages and families, the strong masculine stress on complex hunting and circumcision rites in a system ultimately dependent on women's agricultural and food-processing activities, and the patterning of witchcraft accusations—which are often directed against matrilineal rivals for office or prestige.

I suppose that if I had confined myself to the analysis of numerical data, guided by knowledge of salient kinship principles and political, legal and economic contexts, I would have construed an anthropological narrative informed by what Hayden White (1973:16) in his book *Metahistory* surely would have called "mechanistic" presuppositions. Indeed, this was standard practice in the British School of structuralist-functionalist anthropology in which I was nurtured in the late forties and early fifties. One of its main aims was to exhibit the laws of structure and process which, in a given preliterate society, determine the specific configurations of relationships and institutions detectable by trained observation. The ultimate intent of this school, as formulated by Radcliffe-Brown, was by the comparative method to seek out general laws by successive approximation. Each specific ethnography sought for general principles that appeared in the study of a single society. In other words, idiographic procedures, detailed descriptions of what I actually observed or learned from informants, were pressed into the service of the development of laws. Hypotheses developed out of idiographic research were tested nomothetically, i.e., for the purpose of formulating general sociological laws.

There are, of course, many virtues in this approach. My figures *did* give me some measure of the relative importance of the principles on which Ndembu villages are socially constructed. They pointed to trends in the direction of individual and corporate spatial mobility. They indicated how in some areas particularly exposed to the modern cash economy, a smaller type of residential unit based on the polygynous family, called a "farm," was replacing the traditional circular village whose nucleus was a sibling group of matrilineal kin. The method I used was also employed by colleagues working from the Rhodes-Livingstone Institute and facilitated controlled comparison of village structures belonging to different Central African societies. Differences of kinship and local structures were compared with differences in such variables as the divorce rate, the amount of bridewealth, the mode of subsistence, and so forth.

Nevertheless, this approach has its limitations. As George Spindler (1978:31) has argued, "the idiography of ethnography may be distorted by the nomethetic orientation of the ethnographer." In other words, the general theory you take into the field leads you to select certain data for attention, but blinds you to others perhaps more important for the understanding of the people studied. As I came to know Ndembu well both in stressful and uneventful times as "men and women alive" (to paraphrase D. H. Lawrence), I become increasingly aware of this limitation. Long before I had read a word of Wilhelm Dilthey's I had shared his notion that "structures of experience" are fundamental units in the study of human action. Such structures are irrefrangibly threefold, being at once cognitive, conative, and affective. Each of these terms is itself, of course, a shorthand for a range of processes and capacities. Perhaps this view was influenced by Edward Sapir's celebrated essay in the *Journal of Social Psychology* (1934, 5:410–16), "Emergence of a Concept of Personality in a Study of Culture," in which he wrote: "In spite of the oft-asserted impersonality of culture, a humble truth remains that vast reaches of culture, far from being 'carried' by a group or community . . . are discovered only as the peculiar property of certain individuals, who cannot but give these cultural goods the impress of their own personality" (p. 412). Not only that, but persons will desire and feel as well as think, and their desires and feelings impregnate their thoughts and influence their intentions. Sapir assailed cultural overdeterminism as a reified cognitive construct of the anthropologist, whose "impersonalized" culture is hardly more than "an assembly of loosely overlapping ideas and action systems, which, through verbal habit, can be made to assume the appearance of a closed system of behavior" (p. 411), a position corresponding to some extent with Hayden White's organicist paradigm—as prestigious among American anthropologists as functionalism was among their British contemporaries. It became clear to me that an "anthropology of experience" would have to take into account the psychological properties of individuals as well as the culture which, as Sapir insists, is *never given* to each individual, but, rather, "gropingly discovered," and, I would add, some parts of it quite late in life. We never cease to learn our *own* culture, let alone other cultures, and our own culture is always changing. It also became clear that among the many tasks of the anthropologist lay the duty not only to make structuralist and functionalist analyses of statistical and textual data (censuses and myths), but also to prehend experiential structures in the actual processes of social life. Here my own approach, and that of many other anthropologists, conforms to some extent with White's contextualist model. White, using Pepper's term, sees contextualism as the isolation of some element of the historical field (or, in the anthropological instance, the sociocultural field) as the subject of study, "whether the element be as large as the French Revolution or as small as one day in the life of a specific person. The investigator then proceeds to pick out the 'threads' that link the event to be explained to different areas of the context. The threads are identified and traced outward, into the circumambient natural and social space in which the event occurred, and both backward in time, in order to determine the 'origins' of the event, and forward in time, in order to determine its 'impact' and 'influence' on subsequent events. This tracing operation ends at the point at which the 'threads' either disappear into the 'context' of some other 'event' or 'converge' to cause the occurrence of some new 'event.' The impulse is not to integrate *all* the events and trends that might be identified in the whole historical field, but rather to link them together in a chain of provisional and restricted characterizations of finite provinces of manifestly 'significant' occurrence" (pp. 18–19). It is interesting to pause here for a moment and compare how Sapir and White use the metaphor of "thread." For Sapir points out (op. cit., 411) that the "purely formalized and logically developed schemes" we call ethnographies do not explain behavior until "the *threads* [my emphasis] of symbolism and implication that connect patterns or parts of patterns with others, of an entirely different formal aspect" are discovered. For Sapir these "threads" are *internal* to the sociocultural space studied, and relate to the personality and temperament of individuals, while for White and Pepper, "threads" describe the nature of connections between an "element" or "event" and its significant *environing* sociocultural field viewed, according to White, "synchronically" or "structurally" (p. 19). I find fascinating Sapir's notion that his "threads" are *"symbolic"* and *"implicative";* for symbols, the spawn of such tropes as arise in the interaction of men and women alive, metaphors, synechdoches, metonymies new minted in crises, so to speak, really do come to serve as semiotic connectives among the levels and parts of a system of action and between that system and its significant environment. We have been neglecting the role of symbols in establishing connexity between the different levels of a narrative structure.

But I am anticipating. I shall shortly call attention to a kind or species of "element of the historical field" or "event," in White's terminology, which is cross-culturally isolable and which exhibits, if it is allowed to come to full term, a characteristic processual structure, a structure that holds firm whether one is considering a macro- or micro-historical event of this type. Before I discuss this unit, which I consider to be the social ground of many types of "narrative," and which I have called "social drama," I must first mention for the benefit of my non-anthropologist readers another useful distinction made by anthropologists, that between "emic" and "etic" perspectives, these terms being derived from the distinction made by linguists between *phonemic* and *phonetic,* the former being the study of sounds recognized as distinct *within* a specific language, the latter being the cross-lingual study of distinguishable human sound units. Kenneth Pike, who propounded this dichotomy, should be allowed to formulate it: "Descriptions of analyses from the etic standpoint are 'alien,' with criteria external to the system. Emic descriptions provide an internal view (or an 'inside view' in Hockett's terms), with criteria chosen from within the system. They represent to us the view of one familiar with this system and who knows how to function within it himself" (1954:8). From this standpoint all four of the strategies of explanation proposed by White drawing on Stephen Pepper—formism, organicism, mechanism, and contextualism—would produce "etic" narratives, if they were used to provide accounts of societies outside that Western cultural tradition generatively triangulated by the thinking of Jerusalem, Athens, and Rome, and continued in the philosophical, literary, and social-scientific traditions of Europe, North America, and their cultural offshoots. Indeed, members of such societies (the so-called "Third World") have protested (for example, the Ethiopian anthropologist, Asmarom Legesse, in *Gada,* 1973:283), that Western attempts to "explain" their cultures amount to no more than "cognitive ethnocentrism," diminishing their contribution to the global human reflexivity which modern communicational and informational systems are now making possible, if hardly easy. In other words, what we in the West consider "etic," that is, "nomothetic," "non-culture-bound," "scientific," "objective," they are coming to regard as "emic," the mental product of a portion of world-culture whose bearers could say, rather smugly, until very recently, with Thomas Hardy, but without a trace of his ironical intent, that "We have got the Gatling Gun, and they have not."

There are then *both* etic and emic ways of regarding narrative. An anthropologist, embedded in the life of an at-first-wholly-other culture and separated, save in memory, from his own, has to come to terms with that which invests and invades him. The situation is odd enough. He is tossed into the ongoing life of a parcel of people who not only speak a different language but also classify what we would call "social reality" in ways that are at first quite unexpected. He is compelled to learn, however haltingly, the criteria which provide the "inside view."

I am aware of Hayden White's "theory of the historical work," and that bears importantly upon how to write ethnographies as well as histories, but I am also aware that any discussion of the role of narrative in other cultures requires that an emic description of narrative be made. For the anthropologist's work is deeply involved in what *we* might call "tales," "stories," "folk-tales," "histories," "gossip," and "informants' accounts," types of narrative for which there may be many native names, not all of which coincide with our terms. Indeed, Max Gluckman has commented that the very term "anthropologist" means in Greek "one who talks about men," in other words, a "gossip." In our culture we have many ways of talking about men, descriptive and analytical, formal and informal, traditional and open-ended. Since ours is a literate culture, characterized by a refined division of cultural labor, we have devised numerous specialized genres by means of which we scan, describe, and interpret our behavior towards one another. But the impulse to talk about one another in different ways, in terms of different qualities and levels of mutual consciousness, precedes literacy in all human communities. All human acts and institutions are developed, as Clifford Geertz might say, in webs of interpretive words. Also, of course, we mime and dance one another— we have webs of interpretive nonverbal symbols. And we play one another—beginning as children, and continuing through life to learn new roles and the subcultures of higher statuses to which we aspire, partly seriously, partly ironically.

Ndembu make a distinction, akin to White's division between "chronicle" and "story" as levels of conceptualization in Western culture, between *nsang'u* and *kaheka*. *Nsang'u* may refer, for example, to a purportedly factual record of the migration of the Lunda chiefs and their followers from the Katanga region of Zaire on the Nkalanyi River, their encounter with the autochthonous Mbwela or Lukolwe peoples in Mwinilunga District, battles and marriages between Lunda and Mbwela, the establishment of Ndembu-Lunda chiefdoms, the order of chiefly incumbents down to the present (the praise-names and praise-songs for chiefs themselves amounting to a kind of chronicle), the raids of Luvale and Tchokwe in the nineteenth century to secure indentured labor for the Portuguese in San Tome long after the formal abolition of the slave trade, the coming of the missionaries, followed by the British South Africa Company, and finally British Colonial rule. *Nsang'u* may also denote an autobiographical account, a personal reminiscence, or an eye-witness report of yesterday's interesting happening. *Nsang'u*, like "chronicle," in White's words (*op. cit.:* 5) arranges "the events to be dealt with in the temporal order of their occurrence." Just as a chronicle becomes a "story," in White's usage, "by the further arrangement of the events into components of a 'spectacle' or process of happening, which is thought to possess a discernible beginning, middle, and end . . . in terms of inaugural motifs . . . transitional motifs . . . and terminal motifs," so does *nsang'u* become *kaheka*, chronicle becomes story. This term covers a range of tales which our folklorists would no doubt sort out into a number of "etic" types: myth, folktale, *märchen*, legend, ballad, folk epic, and the like. Their distinctive feature is that they are part told, part sung. At key points in the narration the audience joins in a sung refrain, breaking the spoken sequence. It depends on the context of situation and the mode of framing whether a given set of events is regarded as *nsang'u* or *kaheka*. Take, for example, the series of tales about the ancient Lunda chief Yala Mwaku, his daughter Lweji Ankonde, her lover the Luban hunter-prince Chibinda Ilung'a, and her brothers Ching'uli and Chinyama (I use the Southern Lunda pronunciation of these names), their loves, hates, conflicts and reconciliations, which led, on the one hand, to the establishment of the Lunda nation, and, on the other, to the secession and diaspora of dissident Lunda groups, thereby spreading knowledge of centralized political organization over a wide territory. This sequence may be told by a chief of putative Lunda origin in his court to politically influential visitors as an *nsang'u*, a "chronicle," perhaps to justify his title to his office. But episodes from this chronicle may be transformed into *tuheka* (plural of *kaheka*), "stories," and told by old women to groups of children huddled near the kitchen fire during the cold season. A particular favorite, analyzed recently by the distinguished Belgian structuralist Luc de Heusch in *Le Roi Ivre* relates how the drunken king Yala Mwaku was derided and beaten by his sons, but cared for tenderly by his daughter Lweji Ankonde, whom he rewarded by passing on to her, on his death, the royal bracelet, the *lukanu* (made of human genitalia for the magical maintenance of the fertility of humans, animals, and crops in the whole kingdom), thus rendering her the legitimate monarch of the Lunda. Another tells of how the young queen is told by her maidens that a handsome young hunter, having slain a waterbuck, had camped with his companions on the far side of the Nkalanye River. She summons him to her presence and the two fall in love at once and talk for many hours in a grove of trees (where today a sacred fire, the center of an extensive pilgrimage, burns constantly). She learns that he is the youngest son of a great Luba chief, but that he prefers the free life of a forest hunter to the court. Nevertheless, from love he marries Lweji, and, in time, receives from her the *lukanu*—she has to go into seclusion during menstruation and hands Chibinda the bracelet lest it become polluted—making him the ruler of the Lunda nation. Southern Lunda folk etymology even derives the term "Lunda" from the noun *Wulunda*, "love" or "close friendship." Lweji's turbulent brothers refuse to recognize him, and lead their people away to carve out new kingdoms for themselves and consequently spread the format of political centralization among stateless societies. Jan Vansina, the noted Belgian ethnohistorian, has discussed the relationship between this foundation narrative and the political structures of the many Central African societies who claim that they "came from Mwantiyanvwa," as the new dynasty came to call itself, in his book, *Kingdoms of the Savanna* (1966). He finds in his corpus of stories more than myth, although de Heusch has illuminatingly treated it as such; Vansina finds clues to historical affinities between the scattered societies who assert Lunda origin; indications corroborated by other types of evidence, linguistic, archaeological, and cultural. As in other cultures, the same events may be framed as *nsang'u* or *kaheka*, chronicle or story, often according to their nodal location in the life-process of the group or community that recounts them. It all depends where and when and by whom they are told. Thus, for some purposes the foundation tales of Yala Mwaku and Lweji are treated as chronicle, to advance a political claim, for example, to "Lundahood," as Ian Cunnison calls their assertion of descent from prestigious migrants. For the purpose of entertainment, in the village men's shelter in the evening or women's kitchens, the same tales are defined as "stories," with many rhetorical touches and flourishes as well as songs inserted as evocative embellishment. Incidents may even be cited during processes of litigation to legitimate or reinforce the claims of a plaintiff in a dispute over boundaries or succession to office.

For the anthropologist, however, who is concerned with the study of social action and social process, it is not these formal genres of tale-telling and tale-bearing that most grip his attention, but rather, as we have seen, what we would call "gossip," talk and rumors about the private affairs of others, what the Ndembu and their neighbors, the Luvale, call *kudiyongola,* related to the verb *kuyong'a,* "to crowd together," for much gossip takes place in the central, unwalled shelter of traditional villages, where the circumcised, hence socially "mature," males foregather, to discuss community affairs, and hear the "news" *(nsang'u)* of other communities from wayfarers. The critic Frank Kermode once defined the novel as consisting of two components: scandal and myth. Certainly gossip (which includes scandal) is one of the perennial sources of cultural genres. Gossip does not occur in a vacuum among the Ndembu; it is almost always "plugged in" to the unit of social process that I briefly described in the Introduction—the social drama.

Although it might be argued that the social drama is a "story" in Hayden White's sense, in that it has discernible inaugural, transitional, and terminal motifs, cultural markers that it has a beginning, a middle, and an end, my observations convince me that it is, indeed, a spontaneous unit of social process and a fact of everyone's experience in every human society. My hypothesis, based on repeated observations of such processual units in a range of sociocultural systems, and on my reading in ethnography and history, is that social dramas, "dramas of living," as Kenneth Burke calls them, can be aptly studied as having four phases. These I label: breach, crisis, redress, and *either* reintegration *or* recognition of schism. Social dramas occur within groups bounded by shared values and interests of persons and having a real or alleged common history. Their main actors are persons for whom the group which constitutes the field of dramatic action has a high value priority. Most of us have what I like to call our "star" group or groups to which we owe our deepest loyalty and whose fate is for us of the greatest personal concern. We are all members of many groups, formal or informal, from the family to the nation or some international religious or political institution. Each person makes his/her own subjective evaluation of their respective worth: some are "dear" to one, others it is one's "duty to defend," and so on. Some tragic situations arise from conflicts of loyalty to different "star" groups. A star group is the one with which a person identifies most deeply and in which he finds fulfillment of his major social and personal strivings and desires. There is no *objective* rank order in any culture for such groups. I have known academic colleagues whose supreme star group, believe it or not, was a particular faculty administrative committee, and whose families and recreational groups ranked much lower, others whose love and loyalty were towards the local Philatelic Society. In every culture one is *obliged* to belong to certain groups, usually institutionalized ones—family, age-set, school, firm, professional association, and the like. But such groups are not necessarily one's beloved chosen star groups. It is in one's star group that one looks most for love, recognition, prestige, office, and other tangible and intangible benefits and rewards. In it one achieves self-respect and a sense of belonging with others for whom one has respect. Now every objective group has members some of whom see it as their star group, while others may regard it with indifference, even dislike. Relations among the "star-groupers," as the first category may be called, are often highly ambivalent, resembling those among members of an elementary family for which, perhaps, the star group is an adult substitute. They recognize one another's common attachment to the group, but are jealous of one another over the relative intensity of that attachment or the esteem in which another member is held by the group as a whole. They may contend with each other for the incumbency of high office in the group, not merely to seek power but out of the conviction that they, and they alone, really understand the nature and value of the group and can altruistically advance its interests. In other words, we find symbolic equivalents of sibling rivalry and parent-child competition among "star-groupers."

In several books (1957, 1967, 1968, 1974) I have discussed social dramas at some length, both in small-scale societies, such as Ndembu, at the village level, and on the scale of complex nations, as in the power struggle between Henry II of England and Archbishop Thomas Becket and the Hidalgo Insurrection in early nineteenth century Mexico. Whether it is large affair, like the Dreyfuss Case or Watergate, or a struggle for village headmanship, a social drama first manifests itself as the breach of a norm, the infraction of a rule of morality, law, custom or etiquette in some public arena. This breach may be deliberately, even calculatedly, contrived by a person or party disposed to demonstrate or challenge entrenched authority—for example, the Boston Tea Party—or it may emerge from a scene of heated feelings. Once visible, it can hardly be revoked. Whatever the case, a mounting crisis follows, a momentous juncture or turning point in the relations between components of a social field—at which seeming peace becomes overt conflict and covert antagonisms become visible. Sides are taken, factions are formed, and unless the conflict can be sealed off quickly within a limited area of social interaction, there is a tendency for the breach to widen and spread until it coincides with some dominant cleavage in the widest set of relevant social relations to which the parties in conflict belong. We have seen this process at work in the Iranian crisis following the breach precipitated by the seizure of the U.S. Embassy in Teheran. The phase of crisis exposes the pattern of current factional struggle within the relevant social group, be it village or world community; and beneath it there becomes slowly visible the less plastic, more durable, but nevertheless gradually changing basic social structure, made up of relations which are relatively constant and consistent. For example, I found that among the Ndembu, prolonged social dramas always revealed the related sets of oppositions that give Ndembu social structure its tensile character: matriliny versus virilocality; the ambitious individual versus the wider interlinking of matrilineal kin; the elementary family versus the uterine sibling group (children of one mother); the forwardness of youth versus the domineering elders; status-seeking versus responsibility; sorcerism (*wuloji*)—that is, hostile feelings, grudges, and intrigues—versus friendly respect and generosity towards others. In the Iranian crisis we saw the emergence to public visibility of divisions and coalitions of interests, some of which are surprising and revelatory. Love may be "a many splendored thing," but crisis is certainly a "many-levelled thing" in all cultures. In social dramas, false friendship is winnowed from true communality of interests; the limits of consensus are reached and realized; real power emerges from behind the facade of authority.

In order to limit the contagious spread of *breach* certain adjustive and redressive mechanisms, informal and formal, are brought into operation by leading members of the disturbed group. These mechanisms vary in character with such factors as the depth and significance of the breach, the social inclusiveness of the crisis, the nature of the social group within which the breach took place, and its degree of autonomy in regard to wider systems of social relations. The mechanisms may range from personal advice and informal arbitration, to formal juridical and legal machinery, and to resolve certain kinds of crisis, to the performance of public ritual. Such ritual involves a "sacrifice," literal or moral, a victim as scapegoat for the group's "sin" of redressive violence.

The final phase consists either in the reintegration of the disturbed social group—though, as like as not, the scope and range of its relational field will have altered; the number of its parts will be different; and their size and influence will have changed—or the social recognition of irreparable breach between the contesting parties, sometimes leading to their spatial separation. This may be on the scale of the many Exoduses of history or merely a move of disgruntled villagers to a spot a few miles away. This phase, too, may be registered by a public ceremony or ritual, indicating reconciliation or permanent cleavage between the parties involved.

I am well aware that the social drama is an agonistic model drawn after a recurrent agonistic situation, and I make no claim that there are no other types of processual unit. Gulliver, for example, studying another Central African society, the Ndendeuli of Tanzania, directs attention to the cumulative effect of an endless series of minor incidents, cases, and events that might be quite as significant in affecting and changing social relationships as the more overtly dramatic encounters. Raymond Firth discusses "harmonic" processual units—which I call "social enterprises" that also have recognizable phase structure. These stress "the process of ordering of action and of relations in reference to given social ends" and are often economic in type. Quite often, though, such "enterprises"—as in the case of urban renewal in America—become social dramas, if there is resistance to the aims of their instigators. The resisters perceive the inauguration of the enterprise as "breach," not "progress." Nor does the course of a social drama—like "true love"—always "run smooth." Redressive procedures may break down, with reversion to crisis. Traditional machinery of conciliation or coercion may prove inadequate to cope with new types of issues and problems, and new roles and statuses. And, of course, reconciliation may only seem to have been achieved in phase four, with real conflicts glossed over but not resolved. Moreover, at certain historical junctures in large-scale complex societies, redress may be through rebellion, or even revolution, if the societal value-consensus has broken down, and new unprecedented roles, relationships, and classes have emerged.

Nevertheless, I would persist in arguing that the social drama is a well-nigh universal processual form, and represents a perpetual challenge to all aspirations to perfection in social and political organization. In some cultures its profile is clear-cut and style abrasive: in others, agonistic (contestative) action may be muted or deflected by elaborate codes of etiquette. In yet others conflict may be—to cite Richard Antoun on Arab village politics in Jordan—"low-key," eschewing direct confrontation and encounter in its style. Social dramas are in large measure political processes, that is, they involve competition for scarce ends—power, dignity, prestige, honor, purity—by particular means and by the utilization of resources that are also scarce—goods, territory, money, men and women. Ends, means, and resources are caught up in an interdependent feedback process. Some kinds of resources, for example, land, money, may be converted into others, for instance, honor and prestige (which are simultaneously the needs sought). Or they may be employed to stigmatize rivals and deny them these ends. According to my observations, the political aspect of social dramas is dominated by those I have called "star-groupers." They are the main protagonists, the leaders of factions, the defenders of the faith, the revolutionary vanguard, the arch-reformers. These are the ones who develop to an art the rhetoric of persuasion and influence, who know how and when to apply pressure and force, and are most sensitive to the factors of legitimacy. In Phase Three, redress, the the "star-groupers" who manipulate the machinery of redress, the lawcourts, the procedures of divination and ritual, and impose sanctions on those adjudged to have precipitated crisis, just as it may well be disgruntled or dissident star-groupers who lead rebellions and provoke the initial breach.

The fact that a social drama, as I have analyzed its form, closely corresponds to Aristotle's description of tragedy in the *Poetics,* in that it is "the imitation of an action that is complete, and whole, and of a certain magnitude . . . having a beginning, a middle, and an end," is not, I repeat, because I have tried inappropriately to impose an "etic" Western model of stage action upon the conduct of an African village society, but because there is an interdependent, perhaps dialectic, relationship between social dramas and genres of cultural performance in perhaps all societies. Life, after all, is as much an imitation of art as the reverse. Those who, as children in Ndembu society, have listened to innumerable stories about Yala Mwaku and Luweji Ankonde, know all about "inaugural motifs"—"when the king was drunk and helpless, his sons beat and reviled him"—"transitional" motifs—"his daughter found him near death and comforted and tended him"—and "terminal" motifs—"the king gave his daughter the *lukanu* and excluded his sons from the royal succession." When these same Ndembu, now full-grown, wish to provoke a breach or to claim that some party has crucially disturbed the placid social order, they have a frame available to "inaugurate" a social drama, with a repertoire of "transitional" and "ending" motifs to continue the framing process and channel the subsequent agonistic developments. Just as the story itself still makes important points about family relationships and about the stresses between sex- and age-roles, and appears to be an emic generalization, clothed in metaphor and involving the projection of innumerable specific social dramas generated by these structural tensions, so does it feed back into the social process, providing it with a rhetoric, a mode of employment, and a meaning. Some genres, particularly epic, serve as paradigms which inform the action of important political leaders—stargroupers of encompassing groups such as Church or State—giving them style, direction, and sometimes compelling them subliminally to follow in major public crisis a certain course of action, thus emplotting their lives. I tried to show in *Dramas, Fields, and Metaphors* (1975: chapter 2) how Thomas Becket, after his antagonistic confrontation with both Henry II and the bench of Bishops at the Council of Northampton, seemed to have been almost "taken over," "possessed" by the action-paradigm provided by the *Via Crucis* in Christian belief and ritual, sealing his love-hate relationship with Henry in the conjoined image of martyr and martyrizer—and giving rise to a subsequent host of narratives and aesthetic dramas. By paradigm I do not mean a system of univocal concepts, logically arrayed. I do not mean either a stereotyped set of guidelines for ethical, aesthetic, or conventional action. A paradigm of this sort goes beyond the cognitive and even the moral to the existential domain; and in so doing becomes clothed with allusiveness, implications, and metaphor—for in the stress of action, firm definitional outlines become blurred by the encounter of emotionally charged wills. Paradigms of this type, cultural root paradigms, so to speak, reach down to irreducible life stances of individuals, passing beneath conscious prehension to a fiduciary hold on what they sense to be axiomatic values, matters literally of life and death. Richard Schechner (1977) has sought to express the relationship between social drama and aesthetic or staged drama in the form of a figure eight placed in a horizontal position and then bisected through both loops:

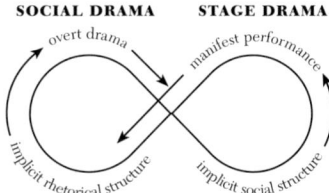

**SOCIAL DRAMA**    **STAGE DRAMA**

overt drama    manifest performance

implicit rhetorical structure    implicit social structure

The left loop represents the social drama; above the line is the overt drama, below it, the implicit rhetorical structure; the right loop represents stage drama; above the line is the manifest performance, below it, the implicit social process, with its structural contradictions. Arrows pointing from left to right represent the course of action. They follow the phases of the social drama above the line in the left loop, descending to cross into the lower half of the right loop where they represent the hidden social infrastructures. The arrows then ascend and, moving now from right to left, pass through the successive phases of a generalized stage drama. At the point of intersection between the two loops, they descend once more to form the hidden aesthetic model underpinning, so to speak, the overt social drama. This model, though effective, is somewhat equilibrist in its implications for my taste, and suggests cyclical rather than linear movement. But it has the merit of pointing up the dynamical relation between social drama and expressive cultural genres. The social drama of Watergate was full of "*stage* business" during every phase, from the Guy Fawkes-like conspiratorial atmosphere of the "breach" episode, signalized by the finding of the incriminating tape of the door, through the tough minded fictionality of the cover-up, and all that went into the "crisis" phase of investigation, with its Deep Throat revelations and combinations of high-minded principle and low-minded political opportunism. The redressive phase was no less implicitly scripted by theatrical and fictional models. I need not describe the Hearings and the Saturday Night Massacre. Now we have plays, films, and novels about Watergate and its *dramatis personae naturalis,* which are shaped—to use the aseptic language of social science—in accord with the structure and properties of the social field environing and penetrating their authors at the time of writing. At the deepest level we may anticipate an interpretive shift towards accommodation of the most acceptable texts to some deeply entrenched paradigm of Americanity. The American "myth," as Sacvan Bercovitch has argued in his book *The American Jeremiad* (1978), periodically produces "jeremiads" (polemical homilies in various cultural genres) against declension into ways of life which reek of the static, corrupt, hierarchical Old World, and obviate movement towards an ever receding but ultimately reachable promised land to be craved from some unsullied wilderness, where an ideal, prosperous democracy can thrive "under God." Watergate is a superb target for the American jeremiad. Paradoxically, many of its personages have become celebrities, but this may not be so surprising after all. Pontius Pilate was canonized by the Ethiopean Church, and if Dean and Ehrlichman will never perhaps be seen as saints, their mere participation in a drama which activated a major cultural paradigm has conferred on them an ambiguous eminence they might otherwise have never achieved. The winners of social dramas positively require cultural performances to continue to legitimate their success. And such dramas generate their "symbolic types" (R. Grathoff, 1970; Don Handelman, 1979): traitors, renegades, villains, martyrs, heroes, faithful, infidels, deceivers, scapegoats. Just to be in the cast of a narrated drama which comes to be taken as exemplary or paradigmatic is some assurance of social immortality.

It is the third phase of a social drama, redress, that has most to do with the genesis and sustentation of cultural genres, both "high" and "folk," oral and literate. In *Schism and Continuity,* I argued that in Ndembu society when conflict emerges from the opposed interests and claims of protagonists acting under a single social principle, say, descent from a common ancestress, judicial institutions can be invoked to meet the crisis, for a rational attempt can be made to adjust claims that are similarly based. But when claims are advanced under different social principles, which are inconsistent with one another even to the point of mutual contradiction, there can be no rational settlement. Here Ndembu have recourse to divination of sorcery or ancestral wrath to account for misfortune, illness, or death occurring before or during the social drama. Ultimately, rituals of reconciliation may be performed, which, in their verbal and nonverbal symbolism, reassert and re-animate the overarching values shared by all Ndembu, despite conflicts of norms and interests on ground level.

Whether juridical or ritual processes of redress are invoked against mounting crisis, the result is an increase in what one might call social or plural *reflexivity,* the ways in which a group tries to scrutinize, portray, understand, and then act on itself. Barbara Myerhoff has written of cultural performances ("Life History Among the Elderly: Performance, Visibility, and Remembering," n.d., p. 5) that they are "*reflective* in the sense of showing ourselves to ourselves. They are also capable of being *reflexive,* arousing consciousness of ourselves as we see ourselves. As heroes in our own dramas, we are made self aware, conscious of our consciousness. At once actor and audience, we may then come into the fullness of our human capability—and perhaps human desire to watch ourselves and enjoy knowing that we know." I tend to regard the social drama in its full formal development, its full phase structure, as a process of converting particular values and ends, distributed over a range of actors, into a system (which is always temporary and provisional) of shared or consensual meaning. It has not yet reached the stage of Myerhoff's enjoying that we know that we know ourselves, but it is a step in that direction. I am inclined to agree with Wilhelm Dilthey (see H. Hodges, 1952:272–3) that *meaning (Bedeutung)* arises in *memory,* in *cognition* of the *past,* and is concerned with negotiation about the "fit" between past and present, whereas *value (Wert)* inheres in the affective enjoyment of the *present,* while the category of *end (Zweck)* or *good (Gut)* arises from *volition,* the power or faculty of using the will, which refers to the *future.* The redressive phase, in which feedback on crisis is provided by the scanning devices of law (secular ritual) and religious ritual, is a liminal time, set apart from the ongoing business of quotidian life, when an interpretation *(Bedeutung)* is constructed to give the appearance of sense and order to the events leading up to and constituting the crisis. It is only the category of meaning, so Dilthey tells us, that enables us to conceive of an intrinsic affinity between the successive events of life, or, one might add, of a social drama. In the redressive phase the meaning of the social life informs the apprehension of itself, while the object to be apprehended enters into and reshapes the apprehending subject. Pure anthropological functionalism, whose aim is to state the conditions of social equilibrium among the components of a social system at a given time, cannot deal with meaning, for meaning always involves retrospection and reflexivity, a past, a history. Meaning is the only category which grasps the full relation of the part to the whole in life, for value, being dominantly affective, belongs essentially to an experience in a conscious present. Such conscious presents, regarded purely as present moments, totally involve the experiencer, even to the extent that they have no intrinsic connection with one another, at least of a systematic, cognitive kind. They stand behind one another in temporal sequence, and, while they may be compared as "values," that is, as having the same epistemological status, they do not form anything like a coherent whole, for they are essentially momentary, transient, insofar as they are values alone; if they are interconnected, the ligatures that bind them belong to another category—that of *meaning,* reflexivity arrived at. In stage drama, values would be the province of actors, meaning that of the producer. Values exist in what Csikszentmihalyi would call the state of "flow." Reflexivity tends to inhibit flow, for it articulates experience. Dilthey eloquently hits off the unarticulated quality of value: "From the standpoint of value, life appears as an infinite assortment of positive and negative existence-values. It is like a chaos of harmonies and discords. Each of these is a tone-structure which fills a present; but they have *no musical relation* to one another" [my emphasis]. To establish such a musical relation, the liminal reflexivity of the redressive phase is necessary if crisis is to be rendered meaningful. Crises are "like a chaos of harmonies and discords." Some modern modalities of music, I think, try to replicate this chaos, let it stand as it is—for the meaning-ligatures inherited from the past no longer bind. Here we must return to narrative.

For both the legal and ritual procedures generate *narratives* from the brute facts, the mere empirical coexistence of experiences, and endeavor to lay hold of the factors making for integration in a given situation. Meaning is apprehended by *looking back* over a temporal process: it is generated in the "narrative" constructed by lawmen and judges in the process of cross-examination from witnesses' evidence, or by diviners from their intuitions into the responses of their clients as framed by their specific hermeneutic techniques. The meaning of every part of the process is assessed by its contribution to the total result.

It will be noted that my basic social drama is agonistic, rife with problem and conflict, and this is not merely because it assumes that sociocultural systems are never logical systems or harmonious *gestalten,* but are fraught with structural contradictions and norm-conflicts. The true opposition should not be defined in these "objectivized" terms. It is between indeterminacy and all modes of determination. Indeterminacy is, so to speak, in the "subjunctive mood," since it is that which is not yet settled, concluded, and known. It is all that may be, might be, could be, perhaps even should be. It is that which terrifies in the breach and crisis phases of a social drama. Sally Falk Moore goes so far as to suggest that "the underlying quality of social life should be considered to be one of theoretical absolute indeterminacy" (1978:48). Social reality is "fluid and indeterminate," though, for her, "regularizing processes" and "processes of situational adjustment," represent human aspirations constantly to transform it into organized or systematic forms. But even where ordering rules and customs are strongly sanctioned, "indeterminacy may be produced and ambiguities within the universe of relatively determinate elements." Such manipulation is characteristic of breach and crisis. It may also help to resolve crisis. The third phase, redress, reveals that "determining" and "fixing" are indeed processes, not permanent states or givens. They proceed by assigning meanings to events and relationships in reflexive narratives. Indeterminacy should not be regarded as the absence of social being; it is not negation, emptiness, privation. Rather it is potentiality, the possibility of becoming. From this point of view social being is finitude, limitation, constraint. Actually it only "exists" as a set of cognitive models in actors' heads or as more or less coherent "objectivized" doctrines and protocols. Ritual and legal procedures mediate between the formed and the indeterminate. As Moore argues, "ritual is a declaration of form against indeterminacy, *therefore* indeterminacy is always present in the background of any analysis of ritual." In 1979 I attended several sessions of the *Umbanda* religion at a cult center *(terreiro)* in Rio de Janeiro and found that the medium-possessing *Orixa* or Entity known as *Exu,* of West African Yoruba origin, where he is the Trickster deity of the Crossroads, in several ways personifies this "meonic" (to use Nicholas Berdyaev's term) indeterminacy. He is sometimes represented on Umbanist altars as a being *(Entitade)* with two heads: one face is that of Christ, the other, Satan's. *Exu,* whose ritual colors are black and red, is the Lord of the Limen and of Chaos, the full ambiguity of the subjunctive mood of culture, representing the indeterminacy that lurks in the cracks and crevices of all sociocultural "constructions of reality," the one who must be kept at bay if the framed formal order of the ritual proceedings is to go forward according to protocol. He is the abyss of possibility; hence his two heads, for he is both potential savior and tempter. He is also destroyer, for in one of his modes he is Lord of the Cemetery. Like Shiva, Creator and Destroyer, he wields a trident. One may see his image and sign in New York and Montreal, if one scans carefully the costumes (known as "fantasies") of the Caribbean *Mardi Gras* carnivals—for he is worshipped in Cuban and Puerto Rican *Santeria* religion, as well as in Brazilian *Candomble* and *Umbanda.* In all major cultural process, from ritual to theatre and the novel, of any complexity of meaning, there are both "sequence and secrets"—to quote Kermode again—"secrets" are those non-sequential bits of creative indeterminacy which get into, and apparently seem to foul up all coherent protocols, scripts, texts, whatsoever little hints of the abyss of subjunctivity, that break in and out like *Exu* and threaten the measured movement towards climax on cultural terms.

The social drama, then, I regard as the experiential matrix from which the many genres of cultural performance, beginning with redressive ritual and juridical procedures, and eventually including oral and literary narrative, have been generated. Breach, crisis, and reintegrative or divisive outcomes provide the content of such later genres, redressive procedures their form. As society complexifies, as the division of labor produces more and more specialized and professionalized modalities of sociocultural action, so do the modes of assigning meaning to social dramas multiply—but the drama remains to the last simple and ineradicable, a fact of everyone's social experience, and a significant node in the developmental cycle of all groups that aspire to continuance. The social drama remains humankind's thorny problem, its undying worm, its Achilles' heel—one can only use cliches for such an obvious and familiar pattern of sequentiality. At the same time it is our native way of manifesting ourselves to ourselves and, of declaring where power and meaning lie and how they are distributed.

In *The Ritual Process* and in these essays, I have discussed van Gennep's discovery of the processual form of the *rite de passage,* and will refer to it again shortly. Rites of passage, like social dramas, involve temporal processes and agonistic relations—novices or initiands are separated (sometimes real or symbolic force is used) from a previous social state or status, compelled to remain in seclusion during the liminal phase, submitted to ordeal by initiated seniors or elders, and re-aggregated to quotidian society in symbolic ways that often show that preritual ties have been irremediably broken and new relationships rendered compulsory. But, like other kinds of rituals, life-crisis rituals, the most transformative kind of rites of passage, already exhibit a marked degree of generalization—they are the fairly late product of social reflexivity. They confer on the actors, by nonverbal as well as verbal means, the experiential understanding that social life is a series of movements in space and time, a series of changes of activity, and a series of transitions in status for individuals. They also inscribe in them the knowledge that such movements, changes, and transitions are not merely marked but also effected by ritual. Ritual and juridical procedures represent germinative components of social drama, from which, I suggest, many performative and narrative modes of complex culture derive. Cultural performances may be viewed as "dialectical dancing partners" (to use Ronald Grimes's phrase) of the perennial social drama, to which they give meaning appropriate to the specificities of time, place, and culture. However, they have their own autonomy and momentum; one genre may generate another; with sufficient evidence in certain cultural traditions one might be able to reconstruct a reasonably accurate genealogy of genres. (I use advisedly these terms derived from the Indo-European root *gan,* "to beget or produce," as metaphors for their ready cultural reproductiveness.) Or one genre might supplant or replace another as the historically or situationally dominant form "social metacommentary" (to use Geertz's illuminating term). New communicative techniques and media may make possible wholly unprecedented genres of cultural performance, making possible new modes of self-understanding. Once a genre has become prominent, however, it is likely to survive or be revived at some level of the sociocultural system, perhaps moving from the elite to the popular culture or vice-versa, gaining and losing audiences and support in the process. Nevertheless, all the genres have to circle, as it were, around the earth of the social drama, and some, like satellites, may exert tidal effects on its inner structure. Since ritual in the so-called "simpler" societies is so complex and many-layered it may not unfittingly be considered an important "source" of later (in cultural evolutionary terms), more specialized, performative genres. Often when ritual perishes as a dominant genre, it dies, a *multipara,* giving birth to ritualized progeny, including the many performative arts.

In earlier publications I defined "ritual" as "prescribed formal behavior for occasions not given over to technological routine, having reference to beliefs in invisible beings or powers regarded as the first and final causes of all effects"—a definition which owes much to those of Auguste Comte, Godfrey and Monica Wilson, and Ruth Benedict. I still find this formulation operationally useful despite Sir Edmund Leach, and other anthropologists of his ilk, who would eliminate the religious component and regard ritual as "stereotyped behavior which is potent in itself in terms of the cultural conventions of the actors, though not potent in a rational technical sense," and which serves to communicate information about a culture's most cherished values. I find it useful, because I like to think of ritual essentially as *performance, enactment,* not primarily as rules or rubrics. The rules "frame" the ritual process, but the ritual process transcends its frame. A river needs banks or it will be a dangerous flood, but banks without a river epitomize aridity. The term "performance" is, of course, derived from Old English *parfournir,* literally "to furnish completely or thoroughly." To perform is thus to bring something about, to consummate something, or to *"carry out"* a play, order, or project. But in the "carrying out," I hold, something new may be generated. The performance transforms itself. True, as I said, the rules may "frame" the performance, but the "flow" of action and interaction within that frame may conduce to hitherto unprecedented insights and even generate new symbols and meanings, which may be incorporated into subsequent performances. Traditional framings may have to be reframed—new bottles made for new wine. It is here that I find the notion of orientation to preternatural and invisible beings and powers singularly apposite. For there is undoubtable transformative capacity in a well-performed ritual, implying an ingress of power into the initial situation; and "performing well" implies the co-involvement of the majority of its performers in a self-transcending flow of ritual events. The power may be drawn from the persons of the drama, but drawn from their human depths, not entirely from their cognitive, "indicative" hold on cultural skills. Even if a rubrical book exists prescribing the order and character of the performance of the rites, this should be seen as a source of channelings, rather than of dictates. The experience of subjective and intersubjective flow in ritual performance, whatever its sociobiological or personalogical concomitants may be, often convinces performers that the ritual situation *is* indeed informed with powers both transcendental and immanent. Moreover, most anthropological definitions of ritual, including my own earlier attempts, have failed to take into account van Gennep's discovery that rituals nearly always "accompany transitions from one situation to another and from one cosmic or social world to another" (*Les Rites de Passage*, p. 13). As is well known he divides these rituals into rites of separation, threshold rites, and rites of re-aggregation, for which he also employs the terms preliminal, liminal, and postliminal. The order in which the ritual events follow one another and must be performed, van Gennep points out, is a religious element of essential importance. To exist at all, writes Nicole Belmont about van Gennep's notion, "a ritual must first and foremost be inscribed in time and space, or rather reinscribed" if it follows a prior model given in myth (*Arnold Van Gennep: The Creator of French Ethnography*, 1979:64). In other words, performative *sequencing* is intrinsic and should be taken into account in any definition of ritual. Here I would query the formal structuralist implication that sequence is an illusion and all is but a permutation and combination of rules and vocabularies already laid down in the deep structures of mind and brain. There *is* a qualitative distinction between successive stages in social dramas and rites of passage which renders them irreversible—their sequence is no illusion—the unidirectional movement is transformative. I have written at some length about the "threshold" or liminal phase of ritual, and found it fruitful to extend the notion of liminality as metaphor to other domains of expressive cultural action than ritual. But liminality must be taken into account in any serious formulation of ritual as performance, for it is in connection with this phase that "emic" folk characterizations of ritual lay strongest stress on the transformative action of "invisible or supernatural beings or powers regarded as the first and final causes of all effects." Without taking liminality into account ritual becomes indistinguishable from "ceremony," "formality," or what Barbara Myerhoff and Sally Moore, in their Introduction to *Secular Ritual* (1977) indeed call "*secular*" ritual." The liminal phase is the essential, *anti*-secular component in ritual *per se*, whether it be labeled "religious" or "magical." Ceremony *indicates*, ritual *transforms*, and transformation occurs most radically in the ritual "pupation" of liminal seclusion—at least in life-crisis rituals. The public liminality of great seasonal feasts exhibits its fantasies and "transforms" (akin here to the linguistic sense of "transform," that is, [a] any of a set of rules for producing grammatical transformations of a kernel sentence; [b] a sentence produced by using such a role) to the eyes of all—and so does postmodern theatre—but that is a matter for a different paper.

I have also argued that ritual in its performative plenitude in tribal and many post-tribal cultures is a matrix from which several other genres of cultural performance, including most of those we tend to think of as "aesthetic" have been derived. It is a late modern Western myth, encouraged perhaps by depth psychologists, and, lately by ethnologists, that ritual has the rigid precision characteristics of the "ritualized" behavior of an obsessive neurotic, or a territory-marking animal or bird, and also encouraged by an early modern Puritan myth that ritual is "mere empty form without true religious content." It is true that rituals may become mere shells or husks at certain historical junctures, but this state of affairs belongs to the senescence or pathology of the ritual process, not to its "normal working." Living ritual may be better likened to artwork than neurosis. Ritual is, in its most typical cross-cultural expressions, a synchronization of many performative genres, and is often ordered by *dramatic* structure, a plot, frequently involving an act of sacrifice or self-sacrifice, which energizes and gives emotional coloring to the interdependent communicative codes which express in manifold ways the meaning inherent in the dramatic *leitmotiv*. In so far as it is "dramatic," ritual contains a distanced and generalized reduplication of the agonistic process of the social drama. Ritual, therefore, is not "threadbare" but "richly textured" by virtue of its varied interweavings of the productions of mind and senses. Participants in the major rituals of vital religions, whether tribal or post-tribal, may be passive and active in turn with regard to the ritual movement, which as van Gennep, and, more recently, Roland Delattre, have shown, draws on biological, climatic, and ecological rhythms, as well as on social rhythms, as models for the processual forms it sequentially employs in its episodic structure. *All* the senses of participants and performers may be engaged; they *hear* music and prayers, *see* visual symbols, *taste* consecrated foods, *smell* incense, and *touch* sacred persons and objects. They also have available the kinesthetic forms of dance and gesture, and perhaps cultural repertoires of facial expression, to bring them into significant performative rapport. Here I should mention in this connection Judith Lynne Hanna's useful book *To Dance is Human: A Theory of Nonverbal Communication* (1979) in which she attempts to construct a sociocultural theory of dance. In song, participants merge (and diverge) in other ordered and symbolic ways. Moreover, few rituals are so completely stereotyped that every word, every gesture, every scene is authoritatively prescribed. Most often, invariant phases and episodes are interdigitated with variable passages, in which, both at the verbal and nonverbal levels, improvisation may not be merely permitted but required. Like the black and white keys of a piano, like the *Yin* and *Yang* interplay in Chinese religious cosmology and Taoist ritual, constancy and mutability make up, in their contrariety, a total instrument for the expression of human meaning, joyous, sorrowful, and both at once, "woven fine," in William Blake's words. Ritual, in fact, far from being merely formal, or formulaic, is a symphony in more than music. It can be—and often is—a symphony or synaesthestic ensemble of expressive cultural genres, or, a synergy of varied symbolic operations, an opus which unlike "opera" (also a multiplicity of genres as Wagner repeatedly emphasized) escapes opera's theatricality, though never life's inexpugnable social drama, by virtue of the seriousness of its ultimate concerns. The "flat" view of ritual must go. So also must the notion, beloved until recently by functionalist anthropologists, that ritual could be best understood as a set of mechanism for promoting a gross group solidarity, as, in fact, a "sort of all-purpose social glue," as Robin Horton characterized this position, and that its symbols were merely "reflections or expressions of components of social structure." Ritual, in its full performative flow, is not only many-leveled, "laminated," but also capable, under conditions of societal change, of creative modification on all or any of its levels. Since it is tacitly held to communicate the deepest values of the group regularly performing it, it has a *"paradigmatic"* function, in both of the senses argued for by Clifford Geertz. As a *"model for"* ritual can anticipate, even generate change; as a *"model of,"* it may inscribe order in the minds, hearts, and wills of participants.

Ritual, in other words, is not only complex and many-layered; it has an *abyss* in it, and indeed, is an effort to make meaningful the dialectical relation of what the Silesian mystic Jakob Boehme, following Meister Eckhart, called "Ground" and "Underground," "Byss and Abyss" ( = the Greek *a-bussos*, ʼαβυσσοσ, from a-"without," and the Ionic variant of the Attic *buthos*, βʹυθοσ, meaning "bottom," or, better, [finite] "depth," especially "of the sea." So "byss" is deep but "abyss" is beyond all depth.) Many definitions of ritual contain the notion of *depth,* but few of *infinite* depth. In the terminology I favor, such definitions are concerned with finite structural depth, not with infinite "antistructural" depth. A homelier analogy, drawn from linguistics, would be to say that the passage form of ritual, as elicited by van Gennep, postulates a unidirectional move from the *"indicative"* mood of cultural process, through culture's *"subjunctive"* mood back to the *"indicative"* mood, though this recovered mood has now been tempered, even transformed, by immersion in subjunctivity; this process roughly corresponds with his preliminal, liminal, and postliminal phases. In preliminal rites of separation the initiand is moved from the indicative quotidian social structure into the subjunctive antistructure of the liminal process and is then returned, transformed by liminal experiences, by the rites of reaggregation to social structural participation in the indicative mood. The subjunctive, according to Webster's Dictionary, is always concerned with "wish, desire, possibility, or hypothesis"; it is a world of "as if," ranging from scientific hypothesis to festive fantasy. It is "if it *were* so," not "it *is* so." The indicative prevails in the world of what in the West we call "actual fact," though this definition can range from a close scientific inquiry into how a situation, event, or agent produces an effect or result, to a lay person's description of the characteristics of ordinary good sense or sound practical judgment. Sally Moore and Barbara Myerhoff, in their introduction to *Secular Ritual,* did not use this pair of terms, "subjunctive" and "indicative," but, rather, saw social process as moving "between the formed and the indeterminate" (p. 17). They are, however, mostly discussing "ceremony" or "secular ritual," not ritual *pur sang.* I agree with them, as I said earlier, that "all collective ceremony can be interpreted as a cultural statement about cultural order as against a cultural void" (p. 16), and that "ceremony is a declaration against indeterminacy. Through form and formality it celebrates man-made meaning, the culturally determinate, the regulated, the named, and the explained. It banishes from consideration the basic questions raised by the made-upness of culture, its malleability and alternability . . . [every ceremony] seeks to state that the cosmos and social world, or some particular small part of them are orderly and explicable and for the moment fixed. A ceremony can allude to such propositions and demonstrate them at the same time . . . Ritual [*sic*, really "ceremony"] is a declaration of form *against* [Moore and Myerhoff's emphasis] indeterminacy, therefore indeterminacy is always present in the background of any analysis of ritual" (pp. 16–17). Roy Rappaport in his book, *Ecology, Meaning, and Religion* (1979:206), adopts a similar standpoint when he writes: "Liturgical orders [whose "sequential dimension," he says, is ritual] bind together disparate entities and processes, and it is this binding together, rather than what is bound together that is peculiar to them. Liturgical orders are meta-orders, or orders of orders . . . they mend ever again worlds forever breaking apart under the blows of usage and the slashing distinctions of language."

While I consider these to be admirably lucid statements about ceremony, which, for me, constitutes an impressive institutionalized performance of indicative, normatively structured social reality, and is also both a model *of* and a model *for* social states and statuses, I do not think such formulations can be applied with equal cogency to ritual. For ritual, as I have said, does not portray a dualistic, almost Manichean, struggle between order and void, cosmos and chaos, formed and indeterminate, with the former always triumphing in the end. Rather is it a transformative self-immolation of order as presently constituted, even sometimes a voluntary *sparagmos* or self-dismemberment of order, in the subjunctive depths of liminality. One thinks of Eliade's studies of the "shaman's journey" where the initiand is broken into pieces then put together again as a being bridging visible and invisible worlds. Only in this way, through destruction and reconstruction, that is, transformation, may an authentic reordering come about. Actuality takes the sacrificial plunge into possibility and emerges as a different kind of actuality. We are not here in the presence of two like but opposed forces as in Manichean myth; rather there is a qualitative incongruence between the contraries engaged, though Jung's daring metaphor of the incestuous marriage of the conscious ego with the unconscious seen as an archetypal mother, poses that relationship in terms of paradoxical kinship and affinity. Subjunctivity is fittingly the mother of indicativity, since any actualization is only one among a myriad possibilities of being, some of which may be actualized in space-time somewhere or somewhen else. The "hard saying" "except ye become as a little child" assumes new meaning. Unless the fixing and ordering processes of the adult, *sociostructural* domain, are liminally abandoned and the initiand submits to being broken down to a generalized *prima materia*, a lump of human clay, he cannot be transformed, reshaped to encounter new experiences.

Ritual's liminal phase, then, approximates to the "subjunctive mood" of sociocultural action. It is, quintessentially, a time and place lodged between all times and spaces defined and governed in any specific biocultural ecosystem (A. Vayda, J. Bennett, and the like) by the rules of law, politics and religion, and by economic necessity. Here the cognitive schemata that give sense and order to everyday life no longer apply, but are, as it were, suspended—in ritual symbolism perhaps even shown as destroyed or dissolved. Gods and goddesses of destruction are adored primarily because they personify an essential phase in an irreversible transformative process. All further growth requires the immolation of that which was fundamental to an earlier stage—"lest one good custom should corrupt the world." Clearly, the liminal space-time "pod" created by ritual action, or today by certain kinds of reflexively ritualized theatre, is potentially perilous. For it may be opened up to energies of the biophysical human constitution normally channeled by socialization into status-role activities, to employ the unwieldy jargon of the social sciences. Nevertheless, the danger of the liminal phase conceded, and respected by hedging it around by ritual interdictions and taboos, it is also held in most cultures to be regenerative, as I mentioned earlier. For in liminality what is mundanely bound in sociostructural form may be unbound and rebound. Of course, if a society is in hairline-precarious subsistence balance with its environment, we are unlikely to find in its liminal zones very much in the way of experimentation—here one does not fool around with the tried and tested. But when a "biocultural ecosystem," to use Vayda's terms, produce significant surpluses, even if these are merely the seasonal boons of a naturally well-endowed environment, the liminality of its major rituals may well generate cultural surpluses too. One thinks of the Kwakiutl and other Northwest Amerindian peoples with their complex iconographies and formerly rich hunting and gathering resources. New meanings and symbols may be introduced—or new ways of portraying or embellishing old models for living, and so of renewing interest in them. Ritual liminality, therefore, contains the potentiality for cultural innovation, as well as the means of effecting structural transformations within a relatively stable sociocultural system. For many transformations are, of course, within the limits of social structure, and have to do with its internal adjustments and external adaptations to environmental changes. Cognitive structuralism can cope best with such relatively cyclical and repetitive societies.

In tribal and agrarian cultures, even relatively complex ones, the innovative potential of ritual liminality seems to have been circumscribed, even dormant, or pressed into the service of maintaining the existing social order. Even so, room for "play," Huizinga's *ludic*, abounds in many kinds of tribal rituals, even in funerary rituals. There is a play of *symbol*-vehicles, leading to the construction of bizarre masks and costumes from elements of mundane life now conjoined in fantastic ways. There is a play of *meanings*, involving the reversal of hierarchical orderings of values and social statuses. There is a play with *words* resulting in the generation of secret initiatory languages, as well as joyful or serious punning. Even the dramatic scenarios which give many rituals their processual armature may be presented as comedic rather than serious or tragic. Riddling and joking may take place, even in the liminal seclusion of initiatory lodges. Recent studies of Pueblo ritual clowns recall to us how widespread the clown role is in tribal and archaic religious culture. Liminality is peculiarly conducive to play, where it is not restricted to games and jokes, but extends to the introduction of new forms of symbolic action, such as word-games or original masks.

But whatever happened to liminality, as societies increased in scale and complexity, particularly Western industrial societies? With deliminalization seems to have gone the powerful *play* component. Other religions of the Book, too, have tended regularly to stress the solemn at the expense of the festive. Religiously connected fairs, fiestas and carnivals do continue to exist, of course, but not as intrinsic parts of liturgical systems. The great Oriental religions—Hinduism, Taoism, Tantric Buddhism, Shintoism, however, still recognize in many public performances that human ritual can be both earnest *and* playful. Eros may sport with Thanatos, not as a grisly Danse Macabre, but to symbolize a complete human reality and a Nature full of oddities.

It would seem that with industrialization, urbanization, spreading literacy, labor migration, specialization, professionalization, bureaucracy, the division of the leisure sphere from the work sphere by the firm's clock, the former integrity of the orchestrated religious *gestalt* that once constituted ritual has burst open and many specialized performative genres have been born from the death of that mighty *opus deorum hominumque*. These genres of industrial leisure would include theatre, ballet, opera, film, the novel, printed poetry, the art exhibition, classical music, rock music, carnivals, processions, folk drama, major sports events and dozens more. Disintegration has been accompanied by secularization. Traditional religions, their rituals denuded of much of their former symbolic wealth and meaning, hence their transformative capacity, persist in the leisure sphere, but have not adapted well to modernity. Modernity means the exaltation of the indicative mood—but in what Ihab Hassan has called the "postmodern turn," we may be seeing a re-turn to subjunctivity and a rediscovery of cultural transformative modes, particularly in some forms of theatre. Dismembering may be a prelude to re-membering. Re-membering is not merely the restoration of some past intact, but setting it in living relationship to the present.

However, there are signs that those nations and cultures which came late to the industrial table, such as Japan, India, the Middle Eastern nations, and much of South and Central America, have succeeded, at least in part, in avoiding the dismemberment of important ritual types, and they have incorporated into their ritual performances many of the issues and problems of modern urban living and succeeded in giving them religious meaning. When industrial development came to much of the Third World it had to confront powerfully consolidated structures of ritual performative genres. In the West similar institutions had been gradually eroded from within, from the revival of learning to the Industrial Revolution. Here the indicative mood triumphed, and subjunctivity was relegated to a reduced domain where admittedly it shone brighter in the arts than in religion.

Religion, like art, *lives* in so far as it is performed, i.e., in so far as its rituals are "going concerns." If you wish to spay or geld religion, first remove its rituals, its generative and regenerative processes. For religion is not a cognitive system, a set of dogmas, alone, it is meaningful experience and experienced meaning. In ritual one *lives through* events, or through the alchemy of its framings and symbolings, *re*lives semiogenetic events, the deeds and words of prophets and saints, or if these are absent, myths and sacred epics.

If, then, we regard narrative as an "emic" Western genre or meta-genre of expressive culture, it has to be seen as one of the cultural grandchildren or great-grandchildren of "tribal" ritual or juridical process. But if we regard narrative, "etically," as the supreme instrument for binding the "values" and "goals," in Dilthey's sense of these terms, which motivate human conduct, particularly when men and women become actors in social drama, into situational structures of "meaning," then we must concede it to be a universal cultural activity, embedded in the very center of the social drama, itself another cross-cultural and trans-temporal unit of social process. "Narrate" is from the Latin *narrare,* "to tell," which is akin to the Latin *gnarus,* "knowing, acquainted with, expert in," both derivative from the Indo-European root, *GNA,* to "know," whence the vast family of words deriving from the Latin *cognoscere,* including "cognition" itself, and "noun" and "pronoun," the Greek *gignóskein,* whence *gnosis,* and the Old English past participle *gecnawan,* whence the Modern English, "know." Narrative is, it would seem, rather an appropriate term for a reflexive activity which seeks to "know" (even in its ritual aspect, to have *gnōsis* about) antecedent events, and about the meaning of those events. *Drama* itself is, of course, derived from the Greek *dran,* "to do, or act," hence narrative is knowledge (and/or *gnosis*) emerging from action, i.e., experiential knowledge. The redressive phase of social drama frames an endeavor to rearticulate a social group broken by sectional or self-serving interests; in like manner, the narrative component in ritual and legal action attempts to rearticulate opposing values and goals in a meaningful structure, the plot of which makes cultural sense. Where historical life itself fails to make cultural sense in terms that formerly held good, narrative and cultural drama may have the task of *poiesis,* that is, of remaking cultural sense, even when they seem to be dismantling ancient edifices of meaning, that can no longer redress our modern "dramas of living"—now ever more on a global and species-threatening scale.

## References

Belmont, Nicole. *Arnold Van Gennep: The Creator of French Ethnography.* Trans. by Derek Coltman. Chicago: Chicago University Press, 1979.

Bercovitch, Sacvan. *The American Jeremiad.* Madison: University of Wisconsin Press, 1978.

Gennep, Arnold van. *The Rites of Passage.* London: Routledge and Kegan Paul, 1960. First published 1908.

Grathoff, R. *The Structure of Social Inconsistencies: A Contribution to a Unified Theory of Play, Game and Social Action.* The Hague: Martinus Nijhoff, 1970.

Handelman, Don. "Is Naven Ludic?" *Social Analysis* (published in Adelaide, Australia), no. 1, 1979.

Hanna, Judith Lynne. *To Dance is Human: A Theory of Nonverbal Communication.* Austin: University of Texas Press, 1979.

Heusch, Luc de. *Le roi ivre ou l'origine de l'Etat.* Paris: Gallimard, 1972.

Hodges, H. A. *The Philosophy of Wilhelm Dilthey.* London: Routledge and Kegan Paul, 1952.

Legesse, Asmarom. *Gada: Three Approaches to the Study of African Society.* New York: Free Press, 1973.

Moore, Sally Falk. *Law as Process.* London: Routledge and Kegan Paul, 1978.

Myerhoff, Barbara. *Life History among the Elderly: Performance, Visibility, and Remembering.* n.d.

————, and Moore, Sally Falk (eds.) *Secular Ritual.*

Amsterdam: Royal van Gorcum, 1977.

Pike, Kenneth L. *Language in Relation to a Unified Theory of the Structure of Human Behavior.* Glendale, California: Summer Institute of Linguistics, 1954.

Rappaport, Roy. *Ecology, Meaning, and Religion.* Richmond, California: North American Books, 1979.

Sapir, Edward. "Emergence of a Concept of Personality in a Study of Cultures." *Journal of Social Psychology,* 5, pp. 410–416, 1934.

Spindler, George D. (ed.) *The Making of Psychological Anthropology.* Berkeley: University of California Press, 1978.

Turner, Victor. *Schism and Continuity in an African Society: A Study of Ndembu Village Life.* Manchester: Manchester University Press, 1957.

————. *The Forest of Symbols: Aspects of Ndembu Ritual.* Ithaca: Cornell University Press, 1967.

————. *The Drums of Affliction: A Study of Religious Processes among the Ndembu of Zambia.* Oxford: The Clarendon Press, 1968.

————. *The Ritual Process: Structure and Anti-Structure.* Chicago: Aldine, 1969.

————. *Dramas, Fields, and Metaphors: Symbolic Action in Human Society.* Ithaca: Cornell University Press, 1974.

Vansina, Jan. *Kingdoms of the Savanna.* Madison: University of Wisconsin Press, 1966.

White, Hayden. *Metahistory: The Historical Imagination in Nineteenth-Century Europe.* Baltimore: Johns Hopkins University Press, 1973.

Raymond
Williams
(1921–1988)

Conclusion FROM Drama
from Ibsen to Brecht
(1968)

*THROUGHOUT his long career, the Marxist cultural critic Raymond Williams wrote often about drama and theater. His first book on drama,* Drama from Ibsen to Eliot, *was published in 1952, then extensively revised in the late 1960s—in part in response to his own work in* Modern Tragedy *(1966). Later in his career, Williams turned to the specific questions of drama's political work on the stage in* Drama in Performance *(1988). Here, in his Conclusion to* Drama from Ibsen to Brecht, *Williams offers a critique of how the forms of modern drama respond to the "structures of feeling" of modern life.*

1      We can now look again at the real relations, in modern drama, between structures of feeling and conventions. These relations imply, analytically, questions of consciousness and audience: of dramatic form and the theatre.

To define the history in this way is a critical choice. We cannot usefully apply, to any modern art, the critical terms and procedures which were discovered for the understanding of earlier work. A theory of kinds, which still haunts dramatic criticism, is now obviously null. Its inherent notions—of hierarchy, separation, fixed rules for each kind—belong to a social and philosophical order built on exactly those principles. The order and the theory have fallen together. The terms that succeeded, in art as in society, were of movements: self-originating movements, which defined their own characteristics. From the manifesto of Strindberg to the manifesto of Brecht; from Ibsen's critical description of his decision to write the "language of real life" to Eliot's critical arguments for dramatic verse; from the self-criticism of theatre in Büchner and Chekhov to a later self-criticism in Pirandello and Anouilh: these bearings indicate our initial survey. It is part of a deep inner history, in repeated struggles, that this century of new drama is directly and indirectly self-conscious: critically aware of its own problems and forms. Very few modern dramatists, whose work has survived their immediate place and time, have failed to write critically about dramatic form and the theatre. Yet no real history can be written from the critical pronouncements alone: there is too much evident tension between the critical positions and the varying creative practices. The substance is always in many hundreds of plays, or, to put it another way (which is already a beginning of history) in the life's work of many scores of dramatists. But then these are interpreted, not only externally but also internally, not in kinds but in movements. It is where a critical survey begins.

It will take us some way, but no longer far enough. It is not only that as the names of movements get known—naturalism, expressionism, epic theatre, the absurd—they harden, inevitably. They acquire external associations; become a shorthand of classification; tend to blur and confuse essentially different practices, and certain necessary connections. About the past, always, they have a look of calm certainty; but in any active present they can decline to meaningless repetition, or become rigid, desperate: a barrier where work is now done. It is also that each of the movements is, intrinsically, a recommendation: an offered completion of the creative effort; a way of forming and training an audience. In the competition of offers there is already confusion: where the kinds stare inertly, from another history, the movements penetrate, organize; find workers, supporters, hangers-on. To accept the terms of those offers is to make any critical history impossible. It is receiving a tradition as opposed to living it. Any real tradition is a selection, a revaluation, a critique of the orthodox survey. Now, when we have looked at the plays, we can go back behind the names, and make our own history, in our own terms.

2      It is commonly said that we have got beyond naturalism. Yet the argument, here, has scarcely even begun. For it is clear, in practice, that naturalism means several different things. In its widest sense, it is an absorbed interest in the contemporary everyday world, and a corresponding rejection or exclusion of any supposed external design or system of values. It is then an absorbed recreation of the ways in which people, within human limits, actually speak, feel, think, behave, act. By these criteria, many of the supposed rejections of naturalism are in fact variations on it. Conventions are changed, not because some other view of the world, or some other creative purpose, is now proposed, but because existing conventions are no longer *true enough*, by essentially similar criteria. It must be obvious that what is meant by the "rejection of naturalism" is ordinarily a rejection of its earliest particular conventions. The most evident emphasis, of those early conventions, was the

dramatic representation, the theatrical reproduction, of "lifelike," "probable" speech, behaviour and environment. It can then seem a rejection of naturalism to use conventions of speech, action and scene which are not, in immediate terms, probable, or superficially lifelike. But these new conventions, normally, have the same central purpose: a true representation of life. Strindberg, proposing his experimental conventions, made the distinction in that way:

> false naturalism, which believes that art consists simply of sketching a piece of nature in a natural manner; . . . true naturalism, which seeks out those points in life where the great conflicts occur, which rejoices in seeing what cannot be seen every day.

These intense isolated moments, and the conventions needed to give them dramatic expression, are then not evidence of an alternative structure of feeling, but of the development of the heart of the original naturalist claim. Strindberg's definition, clearly, could be applied as it stands to Ibsen's major naturalist plays.

Or take Yeats, again recommending quite new conventions:

> There, where no studied lighting, no stage-picture made an artificial world, he was able to recede from us into some more powerful life. Because that separation was achieved by human means alone, he receded, but to inhabit as it were the deeps of the mind . . . Our unimaginative arts are content to set a piece of the world as we know it in a place by itself, to put their photographs, as it were, in a plush or plain frame, but the arts which interest me, while seeming to separate from the world and us a group of figures, images, symbols, enable us to pass for a few moments into a deep of the mind that had hitherto been too subtle for our habitation.

This "deep of the mind," again, is not evidence of an alternative structure of feeling; it is a human discovery, "by human means alone." We can compare it with Ibsen saying:

> My play is no tragedy in the ancient acceptation. My desire was to depict human beings and therefore I would not make them speak the language of the gods.

It is not the creative purpose, but the creative means, that are at issue. We can compare, in this precise respect, Eliot arguing against the kind of speech that Ibsen had chosen, and for a return to dramatic verse:

> The *human* soul, in intense emotion, strives to express itself in verse. It is not for me, but for the neurologists, to discover why this is so, and why and how feeling and rhythm are related. The tendency, at any rate, of prose drama is to emphasise the ephemeral and superficial; if we want to get at the permanent and universal we tend to express ourselves in verse.

The offered contrast is sharp, but the "permanent and universal" is not a world outside man; it is "the *human* soul, in intense emotion," and subject—in a characteristically naturalist reference—to the understanding of the neurologist.

We can evidently, then, avoid some confusion if we make certain initial distinctions about naturalism. Nobody who knows the major naturalist plays can believe, seriously, that their impulse is technical: that their particular conventions for putting human beings and their environment on the stage were a choice of style, subject to rejection by choice of a different style. It is this, above all, that we now underestimate: under the influence, of course, of important arguments for different conventions. The driving force of the great naturalist drama was not the reproduction of rooms or dress or conversation on the stage. It was a passion for truth, in strictly human and contemporary terms. Whatever the later argument, about particular conventions, it was the decisive moment, in all modern drama. A long prepared redefinition, of the sources of human understanding and of the objects of human concern, found at last, in this form, its decisive realization. It is one of the great revolutions, in human consciousness: to confront the human drama in its immediate setting, without reference to "outside" forces and powers. It is so difficult a revolution that it is still, in some ways, incomplete. Dramatic methods and theatrical practices, drawn from an earlier consciousness, persist, as we have seen, in the greatest dramatists: in Ibsen more clearly than anywhere. But, in spite of these difficulties, it is a successful revolution, and it is from its central purposes that nearly all serious modern drama derives. There are important secondary arguments, on the dramatic means of this confrontation, even on the particular sources of this decisive human truth. But it is deeply significant that the creative purpose is now so widely accepted that it is hardly even noticed; indeed that it is often taken for granted.

It can never be taken for granted, as we can show, at once, by considering another meaning of naturalism. There is always a precise internal relation between a structure of feeling and its effective conventions: in the great naturalist drama, between the strictly human definition of truth and the direct representation of human actuality. To achieve this, as we saw in Ibsen, certain external conventions, mechanically persisting from an earlier major consciousness, had to be rejected and altered: conventions deriving ultimately from a design, a fate, outside man, intervening beyond his terms. These were dismissed as "theatrical": an opposition to truth. But the new naturalist conventions had to be established in the theatre; learned as practices. What then happened, in turn, was the establishment of new external conventions: methods and practices without precise relation to the consciousness they had been designed to express. Representation, verisimilitude, probability became, in these terms, self-sufficient. A dramatic setting must be "right"—the sort of room people like this would live in. An actor's movements must give the effect of "the expected"—what that person, in that situation, would probably do. Dramatic speech must be "like conversation"— what those people, in that situation, would say, and no more. These conventions and practices, which in effect still govern our majority drama, can be seen as external because they are self-defining dogmas. We are in fact as likely to see them employed without consideration of the structure of feeling from which they derive, as to see them *necessarily* following from the consciousness of the play. Thus what are authentic conventions, in major naturalist drama, become inauthentic, by simple habit; as can be seen in performances of what are essentially intrigue plays, melodramas, fantasies; in the development of Eliot, where the consciousness and the conventions come to open contradiction; in the ordinary season of Shakespeare. There are then comic paradoxes. A naturalist scene is abandoned but naturalist speech is retained; or naturalist speech abandoned, but naturalist scene and movement retained: yet all, in the jargon, going "beyond naturalism." It is then important to distinguish naturalist drama from what we can call the naturalist habit. It is not in the separated conventions that naturalism defines itself; it is in the structure of feeling to which, as serious conventions, they relate.

3      What is the naturalist structure of feeling? We have described the revolution in which the whole consciousness and concern of modern drama were altered. It was called the naturalist revolution, and the term is still accurate. But a particular distinction, of its earliest phase, needs to be clearly made. In any precise analysis of the structure and its conventions, a particular relation between men and their environment is evidently assumed. If we see, in its detail, the environment men have created, we shall learn the truth about them. That is one way of putting it, and it is deeply relevant to Ibsen and Chekhov, where the dramatic tension, again and again, is between what men feel themselves capable of becoming, and a thwarting, directly present environment. It is even possible to feel that Ibsen had to make rooms on the stage in order to show men trapped in them. For he certainly did not make them in a kind of competition with furnishers. It is perhaps a particular stage of bourgeois society, in which the decisive action is elsewhere, and what is lived out, in these traps of rooms, are the human consequences: in particular, the consequences of a relatively leisured society. To stare from a window at where one's life is being decided: that consciousness is specific, in this great early phase. The rooms are not there to define the people, but to define what they seem to be, what they cannot accept they are. This is of course radically different from the reproduction of a room to try to persuade us (it is usually hard going) that if the room is right the people are real; if the phrasing is right, something is being said; if the gesture is right, it means something.

But then the authentic naturalism, of this early phase, reached a necessary limit. It is what we saw in the discussion of Lawrence's plays, or in the problem of Synge's *Riders to the Sea.* When the action is really elsewhere, and begins to engage the exploring consciousness of a writer, the trap of the room is a real trap; the interior life—not only the domestic interior but the corresponding consciousness, reflecting, reacting—is no longer an adequate truth. There must be a break to action: to a made and making rather than merely received environment; and then the early conventions, within a room and among people waiting and watching, are dangerously in the way. Many of the simple limitations, of this early naturalist form, can be overcome, at once, in a different convention of performance: with the cleared stage, allowing a different range of actions; or with the film or television cameras, offering a new range and mobility. At the same time, the will to move in this way, for dramatic rather than for spectacular reasons, is quite another matter. We have gone on being trapped, by that same early consciousness, in the more crowded and moving streets.

We can perhaps best see that room—the room in which one watches at a window, to which people call saying what is happening in the world, in which one's fate is decided—as intermediate, between two possible dramas. It was a real situation, a real consciousness. It was also an attempt to bridge two radically different worlds, which, for historical reasons, were now difficult to integrate: a world of action, in which an environment is made; and a world of consciousness, in which a consequence is realized. Dramatists have struggled, throughout, to bring these worlds together; but no real integration is within a gift. If the separation were not real, the conventions would not have needed to be changed.

What was at stake, in that early phase, was a more difficult claim: to be representative; to create a unique history which was a general truth. The claim has persisted, yet it belongs, deeply, to a particular history, a particular consciousness. The major and irreversible change, between renaissance and modern drama, is an alteration in the terms of that "typicality" on which all drama depends. The former typicality was "universal" in character: depending at once on a social and metaphysical order, it took the prince (the hero) as in this sense representative of human destiny. The liberal revolution against the social and metaphysical order overthrew any such definition. The insistence on the drama of ordinary life, on the dramatic importance of people without formal rank, altered action and character in a single movement. The change from the "universal" to the "representative" is one way of describing this; each mode has deep ties to other characteristic institutions and forms of thought in its kind of society. Yet each mode, in real situations, is a mystification, or, if we prefer it, an ideal. It would be possible in some simple communities to create a unique history which was also a general truth; but all drama has been made in already complicated societies: it is a willed form, not a self-evident or traditional fact. In the period of early naturalism, the complication was exceptional. It was a class society, in which the "middle" class was dominant. While the drama could remain, by isolation, within a single class, it could offer to be representative, in simple ways; it could assume an effective common understanding of a human situation and human claims. Some isolated popular drama (early Synge and early Lawrence, or Büchner and Hauptmann, are relevant) could make a similar, though always temporary, assumption. The inner history of naturalism is really this: that it developed *as a style*—a characteristic way of handling the world—in bourgeois society, but that it developed *as a form*, capable of major dramatic importance, in a period in which bourgeois society was being fundamentally criticized and rejected, mainly by people who nevertheless belonged in its world. There is then a contradiction in naturalism, but also a tension out of which the great drama of Ibsen directly came. The style assumed an understandable, recognizable, manageable everyday world; the form, while linked to this, discovered a humanity which this same world was frustrating or destroying. It is easy to see, by contrast, how little tension there is in the simple majority drama of what we have called the naturalist habit. Take that explosive discovery away, and the people are indeed as they seem, and everything necessary can be said or, even more crucially, done. There have been hardly any difficulties with naturalism in the majority middle-class theatre and its derivatives; it is a self-evident, though to others mainly boring, tradition. But important naturalist drama developed, historically, in just that period of liberal revolt against orthodox liberalism, of individual revolt against an orthodox "individualist" society, of bourgeois revolt against the forms of bourgeois life. Its means were the "free theatres" which sprang up across Europe (often interwoven with nationalism, but still connecting with each other) between 1860 and 1900. What was becoming available as a style was used to push an action beyond the ordinary terms of the beliefs on which it depended. The self-evident reproductive element in naturalism was joined by the alternative emphasis of direct exposure. The passion for evident truth burst beyond the forms of self-evident truth. We have seen, in detail, what then happened: in Ibsen and in Chekhov; a repeated search for some means of defining the humanity that cannot be lived, in these well-ordered rooms—the forces outside, the white horses or the seagull, the tower or the cherry orchard, which have meaning because there are forces inside these people in these rooms, which can not be realized in any available life. This is the paradox of the unique history which is also a general truth, in early naturalism: that it is of an individual who is breaking away from what is offered as general truth: a uniquely representative figure (representative of "humanity," of "Man") who is in revolt against the representative environment other men have made. The world of action, characteristically, is then the action of others; the world of consciousness is one's own. Out of this separation, and out of its terrible tensions, these men trapped in their rooms make their only possible, their exceptionally powerful, drama.

4     This real contradiction, between style and form, could not last for ever, in serious drama. Ibsen, towards the end, is already breaking, externally, what he had broken internally by sheer tension and force. Strindberg, in a younger generation, soon abandoned the given environment, and made a dramatic form out of the internal struggles. The subsidiary characters—the characters as environment—are excluded, and then, in a new major innovation, a dramatic form is made wholly from the already isolated consciousness: what we call, in defining that kind of early expressionism, the drama of a "single mind." Instead of an understandable, recognizable, manageable everyday world, there is the creation, from separation, of a world which is still everyday—which is still offered for recognition—but which is now unmanageable, strange, hostile. The suppressed tension, of those many trapped rooms, now breaks to a redefinition of what any environment is. A dramatic world is made (and we are still mainly in this phase) in which it is human isolation that has become representative: another unique history, offered, even more paradoxically, as a general truth. What was still, in the patient reproduction of naturalism, a self-evidently man-made world, is now a phantasmagoria, a hostile projection, a parody of order. Out of this structure of feeling—in historical terms, out of the failure of bourgeois revolt against bourgeois society—comes a new confidence: a confidence of despair. The techniques were available, from traditional romantic literature, from the fragments of a supernatural order: visions, transformations, superhuman powers, a malignant nature. But the techniques became conventions by a major creative reworking. It was not now in an order beyond man that these manifestations occurred; it was inside him, deep inside him, in dreams and in visions, in his own irreducible and most personal and significant life. What in orthodox fantasy or romance (of which, in the commercial theatre, there are still many examples) were still theatrical tricks, a kind of conscious play in the relaxation from reality, became now a reality of its own: the direct projection, into a dramatic action, of man's inner history. It is the abandonment of naturalism, in one ordinary sense. Yet the new conventions establish themselves because what is shown is integrated by an inner personality, an inner vision. They are more than techniques because they have this organizing principle: not a way of looking at reality, a way among other ways, but reality itself: what life is like when the external pretences are dropped. We can all see the difference, in dramatic method, between say *Ghosts* and *The Road to Damascus;* but we must also now see the connection. It is in the same passion for a strictly human truth that each play is conceived, but the suspicion of Mrs. Alving—"I sometimes think that we are all ghosts"—has been put directly on the stage, in quite different conventions but in what is really only a development of the structure of feeling. This early expressionism, and the whole powerful drama of "internal vision, external distortion" which has followed from it, is the action that succeeds to, rather than contradicts, the great tensions of the major naturalist play. The person looking from the window of that trapped room is still there; but the room around him has gone, the other people in his direct dimension have gone, and what he sees from the window, now through his own eyes, is not the orthodox world but his own necessary version of it: a look from the window that is now, in essence, the dramatic form.

5     It is not then really surprising that two apparently different forms—serious naturalism and psychological expressionism—should have come to coexist in the same drama: often, indeed, in the same theatres, the same companies, the same actors, the same writers. The conventions are

different, as well as the local techniques, but they relate, essentially, to historically connected structures of feeling. Thus we can turn from what Strindberg was doing, in his late plays, to Stanislavsky's version of the naturalism he developed from and applied to Chekhov:

> This imaginative truth was formerly achieved by us mostly externally; it was the truth of objects, furniture, costumes, stage property, lighting and sound effects, the outward image of the actor and his external physical life.

That is indeed the convention which Joyce mocked in his "writing the mystery of himself in furniture." Stanislavsky moved on to direct human means, in acting, to express what he called an "inner realism" (though in fact he never abandoned the "truth of objects," any more than most modern theatre). Expressionism, on the contrary, moved on to transform, in a surprising way, the "truth of objects," using the stage physically to realize "inner" images. This is basically the completion of the movement we have already discussed: in which there was first a tension, then a separation, between the decisive consciousness and the available world. What was dramatized, in major naturalism, was a tension which still drew much of its force from the physical existence of an unacceptable world, and from the presence in it of others, in the same dimension, with whom the attempt at a common understanding, a common recognition, must continue to be made. (This form, of course, has continued, down to the drama of our own day; it is the naturalist form—as in Pinter—of what is called the drama of "non-communication"). What was dramatized in expressionism was a related tension which remade the world and its persons in its own terms: not for liberation from it—it was still consciousness and not action—but to show what it really was, what it felt like; to expose it.

There are, of course, two clear meanings of exposure, and throughout this history they have both been important. We have already seen how major naturalism was an inherently critical form; it showed the world as unacceptable by showing directly what it was like, and then how impossible it was when people really tried to live in it. Major expressionism was also inherently critical; it said not only "this is what my world is like" but, in a persistent anguish, "because it is like this it is intolerable to me." This is true in naturalism from Ibsen to O'Neill, and in expressionism from Strindberg to Beckett. Yet, in all these cases, though the critique is evident, it is also implicit. It is in tensions within the form that the critique is expressed. What we have now to look at is a succeeding phase, still deeply connected, in which dramatists attempted to make the critique explicit, by a new variation of form, requiring new conventions.

Once again, techniques and methods were in fact available, from earlier drama: chorus, narrator, commentator, raisonneur. Any of these, of course, might be used simply as techniques: available variations of style, as still in many examples. But in some major experiments these methods became true conventions; were related, organically, to an altered structure of feeling. Yet what could this be? The internal critique, like the internal tensions, seems to have depended, historically, on the situation we have described: a "rejection" of bourgeois society which was also, factually, a resigned or angry acceptance of it as inevitable. The dramatists could have done nothing else, from real experience, and yet the nature of the "solution" is one of the reasons for the development of more frankly separated and isolated forms: to speak the whole truth at last, in one's own terms and no others. By definition, of course, there could not be an internal critique, of one's own vision, in the same way: what is present in Ibsen, as a continually implied point of view, is present in late Strindberg or Beckett as an impotent anguish.

What had to be done, to get truly outside? This is the later history, of social expressionism, and of the experiments of Brecht. The isolated consciousness, seeing the world in its own way, had to try to become, to identify itself with, an objectively critical or revolutionary consciousness. This is a phase of profound importance, but it has been more often imitated than achieved. We have seen in Toller, or in Auden and Isherwood, how the conventions can fail, can decline to techniques, if there is any real doubt about the truth of that objective viewpoint; or if it is only negatively identified with a still subjective and anguished consciousness. There have been two main solutions: in summary, those of Pirandello and Brecht. The objective viewpoint, in Pirandello, as in later writers like Ionesco, is a total criticism of the possibility of a knowable world: this is the centre of what is now called "absurdism," though many essentially different things have been confused with it.

Not this society but any society; not this relationship but any relationship; not these words but any words: all these thwart men, inevitably; and that "universal" condition is then critically seen. In Pirandello the critique is formal: against the attempts at reality which prove to be illusions. In Ionesco, the critique is a self-sufficient form: a world openly mocked in a set of cliches and self-deceptions which are the only available words and actions.

The objective viewpoint in Brecht, on the other hand, is revolutionary and historical: the thwarting and destruction are shown, but are then explained, critically: a point of view is established, by what are now not techniques but conventions, and this viewpoint controls the dramatization. We can then see the development—in the rush of work of course very complicated—from naturalism to critical naturalism; from personal expressionism to social expressionism; from an "absurd" private drama to an "absurd" social drama; from the subjective-critical to the objective-critical. It is a development that is still very far from complete, for what has persisted throughout, in a majority of cases, is the original difficulty: of the real experience: of a man trapped in bourgeois society and unable to escape from it; of the conviction, after so long a persistence, that this is not a social but a "universal" condition; of the precarious and often ambiguous character of actual change and revolution.

There have been, of course, certain clear periods of development. There is a clear difference, in action and tone, between the generously angry, the bitterly humane naturalism of the liberal period, at the end and at the turn of the century, and the kinds of despair, contempt and rejection which have multiplied since the first war. There has been a steady development of theories but also processes of illusion and alienation, to the point where they have become an orthodoxy. The preoccupation with violence and degradation has not always been either critical or humane; in a good deal of minority work—now sedulously imitated in commercial entertainment—it is often brutally exposed and even rationalized: a pseudo-tough modernity which is the mark of a broken spirit—a broken general spirit. As it has penetrated the crisis, in new dramatic forms, modern drama has also found ways of playing with it: reducing it back to a trick of theatre. The possibility of a controlling illuminating form, so often glimpsed and in some important cases realized, has been repeatedly contradicted by a kind of sensational displacement. This real history is still a history of crisis.

But then it is also an indication of the character of the crisis that its forms and problems so often recur: that European drama, since 1945, is so close to the world of Strindberg, some fifty years earlier; that, in particular situations, the break to naturalism—the passion for truth, in a real situation, against an artificial theatre—can be still authentically made, as in some of the new English drama of the fifties and sixties; that the trap of a room, of a street, from which a man looks at a world that at once determines and is beyond him, should go on being experienced, in comparable dramatic actions; that certain illusions hold, and can be replayed but newly experienced. Within and across the lines of development, there are these continuities, recurrences, new breaks to an already realized position. It is this double character of the history that defines the nature of the movements: there is a historical succession of naturalism, private expressionism, social expressionism, the theatre of illusion and of the absurd; but there is also a continual coexistence, in authentic work, of each one of these tendencies, in the struggle for a common form.

6     It is then necessary to emphasize the difficult relation between what are not only historical but socially alternative structures of feeling, and the consequently complex relations between conventions, theatrical methods and audiences. My essential argument is on the relation between a structure of feeling and a convention: the first critical task is always that necessary analysis. This brings to our attention, as the first kind of fact, problems of form and method which reveal themselves, ultimately, as problems of content and viewpoint. To clarify these relations is a main critical purpose, for it is then possible to see the choice between structures of feeling, and the consequent choice of conventions, as a substantial and still active history and experience, rather than a random variation of viewpoints and styles.

This is especially important, and especially difficult, in the history of the theatre. For there is a continual attempt to abstract a general "dramatic" method, a "true theatrical use," and this is frequently supported by the prestige of a successful theatre in a particular time and place. It is in fact abundantly clear, from modern drama alone (and of course from the whole wider history of drama and performance) that there is no such special orthodoxy: virtually anything can be done, virtually any method become a convention, in the pressure of actual experience. What is continually but variously defended as the special art of the theatre is always the local materialization of particular conventions, and the history of modern drama is, to a large extent, the repeated breaking and altering of those conventions, to allow a different form to come through. Of course, when this has been done, the theatre itself is usually the first to identify with it; to dismiss, with a fine confidence, old "theatrical" methods, and to reannounce the "true" possibilities of theatre. In practice, of course, the new orthodoxy is simply repeating the position of the old orthodoxy, in relation to newly discovered dramatic forms.

The forms and conventions we have seen in such variety, in so many plays, can not, then, be reduced to varying theatrical styles. Each form and convention has to solve the problem of performance; there is no dramatic solution until that has been done. But the method of performance is not a style applied to the play; it is, in its central importance, the necessary realization of the play's essential form. We cannot then reduce naturalism or expressionism to methods of production: to the look of the stage; to particular kinds of scenery or design; to particular ways of speaking and moving. Given that abstracted autonomy, the methods lack a dimension, and to speak of "going beyond naturalism," or "dropping all that expressionism," will often be a merely external change—a temporary fashion in the theatre—which while giving opportunities to particular kinds of drama will merely frustrate or break the back of other important kinds. What happened to Eliot's drama is a major example of this, but it is only one among many.

This false autonomy of theatrical method is in itself a symptom of the general situation that has been described. It is the absence of a reasonably common form, in modern drama as a whole, that has led both to waves of fashionable emphasis or eclecticism, and to the supposed autonomy of an internally determined production. The repeated tension between dramatists and theatres, which has been so marked in this century, is an aspect of the problems of dramatic form itself. This is especially clear in those movements of literary reform which, concentrating on the problems of dramatic speech, have neglected the central problems of dramatic action. To change a speech convention, but no other convention, is to disintegrate a form which already has its theatrical methods, and so to leave a gap which "production" is forced to fill. The problem, throughout, has been the writing of a whole form, and in the absence of any reasonably common conventions (which are of course not received, but have to be made) this raises severe problems: at root creative, but involving also the method of notation. As we pass from Ibsen's detailed stage directions to Strindberg's writing of a flow of images we see a major example of just this problem. What in orthodox naturalism is stage direction is in later forms either a creation of mood for the reader (and for that crucial reader, the producer) or an attempt to realize an action for which no theatrical notation (as opposed to a dramatic notation) was, as yet, available. Brecht's success is directly related to his willingness to make the notation in practice with a company, and this is obviously admirable. But there are real social reasons why this direct relation is often unavailable, or breaks down: not least the characteristic discontinuity of experimental theatres, and the social failure to support the institutions from which new work can come. We can look back, in this century, at enough successes, where a dramatist worked with a theatre, to see how important this opportunity can be. But we have also to look back at repeated failures and false connections, which have radically affected dramatic development.

The question of convention is, in practice, often, just this question of a relation between form and performance, which the dramatist, where possible collaboratively, has to learn to solve. But to put the matter in this way is to realize also that it is a question of audiences; it is there, in the theatre as a social institution, that conventions are really made. It is then necessary to argue for properly based and continuing dramatic companies, with the necessary time and autonomy, which are now being attempted, in many different ways, in many countries.

But it is also necessary to realize that drama is no longer coexistent with theatre, in the narrow sense. We have been used to their equation, for some centuries, but for half a century now, and with increasing effect, other means and places of performance have been discovered. The largest audience for drama, in our own world, is in the cinema and on television, and in many countries these are explicitly popular forms where the theatre is self-consciously, even willingly, a minority form. It is then very important that many of the developments we have observed, in dramatic forms and conventions, have been, in a deep way, towards these new media. For one particular kind of drama, that of early naturalism, the framed-stage theatre was exactly suited: the group trapped in a room—that substantial experience—could be immediately staged; and the audience, essentially, was in the same position. Of course, as the stage was cleared of its furniture, the frame taken down, the audience encouraged to react and participate rather than sitting trapped, many new conventions were possible. Expressionism, in particular, was well served in this kind of theatre, often with the addition of devices of film projection and broadcasting, allowing new relations between speech and action, or action and real environment. Many of the later experiments in illusion were built directly on this kind of theatrical opportunity, and on the very limitations and contradictions of the theatre. Some important work has been done in this way, but it has been possible, also, to notice a confusion of dramatic illusion with theatrical play: some recent minor work suggests, in a strange recurrence, not men trapped in a room but actors and dramatists trapped in a theatre, seeing what can be done within those accepted limits. It is often a useful exercise, but it can be an evasion, when we look at actual contemporary dramatic possibilities.

In method, film and television offer certain real solutions to many of the recurrent problems of modern dramatic form, though in practice, in ordinary use, they often simply repeat some familiar deadlocks. At the same time, these potentially liberating media, which have already released certain newly mobile forms, are often, by habit, still treated as inferior. They may get audiences, but the important work, it is felt, is still in the culturally warranted form: the theatre, where drama happens, as opposed to film and television, where entertainment happens. I do not know any real country in which this comparison can be seriously made: not only is there now a body of serious drama, in film and television, but also, in most theatres, there is work of at least no higher level than ordinary film and television production. As a cultural convention, however, the contrast persists.

I believe there can be little doubt, when the critical history of the next half-century of drama comes to be written, that the majority of its examples will be taken from these new forms. It is indeed with just this realization, and facing the acute problems of developing a critical method which would be adequate for what is in many ways a wholly new kind of analysis, that I have tried to bring together, at a decisive point of transition, the development of modern drama in its traditionally written forms. I do not of course mean that the theatre will become unimportant: for certain kinds of drama it is still essential, and it is still, in practice, inventive and innovating, so that new forms will almost certainly be developed. Again, in some kinds of work, but only some kinds, "live" performance is an advantage. But as I read the development of modern drama, and as I try to relate it to the continuing social crisis with which, throughout, it has been closely related, I see in film and television the evidence and the promise of new kinds of action, of complex seeing made actual in a directly composed performance, of new kinds of relation between action and speech, of changes in the fundamental concept of dramatic imagery, which open up not simply as techniques (as they are still, on the whole, regarded) but as responses to an altering structure of feeling, and as new and important relations with audiences. There are as many problems, in this new work, as in any of the work we have studied. The position of the writer is already quite different, and not always, in practice, to his advantage. The new relations with audiences can be exploited as often as honestly welcomed and developed. The inherited separation between "verbal" and "visual" dramatic conventions is not easily overcome, and it is possible to waste much energy in a false competition between them. But it has been a record of difficulty and struggle, throughout.

I shall try, in a later essay, to connect the history of modern drama, in its theatrical forms, with the already major achievement of modern film drama, and the already interesting achievement of television drama. But what I have defined, in the present book, is what I believe to be the meaning of the dramatic tradition of the modern theatre: a record of difficulty and struggle; but still primarily, from that first major generation to its many successors, from Ibsen to Brecht, one of the great periods of dramatic history: a major creative achievement, of our own civilization, which gives us a continuing understanding, imagination and courage.

*AN influential novelist, playwright, and literary theorist, Zola became the spokesman for natural-*
*ism in the theater in a series of articles he wrote in the 1870s, collected as* Naturalism in the Theatre *in 1878. In these essays, Zola urged the theater to adopt an attitude of scientific objectivity, an*
*attitude reflected in the development of a new dramatic style. The naturalistic theater asserted such*
*objectivity through its choice of subject matter (middle-class life), its treatment of characters (dri-*
*ven by "physiological" motives, not by "metaphysical" passions), its use of a prosaic, antiliterary*
*language, and by the importance attached to the material environment.*

*I*

Each winter at the beginning of the theatre season I fall prey to the same thoughts. A hope springs
up in me, and I tell myself that before the first warmth of summer empties the playhouses, a
dramatist of genius will be discovered. Our theatre desperately needs a new man who will scour
the debased boards and bring about a rebirth in an art degraded by its practitioners to the simple-
minded requirements of the crowd. Yes, it would take a powerful personality, an innovator's mind,
to overthrow the accepted conventions and finally install the real human drama in place of the
ridiculous untruths that are on display today. I picture this creator scorning the tricks of the clever
hack, smashing the imposed patterns, remaking the stage until it is continuous with the auditorium,
giving a shiver of life to the painted trees, letting in through the backcloth the great, free air of
reality.

Unfortunately, this dream I have every October has not yet been fulfilled, and is not likely to
be for some time. I wait in vain, I go from failure to failure. Is this, then, merely the naive wish of
a poet? Are we trapped in today's dramatic art, which is so confining, like a cave that lacks air and
light? Certainly, if dramatic art by its nature forbids this escape into less restricted forms, it would
indeed be vain to delude ourselves and to expect a renaissance at any moment. But despite the
stubborn assertions of certain critics who do not like to have their standards threatened, it is obvious that dramatic art, like all the arts, has before it an unlimited domain, without barriers of any
kind to left or right. Inability, human incapacity, is the only boundary to an art.

To understand the need for a revolution in the theatre, we must establish clearly where we
stand today. During our entire classical period tragedy ruled as an absolute monarch. It was rigid
and intolerant, never granting its subjects a touch of freedom, bending the greatest minds to its inexorable laws. If a playwright tried to break away from them he was condemned as witless, incoherent and bizarre; he was almost considered a dangerous man. Yet even within the narrow
formula genius did build its monument of marble and bronze. The formula was born during the
Greek and Latin revival; the artists who took it over found in it a pattern that would serve for great
works. Only later, when the imitators—that line of increasingly weaker and punier disciples—
came along, did the faults in the formula show up: outlandish situations, improbabilities, dishonest
uniformity, and uninterrupted, unbearable declaiming. Tragedy maintained such a sway that two
hundred years had to pass before it went out of date. It tried slowly to become more flexible, but
without success, for the authoritarian principles in which it was grounded formally forbade any
concession to new ideas, under pain of death. Just when it was trying to broaden its scope, it was
overturned, after a long and glorious reign.

In the eighteenth century romantic drama was already stirring inside tragedy. On occasion the
three unities were violated, more importance was given to scenery and extras, violent climaxes
were now staged, where formerly they had been described in speeches so that the majestic tranquility of psychological analysis might not be disturbed by physical action. In addition, the passion
of the *grande époque* was replaced by commonplace acting; a grey rain of mediocrity and staleness
soaked the stage. One can visualize tragedy, by the beginning of this century, as a long, pale, ema-
ciated figure without a drop of blood under its white skin, trailing its tattered robes across a gloomy
stage on which the footlights had gone dark of their own accord. A rebirth of dramatic art out of a
new formula was inevitable. It was then that romantic drama noisily planted its standard in front
of the prompter's box. The hour had come; a slow ferment had been at work; the insurrection advanced on to terrain already softened-up for the victory. And never has the word insurrection
seemed more apt, for romantic drama bodily seized the monarch tragedy and, out of hatred for its

**Émile Zola**
(1840–1902)

FROM Naturalism in the
Theatre
(1878)

TRANSLATED BY
ALBERT BERMEL

*Naturalism*

impotence, sought to destroy every memory of its reign. Tragedy did not react; it sat still on its throne, guarding its cold majesty, persisting with its speeches and descriptions. Whereas romantic drama made action its rule, excesses of action that leapt to the four corners of the stage, hitting out to right and left, no longer reasoning or analysing, giving the public a full view of the blood-drenched horror of its climaxes. Tragedy had chosen antiquity for its setting, the eternal Greeks and Romans, immobilizing the action in a room or in front of the columns of a temple; romantic drama chose the Middle Ages, paraded knights and ladies, manufactured strange sets with castles pinnacled over sheer gorges, armories crowded with weapons, dungeons dripping with moisture, ancient forests pocked with moonlight. The war was joined on all fronts; romantic drama ruthlessly made itself the armed adversary of tragedy and assaulted it with every method that defied the old formula.

This raging hostility, which characterized the romantic drama at its high tide, needs to be stressed, for it offers a precious insight. The poets who led the movement undoubtedly talked about putting real passion on stage and laying claim to a vast new realm that would encompass the whole of human life with its contradictions and inconsistencies; it is worth remembering, for example, that romantic drama fought above all for a mixture of laughter and tears in the same play, arguing that joy and pain walk side by side on earth. Yet truth, reality, in fact counted for little—even displeased the innovators. They had only one passion, to overthrow the tragic formula that inhibited them, to crush it once and for all under a stampede of every kind of audacity. They did not want their heroes of the Middle Ages to be more real than the heroes of tragic antiquity; they wanted them to appear as passionate and splendid as their predecessors had appeared cold and correct. A mere skirmish over dress and modes of speech, nothing more: one set of puppets at odds with another. Togas were torn up in favour of doublets; a lady, instead of addressing her lover as "My lord," called him "My lion." After the transition fiction still prevailed; only the setting was different.

I do not want to be unfair to the romantic movement. Its effect has been outstanding and unquestionable; it has made us what we are: free artists. It was, I repeat, a necessary revolution, a violent struggle that arose just in time to sweep away a tragic convention that had become childish. Still, it would be ridiculous to arrest the evolution of dramatic art at romanticism. These days, especially, it is astounding to read certain prefaces in which the 1830 movement is announced as the triumphal entry into human truth. Our forty-year distance is enough to let us see clearly that the alleged truth of the romanticists is a persistent and monstrous exaggeration of reality, a fantasy that has declined into excesses. Tragedy, to be sure, is another type of falseness, but it is not *more* false. Between the characters who pace about in togas, endlessly discussing their passions with confidants, and the characters in doublets who perform great feats and flit about like insects drunk with the sun, there is nothing to choose; both are equally and totally unacceptable. Such people have never existed. Romantic heroes are only tragic heroes bitten by the mardi gras bug, hiding behind false noses, and dancing the dramatic cancan after drinking. For the old sluggish rhetoric the 1830 movement substituted an excited, full-blooded rhetoric, and that is all.

Without believing that art progresses, we can still say that it is continuously in motion, among all civilizations, and that this motion reflects different phases of the human mind. Genius is made manifest in every formula, even in the most primitive and innocent ones, though the formulas become transmuted according to the intellectual breadth of each civilization; that is incontestable. If Aeschylus was great, Shakespeare and Molière showed themselves to be equally great, each within his differing civilization and formula. By this I mean that I set apart the creative genius who knows how to make the most of the formula of his time. There is no progress in human creation but there is a logical succession to the formulas, to methods of thought and expression. Thus, art takes the same strides as humanity, is its very language, goes where it goes, moves with it towards light and truth; but for that, we could never judge whether a creator's efforts were more or less great, depending on whether he comes at the beginning or end of a literature.

In these terms, it is certain that when we left tragedy behind, the romantic drama was a first step in the direction of the naturalistic drama, towards which we are now advancing. The romantic drama cleared the ground, proclaimed the freedom of art. Its love of action, its mixture of laughter and tears, its research into accuracy of costume and setting show the movement's impulse towards real life. Is this not how things happen during every revolution against a secular regime?

One begins by breaking windows, chanting and shouting, wrecking relics of the last regime with hammer blows. There is a first exuberance, an intoxication with the new horizons faintly glimpsed, excesses of all kinds that go beyond the original aims and degenerate into the despotism of the old, hated system, those very abuses the revolution has just fought against. In the heat of the battle tomorrow's truths evaporate. And not until all is calm and the fever has abated is there any regret for the broken windows, any understanding of how the effort has gone awry, how the new laws have been prematurely thrown together so that they are hardly any improvement over the laws that were destroyed. Well, the whole history of romantic drama is there. It may have been the formula necessary for its time, it may have had truthful intuitions, it may have been the form that will always be celebrated because a great poet used it to compose his masterpieces. At the present time it is, nonetheless, a ridiculous, outdated formula, with a rhetoric that offends us. We now wonder why it was necessary to push in windows, wave swords, bellow without a break, to go a scale too shrill in sentiment and language. All that leaves us cold, it bores and annoys us. Our condemnation of the romantic formula is summed up in one severe remark: To destroy one rhetoric it was not necessary to invent another.

Today, then, tragedy and romantic drama are equally old and worn out. And that is hardly to the credit of the latter, it should be said, for in less than half a century it has fallen into the same state of decay as tragedy, which took two centuries to die. There it lies, flattened in its turn, overwhelmed by the same passion it showed in its own battle. Nothing is left. We can only guess at what is to come. Logically all that can grow up on that free ground conquered in 1830 is the formula of naturalism.

2

It seems impossible that the movement of inquiry and analysis, which is precisely the movement of the nineteenth century, can have revolutionized all the sciences and arts and left dramatic art to one side, as if isolated. The natural sciences date from the end of the last century; chemistry and physics are less than a hundred years old; history and criticism have been renovated, virtually recreated since the Revolution; an entire world has arisen; it has sent us back to the study of documents, to experience, made us realize that to start afresh we must first take things back to the beginning, become familiar with man and nature, verify what is. Thenceforward, the great naturalistic school, which has spread secretly, irrevocably, often making its way in darkness but always advancing, can finally come out triumphantly into the light of day. To trace the history of this movement, with the misunderstandings that might have impeded it and the multiple causes that have thrust it forward or slowed it down, would be to trace the history of the century itself. An irresistible current carries our society towards the study of reality. In the novel Balzac has been the bold and mighty innovator who has replaced the observation of the scholar with the imagination of the poet. But in the theatre the evolution seems slower. No eminent writer has yet formulated the new idea with any clarity.

I certainly do not say that some excellent works have not been produced, with characters in them who are ingeniously examined and bold truths taken right on to the stage. Let me, for instance, cite certain plays by M. Dumas *fils,* whose talent I scarcely admire, and M. Émile Augier, the most humane and powerful of all. Still, they are midgets beside Balzac; they lack the genius to lay down the formula. It must be said that one can never tell quite when a movement is getting under way; generally its source is remote and lost in the earlier movement from which it emerged. In a manner of speaking, the naturalistic current has always existed. It brings with it nothing absolutely novel. But it has finally flowed into a period favourable to it; it is succeeding and expanding because the human mind has attained the necessary maturity. I do not, therefore, deny the past; I affirm the present. The strength of naturalism is precisely that it has deep roots in our national literature which contains plenty of wisdom. It comes from the very entrails of humanity; it is that much the stronger because it has taken longer to grow and is found in a greater number of our masterpieces.

Certain things have come to pass and I point them out. Can we believe that *L'Ami Fritz* would have been applauded at the Comédie-Française twenty years ago? Definitely not! This play, in which people eat all the time and the lover talks in such homely language, would have disgusted both the classicists and the romantics. To explain its success we must concede that as the years have gone by a secret fermentation has been at work. Lifelike paintings, which used to repel the public, today attract them. The majority has been won over and the stage is open to every experiment. This is the only conclusion to draw.

So that is where we stand. To explain my point better—I am not afraid of repeating myself—I will sum up what I have said. Looking closely at the history of our dramatic literature, one can detect several clearly separated periods. First, there was the infancy of the art, farces and the mystery plays of the Middle Ages, the reciting of simple dialogues which developed as part of a naïve convention, with primitive staging and sets. Gradually, the plays became more complex but in a crude fashion. When Corneille appeared he was acclaimed most of all for his status as an innovator, for refining the dramatic formula of the time, and for hallowing it by means of his genius. It would be very interesting to study the pertinent documents and discover how our classical formula came to be created. It corresponded to the social spirit of the period. Nothing is solid that is not built on necessity. Tragedy reigned for two centuries because it satisfied the exact requirements of those centuries. Geniuses of differing temperaments had buttressed it with their masterpieces. And it continued to impose itself long afterwards, even when second-rate talents were producing inferior work. It acquired a momentum. It persisted also as the literary expression of that society, and nothing would have overthrown it if the society had not itself disappeared. After the Revolution, after that profound disturbance that was meant to transform everything and give birth to a new world, tragedy struggled to stay alive for a few more years. Then the formula cracked and romanticism broke through. A new formula asserted itself. We must look back at the first half of the century to understand the meaning of this cry for liberty. The young society was in the tremor of its infancy. The excited, bewildered, violently unleashed people were still racked by a dangerous fever; and in the first flush of their new liberty they yearned for prodigious adventures and superhuman love affairs. They gaped at the stars; some committed suicide, a very curious reaction to the social enfranchisement which had just been declared at the cost of so much blood. Turning specifically to dramatic literature, I maintain that romanticism in the theatre was an uncomplicated revolt, the invasion by a victorious group who took over the stage violently with drums beating and flags flying. In these early moments the combatants dreamed of making their imprint with a new form; to one rhetoric they opposed another: the Middle Ages to Antiquity, the exalting of passion to the exalting of duty. And that was all, for only the scenic conventions were altered. The characters remained marionettes in new clothing. Only the exterior aspect and the language were modified. But for the period that was enough. Romanticism had taken possession of the theatre in the name of literary freedom and it carried out its revolutionary task with incomparable bravura. But who does not see today that its role could extend no farther than that? Does romanticism have anything whatever to say about our present society? Does it meet one of our requirements? Obviously not. It is as outmoded as a jargon we no longer follow. It confidently expected to replace classical literature which had lasted for two centuries because it was based on social conditions. But romanticism was based on nothing but the fantasy of a few poets or, if you will, on the passing malady of minds overwhelmed by historical events; it was bound to disappear with the malady. It provided the occasion for a magnificent flowering of lyricism; that will be its eternal glory. Today, however, with the evolution accomplished, it is plain that romanticism was no more than the necessary link between classicism and naturalism. The struggle is over; now we must found a secure state. Naturalism flows out of classical art, just as our present society has arisen from the wreckage of the old society. Naturalism alone corresponds to our social needs; it alone has deep roots in the spirit of our times; and it alone can provide a living, durable formula for our art, because this formula will express the nature of our contemporary intelligence. There may be fashions and passing fantasies that exist outside naturalism but they will not survive for long. I say again, naturalism is the expression of our century and it will not die until a new upheaval transforms our democratic world.

Only one thing is needed now: men of genius who can fix the naturalistic formula. Balzac has done it for the novel and the novel is established. When will our Corneilles, Molières and Racines appear to establish our new theatre? We must hope and wait.

*3*

The period when romantic drama ruled now seems distant. In Paris five or six of its playhouses prospered. The demolition of the old theatres along the Boulevard du Temple was a catastrophe of the first order. The theatres became separated from one another, the public changed, different fashions arose. But the discredit into which the drama has fallen proceeds mostly from the exhaustion of the genre—ridiculous, boring plays have gradually taken over from the potent works of 1830.

To this enfeeblement we must add the absolute lack of new actors who understand and can interpret these kinds of plays, for every dramatic formula that vanishes carries away its interpreters with it. Today the drama, hunted from stage to stage, has only two houses that really belong to it, the Ambigu and the Théâtre-Historique. Even at the Saint-Martin the drama is lucky to win a brief showing for itself, between one great spectacle and the next.

An occasional success may renew its courage. But its decline is inevitable; romantic drama is sliding into oblivion, and if it seems sometimes to check its descent, it does so only to roll even lower afterwards. Naturally, there are loud complaints. The tail-end romanticists are desperately unhappy. They swear that except in the drama—meaning their kind of drama—there is no salvation for dramatic literature. I believe, on the contrary, that we must find a new formula that will transform the drama, just as the writers in the first half of the century transformed tragedy. That is the essence of the matter. Today the battle is between romantic drama and naturalistic drama. By romantic drama I mean every play that mocks truthfulness in its incidents and characterization, that struts about in its puppet-box, stuffed to the belly with noises that flounder, for some idealistic reason or other, in pastiches of Shakespeare and Hugo. Every period has its formula; ours is certainly not that of 1830. We are an age of method, of experimental science; our primary need is for precise analysis. We hardly understand the liberty we have won if we use it only to imprison ourselves in a new tradition. The way is open: we can now return to man and nature.

Finally, there have been great efforts to revive the historical drama. Nothing could be better. A critic cannot roundly condemn the choice of historical subjects, even if his own preferences are entirely for subjects that are modern. It is simply that I am full of distrust. The manager one gives this sort of play to frightens me in advance. It is a question of how history is treated, what unusual characters are presented bearing the names of kings, great captains or great artists, and what awful sauce they are served up in to make the history palatable. As soon as the authors of these concoctions move into the past they think everything is permitted: improbabilities, cardboard dolls, monumental idiocies, the hysterical scribblings that falsely represent local colour. And what strange dialogue—François I talking like a haberdasher straight out of the Rue Saint-Denis, Richelieu using the words of a criminal from the Boulevard du Crime, Charlotte Corday with the weeping sentimentalities of a factory girl.

What astounds me is that our playwrights do not seem to suspect for a moment that the historical genre is unavoidably the least rewarding, the one that calls most strongly for research, integrity, a consummate gift of intuition, a talent for reconstruction. I am all for historical drama when it is in the hands of poets of genius or men of exceptional knowledge who are capable of making the public see an epoch come alive with its special quality, its manners, its civilization. In that case we have a work of prophecy or of profoundly interesting criticism.

But unfortunately I know what it is these partisans of historical drama want to revive: the swaggering and swordplay, the big spectacle with big words, the play of lies that shows off in front of the crowd, the gross exhibition that saddens honest minds. Hence my distrust. I think that all this antiquated business is better left in our museum of dramatic history under a pious layer of dust.

There are, undeniably, great obstacles to original experiments: we run up against the hypocrisies of criticism and the long education in idiocies that has been foisted on the public. This public, which titters at every childishness in melodramas, nevertheless lets itself be carried away by outbursts of fine sentiment. But the public is changing. Shakespeare's public and Molière's are no longer ours. We must reckon with shifts in outlook, with the need for reality which is everywhere getting more insistent. The last few romantics vainly repeat that the public wants this and the public wants that; the day is coming when the public will want the truth.

*4*

The old formulas, classical and romantic, were based on the rearrangement and systematic amputation of the truth. They determined on principle that the truth is not good enough; they tried to draw out of it an essence, a "poetry," on the pretext that nature must be expurgated and magnified.

Up to the present the different literary schools disputed only over the question of the best way to disguise the truth so that it might not look too brazen to the public. The classicists adopted the toga; the romantics fought a revolution to impose the coat of mail and the doublet. Essentially the change of dress made little difference; the counterfeiting of nature went on. But today the naturalistic thinkers are telling us that the truth does not need clothing; it can walk naked. That, I repeat, is the quarrel.

Writers with any sense understand perfectly that tragedy and romantic drama are dead. The majority, though, are badly troubled when they turn their minds to the as-yet-unclear formula of tomorrow. Does the truth seriously ask them to give up the grandeur, the poetry, the traditional epic effects that their ambition tells them to put into their plays? Does naturalism demand that they shrink their horizons and risk not one flight into fantasy?

I will try to reply. But first we must determine the methods used by the idealists to lift their works into poetry. They begin by placing their chosen subject in a distant time. That provides them with costumes and makes the framework of the story vague enough to give them full scope for lying. Next, they generalize instead of particularizing; their characters are no longer living people but sentiments, arguments, passions that have been induced by reasoning. This false framework calls for heroes of marble or cardboard. A man of flesh and bone with his own originality would jar in such a legendary setting. Moreover, when we see the characters in romantic drama or tragedy walking about they are stiffened into an attitude, one representing duty, another patriotism, a third superstition, a fourth maternal love; thus, all the abstract ideas file by. Never the thorough analysis of an organism, never a character whose muscles and brain function as in nature.

These, then, are the mannerisms that writers with epic inclinations do not want to give up. For them poetry resides in the past and in abstraction, in the idealizing of facts and characters. As soon as one confronts them with daily life, with the people who fill our streets, they blink, they stammer, they are afraid; they no longer see clearly; they find everything ugly and not good enough for art. According to them, a subject must enter the lies of legend, men must harden and turn to stone like statues before the artist can accept them and make them fit the disguises he has prepared.

Now, it is at this point that the naturalistic movement comes along and says squarely that poetry is everywhere, in everything, even more in the present and the real than in the past and the abstract. Each event at each moment has its poetic, superb aspect. We brush up against heroes who are great and powerful in different respects from the puppets of the epic-makers. Not one playwright in this century has brought to life figures as lofty as Baron Hulot, Old Grandet, César Birotteau, and all the other characters of Balzac, who are so individual and so alive. Beside these real, giant creations Greek and Roman heroes quake; the heroes of the Middle Ages fall flat on their faces like lead soldiers.

With the superior works being produced in these times by the naturalistic school—works of high endeavour, pulsing with life—it is ridiculous and false to park our poetry in some antiquated temple and bury it in cobwebs. Poetry flows at its full force through everything that exists; the truer to life, the greater it becomes. And I mean to give the word poetry its widest definition, not to pin it down exclusively to the cadence of two rhymes, nor to bury it in a narrow coterie of dreamers, but to restore its real human significance which concerns the expansion and encouragement of every kind of truth.

Take our present environment, then, and try to make men live in it: you will write great works. It will undoubtedly call for some effort; it means sifting out of the confusion of life the simple formula of naturalism. Therein lies the difficulty: to do great things with the subjects and characters that our eyes, accustomed to the spectacle of the daily round, have come to see as small. I am aware that it is more convenient to present a marionette to the public and name it Charlemagne and puff it up with such tirades that the public believes it is watching a colossus; it is more convenient than taking a bourgeois of our time, a grotesque, unsightly man, and drawing sublime poetry out of him, making him, for example, Père Goriot, the father who gives his guts for his daughters, a figure so gigantic with truth and love that no other literature can offer his equal.

Nothing is as easy as persuading the managers with known formulas; and heroes in the classical or romantic taste cost so little labour that they are manufactured by the dozen, and have become standardized articles that clutter up our literature. But it takes hard work to create a real hero, intelligently analysed, alive and performing. That is probably why naturalism terrifies those authors who are used to fishing up great men from the troubled waters of history. They would have to burrow too deeply into humanity, learn about life, go straight for the greatness of reality and make it function with all their power. And let nobody gainsay this true poetry of humanity; it has been sifted out in the novel and can be in the theatre; only the method of adaptation remains to be found.

I am troubled by a comparison; it has been haunting me and I will now free myself of it. For two long months a play called *Les Danicheff* has been running at the Odéon. It takes place in Russia. It has been very successful here, but is apparently so dishonest, so packed with gross improbabilities, that the author, a Russian, has not even dared to show it in his country. What can you think of this work which is applauded in Paris and would be booed in St Petersburg? Well, imagine for a moment that the Romans could come back to life and see a performance of *Rome vaincue*. Can you hear their roars of laughter? Do you think the play would complete one performance? It would strike them as a parody; it would sink under the weight of mockery. And is there one historical play that could be performed before the society it claims to portray? A strange theatre, this, which is plausible only among foreigners, is based on the disappearance of the generations it deals with, and is made up of so much misinformation that it is good only for the ignorant!

The future is with naturalism. The formula will be found; it will be proved that there is more poetry in the little apartment of a bourgeois than in all the empty, worm-eaten palaces of history; in the end we will see that everything meets in the real: lovely fantasies that are free of capriciousness and whimsy, and idylls, and comedies, and dramas. Once the soil has been turned over, the task that seems alarming and unfeasible today will become easy.

I am not qualified to pronounce on the form that tomorrow's drama will take; that must be left to the voice of some genius to come. But I will allow myself to indicate the path I consider our theatre will follow.

First, the romantic drama must be abandoned. It would be disastrous for us to take over its outrageous acting, its rhetoric, its inherent thesis of action at the expense of character analysis. The finest models of the genre are, as has been said, mere operas with big effects. I believe, then, that we must go back to tragedy—not, heaven forbid, to borrow more of its rhetoric, its system of confidants, its declaiming, its endless speeches, but to return to its simplicity of action and its unique psychological and physiological study of the characters. Thus understood, the tragic framework is excellent; one deed unwinds in all its reality, and moves the characters to passions and feelings, the exact analysis of which constitutes the sole interest of the play—and in a contemporary environment, with the people who surround us.

My constant concern, my anxious vigil, has made me wonder which of us will have the strength to raise himself to the pitch of genius. If the naturalistic drama must come into being, only a genius can give birth to it. Corneille and Racine made tragedy. Victor Hugo made romantic drama. Where is the as-yet-unknown author who must make the naturalistic drama? In recent years experiments have not been wanting. But either because the public was not ready or because none of the beginners had the necessary staying-power, not one of these attempts has had decisive results.

In battles of this kind, small victories mean nothing; we need triumphs that overwhelm the adversary and win the public to the cause. Audiences would give way before the onslaught of a really strong man. This man would come with the expected word, the solution to the problem, the formula for a real life on stage, combining it with the illusions necessary in the theatre. He would have what the newcomers have as yet lacked: the cleverness or the might to impose himself and to remain so close to truth that his cleverness could not lead him into lies.

And what an immense place this innovator would occupy in our dramatic literature! He would be at the peak. He would build his monument in the middle of the desert of mediocrity that we are crossing, among the jerry-built houses strewn about our most illustrious stages. He would put everything in question and remake everything, scour the boards, create a world whose elements he would lift from life, from outside our traditions. Surely there is no more ambitious dream that a writer of our time could fulfil. The domain of the novel is crowded; the domain of the theatre is free. At this time in France an imperishable glory awaits the man of genius who takes up the work of Molière and finds in the reality of living comedy the full, true drama of modern society.

*Physiological man\**

. . . In effect, the great naturalistic evolution, which comes down directly from the fifteenth century to ours has everything to do with the gradual substitution of physiological man for metaphysical man. In tragedy metaphysical man, man according to dogma and logic, reigned absolutely. The body did not count; the soul was regarded as the only interesting piece of human machinery; drama took place in the air, in pure mind. Consequently, what use was the tangible world? Why worry about the place where the action was located? Why be surprised at a baroque costume or false declaiming? Why notice that Queen Dido was a boy whose budding beard forced him to wear a mask? None of that mattered; these trifles were not worth stooping to; the play was heard out as if it were a school essay or a law case; it was on a higher plane than man, in the world of ideas, so far away from real man that any intrusion of reality would have spoiled the show.

Such is the point of departure—in Mystery plays, the religious point; the philosophical point in tragedy. And from that beginning natural man, stifling under the rhetoric and dogma, struggled secretly, tried to break free, made lengthy, futile efforts, and in the end asserted himself, limb by limb. The whole history of our theatre is in this conquest by the physiological man, who emerged more clearly in each period from behind the dummy of religious and philosophical idealism. Corneille, Molière, Racine, Voltaire, Beaumarchais and, in our day, Victor Hugo, Émile Augier, Alexandre Dumas *fils*, even Sardou, have had only one task, even when they were not completely aware of it: to increase the reality of our corpus of drama, to progress towards truth, to sift out more and more of the natural man and impose him on the public. And inevitably, the evolution will not end with them. It continues; it will continue forever. Mankind is very young. . . .

*Costume, stage design, speech*

Modern clothes make a poor spectacle. If we depart from bourgeois tragedy, shut in between its four walls, and wish to use the breadth of larger stages for crowd scenes we are embarrassed and constrained by the monotony and the uniformly funereal look of the extras. In this case, I think, we should take advantage of the variety of garb offered by the different classes and occupations. To elaborate: I can imagine an author setting one act in the main marketplace of les Halles in Paris. The setting would be superb, with its bustling life and bold possibilities. In this immense setting we could have a very picturesque ensemble by displaying the porters wearing their large hats, the saleswomen with their white aprons and vividly-coloured scarves, the customers dressed in silk or wool or cotton prints, from the ladies accompanied by their maids to the female beggars on the prowl for anything they can pick up off the street. For inspiration it would be enough to go to les Halles and look about. Nothing is gaudier or more interesting. All of Paris would enjoy seeing this set if it were realized with the necessary accuracy and amplitude.

And how many other settings for popular drama there are for the taking! Inside a factory, the interior of a mine, the gingerbread market, a railway station, flower stalls, a racetrack, and so on. All the activities of modern life can take place in them. It will be said that such sets have already been tried. Unquestionably we have seen factories and railway stations in fantasy plays; but these were fantasy stations and factories. I mean, these sets were thrown together to create an illusion that was at best incomplete. What we need is detailed reproduction: costumes supplied by tradespeople, not sumptuous but adequate for the purposes of truth and for the interest of the scenes. Since everybody mourns the death of the drama our playwrights certainly ought to make a try at this type of popular, contemporary drama. At one stroke they could satisfy the public hunger for spectacle and the need for exact studies which grows more pressing every day. Let us hope, though, that the playwrights will show us real people and not those whining members of the working class who play such strange roles in boulevard melodrama.

As M. Adolphe Jullien has said—and I will never be tired of repeating it—everything is interdependent in the theatre. Lifelike costumes look wrong if the sets, the diction, the plays themselves are not lifelike. They must all march in step along the naturalistic road. When costume becomes more accurate, so do sets; actors free themselves from bombastic declaiming; plays study reality more closely and their characters are more true to life. I could make the same observations about sets I have just made about costume. With them too, we may seem to have reached the

---

\*What precedes is a complete chapter. Two brief excerpts follow from the chapter on Costume..

highest possible degree of truth, but we still have long strides to take. Most of all we would need to intensify the illusion in reconstructing the environments, less for their picturesque quality than for dramatic utility. The environment must determine the character. When a set is planned so as to give the lively impression of a description by Balzac; when, as the curtain rises, one catches the first glimpse of the characters, their personalities and behaviour, if only to see the actual locale in which they move, the importance of exact reproduction in the decor will be appreciated. Obviously, that is the way we are going. Environment, the more truthful, the actors' diction will gain enormously in simplicity and naturalness.

To conclude, I will repeat that the battle of the conventions is far from being finished, and that it will no doubt last forever. Today we are beginning to see clearly where we are going, but our steps are still impeded by the melting slush of rhetoric and metaphysics.

# GLOSSARY

**Absurd** *See* **Theater of the Absurd.**

**actos** Short satirical plays devised by Luis Valdez and El Teatro Campesino in the late 1960s to dramatize the conditions of farmworkers in California.

**alienation effect** A stage technique developed by Bertolt Brecht in the 1920s and 1930s for "estranging" the action of the play. By making characters and their actions seem remarkable, alien, or unusual, Brecht encouraged the audience to question the social realities that produced such events, the political and ideological background of the drama and of its stage production.

**allegory** A literary or dramatic technique that uses actual characters, places, and actions to represent more abstract political, moral, or religious ideas.

**avant-garde** Literally the "advance group," the term usually refers to the most innovative, experimental, or unorthodox artists in a given historical period. Used almost exclusively of late nineteenth- and twentieth-century movements.

**biomechanics** An experimental technique for actor training and performance devised by the Russian director Vsevolod Meyerhold after the Russian Revolution (1917). The technique emphasized the actor's physical training, stressing acrobatic and choreographic elements in production.

**box set** First devised in the 1830s, a set consisting of three practical walls enclosing the stage in a roomlike way.

**cabaret performance** Stage performances in restaurants serving food and drink; especially popular in Europe after World War I, cabarets often were used for innovative kinds of performance.

**canon** An authorized body of texts, such as the "canon" of Shakespeare's known plays; also commonly used to mean a "traditional" body of texts.

**catastrophe** The turning point in the plot of a classical tragedy.

**character** A fictional "person" appearing in a play or other work of fiction; usually conventionalized to some degree.

**comedy** Traditionally a humorous literary form, comedy typically concerns the trials of love and/or ridicules the failings of certain members of society.

**Constructivism, Constructivist theater** A movement in the Soviet theater after World War I, often associated with the director Vsevolod Meyerhold. Adapted from the visual arts, constructivist theater resisted the use of representational sets, using more abstract "constructions" onstage.

**cross-dressing** One of the conventions of cross-gendered acting, in which women play male characters in male costume, and men play female characters in women's clothing.

**cruelty** *See* **Theater of Cruelty.**

**Cubism** A style of painting pioneered by Picasso and others, in which several perspectives on the object are represented on the surface of the painting simultaneously.

**Dada** A nonsense term adopted as the name of a literary and theatrical movement in Europe after World War I; Dada developed an aesthetic of random and irrational art. Dada performances became popular in cabarets of Paris, Zurich, and Berlin in the 1920s.

**deconstruction** Movement in philosophy, and subsequently in literary studies, associated with the work of French philosopher Jacques Derrida. In deconstructive philosophy, the "presence" of metaphysical categories is questioned through a process that interrogates, suspends, or "de-constructs" the way in which those categories have been produced.

**demonstration** Describing "alienation effects," Bertolt Brecht urged his actors to "demonstrate" the roles they played, rather than identifying with them in the mode of Stanislavskian acting. Acting-as-demonstration keeps the audience aware of both the actor *and* the "character" at the same time.

**drama** A literary composition, usually in dialogue form, that centers on the actions of fictional characters.

**emotion memory** A term developed by the Russian director Constantin Stanislavski to describe an actor's "work on himself" in acting. After considering a character's circumstances in the play and his or her own past life leading up to the action of the play, the actor tries to connect the character's situation with important events in his or her own life. This emotional or affectual connection can make the character's display of emotion onstage seem realistic and immediate.

**environmental theater** A term coined by Richard Schechner in the late 1960s to describe performances that do not distinguish between the playing area and the audience; the performance takes place throughout the theatrical environment.

**epic theater** A term associated with the German director Erwin Piscator and theorized by Bertolt Brecht in the late 1920s and 1930s, epic theater uses episodic dramatic action, nonrepresentational staging, and "alienation effects" to demonstrate the political, social, and economic factors governing the lives of the dramatic characters. In the theater, Brecht advocated the use of placards to announce the action, visible lighting, film screens on the stage, and other devices to produce this epic effect.

**episode** Originally, a dramatic scene in a classical Greek tragedy, as distinct from the choral odes; now, usually refers to any incident or event in a play. Plays that are episodic tend not to subordinate episodes to a causal plot, but simply to arrange them in a series.

**existentialism** A philosophical movement associated with Jean-Paul Sartre and Albert Camus, existentialism argues that "existence precedes essence," that individuals must choose, decide their "essential" nature rather than having it given from some transcendent source.

**Expressionism, Expressionist theater** An early twentieth-century movement challenging the verisimilitude of realistic theater by staging individual emotional, unconscious states of mind directly. In expressionist plays, the action is usually abrupt and intense; the characters are usually generalized; the plot is typically symbolic or allegorical.

**extravaganza**  Visual spectacle popular in nineteenth-century theater.

**Fabian Society**  A late nineteenth-century English socialist political society; Marxist in its orientation to social change, the Fabian Society advocated a policy of gradual reform rather than revolution.

**farce**  Usually a short comic play, often relying on a highly coincidental plot.

**film noir**  A genre of black-and-white detective films popular in the 1940s, which frequently used shadowy, nighttime settings to establish an aura of menace and foreboding.

**fourth-wall**  Refers to the style of realistic theater since the late nineteenth century, in which the stage is treated as a room with one wall missing. The audience is not acknowledged or addressed by the actors, but overlooks the scene as a silent, invisible observer.

**Futurism**  An avant-garde movement popular in Italy and the Soviet Union in the 1910s and 1920s, in which the attributes of the machine were glorified—speed, regularity, brilliance.

**genre**  Literally, "kind" or "type," *genre* in literary and dramatic studies refers to the main types of literary form, principally tragedy and comedy. The term can also refer to forms that are more specific to a given historical era, such as "revenge tragedy" or to more specific subgenres of tragedy and comedy, such as "comedy of manners."

**given circumstances**  Term used by Constantin Stanislavski to describe the situation a character finds himself or herself in at the opening of the play, which the actor must construct as his first step in building the character toward performance.

**ideology**  A complex term first used in the eighteenth century to categorize political beliefs and attitudes. Used to mean 1) a body of beliefs, a doctrine; 2) a body of illusory beliefs, a false doctrine; 3) a socially grounded system for producing beliefs and values, a way of producing meanings or doctrines

**Independent Theater Movement**  A late nineteenth-century movement in Europe, in which small theaters gambled on the production of new and unconventional plays—by Ibsen, Shaw, Chekhov—to a small audience, usually outside the theatrical mainstream.

**line of business**  The performance attributes of a stock character-type; the typical demeanor, gestures, and manner of, for example, a comic old man, the leading man, tragic "heavy," would become an actor's "line of business," enabling him or her to specialize in a certain character-type

**Little Negro Theater Movement**  A movement in the U.S. theater in the 1920s to develop theaters owned and operated by African Americans, playing a dramatic repertory by African-American writers.

**Little Theater Movement**  A movement in the American theater in the early twentieth century akin to the Inde-

pendent Theater Movement in Europe. Little Theaters offered new or noncommercial plays to smaller audiences.

**magic if**  Term developed by Constantin Stanislavski to describe the actor's attitude toward a role; to play "as if I were in this situation."

**melodrama**  First used in the late eighteenth century, the term originally referred to highly charged, popular plays using music to reinforce their clear-cut moral action; now refers more generally to plays with a schematic opposition between good and evil, in which good usually prevails.

**metatheater**  A term used to describe plays that self-consciously comment on the process of theater, and so treat the relationship between theater and life. Such plays sometimes use the play-within-the-play device.

**method acting**  A technique of acting developed by Constantin Stanislavski at the turn of the twentieth century, which teaches actors to use emotion memory to enact the character's feelings persuasively and realistically in performance; method acting became especially popular in the United States in the 1930s, 1940s, and 1950s.

**mise-en-scène**  The "putting onstage" of a play, including the setting, scenery, direction, and action.

**mitos**  Lyrical plays on Mexican-American life devised by Luis Valdez and El Teatro Campesino in the late 1960s and 1970s.

**modernism**  A movement in the arts and culture of Europe and the Americas, usually dated from the end of the nineteenth century. Modernist art is generally characterized by a complex, often fragmentary surface; modernist movements in the arts usually stem from an avant-garde opposition to social or artistic conventions.

**modernity**  In philosophical terms, "modernity" refers to the consequences of post-Cartesian rationalism, the sense that human reason is both distinct from the world, and capable of lending it—or discovering within it—a rational order.

**modernization**  The process of human and social organization that arose from philosophical modernity: rationalizing of labor, of spheres of living, of social and cultural life.

**montage**  A technique used in film consisting of a rapid sequence of images.

**Naturalism**  A late nineteenth-century movement that attempted to achieve an objective verisimilitude in art—chiefly in theater and literature—by adopting a "scientific" attitude toward its subject matter. Thematically, naturalism emphasizes the role of society, history, and personality in determining the actions of its characters, usually expressed as a conflict between the characters and their environment.

**nautical shows**  A type of melodrama popular in England in the eighteenth and nineteenth centuries on seafaring subjects; in aquatic dramas, the stage was actually flooded.

**pantomime**  A silent, narrative performance; in England, pantomime refers to a stage show usually performed in the Christmas season featuring a large cast, song and dance numbers, and usually on a fairy-tale theme, performed for children.

**pastiche**   Term used by Fredric Jameson to describe the toneless quotation of earlier artistic styles in contemporary (or postmodern) works.

**performance art**   A late twentieth-century phenomenon, performance art arose in the "happenings" of Alan Kaprow in the 1960s; it is a kind of performance which may be unscripted, is often autobiographical, in which the performer engages in a direct communication with the audience. Performance art is distinguished from drama in that there is no fictive "play" being performed: the performance itself is the work of art.

**plot**   The sequence of events in a play or narrative; differs from the "story," which encompasses earlier events. Some works have several plots.

**political theater**   In conventional usage, theater that seems to question the inequities and injustices of contemporary society. Bertolt Brecht developed a more searching critique of political theater, however, in which the ideology of theatrical representation itself could be seen as the theater's "politics."

**poor theater**   A term coined by Polish director Jerzy Grotowski in the 1960s, poor theater refers to a kind of theater that relies essentially on acting, and on the kind of metaphysical relationship that can be forged between actors and audiences in performance.

**postcolonial**   A term referring to the complicated cultural and political situation facing nations after they have become independent from colonial rule; typically many civil and cultural practices and institutions originally derived from the colonial culture remain, but in altered or contested form.

**postmodern, postmodernism**   A term used to characterize the complex transformation of culture in the late twentieth century. Although the postmodern is not confined to the sphere of art, postmodern works are generally characterized by stylistic "quotation," an invocation and disengagement from history and the fragmentation of artistic surface.

**proscenium**   An arch over the front of the stage. First used in European theaters in the Renaissance; throughout the eighteenth and nineteenth centuries, theater design gradually eliminated the apron that extended in front of the proscenium, and decorated the proscenium arch itself, emphasizing its framelike quality.

**protagonist**   Literally the "first contestant" in the ancient Greek theater, the term referred to the "first" or main actor competing for a prize. In modern usage, refers to the play's main character.

**Realism**   A literary and theatrical practice valuing direct imitation or verisimilitude. Often associated with Naturalism, modern realism is sometimes described as the inheritor of naturalism. In practice, realism is usually more concerned with psychological motives, the "inner reality," and less committed to achieving a superficial verisimilitude alone.

**repertory**   A company that performs several plays in rotation throughout a season is a repertory company; the term also refers to a set of plays.

**role doubling**   The practice of using one actor to play more than one part.

**scenic unity**   The practice of harmonizing acting style, costumes, and sets to create the illusion of a single, unified environment on the stage.

**social realism**   A form of modern realistic drama emphasizing social messages and themes; social realism was the official genre approved by the Communist Party in the Soviet Union after the revolution.

**soliloquy**   A speech delivered by a character alone onstage, speaking to himself or herself, or to the audience.

**soubrette**   A stock character in drama: a young, pert female character.

**subtext**   A term first elaborated by Constantin Stanislavski, *subtext* refers to the unspoken motive for a given line or speech, what the character wants to get or to do by saying the line. It is sometimes now used more generally to suggest a text's underlying sense or meaning.

**Surrealism, Surrealist theater**   A movement originating in Paris in the 1920s attempting to represent subconscious experience directly in art.

**Symbolism, Symbolist theater**   A European movement of the late nineteenth and early twentieth century in reaction to realism and naturalism. Symbolist theater attempted to dramatize more poetic or metaphorical situations, often using unusual stage settings and ethereal dramatic action and language.

**tableau/tableaux (pl.)**   A motionless grouping of actors to represent a "picture" of a dramatic scene; sometimes called *tableau vivant,* a "living picture."

**tableaux vivants**   See tableau; *tableaux vivants* is the plural form of *tableau vivant.*

**theater**   A structure built for the performance of drama; also refers to the institution of dramatic performance.

**theater in the round**   The presentation of a play in an arena setting, in which the audience sits on all sides of the stage area, but is separate from the playing space itself.

**Theater of the Absurd**   A type of late twentieth-century theater and drama, characterized by a relatively abstract setting, and arbitrary and illogical action. It is sometimes said to express the "human condition" in a basic or "existential" way. The term was first coined by Martin Esslin.

**Theater of Cruelty**   Term used by Antonin Artaud to describe his nonrepresentational, mystical, mythological theater.

**theme**   A term used to describe a consistent kind of meaning asserted by a work of literature.

**tragedy**   Originating in the classical Greek theater, tragedy generally refers to serious drama, taking a central character's conflict with himself or herself, with society, or with the gods as its subject. Aristotle first described tragedy in his *Poetics,* and tragedy has undergone almost continual redefinition.

**tragicomedy**   In the English Renaissance, a term describing a dramatic form: a play beginning like a tragedy, but ending happily, like a comedy. In modern usage, the term refers most often to a play's tone or attitude: a play that is ironic, both serious and absurd, leaning toward black comedy or tragic farce.

**verisimilitude**   Verisimilitude refers to the extent to which the drama or stage setting appears to copy the superficial appearance of life offstage.

**well-made play**   A form of drama popularized in the nineteenth century, especially in France. The plot usually turns on the revelation of a secret and includes a character who explains and moralizes the action of the play to others; the plot is often relentlessly coincidental, even mechanically so.

# BIBLIOGRAPHY

## Readings on Drama and Theater

Barish, Jonas. *The Antitheatrical Prejudice.* Berkeley: U of California P, 1981.

Beckerman, Bernard. *Dynamics of Drama.* New York: Drama Book Specialists, 1979.

Bennett, Susan. *Theatre Audiences: A Theory of Production and Reception.* London: Routledge, 1990.

Bentley, Eric. *The Life of the Drama.* New York: Atheneum, 1964.

Herbert Blau, *The Audience.* Baltimore: Johns Hopkins UP, 1990.

Brockett, Oscar G. *History of the Theatre.* Boston: Allyn and Bacon, 1987.

Carlson, Marvin. *Theories of the Theatre: A Historical and Critical Survey, from the Greeks to the Present.* Ithaca: Cornell UP, 1984.

Case, Sue-Ellen. *Feminism and Theatre.* New York: Methuen, 1988.

——, and Janelle Reinelt, eds. *The Performance of Power: Theatrical Discourse and Politics.* Iowa City: U of Iowa P, 1991.

——, ed. *Performing Feminisms: Feminist Critical Theory and Theatre.* Baltimore: Johns Hopkins UP, 1990.

Clark, Barrett H. *European Theories of the Drama.* New York: Crown, 1965.

Cole, Toby, and Helen Krich Chinoy, eds. *Actors on Acting.* New York: Crown, 1970.

——. *Directors on Directing.* Indianapolis: Bobbs-Merrill, 1963.

——. *Playwrights on Playwriting.* New York: Hill and Wang, 1960.

Dukore, Bernard F. *Dramatic Theory and Criticism: Greeks to Grotowski.* New York: Holt Rinehart and Winston, 1974.

Elam, Keir. *The Semiotics of Theatre and Drama.* London: Methuen, 1980.

Fergusson, Francis. *The Idea of a Theater.* Princeton: Princeton UP, 1949.

Frye, Northrop. *Anatomy of Criticism.* Princeton: Princeton UP, 1957.

Goldman, Michael. *The Actor's Freedom.* New York: Viking, 1975.

Kubiak, Anthony. *Stages of Terror: Terrorism, Ideology, and Coercion as Theatre History.* Bloomington: Indiana UP, 1991.

Leacroft, Richard, and Helen Leacroft. *Theatre and Playhouse: An Illustrated Survey of Theatre Building from Ancient Greece to the Present Day.* New York: Methuen, 1984.

Reinelt, Janelle, and Joseph Roach, eds. *Critical Theory and Performance.* Ann Arbor: U of Michigan P, 1992.

States, Bert O. *Great Reckonings in Little Rooms: On the Phenomenology of Theater.* Berkeley: U of California P, 1985.

——. *Irony and Drama.* Ithaca: Cornell UP, 1971.

Steiner, George. *The Death of Tragedy.* New York: Oxford UP, 1961.

Turner, Victor. *From Ritual to Theatre: The Human Seriousness of Play.* New York: Performing Arts Journal Publications, 1982.

Worthen, William B. *The Idea of the Actor: Drama and the Ethics of Performance.* Princeton: Princeton UP, 1984.

## Modern Drama: General

Antoine, André. *Memories of the Théâtre Libre.* Trans. Marvin Carlson. Coral Gables: U of Miami P, 1964.

Artaud, Antonin. *The Theater and Its Double.* Trans. Mary Caroline Richards. New York: Grove, 1958.

Bennett, Benjamin. *Modern Drama and German Classicism: Renaissance from Lessing to Brecht.* Ithaca: Cornell UP, 1979.

——. *Theater as Problem: Modern Drama and Its Place in Literature.* Ithaca: Cornell UP, 1990.

Bentley, Eric. *The Playwright as Thinker: A Study of Drama in Modern Times.* New York: Harcourt, 1946.

——. *Theatre of War.* New York: Viking, 1972.

Betsko, Kathleen, and Rachel Koenig. *Interviews with Contemporary Women Playwrights.* New York: Beech Tree, 1987.

Bigsby, C. W. E. *A Critical Introduction to Twentieth-Century American Drama.* 3 vols. Cambridge: Cambridge UP, 1982–85.

——. "The Language of Crisis in British Theatre: The Drama of Cultural Pathology." *Contemporary English Drama.* Ed. C. W. E. Bigsby. New York: Holmes and Meier, 1981.

Blau, Herbert. *Eye of the Prey: Subversions of the Postmodern.* Bloomington: Indiana UP, 1987.

Bradby, David. *Modern French Drama, 1940–1980.* New York: Grove, 1984.

Brater, Enoch, ed. *Feminine Focus: The New Women Playwrights.* New York: Oxford UP, 1989.

Braun, Edward. *Meyerhold on Theatre.* New York: Hill and Wang, 1969.

Brockett, Oscar G., and Robert R. Findlay. *Century of Innovation: A History of European and American Theatre and Drama Since 1870.* Englewood Cliffs: Prentice-Hall, 1973.

Bronner, Edwin, ed. *The Encyclopedia of the American Theatre 1900–1975.* New York: A. S. Barnes, 1980.

Brook, Peter. *The Empty Space.* New York: Avon, 1968.

Brustein, Robert. *The Theatre of Revolt.* Boston: Little, Brown, 1964.

Bull, John. *New British Political Dramatists.* London: Macmillan, 1984.

Butters, Ronald R., John M. Clum, and Michael Moon, eds. *Displacing Homophobia: Gay Male Perspectives in Literature and Culture.* Durham: Duke UP, 1989.

Calandra, Denis. *New German Dramatists.* New York: Grove, 1983.

Case, Sue-Ellen. "Toward a Butch-Femme Aesthetic." *Making a Spectacle: Feminist Essays on Contemporary Women's Theatre.* Ed. Lynda Hart. Ann Arbor: U of Michigan P, 1989.

Chinoy, Helen Krich, and Linda Walsh Jenkins, eds. *Women in American Theatre.* New York: Crown, 1981.

Chinweizu, Onwuchekwa Jemie, and Ihechukwu Madubuike. *Toward the Decolonization of African Literature.* Vol. 1. Washington: Howard UP, 1983.

Cohn, Ruby. *From Desire to Godot: Pocket Theater of Postwar Paris.* Berkeley: U of California P, 1987.

——. *New American Dramatists, 1960–1980.* New York: Grove, 1982.

Davis, Tracy C. *Actresses as Working Women: Their Social Identity in Victorian Culture.* London: Routledge, 1991.

de Lauretis, Teresa. "Sexual Indifferentiation and Lesbian Representation." *Theatre Journal* 40 (1988): 155–77.

Dolan, Jill. *The Feminist Spectator as Critic.* Ann Arbor: UMI Research Press, 1988.

Driver, Tom. *Romantic Quest and Modern Query: A History of the Modern Theatre.* New York: Delacorte, 1970.

Elsom, John. *Post-War British Theatre.* London: Routledge and Kegan Paul, 1976.

Esslin, Martin. *The Theatre of the Absurd.* New York: Doubleday, 1969.

Finney, Gail. *Women in Modern Drama: Freud, Feminism, and European Theater at the Turn of the Century.* Ithaca: Cornell UP, 1989.

Garza, Roberto, ed. *Contemporary Chicano Theatre.* Notre Dame: U of Notre Dame P, 1976.

Gilman, Richard. *The Making of Modern Drama.* New York: Farrar, Straus and Giroux, 1974.

Grotowski, Jerzy. *Towards a Poor Theatre.* New York: Simon and Schuster, 1968.

Harrison, Paul Carter. *The Drama of Nommo.* New York: Grove, 1972.

Hart, Lynda, ed. *Making a Spectacle: Feminist Essays on Contemporary Women's Theatre.* Ann Arbor: U of Michigan P, 1989.

—— and Peggy Phelan, eds. *Acting Out: Feminist Performances.* Ann Arbor: U of Michigan P, 1992.

Hatch, James V., ed. *Black Theatre USA: Forty-Five Plays by Black Americans 1847–1974.* New York: Macmillan, 1974.

Heilbing, Terry. *Gay and Lesbian Plays Today.* Portsmouth: Heinemann, 1993.

Hill, Errol, ed. *The Theatre of Black Americans.* 2 vols. Englewood Cliffs: Prentice-Hall, 1980.

Huerta, Jorge A. *Chicano Theater: Themes and Forms.* Ypsilanti: Bilingual Press, 1982.

Hunt, Hugh, et al., eds. *The Revels History of Drama in English.* Vol. 7: *1880 to the Present Day.* London: Methuen, 1979.

Jones, David Richard. *Great Directors at Work.* Berkeley: U of California P, 1986.

Kanellos, Nicolás. *Hispanic Theatre in the United States.* Houston: Arte Público Press, 1984.

Kennedy, Andrew. *Six Dramatists in Search of a Language.* Cambridge: Cambridge UP, 1975.

Keyssar, Helene. *Feminist Theatre.* London: Macmillan, 1984.

Kruger, Loren. *The National Stage: Theatre and Cultural Legitimation in England, France, and America.* Chicago: U of Chicago P, 1992.

Marranca, Bonnie, ed. *The Theatre of Images.* New York: Drama Book Specialists, 1977.

Ndlovu, Duma, ed. *Woza Afrika! An Anthology of South African Plays.* New York: Braziller, 1986.

Ngugi wa Thiong'o. *Decolonising the Mind: The Politics of Language in African Literature.* London: James Curey, 1986.

Perkins, Kathy A., ed. *Black Female Playwrights: An Anthology of Plays Before 1950.* Bloomington: Indiana UP, 1989.

Peter, John. *Vladimir's Carrot: Modern Drama and the Modern Imagination.* Chicago: U of Chicago P, 1987.

Phelan, Peggy. *Unmarked: The Politics of Performance.* London: Routledge, 1993.

Postlewait, Thomas, and Bruce A. McConachie, eds. *Interpreting the Theatrical Past: Essays in the Historiography of Performance.* Iowa City: U of Iowa P, 1989.

Quigley, Austin. *The Modern Stage and Other Worlds.* London: Methuen, 1985.

Rosen, Carol. *Plays of Impasse: Contemporary Drama Set in Confining Institutions.* Princeton: Princeton UP, 1983.

Savran, David, ed. *In Their Own Words: Contemporary American Playwrights.* New York: Theatre Communications Group, 1988.

Schechner, Richard. *Environmental Theater.* New York: Hawthorn, 1973.

Seltzer, Daniel, ed. *The Modern Theatre: Readings and Documents.* Boston: Little, Brown, 1967.

Shank, Ted. *American Alternative Theatres.* New York: Grove, 1982.

Shewey, Don, ed. *Out Front: Contemporary Gay and Lesbian Plays.* New York: Grove, 1988.

Stanislavski, Constantin. *An Actor Prepares.* Trans. Elizabeth Reynolds Hapgood. New York: Theatre Arts, 1936.

——. *Building a Character.* Trans. Elizabeth Reynolds Hapgood. New York: Theatre Arts, 1949.

——. *Creating a Role.* Trans. Elizabeth Reynolds Hapgood. New York: Theatre Arts, 1961.

——. *My Life in Art.* Trans. J. J. Robbins. Boston: Little, Brown, 1924.

Styan, J. L. *The Dark Comedy.* Cambridge: Cambridge UP, 1968.

——. *Modern Drama in Theory and Practice.* 3 vols. Cambridge: Cambridge UP, 1980.

Taylor, John Russell. *Anger and After.* London: Methuen, 1969.

——. *The Second Wave: British Drama of the Sixties.* London: Eyre Methuen, 1978.

Wandor, Michelene. *Understudies.* London: Methuen, 1980.

Whitaker, Thomas R. *Fields of Play in Modern Drama.* Princeton: Princeton UP, 1977.

Wiles, Timothy J. *The Theater Event: Modern Theories of Performance.* Chicago: U of Chicago P, 1980.

Williams, Raymond. *Drama from Ibsen to Brecht.* London: Hogarth, 1987.

——. *Modern Tragedy.* Stanford: Stanford UP, 1966.

Worth, Katharine. *Revolutions in Modern English Drama.* London: G. Bell and Sons, 1972.

Worthen, W. B. *Modern Drama and the Rhetoric of Theater.* Berkeley: U of California P, 1992.

## Individual Playwrights

### Samuel Beckett

Acheson, James, and Kateryna Arthur, eds. *Beckett's Later Fiction and Drama: Texts for Company.* New York: St. Martin's, 1987.

Bair, Deirdre. *Samuel Beckett: A Biography.* New York: Harcourt Brace Jovanovich, 1978.

Brater, Enoch, ed. *Beckett at 80/Beckett in Context.* Oxford: Oxford UP, 1986.

——. *Beyond Minimalism: Beckett's Late Style in the Theater.* Oxford: Oxford UP, 1987.

Cohn, Ruby. *Just Play: Beckett's Theater.* Princeton: Princeton UP, 1980.

——. *Samuel Beckett: The Comic Gamut.* New Brunswick: Rutgers UP, 1962.

Gontarski, S. E. *On Beckett: Essays and Criticism.* New York: Grove, 1986.

Graver, Lawrence, and Raymond Federman, eds. *Samuel Beckett: The Critical Heritage.* London: Routledge and Kegan Paul, 1979.

Kalb, Jonathan. *Beckett in Performance.* Cambridge: Cambridge UP, 1989.

Kenner, Hugh. *Samuel Beckett.* Berkeley: U of California P, 1968.

Worth, Katharine. *The Irish Drama of Europe from Yeats to Beckett.* London: Athlone, 1978.

### Edward Bond

Bulman, James C. "Bond, Shakespeare, and the Absurd." *Modern Drama* 29 (1986): 60–70.

Coult, Tony. *The Plays of Edward Bond.* London: Methuen, 1977.

Hay, Malcolm, and Philip Roberts. *Bond: A Study of His Plays.* London: Methuen, 1980.

——. *Edward Bond: A Companion to the Plays.* London: TQ Publications, 1978.

Spencer, Jenny. *Dramatic Strategies in the Plays of Edward Bond.* Cambridge: Cambridge UP, 1992.

### Bertolt Brecht

Benjamin, Walter. *Understanding Brecht.* Trans. Anna Bostock. London: NLB, 1973.

Bentley, Eric. *The Brecht Commentaries 1943–1980.* New York: Grove, 1981.

Brecht, Bertolt. *Brecht on Theatre: The Development of an Aesthetic.* Ed. and Trans. John Willett. New York: Hill and Wang, 1964.

——. *The Messingkauf Dialogues.* Trans. John Willett. London: Methuen, 1965.

Dickson, Keith A. *Towards Utopia: A Study of Brecht.* Oxford: Oxford UP, 1978.

Esslin, Martin. *Brecht: The Man and His Work.* Garden City: Doubleday, 1971.

Ewen, Frederick. *Bertolt Brecht: His Life, His Art and His Times.* New York: Citadel, 1967.

Fuegi, John. *Bertolt Brecht: Chaos According to Plan.* Cambridge: Cambridge UP, 1987.

Lyon, James K. *Bertolt Brecht in America.* Princeton: Princeton UP, 1980.

Wright, Elizabeth. *Postmodern Brecht: A Re-Presentation.* London: Routledge, 1989.

### Anton Chekhov

Chekhov, Anton. *Letters of Anton Chekhov.* Trans. Michael Henry Heim and Simon Karlinsky. New York: Harper and Row, 1973.

Gottlieb, Vera. *Chekhov and the Vaudeville.* Cambridge: Cambridge UP, 1982.

Hingley, Ronald. *Chekhov: A Biographical and Critical Study.* New York: Barnes and Noble, 1966.

Magarshack, David. *Chekhov the Dramatist.* New York: Hill and Wang, 1960.

Peace, Richard. *Chekhov: A Study of the Four Major Plays.* New Haven: Yale UP, 1983.

Pitcher, Henry. *The Chekhov Play.* London: Chatto and Windus, 1973.

Rayfield, Donald. *Chekhov: The Evolution of His Art.* London: Paul Elek, 1975.

Styan, J. L. *Chekhov in Performance.* Cambridge: Cambridge UP, 1971.

### Caryl Churchill

Churchill, Caryl. "The Common Imagination and the Individual Voice." *New Theatre Quarterly* 4 (1988): 3–16.

Diamond, Elin. "Brechtian Theory/Feminist Criticism: Toward a Gestic Feminist Criticism." *Drama Review* 32.1 (1988): 82–94.

——. "(In)Visible Bodies in Churchill's Theatre." *Theatre Journal* 40 (1988): 188–204.

——. "Refusing the Romanticism of Identity: Narrative Interventions in Churchill, Benmussa, Duras." *Theatre Journal* 37 (1985): 273–86.

Kritzer, Amelia H. *Plays of Caryl Churchill: Theatre of Empowerment.* New York: St. Martin's, 1991.

Quigley, Austin E. "Stereotype and Prototype: Character in the Plays of Caryl Churchill." *Feminine Focus: The New Women Playwrights.* Ed. Enoch Brater. New York: Oxford UP, 1989.

Randall, Phyllis R., ed. *Caryl Churchill: A Casebook.* New York: Garland, 1989.

### Marguerite Duras

Diamond, Elin. "Refusing the Romanticism of Identity: Narrative Interventions in Churchill, Benmussa, Duras." *Theatre Journal* 37 (1985): 273–86.

Loufti, Martine. "Duras's India." *Literature/Film Quarterly* 14.3 (1986): 151–53.

Papin, Lilian. "Staging Writing or the Ceremony of the Text in Marguerite Duras." *Modern Drama* 34 (1981): 128–37.

Selous, Trista. *The Other Woman: Feminism and Femininity in the Work of Marguerite Duras.* New Haven: Yale UP, 1988.

Struebig, Patricia. *"India Song / The Vice Consul* of Marguerite Duras: Comparative Techniques in Film and Novel." *Apocalyptic Visions Past and Present.* Ed. JoAnn James and William Cloonan. Tallahassee: Florida State UP, 1988.

## Maria Irene Fornes

Cummings, Scott. "Seeing with Clarity: The Visions of Maria Irene Fornes." *Theater* (Yale) 17.1 (1985): 51–56.

Fornes, Maria Irene. "Interview." *Performing Arts Journal* 2.3 (1978): 106–11.

Marranca, Bonnie. "The Real Life of Maria Irene Fornes." *Theatrewritings.* By Marranca. New York: PAJ Publications, 1984.

Worthen, W. B. *"Still playing games:* Ideology and Performance in the Theater of Maria Irene Fornes." *Feminine Focus: The New Women Playwrights.* Ed. Enoch Brater. New York: Oxford UP, 1989.

## Brian Friel

Dantanus, Ulf. *Brian Friel: A Study.* London: Faber and Faber, 1988.

Deane, Seamus. *Celtic Revivals: Essays in Modern Irish Literature, 1880–1980.* Winston-Salem: Wake Forest UP, 1987.

Maxwell, D. E. S. *Brian Friel.* Lewisburg: Bucknell UP, 1973.

O'Brien, Lance. *Brian Friel.* Boston: Twayne, 1990.

Pine, Richard. *The Diviner: The Art of Brian Friel.* Mullingar: Lilliput Press, 1988.

## Athol Fugard

Fugard, Athol. *Notebooks 1960–1977.* New York: Knopf, 1983.

Gray, Stephen, ed. *Athol Fugard.* Johannesburg: McGraw, 1982.

Kavanagh, Robert Mshengu. *Theatre and Cultural Struggle in South Africa.* London: Zed, 1985.

Vandenbroucke, Russell. *Truths the Hand Can Touch: The Theatre of Athol Fugard.* New York: Theatre Communications Group, 1985.

Walder, Dennis. *Athol Fugard.* New York: Grove, 1985.

## Griselda Gambaro

Cypess, Sandra Messenger. "The Plays of Griselda Gambaro." *Dramatists in Revolt: The New Latin American Theatre.* Ed. Leon F. Lyday and George W. Woodyard. Austin: U of Texas P, 1976. 95–109.

Gambaro, Griselda. *Information for Foreigners: Three Plays by Griselda Gambaro.* Ed. and Trans. Marguerite Feitlowitz. Evanston: Northwestern UP, 1992.

Postma, Rosalea. "Space and Spectator in the Theatre of Griselda Gambaro: *Información para extranjeros." Latin American Theatre Review* 14.1 (1980): 35–45.

Taylor, Diana. "Theater and Terrorism: Griselda Gambaro's Information for Foreigners." *Theatre Journal* 42 (1990): 165–82.

——. *Theatre of Crisis: Drama and Politics in Latin America.* Lexington: UP of Kentucky, 1991.

Simpson, John, and Jana Bennett. *The Disappeared and the Mothers of the Plaza.* New York: St. Martin's, 1985.

## Jean Genet

Brooks, Peter, and Joseph Halpern, eds. *Genet: A Collection of Critical Essays.* Englewood Cliffs: Prentice-Hall, 1979.

Chaudhuri, Una. *No Man's Stage: A Semiotic Study of Jean Genet's Major Plays.* Ann Arbor: UMI Research Press, 1986.

Coe, Richard N. *The Vision of Jean Genet.* New York: Grove, 1968.

Genet, Jean. *Reflections on the Theatre and Other Writings.* Trans. Richard Seaver. London: Faber and Faber, 1972.

Sartre, Jean-Paul. *Saint Genet: Actor and Martyr.* Trans. Bernard Frechtman. New York: Pantheon, 1963.

Sohlich, W. F. "Genet's *The Blacks* and *The Screens:* Dialectic of Refusal and Revolutionary Consciousness." *Comparative Drama* 10 (1969): 216–34.

## Susan Glaspell

Ben-Zvi, Linda. "'Murder, She Wrote': The Genesis of Susan Glaspell's *Trifles." Theatre Journal* 44 (1992): 141–62.

——. "Susan Glaspell's Contributions to Contemporary Women Playwrights." *Feminine Focus: The New Women Playwrights.* Ed. Enoch Brater. New York: Oxford UP, 1989.

Dymkowski, Christine. "On the Edge: The Plays of Susan Glaspell." *Modern Drama* 31 (1988): 91–105.

Kolodny, Annette. "A Map for Rereading: Gender and the Interpretation of Literary Texts." *The New Feminist Criticism: Essays on Women, Literature, and Theory.* Ed. Elaine Showalter. New York: Pantheon, 1985.

Makowsky, Veronica. *Susan Glaspell's Century of American Women: A Critical Interpretation of Her Work.* New York and Oxford: Oxford UP, 1993.

Stein, Karen F. "The Women's World of Glaspell's *Trifles." Women in the American Theatre.* Ed. Helen Krich Chinoy and Linda Walsh Jenkins. New York: Crown, 1981.

## Angelina Weld Grimké

Bradley, Gerald. "Goodbye, Mister Bones." *Drama Critique* 7 (1964): 83.

Davis, Arthur Paul. *From the Dark Tower: Afro-American Writers.* Washington: Howard UP, 1974.

Grimké, Angelina Weld. *Selected Works of Angelina Weld Grimké.* Ed. Carolivia Herron. New York and Oxford: Oxford UP, 1991.

Hull, Gloria. *Color, Sex, and Poetry: Three Women Writers of the Harlem Renaissance.* Bloomington: Indiana UP, 1987.

Perkins, Kathy A., ed. *Black Female Playwrights: An Anthology of Plays Before 1950.* Bloomington: Indiana UP, 1989.

### Peter Handke

Hays, Michael. "Peter Handke and the End of the "'Modern.'" *Modern Drama* 23 (1981): 346–66.

Klinkowitz, Jerome, and James Knowlton. *Peter Handke and the Postmodern Transformation: The Goalie's Journey Home.* Columbia: U of Missouri P, 1983.

Schleuter, June. *The Plays and Novels of Peter Handke.* Pittsburgh: U of Pittsburgh P, 1981.

### David Henry Hwang

Garber, Marjorie. *Vested Interests: Cross-Dressing and Cultural Anxiety.* London: Routledge, 1992.

Hwang, David Henry. Afterword. *M. Butterfly.* By Hwang. New York: New American Library, 1988. 94–100.

——. *F. O. B. New Plays USA 1.* New York: Theatre Communications Group, 1982.

Moy, James S. "David Henry Hwang's *M. Butterfly* and Philip Kan Gotanda's *Yankee Dawg You Die:* Repositioning Chinese American Marginality on the American Stage." *Theatre Journal* 42 (1990): 48–56.

### Henrik Ibsen

Cima, Gay Gibson. "Discovering Signs: The Emergence of the Critical Actor in Ibsen," *Theatre Journal* 35 (1983): 5–22.

Egan, Michael, ed. *Ibsen: The Critical Heritage.* London: Routledge and Kegan Paul, 1972.

Hardwick, Elizabeth. "A Doll's House." *Seduction and Betrayal.* By Hardwick. New York: Random House, 1970.

Lyons, Charles R. *Henrik Ibsen: The Divided Consciousness.* Carbondale: Southern Illinois UP, 1972.

Marker, Frederick J., and Lise-Lone Marker. *Ibsen's Lively Art: A Performance Study of the Major Plays.* Cambridge: Cambridge UP, 1989.

Meyer, Michael. *Henrik Ibsen: A Biography.* Garden City: Doubleday, 1971.

Northam, John. *Ibsen: A Critical Study.* Cambridge: Cambridge UP, 1973.

——. *Ibsen's Dramatic Method: A Study of the Prose Dramas.* London: Faber and Faber, 1953.

Shaw, Bernard. *The Quintessence of Ibsenism.* New York: Hill and Wang, 1957.

Sprinchorn, Evert, ed. *Ibsen: Letters and Speeches.* New York: Hill and Wang, 1964.

### Adrienne Kennedy

Blau, Herbert. "The American Dream in American Gothic: The Plays of Sam Shepard and Adrienne Kennedy." *Modern Drama* 27 (1984): 520–39.

Bryant-Jackson, Paul, and Lois More Overbeck, eds. *Intersecting Boundaries: The Theatre of Adrienne Kennedy.* Minneapolis: U of Minnesota P, 1992.

Cohn, Ruby. *New American Dramatists: 1960–1990.* New York: Grove, 1992.

Harrison, Paul Carter. *The Drama of Nommo.* New York: Grove, 1972.

Tiner, Robert C. "Theatre of Identity: Adrienne Kennedy's Portrait of the Black Woman." *Studies in Black Literature.* 6 (1975): 1–5.

### Tony Kushner

Cheever, Susan. Interview with Tony Kushner. *New York Times* 13 Sept. 1992: II, 7.

### Heiner Müller

Bathrick, David, and Andreas Huyssen. "Producing Revolution: Heiner Müller's *Mauser* as a Learning Play." *New German Critique* 3.2 (1976): 110–21.

Dudley, Robert M. "Being and Non-Being: The Other and Heterotopia in *Hamletmachine.*" *Modern Drama* 35 (1992): 562–70.

Fehervay, Helen. "Enlightenment or Entanglement: History and Aesthetics in Bertolt Brecht and Heiner Müller." *New German Critique* 3.8 (1976): 80–109.

Girshausen, Theo. "'Reject it, in order to possess it:' On Heiner Müller and Bertolt Brecht." *Modern Drama* 23 (1981): 404–21.

Gussow, Mel. "Cranking Up a Powerful *Hamletmachine.*" *New York Times* 5 May 1986: H3.

Rouse, John. "Heiner Müller and the Politics of Memory." *Theatre Journal* 45 (1993): 65–74.

### Eugene O'Neill

Bogard, Travis. *Contour in Time: The Plays of Eugene O'Neill.* Oxford: Oxford UP, 1988.

Cargill, Oscar, N. Bryllion Fagin, and William J. Fisher, eds. *O'Neill and His Plays: Four Decades of Criticism.* New York: New York UP, 1961.

Chothia, Jean. *Forging a Language: A Study of the Plays of Eugene O'Neill.* Cambridge: Cambridge UP, 1979.

Floyd, Virginia, ed. *Eugene O'Neill at Work: Newly Released Ideas for Plays.* New York: Ungar, 1981.

Gelb, Arthur, and Barbara Gelb. *O'Neill.* New York: Harper and Row, 1973.

Sheaffer, Louis. *O'Neill: Son and Playwright.* Boston: Little, Brown, 1968.

Wainscott, Ronald H. *Staging O'Neill: The Experimental Years, 1920–1934.* New Haven: Yale UP, 1988.

### Harold Pinter

Diamond, Elin. *Pinter's Comic Play.* Lewisburg: Bucknell UP, 1985.

Esslin, Martin. *Pinter.* New York: Norton, 1976.

Ganz, Arthur, ed. *Pinter: A Collection of Critical Essays.* Englewood Cliffs: Prentice-Hall, 1972.

Merritt, Susan Hollis. *Pinter in Play: Critical Strategies in the Plays of Harold Pinter.* Durham: Duke UP, 1990.

Postlewait, Thomas. "Pinter's *The Homecoming:* Displacing and Repeating Ibsen." *Comparative Drama* 15 (1981): 195–212.

Quigley, Austin E. *The Pinter Problem.* Princeton: Princeton UP, 1975.

### Luigi Pirandello

Bassnet-McGuire, Susan. *Luigi Pirandello.* New York: Grove, 1983.

Bentley, Eric. *The Pirandello Commentaries.* Evanston:

Northwestern UP, 1986.

Guidice, Gaspare. *Pirandello: A Biography.* Trans. Alastair Hamilton. Oxford: Oxford UP, 1975.

Kennedy, Andrew K. "*Six Characters:* Pirandello's Last Tape." *Modern Drama* 12 (1969): 1–9.

Oliver, Roger W. *Dreams of Passion: The Theater of Luigi Pirandello.* New York: New York UP, 1979.

Paolucci, Anne. *Pirandello's Theater.* Carbondale: Southern Illinois UP, 1974.

Pirandello, Luigi. *On Humor.* Trans. Antonio Illiano and Daniel P. Testa. Chapel Hill: U of North Carolina P, 1974.

Sogluizzo, A. Richard. *Luigi Pirandello, Director: The Playwright in the Theatre.* Metuchen: Scarecrow, 1982.

### Elizabeth Robins

Gates, Joanna E. "Elizabeth Robins and the 1891 Production of *Hedda Gabler.*" *Modern Drama* 28 (1985): 610–19.

Marcus, Jane Conner. "Elizabeth Robins." Diss. Northwestern University, 1973.

Wiley, Catherine. "The matter with manners: The New Woman and the problem play." *Themes in Drama* 11 (1989): 109–27.

Worthen, W. B. *Modern Drama and the Rhetoric of Theater.* Berkeley: U of California P, 1992.

### Ntozake Shange

Richards, Sandra. "Under the 'Trickster's' Sign: Toward a Reading of Ntozake Shange and Femi Osofisan." *Critical Theory and Performance.* Ed. Janelle G. Reinelt and Joseph Roach. Ann Arbor: U of Michigan P, 1992.

Shange, Ntozake. *See No Evil: Prefaces, Essays, and Accounts 1976–1983.* San Francisco: Momo's Press, 1984.

——. *Three Pieces: Spell #7, A Photograph: Lovers in Motion, Boogie Woogie Landscapes.* New York: Penguin, 1982.

### Bernard Shaw

Bentley, Eric. *Bernard Shaw.* New York: Norton, 1976.

Berst, Charles A. *Bernard Shaw and the Art of Drama.* Urbana: U of Illinois P, 1973.

Compton, Louis. *Shaw the Dramatist.* Lincoln: U of Nebraska P, 1969.

Evans, T. F., ed. *Shaw: The Critical Heritage.* London: Routledge and Kegan Paul, 1976.

Goldman, Michael. "Shaw and the Marriage in Dionysus." *The Play and Its Critic: Essays for Eric Bentley.* Ed. Michael Bertin. New York: UP of America, 1986.

Holroyd, Michael. *Bernard Shaw.* 3 vols. New York: Random House, 1988–91.

Meisel, Martin. *Shaw and the Nineteenth-Century Theater.* Princeton: Princeton UP, 1963.

Peters, Margot. *Bernard Shaw and the Actresses.* Garden City: Doubleday, 1980.

Turco, Alfred, Jr. *Shaw's Moral Vision: The Self and Salvation.* Ithaca: Cornell UP, 1976.

Wisenthal, J. L. *The Marriage of Contraries: Bernard Shaw's Middle Plays.* Cambridge: Harvard UP, 1974.

### Sam Shepard

King, Kimball. *Sam Shepard: A Casebook.* New York: Garland, 1988.

Marranca, Bonnie, ed. *American Dreams: The Imagination of Sam Shepard.* New York: Performing Arts Journal Publications, 1981.

Mottram, Ron. *Inner Landscapes: The Theater of Sam Shepard.* Columbia: U of Missouri P, 1984.

Oumano, Ellen. *Sam Shepard: The Life and Work of an American Dreamer.* New York: St. Martin's, 1986.

### Anna Deavere Smith

Case, Sue-Ellen. "Introduction to *Chlorophyll Postmodernism and the Mother Goddess/A Conversation.*" *Women and Performance* 4.8 (1989): 20–25.

Dolan, Jill. "Staking Claims and Positions: The Women and Theatre Program, San Diego, and the Danger Zone." *Women and Performance* 4.8 (1989): 46–57.

Smith, Anna Deavere. *Chlorophyll Postmodernism and the Mother Goddess/A Conversation. Women and Performance* 4.8 (1989): 26–45.

Richards, Sandra L. "Caught in the Act of Social Definition: *On the Road* with Anna Deavere Smith." *Acting Out: Feminist Performances.* Ed. Lynda Hart and Peggy Phelan. Ann Arbor: U of Michigan P, 1993. 35–53.

### Wole Soyinka

Gibbs, James. *Wole Soyinka.* London: Macmillan, 1986.

——, ed. *Critical Perspectives on Wole Soyinka.* Washington: Three Continents, 1980.

——, Ketu H. Katrak, and Henry Louis Gates, Jr., eds. *Wole Soyinka: A Bibliography of Primary and Secondary Sources.* Westport: Greenwood, 1986.

Gugelberger, Georg M., ed. *Marxism and African Literature.* London: James Currey, 1985.

Jones, Eldred Durosimi. *The Writings of Wole Soyinka.* London: James Currey, 1988.

Nazareth, Peter. *An African View of Literature.* Evanston: Northwestern UP, 1974.

Ogunba, Oyin. *The Movement of Transition: A Study of the Plays of Wole Soyinka.* Ibadan: Ibadan UP, 1975.

Soyinka, Wole. "The Fourth Stage." *The Morality of Art: Essays Presented to G. Wilson Knight by His Colleagues and Friends.* Ed. D. W. Jefferson. New York: Barnes and Noble, 1969.

——. *The Man Died.* London: Rex Collings, 1972.

### Split Britches

Case, Sue-Ellen. "From Split Subject to Split Britches." *Feminine Focus: The New Women Playwrights.* Ed. Enoch Brater. New York: Oxford UP, 1989.

——. "Toward a Butch-Femme Aesthetic." *Making a Spectacle: Feminist Essays on Contemporary Women's Theatre.* Ed. Lynda Hart. Ann Arbor: U of Michigan P, 1989.

Davy, Kate. "Constructing the Spectator: Reception, Context, and Address in Lesbian Performance." *Performing Arts Journal* 10.2 (1986): 43–52.

Dolan, Jill. "The Dynamics of Desire: Sexuality and Gender in Pornography and Performance." *Theatre Journal* 39 (1987): 156–74.

Harris, Hillary. Rev. of *Anniversary Waltz,* by Split Britches. *Theatre Journal* 42 (1990): 484–88.

Hart, Lynda. Rev. of *Lesbians Who Kill*, by Split Britches. *Theatre Journal* 44 (1992): 515–17.

Leondar, Gail. Rev. of *Belle Reprieve*, by Bette Bourne, Paul Shaw, Peggy Shaw, Lois Weaver. *Theatre Journal* 43 (1991): 386–88.

## August Strindberg

Carlson, Harry G. *Strindberg and the Poetry of Myth*. Berkeley: U of California P, 1982.

Lucas, F. L. *The Drama of Ibsen and Strindberg*. London: Cassell, 1962.

Reinert, Otto, ed. *Strindberg: A Collection of Critical Essays*. Englewood Cliffs: Prentice-Hall, 1971.

Sprinchorn, Evert. *Strindberg As Dramatist*. New Haven: Yale UP, 1982.

Strindberg, August. *From an Occult Diary*. Trans. Mary Sandbach. New York: Hill and Wang, 1965.

——. *Open Letters to the Intimate Theater*. Trans. Walter Johnson. Seattle: U of Washington P, n.d.

Törnqvist, Egil. *Strindbergian Drama*. Atlantic Highlands: Humanities Press, 1982.

## Luis Valdez and El Teatro Campesino

Broyles González, Yolanda "Toward a Re-Vision of Chicano Theatre History: The Women of El Teatro Campesino." *Making a Spectacle: Feminist Essays on Contemporary Women's Theatre*. Ed. Lynda Hart. Ann Arbor: U of Michigan P, 1989.

Huerta, Jorge A. *Chicano Theater: Themes and Forms*. Ypsilanti: Bilingual Press, 1982.

Kanellos, Nicolas. *Hispanic Theatre in the United States*. Houston: Arte Público, 1984.

Morton, Carlos. "The Teatro Campesino." *Tulane Drama Review* 18.4 (1974): 71–76.

von Bardeleben, Renate, ed. *Missions in Conflict: Essays on U.S.-Mexican Relations and Chicano Culture*. Tubingen: G. Narr, 1986.

Valdez, Luis. *Pensamiento Serpentino*. El Centro Campesino Cultural: Cucaracha, 1973.

Valdez, Luis, and El Teatro Campesino. *Actos*. San Juan Bautista: Menyah Productions, 1971.

## Wendy Wasserstein

Carlson, Susan L. "Comic Textures and Female Communities, 1937 and 1977: Claire Boothe and Wendy Wasserstein." *Modern American Drama: The Female Canon*. Ed. June Schleuter. Rutherford: Fairleigh Dickinson UP, 1990.

Cohen, Esther. "Uncommon Woman: An Interview with Wendy Wasserstein." *Women's Studies: An Interdisciplinary Journal* 15 (1988): 257–70.

Keyssar, Helene. "Drama and the Dialogic Imagination: *The Heidi Chronicles* and *Fefu and Her Friends*." *Modern Drama* 34 (1991): 88–106.

Mandl, Bette. "Feminism, Postfeminism, and *The Heidi Chronicles*." *Studies in the Humanities* 17.2 (1990): 120–28.

## Oscar Wilde

Berggren, Ruth, ed. *The Definitive Four-Act Version of* The Importance of Being Earnest, *A Trivial Comedy for Serious People*. New York: Vanguard, 1987.

Cohen, Ed. "Writing Gone Wilde: Homoerotic Desire in the Closet of Representation." *PMLA* 102 (1987): 801–13.

Craft, Christopher. "Alias Bunbury: Desire and Termination in *The Importance of Being Earnest*." *Representations* No. 31 (1990): 19–46.

Ellman, Richard. *Oscar Wilde*. New York: Knopf, 1988.

Gagnier, Regenia. *Idylls of the Marketplace: Oscar Wilde and the Victorian Public*. Stanford: Stanford UP, 1986.

## Tennessee Williams

Boxill, Roger. *Tennessee Williams*. New York: St. Martin's, 1987.

Devlin, Albert J., ed. *Conversations with Tennessee Williams*. Jackson: U of Mississippi P, 1986.

Leavitt, Richard Freeman, ed. *The World of Tennessee Williams*. New York: Putnam, 1978.

Savran, David. *Communists, Cowboys, and Queers: The Politics of Masculinity in the Work of Arthur Miller and Tennessee Williams*. Minneapolis and London: U of Minnesota P, 1992.

Spoto, Donald. *The Kindness of Strangers: The Life of Tennessee Williams*. Boston: Little, Brown, 1985.

Stanton, Stephen, ed. *Tennessee Williams: A Collection of Critical Essays*. Englewood Cliffs: Prentice-Hall, 1977.

Williams, Tennessee. *Memoirs*. Garden City: Doubleday, 1975.

## August Wilson

Ching, Mei-Ling. "Wrestling against History." *Theater/Yale* 19.3 (1988): 70–71.

Henderson, Heather. "Building Fences: An Interview with Mary Alice and James Earl Jones." *Theater/Yale* 16.3 (1985): 67–70.

Shannon, Sandra G. "The Long Wait: August Wilson's *Ma Rainey's Black Bottom*." *Black American Literature Forum* 25.1 (1991): 135–45.

Wilde, Lisa. "Reclaiming the Past: Narrative and Memory in August Wilson's *Two Trains Running*." *Theatre/Yale* 22.1 (1991): 73–84.

# SELECTED FILM AND VIDEO RECORDINGS

**Bertolt Brecht: *Life of Galileo***
Film. 1975. Directed by Joseph Losey. Cast includes Topol, Edward Fox, Colin Blakeley, John Gielgud.

**Anton Chekhov: *The Three Sisters***
VHS. 1965. Directed by Paul Bogart. Cast includes Shelley Winters, Sandy Dennis, Geraldine Page, Kevin

McCarthy. Film of stage production.

Marguerite Duras: *India Song*
Film. 1975. Directed by Marguerite Duras. Cast includes Delphyne Seyrig, Michael Lonsdale, Marguerite Duras.

Jean Genet: *The Balcony*
VHS, Film. 1965. Film based on Genet's play. Directed by Doseph Strick. Cast includes Peter Falk, Shelley Winters, Lee Grant, Leonard Nimoy.

Henrik Ibsen: *The Wild Duck*
VHS. 1978. Miami Dade Community College. VHS. 1984. Directed by Henri Safran. Cast includes Jeremy Irons, Liv Ullman.

Eugene O'Neill: *The Emperor Jones*
VHS. 1933. Directed by Dudley Murphy. Cast includes Paul Robeson, Dudley Digges.

Harold Pinter: *The Homecoming*
Film. 1973. Directed by Peter Hall. Cast includes Cyril Cusac, Ian Holm, Vivian Merchant.

Luigi Pirandello: *Six Characters in Search of an Author*
VHS. 1978. Miami Dade Community College.

Bernard Shaw: *Heartbreak House*
VHS. 1986. Directed by Arthur Page. Cast includes Rex Harrison, Rosemary Harris, Amy Irving.

Oscar Wilde: *The Importance of Being Earnest*
Film. 1952. Directed by Anthony Asquith. Cast includes Michael Redgrave, Edith Evans, Dorothy Tutin.

Tennessee Williams: *The Glass Menagerie*
Film. 1950. Directed by Irving Rippen. Cast includes Jane Wyman, Kirk Douglas, Arthur Kennedy. Film. 1973. Directed by Anthony Harvey. Cast includes Katherine Hepburn, Sam Waterston, Joanna Miles, Michael Moriarty. VHS. 1987. Directed by Paul Newman. Cast includes John Malkovich, Joanne Woodward, Karen Allen.

ANTONIN ARTAUD  "No More Masterpieces" and "The Theater and Culture" from THE THEATER AND ITS DOUBLE by Antonin Artaud. Copyright © 1958 by Grove Press. Used with the permission of Grove/Atlantic Monthly Press.

AMIRI BARAKA  "The Dutchman" and "The Revolutionary Theatre" from SELECTED PLAYS AND PROSE OF AMIRI BARAKA. Copyright © 1964, 1979 by Amiri Baraka, published by William Morrow and Co. Reprinted by permission of Sterling Lord Literistic, Inc.

SAMUEL BECKETT  "Catastrophe" from CASCANDO AND OTHER SHORT DRAMATIC PIECES by Samuel Beckett. Copyright © 1963 by Samuel Beckett, renewed copyright © 1991 by Edward Beckett. "Endgame" from ENDGAME by Samuel Beckett. Copyright © 1958 by Grove Press, renewed 1986 by Samuel Beckett. From "Dante . . . Bruno. Vico . . Joyce" in DISJECTA by Samuel Beckett. Copyright © 1984 by Grove Press. All used with the permission of Grove/Atlantic Monthly Press.

WALTER BENJAMIN  "What is Epic Theater?" from ILLUMINATIONS by Walter Benjamin. Copyright © 1955 Suhrkamp Verlag, Frankfurt A.M.; English translation copyright © 1968 by Harcourt Brace & Company. Reprinted by permission of the publisher.

KATHLEEN BETSKO AND RACHEL KOENIG  "Interviews with: Griselda Gambaro, Caryl Churchill, Maria Irene Fornes, Ntozake Shange, Wendy Wasserstein, and Adrienne Kennedy" from INTERVIEWS WITH CONTEMPORARY WOMEN PLAYWRIGHTS by Kathleen Betsko and Rachel Koenig. Copyright © 1987 by the authors. Reprinted by permission of William Morrow & Company, Inc.

HOMI K. BHABHA  "Of Mimicry and Man: The Ambivalence of Colonial Discourse" by Homi K. Bhabha from OCTOBER 28 (Spring 1984): 125–33, published by MIT Press. Reprinted by permission of Homi K. Bhabha.

EDWARD BOND "Bingo" and "Introduction to Bingo" by Edward Bond from BINGO AND THE SEA, published by Hill and Wang, a division of Farrar, Straus & Giroux. Copyright © 1975 by Edward Bond. Reprinted by permission of Casarotto Ramsay Ltd. CAUTION: All rights whatsoever in this play are strictly reserved and application for performance, etc., should be made before rehearsal to Casarotto Ramsay Ltd., National House, 60–66 Wardour Street, London W1V 3HP. No performance may be given unless a license has been obtained.

BETTE BOURNE, PEGGY SHAW, PAUL SHAW, AND LOIS WEAVER  "Belle Reprieve" by Bette Bourne, Peggy Shaw, Paul Shaw, and Lois Weaver from GAY AND LESBIAN PLAYS TODAY, selected and introduced by Terry Helbin, published by Heinemann/Portsmouth, N. H. Copyright © 1991, 1993 by Bette Bourne, Peggy Shaw, Paul Shaw, and Lois Weaver. Reprinted by permission of the authors.

BERTHOLT BRECHT GALILEO translated by Charles Laughton. Original work LEBEN DES GALILEI by Bertholt Brecht. Copyright © 1940 by Arvid Englind Teaterforlag, a.b., renewed June 1967 by Stefan S. Brecht; copyright © 1955 by [Su]rkamp Verlag, Frankfurt am Main. Charles Laughton's translation of GALILEO and essay "Building Up a Part" by Bertholt [Brecht] Copyright © 1952 by Bertholt Brecht; renewed by Stefan S.

[c]opyright for "Building Up a Part" © 1980 by Stefan S. [trans]lated from LIFE OF GALILEO by Bertholt Brecht, [J]ohn Willett and edited by John Willett and Ralph [publ]ished by Arcade Publishing, New York, New York.

Reprinted by permission of the publisher.

JUDITH BUTLER  "Performative Acts and Gender Constitution: An Essay in Phenomenology and Feminist Theory" by Judith Butler from PERFORMING FEMINISM: FEMINIST CRITICAL THEORY AND THEATRE, edited by Sue-Ellen Case, pp. 270–282. The Johns Hopkins University Press, Baltimore/London, 1990. Reprinted by permission of The Johns Hopkins University Press.

SUE-ELLEN CASE "From Split Subject to Split Britches" by Sue-Ellen Case from FEMININE FOCUS: THE NEW WOMEN PLAYWRIGHTS, edited by Enoch Brater. Copyright © 1989 by Oxford University Press, Inc. Reprinted by permission of Oxford University Press.

ANTON CHEKHOV  "The Three Sisters" from CHEKHOV: THE MAJOR PLAYS by Anton Chekhov, translated by Ann Dunnigan. Translation copyright © 1964 by Ann Dunnigan. Used by permission of Dutton Signet, a division of Penguin Books USA.

CARYL CHURCHILL CLOUD NINE and "Introduction to CLOUD NINE" copyright © 1979, 1980, 1983, 1984, 1985 by Caryl Churchill. MAD FOREST copyright © 1990, 1991 by Caryl Churchill. Distributed in the USA by Theatre Communications Group, 355 Lexington Avenue, New York, N.Y. 10017. Both plays reproduced by arrangement with Nick Hern Books.

RUBY COHN  "Beckett Directs: Endgame and Krapp's Last Tape" by Ruby Cohn from ON BECKETT: ESSAYS AND CRITICISM, edited by S. E. Gontarski. Copyright © 1986 by S. E. Gontarski. Used with the permission of Grove/Atlantic Monthly Press.

KATE DAVY  "Unpublished Excerpts from Interviews with Peggy Shaw and Lois Weaver." Copyright © 1985, 1992, 1993 by Kate Davy. Reprinted by permission of Kate Davy.

HILARY DEVRIES  "A Playwright Spreads His Wings: An Interview with Tony Kushner" by Hilary Devries from THE LOS ANGELES TIMES, October 25, 1992. Copyright by Hilary Devries. Reprinted by permission of the author.

MARGUERITE DURAS  "India Song" from INDIA SONG by Marguerite Duras. Copyright © 1976 by Marguerite Duras. Used with the permission of Grove/Atlantic Monthly Press. From THE VICE CONSUL by Marguerite Duras. Copyright © 1966 by Editions Gallimard. Translation copyright © 1968 by Hamish Hamilton Ltd. Reprinted by permission of Georges Borchardt, Inc.

FIELD DAY THEATRE COMPANY "Field Day Theatre Company, Program Notes for Brien Friel's "TRANSLATIONS" from MODERN IRISH DRAMA, edited by John P. Harrington, published by W. W. Norton 1991. Copyright Field Day Theatre Company, Ireland. Reprinted by permission of Field Day Theatre Company.

MARIA IRENE FORNES  "The Conduct of Life" by Maria Irene Fornes from MARIA FORNES PLAYS. Copyright © 1986 by Maria Irene Fornes, published by PAJ Publications. Reprinted by permission of Johns Hopkins Press.

SIGMUND FREUD  "Psychopathic Characters on the Stage" by Sigmund Freud from THE STANDARD EDITION OF THE COMPLETE PSYCHOLOGICAL WORKS OF SIGMUND FREUD, Vol. VII., translated and edited by James Strachey. Reprinted by permission of The Institute of Psycho-Analysis and The Hogarth Press.

BRIAN FRIEL  "Translations" by Brian Friel from SELECTED PLAYS OF BRIAN FRIEL. Copyright © 1981 by Brian Friel.